Spanish-English English-Spanish Reference Dictionary

Berlitz Publishing Company, Inc.

Princeton Mexico City Dublin Eschborn Singapore

 Published in the United States by Random House, Inc., New York and simultaneously in Canada by Random House of Canada Limited, Toronto. Dictionary originally published by David McKay Company, Inc., under the title *Modern Spanish-English English-Spanish Dictionary*.

Published by arrangement with Random House Reference & Information Publishing, a division of Random House, Inc.

ISBN 2-8315-7125-1

Printed in Canada

Contents

Preface

New Second Edition

This is a revised Second Edition of *Random House Spanish–English English–Spanish Dictionary,* first published in 1995. New to this edition are pronunciations for all Spanish and English main entries, using IPA (International Phonetic Alphabet) symbols. The IPA symbols are explained in the pronunciation key for English on page viii and for Spanish on page xiv. Also included in this dictionary are detailed guides to the pronunciation of both languages.

Selection of Vocabulary

The aim of this dictionary is to cover as much current vocabulary as possible, as well as certain terms found in standard works of modern Spanish and English literature.

This dictionary includes items often omitted in other bilingual dictionaries—road and street signs, for example—though few things could be as frustrating (and, sometimes, as dangerous) as seeing such signs but not knowing what they mean (in this dictionary, all kinds of public notices are enclosed by the symbols << >> in Spanish and by quotation marks in English). Also, many vocabulary items consisting of more than one word have been covered here (see for instance **do** in the English–Spanish section).

Spanish Spelling and Alphabetization

On January 1, 1959, the Spanish language academies changed certain spelling rules and on April 27, 1994, they eliminated **ch** and **ll** as separate letters of the alphabet. Thus, whereas words like **chico** and **chocolate** were formerly alphabetized under their own letter (**ch,** which came between **c** and **d**) and words like **llamar** and **llegar** were formerly alphabetized under their own letter (**ll,** which came between **l** and **m**), words containing **ch** or **ll,** in whatever part of the word they may appear, are now alphabetized as they would be in English (**chico** therefore now appears under **c** and **llegar** under **l**).

Field Labels

Only essential field labels are given in this dictionary. For example, the label *medicine* or *pathology* is unnecessary at **flebitis** "phlebitis" (in the Spanish–English section) because both the Spanish and English words refer only to the medical condition so called in those languages.

In contrast to that entry, we do need a label at **foca** "seal" (in the Spanish–English section) because English **seal** has several meanings and only the zoological one is intended here. English speakers looking up **foca** thus need the label *zoology* (Spanish speakers need no label because they know that **foca** is the name of an animal, and so they will correctly assume that **seal** is intended only in its zoological sense).

Regional Labels for Spanish

Regional labels are given in this dictionary when a less than universal usage is found in a certain region or country. A regional label should be interpreted as meaning that the usage so labeled is found in that particular place, but it may also be found elsewhere. For instance, the regional label *Mexican* means that the usage so labeled is found in Mexico, but further research would be necessary to determine whether the usage is present or absent in other countries. The label *West. Hem.* is used for Spanish terms that are in general use throughout the Western Hemisphere.

Subentries

If a main entry head is repeated in a subentry in exactly the same form, it is abbreviated to its first letter (for instance, at **fin** in the Spanish–English section we find **a f. de,** which stands for **a fin de**). If the main entry head appears in any other form, the full form is given in the subentry (thus, at **fin,** the subentry head **a fines de** is spelled without abbreviation).

Irregular Spanish Verbs and the Direction "See . . ."

If a Spanish verb is irregular, it has been treated in one of two ways: either its principal parts are shown (see for example the end of the entry for **caber**) or you are referred to an analogous irregular verb for guidance (see for example the end of the entry for **comparecer,** where you are directed to **conocer**). Thus, since the irregular form **conozco** is shown at **conocer** (it being irregular in the sense that it has a **z**), you may infer that **comparecer** has the irregular form **comparezco.**

One of the consequences of the changes in Spanish spelling is that a new kind of orthographically irregular verb has come into existence (for example, **ahijar, ahincar, ahitar, ahuchar, ahumar, ahusar, cohibir, desahuciar, prohibir, prohijar, rehilar, rehusar, sahumar, sobrehilar,** and **trashumar**).

If "See . . ." is all you find at an entry, you are being directed to a synonym. Thus, "**descompasarse** See **descomedirse**" means that the translations of **descomedirse** are those of **descompasarse** too.

Spanish Equivalents of "you"

Today's Spanish, when taken as a whole, has at least six equivalents of "you": **tú, vos, usted** (abbreviated to **Vd.**), **su merced** (all of which are used in addressing one person), **ustedes** (abbreviated to **Vds.**), **vosotros, vosotras,** and **sus mercedes** (all used in addressing more than one person).

When **you** occurs in this dictionary, usually only one of those words has been chosen to translate it, though three are never used here: **su merced, sus mercedes,** because they are now limited to only a small area of the Spanish-speaking world (the Cundinamarca Savanna, in Colombia) and even there they are now obsolescent, and **vos,** because the verb forms corresponding to this pronoun often vary from country to country.

Usually, the selection of one pronoun or another in this dictionary has been arbitrary, in which case any of the others could just as easily have been chosen. For example, for **How are you?** the translation "¿Cómo está Vd.?" is offered, yet any of the other pronouns could appear instead (with, in certain cases, a different verb form, for instance "¿Cómo están Vds.?").

In certain cases, however, not all pronouns (whether actually used or just implicit) would be appropriate. For example, among the translations of **please** . . . are imperative forms of **servirse. . . .** Because **servirse** in this sense is a formal usage (found mostly in impersonal writing like application blanks), it is not found in any familiar form of the imperative. The dictionary therefore gives **¡sírvase . . . !** (where the understood subject is **usted,** a formal pronoun). It could also have given **¡sírvanse . . . !** (where the understood subject is **ustedes,** likewise a formal pronoun), but not any form in which the subject were an informal pronoun.

Masculine and Feminine, Male and Female

As women engage in more and more activities once the domain of men, a growing number of Spanish nouns formerly used only in the masculine gender are being used in the feminine too. This dictionary thus labels **nauta, paracaidista, púgil, pugilista, recluta, reservista,** and **seminarista,** for example, as both masculine and feminine (the gender to be chosen depending on the gender of the person in question). For the user's convenience, the gender of Spanish nouns is indicated not only in the Spanish–English section but also in the English–Spanish one.

Many sample Spanish phrases and sentences in this dictionary can refer to people of either gender. For example, under **wish** in the English–Spanish section the sample sentence **I wished him a Merry Christmas** is translated "Le deseé unas Pascuas muy felices" and "Le felicité las Pascuas." Since they both also mean "I wished her a Merry Christmas," the sentence could as easily have contained **her** rather than **him.** In this dictionary, male and female references have been chosen randomly, hopefully in about equal number.

In other cases, a slight change is needed to turn a male reference into a female one or vice versa. For instance, **He was within an inch of being killed** (under **within,** in the English–Spanish section) is rendered by "Por poco le matan." Changing **he** to **she** and **le** to **la** will yield a correct equivalence referring to a female. With just an elementary knowledge of both languages, users of this dictionary will be able to make the necessary changes and thus have at their disposal many more sample phrases and sentences than it supplies.

Símbolos de Pronunciacíon por los Sonidos del inglés

Pronunciation Symbols for the Sounds of English

Símbolos del AFI IPA Symbols	Ejemplos Key Words
/æ/	*Eng.* h**a**t
/ei/	*Eng.* st**ay**; *Fr.* cit**é**; *Ger.* beq**ue**m; *It.* fr**é**ccia; *Sp.* r**ei**na
/ɛə/ [followed by /r/]	*Eng.* h**ai**r; *Fr.* fr**è**re; *Ger.* m**eh**r; *It.* m**e**rcante; *Sp.* v**e**r
/ɑ/	*Eng.* f**a**ther; *Fr.* t**a**sse; *Ger.* V**a**ter; *It.* p**a**sta; *Sp.* c**a**sa
/ɛ/	*Eng.* b**e**t; *Fr.* gaz**e**lle; *Ger.* B**e**tt; *It.* fresch**e**zza; *Sp.* **e**ntre
/i/	*Eng.* b**ee**; *Fr.* diff**i**c**i**le; *Ger.* W**ie**gen; *It.* l**i**mone; *Sp.* v**i**da
/ɪə/ [followed by /r/]	*Eng.* h**ea**r; *Fr.* r**i**re; *Ger.* h**ie**r
/ɪ/	*Eng.* s**i**t; *Ger.* **i**st
/ai/	*Eng.* tr**y**; *Ger.* z**ei**gen; *It.* oper**ai**o; *Sp.* **ay**
/ɒ/	*Eng.* h**o**t
/o/	*Eng.* b**oa**t; *Fr.* chap**eau**; *Ger.* M**o**nd
/ɔ/	*Eng.* s**aw**; *Fr.* d**o**nner; *Ger.* d**o**ch; *It.* **o**glio; *Sp.* n**o**ta
/ɔi/	*Eng.* t**oy**; *Ger.* D**eu**tsch; *Sp.* h**oy**
/ʊ/	*Eng.* b**oo**k
/u/	*Eng.* t**oo**; *Fr.* t**ou**t; *Ger.* t**u**n; *It.* in**u**tile; *Sp.* l**u**na
/au/	*Eng.* c**ow**; *Ger.* **au**s; *Sp.* p**au**sa
/ʌ/	*Eng.* **u**p
/ɜ/ [followed by /r/]	*Eng.* b**ur**n; *Fr.* fl**eu**r; *Ger.* b**ö**se
/ə/	*Eng.* **a**lone; *Fr.* d**e**main; *Ger.* steh**e**n
/ᵊ/	*Eng.* f**ire** (fiᵊr); *Fr.* bastill**e**
/œ̃/, /ɔ̃/, /ɛ̃/, /ɑ̃/ [A tilde over a vowel shows that it is nasalized]	As in *Fr.* **un** b**on** v**in** bl**an**c
/b/	*Eng.* **b**oy; *Fr.* **b**ête; *Ger.* **b**acken; *It.* **b**uio; *Sp.* **b**oca
/tʃ/	*Eng.* **ch**ild; *It.* **c**ibo; *Sp.* mu**ch**o
/d/	*Eng.* **d**a**d**; *Fr.* **d**anse; *Ger.* **d**ieser; *It.* **d**estra; *Sp.* **d**oy
/f/	*Eng.* **f**or; *Fr.* **f**ête; *Ger.* **f**ahren; *It.* **f**retta; *Sp.* **f**echa
/g/	*Eng.* **g**ive; *Fr.* **g**arde; *Ger.* **g**ut; *It.* se**g**uito; *Sp.* **g**ato

Símbolos del AFI **IPA Symbols**	**Ejemplos** **Key Words**
/h/	*Eng.* **h**appy; *Ger.* **h**eben; *It.* **h**ascisc
/dʒ/	*Eng.* **j**ust; *It.* **g**iugno
/k/	*Eng.* **kick**; *Fr.* **c**apable; *Ger.* **K**irche; *It.* ami**ch**evole; *Sp.* **k**ilogramo
/l/	*Eng.* **l**ove; *Fr.* **l**ait; *Ger.* **l**ieben; *It.* **l**ira; *Sp.* **l**ibro
/m/	*Eng.* **m**other; *Fr.* **m**anger; *Ger.* **M**ann; *It.* **m**eandro; *Sp.* li**m**bo
/n/	*Eng.* **n**ow; *Fr.* **n**oble; *Ger.* **n**ach; *It.* **n**ulla; *Sp.* **n**oche
/ŋ/	*Eng.* si**ng**; *Ger.* si**ng**en; *It.* ve**n**go
/p/	*Eng.* **p**ot; *Fr.* **p**arfum; *Ger.* **P**ost; *It.* **p**ace; *Sp.* **p**a**p**a
/r/	*Eng.* **r**ead; *Fr.* **r**ouge; *Ger.* **R**at; *It.* **r**icco; *Sp.* **p**ara
/s/	*Eng.* **s**ee; *Fr.* **s**anté; *Ger.* e**ss**en; *It.* **s**érpo; *Sp.* ha**s**ta
/ʃ/	*Eng.* **sh**op; *Fr.* **ch**er**ch**er; *Ger.* **Sch**laf; *It.* **sc**elto
/t/	*Eng.* **t**en; *Fr.* **t**ê**t**e; *Ger.* **T**eil; *It.* **t**opo; *Sp.* **t**omar
/θ/	*Eng.* **th**ing; *Sp.* (in Spain) **c**erdo
/ð/	*Eng.* fa**th**er; *Sp.* co**d**o
/v/	*Eng.* **v**ictory; *Fr.* **v**ie; *Ger.* **w**as; *It.* **v**oi; *Sp.* **v**erdad
/w/	*Eng.* **w**itch; *Fr.* **oui**; *It.* g**u**ardare
/y/	*Eng.* **y**es; *Fr.* **y**eux; *Ger.* **j**ung; *Sp.* **y**acer
/z/	*Eng.* **z**ipper; *Fr.* **z**éro; *Ger.* **S**ieg
/ʒ/	*Eng.* plea**s**ure; *Fr.* **j**eune

Los sonidos del inglés americano

Vocales y diptongos

a Cuando representa el sonido /æ/, se pronuncia más cerrada que la *a* de *paro* (por ejemplo: **act, at, bat, hat, marry**); también se encuentra este sonido en palabras deletreadas con: -ah- (d*ah*lia), -ai- (pl*ai*d), -al- (h*al*f), -au- (l*au*gh), -ua- (g*ua*rantee).

a Cuando representa el sonido /ei/, se pronuncia más cerrada que la *e* de *hablé* y como si fuera seguido de *i* (por ejemplo: **age, gate, rate**); también se encuentra este sonido en palabras deletreadas con: -ai- (r*ai*n, *ai*r), -aigh- (str*aigh*t), -au- (g*au*ge), -ay- (s*ay*), -ea- (st*ea*k), -ei- (v*ei*l, w*ei*gh), -ey- (ob*ey*).

a /ɑ/ Equivale aproximadamente a la *a* de *sentado* y *bajo* (por ejemplo: **ah, father, part**); también se encuentra este sonido en palabras deletreadas con: -al- (c*al*m), -e(r)- (s*er*geant), -ea(r)- (h*ear*t), -ua- (g*ua*rd).

a /ə/ Equivale aproximadamente a la *e* de las palabras francesas *de* y *le* (por ejemplo: **alone, about**); también se encuentra este sonido en palabras deletreadas con: -e- (syst*e*m), -i- (eas*i*ly), -o- (gall*o*p), -u- (circ*u*s), -y- (mart*y*r).

e /ɛ/ Equivale aproximadamente a la *e* de *templo* y *perro* (por ejemplo: **edge, set, merry**); también se encuentra este sonido en palabras deletreadas con: a-, -a- (*a*ny, m*a*ny), -ai- (s*ai*d), -ay- (s*ay*s), -ea- (l*ea*ther), -ei- (h*ei*fer), -eo- (j*eo*pardy), -ie- (fr*ie*nd).

e /i/ Equivale aproximadamente a la *i* de *Chile* (por ejemplo: **be, equal, secret**); también se encuentra este sonido en palabras deletreadas con: ea- *(ea*ch, t*ea)*, -ee- (f*ee*, k*ee*p), -ei- (rec*ei*ve), -eo- (p*eo*ple), -ey (k*ey*), -ie- (f*ie*ld), -y (cit*y*).

i /ɪ/ Se pronuncia menos cerrada que la *i* de *Chile* (por ejemplo: **if, big, fit, mirror**); también se encuentra este sonido en palabras deletreadas con: e- (*E*ngland), -ee- (b*ee*n), -ei- (counterf*ei*t), -ia- (carr*ia*ge), -ie- (s*ie*ve), -o- (w*o*men), (b)u(s)- (b*u*siness), -y- (s*y*mpathetic).

i /ai/ Equivale aproximadamente a la *ai* de *aire, baile* (por ejemplo: **bite, ice, pirate**); también se encuentra este sonido en palabras deletreadas con: ais- (*ais*le), -ei- (h*ei*ght, st*ei*n), -eye- *(eye)*, -ie (p*ie*), -igh (h*igh*), is- (*is*land), -uy (b*uy*), -y (c*y*cle, sk*y*), -ye (l*ye*).

o /ou/ Se pronuncia más cerrada que la *o* de *supo* (por ejemplo: **hope, go, oh, over**); también se encuentra este sonido en palabras deletreadas con: -au- (m*au*ve), -aux (f*aux* pas), -eau (b*eau*), -ew (s*ew*), -oa- (r*oa*d), -oe (t*oe*), -oo- (br*oo*ch), -ot (dep*ot*), -ou- (s*ou*l), -ow (fl*ow*), -owe- *(owe)*.

o /ɔ/ Se pronuncia más cerrada que la *o* de *corre* (por ejemplo: **alcohol, order, raw**); también se encuentra este sonido en palabras deletreadas con: -a- (t*a*ll), -al- (w*al*k), au- (*au*thor, v*au*lt), -augh- (c*augh*t), -oa- (br*oa*d), -oo- (fl*oo*r), -ough- (s*ough*t).

oi /oi/ Equivqale aproximadamente a la *oy* de *doy* (por ejemplo: **oil, joint, voice**); también se encuentra este sonido en palabras deletreadas con: -awy- (l*awy*er), -oy- (b*oy*).

oo /ʊ/ Se pronuncia menos cerrada que la *u* de *insulto* (por ejemplo: **book, foot**); también se encuentra este sonido en palabras deletreadas con: -o- (w*o*lf), -ou- (t*ou*r), -u- (p*u*ll).

oo /u/ Se pronuncia más larga que la *u* de *susto* (por ejemplo: **too, ooze, fool**); también se encuentra este sonido en palabras deletreadas con: -eu- (man*eu*ver), -ew (gr*ew*), -o (wh*o*), -o. . .e (m*o*v*e*), -oe (can*oe*), -ou- (tr*ou*pe), -u. . .e (r*u*l*e*), -ue (fl*ue*), -ui- (s*ui*t).

ou /au/ Equivale aproximadamente a la *au* de *aurora* (por ejemplo: **loud, out**); también se encuentra este sonido en palabras deletreadas con -ow (br*ow*, c*ow*, pl*ow*).

u /iu/ Equivale aproximadamente a la *iu* de *ciudad* (por ejemplo: **cue, use, utility**); también se encuentra este sonido en palabras deletreadas con: -eau- (b*eau*ty), -eu- (f*eu*d), -ew (f*ew*), (h)u- (h*u*man), (h)u. . .e (h*u*g*e*), -iew (v*iew*), you *(you)*, yu. . .e *(yule)*.

u /ʌ/ Es sonido intermedio entre la *o* de *borro* y la *a* de *barro*, algo parecido a la pronunciación de la *eu* francesa de *peur;* (por ejemplo: **up, sun, mud**); también se encuentra este sonido en palabras deletreadas con: o- (*o*ther), -o- (s*o*n), -oe- (d*oe*s), o. . .e (l*o*v*e*), -oo- (bl*oo*d), -ou (tr*ou*ble).

Consonantes

b Se pronuncia igual que la *p* española salvo que en la pronunciación de la *b* suenan las cuerdas vocales. La *b* inglesa es más fuerte (más aspirada) que la española. Se encuentra en palabras escritas con *b* **(bed, amber, rub)** y también en palabras deletreadas con -bb- (ho*bb*y).

c Como la *c* española, lleva dos sonidos, /s/ y /k/. La /s/ se pronuncia igual que la *s* española y se encuentra en palabras deletreadas con ce- **(center)** y ci- **(city).** La /k/ es semejante a la *c* española cuando aparece delante de -a, -o, y -u *(católica, cómo, cuándo)* pero se pronuncia más fuerte (más aspirada). La /k/ se encuentra en palabras deletreadas con ca-, co-, y cu- (**cat, account, cut**).

ch Equivale aproximadamente a la *ch* española (por ejemplo: **chief, beach**); también se encuentra en palabras deletreadas con: -tch- (ca*tch*, bu*tch*er), -te- (righ*te*ous), -ti- (ques*ti*on), -tu- (na*tu*ral). A veces equivale a la /š/ de la palabra francese *chèrie* (**chef**), o a la /k/ de *cómo* (**character**).

d Equivale aproximadamente a la *d* de *onda* (por ejemplo: **do, odor, red**); también se encuentra en palabras deletreadas con -dd- (la*dd*er) y -de- (fa*de*). La *d* inglesa es siempre más fuerte (más aspirada) que la española y no se pronuncia nunca /ʤ/ como la *d* de *padre* o las *d*'s de *Madrid.*

f Equivale aproximadamente a la *f* española (por ejemplo: **feed, safe**); también se encuentra en palabras deletreadas con -ff- (mu*ff*in) y -fe (li*fe*).

g Equivale aproximadamente a la *g* de *globo* (por ejemplo: **give, fog**); también se encuentra en palabras deletreadas con -gg (egg), gh- (*gh*ost), y -gue (pla*gue*). La *g* cuando cae delante de -i y -e se pronuncia /ʤ/ (**George, gem, legitimate**). El sonido /ʤ/ es semejante a, pero más fuerte que, la *y* y la *ll* españolas de *yo* y *llevar.* Véase *j.*

h Se pronuncia más aspirada pero menos áspera que la *j* española en *jabón* (por ejemplo: **hit, hope**); tambièn se encuentra en palabras deletreadas con wh- (*wh*o).

j Equivale aproximadamente a la *y* de *yo* en su pronunciación enfática (p.ej. . . . *yo, y yo sólo soy el dueño aquí!*) o como la *y* de *cónyuge* en ciertas modalidades del español (por ejemplo: **just, joke**); también se encuentra en palabras deletreadas con: -dg- (ju*dg*e), -di- (sol*di*er), -ge (sa*ge*), -gg- (exa*gg*erate), gi- (*gi*n). La pronunciación de la *j* y de la *g* delante de -i y -e /ʤ/ es igual que la de la *ch* española, salvo que suenan las cuerdas vocales en la pronunciación del sonido /ʤ/.

k (Por ejemplo: **keep, make, token**) equivale a la *qui-* y *que* españolas pero se pronuncia más fuerte (más aspirada). La *k* inglesa no se pronuncia cuando cae delante de una *n* (**knife, knight, knee**).

l Se pronuncia aproximadamente como la *l* de *lago* (por ejemplo: **leap, sail**); también se encuentra en palabras deletreadas con -le (mi*le*) y -ll (ca*ll*).

m Equivale aproximadamente a la *m* española (por ejemplo: **more, drum, him, summer**). Tengan cuidado de pronunciar la *m* al final de una palabra igual que se pronuncia en medio de la palabra y de no convertir el sonido en *n*.

n Equivale aproximadamente a la *n* de *bueno* (por ejemplo: **now, sunny**); tambièn se encuentra en palabras deletreadas con gn- (*gn*at) y kn- (*kn*ife).

ng (Por ejemplo: **sing, Washington**) equivale aproximadamente a la *n* de *blanco*.

p (Por ejemplo: **pool, spool, supper, stop**) tras consonante equivale aproximadamente a la *p* española, pero lleva más aspiración. La *p* delante de una *s* (**psychologist, psyche**) no se pronuncia.

r Se pronuncia con la punta de la lengua elevada hacia el paladar (sin tocarlo) y doblada para atrás (por ejemplo: **red, hurry, near**); también se encuentra en palabras deletreadas con: -re (pu*re*), rh- (*rh*ythm), y wr- (*wr*ong).

s Equivale aproximadamente a la *s* de *salir,* pero algo más tensa y larga (por ejemplo: **see, kiss**).

sh Equivale aproximadamente a la *ch* de las palabras francesas *changer* and *chapeau* (por ejemplo: **ship, wash**); también se encuentra en palabras deletreadas con: -ce- (o*ce*an), -ch- (ma*ch*ine), -ci- (spe*ci*al), s(u)- (*s*ugar), -sci- (con*sci*ence), -si- (man*si*on), -ss- (ti*ss*ue, mi*ss*ion), -ti- (cap*ti*on).

t (Por ejemplo: **team, ten, steam, bit**) tras consonante equivale aproximadamente a la *t* española salvo con más aspiración; también se encuentra en palabras deletreadas con: -bt (dou*bt*), -cht (ya*cht*), -ed (talk*ed*), -ght (bou*ght*), -te (bi*te*), th- (*th*yme), -tt- (bo*tt*om), tw- (*tw*o).

th (Por ejemplo: **thin, ether, path**) equivale aproximadamente a la *z* española en el norte de España.

th (Por ejemplo: **that, the, either, smooth**) equivale aproximadamente a la *d* de *adoptar.*

v (Por ejemplo: **voice, river, live**) equivale aproximadamente a la *b* de *haba* pero es labiodental en vez de bilabial. La pronunciación de la *v* inglesa es igual que la de la *f,* salvo que suenan las cuerdas vocales en la pronunción de la *v.*

w (Por ejemplo: **west, witch, away**) equivale aproximadamente a la *u* de *puesto.*

y (Por ejemplo: **yes, beyond**) equivale aproximadamente a la *i* de *bien;* también se encuentra en palabras deletreadas con -i- (on*i*on, un*i*on), -j- (hallelu*j*ah), y -ll- (torti*ll*a).

z Tiene dos sonidos: /z/ y /zh/. La /z/, la más común (por ejemplo: **zoo, lazy, zone**), equivale aproximadamente a la *s* de *isla* y *mismo* en ciertas modalidades del español, pero con más sonoridad. Este sonido se pronuncia igual que la *s* española, salvo que en la pronunciación de la /z/ suenan las cuerdas vocales. Se encuentra el sonido /z/ en algunas palabras deletreadas con: -s- (ha*s*), -se (ri*se*), x- (*x*ylophone), y -zz- (bu*zz*ard, fu*zz*). El sonido /zh/ que se encuentra en **azure** y **brazier** equivale aproximadamente a la *ll* del español de la gente mayor de la cuidad de Buenos Aires (o sea, como la *j* de la palabra francesa *bonjour*). El sonido /zh/ también se encuentra en ciertas palabras deletreadas con -ge (gara*ge*, mira*ge*), -si- (vi*si*on), y su- (plea*su*re).

Pronunciation Symbols for the Sounds of Spanish

Símbolos de Pronunciacíon por los Sonidos del español

IPA Symbols Símbolos del AFI	Key Words Ejemplos	Key Words Ejemplos
a	**a**lbo, b**a**nco, cer**a**	f**a**ther, dep**a**rt
e	**e**sto, d**e**l, part**e**	r**ai**n, **eigh**t
i	**i**r, f**i**no, ad**i**ós, mu**y**	b**ee**t, conc**ei**ve
o	**o**ler, fl**o**r, gran**o**	teleph**o**ne, g**oa**l
u	**u**n, l**u**na, c**u**ento	f**oo**l, gr**ou**p
b	**b**ajo, **v**aca	**b**y, a**b**et
β	ha**b**lar, escri**b**ir, la**v**ar	
d	**d**ar, **d**esde, **d**os, **d**ueña	**d**eal, a**d**ept
ð	pe**d**ir, Pe**d**ro, ver**d**a**d**	**th**at, ga**th**er
f	**f**echa, a**f**ectar, gol**f**	**f**an, a**f**ter
g	**g**ato, **g**rave, **g**usto, lar**g**o	**g**arden, u**g**ly
h	**g**emir, **g**iro, **j**unta, ba**j**o, relo**j**es	**h**orse, lo**ch**
k	**c**acao, **c**laro, **c**ura, **c**uenta, **qu**e, **qu**into	**k**ind, a**c**tor
l	**l**ado, **l**ente, hab**l**a, pape**l**	**l**ot, a**l**tar
ʎ	**ll**amar, ca**ll**e, o**ll**a	mi**ll**ion, civi**l**ian
m	**m**al, a**m**or	**m**ore, co**mm**it
n	**n**ada, **n**uevo, ma**n**o, bie**n**	**n**ot, e**n**ter
ɲ	**ñ**aques, a**ñ**o	ca**ny**on, compa**ni**on
ŋ	a**n**gosto, au**n**que	ri**ng**, a**n**chor
p	**p**eso, gua**p**o	**p**ill, a**pp**laud
r	**r**eal, fa**r**o, debe**r**	**r**ice, ca**r**pet
s	**s**ala, e**s**pejo, ma**s**	**s**ay, cla**s**p
θ	**c**ena, ha**c**er, **c**ierto, **c**ine, **z**ar**z**uela, la**z**o, ve**z**	**th**in, my**th**
t	**t**ocar, es**t**ado, ceni**t**	**t**able, a**tt**rac**t**
y	**y**a, a**y**er	**y**ou, vo**y**age
tʃ	**ch**ica, mu**ch**o	**ch**ill, bat**ch**

Diphthongs

ai, ay	b**ai**le, h**ay**	h**igh**, r**ye**
au	**au**ditor, l**au**dar	**ou**t, r**ou**nd
ei	v**ei**nte, s**ei**s	**ai**m, r**ay**
eu	**eu**scaro, d**eu**da	
oi, oy	r**oi**do, h**oy**	c**oi**n, l**oy**al
ue	b**ue**na, s**ue**rte	s**wa**y, q**uai**nt
ie	m**ie**l, tamb**ie**n	f**ie**sta, p**ie**ta

The Basics of Standard Spanish Pronunciation

Whereas the fit between English spelling and pronunciation has for centuries been less than ideal (think, for example, of the various pronunciations of **-ough,** as in **although, bough, cough,** and **slough**), the fit between today's Spanish spelling and pronunciation is quite good, thanks to the regulatory efforts of the Spanish academies.

The following instructions thus take spelling as their starting point. Pronunciation is described in two ways: with phonetic symbols (enclosed in slashes) and by way of approximate comparisons with English. A wavy line separates variants (like **esnob** ~ **snob**). A stress mark (') means that the syllable following it is stressed (as in /re'lo/). An asterisk indicates a nonexistent form (like English ***llion**). A right-facing "arrow" (>), or "greater than" sign, means "became in Spanish" (as in English **rum** and French **rhum** > **ron** ~ **romo**).

As may be expected of a language that has been used for many centuries, over a vast area, and by many diverse people, Spanish is now pronounced in various ways. Of the many current pronunciations, two are offered as most suitable for speakers of Spanish as a second language. The two standards are identical to a large extent, differing chiefly with respect to the pronunciation of **c** before **e; c** before **i; z** in any position; and, optionally, **ll, g,** and **j.**

To the extent that the two standards differ, features belonging to just one of them are labeled either *Standard 1* or *Standard 2* below.

Features labeled *Standard 1* are accepted as standard in Spain but not in the Western Hemisphere. Features labeled *Standard 2* are accepted as standard in the Western Hemisphere but not in Spain. If you speak Spanish mostly with Spaniards or mostly with people from the Western Hemisphere, your choice of standard will thus be straightforward. If you speak with people from both areas, you can either try to master both standards or, if you want to follow just one of them no matter to whom you speak, pick Standard 2.

a is pronounced /a/, which is similar to the second vowel of the English interjection **aha!** and the vowel of the English interjection **ah,** although much shorter in duration. See also "Diphthongs and Triphthongs" below.

b has three pronunciations. At the beginning of an utterance, after /m/ (whether represented by **m** or by **n**), or after /n/ (whether represented by **n** or by **m**), the letter **b** is pronounced /b/, which is similar to the pronunciation of the first consonant of English **beach, broth, pebble,** etc. For example, in the sentence **Bulgaria envió a ambos embajadores en un barco japonés,** each of the four instances of **b** (and the one instance of **v**) is pronounced in this way.

At the end of a word, more than one pronunciation of **b** may be heard. For example, **club** may be /klub/, /kluβ/, or /klu/. Its plural, **clubs,** may be /klups/, /klus/, and possibly /kluβs/, unless the plural **clubes** is used, whose universal pronunciation is /kluβɛs/ (see the next paragraph for interpreting /β/, and **e** for interpreting /ɛ/). All of the foregoing holds for compounds of **club**, like **aeroclub**. In **esnob** ~ **snob**, the final **b** is pronounced /b/.

In all other positions (for example, **hablas, hablar,** and **habré**), **b** is pronounced /β/, a sound absent in English, which is made by bringing the lips close together without letting them touch each other (as if you were blowing dust away or blowing out a match or candle), expelling air through the mouth, and vibrating the vocal cords. This sound is thus similar to /v/ (as in English **very** and **vowel**), except that the latter is made by making the lower lip touch the upper teeth. English-speakers should not mistake Spanish /β/ for English /v/.

It follows from the foregoing that if the position of **b** in the utterance changes, its pronunciation may change. For example, when the word **baba** is pronounced in isolation, the first **b** is rendered /b/ and the second one /β/, but in the phrase **la baba,** the first **b** is no longer at the beginning of an utterance (nor is it preceded by the sounds /m/ or /n/), hence the phrase is pronounced /laβaβa/.

These rules of pronunciation also hold true for the letter **v,** which is pronounced /b/ at the beginning of words, and /β/ in the middle. See also **v.**

c has several pronunciations. If it is followed by **e** or **i,** the letter **c** is pronounced /θ/ in Standard 1 and /s/ in Standard 2. The pronunciation of /θ/ in Spanish is similar to that of **th** in English **thatch, think,** etc., but made with somewhat more protrusion of the tongue. The sound /s/ is similar to the pronunciation of **s** in English **say, simple,** etc.

Although Standard 1 has /θ/ for **c** before **e** or **i,** people who use that pronunciation will not be put off if they hear you pronounce the **c** as /s/, because the latter is widespread (though not standard) in Spain. In the Western Hemisphere, **c** before **e** or **i** is always pronounced /s/ and never /θ/. Speakers of Western Hemispheric Spanish will react to /θ/ either as "the correct pronunciation" ("though we don't use it") or as a pretentious pronunciation (unless it comes from people to the manner born, i.e., many Spaniards). Thus, whereas it is desirable though not obligatory that you use Standard 1 in Spain, you would be well advised to use only Standard 2 in the Western Hemisphere, where /θ/ is bound to elicit a sharp reaction of one kind or another (as sharp as British **drawing pin, lorry,** or **trunk call** instead of **thumbtack, truck,** and **long-distance call** would probably elicit in the United States).

ch, wherever it is found, is always pronounced as /tʃ/, which is similar to the pronunciation of **ch** in English **church, child,** etc.

If **c** ends a syllable (for instance, **accionista, facsimíl,** and **técnico**), **c** is pronounced as /k/. Spanish /k/ is similar to the pronunciation of **c** in English **escape, scandal,** etc. To achieve a good rendition of Spanish /k/, hold your open palm in front of your mouth and pronounce first **cape** and **coop,** then **escape** and **scandal.** When pronouncing the first two words, you felt a noticeable puff of air on your palm, but in the last two words you felt almost no puff at all. A noticeable puff of air accompanying a speech sound is called *aspiration;* sounds pronounced with aspiration are *aspirated,* and those pronounced without it are *unaspirated.* Spanish /k/ (like Spanish /p/ and /t/) is always unaspirated, wherever it occurs. Thus, you should have no trouble with Spanish **escapar** and **escandalo** because here /k/ occurs after /s/, and as an English speaker you will automatically pronounce it as unaspirated, just as you would the **c** of the English cognates of those words: **escape** and **scandal.** It is in other positions that you have to be careful not to aspirate: **claro, crear,** etc. (contrast them with their English cognates, both of which have an aspirated /k/: **clear, create**).

See also **k, ll** (under **l**), **q, s,** and **z.**

d has several pronunciations. At the beginning of an utterance, after /n/, or after /l/, this letter is pronounced /d/, which is similar to the pronunciation of **d** in English **dear, dust,** etc., with this difference: in the production of Spanish /d/, the tongue touches the lower edge of the upper front incisors.

When between two vowels, when preceded by a vowel and followed by **r,** or when at the end of a word and not preceded by **r** (as in **pedir, Pedro,** and

libertad), the letter **d** is pronounced /ð/, which is similar to the pronunciation of **th** in English **that, there,** etc., but less interdental than English /ð/ (in the production of the Spanish sound, the tip of the tongue gently touches the lower edge of the upper incisors).

It follows from the foregoing that if the position of **d** in the utterance changes, its pronunciation may change. Contrast, for example, these three utterances: (1) **Dinamarca mandó embajadores a doce países,** (2) **En Dinamarca viven unos cuantos americanos,** and (3) **Iremos a Dinamarca.** In (1), the **d** of **Dinamarca** is pronounced /d/ because it comes at the beginning of an utterance; in (2) the same **d** is also pronounced /d/ because it comes after /n/; but in (3) the same **d** is pronounced /ð/ because none of the conditions for pronouncing it /d/ is met. Similarly, when the word **dedo** is pronounced in isolation, the first **d** is rendered /d/ (and the second one /ð/), but in the phrase **mi dedo,** the first **d** is no longer at the beginning of an utterance (nor is it preceded by /n/ or /l/); hence the phrase is pronounced /miðeðo/.

e has two pronunciations. The instruction given in some books that **e** is pronounced /e/ when stressed and /ε/ when unstressed does not hold true for today's Spanish and may never have been an accurate description of its pronunciation in any variety of the language.

Here are better guidelines for **e** (except when it is part of a diphthong or triphthong):

If **e** is found in a syllable ending in a consonant (see "Syllabification" below), it is pronounced /ε/, which is similar to the pronunciation of **è** in French or to the vowel of **bet, let, met,** etc., as pronounced in Standard English, that is, with considerable lowering of the jaw, for example, **embaldosar, fresco, hablen,** and **mestizo.**

If **e** ends a syllable and the next one begins with **r, rr,** or **t,** it is pronounced /ε/, for instance, **pero, caballete** (the first **e**), **cerrar,** and **jinete.**

Otherwise, **e** is pronounced /e/, which is similar to the pronunciation of **é** in French, that is, the jaw is lowered only minimally (the closest English comes to having a sound like /e/ is the vowel of **ache, rake, stake,** etc.), for example, **caballete** (the second **e**), **hablé,** and **mesa.** In this dictionary, the sounds /e/ and /ε/ are both represented by /e/.

See also "Diphthongs and Triphthongs" below.

f is pronounced /f/, which is similar to the pronunciation of **f** in English **fate, feet,** etc., for example, **afectar, fecha, golf, golfo, ¡uf!.**

g has several pronunciations. At the beginning of an utterance and when followed by **a, o, u,** or a consonant letter except **n** (as in **gato, goma, gusto,** or **glaciar**), **g** is pronounced /g/, which is similar to the pronunciation of **g** in English **get, go, gumption,** etc.

At the beginning of a word and when followed by **n,** the letter **g** is silent (as in **gnomo**). That pronunciation is in fact so widespread and reputable that a **g**-less spelling is now acceptable and is in fact preferred in this dictionary (see "Miscellaneous" below).

When **g** occurs at the end of a syllable and is preceded by **n,** it is silent, as in **búmerang**. In older borrowings from other languages, that **g** was systematically or sometimes omitted, as in **sterling** > **esterlina, pudding** > **pudín.**

Before **e** or **i** (as in **gemir** and **gigante**), except if it comes at the end of a word, the letter **g** is pronounced /x/, which is absent in most varieties of current English. This sound is similar to the pronunciation of **ch** in German **Bach,** that of **ch** in Israeli Hebrew **zecher,** and that of **ch** in Scots English **loch, Lochaber,** etc. Press the back of the tongue against the soft palate, expel air (as if coughing), and do not vibrate the vocal chords. **g** before **e** or **i** can also be pronounced /h/, as in English **"house,"** which is common in Latin America and in southern Spain. In this dictionary, both /x/ and /h/ are represented by /h/.

If **g** ends a syllable that is not the last syllable of the word (as in **dogma** and the first syllable of **zigzag**), this letter is pronounced /g/. In such cases, the next syllable always begins with a consonant.

Otherwise, **g** is pronounced /ɣ/, a sound absent in English, which is made by bringing the back of the tongue close to the soft palate (without letting them touch), expelling air through the mouth, and vibrating the vocal chords. Examples are **hago** and **hígado.** In this dictionary, both sounds, /g/ and /ɣ/, are represented by /g/.

h is silent.

i is pronounced /i/, which is similar to the vowel of English **beet, feet, sheen,** etc., but shorter (for instance, **dicho, isla,** and **cursi**).

See also **y.**

j is almost always pronounced /x/, although a pronunciation as /h/ is also acceptable in parts of Latin America and southern Spain (see **g** for interpreting these symbols). A notable exception is **reloj,** which many speakers pronounce /re'lo/. That pronunciation of **reloj** is so widespread that **reló** is an alternate spelling of the singular form, but only in informal writing. In the plural, everyone pronounces /x/ or /h/ and therefore writes the **j: relojes.**

See **x.**

k, which is now found only in recent borrowings from other languages, is pronounced /k/ (see **c** for interpreting that symbol). The letter combination **ck** (as in **crack, flashback, shock, snack, stock**) is pronounced /k/.

l when not doubled is pronounced /l/, which is formed by putting the tip of the tongue against the sockets of the upper incisors, the remainder of the tongue lying flat. Spanish /l/ thus does not have the hollow sound of English /l/, in whose formation the back of the tongue rises toward the palate.

ll has two pronunciations, /ʎ/ and /y/, which vary by region and class rather than by placement within a word. /ʎ/, a sound similar to the Italian **gli,** has no real equivalent in English, although the **lli** of **million** comes close. While /λ/ is held to be the "correct" pronunciation by Spanish radio and television guidelines, it is almost never used in Latin America, except among some academics and the very wealthy. In Spain it is only heard in the northern regions of Castile. Much more common, and almost universally accepted today, is the pronunciation /y/, which is similar to our **y** in **yes** or **yam.**

In the Southern Cone of Latin America, a third pronunciation, /ʒ/ (like the French **Geneviève**), is also used.

m is pronounced /m/, which is similar to the pronunciation of **m** in English **make, might,** etc.

Traditionally, Spanish does not have /m/ at the end of a word when it is pronounced in isolation. However, a few words (all learned borrowings from other languages) end in **m** (for example, **álbum, factótum, ídem, médium, memorándum, ultimátum,** and **vademécum**), and that letter always appears in the Spanish names of many places outside Spanish-speaking areas, like **Bírmingham, Búckingham, Siam,** and **Vietnam.** Both /m/ and /n/ are heard in such words, depending on people's ability to pronounce /m/ at the end of a word (as more and more Spanish-speakers study other languages, they find it easier to produce that sound in that position) and their interest in maintaining the supposedly "correct" (i.e., non-Spanish) pronunciation of that letter.

n has several pronunciations. If immediately followed by a labial consonant (represented by **b, f, m, p,** or **v**) whether in the same word or in the next one, it is pronounced /m/ (as in the words **anfitrión, inmediato, anverso,** or the sentences **insiste en bucear, insiste en pelear,** and **en muchos casos hay más**). Since /m/ + /m/ is reduced to a single /m/, **en muchos casos** actually has just one /m/.

However, /m/ + /n/ (as in **insomne**) is not reduced.

Before /k/ or /g/ (as in **aunque** and **angosto**), **n** is pronounced /ŋ/, which is similar to the final consonant of **sing, long,** and **song** as pronounced in English.

In all other positions (as in **Anatolia, andan,** and **nombrar**), **n** is pronounced /n/, which is similar to the pronunciation of **n** in English **hand, near,** etc.

See also **m,** "Stress," and, "Miscellaneous" below.

ñ is pronounced /ɲ/, which is similar to the pronunciation of **ny** in English **canyon** or **ni** in English **onion.**

o is pronounced similarly to the **o** in the English words **tote** and **gloat.** English speakers, however, must be careful not to end the pronunciation of this vowel with an "off-glide" (an "off-glide," in this case, would close the **o** into a **u** sound at the end of the vowel). Thus, the Spanish **no** and the English **no** are not exactly alike, as the Spanish ends in a pure /o/ sound, while the English "off-glides" into a /u/, producing /nou/.

p, where it is pronounced, stands for /p/, which is similar to the pronunciation of **p** in English **space, spare, spook,** etc., but different from that of **p** in English **pike, peak, poke,** etc., in that it is not aspirated (see **c** for definitions of aspirated and unaspirated sounds).

Spanish **ps** at the beginning of a word is pronounced /s/.

q is always followed by **ue** or **ui.** The sequence **que** is pronounced /ke/ and **qui** is pronounced /ki/ (for example, **quince**).

To represent the sound sequences /kue/ and /kui/, Spanish has **cue** and **cui** respectively (as in **cueva** and **cuidar**).

Because **q** is always followed by **u,** if Spanish-speakers borrow words containing just **q** from other languages, that letter is changed to **k.** Thus, the Spanish names of Iraq and Qatar, for example, are **Irak** and **Katar.**

r has two pronunciations. At the beginning of a word or when it comes after **l, n,** or **s** (for example, **reir, alrededor, enrojecer,** and **Israel**), this letter has the same pronunciation as **rr** (see below).

In all other positions, **r** is pronounced with one flip of the upper part of the tongue against the sockets of the upper incisors (for instance, **leer, para, pera, pero, tercero,** and **treinta**).

rr is pronounced with a trill (several flips) of the upper front part of the tongue against the sockets of the upper incisors (for instance, **parra, perra, perro,** and **sierra**). Thus, **para** and **parra** are different words, with different meanings. The same applies to **caro** and **carro, pera** and **perra, pero** and **perro, torero** and **torrero,** and other pairs of words.

s has several pronunciations. When it represents the plural ending of nouns recently borrowed from other languages, it is silent in certain words, like **cabarets, carnets, complots, conforts, superávits, tíckets, trusts, vermuts.**

Before the letters **b, v, d, g** (but only when the letter is not followed by **e** or **i**), **l, m, n,** or **r** (whether any of those eight letters appear in the same word as **s** or they appear in the next word), you have an alternative in both standards if **s** is not the last letter of the word: it may be pronounced /z/ (a sound similar to the pronunciation of **z** in English **zebra, zoo,** etc.) or /s/ (see **c** for interpreting that symbol): **esbelto, esdrújulo, esgrimir, isla, esmalte, Israel, los baúles, los varones, los dedos, los guantes, los lagos, los maestros, los nervios, los ratones,** etc. If **s** is the last letter, only /s/ is found (for instance, in the family name **Pons**).

If **s** is followed by **r** (whether in the same word or in the next one), besides the two pronunciations suggested above, /s/ or /z/, a third possibility is not to pronounce the **s** at all and, as compensation, trill the **r** more. The word **Israel** (and its derivatives) thus has three pronunciations: /isrrael/, /izrrael/, and /irrrael/.

Otherwise, **s** is pronounced /s/ (as in **ese, especial, hablas, hasta, insistir, seco**).

If **s** is followed by **h,** the foregoing paragraph applies, except in the case of Spanish words recently borrowed from other languages or words modeled on such recently borrowed words, in which **sh** constitutes a unit, to be pronounced /ʃ/ (a sound similar to the pronunciation of **sh** in English **shall, sheet, should,** etc.). Thus, in **deshacer,** an old Spanish word not recently borrowed from another language, the instructions about **s** apply and the **h** is silent (hence the first two syllables of that word are /desa/), whereas in **riksha, sh** is pronounced /ʃ/.

See also **b, c, t, z,** and "Syllabification" below.

t is pronounced /t/, which is similar to the pronunciation of **t** in English **stoop, stake, steer,** etc., but different from that of **t** in English **take, teak, took,** etc., in that it is less aspirated (see **c**).

The Spanish /t/ is made by touching the tip of the tongue against the upper incisors (in contrast to English /t/, in whose production the tongue touches the gums). In two positions, **t** may not be pronounced as described above. First, before **l** or **m** in the same word (as in **atleta, aritmético,** and **ritmo**) you have an alternative: **t** may be pronounced as described or it may be pronounced /ð/ (see **d** for interpreting that symbol).

Second, the **t** at the end of a word may be silent. Probably many, most, or all Spanish-speakers pronounce it in **cenit, déficit, fagot, mamut, superavít,** and **el Tíbet** ~ **el Tibet,** whereas in other words the **t** is silent, for instance **cabaret, carnet, complot, tícket, trust,** and **vermut,** which are pronounced as if written ***cabaré, *carné, *compló, *tique, *trus,** and ***vermú** (the plurals are pronounced identically to their singulars). In still other words you have an alternative: **confort** is pronounced either /kom'for/ or /kom'fort/ (the plural **conforts** has both variants too).

u has two pronunciations. In the combinations **gue, gui, que,** and **qui,** the letter **u** is silent, for example, **guedeja** /geðeha/, **quedar** /keðar/, and **quien** /kien/ (see **q** and **e** on the pronunciation of those letters).

In all other cases, it is pronounced /u/, which is similar to the vowel sound of English **who** and **cool.** Thus, **puesto** and **seudonónimo,** for example, are pronounced /puesto/ and /seuðonónimo/.

v has two pronunciations. At the beginning of an utterance or after **n** (which in this position is pronounced /m/), the letter **v** is pronounced /b/, which is similar to the first consonant of English **beach, broth,** etc. In all other positions, this letter is pronounced /β/ (see **b** for interpreting that symbol). For example, in the sentence **¿Es verdad que en el anverso de la medalla se ve un pavo real?,** the second and sixth words have /b/ and the eleventh and thirteenth have /β/.

The instructions for pronouncing **b** and those for pronouncing **v** are identical (depending on the position of those letters in the utterance), as a consequence of which pairs of words like **baca** and **vaca** or **hube** and **uve** are homophones in today's Spanish and, as a further consequence of which, if you hear /b/ or /β/, you cannot tell whether it is to be represented by **b** or by **v** unless you know how to spell the word.

See also **b.**

w, which is found only in borrowings from Germanic languages and French, has several pronunciations. In several words, it is pronounced as if it were **b** or **v** and in such cases alternate spellings with **v** are found too: **wagneriano ~ vagneriano, Westfalia ~ Vestfalia.** The forms with **v** are preferable.

In at least a few words, **w** is pronounced /w/ (a sound similar to the first sound of English **win** and **won**), and for one of them an alternate spelling with **u** exists: **Malawi, Taiwán, Zimbabwe.**

In **whisky,** the letter combination **wh** is pronounced /w/ by those who want to show off their knowledge of English or, alternatively, /gw/.

x has several pronunciations. If **x** occurs before a consonant (as in **experiencia, extremidad,** and **mixto**), pronounce it /ks/. That pronunciation is probably the most frequent in words beginning with the prefix **ex-** followed by a consonant, for example **excelente,** widely pronounced /eksselente/ in Latin America, or /eksθelente/ in Castile.

If **x** occurs between vowels, you have an alternative in certain words (**examen** and **exiguo,** for example, may be pronounced with /ks/ or /gz/, but not in others (for instance, all Spanish-speakers, it seems, now pronounce **sexo** with /ks/).

At the end of a word, the pronunciation of **x** is in flux. In **ántrax, Benelux, dux, fénix, látex,** and **tórax,** /ks/ seems to be the most frequent if not universal pronunciation today, although /s/ is also heard.

At least some exceptions to those pronunciations are heard in words of Native American origin: for example, in **México** and **mexicano,** the **x** is now always pronounced /x/ (those are the spellings official and universal in Mexico; elsewhere, **Méjico** and **mejicano** are used); in **Xochimilco** (a Mexican place name), the **x** is always pronounced /s/.

Further exceptions are certain given and family names, which are found in two variants: one preserving a now archaic spelling with **x** (like **Xavier** and **Ximénez**) and the other spelled in modern fashion with **j** (**Javier** and **Jiménez**). Here, **x** is pronounced /h/, that is, just like **j.**

y has several pronunciations. In the word **y,** it is pronounced /i/ (see **i** for interpreting that symbol).

When it represents the first or last segment of a diphthong or triphthong (see "Diphthongs and Triphthongs" below), as in **ya, yegua, yunque, ley, rey, soy,** and **Paraguay,** the letter **y** is pronounced /y/ (see **ll** for interpreting that symbol).

In certain varieties of Spanish, **y** is pronounced with more occlusion, so that it has come to be close to /ʒ/ if not actually that sound (see **ll** for interpreting the latter symbol); and in still other varieties it is pronounced with so much occlusion that is has come to be close to /dʒ/ if not actually that (/dʒ/ is similar to the first consonant of English **Jacob, Jerusalem, Jew,** etc.)

Certain family names have two spelling variants, an archaic one with **y** and one spelled in modern fashion with **i** (like **Yglesias ~ Iglesias).** Here, **y** is pronounced /i/, that is, just like **i.**

z has several pronunciations. In Standard 1, you have an alternative: (1) In all positions, pronounce it /θ/ (see **c** for interpreting that symbol). Or, (2) Before the letters **b, v, d, g, l, m, n,** or **r** (whether in the same word or in the next one), pronounce it /ð/ (see **d** for interpreting that symbol), and in all other positions pronounce it /θ/.

In Standard 2, you have an alternative: (3) In all positions, pronounce it /s/ (see **c** for interpreting that symbol). Or, (4) Before the letters **b, v, d, g, l, m, n,** or **r** (whether in the same word or in the next one), pronounce it /z/, and in all other positions pronounce it /s/.

Diphthongs and Triphthongs

Spanish has fifteen diphthongs and eight triphthongs.

Eight of the diphthongs begin with a semivowel:

ia /ia/ is spelled **ya** at the beginning of a word, e.g., **desahuciar, yámbico.**

ua /ua/, e.g., **guardar**.

ie /ie/ is spelled **ye** at the beginning of a word, e.g., **agüero, bien, higiene, siete, yema.**

ue /ue/ is spelled **üe** after **g** that is not pronounced /h/, e.g., **huelga, hueste, huevo, vergüenza.**

io /io/ e.g., **biombo, piojo.** The spelling **io** at the beginning of a word is an imitation of Greek.

uo /uo/, e.g., **arduo**.

iu /iu/ is spelled **yu** at the beginning of a word, e.g., **yuca, yugo, triunfo.**

ui /ui/ (spelled **uy** in **muy**), e.g., **cuidar, muy.** For **uy** representing /uy/, see **uy** in the next section.

Take care to pronounce diphthongs beginning with a semivowel as diphthongs and not as two syllables. Thus, whereas English **barrio** has three syllables, Spanish **barrio** has two (**ba-rrio**), pronounced /barrio/.

Seven of the diphthongs end in a semivowel:

ai /ai/ is spelled **ay** at the end of most words; rarely, **ay** is found in the middle of a word, e.g., **aimará ~ aymará, hay, Raimundo, Seychelles.** If **ay** occurs before a vowel in the same word, it represents not a diphthong but /a/ + /y/, and each of those sounds belongs to a different syllable (thus, **aya** and **haya** for example are syllabified **a-ya** and **ha-ya).**

au /au/, e.g., **caudillo**.

ei is almost always pronounced /ey/ and is almost always spelled **ey** at the end of a word, e.g., **reina, rey.** A pronunciation exception is **reir,** which is pronounced as if it is spelled ***reír.** If **ey** occurs before a vowel in the same word, it represents not a diphthong but /e/ + /y/, and each of those sounds belongs to a different syllable (thus, **reyes** and **leyenda** for instance are syllabified **re-yes** and **le-yen-da**).

eu /eu/, e.g., **seudonónimo**.

oi is almost always pronounced /oi/ and is spelled **oy** at the end of a word, e.g., **hoy**, and in certain family names in other positions too (like **Goytisolo**). A pronunciation exception is **oir,** which is pronounced as if spelled ***oír.** If **oy** occurs before a vowel in the same word, it represents not a diphthong but /o/ + /y/ and each of those sounds belongs to a different syllable (thus, **Goya** is syllabified **Go-ya**).

uy, which always occurs at the end of a word, is almost always pronounced /ui/ (as in **¡huy!, Jujuy**). The exception is **muy,** whose pronunciation is given in the previous section. If **uy** occurs before a vowel in the same word, it represents not a diphthong but /u/ + /y/ and each of those sounds belongs to a different syllable (thus, **cuyo** and **tuyas** are syllabified **cu-yo** and **tu-yas**).

The triphthongs are:
iai /iai/ e.g., **despreciáis.**
iau /iau/ e.g., **miau.**
iei /iei/ e.g., **desprecieís.**
uai /uai/ (spelled **uay** at the end of a word), e.g., **evaluáis, Uruguay.**
uau /uau/ e.g., **guau.**
uei /uei/ (spelled **uey** at the end of a word), e.g., **evaluéis, buey.**

Syllabification

Spanish is a consonant-vowel language, that is, syllables preferably end in a vowel (though many exceptions are found). Therefore, a single consonant and the vowel following it usually form a syllable or, expressed otherwise, a single consonant between two vowels usually goes with the following vowel (thus, **ba-jo, ad-he-sión**). Since **ch, ll, ñ,** and **rr** represent a single consonant, the syllabification is, for example, **mu-cha-cho, ha-llar, ni-ño, ba-rrio,** and **haz-me-rreír.**

The consonant clusters **bl, cl, dl, fl, gl, pl, tl, br, cr, dr, fr, gr, pr,** and **tr** form a syllable with the following vowel, for instance, **ha-blar, a-cla-rar, a-flo-jar, a-glo-me-rar, a-pla-zar, a-tle-ta, a-bra-zar, a-cre-di-tar, a-dre-de, a-fran-ce-sar, a-gre-gar,** and **a-pren-der.**

When representing /ʃ/, **sh** is not divided, whereas if a consonant letter + **h** is found in the middle of a word and the **h** is silent, the **h** begins a new syllable: **al-ha-ra-ca, clor-hi-dra-to, des-hi-dra-tar, in-hu-ma-ción.**

All other clusters of two consonants between vowels (including diphthongs and triphthongs) are usually divided, so that the first consonant belongs to the preceding syllable and the second consonant to the following syllable, for example, **a-cos-tar-se, ac-tuar, cuer-do, en-car-gar, es-la-vo, fras-co, Is-ra-el, llan-ta, per-di-ción, sol-da-du-ra,** and **der-vi-che.** Subject to that rule are also instances of double **c** or **n,** as in **per-fec-ción** and **en-ne-gre-cer.**

If a cluster of three or more consonants stands between vowels, the last two consonants are usually **bl, cl, fl, gl, pl, tl, br, cr, dr, fr, gr, pr,** or **tr** and they go with the following syllable, for instance, **tem-blar, ten-dré, ex-plo-tar, tem-pra-no.**

If a cluster of three or more consonants stands between vowels and if the second consonant is **s,** the **s** goes with the preceding syllable, for example **ins-tan-te** and **pers-pec-ti-va.**

If one vowel follows another and they do not constitute a diphthong (see above), they belong to separate syllables, for instance, **ma-es-tro, cre-o, le-er, to-a-lla.** Accordingly, if **i** or **u** (which represent respectively /i/ or /u/ in diphthongs and triphthongs) represents a vowel, it belongs in a separate syllable and that fact is indicated by a stress mark. Thus, **ahínco** (three syllables: **a-hín-co**), **búho** (two syllables: **bú-ho**), **desahúcio** (four syllables: **de-sa-hú-cio**), **traído** (three syllables: **tra-í-do**), **prohíbo** (three syllables: **pro-hí-bo**), **Raúl** (two syllables: **Ra-úl**), **haría** (three syllables: **ha-rí-a**), **haríais** (three syllables: **ha-rí-ais**), etc.

If **y** is preceded and followed by a vowel, it forms a diphthong with the following one and therefore belongs in the following syllable, for instance **ca-yó, tu-yo, cre-yó.** In fact, all diphthongs and triphthongs (see the list above) form syllables of their own. In contrast, identical contiguous vowels (as in **creer**) and vowels that do not form diphthongs or triphthongs (as in **leal**), as well as diphthongs or triphthongs dissolved by the stress mark (see the examples from **ahinco** to **haríais** in the previous paragraph), form separate syllables (thus, **cre-er, le-al,** etc.).

It is permissible but not obligatory to set aside the foregoing rules in the case of prefixes, which one may consider as forming syllables of their own (whether or not such would be the case if the rules were followed) or which one may subject to the rules. For example, **ab-ro-ga-ción** or **a-bro** . . ., **des-a-bro-char** or **de-sa** . . ., **ex-a-cer-ba-ción** or **e-xa** . . ., **sub-li-mar** or **su-bli** . . . (in each pair, the first variant reflects treatment of the prefix as a syllable in its own right, no matter what the rules should require, and the second variant shows syllabification when the rules are applied). The same applies to solid compounds: **no-so-tros, vos-o-tras** or **vo-so-tras,** etc.

The foregoing paragraph notwithstanding, the rules must be followed with respect to a succession of three consonant letters, the second of which is **s,** in which case **s** belongs with the preceding, not the following letter (thus, as already noted, **ins-tan-te, pers-pect-ti-va,** not **in-st** . . ., **per-sp** . . .) and with respect to prefixes if the first letter immediately following them is **h** (thus, **des-ha-cer** and **des-hi-dra-tar,** not **de-sha** . . . or **de-shi** . . .).

Stress

Most Spanish words have only one primary stress, which can be determined from the spelling according to these rules:

(1) If a word is spelled with a stress mark, stress the syllable in which it is found (like **águila, bíceps, fórceps, hablarán, Martínez**).

(2) If a word contains no stress mark:

[2.A] Stress the last syllable if the word ends in:

[2.A.i] a vowel letter + **y** (like **convoy, Uruguay, virrey**),

[2.A.ii] a consonant letter other than **n** or **s** (like **consentir, David, lateral**),

[2.A.iii] **n** not preceded by a vowel letter (like **Isern**),

[2.A.iv] **s** not preceded by a vowel letter (like **Fontanals, Casals**).

[2.B] Stress the next-to-last syllable if the word ends in:

[2.B.i] a vowel letter other than **y** (like **casi, habla, hable, hablo, fatuo, patria, sitio**),

[2.B.ii] a vowel letter + **n** (like **consienten, hablan**),

[2.B.iii] a vowel letter + **s** (like **consientes, hablas**).

The triplets **árbitro, arbitro, arbitró; público, publico, publicó; término, termino, terminó; tráfago, trafago, trafagó;** and **válido, valido, validó** illustrate several possibilities.

Miscellaneous

It is noted above that /m/ + /m/, /n/ + /n/, /p/ + /p/, and /s/ + /s/ are respectively reduced to one /m/, /p/, and /s/. Since the number of instances of /s/ + /s/ is not the same in all varieties of Spanish, the number of reductions to /s/ varies accordingly. For example, **absceso** is pronounced /apseso/ only where **c** before **e** (or **i**) is pronounced /s/ (otherwise it is rendered /apθeso/); see also **excelente** in the remarks on **x.**

Reduction of identical contiguous sounds (whether vowels or consonants) is widespread in Spanish, whether within a word or between two words. Thus, /a/ + /a/ is reduced to /a/ both in the word **portaaviones** and in a phrase like **a ambos;** or, /e/ + /e/ is reduced to /e/ in the word **sobreexcitar.** The spellings **guardagujas, guardalmacén, remplazar, sobrentender,** etc., are in fact used too and they are preferable. In many cases, only spellings reflecting a reduction are now found, for example, **aprensión, prensil,** and **reprensible** (contrast those forms with their English cognates: **apprehension, prehensile,** and **reprehensible**).

English, especially British English, is a stress-timed language (it has a rhythm in which stressed syllables tend to occur at regular intervals of time, regardless of the number of intervening unstressed syllables) whereas Spanish is a syllable-timed language (with rhythm in which syllables are approximately equal in duration and thus tend to follow one another at regular intervals). Consequently, speakers of English, especially British English, tend to reduce unstressed syllables (as in the British pronunciation of **momentary, pattern, secretary**), whereas Spanish-speakers tend to pronounce each syllable distinctly and do not often slur over any of them. Spanish-speakers thus often react to English-accented Spanish as one in which **se comen las vocales** 'the vowels are swallowed up' and speakers of English (especially British English) tend to react to Spanish-accented English as "overly precise." To get an idea of the difference between stress- and syllable-timed languages, contrast American and British pronunciations of **momentary** and **secretary:** Americans pronounce each syllable of those words with more or less the same degree of distinctiveness, whereas the British pronounce only the first syllable distinctly and slur over the others; thus, American English is more syllable-timed and British English more stress-timed. To pronounce Spanish correctly, English-speakers should therefore give each vowel its full value.

Formerly, in the Spanish-speaking world, the pronunciation and spelling of words borrowed from other languages were routinely changed so that they conformed to Spanish norms. Thus for example, **bowline** > **bolina, coolie** > **culi, goal** > **gol,** and **kerosene** > **kerosen.**

Now, however, the trend is to retain non-Spanish spellings, though not necessarily non-Spanish pronunciations, with the result that the good fit between the Spanish spelling and pronunciation is in certain words absent.

List of Abbreviations Used in This Dictionary

a adjective
Abbr. abbreviation
acc accusative
adv adverb
Aer. aeronautics
Agr. agriculture
Anat. anatomy
Archit. architecture
Archeol. archeology
art. article
art art
Astron. astronomy
Astrol. astrology
Auto. automobiles
aux auxiliary
Biol. biology
Bot. botany
Cards. card games
Chem. chemistry
Com. commerce
Compar. comparative
condit conditional
conjunc conjunction
Culin. culinary
Dance. dancing
dat dative
dim diminutive
Eccl. ecclesiastical
Educ. education
Elec. electricity
Engin. engineering
Ent. entomology
Euph. euphemism
f feminine
Fig. figurative
Fig. Inf. used figuratively in informal speech or writing
fut future
gen generally; genitive
Geog. geography
Geol. geology
Geom. geometry
Gram. grammar
Gym. gymnastics
Herald. heraldry
Hist. history
Ichth. ichthyology
imperf imperfect
impers impersonal
indic indicative
indef art indefinite article
Inf. informal
infin infinitive
insep inseparable
interj interjection, exclamation
interr interrogative
Ironic. ironical
irr irregular
Law. law
Ling. linguistics
Lit. literature
m masculine
Mas. masonry
Math. mathematics
Mech. mechanics
Med. medical
Metall. metallurgy
mf masculine or feminine
Mil. military
Mineral. mineralogy
Mus. music
Myth. mythology
n noun
Naut. nautical
Nav. naval
neut neuter
Obs obsolete
Opt. optics
Ornith. ornithology
part participle
Pers. personal; person
Pharm. pharmacy
Philos. philosophy
Phonet. phonetics
Photo. photography
Phys. physics
Physiol. physiology
pl plural
Poet. poetic
Polit. political
Polit. Econ. political economy
poss possessive
prep preposition
pres present
Print. printing
pron pronoun
Psychol. psychology
Radio. radio
Rail. railway
Sew. sewing
sing singular
Spirit. spiritualism
Sports. sports
subjunc subjunctive
Superl superlative
Surg. surgery
Surv. surveying
Tan. tanning
Theat. theater
Theol. theology
v aux auxiliary verb
vi intransitive verb
vr reflexive verb
vt transitive verb
West. Hem. Western Hemispheric Spanish
Zool. zoology

Spanish-English Dictionary

a /a/ *f*, name of the letter A

a /a/ *prep* to; at; on; by; in, into; up to; according to; if, etc. 1. Denotes the direct complement of verb before objects representing specified persons or animals, personified nouns, pronouns referring to specific persons (**alguien, entrambos, cualquiera,** etc.), demonstrative or relative pronouns, collective nouns representing persons (**el público, la muchedumbre,** etc.), names of countries, cities, rivers, etc., except where these invariably take the def. art., e.g. *Dejé a Varsovia,* I left Warsaw, *but Dejé el Perú,* I left Peru. 2. Introduces indirect obj. when this is a noun governed by a verb implying motion, or an emphatic pers. pron., e.g. *Nos conviene a ti y a mí,* It suits both you and me. It is also used before indirect obj. to avoid ambiguity when there is both an indirect and direct obj. 3. Denotes the complement of verb when this is an infin., e.g. *Enseñó a pintar a María,* He taught Mary to paint. 4. Indicates direction or destination, e.g. *Vamos a Edimburgo,* We are going to Edinburgh. 5. Signifies location, or point of time when action takes place, e.g. *Vinieron a las doce.* They came at twelve o'clock. 6. Describes position of persons or things, e.g. *Se sentaron a la puerta,* They sat down at the door. *La casa queda a la derecha,* The house is on the right. 7. Denotes interval of time or place between one thing and another, e.g. *de tres a cinco de la tarde,* from three to five in the afternoon, *de calle a calle,* from street to street. 8. Expresses manner of action, e.g. *a la francesa,* in the French way, *bordado a mano,* embroidered by hand. 9. Indicates rate or price, e.g. *a cuatro pesetas la libra,* at four pesetas the lb. 10. Indicates difference or comparison, e.g. *Va mucho de querer a hacer,* There's a difference between wishing and doing. 11. Sometimes is synonymous with *hasta, según, hacia* and governs almost all parts of speech. Has many idiomatic uses. 12. Before infin. sometimes has conditional sense, e.g. *A haber sabido las noticias no lo hubiéramos hecho,* If we had heard the news we would not have done it. 13. With nouns and adjectives forms adverbial phrases, e.g. *poco a poco,* little by little, *a veces,* sometimes, *a ciegas,* blindly, etc. *A* + *el* becomes *al,* e.g. *al rey,* to the king. *Al* + infin. means when or on, e.g. *al marcharme yo,* when I left (on my leaving)

abacería /aβaθe'ria; aβase'ria/ *f*, grocery shop

abacero /aβa'θero; aβa'sero/ **(-ra)** *n* grocer

ábaco /'aβako/ *m*, *Archit.* abacus; counting frame

abad /a'βað/ *m*, abbot

abadesa /aβa'ðesa/ *f*, abbess

abadía /aβa'ðia/ *f*, abbacy; abbey

abajamiento /a,βaha'miento/ *m*, lowering; letting down

abajar /aβa'har/ *vt* to lower

abajo /a'βaho/ *adv* under; underneath; below; down. Used immediately after noun in adverbial phrases, e.g. *cuesta a., escalera a.,* downhill, downstairs —*interj* Down with! e.g., *¡A. el rey!* Down with the king! *venirse a.,* to fall down; *Fig.* collapse

abalanzamiento /aβa,lanθa'miento; aβa,lansa'miento/ *m*, balancing; rushing upon; dashing

abalanzar /aβalan'θar; aβalan'sar/ *vt* to balance; impel violently; —*vr* throw oneself upon; attack, rush upon; (*with prep a*) rush into, risk. **Se abalanzó hacia ellos,** He rushed toward them

abalorio /aβa'lorio/ *m*, glass bead; bead work

abanderado /aβande'raðo/ *m*, standardbearer; (Argentina) valedictorian

abanderar /aβande'rar/ *vt* to register (a ship)

abanderizar /aβanderi'θar; aβanderi'sar/ *vt* to organize in groups; —*vr* band together

abandonado /aβando'naðo/ *a* deserted; forlorn; helpless; indolent, careless; slovenly

abandonamiento /a,βandona'miento/ *m*, desertion; forlornness; helplessness; carelessness; slovenliness

abandonar /aβando'nar/ *vt* to forsake, desert; neglect; leave; give up; renounce; —*vr* neglect oneself; grow discouraged; (*with prep a*) give oneself over to

abandono /aβan'dono/ *m*, abandonment; defenselessness; forlornness; dilapidation; renunciation; neglect; slovenliness; debauchery

abanicar /aβani'kar/ *vt* to fan

abanico /aβa'niko/ *m*, fan; anything fan-shaped; *Inf.* sword; railway signal; *Naut.* derrick. **en a.,** fan-shaped

abaniqueo /aβani'keo/ *m*, fanning; swinging, oscillation; gesticulation

abaratar /aβara'tar/ *vt* to cheapen, make less expensive; —*vr* fall in price

abarca /a'βarka/ *f*, leather sandal, worn chiefly in the Basque provinces

abarcador /aβarka'ðor/ **(-ra)** *n* one who clasps or embraces; monopolist

abarcadura /aβarka'ðura/ *f*, **abarcamiento** /aβarka'miento/ *m*, inclusion; scope

abarcar /aβar'kar/ *vt* to clasp, encircle; include, comprise; undertake, attempt; monopolize

abarquillar /aβarki'ʎar; aβarki'yar/ *vt* to shape into a roll; roll; curl

abarracar /aβarra'kar/ **(se)** *vi* and *vr Mil.* to go into barracks

abarrancadero /aβarranka'ðero/ *m*, rough road; ravine, precipice; *Fig.* difficult situation

abarrancar /aβarran'kar/ *vt* to ditch; make a ravine; —*vr* fall into a pit; stick (in the mud, etc.); get into difficulties; *Naut.* run aground

abastar /aβas'tar/ see **abastecer**

abastecedor /aβasteθe'ðor; aβastese'ðor/ **(-ra)** *a* provisioning, supplying —*n* provider; purveyor, supplier; caterer

abastecer /aβaste'θer; aβaste'ser/ *vt irr* to supply, provide; purvey. See **conocer**

abastecimiento /aβasteθi'miento; aβastesi'miento/ *m*, providing; supply, provision; catering; supplies

abasto /a'βasto/ *m*, provisions, food; *Com.* supply —*adv* plentifully, abundantly

abatanar /aβata'nar/ *vt* to full (cloth)

abate /a'βate/ *m*, abbé

abatido /aβa'tiðo/ *a* dejected, depressed; spiritless; discouraged; crushed, humbled; *Com.* depreciated

abatimiento /aβati'miento/ *m*, dejection, depression; humiliation; discouragement; falling; lowering; (*Aer. Naut.*) drift

abatir /aβa'tir/ *vt* to knock down; overthrow; demolish; lower, take down; droop; humiliate; discourage; *Naut.* dismantle; —*vi* (*Naut. Aer.*) drift; —*vr* be despondent, despair; humble oneself; swoop down (of birds). **a. el vuelo,** to fly down

ABC /aβe'θe; aβe'se/ *m*, ABCs (e.g. *el ABC de la física,* the ABCs of physics)

abdicación /aβðika'θion; aβðika'sion/ *f*, abdication

abdicar /aβði'kar/ *vt* to abdicate; revoke, cancel; give up (rights, opinions)

abdomen /aβ'ðomen/ *m*, abdomen

abdominal /aβðomi'nal/ *a* abdominal

abecé /aβe'θe; aβe'se/ *m*, ABCs

abecedario /aβeθe'ðario; aβese'ðario/ *m*, ABC, alphabet; reading book, primer

abedul /aβe'ðul/ *m*, birch tree; birch wood

abeja /a'βeha/ *f*, bee. **a. maestra,** queen bee. **a. obrera,** worker

abejar /aβe'har/ *m*, beehive

abejero /aβe'hero/ **(-ra)** *n* beekeeper

abejón /aβe'hon/ *m*, drone; hornet

abejorro /aβe'horro/ *m*, bumblebee

abellacar /aβeʎa'kar; aβeya'kar/ *vt* to make a rogue of; —*vr* become a rogue

aberración /aβerra'θion; aβerra'sion/ *f*, deviation; error, lapse; (*Astron. Phys. Biol.*) aberration

abertura /aβer'tura/ *f*, opening; aperture, gap, hole; fissure, cleft; mountain pass; naturalness, frankness

abeto /a'βeto/ *m*, yew-leaved fir

abetunado /aβetu'naðo/ *a* bituminous

abiertamente /aβierta'mente/ *adv* openly; frankly.

abierto /a'βierto/ *a* free, unobstructed; open, not enclosed; open, full-blown (flowers); frank, sincere —*adv* openly

abigarrado /aβiga'rraðo/ *a* variegated; varied; speckled

abigarrar /aβiga'rrar/ *vt* to variegate; vary; speckle; fleck; spot; dapple

abigotado /aβigo'taðo/ *a* having a thick moustache

abintestato /aβintes'tato/ *a Law.* intestate

abiselar /aβisel'ar/ *vt* to bevel

abismal /aβis'mal/ *a* abysmal

abismar /aβis'mar/ *vt* to plunge into an abyss; depress, sadden; —*vr* despair; be plunged in thought, be abstracted; be amazed

abismo /a'βismo/ *m,* chasm, abyss, gulf; hell

abjuración /aβhura'θion; aβhura'sion/ *f,* abjuration

abjurar /aβhu'rar/ *vt* to forswear, retract

ablactar /aβlak'tar/ *vt* to wean

ablandamiento /aβlanda'miento/ *m,* softening; placating

ablandante /aβlan'dante/ *a* softening; placatory

ablandar /aβlan'dar/ *vt* to soften; appease, placate; loosen; relax; —*vi* and *vr* be softened; be appeased; grow less stormy; (elements) decrease in force

ablandecer /aβlande'θer; aβlande'ser/ *vt irr* to soften. See **conocer**

ablución /aβlu'θion; aβlu'sion/ *f,* ablution

abnegación /aβnega'θion; aβnega'sion/ *f,* abnegation, self-sacrifice

abnegado /aβne'gaðo/ *a* self-sacrificing

abnegarse /aβne'garse/ *vr irr* to deprive oneself, sacrifice oneself. See **cegar**

abobado /aβo'βaðo/ *a* bewildered; foolish-looking, silly

abobar /aβo'βar/ *vt* to daze, bewilder; make stupid

abocado /aβo'kaðo/ *a* full-flavored, pleasant (of wine)

abocar /aβo'kar/ *vt* to seize with the mouth; bring nearer; transfer (contents of one jug to another); —*vr* meet, assemble; —*vi Naut.* enter (a channel, port, etc.). **abocarse (con...),** to contact (...), get in touch (with...)

abocetado /aβoθe'taðo; aβose'taðo/ *a Art.* unfinished; sketchy

abochornado /aβotʃor'naðo/ *a* flushed (of the face); ashamed; embarrassed

abochornar /aβotʃor'nar/ *vt* to overheat, make flushed; shame; embarrass; —*vr* (plants) dry up

abofetear /aβofete'ar/ *vt* to slap, hit; buffet

abogacía /aβoga'θia; aβoga'sia/ *f,* legal profession; practice of law; advocacy

abogado /aβo'gaðo/ **(-da)** *n* lawyer

abogar /aβo'gar/ *vi* to defend at law; intercede for; advocate, champion

abolengo /aβo'leŋgo/ *m,* lineage, descent, family; inheritance

abolición /aβoli'θion; aβoli'sion/ *f,* abolition

abolir /aβo'lir/ *vt* to abolish; cancel; annul

abolladura /aβoʎa'ðura; aβoya'ðura/ *f,* bruise; dent; embossment

abollar /aβo'ʎar; aβo'yar/ *vt* to bruise; dent

abollonar /aβoʎo'nar; aβoyo'nar/ *vt* to emboss, do raised work on; —*vr* (vines) sprout

abombado /aβom'baðo/ *a* convex; domed

abombar /aβom'bar/ *vt* to make convex; *Inf.* deafen, bewilder; —*vr* begin to putrefy; get intoxicated

abominable /aβomi'naβle/ *a* abominable

abominación /aβomina'θion; aβomina'sion/ *f,* abomination; loathing, detestation

abominar /aβomi'nar/ *vt* to abominate, loathe, detest

abonable /aβo'naβle/ *a* subscribable; payable

abonado /aβo'naðo/ **(-da)** *a* trustworthy, reliable; ready, prepared, inclined —*n* subscriber; season ticket holder (for concerts, etc.)

abonanzar /aβonan'θar; aβonan'sar/ *vi impers* to clear up, be fine (weather)

abonar /aβo'nar/ *vt* to guarantee; go surety for; improve, better; manure; ratify, confirm; pay; *Com.* place to the credit of; —*vr* subscribe, become a subscriber; take out (season tickets, etc.)

abonaré /aβona're/ *m, Com.* due bill; promissory note, I.O.U.

abono /a'βono/ *m,* subscription; voucher; guarantee; manure. **a. verde,** leaf mold. **en a. de,** in payment of; in support of

aboquillado /aβoki'ʎaðo; aβoki'yaðo/ *a* tipped (of cigarettes)

abordaje /aβor'ðahe/ *m, Naut.* boarding of a ship

abordar /aβor'ðar/ *vt Naut.* to board a ship; *Naut.* collide, run into; accost, tackle; undertake; —*vi Naut.* put into port

aborigen /aβor'ihen/ *a* aboriginal

aborígenes /aβo'rihenes/ *m pl,* aborigines

aborrachado /aβorra'tʃaðo/ *a* bright red; highly colored; flushed

aborrascarse /aβorras'karse/ *vr* to grow stormy

aborrecedor /aβorreθe'ðor; aβorrese'ðor/ **(-ra)** *a* hateful —*n* hater, loather

aborrecer /aβorre'θer; aβorre'ser/ *vt irr* to hate, loathe; desert offspring (animals, birds). See **conocer**

aborrecible /aβorre'θiβle; aβorre'siβle/ *a* hateful, detestable

aborrecimiento /aβorreθi'miento; aβorresi'miento/ *m,* hate, detestation; dislike

abortar /aβor'tar/ *vt* to abort; foil (a plot); —*vi Med.* miscarry; fail, go awry

abortivo /aβor'tiβo/ *a* abortive

aborto /a'βorto/ *m,* abortion; miscarriage; monster; failure

abotagarse /aβota'garse/ *vr* to swell up, become bloated

abotonador /aβotona'ðor/ *m,* button-hook

abotonar /aβoto'nar/ *vt* to button; —*vi* bud, sprout

abozalar /aβoθa'lar; aβosa'lar/ *vt* to muzzle

abra /'aβra/ *f,* cove, small bay; narrow gorge; fissure, cleft

abrasador /aβrasa'ðor/ *a* burning, flaming

abrasamiento /aβrasa'miento/ *m,* burning; ardor, heat

abrasar /aβra'sar/ *vt* to burn; dry up, parch (plants); squander, waste; shame; —*vi* burn; —*vr* be very hot, glow; burn with passion

abrasión /aβra'sion/ *f,* abrasion

abrasivo /aβra'siβo/ *a* and *m,* abrasive

abrazadera /aβraθa'ðera; aβrasa'ðera/ *f,* clasp; clamp

abrazamiento /aβraθa'miento; aβrasa'miento/ *m,* embracing

abrazar /aβra'θar; aβra'sar/ *vt* to embrace, clasp in one's arms; follow, adopt; engage in; seize, take advantage of; comprise, include; surround; take in hand; clamp; clasp. **abrazarse a,** to clutch, hang on to

abrazo /a'βraθo; a'βraso/ *m,* embrace

abrelatas /aβre'latas/ *m,* can opener

abrevadero /aβreβa'ðero/ *m,* watering place (for cattle)

abrevar /aβre'βar/ *vt* to water cattle; irrigate, water

abreviación /aβreβia'θion; aβreβia'sion/ *f,* abbreviation, shortening; summary; hastening

abreviador /aβreβia'ðor/ *m,* abridger, condenser

abreviar /aβre'βiar/ *vt* to abbreviate, shorten; hasten, accelerate; condense, abridge. **a. tiempo,** to save time. **Y para a....,** And, to cut a long story short...

abreviatura /aβreβia'tura/ *f,* abbreviation, contraction; shorthand

abridor /aβri'ðor/ *m,* opener; ear-ring (for keeping holes in ears open). **a. de guantes,** glove-stretcher. **a. de láminas,** engraving needle. **a. de latas,** can opener

abridura /aβri'ðura/ *f,* (act of) opening (e.g. of a trunk)

abrigada /aβri'gaða/ *f,* **abrigadero** *m,* sheltered place

abrigar /aβri'gar/ *vt* to shelter, protect (against the cold, etc.); defend, help; hold (opinions); nurse (a hope, etc.); cover; —*vr* take shelter; wrap oneself up

abrigo /a'βrigo/ *m,* shelter; defense; protection; help; sheltered place; wrap, coat; *Naut.* haven

abril /a'βril/ *m,* April; youth; *pl Poet.* years

abrillantar /aβriʎan'tar; aβriyan'tar/ *vt* to cut in

facets like a diamond; polish, burnish; cause to shine; *Fig.* improve, add luster to

abrir /a'βrir/ *vt* to open; reveal; unlock; slide the bolt of; extend, spread out; cleave; engrave; clear (the way, etc.); begin; head, lead; separate; dig; inaugurate —*vi* unfold (flowers); expand; **en un abrir y cerrar de ojos,** in the twinkling of an eye, in the wink of an eye; —*vr* open; expand; (*with con*) confide in. **a. el camino (a...),** to pave the way (for...). **abrirse camino,** to make one's way; **abrirse paso a codazos,** to elbow one's way out, (or through)

abrochador /aβrotʃa'ðor/ *m,* button-hook

abrochamiento /aβrotʃa'miento/ *m,* buttoning; fastening

abrochar /aβro'tʃar/ *vt* to button; fasten, clasp; hook up (a dress, etc.); buckle

abrogación /aβroga'θion; aβroga'sion/ *f,* repeal, annulment

abrogar /aβro'gar/ *vt* to repeal, annul

abrojo /a'βroho/ *m,* thistle; *Bot.* caltrops; thorn, prickle; *pl* submerged rocks in sea

abroncar /aβron'kar/ *vt Inf.* to bore, annoy

abrumador /aβruma'ðor/ *a* burdensome, crushing, oppressive; troublesome, tiresome; exhausting

abrumar /aβru'mar/ *vt* to weigh down, overwhelm, oppress; weary, exhaust; —*vr* grow misty

abrupto /a'βrupto/ *a* steep; rough, broken (ground); rugged

absceso /aβ'sθeso; aβ'sseso/ *m,* abscess

absentismo /aβsen'tismo/ *m,* absenteeism

ábside /'aβsiðe/ *mf, Archit.* apse. *m, Astron.* apsis

absolución /aβsolu'θion; aβsolu'sion/ *f,* (*Eccl.* and *Law.*) absolution; remission, pardon

absoluta /aβso'luta/ *f, Mil.* discharge

absolutismo /aβsolu'tismo/ *m,* absolutism

absolutista /aβsolu'tista/ *mf* absolutist

absoluto /aβso'luto/ *a* absolute; categorical; *Inf.* despotic. **en a.,** absolutely

absolver /aβsol'βer/ *vt irr* to absolve; acquit (of a charge). *Law.* **a. de la instancia,** to dismiss the case. See **mover**

absorbente /aβsor'βente/ *a* and *m,* absorbent

absorber /aβsor'βer/ *vt* to absorb; consume, use up; attract, hold (the attention, etc.); imbibe

absorción /aβsor'θion; aβsor'sion/ *f,* absorption

absortar /aβsor'tar/ *vt* to amaze, dumbfound

absorto /aβ'sorto/ *a* amazed, astounded; abstracted, lost in thought

abstemio /aβs'temio/ *a* abstemious

abstención /aβsten'θion; aβsten'sion/ *f,* abstention

abstenerse /aβste'nerse/ *vr irr* to refrain; abstain. See **tener**

abstinencia /aβsti'nenθia; aβsti'nensia/ *f,* abstinence; fasting

abstinente /aβsti'nente/ *a* abstemious; temperate

abstracción /aβstrak'θion; aβstrak'sion/ *f,* abstraction; preoccupation; absent-mindedness

abstracto /aβ'strakto/ *a* abstract. **en a.,** in the abstract

abstraer /aβstra'er/ *vt irr* to abstract; consider separately; —*vi* (*with de*) do without, exclude; —*vr* be preoccupied; let one's thoughts wander. See **traer**

abstraído /aβstra'iðo/ *a* retired, recluse; preoccupied; absent-minded

abstruso /aβ'struso/ *a* abstruse

absurdidad /aβsurði'ðað/ *f,* absurdity; folly, nonsense

absurdo /aβ'surðo/ *a* ridiculous, absurd. *m,* piece of folly, nonsense

abuchear /aβutʃe'ar/ *vt vi* to boo, hoot, jeer

abuela /a'βuela/ *f,* grandmother; old woman, dame

abuelo /a'βuelo/ *m,* grandfather; ancestor (gen. *pl*); old man; *pl* grandparents

abulia /a'βulia/ *f,* lack of will-power, abulia

abúlico /a'βuliko/ *a* abulic, lacking will-power

abultado /aβul'taðo/ *a* bulky, large; voluminous; exaggerated

abultamiento /aβulta'miento/ *m,* bulkiness; enlargement, increase; mound; exaggeration

abultar /aβul'tar/ *vt* to enlarge, increase; exaggerate; model in rough (sculpture); —*vi* be bulky; be large

abundancia /aβun'danθia; aβun'dansia/ *f,* abundance, plenty

abundante /aβun'dante/ *a* abundant, plentiful; abounding (in)

abundar /aβun'dar/ *vi* to be plentiful, abound

abundoso /aβun'doso/ *a* See **abundante**

aburrido /aβu'rriðo/ *a* boring, tedious, dull; tired, weary

aburrimiento /aβurri'miento/ *m,* boredom, dullness; wearisomeness, tediousness

aburrir /aβu'rrir/ *vt* to bore; *Inf.* spend (time, money); (birds) desert the nest; —*vr* grow bored; be weary

abusar /aβu'sar/ *vi* to abuse; exceed one's rights, go too far; (*with de*) take advantage of

abusivo /aβu'siβo/ *a* abusive

abuso /a'βuso/ *m,* abuse. **a. de confianza,** abuse of trust

abyección /aβyek'θion; aβyek'sion/ *f,* degradation, misery; abjectness, servility

abyecto /aβ'yekto/ *a* abject, wretched; servile

acá /a'ka/ *adv* hither, here; at this time, now. **a. y acullá,** hither and thither. **desde ayer a.,** from yesterday until now

acabable /aka'βaβle/ *a* terminable, finishable; achievable

acabado /aka'βaðo/ *a* complete; perfect; expert, consummate; old, worn out; ill, infirm. *m,* finish

acabamiento /akaβa'miento/ *m,* finishing, completion; end; death, decease

acabar /aka'βar/ *vt* to end, terminate; finish; complete, perfect; kill; (*with con*) destroy, finish off; suppress; squander; —*vi* end; die; be destroyed; (*with de + infin*) to have just (e.g. *Acaba de salir,* He has just gone out); —*vr* end, be exhausted, run out of (e.g. *Se le acabó el dinero,* His money ran out); fade, grow weak; be destroyed. **Se les acabaron las dudas,** Their doubts were cleared up. **a. de desconcertar,** to nonplus completely; **a. de decidirse,** to come to a decision; **a. de saber,** to finally learn

acacia /a'kaθia; a'kasia/ *f, Bot.* acacia

academia /aka'ðemia/ *f,* academy

academicismo /akaðemi'θismo; akaðemi'sismo/ *m,* academicism, academism

académico /aka'ðemiko/ **(-ca)** *a* academic —*n* academician. **a. de la lengua,** member of the Royal Spanish Academy

acaecer /akae'θer; akae'ser/ *vi irr* to happen, occur. See **conocer**

acaecimiento /akaeθi'miento; akaesi'miento/ *m,* happening, occurrence, event

acalambrarse /akalam'brarse/ (muscle) to contract with cramps. **Estar acalambrado,** to have cramps

acalenturarse /akalentu'rarse/ *vr* to grow feverish

acallar /aka'ʎar; aka'yar/ *vt* to quieten, hush; soothe, appease

acalorado /akalo'raðo/ *a* hot; fervent; *Fig.* heated

acaloramiento /akalora'miento/ *m,* excitement, agitation, vehemence; ardor

acalorar /akalo'rar/ *vt* to warm; aid, encourage; excite, stimulate; stir, move (to enthusiasm); inflame, rouse; tire (by exercise); —*vr* grow hot; become agitated or excited; become heated (arguments)

acamar /aka'mar/ *vt* to lay flat (plants by the wind); —*vr* be flattened (plants); lie down (animals); go rotten (fruit)

acampar /akam'par/ *vi* and *vt* to encamp

acanalar /akana'lar/ *vt* to groove; striate, flute, corrugate; furrow, channel

acantilado /akanti'laðo/ *a* steep, precipitous; shelving (ocean-bed). *m,* cliff

acanto /a'kanto/ *m,* (*Archit. Bot.*) acanthus

acantonamiento /akantona'miento/ *m,* billeting; cantonment

acantonar /akanto'nar/ *vt* to billet or quarter troops

acaparador /akapara'ðor/ **(-ra)** *n* monopolist

acaparar /akapa'rar/ *vt Com.* to monopolize, corner; seize, take possession of

acápite /a'kapite/ *m, West. Hem.* new paragraph

acaracolado /akarako'laðo/ *a* spiral, winding, twisting

acardenalar /akarðena'lar/ *vt* to bruise; *—vr* be bruised; be covered with livid marks
acarear /akare'ar/ *vt* to face; face up to, meet with courage
acariciador /akariθia'ðor; akarisia'ðor/ **(-ra)** *a* caressing, loving *—n* fondler
acariciar /akari'θiar; akari'siar/ *vt* to caress; brush, touch lightly; cherish, treat affectionately; toy with (a suggestion)
acarreador /akarrea'ðor/ **(-ra)** *n* carrier, carter
acarreamiento, acarreo /akarrea'miento, aka'reo/ *m,* cartage, carting; transport, carriage; occasioning
acarrear /akarre'ar/ *vt* to cart, transport; occasion, bring (gen. evil). **La guerra acarreó la carestía,** The war brought scarcity
acartonado /akarto'naðo/ *a* shriveled; shrunken; of cardboard; *Fig.* forced (dialogue)
acaso /a'kaso/ *m,* chance *—adv* by chance; perhaps, perchance. **por si a.,** in case (e.g. *Por si a. venga,* In case he comes)
acatable /aka'taβle/ *a* venerable, worthy
acatadamente /akataða'mente/ *adv* with respect, humbly
acatamiento /akata'miento/ *m,* respect; reverence; observance
acatar /aka'tar/ *vt* to treat with respect, honor, revere; observe
acatarrarse /akata'rrarse/ *vr* to catch a cold
acaudalado /akauða'laðo/ *a* wealthy, well-to-do
acaudalar /akauða'lar/ *vt* to make money; hoard up wealth; acquire (learning, etc.)
acaudillar /akauði'ʎar; akauði'yar/ *vt Mil.* to command, lead; head (a party, etc.)
acceder /akθe'ðer; akse'ðer/ *vi* (*with prep a*) to concede, grant; accede to, agree to
accesibilidad /ak,θesiβili'ðað; ak,sesiβili'ðað/ *f,* accessibility; approachableness
accesible /akθe'siβle; akse'siβle/ *a* accessible; approachable
accesión /akθe'sion; akse'sion/ *f,* agreement, acquiescence; accession; accessory; feverish attack
acceso /ak'θeso; ak'seso/ *m,* access; paroxysm, outburst; *Med.* attack
accesorio /akθe'sorio; akse'sorio/ *a* accessory
accesorios /akθe'sorios; akse'sorios/ *m pl,* accessories; *Theat.* properties
accidentado /akθiðen'taðo; aksiðen'taðo/ *a* rough, uneven; stormy, troubled (life, etc.)
accidental /akθiðen'tal; aksiðen'tal/ *a* accidental; *m, Mus.* accidental
accidentar /akθiðen'tar; aksiðen'tar/ *vt* to cause (someone) an accident; *—vr* be the victim of an accident; be seized by a fit
accidente /akθi'ðente; aksi'ðente/ *m,* chance; accident, mishap; illness, indisposition; *Med.* fit; *Gram.* accidence; *Mus.* accidental. **a. del trabajo,** accident at work. **por a.,** by chance, accidentally
acción /ak'θion; ak'sion/ *f,* action; battle; skirmish; *Mech.* drive; *Com.* share; gesture; lawsuit; *Lit.* action (of play, etc.); *Art.* posture, pose. **a. de gracias,** thanksgiving; *Com.* **a. liberada,** paid-up share. **a. privilegiada,** preference share
accionar /akθio'nar; aksio'nar/ *vi* to gesture, gesticulate
accionista /akθio'nista; aksio'nista/ *mf Com.* shareholder
acechar /aθe'tʃar; ase'tʃar/ *vt* to spy upon, watch; lie in ambush for
acecho /a'θetʃo; a'setʃo/ *m,* spying upon, watch; waylaying, ambush. **al a.,** in ambush; on the watch
acechona /aθe'tʃona; ase'tʃona/ *f,* waylaying; ambush
acecinar /aθeθi'nar; asesi'nar/ *vt* to salt and dry (meat); *—vr* (persons) wither, dry up
acedar /aθe'ðar; ase'ðar/ *vt* to make bitter, sour; embitter, displease; *—vr* turn sour; wither (plants)
acefalía /aθefa'lia; asefa'lia/ *f,* acephalia, headlessness
acéfalo /a'θefalo; a'sefalo/ *a* acephalous
aceitar /aθei'tar; asei'tar/ *vt* to oil, lubricate; rub with oil
aceite /a'θeite; a'seite/ *m,* olive oil; oil. **a. de hígado de bacalao,** cod-liver oil. **a. de linaza,** linseed oil. **a. de ricino,** castor-oil. **a. de trementina,** oil of turpentine
aceitera /aθei'tera; asei'tera/ *f,* woman who sells oil; oil can; oil bottle; *pl* cruet
aceitero /aθei'tero; asei'tero/ *m,* oil seller *—a* oil
aceitoso /aθei'toso; asei'toso/ *a* oily
aceituna /aθei'tuna; asei'tuna/ *f, Bot.* olive
aceitunado /aθeitu'naðo; aseitu'naðo/ *a* olive-colored
aceitunero /aθeitu'nero; aseitu'nero/ **(-ra)** *n* olive picker; olive seller. *m,* warehouse for storing olives
aceituno /aθei'tuno; asei'tuno/ *m,* olive tree
aceleración /aθelera'θion; aselera'sion/ *f,* speed, haste; acceleration
aceleradamente /aθele,raða'mente; asele,raða'mente/ *adv* hastily, swiftly
acelerador /aθelera'ðor; aselera'ðor/ *a* accelerating. *m,* hastener; *Auto.* accelerator
acelerar /aθele'rar; asele'rar/ *vt* to hasten, speed up; accelerate
acémila /a'θemila; a'semila/ *f,* beast of burden, mule
acendrado /aθen'draðo; asen'draðo/ *a* pure, unblemished, spotless
acendrar /aθen'drar; asen'drar/ *vt* to refine (metals); purify, make spotless
acento /a'θento; a'sento/ *m,* accent; tone, inflection; *Poet.* voice, words. **a. agudo,** acute accent. **a. circunflejo,** circumflex accent. **a. grave,** grave accent. **a. ortográfico,** graphic accent, written accent. **a. tónico,** tonic accent
acentuación /aθentua'θion; asentua'sion/ *f,* accentuation, stress; emphasis
acentuar /aθen'tuar; asen'tuar/ *vt* to accent; stress, emphasize; *—vr* become evident, become marked, be noticeable
aceña /a'θeɲa; a'seɲa/ *f,* water-mill; irrigation waterwheel; chain-well
acepción /aθep'θion; asep'sion/ *f,* meaning, significance, acceptation. **a. de personas,** partiality, preference
acepilladura /aθe,piʎa'ðura; ase,piya'ðura/ *f,* sweeping, brushing; planing; wood-shaving
acepillar /aθepi'ʎar; asepi'yar/ *vt* to sweep, brush; plane; *Inf.* brush up, polish up
aceptabilidad /a,θeptaβili'ðað; a,septaβili'ðað/ *f,* acceptability
aceptable /aθep'taβle; asep'taβle/ *a* acceptable
aceptación /aθepta'θion; asepta'sion/ *f,* acceptance; popularity; approval
aceptador /aθepta'ðor; asepta'ðor/ **(-ra)** *a* accepting *—n* acceptor
aceptar /aθep'tar; asep'tar/ *vt* to accept; approve; accept a challenge; *Com.* honor
acequía /aθe'kia; ase'kia/ *f,* ditch, trench; irrigation channel
acequiero /aθe'kiero; ase'kiero/ *m,* keeper of irrigation ditches
acera /a'θera; a'sera/ *f,* sidewalk, pavement. **a. del sol,** sunny side of the street
acerado /aθe'raðo; ase'raðo/ *a* steel; steel-like; strong, tough; mordant, incisive
acerar /aθe'rar; ase'rar/ *vt* to steel; treat (liquids) with steel; harden, make obdurate
acerbidad /aθerβi'ðað; aserβi'ðað/ *f,* bitterness, acerbity, sourness; harshness, cruelty
acerbo /a'θerβo; a'serβo/ *a* sour, tart, bitter; cruel, harsh
acerca de /a'θerka de; a'serka de/ *adv* about, concerning
acercamiento /aθerka'miento; aserka'miento/ *m,* approach
acercar /aθer'kar; aser'kar/ *vt* to bring nearer; *—vr* be near at hand, draw near; (*with prep a*) approach
acerico /aθe'riko; ase'riko/ *m,* small cushion; pincushion
acero /a'θero; a'sero/ *m,* steel; blade, sword; *pl* bravery, spirit; *Inf.* good appetite. **a. inoxidable,** stainless steel
acérrimo /a'θerrimo; a'serrimo/ *a superl* extremely strong, mighty; most harsh; most resolute, unflinching; very strong (taste, smell)

acerrojar /aθerro'har; aserro'har/ *vt* to lock, padlock; bolt
acertado /aθer'taðo; aser'taðo/ *a* well-aimed; fitting, suitable; wise; successful
acertar /aθer'tar; aser'tar/ *vt irr* to hit the mark; find, come across; succeed (in), achieve; guess, find out; **No acertaba a explicármelo,** I couldn't quite understand it. **a. por chambra,** to make a lucky guess —*vi* be successful; thrive (of plants); (*with prep a + infin*) happen, occur, come to pass —*Pres. Indic.* **acierto, aciertas, acierta, aciertan.** *Pres. Subjunc.* **acierte, aciertes, acierte, acierten**
acertijo /aθer'tiho; aser'tiho/ *m,* riddle
acervo /a'θerβo; a'serβo/ *m,* pile, heap; *Fig.* storehouse, wealth (e.g. of words)
acetato /aθe'tato; ase'tato/ *m,* acetate
acético /a'θetiko; a'setiko/ *a* acetic
acetileno /aθeti'leno; aseti'leno/ *m,* acetylene
achacar /atʃa'kar/ *vt* to attribute, impute, assign. **achacable a,** imputable to
achacoso /atʃa'koso/ *a* ailing, ill, sickly
achantarse /atʃan'tarse/ *vr Inf.* to hide from danger; put up with, bear
achaparrado /atʃapa'rraðo/ *a* stocky
achaque /a'tʃake/ *m,* ailment, illness (permanent); *Inf.* period, menstruation; pregnancy; matter, affair; pretext; failing, bad habit. **En a. de...,** Re..., concerning...
achatamiento /atʃata'miento/ *m,* flattening
achatar /atʃa'tar/ *vt* to flatten, make flat
achicado /atʃi'kaðo/ *a* childish
achicar /atʃi'kar/ *vt* to make smaller, diminish; drain, bail out; depreciate, belittle
achicarse /atʃi'karse/ *Inf.* to sing small
achicharrar /atʃitʃa'rrar/ *vt Cul.* to overcook; overheat; annoy, importune
achicoria /atʃi'koria/ *f,* chicory
achique /a'tʃike/ *m,* bailing, draining
achispado /atʃis'paðo/ *a Inf.* tipsy
achubascarse /atʃuβas'karse/ *vr* to become overcast, grow stormy
achuchar /atʃu'tʃar/ *vt Inf.* to squeeze, hug; jostle, push against
achuchón /atʃu'tʃon/ *m, Inf.* shove, push; hug, squeeze
achulado /atʃu'laðo/ *a Inf.* brazen, tough
aciago /a'θiago; a'siago/ *a* unhappy, ill-omened; fateful
acíbar /a'θiβar; a'siβar/ *m,* aloe tree; bitter aloes; sorrow, bitterness
acibarar /aθiβa'rar; asiβa'rar/ *vt* to add bitter aloes to; embitter, sadden
acicalado /aθika'laðo; asika'laðo/ *a* polished; neat; well-groomed. *m,* polishing, burnishing (of weapons)
acicalador /aθikala'ðor; asikala'ðor/ **(-ra)** *a* polishing —*n* polisher. *m,* burnisher (machine)
acicalar /aθika'lar; asika'lar/ *vt* to burnish (weapons); adorn, deck; —*vr* dress oneself with care
acicate /aθi'kate; asi'kate/ *m,* Moorish spur; incitement, stimulus
acicatear /aθikate'ar; asikate'ar/ *vt* to induce, spur on. **a. la curiosidad,** arouse curiosity
acidez /aθi'ðeθ; asi'ðes/ *f,* acidity, bitterness
acidia /a'θiðia; a'siðia/ *f,* indolence; sluggishness
ácido /'aθiðo; 'asiðo/ *a* acid; sour; harsh. *m,* acid. **a. fénico,** carbolic acid. **a. graso,** fatty acid
acidular /aθiðu'lar; asiðu'lar/ *vt Chem.* to acidulate
acídulo /a'θiðulo; a'siðulo/ *a Chem.* acidulous
acierto /a'θierto; a'sierto/ *m,* good hit, bull's-eye; success; achievement; cleverness; dexterity, skill; wisdom, sense; tact
acimut /aθi'mut; asi'mut/ *m, Astron.* azimuth
aclamación /aklama'θion; aklama'sion/ *f,* acclamation; shout of acclamation. **por a.,** unanimously
aclamador /aklama'ðor/ **(-ra)** *a* acclaiming —*n* applauder, acclaimer
aclamar /akla'mar/ *vt* to acclaim; applaud
aclaración /aklara'θion; aklara'sion/ *f,* explanation; elucidation
aclarado /akla'raðo/ *m,* rinse; rinsing
aclarador, aclaratorio /aklara'ðor, aklara'torio/ *a* explanatory
aclarar /akla'rar/ *vt* to clarify, purify; clear; rinse (clothes); explain; thin; —*vi* clear; (sky) clear up; dawn
aclimatación /aklimata'θion; aklimata'sion/ *f,* acclimatization
aclimatar /aklima'tar/ *vt* to acclimatize
acné /ak'ne/ *m,* acne
acobardar /akoβar'ðar/ *vt* to intimidate, frighten
acocear /akoθe'ar; akose'ar/ *vt* to kick; *Inf.* insult, humiliate
acocharse /ako'tʃarse/ *vr* to squat, crouch
acodalar /akoða'lar/ *vt* to prop
acodiciar /akoði'θiar; akoði'siar/ *vt* to yearn for, covet, desire
acogedizo /akohe'ðiθo; akohe'ðiso/ *a* gathered haphazardly
acogedor /akohe'ðor/ **(-ra)** *a* welcoming, friendly; inviting (e.g. a chair or room); —*n* protector
acoger /ako'her/ *vt* to receive, welcome, admit; protect, harbor; —*vr* take refuge; (*with prep a*) make use of, resort to; **acogerse a sagrado,** seek sanctuary
acogida /ako'hiða/ *f,* reception, welcome; protection, shelter; meeting place; confluence (of waters). **tener buena a.,** to be well received
acogollar /akogo'ʎar; akogo'yar/ *vt* to protect, cover (plants); —*vi* sprout, shoot
acogotar /akogo'tar/ *vt* to fell by a blow on the neck; *Inf.* knock out
acolada /ako'laða/ *f,* accolade
acolitar /akoli'tar/ *vi* to serve as an altar boy, serve as an altar girl
acólito /a'kolito/ *m,* acolyte
acometedor /akomete'ðor/ **(-ra)** *a* capable, enterprising; aggressive —*n* aggressor, attacker
acometer /akome'ter/ *vt* to attack furiously; undertake; take in hand; overcome (of sleep, etc.)
acometida /akome'tiða/ *f,* **acometimiento** *m,* assault, onrush; undertaking
acometividad /akometiβi'ðað/ *f,* aggressiveness
acomodable /akomo'ðaβle/ *a* easily arranged
acomodación /akomoða'θion; akomoða'sion/ *f,* adjustment; adaptation; accommodation
acomodadizo /akomoða'ðiθo; akomoða'ðiso/ *a* accommodating, easy-going
acomodado /akomo'ðaðo/ *a* suitable; convenient; wealthy, well-off; comfort-loving; moderate, low (of price)
acomodador /akomoða'ðor/ **(-ra)** *n* theater attendant, usher
acomodamiento /akomoða'miento/ *m,* agreement, transaction; accommodation
acomodar /akomo'ðar/ *vt* to arrange, adjust, accommodate; adapt; appoint; place; reconcile; employ, take on; equip, provide; lodge; —*vi* suit, be convenient; —*vr* compromise, agree
acomodaticio /akomoða'tiθio; akomoða'tisio/ *a* accommodating
acomodo /ako'moðo/ *m,* post, employment; arrangement; settlement
acompañamiento /akompaɲa'miento/ *m,* accompaniment; following, retinue; *Mus.* accompaniment; *Theat.* crowd, chorus
acompañanta /akompa'ɲanta/ *f,* chaperon; maid, servant
acompañante /akompa'ɲante/ *m, Mus.* accompanist
acompañar /akompa'ɲar/ *vt* to accompany; follow, escort; enclose (a letter, etc.); *Mus.* accompany
acompasado /akompa'saðo/ *a* rhythmic; deliberate, slow
acondicionado /akondiθio'naðo; akondisio'naðo/ *a* conditioned; (*with* **bien** *or* **mal**) in good or bad condition; of good or bad quality; good- or ill-natured. **reflejo acondicionado** *Med.* conditioned reflex
acondicionar /akondiθio'nar; akondisio'nar/ *vt* to prepare; mend, repair; —*vr* condition oneself
acongojar /akongo'har/ *vt* to sadden, grieve; oppress
aconsejable /akonse'haβle/ *a* advisable
aconsejar /akonse'har/ *vt* to advise; —*vr* (*with con*) consult, ask advice of

aconsonantar /akonsonan'tar/ *vt* and *vi* to rhyme
acontecedero /akonteθe'ðero; akontese'ðero/ *a* possible
acontecer /akonte'θer; akonte'ser/ *vi irr impers* to happen. See **conocer**
acontecimiento /akonteθi'miento; akontesi'miento/ *m*, event, occurrence
acopiar /ako'piar/ *vt* to collect, amass, gather
acopio /a'kopio/ *m*, collection, store; accumulation, gathering
acopladura /akopla'ðura/ *f*, **acoplamiento** *m*, (*Mech.*) joint; coupling; yoking; mating (of animals)
acoplar /ako'plar/ *vt* to join, couple; yoke; mate (animals); reconcile (opinions); *—vr Inf.* fall in love
acoquinar /akoki'nar/ *vt Inf.* to intimidate, terrify
acorazado /akora'θaðo; akora'saðo/ *a* (*Nav. Mil.*) armored, iron-clad. *m*, iron-clad, battleship
acorazar /akora'θar; akora'sar/ *vt* (*Nav. Mil.*) to armor
acorcharse /akor'tʃarse/ *vr* to dry up, shrivel; go numb (limbs)
acordadamente /akorˌðaða'mente/ *adv* by common consent, unanimously; deliberately, after due thought
acordar /akor'ðar/ *vt irr* to decide unanimously; resolve; remind; tune; harmonize (colors); *—vi* agree; *—vr* remember; come to an agreement. **Si mal no me acuerdo,** If memory serves me right *—Pres. Indic.* **acuerdo, acuerdas, acuerda, acuerdan.** *Pres. Subjunc.* **acuerde, acuerdes, acuerde, acuerden**
acorde /a'korðe/ *a* agreed; in harmony; in agreement. *m*, *Mus.* chord; harmony
acordeón /akorðe'on/ *m*, accordion; (slang) crib sheet
acordonar /akorðo'nar/ *vt* to lace; cordon off, surround; mill (coins)
acornear /akorne'ar/ *vt* to butt, toss (bulls)
acorralado /akorra'laðo/ *a* at bay, intimidated
acorralamiento /akorrala'miento/ *m*, corralling, penning
acorralar /akorra'lar/ *vt* to corral, pen; confine; corner, silence (in argument); frighten; harass
acorrer /ako'rrer/ *vt* to aid, assist; *—vi* run, hasten; *—vr* take refuge
acortamiento /akorta'miento/ *m*, shortening
acortar /akor'tar/ *vt* to shorten; *—vr* be speechless, be shy. **a. las velas,** to take in sail
acosador /akosa'ðor/ **(-ra)** *a* persecuting *—n* persecutor
acosamiento /akosa'miento/ *m*, persecution
acosar /ako'sar/ *vt* to persecute relentlessly; annoy, harass
acostado /ako'staðo/ *a* in bed; stretched out; *Herald.* couchant
acostar /ako'star/ *vt irr* to lay down, stretch out; put to bed; *—vi* lean, tilt; *—vr* lie down; go to bed; *Naut.* come alongside. See **contar**
acostumbrado /akostum'braðo/ *a* accustomed, usual
acostumbrar /akostum'brar/ *vt* to habituate, accustom; *—vi* be in the habit of (e.g. *Acostumbramos ir a la playa en el verano,* We generally go to the seashore in summer); *—vr* (*with prep a*) become used to
acotación /akota'θion; akota'sion/ *f*, noting; marginal note; stage direction; ordnance survey number
acotar /ako'tar/ *vt* to annotate; mark out boundaries; fix, establish; accept; *Inf.* choose; testify; fill in elevation figures (on a map); *—vr* seek refuge
acotillo /ako'tiʎo; ako'tiyo/ *m*, sledgehammer
acre /'akre/ *a* bitter, sour; harsh; biting, mordant. *m*, acre (land measure)
acrecencia /akre'θenθia; akre'sensia/ *f*, **acrecentamiento** *m*, increase; addition
acrecentar /akreθen'tar; akresen'tar/ *vt irr* to increase; augment; promote, prefer. See **acertar**
acrecer /akre'θer; akre'ser/ *vt irr* to increase; augment. See **conocer**
acreción /akre'θion; akre'sion/ *f*, accretion
acreditado /akreði'taðo/ *a* accredited, well-reputed; respected
acreditar /akreði'tar/ *vt* to prove; verify; accredit; recommend; sanction, authorize; vouch for, guarantee; *Com.* credit
acreedor /akree'ðor/ **(-ra)** *n* creditor; claimant *—a* deserving. **a. hipotecario,** mortgagee
acreencia /akre'enθia; akre'ensia/ *f*, debt; *Com.* claim
acribillar /akriβi'ʎar; akriβi'yar/ *vt* to riddle with holes; wound repeatedly; pelt; torment; *Inf.* pester, harass
acriminación /akrimina'θion; akrimina'sion/ *f*, accusation
acriminador /akrimina'ðor/ **(-ra)** *a* incriminating *—n* accuser
acriminar /akrimi'nar/ *vt* to accuse, charge
acrimonia /akri'monia/ *f*, acrimony
acrisolar /akriso'lar/ *vt* to refine, purify (metals); perfect; clarify, elucidate
acrobacia /akro'βaθia; akro'βasia/ *f*, acrobatics
acróbata /a'kroβata/ *mf* acrobat
acrobático /akro'βatiko/ *a* acrobatic
acromatópsico /akroma'topsiko/ *a* color-blind
acrópolis /a'kropolis/ *f*, acropolis
acróstico /a'krostiko/ *a* and *m*, acrostic
acta /'akta/ *f*, minutes, record; certificate of election (as deputy to Cortes, etc.); *pl* deeds (of a martyr). **a. matrimonial,** marriage register
actitud /akti'tuð/ *f*, attitude
activar /akti'βar/ *vt* to stimulate, make active; accelerate, hasten
actividad /aktiβi'ðað/ *f*, activity; movement, bustle. **en a.,** in action; at work
activo /ak'tiβo/ *a* active. *m*, *Com.* assets
acto /'akto/ *m*, act, deed, action; act, law; act (of a play); public ceremony; *pl* minutes (of a meeting), proceedings (of a conference). **a. continuo** *or* **a. seguido,** immediately afterwards. **a. vandálico,** act of vandalism. **los Actos de los Apóstoles,** Acts of the Apostles. **en a.,** in the act (of doing). **en el a.,** in the act; immediately
actor /ak'tor/ *m*, actor; *Law.* plaintiff
actriz /ak'triθ; ak'tris/ *f*, actress
actuación /aktua'θion; aktua'sion/ *f*, operation, functioning; action; *pl* legal functions, judicial acts
actual /ak'tual/ *a* present; contemporary
actualidad /aktuali'ðað/ *f*, present, present time; topic of interest. **actualidades,** current events. **en la a.,** at the present time
actuar /ak'tuar/ *vt* to operate, set in motion; *—vi* act; exercise legal functions
actuario /ak'tuario/ (**de seguros**) *m*, actuary
acuarela /akua'rela/ *f*, water-color painting
acuarelista /akuare'lista/ *mf* water-colorist
acuario /a'kuario/ *m*, aquarium; Aquarius
acuartelamiento /aˌkuartela'miento/ *m*, billeting (of troops); billet, quarters
acuartelar /akuarte'lar/ *vt* to billet
acuático, acuátil /a'kuatiko, a'kuatil/ *a* aquatic
acuatinta /akua'tinta/ *f*, aquatint
acuchillado /akutʃi'ʎaðo; akutʃi'yaðo/ *a* taught by experience, schooled
acuchillar /akutʃi'ʎar; akutʃi'yar/ *vt* to hack, cut about; stab, put to the sword; slash (sleeves, etc.); *—vr* fight with swords, daggers
acucia /a'kuθia; a'kusia/ *f*, fervor, zeal; yearning, longing
acuciar /aku'θiar; aku'siar/ *vt* to incite; goad; stimulate; encourage
acuciosidad /akuθiosi'ðað; akusiosi'ðað/ *f*, eagerness, fervor, zeal
acucioso /aku'θioso; aku'sioso/ *a* eager, fervent, keen, zealous
acuclillarse /akukli'ʎarse; akukli'yarse/ *vr* to squat, crouch
acudir /aku'ðir/ *vi* to go, repair (to); come; go or come to the aid of; attend, be present; **No me acude ningún ejemplo a la memoria,** No example comes to mind; resort (to), seek protection; reply, respond
acueducto /akue'ðukto/ *m*, aqueduct
acuerdo /a'kuerðo/ *m*, motion, resolution; decision; harmony, agreement; opinion, belief; remembrance; report; meeting (of members of a tribunal); *Art.* harmony (of colors). **de a.,** in agreement, in conformity; unanimously. **estar de a. (con),** to agree (with). **es-**

tar de acuerdo en (+ inf.), to agree to (+ inf.) **ponerse de a.,** to come to an understanding
acuitar /akui'tar/ *vt* to distress, trouble; grieve
acullá /aku'ʎa; aku'ya/ *adv* afar, yonder, in the distance
acumulación /akumula'θion; akumula'sion/ *f,* accumulation, collection
acumulador /akumula'ðor/ **(-ra)** *a* accumulative. *m,* accumulator, storage battery —*n* collector, accumulator
acumulamiento /akumula'miento/ *m,* accumulation (act)
acumular /akumu'lar/ *vt* to accumulate, amass, collect; accuse, charge with
acuñación /akuɲa'θion; akuɲa'sion/ *f,* minting, coining; wedging
acuñador /akuɲa'ðor/ **(-ra)** *n* coiner, stamper; wedge. *m,* coining machine
acuñar /aku'ɲar/ *vt* to mint, stamp, coin; wedge
acuosidad /akuosi'ðað/ *f,* wateriness
acuoso /a'kuoso/ *a* aqueous, watery
acurrucarse /akurru'karse/ *vr* to huddle; curl up; crouch
acusación /akusa'θion; akusa'sion/ *f,* accusation; *Law.* charge; *Law.* prosecution
acusado /aku'saðo/ **(-da)** *a* accused; prominent; well-defined; —*n* accused; *Law.* defendant
acusador /akusa'ðor/ **(-ra)** *a* accusing —*n* accuser; *Law.* prosecutor
acusar /aku'sar/ *vt* to accuse; blame; denounce; *Com.* acknowledge receipt; *Law.* prosecute; *Law.* charge. **acusarle a uno las cuarenta,** *Inf.* to give someone a piece of one's mind
acusatorio /akusa'torio/ *a* accusatory
acusón /aku'son/ **(-ona)** *n Inf.* telltale, sneak, informer
acústica /a'kustika/ *f,* acoustics
acústico /a'kustiko/ *a* acoustic
adagio /a'ðahio; *also for 2* ɑ'dɑdʒio/ *m,* adage; *Mus.* adagio
adalid /aða'lið/ *m,* chieftain; head, leader
adamado /aða'maðo/ *a* effeminate; refined; genteel
adamantino /aðaman'tino/ *a* adamantine
adaptabilidad /aðaptaβili'ðað/ *f,* adaptability
adaptación /aðapta'θion; aðapta'sion/ *f,* adaptation
adaptar /aðap'tar/ *vt* to adapt, make suitable; —*vr* adapt oneself
adarme /a'ðarme/ *m,* tittle, jot. **por adarmes,** in bits and pieces, in drabs and driblets
adecentar /aðeθen'tar; aðesen'tar/ *vt* to make decent; tidy up; —*vr* tidy oneself
adecuación /aðekua'θion; aðekua'sion/ *f,* adequacy; suitability
adecuado /aðe'kuaðo/ *a* adequate; suitable
adecuar /aðe'kuar/ *vt* to proportion, fit; *Fig.* tailor
adefesio /aðe'fesio/ *m, Inf.* folly, absurdity (gen. *pl*); extravagant attire; guy, sight
adelantado /aðelan'taðo/ *a* precocious; forward, pert; fast (clocks); early (of fruit); excellent; capable, proficient. *m, Obs.* provincial governor *or* chief justice *or* captain-general (Spanish history). **por a.,** in advance
adelantamiento /aðelanta'miento/ *m,* promotion, furtherance; progress, advancement; betterment, improvement; *Obs.* office of **adelantado**; anticipation
adelantar /aðelan'tar/ *vt* to advance, move on; hasten; forestall; overtake; put on (the hands of clocks); improve, better; beat, excel; place in front; —*vi* progress, advance, be fast (clocks); grow, develop; —*vr* come forward
adelante /aðe'lante/ *adv* on, forward; further on; straight ahead. **¡A.!** Onward!; Come in! **de hoy en a.,** henceforth, from today
adelanto /aðe'lanto/ *m,* anticipation; progress; *Com.* payment in advance. **el a. de la hora,** moving the clock forward
adelfa /a'ðelfa/ *f, Bot.* rose-bay, oleander
adelgazamiento /aðelˌgaθa'miento; aðelˌgasa'miento/ *m,* loss of weight; slenderness; thinness
adelgazar /aðelga'θar; aðelga'sar/ *vt* to make slender or thin; *Fig.* split hairs; whittle, taper; —*vi* grow slender or thin
ademán /aðe'man/ *m,* posture, attitude; gesture; *pl* behavior, manners
además /aðe'mas/ *adv* besides, in addition; moreover. **a. de,** as well as
adentellar /aðente'ʎar; aðente'yar/ *vt* to bite, sink the teeth into
adentro /a'ðentro/ *adv* inside, within
adentros /a'ðentros/ *m pl,* private thoughts (e.g. *Pensé para mis adentros,* I thought to myself) —*interj* **¡Adentro!** Come in!; Go in!
adepto /a'ðepto/ *a* affiliated; adept, proficient
aderezamiento /aðeˌreθa'miento; aðeˌresa'miento/ *m,* dressing; seasoning; embellishment
aderezar /aðere'θar; aðere'sar/ *vt* to deck, embellish; cook; *Cul.* season; *Cul.* dress; prepare; repair, mend; guide, direct; dress (cloth)
aderezo /aðe'reθo; aðe'reso/ *m,* dressing, adornment; beautifying; finery, ornament; preparation; seasoning; set of jewels; horse's trappings; gum starch (for dressing cloth); equipment
adeudar /aðeu'ðar/ *vt* to owe; be dutiable (goods); *Com.* debit; —*vi* become related (by marriage); —*vr* run into debt
adeudo /a'ðeuðo/ *m,* debt; customs duty; *Com.* debit
adherencia /aðe'renθia; aðe'rensia/ *f,* adherence; adhesion
adherente /aðe'rente/ *a* adhesive; connected, attached. *mf* adherent, follower; *m pl.* **adherentes,** accessories, requisites
adherirse /aðe'rirse/ *vr irr* to adhere, stick; follow; believe (in). See **herir**
adhesión /aðe'sion/ *f,* adhesion; adherence
adhesivo /aðe'siβo/ *a* adhesive
adición /aði'θion; aði'sion/ *f,* addition
adicional /aðiθio'nal; aðisio'nal/ *a* additional, extra
adicionar /aðiθio'nar; aðisio'nar/ *vt* to add up; add to
adicto /a'ðikto/ **(-ta)** *a* addicted, fond; joint —*n* addict; follower, disciple
adiestrador /aðiestra'ðor/ **(-ra)** *n* trainer, coach; guide, teacher
adiestrar /aðies'trar/ *vt* to train, coach; guide, teach; lead; —*vr* practice, perfect oneself
adietar /aðie'tar/ *vt Med.* to put on a diet
adinerado /aðine'raðo/ *a* wealthy, well-off, rich
adiós /a'ðios/ *interj* Good-bye!; Hello, God be with you! (used as greeting). *m,* farewell
adiposo /aði'poso/ *a* adipose
aditamento /aðita'mento/ *m,* addition
adive /a'ðiβe/ *m,* jackal
adivinación /aðiβina'θion; aðiβina'sion/ *f,* divination; guess
adivinador /aðiβina'ðor/ **(-ra)** *a* prophesying, divining —*n* soothsayer
adivinanza /aðiβi'nanθa; aðiβi'nansa/ *f,* divination; riddle; puzzle. **adivinanzas,** guessing games. **no estar para jugar a las a.,** to be in no mood for guessing games
adivinar /aðiβi'nar/ *vt* to prophesy, foretell; divine, guess; solve, guess (riddles, etc.)
adivino /aði'βino/ **(-na)** *n* soothsayer, prophet
adjetivo /aðhe'tiβo/ *a* adjectival. *m,* adjective
adjudicación /aðhuðika'θion; aðhuðika'sion/ *f,* adjudication, award
adjudicador /aðhuðika'ðor/ **(-ra)** *n* adjudicator
adjudicar /aðhuði'kar/ *vt* to adjudge; award; —*vr* appropriate
adjudicatario /aðhuðika'tario/ **(-ia)** *n* recipient (of a prize, etc.); grantee
adjuntar /aðhun'tar/ *vt* to enclose (with a letter, etc.)
adjunto /að'hunto/ *a* attached; enclosed, accompanying; assistant, deputy; adjectival. *m,* addition, supplement
administración /aðministra'θion; aðministra'sion/ *f,* administration; direction, control; administratorship
administrador /aðministra'ðor/ **(-ra)** *a* administrative —*n* administrator. **a. de correos,** postmaster
administrar /aðminis'trar/ *vt* to control, manage; provide, supply; administer. **administrarse el tiempo,** to budget one's time

administrativo /aðministra'tiβo/ *a* administrative, executive
admirable /aðmi'raβle/ *a* admirable
admirablemente /aðmi,raβle'mente/ *adv* admirably, excellently
admiración /aðmira'θion; aðmira'sion/ *f,* amazement; admiration; wonder; exclamation mark
admirador /aðmira'ðor/ **(-ra)** *a* admiring —*n* admirer
admirar /aðmi'rar/ *vt* to admire; surprise, amaze (e.g. *Me admira su acción,* His action surprises me); to see (e.g. *Desde la colina se pueden admirar varios edificios de la ciudad,* From the hill several buildings in the city can be seen); —*vr* (*with de*) be surprised at or by
admirativo /aðmira'tiβo/ *a* admiring; admirable, excellent
admisibilidad /aðmisiβili'ðað/ *f,* allowability, permissibility
admisible /aðmi'siβle/ *a* admissible; permissible
admisión /aðmi'sion/ *f,* admission; acceptance; allowance
admitir /aðmi'tir/ *vt* to admit; receive, accept; tolerate, brook; allow, permit
admonición /aðmoni'θion; aðmoni'sion/ *f,* admonition, warning; reprimand
adobar /aðo'βar/ *vt* to prepare; *Cul.* garnish; pickle (meat); cook; dress (hides)
adobo /a'ðoβo/ *m,* repairing; dressing (for cloth, leather); *Cul.* savory sauce; pickling sauce; make-up, cosmetic
adocenado /aðoθe'naðo; aðose'naðo/ *a* ordinary; narrow-minded
adoctrinar /aðoktri'nar/ *vt* to instruct
adolecer /aðole'θer; aðole'ser/ *vi irr* to fall ill; (*with de*) suffer from (diseases, defects); —*vr* be sorry for, regret. See **conocer**
adolescencia /aðoles'θenθia; aðoles'sensia/ *f,* adolescence
adolescente /aðoles'θente; aðoles'sente/ *a* and *mf* adolescent
adonde /a'ðonde/ *adv* (*interr* **a dónde**) where to, whither (e.g. *¿A dónde fuiste?* Where did you go to?)
adondequiera /a,ðonde'kiera/ *adv* wherever
adopción /aðop'θion; aðop'sion/ *f,* adoption
adoptador /aðopta'ðor/ **(-ra)** *a* adopting —*n* adopter
adoptar /aðop'tar/ *vt* to adopt (children); make one's own, embrace (opinions); take (decisions)
adoptivo /aðop'tiβo/ *a* adoptive
adoquín /aðo'kin/ *m,* cobble-stone; *Fig.* blockhead
adoquinado /aðoki'naðo/ *m,* cobbling, paving. *m,* cobbled pavement
adoquinar /aðoki'nar/ *vt* to pave with cobble-stones
adorable /aðo'raβle/ *a* adorable
adoración /aðora'θion; aðora'sion/ *f,* worship, adoration. **A. de los Reyes,** Adoration of the Magi; Epiphany
adorador /aðora'ðor/ **(-ra)** *a* adoring —*n* adorer
adorar /aðo'rar/ *vt* to adore; worship; (*with en*) dote on; —*vi* pray
adormecedor /aðormeθe'ðor; aðormese'ðor/ *a* soporific, drowsy
adormecer /aðorme'θer; aðorme'ser/ *vt irr* to make drowsy; soothe, lull; hush to sleep; —*vr* go to sleep; (limbs); fall asleep; (*with en*) persist in. See **conocer**
adormecimiento /aðormeθi'miento; aðormesi'miento/ *m,* sleepiness; lulling asleep; numbness
adormitarse /aðormi'tarse/ *vr* to doze, take a nap, snooze
adornamiento /aðorna'miento/ *m,* adornment, decoration
adornar /aðor'nar/ *vt* to deck, beautify; decorate; trim, embellish; adorn (of virtues, etc.)
adorno /a'ðorno/ *m,* decoration, adornment; ornament; trimming. **de a.,** ornamental; flowering (shrubs)
adquiridor /aðkiri'ðor/ **(-ra)** *a* acquiring —*n* acquirer
adquirir /aðki'rir/ *vt irr* to acquire, get; achieve, obtain —*Pres. Indic.* **adquiero, adquieres, adquiere, adquieren.** *Pres. Subjunc.* **adquiera, adquieras, adquiera, adquieran**
adquisición /aðkisi'θion; aðkisi'sion/ *f,* acquirement; acquisition. **poder de a.,** purchasing power
adquisidor /aðkisi'ðor/ **(-ra)** *a* acquiring —*n* acquirer, obtainer
adquisitivo /aðkisi'tiβo/ *a* acquisitive
adquisividad /aðkisiβi'ðað/ *f,* acquisitiveness
adrazo /a'ðraθo; a'ðraso/ *m,* salt-water still
adrede /a'ðreðe/ *adv* on purpose, intentionally
adrenalina /aðrena'lina/ *f,* adrenaline
adriático /a'ðriatiko/ *a* Adriatic
adscribir /aðskri'βir/ *vt* to ascribe, attribute; appoint (to a post, etc.)
adscripción /aðskrip'θion; aðskrip'sion/ *f,* ascription, attribution; appointment
aduana /a'ðuana/ *f,* customs house, customs. **pasar por la a.,** to go through customs
aduanero /aðua'nero/ *a* customs. *m,* customs officer
aducir /aðu'θir; aðu'sir/ *vt irr* to adduce, allege, cite; add. See **conducir**
adueñarse /aðue'ɲarse/ **(-de)** *vr* to appropriate, take possession (of)
adulación /aðula'θion; aðula'sion/ *f,* adulation, flattery
adulador /aðula'ðor/ **(-ra)** *a* fawning —*n* flatterer
adular /aðu'lar/ *vt* to flatter, fawn upon, adulate
adulteración /aðultera'θion; aðultera'sion/ *f,* adulteration; falsification
adulterador /aðultera'ðor/ **(-ra)** *a* adulterant —*n* adulterator; falsifier; coiner
adulterar /aðulte'rar/ *vi* to commit adultery; —*vt* adulterate; falsify
adulterino /aðulte'rino/ *a* adulterous; false
adulterio /aðul'terio/ *m,* adultery
adúltero /a'ðultero/ **(-ra)** *a* adulterous; corrupt —*n* adulterer
adulto /a'ðulto/ **(-ta)** *a* and *n* adult
adunar /aðu'nar/ *vt* to join, unite; unify, combine
adusto /a'ðusto/ *a* extremely hot (of climate); grave, austere; standoffish, reserved
advenedizo /aðβene'ðiθo; aðβene'ðiso/ *a* foreign, alien; strange, unknown; upstart; newly rich
advenimiento /aðβeni'miento/ *m,* advent, arrival; ascension (to the throne)
advenir /aðβe'nir/ *vi irr* to come, arrive; happen, befall. See **venir**
adventicio /aðβen'tiθio; aðβen'tisio/ *a* casual, accidental; *Bot.* adventitious
adverbio /að'βerβio/ *m,* adverb
adversario /aðβer'sario/ **(-ia)** *n* adversary, rival; opponent
adversidad /aðβersi'ðað/ *f,* adversity, misfortune, sorrow
adverso /að'βerso/ *a* unfavorable, contrary, adverse; opposite
advertencia /aðβer'tenθia; aðβer'tensia/ *f,* warning; introduction, preface; remark
advertido /aðβer'tiðo/ *a* capable, clever; experienced; expert
advertir /aðβer'tir/ *vt irr* to observe, notice; warn; advise; feel, be conscious of; point out, indicate; inform; discover. See **sentir**
Adviento /að'βiento/ *m, Eccl.* Advent
adyacente /aðya'θente; aðya'sente/ *a* adjacent, near-by, neighboring
aedo /a'eðo/ *m, Poet.* poet
aeración /aera'θion; aera'sion/ *f,* aeration
aéreo /'aereo/ *a* aerial; airborne; airy; air; aeronautic; unsubstantial, fantastic. **correo a.,** airmail. **línea aérea** airline
aerobismo /aero'βismo/ *m,* aerobics
aerodinámica /aeroði'namika/ *f,* aerodynamics
aeronauta /aero'nauta/ *mf* aeronaut, balloonist
aeronáutica /aero'nautika/ *f,* aeronautics
aeronáutico /aero'nautiko/ *a* aeronautic
aeropuerto /aero'puerto/ *m,* airport
aeróstato /ae'rostato/ *m,* dirigible
afabilidad /afaβili'ðað/ *f,* affability, geniality, friendliness
afable /a'faβle/ *a* affable, genial, pleasant
afamado /afa'maðo/ *a* famous, well-known
afamar /afa'mar/ *vt* to make famous
afán /a'fan/ *m,* effort; manual labor; desire, anxiety **a. de mando,** thirst for power

afanar /afa'nar/ *vt* to press, urge on; filch; *—vr* toil, labor; (*with por*) work hard to, try to
afanoso /afa'noso/ *a* hard, laborious; hard-working, painstaking; eager, anxious
afasia /a'fasia/ *f*, *Med.* aphasia
afear /afe'ar/ *vt* to make ugly; distort, deform; blame; criticize
afección /afek'θion; afek'sion/ *f*, fondness, affection; complaint, ailment, trouble
afectación /afekta'θion; afekta'sion/ *f*, affectation
afectado /afek'taðo/ *a* affected
afectar /afek'tar/ *vt* to feign, assume; affect; move, touch; *Law.* encumber
afectivo /afek'tiβo/ *a* affective
afecto /a'fekto/ *a* fond, affectionate; *Law.* encumbered; (*with prep a*) addicted to. *m*, emotion, sentiment; affection
afectuosidad /afektuosi'ðað/ *f*, affectionateness
afectuoso /afek'tuoso/ *a* affectionate, fond
afeitada /afei'taða/ *f*, shave, shaving
afeitar /afei'tar/ *vt* to shave; make up (one's face); adorn, beautify
afeite /a'feite/ *m*, cosmetic; make-up (for the complexion)
afelpado /afel'paðo/ *a* velvet-like, plushy
afeminación /afemina'θion; afemina'sion/ *f*, effeminacy; weakness, languor
afeminado /afemi'naðo/ *a* effeminate
afeminar /afemi'nar/ *vt* to make effeminate; weaken; *—vr* grow effeminate
aferradamente /aferraða'mente/ *adv* tenaciously, persistently, obstinately
aferramiento /aferra'miento/ *m*, seizing, clutching; *Naut.* furling; *Naut.* grappling; mooring, anchoring; obstinacy
aferrar /afe'rrar/ *vt* to seize, clutch; *Naut.* take in, furl; *Naut.* grapple; *—vi Naut.* anchor; *—vr* (*with con, en, a*) persist in, insist on
afestonado /afesto'naðo/ *a* festooned
Afganistán /afganis'tan/ Afghanistan
afgano /af'gano/ **(-na)** *a* and *n* Afghan
afianzamiento /afianθa'miento; afiansa'miento/ *m*, fastening, fixing; propping; grasping; guarantee, security
afianzar /afian'θar; afian'sar/ *vt* to fasten, fix; prop; consolidate (e.g. one's power); guarantee, be security for; grasp
afición /afi'θion; afi'sion/ *f*, propensity, inclination; fondness. **tomar a. (a),** to take a liking to
aficionado /afiθio'naðo; afisio'naðo/ **(-da)** *a* amateur *—n* amateur, fan, enthusiast. **ser a a.,** to be fond of, have a liking for
aficionar /afiθio'nar; afisio'nar/ *vt* to inspire liking or affection; *—vr* (*with prep a*) take a liking to, grow fond of; become an enthusiast of
afijo /a'fiho/ *m*, *Gram.* affix
afiladera /afila'ðera/ *f*, whetstone, grindstone
afilado /afi'laðo/ *a* sharp, keen (of edges)
afilador /afila'ðor/ *m*, grinder (of scissors, etc.); razor strop
afilalápices /afila'lapiθes; afila'lapises/ *m*, pencil sharpener
afilar /afi'lar/ *vt* to sharpen; grind, whet; taper; *—vr* grow thin; taper
afiliación /afilia'θion; afilia'sion/ *f*, affiliation
afiliar /afi'liar/ *vt* (*with prep a*) to affiliate with; *—vr* (*with prep a*) become affiliated with; join, become a member of
afiligranado /afiligra'naðo/ *a* filigree; delicate, fine; slender
afilón /afi'lon/ *m*, steel, knife sharpener; razor-strop
afín /a'fin/ *a* nearby, contiguous; similar, related. *mf* relative by marriage
afinador /afina'ðor/ *m*, tuning key; tuner (of pianos, etc.)
afinar /afi'nar/ *vt* to finish, perfect; *Fig.* polish, refine; tune (musical instruments); refine (metals); *—vi* sing in tune; *—vr* grow refined
afinidad /afini'ðað/ *f*, affinity, analogy; relationship (by marriage); *Chem.* affinity
afirmación /afirma'θion; afirma'sion/ *f*, affirmation, statement
afirmadamente /afir,maða'mente/ *adv* firmly
afirmar /afir'mar/ *vt* to make firm; fix, fasten; affirm; *—vr* steady oneself; hold on to
afirmativa /afirma'tiβa/ *f*, affirmative
afirmativo /afirma'tiβo/ *a* affirmative
aflicción /aflik'θion; aflik'sion/ *f*, affliction, grief
aflictivo /aflik'tiβo/ *a* sorrowful, grievous
afligidamente /afli,hiða'mente/ *adv* sorrowfully
afligir /afli'hir/ *vt* to sadden; afflict, trouble; *—vr* lament, mourn
aflojamiento /afloha'miento/ *m*, slackening; loosening; diminution
aflojar /aflo'har/ *vt* to slacken; loosen; *—vi* relax, weaken; abate, diminish. **a. el paso,** to slow down
afluencia /a'fluenθia; a'fluensia/ *f*, crowd, concourse; eloquence, fluency
afluente /a'fluente/ *a* fluent, eloquent. *m*, tributary (river)
afluir /aflu'ir/ *vi irr* to crowd, swarm; flow (into). See **huir**
afonía /afo'nia/ *f*, *Med.* aphonia, loss of voice; hoarseness
afónico /a'foniko/ *a* hoarse
aforismo /afo'rismo/ *m*, aphorism
aforrador /aforra'ðor/ **(-ra)** *n* one who lines jackets, etc.
aforrar /afo'rrar/ *vt* to line (clothes, etc.); *—vr* wrap oneself up; *Inf.* gormandize
afortunadamente /afortu,naða'mente/ *adv* luckily, fortunately
afortunado /afortu'naðo/ *a* lucky, fortunate; happy; stormy
afortunar /afortu'nar/ *vt* to bring luck to, make happy
afrancesado /afranθe'saðo; afranse'saðo/ **(-da)** *a* Francophile; Frenchified *—n* Francophile
afrancesamiento /afranθesa'miento; afransesa'miento/ *m*, adoption of the French way of life; servile imitation of everything French
afrancesar /afranθe'sar; afranse'sar/ *vt* to make French, gallicize; Frenchify; *—vr* become a Francophile
afrenta /a'frenta/ *f*, insult, affront; disgrace
afrentar /afren'tar/ *vt* to insult; *—vr* be ashamed
afrentoso /afren'toso/ *a* insulting, outrageous; disgraceful
África /'afrika/ Africa
africanismo /,afrikan'ismo/ *m*, Africanism
africano /afri'kano/ **-na** *a* and *n* African
afrodisíaco /afroði'siako/ *a* and *m*, aphrodisiac
afrontar /afron'tar/ *vt* to place opposite; confront; face (danger, etc.)
afuera /a'fuera/ *adv* outside, out.
afueras /a'fueras/ *f pl*, suburbs, outskirts
agachada /aga'tʃaða/ *f*, crouch, duck; jerk
agachar /aga'tʃar/ *vt Inf.* bend, bow; *—vr Inf.* crouch down; lie low, hide
agalla /a'gaʎa; a'gaya/ *f*, oak-apple; tonsil (gen. *pl*); *Zool.* gill; *Inf.* gall, cheek
ágape /'agape/ *m*, agape; banquet, feast
Agar /a'gar/ Hagar
agárico /a'gariko/ *m*, *Bot.* agaric
agarrada /aga'rraða/ *f*, *Inf.* brawl, scuffle
agarradero /agarra'ðero/ *m*, handle; heft; *Inf.* influence, pull
agarrado /aga'rraðo/ *a Inf.* tight-fisted, mean
agarrar /aga'rrar/ *vt* to grip, grasp; seize, take; *Inf.* nab (jobs); *—vr* grip, hold on
agarro /a'garro/ *m*, hold; grip, grasp
agarrotar /agarro'tar/ *vt* to garrotte; tighten (ropes, etc.); press, squeeze; *—vr* (limbs) go numb
agasajar /agasa'har/ *vt* to indulge, spoil, pet; receive kindly; entertain; caress
agasajo /aga'saho/ *m*, indulgence, kindness; affability, geniality; entertainment; gift, offering
ágata /'agata/ *f*, *Mineral.* agate
agauchado /agau'tʃaðo/ *a* gaucho-like
agazapar /agaθa'par; agasa'par/ *vt Inf.* to nab, catch; *—vr Inf.* squat, crouch

agencia /a'henθia; a'hensia/ *f*, influence, agency
agenciar /ahen'θiar; ahen'siar/ *vt* to negotiate, arrange; procure, manage
agenda /a'henda/ *f*, notebook; agenda
agente /a'hente/ *m*, agent. **a. de bolsa** *or* **a. de cambio**, bill broker. **a. de negocios**, business agent. **a. de policía**, police officer. **a. fiscal**, revenue officer
agerasia /ahe'rasia/ *f*, sickness-free old age
agestado /ahes'taðo/ *a* used generally with advs. **bien** *or* **mal**, well *or* ill-featured
agigantado /ahigan'taðo/ *a* enormous, gigantic; outstanding, extraordinary
ágil /'ahil/ *a* agile, nimble; easy to use (e.g. *un libro ágil*, a book easy to use)
agilidad /ahili'ðað/ *f*, agility, nimbleness
agilizar /ahili'θar; ahili'sar/ *vt* to make agile, limber; refresh one's knowledge of (e.g. *Quiero agilizar mi español*, I want to refresh my knowledge of Spanish); to enable; *—vr* limber up
agitación /ahita'θion; ahita'sion/ *f*, shaking; agitation, excitement
agitador /ahita'ðor/ **(-ra)** *a* stirring; agitating *—n* agitator. *m*, stirrer, stirring rod
agitar /ahi'tar/ *vt* to stir; shake; agitate, excite **a. una cuestión**, raise a question; discuss a question
aglomeración /aglomera'θion; aglomera'sion/ *f*, agglomeration
aglomerado /aglome'raðo/ *m*, briquette
aglomerar /aglome'rar/ *vt* to agglomerate, amass
aglutinación /aglutina'θion; aglutina'sion/ *f*, agglutination
aglutinar(se) /agluti'nar/ *vt* and *vr* to stick, agglutinate
agnosticismo /agnosti'θismo; agnosti'sismo/ *m*, agnosticism
agnóstico /ag'nostiko/ **(-ca)** *a* and *n* agnostic
agobiar /ago'βiar/ *vt* to bow, bend down; *Fig.* weigh down, oppress; *—vr* bend (beneath a weight)
agobio /a'goβio/ *m*, bowing, bending down; oppression, burden, weight
agolparse /agol'parse/ *vr* to rush, crowd, swarm
agonía /ago'nia/ *f*, agony, anguish
agónico /a'goniko/ *a* dying; agonizing
agonizante /agoni'θante; agoni'sante/ *a* dying
agonizar /agoni'θar; agoni'sar/ *vt* to attend a dying person; *Inf.* pester, annoy; *—vi* be dying (gen. **estar agonizando**)
agorar /ago'rar/ *vt* to prophesy, foretell
agorero /ago'rero/ **(-ra)** *a* prophetic; ill-boding *—n* seer, augur
agostarse /agos'tarse/ *vt* and *vr* to dry up, shrivel
agosto /a'gosto/ *m*, August; harvest. *Inf.* **hacer su a.**, to make hay while the sun shines
agotable /ago'taβle/ *a* exhaustible
agotado /ago'taðo/ *a* exhausted; out of print (of books)
agotador /agota'ðor/ *a* exhausting; exhaustive
agotamiento /aˌgota'miento/ *m*, exhaustion
agotar /ago'tar/ *vt* to drain off (water); empty (a glass); exhaust; run through (money); study thoroughly, examine closely (a subject)
agraciado /agra'θiaðo; agra'siaðo/ *a* graceful; pretty
agraciar /agra'θiar; agra'siar/ *vt* to lend grace to; make pretty; favor
agradable /agra'ðaβle/ *a* agreeable, pleasant
agradar /agra'ðar/ *vi* to be pleasing, like, please (e.g. *Me agrada su sinceridad*, I like his sincerity)
agradecer /agraðe'θer; agraðe'ser/ *vt irr* to be grateful for; thank for; *Fig.* repay, requite. See **conocer**
agradecido /agraðe'θiðo; agraðe'siðo/ *a* grateful; thankful
agradecimiento /agraðeθi'miento; agraðesi'miento/ *m*, gratitude; thankfulness
agrado /a'graðo/ *m*, pleasure; desire, liking; amiability, affability
agrandar /agran'dar/ *vt* to enlarge
agrario /a'grario/ *a* agrarian
agravación /agraβa'θion; agraβa'sion/ *f*, **agravamiento** *m*, aggravation, worsening
agravador /agraβa'ðor/ *a* aggravating; worsening; increasing
agravar /agra'βar/ *vt* to aggravate, increase; oppress (taxes, responsibilities); make worse; exaggerate; *—vr* grow worse
agraviador /agraβia'ðor/ **-ra** *a* offensive *—n* offender
agraviar /agra'βiar/ *vt* to offend; wrong; *—vr* take offense, be insulted
agravio /a'graβio/ *m*, offense, insult; wrong, injury
agraz /a'graθ; a'gras/ *m*, unripened grape; verjuice; *Fig.* bitterness
agredir /agre'ðir/ *vt* to attack
agregación /agrega'θion; agrega'sion/ *f*, association, aggregation; total, collection, aggregate
agregado /agre'gaðo/ *m*, aggregate; assistant; attaché
agregar /agre'gar/ *vt* to add; collect, amass; appoint (to a post). **agregarse a...**, to join... (e.g. an association)
agresión /agre'sion/ *f*, aggression
agresivo /agre'siβo/ *a* aggressive
agresor /agre'sor/ **(-ra)** *a* and *n* aggressor
agreste /a'greste/ *a* rural, rustic; wild; uncouth, rude
agriar /a'griar/ *vt* to make bitter or sour; exasperate, provoke
agrícola /a'grikola/ *a* agricultural; *mf* agriculturalist, farmer
agricultura /agrikul'tura/ *f*, agriculture
agridulce /agri'ðulθe; agri'ðulse/ *a* bitter-sweet
agrietarse /agrie'tarse/ *vr* to crack, split
agrimensor /agrimen'sor/ *m*, surveyor
agrimensura /agrimen'sura/ *f*, surveying
agrio /'agrio/ *a* bitter, sour; rough, uneven (ground); brittle; sharp (of color contrast); unsociable; disagreeable
agrisetado /agrise'taðo/ *a* flowered (of materials)
agronomía /agrono'mia/ *f*, agronomy
agrónomo /a'gronomo/ *a* agronomic. *m*, agronomist
agrupación /agrupa'θion; agrupa'sion/ *f*, congregation, assembly; group; crowd; crowding, grouping
agrupar /agru'par/ *vt* to assemble, group; *—vr* crowd, cluster
agrura /a'grura/ *f*, bitterness; sourness; asperity
agua /'agua/ *f*, water; rain; slope of a roof; *pl* shot or watered effect on silks, etc.; medicinal waters; waves; water (of precious stones). **a. abajo**, down-stream. **a. arriba**, upstream. **a. bendita**, holy water. **a. cruda**, hard water. **a. de colonia**, eau de Cologne. **a. dulce**, fresh water. **a. fresca**, cold water. **a. nieve**, sleet. **a. oxigenada**, hydrogen peroxide. *Fig. Inf.* **estar con el a. al cuello**, to be in low water. *Fig. Inf.* **estar entre dos aguas**, to be between two fires. *Naut.* **hacer a.**, to leak. **Todo eso es ya a. pasada**, That's all water under the bridge
aguacero /agua'θero; agua'sero/ *m*, heavy rainfall, shower
aguada /a'guaða/ *f*, water supply on board ship; flood (in mines); watering station; *Art.* water color
aguadero /agua'ðero/ *m*, (animals') watering place
aguado /a'guaðo/ *a* watery; abstemious; watered
aguador /agua'ðor/ **(-ra)** *n* water carrier, water seller; drawer (of water)
aguafiestas /ˌagua'fiestas/ *mf Fig. Inf.* wet blanket
aguafuerte /ˌagua'fuerte/ *f*, etching
aguaje /a'guahe/ *m*, tide, waves; sea current; water supply (on board ship); wake (of a ship)
aguamanil /aguama'nil/ *m*, washstand; pitcher, ewer
aguamanos /agua'manos/ *m*, water for washing hands; pitcher
aguamarina /aguama'rina/ *f*, aquamarine
aguamiel /agua'miel/ *f*, honey and water, hydromel
aguantable /aguan'taβle/ *a* tolerable, bearable
aguantar /aguan'tar/ *vt* to bear, tolerate, endure; restrain, resist, oppose; *—vr* bear in silence, keep quiet
aguante /a'guante/ *m*, patience, endurance; resistance
aguar /a'guar/ *vt* to water down (wine, etc.); spoil (fun, etc.); *—vr* be filled with water; be flooded; become watery or thin
aguardar /aguar'ðar/ *vt* to await; expect; allow time to (debtors)
aguardentería /aguarˌðente'ria/ *f*, liquor shop

aguardentoso /aguarðen'toso/ *a* spirituous, containing; **aguardiente** hoarse, husky (of the voice)
aguardiente /aguar'ðiente/ *m,* liquor. **a. de caña,** rum
aguardo /a'guarðo/ *m,* ambush (for a hunter)
aguarrás /agua'rras/ *m,* oil of turpentine
aguatinta /agua'tinta/ *f,* aquatint
aguatocha /agua'totʃa/ *f,* pump (for water, etc.)
aguaturma /agua'turma/ *f,* Jerusalem artichoke
agudeza /agu'ðeθa; agu'ðesa/ *f,* sharpness; keenness; distinctness; alertness, cleverness; witty sally, repartee; wit; swiftness
agudo /a'guðo/ *a* sharp; alert, clever; (*Geom. Med.*) acute; fine, keen; rapid; high-pitched; strong (of scents, etc.)
agüero /a'guero/ *m,* omen, sign; prophecy, prediction
aguerrido /age'rriðo/ *a* veteran, war-hardened
aguerrir /age'rrir/ *vt defective* to harden to war; toughen
aguijada /agi'haða/ *f,* goad, spur
aguijar /agi'har/ *vt* to prick (with a goad); urge on, encourage (animals); incite, instigate; spur on; *—vi* walk swiftly
aguijón /agi'hon/ *m,* goad; sting; thorn, prickle; spur; incitement, stimulus. **tener aguijones,** to be on pins and needles
aguijonazo /agiho'naθo; agiho'naso/ *m,* prick (with a goad)
águila /'agila/ *f,* eagle; master mind. **a. caudal** *or* **a. real,** royal eagle. **á. o sol,** heads or tails (Mexico)
aguileña /agi'leɲa/ *f, Bot.* columbine
aguileño /agi'leɲo/ *a* aquiline
aguilón /agi'lon/ *m, Archit.* gable; boom (of a crane)
aguinaldo /agi'naldo/ *m,* Christmas present; New Year's gift
aguja /a'guha/ *f,* needle; hand, pointer; hatpin; engraver's burin; switch; *Rail.* point; *Rail.* rail; obelisk; spire; bodkin; knitting needle; crochet hook; (compass) needle *pl Bot.* plumelet. **a. capotera, a. de zurcir,** darning needle. **a. de marear** *Naut.*, binnacle; mariner's compass. **a. de media,** knitting needle. **a. espartera,** packing needle
agujerear /aguhere'ar/ *vt* to perforate, make holes in
agujero /agu'hero/ *m,* hole, aperture; needle maker or seller; needle case
agujeta /agu'heta/ *f,* lace (for shoes, etc.); *pl* muscular pains, aches; tip, gratuity
agusanarse /agusa'narse/ *vr* to become worm-infested
aguzadura /aguθa'ðura; agusa'ðura/ *f,* sharpening, grinding, whetting
aguzar /agu'θar; agu'sar/ *vt* to sharpen; grind, whet; stimulate, encourage; urge on, incite
ahechadura /aetʃa'ðura/ *f,* chaff (of grain)
ahembrado /aem'braðo/ *a* effeminate
aherrojar /aerro'har/ *vt* to put (a prisoner) in irons; oppress
aherrumbrar /aerrum'brar/ *vt* to give the color or taste of iron to; *—vr* taste or look like iron; go rusty
ahí /a'i/ *adv* there; over there. **de a.,** thus, so. **por a.,** somewhere about, near at hand.
ahidalgado /aiðal'gaðo/ *a* gentlemanly; noble, generous
ahijado /ai'haðo/ **(-da)** *n* godchild; protégé
ahijar /ai'har/ *vt* to adopt (children); mother (animals); attribute, impute; *—vi* bring forth offspring; *Bot.* sprout. See **prohibir**
ahincado /ain'kaðo/ *a* earnest, eager
ahincar /ain'kar/ *vt* to urge, press; *—vr* hurry, hasten. See **prohibir**
ahínco /a'inko/ *m,* earnestness, eagerness
ahitar /ai'tar/ *vt* to stuff with food; bore, disgust. See **prohibir**
ahíto /a'ito/ *a* full of food; *Fig.* fed up. *m,* indigestion
ahogado /ao'gaðo/ **(-da)** *a* drowned; suffocated; stuffy, unventilated; stifling *—n* drowned person; victim of suffocation
ahogamiento /aoga'miento/ *m,* drowning; suffocation
ahogar /ao'gar/ *vt* to drown; suffocate; put out (the fire); stifle (yawns, etc.); suppress, extinguish; tire; overwater (plants); *—vr Naut.* sink, founder; drown; suffocate
ahogo /a'ogo/ *m,* anxiety, grief; difficulty in breathing, oppression; asthma; embarrassment; suffocation; straitened circumstances
ahondamiento /aonda'miento/ *m,* in-depth treatment (e.g. *el a. de un problema,* in-depth treatment of a problem)
ahondar /aon'dar/ *vt* to deepen; excavate, dig; go into thoroughly; go deep into, penetrate; *—vr* (earth) subside
ahora /a'ora/ *adv* now; very soon; just now, a short time ago *—conjunc* whether; now. **a. bien,** well now, given that. **a. mismo,** immediately, at once. **por a.,** for the present
ahorcado /aor'kaðo/ **(-da)** *n* hanged man
ahorcar /aor'kar/ *vt* to execute by hanging, hang. *Inf.* **a. los hábitos,** to leave the priesthood, cease to be an ecclesiastic
ahormar /aor'mar/ *vt* to adjust, shape; break in (new shoes); make (a person) see reason
ahorquillar /aorki'ʎar; aorki'yar/ *vt* to prop up (trees) with forks; *—vr* grow forked
ahorrar /ao'rrar/ *vt* to free (slaves); save, economize; avoid, eschew; *—vr* avoid; remove clothing
ahorro /a'orro/ *m,* economy, thrift; *pl* savings
ahuchar /au'tʃar/ *vt* to hoard; expel, drive away. See **desahuciar**
ahuciar /au'θiar; au'siar/ *vt* take possession of (a house)
ahuecar /aue'kar/ *vt* to hollow out; loosen; shake out; puff out, inflate; put on a solemn voice; hoe, dig; *Inf. vr* puff oneself out; put on airs
ahumada /au'maða/ *f,* smoke signal
ahumado /au'maðo/ *a* smoked; smoky
ahumar /au'mar/ *vt* to smoke (herrings, etc.); fill with smoke; *—vi* smoke, burn; *—vr* be full of smoke; taste smoked; *Inf.* get drunk. See **desahuciar**
ahusado /au'saðo/ *a* spindle-shaped
ahuyentar /auyen'tar/ *vt* to frighten off; drive away; dismiss, banish (anxiety, etc.); *—vr* flee
airadamente /airaða'mente/ *adv* wrathfully, angrily
airado /ai'raðo/ *a* angry
airar /ai'rar/ *vt* to annoy, anger; *—vr* grow annoyed
aire /'aire/ *m,* air; atmosphere (sometimes *pl*); breeze, wind; bearing, appearance; vanity; (horse's) gait; futility, frivolity; grace, charm; gracefulness; *Mus.* air; *Mus.* tempo. **a. popular,** popular tune. **al a. libre,** in the open air, outdoors. *Inf.* **beber los aires (por),** to yearn (for)
aireación /airea'θion; airea'sion/ *f,* airing; ventilation
airear /aire'ar/ *vt* to air; ventilate; aerate; *—vr* take the air; catch a chill
airosidad /airosi'ðað/ *f,* gracefulness; jauntiness
airoso /ai'roso/ *a* airy, open; windy, breezy, fresh; graceful; handsome; jaunty; victorious, successful
aislacionamismo /aislaθiona'mismo; aislasiona'mismo/ *m, Polit.* isolationism
aislacionista /aislaθion'ista; aislasion'ista/ *mf Polit.* isolationist
aislado /ais'laðo/ *a* isolated; remote; individual; single; *Elec.* insulated
aislador /aisla'ðor/ *m, Phys.* insulator
aislamiento /aisla'miento/ *m,* isolation; *Phys.* insulation
aislante /ais'lante/ *a* isolating; insulating
aislar /ais'lar/ *vt* to isolate; *Elec.* insulate; *—vr* become a recluse; become isolated
¡ajá! /a'ha/ *interj Inf.* Aha! Good!
ajaquecarse /ahake'karse/ *vr* to have a headache
ajar /a'har/ *vt* to crease, crumple, spoil; humiliate; *—vr* fade, wither (flowers)
ajear /ahe'ar/ *vi* (partridge) to squawk (when cornered)
ajedrecista /aheðre'θista; aheðre'sista/ *mf* chess player
ajedrez /ahe'ðreθ; ahe'ðres/ *m,* chess
ajenjo /a'henho/ *m, Bot.* wormwood; absinthe
ajeno /a'heno/ *a* alien; belonging to another; various, diverse; free, exempt; unsuitable; irrelevant

ajetrear /ahetre'ar/ *vt* to tire out, exhaust; *—vr* be overtired
ajetreo /ahe'treo/ *m,* exhaustion, fatigue
ajo /'aho/ *m,* garlic; *Inf.* make up, paint; disreputable affair, shady business; curse, oath. *Inf.* **revolver el a.,** to stir up trouble
ajorca /a'horka/ *f,* bracelet; slave bangle
ajornalar /ahorna'lar/ *vt* to hire by the day
ajuar /ahu'ar/ *m,* trousseau; household equipment
ajustado /ahus'taðo/ *a* exact; tight-fitting; trim
ajustador /ahusta'ðor/ **(-ra)** *a* adjusting *—n* adjuster. *m,* tight-fitting jacket
ajustamiento /ahusta'miento/ *m,* adjustment; agreement
ajustar /ahus'tar/ *vt* to adjust; fit; arrange; make an agreement about; reconcile; settle (accounts); engage, employ; retain (a barrister); regulate; tune up (a motor); *—vi* fit; *—vr* adapt oneself. *Inf.* **a. cuentas viejas,** to settle old accounts
ajuste /a'huste/ *m,* fitting; adjustment; agreement; arrangement; *Print.* make-up. reconciliation; settlement; regulation; engagement, appointment
ajusticiado /ahusti'θiaðo; ahusti'siaðo/ **(-da)** *n* executed person
ajusticiar /ahusti'θiar; ahusti'siar/ *vt* to put to death
al /al/ (contraction of *a* + *el*). 1 *—prep a* + *m. def. art.,* to the, e.g. *Han ido al mar,* They have gone to the sea. 2 *—prep a* + *el* used as *dem. pron* to that, to the one, e.g. *Mi sombrero se parece mucho al que tiene Vd.,* My hat is very similar to the one you have. *al* + *infin.* means when, as, at the same time as, e.g. *Al llamar a la puerta la vi en el jardín,* As I was knocking at the door, I saw her in the garden
ala /'ala/ *f, Zool.* wing; row, line; brim (of a hat); eaves; (*Archit. Aer. Mil. Bot.*) wing; blade (of propeller); fin (of fish); *pl* courage. **a. del corazón,** *Anat.* auricle. **arrastrar el a.,** to woo, flirt with. *Fig.* **cortar** (*or* **quebrar**) **las alas (a),** to clip a person's wings
Alá /a'la/ *m,* Allah
alabador /alaβa'ðor/ **(-ra)** *n* praiser, extoller
alabanza /ala'βanθa; ala'βansa/ *f,* praise; eulogy
alabar /ala'βar/ *vt* to praise; *—vr* brag, boast
alabarda /ala'βarða/ *f,* halberd
alabardero /alaβar'ðero/ *m,* halberdier; *Theat.* claque, clapper
alabastrino /alaβas'trino/ *a* alabastrine, alabaster
alabastro /ala'βastro/ *m,* alabaster
alacena /ala'θena; ala'sena/ *f,* cupboard; recess; closet; safe (for food)
alacrán /ala'kran/ *m,* scorpion
alacridad /alakri'ðað/ *f,* alacrity, eagerness
alado /a'laðo/ *a* winged; feathered; *Fig.* soaring
alambicado /alambi'kaðo/ *a* sparing, frugal; subtle; euphuistic
alambicar /alambi'kar/ *vt* to distil; examine carefully, scrutinize; make over-subtle or euphuistic (of style)
alambique /alam'bike/ *m,* still
alambrada /alam'braða/ *f, Mil.* wire-entanglement
alambrado /alam'braðo/ *m,* wire-netting; *Mil.* wire-entanglement; wire cover
alambrar /alam'brar/ *vt* to wire (fence)
alambre /a'lambre/ *m,* wire; sheep bells. **a. espinoso,** barbed wire
alambrera /alam'brera/ *f,* wire fence; wire-netting; wire cover
alambrista /alam'brista/ *mf* tight-rope walker; (Mexico) wetback
alameda /ala'meða/ *f,* poplar wood or grove; avenue of poplars
álamo /'alamo/ *m,* poplar. **a. temblón,** aspen tree
alano /a'lano/ *m,* mastiff
alarde /a'larðe/ *m, Mil.* parade; display, ostentation. **hacer a. de,** to brag about
alargamiento /alarga'miento/ *m,* lengthening; stretching
alargar /alar'gar/ *vt* to lengthen; prolong; pass, hand (things); pay out (ropes, etc.); increase; *—vr* go away, depart; be wordy, spread oneself; lengthen
alarido /ala'riðo/ *m,* yell, shout; shriek, scream; howl; yelp; cry (of a seagull)
alarma /a'larma/ *f,* alarm. **a. aérea,** air-raid warning
alarmante /alar'mante/ *a* alarming
alarmar /alar'mar/ *vt* to give the alarm; frighten; *—vr* be alarmed
alarmista /alar'mista/ *mf* alarmist
alazán /ala'θan; ala'san/ *a* sorrel-colored. *m,* sorrel horse
alazo /a'laθo; a'laso/ *m,* flap or stroke of the wings
alba /'alβa/ *f,* dawn; *Eccl.* alb, vestment. **al a.,** at dawn
albacea /alβa'θea; alβa'sea/ *mf* executor, executrix; testator
albanés /alβa'nes/ **(-esa)** *a* and *n* Albanian. *m,* Albanian language
albañil /alβa'ɲil/ *m,* mason, bricklayer
albañilería /alβaɲile'ria/ *f,* masonry; bricklaying
albarda /al'βarða/ *f,* pack-saddle
albardilla /alβar'ðiʎa; alβar'ðiya/ *f,* small saddle; pad; small pillow; *Archit.* coping
albaricoque /alβari'koke/ *m,* apricot
albaricoquero /alβariko'kero/ *m,* apricot tree
albarrada /alβa'rraða/ *f,* stone wall; mud fence
albatros /alβa'tros/ *m,* albatross
albear /alβe'ar/ *vi* to become white, whiten
albedrío /alβe'ðrio/ *m,* free will; fancy, caprice
albéitar /al'βeitar/ *m,* veterinary surgeon; farrier
alberca /al'βerka/ *f,* reservoir, tank; vat; artificial lake
albergar /alβer'gar/ *vt* to shelter; nourish, harbor; *—vi* and *vr* take refuge or shelter; lodge
albergue /al'βerge/ *m,* shelter, refuge; den, lair; hospitality; lodging; asylum
albo /'alβo/ *a* pure white
albóndiga /al'βondiga/ *f,* forced meat ball, rissole
albor /al'βor/ *m,* whiteness; dawnlight, dawn. **a. de la vida,** life's dawning, childhood
alborada /alβo'raða/ *f,* dawn; reveille; *Mil.* dawn attack; *Mus.* aubade
alborear /alβore'ar/ *vi* to grow light, dawn
albornoz /alβor'noθ; alβor'nos/ *m,* burnouse
alborotado /alβoro'taðo/ *a* impulsive; turbulent; noisy; excitable
alborotar /alβoro'tar/ *vt* to disturb; *—vi* make a noise; be gay; *—vr* riot; grow rough (sea)
alboroto /alβo'roto/ *m,* noise; confusion; tumult; riot; rejoicing, gaiety; *pl* popcorn
alborozar /alβoro'θar; alβoro'sar/ *vt* to overjoy, gladden; *—vr* rejoice, be glad
alborozo /alβo'roθo; alβo'roso/ *m,* gladness, rejoicing, joy
albricias /al'βriθias; al'βrisias/ *f pl,* reward for bringer of good tidings *—interj* **¡A.!** Joy! Congratulations!
álbum /'alβum/ *m,* album
albúmina /al'βumina/ *f,* albumin
albur /al'βur/ *m, Ichth.* dace; chance, risk. **al a. de,** at the risk of
alcachofa /alka'tʃofa/ *f,* artichoke
alcahueta /alka'ueta/ *f,* procuress, go-between
alcahuete /alka'uete/ *m,* procurer, go-between, pimp, pander; *Fig. Inf.* protector, screen; *Inf.* scandalmonger
alcahuetear /alkauete'ar/ *vt* to procure, act as a go-between for; *—vi* be a pimp or a procuress
alcaide /al'kaiðe/ *m,* governor of a fortress *Obs.*; governor of a prison
alcalde /al'kalde/ *m,* mayor; magistrate. *Inf.* **tener el padre a.,** to have a friend at court
alcaldesa /alkal'desa/ *f,* mayoress
alcaldía /alkal'dia/ *f,* office or authority of an alcalde
álcali /'alkali/ *m, Chem.* alkali
alcalino /alka'lino/ *a* alkaline
alcaloide /alka'loiðe/ *m, Chem.* alkaloid
alcance /al'kanθe; al'kanse/ *m,* reaching, attainment; range (of firearms, etc.); scope; arm's length or reach; pursuit; stop press *or* extra edition (newspapers); *Com.* deficit; importance; *pl* talent; capacity. **al a. de la voz,** within call. **hombre de cortos alcances,** a limited, dull man. **poner al a. de,** to make available to; make intelligible to
alcancía /alkan'θia; alkan'sia/ *f,* money-box; coin bank, piggy bank
alcanfor /alkan'for/ *m,* camphor
alcanforado /alkanfo'raðo/ *a* camphorated

alcantarilla /alkanta'riʎa; alkanta'riya/ *f*, little bridge; sewer; culvert; bed for electric cable
alcantarillado /alkantari'ʎaðo; alkantari'yaðo/ *m*, sewage system; main sewer
alcanzable /alkan'θaβle; alkan'saβle/ *a* obtainable; attainable
alcanzadizo /alkanθa'ðiθo; alkansa'ðiso/ *a* attainable, easily reached
alcanzar /alkan'θar; alkan'sar/ *vt* to overtake; reach; range (of guns, etc.); attain, achieve; understand; *Fig.* equal (in attainments); live at the same time as, be contemporaneous with; be capable of, be able; —*vi* reach; share, participate in; be enough
alcaparra /alka'parra/ *f*, *Bot.* caper; caper bush
alcaucil /alkau'θil; alkau'sil/ *m*, (in most places) wild artichoke; (in some places) cultivated artichoke
alcazaba /alka'θaβa; alka'saβa/ *f*, fortress (within a walled town or city), casbah
alcázar /al'kaθar; al'kasar/ *m*, fortress; royal residence, castle; *Naut.* quarterdeck
alción /al'θion; al'sion/ *m*, *Ornith.* kingfisher
alcista /al'θista; al'sista/ *mf* speculator (on Stock Exchange)
alcoba /al'koβa/ *f*, bedroom; alcove, recess; Moorish flute
alcohol /al'kool/ *m*, alcohol; galena; eye black (cosmetic); spirits of wine. **a. desnaturalizado,** industrial alcohol, methylated spirit. **a. metílico,** wood alcohol
alcohólico /alko'oliko/ *a* alcoholic
alcoholismo /alkool'ismo/ *m*, alcoholism
alcor /al'kor/ *m*, hill; slope
Alcorán /alko'ran/ *m*, Koran
alcornoque /alkor'noke/ *m*, cork tree; dunderhead, dolt
alcorza /al'korθa; al'korsa/ *f*, *Cul.* icing, sugar-paste
alcorzar /alkor'θar; alkor'sar/ *vt* *Cul.* to ice, cover with sugar; decorate, adorn
alcurnia /al'kurnia/ *f*, lineage, family, descent
alcuza /al'kuθa; al'kusa/ *f*, oil-bottle; oil-can; cruet
aldaba /al'daβa/ *f*, door knocker; bolt, latch; *pl* protectors, influential helpers. *Inf.* **tener buenas aldabas,** to have plenty of pull
aldabada /alda'βaða/ *f*, rap with the knocker; sudden shock
aldabeo /alda'βeo/ *m*, knocking
aldea /al'dea/ *f*, village
aldeano /alde'ano/ **(-na)** *a* village; country, ignorant —*n* villager; countryman, peasant
aldehído /alde'iðo/ *m*, *Chem.* aldehyde
aleación /alea'θion; alea'sion/ *f*, alloy
alear /ale'ar/ *vi* to flutter, beat the wings; flap one's arms; recuperate, grow well; —*vt* alloy
aleatorio /alea'torio/ *a* accidental, fortuitous
aleccionamiento /alekθiona'miento; aleksiona'miento/ *m*, teaching, training, coaching
aleccionar /alekθio'nar; aleksio'nar/ *vt* to teach, train, coach
aledaño /ale'ðaɲo/ *a* adjoining; border. *m*, boundary, border
alegación /alega'θion; alega'sion/ *f*, allegation, statement
alegar /ale'gar/ *vt* to allege, state; cite; —*vi* *Law.* bring forward, adduce
alegato /ale'gato/ *m*, *Law.* speech (for the prosecution or defense)
alegoría /alego'ria/ *f*, allegory
alegórico /ale'goriko/ *a* allegorical
alegorizar /alegori'θar; alegori'sar/ *vt* to interpret allegorically, treat as an allegory
alegrar /ale'grar/ *vt* to make happy, gladden, rejoice; adorn, beautify; stir (fires); —*vr* be glad, rejoice; *Inf.* be merry (tipsy)
alegre /a'legre/ *a* joyful, glad; cheerful, gay; bright (colors, etc.); pretty, attractive; *Inf.* risqué; *Inf.* flirtatious, light
alegría /ale'gria/ *f*, joy, gladness; cheerfulness, gaiety; *pl* public rejoicings
alegrón /ale'gron/ *m*, sudden unexpected joy; *Inf.* flash of light —*a* *Inf.* flirtatious
alejamiento /aleha'miento/ *m*, placing at a distance, removal; withdrawal
Alejandría /alehan'dria/ Alexandria
alejar /ale'har/ *vt* to place at a distance, remove; withdraw; ward off (dangers, etc.); —*vr* depart, go away; withdraw. **alejarse de,** to abandon (a belief, custom, superstition, etc.)
alelar /ale'lar/ *vt* to make silly or stupid
aleluya /ale'luya/ *mf*, alleluia. *m*, Eastertide. *f*, small Easter cake; *Inf.* daub, poor painting; *Inf.* doggerel; joy, rejoicing
alemán /ale'man/ **(-ana)** *a* and *n* German. *m*, German language.
Alemania /ale'mania/ Germany
alentada /alen'taða/ *f*, deep breath
alentado /alen'taðo/ *a* valiant, spirited; proud
alentador /alenta'ðor/ *a* encouraging, inspiring, stimulating
alentar /alen'tar/ *vi irr* to breathe; —*vt* encourage, inspire; —*vr* be encouraged. See **sentar**
alerce /a'lerθe; a'lerse/ *m*, larch tree and wood
alergia /aler'hia/ *f*, allergy
alergólogo /aler'gologo/ *m*, allergist
alero /a'lero/ *m*, projecting roof; splashboard (of carriages); eaves; gable end
alerón /ale'ron/ *m*, *Aer.* aileron
alerta /a'lerta/ *adv* watchfully —*interj* Take care! Look out! **estar ojo a.,** to be on the watch
alerto /a'lerto/ *a* watchful, alert
aleta /a'leta/ *f*, *dim* small wing; fin
aletargado /aletar'gaðo/ *a* lethargic; comatose
aletargamiento /aletarga'miento/ *m*, lethargy
aletargar /aletar'gar/ *vt* to cause lethargy; —*vr* become lethargic
aletazo /ale'taθo; ale'taso/ *m*, flapping, beating (of wings); *Inf.* theft
aletear /alete'ar/ *vi* to flap the wings, flutter; move the arms up and down; become convalescent
aleteo /ale'teo/ *m*, fluttering, flapping of wings; beating, palpitation (of heart)
aleve /a'leβe/ *a* See **alevoso**
alevosía /ale'βosia/ *f*, *Law.* malice; treachery
alevoso /ale'βoso/ *a* *Law.* malicious; treacherous
alfabético /alfa'βetiko/ *a* alphabetical
alfabetización /alfaβetiθa'θion; alfaβetisa'sion/ *f*, literacy work
alfabetizador /alfaβetiθa'ðor; alfaβetisa'ðor/ *m*, literacy worker
alfabeto /alfa'βeto/ *m*, alphabet. **a. manual,** sign language
alfalfa /al'falfa/ *f*, *Bot.* lucerne
alfar /al'far/ *m*, potter's workshop; pottery, earthenware
alfarería /alfare'ria/ *f*, pottery shop; potter's workshop; potter's craft
alfarero /alfa'rero/ *m*, potter
alfeñique /alfe'ɲike/ *m*, *Cul.* icing, sugarpaste; *Inf.* affectation
alférez /al'fereθ; al'feres/ *m*, *Mil.* ensign; second lieutenant; lieutenant. *Nav.* **a. de fragata,** sub-lieutenant. *Nav.* **a. de navío,** lieutenant
alfil /al'fil/ *m*, bishop (in chess)
alfiler /alfi'ler/ *m*, pin; brooch with a pin; tiepin; *pl* pin-money, dress-allowance; *Fig. Inf.* **no estar uno con sus alfileres,** to have a slate loose. *Inf.* **vestido de veinticinco alfileres,** dressed to the nines
alfiletero /alfile'tero/ *m*, needle-case
alfombra /al'fombra/ *f*, carpet; rug
alfombrado /alfom'braðo/ *m*, carpeting
alfombrar /alfom'brar/ *vt* to carpet
alfombrilla eléctrica /alfom'briʎa e'lektrika; alfom'briya e'lektrika/ *f*, electric pad or blanket
alfombrista /alfom'brista/ *m*, carpet merchant; layer of carpets
alforja /al'forha/ *f*, saddle-bag; *Mil.* knapsack
alforza /al'forθa; al'forsa/ *f*, *Sew.* tuck; *Inf.* scar
alforzar /alfor'θar; alfor'sar/ *vt* *Sew.* to tuck
alga /'alga/ *f*, alga, seaweed
algalia /al'galia/ *f*, civet
algarabía /algara'βia/ *f*, Arabic; *Inf.* gibberish; din of voices, uproar
algarada /alga'raða/ *f*, troop of horse; uproar, hubbub; outcry

algarroba /alga'rroβa/ *f, Bot.* carob bean
algazara /alga'θara; alga'sara/ *f,* Moorish war cry; rejoicing, merriment; noise, clamor
álgebra /'alheβra/ *f,* algebra; art of bone setting
algebraico /alhe'βraiko/ *a* algebraic
algebrista /alhe'βrista/ *mf* bonesetter; algebraist
álgido /'alhiðo/ *a* icy cold
algo /'algo/ *indef pron* some, something (e.g. *Se ve que hay a. que le molesta,* You can see that something is irritating him) *—adv* somewhat, a bit. **en a.,** in some way
algodón /algo'ðon/ *m,* cotton plant; cotton flower; cotton fabric; candy floss (UK), cotton candy (USA). **a. en rama,** cotton-wool. **a. hidró-filo,** absorbent cotton wool. **a. pólvora,** nitrocellulose
algodonal /algoðo'nal/ *m,* cotton plantation
algodonero /algoðo'nero/ **(-ra)** *a* cotton *—n* cotton merchant
alguacil /algua'θil; algua'sil/ *m,* policeman, constable; *Obs.* city governor; short-legged spider
alguien /'algien/ *indef pron* someone, somebody, e.g. *Dime si viene a.,* Tell me if anyone comes
algún /al'gun/ *Abbr.* of **alguno** bef. *m sing* noun, e.g. *a. libro*
alguno /al'guno/ *a* (*Abbr.* **algún** bef. *m, sing*) some, any *—indef pron* someone, somebody; *pl* some, some people. **alguno que otro,** a few
alhaja /al'aha/ *f,* jewel; ornament; treasure, precious object; *Inf.* gem, excellent person (also ironic, e.g. *Es una a.,* He's a fine fellow)
alhajar /ala'har/ *vt* to adorn with jewels, bejewel; furnish, equip
alharaca /alar'aka/ *f,* vehemence, demonstration, fuss (gen. *pl*)
alheña /al'eɲa/ *f, Bot.* privet; henna
alhóndiga /al'ondiga/ *f,* corn exchange; public granary
aliado /a'liaðo/ **(-da)** *a* allied *—n* ally
alianza /a'lianθa; a'liansa/ *f,* alliance; pact, agreement; relationship (by marriage); sum total, whole (of factors, etc.); wedding-ring
aliarse /a'liarse/ *vr* to join together, become allies; be associated
alicaído /alika'iðo/ *a* drooping; *Inf.* weak, exhausted; discouraged, downhearted; come down in the world
alicates /ali'kates/ *m pl,* pincers, pliers
aliciente /ali'θiente; ali'siente/ *m,* attraction, inducement
alícuota /a'likuota/ *f, a* aliquot; proportional. **partes alícuotas,** aliquot parts
alienación /aliena'θion; aliena'sion/ *f,* alienation
alienado /alie'naðo/ *a* insane, mad
alienar /alie'nar/ *vt* See **enajenar**
alienista /alie'nista/ *mf Med.* alienist
aliento /a'liento/ *m,* breathing; breath; courage, spirit; encouragement. **el posterior a.,** one's last breath. **cobrar a.,** to regain one's breath; take heart. **de un a.,** in one breath; without stopping
alifafe /ali'fafe/ *m, Inf.* ailment; tumor on horse's hock
aligación /aliga'θion; aliga'sion/ *f,* binding together, alligation
aligeramiento /a,lihera'miento/ *m,* lightening, reduction in weight
aligerar /alihe'rar/ *vt* to lighten, make less heavy; quicken, hasten; ease, alleviate; moderate; shorten, abbreviate
alígero /a'lihero/ *a Poet.* winged; fleet, swift
alimaña /ali'maɲa/ *f,* destructive animal
alimentación /alimenta'θion; alimenta'sion/ *f,* nourishment; feeding
alimentar /alimen'tar/ *vt* to feed; nourish; encourage, foment; assist, aid; keep, support
alimenticio /alimen'tiθio; alimen'tisio/ *a* nourishing; feeding
alimento /ali'mento/ *m,* food, nourishment; stimulus, encouragement; *pl* alimony; allowance
alindar /alin'dar/ *vt* to mark the boundary of; beautify, adorn; *—vi* border, be contiguous
alineación /alinea'θion; alinea'sion/ *f,* alignment
alinear /aline'ar/ *vt* to align, range in line; dress (troops); *—vr* fall into line
aliñar /ali'ɲar/ *vt* to decorate, adorn; *Cul.* season; prepare; set (bones)
aliño /a'liɲo/ *m,* decoration, ornament; preparation; condiment, seasoning; setting (bones)
aliquebrado /alike'βraðo/ *a* broken-winged; *Inf.* down in the mouth
alisador /alisa'ðor/ **(-ra)** *a* smoothing; polishing *—n* polisher
alisar /ali'sar/ *vt* to smooth; polish; sleek; plane; comb lightly
alisios /a'lisios/ *m pl,* trade winds
aliso /a'liso/ *m,* alder tree and wood
alistador /alista'ðor/ *m,* enroller
alistamiento /alista'miento/ *m,* enlistment; conscription; enrolment
alistar /alis'tar/ *vt* to enroll, list; enlist; conscript; prepare, get ready; *—vr* enroll; *Mil.* enlist; get ready
aliviar /ali'βiar/ *vt* to lighten; alleviate, mitigate; relieve; ease; quicken (one's step); hasten, speed up; steal
alivio /a'liβio/ *m,* lightening; relief; alleviation; ease
aljaba /al'haβa/ *f,* quiver (for arrows)
aljibe /al'hiβe/ *m,* tank, cistern; watership or tanker
aljófar /al'hofar/ *m,* small irregular shaped pearl; dew-drop, raindrop, tear drop
aljofifa /alho'fifa/ *f,* floorcloth
allá /a'ʎa; a'ya/ *adv* there; to that place. **más a.,** farther on, beyond. Used in conjunction with phrases of time, indicates remoteness, e.g. *a. en tiempos de los Reyes Católicos,* long ago in the time of the Catholic Monarchs. *a. por 1900,* way back in 1900
allanamiento /aʎana'miento; ayana'miento/ *m,* leveling, flattening; condescension, affability; (police) raid, (police) search acceptance of a judicial finding
allanar /aʎa'nar; aya'nar/ *vt* to level, flatten; overcome (difficulties); soothe; break into (a house, etc.); give entrance to the police; *—vr* collapse (buildings, etc.); abide by, adapt oneself (to); condescend, be affable. **a. el camino (a...),** to pave the way (for...)
allegado /aʎe'gaðo; aye'gaðo/ **(-da)** *a* near, allied; related *—n* follower, ally
allegar /aʎe'gar; aye'gar/ *vt* to gather, collect; draw nearer; *Agr.* reap; add; *—vi* arrive
allende /a'ʎende; a'yende/ *adv* beyond; besides. **de a. el mar,** from beyond the sea
allí /a'ʎi; a'yi/ *adv* there; to that place, thereto; thereupon, then. **por a.,** through there; that way
alma /'alma/ *f,* soul; living person; essence, core; vivacity, animation; energy, vitality; spirit, ghost; core (of a rope). **a. de cántaro,** fool, ninny. **a. de Dios,** simple soul, kind person. **a. en pena,** soul in purgatory. **¡A. mía!** My darling! **con todo el a.,** with all my heart. **Lo siento en el a.,** I feel it deeply
almacén /alma'θen; alma'sen/ *m,* warehouse; store, shop
almacenaje /almaθe'nahe; almase'nahe/ *m,* cost of storage
almacenar /almaθe'nar; almase'nar/ *vt* to store; put in store; hoard
almacenero /almaθe'nero; almase'nero/ *m,* warehouseman, storekeeper
almacenista /almaθe'nista; almase'nista/ *mf* owner of a store; assistant, salesman (saleswoman)
almáciga /al'maθiga; al'masiga/ *f,* mastic; tree plantation or nursery
almagre /al'magre/ *m, Mineral.* red ocher; stain, mark
almanaque /alma'nake/ *m,* calendar, almanac
almeja /al'meha/ *f, Ichth.* clam
almenara /alme'nara/ *f,* beacon fire
almendra /al'mendra/ *f,* almond; kernel; crystal drop (of chandeliers, etc.); cocoon; bean (of cocoa tree, etc.). **a. garapiñada,** sugar almond
almendro /al'mendro/ *m,* almond tree
almendruco /almen'druko/ *m,* green almond
almete /al'mete/ *m,* casque, helmet; helmeted soldier
almiar /al'miar/ *m,* haystack, hayrick
almíbar /al'miβar/ *m,* sugar syrup; nectar
almibarado /almiβa'raðo/ *a* syrupy; *Inf.* sugary

almibarar /almiβa'rar/ *vt* to coat with sugar; preserve (fruit) in syrup; flatter with sweet words

almidón /almi'ðon/ *m,* starch

almidonado /almiðo'naðo/ *a* starched; *Fig. Inf.* stiff, unbending; prim, starchy

almidonar /almiðo'nar/ *vt* to starch

alminar /almi'nar/ *m,* minaret (of mosque)

almiranta /almi'ranta/ *f,* admiral's wife; flagship

almirantazgo /almiran'taθgo; almiran'tasgo/ *m,* Admiralty; admiralship; Admiralty Court

almirante /almi'rante/ *m,* admiral

almizcle /al'miθkle; al'miskle/ *m,* musk

almizcleño /almiθ'kleɲo; almis'kleɲo/ *a* musk (of scents)

almizclero /almiθ'klero; almis'klero/ *a* musky. *m, Zool.* musk-deer

almocafre /almo'kafre/ *m, Agr.* hoe; trowel, dibble

almohada /almo'aða/ *f,* pillow; pillowcase; cushion. *Inf.* **aconsejarse** *or* **consultar con la a.,** to think over (a matter) carefully, sleep on it

almohadilla /almoa'ðiʎa; almoa'ðiya/ *f, dim* small cushion; lace or sewing cushion; pin cushion

almohadillado /almoaði'ʎaðo; almoaði'yaðo/ *a* cushioned; padded

almoneda /almo'neða/ *f,* auction; furniture sale

almonedear /almoneðe'ar/ *vt* to auction; sell off (furniture)

almorranas /almo'rranas/ *f pl,* hemorrhoids

almorzar /almor'θar; almor'sar/ *vi irr* to lunch; breakfast. See **forzar**

almuecín, almuédano /almue'θin, al'mueðano; almue'sin, al'mueðano/ *m,* muezzin

almuerzo /al'muerθo; al'muerso/ *m,* luncheon; breakfast (not so usual)

alocado /alo'kaðo/ *a* feather-brained, reckless; crazy, wild

alocución /aloku'θion; aloku'sion/ *f,* allocution, address, harangue

áloe /'aloe/ *m, Bot.* aloe

alojado /alo'haðo/ **(-da)** *m,* billeted soldier —*n* lodger

alojamiento /aloha'miento/ *m,* lodging; dwelling; *Mil.* billeting; *Naut.* steerage; camp, encampment

alojar /alo'har/ *vt* to lodge; billet, quarter (troops); insert, introduce; —*vi* and *vr* lodge; live, dwell

alondra /a'londra/ *f, Ornith.* lark

alopatía /alopa'tia/ *f, Med.* allopathy

alpaca /al'paka/ *f,* alpaca (animal and fabric); nickel silver

alpargata /alpar'gata/ *f,* sandal with hemp sole

alpargatero /alparga'tero/ **(-ra)** *n* manufacturer or seller of alpargatas

Alpes, los /'alpes, los/ the Alps

alpestre /al'pestre/ *a* Alpine; rock (of plants); mountainous, lofty

alpinismo /alpi'nismo/ *m,* mountaineering

alpinista /alpi'nista/ *mf* mountaineer, climber

alpino /al'pino/ *a* Alpine

alpiste /al'piste/ *m,* bird seed

alpro /'alpro/ *f,* (Alianza para el Progreso)

alquería /alke'ria/ *f,* farmstead

alquiladizo /alkila'ðiθo; alkila'ðiso/ *a* rentable, hirable

alquilador /alkila'ðor/ **(-ra)** *n* hirer

alquilamiento /alkila'miento/ *m,* See **alquiler**

alquilar /alki'lar/ *vt* to rent; hire out; hire; —*vr* hire oneself out, serve on a wage basis

alquiler /alki'ler/ *m,* hiring out; renting; rental; hire; wages. **de a.,** for hire, on hire

alquimia /al'kimia/ *f,* alchemy

alquímico /al'kimiko/ *a* alchemic

alquimista /alki'mista/ *mf* alchemist

alquitrán /alki'tran/ *m,* tar, pitch. **a. mineral,** coal tar

alquitranado /alkitra'naðo/ *a* tarred. *m, Naut.* tarpaulin

alrededor /alreðe'ðor/ *adv* around, round about. **a. de,** around; approximately, about (e.g. *a. de cinco dólares,* about $5)

alrededores /alreðe'ðores/ *m pl,* environs, surrounding country

Alsacia /al'saθia; al'sasia/ Alsace

alsaciano /alsa'θiano; alsa'siano/ **(-na)** *a* and *n* Alsatian

alta /'alta/ *f,* certificate of discharge from hospital

altanería /altane'ria/ *f,* hawking; haughtiness, disdain; superciliousness

altanero /alta'nero/ *a* soaring, high-flying (of birds); supercilious; haughty, disdainful

altar /al'tar/ *m,* altar. **a. mayor,** high altar

altavoz /ˌalta'βoθ; ˌalta'βos/ *m,* loudspeaker; megaphone

altearse /alte'arse/ *vr* to rise, grow steep (of land)

alterabilidad /alteraβili'ðað/ *f,* alterability, changeability

alteración /altera'θion; altera'sion/ *f,* alteration, change; debasement (of coinage); agitation

alterar /alte'rar/ *vt* to change, alter; debase (coinage); disturb, agitate; —*vr* grow angry; become excited

altercación, /alterka'θion; alterka'sion/ *f.* **altercado** *m,* altercation, quarrel

altercar /alter'kar/ **(se)** *vi* and *vr* to quarrel, dispute, altercate

alternación /alterna'θion; alterna'sion/ *f,* alternation

alternado /alter'naðo/ *a* alternate

alternador /alterna'ðor/ *a* alternating. *m, Elec.* alternator

alternante /alter'nante/ *a* alternating

alternar /alter'nar/ *vt* to alternate; make one's debut as a **matador**; —*vi* alternate; (*with con*) have dealings with, know

alternativa /alterna'tiβa/ *f,* alternative, option; service performed by turns; alternation

alternativo /alterna'tiβo/ *a* alternative

alterno /al'terno/ *a* alternative; *Bot.* alternate

alteza /al'teθa; al'tesa/ *f,* altitude, height; sublimity, perfection; **(A.)** Highness (title)

altibajo /alti'βaho/ *m,* embossed velvet; *pl Inf.* rough ground; *Inf.* vicissitudes of fortune

altillo /al'tiʎo; al'tiyo/ *m,* hillock, eminence; garret, attic

altímetro /al'timetro/ *m, Aer.* altimeter

altiplanicie /altipla'niθie; altipla'nisie/ *f,* plateau; highland

altisonante /altiso'nante/ *a* sonorous; sublime; high-flown, pompous

altitud /alti'tuð/ *f,* altitude, height

altivez /alti'βeθ; alti'βes/ *f,* arrogance, haughtiness

altivo /al'tiβo/ *a* arrogant, haughty

alto /'alto/ *a* high; tall; difficult, arduous; sublime; deep; most serious (of crimes, etc.); dear (of price); small, early (hours). *m,* height; eminence, hill; story, floor; *Mil.* halt; red light (traffic light) —*adv* up, above, on high; loudly —*interj* **¡A.!** *Mil.* Halt! *Mil.* **A. Mando,** High Command. **las altas horas de la noche,** the small (or early) hours. **en alta voz,** in a loud voice. **en alto,** on high; up above. **hacer alto,** to halt, stop

altoparlante /ˌaltopar'lante/ *m, Radio.* loudspeaker

altozano /alto'θano; alto'sano/ *m,* mound, hillock; viewpoint, open space

altruismo /altru'ismo/ *m,* altruism

altruista /altru'ista/ *a* altruistic. *mf* altruist

altura /al'tura/ *f,* height; altitude; *Geom.* altitude or height; top, peak; sublimity; tallness

alucinación /aluθina'θion; alusina'sion/ *f,* **alucinamiento,** *m,* hallucination

alucinado /aluθi'naðo; alusi'naðo/ *m,* person suffering from hallucinations

alucinador /aluθina'ðor; alusina'ðor/ *a* hallucinatory, deceptive

alucinar /aluθi'nar; alusi'nar/ *vt* to dazzle, fascinate; deceive

alud /a'luð/ *m,* avalanche

aludir /alu'ðir/ *vi* to allude (to); refer (to), cite

alumbrado /alum'braðo/ *m,* lighting; *pl* illuminati

alumbramiento /alumbra'miento/ *m,* lighting, supply of light; childbirth

alumbrar /alum'brar/ *vt* to light, illuminate; give sight to the blind; instruct, teach; inflict (blows); hoe vine roots; —*vi* give birth to a child; —*vr Inf.* grow tipsy

alumbre /a'lumbre/ *m,* alum
aluminio /alu'minio/ *m,* aluminum
alumno /a'lumno/ **(-na)** *n* ward, adopted child; pupil. **a. externo,** day pupil. **a. interno,** boarder
alunizaje /aluni'θahe; aluni'sahe/ *m,* landing on the moon, moon-landing
alunizar /aluni'θar; aluni'sar/ *vi* to land on the moon
alusión /alu'sion/ *f,* allusion
alusivo /alu'siβo/ *a* allusive, suggestive; hinting
aluvial /alu'βial/ *a* alluvial
aluvión /alu'βion/ *m,* alluvium. **de a.,** alluvial
alza /'alθa; 'alsa/ *f,* rise (of temperature, etc.); increase (in price); front sight (of guns)
alzacuello /alθa'kueʎo; alsa'kueyo/ *m,* high collar, clerical collar; neck stock
alzada /al'θaða; al'saða/ *f,* horse's stature; mountain pasture; *Law.* appeal
alzado /al'θaðo; al'saðo/ *a* fraudulent (of bankruptcy); fixed (of price). *m,* theft; *Archit.* front elevation
alzamiento /alθa'miento; alsa'miento/ *m,* raising, lifting; higher bid (at auction); rising, rebellion; fraudulent bankruptcy
alzaprima /alθa'prima; alsa'prima/ *f,* lever; wedge; bridge (of string instruments)
alzar /al'θar; al'sar/ *vt* to raise; lift up; elevate (the Host); steal, remove; hide; gather in the harvest; build, construct; *Naut.* heave; *—vr* rise (of temperature, mercury, price, etc.); make a fraudulent bankruptcy; *Law.* appeal; (*with con*) run off with, steal. *Naut.* **a. la vela,** to set sail
ama /'ama/ *f,* mistress of the house; owner; housekeeper; wet nurse. **a. de casa,** homemaker, housewife. **a. de leche,** foster-mother. **a. de llaves** *or* **a. de gobierno,** housekeeper. **a. seca,** children's nurse
amabilidad /amaβili'ðað/ *f,* lovableness; kindness; niceness, goodness, helpfulness
amable /a'maβle/ *a* lovable; kind; nice, good, helpful
amador /ama'ðor/ **(-ra)** *a* loving *—n* lover, admirer
amadrigar /amaðri'gar/ *vt* to welcome, receive well; *—vr* go into a burrow or lair; go into seclusion
amaestrar /amaes'trar/ *vt* to train, instruct; tame; break in (horses)
amagar /ama'gar/ *vt* and *vi* to threaten; *—vt* show signs of (diseases, etc.); *—vr Inf.* hide
amago (contra...), /a'mago/ threat (to...), menace (to...)
amainar /amai'nar/ *vt Naut.* to take in the sails; *—vi* drop (of the wind); *—vi* and *vt* relax (efforts, etc.)
amaine /a'maine/ *m,* dropping, abatement (of the wind)
amalgama /amal'gama/ *f, Chem.* amalgam
amalgamación /amalgama'θion; amalgama'sion/ *f,* amalgamation
amalgamar /amalga'mar/ *vt* to amalgamate; *—vr* be amalgamated
amamantamiento /amamanta'miento/ *m,* suckling, nursling
amamantar /amaman'tar/ *vt* to suckle
amancebado /amanθe'βaðo; amanse'βaðo/ *m,* concubine
amancillar /amanθi'ʎar; amansi'yar/ *vt* to discredit, dishonor; tarnish; stain
amanecer /amane'θer; amane'ser/ *vi irr* to dawn; arrive *or* be somewhere *or* be doing, at dawn (e.g. *Amanecimos en el barco,* Dawn came while we were on the ship. *Amanecimos escribiendo la carta,* The day broke as we were writing the letter); appear at daybreak; begin to appear. *m,* dawn, daybreak. See **conocer**
amanerado /amane'raðo/ *a* mannered; affected
amaneramiento /amanera'miento/ *m,* manneredness; mannerism
amanerarse /amane'rarse/ *vr* to acquire mannerisms or tricks of style; become affected
amansador /amansa'ðor/ **(-ra)** *a* soothing, calming *—n* appeaser
amansamiento /amansa'miento/ *m,* taming; appeasement; soothing; breaking in (horses)
amansar /aman'sar/ *vt* to tame; appease, moderate; soothe, pacify; break in (horses)
amante /a'mante/ *a* loving. *mf* lover
amanuense /ama'nuense/ *mf* amanuensis, secretary, clerk
amanzanar /amanθa'nar; amansa'nar/ to lay out the streets of
amañar /ama'ɲar/ *vt* to execute with skill; *—vr* grow skillful
amaño /a'maɲo/ *m,* skill, dexterity; *pl* schemes, intrigues; tools, equipment
amapola /ama'pola/ *f,* poppy
amar /a'mar/ *vt* to love
amaranto /ama'ranto/ *m, Bot.* amaranth
amarar /ama'rar/ *vi* to alight on the water (of hydroplanes)
amargar /amar'gar/ *vi* to taste or be bitter; *—vt* make bitter; embitter
amargo /a'margo/ *a* bitter; embittered; grievous, sad. *m,* bitterness; *pl* bitters
amargor /amar'gor/ *m,* **amargura,** /amar'gura/ *f,* bitter taste, bitterness; trouble, affliction, pain
amaricado /amari'kaðo/ *a Inf.* effeminate
amarilis /ama'rilis/ *f, Bot.* amaryllis; *Poet.* shepherdess
amarillear /amariʎe'ar; amariye'ar/ *vi* to look yellow; turn yellow; tend to yellow
amarillento /amari'ʎento; amari'yento/ *a* yellowish, turning yellow
amarilleo /amari'ʎeo; amari'yeo/ *m,* yellowing
amarillez /amari'ʎeθ; amari'yes/ *f,* yellowness
amarillo /ama'riʎo; ama'riyo/ *a* and *m,* yellow
amarra /a'marra/ *f, Naut.* cable, thick rope
amarradero /amarra'ðero/ *m, Naut.* mooring berth; mooring-post; hitchingpost or ring
amarraje /ama'rrahe/ *m, Naut.* mooring charge
amarrar /ama'rrar/ *vt* to tie up, hitch; moor
amarre /a'marre/ *m,* mooring; hitching
amartelar /amarte'lar/ *vt* to make jealous; court, woo, make love to; *—vr* be jealous; fall madly in love
amartillar /amarti'ʎar; amarti'yar/ *vt* to hammer, knock; cock (firearms)
amasadera /amasa'ðera/ *f,* kneading-trough
amasador /amasa'ðor/ **(-ra)** *a* kneading *—n* kneader
amasar /ama'sar/ *vt* to knead; massage; scheme, plot
amasia /a'masia/ *f,* concubine
amasiato /ama'siato/ *m,* concubinage
amasijo /ama'siho/ *m, Cul.* dough; kneading; portion of plaster or mortar; *Inf.* hotchpotch, mixture; scheme, plot
amatista /ama'tista/ *f,* amethyst
amatorio /ama'torio/ *a* amatory
amazacotado /aˌmaθako'taðo; aˌmasako'taðo/ *a* heavy, dense; *Fig.* stodgy (of writings, etc.)
amazona /ama'θona; ama'sona/ *f,* Amazon; independent woman; woman rider; woman's riding habit
ambages /am'bahes/ *m pl,* maze, intricate paths; circumlocutions
ámbar /'ambar/ *m,* amber. **a. gris,** ambergris
ambarino /amba'rino/ *a* amber
Amberes /am'beres/ Antwerp
ambición /ambi'θion; ambi'sion/ *f,* ambition
ambicionar /ambiθio'nar; ambisio'nar/ *vt* to long for; desire eagerly; be ambitious to
ambicioso /ambi'θioso; ambi'sioso/ *a* ambitious; eager, desirous
ambidextro /ambi'ðekstro/ *a* ambidextrous
ambiente /am'biente/ *a* ambient, surrounding. *m,* air, atmosphere; environment
ambigú /ambi'gu/ *m,* cold buffet; buffet (in theaters, etc.)
ambigüedad /ambigue'ðað/ *f,* ambiguity
ambiguo /am'biguo/ *a* ambiguous
ámbito /'ambito/ *m,* precincts; boundary, limit; compass, scope
amblar /am'blar/ *vi* to pace (of a horse)
ambos, /'ambos,/ *a m pl,* **ambas** *a f pl,* both, e.g. *ambas casas,* both houses
ambulancia /ambu'lanθia; ambu'lansia/ *f,* ambulance. **a. de correos,** railway post office. **a. fija,** field-hospital
ambulante /ambu'lante/ *a* walking; traveling, wandering

amedrentador /ameðrenta'ðor/ *a* frightening; terrible; intimidating
amedrentar /ameðren'tar/ *vt* to frighten, scare; intimidate
ameliorar /amelio'rar/ *vt* to better, improve
amelonado /amelo'naðo/ *a* melon-shaped; *Inf.* madly in love
amén /a'men/ *m,* amen, so be it. **a. de,** besides, in addition to. *Inf.* **en un decir a.,** in a trice
amenaza /ame'naθa; ame'nasa/ *f,* threat
amenazador, amenazante /amenaθa'ðor, amena'θante; amenasa'ðor, amena'sante/ *a* menacing, threatening
amenazar /amena'θar; amena'sar/ *vt* to threaten; *—vt* and *vi* presage, be pending
amenguamiento /amengua'miento/ *m,* lessening, diminution; discredit; loss of prestige
amenguar /amen'guar/ *vt* to lessen, decrease; dishonor, discredit
amenidad /ameni'ðað/ *f,* amenity; agreeableness
amenizar /ameni'θar; ameni'sar/ *vt* to make pleasant or attractive
ameno /a'meno/ *a* pleasant; entertaining; agreeable, delightful
América /a'merika/ America
América del Norte /a'merika del 'norte/ North America
América del Sur /a'merika del sur/ South America
americana /ameri'kana/ *f,* (man's) jacket
americanismo /amerika'nismo/ *m,* usage typical of Western-Hemisphere Spanish
americano /ameri'kano/ *a* American
ameritar /ameri'tar/ *vt West. Hem.* to deserve, merit
ametrallador /ametraʎa'ðor; ametraya'ðor/ *m,* machine-gunner
ametralladora /ametraʎa'ðora; ametraya'ðora/ *f,* machine-gun
amianto /a'mianto/ *m, Mineral.* amianthus, asbestos
amiba /a'miβa/ *f, Zool.* ameba
amicísimo /ami'θisimo; ami'sisimo/ *a superl* **amigo,** most friendly
amiga /a'miga/ *f,* woman friend; mistress, lover; dame, schoolmistress; dame school
amigabilidad /amigaβili'ðað/ *f,* friendliness, amicability
amigable /ami'gaβle/ *a* friendly, amicable; harmonious; suitable
amígdala /a'migðala/ *f,* tonsil
amigdalitis /amigða'litis/ *f,* tonsillitis
amigo /a'migo/ **(-ga)** *a* friendly; fond, addicted *—n* friend. *m,* lover. *Inf.* **ser muy a. de,** to be very friendly with; be very keen on or fond of
amilanado /amila'naðo/ *a* cowed, spiritless
amilanar /amila'nar/ *vt* to terrify, intimidate; *—vr* grow discouraged
aminorar /amino'rar/ *vt* to diminish, lessen
amir /a'mir/ *m,* emir, Arab prince or chief
amistad /amis'tað/ *f,* friendship; liaison; favor; *pl* acquaintances, friends
amistar /amis'tar/ *vt* to introduce, make known to each other; bring about a reconciliation between or with
amistoso /amis'toso/ *a* friendly
amnesia /am'nesia/ *f,* amnesia
amnistía /amnis'tia/ *f,* amnesty
amnistiar /amnisti'ar/ *vt* to concede an amnesty, pardon
amo /'amo/ *m,* head of the house; master; owner; overlord; overseer. **a. de huéspedes,** keeper of a boarding house. **Nuestro A.** Our Lord. *Inf.* **ser el a. del cotarro,** to rule the roost
amodorramiento /amoðorra'miento/ *m,* stupor, deep sleep
amodorrarse /amoðo'rrarse/ *vr* to fall into a stupor; fall into a heavy sleep
amoladera /amola'ðera/ *f,* whetstone
amolador /amola'ðor/ *m,* scissors grinder; knife grinder; sharpener
amoladura /amola'ðura/ *f,* grinding, whetting, sharpening
amolar /amo'lar/ *vt irr* to grind, sharpen; *Inf.* pester, annoy. See **colar**
amoldar /amol'dar/ *vt* to mold; adjust; *—vr* adapt oneself
amonedación /amoneða'θion; amoneða'sion/ *f,* coinage, minting
amonedar /amone'ðar/ *vt* to coin, mint
amonestación /amonesta'θion; amonesta'sion/ *f,* warning; advice. **correr las amonestaciones,** to publish bans of marriage
amonestador /amonesta'ðor/ **(-ra)** *a* warning, admonitory *—n* admonisher
amonestar /amones'tar/ *vt* to warn; advise; rebuke; *Eccl.* publish bans of marriage
amoníaco /amo'niako/ *m,* ammonia
amontillado /amonti'ʎaðo; amonti'yaðo/ *m,* kind of pale, dry sherry
amontonamiento /amontona'miento/ *m,* accumulation; gathering, collection; piling up, heaping
amontonar /amonto'nar/ *vt* to pile up, heap; gather; collect; accumulate; *—vr Inf.* fly into a rage
amor /a'mor/ *m,* love; beloved; willingness, pleasure; *pl* love affairs; caresses. **a. propio,** self-esteem; vanity. *Inf.* **con mil amores,** with great pleasure. **por a. de,** for love of; for the sake of
amoral /amo'ral/ *a* amoral
amoralidad /amorali'ðað/ *f,* amorality
amoratado /amora'taðo/ *a* livid, bluish
amorcillo /amor'θiʎo; amor'siyo/ *m, dim* little love; unimportant love affair; Cupid
amordazamiento /amorðaθa'miento; amorðasa'miento/ *m,* muzzling; gagging
amordazar /amorða'θar; amorða'sar/ *vt* to muzzle; gag; prevent speaking
amorfo /a'morfo/ *a* amorphous
amorío /amo'rio/ *m, Inf.* wooing, love making; *pl* love affairs
amoroso /amo'roso/ *a* loving; gentle; mild, balmy
amorrar /amo'rrar/ *vi Inf.* to hang one's head; sulk, be sullen
amortajar /amorta'har/ *vt* to wrap in a shroud; enshroud
amortiguador /amortigua'ðor/ *m, Mech.* shock absorber. *Auto.* **a. de los muelles,** shock-absorber
amortiguamiento /amortigua'miento/ *m,* softening, deadening; mitigation, lessening
amortiguar /amorti'guar/ *vt* to soften, deaden; absorb (shocks); moderate, mitigate; soften (colors)
amortización /amortiθa'θion; amortisa'sion/ *f,* amortization
amortizar /amorti'θar; amorti'sar/ *vt* to amortize; recover, redeem; suppress, abolish (posts)
amoscarse /amos'karse/ *vr Inf.* to be piqued or annoyed; become agitated
amostazar /amosta'θar; amosta'sar/ *vt Inf.* to annoy; *—vi* become peeved
amotinador /amotina'ðor/ **(-ra)** *a* mutinous, rebellious *—n* rebel, mutineer; rioter
amotinar /amoti'nar/ *vt* to incite to rebellion; unbalance, unhinge (mind); *—vr* rebel; riot; *Fig.* be unhinged
amovible /amo'βiβle/ *a* movable, removable; removable (of officials, etc.)
amovilidad /amoβili'ðað/ *f,* movability, removability; liability to discharge or dismissal
amparador /ampara'ðor/ **(-ra)** *a* protective; sheltering *—n* protector, defender, helper; shelterer
amparar /ampa'rar/ *vt* to protect, favor, help; shelter; *—vr* take refuge, take shelter; defend oneself
amparo /am'paro/ *m,* shelter, refuge; protection, favor, help; defense
amper /am'per/ *m, Elec.* ampere
amperímetro /ampe'rimetro/ *m, Elec.* ammeter
amperio /am'perio/ *m, Elec.* ampere
ampliable /am'pliaβle/ *a* amplifiable
ampliación /amplia'θion; amplia'sion/ *f,* enlargement, increase, extension; *Photo.* enlargement
ampliador /amplia'ðor/ **(-ra)** *a* enlarging *—n* enlarger
ampliadora /amplia'ðora/ *f, Photo.* enlarger
ampliar /amp'liar/ *vt* to extend, enlarge, increase; *Photo.* enlarge

amplificación /amplifika'θion; amplifika'sion/ *f,* extension, amplification; *Photo.* enlargement
amplificar /amplifi'kar/ *vt* to enlarge; extend; increase; amplify, expatiate upon
amplio /'amplio/ *a* wide; extensive; roomy, ample; prolix
amplitud /ampli'tuð/ *f,* extension; width; spaciousness, amplitude
ampolla /am'poʎa; am'poya/ *f,* blister; ampoule; bubble; *Elec.* bulb
ampulosidad /ampulosi'ðað/ *f,* pomposity, redundancy (of style)
ampuloso /ampu'loso/ *a* pompous, high-flown (style)
amputación /amputa'θion; amputa'sion/ *f,* amputation
amputar /ampu'tar/ *vt* to amputate
amuchachado /amutʃa'tʃaðo/ *a* boyish
amueblar /amue'βlar/ *vt* to furnish; provide with furniture
amuleto /amu'leto/ *m,* amulet, charm
amurallar /amura'ʎar; amura'yar/ *vt* to surround with a wall, wall
amusgar /amus'gar/ *vt* and *vi* to flatten the ears (animals); —*vt* screw up the eyes (to see better)
ana /'ana/ *f,* ell (measure)
anabaptismo /anaβap'tismo/ *m,* Anabaptism
anabaptista /anaβap'tista/ *mf* Anabaptist
anacardo /ana'karðo/ *m,* cashew (nut)
anacoreta /anako'reta/ *mf* anchorite, hermit
anacreóntico /anakre'ontiko/ *a* Anacreontic
anacrónico /ana'kroniko/ *a* anachronous
anacronismo /anakro'nismo/ *m,* anachronism
ánade /'anaðe/ *mf* duck
anadear /anaðe'ar/ *vi* to waddle (like a duck)
anadeo /ana'ðeo/ *m,* waddle
anadino /ana'ðino/ **(-na)** *n* duckling
anadón /ana'ðon/ *m,* drake
anáfora /a'nafora/ *f,* anaphora
anafrodisíaco /anafroði'siako/ *a* anaphrodisiac
anagrama /ana'grama/ *m,* anagram
analectas /ana'lektas/ *f, pl* analects
anales /a'nales/ *m, pl* annals
analfabetismo /analfaβe'tismo/ *m,* illiteracy
analfabeto /analfa'βeto/ **(-ta)** *a* and *n* illiterate
analgesia /anal'hesia/ *f,* analgesia
analgésico /anal'hesiko/ *a* and *m, Med.* analgesic
análisis /a'nalisis/ *m,* analysis; *Gram.* parsing
analista /ana'lista/ *mf* analyst
analizar /anali'θar; anali'sar/ *vt* to analyse
analogía /analo'hia/ *f,* analogy
analógico, análogo /ana'lohiko, a'nalogo/ *a* analogous
ananás /ana'nas/ *m,* pineapple
anaquel /ana'kel/ *m,* shelf, ledge
anaranjado /anaran'haðo/ *a* and *m,* orange (color)
anarquía /anar'kia/ *f,* anarchy
anárquico /a'narkiko/ *a* anarchical
anarquismo /anar'kismo/ *m,* anarchism
anarquista /anar'kista/ *mf* anarchist
anatema /ana'tema/ *mf.* anathema
anatematizar /anatemati'θar; anatemati'sar/ *vt* to anathematize, denounce
anatomía /anato'mia/ *f,* anatomy
anatómico /ana'tomiko/ *a* anatomical
anatomista /anato'mista/ *mf* anatomist
anca /'anka/ *f,* croup, hindquarters of a horse
ancho /'antʃo/ *a* wide, broad. *m,* width, breadth. *Inf.* **a mis** (**tus, sus,** etc.) **anchas** *or* **anchos,** at my (your, his, etc.) ease, with complete freedom
anchoa /an'tʃoa/ *f,* anchovy
anchura /an'tʃura/ *f,* width, breadth; ease, freedom; extent
anchuroso /antʃu'roso/ *a* very wide; extensive; spacious
ancianidad /anθiani'ðað; ansiani'ðað/ *f,* old age; seniority; oldness
anciano /an'θiano; an'siano/ **(-na)** *a* old; ancient —*n* old person
ancla /'ankla/ *f,* anchor. **a. de la esperanza,** sheet anchor. **echar anclas,** to anchor
ancladero, anclaje /ankla'ðero, an'klahe/ *m,* anchorage
anclar /an'klar/ *vi* to anchor
áncora /'ankora/ *f,* anchor; refuge, haven
andada /an'daða/ *f,* wandering, roving; hard bread roll; pasture; *pl* trail, tracks. *Fig. Inf.* **volver a las andadas,** to return to one's old tricks
andaderas /anda'ðeras/ *f pl,* go-cart (for learning to walk)
andadoba /anda'ðoβa/ *f,* lansquenet (card game)
andador /anda'ðor/ *a* walking; swift walking; wandering. *m,* walker; garden path; *pl* leading-strings, reins
andadura /anda'ðura/ *f,* walk, gait; pace, step
Andalucía /andalu'θia; andalu'sia/ Andalusia
andaluz /anda'luθ; anda'lus/ **(-za)** *a* and *n* Andalusian
andaluzada /andalu'θaða; andalu'saða/ *f, Inf.* exaggeration, tall story
andamio /an'damio/ *m,* scaffolding; stand, platform
andanada /anda'naða/ *f, Naut.* broadside; cheapest priced seat in a bullring; *Inf.* dressing-down, scolding
andante /an'dante/ *a* walking, strolling; errant (of knights) —*a* and *m, Mus.* andante
andanza /an'danθa; an'dansa/ *f,* happening, occurrence; *pl* doings, deeds. **buena a.,** good fortune
andar /an'dar/ *vi irr* to walk; move; work, operate, run (machines, etc.); progress, get along (negotiations, etc.); be, feel; elapse (of time); be occupied; behave; (*with prep a*) administer (blows, etc.); (*with en*) upset, turn over (papers, etc.); ride in or on (cars, bicycles, etc.); be engaged in; (*with con*) use, handle; —*vt* traverse. *m,* gait, walk. **a. por los cuarenta,** to be in one's forties. **a. con paños tibios,** not to be firm. **a. con pies de plomo,** to be extremely cautious. **a. tras,** to follow, go after; persecute; desire ardently (things). **andarse a la flor del berro,** to sow one's wild oats. *Fig. Inf.* **andarse por las ramas,** to beat about the bush. **¡Anda!** Get along with you!; Hurry up!; You don't say so! **¡Andando!** Let's get going!, Let's get a move on it! *Preterite* **anduve,** etc —*imperf subjunc* **anduviese,** etc.
andariego /anda'riego/ *a* swift walking; wandering, vagrant
andarín (-ina) /anda'rin/ *n* good walker; professional walker
andas /'andas/ *f pl,* kind of stretcher; bier
andén /an'den/ *m,* railway platform
andero /an'dero/ *m,* bearer (of a bier)
andino /an'dino/ *a* Andean
andorrano (-na) /ando'rrano/ *a* and *n* Andorran
andrajo /an'draho/ *m,* rag, wisp of cloth, tatter
andrajoso /andra'hoso/ *a* ragged, tattered
andurriales /andu'rriales/ *m pl,* byways, unfrequented paths; remote places
anécdota /a'nekðota/ *f,* anecdote
anecdótico /anek'ðotiko/ *a* anecdotal
anegación /anega'θion; anega'sion/ *f,* drowning; flooding, inundation
anegar /ane'gar/ *vt* to drown; inundate; shipwreck; —*vr* drown; be flooded
anejo /a'neho/ *a* attached, annexed. *m,* annexed borough
anemia /a'nemia/ *f,* anemia
anémico /a'nemiko/ *a* anemic
anémona, anémone /a'nemona, a'nemone/ *f,* anemone. **anémona de mar,** sea-anemone
anestesia /anes'tesia/ *f,* anesthesia
anestesiador (-ra) /anestesia'ðor/ *n* anesthetist
anestesiar /aneste'siar/ *vt* to anesthetize
anestésico /anes'tesiko/ *a* and *m,* anesthetic
aneurisma /aneu'risma/ *mf Med.* aneurism
anexar /anek'sar/ *vt* to annex
anexión /anek'sion/ *f,* annexation
anexo /a'nekso/ *a* attached, joined. *m,* annex
anfibio /an'fiβio/ *a* amphibious. *m,* amphibian
anfiteatro /anfite'atro/ *m,* amphitheater; operating theater; dissecting room; morgue; *Theat.* dress-circle
anfitrión /anfitri'on/ *m, Inf.* host, one who entertains guests
ánfora /'anfora/ *f,* amphora

angarillas /aŋga'riʎas; aŋga'riyas/ *f pl*, hand barrow; table cruet; yoke and panniers
ángel /'anhel/ *m*, angel. **á. de la guarda,** guardian angel. **estar con los ángeles,** to be in Heaven (euphem. for "to be dead')
angelical, angélico /anheli'kal, an'heliko/ *a* angelic; divine, excellent
angina /an'hina/ *f*, *Med.* angina, tonsillitis. **a. de pecho,** angina pectoris
anglicanismo /aŋglika'nismo/ *m*, Anglicanism
anglicano (-na) /aŋgli'kano/ *a* and *n* Anglican
anglicismo /aŋgli'θismo; aŋgli'sismo/ *m*, anglicism
anglo (-la) /'aŋglo/ *a* and *n* Angle —*a* Anglo-
angloamericano (-na) /ˌaŋgloameri'kano/ *a* and *n* Anglo-American
anglófilo (-la) /aŋ'glofilo/ *n* Anglophile
anglosajón (-ona) /aŋglosa'hon/ *a* and *n* Anglo-Saxon. *m*, Anglo-Saxon language
angostar /aŋgos'tar/ *vi* and *vt* to narrow; tighten
angosto /aŋ'gosto/ *a* narrow; tight
angostura /aŋgos'tura/ *f*, narrowness; tightness; narrow pass; strait; *Fig.* tight corner, fix
anguila /aŋ'gila/ *f*, *Ichth.* eel; *pl Naut.* slipway, slips
angula /aŋ'gula/ *f*, *Ichth.* elver (young eel)
angular /aŋgu'lar/ *a* angular
ángulo /'aŋgulo/ *m*, angle. **á. inferior izquierdo,** lower lefthand corner. **á. inferior derecho,** lower righthand corner. **á. superior izquierdo,** upper lefthand corner. **á. superior derecho,** upper righthand corner. **á. recto,** right angle
anguloso /aŋgu'loso/ *a* angulate; angular, gaunt; cornered
angustia /aŋ'gustia/ *f*, anguish, grief
angustiante /aŋgus'tiante/ *a* distressing
angustiar /aŋgus'tiar/ *vt* to grieve; afflict; —*vr* be full of anguish
anhelación /anela'θion; anela'sion/ *f*, panting, hard breathing; yearning, longing
anhelar /ane'lar/ *vi* to pant, breathe with difficulty; —*vi* and *vt* long for, yearn for, desire
anhélito /a'nelito/ *m*, pant, hard breathing
anhelo (de) /a'nelo/ *m*, longing (for), desire (for), yearning (for)
anheloso /ane'loso/ *a* difficult, labored (of breathing); anxious, longing
anidar /ani'ðar/ *vi* to nest (birds); swell; —*vt* shelter, protect; —*vr* nest; dwell; nestle
anilla /a'niʎa; a'niya/ *f*, curtain ring; *pl* gymnastic rings
anillo /a'niʎo; a'niyo/ *m*, finger ring; small ring; coil (of serpents and ropes). *Inf.* **venir como a. al dedo,** to fit like a glove; come just at the right moment
ánima /'anima/ *f*, soul, spirit; soul in purgatory; bore (of firearms); *pl* prayer bell for the souls of the departed
animación /anima'θion; anima'sion/ *f*, liveliness, gaiety; animation, vivacity; bustle, movement
animal /ani'mal/ *m*, animal; *Inf.* dolt, brute —*a* animal; *Inf.* brutish, doltish
animalada /anima'laða/ *f*, *Inf.* stupidity, foolishness
animalidad /animali'ðað/ *f*, animalism
animar /ani'mar/ *vt* to animate; encourage, incite; invigorate, enliven; make gay, cheer up; make attractive, adorn; —*vr* take heart; make up one's mind; cheer up; grow gay
animismo /ani'mismo/ *m*, animism
ánimo /'animo/ *m*, soul, spirit; courage; endurance, fortitude, will, intention; mind. **con ánimo de + Inf.,** with the intention of + *ger.* **¡Á.!** Courage!
animosidad /animosi'ðað/ *f*, hatred, animosity, dislike
animoso /ani'moso/ *a* spirited, lively; valiant
aniñado /ani'ɲaðo/ *a* childlike, childish
aniquilable /aniki'laβle/ *a* destructible
aniquilación /anikila'θion; anikila'sion/ *f*, destruction, annihilation; suppression; decay
aniquilador (-ra) /anikila'ðor/ *a* destructive, annihilating —*n* destroyer
aniquilamiento /anikila'miento/ *m*, See **aniquilación**
aniquilar /aniki'lar/ *vt* to annihilate, destroy completely; —*vr* waste away, decay
anís /a'nis/ *m*, aniseed, anise; anisette (liqueur)
anisar /ani'sar/ *vt* to flavor with aniseed
anisete /ani'sete/ *m*, anisette
aniversario /aniβer'sario/ *a* annual. *m*, anniversary
Anjeo /an'heo/ Anjou
ano /'ano/ *m*, anus
anoche /a'notʃe/ *adv* last night; the previous night
anochecer /anotʃe'θer; anotʃe'ser/ *vi irr* to grow night; become dark; be in a place *or* be doing something at nightfall (e.g. *Anochecimos en Lérida,* We were in Lerida at nightfall) —*vr Poet.* be obscured or darkened. *m*, nightfall, dusk. See **conocer**
anochecida /anotʃe'θiða; anotʃe'siða/ *f*, dusk, late twilight
anodino /ano'ðino/ *a Med.* anodyne; ineffective, useless; inoffensive. *m*, anodyne
anomalía /anoma'lia/ *f*, anomaly, inconstancy, irregularity; *Astron.* anomaly
anómalo /a'nomalo/ *a* anomalous, abnormal, unusual
anonadar /anona'ðar/ *vt* to destroy, annihilate; suppress; *Fig.* overwhelm, depress; humble
anónimo /a'nonimo/ *a* anonymous. *m*, anonymity; anonymous letter; unsigned literary work
anormal /anor'mal/ *a* abnormal; irregular, unusual. *mf* abnormal person
anormalidad /anormali'ðað/ *f*, abnormality; irregularity, inconsistency
anotación /anota'θion; anota'sion/ *f*, annotation
anotador /anota'ðor/ **(-ra)** *n* annotator
anotar /ano'tar/ *vt* to annotate; note down
anquilostoma /ankilos'toma/ *m*, *Med.* hookworm
ánsar /an'sar/ *m*, goose; drake
ansarino /ansa'rino/ *a* goose. *m*, gosling
anseático /anse'atiko/ *a* Hanseatic
ansia (de) /'ansia/ *f*, anxiety, trouble; grief; longing (for), yearning (for); greed
ansiar /an'siar/ *vt* to long for, yearn for; covet, desire
ansiedad /ansie'ðað/ *f*, anxiety, anguish, worry
ansión /an'sion/ *f*, intense desire
ansioso /an'sioso/ *a* anxious; grievous, painful; eager, desirous; greedy
anta /'anta/ *f*, *Zool.* elk; obelisk
antagónico /anta'goniko/ *a* antagonistic
antagonismo /antago'nismo/ *m*, antagonism
antagonista /antago'nista/ *mf* antagonist, adversary
antaño /an'taɲo/ *adv* last year, yesteryear; long ago
antártico /an'tartiko/ *a* antarctic
ante /'ante/ *m*, *Zool.* elk; suede; buffalo
ante /'ante/ *prep* in the presence of, before; regarding, in the face of (e.g. *a. deber tan alto,* in the face of so noble a duty)
anteado /ante'aðo/ *a* beige, buff-colored, fawn
anteanoche /antea'notʃe/ *adv* the night before last
anteayer /antea'yer/ *adv* the day before yesterday
antebrazo /ante'βraθo; ante'βraso/ *m*, forearm
antecámara /ante'kamara/ *f*, antechamber
antecedente /anteθe'ðente; antese'ðente/ *m*, antecedent. **antecedentes** *m pl* background (of a case, situation, etc.)
antecedentemente /anteθeˌðente'mente; anteseˌðente'mente/ *adv* previously
anteceder /anteθe'ðer; antese'ðer/ *vt* to precede
antecesor /anteθe'sor; antese'sor/ **(-ra)** *a* previous —*n* predecessor. *m*, forebear, ancestor
antecoger /anteko'her/ *vt* to carry in front, lead before, pick too soon
antecomedor /antekome'ðor/ *m*, breakfast nook, breakfast room
antedata /ante'ðata/ *f*, antedate
antedatar /anteða'tar/ *vt* to antedate
antedicho /ante'ðitʃo/ *a* aforementioned, aforesaid
antediluviano /anteðilu'βiano/ *a* antediluvian
antelación /antela'θion; antela'sion/ *f*, advance, anticipation
antemano, de /ante'mano, de/ *adv* in advance, beforehand
antemeridiano /antemeri'ðiano/ *a* antemeridian, forenoon
antena /an'tena/ *f*, antenna; *Radio.* aerial

antenacido /antena'θiðo; antena'siðo/ *a* born prematurely
antenombre /ante'nombre/ *m,* title (placed before name)
anteojera /anteo'hera/ *f,* horse's blinker; eyeglass case
anteojo /ante'oho/ *m,* spy-glass, small telescope; *pl* horse's blinkers; eyeglasses, glasses; spectacles; goggles
antepagar /antepa'gar/ *vt* to pay in advance
antepalco /ante'palko/ *m,* vestibule of a box in a theater
antepasado /antepa'saðo/ *a* previous, past. *m,* ancestor (gen. *pl*)
antepecho /ante'petʃo/ *m,* parapet; windowsill; railing, balustrade; front (of a theater box, etc.); *Naut.* bulwark
antepenúltimo /antepe'nultimo/ *a* antepenultimate, second from the last
anteponer /antepo'ner/ *vt irr* to place before; prefer, favor. See **poner**
anteproyecto /antepro'yekto/ *m,* first sketch, preliminary work or plan
antepuerta /ante'puerta/ *f,* door-curtain, portiere; *Mil.* anteport
anterior /ante'rior/ *a* previous, former; anterior; aforementioned, preceding
anteriormente /anterior'mente/ *adv* beforehand, previously
antes /'antes/ *adv* before; rather, on the contrary; previously. **a. bien,** rather, sooner. **a. con a.** *or* **cuanto a.,** as soon as possible
antesala /ante'sala/ *f,* antechamber
antevíspera /ante'βispera/ *f,* two days previously
antiaéreo /anti'aereo/ *a* antiaircraft. *m pl.* **(cañones) antiaéreos,** A.A. guns
anticiclón /antiθi'klon; antisi'klon/ *m,* anticyclone
anticipación /antiθipa'θion; antisipa'sion/ *f,* anticipation; advance
anticipada /antiθi'paða; antisi'paða/ *f,* foul thrust (in fencing, etc.)
anticipadamente /antiθi,paða'mente; antisi,paða'mente/ *adv* in advance; prematurely
anticipado /antiθi'paðo; antisi'paðo/ *a* in advance; premature
anticipador /antiθipa'ðor; antisipa'ðor/ *a* anticipatory
anticipar /antiθi'par; antisi'par/ *vt* to anticipate; foresee; forestall; advance (money); lend; *—vr* happen before time; (*with prep a*) act in advance of, anticipate; get ahead of oneself
anticipo /anti'θipo; anti'sipo/ *m,* anticipation, advance; advance payment; sum of money lent
anticlerical /antikleri'kal/ *a* anticlerical
anticlímax /anti'klimaks/ *m,* anticlimax
anticonstitucional /antikonstituθio'nal; antikonstitusio'nal/ *a* unconstitutional
Anticristo /anti'kristo/ *m,* Antichrist
anticuado /anti'kuaðo/ *a* antiquated, ancient
anticuario /anti'kuario/ *m,* antiquarian, antique dealer
antídoto /an'tiðoto/ *m,* antidote
antiesclavista /antieskla'βista/ *a* antislavery. *mf* antislavist
antiespasmódico /antiespas'moðiko/ *a* and *m, Med.* antispasmodic
antiestético /anties'tetiko/ *a* unesthetic
antietimológico /antietimo'lohiko/ *a* non-etymological, unetymological
antifaz /anti'faθ; anti'fas/ *m,* mask; face-covering
antiflogístico /antiflo'histiko/ *a* and *m, Med.* antiphlogistic
antigramatical /antigramati'kal/ *a* ungrammatical
antigualla /anti'guaʎa; anti'guaya/ *f,* antique; ancient custom; anything out-of-date
antiguamente /antigua'mente/ *adv* in time past, formerly
antiguamiento /antigua'miento/ *m,* seniority
antigüedad /antigue'ðað/ *f,* antiquity; ancients; length of service (in an employment); *pl* antiquities
antiguo /an'tiguo/ *a* ancient, very old; antique; senior (in an employment); former. *m,* senior member (of a community, etc.). *m pl,* ancients. **A. Testamento,** Old Testament. **de a.,** from ancient times. **en lo antiguo,** in ancient times; in former times, in days of yore
antillano /anti'ʎano; anti'yano/ **(-na)** *a* and *n* of or from the Antilles
Antillas, las /an'tiʎas, las; an'tiyas, las/ the Antilles
antílope /an'tilope/ *m,* antelope
antimacasar /antimaka'sar/ *m,* antimacassar
antimilitarismo /antimilita'rismo/ *m,* antimilitarism
antimilitarista /antimilita'rista/ *a* antimilitaristic
antimonárquico /antimo'narkiko/ *a* antimonarchical
antimonio /anti'monio/ *m, Metall.* antimony
antipalúdico /antipa'luðiko/ *a* antimalarial
antipapa /anti'papa/ *m,* antipope
antipara /anti'para/ *f,* screen, shield
antiparras /anti'parras/ *f pl, Inf.* spectacles, eyeglasses, glasses
antipatía /antipa'tia/ *f,* antipathy
antipático /anti'patiko/ *a* disagreeable; unattractive
antipatriótico /antipa'triotiko/ *a* unpatriotic
antípoda /an'tipoða/ *a* and *m,* or *f,* antipode
antiquísimo /anti'kisimo/ *a superl,* **antiguo,** most ancient
antirrepublicano /antirrepuβli'kano/ *a* antirepublican
antisemita /antise'mita/ *a* anti-Semitic. *mf* anti-Semite
antisemitismo /antisemi'tismo/ *m,* anti-Semitism
antiséptico /anti'septiko/ *a* and *m,* antiseptic
antisifilítico /antisifi'litiko/ *a Med.* anti-syphilitic
antisocial /antiso'θial; antiso'sial/ *a* antisocial
antítesis /an'titesis/ *f,* antithesis
antitético /anti'tetiko/ *a* antithetic, contrasted
antófago /an'tofago/ *a* anthophagous, flower-eating
antojadizo /antoha'ðiθo; antoha'ðiso/ *a* capricious, fanciful, whimsical
antojarse /anto'harse/ *vr* to have a fancy for, want (e.g. *Se me antoja marcharme al campo,* I have a yen to go to the country); suspect, imagine
antojo /an'toho/ *m,* caprice, fancy, whim; desire, will; *pl* birthmark
antología /antolo'hia/ *f,* anthology
antólogo /an'tologo/ *m,* anthologist
antonomasia /antono'masia/ *f,* antonomasia. **por a.,** by analogy, by transference
antorcha /an'tortʃa/ *f,* torch, flambeau
antracita /antra'θita; antra'sita/ *f,* anthracite
ántrax /'antraks/ *m, Med.* anthrax
antro /'antro/ *m,* cave, cavern; *Anat.* antrum
antropofagia /antropo'fahia/ *f,* cannibalism, anthropophagy
antropófago /antro'pofago/ **(-ga)** *a* cannibalistic *—n* cannibal
antropología /antropolo'hia/ *f,* anthropology
antropológico /antropo'lohiko/ *a* anthropological
antropólogo /antro'pologo/ *m,* anthropologist
antropometría /antropome'tria/ *f,* anthropometry
antropomorfo /antropo'morfo/ *a* anthropomorphous
antroposofía /antroposo'fia/ *f,* anthroposophy
antruejo /antru'eho/ *m,* three days of carnival before Lent
anual /a'nual/ *a* yearly, annual
anualidad /anuali'ðað/ *f,* annuity
anuario /a'nuario/ *m,* directory, yearbook, handbook
anubarrado /anuβa'rraðo/ *a* covered with clouds, cloudy
anublado /anu'βlaðo/ *a* lowering, overcast; clouded
anublar /anu'βlar/ *vt* to cloud; darken, obscure; blight (plants); *—vr* cloud over; become blighted or mildewed
anudar /anu'ðar/ *vt* to knot; tie, fasten; join; continue; **a. amistad de,** to strike up a friendship with. **a. la corbata,** to put on one's tie, tie one's tie; *—vr* grow stunted
anulable /anu'laβle/ *a* annulable, voidable
anulación /anula'θion; anula'sion/ *f,* annulment, abrogation
anular /anu'lar/ *a* annular, ring-shaped *—vt* to annul; *Math.* cancel out

anuloso /anu'loso/ *a* annulate, formed of rings

anunciación /anunθia'θion; anunsia'sion/ *f*, *Eccl.* Annunciation; announcement

anunciador /anunθia'ðor; anunsia'ðor/ **(-ra)**, *n* **anunciante** /anun'θiante; anun'siante/ *mf* announcer; advertiser

anunciar /anun'θiar; anun'siar/ *vt* to announce; publish, proclaim; advertise; foretell, presage. **Anuncian lluvia,** The forecast calls for rain

anuncio /a'nunθio; a'nunsio/ *m*, announcement; publication, proclamation; advertisement; presage, omen. **a. luminoso,** sky-sign

anverso /am'berso/ *m*, obverse, face

anzuelo /an'θuelo; an'suelo/ *m*, fish-hook; *Cul.* fritter; *Inf.* attraction, inducement

añadido /aɲa'ðiðo/ *m*, hair-switch; make-weight

añadidura /aɲaði'ðura/ *f*, addition; make-weight, extra

añadir /aɲa'ðir/ *vt* to add; increase

añagaza /aɲa'gaθa; aɲa'gasa/ *f*, decoy bird; enticement, lure

añejo /a'ɲeho/ *a* very old

añicos /a'ɲikos/ *m pl*, fragments, small pieces. **hacer a.,** to break into fragments

añil /a'ɲil/ *m*, indigo, indigo blue

año /'aɲo/ *m*, year; *pl* birthday. **a. bisiesto,** leap-year. **a. económico,** fiscal year. **A. Nuevo,** New Year. **tener (siete) años,** to be (seven) years old. **los Años Bobos,** the period from 1874 to 1898 in Spain

añoranza /aɲo'ranθa; aɲo'ransa/ *f*, homesickness, loneliness; nostalgia

añorar /aɲo'rar/ *vi* to be homesick or lonely

añoso /a'ɲoso/ *a* very old, full of years

añublo /a'ɲuβlo/ *m*, mildew

aojamiento /aoha'miento/ *m*, evil eye, wicked spell

aojar /ao'har/ *vt* to bewitch, place under a spell; spoil, frustrate

aojo /a'oho/ *m*, evil eye; magic spell

aorta /a'orta/ *f*, *Anat.* aorta

aovillarse /aoβi'ʎarse; aoβi'yarse/ *vr* to roll oneself into a ball; curl up

apabullante /apaβu'ʎante; apaβu'yante/ *a* crushing, flattening

apacentadero /apaθenta'ðero; apasenta'ðero/ *m*, grazing land, pasture

apacentamiento /apaθenta'miento; apasenta'miento/ *m*, pasturage; grazing

apacentar /apaθen'tar; apasen'tar/ *vt irr* to put out to grass; teach, instruct; satisfy (one's desires); —*vr* graze (cattle). See **acertar**

apacibilidad /apaθiβili'ðað; apasiβili'ðað/ *f*, agreeableness; mildness; peaceableness

apacible /apa'θiβle; apa'siβle/ *a* agreeable; mild; peaceable; calm, peaceful

apaciguamiento /aˌpaθigua'miento; aˌpasigua'miento/ *m*, appeasement, soothing, pacification

apaciguar /apaθi'guar; apasi'guar/ *vt* to appease, pacify; calm

apadrinar /apaðri'nar/ *vt* to act as godfather to; be best man to (at a wedding); act as a second for (in a duel); sponsor; favor

apagable /apa'gaβle/ *a* extinguishable

apagado /apa'gaðo/ *a* timid, nervous; pale (of colors); dull, lusterless

apagador /apaga'ðor/ **(-ra)** *a* quenching —*n* extinguisher. *m*, candle-snuffer; damper (of a piano)

apagaincendios /aˌpagain'θendios; aˌpagain'sendios/ *m*, ship's fire-extinguisher

apagamiento /apaga'miento/ *m*, quenching, extinguishment

apagar /apa'gar/ *vt* to extinguish, put out; *Fig.* quench, moderate; slake (lime); *Art.* tone down (colors); shut off (engines)

apagarrisas /apaga'rrisas/ *mf* crapehanger, killjoy, wet blanket

apagavelas /apaga'βelas/ *m*, candle-snuffer

apalabrar /apala'βrar/ *vt* to make an appointment with; discuss, consider

apaleamiento /apalea'miento/ *m*, beating; thrashing

apalear /apale'ar/ *vt* to beat, thrash; knock down with a stick

apandillarse /apandi'ʎarse; apandi'yarse/ *vr* to form a gang or group

apañar /apa'ɲar/ *vt* to take away, remove; seize; steal; dress, get ready; *Inf.* wrap up; patch, repair; —*vr Inf.* grow skillful

apaño /a'paɲo/ *m*, dexterity, skill; craft, guile

aparador /apara'ðor/ *m*, shop window; sideboard; workshop; *Eccl.* credence (table)

aparato /apa'rato/ *m*, apparatus; equipment, utensils; pomp, ostentation; symptoms; sign, circumstance, token. **a. digestivo,** digestive system; digestive tract. **a. fonador,** speech apparatus

aparatoso /apara'toso/ *a* showy, ostentatious. **incendio. a.,** conflagration, large fire

aparcería /aparθe'ria; aparse'ria/ *f*, partnership (in a farm)

aparear /apare'ar/ *vt* to match, make equal; pair; mate (animals); —*vr* form up in pairs

aparecer /apare'θer; apare'ser/ **(se)** *vi* and *vr irr* to appear; seem; be. See **conocer**

aparecido /apare'θiðo; apare'siðo/ *m*, apparition, specter

aparejador /apareha'ðor/ *m*, overseer, foreman; *Naut.* rigger

aparejar /apare'har/ *vt* to prepare, make ready; saddle (horses); prime, size; rig (a ship)

aparejo /apa'reho/ *m*, preparation, arrangement; harness, trappings; *Naut.* rigging; *Naut.* gear; priming, sizing; *Mech.* tackle; *pl* equipment

aparentar /aparen'tar/ *vt* to pretend, simulate

aparente /apa'rente/ *a* seeming, apparent; obvious, visible; suitable, proper

aparición /apari'θion; apari'sion/ *f*, appearance, arrival; apparition, phantom

apariencia /apa'rienθia; apa'riensia/ *f*, appearance, looks, probability, likelihood; outward semblance; *pl Theat.* scenery

apartadamente /apartaða'mente/ *adv* apart, in private; secretly

apartadero /aparta'ðero/ *m*, passing place for cars; railway siding; grass verge. **a. ferroviario,** railway marshaling yard

apartado /apar'taðo/ *a* distant, far off; secluded; different. *m*, post-office box; secluded room; smelting house; sorting of cattle; selection of bulls for a bullfight

apartamiento /aparta'miento/ *m*, separation; withdrawal, retiral; seclusion; apartment, flat; *Law.* withdrawal of an action

apartar /apar'tar/ *vt* to separate; remove (e.g. an obstacle), take away; *Rail.* shunt; dissuade; sort; —*vr* obtain a divorce; *Law.* withdraw an action. **apartarse de la tradición,** to depart from tradition

aparte /a'parte/ *adv* aside, on one side; separately; *Theat.* aside; besides; beyond. *m*, *Theat.* aside; paragraph; space between words. **¡Aparte!** Move to one side!

apartidario /aparti'ðario/ *a* non-partisan

apasionado /apasio'naðo/ **(-da)** *a* impassioned; fervent, devoted; passionate; enthusiastic —*n* admirer, lover; enthusiast

apasionamiento /apasiona'miento/ *m*, passion

apasionar /apasio'nar/ *vt* to arouse to passion; pain; —*vr* (*with por*) grow passionately fond of; become enthusiastic for

apatía /apa'tia/ *f*, apathy

apático /a'patiko/ *a* apathetic

apeadero /apea'ðero/ *m*, mounting-block; halt, stopping place; wayside railway station; pied-à-terre, occasional dwelling

apear /ape'ar/ *vt* to dismount; hobble (horse); survey, map out; fell a tree; *Fig.* overcome (difficulties); *Inf.* dissuade; prop; remove, bring down; scotch (a wheel); —*vr* dismount; alight, step off

apechugar /apetʃu'gar/ *vi* to push with the breast; *Inf.* put up with reluctantly

apedazar /apeða'θar; apeða'sar/ *vt* to tear; break; mend, repair

apedrear /apeðre'ar/ *vt* to stone; stone to death; —*vi impers* hail; —*vr* be damaged by hail (crops)

apegarse /ape'garse/ *vr* to grow fond (of), become attached (to)

apego /a'pego/ *m*, fondness, inclination; affection, attachment
apelación /apela'θion; apela'sion/ *f*, *Law*. appeal; *Inf*. doctor's consultation
apelante /ape'lante/ *a* and *mf Law*. appellant
apelar /ape'lar/ *vi Law*. to appeal; (*with prep a*) have recourse to; —*vi* be of the same color (horses)
apellidar /apeʎi'ðar; apeyi'ðar/ *vt* to name, call; acclaim; call to arms; —*vr* be named
apellido /ape'ʎiðo; ape'yiðo/ *m*, surname; nickname; call to arms; clamor; name
apenar /ape'nar/ *vt* to grieve, afflict; cause sorrow
apenas /a'penas/ *adv* scarcely; immediately, as soon as; with trouble or difficulty
apéndice /a'pendiθe; a'pendise/ *m*, appendix, supplement; *Anat*. appendix
apendicitis /apendi'θitis; apendi'sitis/ *f*, appendicitis
Apeninos, los /ape'ninos, los/ the Apennines
apeo /a'peo/ *m*, survey; scaffolding; prop, support
apercibimiento /aperθiβi'miento; apersiβi'miento/ *m*, preparation; provision; warning; *Law*. summons
apercibir /aperθi'βir; apersi'βir/ *vt* to prepare, furnish; warn; *Law*. summon
apergaminado /apergami'naðo/ *a* parchment; parchment-like
apergaminarse /apergami'narse/ *vr Inf*. to shrivel, dry up (with old age, etc.)
aperitivo /aperi'tiβo/ *a* aperitive. *m*, aperient; aperitive, appetizer
apertura /aper'tura/ *f*, opening; inauguration; reading (of a will)
apesadumbrar /apesaðum'brar/ *vt* to sadden, afflict, grieve
apestar /apes'tar/ *vt* to infect with the plague; catch the plague; *Fig*. corrupt; *Inf*. pester, annoy; —*vi* stink
apestoso /apes'toso/ *a* stinking, putrid
apetecer /apete'θer; apete'ser/ *vt irr* to want, desire; attract. See **conocer**
apetecible /apete'θiβle; apete'siβle/ *a* attractive, desirable
apetencia /ape'tenθia; ape'tensia/ *f*, appetite; desire
apetito /ape'tito/ *m*, appetite
apetitoso /apeti'toso/ *a* appetising; tasty, savory; attractive
apiadarse /apia'ðarse/ *vr* (*with de*) to have compassion on, be sorry for
ápice /'apiθe; 'apise/ *m*, apex; peak, summit, top; orthographic accent; iota, tittle; crux (of a problem)
apicultor /apikul'tor/ **(-ra)** *n* apiarist, beekeeper
apicultura /apikul'tura/ *f*, apiculture, beekeeping
apilar /api'lar/ *vt* to pile, heap
apiñado /api'ɲaðo/ *a* crowded, serried
apiñamiento /apiɲa'miento/ *m*, crowding; congestion
apiñar /api'ɲar/ *vt* to group together, crowd; —*vr* crowd
apio /'apio/ *m*, celery
apisonadora /apisona'ðora/ *f*, steam-roller; roller
apisonar /apiso'nar/ *vt* to roll, stamp, flatten, ram down; tamp, pack down (e.g. tobacco in a pipe)
apizarrado /apiθa'rraðo; apisa'rraðo/ *a* slate-colored
aplacable /apla'kaβle/ *a* appeasable, placable
aplacamiento /aplaka'miento/ *m*, appeasement
aplacar /apla'kar/ *vt* to appease, calm; moderate, mitigate
aplacible /apla'θiβle; apla'siβle/ *a* agreeable, pleasant
aplanar /apla'nar/ *vt* to flatten, level; roll (pastry); *Inf*. dumbfound, overwhelm; —*vr* collapse (buildings); lose heart
aplastar /aplas'tar/ *vt* to flatten, squash, crush; *Inf*. squash flat, floor
aplaudir /aplau'ðir/ *vt* to applaud, clap; praise, commend, approve
aplauso /a'plauso/ *m*, applause; clapping, plaudit; approbation, commendation
aplazamiento /aplaθa'miento; aplasa'miento/ *m*, postponement; appointment, summons
aplazar /apla'θar; apla'sar/ *vt* to summon, arrange a meeting; postpone; adjourn
aplicabilidad /aplikaβili'ðað/ *f*, applicability
aplicable /apli'kaβle/ *a* applicable
aplicación /aplika'θion; aplika'sion/ *f*, application; diligence, assiduity; appliqué, ornamentation
aplicado /apli'kaðo/ *a* diligent, hardworking; appliqué
aplicar /apli'kar/ *vt* to apply; impute; intend, destine (for processions); *Law*. adjudge; —*vr* engage in; apply oneself. **a. el oído,** to listen intently. **a. sanciones,** *Polit*. to impose sanctions
aplomado /aplo'maðo/ *a* self-possessed, dignified; leaden, lead-colored
aplomar /aplo'mar/ *vt* and *vi* to plumb, test with a plumb-line; —*vr* collapse, fall down
aplomo /a'plomo/ *m*, self-possession, dignity; sangfroid
apocado /apo'kaðo/ *a* spiritless, timid; base, mean
Apocalipsis /apoka'lipsis/ *m*, Apocalypse
apocalíptico /apoka'liptiko/ *a* apocalyptic
apocamiento /apoka'miento/ *m*, timidity, pusillanimity; depression, discouragement; shyness; baseness, meanness
apocar /apo'kar/ *vt* to diminish, reduce; humiliate, scorn
apócrifo /a'pokrifo/ *a* fictitious, false; apocryphal. **Apócrifos,** Apocrypha
apodar /apo'ðar/ *vt* to nickname
apoderado /apoðe'raðo/ *a* authorized. *m*, attorney; deputy; proxy
apoderar /apoðe'rar/ *vt* to authorize; grant powers of attorney to; —*vr* (*with de*) seize, take possession of
apodo /a'poðo/ *m*, nickname
apogeo /apo'heo/ *m*, *Astron*. apogee; *Fig*. zenith, peak (of fame, etc.)
apolillar /apoli'ʎar; apoli'yar/ *vt* to eat clothes (moths); —*vr* be moth-eaten
apolíneo /apo'lineo/ *a* Apollo-like
apologético /apolo'hetiko/ *a* apologetic
apologista /apolo'hista/ *mf* apologist
apólogo /a'pologo/ *m*, apologue, moral fable
apoltronarse /apoltro'narse/ *vr* to grow idle
apoplejía /apople'hia/ *f*, apoplexy
apoplético /apo'pletiko/ **(-ca)** *a* and *n* apoplectic
aporrear /aporre'ar/ *vt* to beat, cudgel; —*vr* work hard, slog away
aportación /aporta'θion; aporta'sion/ *f*, contribution; occasionment
aportar /apor'tar/ *vt* to cause, occasion; contribute; —*vi Naut*. reach port; **El buque aportó a Nueva York,** The ship reached New York, The ship sailed into New York harbor; arrive at an unexpected place
aposentador /aposenta'ðor/ *m*, usher; *Mil*. billeting officer
aposentar /aposen'tar/ *vt* to lodge, give hospitality to; —*vr* lodge, settle down
aposento /apo'sento/ *m*, room; suite, apartments; lodging, accommodation; *Theat*. box
aposición /aposi'θion; aposi'sion/ *f*, *Gram*. apposition
apósito /a'posito/ *m*, poultice, external application; (medical) dressing
apostadero /aposta'ðero/ *m*, *Naut*. naval station; placing or stationing (of soldiers)
apostar /apos'tar/ *vt irr* to bet; station (soldiers); —*vi* compete, rival. See **contar**
apostasía /aposta'sia/ *f*, apostasy
apóstata /a'postata/ *mf* apostate
apostilla /apos'tiʎa; apos'tiya/ *f*, marginal note, gloss
apóstol /a'postol/ *m*, apostle
apostólico /apos'toliko/ *a* apostolic
apóstrofe /a'postrofe/ *m*, or *f*, apostrophe, hortatory exclamation
apóstrofo /a'postrofo/ *m*, *Gram*. apostrophe
apostura /apos'tura/ *f*, neatness, spruceness
apotegma /apo'tegma/ *m*, apothegm, maxim
apoteosis /apote'osis/ *f*, apotheosis
apoyar /apo'yar/ *vt* (*with en*) to lean against; rest upon; —*vt* uphold, favor; confirm, bear out; droop the head (horses); second (a motion); —*vi* (*with en*) rest on; lean against; —*vr* (*with en*) rest on; lean against; **apoyarse de codos,** to lean on one's elbows; be upheld by; *Fig*. be founded on; *Fig*. depend on, lean on

apoyo /a'poyo/ *m*, support, prop; windowsill, sill; assistance; backing, support
apreciable /apreθia'βle; apresia'βle/ *a* appreciable; estimable; important
apreciación /apreθia'θion; apresia'sion/ *f*, appreciation; valuation, estimate
apreciador /apreθia'ðor; apresia'ðor/ **(-ra)** *a* appreciatory —*n* appreciator
apreciar /apre'θiar; apre'siar/ *vt* to estimate (values); appreciate; like, esteem, have a regard for
apreciativo /apreθia'tiβo; apresia'tiβo/ *a* appreciative
aprecio /a'preθio; a'presio/ *m*, valuation; appreciation, regard
aprehender /apreen'der/ *vt* to apprehend, catch; seize (contraband); understand, grasp
aprehensión /apreen'sion/ *f*, seizure, apprehension
apremiador, apremiante /apremia'ðor, apre'miante/ *a* urgent, pressing
apremiar /apre'miar/ *vt* to hurry; urge, press; force, oblige; burden, oppress (with taxes)
apremio /a'premio/ *m*, insistence, pressure; compulsion; demand note
aprendedor /aprende'ðor/ **(-ra)** *n* learner
aprender /apren'der/ *vt* to learn. **a. de memoria,** to learn by heart
aprendiz /apren'diθ; apren'dis/ **(-za)** *n* apprentice
aprendizaje /aprendi'θahe; aprendi'sahe/ *m*, apprenticeship. **hacer el a.,** to serve an apprenticeship
aprensión /apren'sion/ *f*, capture; fear, apprehension; suspicion, fancy; prejudice, scruple
aprensivo /apren'siβo/ *a* apprehensive, nervous, fearful
apresar /apre'sar/ *vt* to nab, catch; capture (a ship); imprison; fetter
aprestar /apres'tar/ *vt* to prepare, arrange; dress (fabrics)
apresto /a'presto/ *m*, preparation, arrangement; dressing (for cloth)
apresurar /apresu'rar/ *vt* to quicken; —*vr* hasten, be quick
apretado /apre'taðo/ *a* difficult, dangerous; tight; crabbed (of handwriting); clustered (e.g. *casas apretadas alrededor de la sinagoga,* houses clustered around the synagogue). *Inf.* mean, close-fisted. *m*, small close handwriting
apretadura /apreta'ðura/ *f*, tightening, compression
apretar /apre'tar/ *vt irr* to tighten; compress; urge on, press; harass, vex; trouble, worry; speed up; squeeze; press (bells, gun triggers, etc.); —*vi* increase, grow worse (storms, heat, etc.); pinch, hurt (shoes). **a. los pasos,** to quicken one's pace. *Inf.* **a. a correr,** to take to one's heels. **¡Aprieta!** *Inf.* Nonsense! It can't be! See **acertar**
apretón /apre'ton/ *m*, squeeze, grip, pressure; *Inf.* sprint, spurt; *Inf.* fix, pickle. **a. de manos,** handshake
apretujamiento /apretuha'miento/ *m*, squeezing together
apretujar /apretu'har/ *vt Inf.* to squeeze, hug
aprieto /a'prieto/ *m*, crowd, crush; urgency; *Inf.* jam, trouble, fix
aprisa /a'prisa/ *adv* quickly, in a hurry
aprisco /a'prisko/ *m*, cattle-shed; sheepfold
aprisionar /aprisio'nar/ *vt* to imprison; bind, fetter; tie
aprobación /aproβa'θion; aproβa'sion/ *f*, approbation, approval, commendation; ratification (of a bill); pass (in an examination)
aprobado /apro'βaðo/ *m*, pass certificate (in examinations)
aprobar /apro'βar/ *vt irr* to approve; pass (in an examination). See **contar**
apropiación /apropia'θion; apropia'sion/ *f*, appropriation; application; adaptation
apropiado /apro'piaðo/ *a* appropriate, suitable, proper
apropiar /apro'piar/ *vt* to appropriate; adapt, fit; —*vr* appropriate, take possession
aprovechable /aproβe'tʃaβle/ *a* usable, available
aprovechado /aproβe'tʃaðo/ *a* advantageous; assiduous, conscientious; capable; thrifty
aprovechador /aproβetʃa'ðor/ *a* self-seeking
aprovechamiento /aproβetʃa'miento/ *m*, utilization, employment; exploitation; profitable use
aprovechar /aproβe'tʃar/ *vi* to be advantageous or useful; be beneficial; make progress (in studies, etc.); —*vt* use; profit by; —*vr* take advantage of, make use of. **¡Que aproveche!** May it do you good! (said to anyone eating)
aprovisionar /aproβi'sionar/ *vt* to provision, supply
aproximación /aproksima'θion; aproksima'sion/ *f*, approximation; consolation prize (in a lottery)
aproximadamente /aproksimaða'mente/ *adv* approximately; nearly, almost
aproximar /aproksi'mar/ *vt* to bring or draw nearer; —*vr* approach; be almost, be approximately; draw closer
aptitud /apti'tuð/ *f*, aptitude, ability; fitness; propensity
apto /'apto/ *a* suitable, fitting; competent. **no apta para menores,** not suitable for children (of films, etc.)
apuesta /a'puesta/ *f*, bet, wager; competition
apuestas benéficas de fútbol /a'puestas be'nefikas de 'futβol/ football pools
apuesto /a'puesto/ *a* elegant; handsome, well set-up
apuntación /apunta'θion; apunta'sion/ *f*, noting down; note; *Mus.* notation
apuntador /apunta'ðor/ **(-ra)** *n* note-taker; observer. *m, Theat.* prompter; *Theat.* stage-manager
apuntalar /apunta'lar/ *vt* to prop, prop up, underpin, bolster
apuntamiento /apunta'miento/ *m*, summary; *Law.* indictment, minute
apuntar /apun'tar/ *vt* to aim (a gun, etc.); point to, indicate; note down; mark; sketch; sharpen; bet (at cards); fasten temporarily; *Inf.* mend; *Theat.* prompt; suggest, hint (e.g. *La fecha está apuntada en vanos manuscritos,* The date is hinted at in various manuscripts); —*vi* begin to appear. *Inf.* **a. y no dar,** to promise and do nothing
apunte /a'punte/ *m*, abstract; note; annotation; sketch; *Theat.* prompt *or* prompter *or* prompt book *or* cue; stake in a card game
apuñalado /apuɲa'laðo/ *a* dagger-shaped
apuñalar /apuɲa'lar/ *vt* to stab, attack with a dagger
apurado /apu'raðo/ *a* poor, needy; dangerous; difficult; accurate, exact; hurried
apurar /apu'rar/ *vt* to purify; drain; exhaust; finish, conclude; examine closely, scrutinize (e.g. *apurar una materia,* to exhaust a subject, examine a subject thoroughly); irritate, make impatient; urge on, hasten; —*vr* be anxious, fret
apuro /a'puro/ *m*, difficulty, fix; poverty, want; anxiety, worry. **pasar apuros,** to have a hard time
aquejar /ake'har/ *vt* to afflict; weary, beset, harass; —*vr* complain; hurry
aquel, /a'kel,/ *a m* **aquella,** *a f* **aquellos,** *a m pl* **aquellas** *a f pl,* that, those; that or those over there (farther off than **ese**)
aquel /a'kel/ *m*, charm, attraction, it
aquél, aquélla, aquéllos, aquéllas /a'kel, a'keʎa, a'keʎos, a'keʎas; a'kel, a'keya, a'keyos, a'keyas/ *dem pron m, f,* sing. and pl., that, the one, those, those ones; the former. e.g. *La casa que ve usted a lo lejos aquélla es la vivienda de mi tío,* The house that you see in the distance, that is my uncle's dwelling. *Éste no me gusta pero aquél sí,* I do not like the latter, but I like the former
aquelarre /ake'larre/ *m*, witches' sabbath
aquello /a'keʎo; a'keyo/ *dem pron neut* that; the fact; the matter, the affair, the former (remark, idea, etc.). e.g. *Todo a. por fin acabó,* All that came to an end at last. *a. de,* the fact that
aquende /a'kende/ *adv* on this side (rarely used)
aquí /a'ki/ *adv* here. **de a.,** hence the fact that. **¡He a.!** Behold!
aquiescencia /akies'θenθia; akies'sensia/ *f*, consent, acquiescence
aquietar /akie'tar/ *vt* to calm, soothe
aquilatar /akila'tar/ *vt* to assay; scrutinize; examine, weigh up (persons)
aquistar /akis'tar/ *vt* to attain, acquire

ara /'ara/ *f,* altar; **en aras de,** in honor of; for the sake of

árabe /'araβe/ *a* Arab, Arabic. *mf* Arab. *m,* Arabic (language)

arabesco /ara'βesko/ *a* Arabic. *m, Art.* arabesque

Arabia Saudita /a'raβia sau'ðita/ Saudi Arabia

arábigo /a'raβigo/ *a* Arabic. *m,* Arabic (language)

arácnido /a'rakniðo/ *m, Zool.* arachnid

arado /a'raðo/ *m,* plow

arador /ara'ðor/ *a* plowing. *m,* plowman. **a. de la sarna,** *Ent.* scabies mite

aragonés /arago'nes/ **(-esa)** *a* and *n* Aragonese

arahuaco /ara'uako/ *a* and *n* Arawak, Arawakian

arancel /aran'θel; aran'sel/ *m,* tariff, duty, tax

arancelar /aranθe'lar; aranse'lar/ to charge tuition for (e.g. *a. la universidad,* charge tuition for college studies)

arancelario /aranθe'lario; aranse'lario/ *a* tariff, tax, customs

arándano /a'randano/ *m, Bot.* bilberry

arandela /aran'dela/ *f,* candle-dripper; *Mech.* washer; wall candelabrum

araña /a'raɲa/ *f,* spider; chandelier

arañacielos /a,raɲa'θielos; a,raɲa'sielos/ *m,* skyscraper

arañar /ara'ɲar/ *vt* to scratch; *Inf.* scrape together, hoard

arañazo /ara'ɲaθo; ara'ɲaso/ *m,* scratch

arar /a'rar/ *vt* to plough. **a. en el mar,** to labor in vain

arbitrador /arβitra'ðor/ **(-ra)** *n* arbitrator

arbitraje /arβi'trahe/ *m,* arbitration; arbitrament, decision

arbitrar /arβi'trar/ *vt* to judge freely; *Law.* arbitrate, mediate; devise; invent; marshal (money, resources, etc.); draft (a law) *vr* make shift, contrive

arbitrariedad /arβitrarie'ðað/ *f,* arbitrariness

arbitrario /arβi'trario/ *a* arbitral, mediatory; arbitrary, capricious

arbitrio /ar'βitrio/ *m,* free will; arbitration; means, way; discretion; arbitrament, judgment; *pl* rates, municipal taxes

árbitro /'arβitro/ **(-ra)** *a* arbitrary —*n* arbiter. *m, Sports.* umpire; referee

árbol /'arβol/ *m,* tree; *Mech.* shaft; *Naut.* mast; axis of a winding stair. **a. de amor** *or* **a. de Judas,** Judas tree. **a. de la ciencia (del bien y del mal),** Tree of Knowledge (of good and evil). **a. de levas,** *Mech.* camshaft. **a. del pan,** breadfruit tree. *Naut.* **a. mayor,** mainmast. **a. motor** *Mech.*, drivingshaft

arbolado /arβo'laðo/ *a* tree-covered, wooded. *m,* copse, woodland

arboladura /arβola'ðura/ *f, Naut.* masts and spars

arbolar /arβo'lar/ *vt* to hoist (flags); *Naut.* fit with masts; place upright; —*vr* rear, prance (horses)

arboleda /arβo'leða/ *f,* copse, grove, spinney

arbotante /arβo'tante/ *m,* flying buttress

arbusto /ar'βusto/ *m,* shrub, woody plant

arca /'arka/ *f,* chest; money-box, coffer; ark; *pl* (treasury) vaults. **a. caudal,** strong box. **a. de agua,** water-tower. **a. de la alianza.** *or* **a. del testamento,** Ark of the Covenant (Bible). **a. de Noé,** Noah's Ark; lumber box

arcabucero /arkaβu'θero; arkaβu'sero/ *m,* arquebusier; maker of arquebuses

arcabuz /arka'βuθ; arka'βus/ *m,* arquebus

arcada /ar'kaða/ *f,* arcade; series of arches; *pl* sickness, nausea

árcade /ar'kaðe/ *a* and *mf* Arcadian

arcaico /ar'kaiko/ *a* archaic

arcaísmo /arka'ismo/ *m,* archaism

arcángel /ar'kanhel/ *m,* archangel

arcano /ar'kano/ *a* secret. *m,* mystery, arcanum

arce /'arθe; 'arse/ *m, Bot.* maple tree

archifeliz /artʃife'liθ; artʃife'lis/ *a* extremely happy, in bliss

archimandrita /artʃiman'drita/ *m,* archimandrite

archimillonario /artʃimiʎo'nario; artʃimiyo'nario/ **(-ia)** *a* and *n* multimillionaire

archipiélago /artʃi'pielago/ *m,* archipelago

Archipiélago de Colón /artʃi'pielago de ko'lon/ *m,* Galapagos Islands

archivar /artʃi'βar/ *vt* to place in an archive; file (papers)

archivero /artʃi'βero/ *m,* archivist, keeper of the archives; librarian; registrar; (Mexico) file cabinet, filing cabinet

archivista /artʃi'βista/ *mf* archivist; file clerk, filing clerk

archivo /ar'tʃiβo/ *m,* archives

arcilla /ar'θiʎa; ar'siya/ *f,* clay

arcilloso /arθi'ʎoso; arsi'yoso/ *a* clayey, like or full of clay

arcipreste /arθi'preste; arsi'preste/ *m,* archpriest

arco /'arko/ *m, Geom.* arc; *Mil.* bow; bow (of a stringed instrument); hoop (of casks, etc.); *Archit.* arch. **a. del cielo** *or* **a. de San Martín** *or* **a. iris,** rainbow. **a. voltaico,** electric arc. *Mus.* **para a.,** for strings

arder /ar'ðer/ *vi* to burn; shine, gleam; *Fig.* burn (with passion, etc.); —*vt* to set alight, burn

ardid /ar'ðið/ *a* crafty. *m,* trick, stratagem

ardiente /ar'ðiente/ *a* burning; ardent, passionate; vehement; enthusiastic; flame-colored; fiery-red

ardilla /ar'ðiʎa; ar'ðiya/ *f,* squirrel

ardite /ar'ðite/ *m,* ancient Spanish coin of little value; *Fig.* farthing, fig, straw. **no valer un a.,** to be not worth a straw

ardor /ar'ðor/ *m,* great heat; zeal, earnestness; passion, ardor; courage

ardoroso /arðo'roso/ *a* ardorous

arduo /'arðuo/ *a* arduous

área /'area/ *f,* area; small plot of ground; common threshing floor; arc (surface measure)

arena /a'rena/ *f,* sand; arena; grit, gravel. **a. movediza,** quicksand

arenal /are'nal/ *m,* quicksand; sand pit; sandy place

arenero /are'nero/ **(-ra)** *n* sand merchant. *m,* sandbox (carried by railway engines)

arenga /a'reŋga/ *f,* harangue, discourse

arenilla /are'niʎa; are'niya/ *f,* sand (for drying writing)

arenisca /are'niska/ *f,* sandstone

arenisco /are'nisko/ *a* sandy

arenque /a'renke/ *m,* herring

arete /a'rete/ *m,* earring

argamasa /arga'masa/ *f,* mortar

argayo /ar'gayo/ *m,* landslide; (Asturias) **a. de nieve,** avalanche

Árgel /'arhel/ Algiers

Argelia /ar'helia/ Algeria

argelino /arhe'lino/ **(-na)** *a* and *n* Algerian

argentado /arhen'taðo/ *a* silvered; silvery

argénteo /ar'henteo/ *a* silver; silvery

argentífero /arhen'tifero/ *a* silver-yielding

argentino /arhen'tino/ **(-na)** *a* silvery —*a* and *n* Argentinian. *m,* Argentinian gold coin

argento /ar'hento/ *m,* silver. **a. vivo,** mercury

argolla /ar'goʎa; ar'goya/ *f,* thick metal ring (for hitching, etc.); croquet (game); stocks, pillory; hoop, iron arch

argonauta /argo'nauta/ *m, Myth.* Argonaut; *Zool.* paper nautilus, argonaut

argucia /ar'guθia; ar'gusia/ *f,* sophism, quibble; subtlety

argüir /ar'guir/ *vt irr* to deduce, imply; prove; reveal, manifest; accuse; —*vi* argue, debate; dispute, oppose. See **huir**

argumentador /argumenta'ðor/ **(-ra)** *a* argumentative —*n* arguer

argumentar /argumen'tar/ *vi* to argue; dispute; oppose

argumento /argu'mento/ *m,* contention, case; theme (of a book, etc.); argument, discussion

aridez /ari'ðeθ; ari'ðes/ *f,* aridity, dryness; drought; sterility, barrenness; dullness, lack of interest

árido /'ariðo/ *a* dry, arid; sterile, barren; uninteresting, dull

ariete /a'riete/ *m, Mil.* battering ram

ario /'ario/ **(-ia)** *a* and *n* Aryan

arisco /a'risko/ *a* unsociable, surly; wild, shy (animals)
arista /a'rista/ *f, Bot.* arista, awn, beard; pebble; edge, side
aristocracia /aristo'kraθia; aristo'krasia/ *f,* aristocracy
aristócrata /aris'tokrata/ *mf* aristocrat
aristocrático /aristo'kratiko/ *a* aristocratic
aristotélico /aristo'teliko/ *a* Aristotelian
aristotelismo /aristote'lismo/ *m,* Aristotelianism
aritmética /arit'metika/ *f,* arithmetic
aritmético /arit'metiko/ **(-ca)** *a* arithmetical —*n* arithmetician
arlequín /arle'kin/ *m,* harlequin; *Inf.* fool, buffoon; Neapolitan ice-cream
arlequinada /arleki'naða/ *f,* harlequinade; buffoonery
arma /'arma/ *f,* weapon; *Mil.* arm, branch; bull's horn; *pl* troops, army; means, way; arms, coat of arms. **a. arrojadiza,** missile. **a. blanca,** steel weapon. **a. de fuego,** fire-arm. **¡Armas al hombro!** Shoulder Arms! **armas portátiles,** small arms. *Inf.* **de armas tomar,** belligerent; resolute. **pasar por las armas,** *Mil.* to shoot. **presentar las armas,** *Mil.* to present arms. **ser a. de dos filos,** *Fig.* to cut both ways
armada /ar'maða/ *f,* navy, armada; fleet, squadron
armadía /arma'ðia/ *f,* raft, pontoon
armador /arma'ðor/ **(-ra)** *n* supplier, outfitter. *m,* shipowner; pirate, privateer; jacket; assembler, fitter
armadura /arma'ðura/ *f,* armature, armor; frame, framework; skeleton (of a building); skeleton (of vertebrates); *Phys.* armature; plate armor (of persons)
armamento /arma'mento/ *m, Mil.* armament; arms, military equipment
armar /ar'mar/ *vt* to arm; *Mech.* mount; man (guns); put together, assemble; roll (a cigarette); reinforce (concrete); *Inf.* arrange, prepare; *Inf.* occasion (quarrels); *Inf.* outfit; *Naut.* equip; commission (a ship); —*vr* prepare oneself, arm oneself. **a. caballero,** to knight. **a. los remos,** to ship the oars. *Inf.* **armarla,** to cause a row or quarrel
armario /ar'mario/ *m,* cupboard; wardrobe. **a. de luna,** wardrobe with a mirror
armatoste /arma'toste/ *m,* unwieldy piece of furniture; *Fig. Inf.* dead weight, clumsy person; snare
armazón /arma'θon; arma'son/ *f,* frame, framework; ship's hulk. *m, Anat.* skeleton
armenio /ar'menio/ **(-ia)** *a* and *n* Armenian. *m,* Armenian language
armería /arme'ria/ *f,* armory; heraldry; gunsmith's craft or shop
armero /ar'mero/ *m,* gunsmith, armorer; stand for weapons. **a. mayor,** Royal Armorer
armiño /ar'miɲo/ *m,* ermine
armisticio /armis'tiθio; armis'tisio/ *m,* armistice
armón de artillería /ar'mon de artiʎe'ria; ar'mon de artiye'ria/ *m,* gun-carriage
armonía /armo'nia/ *f,* harmony; friendship, concord; *Mus.* harmony
armónica /ar'monika/ **(de boca)** *f,* mouth-organ
armónico /ar'moniko/ *a* harmonious —*a* and *m, Mus.* harmonic
armonio /ar'monio/ *m,* harmonium
armonioso /armo'nioso/ *a* harmonious
armonización /armoniθa'θion; armonisa'sion/ *f, Mus.* harmonization
armonizar /armoni'θar; armoni'sar/ *vt* to bring into harmony; *Mus.* harmonize
arnés /ar'nes/ *m,* armor; harness; *pl* horse trappings; *Inf.* equipment, tools
aro /'aro/ *m,* hoop; rim (of wheel, etc.); napkin-ring; croquet hoop; *Bot.* wild arum; child's hoop. **a. de empaquetadura,** *Mech.* gasket
aroma /a'roma/ *m,* aroma, fragrance; balsam; sweet-smelling herb
aromático /aro'matiko/ *a* aromatic
arpa /'arpa/ *f,* harp. **a. eolia,** Eolian harp
arpar /ar'par/ *vt* to scratch, claw; tear, rend
arpegio /ar'pehio/ *m, Mus.* arpeggio
arpía /ar'pia/ *f,* harpy
arpicordio /arpi'korðio/ *m,* harpsichord
arpista /ar'pista/ *mf* harpist, harp player
arpón /ar'pon/ *m,* harpoon
arponear /arpone'ar/ *vt* to harpoon
arponero /arpo'nero/ *m,* harpooner; harpoon maker
arquear /arke'ar/ *vt* to arch; bend; beat (wool); gauge (ship's capacity); —*vi* retch
arqueo /ar'keo/ *m,* arching; bending, curving; *Naut.* tonnage; gauging (of ship's capacity); *Com.* examination of deposits and contents of safe
arqueología /arkeolo'hia/ *f,* archeology
arqueológico /arkeo'lohiko/ *a* archeological
arqueólogo /arke'ologo/ *m,* archeologist
arquero /ar'kero/ *m, Com.* cashier, treasurer; *Mil.* archer
arquitecto /arki'tekto/ *m,* architect. **a. de jardines,** landscape gardener
arquitectónico /arkitek'toniko/ *a* architectural
arquitectura /arkitek'tura/ *f,* architecture
arquitrabe /arki'traβe/ *m,* architrave
arrabal /arra'βal/ *m,* suburb, district; *pl* outskirts
arracada /arra'kaða/ *f,* pendant-earring
arracimarse /arraθi'marse; arrasi'marse/ *vr* to cluster; group
arraigadamente /arrai,gaða'mente/ *adv* deeply, firmly
arraigado /arrai'gaðo/ *a* deep rooted; firm; convinced
arraigar /arrai'gar/ *vi* to take root; —*vi* and *vr Fig.* become established, take hold; —*vr* settle; take up residence
arraigo /a'rraigo/ *m,* rooting; settlement, establishment; landed property
arrancaclavos /a,rranka'klaβos/ *m,* nail-puller
arrancadero /a,rranka'ðero/ *m, Sports.* starting-point
arrancar /arran'kar/ *vt* to uproot; pull out; wrench; tear off; extirpate; obtain by threats; clear one's throat; —*vt* and *vi Naut.* put on speed; —*vi* start (a race); *Inf.* leave, quit; derive, originate **¡Arrancan!** And they're off! (races)
arranque /a'rranke/ *m,* uprooting; extirpation; wrenching, pulling, seizing; stimulus (of passion); sudden impulse; *Mech.* start; *Mech.* starter. **a. automático,** self-starter
arras /'arras/ *f pl,* dowry; coins given by bridegroom to his bride; earnest money, token
arrasamiento /arrasa'miento/ *m,* demolition, destruction; leveling
arrasar /arra'sar/ *vt* to demolish, destroy; level; fill to the brim; —*vi* and *vr* clear up (sky). **ojos arrasados de lágrimas,** eyes brimming with tears
arrastrado /arras'traðo/ *a Inf.* poverty-stricken, wretched; *Inf.* knavish; unhappy, unfortunate
arrastrar /arras'trar/ *vt* to drag; trail; convince; haul; —*vi* trail along or touch the ground; trump (at cards); —*vr* crawl, creep; shuffle along; humble oneself
arrastre /a'rrastre/ *m,* dragging, trailing; haulage; trumping (at cards)
¡arre! /'arre/ *interj* Gee up! Get along!
arrear /arre'ar/ *vt* to spur on, whip up (horses, etc.) —*interj Inf.* **¡Arrea!** Hurry up! Get on!
arrebañar /arreβa'ɲar/ *vt* to pick clean, clear; eat or drink up
arrebatado /arreβa'taðo/ *a* precipitate, headlong; rash; flushed, red
arrebatador /arreβata'ðor/ *a* overwhelming; violent; bewitching, captivating; delightful
arrebatamiento /arreβata'miento/ *m,* abduction; seizure; fury; ecstasy
arrebatar /arreβa'tar/ *vt* to abduct, carry off; seize, grab; attract, charm; grip (the attention); —*vr* be overcome with rage
arrebatiña /arreβa'tiɲa/ *f,* grab; scuffle, scrimmage
arrebato /arre'βato/ *m,* fit (gen. of anger); ecstasy, rapture
arrebol /arre'βol/ *m,* red flush in the sky; rouge; *pl* red clouds
arrebozar /arreβo'θar; arreβo'sar/ *vt* to muffle; envelop
arrebujarse /arreβu'harse/ *vr* to huddle; wrap oneself up
arrechucho /arre'tʃutʃo/ *m, Inf.* fit of rage; sudden slight ailment

arreciar /arre'θiar; arre'siar/ *vi* to increase in intensity; —*vr* grow strong
arrecife /arre'θife; arre'sife/ *m,* reef (in the sea); stone-paved road
arredrar /arre'ðrar/ *vt* to separate, remove; force back, repel; terrify
arregazar /arrega'θar; arrega'sar/ **(se)** *vt* and *vr* to tuck up one's skirts
arreglado /arre'glaðo/ *a* regular; regulated; ordered; methodical
arreglar /arre'glar/ *vt* to regulate; arrange; adjust, put right; tidy; make up (the face); —*vr* (*with prep a*) conform to; (*with con*) reach an agreement with. **Me voy a a.,** I am going to make myself presentable. *Inf.* **arreglárselas,** to shift for oneself
arreglo /a'rreglo/ *m,* arrangement; rule; regulation; method, order; agreement; adjustment; compromise
arrellanarse /arreʎa'narse; arreya'narse/ *vr* to settle comfortably in one's chair; be happy in one's work
arremangar /arremaŋ'gar/ *vt* to roll up (sleeves, trousers, etc.); —*vr Inf.* make a decision
arremango /arre'maŋgo/ *m,* rolling or tucking up (of sleeve, etc.)
arremetedor /arremete'ðor/ **(-ra)** *n* attacker, assailant
arremeter /arreme'ter/ *vt* to attack, assail; —*vi* launch oneself (at); *Fig.* spoil the view, shock the eye
arremetida /arreme'tiða/ *f,* attack, assault
arremolinarse /arremoli'narse/ *vr* to crowd, cluster, group
arrendador /arrenda'ðor/ **(-ra)** *n* landlord; renter; hirer; tenant
arrendamiento /arrenda'miento/ *m,* letting, renting; hiring; rental; agreement, lease
arrendar /arren'dar/ *vt irr* to let, lease; hire; rent (as a tenant); train (horses); tie up (horses); restrain; mimic, imitate. See **recomendar**
arrendatario /arrenda'tario/ **(-ia)** *a* rent, lease —*n* tenant; lessee; hirer. **a. de contribuciones,** tax farmer
arreo /a'rreo/ *m,* ornament; apparel; *pl* horse trappings; appurtenances, equipment
¡Arrepa! /a'rrepa/ But look!, Hold on!, Hold your horses!, Not so fast!
arrepentimiento /arrepenti'miento/ *m,* repentance
arrepentirse /arrepen'tirse/ *vr irr* to repent. See **sentir**
arrestado /arres'taðo/ *a* courageous, audacious, bold
arrestar /arres'tar/ *vt* to arrest, detain; —*vr* be bold, dare
arresto /a'rresto/ *m,* arrest; detention; imprisonment; audacity, boldness
arriada /a'rriaða/ *f,* lowering (of a boat); taking in (of sail)
arriar /a'rriar/ *vt Naut.* to strike (colors); take in (sail); pay out (ropes, etc.); lower (boats); flood, inundate
arriate /a'rriate/ *m,* garden border; avenue, walk; trellis (for plants)
arriba /a'rriβa/ *adv* up, above; overhead; upstairs; earlier, before; upwards (with prices) —*interj* **¡A.!** Up with!; Long live! **de a. abajo,** from head to foot, from one end to the other; completely, wholly
arribada /arri'βaða/ *f, Naut.* arrival. **de a.,** emergency (port)
arribar /arri'βar/ *vi Naut.* to arrive; put into an emergency port; reach, arrive at; *Inf.* convalesce; attain; *Naut.* drift
arribista /arri'βista/ *mf* social climber
arribo /a'rriβo/ *m,* arrival
arriero /a'rriero/ *m,* farrier; muleteer
arriesgado /arries'gaðo/ *a* dangerous, risky; rash, daring
arriesgar /arries'gar/ *vt* to risk; —*vr* run into danger; dare, risk
arrimar /arri'mar/ *vt* to bring or draw near; abandon (professions, etc.); lay aside, discard; *Inf.* administer (blows); *Naut.* stow (cargo); —*vr* (*with prep a*) lean against, rest on; join, go with; seek the protection of. **Cada cual se arrima a su cada cual,** Birds of a feather flock together
arrimo /a'rrimo/ *m,* bringing or placing near; leaning or resting against; abandonment, giving up; protection; staff, support
arrinconado /arrinko'naðo/ *a* remote, secluded; forgotten, neglected
arrinconar /arrinko'nar/ *vt* to discard, lay aside; corner, besiege; set aside, dismiss; forsake; —*vr* go into retirement, withdraw
arriscado /arris'kaðo/ *a* craggy, rugged; bold, resolute; sprightly, handsome
arro, arro, arro /'arro, 'arro, 'arro/ purrrr (echoic of a cat's purr)
arroba /a'rroβa/ *f,* weight of 25 lb.; variable liquid measure
arrobamiento /arroβa'miento/ *m,* ecstasy, rapture; trance
arrobar /arro'βar/ *vt* to charm, entrance; —*vr* be enraptured; be in ecstasy
arrodillar /arroði'ʎar; arroði'yar/ *vt* to cause to kneel down; —*vi* and *vr* kneel down
arrogancia /arro'ganθia; arro'gansia/ *f,* arrogance; courage; majesty, pride
arrogante /arro'gante/ *a* arrogant, haughty; courageous; proud, majestic
arrogar /arro'gar/ *vt* to adopt (as a son); —*vr* usurp, appropriate
arrojadizo /arroha'ðiθo; arroha'ðiso/ *a* easily cast or hurled; projectile
arrojado /arro'haðo/ *a* bold, determined; rash
arrojar /arro'har/ *vt* to throw, hurl, cast; shed (light, etc.; e.g. *La cuenta arroja un total de cien dólares,* The bill shows a total of a hundred dollars); *Com.* show (a balance, etc.); put out (sprouts); dismiss, send away; —*vr* cast oneself; (*with prep a*) hurl oneself against or upon; undertake, venture upon. **a. de sí (a),** to get rid of, dismiss
arrojo /a'rroho/ *m,* daring, intrepidity; boldness
arrollar /arro'ʎar; arro'yar/ *vt* to roll; make into a roll, roll up; defeat (the enemy); silence, confound; rock to sleep; bear along, carry off
arromar /arro'mar/ *vt* to blunt; flatten
arropamiento /arropa'miento/ *m,* wrapping up, covering, muffling
arropar /arro'par/ *vt* to wrap up, cover
arrostrar /arros'trar/ *vt* to confront, defy, face up to; —*vr* fight hand to hand. **a. las consecuencias,** *Fig.* to face the music
arroyada /arro'yaða/ *f,* gorge, gully; course, channel; flood
arroyo /a'rroyo/ *m,* stream, brook; street gutter; road, street; *Fig.* flood, plenty
arroz /a'rroθ; a'rros/ *m,* rice
arrozal /arro'θal; arro'sal/ *m,* rice field
arruga /a'rruga/ *f,* wrinkle; fold, pleat; crease
arrugamiento /arruga'miento/ *m,* wrinkling; fold, pleating; crumpling, creasing; corrugation
arrugar /arru'gar/ *vt* to wrinkle; pleat; corrugate; crumple, crease. **a. el ceño,** to knit one's brow, scowl
arruinamiento /arruina'miento/ *m,* ruin, decay, decline
arruinar /arrui'nar/ *vt* to ruin; destroy, damage severely
arrullar /arru'ʎar; arru'yar/ *vt* to bill and coo (doves); lull to sleep; *Inf.* whisper sweet words to, make love to
arrullo /a'rruʎo; a'rruyo/ *m,* cooing of doves; lullaby
arrumaco /arru'mako/ *m, Inf.* embrace, caress (gen. *pl*); ornament in bad taste
arrumaje /arru'mahe/ *m, Naut.* stowage; clouds on the horizon
arrurruz /arru'rruθ; arru'rrus/ *m,* arrowroot
arsenal /arse'nal/ *m,* dockyard; arsenal; *Fig.* store (of information, etc.)
arsénico /ar'seniko/ *m,* arsenic
arte /'arte/ *mf,* art; skill; ability, talent; guile, craftiness. **las bellas artes,** fine arts. *Inf.* **no tener a. ni parte en,** to have nothing to do with, have no part in
artefacto /arte'fakto/ *m,* machine, mechanism, apparatus; device, appliance. **a. atómico,** atomic bomb
arteria /ar'teria/ *f, Med.* artery; main line (of communication)
artería /arte'ria/ *f,* craftiness, guile
arterial /arte'rial/ *a* arterial

artesa /ar'tesa/ *f,* wooden trough; kneading bowl
artesano /arte'sano/ **(-na)** *n* artisan; mechanic
artesiano /arte'siano/ *a* artesian
artesón /arte'son/ *m,* bucket, pail; *Archit.* curved ceiling-panel; paneled ceiling
artesonado /arteso'naðo/ *a Archit.* paneled (ceiling). *m,* paneled ceiling
ártico /'artiko/ *a* Arctic
articulación /artikula'θion; artikula'sion/ *f,* joint, articulation; jointing; enunciation, pronunciation
articular /artiku'lar/ *vt* to joint, articulate; enunciate, pronounce clearly
articulista /artiku'lista/ *mf* article writer
artículo /ar'tikulo/ *m,* finger knuckle; heading; article; *Anat.* joint; *Gram.* article; *pl* goods, things. **a. de fondo,** leading article (in a newspaper). **a. de primera necesidad,** prime necessity, essential
artífice /ar'tifiθe; ar'tifise/ *mf* craftsman, artificer; author, creator; forger
artificial /artifi'θial; artifi'sial/ *a* artificial
artificio /arti'fiθio; arti'fiçsio/ *m,* skill, art; appliance, contraption, mechanism; trick, cunning device; guile, craftiness
artificioso /artifi'θioso; artifi'sioso/ *a* skilful; artificial; crafty, cunning
artillería /artiʎe'ria; artiye'ria/ *f,* artillery. **a. de costa,** coastal guns. **a. ligera, a. montada, a. rodada** *or* **a. volante,** field artillery
artillero /arti'ʎero; arti'yero/ *m,* gunner
artimaña /arti'maɲa/ *f,* trick, ruse, stratagem
artista /ar'tista/ *mf* artist; performer
artístico /ar'tistiko/ *a* artistic
artrítico /ar'tritiko/ *a Med.* arthritic
artritis /ar'tritis/ *f, Med.* arthritis
arveja /ar'βeha/ *f, Bot.* vetch
arzobispado /arθoβis'paðo; arsoβis'paðo/ *m,* archbishopric
arzobispo /arθo'βispo; arso'βispo/ *m,* archbishop
as /as/ *m,* Roman copper coin; ace (*Aer.* cards, etc.)
asa /'asa/ *f,* handle; pretext, excuse
asado /a'saðo/ *m, Cul.* roast
asador /asa'ðor/ *m, Cul.* roasting-spit; roaster
asadura /asa'ðura/ *f, Cul.* chitterlings; offal
asalariar /asala'riar/ *vt* to fix a salary for
asaltador /asalta'ðor/ **(-ra)** *a* attacking —*n* assailant, attacker
asaltar /asal'tar/ *vt* to storm, besiege; assault, attack; occur to (ideas); come on suddenly (illness)
asalto /a'salto/ *m,* storming, besieging; assault, attack; bout (in fencing, boxing, wrestling); round (in a fight)
asamblea /asam'βlea/ *f,* congregation, assembly; meeting; legislative assembly; *Mil.* assembly (bugle call)
asambleísta /asamble'ista/ *mf* member of an assembly
asar /a'sar/ *vt Cul.* to roast; grill; —*vr* be burning-hot; *Fig.* burn (with enthusiasm)
asaz /a'saθ; a'sas/ *adv* sufficiently, enough; very; in abundance —*a* sufficient; many
asbesto /as'βesto/ *m,* asbestos
ascalonia /aska'lonia/ *f, Bot.* shallot
ascendencia /asθen'denθia; assen'densia/ *f,* lineage, ancestry, origin
ascendente /asθen'dente; assen'dente/ *a* ascending
ascender /asθen'der; assen'der/ *vi irr* to ascend, climb; be promoted; (*with prep a*) amount to (bills, etc.); —*vt* promote. See **entender**
ascendiente /asθen'diente; assen'diente/ *mf* ancestor, forbear. *m,* influence, ascendancy
ascensión /asθen'sion; assen'sion/ *f,* ascension; promotion; *Astron.* exaltation
ascenso /as'θenso; as'senso/ *m,* ascent; promotion, preferment
ascensor /asθen'sor; assen'sor/ *m,* lift, elevator
ascensorista /asθenso'rista; assenso'rista/ *mf* elevator operator
asceta /as'θeta; as'seta/ *mf* ascetic
ascético /as'θetiko; as'setiko/ *a* ascetic
ascetismo /asθe'tismo; asse'tismo/ *m,* asceticism
asco /'asko/ *m,* nausea; repugnance, loathing; revolting thing. *Inf.* **Me da a.,** It sickens me
ascua /'askua/ *f,* live coal, ember. **estar como una a. de oro,** to be as bright as a new pin. **estar en ascuas,** *Fig.* to be on pins
aseado /ase'aðo/ *a* clean, tidy
asear /ase'ar/ *vt* to tidy, make neat; clean up; decorate, adorn
asechanza /ase'tʃanθa; ase'tʃansa/ *f,* ambush; trick, snare, stratagem
asechar /ase'tʃar/ *vt* to ambush, waylay; *Fig.* lay snares for
asediador /aseðia'ðor/ **(-ra)** *n* besieger
asediar /ase'ðiar/ *vt* to besiege; pester, importune
asedio /a'seðio/ *m,* siege; importunity
asegurado /asegu'raðo/ **(-da)** *a* insured —*n* insured person
asegurador /asegura'ðor/ **(-ra)** *a* insuring —*n* insurer
asegurar /asegu'rar/ *vt* to fasten, make secure; pinion, grip; reassure, soothe; assert, state; *Com.* insure; guarantee; ensure, secure; —*vr Com.* insure oneself; (*with de*) make sure of
asemejar /aseme'har/ *vt* to imitate, copy; make similar to; —*vr* (*with prep a*) be like, be similar to
asenderear /asendere'ar/ *vt* to make a pathway through; persecute, harass
asenso /a'senso/ *m,* assent. **dar a.,** to believe, give credence (to)
asentaderas /asenta'ðeras/ *f pl, Inf.* buttocks, seat
asentado /asen'taðo/ *a* prudent, circumspect; permanent, stable
asentamiento /asenta'miento/ *m,* seating; settlement, residence; prudence, judgment
asentar /asen'tar/ *vt irr* to seat; place; fasten, fix; found; plant (flags); pitch (a tent); establish, make firm; smooth; hone (razors); estimate, budget, arrange, set forth; note down; affirm, believe; *Com.* enter (in an account); —*vi* fit (clothes); —*vr* seat oneself; alight (birds); settle (liquids); *Archit.* settle, subside; to be located (e.g. *El edificio se asienta en una esquina,* The building is located on a corner). **a. la mano en,** to strike hard. See **acertar**
asentimiento /asenti'miento/ *m,* assent; consent, approval
asentir /asen'tir/ *vi irr* to assent, agree; (*with en*) consent to. See **sentir**
aseñorado /aseɲo'raðo/ *a* refined, gentlemanly; ladylike; presumptuous
aseo /a'seo/ *m,* cleanliness, neatness
asepsia /a'sepsia/ *f,* asepsis
asequible /ase'kiβle/ *a* attainable; obtainable
aserción /aser'θion; aser'sion/ *f,* assertion
aserradero /ase'rraðero/ *m,* sawmill; saw-pit
aserrador /aserra'ðor/ **(-ra)** *n* sawyer
aserrar /ase'rrar/ *vt irr* to saw. See **acertar**
aserrín /ase'rrin/ *m,* sawdust
asertivo /aser'tiβo/ *a* assertive
aserto /a'serto/ *m,* assertion
asesinar /asesi'nar/ *vt* to assassinate, murder
asesinato /asesi'nato/ *m,* assassination, murder
asesino /ase'sino/ *mf* assassin, murderer; murderess
asesor /ase'sor/ **(-ra)** *n* assessor
asesorar /aseso'rar/ *vt* to give advice; —*vr* take legal advice; seek advice
asestar /ases'tar/ *vt* to aim (firearms); fire; deal (a blow)
aseveración /aseβera'θion; aseβera'sion/ *f,* assertion, statement
aseveradamente /aseβeraða'mente/ *adv* affirmatively
aseverar /aseβe'rar/ *vt* to affirm, assert
asfaltado /asfal'taðo/ *m,* asphalting; asphalt pavement
asfaltar /asfal'tar/ *vt* to asphalt
asfalto /as'falto/ *m,* asphalt
asfixia /as'fiksia/ *f, Med.* asphyxia
asfixiante /asfik'siante/ *a* asphyxiating
asfixiar /asfik'siar/ *vt* to asphyxiate
asfódelo /as'foðelo/ *m, Bot.* asphodel
así /a'si/ *adv* thus, so, in this way; like this (e.g. *en días a.,* on days like this); even if; so that, therefore. **a. a.,** middling, so-so. **a. como a.,** as well as; as soon

as. **a. las cosas,** that being the case, **a. que,** as soon as, immediately; consequently, thus
Asia Menor /'asia me'nor/ Asia Minor
asiático /a'siatiko/ **(-ca)** *a* and *n* Asiatic
asidero /asi'ðero/ *m,* hold, grasp; handle, haft; pretext, excuse
asido a /a'siðo a/ wedded to (e.g. a belief)
asiduidad /asiðui'ðað/ *f,* assiduity
asiduo /a'siðuo/ *a* assiduous
asiento /a'siento/ *m,* seat; place, position; site; base (of a vase, etc.); lees, sediment; indigestion; *Archit.* subsidence, settling; treaty, pact; contract; note, reminder; *Com.* entry; permanence, stability; prudence; bit (of a bridle); *pl* buttocks, seat. **estar de a.,** to be established (in a place)
asignación /asigna'θion; asigna'sion/ *f,* assignation; appropriation (of money); salary; portion, share
asignar /asig'nar/ *vt* to assign; apportion; destine, intend; appoint
asignatura /asigna'tura/ *f,* subject (of study in schools, etc.)
asilar /asi'lar/ *vt* to give shelter to, receive; put into an institution
asilo /a'silo/ *m,* shelter, refuge; sanctuary, asylum; *Fig.* protection, defense; home, institution
asimetría /asime'tria/ *f,* asymmetry
asimétrico /asi'metriko/ *a* asymmetrical
asimiento /asi'miento/ *m,* hold, grasp; attachment, affection
asimilable /asimi'laβle/ *a* assimilable
asimilación /asimila'θion; asimila'sion/ *f,* assimilation
asimilar /asimi'lar/ *vt* to compare, liken; (*Bot. Zool. Gram.*) assimilate; *—vi* resemble, be like; *Fig.* assimilate, digest (ideas)
asimismo /asi'mismo/ *adv* similarly, likewise
asir /a'sir/ *vt irr* to grasp, take hold of; seize; *—vi* take root (plants); *—vr* (*with de*) lay hold of; take advantage of; make an excuse to *—Pres. Indic.* **asgo, ases,** etc *—Pres. Subjunc.* **asga,** etc.
asirio /a'sirio/ **(-ia)** *a* and *n* Assyrian. *m,* Assyrian language
asistencia /asis'tenθia; asistensia/ *f,* presence, attendance; minimal attendance required (e.g. *Los alumnos tienen que completar una a.,* Pupils must attend a certain number of classes) assistance, help; service, attendance; medical treatment; remuneration; *pl* allowance. **a. pública,** Public Assistance. **a. social,** social work
asistenta /asis'tenta/ *f,* daily maid; waiting-maid
asistente /asis'tente/ *m,* assistant; *Mil.* orderly
asistir /asis'tir/ *vt* to accompany; assist, help; attend, treat; (*with de*) act as; *—vi* (*with prep a*) be present at, attend; follow suit (in cards)
asma /'asma/ *f,* asthma
asmático /as'matiko/ **(-ca)** *a* asthmatic *—n* asthma sufferer
asnal /as'nal/ *a* asinine; brutish, stupid
asno /'asno/ *m,* ass
asociación /asoθia'θion; asosia'sion/ *f,* association; company, partnership; society, fellowship
asociado /aso'θiaðo; aso'siaðo/ **(-da)** *n* associate; member; partner
asociar /aso'θiar; aso'siar/ *vt* to associate; *—vr* associate oneself; join together; form a partnership
asolar /aso'lar/ *vt irr* to destroy, devastate, lay flat; *—vr* wither; settle (liquids). See **contar**
asoldar /asol'dar/ *vt irr* to employ, engage, hire. See **contar**
asolear /asole'ar/ *vt* to expose to the sun; *—vr* sun oneself; become sunburnt
asomada /aso'maða/ *f,* brief appearance; vantage point
asomar /aso'mar/ *vt* to show, allow to appear, put forth; *—vi* begin to show; *—vr* show oneself, appear; *Inf.* be flushed (with wine); (*with prep a, por*) look out of. **asomarse a la ventana,** to show oneself at, or look out of, the window
asombrar /asom'βrar/ *vt* to shade, shadow; darken (a color); terrify; amaze
asombro /a'sombro/ *m,* fright, terror; amazement; wonder, marvel
asombroso /asom'βroso/ *a* amazing; marvelous, wonderful
asonancia /aso'nanθia; aso'nansia/ *f,* assonance; congruity, harmony
asonante /aso'nante/ *a* and *m,* assonant
asordar /asor'ðar/ *vt* to deafen
aspa /'aspa/ *f,* cross; sail of a windmill
aspaviento /aspa'βiento/ *m,* exaggerated display of emotion; gesture (of horror, etc.); **hacer aspavientos,** to make a fuss
aspecto /as'pekto/ *m,* look, appearance; aspect, outlook
aspereza /aspe'reθa; aspe'resa/ *f,* roughness, harshness; ruggedness, rockiness; severity, asperity
áspero /'aspero/ *a* rough, harsh; uneven, rocky; jarring, grating; hard, severe
aspersión /asper'sion/ *f, Eccl.* aspersion; sprinkling
áspid /'aspið/ *m,* asp, viper
aspiración /aspira'θion; aspira'sion/ *f,* breath; breathing; aspiration, desire; *Mus.* pause
aspirador /aspira'ðor/ **(de polvo)** *m,* vacuum cleaner
aspirante /aspi'rante/ *m,* aspirant, novice; office-seeker; applicant
aspirar /aspi'rar/ *vt* to breathe in, inhale; *Gram.* aspirate; (*with prep a*) aspire to, desire
aspirina /aspi'rina/ *f,* aspirin
asquear /aske'ar/ *vi* and *vt* to hate, loathe
asquerosidad /askerosi'ðað/ *f,* filthiness, loathsomeness; vileness, hatefulness
asqueroso /aske'roso/ *a* nauseating; loathsome, revolting; vile, hateful
asta /'asta/ *f,* lance, spear, pike; horn (of bull); antler; flagstaff; shaft. **a media a.,** at half-mast
asterisco /aste'risko/ *m,* asterisk
astigmático /astig'matiko/ *a* astigmatic
astigmatismo /astigma'tismo/ *m,* astigmatism
astil /as'til/ *m,* handle, pole, shaft; bar of a balance; beam feather
astilla /as'tiʎa; as'tiya/ *f,* splinter
astillar /asti'ʎar; asti'yar/ *vt* to splinter, chip
astillero /asti'ʎero; asti'yero/ *m,* shipyard; rack for lances and pikes
astilloso /asti'ʎoso; asti'yoso/ *a* splintery, fragile
astracán /astra'kan/ *m,* astrakhan
astringente /astrin'hente/ *a* astringent
astringir /astrin'hir/ *vt* to tighten up; compress; constrain
astro /'astro/ *m,* heavenly body
astrolatría /astrola'tria/ *f,* astrolatry, star worship
astrología /astrolo'hia/ *f,* astrology
astrológico /astro'lohiko/ *a* astrological
astrólogo /as'trologo/ **(-ga)** *n* astrologist
astronauta /astro'nauta/ *m,* astronaut
astronomía /astrono'mia/ *f,* astronomy
astronómico /astro'nomiko/ *a* astronomical
astrónomo /as'tronomo/ *m,* astronomer
astucia /as'tuθia; as'tusia/ *f,* astuteness, guile, craftiness
asturiano /astu'riano/ **(-na)** *a* and *n* Asturian
astuto /as'tuto/ *a* guileful, crafty, astute
Asuero /a'suero/ Ahasuerus
asueto /a'sueto/ *m,* day's holiday
asumir /asu'mir/ *vt* to assume; adopt, appropriate
asunción /asun'θion; asun'sion/ *f,* assumption
asunto /a'sunto/ *m,* matter, theme, subject; business, affair
asustadizo /asusta'ðiθo; asusta'ðiso/ *a* timid, nervous, easily frightened
asustar /asus'tar/ *vt* to frighten; **que asusta,** terribly (e.g. *Es de una ñoñería que asusta,* It's a terribly timid thing to do) *vr* be frightened
atablar /ata'βlar/ *vt* to roll, flatten (earth)
atacado /ata'kaðo/ *a Inf.* hesitant; mean, stingy
atacador /ataka'ðor/ **(-ra)** *a* attacking *—n* aggressor, attacker
atacar /ata'kar/ *vt* to attack; fasten, button; fit (clothes); ram (guns); *Fig.* press hard, corner (persons). **a. a los nervios,** to jar on the nerves
atadero /ata'ðero/ *m,* rope, tie, cord; hook, ring, etc. (for hitching); hindrance, impediment; hitching or fastening point

atado /a'taðo/ *m,* bundle, roll
atadura /ata'ðura/ *f,* tying, stringing, fastening, tie; knot; connection
atajar /ata'har/ *vi* to take a short cut; *—vt* intercept, cut off; screen off, divide; impede, stop; interrupt (people); **atajarle la palabra a uno,** to cut somebody off, interrupt *vr* be overcome (by fear, shame, etc.)
atajo /a'taho/ *m,* short cut, quick way; cutting, abbreviation; division. *Inf.* **echar por el a.,** to go to the root of (a matter)
atalaya /ata'laya/ *f,* look out, watch tower; observation point. *m,* lookout
atalayar /atala'yar/ *vt* to scan, watch; spy upon
atalón /ata'lon/ *m,* atoll, coral island
atañadero: en lo atañadero a /ataɲa'ðero en lo ataɲa'ðero a/ with regard to, with respect to
atañer /ata'ɲer/ *vi impers* to concern, affect; belong, pertain
ataque /a'take/ *m,* (*Mil. Med.*) attack; quarrel, fight
atar /a'tar/ *vt* to tie; fasten; lace; stop, paralyse; *—vr* get in a fix; confine oneself. **a. cabos,** to put two and two together
atardecer /atarðe'θer; atarðe'ser/ *vi irr impers* to grow dusk. See **conocer**
atardecer /atarðe'θer; atarðe'ser/ *m,* dusk, evening
atarear /atare'ar/ *vt* to set to work, assign work to; *—vr* work hard
atarugar /ataru'gar/ *vt* to wedge; stop up; plug; block; *Inf.* silence, shut up; stuff, cram; *—vr Fig. Inf.* lose one's head
atasajar /atasa'har/ *vt* to cut up, jerk (beef, etc.)
atascadero /ataska'ðero/ *m,* deep rut, boggy place; impediment, obstacle
atascar /atas'kar/ *vt* to plug; block up; stop (a leak); hinder, obstruct; *—vr* stick in the mud; be held up or delayed; *Inf.* get stuck in a speech
atasco /a'tasko/ *m,* obstruction, block
ataúd /ata'uð/ *m,* coffin
Ataulfo /a'taulfo/ Ataulf
ataviar /ata'βiar/ *vt* to deck, apparel, adorn
atavío /ata'βio/ *m,* get-up, dress, apparel; *pl* ornaments
atavismo /ata'βismo/ *m,* atavism
ate /'ate/ *m,* (Mexico) kind of Turkish delight
ateísmo /ate'ismo/ *m,* atheism
atelaje /ate'lahe/ *m,* team, yoke (of horses); trappings, harness; *Inf.* trousseau
atemperación /atempera'θion; atempera'sion/ *f,* moderation, mitigation; tempering
atemperar /atempe'rar/ *vt* to moderate, mitigate; adapt, adjust; temper, cool. **atemperarse a la realidad,** to adjust to reality
Atenas /a'tenas/ Athens
atenazar /atena'θar; atena'sar/ *vt* to grip, grasp; torture
atención /aten'θion; aten'sion/ *f,* attention; solicitude, kindness; courtesy, civility; *pl* business affairs *—interj* **¡A.!** Take care! Look out!; *Mil.* Attention! **en a.** (**a),** taking into consideration. **estar en a.,** (patient) to be under treatment
atender /aten'der/ *vt irr* to await, expect; take care of, look after; *—vi* (*with prep a*) attend to, listen to; *—vi* remember. See **entender**
ateneo /ate'neo/ *m,* atheneum *—a* Athenian
atenerse /ate'nerse/ *vr irr* (*with prep a*) to abide by; resort to, rely on. See **tener**
ateniense /ate'niense/ *a* and *mf* Athenian
atentado /aten'taðo/ *a* prudent, sensible; secret, silent. *m,* infringement, violation; attempt (on a person's life); crime
atentar /aten'tar/ *vt irr* to do illegally; attempt a crime; *—vr* proceed cautiously; restrain oneself. See **acertar**
atento /a'tento/ *a* attentive; courteous, civil *—adv* taking into consideration. **su atenta** (**atta),** *Com.* your favor
atenuación /atenua'θion; atenua'sion/ *f,* attenuation, diminution
atenuante /ate'nuante/ *a* attenuating; extenuating (of circumstances)
atenuar /ate'nuar/ *vt* to attenuate, diminish; extenuate
ateo /a'teo/ **(-ea)** *a* atheistic *—n* atheist
aterciopelado /aterθiope'laðo; atersiope'laðo/ *a* velvety
aterirse /ate'rirse/ *vr defective* to grow stiff with cold
aterrador /aterra'ðor/ *a* terrifying, dreadful
aterraje /ate'rrahe/ *m,* (*Aer. Naut.*) landing
aterramiento /aterra'miento/ *m,* horror, terror; terrorization; *Naut.* landing; ruin, demolition
aterrar /ate'rrar/ *vt irr* to demolish; discourage; cover with earth; *—vi* land; *—vr Naut.* draw near to land. See **acertar**
aterrizaje /aterri'θahe; aterri'sahe/ *m, Aer.* landing. **a. forzoso,** forced landing. **campo de a.,** landing field
aterrizar /aterri'θar; aterri'sar/ *vi Aer.* to land, touch down
aterrorizar /aterrori'θar; aterrori'sar/ *vt* to terrify; terrorize
atesorar /ateso'rar/ *vt* to hoard, treasure up
atestación /atesta'θion; atesta'sion/ *f,* attestation, affidavit
atestar /ates'tar/ *vt irr* to stuff, cram; insert; *Inf.* stuff with food; crowd, fill with people. See **acertar**
atestar /ates'tar/ *vt* to attest, testify
atestiguación /atestigua'θion; atestigua'sion/ *f,* deposition, testimony
atestiguar /atesti'guar/ *vt* to testify, attest
atetar /ate'tar/ *vt* to suckle; *—vi* suck
atezado /ate'θaðo; ate'saðo/ *a* bronzed, sunburnt; black
ático /'atiko/ *a* Attic; *m,* penthouse
atiesar /atie'sar/ *vt* to stiffen
atildar /atil'dar/ *vt* to place a tilde over; blame, criticize; decorate, ornament
atimia /a'timia/ *f,* loss of status
atinado /ati'naðo/ *a* pertinent, relevant
atinar /ati'nar/ *vi* to find by touch; discover by chance; guess; hit the mark
atinente a... /ati'nente a / concerning...
atisbadura /atisβa'ðura/ *f,* watching, spying, prying
atisbar /atis'βar/ *vt* to spy upon, watch
atisbo /a'tisβo/ *m,* prying, watching; suspicion, hint
atisbón /atis'βon/ *a* penetrating (mind, vision)
atizador /atiθa'ðor; atisa'ðor/ *m,* poker (for the fire)
atizar /ati'θar; ati'sar/ *vt* to poke (the fire); dowse, snuff; trim (lamps); excite, rouse; *Inf.* slap, wallop
atlántico /at'lantiko/ *a* Atlantic. *m,* Atlantic Ocean
Atlántida /at'lantiða/ Atlantis
atleta /at'leta/ *m,* athlete
atlético /at'letiko/ *a* athletic
atletismo /atle'tismo/ *m,* athletics
atmósfera /at'mosfera/ *f,* atmosphere
atmosférico /atmos'feriko/ *a* atmospheric
atolladero /atoʎa'ðero; atoya'ðero/ *m,* rut; mud; bog
atolón /ato'lon/ *m,* atoll, coral island
atolondrado /atolon'draðo/ *a* scatter-brained, flighty
atolondramiento /atolondra'miento/ *m,* rashness, recklessness; bewilderment
atolondrar /atolon'drar/ *vt* to bewilder, confuse
atómico /a'tomiko/ *a* atomic
atomización /atomiθa'θion; atomisa'sion/ *f,* atomization
átomo /'atomo/ *m,* atom; speck, particle
atónito /a'tonito/ *a* amazed, astounded
atontar /aton'tar/ *vt* to confuse, daze; make stupid; stun
atormentador /atormenta'ðor/ **(-ra)** *a* torturing *—n* tormentor; torturer
atormentar /atormen'tar/ *vt* to torment; torture; grieve, harass
atorrante /ato'rrante/ *a* and *mf* (Argentina) good-for-nothing
atracadero /atraka'ðero/ *m,* jetty, landingstage
atracar /atra'kar/ *vt Inf.* to stuff with food; *Naut.* tie up, moor; hold up, rob; *—vi Naut.* moor, stop; *—vr Inf.* guzzle, gorge
atracción /atrak'θion; atrak'sion/ *f,* attraction
atraco /a'trako/ **(a)** *m,* hold up (of), ambush (of)
atracón /atra'kon/ *m, Inf.* gorge, fill; surfeit. **darse atracones de,** to gorge oneself on

atractivo /atrak'tiβo/ *a* attractive. *m,* attraction, charm
atractriz /atrak'triθ; atrak'tris/ *a* attracting; *f,* force of attraction; (fig.) lure
atraer /atra'er/ *vt irr* to attract; charm, enchant. See **traer**
atragantarse /atragan'tarse/ *vr* to choke; *Inf.* be at a loss, dry up (in conversation)
atraíble /atra'iβle/ *a* attractable, able to be attracted
atrancar /atran'kar/ *vt* to bar the door; obstruct, block; hinder; *—vi Inf.* stride; skip (in reading)
atrapar /atra'par/ *vt Inf.* grab, seize, catch; net, obtain; deceive
atrás /a'tras/ *adv* behind, back; past; previously. **¡A.!** Back! **años a.,** years ago
atrasado /atra'saðo/ *a* slow (of clocks); backward; old-fashioned; hard-up, poor. **a. mental,** retarded person
atrasar /atra'sar/ *vt* to delay, retard; fix a later date than the true one; put back (clocks) *—vi* be slow (clocks); *—vr* be late; be left behind
atraso /a'traso/ *m,* delay; backwardness, dullness; slowness (clocks); lateness; *pl* arrears. **El reloj lleva cinco minutos de a.,** The watch is five minutes slow
atravesado /atraβe'saðo/ *a* slightly squint-eyed; mongrel, crossbreed; half-caste; ill-intentioned
atravesar /atraβe'sar/ *vt irr* to lay across, put athwart; cross, traverse; pierce; obstruct; *Naut.* lie to; *—vr* be among, mingle (with); interrupt; interfere, take part; quarrel; occur, arise. See **confesar**
atrayente /atra'yente/ *a* attractive
atreverse /atre'βerse/ *vr* to dare, risk, venture; be overbold or insolvent
atrevido /atre'βiðo/ *a* bold, audacious; hazardous, dangerous; brazen, impudent
atribución /atriβu'θion; atriβu'sion/ *f,* attribution; perquisite, attribute
atribuible /atri'βuiβle/ *a* attributable
atribuir /atri'βuir/ *vt irr* to impute, attribute; assign, turn over to; *—vr* take upon oneself, assume. See **huir**
atributo /atri'βuto/ *m,* attribute, quality
atril /a'tril/ *m,* lectern, reading desk; music stand
atrincherar /atrintʃe'rar/ *vt* to protect with entrenchments; *—vr* entrench oneself
atrio /'atrio/ *m,* atrium; hall, vestibule; *Archit.* parvis
atrocidad /atroθi'ðað; atrosi'ðað/ *f,* atrocity, cruelty; *Inf.* terrific amount; enormity, crime
atrofia /a'trofia/ *f,* atrophy
atrofiarse /atro'fiarse/ *vr* to atrophy
atronado /atro'naðo/ *a* harebrained, foolish
atronar /atro'nar/ *vt irr* to deafen, stun with noise; confuse, daze. See **tronar**
atropelladamente /atropeʎaða'mente; atropeyaða'mente/ *adv* in disorder, helter-skelter
atropellado /atrope'ʎaðo; atrope'yaðo/ *a* rash, foolhardy
atropellar /atrope'ʎar; atrope'yar/ *vt* to trample upon; thrust out of the way; knock down; disregard, violate (feelings); insult, abuse; transgress; do hastily; *—vr* act rashly
atropello /atro'peʎo; atro'peyo/ *m,* trampling; road accident; knocking over; upsetting; violation; outrage
atroz /a'troθ; a'ntros/ *a* atrocious, savage; monstrous, outrageous; *Inf.* terrific, enormous
atufar /atu'far/ *vt* to irritate, vex; *—vr* grow irritated; turn sour (wine, etc.)
atún /a'tun/ *m,* tuna
aturdido /atur'ðiðo/ *a* reckless, scatterbrained, silly; thoughtless; stunned
aturdimiento /aturði'miento/ *m,* daze; confusion, bewilderment
aturdir /atur'ðir/ *vt* to daze; confuse, bewilder; amaze; stun
atusar /atu'sar/ *vt* to trim (hair, beard); *Agr.* prune; smooth down (hair); *—vr* dress over-carefully
audacia /au'ðaθia; au'ðasia/ *f,* audacity
audaz /au'ðaθ; au'ðas/ *a* audacious, daring
audibilidad /auðiβili'ðað/ *f,* audibility
audición /auði'θion; auði'sion/ *f,* audition
audiencia /au'ðienθia; au'ðiensia/ *f,* audience, hearing; *Law.* audience; audience chamber
audifono /au'ðifono/ *m,* hearing aid
audioteca /auðio'teka/ *f,* audio library
auditivo /auði'tiβo/ *a* auditory
auditor /auði'tor/ *m,* magistrate, judge
auditorio /auði'torio/ *a* auditory. *m,* audience
auge /'auhe/ *m, Fig.* zenith, height; *Astron.* apogee
augusto /au'gusto/ *a* august, awesome
aula /'aula/ *f,* lecture or class room; *Poet.* palace
aullador /auʎa'ðor; auya'ðor/ *a* howling
aullar /au'ʎar; au'yar/ *vi* to howl; bay
aullido /au'ʎiðo; au'yiðo/ *m,* howl; baying
aumentar /aumen'tar/ **(se)** *vt vi vr* to increase, augment
aumentativo /aumenta'tiβo/ *a Gram.* augmentative
aumento /au'mento/ *m,* increase; progress; enlargement. **ir en a.,** to increase; advance, progress; prosper
aun /a'un/ *adv* even. **A. los que viven lejos han de oíros,** Even those who live far must hear you. **a. así** *or* **a. siendo así,** even so. **a. ayer,** only yesterday. **a. cuando,** even if. **más a.,** even more. **ni a. si,** not even if.
aún /a'un/ *adv* still, yet. **A. no te creen** *or* **No te creen a.,** They still don't believe you **¿A. se lo darás?** *or* **¿Se lo darás a.?** Will you still give it to her?
aunque /'aunke/ *conjunc* although, even if, even though. It takes the Indicative referring to statement of fact and Subjunctive referring to a hypothesis, e.g. *A. vino, no lo hizo,* Although he came, he did not do it. *A. él cantase yo no iría allí,* Even though he sang (were to sing), I should not go there
aura /'aura/ *f,* zephyr, gentle breeze; popularity, approbation; aura. **a. epiléptica,** *Med.* epileptic aura
áureo /'aureo/ *a* gold, gilt; golden
auricular /auriku'lar/ *a* auricular. *m,* little finger; receiver, ear-piece (of a telephone); earphone (radio)
aurífero /au'rifero/ *a* gold-yielding, auriferous
auriga /au'riga/ *m,* charioteer
aurora /au'rora/ *f,* dawn; genesis, beginnings. **a. boreal,** aurora borealis, Northern Lights
auscultación /auskulta'θion; auskulta'sion/ *f, Med.* auscultation
auscultar /auskul'tar/ *vt Med.* to auscultate
ausencia /au'senθia; au'sensia/ *f,* absence. **en ausencia de,** in the absence of
ausentar /ausen'tar/ *vt* to send away; *—vr* absent oneself
ausente /au'sente/ *a* absent. *mf* absent person
auspicio /aus'piθio; aus'pisio/ *m,* augury, prediction; favor, patronage; *pl* auspices
austeridad /austeri'ðað/ *f,* austerity; mortification of the flesh
austero /aus'tero/ *a* austere, ascetic; severe, harsh; honest, upright
austral /aus'tral/ *a* southerly, austral
australiano /austra'liano/ **(-na)** *a* and *n* Australian
austríaco /aus'triako/ **(-ca)** *a* and *n* Austrian
Austrias, los /'austrias, los/ the Hapsburgs (ruling house of Spain, 1516–1700)
austrófilo /aus'trofilo/ *a* and *n* Austrophile
autenticación /autentika'θion; autentika'sion/ *f,* authentication
autenticar /autenti'kar/ *vt* to authenticate, attest; prove genuine
autenticidad /autentiθi'ðað; autentisi'ðað/ *f,* authenticity
auténtico /au'tentiko/ *a* authentic
auto /'auto/ *m, Law.* sentence, decision; *Theat.* one-act allegory (gen. religious); *pl* proceedings. **a. de fe,** auto-da-fé. **a. de reconocimiento,** search-warrant. **a. sacramental,** one-act religious drama on theme of mystery of the Eucharist. **hacer a. de fe de,** to burn
autobiografía /autoβiogra'fia/ *f,* autobiography
autobús /auto'βus/ *m,* motor bus, bus
autocitarse /autoθi'tarse; autosi'tarse/ *vr* to quote from one's own works
autoclave /auto'klaβe/ *m,* pressure cooker
autocracia /auto'kraθia; auto'krasia/ *f,* autocracy
autócrata /au'tokrata/ *mf* autocrat
autocrático /auto'kratiko/ *a* autocratic
autocrueldad /autokruel'dað/ *f,* self-inflicted pain

autodescubrimiento /autoðeskuβri'miento/ *m,* self-discovery
autodidacto /autoði'ðakto/ *a* autodidactic; self-educated, self-taught
autódromo /au'toðromo/ *m,* speedway
autógeno /au'toheno/ *a* autogenous, self-generating
autogiro /auto'hiro/ *m, Aer.* autogyro
autografía /autogra'fia/ *f,* autography
autográfico /auto'grafiko/ *a* autographic, in lithographic reproduction
autógrafo /au'tografo/ *a* autographical. *m,* autograph
autoinducción /autoinduk'θion; autoinduk'sion/ *f,* self-induction
autómata /au'tomata/ *m,* automaton
automático /auto'matiko/ *a* automatic. *m, Sew.* press stud
automatismo /automa'tismo/ *m,* automatism
automejoramiento /autome,hora'miento/ *m,* self-improvement
automóvil /auto'moβil/ *m,* automobile, motor car —*a* automatic
automovilismo /automoβi'lismo/ *m,* motoring
automovilista /automoβi'lista/ *mf* motorist
autonombrarse /autonom'βrarse/ *vr* to call oneself, go by the name of
autonomía /autono'mia/ *f,* autonomy
autónomo /au'tonomo/ *a* autonomous
autopista /auto'pista/ *f,* motor road
autopsia /au'topsia/ *f, Med.* autopsy, post-mortem
autor /au'tor/ **(-ra)** *n* agent, originator; author; inventor; *Law.* perpetrator
autoridad /autori'ðað/ *f,* authority; pomp, show
autoritario /autori'tario/ *a* authoritarian; authoritative
autorización /autoriθa'θion; autorisa'sion/ *f,* authorization
autorizado /autori'θaðo; autori'saðo/ *a* approved, authorized, responsible
autorizar /autori'θar; autori'sar/ *vt* to authorize; *Law.* attest, testify; cite, prove by reference; approve; exalt
autorretratarse /autorretra'tarse/ *vr* to have one's portrait painted, sit for one's portrait
autorretrato /autorre'trato/ *m,* self-portrait
autostopista /autosto'pista/ *mf* hitchhiker (Spain)
autosugestión /autosuhes'tion/ *f,* autosuggestion
auxiliador /auksilia'ðor/ **(-ra)** *a* assistant; helpful —*n* helper, assistant
auxiliar /auksi'liar/ *vt* to help, aid; attend (the dying). *m, Educ.* lecturer —*a* assisting
auxiliaría /auksilia'ria/ *f, Educ.* lectureship
auxilio /auk'silio/ *m,* help, aid, assistance
aval /a'βal/ *m, Com.* endorsement; voucher
avalar /aβa'lar/ *vt* to enhance. **avalado por la tradición,** hallowed by tradition
avalentado /aβalen'taðo/ *a* boastful, bragging
avalorar /aβalo'rar/ *vt* to value, estimate; put spirit into, encourage
avance /a'βanθe; a'βanse/ *m,* advance; advance payment; balance sheet; attack
avanzada /aβan'θaða; aβan'saða/ *f, Mil.* advance guard
avanzado /aβan'θaðo; aβan'saðo/ *a* advanced, progressive
avanzar /aβan'θar; aβan'sar/ *vt* to advance; promote; —*vi* advance; attack; grow late (time)
avanzo /a'βanθo; a'βanso/ *m,* balance sheet; price estimate
avaricia /aβa'riθia; aβa'risia/ *f,* greed, avarice
avaricioso, avariento /aβari'θioso, aβa'riento; aβari'sioso, aβa'riento/ *a* avaricious, greedy
avaro /a'βaro/ **(-ra)** *a* miserly; greedy —*n* miser
avasallador /aβasaʎa'ðor; aβasaya'ðor/ *a* dominating; *Fig.* overwhelming; enslaving
avasallar /aβasa'ʎar; aβasa'yar/ *vt* to subdue, dominate; —*vr* become a vassal; surrender, yield
ave /'aβe/ *f,* bird. **a. de paso,** migratory bird; *Fig.* bird of passage. **a. de rapiña,** bird of prey. **a. fría,** *Ornith.* plover. **ave cantora,** songbird
avecinarse /aβeθi'narse; aβesi'narse/ *vr* to be approaching (e.g. *el año que avecina,* the coming year)
avellana /aβe'ʎana; aβe'yana/ *f,* hazel nut
avellanarse /aβeʎa'narse; aβeya'narse/ *vr* to shrivel
avellano /aβe'ʎano; aβe'yano/ *m, Bot.* hazel
avemaría /aβema'ria/ *f,* Hail Mary (prayer); Angelus; rosary bead. *Inf.* **en un a.,** in a trice
avena /a'βena/ *f,* oats; *Poet.* oaten pipe. **a. loca,** wild oats
avenal /aβe'nal/ *m,* oatfield
avenar /aβe'nar/ *vt* to drain (land); drain off (liquids)
avenencia /aβe'nenθia; aβe'nensia/ *f,* agreement, arrangement; transaction; conformity, harmony
avenida /aβe'niða/ *f,* flood, spate; avenue; abundance; way, approach (to a place)
avenido /aβe'niðo/ *a* (*with bien or mal*) well *or* ill-suited
avenidor /aβeni'ðor/ **(-ra)** *n* arbitrator, mediator
avenir /aβe'nir/ *vt irr* to reconcile; —*vi* happen (used in infinitive and third singular and plural); —*vr* be reconciled; agree; compromise, give way; harmonize (things); (*with con*) get on with, agree with. See **venir**
aventador /aβenta'ðor/ *m, Agr.* winnower; pitchfork
aventajado /aβenta'haðo/ *a* outstanding, talented; advantageous. *m, Mil.* private who enjoys extra pay
aventajar /aβenta'har/ *vt* to improve, better; promote, prefer; excel; —*vr* (*with prep a*) surpass, excel. **Te aventajo en diez años,** I'm ten years older than you
aventamiento /aβenta'miento/ *m,* winnowing
aventar /aβen'tar/ *vt irr* to fan; air, ventilate; winnow; *Inf.* drive away, expel; —*vr* be inflated; *Inf.* flee; smell (bad meat). See **sentar**
aventura /aβen'tura/ *f,* adventure; chance, luck; risk, danger
aventurar /aβentu'rar/ *vt* to risk, hazard
aventurero /aβentu'rero/ **(-ra)** *a* adventurous; unscrupulous, intriguing; undisciplined (of troops) —*n* adventurer
avergonzar /aβergon'θar; aβergon'sar/ *vt irr* to shame; make shy, abash; —*vr* be ashamed; be shy or sheepish —*Pres. Indic.* **avergüenzo, avergüenzas, avergüenza, avergüenzan.** *Pres. Subjunc.* **avergüence, avergüences, avergüence, avergüencen**
avería /aβe'ria/ *f,* aviary; damage (to merchandise); loss, harm; *Elec.* fault; breakdown. **a. gruesa,** general average (marine insurance)
averiarse /aβe'riarse/ *vr* to be damaged; deteriorate; break down
averiguable /aβeri'guaβle/ *a* examinable, investigable; discoverable
averiguación /aβerigua'θion; aβerigua'sion/ *f,* inquiry, investigation; discovery
averiguar /aβeri'guar/ *vt* to investigate, inquire into; discover, ascertain. **¡averígüelo Vargas!** Beats me!, Search me!
averío /aβe'rio/ *m,* flock of birds
Averno /a'βerno/ *m, Poet.* Avernus, Hades
aversión /aβer'sion/ *f,* aversion, repugnance
avestruz /aβes'truθ; aβes'trus/ *m,* ostrich
avetado /aβe'taðo/ *a* veined, mottled, streaked
avezar /aβe'θar; aβe'sar/ *vt* to accustom; —*vr* grow accustomed (to)
aviación /aβia'θion; aβia'sion/ *f,* aviation
aviador /aβia'ðor/ *m,* aviator
aviar /a'βiar/ *vt* to outfit, equip; prepare, make ready; *Inf.* speed up; caulk (ship). *Fig. Inf.* **estar aviado,** to be in a mess
avidez /aβi'ðeθ; aβi'ðes/ *f,* avidity, greed; longing, desire
ávido /'aβiðo/ *a* avid, greedy
avieso /a'βieso/ *a* twisted, crooked; ill-natured; sinister
avillanado /aβiʎa'naðo; aβiya'naðo/ *a* countrified; gross, vulgar; boorish
avinagrado /aβina'graðo/ *a Inf.* crabbed, sour, testy
avío /a'βio/ *m,* preparation, provision; picnic lunch; money advanced (to miners or laborers); *pl Inf.* equipment, tools. **avíos de pesca,** fishing tackle
avión /a'βion/ *m,* airplane; *Ornith.* martin or swift. **a. de bombardeo,** bomber. **a. de caza,** fighter plane. **a. de combate nocturno,** night fighter. **a. de hostigamiento,** interceptor. **a. de reacción,** jet airplane. **a. de transporte,** *Aer.* transport. **a. en picado,** dive-

bomber. **a. taxi,** air taxi. **por a.,** by airmail **«Avión»** "Airmail"
avioneta /aβio'neta/ *f,* light airplane, small airplane
avisado /aβi'saðo/ *a* shrewd, sensible. **mal a.,** ill-advised, imprudent
avisar /aβi'sar/ *vt* to inform, acquaint; warn; advise
aviso /a'βiso/ *m,* notice, announcement; warning; advice; care, caution; attention; shrewdness, prudence. **estar sobre a.,** to be on call; be on the alert
avispa /a'βispa/ *f,* wasp
avispado /aβis'paðo/ *a Inf.* smart, clever, quick; wide-awake
avispar /aβis'par/ *vt* to goad, prick; *Inf.* rouse, incite; *—vr* be uneasy, fret
avispero /aβis'pero/ *m,* wasp's nest; swarm of wasps; *Fig. Inf.* hornet's nest
avispón /aβis'pon/ *m,* hornet
avistamiento /aβista'miento/ *m,* sighting, spotting (e.g. of a ship)
avistar /aβis'tar/ *vt* to descry, sight, spot; *—vr* **avistarse con,** to interview
avituallar /aβitua'ʎar; aβitua'yar/ *vt* to victual, supply with food
avivar /aβi'βar/ *vt* to enliven; stimulate, encourage; stir (fire); trim (wicks); brighten (colors); inflame; vivify, invigorate; *—vi* revive, recover
avizor /aβi'θor; aβi'sor/ *m,* watcher, spy *—a* watchful, vigilant
avizorar /aβiθo'rar; aβiso'rar/ *vt* to watch, spy upon
avutarda /aβu'tarða/ *f,* bustard
axila /ak'sila/ *f, Bot.* axil; *Anat.* axilla, armpit
axioma /ak'sioma/ *m,* axiom
axiomático /aksio'matiko/ *a* axiomatic
¡ay! /ai/ *interj* Alas! Woe is me! *m,* complaint, sigh
aya /'aya/ *f,* governess
ayer /a'yer/ *adv* yesterday; a short while ago; in the past. *m,* past
ayo /'ayo/ *m,* tutor
ayuda /a'yuða/ *f,* help, assistance; enema; clyster; watch dog. *m,* **a. de cámara,** valet
ayudador /ayuða'ðor/ **(-ra)** *a* helping, assisting *—n* helper
ayudante /ayu'ðante/ *m,* assistant; teaching assistant; *Mil.* adjutant. **a. a cátedra,** *Educ.* assistant lecturer. **a. de plaza,** post adjutant
ayudar /ayu'ðar/ *vt* to assist; help, aid; *—vr* make an effort; avail oneself of another's help
ayunador /ayuna'ðor/ **(-ra)** *a* fasting *—n* faster; abstainer
ayunar /ayu'nar/ *vi* to fast
ayuno /a'yuno/ *m,* fast *—a* fasting; ignorant, unaware. **en a.** *or* **en ayunas,** before breakfast, fasting; *Inf.* ignorant, unaware
ayuntamiento /ayunta'miento/ *m,* meeting, assembly; municipal government; town hall; sexual union
azabache /aθa'βatʃe; asaβatʃe/ *m, Mineral.* jet
azada /a'θaða; a'saða/ *f, Agr.* spade; hoe
azadón /aθa'ðon; asa'ðon/ *m, Agr.* hoe
azafata /aθa'fata; asa'fata/ *f,* queen's waiting-maid *Obs.*; flight attendant
azafate /aθa'fate; asa'fate/ *m,* flat basket; small tray
azafrán /aθa'fran; asa'fran/ *m, Bot.* saffron; crocus
azafranado /aθafra'naðo; asafra'naðo/ *a* saffron-colored
azahar /a'θaar; a'saar/ *m,* flower of orange, lemon or sweet lime tree
azar /a'θar; a'sar/ *m,* chance, hazard; unexpected misfortune; losing card or throw of dice
azararse /aθa'rarse; asa'rarse/ *vr* to go wrong, fail (negotiations, etc.); grow nervous; become confused; blush
azaroso /aθa'roso; asa'roso/ *a* unlucky, ill-omened; hazardous
ázimo /'aθimo; 'asimo/ *a* unleavened (bread)
ázoe /'aθoe; 'asoe/ *m,* nitrogen
azogar /aθo'gar; aso'gar/ *vt* to silver (mirrors, etc.); slake lime; *—vr* suffer from mercury poisoning; *Inf.* grow uneasy, be agitated
azogue /a'θoge; a'soge/ *m, Mineral.* mercury, quicksilver; market-place
azolve /a'θolβe; a'solβe/ *m,* silt
azoramiento /aθora'miento; asora'miento/ *m,* alarm, terror; confusion, stupefaction; incitement
azorar /aθo'rar; aso'rar/ *vt* to alarm, terrify; confuse, stun, dumbfound; excite, stimulate; encourage
azotacalles /aθota'kaʎes; asota'kayes/ *mf Inf.* idler, street loafer
azotaina /aθo'taina; aso'taina/ *f, Inf.* whipping, spanking
azotamiento /aθota'miento; asota'miento/ *m,* flogging, beating, whipping
azotar /aθo'tar; aso'tar/ *vt* to whip, beat, flog; scourge, ravage; knock against or strike repeatedly
azotazo /aθo'taθo; aso'taso/ *m,* spank
azote /a'θote; a'sote/ *m,* whip; scourge; lash, blow with a whip; spank, slap; misfortune, disaster. *Inf.* **azotes y galeras,** monotonous diet
azotea /aθo'tea; aso'tea/ *f,* flat terrace roof
azozador /aθoθa'ðor; asosa'ðor/ party whip, whip
azteca /aθ'teka; as'teka/ *a* and *mf* Aztec
azúcar /a'θukar; a'sukar/ *m,* sugar. **a. blanco** *or* **a. de flor,** white sugar. **a. de pilón,** loaf sugar. **a. moreno,** brown sugar. **a. quebrado,** brown sugar. **a. y canela,** sorrel gray (of horses)
azucarado /aθuka'raðo; asuka'raðo/ *a* sugary; sugared, sugar-coated; *Inf.* honeyed, flattering
azucarar /aθuka'rar; asuka'rar/ *vt* to coat with sugar; sweeten; *Inf.* soften, mitigate; *—vr* crystallize; go sugary (jam)
azucarera /aθuka'rera; asuka'rera/ *f,* sugar-basin
azucarero /aθuka'rero; asuka'rero/ *a* sugar-producing (e.g. province)
azucarillo /aθuka'riʎo; asuka'riyo/ *m, Cul.* bar made of white of egg and sugar for sweetening water
azucena /aθu'θena; asu'sena/ *f,* white lily. **a. de agua,** water-lily
azuela /a'θuela; a'suela/ *f,* adze
azufrar /aθu'frar; asu'frar/ *vt* to sulphurate
azufre /a'θufre; a'sufre/ *m,* sulphur
azufroso /aθu'froso; asu'froso/ *a* sulphurous
azul /a'θul; a'sul/ *a* and *m,* blue. **a. celeste,** sky blue, azure. **a. de mar** *or* **a. marino,** navy blue. **a. de ultramar,** ultramarine. **a. turquí,** indigo
azulado /aθu'laðo; asu'laðo/ *a* bluish, blue
azulear /aθule'ar; asule'ar/ *vi* to look bluish, have a blue tint
azulejo /aθu'leho; asu'leho/ *m,* ornamental glazed tile
azumbre /a'θumbre; a'sumbre/ *f,* liquid measure (just over 2 liters)
azuzar /aθu'θar; asu'sar/ *vt* to set on (dogs); irritate, provoke; incite, urge

B

baba /'baβa/ *f,* saliva; secretion (of snails, etc.); viscous fluid (of plants). *Inf.* **caérsele (a uno) la b.,** to ooze satisfaction; be dumbfounded
babador, babero /baβa'ðor, ba'βero/ *m,* bib, feeder
babear /baβe'ar/ *vi* to dribble, slaver; *Fig. Inf.* slobber over, be sloppy
babel /ba'βel/ *m,* babel
babélico /ba'βeliko/ *a* Babelian, Babel-like confusion; unintelligible
Babia, estar en /'baβia, es'tar en/ to be daydreaming
babieca /ba'βieka/ *mf Inf.* stupid person. **Babieca** *f,* the Cid's horse
Babilonia /baβi'lonia/ Babylon
babilónico /baβi'loniko/ *a* Babylonian
bable /'baβle/ *m,* Asturian (language)
babor /ba'βor/ *m, Naut.* larboard, port
babosa /ba'βosa/ *f,* slug; young onion
baboso /ba'βoso/ *a* slavering; *Fig. Inf.* "sloppy"; *Inf.* incompetent, useless
babucha /ba'βutʃa/ *f,* heelless slipper, babouche
babuino /ba'βuino/ *m, Zool.* baboon
baca /'baka/ *f,* luggage carrier (on roof of bus, etc.)
bacalao /baka'lao/ *m,* codfish
bacanales /baka'nales/ *f pl,* Bacchanalia
bacante /ba'kante/ *f,* Bacchante
bacará /baka'ra/ *m,* baccarat (card game)
baceta /ba'θeta; ba'seta/ *f,* pool (in card games)
bache /'batʃe/ *m,* rut (in road); pothole
bacheo /ba'tʃeo/ *m,* repairing of streets
bachiller /batʃi'ʎer; batʃi'yer/ *mf* high-school graduate *m, Inf.* babbler. *f.* **bachillera,** *Inf.* blue-stocking; garrulous woman
bachillerarse /batʃiʎe'rarse; batʃiye'rarse/ *vr* to graduate as a bachelor
bachillerato /batʃiʎe'rato; batʃiye'rato/ *m,* baccalaureate, bachelor's degree
bacía /ba'θia; ba'sia/ *f,* bowl; barber's circular shaving-dish; barber's trade sign
bacilar /baθi'lar; basi'lar/ *a* bacillary
bacilo /ba'θilo; ba'silo/ *m,* bacillus
bacterial, bacteriano /bakte'rial, bakte'riano/ *a* bacterial
bactericida /bakteri'θiða; bakteri'siða/ *m,* bactericide
bacteriología /bakteriolo'hia/ *f,* bacteriology
bacteriológico /bakterio'lohiko/ *a* bacteriological
bacteriólogo /bakte'riologo/ *m,* bacteriologist
báculo /'bakulo/ *m,* staff; walking-stick; *Fig.* support. **b. episcopal,** bishop's crozier
badajo /ba'ðaho/ *m,* clapper (of a bell); chatterbox, gossip
badana /ba'ðana/ *f,* cured sheepskin, chamois leather, washleather; sweat band; *Inf.* **zurrar** (*a uno*) **la b.,** to take the hide off; insult
badén /ba'ðen/ *m,* channel made by rain, furrow; conduit
badil /ba'ðil/ *m,* fire-shovel
badulaque /baðu'lake/ *m, Inf.* good-for-nothing
bagaje /ba'gahe/ *m, Mil.* baggage; beast of burden, transport animal; luggage
bagatela /baga'tela/ *f,* trifle, oddment, bagatelle
bagazo /ba'gaθo; ba'gaso/ *m,* oilcake, bagasse
bagual /ba'gual/ *a West. Hem.* untamed, wild; doltish, dull. *m,* untamed horse, wild horse
bahía /ba'ıa/ *f,* bay, harbor
bailable /bai'laβle/ *a* dance (of music). *m, Theat.* dance number
bailador /baila'ðor/ **(-ra)** *n* dancer
bailar /bai'lar/ *vi* to dance; spin around. **b. al son que le toca,** to adapt oneself to circumstances
bailarín /baila'rin/ *a* dancing. *m,* professional dancer. **b. de cuerda, bailarín de la cuerda floja,** tightrope dancer
bailarina /baila'rina/ *f,* ballerina
baile /'baile/ *m,* dance; ball; ballet. **b. de máscaras, b. de trajes,** fancy-dress ball. **b. de San Vito,** St. Vitus' dance. **b. ruso,** ballet
bailotear /bailote'ar/ *vi* to jig about; dance
baja /'baha/ *f,* drop, diminution; fall (in price, etc.); *Mil.* casualty; discharge. *Inf.* **darse de b.,** to leave an employment
bajada /ba'haða/ *f,* descent, fall; slope, incline; hollow, depression. **b. de aguas,** roof gutter
bajalato /baha'lato/ *m,* pashalik
bajamar /baha'mar/ *f,* low tide
bajamente /baha'mente/ *adv* basely, abjectly
bajar /ba'har/ *vi* to descend; go down; get off; drop; fall, decrease; *—vt* lower, take down, bring down; let down; dismount, alight; bend, droop; drop; reduce (price); *Fig.* lower (voices); humiliate, humble; **b. a tierra,** to step ashore; **b. la cabeza ante,** to submit to (e.g. a judgment) *vr* alight, dismount; humble oneself
bajel /ba'hel/ *m, Naut.* galley, ship
bajeza /ba'heθa; ba'hesa/ *f,* base action; meanness; *Fig.* humble estate, lowliness. **b. de ánimo,** timorousness
bajío /ba'hio/ *m, Naut.* shallows, shoal; depression, hollow
bajista /ba'hista/ *mf* speculator, bear (Stock Exchange)
bajo /'baho/ *a* low; short, not tall; downcast; under; subordinate; pale (of colors); humble (origin); base; coarse, vulgar; cheap (price); low (sounds). *m,* depth; shoal, sand bank; *Mus.* bass; *pl* petticoats, skirts; horses' hoofs *—adv* beneath, below *—prep* under, beneath. **b. juramento,** upon oath. **bajo relieve,** bas relief. **en voz baja,** in a low voice. **planta baja,** ground floor. **por lo b.,** in a whisper; in secret, on the sly
bajolatino /bahola'tino/ *a* Low Latin
bajón /ba'hon/ *m, Mus.* bassoon; bassoon player; *Fig. Inf.* downfall
bajonista /baho'nista/ *mf* bassoon player
bala /'bala/ *f,* bullet, ball; bale. **b. fría,** spent bullet. **b. luminosa,** tracer bullet. **b. perdida,** stray bullet. *Inf.* **como una b.,** like a shot
balada /ba'laða/ *f,* ballad, song
baladí /bala'ði/ *a* worthless, insignificant
baladro /ba'laðro/ *m,* yell, outcry, shout
baladrón /bala'ðron/ *a* braggart
baladronada /balaðro'naða/ *f,* bravado, bragging
balagar /bala'gar/ *m,* straw rick
bálago /'balago/ *m,* straw; soap-ball; straw rick
balance /ba'lanθe; ba'lanse/ *m,* balance; swinging, oscillation; rolling, rocking (of a ship, etc.); doubt, insecurity, *Com.* balance; *Com.* balance sheet
balancear /balanθe'ar; balanse'ar/ *vi* to swing; oscillate; vacillate, hesitate; *—vt* balance; *—vr* balance oneself; rock or swing oneself
balanceo /balan'θeo; balan'seo/ *m,* balancing; rocking; swinging; rolling (of a ship, etc.)
balancín /balan'θin; balan'sin/ *m,* swing-bar; whipple-tree; balance beam; tight-rope dancer's pole; minting-mill; yoke (for carrying pails); *pl Naut.* lifts
balandra /ba'landra/ *f, Naut.* sloop, cutter
balanza /ba'lanθa; ba'lansa/ *f,* balance; scale; judgment; comparison. **b. de comercio,** balance of trade. **en balanzas,** in doubt or danger, in the balance
balar /ba'lar/ *vi* to bleat (sheep)
balasto /ba'lasto/ *m, Rail.* ballast
balaustrada /balaus'traða/ *f,* balustrade
balaustre /bala'ustre/ *m,* baluster
balazo /ba'laθo; ba'laso/ *m,* shot; bullet wound
balbuceo /balβu'θeo; balβu'seo/ *m,* stammering; babbling; lisping; **balbuceos** *Fig.* beginnings, early stages (e.g. *los b. de la literatura yídica,* the beginnings of Yiddish literature)
balbuciente /balβu'θiente; balβu'siente/ *a* stammering; babbling; lisping
balbucir /balβu'θir; balβu'sir/ *vi irr defective* to stammer; lisp; babble; read hesitantly. See **lucir**
Balcanes, los /bal'kanes, los/ the Balkans
balcánico /bal'kaniko/ *a* Balkan

balcón /bal'kon/ *m,* balcony
baldaquín /balda'kin/ *m,* canopy, baldachin
baldar /bal'dar/ *vt* to cripple; impede, obstruct
balde /'balde/ *m,* bucket
balde /'balde/ **(en)** *adv* in vain. **de b.,** gratis, free of charge
baldear /balde'ar/ *vt Naut.* to wash the decks
baldío /bal'dio/ *a* untilled; fallow; useless, worthless; vagrant
baldón /bal'don/ *m,* insult; dishonor
baldonar /baldo'nar/ *vt* to insult
baldosa /bal'dosa/ *f,* paving stone; tile
baldrufa /bal'drufa/ *f,* top, spinning top
balduque /bal'duke/ *m,* red tape
Baleares, las Islas /bale'ares, las 'islas/ the Balearic Islands
baleárico /bale'ariko/ *a* Balearic
balido /ba'liðo/ *m,* bleat, bleating
balística /ba'listika/ *f,* ballistics
baliza /ba'liθa; ba'lisa/ *f, Naut.* buoy, beacon
balizamiento /baliθa'miento; balisa'miento/ *m,* marking with beacons, marking with buoys; traffic signs and signals
ballena /ba'ʎena; ba'yena/ *f,* whale; whalebone
ballenero /baʎe'nero; baye'nero/ *a* whaling. *m,* whaler
ballesta /ba'ʎesta; ba'yesta/ *f,* crossbow; spring (of carriages)
ballestería /baʎeste'ria; bayeste'ria/ *f,* archery; crossbowmen
ballestero /baʎes'tero; bayes'tero/ *m,* archer; crossbowman; crossbow maker
balneario /balne'ario/ *a* pertaining to public baths; bathing; holiday; spa. *m,* watering place, spa
balompié /balom'pie/ *m,* football (game)
balón /ba'lon/ *m,* large ball; football; *Chem.* balloon; bundle; bale. **b. de ensayo,** *Fig.* feeler
baloncesto /balon'θesto; balon'sesto/ *m, Sports.* basketball
balota /ba'lota/ *f,* ballot
balotaje /balo'tahe/ *m,* balloting; run-off election
balotar /balo'tar/ *vi* to ballot
balsa /'balsa/ *f,* pond; raft
balsadera /balsa'ðera/ *f,* ferry
balsámico /bal'samiko/ *a* balmy
bálsamo /'balsamo/ *m,* balm
balsero /bal'sero/ *m,* ferryman; rafter (person fleeing a country by raft, rowboat, etc.)
balso /'balso/ *m, Naut.* sling
báltico /'baltiko/ *a* Baltic. **el Mar Báltico** the Baltic Sea
baluarte /ba'luarte/ *m,* bulwark; bastion; protection, defense
bambalina /bamba'lina/ *f,* fly (theatrical scenery)
bamboleante /bambole'ante/ *a* swaying, swinging; *Fig.* tottering (e.g. empire)
bambolearse /bambole'arse/ *vr* to sway; swing; totter; be shaky; stagger
bamboleo /bambo'leo/ *m,* rocking; swinging; tottering; staggering; reeling
bambolla /bam'βoʎa; bam'βoya/ *f, Inf.* ostentation, swank
bambú /bam'βu/ *m,* bamboo
banal /ba'nal/ *a* banal, commonplace
banana /ba'nana/ *f,* banana
banasta /ba'nasta/ *f,* big basket
banastero /banas'tero/ **(-ra)** *n* basket maker or dealer
banasto /ba'nasto/ *m,* big round basket
banca /'banka/ *f,* bench; card game; stall; *Com.* banking
bancada /ban'kaða/ *f,* rowing seat
bancal /ban'kal/ *m,* oblong garden plot; terrace
bancario /ban'kario/ *a* banking, bank
bancarrota /banka'rrota/ *f,* bankruptcy. **hacer b.,** to go bankrupt
banco /'banko/ *m,* form, bench; rowing seat; settle; seat; bench; *Com.* bank; *Naut.* bar, shoal; school (of fish). **b. azul,** government benches in Spanish Parliament. **b. de arena,** sand-bank. **b. de descuento,** discount bank. **b. de emisión, banco emisor,** bank of issue. **b. de hielo,** iceberg. **b. de nivel,** benchmark
banda /'banda/ *f,* wide ribbon; sash; ribbon, insignia; strip; border; party, group; gang; flock (of birds); zone, belt; side (of ship); *Mus.* band; cushion (billiards); *Herald.* bar, bend. **b. elástica,** rubber band. *Naut.* **dar a la b.,** to lie along
bandada /ban'daða/ *f,* flock (of birds)
bandeja /ban'deha/ *f,* tray, salver
bandera /ban'dera/ *f,* banner, flag; colors, standard. **b. de popa,** ensign. **jurar la b.,** (*Mil. Nav.*) to take the oath of allegiance
banderilla /bande'riʎa; bande'riya/ *f,* banderilla (bullfighting)
banderillear /banderiʎe'ar; banderiye'ar/ *vt* to put banderillas on bulls
banderillero /banderi'ʎero; banderi'yero/ *m,* man who puts banderillas on bulls
banderín /bande'rin/ *m, dim* small flag; recruiting post
banderizo /bande'riθo; bande'riso/ *a* factious; vehement, excitable
banderola /bande'rola/ *f,* banderole, pennon; bannerole
bandido /ban'diðo/ **(-da)** *a* and *n* outlaw, fugitive. *m,* bandit; highwayman; rogue, desperado
bando /'bando/ *m,* proclamation, order; faction, group, party
bandola /ban'dola/ *f, Mus.* pandora, pandore
bandolerismo /bandole'rismo/ *m,* brigandage
bandolero /bando'lero/ *m,* robber, footpad, brigand
bandolín /bando'lin/ *m,* mandolin
bandurria /ban'durria/ *f, Mus.* mandolin
banjo /'banho/ *m,* banjo
banquero /ban'kero/ *m,* banker
banqueta /ban'keta/ *f,* three-legged stool; seat; footstool
banquete /ban'kete/ *m,* banquet, feast
banquetear /bankete'ar/ *vt* and *vi* to banquet
banqueteo /banke'teo/ *m,* banqueting, feasting
bañado /ba'ɲaðo/ *m,* chamber pot; *West. Hem.* marshy land, marsh; **bañados** *pl* marsh
bañador /baɲa'ðor/ **(-ra)** *a* bathing —*n* bather. *m,* bathing dress; bath, vat
bañar /ba'ɲar/ *vt* to bathe; coat, cover; dip; lave, wash; *Fig.* bathe (of sunlight, etc.) —*vr* take a bath; bathe
bañera /ba'ɲera/ *f,* bath attendant; bathtub
bañista /ba'ɲista/ *mf* bather; one who takes spa waters
baño /'baɲo/ *m,* bathing; bath; bathroom; bathtub; bagnio, Turkish prison; covering, coat; *pl* mineral baths, spa. **b. de mar,** sea bath. **b. de María,** double saucepan. **b. de sol,** sunbath. **casa de baños,** public baths. **cuarto de b.,** bathroom
bao /'bao/ *m, Naut.* beam
baptisterio /baptis'terio/ *m,* baptistery; *Eccl.* font
baquelita /bake'lita/ *f,* bakelite
baqueta /ba'keta/ *f,* ramrod; *pl* drumsticks; *Mil.* gauntlet
bar /bar/ *m,* bar; café
barahúnda /bara'unda/ *f,* See **baraúnda**
baraja /ba'raha/ *f,* pack (of cards); game of cards
barajar /bara'har/ *vt* to shuffle (cards); jumble, mix; —*vi* quarrel
baranda /ba'randa/ *f,* handrail, banister; cushion (of billiard table)
barandilla /baran'diʎa; baran'diya/ *f, dim* railing
baratija /bara'tiha/ *f,* (gen. *pl*) trifle, oddment
baratillo /bara'tiʎo; bara'tiyo/ *m,* second-hand article, frippery; second-hand shop or stall; bargain counter
barato /ba'rato/ *a* cheap; easy. *m,* bargain sale —*adv* cheaply
baratura /bara'tura/ *f,* cheapness
baraúnda /bara'unda/ *f,* uproar, confusion
barba /'barβa/ *f,* chin; beard; whiskers; fin; barb (of a feather); *m,* actor who plays old men. *f pl,* fibers of plants. **b. bien poblada,** a thick beard. **barbas de ballena,** whalebone. *Fig. Inf.* **echar a las barbas,** to throw in a person's face. **en la barba, en las barbas,** to ones face (e.g. *Me lo dijeron en las barbas.* They

told me so to my face). **hacer la b.,** to shave; *Inf.* annoy
barbacoa /barβa'koa/ *f, West Hem.* barbecue; trellis (for climbing plants)
barbado /bar'βaðo/ *a* bearded. *m,* shoot; sucker; transplanted plant
barbárico /bar'βariko/ *a* barbarian; barbaric
barbaridad /barβari'ðað/ *f,* barbarity; blunder; atrocity; outrage; *Inf.* huge amount. **¡Qué b.!** How awful! You don't say so!
barbarie /bar'βarie/ *f,* barbarism; barbarity, cruelty
barbarismo /barβa'rismo/ *m,* barbarism; cruelty; barbarians
bárbaro /'barβaro/ **(-ra)** *a* and *n* barbarian —*a* fierce; headstrong; uncivilized. **como un b.,** like crazy (e.g. *estudiar como un b.,* to study like crazy)
barbechar /barβe'tʃar/ *vt* to plow; leave fallow
barbecho /bar'βetʃo/ *m, Agr.* fallow; first plowing
barbería /barβe'ria/ *f,* barber shop
barbero /bar'βero/ *m,* barber
barbihecho /bar'βietʃo/ *a* fresh-shaved
barbilampiño /barβilam'piɲo/ *a* smooth-faced, beardless, clean-shaven
barbilindo /barβi'lindo/ *a* dandified, dappy; *m,* dandy
barbilla /bar'βiʎa; bar'βiya/ *f,* point of the chin; chin. **acariciar la b.** (**de),** to chuck under the chin
barbiquejo /barβi'keho/ *m, Naut.* bobstay; hat-guard
barbudo /bar'βuðo/ *a* heavily bearded
barbulla /bar'βuʎa; bar'βuya/ *f, Inf.* babble, chatter, murmur of voices
barca /'barka/ *f,* small boat, bark; barge. **b. de pasaje,** ferryboat. **b. plantaminas** minelayer
barcada /bar'kaða/ *f,* boat-load; ferry crossing
barcaza /bar'kaθa; bar'kasa/ *f, Naut.* lighter; barge. **b. de desembarco,** landingcraft
barcelonés /barθelo'nes; barselo'nes/ **(-esa)** *a* and *n* of or from Barcelona
barcino /bar'θino; bar'sino/ *a* ruddy (of animals); fawn and white; *Inf.* turncoat (of politicians)
barco /'barko/ *m,* boat; ship; hollow, rut. **b. barredero,** trawler. **b. siembraminas,** minelayer
barda /'barða/ *f,* horse armor; thatch; shingle; (Mexico) cement fence, cement wall
bardal /bar'ðal/ *m,* thatched wall; mud wall
bardar /bar'ðar/ *vt* to thatch
bardo /'barðo/ *m,* poet, bard
bario /'bario/ *m,* barium
barítono /ba'ritono/ *m,* baritone
barloventear /barloβente'ar/ *vi Naut.* to tack; ply to windward; *Inf.* wander about
barlovento /barlo'βento/ *m, Naut.* windward
barnacla /bar'nakla/ *m,* barnacle
barniz /bar'niθ; bar'nis/ *m,* varnish; glaze; smattering, veneer
barnizar /barni'θar; barni'sar/ *vt* to varnish; glaze
barométrico /baro'metriko/ *a* barometric
barómetro /ba'rometro/ *m,* barometer
barón /ba'ron/ *m,* baron
baronesa /baro'nesa/ *f,* baroness
baronía /baro'nia/ *f,* barony
barquero /bar'kero/ *m,* boatman; bargee; *Ent.* waterboatman
barquillero /barki'ʎero; barki'yero/ *m,* seller of wafers; waffle-iron
barquillo /bar'kiʎo; bar'kiyo/ *m,* wafer, cornet
barquín /bar'kin/ *m,* furnace bellows
barra /'barra/ *f,* bar; ingot; railing (in courtroom); sandbank; fault (in cloth); lever, crossbar; (in cricket) bail; *Mus.* bar. **b. de jabón de afeitar,** shaving-stick. **a barras derechas,** without deceit
barrabasada /barraβa'saða/ *f, Inf.* wilfulness, escapade
barraca /ba'rraka/ *f,* cabin, hut; stall; sideshow. **b. de tiro,** shooting gallery
barracón /barra'kon/ *m,* side-show; stall
barragana /barra'gana/ *f,* concubine, mistress
barranca, /ba'rranka,/ *f,* **barranco** *m,* furrow, channel, rut; gorge; difficulty, fix
barrancoso /barran'koso/ *a* rutty, uneven
barredor /barre'ðor/ **(-ra)** *n* sweeper
barredura /barre'ðura/ *f,* sweeping; *pl* sweepings; rubbish
barrena /ba'rrena/ *f,* borer, gimlet, drill, auger. *Aer.* **b. de cola,** tail-spin
barrenar /barre'nar/ *vt* to drill, bore; blast (in quarries)
barrendero /barren'dero/ **(-ra)** *n* sweeper, scavenger
barrenero /barre'nero/ *m,* driller; blaster
barreno /ba'rreno/ *m,* blast hole; bore, drill; vanity
barreño /ba'rreɲo/ *m,* earthenware bowl (for dish washing, etc.)
barrer /ba'rrer/ *vt* to sweep; *Fig.* clear, make a clean sweep
barrera /ba'rrera/ *f,* barrier; barricade; *Fig.* obstacle. **b. de golpe,** automatic gate (at level crossings, etc.). **b. de minas,** minefield
barriada /barria'ða/ *f,* district; quarter (of a city)
barrica /ba'rrika/ *f,* cask; barrel
barricada /barri'kaða/ *f,* barricade
barriga /ba'rriga/ *f, Inf.* belly
barrigón, barrigudo /barri'gon, barri'guðo/ *a* potbellied
barril /ba'rril/ *m,* barrel; cask; water-butt
barrilero /barri'lero/ *m,* cooper
barrilete /barri'lete/ *m, dim* keg; clamp; *Naut.* mouse
barrio /'barrio/ *m,* district, quarter; suburb. **barrios bajos,** slums, back streets. **el otro b.,** the other world, Eternity
barrizal /barri'θal; barri'sal/ *m,* muddy place; claypit
barro /'barro/ *m,* mud; clay; earthenware drinking vessel; *Inf.* money
barroco /ba'rroko/ *a* baroque
barroso /ba'rroso/ *a* muddy; pimpled; mud-colored
barrote /ba'rrote/ *m,* thick iron bar; stave, bond
barruntar /barrun'tar/ *vt* to conjecture; suspect
barrunto /ba'rrunto/ *m,* conjecture; indication, sign
bártulos /'bartulos/ *m pl,* household goods; *Fig.* means, wherewithal
barullo /ba'ruʎo; ba'ruyo/ *m, Inf.* confusion, disorder; mob
basa /'basa/ *f,* base; *Archit.* pedestal; foundation, basis
basalto /ba'salto/ *m,* basalt
basar /ba'sar/ *vt* to base, place on a base; *Fig.* found, base; —*vr* (*with en*) rely upon, base oneself on
basca /'baska/ *f,* (gen. *pl*) nausea; retching; wave of anger
báscula /'baskula/ *f,* weighing-machine, platform-scale; weigh-bridge
base /'base/ *f,* base; (*Chem. Geom. Mil.*) base; basis; *Archit.* pedestal; *Mus.* root. **sin b.,** baseless
básico /'basiko/ *a* basic
Basilea /basi'lea/ Basel, Basle
basílica /ba'silika/ *f,* palace; church, basilica
basilisco /basi'lisko/ *m,* basilisk; antique cannon
basquear /baske'ar/ *vi* to retch; feel squeamish
bastante /bas'tante/ *a* sufficient, enough —*adv* sufficiently; enough; fairly; a good deal; somewhat. **Hace b. calor,** It is quite hot. **Tengo b.,** I have enough. **Tenemos b. tiempo,** We have sufficient time
bastar /bas'tar/ *vi* to suffice. **¡Basta!** Enough! No more! Stop! **¡Basta de...!** Enough of...! **Basta decir que...,** Suffice it to say that...
bastardía /bastar'ðia/ *f,* bastardy, illegitimacy; baseness, meanness
bastardilla /bastar'ðiʎa; bastar'ðiya/ *f, Print.* italics
bastardo /bas'tarðo/ **(-da)** *a* bastard, spurious —*n* bastard
bastear /baste'ar/ *vt Sew.* to baste
bastidor /basti'ðor/ *m,* embroidery frame; *Art.* stretcher (for canvas); *Theat.* wing; *Mech.* underframe; chassis, carriage; frame (of a window). *Fig.* **entre bastidores,** behind the scenes
bastilla /bas'tiʎa; bas'tiya/ *f, Sew.* hem; bastille
bastimentar /bastimen'tar/ *vt* to provision; supply
bastimento /basti'mento/ *m,* supplies; provisioning
bastión /bas'tion/ *m,* bastion
basto /'basto/ *m,* pack-saddle; ace of clubs; clubs (cards) —*a* rude; tough; *Fig.* unpolished, rough
bastón /bas'ton/ *m,* cane, walking-stick; rod (of of-

fice); truncheon. **b. de junquillo,** Malacca cane. **empuñar el b.,** to take control, take over. **meter el b.,** to mediate
bastonear /bastone'ar/ *vt* to cane; stir with a stick
basura /ba'sura/ *f,* rubbish, refuse; dung; sweepings
basurero /basu'rero/ *m,* dustman; dunghill, rubbish dump; kitchen middens; dust-bin
bata /'bata/ *f,* dressing-gown; smoking-jacket; old-fashioned dress; overall, smock
batacazo /bata'kaθo; bata'kaso/ *m,* bump, noise of a fall; *Polit.* dark horse
batahola /bata'ola/ *f, Inf.* hurly-burly, hubbub
batalla /ba'taʎa; ba'taya/ *f,* battle; *Fig.* struggle, conflict; tournament; *Art.* battle-piece. **b. campal,** pitched battle
batallador /bataʎa'ðor; bataya'ðor/ *a* fighting, warlike
batallar /bata'ʎar; bata'yar/ *vi* to battle, fight; dispute, argue; hesitate
batallón /bata'ʎon; bata'yon/ *m,* battalion
batanero /bata'nero/ *m,* fuller
batata /ba'tata/ *f,* sweet potato
batayola /bata'yola/ *f, Naut.* rail
batea /ba'tea/ *f,* wooden tray; punt
batería /bate'ria/ *f,* (*Mil. Elec. Naut.*) battery. **b. de cocina,** kitchen utensils. **b. de pilas secas,** dry battery. **b. de teatro,** stage lights. **b. eléctrica,** electric battery
baticola /bati'kola/ *f,* crupper
batida /ba'tiða/ *f,* game drive; attack; *Metall.* beating
batido /ba'tiðo/ *a* beaten (of metals); shot (of silk); trodden, worn (roads, etc.). *m, Cul.* batter; hunting party
batidor /bati'ðor/ *m,* beater; scout; outrider; hair comb; *Cul.* whisk. **b. de oro** (*or* **de plata**)**,** gold (*or* silver) beater
batiente /ba'tiente/ *m,* jamb (of door, etc.); damper (piano); leaf (of door); place where sea beats against cliffs, etc.
batihoja /bati'oha/ *m,* gold beater; metal worker
batimiento /bati'miento/ *m,* beating
batín /ba'tin/ *m,* smoking-jacket; man's dressing-gown
batintín /batin'tin/ *m,* Chinese gong
batir /ba'tir/ *vt* to beat, slap; demolish; dismantle, take down (stall, etc.); hammer, flatten; batter; *Fig.* beat (of sun, etc.); stir; pound; churn; comb (hair); vanquish, defeat; coin; reconnoiter, beat; throw down or drop; *—vr* fight; swoop (birds of prey). **b. palmas,** to clap, applaud
batista /ba'tista/ *f,* cambric, batiste
baturrillo /batu'rriʎo; batu'rriyo/ *m,* hotchpotch (gen. food); *Inf.* farrago, medley
batuta /ba'tuta/ *f,* baton, conductor's wand. **llevar la b.,** *Inf.* boss the show, call the music, be in charge, to rule the roost
baúl /ba'ul/ *m,* trunk; *Inf.* belly. **b. escaparate** *or* **b. mundo,** wardrobe trunk
bauprés /bau'pres/ *m, Naut.* bowsprit
bausán /bau'san/ **(-ana)** *n* guy, strawman; puppet; fool, idiot; lazybones
bautismo /bau'tismo/ *m,* baptism
bautista /bau'tista/ *m,* baptizer, baptist. **San Juan B.,** St. John the Baptist
bautisterio /bautis'terio/ *m,* baptistery
bautizar /bauti'θar; bauti'sar/ *vt* to baptize, christen; *Inf.* nickname; *Inf.* water (wine); accidentally shower with water
bautizo /bau'tiθo; bau'tiso/ *m,* baptism; christening party
bávaro /'baβaro/ **(-ra)** *a* and *n* Bavarian
baya /'baia/ *f,* berry
bayadera /baya'ðera/ *f,* Indian dancing girl
bayeta /ba'yeta/ *f,* baize; flannel
bayo /'bayo/ **(-ya)** *a* bay (of horses)
Bayona /ba'yona/ Bayonne
bayoneta /bayo'neta/ *f,* bayonet. **b. calada,** fixed bayonet
bayonetazo /bayone'taθo; bayone'taso/ *m,* bayonet thrust
baza /'baθa; 'basa/ *f,* tricks taken (playing cards). *Fig. Inf.* **meter b.,** to stick one's oar in
bazar /ba'θar; ba'sar/ *m,* bazaar; shop, store; department store
bazo /'baθo; 'baso/ *m, Anat.* spleen *—a* yellow-brown
bazucar, bazuquear /baθu'kar, baθuke'ar; basu'kar, basuke'ar/ *vt* to shake or stir (liquids)
bazuqueo /baθu'keo; basu'keo/ *m,* shaking or stirring of liquids
be /be/ *f,* letter B. *m,* baa
beata /be'ata/ *f,* devout woman; *Inf.* pious hypocrite, prude; Sister of Mercy; over-religious woman
beatería /beate'ria/ *f,* sanctimoniousness; bigotry
beatificación /beatifika'θion; beatifika'sion/ *f,* beatification
beatificar /beatifi'kar/ *vt* to make happy; sanctify; beatify
beatífico /bea'tifiko/ *a* beatific
beatitud /beati'tuð/ *f,* blessedness, beatitude; happiness
beato /be'ato/ **(-ta)** *a* happy; blessed, beatified; devout; prudish *—n* devout person; over-pious person
bebé /be'βe/ *m,* baby
bebedero /beβe'ðero/ *a* drinkable. *m,* drinking trough or place
bebedizo /beβe'ðiθo; beβe'ðiso/ *a* drinkable. *m,* draught of medicine; love-potion; poisonous drink
bebedor /beβe'ðor/ **(-ra)** *a* drinkable *—n* drinker; toper
beber /be'βer/ *vt* to drink; absorb; *—vi* toast, drink to the health (of); tipple. *m,* drinking; drink
bebida /be'βiða/ *f,* drink; beverage; alcoholic liquor
beca /'beka/ *f,* academic scarf or sash; scholarship, exhibition
becado, becario /be'kaðo, be'kario/ *m,* exhibitioner, scholarship holder
becerra /be'θerra; be'serra/ *f,* calf; *Bot.* snapdragon
becerro /be'θerro; be'serro/ *m,* bullock; bull calf; calf-skin. **b. marino,** *Zool.* seal
Beda el Venerable /'beða el bene'raβle/ the Venerable Bede
bedel /be'ðel/ *m,* beadle; servitor, university porter
beduino /be'ðuino/ **(-na)** *a* and *n* Bedouin. *m,* savage, bloodthirsty man
befar /be'far/ *vt* to mock, ridicule
befo /'befo/ *a* thick-lipped; knock-kneed. *m,* animal's lip
begonia /be'gonia/ *f, Bot.* begonia
bejín /be'hin/ *m, Bot.* puff-ball; spoiled child
bejuco /be'huko/ *m,* rattan
beldad /bel'dað/ *f,* beauty; belle
beldar /bel'dar/ *vt Agr.* to winnow
Belén /be'len/ Bethlehem
belén /be'len/ *m,* nativity, manager; *Inf.* bedlam; *Inf.* gossip
belfo /'belfo/ *a* thick-lipped
belga /'belga/ *a* and *mf* Belgian
Bélgica /'belhika/ Belgium
bélgico /'belhiko/ *a* Belgian
Belgrado /bel'graðo/ Belgrade
Belice /be'liθe; be'lise/ Belize
belicista /beli'θista; beli'sista/ *adj* war, militaristic; *mf* warmonger
bélico /'beliko/ *a* warlike, military
belicosidad /belikosi'ðað/ *f,* bellicosity
belicoso /beli'koso/ *a* bellicose, aggressive; warlike
beligerancia /belihe'ranθia; belihe'ransia/ *f,* belligerency
beligerante /belihe'rante/ *a* and *mf* belligerent
belitre /be'litre/ *a Inf.* knavish, cunning
bellaco /be'ʎako; be'yako/ **(-ca)** *a* artful, cunning *—n* knave
belladona /beʎa'ðona; beya'ðona/ *f,* belladonna
bellaquería /beʎake'ria; beyake'ria/ *f,* roguery, knavery, cunning
bellasombra /beʎa'sombra; beya'sombra/ *f,* umbra tree
belleza /be'ʎeθa; be'yesa/ *f,* beauty, loveliness, fairness
bello /'beʎo; 'beyo/ *a* beautiful

bellota /be'ʎota; be'yota/ *f,* acorn; carnation bud; ornamental button, knob
bellote /be'ʎote; be'yote/ *m,* round-headed nail
bemol /be'mol/ *a* and *m, Mus.* flat. *Inf.* **tener bemoles,** to be thorny, be difficult
bencina /ben'θina; ben'sina/ *f,* benzine; gasoline
bendecir /bende'θir; bende'sir/ *vt irr* to praise, extol; bless; dedicate, consecrate. See **decir**
bendición /bendi'θion; bendi'sion/ *f,* benediction; blessing; consecration; *pl* marriage ceremony. **b. de la mesa,** grace before meals
bendito /ben'dito/ *a* holy, blessed; fortunate; simple. **ser un b.,** to be a simpleton; be a good soul. **¡Benditos los ojos que te ven!** It's so nice to see you!
benedictino /beneðik'tino/ **(-na)** *a* and *n* Benedictine. *m,* Benedictine liqueur
beneficencia /benefi'θenθia; benefi'sensia/ *f,* beneficence; charitable institutions
beneficiación /benefiθia'θion; benefisia'sion/ *f,* benefaction
beneficiado /benefi'θiaðo; benefi'siaðo/ **(-da)** *n* beneficiary. *m,* incumbent of a benefice
beneficiador /benefiθia'ðor; benefisia'ðor/ **(-ra)** *n* benefactor
beneficiar /benefi'θiar; benefi'siar/ *vt* to benefit; improve; cultivate (land); exploit (mine); purchase (directorship, etc.); sell at a loss (bonds, etc.)
beneficiario /benefi'θiario; benefi'siario/ **(-ia)** *n* beneficiary
beneficiencia /benefi'θienθia; benefi'siensia/ *f,* beneficence, charity
beneficio /bene'fiθio; bene'fisio/ *m,* benefit; profit; cultivation (land, etc.); working (mine); *Eccl.* benefice; *Theat.* benefit
beneficioso /benefi'θioso; benefi'sioso/ *a* beneficial; useful
benéfico /be'nefiko/ *a* beneficent; kind, helpful; charitable
benemérito /bene'merito/ *a* benemeritus, worthy, meritorious
beneplácito /bene'plaθito; bene'plasito/ *m,* approbation; consent
benevolencia /beneβo'lenθia; beneβo'lensia/ *f,* benevolence, goodwill
benévolo /be'neβolo/ *a* benevolent, kind
Bengala /beŋ'gala/ Bengal
bengalí /beŋga'li/ *a* and *mf* Bengali
benignidad /benigni'ðað/ *f,* kindness; mildness (of the weather, etc.)
benigno /be'nigno/ *a* kind; benign; mild; balmy
beodo /be'oðo/ **(-da)** *a* drunk, intoxicated —*n* drunkard
Berbería /berβe'ria/ Barbary
bereber /bere'βer/ *a* and *mf* Berber
berenjena /beren'hena/ *f,* eggplant
bergante /ber'gante/ *m,* rascal, rogue
bergantín /bergan'tin/ *m, Naut.* brig, brigantine
berilo /be'rilo/ *m,* beryl
Berlín /ber'lin/ Berlin
berlinés /ber'lines/ **(-esa)** *a* and *n* of or from Berlin
bermejear /bermehe'ar/ *vi* to be or look reddish
bermejo /ber'meho/ *a* reddish; red; redgold; carroty (of hair)
bermellón /berme'ʎon; berme'yon/ *m,* vermilion
Berna /'berna/ Berne
bernardina /bernar'ðina/ *f,* lie; boast; gibberish
bernardo /ber'narðo/ **(-da)** *a* and *n Eccl.* Bernardine (Order of St. Bernard)
berquelio /ber'kelio/ *m,* berkelium
berrear /berre'ar/ *vi* to low, bellow; yell, squall; shriek; —*vr* reveal, confess
berrido /be'rriðo/ *m,* lowing, bellowing; *Inf.* yell
berrinche /be'rrintʃe/ *m, Inf.* tantrum, fit, fit of sulks
berro /'berro/ *m,* watercress
berroqueña /berro'keɲa/ *f,* granite
berza /'berθa; 'bersa/ *f,* cabbage
besamanos /besa'manos/ *m,* ceremony of kissing royal hand, levee; kissing fingers (in salute)
besar /be'sar/ *vt* to kiss; *Inf.* brush against, touch (of things); —*vr* kiss one another; *Inf.* bang into, knock against one another
beso /'beso/ *m,* kiss; knock, collision
bestia /'bestia/ *f,* quadruped (especially horses or mules); beast. *mf Inf.* nasty piece of work. **b. de carga,** beast of burden. **como una b.,** like a dog (e.g. *Trabajo como una b.* I work like a dog)
bestial /bes'tial/ *a* bestial; brutal; beastly
bestialidad /bestiali'ðað/ *f,* brutality; bestiality; beastliness
bestialismo /bestia'lismo/ *m,* bestiality (sexual orientation)
besuquear /besuke'ar/ *vt Inf.* to cover with kisses; —*vr Inf.* spoon, make love
besuqueo /besu'keo/ *m, Inf.* kissing and spooning
bético /'betiko/ *a* Andalusian
betún /be'tun/ *m,* bitumen; shoe blacking; kind of cement. **b. de Judea** *or* **b. judaico,** asphalt
bey /bei/ *m,* bey
bezo /'beθo; 'beso/ *m,* blubber lip; proud flesh (of a wound)
bezudo /be'θuðo; be'suðo/ *a* thick-lipped
biberón /biβe'ron/ *m,* feeding bottle
Biblia /'biβlia/ *f,* Bible
bíblico /'biβliko/ *a* biblical
bibliófilo /biβli'ofilo/ *m,* bibliophile
bibliografía /biβliogra'fia/ *f,* bibliography
bibliográfico /biβlio'grafiko/ *a* bibliographical
biblioteca /biβlio'teka/ *f,* library; book series. **b. por subscripción,** circulating library
bibliotecario /biβliote'kario/ **(-ia)** *n* librarian
bibliotecnia, bibliotecología, biblioteconomía /biβlio'teknia, biβlioteko'lohia, biβliotekono'mia/ *f,* library science
bicarbonato /bikarβo'nato/ *m,* bicarbonate
bíceps /'biθeps; 'biseps/ *m,* biceps
bicho /'bitʃo/ *m,* any small animal or reptile; quadruped; fighting bull; scarecrow, sight. **b. viviente,** *Inf.* living soul. **mal b.,** rogue
bicicleta /biθi'kleta; bisi'kleta/ *f,* bicycle, bike. **ir** (*or* **andar** *or* **montar**) **en b.,** to bicycle, bike, go by bicycle, go by bike
bicoca /bi'koka/ *f, Inf.* trifle, bagatelle
bicolor /biko'lor/ *a* bicolored
bidé /bi'ðe/ *m,* bidet
biela /'biela/ *f,* axle-tree; connecting-rod; big-end
bielda /'bielda/ *f,* pitchfork; *Agr.* winnowing
bien /bien/ *m,* ideal goodness, perfection; benefit, advantage; welfare; *pl* property, wealth —*adv* well; willingly; happily; perfectly; easily; enough, sufficient; all right! very well! **b. que,** although. **b. de equipo,** capital good. **bienes muebles,** movables, goods and chattels. **bienes raíces,** real estate. **el B. y el Mal,** Good and Evil. **¡Está b.!** All right! **no b.,** scarcely, as soon as. **si b.,** although, even if. **¿Y b.?** And so what? Well, then; What next?
bienal /bie'nal/ *a* biennial
bienamado /biena'maðo/ *a* dearly beloved
bienandante /bienan'dante/ *a* prosperous; happy
bienandanza /bienan'danθa; bienan'dansa/ *f,* happiness, welfare; prosperity
bienaventurado /bienaβentu'raðo/ *a* blessed, holy; happy; *Inf.* over-simple, innocent, foolish
bienaventuranza /bienaβentu'ranθa; bienaβentu'ransa/ *f,* blessedness
bienestar /bienes'tar/ *m,* wellbeing; ease; comfort
bienhablado /biena'βlaðo/ *a* well-spoken; civil, polite
bienhadado /biena'ðaðo/ *a* fortunate, happy
bienhechor /biene'tʃor/ **(-ra)** *a* kind, helpful —*n* benefactor
bienintencionado /bienintenθio'naðo; bienintensio'naðo/ *a* well-meaning
bienio /'bienio/ *m,* biennium, space of two years, period of two years
bienquisto /bien'kisto/ *a* respected; generally esteemed
bienvenida /biembe'niða/ *f,* safe or happy arrival; welcome. **dar la b.,** to welcome
bienvivir /biembi'βir/ *vi* to live comfortably; live decently or uprightly
bies /bies/ *m,* bias, cross; slant
biftec /bif'tek/ *m,* beefsteak

bifurcación /bifurka'θion; bifurka'sion/ *f,* bifurcation; fork, branch, junction
bifurcarse /bifur'karse/ *vr* to fork, branch
bigamia /bi'gamia/ *f,* bigamy
bígamo /'bigamo/ **(-ma)** *a* bigamous —*n* bigamist
bigornia /bi'gornia/ *f,* anvil
bigote /bi'gote/ *m,* moustache; *pl* whiskers
bigotudo /bigo'tuðo/ *a* moustached, whiskered
bikini /bi'kini/ *m,* bikini
bilateral /bilate'ral/ *a* bilateral
bilbaíno /bilβa'ino/ *a* pertaining to or native of Bilbao
bilingüe /bi'liŋgue/ *a* bilingual
bilioso /bi'lioso/ *a* bilious
bilis /'bilis/ *f,* bile
billar /bi'ʎar; bi'yar/ *m,* billiards; billiard table
billete /bi'ʎete; bi'yete/ *m,* note, short letter; ticket; banknote. **b. circular,** excursion ticket. **b. de abono,** season ticket. **b. de andén,** platform ticket. **b. de banco,** banknote. **b. de favor,** free ticket. **b. de ida y vuelta,** round trip ticket. **b. entero,** full fare. **b. kilométrico,** tourist ticket. **b. sencillo,** one-way. **medio b.,** half-fare
billón /bi'ʎon; bi'yon/ *m,* billion
bimestral /bimes'tral/ *a* bimonthly
bimestre /bi'mestre/ *a* bimonthly. *m,* two months' duration; money paid or received at two-monthly intervals
bimotor /bimo'tor/ *a* two-motor. *m,* twin-engined aircraft
binario /bi'nario/ *a* binary
binóculo /bi'nokulo/ *m,* opera glasses
binomio /bi'nomio/ *a* and *m,* binomial
biodiversidad *f,* biodiversity
biofísica /bio'fisika/ *f,* biophysics
biografía /biogra'fia/ *f,* biography
biográfico /bio'grafiko/ *a* biographical
biógrafo /'biografo/ **(-fa)** *n* biographer; (Chile) movie theater (e.g. *¡Vamos al biógrafo!* Let's go to the movies!)
biología /biolo'hia/ *f,* biology
biológico /bio'lohiko/ *a* biological
biólogo /'biologo/ *m,* biologist
biombo /'biombo/ *m,* screen
bioquímica /bio'kimika/ *f,* biochemistry
bioquímico /bio'kimiko/ *m,* biochemist
bipartido /bipar'tiðo/ *a* bipartite
bípedo /'bipeðo/ *a* and *m,* biped
biplano /bi'plano/ *m,* biplane
biplaza /bi'plaθa; biplasa/ *a* two-seater
birla /'birla/ *f,* skittle
birlar /bir'lar/ *vt* to bowl from where the bowl stopped; *Inf.* knock down; snatch away; *Inf.* rob
birlocha /bir'lotʃa/ *f,* child's kite
birlocho /bir'lotʃo/ *m,* barouche
Birmania /bir'mania/ Burma
birmano /bir'mano/ **(-na)** *a* and *n* Burmese
birreta /bi'rreta/ *f,* biretta
birrete /bi'rrete/ *m,* biretta; university cap; cap
bis /bis/ *adv* twice; repeat; encore —*a* duplicate; **B** (in addresses, e.g., *Calle de Alcalá 18bis,* 18b Alcalá St.)
bisabuela /bisa'βuela/ *f,* great-grandmother
bisabuelo /bisa'βuelo/ *m,* great-grandfather
bisagra /bi'sagra/ *f,* hinge; shoemaker's polisher
bisbís /bis'βis/ *m,* game of chance
bisbisar /bisβi'sar/ *vt Inf.* to mutter; whisper
bisbiseo /bisβi'seo/ *m, Inf.* muttering; murmuring; whispering
bisecar /bise'kar/ *vt* to bisect
bisección /bisek'θion; bisek'sion/ *f, Geom.* bisection
bisectriz /bisek'triθ; bisek'tris/ *f,* bisector
bisel /bi'sel/ *m,* bevel, chamfer
bisiesto /bi'siesto/ *a* leap and *m,* leap (year)
bisílabo /bi'silaβo/ *a* two-syllabled
bismuto /bis'muto/ *m,* bismuth
bisnieto /bis'nieto/ **(-ta)** *n* great-grandchild
bisonte /bi'sonte/ *m,* bison
bisoño /bi'soɲo/ **(-ña)** *a* inexperienced, raw —*n* recruit; *Inf.* greenhorn
bistec /bis'tek/ *m,* beef steak
bisturí /bistu'ri/ *m,* surgical knife
bisunto /bi'sunto/ *a* grubby, greasy
bisutería /bisute'ria/ *f,* imitation jewelry
bituminoso /bitumi'noso/ *a* bituminous
bivalvo /bi'βalβo/ *a* bivalve
Bizancio /bi'θanθio; bi'sansio/ Byzantium
bizantinismo /biθanti'nismo; bisanti'nismo/ *m,* Byzantinism
bizantino /biθan'tino; bisan'tino/ *a* Byzantine
bizarría /biθa'rria; bisa'rria/ *f,* handsomeness; dash; verve; gallantry, courage; magnificence; liberality; whim, caprice
bizarro /bi'θarro; bi'sarro/ *a* handsome; dashing; gallant, courageous; liberal; splendid, magnificent
bizcaitarrismo /biθkaita'rrismo; biskaita'rrismo/ *m,* doctrine of Basque autonomy; Basque autonomy movement
bizco /'biθko; 'bisko/ *a* squint-eyed, cross-eyed
bizcocho /biθ'kotʃo; bis'kotʃo/ *m,* biscuit; sponge-cake; bisque
bizma /'biθma; 'bisma/ *f,* poultice. **poner bizmas,** to poultice
biznieto /biθ'nieto; bis'nieto/ *n* See **bisnieto**
blanca /'blanka/ *f,* old Spanish coin; *Inf.* penny; *Mus.* minim. **sin b.,** penniless
blanco /'blanko/ *a* white; fair-skinned; blank, vacant; *Inf.* cowardly. *m,* target; blank left in writing; white person; interval. **b. de España,** whiting. **b. de la uña,** half-moon of the nail. **dar en el b.,** to hit the mark. **en b.,** blank, unused; *Inf.* in vain; uncomprehendingly; (of nights) sleepless
blancor, /blan'kor,/ *m.* **blancura** *f,* whiteness; fairness (of skin)
blandear /blande'ar/ *vt* to moderate, soothe; brandish; —*vi Fig.* give way, yield
blandir /blan'dir/ *vt* to brandish, wield, flourish
blando /'blando/ *a* soft; mild (weather); delicate; kind; peaceable; delicate, effeminate; *Inf.* cowardly
blandón /blan'don/ *m,* wax taper
blandura /blan'dura/ *f,* softness; poultice; blandishment, compliment; mildness (of weather); gentleness, affability; luxury
blanquear /blanke'ar/ *vt* to bleach; whitewash; whiten; —*vi* appear white; show white
blanquecino /blanke'θino; blanke'sino/ *a* whitish
blanqueo /blan'keo/ *m,* whitening; whitewashing; bleaching
blanquizal /blanki'θal; blanki'sal/ *m,* pipe-clay
blasfemador /blasfema'ðor/ **(-ra)** *a* blaspheming —*n* blasphemer
blasfemar /blasfe'mar/ *vi* to blaspheme; curse, swear
blasfemia /blas'femia/ *f,* blasphemy; insult
blasfemo /blas'femo/ **(-ma)** *n* blasphemer —*a* blasphemous
blasón /bla'son/ *m,* heraldry; escutcheon; glory, honor. **una familia con antiguos blasones,** a family of ancient lineage
blasonar /blaso'nar/ *vt* to blazon; —*vi* boast, brag, blazon abroad
bledo /'bleðo/ *m,* blade, leaf. **no importar un b.,** not to matter a straw
blenda /'blenda/ *f, Mineral.* blende
blindado /blin'daðo/ *a Nav.* armored, ironclad
blindaje /blin'dahe/ *m, Nav.* armor-plating; *Mil.* blindage
blindar /blin'dar/ *vt* to plate with armor, to case with steel
blocao /blo'kao/ *m, Mil.* blockhouse
blonda /'blonda/ *f,* blonde (of lace)
blondo /'blondo/ *a* fair, blond, flaxen-haired
bloque /'bloke/ *m,* block, slab
bloquear /bloke'ar/ *vt* to blockade; besiege
bloqueo /blo'keo/ *m,* blockade; siege; blocking; freezing (of assets). **violar el b.,** to run the blockade
blusa /'blusa/ *f,* blouse
boa /'boa/ *f,* boa, large snake. *m,* boa (fur)
boato /boato/ *m,* outward show, ostentation
bobería /boβe'ria/ *f,* foolishness, stupidity
bóbilis, bóbilis /'boβilis, 'boβilis/ **(de)** *adv Inf.* free of charge; without effort

bobina /bo'βina/ *f,* bobbin, spool, reel; *Elec.* coil; spool (of fishing rod)
bobo /'boβo/ **(-ba)** *a* stupid, idiotic; simple, innocent —*n* fool. *m,* clown, jester
boca /'boka/ *f,* mouth; pincers (of crustaceans); entrance or exit; mouth (of a river), gulf, inlet; orifice, opening; muzzle (of guns); cutting edge (of tools); taste (of wine, etc.). **b. abajo,** face down, prone. **b. arriba,** on one's back, face up, supine. **b. del estómago,** pit of the stomach. **b. rasgada,** large mouth. **a b.,** verbally. **a b. de jarro,** point-blank. **a pedir de b.,** just as one would wish. **de b.,** by word of mouth. *Inf.* **sin decir esta b. es mía,** without a word, in silence
bocacalle /boka'kaʎe; boka'kaye/ *f,* entrance (to a street); street junction
Bocacio /bo'kaθio; bo'kasio/ Bocaccio
bocadillo /boka'ðiʎo; boka'ðiyo/ *m,* narrow ribbon; sandwich
bocado /bo'kaðo/ *m,* mouthful. **b. de reyes,** delicacy, exquisite dish (of food); snack; bite; (horse's) bit; bridle; *pl* preserved fruit cut up
bocamanga /boka'maŋga/ *f,* wrist (of sleeve)
bocanada /boka'naða/ *f,* mouthful (of liquid); cloud (of smoke). **b. de aire,** gust of wind
boceto /bo'θeto; bo'seto/ *m,* sketch; outline; roughcast model
bocha /'botʃa/ *f, Sports.* bowl; *pl* bowls
bochorno /bo'tʃorno/ *m,* sultry weather; heat, stuffiness; blush, hot flush; shame
bochornoso /botʃor'noso/ *a* sultry; shameful
bocina /bo'θina; bo'sina/ *f,* trumpet; megaphone; foghorn; hooter; *Auto.* horn; horn (of gramophone); *Astron.* Ursa Minor
bocio /'boθio; 'bosio/ *m, Med.* goiter
bocoy /bo'koi/ *m,* hogshead; large cask
boda /'boða/ *f,* wedding, marriage. **bodas de oro,** fiftieth (golden) anniversary. **bodas de plata,** silver wedding anniversary
bodega /bo'ðega/ *f,* wine-cellar; storeroom; stockroom; granary; *West Hem.* grocery store; *Naut.* hold (of ship)
bodegón /boðe'gon/ *m,* eating-house; tavern; *Art.* still-life; genre picture
bóer /'boer/ *a* and *mf* Boer
bofes /'bofes/ *m pl,* lungs, lights. *Inf.* **echar los b.,** to work oneself to death
bofetada /bofe'taða/ *f.* **bofetón** *m,* blow, slap; box on the ear
boga /'boga/ *f,* rowing; fashion, vogue; *Mech.* bogie. *mf* oarsman, rower. **estar en b.,** to be fashionable
bogador /boga'ðor/ **(-ra)** *n* rower, oarsman
bogar /bo'gar/ *vi* to row
bogavante /boga'βante/ *m,* lobster
bogotano /bogo'tano/ **(-na)** *a* and *n* of or from Bogotá
bohemio /bo'emio/ **(-ia)** *a* and *n* gipsy; bohemian; Bohemian. *m,* archer's short cloak
boicot, boicoteo /boi'kot, boiko'teo/ *m,* boycott
boicotear /boikote'ar/ *vt* to boycott
boina /'boina/ *f,* Basque cap; beret
boj /boh/ *m,* box tree; boxwood, box oak; shoemaker's tool
bola /'bola/ *f,* globe; ball; *Sports.* bowl; *Archit.* balloon; *Inf.* trick, lie; (Cuba) rumor. **b. de nieves,** snowball. *Inf.* **dejar rodar la b.,** to let things slide
bolardo /bo'larðo/ *m,* bollard
bolchevique /boltʃe'βike/ *a* and *mf* bolshevist
bolchevismo /boltʃe'βismo/ *m,* Bolshevism
bolchevista /boltʃe'βista/ *mf* bolshevist
bolea /bo'lea/ *f,* (tennis) volley; throw
bolera /bo'lera/ *f,* bowling alley
bolero /bo'lero/ *m,* bolero; dancer; *Inf.* top hat
boleta /bo'leta/ *f,* admission ticket; billet ticket; warrant, voucher; summons, ticket, traffic ticket
boletín /bole'tin/ *m,* bulletin; admission ticket; pay warrant; *Com.* price list; learned periodical. **b. de noticias,** news bulletin. **b. meteorológico,** weather report
boliche /bo'litʃe/ *m,* jack (in bowls); cup-and-ball toy; small oven (for charcoal); dragnet. **juego de b.,** bowls
bólido /'boliðo/ *m, Astron.* bolide, meteor
bolígrafo /bo'ligrɑfo/ *f,* ballpoint pen
bolillo /bo'liʎo; bo'liyo/ *m,* bobbin (lace making)
bolina /bo'lina/ *f, Naut.* bowline; *Naut.* sounder; *Inf.* uproar, tumult
bolita /bo'lita/ *f,* pellet
boliviano /boli'βiano/ **(-na)** *a* and *n* Bolivian. *m,* silver coin
bollo /'boʎo; 'boyo/ *m,* bread roll; bun; bulge, bruise (in metal); *Med.* lump
bollón /bo'ʎon; bo'yon/ *m,* round-headed or brass-headed nail; *Bot.* bud (especially vines)
bolo /'bolo/ *m,* skittle, ninepin; pillow (for lace making); Cuban coin; *Med.* large pill; *Fig. Inf.* blockhead; *pl* skittles (game of)
boloñés /bolo'ɲes/ **(-esa)** *a* and *n* Bolognese
bolsa /'bolsa/ *f,* purse; bag; footmuff; fold, pucker; pouch; exchange, stock exchange, capital, money; prize money; *Med.* sac; *Mineral.* pocket. **b. de estudio,** scholarship grant. **b. de trabajo,** labor exchange. **b. de valores,** stock exchange. **bajar** (*or* **subir**) **la b.,** to fall (or rise) (of stock exchange quotations). **jugar a la b.,** to speculate on the stock exchange
bolsillo /bol'siʎo; bol'siyo/ *m,* pocket; purse; money
bolsista /bol'sista/ *mf* stock-broker; speculator (on the stock exchange)
bomba /'bomba/ *f, Mech.* pump; pumping engine; bomb; *Mil.* shell; lamp globe; *Inf.* improvised verses; *Inf.* drinking bout. **¡B.!** Listen! Here goes! **b. de incendios,** fire-engine. **b. marina,** waterspout. **b. de mecha atrasada,** time bomb. **b. volante,** flying-bomb. **a prueba de b.,** bombproof. **arrojar bombas,** to bomb. *Inf.* **caer como una b.,** to be a bombshell
bombachos /bom'βatʃos/ *a* baggy, loose-fitting; *m pl,* plus fours
bombardear /bombarðe'ar/ *vt* to bombard; bomb; shell
bombardeo /bombar'ðeo/ *m,* bombardment, bombing; shelling
bombardero /bombar'ðero/ *m,* gunner, bombardier; *Aer.* bomber. **b. pesado,** *Aer.* heavy bomber. **Servicio de b.,** Bomber Command
bombástico /bom'βastiko/ *a* bombastic, high sounding
bombazo /bom'βaθo; bom'βaso/ *m,* bombshell; bomb crater; noise of an exploding bomb
bombear /bombe'ar/ *vt* to pump; bombard, shell; praise
bombero /bom'βero/ *m,* worker of a pressure pump; fireman; mortar, howitzer
bombilla /bom'βiʎa; bom'βiya/ *f, Naut.* lantern; (*Elec. Phys.*) bulb; small pump; straw for drinking maté *West Hem.*
bombillo /bom'βiʎo; bom'βiyo/ *m,* w.c. siphon; handpump
bombo /'bombo/ *m,* big drum or player of it; *Naut.* barge, ferry; ballot box; exaggerated praise
bombón /bom'βon/ *m,* bonbon, sweet
bombonera /bombo'nera/ *f,* box for toffee, etc.
Bona /'bona/ Bonn
bonachón /bona'tʃon/ *a Inf.* genial, good-natured
bonaerense /bonae'rense/ *a* and *mf* of or from the Province of Buenos Aires
Bonaira /bo'naira/ Bonaire
bonancible /bonan'θiβle; bonan'siβle/ *a* calm (of weather, sea)
bonanza /bo'nanθa; bo'nansa/ *f,* fair weather; prosperity
bondad /bon'dað/ *f,* goodness; kindness, helpfulness. **Tenga la b. de...,** Be good enough to..., Please...
bondadoso /bonda'ðoso/ *a* good, kind
bonete /bo'nete/ *m,* academic cap; *Zool.* reticulum (ruminants); *Eccl.* biretta. **gran b.,** important person. *Inf.* **a tente b.,** insistently
bonetero /bone'tero/ **(-ra)** *n* seller or maker of caps and birettas
bonificación /bonifika'θion; bonifika'sion/ *f,* bonus; allowance, discount
bonito /bo'nito/ *a* pretty; graceful; (ironical) fine. *m, Ichth.* bonito

bono /'bono/ *m,* voucher; *Com.* bond, certificate. **b. postal,** postal money order. **bono del gobierno,** government bond
boñiga /bo'ɲiga/ *f,* cow-dung, animal manure
boqueada /boke'aða/ *f,* gasp, opening of the mouth. **dar las boqueadas, estar en las últimas boqueadas,** to be at the last gasp
boquear /boke'ar/ *vi* to gasp; be dying; *Inf.* be at last gasp (of things); *—vt* say, utter
boquera /bo'kera/ *f,* sluice (in irrigation canal)
boquerón /boke'ron/ *m,* large opening; *Ichth.* anchovy (fish); whitebait
boquete /bo'kete/ *m,* narrow entrance, aperture; gap, breach; hole
boquiabierto /bokia'βierto/ *a* open-mouthed; amazed
boquiancho /bo'kiantʃo/ *a* wide-mouthed
boquiasombrado /bokiasom'βraðo/ *a* gaping
boquilla /bo'kiʎa; bo'kiya/ *f, dim* small mouth; mouthpiece (of wind instruments, etc.); cigar- or cigarette-holder; gas-burner; nozzle; tip (of cigarettes)
boquirroto /boki'rroto/ *a Inf.* loquacious, indiscreet
borbollar /borβo'ʎar; borβo'yar/ *vi* to bubble, foam, froth
borbollón, borbotón /borβo'ʎon, borβo'ton; borβo'yon, borβo'ton/ *m,* gushing, bubbling, welling up. **a borbollones,** in a torrent; hastily, impetuously
borbónico /bor'βoniko/ *a* Bourbon
borbotar /borβo'tar/ *vi* to gush out, well up
borceguí /borθe'gi; borse'gi/ *m,* buskin, boot
borda /'borða/ *f,* hut, cabin; *Naut.* gunwale
bordado /bor'ðaðo/ *m,* embroidery
bordador /borða'nðor/ **(-ra)** *n* embroiderer
bordar /bor'ðar/ *vt* to embroider; *Fig.* perform perfectly
borde /'borðe/ *m,* edge; fringe; verge; rim; mount (of a picture); brim (of a hat); side (of ship) *—a* wild (of plants); illegitimate. **estar lleno hasta los bordes,** to be full to the brim
bordear /borðe'ar/ *vt* to border, trim with a bordear; line (a street, e.g. *Diez mil personas bordearon las calles durante el desfile,* Ten thousand people lined the streets during the parade)
bordelés /bor'ðeles/ **(-esa)** *a* and *n* of or from Bordeaux
bordillo /bor'ðiʎo; bor'ðiyo/ *m,* curbstone, curb.
bordo /'borðo/ *m,* side (of ships); border, edge. **a b.,** on board
bordón /bor'ðon/ *m,* pilgrim's staff; monotonous repetition; refrain; *Mus.* bass string; *Fig.* guide, stay
borgoña /bor'goɲa/ *m,* Burgundy wine
borgoñón /borgo'ɲon/ **(-ona)** *a* and *n* Burgundian
bórico /'boriko/ *a* boric
borla /'borla/ *f,* tassel; puff (for powder). *Fig.* **tomar la b.,** to take one's doctorate, graduate
borne /'borne/ *m,* tip (of lance); *Elec.* terminal
bornear /borne'ar/ *vt* to bend, twist; *Archit.* hoist into position; *—vr* warp (wood)
borra /'borra/ *f,* yearling ewe; thickest wool; wad-stuffing; lees, sediment; fluff, dust; *Inf.* trash. **b. de algodón,** cotton-waste
borrachera /borra'tʃera/ *f,* drunkenness; orgy, carousal; *Inf.* blunder
borrachín /borra'tʃin/ **(-ina)** *n* tippler, toper
borrachito /borra'tʃito/ *a* high (on liquor), tipsy
borracho /bo'rratʃo/ **(de)** *a* drunk (on), intoxicated (with); *Inf.* blind (with rage, etc.) *—n* tippler, drunkard
borrador /borra'ðor/ *m,* rough draft. **en borrador,** in the works (e.g. *Tiene dos ensayos en borrador,* She has two essays in the works). **estar en borrador,** to be in the works
borradura /borra'ðura/ *f,* erasure
borrajear /borrahe'ar/ *vt* to scribble
borrar /bo'rrar/ *vt* to erase; cross out; blot out; *Fig.* obliterate
borrasca /bo'rraska/ *f,* storm, tempest; peril, danger; *Inf.* orgy
borrascosidad /borraskosi'ðað/ *f,* storminess
borrascoso /borras'koso/ *a* stormy; disordered, turbulent
borrego /bo'rrego/ **(-ga)** *n* lamb; *Inf.* nincompoop, simpleton; *m pl,* fleecy clouds; white horses (waves)
borrico /bo'rriko/ **(-ca)** *n* donkey; fool. *m,* sawing-horse
borrón /bo'rron/ *m,* blot; rough draft; defect; *Fig.* stigma
borroso /bo'rroso/ *a* blurred, indistinct; full of dregs, muddy
boscaje /bos'kahe/ *m,* grove, group of trees, thicket
Bósforo, el /'bosforo, el/ the Bosporus
bosque /'boske/ *m,* wood, forest
bosquejar /boske'har/ *vt Art.* to sketch; sketch out, draft; model in rough (sculpture); outline
bosquejo /bos'keho/ *m,* outline, sketch; rough plan or idea; unfinished work. **en bosquejo,** grosso modo
bostar /bos'tar/ *m,* ox barn
bostezar /boste'θar; boste'sar/ *vi* to yawn
bostezo /bos'teθo; bos'teso/ *m,* yawning; yawn
bota /'bota/ *f,* small wineskin; barrel, butt; boot. **b. de montar,** riding boot. **botas de campaña,** top-boots. **botas de vadear,** waders
botada, botadura /bo'taða, bota'ðura/ *f,* launching (of a ship)
botador /bota'ðor/ *m,* thrower; boating-pole; nail-puller
botafuego /bota'fuego/ *m, Mil.* linstock; *Inf.* quick-tempered, irascible person
botalón /bota'lon/ *m, Naut.* boom. **b. de foque,** jib-boom
botánica /bo'tanika/ *f,* botany
botánico /bo'taniko/ **(-ca)** *a* botanical *—n* botanist
botar /bo'tar/ *vt* to fling; launch (boat); *Naut.* shift the helm; *—vi* jump; bounce, rebound; rear, prance (horses)
botarate /bota'rate/ *m, Inf.* madcap, devil-may-care
botarel, botarete /bota'rel, bota'rete/ *m, Archit.* abutment, buttress, flying buttress
botarga /bo'targa/ *f,* motley; harlequin
bote /'bote/ *m,* thrust (with lance, etc.); rearing (of horse); rebound; *Aer.* bump; open boat; small bottle, jar. **b. salvavidas,** lifeboat. *Inf.* **de b. en b.,** chockfull
botella /bo'teʎa; bo'teya/ *f,* bottle; bottleful; flask
botica /bo'tika/ *f,* chemist's shop; medicines, remedies; physic; store, shop; medicine chest
boticario /boti'kario/ *m,* apothecary, chemist
botija /bo'tiha/ *f,* earthen jug; *Slang* chunky person
botijo /bo'tiho/ *m,* earthenware jar with spout and handle
botillería /botiʎe'ria; botiye'ria/ *f,* ice-cream bar
botín /bo'tin/ *m,* gaiter; buskin; booty
botiquín /boti'kin/ *m,* first-aid kit; medicine chest
botón /bo'ton/ *m,* bud; button; knob, handle; switch (electric); press button (bell); *Bot.* center; button (on a foil); *Mech.* stud
botonero /boto'nero/ **(-ra)** *n* button maker or seller
bóveda /b'oβeða/ *f, Archit.* vault, arch; crypt; cavern. **b. celeste,** sky
bovino /bo'βino/ *a* bovine
boxeador /boksea'ðor/ *m,* boxer
boxear /bokse'ar/ *vi Sports.* to box
boxeo /bok'seo/ *m, Sports.* boxing
boya /'boya/ *f, Naut.* buoy; float
boyante /bo'yante/ *a* floating; light, buoyant; prosperous
boyar /bo'yar/ *vi Naut.* to float
boyera /bo'yera/ *f,* ox-stall
boyero /bo'yero/ *m,* cowherd
boza /'boθa; 'bosa/ *f,* painter (of a boat)
bozal /bo'θal; bo'sal/ *m,* muzzle; nosebag; harness bells. *mf Inf.* greenhorn; *—a* wild, untamed (horses)
bozo /'boθo; 'boso/ *m,* down which precedes beard; muzzle; headstall; lips, snout
bracero /bra'θero; bra'sero/ *m,* one who offers his arm (to a lady); day laborer; strong man. **de b.,** arm-in-arm
bracete /bra'θete; bra'sete/ *m,* small arm. **de b.,** arm-in-arm
bracmán /brak'man/ *m,* Brahmin
braga /'braga/ *f,* (gen. *pl*) breeches; knickerbockers; hoist or pulley rope

bragazas /bra'gaθas; bra'gasas/ *m, Inf.* weak-willed, fellow, soft specimen
braguero /bra'gero/ *m, Med.* truss
bragueta /bra'geta/ *f,* fly (of breeches)
brahmanismo /brama'nismo/ *m,* Brahmanism
bramante /bra'mante/ *a* roaring. *m,* twine, pack-thread
bramar /bra'mar/ *vi* to roar; rage; *Fig.* howl (of the wind, etc.)
bramido /bra'miðo/ *m,* bellowing; roaring; yell of rage; *Fig.* howling (wind, sea, etc.)
brancada /bran'kaða/ *f,* drag net
branquia /'brankia/ *f,* (gen. *pl*) *Ichth.* gill
branquial /bran'kial/ *a* branchiate
braquicefalia /braˌkiθe'falia; braˌkise'falia/ *f,* brachy-cephaly
braquiotomía /brakioto'mia/ *f, Surg.* brachiotomy, amputation of the arms
brasa /'brasa/ *f,* live coal. **estar como en brasas,** to be like a cat on hot bricks
brasero /bra'sero/ *m,* brazier
Brasil /bra'sil/ Brazil
brasileño /brasi'leɲo/ **(-ña)** *a* and *n* Brazilian
bravata /bra'βata/ *f,* bravado; threat
braveza /bra'βeθa; bra'βesa/ *f,* ferocity, savageness; valor; violence, fury (of elements)
bravío /bra'βio/ *a* savage, untamed; wild (plants); uncultured
bravo /'braβo/ *a* valiant; surly, rude; independent, strong-minded, good, excellent; savage (animals); stormy (sea); rough, rugged; violent, angry; *Inf.* sumptuous, magnificent.
bravura /bra'βura/ *f,* ferocity (animals); courage (persons); boastful threat
braza /'braθa; 'brasa/ *f, Naut.* fathom; stroke (in swimming)
brazado /bra'θaðo; bra'saðo/ *m,* armful
brazal /bra'θal; bra'sal/ *m,* armlet, brassard
brazalete /braθa'lete; brasa'lete/ *m,* bracelet; brassard
brazo /'braθo; 'braso/ *m,* arm; upper arm; front paw; *Mech.* arm; branch (of chandelier, etc.); bough; arm (of chair); power, courage; *pl* protectors; workmen, hands. **b. de mar,** firth, arm of the sea. **a b. partido,** in unarmed fight, man to man. **con los brazos abiertos,** welcomingly; willingly, gladly. **dar los brazos**(**a**)**,** to embrace. *Inf.* **hecho un b. de mar,** dressed up to the nines
brea /'brea/ *f,* pitch, tar; sacking, canvas
brebaje /bre'βahe/ *m,* beverage; unpleasant drink; *Naut.* draft (of beer, grog, etc.)
brecha /'bretʃa/ *f, Mil.* breach; opening; *Fig.* impression (on mind). **morir en la b.,** to fight to the last ditch; die in harness
brécol /'brekol/ *m, Bot.* broccoli
brega /'brega/ *f,* fight; quarrel; disappointment, trick. **andar a la b.,** to work hard. **dar b.,** to play a trick
bregar /bre'gar/ *vi* to fight; work hard; *Fig.* struggle; **bregarse con,** to tackle (a problem)
Brema /'brema/ Bremen
breña /'breɲa/ *f,* rough ground, bramble patch
breñal /bre'ɲal/ *m,* scrub, brushwood
breñoso /bre'ɲoso/ *a* rugged, rocky
Bretaña /bre'taɲa/ Brittany
brete /'brete/ *m,* fetters, shackles; *Fig.* fix, squeeze, tight spot, tight squeeze (e.g. *Estoy en un brete.* I'm in a tight spot)
bretón /bre'ton/ **(-ona)** *a* and *n* Breton. *m,* Breton (language)
breva /'breβa/ *f,* early fig; early acorn; *Fig.* advantage, "plum"; *Inf.* peach (girl); *Inf.* windfall, piece of luck; Havana cigar
breve /'breβe/ *a* brief; concise. *m,* papal brief. *f, Mus.* breve. **en b.,** shortly, concisely; in a short while, soon
brevedad /breβe'ðað/ *f,* brevity
breviario /bre'βiario/ *m,* breviary
brezal /bre'θal; bre'sal/ *m,* heath, moor
brezo /'breθo; 'breso/ *m, Bot.* heath
bribón /bri'βon/ **(-ona)** *n* rogue, ruffian —*a* knavish, dishonest; lazy
bribonada /briβo'naða/ *f,* knavery, mischievous trick
bribonear /briβone'ar/ *vi* to idle; play tricks, be a rogue
bribonería /briβone'ria/ *f,* rascality, vagrant life
brida /'briða/ *f,* bridle
brigada /bri'gaða/ *f, Mil.* brigade; *Naut.* division of fleet; beasts of burden. **brigada millonaria,** (Castroist Cuba) team of thirty sugarcane cutters who cut a million or more arrobas in one harvest
brigadier /briga'ðier/ *m,* brigadier-general
brillante /bri'ʎante; bri'yante/ *a* sparkling, brilliant; *Fig.* outstanding. *m,* diamond
brillantez /briʎan'teθ; briyan'tes/ *f,* brightness, luster; fame; *Fig.* brilliance
brillantina /briʎan'tina; briyan'tina/ *f,* brilliantine
brillar /bri'ʎar; bri'yar/ *vi* to shine, sparkle, gleam, glisten; *Fig.* be brilliant or outstanding
brillo /'briʎo; 'briyo/ *m,* brilliancy, brightness, shine; fame, glory; distinction, brilliance, splendor
brincar /brin'kar/ *vi* to spring, leap, skip, frisk; *Fig. Inf.* skip, omit; *Inf.* grow angry; —*vt* jump a child up and down
brinco /'brinko/ *m,* leap, spring; skip, frolicking
brindar /brin'dar/ *vi* to invite, provoke (of things); (*with prep a or por*) drink the health of, toast; —*vt* and *vi* give, present; offer; —*vr* offer one's services
brindis /'brindis/ *m,* toast (drink)
brío /'brio/ *m,* vigor; spirit, courage; gusto, verve
brioso /'brioso/ *a* vigorous, enterprising; spirited, courageous; dashing, lively
briqueta /bri'keta/ *f,* briquette
brisa /'brisa/ *f,* breeze; grape pressings
británico /bri'taniko/ *a* British
brizna /'briθna; 'brisna/ *f,* shred, paring; blade (grass); filament, fiber; string (of bean-pod, etc.); splinter, chip
broca /'broka/ *f,* reel; tack (shoemaker's); *Mech.* drill, bit
brocado /bro'kaðo/ *m,* brocade —*a* brocade or embroidered like brocade
brocal /bro'kal/ *m,* puteal (of a well); mouthpiece (of wineskin); metal ring (of sword-sheath)
brocamantón /brokaman'ton/ *m,* large jeweled brooch
brocatel /broka'tel/ *m,* imitation brocade
brocha /'brotʃa/ *f,* brush. **b. de afeitar,** shaving brush. **de b. gorda,** crudely painted. **pintor de b. gorda,** decorator
brochada /bro'tʃaða/ *f,* stroke (of the brush)
brochado /bro'tʃaðo/ *a* brocaded, embossed
brochadura /brotʃa'ðura/ *f,* fastening, set of hooks and eyes
broche /'brotʃe/ *m,* clasp, fastening; brooch; hooks and eyes
brochón /bro'tʃon/ *m,* whitewash brush
broma /'broma/ *f,* merriment; joke, jest; ship-worm. **b. literaria,** literary hoax
bromear /brome'ar/ **(se)** *vi* and *vr* to joke, make fun
bromista /bro'mista/ *a* joking, jesting; mischievous. *mf* genial person; prankster, tease
bromo /'bromo/ *m,* bromine
bromuro /bro'muro/ *m,* bromide
bronca /'bronka/ *f, Inf.* shindy
bronce /'bronθe; 'bronse/ *m,* bronze; brass; *Poet.* gun, bell, trumpet; bronze statue; sunburn
bronceado /bronθe'aðo; bronse'aðo/ *a* bronzed; sunburned. *m,* sunburn
broncear /bronθe'ar; bronse'ar/ *vt* to bronze; sunburn
bronco /'bronko/ *a* rough, coarse; brittle; (of metals); harsh (voice, musical instruments); rigid, stiff; surly
bronconeumonía /ˌbronkoneumo'nia/ *f,* broncho-pneumonia
bronquial /bron'kial/ *a* bronchial
bronquio /'bronkio/ *m,* (gen. *pl*) bronchi
bronquitis /bron'kitis/ *f,* bronchitis
broquel /bro'kel/ *m,* shield; *Fig.* protection
broquelero /broke'lero/ *m,* shield maker; quarrelsome man
broqueta /bro'keta/ *f,* skewer

brotadura /brota'ðura/ *f*, budding
brotar /bro'tar/ *vi* to germinate, sprout; gush forth (water); issue forth, burst out; *Fig.* appear (of rash); *Fig.* begin to appear; *—vt* to bring forth; produce (of earth)
brote /'brote/ *m*, bud, sprout; *Fig.* germ, genesis; iota, jot, atom
broza /'broθa; 'brosa/ *f*, garden rubbish; debris; thicket
bruces /'bruθes; 'bruses/ **(a** *or* **de)** *adv* face downwards. **caer de b.,** to fall flat. Also with other verbs: **dar, echarse,** etc.
bruja /'bruha/ *f*, witch; owl; *Inf.* hag
Brujas /'bruhas/ Bruges
brujear /bruhe'ar/ *vi* to practice witchcraft
brujería /bruhe'ria/ *f*, witchcraft
brujo /'bruho/ *m*, magician, wizard
brújula /'bruhula/ *f*, magnetic needle; compass; mariner's compass. **b. de bolsillo,** pocket compass. **b. giroscópica,** gyrocompass
bruma /'bruma/ *f*, haze; sea-mist
brumoso /bru'moso/ *a* misty, hazy
bruno /'bruno/ *a* dark brown
bruñido /bru'ɲiðo/ *m*, polishing; burnish
bruñidor /bruɲi'ðor/ **(-ra)** *a* polishing *—n* burnisher. *m*, polisher (instrument)
bruñir /bru'ɲir/ *vt* to polish, burnish; *Inf.* apply make up
brusco /'brusko/ *a* brusque, rude; blunt; sudden, unexpected; sharp (of bends)
Bruselas /bru'selas/ Brussels
bruselense /bruse'lense/ *a* and *mf* of or from Brussels
brusquedad /bruske'ðað/ *f*, brusquerie, rudeness; bluntness; suddenness, unexpectedness; sharpness (of a bend)
brutal /bru'tal/ *a* brutal
brutalidad /brutali'ðað/ *f*, brutality; *Fig.* brutishness; viciousness
bruto /'bruto/ *a* stupid, unreasonable; vicious; unpolished, rough. *m*, animal (gen. quadruped). **en b.,** in the rough; *Com.* in bulk. **diamante en b.,** an uncut diamond
bruza /'bruθa; 'brusa/ *f*, strong brush; scrubbing brush
Bs. As. /ˌbuenos 'aires/ abbrev. of Buenos Aires
bu /bu/ *m*, *Inf.* bogey man
buba /'buβa/ *f*, pustule; *pl* buboes
bubónico /bu'βoniko/ *a* bubonic
bucal /bu'kal/ *a* buccal
bucanero /buka'nero/ *m*, buccaneer
Bucarest /buka'rest/ Bucharest
búcaro /'bukaro/ *m*, arsenican clay; jar made of arsenican clay
buceador /buθea'ðor; busea'ðor/ *m*, diver
bucear /buθe'ar; buse'ar/ *vi* to work as a diver; swim under water; *Fig.* investigate
bucéfalo /bu'θefalo; bu'sefalo/ *m*, bucephalus; *Inf.* fool, blockhead
buceo /bu'θeo; bu'seo/ *m*, diving; dive; *Fig.* investigation
buche /'butʃe/ *m*, craw or crop; mouthful; wrinkle, pleat; *Inf.* stomach, belly. *Fig. Inf.* inmost heart
bucle /'bukle/ *m*, ringlet, curl
bucólico /bu'koliko/ *a* bucolic
búdico /'buðiko/ *a* Buddhist
budín /bu'ðin/ *m*, pudding
budismo /bu'ðismo/ *m*, Buddhism
budista /bu'ðista/ *a* and *mf* Buddhist
buen /buen/ *a Abbr.* of **bueno,** good. Used before *m*, singular nouns and infinitives used as nouns, e.g. *un b. libro*, a good book. *el b. cantar*, good singing
buenamente /buena'mente/ *adv* easily; comfortably, conveniently; willingly
buenaventura /buenaβen'tura/ *f*, good luck; fortune told from hand
bueno /'bueno/ (see **buen**) *a* good; kind; useful; convenient; pleasant; healthy; large (drink, etc.); simple, innocent; suitable; sufficient; opportune. **¡B.!** Good!; Enough!; All right! **a buenas,** willingly. **de buenas a primeras,** at first sight, from the beginning. **hacer bueno,** to prove, justify (a claim)
buey /buei/ *m*, ox. **b. suelto,** *Inf.* freelance; bachelor
búfalo /'bufalo/ **(-la)** *n* buffalo
bufanda /bu'fanda/ *f*, scarf
bufar /bu'far/ *vi* to bellow; snort; *Inf.* snort with rage
bufete /bu'fete/ *m*, desk, writing table; lawyer's office or practice; sideboard
bufido /bu'fiðo/ *m*, snort; bellow
bufo /'bufo/ *a* comic. *m*, clown, buffoon
bufón /bu'fon/ *m*, buffoon, clown; jester *—a* comical, clownish
bufonada /bufo'naða/ *f*, buffoonery, clowning; raillery, taunt
bufonear /bufone'ar/ **(se)** *vr* and *vi* to joke, jest, parody
bufonería. /bufone'ria/ See **bufonada**
buhardilla /buar'ðiʎa; buar'ðiya/ *f*, garret; skylight
búho /'buo/ *m*, owl; *Inf.* hermit, unsociable person
buhonería /buone'ria/ *f*, peddling, hawking; peddler's wares
buhonero /buo'nero/ *m*, pedler
buido /'buiðo/ *a* sharp-pointed; sharp
buitre /'buitre/ *m*, vulture
bujía /bu'hia/ *f*, candle; candlestick; *Elec.* candlepower; *Auto.* sparking plug
bula /'bula/ *f*, (Papal) bull
bulbo /'bulβo/ *m*, *Bot.* bulb. **b. dentario,** pulp (of teeth)
bulboso /bul'βoso/ *a* bulbous
bulevar /bule'βar/ *m*, boulevard, promenade
búlgaro /'bulgaro/ **(-ra)** *a* and *n* Bulgarian
bulla /'buʎa; 'buya/ *f*, noise; bustle; confusion; fuss. *Inf.* **meter a b.,** to throw into great confusion
bullebulle /buʎe'βuʎe; buye'βuye/ *mf* busybody; madcap
bullente /bu'ʎente; bu'yente/ *adj* boiling, bubbling; frothy (beer); swarming, teeming. **b. de sol,** drenched in sunlight, sun-drenched
bullicio /bu'ʎiθio; bu'yisio/ *m*, noise, bustle; rioting; uproar
bullicioso /buʎi'θioso; buyi'sioso/ *a* noisy, merry, boisterous; rebellious; lively, restless
bullir /bu'ʎir; bu'yir/ *vi* to boil; foam, bubble; *Fig.* seethe; *Fig.* swarm (insects); bustle; *—vt* move, stir; *—vr* stir, give signs of life
bulto /'bulto/ *m*, bulk, mass, size; form of person, etc., seen indistinctly; swelling; bust, statue; bundle, package, piece of luggage; pillowcase. *Fig. Inf.* **poner de b.,** to put clearly, emphasize. **ser de b.,** to be obvious
bumerang /bume'raŋ/ *m*, boomerang
buñolería /buɲole'ria/ *f*, bun or waffle shop
buñuelo /bu'ɲuelo/ *m*, bun; waffle, fritter; *Fig.* botch
buque /'buke/ *m*, ship, vessel; capacity of ship; ship's hull. **b. barreminas,** minesweeper. **b. de guerra,** battleship, man-of-war. **b. de vapor,** steamer. **b. de vela,** sailing ship. **b. escuela,** trainingship. **b. mercante,** merchant vessel. **b. submarino,** submarine. **b. transbordador,** train-ferry
burbuja /bur'βuha/ *f*, bubble
burbujear /burβuhe'ar/ *vi* to bubble
burdel /bur'ðel/ *m*, brothel; *Inf.* untidy, noisy place *—a* lascivious
burdo /'burðo/ *a* coarse, tough
burgalés /burga'les/ **(-esa)** *a* and *n* of or from Burgos
burgo /'burgo/ *m*, borough, burgh
burgomaestre /burgoma'estre/ *m*, burgomaster
burgués /bur'ges/ **(-esa)** *a* and *n* bourgeois
burguesía /burge'sia/ *f*, bourgeoisie
buriel /bu'riel/ *a* dark red
buril /bu'ril/ *m*, burin, engraver's tool
burla /'burla/ *f*, mockery; joke, jest; trick. **b. burlando,** without effort; negligently. **de burlas,** in fun. **entre burlas y veras,** half-jokingly
burlador /burla'ðor/ *a* mocking. *m*, libertine, rake; deceiver
burlar /bur'lar/ *vt* to play a trick on; deceive; disappoint; *—vr* and *vi* (*with de*) make fun of, laugh at, ridicule
burlesco /bur'lesko/ *a* jocular, comic, burlesque

burlón /bur'lon/ **(-ona)** *a* joking; mocking, scoffing —*n* joker; scoffer

buró /bu'ro/ *m,* bureau, writing-desk

burocracia /buro'kraθia; buro'krasia/ *f,* bureaucracy

burócrata /bu'rokrata/ *mf* bureaucrat

burocrático /buro'kratiko/ *a* bureaucratic

burocratismo /burokra'tismo/ *m,* bureaucracy, red tape

burra /'burra/ *f,* she-ass; foolish, unteachable woman; painstaking, patient woman

burrajo /bu'rraho/ *m,* dry stable dung used as fuel

burro /'burro/ *m,* ass, donkey; sawing-horse; card game

bursátil /bur'satil/ *a Com.* relating to the stock exchange; financial

busca /'buska/ *f,* search; hunting party; research; pursuit

buscado /bus'kaðo/ *adj* deliberate, intentional (negligence, etc.)

buscador /buska'ðor/ **(-ra)** *n* searcher; investigator. *m,* finder (of a camera, etc.)

buscapié /buska'pie/ *m,* hint or suggestion; *Fig.* feeler

buscapiés /buska'pies/ *m,* squib, cracker

buscar /bus'kar/ *vt* to search, look for; pursue. **ir a b.,** to go to look for, go and get; bring, fetch

buscarruidos /buska'rruiðos/ *mf Inf.* quarrel maker

buscavidas /buska'βiðas/ *mf Inf.* busybody; *Inf.* go-getter

buscón /bus'kon/ **(-ona)** *n* searcher; pickpocket, thief, swindler, rogue

buscona /bus'kona/ *f,* prostitute

busilis /bu'silis/ *m, Inf.* knotty problem, snag; **ahí está el b.,** there's the rub; core, main point

búsqueda /'buskeða/ **(de)** *f,* search (for)

busto /'busto/ *m, Art.* bust, head and shoulders

butaca /bu'taka/ *f,* armchair; *Theat.* orchestra stall; seat (in movies, etc.)

butifarra /bu'tifarra/ *f,* sausage made principally in Catalonia and the Balearic Islands; *Inf.* badly fitting stocking

buz /buθ; bus/ *m,* respectful kiss

buzo /'buθo; 'buso/ *m,* diver

buzón /bu'θon; bu'son/ *m,* mailbox; letter-box; canal, channel; sluice

C

C. /k/ abbrev. of ciudadano
¡ca! /ka/ *interj* Fancy! Oh no!
cabal /ka'βal/ *a* just, exact; perfect; complete; faultless —*interj* Exactly! **por sus cabales,** according to plan; perfectly
cábala /'kaβala/ *f,* cabala; divination; *Inf.* intrigue. **hacer cábalas,** to venture a guess
cabalgada /kaβal'gaða/ *f,* cavalcade; foray, raid
cabalgador /kaβalga'ðor/ **(-ra)** *n* rider, horseman
cabalgadura /kaβalga'ðura/ *f,* riding horse; beast of burden
cabalgar /kaβal'gar/ *vi* to ride a horse; ride in procession
cabalgata /kaβal'gata/ *f,* cavalcade; troop of horse
cabalístico /kaβa'listiko/ *a* cabalistic; mysterious
caballa /ka'βaʎa; ka'βaya/ *f,* mackerel
caballada /kaβa'ʎaða; kaβa'yaða/ *f,* pack of horses; stud (of horses)
caballeresco /kaβaʎe'resko; kaβaye'resko/ *a* gentlemanly; knightly; chivalrous
caballerete /kaβaʎe'rete; kaβaye'rete/ *m, dim Inf.* foppish young man, dandy
caballería /kaβaʎe'ria; kaβaye'ria/ *f,* riding animal; cavalry; knightly deed or quest; any of Spanish Military Orders; knight-errantry; knighthood; chivalry; share of the spoils of war; horsemanship. **c. andante,** knight-errantry. **c. ligera,** *Mil.* light horse. **c. mayor,** horses, mares, mules. **c. menor,** asses, donkeys
caballeriza /kaβaʎe'riθa; kaβaye'risa/ *f,* stable; stud of horses; staff of a stable
caballerizo /kaβaʎe'riθo; kaβaye'riso/ *m,* head stable-groom. **c. mayor del rey,** Master of the King's Horse
caballero /kaβa'ʎero; kaβa'yero/ *m,* gentleman; cavalier; knight. **c. andante,** knight-errant. *Inf.* **c. de industria,** adventurer, sharper. **el C. de la Mancha,** the Knight of La Mancha. **el C. Sin Miedo y Sin Tacha,** the Seigneur de Bayart. **c. del hábito,** knight of one of the Spanish Military Orders. **c. novel,** untried knight. **armar c.,** to dub a knight
caballerosidad /kaβaʎerosi'ðað; kaβayerosi'ðað/ *f,* gentlemanliness; nobility; generosity; chivalry
caballeroso /kaβaʎe'roso; kaβaye'roso/ *a* gentlemanly; noble; generous; chivalrous
caballete /kaβa'ʎete; kaβa'yete/ *m,* ridge (of a roof); *Mil.* wooden horse; brake (for flax and hemp); *Agr.* furrow; easel; sawing-frame; trestle; bridge (of the nose)
caballito /kaβa'ʎito; kaβa'yito/ *m, dim* little horse; *pl* merry-go-round; automatic horse gambling game; circus equestrian act. **c. del diablo,** dragonfly
caballo /ka'βaʎo; ka'βayo/ *m,* horse; (chess) knight; (Spanish cards) queen; sawing-frame; *pl* cavalry. **c. balancín,** rocking horse. **c. de batalla,** war-horse; *Fig.* hobby-horse; forte; crux. **c. de cartón,** hobby-horse; rocking horse. **c. de carrera,** racehorse. **c. de tiro,** draft-horse. **c. de vapor,** horsepower. **c. marino,** sea-horse. **a c.,** on horseback. **A c. regalado no le mires el diente,** Never look a gift horse in the mouth. **caer bien a c.,** to have a good seat (on a horse). **ser un c. loco en una cacharrería,** to be like a bull in a china shop
cabaña /ka'βaɲa/ *f,* hut, cabin, cottage; flock (of sheep); drove (of mules); *Art.* pastoral scene; balk (billiards)
cabaret /kaβa'ret/ *m,* cabaret, nightclub
cabaretero /kaβare'tero/ *m,* nightclub owner
cabecear /kaβeθe'ar; kaβese'ar/ *vi* to nod; shake the head in disapproval; move the head from side to side; toss the head (horses); (*Aer. Naut.*) pitch; sway (of a carriage); lean; —*vt* refoot (socks); head (wine)
cabeceo /kaβe'θeo; kaβe'seo/ *m,* nod, shake (of head); (*Naut. Aer.*) pitching; lurching (of a carriage, etc.); bight (of river)
cabecera /kaβe'θera; kaβe'sera/ *f,* top, upper portion, head; seat of honor; bed-head; river source; capital (country or county); illustrated chapter heading; pillow; inscription, heading
cabecilla /kaβe'θiʎa; kaβe'siya/ *dim f,* small head. *mf Inf.* hothead. *m,* rebel leader
cabellera /kaβe'ʎera; kaβe'yera/ *f,* head of long hair; hair-switch; tail (of comet)
cabello /ka'βeʎo; ka'βeyo/ *m,* hair; head of hair; silk (of maize). *Fig. Inf.* **asirse de un c.,** to clutch at a straw
cabelludo /kaβe'ʎuðo; kaβe'yuðo/ *a* hairy; *Bot.* fibrous
caber /ka'βer/ *vi irr* to be room for, contain; fit into, go into (e.g. *No cabemos todos en este coche,* There isn't room for all of us in this car); happen, befall, have (e.g. *No les cupo tal suerte,* They did not have such luck--Such luck did not befall them); be possible (e.g. *Todo cabe en Dios,* All things are possible with God). **No cabe más,** There's no room for anything else; *Fig.* That's the limit. *Fig.* **no c. en sí,** to be beyond oneself (with joy, pride, etc.). **No cabe duda de que,** There's no doubt that —*Pres. Indic.* **quepo, cabes,** etc —*Fut.* **cabré,** etc —*Conditional* **cabría,** etc —*Preterite* **cupe, cupiste,** etc —*Pres. Subjunc.* **quepa, quepas,** etc —*Imperf. Subjunc.* **cupiese,** etc.
cabestrar /kaβes'trar/ *vt* to halter
cabestrillo /kaβes'triʎo; kaβes'triyo/ *m,* sling; thin chain (for ornament). **en c.,** in a sling (e.g. *Tenía el brazo en c.,* His arm was in a sling)
cabestro /ka'βestro/ *m,* halter; sling; leading ox
cabeza /ka'βeθa; ka'βesa/ *f,* head; top, upper end; nail-head; brain; mind; judgment; self-control; edge (of book); peak, summit; source, origin; individual, person; head of cattle; capital city. *m,* leader, chief, head. *Mech.* **c. de biela,** big-end. *Inf.* **c. de chorlito,** scatterbrain (person). **c. de hierro,** blockhead. *Mil.* **c. de puente,** bridgehead. **c. de partido,** principal town of a region. **c. de turco,** scapegoat. **irse la c. (a alguien),** to feel giddy. *Fig. Inf.* **meter a uno en la c.,** to put into someone's head. *Inf.* **quebrarse la c.,** to rack one's brains. *Inf.* **quitar a uno de la c. (una cosa),** to dissuade; get an idea out of someone's head
cabezada /kaβe'θaða; kaβe'saða/ *f,* blow with or on the head; nod; headshake; headstall; *Naut.* pitching. **dar cabezadas,** to nod, go to sleep
cabezal /kaβe'θal; kaβe'sal/ *m,* small head pillow; *Surg.* pad; bolster; narrow mattress; *Mech.* head
cabezo /ka'βeθo; ka'βeso/ *m,* summit (of mountain); hill; *Naut.* reef
cabezón /kaβe'θon; kaβe'son/ *m,* tax-register; collar-band; head-opening (of a garment)
cabezudo /kaβe'θuðo; kaβe'suðo/ *a* large-headed; *Inf.* obstinate; *Inf.* heady (of wine). *m,* carnival grotesque
cabida /ka'βiða/ *f,* space, capacity; extent, area
cabildear /kaβilde'ar/ *vi* to canvass votes, lobby
cabildo /ka'βildo/ *m, Eccl.* chapter; municipal council; meeting, or meeting place of council. **c. abierto,** town meeting
cabina /ka'βina/ *f,* cabin. **c. telefónica** phone booth
cabizbajo /kaβiθ'βaho; kaβis'βaho/ *a* crestfallen; pensive, melancholy
cable /'kaβle/ *m,* cable; string (of bridge); cable's length; **c. aéreo,** overhead cable. **c. alimentarlo,** feed line. **c. eléctrico,** electric cable
cabo /'kaβo/ *m,* end, extremity; stump, stub; handle, shaft, haft; leader; *Geog.* cape; end, conclusion; *Naut.* rope; ply (of wool, etc.); *Mil.* corporal; *pl* accessories (clothes); horse's tail and mane. **c. de maestranza,** foreman. **c. de mar,** naval quartermaster. **c. furriel,** *Mil.* quartermaster. **al c.,** in the end. **llevar a c.,** to finish
Cabo de Buena Esperanza /'kaβo de 'buena espe'ranθa; 'kaβo de 'buena espe'ransa/ Cape of Good Hope
Cabo de Hornos /'kaβo de 'ornos/ Cape Horn
cabotaje /kaβo'tahe/ *m, Naut.* coasting trade

cabra /'kaβra/ *f*, nanny-goat; goat. **c. montesa,** wild goat

cabrahigo /kaβra'igo/ *m*, wild fig; wild fig tree

cabrerizo /kaβre'riθo; kaβreriso/ **(-za)** *a* goatish. *m*, goatherd

cabrero /ka'βrero/ **(-ra)** *m*, goatherd

cabrestante /kaβres'tante/ *m*, *Naut.* capstan

cabria /'kaβria/ *f*, winch, hoist

cabrilla /ka'βriʎa; ka'βriya/ *f*, saw-horse; *pl Astron.* Pleiades; burn marks on legs from sitting too near fire; white crests (of waves)

cabrillear /kaβriʎe'ar; kaβriye'ar/ *vi* to foam, froth (the sea)

cabrío /ka'βrio/ *a* goatish. *m*, herd of goats. **macho c.,** male goat, he-goat

cabriola /ka'βriola/ *f*, fouetté (in dancing); spin in the air (acrobats); curvet (horses); caper

cabriolar /kaβrio'lar/ *vi* to curvet; caper, skip

cabriolé /kaβrio'le/ *m*, cabriolet; short cape with or without sleeves

cabritilla /kaβri'tiʎa; kaβri'tiya/ *f*, dressed kid; lambskin, etc.

cabrito /ka'βrito/ *m*, *Zool.* kid; *pl* toasted maize, popcorn

cabrón /ka'βron/ *m*, billy goat, buck, he-goat; *Inf.* complaisant husband, cuckhold; *Chile* owner or operator of a brothel

cabrona /ka'βrona/ *f*, *Chile* bawd, madam

cabruno /ka'βruno/ *a* goatish

cabujón /kaβu'hon/ *m*, *Mineral.* uncut gem; unpolished ruby; *pl* vignettes

cacahual /kaka'ual/ *m*, cacao plantation

cacahuete /kaka'uete/ *m*, *Bot.* peanut, monkey nut

cacao /ka'kao/ *m*, *Bot.* cacao tree; cacaonut

cacarear /kakare'ar/ *vi* to crow, cackle; —*vt Inf.* boast

cacareo /kaka'reo/ *m*, crowing, cackling; *Inf.* boast

cacatúa /kaka'tua/ *f*, cockatoo

cacera /ka'θera; ka'sera/ *f*, irrigation channel

cacería /kaθe'ria; kase'ria/ *f*, hunting party; hunting bag, booty; *Art.* hunting scene

cacerola /kaθe'rola; kase'rola/ *f*, stew-pot, casserole

cachalote /katʃa'lote/ *m*, sperm whale

cachano /ka'tʃano/ *m*, Old Nick

cachar /ka'tʃar/ *vt* to break in fragments; split (wood)

cacharrería /katʃarre'ria/ *f*, crockery store

cacharro /ka'tʃarro/ *m*, coarse earthenware vessel; *Inf.* decrepit, worthless object

cachazudo /katʃa'θuðo; katʃa'suðo/ *a* phlegmatic, slow

cachear /katʃe'ar/ *vt* to search (a person) for weapons

Cachemira /katʃe'mira/ Kashmir

cachemira /katʃe'mira/ *f*, cashmere

cacheo /ka'tʃeo/ *m*, search (of persons) for weapons

cachete /ka'tʃete/ *m*, blow on the head or face with one's fist; cheek (especially fat one)

cachetero /katʃe'tero/ *m*, dagger

cachetina /katʃe'tina/ *f*, hand-to-hand fight

cachiporra /katʃi'porra/ *f*, club, bludgeon

cachivache /katʃi'βatʃe/ *m*, *Inf.* (gen. *pl*) trash; pots, pans, utensils

cacho /'katʃo/ *m*, small slice (gen. of bread or fruit)

cachón /ka'tʃon/ *m*, breaker, wave; small waterfall

cachorro /ka'tʃorro/ **(-rra)** *n* puppy; cub. *m*, small pistol

cachuela /ka'tʃuela/ *f*, Extremaduran pork stew

cacillo /ka'θiʎo; ka'siyo/ *m*, ladle; basting spoon

cacique /ka'θike; ka'sike/ *m*, Indian chief, cacique; *Inf.* political "boss"

caciquismo /kaθi'kismo; kasi'kismo/ *m*, political "bossism"

caco /'kako/ *m*, pickpocket, thief; *Inf.* poltroon

cacofonía /kakofo'nia/ *f*, cacophony

cacografía /kakogra'fia/ *f*, cacography

cacto /'kakto/ *m*, cactus

cacumen /ka'kumen/ *m*, *Inf.* brains, acumen

cada /'kaða/ *a* every, each. **c. cual,** each. **c. que,** whenever; every time that. **c. y cuando que,** whenever

cadalso /ka'ðalso/ *m*, scaffold; platform, stand

cadáver /ka'ðaβer/ *m*, corpse

cadavérico /kaða'βeriko/ *a* cadaverous, ghastly

cadena /ka'ðena/ *f*, chain; link, tie; *Fig.* bond; *Fig.* sequence (of events); *Law.* imprisonment; *Archit.* buttress; grand chain (dancing); **c. de montañas,** range of mountains. **c. perpetua,** life imprisonment

cadencia /ka'ðenθia; ka'ðensia/ *f*, cadence; rhythm; *Mus.* measure, time; *Mus.* cadenza

cadencioso /kaðen'θioso; kaðen'sioso/ *a* rhythmic

cadente /ka'ðente/ *a* falling, declining; decaying, dying; rhythmic

cadera /ka'ðera/ *f*, hip; flank

caderillas /kaðe'riʎas; kaðe'riyas/ *f pl*, bustle, panniers

cadete /ka'ðete/ *m*, *Mil.* cadet

cadi /'kaði/ *mf* caddy

Cádiz /'kaðiθ; 'kaðis/ Cadiz

caducar /kaðu'kar/ *vi* to become senile; become invalid, be annulled; expire, lapse; *Fig.* be worn out

caduceo /kaðu'θeo; kaðu'seo/ *m*, Mercury's wand

caducidad /kaðuθi'ðað; kaðusi'ðað/ *f*, decrepitude; lapse, expiry

caduco /ka'ðuko/ *a* senile; decrepit; perishable; lapsed; obsolete

caduquez /kaðu'keθ; kaðu'kes/ *f*, senility

caedizo /kae'ðiθo; kae'ðiso/ *a* ready to fall; timid, cowardly, weak

caer /ka'er/ *vi irr* to fall, drop; drop out or off; suit, fit, become; fail; fade (colors); *Fig.* drop (voice); (*with sobre*) attack, fall upon; (*with en*) fall in or on to; decay, collapse; understand; (*with preps. a, hacia*) *Fig.* look on to, face; (*with por, en*) *Fig.* fall on, occur on; —*vr Aer.* crash; fly off (buttons, etc.). **c. de cabeza,** to fall head foremost. **c. en conflicto (con),** to come into conflict (with) **c. en las manos de uno,** to come into somebody's possession (come to be owned by somebody). **c. en gracia,** to make a good impression, arouse affection. **caerse de suyo,** to be self-evident. **c. por tierra,** (plan, etc.) to fall through. **Cayó enfermo,** He was taken ill. **cayendo y levantado,** dying *Pres. Indic.* **caigo, caes,** etc —*Pres. Part.* **cayendo.** *Preterite* **cayó cayeron.** *Pres. Subjunc.* **caiga,** etc.

café /ka'fe/ *m*, coffee (tree, berry, drink); café, coffee-house. **c. con leche,** café au lait

cafeína /kafe'ina/ *f*, caffeine

cafetal /kafe'tal/ *m*, coffee plantation

cafetera /kafe'tera/ *f*, coffeepot; *Peru* cab, taxi

cafeto /ka'feto/ *m*, coffee tree

cafiche /ka'fitʃe/ *m*, *Argentina, Chile* pimp

caficultor /kafikul'tor/ *m*, coffee-grower

caficultura /kafikul'tura/ *f*, coffee-growing

cafúa /ka'fua/ *f*, *Argentina* clink, slammer

cagadas /ka'gaðas/ *f pl*, droppings, dung

cagar /ka'gar/ **(se)** *vi vt vr* to evacuate (bowels); —*vt Inf.* spoil, make a botch of

cagarruta /kaga'rruta/ *f*, dung of sheep, deer, rabbits, etc.

caída /ka'iða/ *f*, falling; fall; ruin; failure; close (of day); *Fig.* falling off; hanging (curtains, etc.); diminution; incline; *pl* coarse wool; *Inf.* repartee. **a la c. de la tarde,** at the end of the afternoon. **a la c. del sol,** at sunset

caído /ka'iðo/ **(-da)** *a* debilitated, languid; lapsed; (of a shoulder) sloping. **los caídos,** the fallen, the dead (in war, etc.)

caimán /kai'man/ *m*, alligator; *Inf.* shark, astute person

caja /'kaha/ *f*, box; safe, cash box; coffin; (of a vehicle) body; *Mus.* drum; case (of piano, watch, etc.); cavity; well (of a stair); *Com.* cash; cash-desk; cashier's office; *Bot.* sheath. **c. de ahorros,** savings bank. **c. de caudales,** strong-box. *Print.* **c. de imprenta,** type case. **c. de música,** musical box. **c. de reclutamiento,** recruiting office. **c. de velocidades,** gearbox. **c. registradora,** cash register. **c. torácica,** rib cage, thoracic cage

cajero /ka'hero/ **(-ra)** *m*, boxmaker; —*n Com.* cashier; pedler **c. automático,** automatic teller, automatic teller machine, bank machine, money machine

cajetilla /kahe'tiʎa; kahe'tiya/ *f*, packet (cigarettes, etc.)

cajista /ka'hista/ *mf Print.* compositor

cajón /ka'hon/ *m*, chest, locker, case; drawer. **c. de municiones,** ammunition-box
cajonera /kaho'nera/ *f*, *Eccl.* chest of drawers in sacristy; *Agr.* frame
cal /kal/ *f*, lime. **c. muerta,** slaked lime. **c. viva,** quicklime. *Fig. Inf.* **de c. y canto,** tough, strong
cala /'kala/ *f*, sample slice (of fruit); *Naut.* hold; *Surg.* probe; cove, small bay; *Bot.* iris
calabacera /kalaβa'θera; kalaβa'sera/ *f*, *Bot.* pumpkin or gourd plant
calabacín /kalaβa'θin; kalaβa'sin/ *m*, kind of vegetable marrow; *Inf.* dolt
calabaza /kala'βaθa; kala'βasa/ *f*, *Bot.* pumpkin (plant and fruit); gourd; *Inf.* dolt. **dar calabazas,** to refuse (suitor); flunk (an examinee). *Inf.* **llevar calabazas,** to get the sack; be jilted
calabobos /kala'βoβos/ *m*, *Inf.* drizzle
calabocero /kalaβo'θero; kalaβo'sero/ *m*, jailer
calabozo /kala'βoθo; kala'βoso/ *m*, dungeon; prison cell; pruning knife
calabrés /kala'βres/ **(-esa)** *a* and *n* Calabrian
calada /ka'laða/ *f*, soaking, wetting through; flight of bird of prey; swoop. **dar una c.,** *Fig. Inf.* to dress down
calado /ka'laðo/ *a* soaked, wet through. *m*, *Sew.* open-work; fretwork; *Naut.* draft of a ship; water level; *pl* lace. **c. hasta los huesos,** soaked to the skin; madly in love
calador /kala'ðor/ *m*, one who does open or fretwork; caulking iron; borer; *Surg.* probe
calafate /kala'fate/ *m*, caulker
calafatear /kalafate'ar/ *vt Naut.* to caulk
calamar /kala'mar/ *m*, *Zool.* squid, calamary
calambre /ka'lambre/ *m*, cramp. **c. del escribiente,** writer's cramp
calamidad /kalami'ðað/ *f*, misfortune, calamity
calamina /kala'mina/ *f*, *Mineral.* calamine
calamitoso /kalami'toso/ *a* calamitous; unfortunate, unhappy
cálamo /'kalamo/ *m*, ancient flute; stalk (of grass); *Poet.* pen
calamocano /kalamo'kano/ *a* maudlin, tipsy
calandria /ka'landria/ *f*, *Ornith.* calender, lark; *Mech.* calender; treadmill. *mf Inf.* malingerer
calaña /ka'laɲa/ *f*, sample; model; pattern; kind, quality; temperament; cheap fan
calar /ka'lar/ *vt* to permeate, soak through; pierce; do openwork (in cloth, paper, metal); cut a sample slice from fruit; pull (hat, etc.) well down on head; put down (an eyeshade or visor); fix (bayonets, etc.); *Inf.* understand (persons); *Inf.* guess, realize; *Naut.* let down; *—vi Naut.* draw (water); *—vr* be drenched, wet through; swoop (birds of prey); *Inf.* sneak in *—a* calcareous
calar /ka'lar/ *m*, limestone deposit or region
calavera /kala'βera/ *f*, skull. *m*, dare-devil, madcap; roué
calaverada /kalaβe'raða/ *f*, *Inf.* dare-devilment, foolishness; escapade
calcañar /kalka'ɲar/ *m*, heel (of foot)
calcar /kal'kar/ *vt* to trace (drawing); press with foot; copy servilely, imitate
calcáreo /kal'kareo/ *a* calcareous
calce /'kalθe; 'kalse/ *m*, rim of a wheel; wedge; tire
calcés /kal'θes; kal'ses/ *m*, *Naut.* masthead
calceta /kal'θeta; kal'seta/ *f*, stocking; fetter. *Inf.* **hacer c.,** to knit
calcetería /kalθete'ria; kalsete'ria/ *f*, hosiery shop; hosiery trade
calcetero /kalθe'tero; kalse'tero/ **(-ra)** *n* hosier; hose maker or darner
calcetín /kalθe'tin; kalse'tin/ *m*, sock
calcificación /kalθifika'θion; kalsifika'sion/ *f*, *Med.* calcification
calcinación /kalθina'θion; kalsina'sion/ *f*, calcination
calcinar /kalθi'nar; kalsi'nar/ *vt* to calcine
calcio /'kalθio; 'kalsio/ *m*, calcium
calco /'kalko/ *m*, tracing (drawing)
calcografía /kalkogra'fia/ *f*, chalcography
calcografiar /kalkogra'fiar/ *vt* to transfer; make chalcographies of
calcomanía /kalkoma'nia/ *f*, transfer
calculación /kalkula'θion; kalkula'sion/ *f*, calculation
calculadamente /kalkulaða'mente/ *adv* calculatedly
calculado /kalku'laðo/ *a* calculated
calculador /kalkula'ðor/ *a* calculating. *m*, calculating machine, comptometer
calcular /kalku'lar/ *vt* to calculate
cálculo /'kalkulo/ *m*, calculation; *Math.* estimate; investigation; conjecture; *(Math Med.)* calculus. **c. hepático,** *Med.* gallstone
Calcuta /kal'kuta/ Calcutta
calda /'kalda/ *f*, heating; *pl* hot mineral baths
Caldea /kal'dea/ Chaldea
caldear /kalde'ar/ *vt* to heat
caldeo /kal'deo/ **(-ea)** *a* and *n* Chaldean
caldeo /kal'deo/ *m*, heating
caldera /kal'dera/ *f*, cauldron; cauldron full; *West Hem.* teapot; *Engin.* boiler. **c. de vapor,** steam-boiler
calderería /kaldere'ria/ *f*, coppersmith's trade and shop
calderero /kalde'rero/ *m*, boiler maker; coppersmith; tinker
calderilla /kalde'riʎa; kalde'riya/ *f*, holy water stoup; any copper coin
caldero /kal'dero/ *m*, small cauldron; casserole; kettle
calderón /kalde'ron/ *m*, large cauldron; *Mus.* rest; *Mus.* trill; pause
caldo /'kaldo/ *m*, broth; salad dressing; *pl Agr.* oil, wine, vegetable juices
calefacción /kalefak'θion; kalefak'sion/ *f*, heating. **c. central,** central heating
calendario /kalen'dario/ *m*, calendar. **c. deportivo,** fixture card. **c. gregoriano,** Gregorian calendar
calendas /ka'lendas/ *f pl*, calends. **en las c. griegas,** at the Greek calends
caléndula /ka'lendula/ *f*, marigold
calentador /kalenta'ðor/ *a* heating, warming. *m*, heater; warming-pan
calentamiento /kalenta'miento/ *m*, heating, warming
calentar /kalen'tar/ *vt irr* to heat, warm; rev-up (an engine); hasten; *Inf.* spank; *—vr* warm oneself; be in heat (animals); grow excited. See **acertar**
calentura /kalen'tura/ *f*, fever
calenturiento /kalentu'riento/ *a* feverish
calera /ka'lera/ *f*, lime-pit; lime-kiln; fishing smack
calesa /ka'lesa/ *f*, calash, calèche, chaise (two-wheeled carriage)
caleta /ka'leta/ *f*, cove, creek
caletre /ka'letre/ *m*, *Inf.* discernment, head, sense
calibrar /kali'βrar/ *vt* to calibrate; gauge
calibre /ka'liβre/ *m*, *Mech.* gauge; bore, caliber; diameter (tubes, pipes, etc.)
calidad /kali'ðað/ *f*, quality; role; character, temperament; condition, requisite; importance, gravity; personal particulars; nobility; *pl* qualities of the mind. **c. originaria,** rank and birth. **c. de oficio,** justification for action. **en c. de,** in the capacity of
cálido /'kaliðo/ *a* warm, hot; warming, heating; vehement, ardent; *Art.* warm
calidoscópico /kaliðos'kopiko/ *a* kaleidoscopic
calidoscopio /kaliðos'kopio/ *m*, kaleidoscope
calientalibros /kalienta'liβros/ *m*, bookworm (person)
calientapiés /kalienta'pies/ *m*, footwarmer
calientaplatos /kalienta'platos/ *m*, hot plate, platewarmer
caliente /ka'liente/ *a* warm, hot; excited; *Art.* warm
calientito /kalien'tito/ *a* piping hot
califa /ka'lifa/ *m*, caliph
califal /kali'fal/ *a* caliphal
califato /kali'fato/ *m*, caliphate
calificable /kalifi'kaβle/ *a* classifiable; qualifiable
calificación /kalifika'θion; kalifika'sion/ *f*, classification; qualification; judgment; mark, place (examinations)
calificar /kalifi'kar/ *vt* to class; authorize; judge (qualities); *Fig.* ennoble; *—vr* prove noble descent
calificativo /kalifika'tiβo/ *a Gram.* qualifying. *m*, epithet

californio /kali'fornio/ **(-ia)** *a* and *n* Californian
caliginoso /kalihi'noso/ *a* murky, dark
caligrafía /kaligra'fia/ *f,* calligraphy
calígrafo /ka'ligrafo/ *m,* calligraphist
calinoso /kali'noso/ *a* hazy
caliqueño /kali'keɲo/ *m,* cheroot
calistenia /kalis'tenia/ *f,* callisthenics
cáliz /'kaliθ; 'kalis/ *m,* chalice; *Poet.* cup; *Bot.* calyx
caliza /ka'liθa; ka'lisa/ *f,* limestone
calizo /ka'liθo; ka'liso/ *a* calcareous
callado /ka'ʎaðo; ka'yaðo/ *a* silent; reserved; secret
callar /ka'ʎar; ka'yar/ **(se)** *vi* and *vr* to say nothing, keep silent; stop speaking; stop making any sound (persons, animals, things); —*vt* conceal, keep secret; omit, leave out; *Inf. interj* **¡Calle!** You don't say so! **Quien calla otorga,** Silence gives consent
calle /'kaʎe; 'kaye/ *f,* street. *Inf.* **abrir c.,** to clear the way. *Inf.* **dejar en la c.,** to leave destitute. *Inf.* **echar a la c.,** put out of the house, to throw out of the house; make known, publish. **ponerse en la c.,** to go out
calleja, callejuela /ka'ʎeha, kaʎe'huela; ka'yeha, kaye'huela/ *f,* small street, alley, side street
callejear /kaʎehe'ar; kayehe'ar/ *vi* to walk the streets, wander about the streets, loaf around the streets
callejero /kaʎe'hero; kaye'hero/ *a* fond of gadding. *m,* street directory
callejón /kaʎe'hon; kaye'hon/ *m,* alley, lane. **c. sin salida,** cul-de-sac; *Fig.* impasse
callicida /kaʎi'θiða; kayi'siða/ *m,* corn cure
callista /ka'ʎista; ka'yista/ *mf* chiropodist
callo /'kaʎo; 'kayo/ *m,* corn, callosity; *Med.* callus; *pl* tripe
calloso /ka'ʎoso; ka'yoso/ *a* callous, horny
calma /'kalma/ *f,* calm, airlessness; serenity, composure; quiet, tranquillity, peace. **c. chicha,** dead calm. **en c.,** at peace; tranquil; calm (of the sea)
calmante /kal'mante/ *a* calming, soothing. *Med. a* and *m,* sedative, tranquilizer
calmar /kal'mar/ *vt* to soothe, calm; moderate, mitigate; pacify; quench (thirst); —*vi* grow calm; moderate; be becalmed
calmoso /kal'moso/ *a* calm, tranquil; *Inf.* sluggish, lazy; imperturbable
calor /ka'lor/ *m,* heat; ardor, vehemence; cordiality; *Fig.* heat (of battle); excitement
caloría /kalo'ria/ *f, Phys.* calorie
calórico /ka'loriko/ *a Phys.* caloric, thermic
calorífero /kalo'rifero/ *a* heat-giving. *m,* heater, radiator
calorífico /kalo'rifiko/ *a* calorific
calumnia /ka'lumnia/ *f,* calumny; *Law.* slander
calumniador /kalumnia'ðor/ **(-ra)** *a* slandering —*n* calumniator, slanderer
calumniar /kalumni'ar/ *vt* to calumniate; *Law.* slander
calumnioso /kalum'nioso/ *a* calumnious, slanderous
caluroso /kalu'roso/ *a* hot, warm; cordial, friendly; enthusiastic; ardent, impassioned; excited
calva /'kalβa/ *f,* bald patch on head; worn place (cloth, etc.); bare spot, clearing (trees, etc.)
Calvario /kal'βario/ *m,* Calvary; *Inf.* series of disasters; *Inf.* debts
calvero /kal'βero/ *m,* clearing (in a wood); chalk or marl pit
calvicie /kal'βiθie; kalβisie/ *f,* baldness
calvinismo /kalβi'nismo/ *m,* Calvinism
calvinista /kalβi'nista/ *mf* Calvinist —*a* Calvinistic
calvo /'kalβo/ *a* bald; bare, barren (land); worn (cloth, etc.)
calza /'kalθa; 'kalsa/ *f,* breeches (gen. *pl*); wedge; *Inf.* stocking. *Inf.* **tomar calzas,** to beat it
calzada /kal'θaða; kal'saða/ *f,* roadway. **c. romana,** Roman road
calzado /kal'θaðo; kal'saðo/ *m,* footwear, shoes
calzador /kalθa'ðor; kalsa'ðor/ *m,* shoehorn
calzadura /kalθa'ðura; kalsa'ðura/ *f,* wedging (of a wheel); act of putting on shoes; felloe of a wheel
calzar /kal'θar; kal'sar/ *vt* to put on shoes; wear (spurs, gloves, etc.); wedge, block (wheel); scotch (a wheel). *Fig. Inf.* **c. el coturno,** don the buskin; write in the sublime style; write a tragedy, write tragedies. **calzarse a una persona,** to have a person in one's pocket
calzón /kal'θon; kal'son/ *m,* breeches (gen. *pl*). *Fig. Inf.* **ponerse los calzones,** to wear the breeches (of a woman)
calzonazos /kalθo'naθos; kalso'nasos/ *m, Inf.* weak-willed, easily led fellow
calzoncillos /kalθon'θiʎos; kalson'siyos/ *m pl,* drawers, pants
cama /'kama/ *f,* bed; bedstead; bedhanging; lair, form; floor (of a cart); check (of bridle) (gen. *pl*). **c. de campaña,** camp bed. **c. de matrimonio,** double bed. **c. de monja,** single bed. **c. de operaciones,** operating table. **c. turca,** settee-bed. **guardar c.,** to stay in bed
camada /ka'maða/ *f,* brood, litter; *Inf.* gang
camafeo /kama'feo/ *m,* cameo
camaleón /kamale'on/ *m,* chameleon; *Inf.* changeable person
cámara /'kamara/ *f,* chamber; hall; house (of deputies); granary; *Naut.* state room; chamber (firearms, mines); *Phys.* camera; human excrement; *Auto.* inner tube. **c. acorazada,** strong-room. **c. alta,** Upper House, **c. baja** *or* **c. de los comunes,** lower house, house of commons. **c. de comercio,** chamber of commerce. **c. oscura,** (optics) dark room
camarada /kama'raða/ *mf* pal, companion, comrade
camaradería /kamaraðe'ria/ *f,* comradeship, companionship
camarera /kama'rera/ *f,* waiting-maid; waitress; chambermaid; stewardess
camarero /kama'rero/ *m,* waiter; papal chamberlain; chamberlain; steward; valet. **c. mayor,** lord chamberlain
camarilla /kama'riʎa; kama'riya/ *f,* palace or other clique, coterie; *Inf.* back-scratch
camarín /kama'rin/ *m, Theat.* dressing-room; closet; boudoir; cage (of a lift); niche
camarón /kama'ron/ *m,* prawn, shrimp; tip, reward
camarote /kama'rote/ *m,* cabin; berth
cambalachear /kambalatʃe'ar/ *vt Inf.* to barter
cámbaro /'kambaro/ *m,* sea-crab
cambiable /kam'βiaβle/ *a* exchangeable; changeable
cambiante /kam'βiante/ *a* exchanging; changing. *m,* sheen, luster (gen. *pl*); money changer
cambiar /kam'βiar/ *vt* to exchange; convert —*vt* and *vi* change, alter; —*vi* and *vr* to veer (wind). **c. de aguas,** *Poet.* to move (change one's residence). **c. de aire,** get a change of scenery. **c. de frente,** to face about; *Fig.* change front
cambio /'kambio/ *m,* exchange; change; *Com.* rate of exchange; money change; *Com.* premium on bills of exchange. **a c. de, en c. de,** in exchange for; instead of. **en c.,** instead, on the other hand. **c. de velocidad,** *Auto.* gear-changing. **letra de c.,** bill of exchange. **libre c.,** free trade
cambista /kam''βista/ *mf* money changer. *m,* banker
Camboya /kam'βoia/ Cambodia
Cambrige /kam'βrihe/ Cambridge
camelar /kame'lar/ *vt Inf.* to woo; seduce
camelia /ka'melia/ *f,* camelia. **c. japonesa,** japonica
camellero /kame'ʎero; kame'yero/ *m,* camel keeper or driver
camello /ka'meʎo; ka'meyo/ *m,* camel. **c. pardal,** giraffe
camellón /kame'ʎon; kame'yon/ *m,* furrow; drinking trough; *Mexico* island, traffic island, median strip
camelo /ka'melo/ *m, Inf.* eyewash
Camerún /kame'run/ Cameroon
camilla /ka'miʎa; ka'miya/ *f,* couch; small round skirted table with brazier underneath; stretcher, litter
camillero /kami'ʎero; kami'yero/ *m, Mil.* stretcher-bearer
caminador /kamina'ðor/ *a* in the habit of walking a great deal
caminante /kami'nante/ *mf* walker, traveler
caminar /kami'nar/ *vi* to travel; walk; *Fig.* move on, go (inanimate things). *Fig. Inf.* **c. derecho,** to walk uprightly
caminata /kami'nata/ *f,* long, tiring walk; excursion

caminejo /kami'neho/ *m,* worn path
camino /ka'mino/ *m,* road; route; journey; way, means; **c. de hierro,** railway. **c. de mesa,** table-runner. **c. de sirga,** towpath. **c. real,** highway, main road. **de c.,** on the way, in passing. **ponerse en c.,** to set out
camión /ka'mion/ *m,* truck. **c. de volteo, c. volquete** dump truck; *Mexico* bus
camioneta /kamio'neta/ *f,* light truck, pick-up truck; *West. Hem.* station wagon
camisa /ka'misa/ *f,* shirt, stiff shirt; thin skin (of fruit); sloughed skin of snakes; coat (of whitewash, etc.); *Mech.* jacket; mantle (gas). **c. de fuerza,** strait-jacket. **dejar sin c.,** *Inf.* to leave penniless
camisería /kamise'ria/ *f,* shirt shop or factory
camisero /kami'sero/ **(-ra)** *n* shirt maker or seller
camiseta /kami'seta/ *f,* vest, T-shirt. **c. de fútbol,** soccer player's jersey
camisola /kami'sola/ *f,* stiff shirt; ruffled shirt
camisón /kami'son/ *m,* large wide shirt; night shirt
camomila /kamo'mila/ *f,* chamomile
camorra /ka'morra/ *f, Inf.* brawl, shindy. **armar c.,** to start a row
campal /kam'pal/ *a* field, country
campamento /kampa'mento/ *m,* camping; *Mil.* encampment; camp; jamboree
campana /kam'pana/ *f,* bell; anything bell-shaped; church, parish. **c. de chimenea,** mantelpiece. **c. de hogar,** hood, shutter (of a fireplace)
campanada /kampa'naða/ *f,* peal of a bell; scandal
campanario /kampa'nario/ *m,* belfry, bell tower
campanear /kampane'ar/ *vi* to ring bells frequently
campaneo /kampa'neo/ *m,* bell-ringing; chime
campanero /kampa'nero/ *m,* bell-founder; bell ringer
campanil /kampa'nil/ *m,* small belfry, campanile
campanilla /kampa'niʎa; kampa'niya/ *f,* hand-bell; bubble; any bell-shaped flower
campanillazo /kampani'ʎaθo; kampani'yaso/ *m,* loud peal of a bell
campante /kam'pante/ *a* outstanding; *Inf.* proud, satisfied
campanudo /kampa'nuðo/ *a* bell-shaped; sonorous (of words); pompous (of speech)
campaña /kam'paɲa/ *f,* level country; campaign. *Naut.* voyage, cruise. **correr la c.,** to reconnoiter. **la C. del Desierto,** the War against the Gauchos (in Argentina)
campar /kam'par/ *vi* to camp. *Inf.* **c. por sus respetos,** to stand on one's own feet
campeador /kampea'ðor/ *a* mighty in battle
campear /kampe'ar/ *vi* to go out to graze; grow green (crops); excel; *Mil.* be engaged in a campaign, reconnoiter
campechano /kampe'tʃano/ *a Inf.* hearty; frank; cheerful; generous
campeche /kam'petʃe/ *m, Bot.* logwood
campeón /kampe'on/ *m,* champion; advocate, defender
campeonato /kampeo'nato/ *m,* championship
campesinado /kampesi'naðo/ *m,* peasantry
campesino /kampe'sino/ **(-na)** *a* rural, rustic —*n* country dweller
campestre /kam'pestre/ *a* rural
campiña /kam'piɲa/ *f,* expanse of cultivated land; countryside, landscape
campo /'kampo/ *m,* country (as opposed to urban areas); field; *Fig.* sphere, province; (*Phys. Herald. Mil.*) field; *Art.* ground; *Mil.* camp, army; plain ground (of silks, etc.). **«C. Abierto»,** "Miscellaneous" (e.g. as the title of a section in a book catalog). **c. de aterrizaje,** *Aer.* landing-field. **c. de batalla,** battlefield. **c. de concentración,** concentration camp. **c. de experimentación,** testing ground. **c. de golf,** golf course. **c. de prisioneros** *Mil.* prison camp. **c. de tiro,** rifle-range. **c. santo,** graveyard. **c. visual,** field of vision. **a c. abierto,** in the open air. **a c. travieso,** cross-country
camuflaje /kamu'flahe/ *m,* camouflage
camuflar /kamu'flar/ *vt* to camouflage
can /kan/ *m,* dog; trigger; *Archit.* modillion; *Astron.* Dog Star
cana /'kana/ *f,* gray hair
Canadá /kana'ða/ Canada
canadiense /kana'ðiense/ *a* and *mf* Canadian
canal /ka'nal/ *m,* canal. *mf, Geol.* subterranean waterway; channel; *Anat.* canal, duct; defile, narrow valley; gutter; drinking trough; animal carcass. **abrir en c.,** to open up, split open
Canal de la Mancha /ka'nal de la 'mantʃa/ English Channel
canalera /kana'lera/ *f,* roof gutter
canaleta /kana'leta/ *f,* (wooden) trough; gutter (on roof)
canalete /kana'lete/ *m,* paddle
canalización /kanaliθa'θion; kanalisa'sion/ *f,* canalization; *Elec.* main, mains; piping, tubing
canalizar /kanali'θar; kanali'sar/ *vt* to make canals or channels; regulate waters of rivers, etc.; canalize
canalla /ka'naʎa; ka'naya/ *f, Inf.* mob, rabble. *m, Inf.* scoundrel
canallesco /kana'ʎesko; kana'yesko/ *a* scoundrelly, knavish; despicable
canalón /kana'lon/ *m,* gutter, spout; shovel hat; pantile
canana /ka'nana/ *f,* cartridge belt
canapé /kana'pe/ *m,* sofa
Canarias, las Islas /ka'narias, las 'islas/ the Canary Islands
canario /ka'nario/ **(-ia)** *m,* canary —*a* and *n* pertaining to or native of the Canary Islands.
canasta /ka'nasta/ *f,* hamper, basket; card game
canastilla /kanas'tiʎa; kanas'tiya/ *f,* small basket; layette
canastillo /kanas'tiʎo; kanas'tiyo/ *m,* basket-work tray
cáncamo /'kankamo/ *m,* ring-bolt
cancamusa /kanka'musa/ *f, Inf.* trick, deception
cancel /kan'θel; kan'sel/ *m,* draftscreen; *Eccl.* screen
cancela /kan'θela; kan'sela/ *f,* wrought-iron door
cancelación /kanθela'θion; kansela'sion/ *f,* cancellation; expunging
cancelar /kanθe'lar; kanse'lar/ *vt* to cancel; expunge, annul; abolish, blot out; pay off, clear (a mortgage)
cancelaría /kanθe'laria; kanse'laria/ *f,* papal chancery
cancelario /kanθe'lario; kanse'lario/ *m,* chancellor (universities)
cáncer /'kanθer; 'kanser/ *m,* cancer
cancerar /kanθe'rar; kanse'rar/ *vt* to consume; weaken; mortify; —*vr* suffer from cancer; become cancerous
cancerbero /kanθer'βero; kanser'βero/ *m, Myth.* Cerberus; *Fig.* unbribable guard
canceroso /kanθe'roso; kanse'roso/ *a* cancerous
cancha /'kantʃa/ *f, Sports.* fronton; (tennis) court; cockpit; yard; hippodrome; widest part of a river; road; toasted maize
canciller /kanθi'ʎer; kansi'yer/ *m,* chancellor; foreign minister; assistant vice-consul
cancillería /kanθiʎe'ria; kansiye'ria/ *f,* chancellorship; chancellery; foreign ministry
canción /kan'θion; kan'sion/ *f,* song; lyric poem; musical accompaniment; old name for any poetical composition. **volver a la misma c.,** *Fig.* to be always harping on the same theme
cancionero /kanθio'nero; kansio'nero/ *m,* collection of songs and verses; songbook
cancionista /kanθio'nista; kansio'nista/ *mf* singer; song writer
candado /kan'daðo/ *m.* padlock; earring
candeal /kande'al/ *a* white (of bread)
candela /kan'dela/ *f,* candle; horse-chestnut flower; candlestick; *Inf.* fire. **en c.,** *Naut.* vertical (of masts, etc.)
candelabro /kande'laβro/ *m,* candelabrum
candelaria /kande'laria/ *f,* Candlemas
candelero /kande'lero/ *m,* candlestick; lamp; candle maker or seller; *Naut.* stanchion
candente /kan'dente/ *a* candescent, red-hot
candidatear /kandiðate'ar/ *vi* to run (for office)
candidato /kandi'ðato/ **(-ta)** *n* candidate
candidatura /kandiða'tura/ *f,* candidature
candidez /kandi'ðeθ; kandi'ðes/ *f,* simplicity, ingenuousness; candidness

cándido /'kandiðo/ *a* white; simple, ingenuous; candid, frank

candil /kan'dil/ *m,* oil lamp; Greek lamp; tips of stag's horns; *Inf.* cock of a hat

candileja /kandi'leha/ *f,* oil reservoir of lamp; *pl* footlights, floats

candor /kan'dor/ *m,* extreme whiteness; sincerity, candor; simplicity, innocence

candoroso /kando'roso/ *a* candid, open; simple, honest

canela /ka'nela/ *f, Bot.* cinnamon; *Fig.* anything exquisitely perfect

canelo /ka'nelo/ *m,* cinnamon tree —*a* cinnamon-colored

cangilón /kanhi'lon/ *m,* pitcher, jar; bucket (for water); dredging bucket

cangreja /kaŋ'greha/ *f, Naut.* gaffsail. **c. de mesana,** *Naut.* jigger

cangrejo /kaŋ'greho/ *m,* crab. **c. de mar,** sea-crab. **c. ermitaño,** hermit crab

canguro /kaŋ'guro/ *m,* kangaroo

caníbal /ka'niβal/ *a* and *mf* cannibal

canibalismo /kaniβa'lismo/ *m,* cannibalism

canica /ka'nika/ *f,* marble (for playing with)

canícula /ka'nikula/ *f,* dog days; *Astron.* Dog star

caniculares /kaniku'lares/ *m pl* dog days

canijo /ka'niho/ *a Inf.* delicate, sickly; anemic, stunted

canilla /ka'niʎa; ka'niya/ *f,* long bone of leg or arm; any principal bones in bird's wing; tap, faucet; spool, reel; fault (in cloth)

canino /ka'nino/ *a* canine

canje /'kanhe/ *m,* (diplomacy, *Mil.*, *Com.*) exchange, substitution. **c. de prisioneros,** exchange of prisoners

canjear /kanhe'ar/ *vt* to exchange

cano /'kano/ *a* white-haired, hoary; ancient; *Poet.* white

canoa /ka'noa/ *f,* canoe; launch. **c. automóvil,** motor launch

canódromo /ka'noðromo/ *m,* dog-race track

canoero /kano'ero/ **(-ra)** *n* canoeist

canon /'kanon/ *m,* rule; (*Eccl. Print.*) canon; catalog; part of the Mass; *Mus.* canon, catch; tax *pl* canon law

canonesa /kano'nesa/ *f,* canoness

canónico /ka'noniko/ *a* canonic, canonical

canónigo /ka'nonigo/ *m,* canon; prebendary

canonización /kanoniθa'θion; kanonisa'sion/ *f,* canonization

canonizar /kanoni'θar; kanoni'sar/ *vt* to canonize; extol, exalt; approve, acclaim

canonjía /kanon'hia/ *f,* canonry, canonship; *Inf.* sinecure

canoso /ka'noso/ *a* white-haired, hoary

cansado /kan'saðo/ **(-da)** *a* tired; weary; exhausted; decadent; tiresome; *Inf.* fed up —*n* bore, tedious person

cansancio /kan'sanθio; kan'sansio/ *m,* fatigue, weariness

cansar /kan'sar/ *vt* to tire, weary; *Agr.* exhaust soil; bore; badger, annoy; —*vr* be tired; grow weary

cansino /kan'sino/ *a* worn-out (of horses, etc.)

cantable /kan'taβle/ *a* singable; *Mus.* cantabile

cantábrico /kan'taβriko/ **(-ca)** *a* and *n* Cantabrian

cantante /kan'tante/ *a* singing. *mf* professional singer

cantar /kan'tar/ *vi* to sing; twitter, chirp; extol; *Inf.* squeak, creak; *Fig.* call (cards); *Inf.* squeal, confess. *m,* song. **C. de los Cantares,** Song of Songs. **cantar las claras,** to call a spade a spade

cántara /'kantara/ *f,* pitcher, jug

cantárida /kan'tariða/ *f,* Spanish fly

cántaro /'kantaro/ *m,* pitcher, jug; jugful; varying wine measure; ballot box; tax on spirits and oil

cantata /kan'tata/ *f,* cantata

cantatriz /kanta'triθ; kanta'tris/ *f,* singer, prima donna

cante /'kante/ *m,* song; singing

cantera /kan'tera/ *f, Mineral.* quarry; capacity, talent

cantería /kante'ria/ *f,* stone-cutting; quarrying; building made of hewn stone

cantero /kan'tero/ *m,* stone-cutter; quarryman

cántico /'kantiko/ *m, Eccl.* canticle; *Poet.* poem

cantidad /kanti'ðað/ *f,* quantity; large part; portion; sum of money; quantity (prosody). **c. llovida,** rainfall

cantiga /kan'tiga/ *or* **cántiga** /'kantiga/ *f,* old poetic form designed to be sung

cantil /kan'til/ *m,* cliff; steep rock

cantimplora /kantim'plora/ *f,* water cooler; canteen (of water); siphon

cantina /kan'tina/ *f,* wine cellar; canteen; refreshment room

cantinero /kanti'nero/ *m,* sutler; owner of a canteen

canto /'kanto/ *m,* singing; song; canto; epic or other poem; end, rim, edge; non-cutting edge (knives, swords); pebble, stone; angle (of a building). *Mus.* **c. llano,** plain-song. **al c. del gallo,** at cockcrow. **de c.,** on edge

cantón /kan'ton/ *m,* province, region; corner (of a street); cantonment; *Herald.* canton, quartering

cantonera /kanto'nera/ *f,* corner-piece (books, furniture, etc., as ornament); angle-iron; bracket, small shelf

cantor /kan'tor/ **(-ra)** *a* singing —*n* singer; song-bird

Cantórbery /kan'torβeri/ Canterbury

canturía /kantu'ria/ *f,* singing exercise; vocal music; monotonous song; droning; *Mus.* execution, technique

canturreo, /kantu'rreo,/ *m,* **canturria** *f,* humming; droning

canturriar /kantu'rriar/ *vi Inf.* to hum, sing under one's breath

caña /'kaɲa/ *f,* stalk; reed; bone of arm or leg; leg (of a trouser, stocking, boot, etc.); marrow; *Bot.* cane; tumbler, glass; wine measure; gallery (of mine); *pl* mock joust on horseback using **cañas** as spears. **c. de azúcar,** sugar-cane. **c. de pescar,** fishing rod. **c. del timón,** tiller *Naut.*

cañada /ka'ɲaða/ *f,* glen, gulch, gully, hollow, ravine, vale, cattle path; *West. Hem.* brook, cattle track

cañal /ka'ɲal/ *m,* cane-break; weir (for fish)

cañamazo /kaɲa'maθo; kaɲa'maso/ *m,* hempen canvas; embroidery canvas; embroidered canvas

cañamelar /kaɲame'lar/ *m,* sugar-cane plantation

cáñamo /'kaɲamo/ *m,* hemp

cañamón /kaɲa'mon/ *m,* hemp-seed

cañar /ka'ɲar/ *m,* canebrake; growth of reeds; fish-garth made of reeds

cañavalera /kaɲaβa'lera/ *f,* canefield

cañaveral /kaɲaβe'ral/ *m,* cane-brake; *West Hem.* bamboo field

cañazo /ka'ɲaθo; ka'ɲaso/ *m,* blow with a cane

cañería /kaɲe'ria/ *f,* conduit; pipe; piping

cañero /ka'ɲero/ *m,* pipe layer

caño /'kaɲo/ *m,* pipe, tube, sewer; organ pipe; jet (of water); mine gallery

cañón /ka'ɲon/ *m,* pipe, cylindrical tube; flue; quill (of birds); cannon; soft down; *Archit.* shaft (of column); stack (of a chimney). **c. antiaéreo,** A.A. gun. **c. antitanque,** anti-tank gun. **c. de escalera,** well of a staircase; *Slang.* terrific-looking, absolutely gorgeous (e.g. mujer cañón)

cañonazo /kaɲo'naθo; kaɲo'naso/ *m,* cannon shot; roar of a cannon

cañonear /kaɲone'ar/ *vt* to bombard

cañoneo /kaɲo'neo/ *m,* cannonade; bombardment

cañonera /kaɲo'nera/ *f,* embrasure (for cannon)

cañonería /kaɲone'ria/ *f, Mil.* group of cannon; *Mus.* set of organ pipes

cañonero /kaɲo'nero/ *m,* gunboat

cañuto /ka'ɲuto/ *m, Bot.* internode; small pipe or tube; *Inf.* tale-bearer

caoba /ka'oβa/ *f, Bot.* mahogany

caos /'kaos/ *m,* chaos; confusion

caótico /ka'otiko/ *a* chaotic

capa /'kapa/ *f,* cloak; cape; *Eccl.* cope; coating; layer; cover; coat (animals); *Fig.* cloak, disguise; *Geol.* stratum. **la c. del cielo,** the canopy of heaven. *Fig. Inf.* **echar la c. al toro,** to throw one's cap over the windmill. *Naut.* **estarse** (*or* **ponerse**) **a la c.,** to lie to

capacete /kapa'θete; kapa'sete/ *m,* helmet

capacidad /kapaθi'ðað; kapasi'ðað/ *f,* capacity; extension, space; mental capacity, talent; opportunity,

means; *Law.* capacity. **c. de compra,** buying power, purchasing power. **c. de producción,** output
capacitación /kapaθita'θion; kapasita'sion/ *f,* qualification, (act of) qualifying; (act of) training
capacitar /kapaθi'tar; kapasi'tar/ *vt* to capacitate, qualify, enable
capadura /kapa'ðura/ *f,* castration
capar /ka'par/ *vt* to castrate, geld; *Inf.* diminish, reduce
caparazón /kapara'θon; kapara'son/ *m,* caparison, horse blanket; waterproof cover; hood (of carriages); nosebag; shell (insects, crustaceans)
capataz /kapa'taθ; kapa'tas/ *m,* foreman; steward; overseer
capaz /ka'paθ; ka'pas/ *a* capacious; large, spacious; capable, competent; *Law.* able
capcioso /kap'θioso; kap'sioso/ *a* deceitful, artful; captious, carping
capear /kape'ar/ *vt* to steal a cape; play the bull with a cape (bullfighting); *Inf.* put off with excuses, deceive; *Naut.* lie to
capellán /kape'ʎan; kape'yan/ *m,* chaplain; any ecclesiastic
capellanía /kapeʎa'nia; kapeya'nia/ *f,* chaplaincy
capelo /ka'pelo/ *m,* cardinal's hat; cardinalate
capeo /ka'peo/ *m,* playing the bull with a cape (bullfighting)
caperuza /kape'ruθa; kape'rusa/ *f,* hood, pointed cap; *Archit.* coping-stone
capigorrón /kapigo'rron/ *a Inf.* loafing. *m,* loafer, idler
capilar /kapi'lar/ *a* capillary
capilaridad /kapilari'ðað/ *f,* capillarity
capilla /ka'piʎa; ka'piya/ *f,* cowl, hood; chapel; *Eccl.* chapter; *Eccl.* choir. **c. ardiente,** chapelle ardente. **estar en c.,** to await execution (criminals); *Inf.* be in suspense, await anxiously
capillero /kapi'ʎero; kapi'yero/ *m,* sexton; churchwarden
capillo /ka'piʎo; ka'piyo/ *m,* baby's bonnet; cocoon of silkworm; flowerbud
capirotazo /kapiro'taθo; kapiro'taso/ *m,* box on the ear; fillip
capirote /kapi'rote/ *m,* academic hood and cap; hood (falconry); tall pointed cap. **ser tonto de c.,** *Inf.* to be a complete fool
capitación /kapita'θion; kapita'sion/ *f,* poll-tax, capitation
capital /kapi'tal/ *a* relating to the head; capital (sins, etc.); main, principal. *m,* capital, patrimony; *Com.* capital stock. *f,* capital (city). **c. pagado,** paid-in capital stock
capitalismo /kapita'lismo/ *m,* capitalism
capitalista /kapita'lista/ *a* capitalistic. *mf* capitalist
capitalización /kapitaliθa'θion; kapitalisa'sion/ *f,* capitalization
capitalizar /kapitali'θar; kapitali'sar/ *vt* to capitalize
capitán /kapi'tan/ *m,* captain, skipper; chief, leader; ringleader. *Aer.* **c. de aviación,** group captain. **c. de fragata,** *Nav.* commander. **c. de puerto,** harbor master. **c. general de ejército,** field-marshal
capitana /kapi'tana/ *f,* admiral's ship; *Inf.* captain's wife
capitanear /kapitane'ar/ *vt* to captain, command; *Fig.* guide, lead
capitanía /kapita'nia/ *f,* captaincy; captainship
capitel /kapi'tel/ *m, Archit.* capital
capitolio /kapi'tolio/ *m,* dignified building; *Archit.* acropolis; Capitol
capitulación /kapitula'θion; kapitula'sion/ *f,* agreement, pact; capitulation; *pl* marriage articles
capitular /kapitu'lar/ *a* capitulary, belonging to a Chapter. *m,* capitular, member of a Chapter —*vi* to make an agreement; capitulate; sing prayers; arrange order
capítulo /ka'pitulo/ *m, Eccl.* Chapter; meeting of town council, etc.; chapter (of book); item (in a budget); determination, decision
capó /ka'po/ *m, Auto.* hood
capón /ka'pon/ *a* castrated; gelded. *m,* capon; bundle of firewood or vines
caponera /kapo'nera/ *f,* coop for fattening capons; *Inf.* gaol; *Inf.* place where one lives well free of charge
capota /ka'pota/ *f, Bot.* head of teasel; bonnet; hood (of vehicles)
capote /ka'pote/ *m,* short, brightly colored cape (used by bullfighters); cape coat; (cards) slam; *Inf.* scowl
capricho /ka'pritʃo/ *m,* caprice, fancy; strong desire
caprichoso /kapri'tʃoso/ *a* capricious; whimsical
caprichudo /kapri'tʃuðo/ *a* headstrong; capricious
Capricornio /kapri'kornio/ *m,* Capricorn
cápsula /'kapsula/ *f,* cartridge-case; bottlecap; (*Bot. Med. Chem. Zool.*) capsule
captar /kap'tar/ *vt* gain, attract (goodwill, attention, etc.); *Mech.* collect; monitor (foreign broadcasts)
captor /kap'tor/ *m,* capturer
captura /kap'tura/ *f, Law.* capture; seizing, arrest
capturar /kaptu'rar/ *vt* to capture; arrest, apprehend
capucha /ka'putʃa/ *f,* hood; cowl; *Print.* circumflex accent
capuchina /kapu'tʃina/ *f,* Capuchin nun; *Bot.* nasturtium; table-lamp with an extinguisher
capuchino /kapu'tʃino/ **(-na)** *a* and *n* Capuchin
capucho /ka'putʃo/ *m,* cowl
capullo /ka'puʎo; ka'puyo/ *m,* cocoon; flower bud; acorn cup; *Anat.* prepuce
caqui /'kaki/ *m,* khaki; khaki color
cara /'kara/ *f,* face; likeness, aspect; façade, front; surface; side (of metal, etc.); mien. **c. a c.,** face to face; frankly; openly. *Inf.* **c. de juez,** severe face. *Inf.* **c. de pascua,** smiling face. *Inf.* **c. de vinagre,** sour face. **c. o cruz,** heads or tails. **de c.,** opposite. **hacer a dos caras,** to be deceitful, be two-faced. **hacer c.(a),** to stand up to
caraba /ka'raβa/ *f, Slang.* 25-centimo coin
cárabe /'karaβe/ *m,* amber
carabina /kara'βina/ *f,* carbine; rifle
carabinazo /karaβi'naθo; karaβi'naso/ *m,* report of a carbine
carabinero /karaβi'nero/ *m,* carabineer; customs' guard, revenue guard; customs officer, customs official
caracol /kara'kol/ *m,* snail; snail's shell; cure; *Zool.* cochlea; winding stair. **c. marino,** periwinkle. **¡Caracoles!** Fancy!
caracola /kara'kola/ *f,* conch shell used as a horn
caracolear /karakole'ar/ *vi* to prance from side to side (horses)
carácter /ka'rakter/ *m,* sign, mark; character, writing (gen. *pl*); style of writing; brand (animals); nature, temperament; character, individuality, strong-mindedness, energy, firmness; condition, state, capacity. **comedia de c.,** psychological play. **en su c. de,** as in one's capacity as. **caracteres de imprenta,** printing types
característica /karakte'ristika/ *f,* quality, characteristic; *Math.* characteristic; actress who plays the part of an old woman
característico /karakte'ristiko/ *a* characteristic, distinctive. *m,* actor who plays roles of old men
caracterización /karakteriθa'θion; karakterisa'sion/ *f,* characterization; *Theat.* make-up
caracterizar /karakteri'θar; karakteri'sar/ *vt* to characterize; confer an office, honor, dignity, on; *Theat.* create a character; —*vr Theat.* to make up, dress as, a character
caraísmo /kara'ismo/ *m,* Karaism
caraíta /kara'ita/ *a* and *mf* Karaite
¡caramba! /ka'ramba/ *interj* gosh!; blast!
carámbano /ka'rambano/ *m,* icicle
carambola /karam'βola/ *f,* cannon (billiards); *Inf.* double effect; *Inf.* trick, deception
caramelo /kara'melo/ *m,* caramel; toffee
caramillo /kara'miʎo; kara'miyo/ *m,* flageolet; small flute, pipe; gossip, intrigue
carantamaula /karanta'maula/ *f, Inf.* hideous mask; ugly person
carapacho /kara'patʃo/ *m,* carapace, shell
carátula /ka'ratula/ *f,* mask; *Fig.* dramatic art, the theater
caravana /kara'βana/ *f,* caravan, group of traders, pil-

grims, etc. (especially in East); *Inf.* crowd of excursionists, picnickers, etc.

¡caray! /ka'rai/ *interj* blast!; gosh!

carbólico /kar'βoliko/ *a* carbolic

carbón /kar'βon/ *m,* coal; charcoal; black chalk, crayon. **c. bituminoso,** soft coal. **c. de coque,** coke. **c. de leña,** charcoal. **c. mineral,** coal, anthracite. **mina de c.,** coal-mine

carboncillo /karβon'θiʎo; karβon'siyo/ *m,* charcoal crayon

carbonear /karβone'ar/ *vt* to turn into charcoal; *Naut.* coal

carboneo /karβo'neo/ *m,* coaling

carbonera /karβo'nera/ *f,* coal-cellar, coal-house, etc.; coal-scuttle; woman who sells charcoal or coal; charcoal burner

carbonería /karβone'ria/ *f,* coal or charcoal merchant's office

carbonero /karβo'nero/ *a* relating to coal or charcoal. *m,* collier; charcoal maker; coal merchant; *Naut.* coal-ship

carbónico /kar'βoniko/ *a Chem.* carbonic

carbonífero /karβo'nifero/ *a* carboniferous

carbonizar /karβoni'θar; karβoni'sar/ *vt* to carbonize

carbono /kar'βono/ *m, Chem.* carbon

carbonoso /karβo'noso/ *a* carbonaceous; coaly

carbunco /kar'βunko/ *m, Med.* carbuncle

carbúnculo /kar'βunkulo/ *m,* carbuncle, ruby

carburador /karβura'ðor/ *m,* carburetor

carcaj /kar'kah/ *m,* quiver (for arrows)

carcajada /karka'haða/ *f,* burst of laughter, guffaw. **reírse a carcajadas,** to roar with laughter

carcajearse /karkahe'arse/ *vi* to guffaw

carcamal /karka'mal/ *m, Inf.* dotard

cárcel /'karθel; 'karsel/ *f,* prison, jail

carcelario /karθe'lario; karse'lario/ *a* prison, jail

carcelero /karθe'lero; karse'lero/ **(-ra)** *a* jail —*n* jailer

cárcola /'karkola/ *f,* treadle (of a loom)

carcoma /kar'koma/ *f,* wood-worm; dry rot; *Fig.* gnawing care; spendthrift

carcomer /karko'mer/ *vt* to gnaw wood (worms); *Fig.* undermine (health, etc.); —*vr* be worm-eaten

carda /'karða/ *f,* card, carding; teasel head; card brush; *Inf.* reprimand

cardador /karða'ðor/ **(-ra)** *n* carder, comber

cardadura /karða'ðura/ *f,* carding; carding frame

cardar /kar'ðar/ *vt* to card, tease; brush up (felt, etc.)

cardenal /karðe'nal/ *m,* cardinal; cardinal bird; bruise

cardenalato /karðena'lato/ *m,* cardinalate, cardinalship

cardenillo /karðe'niʎo; karðe'niyo/ *m,* verdigris; *Art.* verditer

cárdeno /'karðeno/ *a* livid

cardíaco /kar'ðiako/ *a Med.* cardiac

cardinal /karði'nal/ *a* principal; cardinal (point); *Gram.* cardinal (number)

cardiógrafo /kar'ðiografo/ *m, Med.* cardiograph

cardiograma /karðio'grama/ *m, Med.* cardiogram

cardizal /karði'θal; karði'sal/ *m,* waste land covered with thistles and weeds

cardo /'karðo/ *m, Bot.* thistle

carear /kare'ar/ *vt* to confront; compare; —*vi* turn towards, face; —*vr* meet; come together

carecer /kare'θer; kare'ser/ *vi irr* to be short; lack, need (e.g. *Carece de las condiciones necesarias,* It lacks the necessary conditions). See **conocer**

carena /ka'rena/ *f, Naut.* bottom; careening

carenar /kare'nar/ *vt* to careen

carencia /ka'renθia; ka'rensia/ *f,* shortage, lack

carestía /kares'tia/ *f,* shortage, scarcity; famine; dearness, high price

careta /ka'reta/ *f,* mask; beekeeper's veil; fencing mask. *Fig.* **quitar la c. (a),** to unmask

carey /ka'rei/ *m, Zool.* shell turtle; tortoise-shell

carga /'karga/ *f,* loading; *Elec.* charging, charge; load; burden, weight; cargo; explosive charge; *Fig.* imposition; tax; duty, obligation. *Naut.* **c. de profundidad,** depth charge

cargadero /karga'ðero/ *m,* place where goods are loaded or unloaded

cargado /kar'gaðo/ *a* loaded; heavy, sultry; strong (tea, coffee). **c. de cadenas,** (prisoner, etc.) in chains. **c. de espaldas,** round-shouldered

cargador /karga'ðor/ *m,* loader; porter; dockhand; pitchfork; rammer; *Mech.* stoker; *Elec.* charger

cargamento /karga'mento/ *m, Naut.* cargo, freight, shipload

cargar /kar'gar/ *vt* to load; charge (guns, etc.); stoke; overburden; tax, impose; blame for, charge with; *Inf.* annoy, bore; *Argentina Inf.* to kid, tease; *Com.* charge, book; *Mil.* attack; (football) tackle; —*vi* tip, slope; (*with con*) carry away; be loaded with (fruit); assume responsibility; (*with sobre*) importune, urge; lean against; —*vr* turn (head, etc.); lower, grow darker (sky); (*with de*) be abundant (in or with); load oneself with

cargazón /karga'θon; karga'son/ *f,* cargo; loading; heaviness; darkness (of the sky)

cargo /'kargo/ *m,* loading; load, weight; post, office; duty, obligation; management, charge; care; *Com.* debit; accusation. *Com.* **el c. y la data,** debit and credit. **hacerse c. de,** to take charge of; understand; consider carefully. **ser en c. (a),** to be debtor (to)

cariacontecido /kariakonte'θiðo; kariakonte'siðo/ *a* crestfallen, disappointed; glum

cariancho /kari'antʃo/ *a Inf.* broadfaced

cariarse /ka'riarse/ *vr* to become carious

cariátide /kari'atiðe/ *f, Archit.* caryatid

caribe /ka'riβe/ *a* Caribbean. *mf* cannibal, savage

caricatura /karika'tura/ *f,* caricature

caricaturesco /karikatu'resko/ *a* caricaturish

caricaturista /karikatu'rista/ *mf* caricaturist

caricaturizar /karikaturi'θar; karikaturi'sar/ *vt* to caricature

caricia /ka'riθia; ka'risia/ *f,* caress

caridad /kari'ðað/ *f,* charity; charitableness; alms

caries /'karies/ *f,* caries

carilargo /kari'largo/ *a Inf.* long-faced

carilla /ka'riʎa; ka'riya/ *f, dim* small face; mask; page (of a book)

carilleno /kari'ʎeno; kari'yeno/ *a Inf.* plump-faced, round-faced

carillón /kari'ʎon; kari'yon/ *m,* peal (of bells)

cariño /ka'riɲo/ *m,* affection; love; caress affectionately (gen. *pl*); fondness, inclination. **con c.,** affectionately

cariñoso /kari'ɲoso/ *a* affectionate; loving; kind

carirredondo /karirre'ðondo/ *a Inf.* roundfaced

carismático /karis'matiko/ *a* charismatic

caritativo /karita'tiβo/ *a* charitable

cariz /ka'riθ; ka'ris/ *m,* appearance of the sky; look, face; aspect; *Inf.* outlook (for a business deal, etc.)

carlista /kar'lista/ *a* and *mf* Carlist

carmelita /karme'lita/ *a* and *mf* Carmelite

carmen /'karmen/ *m,* country house and garden (Granada); song; poem

carmesí /karme'si/ *a* crimson. *m,* crimson color; cramoisy

carmín /kar'min/ *m,* red, carmine color; red wild rose-tree and flower

carnada /kar'naða/ *f,* bait

carnaje /kar'nahe/ *m,* salted meat

carnal /kar'nal/ *a* carnal; lascivious; materialistic, worldly; related by blood

carnalidad /karnali'ðað/ *f,* carnality

carnaval /karna'βal/ *m,* carnival. **martes de c.,** Shrove Tuesday

carnavalesco /karnaβa'lesko/ *a* carnival

carne /'karne/ *f,* flesh; meat; pulpy part of fruit; carnality, **c. concentrada,** meat extract. **c. congelada,** frozen meat. **c. de gallina** *Fig.* gooseflesh. **c. de membrillo,** quince cheese or conserve. **c. y hueso,** *Fig.* flesh and blood. *Inf.* **cobrar carnes,** to put on weight. **poner toda la c. en el asador,** *Inf.* to put all one's eggs in one basket

carnerada /karne'raða/ *f,* flock of sheep

carnerero /karne'rero/ **(-ra)** *n* shepherd

carnero /kar'nero/ *m,* sheep; mutton; mortuary; charnel-house; family burial vault. **c. marino,** *Zool.* seal

carnestolendas /karnesto'lendas/ *f pl* three days of carnival before Ash Wednesday
carnet /kar'net/ *m*, notebook, diary; identity card; membership card, pass. **c. de chófer,** driving license
carnicería /karniθe'ria; karnise'ria/ *f*, butcher's shop; carnage, slaughter
carnicero /karni'θero; karni'sero/ *a* carnivorous; inhuman, cruel. *m*, butcher
carnívoro /kar'niβoro/ *a* carnivorous. *m*, carnivore
carnosidad /karnosi'ðað/ *f*, proud flesh; local fat; fatness
carnoso /kar'noso/ *a* meaty; fleshy; full of marrow; *Bot.* pulpy, juicy
caro /'karo/ *a* beloved; expensive; dear —*adv* expensively; dear
carolingio /karo'linhio/ **(-ia)** *a* and *n* Carolingian
carótida /ka'rotiða/ *f*, carotid artery
carpa /'karpa/ *f*, *Ichth.* carp. **c. dorada,** goldfish
carpanta /kar'panta/ *f*, *Inf.* violent hunger
Cárpatos, los Montes /'karpatos, los 'montes/ the Carpathian Mountains
carpeta /kar'peta/ *f*, table or chest cover, doily; writing case; portfolio; docket, letter file
carpetazo, dar /karpe'taθo, dar; karpe'taso, dar/ *vt* to shelve (a project, etc.)
carpintear /karpinte'ar/ *vi* to carpenter
carpintería /karpinte'ria/ *f*, carpenter's shop; carpentry
carpinteril /karpinte'ril/ *a* carpentering
carpintero /karpin'tero/ *m*, carpenter, joiner; *Theat.* scene-shifter. **c. de carretas,** wheelwright. **c. de ribera,** shipwright
carraca /ka'rraka/ *f*, rattle; ratchet-drill
Carrapempe /karra'pempe/ *m*, Old Nick
carrascal /karras'kal/ *m*, field of pinoaks
carraspear /karraspe'ar/ *vi* to clear one's throat, cough
carraspera /karras'pera/ *f*, *Inf.* hoarseness
carraspique /karras'pike/ *m*, *Bot.* candytuft
carrera /ka'rrera/ *f*, run; race; racing; racecourse; *Astron.* course; high road; route; *Mas.* layer, course; line, row; *Fig.* ladder (in stockings, etc.); course; duration (of life); career, profession; conduct; girder. **c. de fondo,** long-distance race. **c. de relevos, c. de equipos,** relay race. **a c. abierta, a c. tendida,** at full speed
carrerista /karre'rista/ *mf* racing enthusiast; professional racer
carreta /ka'rreta/ *f*, long, narrow two-wheeled cart; wagon; tumbril
carretada /karre'taða/ *f*, cart-load; *Inf.* great deal, mass
carretaje /karre'tahe/ *m*, cartage; carriage, transport
carrete /ka'rrete/ *m*, spool, reel, bobbin; fishing reel; *Elec.* coil; *Photo.* film spool
carretear /karrete'ar/ *vt* to cart; drive a cart
carretela /karre'tela/ *f*, calash
carretera /karre'tera/ *f*, high road
carretería /karrete'ria/ *f*, number of carts; carting trade; cartwright's yard
carretero /karre'tero/ *m*, cartwright; carter, driver
carretilla /karre'tiʎa; karre'tiya/ *f*, wheelbarrow; hand cart; railway truck; squib. **de c.,** *Inf.* mechanically, without thought; (*with saber, repetir,* etc.) by rote
carretón /karre'ton/ *m*, truck, trolley; hand cart
carril /ka'rril/ *m*, wheel mark; furrow, rut; cart road, narrow road; rail (railways, etc.)
carrillera /karri'ʎera; karri'yera/ *f*, jaw (of some animals); chin strap; *pl* bonnet strings, etc.
carrillo /ka'rriʎo; ka'rriyo/ *m*, cheek; jowl
carriola /ka'rriola/ *f*, truckle bed; curricle
carro /'karro/ *m*, cart; cartload; car, chariot; carriage (of a typewriter, etc.); chassis; *Astron.* Plow, Great Bear. *Mil.* **c. blindado,** armored car. *Mil.* **c. de asalto,** tank. **c. de mudanzas,** moving van. **c. de regar,** watercart
carrocería /karroθe'ria; karrose'ria/ *f*, place where carriages are made, sold, repaired; *Auto.* coachwork, body shop
carrocha /ka'rrotʃa/ *f*, eggs (of insects)
carrochar /karro'tʃar/ *vi* to lay eggs (insects)
carromato /karro'mato/ *m*, road wagon; covered wagon
carroña /ka'rroɲa/ *f*, putrid flesh, carrion
carroza /ka'rroθa; ka'rrosa/ *f*, elegant coach; state coach; carriage; float (for tableaux, etc.); *Naut.* awning
carruaje /ka'rruahe/ *m*, carriage; any vehicle
carta /'karta/ *f*, letter; charter; royal order; playing card; chart, map. **c. certificada,** registered letter. **c. de amparo,** safe-conduct. **c. de crédito,** *Com.* letter of credit. **c. de marear,** sea chart. **c. de naturaleza,** naturalization papers. **c. de pésame,** letter of condolence. **c. de venta,** *Com.* bill of sale. **c. ejecutoria de hidalguía,** letters patent of nobility. **carta-poder,** letter of proxy, proxy. **cartas rusas,** (game of) consequences. **poner las cartas boca arriba,** *Fig.* to lay one's cards on the table
cartabón /karta'βon/ *m*, set-square; shoemaker's slide; quadrant
cartaginés /kartahi'nes/ **(-esa)** *a* and *n* Carthaginian
Cartago /'kartago/ Carthage
cartapacio /karta'paθio; karta'pasio/ *m*, note-book; schoolbag, satchel; file, batch of papers
cartear /karte'ar/ *vi Cards.* to play low; —*vr* to correspond by letter
cartel /kar'tel/ *m*, placard, poster; cartel; pasquinade, lampoon. **fijar carteles,** to placard
cartela /kar'tela/ *f*, tablet (for writing); slip (of paper, etc.); *Archit.* console, bracket
cartelera /karte'lera/ *f*, billboard
cartelero /karte'lero/ *m*, billpaster, billsticker
carteo /kar'teo/ *m*, correspondence (by letter)
cartera /kar'tera/ *f*, pocketbook; wallet; dispatch-case; portfolio; notebook; pocket flap; office of a cabinet minister; *Com.* shares
cartería /karte'ria/ *f*, sorting room (in a post-office)
carterista /karte'rista/ *mf* pickpocket
cartero /kar'tero/ *m*, mail carrier, postman
cartesiano /karte'siano/ **(-na)** *a* and *n* Cartesian
Cartesio /kar'tesio/ Descartes
carteta /kar'teta/ *f*, lansquenet (card game)
cartilaginoso /kartilahi'noso/ *a* cartilaginous
cartílago /kar'tilago/ *m*, cartilage
cartilla /kar'tiʎa; kar'tiya/ *f*, first reading book; primer; certificate of ordination; note-book; liturgical calendar. **c. de racionamiento,** ration book
cartografía /kartogra'fia/ *f*, cartography
cartógrafo /kar'tografo/ *m*, map maker
cartón /kar'ton/ *m*, pasteboard, cardboard; *Archit.* bracket; *Art.* cartoon, design
cartuchera /kartu'tʃera/ *f*, cartridge-pouch; cartridge-belt
cartucho /kar'tutʃo/ *m*, cartridge; paper cone
cartuja /kar'tuha/ *f*, Carthusian Order or monastery
cartujano /kartu'hano/ *a* Carthusian
cartujo /kar'tuho/ *m*, Carthusian monk; *Inf.* taciturn, reserved man
cartulina /kartu'lina/ *f*, Bristol board, oaktag, pasteboard, card
carúncula /ka'runkula/ *f*, caruncle, comb of cock, etc.
casa /'kasa/ *f*, house; home; household; residence, dwelling; family house; *Com.* firm. **c. consistorial,** town hall. **c. cuna,** crèche. **c. de campo,** country-house. **c. de empeño,** pawnshop. **c. de huéspedes,** boarding house, lodging-house. **c. de los sustos,** haunted house (at amusement park). **c. de moneda,** mint. **c. de socorro,** First Aid Post. **c. de vecindad,** tenement. **c. mala,** house of ill repute. **c. solar** *or* **c. solariega,** family seat. **en c.,** at home (also sport usage). **poner c.,** to set up house
casaca /ka'saka/ *f*, dress coat. **volver la c.,** to become a turncoat, change one's allegiance
casación /kasa'θion; kasa'sion/ *f*, *Law.* cassation
casadero /kasa'ðero/ *a* marriageable
casadoro /kasa'ðoro/ *m*, *Costa Rica* bus
casamata /kasa'mata/ *f*, *Mil.* casemate
casamiento /kasa'miento/ *m*, marriage; wedding
casar /ka'sar/ *vt* to marry (of a priest); *Law.* repeal; *Inf.* marry off; join; match, harmonize; —*vi* and *vr* (*with con*) to get married

casar /ka'sar/ *m,* group of houses

casca /'kaska/ *f,* grape skin; tan (bark); shell, peel, rind

cascabel /kaska'βel/ *m,* small bell (for harness, etc.). **serpiente de c.,** rattlesnake. *Inf.* **ser un c.,** to be feather-brained

cascabeleo /kaska'βeleo/ *m,* jingling of bells

cascabillo /kaska'βiʎo; kaska'βiyo/ *m,* husk (of cereals)

cascada /kas'kaða/ *f,* cascade; waterfall

cascadura /kaska'ðura/ *f,* cracking, crack

cascajo /kas'kaho/ *m,* gravel, shingle; *Inf.* broken, old things, junk; nuts

cascanueces /kaska'nueθes; kaska'nueses/ *m,* nutcrackers

cascar /kas'kar/ *vt* to crack, split, break; *Inf.* beat; *Fig. Inf.* break down (of health); —*vi Inf.* talk, chatter

cáscara /'kaskara/ *f,* shell; peel, rind; bark. *Med.* **c. sagrada,** cascara

cascarón /kaska'ron/ *m,* eggshell; *Archit.* vault

cascarrabias /kaska'rraβias/ *mf Inf.* spitfire

casco /'kasko/ *m,* cranium; broken fragment of china, glass, etc.; crown of hat; helmet; tree of saddle; bottle; tank, pipe; barrel; *Naut.* hull; hoof; quarter (of fruit), *pl Inf.* head. **c. colonial,** sun-helmet. **c. respiratorio,** smoke-helmet

cascote /kas'kote/ *m,* rubble, ruins

caseoso /kase'oso/ *a* cheesy

caserío /kase'rio/ *m,* group of houses; country house

casero /ka'sero/ *a* home made; home bred; familiar; informa; *Inf.* domesticated, home-loving; domestic. *m, landlord;* caretaker; tenant

caserón /kase'ron/ *m,* large tumbledown house, mansion, hall

caseta /ka'seta/ *f,* hut; cottage; booth, stall. **c. de baños,** bathing van

casi /'kasi/ *adv* almost, nearly. **c. c.,** very nearly

casilla /ka'siʎa; ka'siya/ *f,* hut; cabin; lodge; ticket office; pigeon-hole. *Aer.* **c. del piloto,** cockpit

casillero /kasi'ʎero; kasi'yero/ *m,* file cabinet, filing cabinet; locker (as in a locker room); set of pigeonholes; *Sports.* scoreboard; *Rail.* crossing guard

casino /ka'sino/ *m,* casino; club

caso /'kaso/ *m,* happening, event; chance, hazard; occasion, opportunity; case, matter; (*Med. Gram.*) case. **en el c. de,** in a position to (e.g. *No estamos en el c. de pagar tanto dinero.* We are in no position to pay so much money). **en tal c.,** in such a case. **en todo c.,** in any case. **no hacer c. de,** to take no notice of. **venir al c.,** to be opportune

caspa /'kaspa/ *f,* dandruff; scab

caspio /'kaspio/ *a* Caspian

¡cáspita! /'kaspita/ *interj* Amazing! Wonderful!

casquete /kas'kete/ *m,* helmet; skullcap; half wig

casquijo /kas'kiho/ *m,* gravel

casquillo /kas'kiʎo; kas'kiyo/ *m,* tip, cap, ferrule; socket; arrow-head; metal cartridge-case

casquivano /kaski'βano/ *a Inf.* giddy, feather-brained

casta /'kasta/ *f,* race; caste; breed (animals); kind, species, quality. **de buena c.,** pedigree (e.g. *perros de buena c.,* pedigree dogs)

castaña /kas'taɲa/ *f, Bot.* chestnut; knot, bun (of hair)

castañar /kasta'ɲar/ *m,* chestnut plantation or grove

castañetear /kastaɲete'ar/ *vi* to play the castanets; snap one's fingers; chatter (of teeth); knock together (of knees)

castaño /kas'taɲo/ *a* chestnut-colored. *m,* chestnut tree; chestnut wood. **c. de Indias,** horse-chestnut tree

castañuela /kasta'ɲuela/ *f,* castanet. **tocar las castañuelas,** to play the castanets

castellán /kaste'ʎan; kaste'yan/ *m,* castellan

castellano /kaste'ʎano; kaste'yano/ **(-na)** *n* Castilian; Spaniard. *m,* Spanish (language); castellan —*a* Castilian; Spanish

casticismo /kasti'θismo; kasti'sismo/ *m,* purity (of language); Spanish spirit; traditionalism

castidad /kasti'ðað/ *f,* chastity

castigador /kastiga'ðor/ *a* punishing. *m,* punisher; *Inf.* lady-killer

castigadora /kastiga'ðora/ *f, Inf.* man-hunter

castigar /kasti'gar/ *vt* to punish; chastise; chasten, advise; pain, grieve; correct, edit; decrease (expenses); *Com.* allow a discount

castigo /kas'tigo/ *m,* punishment; emendation, correction

Castilla /kas'tiʎa; kas'tiya/ Castile

castillo /kas'tiʎo; kas'tiyo/ *m,* castle; howdah. **c. de naipes,** house of cards. **c. de proa,** *Naut.* forecastle. **c. fuerte,** fortified castle. *Inf.* **hacer castillos en el aire,** to build castles in the air or in Spain

castizo /kas'tiθo; kas'tiso/ *a* pure-blooded; prolific; pure (of language); typically Spanish; traditional

casto /'kasto/ *a* chaste; pure, unsullied

castor /kas'tor/ *m, Zool.* beaver (animal and fur); soft, woollen cloth

castración /kastra'θion; kastra'sion/ *f,* castration, gelding

castrado /kas'traðo/ *a* castrated. *m, Inf.* eunuch

castrador /kastra'ðor/ *m,* castrator, gelder

castrapo /kas'trapo/ *m,* mixed Spanish and Galician spoken in Galicia, Spain

castrar /kas'trar/ *vt* to castrate, geld; prune; remove honeycomb from hives; weaken

castrense /kas'trense/ *a* military

castrista /kas'trista/ *v* and *mf* Castroite

casual /ka'sual/ *a* accidental, casual

casualidad /kasuali'ðað/ *f,* chance, coincidence. **por c.,** by chance. **ser mucha c. que...,** to be too much of a coincidence that...

casucha /ka'sutʃa/ *f, Inf.* tumbledown hut

casuista /ka'suista/ *a* casuistic. *mf* casuist

casuística /ka'suistika/ *f,* casuistry

casulla /ka'suʎa; ka'suya/ *f,* chasuble

cata /'kata/ *f,* tasting; taste, sample

catabolismo /kataβo'lismo/ *m,* catabolism

cataclismo /kata'klismo/ *m,* cataclysm

catacumbas /kata'kumbas/ *f pl,* catacombs

catador /kata'ðor/ *m,* taster, sampler

catadura /kata'ðura/ *f,* tasting; look, countenance (gen. qualified)

catafalco /kata'falko/ *m,* catafalque

catalán /kata'lan/ **(-ana)** *a* and *n* Catalan, Catalonian. *m,* Catalan (language)

catalejo /kata'leho/ *m,* telescope

cataléptico /kata'leptiko/ *a* cataleptic

catálisis /ka'talisis/ *f, Chem.* catalysis

catalítico /kata'litiko/ *a* catalytic

catalogar /katalo'gar/ *vt* to catalog, list

catálogo /ka'talogo/ *m,* catalog, list

Cataluña /kata'luɲa/ Catalonia

cataplasma /kata'plasma/ *f,* cataplasm

catapulta /kata'pulta/ *f,* catapult

catar /ka'tar/ *vt* to taste, sample; see, examine; inspect; regard

catarata /kata'rata/ *f,* cataract, waterfall; *Med.* cataract (of the eyes)

catarral /kata'rral/ *a* catarrhal

catarro /ka'tarro/ *m,* catarrh; common cold

catástrofe /ka'tastrofe/ *f, Lit.* tragic climax; catastrophe

catastrófico /katas'trofiko/ *a* catastrophic

catavino /kata'βino/ *m,* taster (cup)

catavinos /kata'βinos/ *m,* professional wine taster; *Inf.* tippler, tavern haunter

cate /'kate/ *m, Slang* flunk (failure in a course at school)

catecismo /kate'θismo; kate'sismo/ *m,* catechism

catecúmeno /kate'kumeno/ **(-na)** *n* catechumen

cátedra /'kateðra/ *f,* university chair; chair in a Spanish **instituto**; professorship; university lecture room; subject taught by professor; reading desk, lectern; *Eccl.* throne; *Eccl.* see. **c. del espíritu santo,** pulpit. **c. de San Pedro,** Holy See

catedral /kate'ðral/ *f,* and *a* cathedral

catedrático /kate'ðratiko/ **(-ca)** *n* professor

categoría /katego'ria/ *f, Philos.* category; class, rank

categórico /kate'goriko/ *a* categorical, downright

cateo /ka'teo/ *m, West. Hem.* sampling; prospecting; house search (by the police)

catequismo /kate'kismo/ *m,* catechism; question and answer method of teaching

catequista /kate'kista/ *mf* catechist
catequizar /kateki'θar; kateki'sar/ *vt* to catechize; persuade, induce
caterva /ka'terβa/ *f*, crowd, throng; jumble, collection
catéter /ka'teter/ *m*, *Surg.* probe; catheter
catódico /ka'toðiko/ *a Elec.* cathodic
cátodo /'katoðo/ *m*, cathode
catolicidad /katoliθi'ðað; katolisi'ðað/ *f*, catholicity; catholic world
catolicismo /katoli'θismo; katoli'sismo/ *m*, Catholicism
católico /ka'toliko/ **(-ca)** *a* universal, catholic; infallible —*a* and *n* Catholic (by religion)
catorce /ka'torθe; ka'torse/ *a* fourteen; fourteenth. *m*, number fourteen; fourteenth (of days of month)
catorzavo /kator'θaβo; kator'saβo/ *a* fourteenth
catre /'katre/ *m*, camp-bed; truckle-bed; cot
caucáseo /kau'kaseo/ **(-ea)** *a* and *n* Caucasian
Cáucaso, el /'kaukaso, el/ the Caucasus
cauce /'kauθe; 'kause/ *m*, river or stream bed; ditch, irrigation canal
cauchal /kau'tʃal/ *m*, rubber plantation
cauchera /kau'tʃera/ *f*, rubber tree
cauchero /kau'tʃero/ *m*, rubber planter
caucho /'kautʃo/ *m*, caoutchouc, rubber
caución /kau'θion; kau'sion/ *f*, caution, precaution; surety; security
caucional /kauθio'nal; kausio'nal/ *a* See **libertad**
caudal /kau'ðal/ *m*, wealth, capital; flow, volume (of water); plenty, abundance (e.g. *un c. de conocimientos*, a wealth of knowledge)
caudaloso /kauða'loso/ *a* carrying much water; wealthy; abundant
caudillo /kau'ðiʎo; kau'ðiyo/ *m*, head, leader; chieftain. **el C.**, (title of Francisco Franco)
causa /'kausa/ *f*, cause; reason, motive; lawsuit; *Law.* trial. **c. final,** *Philos.* final cause. **c. pública,** public welfare. **ser c. bastante para...,** to be reason enough to...
causador /kausa'ðor/ **(-ra)** *a* motivating —*n* occasioner, originator
causalidad /kausali'ðað/ *f*, causality
causante /kau'sante/ *a* causative, causing. *m*, *Law.* principal; *Mexico* taxpayer
causar /kau'sar/ *vt* to cause; occasion
causticidad /kaustiθi'ðað; kaustisi'ðað/ *f*, causticity; mordacity
cáustico /'kaustiko/ *a* burning, caustic; scathing; mordant; *Surg.* caustic
cautela /kau'tela/ *f*, caution; astuteness, cunning
cauteloso /kaute'loso/ *a* cautious; cunning
cauterio /kau'terio/ *m*, cautery
cauterización /kauteriθa'θion; kauterisa'sion/ *f*, cauterization
cauterizar /kauteri'θar; kauteri'sar/ *vt* to cauterize
cautivar /kauti'βar/ *vt* to capture; captivate, charm; attract; —*vi* become a prisoner
cautiverio /kauti'βerio/ *m*, captivity
cautivo /kau'tiβo/ **(-va)** *a* and *n* captive
cauto /'kauto/ *a* cautious; prudent; sly
cava /'kaβa/ *f*, digging (especially vines); wine cellar in royal palaces
cavador /kaβa'ðor/ **(-ra)** *n* digger, hoer
cavadura /kaβa'ðura/ *f*, digging, hoeing; sinking (wells)
cavar /ka'βar/ *vt* to dig, hoe; sink (wells); —*vi* hollow; *Fig.* go deeply into a thing
caverna /ka'βerna/ *f*, cavern, cave; *Med.* cavity (generally in the lung)
cavernícola /kaβer'nikola/ *a* cave. **hombre c.,** caveman
cavernoso /kaβer'noso/ *a* cavernous; caverned; *Fig.* hollow (cough, etc.); deaf
cavidad /kaβi'ðað/ *f*, cavity; sinus; cell
cavilación /kaβila'θion; kaβila'sion/ *f*, caviling
cavilar /kaβi'lar/ *vt* to cavil; criticize
caviloso /kaβi'loso/ *a* captious
cayado /ka'yaðo/ *m*, crook; bishop's crozier
caz /kaθ; kas/ *m*, channel, canal; head-race, flume
caza /'kaθa; 'kasa/ *f*, hunting; hunt, chase; game. *m*, *Aer.* fighter. *Aer.* **c. lanzacohetes,** rocket-launching aircraft. **c. nocturno,** night fighter. *Naut.* **dar c.,** to pursue
cazaautógrafos /ˌkaθaau'tografos; ˌkasaau'tografos/ *m*, autograph hunter
cazabombardero /ˌkaθaβombar'ðero; ˌkasaβombar'ðero/ *m*, *Aer.* fighter bomber
cazadero /kaθa'ðero; kasa'ðero/ *m*, hunting ground
cazador /kaθa'ðor; kasa'ðor/ *a* hunting. *m*, *Mil.* chasseur; huntsman
cazadora /kaθa'ðora; kasa'ðora/ *f*, huntress; jacket; forage cap
cazadotes /kaθa'ðotes; kasa'ðotes/ *m*, dowry hunter
cazafortunas /kaθafor'tunas; kasafor'tunas/ *mf* fortune hunter
cazar /ka'θar; ka'sar/ *vt* to hunt, chase; *Fig. Inf.* run to earth; *Fig. Inf.* catch out; *Inf.* overcome by flattery
cazasubmarino /kaθasuβma'rino; kasasuβma'rino/ *m*, submarine chaser
cazatorpedero /kaθatorpe'ðero; kasatorpe'ðero/ *m*, *Naut.* torpedo-boat destroyer
cazo /'kaθo; 'kaso/ *m*, ladle; dipper
cazolada /kaθo'laða; kaso'laða/ *f*, panful
cazoleta /kaθo'leta; kaso'leta/ *f*, small pan; bowl (of pipe, etc.); sword guard; boss of a shield; pan (of a firelock)
cazuela /ka'θuela; ka'suela/ *f*, earthenware cooking dish; stew-pot; part of theater formerly reserved for women; *Theat.* gallery
cazumbrón /kaθum'βron; kasum'βron/ *m*, cooper
cazurro /ka'θurro; ka'surro/ *a Inf.* unsociable; surly, boorish
c.c.p. /θeθe'pe; sese'pe/ abbrev. of **con copia para**
ce /θe; se/ *f*, name of the letter C —*interj* Look! Chist! **ce por be,** in detail
cebada /θe'βaða; se'βaða/ *f*, barley (plant and grain). **c. perlada,** pearl barley
cebadal /θeβa'ðal; seβa'ðal/ *m*, barley field
cebadera /θeβa'ðera; seβa'ðera/ *f*, nose-bag; barley bin
cebadero /θeβa'ðero; seβa'ðero/ *m*, barley dealer
cebado /θe'βaðo; se'βaðo/ *a* on the prowl; having tasted human flesh (animal)
cebar /θe'βar; se'βar/ *vt* to feed or fatten (animals); fuel, feed (furnace, etc.); prime, charge (firearms, etc.); start up (machines); bait (fish hook); stimulate (passion, etc.); —*vi* stick in, penetrate (nails, screws, etc.); —*vr* put one's mind to; grow angry. **cebarse en vanas esperanzas,** to nurture vain hopes
cebo /'θeβo; 'seβo/ *m*, fodder; detonator; encouragement, food; bait
cebolla /θe'βoʎa; se'βoya/ *f*, onion; onion bulb; any bulbous stem; oil bulb (of lamp). **c. escalonia,** shallot
cebollana /θeβo'ʎana; seβo'yana/ *f*, chive
cebollero /θeβo'ʎero; seβo'yero/ **(-ra)** *n* onion seller
cebolleta /θeβo'ʎeta; seβo'yeta/ *f*, leek; young onion
cebollino /θeβo'ʎino; seβo'yino/ *m*, onion seed; onion bed; chive
cebra /'θeβra; 'seβra/ *f*, zebra
ceca /'θeka; 'seka/ *f*, mint (for coining money); name of mosque in Cordova. **de C. en Meca,** from pillar to post, hither and thither
cecear /θeθe'ar; sese'ar/ *vi* to lisp
ceceo /θe'θeo; se'seo/ *m*, lisping
ceceoso /θeθe'oso; sese'oso/ *a* lisping
cecial /θe'θial; se'sial/ *m*, dried fish
cecina /θe'θina; se'sina/ *f*, dried salt meat
cedazo /θe'ðaθo; se'ðaso/ *m*, sieve, strainer
ceder /θe'ðer; se'ðer/ *vt* to cede, give up; transfer; —*vi* give in, yield; diminish, decrease (fever, storm, etc.); fail, end; happen, turn out; sag, give, stretch. **No c. la fama a,** to be no less famous than
cedro /'θeðro; 'seðro/ *m*, cedar tree; cedar wood. **c. dulce,** red cedar
cédula /'θeðula; 'seðula/ *f*, document, certificate, card. *Eccl.* **c. de comunión,** Communion card. **c. personal,** identity card. **c. real,** royal letters patent
céfiro /'θefiro; 'sefiro/ *m*, west wind; *Poet.* zephyr
cegajoso /θega'hoso; sega'hoso/ *a* blear-eyed
cegar /θe'gar; se'gar/ *vi irr* to become blind; —*vt* to put out the eyes; *Fig.* blind; wall up, close up, stop

up; infatuate —*Pres. Indic.* **ciego, ciegas, ciega, ciegan.** *Pres. Subjunc.* **ciegue, ciegues, ciegue, cieguen**
cegato /θe'gato; se'gato/ *a Inf.* short-sighted
ceguedad, ceguera /θege'ðað, θe'gera; sege'ðað, se'gera/ *f,* blindness; delusion; ignorance
Ceilán /θei'lan; sei'lan/ Ceylon
ceja /'θeha; 'seha/ *f,* eyebrow; cloud cap; mountain peak; *Mus.* bridge (of stringed instruments). *Fig.* **quemarse las cejas,** to burn the midnight oil
cejar /θe'har; se'har/ *vi* to go backwards; give way, hesitate
cejijunto /θehi'hunto; sehi'hunto/ *a* having eyebrows that almost meet, beetle-browed
cejo /'θeho; 'seho/ *m,* river mist
cejudo /θe'huðo; se'huðo/ *a* having long thick eyebrows
celada /θe'laða; se'laða/ *f,* helmet; ambush; fraud, trick
celador /θela'ðor; sela'ðor/ **(-ra)** *a* watchful, zealous —*n* supervisor; caretaker; guard (at a museum, etc.)
celaje /θe'lahe; se'lahe/ *m,* sky with scudding clouds (gen. *pl*); skylight, window; promising sign, presage
celar /θe'lar; se'lar/ *vt* to be zealous in discharge of duties; spy upon; watch; oversee, superintend; conceal; engrave
celda /'θelda; 'selda/ *f,* cell
celdilla /θel'diʎa; sel'diya/ *f,* cell (bees, wasps, etc.); (*Zool. Bot.*) cell; *Bot.* capsule
celebérrimo, /θele'βerrimo; sele'βerrimo,/ *a superl* **célebre** most celebrated
celebración /θeleβra'θion; seleβra'sion/ *f,* celebration; applause
celebrador /θeleβra'ðor; seleβra'ðor/ **(-ra)** *n* celebrator; applauder
celebrante /θele'βrante; sele'βrante/ *a* celebrating. *m, Eccl.* celebrant
celebrar /θele'βrar; sele'βrar/ *vt* to celebrate; applaud; praise; venerate; hold, conduct; **c. que** + *subj,* to be happy that, be glad that —*vt* and *vi Eccl.* officiate; —*vr* take place
célebre /'θeleβre; 'seleβre/ *a* famous
celebridad /θeleβri'ðað; seleβri'ðað/ *f,* fame, celebrity; magnificence, show, pomp
celeridad /θeleri'ðað; seleri'ðað/ *f,* celerity
celeste /θe'leste; se'leste/ *a* celestial, heavenly
celestial /θeles'tial; seles'tial/ *a* celestial, heavenly; perfect, delightful; *Inf.* foolish (ironical)
celestina /θeles'tina; seles'tina/ *f,* procuress (allusion to *Tragicomedia de Calixto y Melibea*)
celestinaje /θelesti'nahe; selesti'nahe/ *m,* pandering, procuring
celibato /θeli'βato; seli'βato/ *m,* celibacy; *Inf.* bachelor
célibe /'θeliβe; 'seliβe/ *a* celibate, unmarried. *mf* unmarried person
celo /'θelo; 'selo/ *m,* enthusiasm, ardor; religious zeal; devotion; jealousy; heat, rut; *pl* jealousy, suspicion. **dar celos (a),** to make jealous
celosía /θelo'sia; selo'sia/ *f,* lattice; Venetian blind
celoso /θe'loso; se'loso/ *a* zealous; jealous; suspicious
celta /'θelta; 'selta/ *a* Celtic. *mf* Celt
célula /'θelula; 'selula/ *f,* cell
celular /θelu'lar; selu'lar/ *a* cellular —*m,* cellular phone.
celuloide /θelu'loiðe; selu'loiðe/ *f,* celluloid
celulosa /θelu'losa; selu'losa/ *f,* cellulose
celuloso /θelu'loso; selu'loso/ *a* cellular
cementación /θementa'θion; sementa'sion/ *f,* cementation
cementar /θemen'tar; semen'tar/ *vt* to cement
cementerio /θemen'terio; semen'terio/ *m,* cemetery
cemento /θe'mento; se'mento/ *m,* cement
cena /'θena; 'sena/ *f,* evening meal; supper; Last Supper
cenacho /θe'natʃo; se'natʃo/ *m,* marketing bag
cenáculo /θe'nakulo; se'nakulo/ *m,* cenacle
cenador /θena'ðor; sena'ðor/ *m,* diner out; arbor, pergola
cenagal /θena'gal; sena'gal/ *m,* quagmire; *Fig.* impasse
cenagoso /θena'goso; sena'goso/ *a* miry, muddy
cenar /θe'nar; se'nar/ *vi* to dine, sup; —*vt* eat for evening meal, sup off
cenceño /θen'θeɲo; sen'seɲo/ *a* slim, thin
cencerrada /θenθe'rraða; sense'rraða/ *f,* noisy mock serenade given to widows or widowers on the first night of their new marriage
cencerrear /θenθerre'ar; senserre'ar/ *vi* to jingle; *Inf.* play out of tune; bang in the wind, rattle; squeak
cencerreo /θenθe'rreo; sense'rreo/ *m,* jingling; jangle; rattling; squeaking
cencerro /θen'θerro; sen'serro/ *m,* cow-bell
cendal /θen'dal; sen'dal/ *m,* gauze; *Eccl.* stole; barbs of a feather
cenefa /θe'nefa; se'nefa/ *f,* border; valance, flounce; edging
cenicero /θeni'θero; seni'sero/ *m,* ash-pan; ash-pit; ash-tray
ceniciento /θeni'θiento; seni'siento/ *a* ash colored, ashen. **la Cenicienta,** Cinderella
cenit /'θenit; 'senit/ *m, Astron.* zenith; *Fig.* peak, summit
ceniza /θe'niθa; se'nisa/ *f,* ash, cinders
cenotafio /θeno'tafio; seno'tafio/ *m,* cenotaph
censo /'θenso; 'senso/ *m,* census; agreement for settlement of an annuity; annual ground rent; leasehold
censor /θen'sor; sen'sor/ *m,* censor; censorious person; *Educ.* proctor
censual /θen'sual; sen'sual/ *a* pertaining to census, annuity, rents
censualista /θensua'lista; sensua'lista/ *mf* annuitant
censura /θen'sura; sen'sura/ *f,* censorship; criticism; blame, reproach; scandal, gossip; *Psychol.* censorship
censurable /θensu'raβle; sensu'raβle/ *a* reprehensible; censorable
censurar /θensu'rar; sensu'rar/ *vt* to judge; censure; criticize
centauro /θen'tauro; sen'tauro/ *m, Myth.* centaur
centavo /θen'taβo; sen'taβo/ *m,* hundredth part; cent
centella /θen'teʎa; sen'teya/ *f,* lightning; spark; flash; *Fig.* spark (of anger, affection, etc.)
centellador /θenteʎa'ðor; senteya'ðor/ *a* flashing
centellear /θenteʎe'ar; senteye'ar/ *vi* to flash; twinkle; sparkle
centelleo /θente'ʎeo; sente'yeo/ *m,* scintillation; sparkle; flash
centén /θen'ten; sen'ten/ *m,* Spanish gold coin once worth 100 reals and later 25 pesetas
centena /θen'tena; sen'tena/ *f,* hundred
centenal, centenar /θente'nal, θente'nar; sente'nal, sente'nar/ *m,* hundred; centenary; rye field. **a centenares,** by the hundred, in crowds
centenario /θente'nario; sente'nario/ **(-ia)** *a* centenary —*n* centenarian. *m,* centenary
centeno /θen'teno; sen'teno/ *m, Bot.* rye
centésimo /θen'tesimo; sen'tesimo/ *a* and *m,* hundredth
centígrado /θen'tigraðo; sen'tigraðo/ *a* centigrade
centigramo /θenti'gramo; senti'gramo/ *m,* centigram
centilitro /θenti'litro; senti'litro/ *m,* centiliter
centímetro /θenti'metro; senti'metro/ *m,* centimeter. **c. cúbico,** cubic centimeter, milliliter
céntimo /'θentimo; 'sentimo/ *a* hundredth. *m,* centime (coin)
centinela /θenti'nela; senti'nela/ *mf Mil.* sentry, sentinel; person on watch. **estar de c.,** to be on sentry duty; be on guard
centolla /θen'toʎa; sen'toya/ *f,* marine crab
centón /θen'ton; sen'ton/ *m,* patchwork quilt
central /θen'tral; sen'tral/ *a* central; centric. *f,* head office; central depot; mother house. **c. de fuerza,** power-house. **c. telefónica,** telephone exchange
centralilla, centralita /θentra'liʎa, θentra'lita; sentra'liya, sentra'lita/ *f,* local exchange, private exchange
centralismo /θentra'lismo; sentra'lismo/ *m,* centralism
centralista /θentra'lista; sentra'lista/ *a* centralistic. *mf* centralist

centralización /θentraliθa'θion; sentralisa'sion/ *f,* centralization
centralizador /θentraliθa'ðor; sentralisa'ðor/ *a* centralizing
centralizar /θentrali'θar; sentrali'sar/ *vt* to centralize
centrar /θen'trar; sen'trar/ *vt* to center
céntrico /'θentriko; 'sentriko/ *a* central, centric; centrally located; downtown
centrífugo /θen'trifugo; sen'trifugo/ *a* centrifugal
centrípeto /θen'tripeto; sen'tripeto/ *a* centripetal
centro /'θentro; 'sentro/ *m,* center; headquarters, meeting place, club; center, hub; middle; core (of a rope); *Fig.* focus. *Phys.* **c. de gravedad,** center of gravity. **c. de mesa,** table center-piece. *Anat.* **centro nervioso,** nerve center
centroamericano /θentroameri'kano; sentroameri'kano/ **(-na)** *a* and *n* Central American
céntuplo /'θentuplo; 'sentuplo/ *a* centuple
centuria /θen'turia; sen'turia/ *f,* century
centurión /θentu'rion; sentu'rion/ *m,* centurion
ceñidamente /θeɲiða'mente; seɲiða'mente/ tightly (e.g. *un argumento c. organizado,* a tightly organized plot)
ceñido /θe'ɲiðo; se'ɲiðo/ *a* thrifty; wasp-waisted, slender waisted; fitting (of garments)
ceñidor /θeɲi'ðor; seɲi'ðor/ *m,* girdle, belt
ceñir /θe'ɲir; se'ɲir/ *vt irr* to girdle; surround; shorten, abbreviate; *—vr* be moderate (speech, expenditure, etc.); conform, confine oneself (to). **ceñirse a las reglas,** to abide by the rules *—Pres. Indic.* **ciño, ciñes, ciñen.** *Pres. Part.* **ciñendo.** *Preterite* **ciñó, ciñeron.** *Pres. Subjunc.* **ciña,** etc *—Imperf. Subjunc.* **ciñese,** etc.
ceño /'θeɲo; 'seɲo/ *m,* band, hoop; frown; *Fig.* dark outlook
ceñudo /θe'ɲuðo; se'ɲuðo/ *a* frowning
cepa /'θepa; 'sepa/ *f,* stump; vine-stock; root (tails, antlers, etc.); *Fig.* origin, trunk (of a family); *Biol.* strain. **de la más pura c.,** of the best quality
cepillar /θepi'ʎar; sepi'yar/ *vt* to brush; plane; smooth
cepillo /θe'piʎo; se'piyo/ *m,* brush; plane; poor-box, offertory-box. **c. para los dientes,** toothbrush. **c. para ropa,** clothes-brush. **c. para el suelo,** scrubbing-brush. **c. para las uñas,** nail-brush
cepo /'θepo; 'sepo/ *m,* bough; wooden stocks; snare; trap; poor-box; collecting-box
cera /'θera; 'sera/ *f,* beeswax; wax; wax candles, etc., used at a function. *Inf.* **ser como una c.,** to be like wax (in the hands of)
cerador /θera'ðor; sera'ðor/ *m,* floor waxer (person)
ceradora /θera'ðora; sera'ðora/ *f,* floor waxer (machine)
cerámica /θe'ramika; se'ramika/ *f,* ceramics; ceramic art, pottery
cerámico /θe'ramiko; se'ramiko/ *a* ceramic
cerbatana /θerβa'tana; serβa'tana/ *f,* blow-pipe, popgun; pea-shooter; ear-trumpet
cerca /'θerka; 'serka/ *f,* fence, wall
cerca /'θerka; 'serka/ *adv* near. **c. de,** near to; almost, nearly (e.g. *c. de las once,* nearly eleven o'clock)
cercado /θer'kaðo; ser'kaðo/ *m,* enclosure, fenced in place; fence
cercanía /θerka'nia; serka'nia/ *f,* nearness, proximity; (gen. *pl*) outskirts, surroundings
cercano /θer'kano; ser'kano/ *a* near, neighboring; impending, early
cercar /θer'kar; ser'kar/ *vt* to enclose; build a wall or fence round; to lay siege to; crowd round; *Mil.* surround
cercenamiento /θerθena'miento; sersena'miento/ **(a)** *m,* curtailment (of)
cercenar /θerθe'nar; serse'nar/ *vt* to lop off the ends, clip; curtail, diminish; abridge; whittle
cerciorar /θerθio'rar; sersio'rar/ *vt* to assure, confirm; *—vr* make sure
cerco /'θerko; 'serko/ *m,* ring, hoop; fence; siege; small conversational circle; spin, circling; halo (sun, moon); frame; sash (of a window). **poner c. (a),** to lay siege to, blockade
cerda /'θerða; 'serða/ *f,* sow; bristle
Cerdeña /θer'ðeɲa; ser'ðeɲa/ Sardinia
cerdo /'θerðo; 'serðo/ *m,* pig, hog
cerdoso /θer'ðoso; ser'ðoso/ *a* bristly
cereal /θere'al; sere'al/ *a* and *m,* cereal
cerebelo /θere'βelo; sere'βelo/ *m, Anat.* cerebellum
cerebral /θere'βral; sere'βral/ *a* cerebral
cerebro /θe'reβro; se'reβro/ *m,* cerebrum; brain; intelligence
cerebro-espinal /θe'reβro-espi'nal; se'reβro-espi'nal/ *a* cerebrospinal
ceremonia /θere'monia; sere'monia/ *f,* ceremony; function, display; formality. **de c.,** ceremonial; formally. **por c.,** for politeness' sake
ceremonial /θeremo'nial; seremo'nial/ *a* ceremonial. *m,* ceremony; rite; protocol (rules of behavior)
ceremonioso /θeremo'nioso; seremo'nioso/ *a* ceremonious; formal, over-courteous
cerero /θe'rero; se'rero/ *m,* wax-chandler
cereza /θe'reθa; se'resa/ *f,* cherry
cerezal /θere'θal; sere'sal/ *m,* cherry orchard
cerezo /θe'reθo; se'reso/ *m,* cherry tree; cherry wood
cerilla /θe'riʎa; se'riya/ *f,* wax taper; match; ear wax
cerner /θer'ner; ser'ner/ *vt irr* to sieve; watch, observe; *Fig.* sift, clarify; *—vi* bolt (of plants); drizzle; *—vr* waddle; hover; threaten (of evil, etc.) *—Pres. Indic.* **cierno, ciernes, cierne, ciernen.** *Pres. Subjunc.* **cierna, ciernas, cierna, ciernan**
cernícalo /θer'nikalo; ser'nikalo/ *m, Ornith.* kestrel; *Inf.* lout
cernidillo /θerni'ðiʎo; serni'ðiyo/ *m,* drizzle; teetering walk
cernido /θer'niðo; ser'niðo/ *m,* sifting, sieving; sifted flour
cerniduras /θerni'ðuras; serni'ðuras/ *f pl,* siftings
cero /'θero; 'sero/ *m, Math.* zero; naught; (tennis) love. *Fig. Inf.* **ser un c.,** to be a mere cipher
cerote /θe'rote; se'rote/ *m,* cobbler's wax. *Inf.* fear
cerquillo /θer'kiʎo; ser'kiyo/ *m,* tonsure; welt (of a shoe)
cerquita /θer'kita; ser'kita/ *adv* very near, hard by
cerradero, /θerra'ðero; serra'ðero,/ *m,* **cerradera** *f,* bolt staple; catch of a lock; clasp or strings of a purse
cerradizo /θerra'ðiθo; serra'ðiso/ *a* closable, lockable
cerrado /θe'rraðo; se'rraðo/ *a* closed; compact; incomprehensible, obscure; overcast, cloudy; *Inf.* taciturn; secretive. *m,* enclosure
cerradura /θerra'ðura; serra'ðura/ *f,* fastening, lock; closing, locking
cerraja /θe'rraha; se'rraha/ *f,* lock (of a door); bolt
cerrajería /θerrahe'ria; serrahe'ria/ *f,* locksmith's craft; locksmith's workshop or shop
cerrajero /θerra'hero; serra'hero/ *m,* locksmith
cerramiento /θerra'miento; serra'miento/ *m,* closing, locking up; fence; enclosure, shooting preserve; partition wall
cerrar /θe'rrar; se'rrar/ *vt irr* to close; lock, fasten, bolt; shut up; *Mech.* shut off, turn off; fold up; block or stop up; seal (letters, etc.); close down; terminate; obstruct; (*with con*) attack; *—vi* close; close in (of night, etc.); *—vr* heal up (wounds); close (flowers); *Radio.* close down; crowd together; *Fig.* stand firm. *Inf.* **cerrarse la espuela,** to take a nightcap, have a last drink. **c. la marcha,** to bring up the rear. **al c. la edición,** stop press. See **acertar**
cerrazón /θerra'θon; serra'son/ *f,* dark, overcast sky heralding a storm
cerril /θe'rril; se'rril/ *a* rough, rocky; wild, untamed (cattle, horses); *Inf.* boorish
cerrillar /θerri'ʎar; serri'yar/ *vt* to mill coins
cerro /'θerro; 'serro/ *m,* neck of an animal; spine, backbone; hill. *Fig.* **irse por los cerros de Úbeda,** to go off the track, indulge in irrelevancies
cerrojo /θe'rroho; se'rroho/ *m,* bolt (of a door, etc.); lock (of a door, gun, etc.)
certamen /θer'tamen; ser'tamen/ *m,* contest; competition; match
certero /θer'tero; ser'tero/ *a* well-aimed; sure, well-timed; knowledgeable, sure
certeza, certidumbre /θer'teθa, θerti'ðumbre; ser'tesa, serti'ðumbre/ *f,* certitude, assurance
certificación /θertifika'θion; sertifika'sion/ *f,* certification; certificate; affidavit

certificado /θertifi'kaðo; sertifi'kaðo/ *a* certified; registered. *m,* registered letter; certificate
certificar /θertifi'kar; sertifi'kar/ *vt* to certify; register (letter, etc.)
certificatorio /θertifika'torio; sertifika'torio/ *a* certifying or serving to certify
certísimo /θer'tisimo; ser'tisimo/ *a* learned form of the superlative of **cierto** (see **certísimo**)
certitud /θerti'tuð; serti'tuð/ *f,* certitude
cervantino /θerβan'tino; serβan'tino/ *a* Cervantine
cervato /θer'βato; ser'βato/ *m,* fawn
cervecería /θerβeθe'ria; serβese'ria/ *f,* brewery; alehouse
cervecero /θerβe'θero; serβe'sero/ **(-ra)** *n* brewer; beer seller
cerveza /θer'βeθa; ser'βesa/ *f,* beer, ale. **c. negra,** stout
cerviz /θer'βiθ; ser'βis/ *f,* cervix, nape (of neck). **doblar** (*or* **bajar**) **la c.,** to humble oneself
cesación /θesa'θion; sesa'sion/ *f,* cessation, stopping
cesante /θe'sante; se'sante/ *a* dismissed; pensioned off. **declarar c.** (**a**), to dismiss (a person from a post). **estar c.,** to be out of a job
cesantía /θesan'tia; sesan'tia/ *f,* status of dismissed or retired official, retirement pension
cesar /θe'sar; se'sar/ *vi* to cease, stop, end; leave an employment; desist; retire
cesáreo /θe'sareo; se'sareo/ *a* Cesarean; imperial
cese /'θese; 'sese/ *m,* stopping of payment for an employment
cesión /θe'sion; se'sion/ *f,* cession; transfer; resignation; *Law.* release
cesionario /θesio'nario; sesio'nario/ **(-ia)** *n* cessionary, transferee
cesionista /θesio'nista; sesio'nista/ *mf* grantor, transferer
césped /'θespeð; 'sespeð/ *m,* grass, sward; sod, lawn
cesta /'θesta; 'sesta/ *f,* basket, hamper; *Sports.* racket; cradle (for a wine bottle)
cestada /θes'taða; ses'taða/ *f,* basketful
cestería /θeste'ria; seste'ria/ *f,* basketmaking, basketweaving; basket factory; basket shop; basketwork
cestero /θes'tero; ses'tero/ **(-ra)** *n* basket maker or seller
cesto /'θesto; 'sesto/ *m,* basket, hamper, skip
cesura /θe'sura; se'sura/ *f,* cesura
cetáceo /θe'taθeo; se'taseo/ *a* and *m, Zool.* cetacean
cetorrino /θeto'rrino; seto'rrino/ *m,* basking shark
cetrería /θetre'ria; setre'ria/ *f,* falconry
cetrino /θe'trino; se'trino/ *a* greenish-yellow; sallow; citrine; melancholy; reserved, aloof
cetro /'θetro; 'setro/ *m,* scepter; verge; reign
Cevenes, los /θe'βenes, los; se'βenes, los/ the Cevennes
chabacanería /tʃaβakane'ria/ *f,* bad taste; vulgarity
chabacano /tʃaβa'kano/ *a* vulgar, common; rude, uncouth
chacal /tʃa'kal/ *m, Zool.* jackal
cháchara /'tʃatʃara/ *f, Inf.* empty chatter; verbiage
chacharear /tʃatʃare'ar/ *vi* to chatter; gabble, cackle
chacharero /tʃatʃa'rero/ *a Inf.* chattering; talkative
chacolotear /tʃakolote'ar/ *vi* to clatter, clink (loose horseshoe)
chacota /tʃa'kota/ *f,* merriment, mirth
chacotear /tʃakote'ar/ *vi Inf.* to be merry, have fun
chacotón /tʃako'ton/ *a* of a boisterous humor
chafado /tʃa'faðo/ *a* taken aback; disappointed
chafallar /tʃafa'ʎar; tʃafa'yar/ *vt Inf.* to mend carelessly, botch
chafandín /tʃafan'din/ *m,* vain fool
chafar /tʃa'far/ *vt* to flatten; crumple, crease (clothes); *Inf.* heckle
chafarrinar /tʃafarri'nar/ *vt* to stain, mark, blot
chaflán /tʃa'flan/ *m,* bevel edge, chamfer
chagrén /tʃa'gren/ *m,* shagreen leather
chal /tʃal/ *m,* shawl
chalán /tʃa'lan/ *m,* horse-dealer
chalana /tʃa'lana/ *f, Naut.* wherry, lighter
chalanear /tʃalane'ar/ *vt* to bargain; indulge in sharp practice
chalar /tʃa'lar/ *vt* to drive mad; enamor
chaleco /tʃa'leko/ *m,* waistcoat; cardigan
chalina /tʃa'lina/ *f,* flowing scarf, artist's bow
Chalo /'tʃalo/ pet form of the male given name *Carlos* "Charles', hence = English *Chuck; Bud, Mac* (in direct address to a male whose name one does not know)
chalote /tʃa'lote/ *m,* shallot
chalupa /tʃa'lupa/ *f,* shallop; launch; canoe; long boat, ship's boat
chamar /tʃa'mar/ *vt Inf.* to palm off, barter
chamarasca /tʃama'raska/ *f,* brushwood, tinder
chamarilero /tʃamari'lero/ **(-ra)** *n* secondhand dealer
chamarreta /tʃama'rreta/ *f,* sheepskin jacket; *Mexico* jacket
chambelán /tʃambe'lan/ *m,* court chamberlain
chambergo /tʃam'βergo/ *a* pertaining to the Chambergo regiment. *m,* broad-brimmed hat
chambón /tʃam'βon/ *a Inf.* awkward, clumsy; lucky
chambonada /tʃambo'naða/ *f, Inf.* blunder; fluke, chance
chambra /'tʃambra/ *f,* dressing-jacket, peignoir, negligee
chamicera /tʃami'θera; tʃami'sera/ *f,* piece of scorched earth (woodland, etc.)
chamorro /tʃa'morro/ *a* close-cropped, shorn (hair)
champán /tʃam'pan/ *m,* champagne. **c. obrero,** *humorous* cider
champaña /tʃam'paɲa/ *m,* champagne
champar /tʃam'par/ *vt Inf.* to cast in a person's face, remind
champú /tʃam'pu/ *m,* shampoo
chamuscar /tʃamus'kar/ *vt* to scorch; singe
chamusquina /tʃamus'kina/ *f,* scorching; singeing; *Inf.* brawl
chanada /tʃa'naða/ *f, Inf.* trick, mischievous act
chancearse /tʃanθe'arse; tʃanse'arse/ *vr* to joke
chancero /tʃan'θero; tʃan'sero/ *a* joking, facetious
chanchollada /tʃantʃo'ʎaða; tʃantʃo'yaða/ *f,* dirty trick, foul play, trick
chanchullo /tʃan'tʃuʎo; tʃan'tʃuyo/ *m, Inf.* fraud
chanciller /tʃanθi'ʎer; tʃansi'yer/ *m,* chancellor
chancillería /tʃanθiʎe'ria; tʃansiye'ria/ *f,* chancery
chancla /'tʃankla/ *f,* down at heel shoe; heelless slipper
chancleta /tʃan'kleta/ *f,* heelless slipper, babouche. *mf Inf.* ninny
chancleteo /tʃankle'teo/ *m,* clicking of heelless slippers
chanclo /'tʃanklo/ *m,* overshoe; Wellington
chanfaina /tʃan'faina/ *f, Cul.* savory fricassee
chanflón /tʃan'flon/ *a* tough, coarse; ungainly
chantaje /tʃan'tahe/ *m,* blackmail
chantajista /tʃanta'hista/ *mf* blackmailer
chantar /tʃan'tar/ *vt* to put on, clothe; *Inf.* tell plainly. *Inf.* **c. sus verdades,** to tell hometruths
chanza /'tʃanθa; 'tʃansa/ *f,* joke, jest
chanzoneta /tʃanθo'neta; tʃanso'neta/ *f,* canzonetta; *Inf.* joke
chapa /'tʃapa/ *f,* plate, sheet; veneer; clasp; *Inf.* prudence, common sense; rouge. **c. de hierro,** sheet-iron. **c. de identidad,** number plate
chapado a la antigua /tʃa'paðo a la an'tigua/ *a* old-fashioned
chapalear /tʃapale'ar/ *vi* to dabble in water; splash; clatter (of a horseshoe)
chapaleo /tʃapa'leo/ *m,* dabbling, paddling; splash; clattering, clink (of a horseshoe)
chapaleteo /tʃapale'teo/ *m,* lapping of water; splashing (of rain)
chaparrear /tʃaparre'ar/ *vi* to pour with rain
chaparrón /tʃapa'rron/ *m,* heavy shower of rain, downpour
chapear /tʃape'ar/ *vt* to veneer; —*vi* clatter (loose horseshoe)
chapeo /tʃa'peo/ *m,* hat
chaperón /tʃape'ron/ *m,* hood
chapeta /tʃa'peta/ *f, dim* clasp; red flush or spot on cheek
chapetón /tʃape'ton/ **(-ona)** *n West Hem.* recently arrived European, especially Spaniard

chapín /tʃa'pin/ *m,* cork-soled leather overshoe (for women) *Obs.*
chapino /tʃa'pino/ *a* and *m, Mexico contemptuous* Guatemalan
chapitel /tʃapi'tel/ *m, Archit.* capital; spire
chapodar /tʃapo'ðar/ *vt* to prune, lop off branches; cut down, reduce
chapotear /tʃapote'ar/ *vt* to sponge, moisten, damp; *—vi* paddle, splash; dabble or trail the hands (in water)
chapoteo /tʃapo'teo/ *m,* moistening, sponging; paddling, splashing; dabbling
chapucear /tʃapuθe'ar; tʃapuse'ar/ *vt* to botch, do badly; bungle
chapuceramente /tʃapuθera'mente; tʃapusera'mente/ *adv* awkwardly. **hablar el japonés c.,** to speak broken Japanese
chapucería /tʃapuθe'ria; tʃapuse'ria/ *f,* roughness, poor workmanship; botch
chapucero /tʃapu'θero; tʃapu'sero/ *a* rough, badly finished; bungling, clumsy, awkward
chapurrado /tʃapu'rraðo/ *a* broken (e.g. *hablar un italiano c.,* to speak broken Italian)
chapurrar, chapurrear /tʃapu'rrar, tʃapurre'ar/ *vt* to speak badly (a language); jabber; *Inf.* mix (drinks)
chapuz /tʃa'puθ; tʃa'pus/ *m,* ducking, submerging; plunge; unimportant job; clumsiness
chapuzar /tʃapu'θar; tʃapu'sar/ *vt* to duck, submerge; plunge
chaqué /tʃa'ke/ *m,* morning coat; morning suit
chaqueta /tʃa'keta/ *f,* jacket; *Mech.* casing
chaquete /tʃa'kete/ *m,* backgammon
chaquetilla /tʃake'tiʎa; tʃake'tiya/ *f,* short jacket; coatee; blazer
chaquetón /tʃake'ton/ *m,* short coat. **c. de piloto,** *Aer.* pea-jacket
charabán /tʃara'βan/ *m,* charabanc
charada /tʃa'raða/ *f,* charade
charanguero /tʃaraŋ'guero/ *a* rough, badly finished; clumsy. *m,* Andalusian boat
charca /'tʃarka/ *f,* pond, pool; reservoir
charco /'tʃarko/ *m,* puddle; *Inf.* sea
charla /'tʃarla/ *f, Inf.* chatter; conversation; talk, informal lecture
charlar /'tʃarlar/ *vi Inf.* to prattle, chatter; chat, converse; give a talk (on)
charlatán /tʃarla'tan/ **(-ana)** *a* loquacious, garrulous; indiscreet; fraudulent, false *—n* charlatan; chatterer
charlatanería /tʃarlatane'ria/ *f,* loquacity, garrulity; quackery
charlatanismo /tʃarlata'nismo/ *m,* charlatanism, quackery
charnela /tʃar'nela/ *f,* hinge; hinged joint
charol /tʃa'rol/ *m,* japan, varnish; patent leather
charolar /tʃaro'lar/ *vt* to japan, varnish
charolista /tʃaro'lista/ *m,* varnisher
charpa /'tʃarpa/ *f,* pistol-belt; sling
charrán /tʃa'rran/ **(-ana)** *n* rogue, trickster
charranada /tʃarra'naða/ *f,* roguery, knavery
charrería /tʃarre'ria/ *f,* tawdriness; gaudiness
charretera /tʃarre'tera/ *f, Mil.* epaulet; garter
charro /'tʃarro/ *a* churlish, coarse; flashy, tawdry
chasca /'tʃaska/ *f,* brushwood, firewood
chascar /tʃas'kar/ *vi* to creak, crack; clack (the tongue); swallow
chascarrillo /tʃaska'rriʎo; tʃaska'rriyo/ *m, Inf.* amusing anecdote, good story
chasco /'tʃasko/ *m,* trick, practical joke; disappointment. **llevarse un c.,** to meet with a disappointment
chasis /'tʃasis/ *m, Auto.* chassis; *Photo.* plate-holder; *Mech.* underframe
chasquear /tʃaske'ar/ *vt* to play a trick on; wag (one's tongue); crack (a whip, one's knuckles); break a promise, disappoint; *—vi* creak, crack; meet with a disappointment
chasquido /tʃas'kiðo/ *m,* crack (of whip); creaking (of wood); click (of the tongue)
chatarra /tʃa'tarra/ *f,* scrap iron; junk
chato /'tʃato/ *a* flat-nosed; flat
chauvinismo /tʃauβi'nismo/ *m,* chauvinism
chaval /tʃa'βal/ *a Inf.* young. *m,* lad
chaveta /tʃa'βeta/ *f, Mech.* bolt, pin, peg, cotter, key
che /tʃe/ *f,* name of the letter *ch*
checo /'tʃeko/ **(-ca)** *a* and *n* Czech. Czech (language)
checoslovaco /tʃekoslo'βako/ **(-ca)** *a* Czechoslovakian *—n* Czechoslovak
Checoslovaquia /tʃekoslo'βakia/ Czechoslovakia
Chejov /tʃe'hoβ/ Chekov
chelín /tʃe'lin/ *m,* shilling
Chengis-Jan /tʃenhis-'han/ Genghis Khan
chepa /'tʃepa/ *f, Inf.* hunch (back); hump
cheque /'tʃeke/ *m,* check. **c. cruzado,** crossed check
chica /'tʃika/ *f,* girl; *Inf.* dear
chicana /tʃi'kana/ *f,* chicanery
chicano /tʃi'kano/ **(-na)** *a* and *n* Chicano, American of Mexican ancestry
chícharo /'tʃitʃaro/ *m,* pea
chicharrón /tʃitʃa'rron/ *m, Cul.* crackling; burnt meat; *Inf.* sunburnt person
chichón /tʃi'tʃon/ *m,* bruise, bump
chichonera /tʃitʃo'nera/ *f,* child's protective hat (something like a straw crash-helmet)
chicle /'tʃikle/ *m,* chewing gum
chiclero /tʃi'klero/ *m,* chicle-gatherer
chico /'tʃiko/ *a* little, small; young. *m,* little boy; youth; *Inf.* old boy, dear. **Es un buen c.,** He's a good fellow
chicoleo /tʃiko'leo/ *m, Inf.* compliment
chicote /tʃi'kote/ *mf* sturdy child. *m, Inf.* cigar
chifla /'tʃifla/ *f,* whistling, whistle; tanner's paring knife
chiflado /tʃi'flaðo/ *a Inf.* cracked, daft; crack-brained
chifladura /tʃifla'ðura/ *f,* whistling; *Inf.* whim, mania, hobby
chiflar /tʃi'flar/ *vi* to whistle; *—vt* to make fun of, hiss; pare or scrape leather; *Inf.* swill, tipple; *—vr Inf.* have a slate loose; be slightly mad; *Inf.* lose one's head over, adore
chifle /'tʃifle/ *m,* whistle, whistling; decoy call (birds)
chile /'tʃile/ *m, Bot.* red pepper, chilli
chileno /tʃi'leno/ **(-na)** *a* and *n* Chilean
chillador /tʃiʎa'ðor; tʃiya'ðor/ *a* screaming, shrieking
chillar /tʃi'ʎar; tʃi'yar/ *vi* to scream, shriek; creak; squeak; jabber (monkeys, etc.); *Art.* be strident (of colors)
chillería /tʃiʎe'ria; tʃiye'ria/ *f,* shrieking, screaming
chillido /tʃi'ʎiðo; tʃi'yiðo/ *m,* scream, shriek; squeak (of mice, etc.); jabber (of monkeys, etc.)
chillón /tʃi'ʎon; tʃi'yon/ *a Inf.* screaming, yelling; strident, piercing; crude, loud (colors)
chimenea /tʃime'nea/ *f,* chimney; funnel; fireplace; kitchen range
chimpancé /tʃimpan'θe; tʃimpan'se/ *m,* chimpanzee
china /'tʃina/ *f,* pebble; porcelain, china; Chinese silk
chinche /'tʃintʃe/ *f,* bedbug; thumbtack, drawing-pin. *mf Inf.* bore
chinchona /tʃin'tʃona/ *f,* quinine
chinchorrería /tʃintʃorre'ria/ *f, Inf.* impertinence, tediousness; gossip
chinela /tʃi'nela/ *f,* mule, slipper; overshoe, patten *Obs.*
chinero /tʃi'nero/ *m,* china cupboard
chinesco /tʃi'nesko/ *a* Chinese. **a la chinesca,** in Chinese fashion
chino /'tʃino/ **(-na)** *a* and *n* Chinese. *m,* Chinese (language)
Chipre /'tʃipre/ Cyprus
chipriota /tʃi'priota/ *a* and *mf* Cypriot
chiquero /tʃi'kero/ *m,* pigsty; stable for bulls
chiquillada /tʃiki'ʎaða; tʃiki'yaða/ *f,* childishness, puerility
chiquillería /tʃikiʎe'ria; tʃikiye'ria/ *f, Inf.* crowd of children
chiquillo /tʃi'kiʎo; tʃi'kiyo/ **(-lla)** *n* small boy
chiquito /tʃi'kito/ **(-ta)** *a dim* **chico,** tiny, very small *—n* little one, small boy
chirimía /tʃiri'mia/ *f,* flageolet. *m,* flageolet player
chiripa /tʃi'ripa/ *f,* (billiards) fluke; *Inf.* happy coincidence, stroke of luck; lucky guess
chirivía /tʃiri'βia/ *f, Bot.* parsnip; *Ornith.* wagtail
chirlar /tʃir'lar/ *vi Inf.* to gabble, talk loudly
chirlo /'tʃirlo/ *m,* knife wound, sabre cut; knife scar

chirona /tʃi'rona/ *f, Inf.* jail

chirriador /tʃirria'ðor/ *a* sizzling, crackling; creaking, squeaking

chirriar /tʃi'rriar/ *vi* to sizzle, crackle; creak, squeak; squawk; *Inf.* croak, sing out of tune

chirrido /tʃi'rriðo/ *m,* squawk; croaking; noise of grasshoppers; squeaking; creaking, creak

¡chis! /tʃis/ *interj* Shh! Silence!

chisme /'tʃisme/ *m,* gossip, tale; *Inf.* small household utensil, trifle

chismear /tʃisme'ar/ *vt* to tell tales, gossip

chismero /tʃis'mero/ **(-ra), chismoso (-sa)** *a* gossiping, talebearing *—n* gossip, tale bearer

chispa /'tʃispa/ *f,* spark; ember; *Elec.* spark; tiny diamond; small particle; wit; quickwittedness; *Inf.* drunkenness. **c. del encendido,** ignition spark

chispazo /tʃis'paθo; tʃis'paso/ *m,* flying out of a spark, sparking; damage done by spark; *Inf.* gossip, rumor

chispeante /tʃispe'ante/ *a* sparking; sparkling; *Fig.* scintillating (with wit etc.)

chispear /tʃispe'ar/ *vi* to throw out sparks, spark; sparkle, gleam; *Fig.* scintillate; drizzle gently

chisporrotear /tʃisporrote'ar/ *vi Inf.* to sputter; fizz

chisporroteo /tʃisporro'teo/ *m, Inf.* sputtering; fizz

chisposo /tʃis'poso/ *a* sputtering, throwing out sparks

chistar /tʃis'tar/ *vi* to speak, break silence (gen. used negatively)

chiste /'tʃiste/ *m,* witticism, bon mot; amusing incident; joke

chistera /tʃis'tera/ *f,* creel (for fish); *Inf.* top-hat, tile

chistoso /tʃis'toso/ *a* joking; amusing, funny

chiticallando /tʃitika'ʎando; tʃitika'yando/ *adv* quietly, stealthily; *Inf.* on the quiet, in secret

¡chito! ¡chitón! /'tʃito; tʃi'ton/ *interj* Hush! Sh!

chiva /'tʃiβa/ *f, Panama* bus

chivo /'tʃiβo/ *n Zool.* kid. **c. expiatorio,** scapegoat

chocante /tʃo'kante/ *a* colliding; provoking; shocking; surprising

chocar /tʃo'kar/ *vi* to collide; strike (against); run into; fight, clash; *—vt* clink (glasses); provoke, annoy; surprise, shock. **¡Choca cinco!** Clasp five!, Gimme five!, Put it there!, Give some skin! (invitation to shake hands)

chocarrería /tʃokarre'ria/ *f,* coarse joke

chochear /tʃotʃe'ar/ *vi* to be senile; *Fig. Inf.* dote (on)

chocho /'tʃotʃo/ *a* senile; *Fig. Inf.* doting

choco /'tʃoko/ *m,* small hump, hunchback

chocolate /tʃoko'late/ *m,* chocolate; drinking chocolate. **c. a la española,** thick chocolate. **c. a la francesa,** French drinking chocolate

chocolatería /tʃokolate'ria/ *f,* chocolate factory or shop

chocolatero /tʃokola'tero/ **(-ra)** *a* fond of chocolate *—n* chocolate maker or seller

chófer /'tʃofer/ *m,* chauffeur; driver

chopera /tʃo'pera/ *f,* grove or plantation of black poplar trees

chopo /'tʃopo/ *m, Bot.* black poplar; *Inf.* gun

choque /'tʃoke/ *m,* collision; shock; jar; *Med.* concussion; fight; clink (of glasses); clash; *Mil.* skirmish

choricera /tʃori'θera; tʃori'sera/ *f,* sausage-making machine

choricero /tʃori'θero; tʃori'sero/ **(-ra)** *n* sausage maker

chorizo /tʃo'riθo; tʃo'riso/ *m,* kind of pork sausage; counterweight

chorrear /tʃorre'ar/ *vi* to spout, jet; drip; *Fig. Inf.* trickle, arrive slowly

chorreo /tʃo'rreo/ *m,* drip, dripping; spouting, gushing

chorrera /tʃo'rrera/ *f,* spout; drip; jabot, lace front

chorro /'tʃorro/ *m,* jet; stream (of water, etc.); *Fig.* shower. **a chorros,** in a stream; in abundance, plentifully

chova /'tʃoβa/ *f,* rook; carrion crow; jackdaw

choza /'tʃoθa; 'tʃosa/ *f,* hut, cabin; cottage

chubasco /tʃu'βasko/ *m,* squall, downpour; storm; transitory misfortune

chuchería /tʃutʃe'ria/ *f,* gewgaw, trinket; savory titbit; snaring, trapping

chucruta /tʃu'kruta/ *f,* sauerkraut

chueca /'tʃueka/ *f,* round head of a bone; small ball; game like shinty; *Inf.* practical joke

chufa /'tʃufa/ *f, Bot.* chufa; *Inf.* joke, trick

chufería /tʃufe'ria/ *f,* place where drink made of **chufas** is sold

chufla /'tʃufla/ *f,* flippant remark

chufleta /tʃu'fleta/ *f, Inf.* joke; taunt

chulada /tʃu'laða/ *f,* mean trick, base action; drollery

chulería /tʃule'ria/ *f,* drollness; attractive personality

chuleta /tʃu'leta/ *f, Cul.* cutlet, chop; mutton-chop; *Inf.* slap

chulo /'tʃulo/ *a* droll, amusing; attractive. *m,* slaughterhouse worker; bullfighter's assistant; pimp; rogue

chumbera /tʃum'βera/ *f,* prickly pear; Indian fig

chunga /'tʃuŋga/ *f, Inf.* banter, teasing

chupada /tʃu'paða/ *f,* sucking; suck; suction

chupado de cara, c. de mofletes /tʃu'paðo de 'kara; mof'letes/ *a* lantern-jawed

chupador /tʃupa'ðor/ *a* sucking. *m,* baby's comforter or dummy

chupar /tʃu'par/ *vt* to suck; absorb (of plants); *Fig. Inf.* drain, rob; *—vr* grow thin. **chuparse los dedos,** *Inf.* to lick one's lips; be delighted

chupatintas /tʃupa'tintas/ *m, Inf.* scrivener, clerk (scornful)

churdón /tʃur'ðon/ *m,* raspberry cane; raspberry; raspberry vinegar

churrería /tʃurre'ria/ *f,* place where **churros** are made or sold

churrero /tʃu'rrero/ **(-ra)** *n* maker or seller of **churros**

churrigueresco /tʃurrige'resko/ *a* Churrigueresque

churro /'tʃurro/ *a* coarse (of wool). *m, Cul.* a kind of fritter eaten with chocolate, coffee, etc.

churumbela /tʃurum'βela/ *f, Mus.* pipe; reed for drinking mate *West Hem.*

chusco /'tʃusko/ *a* droll, witty, amusing

chusma /'tʃusma/ *f,* galley hands, crew; rabble, mob

chutar /tʃu'tar/ *vt Sports.* to shoot (a goal)

chuzo /'tʃuθo; 'tʃuso/ *m, Mil.* pike

chuzón /tʃu'θon; tʃu'son/ *a* wily, suspicious, cunning

cianuro /θia'nuro; sia'nuro/ *m,* cyanide

ciar /θiar; siar/ *vi* to go backwards; *Naut.* row backwards; *Fig.* make no headway (negotiations)

ciática /'θiatika; 'siatika/ *f,* sciatica

ciático /'θiatiko; 'siatiko/ *a* sciatic

ciberespacio *m,* cyberspace

ciborio /θi'βorio; si'βorio/ *m,* ciborium

cicatería /θikate'ria; sikate'ria/ *f,* niggardliness, avarice

cicatero /θika'tero; sika'tero/ *a* avaricious, niggardly, mean

cicatriz /θika'triθ; sika'tris/ *f,* cicatrice; *Fig.* scar, mark, impression

cicatrización /θikatriθa'θion; sikatrisa'sion/ *f,* cicatrization

cicatrizar /θikatri'θar; sikatri'sar/ *vt* to cicatrize, heal; *—vr* scar over

ciclamino /θikla'mino; sikla'mino/ *m,* cyclamen

cíclico /'θikliko; 'sikliko/ *a* cyclic, cyclical

ciclismo /θi'klismo; si'klismo/ *m,* bicycling

ciclista /θi'klista; si'klista/ *mf* cyclist

ciclo /'θiklo; 'siklo/ *m,* cycle (of time). **c. artúrico, c. de Artús,** Arthurian Cycle. **c. de conferencias,** series of lectures

ciclón /θi'klon; si'klon/ *m,* cyclone

ciclópeo /θi'klopeo; si'klopeo/ *a* cyclopean

ciclostilo /θiklos'tilo; siklos'tilo/ *m,* cyclostyle

cicuta /θi'kuta; si'kuta/ *f,* hemlock

cid /θið; sið/ *m,* great warrior, chief. **el Cid,** national hero of Spanish wars against the Moors

cidra /'θiðra; 'siðra/ *f,* citron

cidro /'θiðro; 'siðro/ *m,* citron tree

ciego /'θiego; 'siego/ *a* blind; dazed, blinded; choked up. *m,* blind man; *Anat.* cæcum. **a ciegas,** blindly; heedlessly

cielo /'θielo; 'sielo/ *m,* sky, firmament; atmosphere; climate; paradise; Providence; bliss, glory; roof, canopy; *Inf.* darling. **a c. abierto,** in the open air. **parecer un c.,** to be heavenly

ciempiés /θiem'pies; siem'pies/ *m,* centipede

cien /θien; sien/ *a* abb. **ciento,** hundred. Used always before substantives (e.g. *c. hombres,* 100 men)
ciénaga /'θienaga; 'sienaga/ *f,* swamp; morass
ciencia /'θienθia; 'siensia/ *f,* science; knowledge; erudition, ability. **ciencias naturales,** natural science. **a c. cierta,** for certain, without doubt (gen. with *saber*)
cienmilésimo /θiemi'lesimo; siemi'lesimo/ *a* hundred-thousandth
cieno /'θieno; 'sieno/ *m,* slime, mud; silt
científico /θien'tifiko; sien'tifiko/ *a* scientific. *m,* scientist
ciento /'θiento; 'siento/ (cf. **cien**) *a* hundred; hundredth. *m,* hundred. **por c.,** per cent.
cierne, en /'θierne, en; 'sierne, en/ in flower; *Fig.* in the early stages, in embryo
cierre /'θierre; 'sierre/ *m,* closing, shutting; closing time of shops, etc.; fastening; fastener; clasp (of a necklace, handbag, etc.). **c. cremallera,** zip fastener. **c. metálico,** doorshutter
ciertamente /θierta'mente; sierta'mente/ *adv* certainly; undoubtedly; indeed
ciertísimo /θier'tisimo; sier'tisimo/ *a* everyday form of the superlative of **cierto** (see **certísimo**)
cierto /'θierto; 'sierto/ *a* certain, sure; true; particular (e.g. *c. hombre,* a certain man (note no *def. art.*)). **un c. sabor,** a special flavor. **una cosa cierta,** something certain. **no, por c.,** no, certainly not. **por c.,** truly, indeed
cierva /'θierβa; 'sierβa/ *f,* hind
ciervo /'θierβo; 'sierβo/ *m,* stag. **c. volante,** stag-beetle
cierzo /'θierθo; 'sierso/ *m,* northerly wind
cifra /'θifra; 'sifra/ *f,* number; figure; sum total; cipher, code; monogram; abbreviation
cifrar /θi'frar; si'frar/ *vt* to write in cipher; summarize, abridge; (*with en*) be dependent on; depend on
cigarra /θi'garra; si'garra/ *f, Ent.* cicada, harvest fly
cigarral /θiga'rral; siga'rral/ *m,* (Toledo) country-house and garden or orchard
cigarrera /θiga'rrera; siga'rrera/ *f,* woman who makes or sells cigars; cigar-cabinet; cigar-case
cigarrillo /θiga'rriʎo; siga'rriyo/ *m,* cigarette
cigarro /θi'garro; si'garro/ *m,* cigar
cigüeña /θi'gueɲa; si'gueɲa/ *f, Ornith.* stork; *Mech.* crank
ciliar /θi'liar; si'liar/ *a* ciliary
cilicio /θi'liθio; si'lisio/ *m,* hairshirt
cilindrar /θilin'drar; silin'drar/ *vt* to roll; calendar; bore
cilindrero /θilin'drero; silin'drero/ *m,* organ grinder
cilíndrico /θi'lindriko; si'lindriko/ *a* cylindrical
cilindro /θi'lindro; si'lindro/ *m,* cylinder; roller
cima /'θima; 'sima/ *f,* summit; top of trees; apex; *Archit.* coping; head (thistle, etc.); *Fig.* aim, goal, end
cimbalero /θimba'lero; simba'lero/ **(-ra)** *n* cymbalist
címbalo /'θimbalo; 'simbalo/ *m,* cymbal
cimborrio /θim'βorrio; sim'βorrio/ *m, Archit.* cupola; cimborium
cimbrar, cimbrear /θim'βrar, θimbre'ar; sim'βrar, simbre'ar/ *vt* to bend; brandish; *—vr* sway (in walking)
cimbreño /θim'βreɲo; sim'βreɲo/ *a* graceful, lithe, willowy
cimbreo /θim'βreo; sim'βreo/ *m,* swaying, bending
cimentar /θimen'tar; simen'tar/ *vt irr* to lay foundations; refine (gold, metals, etc.); found; *Fig.* ground (in virtue, etc.). See **acertar**
cimera /θi'mera; si'mera/ *f,* crest of helmet
cimiento /θi'miento; si'miento/ *m,* foundation (of a building); bottom; groundwork; origin, base. **abrir los cimientos,** to lay the foundations
cimitarra /θimi'tarra; simi'tarra/ *f,* scimitar
cinabrio /θi'naβrio; si'naβrio/ *m,* cinnabar; vermilion
cinc /θink; sink/ *m,* zinc
cincel /θin'θel; sin'sel/ *m,* chisel; burin, engraver
cincelador /θinθela'ðor; sinsela'ðor/ **(-ra)** *n* engraver; chiseler
cincelar /θinθe'lar; sinse'lar/ *vt* to chisel; carve; engrave
cincha /'θintʃa; 'sintʃa/ *f,* girth of a saddle
cinchar /θin'tʃar; sin'tʃar/ *vt* to tighten the saddle girths
cincho /'θintʃo; 'sintʃo/ *m,* belt, girdle; iron hoop
cinco /'θinko; 'sinko/ *a* and *m,* five; fifth. **a las c.,** at five o'clock
cincuenta /θin'kuenta; sin'kuenta/ *a* and *m,* fifty; fiftieth
cincuentavo /θinkuen'taβo; sinkuen'taβo/ *a* fiftieth
cincuentenario /θinkuente'nario; sinkuente'nario/ *m,* fiftieth anniversary
cincuentón /θinkuen'ton; sinkuen'ton/ **(-ona)** *a* and *n* fifty years old (person)
cine, cinema /'θine, θi'nema; 'sine, si'nema/ *m,* cinema, movies. **c. sonoro,** sound film
cinemática /θine'matika; sine'matika/ *f, Phys.* kinematics
cinematografía /θinematogra'fia; sinematogra'fia/ *f,* cinematography
cinematografiar /θinematogra'fiar; sinematogra'fiar/ *vt* to film
cinematográfico /θinemato'grafiko; sinemato'grafiko/ *a* cinematographic
cinematógrafo /θinema'tografo; sinema'tografo/ *m,* motion-picture camera; cinema
cínico /'θiniko; 'siniko/ *a* cynical; impudent; untidy. *m,* cynic
cinismo /θi'nismo; si'nismo/ *m,* cynicism
cinta /'θinta; 'sinta/ *f,* ribbon; tape; strip; film (cinematograph). **c. métrica,** tape-measure
cintillo /θin'tiʎo; sin'tiyo/ *m,* hatband; small ring set with gems
cinto /'θinto; 'sinto/ *m,* belt, girdle. **c. de pistolas,** pistol-belt
cintoteca /θinto'teka; sinto'teka/ *f,* tape library
cintura /θin'tura; sin'tura/ *f,* waist; belt, girdle
cinturón /θintu'ron; sintu'ron/ *m,* large waist; belt girdle; sword-belt; that which encircles or surrounds. **c. de seguridad,** seat belt
ciprés /θi'pres; si'pres/ *m, Bot.* cypress tree or wood
cipresal /θipre'sal; sipre'sal/ *m,* cypress grove
cipresino /θipre'sino; sipre'sino/ *a* cypress; cypress-like
circasiano /θirka'siano; sirka'siano/ **(-na)** *a* and *n* Circassian
circo /'θirko; 'sirko/ *m,* circus; amphitheater
circón /θir'kon; sir'kon/ *m,* zircon
circuir /θir'kuir; sir'kuir/ *vt. irr* to surround, encircle. See **huir**
circuito /θir'kuito; sir'kuito/ *m,* periphery; contour; (*Elec. Phys.*) circuit. **corto c.,** short circuit
circulación /θirkula'θion; sirkula'sion/ *f,* circulation; traffic. **c. de la sangre,** circulation of the blood. **calle de gran c.,** busy street
circular /θirku'lar; sirku'lar/ *a* circular. *f,* circular *—vt* to pass round; *—vi* circle; circulate; move in a circle; move about; run, travel (traffic)
circulatorio /θirkula'torio; sirkula'torio/ *a* circulatory
círculo /'θirkulo; 'sirkulo/ *m,* circle; circumference; circuit; casino, social club
circuncidar /θirkunθi'ðar; sirkunsi'ðar/ *vt* to circumcise; modify, reduce
circuncisión /θirkunθi'sion; sirkunsi'sion/ *f,* circumcision
circunciso /θirkun'θiso; sirkun'siso/ *a* circumcised
circundar /θirkun'dar; sirkun'dar/ *vt* to surround
circunferencia /θirkunfe'renθia; sirkunfe'rensia/ *f,* circumference
circunflejo /θirkun'fleho; sirkun'fleho/ *a* circumflex. **acento c.,** circumflex accent
circunlocución /θirkunloku'θion; sirkunloku'sion/ *f,* circumlocution
circunnavegación /θirkunnaβega'θion; sirkunnaβega'sion/ *f,* circumnavigation
circunnavegar /θirkunnaβe'gar; sirkunnaβe'gar/ *vt* to circumnavigate
circunscribir /θirkunskri'βir; sirkunskri'βir/ *vt* to circumscribe *—Past Part.* **circunscrito**
circunscripción /θirkunskrip'θion; sirkunskrip'sion/ *f,* circumscription
circunspección /θirkunspek'θion; sirkunspek'sion/ *f,* circumspection; seriousness, dignity

circunspecto /θirkuns'pekto; sirkuns'pekto/ *a* circumspect; serious, dignified
circunstancia /θirkuns'tanθia; sirkuns'tansia/ *f*, circumstance; incident, detail; condition. **c. agravante,** aggravating circumstance. **c. atenuante,** extenuating circumstance. **bajo las circunstancias,** in the circumstances. **de circunstancias,** occasional (e.g. *poesías de circunstancias,* occasional verse). **estar al nivel de las circunstancias,** to rise to the occasion
circunstanciado /θirkunstan'θiaðo; sirkunstan'siaðo/ *a* circumstantiated, detailed
circunstancial /θirkunstan'θial; sirkunstan'sial/ *a* circumstantial; occasional (e.g. *poesías circunstanciales,* occasional verse)
circunstante /θirkuns'tante; sirkuns'tante/ *a* surrounding; present. *mf* person present, bystander
circunvecino /θirkumbe'θino; sirkumbe'sino/ *a* adjacent, neighboring
circunvolución /θirkumbolu'θion; sirkumbolu'sion/ *f*, circumvolution
cirial /θi'rial; si'rial/ *m*, processional candlestick
cirio /'θirio; 'sirio/ *m*, wax candle
cirro /'θirro; 'sirro/ *m*, *Med.* scirrhus; *Bot.* tendril; *Zool.* cirrus
cirrosis /θi'rrosis; si'rrosis/ *f*, cirrhosis
cirroso /θi'rroso; si'rroso/ *a Med.* scirrhous; (*Zool. Bot.*) cirrose
ciruela /θi'ruela; si'ruela/ *f*, plum; prune. **c. claudia, c. veidal,** greengage. **c. damascena,** damson
ciruelo /θi'ruelo; si'ruelo/ *m*, plum tree
cirugía /θiru'hia; siru'hia/ *f*, surgery
cirujano /θiru'hano; siru'hano/ *m*, surgeon
cisco /'θisko; 'sisko/ *m*, coal dust, slack coal; *Inf.* hubbub, quarrel
cisma /'θisma; 'sisma/ *m*, or *f*, schism; disagreement, discord. **el C. de Occidente,** the Western Schism
cismático /θis'matiko; sis'matiko/ *a* schismatic; discordant, inharmonious
cisne /'θisne; 'sisne/ *m*, swan
cisterciense /θister'θiense; sister'siense/ *a* Cistercian
cisterna /θis'terna; sis'terna/ *f*, water-tank, cistern
cístico /'θistiko; 'sistiko/ *a* cystic
cistitis /θis'titis; sis'titis/ *f*, cystitis
cita /'θita; 'sita/ *f*, appointment; quotation, citation
citable /θi'taβle; si'taβle/ *a* quotable
citación /θita'θion; sita'sion/ *f*, quotation; *Law.* summons
citar /θi'tar; si'tar/ *vt* to make an appointment; cite, quote; *Law.* summon. **c. en comparecencia,** to summon to appear in court
cítara /'θitara; 'sitara/ *f*, *Mus.* zither
citatorio /θita'torio; sita'torio/ *m*, summons
citerior /θite'rior; site'rior/ *a* hither, nearer
citrato /θi'trato; si'trato/ *m*, *Chem.* citrate
cítrico /'θitriko; 'sitriko/ *a* citric
ciudad /θiu'ðað; siu'ðað/ *f*, city; municipal body. **la c. señorial,** the Aristocratic City (Ponce, Puerto Rico)
ciudadanía /θiuðaða'nia; siuðaða'nia/ *f*, citizenship
ciudadano /θiuða'ðano; siuða'ðano/ **(-na)** *a* city; civic, born in or belonging to a city —*n* citizen; burgess; bourgeois. **c. de honor,** freeman (of a city)
ciudadela /θiuða'ðela; siuða'ðela/ *f*, citadel
cívico /'θiβiko; 'siβiko/ *a* civic; patriotic
civicultura /θiβikul'tura; siβikul'tura/ *f*, raising of civets
civil /θi'βil; si'βil/ *a* civil; civilian; polite
civilidad /θiβili'ðað; siβili'ðað/ *f*, politeness, civility
civilización /θiβiliθa'θion; siβilisa'sion/ *f*, civilization
civilizador /θiβiliθa'ðor; siβilisa'ðor/ *a* civilizing
civilizar /θiβili'θar; siβili'sar/ *vt* to civilize; educate; —*vr* grow civilized; be educated
civismo /θi'βismo; si'βismo/ *m*, civism; patriotism; civics
cizalla /θi'θaʎa; si'saya/ *f*, shears, shearing machine; metal filings
cizaña /θi'θaɲa; si'saɲa/ *f*, *Bot.* darnel, tare; vice, evil; dissension, discord (gen. with *meter* and *sembrar*)
clac /klak/ *m*, opera-hat; tricorne
clamar /kla'mar/ *vi* to cry out; *Fig.* demand (of inanimate things); vociferate; speak solemnly
clamor /kla'mor/ *m*, outcry, shouting; shriek, complaint; knell, tolling of bells
clamorear /klamore'ar/ *vt* to implore, clamor (for); —*vi* toll (of bells)
clamoroso /klamo'roso/ *a* noisy, clamorous
clandestino /klandes'tino/ *a* clandestine, secret
clangor /klaŋ'gor/ *m*, *Poet.* blare, bray (of trumpet)
claqué /kla'ke/ *m*, tap-dance
clara /'klara/ *f*, white of egg; bald patch (in fur); *Inf.* fair interval on a rainy day
claraboya /klara'βoya/ *f*, skylight; *Archit.* clerestory
claramente /klara'mente/ *adv* clearly, evidently
clarear /klare'ar/ *vt* to clear; give light to; —*vi* to dawn; grow light; —*vr* be transparent; *Inf.* reveal secrets unwittingly
clarete /kla'rete/ *m*, claret (wine); claret color —*a* claret; claret-colored
claridad /klari'ðað/ *f*, clearness; transparency; lightness, brightness; distinctness; clarity; good reputation, renown; plain truth, home truth (gen. *pl*)
clarificación /klarifika'θion; klarifika'sion/ *f*, clarification; purifying, refining
clarificar /klarifi'kar/ *vt* to illuminate; clarify, purify; refine (sugar, etc.)
clarín /kla'rin/ *m*, bugle; clarion; organ stop, bugler
clarinete /klari'nete/ *m*, clarinet; clarinet player
clarión /kla'rion/ *m*, white chalk, crayon
clarividencia /klariβi'ðenθia; klariβi'ðensia/ *f*, perspicuity, clear-sightedness
clarividente /klariβi'ðente/ *a* perspicacious, clear-sighted
claro /'klaro/ *a* clear; light, bright; distinct; pure, clean; transparent, translucent; light (of colors); easily understood; evident, obvious; frank; cloudless; shrewd, quick-thinking; famous. *m*, skylight; space between words; break in a speech; space in procession, etc.; *Art.* (gen. *pl*) high lights —*interj* **¡C.!** or **¡C. está!** Of course! **a las claras,** openly, frankly
claroscuro /klaros'kuro/ *m*, chiaroscuro; monochrome
clase /'klase/ *f*, class, group; kind, sort, quality; class (school, university); lecture room; lecture, lesson; order, family. **c. dirigente,** ruling class. **c. media,** middle class. **c. social,** social class
clasicismo /klasi'θismo; klasi'sismo/ *m*, classicism
clasicista /klasi'θista; klasi'sista/ *a* and *mf* classicist
clásico /'klasiko/ *a* classic; notable; classical. *m*, classic
clasificación /klasifika'θion; klasifika'sion/ *f*, classification
clasificador /klasifika'ðor/ **(-ra)** *n* classifier. **c. de billetes,** ticket-punch
clasificar /klasifi'kar/ *vt* to classify, arrange. **c. correspondencia,** to file letters
claudicación /klauðika'θion; klauðika'sion/ *f*, limping; negligence; hesitancy, weakness; backing down
claudicar /klauði'kar/ *vi* to limp; be negligent; hesitate, give way
claustral /klaus'tral/ *a* cloistral
claustro /'klaustro/ *m*, cloister; council, faculty, senate (of university); monastic rule
claustrofobia /klaustro'foβia/ *f*, claustrophobia
cláusula /'klausula/ *f*, clause. **c. de negación implícita,** contrary-to-fact clause. **c. principal,** main clause. **c. subordinada,** dependent clause, subordinate clause. **c. sustantiva,** noun clause
clausura /klau'sura/ *f*, sanctum of convent; claustration; solemn ending ceremony of tribunal, etc. **la vida de c.,** monastic or conventual life
clava /'klaβa/ *f*, club, truncheon; *Naut.* scupper
clavadizo /klaβa'ðiθo; klaβa'ðiso/ *a* nail studded (doors, etc.)
clavar /kla'βar/ *vt* to nail; fasten with nails; pierce, prick; set gems (jeweler); spike (cannon, gum); *Fig.* fix (eyes, attention, etc.); *Inf.* cheat
clave /'klaβe/ *m*, clavichord. *f*, code, key; *Mus.* clef; *Archit.* keystone; plug (telephones); **c. (de),** key to. *Mus.* **c. de sol,** treble clef
clavel /kla'βel/ *m*, *Bot.* carnation plant and flower
clavelito /klaβe'lito/ *m*, *Bot.* pink plant and flower
clavero /kla'βero/ **(-ra)** *n* keeper of the keys. *m*, clove tree

clavetear /klaβete'ar/ *vt* to stud with nails; *Fig.* round off (business affairs)
clavicordio /klaβi'korðio/ *m,* clavichord
clavícula /kla'βikula/ *f,* clavicle
clavija /kla'βiha/ *f,* peg, pin; plug; peg of stringed instrument; axle-pin
clavo /'klaβo/ *m,* nail, spike, peg; corn (on foot); anguish. **c. de especia,** clove. **c. de herradura,** hob-nail
claymore /klai'more/ *f,* claymore
clemátide /kle'matiðe/ *f, Bot.* clematis
clemencia /kle'menθia; kle'mensia/ *f,* mildness; clemency; mercy
clemente /kle'mente/ *a* mild; clement; merciful
cleptomanía /kleptoma'nia/ *f,* kleptomania
cleptómano /klep'tomano/ **(-na)** *a* and *n* kleptomaniac
clerecía /klere'θia; klere'sia/ *f,* clergy
clerical /kleri'kal/ *a* belonging to the clergy; clerical
clericalismo /klerika'lismo/ *m,* clericalism
clerigalla /kleri'gaʎa; kleri'gaya/ *f,* (*contemptuous*) dog-collar men
clérigo /'klerigo/ *m,* cleric, clergyman; clerk (in Middle Ages)
clero /'klero/ *m,* clergy
cliente /'kliente/ *mf* client, customer; protégé, ward
clientela /klien'tela/ *f,* patronage, protection; clientele
clima /'klima/ *m,* climate, clime
climatérico /klima'teriko/ *a* climacteric
climático /kli'matiko/ *a* climatic
climatología /klimatolo'hia/ *f,* climatology
clímax /'klimaks/ *m,* climax
clínica /'klinika/ *f,* clinic, nursing home; department of medicine or surgery
clínico /'kliniko/ *a* clinical
clíper /'kliper/ *m,* (*Aer.* and *Naut.*) clipper
clisar /kli'sar/ *vt Print.* to cast from a mold, stereotype
clisé /kli'se/ *m, Print.* stereotype plate
cloaca /klo'aka/ *f,* sewer, drain; *Zool.* cloaca
cloquear /kloke'ar/ *vi* to go broody (hen); cluck
cloqueo /klo'keo/ *m,* cluck, clucking
cloquera /klo'kera/ *f,* broodiness (hens)
clorato /klo'rato/ *m,* chlorate
clorhidrato /klori'ðrato/ *m,* hydrochloride
clorhídrico /klor'iðriko/ *a* hydrochloric
cloro /'kloro/ *m,* chlorine
clorofila /kloro'fila/ *f,* chlorophyll
cloroformizar /kloroformi'θar; kloroformi'sar/ *vt* to chloroform
cloroformo /kloro'formo/ *m,* chloroform
clorosis /klo'rosis/ *f,* chlorosis
cloruro /klo'ruro/ *m,* chloride
club /kluβ/ *m,* club
clueca /'klueka/ *f,* broody hen
clueco /'klueko/ *a* broody (hens); *Inf.* doddering
C.N.T. /knt/ initialism of Confederación Nacional de Trabajo
coacción /koak'θion; koak'sion/ *f,* coercion
coactivo /koak'tiβo/ *a* coercive
coadjutor /koaðhu'tor/ *m,* co-worker, assistant
coadunar /koaðu'nar/ *vt* to join or mingle together
coadyuvar /koaðyu'βar/ *vt* to assist
coagulación /koagula'θion; koagula'sion/ *f,* coagulation
coagular /koagu'lar/ *vt* to coagulate; clot; curdle
coágulo /ko'agulo/ *m,* clot; coagulation; congealed blood
coalición /koali'θion; koali'sion/ *f,* coalition
coartada /koar'taða/ *f,* alibi. **probar la c.,** to prove an alibi
coartar /koar'tar/ *vt* to limit, restrict
coautor /koau'tor/ **(-ra)** *n* co-author
cobalto /ko'βalto/ *m,* cobalt
cobarde /ko'βarðe/ *a* cowardly; irresolute. *m,* coward
cobardía /koβar'ðia/ *f,* cowardice
cobayo /ko'βayo/ *m,* guinea-pig
cobertera /koβer'tera/ *f,* lid, cover
cobertizo /koβer'tiθo; koβer'tiso/ *m,* overhanging roof; shack, shed, hut. **c. de aeroplanos,** *Aer.* hangar
cobertura /koβer'tura/ *f,* covering; coverlet; wrapping
cobija /ko'βiha/ *f,* imbrex tile; cover
cobijar /koβi'har/ *vt* to cover; shelter
cobra /'koβra/ *f, Zool.* cobra; rope or thong for yoking oxen; retrieval (of game)
cobradero /koβra'ðero/ *a* that which can be collected, recoverable
cobrador /koβra'ðor/ *m,* collector, receiver —*a* collecting. **c. de tranvía,** tram conductor
cobranza /ko'βranθa; ko'βransa/ *f,* receiving, collecting; collection of fruit or money
cobrar /ko'βrar/ *vt* to collect (what is owed); charge; earn; regain, recover; feel, experience (emotions); wind, pull in (ropes, etc.); gain, acquire; retrieve (game); —*vr* recuperate. **c. ánimo,** to take courage. **c. cariño (a),** to grow fond of. **c. fuerzas,** to gather strength. **c. importancia,** to gain importance. **¿Cuánto cobra Vd.?** How much do you charge?; How much do you earn?
cobre /'koβre/ *m, Mineral.* copper; copper kitchen utensils; *pl Mus.* brass
cobrizo /ko'βriθo; ko'βriso/ *a* containing copper; copper-colored
cocacolismo /kokako'lismo/ *n Inf.* economic dependence on the United States and adoption of its pop culture
cocacolonización /kokakoloniθa'θion; kokakolonisa'sion/ *f,* economic domination by the United States and introduction of its pop culture
cocacolonizar /kokakoloni'θar; kokakoloni'sar/ *vt* (United States) to gain economic control of... and introduce into its pop culture
cocaína /koka'ina/ *f,* cocaine
cocción /kok'θion; kok'sion/ *f,* coction
coceador /koθea'ðor; kosea'ðor/ *a* inclined to kick; kicking (animals)
coceadura /koθea'ðura; kosea'ðura/ *f,* kicking
cocear /koθe'ar; kose'ar/ *vi* to kick; *Inf.* kick against, oppose
cocedero /koθe'ðero; kose'ðero/ *a* easily cooked
cocer /ko'θer; ko'ser/ *vt. irr* to boil; cook; bake (bricks, etc.); digest; *Surg.* suppurate; —*vi* boil (of a liquid); ferment; —*vr* suffer pain or inconvenience over a long period —*Pres. Indic.* **cuezo, cueces, cuece, cuecen.** *Pres. Subjunc.* **cueza, cuezas, cueza, cuezan**
coche /'kotʃe/ *m,* carriage, car. **c. camas,** sleeping car. **c. -camioneta,** station wagon. **c. cerrado,** *Auto.* sedan. **c. de muchos caballos,** high-powered car. **c. de plaza,** hackney-carriage. **c. fúnebre,** hearse. **c. -línea,** intercity bus. *f, Ecuador* puddle
cochera /ko'tʃera/ *f,* coach house; tramway depot
cochero /ko'tʃero/ *m,* coachman; driver —*a* easily cooked
¡cochi! /'kotʃi/ (call to pigs)
cochina /ko'tʃina/ *f,* sow
cochinería /kotʃine'ria/ *f, Inf.* filthiness; mean trick
cochinilla /kotʃi'niʎa; kotʃi'niya/ *f,* wood louse; cochineal insect; cochineal
cochinillo /kotʃi'niʎo; kotʃi'niyo/ *m,* sucking-pig. **c. de Indias,** guinea-pig
cochino /ko'tʃino/ *m,* pig; *Inf.* filthy person —*a* filthy
cocido /ko'θiðo; ko'siðo/ *a* boiled, cooked, baked. *m,* dish of stewed meat, pork, chicken, with peas, etc.
cociente /ko'θiente; ko'siente/ *m,* quotient
cocimiento /koθi'miento; kosi'miento/ *m,* cooking; decoction
cocina /ko'θina; ko'sina/ *f,* kitchen; pottage; broth; cookery. **c. de campaña,** field-kitchen. **c. económica,** cooking range
cocinar /koθi'nar; kosi'nar/ *vt* to cook; —*vi Inf.* meddle, interfere
cocinería /koθine'ria; kosine'ria/ *f, Naut.* galley
cocinero /koθi'nero; kosi'nero/ **(-ra)** *n* cook, chef
cocinilla /koθi'niʎa; kosi'niya/ *f,* spirit-stove
coco /'koko/ *m, Bot.* coconut tree and fruit; coconut shell; grub, maggot; bogeyman; hobgoblin; *Inf.* grimace. *Inf.* **ser un c.,** to be hideously ugly
cocodrilo /koko'ðrilo/ *m,* crocodile
cócora /'kokora/ *mf Inf.* bore, nosy Parker
cocotal /koko'tal/ *m,* grove of coconut palms
cocotero /koko'tero/ *m,* coconut palm
coctel /kok'tel/ *m,* cocktail

cocuyo /ko'kuyo/ *m*, firefly
codal /ko'ðal/ *a* cubital. *m*, shoot of a vine; prop, strut; frame of a hand-saw
codazo /ko'ðaθo; ko'ðaso/ *m*, blow or nudge of the elbow. **dar codazos,** to elbow, shoulder out of the way
codear /koðe'ar/ *vi* to jostle; elbow, nudge; —*vr* be on terms of equality with
codeína /koðe'ina/ *f*, codeine
codelincuente /koðelin'kuente/ *mf* partner in crime, accomplice
codera /ko'ðera/ *f*, elbow rash; elbow-piece or patch
codeso /ko'ðeso/ *m*, laburnum
códice /'koðiθe; 'koðise/ *m*, codex
codicia /ko'ðiθia; ko'ðisia/ *f*, covetousness; greed
codiciar /koðiθi'ar; koðisi'ar/ *vt* to covet
codicilo /koði'θilo; koði'silo/ *m*, codicil
codicioso /koðiθi'oso; koðisi'oso/ **(-sa)** *a* covetous; *Inf.* hardworking —*n* covetous person
codificación /koðifika'θion; koðifika'sion/ *f*, codification
codificar /koðifi'kar/ *vt* to codify, compile
código /'koðigo/ *m*, code of laws. **c. civil,** civil laws. **c. de la circulación, c. de la vía pública,** highway code, traffic code. *Naut.* **c. de señales,** signal code. **c. penal,** criminal laws. **c. postal,** zip code
codillo /ko'ðiʎo; ko'ðiyo/ *m*, knee (of quadrupeds); shaft (of branch); bend (pipe, tube); stirrup
codo /'koðo/ *m*, elbow; angle, bend (pipe, tube); cubit. *Inf.* **hablar por los codos,** to chatter
codorniz /koðor'niθ; koðor'nis/ *f*, *Ornith.* quail
coeducación /koeðuka'θion; koeðuka'sion/ *f*, coeducation
coeficiente /koefi'θiente; koefi'siente/ *m*, coefficient
coercer /koer'θer; koer'ser/ *vt* to restrain, coerce
coerción /koer'θion; koer'sion/ *f*, *Law.* coercion
coercitivo /koerθi'tiβo; koersi'tiβo/ *a* coercive
coetáneo /koe'taneo/ **(-ea)** *a* contemporaneous —*n* contemporary
coevo /ko'eβo/ *a* coeval
coexistencia /koeksis'tenθia; koeksis'tensia/ *f*, coexistence
coexistir /koeksis'tir/ *vi* to co-exist
cofia /'kofia/ *f*, hairnet; coif
cofín /ko'fin/ *m*, basket
cofradía /kofra'ðia/ *f*, confraternity, brotherhood or sisterhood **c. de gastronomía,** eating club (US), dining society (UK)
cofre /'kofre/ *m*, trunk, chest (for clothes); coffer
cogedor /kohe'ðor/ *m*, collector, gatherer; dustpan; coal-shovel
coger /ko'her/ *vt* to seize, hold; catch; take, collect, gather; have room for; take up or occupy space; find; catch in the act; attack, surprise; reach; **c. un berrinche,** have a fit, have a tantrum —*vi* have room, fit
cogida /ko'hiða/ *f*, gathering, picking; *Inf.* fruit harvest; toss (bullfighting)
cogido /ko'hiðo/ *m*, pleat, fold; crease. **estar c. de tiempo** to be pressed for time.
cogitabundo /kohita'βundo/ *a* very pensive
cognación /kogna'θion; kogna'sion/ *f*, cognation; kinship
cognoscitivo /kognosθi'tiβo; kognossi'tiβo/ *a* cognitive
cogollo /ko'goʎo; ko'goyo/ *m*, heart (of lettuce, etc.); shoot; topmost branches of pine tree
cogote /ko'gote/ *m*, nape (of neck)
cogulla /ko'guʎa; ko'guya/ *f*, monk's habit
cohabitación /koaβita'θion; koaβita'sion/ *f*, cohabitation
cohabitar /koaβi'tar/ *vt* to cohabit
cohechador /koetʃa'ðor/ **(-ra)** *a* bribing —*n* briber
cohechar /koe'tʃar/ *vt* to bribe, corrupt, suborn
cohecho /ko'etʃo/ *m*, bribing; bribe
coheredero /koere'ðero/ **(-ra)** *n* co-heir
coherencia /koe'renθia; koe'rensia/ *f*, coherence, connection
coherente /koe'rente/ *a* coherent
cohesión /koe'sion/ *f*, cohesion
cohesivo /koe'siβo/ *a* cohesive
cohete /ko'ete/ *m*, rocket
cohetero /koe'tero/ *m*, firework manufacturer
cohibir /koi'βir/ *vt* to restrain; repress. See **Prohibir**.
cohombrillo /koom'briʎo; koom'briyo/ *m*, *dim* gherkin
cohombro /ko'ombro/ *m*, cucumber
cohonestar /koones'tar/ *vt Fig.* to gloss over, cover up; make appear decent (actions, etc.)
cohorte /ko'orte/ *f*, cohort
coincidencia /koinθi'ðenθia; koinsi'ðensia/ *f*, coincidence
coincidir /koinθi'ðir; koinsi'ðir/ *vt* to coincide; (two or more people) be in the same place at the same time. **c. con que...** to agree that...
coito /'koito/ *m*, coitus
cojear /kohe'ar/ *vi* to limp; wobble, be unsteady (of furniture); *Fig. Inf.* go wrong or astray; *Inf.* suffer from (vice, bad habit)
cojera /ko'hera/ *f*, lameness, limp
cojijoso /kohi'hoso/ *a* peevish
cojín /ko'hin/ *m*, cushion; pad; pillow (for lacemaking)
cojinete /kohi'nete/ *m*, small cushion; *Mech.* bearing. **c. de bolas,** ball-bearing
cojo /'koho/ *a* lame; unsteady, wobbly (of furniture, etc.)
col /kol/ *f*, cabbage. **c. de Bruselas,** Brussels sprouts
cola /'kola/ *f*, tail; train (of gown); shank (of a button); queue; tailpiece (of a violin, etc.); appendage; glue. **c. de milano,** dovetail. **c. de pescado,** isinglass. **formar c.,** to line up, queue up
colaboración /kolaβora'θion; kolaβora'sion/ *f*, collaboration. **en c.,** joint (e.g. *obra en colaboración*, joint work)
colaboracionista /kolaβoraθio'nista; kolaβorasio'nista/ *mf* collaborationist
colaborador /kolaβora'ðor/ **(-ra)** *n* collaborator
colaborar /kolaβo'rar/ *vt* to collaborate
colación /kola'θion; kola'sion/ *f*, conferment of a degree; collation (of texts); light repast; cold supper; area of a parish
colada /ko'laða/ *f*, wash; bleaching; mountain path; *Metall.* casting; *Inf.* trusty sword (allusion to name of one of the Cid's swords)
coladero /kola'ðero/ *m*, colander, sieve, strainer; narrow path
colador /kola'ðor/ *m*, colander
coladura /kola'ðura/ *f*, straining, filtration; *Inf.* untruth; *Inf.* howler, mistake
colapso /ko'lapso/ *m*, *Med.* prostration, collapse
colar /ko'lar/ *vt irr* to filter, strain; bleach; *Metall.* cast; —*vi* go through a narrow place; *Inf.* drink wine; —*vr* thread one's way; *Inf.* enter by stealth, steal in; *Inf.* tell untruths —*Pres. Indic.* **cuelo, cuelas, cuela, cuelan.** *Pres. Subjunc.* **cuele, cueles, cuele, cuelen**
colateral /kolate'ral/ *a* collateral
colcha /'koltʃa/ *f*, bedspread, counterpane, quilt
colchadura /koltʃa'ðura/ *f*, quilting
colchero /kol'tʃero/ *m*, quilt maker
colchón /kol'tʃon/ *m*, mattress. **c. de muelles,** spring-mattress. **c. de viento,** air-bed
colchonero /koltʃo'nero/ *m*, mattress maker or seller
colchoneta /koltʃo'neta/ *f*, pad, thin mattress
coleada /kole'aða/ *f*, wag of the tail
colear /kole'ar/ *vi* to wag the tail
colección /kolek'θion; kolek'sion/ *f*, collection
coleccionador /kolekθiona'ðor; koleksiona'ðor/ **(-ra)** *n* collector
coleccionar /kolekθio'nar; koleksio'nar/ *vt* to collect
coleccionista /kolekθio'nista; koleksio'nista/ *mf* collector
colecta /ko'lekta/ *f*, assessment; collection (of donations); *Eccl.* collect; voluntary offering
colectivero /kolekti'βero/ *m*, bus driver
colectividad /kolektiβi'ðað/ *f*, collectivity; body of people
colectivismo /kolekti'βismo/ *m*, collectivism
colectivista /kolekti'βista/ *a* collectivist
colectivo /kolek'tiβo/ *a* collective; *Argentina* (local) bus
colector /kolek'tor/ *m*, gatherer; collector; tax-

collector; water-pipe; water-conduit; *Elec.* commutator, collector
colega /ko'lega/ *m,* colleague
colegiado /kole'hiaðo/ *a* collegiate
colegial /kole'hial/ **(-la)** *a* college, collegiate —*n* student; pupil; *Fig. Inf.* novice.
colegiarse /kole'hiarse/ *vr* to meet as an association (professional, etc.)
colegiata /kole'hiata/ *f,* college church
colegiatura /kolehia'tura/ *f,* scholarship, fellowship (money granted a student); tuition (fee paid by a student), tuition fee, tuition fees
colegio /ko'lehio/ *m,* college; school; academy; association (professional); council, convocation; college or school buildings. **c. de abogados,** bar association. **c. de cardenales,** College of Cardinals. **c. electoral,** polling-booth. **c. militar,** military academy
colegir /kole'hir/ *vt irr* to collect, gather; deduce, infer. See **elegir**
cólera /'kolera/ *f,* bile, anger. *m,* cholera. **montar en c.,** to fly into a rage
colérico /ko'leriko/ *a* angry; choleric; suffering from cholera
colesterina /koleste'rina/ *f, Chem.* cholesterol
coleta /ko'leta/ *f,* pigtail; queue; *Inf.* postscript
coletazo /kole'taθo; kole'taso/ *m,* blow with one's tail, lash with one's tail; lash of a dying fish; *Fig.* last hurrah
coleto /ko'leto/ *m,* leather jerkin; *Inf.* body of a man
colgadero /kolga'ðero/ *a* able to be hung up. *m,* coat-hanger, hook
colgadizo /kolga'ðiθo; kolga'ðiso/ *a* hanging. *m,* overhanging roof
colgadura /kolga'ðura/ *f,* hangings, drapery, tapestries. **c. de cama,** bedhangings
colgajo /kol'gaho/ *m,* tatter; bunch (of grapes, etc.); *Surg.* skin lap
colgar /kol'gar/ *vt irr* to hang up; decorate with hangings; *Inf.* hang, kill; —*vi* hang, be suspended; *Fig.* be dependent. See **contar**
colibrí /koli'βri/ *m,* hummingbird
cólico /'koliko/ *m,* colic
colicuar /koli'kuar/ *vt* to dissolve
coliflor /koli'flor/ *f,* cauliflower
coligarse /koli'garse/ *vr* to confederate, unite
colilla /ko'liʎa; ko'liya/ *f,* stub (of a cigar or cigarette)
colina /ko'lina/ *f,* hill; cabbage seed; *Chem.* choline
colindante /kolin'dante/ *a* adjacent, contiguous
coliseo /koli'seo/ *m,* coliseum; theater
colisión /koli'sion/ *f,* collision; abrasion, bruise; *Fig.* clash (of ideas)
colitis /ko'litis/ *f,* colitis
collado /ko'ʎaðo; ko'yaðo/ *m,* hill, hillock
collar /ko'ʎar; ko'yar/ *m,* necklace; chain of office or honor; collar (dogs, etc.)
collera /ko'ʎera; ko'yera/ *f,* **collerón,** *m,* horse collar
colmado /kol'maðo/ *a* abundant. *m,* provision shop
colmar /kol'mar/ *vt* to fill to overflowing; bestow generously, heap upon
colmena /kol'mena/ *f,* beehive
colmenero /kolme'nero/ **(-ra)** *n* beekeeper
colmillo /kol'miʎo; kol'miyo/ *m,* canine tooth; tusk; fang
colmilludo /kolmi'ʎuðo; kolmi'yuðo/ *a* having large canine teeth; tusked; fanged; sagacious
colmo /'kolmo/ *m,* overflow; highest point; completion, limit, end. **ser el c.,** *Inf.* to be the last straw. **el c. de los colmos,** the absolute limit
colocación /koloka'θion; koloka'sion/ *f,* placing, putting; situation, place; employment; *Sports.* placing; order, arrangement; *Ling.* collocation
colocar /kolo'kar/ *vt* to place, put, arrange; place in employment. **c. bajo banderas,** to draft (into the armed forces) —*vr* place oneself
colofón /kolo'fon/ *m, Print.* colophon
colofonia /kolo'fonia/ *f,* solid resin (for bows of stringed instruments, etc.)
coloide /ko'loiðe/ *a* and *m,* colloid
colombiano /kolom'biano/ **(-na)** *a* and *n* Colombian
colombina /kolom'bina/ *f,* columbine
colombofilia /kolombo'filia/ *f,* pigeon fancying
colonia /ko'lonia/ *f,* colony; plantation
colonial /kolo'nial/ *a* colonial
colonización /koloniθa'θion; kolonisa'sion/ *f,* colonization
colonizador /koloniθa'ðor; kolonisa'ðor/ **(-ra)** *a* colonizing —*n* colonizer
colonizar /koloni'θar; koloni'sar/ *vt* to colonize; settle
colono /ko'lono/ *m,* settler, colonist; farmer
coloquio /ko'lokio/ *m,* colloquy, conversation, talk; colloquium
color /ko'lor/ *m,* color; dye; paint; rouge; coloring; pretext, excuse; character, individuality; *pl* natural colors. **c. estable, c. sólido,** fast color. **mudar de c.,** to change color. **de c.,** colored. **so c.,** under the pretext. **ver las cosas c. de rosa,** to see things through rose-colored glasses
coloración /kolora'θion; kolora'sion/ *f,* coloration, painting
colorado /kolo'raðo/ *a* colored. *West Hem.* red, reddish; *Inf.* blue, obscene; specious
colorante /kolo'rante/ *a* coloring. *m,* dyestuff; coloring (substance)
colorar /kolo'rar/ *vt* to color; dye
colorear /kolore'ar/ *vt* to color; pretext; *Fig.* whitewash, excuse; —*vi* show color; be reddish; grow red, ripe (tomatoes, cherries, etc.)
colorero /kolo'rero/ *m,* dyer
colorete /kolo'rete/ *m,* rouge
colorido /kolo'riðo/ *m,* coloring, color
colorín /kolo'rin/ *m,* goldfinch; bright color
colorista /kolo'rista/ *a* and *mf* colorist
colosal /kolo'sal/ *a* colossal, enormous; extraordinary, excellent
coloso /ko'loso/ *m,* colossus; *Fig.* outstanding person or thing, giant; **el C. del Norte, el Gran C. del Norte,** (contemptuous epithet for the United States of America)
columbino /kolum'bino/ *a* pertaining to a dove; dovelike; candid, innocent; purply-red
columbrar /kolum'brar/ *vt* to discern in the distance, glimpse; conjecture, guess
columna /ko'lumna/ *f, Mil. Archit. Print.* column; *Fig.* protection, shelter; *Naut.* stanchion. **c. cerrada,** *Mil.* etc. mass formation. **c. de los suspiros,** agony column (in a newspaper)
columnata /kolum'nata/ *f,* colonnade
columpiar /kolum'piar/ *vt* to swing; dangle (one's feet); —*vr Inf.* sway in walking; swing
columpio /ko'lumpio/ *m,* swing
colusión /kolu'sion/ *f,* collusion
colusorio /kolu'sorio/ *a* collusive
coma /'koma/ *f, Gram.* comma. *m, Med.* coma
comadre /ko'maðre/ *f,* midwife; *Inf.* procuress, go-between; *Inf.* pal, gossip
comadrear /komaðre'ar/ *vi Inf.* to gossip
comadreja /koma'ðreha/ *f, Zool.* weasel
comadrón /koma'ðron/ *m,* accoucheur
comadrona /koma'ðrona/ *f,* midwife
comandancia /koman'danθia; koman'dansia/ *f, Mil.* command; commandant's H.Q.
comandante /koman'dante/ *m,* commandant; commander; major; squadron-leader —*a Mil.* commanding. **c. en jefe,** commanding officer
comandar /koman'dar/ *vt Mil.* to command
comandita /koman'dita/ *f, Com.* sleeping partnership; private company
comando /ko'mando/ *m, Mil.* commando
comarca /ko'marka/ *f,* district, region
comatoso /koma'toso/ *a* comatose
comba /'komba/ *f,* bend, warping; jump rope, skipping-rope; camber (of road)
combadura /komba'ðura/ *f,* curvature; warping; camber (of a road)
combar /kom'bar/ *vt* to bend; twist; warp; camber
combate /kom'bate/ *m,* fight, combat; mental strife; contradiction, opposition. **c. judicial,** trial by combat. **dejar fuera de c.,** (a) (boxing) to knock out
combatiente /komba'tiente/ *m,* combatant, soldier
combatir /komba'tir/ *vi* to fight; —*vt* attack; struggle

against (winds, water, etc.); contradict, oppose; *Fig.* disturb, trouble (emotions)

combinación /kombina'θion; kombina'sion/ *f,* combination; list of words beginning with same letter; project; concurrence; underskirt, petticoat. **estar en c.** (**con**), to be in cahoots (with), connive (with)

combinar /kombi'nar/ *vt* to combine; (*Mil. Nav.*) join forces; arrange, plan; *Chem.* combine; **combinar para + inf.** (two or more people) to make arrangements to + inf.

combustible /kombus'tiβle/ *a* combustible. *m,* fuel

combustión /kombus'tion/ *f,* combustion. **c. activa,** rapid combustion. **c. espontánea,** spontaneous combustion

comedero /kome'ðero/ *a* edible. *m,* feeding-trough; dining-room

comedia /ko'meðia/ *f,* comedy; play; theater; comic incident; *Fig.* play-acting, theatricalism. **c. alta,** art theater. **c. de costumbres,** comedy of manners. **c. de enredo,** play with very involved plot. *Inf.* **hacer la c.,** to play-act, pretend

comedianta /kome'ðianta/ *f,* actress

comediante /kome'ðiante/ *m,* actor; *Inf.* dissembler.

comedido /kome'ðiðo/ *a* courteous; prudent; moderate

comedimiento /komeði'miento/ *m,* courtesy; moderation; prudence

comedir /kome'ðir/ *vt irr* to prepare, premeditate; *—vr* restrain oneself, be moderate; offer one's services. See **pedir**

comedor /kome'ðor/ *a* voracious. *m,* dining-room

comendador /komenda'ðor/ *m,* knight commander

comendatorio /komenda'torio/ *a* commendatory (of letters)

Comenio /ko'menio/ Comenius

comensal /komen'sal/ *mf* table companion

comentador /komenta'ðor/ **(-ra)** *n* commentator

comentar /komen'tar/ *vt* explain (document); *Inf.* comment

comentario /komen'tario/ **(a)** *m,* commentary (on)

comentarista /komenta'rista/ *mf* commentator

comento /ko'mento/ *m,* comment; commentary

comenzante /komen'θante; komen'sante/ *mf* beginner, novice *—a* initial

comenzar /komen'θar; komen'sar/ *vt vi irr* to begin, commence. See **empezar**

comer /ko'mer/ *m,* eating; food *—vi* to eat; feed; dine *—vt* eat; *Inf.* enjoy an income; waste (patrimony); consume, exhaust; fade (of colors); *—vr* be troubled, uneasy, remorseful. **ser de buen c.,** to have a good appetite; taste good. **tener que c.,** to be obliged to eat; have to eat; have enough to eat

comerciable /komer'θiaβle; komer'siaβle/ *a* marketable; sociable, pleasant (of persons)

comercial /komer'θial; komer'sial/ *a* commercial

comerciante /komer'θiante; komer'siante/ *a* trading. *mf* merchant, trader

comerciar /komer'θiar; komer'siar/ *vt* to trade; have dealings (with)

comercio /ko'merθio; ko'mersio/ *m,* trade, commerce; intercourse, traffic; illicit sexual intercourse; shop, store; tradesmen; commercial quarter of town

comestible /komes'tiβle/ *a* edible, eatable. *m,* (gen. *pl*) provisions

cometa /ko'meta/ *m, Astron.* comet. *f,* kite (toy). **c. celular,** box-kite

cometedor /komete'ðor/ **(-ra)** *n* perpetrator

cometer /kome'ter/ *vt* to entrust, hand over to; commit (crime, sins, etc.); *Com.* order

cometido /kome'tiðo/ *m,* charge, commission; moral obligation; function

comezón /kome'θon; kome'son/ *f,* itching, irritation; hankering, longing

comicidad /komiθi'ðað; komisi'ðað/ *f,* comic element; comic spirit

cómico /'komiko/ *a* comic; funny, comical. *m,* actor; comedian. **c. de la legua,** strolling player

comida /ko'miða/ *f,* food; meal; dinner; eating. **c. de gala,** state banquet. **c. de prueba,** *Med.* test meal

comienzo /ko'mienθo; ko'mienso/ *m,* beginning, origin

comillas /ko'miʎas; ko'miyas/ *f pl, Gram.* inverted commas

comilón /komi'lon/ **(-ona)** *a Inf.* gluttonous *—n* glutton

comino /ko'mino/ *m, Bot.* cumin. **no valer un c.,** to be not worth a jot

comisar /komi'sar/ *vt* to confiscate, sequestrate

comisaría /komisa'ria/ *f,* commissaryship; commissariat. **c. de policía,** police station

comisario /komi'sario/ *m,* deputy, agent; commissary, head of police; commissioner. **alto c.,** high commissioner. **c. propietario,** stockholders' representative

comisión /komi'sion/ *f,* perpetration, committal; commission; committee; *Com.* commission

comisionado /komisio'naðo/ **(-da)** *a* commissioned. *m,* commissary

comisionar /komisio'nar/ *vt* to commission

comisionista /komisio'nista/ *mf Com.* commission agent

comiso /ko'miso/ *m, Law.* confiscation, sequestration; contraband

comité /komi'te/ *m,* committee

comitiva /komi'tiβa/ *f,* retinue, following

como /'komo/ *adv* like, as; in the same way; thus, accordingly; in the capacity of; so that; since *—conjunc* if (*followed by subjunc.*); because. **c. no,** unless. **¿Cómo?** How? In what way? Why? Pardon? What did you say? *interj* **¡Cómo!** What! You don't say! **¡Cómo no!** Why not! Of course! Surely! **¿Cómo que...?** What do you mean that...?

cómo /'komo/ *m,* the wherefore. **no saber el porqué ni el c.,** not to know the why or wherefore

cómoda /'komoða/ *f,* chest of drawers

comodidad /komoði'ðað/ *f,* comfort; convenience; advantage; utility, interest

comodín /komo'ðin/ *m,* (in cards) joker

cómodo /'komoðo/ *a* comfortable; convenient; opportune

comodón /komo'ðon/ *a Inf.* comfort-loving; easy-going; egoistical

comodoro /komo'ðoro/ *m, Naut.* commodore

comoquiera que /komo'kiera ke/ *adv* by any means that, anyway; whereas, given that

compacidad /kompaθi'ðað; kompasi'ðað/ *f,* compactness

compacto /kom'pakto/ *a* compact, dense; close (type)

compadecer /kompaðe'θer; kompaðe'ser/ *vt irr* to pity; *—vr* (*with* **de**) sympathize with; pity; harmonize, agree with. See **conocer**

compadre /kom'paðre/ *m, Inf.* pal

compaginación /kompahina'θion; kompahina'sion/ *f,* joining, fixing; *Print.* making-up

compaginar /kompahi'nar/ *vt* to fit together; join, put in order; harmonize, square (e.g. *compaginé una cuenta con la otra,* I squared one account with the other); *Print.* make up

compañero /kompa'ɲero/ **(-ra)** *n* companion, comrade; fellow-member; partner (games); *Fig.* pair, fellow, mate (things). **c. de armas,** brother-in-arms, companion-at-arms. **c. de cabina,** boothmate. **c. de exilio,** companion in exile, fellow exile. **c. de generación,** contemporary, person of the same generation. **c. de viaje,** traveling companion; *Polit.* fellow traveler (communist sympathizer)

compañía /kompa'ɲia/ *f,* company; society, association; theatrical company; (*Com. Mil.*) company. **C. de Jesús,** Order of Jesus. **c. de la zarza,** guild of guards and woodcutters for autos de fe. **c. de navegación,** shipping company. **c. por acciones,** joint stock company

comparable /kompa'raβle/ *a* comparable

comparación /kompara'θion; kompara'sion/ *f,* comparison

comparar /kompa'rar/ *vt* to compare; collate

comparativo /kompara'tiβo/ *a* comparative

comparecencia /kompare'θenθia; kompare'sensia/ *f,* (gen. *Law.*) appearance

comparecer /kompare'θer; kompare'ser/ *vi irr Law.* to appear (before tribunal, etc.); present oneself. See **conocer**

comparendo /kompa'rendo/ *m, Law.* summons

comparsa /kom'parsa/ *f,* retinue; *Theat.* chorus; troop of carnival revelers dressed alike. *mf Theat.* supernumerary actor
comparte /kom'parte/ *mf Law.* partner; accomplice
compartimiento /komparti'miento/ *m,* share, division; railway carriage. *Naut.* **c. estanco,** compartment
compartir /kompar'tir/ *vt* to share out, divide; participate
compás /kom'pas/ *m,* compasses; callipers; size; compass, time; range of voice; (*Naut. Mineral.*) compass; *Mus.* time, rhythm, bar, marking time. **c. de mar,** mariner's compass. **c. de puntas,** dividers, callipers. **fuera de c.,** *Mus.* out of time; out of joint (of the times). *Mus.* **llevar el c.,** to beat time
compasar /kompa'sar/ *vt* to measure with compasses; arrange or apportion accurately; *Mus.* put into bars
compasillo /kompa'siʎo; kompa'siyo/ *m, Mus.* $\frac{4}{4}$ measure
compasivo /kompa'siβo/ *a* compassionate; tenderhearted
compatibilidad /kompatiβili'ðað/ *f,* compatibility
compatible /kompa'tiβle/ *a* compatible
compatriota /kompa'triota/ *mf* compatriot
compeler /kompe'ler/ *vt* to compel, force
compendiar /kompen'diar/ *vt* to abridge, summarize
compendio /kom'pendio/ *m,* compendium. **en c.,** briefly
compendioso /kompen'dioso/ *a* summary, condensed; compendious
compenetración /kompenetra'θion; kompenetra'sion/ *f,* co-penetration; intermingling
compenetrado /kompene'traðo/ **(de)** *a* thoroughly convinced (of)
compenetrarse /kompene'trarse/ *vr* to co-penetrate; intermingle
compensación /kompensa'θion; kompensa'sion/ *f,* compensating; compensation
compensar /kompen'sar/ *vt* to equalize, counterbalance; compensate
compensatorio /kompensa'torio/ *a* compensatory; equalizing
competencia /kompe'tenθia; kompe'tensia/ *f,* competition, contest; rivalry; competence; aptitude; *Law.* jurisdiction
competente /kompe'tente/ *a* adequate, opportune; rightful, correct; apt, suitable; learned, competent
competer /kompe'ter/ *vi irr* to belong to; devolve on; concern. See **pedir**
competición /kompeti'θion; kompeti'sion/ *f,* competition
competidor /kompeti'ðor/ **(-ra)** *n* competitor
competir /kompe'tir/ *vi irr* to compete, contest; be equal (to), vie (with). See **pedir**
compilación /kompila'θion; kompila'sion/ *f,* compilation
compilador /kompila'ðor/ **(-ra)** *n* compiler —*a* compiling
compilar /kompi'lar/ *vt* to compile
compinche /kom'pintʃe/ *mf Inf.* pal, chum
complacencia /kompla'θenθia; kompla'sensia/ *f,* satisfaction, pleasure
complacer /kompla'θer; kompla'ser/ *vt irr* to oblige, humor; —*vr* (*with en*) be pleased or satisfied with; delight in, like to. See **nacer**
complaciente /kompla'θiente; kompla'siente/ *a* pleasing; obliging, helpful
complejidad /komplehi'ðað/ *f,* complexity
complejo /kom'pleho/ *a* complex; intricate. *m,* complex. **c. de inferioridad,** inferiority complex
complementario /komplemen'tario/ *a* complementary
complemento /komple'mento/ *m,* complement (all meanings)
completar /komple'tar/ *vt* to complete; perfect
completo /kom'pleto/ *a* full; finished; perfect
complexión /komplek'sion/ *f,* physical constitution
complexo /kom'plekso/ *a* complex; intricate
complicación /komplika'θion; komplika'sion/ *f,* complication
complicar /kompli'kar/ *vt* to complicate; muddle, confuse; —*vr* be complicated; be muddled or confused
cómplice /'kompliθe; 'komplise/ *mf* accomplice
complicidad /kompliθi'ðað; komplisi'ðað/ *f,* complicity
complot /kom'plot/ *m, Inf.* conspiracy, plot, intrigue
complutense /komplu'tense/ *a* native of, or belonging to, Alcalá de Henares
componedor /kompone'ðor/ **(-ra)** *n* repairer; arbitrator; bone-setter; *Mus.* composer; writer, author, compiler; *Print.* compositor
componenda /kompo'nenda/ *f,* mending, repair; *Inf.* settlement; compromise, arbitration; *Inf.* shady business
componente /kompo'nente/ *a* and *m,* component
componer /kompo'ner/ *vt irr* to construct, form; *Mech.* resolve; compose, create; *Print.* compose; prepare, concoct, mend, repair; settle (differences); remedy; trim; correct, adjust; *Lit. Mus.* compose; add up to, amount to; —*vi* write (verses); *Mus.* compose; —*vr* dress oneself up. **c. el semblante,** to compose one's features; *Inf.* **componérselas,** to fix matters, use one's wits. See **poner**
componible /kompo'niβle/ *a* reparable, mendable; able to be arranged or adjusted
comportamiento /komporta'miento/ *m,* conduct; deportment
comportar /kompor'tar/ *vt* to tolerate; —*vr* behave, comport oneself
composición /komposi'θion; komposi'sion/ *f,* composition; repair; arrangement, compromise; *Print.* composition; *Gram.* compound; *Chem.* constitution; *Mech.* resolution
compositor /komposi'tor/ **(-ra)** *n Mus.* composer; *Print.* compositor
Compostela /kompos'tela/ Compostella
compostura /kompos'tura/ *f,* composition, structure; repair; neatness (of person); adulteration; arrangement, agreement; discretion, modesty
compota /kom'pota/ *f,* fruit preserve, compote; thick sauce
compotera /kompo'tera/ *f,* jam or preserve dish
compra /'kompra/ *f,* buying; marketing, shopping; purchase. **estar de compras,** *Euph.* to be in the family way. **ir de compras,** to go shopping
comprable /kom'praβle/ *a* purchasable
comprador /kompra'ðor/ **(-ra)** *a* purchasing —*n* purchaser; buyer; shopper
comprar /kom'prar/ *vt* to buy; bribe
comprender /kompren'der/ *vt* to encircle, surround; include, comprise, contain; understand
comprensible /kompren'siβle/ *a* comprehensible
comprensión /kompren'sion/ *f,* comprehension, understanding
comprensivo /kompren'siβo/ *a* understanding; comprehensive
compresa /kom'presa/ *f, Med.* compress, swab; pack (for the face, etc.)
compresión /kompre'sion/ *f,* compression; squeeze
compresivo /kompre'siβo/ *a* compressive
compresor /kompre'sor/ *m,* compressor; *Auto. Aer.* supercharger
comprimido /kompri'miðo/ *m,* tablet, pill
comprimir /kompri'mir/ *vt* to compress; squeeze; restrain; —*vr* restrain oneself
comprobación /komproβa'θion; komproβa'sion/ *f,* verification; checking; proof
comprobante /kompro'βante/ *a* verifying; confirmatory
comprobar /kompro'βar/ *vt irr* to verify, check; confirm, prove. See **probar**
comprobatorio /komproβa'torio/ *a* confirmatory; verifying; testing
comprometedor /kompromete'ðor/ *a Inf.* compromising; jeopardizing
comprometer /komprome'ter/ *vt* to submit to arbitration; compromise; imperil, jeopardize; —*vr* pledge oneself; *Inf.* compromise oneself
comprometido /komprome'tiðo/ *a* awkward, embarrassing; (e.g. literature of a writer) committed, engagé
compromiso /kompro'miso/ *m,* compromise, agree-

ment, arbitration, commitment, obligation; appointment, engagement; jeopardy; difficulty
compuerta /kom'puerta/ *f,* half-door, wicket, hatch; floodgate, sluice. **c. flotante,** floating dam
compuesto /kom'puesto/ *a* and *past part* made-up, built-up; composite; circumspect; *Bot. Gram.* compound. *m,* composite; preparation, compound
compulsar /kompul'sar/ *vt* to collate; *Law.* make a transcript of
compulsivo /kompul'siβo/ *a* compelling
compunción /kompun'θion; kompun'sion/ *f,* compunction
compungir /kompun'hir/ *vt* to cause remorse or pity; *—vr* repent; sympathize with, pity
computable /kompu'taβle/ *a* computable
computación /komputa'θion; komputa'sion/ *f,* **cómputo** *m,* calculation, computation
computador /komputa'ðor/ **(-ra)** *n* computer
computar /kompu'tar/ *vt* to compute
computista /kompu'tista/ *mf* computer
cómputo /'komputo/ *m,* computation; estimate
comulgar /komul'gar/ *vt* to administer Holy Communion; *—vi* receive Holy Communion
comulgatorio /komulga'torio/ *m,* communion rail, altar rail
común /ko'mun/ *a* general, customary, ordinary; public, communal; universal, common; vulgar, low. *m,* community, population; water-closet. **en c.,** in common; generally. **por lo c.,** generally. **sentido c.,** common sense
comunal /komu'nal/ *a* communal; common. *m,* commonalty
comunero /komu'nero/ *a* popular, affable, democratic. *m,* joint owner; commoner; *Hist.* commune
comunicable /komuni'kaβle/ *a* communicable; communicative, sociable
comunicación /komunika'θion; komunika'sion/ *f,* communication; (telephone) call, message; letter (to the press); *Mil.* communiqué; *pl* lines of communication, transport
comunicado /komuni'kaðo/ *m,* official communication, communiqué; letter (to the press)
comunicante /komuni'kante/ *a* communicating
comunicar /komuni'kar/ *vt* to communicate; transmit; impart, share; *—vr* **comunicarse con,** (door) to open onto (e.g. *Esta puerta se comunica con el jardín.* This door opens onto the garden); communicate, converse, correspond with each other
comunicativo /komunika'tiβo/ *a* communicative; talkative, not reserved
comunidad /komuni'ðað/ *f,* the common people; community; generality, majority; *pl Hist.* Commune
comunión /komu'nion/ *f,* communion; intercourse, fellowship; *Eccl.* Communion
comunismo /komu'nismo/ *m,* communism
comunista /komu'nista/ *a* and *mf* communist
comunistófilo, comunistoide /komunis'tofilo, komunis'toiðe/ *a* fellow-traveling; *—n* fellow traveler
comúnmente /komu'mente/ *adv* commonly, generally; frequently
con /kon/ *prep* with; by means of; in the company of; towards, to; although (followed by *infin.*, but generally translated by an inflected verb, e.g. *C. ser almirante, no le gusta el mar,* Although he is an admiral, he doesn't like the sea); by (followed by *infin.* and generally translated by a gerund, e.g. *c. hacer todo esto,* by doing all this). **c. bien,** safe and sound, safely (e.g. *Llegamos con bien.* We arrived safely.) **c. cuentagotas,** sparingly; stingily. **c. que,** so, then. **c. tal que,** provided that, on condition that. **c. todo,** nevertheless. **¿Con...?** Is this...? (on the telephone, e.g. *¿Con el Sr. Piñangos?* Is this Mr. Piñangos?)
conato /ko'nato/ *m,* effort, endeavor; tendency; *Law.* attempted crime
concatenación /konkatena'θion; konkatena'sion/ *f,* concatenation
concavidad /konkaβi'ðað/ *f,* concavity; hollow
cóncavo /'konkaβo/ *a* concave. *m,* concavity; hollow
concebible /konθe'βiβle; konse'βiβle/ *a* conceivable
concebimiento /konθeβi'miento; konseβi'miento/ *m.* See **concepción**
concebir /konθe'βir; konse'βir/ *vi irr* to become pregnant; conceive, imagine; understand; *—vt* conceive, acquire (affection, etc.). See **pedir**
concedente /konθe'ðente; konse'ðente/ *a* conceding
conceder /konθe'ðer; konse'ðer/ *vt* to confer, grant; concede; agree to
concejal /konθe'hal; konse'hal/ *m,* councillor; alderman
concejil /konθe'hil; konse'hil/ *a* pertaining to a municipal council; public
concejo /kon'θeho; kon'seho/ *m,* town council; town hall; council meeting
concentración /konθentra'θion; konsentra'sion/ *f,* concentration
concentrado /konθen'traðo; konsen'traðo/ *a* concentrated; (of persons) reserved
concentrar /konθen'trar; konsen'trar/ *vt* to concentrate
concéntrico /kon'θentriko; kon'sentriko/ *a* concentric
concepción /konθep'θion; konsep'sion/ *f,* conception; idea, concept; *Eccl.* Immaculate Conception
conceptismo /konθep'tismo; konsep'tismo/ *m, Lit.* Concetism (cf. **Euphuism**)
conceptista /konθep'tista; konsep'tista/ *a* and *mf* concettist
concepto /kon'θepto; kon'septo/ *m,* idea, concept; epigram; opinion. **en mi c.,** in my opinion; judgment. **por c. de,** in payment of
conceptualismo /konθeptua'lismo; konseptua'lismo/ *m,* conceptualism
conceptuar /konθep'tuar; konsep'tuar/ *vt* to judge, take to be; believe; imagine
conceptuoso /konθep'tuoso; konsep'tuoso/ *a* witty, ingenious
concernencia /konθer'nenθia; konser'nensia/ *f,* respect, relation
concerniente /konθer'niente; konser'niente/ *a* concerning
concernir /konθer'nir; konser'nir/ *vi irr defective* to concern. See **discernir**
concertadamente /konθertaða'mente; konsertaða'mente/ *adv* methodically, orderly; by arrangement, or agreement
concertar /konθer'tar; konser'tar/ *vt irr* to arrange, settle, adjust; bargain; conclude (business deal); harmonize; compare, correlate; tune instruments; *—vi* reach an agreement. See **acertar**
concertina /konθer'tina; konser'tina/ *f,* concertina
concertista /konθer'tista; konser'tista/ *mf Mus.* performer, soloist; *Mus.* manager. **c. de piano,** concert pianist
concesión /konθe'sion; konse'sion/ *f,* conceding, grant; concession; lease
concesionario /konθesio'nario; konsesio'nario/ *m, Law.* concessionaire, leaseholder
concha /'kontʃa/ *f,* shell; turtle-shell; prompter's box; cove, creek; anything shell-shaped. *Fig.* **meterse en su c.,** to retire into one's shell. *Inf.* **tener más conchas que un galápago,** to be very cunning
conchado /kon'tʃaðo/ *a* scaly, having a shell
conciencia /kon'θienθia; kon'siensia/ *f,* consciousness; conscience; conscientiousness. **c. doble,** dual personality. **ancho de c.,** broad-minded. **a c.,** conscientiously
concienzudo /konθien'θuðo; konsien'suðo/ *a* of a delicate conscience, scrupulous; conscientious
concierto /kon'θierto; kon'sierto/ *m,* methodical arrangement; agreement; *Mus.* concert; *Mus.* concerto. **de c.,** by common consent
conciliable /konθi'liaβle; konsi'liaβle/ *a* reconcilable, compatible
conciliábulo /konθi'liaβulo; konsi'liaβulo/ *m,* conclave, private meeting; secret meeting
conciliación /konθilia'θion; konsilia'sion/ *f,* conciliation; similarity, affinity; protection, favor
conciliador /konθilia'ðor; konsilia'ðor/ *a* conciliatory
conciliar /konθi'liar; konsi'liar/ *m,* councilor *—vt* to conciliate; *Fig.* reconcile (opposing theories, etc.). **c. el sueño,** to induce sleep, woo sleep *—vr* win liking (or sometimes dislike)
concilio /kon'θilio; kon'silio/ *m,* council; *Eccl.* assembly; conciliary decree; findings of council

concinidad /konθini'ðað; konsini'ðað/ *f,* concinnity
concino /kon'θino; kon'sino/ *a* concinnous
concisión /konθi'sion; konsi'sion/ *f,* conciseness, brevity
conciso /kon'θiso; kon'siso/ *a* concise
concitar /konθi'tar; konsi'tar/ *vt* to stir up, foment
conciudadano /konθiuða'ðano; konsiuða'ðano/ **(-na)** *n* fellow citizen; fellow countryman
cónclave /'konklaβe/ *m,* conclave; meeting
concluir /kon'kluir/ *vt irr* to conclude, finish; come to a conclusion, decide; infer, deduce; convince by reasoning; *Law.* close legal proceedings; *—vr* expire, terminate. **c. con,** to put an end to. See **huir**
conclusión /konklu'sion/ *f,* finish, end; decision; close, denouement; theory, proposition (gen. *pl*); deduction, inference; *Law.* close. **en c.,** in conclusion
conclusivo /konklu'siβo/ *a* final; conclusive
concluyente /konklu'yente/ *a* concluding; convincing; conclusive
concomer /konko'mer/ *vi Inf.* to give a shrug, shrug one's shoulders; fidget with an itch. **c. de placer,** to itch with pleasure
concomitancia /konkomi'tanθia; konkomi'tansia/ *f,* concomitance
concomitante /konkomi'tante/ *a* and *m,* concomitant
concordable /konkor'ðaβle/ *a* conformable
concordador /konkorða'ðor/ **(-ra)** *a* peacemaking *—n* peacemaker
concordancia /konkor'ðanθia; konkor'ðansia/ *f,* harmony, agreement; (*Mus. Gram.*) concord; *pl* concordance
concordar /konkor'ðar/ *vt irr* to bring to agreement; *—vi* agree. See **acordar**
concordato /konkor'ðato/ *m,* concordat
concorde /kon'korðe/ *a* agreeing; harmonious
concordia /kon'korðia/ *f,* concord, agreement, harmony; written agreement
concreción /konkre'θion; konkre'sion/ *f,* concretion
concretar /konkre'tar/ *vt* to combine, bring together; make concise; resume; *—vr Fig.* confine oneself (to a subject) to hammer out, work out (an agreement)
concreto /kon'kreto/ *a* concrete, real, not abstract. **en c.,** in definite terms; finally, to sum up
concubina /konku'βina/ *f,* concubine, mistress
concubinato /konkuβi'nato/ *m,* concubinage
conculcación /konkulka'θion; konkulka'sion/ *f,* trampling, treading; violation
conculcador /konkulka'ðor/ *m,* violator
conculcar /konkul'kar/ *vt* to trample under foot, tread on; break, violate
concupiscencia /konkupis'θenθia; konkupis'sensia/ *f,* concupiscence, lust; greed
concupiscente /konkupis'θente; konkupis'sente/ *a* concupiscent, lustful; greedy
concurrencia /konku'rrenθia; konku'rrensia/ *f,* assembly; coincidence; attendance; help, influence
concurrido /konku'rriðo/ *a* crowded; busy; frequented
concurrir /konku'rrir/ *vi* to coincide; contribute; meet together; agree, be of same opinion; compete (in an examination, etc.)
concurso /kon'kurso/ *m,* crowd, concourse; conjunction, coincidence; help; competition; (tennis) tournament; competitive examination; invitation to offer tenders. **c. de acreedores,** creditors' meeting. **c. interno,** competitive examination for a position open to staff members only
concusión /konku'sion/ *f,* concussion; shock; extortion
condado /kon'daðo/ *m,* earldom; county
condal /kon'dal/ *a* of an earl, earl's; of a count, count's; of Barcelona
conde /'konde/ *m,* earl; king of the gypsies
condecir /konde'θir; konde'sir/ **(con)** *vi* to agree (with)
condecoración /kondekora'θion; kondekora'sion/ *f,* conferment of an honor, decoration; medal
condecorar /kondeko'rar/ *vt* to confer a decoration or medal
condena /kon'dena/ *f, Law.* sentence; punishment; penalty
condenable /konde'naβle/ *a* culpable, guilty; worthy of damnation
condenado /konde'naðo/ **(-da)** *a* damned; wicked, harmful *—n Law.* convicted criminal
condenador /kondena'ðor/ *a* condemning; incriminating; blaming
condenar /konde'nar/ *vt Law.* to pronounce sentence (on), convict; condemn; disapprove; wall or block or close up. **c. a galeras,** to condemn to the gallies *—vr* blame oneself; be eternally damned
condenatorio /kondena'torio/ *a* condemnatory; incriminating
condensación /kondensa'θion; kondensa'sion/ *f,* condensation
condensador /kondensa'ðor/ *a* condensing. *m,* (*Elec. Mech. Chem.*) condenser
condensante /konden'sante/ *a* condensing
condensar /konden'sar/ *vt* to condense; thicken; abridge
condesa /kon'desa/ *f,* countess
condescendencia /kondesθen'denθia; kondessen'densia/ *f,* affability, graciousness
condescender /kondesθen'der; kondessen'der/ *vi irr* to be obliging, helpful, agreeable. See **entender**
condescendiente /kondesθen'diente; kondessen'diente/ *a* affable, gracious
condestable /kondes'taβle/ *m, Hist.* constable, commander-in-chief
condición /kondi'θion; kondi'sion/ *f,* condition; quality; temperament, character; (social) position; rank, family; nobility, circumstance; stipulation, condition, requirement. **estar en condiciones de,** to be in a position to. **no estar en condiciones de,** to be in no condition to
condicional /kondiθio'nal; kondisio'nal/ *a* conditional
condicionar /kondiθio'nar; kondisio'nar/ *vi* to come to an agreement, arrange; *—vt* impose conditions
condigno /kon'digno/ *a* condign
condimentación /kondimenta'θion; kondimenta'sion/ *f, Cul.* seasoning
condimentar /kondimen'tar/ *vt* to flavor, season (food)
condimento /kondi'mento/ *m,* condiment, flavoring
condiscípulo /kondis'θipulo; kondis'sipulo/ *m,* schoolfellow
condolencia /kondo'lenθia; kondo'lensia/ *f,* compassion; condolence
condolerse /kondo'lerse/ *vr* (*with de*) to sympathize with, be sorry for. See **doler**
condonar /kondo'nar/ *vt* to condone
conducción /konduk'θion; konduk'sion/ *f.* **conducencia,** *f,* transport, conveyance, carriage; guiding; direction, management; *Phys.* conduction; *Mech.* control-gear. *Auto.* **c. a izquierda,** left-hand drive
conducente /kondu'θente; kondu'sente/ *a* conducting, conducive
conducir /kondu'θir; kondu'sir/ *vt irr* to transport, convey, carry; *Phys.* conduct; guide, lead; manage, direct; *Auto.* drive; conduce; *—vi* be suitable; *—vr* behave, conduct oneself *—Pres. Indic.* **conduzco, conduces,** etc *—Preterite* **conduje, condujiste,** etc *—Pres. Subjunc.* **conduzca, conduzcas,** etc *—Imperf. Subjunc.* **condujese,** etc.
conducta /kon'dukta/ *f,* transport, conveyance; management, conduct, direction; behavior
conductibilidad /konduktiβili'ðað/ *f, Phys.* conductivity
conductivo /konduk'tiβo/ *a* conductive
conducto /kon'dukto/ *m,* pipe, conduit, drain, duct; *Fig.* channel, means; *Anat.* tube
conductor /konduk'tor/ **(-ra)** *n* guide; leader; driver (vehicles); *m, Phys.* conductor. **c. de caballos,** teamster. **c. de entrada,** *Radio.* lead-in. **c. del calor,** heat-conductor. **c. eléctrico,** electric wire or cable
conectar /konek'tar/ *vt Elec.* to connect, switch on; couple; attach, join
conectivo /konek'tiβo/ *a* connective; (*Elec. Mech.*) connecting

conejera /kone'hera/ *f*, rabbit-warren; *Inf.* low dive or haunt
conejillo de Indias /kone'hiʎo de 'indias; kone'hiyo de 'indias/ *m*, guineapig
conejo /ko'neho/ *m*, rabbit
conejuna /kone'huna/ *f*, rabbit fur, coney
conejuno /kone'huno/ *a* rabbit, rabbit-like
conexión /konek'sion/ *f*, connection; *Elec.* switching on, connection; joint; joining; *pl* friends, connections; *Elec.* wiring
conexo /ko'nekso/ *a* connected
confabulación /konfaβula'θion; konfaβula'sion/ *f*, confabulation, conspiracy
confabular /konfaβu'lar/ *vi* to confer; —*vr* scheme, plot
confalón /konfa'lon/ *m*, standard, banner
confección /konfek'θion; konfek'sion/ *f*, making; confection; making-up; concoction, remedy; ready-made garment
confeccionador /konfekθiona'ðor; konfeksiona'ðor/ **(-ra)** *n* maker (of clothes, etc.)
confeccionar /konfekθio'nar; konfeksio'nar/ *vt* to make; prepare; make up (pharmaceuticals)
confederación /konfeðera'θion; konfeðera'sion/ *f*, alliance, pact; confederacy, federation
confederarse /konfeðe'rarse/ *vr* to confederate, be allied
conferencia /konfe'renθia; konfe'rensia/ *f*, conference, meeting; lecture; (telephone) long-distance call (US), trunk call (UK)
conferenciante /konferen'θiante; konferen'siante/ *mf* lecturer
conferenciar /konferen'θiar; konferen'siar/ *vi* to confer
conferir /konfe'rir/ *vt irr* to grant, concede; consider, discuss; compare, correlate. See **herir**
confesable /konfe'saβle/ *a* acknowledgeable, avowable
confesar /konfe'sar/ *vt irr* to avow, declare; acknowledge, admit; *Eccl.* hear confession; —*vr Eccl.* confess —*Pres. Indic.* **confieso, confiesas, confiesa, confiesan.** *Pres. Subjunc.* **confiese, confieses, confiese, confiesen**
confesión /konfe'sion/ *f*, confession
confesional /konfesio'nal/ *a* confessional
confesionario, confesonario, confesorio /konfesio'nario, konfeso'nario, konfe'sorio/ *m*, *Eccl.* confessional
confeso /kon'feso/ *a* confessed; converted (of Jews). *m*, *Eccl.* lay brother
confesor /konfe'sor/ *m*, confessor
confeti /kon'feti/ *m*, confetti
confianza /kon'fianθa; kon'fiansa/ *f*, confidence, trust; assurance, courage; over-confidence, conceit; intimacy; familiarity. **de c.,** reliable (e.g. *persona de c.*, reliable person); informal (e.g. *reunión de c.*, informal meeting). **en c.,** in confidence, confidentially
confianzudo /konfian'θuðo; konfian'suðo/ *a Inf.* overconfident
confiar /kon'fiar/ *vi* (*with en*) to trust in, hope; —*vt* (*with prep a* or *en*) entrust, commit to the care of; confide in
confidencia /konfi'ðenθia; konfi'ðensia/ *f*, trust; confidence; confidential information
confidencial /konfiðen'θial; konfiðen'sial/ *a* confidential
confidente /konfi'ðente/ **(-ta)** *a* trustworthy, true. *m*, seat for two *n* confidant(e); spy
configuración /konfigura'θion; konfigura'sion/ *f*, configuration, form, lie
configurar /konfigu'rar/ *vt* to shape
confín /kon'fin/ *m*, boundary, frontier; limit —*a* boundary
confinado /konfi'naðo/ *a* banished. *m*, *Law.* prisoner
confinar /konfi'nar/ *vi* (*with con*) to be bounded by, contiguous to; —*vt* banish; place in confinement
confirmación /konfirma'θion; konfirma'sion/ *f*, corroboration; *Eccl.* confirmation
confirmar /konfir'mar/ *vt* to corroborate; uphold; *Eccl.* confirm
confirmatorio /konfirma'torio/ *a* confirmatory
confiscación /konfiska'θion; konfiska'sion/ *f*, confiscation
confiscar /konfis'kar/ *vt* to confiscate
confitar /konfi'tar/ *vt* to candy, crystallize or preserve (fruit, etc.); *Fig.* sweeten
confite /kon'fite/ *m*, bonbon, sugared almond, etc.
confitería /konfite'ria/ *f*, confectionery
confitero /konfi'tero/ **(-ra)** *n* confectioner
confitura /konfi'tura/ *f*, preserve, jam
conflagración /konflagra'θion; konflagra'sion/ *f*, conflagration, blaze; uprising, rebellion
conflicto /kon'flikto/ *m*, strife, struggle; spiritual conflict; *Fig.* difficult situation
confluencia /kon'fluenθia; kon'fluensia/ *f*, confluence; crowd
confluir /kon'fluir/ *vi irr* to meet, flow together (rivers); run together (roads); crowd. See **huir**
conformación /konforma'θion; konforma'sion/ *f*, conformation; make-up, structure (e.g. of an organization)
conformar /konfor'mar/ *vt* to fit, adjust; —*vr* agree, be of the same opinion; submit, comply; to make up (e.g. *los grupos sociales que conforman este país*, the social groups who make up this country)
conforme /kon'forme/ *a* similar, alike; consistent; in agreement; long-suffering, resigned —*adv* according (to), in proportion (to)
conformidad /konformi'ðað/ *f*, conformity; similarity; resignation; agreement, harmony; proportion, symmetry. **de c.,** by common consent. **en c.,** according to
confort /kon'fort/ *m*, comfort
confortante /konfor'tante/ *a* comforting; consoling; strengthening (of beverages)
confortar /konfor'tar/ *vt* to comfort, reassure; encourage; console
confortativo /konforta'tiβo/ *a* comforting; comfortable; strengthening, warming (of beverages); encouraging, cheering
confrontación /konfronta'θion; konfronta'sion/ *f*, confrontment; comparison (of texts, etc.)
confrontar /konfron'tar/ *vt* to bring face to face; compare, correlate; —*vi* face; (*with con*) be contiguous to, border on
confucianismo /konfuθia'nismo; konfusia'nismo/ *m*, Confucianism
confundible /konfun'diβle/ *a* mistakable, liable to be confused
confundimiento /konfundi'miento/ *m*, confounding; mistaking; confusion
confundir /konfun'dir/ *vt* to mix, confuse; jumble together; mistake; *Fig.* confound (in argument); humble; bewilder, perplex; —*vr* be mixed together; mistake, confuse; be ashamed; be bewildered
confusión /konfu'sion/ *f*, confusion; perplexity; shame; jumble
confuso /kon'fuso/ *a* mixed, upset; jumbled; obscure; indistinct; blurred; bewildered
confutación /konfuta'θion; konfuta'sion/ *f*, confutation
confutar /konfu'tar/ *vt* to confute
conga /'koŋga/ *f*, conga (dance; drum)
congelación /konhela'θion; konhela'sion/ *f*, freezing; congealment. **punto de c.,** freezing point
congelar /konhe'lar/ *vt* to congeal; freeze
congeniar /konhe'niar/ *vi* to be congenial
congénito /kon'henito/ *a* congenital
congestión /konhes'tion/ *f*, *Med.* congestion
congestionar /konhestio'nar/ *vt* to congest; —*vr* *Med.* be overcharged (with blood)
conglomeración /koŋglomera'θion; koŋglomera'sion/ *f*, conglomeration
conglomerar /koŋglome'rar/ *vt* to conglomerate
congoja /koŋ'goha/ *f*, anguish, anxiety, grief
congraciarse /koŋgra'θiarse; koŋgra'siarse/ (*con*), *vr* to ingratiate oneself (with), get into the good graces (of)
congratulación /koŋgratula'θion; koŋgratula'sion/ *f*, congratulation
congratular /koŋgratu'lar/ *vt* to congratulate; —*vr* congratulate oneself

congratulatorio /koŋgratula'torio/ *a* congratulatory
congregación /koŋgrega'θion; koŋgrega'sion/ *f,* gathering, meeting, congregation; brotherhood, guild
congregar /koŋgre'gar/ **(se)** *vt* and *vr* to meet, assemble
congresista /koŋgre'sista/ *mf* member of a congress
congreso /koŋ'greso/ *m,* congress; conference, meeting; sexual intercourse
congrio /'koŋgrio/ *m,* conger eel
congruencia /koŋ'gruenθia; koŋ'gruensia/ *f,* suitability, convenience; *Math.* congruence
congruente /koŋ'gruente/ *a* convenient, opportune; *Math.* congruent
cónico /'koniko/ *a* conical, tapering *Math.* conic
conífera /ko'nifera/ *f,* conifer
conífero /ko'nifero/ *a* coniferous
conjetura /konhe'tura/ *f,* conjecture
conjetural /konhetu'ral/ *a* conjectural
conjeturar /konhetu'rar/ *vt* to conjecture, surmise
conjugación /konhuga'θion; konhuga'sion/ *f,* conjugation
conjugar /konhu'gar/ *vt* to conjugate
conjunción /konhun'θion; konhun'sion/ *f,* connection, union association; (*Astron. Gram.*) conjunction
conjuntivitis /konhunti'βitis/ *f,* conjunctivitis
conjunto /kon'hunto/ *a* united, associated adjoining; mingled, mixed (with) bound, affiliated. *m,* whole; combo, ensemble (of musicians). **c. habitacional,** housing complex, housing project
conjura, conjuración /kon'hura, konhura'θion; kon'hura, konhura'sion/ *f,* conspiracy, plot
conjurador /konhura'ðor/ **(-ra)** *n* conspirator, plotter; exorcist
conjurar /konhu'rar/ *vi* to conspire, plot *vt* swear, take an oath; exorcise; implore, beg; ward off (danger)
conjuro /kon'huro/ *m,* plot, conspiracy, spell, incantation; entreaty
conllevar /konʎe'βar; konye'βar/ *vt* to share (troubles) bear, put up with; endure
conmemoración /komemora'θion; komemora'sion/ *f,* commemoration
conmemorar /komemo'rar/ *vt* to commemorate
conmemorativo /komemora'tiβo/ *a* commemorative
conmensurable /komensu'raβle/ *a* commensurable
conmigo /ko'migo/ *pers pron* 1st pers. sing. *mf* with myself, with me
conminar /komi'nar/ *vt* to threaten
conminatorio /komina'torio/ *a* threatening
conmiseración /komisera'θion; komisera'sion/ *f,* commiseration, compassion, pity
conmoción /komo'θion; komo'sion/ *f,* disturbance (mind or body); upheaval, commotion. **c. eléctrica,** electric shock
conmovedor /komoβe'ðor/ *a* moving, pitiful; stirring, thrilling
conmover /komo'βer/ *vt irr* to perturb, stir; move to pity. **c. los cimientos de,** to shake the foundations of; *—vr* be emotionally moved. See **mover**
conmutable /komu'taβle/ *a* commutable
conmutación /komuta'θion; komuta'sion/ *f,* commutation
conmutador /komuta'ðor/ *m, Elec.* commutator; change-over switch
conmutar /komu'tar/ *vt* to commute; *Elec.* switch, convert
conmutatriz /komuta'triθ; komuta'tris/ *f, Elec.* converter
connato /kon'nato/ *a* contemporary
connatural /konnatu'ral/ *a* innate, inborn
connaturalizar /konnaturali'θar; konnaturali'sar/ *vt* to connaturalize
connaturalizarse /konnaturali'θarse; konnaturali'sarse/ **(con)** *vr* to become accustomed (to), become acclimated (to)
connivencia /konni'βenθia; konni'βensia/ *f,* connivance
connotación /konnota'θion; konnota'sion/ *f,* connotation
connotar /konno'tar/ *vt* to connote
cono /'kono/ *m,* (*Geom. Bot.*) cone. **el C. Sur,** the Southern Cone
conocedor /konoθe'ðor; konose'ðor/ **(-ra)** *n* one who knows; connoisseur; expert
conocer /kono'θer; kono'ser/ *vt irr* to know; understand; observe, perceive; be acquainted (with); conjecture; confess, acknowledge; know carnally; *—vr* know oneself; know one another. **conocerle a uno la voz,** to recognize somebody's voice (e.g. *Le conozco la voz.* I recognize her by her voice.) **conocerle a uno en su manera de andar,** to recognize somebody by his gait, recognize somebody by his walk *—Pres. Indic.* **conozco, conoces,** etc *—Pres. Subjunc.* **conozca,** etc.
conocido /kono'θiðo; kono'siðo/ **(-da)** *a* illustrious, distinguished *—n* acquaintance
conocimiento /konoθi'miento; konosi'miento/ *m,* knowledge; understanding; intelligence; acquaintance (*not* friend); consciousness; *Com.* bill of lading; *pl* knowledge, learning
conque /'konke/ *conjunc* so, so that (e.g. *¿C. Juan se va?* So John's going away?)
conquista /kon'kista/ *f,* conquest
conquistador /konkista'ðor/ **(-ra)** *a* conquering *—n* conqueror
conquistar /konkis'tar/ *vt* to conquer; *Fig.* captivate, win
consabido /konsa'βiðo/ *a* aforesaid, beforementioned
consagración /konsagra'θion; konsagra'sion/ *f,* consecration; dedication
consagrar /konsa'grar/ *vt* to consecrate; dedicate, devote; deify; *—vr* (*with prep a*) dedicate oneself to, engage in
consanguíneo /konsaŋ'guineo/ *a* consanguineous
consanguinidad /konsaŋguini'ðað/ *f,* consanguinity
consciente /kons'θiente; kons'siente/ *a* conscious; aware; sane. *m, Psychol.* conscious
conscripción /konskrip'θion; konskrip'sion/ *f,* conscription
conscripto /kons'kripto/ *m,* conscript
consecución /konseku'θion; konseku'sion/ *f,* obtainment; attainment
consecuencia /konse'kuenθia; konse'kuensia/ *f,* consequence, outcome; logical consequence, conclusion; importance; consistence (of people)
consecuente /konse'kuente/ *a* consequent, resultant; consistent. **c. consigo mismo,** self-consistent *m,* consequence; *Math.* consequent
consecutivo /konseku'tiβo/ *a* consecutive, successive
conseguir /konse'gir/ *vt irr* to obtain, achieve. See **seguir**
conseja /kon'seha/ *f,* story, fairy-tale; old wives' tale
consejero /konse'hero/ **(-ra)** *n* adviser; member of council. *m.* **c. de estado,** counselor of state
consejo /kon'seho/ *m,* advice; council, commission, board; council chamber or building. **c. de administración,** board of directors. **c. de guerra,** council of war. **c. del reino,** council of the realm. **c. privado,** privy council
consenso /kon'senso/ *m,* consensus of opinion, unanimity
consentido /konsen'tiðo/ *a* complaisant (of husband); spoiled, over-indulged
consentimiento /konsenti'miento/ *m,* consent; assent
consentir /konsen'tir/ *vt irr* to permit, allow; believe; tolerate, put up with; over-indulge, spoil; *—vr* crack, give way (furniture, etc.). **c. en,** to consent to; to agree to. See **sentir**
conserje /kon'serhe/ *m,* concierge, porter; warden or keeper (of castle, etc.)
conserjería /konserhe'ria/ *f,* conciergerie, porter's lodge; warden's dwelling (in castles, etc.)
conserva /kon'serβa/ *f,* jam; preserve; pickles; *Naut.* convoy. **en c.,** preserved, tinned
conservación /konserβa'θion; konserβa'sion/ *f,* upkeep; preservation, maintenance; *Cul.* preserving; conservation. **c. refrigerada,** cold storage
conservador /konserβa'ðor/ **(-ra)** *a* keeping, preserving *—a* and *n* preserver; *Polit.* conservative; traditionalist. *m,* curator

conservadurismo /konserβaðu'rismo/ *m,* conservatism
conservar /konser'βar/ *vt* to keep, maintain, preserve; keep up (custom, etc.); guard; *Cul.* preserve. **c. en buen estado,** to keep in repair
conservatorio /konserβa'torio/ *m,* conservatoire; academy. **c. de música,** academy of music, conservatoire
considerable /konsiðe'raβle/ *a* considerable; worthy of consideration, powerful; numerous; large; important
consideración /konsiðera'θion; konsiðera'sion/ *f,* consideration, attention; reflection, thought; civility; importance. **en c. de,** considering
considerado /konsiðe'raðo/ *a* considerate; prudent; distinguished; important
considerar /konsiðe'rar/ *vt* to consider, reflect upon; treat with consideration (persons); judge, estimate, feel (e.g. *Considero que...* I feel that...)
consigna /kon'signa/ *f, Mil.* watchword; left luggage office
consignador /konsigna'ðor/ **(-ra)** *n Com.* consigner, sender
consignar /konsig'nar/ *vt* to assign, lay aside; deposit; *Com.* consign; entrust, commit; put in writing, *Law.* deposit in trust; book (a suspect)
consignatario /konsigna'tario/ *m, Law.* trustee; mortgagee; *Com.* consignee. **c. de buques,** shipping agent
consigo /kon'sigo/ *pers pron* 3rd sing. and pl. *mf* with himself, herself, oneself, yourself, yourselves, themselves
consiguiente /konsi'giente/ *a* consequent, resulting. *m,* consequence. **por c.,** in consequence
consistencia /konsis'tenθia; konsis'tensia/ *f,* solidity; consistence, density; consistency, congruity, relevance
consistente /konsis'tente/ *a* of a certain consistency; solid
consistir /konsis'tir/ *vi* (*with en*) to consist in; be comprised of; be the result of
consistorio /konsis'torio/ *m,* consistory; municipal council (in some Spanish towns); town hall
consola /kon'sola/ *f,* console table; piertable; *Mech.* bracket
cónsola /'konsola/ *f,* radio cabinet
consolable /konso'laβle/ *a* consolable
consolación /konsola'θion; konsola'sion/ *f,* consolation
consolador /konsola'ðor/ **(-ra)** *n* comforter, consoler
consolar /konso'lar/ *vt irr* to comfort, console. **consolarse de + inf.,** to console oneself for + *pp.* See **contar**
consolidación /konsoliða'θion; konsoliða'sion/ *f,* consolidation; stiffening
consolidar /konsoli'ðar/ *vt* to consolidate; strengthen; combine, unite; *—vr Law.* unite
consomé /konso'me/ *m,* consommé
consonancia /konso'nanθianb; konso'nansia/ *f,* harmony; agreement
consonante /konso'nante/ *a* consonant, consistent. *m,* rhyme. *f, Gram.* consonant
consonantismo /konsonan'tismo/ *m,* consonantism, consonant system
consorcio /kon'sorθio; kon'sorsio/ *m,* partnership; trust; intimacy, common life
consorte /kon'sorte/ *mf* consort; companion, associate, partner; spouse
conspicuo /kons'pikuo/ *a* outstanding, distinguished; conspicuous
conspiración /konspira'θion; konspira'sion/ *f,* conspiracy
conspirador /konspira'ðor/ **(-ra)** *n* conspirator
conspirar /konspi'rar/ *vi* to conspire; plot, scheme; tend, combine
constancia /kons'tanθia; kons'tansia/ *f,* constancy, steadfastness; stability, steadiness; transcript (of grades). **c. de estudios,** transcript (of grades)
constante /kons'tante/ *a* constant; durable; *Mech.* steady, non-oscillating. *m,* constant
Constantinopla /konstanti'nopla/ Constantinople
Constanza /kons'tanθa; kons'tansa/ Constance (female given name and lake)
constar /kons'tar/ *vi* to be evident, be clear; (*with de*) be composed of, consist of, comprise
constelación /konstela'θion; konstela'sion/ *f, Astron.* constellation; climate
consternación /konsterna'θion; konsterna'sion/ *f,* dismay, alarm
consternarse /konster'narse/ *vr* to be dismayed or alarmed
constipado /konsti'paðo/ *m, Med.* cold; chill
constiparse /konsti'parse/ *vr* to catch a cold or chill
constitución /konstitu'θion; konstitu'sion/ *f,* constitution; composition, make-up (e.g. *la c. del suelo,* the make-up of the soil)
constitucional /konstituθio'nal; konstitusio'nal/ *a* constitutional
constituir /konsti'tuir/ *vt irr* to constitute, form; found, establish; (*with en*) appoint, nominate; *Fig.* place in (a difficult situation, etc.); *—vr* (*with en* or *por*) be appointed or authorized; be under (an obligation). See **huir**
constituyente, constitutivo /konstitu'yente, konstitu'tiβo/ *a* and *m,* constituent
constreñir /konstre'ɲir/ *vt irr* to constrain, oblige; constrict; constipate. See **ceñir**
constricción /konstrik'θion; konstrik'sion/ *f,* constriction; contraction, shrinkage
construcción /konstruk'θion; konstruk'sion/ *f,* construction; art or process of construction; fabric, structure; *Gram.* construction; building, erection. **c. de caminos,** road making. **c. naval,** shipbuilding
constructor /konstruk'tor/ **(-ra)** *a* building, constructive *—n* builder; constructor
construir /kons'truir/ *vt irr* to construct; build, make; *Gram.* construct. See **huir**
consuelo /kon'suelo/ *m,* consolation; comfort, solace; joy, delight
cónsul /'konsul/ *m,* consul
consulado /konsu'laðo/ *m,* consulate. **c. general,** consulate general
consulta /kon'sulta/ *f,* deliberation, consideration; advice; reference; conference, consultation
consultar /konsul'tar/ *vt* to discuss, consider; seek advice, consult. **consultarlo con la almohada,** *Fig.* to sleep on it, think it over, mull it over
consultor /konsul'tor/ **(-ra)** *a* consultative, advisory; consulting *—n* consultant; adviser. **c. externo,** outside consultant
consultorio /konsul'torio/ *m, Med.* consulting rooms; surgery; technical information bureau
consumación /konsuma'θion; konsuma'sion/ *f,* consummation; completion, attainment; extinction, end
consumado /konsu'maðo/ *a* consummate; *Inf.* thorough, perfect
consumar /konsu'mar/ *vt* to consummate; complete, accomplish, perfect
consumido /konsu'miðo/ *a Inf.* emaciated, wasted away; timid, spiritless
consumidor /konsumi'ðor/ **(-ra)** *a* consuming *—n* consumer, user
consumir /konsu'mir/ *vt* to destroy; consume, use; waste away, wear away; *Eccl.* take communion; *Inf.* grieve; *—vr* be destroyed; *Inf.* be consumed with grief
consumo /kon'sumo/ *m,* consumption; demand. **c. de combustible,** fuel consumption
contabilidad /kontaβili'ðað/ *f,* bookkeeping; accounts; accounting
contable /kon'taβle/ *m,* bookkeeper
contacto /kon'takto/ *m,* contact (also *Elec. Mil.*). **en c.,** in common (e.g. *Los dos libros tienen mucho en c.* The two books have much in common.)
contado /kon'taðo/ *a* few; infrequent; rare. **al c.,** *Com.* cash down. **por de c.,** presumably; of course, naturally
contador /konta'ðor/ *a* counting. *m,* accountant; *Law.* auditor; counter (in banks); *Elec.* meter, counter; *Naut.* purser. **c. oficial,** *Argentina* certified public accountant. **c. público titulado,** certified public accountant
contaduría /kontaðu'ria/ *f,* accountancy; counting house; accountant's office; auditorship; *Theat.* box-office; *Naut.* purser's office

contagiar /konta'hiar/ *vt* to infect; corrupt, pervert; *—vr* (*with con, de* or *por*) be infected by or through
contagio /kon'tahio/ *m*, infection; contagious disease; *Fig.* contagion, perversion, corruption
contagioso /konta'hioso/ *a* infectious; *Fig.* catching, contagious
contaminación /kontamina'θion; kontamina'sion/ *f*, contamination, pollution
contaminar /kontami'nar/ *vt* to pollute, contaminate; infect; *Fig.* corrupt
contante /kon'tante/ *a* ready (of money)
contar /kon'tar/ *vt irr* to count; recount, tell; place to account; include, count among; *—vi* calculate, compute. **contarle a uno las cuarenta,** *Inf.* to give someone a piece of one's mind. **c. con,** to rely upon; reckon upon *—Pres. Indic.* **cuento, cuentas, cuenta, cuentan.** *Pres. Subjunc.* **cuente, cuentes, cuente, cuenten**
contemplación /kontempla'θion; kontempla'sion/ *f*, meditation, contemplation; consideration
contemplar /kontem'plar/ *vt* to consider, reflect upon; look at, contemplate; indulge, please
contemplativo /kontempla'tiβo/ *a Eccl.* contemplative; reflective, thoughtful; kind, indulgent
contemporáneo /kontempo'raneo/ **(de)** *a* contemporaneous (to *or* with) *n* contemporary
contemporizar /kontempori'θar; kontempori'sar/ *vi* to temporize, gain time
contencioso /konten'θioso; konten'sioso/ *a* contentious, argumentative; *Law.* litigious
contender /konten'der/ *vi irr* to contain; restrain, hold back; comprise; *—vr* control oneself. See **entender**
contendiente /konten'diente/ *mf* contestant
contener /konte'ner/ *vt irr* to contain; include; comprise; hold back; restrain; check, repress; hold down, subdue; suppress, put down; *—vr* contain oneself; keep one's temper; keep quiet; refrain. See **tener**
contenido /konte'niðo/ *m*, contents *—a* contained; *Fig.* restrained; reserved (of persons)
contentamiento /kontenta'miento/ *m*, contentment
contentar /konten'tar/ *vt* to satisfy, please; *Com.* endorse; *—vr* be pleased or satisfied
contento /kon'tento/ *a* happy; content; satisfied; pleased. *m*, pleasure; contentment. **no caber de c.,** to be overjoyed
contestación /kontesta'θion; kontesta'sion/ *f*, reply, answer; discussion, argument, dispute
contestar /kontes'tar/ *vt* to reply, answer; confirm, attest; *—vi* accord, harmonize
contexto /kon'teksto/ *m*, context
contextura /konteks'tura/ *f*, structure; context; physique, frame
contienda /kon'tienda/ *f*, struggle, fight; quarrel, dispute; discussion
contigo /kon'tigo/ *pers pron* 2nd sing. *mf* with thee, with you
contigüidad /kontigui'ðað/ *f*, proximity, nearness
contiguo /kon'tiguo/ *a* adjacent, near
continencia /konti'nenθia; konti'nensia/ *f*, moderation, self-restraint; continence; chastity; containing
continental /konti'nental/ *a* continental. *m*, express messenger service; *Puerto Rico* person from the mainland United States
continente /konti'nente/ *a* continent. *m*, container; demeanor, bearing; *Geog.* continent; mainland
contingencia /kontin'henθia; kontin'hensia/ *f*, contingency; risk, danger
contingente /kontin'hente/ *a* incidental; fortuitous; dependent; *m*, *Mil.* taskforce, contingent
continuación /kontinua'θion; kontinua'sion/ *f*, continuation; prolongation; sequel (of a story, etc.)
continuador /kontinua'ðor/ **(-ra)** *n* continuer
continuar /konti'nuar/ *vt* to continue; *—vi* continue; last, remain, go on; *—vr* be prolonged
continuidad /kontinui'ðað/ *f*, continuity
continuo /kon'tinuo/ *a* continuous, steady, uninterrupted; persevering, tenacious; persistent, lasting, unremitting. *m*, a united whole. **de c.,** continuously
contonearse /kontone'arse/ *vr* to swing the hips (in walking); strut
contorno /kon'torno/ *m*, contour, outline; (gen. *pl*) environs, surrounding district
contorsión /kontor'sion/ *f*, contortion
contorsionista /kontorsio'nista/ *mf* contortionist
contra /'kontra/ *prep* against, counter, athwart; opposed to, hostile to; in front of, opposite; towards. *m*, opposite view or opinion. *f*, *Inf.* difficulty, trouble. **c. la corriente,** upstream. **el pro y el c.,** the pros and cons. **en c.,** in opposition, against
contraalmirante /kontraalmi'rante/ *m*, rear admiral
contraataque /kontraa'take/ *m*, counterattack
contraaviso /kontraa'βiso/ *m*, countermand
contrabajo /kontra'βaho/ *m*, doublebass; player of this instrument; deep bass voice
contrabalancear /kontraβalanθe'ar; kontraβalanse'ar/ *vt* to counterbalance; *Fig.* compensate
contrabandista /kontraβan'dista/ *a* smuggling. *mf* smuggler
contrabando /kontra'βando/ *m*, contraband; smuggling
contracción /kontrak'θion; kontrak'sion/ *f*, contraction; shrinkage; abridgment; abbreviation
contracubierta /kontraku'βierta/ *f*, book jacket, jacket
contradanza /kontra'ðanθa; kontra'ðansa/ *f*, square dance
contradecir /kontraðe'θir; kontraðe'sir/ *vt irr* to contradict; *—vr* contradict oneself. See **decir**
contradicción /kontraðik'θion; kontraðik'sion/ *f*, contradiction
contradictorio /kontraðik'torio/ *a* contradictory
contraer /kontra'er/ *vt irr* to shrink, reduce in size, shorten; abridge; contract (matrimony, obligations); *Fig.* acquire (diseases, habits); *—vr* shorten, contract, shrink. See **traer**
contrafuerte /kontra'fuerte/ *m*, buttress, counterfort, abutment; *Geog.* spur
contrahacer /kontraa'θer; kontraa'ser/ *vt irr* to forge, counterfeit; mimic; imitate. See **hacer**
contrahecho /kontra'etʃo/ *a* deformed
contralor /kontra'lor/ *m*, comptroller
contraloría /kontralo'ria/ *f*, comptrollership, office of comptroller (position); comptroller's office (place)
contralto /kon'tralto/ *m*, contralto (voice)
contraluz /kontra'luθ; kontra'lus/ *f*, counterlight
contramaestre /kontrama'estre/ *m*, *Naut.* boatswain; overseer, superintendent, foreman
contramarcha /kontra'martʃa/ *f*, retrogression; *Mil.* countermarch
contramedida /kontrame'ðiða/ *f*, counter-measure
contraorden /kontra'orðen/ *f*, countermand
contrapedalear /kontrapeðale'ar/ *vi* to backpedal
contrapelo /kontra'pelo/ *a adv* the wrong way of the hair, against the grain; *Inf.* reluctantly, distastefully
contrapeso /kontra'peso/ *m*, counterpoise, counterweight; balancing-pole (acrobats); *Fig.* counterbalance; makeweight
contraponer /kontrapo'ner/ *vt irr* to compare; place opposite; oppose. See **poner**
contraproducente /kontraproðu'θente; kontraproðu'sente/ *a* counteractive, counterproductive, unproductive, self-deceiving; self-defeating
contrapuesto /kontra'puesto/ *a* opposing, divergent
contrapunto /kontra'punto/ *m*, counterpoint
contrariar /kontra'riar/ *vt* to counter, oppose; impede; vex, annoy
contrariedad /kontrarie'ðað/ *f*, contrariety, opposition; obstacle; vexation, trouble
contrario /kon'trario/ **(-ia)** *a* opposite; hostile, opposed; harmful; adverse, contrary *—n* adversary; opponent. *m*, obstacle. *f*. **contraria,** contrary, opposite. **al contrario,** on the contrary. **llevar la contraria (a),** to oppose; contradict
contrarreforma /kontrarre'forma/ *f*, counter-Reformation
contrasentido /kontrasen'tiðo/ *m*, wrong sense, opposite sense (of words); contradiction of initial premise; self-contradiction; nonsense
contraseña /kontra'seɲa/ *f*, countersign; *Mil.* password
contrastar /kontras'tar/ *vt* to contrast; oppose, resist;

check (weights and measures); assay; *Mech.* calibrate, gauge; —*vi* contrast
contraste /kon'traste/ *m,* contrast; opposition, difference; weights and measures inspector; dispute, clash. **en c. a,** in contrast to
contrata /kon'trata/ *f,* **contrato,** *m,* contract. **contrato de arrendamiento,** lease
contratación /kontrata'θion; kontrata'sion/ *f,* hiring; *Com.* transaction; commerce, trade
contratapa /kontra'tapa/ *f,* back cover (of a periodical, etc.)
contratar /kontra'tar/ *vt* to contract, enter into an agreement; make a bargain (with), deal (with); hire, contract
contratiempo /kontra'tiempo/ *m,* mishap, accident
contratista /kontra'tista/ *mf* contractor
contratorpedero /kontratorpe'ðero/ *m,* torpedoboat destroyer
contravención /kontraβen'θion; kontraβen'sion/ *f,* contravention; violation. **en c. a,** in violation of
contraveneno /kontraβe'neno/ *m, Med.* antidote; remedy, precaution
contravenir /kontraβe'nir/ *vt irr* to infringe, contravene. See **venir**
contraventana /kontraβen'tana/ *f,* shutter (for windows)
contravidriera /kontraβið'riera/ *f,* storm window
contrayente /kontra'yente/ *a* contracting. *mf* contracting party (used of matrimony)
contribución /kontriβu'θion; kontriβu'sion/ *f,* contribution; tax. **c. sobre la propiedad,** property tax
contribuir /kontri'βuir/ *vt irr* to pay (taxes); contribute. See **huir**
contribuyente /kontriβu'yente/ *a* contributing; contributory. *mf* contributor; taxpayer
contrición /kontri'θion; kontri'sion/ *f,* contrition
contrincante /kontrin'kante/ *m,* competitor, candidate (public examinations); rival, opponent
contrito /kon'trito/ *a* contrite
control /kon'trol/ *m,* control; checking. **c. de precios,** price control
controlar /kontro'lar/ *vt* to control
controversia /kontro'βersia/ *f,* controversy
controvertir /kontroβer'tir/ *vi* and *vt irr* to dispute, argue against, deny. See **sentir**
contumacia /kontu'maθia; kontu'masia/ *f,* obstinacy; *Law.* contumacy
contumaz /kontu'maθ; kontu'mas/ *a* stubborn; impenitent; *Law.* contumacious; *Med.* obstinate, resistant (to cure)
contumelia /kontu'melia/ *f,* contumely
conturbar /kontur'βar/ *vt* to perturb, make anxious, disturb; —*vr* be perturbed
contuso /kon'tuso/ *a* contused, bruised
convalecencia /kombale'θenθia; kombale'sensia/ *f,* convalescence; convalescent home
convalecer /kombale'θer; kombale'ser/ *vi irr* to convalesce, get better; *Fig.* recover, regain (influence, etc.). See **conocer**
convaleciente /kombale'θiente; kombale'siente/ *a* and *mf* convalescent
convalidar /kombali'ðar/ *vt* to ratify, confirm
convecino /kombe'θino; kombe'sino/ *a* nearby; neighboring
convencedor /kombenθe'ðor; kombense'ðor/ *a* convincing
convencer /komben'θer; komben'ser/ *vt* to convince; prove beyond doubt, demonstrate to (persons); be convincing (e.g. *No convence,* It's not convincing; He's not convincing.) *vr* be convinced
convencimiento /kombenθi'miento; kombensi'miento/ *m,* conviction, belief, assurance
convención /komben'θion; komben'sion/ *f,* pact, formal agreement; harmony, conformity; convention
convencional /kombenθio'nal; kombensio'nal/ *a* conventional (all meanings)
convencionalismo /kombenθiona'lismo; kombensiona'lismo/ *m,* conventionality
convenido /kombe'niðo/ *a* agreed
conveniencia /kombe'nienθia; kombe'niensia/ *f,* conformity, harmony, adjustment; experience, suitability, convenience; advantage; agreement, pact; post as domestic; ease, comfort; *pl* income; social conventions
conveniente /kombe'niente/ *a* convenient, opportune; suitable, fitting; profitable; useful; decorous. **tener por c. + inf,** to think it fitting to + *inf,* find it appropriate to + *Inf.*
convenio /kom'benio/ *m,* pact, treaty; *Com.* agreement, contract
convenir /kombe'nir/ *vi irr* to agree; assemble, congregate; belong; be suitable; —*vr* agree; suit oneself. **No me conviene salir esta tarde,** It does not suit me to go out this afternoon. **Me convendría pasar un mes allí,** It would be a good idea (or a wise thing) for me to spend a month there. See **venir**
convento /kom'bento/ *m,* convent; monastery; religious community
conventual /komben'tual/ *a* conventual; monastic. *m, Eccl.* conventual
convergencia /komber'henθia; komber'hensia/ *f,* convergence
convergir /komber'hir/ *vi* to converge; *Fig.* coincide (views, etc.)
conversación /kombersa'θion; kombersa'sion/ *f,* conversation; intercourse, company; *Law.* criminal conversation
conversar /komber'sar/ *vi* to converse; chat; live with others; know socially
conversión /komber'sion/ *f,* conversion; change, transformation; *Com.* conversion; *Mil.* wheel; wheeling
converso /kom'berso/ **(-sa)** *n* convert
convertible /komber'tiβle/ *a* convertible
convertir /komber'tir/ *vt irr* to change, transform; convert; reform; —*vr* be transformed; be converted; be reformed. See **sentir**
convexidad /kombeksi'ðað/ *f,* convexity
convexo /kom'bekso/ *a* convex
convicción /kombik'θion; kombik'sion/ *f,* conviction; certitude; *Law.* conviction
convicto /kom'bikto/ **(-ta)** *a* and *n Law.* convict
convidado /kombi'ðaðo/ **(-da)** *n* guest
convidar /kombi'ðar/ *vt* to invite (persons); encourage, provoke; entice, attract; —*vr* invite oneself; offer one's services
convincente /kombin'θente; kombin'sente/ *a* convincing
convite /kom'bite/ *m,* invitation; banquet; party
convivencia /kombi'βenθia; kombi'βensia/ *f,* coexistence, common life, life together. **c. pacífica,** peaceful coexistence
convivial /kombi'βial/ *a* convivial
convivir /kombi'βir/ *vi* to live together, live under the same roof
convocación /komboka'θion; komboka'sion/ *f,* convocation
convocar /kombo'kar/ *vt* to convene, convoke
convoy /kom'boi/ *m,* convoy; escort; following; cruet-stand
convoyar /kombo'yar/ *vt* to convoy, escort
convulsión /kombul'sion/ *f,* convulsion
convulsivo /kombul'siβo/ *a* convulsive
conyugal /konyu'gal/ *a* conjugal
cónyuge /'konyuhe/ *mf* husband or (and) wife (used gen. in *pl*)
coñac /ko'ɲak/ *m,* brandy
cooperación /koopera'θion; koopera'sion/ *f,* cooperation
cooperador /koopera'ðor/ **(-ra)** *a* cooperative —*n* cooperator, collaborator
cooperar /koope'rar/ *vt* to cooperate
cooperativa /koopera'tiβa/ *f,* cooperative society
cooperativo /koopera'tiβo/ *a* cooperative
coordenada /koorðe'naða/ *f,* coordinate
coordinación /koorðina'θion; koorðina'sion/ *f,* coordination
coordinar /koorði'nar/ *vt* to coordinate, classify
copa /'kopa/ *f,* wineglass, goblet; glassful; top branches (of trees); crown (of hat); *Cards.* heart; gill (liquid measure); *Inf.* drink, glass; *pl Cards.* hearts (in Spanish pack, goblets)

copartícipe /kopar'tiθipe; kopar'tisipe/ *mf* co-partner, partaker, participant
copec /'kopek/ *m*, kopeck
Copenhague /kope'nage/ Copenhagen
copernicano /koperni'kano/ *a* Copernican
copero /ko'pero/ *m*, cupbearer; sideboard; cocktail cabinet
copete /ko'pete/ *m*, lock, tress (hair); tuft, crest; forelock (horses); head, top (ice-cream, drinks); *Inf.* **de alto c.,** aristocratic; socially prominent
copia /'kopia/ *f*, abundance, plenty; copy, reproduction; transcript; imitation
copiador /kopia'ðor/ **(-ra)** *a* copying —*n* copier; transcriber. *m*, copybook
copiar /ko'piar/ *vt* to copy
copioso /ko'pioso/ *a* abundant, plentiful
copla /'kopla/ *f*, couplet; popular four-line poem; couple, pair; *pl Inf.* verses
coplero /kop'lero/ **(-ra)** *n* balladmonger; poetaster
copo /'kopo/ *m*, cop (of a spindle); snowflake
copón /ko'pon/ *m*, large goblet; *Eccl.* ciborium, chalice
coprófago /ko'profago/ *a* coprophagous
copropietario /kopropie'tario/ **(-ia)** *n* coproprietor, coowner
cóptico /'koptiko/ *a* Coptic. *m*, Coptic (language)
copto /'kopto/ **(-ta)** *n* Copt
cópula /'kopula/ *f*, connection; coupling; joining; copulation
copularse /kopu'larse/ *vr* to copulate
coque /'koke/ *m*, coke
coqueluche /koke'lutʃe/ *f*, whooping cough
coqueta /ko'keta/ *f*, coquette, flirt
coquetear /kokete'ar/ *vi* to flirt
coqueteo /koke'teo/ *m*, coquetry; flirtation
coquetería /kokete'ria/ *f*, coquetry
coquetón /koke'ton/ *a* coquettish
coracero /kora'θero; kora'sero/ *m*, cuirassier
coraje /ko'rahe/ *m*, courage, valor; anger
coral /ko'ral/ *m*, coral. *f*, coral snake. *m*, *Bot.* coral tree; *pl* coral beads
coral /ko'ral/ *a* choral
coralina /kora'lina/ *f*, coral (polyp).
coraza /ko'raθa; ko'rasa/ *f*, cuirass; shell (of tortoise); armor-plate, armor (ships, etc.)
corazón /kora'θon; kora'son/ *m*, heart; courage, spirit; love, tenderness; goodwill, benevolence; core (of a fruit); *Fig.* pith. **de c.,** sincerely. **tener el c. en la mano,** to wear one's heart on one's sleeve
corazonada /koraθo'naða; koraso'naða/ *f*, feeling, instinct; presentiment, apprehension
corbata /kor'βata/ *f*, necktie; scarf; ribbon (insignia)
corbatería /korβate'ria/ *f*, necktie shop
corbatero /korβa'tero/ *m*, necktie maker; necktie dealer; tie rack
corbeta /kor'βeta/ *f*, corvette
Córcega /'korθega; 'korsega/ Corsica
corcel /kor'θel; kor'sel/ *m*, charger or battle horse
corchea /kor'tʃea/ *f*, *Mus.* quaver
corchete /kor'tʃete/ *m*, *Sew.* hook and eye; hook
corcho /'kortʃo/ *m*, *Bot.* cork, cork bark; stopper, cork; cork mat; bee hive
corcova /kor'koβa/ *f*, hump, abnormal protuberance
corcovado /korko'βaðo/ **(-da)** *a* hunchbacked, crooked —*n* hunchback
corcovear /korkoβe'ar/ *vi* to curvet, caper
cordaje /kor'ðahe/ *m*, *Naut.* cordage, tackling, rope
cordel /kor'ðel/ *m*, cord; *Naut.* line. **a c.,** in a straight line
cordelería /korðele'ria/ *f*, rope making; ropeyard; cordage
cordelero /korðe'lero/ **(-ra)** *n* rope maker
cordera /kor'ðera/ *f*, ewe lamb; sweet, gentle woman
cordero /kor'ðero/ *m*, lamb; dressed lambskin; peaceable, mild man; Jesus (gen. **Divino C.**)
cordial /kor'ðial/ *a* warming, invigorating; affectionate, loving, friendly. *m*, *Med.* cordial
cordialidad /korðiali'ðað/ *f*, cordiality, friendliness
cordillera /korði'ʎera; korði'yera/ *f*, mountain range
Córdoba /'korðoβa/ Cordova
cordobán /korðo'βan/ *m*, cured goatskin; Cordovan leather, Spanish leather
cordobés /korðo'βes/ **(-esa)** *a* and *n* Cordovan
cordón /kor'ðon/ *m*, cord; cordon; *Eccl.* rope girdle; *Archit.* string-course
cordoncillo /korðon'θiʎo; korðon'siyo/ *m*, rib (in cloth); ridge, milling (of coins); *Sew.* piping
cordura /kor'ðura/ *f*, good sense, prudence
Corea /ko'rea/ Korea
corego, corega /ko'rego, ko'rega/ *m*, choragus
coreografía /koreogra'fia/ *f*, choreography; art of dancing
coreográfico /koreo'grafiko/ *a* choreographic
coreógrafo /kore'ografo/ *m*, choreographer
corintio /ko'rintio/ **(-ia)** *a* and *n* Corinthian
Corinto /ko'rinto/ Corinth
corista /ko'rista/ *m*, *Eccl.* chorister. *mf Theat.* member of the chorus
cornada /kor'naða/ *f*, horn thrust or wound (bulls, etc.)
cornalina /korna'lina/ *f*, *Mineral.* cornelian
cornamenta /korna'menta/ *f*, horns (bulls, deer, etc.)
córnea /'kornea/ *f*, cornea
corneja /kor'neha/ *f*, carrion or black crow
córneo /'korneo/ *a* horny, corneous
corneta /kor'neta/ *f*, *Mus.* bugle; *Mus.* cornet; swineherd's horn; *Mil.* pennon. *m*, bugler; *Mil.* cornet. **c. de monte,** hunting horn
cornetín /korne'tin/ *m*, *dim* **corneta,** *Mus.* cornet; cornet player
cornezuelo /korne'θuelo; korne'suelo/ *m*, *dim* little horn; *Med.* ergot; *Bot.* variety of olive
cornisa /kor'nisa/ *f*, cornice
cornucopia /kornu'kopia/ *f*, cornucopia, horn of plenty; sconce; mirror
cornudo /kor'nuðo/ *a* horned. *m*, cuckold. **el C.,** the Devil
coro /'koro/ *m*, choir; chorus; *Archit.* choir. **hacer c. (a),** to listen to, support. **saber de c.,** to know by heart
corolario /koro'lario/ *m*, corollary
corona /ko'rona/ *f*, garland, wreath; halo; (*Astron. Archit.*) corona; crown (of tooth); crown (of head); tonsure; crown (coin); royal power; kingdom; triumph; reward; summit, height, peak; circlet (for candles)
coronación /korona'θion; korona'sion/ *f*, coronation; coping stone
coronamiento /korona'miento/ *m*, coronation; coping stone; *Fig.* crowning touch; *Naut.* taffrail
coronar /koro'nar/ *vt* to crown; crown (in draughts); complete, round off; —*vr* be crowned; crown oneself; be tipped or capped
coronel /koro'nel/ *m*, colonel
coronela /koro'nela/ *f*, *Inf.* colonel's wife
coronelía /korone'lia/ *f*, colonelcy
coronilla /koro'niʎa; koro'niya/ *f*, *dim* small crown; crown of head; *Fig. Inf.* **estar hasta la c.,** to be fed up
coroza /ko'roθa; ko'rosa/ *f*, dunce's cap
corpiño /kor'piɲo/ *m*, bodice
corporación /korpora'θion; korpora'sion/ *f*, corporation, body, association
corporal /korpo'ral/ *a* and *m*, *Eccl.* corporal
corporativo /korpora'tiβo/ *a* corporate, corporative
corpóreo /kor'poreo/ *a* corporeal
corporizar /korpori'θar; korpori'sar/ *vt* to embody
corpulento /korpu'lento/ *a* corpulent, stout
Corpus /'korpus/ *m*, Corpus Christi
corpúsculo /kor'puskulo/ *m*, corpuscle
corral /ko'rral/ *m*, yard; pen, enclosure, corral; old-time theater. **c. de madera,** timber yard. *Inf.* **hacer corrales,** to play truant
correa /ko'rrea/ *f*, leather strap or thong; flexibility; *Mech.* belt, band
corrección /korrek'θion; korrek'sion/ *f*, correction; correctness; punishment; emendation. **c. de pruebas,** proofreading, proofing, reading proof
correcional /korre'θional; korre'sional/ *a* correctional. *m*, reformatory
correctivo /korrek'tiβo/ *a* and *m*, corrective

correcto /ko'rrekto/ *a* correct; well-bred; unexceptionable, irreproachable; regular (of features)

corredera /korre'ðera/ *f,* link (engines); *Mech.* slide; *Naut.* log; racecourse; *Inf.* procuress

corredizo /korre'ðiθo; korre'ðiso/ *a* easy to untie; running (of knots); sliding

corredor /korre'ðor/ **(-ra)** *n* runner. *m, Com.* broker; corridor; *Inf.* meddler; *Inf.* procurer, pimp *—a* running. **c. de bolsa,** stockbroker

corregible /korre'hiβle/ *a* corrigible

corregidor /korrehi'ðor/ *m,* Spanish magistrate; *Obs.* mayor

corregidora /korrehi'ðora/ *f,* wife of corregidor; mayoress

corregir /korre'hir/ *vt irr* to correct; scold, punish; moderate, counteract; *Mech.* adjust; *—vr* mend one's ways. **c. pruebas,** to read proof *—Pres. Indic.* **corrijo, corriges, corrige, corrigen.** *Pres. Part.* **corrigiendo.** *Pres. Subjunc.* **corrija, corrijas,** etc *—Imperf. Subjunc.* **corrigiese,** etc.

correlación /korrela'θion; korrela'sion/ *f,* correlation

correligionario /korrelihio'nario/ **(-ia)** *n* coreligionist; fellow-supporter or believer

correo /ko'rreo/ *m,* courier; mail; post-office; letters. **c. aéreo,** air-mail. **c. certificado,** registered mail. **c. electrónico,** e-mail. **a vuelta de c.,** by return of mail. **tren c.,** mail train

correr /ko'rrer/ *vi* to run; race; sail, steam; flow; blow; flood; extend, stretch; pass (of time); fall due (salary, etc.); be current or general; (*with con*) be in charge of or responsible for; *—vt* run (a horse); fasten, slide (bolts, etc.); draw (curtains); undergo, suffer; sell, auction; *Inf.* steal; *Fig.* embarrass; spread (a rumor, etc.); catch, make (bus, train, etc.); *—vr* slide, glide, slip; run (of colors); *Inf.* spread oneself, talk too much. **c. cañas,** to participate in a mock joust using reeds as spears

correría /korre'ria/ *f,* raid, foray; excursion, trip

correspondencia /korrespon'denθia; korrespon'densia/ *f,* relationship, connection; intercourse, communication; correspondence, letters; equivalence, exact translation

corresponder /korrespon'der/ *vi* to requite, repay; be grateful; belong to, concern; devolve upon, fall to; suit, harmonize (with); fit; *—vr* correspond by letters; like or love each other

correspondiente /korrespon'diente/ *a* suitable; proportionate; corresponding. *mf* correspondent

corresponsal /korrespon'sal/ *mf* correspondent (especially professional); *Com.* agent

corretear /korrete'ar/ *vi* to wander about the streets; gad

correveidile /korreβei'ðile/ *mf Inf.* tale-bearer, gossip

corrida /ko'rriða/ *f,* race, run; *Aer.* taxying; bull fight (abb. for **c. de toros**)

corrido /ko'rriðo/ *a* extra, over (of weight); embarrassed; experienced

corriente /ko'rriente/ *a* current, present; well-known; usual, customary; fluent (style); ordinary, average; easy. *f,* flow, stream; *Fig.* course (of events, etc.); *Elec.* current *—adv* quite, exactly. *Elec.* **c. alterna,** alternating current. **c. continua,** direct current. **c. de aire,** draft. **estar al c.,** to be informed (of something)

Corriente del Golfo /ko'rriente del 'golfo/ Gulf Stream

corrillo /ko'rriʎo; ko'rriyo/ *m,* knot, group, huddle (of people)

corro /'korro/ *m,* circle, group; ring (for children's games)

corroboración /korroβora'θion; korroβora'sion/ *f,* corroboration, confirmation

corroborar /korroβo'rar/ *vt* to fortify; corroborate, support

corroborativo /korroβora'tiβo/ *a* corroborative

corroer /korro'er/ *vt irr* to corrode, waste away; *Fig.* gnaw. See **roer**

corromper /korrom'per/ *vt* to rot; mar; spoil, ruin; seduce; corrupt (texts); bribe; *Fig.* contaminate, corrupt; *—vi* stink; *—vr* putrefy, rot; be spoiled; *Fig.* be corrupted

corrosión /korro'sion/ *f,* corrosion

corrosivo /korro'siβo/ *a* corrosive

corrugación /korruga'θion; korruga'sion/ *f,* corrugation, wrinkling

corrupción /korrup'θion; korrup'sion/ *f,* rot, putrefaction; corruption, depravity; decay; stink; bribery; falsification (of texts); corruption (of language, etc.)

corrupto /ko'rrupto/ *a* corrupt

corruptor /korrup'tor/ **(-ra)** *n* corrupter

corsario /kor'sario/ *m,* pirate; privateer

corsé /kor'se/ *m,* corset

corsetería /korsete'ria/ *f,* corset shop or manufactory

corso /'korso/ **(-sa)** *a* and *n* Corsican

corta /'korta/ *f,* felling, cutting

cortacircuitos /kortaθir'kuitos; kortasir'kuitos/ *m, Elec.* circuit breaker, cut-out; disconnecting switch

cortado /kor'taðo/ *a* fitting, proportioned; disjointed (style); confused, shamefaced

cortador /korta'ðor/ *m,* cutter; cutter-out (dresses, etc.); butcher

cortadura /korta'ðura/ *f,* cut, wound; cutting (from periodicals); defile; *pl* clippings, cuttings

cortafrío /korta'frio/ *m,* cold chisel; hammer-head chisel

cortalápices /korta'lapiθes; korta'lapises/ *m,* pencil sharpener

cortante /kor'tante/ *a* cutting, sharp; piercing (of wind, etc.); trenchant

cortapapel /kortapa'pel/ *m,* paper-knife

cortapisa /korta'pisa/ *f,* condition, stipulation

cortaplumas /korta'plumas/ *m,* penknife

cortapuros /korta'puros/ *m,* cigar cutter

cortar /kor'tar/ *vt* to cut; cut out (dresses, etc.); switch off, shut off (water, electricity, etc.); cleave, divide; cut (cards); pierce (wind, etc.); interrupt, impede; omit, cut; *Fig.* interrupt (conversation); decide, determine; *—vr* be confused or shamefaced; curdle, turn sour (e.g. *Se cortó la leche,* The milk turned sour); split, fray; chap

cortavidrios /korta'βiðrios/ *m,* diamond, glasscutter

cortaviento /korta'βiento/ *m,* windscreen

corte /'korte/ *f,* court (royal); retinue; yard; *pl* Spanish parliament. *m,* cutting, cut; blade, cutting edge; cutting out, dressmaking; length, material required for garment, shoes, etc.; cut, fit; style; book edge; *Archit.* section; means, expedient; counting of money (in a till). **c. de caja,** counting of money (in a till). **c. trasversal,** side view

cortedad /korte'ðað/ *f,* shortness, brevity; smallness; stupidity, dullness; timidity, shyness. **c. de fuerzas,** lack of strength

cortejar /korte'har/ *vt* to accompany, escort; woo, court

cortejo /kor'teho/ *m,* courtship, wooing; suite, accompaniment; gift, present; homage, attention; *Inf.* lover, beau

cortés /kor'tes/ *a* polite, attentive, courteous, civil

cortesana /korte'sana/ *f,* courtesan

cortesano /korte'sano/ *a* court; courtly. *m,* courtier

cortesía /korte'sia/ *f,* politeness, courtesy; attentiveness; civility; gift, present; favor. **c. internacional,** courtesy of nations. **c. de boca mucho vale y poco cuesta.** Courtesy is worth much and costs little

corteza /kor'teθa; kor'tesa/ *f, Bot.* bark; *Anat.* cortex; skin, peel, crust; aspect, appearance; roughness. **c. terrestre,** Earth's crust, crust of the Earth. **de c.,** superficial (e.g. explanation)

cortijo /kor'tiho/ *m,* farmhouse and land

cortina /kor'tina/ *f,* curtain; *Fig.* veil; *Inf.* heel taps; *Mil.* curtain, screen. **c. de fuego de artillería,** antiaircraft barrage. **c. de globos de intercepción,** balloon barrage. **c. de humo,** smoke screen. **c. metálica,** metal shutter

cortinaje /korti'nahe/ *m,* curtains, hangings

corto /'korto/ *a* short, brief; timid, bashful; concise; defective; stupid, dull; tongue-tied, inarticulate. **c. circuito,** *Elec.* short-circuit. **c. de alcances,** dull-witted. **c. de vista,** short-sighted

coruscar /korus'kar/ *vi* to glitter, shine

corvadura /korβa'ðura/ *f,* bend; curvature

corvea /kor'βea/ *f,* corvée

corveta /kor'βeta/ *f,* curvet, prancing

corvetear /korβete'ar/ *vi* to curvet

corzo /'korθo; 'korso/ *m,* roe-deer, fallow-deer

cosa /'kosa/ *f*, thing. **c. rara,** strange to relate; an extraordinary thing. **como si tal c.,** as though nothing had happened. *Inf.* **poquita c.,** a person of no account

cosaco /ko'sako/ **(-ca)** *a* and *n* Cossack

coscorrón /kosko'rron/ *m*, blow on the head, cuff

cosecha /ko'setʃa/ *f*, harvest; harvest time; reaping, gathering, lifting; yield, produce; crop, shower (of honors, etc.). **c. de vino,** vintage

cosechar /kose'tʃar/ *vi* and *vt* to harvest, reap

coseno /ko'seno/ *m*, cosine

coser /ko'ser/ *vt* to sew, stitch; join, unite; press together (lips, etc.). **c. a puñaladas,** to stab repeatedly

Cosme /'kosme/ Cosmo

cosmético /kos'metiko/ *a* and *m*, cosmetic

cósmico /'kosmiko/ *a* cosmic

cosmografía /kosmogra'fia/ *f*, cosmography

cosmógrafo /kos'mografo/ *m*, cosmographer

cosmonave /kosmo'naβe/ *f*, spaceship

cosmopolita /kosmopo'lita/ *a* and *mf* cosmopolitan

cosmopolitismo /kosmopoli'tismo/ *m*, cosmopolitanism

cosmos /'kosmos/ *m*, cosmos

cospel /kos'pel/ *m*, blank (from which to stamp coins); to ken; subway to ken

cosquillas /kos'kiʎas; kos'kiyas/ *f pl*, tickling. **hacer c. (a),** to tickle

cosquillear /koskiʎe'ar; koskiye'ar/ *vt* to tickle

cosquilleo /koski'ʎeo; koski'yeo/ *m*, tickle, tickling

cosquilloso /koski'ʎoso; koski'yoso/ *a* ticklish; hypersensitive, touchy

costa /'kosta/ *f*, cost; expense; coast; *pl Law.* costs. **a c. de,** by dint of; at the cost of. **a toda c.,** at all costs

Costa del Oro, la /'kosta del 'oro, la/ the Gold Coast

Costa de Marfil /'kosta de mar'fil/ Ivory Coast

costado /kos'taðo/ *m*, *Anat.* side; *Mil.* flank; side; *pl* line of descent, genealogy. *Naut.* **dar el c.,** to be broadside on

costal /kos'tal/ *m*, sack, bag

costanero /kosta'nero/ *a* sloping; coast, coastal

costar /kos'tar/ *vi irr* to cost; cause. See **contar**

costarriqueño /kostarri'keɲo/ **(-ña)** *a* and *n* Costa Rican

coste /'koste/ *m*, cost, price

costear /koste'ar/ *vt* to pay for, defray the expense of; *Naut.* coast; *—vr* pay (for itself)

costilla /kos'tiʎa; kos'tiya/ *f*, (*Anat. Aer. Naut. Archit.*) rib; *Fig. Inf.* better half, wife; *pl Inf.* back, behind

costillaje, costillar /kosti'ʎahe, kosti'ʎar; kosti'yahe, kosti'yar/ *m*, *Anat.* ribs; *Naut.* ship's frame

costoso /kos'toso/ *a* expensive, costly; valuable; dear, costly, difficult

costra /'kostra/ *f*, crust; scab; rind (of cheese)

costumbre /kos'tumbre/ *f*, habit; custom

costumbrista /kostum'brista/ *mf* writer on everyday life and customs *—a* (of literary work) dealing with life and customs

costura /kos'tura/ *f*, sewing; seam; needlework; joint; riveting

costurera /kostu'rera/ *f*, seamstress

costurero /kostu'rero/ *m*, work-box, sewing bag

cota /'kota/ *f*, *Surv.* elevation, height; coat (of mail); quota. **c. de malla,** chain-mail

cotangente /kotan'hente/ *f*, cotangent

cotejar /kote'har/ *vt* to compare; collate

cotejo /ko'teho/ *m*, comparison; collation

cótel /'kotel/ *m*, cocktail, drink

cotelera /kote'lera/ *f*, cocktail shaker

cotí /ko'ti/ *m*, ticking (cloth)

cotidiano /koti'ðiano/ *a* daily

cotillón /koti'ʎon; koti'yon/ *m*, cotillion

cotizable /koti'θaβle; koti'saβle/ *a* valued at; (of prices, shares) quoted

cotización /kotiθa'θion; kotisa'sion/ *f*, *Com.* quotation; *Com.* rate. **boletín de c.,** price list (of shares, etc.)

cotizar /koti'θar; koti'sar/ *vt Com.* to quote (prices, rates)

coto /'koto/ *m*, enclosed ground; boundary stone; preserve, covert; hand's breadth; end, stop, limit. **c. de caza,** game preserve

cotorra /ko'torra/ *f*, small green parrot; magpie; *Inf.* chatterbox

cotufa /ko'tufa/ *f*, earthnut; titbit; *Inf.* **pedir cotufas en el golfo,** to ask for the moon

coturno /ko'turno/ *m*, buskin

coyote /ko'yote/ *m*, coyote, prairie wolf; *Mexico* fixer (anyone who can pull strings to cut red tape or achieve something illegally); smuggler (of goods or people)

coyuntura /koyun'tura/ *f*, *Anat.* joint; juncture, occasion

coz /koθ; kos/ *f*, kick, recoil (of gun); butt (of a rifle); *Inf.* slap in the face, unprovoked rudeness. **dar coces,** to kick

craneal /krane'al/ *a* cranial

cráneo /'kraneo/ *m*, cranium, skull

crápula /'krapula/ *f*, drunkenness; depravity, immorality, debauchery

craquear /krake'ar/ *vt* to crack (petroleum)

crasitud /krasi'tuð/ *f*, greasiness; fatness; crassness

craso /'kraso/ *a* fat, greasy; thick; unpardonable, crass (often with *ignorancia*). *m*, fatness; ignorance

creación /krea'θion; krea'sion/ *f*, creation; universe, world; foundation, establishment; appointment (dignitaries)

creador /krea'ðor/ **(-ra)** *n* creator, originator. *m*, God *—a* creative

crear /kre'ar/ *vt* to create; found, institute, establish; make, appoint

crecer /kre'θer; kre'ser/ *vi irr* to grow; grow up; increase in size; grow longer; wax (moon); come in (of the tide); increase in value (money); *—vr* become more sure of oneself; swell with pride; grow in authority. See **nacer**

creces /'kreθes; 'kreses/ *f pl*, increase, interest. **con c.,** fully, amply. **pagar con c.,** *Fig.* to pay with interest

crecida /kre'θiða; kre'siða/ *f*, swollen river or stream; food; rising (of the tide)

crecido /kre'θiðo; kre'siðo/ *a* grown up; considerable; abundant, plentiful; large; full; serious, important

crecidos /kre'θiðos; kre'siðos/ *m pl*, widening stitches (knitting)

creciente /kre'θiente; kre'siente/ *a* growing; rising (of the tide); crescent (moon). *m*, *Herald.* crescent. *f*, rising of the tide; crescent moon

crecimiento /kreθi'miento; kresi'miento/ *m*, growing; growth, development; increase (in value, money); waxing (of moon)

credencial /kreðen'θial; kreðen'sial/ *a* accrediting

credenciales /kreðen'θiales; kreðen'siales/ *f pl*, credentials

credibilidad /kreðiβili'ðað/ *f*, credibility

crédito /'kreðito/ *m*, belief, credence; assent, acquiescence; reputation, name; favor, popularity, acceptance; *Com.* credit; *Com.* letter of credit. **créditos activos,** assets. **créditos pasivos,** liabilities. **a c.,** on credit

credo /'kreðo/ *m*, creed. *Inf.* **en un c.,** in a jiffy

credulidad /kreðuli'ðað/ *f*, credulity

crédulo /'kreðulo/ *a* credulous

creencia /kre'enθia; kre'ensia/ *f*, belief; religion, sect, faith

creer /kre'er/ *vt irr* to believe; think, consider, opine; think likely or probable. **¡Ya lo creo!** I should just think so! Rather! **creerse la divina garza,** *Mexico* to think one is God's gift to the world. **creerse descender del sobaco de Jesucristo,** to think one is God's gift to the world *—Pres. Part.* **creyendo.** *Preterite* **creyó, creyeron.** *Imperf. Subjunc.* **creyese,** etc.

creíble /kre'iβle/ *a* credible

crema /'krema/ *f*, cream (off milk); custard mold, cream, shape; face cream; cold cream; elect, flower (of society, etc.)

cremación /krema'θion; krema'sion/ *f*, cremation; burning, incineration

cremallera /krema'ʎera; krema'yera/ *f*, *Mech.* rack, ratch; zip fastener. **colgar la c.,** to give a house-warming

crematístico /krema'tistiko/ *a* economic, financial

crematorio /krema'torio/ *m,* crematorium —*a* burning; cremating
cremor /kre'mor/ *m, Chem.* cream of tartar
cremoso /kre'moso/ *a* creamy
crencha /'krentʃa/ *f,* parting (of the hair); each side of parting
creosota /kreo'sota/ *f,* creosote
crepitación /krepita'θion; krepita'sion/ *f,* crackling, sputtering; hissing; roar (of a fire); *Med.* crepitation
crepitar /krepi'tar/ *vi* to crackle; sputter; hiss; roar (of a fire); *Med.* crepitate
crepuscular /krepusku'lar/ *a* twilight
crepúsculo /kre'puskulo/ *m,* twilight, half light
cresa /'kresa/ *f,* maggot; cheese-mite; fly's egg
Creso /'kreso/ Croesus
crespo /'krespo/ *a* curly, frizzy (hair); rough (of animal's fur); curled (leaves); artificial, involved (style)
crespón /kres'pon/ *m,* crape
cresta /'kresta/ *f,* comb (of cock, etc.); tuft, topknot (birds); plume; summit, top (of mountains); crest (of a wave); *Herald.* crest
crestado /kres'taðo/ *a* crested
Creta /'kreta/ Crete
creta /'kreta/ *f,* chalk
cretense /kre'tense/ *a* Cretan
cretinismo /kreti'nismo/ *m,* cretinism
cretino /kre'tino/ **(-na)** *a* and *n* cretin
creyente /kre'yente/ *a* believing; religious. *mf* believer
cría /'kria/ *f,* rearing; bringing up; nursing; suckling; breeding; brood; litter
criada /kri'aða/ *f,* servant, maid
criadero /kria'ðero/ *m, Mineral.* vein, deposit; tree nursery, plantation; breeding farm or place —*a* prolific
criado /kri'aðo/ *m,* servant —*a* bred, brought up (used with *bien* or *mal,* well *or* badly brought up)
criador /kria'ðor/ **(-ra)** *n* breeder, keeper, raiser —*a* creating; rearing; creative; fertile, rich
crianza /kri'anθa; kri'ansa/ *f,* feeding, suckling; lactation; manners. **buena** (or **mala**) c., good (or bad) breeding or upbringing
criar /kri'ar/ *vt* to create; procreate; rear, educate, bring up; feed, nurse, suckle; raise (birds, animals); inspire, give rise to. **Me crié raquítico,** I grew up delicate
criatura /kria'tura/ *f,* being, creature; man, human being; infant; small child; fetus; *Fig.* puppet, tool
criba /'kriβa/ *f,* sieve, cribble
cribar /kri'βar/ *vt* to sieve; riddle (earth, etc.)
crimen /'krimen/ *m,* crime. **c. pasional,** crime of passion
criminal /krimi'nal/ *a* and *m,* criminal
criminalidad /kriminali'ðað/ *f,* guilt; crime ratio; delinquency
criminalista /krimina'lista/ *mf* criminal lawyer; criminologist
criminología /kriminolo'hia/ *f,* criminology
crin /krin/ *f,* horsehair; (gen. *pl*) mane
crinolina /krino'lina/ *f,* crinoline
crío /'krio/ *m, Inf.* kid, brat
criollo /'krioʎo; 'krioyo/ **(-lla)** *a* and *n* creole —*a* indigenous, native
cripta /'kripta/ *f,* crypt
criptografía /kriptogra'fia/ *f,* cryptography
criquet /kri'ket/ *m, Sports.* cricket
crisálida /kri'saliða/ *f,* chrysalis
crisantemo /krisan'temo/ *m,* chrysanthemum
crisis /'krisis/ *f,* crisis. **c. de desarrollo,** growing pains. **c. de vivienda,** housing shortage
crisma /'krisma/ *m,* or *f,* chrism
crisol /kri'sol/ *m,* crucible; melting pot
crispado /kris'paðo/ *a* stiffened
crispar /kris'par/ *vt* to cause to contract or twitch; —*vr* twitch. *Inf.* **Se me crispan los nervios,** My nerves are all on edge
cristal /kri'stal/ *m,* crystal; glass; windowpane; mirror; water. **c. tallado,** cut glass
cristalería /kristale'ria/ *f,* glassware; glass manufacture; glass panes; glass and china shop
cristalino /krista'lino/ *a* crystalline. *m,* lens (of the eye)
cristalización /kristaliθa'θion; kristalisa'sion/ *f,* crystallization
cristalizar /kristali'θar; kristali'sar/ *vi* to crystallize; *Fig.* take shape; —*vt* cause to crystallize
cristalografía /kristalogra'fia/ *f,* crystallography
cristiandad /kristian'dað/ *f,* Christendom
cristianismo /kristia'nismo/ *m,* Christianity; Christendom
cristianizar /kristiani'θar; kristiani'sar/ *vt* to convert to Christianity, christianize
cristiano /kris'tiano/ **(-na)** *a* and *n* Christian —*a Inf.* watered (of wine). *m, Inf.* Spanish (contrasted with other languages); *Inf.* soul, person
cristino /kris'tino/ **(-na)** *a* and *n* supporting, or follower of, Queen Regent Maria Cristina during Carlist wars
cristo /'kristo/ *m,* Christ; crucifix. *Inf.* **donde C. dio las tres voces,** in the middle of nowhere
cristus /'kristus/ *m,* Christ-cross; alphabet. **no saber el c.,** to be extremely ignorant
criterio /kri'terio/ *m,* criterion, standard; judgment, discernment; opinion. **a c. de,** in the opinion of. **según mi c.,** in my opinion
crítica /'kritika/ **(a)** *f,* criticism (of)
criticar /kriti'kar/ *vt* to criticize; censure, find fault with, blame
crítico /'kritiko/ *a* critical; censorious; dangerous, difficult; *Med.* critical. *m,* critic; fault-finder
criticón /kriti'kon/ **(-ona)** *a* censorious, hyper-critical —*n* fault-finder
Croacia /kro'aθia; kro'asia/ Croatia
croar /kro'ar/ *vi* (frog) to croak
croata /kro'ata/ *a* and *mf* Croatian
croché /kro'tʃe/ *m,* crochet work
crol /krol/ *m,* crawl (swimming)
cromado /kro'maðo/ *a* chromium-plated
cromático /kro'matiko/ *a* chromatic
cromato /kro'mato/ *m,* chromate
crómico /'kromiko/ *a* chromic
cromo /'kromo/ *m,* chrome; chromium; chromolithograph
crónica /'kronika/ *f,* chronicle; diary of events
crónico /'kroniko/ *a* chronic; inveterate
cronista /kro'nista/ *mf* chronicler
cronología /kronolo'hia/ *f,* chronology
cronológico /krono'lohiko/ *a* chronological
cronómetro /kro'nometro/ *m,* stop-watch
croqueta /kro'keta/ *f,* croquette
croquis /'krokis/ *m,* sketch, outline, drawing. **c. de nivel,** (optical) foresight
crótalo /'krotalo/ *m,* rattlesnake; snapper (kind of castanet)
cruce /'kruθe; 'kruse/ *m,* crossing; point of intersection; crossroads
crucero /kru'θero; kru'sero/ *m, Eccl.* cross-bearer; crossroads; *Archit.* transept; *Astron.* Cross; *Naut.* cruiser
crucificar /kruθifi'kar; krusifi'kar/ *vt* to crucify; *Fig. Inf.* torment, torture
crucifijo /kruθi'fiho; krusi'fiho/ *m,* crucifix
crucifixión /kruθifik'sion; krusifik'sion/ *f,* crucifixion
cruciforme /kruθi'forme; krusi'forme/ *a* cruciform
crucigrama /kruθi'grama; krusi'grama/ *m,* crossword puzzle
cruda /'kruða/ *f, Mexico* hangover
crudelísimo /kruðe'lisimo/ *a superl* **cruel,** most cruel, exceedingly cruel
crudeza /kru'ðeθa; kru'ðesa/ *f,* rawness, uncookedness; unripeness; rawness (silk, etc.); crudeness; harshness; *Inf.* boasting
crudo /'kruðo/ *a* uncooked, raw; green, unripe; indigestible; raw, natural, unbleached; harsh, cruel; cold, raw; *Inf.* boastful. **crudos de petróleo,** *m pl* crude oil
crueldad /kruel'dað/ *f,* cruelty; harshness
cruento /'kruento/ *a* bloody
crujía /kru'hia/ *f,* passage, corridor; *Naut.* midship gangway
crujidero /kruhi'ðero/ *a* crackling; creaking; crispy; clattering; rustling; chattering

crujido /kru'hiðo/ *m,* creak, crack, crackling, rustle
crujir /kru'hir/ *vi* to creak, crackle, rustle
crup /krup/ *m,* croup
crupié /kru'pie/ *m,* croupier
crustáceo /krus'taθeo; krus'taseo/ *a* and *m,* crustacean
crux /kruks/ *f,* cross; tails (of coin); withers (of animals); insignia, decoration; affliction, trouble; *Astron.* Southern Cross; *Print.* dagger, obelisk, obelus. **c. doble,** diesis, double dagger. **c. de mayo,** May cross. **c. gamada,** swastika. *Inf.* **¡C. y raya!** An end to this! **en c.,** in the shape of a cross. *Inf.* **hacerse cruces,** to be left speechless, be dumbfounded
cruzada /kru'θaða; kru'saða/ *f,* crusade; crossroads; campaign
cruzado /kru'θaðo; kru'saðo/ *a* cross; double-breasted (of coats). *m,* crusader; member of military order
cruzamiento /kruθa'miento; krusa'miento/ *m,* crossing; intersection
cruzar /kru'θar; kru'sar/ *vt* to cross; intersect; interbreed; bestow a cross upon; *Naut.* cruise; *—vr* take part in a crusade; cross one another; coincide; *Geom.* intersect
cu /ku/ *f,* name of the letter Q
cuacuac /kua'kuak/ *m,* quack (of a duck)
cuaderna /kua'ðerna/ *f, Naut.* ship's frame, timber; double fours (backgammon)
cuaderno /kua'ðerno/ *m,* notebook, jotter, account book; *Inf.* card pack. *Naut.* **c. de bitácora,** logbook
cuadra /'kuaðra/ *f,* stable; ward, dormitory; hall, large room; quarter of a mile
cuadrado /kua'ðraðo/ *a* square; perfect, exact. *m,* square; (*Mil. Math.*) square; window-frame; clock (of a stocking)
cuadragenario /kuaðrahe'nario/ *a* forty years old
cuadragésima /kuaðra'hesima/ *f,* Quadragesima
cuadragésimo /kuaðra'hesimo/ *a* fortieth
cuadrángulo /kua'ðraŋgulo/ *m,* quadrangle
cuadrante /kua'ðrante/ *m,* quadrant; dial, face
cuadrar /kua'ðrar/ *vt* (*Math.*) to square; make square; *—vi* correspond, tally; fit, be appropriate *—vr Mil.* stand at attention; *Fig. Inf.* dig one's heels in
cuadrática /kua'ðratika/ *f,* quadratic equation
cuadrático /kua'ðratiko/ *a* quadratic
cuadratura /kuaðra'tura/ *f,* squareness; (*Math. Astron.*) quadrature
cuadrienio /kua'ðrienio/ *m,* space of four years
cuadriga /kua'ðriga/ *f,* quadriga
cuadrilátero /kuaðri'latero/ *m,* quadrilateral; boxing ring *—a* quadrilateral
cuadrilla /kua'ðriʎa; kua'ðriya/ *f,* gang; company, band, group; police patrol; quadrille (dance); matadors and their assistants (at a bull fight). **c. carrillana,** track gang
cuadrilongo /kuaðri'loŋgo/ *a* and *m,* oblong
cuadrimotor /kuaðrimo'tor/ *a Aer.* four-engined
cuadrivio /kua'ðriβio/ *m,* quadrivium
cuadro /'kuaðro/ *m,* square; picture-frame; frame (of bicycle); flowerbed; *Theat.* tableau, scene; spectacle, sight; board (of instruments); description (in novel, etc.); *Mil.* command, officers; square (of troops). **c. de distribución,** *Elec.* main switchboard. **c. enrejado,** play pen. **cuadro de costumbres,** word-picture of everyday life and customs. **cuadro vivo,** tableau vivant. **a cuadros,** checked, in squares
cuadrúpedo /kua'ðrupeðo/ **(-da)** *a* and *n* quadruped
cuadruple /kua'ðruplc/ *a* quadruple
cuadruplicar /kuaðrupli'kar/ *vt* to quadruple
cuajada /kua'haða/ *f,* curd (of milk)
cuajar /kua'har/ *m,* maw (of a ruminant)
cuajar /kua'har/ *vt* to coagulate; curdle; *—vi Inf.* achieve, get away with; *—vr* be coagulated or curdled; *Inf.* be packed or chock full; get stuck (e.g. a piece of food in one's throat)
cuajarón /kuaha'ron/ *m,* clot (of blood, etc.)
cuajo /'kuaho/ *m,* rennet; coagulation; curdling; *Anat.* abomasum
cual /kual/ *rel pron* sing. *mf* and *neut pl* **cuales,** which; who; such as (e.g. *Le detuvieron sucesos cuales suelen ocurrir,* He was detained by events such as usually happen). **a c. mas,** vying (with) (e.g. *Los dos canónigos a c. más grueso,* The two canons each fatter (vying in fatness) than the other). **c.** is used with *def art* **el (la, lo, los, las) cual(es),** who; which, when the antecedent is a noun (e.g. *Juan saltó en el barco, el c. zarpó en seguida,* John jumped into the boat which sailed at once). **por lo c.,** for which reason *—adv* like (gen. literary or poet.). **¿cuál?** *interr. pron* (no article) which? what? e.g. *Aquí tienes dos cuadros, ¿cuál de ellos te gusta?* Here are two pictures, which one do you like? Also expresses an implicit question, e.g. *No sé cuál te guste,* I don't know which you will like. *¡cuál! adv interj* how! *c.... c. indef pron* some... some
cualesquier /kuales'kier/ *a pl* of **cualquier**
cualesquiera /kuales'kiera/ *a pl* of **cualquiera**
cualidad /kuali'ðað/ *f,* quality; characteristic; talent
cualitativo /kualita'tiβo/ *a* qualitative
cualquier /kual'kier/ *Abbr.* **of cualquiera,** any; *pl* **cualesquier.** Only used as abb. *before* noun
cualquiera /kual'kiera/ *a mf* any, e.g. *una canción c.,* any song *—pron* anybody, each, anyone whatsoever, whoever (e.g. *¡C. diría que no te gusta!* Anyone would say you don't like it!) *Inf.* **un c.,** a nobody
cuán /ku'an/ *adv* how (e.g. *¡C. bello es!* How beautiful it is). Used only before *a* or *adv.* Abb. of **cuánto**
cuando /'kuando/ *adv* when; if *—interr* **¿cuándo?** *conjunc* although; since; sometimes; *—prep* during (e.g. *c. la guerra,* during the war) **c. más,** at most, at best. **c. menos,** at the least. **c. no,** if not (e.g. *Es agnóstica cuando no atea,* She's an agnostic, if not an atheist) **de c. en c.,** from time to time
cuandoquiera /kuando'kiera/ *adv* whenever
cuanta, teoría de la /'kuanta, teo'ria de la/ *f,* quantum theory
cuantía /kuan'tia/ *f,* quantity, amount; importance, rank, distinction
cuantiar /kuan'tiar/ *vt* to value, estimate; tax
cuantidad /kuanti'ðað/ *f,* quantity
cuantioso /kuan'tioso/ *a* large, considerable; numerous; plentiful, abundant
cuantitativo /kuantita'tiβo/ *a* quantitative
cuanto /'kuanto/ *a* as much as, all the; *pl* as many as, all the (e.g. *Te daré cuantas muñecas veas allí,* I'll give you all the dolls you see there) *—a correlative* the... the, as... as (e.g. *C. más tanto, mejor,* The more the better). **cuánto,** *a* and *pron interr* and *interj* how much; *pl* how many (e.g. *¡Cuánto tiempo sin verla!* How long without seeing her!) *pron neut* **cuanto,** as much as, all that (e.g. *Te daré c. quieras,* I shall give you all that you wish) *—adv* **cuanto,** as soon as. **c. antes,** as soon as possible. **c. a** *or* **en c. a,** concerning *—adv* and *conjunc* **c. más,** all the more (e.g. *Se lo diré c. más que tenía esa intención,* I shall tell him all the more because I meant to do so) *—adv* **en c.,** as soon as, immediately (e.g. *Lo haré en c. venga,* I shall do it immediately he comes). **en c. a,** with regard to. **por c.,** inasmuch, for this reason *—adv interr* **¿Cuánto?** How much? How long? *adv interj* How! How much! (e.g. *¡Cuánto me gustaría ir!* How much I should like to go!)
cuaquerismo /kuake'rismo/ *m,* Quakerism
cuáquero /'kuakero/ **(-ra)** *n* Quaker
cuarenta /kua'renta/ *a* and *m,* forty; fortieth
cuarentena /kuaren'tena/ *f,* fortieth; period of forty days, months or years; Lent; quarantine
cuarentón /kuaren'ton/ **(-ona)** *n* person forty years old
cuaresma /kua'resma/ *f,* Lent
cuaresmal /kuares'mal/ *a* Lenten
cuarta /'kuarta/ *f,* quarter, fourth; hand's breadth; *Mus.* fourth; *Astron.* quadrant
cuartana /kuar'tana/ *f,* quartan (fever)
cuarteadura /kuartea'ðura/ *f,* crack
cuartear /kuarte'ar/ *vt* to quarter, divide into quarters; cut or divide into pieces
cuartel /kuar'tel/ *m,* barracks; *Naut.* hatch; quarter, fourth; *Herald.* quarter; district, ward; flowerbed; *Inf.* house, accommodation; *Mil.* quarter, mercy; *Mil.* billet, station. *Mil.* **c. general,** general headquarters
cuartelada /kuarte'laða/ *f, Naut.* quarter; military rebellion, military uprising, mutiny
cuartelar /kuarte'lar/ *vt Herald.* to quarter

cuartelazo /kuarte'laθo; kuarte'laso/ *m*, military rebellion, military uprising, mutiny
cuarterón /kuarte'ron/ **(-ona)** *n* quadroon
cuarteta /kuar'teta/ *f*, quatrain
cuarteto /kuar'teto/ *m*, *Mus.* quartet; *Poet.* quatrain
cuartilla /kuar'tiʎa; kuar'tiya/ *f*, sheet of paper; liquid measure; quarter of an arroba; pastern (horses)
cuarto /'kuarto/ *m*, room; quarter, fourth; point (of compass); watch (on battleships); *Astron.* quarter, phase; portion, quarter; joint (of meat); *pl* quarters (of animals); *Inf.* penny, farthing —*a* quarter, fourth. **c. creciente,** first phase (of moon). **c. de hora,** quarter of an hour. **en c.,** *Print.* in quarto. *Inf.* **no tener un c.,** to be broke
cuarzo /'kuarθo; 'kuarso/ *m*, quartz
cuasi /'kuasi/ *adv* almost, nearly, quasi
cuasidelito /kuasiðe'lito/ *m*, *Law.* technical offense
cuasimodo /kuasi'moðo/ *m*, *Eccl.* Low Sunday, Quasimodo
cuaterna /kua'terna/ *f*, quaternion
cuatrillón /kuatri'ʎon; kuatri'yon/ *m*, quadrillion
cuatrimestre /kuatri'mestre/ *a* of four months' duration. *m*, space of four months
cuatrimotor /kuatrimo'tor/ *m*, *Aer.* four-engine airplane
cuatrisílabo /kuatri'silaβo/ *a* quadrisyllabic
cuatro /'kuatro/ *a* four; fourth. *m*, figure four; fourth (of days of months); playing-card with four spots; *Mus.* quartet. **el c. de mayo,** the fourth of May. **Son las c.,** It is four o'clock
cuatrocientos /kuatro'θientos; kuatro'sientos/ *a* four hundred; four hundredth.
cuba /'kuβa/ *f*, barrel, cask; tub, vat; *Inf.* pot-bellied person; *Inf.* drunkard, toper
cubano /ku'βano/ **(-na)** *a* and *n* Cuban
cubería /kuβe'ria/ *f*, cooperage
cubeta /ku'βeta/ *f*, *dim* keg, small cask; bucket, pail; *Photo.* developing dish
cubicar /kuβi'kar/ *vt Math.* to cube; *Geom.* measure the volume of
cúbico /'kuβiko/ *a* cubic
cubículo /ku'βikulo/ *m*, cubicle
cubierta /ku'βierta/ *f*, cover; envelope; casing; deck (of ship); tire cover; book-jacket; pretext, excuse. **c. de escotilla,** *Naut.* companion-hatch. **c. de paseo,** promenade deck
cubierto /ku'βierto/ *m*, cover, place at table; course (of a meal); table d'hôte, complete meal; roof. **un c. de doscientas pesetas,** a two hundred peseta meal
cubil /ku'βil/ *m*, lair, den (of animals)
cubilete /kuβi'lete/ *m*, *Cul.* mold; dice box; conjurer's cup
cubismo /ku'βismo/ *m*, cubism
cubista /ku'βista/ *mf* cubist —*a* cubistic
cubo /'kuβo/ *m*, bucket, pail; *Mech.* socket; *Math.* cube; hub (of a wheel); mill-pond
cubrecama /kuβre'kama/ *m*, bedspread
cubrecorsé /kuβrekor'se/ *m*, camisole
cubrimiento /kuβri'miento/ *m*, covering
cubrir /ku'βrir/ *vt* to cover; *Mil.* defend; spread over, extend over; conceal, hide; *Com.* cover; dissemble; *Archit.* roof; —*vr* cover one's head; pay, meet (debts, etc.); cover or protect oneself (by insurance, etc.) —*Past Part.* **cubierto**
cucaña /ku'kaɲa/ *f*, greasy pole; *Inf.* snip, cinch, bargain
cucaracha /kuka'ratʃa/ *f*, cockroach
cuchara /ku'tʃara/ *f*, spoon; ladle; *Naut.* boat scoop; scoop, dipper. *Fig.* **meter c.,** to stick one's oar in
cucharada /kutʃa'raða/ *f*, spoonful; ladleful
cuchicheador /kutʃitʃea'ðor/ **(-ra)** *n* whisperer
cuchichear /kutʃitʃe'ar/ *vi* to whisper
cuchicheo /kutʃi'tʃeo/ *m*, whisper; whispering; murmur
cuchillada /kutʃi'ʎaða; kutʃi'yaða/ *f*, knife thrust or wound; *pl* (in sleeves, etc.) slashes; fight, blows
cuchillería /kutʃiʎe'ria; kutʃiye'ria/ *f*, cutlery; cutler's shop
cuchillero /kutʃi'ʎero; kutʃi'yero/ *m*, cutler
cuchillo /ku'tʃiʎo; ku'tʃiyo/ *m*, knife; *Sew.* gore, gusset (gen. *pl*); authority, power; anything triangular in shape. **pasar a c.,** to put to the sword
cuclillas, en /ku'kliʎas, en; ku'kliyas, en/ *adv* in a squatting position
cuclillo /ku'kliʎo; ku'kliyo/ *m*, *Ornith.* cuckoo; *Inf.* cuckold
cuco /'kuko/ *a Inf.* pretty, cute; crafty, smart
cucú /ku'ku/ *m*, cry of the cuckoo
Cucufo /ku'kufo/ *m*, the Devil
cuculla /ku'kuʎa; ku'kuya/ *f*, cowl, hood
cucurucho /kuku'rutʃo/ *m*, paper cornet
cuello /'kueʎo; 'kueyo/ *m*, *Anat.* neck; neck (of bottle, etc.); *Sew.* neck; collar; necklet (of fur, etc.)
cuenca /'kuenka/ *f*, socket (of eye); *Geog.* catchment-basin; gorge, deep valley. **c. de un río,** river-basin
cuenta /'kuenta/ *f*, count, counting; calculation; account; bead; charge, responsibility; reckoning; explanation, reason; *Com.* bill. **c. a cero, c. a la inversa, c. atrás,** countdown. **c. corriente,** current account. **cuentas alegres, cuentas galanas,** *Inf.* idle dreams, illusions. **c. pendiente,** outstanding account. *Inf.* **caer en la c.,** to tumble to, realize. **llevar la c.,** to reckon, keep account. **sin c.,** countless. **tener en c.,** to bear in mind
cuentacorrentista /kuentakorren'tista/ *mf* one who has a bank account
cuentagotas /kuenta'gotas/ *m*, dropper, dropping tube
cuentakilómetros /kuentaki'lometros/ *m*, speedometer
cuentapasos /kuenta'pasos/ *m*, pedometer
cuentista /kuen'tista/ *mf* storyteller; *Inf.* gossip
cuento /'kuento/ *m*, story, tale; narrative; calculation; *Inf.* gossip, fairytale; *Math.* million. **c. de viejas,** old wives' tale. *Fig. Inf.* **dejarse de cuentos,** to go straight to the point. *Inf.* **Va de c.,** It is told, they say
cuerda /'kuerða/ *f*, rope; cord; string; *Geom.* chord; *Mus.* string; catgut; chain (of clock); *Mus.* chord; vocal range. **dar c. (a),** to wind up (a watch); lead on, make talk. **de cuerdas cruzadas,** overstrung (of a piano)
cuerdo /'kuerðo/ *a* sane; prudent; levelheaded
cuerno /'kuerno/ *m*, *Anat.* horn; feeler, antenna; *Mus.* horn; horn (of the moon). **c. de abundancia,** horn of plenty. *Inf.* **poner en los cuernos de la luna,** to praise to the skies
cuero /'kuero/ *m*, hide, pelt; leather. **c. charolado,** patent leather. **en cueros,** stark naked
cuerpo /'kuerpo/ *m*, *Anat.* body or trunk; flesh (as opposed to spirit); bodice; volume, book; main portion; collection; size, volume; physical appearance; corpse; group, assembly; corporation, association; *Geom.* solid; *Chem.* element; thickness, density; *Mil.* corps. **c. de bomberos,** fire brigade. **c. de guardia,** guardhouse. **c. de la vida,** staff of life; *Inf.* **dar con el c. en tierra,** to fall flat. **de c. entero,** *Art.* full-length (portrait). **en c.,** without a coat, lightly clad. **un c. a c.,** a clinch (in wrestling)
cuervo /'kuerβo/ *m*, raven; crow
cuesco /'kuesko/ *m*, stone, seed, pip
cuesta /'kuesta/ *f*, slope, incline, gradient. **c. abajo (arriba),** down (up) hill. **a cuestas,** on one's back; having the responsibility of
cuestión /kues'tion/ *f*, problem, question; quarrel, disagreement; affair, matter; torture
cuestionable /kuestio'naβle/ *a* doubtful, questionable
cuestionar /kuestio'nar/ *vt* to discuss, debate
cuestionario /kuestio'nario/ *m*, questionnaire
cueva /'kueβa/ *f*, cave, cavern; basement, cellar. *Fig.* **c. de ladrones,** den of thieves
cuévano /'kueβano/ *m*, hamper, basket
cuidado /kui'ðaðo/ *m*, carefulness, pains; attention; charge, care, responsibility; anxiety, fear —*interj* **¡C.!** Careful! Look out! **Me tiene sin c. su opinión,** I am not interested in his (your) opinion. *Inf.* **estar al c. de,** to be under the direction of. **estar de c.,** to be dangerously ill
cuidadoso /kuiða'ðoso/ **(de)** *a* careful (about *or* with); anxious (about); concerned (with); watchful; conscientious
cuidar /kui'ðar/ *vt* to care for; tend; take care of, look after; mind, be careful of; —*vr* look after oneself

cuita /'kuita/ *f,* misfortune, anxiety, trouble

cuitado /kui'taðo/ *a* unfortunate, worried; timid, bashful, humble

culata /ku'lata/ *f, Anat.* haunch; butt (of fire-arms); back, rear; *Auto.* sump

culatazo /kula'taθo; kula'taso/ *m,* recoil (of fire-arms)

culebra /ku'leβra/ *f,* snake; *Inf.* trick, joke; *Inf.* sudden uproar. **hacer c.,** to stagger along

culebrear /kuleβre'ar/ *vi* to wriggle; grovel; meander, wind

culebreo /kule'βreo/ *m,* wriggling; meandering, winding

culí /ku'li/ *m,* coolie

culinario /kuli'nario/ *a* culinary

culminación /kulmina'θion; kulmina'sion/ *f,* culmination, peak; *Astron.* zenith

culminante /kulmi'nante/ *a* culminating, *Fig.* outstanding

culminar /kulmi'nar/ *vi* to culminate (in)

culo /'kulo/ *m,* buttocks, seat; rump; anus; base, bottom. **c. de lámpara,** *Archit.* pendant; *Print.* tail-piece

culpa /'kulpa/ *f,* fault; blame. **echar la c.** (**a**), to blame. **por c. de,** through the fault of. **tener la c.,** to be to blame

culpabilidad /kulpaβili'ðað/ *f,* guilt

culpable /kul'paβle/ *a* culpable

culpado /kul'paðo/ **(-da)** *n* culprit

culpar /kul'par/ *vt* to blame, accuse; criticize, censure

culteranismo, cultismo /kultera'nismo, kul'tismo/ *m,* involved literary style (cf. **Euphuism**)

cultígeno /kul'tiheno/ *m,* cultigen

cultismo /kul'tismo/ *m,* cultism (Gongorism); learned form, learnedism, learned word

cultivable /kulti'βaβle/ *a* cultivable

cultivación /kultiβa'θion; kultiβa'sion/ *f,* cultivation; culture

cultivador /kultiβa'ðor/ **(-ra)** *n* cultivator; planter

cultivar /kulti'βar/ *vt* to cultivate; develop; exercise, practice (professions); culture (bacteriology)

cultivo /kul'tiβo/ *m,* cultivation; farming; culture (bacteriological)

culto /'kulto/ *a* cultivated; educated; cultured; elegant, artificial (style). *m,* worship; cult; religion, creed; homage

cultura /kul'tura/ *f,* cultivation; culture. **de c. universitaria,** college-educated

cultural /kultu'ral/ *a* cultural

cumbre /'kumbre/ *f,* peak, crest, summit; *Fig.* zenith, acme

cumpleaños /kumple'aɲos/ *m,* birthday

cumplidamente /kumpliða'mente/ *adv* fully, completely

cumplido /kum'pliðo/ *a* complete; thorough; long; plentiful; courteous, punctilious; fulfilled. *m,* courtesy, attention; formality. **gastar cumplidos,** to stand on ceremony; be formal

cumplimentar /kumplimen'tar/ *vt* to congratulate; perform, carry out

cumplimentero /kumplimen'tero/ *a* over-complimentary; *Inf.* gushing

cumplimiento /kumpli'miento/ *m,* fulfillment, performance; courtesy, formality; completion; complement

cumplir /kum'plir/ *vt* to perform, carry into effect; reach (of age); keep (promises). **c. su palabra,** to keep one's word; —*vi* perform a duty; expire, fall due; serve the required term of military service; be necessary, behove; —*vr* be fulfilled, come true. **por c.,** as a matter of form

cumulativo /kumula'tiβo/ *a* cumulative

cúmulo /'kumulo/ *m,* heap, pile; great many, host, mass, myriad; (cloud) cumulus, thunderhead

cuna /'kuna/ *f,* cradle; foundling hospital; birthplace; origin, genesis; *pl* cat's cradle (game)

cundir /kun'dir/ *vi* to extend, spread (gen. liquids); be diffused (news); expand, grow

cuneiforme /kunei'forme/ *a* wedge-shaped, cuneiform

cunero /ku'nero/ **(-ra)** *n* foundling, orphan

cuña /'kuɲa/ *f,* wedge; *Mech.* quoin. *Mil.* **practicar una c.,** to make a wedge

cuñada /ku'ɲaða/ *f,* sister-in-law

cuñado /ku'ɲaðo/ *m,* brother-in-law

cuño /'kuɲo/ *m,* die, stamp; *Fig.* impression; mark on silver, hallmark. **de viejo c.,** old-guard (e.g. socialites)

cuota /'kuota/ *f,* quota; share; subscription; fee

cupé /ku'pe/ *m,* coupé

Cupido /ku'piðo/ *m,* Cupid; philanderer

cuplé /ku'ple/ *m,* couplet; song

cupo /'kupo/ *m,* quota; share; tax rate; *Mil.* contingent

cupón /ku'pon/ *m,* coupon

cúpula /'kupula/ *f, Archit.* dome, cupola; *Bot.* cup

cuquería /kuke'ria/ *f,* craftiness, smartness; cuteness, prettiness

cura /'kura/ *m,* parish priest; *Inf.* Roman Catholic priest. *f,* cure (e.g. *La enfermedad tiene c.,* The illness can be cured); healing; remedy. **c. de almas,** cure of souls. **primera c.,** first aid. *Inf.* **c. de misa y olla,** ignorant priest

curable /ku'raβle/ *a* curable

curación /kura'θion; kura'sion/ *f,* cure, remedy; healing

curador /kura'ðor/ **(-ra)** *n* curer, salter. *m,* (*Scots law*) curator —*a* curing; healing

curaduría /kuraðu'ria/ *f, Law.* guardianship

curanderismo /kurande'rismo/ *m,* quackery, charlatanism; quack medicine

curandero /kuran'dero/ **(-ra)** *n* quack doctor; charlatan

curar /ku'rar/ *vi* to heal, cure; (*with de*) take care of; care about, mind; —*vt* cure, salt; treat medically (bandage, give medicines, etc.); cure (leather); bleach (cloth); season (timber); *Fig.* remedy (an evil)

curasao /kura'sao/ *m,* curaçao (drink)

curativo /kura'tiβo/ *a* curative

curato /ku'rato/ *m, Eccl.* parish, cure

Curazao /kura'θao; kura'sao/ Curaçao

cúrcuma /'kurkuma/ *f,* turmeric

curdo, /'kurðo,/ **(-da)** *a* Kurdish —*n* Kurd

cureña /ku'reɲa/ *f,* gun-carriage

curia /'kuria/ *f, Law.* bar; tribunal; *Eccl.* curia; care, attention

curiana /ku'riana/ *f,* cockroach

curiche /ku'ritʃe/ *m,* swamp

curiosamente /kuriosa'mente/ *adv* curiously; carefully, attentively; neatly

curiosear /kuriose'ar/ *vi* to pry; be curious (about); meddle, be a busybody

curiosidad /kuriosi'ðað/ *f,* curiosity; inquisitiveness, meddlesomeness; neatness; carefulness, conscientiousness; curio

curioso /ku'rioso/ *a* curious; inquisitive; interesting, odd; neat, clean; conscientious, careful

Curita /ku'rita/ *f, trademark* Band-Aid

cursado /kur'saðo/ *a* experienced, versed

cursante /kur'sante/ *m,* student

cursar /kur'sar/ *vt* to frequent, visit; do repeatedly; study, attend classes, take courses (e.g. *¿En qué escuela cursan?* At what school are you studying?); expedite (public admin.)

cursi /'kursi/ *a Inf.* vulgar, in bad taste; loud, crude

cursilería /kursile'ria/ *f, Inf.* vulgarity, bad taste

cursillo /kur'siʎo; kursiyo/ *m,* minicourse, short course; short series of lectures

cursiva /kur'siβa/ *f,* italics. **en c.,** in italics, italicized

cursivo /kur'siβo/ *a* cursive

curso /'kurso/ *m,* course, direction; duration, passage (time); progress; route; course of study; academic year; succession, series; *Com.* tender

curtido /kur'tiðo/ *m,* tanning; leather; tanned leather (gen. *pl*)

curtidor /kurti'ðor/ *m,* tanner

curtiduría /kurtiðu'ria/ *f,* tannery

curtimiento /kurti'miento/ *m,* tanning; effect of weather on the complexion; toughening-up; hardening

curtir /kur'tir/ *vt* to tan; *Fig.* bronze (complexions); make hardy, harden up; —*vr* be weatherbeaten; be hardy. *Inf.* **estar curtido en,** to be experienced in; be expert at

curul /ku'rul/ *a* **curule** *m*, seat (in parliament)

curva /'kurβa/ *f*, curve; bend. *Surv.* **c. de nivel,** contour line

curvatura, curvidad /kurβa'tura, kurβi'ðað/ *f*, curvature

curvilíneo /kurβi'lineo/ *a* curvilinear

curvo /'kurβo/ *a* curved; bent. *m*, curve

cúspide /'kuspiðe/ *f*, peak, summit; (*Geom. Archit.*) cusp

custodia /kus'toðia/ *f*, custody; guardianship, care; *Eccl.* monstrance; custodian, keeper; guardian; guard

custodiar /kusto'ðiar/ *vt* to watch, guard; look after, care for; *Naut.* convoy

custodio /kus'toðio/ *a* guardian; guarding; custodial. *m*, custodian; guard. **angel c.,** guardian angel

cutáneo /ku'taneo/ *a* cutaneous, skin

cúter /'kuter/ *m*, *Naut.* cutter

cutícula /ku'tikula/ *f*, cuticle

cutis /'kutis/ *m*, complexion; skin (sometimes *f*)

cuyo /'kuyo/ (**cuya, cuyos, cuyas**) *rel pron poss* whose, of which (e.g. *el viejo cuya barba era más blanca que la nieve,* the old man whose beard was whiter than snow) —*interr* **¿Cúyo?** Whose? (e.g. *¿Cúyos son estos lápices?* Whose pencils are these?) (gen. **de quién** or **de quiénes** is used rather than **cúyo**). *m*, beau, lover

D

dable /'daβle/ *a* practicable, possible
daca /'daka/ Give me!
dactilografía /daktilogra'fia/ *f*, typewriting
dactilógrafo /dakti'lografo/ **(-fa)** *n* typist
dactilología /daktilolo'hia/ *f*, dactylology
dádiva /'daðiβa/ *f*, gift, present
dadivosidad /daðiβosi'ðað/ *f*, generosity
dadivoso /daði'βoso/ *a* generous, liberal
dado /'daðo/ *m*, die; *Archit.* dado —*conjunc* **d. que,** given that, supposing that. **cargar los dados,** to load the dice
dador /da'ðor/ **(-ra)** *n* giver, donor. *m*, *Com.* bearer; *Com.* drawer (of a bill of exchange)
daga /'daga/ *f*, dagger
daguerrotipo /dagerro'tipo/ *m*, daguerreotype
daifa /'daifa/ *f*, concubine
¡dale! /'dale/ *interj* Stop! No more about...!
dalia /'dalia/ *f*, *Bot.* dahlia
dallar /da'ʎar; da'yar/ *vt* to scythe (grass)
dalle /'daʎe; 'daye/ *m*, scythe
dálmata /'dalmata/ *a* and *mf* Dalmatian
dalmática /dal'matika/ *f*, dalmatic, loose tunic or vestment
dalmático /dal'matiko/ **(-ca)** *a* and *n* Dalmatian
daltoniano /dalto'niano/ *a* color-blind
daltonismo /dalto'nismo/ *m*, color-blindness
dama /'dama/ *f*, lady; noblewoman; lady-in-waiting; lady-love; mistress, concubine; queen (chess); king (checkers); *Theat.* **d. primera,** leading lady
damajuana /dama'huana/ *f*, demijohn
damas /'damas/ *f pl*, checkers (game)
damasceno /damas'θeno; damas'seno/ **(-na)** *a* and *n* Damascene
Damasco /da'masko/ Damascus
damasco /da'masko/ *m*, damask
damasquino /damas'kino/ *a* damascened (swords, etc.)
damería /dame'ria/ *f*, prudery, affectation
damisela /dami'sela/ *f*, damsel; *Inf.* woman of the town
damnificar /damnifi'kar/ *vt* to injure
dandi /'dandi/ *m*, dandy
dandismo /dan'dismo/ *m*, dandyism
danés /da'nes/ **(-esa)** *a* Danish —*n* Dane. *m*, Danish (language)
danta /'danta/ *f*, *Zool.* tapir
dantesco /dan'tesko/ *a* Dantesque
danubiano /da'nuβiano/ *a* Danubian
Danubio, el /da'nuβio, el/ the Danube
danza /'danθa; 'dansa/ *f*, dance; set (of dancers); *Fig. Inf.* dirty business. **d. de arcos,** dance of the arches. **d. de cintas,** maypole dance. **d. de monos,** amusing spectacle
danzador /danθa'ðor; dansa'ðor/ **(-ra)** *n* dancer; —*a* dancing
danzante /dan'θante; dan'sante/ **(-ta)** *n* dancer; *Fig. Inf.* live wire; *Inf.* busybody
danzar /dan'θar; dan'sar/ *vt* and *vi* to dance; —*vi* jump up and down, rattle; *Inf.* interfere, meddle
danzarín /danθa'rin; dansa'rin/ **(-ina)** *n* good dancer; *Inf.* meddler; *Inf.* playboy
danzón /dan'θon; dan'son/ *m*, Cuban dance
dañable /da'ɲaβle/ *a* harmful; worthy of condemnation
dañado /da'ɲaðo/ *a* evil, perverse; damned; spoiled, damaged
dañador /daɲa'ðor/ **(-ra)** *a* harmful —*n* injurer, offender
dañar /da'ɲar/ *vt* to hurt, harm; damage, spoil; —*vr* spoil, deteriorate
dañino /da'ɲino/ *a* destructive (often of animals); hurtful, harmful. **animales dañinos,** vermin, pests
daño /'daɲo/ *m*, hurt; damage; loss. *Law.* **daños y perjuicios,** damages. **hacerse d.,** to hurt oneself
dañoso /da'ɲoso/ *a* hurtful, harmful
dar /dar/ *vt irr* to give; wish, express (congratulations, etc.); hand over; concede, grant; inspire; produce, yield; cause, create; sacrifice; propose, put forward; take (a walk); believe, consider; deliver (blows, etc.); administer (medicine); provide with; apply, coat with; occasion; perform (plays); propose (a toast); give forth, emit; set (norms), render (thanks, etc.); hold (banquets, etc.); proffer, hold out; —*vi* to strike (clocks); (*with prep a*) overlook, look on to (e.g. *Su ventana da a la calle,* His window looks on to the street); (*with con*) find, meet (things, persons); (*with de*) fall on, fall down (e.g. *Dio de cabeza,* He fell head first. *Dio de espaldas,* He fell on his back); (*with en*) fall into, incur; insist on or persist in (doing something); acquire the habit of (e.g. *Dieron en no venir a vernos,* They took to not coming to see us); solve, guess (riddles, etc.); strike, wound, hurt (e.g. *La bala le dio en el brazo,* The bullet struck him in the arm); (*with por*) decide on (e.g. *Di por no hacerlo,* I decided not to do it) —*vr* to yield, give in; (*with prep a*) engage in, devote oneself to; (*with por*) think or consider oneself (e.g. *Me di por muerto,* I gave myself up for dead). **d. alas a,** to propagate, spread (a belief). **darse a la vela,** to set sail. **darse la mano,** to shake hands. **darse por buenos,** to make up a quarrel, be friends. **darse prisa,** to hurry up, make haste. **darse uno a conocer,** to make oneself known. **darse uno por entendido,** to show that one understands; be grateful. **No se me da un bledo,** I don't care a straw. **d. abajo,** to fall down. **d. bien por mal,** to return good for evil. **d. a conocer,** to make known. **d. a entender,** to suggest, hint. **d. a luz,** to give birth; publish, issue. **d. cuenta de,** to give an account of. **d. de baja,** *Mil.* to muster out, discharge. **d. de comer,** to feed. **d. de sí,** to stretch, expand; produce, yield; give of itself (oneself, himself, themselves) (either in good or bad sense). **d. diente con diente,** to chatter (of teeth), shiver. **d. el pésame,** to tender condolences. **d. en cara,** *Fig. Inf.* to throw in one's face. **d. en el clavo,** *Fig.* to hit the mark. **d. en qué pensar,** to make suspicious, cause to think. **d. fe,** to certify, attest. **d. fiado,** to give on credit. **d. fianza,** to give security. **d. fin a,** to finish. **d. licencia,** to permit, allow. **d. los buenos días,** to wish good day or good morning. **d. mal,** to have bad luck at cards. **d. parte de,** to announce; issue a communiqué about (e.g. *Dieron parte de la pérdida del buque,* They announced the loss of the ship). **d. prestado,** to lend. **d. qué decir,** to cause a scandal. **d. qué hacer,** to cause trouble. **d. razón de,** to give an account of. **d. sobre uno,** to assault a person. **d. un abrazo,** to embrace. **d. voces,** to shriek; call out. *Inf.* **Donde las dan las toman,** It's only tit-for-tat. *Inf.* **No me da la real gana,** I darn well don't want to —*Pres. Indic.* **doy, das,** etc —*Preterite* **di, diste,** etc —*Pres. Subjunc.* **dé,** etc —*Imperf. Subjunc.* **diese,** etc.
Dardanelos, los /darða'nelos, los/ the Dardanelles
dardo /'darðo/ *m*, (*Mil. Sports.*) dart; *Ichth.* dace; lampoon
dares y tomares /dares i tomares/ *m, pl* give and take; *Inf.* back-chat. Generally used with *andar, haber* or *tener*
dársena /'darsena/ *f*, *Naut.* dock
darviniano /darβi'niano/ *a* Darwinian
darvinismo /darβi'nismo/ *m*, Darwinism
darvinista /darβi'nista/ *mf* Darwinian
data /'data/ *f*, date (calendar); *Com.* credit
datar /'datar/ *vt* to date; —*vi* (*with de*) date from; —*vr Com.* credit
dátil /'datil/ *m*, *Bot.* date
datilado /datil'aðo/ *a* date-like or date-colored
datilera /datil'era/ *f*, *Bot.* date-palm
dativo /da'tiβo/ *m*, *Gram.* dative
dato /'dato/ *m*, datum; basis, fact
davídico /da'βiðiko/ *a* Davidic
de /de/ *f*, name of letter D —*prep* of (possessive) (e.g. *Este cuadro es de Vd.*, This picture is yours); from (place and time) (e.g. *Vengo de Madrid,* I come from

Madrid. *de vez en cuando,* from time to time); with, of, from, as the result of (e.g. *Lloraban de miedo,* They were crying with fright. *Murió de un ataque del corazón,* He died from a heart attack); for, to (e.g. *Es hora de marchar,* It is time to leave); with (of characteristics) (e.g. *el señor de los lentes,* the gentleman with the eyeglasses. *el cuarto de la alfombra azul,* the room with the blue carpet); when, as (e.g. *De niños nos gustaban los juguetes,* When we were children we liked toys); by (e.g. *Es un ensayo del mismo autor,* It is an essay by the same author. *Fue amado de todos,* He was loved by all. *Es hidalgo de nacimiento,* He is a gentleman by birth). Indicates the material of which a thing is made (e.g. *La mesa es de mármol,* The table is marble). Indicates contents of a thing (e.g. *un vaso de leche,* a glass of milk). Shows manner in which an action is performed (e.g. *Lo hizo de prisa,* He did it hurriedly). Shows the use to which an article is put (e.g. *una mesa de escribir,* a writing-table. *una máquina de coser,* a sewing-machine. *un caballo de batalla,* a war-horse). Sometimes used for emphasis (e.g. *El tonto de tu secretario,* That fool of a secretary of yours). Used by Spanish married women before husband's family name (e.g. *Señora Martínez de Cabra,* Mrs. Cabra (nee Martinez)). Used after many adverbs (generally of time or place) to form prepositional phrases (e.g. *detrás de,* behind. *enfrente de,* opposite to; in front of. *de acá para allá,* here and there. *de allí a poco,* shortly afterward. *de allí a pocos días,* a few days later. *de bamba,* by chance. *de cabo a rabo,* from cover to cover. *además de,* besides, etc.). Used at beginning of various adverbial phrases (e.g. *de noche,* at night. *de día,* by day. *de antemano,* previously, *la persona de mi derecha* the person at my right, etc.). Used partitively before nouns, pronouns, adjectives (e.g. *Estas historias tienen algo de verdad,* These stories have some truth in them. *¿Qué hay de nuevo?* What's the news?) Forms many compound words (e.g. *deponer, denegar,* etc.). With **"uno"** means "at" (e.g. *Lo cogió de un salto,* He caught it at one bound). **de a** is used before expressions of price, weight, etc. (e.g. *un libro de a cinco pesetas,* a five-peseta book)

dea /dea/ *f, Poet.* goddess

deán /de'an/ *m,* dean

debajo /de'βaho/ *adv* underneath; below

debate /de'βate/ *m,* discussion, debate; dispute

debatible /deβa'tiβle/ *a* debatable

debatir /deβa'tir/ *vt* to discuss, debate, argue

debe /'deβe/ *m, Com.* debtor

debelación /deβela'θion; deβela'sion/ *f,* conquest

debelador /deβela'ðor/ **(-ra)** *a* conquering *—n* conqueror

debelar /deβe'lar/ *vt* to conquer, overthrow

deber /de'βer/ *vt* to owe (e.g. *Le debo mil pesetas,* I owe him one thousand pesetas). Used as auxiliary verb followed by infinitive, ought to, be obliged to (e.g. *Debía haberlo hecho,* I ought to have done it. *Deberá hacerlo,* He will have to do it); be destined to (e.g. *La princesa que más tarde debió ser reina,* The princess who later was destined to be queen); be essential, must (e.g. *La cuestión debe ser resuelta,* The question must be settled); (*with de + infin.*) be probable (indicates supposition) (e.g. *Debe de tener cincuenta años,* He is probably about fifty. *Debía de sufrir del corazón,* He probably suffered from heart trouble); (preceded by a negative *with de + infin.*) be impossible (e.g. *No debe de ser verdad,* It can't be true)

deber /de'βer/ *m,* duty, obligation; debt. **hacer su d.,** to do one's duty

debidamente /deβiða'mente/ *adv* justly, rightly; duly

debido /de'βiðo/ *a* correct, due. **d. a,** owing to, because of

débil /'deβil/ *a* weak; *Fig.* spineless; frail

debilidad /deβili'ðað/ *f,* weakness; feebleness

debilitación /deβilita'θion; deβilitasion/ *f,* debilitation

debilitante /deβili'tante/ *a* weakening

debilitar /deβili'tar/ *vt* to weaken; *—vr* become weak

débito /'deβito/ *m,* debit, debt; duty

debutar /deβu'tar/ *vi* to appear for the first time, make one's début

década /'dekaða/ *f,* decade

decadencia /deka'ðenθia; dekaðensia/ *f,* decadence, decline

decadente /deka'ðente/ *a* decadent, decaying

decaer /deka'er/ *vi irr* to fail (persons); decay, decline. See **caer**

decagramo /deka'gramo/ *m,* decagram

decaimiento /dekai'miento/ *m,* decadence; *Med.* prostration

decalaje /deka'lahe/ *m, Aer.* stagger

decalitro /deka'litro/ *m,* decaliter

decálogo /de'kalogo/ *m,* decalogue, the Ten Commandments

decámetro /de'kametro/ *m,* decameter

decampar /de'kampar/ *vi Mil.* to decamp

decanato /dekan'ato/ *m,* deanery; *Educ.* dean's rooms

decano /de'kano/ *m,* senior member; *Educ.* dean

decantación /dekanta'θion; dekantasion/ *f,* decantation

decantar /dekan'tar/ *vt* to decant (wines); praise

decapitación /dekapita'θion; dekapitasion/ *f,* decapitation

decapitar /dekapi'tar/ *vt* to decapitate, behead

decena /de'θena; de'sena/ *f,* ten; *Mus.* tenth

decenal /de'θenal; de'senal/ *a* decennial

decenario /deθe'nario; dese'nario/ *m,* decade

decencia /de'θenθia; de'sensia/ *f,* propriety, decency; decorum, modesty

decenio /de'θenio; de'senio/ *m,* decade

deceno /de'θeno; de'seno/ *a* tenth

decentar /deθen'tar; desen'tar/ *vt irr* to begin, cut (loaves, etc.); *Fig.* undermine (health, etc.); *—vr* suffer from bedsores. See **acertar**

decente /de'θente; de'sente/ *a* decent, honest; respectable; suitable; tidy

decepción /deθep'θion; desep'sion/ *f,* disillusionment, disappointment

dechado /de'tʃaðo/ *m,* model, ideal; *Sew.* sampler; exemplar, ideal

decible /de'θiβle; de'siβle/ *a* expressible

decidero /de'θiðero; de'siðero/ *a* that which can be safely said

decidido /deθi'ðiðo; desi'ðiðo/ *a* decided; resolute, determined

decidir /deθi'ðir; desi'ðir/ *vt* to resolve, decide; *—vr* make up one's mind

decidor /deθi'ðor; desi'ðor/ **(-ra)** *a* talkative, fluent, eloquent *—n* good talker

decigramo /deθi'gramo; desi'gramo/ *m,* decigram

décima /'deθima; 'desima/ *f,* tenth; tithe; ten-line stanza of eight-syllable verse

decimal /deθi'mal; desi'mal/ *a* decimal; pertaining to tithes. **sistema d.,** metric system

decímetro /de'θimetro; de'simetro/ *m,* decimeter

décimo /'deθimo; 'desimo/ *a* tenth. *m,* tenth part; tenth of a lottery ticket

decimoctavo /deθimok'taβo; desimok'taβo/ *a* eighteenth

decimocuarto /deθimo'kuarto; desimo'kuarto/ *a* fourteenth

decimonono /deθimo'nono; desimo'nono/ *a* nineteenth

decimoquinto /deθimo'kinto; desimo'kinto/ *a* fifteenth

decimoséptimo /deθimo'septimo; desimo'septimo/ *a* and *m,* seventeenth

decimosexto /deθimo'seksto; desimo'seksto/ *a* sixteenth

decimotercio /deθimoter'θio; desimoter'sio/ *a* thirteenth

decir /de'θir; de'sir/ *vt irr* to say; name; indicate, show; tell. **d. bien,** to go with, suit; speak the truth; be eloquent. **d. entre** (or **para**) **sí,** to say to oneself. *Inf.* **d. nones,** to refuse. **¡Diga!** Hello! (telephone). *Inf.* **el que dirán,** public opinion (what will people say!). **Es d.,** That is to say. **Se dice,** It is said, people say *—Pres. Ind.* **digo, dices,** etc *—Pres. Part.* **diciendo.** *Past Part.* **dicho.** *Fut.* **diré,** etc *—Condit.*

diría, etc —*Preterite* **dije,** etc —*Pres. Subjunc.* **diga,** etc —*Imperf. Subjunc.* **dijese,** etc.
decir /de'θir; de'sir/ *m,* saying, saw; maxim, witticism (often *pl.*)
decisión /deθi'sion; desi'sion/ *f,* decision, resolution; *Law.* judgment; firmness, strength (of character)
decisivo /deθi'siβo; desi'siβo/ *a* decisive
declamación /deklama'θion; deklama'sion/ *f,* declamation, oration; *Theat.* delivery; recitation
declamador /deklama'ðor/ **(-ra)** *a* declamatory —*n* reciter; orator
declamar /dekla'mar/ *vi* to make a speech, declaim; recite
declamatorio /deklama'torio/ *a* declamatory, rhetorical
declaración /deklara'θion; deklara'sion/ *f,* declaration; exposition, explanation; confession; statement; *Law.* deposition. **d. jurada,** affidavit, sworn statement
declaradamente /deklaraða'mente/ *adv* avowedly
declarante /dekla'rante/ *a* declaring. *mf Law.* deponent
declarar /dekla'rar/ *vt* to declare; make clear, explain; *Law.* find; —*vi Law.* give evidence; —*vr* avow, confess (one's sentiments, etc.); show, reveal itself
declarativo, declaratorio /deklara'tiβo, deklara'torio/ *a* explanatory, declarative.
declinación /deklina'θion; deklina'sion/ *f,* fall, descent; decadence, decay; *Astron.* declination; *Gram.* declension. *Inf.* **no saber las declinaciones,** not to know one's ABC, be very ignorant
declinante /dekli'nante/ *a* declining; sloping
declinar /dekli'nar/ *vi* to slope; diminish, fall; decline, deteriorate; *Fig.* near the end; —*vt Gram.* decline
declive, /de'kliβe,/ *m.* **declividad** *f,* slope, incline; gradient
decocción /dekok'θion; dekok'sion/ *f,* decoction
decoloración /dekolora'θion; dekolora'sion/ *f,* decoloration; decolorization
decomisar /dekomi'sar/ *vt* to confiscate, seize
decoración /dekora'θion; dekora'sion/ *f,* decoration; ornament, embellishment; *Theat.* scenery
decorado /deko'raðo/ *m, Theat.* scenery, décor
decorador /dekora'ðor/ *m,* decorator
decorar /deko'rar/ *vt* to adorn, ornament; *Poet.* decorate, honor
decorativo /dekora'tiβo/ *a* decorative
decoro /de'koro/ *m,* respect, reverence; prudence, circumspection; decorum, propriety; integrity, decency; *Archit.* decoration
decoroso /deko'roso/ *a* decorous, honorable, decent
decrecer /dekre'θer; dekre'ser/ *vi irr* to decrease, grow less. See **conocer**
decreciente /dekre'θiente; dekre'siente/ *a* decreasing
decrepitación /dekrepita'θion; dekrepita'sion/ *f, Chem.* decrepitation, crackling
decrepitar /dekrepi'tar/ *vi Chem.* to decrepitate, crackle
decrépito /de'krepito/ *a* decrepit
decrepitud /dekrepi'tuð/ *f,* decrepitude
decretar /dekre'tar/ *vt* to decree, decide; *Law.* give a judgment (in a suit)
decreto /de'kreto/ *m,* decree, order; judicial decree
decuplar, decuplicar /dekup'lar, dekupli'kar/ *vt* to multiply by ten
décuplo /'dekuplo/ *a* tenfold
decurso /de'kurso/ *m,* course, lapse (of time)
dedada /de'ðaða/ *f,* thimbleful, finger; pinch
dedal /de'ðal/ *m,* thimble; finger-stall
dédalo /'deðalo/ *m,* labyrinth
dedeo /de'ðeo/ *m, Mus.* touch
dedicación /deðika'θion; deðika'sion/ *f,* dedication (all meanings)
dedicar /deði'kar/ *vt* to dedicate; devote; consecrate; —*vr* (*with prep a*) dedicate oneself to, engage in
dedicatoria /deðika'toria/ *f,* dedication (of a book, etc.)
dedicatorio /deðika'torio/ *a* dedicatory
dedil /'deðil/ *m,* finger-stall
dedillo, saber al /de'ðiʎo, saβer al; de'ðiyo, saβer al/ *Fig.* to have at one's fingertips, know perfectly
dedo /'deðo/ *m,* finger; toe; finger's breadth. **d. anular,** third (ring) finger. **d. de en medio** *or* **del corazón,** middle finger. **d. índice,** forefinger. **d. meñique,** little finger. **d. pulgar,** thumb or big toe. *Fig. Inf.* **a dos dedos de,** within an inch of. *Fig. Inf.* **chuparse los dedos,** to smack one's lips over. *Inf.* **estar unidos como los dedos de la mano,** to be as thick as thieves
deducción /deðuk'θion; deðuk'sion/ *f,* inference, deduction; derivation; (*Mus. Math.*) progression
deduciente /deðu'θiente; deðu'siente/ *a* deductive
deducir /deðu'θir; deðu'sir/ *vt irr* to deduce, infer; deduct, subtract; *Law.* plead, allege in pleading. See **conducir**
deductivo /deðuk'tiβo/ *a* deductive
defecación /defeka'θion; defeka'sion/ *f,* purification; defecation
defecar /defe'kar/ *vt* to clarify, purify; defecate
defección /defek'θion; defek'sion/ *f,* defection
defectible /defek'tiβle/ *a* deficient; imperfect
defecto /de'fekto/ *m,* defect, fault; imperfection
defectuoso /defek'tuoso/ *a* imperfect, defective
defender /defen'der/ *vt irr* to defend, protect; maintain, uphold; forbid; hinder; —*vr* defend oneself. See **entender**
defendible /defen'diβle/ *a* defensible
defensa /de'fensa/ *f,* defence; protection; (hockey) pad; *Law.* defense; *Sports.* back; *pl Mil.* defenses; *Naut.* fenders. **d. química,** chemical warfare. *Mil.* **defensas costeras,** coastal defenses
defensiva /defen'siβa/ *f,* defensive
defensivo /defen'siβo/ *a* defensive. *m,* safeguard
defensor /defen'sor/ **(-ra)** *n* defender. *m, Law.* counsel for the defense
deferencia /defe'renθia; deferensia/ *f,* deference
deferente /defe'rente/ *a* deferential
deferir /defe'rir/ *vi irr* to defer, yield; —*vt* delegate —*Pres. Indic.* **defiero, defieres, defiere, defieren.** *Pres. Part.* **defiriendo.** *Preterite* **defirió, defirieron.** *Pres. Subjunc.* **defiera,** etc —*Imperf. Subjunc.* **defiriese,** etc.
deficiencia /defi'θienθia; defi'siensia/ *f,* defect, deficiency
deficiente /defi'θiente; defi'siente/ *a* faulty, deficient
déficit /'defiθit; 'defisit/ *m,* deficit
definible /defi'niβle/ *a* definable
definición /defini'θion; defini'sion/ *f,* definition; decision
definido /defi'niðo/ *a* definite
definir /defi'nir/ *vt* to define; decide
definitivo /defini'tiβo/ *a* definitive. **en definitiva,** definitely; in short
deflagración /deflagra'θion; deflagra'sion/ *f,* sudden blaze, deflagration
deflagrador /deflagra'ðor/ *m, Elec.* deflagrator
deflagrar /defla'grar/ *vi* to go up in flames
deformación /deforma'θion; deforma'sion/ *f,* deformation; *Radio.* distortion
deformado /defor'maðo/ *a* deformed; misshapen
deformador /deforma'ðor/ **(-ra)** *a* disfiguring, deforming —*n* disfigurer
deformar /defor'mar/ *vt* to deform; —*vr* become deformed or misshapen
deformidad /deformi'ðað/ *f,* deformity; gross error; vice, lapse
defraudación /defrauða'θion; defrauða'sion/ *f,* defrauding; deceit
defraudador /defrauða'ðor/ **(-ra)** *n* defrauder
defraudar /defrau'ðar/ *vt* to defraud; usurp; frustrate, disappoint; impede
defuera /de'fuera/ *adv* outwardly, externally
defunción /defun'θion; defun'sion/ *f,* decease, death
degeneración /dehenera'θion; dehenera'sion/ *f,* degeneration. **d. grasienta,** fatty degeneration
degenerado /dehene'raðo/ **(-da)** *a* and *n* degenerate
degenerar /dehene'rar/ *vi* to degenerate
deglución /deglu'θion; deglu'sion/ *f,* swallowing, deglutition
deglutir /deglu'tir/ *vi* and *vt* to swallow
degollación /degoʎa'θion; degoya'sion/ *f,* decollation, throat slitting

degolladero /degoʎa'ðero; degoya'ðero/ *m*, slaughterhouse; execution block
degollador /degoʎ'aðor; degoya'ðor/ *m*, executioner
degolladura /degoʎa'ðura; degoya'ðura/ *f*, slitting of the throat
degollar /dego'ʎar; dego'yar/ *vt irr* to behead; slit the throat; *Fig.* destroy; (*Fig. Theat.*) murder; *Inf.* annoy, bore —*Pres. Indic.* **degüello, degüellas, degüella, degüellan.** *Pres. Subjunc.* **degüelle, degüelles, degüelle, degüellen**
degollina /dego'ʎina; dego'yina/ *f*, *Inf.* massacre
degradación /degraða'θion; degraða'sion/ *f*, degradation; humiliation, debasement; *Art.* gradation, shading (colors, light)
degradante /degra'ðante/ *a* degrading, humiliating
degradar /degra'ðar/ *vt* to degrade; humiliate; *Art.* grade, blend; —*vr* degrade oneself
degüello /de'gueʎo; de'gueyo/ *m*, decollation; havoc, destruction; haft (of swords, etc.)
degustación /degusta'θion; degusta'sion/ *f*, act of tasting or sampling
dehesa /de'esa/ *f*, pasture, meadow
deicida /dei'θiða; dei'siða/ *mf* deicide (person)
deicidio /dei'θiðio; dei'siðio/ *m*, deicide (act)
deidad /dei'ðað/ *f*, divinity; deity, idol
deificación /deifika'θion; deifika'sion/ *f*, deification
deificar /deifi'kar/ *vt* to deify; overpraise
deífico /de'ifiko/ *a* deific, divine
deísmo /de'ismo/ *m*, Deism
deísta /de'ista/ *mf* deist —*a* deistic
dejación /deha'θion; deha'sion/ *f*, relinquishment, abandonment
dejadez /deha'ðeθ; deha'ðes/ *f*, slovenliness; neglect; laziness; carelessness
dejado /de'haðo/ *a* lazy; neglectful; slovenly; discouraged, depressed
dejamiento /deha'miento/ *m*, relinquishment; negligence; lowness of spirits; indifference
dejar /de'har/ *vt* to leave; omit, forget, allow, permit (e.g. *Déjame salir,* Let me go out); yield, produce, entrust, leave in charge; believe, consider; intend, appoint; cease, stop; forsake, desert; renounce, relinquish; bequeath; give away; —*vr* neglect oneself; engage (in); lay oneself open to, allow oneself; abandon oneself (to), fling oneself (into); *Fig.* be depressed or languid; (*with de + infin.*) cease to (e.g. *Se dejó de hacerlo,* He stopped doing it); —*vi* (*with de + adjective*) be none the less, be rather (e.g. *No deja de ser sorprendente,* It isn't any the less surprising). **d. aparte,** to omit, leave out. **d. atrás,** to overtake; *Fig.* leave behind, beat. **d. caer,** to let fall. **dejarse caer,** to let oneself fall; *Fig. Inf.* to let fall, utter; appear suddenly. **dejarse vencer,** to give way, allow oneself to be persuaded
dejo /'deho/ *m*, relinquishment; end; accent (of persons); savor, after-taste; negligence; *Fig.* touch, flavor
del /del/ contraction of **de + el,** (*def. art. m.*) of the (e.g. *del perro,* of the dog)
delación /dela'θion; dela'sion/ *f*, accusation, denunciation
delantal /delan'tal/ *m*, apron
delante /de'lante/ *adv* before, in front, in the presence (of)
delantera /delan'tera/ *f*, front, front portion; *Theat.* orchestra stall, front seat; front (of garment). **tomar la d.,** to take the lead; *Inf.* steal a march on
delantero /delan'tero/ *a* fore, front. *m*, postilion; *Sports.* forward. **d. centro,** *Sports.* centerforward
delatable /dela'taβle/ *a* impeachable; blameworthy
delatar /dela'tar/ *vt* to inform against, accuse; impeach
delator /dela'tor/ **(-ra)** *a* denunciatory, accusing —*n* denouncer, informer
delectación /delekta'θion; delekta'sion/ *f*, delectation, pleasure
delegación /delega'θion; delega'sion/ *f*, delegation; proxy
delegado /dele'gaðo/ **(-da)** *n* delegate; proxy
delegar /dele'gar/ *vt* to delegate
deleitable /delei'taβle/ *a* delightful
deleitar /delei'tar/ *vt* to delight, charm, please; —*vr* delight (in)
deleite /de'leite/ *m*, delight; pleasure
deleitoso /delei'toso/ *a* delightful, pleasant
deletéreo /dele'tereo/ *a* deleterious; poisonous
deletrear /deletre'ar/ *vi* to spell; *Fig.* decipher
deletreo /dele'treo/ *m*, spelling; *Fig.* decipherment
deleznable /deleθ'naβle; deles'naβle/ *a* fragile, brittle; slippery; brief, fugitive, transitory
délfico /'delfiko/ *a* Delphic
delfín /del'fin/ *m*, (*Ichth. Astron.*) dolphin; dauphin
delfina /del'fina/ *f*, dauphiness
Delfos /'delfos/ Delphi
delgadez /delga'ðeθ; delgaðes/ *f*, thinness; slenderness, leanness
delgado /del'gaðo/ *a* slim; thin; scanty; poor (of land); sharp, perspicacious
delgaducho /delga'ðutʃo/ *a* slenderish, somewhat thin
deliberación /deliβera'θion; deliβera'sion/ *f*, deliberation; consideration; discussion
deliberadamente /deliβeraða'mente/ *adv* deliberately
deliberante /deliβe'rante/ *a* deliberative, considering
deliberar /deliβe'rar/ *vi* to deliberate, consider; —*vt* decide after reflection; discuss
delicadez /delika'ðeθ; delika'ðes/ *f*, weakness; delicacy; hypersensitiveness; amiability
delicadeza /delika'ðeθa; delika'ðesa/ *f*, delicacy; fastidiousness; refinement, subtlety; sensitiveness; consideration, tact; scrupulosity
delicado /deli'kaðo/ *a* courteous; tactful; fastidious; weak, delicate; fragile, perishable; delicious, tasty; exquisite; difficult, embarrassing; refined, discriminating, sensitive; scrupulous; subtle; hypersensitive, suspicious. **d. de salud,** in poor health
delicia /deli'θia; deli'sia/ *f*, pleasure, delight; sensual pleasure
delicioso /deli'θioso; deli'sioso/ *a* delightful, agreeable, pleasant
delimitar /delimi'tar/ *vt* to delimit
delincuencia /delin'kuenθia; delin'kuensia/ *f*, delinquency
delincuente /delin'kuente/ *a* and *mf* delinquent
delineación /delinea'θion; delinea'sion/ *f*, delineation; diagram, design, plan
delineador /delinea'ðor/ **(-ra),** *n* **delineante** *m*, draftsman, designer
delineamiento /delinea'miento/ *m*, delineation
delinear /deline'ar/ *vt* to delineate; sketch; describe
delinquimiento /delinki'miento/ *m*, delinquency; crime
delinquir /delin'kir/ *vi irr* to commit a crime —*Pres. Indic.* **delinco.** *Pres. Subjunc.* **delinca**
deliquio /deli'kio/ *m*, faint, swoon
delirante /deli'rante/ *a* delirious
delirar /deli'rar/ *vi* to be delirious; act or speak foolishly
delirio /de'lirio/ *m*, delirium; frenzy; foolishness, nonsense. **d. de grandezas,** illusions of grandeur
delito /de'lito/ *m*, delict, offense against the law, crime
delta /'delta/ *f*, fourth letter of Greek alphabet. *m*, delta (of a river)
delusorio /delu'sorio/ *a* deceptive
demacración /demakra'θion; demakrasion/ *f*, emaciation
demacrado /dema'kraðo/ *a* emaciated
demacrarse /dema'krarse/ *vr* to become emaciated
demagogia /dema'gohia/ *f*, demagogy
demagógico /dema'gohiko/ *a* demagogic
demagogo /dema'gogo/ **(-ga)** *n* demagogue
demanda /de'manda/ *f*, petition, request; collecting (for charity); collecting box; want ad; question; search; undertaking; *Com.* order or demand; *Law.* claim
demandadero /demanda'ðero/ **(-ra)** *n* convent or prison messenger; errandboy
demandado /deman'daðo/ **(-da)** *n* *Law.* defendant; *Law.* respondent
demandante /deman'dante/ *mf* *Law.* plaintiff
demandar /deman'dar/ *vt* to ask, request; desire, yearn for; question; *Law.* claim

demarcación /demarka'θion; demarka'sion/ *f*, demarcation, limit
demarcar /demar'kar/ *vt* to fix boundaries, demarcate
demás /de'mas/ *a* other —*adv* besides. **lo d.,** the rest. **los** (**las**) **d.,** the others. **por d.,** useless; superfluous. **por lo d.,** otherwise; for the rest
demasía /dema'sia/ *f*, excess; daring; insolence; guilt, crime. **en d.,** excessively
demasiado /dema'siaðo/ *a* too; too many; too much —*adv* excessively
demencia /de'menθia; de'mensia/ *f*, madness, insanity
demencial /demen'θial; demen'sial/ *a* insane
dementar /demen'tar/ *vt* to render insane; —*vr* become insane
demente /de'mente/ *a* insane, mad. *mf* lunatic
demérito /de'merito/ *m*, demerit, fault
demeritorio /demeri'torio/ *a* undeserving, without merit
demisión /demi'sion/ *f*, submission, acquiescence
democracia /demo'kraθia; demo'krasia/ *f*, democracy
demócrata /de'mokrata/ *mf* democrat
democrático /demo'kratiko/ *a* democratic
democratizar /demokrati'θar; demokrati'sar/ *vt* to make democratic
demoledor /demole'ðor/ **(-ra)** *a* demolition —*n* demolisher
demoler /demo'ler/ *vt irr* to demolish, destroy, dismantle. See **moler**
demolición /demoli'θion; demoli'sion/ *f*, demolition, destruction, dismantling
demoníaco /demo'niako/ *a* devilish; possessed by a demon
demonio /de'monio/ *m*, devil; evil spirit —*interj* **¡Demonios!** Deuce take it! *Inf.* **tener el d. en el cuerpo,** to be always on the move, be very energetic
demontre /de'montre/ *m*, *Inf.* devil
demora /de'mora/ *f*, delay; *Naut.* bearing; *Com.* demurrage
demorar /demo'rar/ *vt* to delay; —*vi* stay, remain, tarry; *Naut.* bear
demostrable /demos'traβle/ *a* demonstrable
demostración /demostra'θion; demostra'sion/ *f*, demonstration; proof
demostrador /demostra'ðor/ **(-ra)** *a* demonstrating —*n* demonstrator
demostrar /demos'trar/ *vt irr* to demonstrate, explain; prove; teach. See **mostrar**
demostrativo /demostra'tiβo/ *a* demonstrative. *Gram.* **pronombre d.,** demonstrative pronoun
demudación /demuða'θion; demuða'sion/ *f*, change; alteration
demudar /demu'ðar/ *vt* to change, vary; alter, transform; —*vr* change suddenly (color, facial expression, etc.); grow angry
denario /de'nario/ *a* denary. *m*, denarius
denegación /denega'θion; denega'sion/ *f*, denial; refusal
denegar /dene'gar/ *vt irr* to deny, refuse. See **acertar**
dengoso /deŋ'goso/ *a* fastidious, finicky
dengue /'deŋgue/ *m*, affectation, faddiness, fastidiousness
denigrable /deni'graβle/ *a* odious
denigración /denigra'θion; denigra'sion/ *f*, slander, defamation (of character)
denigrante /deni'grante/ *a* slanderous
denigrar /deni'grar/ *vt* to slander; insult
denodado /deno'ðaðo/ *a* valiant, daring
denominación /denomina'θion; denomina'sion/ *f*, denomination
denominador /denomina'ðor/ *a* denominating *m*, *Math.* denominator
denominar /denomi'nar/ *vt* to name, designate
denostada /denos'taða/ *f*, insult
denostar /denos'tar/ *vt irr* to revile, insult. See **acordar**
denotar /deno'tar/ *vt* to denote, indicate
densidad /densi'ðað/ *f*, density; closeness, denseness; *Phys.* specific gravity; obscurity
denso /'denso/ *a* compact, close; thick, dense; crowded; dark, confused
dentado /den'taðo/ *a* toothed; pronged; dentate
dentadura /denta'ðura/ *f*, set of teeth (real or false). **d. de rumiante,** teeth like an ox. **d. postiza,** false teeth
dental /den'tal/ *a* dental
dentar /den'tar/ *vt irr* to provide with teeth, prongs, etc.; —*vi* cut teeth. See **sentar**
dentellada /dente'ʎaða; dente'yaða/ *f*, gnashing or chattering of teeth; bite; toothmark
dentellar /dente'ʎar; dente'yar/ *vt* to chatter, grind, gnash (teeth)
dentellear /denteʎe'ar; denteye'ar/ *vt* to bite, sink the teeth into
dentera /den'tera/ *f*, (**dar**) to set one's teeth on edge; *Fig. Inf.* make one's mouth water
dentición /denti'θion; denti'sion/ *f*, teething, dentition
dentífrico /den'tifriko/ *m*, toothpaste
dentista /den'tista/ *mf* dentist
dentro /'dentro/ *adv* within, inside. **d. de poco,** soon, shortly. **por d.,** from the inside; on the inside
dentudo /den'tuðo/ *a* having large teeth
denudación /denuða'θion; denuða'sion/ *f*, denudation; *Geol.* erosion
denudar /denu'ðar/ *vt* to denude
denuedo /de'nueðo/ *m*, courage, daring
denuesto /de'nuesto/ *m*, insult
denuncia /de'nunθia; de'nunsia/ *f*, denunciation, accusation
denunciante /denun'θiante; denun'siante/ *a* accusing. *mf Law.* denouncer
denunciar /denun'θiar; denun'siar/ *vt* to give notice, inform; herald, presage; declare, proclaim; denounce; *Law.* accuse
denunciatorio /denunθia'torio; denunsia'torio/ *a* denunciatory
deparar /depa'rar/ *vt* to furnish, offer, present
departamental /departamen'tal/ *a* departmental
departamento /departa'mento/ *m*, department; compartment (railway); branch, section. **d. de lactantes,** nursery (in a hospital)
departir /depar'tir/ *vi* to converse
depauperación /depaupera'θion; depaupera'sion/ *f*, impoverishment; *Med.* emaciation
depauperar /depaupe'rar/ *vt* to impoverish; —*vr* *Med.* grow weak, become emaciated
dependencia /depen'denθia; depen'densia/ *f*, dependence; subordination; dependency; *Com.* branch; firm, agency; business affair; kinship or affinity; *pl Archit.* offices; *Com.* staff; accessories
depender /depen'der/ *vi* (*with de*) to be subordinate to; depend on; be dependent on, need
dependiente /depen'diente/ **(-ta)** *a* and *n* dependent, subordinate. *m*, employee; shop assistant
depilación /depila'θion; depila'sion/ *f*, depilation
depilar /depi'lar/ *vt* to depilate
depilatorio /depila'torio/ *m*, depilatory
deplorar /deplo'rar/ *vt* to deplore, lament
deponente /depo'nente/ *a* deposing; affirming. *mf* deponent. *Gram.* **verbo d.,** deponent verb
deponer /depo'ner/ *vt irr* to lay aside; depose, oust; affirm, testify; remove, take from its place; *Law.* depose. See **poner**
deportación /deporta'θion; deporta'sion/ *f*, deportation
deportar /depor'tar/ *vt* to exile; deport
deporte /de'porte/ *m*, sport; *pl* games. **d. de vela,** sailing; boating
deportismo /depor'tismo/ *m*, sport
deportista /depor'tista/ *a* sporting. *mf* sportsman (sportswoman)
deportivo /depor'tiβo/ *a* sporting
deposición /deposi'θion; deposi'sion/ *f*, affirmation, statement; *Law.* deposition; degradation, removal (from office, etc.)
depositador /deposita'ðor/ **(-ra)** *a* depositing —*n* depositor
depositar /deposi'tar/ *vt* to deposit; place in safety; entrust; lay aside, put away; —*vr Chem.* settle

depositaría /deposita'ria/ *f,* depository; trusteeship; accounts office

depositario /deposi'tario/ **(-ia)** *a* pertaining to a depository —*n* depositary, trustee

depósito /de'posito/ *m,* deposit; depository; *Com.* depot, warehouse; *Chem.* deposit, sediment; tank, reservoir; *Mil.* depot. **d. de bencina, d. de gasolina,** gas tank; service station. **d. de municiones,** munitions dump. *Com.* **en d.,** in bond. **Queda hecho el d. que marca la ley,** Copyright reserved

depravación /depraβa'θion; depraβa'sion/ *f,* depravity

depravar /depra'βar/ *vt* to deprave, corrupt; —*vr* become depraved

deprecación /depreka'θion; depreka'sion/ *f,* supplication, petition; deprecation

deprecar /depre'kar/ *vt* to supplicate, petition; deprecate

depreciación /depreθia'θion; depresia'sion/ *f,* depreciation, fall in value

depreciar /depre'θiar; depre'siar/ *vt* to depreciate, reduce the value (of)

depredación /depreða'θion; depreða'sion/ *f,* depredation, robbery

depredar /depre'ðar/ *vt* to pillage

depresión /depre'sion/ *f,* depression. **d. nerviosa,** nervous breakdown

depresivo /depre'siβo/ *a* depressive; humiliating

deprimir /depri'mir/ *vt* to depress, compress, press down; depreciate, belittle; —*vr* be compressed

depuración /depura'θion; depura'sion/ *f,* cleansing, purification; *Polit.* purge

depurar /depu'rar/ *vt* to cleanse, purify; *Polit.* purge

derecha /de'retʃa/ *f,* right hand; *Polit.* (gen. *pl*) Right. *Mil.* **¡D.!** Right Turn! **a la d.,** on the right

derechamente /deretʃa'mente/ *adv* straight, directly; prudently, justly; openly, frankly

derechera /dere'tʃera/ *f,* direct road

derechista /dere'tʃista/ *mf Polit.* rightist

derecho /de'retʃo/ *a* straight; upright; right (not left); just, reasonable; *Sports.* forehand —*adv* straightaway. *m,* right; law; just claim; privilege; justice, reason; exemption; right side (cloth, etc.); *pl* dues, taxes; fees. **d. a la vía,** right of way. **d. de apelación,** right to appeal. **d. de visita,** (international law) right of search. **derechos de aduana,** customhouse duties. **derechos de entrada,** import duties. **según d.,** according to law. **usar de su d.,** to exercise one's right

derechura /dere'tʃura/ *f,* directness, straightness; uprightness

deriva /de'riβa/ *f,* (*Naut. Aer.*) drift, leeway

derivación /deriβa'θion; deriβa'sion/ *f,* origin, derivation; inference, consequence; *Gram.* derivation

derivar /deri'βar/ *vi* to originate; *Naut.* drift; —*vt* conduct, lead; *Gram.* derive; *Elec.* tap

derivativo /deriβa'tiβo/ *a* derivative

dermatitis /derma'titis/ *f,* dermatitis

dermatología /dermatolo'hia/ *f,* dermatology

dermatólogo /derma'tologo/ *m,* dermatologist

derogación /deroga'θion; deroga'sion/ *f,* repeal, annulment; deterioration

derogar /dero'gar/ *vt* to annul, repeal; destroy, suppress

derogatorio /deroga'torio/ *a Law.* repealing

derrama /de'rrama/ *f,* apportionment of tax

derramado /derra'maðo/ *a* extravagant, wasteful

derramamiento /derrama'miento/ *m,* pouring out; spilling; scattering

derramar /derra'mar/ *vt* to pour out; spill; scatter; apportion (taxes); publish abroad, spread; —*vr* be scattered; overflow

derrame /de'rrame/ *m,* spilling; leakage; overflow; scattering; slope

derredor /derre'ðor/ *m,* circumference. **al** (*or* **en**) **d.,** round about

derrelicto /derre'likto/ *a* abandoned; derelict. *m, Naut.* derelict

derrengado /derreŋ'gaðo/ *a* crooked; crippled

derretimiento /derreti'miento/ *m,* melting; thaw; liquefaction; *Inf.* burning passion

derretir /derre'tir/ *vt irr* to melt, liquefy; waste, dissipate; —*vr* be very much in love; *Inf.* be susceptible (to love); *Inf.* long, be impatient. See **pedir**

derribar /derri'βar/ *vt* to demolish; knock down; fell; throw down; *Aer.* shoot down; throw (in wrestling); *Fig.* overthrow; demolish, explode (a myth); control (emotions); —*vr* fall down; prostrate oneself; throw oneself down. **d. el chapeo,** *humorous* to doff one's hat

derribo /de'rriβo/ *m,* demolition; debris, rubble; throw (in wrestling)

derrocadero /derroka'ðero/ *m,* rocky precipice

derrocar /derro'kar/ *vt* to throw down from a rock; demolish (buildings); overthrow, oust

derrochador /derrotʃa'ðor/ **(-ra)** *a* wasteful, extravagant —*n* spendthrift

derrochar /derro'tʃar/ *vt* to waste, squander

derroche /de'rrotʃe/ *m,* squandering

derrota /de'rrota/ *f,* road; route, path; *Naut.* course; *Mil.* defeat

derrotar /derro'tar/ *vt* to squander; destroy, harm; *Mil.* defeat; —*vr Naut.* drift, lose course

derrotero /derro'tero/ *m, Naut.* course; *Naut.* ship's itinerary; number of sea charts; means to an end, course of action

derrotismo /derro'tismo/ *m,* defeatism

derrotista /derro'tista/ *mf* defeatist

derruir /de'rruir/ *vt irr* to demolish (a building). See **huir**

derrumbadero /derrumba'ðero/ *m,* precipice; risk, danger

derrumbamiento /derrumba'miento/ *m,* landslide; collapse, downfall

derrumbar /derrum'bar/ *vt* to precipitate; —*vr* throw oneself down, collapse, tumble down (buildings, etc.)

derrumbe /de'rrumbe/ *m,* collapse; subsidence

derviche /der'βitʃe/ *m,* dervish

desabarrancar /desaβarran'kar/ *vt* to pull out of a ditch or rut; extricate (from a difficulty)

desabillé /desaβi'ʎe; desaβi'ye/ *m,* deshabille

desabor /desa'βor/ *m,* insipidity

desabotonar /desaβoto'nar/ *vt* to unbutton; —*vi* open (flowers)

desabrido /desa'βriðo/ *a* insipid, poor-tasting; inclement (weather); disagreeable; unsociable; homely, plain (woman)

desabrigar /desaβri'gar/ *vt* to uncover; leave without shelter

desabrigo /desa'βrigo/ *m,* want of clothing or shelter; poverty, destitution

desabrimiento /desaβri'miento/ *m,* insipidity; harshness, disagreeableness; melancholy, depression

desabrir /desa'βrir/ *vt* to give a bad taste (to food); annoy, trouble

desabrochar /desaβro'tʃar/ *vt* to unbutton, untie; open; —*vr Inf.* confide, open up

desacatar /desaka'tar/ *vt* to behave disrespectfully (towards); lack reverence

desacato /desa'kato/ *m,* irreverence; disrespect

desacertado /desaθer'taðo; desaser'taðo/ *a* wrong, erroneous; imprudent

desacertar /desaθer'tar; desaser'tar/ *vi irr* to be wrong; act imprudently. See **acertar**

desacierto /desa'θierto; desa'sierto/ *m,* mistake, miscalculation, blunder

desacomodado /desakomo'ðaðo/ *a* lacking means of subsistence; poor; unemployed (servants); troublesome

desacomodar /desakomo'ðar/ *vt* to incommode, make uncomfortable, inconvenience; dismiss, discharge

desaconsejado /desakonse'haðo/ *a* ill-advised

desaconsejar /desakonse'har/ *vt* to advise against, dissuade

desacoplar /desakop'lar/ *vt* to disconnect

desacordar /desakor'ðar/ *vt irr Mus.* to put out of tune; —*vr* (*with de*) forget. See **acordar**

desacorde /desa'korðe/ *a* discordant, inharmonious; *Mus.* out of tune

desacostumbrado /desakostum'braðo/ *a* unaccustomed; unusual

desacostumbrar /desakostum'brar/ *vt* to break of a habit

desacotar /desako'tar/ *vt* to remove (fences); refuse, deny; *—vi* withdraw (from agreement, etc.)

desacreditar /desakreði'tar/ *vt* to discredit

desacuerdo /desa'kuerðo/ *m*, disagreement, discord; mistake; forgetfulness; swoon, loss of consciousness

desadeudar /desaðeu'ðar/ *vt* to free from debt

desadornar /desaðor'nar/ *vt* to denude of ornaments

desadorno /desa'ðorno/ *m*, lack of ornaments; bareness

desafecto /desa'fekto/ *a* disaffected; hostile. *m*, disaffection

desaferrar /desafe'rrar/ *vt irr* to untie, unfasten; *Fig.* wean from; *Naut.* weigh anchor. See **acertar**

desafiador /desafia'ðor/ **(-ra)** *a* challenging *—n* challenger. *m*, duelist

desafiar /desafi'ar/ *vt* to challenge; compete with; oppose

desafinar /desafi'nar/ *vi Mus.* to go out of tune; *Fig. Inf.* speak out of turn

desafío /desa'fio/ *m*, challenge; competition; duel

desaforado /desafo'raðo/ *a* lawless; outrageous; enormous

desaforar /desafo'rar/ *vt* to infringe (laws, etc.); *—vr* be disorderly

desaforrar /desafo'rrar/ *vt* to remove the lining of or from

desafortunado /desafortu'naðo/ *a* unfortunate

desafuero /desa'fuero/ *m*, act of injustice; outrage, excess

desagarrar /desaga'rrar/ *vt Inf.* to release, loosen; unhook

desagraciado /desagra'θiaðo; desagra'siaðo/ *a* ugly, unsightly

desagraciar /desagra'θiar; desagra'siar/ *vt* to disfigure, make ugly

desagradable /desagra'ðaβle/ *a* disagreeable; unpleasant

desagradar /desagra'ðar/ *vi* to be disagreeable, displease (e.g. *Me desagrada su voz,* I find his voice unpleasant)

desagradecer /desagraðe'θer; desagraðe'ser/ *vt irr* to be ungrateful (for). See **conocer**

desagradecido /desagraðe'θiðo; desagraðe'siðo/ *a* ungrateful

desagradecimiento /desagraðeθi'miento; desagraðesimiento/ *m*, ingratitude

desagrado /desa'graðo/ *m*, displeasure, dislike, dissatisfaction

desagraviar /desagra'βiar/ *vt* to make amends, apologize; indemnify

desagravio /desa'graβio/ *m*, satisfaction, reparation; compensation

desagregar /desagre'gar/ **(se)** *vt* and *vr* to separate

desaguadero /desagua'ðero/ *m*, drain, waste pipe

desaguar /desa'guar/ *vt* to drain off; dissipate; *—vi* flow (into sea, etc.)

desagüe /de'sague/ *m*, drainage; outlet, drain; catchment

desaguisado /desagi'saðo/ *a* outrageous, lawless. *m*, offense, insult

desahogado /desao'gaðo/ *a* brazen, insolent; clear, unencumbered; in comfortable circumstances

desahogar /desao'gar/ *vt* to ease, relieve; *—vr* unburden oneself; recover (from illness, heat, etc.); get out of debt; speak one's mind

desahogo /desa'ogo/ *m*, relief, alleviation; ease; comfort, convenience; freedom, frankness; unburdening (of one's mind). *Inf.* **vivir con d.,** to be comfortably off

desahuciar /desau'θiar; desau'siar/ *vt* to banish all hope; give up, despair of the life of; put out (tenants). When the third syllable of this verb is stressed, it is spelled with **ú:** *Pres. Indic.* **desahúcio, desahúcias, desahúcia, desahúcian.** *Pres. Subj.* **desahúcie, desahúcies, desahúcie, desahúcien.** *Imperf.* **desahúcia, desahúcie, desahúcien**

desahúcio /desa'uθio; desa'usio/ *m*, ejection, dispossession (of tenants)

desahumar /desau'mar/ *vt* to clear of smoke

desairado /desai'raðo/ *a* unattractive, graceless, ugly; unsuccessful, crestfallen; slighted

desairar /desai'rar/ *vt* to disdain, slight, disregard; underrate (things)

desaire /des'aire/ *m*, gracelessness, ugliness; insult, slight

desalabanza /desala'βanθa; desala'βansa/ *f*, disparagement; criticism

desalabar /desala'βar/ *vt* to censure, disparage

desalación /desala'θion; desala'sion/ *f*, desalinization

desalado /desa'laðo/ *a* anxious, precipitate, hasty

desalar /desa'lar/ *vt* to remove the salt from; take off wings; *—vr* walk or run at great speed; long for, yearn

desalentar /desalen'tar/ *vt irr* to make breathing difficult (work, fatigue); discourage; *—vr* be depressed or sad. See **sentar**

desaliento /desa'liento/ *m*, depression, discouragement, dismay

desalinear /desaline'ar/ *vt* to throw out of the straight

desaliñado /desali'ɲaðo/ *a* slovenly; slipshod

desaliñar /desali'ɲar/ *vt* to disarrange, make untidy, crumple

desaliño /desa'liɲo/ *m*, untidiness, slovenliness; negligence, carelessness

desalmado /desal'maðo/ *a* soulless, conscienceless; cruel

desalmamiento /desalma'miento/ *m*, inhumanity, consciencelessness; cruelty

desalmidonar /desalmiðo'nar/ *vt* to remove starch from

desalojamiento /desaloha'miento/ *m*, dislodgement, ejection

desalojar /desalo'har/ *vt* to dislodge, remove, eject; *—vi* move out, remove

desalquilado /desalki'laðo/ *a* untenanted, vacant

desalquilar /desalki'lar/ *vt* to leave, or cause to leave, rented premises

desalterar /desalte'rar/ *vt* to soothe, calm

desamar /desa'mar/ *vt* to cease to love; hate

desamarrar /desama'rrar/ *vt* to untie; separate; *Naut.* unmoor

desamor /desa'mor/ *m*, indifference; lack of sentiment or affection; hatred

desamotinarse /desamoti'narse/ *vr* to cease from rebellion; submit

desamparar /desampa'rar/ *vt* to abandon, forsake; leave (a place)

desamparo /desam'paro/ *m*, desertion; need

desamueblado /desamue'βlaðo/ *a* unfurnished

desamueblar /desamue'βlar/ *vt* to empty of furniture

desandar lo andado /desan'dar lo an'daðo/ *vt irr* to retrace one's steps. See **andar**

desangrar /desaŋ'grar/ *vt Med.* to bleed; drain (lake, etc.); impoverish, bleed; *—vr* lose much blood

desanidar /desani'ðar/ *vi* to leave the nest; *—vt* eject, expel

desanimado /desani'maðo/ *a* downhearted; (of places) dull, quiet

desanimar /desani'mar/ *vt* to discourage, depress

desanublar, /desanu'βlar,/ *vt* **desanublarse** *vr* to clear up (weather)

desanudar /desanu'ðar/ *vt* to untie; disentangle

desaojar /desao'har/ *vt* to cure of the evil eye

desapacibilidad /desapaθiβili'ðað; desapasiβili'ðað/ *f*, disagreeableness, unpleasantness

desapacible /desapa'θiβle; desapa'siβle/ *a* disagreeable; unpleasant; unsociable

desaparecer /desapare'θer; desapare'ser/ *vt irr* to cause to disappear; *—vi* and *vr* disappear. See **conocer**

desaparecido /desapare'θiðo; desapare'siðo/ *a* late (deceased); *Mil.* missing

desaparejar /desapare'har/ *vt* to unharness

desaparición /desapari'θion; desapari'sion/ *f*, disappearance

desapegar /desape'gar/ *vt* to unstick, undo; *—vr* be indifferent, cast off a love or affection

desapego /desa'pego/ *m*, lack of affection or interest, coolness

desapercibido /desaperθi'βiðo; desapersi'βiðo/ *a* unnoticed; unprovided, unprepared
desapercibimiento /desaperθiβi'miento; desapersiβi'miento/ *m,* unpreparedness
desapestar /desapes'tar/ *vt* to disinfect
desapiadado /desapia'ðaðo/ *a* merciless
desaplicación /desaplika'θion; desaplika'sion/ *f,* laziness, lack of application; carelessness, negligence
desaplicado /desapli'kaðo/ *a* lazy; careless
desapoderado /desapoðe'raðo/ *a* precipitate, uncontrolled; furious, violent
desapoderar /desapoðe'rar/ *vt* to dispossess, rob; remove from office
desapolillar /desapoli'ʎar; desapoli'yar/ *vt* to free from moths; *—vr Inf.* take an airing
desaposentar /desaposen'tar/ *vt* to evict; drive away
desapreciar /desapre'θiar; desapre'siar/ *vt* to scorn
desaprender /desapren'der/ *vt* to unlearn
desaprensivo /desapren'siβo/ *a* unscrupulous
desapretar /desapre'tar/ **(se)** *vt* and *vr irr* to slacken. See **acertar**
desaprisionar /desaprisio'nar/ *vt* to release from prison
desaprobación /desaproβa'θion; desaproβa'sion/ *f,* disapproval
desaprobar /desapro'βar/ *vt irr* to disapprove; disagree with. See **probar**
desapropiamiento /desapropia'miento/ *m,* renunciation or transfer of property
desapropiarse /desapropi'arse/ *vr* to renounce or transfer (property)
desaprovechado /desaproβe'tʃaðo/ *a* unprofitable; backward; unintelligent
desaprovechar /desaproβe'tʃar/ *vt* to take no advantage of, waste; *—vi Fig.* lose ground, lose what one has gained
desapuntar /desapun'tar/ *vt* to unstitch; lose one's aim
desarbolar /desarβo'lar/ *vt Naut.* to unmast
desarenar /desare'nar/ *vt* to clear of sand
desarmar /desar'mar/ *vt* to disarm; dismantle, dismount; appease
desarme /de'sarme/ *m,* disarming; disarmament
desarraigar /desarrai'gar/ *vt* to pull up by root (plants); extirpate, suppress; eradicate (opinion, etc.); exile
desarraigo /desa'rraigo/ *m,* uprooting; extirpation; eradication; exile
desarrebujar /desarreβu'har/ *vt* to disentangle, uncover; explain
desarreglado /desarre'glaðo/ *a* disarranged; untidy; intemperate, immoderate
desarreglar /desarre'glar/ *vt* to disarrange
desarreglo /desa'rreglo/ *m,* disorder; disarrangement; irregularity
desarrendar /desarren'dar/ *vt irr* to unbridle a horse; end a tenancy or lease. See **recomendar**
desarrollar /desarro'ʎar; desarro'yar/ *vt* to unroll; increase, develop, grow, unfold; explain (theory); *—vr* develop, grow
desarrollo /desa'rroʎo; des'arroyo/ *m,* unrolling; development, growth; explanation
desarropar /desarro'par/ *vt* to uncover, remove the covers, etc. from
desarrugar /desarru'gar/ *vt* to take out wrinkles or creases
desarticulación /desartikula'θion; desartikula'sion/ *f,* disarticulation
desarticular /desartiku'lar/ *vt* to disarticulate; *Mech.* disconnect
desaseado /desase'aðo/ *a* dirty; unkempt, slovenly
desaseo /desa'seo/ *m,* dirtiness; slovenliness
desasimiento /desasi'miento/ *m,* loosening; liberality; disinterestedness; indifference, coldness
desasir /desa'sir/ *vt irr* to loosen, undo *—vr* disengage oneself. See **asir**
desasnar /desas'nar/ *vt Inf.* to instruct, educate, polish
desasosegar /desasose'gar/ *vt irr* to disturb, make anxious. See **cegar**
desasosiego /desaso'siego/ *m,* uneasiness, disquiet
desastre /de'sastre/ *m,* disaster, calamity
desastroso /desas'troso/ *a* unfortunate, calamitous
desatacar /desata'kar/ *vt* to unfasten, undo, unbutton
desatadura /desata'ðura/ *f,* untying
desatar /desa'tar/ *vt* to untie; melt, dissolve; elucidate, explain; *—vr* loosen the tongue; lose self control; lose all reserve; unbosom oneself
desatascar /desatas'kar/ *vt* to pull out of the mud; free from obstruction; extricate from difficulties
desataviar /desata'βiar/ *vt* to strip of ornaments
desatavío /desata'βio/ *m,* carelessness in dress, slovenliness
desatención /desaten'θion; desaten'sion/ *f,* inattention, abstraction; incivility
desatender /desaten'der/ *vt irr* to pay no attention to; disregard, ignore. See **entender**
desatentado /desaten'taðo/ *a* imprudent, ill-advised; excessive, immoderate
desatento /desa'tento/ *a* inattentive, abstracted; discourteous
desatinado /desati'naðo/ *a* foolish, imprudent, wild
desatinar /desati'nar/ *vt* to bewilder; *—vi* behave foolishly; lose one's bearings
desatino /desa'tino/ *m,* folly, foolishness, imprudence, rashness; blunder, faux pas, mistake
desatracar /desatra'kar/ *vi Naut.* to push off
desatrancar /desatran'kar/ *vt* to unbar the door; remove obstacles
desaturdir /desatur'ðir/ *vt* to rouse (from torpor, etc.)
desautorizar /desautori'θar; desautori'sar/ *vt* to remove from authority; discredit
desavenencia /desaβe'nenθia; desaβe'nensia/ *f,* disharmony, disagreement
desavenido /desaβe'niðo/ *a* disagreeing, discordant
desavenir /desaβe'nir/ *vt irr* to upset. See **venir**
desaventajado /desaβenta'haðo/ *a* disadvantageous; unfavorable, inferior
desaviar /desa'βiar/ *vt* to lead astray; deprive of a necessity; *—vr* lose one's way
desavisado /desaβi'saðo/ *a* unaware, unprepared
desavisar /desaβi'sar/ *vt* to take back one's previous advice
desayunador /desayuna'ðor/ *m,* breakfast nook
desayunarse /desayu'narse/ *vr* to have breakfast, eat breakfast
desayuno /desa'yuno/ *m,* breakfast
desazón /desa'θon; desa'son/ *f,* insipidity, lack of flavor; poorness (soil); anxiety, trouble; vexation
desazonar /desaθo'nar; desaso'nar/ *vt* to make insipid; make anxious, worry; vex; *—vr* feel out of sorts
desbancar /desβan'kar/ *vt* to break the bank (gambling); supplant
desbandada /desβan'daða/ *f,* dispersal, rout. **a la d.,** in confusion or disorder
desbandarse /desβan'darse/ *vr* to disband, retreat in disorder; *Mil.* desert
desbaratado /desβara'taðo/ *a Inf.* corrupt, vicious
desbaratar /desβara'tar/ *vt* to spoil, destroy; dissipate, waste; foil, thwart (a plot); *Mil.* rout; *—vi* talk foolishly; *—vr* go too far, behave badly
desbarbado /desβar'βaðo/ *a* beardless
desbastar /desβas'tar/ *vt* to plane, dress; polish, refine, civilize
desbocado /desβo'kaðo/ *a* (of tools) blunt; runaway (of a horse); *Inf.* foul-tongued
desbocar /desβo'kar/ *vt* to break the spout or neck (of jars, etc.); *—vi* run (into) (of streets, etc.); *—vr* bolt (horses); curse, swear
desboquillar /desβoki'ʎar; desβoki'yar/ *vt* to remove or break a stem or mouthpiece
desbordamiento /desβorða'miento/ *m,* overflowing, flood
desbordarse /desβor'ðarse/ *vr* to overflow; lose self-control. **d. en alabanzas para,** to heap praise on
desbravar /desβra'βar/ *vt* to break in (horses, etc.); *—vi* grow less savage; lose force, decrease
desbrozar /desβro'θar; desβro'sar/ *vt* to free of rubbish, clear up
descabalgadura /deskaβalga'ðura/ *f,* alighting (from horses, etc.)

descabalgar /deskaβal'gar/ *vi* to alight (from horse); —*vt* dismantle (gun)
descabellado /deskaβe'ʎaðo; deskaβe'yaðo/ *a* disheveled; ridiculous, foolish
descabellar /deskaβe'ʎar; deskaβe'yar/ *vt* to disarrange, ruffle (hair)
descabezado /deskaβe'θaðo; deskaβe'saðo/ *a* headless; rash, impetuous
descabezar /deskaβe'θar; deskaβe'sar/ *vt* to behead; cut the top off (trees, etc.); *Fig. Inf.* break the back of (work); —*vi* abut, join; —*vr* (*with con* or *en*) rack one's brains about
descalabazarse /deskalaβa'θarse; deskalaβa'sarse/ *vr Inf.* to rack one's brains
descalabradura /deskalaβra'ðura/ *f,* head wound or scar
descalabrar /deskala'βrar/ *vt* to wound in the head; wound; harm
descalabro /deska'laβro/ *m,* misfortune, mishap
descalzar /deskal'θar; deskal'sar/ *vt* to remove the shoes and stockings; undermine; —*vr* remove one's shoes and stockings; lose a shoe (horses)
descalzo /des'kalθo; des'kalso/ *a* barefoot
descaminar /deskami'nar/ *vt* to lead astray; pervert, corrupt
descamisado /deskami'saðo/ **(-da)** *a Inf.* shirtless; ragged, poor —*n Inf.* down and out, outcast; vagabond
descansadero /deskansa'ðero/ *m,* resting place
descansado /deskan'saðo/ *a* rested, refreshed; tranquil
descansar /deskan'sar/ *vi* to rest, repose oneself; have relief (from anxiety, etc.); sleep; *Agr.* lie fallow; sleep in death; (*with en*) trust, have confidence in; (*with sobre*) lean on or upon; —*vt* (*with sobre*) rest (a thing) on another. **¡Que en paz descanse!** May he rest in peace!
descanso /des'kanso/ *m,* rest, repose; relief (from care); landing of stairs; *Mech.* bench, support; *Mil.* stand easy
descarado /deska'raðo/ *a* impudent, brazen
descararse /deska'rarse/ *vr* to behave impudently
descarbonizar /deskarβoni'θar; deskarβoni'sar/ *vt* to decarbonize
descarburación /deskarβura'θion; deskarβura'sion/ *f,* decarbonization
descarga /des'karga/ *f,* unloading; *Naut.* discharge of cargo; *Elec.* discharge; *Mil.* volley. **d. cerrada,** dense volley, fusillade
descargadero /deskarga'ðero/ *m,* wharf
descargador /deskarga'ðor/ *m,* unloader, docker; *Elec.* discharger
descargar /deskar'gar/ *vt* to unload; *Mil.* fire; unload (fire-arms); *Elec.* discharge; rain (blows) upon; *Fig.* free, exonerate; —*vi* disembogue (of rivers); burst (clouds); —*vr* relinquish (employment); shirk responsibility; *Law.* clear oneself
descargo /des'kargo/ *m,* unloading; *Com.* acquittance; *Law.* answer to an impeachment
descargue /des'karge/ *m,* unloading
descarnado /deskar'naðo/ *a* fleshless; scraggy; spare, lean
descarnador /deskarna'ðor/ *m,* dental scraper; tanner's scraper
descarnar /deskar'nar/ *vt* to scrape off flesh; corrode; inspire indifference to earthly things
descaro /des'karo/ *m,* impudence
descarriar /deska'rriar/ *vt* to lead astray; —*vr* be lost, be separated (from others); *Fig.* go astray
descarrilamiento /deskarrila'miento/ *m,* derailment
descarrilar /deskarri'lar/ *vi* to run off the track, be derailed
descarrío /deska'rrio/ *m,* losing one's way
descartar /deskar'tar/ *vt* to put aside; —*vr* discard (cards); shirk, make excuses
descarte /des'karte/ *m,* discard (cards); excuse, pretext
descascarar /deskaska'rar/ *vt* to peel; shell; —*vr* peel off
descendencia /desθen'denθia; dessen'densia/ *f,* descendants, offspring; lineage, descent
descender /desθen'der; dessen'der/ *vi irr* to descend; flow (liquids); (*with de*) descend from, derive from; —*vt* lower, let down. See **entender**
descendiente /desθen'diente; dessen'diente/ *mf* descendant, offspring —*a* descending
descendimiento /desθendi'miento; dessendi'miento/ *m,* descent
descenso /des'θenso; des'senso/ *m,* descent; lowering, letting down; degradation
descentralización /desθentraliθa'θion; dessentralisa'sion/ *f,* decentralization
descentralizar /desθentrali'θar; dessentrali'sar/ *vt* to decentralize
desceñir /desθe'ɲir; desse'ɲir/ **(se)** *vt* and *vr irr* to ungird, remove a girdle, etc. See **ceñir**
descepar /desθe'par; desse'par/ *vt* to tear up by the roots; *Fig.* extirpate
descercado /desθer'kaðo; desser'kaðo/ *a* unfenced, open
descercar /desθer'kar; desser'kar/ *vt* to pull down a wall or fence; *Mil.* raise a siege
descerrajar /desθerra'har; desserra'har/ *vt* to remove the locks (of doors, etc.)
descifrable /desθi'fraβle; dessi'fraβle/ *a* decipherable
descifrador /desθifra'ðor; dessifra'ðor/ *m,* decipherer, decoder
descifrar /desθi'frar; dessi'frar/ *vt* to decipher; decode
descinchar /desθin'tʃar; dessin'tʃar/ *vt* to loosen or remove girths (of horse)
desclavar /deskla'βar/ *vt* to remove nails; unnail, unfasten
descoagular /deskoagu'lar/ *vt* to liquefy, dissolve, melt
descobijar /deskoβi'har/ *vt* to uncover; undress
descocado /desko'kaðo/ *a Inf.* brazen, saucy
descoco /des'koko/ *m, Inf.* impudence
descogollar /deskogo'ʎar; deskogo'yar/ *vt* to prune a tree of shoots; remove hearts (of lettuces, etc.)
descolar /desko'lar/ *vt irr* to cut off or dock an animal's tail. See **colar**
descolgar /deskol'gar/ *vt irr* to unhang; lower; —*vr* lower oneself (by rope, etc.); come down, descend; *Inf.* come out (with), utter. See **volcar**
descollar /desko'ʎar; desko'yar/ *vi irr* to excel, be outstanding. See **degollar**
descoloramiento /deskolora'miento/ *m,* discoloration
descolorar /deskolo'rar/ *vt* to discolor; —*vr* be discolored
descolorido /deskolo'riðo/ *a* discolored; pale-colored; pallid
descomedido /deskome'ðiðo/ *a* excessive, disproportionate; rude
descomedimiento /deskomeði'miento/ *m,* disrespect, lack of moderation, rudeness
descomedirse /deskome'ðirse/ *vr irr* to be disrespectful or rude. See **pedir**
descompasarse /deskompa'sarse/ *vr* See **descomedirse**
descomponer /deskompo'ner/ *vt irr* to disorder, disarrange; *Chem.* decompose; unsettle; —*vr* go out of order; rot, putrefy; be ailing; lose one's temper. See **poner**
descomposición /deskomposi'θion; deskomposi'sion/ *f,* disorder, confusion; discomposure; *Chem.* decomposition; putrefaction
descompostura /deskompos'tura/ *f,* decomposition; slovenliness, dirtiness, untidiness; impudence, rudeness
descompuesto /deskom'puesto/ *a* rude, impudent
descomunal /deskomu'nal/ *a* enormous, extraordinary
desconcertar /deskonθer'tar; deskonser'tar/ *vt irr* to disorder, disarrange; dislocate (bones); disconcert, embarrass; —*vr* disagree; be impudent. See **acertar**
desconcharse /deskon'tʃarse/ *vr* to flake off, peel
desconcierto /deskon'θierto; deskon'sierto/ *m,* disorder, disarrangement; dislocation; embarrassment; disagreement; impudence
desconectar /deskonek'tar/ *vt* to disconnect; switch off

desconfianza /deskon'fianθa; deskon'fiansa/ *f,* lack of confidence
desconfiar /deskon'fiar/ *vi* to lack confidence
desconformidad /deskonformi'ðað/ *f,* See **disconformidad**
desconformismo /deskonfor'mismo/ *m,* nonconformism
desconocer /deskono'θer; deskono'ser/ *vt irr* to forget; be unaware of; deny, disown; pretend ignorance; not to understand (persons, etc.). See **conocer**
desconocido /deskono'θiðo; deskonos'iðo/ **(-da)** *a* unknown; ungrateful *—n* stranger; ingrate
desconocimiento /deskonoθi'miento; deskonosi'miento/ *m,* unawareness; ignorance; ingratitude
desconsiderado /deskonsiðe'raðo/ *a* inconsiderate; discourteous; rash
desconsolación /deskonsola'θion; deskonsola'sion/ *f,* affliction, trouble
desconsolar /deskonso'lar/ *vt irr* to afflict, make disconsolate; *—vr* grieve, despair. See **colar**
desconsuelo /deskon'suelo/ *m,* anguish, affliction, despair
descontar /deskon'tar/ *vt irr Com.* to make a discount; ignore, discount; take for granted, leave aside. See **contar**
descontentadizo /deskontenta'ðiθo; deskontenta'ðiso/ *a* discontented, difficult to please; fastidious, finicky
descontentar /deskonten'tar/ *vt* to displease; *—vr* be dissatisfied
descontento /deskon'tento/ *m,* discontent, dissatisfaction
descontextualizar /deskontekstuali'θar; deskontekstuali'sar/ *vt* to take out of context
descontrolarse /deskontro'larse/ *vr* to lose control, lose control of oneself.
desconveniencia /deskombe'nienθia; deskombe'niensia/ *f,* inconvenience, unsuitability, disagreement
desconvenir /deskombe'nir/ *vi irr* to disagree; be unsuitable, unsightly or odd (things). See **venir**
descorazonamiento /deskoraθona'miento; deskorasona'miento/ *m,* depression, despair
descorazonar /deskoraθo'nar; deskoraso'nar/ *vt* to tear out the heart; depress, discourage
descorchar /deskor'tʃar/ *vt* to take the cork from cork tree; draw a cork (bottles); force, break into (safes)
descorrer /desko'rrer/ *vt* to re-run (race, etc.); draw back (curtains, etc.); *—vi* run, flow (liquids)
descorrimiento /deskorri'miento/ *m,* overflow (liquids)
descortés /deskor'tes/ *a* impolite
descortesía /deskorte'sia/ *f,* impoliteness, discourtesy
descortezadura /deskorteθa'ðura; deskortesa'ðura/ *f,* peeling (of bark)
descortezar /deskorte'θar; deskorte'sar/ *vt* to decorticate; remove crust (bread, etc.); polish, civilize
descoser /desko'ser/ *vt Sew.* to unpick; *—vr* be unpicked; be indiscreet or tactless
descosido /desko'siðo/ *a* tactless, talkative; *Fig.* disjointed; desultory; unsewn. *m, Sew.* rent, hole
descoyuntamiento /deskoyunta'miento/ *m,* dislocation (bones); irritation, bore; ache, pain
descoyuntar /deskoyun'tar/ *vt* to dislocate (bones); bore, annoy; *—vr* be dislocated
descrédito /des'kreðito/ *m,* fall in value (things); discredit (persons)
descreer /deskre'er/ *vt irr* to disbelieve; depreciate, disparage (persons). See **creer**
descreído /deskre'iðo/ **(-da)** *a* unbelieving *—n* unbeliever; infidel
describir /deskri'βir/ *vt* to describe; outline, sketch *—Past Part.* **descrito**
descripción /deskrip'θion; deskrip'sion/ *f,* description; *Law.* inventory
descriptible /deskrip'tiβle/ *a* describable
descriptivo /deskrip'tiβo/ *a* descriptive
descuajar /deskua'har/ *vt* to liquefy; *Inf.* discourage; *Agr.* pull up by the root
descuartizar /deskuarti'θar; deskuarti'sar/ *vt* to quarter; joint (meat); *Inf.* carve, cut into pieces, break up
descubierto /desku'βierto/ *a* bareheaded; exposed. *m,* deficit. **al d.,** openly; in the open, without shelter. **girar en d.,** to overdraw (a bank account)
descubridero /deskuβri'ðero/ *m,* viewpoint, lookout
descubridor /deskuβri'ðor/ **(-ra)** *n* discoverer; inventor; explorer. *m, Mil.* scout
descubrimiento /deskuβri'miento/ *m,* find; discovery; revelation; newly discovered territory
descubrir /desku'βrir/ *vt* to reveal; show; discover; learn; unveil (memorials, etc.); *—vr* remove one's hat; show oneself, reveal one's whereabouts *—Past Part.* **descubierto**
descuello /des'kueʎo; des'kueyo/ *m,* extra height; *Fig.* pre-eminence; arrogance
descuento /des'kuento/ *m,* reduction; *Com.* rebate, discount
descuidado /deskui'ðaðo/ *a* negligent; careless; untidy; unprepared
descuidar /deskui'ðar/ *vt* to relieve (of responsibility, etc.); distract, occupy (attention, etc.); *—vi* and *vr* be careless; *—vr* (*with de* or *en*) neglect
descuido /des'kuiðo/ *m,* carelessness, negligence; oversight, mistake; incivility; forgetfulness; shameful act
desde /'desðe/ *prep* since, from (time or space); after (e.g. *d. hoy,* from today). **d. la ventana,** from the window. **d. allá,** from the other world. **d. aquella época,** since that time
desdecir /desðe'θir; desðe'sir/ *vi irr* (*with de*) to degenerate, be less good than; be discordant, clash; be unworthy of; *—vr* unsay one's words, retract. See **decir**
desdén /des'ðen/ *m,* indifference, coldness; disdain, scorn
desdentado /desðen'taðo/ *a* toothless; *Zool.* edentate
desdentar /desðen'tar/ *vt* to remove teeth
desdeñar /desðe'ɲar/ *vt* to scorn; *—vr* (*with de*) dislike, be reluctant
desdeñoso /desðe'ɲoso/ *a* disdainful, scornful
desdevanar /desðeβa'nar/ *vt* to unwind thread, etc.
desdibujado /desðiβu'haðo/ *a* badly drawn; blurred, confused
desdicha /des'ðitʃa/ *f,* misfortune; extreme poverty, misery. **por d.,** unfortunately
desdichado /desði'tʃaðo/ *a* unfortunate; *Inf.* timid, weak-kneed
desdicharse /desði'tʃarse/ *vr* to bewail one's fate
desdinerarse una fortuna /desðine'rarse 'una for'tuna/ *vr* to spend a fortune
desdoblar /desðo'βlar/ *vt* to unfold
desdorar /desðo'rar/ *vt* to remove the gilt; *Fig.* tarnish, sully
desdoro /des'ðoro/ *m,* discredit, dishonor
deseable /dese'aβle/ *a* desirable
desear /dese'ar/ *vt* to desire; yearn or long for
desecar /dese'kar/ *vt* to dry; *—vr* be desiccated
desechar /dese'tʃar/ *vt* to reject, refuse; scorn; cast out, expel; put away (thoughts, etc.); cast off (old clothes); turn (key); give up
desecho /de'setʃo/ *m,* residue, rest, remains; cast-off; scorn
desembalar /desemba'lar/ *vt* to unpack
desembanastar /desembana'star/ *vt* to take out of a basket; *Inf.* unsheath (sword); *—vr* break loose (animals); *Inf.* get out, alight
desembarazar /desembara'θar; desembara'sar/ *vt* to clear of obstruction; disembarrass, free; vacate; *—vr Fig.* rid oneself of obstacles
desembarazo /desemba'raθo; desemba'raso/ *m,* freedom, insouciance, naturalness
desembarcadero /desembarka'ðero/ *m,* landing-stage
desembarcar /desembar'kar/ *vt* to unload; *—vi* disembark; alight from vehicle
desembarco /desem'barko/ *m,* disembarkation, landing; staircase landing
desembargar /desembar'gar/ *vt* to free of obstacles or impediments; *Law.* remove an embargo
desembargo /desem'bargo/ *m, Law.* removal of an embargo
desembarque /desem'barke/ *m,* disembarkation, landing
desembarrancar /desembarran'kar/ *vt* and *vi Naut.* to refloat

desembaular /desembau'lar/ *vt* to unpack from a trunk; disinter, empty; *Inf.* unbosom oneself
desembocadero /desemboka'ðero/ *m,* exit, way out; mouth (rivers, etc.)
desembocadura /desemboka'ðura/ *f,* mouth (rivers, etc.); street opening
desembocar /desembo'kar/ *vi* (*with en*) to lead to, end in; flow into (rivers)
desembolsar /desembol'sar/ *vt* to take out of a purse; pay, spend
desembolso /desem'bolso/ *m,* disbursement; expenditure
desemboscarse /desembos'karse/ *vr* to get out of the wood; extricate oneself from an ambush
desembozar /desembo'θar; desembo'sar/ *vt* to unmuffle
desembozo /desem'boθo; desem'boso/ *m,* uncovering of the face
desembragar /desembra'gar/ *vt Mech.* to disengage (the clutch, etc.)
desembravecer /desembraβe'θer; desembraβe'ser/ *vt irr* to tame, domesticate. See **conocer**
desembriagar /desembria'gar/ **(se)** *vt* and *vr* to sober up (after a drinking bout)
desembrollar /desembro'ʎar; desembro'yar/ *vt Inf.* to disentangle, unravel
desemejanza /deseme'hanθa; deseme'hansa/ *f,* unlikeness
desemejar /deseme'har/ *vi* to be unlike; —*vt* disfigure, deform
desempacar /desempa'kar/ *vt* to unpack
desempapelar /desempape'lar/ *vt* to unwrap, remove the paper from; remove wallpaper
desempaquetar /desempake'tar/ *vt* to unpack
desemparejar /desempare'har/ *vt* to split (a pair); make unequal
desemparentado /desemparen'taðo/ *a* without relatives
desempedrar /desempe'ðrar/ *vt irr* to take up the flags (of a pavement). See **acertar**
desempeñar /desempe'ɲar/ *vt* to redeem (pledges); free from debt; fulfil (obligations, etc.); take out of pawn; hold, fill (an office); extricate (from difficulties, etc.); perform, carry out; *Theat.* act
desempeño /desempe'ɲo/ *m,* redemption of a pledge; fulfillment (of an obligation, etc.); performance, accomplishment; *Theat.* acting of a part
desempolvar /desempol'βar/ *vt* to free from dust, dust
desenamorar /desenamo'rar/ *vt* to kill the affection of; —*vr* fall out of love
desencadenar /desenkaðe'nar/ *vt* to unchain, unfetter; *Fig.* unleash, let loose; —*vr Fig.* break loose
desencajamiento /desenkaha'miento/ *m,* disjointedness, dislocation; ricketiness, broken-down appearance
desencajar /desenka'har/ *vt* to disconnect, disjoint; dislocate; —*vr* be out of joint; be contorted (of the face); be tired looking
desencaje /desen'kahe/ *m,* See **desencajamiento**
desencallar /desenka'ʎar; desenka'yar/ *vt Naut.* to float a grounded ship
desencantar /desenkan'tar/ *vt* to disenchant
desencanto /desen'kanto/ *m,* disenchantment; disillusionment
desencerrar /desenθe'rrar; desense'rrar/ *vt irr* to set at liberty; unlock; disclose, reveal. See **acertar**
desenchufar /desentʃu'far/ *vt* to disconnect, unplug (electric plugs, etc.)
desenclavijar /desenklaβi'har/ *vt* to remove the pegs or pins; disconnect, disjoint
desencoger /desenko'her/ *vt* to unfold, spread out; —*vr* grow bold
desencolerizar /desenkoleri'θar; desenkoleri'sar/ *vt* to placate; —*vr* lose one's anger, grow calm
desenconar /desenko'nar/ *vt* to reduce (inflammation); appease (anger, etc.); —*vr* become calm
desencono /desen'kono/ *m,* reduction of inflammation; appeasement (of anger, etc.)
desencordelar /desenkorðe'lar/ *vt* to untie the ropes (of), unstring
desencorvar /desenkor'βar/ *vt* to straighten (curves, etc.)
desenfadado /desenfa'ðaðo/ *a* expeditious; natural, at ease; gay; forward, bold; wide, spacious
desenfadar /desenfa'ðar/ *vt* to appease, make anger disappear
desenfado /desen'faðo/ *m,* freedom; ease; unconcern, frankness
desenfardar /desenfar'ðar/ *vt* to unpack bales
desenfrailar /desenfrai'lar/ *vi* to leave the cloister, become secularized; *Inf.* emancipate oneself
desenfrenar /desenfre'nar/ *vt* to unbridle (horses); —*vr* give rein to one's passions, etc.; break loose (storms, etc.)
desenfreno /desen'freno/ *m,* license, lasciviousness; complete freedom from restraint
desengalanar /deseŋgala'nar/ *vt* to strip of ornaments
desenganchar /deseŋgan'tʃar/ *vt* to unhook; uncouple; unfasten; unharness
desengañador /deseŋgaɲa'ðor/ *a* undeceiving
desengañar /deseŋga'ɲar/ *vt* to undeceive, disillusion
desengaño /deseŋ'gaɲo/ *m,* undeceiving, disabuse; disillusionment
desengarzar /deseŋgar'θar; deseŋgar'sar/ *vt* to loosen from its setting; unlink, unhook, unclasp
desengastar /deseŋgas'tar/ *vt* to remove from its setting (jewelry, etc.)
desengrasar /deseŋgra'sar/ *vt* to remove the grease from, clean; —*vi Inf.* grow thin
desenlace /desen'laθe; desen'lase/ *m,* loosening, untying; *Lit.* denouement, climax (of play, etc.)
desenlazar /desenla'θar; desenla'sar/ *vt* to untie, unloose; *Lit.* unravel (a plot)
desenlosar /desenlo'sar/ *vt* to remove flagstones
desenmarañar /desemara'ɲar/ *vt* to disentangle; *Fig.* straighten out
desenmascarar /desemaska'rar/ *vt* to remove the mask from; *Fig.* unmask
desenmudecer /desemuðe'θer; desemuðe'ser/ *vi irr* to be freed of a speech impediment; break silence, speak. See **conocer**
desenojar /deseno'har/ *vt* to soothe, appease; —*vr* distract oneself, amuse oneself
desenojo /dese'noho/ *m,* relenting, abatement of anger
desenredar /desenre'ðar/ *vt* to disentangle; *Fig.* set right; straighten out; —*vr* extricate oneself, get out of a difficulty
desenredo /desen'reðo/ *m,* disentanglement; *Lit.* climax
desentablar /desenta'βlar/ *vt* to tear up planks or boards; disorder, disrupt
desentenderse /desenten'derse/ *vr irr* (*with de*) to pretend to be ignorant of; take no part in. See **entender**
desenterrador /desenterra'ðor/ *m,* disinterrer, unearther
desenterramiento /desenterra'miento/ *m,* disinterment; *Fig.* unearthing, recollection
desenterrar /desente'rrar/ *vt irr* to unbury, disinter; rummage out; *Fig.* unearth, bring up, recall. See **acertar**
desentoldar /desentol'dar/ *vt* to take away an awning; *Fig.* strip of ornament
desentonar /desento'nar/ *vt* to humiliate; —*vi Mus.* be out of tune; speak rudely; —*vr* be inharmonious; raise the voice (anger, etc.), behave badly
desentono /desen'tono/ *m,* bad behavior, rudeness; *Mus.* discord; grating quality or harshness (of voice)
desentorpecer /desentorpe'θer; desentorpe'ser/ *vt irr* to restore feeling to (numbed limbs); free from torpor; —*vr* become bright and intelligent. See **conocer**
desentramparse /desentram'parse/ *vr Inf.* free oneself from debt
desentrañar /desentra'ɲar/ *vt* to disembowel; *Fig.* unravel, penetrate; —*vr* give away one's all
desentronizar /desentroni'θar; desentroni'sar/ *vt* to dethrone; dismiss from office
desentumecer /desentume'θer; desentume'ser/ *vt irr*

to free from numbness (limbs); *—vr* be restored to feeling (numb limbs). See **conocer**

desenvainar /desembai'nar/ *vt* to unsheath; *Inf.* reveal, bring into the open

desenvoltura /desembol'tura/ *f,* naturalness, ease, freedom; eloquence, facility (of speech); effrontery, audacity, shamelessness (especially in women)

desenvolver /desembol'βer/ *vt irr* to unroll; unfold; *Fig.* unravel, explain; *Fig.* develop, work out (theories, etc.); *—vr* unroll; unfold; lose one's timidity, blossom out; be over-bold; extricate oneself (from a difficulty). See **resolver**

desenvuelto /desem'buelto/ *a* natural, easy; impudent, bold

deseo /de'seo/ *m,* desire, will, wish

deseoso /dese'oso/ *a* desirous, wishful

desequilibrar /desekili'βrar/ **(se)** *vt* and *vr* to unbalance

desequilibrio /deseki'liβrio/ *m,* lack of balance; confusion, disorder; mental instability

deserción /deser'θion; deser'sion/ *f, Mil.* desertion. **d. estudiantil,** school dropout

desertar /deser'tar/ *vt Mil.* to desert; *Inf.* quit

desertor /deser'tor/ *m, Mil.* deserter; *Inf.* quitter

deservicio /deser'βiθio; deser'βisio/ *m,* disservice

desesperación /desespera'θion; desespera'sion/ *f,* desperation, despair; frenzy, violence

desesperado /desespe'raðo/ *a* desperate, hopeless; frenzied

desesperanza /desespe'ranθa; desespe'ransa/ *f,* despair; hopelessness

desesperanzar /desesperan'θar; desesperan'sar/ *vt* to render hopeless; *—vr* despair, lose hope

desesperar /desespe'rar/ *vt* to make hopeless; *Inf.* annoy, make furious; *—vr* lose hope, despair; be frenzied

desestañar /desesta'ɲar/ *vt* to unsolder

desestimación /desestima'θion; desestima'sion/ *f,* disrespect, lack of esteem; rejection

desestimar /desesti'mar/ *vt* to scorn; reject

desfachatado /desfatʃa'taðo/ *a Inf.* impudent, brazen

desfachatez /desfatʃa'teθ; desfatʃa'tes/ *f, Inf.* effrontery, cheek

desfalcador /desfalka'ðor/ **(-ra)** *a* embezzling *—n* embezzler

desfalcar /desfal'kar/ *vt* to remove a part of; embezzle

desfalco /des'falko/ *m,* diminution, reduction; embezzlement

desfallecer /desfaʎe'θer; desfaye'ser/ *vt irr* to weaken; *—vi* grow weak; faint, swoon. See **conocer**

desfallecimiento /desfaʎeθi'miento; desfayesi'miento/ *m,* weakness, languor; depression, discouragement; faint, swoon

desfavorable /desfaβo'raβle/ *a* unfavorable; hostile, contrary

desfavorecer /desfaβore'θer; desfaβore'ser/ *vt irr* to withdraw one's favor, scorn; disfavor; oppose. See **conocer**

desfiguración /desfigura'θion; desfigura'sion/ *f,* deformation; disfigurement

desfigurar /desfigu'rar/ *vt* to deform, misshape; disfigure; *Fig.* disguise, mask; obscure, darken; distort, misrepresent; *—vr* be disfigured (by rage, etc.)

desfijar /desfi'har/ *vt* to unfix, pull off, remove

desfiladero /desfila'ðero/ *m,* defile, gully

desfilar /desfi'lar/ *vi* to walk in file; *Inf.* file out; *Mil.* file or march past

desfile /des'file/ *m, Mil.* march past; parade; walk past; procession

desflecarse /desfle'karse/ **(en)** *vr* to disintegrate (into)

desfloración /desflora'θion; desflora'sion/ *f,* defloration

desflorar /desflo'rar/ *vt* to tarnish, stain; deflower, violate; *Fig.* touch upon, deal lightly with

desfortalecer /desfortale'θer; desfortale'ser/ *vt irr Mil.* to dismantle a fortress. See **conocer**

desfruncir /desfrun'θir; desfrun'sir/ *vt* to unfold, shake out

desgaire /des'gaire/ *m,* untidiness, slovenliness; affectation of carelessness (in dress); scornful gesture. **al d.,** with an affectation of carelessness, negligently

desgajar /desga'har/ *vt* to tear off a tree branch; break; *—vr* break off; dissociate oneself (from)

desgalgar /desgal'gar/ *vt* to throw headlong

desgana /des'gana/ *f,* lack of appetite; lack of interest, indifference; reluctance

desganar /desga'nar/ *vt* to dissuade; *—vr* lose one's appetite; become bored or indifferent, lose interest

desgarbado /desgar'βaðo/ *a* slovenly, slatternly; gawky, graceless

desgarrado /desga'rraðo/ *a* dissolute, vicious; impudent, brazen

desgarrador /desgarra'ðor/ *a* tearing; heart-rending

desgarrar /desga'rrar/ *vt* to tear; *—vr* leave, tear oneself away

desgarro /des'garro/ *m,* tearing; rent, breach; boastfulness, impudence, effrontery

desgastar /desgas'tar/ *vt* to corrode, wear away; spoil, corrupt; *—vr* lose one's vigor, grow weak; wear away

desgaste /des'gaste/ *m,* attrition; wearing down or away; corrosion; wear and tear

desgobernado /desgoβer'naðo/ *a* uncontrolled (of persons)

desgobernar /desgoβer'nar/ *vt irr* to upset or rise against the government; dislocate (bones); *Naut.* neglect the tiller; *—vr* affect exaggerated movements in dancing. See **recomendar**

desgobierno /desgo'βierno/ *m,* misgovernment; mismanagement; maladministration; disorder, tumult

desgomar /desgo'mar/ *vt* to ungum (fabrics)

desgorrarse /desgo'rrarse/ *vr* to doff one's cap, doff one's hat

desgoznar /desgoθ'nar; desgos'nar/ *vt* to unhinge; *—vr Fig.* lose one's self-control

desgracia /des'graθia; des'grasia/ *f,* misfortune, adversity; mishap, piece of bad luck; disgrace, disfavor; disagreeableness, brusqueness; ungraciousness. **por d.,** unhappily, unfortunately

desgraciado /desgra'θiaðo; desgra'siaðo/ *a* unfortunate, unhappy; unlucky; dull, boring; disagreeable

desgraciar /desgra'θiar; desgra'siar/ *vt* to displease; spoil the development (of), destroy; maim; *—vr* fall out of friendship; be out of favor; turn out badly, fail; be destroyed or spoiled; be maimed

desgranar /desgra'nar/ *vt Agr.* to thresh, flail; *—vr* break (string of beads, etc.)

desgrasante /desgra'sante/ *m,* grease remover

desgreñar /desgre'ɲar/ *vt* to dishevel the hair; *—vr Inf.* pull each other's hair, come to blows

desguarnecer /desguarne'θer; desguarne'ser/ *vt irr* to strip of trimming; *Mil.* demilitarize; *Mil.* disarm; dismantle; unharness. See **conocer**

desguazar /desgua'θar; desgua'sar/ *vt* to break up (ships)

deshabitado /desaβi'taðo/ *a* uninhabited, empty

deshabitar /desaβi'tar/ *vt* to desert, quit, leave (a place)

deshabituar /desaβi'tuar/ *vt* to disaccustom; *—vr* lose the habit, become unaccustomed

deshacer /desa'θer; desa'ser/ *vt irr* to undo; destroy; *Mil.* rout, defeat; take to pieces; melt; pulp (paper); untie (knots, etc.); open (parcels); diminish, decrease; break in pieces, smash; *Fig.* obstruct, spoil; *—vr* be wasted or spoiled; be full of anxiety; vanish; try or work very hard; injure oneself; be emaciated, grow extremely thin; (*with de*) part with. **d. agravios,** to right wrongs. See **hacer**

desharrapado /desarra'paðo/ *a* tattered, shabby

deshebillar /deseβi'ʎar; deseβi'yar/ *vt* to unbuckle

deshebrar /dese'βrar/ *vt* to unravel; shred

deshecha /des'etʃa/ *f,* pretense, evasion; courteous farewell; obligatory departure

deshechizar /desetʃi'θar; desetʃi'sar/ *vt* to disenchant

deshelar /dese'lar/ *vt irr* to thaw, melt. See **acertar**

desherbar /deser'βar/ *vt irr* to pull up weeds. See **acertar**

desheredación /desereða'θion; desereða'sion/ *f,* disinheritance

desheredar /desere'ðar/ *vt* disinherit; *—vr Fig.* lower oneself

desherrar /dese'rrar/ *vt irr* to unfetter, unchain; strike off horseshoes; —*vr* lose a shoe (horses). See **acertar**
desherrumbrar /deserrum'brar/ *vt* to remove the rust from; clean off rust from
deshidratación /desiðrata'θion; desiðrata'sion/ *f,* dehydration
deshidratar /desiðra'tar/ *vt* to dehydrate
deshielo /des'ielo/ *m,* thaw
deshilado /desi'laðo/ *a* in single file. *m, Sew.* drawn-thread work (gen. *pl*). **a la deshilada,** *Mil.* in file formation; secretly
deshiladura /desila'ðura/ *f,* unraveling
deshilar /desi'lar/ *vt* to unravel; *Sew.* draw threads; *Cul.* shred, grate
deshilvanado /desilβa'naðo/ *a Fig.* disjointed, disconnected
deshilvanar /desilβa'nar/ *vt Sew.* to remove the tacking threads
deshincar /desin'kar/ *vt* to pull out, remove, draw out
deshinchar /desin'tʃar/ *vt* to remove a swelling; deflate; lessen the anger of; —*vr* decrease, subside (swellings); deflate; *Inf.* grow humble
deshojar /deso'har/ *vt* to strip off leaves or petals
deshollejar /desoʎe'har; desoye'har/ *vt* to skin, peel (fruit); shell (peas, etc.)
deshollinador /desoʎina'ðor; desoyina'ðor/ *m,* chimney-sweep; wall-brush; chemical chimney cleaner
deshollinar /desoʎi'nar; desoyi'nar/ *vt* to sweep chimneys; clean down walls; *Inf.* examine closely
deshonestidad /desonesti'ðað/ *f,* immodesty, shamelessness; indecency
deshonesto /deso'nesto/ *a* shameless, immodest; dissolute, vicious; indecent
deshonor /deso'nor/ *m,* dishonor; disgrace, insult
deshonra /de'sonra/ *f,* dishonor
deshonrabuenos /desonra'βuenos/ *mf Inf.* slanderer; degenerate
deshonrador /desonra'ðor/ **(-ra)** *a* dishonorable —*n* dishonorer
deshonrar /deson'rar/ *vt* to dishonor; insult; seduce (women)
deshonroso /deson'roso/ *a* dishonorable, insulting, indecent
deshora /de'sora/ *f,* inconvenient time. **a d.,** *or* **a deshoras,** at an inconvenient time, unseasonably; extempore
deshuesar /desue'sar/ *vt* to bone, remove the bone (from meat); stone (fruit)
deshumedecer /desumeðe'θer; desumeðe'ser/ *vt irr* to dry; —*vr* become dry. See **conocer**
desidia /de'siðia/ *f,* negligence; laziness
desidioso /desi'ðioso/ *a* negligent; lazy
desierto /de'sierto/ *a* deserted, uninhabited, solitary. *m,* desert; wilderness
designación /designa'θion; designa'sion/ *f,* designation; appointment
designar /desig'nar/ *vt* to plan, intend; designate; appoint
designio /de'signio/ *m,* intention, idea
desigual /desi'gual/ *a* unequal; uneven (ground); rough; arduous, difficult; changeable
desigualar /desigua'lar/ *vt* to make unequal; —*vr* prosper
desigualdad /desigual'dað/ *f,* inequality; unevenness, rockiness; *Fig.* changeability; variability
desilusión /desilu'sion/ *f,* disillusionment; disappointment
desilusionar /desilusio'nar/ *vt* to disillusion; —*vr* become disillusioned; be undeceived
desinclinar /desinkli'nar/ *vt* to dissuade
desinfección /desinfek'θion; desinfek'sion/ *f,* disinfection
desinfectante /desinfek'tante/ *a* and *m,* disinfectant
desinfectar /desinfek'tar/ *vt* to disinfect
desinflación /desinfla'θion; desinfla'sion/ *f,* deflation
desinflar /desin'flar/ *vt* to deflate
desinterés /desinte'res/ *m,* disinterestedness
desinteresado /desintere'saðo/ *a* disinterested; generous
desinteresarse /desintere'sarse/ *vr* to lose interest, grow indifferent
desistencia, /desis'tenθia,; desis'tensia,/ *f,* **desistimiento** *m,* desistance, ceasing
desistir /desis'tir/ *vi* to desist; cease; *Law.* renounce
desjuntamiento /deshunta'miento/ *m,* separation; division
desjuntar /deshun'tar/ **(se)** *vt* and *vr* to separate; divide
deslavado /desla'βaðo/ *a* brazen, impudent
deslavar /desla'βar/ *vt* to wash superficially; spoil by washing, take away the body of (cloth, etc.)
desleal /desle'al/ *a* disloyal, treacherous
deslealtad /desleal'tað/ *f,* disloyalty
desleír /desle'ir/ *vt irr* to dissolve; dilute. See **reír**
deslenguado /desleŋ'guaðo/ *a* shameless, foul-mouthed
deslenguar /desleŋ'guar/ *vt* to remove the tongue; —*vr Inf.* be insolent
desliar /des'liar/ *vt* to untie, undo, unloose
desligadura /desliga'ðura/ *f,* untying, loosening
desligar /desli'gar/ *vt* to unfasten, unbind; *Fig.* solve, unravel; relieve of an obligation; *Mus.* play staccato; —*vr* come unfastened, grow loose. **desligarse de,** to weasel out of, wiggle out of (a promise)
deslindador /deslinda'ðor/ *m,* one who fixes boundaries or limits
deslindar /deslin'dar/ *vt* to fix the boundaries (of); limit, circumscribe
deslinde /des'linde/ *m,* demarcation, boundary
desliz /des'liθ; des'lis/ *m,* slipping, slip, slide; skid; indiscretion, slip; peccadillo, trifling fault
deslizadero /desliθa'ðero; deslisa'ðero/ *m,* slippery place; chute
deslizadizo /desliθa'ðiθo; deslisa'ðiso/ *a* slippery
deslizar /desli'θar; desli'sar/ *vt* to slip, slide; skid; —*vr* commit an indiscretion; speak or act unwisely; escape, slip away; slip; skid
deslucido /des'luθiðo; des'lusiðo/ *a* fruitless, vain; stupid, clumsy, awkward; discolored; tarnished, dull; unsuccessful
deslucimiento /desluθi'miento; deslusi'miento/ *m,* clumsiness, gracelessness; failure, lack of success
deslucir /deslu'θir; deslu'sir/ *vt irr* to fade; discolor, stain; tarnish; spoil; sully the reputation of; —*vr* do a thing badly, fail at. See **lucir**
deslumbrador /deslumbra'ðor/ *a* dazzling
deslumbramiento /deslumbra'miento/ *m,* brilliant light, glare, dazzle; bewilderment, confusion
deslumbrar /deslumb'rar/ *vt* to dazzle; confuse, bewilder; *Fig.* daze (with magnificence)
deslustrar /deslus'trar/ *vt* to dull, dim, tarnish; frost (glass); discredit, sully (reputation)
deslustre /des'lustre/ *m,* dullness, tarnish; frosting (of glass); disgrace, stigma
deslustroso /deslus'troso/ *a* ugly, unsuitable, unbecoming
desmadejar /desmaðe'har/ *vt* to debilitate, enervate
desmán /des'man/ *m,* outrageous behavior; disaster, misfortune
desmandado /desman'daðo/ *a* disobedient
desmandar /desman'dar/ *vt* to cancel, revoke (orders); withdraw (an offer) —*vr* behave badly; stray
desmantelado /desmante'laðo/ *a* dismantled, dilapidated
desmantelamiento /desmantela'miento/ *m,* dismantling; dilapidation
desmantelar /desmante'lar/ *vt* to dismantle; abandon, forsake
desmaña /des'maɲa/ *f,* lack of dexterity, clumsiness, awkwardness
desmañado /desma'ɲaðo/ *a* clumsy, awkward, unhandy
desmayado /desma'yaðo/ *a* pale, faint (of colors); weak (of a voice)
desmayar /desma'yar/ *vt* to cause to faint; —*vi* grow discouraged, lose heart; —*vr* swoon, faint

desmayo /des'mayo/ *m*, depression, discouragement; faint, swoon
desmedido /desme'ðiðo/ *a* disproportionate; excessive
desmedirse /desme'ðirse/ *vr* to misbehave, go too far
desmedrado /desme'ðraðo/ *a* thin, emaciated; deteriorated, spoiled
desmedrar /desme'ðrar/ *vt* to spoil, ruin; *—vi* deteriorate; decline
desmedro /des''meðro/ *m*, impairment; decline, deterioration. **en d. de,** to the detriment of
desmejora /desme'hora/ *f*, deterioration
desmejorar /desmeho'rar/ *vt* to spoil, impair, cause to deteriorate; *—vr* deteriorate; *—vi* and *vr* decline in health; lose one's beauty
desmelenar /desmele'nar/ *vt* to ruffle or dishevel the hair
desmembración /desmembra'θion; desmembrasion/ *f*, dismemberment
desmembrar /desmem'brar/ *vt* to dismember; separate, divide
desmemoriarse /desmemo'riarse/ *vr* to forget, lose one's memory
desmenguar /desmeŋ'guar/ *vt* to reduce, decrease; *Fig.* diminish
desmentida /desmen'tiða/ *f*, action of giving the lie to
desmentir /desmen'tir/ *vt irr* to give the lie to; contradict, deny; lower oneself; behave unworthily; *—vi* deviate (from right direction, etc.). See **sentir**
desmenuzar /desmenu'θar; desmenu'sar/ *vt* to crumble, break into small pieces; *Fig.* examine in detail; *—vr* be broken up
desmeollar /desmeo'ʎar; desmeo'yar/ *vt* to remove the marrow of
desmerecedor /desmereθe'ðor; desmerese'ðor/ *a* unworthy
desmerecer /desmere'θer; desmere'ser/ *vt irr* to become undeserving of; *—vi* deteriorate; be inferior to. See **conocer**
desmesura /desme'sura/ *f*, insolence; disproportion; excess
desmesurado /desmesu'raðo/ *a* disproportionate; excessive, enormous; insolent, uncivil
desmesurar /desmesu'rar/ *vt* to disarrange, disorder; *—vr* be insolent
desmigajar /desmiga'har/ **(se)** *vt* and *vr* to crumble
desmigar /desmi'gar/ *vt Cul.* to make breadcrumbs
desmilitarizar /desmilitari'θar; desmilitari'sar/ *vt* to demilitarize
desmochar /desmo'tʃar/ *vt* to lop off the top; pollard (trees)
desmonetización /desmonetiθa'θion; desmonetisa'sion/ *f*, demonetization; conversion of coin into bullion
desmonetizar /desmoneti'θar; desmoneti'sar/ *vt* to convert money into bullion; demonetize; *—vr* depreciate (shares, etc.)
desmontable /desmon'taβle/ *a* movable; sectional
desmontadura /desmonta'ðura/ *f*, clearing; deforestation; leveling; demounting, dismounting
desmontar /desmon'tar/ *vt* to clear wholly or partly of trees or shrubs; clear up (rubbish); level (ground); dismantle; dismount; uncock (firearms); *—vi* and *vr* dismount (from horse, etc.)
desmonte /des'monte/ *m*, clearing of trees and shrubs; clearing, cleared ground; timber remaining
desmoralización /desmoraliθa'θion; desmoralisa'sion/ *f*, demoralization, corruption
desmoralizador /desmoraliθa'ðor; desmoralisa'ðor/ *a* demoralizing
desmoralizar /desmorali'θar; desmorali'sar/ *vt* to demoralize, corrupt
desmoronamiento /desmorona'miento/ *m*, crumbling; decay, ruin
desmoronar /desmoro'nar/ *vt* to destroy, decay; crumble; *—vr* crumble away, fall into ruin; decline, decay; wane, fade (power, etc.)
desmovilización /desmoβiliθa'θion; desmoβilisa'sion/ *f*, demobilization
desmovilizar /desmoβili'θar; desmoβili'sar/ *vt* to demobilize
desnacificación /desnaθifika'θion; desnasifika'sion/ *f*, denazification
desnatar /desna'tar/ *vt* to skim; *Fig.* take the cream or best
desnaturalización /desnaturaliθa'θion; desnaturalisa'sion/ *f*, denaturalization
desnaturalizar /desnaturali'θar; desnaturali'sar/ *vt* to denaturalize; exile; deform, disfigure, pervert; *—vr* give up one's country
desnivel /desni'βel/ *m*, unevenness; slope, drop
desnivelar /desniβe'lar/ **(se)** *vi* and *vr* to become uneven
desnudar /desnu'ðar/ *vt* to undress; *Fig.* despoil, strip, denude; *—vr* undress oneself; deprive oneself
desnudez /desnu'ðeθ; desnu'ðes/ *f*, nudity; nakedness; bareness; plainness
desnudo /des'nuðo/ *a* nude; ill-clad; bare, naked; clear, patent; *Fig.* destitute (of grace, etc.). *m*, *Art.* nude
desnutrición /desnutri'θion; desnutri'sion/ *f*, malnutrition
desobedecer /desoβeðe'θer; desoβeðe'ser/ *vt irr* to disobey. See **conocer**
desobediencia /desoβeðien'θia; desoβeðien'sia/ *f*, disobedience
desobediente /desoβe'ðiente/ *a* disobedient
desobligar /desoβli'gar/ *vt* to free from obligation; offend, hurt
desocupación /desokupa'θion; desokupa'sion/ *f*, lack of occupation; leisure
desocupado /desoku'paðo/ *a* idle; vacant, unoccupied
desocupar /desoku'par/ *vt* to empty; vacate; *—vr* give up an employment or occupation
desodorante /desoðo'rante/ *a* and *m*, deodorant
desoir /deso'ir/ *vt irr* to pay no attention, pretend not to hear. See **oir**
desojar /deso'har/ *vt* to break the eye of (needles, etc.); *—vr* gaze intently
desolación /desola'θion; desola'sion/ *f*, destruction, desolation; affliction
desolador /desola'ðor/ *a* desolate; grievous
desolar /deso'lar/ *vt irr* to lay waste, destroy; *—vr* grieve, be disconsolate. See **contar**
desoldar /desol'dar/ *vt* to unsolder; *—vr* become unsoldered
desolladero /desoʎa'ðero; desoya'ðero/ *m*, slaughterhouse
desollado /deso'ʎaðo; deso'yaðo/ *a Inf.* impertinent, barefaced. *m*, carcass
desolladura /desoʎa'ðura; desoya'ðura/ *f*, flaying, skinning; *Inf.* slander
desollar /deso'ʎar; deso'yar/ *vt irr* to flay, skin; harm, discredit. **d. vivo,** *Inf.* to extort an exorbitant price; slander. See **contar**
desopinado /desopi'naðo/ *a* discredited
desopinar /desopi'nar/ *vt* to discredit, defame
desorden /de'sorðen/ *m*, disorder, disarray; confusion; excess
desordenado /desorðe'naðo/ *a* disordered; vicious; licentious
desordenar /desorðe'nar/ *vt* to disorder; confuse; *—vr* go beyond the just limits; behave badly; be impertinent
desorganización /desorganiθa'θion; desorganisa'sion/ *f*, disorganization
desorganizador /desorganiθa'ðor; desorganisa'ðor/ *a* disorganizing
desorganizar /desorgani'θar; desorgani'sar/ *vt* to disorganize; disband
desorientación /desorienta'θion; desorienta'sion/ *f*, disorientation, loss of bearings; lack of method, confusion
desorientar /desorien'tar/ *vt* to disorient; perplex, confuse; *—vr* lose one's way; be disoriented
desovar /deso'βar/ *vi* to spawn
desove /de'soβe/ *m*, spawning; spawning season
desovillar /desoβi'ʎar; desoβi'yar/ *vt* to unwind; uncoil; uncurl; explain, clarify
despabiladeras /despaβila'ðeras/ *f pl*, snuffers

despabilado /despaβi'laðo/ *a* alert, wide-awake; watchful, vigilant
despabiladura /despaβila'ðura/ *f,* snuff of a candle, lamp, etc.
despabilar /despaβi'lar/ *vt* to snuff (a candle); trim (lamps); hasten, expedite; finish quickly; steal, rob; *Fig.* quicken (intelligence, etc.); *Inf.* kill; *—vr* rouse oneself, wake up
despachador /despatʃa'ðor/ **(-ra)** *n* dispatcher, sender
despachar /despa'tʃar/ *vt* to expedite; dispatch, conclude; forward, send; attend to correspondence; sell; dismiss; *Inf.* serve in a shop; *Inf.* kill; *—vi* hasten; carry letters to be signed (in offices, etc.); *—vr* get rid of
despacho /despa'tʃo/ *m,* transaction, execution; study; office, room; department; booking-office; dispatch, shipment; expedient; commission, warrant; dispatch (diplomatic); telegram; telephone message. **d. particular,** private office
despachurrar /despa'tʃurrar/ *vt Inf.* to crush, squash; recount in a muddled fashion; *Fig.* squash flat, confound
despacio /des'paθio; des'pasio/ *adv* slowly, little by little; deliberately, leisurely *—interj* Careful! Gently now!
despacito /despa'θito; despa'sito/ *adv Inf.* very slowly
despalmador /despalma'ðor/ *m,* dockyard
despalmar /despal'mar/ *vt Naut.* to careen, caulk
despampanar /despampa'nar/ *vt Agr.* to prune vines; *Inf.* amaze, stun, astound; *—vi Inf.* relieve one's feelings; *—vr Inf.* receive a serious injury (through falling)
desparpajar /desparpa'har/ *vt* to spoil; *—vi Inf.* chatter
desparpajo /despar'paho/ *m, Inf.* loquaciousness, pertness; disorder, muddle
desparramar /desparra'mar/ *vt* to disperse, scatter; squander, waste (money, etc.); *—vr* amuse oneself; be dissipated
despavorido /despaβo'riðo/ *a* terrified, panicstricken
despechar /despe'tʃar/ *vt* to anger; make despair; *Inf.* wean; *—vr* be angry; be in despair
despecho /des'petʃo/ *m,* rancor, malice; despair. **a d. de,** in spite of
despechugar /despetʃu'gar/ *vt* to cut off the breast (fowls); *—vr Inf.* show the bosom
despectivo /despek'tiβo/ *a* contemptuous, depreciatory
despedazar /despeða'θar; despeða'sar/ *vt* to cut or break into pieces; *Fig.* break (heart, etc.)
despedida /despe'ðiða/ *f,* dismissal, discharge; seeing off (a visitor, etc.); farewell, good-by
despedir /despe'ðir/ *vt irr* to throw out, emit, cast up; dismiss, discharge; see off (on a journey or after a visit); banish (from the mind); get rid of; *—vr* say good-by; leave (employment). See **pedir**
despedregar /despeðre'gar/ *vt* to clear of stones
despegadamente /despegaða'mente/ *adv* uninterestedly, unconcernedly, indifferently
despegado /despe'gaðo/ *a Inf.* indifferent, unconcerned, cold
despegar /despe'gar/ *vt* to unstick; unglue; separate, detach; *—vr* become estranged; come apart or unstuck; *—vi Aer.* take off. **sin d. los labios,** without saying a word
despegue /des'pege/ *m, Aer.* take-off
despeinar /despei'nar/ *vt* to disarrange the hair; undo the coiffure
despejado /despe'haðo/ *a* lively, sprightly; logical, clear-cut; cloudless; spacious, unobstructed, clear
despejar /despe'har/ *vt* to clear, free of obstacles; **d. el camino de,** to clear the way for; *Fig.* elucidate, solve; *Math.* find the value of; *—vr* smarten up, grow gay; amuse oneself; clear up (weather, sky, etc.); improve (a patient)
despejo /des'peho/ *m,* freeing of obstacles; smartness, gaiety; grace, elegance; perkiness; clear-sightedness, intelligence
despellejar /despe'ʎehar; despe'yehar/ *vt* to flay, skin; slander
despeluzar /despelu'θar; despelu'sar/ *vt* to disorder the hair; cause the hair to stand on end; horrify; *—vr* stand on end (hair); be horrified or terrified
despeluznante /despeluθ'nante; despelus'nante/ *a* hair-raising, terrifying
despendedor /despende'ðor/ **(-ra)** *n* spendthrift, waster
despender /despen'der/ *vt* to spend; waste
despensa /des'pensa/ *f,* larder, pantry; store (of food); *Naut.* steward's room; stewardship
despensero /despen'sero/ **(-ra)** *n* steward; caterer; victualler; *Naut.* steward
despeñadero /despeɲa'ðero/ *m,* precipice, crag; dangerous undertaking, risk *—a* steep, precipitous
despeñar /despe'ɲar/ *vt* to precipitate, fling down from a height, hurl down; *—vr* fling oneself headlong; throw oneself into (vices, etc.)
despeño /des'peɲo/ *m,* precipitation; headlong fall; *Fig.* collapse, ruin
despepitar /despepi'tar/ *vt* to remove seeds or pips; *—vr* vociferate; act wildly; *Inf.* desire, long (for)
desperdiciador /desperði'θiaðor; desperði'siaðor/ **(-ra)** *a* squandering, wasting *—n* squanderer
desperdiciar /desperði'θiar; desperði'siar/ *vt* to squander; *Fig.* misspend, waste
desperdicio /desper'ðiθio; desper'ðisio/ *m,* waste; remains, leftovers (gen. *pl*)
desperdigar /desperði'gar/ *vt* to separate, sever; scatter
desperecerse /despere'θerse; despere'serse/ *vr irr* to crave, yearn (for). See **conocer**
desperezarse /despere'θarse; despere'sarse/ *vr* to stretch oneself
desperfecto /desper'fekto/ *m,* imperfection, flaw; slight deterioration
despernado /desper'naðo/ *a* weary, footsore
despertador /desperta'ðor/ **(-ra)** *a* awakening *—n* awakener. *m,* alarm clock; incentive, stimulus
despertar /desper'tar/ *vt irr* to awaken; bring to mind, recall; incite, stimulate; *—vi* waken; *Fig.* wake up, become more intelligent. See **acertar**
despiadado /despia'ðaðo/ *a* cruel, merciless
despicar /despi'kar/ *vt* to satisfy, content; *—vr* revenge oneself
despierto /des'pierto/ *a* wide-awake, clever
despilfarrado /despilfa'rraðo/ *a* ragged, shabby; wasteful; spendthrift
despilfarrar /despilfa'rrar/ *vt* to squander, waste
despilfarro /despil'farro/ *m,* slovenliness; waste, extravagance; mismanagement, maladministration
despintar /despin'tar/ *vt* to paint out; wash off the paint; efface, blot out; disfigure, deform; *—vi* be unlike or unworthy (of); *—vr* fade (colors); forget
despiojar /despio'har/ *vt* to remove lice, delouse; *Inf.* rescue from misery
despique /des'pike/ *m,* vengeance, revenge
despistar /despis'tar/ *vt* to throw off the scent; mislead
desplacer /despla'θer; despla'ser/ *vt irr* to displease. *m,* disgust, displeasure, sorrow. See **placer**
desplantar /desplan'tar/ **(se)** *vt* and *vr* to deviate from the vertical
desplazamiento /desplaθa'miento; desplasa'miento/ *m, Naut.* displacement
desplegadura /desplega'ðura/ *f,* unfolding
desplegar /desple'gar/ *vt irr* to unfold; spread open; *Fig.* reveal, disclose, explain; evince, display; *Mil.* deploy troops; *—vr* unfold, open (flowers, etc.); *Mil.* deploy. See **cegar**
despliegue /des'pliege/ *m,* unfolding; spreading out; evincing, demonstration; *Mil.* deployment
desplomar /desplo'mar/ *vt* to put out of the straight, cause to lean (walls, buildings); *—vr* lean, tilt (buildings); topple, fall down (walls, etc.); collapse (people); be ruined
desplome /des'plome/ *m,* collapse
desplomo /des'plomo/ *m,* tilt, cant, deviation from vertical
desplumar /desplu'mar/ *vt* to remove feathers, pluck; rob, despoil
despoblación /despoβla'θion; despoβla'sion/ *f,* depopulation. **d. forestal,** deforestation

despoblado /despo'βlaðo/ *m,* wilderness; deserted place
despoblar /despo'βlar/ *vt* to depopulate; despoil, rob; —*vr* become depopulated
despojador /despoha'ðor/ **(-ra)** *a* robbing, despoiling —*n* despoiler
despojar /despo'har/ *vt* to plunder, despoil; dispossess; —*vr* (*with de*) remove (garments, etc.); relinquish, give up
despojo /des'poho/ *m,* pillaging, spoliation; booty, plunder; butcher's offal; *pl* remains, leavings; debris, rubble; corpse
despolvorear /despolβore'ar/ *vt* to remove dust; *Fig.* shake off
desposado /despo'saðo/ *a* recently married; fettered, handcuffed. **los desposados,** the newlyweds
desposar /despo'sar/ *vt* to perform the marriage ceremony; —*vr* become betrothed; marry
desposeer /despose'er/ *vt* to dispossess; —*vr* renounce one's possessions. See **creer**
desposeimiento /desposei'miento/ *m,* dispossession
desposorio /despo'sorio/ *m,* betrothal, promise of marriage; (gen. *pl*) wedding, marriage
déspota /'despota/ *m,* despot, tyrant
despótico /des'potiko/ *a* tyrannical
despotismo /despo'tismo/ *m,* despotism
despotricarse /despotri'karse/ *vr* to rave (against), rail (against)
despreciable /despre'θiaβle; despre'siaβle/ *a* worthless, contemptible
despreciar /despre'θiar; despre'siar/ *vt* to scorn, despise; —*vr* despise oneself
despreciativo /despreθia'tiβo; despresia'tiβo/ *a* contemptuous, scornful
desprecio /des'preθio; des'presio/ *m,* contempt, scorn
desprender /despren'der/ *vt* to loosen, remove, unfix; give off (gases, etc.); —*vr* work loose, give way; deduce, infer; give away, deprive oneself (of)
desprendido /despren'diðo/ *a* disinterested; generous
desprendimiento /desprendi'miento/ *m,* loosening; removal, separation; emission; indifference, lack of interest; generosity; impartiality
despreocupación /despreokupa'θion; despreokupa'sion/ *f,* fair mindedness, impartiality; lack of interest
despreocupado /despreoku'paðo/ *a* unprejudiced, broadminded; indifferent, uninterested
despreocuparse /despreoku'parse/ *vr* to shake off prejudice; (*with de*) pay no attention to; set aside
desprestigiar /despresti'hiar/ *vt* to discredit; —*vr* lose prestige; lose caste
desprestigio /despres'tihio/ *m,* loss of prestige, discredit
desprevenido /despreβe'niðo/ *a* unprepared, improvident
desproporción /despropor'θion; despropor'sion/ *f,* disproportion
desproporcionado /desproporθio'naðo; desproporsio'naðo/ *a* disproportionate; out of proportion
despropósito /despro'posito/ *m,* nonsense, absurdity
desproveer /desproβe'er/ *vt irr* to deprive of necessities. See **creer**
despueble /des'pueβle/ *m,* depopulation
después /des'pues/ *adv* afterwards, after, next (of time and place) (e.g. *Vendrá d. de Pascua,* He will come after Easter. *Zaragoza viene d. de Madrid,* Saragossa comes after Madrid)
despuntar /despun'tar/ *vt* to blunt the point; *Naut.* double, sail round; —*vi* show green, sprout; appear (the dawn); grow clever; *Fig.* stand out, excel
desquiciamiento /deskiθia'miento; deskisia'miento/ *m,* unhinging; disconnecting; *Fig.* upsetting, throwing out of gear; downfall, fall from favor
desquiciar /deski'θiar; deski'siar/ *vt* to unhinge; disconnect; *Fig.* throw out of gear, upset; banish from favor; —*vr* become unhinged; *Fig.* be disordered; upset
desquitar /deski'tar/ **(se)** *vt* and *vr* to retrieve a loss; take revenge, retaliate
desquite /des'kite/ *m,* compensation; revenge
destacamento /destaka'mento/ *m, Mil.* detachment
destacar /desta'kar/ *vt Mil.* to detach; —*vr* excel; be prominent; be conspicuous; *Art.* stand out
destajador /destaha'ðor/ *m,* smith's hammer
destajar /desta'har/ *vt* to cut (cards); set forth conditions, stipulate, contract
destajista /desta'hista/ *mf* pieceworker; jobber (worker)
destajo /des'taho/ *m,* piecework; job. **a d.,** quickly and diligently. *Inf.* **hablar a d.,** to chatter, talk too much
destapar /desta'par/ *vt* to remove the cover or lid; reveal, uncover; —*vr* be uncovered; reveal oneself. **no destaparse,** to keep quiet, be mum
destartalado /destarta'laðo/ *a* tumble-down, rickety; poverty-stricken
destechado /deste'tʃaðo/ *a* roofless
destejar /deste'har/ *vt* to remove tiles or slates; leave unprotected
destejer /deste'her/ *vt* to unweave, unravel; *Fig.* undo, spoil
destello /des'teʎo; deste'yo/ *m,* gleam, sparkle, brilliance; flash, beam, ray; *Fig.* gleam (of talent)
destemplado /destem'plaðo/ *a* out of tune; inharmonious; intemperate; *Art.* inharmonious; *Inf.* out of sorts, indisposed
destemplanza /destem'planθa; destem'plansa/ *f,* inclemency, rigor (weather); intemperance, excess, abuse; *Inf.* indisposition; lack of moderation (actions, speech)
destemplar /destem'plar/ *vt* to disturb, upset, alter; *Mus.* put out of tune; put to confusion; —*vr* be unwell; *Fig.* go too far, behave badly; lose temper (metals)
destemple /des'temple/ *m, Mus.* being out of tune; *Med.* indisposition; uncertainty (weather); lack of temper (metals); disturbance, disorder; intemperance, excess, confusion
desternillarse de risa /desterni'ʎarse de 'rrisa; desterni'yarse de 'rrisa/ to shake with laughter
desterrado /deste'rraðo/ **(-da)** *a* exiled —*n* exile
desterrar /deste'rrar/ *vt irr* to exile; shake off the soil; *Fig.* discard, lay aside; extirpate (an error). See **recomendar**
destetar /deste'tar/ *vt* to wean
destete /des'tete/ *m,* weaning
destiempo, a /des'tiempo, a/ *adv* untimely, inopportunely
destierro /des'tierro/ *m,* banishment, exile; place of exile; remote place
destilación /destila'θion; destila'sion/ *f,* distillation
destilador /destila'ðor/ **(-ra)** *n* distiller. *m,* still
destilar /desti'lar/ *vt* to distill; filter; —*vi* to drip
destilatorio /destila'torio/ *a* distilling. *m,* distillery; still
destilería /destile'ria/ *f,* distillery
destinación /destina'θion; destina'sion/ *f,* destination
destinar /desti'nar/ *vt* to destine; appoint; assign
destino /des'tino/ *m,* fate, destiny; post, appointment; destination. **con d. a,** going to, bound for
destitución /destitu'θion; destitu'sion/ *f,* destitution; discharge, dismissal
destituir /destitu'ir/ *vt irr* (*with de*) to dismiss or discharge from (employment); deprive of. See **huir**
destorcer /destor'θer; destor'ser/ *vt irr* to untwist; straighten out; —*vr Naut.* drift. See **torcer**
destornillado /destorni'ʎaðo; destorni'yaðo/ *a* reckless; *Fig. Inf.* with a screw loose
destornillador /destorni'ʎaðor; destorni'yaðor/ *m,* screwdriver
destornillamiento /destorniʎa'miento; destorniya'miento/ *m,* unscrewing
destornillar /destorni'ʎar; destorni'yar/ *vt* to unscrew; —*vr* act rashly
destrenzar /destren'θar; destren'sar/ *vt* to unplait. **destrenzarse las cintas,** to unlace one's shoes
destreza /des'treθa; des'tresa/ *f,* dexterity; agility
destrón /des'tron/ *m,* blind person's guide
destronamiento /destrona'miento/ *m,* dethronement
destronar /destro'nar/ *vt* to dethrone, depose; oust

destroncamiento /destronka'miento/ *m*, detruncation
destroncar /destron'kar/ *vt* to lop, detruncate (trees); dislocate, disjoint; mutilate; *Fig.* ruin, seriously harm; tire out; —*vr* be exhausted or tired
destrozar /destro'θar; destro'sar/ *vt* to destroy; break in pieces, shatter; *Mil.* wipe out, annihilate; squander, dissipate
destrozo /des'troθo; des'troso/ *m*, destruction, ruin; shattering; *Mil.* rout; dissipation, waste
destrozón /destro'θon; destro'son/ *a* hard on wearing apparel, shoes, etc.
destrucción /destruk'θion; destruk'sion/ *f*, destruction; ruin, irreparable loss
destructible /destruk'tiβle/ *a* destructible
destructivo /destruk'tiβo/ *a* destructive
destructor /destruk'tor/ **(-ra)** *a* destructive —*n* destroyer. *m*, *Nav.* destroyer
destruible /destruiβle/ *a* destructible
des'truir /destruir/ *vt irr* to destroy, ruin, annihilate; frustrate, blast, disappoint; deprive of means of subsistence; squander, waste; —*vr Math.* cancel. See **huir**
desuello /desue'ʎo; desue'yo/ *m*, flaying, skinning; forwardness, impertinence; extortion, fleecing. *Fig. Inf.* **¡Es un d.!** It's highway robbery!
desu'nión /desu'nion/ *f*, disunion, separation; *Fig.* discord, disharmony
desunir /desu'nir/ *vt* to disunite, separate; *Fig.* cause discord or disharmony
desusarse /desu'sarse/ *vr* to fall into disuse, become obsolete
desuso /de'suso/ *m*, disuse
desvaído /desβa'iðo/ *a* gaunt, lanky; pale, faded, dull (of colors)
desvainar /desβai'nar/ *vt* to shell (peas, beans)
desvalido /des'βaliðo/ *a* unprotected, helpless
desvalijar /desβali'har/ *vt* to rifle (a suitcase, etc.); swindle
desvalimiento /desβali'miento/ *m*, defenselessness, lack of protection; lack of favor; desertion, abandonment
desvalorización /desβaloriθa'θion; desβalorisa'sion/ *f*, devaluation
desván /des'βan/ *m*, garret
desvanecer /desβane'θer; desβane'ser/ *vt irr* to cause to disappear; disintegrate; make vain; remove; —*vr* evaporate; faint, swoon; grow vain or conceited. See **conocer**
desvanecimiento /desβaneθi'miento; desβanesimiento/ *m*, faintness, loss of consciousness; vanity, conceit
desvarar /desβa'rar/ *vt* to slip, slide; *Naut.* refloat
desvariar /desβa'riar/ *vi* to be delirious; rave, talk wildly
desvarío /desβa'rio/ *m*, foolish action, absurdity; delirium; monstrosity; whim, caprice
desvedar /desβe'ðar/ *vt* to raise a ban or prohibition
desvelar /desβe'lar/ *vt* to keep awake; —*vr* be sleepless; (*with por*) take great care over
desvelo /des'βelo/ *m*, sleeplessness, vigil; care, attention, vigilance; anxiety. **con d.,** watchfully
desvencijar /desβenθi'har; desβensi'har/ *vt* to loosen, disconnect, disjoint; —*vr* work loose, become disjointed
desventaja /desβen'taha/ *f*, disadvantage. **estar en d.,** to be at a disadvantage
desventajoso /desβenta'hoso/ *a* disadvantageous
desventura /desβen'tura/ *f*, misfortune
desventurado /desβentu'raðo/ *a* unfortunate; timid, faint-hearted; miserly
desvergonzado /desβergon'θaðo; desβergonsaðo/ *a* shameless, brazen, impudent
desvergonzarse /desβergon'θarse; desβergon'sarse/ *vr irr* to be brazen, be impudent. See **avergonzar**
desvergüenza /desβer'guenθa; desβer'guensa/ *f*, insolence; shamelessness
desvestir /desβes'tir/ **(se)** *vt* and *vr irr* to undress. See **pedir**
desviación /desβia'θion; desβia'sion/ *f*, deviation, deflection
desviadero /desβia'ðero/ *m*, diversion; *Rail.* siding
desviar /des'βiar/ *vt* to divert, deflect; dissuade
desvío /des'βio/ *m*, deviation; indifference, coldness; repugnance
desvirgar /desβir'gar/ *vt* to deflower
desvirtuar /desβir'tuar/ *vt* to decrease in strength or merit
desvivirse /desβi'βirse/ *vr* (*with por*) to adore, love dearly; yearn for, be dying to; do one's best to please, (e.g. *Juan se desvive por servirme*, John does his best to help me)
detallar /deta'ʎar; deta'yar/ *vt* to tell in detail; relate
detalle /de'taʎe; de'taye/ *m*, detailed account; detail, particular
detallismo /deta'ʎismo; deta'yismo/ *m*, meticulous attention to details
detective /de'tektiβe/ *mf* detective
detector /detek'tor/ *m*, detector; *Radio.* catwhisker
detención /deten'θion; deten'sion/ *f*, stop, halt; delay; prolixity; arrest, detention. **con d.,** carefully, meticulously
detener /dete'ner/ *vt irr* to detain, stop; arrest; retain, keep; —*vr* go slowly; tarry; halt, stop; (*with en*) pause over, stop at. See **tener**
detenido /dete'niðo/ *a* timid, irresolute; miserable, mean
deterioración /deteriora'θion; deteriora'sion/ *f*, deterioration
deteriorar /deterio'rar/ **(se)** *vt* and *vr* to deteriorate
determinación /determina'θion; determina'sion/ *f*, determination; daring; decision
determinado /determi'naðo/ *a* resolute, determined
determinar /determi'nar/ *vt* to determine, limit; discern, distinguish; specify, appoint; decide, resolve; *Law.* define, judge; —*vr* make up one's mind
determinativo /determina'tiβo/ *a* determining
determinismo /determi'nismo/ *m*, determinism
determinista /determi'nista/ *mf* determinist —*a* deterministic
detersorio /deter'sorio/ *a* and *m*, detergent
detestable /detes'taβle/ *a* detestable
detestación /detesta'θion; detesta'sion/ *f*, detestation
detestar /detes'tar/ *vt* to abominate, detest
detonación /detona'θion; detona'sion/ *f*, detonation
detonador /detona'ðor/ *m*, detonator
detonar /deto'nar/ *vi* to detonate
detracción /detrak'θion; detrak'sion/ *f*, detraction
detractor /detrak'tor/ **(-ra)** *a* slandering *n* detractor, slanderer
detraer /detra'er/ *vt irr* to detract, take away; separate; slander. See **traer**
detrás /de'tras/ *adv* behind, after (place). **por d.,** in the rear; *Fig.* behind one's back
detrimento /detri'mento/ *m*, detriment; moral harm. **en d. de,** to the detriment of
deuda /'deuða/ *f*, debt; fault, offense; sin. **d. exterior,** foreign debt. **estar en d. con,** to be indebted to. **Perdónanos nuestras deudas,** Forgive us our trespasses
deudo /'deuðo/ *m*, relative, kinsman; kinship, relationship
deudor /deu'ðor/ **(-ra)** *a* indebted —*n* debtor. **d. hipotecario,** mortgagor
devanadera /deβana'ðera/ *f*, bobbin, reel, spool; winder (machine)
devanador /deβana'ðor/ **(-ra)** *n* winder (person). *m*, spool, bobbin
devanar /deβa'nar/ *vt* to reel, wind. *Inf.* **devanarse los sesos,** to rack one's brains
devanear /deβane'ar/ *vi* to rave, talk nonsense
devaneo /deβa'neo/ *m*, delirium; foolishness, nonsense; dissipation; love affair
devastación /deβasta'θion; deβasta'sion/ *f*, devastation
devastar /deβas'tar/ *vt* to devastate, lay waste; *Fig.* destroy, ruin
develador /deβela'ðor/ *m*, betrayer
devengar /deβeŋ'gar/ *vt* to have a right to, earn (salary, interest, etc.)
devoción /deβo'θion; deβo'sion/ *f*, piety; affection, love; pious custom; prayer

devocionario /deβoθio'nario; deβosio'nario/ *m*, prayer book
devolución /deβolu'θion; deβolu'sion/ *f*, restitution, return; its devolution
devolutivo /deβolu'tiβo/ *a Law*. returnable
devolver /deβol'βer/ *vt irr* to restore to original state; return, give back; repay. See **resolver**
devorador /deβora'ðor/ **(-ra)** *a* devouring *—n* devourer
devorar /deβo'rar/ *vt* to devour; destroy, consume
devoto /de'βoto/ **(-ta)** *a* devout, pious; devoted, fond *—n* devotee. *m*, object of devotion
día /dia/ *m*, day; daylight; *pl* name or saint's day; birthday (e.g. *Hoy son los días de María*, This is Mary's saint's day (or birthday)). **d. de Año Nuevo,** New Year's Day. **d. de asueto,** day off. **d. de ayuno** or **de vigilia,** fast day. **d. del cura,** *humorous* wedding day. **d. del juicio,** Day of Judgment. **d. de los difuntos,** All Souls' Day. **d. de recibo,** at home day. **d. de Reyes,** Epiphany (when Spanish children receive their Christmas presents). **d. de trabajo** or **d. laborable,** working day. **d. por medio,** every other day. **días caniculares,** dog days. **d. por d.,** day by day. **al d.,** up to date; per day. **al otro d.,** next day. **¡Buenos días!** Good morning! Good day! **de d.,** by day. **de d. en d.,** from day to day. **de un d. a otro,** any time now, very soon. **el d. de mañana,** tomorrow, the near future. **un d. sí y otro no,** every other day. **vivir al d.,** to live up to one's income
diabético /dia'βetiko/ *a* diabetic
diablillo /dia'βliʎo; dia'βliyo/ *m, dim* devilkin, imp; *Inf.* madcap
diablo /'diaβlo/ *m*, devil; Satan; *Fig.* fiend. *Inf.* **d. cojuelo,** mischievous devil; *Fig. Inf.* imp. *Inf.* **Anda el d. suelto,** The Devil's abroad, there's trouble. *Inf.* **tener el d. en el cuerpo,** to be as clever as the Devil; be mischievous
diablura /dia'βlura/ *f*, mischief, prank; devilry
diabólico /dia'βoliko/ *a* diabolical, devilish; *Inf.* fiendish, iniquitous
diaconisa /dia'konisa/ *f*, deaconess
diácono /'diakono/ *m*, deacon
diadema /dia'ðema/ *f*, diadem; crown; tiara
diafanidad /diafani'ðað/ *f*, transparency
diáfano /'diafano/ *a* transparent, diaphanous
diafragma /dia'fragma/ *m*, *Anat. Mech.* diaphragm; sound-box (of a phonograph)
diagnosticar /diagnosti'kar/ *vt Med.* to diagnose
diagnóstico /diag'nostiko/ *a* diagnostic. *m*, diagnosis. **d. precoz,** early diagnosis
diagonal /diago'nal/ *a* diagonal; oblique
diagrama /dia'grama/ *m*, diagram
diagramación /diagrama'θion; diagrama'sion/ *f*, layout (of a publication)
dialectal /dialek'tal/ *a* dialect
dialéctica /dia'lektika/ *f*, dialectic
dialéctico /dia'lektiko/ *a* dialectic. *m*, logician
dialecto /dia'lekto/ *m*, dialect
dialogar /dialo'gar/ *vi* to hold dialogue, converse; *—vt* write dialogue
diálogo /'dialogo/ *m*, dialogue
diamante /dia'mante/ *m*, diamond; miner's lamp; glass-cutting diamond. **d. bruto,** rough diamond
diamantífero /diaman'tifero/ *a* diamond-bearing
diamantino /diaman'tino/ *a* diamantine; *Poet.* adamant
diamantista /diaman'tista/ *mf* diamond-cutter; diamond merchant
diametral /diame'tral/ *a* diametrical
diámetro /'diametro/ *m*, diameter
diana /'diana/ *f*, *Mil.* reveille; bull's-eye (of a target); the moon
¡diantre! /'diantre/ *interj Inf.* the deuce!
diapasón /diapa'son/ *m*, *Mus.* tuning fork; diapason; neck (of violins, etc.). **d. normal,** tuning fork. **d. vocal,** pitch-pipe
diapositiva /diaposi'tiβa/ *f*, *Photo.* diapositive; (lantern) slide
diario /'diario/ *a* daily. *m*, diary; daily paper; daily expenses. **d. de navegación,** ship's log. **d. de viaje,** travel diary, trip journal
diarista /dia'rista/ *mf* journalist, diarist
diarrea /dia'rrea/ *f*, diarrhea
diatónico /dia'toniko/ *a Mus.* diatonic
diatriba /dia'triβa/ *f*, diatribe
diávolo /'diaβolo/ *m*, diabolo (game)
dibujante /diβu'hante/ *m*, sketcher; draftsman; designer
dibujar /diβu'har/ *vt Art.* to draw; describe, depict; *—vr* appear, be revealed; be outlined, stand out
dibujo /di'βuho/ *m*, drawing; sketch, design, pattern; depiction, description. **d. a la pluma,** pen-and-ink drawing. **d. a pulso,** freehand drawing. **d. del natural,** drawing from life
dicción /dik'θion; dik'sion/ *f*, word; diction, language, style
diccionario /dikθio'nario; diksio'nario/ *m*, dictionary
díceres /'diθeres; 'diseres/ *m pl West. Hem.* news
dicha /'ditʃa/ *f*, happiness; good fortune. **por d.,** by chance; fortunately
dicharacho /ditʃa'ratʃo/ *m*, *Inf.* vulgar expression, slangy expression
dicho /'ditʃo/ *m*, saying, phrase, expression; witty remark; *Law.* declaration; *Inf.* insult *—a* said, aforementioned *—past part* **decir,** "said." **D. y hecho,** No sooner said than done. **Del d. al hecho hay muy gran trecho,** There's many a slip 'twixt the cup and the lip. **Lo d. d.,** The agreement stands
dichoso /di'tʃoso/ *a* happy; lucky; *Inf.* blessed, wretched, darn
diciembre /di'θiembre; di'siembre/ *m*, December
dictado /dik'taðo/ *m*, title of honor; dictation; *pl* promptings (of heart, etc.). **escribir al d.,** to write to dictation
dictador /dikta'ðor/ *m*, dictator
dictadura /dikta'ðura/ *f*, dictatorship
dictáfono /dik'tafono/ *m*, dictaphone
dictamen /dik'tamen/ *m*, judgment, opinion
dictaminar /diktami'nar/ *vi* to give judgment or opinion
dictar /dik'tar/ *vt* to dictate; suggest, inspire. **dictar fallo,** to hand down a decision, render judgment
dictatorial, dictatorio /diktato'rial, dikta'torio/ *a* dictatorial
dicterio /dik'terio/ *m*, taunt, insult
didáctica /di'ðaktika/ *f*, didactics
didáctico /di'ðaktiko/ *a* didactic
diecinueve /dieθi'nueβe; diesi'nueβe/ *a* and *m*, nineteen
diecinueveavo /dieθinueβe'aβo; diesinueβe'aβo/ *a* and *m*, nineteenth
dieciochavo /dieθio'tʃaβo; diesio'tʃaβo/ *a* and *m*, eighteenth
dieciocheno /dieθio'tʃeno; diesio'tʃeno/ *a* See **décimoctavo**
dieciocho /die'θiotʃo; die'siotʃo/ *a* and *m*, eighteen
dieciséis /dieθi'seis; diesi'seis/ *a* and *m*, sixteen
dieciseisavo /dieθisei'saβo; diesisei'saβo/ *a* and *m*, sixteenth
dieciseiseno /dieθisei'seno; diesisei'seno/ *a* See **décimosexto**
diecisiete /dieθi'siete; diesi'siete/ *a* and *m*, seventeen
diecisieteavo /dieθisiete'aβo; diesisiete'aβo/ *a* and *m*, seventeenth
diente /diente/ *m*, tooth; tooth (of saw, etc.); tusk; cog (of wheel); prong (of fork); tongue (of a buckle). **d. de leche,** milk-tooth. *Bot.* **d. de león,** dandelion. **d. de perro,** *Sew.* feather-stitch. *Inf.* **dar d. con d.,** to chatter (teeth). *Fig. Inf.* **enseñar** (*or* **mostrar**) **los dientes,** to show one's teeth; threaten. *Inf.* **estar a d.,** to be famished. **hablar entre dientes,** to mutter; fume, grumble. *Inf.* **tener buen d.,** to have a good appetite. **traer a uno entre dientes,** to loathe someone; speak scandal of
Diepa /'diepa/ Dieppe
diestra /'diestra/ *f*, right hand; protection
diestro /'diestro/ *a* right (hand); skillful, dextrous; shrewd; astute, cunning; favorable, happy. *m*, expert fencer; bullfighter; halter; bridle
dieta /'dieta/ *f*, *Med.* diet; *Inf.* fast, abstinence; legislative assembly; travel allowance (gen. *pl*); day's journey of ten leagues; daily fee (gen. *pl*)
dietario /die'tario/ *m*, household accounts' book

dietética /die'tetika/ *f*, dietetics
dietético /die'tetiko/ *a* dietetic
dietista /die'tista/ *mf* dietician
diez /dieθ; dies/ *a* ten; tenth. *m*, ten; decade of rosary
diezmar /dieθ'mar; dies'mar/ *vt* to tithe; decimate; punish every tenth person
diezmero /dieθ'mero; dies'mero/ **(-ra)** *n* tax-gatherer
diezmesino /dieθme'sino; diesme'sino/ *a* ten months old
diezmilésimo /dieθmi'lesimo; diesmi'lesimo/ *a* ten-thousandth
diezmo /'dieθmo; 'diesmo/ *m*, ten per cent tax; tithe
difamación /difama'θion; difama'sion/ *f*, defamation, libel
difamador /difama'ðor/ **(-ra)** *a* libeling —*n* libeler
difamar /difa'mar/ *vt* to libel; denigrate
difamatorio /difama'torio/ *a* libelous, defamatory
diferencia /dife'renθia; dife'rensia/ *f*, unlikeness, dissimilarity; *Math.* difference; dissension, disagreement. **a d. de,** unlike; in contrast to
diferenciación /diferenθia'θion; diferensia'sion/ *f*, differentiation. **d. del trabajo,** division of labor
diferencial /diferen'θial; diferen'sial/ *a* differential
diferenciar /diferen'θiar; diferen'siar/ *vt* to differentiate; change the function (of); —*vi* dissent, disagree; —*vr* be different, differ; distinguish oneself
diferente /dife'rente/ *a* different, various
diferir /dife'rir/ *vt irr* to delay, retard; postpone; suspend, interrupt; —*vi* be different. See **discernir**
difícil /di'fiθil; di'fisil/ *a* difficult
dificultad /difikul'tað/ *f*, difficulty; impediment, obstacle; objection
dificultar /difikul'tar/ *vt* to raise difficulties; put obstacles in the way; —*vi* think difficult (of achievements)
dificultoso /difikul'toso/ *a* difficult; *Inf.* ugly (face, figure, etc.)
difidencia /difi'ðenθia; difi'ðensia/ *f*, mistrust; lack of faith, doubt
difidente /difi'ðente/ *a* mistrustful
difracción /difrak'θion; difrak'sion/ *f*, diffraction
difractar /difrak'tar/ *vt* to diffract
difteria /dif'teria/ *f*, diphtheria
difundir /difun'dir/ *vt* to diffuse (fluids); spread, publish, divulge; *Radio.* broadcast
difunto /di'funto/ **(-ta)** *a* and *n* deceased. *m*, corpse
difusión /difu'sion/ *f*, diffusion; prolixity; *Radio.* broadcasting
difusivo /difu'siβo/ *a* diffusive
difuso /di'fuso/ *a* widespread, diffuse; prolix, wordy
digerible /dihe'riβle/ *a* digestible
digerir /dihe'rir/ *vt irr* to digest; bear patiently; consider carefully; *Chem.* digest. See **sentir**
digestible /dihes'tiβle/ *a* easily digested
digestivo /dihes'tiβo/ *a* digestive
digesto /di'hesto/ *m*, *Law.* digest
digitación /dihita'θion; dihita'sion/ *f*, *Mus.* fingering
digital /dihi'tal/ *a* digital. *f*, *Bot.* foxglove, digitalis
dígito /'dihito/ *a* digital. *m*, (*Astron. Math.*) digit
dignación /digna'θion; digna'sion/ *f*, condescension
dignarse /dig'narse/ *vr* to deign, condescend
dignatario /digna'tario/ *m*, dignitary
dignidad /digni'ðað/ *f*, dignity, stateliness; serenity, loftiness; high office or rank; high repute, honor; *Eccl.* dignitary
dignificar /dignifi'kar/ *vt* to dignify
digno /'digno/ *a* worthy, deserving; upright, honorable; fitting, suitable, appropriate
digresión /digre'sion/ *f*, digression
dije /'dihe/ *m*, charm; trinket, any small piece of jewelry; *Inf.* person of excellent qualities, jewel
dilacerar /dilaθe'rar; dilase'rar/ *vt* to lacerate, tear flesh; *Fig.* discredit
dilación /dila'θion; dila'sion/ *f*, delay
dilapidación /dilapiða'θion; dilapi'ðasion/ *f*, waste, dissipation, squandering
dilapidar /dilapi'ðar/ *vt* to waste, squander
dilatación /dilata'θion; dilata'sion/ *f*, expansion; enlargement, widening; prolongation; *Surg.* dilatation; respite (in trouble)
dilatador /dilata'ðor/ *a* dilating. *m*, *Surg.* dilater
dilatar /dila'tar/ *vt* to dilate, enlarge; expand; delay, postpone; spread, publish abroad; prolong; —*vr* expand; be prolix, spread oneself
dilatorio /dila'torio/ *a* procrastinating, dilatory
dilección /dilek'θion; dilek'sion/ *f*, affection, love
dilema /di'lema/ *m*, dilemma
diletantismo /diletan'tismo/ *m*, dilettantism
diligencia /dili'henθia; dili'hensia/ *f*, care, conscientiousness, industry; haste, briskness; diligence (coach); *Inf.* business, occupation. **hacer sus diligencias,** to try one's best
diligenciar /dilihen'θiar; dilihen'siar/ *vt* to set on foot, put into motion
diligente /dili'hente/ *a* diligent, conscientious, industrious; speedy, prompt
dilucidación /diluθiða'θion; dilusiða'sion/ *f*, elucidation, clarification
dilucidar /diluθi'ðar; dilusi'ðar/ *vt* to elucidate, clarify
dilución /dilu'θion; dilu'sion/ *f*, dilution
diluir /di'luir/ *vt irr* to dilute. See **huir**
diluviano /dilu'βiano/ *a* diluvian
diluviar /dilu'βiar/ *vi* to teem with rain
diluvio /di'luβio/ *m*, flood, inundation; *Inf.* very heavy rain, deluge; overabundance
dimanación /dimana'θion; dimana'sion/ *f*, emanation, source
dimanar /dima'nar/ *vi* (*with de*) to rise in (rivers); proceed from, originate in
dimensión /dimen'sion/ *f*, dimension; size, extent
dimes y diretes /'dimes i di'retes/ *m pl*, *Inf.* back-chat
diminutivo /diminu'tiβo/ *a* diminutive; diminishing; *Gram.* diminutive
diminuto /dimi'nuto/ *a* defective, incomplete; minute, very small
dimisión /dimi'sion/ *f*, resignation (of office, etc.)
dimisorias /dimi'sorias/ *f pl*, *Eccl.* letter dimissory. *Inf.* **dar d. a uno,** to give a person his marching orders, dismiss
dimitente /dimi'tente/ *a* resigning; retiring. *mf* resigner (of a post)
dimitir /dimi'tir/ *vt* to resign (office, post, etc.)
Dinamarca /dina'marka/ Denmark
dinamarqués /dinamar'kes/ **(-esa)** *a* Danish —*n* Dane
dinámica /di'namika/ *f*, dynamics
dinámico /di'namiko/ *a* dynamic
dinamita /dina'mita/ *f*, dynamite
dinamo /'dinamo/ *f*, dynamo
dinasta /di'nasta/ *mf* dynast
dinastía /dinas'tia/ *f*, dynasty
dinástico /di'nastiko/ *a* dynastic
dineral /dine'ral/ *m*, large amount of money, fortune
dinero /di'nero/ *m*, money; Peruvian coin; wealth, fortune; currency. **d. contante, d. junto,** ready cash, **Poderoso caballero es Don D.,** Money talks
dinosauro /dino'sauro/ *m*, dinosaur
dintel /'dintel/ *m*, lintel
diocesano /dioθe'sano; diose'sano/ *a* diocesan
diocesis /'dioθesis; 'diosesis/ *f*, diocese
Dios /dios/ *m*, God; deity. **¡D. le guarde!** God keep you! **¡D. lo quiera!** God grant it! **D. mediante,** God willing (D.V.). **¡D. mío!** Good gracious! **De menos nos hizo D.,** Nothing is impossible, Never say die. *Inf.* **haber** (*or* **armarse**) **la de D. es Cristo,** to be the deuce of a row. **¡No lo quiera D.!** God forbid! **¡Plegue a D.!** Please God! **¡Por D.!** For goodness sake! Heavens! **¡Válgame D.!** Bless me! **¡Vaya Vd. con D.!** Goodbye! Off with you! Depart! **¡Vive D.!** By God!
diosa /'diosa/ *f*, goddess
diploma /di'ploma/ *m*, license, bull; diploma. **d. de suficiencia,** general diploma
diplomacia /diplo'maθia; diplo'masia/ *f*, diplomacy; tactfulness; *Inf.* astuteness
diplomático /diplo'matiko/ *a* diplomatic; tactful; *Inf.* astute. *m*, diplomat. **cuerpo d.,** diplomatic corps
dipsomanía /dipsoma'nia/ *f*, dipsomania
dipsómano /dip'somano/ **(-na)** *n* dipsomaniac

diptongo /dip'toŋgo/ *m,* diphthong

diputación /diputa'θion; diputa'sion/ *f,* deputation; mission

diputado /dipu'taðo/ **(-da)** *n* deputy, delegate. **d. a Cortes,** member of the Spanish Parliament, congressman

diputar /dipu'tar/ *vt* to appoint, depute; delegate; empower

dique /'dike/ *m,* dike; dam; dry dock; *Fig.* bulwark, check; **d. flotante,** floating dock

dirección /direk'θion; direk'sion/ *f,* direction; management, control, guidance; directorate; instruction; information; order, wish, command; editorial board; directorship, managership; (postal) address; managerial office. **d. cablegráfica,** cable address. **d. particular,** home address

directiva /direk'tiβa/ *f,* board, governing body

directivo /direk'tiβo/ *a* directive, control, ling, guiding, managing

directo /di'rekto/ *a* direct; straight

director /direk'tor/ **(-ra)** *a* directing, controlling —*n* director; manager; principal, head (schools, etc.); editor. **d. del ceremonial,** chief of protocol. **d. de escena,** stagemanager. **d. espiritual,** *Eccl.* father confessor. **d. gerente,** managing director

directorio /direk'torio/ *a* directory, advising. *m,* directory; directorate, board of directors

dirigible /diri'hiβle/ *m,* airship

dirigir /diri'hir/ *vt* to direct; regulate; govern; supervise; guide; *Mus.* conduct; address (an envelope, etc.); keep (a shop, etc.); edit; put (a question); point (a gun); cast (a glance); —*vr* go; wend one's way. **d. la palabra** (**a),** to speak to, address. **d. la vista a,** to look towards, look in the direction of, turn towards, turn in the direction of. **dirigirse a,** to go towards; make one's way to

dirimir /diri'mir/ *vt* to annul, make void; break, dissolve; settle (disputes, etc.)

discernidor /disθerni'ðor; disserni'ðor/ **(-ra)** *n* discerner —*a* discerning

discernimiento /disθerni'miento; disserni'miento/ *m,* discernment; judgment; discrimination

discernir /disθer'nir; disser'nir/ *vt irr* to discern, distinguish —*Pres. Indic.* **discierno, disciernes, discierne, disciernen.** *Pres. Subjunc.* **discierna, disciernas, discierna, disciernan**

disciplina /disθi'plina; dissi'plina/ *f,* discipline; system, philosophy, education; submission, obedience; subject (arts or science); *pl* scourge

disciplinante /disθipli'nante; dissipli'nante/ *a* disciplinary. *m,* scourge

disciplinar /disθipli'nar; dissipli'nar/ *vt* to train; educate; scourge, beat; discipline; —*vr* scourge oneself

disciplinario /disθipli'nario; dissipli'nario/ *a* disciplinary

discipulado /disθipu'laðo; dissipu'laðo/ *m,* pupilship, studentship; education, teaching; discipleship; body of pupils (of a school, etc.)

discípulo /dis'θipulo; dis'sipulo/ **(-la)** *n* pupil, student; disciple, follower

disco /'disko/ *m,* discus; disk; phonograph record; *Astron.* disk. **d. compacto,** compact disc. **d. de señales,** railway signal. **d. giratorio,** turntable (of a phonograph)

discóbolo /dis'koβolo/ *m,* discus thrower

díscolo /'diskolo/ *a* willful, unmanageable

disconformidad /diskonformi'ðað/ *f,* disagreement; disconformity

discontinuo /diskon'tinuo/ *a* intermittent, discontinuous

discordancia /diskor'ðanθia; diskor'ðansia/ *f,* discord, disagreement

discordar /diskor'ðar/ *vi* to be discordant; disagree; *Mus.* be out of tune

discorde /dis'korðe/ *a* discordant; *Mus.* dissonant

discordia /dis'korðia/ *f,* discord, disagreement

discreción /diskre'θion; diskre'sion/ *f,* discretion; circumspection; prudence, good sense; shrewdness; pithy or clever saying. **a d.,** at discretion; at will; voluntarily. *Mil.* **darse** (*or* **entregarse) a d.,** to surrender unconditionally

discrecional /diskreθio'nal; diskresio'nal/ *a* optional, voluntary

discrepancia /diskre'panθia; diskre'pansia/ *f,* discrepancy; disagreement

discrepar /diskre'par/ *vi* to be discrepant; differ; disagree

discreto /dis'kreto/ *a* discreet; ingenious, witty

disculpa /dis'kulpa/ *f,* excuse

disculpabilidad /diskulpaβili'ðað/ *f,* pardonableness

disculpable /diskul'paβle/ *a* excusable

disculpar /diskul'par/ *vt* to excuse; forgive, pardon; —*vr* apologize; excuse oneself

discurrir /disku'rrir/ *vi* to wander, roam; flow, run (rivers, etc.); (*with en*) consider, think about; (*with sobre*) discourse on; —*vt* invent; conjecture

discursivo /diskur'siβo/ *a* discursive; thoughtful, reflective

discurso /dis'kurso/ *m,* reasoning power; oration, discourse; consideration, reflection; speech, conversation; dissertation. **d. aceptatorio,** acceptance speech

discusión /disku'sion/ *f,* discussion

discutible /disku'tiβle/ *a* debatable; disputable

discutir /disku'tir/ *vt* to discuss, debate, consider

disecar /dise'kar/ *vt Anat.* to dissect; stuff animals, mount plants

disección /disek'θion; disek'sion/ *f,* dissection

disector /disek'tor/ *m,* dissector, anatomist

diseminación /disemina'θion; disemina'sion/ *f,* dissemination

diseminar /disemi'nar/ *vt* to disseminate; spread

disensión /disen'sion/ *f,* dissension

disentería /disente'ria/ *f,* dysentery

disentimiento /disenti'miento/ *m,* dissent

disentir /disen'tir/ *vi irr* to dissent; disagree. See **sentir**

diseñador /diseɲa'ðor/ *m,* delineator, drawer

diseñar /dise'ɲar/ *vt* to outline, sketch

diseño /di'seɲo/ *m,* outline, sketch; plan; description

disertación /diserta'θion; diserta'sion/ *f,* dissertation

disertar /diser'tar/ *vi* (*with sobre*) to discourse on, discuss, treat of

diserto /di'serto/ *a* eloquent

disfavor /disfa'βor/ *m,* disfavor, discourtesy, slight

disforme /dis'forme/ *a* deformed; ugly; enormous

disfraz /dis'fraθ; dis'fras/ *m,* disguise; mask; fancy dress; pretense

disfrazar /disfra'θar; disfra'sar/ *vt* to disguise; dissemble, misrepresent; —*vr* disguise oneself; wear fancy dress

disfrutar /disfru'tar/ *vt* to enjoy (health, comfort, friendship, etc.); reap the benefit of; —*vi* take pleasure in, enjoy

disfrute /dis'frute/ *m,* enjoyment, use, benefit

disgregación /disgrega'θion; disgrega'sion/ *f,* separation, disjunction

disgregar /disgre'gar/ *vt* to separate, disjoin

disgustado /disgus'taðo/ *a* annoyed; discontented, dissatisfied; melancholy, depressed

disgustar /disgus'tar/ *vt* to displease, dissatisfy; annoy; *Fig.* depress; —*vr* quarrel, fall out. **Me disgusta la idea de marcharme,** I don't like the idea of going away

disgusto /dis'gusto/ *m,* displeasure, dissatisfaction; discontent; annoyance; affliction, sorrow, trouble; quarrel; boredom; repugnance

disidente /disi'ðente/ *a* dissenting. *mf* dissenter, nonconformist

disidir /disi'ðir/ *vi* to dissent

disímil /di'simil/ *a* dissimilar, different, unlike

disimulación /disimula'θion; disimula'sion/ *f,* dissimulation, pretense

disimulado /disimu'laðo/ *a* feigned, pretended

disimular /disimu'lar/ *vt* to dissemble; pretend, feign; put up with, tolerate; misrepresent, misinterpret

disimulo /di'simulo/ *m,* pretense, dissimulation; tolerance, patience

disipación /disipa'θion; disipa'sion/ *f,* dispersion; dissipation, frivolity; immorality

disipado /disi'paðo/ *a* spendthrift; dissipated, frivolous

disipar /disi'par/ *vt* to disperse; squander; *—vr* evaporate; vanish, fade, disappear
dislate /di'slate/ *m*, absurdity, nonsense
dislocación /disloka'θion; disloka'sion/ *f*, dislocation
dislocar /dislo'kar/ *vt* to dislocate; *—vr* dislocate; sprain
disminución /disminu'θion; disminu'sion/ *f*, diminution. **ir (una cosa) en d.,** to diminish, decrease; taper, grow to a point
disminuido físico /dismi'nuiðo 'fisiko/ *m*, physically impaired person, physically handicapped person
disminuir /dismi'nuir/ *vt* and *vi irr* to diminish, decrease. See **huir**
disociación /disoθia'θion; disosia'sion/ *f*, dissociation. **d. nuclear,** nuclear fission
disociar /diso'θiar; diso'siar/ *vt* to dissociate, separate; *Chem.* dissociate
disoluble /diso'luβle/ *a* disoluble
disolución /disolu'θion; disolu'sion/ *f*, dissolution; immorality, laxity; disintegration; loosening, relaxation
disolutivo /disolu'tiβo/ *a* dissolvent, solvent
disoluto /diso'luto/ *a* dissolute, vicious
disolvente /disol'βente/ *m*, dissolvent, solvent
disolver /disol'βer/ *vt irr* to loosen, undo; *Chem.* dissolve; separate, disintegrate; annul. See **resolver**
disonancia /diso'nanθia; diso'nansia/ *f*, dissonance; disagreement; *Mus.* dissonant
disonante /diso'nante/ *a* dissonant; discordant, inharmonious
disonar /diso'nar/ *vi irr* to be inharmonious; disagree. See **sonar**
dísono /di'sono/ *a* dissonant
dispar /dis'par/ *a* unequal; unlike, different
disparadero /dispara'ðero/ *m*, trigger of a firearm
disparador /dispara'ðor/ *m*, shooter, firer; trigger (of firearms); ratchet (of watch)
disparar /dispa'rar/ *vt* to shoot, fire; throw or discharge with violence; *—vr* run precipitately; rush (towards); bolt (horses); race (of a machine); explode, go off; *Inf.* go too far, misbehave
disparatado /dispara'taðo/ *a* foolish; absurd, unreasonable
disparatar /dispara'tar/ *vi* to act or speak foolishly
disparate /dispa'rate/ *m*, foolishness, nonsense
disparidad /dispari'ðað/ *f*, disparity, dissimilarity
disparo /dis'paro/ *m*, shooting; explosion; racing (of an engine); discharge; foolishness
dispendio /dis'pendio/ *m*, squandering, extravagance
dispendioso /dispen'dioso/ *a* costly, expensive
dispensa /dis'pensa/ *f*, dispensation; privilege
dispensable /dispen'saβle/ *a* dispensable; excusable
dispensación /dispensa'θion; dispensa'sion/ *f*, dispensation; exemption
dispensar /dispen'sar/ *vt* to grant, concede, distribute; exempt; excuse, forgive
dispensario /dispen'sario/ *m*, dispensary
dispepsia /dis'pepsia/ *f*, dyspepsia
dispéptico /dis'peptiko/ **(-ca)** *a* and *n* dyspeptic
dispersar /disper'sar/ *vt* to disperse, scatter, separate; *Mil.* rout
dispersión /disper'sion/ *f*, dispersion
disperso /dis'perso/ *a* dispersed, scattered; *Mil.* separated from regiment
displicencia /displi'θenθia; displi'sensia/ *f*, disagreeableness, coldness; hesitation, lack of enthusiasm
displicente /displi'θente; displi'sente/ *a* unpleasant, disagreeable; difficult, peevish
disponer /dispo'ner/ *vt irr* to arrange, dispose; direct, order; decide; prepare, get ready; *—vi* (*with de*) dispose of, make free with; possess; have at one's disposal; *—vr* prepare oneself to die; make one's will; get ready. See **poner**
disponible /dispo'niβle/ *a* disposable; available
disposición /disposi'θion; disposi'sion/ *f*, arrangement; order, instruction; decision; preparation; aptitude, talent; disposal; condition of health; temperament; grace of bearing; promptitude, competence; measure, step, preliminary; *Archit.* plan; proviso, stipulation; symmetry. **A la d. de Vd,** I (we, he, it, etc.) am at your disposal. **hallarse en d. de hacer una cosa,** to be ready to do something. **última d.,** last will and testament
dispositivo /disposi'tiβo/ *a* directory, advisory
dispuesto /dis'puesto/ *a* ready, prepared; handsome, gallant; clever, wide-awake. **bien d.,** well-disposed; well, healthy. **mal d.,** ill-disposed; disinclined; out of sorts, indisposed
disputa /dis'puta/ *f*, dispute. **sin d.,** undoubtedly
disputar /dispu'tar/ *vt* to argue, debate; dispute, question; *Fig.* fight for
disquisición /diskisi'θion; diskisi'sion/ *f*, disquisition
distancia /dis'tanθia; dis'tansia/ *f*, distance; interval of time; difference, dissimilarity; unfriendliness, coolness
distanciar /distan'θiar; distan'siar/ *vt* to separate, place farther apart
distante /dis'tante/ *a* separated; distant; far off
distar /dis'tar/ *vi* to be distant (time and place); be different, unlike
distender /disten'der/ **(se)** *vt* and *vr Med.* to distend, swell
distinción /distin'θion; distin'sion/ *f*, distinction, differentiation; difference, individuality; privilege, honor; clarity, order; distinction (of bearing or mind). **a d. de,** unlike, different from
distinguible /distiŋ'guiβle/ *a* distinguishable
distinguido /distiŋ'guiðo/ *a* distinguished, illustrious
distinguir /distiŋ'guir/ *vt* to distinguish, discern; differentiate; characterize; esteem, honor, respect; discriminate; see with difficulty; make out; *—vr* be different; excel, distinguish oneself
distintivo /distin'tiβo/ *a* distinguishing; distinctive. *m*, distinguishing mark
distinto /dis'tinto/ *a* different; distinct; clear
distracción /distrak'θion; distrak'sion/ *f*, distraction; abstraction, heedlessness, absentmindedness; pleasure, amusement; licentiousness
distraer /distra'er/ *vt irr* to lead astray; distract (attention); influence for bad; amuse *—vr* be absentminded; amuse oneself. See **traer**
distraído /distra'iðo/ *a* abstracted, absentminded; inattentive; licentious
distribución /distriβu'θion; distriβu'sion/ *f*, distribution; (gen. *pl*) share
distribuidor /distriβui'ðor/ **(-ra)** *a* distributing *—n* distributor
distribuir /distri'βuir/ *vt irr* to distribute; share out, divide. See **huir**
distributivo /distriβu'tiβo/ *a* distributive
distrito /dis'trito/ *m*, district
disturbio /dis'turβio/ *m*, disturbance
disuadir /disua'ðir/ *vt* to dissuade
disuasión /disua'sion/ *f*, dissuasion
disuasivo /disua'siβo/ *a* dissuasive
disyunción /disyun'θion; disyun'sion/ *f*, disjunction
ditirambo /diti'rambo/ *m*, dithyramb; excessive praise
diurético /diu'retiko/ *a* diuretic
diurno /'diurno/ *a* diurnal
diva /'diβa/ *f*, prima donna; woman singer
divagación /diβaga'θion; diβaga'sion/ *f*, wandering, roaming; digression
divagar /diβa'gar/ *vi* to wander, roam; digress
diván /di'βan/ *m*, divan (Turkish supreme council); divan, sofa; collection of Arabic, Persian or Turkish poems
divergencia /diβer'henθia; diβer'hensia/ *f*, divergence; disagreement
divergente /diβer'hente/ *a* divergent; conflicting, dissentient
divergir /diβer'hir/ *vi* to diverge; dissent
diversidad /diβersi'ðað/ *f*, diversity, unlikeness, difference; variety
diversificar /diβersifi'kar/ *vt* to differentiate; vary
diversión /diβer'sion/ *f*, pastime, amusement; *Mil.* diversion
diverso /di'βerso/ *a* diverse, unlike; *pl* various, many
divertido /diβer'tiðo/ *a* amusing, funny, entertaining
divertir /diβer'tir/ *vt irr* to lead astray, turn aside; entertain; *Mil.* create a diversion *—vr* amuse oneself. See **sentir**

dividendo /diβi'ðendo/ *m,* dividend. *Com.* **d. activo,** dividend
dividir /diβi'ðir/ *vt* to divide; distribute; stir up discord; *—vr* (*with de*) part company with, leave
divieso /di'βieso/ *m, Med.* boil
divinamente /diβina'mente/ *adv* divinely; excellently, admirably, perfectly
divinidad /diβini'ðað/ *f,* divinity, Godhead; person or thing of great beauty
divinizar /diβini'θar; diβini'sar/ *vt* to deify; sanctify; extol
divino /di'βino/ *a* divine; excellent, admirable, superb
divisa /di'βisa/ *f,* badge, emblem; *Herald.* motto
divisar /diβi'sar/ *vt* to glimpse, descry
divisibilidad /diβisiβili'ðað/ *f,* divisibility
divisible /diβi'siβle/ *a* divisible
división /diβi'sion/ *f,* division, partition; discord; (*Math. Mil.*) division; hyphen; apportionment; district, ward
divisor /diβi'sor/ **(-ra)** *a* dividing, separating. *m, Math.* divisor *—n* divider, separator
divisoria /diβi'soria/ *f,* dividing line
divisorio /diβi'sorio/ *a* dividing
divorciar /diβor'θiar; diβor'siar/ *vt* to divorce; separate; *—vr* be divorced, be separated
divorcio /di'βorθio; di'βorsio/ *m,* divorce
divulgación /diβulga'θion; diβulga'sion/ *f,* spreading, publication, propagation
divulgar /diβul'gar/ **(se)** *vt* and *vr* to spread abroad, publish
do /do/ *m, Mus.* doh, C. *Poet.* where
dobladillo /doβla'ðiʎo; doβla'ðiyo/ *m, Sew.* hem; turn-up (of a trouser)
doblado /do'βlaðo/ *a* stocky, thickset, sturdy; rocky, rough, uneven; dissembling. *m,* garret
dobladura /doβla'ðura/ *f,* fold, crease; crease mark
doblamiento /doβla'miento/ *m,* doubling; folding
doblar /do'βlar/ *vt* to double, multiply by two; fold, double; bend; persuade, induce; *Naut.* double, sail round; turn, walk round; *—vi Eccl.* ring the passing bell; *Theat.* double a role; *—vr* fold, double; bend; bow; stoop; allow oneself to be persuaded
doble /'doβle/ *a* double, twofold; duplicate; insincere, false; thick (cloth); *Bot.* double (flowers); hardy, robust. *m,* fold, crease; *Eccl.* passing-bell; Spanish dance step *—adv* double, twice. *Eccl.* **rito d.,** full rites
doblegar /doβle'gar/ *vt* to fold; bend; brandish; dissuade in favor of another proposition; *—vr* submit, give way, acquiesce
doblete /doβ'lete/ *a* of medium thickness. *m,* imitation jewel
doblez /do'βleθ; doβles/ *m,* fold, crease; fold mark. *mf,* double dealing, treachery
doblilla /do'βliʎa; do'βliya/ *f,* twenty-real coin
doblón /do'βlon/ *m,* doubloon
doce /'doθe; 'dose/ *a* twelve. *m,* twelve; twelfth (of the month). **las d.,** twelve o'clock
docena /do'θena; do'sena/ *f,* dozen. **la d. del fraile,** baker's dozen
docente /do'θente; do'sente/ *a* teaching
dócil /'doθil; 'dosil/ *a* docile; obedient; flexible, easily worked (metals, etc.)
docilidad /doθili'ðað; dosili'ðað/ *f,* docility; obedience; flexibility
docto /'dokto/ *a* learned, erudite
doctor /dok'tor/ **(-ra)** *n* doctor; physician; teacher. *f, Inf.* blue-stocking
doctorado /dokto'raðo/ *m,* doctorate
doctorarse /dokto'rarse/ *vr* to get one's doctorate
doctrina /dok'trina/ *f,* doctrine; instruction, teaching; theory, conception; *Eccl.* sermon
doctrinar /doktri'nar/ *vt* to teach, instruct
documentación /dokumenta'θion; dokumenta'sion/ *f,* documentation; collection of documents, papers
documental /dokumen'tal/ *a* documental. *m,* documentary film
documentar /dokumen'tar/ *vt* to document
Dodecaneso, el /doðeka'neso, el/ the Dodecanese
dogal /do'gal/ *m,* halter; noose; slipknot. *Fig.* **estar con el d. a la garganta,** to be in a fix
dogma /'dogma/ *m,* dogma
dogmático /dog'matiko/ *a* dogmatic
dogmatizar /dogmati'θar; dogmati'sar/ *vt* to teach heretical doctrines; dogmatize
dólar /'dolar/ *m,* dollar
dolencia /do'lenθia; do'lensia/ *f,* ailment; pain; ache
doler /do'ler/ *vi irr* to be in pain; be reluctant; *—vr* be sorry, regretful; grieve; sympathize, be compassionate; complain *—Pres. Indic.* **duelo, dueles, duele, duelen.** *Pres. Subjunc.* **duela, duelas, duela, duelan**
doliente /do'liente/ *a* suffering; ill; afflicted, sad. *mf* sufferer, ill person. *m,* chief mourner
dolo /'dolo/ *m,* fraud; deception; deceit; *Law.* premeditation
dolor /do'lor/ *m,* pain, ache; mental suffering. **d. sordo,** dull pain
dolorido /dolo'riðo/ *a* painful; afflicted, sad
doloroso /dolo'roso/ *a* sad, regrettable; mournful, sorrowful; pitiful; painful
doloso /do'loso/ *a* deceitful, fraudulent
domable /do'maβle/ *a* tamable; controllable
domador /doma'ðor/ **(-ra)** *n* subduer, controller; wild animal tamer; horsebreaker
domadura /doma'ðura/ *f,* taming, breaking in; controlling (emotions)
domar /do'mar/ *vt* to tame, break in; control, repress (emotions)
domesticable /domesti'kaβle/ *a* tamable; domesticable
domesticar /domesti'kar/ *vt* to tame; domesticate; *—vr* grow tame; become domesticated
domesticidad /domestiθi'ðað; domestisi'ðað/ *f,* domesticity
doméstico /do'mestiko/ **(-ca)** *a* domestic, domesticated; tame *—n* domestic worker
domiciliar /domiθi'liar; domisi'liar/ *vt* to domicile; *—vr* become domiciled, settle down
domiciliario /domiθi'liario; domisi'liario/ *a* domiciliary
domicilio /domi'θilio; domi'silio/ *m,* domicile; house
dominación /domina'θion; domina'sion/ *f,* domination; power, authority; command (of a military position, etc.); *Mil.* high ground; *pl* dominions, angels
dominador /domina'ðor/ *a* dominating; overbearing
dominante /domi'nante/ *a* dominating; overbearing, domineering; dominant. *f, Mus.* dominant
dominar /domi'nar/ *vt* to dominate; repress, subdue; *Fig.* master (branch of knowledge); *—vi* stand out; *—vr* control oneself
dómine /'domine/ *m, Inf.* teacher; pedant, know-all
domingo /do'miŋgo/ *m,* Sunday. **d. de Cuasimodo,** Low Sunday. **d. de Pentecostés,** Whitsuntide Sunday. **d. de Ramos,** Palm Sunday. **d. de Resurrección,** Easter Sunday
dominguero /domiŋ'guero/ *a Inf.* Sunday; special, excursion (trains)
dominicano /domini'kano/ **(-na)** *a* and *n* Dominican; native of Santo Domingo
dominio /'dominio/ *m,* authority, power; rule, sovereignty; dominion (country); domain
dominó /domi'no/ *m,* domino; game of dominoes
don /don/ *m,* gift; quality, characteristic; talent. **d. de gentes,** the human touch; charm
don /don/ *m,* title of respect equivalent to English Mr. or Esquire. Used only before given name and *not* before a family name, e.g. *don Juan Martínez, or don Juan*
donación /dona'θion; dona'sion/ *f,* donation, gift, grant
donador /dona'ðor/ **(-ra)** *a* donating *—n* donor
donaire /do'naire/ *m,* discretion, wit; witticism; gracefulness, elegance
donar /do'nar/ *vt* to bestow, give; transfer; grant
donatario /dona'tario/ *m,* recipient, grantee
donativo /dona'tiβo/ *m,* gift, present, donation
doncel /don'θel; don'sel/ *m,* squire, youth not yet armed; knight; male virgin; king's page

doncella /don'θeʎa; don'seya/ *f,* virgin, maid; maidservant; lady's maid
doncellez /donθe'ʎeθ; donse'yes/ *f,* virginity; maidenhood
donde /'donde/ *adv* where, wherein. Sometimes used as relative pronoun "in which" (e.g. *La casa d. estaba,* The house in which I was) *—interr* **¿dónde? ¿A dónde va Vd.?** Where are you going to? **¿De dónde viene Vd.?** Where do you come from? **¿Por dónde se va a Madrid?** Which is the way to Madrid?
dondequiera /donde'kiera/ *adv* wherever, anywhere, everywhere
donoso /do'noso/ *a* witty; graceful
donostiarra /donos'tiarra/ *a* and *mf* of or from San Sebastian (N. Spain)
donosura /dono'sura/ *f,* wit; grace; dash, verve
doña /'doɲa/ *f,* feminine equivalent of **don** (e.g. *D. Catalina Palacios*)
dorado /do'raðo/ *a* golden, gilded; fortunate, happy. *m,* gilding
dorador /dora'ðor/ *m,* gilder
doradura /dora'ðura/ *f,* gilding
dorar /do'rar/ *vt* to gild; make golden; *Fig.* gild the pill; *Cul.* toast lightly; *—vr* become golden
dórico /'doriko/ *a* Doric
dormidero /dormi'ðero/ *a* soporiferous, narcotic
dormilón /dormi'lon/ **(-ona)** *a Inf.* sleepy *—n* sleepyhead
dormir /dor'mir/ *vi irr* to sleep; spend the night; *Fig.* grow calm; sleep (tops); (*with sobre*) sleep on, consider; *—vt* put to sleep; *—vr* go to sleep; go slow over, neglect; be dormant; go numb (limbs). **d. como un lirón,** to sleep like a top. *Inf.* **d. la mona,** to sleep oneself sober. **entre duerme y vela,** half-awake *—Pres. Indic.* **duermo, duermes, duerme, duermen.** *Pres. Part.* **durmiendo.** *Preterite* **durmió, durmieron.** *Pres. Subjunc.* **duerma, duermas, duerma, duerman**
dormitar /dormi'tar/ *vi* to doze
dormitivo /dormi'tiβo/ *a* and *m,* sedative
dormitorio /dormi'torio/ *m,* dormitory; bedroom
dorsal /dor'sal/ *a* dorsal
dorso /'dorso/ *m,* back; dorsum
dos /dos/ *a* two. *m,* two; second (of the month). **las d.,** two o'clock. **d. a d.,** two against two. **de d. en d.,** two by two. *Inf.* **en un d. por tres,** in a twinkling
doscientos /dos'θientos; dos'sientos/ *a* and *m,* two hundred; two hundredth
dosel /do'sel/ *m,* canopy; dais
dosis /'dosis/ *f,* dose; quantity
dotación /dota'θion; dota'sion/ *f,* endowment; *Naut.* crew; staff, workers; equipment
dotar /do'tar/ *vt* to give as dowry; endow, found; *Fig.* endow (with talents, etc.); equip; apportion (salary)
dote /'dote/ *mf,* dowry. *f,* (gen. *pl*) gifts, talents. **dotes de mando,** capacity for leadership
dracma /'drakma/ *f,* drachma; dram
draga /'draga/ *f,* dredger
dragado /dra'gaðo/ *m,* dredging
dragaminas /draga'minas/ *m, Nav.* minesweeper
dragar /dra'gar/ *vt* to dredge
dragón /dra'gon/ *m,* dragon; *Bot.* snapdragon; *Mil.* dragoon; *Zool.* dragon, giant lizard; *Astron.* Draco
dragona /dra'gona/ *f,* female dragon; *Mil.* shoulder-strap
drama /'drama/ *m,* play; drama. **d. lírico,** opera
dramática /dra'matika/ *f,* dramatic art
dramático /dra'matiko/ *a* dramatic; vivid, unexpected, moving
dramaturgo /drama'turgo/ *m,* dramatist, playwright
drenaje /dre'nahe/ *m,* drainage (of land and wounds)
Dresde /'dresðe/ Dresden
dril /dril/ *m,* drill, cotton cloth
droga /'droga/ *f,* drug; falsehood, deception; nuisance
droguería /droge'ria/ *f,* chemist's shop; drug trade
droguero /dro'gero/ **(-ra)** *n* chemist, druggist
dromedario /drome'ðario/ *m, Zool.* dromedary
druida /'druiða/ *m,* Druid
dualidad /duali'ðað/ *f,* duality
ducado /du'kaðo/ *m,* dukedom; duchy; ducat
ducentésimo /duθen'tesimo; dusen'tesimo/ *a* two hundredth
ducha /'dutʃa/ *f,* shower-bath; douche; stripe in cloth; furrow
ducho /'dutʃo/ *a* experienced, skillful
dúctil /'duktil/ *a* ductile (metals); adaptable, docile, flexible
ductilidad /duktili'ðað/ *f,* ductility; adaptability
duda /'duða/ *f,* doubt, hesitation; problem. **sin d.,** doubtless
dudable /du'ðaβle/ *a* doubtful
dudar /du'ðar/ *vi* to be in doubt; *—vt* doubt, disbelieve
dudoso /du'ðoso/ *a* doubtful; uncertain, not probable
duela /'duela/ *f,* hoop, stave
duelista /due'lista/ *mf* dueler; duelist
duelo /'duelo/ *m,* sorrow, grief; mourning; mourners; duel; (gen. *pl*) troubles, trials. **duelos y quebrantos,** *Cul.* fried offal. **sin d.,** in abundance
duende /'duende/ *m,* imp, elf, sprite, ghost
dueña /'dueɲa/ *f,* owner, proprietress, mistress; duenna; married lady *Obs.*
dueño /'dueɲo/ *m,* owner, proprietor; master (of servants). **d. de sí mismo,** self-controlled
Duero, el /'duero, el/ the Douro
duetista /due'tista/ *mf* duetist
dula /'dula/ *f,* common pasture ground or herds
dulce /'dulθe; dulse/ *a* sweet; fresh, pure; fresh, not salty; fragrant; melodious; pleasant, agreeable; tender, gentle; soft (metals). *m,* sweetmeat, bonbon. **d. de almíbar,** preserved fruit.
dulcedumbre /dulθe'ðumbre; dulse'ðumbre/ *f,* sweetness; softness
dulcémele /dulθe'mele; dulse'mele/ *m,* dulcimer
dulcera /dul'θera; dul'sera/ *f,* preserve dish, fruit dish
dulcería /dulθe'ria; dulse'ria/ *f,* See **confitería**
dulcificar /dulθifi'kar; dulsifi'kar/ *vt* to make sweet; alleviate, sweeten
dulcinea /dul'θinea; dul'sinea/ *f, Inf.* sweetheart; ideal
dulzaina /dul'θaina; dul'saina/ *f, Mus.* flageolet
dulzura /dul'θura; dul'sura/ *f,* sweetness; gentleness; pleasure; meekness; agreeableness
duna /'duna/ *f,* (gen. *pl*) sand dune
Dunas, las /'dunas, las/ the Downs
Dunquerque /dun'kerke/ Dunkirk
dúo /'duo/ *m, Mus.* duet
duodécimo /duo'ðeθimo; duoðesimo/ *a* twelfth
duodeno /duo'ðeno/ *a* twelfth. *m, Anat.* duodenum
duplicación /duplika'θion; duplika'sion/ *f,* duplication
duplicado /dupli'kaðo/ *m,* duplicate
duplicar /dupli'kar/ *vt* to duplicate; double
duplicidad /dupliθi'ðað; duplisi'ðað/ *f,* duplicity, falseness
duplo /'duplo/ *a* double
duque /'duke/ *m,* duke
duquesa /du'kesa/ *f,* duchess
duración /dura'θion; dura'sion/ *f,* duration; durability
duradero /dura'ðero/ *a* lasting; durable
durante /du'rante/ *adv* during
durar /du'rar/ *vi* to continue; endure, last
dureza /du'reθa; du'resa/ *f,* hardness; *Med.* callosity, severity, harshness
durmiente /dur'miente/ *a* sleeping. *mf* sleeper; *m, Archit.* dormant
duro /'duro/ *a* hard; firm, unyielding; vigorous, robust; severe, inclement; exacting, cruel; *Mus.* metallic, harsh; *Art.* crude, too sharply defined; miserly, avaricious; obstinate; self-opinionated; unbearable, intolerable; merciless, hard; harsh (style). *m,* Spanish coin worth five pesetas
dux /duks/ *m,* doge

E

e /e/ *f,* letter E —*conjunc* used instead of *y* (and) before words beginning with *i* or *hi,* provided this last is not followed by a diphthong (e.g. *e invierno, e hijos, but y hierro*)
¡ea! /'ea/ *interj* Well!; Come on!; Let's see! (often used with **pues**)
ebanista /eβa'nista/ *mf* cabinetmaker
ebanistería /eβaniste'ria/ *f,* cabinetmaker's shop; cabinetmaking or work
ébano /'eβano/ *m,* ebony
ebonita /eβo'nita/ *f,* ebonite, vulcanite
ebrio /'eβrio/ *a* intoxicated, inebriated
ebullición /eβuʎi'θion; eβuyi'sion/ *f,* boiling, ebullition
ebúrneo /e'βurneo/ *a* eburnine, ivory-like
echada /e'tʃaða/ *f,* throw, cast; pitch; fling; length of a man
echador /etʃa'ðor/ **(-ra)** *n* thrower. *m, Inf.* chucker-out
echadura /etʃa'ðura/ *f,* sitting on eggs to hatch them; (gen. *pl*) gleanings
echamiento /etʃa'miento/ *m,* throw, fling; throwing, casting; expulsion; rejection
echar /e'tʃar/ *vt* to throw, fling; eject, drive away; cast out, expel; put forth, sprout; emit, give forth; cut (teeth); dismiss, discharge; couple (animals); pour (liquids); place, apply; put into, fill; turn (keys, locks); impute; attribute; impose (penalty, taxes, etc.); play (game); try one's luck; distribute; publish, make known; perform (plays); (*with por*) go in direction of; (*with prep a + infin.*) begin to (**e. a andar,** to begin to walk); —*vr* throw oneself down, lie down; sit on eggs (birds); abate, calm (wind); apply oneself, concentrate on; rush (towards), fling oneself (upon). **e. abajo,** to overthrow; demolish. **e. aceite al fuego,** to add fuel to the flames. **e. a perder,** to spoil, deteriorate. *Naut.* **e. a pique,** to sink. **e. a vuelo,** to ring (bells). **e. carnes,** to put on weight, grow fat. **e. cuentas,** to reckon up. **e. de menos,** to miss; mourn absence of. **e. de ver,** to notice. *Fig.* **e. en cara,** to throw in one's face, reproach. **echarla de majo,** to play the gallant. **e. las cartas al correo,** to post the letters. **e. las cartas,** to tell fortunes. **e. el pie atrás,** *Fig.* to climb down; *Fig.* back out. **e. raíces,** to take root; **e. las bases de, e. los cimientos de,** to lay the foundation of, lay the foundation for. *Fig.* become established. **e. rayos por la boca,** to fly into a rage. **e. suertes,** to draw lots. **echarlo todo a rodar,** to spoil everything. **e. una mano,** to lend a hand
echazón /etʃa'θon; etʃa'son/ *f,* throw, cast; jetsam
eclecticismo /eklekti'θismo; eklekti'sismo/ *m,* eclecticism
ecléctico /e'klektiko/ **(-ca)** *a* and *n* eclectic
eclesiástico /ekle'siastiko/ *a* ecclesiastical. *m,* ecclesiastic, clergyman; Ecclesiasticus
eclipsar /eklip'sar/ *vt Astron.* to eclipse; surpass, outvie; —*vr Astron.* be in eclipse; disappear
eclipse /e'klipse/ *m, Astron.* eclipse; retirement, withdrawal
écloga /'ekloga/ *f,* eclogue
eco /'eko/ *m,* echo; verse-echo; muffled sound; slavish imitation or imitator
economato /ekono'mato/ *m,* trusteeship; cooperative store
econometría /ekonome'tria/ *f,* econometrics
economía /ekono'mia/ *f,* economy, thrift; structure, organization; poverty, shortage; saving (of time, labor, etc.); *pl* savings. **e. dirigida,** planned economy. **e. doméstica,** domestic economy. **e. política,** political economy
económico /eko'nomiko/ *a* economic; thrifty; avaricious; cheap
economista /ekono'mista/ *mf* economist
economizar /ekonomi'θar; ekonomi'sar/ *vt* to economize; save
ecónomo /e'konomo/ *m,* trustee, guardian
ecuación /ekua'θion; ekua'sion/ *f,* (*Math.* and *Astron.*) equation. **e. personal,** personal equation
ecuador /ekua'ðor/ *m,* equator
ecuánime /ekua'nime/ *a* calm, unruffled; impartial
ecuanimidad /ekuanimi'ðað/ *f,* calmness, serenity; impartiality
ecuatorial /ekuato'rial/ *a* equatorial
ecuatoriano /ekuato'riano/ **(-na)** *a* and *n* Ecuadorian
ecuestre /e'kuestre/ *a* equestrian
ecuménico /eku'meniko/ *a* ecumenical
eczema /'ekθema; 'eksema/ *m,* eczema
edad /e'ðað/ *f,* age; epoch; period. **e. de piedra,** Stone Age. **e. media,** Middle Ages. **de cierta e.,** middle-aged. **ser mayor de e.,** to have attained one's majority. **ser menor de e.,** to be a minor
edecán /eðe'kan/ *m,* aide-de-camp
edema /e'ðema/ *m,* edema
Edén /e'ðen/ *m,* Eden; *Fig.* paradise
edición /eði'θion; eði'sion/ *f,* edition. **e. diamante,** miniature edition. **e. príncipe,** first edition
edicto /e'ðikto/ *m,* edict, decree; public notice
edificación /eðifika'θion; eðifika'sion/ *f,* building, construction; edification
edificador /eðifika'ðor/ **(-ra)** *a* uplifting, edifying; building —*n* builder
edificante /eðifi'kante/ *a* building, constructing; edifying
edificar /eðifi'kar/ *vt* to build, construct; edify
edificio /eði'fiθio; eði'fisio/ *m,* building, structure, fabric
Edimburgo /eðim'burgo/ Edinburgh
editar /eði'tar/ *vt* (of a publisher) to publish; edit
editor /eði'tor/ **(-ra)** *n* publisher; editor
editorial /eðito'rial/ *a* publishing; editorial. *m,* editorial, leading article
edredón /eðre'ðon/ *m,* down of an eiderduck; eiderdown, quilt
eduardiano /eðuar'ðiano/ **(-na)** *a* and *n* Edwardian
educable /eðu'kaβle/ *a* educable
educación /eðuka'θion; eðuka'sion/ *f,* upbringing; education; good breeding, good manners
educado /eðu'kaðo/ *a* educated. **ser mal e.,** to be badly brought up; be ill-mannered
educador /eðuka'ðor/ **(-ra)** *a* educating —*n* educator
educando /eðu'kando/ **(-da)** *n* pupil
educar /eðu'kar/ *vt* to educate; bring up, train, teach, develop
educativo /eðuka'tiβo/ *a* educational, educative
educción /eðuk'θion; eðuk'sion/ *f,* eduction; inference, deduction
educir /eðu'θir; eðu'sir/ *vt irr* to educe; infer, deduce. See **conducir**
efe /'efe/ *f,* name of letter F
efectismo /efek'tismo/ *m,* sensationalism; striving after effect
efectista /efek'tista/ *a* (*Art. Lit.*) striking, sensational
efectivo /efek'tiβo/ *a* effective; real. *m,* cash. **hacer e.,** to put into effect
efecto /e'fekto/ *m,* effect, result; purpose, intent; impression; *pl* assets; goods, chattels. **efectos de escritorio,** stationery. **efectos públicos,** public securities. **en e.,** in fact, actually. **llevar a e.,** to put into effect; make effective
efectuación /efektua'θion; efektua'sion/ *f,* accomplishment, execution
efectuar /efek'tuar/ *vt* to accomplish, effect; make (a payment); —*vr* be effected; happen, take place
eferente /efe'rente/ *a* efferent
efervescencia /eferβes'θenθia; eferβes'sensia/ *f,* effervescence; excitement, enthusiasm
efervescente /eferβes'θente; eferβes'sente/ *a* effervescent
Éfeso /e'feso/ Ephesus
eficacia /efi'kaθia; efi'kasia/ *f,* efficacy; effectiveness
eficaz /efi'kaθ; efi'kas/ *a* efficacious; effective
eficiencia /efi'θienθia; efi'siensia/ *f,* efficiency

eficiente /efi'θiente; efi'siente/ *a* efficient, effective
efigie /e'fihie/ *f*, effigy; image, representation, symbol
efímero /e'fimero/ *a* ephemeral; brief
eflorescencia /eflores'θenθia; eflores'sensia/ *f*, *Chem*. efflorescence
efluvio /e'fluβio/ *m*, effluvium; exhalation
efugio /e'fuhio/ *m*, subterfuge, evasion
efusión /efu'sion/ *f*, effusion; *Fig*. spate (of words, etc.)
efusivo /efu'siβo/ *a* effusive, expansive
Egeo, Mar /e'heo, mar/ Aegean Sea
égida /'ehiða/ *f*, shield; egis, protection
egipcíaco /ehip'θiako; ehip'siako/ **(-ca), egipcio (-ia)** *a* and *n* Egyptian
Egipto /e'hipto/ Egypt
egiptólogo /ehip'tologo/ **(-ga)** *n* Egyptologist
égloga /'egloga/ *f*, eclogue
egoísmo /ego'ismo/ *m*, egoism
egoísta /ego'ista/ *a* egoistic. *mf* egoist
egolatría /egola'tria/ *f*, self-love
egotismo /ego'tismo/ *m*, egotism
egotista /ego'tista/ *a* egotistical. *mf* egotist
egregio /e'grehio/ *a* distinguished, celebrated
egresado /egre'saðo/ *m*, graduate (of a certain school)
eje /'ehe/ *m*, axis; axle-tree; shaft; pivot, fundamental idea. **e. trasero,** rear-axle
ejecución /eheku'θion; eheku'sion/ *f*, accomplishment, performance; execution, technique; death penalty
ejecutable /eheku'taβle/ *a* feasible, practicable
ejecutante /eheku'tante/ *mf Mus*. executant, performer
ejecutar /eheku'tar/ *vt* to discharge, perform; put to death; (*Art. Mus*.) execute; serve (a warrant, etc.); *Law*. seize (property)
ejecutivo /eheku''tiβo/ *a* executive; urgent
ejecutor /eheku'tor/ *m*, executor
ejecutoria /eheku'toria/ *f*, letters patent of nobility; *Law*. judgment, sentence
ejecutoría /ehekuto'ria/ *f*, executorship
ejemplar /ehem'plar/ *a* exemplary. *m*, copy, specimen; precedent; example; warning
ejemplificar /ehemplifi'kar/ *vi* to exemplify
ejemplo /e'hemplo/ *m*, example, precedent; illustration, instance; specimen. **dar e.,** to set an example. **por e.,** for example
ejercer /eher'θer; eher'ser/ *vt* to practice (a profession); perform, fulfill; exercise, use
ejercicio /eher'θiθio; eher'sisio/ *m*, exercise; practice; performance; exertion, effort; *Mil*. exercises (gen. *pl*). **ejercicios espirituales,** spiritual exercises. **ejercicios físicos,** physical training
ejercitar /eherθi'tar; ehersi'tar/ *vt* to exercise; train, teach; *—vr* exercise; practice
ejército /e'herθito; e'hersito/ *m*, army
el /el/ *def art m, sing* the
él /el/ *pers pron sing m*, he; it (*f*. **ella.** *neut* **ello**) (e.g. *Lo hizo él, He* did it). Also used with prep. (e.g. *Lo hicimos por él,* We did it for him)
elaboración /elaβora'θion; elaβora'sion/ *f*, elaboration, working out
elaborado /elaβo'raðo/ *a* elaborate
elaborar /elaβo'rar/ *vt* to elaborate; produce, work out
elasticidad /elastiθi'ðað; elastisi'ðað/ *f*, elasticity; adaptability
elástico /e'lastiko/ *a* elastic; adaptable. *m*, elastic tape; elastic material
ele /'ele/ *f*, name of letter L
elección /elek'θion; elek'sion/ *f*, choice; election; selection; discrimination
electivo /elek'tiβo/ *a* elective
electo /e'lekto/ *m*, elect, candidate elect
elector /elek'tor/ **(-ra)** *n* elector, voter. *m*, German prince *Obs*.
electorado /elekto'raðo/ *m*, electorate
electoral /elekto'ral/ *a* electoral
electricidad /elektriθi'ðað; elektrisi'ðað/ *f*, electricity
electricista /elektri'θista; elektri'sista/ *mf* electrician
eléctrico /e'lektriko/ *a* electric; electrical
electrificación /elektrifika'θion; elektrifika'sion/ *f*, electrification
electrificar /elektrifi'kar/ *vt* to electrify
electrizar /elektri'θar; elektri'sar/ *vt* to electrify; startle; *—vr* be electrified
electrocución /elektroku'θion; elektroku'sion/ *f*, electrocution
electrocutar /elektroku'tar/ *vt* to electrocute
electrodinámica /elektroði'namika/ *f*, electrodynamics
electrodo /elek'troðo/ *m*, electrode
electroimán /elektroi'man/ *m*, electromagnet
electrólisis /elek'trolisis/ *f*, electrolysis
electrólito /elek'trolito/ *m*, electrolyte
electrolizar /elektroli'θar; elektroli'sar/ *vt* to electrolyze
electromagnético /elektromag'netiko/ *a* electromagnetic
electromotriz /elektro'motriθ; elektro'motris/ *a* electromotive. **fuerza e.,** electromotive force
electrón /elek'tron/ *m*, electron
electroquímica /elektro'kimika/ *f*, electrochemistry
electroscopio /elektro'skopio/ *m*, electroscope
electrotecnia /elektro'teknia/ *f*, electrical engineering
electroterapia /elektrote'rapia/ *f*, *Med*. electrotherapy
elefante /ele'fante/ **(-ta)** *n* elephant
elefantíasis /elefan'tiasis/ *f*, elephantiasis
elefantino /elefan'tino/ *a* elephantine
elegancia /ele'ganθia; ele'gansia/ *f*, elegance, grace; fashionableness; *Lit*. beauty of style
elegante /ele'gante/ *a* elegant; graceful, lovely; fashionable, stylish
elegía /ele'hia/ *f*, elegy
elegíaco /ele'hiako/ *a* elegiac
elegibilidad /elehiβili'ðað/ *f*, eligibility
elegible /ele'hiβle/ *a* eligible
elegir /ele'hir/ *vt irr* to select, prefer; elect *—Pres. Indic*. **elijo, eliges, elige, eligen.** *Pres. Part*. **eligiendo.** *Preterite* **eligió, eligieron.** *Pres. Subj*. **elija,** etc.
elemental /elemen'tal/ *a* elemental; fundamental; elementary
elemento /ele'mento/ *m*, element; component, constituent; *Elec*. element; *pl* rudiments. *Mil*. **elementos de choque,** shock troops
elevación /eleβa'θion; eleβa'sion/ *f*, lifting, raising; height, high ground; elevation; altitude; *Fig*. eminence; elevation, advancement; ecstasy; raising (of the voice)
elevado /ele'βaðo/ *a* sublime, lofty
elevar /ele'βar/ *vt* to raise, lift; *Fig*. exalt; *—vr* be in ecstasy, be transported. **elevarse de categoría,** to rise in status
elfo /'elfo/ *m*, elf
elidir /eli'ðir/ *vt* (phonetics) to elide
eliminación /elimina'θion; elimina'sion/ *f*, elimination
eliminador /elimina'ðor/ *a* eliminatory. *m*, eliminator
eliminar /elimi'nar/ *vt* to eliminate
elipse /e'lipse/ *f*, ellipse
elipsis /e'lipsis/ *f*, ellipsis
elíptico /e'liptiko/ *a* elliptic
elíseo /e'liseo/ *m*, Elysium *—a* Elysian. **campos elíseos,** Elysian fields
ella /'eʎa; 'eya/ *pers pron 3rd sing f* she; it. See **él**
elle /'eʎe; 'eye/ *f*, name of letter LL
ello /'eʎo; 'eyo/ *pers pron 3rd sing neut* that, the fact, it. **Ello es que...,** The fact is that... **No tengo tiempo para ello,** I have no time for that
ellos, ellas /'eʎos, 'eʎas; 'eyos, 'eyas/ *pers pron 3rd pl m* and *f*, they. See **él**
elocución /eloku'θion; eloku'sion/ *f*, elocution; style of speech
elocuencia /elo'kuenθia; elo'kuensia/ *f*, eloquence
elocuente /elo'kuente/ *a* eloquent
elogiador /elohia'ðor/ **(-ra)** *a* eulogistic *—n* eulogist
elogiar /elo'hiar/ *vt* to eulogize, praise
elogio /e'lohio/ *m*, eulogy, praise. **«Elogio de la Locura»,** "In Praise of Folly"
elucidación /eluθiða'θion; elusiða'sion/ *f*, elucidation, explanation

elucidar /eluθi'ðar; elusi'ðar/ *vt* to elucidate, clarify
eludible /elu'ðiβle/ *a* escapable, avoidable
eludir /elu'ðir/ *vt* to elude, avoid
emaciación /emaθia'θion; emasia'sion/ *f,* emaciation
emanación /emana'θion; emana'sion/ *f,* emanation; effluvium
emanar /ema'nar/ *vi* to emanate (from), originate (in)
emancipación /emanθipa'θion; emansipa'sion/ *f,* emancipation; enfranchisement
emancipador /emanθipa'ðor; emansipa'ðor/ **(-ra)** *a* emancipatory *—n* emancipator
emancipar /emanθi'par; emansi'par/ *vt* to emancipate, free; enfranchise; *—vr* emancipate oneself; become independent; free oneself
emascular /emasku'lar/ *vt* to emasculate
embadurnar /embaður'nar/ *vt* to smear, smudge, daub
embajada /emba'haða/ *f,* embassy; ambassadorship; embassy building; *Inf.* message
embajador /embaha'ðor/ *m,* ambassador; emissary
embajadora /embaha'ðora/ *f,* wife of ambassador; woman ambassador
embalador /embala'ðor/ *m,* packer
embalaje /emba'lahe/ *m,* packing; bale; wrapper; packing charge
embalar /emba'lar/ *vt* to pack
embaldosado /embaldo'saðo/ *m,* tiled pavement or floor
embaldosar /embaldo'sar/ *vt* to tile, pave with tiles
embalsamador /embalsama'ðor/ *a* embalming. *m,* embalmer
embalsamar /embalsa'mar/ *vt* to embalm; perfume
embalse /em'balse/ *m,* dam; damming, impounding (of water)
embanastar /embanas'tar/ *vt* to place in a basket; crowd, squeeze
embarazada /embara'θaða; embara'saða/ *a f,* pregnant
embarazar /embara'θar; embara'sar/ *vt* to impede, hinder, embarrass; *—vr* be hindered or embarrassed; be pregnant
embarazo /emba'raθo; emba'raso/ *m,* difficulty, impediment; pregnancy; timidity, embarrassment
embarazoso /embara'θoso; embara'soso/ *a* embarrassing; inconvenient; difficult, troublesome
embarcación /embarka'θion; embarka'sion/ *f,* ship, vessel; embarkation
embarcadero /embarka'ðero/ *m,* wharf, dock; quay; pier; jetty
embarcador /embarka'ðor/ *m,* shipper
embarcar /embar'kar/ *vt* to embark, ship; board (boat, train, etc.); *—vr* embark; board
embarco /em'barko/ *m,* embarking, embarkation
embargar /embar'gar/ *vt* to obstruct, impede; *Law.* seize; suspend, paralyse
embargo /em'bargo/ *m, Law.* seizure; embargo. **sin e.,** nevertheless, however
embarque /em'barke/ *m,* loading, embarkation (goods)
embarrancar /embarran'kar/ *vi Naut.* to run aground; *—vr Naut.* be stuck on a reef or in the mud
embarrilar /embarri'lar/ *vt* to barrel
embarullar /embaru'ʎar; embaru'yar/ *vt Inf.* to mix up, muddle; do hastily and badly
embasamiento /embasa'miento/ *m, Archit.* foundation
embastar /embas'tar/ *vt Sew.* to baste; tack
embaste /em'baste/ *m, Sew.* basting; tacking stitch
embate /em'bate/ *m,* beating of the waves; sudden attack; unexpected misfortune
embaucamiento /embauka'miento/ *m,* trick, deception
embaucar /embau'kar/ *vt* to deceive, hoodwink
embaular /embau'lar/ *vt* to pack in a trunk; *Inf.* stuff with food
embazar /emba'θar; emba'sar/ *vt* to dye brown; hinder; amaze; *—vr* be amazed; be tired or bored; be satiated
embebecer /embeβe'θer; embeβe'ser/ *vt irr* to entertain, amuse; engross, fascinate; *—vr* be dumbfounded. See **conocer**
embebecimiento /embeβeθi'miento; embeβesi'miento/ *m,* astonishment; absorption, engrossment
embeber /embe'βer/ *vt* to absorb; contain; shrink, contract; saturate; insert, introduce; incorporate; *—vi* shrink; *—vr* be amazed; master or absorb (a subject). **embebido en sus pensamientos,** absorbed in thought
embelecar /embele'kar/ *vt* to dupe, deceive, trick
embeleco /embe'leko/ *m,* deception, fraud
embelesar /embele'sar/ *vt* to astonish; fascinate, enchant; *—vr* be astonished or fascinated
embeleso /embe'leso/ *m,* astonishment; fascination; charm
embellecer /embeʎe'θer; embeye'ser/ *vt irr* to embellish; *—vr* beautify oneself. See **conocer**
embellecimiento /embeʎeθi'miento; embeyesi'miento/ *m,* beautifying, embellishment
emberizo /embe'riθo; embe'riso/ *m, Ornith.* yellowhammer
embermejecer /embermehe'θer; embermehe'ser/ *vt irr* to dye red; shame, make blush; *—vi* turn red or reddish; *—vr* blush. See **conocer**
embestida /embes'tiða/ *f,* assault, attack, onrush, *Inf.* importunity
embestir /embes'tir/ *vt irr* to rush upon, assault; *Inf.* importune, be a nuisance to; *—vi Fig. Inf.* clash, be inharmonious. See **pedir**
emblema /em'blema/ *m,* emblem; symbol; badge
emblemático /emble'matiko/ *a* emblematic; symbolical
embobamiento /emboβa'miento/ *m,* stupefaction, amazement
embobar /embo'βar/ *vt* to entertain, fascinate; *—vr* be dumbfounded
embobecer /emboβe'θer; emboβe'ser/ *vt irr* to make stupid. See **conocer**
embobecimiento /emboβeθi'miento; emboβesi'miento/ *m,* stupefaction
embocadero /emboka'ðero/ *m,* narrow entrance, bottleneck; mouth of a channel
embocadura /emboka'ðura/ *f,* entrance by a narrow passage; *Mus.* mouthpiece; flavor (of wine); estuary, mouth of a river; *Theat.* proscenium
embocar /embo'kar/ *vt* to put in the mouth; go through a narrow passage; deceive; *Inf.* devour, wolf; initiate a business deal
embolia /em'bolia/ *f,* embolism
émbolo /'embolo/ *m, Mech.* piston, plunger
embolsar /embol'sar/ *vt* to place money in a purse; collect (a debt, etc.)
emborrachar /emborra'tʃar/ *vt* to intoxicate; daze, stupefy; *—vr* become intoxicated; run (of dyes)
emborrascarse /emborras'karse/ *vr* to be furious; become stormy (weather); *Fig.* go downhill (business concern)
emborronar /emborro'nar/ *vt* to blot; scribble, write hastily
emboscada /embos'kaða/ *f,* ambuscade, ambush; intrigue, spying
emboscar /embos'kar/ *vt Mil.* to set an ambush; *—vr* lie in ambush
embosquecer /emboske'θer; emboske'ser/ *vi irr* to become wooded. See **conocer**
embotar /embo'tar/ *vt* to blunt (cutting edge); *—vi Fig.* weaken; *—vr* become blunt
embotellado /embote'ʎaðo; embote'yaðo/ *m,* bottling; *Fig.* bottleneck
embotellador /embote'ʎaðor; embote'yaðor/ **(-ra)** *n* bottler. *f.* **embotelladora,** bottling outfit
embotellar /embote'ʎar; embote'yar/ *vt* to bottle; bottle up, prevent from escaping
embotijar /emboti'har/ *vt* to put into jars; *—vr Inf.* be enraged
embozar /embo'θar; embo'sar/ *vt Fig.* to cloak, dissemble; muffle; *—vr* muffle oneself up
embozo /em'boθo; em'boso/ *m,* anything used to cover or muffle the face; pretense, pretext; facings (gen. *pl*); yashmak
embragar /embra'gar/ *vt* to sling, lift; *Mech.* let in the clutch

embrague /em'brage/ *m*, hoisting, slinging; *Mech.* clutch
embravecer /embraβe'θer; embraβe'ser/ *vt irr* to infuriate; *—vr* be enraged; be boisterous (sea). See **conocer**
embravecimiento /embraβeθi'miento; embraβesi'miento/ *m*, fury, rage
embrazadura /embraθa'ðura; embrasa'ðura/ *f*, grasping, clasping; handle, clasp
embreadura /embrea'ðura/ *f*, tarring
embrear /embre'ar/ *vt* to tar, paint with pitch
embriagador /embriaga'ðor/ *a* intoxicating
embriagar /embria'gar/ *vt* to intoxicate; enrapture; *—vr* become inebriated
embriaguez /embria'geθ; embria'ges/ *f*, intoxication, inebriation; rapture
embriología /embriolo'hia/ *f*, embryology
embrión /em'brion/ *m*, embryo; germ, rough idea
embrionario /embrio'nario/ *a* embryonic
embrocación /embroka'θion; embroka'sion/ *f*, *Med.* embrocation
embrollar /embro'ʎar; embro'yar/ *vt* to entangle; embroil
embrollo /em'broʎo; em'broyo/ *m*, tangle; falsehood; difficult situation
embromar /embro'mar/ *vt* to tease, chaff; trick, deceive; waste the time of; annoy; harm
embrujar /embru'har/ *vt* to bewitch
embrutecer /embrute'θer; embrute'ser/ *vt irr* to make brutish or stupid; *—vr* become brutish. See **conocer**
embudo /em'buðo/ *m*, *Chem.* funnel
embuste /em'buste/ *m*, lie, fraud; *pl* trinkets
embustero /embus'tero/ **(-ra)** *a* deceitful, knavish *—n* liar, cheat, trickster
embutido /embu'tiðo/ *m*, inlaid work; *Cul.* sausage
embutir /embu'tir/ *vt* to inlay; stuff full, cram; *—vt* and *vr Inf.* stuff with food
eme /'eme/ *f*, name of letter M
emergencia /emer'henθia; emer'hensia/ *f*, emergence; accident, emergency
emergente /emer'hente/ *a* emergent
emerger /emer'her/ *vi* to emerge; have its source (rivers, etc.)
emérito /e'merito/ *a* emeritus
emético /e'metiko/ *a* and *m*, emetic
emigración /emigra'θion; emigra'sion/ *f*, emigration; migration; number of emigrants
emigrado /emi'graðo/ *m*, emigrant, emigré
emigrante /emi'grante/ *a* and *mf* emigrant
emigrar /emi'grar/ *vi* to emigrate; migrate
emigratorio /emigra'torio/ *a* emigration
eminencia /emi'nenθia; emi'nensia/ *f*, highland; importance, prominence; outstanding personality, genius; title given to cardinals
eminente /emi'nente/ *a* high, elevated; prominent, illustrious
emirato /emi'rato/ *m*, emirate
emisario /emi'sario/ **(-ia)** *n* emissary
emisión /emi'sion/ *f*, emission; *Radio.* broadcast; *Com.* issue (bonds, etc.); floating (of a loan)
emisor /emi'sor/ *m*, *Elec.* transmitter.
emisora /emi'sora/ *f*, *Radio.* broadcasting station
emitir /emi'tir/ *vt* to emit; *Radio.* broadcast; *Com.* issue (bonds, paper money, etc.); utter, give voice to
emoción /emo'θion; emo'sion/ *f*, emotion
emocional /emo'θional; emo'sional/ *a* emotional; emotive
emocionante /emoθio'nante; emosio'nante/ *a* moving, causing emotion; thrilling
emocionar /emoθio'nar; emosio'nar/ *vt* to cause emotion, move; *—vr* be stirred by emotion; be thrilled
emoliente /emo'liente/ *a* and *m*, emollient
emolumento /emolu'mento/ *m*, emolument (gen. *pl*)
emotivo /emo'tiβo/ *a* emotive
empachado /empa'tʃaðo/ *a* awkward, clumsy
empachar /empa'tʃar/ *vt* to hinder, impede; disguise, dissemble; *—vr* overeat, stuff; be bashful
empacho /em'patʃo/ *m*, bashfulness, timidity; embarrassment, impediment; indigestion, satiety
empadronamiento /empaðrona'miento/ *m*, census
empadronar /empaðro'nar/ *vt* to take the census
empalagar /empala'gar/ *vt* to cloy (of food); tire, annoy
empalagoso /empala'goso/ *a* sickly, oversweet; cloying; *Fig.* sugary, honeyed
empalar /empa'lar/ *vt* to impale
empalizada /empali'θaða; empali'saða/ *f*, stockade, fencing
empalmar /empal'mar/ *vt* to dovetail; splice (ropes); clamp; *Fig.* combine (plans, actions, etc.); *—vi* join (railroad lines); couple (railroad trains); *—vr* palm (as in conjuring)
empalme /em'palme/ *m*, connection; splicing; *Fig.* combination (of plans, etc.); railroad junction; continuation; palming, secreting
empanada /empa'naða/ *f*, savory turnover or pie; secret negotiations, intrigue
empanar /empa'nar/ *vt* to bread; *Cul.* cover with breadcrumbs; *Agr.* sow grain
empantanar /empanta'nar/ *vt* to turn into marsh; embog; delay, embarrass
empañar /empa'ɲar/ *vt* to swaddle; tarnish, dim; blur; *Fig.* sully (fame, etc.)
empapar /empa'par/ *vt* to saturate; absorb; impregnate; *—vr* be saturated; absorb; *Fig.* be imbued
empapelado /empape'laðo/ *m*, paperhanging; wallpaper
empapelador /empapela'ðor/ *m*, paperhanger
empapelar /empape'lar/ *vt* to wrap in paper; paper (a room, etc.)
empaque /em'pake/ *m*, packing; paneling; *Inf.* mien, air; pomposity
empaquetador /empaketa'ðor/ **(-ra)** *n* packer
empaquetar /empake'tar/ *vt* to pack; make up parcels or packages; overcrowd
emparedado /empare'ðaðo/ **(-da)** *a* cloistered, reclusive *—n* recluse. *m*, *Cul.* sandwich
emparedar /empare'ðar/ *vt* to shut up, immure; *—vr* become a recluse
emparejar /empare'har/ *vt* to pair, match; equalize, make level; *—vi* come abreast (of); be equal
emparentar /emparen'tar/ *vi irr* to become related by marriage. See **acertar**
emparrado /empa'rraðo/ *m*, vine arbor; vine prop; pergola
empastadura /empasta'ðura/ *f*, filling (of teeth)
empastar /empas'tar/ *vt* to cover with glue or paste; bind in boards (books); fill (teeth). **empastado en tela,** clothbound
empaste /em'paste/ *m*, pasting, gluing; filling (teeth)
empatar /empa'tar/ *vt* to equal, tie with
empate /em'pate/ *m*, tie, draw; dead heat
empecatado /empeka'taðo/ *a* willful; evil-minded, wicked; incorrigible, impenitent; extremely unlucky
empecer /empe'θer; empe'ser/ *vt irr* to harm, damage; *—vi* hinder. See **conocer**
empedernido /empeðer'niðo/ *a* stony-hearted, cruel
empedrado /empe'ðraðo/ *a* dappled (horses); *Fig.* flecked (with clouds). *m*, paving; pavement
empedrador /empeðra'ðor/ *m*, stone paver
empedrar /empe'ðrar/ *vt irr* to pave with stones. See **acertar**
empegadura /empega'ðura/ *f*, coat of pitch
empegar /empe'gar/ *vt* to coat with pitch; mark with pitch (sheep)
empeine /em'peine/ *m*, groin; instep
empellar /empe'ʎar; empe'yar/ *vt* to push, jostle
empellón /empe'ʎon; empe'yon/ *m*, hard push. *Inf.* **a empellones,** by pushing and shoving
empenachado /empena'tʃaðo/ *a* plumed
empeñado /empe'ɲaðo/ *a* violent, heated (of disputes)
empeñar /empe'ɲar/ *vt* to pledge, leave as surety; pawn; oblige, compel; appoint as mediator; *—vr* bind oneself, be under an obligation; (*with en*) insist on; persist in; *—vr* intercede; mediate; *Mil.* begin (a battle). **empeñado en,** determined to, intent on
empeño /em'peɲo/ *m*, pledge, surety; obligation, engagement; fervent desire; purpose, intention; determination, resolve; guarantor; *Inf.* influence, favor

empeoramiento /empeora'miento/ *m,* worsening; deterioration

empeorar /empeo'rar/ *vt* to make worse; *—vi* and *vr* deteriorate, grow worse

empequeñecer /empekeɲe'θer; empekeɲe'ser/ *vt irr* to diminish, lessen; make smaller; belittle. See **conocer**

emperador /empera'ðor/ *m,* emperor

emperatriz /empera'triθ; empera'tris/ *f,* empress

emperezar /empere'θar; empere'sar/ *vt* to obstruct, hinder; *—vr* be lazy

empernar /emper'nar/ *vt* to peg, bolt

empero /em'pero/ *conjunc* but; nevertheless

empezar /empe'θar; empe'sar/ *vt irr* to begin, commence; initiate; *—vi* begin *—Pres. Indic.* **empiezo, empiezas, empieza, empiezan.** *Preterite* **empecé, empezaste,** etc *—Pres. Subjunc.* **empiece, empieces, empiece, empecemos, empecéis, empiecen**

empicotar /empiko'tar/ *vt* to pillory

empinado /empi'naðo/ *a* steep; lofty; arrogant; exalted

empinar /empi'nar/ *vt* to raise; tip, tilt (drinking vessels); *—vr* stand on tiptoe; rear, prance; tower, rise; *Aer.* zoom, climb steeply. *Inf.* **e. el codo,** to lift the elbow, tipple

empingorotado /empiŋgoro'taðo/ *a* important, prominent; *Inf.* stuck-up

empíreo /em'pireo/ *a* empyreal; heavenly, divine. *m,* empyrean

empírico /em'piriko/ **(-ca)** *a* empiric *—n* quack, charlatan

empirismo /empi'rismo/ *m,* empiricism

empizarrado /empiθa'rraðo; empisa'rraðo/ *m,* slate roof

empizarrar /empiθa'rrar; empisa'rrar/ *vt* to roof with slate

emplastar /emplas'tar/ *vt Med.* to apply plasters; make up; paint; *Inf.* hinder, obstruct; *—vr* be smeared

emplasto /em'plasto/ *m, Med.* plaster; poultice; *Inf.* put-up job, fraud

emplazamiento /emplaθa'miento; emplasa'miento/ *m,* placing, location; site; *Law.* summons; *Naut.* berth

emplazar /empla'θar; empla'sar/ *vt* to convene, arrange a meeting; *Law.* summon

empleado /emple'aðo/ **(-da)** *n* employee; clerk. **e. público,** civil servant

emplear /em'plear/ *vt* to employ; lay out, invest (money); use; *—vr* be employed or occupied

empleo /em'pleo/ *m,* employment; investment, laying out (of money); occupation; post, office

emplomar /emplo'mar/ *vt* to lead, solder or cover with lead; affix lead seals on or to; weight (a stick, etc.)

emplumar /emplu'mar/ *vt* to feather; decorate with feathers; tar and feather

emplumecer /emplume'θer; emplume'ser/ *vi irr* to fledge, grow feathers. See **conocer**

empobrecer /empoβre'θer; empoβre'ser/ *vt irr* to impoverish; *—vi* and *vr* become poor; decay. See **conocer**

empobrecimiento /empoβreθi'miento; empoβresi'miento/ *m,* impoverishment

empollar /empo'ʎar; empo'yar/ *vt* to hatch; *—vi* produce a brood (of bees); *Inf.* brood on, consider; *Inf.* grind, cram, swot (of students)

empollón /empo'ʎon; empo'yon/ **(-ona)** *n Inf* plodder, grind, swot

empolvar /empol'βar/ *vt* to cover with dust; powder

emponzoñamiento /emponθoɲa'miento; emponsoɲa'miento/ *m,* poisoning

emponzoñar /emponθo'ɲar; emponso'ɲar/ *vt* to poison; pervert, corrupt

emporio /em'porio/ *m,* emporium

empotrar /empo'trar/ *vt* to embed, implant; fix down

emprendedor /emprende'ðor/ *a* capable, efficient, enterprising

emprender /empren'der/ *vt* to undertake; (*with prep a or con*) *Inf.* accost, tackle, buttonhole

empresa /em'presa/ *f,* undertaking, task; motto, device; intention, design; management, firm; enterprise, deal

empresarial /empresa'rial/ *a* entrepreneurial

empresario /empre'sario/ *m,* contractor; theatrical manager

empréstito /em'prestito/ *m,* loan

empujar /empu'har/ *vt* to push; *Fig.* exert pressure, influence

empuje /em'puhe/ *m,* push; *Archit.* pressure; energy; power, influence

empujón /empu'hon/ *m,* violent thrust or push. *Inf.* **a empujones,** by pushing and shoving; intermittently

empuñadura /empuɲa'ðura/ *f,* hilt (of a sword); *Inf.* preamble

empuñar /empu'ɲar/ *vt* to grasp; grip; clutch

emu /'emu/ *m,* emu

emulación /emula'θion; emula'sion/ *f,* emulation, competition, rivalry

emulador /emula'ðor/ *a* emulative

emular /emu'lar/ *vt* to emulate, rival, compete with

émulo /'emulo/ **(-la)** *a* emulative, rival *—n* competitor, rival

emulsión /emul'sion/ *f,* emulsion

emulsivo /emul'siβo/ *a* emulsive

en /en/ *prep* in, into, on, upon; at; by. **en Madrid,** in Madrid. **en junio,** in June. **Se echó en un sillón,** He threw himself into an armchair. **Se transformó en mariposa,** It turned into a butterfly. **Hay un libro en la mesa,** There is a book on the table. **María está en casa,** Mary is at home. **en un precio muy alto,** at a very high price. **El número de candidatos ha disminuido en un treinta por ciento,** The number of candidates has decreased by thirty percent. **En** appears in a number of adverbial phrases, e.g. *en particular,* in particular, *en secreto,* in secret, *en seguida,* immediately. When it is used with a gerund, it means after, as soon as, when, e.g. *En llegando a la puerta llamó,* When he arrived at the door, he knocked. *En todas partes se cuecen habas,* That happens everywhere; It happens in the best of families

enagua /e'nagua/ *f,* slip, crinoline, petticoat

enajenación /enahena'θion; enahena'sion/ *f,* transference, alienation (property); abstraction, absentmindedness. **e. mental,** lunacy

enajenar /enahe'nar/ *vt* to transfer (property)

enaltecer /enalte'θer; enalte'ser/ *vt irr* to elevate, raise; exalt. See **conocer**

enamoradizo /enamora'ðiθo; enamora'ðiso/ *a* susceptible, easily enamored; fickle

enamorado /enamo'raðo/ *a* in love, lovesick; easily enamored

enamorar /enamo'rar/ *vt* to arouse love in; court, make love to; *—vr* fall in love; (with *de*) become fond of (things)

enano /e'nano/ **(-na)** *a* small, dwarf *—n* dwarf

enarbolar /enarβo'lar/ *vt* to hoist (flags); *—vr* prance (horses); become angry

enardecer /enarðe'θer; enarðe'ser/ *vt irr* to kindle, stimulate (passion, quarrel, etc.); *—vr* be afire (with passion); *Med.* be inflamed. See **conocer**

encabestrar /enkaβe'strar/ *vt* to halter; lead, dominate

encabezamiento /enkaβeθa'miento; enkaβesa'miento/ *m,* census taking; tax register; tax assessment; heading, inscription, running head

encabezar /enkaβe'θar; enkaβe'sar/ *vt* to take the census of; put on the tax register; open a subscription list; put a heading or title to; lead, head; *—vr* compound, settle by agreement (taxes, etc.)

encabritarse /enkaβri'tarse/ *vr* to rear, prance (horses)

encadenamiento /enkaðena'miento/ *m,* fettering, chaining; connection, link, relation

encadenar /enkaðe'nar/ *vt* to chain, fetter; *Fig.* link up, connect; *Fig.* paralyze. **encadenar el interés de,** to capture the interest of

encajar /enka'har/ *vt* to insert, fit one thing inside another; force in; fit tightly; *Inf.* be opportune, fit in (often with *bien*); *—vr* squeeze or crowd in; *Inf.* butt in, interfere

encaje /en'kahe/ *m,* fitting, insertion; socket, groove; joining; lace; inlay, mosaic

encajera /enka'hera/ *f,* lace maker or seller
encaladura /enkala'ðura/ *f,* whitewashing
encalar /enka'lar/ *vt* to whitewash
encalladero /enkaʎa'ðero; enkaya'ðero/ *m, Naut.* sandbank, reef, shoal
encallar /enka'ʎar; enka'yar/ *vi Naut.* to run aground; *Fig.* be held up (negotiations, etc.)
encalmado /enkal'maðo/ *a* calm; *Com.* dull
encalmarse /enkal'marse/ *vr* to become calm (wind, weather)
encalvecer /enkalβe'θer; enkalβe'ser/ *vi irr* to grow bald. See **conocer**
encamado /enka'maðo/ *a* bedridden, confined to one's bed; *m,* person confined to his bed
encamarse /enka'marse/ *vr* to go to bed (gen. illness); be laid flat (grain, etc.); crouch
encaminadura /enkamina'ðura/ *f,* **encaminamiento** *m,* directing, forwarding, routing
encaminar /enkami'nar/ *vt* to guide; direct; regulate; manage; promote, advance; *—vr* (*with prep a*) make for, go in the direction of
encandecer /enkande'θer; enkande'ser/ *vt irr* to make incandescent. See **conocer**
encandilar /enkandi'lar/ *vt* to dazzle; mislead; *Inf.* poke (the fire); *—vr* be bloodshot (eyes)
encanecer /enkane'θer; enkane'ser/ *vi irr* to grow gray- or white-haired; grow mold; grow old. See **conocer**
encanijar /enkani'har/ *vt* to make weak, sickly (gen. of babies); *—vr* be delicate or ailing
encantado /enkan'taðo/ *a Inf.* daydreaming, abstracted; haunted; rambling (of houses)
encantador /enkanta'ðor/ *a* captivating, bewitching, delightful. *m,* sorcerer, magician. **e. de serpientes,** snake charmer
encantamiento /enkanta'miento/ *m,* enchantment, spell, charm
encantar /enkan'tar/ *vt* to enchant, weave a spell; delight, captivate, charm
encañada /enka'ɲaða/ *f,* gorge, ravine
encañado /enka'ɲaðo/ *m,* trellis; pipeline
encañar /enka'ɲar/ *vt* to run water through a pipe; stake plants; wind thread on a spool
encañonar /enkaɲo'nar/ *vt* to run into pipes; pleat, fold
encapotarse /enkapo'tarse/ *vr* to muffle oneself in a cloak; scowl; be overcast; lower (sky)
encapricharse /enkapri'tʃarse/ *vr* to take a fancy (to); insist on having one's own way, be stubborn
encapuchar /enkapu'tʃar/ *vt* to cover or hide with a hood
encaramar /enkara'mar/ *vt* to raise, lift; climb; praise, extol. **e. al poder,** to put in power (e.g. a dictator). **encaramarse por,** to climb up
encarar /enka'rar/ *vt* to place face to face; aim (at); *—vt* and *vr* face; come face to face
encarcelación /enkarθela'θion; enkarsela'sion/ *f,* incarceration
encarcelar /enkarθe'lar; enkarse'lar/ *vt* to imprison, jail; clamp
encarecer /enkare'θer; enkare'ser/ *vt irr* to raise the price; overpraise, exaggerate; recommend strongly; *—vi* and *vr* increase in price. See **conocer**
encarecimiento /enkareθi'miento; enkaresi'miento/ *m,* increase (in price); enhancement; exaggeration. **con e.,** insistently, earnestly
encargado /enkar'gaðo/ *m,* person in charge; manager; agent, representative. **e. de negocios,** chargé d'affaires
encargar /enkar'gar/ *vt* to enjoin; commission; recommend; advise; *Com.* order
encargo /en'kargo/ *m,* charge, commission; order; office, employ; responsibility
encariñarse /enkari'ɲarse/ (*con*), *vi* to become fond (of)
encarnación /enkarna'θion; enkarna'sion/ *f,* incarnation
encarnadino /enkarna'ðino/ *a* incarnadine
encarnado /enkar'naðo/ *a* incarnate; flesh-colored; red
encarnar /enkar'nar/ *vi* to incarnate; pierce the flesh; *Fig.* leave a strong impression; *—vt* symbolize, personify; *—vr* mingle, blend
encarnizado /enkarni'θaðo; enkarni'saðo/ *a* bloodshot (eyes); flesh-colored; bloody, cruel (gen. of battles)
encarnizamiento /enkarniθa'miento; enkarnisa'miento/ *m,* cruelty, fury
encarnizar /enkarni'θar; enkarni'sar/ *vt* to infuriate; *—vr* devour flesh (animals); persecute, ill-treat
encaro /en'karo/ *m,* stare, gaze; aim
encarrilar /enkarri'lar/ *vt* to set on the track or rails (vehicles); *Fig.* put right, set on the right track
encartamiento /enkarta'miento/ *m,* proscription; charter
encartar /enkar'tar/ *vt* to proscribe, outlaw; place on the tax register; *Law.* summon, cite
encartonar /enkarto'nar/ *vt* to cover with cardboard; bind in boards (books)
encasar /enka'sar/ *vt Surg.* to set (a bone)
encasillado /enkasi'ʎaðo; enkasi'yaðo/ *m,* set of pigeonholes
encasillar /enkasi'ʎar; enkasi'yar/ *vt* to pigeonhole; file, classify
encasquetar /enkaske'tar/ **(se)** *vt* and *vr* to pull a hat well down on the head; *—vr* get a fixed idea
encastillar /enkasti'ʎar; enkasti'yar/ *vt* to fortify with castles; *—vr* retire to a castle; be headstrong, obstinate
encauzamiento /enkauθa'miento; enkausa'miento/ *m,* channeling; *Fig.* direction
encauzar /enkau'θar; enkau'sar/ *vt* to channel; *Fig.* direct, guide
encefalitis /enθefa'litis; ensefa'litis/ *f,* encephalitis. **e. letárgica,** encephalitis lethargica, sleeping sickness.
encéfalo /en'θefalo; en'sefalo/ *m, Anat.* brain
encenagarse /enθena'garse; ensena'garse/ *vr* to wallow in mire; muddy oneself; take to vice
encendedor /enθende'ðor; ensende'ðor/ *a* lighting. *m,* lighter. **e. de bolsillo,** pocket lighter
encender /enθen'der; ensen'der/ *vt irr* to light; switch on; set fire to, kindle; arouse (emotions); inflame, incite; *—vr* blush. See **entender**
encendido /enθen'diðo; ensen'diðo/ *a* high-colored; inflamed; ardent. *m, Auto.* ignition
encerado /enθe'raðo; ense'raðo/ *a* wax-colored. *m,* oilskin; sticking plaster; blackboard; tarpaulin
enceramiento /enθera'miento; ensera'miento/ *m,* waxing
encerar /enθe'rar; ense'rar/ *vt* to wax, varnish with wax; stain with wax; inspissate (lime)
encerotar /enθero'tar; ensero'tar/ *vt* to wax (thread)
encerrar /enθe'rrar; ense'rrar/ *vt irr* to shut up, imprison; include, contain; *—vr* go into seclusion. See **acertar**
encerrona /enθe'rrona; ense'rrona/ *f, Inf.* voluntary retreat; *Fig. Inf.* tight corner
encespedar /enθespe'ðar; ensespe'ðar/ *vt* to cover with sod
enchufar /entʃu'far/ *vt* to connect tubes; *Fig.* combine (jobs, etc.); *Elec.* plug, connect
enchufe /en'tʃufe/ *m,* joint, fitting together (of tubes); *Elec.* wall socket, plug; part-time post; *Inf.* cushy job. **e. de reducción,** *Elec.* adapter
encía /en'θia; en'sia/ *f,* gum (of the mouth)
encíclica /en'θiklika; en'siklika/ *f,* encyclical
enciclopedia /enθiklo'peðia; ensiklo'peðia/ *f,* encyclopedia
enciclopédico /enθiklo'peðiko; ensiklo'peðiko/ *a* encyclopedic
encierro /en'θierro; en'sierro/ *m,* act of closing or shutting up; prison; retreat, confinement
encima /en'θima; en'sima/ *adv* over; above; at the top; besides; (*with de*) on, on top of. **por e. de esto,** over and above this, besides this
encina /en'θina; en'sina/ *f, Bot.* evergreen or holm oak
encinar /enθi'nar; ensi'nar/ *m,* grove of evergreen or holm oaks
encinta /en'θinta; en'sinta/ *a f,* pregnant
encintar /enθin'tar; ensin'tar/ *vt* to decorate with ribbons

enclavar /enkla'βar/ *vt* to nail; pierce; embed; *Inf.* deceive

enclenque /en'klenke/ *a* ailing, weak; puny, anemic

enclocar /enklo'kar/ *vi irr* to begin to brood (hens). See **contar**

encobar /enko'βar/ *vi* to hatch eggs

encoger /enko'her/ *vt* to shrink, contract, recoil; discourage; *—vi* shrink (wood, cloth, etc.); *—vr* shrink from, recoil; be discouraged; be timid or bashful

encogimiento /enkohi'miento/ *m,* shrinkage; contraction; depression, discouragement; timidity; bashfulness

encoladura /enkola'ðura/ *f.* **encolamiento** *m,* gluing; sizing

encolerizar /enkoleri'θar; enkoleri'sar/ *vt* to anger; *—vr* be angry

encomendar /enkomen'dar/ *vt irr* to charge with, entrust; recommend, commend; *—vr* (*with prep a*) put one's trust in; send greetings to. See **acertar**

encomiar /enko'miar/ *vt* to eulogize, praise

encomiástico /enko'miastiko/ *a* encomiastic

encomienda /enko'mienda/ *f,* commission, charge; knight commandership; insignia of knight commander; land formerly granted in America to *conquistadores*; recommendation, commendation, protection, defense; *pl* greetings, compliments, messages

encomio /en'komio/ *m,* eulogy; strong recommendation

enconar /enko'nar/ *vt* to irritate, exasperate; *—vr Med.* be inflamed; be exasperated; (*with en*) burden one's conscience with

encono /en'kono/ *m,* rancor, resentment, ill will

encontrado /enkon'traðo/ *a* facing, opposite, in front; hostile, inimical, opposed (to)

encontrar /enkon'trar/ *vt irr* to meet; find; *—vi* meet; encounter unexpectedly; (*with con*) run into, collide with; *—vr* be antagonistic; find; feel, be; differ, disagree (opinions); (*with con*) meet, come across. **e. eco,** to strike a responsive chord. **encontrarse con el cura de su pueblo,** to find someone who knows all about, meet someone who knows all about. **¿Cómo se encuentra Vd?** How are you? *Pres. Indic.* **encuentro,** etc *—Pres. Subjunc.* **encuentre,** etc.

encontrón /enkon'tron/ *m,* collision, violent impact

encopetado /enkope'taðo/ *a* conceited, proud; of noble descent; prominent, important

encorajar /enkora'har/ *vt* to encourage, inspire, hearten; *—vr* be angry

encordelar /enkorðe'lar/ *vt* to cord, rope

encorsetar /enkorse'tar/ *vt* to correct

encorvadura /enkorβa'ðura/ *f,* bending, curving

encorvar /enkor'βar/ *vt* to bend, curve; *—vr* have a leaning toward, favor

encostrar /enkos'trar/ *vt* to cover with a crust; *—vr* form a crust

encrespador /enkrespa'ðor/ *m,* curling irons

encrespar /enkres'par/ *vt* to curl (hair); enrage; *—vr* be curly (hair); stand on end (hair, feathers, from fright); be angry; grow rough (sea); become complicated, entangled

encrestado /enkres'taðo/ *a* crested; haughty, arrogant

encrestarse /enkres'tarse/ *vr* to stiffen the comb or crest (birds)

encrucijada /enkruθi'haða; enkrusi'haða/ *f,* crossroad, intersection; ambush

encrudecer /enkruðe'θer; enkruðe'ser/ *vt irr* to make raw-looking; annoy; *—vr* be annoyed. See **conocer**

encuadernación /enkuaðerna'θion; enkuaðerna'sion/ *f,* bookbinding; binding (of a book); bookbinder's workshop. **e. en tela,** cloth binding

encuadernador /enkuaðerna'ðor/ **(-ra)** *n* bookbinder

encuadernar /enkuaðer'nar/ *vt* to bind (a book)

encuadrar /enkuað'rar/ *vt* to frame; fit one thing into another, insert; limit; *Mil.* enlist

encubar /enku'βar/ *vt* to put into casks (wine, etc.)

encubiertamente /enkuβierta'mente/ *adv* secretly; deceitfully

encubierto /enku'βierto/ *a* concealed; secret

encubridor /enkuβri'ðor/ **(-ra)** *a* concealing, hiding *—n* hider; harborer; accomplice; receiver (of stolen goods); *Law.* accessory after the fact

encubrimiento /enkuβri'miento/ *m,* hiding, concealment; *Law.* accessory before (after) the fact; receiving (of stolen goods)

encubrir /enkuβ'rir/ *vt* to conceal; receive (stolen goods); *Law.* prosecute as an accessory. *Past. Part.* **encubierto**

encuentro /en'kuentro/ *m,* collision; meeting, encounter; opposition, hostility; *Mil.* fight, skirmish; *Archit.* angle. **ir al e. de,** to go in search of. **salir al e. (de),** to go to meet; resist

encuesta /en'kuesta/ *f,* investigation, examination

encumbrado /enkum'braðo/ *a* elevated, high

encumbramiento /enkumbra'miento/ *m,* act of elevating; height; aggrandizement, advancement

encumbrar /enkum'brar/ *vt* to raise, elevate; exalt, promote; ascend, climb to the top; *—vr* be proud; be lofty, tower

encurtido /enkur'tiðo/ *m,* pickle

encurtir /enkur'tir/ *vt* to pickle

ende /'ende/ *adv Obs.* there. **por e.,** therefore

endeble /en'deβle/ *a* weak, frail

endeblez /ende'βleθ; ende'βles/ *f,* weakness

endecha /en'detʃa/ *f,* dirge

endémico /en'demiko/ *a Med.* endemic

endemoniado /endemo'niaðo/ *a* devil-possessed; *Inf.* fiendish, malevolent

endemoniar /endemo'niar/ *vt* to possess with a devil; *Inf.* enrage

endentar /enden'tar/ *vt irr Mech.* to cut the cogs (of a wheel); engage, interlock (gears, wheels, etc.). See **regimentar**

endentecer /endente'θer; endente'ser/ *vi irr* to cut teeth. See **conocer**

enderezamiento /endereθa'miento; enderesa'miento/ *m,* straightening; directing, guiding; putting right, correction

enderezar /endere'θar; endere'sar/ *vt* to straighten; direct, guide; put right, correct; *—vi* take the right road; *—vr* straighten oneself; prepare to

endeudarse /endeu'ðarse/ *vr* to contract debts; be under an obligation

endiablado /endia'βlaðo/ *a* ugly, monstrous; *Inf.* fiendish

endiosar /endio'sar/ *vt* to deify; *—vr* be puffed up with pride; be abstracted or lost in ecstasy

endocrino /endo'krino/ *a* endocrine

endocrinología /endokrinolo'hia/ *f,* endocrinology

endomingarse /endomiŋ'garse/ *vr* to put on one's Sunday best

endosante /endo'sante/ *m,* endorser

endosar /endo'sar/ *vt Com.* to endorse; transfer, pass on

endoso /en'doso/ *m, Com.* endorsement

endrino /en'drino/ *m,* sloe tree *—a* blue-black, sloe-colored

endulzar /endul'θar; endul'sar/ *vt* to sweeten; soften, mitigate

endurecer /endure'θer; endure'ser/ *vt irr* to harden; toughen, inure; make severe or cruel; *—vr* grow hard; become hardened or robust; be harsh or cruel. **endurecerse al trabajo,** to become hardened to work. See **conocer**

endurecimiento /endureθi'miento; enduresi'miento/ *m,* hardness; obstinacy, tenacity

ene /'ene/ *f,* name of letter N

enemiga /ene'miga/ *f,* hostility, enmity

enemigo /ene'migo/ **(-ga)** *a* hostile *—n* enemy; antagonist. *m,* devil

enemistad /enemis'tað/ *f,* enmity, hostility

enemistar /enemis'tar/ *vt* to make enemies of; *—vr* (*with con*) become an enemy of; cease to be friendly with

energía /ener'hia/ *f,* energy, vigor

enérgico /e'nerhiko/ *a* energetic, vigorous

energúmeno /ener'gumeno/ **(-na)** *n* energumen

enero /e'nero/ *m,* January

enervación /enerβa'θion; enerβa'sion/ *f,* enervation

enervar /ener'βar/ *vt* to enervate, weaken; *Fig.* take the force out of (reasons, etc.)

enfadar /enfa'ðar/ *vt* to make angry; *—vr* become angry

enfado /en'faðo/ *m*, anger; annoyance; trouble, toil
enfadoso /enfa'ðoso/ *a* vexatious; troublesome, wearisome
enfaldada /enfal'daða/ *f*, skirtful
enfaldar /enfal'dar/ *vt* to tuck up the skirts; lop off lower branches (of trees)
enfangarse /enfaŋ'garse/ *vr* to cover oneself with mud; *Inf.* dirty one's hands, sully one's reputation; wallow in vice
enfardar /enfar'ðar/ *vt* to pack; make bales or bundles
énfasis /'enfasis/ *m*, or *f*, emphasis
enfático /en'fatiko/ *a* emphatic
enfermar /enfer'mar/ *vi* to fall ill; *—vt* cause illness; *Fig.* weaken. **Enfermó del corazón,** He fell ill with heart trouble.
enfermedad /enferme'ðað/ *f*, illness; *Fig.* malady, distemper. **e. del sueño,** sleeping sickness
enfermera /enfer'mera/ *f*, nurse
enfermería /enferme'ria/ *f*, infirmary; hospital; first-aid station
enfermero /enfer'mero/ *m*, nurse
enfermizo /enfer'miθo; enfer''miso/ *a* ailing, delicate; unhealthy, unwholesome
enfermo /en'fermo/ **(-ma)** *a* ill; *Fig.* corrupt, diseased; delicate, sickly *—n* patient. **e. venéreo,** person with a venereal disease
enfilar /enfi'lar/ *vt* to place in line; string; *Mil.* enfilade
enflaquecer /enflake'θer; enflake'ser/ *vt irr* to make thin; weaken, enervate; *—vi* grow thin; lose heart. See **conocer**
enflaquecimiento /enflakeθi'miento; enflakesi'miento/ *m*, loss of flesh; discouragement
enfocar /enfo'kar/ *vt* to focus; envisage
enfoque /en'foke/ *m*, focus
enfoscado /enfos'kaðo/ *a* ill-humored; immersed in business matters
enfrascar /enfras'kar/ *vt* to bottle; *—vr* (*with en*) plunge into, entangle oneself in (undergrowth, etc.); become engrossed or absorbed in
enfrenar /enfre'nar/ *vt* to bridle; curb (a horse); restrain, repress; check
enfrente /en'frente/ *adv* in front, opposite, facing; in opposition
enfriadero /enfria'ðero/ *m*, cooling place, cold cellar, root cellar
enfriamiento /enfria'miento/ *m*, cooling
enfriar /enf'riar/ *vt* to cool; *Fig.* chill, make indifferent; *—vr* grow cold; *Fig.* grow stormy (weather)
enfurecer /enfure'θer; enfure'ser/ *vt irr* to enrage. See **conocer**
enfurecimiento /enfureθi'miento; enfuresi'miento/ *m*, fury
enfurruñarse /enfurru'ɲarse/ *vr Inf.* to fume, be angry; be disgruntled
engalanar /eŋgala'nar/ *vt* to decorate, embellish. **engalanado como nunca,** dressed to the nines, dressed to kill
enganchar /eŋgan'tʃar/ *vt* to hook; couple, connect; hitch, harness, yoke; *Inf.* seduce, hook; *Mil.* bribe into army; *—vr* be hooked or caught on a hook; *Mil.* enlist
enganche /eŋ'gantʃe/ *m*, hooking; coupling (of railroad trains, etc.); connection; yoke, harness; hook; *Inf.* enticement; *Mil.* enlistment
engañifa /eŋga'ɲifa/ *f*, *Inf.* swindle, fraud
engañadizo /eŋgaɲa'ðiθo; eŋgaɲaðiso/ *a* easily deceived, simple
engañador /eŋgaɲa'ðor/ **(-ra)** *a* deceiving; deceptive *—n* deceiver, impostor
engañar /eŋga'ɲar/ *vt* to deceive; defraud, cheat; beguile, while away; hoax, humbug; *—vr* be mistaken; deceive oneself. **e. como a un chino,** *Inf.* to pull the wool over a person's eyes. **Las apariencias engañan,** Appearances are deceptive
engañifa /eŋga'nhook;ifa/ *f*, *Inf.* swindle, fraud
engaño /eŋ'gaɲo/ *m*, deceit; deception, illusion; fraud; falsehood
engañoso /eŋga'ɲoso/ *a* deceitful, false; fraudulent; deceptive, misleading
engarabatar /eŋgaraβa'tar/ *vt Inf.* to hook; *—vr* become hooked, curved, crooked
engarce /eŋ'garθe; eŋgarse/ *m*, hooking; coupling; setting (of jewels)
engarzar /eŋgar'θar; eŋgar'sar/ *vt* to link, couple, enchain; hook; curl; set (jewels)
engastar /eŋgas'tar/ *vt* to set (jewels)
engaste /eŋ'gaste/ *m*, setting (of jewels)
engatusar /eŋgatu'sar/ *vt Inf.* to wheedle, coax, flatter
engendrador /enhendra'ðor/ **(-ra)** *a* engendering; original *—n* begetter
engendrar /enhen'drar/ *vt* to procreate; engender, produce, cause
engendro /en'hendro/ *m*, fetus; abnormal embryo; literary monstrosity
englobar /eŋglo'βar/ *vt* to include, comprise, embrace
engolfarse /eŋgol'farse/ *vr* to sail out to sea; (*with en*) *Fig.* be absorbed in
engomar /eŋgo'mar/ *vt* to gum
engordar /eŋgor'ðar/ *vt* to fatten; *—vi* grow fat; *Inf.* prosper, grow rich
engorde /eŋ'gorðe/ *m*, fattening (of stock)
engorro /eŋ'gorro/ *m*, impediment, obstacle, difficulty
engorroso /eŋgo'rroso/ *a* difficult, troublesome
engranaje /eŋgra'nahe/ *m*, *Mech.* gearing, gear; *Fig.* connection, link
engrandecer /eŋgrande'θer; eŋgrande'ser/ *vt irr* to enlarge; augment; eulogize; promote, exalt. See **conocer**
engrandecimiento /eŋgrandeθi'miento; eŋgrandesi'miento/ *m*, enlargement; increase; exaggeration, eulogization; advancement, promotion
engrasado /eŋgra'saðo/ *m*, oiling; greasing
engrasador /eŋgrasa'ðor/ *m*, greaser, lubricator; oiler
engrasar /eŋgra'sar/ *vt* to grease; lubricate, oil; manure; stain with grease
engreimiento /eŋgrei'miento/ *m*, conceit, vanity
engreír /eŋgre'ir/ *vt irr* to make conceited; *—vr* become vain or conceited. See **reír**
engrescar /eŋgres'kar/ **(se)** *vt* and *vr* to start a quarrel
engrosar /eŋgro'sar/ *vt irr* to fatten, thicken; *Fig.* increase, swell; manure; *—vi* put on weight, grow fat. See **contar**
engrudar /eŋgru'ðar/ *vt* to paste, glue
engrudo /eŋ'gruðo/ *m*, paste, glue
enguantarse /eŋ'guantarse/ *vr* to put on one's gloves
enguijarrado /eŋguiha'rraðo/ *a* pebbled. *m*, pebbled path
engullir /eŋgu'ʎir; eŋgu'yir/ *vt* to gobble, swallow
enhebrar /ene'βrar/ *vt* to thread (needles); string
enhestar /enes'tar/ *vt irr* to erect; set upright; *—vr* rise; rear up; straighten oneself up. See **acertar**
enhiesto /en'iesto/ *a* upright, erect
enhorabuena /enora'βuena/ *f*, congratulation *—adv* well and good. **dar la e.,** to congratulate
enhoramala /enora'mala/ *adv* in an evil hour. *Inf.* **¡Vete e.!** Go to the devil!
enhorquetado /enorke'taðo/ *a* in the saddle
enhuerar /enue'rar/ *vt* to addle; *—vi* become addled
enigma /e'nigma/ *m*, enigma
enigmático /enig'matiko/ *a* enigmatical
enjabonar /enhaβo'nar/ *vt* to soap; *Inf.* soap down, flatter
enjaezar /enhae'θar; enhae'sar/ *vt* to harness (a horse)
enjalbegar /enhalβe'gar/ *vt* to whitewash
enjambrar /enhamb'rar/ *vt* to hive bees; *—vi* multiply, increase
enjambre /en'hambre/ *m*, swarm (of bees); crowd
enjaretado /enhare'taðo/ *m*, latticework
enjaular /enhau'lar/ *vt* to cage; *Inf.* jail
enjoyar /enho'yar/ *vt* to adorn with jewels; beautify; set with precious stones
enjuagadura /enhuaga'ðura/ *f*, rinsing (the mouth); rinse water; mouthwash
enjuagar /enhua'gar/ *vt* to rinse; *—vr* rinse the mouth

enjuague /en'huage/ *m,* rinse; rinsing; mouthwash; tooth mug; scheme, plan

enjugar /enhu'gar/ *vt* to dry; cancel, write off; wipe, mop (perspiration, tears, etc.); *—vr* grow lean

enjuiciar /enhui'θiar; enhui'siar/ *vt* to submit a matter to arbitration; *Law.* prosecute; *Law.* render judgment; *Law.* adjudicate (a case)

enjundia /en'hundia/ *f,* animal fat or grease; *Fig.* substance, meat; strength, vigor; constitution, temperament

enjuto /en'huto/ *a* dry; lean. *m pl,* brushwood; *Cul.* canapés, savories

enlace /en'laθe; en'lase/ *m,* connection; link; tie; *Chem.* bond; alliance, relationship; marriage

enladrillado /enlaðri'ʎaðo; enlaðri'yaðo/ *m,* brick floor or pavement

enlardar /enlar'ðar/ *vt Cul.* to baste

enlazar /enla'θar; enla'sar/ *vt* to tie, bind; join, link; lasso; *—vr* marry; be allied, related. **e. con,** to connect with (of trains); link up with

enlentecerse /enlente'θerse; enlente'serse/ *vr* to decelerate, go slow, slow down

enlodar /enlo'ðar/ *vt* to muddy; *Fig.* smirch, sully

enloquecer /enloke'θer; enloke'ser/ *vt irr* to drive insane; *—vi* go mad. See **conocer**

enlosado /enlo'saðo/ *m,* tile floor

enlosar /enlo'sar/ *vt* to pave with flags

enlucir /enlu'θir; enlu'sir/ *vt irr* to plaster (walls); polish (metals). See **lucir**

enlutar /enlu'tar/ *vt* to put in mourning, drape with crepe; darken, obscure; sadden; *—vr* go into mourning; become dark

enmaderar /emaðe'rar/ *vt* to panel in wood, board up

enmarañar /emara'ɲar/ *vt* to tangle, disorder (hair, etc.); complicate, confuse; *—vr* be tangled; be sprinkled with clouds

enmaridar /emari'ðar/ *vi* to become a wife

enmarillecerse /emariʎe'θerse; emariye'serse/ *vr irr* to grow yellow. See **conocer**

enmascarar /emaska'rar/ *vt* to mask; disguise, dissemble; *—vr* be masked

enmasillar /emasi'ʎar; emasi'yar/ *vt* to putty

enmendar /emen'dar/ *vt irr* to correct, improve; reform; compensate, indemnify; *Law.* repeal; *—vr* be improved or corrected; mend one's ways. See **acertar**

enmienda /e'mienda/ *f,* correction; reform; indemnity; compensation; amendment; *pl Agr.* fertilizers

enmohecer /emoe'θer; emoe'ser/ *vt irr* to rust; *—vr* become moldy. See **conocer**

enmudecer /emuðe'θer; emuðe'ser/ *vt irr* to silence; *—vi* become dumb; be silent. See **conocer**

enmugrecer /emugre'θer; emugre'ser/ *vt irr* to cover with grime; *—vr* be grimy, dirty. See **conocer**

ennegrecer /ennegre'θer; ennegre'ser/ *vt irr* to dye black; make black; *—vr* become black; become dark or cloudy. See **conocer**

ennoblecer /ennoβle'θer; ennoβle'ser/ *vt irr* to ennoble; enrich, embellish; adorn, befit. See **conocer**

ennoblecimiento /ennoβleθi'miento; ennoβlesi'miento/ *m,* ennoblement; enrichment

enojadizo /enoha'ðiθo; enoha'ðiso/ *a* irritable, peevish

enojar /eno'har/ *vt* to anger; annoy, irritate; *—vr* be angry; rage, be rough (wind, sea)

enojo /e'noho/ *m,* anger; resentment; vexations, troubles, trials (gen. *pl*). **con gran e. de,** much to the annoyance of

enojoso /eno'hoso/ *a* annoying; troublesome, tiresome

enorgullecer /enorguʎe'θer; enorguye'ser/ *vt irr* to make proud; *—vr* be proud. See **conocer**

enorme /e'norme/ *a* enormous, huge; monstrous, heinous

enormidad /enormi'ðað/ *f,* hugeness; enormity; wickedness

enramar /enra'mar/ *vt* to intertwine branches; embower; *—vi* branch (trees)

enramidad /enrami'ðað/ *f,* bower; thick foliage

enrarecer /enrare'θer; enrare'ser/ *vt irr* to rarefy; *—vr* become rarefied; grow rare. See **conocer**

enrarecimiento /enrareθi'miento; enraresi'miento/ *m,* rarefaction

enredadera /enreða'ðera/ *f,* convolvulus *—a f,* climbing, twining (plant)

enredador /enreða'ðor/ **(-ra)** *a* mischievous, willful; intriguing, scheming; *Inf.* gossiping, meddlesome *—n* intriguer; *Inf.* meddler

enredar /enre'ðar/ *vt* to catch in a net; put down nets or snares; entangle; sow discord; compromise, involve (in difficulties); *—vi* be mischievous; *—vr* be entangled; be involved (in difficulties)

enredo /en'reðo/ *m,* tangle; mischief, prank; intrigue, malicious falsehood; difficult situation; plot

enredoso /enre'ðoso/ *a* tangled; fraught with difficulties

enrejado /enre'haðo/ *m,* railing, paling; trellis or latticework; *Sew.* openwork

enrejar /enre'har/ *vt* to fence with a railing; cover with grating

enriquecer /enrike'θer; enrike'ser/ *vt irr* to enrich; exalt, aggrandize; *—vi* grow rich; prosper, flourish. See **conocer**

enriscado /enris'kaðo/ *a* craggy, rocky

enriscar /enris'kar/ *vt* to raise; *—vr* hide among crags

enristrar /enris''trar/ *vt* to couch (a lance); string (onions, etc.); *Fig.* surmount (difficulties); go straight to (a place)

enrojecer /enrohe'θer; enrohe'ser/ *vt irr* to redden; make blush; *—vr* grow red; blush. See **conocer**

enroscar /enros'kar/ *vt* to twist, twine; *—vr* turn (screw); twist; coil

ensaimada /ensai'maða/ *f,* Spanish pastry cake

ensalada /ensa'laða/ *f,* salad; hodgepodge

ensaladera /ensala'ðera/ *f,* salad bowl

ensalmar /ensal'mar/ *vt Surg.* to set (bones); cure by spells

ensalmo /en'salmo/ *m,* spell, charm. **por e.,** as if by magic, rapidly

ensalzar /ensal'θar; ensal'sar/ *vt* to exalt, promote; praise

ensamblador /ensambla'ðor/ *m,* joiner, assembler

ensambladura /ensambla'ðura/ *f,* assemblage, joinery; joining; dovetailing

ensamblar /ensam'blar/ *vt* to assemble; join, dovetail, mortise

ensanchador /ensantʃa'ðor/ *m,* glove stretcher

ensanchar /ensan'tʃar/ *vt* to widen, enlarge, extend; *Sew.* let out, stretch; *—vr* put on airs

ensanche /en'santʃe/ *m,* dilatation, widening; stretch; extension; *Sew.* turnings, letting out; (city) extension

ensangrentar /ensaŋgren'tar/ *vt irr* to stain with blood; *—vr* be bloodstained; be overhasty. See **regimentar**

ensañar /ensa'ɲar/ *vt* to irritate, infuriate; *—vr* be merciless (with vanquished)

ensartar /ensar'tar/ *vt* to string (beads); thread (needles); spit, pierce; tell a string (of falsehoods)

ensayador /ensaia'ðor/ *m,* metal assayer

ensayar /ensa'yar/ *vt* to try out; *Chem.* test; *Theat.* rehearse; assay

ensaye /en'saye/ *m,* assaying (of metals)

ensayista /ensa'yista/ *mf* essayist

ensayo /ensa'yo/ *m,* test, trial; *Lit.* essay; assay; experiment; rehearsal. **e. general,** dress rehearsal

ensenada /ense'naða/ *f,* cove, inlet

enseña /en'seɲa/ *f,* ensign, standard

enseñanza /ense'ɲanθa; enseɲansa/ *f,* teaching; education; example, experience. **e. primaria,** elementary education. **e. secundaria,** secondary education. **e. superior,** higher education

enseñar /ense'ɲar/ *vt* to teach, instruct; train; point out; exhibit, show; *—vr* become accustomed. **e. la oreja,** *Fig.* to show the cloven hoof

enseñorearse /enseɲore'arse/ *vr* to take possession (of)

enseres /en'seres/ *m pl,* household goods; utensils; equipment

ensilladero /ensiʎa'ðero; ensiya'ðero/ *m,* paddock

ensillar /ensi'ʎar; ensi'yar/ *vt* to saddle

ensimismarse /ensimis'marse/ *vr* to be lost in thought

ensoberbecer /ensoβerβe'θer; ensoβerβe'ser/ *vt irr* to make haughty; *—vr* become arrogant; grow rough (sea). See **conocer**
ensordecedor /ensorðeθe'ðor; ensorðese'ðor/ *a* deafening
ensordecer /ensorðe'θer; ensorðe'ser/ *vt irr* to deafen; *—vi* become deaf; keep silent, refuse to reply. See **conocer**
ensuciar /ensu'θiar; ensu'siar/ *vt* to soil, dirty; *Fig.* sully; *—vr* be dirty; *Inf.* accept bribes
ensueño /en'sueɲo/ *m,* dream; illusion, fancy
entablado /enta'βlaðo/ *m,* stage, dais; wooden floor; planking
entablar /enta'βlar/ *vt* to plank, floor with boards; board up; *Surg.* splint; undertake, initiate (negotiations, etc.); begin (conversations, etc.); *—vr* settle (winds). **e. acción judicial,** to take legal action
entalegar /entale'gar/ *vt* to put into sacks or bags; hoard (money)
entalladura /entaʎa'ðura; entaya'ðura/ *f,* carving; sculpture; mortise, notch
entallar /enta'ʎar; enta'yar/ *vt* to carve; sculpture; engrave; notch, groove; tap (trees); fit (well or ill) at the waist
entallecer /entaʎe'θer; entaye'ser/ *vi irr* to sprout (plants). See **conocer**
entapizar /entapi'θar; entapi'sar/ *vt* to hang with tapestry; upholster; *Fig.* cover, carpet
entarimado /entari'maðo/ *m,* wooden floor; dais
ente /'ente/ *m,* entity, being; *Inf.* object, individual
enteco /en'teko/ *a* sickly, ailing, delicate
entendederas /entende'ðeras/ *f pl, Inf.* understanding
entendedor /entende'ðor/ **(-ra)** *a* understanding, comprehending *—n* one who understands. **A buen e. pocas palabras,** A word to the wise is sufficient
entender /enten'der/ *vt irr* to comprehend, understand; know; deduce, infer; intend; believe; (*with de*) be familiar with or knowledgeable about; (*with en*) have as a profession or trade; be engaged in; have authority in; *—vr* understand oneself; have a reason (for behavior); understand each other; have an amatory understanding; be meant, signify; (*with con*) have an understanding with. **a mi e.,** in my opinion, as I see it *—Pres. Indic.* **entiendo, entiendes, entiende, entienden.** *Pres. Subjunc.* **entienda, entiendas, entienda, entiendan**
entendido /enten'diðo/ *a* learned, knowledgeable
entendimiento /entendi'miento/ *m,* understanding; mind, reason, intelligence
enteramente /entera'mente/ *adv* completely, entirely, wholly
enterar /ente'rar/ *vt* to inform, advise
entereza /ente'reθa; enteresa/ *f,* entirety; completeness; impartiality, integrity; fortitude, constancy; strictness, rigor
enternecer /enterne'θer; enterne'ser/ *vt irr* to soften, make tender; move to pity; *—vr* be touched by compassion. See **conocer**
enternecimiento /enterneθi'miento; enternesi'miento/ *m,* compassion, pity; tenderness
entero /en'tero/ *a* entire; whole; robust, healthy; upright, just; constant, loyal; virgin; pure; *Inf.* strong, tough (cloth); *Math.* integral
enterrador /enterra'ðor/ *m,* gravedigger
enterrar /ente'rrar/ *vt irr* to inter; outlive; bury, forget. See **acertar**
entibiar /enti'βiar/ *vt* to make lukewarm; *Fig.* cool, temper
entidad /enti'ðað/ *f,* entity; value, importance
entierro /en'tierro/ *m,* interment, burial; grave; funeral; buried treasure
entoldar /entol'dar/ *vt* to cover with an awning; hang with tapestry, etc., drape; cover (sky, clouds)
entomología /entomolo'hia/ *f,* entomology
entomológico /entomo'lohiko/ *a* entomological
entomólogo /ento'mologo/ *m,* entomologist
entonación /entona'θion; entona'sion/ *f,* intonation; modulation (voice); conceit
entonado /ento'naðo/ *m,* haughty, conceited
entonar /ento'nar/ *vt* to modulate (voice); intone; blow (organ bellows); lead (song); *Med.* tone up; *Art.* harmonize; *—vr* become conceited; *Com.* improve, harden (stock, etc.)
entonces /en'tonθes; entonses/ *adv* then, at that time; in that case, that being so
entonelar /entone'lar/ *vt* to put in barrels or casks
entontecer /entonte'θer; entonteser/ *vt irr* to make stupid or foolish; *—vr* become stupid. See **conocer**
entornar /entor'nar/ *vt* to leave ajar; half-close; upset, turn upside down
entorpecer /entorpe'θer; entorpe'ser/ *vt irr* to numb, make torpid; confuse, daze; obstruct, delay; *—vr* go numb; be confused. See **conocer**
entorpecimiento /entorpeθi'miento; entorpesi'miento/ *m,* numbness, torpidity; stupidity, dullness; delay, obstruction
entrada /en'traða/ *f,* entrance; door, gate; admission; *Cul.* entree; admission ticket; *Theat.* house; takings, gate; *Mil.* entry; beginnings (of month, etc.); intimacy; right of entry. **entradas y salidas,** comings and goings; collusion; *Com.* ingoing and outgoing
entrampar /entram'par/ *vt* to trap (animals); swindle; *Fig. Inf.* entangle (business affairs); *Inf.* load with debts; *—vr* be bogged down; *Inf.* be in debt
entrante /en'trante/ *a* incoming, entrant; next, coming (month)
entraña /en'traɲa/ *f,* entrail; *pl* heart; *Fig.* center, core; humaneness; temperament. *Inf.* **no tener entrañas,** to be heartless, be without feeling
entrañable /entra'ɲaβle/ *a* intimate; dearly loved
entrar /en'trar/ *vi* (*with en*) to enter, go into, come in; flow into; *Fig.* have access to; join, become a member; *Fig.* be taken by (fever, panic, etc.); *Mil.* enter; be an ingredient of; (*with por, en*) penetrate, pierce; (*with de*) embrace (professions, etc.); (*with prep a + infin*) begin to; (*with en + noun*) begin to be (e.g. *e. en calor,* begin to be hot) or begin to take part in (e.g. *e. en lucha,* begin to fight); *—vt* introduce, make enter; *Mil.* (*with en*) occupy; *—vr* (*with en*) squeeze in. **e. en apetito,** to work up an appetite, get an appetite. *Inf.* **no e. ni salir en,** to take no part in. *Inf.* **No me entra,** I don't understand it
entre /'entre/ *prep* between; among; to. **e. joyas,** among jewels. **E. las dos se escribió la carta,** Between them, they wrote the letter. **Dije e. mí,** I said to myself. **los días de e. semana,** weekdays. **e. tanto,** in the meanwhile.
entreabrir /entrea'βrir/ *vt* to leave ajar; half-open *—Past Part.* **entreabierto**
entreacto /entre'akto/ *m,* interval, entr'acte; small cigar
entrecano /entre'kano/ *a* going gray, grayish (hair)
entrecejo /entre'θeho; entre'seho/ *m,* space between the eyebrows; frown
entrecoger /entreko'her/ *vt* to intercept, catch; constrain, compel
entrecortado /entrekor'taðo/ *a* intermittent (sounds); faltering, broken (voice)
entrecubiertas /entreku'βiertas/ *f pl, Naut.* between decks
entredicho /entre'ðitʃo/ *m,* prohibition; *Eccl.* interdiction
entredós /en'treðos/ *m, Sew.* insertion
entrefino /entre'fino/ *a* middling, fairly fine
entrega /en'trega/ *f,* handing over; delivery; *Lit.* part, serial; installment. **por entregas,** as a serial, serial (of stories)
entregar /entre'gar/ *vt* to hand over; deliver; surrender; *—vr* give oneself up; surrender; submit; (*with prep a*) engage in, be absorbed in; (*with prep a* or *en*) give oneself over to (vice, etc.)
entreguista /entre'gista/ *mf* defeatist
entrelazar /entrela'θar; entrela'sar/ *vt* to interlace, intertwine; interweave
entrelistado /entrelis'taðo/ *a* striped
entrelucir /entrelu'θir; entrelu'sir/ *vi irr* to show through, be glimpsed. See **lucir**
entremedias /entre'meðias/ *adv* in between, halfway; in the meantime
entremés /entre'mes/ *m,* hors d'oeuvres (gen. *pl*); interlude, one-act farce

entremesista /entreme'sista/ *mf* author of, or actor in, one-act farces
entremeter /entreme'ter/ *vt* to place between or among; —*vr* intrude; meddle, pry
entremetido /entreme'tiðo/ **(-da)** *a* meddlesome —*n* busybody, meddler
entremetimiento /entremeti'miento/ *m*, meddlesomeness
entremezclar /entremeθ'klar; entremes'klar/ *vt* to intermingle
entrenador /entrena'ðor/ **(-ra)** *n* trainer; *Sports.* coach
entrenamiento /entrena'miento/ *m*, training, exercise
entrenar /entre'nar/ **(se)** *vt* and *vr* to train; exercise; *Sports.* coach
entreoír /entreo'ir/ *vt* to overhear; hear imperfectly
entrepaño /entre'paɲo/ *m*, *Archit.* panel; pier (between windows, etc.)
entrepiernas /entre'piernas/ *f pl*, crotch
entrepuente /entre'puente/ *m*, *Naut.* between decks; steerage quarters
entresacar /entresa'kar/ *vt* to choose or pick out; thin out (plants); thin (hair)
entresuelo /entre'suelo/ *m*, mezzanine, entresol; ground floor
entresueño /entre'sueɲo/ *m*, daydream
entretalladura /entretaʎa'ðura; entretayae'th;ura/ *f*, bas-relief
entretallar /entreta'ʎar; entreta'yar/ *vt* to carve in bas-relief; engrave; *Sew.* do openwork; intercept; —*vr* connect, dovetail
entretejer /entrete'her/ *vt* to interweave; interlace; *Lit.* insert
entretela /entre'tela/ *f*, *Sew.* interlining
entretener /entrete'ner/ *vt irr* to keep waiting; make more bearable; amuse, entertain; delay, postpone; maintain, upkeep; —*vr* amuse oneself. See **tener**
entretenido /entrete'niðo/ *a* amusing, entertaining
entretenimiento /entreteni'miento/ *m*, amusement; pastime, diversion; upkeep, maintenance
entretiempo /entre'tiempo/ *m*, between seasons, spring or autumn
entreventana /entreβen'tana/ *f*, space between windows
entreverado /entreβe'raðo/ *a* variegated; streaky (of bacon)
entreverar /entreβe'rar/ *vt* to intermingle
entrevía /entre'βia/ *f*, railroad gauge
entrevista /entre'βista/ *f*, meeting, interview
entristecer /entriste'θer; entriste'ser/ *vt irr* to sadden; —*vr* grieve. See **conocer**
entristecimiento /entristeθi'miento; entristesi'miento/ *m*, sadness
entrometer /entrome'ter/ *vt* See **entremeter**
entronar /entro'nar/ *vt* See **entronizar**
entroncar /entron'kar/ *vt* to prove descent; —*vi* be related, or become related (by marriage)
entronerar /entrone'rar/ *vt* to pocket (in billiards)
entronización /entroniθa'θion; entronisa'sion/ *f*, enthronement
entronizar /entroni'θar; entroni'sar/ *vt* to enthrone; exalt
entronque /entron'ke/ *m*, blood relationship, cognation; junction
entumecer /entume'θer; entume'ser/ *vt irr* to numb; —*vr* go numb; swell, rise (sea, etc.). See **conocer**
enturbiar /entur'βiar/ *vt* to make turbid or cloudy; confuse, disorder; —*vr* become turbid; be in disorder
entusiasmar /entusias'mar/ *vt* to inspire enthusiasm; —*vr* be enthusiastic
entusiasmo /entu'siasmo/ *m*, enthusiasm
entusiasta /entu'siasta/ *a* enthusiastic. *mf* enthusiast
enumeración /enumera'θion; enumera'sion/ *f*, enumeration
enumerar /enume'rar/ *vt* to enumerate
enunciación /enunθia'θion; enunsia'sion/ *f*, statement, declaration, enunciation
enunciar /enun'θiar; enun'siar/ *vt* to state clearly, enunciate
envainar /embai'nar/ *vt* to sheathe
envalentonamiento /embalentona'miento/ *m*, boldness; braggadocio, bravado
envalentonar /embalento'nar/ *vt* to make bold (gen. in a bad sense); —*vr* strut, brag; take courage
envanecer /embane'θer; embane'ser/ *vt irr* to make vain or conceited; —*vr* be vain; be conceited
envanecimiento /embaneθimiento; embanesi'miento/ *m*, conceit, vanity
envasador /embasa'ðor/ **(-ra)** *n* packer. *m*, funnel
envasar /emba'sar/ *vt* to bottle; barrel; sack (grain, etc.); pack in any container; pierce (with sword)
envase /em'base/ *m*, bottling; filling; container; packing
envejecer /embehe'θer; embehe'ser/ *vt irr* to make old, wear out; —*vi* grow old. See **conocer**
envenenador /embenena'ðor/ **(-ra)** *n* poisoner
envenenamiento /embenena'miento/ *m*, poisoning
envenenar /embene'nar/ *vt* to poison; corrupt, pervert; put a malicious interpretation on; embitter; —*vr* take poison
envergadura /emberga'ðura/ *f*, wingspan
envés /em'bes/ *m*, wrong side of anything; *Inf.* back. **al e.,** wrong side out
enviado /em'biaðo/ *m*, messenger; envoy. **e. extraordinario,** special envoy
enviar /em'biar/ *vt* to send, dispatch
enviciar /embi'θiar; embi'siar/ *vt* to corrupt, make vicious; —*vr* (*with con, en*) take to (drink, etc.)
envidia /em'biðia/ *f*, envy; emulation; desire (to possess)
envidiable /embi'ðiaβle/ *a* enviable
envidiar /embi'ðiar/ *vt* to envy, grudge; emulate
envidioso /embi'ðioso/ *a* envious
envilecer /embile'θer; embile'ser/ *vt irr* to debase; —*vr* degrade oneself. See **conocer**
envío /em'bio/ *m*, *Com.* remittance; consignment
envite /em'bite/ *m*, stake (at cards); offer; push, shove
enviudar /embiu'ðar/ *vi* to become a widow or widower
envoltorio /embol'torio/ *m*, bundle
envoltura /embol'tura/ *f*, swaddling clothes; covering; wrapping
envolver /embol'βer/ *vt irr* to enfold; envelop; wrap up, parcel; *Fig.* contain, enshrine; swaddle, swathe; roll into a ball; confound (in argument); *Mil.* outflank; implicate (person). See **mover**
enyesado /enye'saðo/ *m*, plastering; stucco
enyesar /enye'sar/ *vt* to plaster; *Surg.* apply a plaster bandage
enzarzar /enθar'θar; ensar'sar/ *vt* to fill or cover with brambles; —*vr* be caught on brambles; set one person against another; get in difficulties; quarrel
eñe /'eɲe/ *f*, name of letter Ñ
eón /e'on/ *m*, eon
eperlano /eper'lano/ *m*, smelt
épica /'epika/ *f*, epic
épico /'epiko/ *a* epic
epicúreo /epi'kureo/ **(-ea)** *a* epicurean; sensual, voluptuous —*n* epicure
epidemia /epi'ðemia/ *f*, epidemic
epidémico /epi'ðemiko/ *a* epidemic
epifanía /epifa'nia/ *f*, Epiphany, Twelfth Night
epiglotis /epi'glotis/ *f*, epiglottis
epígrafe /epi'grafe/ *m*, epigraph, inscription; title, motto
epigrafía /epigra'fia/ *f*, epigraphy
epigrama /epi'grama/ *m*, inscription; epigram
epigramático /epigra'matiko/ **(-ca)** *a* epigrammatic —*n* epigrammatist
epilepsia /epi'lepsia/ *f*, epilepsy
epiléptico /epi'leptiko/ **(-ca)** *a* and *n* epileptic
epilogar /epilo'gar/ *vt* to summarize, recapitulate
epílogo /e'pilogo/ *m*, recapitulation; summary, digest; epilogue
episcopado /episko'paðo/ *m*, episcopate; bishopric
episódico /epi'soðiko/ *a* episodic
episodio /epi'soðio/ *m*, episode; digression
epístola /e'pistola/ *f*, epistle
epistolar /episto'lar/ *a* epistolary
epitafio /epi'tafio/ *m*, epitaph

epíteto /e'piteto/ *m*, epithet
epítome /e'pitome/ *m*, epitome; summary, abstract
época /'epoka/ *f*, epoch, period; space of time. **é. de celo,** mating season. **é. de lluvias,** rainy season. **é. de secas,** dry season. **en aquella é.,** at that time
épodo /'epoðo/ *m*, *Poet.* epode
epopeya /epo'peya/ *f*, epic poem; *Fig.* epic
equidad /eki'ðað/ *f*, fairness; reasonableness; equity
equidistancia /ekiðis'tanθia; ekiðistansia/ *f*, equidistance
equidistante /ekiðis'tante/ *a* equidistant
equilibrar /ekili'βrar/ *vt* to balance; *Fig.* maintain in equilibrium, counterbalance
equilibrio /eki'liβrio/ *m*, equilibrium; equanimity; *Fig.* balance
equilibrista /ekili'βrista/ *mf* equilibrist, tightrope walker
equino /e'kino/ *a* equine. *m*, *Archit.* echinus; sea urchin
equinoccio /eki'nokθio; ekinoksio/ *m*, equinox
equipaje /eki'pahe/ *m*, luggage, baggage; *Naut.* crew
equipar /eki'par/ *vt* to equip, furnish
equipo /e'kipo/ *m*, outfitting, furnishing; equipment; team; trousseau
equis /'ekis/ *f*, name of letter X
equitación /ekita'θion; ekita'sion/ *f*, horsemanship, riding
equitativo /ekita'tiβo/ *a* equitable, just, fair
equivalencia /ekiβa'lenθia; ekiβalensia/ *f*, equivalence, equality
equivalente /ekiβa'lente/ *a* equivalent
equivaler /ekiβa'ler/ *vi irr* to be equivalent; *Geom.* be equal. See **valer**
equivocación /ekiβoka'θion; ekiβoka'sion/ *f*, error, mistake
equivocadamente /ekiβokaða'mente/ *adv* mistakenly, by mistake
equivocar /ekiβo''kar/ *vt* to mistake; *—vr* be mistaken or make a mistake. **equivocarse de medio a medio,** to be off by a long shot
equívoco /e'kiβoko/ *a* equivocal, ambiguous. *m*, equivocation
era /'era/ *f*, era; threshing floor; vegetable or flower bed
erario /e'rario/ *m*, public treasury, exchequer
erección /erek'θion; erek'sion/ *f*, raising; erection, elevation; foundation, institution
eremita /ere'mita/ *mf* hermit
ergio /'erhio/ *m*, erg
erguir /er'gir/ *vt irr* to raise; straighten; lift up; *—vr* straighten up; tower; grow proud *—Pres. Indic.* **irgo** (or **yergo**), **irgues, irguen.** *Pres. Part.* **irguiendo.** *Preterite* **irguió, irguieron.** *Pres. Subjunc.* **irga** or **yerga,** etc.
erial /e'rial/ *m*, uncultivated land
erigir /eri'hir/ *vt* to found, establish; promote, exalt. **erigirse contra,** to rise up against
erisipela /erisi'pela/ *f*, erysipelas
erizado /eri'θaðo; eri'saðo/ *a* standing on end (of hair); prickly, covered with bristles or quills. **e. de espinas,** bristling with thorns; covered with bristles or quills
erizar /eri'θar; eri'sar/ *vt* to set on end (hair); beset with difficulties; *—vr* stand on end, bristle (hair, quills, etc.)
erizo /e'riθo; e'riso/ *m*, hedgehog; husk (of some fruits); *Inf.* touch-me-not, unsociable person; *Mech.* sprocket wheel. **e. de mar,** sea urchin
ermita /er'mita/ *f*, hermitage
ermitaño /ermi'taɲo/ *m*, hermit
erosión /ero'sion/ *f*, erosion
erótico /e'rotiko/ *a* erotic
errabundo /erra'βundo/ *a* wandering, errant, vagrant
erradamente /erraða'mente/ *adv* erroneously
erradicable /erraði'kaβle/ *a* eradicable
erradicación /erraðika'θion; erraðika'sion/ *f*, eradication
erradicar /erraði'kar/ *vt* to eradicate
errante /e'rrante/ *a* wandering; erring; errant
errar /e'rrar/ *vi irr* to err, fail; rove, roam; wander (attention, etc.); *—vr* be mistaken. *Auto.* **e. el encendido,** to misfire *—Pres. Indic.* **yerro, yerras, yerra, yerran.** *Pres. Subjunc.* **yerre, yerres, yerre, yerren**
errata /e'rrata/ *f*, misprint
errático /e'rratiko/ *a* wandering, vagrant; *Med.* erratic
erre /'erre/ *f*, name of letter R
erróneo /e'rroneo/ *a* erroneous, mistaken
error /e'rror/ *m*, error. **error de más,** an overestimate. **error de menos,** an underestimate
eructar /eruk'tar/ *vi* to eructate, belch
eructo /e'rukto/ *m*, eructation, belching
erudición /eruði'θion; eruði'sion/ *f*, erudition
erudito /eru'ðito/ *a* learned, erudite. *m*, scholar. **e. a la violeta,** pseudo-learned
erupción /erup'θion; erup'sion/ *f*, *Med.* rash; eruption
eruptivo /erup'tiβo/ *a* eruptive
es /es/ *irr 3rd pers. sing Pres. Indic.* of ser, is
esa /'esa/ *f*, *dem a* that. **ésa,** *f*, *dem. pron* that one; the former; the town in which you are (e.g. *Iré a é. mañana,* I shall come to your town tomorrow). Used generally in letters. See **ése**
esbeltez /esβel'teθ; esβel'tes/ *f*, slenderness
esbelto /es'βelto/ *a* tall and slim and graceful, willowy
esbozar /esβo'θar; esβo'sar/ *vt* to sketch, outline
esbozo /es'βoθo; es'βoso/ *m*, sketch; outline, rough plan, first draft
escabechar /eskaβe'tʃar/ *vt* to pickle; dye (the hair, etc.); *Inf.* kill in anger; *Inf.* fail (an examination)
escabeche /eska'βetʃe/ *m*, *Cul.* pickle; hair dye
escabechina /eskaβe'tʃina/ *f*, *Inf.* heavy failure (in an examination)
escabel /eska'βel/ *m*, footstool; small backless chair; *Fig.* steppingstone
escabioso /eska'βioso/ *a* scabby, scabious
escabro /es'kaβro/ *m*, scab, mange
escabroso /eska'βroso/ *a* rough; rocky; uneven; rude, unpolished, uncivil; risqué, improper
escabullirse /eskaβu'ʎirse; eskaβu'yirse/ *vr irr* to escape; run away; slip out unnoticed. See **mullir**
escafandra /eska'fandra/ *f*, diving suit, diving outfit
escala /es'kala/ *f*, ladder; (*Mus. Math.*) scale; dial (of machines); proportion, ratio; stage, stopping place; measuring rule; *Naut.* port of call. **e. de toldilla,** companion ladder. *Mus.* **e. mayor,** major scale. **e. menor,** minor scale. *Naut.* **hacer e. en un puerto,** to call at a port
escalada /eska'laða/ *f*, escalade
escalafón /eskala'fon/ *m*, salary scale; roll, list
escalamiento /eskala'miento/ *m*, scaling, climbing; storming
escalar /eska'lar/ *vt* to scale; climb, ascend; storm, assail, enter or leave violently
escaldadura /eskalda'ðura/ *f*, scalding; scald
escaldar /eskal'dar/ *vt* to scald; make red-hot; *—vr* scald or burn oneself. **Gato escaldado del agua fría huye,** Once bitten, twice shy
escalera /eska'lera/ *f*, staircase; stair. **e. abajo,** below stairs. **e. de caracol,** spiral staircase. **e. de mano,** ladder. **e. de tijera,** stepladder. **e. móvil,** escalator
escalfar /eskal'far/ *vt* to poach (eggs); burn (bread)
escalinata /eskali'nata/ *f*, outside staircase or flight of steps, perron
escalofrío /eskalo'frio/ *m*, (gen. *pl*) shiver, shudder
escalón /eska'lon/ *m*, step, stair; rung (of a ladder); *Fig.* steppingstone; grade, rank. **en escalones,** in steps
escalpar /eskal'par/ *vt* to scalp
escalpelo /eskal'pelo/ *m*, scalpel
escama /es'kama/ *f*, *Zool.* scale; anything scale-shaped; flake; suspicion, resentment
escamar /eska'mar/ *vt* to scale (fish); make suspicious *—vr Inf.* be suspicious or disillusioned
escamondar /eskamon'dar/ *vt Agr.* to prune
escamoso /eska'moso/ *a* scaly
escamotear /eskamote'ar/ *vt* to make disappear; palm (in conjuring); steal
escamoteo /eskamo'teo/ *m*, disappearance; stealing
escampada /eskam'paða/ *f*, *Inf.* clear interval on a rainy day

escampar /eskam'par/ *vi* to cease raining; clear up (of the weather, sky); stop (work, etc.)
escamujar /eskamu'har/ *vt Agr.* to cut out superfluous wood (of trees, etc.)
escanciar /eskan'θiar; eskan'siar/ *vt* to pour out wine; *—vi* drink wine
escandalizar /eskandali'θar; eskandali'sar/ *vt* to shock, scandalize; disturb with noise; *—vr* be vexed or irritated
escandallo /eskan'daʎo; eskan'dayo/ *m, Naut.* deep-sea lead; random test
escándalo /es'kandalo/ *m,* scandal; commotion, uproar; bad example; viciousness; astonishment
escandaloso /eskanda'loso/ *a* disgraceful, scandalous; turbulent
Escandinavia /eskandi'naβia/ Scandinavia
escandinavo /eskandi'naβo/ **(-va)** *a* and *n* Scandinavian
escandir /eskan'dir/ *vt* to scan (verse)
escansión /eskan'sion/ *f,* scansion
escantillón /eskanti'ʎon; eskanti'yon/ *m,* template, pattern; rule
escaño /es'kaɲo/ *m,* bench with a back
escapada /eska'paða/ *f,* escape; escapade
escapar /eska'par/ *vt* to spur on (a horse); *—vi* escape; flee; avoid, evade; *—vr* escape; leak (gas, etc.). **Se me escapó su nombre,** His name escaped me. **e. por un pelo,** to have a narrow escape
escaparate /eskapa'rate/ *m,* showcase, cabinet; shop window
escapatoria /eskapa'toria/ *f,* escape, flight; *Inf.* way out, loophole
escape /es'kape/ *m,* flight; evasion; escape (gas, etc.); *Auto.* exhaust. **a e.,** at full speed
escápula /es'kapula/ *f,* scapula
escaque /es'kake/ *m,* square (chessboard or checkerboard); *pl* chess
escaqueado /eskake'aðo/ *a* checked, worked in squares
escara /es'kara/ *f,* scar
escarabajo /eskara'βaho/ *m,* beetle, scarab; *Fig. Inf.* dwarf; *pl Inf.* scrawl
escaramuza /eskara'muθa; eskara'musa/ *f,* skirmish
escaramuzar /eskaramu'θar; eskaramu'sar/ *vi* to skirmish
escarapela /eskara'pela/ *f,* cockade, rosette; brawl
escarbadientes /eskarβa'ðientes/ *m,* toothpick
escarbar /eskar'βar/ *vt* to scratch, scrabble (fowls); root, dig; rake out (the fire); inquire into
escarcha /es'kartʃa/ *f,* hoarfrost
escarchar /eskar'tʃar/ *vt Cul.* to frost, ice; spread with frosting; *—vi* freeze lightly
escarda /es'karða/ *f,* weeding; *Fig.* weeding out
escardador /eskarða'ðor/ **(-ra)** *n* weeder
escardar /eskar'ðar/ *vt* to weed; *Fig.* separate good from bad
escarificación /eskarifika'θion; eskarifika'sion/ *f,* scarification
escarlata /eskar'lata/ *f,* scarlet; scarlet cloth
escarlatina /eskarla'tina/ *f,* scarlet fever
escarmentar /eskarmen'tar/ *vt irr* to reprehend or punish severely; *—vi* learn from experience, be warned. See **acertar**
escarmiento /eskar'miento/ *m,* disillusionment, experience; warning; punishment, fine
escarnecedor /eskarneθe'ðor; eskarneseðor/ **(-ra)** *a* mocking *—n* mocker
escarnecer /eskarne'θer; eskarne'ser/ *vt irr* to mock. See **conocer**
escarnio /es'karnio/ *m,* gibe, jeer
escarola /eska'rola/ *f,* endive; frilled ruff
escarpa /es'karpa/ *f,* steep slope, declivity; escarpment
escarpado /eskar'paðo/ *a* steep, precipitous
escarpín /eskar'pin/ *m,* pump, slipper
escasear /eskase'ar/ *vt* to dole out, give grudgingly; save, husband; *—vi* be scarce or short; grow less
escasez /eska'seθ; eska'ses/ *f,* meanness, frugality; want; shortage, scarcity
escaso /es'kaso/ *a* scarce; short; bare; parsimonious
escatimar /eskati'mar/ *vt* to cut down, curtail
escatimoso /eskati'moso/ *a* malicious, guileful
escayola /eska'yola/ *f,* plaster of Paris
escena /es'θena; es'sena/ *f, Theat.* stage; scene; scenery; theater, drama; spectacle, sight; episode, incident. **director de e.,** producer. **poner en e.,** *Theat.* to produce
escenario /esθe'nario; esse'nario/ *m, Theat.* stage; scenario
escénico /es'θeniko; es'seniko/ *a* scenic
escenografía /esθenogra'fia; essenogra'fia/ *f,* scenography
escenógrafo /esθe'nografo; esse'nografo/ **(-fa)** *n* scenographer, scene painter
escepticismo /esθepti'θismo; essepti'sismo/ *m,* scepticism
escéptico /es'θeptiko; es'septiko/ **(-ca)** *a* sceptical *—n* sceptic
escindir /esθin'dir; essin'dir/ *vt* to split
escisión /esθi'sion; essi'sion/ *f,* cleavage, split; splitting; schism; disagreement
esclarecer /esklare'θer; esklare'ser/ *vt irr* to illuminate; ennoble, make illustrious; *Fig.* enlighten; elucidate; *—vi* dawn. See **conocer**
esclarecido /esklare'θiðo; esklare'siðo/ *a* distinguished, illustrious
esclavina /eskla'βina/ *f,* short cape
esclavitud /esklaβi'tuð/ *f,* slavery; fraternity
esclavizar /esklaβi'θar; esklaβi'sar/ *vt* to enslave
esclavo /es'klaβo/ **(-va)** *n* slave; member of a brotherhood *—a* enslaved. *f,* slave bracelet; ID bracelet
esclerosis /eskle'rosis/ *f,* sclerosis
esclerótica /eskle'rotika/ *f,* sclerotic
esclusa /es'klusa/ *f,* lock; sluice gate; weir
esclusero /esklu'sero/ *m,* lock keeper
escoba /es'koβa/ *f,* broom, brush; *Bot.* yellow broom
escobada /esko'βaða/ *f,* sweep, stroke (of a broom)
escobar /esko'βar/ *vt* to sweep with a broom
escobazo /esko'βaθo; esko'βaso/ *m,* brush with a broom
escobero /esko'βero/ *m,* brush maker or seller
escobilla /esko'βiʎa; esko'βiya/ *f,* brush
escobina /esko'βina/ *f,* metal filing; woodshaving
escocer /esko'θer; esko'ser/ *vi irr* to smart; *Fig.* sear; *—vr* hurt, smart; be chafed. See **mover**
escocés /esko'θes; esko'ses/ **(-esa)** *a* Scots, Scottish *—n* Scot
Escocia /es'koθia; eskosia/ Scotland
escoda /es'koða/ *f,* claw hammer
escofina /esko'fina/ *f,* rasp, file
escoger /esko'her/ *vt* to choose, select
escogido /esko'hiðo/ *a* choice, select
escolar /esko'lar/ *a* school; pupil. *m,* pupil
escolasticismo /eskolasti'θismo; eskolasti'sismo/ *m,* scholasticism
escolástico /esko'lastiko/ *a* scholastic
escollera /esko'ʎera; esko'yera/ *f,* breakwater, sea wall, jetty
escollo /es'koʎo; es'koyo/ *m,* reef; danger, risk; difficulty, obstacle
escolopendra /eskolo'pendra/ *f,* centipede; hart's-tongue fern
escolta /es'kolta/ *f,* escort, guard
escoltar /eskol'tar/ *vt* to escort; guard, conduct
escombrar /eskom'brar/ *vt* to remove obstacles, free of rubbish; *Fig.* clean up
escombro /es'kombro/ *m,* debris, rubble, rubbish; mackerel
esconder /eskon'der/ *vt* to hide, conceal; *Fig.* contain, embrace; *—vr* hide
escondidas, a /eskon'diðas, a/ *adv* secretly
escondite, escondrijo /eskon'dite, eskon'driho/ *m,* hiding place. **jugar al escondite,** to play hide-and-seek
escopeta /esko'peta/ *f,* shotgun. **e. de aire comprimido,** air gun, popgun. **e. de pistón,** repercussion gun. **e. de viento,** air gun
escopetazo /eskope'taθo; eskope'taso/ *m,* gunshot; gunshot wound; *Fig.* bombshell
escopetear /eskopete'ar/ *vt* to shoot repeatedly
escopetero /eskope'tero/ *m,* musketeer; gunsmith; man with a gun

escoplear /eskople'ar/ *vt* to notch; chisel; gouge

escoplo /es'koplo/ *m,* chisel

escorbuto /eskor'βuto/ *m,* scurvy

escoria /es'koria/ *f,* dross, slag; scoria, volcanic ash; *Fig.* dregs

escorial /esko'rial/ *m,* slag heap

escorpión /eskor'pion/ *m,* scorpion; Scorpio

escorzo /es'korθo; es'korso/ *m, Art.* foreshortening

escotado /eskotaðo/ *a* low-cut (of dresses)

escotadura /eskota'ðura/ *a* low neck (of a dress); piece cut out of something; *Theat.* large trapdoor; recess

escotar /esko'tar/ *vt* to cut low in the neck (of dresses); pay one's share (of expenses)

escote /es'kote/ *m,* low neck (of a dress); shortness (of sleeves); share (of expenses); lace yoke

escotilla /esko'tiʎa; esko'tiya/ *f, Naut.* hatch

escozor /esko'θor; esko'sor/ *m,* smart, pricking pain; irritation, prickle; heartache

escriba /es'kriβa/ *m,* (*Jewish hist.*) scribe

escribanía /eskriβa'nia/ *f,* secretaryship; notaryship; bureau, office; writing case; inkstand

escribano /eskri'βano/ *m,* notary public; secretary

escribiente /eskri'βiente/ *mf* clerk

escribir /eskri'βir/ *vt* to write; —*vr* enlist; enroll; correspond by writing —*Past Part.* **escrito**

escrito /es'krito/ *m,* writing, manuscript; literary or scientific work; *Law.* writ. **por e.,** in writing

escritor /eskri'tor/ **(-ra)** *n* writer, author

escritorio /eskri'torio/ *m,* escritoire; office

escritura /eskri'tura/ *f,* writing; handwriting; *Law.* deed; literary work. **Sagrada E.,** Holy Scripture

escrófula /es'krofula/ *f,* scrofula

escrofuloso /eskrofu'loso/ *a* scrofulous

escroto /es'kroto/ *m,* scrotum

escrúpulo /es'krupulo/ *m,* scruple, qualm; conscientiousness; scruple (pharmacy)

escrupulosidad /eskrupulosi'ðað/ *f,* conscientiousness, scrupulousness

escrupuloso /eskrupu'loso/ *a* scrupulous; exact, accurate

escrutador /eskruta'ðor/ **(-ra)** *n* scrutinizer —*a* examining, inspecting

escrutar /eskru'tar/ *vt* to scrutinize, examine; count (votes)

escrutinio /eskru'tinio/ *m,* scrutiny, examination; count (votes)

escuadra /es'kuaðra/ *f,* carpenter's square; architect's square; *Nav.* fleet; *Aer.* squadron; *Mil.* squad. **e. de agrimensor,** *Surv.* cross-staff

escuadrar /eskuað'rar/ *vt* (and *Mas.*) to square

escuadrilla /eskuað'riʎa; eskuað'riya/ *f,* squadron (airplanes, small ships)

escuadrón /eskuað'ron/ *m,* squadron

escualidez /eskuali'ðeθ; eskuali'ðes/ *f,* squalor, sordidness

escuálido /es'kualiðo/ *a* filthy, squalid; sordid; thin

escucha /es'kutʃa/ *f,* listening; peephole; *Mil.* sentinel

escuchar /esku'tʃar/ *vt* to listen; attend to, heed; —*vr* like the sound of one's own voice

escudar /esku'ðar/ *vt* to shield, protect

escudero /esku'ðero/ *m,* squire, page; gentleman; shield maker

escudete /esku'ðete/ *m,* escutcheon; shield; gusset; white water lily

escudilla /esku'ðiʎa; esku'ðiya/ *f,* bowl

escudo /es'kuðo/ *m,* shield; escudo; escutcheon; protection, defense; ward (of a keyhole)

escudriñador /eskuðriɲa'ðor/ **(-ra)** *a* searching; curious, prying —*n* scrutinizer; pryer

escudriñar /eskuðri'ɲar/ *vt* to scrutinize; scan; investigate; pry into

escuela /es'kuela/ *f,* school; school building; style; (*Lit.* and *Art.*) school. **e. de artes y oficios,** industrial school. **e. industrial,** technical school. **e. normal,** normal school

escueto /es'kueto/ *a* dry, bare, unadorned; simple, exact; unencumbered

esculpir /eskul'pir/ *vt* to sculpture; engrave

escultor /eskul'tor/ **(-ra)** *n* sculptor

escultórico /eskul'toriko/ *a* sculptural

escultura /eskul'tura/ *f,* sculpture; carving; modeling

escupidera /eskupi'ðera/ *f,* spittoon

escupir /esku'pir/ *vi* to expectorate; —*vt Fig.* spit out; cast away, throw out

escurreplatos /eskurre'platos/ *m,* dishrack, draining rack

escurrido /esku'rriðo/ *a* narrow-hipped; skintight (of skirts)

escurridor /eskurri'ðor/ *m,* colander, sieve; dishrack; drainingboard

escurriduras /eskurri'ðuras/ *f pl,* lees, dregs

escurrir /esku'rrir/ *vt* to drain to the dregs; wring, press out, drain; —*vi* trickle, drip; slip, slide; —*vr* slip away, edge away; escape, slip out; skid

esdrújulo /esðru'hulo/ *a Gram.* of words where the accent falls on the antepenultimate syllable

ese /'ese/ *f,* name of letter S; S-shaped link (in a chain). *Inf.* **andar haciendo eses,** to reel about drunkenly

ese /'ese/ *m, dem a* (*f,* **esa.** *pl* **esos, esas**) that; those. **ése,** *m, dem pron* (*f,* **ésa.** *neut* **eso.** *pl* **ésos, ésas**) that one; the former (e.g. *Me gusta éste, pero ése no me gusta,* I like this one, but I do not like that one

esencia /e'senθia; e'sensia/ *f,* essence, nature, character; extract; *Chem.* essence

esencial /esen'θial; esen'sial/ *a* essential

esfera /es'fera/ *f, Geom.* sphere, globe, ball; sky; rank; face, dial; province, scope

esférico /es'feriko/ *a* spherical

esfinge /es'finhe/ *f,* sphinx

esforzado /esfor'θaðo; esfor'saðo/ *a* valiant, courageous; spirited

esforzador /esforθa'ðor; esforsa'ðor/ *a* encouraging

esforzar /esfor'θar; esfor'sar/ *vt irr* to encourage; invigorate; —*vr* make an effort. See **contar**

esfuerzo /es'fuerθo; es'fuerso/ *m,* effort; courage; spirit; vigor; exertion, strain; *Mech.* stress. **sin e.,** effortless

esfumar /esfu'mar/ *vt Art.* shade; *Art.* stump; dim; —*vr* disappear

esfumino /esfu'mino/ *m, Art.* stump

esgrima /es'grima/ *f,* (art of) fencing

esgrimidor /esgrimi'ðor/ *m,* fencer, swordsman

esgrimir /esgri'mir/ *vt* to fence; fend off

esguazar /esgua'θar; esgua'sar/ *vt* to ford (a river)

esguince /es'ginθe; es'ginse/ *m,* dodging, twist; expression or gesture of repugnance; *Med.* sprain

eslabón /esla'βon/ *m,* link (in a chain); steel for producing fire. **e. perdido,** *Fig.* missing link

eslabonar /eslaβo'nar/ *vt* to link; connect, unite

eslavo /es'laβo/ **(-va)** *a* Slavic —*n* Slav

eslora /es'lora/ *f, Naut.* length (of a ship)

eslovaco /eslo'βako/ **(-ca)** *a* Slovakian —*n* Slovak

esloveno /eslo'βeno/ **(-na)** *a* and *n* Slovene

esmaltador /esmalta'ðor/ **(-ra)** *n* enameler

esmaltar /esmal'tar/ *vt* to enamel; decorate, adorn

esmalte /es'malte/ *m,* enamel; enamelwork; smalt; brilliance

esmerado /esme'raðo/ *a* careful, painstaking

esmeralda /esme'ralda/ *f,* emerald

esmerar /esme'rar/ *vt* to polish; —*vr* (*with en*) take great pains with (or to)

esmeril /es'meril/ *m,* emery

esmerilar /esmeri'lar/ *vt* to polish with emery

esmero /es'mero/ *m,* great care, conscientiousness

esmoladera /esmola'ðera/ *f,* grindstone

esnob /es'noβ/ *a* snobbish. *mf* snob

eso /'eso/ *neut dem pron* that; the fact that; that idea, affair, etc.; about (of time) (e.g. *Vendrá a e. de las nueve,* He will come about nine o'clock). **Eso** refers to an abstraction, never to one definite object. **No me gusta e.,** I don't like that kind of thing. **e. es,** that's it. **por e.,** therefore, for that reason

esófago /e'sofago/ *m,* esophagus

esotérico /eso'teriko/ *a* esoteric

espaciar /espa'θiar; espa'siar/ *vt* to space; *Print.* lead; —*vr* spread oneself, enlarge (upon)

espacio /es'paθio; es'pasio/ *m,* space; capacity; interval, duration; slowness; *Print.* lead

espaciosidad /espaθiosi'ðað; espasiosi'ðað/ *f,* spaciousness; capacity

espada /es'paða/ *f,* sword; matador; swordsman; (cards) spade. **entre la e. y la pared,** *Fig.* between a rock and a hard place; between undesirable alternatives.

espadachín /espaða'tʃin/ *m,* good swordsman; bully, quarrelsome fellow

espadaña /espa'ðaɲa/ *f,* open belfry; gladiolus

espadería /espaðe'ria/ *f,* sword cutler's workshop or shop

espadero /espa'ðero/ *m,* sword cutler

espadín /espa'ðin/ *m,* small dress sword

espahi /es'pai/ *m,* spahi

espalda /es'palda/ *f, Anat.* back (often *pl*); *pl* rear, back portion; *Mil.* rear guard. **de espaldas,** with one's (its, his, etc.) back turned; on one's (its, etc.) back

espaldar /espal'dar/ *m,* backpiece of a cuirass; back (of chair); garden trellis, espalier

espaldarazo /espalda'raθo; espalda'raso/ *m,* accolade

espaldera /espal'dera/ *f,* espalier, trellis

espantadizo /espanta'ðiθo; espanta'ðiso/ *a* easily frightened

espantapájaros /espanta'paharos/ *m,* scarecrow

espantar /espan'tar/ *vt* to frighten, terrify; chase off; *—vr* be amazed; be scared

espanto /es'panto/ *m,* terror, panic; dismay; amazement; threat

espantoso /espan'toso/ *a* horrible, terrifying, awesome; amazing

España /es'paɲa/ Spain

español /espa'ɲol/ **(-la)** *a* Spanish *—n* Spaniard. *m,* Spanish (language). **a la española,** in Spanish fashion

españolía /espaɲo'lia/ *f,* Spanish colony, Spanish community (outside Spain)

españolismo /espaɲo'lismo/ *m,* love of things Spanish; Hispanism

españolizar /espaɲoli'θar; espaɲoli'sar/ *vt* to hispanize; *—vr* adopt Spanish customs

esparadrapo /espara'ðrapo/ *m,* court plaster

esparavel /espara'βel/ *m,* casting net

esparcimiento /esparθi'miento; esparsi'miento/ *m,* scattering; naturalness, frankness; geniality

esparcir /espar'θir; espar'sir/ *vt* to scatter, sprinkle, disperse; spread, publish abroad; entertain; *—vr* be scattered; amuse oneself

espárrago /es'parrago/ *m,* asparagus

esparraguera /esparra'gera/ *f,* asparagus plant; asparagus bed; asparagus dish

Esparta /es'parta/ Sparta

espartano /espar'tano/ **(-na)** *a* and *n* Spartan

espartería /esparte'ria/ *f,* esparto industry, esparto shop

esparto /es'parto/ *m,* esparto grass

espasmo /es'pasmo/ *m,* spasm

espasmódico /espas'moðiko/ *a* spasmodic

espátula /es'patula/ *f,* spatula; palette knife

especia /es'peθia; es'pesia/ *f,* spice. **nuez de e.,** nutmeg

especial /espe'θial; espe'sial/ *a* special; particular

especialidad /espeθiali'ðað; espesiali'ðað/ *f,* specialty; branch (of learning)

especialista /espeθia'lista; espesia'lista/ *mf* specialist

especialización /espeθialiθa'θion; espesialisa'sion/ *f,* specialization

especializarse /espeθiali'θarse; espesiali'sarse/ *vr* to specialize

especie /es'peθie; es'pesie/ *f,* class, kind; species; affair, matter, case; idea, image; news; pretext, appearance

especiería /espeθie'ria; espesie'ria/ *f,* spice trade; spice shop

especiero /espe'θiero; espe'siero/ **(-ra)** *n* spice merchant; spice rack

especificación /espeθifika'θion; espesifika'sion/ *f,* specification. **e. normalizada,** standard specification

especificar /espeθifi'kar; espesifi'kar/ *vt* to specify, particularize

específico /espe'θifiko; espe'sifiko/ *a* and *m,* specific patent medicine

espécimen /es'peθimen; es'pesimen/ *m,* specimen, sample

especioso /espe'θioso; espe'sioso/ *a* lovely, perfect; specious

espectacular /espektaku'lar/ *a* spectacular

espectáculo /espek'takulo/ *m,* spectacle, sight; show, display

espectador /espekta'ðor/ **(-ra)** *n* spectator

espectral /espek'tral/ *a* spectral; faint, dim

espectro /es'pektro/ *m,* phantom, specter; *Phys.* spectrum

especulación /espekula'θion; espekula'sion/ *f,* conjecture; *Com.* speculation

especulador /espekula'ðor/ **(-ra)** *n* speculator

especular /espeku'lar/ *vt* to examine, look at; (*with en*) reflect on, consider; *—vi Com.* speculate

especulativo /espekula'tiβo/ *a* speculative; thoughtful, meditative

espejería /espehe'ria/ *f,* mirror shop or factory

espejero /espe'hero/ *m,* mirror manufacturer or seller

espejismo /espe'hismo/ *m,* mirage; illusion

espejo /es'peho/ *m,* mirror; *Fig.* model. **e. de cuerpo entero,** full-length mirror. **e. retrovisor,** rearview mirror

espejuelo /espe'huelo/ *m,* small mirror; *Mineral.* selenite; *Mineral.* sheet of talc; *pl* lenses, eyeglasses

espeluznante /espeluθ'nante; espelus'nante/ *a* hair-raising

espeluznar /espeluθ'nar; espelus'nar/ *vt* to dishevel; untidy (hair, etc.); *—vr* stand on end (hair)

espera /es'pera/ *f,* waiting; expectation; *Law.* adjournment; caution, restraint; *Law.* respite

esperantista /esperan'tista/ *mf* Esperantist

esperanto /espe'ranto/ *m,* Esperanto

esperanza /espe'ranθa; espe'ransa/ *f,* hope

esperanzar /esperan'θar; esperan'sar/ *vt* to inspire hope in

esperar /espe'rar/ *vt* to hope; expect; await; (*with en*) have faith in. **e. sentado,** *Fig. Inf.* to whistle for

esperma /es'perma/ *f,* sperm, semen. **e. de ballena,** spermaceti

esperpento /esper'pento/ *m, Inf.* scarecrow, grotesque; folly, madness; fantastic dramatic composition

espesar /espe'sar/ *vt* to thicken; make closer; tighten (fabrics); *—vr* thicken; grow denser or thicker

espeso /es'peso/ *a* thick; dense; greasy, dirty

espesor /espe'sor/ *m,* thickness; density

espesura /espe'sura/ *f,* thickness; density; thicket; filth

espetar /espe'tar/ *vt Cul.* to spit, skewer; pierce; *Inf.* utter, give; *—vr* be stiff or affected; *Inf.* push oneself in, intrude

espetera /espe'tera/ *f,* kitchen or pot rack

espetón /espe'ton/ *m, Cul.* spit; poker; large pin

espía /es'pia/ *mf* spy. *f, Naut.* warp

espiar /es'piar/ *vt* to spy upon, watch; *—vi Naut.* warp

espiche /es'pitʃe/ *m,* sharp-pointed weapon or instrument; spit, spike

espiga /es'piga/ *f, Bot.* spike, ear; sprig; peg; tang, shank (of sword); tenon, dowel; *Naut.* masthead; *Herald.* garb

espigador /espiga'ðor/ **(-ra)** *n* gleaner

espigar /espi'gar/ *vt* to glean; tenon; *—vi Bot.* begin to show the ear or spike; *—vr Bot.* bolt; shoot up, grow (persons)

espigón /espi'ɣon/ *m,* sting; sharp point; breakwater; bearded spike (corn, etc.)

espigueo /espi'geo/ *m,* gleaning

espín /es'pin/ *m,* porcupine

espina /es'pina/ *f,* thorn; prickle; splinter; fish bone; *Anat.* spine; suspicion, doubt

espinaca /espi'naka/ *f,* spinach

espinal /espi'nal/ *a* spinal

espinar /espi'nar/ *m,* thorn brake; *Fig.* awkward position *—vt* to prick, wound, hurt

espinazo /espi'naθo; espi'naso/ *m,* backbone

espineta /espi'neta/ *f,* spinet; virginals

espinilla /espi'niʎa; espi'niya/ *f,* shinbone; blackhead

espinoso /espi'noso/ *a* thorny; difficult, intricate
espión /es'pion/ *m*, See **espía**
espionaje /espio'nahe/ *m*, espionage; spying
espira /es'pira/ *f*, (*Geom. Archit.*) helix; turn, twist (of winding stairs); whorl (of a shell)
espiración /espira'θion; espira'sion/ *f*, expiration; respiration
espiral /espi'ral/ *a* spiral. *f*, *Geom.* spiral; spiral watchspring
espirar /espi'rar/ *vt* to exhale, breathe out; inspire; encourage; —*vi* breathe; breathe out; *Poet.* blow (wind)
espiritisimo /espiri'tisimo/ *m*, spiritualism
espiritista /espiri'tista/ *a* spiritualist. *mf* spiritualist
espiritoso /espiri'toso/ *a* lively, active, spirited; spirituous
espíritu /es'piritu/ *m*, spirit; apparition, specter; soul; intelligence, mind; mood, temper, outlook; underlying principle, spirit; devil (gen. *pl*) vigor, ardor, vivacity; *Chem.* essence; *Chem.* spirits; turn of mind. **E. Santo,** Holy Ghost
espiritual /espiri'tual/ *a* spiritual
espiritualidad /espirituali'ðað/ *f*, spirituality
espiritualismo /espiritua'lismo/ *m*, *Philos.* spiritualism
espiritualizar /espirituali'θar; espirituali'sar/ *vt* to spiritualize
espita /es'pita/ *f*, spigot, tap; *Inf.* tippler
esplender /esplen'der/ *vi Poet.* to shine
esplendidez /esplendi'ðeθ; esplendiðes/ *f*, liberality, abundance; splendor, pomp
espléndido /es'plendiðo/ *a* magnificent; liberal; resplendent (gen. *pl*)
esplendor /esplen'dor/ *m*, splendor, brilliance; distinction, nobility
esplendoroso /esplendo'roso/ *a* splendid, brilliant, radiant
espliego /es'pliego/ *m*, lavender
esplín /es'plin/ *m*, spleen, melancholy
espolada /espo'laða/ *f*, prick with the spur
espolear /espole'ar/ *vt* to prick with the spur; encourage, stimulate
espoleta /espo'leta/ *f*, fuse (of explosives); breastbone (of fowls); wishbone. **e. de tiempo, e. graduada,** time fuse. **e. de seguridad,** safety fuse
espolón /espo'lon/ *m*, spur (of a bird or mountain range); *Naut.* ram; breakwater; buttress; *Naut.* fender
espolvorear /espolβore'ar/ *vt* to sprinkle with powder
espondeo /espon'deo/ *m*, (metrical foot) spondee
esponja /es'ponha/ *f*, sponge
esponjadura /esponha'ðura/ *f*, sponging
esponjar /espon'har/ *vt* to make spongy; sponge; —*vr* swell with pride; *Inf.* bloom with health
esponjera /espon'hera/ *f*, sponge holder
esponjosidad /esponhosi'ðað/ *f*, sponginess
esponjoso /espon'hoso/ *a* spongy, porous
esponsales /espon'sales/ *m pl*, betrothal; marriage contract
espontaneidad /espontanei'ðað/ *f*, spontaneity
espontáneo /espon'taneo/ *a* spontaneous
espora /es'pora/ *f*, spore
esporádico /espo'raðiko/ *a* sporadic
esportillo /espor'tiʎo; espor'tiyo/ *m*, bass, frail
esposa /es'posa/ *f*, wife; *pl* handcuffs
esposo /es'poso/ *m*, husband; *pl* husband and wife
espuela /es'puela/ *f*, spur; stimulus; (*Ornith. Bot.*) spur. **e. de caballero,** larkspur
espulgar /espul'gar/ *vt* to delouse; examine carefully
espuma /es'puma/ *f*, froth, foam; *Cul.* scum; *Fig.* the best of anything, flower; *Fig. Inf.* **crecer como la e.,** to flourish like weeds
espumadera /espuma'ðera/ *f*, skimming ladle
espumajear /espumahe'ar/ *vi* to foam at the mouth
espumajoso /espuma'hoso/ *a* frothy, foaming
espumar /espu'mar/ *vt* to skim (soup, etc.); —*vi* foam; increase rapidly
espumoso /espu'moso/ *a* frothy, foaming
espurio /es'purio/ *a* bastard; spurious
esputo /es'puto/ *m*, sputum
esqueje /es'kehe/ *m*, *Agr.* cutting
esquela /es'kela/ *f*, note; (printed) card
esqueleto /eske'leto/ *m*, skeleton; *Inf.* skinny person; framework
esquema /es'kema/ *f*, diagram, layout sketch; scheme, plan. **e. de una máquina,** drawing of a machine
esquemático /eske'matiko/ *a* schematic; diagrammatic
esquematizar /eskemati'θar; eskemati'sar/ *vt* to plan, outline
esquí /es'ki/ *m*, ski, snowshoe
esquiador /eskia'ðor/ *m*, skier
esquiar /es'kiar/ *vi* to ski
esquife /es'kife/ *m*, skiff
esquila /es'kila/ *f*, cattle bell; small bell, hand bell; sheep shearing; (*Ichth. Bot.*) squill
esquilador /eskila'ðor/ *a* shearing. *m*, sheep shearer
esquiladora /eskila'ðora/ *f*, shearing machine
esquilar /eski'lar/ *vt* to shear, clip (sheep, etc.)
esquileo /eski'leo/ *m*, shearing; shearing time or place
esquilmar /eskil'mar/ *vt* to harvest; impoverish
esquilmo /es'kilmo/ *m*, harvest
esquimal /eski'mal/ *a* and *mf* Eskimo
esquina /es'kina/ *f*, corner
esquinado /eski'naðo/ *a* having corners; *Fig.* difficult to approach (people)
esquirla /es'kirla/ *f*, splinter (of a bone); shrapnel
esquirol /eski'rol/ *m*, *Inf.* strikebreaker, blackleg
esquisto /es'kisto/ *m*, *Mineral.* slate; shale
esquivar /eski'βar/ *vt* to avoid; —*vr* slip away, disappear; excuse oneself
esquivez /eski'βeθ; eskiβes/ *f*, unsociableness; unfriendliness, aloofness
esquivo /es'kiβo/ *a* unsociable, elusive, aloof
esquizado /eski'θaðo; eskisaðo/ *a* mottled (of marble)
estabilidad /estaβili'ðað/ *f*, stability; fastness (of colors)
estabilizar /estaβili'θar; estaβili'sar/ *vt* to stabilize
estable /es'taβle/ *a* stable; fast (of colors)
establecer /estaβle'θer; estaβle'ser/ *vt irr* to establish, found, institute; decree; —*vr* take up residence; open (a business firm). See **conocer**
establecimiento /estaβleθi'miento; estaβlesi'miento/ *m*, law, statute; foundation, institution; establishment
establero /estaβ'lero/ *m*, stablegroom
establo /es'taβlo/ *m*, stable
estaca /es'taka/ *f*, stake, pole; *Agr.* cutting; cudgel
estacada /esta'kaða/ *f*, fence; *Mil.* palisade; place fixed for a duel
estacar /esta'kar/ *vt* to stake; fence; tie to a stake; —*vr Fig.* be as still as a post
estación /esta'θion; esta'sion/ *f*, position, situation; season; station (railroad, etc.); depot; time, period; stop, halt; building, headquarters; *Bot.* habitat; (*Surv. Geom. Eccl.*) station
estacional /estaθio'nal; estasio'nal/ *a* seasonal; *Astron.* stationary
estacionamiento /estaθiona'miento; estasiona'miento/ *m*, stationariness; *Auto.* parking
estacionar /estaθio'nar; estasio'nar/ *vt* to station, place; *Auto.* park (a car); —*vr* remain stationary; place oneself
estacionario /estaθio'nario; estasio'nario/ *a* motionless; *Astron.* stationary. *m*, stationer
estada /es'taða/ *f*, sojourn
estadía /esta'ðia/ *f*, stay, sojourn; *Art.* sitting (of a model)
estadio /es'taðio/ *m*, racetrack; stadium; furlong
estadista /esta'ðista/ *mf*. statistician; statesman, stateswoman
estadística /esta'ðistika/ *f*, statistics
estadístico /esta'ðistiko/ *a* statistical
estadizo /esta'ðiθo; estaðiso/ *a* stagnant
estado /es'taðo/ *m*, state; condition; rank, position; *Polit.* state; profession; status; *Com.* statement. **e. de guerra,** state of war; martial law. **e. mayor central,** (*Nav. Mil.*) general staff. **e. tapón,** *Polit.* buffer state. **tomar e.,** to marry; *Eccl.* profess; be ordained a priest

Estados Unidos de América /es'taðos u'niðos de a'merika/ United States of America
estadounidense /estaðouni'ðense/ *a* United States
estafa /es'tafa/ *f,* swindle
estafador /estafa'ðor/ **(-ra)** *n* swindler
estafar /esta'far/ *vt* to swindle
estafeta /esta'feta/ *f,* courier, messenger; branch post office; diplomatic pouch
estafilococo /estafilo'koko/ *m,* staphylococcus
estagnación /estagna'θion; estagna'sion/ *f,* stagnation
estalactita /estalak'tita/ *f,* stalactite
estalagmita /estalag'mita/ *f,* stalagmite
estallar /esta'ʎar; esta'yar/ *vi* to explode; burst; *Fig.* break out
estallido /esta'ʎiðo; esta'yiðo/ *m,* explosion, report; crash, crack; *Fig.* outbreak; *Auto.* **e. de un neumático,** blowout (of a tire)
estambre /es'tambre/ *m,* woolen yarn, worsted; stamen
estameña /esta'meɲa/ *f,* serge
estampa /es'tampa/ *f,* illustration, picture; print; aspect; printing press; track, step; *Metall.* boss, stud
estampación /estampa'θion; estampa'sion/ *f,* stamping; printing; imprinting. **e. en seco,** tooling (of a book)
estampado /estam'paðo/ *a* printed (of textiles). *m,* textile printing; printed fabric
estampar /estam'par/ *vt* to print, stamp; leave the print (of); bestow, imprint. **e. en relieve,** to emboss. **e. en seco,** to tool (a book)
estampería /estampe'ria/ *f,* print or picture shop; trade in prints
estampero /estam'pero/ *m,* print dealer, picture dealer
estampido /estam'piðo/ *m,* report, bang, detonation; crash
estampilla /estam'piʎa; estam'piya/ *f,* rubber stamp; seal
estampillar /estampi'ʎar; estampi'yar/ *vt* to stamp, imprint
estancación /estanka'θion; estanka'sion/ *f,* stagnation
estancado /estan'kaðo/ *a* stagnant; blocked, held up
estancar /estan'kar/ *vt* to check, stem; set up a monopoly; *Fig.* hold up (negotiations, etc.); *—vr* be stagnant
estancia /es'tanθia; es'tansia/ *f,* stay, residence; dwelling; lounge, livingroom; stanza; *West Hem.* farm
estanciero /estan'θiero; estan'siero/ *m, West Hem.* farmer
estanco /es'tanko/ *a Naut.* watertight. *m,* monopoly; shop selling government monopoly goods; archive
estandarte /estan'darte/ *m,* standard, flag. **e. real,** royal standard
estanque /es'tanke/ *m,* tank; pool; reservoir
estanquero /estan'kero/ **(-ra)** *n* seller of government monopoly goods (tobacco, matches, etc.)
estante /es'tante/ *a* present; extant; permanent. *m,* shelf; bookcase; bin (for wine)
estantería /estante'ria/ *f,* shelving; shelves, bookcase
estantigua /estan'tigua/ *f,* hobgoblin, specter; *Fig. Inf.* scarecrow
estañador /estaɲa'ðor/ *m,* tinsmith
estañar /esta'ɲar/ *vt* to tin; solder
estaño /es'taɲo/ *m,* tin
estaquilla /esta'kiʎa; esta'kiya/ *f,* peg, cleat
estar /es'tar/ *vi irr* to be. Indicates: 1. Position or place (e.g. *Está a la puerta,* He is at the door). 2. State (e.g. *Las flores están marchitas,* The flowers are faded). 3. Used to form the continuous or progressive tense (e.g. **Siempre está (estaba) escribiendo,** He is (was) always writing). 4. In contrast to verb *ser,* indicates impermanency (e.g. *Está enfermo,* He is ill). 5. **Estar** forms an apparent passive where no action is implied (e.g. *El cuadro está pintado al óleo,* The picture is painted in oils). 6. Used in some impersonal expressions (e.g. *¡Bien está!* All right! *¡Claro está!* Of course! etc.). **e. de,** to be in, or on, or acting as (e.g. *e. de prisa,* to be in a hurry. *e. de capitán,* to be acting as a captain). **e. para,** to be on the point of; to be nearly; to be in the mood for. **e. para llover,** to be on the point of raining. **e. por,** to remain to be done; have a mind to (e.g. *La historia está por escribir,* The story remains to be written). **e. bien,** to be well (healthy). *Mech.* **e. bajo presión,** to have the steam up. *Polit.* **e. en el poder,** to be in office. **e. en una cuenca,** *Dominican Republic* to be broke. **¿A cómo** (*or* **A cuántos**) **estamos?** What is the date? *Pres. Ind.* **estoy, estás, está, estamos, estáis, están.** *Preterite* **estuve,** etc *—Pres. Subjunc.* **esté, estés, esté, estén.** *Imperf. Subjunc.* **estuviese,** etc.
estarcir /estar'θir; estar'sir/ *vt* to stencil
estatal /esta'tal/ *a* state
estática /es'tatika/ *f, Mech.* statics
estático /es'tatiko/ *a* static
estatua /es'tatua/ *f,* statue
estatuaria /esta'tuaria/ *f,* statuary
estatuir /esta'tuir/ *vt irr* to establish, order. See **huir**
estatura /esta'tura/ *f,* stature, height (of persons)
estatuto /esta'tuto/ *m,* statute, law
estay /es'tai/ *m, Naut.* stay. **e. mayor,** *Naut.* mainstay
este /'este/ *m,* east
este /'este/ *m, dem a* this (*f,* **esta,** *pl* **estos, estas,** these). **éste,** *m, dem pron* this one; the latter. (*f,* **ésta,** *neut* **esto,** *pl* **éstos, éstas,** these ones; the latter) (e.g. *Aquel cuadro no es tan hermoso como éste,* That picture is not as beautiful as this one)
estela /es'tela/ *f,* wake, track (of a ship)
estenografía /estenogra'fia/ *f,* shorthand
estenográfico /esteno'grafiko/ *a* shorthand
estenógrafo /este'nografo/ **(-fa)** *n* stenographer
estenordeste /estenor'ðeste/ *m,* east-northeast
estentóreo /esten'toreo/ *a* stentorian
estepa /es'tepa/ *f,* steppe, arid plain
estera /es'tera/ *f,* matting
esterar /este'rar/ *vt* to cover with matting; *—vi Inf.* muffle oneself up
estercoladura /esterkola'ðura/ *f,* manuring
estercolar /esterko'lar/ *vt* to manure
estercolero /esterko'lero/ *m,* manure pile; driver of a dung cart
estereoscopio /estereo'skopio/ *m,* stereoscope
esterería /estere'ria/ *f,* matting factory, matting shop
esterero /este'rero/ **(-ra)** *n* matting maker, matting seller
estéril /es'teril/ *a* sterile, barren; unfruitful, unproductive
esterilidad /esterili'ðað/ *f,* sterility; barrenness, unfruitfulness
esterilización /esteriliθa'θion; esterilisa'sion/ *f,* sterilization
esterilizador /esteriliθa'ðor; esterilisa'ðor/ *a* sterilizing. *m,* sterilizer
esterilizar /esterili'θar; esterili'sar/ *vt* to make barren; *Med.* sterilize
esterilla /este'riʎa; este'riya/ *f,* mat, matting
esterlina /ester'lina/ *a f,* sterling. **libra e.,** pound sterling
esternón /ester'non/ *m,* sternum
estero /es'tero/ *m,* salt marsh
estertor /ester'tor/ *m,* stertorous breathing, rattle
estesudeste /estesu'ðeste/ *m,* east-southeast
estética /es'tetika/ *f,* aesthetics *—a* aesthete
estético /es'tetiko/ *a* aesthetic *m,* aesthete
estetoscopio /esteto'skopio/ *m,* stethoscope
esteva /es'teβa/ *f,* plow handle
estevado /este'βaðo/ *a* bandy-legged
estiaje /es'tiahe/ *m,* low water level (of rivers)
estibador /estiβa'ðor/ *m,* stevedore, dock worker
estibar /esti'βar/ *vt Naut.* to stow
estiércol /es'tierkol/ *m,* dung; manure
estigio /es'tihio/ *a* Stygian; (*Fig. Poet.*) infernal
estigma /es'tigma/ *m,* stigma
estigmatizar /estigmati'θar; estigmati'sar/ *vt* to brand; stigmatize; insult
estilar /esti'lar/ *vi* to be accustomed; *—vt* draw up (document)
estilete /esti'lete/ *m,* stiletto, dagger; needle, hand, pointer; *Med.* stylet
estilista /esti'lista/ *mf* stylist

estilística /esti'listika/ *f*, stylism, stylistics
estilizar /estili'θar; estili'sar/ *vt* to stylize
estilo /es'tilo/ *m*, (*Art. Archit. Lit.*) style, writing instrument; gnomon, pointer; manner, way; *Bot.* style. **por el e.,** in some such way, like that
estilográfico /estilo'grafiko/ *a* stylographic. **pluma estilográfica,** fountain pen
estima /es'tima/ *f*, appreciation, esteem, consideration
estimable /esti'maβle/ *a* estimable
estimación /estima'θion; estima'sion/ *f*, valuation, estimate; regard, esteem. **e. prudente,** conservative estimate
estimar /esti'mar/ *vt* to value, estimate; esteem, judge
estimulante /estimu'lante/ *m*, *Med.* stimulant —*a* stimulating
estimular /estimu 'lar/ *vt* to stimulate, excite; goad on, encourage, incite
estímulo /es'timulo/ *m*, stimulus; incitement, encouragement
estío /es'tio/ *m*, summer
estipendiar /estipen'diar/ *vt* to pay a stipend to
estipendiario /estipen'diario/ *m*, stipendiary
estipendio /esti'pendio/ *m*, stipend, pay, remuneration
estipulación /estipula'θion; estipula'sion/ *f*, stipulation; *Law.* clause, condition
estipular /estipu'lar/ *vt* to stipulate; arrange terms; *Law.* covenant
estirado /esti'raðo/ *a* stretched out; tight, stiff; wire-drawn (metals); stiff, pompous; parsimonious
estirador /estira'ðor/ *m*, wire drawer
estirar /esti'rar/ *vt* to stretch; iron roughly (clothes); *Metall.* wire-draw; dole out (money); *Fig.* stretch, go beyond the permissible; —*vr* stretch oneself
estirpe /es'tirpe/ *f*, race, stock, lineage
estival /esti'βal/ *a* summer
esto /'esto/ *dem pron neut* this, this matter, this idea, etc. Always refers to abstractions, never to a definite object. **e. de,** the matter of. **e. es,** that's it; namely. **por e.,** for this reason. **a todo e.,** meanwhile
estocada /esto'kaða/ *f*, sword thrust
Estocolmo /esto'kolmo/ Stockholm
estofa /es'tofa/ *f*, *Sew.* quilting; kind, quality
estofado /esto'faðo/ *m*, stew —*a Sew.* quilted; stewed
estofar /esto'far/ *vt Sew.* to quilt; make a stew
estoicismo /estoi'θismo; estoi'sismo/ *m*, stoicism
estoico /es'toiko/ **(-ca)** *n* stoic —*a* stoical
estolidez /estoli'ðeθ; estoli'ðes/ *f*, idiocy
estólido /es'toliðo/ **(-da)** *a* idiotic —*a* idiot
estomacal /estoma'kal/ *a* stomach
estómago /es'tomago/ *m*, stomach
estomático /esto'matiko/ *a* pertaining to the mouth, oral
estomatitis /estoma'titis/ *f*, stomatitis
estonio /es'tonio/ **(-ia)** *a* and *n* Estonian. *m*, Estonian (language)
estopa /es'topa/ *f*, tow; oakum
estopilla /esto'piʎa; esto'piya/ *f*, batiste, lawn; calico, cotton cloth
estopín /esto'pin/ *m*, *Mil.* quick march
estoque /es'toke/ *m*, rapier; narrow sword
estoquear /estoke'ar/ *vt* to wound or kill with a rapier
estoqueo /esto''keo/ *m*, swordplay
estorbador /estorβa'ðor/ **(-ra)** *a* obstructive —*n* obstructer
estorbar /estor'βar/ *vt* to obstruct, impede; hinder
estorbo /es'torβo/ *m*, obstruction; hindrance, nuisance
estornino /estor'nino/ *m*, starling
estornudar /estornu'ðar/ *vi* to sneeze
estornudo /estor'nuðo/ *m*, sneezing; sneeze
estrabismo /estra'βismo/ *m*, *Med.* strabismus, squint, cast
estrada /es'traða/ *f*, road, highway
estrado /es'traðo/ *m*, dais
estrafalario /estrafa'lario/ *a Inf.* slovenly, untidy; *Inf.* eccentric, odd
estragar /estra'gar/ *vt* to corrupt, spoil, vitiate; ruin, destroy
estrago /es'trago/ *m*, devastation, destruction, ruin, havoc
estrambote /estram'bote/ *m*, refrain
estrambótico /estram'botiko/ *a Inf.* eccentric
estrangul /estraŋ'gul/ *m*, *Mus.* mouthpiece
estrangulación /estraŋgula'θion; estraŋgula'sion/ *f*, strangulation; *Auto.* throttling
estrangulador /estraŋgula'ðor/ **(-ra)** *a* strangling —*n* strangler. *m*, *Auto.* throttle
estrangular /estraŋgu'lar/ *vt* to strangle
estraperlista /estraper'lista/ *mf* black marketeer
estraperlo /estra'perlo/ *m*, black market
Estrasburgo /estras'βurgo/ Strasbourg
estratagema /estrata'hema/ *f*, stratagem, trick
estrategia /estra'tehia/ *f*, strategy
estratégico /estra'tehiko/ *a* strategic
estratego /estra'tego/ *m*, strategist
estratificación /estratifika'θion; estratifika'sion/ *f*, stratification
estrato /es'trato/ *m*, *Geol.* stratum
estratosfera /estratos'fera/ *f*, stratosphere
estraza /es'traθa; es'trasa/ *f*, rag. **papel de e.,** brown paper
estrechar /estre'tʃar/ *vt* to make narrower, tighten; hold tightly, clasp; compel, oblige; —*vr* tighten oneself up; reduce one's expenses; *Fig.* tighten the bonds (of friendship, etc.). **e. la mano,** to shake hands
estrechez /estre'tʃeθ; estre'tʃes/ *f*, narrowness; tightness; scantiness; poverty, want. **e. de miras,** narrow-mindedness
estrecho /es'tretʃo/ *a* narrow; tight; intimate, close; austere, rigid; meanspirited. *m*, *Geog.* strait
estregadera /estrega'ðera/ *f*, shoe scraper; scourer
estregar /estre'gar/ *vt irr* to rub, scour, scrub, scrape, scratch. See **cegar**
estrella /es'treʎa; es'treya/ *f*, star; fortune, fate; anything star-shaped; *Fig.* star. **e. de la pantalla,** movie star. **e. de mar,** starfish. **e. de rabo,** comet. **e. fugaz,** shooting star. **tener e.,** to be born under a lucky star
estrellado /estre'ʎaðo; estre'yaðo/ *a* star-shaped; full of stars, starry; shattered, broken; fried (eggs)
estrellamar /estreʎa'mar; estreya'mar/ *f*, starfish
estrellar /estre'ʎar; estre'yar/ *vt Inf.* to shatter, break into fragments; fry (eggs); —*vr* be starry or sprinkled with stars; be dashed against; fail in, come up against
estrellón /estre'ʎon; estre'yon/ *m*, large, artificial star (painted or otherwise); star-like firework
estremecer /estreme'θer; estreme'ser/ *vt irr* to cause to tremble; perturb; —*vr* shudder, tremble. See **conocer**
estremecimiento /estremeθi'miento; estremesi'miento/ *m*, shudder, trembling; agitation
estrenar /estre'nar/ *vt* to use or do for the first time; inaugurate; give the first performance of (plays, etc.); —*vr* do for the first time; *Com.* make the first sale of the day
estreno /es'treno/ *m*, commencement, inauguration; first appearance; *Theat.* first performance, opening night, premiere
estrenque /es'trenke/ *m*, strong esparto rope
estrenuo /es'trenuo/ *a* strong, energetic, agile
estreñimiento /estreɲi'miento/ *m*, constipation
estreñir /estre'ɲir/ *vt* to constipate
estrépito /es'trepito/ *m*, clamor, din, great noise; fuss, show
estrepitoso /estrepi'toso/ *a* noisy, clamorous
estreptococo /estrepto'koko/ *m*, streptococcus
estreptomicina /estreptomi'θina; estreptomi'sina/ *f*, streptomycin
estría /es'tria/ *f*, *Archit.* fluting, stria
estribadero /estriβa'ðero/ *m*, prop, support, strut
estribar /estri'βar/ *vi* (*with en*) to lean on, rest on, be supported by; *Fig.* be based on
estribillo /estri'βiʎo; estri'βiyo/ *m*, refrain
estribo /es'triβo/ *m*, stirrup; footboard, step, running board (of vehicles); *Archit.* buttress or pier; *Fig.* stay, support; *Anat.* stapes; *Mech.* stirrup piece. **perder los estribos,** to lose patience, forget oneself

estribor /estri'βor/ *m,* starboard
estricnina /estrik'nina/ *f,* strychnine
estricto /es'trikto/ *a* strict, exact; unbending, severe
estridente /estri'ðente/ *a* strident, shrill
estridor /estri'ðor/ *m,* strident or harsh sound; screech; creak
estro /'estro/ *m,* inspiration
estrofa /es'trofa/ *f,* strophe; verse, stanza
estropajo /estro'paho/ *m,* scourer, dishcloth; worthless person or thing
estropajoso /estropa'hoso/ *a Inf.* indistinct, stammering; dirty and ragged; tough (meat, etc.)
estropear /estrope'ar/ *vt* to spoil, damage; ruin, undo, spoil (plans, effects, etc.); ill-treat, maim; *—vr* hurt oneself, be maimed; spoil, deteriorate
estropicio /estro'piθio; estro'pisio/ *m, Inf.* crash (of china, etc.)
estructura /estruk'tura/ *f,* fabric, structure; *Fig.* construction
estructural /estruktu'ral/ *a* structural
estruendo /es'truendo/ *m,* din, clatter; clamor, noise; ostentation
estruendoso /estruen'doso/ *a* noisy
estrujar /estru'har/ *vt* to squeeze, crush (fruit); hold tightly, press, squeeze, bruise; *Fig. Inf.* squeeze dry
estrujón /estru'hon/ *m,* squeeze, pressure; final pressing (grapes)
estuario /es'tuario/ *m,* estuary
estucado /estu'kaðo/ *m,* stucco
estucar /estu'kar/ *vt* to stucco
estuche /es'tutʃe/ *m,* case; casket, box; cover; sheath
estuco /es'tuko/ *m,* stucco; plaster
estudiante /estu'ðiante/ *mf* student
estudiantil /estuðian'til/ *a Inf.* student
estudiantina /estuðian'tina/ *f,* strolling band of students playing and singing, generally in aid of charity
estudiantino /estuðian'tino/ *a Inf.* student
estudiantón /estuðian'ton/ *m, Inf.* grind
estudiar /estu'ðiar/ *vt* to study. **e. de,** study to be a (e.g. *e. de rabino,* study to be a rabbi); learn; *Art.* copy
estudio /es'tuðio/ *m,* study; sketch; disquisition, dissertation; studio; diligence; *Art.* study; reading room, den
estudiosidad /estuðiosi'ðað/ *f,* studiousness
estudioso /estu'ðioso/ *a* studious
estufa /es'tufa/ *f,* heating stove; hothouse; hot room (in bathhouses); drying chamber; *Elec.* heater
estufador /estufa'ðor/ *m,* stewpot or casserole
estufilla /estu'fiʎa; estu'fiya/ *f,* muff; small brazier
estufista /estu'fista/ *mf* stove maker or repairer, stove seller
estulto /es'tulto/ *a* foolish
estupefacción /estupefak'θion; estupefak'sion/ *f,* stupefaction
estupefacto /estupe'fakto/ *a* stupefied, stunned, amazed
estupendo /estu'pendo/ *a* wonderful, marvelous
estupidez /estupi'ðeθ; estupi'ðes/ *f,* stupidity
estúpido /es'tupiðo/ *a* stupid
estupor /estu'por/ *m, Med.* stupor; astonishment
estupro /es'tupro/ *m, Law.* rape
estuque /es'tuke/ *m,* stucco
estuquería /estuke'ria/ *f,* stuccowork
esturión /estu'rion/ *m,* sturgeon
esvástica /es'βastika/ *f,* swastika
etapa /e'tapa/ *f, Mil.* field ration; *Mil.* halt, camp; stage, juncture. **a pequeñas etapas,** by easy stages (of a journey)
etcétera /et'θetera; et'setera/ etcetera
éter /'eter/ *m,* ether; *Poet.* sky
etéreo /e'tereo/ *a* etheric; ethereal
eterizar /eteri'θar; eteri'sar/ *vt* to etherize
eternidad /eterni'ðað/ *f,* eternity
eternizar /eterni'θar; eterni'sar/ *vt* to drag out, prolong; eternize, perpetuate
eterno /e'terno/ *a* eternal, everlasting; lasting, enduring
ética /'etika/ *f,* ethics
ético /'etiko/ *a* ethical. *m,* moralist
etimología /etimolo'hia/ *f,* etymology
etimológico /etimo'lohiko/ *a* etymological
etimologista /etimolo'hista/ *mf* etymologist
etimólogo /eti'mologo/ *m,* etymologist
etiología /etiolo'hia/ *f,* etiology
etíope /e'tiope/ *a* and *mf* Ethiopian
Etiopía /etio'pia/ Ethiopia
etiqueta /eti'keta/ *f,* etiquette; label
etiquetero /etike'tero/ *a* ceremonious, stiff; prim
étnico /'etniko/ *a* ethnic; heathen
etnografía /etnogra'fia/ *f,* ethnography
etnográfico /etno'grafiko/ *a* ethnographic
etnología /etnolo'hia/ *f,* ethnology
etnólogo /et'nologo/ *m,* ethnologist
etrusco /e'trusko/ **(-ca)** *a* and *n* Etruscan
eubolia /eu'βolia/ *f,* discretion in speech
eucalipto /euka'lipto/ *m,* eucalyptus
Eucaristía /eukaris'tia/ *f,* Eucharist
euclídeo /eu'kliðeo/ *a* Euclidean
eufemismo /eufe'mismo/ *m,* euphemism
eufonía /eufo'nia/ *f,* euphony
eufónico /eu'foniko/ *a* euphonious
euforia /eu'foria/ *f,* resistance to disease; buoyancy, well-being
eufuismo /eu'fuismo/ *m,* euphuism
eugenesia /euhe'nesia/ *f,* eugenics
eugenésico /euhe'nesiko/ *a* eugenic
eunuco /eu'nuko/ *m,* eunuch
euritmia /eu'ritmia/ *f,* eurythmics
eurítmico /eu'ritmiko/ *a* eurythmic
euro /'euro/ *m, Poet.* east wind
Europa /eu'ropa/ Europe
europeizar /europei'θar; europei'sar/ *vt* to Europeanize
europeo /euro'peo/ **(-ea)** *a* and *n* European
éuscaro /'euskaro/ *a* Basque. *m,* Basque (language)
eutanasia /euta'nasia/ *f,* euthanasia
evacuación /eβakua'θion; eβakua'sion/ *f,* evacuation
evacuar /eβa'kuar/ *vt* to vacate; evacuate, empty; finish, conclude (a business deal, etc.)
evadir /eβa'ðir/ *vt* to avoid, elude; *—vr* escape; elope
evaluación /eβalua'θion; eβalua'sion/ *f,* valuation; estimation
evaluar /eβa'luar/ *vt* to evaluate, estimate; gauge; value
evangélico /eβan'heliko/ *a* evangelical
evangelio /eβan'helio/ *m,* Gospel; Christianity; *Inf.* indisputable truth
evangelista /eβanhe'lista/ *m,* evangelist
evangelizar /eβanheli'θar; eβanheli'sar/ *vt* to evangelize
evaporación /eβapora'θion; eβapora'sion/ *f,* evaporation
evaporar /eβapo'rar/ **(se)** *vt* and *vr* to evaporate; disappear, vanish
evasión, evasiva /eβa'sion, eβa'siβa/ *f,* subterfuge, evasion; flight, escape
evasivo /eβa'siβo/ *a* evasive
evento /e'βento/ *m,* happening, event; contingency
eventual /eβen'tual/ *a* possible, fortuitous; accidental (expenses); extra (emoluments)
eventualidad /eβentuali'ðað/ *f,* eventuality
evicción /eβik'θion; eβik'sion/ *f, Law.* eviction
evidencia /eβi'ðenθia; eβiðensia/ *f,* proof, evidence. **ponerse en e.,** to put oneself forward
evidenciar /eβiðen'θiar; eβiðen'siar/ *vt* to show, make obvious
evidente /eβi'ðente/ *a* obvious, evident
evitable /eβi'taβle/ *a* avoidable
evitación /eβita'θion; eβita'sion/ *f,* avoidance
evitar /eβi'tar/ *vt* to avoid; shun, eschew
evocación /eβoka'θion; eβoka'sion/ *f,* evocation
evocador /eβoka'ðor/ *a* evocative
evocar /eβo'kar/ *vt* to evoke
evolución /eβolu'θion; eβolu'sion/ *f,* evolution; development; (*Mil. Nav.*) maneuver; change; *Geom.* involution
evolucionar /eβoluθio'nar; eβolusio'nar/ *vi* to evolve; (*Nav. Mil.*) maneuver; change, alter
evolucionismo /eβoluθio'nismo; eβolusio'nismo/ *m,* evolutionism
evolutivo /eβolu'tiβo/ *a* evolutional

ex /eks/ *prefix* out of; from; formerly
exacción /eksak'θion; eksak'sion/ *f*, exaction; tax
exacerbación /eksaθerβa'θion; eksaserβa'sion/ *f*, exacerbation
exacerbar /eksaθer'βar; eksaser'βar/ *vt* to exasperate; exacerbate
exactitud /eksakti'tuð/ *f*, exactitude; correctness; punctuality
exacto /ek'sakto/ *a* exact; correct; punctual
exactor /eksak'tor/ *m*, tax collector; tyrant, oppressor
exageración /eksahera'θion; eksahera'sion/ *f*, exaggeration
exagerador /eksahera'ðor/ **(-ra)** *a* given to exaggerating *—n* exaggerater
exagerar /eksahe'rar/ *vt* to exaggerate
exaltación /eksalta'θion; eksalta'sion/ *f*, exaltation
exaltar /eksal'tar/ *vt* to exalt, elevate; extol; *—vr* grow excited or agitated
examen /ek'samen/ *m*, inquiry; investigation, research; examination; *Geol.* survey. **e. parcial,** quiz (at school)
examinador /eksamina'ðor/ **(-ra)** *n* examiner
examinando /eksami'nando/ **(-da)** *n* candidate, examinee
examinar /eksami'nar/ *vt* to inquire into; investigate; inspect; examine; *—vr* take an examination
exangüe /ek'saŋgue/ *a* bloodless, pale; exhausted, weak; dead
exánime /eksa'nime/ *a* lifeless; spiritless, weak
exasperación /eksaspera'θion; eksaspera'sion/ *f*, exasperation
exasperador, exasperante /eksaspera'ðor, eksaspe'rante/ *a* exasperating
exasperar /eksaspe'rar/ *vt* to exasperate; irritate, annoy
excarcelar /ekskarθe'lar; ekskarse'lar/ *vt* to release from jail
excavación /ekskaβa'θion; ekskaβa'sion/ *f*, excavation
excavador /ekskaβa'ðor/ **(-ra)** *n* excavator. *f*, *Mech.* excavator
excavar /ekska'βar/ *vt* to hollow; excavate; *Agr.* hoe (roots of plants)
excedente /eksθe'ðente; eksse'ðente/ *a* exceeding; excessive; surplus
exceder /eksθe'ðer; eksse'ðer/ *vt* to exceed; *—vr* forget oneself, go too far
excelencia /eksθe'lenθia; eksse'lensia/ *f*, excellence, superiority; Excellency (title)
excelente /eksθe'lente; eksse'lente/ *a* excellent; *Inf.* first-rate
excelso /eks'θelso; eks'selso/ *a* lofty, high; eminent, mighty; sublime
excentricidad /eksθentriθi'ðað; ekssentrisi'ðað/ *f*, eccentricity
excéntrico /ek'θentriko; eks'sentriko/ *a* unconventional; erratic; *Geom.* eccentric
excepción /eksθep'θion; ekssep''sion/ *f*, exception
excepcional /eksθepθio'nal; ekssepsio'nal/ *a* exceptional
exceptuar /eksθep'tuar; ekssep'tuar/ *vt* to except
excerpta, excerta /eks'θerpta, eks'θerta; eks'serpta, eks'serta/ *f*, excerpt, extract
excesivo /eksθe'siβo; eksse'siβo/ *a* excessive
exceso /eks'θeso; eks'seso/ *m*, excess; *Com.* surplus; *pl* crimes, excesses. **e. de peso** *or* **e. de equipaje,** excess baggage
excipiente /eksθi'piente; ekssi'piente/ *m*, excipient
excisión /eksθi'sion; ekssi'sion/ *f*, excision
excitabilidad /eksθitaβili'ðað; ekssitaβili'ðað/ *f*, excitability
excitable /eksθi'taβle; ekssi'taβle/ *a* excitable, highstrung
excitación /eksθita'θion; ekssita'sion/ *f*, excitation; excitement
excitador /eksθita'ðor; ekssita'ðor/ *a* exciting, stimulating. *m*, *Phys.* exciter
excitar /eksθi'tar; ekssi'tar/ *vt* to excite, stimulate, provoke; *Elec.* energize; *—vr* become agitated or excited
exclamación /eksklama'θion; eksklama'sion/ *f*, exclamation, interjection
exclamar /ekskla'mar/ *vi* to exclaim
exclamatorio /eksklama'torio/ *a* exclamatory
excluir /eksk'luir/ *vt irr* to exclude, keep out; reject, bar. See **huir**
exclusiva /eksklu'siβa/ *f*, exclusion; special privilege, sole right
exclusive /eksklu'siβe/ *adv* exclusively; excluded
exclusivismo /eksklusi'βismo/ *m*, exclusivism
exclusivista /eksklusi'βista/ *a* exclusive. *mf* exclusivist
exclusivo /eksklu'siβo/ *a* exclusive
excomulgado /ekskomul'gaðo/ **(-da)** *a* and *n Eccl.* excommunicate; *Inf.* wicked (person)
excomulgar /ekskomul'gar/ *vt* to excommunicate
excomunión /ekskomu'nion/ *f*, excommunication
excoriar /eksko'riar/ *vt* to flay, excoriate; *—vr* graze oneself
excrecencia /ekskre'θenθia; ekskre'sensia/ *f*, excrescence
excreción /ekskre'θion; ekskre'sion/ *f*, excretion
excremento /ekskre'mento/ *m*, excrement
excretar /ekskre'tar/ *vi* to excrete
excretorio /ekskre'torio/ *a* excretory
exculpación /ekskulpa'θion; ekskulpa'sion/ *f*, exoneration
exculpar /ekskul'par/ **(se)** *vt* and *vr* to exonerate
excursión /ekskur'sion/ *f*, excursion, trip; *Mil.* incursion
excursionismo /ekskursio'nismo/ *m*, sightseeing; hiking
excursionista /ekskursio'nista/ *mf* excursionist; hiker
excusa /eks'kusa/ *f*, excuse
excusabaraja /ekskusaβa'raha/ *f*, basket with a lid
excusado /eksku'saðo/ *a* excused; exempt; unnecessary, superfluous; reserved, private. *m*, lavatory, toilet
excusar /eksku'sar/ *vt* to excuse; avoid, ward off, prevent; exempt; *—vr* excuse oneself
execración /eksekra'θion; eksekra'sion/ *f*, execration
execrar /ekse'krar/ *vt* to execrate; denounce; loathe
exención /eksen'θion; eksen'sion/ *f*, exemption
exentar /eksen'tar/ *vt* to exempt
exento /ek'sento/ *a* exempt; free, liberated; open (of buildings, etc.)
exequias /ekse'kias/ *f pl*, obsequies
exfoliar /eksfo'liar/ *vt* to strip off; *—vr* flake off
exhalación /eksala'θion; eksala'sion/ *f*, exhalation; shooting star; lightning; emanation, effluvium
exhalar /eksa'lar/ *vt* to exhale, give off; *Fig.* give vent to
exhausto /ek'sausto/ *a* exhausted
exhibición /eksiβi'θion; eksiβi'sion/ *f*, exhibition
exhibicionismo /eksiβiθio'nismo; eksiβisio'nismo/ *m*, exhibitionism
exhibicionista /eksiβiθio'nista; eksiβisio'nista/ *mf* exhibitionist
exhibir /eksi'βir/ *vt* to exhibit, show
exhortación /eksorta'θion; eksorta'sion/ *f*, exhortation
exhortar /eksor'tar/ *vt* to exhort
exhumación /eksuma'θion; eksuma'sion/ *f*, exhumation
exhumar /eksu'mar/ *vt* to exhume, disinter
exigencia /eksi'henθia; eksi'hensia/ *f*, exigency; demand
exigente /eksi'hente/ *a* exigent
exigir /eksi'hir/ *vt* to exact, collect; need, require; demand
exigüidad /eksigui'ðað/ *f*, exiguousness
exiguo /ek'siguo/ *a* exiguous, meager
eximio /ek'simio/ *a* most excellent; illustrious
eximir /eksi'mir/ *vt* to exempt
existencia /eksis'tenθia; eksis'tensia/ *f*, existence; *pl Com.* stock on hand
existir /eksis'tir/ *vi* to exist, be; live
éxito /'eksito/ *m*, success; result, conclusion
éxodo /'eksoðo/ *m*, Exodus; exodus, emigration. **é. rural,** rural depopulation
exoneración /eksonera'θion; eksonera'sion/ *f*, exoneration

exonerar /eksone'rar/ *vt* to exonerate; discharge (from employment)
exorbitancia /eksorβi'tanθia; eksorβi'tansia/ *f*, exorbitance
exorbitante /eksorβi'tante/ *a* exorbitant, excessive
exorcismo /eksor'θismo; eksor'sismo/ *m*, exorcism
exorcista /eksor'θista; eksor'sista/ *m*, exorcist
exorcizar /eksorθi'θar; eksorsi'sar/ *vt* to exorcize
exordio /ek'sorðio/ *m*, exordium, introduction
exornar /eksor'nar/ *vt* to adorn; embellish (*Lit.* style)
exótico /ek'sotiko/ *a* exotic, rare
expandir /ekspan'dir/ *vt* to expand
expansibilidad /ekspansiβili'ðað/ *f*, *Phys.* expansibility
expansión /ekspan'sion/ *f*, expansion; recreation, hobby
expansivo /ekspan'siβo/ *a* expansive; communicative, frank
expatriación /ekspatria'θion; ekspatria'sion/ *f*, expatriation
expatriarse /ekspa'triarse/ *vr* to emigrate, leave one's country
expectación /ekspekta'θion; ekspekta'sion/ *f*, expectation; expectancy
expectante /ekspek'tante/ *a* expectant
expectativa /ekspekta'tiβa/ *f*, expectancy; expectation
expectoración /ekspektora'θion; ekspektora'sion/ *f*, expectoration
expectorar /ekspekto'rar/ *vt* to expectorate
expedición /ekspeði'θion; ekspeði'sion/ *f*, expedition; speed, promptness; *Eccl.* bull, dispensation; excursion; forwarding, dispatch
expediente /ekspe'ðiente/ *m*, *Law.* proceedings; file of documents; expedient, device, means; expedition, promptness; motive, reason; provision
expedir /ekspe'ðir/ *vt irr* to expedite; forward, send, ship; issue, make out (checks, receipts, etc.); draw up (documents); dispatch, deal with. See **pedir**
expedito /ekspe'ðito/ *a* expeditious, speedy
expeler /ekspe'ler/ *vt* to expel, discharge, emit
expendedor /ekspende'ðor/ **(-ra)** *a* spending —*n* spender; agent; retailer; seller; *Law.* **e. de moneda falsa,** distributor of counterfeit money
expendeduría /ekspendeðu'ria/ *f*, shop where government monopoly goods are sold (tobacco, stamps, etc.)
expender /ekspen'der/ *vt* to spend (money); *Com.* retail; *Com.* sell on commission; *Law.* distribute counterfeit money
expensas /ek'spensas/ *f pl*, costs, charges
experiencia /ekspe'rienθia; ekspe'riensia/ *f*, experience; practice, experiment
experimentación /eksperimenta'θion; eksperimenta'sion/ *f*, experiencing
experimentar /eksperimen'tar/ *vt* to test, try; experience; feel
experimento /eksperi'mento/ *m*, experiment
experto /ek'sperto/ **(-ta)** *a* practiced, expert —*n* expert
expiación /ekspia'θion; ekspia'sion/ *f*, expiation
expiar /eks'piar/ *vt* to expiate, atone for; pay the penalty of; *Fig.* purify
expiatorio /ekspia'torio/ *a* expiatory
expiración /ekspira'θion; ekspira'sion/ *f*, expiration
expirar /ekspi'rar/ *vi* to die; *Fig.* expire; die down; exhale, expire
explanación /eksplana'θion; eksplana'sion/ *f*, leveling; explanation, elucidation
explanada /ekspla'naða/ *f*, esplanade; *Mil.* glacis
explanar /ekspla'nar/ *vt* to level; explain
explayar /ekspla'yar/ *vt* to extend, enlarge; —*vr* spread oneself, enlarge (upon); enjoy an outing; confide (in)
explicación /eksplika'θion; eksplika'sion/ *f*, explanation; elucidation
explicar /ekspli'kar/ *vt* to explain; expound; interpret, elucidate; —*vr* explain oneself
explicativo /eksplika'tiβo/ *a* explanatory
explícito /eks'pliθito; eksplisito/ *a* explicit, clear
exploración /eksplora'θion; eksplorasion/ *f*, exploration
explorador /eksplora'ðor/ *a* exploring. *m*, explorer; prospector; boy scout; *Mil.* scout
explorar /eksplo'rar/ *vt* to explore; investigate; *Med.* probe
exploratorio /eksplora'torio/ *a* exploratory
explosión /eksplo'sion/ *f*, explosion; outburst, outbreak. **hacer falsas explosiones,** *Mech.* to misfire
explosivo /eksplo'siβo/ *a* and *m*, explosive. **e. violento,** high explosive
explotación /eksplota'θion; eksplota'sion/ *f*, development, exploitation
explotar /eksplo'tar/ *vt* to work (mines); *Fig.* exploit
expoliación /ekspolia'θion; ekspolia'sion/ *f*, spoliation
expoliar /ekspo'liar/ *vt* to despoil
exponente /ekspo'nente/ *a* and *mf* exponent. *m*, *Math.* index
exponer /ekspo'ner/ *vt irr* to show, expose; expound, interpret; risk, jeopardize; abandon (child). See **poner**
exportación /eksporta'θion; eksporta'sion/ *f*, exportation; export
exportador /eksporta'ðor/ **(-ra)** *a* export —*n* exporter
exportar /ekspor'tar/ *vt* to export
exposición /eksposi'θion; eksposi'sion/ *f*, exposition, demonstration; petition; exhibition; *Lit.* exposition; *Photo.* exposure; orientation, position
expósito /eks'posito/ **(-ra)** *a* and *n* foundling
expositor /eksposi'tor/ **(-ra)** *a* and *n* exponent —*n* exhibitor
expremijo /ekspre'miho/ *m*, cheese vat
exprés /eks'pres/ *a* express. *m*, messenger or delivery service; express train; transport office
expresar /ekspre'sar/ *vt* to express (all meanings)
expresión /ekspre'sion/ *f*, statement, utterance; phrase, wording; expression; presentation; manifestation; gift, present; squeezing; pressing (of fruits, etc.)
expresivo /ekspre'siβo/ *a* expressive; affectionate
expreso /eks'preso/ *a* express; clear, obvious. *m*, courier, messenger
exprimelimones /eksprimeli'mones/ *m*, **exprimidera,** *f*, lemon squeezer
exprimidor de la ropa /eksprimi'ðor de la 'rropa/ *m*, wringer, mangle
exprimir /ekspri'mir/ *vt* to squeeze, press (fruit); press, hold tightly; express, utter
expropiación /ekspropia'θion; ekspropia'sion/ *f*, expropriation
expropiar /ekspro'piar/ *vt* to expropriate; commandeer
expugnar /ekspug'nar/ *vt Mil.* to take by storm
expulsar /ekspul'sar/ *vt* to expel, eject, dismiss
expulsión /ekspul'sion/ *f*, expulsion
expurgar /ekspur'gar/ *vt* to cleanse, purify; expurgate
expurgatorio /ekspurga'torio/ *a* expurgatory. *m*, *Eccl.* index
exquisitez /ekskisi'teθ; ekskisi'tes/ *f*, exquisiteness
exquisito /eks'kisito/ *a* exquisite, choice; delicate, delicious
extasiarse /eksta'siarse/ *vr* to fall into ecstasy; marvel (at), delight (in)
éxtasis /'ekstasis/ *m*, ecstasy; rapture
extático /eks'tatiko/ *a* ecstatic
extemporáneo /ekstempo'raneo/ *a* untimely; inopportune, inconvenient
extender /eksten'der/ *vt irr* to spread; reach, extend; elongate; enlarge, amplify; unfold, open out, stretch; draw up (documents); make out (checks, etc.); —*vr* stretch out; lie down; spread, be generalized; extend; last (of time); record; stretch, open out. **extenderse en,** to expatiate on. See **entender**
extensión /eksten'sion/ *f*, extension; expanse; length; extent; duration; extension (logic)
extensivo /eksten'siβo/ *a* extensive, spacious; extensible
extenso /eks'tenso/ *a* extensive, vast
extensor /eksten'sor/ *a* extensor. *m*, chest expander
extenuación /ekstenua'θion; ekstenua'sion/ *f*, emaciation, weakness; extenuation

extenuar /ekste'nuar/ *vt* to exhaust, weaken; —*vr* become weak
exterior /ekste'rior/ *a* external; foreign (trade, etc.). *m*, outside, exterior; outward appearance
exterioridad /eksteriori'ðað/ *f*, cutward appearance; outside, externality; *pl* ceremonies, forms; ostentation
exteriorizar /eksteriori'θar; eksteriori'sar/ *vt* to exteriorize, reveal
exterminador /ekstermina'ðor/ **(-ra)** *a* exterminating —*n* exterminator
exterminar /ekstermi'nar/ *vt* to exterminate; devastate
exterminio /ekster'minio/ *m*, extermination; devastation
externado /ekster'naðo/ *m*, day school
externarse /ekster'narse/ *vr* to stand out
externo /eks'terno/ **(-na)** *a* external —*n* day
extinción /ekstin'θion; ekstin'sion/ *f*, extinction; extinguishment; abolition, cancellation
extinguir /ekstiŋ'guir/ *vt* to extinguish; destroy
extintor /ekstin'tor/ *m*, fire extinguisher
extirpación /ekstirpa'θion; ekstirpa'sion/ *f*, extirpation
extirpador /ekstirpa'ðor/ **(-ra)** *a* extirpating —*n* extirpator
extirpar /ekstir'par/ *vt* to extirpate; *Fig.* eradicate
extorsión /ekstor'sion/ *f*, extortion
extorsionar /ekstorsio'nar/ *vt* to extort
extra /'ekstra/ *prefix* outside, without, beyond —*prep* besides —*a* extremely, most. *m*, *Inf.* extra
extracción /ekstrak'θion; ekstrak'sion/ *f*, extraction; drawing (lottery); origin, lineage; exportation
extractar /ekstrak'tar/ *vt* to abstract, summarize
extracto /eks'trakto/ *m*, abstract, summary; *Chem.* extract
extractor /ekstrak'tor/ *a* extracting. *m*, extractor
extradición /ekstraði'θion; ekstraði'sion/ *f*, extradition
extraer /ekstra'er/ *vt irr* to extract; draw out; export; *Chem.* extract. See **traer**
extranjero /ekstran'hero/ **(-ra)** *a* alien, foreign —*n* foreigner. *m*, abroad, foreign country
extrañar /ekstra'ɲar/ *vt* to exile; alienate, estrange; wonder at; miss, feel the loss of; —*vr* be exiled; be estranged; be amazed (by); refuse (to do a thing)
extrañeza /ekstra'ɲeθa; ekstra'ɲesa/ *f*, strangeness; estrangement; surprise
extraño /eks'traɲo/ *a* strange, unusual; foreign, extraneous
extraoficial /ekstraofi'θial; ekstraofi'sial/ *a* unofficial
extraordinario /ekstraorði'nario/ *a* extraordinary; special. *m*, *Cul.* extra course
extraterritorialidad /ekstraterritoriali'ðað/ *f*, exterritoriality
extravagancia /ekstraβa'ganθia; ekstraβa'gansia/ *f*, eccentricity; queerness; folly
extravagante /ekstraβa'gante/ *a* eccentric; queer, strange; absurd
extravertido /ekstraβer'tiðo/ *m*, extrovert
extraviar /ekstra'βiar/ *vt* to mislead; mislay; —*vr* lose one's way; be lost (of things); *Fig.* go astray
extravío /ekstra'βio/ *m*, deviation, divergence; error; aberration, lapse
extremado /ekstre'maðo/ *a* extreme
extremar /ekstre'mar/ *vt* to take to extremes; —*vr* do one's best
extremaunción /ekstremaun'θion; ekstremaun'sion/ *f*, extreme unction
extremeño /ekstre'meɲo/ **(-ña)** *a* and *n* Extremaduran
extremidad /ekstremi'ðað/ *f*, end; extremity; remotest part; edge; limit; *pl* extremities
extremista /ekstre'mista/ *a* and *mf* extremist
extremo /eks'tremo/ *a* last, ultimate; extreme; furthest; great, exceptional; utmost. *m*, end, extreme; highest degree; extreme care; *pl* excessive emotional display
extremoso /ekstre'moso/ *a* immoderate, exaggerated; very affectionate
extrínseco /ekstrin'seko/ *a* extrinsic
exuberancia /eksuβe'ranθia; eksuβeransia/ *f*, abundance; exuberance
exuberante /eksuβe'rante/ *a* abundant, copious; exuberant
exudar /eksu'ðar/ *vi* and *vt* to exude
exultación /eksulta'θion; eksulta'sion/ *f*, exultation; rejoicing
exultante /eksul'tante/ *a* exultant
exultar /eksul'tar/ *vi* to exult
exvoto /eks'βoto/ *m*, votive offering
eyaculación /eyakula'θion; eyakula'sion/ *f*, *Med.* ejaculation
eyacular /eyaku'lar/ *vt Med.* to ejaculate

F

fa /fa/ *m, Mus.* fa, F
fabada /fa'βaða/ *f,* dish of broad beans with pork, sausage or bacon
fábrica /'faβrika/ *f,* manufacture; making; factory, works; fabric, structure, building; creation; invention. **f. de papel,** paper mill. **marca de f.,** trademark
fabricación /faβrika'θion; faβrika'sion/ *f,* make; making; construction. **f. en serie,** mass production
fabricador /faβrika'ðor/ **(-ra)** *a* creative, inventive —*n* fabricator; maker
fabricante /faβri'kante/ *a* manufacturing. *m,* manufacturer; maker
fabricar /faβri'kar/ *vt* to manufacture; make; construct, build; devise; invent, create
fabril /fa'βril/ *a* manufacturing
fabriquero /faβri'kero/ *m,* manufacturer; churchwarden; charcoal burner
fábula /'faβula/ *f,* rumor, gossip; fiction; fable; story, plot; mythology; myth; laughingstock; falsehood.
fabulista /faβu'lista/ *mf* fabulist, mythologist
fabulosidad /faβulosi'ðað/ *f,* fabulousness
fabuloso /faβu'loso/ *a* fabulous; fictitious; incredible, amazing
faca /''faka/ *f,* jackknife
facción /fak'θion; fak'sion/ *f,* rebellion; faction, party, band; feature (of the face) (gen. *pl*); military exploit; any routine military duty
faccionario /fakθio'nario; faksio'nario/ *a* factional
faccioso /fak'θioso; fak'sioso/ **(-sa)** *a* factional; factious, seditious —*n* rebel
faceta /fa'θeta; fa'seta/ *f,* facet (gems); aspect, view
facha /'fatʃa/ *f, Inf.* countenance, look, face; guy, scarecrow. *Naut.* **ponerse en f.,** to lie to
fachada /fa'tʃaða/ *f,* facade, front (of a building, ship, etc.); *Inf.* build, presence (of a person); frontispiece (of a book)
fachenda /fa'tʃenda/ *f, Inf.* boastfulness, vanity
facial /fa'θial; fa'sial/ *a* facial; intuitive
fácil /'faθil; 'fasil/ *a* easy; probable; easily led; docile; of easy virtue (women) —*adv* easy
facilidad /faθili'ðað; fasili'ðað/ *f,* easiness; facility, aptitude; ready compliance; opportunity
facilitación /faθilita'θion; fasilita'sion/ *f,* facilitation
facilitar /faθili'tar; fasili'tar/ *vt* to facilitate, expedite; provide, deliver
facineroso /faθine'roso; fasine'roso/ *a* criminal, delinquent. *m,* criminal; villain
facistol /faθis'tol; fasis'tol/ *m, Eccl.* lectern; chorister's stand
facsímile /fak'simile/ *m,* facsimile
factibilidad /faktiβili'ðað/ *f,* feasibility, practicability
factible /fak'tiβle/ *a* feasible, practicable
facticio /fak'tiθio; fak'tisio/ *a* factitious, artificial
factor /fak'tor/ *m, Com.* factor, agent; *Math.* factor; element; consideration
factoría /fakto'ria/ *f,* agency; factorage; factory; merchants' trading post, especially in a foreign country
factótum /fak'totum/ *m, Inf.* factotum, handyman; *Inf.* busybody; confidential agent or deputy
factura /fak'tura/ *f, Com.* invoice, bill, account; *Art.* execution; workmanship; making
facturar /faktu'rar/ *vt Com.* to invoice; register (luggage on a railroad)
facultad /fakulta'ð/ *f,* faculty; mental or physical aptitude, capability; authority, right; science, art; *Educ.* faculty; license
facultar /fakul'tar/ *vt* to authorize, permit
facultativo /fakulta'tiβo/ *a* belonging to a faculty; optional, permissive. *m,* physician
facundia /fa'kundia/ *f,* eloquence
facundo /fa'kundo/ *a* eloquent
faena /fa'ena/ *f,* manual labor; mental work; business affairs (gen. *pl*)
faetón /fae'ton/ *m,* phaeton
fagocito /fago'θito; fago'sito/ *m,* phagocyte
fagot /fa'got/ *m,* bassoon
fagotista /fago'tista/ *mf* bassoon player
faisán /fai'san/ **(-ana)** *Ornith.* cock (hen) pheasant
faisanera /faisa'nera/ *f,* pheasantry
faja /'faha/ *f,* belt; sash, scarf; corset, girdle; *Geog.* zone; newspaper wrapper; *Archit.* fascia; swathing band
fajar /fa'har/ *vt* to swathe; swaddle (a child)
fajero /fa'hero/ *m,* swaddling band
fajín /fa'hin/ *m,* ceremonial ribbon or sash worn by generals, etc.
fajina /fa'hina/ *f,* stack; brushwood; (*fort.*) fascine
fajo /'faho/ *m,* bundle, sheaf; *pl* swaddling clothes
falacia /fa'laθia; fa'lasia/ *f,* fraud, deceit; deceitfulness; fallacy
falange /fa'lanhe/ *f, Mil.* phalanx; *Anat.* phalange; (*Spanish pol.*) Falange
falangista /falan'hista/ *a* and *mf* Falangist
falaz /fa'laθ; fa'las/ *a* deceitful; fallacious
falda /'falda/ *f,* skirt; lap, flap, panel (of a dress); slope (of a hill); the lap; loin (of beef, etc.); brim of a hat; *pl Inf.* petticoats, women. **f. escocesa,** kilt. **f.-pantalón,** divided skirt, culottes.
faldellín /falde'ʎin; falde'yin/ *m,* skirt; underskirt
faldero /fal'dero/ *a* lap (dog); fond of the company of women
faldillas /fal'diʎas; fal'diyas/ *f pl,* coattails
faldistorio /faldis'torio/ *m,* faldstool
faldón /fal'don/ *m,* long, flowing skirt; shirttail; coattail
falibilidad /faliβili'ðað/ *f,* fallibility
falible /fa'liβle/ *a* fallible
falla /'faʎa; faya/ *f,* deficiency, defect; failure; *Geol.* displacement; bonfire (Valencia); *Mineral.* slide
fallar /fa'ʎar; fa'yar/ *vt Law.* to pass sentence; —*vi* be deficient
falleba /fa'ʎeβa; fa'yeβa/ *f,* shutter bolt
fallecer /faʎe'θer; faye'ser/ *vi irr* to die; fail. See **conocer**
fallecimiento /faʎeθi'miento; fayesi'miento/ *m,* death, decease
fallido /fa'ʎiðo; fa'yiðo/ *a* frustrated; bankrupt
fallo /'faʎo; 'fayo/ *m, Law.* verdict; judgment
falsario /fal'sario/ *a* falsifying, forging, counterfeiting; deceiving, lying. *m,* falsifier, forger, counterfeiter
falseamiento /falsea'miento/ *m,* falsifying; forging
falsear /false'ar/ *vt* to falsify; forge; counterfeit; penetrate; —*vi* weaken; *Mus.* be out of tune (strings)
falsedad /false'ðað/ *f,* falseness; falsehood
falsete /fal'sete/ *m,* spigot; *Mus.* falsetto voice
falsificación /falsifika'θion; falsifika'sion/ *f,* falsification; forgery
falsificador /falsifika'ðor/ *a* falsifying; forging. *m,* falsifier; forger
falsificar /falsifi'kar/ *vt* to forge, counterfeit; falsify
falso /'falso/ *a* false; forged, counterfeit; treacherous, untrue, deceitful; incorrect; sham; vicious (horses). **de f.,** falsely; deceitfully
falta /'falta/ *f,* lack, shortage; defect; mistake; *Sports.* fault; shortcoming; nonappearance, absence; deficiency in legal weight of coin; *Law.* offense. **f. de éxito,** failure. **hacer f.,** to be necessary. **sin f.,** without fail
faltar /fal'tar/ *vi* to be lacking; fail, die; fall short; be absent from an appointment; not to fulfill one's obligations. **f. a,** to be unfaithful to, break (e.g. *Faltó a su palabra,* He broke his promise). *Inf.* **¡No faltaba más!** I should think not!; That's the limit!
falto /'falto/ *a* lacking, wanting; defective; wretched, mean, timid. **f. de personal,** short-handed
faltriquera /faltri'kera/ *f,* pocket; hip pocket
falúa /fa'lua/ *f, Naut.* tender; longboat
falucho /fa'lutʃo/ *m,* felucca
fama /'fama/ *f,* rumor, report; reputation; fame
famélico /fa'meliko/ *a* ravenous
familia /fa'milia/ *f,* family; household; kindred. **ser de f.,** to run in the family

familiar /fami'liar/ *a* family; familiar; well known; unceremonious; plain, simple; colloquial (language). *m, Eccl.* familiar; servant; intimate friend; familiar spirit
familiaridad /familiari'ðað/ *f,* familiarity
familiarizar /familiari'θar; familiari'sar/ *vt* to familiarize; *—vr* become familiar; accustom oneself
familiarmente /familiar'mente/ *adv* familiarly
famoso /fa'moso/ *a* famous; notorious; *Inf.* excellent, perfect; *Inf.* conspicuous
fámula /'famula/ *f, Inf.* female servant
fámulo /'famulo/ *m,* servant of a college; *Inf.* servant
fanal /fa'nal/ *m,* lantern (of a lighthouse); *Naut.* poop lantern; lantern; lamp glass
fanático /fa'natiko/ **(-ca)** *a* fanatical *—n* fanatic; *Inf.* fan, enthusiast
fanatismo /fana'tismo/ *m,* fanaticism
fanatizar /fanati'θar; fanati'sar/ *vt* to make fanatical; turn into a fanatic
fandango /fan'daŋgo/ *m,* lively Andalusian dance
fanega /fa'nega/ *f,* grain measure about the weight of 1.60 bushel; land measure (about $1\frac{1}{2}$ acres)
fanfarrón /fanfa'rron/ **(-ona)** *a Inf.* boastful; swaggering *—n* swashbuckler; boaster
fanfarronear /fanfarrone'ar/ *vi* to swagger; brag
fanfarronería /fanfarrone'ria/ *f,* bragging
fango /'faŋgo/ *m,* mud, mire; degradation
fangoso /faŋ'goso/ *a* muddy, miry
fantasear /fantase'ar/ *vi* to let one's fancy roam; boast
fantasía /fanta'sia/ *f,* fancy, imagination; fantasy; caprice; fiction; *Inf.* presumption; *Mus.* fantasia
fantasma /fan'tasma/ *m,* ghost, phantom; vision; image, impression; presumptuous person. *f, Inf.* scarecrow; apparition
fantasmagoría /fantasmago'ria/ *f,* phantasmagoria
fantasmagórico /fantasma'goriko/ *a* phantasmagoric
fantástico /fan'tastiko/ *a* fanciful, imaginary; fantastic, imaginative; presumptuous, conceited
fantoche /fan'totʃe/ *m,* puppet; *Inf.* yes-man, mediocrity
faquín /fa'kin/ *m,* porter, carrier
faquir /fa'kir/ *m,* fakir
faradio /fa'raðio/ *m,* farad
faralá /fara'la/ *m,* flounce, frill
farándula /fa'randula/ *f,* profession of low comedian; troupe of strolling players; cunning trick
farandulero /farandu'lero/ *m,* actor, strolling player *—a Inf.* plausible
faraón /fara'on/ *m,* pharaoh; faro (card game)
fardel /far'ðel/ *m,* bag, knapsack; bundle
fardo /far'ðo/ *m,* bundle, bale, package
farfulla /far'fuʎa; far'fuya/ *f, Inf.* mumbling; gibbering. *mf Inf.* mumbler
farfullar /farfu'ʎar; farfu'yar/ *vt Inf.* to mumble; gibber; *Inf.* act in haste
faringe /fa'rinhe/ *f,* pharynx
faríngeo /fa'rinheo/ *a* pharyngeal
faringitis /farin'hitis/ *f,* pharyngitis
farisaico /fari'saiko/ *a* pharisaical
fariseísmo /farise'ismo/ *m,* cant, hypocrisy
fariseo /fari'seo/ *m,* Pharisee; hypocrite
farmacéutico /farma'θeutiko; farma'seutiko/ *a* pharmaceutical. *m,* pharmacist
farmacia /far'maθia; far'masia/ *f,* pharmacy
farmacología /farmakolo'hia/ *f,* pharmacology
farmacológico /farmako'lohiko/ *a* pharmacological
farmacólogo /farma'kologo/ *m,* pharmacologist
faro /'faro/ *m,* lighthouse; beacon, guide; *Auto.* headlight
farol /fa'rol/ *m,* lantern, lamp; streetlamp; cresset
farola /fa'rola/ *f,* lamppost (generally with several branches); lantern
farolero /faro'lero/ *m,* lantern maker; lamplighter; lamp tender *—a Inf.* swaggering, braggart
fárrago /'farrago/ *m,* hodgepodge
farsa /'farsa/ *f,* old name for a play; farce; theatrical company; poor, badly constructed play; sham, trick, deception
farsante /far'sante/ *m,* comedian; *Obs.* actor; *Fig. Inf.* humbug
fascinación /fasθina'θion; fassina'sion/ *f,* evil eye; enchantment, fascination
fascinador /fasθina'ðor; fassina'ðor/ **(-ra)** *a* bewitching; fascinating *—n* charmer
fascinante /fasθi'nante; fassi'nante/ *a* fascinating
fascinar /fasθi'nar; fassi'nar/ *vt* to bewitch, place under a spell; deceive, impose upon; attract, fascinate
fascismo /fas'θismo; fas'sismo/ *m,* fascism
fascista /fas'θista; fas'sista/ *a* and *mf* fascist
fase /'fase/ *f,* phase; aspect
fastidiar /fasti'ðiar/ *vt* to disgust, bore; annoy; *—vr* be bored
fastidio /fasti'ðio/ *m,* sickness, squeamishness; annoyance, boredom, dislike, repugnance
fastidioso /fasti'ðioso/ *a* disgusting, sickening; annoying; boring, tiresome
fastuoso /fas'tuoso/ *a* ostentatious; pompous
fatal /fa'tal/ *a* fatal, mortal; predetermined, inevitable; ill-fated, unhappy, disastrous; evil
fatalidad /fatali'ðað/ *f,* fatality; inevitability; disaster, ill-fatedness
fatalismo /fata'lismo/ *m,* fatalism
fatalista /fata'lista/ *a* fatalistic. *mf* fatalist
fatalmente /fatal'mente/ *adv* inevitably, unavoidably; unhappily, unfortunately; extremely badly
fatídico /fa'tiðiko/ *a* prophetic (gen. of evil)
fatiga /fa'tiga/ *f,* fatigue; toil; difficult breathing; hardship, troubles (gen. *pl*)
fatigar /fati'gar/ *vt* to tire; annoy; *—vr* be tired
fatigoso /fati'goso/ *a* tired; tiring; tiresome, annoying
fatuidad /fatui'ðað/ *f,* fatuousness, inanity, foolishness; conceit; priggishness
fatuo /fa'tuo/ *a* fatuous, foolish; conceited; priggish. *m,* self-satisfied fool. **fuego f.,** will-o'-the-wisp
fauces /'fauθes; 'fauses/ *f pl,* gullet
fauna /'fauna/ *f,* fauna
fauno /'fauno/ *m,* faun
fausto /'fausto/ *m,* pomp, magnificence, ostentation *—a* fortunate, happy
fautor /fau'tor/ *m,* protector, helper; accomplice. **f. de guerra,** warmonger
favonio /fa'βonio/ *m, Poet.* zephyr, westerly wind
favor /fa'βor/ *m,* aid, protection, support; favor, honor, service; love favor, sign of favor. **a f. de,** in favor of; on behalf of
favorable /faβo'raβle/ *a* kind, helpful; favorable
favorecedor /faβoreθe'ðor; faβorese'ðor/ **(-ra)** *a* favoring, helping *—n* helper; protector
favorecer /faβore'θer; faβore'ser/ *vt irr* to aid, protect, support; favor; do a service, grant a favor. See **conocer**
favoritismo /faβori'tismo/ *m,* favoritism
favorito /faβo'rito/ **(-ta)** *a* and *n* favorite
fayenza /fa'yenθa; fa'yensa/ *f,* faience
faz /faθ; fas/ *f,* face; external surface of a thing, side; frontage
fe /fe/ *f,* faith; confidence, trust, good opinion; belief; solemn promise; assertion; certificate, attestation; faithfulness. **f. de erratas,** *Print.* errata. **dar f.,** *Law.* to testify. **de buena f.,** in good faith. **en f.,** in proof
fealdad /feal'dað/ *f,* ugliness; base action
febo /'feβo/ *m,* Phoebus; *Poet.* sun
febrero /fe'βrero/ *m,* February
febril /fe'βril/ *a* feverish; ardent, violent; passionate
fecal /fe'kal/ *a* fecal
fecha /'fetʃa/ *f,* date. **a la f.,** at present, now. **hasta la f.,** up to the present (day)
fechar /fe'tʃar/ *vt* to date, write the date
feculento /feku'lento/ *a* starchy; dreggy
fecundación /fekunda'θion; fekunda'sion/ *f,* fecundation
fecundar /fekun'dar/ *vt* to fertilize; fecundate
fecundidad /fekundi'ðað/ *f,* fecundity; fertility, fruitfulness
fecundizar /fekundi'θar; fekundi'sar/ *vt* to fertilize; make fruitful
fecundo /fe'kundo/ *a* fertile, fecund, prolific; abundant
federación /feðera'θion; feðera'sion/ *f,* federation, league

federal /feðe'ral/ *a* federal. *mf* federalist
federalismo /feðera'lismo/ *m,* federalism
federalista /feðera'lista/ *a* federal, federalist. *mf* federalist
federativo /feðera'tiβo/ *a* federative
fehaciente /fea'θiente; fea'siente/ *a Law.* authentic, attested
feldespato /feldes'pato/ *m,* feldspar
felicidad /feliθi'ðað; felisi'ðað/ *f,* happiness; contentment, satisfaction; good fortune
felicitación /feliθita'θion; felisita'sion/ *f,* congratulation
felicitar /feliθi'tar; felisi'tar/ *vt* to congratulate; wish well; —*vr* congratulate oneself
feligrés /feli'gres/ **(-esa)** *n* parishioner
feligresía /feligre'sia/ *f,* parish
felino /fe'lino/ *a* and *m,* feline
feliz /fe'liθ; fe'lis/ *a* happy; fortunate; skillful, felicitous (of phrases, etc.)
felón /fe'lon/ **(-ona)** *n* felon
felonía /felo'nia/ *f,* felony
felpa /'felpa/ *f,* plush; *Inf.* drubbing, beating
felpilla /fel'piʎa; fel'piya/ *f,* chenille
felpudo /fel'puðo/ *a* plush
femenino /feme'nino/ *a* feminine; female; *Fig.* weak
fementido /femen'tiðo/ *a* sly, false, treacherous, unfaithful
feminismo /femi'nismo/ *m,* feminism
feminista /femi'nista/ *a* feminist. *mf* feminist
fémur /'femur/ *m,* femur, thigh bone
fenecer /fene'θer; fene'ser/ *vt irr* to conclude, finish; —*vi* die; be ended. See **conocer**
fenecimiento /feneθi'miento; fenesi'miento/ *m,* end; death
fenicio /fe'niθio; fe'nisio/ **(-ia)** *a* and *n* Phoenician
fénico /'feniko/ *a* phenic, carbolic
fénix /'feniks/ *f,* phoenix
fenomenal /fenome'nal/ *a* phenomenal; *Inf.* terrific
fenómeno /fe'nomeno/ *m,* phenomenon; *Inf.* something of great size
feo /'feo/ *a* ugly; alarming, horrid; evil. *m, Inf.* slight, insult
feraz /'feraθ; 'feras/ *a* fruitful, fertile
féretro /'feretro/ *m,* coffin; bier
feria /'feria/ *f,* fair, market; workday; holiday; rest
feriar /fe'riar/ *vt* to buy at a fair; bargain —*vi* cease work, take a holiday
fermentación /fermenta'θion; fermenta'sion/ *f,* fermentation
fermentar /fermen'tar/ *vi* to ferment; be agitated; —*vt* cause to ferment
fermento /fer'mento/ *m,* ferment; leaven; *Chem.* enzyme
ferocidad /feroθi'ðað; ferosi'ðað/ *f,* ferocity, cruelty
feroz /fe'roθ; fe'ros/ *a* ferocious, cruel
férreo /'ferreo/ *a* ferrous; hard, tenacious. **línea férrea,** railroad
ferrería /ferre'ria/ *f,* ironworks
ferretería /ferrete'ria/ *f,* ironworks; ironmonger's shop; ironware, hardware
férrico /'ferriko/ *a* ferric
ferrífero /fe'rrifero/ *a* iron-bearing
ferrocarril /ferroka'rril/ *m,* railroad, railway; railroad train. **f. de cremallera,** rack railroad. **f. funicular,** funicular railway
ferroso /fe'rroso/ *a* ferrous
ferroviario /ferro'βiario/ *a* railroad, railway. *m,* railroad employee
fértil /'fertil/ *a* fertile; fruitful, productive
fertilidad /fertili'ðað/ *f,* fertility
fertilización /fertiliθa'θion; fertilisa'sion/ *f,* fertilization
fertilizar /fertili'θar; fertili'sar/ *vt* to fertilize, make fruitful
férula /'ferula/ *f,* ferule; *Surg.* splint; *Fig.* yoke, rule
fervor /fer'βor/ *m,* intense heat; fervor, devotion; zeal
fervoroso /ferβo'roso/ *a* fervent, zealous, devoted
festejar /feste'har/ *vt* to feast, entertain; woo; celebrate; —*vr* amuse oneself
festejo /feste'ho/ *m,* feast, entertainment; courtship, wooing; *pl* public celebrations
festín /fes'tin/ *m,* private dinner or party; sumptuous banquet
festival /festi'βal/ *m,* musical festival; festival
festividad /festiβi'ðað/ *f,* festivity; *Eccl.* celebration, solemnity; witticism
festivo /fes'tiβo/ *a* joking, witty; happy, gay; solemn, worthy of celebration. **día f.,** holiday
festón /fes'ton/ *m,* garland, wreath; festoon; border; scalloped edging
festonear /festone'ar/ *vt* to garland, festoon; border
fetal /fe'tal/ *a* fetal
fetiche /fe'titʃe/ *m,* fetish
fetichismo /feti'tʃismo/ *m,* fetishism
fetidez /feti'ðeθ; feti'ðes/ *f,* fetidness, fetor, stink
fétido /'fetiðo/ *a* stinking, fetid
feto /'feto/ *m,* fetus
feudal /feu'ðal/ *a* feudal; despotic
feudalismo /feuða'lismo/ *m,* feudalism
feudo /'feuðo/ *m,* fief; fee. **f. franco,** freehold
fez /feθ; fes/ *m,* fez
fiado, al /'fiaðo, al/ *adv* on credit. **en f.,** on bail
fiador /fia'ðor/ **(-ra)** *n* guarantor; bail. *m,* fastener, loop (of a coat, clock, etc.); safety catch, bolt. **salir f.,** to be surety (for); post bail
fiambre /'fiambre/ *m,* cold meat, cold dish; *Inf.* stale, out-of-date news, etc.; *Inf.* corpse
fiambrera /fiam'brera/ *f,* lunchbox, lunchpail
fianza /'fianθa; 'fiansa/ *f,* guarantee, bail; surety; security. *Law.* **dar f.,** to guarantee; post bail
fiar /fi'ar/ *vt* to go surety for, post bail; sell on credit; trust; confide; —*vr* (*with de*) confide in; trust
fibra /'fiβra/ *f,* fiber; filament; energy, strength; *Mineral.* vein; grain (of wood)
fibroso /fi'βroso/ *a* fibrous; fibroid
ficción /fik'θion; fik'sion/ *f,* falsehood; invention; fiction, imaginative creation; pretense
ficha /'fitʃa/ *f,* chip, counter; domino; index card, filing card. **f. antropométrica,** personal particulars card
fichar /fi'tʃar/ *vt* to record personal particulars on a filing card; file, index
fichero /fi'tʃero/ *m,* filing cabinet; card catalog
fichú /fi'tʃu/ *m,* fichu, scarf
ficticio /fik'tiθio; fik'tisio/ *a* fictitious
fidedigno /fiðe'ðigno/ *a* trustworthy, bona fide
fideicomisario /fiðeikomi'sario/ *m, Law.* fiduciary, trustee
fideicomiso /fiðeiko'miso/ *m, Law.* trust
fidelidad /fiðeli'ðað/ *f,* fidelity, honesty; loyalty; punctiliousness
fideos /fi'ðeos/ *m pl,* vermicelli. *m, Inf.* scraggy person
fiduciario /fiðu'θiario; fiðu'siario/ *a Law.* fiduciary. *m, Law.* trustee
fiebre /'fieβre/ *f,* fever; great agitation, excitement. **f. de oro,** gold fever. **f. palúdica,** malarial fever. **f. puerperal,** puerperal fever. **f. tifoidea,** typhoid fever
fiel /fiel/ *a* faithful, loyal; true, exact. *m,* axis; pointer (of a scale or balance)
fieltro /'fieltro/ *m,* felt
fiera /'fiera/ *f,* wild beast; cruel person
fiereza /fie'reθa; fie'resa/ *f,* savageness, wildness; cruelty, fierceness; deformity
fiero /'fiero/ *a* wild, savage; ugly; huge, enormous; horrible, alarming; haughty
fiesta /'fiesta/ *f,* merriment, gaiety; entertainment, feast; *Inf.* joke; festivity, celebration; public holiday; caress, cajolery (gen. *pl*); *pl* holidays. **f. fija** *Eccl.* immovable feast. *Inf.* **estar de f.,** to be making merry. **hacer f.,** to take a holiday. *Inf.* **Se acabó la f.,** It's all over and done with
figón /fi'gon/ *m,* eating house, diner
figulino /figu'lino/ *a* fictile, made of terra cotta
figura /fi'gura/ *f,* shape, form; face; *Art.* image, figure; *Law.* form; court card; *Mus.* note; *Theat.* character, role; (*Geom. Gram. Dance.*) figure. **f. de nieve,** snowman. *Naut.* **f. de proa,** figurehead. *Fig.* **f. decorativa,** figurehead. *Fig.* **hacer f.,** to cut a figure
figurado /fi'guraðo/ *a* figurative; rhetorical
figurar /figu'rar/ *vt* to shape, mold; simulate, pre-

tend; represent; —*vi* be numbered among; cut a figure; —*vr* imagine

figurativo /figura'tiβo/ *a* figurative; symbolical

figurilla /figu'riʎa; figu'riya/ *mf Inf.* ridiculous, dwarfish figure. *f, Art.* statuette

figurín /figu'rin/ *m,* fashion plate or model

fijación /fiha'θion; fiha'sion/ *f,* fixing; nailing; sticking, posting; attention, fixity; *Chem.* fixation; firmness, stability

fijador /fiha'ðor/ *m,* (*Med. Photo.*) fixative; setting lotion; *Art.* varnish —*a* fixing

fijamente /fiha'mente/ *adv* firmly; attentively

fijar /fi'har/ *vt* to fix; glue, stick; nail; make firm; settle, appoint (a date); fix, concentrate (attention, gaze); (*Photo. Med.*) fix; —*vr* decide; notice (e.g. *No me había fijado,* I hadn't noticed). **f. anuncios,** to post bills

fijeza /fi'heθa; fi'hesa/ *f,* fixedness; firmness, stability; constancy, steadfastness

fijo /'fiho/ *a* firm; fixed; stable; steadfast; permanent; exact. **de f.,** certainly, without doubt

fila /'fila/ *f,* line, row; *Mil.* rank; antipathy, hatred. **en f.,** in a line

filacteria /filak'teria/ *f,* phylactery

filamento /fila'mento/ *m,* filament

filantropía /filantro'pia/ *f,* philanthropy

filantrópico /filan'tropiko/ *a* philanthropic

filántropo /fi'lantropo/ *m,* philanthropist

filarmónico /filar'moniko/ *a* philharmonic

filatelia /fila'telia/ *f,* philately, stamp collecting

filatélico /fila'teliko/ *a* philatelic

filatelista /filate'lista/ *mf* philatelist, stamp collector

filete /fi'lete/ *m, Archit.* filet; *Cul.* small spit; filet (of meat or fish); thread of a screw; *Sew.* hem

filiación /filia'θion; filia'sion/ *f,* filiation, affiliation, relationship; *Mil.* regimental register

filial /fi'lial/ *a* filial; affiliated

filibustero /filiβus'tero/ *m,* filibuster

filiforme /fili'forme/ *a* filamentous

filigrana /fili'grana/ *f,* filigree; watermark (of paper); *Fig.* delicate creation

filípica /fili'pika/ *f,* philippic

Filipinas, las /fili'pinas, las/ the Philippines

filipino /fili'pino/ **(-na)** *a* and *n* Philippine

filisteo /filis'teo/ **(-ea)** *a* and *n* philistine

filmar /fil''mar/ *vt* to film

filme /'filme/ *m,* (cinema) film

filo /'filo/ *m,* cutting edge; dividing line

filología /filolo'hia/ *f,* philology

filológico /filo'lohiko/ *a* philological

filólogo /fi'lologo/ *m,* philologist

filomela /filo'mela/ *f, Poet.* nightingale

filón /fi'lon/ *m, Mineral.* vein, lode; *Fig.* gold mine

filosofar /filoso'far/ *vi* to philosophize

filosofía /filoso'fia/ *f,* philosophy. **f. moral,** moral philosophy. **f. natural,** natural philosophy

filosófico /filo'sofiko/ *a* philosophic

filósofo /fi'losofo/ *m,* philosopher —*a* philosophic

filoxera /filo'ksera/ *f,* phylloxera

filtración /filtra'θion; filtra'sion/ *f,* filtration

filtrar /fil'trar/ *vt* to filter; —*vi* filter through, percolate; —*vr Fig.* disappear (of money, etc.)

filtro /'filtro/ *m,* filter, strainer; love potion, philter

fin /fin/ *m,* finish, end, conclusion; purpose, goal, aim; limit, extent. **a f. de,** in order to, so that. **a fines de,** toward the end of (with months, years, etc.) (e.g. *a fines de octubre,* toward the end of October). **en f.,** at last; in fine; well then! **por f.,** finally

finado /fi'naðo/ **(-da)** *n* deceased, dead person

final /fi'nal/ *a* final. *m,* end, finish; *Sports.* final (gen. *pl*)

finalidad /finali'ðað/ *f,* finality; purpose

finalista /fina'lista/ *mf Sports.* finalist

finalizar /finali'θar; finali'sar/ *vt* to conclude, finish; —*vi* be finished; close (stock exchange)

finalmente /final'mente/ *adv* finally

financiar /finan'θiar; finan'siar/ *vt* to finance

financiero /finan'θiero; finan'siero/ *a* financial. *m,* financier

finanzas /fi'nanθas; fi'nansas/ *f pl,* finance

finar /fi'nar/ *vi* to die; —*vr* desire, long for a thing

finca /'finka/ *f,* land, real estate; house property, country house, ranch

fineza /fi'neθa; fi'nesa/ *f,* fineness; excellence, goodness; kindness, expression of affection; good turn, friendly act; gift; beauty, delicacy

fingido /fin'hiðo/ *a* pretended; assumed; feigned; sham

fingimiento /finhi'miento/ *m,* pretense; affectation, assumption

fingir /fin'hir/ *vt* to pretend, feign; imagine

finiquitar /finiki'tar/ *vt* to close and pay up an account; *Inf.* end

finiquito /fini'kito/ *m,* closing of an account; final receipt, quittance; quietus

finito /fi'nito/ *a* finite

finlandés /finlan'des/ **(-esa)** *a* Finnish —*n* Finn. *m,* Finnish (language)

Finlandia /fin'landia/ Finland

fino /'fino/ *a* fine; excellent, good; slim, slender, thin; delicate, subtle; dainty (of people); cultured, polished; constant, loving; sagacious, shrewd; *Mineral.* refined

finta /'finta/ *f,* feint (in fencing); menace, threat

finura /fi'nura/ *f,* fineness; excellence; delicacy; courtesy

fiordo /'fiorðo/ *m,* fjord

firma /'firma/ *f,* signature; act of signing; *Com.* firm name, firm

firmamento /firma'mento/ *m,* firmament

firmante /fir'mante/ *a* signing. *mf* signatory

firmar /fir'mar/ *vt* to sign

firme /'firme/ *a* firm; hard; steady, solid; constant, resolute, loyal. *m,* foundation, base. *Mil.* **¡Firmes!** Attention! **batir de f.,** to strike hard

firmeza /fir'meθa; fir'mesa/ *f,* stability, firmness; constancy, resoluteness, loyalty

fiscal /fis'kal/ *a* fiscal. *m,* attorney general; public prosecutor; meddler. **f. de quiebras,** official receiver

fiscalizar /fiskali'θar; fiskali'sar/ *vt* to prosecute; pry into; meddle with; censure, criticize

fisco /'fisko/ *m,* national treasury, exchequer, revenue

fisgar /fis'gar/ *vt* to harpoon; pry; —*vi* mock, make fun of

fisgón /fis'gon/ **(-ona)** *a* prying; mocking —*n* pryer; mocker; eavesdropper

fisgoneo /fisgo'neo/ *m,* prying; eavesdropping

física /'fisika/ *f,* physics

físico /'fisiko/ *a* physical. *m,* physicist; physician; physique

fisiología /fisiolo'hia/ *f,* physiology

fisiológico /fisio'lohiko/ *a* physiological

fisiólogo /fisi'ologo/ *m,* physiologist

fisioterapia /fisiote'rapia/ *f,* physiotherapy

fisonomía /fisono'mia/ *f,* physiognomy

fístula /'fistula/ *f,* pipe, conduit; *Mus.* pipe; *Surg.* fistula

fisura /fi'sura/ *f,* fissure

flaccidez /flakθi'ðeθ; flaksi'ðes/ *f,* flabbiness

fláccido /'flakθiðo; 'flaksiðo/ *a* flaccid, soft, flabby

flaco /'flako/ *a* thin; weak, feeble; *Fig.* weak-minded; dispirited. *m,* failing, weakness. *Inf.* **hacer un f. servicio,** to do an ill turn. **estar f. de memoria,** to have a weak memory

flagelación /flahela'θion; flahela'sion/ *f,* flagellation

flagelante /flahe'lante/ *m,* flagellant

flagelar /flahe'lar/ *vt* to scourge; *Fig.* lash

flagelo /fla'helo/ *m,* whip, scourge

flagrante /fla'grante/ *a Poet.* refulgent; present; actual. **en f.,** in the very act, flagrante delicto

flagrar /fla'grar/ *vi Poet.* to blaze, be refulgent

flamante /fla'mante/ *a* resplendent; brand-new; fresh, spick-and-span

flamenco /fla'menko/ **(-ca)** *m, Ornith.* flamingo —*a* and *n* Flemish —*a* Andalusian; gypsy; buxom, fresh

flan /flan/ *m,* baked custard, creme caramel. **estar como un f.,** to shake like a leaf, be nervous

flanco /'flanko/ *m,* side; *Mil.* flank

Flandes /'flandes/ Flanders

flanquear /flanke'ar/ *vt Mil.* to flank

flanqueo /flan'keo/ *m, Mil.* outflanking

flaquear /flake'ar/ *vi* to grow weak; weaken; totter (buildings, etc.); be disheartened, flag
flaqueza /fla'keθa; fla'kesa/ *f,* weakness; thinness; faintness, feebleness; frailty, fault; loss of zeal
flato /'flato/ *m,* flatulence, gas
flatulento /flatu'lento/ *a* flatulent, gassy
flauta /'flauta/ *f,* flute
flautín /flau'tin/ *m,* piccolo
flautista /flau'tista/ *mf* flutist
flebitis /fle'βitis/ *f,* phlebitis
flebotomía /fleβoto'mia/ *f,* phlebotomy, bloodletting
flecha /'fletʃa/ *f,* arrow, dart
flechar /fle'tʃar/ *vt* to shoot an arrow or dart; wound or kill with arrows; *Inf.* inspire love; *—vi* bend a bow to shoot
flechazo /fle'tʃaθo; fle'tʃaso/ *m,* wound with an arrow; *Inf.* love at first sight
flechero /fle'tʃero/ *m,* archer; arrow maker
fleco /'fleko/ *m,* fringe; fringe (of hair)
fleje /'flehe/ *m,* iron hoop (for barrels, etc.)
flema /'flema/ *f,* phlegm; sluggishness
flemático /fle'matiko/ *a* phlegmatic; sluggish
flemón /fle'mon/ *m,* gumboil; abscess
flequillo /fle'kiʎo; fle'kiyo/ *m,* fringe (of hair)
fletamento /fleta'mento/ *m,* chartering (a ship)
fletar /fle'tar/ *vt* to charter a ship; embark merchandise or people
flete /'flete/ *m,* freightage; cargo, freight
flexibilidad /fleksiβili'ðað/ *f,* flexibility; suppleness, adaptability
flexible /fle'ksiβle/ *a* pliant, supple; flexible, adaptable. *m, Elec.* flex
flexión /fle'ksion/ *f,* flexion; bend, bending; deflection
flirtear /flirte'ar/ *vi* to flirt
flirteo /flir'teo/ *m,* flirtation
flojedad /flohe'ðað/ *f,* flabbiness; weakness, feebleness; laziness, negligence
flojo /'floho/ *a* flabby; slack, loose; weak, feeble; lazy, slothful; poor (of a literary work, etc.)
floqueado /floke'aðo/ *a* fringed
flor /flor/ *f,* flower; best (of anything); bloom (on fruit); virginity; grain (of leather); compliment (gen. *pl*); menstruation (gen. *pl*). **f. de especia,** mace. **f. de la edad,** prime, youth. **f. del cuclillo,** mayflower. **f. del estudiante,** French marigold. **flores de mano,** artificial flowers. **flores de oblón,** hops. **a f. de,** on the surface of, level with. **andarse en flores,** *Fig.* to beat about the bush. **echar flores,** to pay compliments. **en f.,** in bloom
flora /'flora/ *f,* flora
floración /flora'θion; flora'sion/ *f,* flowering
floral /flo'ral/ *a* floral. **juegos florales,** poetry contest
florear /flore'ar/ *vt* to adorn with flowers; *—vi* execute a flourish on the guitar
florecer /flore'θer; flore'ser/ *vi irr* to flower, bloom; flourish, prosper; *—vr* grow mold (of cheese, etc.). See **conocer**
floreciente /flore'θiente; flore'siente/ *a* flowering; prosperous
florecimiento /floreθi'miento; floresi'miento/ *m,* flowering; prosperity
Florencia /flo'renθia; flo'rensia/ Florence
florentino /floren'tino/ **(-na)** *a* and *n* Florentine
floreo /flo'reo/ *m,* witty conversation; flourish (on the guitar or in fencing)
florero /flo'rero/ *m,* vase; flower pot; *Art.* flower piece
florescencia /flores'θenθia; flores'sensia/ *f,* flowering; flowering season, florescence
floresta /flo'resta/ *f,* grove, wooded park, woodland; *Fig.* collector of beautiful things; anthology
florete /flo'rete/ *m,* fencing foil
floricultor /florikul'tor/ **(-ra)** *n* floriculturist
floricultura /florikul'tura/ *f,* floriculture
floridamente /floriða'mente/ *adv* elegantly, with a flourish
florido /flo'riðo/ *a* flowery; best, most select; florid, ornate
florilegio /flori'lehio/ *m,* anthology, collection
florín /flo'rin/ *m,* florin
florista /flo'rista/ *mf* artificial-flower maker; florist; flower seller
florón /flo'ron/ *m,* large flower; *Archit.* fleuron; honorable deed
flósculo /'floskulo/ *m, Bot.* floret
flota /'flota/ *f,* fleet of merchant ships. **f. aérea,** air force
flotación /flota'θion; flota'sion/ *f,* floating. *Naut.* **línea de f.,** water line
flotador /flota'ðor/ *a* floating. *m,* float
flotamiento /flota'miento/ *m,* floating
flotante /flo'tante/ *a* floating
flotar /flo'tar/ *vi* to float on water or in air
flote /'flote/ *m,* floating. **a f.,** afloat; independent, solvent
flotilla /flo'tiʎa; flo'tiya/ *f,* flotilla; fleet of small ships. **f. aérea,** air fleet
fluctuación /fluktua'θion; fluktua'sion/ *f,* fluctuation; hesitation, vacillation
fluctuante /fluk'tuante/ *a* fluctuating
fluctuar /fluktu'ar/ *vi* to fluctuate; be in danger (things); vacillate, hesitate; undulate; oscillate
fluidez /flui'ðeθ; flui'ðes/ *f,* fluidity
flúido /'fluiðo/ *a* fluid; fluent. *m,* fluid; *Elec.* current
fluir /flu'ir/ *vi irr* to flow. See **huir**
flujo /'fluho/ *m,* flow, flux; rising tide. **f. de sangre,** hemorrhage
fluorescencia /fluores'θenθia; fluores'sensia/ *f,* fluorescence
fluorescente /fluores'θente; fluores'sente/ *a* fluorescent
fluvial /flu'βial/ *a* fluvial
flux /fluks/ *m,* flush (in cards)
foca /'foka/ *f, Zool.* seal
focal /fo'kal/ *a* focal
foco /'foko/ *m,* focus; center; origin; source; *Theat.* spotlight; core (of an abscess)
fofo /'fofo/ *a* spongy, soft; flabby
fogata /fo'gata/ *f,* bonfire
fogón /fo'gon/ *m,* fire, cooking area, kitchen range, kitchen stove; furnace of a steamboiler; vent of a firearm
fogonazo /fogo'naθo; fogo'naso/ *m,* powder flash
fogonero /fogo'nero/ *m,* stoker
fogosidad /fogosi'ðað/ *f,* enthusiasm; vehemence; ardor
fogoso /fo'goso/ *a* ardent; vehement; enthusiastic
folclórico /fol'kloriko/ *a* pertaining to folklore
folclorista /folklo'rista/ *mf* folklorist
foliar /fo'liar/ *vt* to number the pages of a book
folículo /fo'likulo/ *m,* follicle
folio /'folio/ *m,* leaf of a book or manuscript, folio. **en f.,** in folio
follaje /fo'ʎahe; fo'yahe/ *m,* foliage; leafy ornamentation; crude, unnecessary decoration; verbosity
folletín /foʎe'tin; foye'tin/ *m,* feuilleton, literary article; serial story; *Inf.* dime novel, potboiler
folletinista /foʎeti'nista; foyeti'nista/ *mf* pamphleteer
folleto /fo'ʎeto; fo'yeto/ *m,* pamphlet, leaflet
follón /fo'ʎon; fo'yon/ *a* lazy; caddish; craven
fomentación /fomenta'θion; fomenta'sion/ *f, Med.* fomentation, poultice
fomentador /fomenta'ðor/ *a* fomenting. *m,* fomenter
fomentar /fomen'tar/ *vt* to warm, foment; incite, instigate; *Med.* apply poultices
fomento /fo'mento/ *m,* heat, shelter; fuel; protection, encouragement; *Med.* fomentation
fonda /'fonda/ *f,* inn; restaurant
fondeadero /fondea'ðero/ *m,* anchorage, anchoring ground
fondear /fonde'ar/ *vt Naut.* to sound; search a ship; examine carefully; *—vi Naut.* anchor
fondillos /fon'diʎos; fon'diyos/ *m pl,* seat (of the trousers)
fondista /fon'dista/ *mf* owner of an inn or restaurant
fondo /'fondo/ *m,* bottom (of a well, etc.); bed (of the sea, etc.); depth; rear, portion at the back; ground (of fabrics); background; *Com.* capital; *Com.* stock; *Fig.* fund (of humor, etc.); character, nature; temperament; *Fig.* substance, core, essence; *Naut.*

bottom; *pl Com.* resources, funds. **f. de amortización,** sinking fund. **f. doble** *or* **f. secreto,** false bottom. **f. muerto, f. perdido** *or* **f. vitalicio,** life annuity. *Com.* **fondos inactivos,** idle capital. **a fondo,** completely, thoroughly. **artículo de f.,** editorial, lead article. *Sports.* **carrera de f.,** long-distance race. *Naut.* **irse a f.,** to sink, founder

fonética /fo'netika/ *f,* phonetics

fonético /fo'netiko/ *a* phonetic

fonetista /fone'tista/ *mf* phonetician

fonógrafo /fo'nografo/ *m,* phonograph

fonología /fonolo'hia/ *f,* phonology

fonológico /fono'lohiko/ *a* phonological

fontanar /fonta'nar/ *m,* spring, stream

fontanería /fontane'ria/ *f,* pipe laying, plumbing

fontanero /fonta'nero/ *m,* pipe layer; plumber

forajido /fora'hiðo/ **(-da)** *a* fugitive, outlawed —*n* robber, fugitive

forastero /foras'tero/ **(-ra)** *a* strange, foreign; alien, exotic —*n* stranger

forcejear /forθehe'ar; forsehe'ar/ *vi* to struggle; try, strive; oppose, contradict

forcejo /for'θeho; for'seho/ *m,* struggle; endeavor; opposition, hostility

fórceps /'forθeps; 'forseps/ *m pl,* forceps

forense /fo'rense/ *a* forensic

forestal /fores'tal/ *a* forestal

forillo /fo'riʎo; fo'riyo/ *m, Theat.* backdrop

forja /'forha/ *f,* forge

forjador /forha'ðor/ *m,* smith, ironworker

forjar /for'har/ *vt* to forge; fabricate; create; counterfeit

forma /'forma/ *f,* shape, form; arrangement; method; style; manifestation, expression; formula, formulary; ceremonial; *Print.* form; manner; means, way; mold, matrix; style of handwriting. *Law.* **en debida f.,** in due form

formación /forma'θion; forma''sion/ *f,* formation; form, contour, shape; (*Mil. Geol.*) formation. **f. del censo,** census taking

formador /forma'ðor/ *a* forming, shaping

formal /for'mal/ *a* apparent, formal; serious, punctilious, steady; truthful, reliable; sedate; orderly, regular, methodical

formaldehído /formalde'iðo/ *m,* formaldehyde

formalidad /formali'ðað/ *f,* orderliness, propriety; formality; requirement, requisite; ceremony; seriousness, sedateness; punctiliousness

formalismo /forma'lismo/ *m,* formalism; bureaucracy, red tape

formalizar /formali'θar; formali'sar/ *vt* to put into final form; legalize; formulate, enunciate; —*vr* take seriously (a joke)

formar /for'mar/ *vt* to shape; form; educate, mold; *Mil.* form. **formarle causa a uno,** to bring charges against someone —*vr* develop, grow

formativo /forma'tiβo/ *a* formative

formato /for'mato/ *m, Print.* format; *Chem.* formate

formidable /formi'ðaβle/ *a* formidable, awe-inspiring; huge, enormous

fórmula /'formula/ *f,* formula; prescription; mode of expression. (*Math. Chem.*) **f. clásica,** standard formula

formular /formu'lar/ *vt* to formulate; prescribe

formulario /formu'lario/ *m, Law.* formulary; handbook

formulismo /formu'lismo/ *m,* formulism; bureaucracy, red tape

fornicación /fornika'θion; fornika'sion/ *f,* fornication

fornicador /fornika'ðor/ **(-ra)** *a* and *n* fornicator

fornicar /forni'kar/ *vi* to fornicate

fornido /for'niðo/ *a* stalwart, muscular, strong

foro /'foro/ *m,* forum; law courts; law, bar, legal profession; *Theat.* back scenery; leasehold

forraje /fo'rrahe/ *m,* forage, fodder; foraging

forrajeador /forrahea'ðor/ *m,* forager

forrajear /forrahe'ar/ *vt* to gather forage, go foraging

forrar /fo'rrar/ *vt Sew.* to line; cover, encase, make a cover for

forro /'forro/ *m,* lining, inner covering; cover (of a book)

fortalecedor /fortaleθe'ðor; fortalese'ðor/ *a* fortifying

fortalecer /fortale'θer; fortale'ser/ *vt irr* to fortify. See **conocer**

fortaleza /forta'leθa; forta'lesa/ *f,* vigor; fortitude; fortress; natural defense. *Aer.* **f. volante,** flying fortress

fortificable /fortifi'kaβle/ *a* fortifiable

fortificación /fortifika'θion; fortifika'sion/ *f,* fortification

fortificador /fortifika'ðor/ *a* fortifying

fortificar /fortifi'kar/ *vt* to fortify

fortísimo /for'tisimo/ *a superl* **fuerte** extremely strong

fortuito /for'tuito/ *a* fortuitous, chance

fortuna /for'tuna/ *f,* fate, destiny; fortune, capital, estate; tempest. **por f.,** fortunately. **probar f.,** to try one's luck

forzado /for'θaðo; for'saðo/ *a* forced, obliged. *m,* convict condemned to the galleys

forzador /forθa'ðor; forsa'ðor/ *m,* violator, seducer

forzar /for'θar; for'sar/ *vt irr* to force, break open; take by force; rape, ravish; oblige, compel —*Pres. Indic.* **fuerzo, fuerzas, fuerza, fuerzan.** *Preterite* **forcé, forzaste,** etc —*Pres. Subjunc.* **fuerce, fuerces, fuerce, forcemos, forcéis, fuercen**

forzoso /for'θoso; for'soso/ *a* obligatory, unavoidable, necessary

forzudo /for'θuðo; for'suðo/ *a* brawny, stalwart

fosa /'fosa/ *f,* grave; socket (of a joint). **f. común,** potter's field.

fosar /fo'sar/ *vt* to undermine; dig a trench around

fosfato /fos'fato/ *m,* phosphate

fosforecer /fosfore'θer; fosfore'ser/ *vi irr* to phosphoresce. See **conocer**

fosforera /fosfo'rera/ *f,* matchbox

fosforero /fosfo'rero/ **(-ra)** *n* match seller

fosforescencia /fosfores'θenθia; fosfores'sensia/ *f,* phosphorescence

fosforescente /fosfores'θente; fosfores'sente/ *a* phosphorescent

fósforo /'fosforo/ *m,* phosphorus; match; morning star

fósil /'fosil/ *a* and *m,* fossil; *Inf.* antique

fosilizarse /fosili'θarse; fosili'sarse/ *vr* to become fossilized

foso /'foso/ *m,* hole, hollow, pit; trench; pit (in garages); *Theat.* room under the stage.

foto /'foto/ *f,* snapshot, photo

fotocopia /foto'kopia/ *f,* photocopy

fotogénico /foto'heniko/ *a* photogenic

fotograbado /fotogra'βaðo/ *m,* photogravure

fotografía /fotogra'fia/ *f,* photography; photograph

fotografiar /fotogra'fiar/ *vt* to photograph

fotográfico /foto'grafiko/ *a* photographic

fotógrafo /fo'tografo/ *m,* photographer

fotograma /foto'grama/ *m,* (cinema) shot

fotoquímica /foto'kimika/ *f,* photochemistry

fotostato /foto'stato/ *m,* photostat

frac /frak/ *m,* tail coat

fracasar /fraka'sar/ *vi* to break, crumble, be shattered; collapse (of plans, etc.); fail; be disappointed

fracaso /fra'kaso/ *m,* shattering; collapse (of plans, etc.); disaster; failure, disappointment, downfall

fracción /frak'θion; frak'sion/ *f,* division into parts; fraction. **f. impropia,** *Math.* improper fraction

fractura /frak'tura/ *f,* fracture. **f. conminuta,** compound fracture

fracturar /fraktu'rar/ *vt* to fracture

fragancia /fra'ganθia; fra'gansia/ *f,* fragrance, perfume; renown, good name

fragante /fra'gante/ *a* fragrant; perfumed; flagrant

fragata /fra'gata/ *f,* frigate

frágil /'frahil/ *a* fragile, brittle; perishable, frail; weak, sinful

fragilidad /frahili'ðað/ *f,* fragility; frailty, sinfulness

fragmentario /fragmen'tario/ *a* fragmentary

fragmento /frag'mento/ *m,* fragment

fragor /fra'gor/ *m,* noise, crash

fragosidad /fragosi'ðað/ *f,* roughness, rockiness, unevenness

fragoso /fra'goso/ *a* craggy, rocky; rough; noisy, clamorous
fragua /'fragua/ *f*, forge
fraguado /fra'guaðo/ *m*, forging; *Mas.* setting
fraguar /fra'guar/ *vt* to forge, work; plot, scheme; —*vi* set (concrete, etc.)
fraile /'fraile/ *m*, friar, monk. *Inf.* **f. de misa y olla,** ignorant friar
frailesco /frai'lesko/ *a Inf.* pertaining to friars, friarlike
frambuesa /fram'buesa/ *f*, raspberry
francachela /franka'tʃela/ *f*, *Inf.* binge
francés /fran'θes; fran'ses/ **(-esa)** *a* French —*n* Frenchman (-woman). *m*, French (language). **a la francesa,** in French fashion
francesilla /franθe'siʎa; franse'siya/ *f*, *Cul.* French roll
Francia /'franθia; 'fransia/ France
franciscano /franθis'kano; fransis'kano/ **(-na)** *a* and *n* Franciscan
francmasón /frankma'son/ **(-ona)** *n* Freemason
francmasonería /frankmasone'ria/ *f*, freemasonry
franco /'franko/ *a* generous, liberal; exempt; sincere, genuine, frank; duty-free; Frank; Franco (in compound words). *m*, franc (coin). **f. de porte,** post-free; prepaid
Franco-Condado /'franko-kon'daðo/ Franche-Comté
francotirador /frankotira'ðor/ *m*, sharpshooter, franc tireur
franela /fra'nela/ *f*, flannel
frangir /fran'hir/ *vt* to divide, quarter
frangollar /fraŋgo'ʎar; fraŋgo'yar/ *vt* to scamp, skimp (work); botch, bungle
franja /'franha/ *f*, fringe; border, trimming; stripe. *Radio.* **f. undosa,** wave band
franjar /fran'har/ *vt Sew.* to fringe, trim
franqueadora /frankea'ðora/ *f*, postage meter
franquear /franke'ar/ *vt* to exempt; make free, make a gift of; clear the way; stamp, prepay; free (slaves); —*vr* fall in easily with others' plans; make confidences
franqueo /fran'keo/ *m*, exemption; bestowal, making free; postage, stamping; enfranchisement (of slaves)
franqueza /fran'keθa; fran'kesa/ *f*, exemption, freedom; generosity, liberality; sincerity, frankness
franquicia /fran'kiθia; fran'kisia/ *f*, exemption from excise duties
franquista /fran'kista/ *mf* Franquist, supporter of Franco
frasco /'frasko/ *m*, bottle, flask; powder flask or horn. **f. cuentagotas,** drop bottle
frase /'frase/ *f*, sentence; phrase; epigram; idiom, style. **f. hecha,** cliché
frasear /frase'ar/ *vt* to phrase
fraseología /fraseolo'hia/ *f*, phraseology; wording
fratás /fra'tas/ *m*, plastering trowel
fraternal /frater'nal/ *a* brotherly
fraternidad /fraterni'ðað/ *f*, fraternity, brotherhood
fraternizar /fraterni'θar; fraterni'sar/ *vi* to fraternize
fraterno /fra'terno/ *a* fraternal
fratricida /fratri'θiða; fratri'siða/ *a* fratricidal. *mf* fratricide
fratricidio /fratri'θiðio; fratri'siðio/ *m*, fratricide (act)
fraude /'frauðe/ *m*, fraud, deception
fraudulento /frauðu'lento/ *a* fraudulent
fray /frai/ *m*, *Abbr.* **fraile.** Always followed by a proper name (e.g. *F. Bartolomé,* Friar Bartholomew)
frazada /fra'θaða; fra'saða/ *f*, blanket
frecuencia /fre'kuenθia; fre'kuensia/ *f*, frequency. **f. radioeléctrica,** radiofrequency
frecuentación /frekuenta'θion; frekuenta'sion/ *f*, frequenting, visiting
frecuentador /frekuenta'ðor/ **(-ra)** *n* frequenter
frecuentar /frekuen'tar/ *vt* to frequent
frecuente /fre'kuente/ *a* frequent
fregadero /frega'ðero/ *m*, kitchen sink
fregado /fre'gaðo/ *m*, scrubbing; rubbing; scouring; washing; *Inf.* murky business
fregador /frega'ðor/ *m*, kitchen sink; scrub brush; dishcloth. **f. mecánico de platos,** dishwasher
fregar /fre'gar/ *vt irr* to rub; scour; wash (dishes). See **cegar**
fregona /fre'gona/ *f*, kitchen maid
fregotear /fregote'ar/ *vt Inf.* to clean or scour inefficiently
freiduría /freiðu'ria/ *f*, fried-fish shop
freír /fre'ir/ *vt irr Cul.* to fry. See **reír**
fréjol /'frehol/ *m*, kidney bean
frenar /fre'nar/ *vt* to restrain, hold back; bridle, check; *Mech.* brake
frenesí /frene'si/ *m*, madness, frenzy; vehemence, exaltation
frenético /fre'netiko/ *a* mad, frenzied; vehement, exalted
freno /'freno/ *m*, bridle; *Mech.* brake; restraint, check. **f. de pedal,** foot brake. **f. neumático,** vacuum brake, pneumatic brake
frente /'frente/ *f*, brow, forehead; front portion; countenance; head; heading; beginning (of a letter, etc.). *m*, *Mil.* front. *mf* facade; front; obverse (of coins) —*adv* in front, opposite. **f. a f.,** face to face. **con la f. levantada,** with head held high; proudly; insolently. **de f.,** abreast
freo /'freo/ *m*, strait, narrow channel
fresa /'fresa/ *f*, strawberry plant and fruit (especially small or wild varieties); *Mech.* milling cutter, miller
fresadora /fresa'ðora/ *f*, milling machine
fresal /fre'sal/ *m*, strawberry bed
fresca /'freska/ *f*, cool air; fresh air; *Inf.* home truth
fresco /'fresko/ *a* cool; fresh, new; recent; buxom, fresh-colored; calm, serene; *Inf.* impudent, cheeky, bold; thin (cloths). *m*, coolness; fresh air; *Art.* fresco. **al f.,** in the open air. **hacer f.,** to be cool or fresh
frescote /fres'kote/ *a Inf.* ruddy and corpulent
frescura /fres'kura/ *f*, coolness; freshness; pleasant verdure and fertility; *Inf.* cheek, nerve; piece of insolence; unconcern, indifference; calmness, serenity
fresero /fre'sero/ **(-ra)** *n* strawberry seller
fresneda /fres'neða/ *f*, ash grove
fresno /'fresno/ *m*, *Bot.* ash
fresón /fre'son/ *m*, strawberry (large, cultivated varieties)
fresquera /fres'kera/ *f*, meat locker; cool place
fresquista /fres'kista/ *mf* fresco painter
friable /'friaβle/ *a* brittle; friable, powdery
frialdad /frial'dað/ *f*, coldness, chilliness; *Med.* frigidity; indifference, lack of interest; foolishness; negligence
fríamente /fria'mente/ *adv* coldly; coolly, with indifference; dully, flatly
fricción /frik'θion; frik'sion/ *f*, friction
friccionar /frikθio'nar; friksio'nar/ *vt* to rub; give a massage
friega /'friega/ *f*, friction, massage
frigidez /frihi'ðeθ; frihi'ðes/ *f*, See **frialdad**
frígido /'frihiðo/ *a* frigid
frigio /'frihio/ *a* and *n* Phrygian
frigorífico /frigo'rifiko/ *a* refrigerative. *m*, refrigerator, cold-storage locker
frío /'frio/ *a* cold; *Med.* frigid; indifferent, uninterested; dull, uninteresting; inefficient. *m*, coldness, chill; cold
friolera /frio'lera/ *f*, bagatelle, trifle, mere nothing
friolero /frio'lero/ *a* sensitive to cold
frisa /'frisa/ *f*, frieze cloth
frisar /fri'sar/ *vt* to frizz, curl (cloth); scrub, rub; —*vi* approach, be nearly (e.g. *Frisa en los setenta años,* He's nearly seventy)
Frisia /'frisia/ Friesland
friso /'friso/ *m*, frieze; dado, border
frisón /fri'son/ **(-ona)** *a* and *n* Frisian
fritada /fri'taða/ *f*, *Cul.* fry, fried food
frito /'frito/ *a* fried
fritura /fri'tura/ *f*, frying; fried food
frivolidad /friβoli'ðað/ *f*, frivolity
frivolité /friβoli'te/ *m*, *Sew.* tatting
frívolo /'friβolo/ *a* frivolous, superficial; futile, unconvincing
fronda /'fronda/ *f*, *Bot.* leaf; frond (of ferns); *pl* foliage
frondosidad /frondosi'ðað/ *f*, luxuriance of foliage

frondoso /fron'doso/ *a* leafy
frontera /fron'tera/ *f,* frontier; facade
fronterizo /fronte'riθo; fronte'riso/ *a* frontier; facing, opposite
frontero /fron'tero/ *a* facing, opposite. *m,* (*Obs. Mil.*) frontier commander
frontispicio /frontis'piθio; frontis'pisio/ *m,* frontispiece; facade; *Fig. Inf.* face, dial
frontón /fron'ton/ *m,* pelota court; jai alai court; *Archit.* pediment
frotamiento, frote /frota'miento, 'frote/ *m,* rubbing, friction
frotar /fro'tar/ *vt* to rub
frotis /'frotis/ *m, Med.* smear
fructífero /fruk'tifero/ *a* fruitful, fructiferous
fructuoso /fruk'tuoso/ *a* fruitful, fertile; useful
frufrú /fru'fru/ *m,* rustle (of silk, etc.)
frugal /fru'gal/ *a* frugal; saving, economical
frugalidad /frugali'ðað/ *f,* frugality, abstemiousness, moderation
fruición /frui'θion; frui'sion/ *f,* enjoyment; fruition; satisfaction
fruir /fruir/ *vi irr* to enjoy what one has long desired. See **huir**
frunce /'frunθe; 'frunse/ *m, Sew.* shirring; gather; ruffling; tuck; pucker; wrinkle
fruncimiento /frunθi'miento; frunsi'miento/ *m,* wrinkling; puckering; *Sew.* shirring
fruncir /frun'θir; frun'sir/ *vt* to frown; purse (the lips); pucker; *Sew.* shirr, pleat, gather; reduce in size; conceal the truth; —*vr* pretend to be prudish. **f. el ceño,** to knit one's brow, scowl
fruslería /frusle'ria/ *f,* trifle, nothing
frustración /frustra'θion; frustra'sion/ *f,* frustration
frustrar /frus'trar/ *vt* to disappoint; frustrate, thwart
fruta /'fruta/ *f,* fruit; *Inf.* consequence, result. **f. de hueso,** stone fruit. *Cul.* **f. de sartén,** fritter
frutal /fru'tal/ *a* fruit-bearing. *m,* fruit tree
frutar /fru'tar/ *vi* to bear fruit
frutería /frute'ria/ *f,* fruit
frutero /fru'tero/ **(-ra)** *a* fruit —*n* fruit seller. *m,* fruit dish; *Art.* painting of fruit; basket of imitation fruit
frútice /'frutiθe; frutise/ *m,* bush, shrub
fruticultura /frutikul'tura/ *f,* fruit farming
fruto /'fruto/ *m,* fruit; product, result; profit, proceeds; *Agr.* grain
fu /fu/ spitting (of cats) —*interj* expression of scorn. *Inf.* **ni f. ni fa,** neither one thing nor the other
fucilazo /fuθi'laθo; fusi'laso/ *m,* heat lightning
fucsia /'fuksia/ *f,* fuchsia
fuego /'fuego/ *m,* fire; conflagration; firing (of firearms); beacon; hearth, home; rash; ardor; heat (of an argument, etc.); —*interj* **¡F.!** *Mil.* Fire! **fuegos artificiales,** fireworks. **a sangre y f.,** by fire and sword. *Mil.* **hacer f.,** to fire (a weapon). **pegar f.,** to set on fire
fuelle /'fueʎe; 'fueye/ *m,* bellows; bag (of a bagpipe); *Sew.* pucker, wrinkle; hood (of a carriage, etc.); wind cloud; *Inf.* talebearer. **f. de pie,** foot pump
fuente /'fuente/ *f,* stream, spring; fountain; meat dish; genesis, origin; source, headwaters; tap
fuera /'fuera/ *adv* outside, out —*interj* get out! **f. de,** besides, in addition to. **f. de alcance,** out of reach. **f. de sí,** beside oneself (with rage, etc.). **de f.,** from the outside. **por f.,** on the outside, externally
fuero /'fuero/ *m,* municipal charter; jurisdiction; compilation of laws; legal right or privilege; *pl Inf.* arrogance. **los fueros de León,** the laws of León
fuerte /'fuerte/ *a* strong, resistant; robust; spirited, vigorous; hard (of diamonds, etc.); rough, uneven; impregnable; terrible, tremendous; overweight (of coins); active; efficacious, effective; expert, knowledgeable; *Gram.* strong; intense; loud; tough. *m,* fort; talent, strong point; *Mus.* forte —*adv* strongly; excessively. **tener genio f.,** to be quick-tempered
fuerza /'fuerθa; 'fuersa/ *f,* strength; power, might; force; efficacy; fortress; *Sew.* stiffening; *Mech.* power; violence; toughness, durability, solidity; potency; authority; courage; vigor; *pl Fig. Inf.* livewires, influential people. **a f. de,** by means of, by dint of. **a la f.,** forcibly. **en f. de,** because of, on account of. **por f. mayor,** by main force. **ser f.,** to be necessary
fuga /'fuga/ *f,* flight, escape, running away; leak (gas, etc.); elopement; *Mus.* fugue; ardor, strength. **f. de cerebros,** brain drain
fugarse /fu'garse/ *vr* to run away; elope; escape
fugaz /fu'gaθ; fu'gas/ *a* fugitive; fleeting, brief
fugitivo /fuhi'tiβo/ **(-va)** *a* fugitive; runaway, escaping; transient —*n* fugitive
fulano /fu'lano/ **(-na)** *n* so-and-so, such a person **f., zutano, y mengano,** *Inf.* Tom, Dick, and Harry
fulcro /'fulkro/ *m,* fulcrum
fulgente, fúlgido /ful'hente, 'fulhiðo/ *a* brilliant, shining
fulgor /ful'gor/ *m,* brilliance, brightness
fulgurar /fulgu'rar/ *vi* to shine, be resplendent, scintillate; flare
fulguroso /fulgu'roso/ *a* shining, sparkling
fúlica /'fulika/ *f, Ornith.* coot
fullería /fuʎe'ria; fuye'ria/ *f,* cheating at play; craftiness, low guile
fullero /fu'ʎero; fu'yero/ **(-ra)** *a* cheating; crafty, astute —*n* cheat, cardsharper
fulminante /fulmi'nante/ *a Med.* fulminant; fulminating; thundering. *m,* percussion cap
fulminar /fulmi'nar/ *vt* to fulminate (all meanings)
fulminato /fulmi'nato/ *m, Chem.* fulminate
fulmíneo, fulminoso /ful'mineo, fulmi'noso/ *a* fulminous, pertaining to lightning
fumadero /fuma'ðero/ *m,* smoking room
fumador /fuma'ðor/ **(-ra)** *a* smoking —*n* smoker. **«No fumadores»,** "Nonsmoking" (area)
fumar /fu'mar/ *vi* to smoke; —*vr Inf.* dissipate, waste
fumarola /fuma'rola/ *f,* fumarole
fumigación /fumiga'θion; fumiga'sion/ *f,* fumigation
fumigador /fumiga'ðor/ **(-ra)** *n* fumigator
fumigar /fumi'gar/ *vt* to fumigate
fumigatorio /fumiga'torio/ *a* fumigatory. *m,* perfume burner
fumista /fu'mista/ *m,* stove maker or seller
fumistería /fumiste'ria/ *f,* stove factory or store
funámbulo /fu'nambulo/ *n* tightrope walker, acrobat
función /fun'θion; fun'sion/ *f,* function; working, operation; *Theat.* performance; activity, duty; ceremony; celebration; *Math.* function; *Mil.* battle
funcional /funθio'nal; funsio'nal/ *a* functional
funcionamiento /funθiona'miento; funsiona'miento/ *m,* functioning
funcionar /funθio'nar; funsio'nar/ *vi* to function, work. **«No funciona»,** "Out of order"
funcionario /funθio'nario; funsio'nario/ *m,* functionary, official; civil servant
funda /'funda/ *f,* case, cover, sheath; hold-all. **f. de almohada,** pillowcase
fundación /funda'θion; funda'sion/ *f,* foundation
fundadamente /fundaða'mente/ *adv* with reason, on good evidence
fundador /funda'ðor/ **(-ra)** *n* founder, creator; originator
fundamental /funda'mental/ *a* fundamental
fundamento /funda'mento/ *m, Mas.* foundation; basis; basic principle, reason; origin, root
fundar /fun'dar/ *vt* to build, erect; base; found, institute; create, establish; —*vr* (*with en*) found, base upon. **f. una compañía,** *Com.* to float a company
fundición /fundi'θion; fundi'sion/ *f,* foundry; smelting, founding, casting; cast iron; *Print.* font
fundido fotográfico /fun'diðo foto'grafiko/ *m,* composite photograph
fundidor /fundi'ðor/ *m,* founder, smelter.
fundir /fun'dir/ *vt* to melt; found, smelt; cast (metals); —*vr* join together, unite; *Elec.* blow (fuses)
fúnebre /'funeβre/ *a* funeral; dismal, lugubrious, mournful
funeral /fune'ral/ *a* funeral
funerala, /fune'rala,/ (**a la**) *adv Mil.* with reversed arms
funerales /fune'rales/ *m pl,* funeral; *Eccl.* memorial masses
funeraria /fune'raria/ *f,* funeral home, undertaker
funerario /fune'rario/ *a* funeral
funéreo /fu'nereo/ *a* funereal, mournful

funesto /fu'nesto/ *a* unlucky, unfortunate; mournful, melancholy, sad
fungoso /fuŋ'goso/ *a* spongy, fungous
funicular /funiku'lar/ *a* funicular
furgón /fur'gon/ *m,* wagon; van; guard's van, baggage car, luggage cart. **f. postal,** mail truck
furia /'furia/ *f, Myth.* fury; rage, wrath; fit of madness; raging, violence (of the elements); speed, haste
furibundo /furi'βundo/ *a* frantic, furious; raging
fúrico /'furiko/ *a* stark raving mad
furioso /fu'rioso/ *a* furious, enraged; mad, insane; violent, terrible; enormous, excessive
furor /fu'ror/ *m,* fury, rage; poetic frenzy; violence; furor
furriel /fu'rriel/ *m,* quartermaster
furtivo /fur'tiβo/ *a* furtive; covert, clandestine; pirate (editions)
fusa /'fusa/ *f,* demisemiquaver
fusco /'fusko/ *a* dark
fuselado /fuse'laðo/ *a* streamlined
fuselaje /fuse'lahe/ *m,* fuselage
fusible /fu'siβle/ *a* fusible. *m, Elec.* fuse; fuse wire
fusil /fu'sil/ *m,* rifle
fusilamiento /fusila'miento/ *m,* execution by shooting
fusilar /fusi'lar/ *vt* to execute by shooting; *Inf.* plagiarize
fusilazo /fusi'laθo; fusi'laso/ *m,* rifle shot
fusión /fu'sion/ *f,* melting, liquefying; fusion, blending; mixture, union; *Com.* merger, amalgamation
fusionar /fusio'nar/ *vt* to blend, fuse, merge; *—vr Com.* combine, form a merger
fusta /'fusta/ *f,* brushwood; whip
fuste /'fuste/ *m,* wood, timber; *Poet.* saddle; *Fig.* core, essence; importance, substance; shaft of a lance; *Archit.* shaft. **hombre de buen f.,** a man with a good (physical) constitution
fustigar /fusti'gar/ *vt* to whip, lash; rebuke harshly
fútbol /'futβol/ *m,* football; soccer
futbolista /futβo'lista/ *mf* football player; soccer player
fútil /'futil/ *a* futile, ineffectual, worthless
futilidad /futili'ðað/ *f,* futility, worthlessness
futura /fu'tura/ *f, Law.* reversion (of offices); *Inf.* fiancée
futurismo /futu'rismo/ *m,* futurism
futurista /futu'rista/ *mf* futurist
futurístico /futu'ristiko/ *a* futuristic
futuro /fu'turo/ **(-ra)** *a* future. *m,* future *—n Inf* betrothed

G

gabacho /ga'βatʃo/ **(-cha)** *a* and *n* (*Inf.* scornful) Frenchman
gabán /ga'βan/ *m*, overcoat; cloak
gabardina /gaβar'ðina/ *f*, gabardine; weatherproof coat
gabarra /ga'βarra/ *f*, *Naut.* lighter, gabbard, barge
gabarro /ga'βarro/ *m*, flaw (in cloth); knot (in stone); snag, drawback; slip, error (in accounts)
gabela /ga'βela/ *f*, duty, tax; imposition, burden
gabinete /gaβi'nete/ *m*, study, library; sitting room; den; *Polit.* cabinet; collection, museum, gallery; laboratory; boudoir; studio; display cabinet. **g. de lectura,** reading room
gablete /ga'βlete/ *m*, *Archit.* gable
gaceta /ga'θeta; ga'seta/ *f*, bulletin, review, record; newspaper; gazette (official Spanish government organ); *Inf.* newshound
gacetero /gaθe'tero; gase'tero/ **(-ra)** *n* newsdealer. *m*, news reporter
gacetilla /gaθe'tiʎa; gase'tiya/ *f*, news in brief, miscellany column, society news; gossip column; *Inf.* newshound
gacetillero /gaθeti'ʎero; gaseti'yero/ *m*, paragrapher, penny-a-liner; reporter
gacha /'gatʃa/ *f*, unglazed crock; *pl* pap; porridge
gaché /ga'tʃe/ *m*, (among the Romany) Andalusian; *Inf.* fellow
gacho /'gatʃo/ *a* drooping, bent downward; slouch (hat); (of ears) lop
gachón /ga'tʃon/ *a Inf.* attractive, charming
gaditano /gaði'tano/ **(-na)** *a* and *n* native of, or pertaining to, Cadiz
gaélico /ga'eliko/ *a* and *m*, Gaelic
gafar /ga'far/ *vt* to claw; seize with a hook, hook; mend with a bracket (pottery)
gafas /'gafas/ *f pl*, spectacles; goggles; spectacle earhooks; grapplehooks
gafete /ga'fete/ *m*, hook and eye; clasp
gaita /'gaita/ *f*, bagpipe; hand organ; kind of clarinet; *Inf.* neck. **g. gallega,** bagpipe
gaitería /gaite'ria/ *f*, crude, gaudy garment or ornament
gaitero /gai'tero/ *a Inf.* overmerry; loud, crude. *m*, piper
gajes /'gahes/ *m pl*, salary; emoluments; perquisites
gajo /'gaho/ *m*, branch, bough (gen. cut); little cluster (of grapes); bunch (of fruit); quarter (of oranges, etc.); prong (of forks, etc.)
gala /'gala/ *f*, evening or full dress; grace, wit; flower, cream, best; gala; *pl* finery; trappings; wedding presents. **de g.,** full dress. **hacer g. de,** to glory in, boast of
galactita /galak'tita/ *f*, fuller's earth
galaico /ga'laiko/ *a* See **gallego**
galán /ga'lan/ *m*, handsome, well-made man; lover, wooer, gallant; *Theat.* leading man or one of leading male roles
galancete /galan'θete; galan'sete/ *m*, handsome little man; *Theat.* male juvenile lead
galano /ga'lano/ *a* smart, well-dressed; agreeable, pleasing; beautiful; ornamented; *Fig.* elegant (speech, style, etc.)
galante /ga'lante/ *a* gallant, courtly, attentive; flirtatious (of women); licentious
galanteador /galantea'ðor/ *a* flirtatious. *m*, philanderer; wooer
galantear /galante'ar/ *vt* to court; flirt with; make love to; *Fig.* procure assiduously
galanteo /galan'teo/ *m*, courtship; flirtation; lovemaking; wooing
galantería /galante'ria/ *f*, courtesy; attention, compliment; elegance, grace; gallantry; generosity, liberality
galanura /gala'nura/ *f*, showiness, gorgeousness; elegance, grace; prettiness
galápago /ga'lapago/ *m*, freshwater tortoise; cleat
galardón /galar'ðon/ *m*, reward, recompense, prize
galardonar /galarðo'nar/ *vt* to reward, recompense
gálata /'galata/ *a* and *mf* Galatian
galbana /gal'βana/ *f*, *Inf.* laziness, inertia
galbanoso /galβa'noso/ *a Inf.* slothful
galdrufa /gal'drufa/ *f*, top, spinning top
galeote /gale'ote/ *m*, galley slave
galera /ga'lera/ *f*, van, wagon, cart; *Naut.* galley; prison for women; *Print.* galley. **echar a galeras,** to condemn to the galleys
galerada /gale'raða/ *f*, galley proof
galería /gale'ria/ *f*, gallery; corridor, passage; collection of paintings; *Mineral.* gallery, drift; *Theat.* gallery
galerna /ga'lerna/ *f*, tempestuous northwest wind (gen. on Spanish north coast)
Gales /'gales/ Wales
galés /ga'les/ **(-esa)** *a* Welsh —*n* Welshman. *m*, Welsh (language)
galga /'galga/ *f*, boulder, rolling stone; greyhound bitch
galgo /'galgo/ *m*, greyhound. **g. ruso,** borzoi
Galia /'galia/ Gaul
gálibo /'galiβo/ *m*, *Naut.* mold; elegance
galicado /gali'kaðo/ *a* gallicized
galicismo /gali'θismo; gali'sismo/ *m*, gallicism
gálico /'galiko/ *m*, syphilis —*a* gallic
Galilea /gali'lea/ Galilee
galileo /gali'leo/ **(-ea)** *a* and *n* Galilean
galimatías /galima'tias/ *m*, *Inf.* gibberish, nonsense
gallardear /gaʎarðe'ar; gayarðe'ar/ *vi* to behave with ease and grace
gallardete /gaʎar'ðete; gayar'ðete/ *m*, pennant; bunting
gallardía /gaʎar'ðia; gayar'ðia/ *f*, grace, dignity; spirit, dash; courage; liveliness
gallardo /ga'ʎarðo; ga'yarðo/ *a* handsome, upstanding; gallant; spirited; fine, noble; lively
gallear /gaʎe'ar; gaye'ar/ *vi Inf.* to put on airs; be a bully; shout, bawl (with anger, etc.); *Fig. Inf.* stand out
gallego /ga'ʎego; ga'yego/ **(-ga)** *a* and *n* Galician. *m*, Galician (language)
galleta /ga'ʎeta; ga'yeta/ *f*, biscuit; *Inf.* slap; anthracite, lump coal; small jar or vessel
gallina /ga'ʎina; ga'yina/ *f*, hen. *mf Inf.* coward. **g. ciega,** blindman's buff. *Inf.* **acostarse con las gallinas,** to go to bed early
gallinaza /gaʎi'naθa; gayi'nasa/ *f*, hen dung
gallinero /gaʎi'nero; gayi'nero/ **(-ra)** *n* poultry dealer. *m*, henhouse; brood of hens; *Theat.* gallery; babel, noisy place
gallito /ga'ʎito; ga'yito/ *m*, small cock; cock of the walk; bully
gallo /ga'ʎo; ga'yo/ *m*, *Ornith.* cock; *Inf.* false note (in singing); *Inf.* boss, chief. **g. de viento,** weathercock. *Inf.* **alzar el g.,** to put on airs, boast. **Cada g. canta en su muladar,** Every man is boss in his own house. *Inf.* **Otro g. nos cantara,** Our lot (or fate) would have been very different
gallofero /gaʎo'fero; gayo'fero/ **(-ra)** *a* mendicant, vagabond —*n* beggar
galocha /ga'lotʃa/ *f*, patten, clog; cap with earflaps
galón /ga'lon/ *m*, galloon, braid; *Mil.* stripe; gallon (measure)
galoneadura /galonea'ðura/ *f*, braiding, trimming
galonear /galone'ar/ *vt* to trim with braid
galop /ga'lop/ *m*, galop; gallopade
galopante /galo'pante/ *a* galloping (of consumption, etc.)
galopar /galo'par/ *vi* to gallop; *Mech.* wobble
galope /ga'lope/ *m*, gallop. **a** or **de g.,** at the gallop; on the run, quickly. **andar a g. corto,** to canter
galopillo /galo'piʎo; galopiyo/ *m*, scullion
galopín /galo'pin/ *m*, ragamuffin, urchin; rogue, knave; *Inf.* clever rogue; *Naut.* cabin boy
galvanización /galβaniθa'θion; galβanisa'sion/ *f*, galvanization

galvanizar /galβani'θar; galβani'sar/ *vt Elec.* to galvanize; electroplate; *Fig.* shock into life

gama /'gama/ *f, Mus.* scale; gamut, range; doe

gambito /gam'bito/ *m,* gambit (in chess)

gamella /ga'meʎa; ga'meya/ *f,* trough (for washing, feeding animals, etc.)

gamo /'gamo/ *m,* buck (of the fallow deer)

gamuza /ga'muθa; ga'musa/ *f,* chamois; chamois leather

gana /'gana/ *f,* appetite; wish, desire. **de buena g.,** willingly. **de mala g.,** reluctantly. **tener g.** (**de**), to wish, desire, want. **no tener g.,** to have no appetite, not be hungry. **No me da la g.,** I don't want (to), I won't

ganable /ga'naβle/ *a* attainable; earnable

ganadería /ganaðe'ria/ *f,* livestock; strain (of cattle); cattle raising; stock farm; cattle dealing

ganadero /gana'ðero/ *m,* cattle raiser or dealer; herdsman

ganado /ga'naðo/ *m,* livestock, herd; flock; hive (of bees); *Inf.* mob. **g. mayor,** cattle, mules, horses. **g. menor,** sheep, goats, etc. **g. moreno,** hogs, swine. **g. vacuno,** cattle

ganador /gana'ðor/ **(-ra)** *a* winning —*n* winner

ganancia /ga'nanθia; ga'nansia/ *f,* winning, gain, profit

ganancial, ganancioso /ganan'θial, ganan'θioso; ganan'sial, ganan'sioso/ *a* gainful, profitable; lucrative

ganapán /gana'pan/ *m,* laborer; porter; *Inf.* boor

ganar /ga'nar/ *vt* to gain; win; conquer; arrive at; earn; surpass, beat; achieve; acquire; —*vi* prosper

ganchero /gan'tʃero/ *m,* lumberjack

ganchillo /gan'tʃiʎo; gan'tʃiyo/ *m,* crochet hook; crochet. **hacer g.,** to crochet

gancho /'gantʃo/ *m,* hook; stump (of a branch); shepherd's crook; crochet hook; *Inf.* trickster, pimp; *Inf.* scribble

ganchoso /gan'tʃoso/ *a* hooked; bent; curved

gandujar /gandu'har/ *vt Sew.* to pleat, tuck, shirr

gandul /gan'dul/ **(-la)** *a Inf.* lazy —*n* lazybones, loafer

gandulería /gandule'ria/ *f,* loafing, idleness

ganga /'gaŋga/ *f, Mineral.* gangue, matrix; bargain, cinch

ganglio /'gaŋglio/ *m,* ganglion

gangoso /gaŋ'goso/ *a* nasal; with a twang (of speech)

gangrena /gaŋ'grena/ *f,* gangrene

gangrenarse /gaŋgre'narse/ *vr* to become gangrenous, mortify

gangrenoso /gaŋgre'noso/ *a* gangrenous

ganguear /gaŋgue'ar/ *vi* to speak nasally, or with a twang

ganoso /ga'noso/ *a* wishful, desirous, anxious

gansada /gan'saða/ *f, Inf.* impertinence, foolishness

ganso /'ganso/ **(-sa)** *n* goose, gander; slow-moving person; yokel, bumpkin

Gante /'gante/ Ghent

ganzúa /gan'θua; gan'sua/ *f,* skeleton key; *Inf.* picklock, burglar; *Inf.* pumper, inquisitive person

gañán /ga'ɲan/ *m,* farm worker; day laborer; brawny fellow

gañido /ga'ɲiðo/ *m,* yowl, yelp, howl

gañir /ga'ɲir/ *vi irr* to yowl, yelp, howl (of dogs, etc.); crow, croak; *Inf.* talk hoarsely. See **mullir**

garabatear /garaβate'ar/ *vi* to hook, catch with hooks; scribble; *Fig. Inf.* beat around the bush

garabateo /garaβa'teo/ *m,* hooking; scribbling

garabato /gara'βato/ *m,* hook; *Agr.* weed clearer; scrawl, scribble; *Inf.* charm, sex appeal; pothook; boat hook; *pl* gestures, movements (with the hands)

garaje /ga'rahe/ *m,* garage

garambaina /garam'baina/ *f,* tawdry finery gaudiness; *pl Inf.* grimaces of affectation; *Inf.* scribble, scrawl

garante /ga'rante/ *mf* guarantor; reference (person) —*a* responsible, guaranteeing

garantía /garan'tia/ *f,* guarantee; security, pledge; *Law.* warranty

garantir /garan'tir/ *vt* to guarantee; warrant, vouch for

garapiñar /garapi'ɲar/ *vt* to ice, freeze (drinks, syrups, etc.); *Cul.* candy, coat with sugar

garapiñera /garapi'ɲera/ *f,* ice-cream freezer

garbanzo /gar'βanθo; gar'βanso/ *m,* chickpea. **g. negro,** *Fig.* black sheep

garbillar /garβi'ʎar; garβi'yar/ *vt Agr.* to sift; *Mineral.* riddle

garbo /'garβo/ *m,* jaunty air; grace, elegance; frankness; generosity, liberality

garboso /gar'βoso/ *a* attractive; handsome, sprightly, gay; graceful; munificent

garduña /gar'ðuɲa/ *f,* weasel; marten

garduño /gar'ðuɲo/ **(-ña)** *n Inf.* sneak thief

garete /ga'rete/ (**ir** *or* **irse al**) *Naut.* to be adrift

garfa /'garfa/ *f,* claw (of a bird or animal)

garfear /garfe'ar/ *vi* to catch with a hook, hook

garfio /'garfio/ *m,* grappling iron, hook, drag hook, cramp; gaff

gargajear /gargahe'ar/ *vi* to expectorate

gargajo /gar'gaho/ *m,* phlegm

garganta /gar'ganta/ *f,* throat; gullet; instep; defile; neck, shaft, narrowest part

gargantear /gargante'ar/ *vi* to warble, trill

gárgara /'gargara/ *f,* gargling (gen. *pl*). **hacer gárgaras,** to gargle

gargarismo /garga'rismo/ *m,* gargling; gargle

gárgol /'gargol/ *a* rotten (eggs). *m,* groove, mortise

gárgola /'gargola/ *f, Archit.* gargoyle; linseed

garguero /gar'gero/ *m,* windpipe; esophagus

garita /ga'rita/ *f,* sentry box; porter's lodge; hut; cabin. **g. de señales,** (railroad) signal box

garitero /gari'tero/ *m,* gambling house keeper; gambler

garito /ga'rito/ *m,* gambling house; profits of a gambling house

garra /'garra/ *f,* paw with claws; talon; hand; *Mech.* clamp, claw. *Fig.* **caer en las garras de,** to fall into the clutches (of)

garrafa /ga'rrafa/ *f,* decanter, carafe; carboy

garrapata /garra'pata/ *f, Ent.* tick

garrapatear /garrapate'ar/ *vi* to scribble

garrapato /garra'pato/ *m,* scribble, scrawl

garrido /ga'rriðo/ *a* handsome; gallant; elegant; graceful

garroba /ga'rroβa/ *f,* carob bean

garrocha /ga'rrotʃa/ *f,* goad. **salto a la g.,** pole jumping

garrotazo /garro'taθo; garro'taso/ *m,* blow with a truncheon or cudgel. **dar garrotazos de ciego,** to lay about one

garrote /ga'rrote/ *m,* truncheon, club; *Med.* tourniquet; garrote. **dar g.** (**a**), to strangle

garrotillo /garro'tiʎo; garro'tiyo/ *m,* croup

garrucha /ga'rrutʃa/ *f,* pulley; *Mech.* gin block

garrulidad /garruli'ðað/ *f,* garrulity, loquaciousness

gárrulo /'garrulo/ *a* twittering, chirping (birds); garrulous; murmuring, babbling (wind, water, etc.)

garza /'garθa; 'garsa/ *f,* heron

garzo /'garθo; 'garso/ *a* blue (gen. of eyes)

gas /gas/ *m,* gas; fumes. **g. asfixiante,** poison gas. **cámara de g.,** gasbag, gas chamber

gasa /'gasa/ *f,* gauze. **tira de g.,** black mourning band

gascón /gas'kon/ **(-ona)** *a* and *n* Gascon

gasconada /gasko'naða/ *f,* bravado, gasconade

gaseosa /gase'osa/ *f,* aerated water

gaseoso /gase'oso/ *a* gaseous

gasista /ga'sista/ *mf* gas fitter; gasman

gasolina /gaso'lina/ *f,* gasoline, petrol

gasómetro /ga'sometro/ *m,* gas meter; gasometer

gastado /gas'taðo/ *a* worn; worn-out; exhausted

gastador /gasta'ðor/ **(-ra)** *a* extravagant, wasteful —*n* spendthrift. *m, Mil.* sapper; convict condemned to hard labor

gastar /gas'tar/ *vt* to spend (money); wear out; exhaust; ruin, destroy; display or have habitually; possess, use, wear; —*vr* wear out; run down (of a battery)

gasto /'gasto/ *m,* spending; expenditure; consumption (of gas, etc.); expense, cost, charge; wear (and tear). **g. suplementario,** extra charge

gástrico /'gastriko/ *a* gastric
gastritis /gas'tritis/ *f*, gastritis
gastronomía /gastrono'mia/ *f*, gastronomy
gastronómico /gastro'nomiko/ *a* gastronomic
gastrónomo /gas'tronomo/ **(-ma)** *n* gastronome
gata /'gata/ *f*, she-cat; wreath of mist; *Inf.* Madrilenian woman. **a gatas,** on all fours
gatada /ga'taða/ *f*, *Inf.* sly trick
gatear /gate'ar/ *vi* to climb like a cat; *Inf.* crawl on all fours; —*vt Inf.* scratch (of a cat); steal, pinch
gatera /ga'tera/ *f*, cat hole (in a door, etc.)
gatillo /ga'tiʎo; ga'tiyo/ *m*, *dim* small cat; dental forceps; trigger (of gun); *Inf.* juvenile petty thief
gato /'gato/ *m*, cat; tomcat; moneybag or its contents; *Mech.* jack; mousetrap; *Inf.* cat burglar, sneak thief; *Inf.* Madrilenian; clamp. **g. atigrado,** tiger cat. **g. de algalia,** civet cat. **g. de Angora,** Persian cat. **g. montés,** wildcat. **g. romano,** tabby cat **dar g. por liebre,** to serve cat for hare, to deceive; misrepresent. *Inf.* **Hay g. encerrado,** There's more to this than meets the eye
gatuno /ga'tuno/ *a* feline
gaucho /'gautʃo/ **(-cha)** *n* gaucho; cowboy, rider
gaveta /ga'βeta/ *f*, drawer (of a desk)
gavia /'gaβia/ *f*, main topsail; *pl* topsails; crow's-nest
gavilán /gaβi'lan/ *m*, sparrow hawk; thistle flower
gavilla /ga'βiʎa; ga'βiya/ *f*, sheaf (of corn, etc.); gang, rabble
gaviota /ga'βiota/ *f*, seagull
gavota /ga'βota/ *f*, gavotte
gayo /'gayo/ *a* gay, happy; showy, attractive. **gaya ciencia,** minstrelsy, art of poetry
gazapera /gaθa'pera; gasa'pera/ *f*, rabbit warren; *Inf.* thieves' den; *Inf.* brawl
gazapo /ga'θapo; ga'sapo/ *m*, young rabbit; *Inf.* cunning fellow; fib, lie; slip, blunder
gazmoñería /gaθmoɲe'ria; gasmoɲe'ria/ *f*, prudery, priggish affectation
gazmoño /gaθ'moɲo; gas'moɲo/ *a* hypocritical, prudish, priggish
gaznápiro /gaθ'napiro; gas'napiro/ **(-ra)** *n* ninny, simpleton
gaznate /gaθ'nate; gas'nate/ *m*, windpipe
gazpacho /gaθ'patʃo; gas'patʃo/ *m*, cold soup containing bread, onions, vinegar, olive oil, garlic, etc.
ge /he/ *f*, name of the letter G
gehena /he'ena/ *m*, gehenna, hell
géiser /'heiser/ *m*, geyser
gelatina /hela'tina/ *f*, gelatin. **g. incendiaria,** napalm. **g. seca,** cooking gelatin
gelatinoso /helati'noso/ *a* gelatinous
gélido /'heliðo/ *a Poet.* icy; very cold
gema /'hema/ *f*, gem; *Bot.* bud
gemelo /he'melo/ **(-la)** *a* and *n* twin. *m pl,* field or opera glasses, binoculars; cuff links; *Astron.* Gemini
gemido /he'miðo/ *m*, groan, lament, moan
gemidor /hemi'ðor/ *a* groaning, moaning; wailing (of the wind, etc.)
gemir /he'mir/ *vi irr* to moan, groan, lament; *Fig.* wail, howl. See **pedir**
gene /'hene/ *m*, gene
genealogía /henealo'hia/ *f*, genealogy
genealógico /henea'lohiko/ *a* genealogical
genealogista /henealo'hista/ *mf* genealogist
generación /henera'θion; henera'sion/ *f*, generation, reproduction; species; generation
generador /henera'ðor/ *a* generative. *m*, *Mech.* generator
general /hene'ral/ *a* general; universal; widespread; common, usual. *m*, (*Mil. Eccl.*) general. **g. de división,** *Mil.* major general. **en** *or* **por lo g.,** generally
generalato /henera'lato/ *m*, generalship
generalidad /henerali'ðað/ *f*, majority, bulk; generality
generalísimo /henera'lisimo/ *m*, generalissimo, commander in chief
generalización /heneraliθa'θion; heneralisa'sion/ *f*, generalization
generalizar /henerali'θar; henerali'sar/ *vt* to generalize; —*vr* become widespread or general
generar /hene'rar/ *vt* to generate
genérico /he'neriko/ *a* generic
género /'henero/ *m*, kind; class; way, mode; *Com.* goods; species, genus; *Gram.* gender; cloth, material. **g. chico,** short theatrical pieces (gen. one act). **g. humano,** humankind
generosidad /henerosi'ðað/ *f*, hereditary nobility; generosity, magnanimity; liberality, munificence; courage
generoso /hene'roso/ *a* noble (by birth); magnanimous; generous (of wine); munificent; courageous; excellent
genésico /he'nesiko/ *a* genetic
génesis /'henesis/ *m*, Genesis. *f*, beginning, origin
genial /he'nial/ *a* of genius; highly talented; brilliant; characteristic, individual; pleasant; cheerful
genialidad /heniali'ðað/ *f*, genius; talent; brilliance; eccentricity, oddity
genio /'henio/ *m*, nature, individuality, temperament; temper; character; talent; genius; genie, spirit. **corto de g.,** unintelligent. **mal g.,** bad temper
genital /heni'tal/ *a* genital. *m*, testicle (gen. *pl*)
genitivo /heni'tiβo/ *a* reproductive, generative. *m*, *Gram.* genitive
Génova /'henoβa/ Genoa
genovés /heno'βes/ **(-esa)** *a* and *n* Genoese
gente /'hente/ *f*, people, a crowd; nation; army; *Inf.* family; followers, adherents. **g. baja,** rabble. **g. de bien,** honest folk; respectable people. **g. de paz,** friends (reply to sentinel's challenge). **g. fina,** nice, cultured people. **g. menuda,** children, small fry
gentecilla /hente'θiʎa; hente'siya/ *f*, *dim Inf.* rabble; contemptible people
gentil /hen'til/ *a* pagan, idolatrous; spirited, dashing, handsome; notable, extraordinary; graceful, charming
gentileza /henti'leθa; henti'lesa/ *f*, grace; elegance; beauty; verve, sprightliness; courtesy; show, ostentation
gentilhombre /hentil'ombre/ *m*, gentleman; handsome man; kind sir! **gentileshombres de cámara,** gentlemen-in-waiting
gentilicio /henti'liθio; henti'lisio/ *a* national; family
gentílico /hen'tiliko/ *a* pagan, idolatrous
gentilidad /hentili'ðað/ *f*, idolatry, paganism; heathendom
gentío /hen'tio/ *m*, crowd, throng
gentualla, gentuza /hen'tuaʎa, hen'tuθa; hen'tuaya, hen'tusa/ *f*, canaille, rabble
genuflexión /henuflek'sion/ *f*, genuflection
genuino /he'nuino/ *a* pure; authentic, genuine
geodesia /heo'ðesia/ *f*, geodesy
geodésico /heo'ðesiko/ *a* geodesic
geofísico /heo'fisiko/ *m*, geophysicist
geografía /heogra'fia/ *f*, geography
geográfico /heo'grafiko/ *a* geographical
geógrafo /he'ografo/ *m*, geographer
geología /heolo'hia/ *f*, geology
geológico /heo'lohiko/ *a* geological
geólogo /he'ologo/ *m*, geologist
geometría /heome'tria/ *f*, geometry. **g. del espacio,** solid geometry
geométrico /heo'metriko/ *a* geometrical
geranio /he'ranio/ *m*, geranium
gerencia /he'renθia; he'rensia/ *f*, *Com.* managership; manager's office; management
gerente /he'rente/ *m*, *Com.* manager
germanía /herma'nia/ *f*, thieves' slang; association of thieves; sixteenth-century political brotherhood
germánico /her'maniko/ *a* germanic
germanófilo /herma'nofilo/ **(-la)** *a* and *n* germanophile
germen /'hermen/ *m*, germ, sprout; *Bot.* embryo; genesis, origin
germinación /hermina'θion; hermina'sion/ *f*, germination
germinar /hermi'nar/ *vi* to germinate, sprout; develop, grow
germinativo /hermina'tiβo/ *a* germinative
gerundio /he'rundio/ *m*, *Gram.* gerund; *Inf.* pompous ass; *Inf.* tub-thumper
gesta /'hesta/ *f*, heroic deed. **cantar de g.,** epic or heroic poem

gestación /hesta'θion; hesta'sion/ *f*, gestation
gestear /heste'ar/ *vi* to gesture, grimace
gesticulación /hestikula'θion; hestikula'sion/ *f*, gesticulation; grimace
gesticular /hestiku'lar/ *vi* to grimace, gesticulate —*a* gesticulatory
gestión /hes'tion/ *f*, negotiation; management, conduct; effort, exertion; measure
gestionar /hestio'nar/ *vt* to negotiate; conduct; undertake; take steps to attain
gesto /'hesto/ *m*, gesture; facial expression; grimace; face, visage
gestor /hes'tor/ **(-ra)** *n* manager; partner; promoter —*a* managing
Getsemaní /hetsema'ni/ Gethsemane
giba /'hiβa/ *f*, hump, hunchback; *Inf.* nuisance, inconvenience
gibón /hi'βon/ *m*, gibbon
giboso /hi'βoso/ *a* hunchbacked
gibraltareño /hiβralta'reɲo/ *a* Gibraltarian
giganta /hi'ganta/ *f*, giantess
gigante /hi'gante/ *a* gigantic. *m*, giant.
gigantesco /higan'tesko/ *a* giant, gigantic; *Fig.* outstanding
gigantez /higan'teθ; higan'tes/ *f*, gigantic size
gigantón /higan'ton/ **(-ona)** *n* enormous giant; carnival grotesque
gimnasia /him'nasia/ *f*, gymnastics
gimnasio /him'nasio/ *m*, gymnasium; school, academy
gimnasta /him'nasta/ *mf* gymnast
gimnástico /him'nastiko/ *a* gymnastic
gimotear /himote'ar/ *vi Inf.* to whine (often used scornfully)
gimoteo /himo'teo/ *m*, *Inf.* whining, whimpering
ginebra /hi'neβra/ *f*, gin (drink); confusion; babble, din
ginebrés /hine'βres/ **(-esa), ginebrino (-na)** *a* and *n* Genevan
gineceo /hine'θeo; hine'seo/ *m*, (*Bot.* and in ancient Greece) gynaecium
ginecología /hinekolo'hia/ *f*, gynecology
ginecológico /hineko'lohiko/ *a* gynecological
ginecólogo /hine'kologo/ **(-ga)** *n* gynecologist
girado /hi'raðo/ *m*, *Com.* drawee
girador /hira'ðor/ *m*, *Com.* drawer
giralda /hi'ralda/ *f*, weathercock in the shape of a person or animal; tower at Seville
girar /hi'rar/ *vi* to revolve; deal (with), concern; turn, branch (streets, etc.); *Com.* trade; *Mech.* turn on, revolve; —*vt* and *vi Com.* draw, cash. **g. en descubierto,** *Com.* to overdraw
girasol /hira'sol/ *m*, sunflower
giratorio /hira'torio/ *a* revolving, gyrating; swiveling
giro /'hiro/ *m*, revolution, turn; revolving; trend; course (of affairs); style, turn (of phrase); threat; knife gash; *Com.* draft, drawing; *Com.* line of business, specialty. **g. postal,** postal order
giroscopio /hiro'skopio/ *m*, gyroscope
gitanería /hitane'ria/ *f*, cajolery, wheedling; gypsies; gypsy saying or action
gitanesco /hita'nesko/ *a* gypsy, gypsy-like
gitano /hi'tano/ **(-na)** *a* gypsy; gypsy-like; seductive, attractive; sly —*n* gypsy
glaciar /gla'θiar; gla'siar/ *m*, glacier
gladiador /glaðia'ðor/ *m*, gladiator
gladiatorio /glaðia'torio/ *a* gladiatorial
glándula /'glandula/ *f*, gland
glicerina /gliθe'rina; glise'rina/ *f*, glycerin, glycerol
globo /'gloβo/ *m*, *Geom.* sphere; globe, world; globe (*Elec. Gas.*); balloon. **g. aerostático,** air balloon. **g. terrestre,** world; geographical globe
globular /gloβu'lar/ *a* globular
glóbulo /'gloβulo/ *m*, globule.
globuloso /gloβu'loso/ *a* globulous
gloria /'gloria/ *f*, heavenly bliss; fame, glory; delight, pleasure; magnificence, splendor; *Art.* apotheosis, glory. *m*, *Eccl.* doxology
gloriar /glo'riar/ *vt* to praise; —*vr* (*with de or en*) boast about; be proud of, rejoice in
glorieta /glo'rieta/ *f*, bower, arbor; open space in a garden; street square
glorificación /glorifika'θion; glorifika'sion/ *f*, glorification
glorificador /glorifika'ðor/ *a* glorifying
glorificar /glorifi'kar/ *vt* to exalt, raise up; glorify, extol; —*vr* (*with de or en*) be proud of; glory in; boast of
glorioso /glo'rioso/ *a* glorious; *Eccl.* blessed; boastful, bragging
glosa /'glosa/ *f*, gloss; explanation, note
glosador /glosa'ðor/ **(-ra)** *n* glossator; commentator —*a* explanatory
glosar /glo'sar/ *vt Lit.* to gloss
glosario /glo'sario/ *m*, glossary
glosopeda /gloso'peða/ *f*, foot-and-mouth disease
glotón /glo'ton/ **(-ona)** *a* greedy, gluttonous —*n* glutton
glotonería /glotone'ria/ *f*, gluttony, greed
glucosa /glu'kosa/ *f*, glucose
glúteo /'gluteo/ *a* gluteal
glutinoso /gluti'noso/ *a* glutinous
gn- /gn-/ For words so beginning, see spellings without **g.**
gobernación /goβerna'θion; goβerna'sion/ *f*, government; governor's office or building; ministry of the interior, home office (abb. for **ministerio de G.**)
gobernador /goβerna'ðor/ **(-ra)** *a* governing, *n* governor
gobernalle /goβer'naʎe; goβer'naye/ *m*, helm
gobernante /goβer'nante/ *a* governing. *m*, *Inf.* self-appointed director or manager
gobernar /goβer'nar/ *vt irr* to govern, rule; lead, conduct; manage; steer; control; —*vi* govern; *Naut.* obey the tiller. See **recomendar**
gobierno /go'βierno/ *m*, government (all meanings); *Naut.* helm; control (of machines, business, etc.)
goce /'goθe; 'gose/ *m*, enjoyment; possession
godo /'goðo/ **(da)** *a* Gothic; aristocratic, noble —*n* Goth; aristocrat
gol /gol/ *m*, *Sports.* goal
gola /'gola/ *f*, throat; gullet; gorget; tucker, bib
goleta /go'leta/ *f*, schooner
golf /golf/ *m*, golf. **palo de g.,** golf club
golfear /golfe'ar/ *vi* to loaf
golfería /golfe'ria/ *f*, loafing; vagabondage; loafers
golfo /'golfo/ **(-fa)** *m*, *Geog.* gulf; sea, ocean —*n* ragamuffin, urchin. *m*, *Inf.* loafer; lounge lizard, wastrel
Golfo Pérsico /'golfo 'persiko/ Persian Gulf
golilla /go'liʎa; go'liya/ *f*, ruff; *m*, *Inf.* magistrate
gollería /goʎe'ria; goye'ria/ *f*, dainty, tidbit; *Inf.* affectation, persnicketiness
gollete /go'ʎete; go'yete/ *m*, gullet; neck (of a bottle, etc.); *Mech.* nozzle
golondrina /golon'drina/ *f*, *Ornith.* swallow. **g. de mar,** tern
golosina /golo'sina/ *f*, tidbit, delicacy; desire, caprice; pleasant useless thing
goloso /go'loso/ *a* fond of sweet things; greedy, desirous; appetizing
golpe /'golpe/ *m*, blow, knock; pull (at the oars); ring (of a bell); *Mech.* stroke; crowd; fall (of rain, etc.); mass, torrent; misfortune; shock, collision; spring lock; beating (of the heart); flap (of a pocket); *Sew.* passementerie; surprise; point, wit; bet. **g. de estado,** coup d'état. **g. de fortuna,** stroke of fortune. **g. de mano,** rising, insurrection. **g. en vago,** blow in the air; disappointment. **g. franco,** *Sports.* free kick. **de g.,** suddenly; quickly
golpeadura /golpea'ðura/ *f.* **golpeo** *m*, knocking, striking; beating, throbbing
golpear /golpe'ar/ *vt* and *vi* to knock, strike; beat, throb
goma /'goma/ *f*, gum, rubber; India rubber; rubber band
gomería /gome'ria/ *f*, tire store
gomero /go'mero/ *a* gum; rubber. *m*, *West Hem.* rubber planter
gomorresina /gomorre'sina/ *f*, gum resin
gomoso /go'moso/ *a* gummy; gum

gónada /'gonaðа/ *f,* gonad
góndola /'gondola/ *f,* gondola
gondolero /gondo'lero/ *m,* gondolier
gongorino /goŋgo'rino/ *a* gongoristic, euphuistic
gonorrea /gono'rrea/ *f,* gonorrhea
gordo /'gorðo/ *a* fat, stout; greasy, oily; thick (thread, etc.). *m,* animal fat, suet. *Inf.* **ganar el g.,** to win first prize (in a lottery, etc.)
gordura /gor'ðura/ *f,* grease, fat; stoutness, corpulence
gorgojo /gor'goho/ *m,* weevil; *Fig.* dwarf
gorgoritear /gorgorite'ar/ *vi Inf.* to trill, quaver
gorgorito /gorgo'rito/ *m, Inf.* quaver, tremolo, trill (gen. *pl*)
gorgoteo /gorgo'teo/ *m,* gurgle
gorjear /gorhe'ar/ *vi* to trill, warble; twitter; *—vr* crow (of a baby)
gorjeo /gor'heo/ *m,* trill, shake; warbling, twitter; crowing, lisping (of a child)
gorra /'gorra/ *f,* cap; bonnet; *Mil.* busby; hunting cap. **vivir de g.,** *Inf.* to sponge
gorrión /go'rrion/ *m,* sparrow
gorrista /go'rrista/ *mf Inf.* parasite; sponger
gorro /'gorro/ *m,* cap; bonnet
gorrón /go'rron/ *m,* smooth, round pebble; *Mech.* pivot, gudgeon; sponger, waster *—a* parasitical
gota /'gota/ *f,* drop (of liquid); gout
gotear /gote'ar/ *vi* to drop, trickle, drip; leak; drizzle; give or receive in driblets
goteo /go'teo/ *m,* trickling, dripping
gotera /go'tera/ *f,* dripping; trickle; leak; leakage; valance
gótico /'gotiko/ *a* Gothic; noble, illustrious
gotoso /go'toso/ **(-sa)** *a* gouty *—n* sufferer from gout
goyesco /go'yesko/ *a* Goyesque
gozar /go'θar; go'sar/ *vt* to enjoy, have; take pleasure (in), delight (in); know carnally; *—vi* (*with de*) enjoy; have, possess
gozne /'goθne; 'gosne/ *m,* hinge
gozo /'goθo; 'goso/ *m,* enjoyment, possession; gladness, joy; *pl* couplets in honor of the Virgin Mary or a saint. *Inf.* **¡Mi g. en el pozo!** I'm sunk! All is lost!
gozoso /go'θoso; go'soso/ *a* glad, happy *—adv* gladly; with pleasure
grabado /gra'βaðo/ *m,* engraver's art; engraving; illustration, picture. **g. al agua fuerte,** etching. **g. al agua tinta,** aquatint
grabador /graβa'ðor/ **(-ra)** *n* engraver
grabadura /graβa'ðura/ *f,* act of engraving
grabar /gra'βar/ *vt* to engrave; *Fig.* leave a deep impression
gracejo /gra'θeho; gra'seho/ *m,* humor, wit; cheerfulness
gracia /'graθia; 'grasia/ *f,* grace; attraction, grace; favor; kindness; jest, witticism; pardon, mercy; pleasant manner; obligingness, willingness; *pl* thanks, thank you. **gracias a,** thanks to. **¡Gracias a Dios!** Thank God! Thank goodness! **las Gracias,** the Three Graces
grácil /'graθil; 'grasil/ *a* slender; small
graciosidad /graθiosi'ðað; grasiosi'ðað/ *f,* beauty, perfection, grace
gracioso /gra'θioso; gra'sioso/ **(-sa)** *a* attractive, graceful, elegant; witty, humorous; free, gratis *—n Theat.* comic role; *m, Theat.* fool
grada /'graða/ *f,* step, stair; gradin, seat; stand, gallery; *Agr.* harrow; *Naut.* runway; *pl* perron, flight of stairs
gradación /graða'θion; graða'sion/ *f,* gradation; climax
gradería /graðe'ria/ *f,* flight of steps
grado /'graðo/ *m,* step, stair; degree (of relationship); university degree; grade, class (in schools); (*Fig. Geom. Phys.*) degree; will, desire. **de buen g.,** willingly. **en sumo g.,** in the highest degree
graduación /graðua'θion; graðua'sion/ *f,* graduation; *Mil.* rank; rating (of a ship's company). **g. de oficial,** *Mil.* commission
graduado /gra'ðuaðo/ *a* graded; *Mil.* brevet. *m,* graduate
gradual /gra'ðual/ *a* gradual
graduar /gra'ðuar/ *vt* to classify; *Mil.* grade; confer a degree on; measure; test; *Com.* standardize; *Mech.* calibrate; *—vr* graduate, receive a degree. **g. la vista,** to test the eyes. **graduarse de oficial,** *Mil.* to get one's commission
gráfica /'grafika/ *f,* graph
gráfico /'grafiko/ *a* graphic; vivid
grafito /gra'fito/ *m,* graphite
grafología /grafolo'hia/ *f,* graphology
grajear /grahe'ar/ *vi* to caw; gurgle, burble (of infants)
grajo /'graho/ *m, Ornith.* rook
gramática /gra'matika/ *f,* grammar. *Inf.* **g. parda,** horse sense
gramático /gra'matiko/ *a* grammatical. *m,* grammarian
gramo /'gramo/ *m,* gram
gramófono /gra'mofono/ *m,* phonograph
gran /gran/ *a Abbr.* See **grande.** Used before a singular noun. big; great; grand
grana /'grana/ *f,* grain, seed; seed time; cochineal; kermes; red
granada /gra'naða/ *f, Mil.* grenade, shell; pomegranate
granadero /grana'ðero/ *m,* grenadier; *Inf.* very tall person
granadilla /grana'ðiʎa; grana'ðiya/ *f,* passionflower
granadina /grana'ðina/ *f,* grenadine
granar /gra'nar/ *vi Agr.* to seed; run to seed
granate /gra'nate/ *m,* garnet; dark red
Gran Bretaña /gran bre'taɲa/ Great Britain
Gran Canaria /gran ka'naria/ Grand Canary
grande /'grande/ *a* big, large; great, illustrious; grand. *m,* great man; grandee. **en g.,** in a large size; as a whole; in style, lavishly
grandeza /gran'deθa; gran'desa/ *f,* largeness; greatness, magnificence; grandeeship; vastness, magnitude
grandilocuencia /grandilo'kuenθia; grandilo'kuensia/ *f,* grandiloquence
grandílocuo /gran'dilokuo/ *a* grandiloquent
grandiosidad /grandiosi'ðað/ *f,* grandeur, greatness
grandioso /gran'dioso/ *a* grandiose, magnificent
grandor /gran'dor/ *m,* size
granear /grane'ar/ *vt Agr.* to sow; grain (of leather)
granero /gra'nero/ *m,* granary; grain-producing country
granito /gra'nito/ *m, dim* small grain; granite; small pimple
granizar /grani'θar; grani'sar/ *vi* to hail, sleet; *—vi* and *vt Fig.* shower down, deluge
granizo /gra'niθo; gra'niso/ *m,* hail, sleet; hailstorm; *Fig.* shower, deluge
granja /'granha/ *f,* farm; farmhouse; dairy farm, dairy
granjear /granhe'ar/ *vt* to trade, profit, earn; obtain, acquire; *—vr* gain, win
granjería /granhe'ria/ *f,* farming; agricultural profits; earnings, profits
granjero /gran'hero/ **(-ra)** *n* farmer
Gran Lago Salado, el /gran 'lago sa'laðo, el/ the Great Salt Lake
grano /'grano/ *m, Agr.* grain; seed; bean (coffee, etc.); particle; markings, grain (of wood, etc.); pimple; grain (measure). *Fig. Inf.* **ir al g.,** to go to the root of the matter; come to the point
granuja /gra'nuha/ *f,* grape pit. *m, Inf.* urchin, scamp; knave, rogue
granujiento /granu'hiento/ *a* pimply
gránulo /'granulo/ *m,* granule
granuloso /granu'loso/ *a* granulous
grapa /'grapa/ *f,* cramp, dowel, clamp; block hook; *Elec.* cleat; staple
grasa /'grasa/ *f,* fat; grease; oil; dripping, suet
grasiento /gra'siento/ *a* greasy; grubby, dirty
gratificación /gratifika'θion; gratifika'sion/ *f,* monetary reward; fee, remuneration; gratuity
gratificar /gratifi'kar/ *vt* to recompense; please, gratify
gratis /'gratis/ *a* and *adv* gratis
gratitud /grati'tuð/ *f,* gratitude
grato /'grato/ *a* pleasing, agreeable; free, gratuitous

gratuito /gra'tuito/ *a* gratuitous, free; baseless, unfounded
grava /'graβa/ *f,* gravel; stone chip, pebble; metal (of a road)
gravamen /gra'βamen/ *m,* obligation; burden; tax
gravar /gra'βar/ *vt* to burden, weigh upon; tax
grave /'graβe/ *a* heavy; important, momentous; grave; dignified, serious; sedate; tiresome; low-pitched, low; *Gram.* grave accent
gravedad /graβe'ðað/ *f, Phys.* gravity
gravitación /graβita'θion; graβita'sion/ *f, Phys.* gravitation; seriousness; sedateness; importance; enormity, gravity
gravitar /graβi'tar/ *vi* to gravitate; lean or rest (upon)
gravoso /gra'βoso/ *a* grievous, oppressive; onerous; costly
graznar /graθ'nar; gras'nar/ *vi* to caw; cackle; quack; croak; sing stridently, screech
graznido /graθ'niðo; gras'niðo/ *m,* caw; cackle; croaking; quack; screech
Grecia /'greθia; 'gresia/ Greece
greco /'greko/ **(-ca)** *a* and *n* Greek
grecorromano /grekorro'mano/ *a* Greco-Roman
gregario /gre'gario/ *a* gregarious
gregoriano /grego'riano/ *a* Gregorian
gregüescos /gre'gueskos/ *m pl,* wide breeches (sixteenth and seventeenth centuries)
gremial /gre'mial/ *a* pertaining to a guild, union, or association. *m,* member of a guild, union, or association
gremio /'gremio/ *m,* guild, corporation, union; society, association; (univ.) general council
greña /'greɲa/ *f,* tangled lock (of hair) (gen. *pl*); tangle, confused mass
gresca /'greska/ *f,* uproar, tumult; fight, row
grey /grei/ *f,* flock, drove, herd; *Eccl.* flock, company; people, nation
grial /grial/ *m,* grail
griego /'griego/ **(-ga)** *a* and *n* Greek. *m,* Greek (language); *Inf.* gibberish
grieta /'grieta/ *f,* fissure; crevice; chink; split; flaw; vein (in stone, etc.); *Mech.* leak
grietado /grie'taðo/ *a* fissured; cracked
grifo /'grifo/ *m,* griffin; tap; cock
grillo /'griʎo; 'griyo/ *m,* cricket; *Bot.* shoot; *pl* fetters, irons, chains; *Fig.* shackles
grima /'grima/ *f,* revulsion, horror
gringo /'griŋgo/ **(-ga)** *n Inf.* foreigner (scornful)
gripe /'gripe/ *f,* influenza; grippe
gris /gris/ *a* and *m,* gray
grisú /gri'su/ *m,* firedamp
gritador /grita'ðor/ **(-ra)** *a* shouting —*n* shouter
gritar /gri'tar/ *vi* to shout, yell, scream; howl down; hoot
gritería /grite'ria/ *f,* shouting, yelling, clamor
grito /'grito/ *m,* shout, yell, shriek, scream. *Inf.* **poner el g. en el cielo,** to cry to high heaven, complain
groenlandés /groenlan'des/ **(-esa)** *a* Greenland —*n* Greenlander
Groenlandia /groen'landia/ Greenland
grog /grog/ *m,* grog
grosella /gro'seʎa; gro'seya/ *f,* currant. **g. blanca,** gooseberry
grosería /grose'ria/ *f,* rudeness; roughness (of workmanship); ignorance; rusticity
grosero /gro'sero/ *a* coarse; rough; thick; unpolished, rude
grotesco /gro'tesko/ *a* grotesque, absurd
grúa /'grua/ *f, Mech.* crane, hoist, derrick. **g. de pescante,** jib crane. **g. móvil,** traveling crane
gruesa /'gruesa/ *f,* twelve dozen, gross
grueso /'grueso/ *a* stout, corpulent; large. *m,* bulk, body; major portion, majority; thick stroke (of a letter); thickness, density. **en g.,** in bulk
grulla /'gruʎa; 'gruya/ *f, Ornith.* crane
grumete /gru'mete/ *m,* ship's boy, cabin boy
grumo /'grumo/ *m,* clot; heart (of vegetables); bunch, cluster; bud
gruñido /gru'ɲiðo/ *m,* grunt; growl
gruñidor /gruɲi'ðor/ *a* grunting; growling
gruñir /gru'ɲir/ *vi* to grunt; growl; grumble; squeak, creak (doors, etc.) —*Pres. Part.* **gruñendo.** *Pres. Indic.* **gruño, gruñes,** etc.
grupa /'grupa/ *f,* croup (of a horse); pillion (of a motorcycle)
grupera /gru'pera/ *f,* pillion (of a horse, etc.)
grupo /'grupo/ *m,* knot, cluster; band, group; *Art.* group; *Mech.* set
gruta /'gruta/ *f,* cavern, grotto
guacamayo /guaka'mayo/ *m,* macaw
guadamecí /guaðame'θi; guaðame'si/ *m,* embossed decorated leather
guadaña /gua'ðaɲa/ *f,* scythe
guagua /'guagua/, *f Caribbean* bus
gualdo /'gualdo/ *a* yellow, golden
gualdrapa /gual'drapa/ *f,* saddlecloth, trappings; *Inf.* tatter, rag
guante /'guante/ *m,* glove. **g. con puño,** gauntlet glove. **g. de boxeo,** boxing glove. **g. de cabritilla,** kid glove. **arrojar el g.,** to throw down the gauntlet; challenge, defy
guantelete /guante'lete/ *m,* gauntlet
guantería /guante'ria/ *f,* glove trade, shop, or factory
guantero /guan'tero/ **(-ra)** *n* glove maker or seller, glover
guapear /guape'ar/ *vi Inf.* to make the best of a bad job; *Inf.* pride oneself on being well dressed
guapeza /gua'peθa; gua'pesa/ *f,* prettiness; *Inf.* resolution, courage; *Inf.* smartness or showiness of dress; boastful act or behavior
guapo /'guapo/ *a* pretty; handsome; *Inf.* daring, enterprising; *Inf.* smart, well-dressed, foppish; *Inf.* handsome. *m,* braggart, brawler; beau, lover; *Inf.* fine fellow, son of a gun
guarda /'guarða/ *mf* keeper, guard. *f,* guarding, keeping, custodianship, preservation; guardianship; observance, fulfillment; flyleaf, end page (books); warder (of locks or keys); *Mech.* guard; guard (of a fan)
guardabarrera /guarðaβa'rrera/ *mf* gatekeeper at a level crossing (railroad)
guardabarro /guarða'βarro/ *m,* mudguard
guardabosque /guarða'βoske/ *mf* gamekeeper
guardabrisa /guarða'βrisa/ *m, Auto.* windshield; glass candle shield
guardacostas /guarða'kostas/ *m,* coast guard; *Naut.* revenue cutter
guardafrenos /guarða'frenos/ *m,* brakeman (railroad)
guardagujas /guarða'guhas/ *m,* pointsman (railroad)
guardainfante /guarðain'fante/ *m,* farthingale, crinoline
guardalmacén /guarðalma'θen; guarðalma'sen/ *mf* storekeeper
guardameta /guarða'meta/ *mf* goalkeeper
guardamuebles /guarða'mueβles/ *m,* furniture warehouse
guardapelo /guarða'pelo/ *m,* locket
guardapolvo /guarða'polβo/ *m,* dustcover; light overcoat; inner case of a pocket watch
guardar /guar'ðar/ *vt* to keep; preserve, retain; maintain, observe; save, put aside, lay away; defend, protect; guard; —*vr* (*with de*) avoid, guard against. **g. compás con,** to be in tune with. **guardarse mucho,** to think twice before. **g. silencio,** to keep silent. **¡Guarda!** Take care! **¡Guárdate del agua mansa!** Still waters run deep!
guardarropa /guarða'rropa/ *m,* cloakroom. *mf* cloakroom attendant; keeper of the wardrobe. *m,* wardrobe, clothes closet
guardarropía /guarðarro'pia/ *f,* theatrical wardrobe
guardavía /guarða'βia/ *m,* signalman (railroad)
guardería /guarðe'ria/ *f,* day nursery, day-care center
guardia /'guarðia/ *f,* guard, escort; protection; (*Mil. Naut.*) watch; regiment, body (of troops); guard (fencing). *m,* guardsman; policeman. **g. de asalto,** armed police. **g. de corps,** royal bodyguard. **g. civil,** civil guard. **g. marina,** midshipman. **g. municipal,** city police. *Mil.* **montar la g.,** to mount guard
guardián /guar'ðian/ **(-ana)** *n* keeper; custodian; warden. *m,* watchman; jailer
guardilla /guar'ðiʎa; guar'ðiya/ *f,* attic, garret

guarecer /guare'θer; guare'ser/ *vt irr* to shelter, protect, aid; preserve, keep; cure; *—vr* take shelter. See **conocer**
guarida /gua'riða/ *f,* lair, den; refuge, shelter; haunt, resort
guarismo /gua'rismo/ *m, Math.* figure; number, numeral
guarnecer /guarne'θer; guarne'ser/ *vt irr* to decorate, adorn; *Sew.* trim, face, border; *Mil.* garrison; *Mas.* plaster. See **conocer**
guarnecido /guarne'θiðo; guarne'siðo/ *m, Mas.* plastering
guarnición /guarni'θion; guarni'sion/ *f, Sew.* trimming, ornament, border, fringe; *Mech.* packing; *Mil.* garrison; setting (of jewels); guard (of a sword, etc.); *pl* harness; fittings
guarnir /guar'nir/ *vt Naut.* to reeve
guasa /'guasa/ *f, Inf.* dullness, boringness; joke. **de g.,** jokingly
guasón /gua'son/ *a Inf.* dull, tedious; humorous, jocose
guatemalteco /guatemal'teko/ **(-ca)** *a* and *n* Guatemalan
guau /guau/ *m,* bowwow, bark of a dog
guayaba /gua'yaβa/ *f,* guava; guava jelly
Guayana /gua'yana/ Guiana
gubernamental /guβernamen'tal/ *a* governmental
gubernativo /guβerna'tiβo/ *a* governmental; administrative
gubia /'guβia/ *f,* chisel; gouge
guedeja /ge'ðeha/ *f,* long tress or lock of hair; forelock; lion's mane
Guernesey /gerne'sei/ Guernsey
guerra /'gerra/ *f,* war; struggle, fight; *Fig.* hostility. *Inf.* **dar g.,** to give trouble, annoy. **en g. con,** at war with. **la g. de Cuba,** the Spanish-American War
guerrear /gerre'ar/ *vi* to make war, fight; oppose
guerrero /ge'rrero/ **(-ra)** *a* war, martial; warrior; *Inf.* troublesome, annoying *—n* fighter. *m,* warrior, soldier
guerrillear /gerriʎe'ar; gerriye'ar/ *vi* to wage guerrilla warfare; fight as a guerrilla
guerrillero /gerri'ʎero; gerri'yero/ *m,* guerrilla fighter
guía /'gia/ *mf* guide, conductor; adviser, director. *f,* guide, aid; guidebook; *Mech.* guide, slide; directory; signpost. **g. de ferrocarriles,** train schedule, railroad timetable. **g. de teléfonos,** telephone directory
guiar /giar/ *vt* to guide; lead, conduct; *Mech.* work, control; *Auto.* drive; pilot; teach, direct, govern
guija /'giha/ *f,* pebble
guijarro /gi'harro/ *m,* smooth, round pebble; boulder; cobblestone
guijarroso /giha'rroso/ *a* pebbly, cobbled
guijo /'giho/ *m,* gravel; granite chips; pebble
guillotina /giʎo'tina; giyo'tina/ *f,* guillotine; paper-cutting machine
guillotinar /giʎoti'nar; giyoti'nar/ *vt* to guillotine, decapitate
guinda /'ginda/ *f,* mazard cherry; *Naut.* height of masts
guinea /gi'nea/ *f,* guinea
guinga /'giŋga/ *f,* gingham
guiñada /gi'ɲaða/ *f,* wink; blink; *Naut.* yaw
guiñapo /gi'ɲapo/ *m,* rag, tatter; sloven, ragamuffin
guiñar /gi'ɲar/ *vt* to wink; blink; *Naut.* yaw; *—vr* wink at each other
guiño /'giɲo/ *m,* wink
guión /gi'on/ *m,* royal standard; banner; summary; leader of a dance; *Gram.* hyphen; subtitle (in films). **g. mayor,** *Gram.* dash
guipuzcoano /gipuθ'koano; gipus'koano/ **(-na)** *a* and *n* Guipuzcoan
guirigay /giri'gai/ *m, Inf.* gibberish; uproar, babble
guirnalda /gir'nalda/ *f,* garland, wreath
guisa /'gisa/ *f,* way, manner; will, desire. **a g. de,** in the manner or fashion of
guisado /gi'saðo/ *m, Cul.* stew; cooked dish
guisante /gi'sante/ *m, Agr.* pea; pea plant. **g. de olor,** sweetpea
guisar /gi'sar/ *vt* to cook; stew; *Cul.* prepare, dress; adjust, arrange
guiso /'giso/ *m,* cooked dish
guitarra /gi'tarra/ *f,* guitar
guitarrista /gita'rrista/ *mf* guitar player
guito /'gito/ *a* vicious (horses, mules)
gula /'gula/ *f,* greed, gluttony
gusaniento /gusa'niento/ *a* worm-eaten; maggoty
gusano /gu'sano/ *m,* worm; caterpillar; maggot; meek, downtrodden person. **g. de seda,** silkworm
gusanoso /gusa'noso/ *a* wormy
gustar /gus'tar/ *vt* to taste, savor; try; *—vi* be pleasing, give pleasure; like. **Me gusta el libro,** I like the book. **La película no me gustó,** I didn't like the film. **g. de,** to like, is used only when a person is the subject
gusto /'gusto/ *m,* taste; flavor, savor; pleasure, delight; will, desire; discrimination, taste, style, fashion, manner; whim, caprice. **a g.,** to taste; according to taste. **con mucho g.,** with great pleasure. **dar g.,** to please. **de buen g.,** in good taste
gustoso /gus'toso/ *a* savory, palatable; willingly, with pleasure; pleasant, agreeable
gutagamba /guta'gamba/ *f,* gamboge (yellow)
gutapercha /guta'pertʃa/ *f,* guttapercha
gutural /gutu'ral/ *a* guttural

H

haba /'aβa/ *f,* broad bean; bean (coffee, cocoa, etc.). **h. de las Indias,** sweetpea. **Esas son habas contadas,** That's a certainty
Habana, la /a'βana, la/ Havana
habanero /aβa'nero/ **(-ra), habano (-na)** *a* and *n* Havanese, from Havana. *m.* **habano,** Havana cigar
habar /a'βar/ *m,* bean field
haber /a'βer/ *m,* estate, property (gen. *pl*); income; *Com.* credit balance. **h. monedado,** specie
haber /a'βer/ *vt irr* to have; catch, lay hands on (e.g. *El reo fue habido,* The criminal was caught) *—v aux* (e.g. *Hemos escrito la carta,* We have written the letter) *—v impers* to happen, take place; be *—3rd pers. sing Pres. Indic.* **ha** is replaced by **hay,** meaning there is or there are (e.g. *No hay naranjas en las tiendas,* There are no oranges in the shops). In certain weather expressions, **hay** means it is (e.g. *Hay luna,* It is moonlight). Used of expressions of time, **haber** means to elapse and **ha** (*3rd pers. sing Pres. Indic.*) has adverbial force of "ago' (e.g. *muchos días ha,* many days ago). **h. de,** to be necessary (less strong than **h. que**) (e.g. *Hemos de verle mañana,* We must see him tomorrow. *He de hacer el papel de Manolo,* I am to play the part of Manolo). **h. que,** to be unavoidable, be essential. With this construction the form **hay** is used (e.g. *Hay que darse prisa,* We (or one) must hurry. **No hay que enojarse,** There's no need to get annoyed). **no h., más que pedir,** to leave nothing to be desired. **no h. tal,** to be no such thing. *Inf.* **habérselas con,** to quarrel or fall out with. **Hubo una vez...,** Once upon a time... **¡No hay de qué!,** Don't mention it!; Not at all!; You're welcome! **No hay para que...,** There's no point in.... **poco tiempo ha,** a little while ago. **¿Qué hay?** What's the matter?; What's new? **¿Qué hay de nuevo?** What's new? *Pres. Indic.* **he, has, ha, hemos, habéis, han.** *Fut.* **habré,** etc *—Condit.* **habría,** etc *—Preterite* **hube, hubiste, hubo, hubimos, hubisteis, hubieron.** *Pres. Subjunc.* **haya,** etc *—Imperf. Subjunc.* **hubiese,** etc.
habichuela /aβi'tʃuela/ *f,* kidney bean
hábil /'aβil/ *a* clever; skillful; able; lawful
habilidad /aβili'ðað/ *f,* ability; skill; accomplishment; craftsmanship, workmanship
habilidoso /aβili'ðoso/ *a* accomplished; able; skillful
habilitación /aβilita'θion; aβilita'sion/ *f,* habilitation; paymastership; equipment; furnishing
habilitado /aβili'taðo/ *m,* paymaster
habilitar /aβili'tar/ *vt* to qualify; equip; furnish; habilitate; enable; *Com.* capitalize
habitabilidad /aβitaβili'ðað/ *f,* habitability
habitable /aβi'taβle/ *a* habitable
habitación /aβita'θion; aβita'sion/ *f,* habitation, dwelling; room in a house; residence; (*Bot. Zool.*) habitat; caretaking
habitante /aβi'tante/ *m,* inhabitant
habitar /aβi'tar/ *vt* to inhabit, reside in
hábito /'aβito/ *m,* attire; *Eccl.* habit; use, custom; skill, facility; *pl* vestments; gown, robe. **tomar el h.,** to become a monk or nun
habitual /aβi'tual/ *a* habitual, usual
habituar /aβi'tuar/ *vt* to accustom; *—vr* accustom oneself; grow used (to)
habitud /aβi'tuð/ *f,* habit, custom; relationship
habla /'aβla/ *f,* speech; language; dialect; discourse.
hablado /a'βlaðo/ *a* spoken. **bien h.,** well-spoken; courteous. **mal h.,** ill-spoken; rude
hablador /aβla'ðor/ **(-ra)** *a* talkative; gossipy *—n* chatterbox; gossip
habladuría /aβlaðu'ria/ *f,* gossip; impertinent chatter
hablanchín /aβlan'tʃin/ *a Inf.* chattering, gossiping
hablar /a'βlar/ *vi* to speak; converse; express oneself; arrange; (*with de*) speak about, discuss; gossip about, criticize; (*with por*) intercede on behalf of; *—vt* speak (a language); say, speak; *—vr* speak to one another. **no hablarse,** to not be on speaking terms. **h. a gritos,** to shout. **h. alto,** to speak loudly or in strong terms. **h. bien** (*or* **mal**), to be well- (or ill-) spoken; be polite (or rude). **h. claro,** to speak frankly. **h. consigo** *or* **h. entre sí,** to talk to oneself. *Inf.* **h. cristiano, h. en cristiano,** to speak clearly or intelligibly; speak frankly. **hablarlo todo,** to talk too much. **h. por h.,** to talk for talking's sake. *Inf.* **h. por los codos,** to chatter. **h. sin ton ni son,** to speak foolishly
hablilla /a'βliʎa; a'βliya/ *f,* rumor, tittletattle, gossip
hacecillo /aθe'θiʎo; ase'siyo/ *m,* small sheaf; small bundle; *Bot.* fascicle; beam (of light)
hacedero /aθe'ðero; ase'ðero/ *a* feasible, practicable
hacedor /aθe'ðor; ase'ðor/ *m,* maker; steward, manager; Creator
hacendado /aθen'daðo; asen'daðo/ **(-da)** *a* landed *—n* landowner; *West Hem.* cattle rancher
hacendista /aθen'dista; asen'dista/ *mf* political economist
hacendoso /aθen'doso; asen'doso/ *a* diligent, hardworking
hacer /a'θer; a'ser/ *vt irr* to make; fashion, form, construct; do, perform; cause, effect; arrange, put right; contain; accustom, harden; pack (luggage); imagine, invent, create; improve, perfect; compel, oblige; deliver (speeches); compose; earn; *Math.* add up to; suppose, imagine (e.g. *Sus padres hacían a María en casa,* Her parents imagined that Mary was at home); put into practice, execute; play the part of or act like (e.g. *h. el gracioso,* to play the buffoon); shed, cast (e.g. *El roble hace sombra,* The oak casts a shadow); assemble, convoke (meetings, gatherings); give off, produce (e.g. *La chimenea hace humo,* The chimney is smoking); perform (plays); (*with el, la, lo, and some nouns*) pretend to be (e.g. *Se hizo el desconocido,* He pretended to be ignorant). (**h.** followed by infin. is sometimes translated by a past participle in English (e.g. *Lo hice h.,* I had it done).) *vi* to matter, be important, signify (e.g. *Su llegada no hace nada al caso,* His arrival makes no difference to the case. *Se me hace muy poco...,* It matters to me very little...); be fitting or suitable; concern, be pertinent; match, go with; agree, be in harmony; (*with de*) act as, discharge duties of temporarily (e.g. *h. de camarero,* to be a temporary waiter); (*with por*) try to, attempt to (e.g. *Haremos por decírselo,* We shall try to tell him) *—vi impers* Used in expressions concerning: 1. the weather. 2. lapse of time. English uses the verb "to be' in both cases, e.g.:
1. *hace buen* (*or mal*) **tiempo,** it is fine (or bad) weather. **hace mucho frío,** it is very cold. **hace sol,** it is sunny. **hace viento,** it is windy. **¿Qué tiempo hace?** What is the weather like?
2. **hace** + an expression of time is followed by **que** introducing a clause (e.g. *Hace dos horas que llegamos,* It is two hours since we arrived) or **hace** + an expression of time may be followed by **desde** + a noun (e.g. *Hace dos años desde aquel día,* It is two years since that day)
When an action or state that has begun in the past is still continuing in the present, the Spanish verb is in the Pres. Ind., whereas the English verb is in the Perfect (e.g. *Hace un mes que la veo todos los días,* I have been seeing her every day for a month). This rule holds good with other tenses. English Pluperfect, Future Perfect, Conditional Perfect become in Spanish Imperfect, Future, Conditional, respectively. *Naut.* **h. agua,** to leak. **h. aguas,** to pass water, urinate. **h. alarde de,** to boast of. **h. el amor a,** to make love to, court, woo. **h. autoridad,** to be authoritative. **h. a todo,** to have many uses; be adaptable. **h. bancarrota,** to go bankrupt. **h. un berrinche, hacerse un berrinche,** to have a fit, have a tantrum. *Fig. Inf.* **h. buena,** to justify. **h. calceta,** to knit. **h. cara** or **frente a,** to face; resist. **h. caso,** to take notice, mind (e.g. *¡No hagas caso!* Never mind!). **h. causas,** to bring charges, institute proceedings. **h. cuentas,** to reckon up. **h. daño,** to harm. *Inf.* **h. de las suyas,** to behave in his usual manner or play one of his usual

tricks. **h. diligencias por,** to endeavor to. **h. fiesta,** to take a holiday. **h. fuerza,** to struggle. **h. fuerza a,** *Fig.* to do violence to (e.g. *Hizo fuerza a sus creencias,* He did violence to his beliefs). **h. h.,** to cause to be made (e.g. *He hecho hacer un vestido,* I have had a dress made). **h. juego,** to make a set, match (e.g. *El sombrero hace juego con el traje,* The hat goes with the dress). **h. la corte (a),** to court, woo. *Fig. Inf.* **h. la vista gorda,** to turn a blind eye. **h. la vida del claustro,** to lead a cloistered existence. **h. mal,** to do wrong; be harmful (food, etc.). **h. pedazos,** to break. **h. pinos** (or **pinitos**) to totter; toddle; stagger. *Aer.* **h. rizos,** to loop the loop. **h. saber,** to make known; notify. **h. seguir,** to forward (letters). **h. señas,** to make signs (wave, beckon, etc.). *Inf.* **h. una que sea sonada,** to cause a big scandal. **¡Hágame el favor!** Please! *Pres. Indic.* **hago, haces,** etc —*Fut.* **haré,** etc —*Condit.* **haría,** etc —*Imperat.* **haz, haga, hagamos, haced, hagan.** *Preterite* **hice, hiciste, hizo, hicimos, hicisteis, hicieron.** *Pres. Subjunc.* **haga,** etc —*Imperf. Subjunc.* **hiciese,** etc.

hacerse /a'θerse; a'serse/ *vr irr* to become (e.g. *Se ha hecho muy importante,* It (or he) has become very important); grow up (e.g. *Miguel se ha hecho hombre,* Michael has grown up (become a man)); develop, mature; pass oneself off as, pretend to be; (*with prep a*) become accustomed to or used to (e.g. *Me haré a este clima,* I shall grow used to this climate); withdraw or retire to (of places); (*with de or con*) provide oneself with. **h. a la vela,** to set sail. **h. a (uno),** to seem (e.g. *Eso que me cuentas se me hace increíble,* What you tell me seems incredible). *Inf.* **h. chiquito,** to be modest. **h. tarde,** to grow late; *Fig.* be too late. See **hacer**

hacha /'atʃa/ *f,* large candle; torch; ax. **h. pequeña,** hatchet

hachazo /a'tʃaθo; a'tʃaso/ *m,* stroke of an ax

hache /'atʃe/ *f,* name of the letter H

hachero /a'tʃero/ *m,* candlestick; woodcutter, axman

hacho /'atʃo/ *m,* torch; beacon

hacia /'aθia; 'asia/ *prep* toward, near, about. **h. adelante,** forward, onward

hacienda /a'θienda; a'sienda/ *f,* country estate, land; property; *pl* domestic tasks; cattle. **h. pública,** public funds. **ministerio de h.,** national treasury, exchequer

hacina /a'θina; a'sina/ *f, Agr.* stack; heap, pile

hacinamiento /aθina'miento; asina'miento/ *m,* stacking, piling; accumulation

hacinar /aθi'nar; asi'nar/ *vt Agr.* to stack sheaves; accumulate, amass; pile up, heap

hada /'aða/ *f,* fairy

hado /'aðo/ *m,* fate; destiny

hagiografía /ahiogra'fia/ *f,* hagiography

hagiógrafo /a'hiografo/ *m,* hagiographer

Haití /ai'ti/ Haiti

haitiano /ai'tiano/ **(-na)** *a* and *n* Haitian

halagar /ala'gar/ *vt* to caress; flatter; coax; please, delight

halago /a'lago/ *m,* flattery; coaxing; caress; source of pleasure, delight

halagüeño /ala'gueɲo/ *a* flattering; pleasing; caressing; hopeful, promising

halar /a'lar/ *vt Naut.* to haul, tow

halcón /al'kon/ *m,* falcon

halconero /alko'nero/ *m,* hawker, hunter

hálito /'alito/ *m,* breath; vapor; *Poet.* breeze

hallado /a'ʎaðo; a'yaðo/ *a* and *Past Part.* found, met. **bien h.,** welcome; happy, contented. **mal h.,** unwelcome; uneasy, discontented

hallador /aʎa'ðor; aya'ðor/ **(-ra)** *n* finder

hallar /a'ʎar; a'yar/ *vt* to find; meet; observe; discover; find out; —*vr* be present; be, find oneself

hallazgo /a'ʎaθgo; a'yasgo/ *m,* finding; thing found; finder's reward

halo /'alo/ *m,* halo

halterofilia /altero'filia/ *f,* weightlifting

hamaca /a'maka/ *f,* hammock

hamadríade /ama'ðriaðe/ *f,* hamadryad

hambre /'ambre/ *f,* hunger; famine; desire, yearning. **tener h.,** to be hungry

hambriento /am'briento/ *a* hungry; famished; *Fig.* starved (of affection, etc.)

Hamburgo /am'burgo/ Hamburg

hamo /'amo/ *m,* fishhook

hampa /'ampa/ *f,* rogue's life; gang of rogues; underworld, slum

hangar /aŋ'gar/ *m,* hangar

hanseático /anse'atiko/ *a* Hanseatic

haragán /ara'gan/ **(-ana)** *a* lazy, idle —*n* idler, lazybones

harapiento /ara'piento/ *a* ragged

harapo /a'rapo/ *m,* tatter, rag

haraposo /ara'poso/ *a* ragged

harén /a'ren/ *m,* harem

harina /a'rina/ *f,* flour; powder; farina. *Inf.* **ser h. de otro costal,** to be a horse of another color

harinero /ari'nero/ *a* relating to flour. *m,* flour merchant; flour bin

harinoso /ari'noso/ *a* floury, mealy; farinaceous

harmónica /ar'monika/ *f,* (*Phys. Math.*) harmonic

harmonizar /armoni'θar; armoni'sar/ *vt* to arrange (music)

harnero /ar'nero/ *m,* sieve

harón /a'ron/ *a* slothful, slow; lazy, idle

harpillera /arpi'ʎera; arpi'yera/ *f,* sackcloth, sacking

hartar /ar'tar/ *vt* to satiate; tire, annoy; satisfy the appetite; shower (with blows, etc.)

hartazgo /ar'taθgo; ar'tasgo/ *m,* satiety

harto /'arto/ *a* satiated; tired (of), *adv* enough

hartura /ar'tura/ *f,* satiety; abundance

hasta /'asta/ *prep* until; as far as; down or up to —*conjunc* also, even. **h. la vista,** See you! Ciaio! Au revoir! **h. mañana,** until tomorrow

hastial /as'tial/ *m,* gable, end wall; boor, lout

hastío /as'tio/ *m,* loathing; distaste; nausea

hato /'ato/ *m,* personal clothing; herd of cattle; gang (of suspicious characters); crowd, mob; *Inf.* group, party. *Inf.* **liar el h.,** to pack up

Hawai /'awai/ Hawaii

hay /ai/ there is; there are. See **haber**

haya /'aya/ *f,* beech tree; beechwood

Haya, La /'aya, la/ The Hague

hayal /a'yal/ *m,* wood of beech trees, beech plantation

hayuco /a'yuko/ *m,* beech mast

haz /aθ; as/ *m,* bundle, sheaf; *Mil.* file; *pl* fasces. *f,* visage; surface, face. **h. de la tierra,** face of the earth. **h. de luz,** beam of light. *Fig.* **ser de dos haces,** to be two-faced

haz /aθ; as/ *2nd pers imperat* **hacer**

hazaña /a'θaɲa; a'saɲa/ *f,* exploit, prowess

hazañoso /aθa'ɲoso; asa'ɲoso/ *a* heroic, dauntless, courageous

hazmerreír /aθmerre'ir; asmerre'ir/ *m, Inf.* laughingstock

he /e/ *interj* and *adv* Hallo! Hist!; Behold! **¡Heme aquí!** Here I am. **he aquí,** here is...

hebilla /e'βiʎa; e'βiya/ *f,* buckle

hebra /'eβra/ *f,* thread; fiber; flesh; *Mineral.* vein, streak; filament (textiles); grain (of wood); *pl Poet.* hair. *Inf.* **pegar la h.,** to start a conversation

hebraísmo /eβra'ismo/ *m,* Hebraism

hebraísta /eβra'ista/ *m,* Hebraist

hebreo /e'βreo/ **(-ea)** *a* Hebraic, Jewish —*n* Jew. *m,* Hebrew (language)

Hébridas, las /'eβriðas, las/ the Hebrides

hecatombe /eka'tombe/ *f,* hecatomb; slaughter, massacre

hechicería /etʃiθe'ria; etʃise'ria/ *f,* sorcery; spell, enchantment

hechicero /etʃi'θero; etʃi'sero/ *a* bewitching, magic; charming, attractive

hechizar /etʃi'θar; etʃi'sar/ *vt* to bewitch; charm, attract, delight

hechizo /e'tʃiθo; e'tʃiso/ *m,* magic spell; fascination, charm; delight, pleasure

hecho /'etʃo/ *a* developed, mature; accustomed, used; perfected, finished; ready-made. **h. una furia,** like a fury, very angry. **bien h.,** well-made, well-proportioned; well or rightly done

hecho /etʃo/ *m,* deed, action; fact; happening, event. **los Hechos de los Apóstoles,** the Acts of the Apostles

hechura /e'tʃura/ *f*, making, make; creation; form; figure, statue; *Lit.* composition; build (of body); *Fig.* puppet, creature; *pl* price paid for work done. **de h. sastre,** *a* tailor-made
hectárea /ekta'rea/ *f*, hectare
hectógrafo /ek'tografo/ *m*, hectograph
hectogramo /ekto'gramo/ *m*, hectogram
hectolitro /ekto'litro/ *m*, hectoliter
heder /e'ðer/ *vi irr* to stink; be intolerable. See **entender**
hediondez /eðion'deθ; eðion'des/ *f*, stink, stench
hediondo /e'ðiondo/ *a* stinking; intolerable, pestilential; obscene
hedonismo /eðo'nismo/ *m*, hedonism
hedonista /eðo'nista/ *mf* hedonist
hegeliano /ehe'liano/ *a* Hegelian
hegemonía /ehemo'nia/ *f*, hegemony
helada /e'laða/ *f*, frost. **h. blanca,** hoarfrost
heladera /ela'ðera/ *f*, refrigerator
helado /e'laðo/ *a* frozen; ice-cold; astounded, disdainful. *m*, iced drink; sherbet, ice cream
helamiento /ela'miento/ *m*, icing; freezing
helar /e'lar/ *vt irr* to freeze; ice, chill; astound; discourage; *—vr* become iced; freeze; become ice-cold *—v impers* to freeze. See **acertar**
helecho /e'letʃo/ *m*, fern
helenismo /ele'nismo/ *m*, Hellenism
hélice /'eliθe; 'elise/ *f*, spiral, helical line; screw, propeller; *Geom.* helix; *Astron.* Ursa Major
helicóptero /eli'koptero/ *m*, *Aer.* helicopter
helio /'elio/ *m*, helium
heliógrafo /e'liografo/ *m*, heliograph
helioscopio /elio'skopio/ *m*, helioscope
helióstato /e'liostato/ *m*, heliostat
helioterapia /eliote'rapia/ *f*, heliotherapy
heliotropismo /eliotro'pismo/ *m*, heliotropism
heliotropo /elio'tropo/ *m*, heliotrope; agate
helvecio /el'βeθio; el'βesio/ **(-ia)** *a* and *n* Helvetian
hembra /'embra/ *f*, female; *Inf.* woman; nut of a screw; eye of a hook
hemiciclo /emi'θiklo; emi'siklo/ *m*, hemicycle; floor (of a legislative building)
hemisférico /emis'feriko/ *a* hemispherical
hemisferio /emis'ferio/ *m*, hemisphere
hemofilia /emo'filia/ *f*, hemophilia.
hemoglobina /emoglo'βina/ *f*, hemoglobin
hemorragia /emo'rrahia/ *f*, hemorrhage
hemorroides /emo'rroiðes/ *f*, hemorrhoids
henchido /en'tʃiðo/ *a* swollen
henchimiento /entʃi'miento/ *m*, swelling; inflation; filling
henchir /en'tʃir/ *vt irr* to fill; stuff; swell *—Pres. Indic.* **hincho, hinches, hinche, hinchen.** *Pres. Part.* **hinchiendo.** *Pres. Subjunc.* **hincha,** etc *—Imperf. Subjunc.* **hinchiese,** etc *—Imperat.* **hinche, hincha, hinchamos, henchid, hinchan**
hendedura /ende'ðura/ *f*, fissure; rift
hender /en'der/ *vt irr* to split, crack; *Fig.* cleave (air, water, etc.); make one's way through. See **entender**
hendidura /endi'ðura/ *f*, split, fissure, crack, chink
henil /e'nil/ *m*, hayloft
heno /'eno/ *m*, hay
hepático /e'patiko/ *a* hepatic
heráldica /e'raldika/ *f*, heraldry
heráldico /e'raldiko/ *a* heraldic
heraldo /e'raldo/ *m*, herald; harbinger
herbaje /er'βahe/ *m*, herbage; pasture, grass; thick woolen cloth
herbario /er'βario/ *m*, herbalist, botanist; herbarium *—a* herbal
herbívoro /er'βiβoro/ *a* herbivorous
herbolaria /erβo'laria/ *f*, herbal
hercúleo /er'kuleo/ *a* herculean
heredad /ere'ðað/ *f*, landed property; country estate
heredar /ere'ðar/ *vt* to inherit; make a deed of gift to; inherit characteristics, etc.; take as heir
heredero /ere'ðero/ **(-ra)** *m*, heir; inheritor. **h. aparente,** heir apparent. **presunto h.,** heir presumptive
hereditario /ereði'tario/ *a* hereditary
hereje /e'rehe/ *mf* heretic
herejía /ere'hia/ *f*, heresy
herencia /e'renθia; e'rensia/ *f*, inheritance; heredity; heritage
heresiarca /ere'siarka/ *mf* heresiarch
herético /e'retiko/ *a* heretical
herida /e'riða/ *f*, wound; insult; anguish. **h. contusa,** contusion. **h. penetrante,** deep wound
herir /e'rir/ *vt irr* to wound; strike, harm; *Fig.* pierce (of sun's rays); *Fig.* pluck (strings of a musical instrument); impress (the senses); affect (the emotions); offend (gen. of words) *—Pres. Part.* **hiriendo.** *Pres. Indic.* **hiero, hieres, hiere, hieren.** *Preterite* **hirió, hirieron.** *Pres. Subjunc.* **hiera, hieras, hiera, hiramos, hiráis, hieran.** *Imperf. Subjunc.* **hiriese,** etc.
hermafrodita /ermafro'ðita/ *a* and *mf* hermaphrodite
hermana /er'mana/ *f*, sister; twin, pair (of things). **h. de leche,** foster sister. **h. política,** sister-in-law
hermanar /erma'nar/ *vt* to join; mate; harmonize; *—vt* and *vr* be the spiritual brother of, be compatible
hermanastra /erma'nastra/ *f*, stepsister
hermanastro /erma'nastro/ *m*, stepbrother
hermandad /erman'dað/ *f*, brotherhood; friendship, intimacy; relationship (of one thing to another); confraternity. **Santa H.,** Spanish rural police force instituted in the fifteenth century
hermano /er'mano/ *m*, brother; pair, twin (of things); *Eccl.* brother. **h. de raza,** member of the same race. **h. político,** brother-in-law
hermético /er'metiko/ *a* hermetic
hermosear /ermose'ar/ *vt* to embellish, beautify, adorn
hermoso /er'moso/ *a* beautiful; shapely; handsome; fine, wonderful (weather, view, etc.)
hermosura /ermo'sura/ *f*, beauty; pleasantness, attractiveness, perfection of form; belle
hernia /'ernia/ *f*, hernia
héroe /'eroe/ *m*, hero
heroicidad /eroiθi'ðað; eroisi'ðað/ *f*, heroism
heroico /e'roiko/ *a* heroic
heroína /ero'ina/ *f*, heroine
heroismo /ero'ismo/ *m*, heroism
herpes /'erpes/ *m pl*, or *f pl*, herpes
herrada /e'rraða/ *f*, pail
herradero /erra'ðero/ *m*, branding of livestock
herrador /erra'ðor/ *m*, blacksmith
herradura /erra'ðura/ *f*, horseshoe
herraje /e'rrahe/ *m*, ironwork
herramienta /erra'mienta/ *f*, tool; set of tools
herrar /e'rrar/ *vt irr* to shoe horses; brand (cattle); decorate with iron. See **acertar**
herrería /erre'ria/ *f*, forge; ironworks; blacksmith's shop; clamor, tumult, confusion
herrero /e'rrero/ *m*, smith
herrete /e'rrete/ *m*, ferrule, tag
herrumbre /e'rrumbre/ *f*, rust; taste of iron
herrumbroso /errum'broso/ *a* rusty
hervidero /erβi'ðero/ *m*, boiling, bubbling; *Fig.* ebullition; swarm, crowd
hervir /er'βir/ *vi irr* to boil; foam and froth (sea); seethe (emotions); surge (crowds); (*with en*) abound in, swarm with. See **sentir**
hervor /er'βor/ *m*, boiling; ebullition, vigor, zest; seething, agitation
hesitación /esita'θion; esita'sion/ *f*, hesitation, doubt, uncertainty
hesitar /esi'tar/ *vi* to hesitate, vacillate
heteo /e'teo/ **(-ea)** *a* and *n* Hittite
heterodina /etero'ðina/ *a f*, *Radio.* heterodyne
heterodoxia /etero'ðoksia/ *f*, heterodoxy
heterodoxo /etero'ðokso/ *a* heterodox
heterogeneidad /eterohenei'ðað/ *f*, heterogeneity
heterogéneo /etero'heneo/ *a* heterogeneous
hético /'etiko/ *a* hectic, consumptive
hexagonal /eksago'nal/ *a* hexagonal
hexágono /e'ksagono/ *m*, hexagon
hexámetro /e'ksametro/ *m*, hexameter
hez /eθ; es/ *f*, (gen. *pl* **heces**) lees, dregs
hiato /'iato/ *m*, hiatus
hibernal /'iβernal/ *a* wintry
hibernés /iβer'nes/ *a* Hibernian
hibisco /i'βisko/ *m*, hibiscus
hibridación /iβriða'θion; iβriða'sion/ *f*, hybridization

hibridismo /iβri'ðismo/ *m,* hybridism

híbrido /'iβriðo/ *a* and *m,* hybrid

hidalgo /i'ðalgo/ **(-ga)** *n* noble, aristocrat —*a* noble; illustrious; generous

hidalguía /iðal'gia/ *f,* nobility; generosity, nobility of spirit

hidra /'iðra/ *f, Zool.* hydra; poisonous snake; *Astron.* Hydra

hidratar /iðra'tar/ *vt Chem.* to hydrate

hidrato /i'ðrato/ *m,* hydrate. **h. de carbono,** carbohydrate

hidráulica /i'ðraulika/ *f,* hydraulics

hidráulico /i'ðrauliko/ *a* hydraulic

hidroavión /iðroa'βion/ *m,* flying boat

hidrocarburo /iðrokar'βuro/ *m,* hydrocarbon

hidrocéfalo /iðro'θefalo; iðro'sefalo/ *a* hydrocephalic

hidrodinámica /iðroði'namika/ *f,* hydrodynamics

hidroeléctrico /iðroe'lektriko/ *a* hydroelectric

hidrofobia /iðro'foβia/ *f,* hydrophobia; rabies

hidrógeno /i'ðroheno/ *m,* hydrogen

hidrografía /iðrogra'fia/ *f,* hydrography

hidrología /iðrolo'hia/ *f,* hydrology

hidropesía /iðrope'sia/ *f,* dropsy

hidrópico /i'ðropiko/ *a* dropsical

hidroplano /iðro'plano/ *m,* seaplane

hidroquinona /iðroki'nona/ *f,* hydroquinone

hidroscopio /iðro'skopio/ *m,* hydroscope

hidrostática /iðro'statika/ *f,* hydrostatics

hidroterapia /iðrote'rapia/ *f,* hydrotherapy

hiedra /'ieðra/ *f,* ivy

hiel /iel/ *f,* gall, bile, bitterness, affliction; *pl* troubles

hielo /'ielo/ *m,* ice, frost; freezing, icing; stupefaction; indifference, coldness. *Inf.* **estar hecho un h.,** to be as cold as ice

hiena /'iena/ *f,* hyena

hierático /ie'ratiko/ *a* hieratical

hierba /'ierβa/ *f,* grass; small plant; herb. **h. cana,** groundsel. **mala h.,** weed

hierbabuena /ierβa'βuena/ *f, Bot.* mint

hierofante /iero'fante/ *m,* hierophant

hierra /'ierra/ *f,* branding time

hierro /'ierro/ *m,* iron; brand with hot iron; iron or steel head of a lance, etc.; instrument or shape made of iron; weapon of war *pl* fetters. **h. colado,** cast iron. **h. dulce,** wrought iron. **h. en planchas,** sheet iron. **h. viejo,** scrap iron

hígado /'igaðo/ *m,* liver; courage

higiene /i'hiene/ *f,* hygiene; cleanliness, neatness. **h. privada,** personal hygiene. **h. pública,** public health

higiénico /i'hieniko/ *a* hygienic

higo /'igo/ *m,* fig. **h. chumbo,** prickly pear

higrómetro /i'grometro/ *m,* hygrometer

higuera /i'gera/ *f,* fig tree

hija /'iha/ *f,* daughter; native of a place; offspring

hijastro /i'hastro/ **(-ra)** *n* stepchild

hijo /'iho/ *m,* son; child; native of a place; offspring; shoot, sprout; *pl* descendants. **h. de la cuna,** foundling. **h. de leche,** foster child. **h. natural,** natural child. **h. político,** son-in-law

hijuela /i'huela/ *f,* little daughter; small mattress; small drain; side road; accessory, subordinate thing; piece of material for widening a garment; *Law.* part of an inheritance

hila /'ila/ *f,* row, line; gut; *Surg.* lint (gen. *pl*)

hilacha /i'latʃa/ *f,* thread raveled from cloth; fiber, filament. **h. de vidrio,** spun glass

hilado /i'laðo/ *m,* spinning; thread, yarn

hilandería /ilande'ria/ *f,* spinning; spinning mill; mill. **h. de algodón,** cotton mill

hilandero /ilan'dero/ **(-ra)** *n* spinner

hilar /i'lar/ *vt* to spin; reason, infer, discourse

hilaridad /ilari'ðað/ *f,* hilarity; quiet happiness

hilaza /i'laθa; i'lasa/ *f,* yarn

hilera /i'lera/ *f,* line, file, row; fine yarn; *Mil.* file, rank; *Metall.* wire drawer; *Mas.* course (of bricks)

hilo /'ilo/ *m,* thread; linen; wire; mesh (spiders, silkworm's web, etc.); edge (of a blade); thin stream (of liquid); thread (of discourse)

hilván /il'βan/ *m, Sew.* basting; tack

hilvanar /ilβa'nar/ *vt Sew.* to baste

himalayo /ima'layo/ *a* Himalayan

himen /'imen/ *m,* hymen

himeneo /ime'neo/ *m,* marriage, wedding

himnario /im'nario/ *m,* hymnal

himno /'imno/ *m,* hymn

hin /in/ *m,* whinny, neigh

hincapié /inka'pie/ *m,* foothold. **hacer h.,** to insist, make a stand

hincar /in'kar/ *vt* to thrust in; drive in, sink; —*vr* kneel. **h. el diente,** to bite. **h. la uña,** to scratch. **hincarse de rodillas,** to kneel down

hinchado /in'tʃaðo/ *a* puffed up, vain; pompous, high-flown, redundant (style)

hinchar /in'tʃar/ *vt* to inflate; puff out (the chest); swell (of a river, etc.); exaggerate (events); —*vr* swell; grow vain, be puffed up

hinchazón /intʃa'θon; intʃa'son/ *f,* swelling; vanity, presumption; pomposity, euphuism (style)

hiniesta /i'niesta/ *f,* Spanish broom

hinojo /i'noho/ *m, Bot.* fennel; knee. **de hinojos,** on bended knee

hipar /i'par/ *vi* to hiccup; pant (of dogs); be overanxious; be overtired; sob, cry

hipérbole /i'perβole/ *f,* hyperbole

hiperbólico /iper'βoliko/ *a* hyperbolical

hipercrítico /iper'kritiko/ *m,* hypercritic —*a* hypercritical

hipertrofiarse /ipertro'fiarse/ *vr* to hypertrophy

hípico /'ipiko/ *a* equine

hipnosis /ip'nosis/ *f,* hypnosis

hipnótico /ip'notiko/ *a* hypnotic. *m,* hypnotic drug

hipnotismo /ipno'tismo/ *m,* hypnotism

hipnotización /ipnotiθa'θion; ipnotisa'sion/ *f,* hypnotization

hipnotizar /ipnoti'θar; ipnoti'sar/ *vt* to hypnotize

hipo /'ipo/ *m,* hiccup; sob; longing, desire; dislike, disgust

hipocondría /ipokon'dria/ *f,* hypochondria

hipocondríaco /ipokon'driako/ **(-ca)** *a* hypochondriacal —*n* hypochondriac

hipocrático /ipo'kratiko/ *a* Hippocratic

hipocresía /ipokre'sia/ *f,* hypocrisy

hipócrita /i'pokrita/ *a* hypocritical. *mf* hypocrite

hipodérmico /ipo'ðermiko/ *a* hypodermic

hipódromo /i'poðromo/ *m,* hippodrome, racetrack

hipopótamo /ipo'potamo/ *m,* hippopotamus

hipostático /ipo'statiko/ *a* hypostatic

hipoteca /ipo'teka/ *f,* mortgage

hipotecar /ipote'kar/ *vt* to mortgage

hipotenusa /ipote'nusa/ *f,* hypotenuse

hipótesis /i'potesis/ *f,* hypothesis

hipotético /ipo'tetiko/ *a* hypothetical

hirsuto /ir'suto/ *a* hirsute, hairy

hirviente /ir'βiente/ *a* boiling

hisca /'iska/ *f,* birdlime

hisopear /isope'ar/ *vt Eccl.* to sprinkle, asperse

hisopo /i'sopo/ *m, Bot.* hyssop; *Eccl.* hyssop, sprinkler

hispánico /is'paniko/ *a* Spanish

hispanismo /ispa'nismo/ *m,* Hispanism

hispanista /ispa'nista/ *mf* Hispanist

hispanoamericano /ispanoameri'kano/ **(-na)** *a* and *n* Spanish-American, Hispano-American

histeria /is'teria/ *f,* hysteria

histérico /is'teriko/ *a* hysterical; hysteric

histerismo /iste'rismo/ *m, Med.* hysteria

histología /istolo'hia/ *f,* histology

histólogo /is'tologo/ *m,* histologist

historia /is'toria/ *f,* history; narrative, story; tale; *Inf.* gossip (gen. *pl*); *Art.* historical piece. **h. natural,** natural history. **h. sagrada,** biblical history. *Fig. Inf.* **dejarse de historias,** to stop beating around the bush

historiador /istoria'ðor/ **(-ra)** *n* historian

historiar /isto'riar/ *vt* to narrate, relate; record, chronicle

histórico /is'toriko/ *a* historical; historic

historieta /isto'rieta/ *f,* short story; anecdote

historiografía /istoriogra'fia/ *f,* historiography

historiógrafo /isto'riografo/ *m,* historiographer

histriónico /ist'rioniko/ *a* histrionic

hitlerismo /itle'rismo/ *m,* Hitlerism

hito /'ito/ *m,* milestone; boundary mark; *Fig.* mark, target. **de h. en h.,** from head to foot
hocico /o'θiko; o'siko/ *m,* snout; *Inf.* face, mug; *Inf.* angry gesture; *Naut.* prow. **meter el h.,** to stick one's nose into other people's business
hogaño /o'gaɲo/ *adv Inf.* during this year; at the present time
hogar /o'gar/ *m,* hearth, fireplace; home, house; family life; firebox (of a locomotive)
hoguera /o'gera/ *f,* bonfire
hoja /'oha/ *f, Bot.* leaf; petal; sheet (metal, paper, etc.); page (of book); blade (sharp instruments); leaf (door, window); sword. **h. de cálculo,** spreadsheet. **h. de servicios,** service or professional record. **h. de tocino,** side of bacon. **h. extraordinaria,** extra, special edition (of a newspaper). **h. volante,** handbill, supplement. **volver la h.,** to turn over (pages); change one's opinion; turn the conversation
hojalata /oha'lata/ *f,* tin plate
hojalatería /ohalate'ria/ *f,* tinware; tin shop
hojalatero /ohala'tero/ *m,* tinsmith
hojaldre /o'haldre/ *m,* or *f,* puff pastry
hojarasca /oha'raska/ *f,* withered leaves; excessive foliage; rubbish, trash
hojear /ohe'ar/ *vt* to turn the leaves of a book; skip, skim, read quickly; *—vi* exfoliate
hojuela /o'huela/ *f, dim* little leaf; *Bot.* leaflet; pancake
¡hola! /'ola/ *interj* Hallo! Goodness!
Holanda /o'landa/ Holland
holandés /olan'des/ **(-esa)** *a* and *n* Dutchman (-woman) *m,* Dutch (language)
holgado /ol'gaðo/ *a* leisured, free; loose, wide; comfortable; well-off, rich
holganza /ol'ganθa; ol'gansa/ *f,* repose, leisure, ease; idleness; pleasure
holgar /ol'gar/ *vi irr* to rest; be idle; be glad; be unused or unnecessary (things) *—vr* enjoy oneself, amuse oneself; be glad. See **contar**
holgazán /olga'θan; olga'san/ **(-ana)** *a* idle *—n* idler
holgazanear /olgaθane'ar; olgasane'ar/ *vi* to idle
holgazanería /olgaθane'ria; olgasane'ria/ *f,* idleness, sloth
holgorio /ol'gorio/ *m,* rejoicing, festivity, merriment
holgura /ol'gura/ *f,* enjoyment, merrymaking; width; comfort, ease; *Mech.* free play
hollar /o'ʎar; o'yar/ *vt irr* to trample under foot; humiliate. See **degollar**
hollejo /o'ʎeho; o'yeho/ *m,* peel, thin skin (of fruit); *Agr.* chaff
hollín /o'ʎin; o'yin/ *m,* soot
holocausto /olo'kausto/ *m,* holocaust
hológrafo /o'lografo/ *m,* holograph
hombradía /ombra'ðia/ *f,* manliness; courage
hombre /'ombre/ *m,* man; adult; omber (cards) *—interj* **¡h.!** *Inf.* Old fellow! You don't say so! **¡h. al agua!** Man overboard! **h. de bien,** honest, honorable man. **h. de estado,** statesman. **h. de muchos oficios,** jack-of-all-trades. **h. de negocios,** businessman; man of affairs. **h. de pro,** worthy man; famous man. **ser muy h.,** to be a real man, be very manly
hombrera /om'brera/ *f,* epaulette; shoulderpad
hombro /'ombro/ *m,* shoulder. **echar al h.,** to shoulder; undertake, take the responsibility of. **encogerse de hombros,** to shrug one's shoulders; be indifferent or uninterested
hombruno /om'bruno/ *a Inf.* mannish (of a woman)
homenaje /ome'nahe/ *m,* allegiance; homage; veneration, respect
homeópata /ome'opata/ *a* homeopathic. *mf* homeopath
homeopatía /omeopa'tia/ *f,* homeopathy
homérico /o'meriko/ *a* Homeric
homicida /omi'θiða; omi'siða/ *a* murderous, homicidal. *mf* murderer (-ess)
homicidio /omi'θiðio; omi'siðio/ *m,* homicide (act)
homilía /omi'lia/ *f,* homily
homogeneidad /omohenei'ðað/ *f,* homogeneity
homogéneo /omo'heneo/ *a* homogeneous
homólogo /o'mologo/ *a* homologous
homónimo /o'monimo/ *a* homonymous. *m,* homonym
homosexual /omose'ksual/ *a* and *mf* homosexual
honda /'onda/ *f,* sling, catapult
hondear /onde'ar/ *vt Naut.* to sound, plumb; *Naut.* unload
hondo /'ondo/ *a* deep; low; *Fig.* profound; deep, intense (emotion). *m,* depth
hondón /on'don/ *m,* depth, recess
hondonada /ondo'naða/ *f,* hollow; glen; valley
hondura /on'dura/ *f,* depth
hondureño /ondu'reɲo/ **(-ña)** *a* and *n* Honduran
honestidad /onesti'ðað/ *f,* honorableness; virtue; respectability; modesty; courtesy
honesto /o'nesto/ *a* honorable, virtuous; modest; honest, just
hongo /'oŋgo/ *m,* fungus; toadstool; bowler hat
honor /o'nor/ *m,* honor; fame; reputation (women); modesty (women); praise; *pl* rank, position; honors
honorable /ono'raβle/ *a* honorable
honorario /ono'rario/ *a* honorary. *m,* honorarium, fee
honorífico /ono'rifiko/ *a* honorary; honorable
honra /'onra/ *f,* self respect, honor, personal dignity, reputation; chastity and modesty (women); *pl* obsequies
honradez /onra'ðeθ; onra'ðes/ *f,* honesty; honorableness, integrity; respectability
honrado /on'raðo/ *a* honest; honorable
honrar /on'rar/ *vt* to respect; honor; *—vr* to be honored
honroso /on'roso/ *a* honor-giving, honorable
hora /'ora/ *f,* hour; opportune moment; *pl* book of hours. **horas hábiles,** working hours. **horas muertas,** wee hours; wasted time. **a última h.,** at the last minute. **dar la h.,** to strike the hour. **¿Qué h. es?** What time is it?
horaciano /ora'θiano; ora'siano/ *a* Horatian
horadar /ora'ðar/ *vt* to bore, pierce
horario /o'rario/ *a* hourly. *m,* timetable; hour hand of a clock; watch
horca /'orka/ *f,* gibbet, gallows; *Agr.* pitchfork; fork; prop for trees
horcajadas /orka'haðas/ (**a**) *adv* astride
horcajadura /orkaha'ðura/ *f,* crotch
horchata /or'tʃata/ *f,* drink made of chufas or crushed almonds
horda /'orða/ *f,* horde
horizontal /oriθon'tal; orison'tal/ *a* horizontal
horizonte /ori'θonte; ori'sonte/ *m,* horizon. **nuevos horizontes,** new opportunities
horma /'orma/ *f,* mold; cobbler's last; stone wall. *Fig. Inf.* **hallar la h. de su zapato,** to find what suits one; meet one's match
hormiga /or'miga/ *f,* ant
hormigón /ormi'gon/ *m,* concrete. **h. armado,** ferroconcrete
hormiguear /ormige'ar/ *vi* to itch; crowd, swarm
hormiguero /ormi'gero/ *m,* anthill; crowd, swarm
hormona /or'mona/ *f,* hormone
hornero /or'nero/ **(-ra)** *n* baker
horno /'orno/ *m,* oven; furnace; kiln; bakery. **h. alfarero,** firing oven (for pottery). **h. de cocina,** kitchen stove. **h. de cuba,** blast furnace. **h. de ladrillo,** brick kiln. **alto h.,** iron-smelting furnace
horóscopo /o'roskopo/ *m,* horoscope
horquilla /or'kiʎa; or'kiya/ *f,* forked stick; hairpin, hatpin; *Agr.* fork; hook. **viraje en h.,** hairpin turn
horrendo /o'rrendo/ *a* horrible, frightful
hórreo /'orreo/ *m,* granary, barn
horribilidad /orriβili'ðað/ *f,* horribleness
horribilísimo /orriβi'lisimo/ *a superl* most horrible, exceedingly horrible
horrible /o'rriβle/ *a* horrible
horrífico /o'rrifiko/ *a* horrific
horripilante /orripi'lante/ *a* hair-raising, horrifying
horrísono /o'rrisono/ *a Poet.* horrid-sounding, terrifying
horror /o'rror/ *m,* horror; horribleness; atrocity, enormity

horrorizar /orrori'θar; orrori'sar/ *vt* to horrify; *—vr* be horrified, be terrified
horroroso /orro'roso/ *a* dreadful, horrible; horrid; *Inf.* hideous, most ugly
hortaliza /orta'liθa; orta'lisa/ *f,* green vegetable, garden produce
hortelano /orte'lano/ *m,* market gardener
hortensia /or'tensia/ *f,* hydrangea
horticultor /ortikul'tor/ **(-ra)** *n* horticulturalist
horticultura /ortikul'tura/ *f,* horticulture
horticultural /ortikultu'ral/ *a* horticultural
hosanna /o'sanna/ *m,* hosanna
hosco /'osko/ *a* dark brown; unsociable, sullen; crabbed
hospedaje /ospe'ðahe/ *m,* lodging; board, payment
hospedar /ospe'ðar/ *vt* to lodge, receive as a guest; *—vr* and *vi* lodge, stay
hospedería /ospeðe'ria/ *f,* hostelry, inn; lodging
hospedero /ospe'ðero/ **(-ra)** *n* innkeeper
hospicio /os'piθio; os'pisio/ *m,* hospice; almshouse, workhouse; lodging; orphanage
hospital /ospi'tal/ *m,* hospital; hospice. **h. de sangre,** field hospital
hospitalario /ospita'lario/ *a* hospitable
hospitalidad /ospitali'ðað/ *f,* hospitality; hospitableness; hospital
hostelero /oste'lero/ **(-ra)** *n* innkeeper
hostería /oste'ria/ *f,* hostelry; inn
hostia /'ostia/ *f, Eccl.* wafer, Host; sacrificial victim
hostigamiento /ostiga'miento/ *m,* harassment. **h. sexual,** sexual harassment
hostigar /osti'gar/ *vt* to chastise; harass; tease, annoy
hostil /'ostil/ *a* hostile
hostilidad /ostili'ðað/ *f,* hostility
hostilizar /ostili'θar; ostili'sar/ *vt* to commit hostile acts against; antagonize
hotel /'otel/ *m,* hotel; villa
hotelero /ote'lero/ **(-ra)** *n* hotelkeeper
hoy /oi/ *adv* today; at present. **h. día** *or* **h. en día,** today. **h. por h.,** day by day; at the present time. **de h. en adelante,** from today forward
hoya /'oya/ *f,* hole; grave; valley, glen; bed (of a river)
hoyo /'oyo/ *m,* hole; pockmark; grave; hollow
hoyuelo /o'yuelo/ *m, dim* little hole; dimple
hoz /oθ; os/ *f,* sickle; defile
hozar /o'θar; o'sar/ *vt* to root (pigs, etc.)
hucha /'utʃa/ *f,* large chest; strongbox; savings
hueco /'ueko/ *a* empty; hollow; vain; hollow (sound); pompous (style); spongy, soft; inflated. *m,* hollow; interval of time or place; *Inf.* vacancy; gap in a wall, etc.
huelga /'uelga/ *f,* strike; leisure; lying fallow; merrymaking. **h. de brazos caídos,** sit-down strike. **h. patronal,** lockout strike
huelguista /uel'gista/ *mf* striker
huella /'ueʎa; 'ueya/ *f,* footprint, track; footstep; tread (of stairs); *Print.* impression; vestige, trace. **h. digital,** fingerprint
huérfano /'uerfano/ **(-na)** *n* orphan *—a* unprotected, uncared for
huero /'uero/ *a* addled; empty, hollow
huerta /'uerta/ *f,* kitchen garden; orchard; irrigation land
huerto /'uerto/ *m,* orchard; kitchen garden
hueso /'ueso/ *m,* bone; stone (of fruit); kernel, core; drudgery; cheap, useless thing of poor quality. *Inf.* **no dejar un h. sano,** to tear (a person) to pieces. **tener los huesos molidos,** to be tired out; be bruised
huésped /'uespeð/ **(-da)** *n* guest; host; innkeeper
hueste /'ueste/ *f,* (gen. *pl*) army on the march, host; party, supporters
huesudo /ue'suðo/ *a* bony
hueva /'ueβa/ *f,* fish roe
huevera /ue'βera/ *f,* egg seller; eggcup
huevo /'ueβo/ *m,* egg. **h. duro,** hard-boiled egg. **h. estrellado,** fried egg. **h. pasado por agua,** soft-boiled egg. **huevos revueltos,** scrambled eggs
hugonote /ugo'note/ **(-ta)** *a* and *n* Huguenot
huida /'uiða/ *f,* flight, escape; bolting (of a horse); outlet
huir /uir/ *vi irr* to flee; fly (of time); elope; run away, bolt; (*with de*) avoid *—Pres. Part.* **huyendo.** *Pres. Indic.* **huyo, huyes, huyen.** *Preterite* **huyó, huyeron.** *Pres. Subjunc.* **huya,** etc *—Imperf. Subjunc.* **huyese,** etc.
hule /'ule/ *m,* oilcloth; rubber
hulla /'uʎa; 'uya/ *f,* coal mine, coal, soft coal
hullera /u'ʎera; u'yera/ *f,* colliery, coal mine
humanidad /umani'ðað/ *f,* humanity; human nature; human weakness; compassion; affability; *Inf.* stoutness; *pl* study of humanities
humanismo /uma'nismo/ *m,* humanism
humanista /uma'nista/ *mf* humanist *—a* humanistic
humanitario /umani'tario/ *a* humanitarian
humanizar /umani'θar; umani'sar/ *vt* to humanize
humano /u'mano/ *a* human; understanding, sympathetic. *m,* human being
humareda /uma'reða/ *f,* cloud of smoke
humeante /ume'ante/ *a* smoking; smoky
humear /ume'ar/ *vi* to give forth smoke; give oneself airs
humedad /ume'ðað/ *f,* humidity; dampness; moisture
humedecer /umeðe'θer; umeðe'ser/ *vt irr* to moisten, wet, damp; *—vr* grow moist. See **conocer**
húmedo /'umeðo/ *a* humid; damp; wet
húmero /'umero/ *m,* humerus
humildad /umil'dað/ *f,* humility; lowliness; humbleness
humilde /u'milde/ *a* meek; lowly; humble
humillación /umiʎa'θion; umiya'sion/ *f,* humiliation
humillante /umi'ʎante; umi'yante/ *a* humiliating; debasing; mortifying
humillar /umi'ʎar; umi'yar/ *vt* to humble; humiliate; *—vr* humble oneself
humo /'umo/ *m,* smoke; vapor, fume; vanity, airs
humor /u'mor/ *m, Med.* humor; temperament, disposition; mood. **de buen h.,** good-tempered. **de mal h.,** ill-tempered
humorada /umo'raða/ *f,* humorous saying, extravagance, witticism
humorismo /umo'rismo/ *m,* humor, comic sense; humorousness
humorista /umo'rista/ *mf* humorist
humorístico /umo'ristiko/ *a* humorous
humoso /u'moso/ *a* smoky, reeky
hundible /un'diβle/ *a* sinkable
hundido /un'diðo/ *a* sunken (of cheeks, etc.); hollow, deep-set (of eyes)
hundimiento /undi'miento/ *m,* sinking; collapse; subsidence (of earth)
hundir /un'dir/ *vt* to sink; oppress; confound; destroy, ruin; *—vr* collapse (building); sink; *Fig. Inf.* disappear
húngaro /'uŋgaro/ **(-ra)** *a* and *n* Hungarian. *m,* Hungarian (language)
Hungría /uŋ'gria/ Hungary
huno /'uno/ **(-na)** *n* Hun
huracán /ura'kan/ *m,* hurricane
hurañía /ura'ɲia/ *f,* shyness, unsociableness; diffidence; wildness (of animals, etc.)
huraño /u'raɲo/ *a* shy, unsociable; diffident; wild (of animals, etc.)
hurgar /ur'gar/ *vt* to stir; poke, rake; touch; rouse, incite *—vr* pick one's nose
hurgón /ur'gon/ *m,* fire rake, poker; *Inf.* sword
hurgonada /urgo'naða/ *f,* raking (of the fire, etc.)
hurí /u'ri/ *f,* houri
hurón /u'ron/ **(-ona)** *n* ferret *—a* shy, unsociable
¡hurra! /'urra/ *interj* Hurrah!
hurtadillas /urta'ðiʎas; urta'ðiyas/ **(a)** *adv* by stealth, secretly
hurtar /ur'tar/ *vt* to steal; encroach (sea, river); plagiarize; *—vr* hide oneself
hurto /'urto/ *m,* theft. **coger con el h. en las manos,** *Fig.* to catch red-handed
husmear /usme'ar/ *vt* to sniff out; *Inf.* pry; *—vi* smell bad (of meat)
huso /'uso/ *m,* spindle; bobbin
¡huy! /'ui/ *interj* (denoting pain or surprise) Oh!

I

ibérico /i'βeriko/ *a* Iberian
ibero /i'βero/ **(-ra)** *a* and *n* Iberian
íbice /'iβiθe; 'iβise/ *m,* ibex
icnografía /iknogra'fia/ *f,* ichnography
icnográfico /ikno'grafiko/ *a* ichnographical
icono /i'kono/ *m,* icon
iconoclasta /ikono'klasta/ *a* iconoclastic. *mf* iconoclast
iconografía /ikonogra'fia/ *f,* iconography
ictericia /ikte'riθia; ikte'risia/ *f,* jaundice
ictiología /iktiolo'hia/ *f,* ichthyology
ictiólogo /ik'tiologo/ *m,* ichthyologist
ida /'iða/ *f,* setting out, departure, going; impetuous action; precipitancy; track, trail (of animals). **de i. y vuelta,** round trip (of tickets)
idea /i'ðea/ *f,* idea. *Inf.* **¡Qué ideas tienes!** What (odd) ideas you have!
ideación /iðea'θion; iðea'sion/ *f,* ideation
ideal /i'ðeal/ *a* ideal; perfect. *m,* model; ideal
idealidad /iðeali'ðað/ *f,* ideality
idealismo /iðea'lismo/ *m,* idealism
idealista /iðea'lista/ *a* idealistic. *mf* idealist
idealización /iðealiθa'θion; iðealisa'sion/ *f,* idealization
idealizar /iðeali'θar; iðeali'sar/ *vt* to idealize
idealmente /iðeal'mente/ *adv* ideally
idear /iðe'ar/ *vt* to imagine; devise; plan; design; draft, draw up
ídem /'iðem/ *adv* idem
idéntico /i'ðentiko/ *a* identical
identidad /iðenti'ðað/ *f,* identity
identificable /iðentifi'kaβle/ *a* identifiable
identificación /iðentifika'θion; iðentifika'sion/ *f,* identification
identificar /iðentifi'kar/ *vt* to identify; recognize; *—vr* (*with con*) identify oneself with
ideografía /iðeogra'fia/ *f,* ideography
ideograma /iðeo'grama/ *m,* ideogram
ideología /iðeolo'hia/ *f,* ideology. **i. racista,** racial ideology
ideológico /iðeo'lohiko/ *a* ideological
ideólogo /iðe'ologo/ **(-ga)** *n* ideologist; dreamer, planner
idílico /i'ðiliko/ *a* idyllic
idilio /i'ðilio/ *m,* idyll
idioma /i'ðioma/ *m,* language, tongue
idiomático /iðio'matiko/ *a* idiomatic
idiosincrasia /iðiosin'krasia/ *f,* idiosyncrasy
idiosincrásico /iðiosin'krasiko/ *a* idiosyncratic
idiota /i'ðiota/ *a* idiot; idiotic. *mf* idiot
idiotez /iðio'teθ; iðio'tes/ *f,* idiocy
idiotismo /iðio'tismo/ *m, Gram.* idiom; ignorance
idólatra /iðo'latra/ *a* idolatrous; adoring. *mf* idolater, heathen
idolatrar /iðola'trar/ *vt* to idolize; worship, love excessively
idolatría /iðola'tria/ *f,* idolatry; adoration, idolization
ídolo /'iðolo/ *m,* idol
idoneidad /iðonei'ðað/ *f,* fitness, suitability; competence; capacity
idóneo /i'ðoneo/ *a* suitable; competent, fit
idus /i'ðus/ *m pl,* ides
iglesia /i'glesia/ *f,* church. **i. colegial,** collegiate church. **cumplir con la i.,** to discharge one's religious duties. **llevar a una mujer a la i.,** to lead a woman to the altar
ígneo /'igneo/ *a* igneous
ignición /igni'θion; igni'sion/ *f,* ignition
ignominia /igno'minia/ *f,* ignominy, disgrace
ignominioso /ignomi'nioso/ *a* ignominious
ignorancia /igno'ranθia; igno'ransia/ *f,* ignorance. **pretender i.,** to plead ignorance
ignorante /igno'rante/ *a* ignorant; unaware, uninformed. *mf* ignoramus
ignorar /igno'rar/ *vt* to be unaware of, not to know
ignoto /ig'noto/ *a* unknown, undiscovered
igual /i'gual/ *a* equal; level; even, smooth; very similar; alike; uniform; proportionate; unchanging; constant; indifferent; same. *mf* equal. *m, Math.* equal sign. **al i.,** equally. **sin i.,** peerless, without equal. **Me es completamente i.,** It's all the same to me
iguala /i'guala/ *f,* equalizing; leveling; agreement, arrangement; cash adjustment
igualación /iguala'θion; iguala'sion/ *f,* equalization; leveling; arrangement, agreement; matching; *Math.* equation
igualador /iguala'ðor/ *a* equalizing; leveling
igualar /igua'lar/ *vt* to equalize, make equal; match; pair; level, flatten; smooth; adjust; arrange, agree upon; weigh, consider; *Math.* equate; *—vi* be equal
igualdad /igual'dað/ *f,* equality; uniformity, harmony; evenness; smoothness; identity, sameness. **i. de ánimo,** equability, equanimity
igualitario /iguali'tario/ *a* equalizing; egalitarian
igualmente /igual'mente/ *adv* equally; the same, likewise
ijada /i'haða/ *f,* side, flank; pain in the side
ijadear /ihaðe'ar/ *vt* to pant
ijar /i'har/ *m,* See **ijada**
ilación /ila'θion; ila'sion/ *f,* connection, reference
ilegal /ile'gal/ *a* illegal
ilegalidad /ilegali'ðað/ *f,* illegality
ilegible /ile'hiβle/ *a* illegible, unreadable
ilegitimidad /ilehitimi'ðað/ *f,* illegitimacy
ilegítimo /ile'hitimo/ *a* illegitimate; false
íleon /'ileon/ *m,* ilium
ileso /i'leso/ *a* unharmed, unhurt
iletrado /ile'traðo/ *a* unlettered, uncultured
Ilíada /i'liaða/ *f,* Iliad
iliberal /iliβe'ral/ *a* illiberal; narrow-minded
iliberalidad /iliβerali'ðað/ *f,* illiberality; narrow-mindedness
ilícito /i'liθito; i'lisito/ *a* illicit
ilicitud /iliθi'tuð; ilisi'tuð/ *f,* illicitness
ilimitado /ilimi'taðo/ *a* unlimited, boundless
iliterato /ilite'rato/ *a* illiterate, uncultured
ilógico /i'lohiko/ *a* illogical
ilota /i'lota/ *mf* helot
iluminación /ilumina'θion; ilumina'sion/ *f,* illumination; lighting. **i. intensiva,** floodlighting
iluminador /ilumina'ðor/ **(-ra)** *a* lighting; illuminating *—n Art.* illuminator
iluminar /ilumi'nar/ *vt* to illuminate; light; *Art.* illuminate; enlighten
iluminativo /ilumina'tiβo/ *a* illuminating
ilusión /ilu'sion/ *f,* illusion; illusoriness; hope; dream
ilusionarse /ilusio'narse/ *vr* to harbor illusions
ilusivo /ilu'siβo/ *a* deceptive, illusive
iluso /i'luso/ *a* deceived, deluded; dreamy; visionary
ilusorio /ilu'sorio/ *a* illusory; deceptive; null
ilustración /ilustra'θion; ilustra'sion/ *f,* illustration, picture; enlightenment; explanation; illustrated newspaper or magazine; erudition, knowledge; example, illustration
ilustrado /ilu'straðo/ *a* erudite, learned; knowledgeable, well-informed
ilustrador /ilustra'ðor/ **(-ra)** *a* illustrative *—n* illustrator
ilustrar /ilus'trar/ *vt* to explain, illustrate; enlighten, instruct; illustrate (books); make illustrious; inspire with divine light
ilustrativo /ilustra'tiβo/ *a* illustrative
ilustre /i'lustre/ *a* illustrious, distinguished
ilustrísimo /ilus'trisimo/ *a superl* most illustrious (title of bishops, etc.)
imagen /i'mahen/ *f,* image; effigy, statue; idea; metaphor, simile. **i. nítida,** sharp image
imaginable /imahi'naβle/ *a* imaginable
imaginación /imahina'θion; imahina'sion/ *f,* imagination
imaginar /imahi'nar/ *vi* to imagine; *—vt* suppose,

conjecture; discover, invent; imagine. **¡Imagínese!** Just imagine!
imaginario /imahi'nario/ *a* imaginary
imaginativa /imahina'tiβa/ *f*, imagination; common sense
imaginativo /imahina'tiβo/ *a* imaginative
imaginería /imahine'ria/ *f*, imagery
imán /i'man/ *m*, magnet; attraction, charm; imam
imanación /imana'θion; imana'sion/ *f*, magnetization
imanar /ima'nar/ *vt* to magnetize
imbécil /im'beθil; im'besil/ *a* imbecile; stupid, idiotic. *mf* imbecile
imbecilidad /imbeθili'ðað; imbesili'ðað/ *f*, imbecility; folly, stupidity
imberbe /im'berβe/ *a* beardless. *Inf.* **joven i.,** stripling
imbibición /imbiβi'θion; imbiβi'sion/ *f*, imbibing, absorption
imborrable /imbo'rraβle/ *a* ineffaceable
imbuir /im'buir/ *vt irr* to imbue. See **huir**
imitable /imi'taβle/ *a* imitable
imitación /imita'θion; imita'sion/ *f*, imitation; reproduction, copy
imitado /imi'taðo/ *a* imitation; imitated
imitador /imita'ðor/ **(-ra)** *a* imitation; imitative *—n* imitator
imitar /imi'tar/ *vt* to imitate; counterfeit
imitativo /imita'tiβo/ *a* imitative
impacción /impak'θion; impak'sion/ *f*, impact
impaciencia /impa'θienθia; impa'siensia/ *f*, impatience
impacientar /impaθien'tar; impasien'tar/ *vt* to make impatient, annoy; *—vr* grow impatient
impaciente /impa'θiente; impa'siente/ *a* impatient
impacto /im'pakto/ *m*, impact. **i. de lleno,** direct hit
impalpabilidad /impalpaβili'ðað/ *f*, impalpability
impalpable /impal'paβle/ *a* impalpable
impar /im'par/ *a* odd; unpaired; single, uneven. **número impar,** odd number
imparcial /impar'θial; impar'sial/ *a* impartial
imparcialidad /imparθiali'ðað; imparsiali'ðað/ *f*, impartiality
imparisilábico /imparisi'laβiko/ *a* imparisyllabic
impartible /impar'tiβle/ *a* indivisible
impasibilidad /impasiβili'ðað/ *f*, impassivity, indifference
impasible /impa'siβle/ *a* impassive
impavidez /impaβi'ðeθ; impaβi'ðes/ *f*, dauntlessness; serenity in the face of danger
impávido /im'paβiðo/ *a* dauntless; calm, composed, imperturbable
impecabilidad /impekaβili'ðað/ *f*, impeccability, perfection
impecable /impe'kaβle/ *a* impeccable, perfect
impedido /impe'ðiðo/ *a* disabled
impedimento /impeði'mento/ *m*, obstacle; hindrance; *Law.* impediment
impedir /impe'ðir/ *vt irr* to impede; obstruct; prevent; thwart; disable; delay; *Poet.* amaze. See **pedir**
impeler /impe'ler/ *vt* to push; incite; drive; urge
impender /impen'der/ *vt* to spend money
impenetrabilidad /impenetraβili'ðað/ *f*, impenetrability; imperviousness; obscurity, difficulty
impenetrable /impene'traβle/ *a* impenetrable, dense; impervious; *Fig.* unfathomable; obscure
impenitencia /impeni'tenθia; impeni'tensia/ *f*, impenitence
impenitente /impeni'tente/ *a* impenitent
impensado /impen'saðo/ *a* unexpected, unforeseen
imperante /impe'rante/ *a* ruling, dominant
imperar /impe'rar/ *vi* to rule; command
imperativo /impera'tiβo/ *a* commanding *—a* and *m*, *Gram.* imperative
imperatorio /impera'torio/ *a* imperial, imperatorial
imperceptible /imperθep'tiβle; impersep'tiβle/ *a* imperceptible
imperdible /imper'ðiβle/ *m*, safety pin
imperdonable /imperðo'naβle/ *a* unpardonable, inexcusable
imperecedero /impereθe'ðero; imperese'ðero/ *a* undying, eternal, everlasting
imperfección /imperfek'θion; imperfek'sion/ *f*, imperfection, inadequacy; fault, blemish; weakness
imperfecto /imper'fekto/ *a* imperfect; inadequate; faulty *—a* and *m*, *Gram.* imperfect
imperial /impe'rial/ *a* imperial. *f*, upper deck of a bus or streetcar
imperialismo /imperia'lismo/ *m*, imperialism
imperialista /imperia'lista/ *a* imperialistic. *mf* imperialist
impericia /impe'riθia; impe'risia/ *f*, inexpertness; unskillfulness, unhandiness
imperio /im'perio/ *m*, empire; rule, reign; command, sway; imperial dignity; arrogance, haughtiness. *Fig. Inf.* **valer un i.,** to be priceless
imperioso /impe'rioso/ *a* imperious
imperito /impe'rito/ *a* inexpert; clumsy, unskilled
impermeabilidad /impermeaβili''ðað/ *f*, watertightness; imperviousness; impermeability
impermeabilizar /impermeaβili'θar; impermeaβili'sar/ *vt* to waterproof
impermeable /imperme'aβle/ *a* watertight, impermeable; impervious. *m*, raincoat, mackintosh
impersonal /imperso'nal/ *a* impersonal
impertérrito /imper'territo/ *a* unafraid, dauntless
impertinencia /impertinen'θia; impertinen'sia/ *f*, impertinence, insolence; peevishness; fancy, whim; overexactness, meticulousness; interference, intrusion
impertinente /imperti'nente/ *a* impertinent; irrelevant; inopportune; officious, interfering
impertinentes /imperti'nentes/ *m pl*, lorgnettes
imperturbabilidad /imperturβaβili'ðað/ *f*, imperturbability
imperturbable /impertur'βaβle/ *a* calm, imperturbable
impetrar /impe'trar/ *vt* to obtain by entreaty; implore
ímpetu /'impetu/ *m*, impetus, momentum; speed, swiftness; violence
impetuosidad /impetuosi'ðað/ *f*, impetuosity
impetuoso /impe'tuoso/ *a* impetuous; precipitate
impiedad /impie'ðað/ *f*, cruelty, harshness; irreligion
impío /im'pio/ *a* impious, wicked; irreverent, irreligious
implacabilidad /implakaβili'ðað/ *f*, implacability, relentless
implacable /impla'kaβle/ *a* implacable
implantación /implanta'θion; implanta'sion/ *f*, inculcation, implantation
implantar /implan'tar/ *vt* to inculcate, implant (ideas, etc.)
implicación /implika'θion; implika'sion/ *f*, implication; contradiction (in terms); complicity
implicar /impli'kar/ *vt* to implicate; imply, infer; involve, entangle; *—vi* imply contradiction (gen. with negatives)
implicatorio /implika'torio/ *a* contradictory; implicated (in crime)
implícito /im'pliθito; im'plisito/ *a* implicit; implied
implorante /implo'rante/ *a* imploring
implorar /implo'rar/ *vt* to implore, entreat
implume /im'plume/ *a* without feathers, unfeathered
impolítico /impo'litiko/ *a* impolitic; unwise, inexpedient; tactless
impoluto /impo'luto/ *a* unpolluted, spotless, pure
imponderabilidad /imponderaβili'ðað/ *f*, imponderability
imponderable /imponde'raβle/ *a* imponderable, immeasurable; most excellent
imponente /impo'nente/ *a* imposing; awe-inspiring
imponer /impo'ner/ *vt irr* to exact; impose; malign, accuse falsely; instruct, acquaint; *Fig.* impress (with respect, etc.); invest or deposit (money); *Print.* impose; give, bestow (a name) *—vr* assert oneself. See **poner**
imponible /impo'niβle/ *a* taxable; ratable
impopular /impopu'lar/ *a* unpopular
impopularidad /impopulari'ðað/ *f*, unpopularity
importable /impor'taβle/ *a* importable
importación /importa'θion; importa'sion/ *f*, *Com.* importation; import

importador /importa'ðor/ **(-ra)** *a* import, importing —*n* importer

importancia /impor'tanθia; impor'tansia/ *f,* importance; magnitude

importante /impor'tante/ *a* important

importar /impor'tar/ *vi* to matter; be important; concern, interest; —*vt* amount to; import; include, comprise. **¡No importa!** It doesn't matter! Never mind!

importe /im'porte/ *m,* amount; value, cost. **i. bruto,** gross or total amount. **i. líquido** *or* **neto,** net amount

importunación /importuna'θion; importuna'sion/ *f,* importuning; importunity

importunadamente /importunaða'mente/ *adv* importunately

importunar /importu'nar/ *vt* to importune, pester

importunidad /importuni'ðað/ (*also* **importunación**) *f,* importunity

importuno /impor'tuno/ *a* importunate, inopportune, ill-timed; persistent; tedious

imposibilidad /imposiβili'ðað/ *f,* impossibility

imposibilitado /imposiβili'taðo/ *a* disabled, crippled; incapable, unable

imposibilitar /imposiβili'tar/ *vt* to disable; render unable; make impossible

imposible /impo'siβle/ *a* impossible

imposición /imposi'θion; imposi'sion/ *f,* imposition; exaction; tax, duty, tribute; *Print.* makeup **i. de manos,** *Eccl.* laying on of hands

impostor /impos'tor/ **(-ra)** *n* impostor

impostura /impos'tura/ *f,* swindle, imposture; aspersion, slur, imputation

impotable /impo'taβle/ *a* undrinkable

impotencia /impo'tenθia; impo'tensia/ *f,* impotence

impotente /impo'tente/ *a* impotent; powerless

impracticabilidad /impraktikaβili'ðað/ *f,* impracticability; impassability (of roads, etc.)

impracticable /imprakti'kaβle/ *a* impracticable; impossible; impassable (roads, etc.)

imprecación /impreka'θion; impreka'sion/ *f,* imprecation; curse, malediction

imprecar /impre'kar/ *vt* to imprecate, curse

impregnación /impregna'θion; impregna'sion/ *f,* impregnation, permeation, saturation

impregnar /impreg'nar/ *vt* impregnate; to permeate; —*vr* become impregnated

impremeditado /impremeði'taðo/ *a* unpremeditated

imprenta /im'prenta/ *f,* printing; printing house or office; print; letterpress

impreparación /imprepara'θion; imprepara'sion/ *f,* unpreparedness

imprescindible /impresθin'diβle; impressin'diβle/ *a* indispensable, essential

impresión /impre'sion/ *f,* printing; impression; effect; influence; imprint, stamp; *Print.* impression; print. **impresión digital,** fingerprint

impresionable /impresio'naβle/ *a* impressionable, susceptible

impresionante /impresio'nante/ *a* imposing; moving, affecting

impresionar /impresio'nar/ *vt* to impress; affect; fix in the mind; *Fig.* move deeply, stir; (*Radio.* cinema) record

impresionismo /impresio'nismo/ *m,* impressionism

impresionista /impresio'nista/ *mf* impressionist —*a* impressionistic

impreso /im'preso/ *m,* (gen. *pl*) printed matter

impresor /impre'sor/ *m,* printer

imprevisión /impreβi'sion/ *f,* lack of foresight; im providence

imprevisto /impre'βisto/ *a* unforeseen, unexpected, sudden

imprevistos /impre'βistos/ *m pl,* incidental expenses

imprimación /imprima'θion; imprima'sion/ *f,* priming (of paint, etc.)

imprimar /impri'mar/ *vt* to prime (of paint)

imprimir /impri'mir/ *vt* to print; stamp; impress upon (the mind)

improbabilidad /improβaβili'ðað/ *f,* improbability

improbable /impro'βaβle/ *a* improbable

improbo /im'proβo/ *a* vicious, corrupt, dishonest; hard, arduous

improductivo /improðuk'tiβo/ *a* unproductive; unprofitable, fruitless

impronta /im'pronta/ *f, Art.* cast, mold

impronunciable /impronun'θiaβle; impronun'siaβle/ *a* unpronounceable; ineffable

improperio /impro'perio/ *m,* insult, affront

impropiedad /impropie'ðað/ *f,* inappropriateness; unsuitableness; impropriety

impropio /im'propio/ *a* unsuitable; inappropriate; inadequate; improper

improporcionado /improporθio'naðo; improporsio'naðo/ *a* disproportionate, out of proportion

impróvido /im'proβiðo/ *a* improvident, heedless

improvisación /improβisa'θion; improβisa'sion/ *f,* improvisation

improvisador /improβisa'ðor/ **(-ra)** *n* improviser

improvisamente /improβisa'mente/ *adv* unexpectedly, suddenly

improvisar /improβi'sar/ *vt* to improvise

improviso, improvisto /impro'βiso, impro'βisto/ *a* unexpected, unforeseen. **al** (*or* **de**) **improviso,** unexpectedly

imprudencia /impru'ðenθia; impru'ðensia/ *f,* imprudence, rashness, indiscretion

imprudente /impru'ðente/ *a* imprudent, unwise, rash

impúbero /im'puβero/ *a* below the age of puberty

impudencia /impu'ðenθia; impu'ðensia/ *f,* impudence, impertinence

impudente /impu'ðente/ *a* brazen, impudent

impudicia /impu'ðiθia; impu'ðisia/ *f,* immodesty, brazenness

impúdico /im'puðiko/ *a* immodest, brazen

impuesto /im'puesto/ *m,* tax; duty. **i. de utilidades,** income tax. **i. sucesorio,** inheritance tax

impugnable /impug'naβle/ *a* impugnable, refutable

impugnación /impugna'θion; impugna'sion/ *f,* refutation; contradiction

impugnar /impug'nar/ *vt* to refute, contradict; oppose; criticize

impulsar /impul'sar/ *vt* to impel; prompt, cause; drive, operate, propel

impulsión /impul'sion/ *f,* impulse; impetus; *Mech.* operation, driving; propulsion

impulsivo /impul'siβo/ *a* impulsive; irreflexive, precipitate

impulso /im'pulso/ *m,* stimulus, incitement; impulse, desire; *Mech.* drive, impulse

impulsor /impul'sor/ **(-ra)** *a* driving, impelling —*n* driver, operator

impune /im'pune/ *a* unpunished

impunemente /impune'mente/ *adv* with impunity

impunidad /impuni'ðað/ *f,* impunity

impureza /impu'reθa; impu'resa/ *f,* impurity; lack of chastity; obscenity, indecency

impurificar /impurifi'kar/ *vt* to defile; make impure; adulterate

impuro /im'puro/ *a* impure; adulterated; polluted; immoral, unchaste

imputable /impu'taβle/ *a* imputable

imputación /imputa'θion; imputa'sion/ *f,* imputation

imputador /imputa'ðor/ **(-ra)** *n* imputer, attributer

imputar /impu'tar/ *vt* to impute; attribute

inacabable /inaka'βaβle/ *a* endless, interminable, ceaseless; wearisome

inaccesibilidad /inakθesiβili'ðað; inaksesiβili'ðað/ *f,* inaccessibility

inaccesible /inakθe'siβle; inakse'siβle/ *a* inaccessible; incomprehensible

inacción /inak'θion; inak'sion/ *f,* inaction

inaceptable /inaθep'taβle; inasep'taβle/ *a* unacceptable

inactividad /inaktiβi'ðað/ *f,* inactivity; quiescence; idleness

inactivo /inak'tiβo/ *a* inactive; idle; unemployed; *Naut.* laid-up

inadaptable /inaðap'taβle/ *a* inadaptable

inadecuado /inaðe'kuaðo/ *a* inadequate, insufficient

inadmisible /inaðmi'siβle/ *a* inadmissible

inadvertencia /inaðβer'tenθia; inaðβer'tensia/ *f,* inadvertence; oversight, mistake, slip
inadvertido /inaðβer'tiðo/ *a* unnoticed; inattentive; inadvertent, unintentional; negligent
inafectado /inafek'taðo/ *a* unaffected, natural
inagotable /inago'taβle/ *a* inexhaustible, unfailing; abundant
inaguantable /inaguan'taβle/ *a* unbearable, intolerable
inajenable /inahe'naβle/ *a* inalienable
inalámbrica /ina'lambrika/ *f,* radio station
inalienable /inalie'naβle/ *a* inalienable
inalterable /inalte'raβle/ *a* unalterable
inamovibilidad /inamoβiβili'ðað/ *f,* immovability
inamovible /inamo'βiβle/ *a* immovable
inanición /inani'θion; inani'sion/ *f,* inanition
inanimado /inani'maðo/ *a* inanimate
inapagable /inapa'gaβle/ *a* inextinguishable
inapelable /inape'laβle/ *a* unappealable; irremediable, inevitable
inapetencia /inape'tenθia; inape'tensia/ *f,* lack of appetite
inaplazable /inapla'θaβle; inapla'saβle/ *a* undeferable, unable to be postponed
inaplicable /inapli'kaβle/ *a* inapplicable
inaplicación /inaplika'θion; inaplika'sion/ *f,* laziness, inattention, negligence
inaplicado /inapli'kaðo/ *a* lazy; inattentive; careless
inapreciable /inapre'θiaβle; inapre'siaβle/ *a* inappreciable; invaluable
inarmónico /inar'moniko/ *a* unharmonious, discordant
inarticulado /inartiku'laðo/ *a* inarticulate
inasequible /inase'kiβle/ *a* unattainable; out of reach
inaudible /inau'ðiβle/ *a* inaudible
inaudito /inau'ðito/ *a* unheard of, unprecedented; extraordinary, strange
inauguración /inaugura'θion; inaugura'sion/ *f,* inauguration; induction; inception, commencement
inaugural /inaugu'ral/ *a* inaugural
inaugurar /inaugu'rar/ *vt* to inaugurate; induct
inaveriguable /inaβeri'guaβle/ *a* unascertainable
inca /'inka/ *mf* Inca
incaico /in'kaiko/ *a* Incan
incalculable /inkalku'laβle/ *a* incalculable; innumerable
incalificable /inkalifi'kaβle/ *a* indescribable, unclassable; vile
incandescencia /inkandes'θenθia; inkandes'sensia/ *f,* incandescence, white heat
incandescente /inkandes'θente; inkandes'sente/ *a* incandescent
incansable /inkan'saβle/ *a* indefatigable; unflagging; unwearying
incapacidad /inkapaθi'ðað; inkapasi'ðað/ *f,* incapacity; incompetence
incapacitar /inkapaθi'tar; inkapasi'tar/ *vt* to incapacitate; disable
incapaz /inka'paθ; inka'pas/ *a* incapable, incompetent; inefficient
incasable /inka'saβle/ *a* unmarriageable; antimarriage
incautarse /inkau'tarse/ *vr* to seize, take possession (of)
incauto /in'kauto/ *a* incautious; unwary
incendiar /inθen'diar; insen'diar/ *vt* to set on fire, set alight
incendiario /inθen'diario; insen'diario/ **(-ia)** *a* and *n* incendiary
incendiarismo /inθendia'rismo; insendia'rismo/ *m,* incendiarism
incendio /in'θendio; in'sendio/ *m,* conflagration, fire; consuming passion
incensar /inθen'sar; insen'sar/ *vt irr Eccl.* to cense, incense; flatter. See **acertar**
incensario /inθen'sario; insen'sario/ *m,* incense burner, incensory
incentivo /inθen'tiβo; insen'tiβo/ *m,* incentive; encouragement
incertidumbre /inθerti'ðumbre; inserti'ðumbre/ *f,* uncertainty, incertitude
incesable, incesante /inθe'saβle, inθe'sante; inse'saβle, inse'sante/ *a* incessant, continuous
incesto /in'θesto; in'sesto/ *m,* incest
incestuoso /inθes'tuoso; inses'tuoso/ *a* incestuous
incidencia /inθi'ðenθia; insi'ðensia/ *f,* incidence
incidental /inθiðen'tal; insiðen'tal/ *a* incidental
incidente /inθi'ðente; insi'ðente/ *a* incidental. *m,* incident, event, occurrence
incidir /inθi'ðir; insi'ðir/ *vi* (*with en*) to incur, fall into (e.g. *Incidió en el pecado,* He fell into sin)
incienso /in'θienso; in'sienso/ *m,* incense; flattery
incierto /in'θierto; in'sierto/ *a* untrue, false; uncertain; unknown
incineración /inθinera'θion; insinera'sion/ *f,* incineration
incinerador /inθinera'ðor; insinera'ðor/ *m,* incinerator
incinerar /inθine'rar; insine'rar/ *vt* incinerate, reduce to ashes
incipiente /inθi'piente; insi'piente/ *a* incipient
incircunciso /inθirkun'θiso; insirkun'siso/ *a* uncircumcised
incisión /inθi'sion; insi'sion/ *f,* incision
incisivo /inθi'siβo; insi'siβo/ *a* sharp, keen; incisive, sarcastic, caustic
inciso /in'θiso; in'siso/ *m,* clause; comma
incitación /inθita'θion; insita'sion/ *f,* incitement; *Fig.* spur, stimulus
incitar /inθi'tar; insi'tar/ *vt* to incite; stimulate, encourage
incivil /inθi'βil; insi'βil/ *a* rude, discourteous, uncivil
incivilidad /inθiβili'ðað; insiβili'ðað/ *f,* rudeness, incivility
inclasificable /inklasifi'kaβle/ *a* unclassifiable
inclemencia /inkle'menθia; inkle'mensia/ *f,* harshness, severity; inclemency (of the weather). **a la i.,** at the mercy of the elements
inclemente /inkle'mente/ *a* inclement
inclinación /inklina'θion; inklina'sion/ *f,* inclination; slope; slant; tendency, propensity; predilection, fondness; bow (in greeting); *Geom.* inclination
inclinar /inkli'nar/ *vt* to incline, tilt, slant; bow; bend; influence; persuade; —*vi* resemble; —*vr* lean; stoop; tilt; tend, incline (to), view favorably (e.g. *Me inclino a creerlo,* I am inclined to believe it)
ínclito /in'klito/ *a* famous, celebrated
incluir /in'kluir/ *vt irr* to comprise, embrace, contain; include, take into account. See **huir**
inclusa /in'klusa/ *f,* foundling home
inclusión /inklu'sion/ *f,* inclusion; relationship, intercourse, friendship
inclusive /inklu'siβe/ *adv* including
inclusivo /inklu'siβo/ *a* inclusive
incluso /in'kluso/ *adv* including, inclusive —*prep* even
incoar /inko'ar/ *vt* to begin (especially lawsuits)
incoativo /inkoa'tiβo/ *a* inceptive
incobrable /inko'βraβle/ *a* irrecoverable; irredeemable
incógnita /in'kognita/ *f, Math.* X; unknown quantity; secret motive; unknown lady
incógnito /in'kognito/ *a* unknown. *m,* incognito, assumed name, disguise
incoherencia /inkoe'renθia; inkoe'rensia/ *f,* incoherence
incoherente /inkoe'rente/ *a* incoherent, disconnected, illogical
íncola /'inkola/ *mf* resident, dweller, inhabitant
incoloro /inko'loro/ *a* colorless, uncolored
incólume /in'kolume/ *a* unharmed, unscathed; untouched, undamaged
incombustibilidad /inkombustiβili'ðað/ *f,* incombustibility
incommensurabilidad /inkommensuraβili'ðað/ *f,* incommensurability
incommutable /inkommu'taβle/ *a* unalterable, immutable, unchangeable
incomodar /inkomo'ðar/ *vt* to disturb, incommode, inconvenience; annoy; —*vr* disturb oneself, put oneself out; grow angry. **¡No se incomode!** Please don't move!; Please don't be angry!

incomodidad /inkomoði'ðað/ *f*, discomfort; inconvenience; trouble, upset; annoyance
incómodo /in'komoðo/ *a* uncomfortable; inconvenient; troublesome, tiresome. *m*, discomfort; inconvenience
incomparable /inkompa'raβle/ *a* incomparable
incompartible /inkompar'tiβle/ *a* indivisible
incompasivo /inkompa'siβo/ *a* unsympathetic, hard
incompatibilidad /inkompatiβili'ðað/ *f*, incompatibility
incompatible /inkompa'tiβle/ *a* incompatible
incompetencia /inkompe'tenθia; inkompe'tensia/ *f*, incompetence
incompetente /inkompe'tente/ *a* incompetent
incomplejo, incomplexo /inkom'pleho, inkom'plekso/ *a* noncomplex, simple
incompleto /inkom'pleto/ *a* incomplete
incomponible /inkompo'niβle/ *a* unrepairable, unmendable
incomprensibilidad /inkomprensiβili'ðað/ *f*, incomprehensibility
incomprensible /inkompren'siβle/ *a* incomprehensible
incomprensión /inkompren'sion/ *f*, incomprehension
incomunicado /inkomuni'kaðo/ *a* in solitary confinement (of a prisoner)
incomunicar /inkomuni'kar/ *vt* to sentence to solitary confinement; isolate, deprive of means of communication; *—vr* become a recluse
inconcebible /inkonθe'βiβle; inkonseβiβle/ *a* inconceivable
inconciliable /inkonθi'liaβle; inkonsi'liaβle/ *a* irreconcilable
incondicional /inkondiθio'nal; inkondisio'nal/ *a* unconditional
inconexión /inkone'ksion/ *f*, disconnectedness
inconexo /inkone'kso/ *a* unconnected; incoherent
inconfeso /inkon'feso/ *a* unconfessed
incongruencia /inkoŋgru'enθia; inkoŋgru'ensia/ *f*, incongruity
incongruente /inkoŋgru'ente/ *a* incongruous, inappropriate
inconmovible /inkomo'βiβle/ *a* immovable; unflinching, unshakable
inconquistable /inkonkis'taβle/ *a* unconquerable; *Fig.* resolute, inflexible
inconsciencia /inkon'sθienθia; inkonssiensia/ *f*, unconsciousness; subconscious
inconsciente /inkon'sθiente; inkons'siente/ *a* unconscious, involuntary; subconscious
inconsecuencia /inkonse'kuenθia; inkonse'kuensia/ *f*, inconsequence; inconsistency
inconsecuente /inkonse'kuente/ *a* inconsequential; inconsistent
inconsideración /inkonsiðera'θion; inkonsiðera'sion/ *f*, thoughtlessness
inconsiderado /inkonsiðe'raðo/ *a* thoughtless; heedless, selfish
inconsiguiente /inkonsi'giente/ *a* illogical, inconsistent
inconsistencia /inkonsis'tenθia; inkonsis'tensia/ *f*, inconsistency
inconsistente /inkonsis'tente/ *a* inconsistent
inconsolable /inkonso'laβle/ *a* inconsolable
inconstancia /inkons'tanθia; inkons'tansia/ *f*, inconstancy, infidelity
inconstante /inkons'tante/ *a* inconstant, fickle
inconstitucional /inkonstituθio'nal; inkonstitusio'nal/ *a* unconstitutional
incontaminado /inkontami'naðo/ *a* uncontaminated
incontestable /inkontes'taβle/ *a* undeniable, unquestionable
incontinencia /inkonti'nenθia; inkonti'nensia/ *f*, incontinence
incontinente /inkonti'nente/ *a* incontinent
incontrastable /inkontras'taβle/ *a* insuperable, invincible; undeniable, unanswerable; *Fig.* unshakable, inconvincible
incontrovertible /inkontroβer'tiβle/ *a* undeniable, incontrovertible
inconvencible /inkomben'θiβle; inkomben'siβle/ *a* inconvincible
inconveniencia /inkombe'nienθia; inkombe'niensia/ *f*, discomfort; inconvenience; unsuitability
inconveniente /inkombe'niente/ *a* awkward, inconvenient; uncomfortable; inappropriate. *m*, inconvenience; obstacle, impediment; disadvantage
inconvertible /inkomber'tiβle/ *a* inconvertible
incorporación /inkorpora'θion; inkorpora'sion/ *f*, incorporation
incorporar /inkorpo'rar/ *vt* to incorporate; cause to sit up, lift up; *—vr* sit up, raise oneself; become a member, join (associations); be incorporated; blend, mix
incorporeidad /inkorporei'ðað/ *f*, incorporeity
incorpóreo /inkor'poreo/ *a* incorporeal; immaterial
incorrección /inkorrek'θion; inkorrek'sion/ *f*, incorrectness; indecorum, impropriety
incorrecto /inko'rrekto/ *a* incorrect; indecorous, unbecoming, improper
incorregible /inkorre'hiβle/ *a* incorrigible
incorrupción /inkorrup'θion; inkorrup'sion/ *f*, incorruption; purity; integrity; wholesomeness
incorrupto /inko'rrupto/ *a* incorrupt; pure; chaste
incredibilidad /inkreðiβili'ðað/ *f*, incredibility
incredulidad /inkreðuli'ðað/ *f*, incredulity, scepticism
incrédulo /in'kreðulo/ **(-la)** *a* incredulous; atheistic *—n* atheist; unbeliever, sceptic
increíble /inkre'iβle/ *a* incredible; marvelous, extraordinary
incremento /inkre'mento/ *m*, increment, increase
increpación /inkrepa'θion; inkrepa'sion/ *f*, scolding, harsh rebuke
increpar /inkre'par/ *vt* to scold, rebuke harshly
incriminante /inkrimi'nante/ *a* incriminating
incriminar /inkrimi'nar/ *vt* to incriminate, accuse; exaggerate (a charge, etc.)
incruento /inkru'ento/ *a* bloodless, unstained with blood
incrustación /inkrusta'θion; inkrusta'sion/ *f*, incrustation; *Art.* inlay
incubación /inkuβa'θion; inkuβa'sion/ *f*, hatching; *Med.* incubation
incubadora /inkuβa'ðora/ *f*, incubator (for chickens)
incubar /inku'βar/ *vi* to sit on eggs (of hens); *—vt* hatch; *Med.* incubate
inculcación /inkulka'θion; inkulka'sion/ *f*, inculcation, instillment
inculcar /inkul'kar/ *vt* to press one thing against another; instill, inculcate; *—vr* grow more fixed in one's views
inculpable /inkul'paβle/ *a* blameless, innocent
inculpar /inkul'par/ *vt* to blame; accuse
incultivable /inkulti'βaβle/ *a* uncultivatable; untillable
inculto /in'kulto/ *a* uncultivated, untilled; uncultured; uncivilized
incultura /inkul'tura/ *f*, lack of cultivation; lack of culture
incumbencia /inkum'benθia; inkumbensia/ *f*, obligation, moral responsibility, duty
incumbir /inkum'bir/ *vi* to be incumbent on; concern
incumplimiento /inkumpli'miento/ *m*, nonfulfilment
incurable /inku'raβle/ *a* incurable; inveterate, hopeless
incuria /in'kuria/ *f*, negligence, carelessness
incurioso /inku'rioso/ *a* incurious
incurrir /inku'rrir/ *vi* (*with en*) to fall into (error, etc.); incur (dislike, etc.)
incursión /inkur'sion/ *f*, incursion; inroad
indagación /indaga'θion; indaga'sion/ *f*, investigation, inquiry
indagador /indaga'ðor/ **(-ra)** *a* investigating, inquiring *—n* investigator
indagar /inda'gar/ *vt* to investigate, examine; inquire. **i. precios,** to inquire about prices
indebido /inde'βiðo/ *a* undue, immoderate improper; illegal, illicit
indecencia /inde'θenθia; inde'sensia/ *f*, indecency; obscenity; impropriety

indecente /inde'θente; inde'sente/ *a* indecent; obscene; improper
indecible /inde'θiβle; inde'siβle/ *a* unutterable, ineffable, unspeakable
indeciso /inde'θiso; inde'siso/ *a* undecided; hesitant, irresolute; vague; noncommittal
indeclinable /indekli'naβle/ *a* obligatory; unavoidable; *Gram.* indeclinable, uninflected
indecoro /inde'koro/ *m,* impropriety, indecorum
indecoroso /indeko'roso/ *a* indecorous, unbecoming; base, mean
indefectible /indefek'tiβle/ *a* unfailing; perfect
indefectiblemente /indefektiβle'mente/ *adv* invariably
indefendible /indefen'diβle/ *a* indefensible
indefenso /inde'fenso/ *a* unprotected, defenseless
indefinible /indefi'niβle/ *a* indefinable, vague; indescribable
indefinido /indefi'niðo/ *a* indefinite, vague; undefined; *Gram.* indefinite
indeleble /inde'leβle/ *a* indelible
indeliberado /indeliβe'raðo/ *a* unpremeditated; unconsidered
indemme /in'demme/ *a* unharmed, undamaged
indemnidad /indemni'ðað/ *f,* indemnity
indemnización /indemniθa'θion; indemnisa'sion/ *f,* compensation, indemnification; indemnity
indemnizar /indemni'θar; indemni'sar/ *vt* to indemnify, compensate
indemostrable /indemo'straβle/ *a* indemonstrable, incapable of demonstration
independencia /indepen'denθia; indepen'densia/ *f,* independence
independiente /indepen'diente/ *a* independent; self-contained
indescifrable /indesθi'fraβle; indessi'fraβle/ *a* undecipherable; illegible
indestructible /indestruk'tiβle/ *a* indestructible
indeterminado /indetermi'naðo/ *a* indeterminate; vague, doubtful, uncertain; hesitant, irresolute; *Math.* indeterminate
indiano /in'diano/ **(-na)** *a* and *n* Indian; East Indian; West Indian. *m,* nouveau riche, one who returns rich from the Western Hemisphere
indicación /indika'θion; indika'sion/ *f,* indication; sign, evidence; intimation, hint
indicador /indika'ðor/ *a* indicative. *m,* indicator. **i. del nivel de gasolina,** gas gauge
indicar /indi'kar/ *vt* to indicate; show; point out; simply, suggest; intimate
indicativo /indika'tiβo/ *a* indicative —*a* and *m, Gram.* indicative
índice /'indiθe; 'indise/ *m,* index; indication, sign; library catalog; catalog room; hand (of a clock); pointer, needle (of instruments); gnomon (of a sundial); *Math.* index; forefinger. **I. expurgatorio,** the Index
indicio /in'diθio; in'disio/ *m,* indication; sign; evidence. **indicios vehementes,** circumstantial evidence
índico /'indiko/ *a* Indian
indiferencia /indife'renθia; indife'rensia/ *f,* indifference
indiferente /indife'rente/ *a* indifferent
indígena /in'dihena/ *a* native, indigenous. *mf* native
indigencia /indi'henθia; indi'hensia/ *f,* destitution, indigence; impecuniosity
indigente /indi'hente/ *a* destitute, indigent; impecunious
indigestión /indihes'tion/ *f,* indigestion
indigesto /indi'hesto/ *a* indigestible; *Lit.* muddled, confused; unsociable, brusque
indignación /indigna'θion; indigna'sion/ *f,* indignation, anger
indignado /indig'naðo/ *a* indignant
indignar /indig'nar/ *vt* to anger, make indignant; —*vr* grow angry
indignidad /indigni'ðað/ *f,* unworthiness; indignity; personal affront
indigno /in'digno/ *a* unworthy; base, despicable
índigo /'indigo/ *m,* indigo
indio /'indio/ **(-ia)** *a* Indian; blue —*n* Indian. *m,* indium
indirecta /indi'rekta/ *f,* hint, covert suggestion, innuendo. *Inf.* **i. del padre Cobos,** strong hint
indirecto /indi'rekto/ *a* indirect
indisciplina /indisθi'plina; indissi'plina/ *f,* indiscipline
indisciplinado /indisθipli'naðo; indissipli'naðo/ *a* undisciplined
indiscreción /indiskre'θion; indiskre'sion/ *f,* indiscretion
indiscreto /indis'kreto/ *a* indiscreet
indiscutible /indisku'tiβle/ *a* unquestionable, undeniable
indisoluble /indiso'luβle/ *a* indissoluble
indispensable /indispen'saβle/ *a* indispensable
indisponer /indispo'ner/ *vt irr* to make unfit or incapable; indispose, make ill; (*with con or contra*) set against, make trouble with; —*vr* be indisposed; (*with con or contra*) quarrel with. See **poner**
indisposición /indisposi'θion; indisposi'sion/ *f,* reluctance, disinclination; indisposition, brief illness
indisputable /indispu'taβle/ *a* indisputable
indistinguible /indistiŋ'guiβle/ *a* undistinguishable
indistinto /indis'tinto/ *a* indistinct; indeterminate; vague
individual /indiβi'ðual/ *a* individual; peculiar, characteristic. *m,* (tennis) single
individualidad /indiβiðuali'ðað/ *f,* individuality
individualismo /indiβiðua'lismo/ *m,* individualism
individualista /indiβiðua'lista/ *a* individualistic. *mf* individualist
individuo /indi'βiðuo/ **(-ua)** *a* individual; indivisible. *m,* individual; member, associate; *Inf.* self —*n Inf.* person
indivisibilidad /indiβisiβili'ðað/ *f,* indivisibility
indivisible /indiβi'siβle/ *a* indivisible
indiviso /indi'βiso/ *a* undivided
indochino /indo'tʃino/ **(-na)** *a* and *n* Indochinese
indócil /in'doθil; in'dosil/ *a* unmanageable; disobedient; brittle, unpliable (of metals)
indocilidad /indoθili'ðað; indosili'ðað/ *f,* indocility; disobedience; brittleness (of metals)
indoeuropeo /indoeuro'peo/ *a* Indo-European
indoísmo /indo'ismo/ *m,* Hinduism
índole /'indole/ *f,* temperament, nature; kind, sort
indolencia /indo'lenθia; indo'lensia/ *f,* idleness, indolence
indolente /indo'lente/ *a* nonpainful; indifferent, insensible; idle, indolent
indoloro /indo'loro/ *a* painless
indomable /indo'maβle/ *a* untamable; invincible; indomitable; ungovernable, unmanageable
indomado /indo'maðo/ *a* untamed
indómito /in'domito/ *a* untamed; untamable; unmanageable, unruly; indomitable
indonesio /indo'nesio/ **(-ia)** *a* and *n* Indonesian
indostanés /indosta'nes/ *a* Hindustani
indostani /indos'tani/ *m,* Hindustani (language)
indubitable /induβi'taβle/ *a* unquestionable
inducción /induk'θion; induk'sion/ *f,* persuasion; *Phys.* induction
inducir /indu'θir; indu'sir/ *vt irr* to persuade, prevail upon; induce; infer, conclude. See **conducir**
inductivo, inductor /induk'tiβo, induk'tor/ *a* inductive
indudable /indu'ðaβle/ *a* indubitable
indulgencia /indul'henθia; indul'hensia/ *f,* overkindness, tenderness; *Eccl.* indulgence
indulgente /indul'hente/ *a* indulgent, tender; tolerant
indultar /indul'tar/ *vt* to pardon; exempt
indulto /in'dulto/ *m,* amnesty; exemption; forgiveness; *Eccl.* indult
indumentaria /indumen'taria/ *f,* clothing; outfit (of clothes)
industria /in'dustria/ *f,* assiduity, industriousness; pains, effort, ingenuity; industry. **i. pesada,** heavy industry. **i. cárnica,** meat industry. **i. extractivos,** mining industry
industrial /indus'trial/ *a* industrial. *m,* industrialist

industrialismo /industria'lismo/ *m,* industrialism
industrialización /industriali θa'θion; industrialisa'sion/ *f,* industrialization
industriar /indus'triar/ *vt* to teach, train; *—vr* find a way, manage, succeed in
industrioso /indus'trioso/ *a* industrious; diligent, assiduous
inédito /i'neðito/ *a* unpublished; unedited
inefable /ine'faβle/ *a* ineffable
ineficacia /inefi'kaθia; inefi'kasia/ *f,* inefficiency; ineffectiveness
ineficaz /inefi'kaθ; inefi'kas/ *a* ineffective; inefficient
ineludible /inelu'ðiβle/ *a* unavoidable
ineptitud /inepti'tuð/ *f,* ineptitude
inepto /i'nepto/ *a* inept, incompetent; unfit, unsuitable
inequívoco /ine'kiβoko/ *a* unequivocal
inercia /i'nerθia; i'nersia/ *f,* inertia
inerme /i'nerme/ *a* defenseless, unprotected; (*Bot. Zool.*) unarmed
inerte /i'nerte/ *a* inert
inescrutable /ineskru'taβle/ *a* inscrutable, unfathomable
inesperado /inespe'raðo/ *a* unexpected, sudden
inestabilidad /inestaβili'ðað/ *f,* instability
inestable /ines'taβle/ *a* unstable
inestimable /inesti'maβle/ *a* inestimable
inevitable /ineβi'taβle/ *a* inevitable
inexactitud /ineksakti'tuð/ *f,* inexactitude, inaccuracy; error, mistake
inexacto /ine'ksakto/ *a* inexact, inaccurate; erroneous
inexcusable /ineksku'saβle/ *a* inexcusable, unforgivable; indispensable
inexhausto /ineks'austo/ *a* inexhaustible
inexistente /ineksis'tente/ *a* nonexistent
inexorable /inekso'raβle/ *a* inexorable
inexperiencia /inekspe'rienθia; inekspe'riensia/ *f,* inexperience
inexperto /ineks'perto/ *a* inexperienced; inexpert
inexplicable /inekspli'kaβle/ *a* inexplicable
inexplorado /ineksplo'raðo/ *a* unexplored
inexplosible /ineksplo'siβle/ *a* inexplosive
inexpresivo /inekspre'siβo/ *a* inexpressive; reticent
inexpugnable /inekspug'naβle/ *a* impregnable; *Fig.* unshakable, firm; obstinate
inextinguible /inekstiŋ'guiβle/ *a* inextinguishable; everlasting, perpetual
infalibilidad /infaliβili'ðað/ *f,* infallibility
infalible /infa'liβle/ *a* infallible
infamación /infama'θion; infama'sion/ *f,* defamation
infamador /infama'ðor/ **(-ra)** *a* slandering *—n* slanderer
infamar /infa'mar/ *vt* to defame, slander
infame /in'fame/ *a* infamous, vile
infamia /in'famia/ *f,* infamy; baseness, vileness
infancia /in'fanθia; in'fansia/ *f,* infancy, babyhood; childhood
infanta /in'fanta/ *f,* female child under seven years; infanta, any Spanish royal princess; wife of a Spanish royal prince
infantado /infan'taðo/ *m,* land belonging to an *infante* or *infanta*
infante /in'fante/ *m,* male child under seven years; infante, any Spanish royal prince except an heir-apparent; infantryman. **i. de coro,** choir boy
infantería /infante'ria/ *f,* infantry
infanticida /infanti'θiða; infanti'siða/ *a* infanticidal. *mf* infanticide (person)
infanticidio /infanti'θiðio; infanti'siðio/ *m,* infanticide (act)
infantil /infan'til/ *a* infantile, babyish; innocent, candid
infatigable /infati'gaβle/ *a* unwearying, indefatigable
infatuación /infatua'θion; infatua'sion/ *f,* infatuation
infatuar /infa'tuar/ *vt* to infatuate; *—vr* become infatuated
infausto /in'fausto/ *a* unlucky, unfortunate
infección /infek'θion; infek'sion/ *f,* infection
infeccioso /infek'θioso; infek'sioso/ *a* infectious
infectar /infek'tar/ *vt* to infect; corrupt, pervert; *—vr* become infected; be corrupted
infecto /in'fekto/ *a* infected; corrupt, perverted; tainted
infecundidad /infekundi'ðað/ *f,* sterility
infecundo /infe'kundo/ *a* sterile, barren
infelice /infe'liθe; infe'lise/ *a Poet.* unhappy, unfortunate
infelicidad /infeliθi'ðað; infelisi'ðað/ *f,* unhappiness
infeliz /infe'liθ; infe'lis/ *a* unhappy; unfortunate; *Inf.* simple, good-hearted
inferencia /infe'renθia; infe'rensia/ *f,* inference, connection
inferior /infe'rior/ *a* inferior; lower; second-rate; subordinate. *mf* inferior, subordinate
inferioridad /inferiori'ðað/ *f,* inferiority
inferir /infe'rir/ *vt irr* to infer, deduce; involve, imply; occasion; inflict. See **sentir**
infernáculo /infer'nakulo/ *m,* hopscotch
infernal /infer'nal/ *a* infernal; devilish, fiendish; wicked, inhuman; *Inf.* confounded
inferno /in'ferno/ *a Poet.* infernal
infértil /in'fertil/ *a* infertile
infestación /infesta'θion; infesta'sion/ *f,* infestation
infestar /infes'tar/ *vt* to infest, swarm in; infect; injure, damage
infesto /in'festo/ *a Poet.* harmful, dangerous
inficionar /infiθio'nar; infisio'nar/ *vt* to infect; pervert, corrupt
infidelidad /infiðeli'ðað/ *f,* faithlessness, infidelity; disbelief in Christian religion; unbelievers, infidels
infidelísimo /infiðe'lisimo/, *a superl* **infiel** most disloyal; most incorrect; most incredulous, faithless
infidencia /infi'ðenθia; infi'ðensia/ *f,* disloyalty, faithlessness
infiel /in'fiel/ *a* unfaithful, disloyal; inaccurate, incorrect; infidel, unbelieving. *mf* infidel, nonbeliever
infierno /in'fierno/ *m,* hell; hades (gen. *pl*); *Fig. Inf.* inferno. **en el quinto i.,** very far off, at the end of the world. **en los quintos infiernos,** at the end of nowhere
infiltración /infiltra'θion; infiltra'sion/ *f,* infiltration; inculcation, implantation
infiltrar /infil'trar/ *vt* to infiltrate; imbue, inculcate
ínfimo /'infimo/ *a* lowest; meanest, vilest, most base; cheapest, poorest (in quality)
infinidad /infini'ðað/ *f,* infinity; infinitude; great number
infinitivo /infini'tiβo/ *a* and *m, Gram.* infinitive
infinito /infi'nito/ *a* infinite; endless; boundless; countless. *m, Math.* infinite *—adv* excessively, immensely
infinitud /infini'tuð/ *f,* See **infinidad**
inflación /infla'θion; infla'sion/ *f,* inflation; distension; pride, vanity
inflacionismo /inflaθio'nismo; inflasio'nismo/ *m,* inflationism
inflacionista /inflaθio'nista; inflasio'nista/ *mf* inflationist
inflamabilidad /inflamaβili'ðað/ *f,* inflammability
inflamable /infla'maβle/ *a* inflammable
inflamación /inflama'θion; inflama'sion/ *f,* inflammation; *Engin.* ignition
inflamador /inflama'ðor/ *a* inflammatory
inflamar /infla'mar/ *vt* to set on fire; *Fig.* inflame, excite; *—vr* take fire; *Med.* become inflamed; grow hot or excited
inflamatorio /inflama'torio/ *a Med.* inflammatory
inflar /in'flar/ *vt* to inflate; blow up, distend; throw out (one's chest); exaggerate; make haughty or vain; *—vr* be swollen or inflated; be puffed up with pride
inflexibilidad /infleksiβili'ðað/ *f,* inflexibility; rigidity; immovability, constancy
inflexible /infle'ksiβle/ *a* inflexible
inflexión /infle'ksion/ *f,* bending, flexion; diffraction (optics); inflection
infligir /infli'hir/ *vt* to impose, inflict (penalties)
influencia /influ'enθia; influ'ensia/ *f,* influence; power, authority; *Elec.* charge
influir /in'fluir/ *vt irr* to influence; affect; (*with en*) cooperate in, assist with. See **huir**

influjo /in'fluho/ *m,* influence; flux, inflow of the tide
influyente /influ'yente/ *a* influential
infolio /in'folio/ *m,* folio
información /informa'θion; informa'sion/ *f,* information; legal inquiry; report; research, investigation
informador /informa'ðor/ **(-ra)** *a* informing, acquainting —*n* informant
informal /infor'mal/ *a* informal, irregular; unreliable (of persons); unconventional
informalidad /informali'ðað/ *f,* irregularity; unconventionality; unreliability
informante /infor'mante/ *mf* informant
informar /infor'mar/ *vt* to inform, acquaint with; —*vi Law.* plead; —*vr* (*with de, en, or sobre*) find out about, investigate
informática /infor'matika/ *f,* information sciences
informativo /informa'tiβo/ *a* informative
informe /in'forme/ *a* formless, shapeless. *m,* report, statement; information; *Law.* plea; *pl* data, particulars; references
infortificable /infortifi'kaβle/ *a* unfortifiable
infortuna /infor'tuna/ *f, Astrol.* evil influence
infortunado /infortu'naðo/ *a* unfortunate
infortunio /infor'tunio/ *m,* misfortune; unhappiness, adversity; mischance, ill luck
infracción /infrak'θion; infrak'sion/ *f,* transgression, infringement
infracto /in'frakto/ *a* imperturbable
infractor /infrak'tor/ **(-ra)** *a* infringing —*n* transgressor, infringer
infrangible /infran'hiβle/ *a* unbreakable
infranqueable /infranke'aβle/ *a* insuperable, unsurmountable
infrarrojo /infra'rroho/ *a* infrared
infrascrito /infras'krito/ *a* undersigned; undermentioned
infrecuente /infre'kuente/ *a* infrequent
infringir /infrin'hir/ *vt* to infringe, transgress, break
infructífero /infruk'tifero/ *a* unfruitful; worthless, useless
infructuosidad /infruktuosi'ðað/ *f,* unfruitfulness; worthlessness, uselessness
infructuoso /infruk'tuoso/ *a* fruitless; useless, worthless
infumable /infu'maβle/ *a* unsmokable (of tobacco)
infundado /infun'daðo/ *a* unfounded, groundless
infundio /in'fundio/ *m, Inf.* nonsense, untruth
infundir /infun'dir/ *vt* to infuse, imbue with
infusión /infu'sion/ *f,* infusion
ingeniar /inhe'niar/ *vt* to devise, concoct, plan; —*vr* contrive, find a way, manage
ingeniería /inhenie'ria/ *f,* engineering
ingeniero /inhe'niero/ *m,* engineer. **i. agrónomo,** agricultural engineer. **i. de caminos, canales y puertos,** civil engineer. **i. radiotelegrafista,** radio engineer. **cuerpo de ingenieros,** royal engineers
ingenio /in'henio/ *m,* mind; inventive capacity; imaginative talent; man of genius; talent, cleverness; ingeniousness; machine; guillotine (bookbinding)
ingeniosidad /inheniosi'ðað/ *f,* ingeniousness; witticism, clever remark
ingenioso /inhe'nioso/ *a* talented, clever; ingenious
ingénito /in'henito/ *a* unengendered, unconceived; innate, inborn
ingente /in'hente/ *a* huge, enormous
ingenuidad /inhenui'ðað/ *f,* ingenuousness, naiveté
ingenuo /in'henuo/ *a* ingenuous, naive, artless, unaffected
Inglaterra /iŋgla'terra/ England
ingle /'iŋgle/ *f,* groin
inglés /iŋ'gles/ **(-esa)** *a* English; British —*n* Englishman; Briton. *m,* English (language); *Inf.* creditor. **a la inglesa,** in English fashion. **marcharse a la inglesa,** *Inf.* to take French leave
inglesismo /iŋgle'sismo/ *m,* Anglicism
ingobernable /iŋgoβer'naβle/ *a* ungovernable, unruly
ingratitud /iŋgrati'tuð/ *f,* ingratitude
ingrato /iŋ'grato/ *a* ungrateful; irksome, thankless; disagreeable
ingrávido /iŋ'graβiðo/ *a* light weight
ingrediente /iŋgre'ðiente/ *m,* ingredient
ingresar /iŋgre'sar/ *vi* to return, come in (money); (*with en*) join, become a member of, enter
ingreso /iŋ'greso/ *m,* joining, entering, admission; *Com.* money received; opening, commencement; *pl* earnings, takings, revenue
ingurgitación /iŋgurhita'θion; iŋgurhita'sion/ *f, Med.* ingurgitation
ingurgitar /iŋgurhi'tar/ *vt* to ingurgitate, swallow
inhábil /in'aβil/ *a* unskillful; unpracticed; incompetent, unfit; unsuitable, ill-chosen
inhabilidad /inaβili'ðað/ *f,* unskillfulness; incompetence; unsuitability; inability
inhabilitación /inaβilita'θion; inaβilita'sion/ *f,* incapacitation; disqualification; disablement
inhabilitar /inaβili'tar/ *vt* to make ineligible; disqualify; incapacitate, make unfit; —*vr* become ineligible; be incapacitated
inhabitable /inaβi'taβle/ *a* uninhabitable
inhabitado /inaβi'taðo/ *a* uninhabited, deserted
inhalación /inala'θion; inala'sion/ *f,* inhalation
inhalador /inala'ðor/ *m, Med.* inhaler
inhalar /ina'lar/ *vt* to inhale
inhallable /ina'ʎaβle; ina'yaβle/ *a* nowhere to be found, unfindable
inheredítable /inereði'taβle/ *a* uninheritable
inherencia /ine'renθia; ine'rensia/ *f,* inherency
inherente /ine'rente/ *a* inherent, innate
inhestar /ines'tar/ *vt irr* to raise, lift up; erect. See **acertar**
inhibición /iniβi'θion; iniβi'sion/ *f,* inhibition
inhibir /ini'βir/ *vt Law.* to inhibit; —*vr* inhibit or restrain oneself. See **prohibir**
inhibitorio /iniβi'torio/ *a Law.* inhibitory
inhonesto /ino'nesto/ *a* indecent, obscene; immodest
inhospedable, inhospitalario /inospe'ðaβle, inospita'lario/ *a* inhospitable; bleak, uninviting; exposed
inhospitalidad /inospitali'ðað/ *f,* inhospitality
inhumación /inuma'θion; inuma'sion/ *f,* inhumation, burial
inhumadora /inuma'ðora/ *f,* crematory
inhumanidad /inumani'ðað/ *f,* inhumanity; brutality
inhumano /inu'mano/ *a* inhuman; brutal, barbarous
inhumar /inu'mar/ *vt* to bury, inter
iniciación /iniθia'θion; inisia'sion/ *f,* initiation
iniciador /iniθia'ðor; inisia'ðor/ **(-ra)** *a* initiating; —*n* initiator
inicial /ini'θial; ini'sial/ *a* and *f,* initial
iniciar /ini'θiar; ini'siar/ *vt* to initiate; admit, introduce; originate; —*vr* be initiated; *Eccl.* take minor or first orders
iniciativa /iniθia'tiβa; inisia'tiβa/ *f,* initiative
inicuo /ini'kuo/ *a* iniquitous, most unjust, wicked
inimaginable /inimahi'naβle/ *a* inconceivable
inimicísimo /inimi'θisimo; inimi'sisimo/ *a superl* **enemigo** most hostile
inimitable /inimi'taβle/ *a* inimitable
ininteligible /ininteli'hiβle/ *a* unintelligible
iniquidad /iniki'ðað/ *f,* iniquity, wickedness
injerir /inhe'rir/ *vt irr* to insert, place within, introduce; interpolate; —*vr* meddle. See **sentir**
injertar /inher'tar/ *vt Agr.* to graft
injerto /in'herto/ *m, Agr.* graft; grafting; grafted plant, briar, or tree
injuria /in'huria/ *f,* insult; slander; outrage; wrong, injustice; harm, damage
injuriador /inhuria'ðor/ **(-ra)** *a* insulting —*n* offender, persecutor
injuriar /inhu'riar/ *vt* to insult; slander; outrage; wrong, persecute; harm, damage
injurioso /inhu'rioso/ *a* insulting; slanderous; offensive, abusive; harmful
injusticia /inhus'tiθia; inhus'tisia/ *f,* injustice; lack of justice; unjust action
injustificable /inhustifi'kaβle/ *a* unjustifiable
injustificado /inhustifi'kaðo/ *a* unjustified
injusto /in'husto/ *a* unjust; unrighteous
inllevable /inʎe'βaβle; inye'βaβle/ *a* unbearable, intolerable

inmaculado /imaku'laðo/ *a* immaculate, pure
inmanejable /imane'haβle/ *a* unmanageable; uncontrollable
inmanencia /ima'nenθia; ima'nensia/ *f,* immanence
inmanente /ima'nente/ *a* immanent
inmarcesible, inmarchitable /imarθe'siβle, imartʃi'taβle; imarsesiβle, imartʃitaβle/ *a* unfading, imperishable
inmaterial /imate'rial/ *a* incorporeal; immaterial
inmaterialidad /imateriali'ðað/ *f,* incorporeity; immateriality
inmaturo /ima'turo/ *a* immature; unripe
inmediación /imeðia'θion; imeðia'sion/ *f,* nearness, proximity; contact; *pl* outskirts, neighborhood, environs
inmediatamente /imeðiata'mente/ *adv* near; immediately, at once
inmediato /ime'ðiato/ *a* adjoining, close, nearby; immediate, prompt
inmejorable /imeho'raβle/ *a* unsurpassable, unbeatable
inmemorable, inmemorial /imemo'raβle, imemo'rial/ *a* immemorial
inmensidad /imensi'ðað/ *f,* vastness, huge extent; infinity; infinite space; immensity; huge number
inmenso /i'menso/ *a* vast; infinite; immense; innumerable
inmensurable /imensu'raβle/ *a* immeasurable, incalculable
inmerecido /imere'θiðo; imere'siðo/ *a* undeserved, unmerited
inmérito /i'merito/ *a* wrongful, unjust
inmeritorio /imeri'torio/ *a* unmeritorious, unpraiseworthy
inmersión /imer'sion/ *f,* immersion; dip
inmigración /imigra'θion; imigra'sion/ *f,* immigration
inmigrante /imi'grante/ *a* and *mf* immigrant
inmigrar /imi'grar/ *vi* to immigrate
inminencia /imi'nenθia; imi'nensia/ *f,* imminence
inminente /imi'nente/ *a* imminent
inmiscuir /imis'kuir/ *vt* to mix; *—vr* meddle. May be conjugated regularly or like **huir**
inmisión /imi'sion/ *f,* inspiration
inmobiliario /imoβi'liario/ *a* concerning real estate
inmoble /i'moβle/ *a* immovable; motionless, immobile, stationary; *Fig.* unshakable, unflinching
inmoderación /imoðera'θion; imoðera'sion/ *f,* immoderateness, excess
inmoderado /imoðe'raðo/ *a* immoderate; unrestrained, excessive
inmodestia /imo'ðestia/ *f,* immodesty
inmodesto /imo'ðesto/ *a* immodest
inmolación /imola'θion; imola'sion/ *f,* immolation
inmolador /imola'ðor/ **(-ra)** *a* sacrificing *—n* immolator
inmolar /imo'lar/ *vt* to immolate; *Fig.* sacrifice, give up; *—vr Fig.* sacrifice oneself
inmoral /imo'ral/ *a* immoral
inmoralidad /imorali'ðað/ *f,* immorality
inmortal /imor'tal/ *a* immortal
inmortalidad /imortali'ðað/ *f,* immortality
inmortalizar /imortali'θar; imortali'sar/ *vt* to immortalize
inmotivado /imoti'βaðo/ *a* unfounded, without reason
inmoto /i'moto/ *a* motionless, stationary
inmóvil /i'moβil/ *a* immovable, fixed; motionless; steadfast, constant
inmovilidad /imoβili'ðað/ *f,* immovability; immobility; constancy, steadfastness
inmovilizar /imoβili'θar; imoβili'sar/ *vt* to immobilize
inmueble /i'mueβle/ *m, Law.* immovable estate
inmundicia /imun'diθia; imun'disia/ *f,* filth, nastiness; dirt; rubbish, refuse; obscenity, indecency
inmundo /i'mundo/ *a* dirty, filthy; obscene, indecent; unclean
inmune /i'mune/ *a* exempt; *Med.* immune
inmunidad /imuni'ðað/ *f,* exemption; immunity
inmunizar /imuni'θar; imuni'sar/ *vt* to immunize
inmutabilidad /imutaβili'ðað/ *f,* immutability, changelessness; imperturbability
inmutable /imu'taβle/ *a* immutable, unchangeable; imperturbable
inmutación /imuta'θion; imuta'sion/ *f,* change, alteration, difference
inmutar /imu'tar/ *vt* to change, alter, vary; *—vr* change one's expression (through fear, etc.)
innato /in'nato/ *a* innate; inherent; instinctive, inborn
innatural /innatu'ral/ *a* unnatural
innavegable /innaβe'gaβle/ *a* unnavigable; unseaworthy (of ships)
innecesario /inneθe'sario; innese'sario/ *a* unnecessary
innegable /inne'gaβle/ *a* undeniable; indisputable, irrefutable
innoble /in'noβle/ *a* plebeian; ignoble
innocuo /inno'kuo/ *a* harmless, innocuous
innovación /innoβa'θion; innoβa'sion/ *f,* innovation
innovador /innoβa'ðor/ **(-ra)** *a* innovatory *—n* innovator
innovar /inno'βar/ *vt* to introduce innovations
innumerabilidad /innumeraβili'ðað/ *f,* countless number, multitude
innumerable /innume'raβle/ *a* innumerable, countless
innúmero /in'numero/ *a* countless, innumerable
inobediencia /inoβe'ðienθia; inoβe'ðiensia/ *f,* disobedience
inobediente /inoβe'ðiente/ *a* disobedient
inobservable /inoβser'βaβle/ *a* unobservable
inobservancia /inoβser'βanθia; inoβser'βansia/ *f,* inobservance
inobservante /inoβser'βante/ *a* unobservant
inocencia /ino'θenθia; ino'sensia/ *f,* innocence; simplicity, candor; harmlessness
inocentada /inoθen'taða; inosen'taða/ *f, Inf.* naïve remark or action; fool's trap; practical joke
inocente /ino'θente; ino'sente/ *a* innocent; candid, simple; harmless; easily deceived
inocentón /inoθen'ton; inosen'ton/ *a Inf.* extremely credulous and easily taken in
inocuidad /inokui'ðað/ *f,* innocuousness
inoculación /inokula'θion; inokula'sion/ *f,* inoculation
inoculador /inokula'ðor/ *m,* inoculator
inocular /inoku'lar/ *vt* to inoculate; pervert, corrupt; contaminate
inodoro /ino'ðoro/ *a* odorless. *m,* toilet, lavatory
inofensivo /inofen'siβo/ *a* inoffensive, harmless
inolvidable /inolβi'ðaβle/ *a* unforgettable
inoperable /inope'raβle/ *a* inoperable
inopia /i'nopia/ *f,* poverty; scarcity
inopinable /inopi'naβle/ *a* indisputable, unquestionable
inopinado /inopi'naðo/ *a* unexpected, sudden
inoportunidad /inoportuni'ðað/ *f,* inopportuneness, unseasonableness; unsuitability
inoportuno /inopor'tuno/ *a* inopportune, untimely
inordenado /inorðe'naðo/ *a* inordinate, immoderate, excessive
inorgánico /inor'ganiko/ *a* inorganic
inoxidable /inoksi'ðaβle/ *a* rustless
inquebrantable /inkeβran'taβle/ *a* unbreakable; final, irrevocable
inquietador /inkieta'ðor/ **(-ra)** *a* disturbing *—n* disturber
inquietar /inkie'tar/ *vt* to disturb; trouble, make anxious, worry; *—vr* be disquieted, worry
inquieto /in'kieto/ *a* restless; unquiet; fidgety; disturbed, anxious, worried, uneasy
inquietud /inkie'tuð/ *f,* restlessness; uneasiness; worry; trouble, care, anxiety
inquilinato /inkili'nato/ *m,* tenancy; rent; *Law.* lease; (rental) rates
inquilino /inki'lino/ **(-na)** *n* tenant; lessee
inquina /in'kina/ *f,* dislike, grudge
inquinar /inki'nar/ *vt* to contaminate, corrupt, infect
inquiridor /inkiri'ðor/ **(-ra)** *a* inquiring, examining *—n* investigator

inquirir /inki'rir/ *vt irr* to inquire; examine, look into. See **adquirir**
inquisición /inkisi'θion; inkisi'sion/ *f,* inquiry, investigation; *Eccl.* Inquisition
inquisidor /inkisi'ðor/ **(-ra)** *a* inquiring, investigating —*n* investigator. *m, Eccl.* inquisitor; judge
inquisitorial /inkisito'rial/ *a* inquisitorial
insaciabilidad /insaθiaβili'ðað; insasiaβili'ðað/ *f,* insatiability
insaciable /insa'θiaβle; insa'siaβle/ *a* insatiable
insalivación /insaliβa'θion; insaliβa'sion/ *f,* insalivation
insalubre /insa'luβre/ *a* unhealthy
insanable /insa'naβle/ *a* incurable
insania /in'sania/ *f,* insanity
insano /in'sano/ *a* insane, mad
inscribir /inskri'βir/ *vt* to inscribe; record; enter (a name on a list, etc.), register, enroll; engrave; *Geom.* inscribe —*Past Part.* **inscrito**
inscripción /inskrip'θion; inskrip'sion/ *f,* inscription; record, enrollment; registration; government bond
insecable /inse'kaβle/ *a* undryable, undrying
insecticida /insekti'θiða; insekti'siða/ *a* insecticide
insectívoro /insek'tiβoro/ *a* insectivorous
insecto /in'sekto/ *m,* insect
inseguridad /inseguri'ðað/ *f,* insecurity
inseguro /inse'guro/ *a* insecure; unsafe; uncertain
insensatez /insensa'teθ; insensa'tes/ *f,* folly, foolishness
insensato /insen'sato/ *a* foolish, stupid, mad
insensibilidad /insensiβili'ðað/ *f,* insensibility; imperception; callousness, hard-heartedness
insensibilizar /insensiβili'θar; insensiβili'sar/ *vt* to make insensible (to sensations)
insensible /insen'siβle/ *a* insensible; imperceptive, insensitive; unconscious, senseless; imperceptible, inappreciable; callous
inseparabilidad /inseparaβili'ðað/ *f,* inseparability
inseparable /insepa'raβle/ *a* inseparable
insepulto /inse'pulto/ *a* unburied (of the dead)
inserción /inser'θion; inser'sion/ *f,* insertion; interpolation; grafting
insertar /inser'tar/ *vt* to insert; introduce; interpolate; —*vr* (*Bot. Zool.*) become attached
inservible /inser'βiβle/ *a* useless; unfit; unsuitable
insidia /in'siðia/ *f,* insidiousness; snare, ambush
insidiador /insiðia'ðor/ **(-ra)** *a* ensnaring —*n* schemer, ambusher
insidiar /insi'ðiar/ *vt* to waylay, ambush; set a trap for; scheme against
insidioso /insi'ðioso/ *a* insidious; treacherous; scheming, guileful
insigne /in'signe/ *a* illustrious, famous; distinguished
insignia /in'signia/ *f,* symbol; badge; token; banner, standard; *Naut.* pennant; *pl* insignia
insignificancia /insignifi'kanθia; insignifi'kansia/ *f,* meaninglessness; unimportance, triviality; insignificance, insufficiency
insignificante /insignifi'kante/ *a* meaningless; unimportant; insignificant, small
insinuación /insinua'θion; insinua'sion/ *f,* insinuation; hint; implication; suggestion
insinuador /insinua'ðor/ *a* insinuating; suggestive, implicative
insinuar /insi'nuar/ *vt* to insinuate; suggest, hint; —*vr* ingratiate oneself; creep in
insinuativo /insinua'tiβo/ *a* insinuative
insipidez /insipi'ðeθ; insipi'ðes/ *f,* tastelessness, insipidity; *Fig.* dullness
insípido /in'sipiðo/ *a* tasteless, insipid; dull, uninteresting, boring
insistencia /insis'tenθia; insis'tensia/ *f,* insistence
insistente /insis'tente/ *a* insistent
insistir /insis'tir/ *vi* (*with en or sobre*) to lay stress upon, insist on; persist in
ínsito /'insito/ *a* inherent, innate
insociabilidad /insoθiaβili'ðað; insosiaβili'ðað/ *f,* unsociability
insociable /inso'θiaβle; inso'siaβle/ *a* unsociable
insolación /insola'θion; insola'sion/ *f,* insolation, exposure to the sun; sunstroke
insolar /inso'lar/ *vt* to expose to the sun's rays; —*vr* contract sunstroke
insoldable /insol'daβle/ *a* unsolderable, unable to be soldered
insolencia /inso'lenθia; inso'lensia/ *f,* insolence; impudence, impertinence
insolentarse /insolen'tarse/ *vr* to grow insolent; be impudent
insolente /inso'lente/ *a* insolent; impudent, impertinent
insólito /in'solito/ *a* unaccustomed; infrequent; unusual; unexpected
insolubilidad /insoluβili'ðað/ *f,* insolubility
insoluble /inso'luβle/ *a* insoluble
insoluto /inso'luto/ *a* unpaid, outstanding
insolvencia /insol'βenθia; insol'βensia/ *f,* insolvency
insolvente /insol'βente/ *a* insolvent
insomne /in'somne/ *a* sleepless
insomnio /in'somnio/ *m,* insomnia
insondable /inson'daβle/ *a* unfathomable, bottomless; inscrutable, secret
insoportable /insopor'taβle/ *a* intolerable, unbearable
insostenible /insoste'niβle/ *a* indefensible; arbitrary, baseless
inspección /inspek'θion; inspek'sion/ *f,* inspection; supervision; examination; inspectorship; inspector's office
inspeccionar /inspekθio'nar; inspeksio'nar/ *vt* to inspect; survey, examine. **i. una casa,** to view a house
inspector /inspek'tor/ **(-ra)** *a* inspecting, examining —*n* supervisor. *m,* inspector; surveyor
inspiración /inspira'θion; inspira'sion/ *f,* inspiration; inhalation
inspirador /inspira'ðor/ **(-ra)** *a* inspiring —*n* inspirer
inspirar /inspi'rar/ *vt* to breathe in, inhale; blow (of the wind); inspire; —*vr* be inspired; (*with en*) find inspiration in, imitate
instabilidad /instaβili'ðað/ *f,* instability; unsteadiness; shakiness; unreliability, inconstancy
instable /ins'taβle/ *a* unstable
instalación /instala'θion; instala'sion/ *f,* plant, apparatus; erection, fitting; induction; installment, settling in
instalador /instala'ðor/ **(-ra)** *n* fitter; one who installs (electricity, etc.)
instalar /insta'lar/ *vt* to appoint, induct; erect (a plant, etc.); install, put in; lay on; *Elec.* wire; —*vr* install oneself, settle down
instancia /ins'tanθia; ins'tansia/ *f,* instance; argument; suggestion; supplication; request; formal petition. **de primera i.,** in the first instance, firstly
instantánea /instan'tanea/ *f, Photo.* snapshot
instantáneo /instan'taneo/ *a* instantaneous
instante /ins'tante/ *a* urgent. *m,* second; instant, moment. **a cada i.,** every minute; frequently. **al i.,** at once, immediately. **por instantes,** continually; immediately
instar /ins'tar/ *vt* to press; persuade; insist upon; —*vi* be urgent, press
instauración /instaura'θion; instaura'sion/ *f,* restoration; renewal; renovation
instaurador /instaura'ðor/ **(-ra)** *a* renovating, renewing —*n* restorer, renovator
instaurar /instau'rar/ *vt* to restore; repair; renovate, renew
instaurativo /instaura'tiβo/ *a* restorative
instigación /instiga'θion; instiga'sion/ *f,* instigation, incitement
instigador /instiga'ðor/ **(-ra)** *n* instigator
instigar /insti'gar/ *vt* to instigate, incite; induce
instilación /instila'θion; instila'sion/ *f,* instillment, pouring drop by drop; inculcation, implantation
instilar /insti'lar/ *vt Chem.* instill; implant, inculcate
instintivo /instin'tiβo/ *a* instinctive
instinto /ins'tinto/ *m,* instinct. **por i.,** by instinct, naturally
institución /institu'θion; institu'sion/ *f,* setting up, establishment; institution; teaching, instruction; *pl* institutes, digest

institucional /instituθio'nal; institusio'nal/ *a* institutional

instituir /insti'tuir/ *vt irr* to found, establish; institute; instruct, teach. See **huir**

instituto /insti'tuto/ *m*, institute; secondary school. **i. de belleza,** beauty parlor, beauty salon

institutor /institu'tor/ *m*, founder, instituter; tutor

institutriz /institu'triθ; institu'tris/ *f*, governess

instrucción /instruk'θion; instruk'sion/ *f*, teaching, instruction; knowledge, learning; education; *pl* orders; rules; instruction. **i. primaria,** primary education. **i. pública,** public education

instructivo /instruk'tiβo/ *a* instructive

instructor /instruk'tor/ **(-ra)** *a* instructive —*n* instructor

instruido /ins'truiðo/ *a* cultured, well-educated; knowledgeable

instruir /ins'truir/ *vt irr* to teach, instruct; train; inform, acquaint with; *Law.* formulate. See **huir**

instrumentación /instrumenta'θion; instrumenta'sion/ *f*, *Mus.* instrumentation

instrumental /instrumen'tal/ *a* instrumental

instrumentar /instrumen'tar/ *vt Mus.* to score

instrumentista /instrumen'tista/ *mf Mus.* instrumentalist; instrument maker

instrumento /instru'mento/ *m*, tool, implement; machine, apparatus; *Mus.* instrument; means, medium; legal document. **i. de cuerda,** string instrument. **i. de percusión,** percussion instrument. **i. de viento,** wind instrument

insuave /in''suaβe/ *a* unpleasant (to the senses); rough

insubordinación /insuβorðina'θion; insuβorðina'sion/ *f*, insubordination, rebellion

insubordinado /insuβorði'naðo/ *a* insubordinate, unruly

insubordinar /insuβorði'nar/ *vt* to rouse to rebellion; —*vr* become insubordinate, rebel

insubsistencia /insuβsis'tenθia; insuβsis'tensia/ *f*, instability

insubsistente /insuβsis'tente/ *a* unstable; groundless, unfounded

insubstancial /insuβstan'θial; insuβstan'sial/ *a* insubstantial, unreal, illusory; pointless, worthless, superficial

insubstancialidad /insuβstanθiali'ðað; insuβstansiali'ðað/ *f*, superficiality, worthlessness

insuficiencia /insufi'θienθia; insufi'siensia/ *f*, insufficiency, shortage; incompetence, inefficiency

insuficiente /insufi'θiente; insufi'siente/ *a* insufficient, scarce, inadequate

insufrible /insu'friβle/ *a* insufferable, unbearable, intolerable

insular /insu'lar/ *a* insular

insulina /insu'lina/ *f*, insulin

insulsez /insul'seθ; insul'ses/ *f*, insipidity, tastelessness; dullness; tediousness

insulso /in'sulso/ *a* insipid, tasteless; tedious; dull

insultador /insulta'ðor/ **(-ra)** *a* insulting —*n* insulter

insultante /insul'tante/ *a* insulting

insultar /insul'tar/ *vt* to insult; call names; —*vr* take offense

insulto /in'sulto/ *m*, insult; sudden attack; sudden illness, fit

insumable /insu'maβle/ *a* incalculable; excessive, exorbitant

insumergible /insumer'hiβle/ *a* unsinkable

insumiso /insu'miso/ *a* rebellious

insuperable /insupe'raβle/ *a* insuperable

insurgente /insur'hente/ *a* insurgent, rebellious. *m*, rebel

insurrección /insurrek'θion; insurrek'sion/ *f*, insurrection

insurreccionar /insurrekθio'nar; insurreksio'nar/ *vt* to incite to rebellion; —*vr* rise in rebellion

insurrecto /insu'rrekto/ **(-ta)** *n* rebel

insustancial /insustan'θial; insustan'sial/ *a* See **insubstancial**

insustituible /insusti'tuiβle/ *a* indispensable

intachable /inta'tʃaβle/ *a* irreproachable; impeccable, perfect

intacto /in'takto/ *a* untouched; intact, uninjured; whole, entire; complete; pure

intangibilidad /intanhiβili'ðað/ *f*, intangibility

intangible /intan'hiβle/ *a* intangible

integración /integra'θion; integra'sion/ *f*, integration

integral /inte'gral/ *a* integral

integrar /inte'grar/ *vt* to integrate; *Com.* repay

integridad /integri'ðað/ *f*, wholeness; completeness; integrity, probity, honesty; virginity

íntegro /'integro/ *a* integral, whole; upright, honest

integumento /integu'mento/ *m*, integument; pretense, simulation

intelectiva /intelek'tiβa/ *f*, understanding

intelecto /inte'lekto/ *m*, intellect

intelectual /intelek'tual/ *a* intellectual

intelectualidad /intelektuali'ðað/ *f*, understanding, intellectuality; intelligentsia

intelectualismo /intelektua'lismo/ *m*, intellectualism

inteligencia /inteli'henθia; inteli'hensia/ *f*, intelligence; intellect; mental alertness; mind; meaning, sense; experience, skill; understanding, secret agreement; information, knowledge; Intelligence, Secret Service

inteligente /inteli'hente/ *a* intelligent, clever, skillful; capable, competent

inteligibilidad /intelihiβili'ðað/ *f*, intelligibility

inteligible /inteli'hiβle/ *a* intelligible; understandable; able to be heard

intemperancia /intempe'ranθia; intempe'ransia/ *f*, intemperance, lack of moderation

intemperante /intempe'rante/ *a* intemperate

intemperie /intem'perie/ *f*, stormy weather. **a la i.,** at the mercy of the elements; in the open air

intempestivo /intempes'tiβo/ *a* inopportune, ill-timed

intención /inten'θion; inten'sion/ *f*, intention; determination, purpose; viciousness (of animals); caution. *Inf.* **con segunda i.,** with a double meaning, slyly

intencionado /intenθio'naðo; intensio'naðo/ *a* intentioned, disposed

intencional /intenθio'nal; intensio'nal/ *a* intentional, designed, premeditated

intendencia /inten'denθia; inten'densia/ *f*, management; supervision; administration; *Polit.* intendancy. *Mil.* **cuerpo de i.,** quartermaster corps, army supply corps

intendente /inten'dente/ *m*, director; manager; *Polit.* intendant. **i. de ejército,** quartermaster general

intensar /inten'sar/ *vt* to intensify

intensidad /intensi'ðað/ *f*, intensity; ardor; vehemence

intensificar /intensifi'kar/ *vt* to intensify

intensivo /inten'siβo/ *a* intensive

intenso /in'tenso/ *a* intense; ardent; fervent, vehement

intentar /inten'tar/ *vt* to intend, mean; propose; try, endeavor; initiate. **i. fortuna,** to try one's luck

intento /in'tento/ *m*, intention, determination, purpose. **de i.,** on purpose; knowingly

intentona /inten'tona/ *f*, *Inf.* foolhardy attempt

interacción /interak'θion; interak'sion/ *f*, interaction; reciprocal effect; *Chem.* reaction

intercalación /interkala'θion; interkala'sion/ *f*, interpolation; insertion

intercalar /interka'lar/ *vt* to intercalate; interpolate, include, insert

intercambiable /interkam'biaβle/ *a* interchangeable

intercambio /inter'kambio/ *m*, interchange

interceder /interθe'ðer; interse'ðer/ *vi* to intercede, plead for

interceptación /interθepta'θion; intersepta'sion/ *f*, interception

interceptar /interθep'tar; intersep'tar/ *vt* to intercept; interrupt; hinder

intercesión /interθe'sion; interse'sion/ *f*, intercession

intercesor /interθe'sor; interse'sor/ **(-ra)** *a* interceding —*n* intercessor

intercutáneo /interku'taneo/ *a* intercutaneous

interdecir /inter'ðeθir; inter'ðesir/ *vt irr* to forbid, prohibit. See **decir**

interdicción /interðik'θion; interðik'sion/ *f*, interdiction, prohibition
interdicto /inter'ðikto/ *m*, interdict
interés /inte'res/ *m*, interest; yield, profit; advantage; *Com.* interest; inclination, fondness; attraction, fascination; *pl* money matters. **i. compuesto,** compound interest. **intereses creados,** bonds of interest; vested interests
interesado /intere'saðo/ *a* involved, concerned; biased; selfish
interesante /intere'sante/ *a* interesting
interesar /intere'sar/ **(se)** *vi* and *vr* to be interested; —*vt Com.* invest; interest
interfecto /inter'fekto/ **(-ta)** *n Law.* victim (of murder)
interferencia /interfe'renθia; interfe'rensia/ *f*, *Phys.* interference
interfoliar /interfo'liar/ *vt* to interleave (of books)
ínterin /'interin/ *m*, interim —*adv* meanwhile, in the meantime
interinamente /interina'mente/ *adv* in the interim; provisionally
interinar /interi'nar/ *vt* to discharge (duties) provisionally, act temporarily as
interino /inte'rino/ *a* acting, provisional, temporary
interior /inte'rior/ *a* interior; inner; inside; indoor; inland; internal, domestic (policies, etc.); inward, spiritual. *m*, interior, inside; mind, soul; *pl* entrails
interjección /interhek'θion; interhek'sion/ *f*, *Gram.* interjection, exclamation
interlinear /interline'ar/ *vt* to write between the lines; *Print.* lead
interlocución /interloku'θion; interloku'sion/ *f*, dialogue, conversation
interlocutorio /interloku'torio/ *a Law.* interlocutory
intérlope /in'terlope/ *a* interloping. *mf* interloper
interludio /inter'luðio/ *m*, interlude
intermediario /interme'ðiario/ **(-ia)** *a* and *n* intermediary. *m*, *Com.* middleman
intermedio /inter'meðio/ *a* intermediate. *m*, interim; *Theat.* interval. **por i. de,** through, by the mediation of
intermisión /intermi'sion/ *f*, intermission, interval
intermitencia /intermi'tenθia; intermi'tensia/ *f*, intermittence
intermitente /intermi'tente/ *a* intermittent
intermitir /intermi'tir/ *vt* to interrupt, suspend, discontinue
internación /interna'θion; interna'sion/ *f*, going inside; penetration; taking into
internacional /internaθio'nal; internasio'nal/ *a* international
internacionalismo /internaθiona'lismo; internasiona'lismo/ *m*, internationalism
internacionalista /internaθiona'lista; internasiona'lista/ *mf* internationalist
internacionalización /internaθionaliθa'θion; internasionalisa'sion/ *f*, internationalization
internado /inter'naðo/ *m*, boarding school
internamiento /interna'miento/ *m*, internment
internar /inter'nar/ *vt* to take or send inland; —*vi* penetrate; —*vr* (*with en*) go into the interior of (a country); get into the confidence of; study deeply (a subject)
Internet *m*, **el,** the Internet.
interno /in'terno/ **(-na)** *a* interior; internal; inner; inside; boarding (student) —*n* boarding school student; *Med.* intern
internodio /inter'noðio/ *m*, internode
internuncio /inter'nunθio; inter'nunsio/ *m*, *Eccl.* internuncio; interlocutor; representative
interoceánico /interoθe'aniko; interose'aniko/ *a* interoceanic
interpaginar /interpahi'nar/ *vt* to interleave (of books)
interpelación /interpela'θion; interpela'sion/ *f*, *Law.* interpellation; appeal
interpelar /interpe'lar/ *vt Law.* to interpellate; appeal to, ask protection from
interpolación /interpola'θion; interpola'sion/ *f*, interpolation, insertion; interruption
interpolador /interpola'ðor/ **(-ra)** *n* interpolator; interrupter
interpolar /interpo'lar/ *vt* to interpolate; interject
interponer /interpo'ner/ *vt irr* to interpose, insert, intervene; designate as an arbitrator; —*vr* intervene. See **poner**
interposición /interposi'θion; interposi'sion/ *f*, interposition; intervention; mediation, arbitration
interpresa /inter'presa/ *f*, *Mil.* surprise attack
interpretación /interpreta'θion; interpreta'sion/ *f*, interpretation; translation
interpretador /interpreta'ðor/ **(-ra)** *a* interpretative —*n* interpreter
interpretar /interpre'tar/ *vt* to interpret; translate; attribute; expound, explain. **i. mal,** to misconstrue; translate wrongly
interpretativo /interpreta'tiβo/ *a* interpretative
intérprete /in'terprete/ *mf* interpreter
interregno /inte'rregno/ *m*, interregnum. **i. parlamentario,** parliamentary recess
interrogación /interroga'θion; interroga'sion/ *f*, interrogation, question; *Gram.* question mark
interrogador /interroga'ðor/ **(-ra)** *n* questioner
interrogante /interro'gante/ *a* interrogating. *m*, *Print.* question mark
interrogar /interro'gar/ *vt* to interrogate, question
interrogativo /interroga'tiβo/ *a* interrogative
interrogatorio /interroga'torio/ *m*, interrogatory
interrumpir /interrum'pir/ *vt* to interrupt; hinder, obstruct; *Elec.* break contact
interrupción /interrup'θion; interrup'sion/ *f*, interruption; stoppage (of work); *Elec.* break
interruptor /interrup'tor/ **(-ra)** *a* interrupting —*n* interrupter. *m*, *Elec.* switch, interruptor. **i. de dos direcciones,** *Elec.* two-way switch
intersecarse /interse'karse/ *vr Geom.* to intersect
intersección /intersek'θion; intersek'sion/ *f*, *Geom.* intersection
intersticio /inter'stiθio; inter'stisio/ *m*, interstice, crack, crevice; interval, intervening space
intervalo /inter'βalo/ *m*, interval
intervención /interβen'θion; interβen'sion/ *f*, intervention; mediation, intercession; auditing (of accounts)
intervenir /interβe'nir/ *vi irr* to take part (in); intervene, interfere; arbitrate, mediate; happen, occur; —*vt Com.* audit. See **venir**
interventor /interβen'tor/ **(-ra)** *a* intervening —*n* one who intervenes. *m*, auditor; inspector
intervocálico /interβo'kaliko/ *a* intervocalic
intestado /intes'taðo/ **(-da)** *a* and *n Law.* intestate
intestinal /intesti'nal/ *a* intestinal
intestino /intes'tino/ *a* intestinal. *m*, intestine
íntima, intimación /'intima, intima'θion; 'intima, intima'sion/ *f*, intimation, notification
intimar /inti'mar/ *vt* to intimate; inform, notify; —*vr* penetrate; —*vr* and *vi* become intimate or friendly
intimidación /intimiða'θion; intimiða'sion/ *f*, intimidation, terrorization
intimidad /intimi'ðað/ *f*, intimacy
intimidar /intimi'ðar/ *vt* to intimidate, terrorize, cow
íntimo /'intimo/ *a* intimate; deep-seated, inward; private, personal
intitular /intitu'lar/ *vt* to give a title to, entitle, call; —*vr* call oneself
intolerable /intole'raβle/ *a* intolerable; unbearable
intolerancia /intole'ranθia; intole'ransia/ *f*, narrow-mindedness, intolerance, bigotry
intolerante /intole'rante/ *a* narrow-minded, illiberal; *Med.* intolerant
intonso /in'tonso/ *a* long-haired, unshorn; boorish, ignorant
intoxicación /intoksika'θion; intoksika'sion/ *f*, poisoning
intoxicar /intoksi'kar/ *vt* to poison
intraducible /intraðu'θiβle; intraðu'siβle/ *a* untranslatable
intramuros /intra'muros/ *adv* within the town walls, within the city
intranquilidad /intrankili'ðað/ *f*, disquiet, restlessness; anxiety

intranquilizador /intrankiliθa'ðor; intrankilisa'ðor/ *a* disquieting, perturbing
intranquilizar /intrankili'θar; intrankili'sar/ *vt* to disquiet, make uneasy, worry
intranquilo /intran'kilo/ *a* uneasy, anxious
intransferible /intransfe'riβle/ *a* untransferable, not transferable
intransigencia /intransi'henθia; intransi'hensia/ *f,* intolerance, intransigence
intransigente /intransi'hente/ *a* intolerant, intransigent
intransitable /intransi'taβle/ *a* impassable; unsurmountable
intransitivo /intransi'tiβo/ *a* intransitive
intratable /intra'taβle/ *a* intractable; impassable; rough; unsociable, difficult
intrauterino /intraute'rino/ *a* intrauterine
intravenoso /intraβe'noso/ *a* intravenous
intrepidez /intrepi'ðeθ; intrepi'ðes/ *f,* intrepidity, dauntlessness, gallantry
intrépido /in'trepiðo/ *a* intrepid, dauntless, gallant
intriga /in'triga/ *f,* scheme, intrigue; entanglement; *Lit.* plot
intrigante /intri'gante/ *mf* intriguer, schemer
intrigar /intri'gar/ *vt* to intrigue, scheme, plot
intrincación /intrinka'θion; intrinka'sion/ *f,* intricacy
intrincado /intrin'kaðo/ *a* intricate
intrincar /intrin'kar/ *vt* to complicate; obscure, confuse
intríngulis /in'triŋgulis/ *m, Inf.* ulterior motive
intrínseco /in'trinseko/ *a* intrinsic, inherent; essential
introducción /introðuk'θion; introðuk'sion/ *f,* introduction
introducir /introðu'θir; introðu'sir/ *vt irr* to introduce; insert; fit in; drive in; present, introduce; bring into use; cause, occasion; show in, bring in; —*vr* interfere, meddle; enter. See **conducir**
introductor /introðuk'tor/ **(-ra)** *n* introducer
intromisión /intromi'sion/ *f,* intromission; interference; *Geol.* intrusion
introspección /introspek'θion; introspek'sion/ *f,* introspection
introverso /intro'βerso/ *a* introvert
intruso /in'truso/ **(-sa)** *a* intruding, intrusive —*n* intruder
intuición /intui'θion; intui'sion/ *f,* intuition
intuir /in'tuir/ *vt irr* to know by intuition. See **huir**
intuitivo /intui'tiβo/ *a* intuitive
intuito /in'tuito/ *m,* glance, look, view
intumescencia /intumes'θenθia; intumes'sensia/ *f,* intumescence
inulto /i'nulto/ *a Poet.* unavenged, unpunished
inundación /inunda'θion; inunda'sion/ *f,* flood; flooding; excess, superabundance
inundar /inun'dar/ *vt* to flood; swamp; *Fig.* inundate, overwhelm
inurbanidad /inurβani'ðað/ *f,* discourtesy, impoliteness
inurbano /inur'βano/ *a* discourteous, uncivil, impolite
inusitado /inusi'taðo/ *a* unusual, unaccustomed; rare
inútil /i'nutil/ *a* useless
inutilidad /inutili'ðað/ *f,* uselessness
inutilizar /inutili'θar; inutili'sar/ *vt* to render useless; disable, incapacitate; spoil, damage
invadeable /imbaðe'aβle/ *a* impassable, unfordable
invadir /imba'ðir/ *vt* to invade
invaginación /imbahina'θion; imbahina'sion/ *f,* invagination
invalidación /imbaliða'θion; imbaliða'sion/ *f,* invalidation
invalidar /imbali'ðar/ *vt* to invalidate
invalidez /imbali'ðeθ; imbali'ðes/ *f,* invalidity; disablement; infirmity
inválido /im'baliðo/ **(-da)** *a* weak, infirm; invalid, null; disabled —*n* invalid; disabled soldier
invariabilidad /imbariaβili'ðað/ *f,* invariability
invariable /imba'riaβle/ *a* invariable
invariación /imbaria'θion; imbaria'sion/ *f,* invariableness
invariante /imba'riante/ *m,* invariant
invasión /imba'sion/ *f,* invasion, encroachment, incursion
invasor /imba'sor/ **(-ra)** *a* invading; *Med.* attacking —*n* invader
invectiva /imbek'tiβa/ *f,* invective
invencibilidad /imbenθiβili'ðað; imbensiβili'ðað/ *f,* invincibility
invencible /imben'θiβle; imben'siβle/ *a* invincible
invención /imben'θion; imben'sion/ *f,* invention, discovery; deception, fabrication, lie; creative imagination; finding (e.g. *i. de la Santa Cruz,* Invention of the Holy Cross)
invencionero /imbenθio'nero; imbensio'nero/ **(-ra)** *n* inventor; schemer, deceiver
invendible /imben'diβle/ *a* unsalable
inventar /imben'tar/ *vt* to invent; create; imagine; concoct, fabricate (lies, etc.)
inventariar /imbenta'riar/ *vt* to make an inventory of; *Com.* take stock of
inventario /imben'tario/ *m,* inventory; *Com.* stock taking
inventiva /imben'tiβa/ *f,* inventiveness, ingenuity; creativeness
inventivo /imben'tiβo/ *a* inventive
invento /im'bento/ *m,* See **invención**
inventor /imben'tor/ **(-ra)** *n* inventor, discoverer; liar, storyteller
inverecundia /imbere'kundia/ *f,* impertinence, impudence
inverecundo /imbere'kundo/ *a* shameless, brazen
inverisímil /imberi'simil/ *a* See **inverosímil**
invernáculo /imber'nakulo/ *m,* greenhouse; conservatory
invernada /imber'naða/ *f,* winter season; hibernation
invernadero /imberna'ðero/ *m,* winter quarters; greenhouse
invernal /imber'nal/ *a* wintry; winter
invernar /imber'nar/ *vi irr* to winter; hibernate; be wintertime. See **acertar**
invernizo /imber'niθo; imber'niso/ *a* wintry, winter
inverosímil /imbero'simil/ *a* unlikely, improbable
inverosimilitud /imberosimili'tuð/ *f,* improbability
inversamente /imbersa'mente/ *adv* inversely
inverso /im'berso/ *a* inverse; inverted
invertebrado /imberte'βraðo/ *a* and *m,* invertebrate
invertir /imber'tir/ *vt irr* to invert, transpose; reverse; *Com.* invest; spend (time). See **sentir**
investidura /imbesti'ðura/ *f,* investiture
investigación /imbestiga'θion; imbestiga'sion/ *f,* investigation, examination; research; inquiry
investigador /imbestiga'ðor/ **(-ra)** *a* investigating —*n* investigator; researcher
investigar /imbesti'gar/ *vt* to investigate, examine; research on
investir /imbes'tir/ *vt irr* to confer upon, decorate with; invest, appoint. See **pedir**
inveterado /imbete'raðo/ *a* inveterate
inviable /im'biaβle/ *a* unfeasible
invicto /im'bikto/ *a* invincible; unconquered
invierno /im'bierno/ *m,* winter; rainy season
inviolabilidad /imbiolaβili'ðað/ *f,* inviolability. **i. parlamentaria,** parliamentary immunity
inviolable /imbio'laβle/ *a* inviolable; infallible
inviolado /imbio'laðo/ *a* inviolate
invisibilidad /imbisiβili'ðað/ *f,* invisibility
invisible /imbi'siβle/ *a* invisible
invitación /imbita'θion; imbita'sion/ *f,* invitation
invitado /imbi'taðo/ **(-da)** *n* guest
invitar /imbi'tar/ *vt* to invite; urge, request; allure, attract
invocación /imboka'θion; imboka'sion/ *f,* invocation
invocador /imboka'ðor/ **(-ra)** *n* invoker
invocar /imbo'kar/ *vt* to invoke
involucro /imbo'lukro/ *m,* involucre
involuntariedad /imboluntarie'ðað/ *f,* involuntariness
involuntario /imbolun'tario/ *a* involuntary
invulnerabilidad /imbulneraβili'ðað/ *f,* invulnerability
invulnerable /imbulne'raβle/ *a* invulnerable

inyección /inyek'θion; inyek'sion/ *f,* injection
inyectado /inyek'taðo/ *a* bloodshot (of eyes)
inyectar /inyek'tar/ *vt* to inject
ipecacuana /ipeka'kuana/ *f,* ipecac
iperita /i'perita/ *f,* mustard gas
ir /ir/ *vi irr* to go; bet (e.g. *Van cinco pesetas que no lo hace,* I bet five pesetas he doesn't do it); be different, be changed (e.g. *¡Qué diferencia va entre esto y aquello!* What a difference there is between this and that!); suit, be becoming, fit (e.g. *El vestido no te va bien,* The dress doesn't suit you); extend; lead, go in the direction of (e.g. *Este camino va a Lérida,* This road leads to Lerida); get along, do, proceed, be (e.g. *¿Cómo te va estos días?* How are you getting along these days?); come (e.g. *Ahora voy,* I'm coming now); *Math.* carry (e.g. *siete y van cuatro,* seven, and four to carry); *Math.* leave (e.g. *De quince a seis van nueve,* Six from fifteen leaves nine). With a gerund, **ir** indicates the continuance of the action, or may mean to become or to grow (e.g. *Iremos andando hacia el mar,* We shall go on walking toward the sea, or *Entre tanto iba amaneciendo,* In the meanwhile it was growing light). With a past participle, **ir** means "to be' (e.g. *Voy encantado de lo que he visto,* I am delighted with what I have seen). With *prep a + infin,* **ir** means to prepare (to do) or to intend (to do) or to be on the point of doing (e.g. *Van a cantar la canción que te gusta,* They are going (or preparing) to sing the song you like). With *prep a + noun,* **ir** indicates destination (e.g. *Voy al cine,* I'm going to the cinema. *¿A dónde vamos?* Where are we going to?). **ir** + *con* means to go in the company of, or to do a thing in a certain manner (e.g. *Hemos de ir con cuidado,* We must go carefully). **ir** + *en* means to concern, interest (e.g. *¿Qué le va a él en este asunto?* What has this affair to do with him?). **ir** + *por* means to follow the career of, become (e.g. *Juan va por abogado,* John is going to be a lawyer). It also means to go and bring, or to go for (e.g. *Iré por agua,* I shall go and bring (or for) water) *—vr* to go away, leave, depart; die; leak (of liquids); evaporate; overbalance, slip (e.g. *Se le fueron los pies,* He slipped (and lost his balance)); be worn out, grow old, deteriorate; be incontinent; *Fig. Inf.* **írsele a uno una cosa,** not to notice or not to understand a thing. *Naut.* **irse a pique,** to founder, sink. **Se le fueron los ojos tras María,** He couldn't keep his eyes off Mary. **i. a caballo,** to ride, go on horseback. **i. adelante,** to go on ahead, lead; *Fig. Inf.* forge ahead, go ahead. **i. al cuartel,** to go into the army. **i. a una,** to cooperate in. **i. bien** *Fig. Inf.* to go on well; be well. **i. de brazo,** to walk arm in arm. **i. de compras,** to go shopping. **i. de juerga** *Inf.* to go on a binge. **i. de bicicleta** *or* **en coche,** to go by bicycle or to ride (in a car or carriage). **i. por,** to do things in order, take one thing at a time. *Fig. Inf.* **i. tirando,** to carry on, manage. **¿Cómo le va?** How are things with you? How are you getting along? *Inf.* **no irle ni venirle a uno nada en un asunto,** to be not in the least concerned in (an affair). **¡Qué va!** Rubbish! Nothing of the sort! **¿Quién va?** *Mil.* Who goes there? **Vamos,** Let's go (also used as an exclamation: Good gracious! You don't say so! Well!) **Vamos a ver...,** Let's see.... **¡Vaya!** What a...!; Come now! Never mind! **¡Vaya a paseo!** *or* **¡Vaya con su música a otra parte!** Take yourself off! Get out! **¡Vaya con Dios!** God keep you! Good-bye! *Pres. Ind.* **voy, vas, va, vamos, váis, van.** *Pres. Part.* **yendo.** *Preterite* **fui, fuiste, fue, fuimos, fuisteis, fueron.** *Imperf.* **iba,** etc *—Pres. Subjunc.* **vaya,** etc *—Imperf. Subjunc.* **fuese,** etc *—Imperat.* **vé**
ira /'ira/ *f,* wrath, anger; vengeance; raging, fury (of elements); *pl* cruelties, acts of vengeance
iracundia /ira'kundia/ *f,* irascibility, irritability; anger
iracundo /ira'kundo/ *a* irascible, irritable, choleric; angry; raging, tempestuous
Irak /i'rak/ Iraq
iranio /i'ranio/ **(-ia)** *a* and *n* Iranian
irascibilidad /irasθiβili'ðað; irassiβili'ðað/ *f,* irascibility; petulance
iridiscencia /iriðis'θenθia; iriðis'sensia/ *f,* iridescence
iridiscente /iriðis'θente; iriðis'sente/ *a* iridescent
iris /'iris/ *m,* rainbow; *Anat.* iris (of the eye)
irisación /irisa'θion; irisa'sion/ *f,* irisation
irisar /iri'sar/ *vi* to be iridescent
Irlanda /ir'landa/ Ireland
irlandés /irlan'des/ **(-esa)** *a* and *n* Irishman (woman)
ironía /iro'nia/ *f,* irony
irónico /i'roniko/ *a* ironical
iroqués /iro'kes/ **(-esa)** *a* and *n* Iroquois
irracional /irraθio'nal; irrasio'nal/ *a* irrational; illogical, unreasonable; *Math.* irrational, absurd
irracionalidad /irraθionali'ðað; irrasionali'ðað/ *f,* irrationality, unreasonableness
irradiación /irraðia'θion; irraðia'sion/ *f,* radiation, irradiation
irradiar /irra'ðiar/ *vt* to radiate, irradiate
irrazonable /irraθo'naβle; irraso'naβle/ *a* unreasonable
irreal /irre'al/ *a* unreal
irrealidad /irreali'ðað/ *f,* unreality
irrealizable /irreali'θaβle; irreali'saβle/ *a* unachievable, unattainable
irrebatible /irreβa'tiβle/ *a* irrefutable, evident
irreconciliable /irrekonθi'liaβle; irrekonsi'liaβle/ *a* irreconcilable, intransigent
irrecuperable /irrekupe'raβle/ *a* irretrievable
irredimible /irreði'miβle/ *a* irredeemable
irreemplazable /irreempla'θaβle; irreempla'saβle/ *a* irreplaceable
irreflexión /irreflek'sion/ *f,* thoughtlessness; impetuosity
irreflexivo /irreflek'siβo/ *a* thoughtless; rash, impetuous
irreformable /irrefor'maβle/ *a* unreformable
irrefragable /irrefra'gaβle/ *a* indisputable, unquestionable
irrefrenable /irrefre'naβle/ *a* unmanageable, uncontrollable
irrefutable /irrefu'taβle/ *a* irrefutable
irregular /irregu'lar/ *a* irregular; infrequent, rare
irregularidad /irregulari'ðað/ *f,* irregularity; abnormality; *Inf.* moral lapse
irreligión /irreli'hion/ *f,* irreligion
irreligiosidad /irrelihiosi'ðað/ *f,* impiety, godlessness
irreligioso /irreli'hioso/ *a* irreligious, impious
irremediable /irreme'ðiaβle/ *a* irremediable
irremediablemente /irremeðiaβle'mente/ *adv* unavoidably; hopelessly
irremisible /irremi'siβle/ *a* unpardonable, inexcusable
irremunerado /irremune'raðo/ *a* unremunerated, gratuitous
irreparable /irrepa'raβle/ *a* irreparable
irreprensible /irrepren'siβle/ *a* blameless, unexceptionable
irreprochable /irrepro'tʃaβle/ *a* irreproachable
irresistible /irresis'tiβle/ *a* irresistible; ravishing
irresolución /irresolu'θion; irresolu'sion/ *f,* vacillation, indecision
irresoluto /irreso'luto/ *a* hesitant, irresolute
irrespetuoso /irrespe'tuoso/ *a* disrespectful
irresponsabilidad /irresponsaβili'ðað/ *f,* irresponsibility
irresponsable /irrespon'saβle/ *a* irresponsible
irreverencia /irreβe'renθia; irreβe'rensia/ *f,* irreverence
irreverente /irreβe'rente/ *a* irreverent
irrevocabilidad /irreβokaβili'ðað/ *f,* irrevocability, finality
irrevocable /irreβo'kaβle/ *a* irrevocable
irrigación /irriga'θion; irriga'sion/ *f,* irrigation
irrigador /irriga'ðor/ *m,* spray, sprinkler; *Med.* syringe, spray
irrigar /irri'gar/ *vt* (*Med. Agr.*) to irrigate
irrisible /irri'siβle/ *a* ridiculous, laughable, absurd
irrisión /irri'sion/ *f,* derision; laughingstock
irrisorio /irri'sorio/ *a* ridiculous; derisive
irritabilidad /irritaβili'ðað/ *f,* irritability, petulance, irascibility
irritable /irri'taβle/ *a* irritable
irritación /irrita'θion; irrita'sion/ *f, Med.* irritation; petulance, exasperation
irritador /irrita'ðor/ *a* irritating; exasperating. *m,* irritant

irritante /irri'tante/ *a* irritating; exasperating
irritar /irri'tar/ *vt* to exasperate, annoy; provoke, inflame; (*Med. Law.*) irritate
írrito /'irrito/ *a Law.* null, void
irrogar /irro'gar/ *vt* to occasion (damage, harm)
irrompible /irrom'piβle/ *a* unbreakable
irrumpir /irrum'pir/ *vi* to enter violently, break in
irrupción /irrup'θion; irrup'sion/ *f,* irruption, incursion, invasion
irruptor /irrup'tor/ *a* invading, attacking
isabelino /isaβe'lino/ *a* Isabelline (pertaining to Spanish Queen Isabella II (reigned 1830–68)); bay (of horses)
isla /'isla/ *f,* island; block (of houses)
islámico /is'lamiko/ *a* Islamic
islamismo /isla'mismo/ *m,* Islam
islamita /is'lamita/ *a* and *mf* Muslim
islandés /islan'des/ **(-esa)**, **islándico (-ca)** *a* Icelandic —*n* Icelander. *m,* Icelandic (language)
Islandia /is'landia/ Iceland
isleño /is'leɲo/ **(-ña)** *a* island —*n* islander; native of the Canary Islands
isleta /is'leta/ *f,* islet
islote /is'lote/ *m,* barren islet
ismaelita /ismae'lita/ *a* and *mf* Ishmaelite
isométrico /iso'metriko/ *a* isometric
isomorfo /iso'morfo/ *a* isomorphic
isotermo /iso'termo/ *a* isothermal
isótope, isótopo /i'sotope, i'sotopo/ *m,* isotope
israelita /israe'lita/ *mf* Israelite —*a* Israeli
istmeño /ist'meɲo/ **(-ña)** *n* native of an isthmus
ístmico /'istmiko/ *a* isthmian
istmo /'istmo/ *m,* isthmus
Istmo de Suez, el /'istmo de 'sueθ, el; 'istmo de 'sues, el/ the Suez Canal
Ítaca /'itaka/ Ithaca
Italia /i'talia/ Italy
italianismo /italia'nismo/ *m,* Italianism
italianizar /italiani'θar; italiani'sar/ *vt* to italianize
italiano /ita'liano/ **(-na)** *a* and *n* Italian. *m,* Italian (language)
itálico /i'taliko/ *a* italic
iteración /itera'θion; itera'sion/ *f,* iteration, repetition
iterar /ite'rar/ *vt* to repeat, reiterate
iterativo /itera'tiβo/ *a* iterative, repetitive
itinerario /itine'rario/ *a* and *m,* itinerary
izar /i'θar; i'sar/ *vt Naut.* to hoist
izote /i'θote; i'sote/ *m,* yucca
izquierda /iθ'kierða; is'kierða/ *f,* left, left-hand side; *Polit.* left. **¡I.!** *Mil.* Left face! **a la I.,** on the left
izquierdo /iθ'kierðo; is'kierðo/ *a* left, left-hand; left-handed; bent, twisted, crooked

JK

¡ja, ja, ja! /ha, ha, ha/ *interj* Ha! ha! ha!

jabalí /haβa'li/ *m,* wild boar

jabalina /haβa'lina/ *f,* sow of wild boar; javelin

jabato /ha'βato/ *m,* young wild boar

jabón /ha'βon/ *m,* soap. **j. blando,** soft soap. **j. de olor** *or* **j. de tocador,** toilet soap. **j. de sastre,** French chalk, steatite

jabonadura /haβona'ðura/ *f,* soaping; *pl* soapsuds, lather

jabonar /haβo'nar/ *vt* to soap; wash; *Inf.* dress down, scold

jaboncillo /haβon'θiʎo; haβon'siyo/ *m,* toilet soap; steatite

jabonera /haβo'nera/ *f,* soapdish or box; soapwort

jabonería /haβone'ria/ *f,* soap factory or shop

jabonoso /haβo'noso/ *a* soapy

jaca /'haka/ *f,* pony; filly

jácara /'hakara/ *f,* gay, roguish ballad; song and dance

jácena /'haθena; 'hasena/ *f, Archit.* beam, girder

jacinto /ha'θinto; ha'sinto/ *m,* hyacinth; jacinth. **j. de ceilán,** zircon. **j. occidental,** topaz. **j. oriental,** ruby

jaco /'hako/ *m,* short coat of mail; hack, jade

jacobinismo /hakoβi'nismo/ *m,* Jacobinism

jacobino /hako'βino/ **(-na)** *n* Jacobin

jactancia /hak'tanθia; hak'tansia/ *f,* bragging, boasting

jactancioso /haktan'θioso; haktan'sioso/ **(-sa)** *a* boastful —*n* braggart

jactarse /hak'tarse/ *vr* to brag, boast

jaculatoria /hakula'toria/ *f,* ejaculatory prayer

jaculatorio /hakula'torio/ *a* ejaculatory

jade /'haðe/ *m, Mineral.* jade

jadeante /haðe'ante/ *a* panting

jadear /haðe'ar/ *vi* to pant

jadeo /ha'ðeo/ *m,* pant; panting; hard breathing

jaez /ha'eθ; ha'es/ *m,* harness (gen. *pl*); kind, sort; *pl* trappings

jaguar /ha'guar/ *m,* jaguar

jalbegar /halβe'gar/ *vt* to whitewash; make up the face

jalbegue /hal'βege/ *m,* whitewash

jalde /'halde/ *a* bright yellow

jalea /ha'lea/ *f,* jelly. **j. de membrillo,** quince jelly

jalear /hale'ar/ *vt* to encourage, urge on (by shouts, etc.)

jaleo /ha'leo/ *m,* act of encouraging dancers by clapping, shouting, etc.; Andalusian song and dance, *Inf.* uproar

jalón /ha'lon/ *m,* surveying rod

jamaicano /hamai'kano/ **(-na)** *a* and *n* Jamaican

jamás /ha'mas/ *adv* never. **nunca j.,** never. **por siempre j.,** for always, forever

jamba /'hamba/ *f,* jamb (of a door or window)

jamelgo /ha'melgo/ *m,* sorry nag, miserable hack

jamón /ha'mon/ *m,* ham

jamona /ha'mona/ *f, Inf.* plumpish middle-aged woman

jansenismo /hanse'nismo/ *m,* Jansenism

jansenista /hanse'nista/ *mf* and *a* Jansenist

Japón /ha'pon/ Japan

japonés /hapo'nes/ **(-esa)** *a* and *n* Japanese. *m,* Japanese (language)

jaque /'hake/ *m,* check (in chess); braggart. **j. mate,** checkmate. **en j.,** at bay

jaquear /hake'ar/ *vt* to check (in chess); *Mil.* harass the enemy

jaqueca /ha'keka/ *f,* migraine, sick headache. *Inf.* **dar una j.,** to annoy

jarabe /ha'raβe/ *m,* syrup. **j. tapatío,** Mexican hat dance

jarana /ha'rana/ *f,* roundhouse; *Inf.* revelry; fight, roughhouse; trick, deception

jarcia /'harθia; 'harsia/ *f,* equipment; *Naut.* tackle, rigging (gen. *pl*); fishing tackle; *Inf.* heap, mixture, medley

jardín /har'ðin/ *m,* garden

jardinar /harði'nar/ *vt* to landscape

jardinera /harði'nera/ *f,* plant stand, jardiniere; open streetcar

jardinería /harðine'ria/ *f,* gardening

jardinero /harði'nero/ **(-ra)** *n* gardener

jareta /ha'reta/ *f, Sew.* running hem; *Naut.* netting

jarra /'harra/ *f,* jar, jug. **en jarras,** arms akimbo

jarrero /ha'rrero/ *m,* jug seller or manufacturer

jarrete /ha'rrete/ *m,* calf (of the leg)

jarretera /harre'tera/ *f,* garter. **Orden de la J.,** Order of the Garter

jarro /'harro/ *m,* pitcher; jug; jar; vase

jarrón /ha'rron/ *m,* garden urn; vase

jaspe /'haspe/ *m,* jasper

jaspeado /haspe'aðo/ *a* marbled, mottled; dappled; frosted (of glass)

jauja /'hauha/ *f, Fig.* paradise, land of milk and honey

jaula /'haula/ *f,* cage; crate; miner's cage

jauría /hau'ria/ *f,* pack of hounds

javanés /haβa'nes/ **(-esa)** *a* and *n* Javanese

jazmín /haθ'min; has'min/ *m,* jasmine. **j. amarillo,** yellow jasmine. **j. de la India,** gardenia

jefa /'hefa/ *f,* forewoman; manager; leader, head

jefatura /hefa'tura/ *f,* chieftainship; managership; leadership. **j. de policía,** police station or headquarters

jefe /'hefe/ *m,* chief; head, leader; manager; *Mil.* commanding officer. *Mil.* **j. de estado mayor,** chief of staff. **j. del tren,** railroad guard

jengibre /hen'hiβre/ *m,* ginger

jeque /'heke/ *m,* sheik

jerarca /he'rarka/ *m,* hierarch

jerarquía /herar'kia/ *f,* hierarchy

jerárquico /he'rarkiko/ *a* hierarchical

jeremiada /here'miaða/ *f,* lamentation

jerez /he'reθ; he'res/ *m,* sherry

jerga /'herga/ *f,* thick frieze cloth; jargon

jergón /her'gon/ *m,* straw or hay mattress, pallet; misfit (garments); *Inf.* fat, lazy person

Jericó /heri'ko/ Jericho

jerigonza /heri'gonθa; heri'gonsa/ *f,* jargon; gibberish

jeringa /he'riŋga/ *f,* syringe

jeringar /heriŋ'gar/ *vt* to inject; syringe; *Inf.* annoy

jeringuilla /heriŋ'guiʎa; heriŋ'guiya/ *f,* small syringe; mock orange

jeroglífico /hero'glifiko/ *a* hieroglyphic. *m,* hieroglyph

jersey /her'sei/ *m,* jersey, sweater

Jerusalén /herusa'len/ Jerusalem

jesuita /he'suita/ *m,* Jesuit

jesuita, jesuítico /he'suita, he'suitiko/ *a* jesuitical

Jesús /he'sus/ *m,* Jesus —*interj* Goodness!; Bless you! (said to someone after sneezing). **¡ay J.!** Alas! *Inf.* **en un decir J.,** in a trice

jeta /'heta/ *f,* hog's snout; blubber lip; *Inf.* face, mug

jibia /'hiβia/ *f,* cuttlefish

jícara /'hikara/ *f,* small cup

jifa /'hifa/ *f,* meat offal

jifia /'hifia/ *f,* swordfish

jilguero /hil'gero/ *m,* goldfinch

jinete /hi'nete/ *m,* horseman, rider; horse soldier, cavalryman

jingoísmo /hiŋgo'ismo/ *m,* jingoism

jip /hip/ *m,* jeep

jipijapa /hipi'hapa/ *f,* very fine straw. **sombrero de j.,** panama hat

jira /'hira/ *f,* strip of cloth; picnic; tour

jirafa /hi'rafa/ *f,* giraffe

jirón /hi'ron/ *m,* rag; piece of a dress, etc.; portion of a whole

jiujitsu /hiu'hitsu/ *m,* jujitsu
jocosidad /hokosi'ðað/ *f,* pleasantry, jocularity; joke
jocoso /ho'koso/ *a* waggish; jocose, joyous
jocundidad /hokundi'ðað/ *f,* jocundity
jocundo /ho'kundo/ *a* jocund
jofaina /ho'faina/ *f,* washbowl
jónico /'honiko/ **(-ca)** *a* Ionic —*n* Ionian. *m,* (metrics) Ionic foot
Jordán /hor'ðan/ Jordan (river)
Jordania /hor'ðania/ Jordan (country)
jornada /hor'naða/ *f,* day's journey; journey, trip; *Mil.* expedition; duration of a working day; opportunity; span of life; act of a drama. **a grandes jornadas,** by forced marches, rapidly
jornal /hor'nal/ *m,* day's wages or labor
jornalear /hornale'ar/ *vi* to work by the day
jornalero /horna'lero/ **(-ra)** *n* day laborer; wage earner
joroba /ho'roβa/ *f,* hump; *Inf.* impertinence, nuisance
jorobado /horo'βaðo/ **(-da)** *a* humpbacked —*n* hunchback
jota /'hota/ *f,* name of letter J; popular Spanish dance; jot, tittle (always used negatively). **no saber j.,** to be completely ignorant
joven /'hoβen/ *a* young. *mf* young man or woman
jovenzuelo /hoβen'θuelo; hoβen'suelo/ **(-la)** *n* youngster, boy
jovialidad /hoβiali'ðað/ *f,* joviality, cheerfulness
joya /'hoia/ *f,* jewel; present; *Archit.* astragal; *Fig.* a jewel of a person
joyería /hoie'ria/ *f,* jeweler's shop or workshop
joyero /ho'iero/ *m,* jeweler; jewel box
juanete /hua'nete/ *m,* bunion; prominent cheekbone; *Naut.* topgallant sail
juanetudo /huane'tuðo/ *a* having bunions; with prominent cheekbones
jubilación /huβila'θion; huβila'sion/ *f,* retirement; pensioning off; pension
jubilado /huβi'laðo/ *a* retired
jubilar /huβi'lar/ *vt* to pension off; excuse from certain duties; *Inf.* put aside as useless (things); —*vr* rejoice; retire or be pensioned off
jubileo /huβi'leo/ *m,* jubilee
júbilo /'huβilo/ *m,* rejoicing, merriment. **j. de vivir,** joie de vivre
jubiloso /huβi'loso/ *a* jubilant, happy
jubón /hu'βon/ *m,* doublet; bodice
judaico /hu'ðaiko/ *a* Judaic
judaísmo /huða'ismo/ *m,* Judaism
judas /'huðas/ *m,* Judas; traitor
judería /huðe'ria/ *f,* Jewry
judesmo /hu'ðesmo/ *m,* Judezmo (Romance language of Jews)
judía /hu'ðia/ *f,* Jew (female); Jewish quarter, Jewish neighborhood; haricot bean. **judías verdes,** string beans
judicatura /huðika'tura/ *f,* judicature; judgeship; judiciary
judío /hu'ðio/ **(-ía)** *a* Jewish —*n* Jew. **j. errante,** wandering Jew
juego /'huego/ *m,* play, sport; gambling; hand (of cards); set; suite; *Mech.* play, working. **j. de café,** coffee set. **j. de los cientos,** piquet. **j. de manos,** sleight of hand, conjuring. **j. de naipes,** game of cards. **j. limpio,** fair play. **j. sencillo,** single (at tennis). **j. sucio,** foul play. **juegos florales,** floral games, poetry contest. **juegos malabares,** juggling. **en j.,** in operation, at stake. **entrar en j.,** to come into play. **hacer j.,** to match. **hacer juegos malabares,** to juggle
juerga /'huerga/ *f, Inf.* spree, binge. **ir de j.,** *Inf.* to go on a binge
jueves /'hueβes/ *m,* Thursday. **¡No es cosa del otro j.!** *Inf.* It's no great shakes! It's nothing to write home about!
juez /hueθ; hues/ *m,* judge. **j. arbitrador,** arbitrator; referee. **j. municipal,** magistrate
jugada /hu'gaða/ *f,* play; playing; move, throw; *Fig.* bad turn
jugador /huga'ðor/ **(-ra)** *a* gambling; playing —*n* gambler; player. **j. de manos,** conjurer
jugar /hu'gar/ *vi irr* to play; frolic; take part in a game; gamble; make a move (in a game); *Mech.* work; handle (a weapon); *Com.* intervene; —*vt* play (a match); bet; handle (a weapon); risk. **j. el lance,** *Fig.* to play one's cards well. **j. limpio,** to play fair; *Fig. Inf.* be straightforward. **j. sucio,** to play foul. **jugarse el todo por el todo,** to stake everything —*Pres. Indic.* **juego, juegas, juega, juegan.** *Pres. Subjunc.* **juegue, juegues, juegue, jueguen**
jugarreta /huga'rreta/ *f, Inf.* bad play; dirty trick
juglar /hug'lar/ *m,* entertainer; buffoon, juggler; minstrel
juglaresco /hugla'resko/ *a* pertaining to minstrels
jugo /'hugo/ *m,* sap; juice; *Fig.* essence. **j. de muñeca,** elbow grease
jugosidad /hugosi'ðað/ *f,* juiciness, succulence; *Fig.* pithiness
jugoso /hu'goso/ *a* juicy, succulent; *Fig.* pithy
juguete /hu'gete/ *m,* toy; plaything; *Fig.* puppet
juguetear /hugete'ar/ *vi* to frolic, gambol
jugueteo /huge'teo/ *m,* gamboling; play, dalliance
juguetería /hugete'ria/ *f,* toy trade; toy shop
juguetón /huge'ton/ *a* playful
juicio /'huiθio; 'huisio/ *m,* judgment; wisdom, prudence; sanity, right mind; opinion; horoscope. **j. final,** Last Judgment. **j. sano,** right mind. **asentar el j.,** to settle down, become sensible. **estar fuera de j.,** to be insane. **pedir en j.,** to sue at law
juicioso /hui'θioso; hui'sioso/ *a* judicious; prudent
julio /'hulio/ *m,* July; *Elec.* joule
jumento /hu'mento/ *m,* ass; beast of burden
juncal /hun'kal/ *a* reedy; rushy; *Inf.* slim, lissome
juncar /hun'kar/ *m,* reedy ground
junco /'hunko/ *m, Bot.* rush, reed; *Naut.* junk
juncoso /hun'koso/ *a* reed-like; rushy; reedy
junio /'hunio/ *m,* June
junquillo /hun'kiʎo; hun'kiyo/ *m,* jonquil; *Archit.* reed molding
junta /'hunta/ *f,* joint; assembly, council; committee; union, association; session, sitting; entirety, whole; board, management. **j. de comercio,** board of trade. **j. directiva,** managerial board
juntamente /hunta'mente/ *adv* jointly; simultaneously
juntar /hun'tar/ *vt* to join, unite (*with prep a or con*); couple; assemble; amass; leave ajar (door); —*vr* (*with con*) frequent company of; meet; join; copulate
junto /'hunto/ *a* united, together —*adv* (*with prep a*) near; —*adv* together, simultaneously. **en j.,** altogether, in all
juntura /hun'tura/ *f,* joining; joint; seam; juncture
jura /'hura/ *f,* solemn oath; swearing
jurado /hu'raðo/ *m,* jury; jury
juramentar /huramen'tar/ *vt* to swear in; —*vr* take an oath
juramento /hura'mento/ *m,* oath; curse, imprecation. **j. falso,** perjury, **prestar j.,** to take an oath
jurar /hu'rar/ *vt* to swear an oath; swear allegiance; —*vi* curse, be profane
jurídico /hu'riðiko/ *a* juridical, legal
jurisconsulto /huriskon'sulto/ *m,* jurisconsult
jurisdicción /urisðik'θion; hurisðik'sion/ *f, Law.* jurisdiction; boundary; authority
jurisprudencia /hurispru'ðenθia; hurispru'ðensia/ *f,* jurisprudence
jurista /hu'rista/ *mf* jurist
justa /'husta/ *f,* joust; tournament; contest
justar /hus'tar/ *vi* to joust
justicia /hus'tiθia; hus'tisia/ *f,* justice; equity, right; penalty, punishment; righteousness; court of justice; *Inf.* death penalty, execution. **administrar j.,** to dispense justice
justiciero /husti'θiero; husti'siero/ *a* just
justificable /hustifi'kaβle/ *a* justifiable
justificación /hustifika'θion; hustifika'sion/ *f,* justification, impartiality, fairness; convincing proof
justificar /hustifi'kar/ *vt* to justify, vindicate; adjust, regulate; prove innocent; —*vr* justify oneself; prove one's innocence
justillo /hus'tiʎo; hus'tiyo/ *m,* jerkin
justipreciar /hustipre'θiar; hustipre'siar/ *vt* to appraise, value

justiprecio /husti'preθio; husti'presio/ *m,* appraisement, valuation
justo /'husto/ *a* just; righteous, virtuous; exact, accurate; tight-fitting, close —*adv* justly; exactly; tightly
Jutlandia /hut'landia/ Jutland
juvenil /huβe'nil/ *a* young
juventud /huβen'tuð/ *f,* youthfulness, youth; younger generation
juzgado /huθ'gaðo; hus'gaðo/ *m,* court of law; jurisdiction; judgeship
juzgar /huθ'gar; hus'gar/ *vt* to judge, pass sentence on; decide, consider
ka /ka/ *f,* name of the letter K
káiser /'kaiser/ *m,* kaiser
kan /kan/ *m,* khan
kantiano /kan'tiano/ *a* Kantian
Kenia /'kenia/ Kenya
kermese /ker'mese/ *f,* kermis, festival
kerosén /kero'sen/ *m,* kerosene
kilo /'kilo/ *prefix* meaning a thousand. *m, Abbr.* kilogram
kilociclo /kilo'θiklo; kilo'siklo/ *m, Elec.* kilocycle
kilogramo /kilo'gramo/ *m,* kilogram (2.17 lb.)
kilolitro /kilo'litro/ *m,* kiloliter
kilometraje /kilome'trahe/ *m,* number of kilometers; mileage
kilométrico /kilo'metriko/ *a* kilometric. **billete k.,** tourist ticket
kilómetro /ki'lometro/ *m,* kilometer (about $\frac{5}{8}$ mile)
kilovatio /kilo'βatio/ *m, Elec.* kilowatt
kiosco /'kiosko/ *m,* kiosk

L

la /la/ *def art f, sing* the (e.g. *la mesa,* the table). **la** is replaced by el *m, sing* before feminine nouns beginning with stressed *a* or *ha* (e.g. *el hambre,* hunger). **la** is sometimes used before names of famous women (e.g. *la Juana de Arco, la Melba* (Joan of Arc, Melba)) and is generally not translated *—pers pron acc f sing* her; it (e.g. *La veo venir,* I see her coming) *—dem. pron* followed by *de,* or by *que* introducing relative clause, that of, that which, the one that, she who (e.g. *La casa está lejos de la en que escribo,* The house is far from the one in which I write). **la de** is used familiarly for Mrs. (e.g. *la de Jiménez,* Mrs. Jimenez). **la** means some, any, one, as substitution for noun already given (e.g. *Su hija lo haría si la tuviera,* Her daughter would do it if she had one)
lábaro /'laβaro/ *m,* labarum, standard
laberíntico /laβe'rintiko/ *a* labyrinthine
laberinto /laβe'rinto/ *m,* labyrinth; *Fig.* tangle, complication; *Anat.* labyrinth of the ear
labia /'laβia/ *f, Inf.* blarney, gab
labial /la'βial/ *a* labial
labihendido /laβien'diðo/ *a* harelipped
labio /'laβio/ *m,* lip; rim, edge. **l. leporino,** harelip. **cerrar los labios,** to close one's lips; keep silent
labor /la'βor/ *f,* work, toil; sewing; needlework; husbandry, farming; silkworm egg; *Mineral.* working; trimming; plowing, harrowing
laborable /laβo'raβle/ *a* workable; cultivable, tillable. **día l.,** workday
laborar /laβo'rar/ *vt* to work; till; plow; construct; *—vi* scheme, plot, plan
laboratorio /laβora'torio/ *m,* laboratory
laborear /laβore'ar/ *vt* to work; till, cultivate; *Naut.* reeve
laboreo /laβo'reo/ *m,* tilling, cultivation; working, development (of mines, etc.)
laboriosidad /laβoriosi'ðað/ *f,* laboriousness, diligence
laborioso /laβo'rioso/ *a* industrious, diligent; laborious, tedious, hard
laborista /laβo'rista/ *a* and *mf* belonging to the Labor Party
labra /'laβra/ *f,* stonecutting; carving or working (metal, stone, or wood)
labrada /la'βraða/ *f,* fallow land ready for sowing
labradero /laβra'ðero/ *a* workable; cultivable, tillable
labrado /la'βraðo/ *a* and *past part* worked; fashioned; carved; embroidered; figured, patterned. *m,* (gen. *pl*) cultivated ground
labrador /laβra'ðor/ *m,* laborer, worker; farmer; peasant
labradora /laβra'ðora/ *f,* peasant girl; farm girl
labradoresco, labradoril /laβraðo'resko, laβraðo'ril/ *a* rustic, peasant, farming
labrandera /laβran'dera/ *f,* seamstress
labrantío /labran'βtio/ *a* tillable, cultivable. *m,* farming
labranza /la'βranθa; la'βransa/ *f,* tillage, cultivation; farm; farmland; farming; employment, work
labrar /la'βrar/ *vt* to work, do; carve; fashion, construct, make; *Agr.* cultivate, till; plow; embroider; sew; bring about, cause; *—vi Fig.* impress deeply, leave a strong impression
labriego /la'βriego/ **(-ga)** *n* agricultural laborer; peasant
laca /'laka/ *f,* lac; lacquer, varnish; *Art.* lake (pigment)
lacayo /la'kaio/ *m,* groom; lackey, footman
lacear /laθe'ar; lase'ar/ *vt Sew.* to trim with bows; tie, lace; snare, trap
laceración /laθera'θion; lasera'sion/ *f,* laceration
lacerado /laθe'raðo; lase'raðo/ *a* unhappy, unfortunate; leprous
lacerar /laθe'rar; lase'rar/ *vt* to lacerate, mangle, tear; distress, wound the feelings of
lacería /laθe'ria; lase'ria/ *f,* poverty, misery; toil, drudgery; trouble, affliction
lacero /la'θero; la'sero/ *m,* cowboy, one who uses a lasso; poacher
lacio /'laθio; 'lasio/ *a* drooping, limp; withered, faded; straight (hair)
lacónico /la'koniko/ *a* laconic; concise; Laconian
lacra /'lakra/ *f,* aftereffect, trace (of illness); vice; fault
lacrar /la'krar/ *vt* to impair the health; infect with an illness; injure, prejudice (the interests, etc.); seal with sealing wax
lacre /'lakre/ *m,* sealing wax *—a* red
lacrimal /lakri'mal/ *a* lachrymal
lacrimoso /lakri'moso/ *a* tearful, lachrymose
lactancia /lak'tanθia; lak'tansia/ *f,* lactation
lactar /lak'tar/ *vt* to suckle; feed with milk; *—vi* take or drink milk
lácteo /'lakteo/ *a* lacteal; milky
lacustre /la'kustre/ *a* lacustrine, lake
ladear /laðe'ar/ *vt* to incline; tilt; turn aside, twist; skirt, pass close to; reach by a roundabout way, go indirectly to; *—vr* tilt; be in favor of, incline to; be equal to
ladeo /la'ðeo/ *m,* tilt; sloping; turning aside
ladera /la'ðera/ *f,* slope, incline; hillside
ladería /laðe'ria/ *f,* terrace on a hillside
ladero /la'ðero/ *a* lateral
ladilla /la'ðiʎa; la'ðiya/ *f,* crab louse
ladino /la'ðino/ *a* eloquent; versatile linguistically; wily, crafty; *m,* Ladino (variety of Judezmo)
lado /'laðo/ *m,* side; edge, margin; slope, declivity; faction, party; side, flank; face (of a coin); *Fig.* aspect, view; line of descent; means, way; favor, protection; *pl* helpers, protectors; advisers. **al l.,** near at hand. *Inf.* **dar de l. (a),** to cool off, fall out with. **dejar a un l. (una cosa),** to omit, pass over (a thing). **mirar de l.** *or* **de medio l.,** to look upon with disapproval; steal a look at
ladrador /laðra'ðor/ *a* barking
ladrar /la'ðrar/ *vi* to bark; *Inf.* threaten without hurting
ladrido /la'ðriðo/ *m,* bark, barking; slander, gossip
ladrillado /laðri'ʎaðo; laðri'yaðo/ *m,* brick floor or pavement
ladrillar /laðri'ʎar; laðri'yar/ *vt* to floor or pave with bricks. *m,* brickyard; brickkiln
ladrillero /laðri'ʎero; laðri'yero/ **(-ra)** *n* brickmaker
ladrillo /la'ðriʎo; la'ðriyo/ *m,* brick; tile
ladrón /la'ðron/ **(-ona)** *a* robbing, thieving *—n* thief, robber; burglar. *m.* **l. de corazones,** ladykiller
ladronera /laðro'nera/ *f,* thieves' den; thieving, pilfering; strongbox
lagar /la'gar/ *m,* wine or olive press
lagarta /la'garta/ *f,* female lizard; *Inf.* she-serpent, cunning female
lagartera /lagar'tera/ *f,* lizard hole
lagartija /lagar'tiha/ *f,* wall lizard, small lizard
lagarto /la'garto/ *m,* lizard; *Inf.* sly, artful person, fox; *Inf.* insignia of Spanish Military Order of Santiago
lago /'lago/ *m,* lake
lagotear /lagote'ar/ *vi Inf.* to wheedle, play up to
lagotería /lagote'ria/ *f,* wheedling, coaxing, flattery
lágrima /'lagrima/ *f,* tear; drop (of liquid); exudation, ozzing (from trees)
lagrimal /lagri'mal/ *a* lachrymal
lagrimear /lagrime'ar/ *vi* to shed tears
lagrimeo /lagri'meo/ *m,* weeping, crying; watering of the eyes
lagrimoso /lagri'moso/ *a* tearful; watery (of eyes); sad, tragic
laguna /la'guna/ *f,* small lake, lagoon; lacuna; gap, hiatus
lagunoso /lagu'noso/ *a* boggy, marshy
laical /lai'kal/ *a* lay, secular
laicismo /lai'θismo; lai'sismo/ *m,* secularism

laico /'laiko/ *a* lay, secular
lama /'lama/ *f,* ooze, slime. *m,* lama, Buddhist priest
lamaísmo /lama'ismo/ *m,* lamaism
lameculos /lame'kulos/ *mf Inf.* toady
lamedura /lame'ðura/ *f,* licking; lapping
lamentable /lamen'taβle/ *a* lamentable
lamentación /lamenta'θion; lamenta'sion/ *f,* lamentation; lament
lamentador /lamenta'ðor/ **(-ra)** *a* lamenting, wailing —*n* wailer, mourner
lamentar /lamen'tar/ *vt* to mourn, lament, bewail; —*vr* bemoan, bewail
lamento /la'mento/ *m,* lament
lamentoso /lamen'toso/ *a* lamenting, afflicted; lamentable
lamer /la'mer/ *vt* to lick; pass the tongue over; touch lightly; lap
lámina /'lamina/ *f,* sheet (of metal); lamina; engraving; illustration, picture; engraving plate
laminación /lamina'θion; lamina'sion/ *f,* lamination, rolling (of metals)
laminado /lami'naðo/ *a* laminate; rolled (metals). *m,* rolling (of metals)
laminador /lamina'ðor/ *m,* rolling mill (for metals)
laminar /lami'nar/ *a* laminate; laminated —*vt* to roll (metals); laminate; lick
lámpara /'lampara/ *f,* lamp; radiance, light, luminous body; grease spot. **l. de los mineros** *or* **l. de seguridad,** safety lamp. **l. de soldar,** blowpipe. **l. termiónica,** *Radio.* thermionic valve. **atizar la l.,** to trim the lamp; *Inf.* refill drinking glasses
lamparería /lampare'ria/ *f,* lamp factory; lamp shop
lamparero /lampa'rero/ **(-ra),** *n* **lamparista** *mf* lamplighter; lamp maker or seller
lamparilla /lampa'riʎa; lampa'riya/ *f,* night-light; *Bot.* aspen; small lamp
lamparón /lampa'ron/ *m,* scrofula, king's evil; tumor (disease of horses)
lampiño /lam'piɲo/ *a* beardless, clean-shaven; smooth-faced; *Bot.* nonhirsute
lampista /lam'pista/ *mf* See **lamparero**
lamprea /lam'prea/ *f,* lamprey
lana /'lana/ *f,* wool; fleece; woolen garments or cloth; woolen trade (gen. *pl*)
lanar /la'nar/ *a* wool; wool-bearing. **ganado l.,** sheep
lance /'lanθe; 'lanse/ *m,* throw, cast; casting a fishing line; catch of fish; crisis, difficult moment; *Lit.* episode; quarrel; move (in a game). *Fig.* **l. apretado,** difficult position, tight corner. **l. de fortuna,** chance, fate. **l. de honor,** affair of honor; duel
lancear /lanθe'ar; lanse'ar/ *vt* to wound with a lance; lance
lancero /lan'θero; lan'sero/ *m, Mil.* lancer; *pl* lancers (dance and music)
lanceta /lan'θeta; lan'seta/ *f,* lancet
lancha /'lantʃa/ *f, Naut.* launch; lighter; ship's boat; small boat; flagstone. **l. bombardera** *or* **l. cañonera,** gunboat. **l. de salvamento,** ship's lifeboat. **l. escampavía,** patrol boat
lancinar /lanθi'nar; lansi'nar/ *vt Med.* to lance
landa /'landa/ *f,* lande
landó /lan'do/ *m,* landau
lanero /la'nero/ *a* woolen. *m,* wool merchant; wool warehouse
langosta /laŋ'gosta/ *f,* locust; lobster. **l. migratoria,** locust
langostín /laŋgos'tin/ *m,* crayfish
languidecer /laŋguiðe'θer; laŋguiðe'ser/ *vi irr* to languish, pine. See **conocer**
languidez /laŋgui'ðeθ; laŋgui'ðes/ *f,* lassitude, inertia; languor
lánguido /'laŋguiðo/ *a* listless, weak, languid; halfhearted; languishing, languorous
lanolina /lano'lina/ *f,* lanolin
lanosidad /lanosi'ðað/ *f,* woolliness; down (on leaves, etc.)
lanoso, lanudo /la'noso, la'nuðo/ *a* woolly
lanza /'lanθa; 'lansa/ *f,* lance, spear; lancer; nozzle (of a hosepipe). **correr lanzas,** to joust (in a tournament). **estar con la l. en ristre,** to have the lance in rest; be prepared or ready. *Inf.* **ser una l.,** to be very clever
lanzabombas /lanθa'βombas; lansa'βombas/ *m,* (*Aer. Nav.*) bomb release
lanzada /lan'θaða; lan'saða/ *f,* lance or spear thrust
lanzadera /lanθa'ðera; lansa'ðera/ *f,* weaver's shuttle; sewing machine shuttle. *Inf.* **parecer una l.,** to be constantly on the go
lanzador /lanθa'ðor; lansa'ðor/ **(-ra)** *m,* batsman —*n* thrower, caster, tosser
lanzallamas /lanθa'ʎamas; lansa'yamas/ *m,* flamethrower
lanzamiento /lanθa'miento; lansa'miento/ *m,* throwing; cast, throw; *Law.* dispossession; *Naut.* launching
lanzaminas /lanθa'minas; lansa'minas/ *m,* minelayer
lanzar /lan'θar; lan'sar/ *vt* to throw, cast, hurl; *Naut.* launch; vomit; *Law.* dispossess; *Agr.* take root; —*vr* hurl oneself, rush; take (to), embark (upon)
lanzatorpedos /lanθator'peðos; lansator'peðos/ **(tubo)** *m,* torpedo tube
lañar /la'ɲar/ *vt* to clamp; clean fish (for salting)
lapa /'lapa/ *f,* barnacle, limpet
lapicero /lapi'θero; lapi'sero/ *m,* pencil holder, pencil case; mechanical pencil
lápida /'lapiða/ *f,* memorial tablet; gravestone
lapidación /lapiða'θion; lapiða'sion/ *f,* lapidation, stoning
lapidar /lapi'ðar/ *vt* to stone, lapidate; throw stones at
lapidario /lapi'ðario/ *a* lapidary
lapislázuli /lapis'laθuli; lapis'lasuli/ *m,* lapis lazuli
lápiz /'lapiθ; 'lapis/ *m,* graphite; pencil; crayon. **l. para los labios,** lipstick
lapizar /lapi'θar; lapi'sar/ *m,* graphite mine —*vt* to pencil
lapón /la'pon/ **(-ona)** *a* Lappish —*n* Laplander. *m,* Sami (language)
Laponia /la'ponia/ Lapland
lapso /'lapso/ *m,* lapse, period, passage; slip, error, failure
laquear /lake'ar/ *vt* to lacquer, paint
lar /lar/ *m,* home; *pl* lares
lardear /larðe'ar/ *vt Cul.* to baste
lardo /'larðo/ *m,* lard; animal fat
lardoso /lar'ðoso/ *a* greasy; fat; oily
larga /'larga/ *f,* longest billiard cue; delay (gen. *pl*). **a la l.,** in the long run
largamente /larga'mente/ *adv* fully, at length; generously; widely, extensively; comfortably
largar /lar'gar/ *vt* to slacken, loosen; *Naut.* unfurl; set at liberty; *Fig. Inf.* let fly (oaths, etc.); administer (blows, etc.); —*vr Inf.* quit, leave (in a hurry or secretly); *Naut.* set sail
largo /'largo/ *a* long; generous, liberal; abundant, plentiful; protracted; prolonged; expeditious; *pl* many long (e.g. *por largos años,* for many long years). *m, Mus.* largo; length. *Inf.* **¡L. de aquí!** Get out! **a la larga,** in length; eventually, finally; slowly; with many digressions. **a lo l.,** lengthwise; along the length (of); in the distance, far off; along, the length (of). *Fig.* **ponerse de l.,** to make one's debut in society; come of age
largor /lar'gor/ *m,* **largura** *f,* length
largueza /lar'geθa; lar'gesa/ *f,* length; generosity, munificence
largura /lar'gura/ *f,* length
laringe /la'rinhe/ *f,* larynx
laríngeo /la'rinheo/ *a* laryngeal
laringitis /larin'hitis/ *f,* laryngitis
larva /'larβa/ *f,* larva; worm, grub; specter, phantom
las /las/ *def art. f pl,* of **la** the —*pers pron acc f pl,* of **la,** them
lascivia /las'θiβia; las'siβia/ *f,* lasciviousness
lascivo /las'θiβo; las'siβo/ *a* lascivious, lewd; wanton
lasitud /lasi'tuð/ *f,* lassitude, weariness, exhaustion
laso /'laso/ *a* weary, exhausted; weak; untwisted (of silk, etc.)
lástima /'lastima/ *f,* compassion, pity; pitiful sight; complaint, lamentation. **dar l.,** to cause pity. **Es l.,** It's a pity. **tener l.** (**a** *or* **de**) to be sorry for (persons)

lastimador /lastima'ðor/ *a* harmful, injurious; painful

lastimar /lasti'mar/ *vt* to hurt, harm, injure; pity; *Fig.* wound, distress; *—vr* (*with de*) be sorry for or about; complain, lament

lastimero /lasti'mero/ *a* pitiful; mournful; injurious, harmful

lastimoso /lasti'moso/ *a* pitiful, heartbreaking; mournful

lastrar /las'trar/ *vt* to ballast

lastre /'lastre/ *m,* ballast; good sense, prudence

lata /'lata/ *f,* can, tin; tin plate; can of food. **en l.,** canned, tinned (of food). *Inf.* **Es una l.,** It's a bore, It's an awful nuisance

latamente /lata'mente/ *adv* extensively, at length; broadly

latente /la'tente/ *a* latent

lateral /late'ral/ *a* lateral

látex /'lateks/ *m,* latex

latido /la'tiðo/ *m,* yelp, bark; beat; throb; palpitation

latifundios /lati'fundios/ *m pl,* latifundia (large agricultural estates)

latigazo /lati'gaθo; lati'gaso/ *m,* lash; crack of a whip; sudden blow of fate; *Inf.* draft (of wine, etc.); harsh scolding; *Naut.* jerk or flapping (of sails)

látigo /'latigo/ *m,* whip, lash; cinch, girth of a saddle

latín /la'tin/ *m,* Latin. **bajo l.,** low Latin. *Inf.* **saber l.,** to know the score; be smart

latinajo /lati'naho/ *m, Inf.* bad Latin

latinidad /latini'ðað/ *f,* Latinity

latinismo /lati'nismo/ *m,* Latinism

latinista /lati'nista/ *mf* Latinist

latinizar /latini'θar; latini'sar/ *vt* to latinize; *—vi Inf.* use Latin phrases

latino /la'tino/ *a* Latin; lateen sail

latinoamericano /latinoameri'kano/ **(-na)** *a* and *n* Latin-American

latir /la'tir/ *vi* to yelp, howl; bark; throb, palpitate, beat

latitud /lati'tuð/ *f,* latitude; area, extent; breadth

latitudinario /lati,tuði'nario/ *a* latitudinarian

lato /'lato/ *a* extensive; large; broad (of word meanings)

latón /la'ton/ *m,* brass

latonería /latone'ria/ *f,* brassworks; brass shop

latoso /la'toso/ *a* boring, troublesome, annoying

latrocinio /latro'θinio; latro'sinio/ *m,* larceny

latvio /'latβio/ **(-ia)** *a* and *n* Latvian

laúd /la'uð/ *m,* lute

laudable /lau'ðaβle/ *a* praiseworthy, laudable

láudano /'lauðano/ *m,* laudanum

laudatorio /lauða'torio/ *a* laudatory

laurear /laure'ar/ *vt* to crown with laurel; honor, reward

laurel /lau'rel/ *m,* bay tree. **l. cerezo,** laurel. **l. rosa,** rosebay, oleander

láureo /'laureo/ *a* laurel

lauréola /lau'reola/ *f,* laurel wreath

lauro /'lauro/ *m,* bay tree; glory, triumph

Lausana /lau'sana/ Lausanne

lava /'laβa/ *f,* lava

lavable /la'βaβle/ *a* washable

lavabo /la'βaβo/ *m,* washstand; cloakroom, lavatory

lavada /la'βaða/ *f,* load of wash, load

lavadedos /laβa'ðeðos/ *m,* fingerbowl

lavadero /laβa'ðero/ *m,* washing place; laundry

lavado /la'βaðo/ *m,* washing; cleaning; wash. **l. al seco,** dry cleaning

lavadura /laβa'ðura/ *f,* washing

lavamanos /laβa'manos/ *m,* washstand; lavatory

lavamiento /laβa'miento/ *m,* washing, cleansing, ablution

lavanda /la'βanda/ *f,* lavender

lavandera /laβan'dera/ *f,* laundress; washerwoman

lavandería /laβande'ria/ *f,* laundry

lavandero /laβan'dero/ *m,* laundry; laundryman

lavaplatos /laβa'platos/ *m,* dishwasher

lavar /la'βar/ *vt* to wash; *Fig.* wipe out, purify; paint in watercolors. **l. al seco,** to dry-clean

lavativa /laβa'tiβa/ *f,* enema; syringe, clyster; *Inf.* nuisance, bore

lavatorio /laβa'torio/ *m,* washing, lavation; *Eccl.* lavabo; lavatory, washing place; *Eccl.* maundy

lavazas /la'βaθas; la'βasas/ *f pl,* dirty soapy water

laxante /lak'sante/ *a* and *m,* laxative

laxar /lak'sar/ *vt* to loosen, relax; soften

laxitud /laksi'tuð/ *f,* laxity

laxo /'lakso/ *a* lax; slack

laya /'laia/ *f, Agr.* spade; kind, sort, class

layar /la'iar/ *vt Agr.* to fork

lazar /la'θar; la'sar/ *vt* to lasso

lazareto /laθa'reto; lasa'reto/ *m,* leper hospital; quarantine hospital

lazarillo /laθa'riʎo; lasa'riyo/ *m,* boy who guides a blind person

lazarino /laθa'rino; lasa'rino/ *a* leprous

lázaro /'laθaro; 'lasaro/ *m,* lazar, beggar

lazo /'laθo; 'laso/ *m,* bow; knot of ribbons; tie; ornamental tree; figure (in dancing); lasso; rope, bond; lace (of a shoe); *Fig.* trap, snare; bond, obligation; slipknot. **l. corredizo,** running knot. *Fig. Inf.* **armar l.,** to set a trap. *Inf.* **caer en el l.,** to fall into the trap, be deceived

le /le/ *pers pron dat m,* or *f, 3rd pers sing* to him, to her, to it, to you (e.g. *María le dio el perro,* Mary gave him (her, you) the dog). Clarity may require the addition of **a él, a ella, a usted** (e.g. *Le dio el perro a ella,* etc.) *—pers pron acc m, 3rd pers sing* him (e.g. *Le mandé a casa,* I sent him home)

leal /le'al/ *a* loyal; faithful (animals)

lealtad /leal'tað/ *f,* loyalty; faithfulness; sincerity, truth

lebrel /le'βrel/ *m,* greyhound

lección /lek'θion; lek'sion/ *f,* reading; lesson; oral test; warning, example. **l. práctica,** object lesson. **dar l.,** to give a lesson. **tomar la l.,** to hear a lesson

leccionista /lekθio'nista; leksio'nista/ *mf* private teacher, coach, tutor

lechas /'letʃas/ *f pl,* soft roe; milt

leche /'letʃe/ *f,* milk; milky fluid of some plants and seeds. *Inf.* **estar con la l. en los labios,** to be young and inexperienced

lechera /le'tʃera/ *f,* milkmaid; milk can or jug

lechería /letʃe'ria/ *f,* dairy; dairy shop

lechero /le'tʃero/ **(-ra)** *a* dairy, milk; milky; milch, milk-giving *—n* milk seller. **industria lechera,** dairy farming

lecho /'letʃo/ *m,* bed; couch; animal's bed, litter; riverbed; bottom of the sea; layer; *Geol.* stratum

lechón /le'tʃon/ *m,* suckling pig; hog; *Inf.* slovenly man

lechoso /le'tʃoso/ *a* milky

lechuga /le'tʃuga/ *f,* lettuce; frill, flounce. *Inf.* **como una l.,** as fresh as a daisy

lechuguero /letʃu'gero/ **(-ra)** *n* lettuce seller

lechuguilla /letʃu'giʎa; letʃu'giya/ *f,* ruff; ruche

lechuguina /letʃu'gina/ *f, Inf.* affected, overdressed young woman

lechuguino /letʃu'gino/ *m,* lettuce plant; *Inf.* young blood, gallant; *Inf.* foppish young man

lechuza /le'tʃuθa; le'tʃusa/ *f,* barn owl

lector /lek'tor/ **(-ra)** *n* reader; lecturer

lectura /lek'tura/ *f,* reading; lecture; culture, knowledge

ledo /'leðo/ *a* happy, content

leer /le'er/ *vt irr* to read; explain, interpret; teach; take part in an oral test. See **creer**

lega /'lega/ *f, Eccl.* lay sister

legación /lega'θion; lega'sion/ *f, Eccl.* legateship, legation

legado /le'gaðo/ *m,* legacy; legate

legajo /le'gaho/ *m,* bundle, docket; file

legal /le'gal/ *a* legal; legitimate; upright, trustworthy

legalidad /legali'ðað/ *f,* legality

legalización /legaliθa'θion; legalisa'sion/ *f,* legalization

legalizar /legali'θar; legali'sar/ *vt* to legalize

legamente /lega'mente/ *adv* ignorantly, stupidly

légamo /'legamo/ *m,* mud, slime

legamoso /lega'moso/ *a* slimy

legaña /le'gaɲa/ *f,* bleariness (of the eyes)

legañoso /lega'ɲoso/ *a* bleary-eyed

legar /le'gar/ *vt* to bequeath; send as a legate
legatario /lega'tario/ **(-ia)** *n* legatee, one to whom a legacy is bequeathed
legendario /lehen'dario/ *a* legendary
legibilidad /lehiβili'ðað/ *f,* legibility
legible /le'hiβle/ *a* legible
legión /le'hion/ *f,* legion
legionario /lehio'nario/ *a* and *m,* legionary
legislación /lehisla'θion; lehisla'sion/ *f,* legislation
legislador /lehisla'ðor/ **(-ra)** *a* legislative —*n* legislator
legislar /lehis'lar/ *vi* to legislate
legislativo /lehisla'tiβo/ *a* legislative
legislatura /lehisla'tura/ *f,* legislature
legista /le'hista/ *mf* jurist; student of law
legítima /le'hitima/ *f,* portion of a married man's estate that cannot be willed away from his wife and children
legitimación /lehitima'θion; lehitima'sion/ *f,* legitimation
legitimar /lehiti'mar/ *vt* to legitimize
legitimidad /lehitimi'ðað/ *f,* legitimacy
legítimo /le'hitimo/ *a* legitimate; real, true
lego /'lego/ *a* lay, secular. *m,* layman
legua /'legua/ *f,* league (approximately 5.573 meters). **a la l., de cien leguas, desde media l.,** from afar
legumbre /le'gumbre/ *f,* pulse; vegetable
leguminoso /legumi'noso/ *a* leguminous
leído /le'iðo/ *a* well-read
leila /'leila/ *f,* nocturnal Moorish merrymaking or dance
lejanía /leha'nia/ *f,* distance
lejano /le'hano/ *a* distant, remote, far off
lejía /le'hia/ *f,* lye; bleaching solution; *Inf.* dressing-down, scolding
lejos /'lehos/ *adv* far off, far, distant. *m,* perspective, view from afar; *Art.* background. **a lo l.,** far off, in the distance. **de** *or* **desde l.,** from afar, from a distance
lelo /'lelo/ *a* stupid; fatuous, inane
lema /'lema/ *m,* chapter heading; argument, summary; motto; theme, subject
lémur /'lemur/ *m,* lemur
lencería /lenθe'ria; lense'ria/ *f,* linen goods; linen merchant's shop; linen closet
lencero /len'θero; len'sero/ *m,* linen merchant
lene /'lene/ *a* smooth, soft; kind, sweet, gentle; lightweight
lengua /'leŋgua/ *f, Anat.* tongue; mother tongue, language; clapper of a bell; information. *mf* spokes. **l. de escorpión** *or* **mala l.,** scandalmonger, backbiter. **l. de fuego,** *Eccl.* tongue of fire, flame. **l. del agua,** waterline, tidemark. **l. de oc,** langue d'oc. **l. de oil,** langue d'oil. **l. de tierra,** neck of land, promontory. **l. viva,** modern language. *Inf.* **andar en lenguas,** to be on every lip, be famous. *Inf.* **hacerse lenguas de,** to praise to the skies. *Inf.* **irse (a uno) la l.,** to be indiscreet, talk too much. **poner l.** *or* **lenguas en,** to gossip about. *Inf.* **tener mucha l.,** to be very talkative. **tomar l.** *or* **lenguas,** to find out about, inform oneself on
lenguado /leŋ'guaðo/ *m, Ichth.* sole
lenguaje /leŋ'guahe/ *m,* language; style; speech, idiom. **l. vulgar,** common speech
lengüeta /leŋ'gueta/ *f, dim* little tongue; *Mus.* tongue (of wind instruments); barb (of an arrow); needle (of a balance)
lenidad /leni'ðað/ *f,* lenience, indulgence, mercy
Leningrado /leniŋ'graðo/ Leningrad
lenitivo /leni'tiβo/ *a* lenitive; soothing. *m, Med.* lenitive; *Fig.* balm (of sorrow, etc.)
lente /'lente/ *m,* lens; *pl* eyeglasses. **l. de aumento,** magnifying glass
lenteja /len'teha/ *f,* lentil; lentil plant
lentejuela /lente'huela/ *f,* sequin
lentitud /lenti'tuð/ *f,* lentitude; slowness, deliberation
lento /'lento/ *a* slow, deliberate; sluggish, heavy; *Med.* glutinous, adhesive
leña /'leɲa/ *f,* firewood; *Inf.* beating, birching. *Fig.* **echar l. al fuego,** to add fuel to the flame. *Fig.* **llevar l. al monte,** to carry coals to Newcastle
leñador /leɲa'ðor/ **(-ra)** *n* woodcutter; firewood dealer
leñera /le'ɲera/ *f,* woodpile; woodshed
leño /'leɲo/ *m,* wooden log; wood, timber; *Poet.* ship; *Inf.* blockhead
leñoso /le'ɲoso/ *a* woody, ligneous
león /le'on/ *m,* lion. *Astron.* Leo; valiant man. **l. marino,** sea lion
leona /le'ona/ *f,* lioness
leonera /leo'nera/ *f,* lion cage; lion's den; *Inf.* gambling den; *Inf.* lumber room
leonero /leo'nero/ **(-ra)** *n* lionkeeper; *Inf.* keeper of a gambling house
leonés /leo'nes/ **(-esa)** *a* and *n* Leonese
leonino /leo'nino/ *a* leonine
leopardo /leo'parðo/ *m,* leopard
lepra /'lepra/ *f,* leprosy
leproso /le'proso/ *a* leprous
lerdo /'lerðo/ *a* slow, lumbering (gen. horses); stupid, slow-witted, dull
les /les/ *pers pron dat 3rd pers pl mf,* to them (e.g. *Les dimos las flores,* We gave them flowers. *Les hablé del asunto,* I spoke to them about the matter)
lesbio /'lesβio/ **(-ia)** *a* and *n* lesbian
lesión /le'sion/ *f,* lesion, wound; *Fig.* injury
lesionar /lesio'nar/ *vt* to wound; *Fig.* injure
lesna /'lesna/ *f,* awl
leso /'leso/ *a* wounded, hurt; offensive, injurious; *Fig.* unbalanced, perturbed (of the mind). **crimen de lesa majestad,** crime of lèse-majesté
letal /le'tal/ *a* lethal; deadly
letanía /leta'nia/ *f, Eccl.* litany
letargia /le'tarhia/ *f, Med.* lethargy
letárgico /le'tarhiko/ *a* lethargic
letargo /le'targo/ *m,* lethargy; indifference, apathy
Letonia /le'tonia/ Latvia
letra /'letra/ *f,* letter (of alphabet); *Print.* type; penmanship, hand; *Fig.* letter, literal meaning; words (of a song); inscription; *Com.* bill, draft; cunning, shrewdness; *pl* learning, knowledge. **l. abierta,** *Com.* open credit. **l. de cambio,** *Com.* bill of exchange. **l. gótica,** Gothic characters. **l. itálica,** italics. **l. mayúscula,** capital letter. **l. paladial,** palatal. **facultad de letras,** faculty of arts. **La l. con sangre entra,** Learning is acquired with pain. **primeras letras,** early education, first letters
letrado /le'traðo/ *a* learned, educated; *Inf.* presumptuous; pedantic. *m,* lawyer
letrero /le'trero/ *m,* label; inscription; poster, bill; sign, indicator. **l. luminoso,** illuminated sign
letrilla /le'triʎa; le'triya/ *f,* short poem, often set to music
letrina /le'trina/ *f,* latrine
leucocito /leuko'θito; leuko'sito/ *m,* leucocyte
leva /'leβa/ *f, Naut.* weighing anchor; *Mil.* levy, forced enrollment; tappet; *Mech.* lever; *Mech.* cam; *Inf.* **irse a l. y a monte,** to flee, beat it, quit
levadizo /leβa'ðiθo; leβa'ðiso/ *a* able to be raised or lowered (bridges). **puente l.,** drawbridge
levadura /leβa'ðura/ *f,* leaven, yeast; rising (of bread)
levantada /leβan'taða/ *f,* act of rising from bed
levantamiento /leβanta'miento/ *m,* raising, lifting; rebellion, revolt; ennoblement, elevation; settlement of accounts
levantar /leβan'tar/ *vt* to raise, lift; pick up; build, construct; cancel, remove; encourage, rouse; recruit, enlist; cut (cards); leave, abandon; survey; disturb (game); produce, raise (a swelling); found, institute; increase (prices); raise (the voice); *Fig.* ennoble, elevate; cause, occasion; libel, accuse falsely; —*vr* rise; get up; stand up; stand out, be prominent; rebel; leave one's bed after an illness. **l. bandera,** to rebel. **l. el campo,** to break camp. **levantarse del izquierdo,** *Inf.* to get out of bed on the wrong side
levante /le'βante/ *m,* east; Levant; east wind
levantino /leβan'tino/ **(-na)** *a* and *n* Levantine
levar /le'βar/ *vt Naut.* to weigh anchor; —*vr* set sail
leve /'leβe/ *a* light (in weight); unimportant, trifling

levedad /leβe'ðað/ *f,* lightness (in weight); unimportance, levity, flippancy
leviatán /leβia'tan/ *m,* leviathan
levita /le'βita/ *m,* Levite; deacon. *f,* frock coat
levitación /leβita'θion; leβita'sion/ *f,* levitation
levítico /le'βitiko/ *a* Levitical. *m,* Leviticus
levitón /leβi'ton/ *m,* frock coat
léxico /'leksiko/ *m,* lexicon
lexicografía /leksikogra'fia/ *f,* lexicography
lexicógrafo /leksi'kografo/ *m,* lexicographer
lexicólogo /leksi'kologo/ *m,* lexicologist
ley /lei/ *f,* law; precept; regulation, rule; doctrine; loyalty, faithfulness; affection, love; legal standard (weights, measures, quality); ratio of gold or silver in coins, jewelry; statute, ordinance; *pl* the Law. **l. de préstamo y arriendo,** Lend-Lease Act. **ley suntuaria,** sumptuary law. *Inf.* **a la l.,** with care and decorum. **a l. de caballero,** on the word of a gentleman. **de buena l.,** *a* excellent; *—adv* genuinely; in good faith. **de mala l.,** *a* disreputable, base; *—adv* in bad faith
leyenda /le'ienda/ *f,* legend; inscription; story, tale
leyente /le'iente/ *a* reading. *mf* reader
lezna /'leθna; 'lesna/ *f,* awl
lía /'lia/ *f,* plaited esparto rope; *pl* lees, dregs
liar /li'ar/ *vt* to fasten or tie up; wrap up, parcel; roll (a cigarette); *Inf.* entangle, embroil; *—vr* take a lover, enter on a liaison. *Inf.* **liarlas,** to quit, sneak off; *Inf.* kick the bucket, die
libación /liβa'θion; liβa'sion/ *f,* libation
Líbano, el /'liβano, el/ Lebanon
libar /li'βar/ *vt* to suck; perform a libation; sip, taste; sacrifice
libelista /liβe'lista/ *mf* libeler
libelo /li'βelo/ *m,* libel; *Law.* petition
libélula /li'βelula/ *f,* dragonfly
liberación /liβera'θion; liβera'sion/ *f,* liberation, freeing; receipt, quittance; *Law.* reconveyance (of mortgages)
liberador /liβera'ðor/ **(-ra)** *a* liberating, freeing *—n* liberator
liberal /liβe'ral/ *a* generous, openhanded; liberal, tolerant; learned (of professions) *—a* and *mf Polit.* liberal
liberalidad /liβerali'ðað/ *f,* generosity, magnanimity
liberalismo /liβera'lismo/ *m,* liberalism
liberalizar /liβerali'θar; liβerali'sar/ *vt* to liberalize, make liberal
liberar /liβe'rar/ *vt* to liberate
libérrimo /li'βerrimo/ *a superl* extremely free, most free
libertad /liβer'tað/ *f,* liberty, freedom; independence; privilege, right (gen. *pl*); exemption; licentiousness; forwardness, familiarity; naturalness, ease of manner; facility, capacity; immunity. **l. caucional,** freedom on bail, release on bail. **l. de cultos,** freedom of worship; religious toleration. **l. vigilada,** *Law.* probation. **poner en l.,** to set at liberty; (*with de*) *Fig.* free from
libertador /liβerta'ðor/ **(-ra)** *a* liberating, freeing *—n* liberator, deliverer
libertar /liβer'tar/ *vt* to liberate, free; save, deliver; exempt
libertario /liβer'tario/ **(-ia)** *a* anarchistic *—n* anarchist
libertinaje /liβerti'nahe/ *m,* libertinage, licentiousness
libertino /liβer'tino/ **(-na)** *a* debauched, licentious. *m,* libertine *—n* child of a freed slave
liberto /li'βerto/ **(-ta)** *n* freed slave, freedman
Libia /'liβia/ Libya
libídine /li'βiðine/ *f,* lust
libidinoso /liβiði'noso/ *a* libidinous, lustful
libio /'liβio/ **(-ia)** *a* and *n* Libyan
libra /'liβra/ *f,* pound (measure, coinage); *Astron.* Libra. **l. esterlina,** pound sterling. **l. medicinal,** pound troy
libración /liβra'θion; liβra'sion/ *f,* oscillation; *Astron.* libration
librador /liβra'ðor/ **(-ra)** *a* freeing, liberating *—n* deliverer, liberator. *m, Com.* drawer (of bill of exchange, etc.)
libramiento /liβra'miento/ *m,* liberation, deliverance; *Com.* delivery; order of payment
libranza /li'βranθa; li'βransa/ *f, Com.* draft
librar /li'βrar/ *vt* to liberate, free; protect (from misfortune); *Com.* draw (a draft); *Com.* deliver; place confidence in; issue, enact; *—vi* bring forth children; *—vr* (*with de*) escape from; get rid of
libre /'liβre/ *a* free; at liberty, disengaged; unhampered, untrammeled; independent; bold, brazen; dissolute, vicious; exempt; vacant, unoccupied; unmarried; clear, free; mutinous, rebellious; isolated, remote; innocent; unharmed. **l. cambio,** free trade
librea /li'βrea/ *f,* livery
librecambio /liβre'kambio/ *m,* free trade
librecambista /liβrekam'βista/ *a* free trade. *mf* free trader
librepensador /liβrepensa'ðor/ **(-ra)** *a* freethinking *—n* freethinker
librepensamiento /liβrepensa'miento/ *m,* free thought
librería /liβre'ria/ *f,* bookshop; book trade, bookselling; bookcase
librero /li'βrero/ *m,* bookseller. **l. anticuario,** antiquarian bookseller; rare-book dealer
libreta /li'βreta/ *f, Cul.* 1-lb. loaf; notebook; passbook, bankbook
libretista /liβre'tista/ *mf* librettist
libreto /li'βreto/ *m,* libretto
librillo /li'βriʎo; li'βriyo/ *m, dim* small book; book of cigarette papers; tub, pail; *Zool.* omasum
libro /'liβro/ *m,* book; *Mus.* libretto; *Zool.* omasum. **l. copiador,** *Com.* letter book. **l. de actas,** minute book. **l. de caja,** *Com.* cash book. **l. de cheques,** checkbook. **l. de facturas,** *Com.* invoice book. **l. de reclamaciones,** complaint book. **l. de texto,** textbook. **l. diario,** *Com.* daybook. **l. mayor,** ledger. **l. talonario,** receipt book. *Fig. Inf.* **hacer l. nuevo,** to turn over a new leaf; introduce innovations
licencia /li'θenθia; li'sensia/ *f,* permission, license; licentiousness; boldness, insolence; *Educ.* bachelor's degree, licentiate. **l. absoluta,** *Mil.* discharge
licenciado /liθen'θiaðo; lisen'siaðo/ **(-da)** *a* pedantic; free, exempt; licensed *—n Educ.* bachelor; licentiate. *m,* discharged soldier
licenciar /liθen'θiar; lisen'siar/ *vt* to allow, permit; license; dismiss, discharge; confer degree of bachelor or licentiate; *Mil.* discharge; *—vr* become licentious; receive bachelor's degree or licentiate
licenciatura /liθenθia'tura; lisensia'tura/ *f,* degree of licentiate or bachelor; graduation as such; licentiate course of study
licencioso /liθen'θioso; lisen'sioso/ *a* licentious, dissolute
liceo /li'θeo; li'seo/ *m,* lyceum
licitación /liθita'θion; lisita'sion/ *f,* bidding (at auction)
licitador /liθita'ðor; lisita'ðor/ *m,* bidder (at auction)
licitar /liθi'tar; lisi'tar/ *vt* to bid for (at auction)
lícito /'liθito; 'lisito/ *a* permissible, lawful
licor /li'kor/ *m,* liquor, alcoholic drink; liquid
licorera /liko'rera/ *f,* liqueur set; decanter
licoroso /liko'roso/ *a* aromatic, generous (of wines)
licuadora /likua'ðora/ *f,* blender
licuar /li'kuar/ *vt* to liquefy
licuefacción /likuefak'θion; likuefak'sion/ *f,* liquefaction
lid /lið/ *f,* combat, fight; dispute, controversy. **en buena l.,** in fair fight; by fair means
líder /'liðer/ *m,* leader; chief
lidia /'liðia/ *f,* fighting; bullfight
lidiador /liðia'ðor/ **(-ra)** *n* combatant, fighter
lidiar /li'ðiar/ *vi* to fight; *Fig.* struggle; (*with contra or con*) oppose, fight against; *—vt* fight (a bull). **¡Cuánto tienen que l. con...!** *Fig.* What a struggle they have with...!
liebre /'lieβre/ *f,* hare
liendre /'liendre/ *f,* nit
lienza /'lienθa; liensa/ *f,* narrow strip (of cloth)
lienzo /'lienθo; 'lienso/ *m,* linen; cotton; cambric; hemp cloth; *Art.* canvas
liga /'liga/ *f,* garter; bandage; birdlime; mixture, blend; *Metall.* alloy; alliance, coalition; league (football, etc.)
ligación /liga'θion; liga'sion/ *f,* tying; binding; union

ligado /li'gaðo/ *m, Mus.* legato; *Mus.* tie
ligadura /liga'ðura/ *f,* bond, tie; binding, fastening; *Fig.* shackle, link; (*Surg. Mus.*) ligature; *Naut.* lashing
ligamento /liga'mento/ *m,* tie, bond; mixture; *Anat.* ligament
ligar /li'gar/ *vt* to tie, bind; *Metall.* alloy; join, connect; render impotent by sorcery; *Mus.* slur (notes); *—vr* ally, join together; *Fig.* bind oneself. **l. cabos,** to put two and two together
ligazón /liga'θon; liga'son/ *f,* fastening; union; bond
ligereza /lihe'reθa; lihe'resa/ *f,* lightness (of weight); swiftness, nimbleness; fickleness; tactless remark, indiscretion
ligero /li'hero/ *a* light (in weight); swift, nimble; light (sleep); unimportant, insignificant; easily digested (food); thin (fabrics, etc.); fickle, changeable. **l. de cascos,** frivolous, gay. **a la ligera,** lightly; quickly; without fuss. **de l.,** impetuously, thoughtlessly; easily, with ease
lignito /lig'nito/ *m,* lignite
lija /'liha/ *f,* dogfish; sandpaper
lijar /li'har/ *vt* to sandpaper
lila /'lila/ *f,* lilac bush and flower; lilac color *—a Inf.* foolish, vain
liliputiense /lilipu'tiense/ *a* and *mf* Lilliputian
lima /'lima/ *f,* sweet lime, citron fruit; lime tree; file (tool); filing, polishing
limadura /lima'ðura/ *f,* filing; polishing; *pl* filings
limar /li'mar/ *vt* to file, smooth with a file; *Fig.* touch up, polish
limazo /li'maθo; li'maso/ *m,* slime, viscosity (especially of snails, etc.)
limbo /'limbo/ *m,* limbo; edge, hem; (*Astron. Bot.*) limb; limb (of a quadrant, etc.). *Inf.* **estar en el l.,** to be bewildered or abstracted
limen /'limen/ *m, Poet.* threshold; *Psychol.* limen
limeño /li'meɲo/ **(-ña)** *a* and *n* native of or belonging to Lima (Peru)
limero /li'mero/ **(-ra)** *n* seller of sweet limes. *m,* sweet lime tree (citron)
limitación /limita'θion; limita'sion/ *f,* limitation; limit, extent, bound; district, area
limitado /limi'taðo/ *a* dull-witted, limited
limitáneo /limi'taneo/ *a* bordering
limitar /limi'tar/ *vt* to limit; curb, restrict; bound
límite /'limite/ *m,* limit, extent; boundary, border; end, confine
limítrofe /li'mitrofe/ *a* bordering, contiguous
limo /'limo/ *m,* mud, mire, slime
limón /li'mon/ *m,* lemon; lemon tree
limonada /limo'naða/ *f,* lemonade. **l. seca,** lemonade powder
limonar /limo'nar/ *m,* lemon grove
limonero /limo'nero/ **(-ra)** *n* lemon seller. *m,* lemon tree
limosna /li'mosna/ *f,* alms
limosnear /limosne'ar/ *vi* to beg, ask alms
limosnero /limos'nero/ *a* charitable, generous. *m,* almoner
limoso /li'moso/ *a* slimy, muddy
limpiabarros /limpia'βarros/ *m,* shoe scraper
limpiabotas /limpia'βotas/ *m,* bootblack (person)
limpiachimeneas /limpiatʃime'neas/ *m,* chimneysweep
limpiador /limpia'ðor/ **(-ra)** *a* cleaning *—n* cleaner
limpiadura /limpia'ðura/ *f,* cleaning; *pl* rubbish
limpiamente /limpia'mente/ *adv* cleanly; dexterously, neatly; sincerely, candidly; generously, charitably
limpiametales /limpiame'tales/ *m,* metal polish
limpiaparabrisas /limpiapara'βrisas/ *m,* windshield wiper
limpiapipas /limpia'pipas/ *m,* pipe cleaner
limpiar /lim'piar/ *vt* to clean; *Fig.* cleanse, clear; empty, free (from); *Agr.* thin out; *Inf.* steal, pinch; *Inf.* win (gambling); *—vr* clean oneself
limpiauñas /limpia'uɲas/ *m,* orange stick (for fingernails)
limpidez /limpi'ðeθ; limpi'ðes/ *f, Poet.* limpidity
límpido /'limpiðo/ *a Poet.* limpid
limpieza /lim'pieθa; lim'piesa/ *f,* cleanliness; cleaning; chastity; purity; altruism; uprightness, integrity; neatness, tidiness; dexterity, skill, precision; fair play
limpio /'limpio/ *a* clean; pure, unalloyed, unmixed; neat, tidy; pure-blooded; unharmed, free. **en l.,** in substance; as a fair copy; clearly; *Com.* net
linaje /li'nahe/ *m,* lineage, family; offspring; kind; sort, quality
linajudo /lina'huðo/ **(-da)** *a* highborn *—n* noble, aristocrat; one who alleges his noble descent
linar /li'nar/ *m,* field of flax
linaza /li'naθa; li'nasa/ *f,* linseed
lince /'linθe; 'linse/ *m,* lynx; fox, crafty person
linchamiento /lintʃa'miento/ *m,* lynching
linchar /lin'tʃar/ *vt* to lynch
lindar /lin'dar/ *vi* to run together, be contiguous
linde /'linde/ *mf* limit, extent; boundary
lindero /lin'dero/ *a* bordering, contiguous. *m,* boundary. *Inf.* **con linderos y arrabales,** with many digressions
lindeza /lin'deθa; lin'desa/ *f,* beauty, loveliness; witticism; *pl* (*Inf. ironical*) insults
lindo /'lindo/ *a* lovely, beautiful; perfect, exquisite. *m, Inf.* fop (gen. **lindo don Diego**)
línea /'linea/ *f,* line; kind, class; ancestry, lineage; limit, extent; *Mil.* file; equator. **l. aérea,** airline. *Naut.* **l. de flotación,** waterline. **l. de toque,** touchline (in soccer). **l. recta,** direct line (of descent)
lineal /line'al/ *a* lineal
lineamento /linea'mento/ *m,* lineament
linear /line'ar/ *a* linear *—vt* to line, mark with lines; *Art.* sketch
linfa /'linfa/ *f, Med.* lymph; vaccine; *Poet.* water
linfático /lin'fatiko/ *a* lymphatic
lingote /liŋ'gote/ *m,* ingot; bar (of iron). **l. de fundición,** pig iron
lingüista /liŋ'guista/ *mf* linguist
lingüística /liŋ'guistika/ *f,* linguistics
lingüístico /liŋ'guistiko/ *a* linguistic
linimento /lini'mento/ *m,* liniment
lino /'lino/ *m, Bot.* flax; linen; *Poet.* ship's sail, canvas
linóleo /li'noleo/ *m,* linoleum
linotipia /lino'tipia/ *f,* linotype
linterna /lin'terna/ *f,* lantern; lighthouse; lamp. **l. sorda,** dark lantern
lío /'lio/ *m,* bundle; *Inf.* muddle, imbroglio; *Inf.* liaison, amour. *Inf.* **armar un l.,** to make a muddle, cause trouble. *Inf.* **hacerse un l.,** to get in a fix; get in a muddle
liquen /'liken/ *m,* lichen
liquidable /liki'ðaβle/ *a* liquefiable
liquidación /likiða'θion; likiða'sion/ *f,* liquefaction; *Com.* clearance, sale; *Com.* settlement
liquidar /liki'ðar/ *vt* to liquefy; *Com.* settle; *Com.* liquidate; finish; *—vr* liquefy
liquidez /liki'ðeθ; liki'ðes/ *f,* liquidness
líquido /'likiðo/ *a* liquid; *Com.* net. *m,* liquid; *Com.* net profit
lira /'lira/ *f, Mus.* lyre; *Astron.* Lyra; lira (coin)
lírica /'lirika/ *f,* lyrical verse, lyric
lírico /'liriko/ *a* lyrical
lirio /'lirio/ *m,* lily. **l. cárdeno,** yellow flag (iris). **l. de los valles,** lily of the valley
lirismo /li'rismo/ *m,* lyricism
lirón /li'ron/ *m, Zool.* dormouse; *Inf.* sleepyhead
Lisboa /lis'βoa/ Lisbon
lisbonense /lisβo'nense/ *a* and *mf* **lisbonés (-esa)** *a* and *n* Lisboan
lisiado /li'siaðo/ *a* lame, crippled
lisiar /li'siar/ *vt* to cripple, lame; *—vr* be disabled; be lame
liso /'liso/ *a* smooth; sleek; unadorned, plain; unicolored
lisonja /li'sonha/ *f,* flattery, adulation
lisonjear /lisonhe'ar/ *vt* to flatter; fawn upon; *Fig.* delight (the ear). **lisonjearse de...,** to flatter oneself on...
lisonjero /lison'hero/ **(-ra)** *a* flattering; sweet, pleasant (sounds) *—n* flatterer
lista /'lista/ *f,* strip of cloth; streak; rib; stripe; catalog, list. **l. de correos,** general delivery, poste re-

stante. **l. de platos,** bill of fare. **pasar l.,** to call the roll; check the list
listado /lis'taðo/ *a* streaked; striped; ribbed
listo /'listo/ *a* clever; expeditious, diligent; ready, prepared
listón /lis'ton/ *m,* ribbon; strip (of wood)
lisura /li'sura/ *f,* smoothness; sleekness; flatness; sincerity
litera /li'tera/ *f,* litter; *Naut.* berth
literal /lite'ral/ *a* literal
literario /lite'rario/ *a* literary
literatear /literate'ar/ *vi* to write on literary subjects
literato /lite'rato/ **(-ta)** *a* literary *—n* writer, litterateur
literatura /litera'tura/ *f,* literature
litigación /litiga'θion; litiga'sion/ *f,* litigation
litigante /liti'gante/ *mf* litigant
litigar /liti'gar/ *vt* to litigate; *—vi* dispute, argue
litigio /li'tihio/ *m,* lawsuit; dispute, argument
litigioso /liti'hioso/ *a* litigious; quarrelsome, disputatious
litisexpensas /litiseks'pensas/ *f pl, Law.* costs of a suit; legal expenses
litografía /litogra'fia/ *f,* lithography
litografiar /litogra'fiar/ *vt* to lithograph
litográfico /lito'grafiko/ *a* lithographic
litoral /lito'ral/ *a* and *m,* littoral
litro /'litro/ *m,* liter
Lituania /li'tuania/ Lithuania
lituano /li'tuano/ **(-na)** *a* and *n* Lithuanian. *m,* Lithuanian (language)
liturgia /li'turhia/ *f,* liturgy
litúrgico /li'turhiko/ *a* liturgical
liviandad /liβian'dað/ *f,* lightness (of weight); fickleness; unimportance; frivolity; lewdness; act of folly, indiscretion
liviano /li'βiano/ *a* light weight; fickle; unimportant, trifling, frivolous; lascivious
lividez /liβi'ðeθ; liβi'ðes/ *f,* lividness
lívido /'liβiðo/ *a* livid
liza /'liθa; 'lisa/ *f,* list (at a tournament); arena
llaga /'ʎaga; 'yaga/ *f,* ulcer; sore; grief, affliction; *Fig.* thorn in the flesh
llagar /ʎa'gar; ya'gar/ *vt* to ulcerate; make or produce sores; *Fig.* wound; *—vr* be covered with sores
llama /'ʎama; 'yama/ *f,* flame; ardor, vehemence; marsh; *Zool.* llama
llamada /ʎa'maða; ya'maða/ *f,* call; *Mil.* call-to-arms, call. **l. molestosa,** annoyance call, nuisance call
llamado /ʎa'maðo; ya'maðo/ *a* called; so-called
llamador /ʎama'ðor; yama'ðor/ **(-ra)** *n* caller. *m,* door knocker; doorbell
llamamiento /ʎama'miento; yama'miento/ *m,* calling; call; divine summons, inspiration; invocation, appeal; summons, convocation
llamar /ʎa'mar; ya'mar/ *vt* to call; invoke, call upon; summon, convoke; name; attract; *—vi* knock (at a door); ring (a bell); *—vr* be named, be called; *Naut.* veer (wind). **Se llama Pedro,** His name is Peter
llamarada /ʎama'raða; yama'raða/ *f,* flame, flash; blaze, flare (of anger, etc.)
llamativo /ʎama'tiβo; yama'tiβo/ *a* striking, showy; provocative
llamear /ʎame'ar; yame'ar/ *vi* to throw out flames, blaze
llana /'ʎana; 'yana/ *f,* mason's trowel; plain; surface of a page
llanada /ʎa'naða; ya'naða/ *f,* plain
llanamente /ʎana'mente; yana'mente/ *adv* frankly, plainly; naturally, simply; candidly, sincerely
llanero /ʎa'nero; ya'nero/ **(-ra)** *n* plain dweller
llaneza /ʎa'neθa; ya'nesa/ *f,* naturalness; candor; familiarity; simplicity (of style)
llano /'ʎano; 'yano/ *a* flat, level; smooth, even; shallow (of receptacles); unaffected, homely, natural; plain (of dresses); manifest, evident; easy; straightforward, candid; informal; simple (of style). *m,* plain; level stretch of ground
llanta /'ʎanta; 'yanta/ *f, Auto.* tire; rim, felloe. **l. de rueda,** wheel, rim
llanto /'ʎanto; 'yanto/ *m,* weeping, flood of tears
llanura /ʎa'nura; ya'nura/ *f,* smoothness, evenness, levelness; plain
llar /ʎar; yar/ *m,* hearth
llave /'ʎaβe; 'yaβe/ **(de)** *f,* key (to); spigot (of), faucet (of), tap (of); spanner, wrench; *Elec.* switch; clock winder; *Mus.* key, clef; *Archit.* keystone; *Print.* brace; *Mech.* wrench; lock (of a gun); tuning key; piston (of musical instruments); lock (in wrestling); *Fig.* key (of a problem or a study). **l. de transmisión,** sender (telegraphy). **l. inglesa,** monkey-wrench, spanner. **l. maestra,** master key, skeleton key. **echar la l.,** to lock. **torcer la l.,** to turn the key
llavero /ʎa'βero; ya'βero/ **(-ra)** *n* keeper of the keys. *m,* key ring. **l. de cárcel,** turnkey
llavín /ʎa'βin; ya'βin/ *m,* yale key, latchkey
llegada /ʎe'gaða; ye'gaða/ *f,* arrival, advent
llegar /ʎe'gar; ye'gar/ *vi* to arrive; last, endure; reach; achieve a purpose; be sufficient, suffice; amount (to), make; *—vt* bring near, draw near; gather; *—vr* come near, approach; adhere. **l. a ser,** to become. **l. a un punto muerto,** to reach a deadlock. **l. hasta...,** to stretch as far as...
llena /'ʎena; 'yena/ *f,* spate, overflow
llenar /ʎe'nar; ye'nar/ *vt* to fill; occupy (a post); satisfy, please; fulfill; satiate; pervade; fill up (a form); *—vi* be full (of the moon); *—vr Inf.* stuff, overeat; *Fig. Inf.* be fed-up
lleno /'ʎeno; 'yeno/ *a* full; replete; abundant; complete. *m,* full moon; *Theat.* full house; *Inf.* glut, abundance; perfection. **de l., de l. en l.,** entirely, completely
llenura /ʎe'nura; ye'nura/ *f,* abundance, plenty
lleva, llevada /'ʎeβa, ʎe'βaða; 'yeβa, ye'βaða/ *f,* carrying, bearing
llevadero /ʎeβa'ðero; yeβa'ðero/ *a* tolerable, bearable
llevar /ʎe'βar; ye'βar/ *vt* to carry, transport; charge (a price); yield, produce; carry off, take away; endure, bear; persuade; guide, take; direct; wear (clothes); carry (a handbag, etc.); introduce, present; gain, achieve; manage (a horse); pass, spend (of time); (*with past part*) have (e.g. *Llevo escrita la carta,* I have written the letter); *Math.* carry; (*with prep. a*) surpass, excel. **l. a cabo,** to accomplish. **l. a cuestas,** to carry on one's back; support. **l. la correspondencia,** to look after the correspondence. **l. la delantera,** to take the lead. **l. luto,** to be in mourning. **llevarse bien,** to get on well, agree
llorar /ʎo'rar; yo'rar/ *vi* to weep, cry; drip; water (eyes); *—vt* lament, mourn; bewail one's troubles
lloriquear /ʎorike'ar; yorike'ar/ *vi* to whine, snivel
lloriqueo /ʎori'keo; yori'keo/ *m,* whining, sniveling
lloro /'ʎoro; 'yoro/ *m,* weeping, crying; flood of tears
llorón /ʎo'ron; yo'ron/ *a* weeping; sniveling, whining. *m,* long plume. **niño llorón,** crybaby
lloroso /ʎo'roso; yo'roso/ *a* tearful; grievous, sad; sorrowful
llovedizo /ʎoβe'ðiθo; yoβe'ðiso/ *a* leaky; rainy
llover /ʎo'βer; yo'βer/ *vi impers irr* to rain; come in abundance (of troubles, etc.); *—vr* leak (roofs, etc.). **l. a cántaros,** to rain in torrents, rain cats and dogs. **l. sobre mojado,** to add insult to injury. **como llovido,** unexpectedly. See **mover**
llovido /ʎo'βiðo; yo'βiðo/ *m,* stowaway
llovizna /ʎo'βiθna; yo'βisna/ *f,* drizzle, fine rain
lloviznar /ʎoβiθ'nar; yoβis'nar/ *vi* to drizzle
lluvia /'ʎuβia; 'yuβia/ *f,* rain; rainwater; *Fig.* shower; rose (of watering can)
lluvioso /ʎu'βioso; yu'βioso/ *a* rainy, showery
lo /lo/ *def art. neut* the thing, part, fact, what, that which. Used before adjectives, past participles, sometimes before nouns and adverbs (e.g. *Lo barato es caro,* Cheap things are dear (in the long run).) **Lo mío es mío, pero lo tuyo es de ambos,** What's mine is mine, but what is yours belongs to both of us. **Juan siente mucho lo ocurrido,** John is very sorry for what has happened. **a lo lejos,** in the distance). **lo... que,** how (e.g. *No sabes lo bueno que es,* You don't know how good he is) *—pers pron acc m,* or *neut* him, it; that, it (e.g. *Lo harán mañana,* They will do it tomorrow). Means some, any, one, as substitute for noun already mentioned (e.g. *Carecemos de azúcar;*

no lo hay, We are short of sugar; there isn't any). **Lo cortés no quita lo valiente,** One can be courteous and still insistent

loa /'loa/ *f*, praise, eulogy; *Theat.* prologue; short dramatic piece; *Obs.*; dramatic eulogy

loable /lo'aβle/ *a* praiseworthy

loador /loa'ðor/ **(-ra)** *a* eulogizing —*n* eulogist

loar /lo'ar/ *vt* to praise; commend

lobero /lo'βero/ *a* wolf; wolfish

lobezno /lo'βeθno; lo'βesno/ *m*, wolf cub

lobo /'loβo/ **(-ba)** *n* wolf. *m*, (*Bot. Anat.*) lobe; *Inf.* drinking fit. **l. marino,** *Zool.* seal. *Inf.* **pillar un l.,** to get drunk

lóbrego /'loβrego/ *a* murky, dark; dismal; mournful, lugubrious

lobreguez /loβre'geθ; loβre'ges/ *f*, obscurity, gloom, darkness

lóbulo /'loβulo/ *m*, lobe

lobuno /lo'βuno/ *a* wolf, wolfish

locación /loka'θion; loka'sion/ *f*, *Law.* lease; agreement, contract

local /lo'kal/ *a* local. *m*, premises; place, spot, scene

localidad /lokali'ðað/ *f*, location; locality; place, spot; seat (in theaters, etc.)

localización /lokaliθa'θion; lokalisa'sion/ *f*, localization, placing; place

localizar /lokali'θar; lokali'sar/ *vt* to localize

locamente /loka'mente/ *adv* insanely, madly; extraordinarily, extremely

loción /lo'θion; lo'sion/ *f*, lotion

loco /'loko/ **(-ca)** *a* insane, mad; rash, foolish, crazy; excessive, enormous; amazing; extraordinary; infatuated —*n* lunatic; rash person. *Fig. Inf.* **Es un l. de atar,** He's completely crazy!

locomoción /lokomo'θion; lokomo'sion/ *f*, locomotion

locomotor /lokomo'tor/ *a* locomotive

locomotora /lokomo'tora/ *f*, locomotive

locomóvil /loko'moβil/ *a* and *f*, locomotive

locuacidad /lokuaθi'ðað; lokuasi'ðað/ *f*, loquacity

locuaz /lo'kuaθ; lo'kuas/ *a* loquacious

locución /loku'θion; loku'sion/ *f*, style of speech; phrase, idiom; *Gram.* locution

locuelo /lo'kuelo/ **(-la)** *n* madcap

locura /lo'kura/ *f*, insanity, lunacy; madness, fury; folly, foolishness

locutor /loku'tor/ **(-ra)** *n* (radio) announcer; commentator

locutorio /loku'torio/ *m*, locutory; phone booth

lodazal, lodazar /loða'θal, loða'θar; loða'sal, loða'sar/ *m*, muddy place; quagmire

lodo /'loðo/ *m*, mud

lodoso /lo'ðoso/ *a* muddy

logarítmico /loga'ritmiko/ *a* logarithmic

logaritmo /loga'ritmo/ *m*, logarithm

logia /'lohia/ *f*, (Freemason's) lodge

lógica /'lohika/ *f*, logic. *Inf.* **l. parda,** common sense

lógico /'lohiko/ **(-ca)** *a* logical —*n* logician

logística /lo'histika/ *f*, logistics

lograr /lo'grar/ *vt* to achieve, attain, obtain; enjoy; (*with infin*) succeed in; —*vr* succeed in, achieve; reach perfection

logrear /logre'ar/ *vi* to borrow or lend at interest

logrero /lo'grero/ **(-ra)** *n* moneylender; monopolist, profiteer

logro /'logro/ *m*, achievement, attainment; profit, gain; usury, money-lending

loma /'loma/ *f*, knoll, hill

lombarda /lom'βarða/ *f*, red cabbage

Lombardía /lombar'ðia/ Lombardy

lombardo /lom'βarðo/ **(-da)** *a* of or from Lombardy —*n* native of Lombardy (Italy). *m*, mortgage bank

lombriz /lom'βriθ; lom'βris/ *f*, earthworm, common worm. **l. intestinal,** intestinal worm. **l. solitaria,** tapeworm

lomo /'lomo/ *m*, loin, back of a book; ridge between furrows; *pl* ribs; loins

lona /'lona/ *f*, canvas, sailcloth

londinense /londi'nense/ *a* London. *mf* Londoner

Londres /'londres/ London

longanimidad /loŋganimi'ðað/ *f*, longanimity, fortitude

longaniza /loŋga'niθa; loŋga'nisa/ *f*, *Cul.* pork sausage

longevidad /lonheβi'ðað/ *f*, longevity

longevo /lon'heβo/ *a* long-lived

longísimo /lon'hisimo/ *a superl* **luengo** exceedingly long

longitud /lonhi'tuð/ *f*, length; longitude. **l. de onda,** *Radio.* wavelength

lonja /'lonha/ *f*, slice, rasher; *Com.* exchange; market; grocery store; woolen warehouse

lonjista /lon'hista/ *mf* provision merchant, grocer

lontananza /lonta'nanθa; lonta'nansa/ *f*, distance (also *Art.*). **en l.,** in the distance, far off

loor /lo'or/ *m*, praise

loquear /loke'ar/ *vi* to play the fool; romp

lord /lorð/ *m*, lord; *pl* **lores,** lords

loro /'loro/ *m*, *Ornith.* parrot

los /los/ *def art m pl*, the (e.g. *l. sombreros*, the hats) —*pers pron acc 3rd pers m pl*, them. **Tus cigarrillos no están sobre la mesa; los tengo en mi bolsillo,** Your cigarettes are not on the table; I have them in my pocket. Means some, any, ones, as substitution for noun already stated (e.g. *Los cigarros están en la caja si los hay*, The cigars are in the box, if there are any). Used demonstratively followed by *de* or *que* introducing relative clause, those of; those which, those who; the ones that (who) (e.g. *Estaba leyendo algunos libros de los que tienes en tu cuarto*, I was reading some books from among those which you have in your room)

losa /'losa/ *f*, flagstone; slab; tombstone

lote /'lote/ *m*, lot, portion, share

lotería /lote'ria/ *f*, lottery; lotto (game); lottery office

lotero /lo'tero/ **(-ra)** *n* seller of lottery tickets

loto /'loto/ *m*, lotus; lotus flower or fruit

loza /'loθa; 'losa/ *f*, porcelain, china

lozanía /loθa'nia; losa'nia/ *f*, luxuriance (of vegetation); vigor, lustiness; arrogance

lozano /lo'θano; lo'sano/ *a* luxuriant, exuberant; vigorous, lusty; arrogant

lubricación /luβrika'θion; luβrika'sion/ *f*, lubrication

lubricador /luβrika'ðor/ *m*, lubricator

lubricante /luβri'kante/ *a* lubricant

lubricar /luβri'kar/ *vt* to lubricate

lúbrico /'luβriko/ *a* slippery, smooth; lascivious, lustful

lucera /lu'θera; lu'sera/ *f*, skylight

Lucerna /lu'θerna; lu'serna/ Lucerne

lucerna /lu'θerna; lu'serna/ *f*, large chandelier; skylight

lucero /lu'θero; lu'sero/ *m*, evening star; any bright star; white star (on a horse's head); brilliance, radiance; *pl Poet.* eyes, orbs. **l. del alba,** morning star

lucha /'lutʃa/ *f*, fight; struggle; wrestling match; argument, disagreement. **l. grecorromana,** wrestling. **l. igualada,** close fight. **l. libre,** catch-as-catch-can

luchador /lutʃa'ðor/ **(-ra)** *n* fighter; struggler

luchar /lu'tʃar/ *vi* to fight hand to hand; wrestle; fight; struggle; argue

lucidez /luθi'ðeθ; lusi'ðes/ *f*, brilliance, shine; lucidity, clarity

lucido /lu'θiðo; lu'siðo/ *a* splendid, brilliant; sumptuous; fine, elegant

lúcido /'luθiðo; 'lusiðo/ *a Poet.* brilliant; lucid; clear

luciente /lu'θiente; lu'siente/ *a* bright, shining

luciérnaga /lu'θiernaga; lu'siernaga/ *f*, glowworm

lucimiento /luθi'miento; lusi'miento/ *m*, brilliance, luster; success, triumph; elegance; display, ostentation

lucir /lu'θir; lu'sir/ *vi irr* to shine, scintillate; excel, outshine; be successful; —*vt* illuminate; display, show off; show; —*vr* dress elegantly; be successful; excel, be brilliant —*Pres. Indic.* **luzco, luces,** etc —*Pres. Subjunc.* **luzca,** etc.

lucrativo /lukra'tiβo/ *a* lucrative

lucro /'lukro/ *m*, gain, profit

lucroso /lu'kroso/ *a* profitable

luctuoso /luk'tuoso/ *a* lugubrious, mournful

lucubración /lukuβra'θion; lukuβra'sion/ *f,* lucubration
ludibrio /lu'ðiβrio/ *m,* mockery, ridicule
luego /'luego/ *adv* immediately; afterward, later; then; soon, presently *—conjunc* therefore. **l. que,** as soon as. **desde l.,** immediately, at once; of course, naturally; in the first place. **hasta l.,** au revoir, good-by for the present
luengo /'lueŋgo/ *a* long
lugar /lu'gar/ *m,* place; spot; village, town, city; region, locality; office, post; passage, text; opportunity, occasion; cause, motive; place on a list; room, space; seat. **l. común,** commonplace. **en l. de,** instead of. **en primer l.,** firstly, in the first place. **hacer l.,** to make room, make way. *Law.* **No ha l.,** The petition is refused. **tener l.,** to take place; have the time or opportunity (to)
lugarejo /luga'reho/ *m,* hamlet
lugareño /luga'reɲo/ **(-ña)** *a* peasant, regional *—n* villager, peasant
lugarteniente /lugarte'niente/ *m,* lieutenant; substitute, deputy
lúgubre /'luguβre/ *a* lugubrious, dismal, mournful
luis /'luis/ *m,* louis (French coin)
lujo /'luho/ *m,* luxury; abundance, profusion. **artículos de l.,** luxury goods
lujoso /lu'hoso/ *a* luxurious; abundant, profuse
lujuria /lu'huria/ *f,* lasciviousness; excess, intemperance
lujuriante /luhu'riante/ *a* luxuriant, abundant, profuse
lujurioso /luhu'rioso/ *a* lascivious, voluptuous
lumbago /lum'βago/ *m,* lumbago
lumbre /'lumbre/ *f,* fire; light; splendor, lustre; transom window, opening, skylight; *pl* tinderbox
lumbrera /lum'βrera/ *f,* luminary; skylight; dormer window; eminent authority
luminar /lumi'nar/ *m,* luminary (also *Fig.*)
luminaria /lumi'naria/ *f,* illumination; fairy lamp, small light; lamp burning before the Sacrament in Catholic churches
luminosidad /luminosi'ðað/ *f,* luminosity
luminoso /lumi'noso/ *a* luminous; bright
luna /'luna/ *f,* moon; mirror; satellite; sheet of plate glass. **l. creciente,** new or rising moon. **l. de miel,** honeymoon. **l. llena,** full moon. **l. menguante,** waning moon. **media l.,** crescent moon
lunado /lu'naðo/ *a* half-moon, crescent
lunar /lu'nar/ *m,* beauty spot; *Fig.* stain, blot (on reputation, etc.); blemish, slight imperfection *—a* lunar
lunático /lu'natiko/ **(-ca)** *a* and *n* lunatic
lunes /'lunes/ *m,* Monday
luneta /lu'neta/ *f,* lens (of eyeglasses), *Theat.* orchestra stall; (*Archit. Mil.*) lunette
lupa /'lupa/ *f,* magnifying glass
lupanar /lupa'nar/ *m,* brothel
lupino /lu'pino/ *a* wolf-like, lupine. *m, Bot.* lupine
lúpulo /'lupulo/ *m, Bot.* hop
lusitano /lusi'tano/ **(-na)** *a* and *n* Lusitanian
lustrador /lustra'ðor/ *m,* polisher. **l. de piso,** floor polisher
lustrar /lus'trar/ *vt* to lustrate, purify; polish, burnish; roam, journey
lustre /'lustre/ *m,* polish, sheen, gloss; glory, luster
lustro /'lustro/ *m,* lustrum, period of five years; chandelier
lustroso /lus'troso/ *a* shining, glossy; brilliant; glorious, noble
luteranismo /lutera'nismo/ *m,* Lutheranism
luterano /lute'rano/ **(-na)** *a* and *n* Lutheran
luto /'luto/ *m,* mourning; grief, affliction; *pl* mourning draperies. **estar de l.,** to be in mourning
luxación /luksa'θion; luksa'sion/ *f, Surg.* luxation, dislocation
Luxemburgo /luksem'βurgo/ Luxembourg
luz /luθ; lus/ *f,* light; glow; brightness, brilliance; information, news; *Fig.* luminary; day, daylight; *pl* culture, learning; windows. **luces de estacionamiento,** parking lights. **a buena l.,** in a good light; in a favorable light; after due consideration. **a primera l.,** at dawn. **dar a l.,** to publish (a book); bring forth (children); reveal. **entre dos luces,** in the dawn light; in the twilight; *Inf.* tipsy. **media l.,** half-light, twilight

M

maca /'maka/ *f,* bruise or blemish on fruit; defect, flaw; *Inf.* fraud, swindle
macabro /ma'kaβro/ *a* macabre
macadán /maka'ðan/ *m,* macadam
macagua /ma'kagua/ *f, Ornith.* macaw
macanudo /maka'nuðo/ *a* (*Inf. West. Hem.*) extraordinary; enormous; robust; fine, excellent
macareno /maka'reno/ **(-na)** *n* inhabitant of the Macarena district of Seville. *m, Inf.* braggart
macarrones /maka'rrones/ *m pl,* macaroni; *Naut.* stanchions
macarrónico /maka'rroniko/ *a* macaronic, recondite, stylized
macarse /ma'karse/ *vr* to go bad, rot (fruit)
macedón /maθe'ðon; mase'ðon/ **(-ona), macedonio (-ia)** *a* and *n* Macedonian
maceración /maθera'θion; masera'sion/ *f,* maceration; steeping, soaking; mortification of the flesh
macerar /maθe'rar; mase'rar/ *vt* to macerate; steep, soak; mortify
macero /ma'θero; ma'sero/ *m,* mace bearer
maceta /ma'θeta; ma'seta/ *f, dim* small mace; handle, haft (of tools); stonecutter's hammer; flowerpot
macetero /maθe'tero; mase'tero/ *m,* flowerpot stand
machaca /ma'tʃaka/ *f,* pestle; pulverizer. *mf Inf.* bore, tedious person
machacador /matʃaka'ðor/ **(-ra)** *a* crushing, pounding —*n* beater, crusher, pounder
machacar /matʃa'kar/ *vt* to crush, pound; —*vi* importune; harp on a subject
machacón /matʃa'kon/ *a* tiresome, prolix
machado /ma'tʃaðo/ *m,* hatchet, ax
machetero /matʃe'tero/ *m,* one who cuts sugarcane with a machete
machihembrar /matʃiem'βrar/ *vt* to dovetail
machina /ma'tʃina/ *f,* derrick, crane; pile driver
macho /'matʃo/ *m,* male; male animal (he-goat, stallion, etc.); male plant; hook (of hook and eye); screw; *Metall.* core; tap (tool); *Inf.* dunderhead, fool; *Archit.* buttress —*a* male; stupid, ignorant; vigorous, strong. **m. cabrío,** he-goat
machucadura /matʃuka'ðura/ *f,* **machucamiento** *m,* pounding, crushing; bruising
machucar /matʃu'kar/ *vt* to crush, pound; bruise
machucho /ma'tʃutʃo/ *a* prudent, sensible; adult, mature
macicez /maθi'θeθ; masi'ses/ *f,* solidity; massiveness; thickness
macilento /maθi'lento; masi'lento/ *a* thin, lean, emaciated
macillo /ma'θiʎo; ma'siyo/ *m, dim* small mace; hammer (of a piano)
macis /'maθis; 'masis/ *f, Cul.* mace
macizar /maθi'θar; masi'sar/ *vt* to block up, fill up
macizo /ma'θiθo; ma'siso/ *a* massive; compact, solid; *Fig.* well-founded, unassailable; thick; strong. *m,* solidity, compactness; bulk, volume; flowerbed; solid tire
macrocosmo /makro'kosmo/ *m,* macrocosm
mácula /'makula/ *f,* stain, spot; *Fig.* blot, blemish; *Inf.* trick, deception; *Astron.* macula
macuquero /maku'kero/ *m,* unauthorized worker of abandoned mines
madeja /ma'ðeha/ *f,* skein, hank; lock of hair; *Inf.* dummy, useless person
madera /ma'ðera/ *f,* wood; timber; *Inf.* kind, sort; *Mus.* wind instruments. **m. contrachapada,** plywood. **m. de construcción,** timber. **maderas de sierra,** lumber wood. *Inf.* **ser de mala m.,** to be a ne'er-do-well
maderada /maðe'raða/ *f,* lumber wood
maderaje /maðe'rahe/ *m,* woodwork, timber work
maderero /maðe'rero/ *m,* timber merchant; lumberjack; carpenter
madería /maðe'ria/ *f,* timber yard
madero /ma'ðero/ *m,* wooden beam; log, piece of lumber; ship, vessel; *Inf.* blockhead or insensible person
madrastra /ma'ðrastra/ *f,* stepmother; anything unpleasant
madraza /ma'ðraθa; ma'ðrasa/ *f, Inf.* overindulgent mother
madre /'maðre/ *f,* mother; matron; cause, genesis; *Inf.* dame, mother; riverbed; dam; womb; main sewer; chief irrigation channel. **m. de familia,** mother; housewife. **m. de leche,** wet nurse. **m. política,** mother-in-law; stepmother. *Inf.* **sacar de m. (a),** to provoke, irritate (a person)
madreperla /maðre'perla/ *f,* mother-of-pearl
madrépora /ma'ðrepora/ *f,* white coral, madrepore
madreselva /maðre'selβa/ *f,* honeysuckle
madrigado /maðri'gaðo/ *a* twice-married (women); *Inf.* experienced, wide-awake
madrigal /maðri'gal/ *m,* madrigal
madriguera /maðri'gera/ *f,* rabbit warren; burrow, den, hole, lair; haunt of thieves, etc.
madrileño /maðri'leɲo/ **(-ña)** *a* and *n* Madrilenian
madrina /ma'ðrina/ *f,* godmother; matron of honor or bridesmaid; sponsor; patroness; prop; stanchion
madroncillo /maðron'θiʎo; maðron'siyo/ *m,* strawberry
madroño /ma'ðroɲo/ *m,* strawberry tree; tuft, spot; tassel
madrugada /maðru'gaða/ *f,* dawn, daybreak; early rising. **de m.,** at dawn
madrugador /maðruga'ðor/ **(-ra)** *a* early rising —*n* early riser
madrugar /maðru'gar/ *vi* to get up early; gain time; anticipate, be beforehand
maduración /maðura'θion; maðura'sion/ *f,* ripening; mellowing; preparation; ripeness; maturity
madurador /maðura'ðor/ *a* ripening; maturing
maduramente /maðura'mente/ *adv* maturely; sensibly
madurar /maðu'rar/ *vt* to ripen; mature; think out; —*vi* ripen; grow mature, learn wisdom
madurez /maðu'reθ; maðu'res/ *f,* ripeness; maturity; mellowness; wisdom
maduro /ma'ðuro/ *a* ripe; mature; mellow; adult; wise
maestra /ma'estra/ *f,* schoolmistress; teacher, instructor; queen bee; guide, model
maestral /maes'tral/ *a* referring to the grand master of one of the Spanish military orders; teaching, pedagogic. *m,* mistral (wind); cell of a queen bee
maestrear /maestre'ar/ *vt* to direct, control, manage; prune vines; —*vi Inf.* bully, domineer
maestría /maes'tria/ *f,* mastery, skill; *Educ.* master's degree
maestril /maes'tril/ *m,* queen cell (of bees)
maestro /ma'estro/ *a* masterly; excellent; chief, main; midship. *m,* master, expert; teacher; instructor; master craftsman; *Educ.* master; *Mus.* composer; *Naut.* mainmast. **m. de armas,** fencing master. **m. de capilla,** *Eccl.* choirmaster. **m. de obras,** building contractor; master builder. **El ejercicio hace m.,** Practice makes perfect
Magallanes, Estrecho de /maga'ʎanes, es'tretʃo de; maga'yanes, es'tretʃo de/ Straits of Magellan
magdalena /magða'lena/ *f,* madeleine (cake); magdalen, penitent. *Inf.* **estar hecha una M.,** to be inconsolable
magia /'mahia/ *f,* magic
mágica /'mahika/ *f,* magic; enchantress, sorceress
mágico /'mahiko/ *a* magic; marvelous, wonderful. *m,* magician; enchanter, wizard
magín /ma'hin/ *m, Inf.* imagination; head, mind
magisterio /mahis'terio/ *m,* teaching profession; teaching diploma; teaching post; pedantry, pompousness. **ejercer su m. en,** to be employed as a teacher in
magistrado /mahis'traðo/ *m,* magistrate; magistracy

magistral /mahis'tral/ *a* magistral; authoritative, magisterial; pedantic, pompous
magistratura /mahistra'tura/ *f,* magistracy
magnanimidad /magnanimi'ðað/ *f,* magnanimity; generosity, liberality
magnánimo /mag'nanimo/ *a* magnanimous, generous, noble
magnate /mag'nate/ *m,* magnate
magnesia /mag'nesia/ *f,* magnesia
magnesio /mag'nesio/ *m,* magnesium
magnético /mag'netiko/ *a* magnetic
magnetismo /magne'tismo/ *m,* magnetism
magnetizar /magneti'θar; magneti'sar/ *vt* to magnetize; mesmerize
magneto /mag'neto/ *m,* magneto
magnificar /magnifi'kar/ *vt* to magnify, enlarge; praise, extol
magnificencia /magnifi'θenθia; magnifi'sensia/ *f,* magnificence, pomp, splendor
magnífico /mag'nifiko/ *a* magnificent; splendid, wonderful, fine; excellent
magnitud /magni'tuð/ *f,* magnitude; quantity; importance
magno /'magno/ *a* great; famous. **Alejandro M.,** Alexander the Great
magnolia /mag'nolia/ *f,* magnolia
mago /'mago/ *m,* magician; *pl* magi
magra /'magra/ *f,* rasher (of bacon, ham)
magrez, magrura /ma'greθ, ma'grura; ma'gres, ma'grura/ *f,* leanness; scragginess
magro /'magro/ *a* lean; scraggy. *m, Inf.* lean pork
magulladura /maguʎa'ðura; maguya'ðura/ *f,* **magullamiento** *m,* bruising; bruise, contusion
magullar /magu'ʎar; magu'yar/ *vt* to bruise
mahometano /maome'tano/ **(-na)** *a* and *n* Muslim
mahometismo /maome'tismo/ *m,* Islam
mahonesa /mao'nesa/ *f,* mayonnaise
maíz /ma'iθ; ma'is/ *m,* corn
maizal /mai'θal; mai'sal/ *m,* cornfield
maja /'maha/ *f,* belle
majada /ma'haða/ *f,* sheepfold; dung
majadería /mahaðe'ria/ *f,* impertinence, insolence
majadero /maha'ðero/ *a* persistent, tedious. *m,* bobbin (for lace making); pestle —*n* fool, bore
majador /maha'ðor/ *m,* pestle
majar /ma'har/ *vt* to pound, crush; *Inf.* importune, annoy
majestad /mahes'tað/ *f,* majesty (title); dignity; stateliness
majestuosidad /mahestuosi'ðað/ *f,* majesty; dignity
majestuoso /mahes'tuoso/ *a* majestic; stately; dignified
majo /'maho/ *a* arrogant, aggressive; gaudily attired, smart; dashing, handsome; attractive, pretty; elegant, well-dressed. *m,* beau, gallant, man about town
majuelo /ma'huelo/ *m,* new vine; species of white hawthorn
mal /mal/ *a Abbr.* **malo.** Used only before *m sing* nouns (e.g. *un m. cuarto de hora,* a bad quarter of an hour). *m,* evil; damage; harm; misfortune; illness, disease; trouble (e.g. *El m. es,* The trouble is). **m. de altura,** air sickness. **m. de ojo,** evil eye. **m. de piedra,** lithiasis, stone. **m. francés,** syphilis. **el m. menor,** the lesser of two evils —*interj* **¡M. haya!** A curse upon! **echar a m.,** to scorn (things); waste, squander. **llevar a m. (una cosa),** to take (a thing) badly, complain. **No hay m. que por bien no venga,** It's an ill wind that blows no one any good, Every cloud has a silver lining. **parar en m.,** to come to a bad end
mal /mal/ *adv* badly; unfavorably; wrongly; wickedly; with difficulty; scarcely, barely. **m. que bien,** willingly or unwillingly; rightly or wrongly. **de m. en peor,** from bad to worse
mala /'mala/ *f,* mail, post. **m. real,** royal mail
malabarista /malaβa'rista/ *mf* juggler
malaconsejado /malakonse'haðo/ *a* ill-advised; imprudent
malacostumbrado /malakostum'βraðo/ *a* badly trained, spoiled; having bad habits
malagueña /mala'geɲa/ *f,* popular song of lament
malagueño /mala'geɲo/ *a* of or from Málaga
malandante /malan'dante/ *a* evildoing; unfortunate, miserable; poor
malandanza /malan'danθa; malan'dansa/ *f,* evildoing; misfortune, misery; poverty
malandrín /malan'drin/ *a* wicked, ill-disposed. *m,* scoundrel, miscreant
malaquita /mala'kita/ *f,* malachite
malaria /ma'laria/ *f,* malaria
malaventura /malaβen'tura/ *f,* misfortune, adversity, bad luck
malaventurado /malaβentu'raðo/ *a* unfortunate, unlucky
malayo /ma'laio/ **(-ya)** *a* Malay —*n* Malayan
malbaratador /malβarata'ðor/ **(-ra)** *a* wasteful, spendthrift —*n* squanderer, spendthrift
malbaratar /malβara'tar/ *vt* to squander, waste; sell at a loss
malcasado /malka'saðo/ *a* adulterous, unfaithful
malcasar /malka'sar/ **(se)** *vt* and *vr* to marry badly
malcomido /malko'miðo/ *a* underfed
malcontento /malkon'tento/ **(-ta)** *a* dissatisfied, discontented; rebellious —*n* malcontent, rebel
malcriado /mal'kriaðo/ *a* badly brought up; ill-bred; spoiled, peevish
maldad /mal'dað/ *f,* badness; depravity, wickedness
maldecidor /maldeθi'ðor; maldesi'ðor/ **(-ra)** *a* slanderous —*n* scandalmonger, slanderer
maldecir /malde'θir; malde'sir/ *vt irr* to curse; —*vt* and *vi* slander, backbite. See **decir**
maldiciente /maldi'θiente; maldi'siente/ *a* defamatory, slanderous; cursing, reviling. *m,* slanderer; curser
maldición /maldi'θion; maldi'sion/ *f,* malediction; curse, imprecation
maldispuesto /maldis'puesto/ *a* indisposed, ill; reluctant
maldita /mal'dita/ *f, Inf.* tongue. *Inf.* **soltar la m.,** to say too much, go too far
maldito /mal'dito/ *a* accursed; wicked; damned; poor (of quality); *Inf.* not a...
maleabilidad /maleaβili'ðað/ *f,* malleability, flexibility
maleable /male'aβle/ *a* malleable, flexible
maleante /male'ante/ *a* rascally, villainous. *mf* evildoer
malecón /male'kon/ *m,* breakwater
maledicencia /maleði'θenθia; maleði'sensia/ *f,* slander, abuse, backbiting; cursing
maleficencia /malefi'θenθia; malefi'sensia/ *f,* wrongdoing
maleficio /male'fiθio; male'fisio/ *m,* (magic) curse; spell; charm
maléfico /ma'lefiko/ *a* malefic, harmful. *m,* sorcerer
malestar /males'tar/ *m,* indisposition, slight illness; discomfort
maleta /ma'leta/ *f,* suitcase, valise, grip; *m, Inf.* clumsy matador; duffer (at games, etc.). **hacer la m.,** to pack a suitcase; *Inf.* prepare for a journey, get ready to leave
maletero /male'tero/ *m,* seller or maker of traveling bags; porter
maletín /male'tin/ *m,* small suitcase or valise
malevolencia /maleβo'lenθia; maleβo'lensia/ *f,* malevolence, hatred, malice
malévolo /ma'leβolo/ *a* malevolent, malicious
maleza /ma'leθa; ma'lesa/ *f,* weeds, undergrowth, thicket
malgastador /malgasta'ðor/ **(-ra)** *a* thriftless, wasteful —*n* squanderer
malgastar /malgas'tar/ *vt* to waste (time); squander, throw away (money)
malhablado /mala'βlaðo/ *a* foul-tongued, indecent
malhadado /mala'ðaðo/ *a* ill-fated, unhappy
malhecho /mal'etʃo/ *a* deformed, twisted (persons). *m,* evil deed, wrongdoing
malhechor /male'tʃor/ **(-ra)** *n* malefactor; evildoer
malhumorado /malumo'raðo/ *a* ill-humored, bad-tempered
malicia /ma'liθia; ma'lisia/ *f,* wickedness, evil; mal-

ice, maliciousness; acuteness, subtlety, shrewdness; craftiness, guile; *Inf.* suspicion
maliciar /mali'θiar; mali'siar/ *vt* to suspect; spoil, damage; hurt, harm
malicioso /mali'θioso; mali'sioso/ *a* malicious; vindictive; wicked; shrewd, clever; *Inf.* suspicious; artful
malignidad /maligni'ðað/ *f,* malignancy, spite, ill will
maligno /ma'ligno/ *a* malignant, spiteful; wicked; *Med.* malignant
malintencionado /malintenθio'naðo; malintensio'naðo/ *a* ill-intentioned, badly disposed
malla /'maʎa; 'maya/ *f,* mesh (of a net); coat of mail; *pl Theat.* tights. **m. de alambre,** wire netting. **cota de m.,** coat of mail
Mallorca /ma'ʎorka; ma'yorka/ Majorca
mallorquín /maʎor'kin; mayor'kin/ **(-ina)** *a* and *n* Majorcan. *m,* Majorcan (variety of Catalan or Spanish)
malmandado /malman'daðo/ *a* disobedient; reluctant, unwilling
malmaridada /malmari'ðaða/ *f,* adultress, faithless wife
malo /'malo/ *a* bad; wicked; evil; injurious; harmful; illicit; licentious; ill; difficult; troublesome, annoying; *Inf.* mischievous; knavish; rotten, decaying *—interj* **¡M.!** That's bad!; You shouldn't have done that!; That's a bad sign! **de malas,** unluckily, unhappily. **el M.,** the Evil One, the Devil. **estar m.,** to be ill. **Lo m. es,** The trouble is, The worst of it is. **por malas o por buenas,** willy-nilly, willingly or unwillingly. **ser m.,** to be wicked; be evil; behave badly (children)
malograr /malo'grar/ *vt* to lose (time); waste, throw away (opportunities); *—vr* fall through, fail; wither, fade; die early, come to an untimely end
malogro /ma'logro/ *m,* loss, waste (time, opportunity); frustration; decline, fading; untimely death
malparar /malpa'rar/ *vt* to ill-treat; damage. **quedar malparado,** to get the worst of
malparir /malpa'rir/ *vt Med.* to miscarry
malparto /mal'parto/ *m,* miscarriage; abortion
malquerencia /malke'renθia; malke'rensia/ *f,* ill will, aversion, dislike
malquistar /malkis'tar/ *vt* to stir up trouble; make unpopular; estrange; *—vr* make oneself disliked
malquisto /mal'kisto/ *a* unpopular, disliked
malsano /mal'sano/ *a* unhealthy
malta /'malta/ *m,* malt
maltés /mal'tes/ **(-esa)** *a* and *n* Maltese
maltraer /maltra'er/ *vt irr* to ill-treat; insult. See **traer**
maltratamiento /maltrata'miento/ *m,* abuse, ill usage; damage, deterioration
maltratar /maltra'tar/ *vt* to ill-treat; abuse, insult; misuse, spoil, damage
maltrato /mal'trato/ *m,* maltreatment; misuse
maltrecho /mal'tretʃo/ *a* ill-treated, bruised; abused, insulted; damaged
maltusianismo /maltusia'nismo/ *m,* Malthusianism
maltusiano /maltu'siano/ *a* Malthusian
Malucas, las /ma'lukas, las/ the Moluccas
malucho /ma'lutʃo/ *a Inf.* off-color, below par, not well
malva /'malβa/ *f,* mallow. **m. real, m. rosa,** *or* **m. loca,** hollyhock. **ser como una m.,** *Fig. Inf.* to be a clinging vine
malvado /mal'βaðo/ *a* evil, malevolent, fiendish *—n* villain, fiend
malvasía /malβa'sia/ *f, Bot.* malvasia; malmsey (wine)
malvavisco /malβa'βisko/ *m, Bot.* marshmallow
malvender /malβen'der/ *vt* to sell at a loss
malversación /malβersa'θion; malβersa'sion/ *f,* malversation, maladministration; misappropriation (of funds)
malversador /malβersa'ðor/ **(-ra)** *n* bad or corrupt administrator
malversar /malβer'sar/ *vt* to misappropriate (funds)
mama /'mama/ *f, Inf.* mamma, mommy; breast; udder
mamá /ma'ma/ *f,* mamma
mamar /ma'mar/ *vt* to suck (the breast); *Inf.* wolf, swallow; learn from an early age; enjoy, obtain unfairly; *—vr* get drunk
mamario /ma'mario/ *a* mammary
mamarracho /mama'rratʃo/ *m, Inf.* scarecrow, dummy; anything grotesque looking
mameluco /mame'luko/ *m,* mameluke; *Inf.* ninny, fool
mamífero /ma'mifero/ *a* mammalian. *m,* mammal
mamotreto /mamo'treto/ *m,* notebook, memorandum; *Inf.* large book or bulky file of papers
mampara /mam'para/ *f,* folding screen; screen; partition
mamparo /mam'paro/ *m,* bulkhead
mampostería /mamposte'ria/ *f,* masonry, stonemasonry
mampostero /mampos'tero/ *m,* stonemason
mamut /ma'mut/ *m,* mammoth
maná /ma'na/ *m,* manna
manada /ma'naða/ *f,* handful; herd, flock; group, drove, crowd
manadero /mana'ðero/ *m,* herdsman, drover; spring, stream
manantial /manan'tial/ *m,* fountain, source, spring; head (of a river)
manar /ma'nar/ *vi* to flow, stream; be plentiful
manatí /mana'ti/ *m,* sea cow, manatee
mancar /man'kar/ *vt* to injure, maim; *—vi* grow calm (elements)
manceba /man'θeβa; man'seβa/ *f,* concubine; girl
mancebía /manθe'βia; manse'βia/ *f,* brothel; youth, young days
mancebo /man'θeβo; man'seβo/ *m,* youth, stripling; bachelor; shop assistant
mancha /'mantʃa/ *f,* spot, smear, stain; blotch; plot of ground; patch of vegetation; stigma, disgrace
manchar /man'tʃar/ *vt* to stain; smear; spot; speckle; disgrace; tarnish
manchego /man'tʃego/ **(-ga)** *a* and *n* of or from La Mancha (Spain)
manchuriano /mantʃu'riano/ **(-na)** *a* and *n* Manchurian
mancilla /man'θiʎa; man'siya/ *f,* stain; slur
mancillar /manθi'ʎar; mansi'yar/ *vt* to stain; *Fig.* smirch
manco /'manko/ **(-ca)** *a* maimed, disabled; one-handed; one-armed; armless; handless; incomplete, faulty *—n* disabled person
mancomunidad /mankomuni'ðað/ *f,* association, society; community, union; commonwealth; regional legislative assembly
manda /'manda/ *f,* offer, suggestion, proposition; legacy
mandadero /manda'ðero/ **(-ra)** *n* convent or prison messenger; errand boy (girl)
mandado /man'daðo/ *m,* order, command; errand
mandamiento /manda'miento/ *m,* order, command; *Eccl.* commandment; *Law.* writ; *pl Inf.* one's five fingers
mandar /man'dar/ *vt* to order, command; bequeath, will; send; control, drive; promise, offer; order (e.g. *Mandó hacerse un traje,* He ordered a suit to be made); *—vr* walk unaided (convalescents, etc.); lead into one another (rooms, etc.); **¿Quién manda aquí?** Who is in charge here?
mandarín /manda'rin/ *m,* mandarin; *Inf.* bureaucrat
mandarina /manda'rina/ *f,* mandarin (classical Chinese); mandarin orange
mandatario /manda'tario/ *m,* mandatary
mandato /man'dato/ *m,* mandate; command; *Eccl.* maundy. *Polit.* mandate. **cuarto m.,** fourth term (of President, Governor, etc.)
mandíbula /man'diβula/ *f,* jaw; jawbone, mandible
mandil /man'dil/ *m,* long leather apron; apron; Freemason's apron; close-meshed fishing net
mandilón /mandi'lon/ *m, Inf.* coward, nincompoop
mandioca /man'dioka/ *f,* manioc, cassava; tapioca
mando /'mando/ *m,* authority, power; (*Mil. Nav.*) command; *Engin.* regulation; controls (of a machine, etc.). **m. a distancia,** remote control. *Aer.* **m. de dos pilotos,** dual-controlled. **mandos gemelos,** dual con-

trol. **al m. de,** under the command of; under the direction of
mandolín /mando'lin/ *m.* **mandolina** *f,* mandolin
mandón /man'don/ *a* domineering, bossy
mandrágora /man'dragora/ *f,* mandrake
mandril /man'dril/ *m, Mech.* mandrel, chuck; *Zool.* mandrill
manear /mane'ar/ *vt* to hobble (a horse); manage, control
manecilla /mane'θiʎa; mane'siya/ *f, dim* little hand; hand of a clock; *Print.* fist
manejable /mane'haβle/ *a* manageable, controllable
manejar /mane'har/ *vt* to handle; use, wield; control; manage, direct; ride (horses); —*vr* manage to move around (after an accident, illness)
manejo /ma'neho/ *m,* handling; use, wielding; control; management, direction; horsemanship; intrigue
maneota /mane'ota/ *f,* hobble, shackle
manera /ma'nera/ *f,* manner, way, means; behavior, style (gen. *pl*); class (of people); *Art.* style, manner. **a la m. de,** like, in the style of. **de esa m.,** in that way; according to that, in that case. **de m. que,** so that. **en gran m.,** to a great extent. **sobre m.,** exceedingly
manga /'maŋga/ *f,* sleeve; bag; grip; handle; pipe (of a hose); strainer; waterspout; body of troops; beam, breadth of a ship; *pl* profits. **m. de viento,** whirlwind. **echar de m. a,** to make use of a person. *Inf.* **estar de m.,** to be in league. **tener m. ancha,** to be broad-minded. *Fig. Inf.* **traer** (**una cosa**) **en la m.,** to have (something) up one's sleeve
mangana /maŋ'gana/ *f,* lasso
manganeso /maŋga'neso/ *m,* manganese
manganilla /maŋga'niʎa; maŋga'niya/ *f,* sleight of hand; hoax, trick
mangle /'maŋgle/ *m,* mangrove tree
mango /'maŋgo/ *m,* handle, haft, stock; mango. **m. de cuchillo,** knife handle
mangonear /maŋgone'ar/ *vi Inf.* to loaf, roam about; interfere, meddle
mangonero /maŋgo'nero/ *a Inf.* meddlesome
mangosta /maŋ'gosta/ *f,* mongoose
mangote /maŋ'gote/ *m, Inf.* long, wide sleeve; black oversleeve
manguera /maŋ'guera/ *f,* hose; sleeve, tube; airshaft; waterspout
manguero /maŋ'guero/ *m,* fireman; hoseman
manguito /maŋ'guito/ *m,* muff; black oversleeve; wristlet, cuff; *Mech.* bush, sleeve
manía /ma'nia/ *f,* mania, obsession; whim, fancy
maníaco /ma'niako/ **(-ca)** *a* maniacal; capricious, extravagant —*n* maniac
maniatar /mania'tar/ *vt* to handcuff; hobble (a cow, etc.)
maniático /ma'niatiko/ **(-ca)** *a* maniacal; capricious; faddy, fussy —*n* crank
manicomio /mani'komio/ *m,* insane asylum, mental hospital
manicura /mani'kura/ *f,* manicure
manicuro /mani'kuro/ **(-ra)** *n* manicurist
manida /ma'niða/ *f,* lair, den; dwelling, habitation
manifestación /manifesta'θion; manifesta'sion/ *f,* declaration, statement; exhibition; demonstration; *Eccl.* exposition (of the Blessed Sacrament)
manifestante /manifes'tante/ *mf* demonstrator
manifestar /manifes'tar/ *vt irr* to declare, make known, state; exhibit, show; *Eccl.* to expose (the Blessed Sacrament). See **acertar**
manifiesto /mani'fiesto/ *a* obvious, evident. *m,* manifesto; *Naut.* manifest; *Eccl.* exposition of the Blessed Sacrament. **poner de m.,** to show; make public; reveal
manigua /ma'nigua/ *f,* thicket, jungle (in Cuba)
manija /ma'niha/ *f,* handle, stock, haft; hand lever; clamp; tether (for horses, etc.)
manileño /mani'leɲo/ **(ña)** *a* and *n* Manilan
manilla /ma'niʎa; ma'niya/ *f,* bracelet; handcuff, manacle
maniobra /ma'nioβra/ *f,* operation, process; *Mil.* maneuver; intrigue; tackle, gear; handling, management; *Naut.* working of a ship; *pl* shunting (trains)
maniobrar /manio'βrar/ *vi Mil.* to maneuver; *Naut.* handle, work (ships)
manipulación /manipula'θion; manipula'sion/ *f,* handling; manipulation; control, management
manipulador /manipula'ðor/ *a* manipulative. *m,* sending key (telegraphy)
manipular /manipu'lar/ *vt* to handle; manipulate; manage, direct
manípulo /ma'nipulo/ *m,* maniple
maniqueo /mani'keo/ **(-ea)** *a* Manichean *n* Manichee
maniquete /mani'kete/ *m,* black lace mitten
maniquí /mani'ki/ *m,* mannequin; dummy; *Inf.* puppet, weak person
manirroto /mani'rroto/ **(-ta)** *a* wasteful, extravagant —*n* spendthrift
manivela /mani'βela/ *f, Mech.* crank, lever
manjar /man'har/ *m,* dish, food; pastime, recreation, pleasure. **m. blanco,** blancmange
mano /'mano/ *f,* hand; coat, coating; quire (of paper); front paw (animals); elephant's trunk; side, hand; hand (of a clock); game (of cards, etc.); lead (at cards); way, means; ability; power; protection, favor; compassion; aid, help; scolding; *Mus.* scale; pestle; workers. *Inf.* editing, correction of a literary work (gen. by a person more skilled than the author). **m. de mortero,** pestle. **m. de obra,** (manual) labor. **manos muertas,** *Law.* mortmain. **m. sobre m.,** with folded hands; lazily, indolently. **a la m.,** at hand, nearby; within one's grasp. **a manos llenas,** in abundance, abundantly. **bajo m.,** in an underhand manner, secretly. **buenas manos,** cleverness, ability; dexterity. **de primera m.,** first-hand, new. **estar dejado de la m. de Dios,** to be very unlucky; be very foolish. **poner la m. en,** to ill-treat; slap, buffet. **Si a m. viene...,** If by chance... **tender la m.,** to put out one's hand, shake hands. **traer entre manos,** to have on hand, be engaged in
manojo /ma'noho/ *m,* bunch, handful. **a manojos,** in handfuls; plentifully, in abundance
manolo /ma'nolo/ **(-la)** *n* inhabitant of low quarters of Madrid noted for pride, gaiety, quarrelsomeness, and wit
manopla /ma'nopla/ *f,* gauntlet
manoseado /manose'aðo/ *a* hackneyed
manosear /manose'ar/ *vt* to handle; paw, touch repeatedly; finger
manoseo /mano'seo/ *m,* handling; fingering; *Inf.* pawing, feeling
manotada /mano'taða/ *f,* slap, cuff
manotear /manote'ar/ *vt* to slap, cuff; —*vi* gesticulate, gesture with the hands
manoteo /mano'teo/ *m,* gesticulation with the hands
manquedad /manke'ðað/ *f,* disablement of hand or arm; lack of one of these; defect; incompleteness
mansalva /man'salβa/ (**a**) *adv* without danger
mansedumbre /manse'ðumbre/ *f,* meekness; kindness; gentleness
mansión /man'sion/ *f,* stay, visit; dwelling, abode; mansion
manso /'manso/ *a* soft, gentle; meek, mild; tame; peaceable, amiable; calm
manta /'manta/ *f,* blanket; horse blanket; traveling rug; *Inf.* hiding, thrashing. **m. de viaje,** traveling rug. *Inf.* **a m. de Dios,** in abundance. **dar una m.,** to toss in a blanket. *Fig. Inf.* **tirar de la m.,** to let the cat out of the bag
manteamiento /mantea'miento/ *m,* tossing in a blanket
mantear /mante'ar/ *vt* to toss in a blanket
manteca /man'teka/ *f,* lard; cooking fat; grease; *Argentina* butter. **como m.,** as mild as milk, as soft as butter
mantecada /mante'kaða/ *f,* buttered toast
mantecado /mante'kaðo/ *m,* French ice cream
mantecoso /mante'koso/ *a* greasy
mantel /man'tel/ *m,* tablecloth; altar cloth
mantelería /mantele'ria/ *f,* table linen
mantelete /mante'lete/ *m,* (*Eccl. Mil.*) mantlet
mantener /mante'ner/ *vt irr* to maintain; keep, feed; support; continue, persevere with; uphold, affirm; keep up; —*vr* support oneself; remain in a place; (*with en*) continue to uphold (views, etc.), persevere

in. **mantenerse firme,** *Fig.* to stand one's ground. See **tener**

mantenimiento /manteni'miento/ *m,* maintenance; support; sustenance, nourishment; affirmation; upkeep; livelihood

manteo /man'teo/ *m,* tossing in a blanket; long cloak

mantequera /mante'kera/ *f,* churn; dairymaid; butter dish

mantequero /mante'kero/ *m,* dairyman; butter dish

mantequilla /mante'kiʎa; mante'kiya/ *f,* butter

mantero /man'tero/ *m,* blanket seller or maker

mantilla /man'tiʎa; man'tiya/ *f,* mantilla; saddlecloth *pl* baby's long clothes. **estar en mantillas,** to be in swaddling clothes; *Fig.* be in early infancy

manto /'manto/ *m,* cloak; cover, disguise; *Zool.* mantle; *Mineral.* layer

mantón /man'ton/ *m,* shawl. **m. de Manila,** Manila shawl

mantuano /man'tuano/ **(-na)** *a* and *n* Mantuan

manuable /ma'nuaβle/ *a* easy to handle or use, handy

manual /ma'nual/ *a* manual; handy, easy to use; docile, peaceable. *m,* manual, textbook; *Eccl.* book of ritual; notebook

manubrio /ma'nuβrio/ *m,* handle, crank

manuela /ma'nuela/ *f,* open carriage (Madrid)

manufactura /manufak'tura/ *f,* manufacture; manufactured article; factory

manufacturar /manufaktu'rar/ *vt* to manufacture

manufacturero /manufaktu'rero/ *a* manufacturing

manumisión /manumi'sion/ *f,* freeing (of a slave), manumission

manumitir /manumi'tir/ *vt Law.* to free, enfranchise (slaves)

manuscrito /manus'krito/ *a* and *m,* manuscript

manutención /manuten'θion; manuten'sion/ *f,* maintenance; upkeep; protection

manzana /man'θana; man'sana/ *f,* apple; block (of houses); city square; Adam's apple

manzanal /manθa'nal; mansa'nal/ *m,* apple orchard; apple tree

manzanar /manθa'nar; mansa'nar/ *m,* apple orchard

manzanilla /manθa'niʎa; mansa'niya/ *f,* white sherry wine; *Bot.* chamomile; chamomile tea; knob, ball (on furniture); pad (on an animal's foot)

manzano /man'θano; man'sano/ *m,* apple tree

maña /'maɲa/ *f,* skill, dexterity; craftiness, guile; vice, bad habit (gen. *pl*). **darse m. para,** to contrive to

mañana /ma'ɲana/ *f,* morning; tomorrow. *m,* future, tomorrow *—adv* tomorrow; in time to come; soon. **¡M.!** Tomorrow! Another day! Not now! (generally to beggars). **de m.,** early in the morning. **muy de m.,** very early in the morning. **pasado m.,** the day after tomorrow

mañanica /maɲa'nika/ *f,* early morning

mañear /maɲe'ar/ *vt* to arrange cleverly; *—vi* behave shrewdly

mañero /ma'ɲero/ *a* shrewd, clever; easily worked; handy

mañoso /ma'ɲoso/ *a* clever, skillful; crafty; vicious, with bad habits

mañuela /ma'ɲuela/ *f,* low guile

mapa /'mapa/ *m,* map; card. **m. en relieve,** relief map. **m. del estado mayor,** ordnance map. *Inf.* **no estar en el m.,** to be off the map; be most unusual (of things)

mapache /ma'patʃe/ *m,* raccoon

mapamundi /mapa'mundi/ *m,* map of the world

maqueta /ma'keta/ *f,* (*Art. Archit.*) model

maquiavélico /makia'βeliko/ *a* Machiavellian

maquiavelismo /makiaβe'lismo/ *m,* Machiavellism

maquillaje /maki'ʎahe; maki'yahe/ *m,* makeup, cosmetics; making up (of the face)

maquillar /maki'ʎar; maki'yar/ **(se)** *vt* and *vr* to make up (the face, etc.)

máquina /'makina/ *f,* machine, mechanism; engine; apparatus; plan, scheme; machine, puppet; *Inf.* mansion, palace; plenty; locomotive; fantasy, product of the imagination. **m. de vapor,** steam engine. **m. de arrastre,** traction engine; tractor. **m. de coser,** sewing machine. **m. de escribir,** typewriter. **m. fotográfica,** camera. **m. de impresionar,** movie camera. **m. de imprimir,** printing machine. **m. herramienta,** machine tool. **m. neumática,** air pump

maquinación /makina'θion; makina'sion/ *f,* intrigue, machination

maquinador /makina'ðor/ **(-ra)** *n* intriguer, schemer

maquinal /maki'nal/ *a* mechanical

maquinar /maki'nar/ *vt* to intrigue, scheme, plot

maquinaria /maki'naria/ *f,* machinery; applied mechanics; mechanism

maquinista /maki'nista/ *mf* driver, enginer; mechanic; machinist; locomotive driver

mar /mar/ *mf* sea; great many, abundance. **m. bonanza** *or* **m. en calma,** calm sea. **m. de fondo** *or* **m. de leva,** swell. **alta m.,** high seas. **a mares,** plentifully. **arar en el m.,** to labor in vain. *Naut.* **hacerse a la m.,** to put out to sea. **la m. de historias,** a great number of stories

maraña /ma'raɲa/ *f,* undergrowth; tangle; *Fig.* difficult position; intrigue; silk waste

marasmo /ma'rasmo/ *m, Med.* marasmus, atrophy; inactivity, paralysis

maravedí /maraβe'ði/ *m,* maravedi (old Spanish coin of fluctuating value)

maravilla /mara'βiʎa; mara'βiya/ *f,* marvel, wonder; admiration; amazement; marigold. **a m.,** wonderfully. **a las mil maravillas,** to perfection, excellently. **por m.,** by chance; occasionally

maravillar /maraβi'ʎar; maraβi'yar/ *vt* to amaze, cause admiration; *—vr* (*with de*) marvel at, admire; be amazed by

maravilloso /maraβi'ʎoso; maraβi'yoso/ *a* marvelous, wonderful

marbete /mar'βete/ *m,* label, tag; edge, border

marca /'marka/ *f,* mark, sign; brand; frontier zone, border country; standard, norm (of size); make, brand; measuring rule; *Sports.* record. **m. de fábrica,** brand, trademark. **m. de ley,** hallmark. **m. registrada,** registered name. **de m.,** excellent, of excellent quality

marcado /mar'kaðo/ *a* marked; pronounced; strong (of accents)

marcador /marka'ðor/ *a* marking. *m,* marker; scoreboard; bookmark

marcar /mar'kar/ *vt* to mark; brand; embroider initials on linen; tell the time (watches); show the amount (cash register, etc.); dial (telephone); *Sports.* score (a goal); notice, observe; set aside, earmark; *—vr Naut.* check the course. **m. el compás** to beat time

Mar Caspio /'mar 'kaspio/ Caspian Sea

marcha /'martʃa/ *f,* departure; running, working; *Mil.* march; speed (of trains, ships, etc.); *Mus.* march; progress, course (of events). **m. atrás,** backing, reversing. **m. de ensayo,** trial run. **m. forzada,** *Mil.* forced march. **a largas marchas,** with all speed. **a toda m.,** at top speed; full speed ahead; by forced marches; *Mil.* **batir la m.,** to strike up a march. **en m.,** underway; working; in operation

marchamero /martʃa'mero/ *m,* customs official who checks and marks goods

marchamo /mar'tʃamo/ *m,* customs mark on checked goods

marchar /mar'tʃar/ *vi* to run; work; function; go; leave, depart; progress, proceed; *Mil.* march; go (clocks); *—vr* leave, go away

marchitable /martʃi'taβle/ *a* perishable, fragile

marchitamiento /martʃita'miento/ *m,* withering

marchitar /martʃi'tar/ *vt* to wither, fade; blight, spoil; weaken; *—vr* wither; be blighted

marchitez /martʃi'teθ; martʃi'tes/ *f,* witheredness; fadedness

marchito /mar'tʃito/ *a* withered; faded; blighted, frustrated

marcial /mar'θial; mar'sial/ *a* martial; courageous, militant

marcialidad /marθiali'ðað; marsiali'ðað/ *f,* war-like spirit, militancy

marciano /mar'θiano; mar'siano/ *a* Martian

marco /'marko/ *m,* mark (German coin); boundary

mark; frame (of a picture, etc.). **m. de ventana,** window frame
Mar de las Indias /'mar de las 'indias/ Indian Ocean
Mar del Norte /'mar del 'norte/ North Sea
marea /ma'rea/ *f,* tide; strand, water's edge; light breeze; drizzle; dew; street dirt. **m. creciente,** flood tide. **m. menguante,** ebb tide. **m. muerta,** neap tide
mareaje /ma'reahe/ *m,* seamanship; ship's course
marear /mare'ar/ *vt* to navigate; sell; sell publicly; *Inf.* annoy; *—vr* be seasick; feel faint; feel giddy; be damaged at sea (goods)
marejada /mare'haða/ *f,* surge, swell; high sea; tidal wave; commotion, uproar
mareo /ma'reo/ *m,* seasickness; nausea, dizziness; *Inf.* irritation, tediousness
mareta /ma'reta/ *f,* movement of the waves; sound, noise (of a crowd)
marfil /mar'fil/ *m,* ivory
marfileño /marfi'leɲo/ *a* ivory; ivory-like
marfuz /mar'fuθ; mar'fus/ *a* spurned, rejected; deceitful
marga /'marga/ *f,* loam, marl
margarina /marga'rina/ *f,* margarine
margarita /marga'rita/ *f,* pearl; marguerite, oxeye daisy; daisy; periwinkle
margen /'marhen/ *mf* edge, fringe, border, verge; margin (of a book); opportunity; marginal note. **dar m. para,** to provide an opportunity for; give rise to
marginal /marhi'nal/ *a* marginal
margoso /mar'goso/ *a* loamy, marly
marica /ma'rika/ *f,* magpie. *m,* (*offensive*) homosexual; milksop
maricón /mari'kon/ *m,* (*offensive*) homosexual
maridable /mari'ðaβle/ *a* marital, matrimonial
maridaje /mari'ðahe/ *m,* conjugal union and harmony; intimate relationship (between things)
maridar /mari'ðar/ *vi* to get married; mate, live as husband and wife; *—vt* unite, link, join together
marido /ma'riðo/ *m,* husband
marihuana /mari'uana/ *f,* marijuana
marimacho /mari'matʃo/ *m, Inf.* mannish woman
marina /ma'rina/ *f,* coast, seashore; *Art.* seascape; seamanship; navy, fleet. **m. de guerra,** navy. **m. mercante,** merchant navy
marinera /mari'nera/ *f,* sailor's blouse
marinería /marine'ria/ *f,* profession of a sailor; seamanship; crew of a ship; sailors (as a class)
marinero /mari'nero/ *m,* sailor, seaman. **m. de agua dulce,** freshwater sailor (a novice). **m. práctico,** able seaman. **a la marinera,** in a seaman-like fashion
marinesco /mari'nesko/ *a* seamanly
marino /ma'rino/ *a* marine, sea; seafaring; shipping. *m,* sailor, mariner
marioneta /mario'neta/ *f,* marionette, puppet
mariposa /mari'posa/ *f,* butterfly; night-light
mariposear /maripose'ar/ *vi* to flutter, flit, fly about; flirt, be fickle; follow about, dance attendance on
mariquita /mari'kita/ *f, Ent.* ladybird; parakeet.
marisabidilla /marisaβi'ðiʎa; marisaβi'ðiya/ *f, Inf.* blue-stocking, know-it-all
mariscal /maris'kal/ *m, Mil.* marshal; field marshal; blacksmith
marisco /ma'risko/ *m,* shellfish
marisma /ma'risma/ *f,* bog, morass, swamp
marital /mari'tal/ *a* marital
marítimo /ma'ritimo/ *a* maritime, sea
marjal /mar'hal/ *m,* marshland, fen
marmita /mar'mita/ *f,* stewpot, copper, boiler
marmitón /marmi'ton/ *m,* kitchen boy, scullion
mármol /'marmol/ *m,* marble; work executed in marble
marmolería /marmole'ria/ *f,* marble works; work executed in marble
marmolista /marmo'lista/ *mf* marble cutter; dealer in marble
marmóreo /mar'moreo/ *a* marble; *Poet.* marmoreal
marmota /mar'mota/ *f, Zool.* marmot; sleepyhead, dormouse
Mar Muerto /mar 'muerto/ Dead Sea
maroma /ma'roma/ *f,* rope, hawser
marqués /mar'kes/ *m,* marquis
marquesa /mar'kesa/ *f,* marchioness
marquesina /marke'sina/ *f,* marquee
marquetería /markete'ria/ *f,* marquetry
marrana /ma'rrana/ *f,* sow; *Inf.* slattern, slut
marrano /ma'rrano/ *m,* pig, hog; Marrano
marras /'marras/ (**de**) *adv* long ago, in the dim past
marrasquino /marras'kino/ *m,* maraschino liqueur
marro /'marro/ *m,* tick, tag (game)
Mar Rojo /mar 'rroho/ Red Sea
marrón /ma'rron/ *a* maroon; brown. *m,* brown color; maroon color; quoit
marroquí /marro'ki/ *a* and *mf* Moroccan. *m,* Morocco leather
marroquín /marro'kin/ **(-ina), marrueco (-ca)** *a* and *n* Moroccan
Marruecos /ma'rruekos/ Morocco
marrullería /marruʎe'ria; marruye'ria/ *f,* flattery, cajolery
marrullero /marru'ʎero; marru'yero/ **(-ra)** *a* wheedling, flattering *—n* wheedler, cajoler
Marsella /mar'seʎa; mar'seya/ Marseilles
marsellés /marse'ʎes; marse'yes/ **(-esa)** *a* and *n* of or from Marseilles. *f.* **la Marsellesa,** the Marseillaise
marsopa /mar'sopa/ *f,* porpoise
marta /'marta/ *f,* sable; marten
Marte /'marte/ *m,* Mars
martes /'martes/ *m,* Tuesday. **m. de carnaval,** mardi gras
martillar /marti'ʎar; marti'yar/ *vt* to hammer; oppress
martillazo /marti'ʎaθo; marti'yaso/ *m,* hammer blow
martilleo /marti'ʎeo; marti'yeo/ *m,* hammering; noise of the hammer; clink, clatter
martillo /mar'tiʎo; mar'tiyo/ *m,* hammer; oppressor, tyrant; auction rooms. **a m.,** by hammering. **de m.,** wrought (of metals)
martinete /marti'nete/ *m,* hammer (of a pianoforte); pile driver; drop hammer. **m. de báscula,** tilt hammer
Martinica /marti'nika/ Martinique
martín pescador /mar'tin peska'ðor/ *m,* kingfisher
mártir /'martir/ *mf* martyr
martirio /mar'tirio/ *m,* martyrdom
martirizar /martiri'θar; martiri'sar/ *vt* to martyr; torture, torment, martyrize; tease, annoy
martirologio /martiro'lohio/ *m,* martyrology
marxismo /mark'sismo/ *m,* Marxism
marxista /mark'sista/ *a* and *mf* Marxist
marzo /'marθo; 'marso/ *m,* March
mas /mas/ *conjunc* but; yet
más /mas/ *adv compar* more; in addition, besides; rather, preferably. *Math.* plus. **el** (**la,** etc.) **más,** *adv superl* the most, etc. **m. bien,** more; rather; preferably. **m. que,** only; but; more than; although, even if. **a lo m.,** at the most; at the worst. **a m.,** besides, in addition. **de m.,** superfluous, unnecessary, unwanted. **no... m. que,** only. **por m. que,** however; even if. **sin m. ni m.,** without further ado. **M. vale un mal arreglo que un buen pleito,** A bad peace is better than a good war
masa /'masa/ *f,* mass; dough; whole, aggregate; majority (of people); mortar. **en la m. de la sangre,** *Fig.* in the blood, in a person's nature
masada /ma'saða/ *f,* farmhouse and stock
masadero /masa'ðero/ *m,* farmer; farm laborer
masaje /ma'sahe/ *m,* massage
masajista /masa'hista/ *mf* masseur; masseuse
mascadura /maska'ðura/ *f,* chewing
mascar /mas'kar/ *vt* to chew; masticate; *Inf.* mumble, mutter
máscara /'maskara/ *f,* mask; fancy dress; pretext, excuse. *mf* masquerader, reveler; *pl* masquerade. **m. para gases,** gas mask
mascarada /maska'raða/ *f,* masquerade; company of revelers
mascarero /maska'rero/ **(-ra)** *n* theatrical costumer, fancy-dress dealer
mascarilla /maska'riʎa; maska'riya/ *f,* death mask
mascarón /maska'ron/ *m,* large mask; *Archit.* gargoyle. **m. de proa,** *Naut.* figurehead
mascota /mas'kota/ *f,* mascot

masculinidad /maskulini'ðað/ *f*, masculinity
masculino /masku'lino/ *a* masculine; male; manly, vigorous
mascullar /masku'ʎar; masku'yar/ *vt Inf.* to chew; mutter, mumble
masera /ma'sera/ *f*, kneading bowl; cloth for covering dough
masilla /ma'siʎa; ma'siya/ *f*, mastic, putty
masón /ma'son/ **(-ona)** *n* Freemason
masonería /masone'ria/ *f*, freemasonry
masónico /ma'soniko/ *a* masonic
masoquismo /maso'kismo/ *m*, masochism
mastelero /maste'lero/ *m*, *Naut.* topmast
masticación /mastika'θion; mastika'sion/ *f*, mastication
masticar /masti'kar/ *vt* to masticate, eat; *Inf.* chew upon, consider
masticatorio /mastika'torio/ *a* masticatory
mástil /'mastil/ *m*, *Naut.* mast; upright, stanchion; pole (of a tent); stem, trunk; neck (of a guitar, etc.)
mastín /mas'tin/ *m*, mastiff
mastodonte /masto'ðonte/ *m*, mastodon
mastoides /mastoi'ðes/ *a* mastoid
mastuerzo /mas'tuerθo; mas'tuerso/ *m*, watercress; fool, blockhead
masturbación /masturβa'θion; masturβa'sion/ *f*, masturbation
masturbarse /mastur'βarse/ *vr* to masturbate
mata /'mata/ *f*, plant, shrub; stalk, sprig; grove, copse. **m. de pelo,** mat of hair
matacandelas /matakan'delas/ *m*, candle snuffer
matachín /mata'tʃin/ *m*, mummer; butcher; *Inf.* swashbuckler
matadero /mata'ðero/ *m*, slaughterhouse, abattoir
matadura /mata'ðura/ *f*, sore (on animals)
matafuego /mata'fuego/ *m*, fire extinguisher; fireman
matalotaje /matalo'tahe/ *m*, ship's supplies, stores; *Inf.* hodgepodge
matamoros /mata'moros/ *a* swashbuckling, swaggering
matamoscas /mata'moskas/ *m*, fly swatter
matanza /ma'tanθa; ma'tansa/ *f*, killing, massacre, slaughter; butchery (animals); *Inf.* persistence, determination
matar /ma'tar/ *vt* to kill; quench (thirst); put out (fire, light); slake (lime); tarnish (metal); bevel (corners, etc.); pester, importune; suppress; compel; *Art.* tone down; *—vr* kill oneself; be disappointed, grieve; overwork. **estar a m.,** to be at daggers drawn. **matarse por,** to try hard to; work hard for
matasanos /mata'sanos/ *m*, *Inf.* quack (doctor); bad doctor
matasellos /mata'seʎos; mata'seyos/ *m*, cancellation, postmark
mate /'mate/ *a* matte, unpolished, dull. *m*, checkmate (chess); maté, Paraguayan tea; gourd; vessel made from gourd, coconut, etc.
maté /ma'te/ *m*, maté, Paraguayan tea
matemáticas /mate'matikas/ *f pl*, mathematics. **m. prácticas,** applied mathematics. **m. teóricas,** pure mathematics
matemático /mate'matiko/ *a* mathematical; exact. *m*, mathematician
materia /ma'teria/ *f*, matter; theme, subject matter; subject (of study); matter, stuff, substance; pus, matter; question, subject; reason, occasion. **m. colorante,** dye. **materias plásticas,** plastics. **materias primas,** raw materials. **en m. de,** concerning; in the matter of
material /mate'rial/ *a* material; dull, stupid, limited. *m*, material; ingredient; plant, factory; equipment. **m. móvil ferroviario,** rolling stock (railroads)
materialidad /materiali'ðað/ *f*, materiality; external appearance (of things)
materialismo /materia'lismo/ *m*, materialism
materialista /materia'lista/ *a* materialistic. *mf* materialist
materializar /materiali'θar; materiali'sar/ *vt* to materialize; *—vr* materialize; grow materialistic, grow less spiritual
maternidad /materni'ðað/ *f*, maternity, motherhood
materno /ma'terno/ *a* maternal
matiz /ma'tiθ; ma'tis/ *m*, combination of colors; tone, hue; shade (of meaning, etc.)
matizar /mati'θar; mati'sar/ *vt* to combine, harmonize (colors); tint, shade; tinge (words, etc.)
matojo /ma'toho/ *m*, shrub, bush
matorral /mato'rral/ *m*, thicket, bush, undergrowth
matraca /ma'traka/ *f*, rattle; *Inf.* scolding, dressing-down; insistence, importunity
matraquear /matrake'ar/ *vi* to make a noise with a rattle; *Inf.* scold
matriarcado /matriar'kaðo/ *m*, matriarchy
matricida /matri'θiða; matri'siða/ *mf* matricide (person)
matricidio /matri'θiðio; matri'siðio/ *m*, matricide (crime)
matrícula /ma'trikula/ *f*, list, register; matriculation; registration number (of a car, etc.). **m. de buques,** maritime register. **m. de mar,** mariner's register; maritime register
matriculación /matrikula'θion; matrikula'sion/ *f*, matriculation; registration
matricular /matriku'lar/ *vt* to matriculate; enrol; *Naut.* register; *—vr* matriculate; enroll, register
matrimonial /matrimo'nial/ *a* matrimonial
matrimonio /matri'monio/ *m*, marriage, matrimony; married couple. **m. a yuras,** secret marriage. **m. de la mano izquierda** *or* **m. morganático,** morganatic marriage. **contraer m.,** to get married
matritense /matri'tense/ *a* and *mf* Madrilenian
matriz /ma'triθ; ma'tris/ *f*, uterus, womb; matrix, mold; *Mineral.* matrix; nut, female screw
matrona /ma'trona/ *f*, married woman; matron; midwife; female customs officer
matusalén /matusa'len/ *m*, Methuselah, very old man
matute /ma'tute/ *m*, smuggling; contraband; gambling den
matutero /matu'tero/ **(-ra)** *n* smuggler, contrabandist
matutino /matu'tino/ *a* matutinal, morning
maula /'maula/ *f*, trash; remnant; deception, fraud, trick. *mf Inf.* good-for-nothing; lazybones. *Inf.* **ser buena m.,** to be a trickster or a fraud
maulería /maule'ria/ *f*, remnant stall; trickery
maullar /mau'ʎar; mau'yar/ *vi* to meow, mew (cats)
maullido /mau'ʎiðo; mau'yiðo/ *m*, meow, cry of the cat
Mauricio, Isla de /mau'riθio, 'isla de; mau'risio, 'isla de/ Mauritius
mauritano /mauri'tano/ **(-na)** *a* and *n* Mauritian
mausoleo /mauso'leo/ *m*, mausoleum
maxilar /maksi'lar/ *a* maxillary. *m*, jaw
máxima /'maksima/ *f*, maxim, rule, precept, principle
máxime /'maksime/ *adv* principally, chiefly
máximo /'maksimo/ *a superl* **grande** greatest, maximum, top. *m*, maximum
maya /'maya/ *f*, common daisy; May queen
mayal /ma'yal/ *m*, flail
mayo /'mayo/ *m*, May; maypole; bouquet, wreath of flowers; *pl* festivities on eve of May Day
mayólica /ma'yolika/ *f*, majolica
mayonesa /mayo'nesa/ *f*, mayonnaise
mayor /ma'yor/ *a compar* **grande** bigger; greater; elder; main, principal; older; high (mass, etc.); *Mus.* major. *mf* major (of full age) *—a superl* **grande. el, la, lo mayor, los (las) mayores,** the biggest, greatest; eldest; chief, principal. **por m.,** in short, briefly; *Com.* wholesale
mayor /ma'yor/ *m*, head, director; chief clerk; *Mil.* major; *pl* ancestors
mayoral /mayo'ral/ *m*, head shepherd; coachman, driver; foreman, overseer, supervisor, steward
mayorazgo /mayo'raθgo; mayo'rasgo/ *m*, *Law.* entail; entailed estate; heir (to an entail); eldest son; right of primogeniture
mayordoma /mayor'ðoma/ *f*, steward's wife; housekeeper; stewardess
mayordomo /mayor'ðomo/ *m*, steward, superintendent; butler; major-domo, royal chief steward
mayoría /mayo'ria/ *f*, majority

mayormente /mayor'mente/ *adv* chiefly; especially

mayúscula /ma'yuskula/ *f,* capital letter, upper-case letter

mayúsculo /ma'yuskulo/ *a* large; capital (letters). **letra mayúscula,** capital letter, upper-case letter

maza /'maθa; 'masa/ *f,* mallet; club, bludgeon; mace; bass drum stick; pile driver; bone, stick, etc., tied to dog's tail in carnival; *Inf.* pedant, bore; important person, authority. **m. de polo,** polo mallet

mazacote /maθa'kote; masa'kote/ *m,* concrete; roughhewn work of art; *Inf.* stodgy overcooked dish; bore, tedious person

mazamorra /maθa'morra; masa'morra/ *f,* dish made of cornmeal; biscuit crumbs; broken fragments, remains

mazapán /maθa'pan; masa'pan/ *m,* marzipan

mazmorra /maθ'morra; mas'morra/ *f,* dungeon

mazo /'maθo; 'maso/ *m,* mallet; bundle, bunch; importunate person; clapper (of a bell)

mazonería /maθone'ria; masone'ria/ *f,* stonemasonry

mazonero /maθo'nero; maso'nero/ *m,* stonemason

mazorca /ma'θorka; ma'sorka/ *f,* spindleful; spike, ear (of corn); cocoa berry; camarilla, group

mazurca /ma'θurka; ma'surka/ *f,* mazurka

me /me/ *pers pron acc* or *dat 1st sing mf* me; to me

meandro /me'andro/ *m,* meandering, twisting, winding; wandering

meato /me'ato/ *m,* meatus

Meca, la /'meka, la/ Mecca

mecánica /me'kanika/ *f,* mechanics; mechanism, machinery; *Inf.* worthless thing; mean action

mecánico /me'kaniko/ *a* mechanical; power-operated; base, ill-bred. *m,* engineer; mechanic

mecanismo /meka'nismo/ *m,* mechanism; works, machinery

mecanizar /mekani'θar; mekani'sar/ *vt* to mechanize

mecanografía /mekanogra'fia/ *f,* typewriting

mecanografiar /mekanografi'ar/ *vt* to typewrite, type

mecanográfico /mekano'grafiko/ *a* typewriting, typing; typewritten, typed

mecanografista /mekanogra'fista/ *mf* **mecanógrafo (-fa)** *n* typist

mecedor /meθe'ðor; mese'ðor/ *a* rocking, swaying. *m,* swing

mecedora /meθe'ðora; mese'ðora/ *f,* rocking chair

mecenas /me'θenas; me'senas/ *m,* Maecenas, patron

mecer /me'θer; me'ser/ *vt* to stir, mix; shake; rock; swing

mecha /'metʃa/ *f,* wick; bit, drill; fuse (of explosives); match (for cannon, etc.); fat bacon (for basting); lock of hair; skein, twist

mechar /me'tʃar/ *vt Cul.* to baste, lard

mechero /me'tʃero/ *m,* gas burner; pocket lighter; socket of a candlestick

mechón /me'tʃon/ *m,* tuft, skein, bundle; lock of hair; wisp

medalla /me'ðaʎa; me'ðaya/ *f,* medal; medallion; plaque, round panel; *Inf.* piece of eight (coin)

medallón /meða'ʎon; me'ðayon/ *m,* large medal; medallion; locket

médano /'meðano/ *m,* sand dune

media /'meðia/ *f,* stocking

mediación /meðia'θion; meðia'sion/ *f,* mediation, arbitration; intercession

mediado /me'ðiaðo/ *a* half-full. **a mediados (del mes,** etc.**),** toward the middle (of the month, etc.)

mediador /meðia'ðor/ **(-ra)** *n* mediator, arbitrator; intercessor

medianamente /meðiana'mente/ *adv* moderately; passably, fairly well

medianero /meðia'nero/ **(-ra)** *a* middle; intervening, intermediate; mediatory —*n* mediator. *m,* owner of a semidetached house or of one in a row

medianía /meðia'nia/ *f,* average; medium, mediocrity; moderate wealth or means

mediano /me'ðiano/ *a* medium, average; moderate; *Inf.* middling, passable, fair

medianoche /meðia'notʃe/ *f,* midnight

mediante /me'ðiante/ *a* mediatory —*adv* by means of, by, through

mediar /me'ðiar/ *vi* to reach the middle; get halfway; elapse half a given time; intercede, mediate; arbitrate; be in between or in the middle; intervene, take part

medicación /meðika'θion; meðika'sion/ *f,* medication

medicamento /meðika'mento/ *m,* medicament, medicine, remedy

medicar /meði'kar/ *vt* to medicate

medicastro /meði'kastro/ *m,* unskilled physician; quack, charlatan

medicina /meði'θina; meði'sina/ *f,* medicine; medicament

medicinar /meðiθi'nar; meðisi'nar/ *vt* to attend; treat (patients)

medición /meði'θion; meði'sion/ *f,* measuring; measurements; survey (land); scansion

médico /'meðiko/ **(-ca)** *a* medical —*n* doctor of medicine. **m. de cabecera,** family doctor. **m. general,** general practitioner

medida /me'ðiða/ *f,* measurement; measuring stick; measure, precaution (gen. with *tomar, adoptar,* etc.); gauge; judgment, wisdom; meter; standard. **a m. que,** while, at the same time as. **tomar las medidas (a),** *Fig.* to take a person's measure, sum him up. **tomar sus medidas,** to take his (their) measurements, take the necessary measures. **un traje hecho a m.,** a suit made to measure

medieval /meðie'βal/ *a* medieval

medio /'meðio/ *a* half; middle; intermediate; halfway. *m,* half; middle; *Art.* medium; spiritualist medium; proceeding, measure, precaution; environment, medium; middle way, mean; *Sports.* halfback. **m. galope,** canter. **m. tiempo,** *Sports.* halftime. **a medias,** by halves; half, partly. **de por m.,** by halves; in between; in the way. **estar de por m.,** to be in the way; take part in. *Inf.* **quitar de en m.,** to get rid of. *Inf.* **quitarse de en m.,** to go away, remove oneself

mediocre /me'ðiokre/ *a* mediocre

mediocridad /meðiokri'ðað/ *f,* mediocrity; insignificance

mediodía /meðio'ðia/ *m,* noon, meridian; south

medioeval /meðioe'βal/ *a* medieval

mediopelo /meðio'pelo/ *m,* lower middle class

mediquillo /meði'kiʎo; meði'kiyo/ *m, Inf.* quack; medicine man (in the Philippines)

medir /me'ðir/ *vt irr* to measure; (metrics) scan; survey (land); compare; —*vr* measure one's words; act with restraint. See **pedir**

meditabundo /meðita'βundo/ *a* pensive, meditative, thoughtful

meditación /meðita'θion; meðita'sion/ *f,* meditation, consideration, reflection

meditador /meðita'ðor/ *a* meditative, thoughtful

meditar /meði'tar/ *vt* to meditate, consider, muse

meditativo /meðita'tiβo/ *a* meditative

mediterráneo /meðite'rraneo/ *a* mediterranean; inland, landlocked

médium /'meðium/ *m, Spirit.* medium

medra /'meðra/ *f,* progress; improvement, betterment; growth; prosperity

medrar /'meðrar/ *vi* to flourish, grow; become prosperous or improve one's position

medro /'meðro/ *m,* improvement, progress. See **medra**

medroso /me'ðroso/ *a* timid, frightened; frightful, horrible

médula /'meðula/ *f,* marrow; *Bot.* pith; *Fig.* essence, core

medusa /me'ðusa/ *f,* jellyfish

mefistofélico /mefisto'feliko/ *a* Mephistophelian

mefítico /me'fitiko/ *a* noxious, mephitic, poisonous

megáfono /me'gafono/ *m,* megaphone

megalómano /mega'lomano/ **(-na)** *n* megalomaniac

mejicano /mehi'kano/ **(-na)** *a* and *n* Mexican

Méjico /'mehiko/ Mexico

mejilla /me'hiʎa; me'hiya/ *f, Anat.* cheek

mejillón /mehi'ʎon; mehi'yon/ *m,* sea mussel

mejor /me'hor/ *a compar* **bueno** better —*adv* better; rather; sooner; preferably —*a superl* **bueno. el, la, lo mejor; los, las mejores,** the best; most preferable. **m. que m.,** better and better. *Inf.* **a lo m.,** probably, in all probability. **tanto m.,** so much the better

mejora /me'hora/ *f,* improvement; bettering; progress; higher bid (at auctions)
mejorable /meho'raβle/ *a* improvable
mejoramiento /mehora'miento/ *m,* betterment, improvement
mejorar /meho'rar/ *vt* to improve; better; outbid; —*vi* grow better (in health); improve (weather); make progress; rally (of markets). **Mejorando lo presente,** Present company excepted
mejoría /meho'ria/ *f,* improvement, progress; betterment; superiority; advantage, profit
mejunje /me'hunhe/ *m, Inf.* brew, potion, cure-all, stuff
melado /me'laðo/ *a* honey-colored. *m,* cane syrup
melancolía /melanko'lia/ *f,* melancholia; sadness, depression, melancholy
melancólico /melan'koliko/ *a* melancholy, sad; depressing
melaza /me'laθa; me'lasa/ *f,* molasses
melena /me'lena/ *f,* long side whiskers; loose, flowing hair (in women); overlong hair (in men); lion's mane. *Inf.* **andar a la m.,** to start a fight or quarrel. *Inf.* **traer a la m.,** to drag by the hair, force
melifluidad /meliflui'ðað/ *f,* mellifluence, sweetness
melifluo /me'lifluo/ *a* mellifluous, sweet-voiced; honeyed
melindre /me'lindre/ *m,* honey fritter; affectation, scruple, fastidiousness; narrow ribbon
melindroso /melin'droso/ *a* overfastidious, affected, prudish
mella /'meʎa; 'meya/ *f,* nick, notch; dent; gap; harm, damage (to reputation, etc.). **hacer m.,** *Fig.* to make an impression (on the mind); *Mil.* breach, drive a wedge
mellar /me'ʎar; me'yar/ *vt* to nick, notch; dent; damage
mellizo /me'ʎiθo; me'yiso/ **(-za)** *a* and *n* twin
melocotón /meloko'ton/ *m,* peach; peach tree
melocotonero /melokoto'nero/ *m,* peach tree
melodía /melo'ðia/ *f,* melody, tune; melodiousness
melódico /me'loðiko/ *a* melodic, melodious
melodioso /melo'ðioso/ *a* melodious, tuneful, sweet-sounding
melodrama /melo'ðrama/ *m,* melodrama
melodramático /meloðra'matiko/ *a* melodramatic
melón /me'lon/ *m,* melon
melosidad /melosi'ðað/ *f,* sweetness
meloso /me'loso/ *a* honeyed; sweet; gentle; mellifluous
membrana /mem'brana/ *f,* membrane
membrete /mem'brete/ *m,* note, memorandum; note or card of invitation; superscription, heading; address (of person)
membrillo /mem'briʎo; mem'briyo/ *m,* quince tree; quince; quince jelly
membrudo /mem'bruðo/ *a* brawny, strong, muscular
memo /'memo/ *a* silly, stupid
memorable /memo'raβle/ *a* memorable
memorándum /memo'randum/ *m,* notebook, jotter; memorandum
memorar /memo'rar/ **(se)** *vt* and *vr* to remember, recall
memoria /me'moria/ *f,* memory; remembrance, recollection; monument; memorial; report; essay, article; codicil; memorandum; record, chronicle; *pl* regards, compliments, greetings; memoirs; memoranda. *Inf.* **m. de grillo,** poor memory. **de m.,** by heart. **flaco de m.,** forgetful. **hacer m.,** to remember
memorial /memo'rial/ *m,* notebook; memorial, petition
memorialista /memoria'lista/ *mf* secretary, amanuensis
memorioso /memo'rioso/ *a* mindful, unforgetful
mena /'mena/ *f, Mineral.* ore
menaje /me'nahe/ *m,* household or school equipment or furniture
mención /men'θion; men'sion/ *f,* mention. **m. honorífica,** honorable mention. **hacer m. de,** to mention
mencionar /menθio'nar; mensio'nar/ *vt* to mention
mendacidad /mendaθi'ðað; mendasi'ðað/ *f,* mendacity, untruthfulness
mendaz /men'daθ; men'das/ *a* mendacious, untruthful
mendelismo /mende'lismo/ *m,* Mendelism
mendicante /mendi'kante/ *a* begging; *Eccl.* mendicant. *mf* beggar
mendicidad /mendiθi'ðað; mendisiða'ð/ *f,* mendicancy, begging
mendigar /mendi'gar/ *vt* to beg for alms; entreat, supplicate
mendigo /men'digo/ **(-ga)** *n* beggar
mendoso /men'doso/ *a* mendacious, untruthful; mistaken
mendrugo /men'drugo/ *m,* crust of bread
menear /mene'ar/ *vt* to sway, move; wag; shake; manage, control, direct; —*vr Inf.* get a move on; sway, move; wriggle
meneo /me'neo/ *m,* swaying movement; wagging; shaking; wriggling; management, direction; *Aer.* bump; *Inf.* spanking
menester /menes'ter/ *m,* lack, shortage; necessity; occupation, employment; *pl* physical necessities; *Inf.* tools, implements, equipment. **haber m.,** to need, require. **ser m.,** to be necessary or requisite
menesteroso /meneste'roso/ *a* indigent, poverty-stricken, needy
menestra /me'nestra/ *f,* vegetable soup; dried vegetable (gen. *pl*)
menestral /menes'tral/ **(-la)** *n* artisan; worker; mechanic
mengano /meŋ'gano/ **(-na)** *n* so-and-so (used instead of the name of the person)
mengua /'meŋgua/ *f,* decrease; lack, shortage; waning (of the moon, etc.); dishonor, disgrace; poverty
menguado /meŋ'guaðo/ **(-da)** *a* timid, cowardly; silly, stupid; mean, avaricious —*n* coward; fool; skinflint. *m,* narrowing stitch when knitting socks
menguante /meŋ'guante/ *a* ebb; waning; decreasing. *f,* ebb tide; decadence, decline. **m. de la luna,** waning of the moon
menguar /meŋ'guar/ *vi* to decrease; decline, decay; wane; ebb; narrow (socks); —*vt* diminish; disgrace, discredit
menina /me'nina/ *f,* child attendant (on Spanish royalty)
menino /me'nino/ *m,* Spanish royal page; little dandy
menjurje /men'hurhe/ *m,* See **mejunje**
menopausia /meno'pausia/ *f,* menopause
menor /me'nor/ *a compar* less, smaller; younger, minor; *Mus.* minor. *m,* minor. *f,* (logic) minor —*a superl* **el, la, lo m.; los, las menores,** the least; smallest; youngest. **m. de edad,** minor (in age). **por m.,** at retail; in detail
Menorca /me'norka/ Minorca
menoría /meno'ria/ *f,* subordination, dependence; inferiority; minority (underage); childhood, youth
menos /'menos/ *adv* less; minus; least; except. **m. de** *or* **m. que,** less than. **al m., por lo m.,** at least. **a m. que,** unless. **De m. nos hizo Dios,** Never say die, Nothing is impossible. **poco más o m.,** more or less, about
menoscabar /menoska'βar/ *vt* to lessen, diminish, decrease; deteriorate, damage; disgrace, discredit
menoscabo /menos'kaβo/ *m,* decrease, diminishment; harm, damage, loss
menospreciable /menospre'θiaβle; menospre'siaβle/ *a* despicable, contemptible
menospreciador /menospreθia'ðor; menospresia'ðor/ **(-ra)** *a* scornful —*n* scorner, despiser
menospreciar /menospre'θiar; menospre'siar/ *vt* to despise, scorn; underestimate, have a poor opinion of
menospreciativo /menospreθia'tiβo; menospresia'tiβo/ *a* scornful, slighting, derisive
menosprecio /menos'preθio; menos'presio/ *m,* scorn, derision; underestimation
mensaje /men'sahe/ *m,* message; official communication
mensajería /mensahe'ria/ *f,* carrier service; steamship line
mensajero /mensa'hero/ **(-ra)** *n* messenger; errand boy

menstruación /menstrua'θion; menstrua'sion/ *f,* menstruation
menstruar /menstru'ar/ *vi* to menstruate
mensual /men'sual/ *a* monthly
mensualidad /mensuali'ðað/ *f,* monthly salary, monthly payment
mensurable /mensu'raβle/ *a* measurable
mensurar /mensu'rar/ *vt* to measure
menta /'menta/ *f,* menthe, mint; peppermint
mentado /men'taðo/ *a* celebrated, distinguished, famous
mental /men'tal/ *a* mental
mentalidad /mentali'ðað/ *f,* mentality
mentalmente /mental'mente/ *adv* mentally
mentar /men'tar/ *vt irr* to mention. See **sentar**
mente /'mente/ *f,* mind; intelligence, understanding; will, intention
mentecatería /mentekate'ria/ *f,* folly, stupidity
mentecato /mente'kato/ **(-ta)** *a* foolish, silly; feeble-minded, simple —*n* fool, idiot
mentir /men'tir/ *vi irr* to lie, be untruthful; deceive, mislead; falsify; *Poet.* belie; disagree, be incompatible; —*vt* break a promise, disappoint. **m. como un bellaco,** to lie like a trooper See **sentir**
mentira /men'tira/ *f,* lie, falsehood, error (in writing); *Inf.* white spot (on a fingernail); cracking (of fingerjoints). **m. oficiosa,** white lie. **Parece m.,** It seems incredible
mentiroso /menti'roso/ *a* lying, false; full of errors (literary works); deceptive
mentís /men'tis/ *m,* giving the lie (literally, you lie); proof, demonstration (of error)
mentol /'mentol/ *m,* menthol
mentón /men'ton/ *m,* chin
mentonera /mento'nera/ *f,* chin rest
menú /me'nu/ *m,* menu
menudamente /menuða'mente/ *adv* minutely; in detail, circumstantially
menudear /menuðe'ar/ *vt* to do frequently; do repeatedly; —*vi* happen frequently; describe in detail; *Com.* sell by retail
menudencia /menu'ðenθia; menu'ðensia/ *f,* minuteness, smallness; exactness, care, accuracy; trifle, worthless object; small matter; *pl* offal; pork sausages
menudeo /menu'ðeo/ *m,* repetition; description in detail; *Com.* retail. **al m.,** at retail
menudillos /menu'ðiʎos; menu'ðiyos/ *m pl,* giblets; offal
menudo /menu'ðo/ *a* minute, tiny; despicable; thin; small; vulgar; meticulous, exact; small (money). *m,* small coal; *m pl,* offal, entrails; small change (money). **a m.,** often, frequently. **por m.,** in detail, carefully; *Com.* in small lots
meñique /me'ɲike/ *a Inf.* very small. *m,* little finger (in full, **dedo m.**)
meollo /me'oʎo; me'oyo/ *m,* brain; *Anat.* marrow; *Fig.* essence, core, substance; understanding; *Inf.* **no tener m.** (**una cosa**)**,** to be worthless, unsubstantial (things)
mequetrefe /meke'trefe/ *m, Inf.* coxcomb, whippersnapper
meramente /mera'mente/ *adv* solely, simply, merely
mercachifle /merkat'ʃifle/ *m,* peddler; small merchant
mercadear /merkaðe'ar/ *vi* to trade, traffic
mercadeo /merka'ðeo/ *m,* marketing (study of markets)
mercader /merka'ðer/ *m,* dealer, merchant, trader. **m. de grueso,** wholesaler
mercadería /merkaðe'ria/ *f,* See **mercancía**
mercado /mer'kaðo/ *m,* market; marketplace
mercancía /merkan'θia; merkan'sia/ *f,* goods, merchandise; commerce, trade, traffic
mercante /mer'kante/ *a* trading; commercial. *m,* merchant, dealer, trader
mercantil /merkan'til/ *a* mercantile, commercial
mercantilismo /merkanti'lismo/ *m,* mercantilism
merced /mer'θeð; mer'seð/ *f,* salary, remuneration; favor, benefit, kindness; will, desire, pleasure; mercy, grace; courtesy title given to untitled person (e.g. *vuestra m.,* your honor. Has now become *usted* and is universally used). **m. a,** thanks to. **estar uno a m. de,** to live at someone else's expense, be dependent on
mercenario /merθe'nario; merse'nario/ **(-ia)** *n Eccl.* member of the Order of la Merced. *m, Mil.* mercenary; day laborer —*a* mercenary
mercería /merθe'ria; merse'ria/ *f,* haberdashery, mercery
mercerizar /merθeri'θar; merseri'sar/ *vt* to mercerize
mercero /mer'θero; mer'sero/ *m,* haberdasher, mercer
mercurio /mer'kurio/ *m,* mercury, quicksilver; *Astron.* Mercury
merecedor /mereθe'ðor; merese'ðor/ *a* deserving, worthy
merecer /mere'θer; mere'ser/ *vt irr* to deserve, be worthy of; attain, achieve; be worth; —*vi* deserve, be deserving. **m. bien de,** to deserve well of; have a claim on the gratitude of. See **conocer**
merecido /mere'θiðo; mere'siðo/ *m,* due reward
merecimiento /mereθi'miento; meresi'miento/ *m,* desert; merit
merendar /meren'dar/ *vi irr* to have lunch; pry into another's affairs, —*vi* have (a certain food) for lunch. *Inf.* **merendarse** (**una cosa**)**,** to obtain (a thing), have it in one's pocket. See **recomendar**
merendero /meren'dero/ *m,* lunchroom; tearoom
merengue /me'reŋgue/ *m, Cul.* meringue
meretriz /mere'triθ; mere'tris/ *f,* prostitute
meridiana /meri'ðiana/ *f,* daybed, chaise longue; siesta
meridiano /meri'ðiano/ *a* meridian. *m,* meridian. **a la meridiana,** at noon
meridional /meriðio'nal/ *a* meridional, southern
merienda /me'rienda/ *f,* tea, snack; lunch; *Inf.* hunchback. *Inf.* **juntar meriendas,** to join forces, combine interests
merino /me'rino/ *a* merino. *m,* merino wool; shepherd of merino sheep
meritísimo /meri'tisimo/ *a superl* most worthy, most deserving
mérito /'merito/ *m,* merit; desert; worth, excellence. **de m.,** excellent, notable. **hacer m. de,** to mention
meritorio /meri'torio/ *a* meritorious. *m,* unpaid worker, learner
merluza /mer'luθa; mer'lusa/ *f,* hake; *Inf.* drinking bout. *Inf.* **pescar una m.,** to get drunk
merma /'merma/ *f,* decrease, drop; loss, waste, reduction; leakage
mermar /mer'mar/ *vi* to diminish, waste away, decrease; evaporate; leak; —*vt* filch, pilfer; reduce, decrease
mermelada /merme'laða/ *f,* conserve, preserve; jam; marmalade
mero /'mero/ *a* mere; simple; plain
merodeador /meroðea'ðor/ *a* marauding. *m,* marauder, raider
merodear /meroðe'ar/ *vi* to maraud, raid
merodeo /mero'ðeo/ *m,* raiding, marauding
mes /'mes/ *m,* month; menses, menstruation
mesa /'mesa/ *f,* table; board, directorate; meseta, tableland; staircase landing; flat (of a sword, etc.); game of billiards. **m. de batalla,** post office sorting table. **m. de caballete,** trestle table. **m. de noche,** bedside table. **m. de tijeras,** folding table. **m. giratoria,** turntable. **alzar** (*or* **levantar**) **la m.,** to clear the table. **cubrir** (*or* **poner**) **la m.,** to set the table
mesada /me'saða/ *f,* monthly wages, monthly payment
mesadura /mesa'ðura/ *f,* tearing of the hair or beard
mesarse /me'sarse/ *vr* to tear one's hair or beard
mesenterio /mesen'terio/ *m,* mesentery
meseta /me'seta/ *f,* staircase landing; plateau, tableland
mesiánico /me'sianiko/ *a* Messianic
Mesías /me'sias/ *m,* Messiah
mesilla /me'siʎa; me'siya/ *f,* small table; laughing admonition; landing (of a stair)
mesmerismo /mesme'rismo/ *m,* mesmerism
mesnada /mes'naða/ *f,* association, company, society

mesocracia /meso'kraθia; meso'krasia/ *f*, mesocracy; middle class, bourgeoisie
mesón /me'son/ *m*, inn, tavern
mesonero /meso'nero/ **(-ra)** *n* innkeeper
mesta /'mesta/ *f*, ancient order of sheep farmers; *pl* confluence, meeting (of rivers)
mester /'mester/ *m*, craft, occupation. **m. de clerecía,** learned poetic meter of the Spanish Middle Ages. **m. de juglaría,** popular poetry and troubadour songs
mestizo /mes'tiθo; mes'tiso/ *a* half-breed; hybrid; cross-breed
mesura /me'sura/ *f*, sedateness; dignity; courtesy; moderation
mesurado /mesu'raðo/ *a* sedate; dignified; moderate, restrained, temperate
meta /'meta/ *f*, goalpost *Fig.* aim, end; goal; goalkeeper
metabolismo /metaβo'lismo/ *m*, metabolism
metafísica /meta'fisika/ *f*, metaphysics
metafísico /meta'fisiko/ *a* metaphysical. *m*, metaphysician
metáfora /me'tafora/ *f*, metaphor
metafórico /meta'foriko/ *a* metaphorical
metal /me'tal/ *m*, metal; brass; timbre of the voice; state, condition; quality, substance; *Herald.* gold or silver; *Mus.* brass (instruments)
metalario /meta'lario/ *m*, metalworker
metálico /me'taliko/ *a* metallic. *m*, metalworker; coin, specie; bullion
metalistería /metaliste'ria/ *f*, metalwork
metalizar /metali'θar; metali'sar/ *vt* to metallize, make metallic; **—***vr* become metallized; grow greedy for money
metalurgia /metalur'hia/ *f*, metallurgy
metalúrgico /meta'lurhiko/ *a* metallurgical. *m*, metallurgist
metamorfosis /metamor'fosis/ *f*, metamorphosis
metano /me'tano/ *m*, methane
metatarso /meta'tarso/ *m*, metatarsus
metátesis /me'tatesis/ *f*, metathesis
metedor /mete'ðor/ **(-ra)** *n* placer, inserter; smuggler, contrabandist
metempsicosis /metempsi'kosis/ *f*, metempsychosis
metemuertos /mete'muertos/ *Inf.* meddler, Nosy Parker
meteórico /mete'oriko/ *a* meteoric
meteorito /meteo'rito/ *m*, meteorite
meteoro /mete'oro/ *m*, meteor
meteorología /meteorolo'hia/ *f*, meteorology
meteorológico /meteoro'lohiko/ *a* meteorological
meteorologista /meteorolo'hista/ *mf* meteorologist; weather forecaster
meter /me'ter/ *vt* to place; put; introduce, insert; stake (gambling); smuggle; cause, occasion; place close together; persuade to take part in; *Sew.* take in fullness; deceive, humbug; cram in, pack tightly; *Naut.* take in sail; **—***vr* interfere, butt in; meddle (with); take up, follow (occupations); be overfamiliar; disembogue, empty itself (rivers, etc.); attack with the sword; (*with prep a*) follow (occupations); become, turn (e.g. *meterse a predicar,* to turn preacher); (*with con*) pick a quarrel with. **meterse en precisiones,** to go into details. *Inf.* **meterse en todo,** to be very meddlesome
metesillas y sacamuertos /mete'siʎas i saka'muertos; mete'siyas i saka'muertos/ *m*, scene shifter, stagehand
meticulosidad /metikulosi'ðað/ *f*, meticulosity; timorousness
meticuloso /metiku'loso/ *a* meticulous, fussy; timid, nervous
metido /me'tiðo/ *a* tight; crowded; crabbed (of handwriting). *m*, *Sew.* material for letting out (seams). **m. en años,** quite old (person)
metílico /me'tiliko/ *a* methylic
metimiento /meti'miento/ *m*, insertion, introduction; influence, sway
metódico /me'toðiko/ *a* methodical
metodismo /meto'ðismo/ *m*, Methodism
metodista /meto'ðista/ *a* methodistic. *mf* Methodist
método /'metoðo/ *m*, method
metodología /metoðolo'hia/ *f*, methodology
metralla /me'traʎa; me'traya/ *f*, *Mil.* grapeshot, shrapnel
métrica /'metrika/ *f*, metrics
métrico /'metriko/ *a* metric; metrical
metro /'metro/ *m*, (verse) meter; meter (measurement); subway, underground railway
metrónomo /me'tronomo/ *m*, metronome
metrópoli /me'tropoli/ *f*, metropolis, capital; see of a metropolitan bishop; mother country
metropolitano /metropoli'tano/ *a* metropolitan. *m*, metropolitan bishop
México /'mehiko/ Mexico
mezcla /'meθkla; 'meskla/ *f*, mixture; blend, combination; mixed cloth, tweed; mortar
mezclar /meθ'klar; mes'klar/ *vt* to mix, blend, combine; **—***vr* mix, mingle; take part; interfere, meddle; intermarry
mezcolanza /meθko'lanθa; mesko'lansa/ *f*, *Inf.* hodgepodge
mezquindad /meθkin'dað; meskin'dað/ *f*, poverty; indigence; miserliness; paltriness; meanness, poorness
mezquino /meθ'kino; mes'kino/ *a* needy, impoverished; miserly, stingy; small, diminutive; unhappy; mean, paltry
mezquita /meθ'kita; mes'kita/ *f*, mosque
mi /'mi/ *poss pron* my. *m*, *Mus.* mi, E
mí /'mi/ *pers pron acc gen dat 1st pers sing* me. Used only after prepositions (e.g. *Lo hicieron por mí,* They did it for me)
miaja /'miaha/ *f*, See **migaja**
miasma /'miasma/ *m*, miasma
miasmático /mias'matiko/ *a* miasmatic, malarious
miau /'miau/ *m*, meow
mica /'mika/ *f*, *Mineral.* mica; coquette, flirt
micción /mik'θion; mik'sion/ *f*, micturition
micho /'mitʃo/ **(-cha)** *n Inf.* puss, pussycat
micología /mikolo'hia/ *f*, mycology
micra /'mikra/ *f*, micron, thousandth part of a millimeter
microbiano /mikro'βiano/ *a* microbial, microbic
microbio /mi'kroβio/ *m*, microbe
microbiología /mikroβiolo'hia/ *f*, microbiology
microbrigada /mikroβri'gaða/ *f*, team of volunteer workers (Castroist Cuba)
microcéfalo /mikro'θefalo; mikro'sefalo/ *a* microcephalous
microcosmo /mikro'kosmo/ *m*, microcosm
micrófono /mi'krofono/ *m*, microphone
microonda /mikro'onda/ *f*, microwave
microscópico /mikros'kopiko/ *a* microscopic
microscopio /mikros'kopio/ *m*, microscope
miedo /'mieðo/ *m*, fear, apprehension, terror. **m. al público,** stagefright. **tener m.,** to be afraid
miedoso /mie'ðoso/ *a Inf.* fearful, nervous
miel /miel/ *f*, honey. **m. de caña,** sugarcane syrup. *Inf.* **quedarse a media m.,** to see one's pleasure snatched away. *Inf.* **ser de mieles,** to be most pleasant or agreeable
mielitis /mie'litis/ *f*, myelitis
miembro /mi'embro/ *m*, *Anat.* limb; penis; member, associate; part, portion, section; *Math.* member
miente /'miente/ *f*, thought, imagination, mind. **parar** *or* **poner mientes en,** to consider, think about. **venírsele a las mientes,** to occur to one's mind
mientras /'mientras/ *adv* while. **m. más...,** the more.... **m. que,** while (e.g. *m. que esperaba en el jardín,* while he was waiting in the garden). **m. tanto,** in the meanwhile
miércoles /'mierkoles/ *m*, Wednesday. **m. de ceniza,** Ash Wednesday
mierda /'mierða/ *f*, (*vulgar*) shit; *Inf.* filth
mies /'mies/ *f*, cereal plant, grain; harvest time; *pl* grain fields
miga /'miga/ *f*, breadcrumb; crumb; *Inf.* essence, core; substance; bit, scrap; *pl* fried breadcrumbs. *Inf.* **hacer buenas** (*or* **malas**) **migas,** to get on well (*or* badly) together
migaja /mi'gaha/ *f*, breadcrumb; bit, scrap; trifle,

mere nothing; *pl* crumbs (from the table); remains, remnants

migajón /miga'hon/ *m,* crumb (of a loaf): *Fig. Inf.* essence, substance, core

migración /migra'θion; migra'sion/ *f,* migration; emigration

migraña /mi'graɲa/ *f,* migraine

migratorio /migra'torio/ *a* migratory

mijo /'miho/ *m,* millet; maize

mil /mil/ *a* thousand; thousandth; many, large number. *m,* thousand; thousandth. *Inf.* **Son las m. y quinientas,** It's extremely late (of the hour)

miladi /mi'laði/ *f,* my lady

milagrero /mila'grero/ *a Inf.* miraculous

milagro /mi'lagro/ *m,* miracle; marvel, wonder. **¡M.!** Amazing! Just fancy!

milagroso /mila'groso/ *a* miraculous; marvelous, wonderful

milanés /mila'nes/ **(-esa)** *a* and *n* Milanese

milano /mi'lano/ *m, Ornith.* kite

mildeu /'mildeu/ *m,* mildew

milenario /mile'nario/ *a* millenary; millennial. *m,* millenary; millennium

milésimo /mi'lesimo/ *a* thousandth

milicia /mi'liθia; mi'lisia/ *f,* militia; military; art of war; military profession

miliciano /mili'θiano; mili'siano/ *a* military. *m,* militiaman

miligramo /mili'gramo/ *m,* milligram

mililitro /mili'litro/ *m,* milliliter

milímetro /mi'limetro/ *m,* millimeter

militante /mili'tante/ *a* militant

militar /mili'tar/ *a* military. *m,* soldier —*vi* to fight in the army; struggle (for a cause); *Fig.* militate (e.g. *Las circunstancias militan en favor de* (*or contra*) **sus ideas,** Circumstances militate against his ideas)

militarismo /milita'rismo/ *m,* militarism

militarista /milita'rista/ *a* militaristic. *mf* militarist

militarizar /militari'θar; militari'sar/ *vt* to militarize; make war-like

milla /'miʎa; 'miya/ *f,* mile

millar /mi'ʎar; mi'yar/ *m,* thousand; vast number (gen. *pl*)

millón /mi'ʎon; mi'yon/ *m,* million

millonario /miʎo'nario; miyo'nario/ **(-ia)** *a* and *n* millionaire

millonésimo /miʎo'nesimo; miyo'nesimo/ *a* millionth

milmillonésimo /milmiʎo'nesimo; milmiyo'nesimo/ *a* billionth

milord /mi'lorð/ *m,* my lord *pl* **milores,** my lords

mimar /mi'mar/ *vt* to spoil, overindulge; caress, fondle

mimbre /'mimbre/ *mf* osier; willow tree. *m,* wicker

mimbrear /mimbre'ar/ *vi* to sway, bend

mimbrera /mim'brera/ *f,* osier; osier bed; willow

mímica /'mimika/ *f,* mimicry; mime

mímico /'mimiko/ *a* mimic

mimo /'mimo/ *m,* mimic, buffoon; mime; caress, expression of affection, tenderness; overindulgence

mimoso /mi'moso/ *a* affectionate, demonstrative

mina /'mina/ *f,* mine; excavation, mining; underground passage; lead (in a pencil); (*Mil. Nav.*) mine; *Fig.* gold mine. *Mil.* **m. terrestre,** landmine

minador /mina'ðor/ *m,* excavator; *Nav.* minelayer; *Mil.* sapper

minar /mi'nar/ *vt* to excavate, mine; *Fig.* undermine; (*Mil. Nav.*) mine; work hard for

minarete /mina'rete/ *m,* minaret

mineraje /mine'rahe/ *m,* exploitation of a mine, mining; mineral products

mineral /mine'ral/ *a* and *m,* mineral

mineralogía /mineralo'hia/ *f,* mineralogy

mineralógico /minera'lohiko/ *a* mineralogical

mineralogista /mineralo'hista/ *mf* mineralogist

minería /mine'ria/ *f,* mining, mineworking; mineworkers

minero /mi'nero/ *a* mining. *m,* miner, mineworker; source, origin

miniar /mini'ar/ *vt Art.* to illuminate

miniatura /minia'tura/ *f,* miniature

miniaturista /miniatu'rista/ *mf* miniaturist

mínima /'minima/ *f, Mus.* minim; very small thing or portion

mínimo /'minimo/ *a superl* **pequeño** smallest; minimum; meticulous, precise. *m,* minimum; (meteorological) trough

ministerial /ministe'rial/ *a* ministerial

ministerio /minis'terio/ *m,* office, post; *Polit.* cabinet; ministry; government office; government department.

ministrar /minis'trar/ *vt* and *vi* to fill; administer (an office); —*vt* minister to; give, provide

ministro /mi'nistro/ *m,* instrument, agency; minister of state, cabinet minister; clergyman, minister; minister plenipotentiary; policeman. **m. de estado,** secretary of state. **m. de gobernación,** secretary of the interior. **m. de hacienda,** treasurer. **m. de relaciones extranjeras,** foreign secretary. **primer m.** prime minister

minoración /minora'θion; minora'sion/ *f,* reduction, decrease

minorar /mino'rar/ *vt* to diminish, decrease

minoría /mino'ria/ *f,* minority, smaller number; minority (of age)

minoridad /minori'ðað/ *f,* minority (of age)

minucia /minu'θia; minu'sia/ *f,* smallness; morsel, mite; *pl* details, trifles, minutiae

minuciosidad /minuθiosi'ðað; minusiosi'ðað/ *f,* meticulousness, minuteness, precision

minucioso /minu'θioso; minu'sioso/ *a* meticulous, precise, minute

minué /mi'nue/ *m,* minuet

minúsculo /mi'nuskulo/ *a* minute, very small

minuta /mi'nuta/ *f,* memorandum, minute; note; list, catalog

minutario /minu'tario/ *m,* minute book

minutero /minu'tero/ *m,* minute hand (of a clock)

minuto /mi'nuto/ *a* minute, very small. *m,* minute

mío /'mio/ *m.* **mía,** *f,* (*m pl.* **míos,** *f pl.* **mías**) *poss pron* mine (e.g. *Las flores son mías,* The flowers are mine). **Mi** is used before nouns, *not* **mío.** Also used with article (e.g. *Este sombrero no es el mío,* This hat is not mine (my one)). **de mío,** by myself, without help. *Inf.* **¡Esta es la mía!** This is my chance!

miope /mi'ope/ *a* myopic. *mf* myopic person

miopía /mio'pia/ *f,* shortsightedness

miosota /mio'sota/ *f,* myosotis, forget-me-not

mira /'mira/ *f,* sight (optical instruments, guns); intention, design; *Mil.* watchtower; care, precaution. **andar, estar** *or* **quedar a la m.,** to be vigilant, be on the lookout

mirada /mi'raða/ *f,* look; gaze. **lanzar miradas de carnero degollado** (**a**), to cast sheep's eyes at

miradero /mira'ðero/ *m,* object of attention, cynosure; observation post, lookout

mirador /mira'ðor/ **(-ra)** *n* spectator. *m, Archit.* oriel; enclosed balcony; observatory

miramiento /mira'miento/ *m,* observation, gazing; scruple, consideration; precaution, care; thoughtfulness

mirar /mi'rar/ *vt* to look at, gaze at; observe, behold; watch; consider, look after; value, appreciate; concern; believe, think; (*with prep a*) overlook, look on to; face; (*with por*) care for, protect; look after, consider. **m. contra el gobierno,** *Inf.* to be squint-eyed. **m. de hito en hito,** to look over, stare at. **mirarse en** (**una cosa**), to consider (a matter) carefully

miríada /mi'riaða/ *f,* myriad, huge number

mirilla /mi'riʎa; mi'riya/ *f,* peephole

miriñaque /miri'ɲake/ *m,* trinket, ornament; crinoline

mirlarse /mir'larse/ *vr Inf.* to give oneself airs

mirlo /'mirlo/ *m,* blackbird; *Inf.* pompous air

mirón /mi'ron/ *a* inquisitive, curious

mirra /'mirra/ *f,* myrrh

mirto /'mirto/ *m,* myrtle

misa /'misa/ *f,* (*Eccl. Mus.*) mass. **m. de difuntos,** requiem mass. **m. del gallo,** midnight mass. **m. mayor,** high mass. **m. rezada,** low mass. **como en m.,** in profound silence. **oír m.,** to attend mass

misal /mi'sal/ *m,* missal

misantropía /misantro'pia/ *f,* misanthropy

misantrópico /misan'tropiko/ *a* misanthropic

misántropo /mi'santropo/ *m*, misanthrope

miscelánea /misθe'lanea; misse'lanea/ *f*, medley, assortment, miscellany

misceláneo /misθe'laneo; misse'laneo/ *a* assorted, miscellaneous, mixed

miscible /mis'θiβle; mis'siβle/ *a* mixable

miserable /mise'raβle/ *a* miserable, unhappy; timid, pusillanimous; miserly, mean; despicable

miseria /mi'seria/ *f*, misery; poverty, destitution; avarice, miserliness; *Inf.* poor thing, trifle

misericordia /miseri'korðia/ *f*, mercy, compassion

misericordioso /miserikor'ðioso/ *a* merciful, compassionate

mísero /'misero/ *a Inf.* fond of churchgoing

misérrimo /mi'serrimo/ *a superl* most miserable

misión /mi'sion/ *f*, mission; vocation; commission, duty, errand

misionar /misio'nar/ *vi* to missionize, act as a missionary; *Eccl.* conduct a mission

misionero /misio'nero/ *m*, missioner; missionary

Misisipi, el /misi'sipi, el/ the Mississippi

misiva /mi'siβa/ *f*, missive

mismo /'mismo/ *a* same; similar; self (e.g. *ellos mismos*, they themselves); very, same (e.g. *Ahora m. voy*, I'm going this very minute). **Me da lo m.,** It makes no difference to me. **por lo m.,** for that selfsame reason

misógamo /mi'sogamo/ **(-ma)** *n* misogamist

misógino /mi'sohino/ *m*, misogynist

misterio /mis'terio/ *m*, mystery

misterioso /miste'rioso/ *a* mysterious

mística /'mistika/ *f*, **misticismo** *m*, mysticism

místico /'mistiko/ *a* mystic

mistificación /mistifika'θion; mistifika'sion/ *f*, mystification; mystery; deception

mistificar /mistifi'kar/ *vt* to mystify; deceive

Misuri, el /mi'suri, el/ the Missouri

mitad /mi'tað/ *f*, half; middle, center. *Fig. Inf.* **cara m.,** better half. *Inf.* **mentir por la m. de la barba,** to lie barefacedly

mítico /'mitiko/ *a* mythical

mitigación /mitiga'θion; mitiga'sion/ *f*, mitigation

mitigador /mitiga'ðor/ **(-ra)** *a* mitigatory —*n* mitigator

mitigar /miti'gar/ *vt* to mitigate, moderate, alleviate; appease

mitin /'mitin/ *m*, mass meeting

mito /'mito/ *m*, myth

mitología /mitolo'hia/ *f*, mythology

mitológico /mito'lohiko/ *a* mythological

mitologista, mitólogo /mitolo'hista, mi'tologo/ *m*, mythologist

mitón /mi'ton/ *m*, mitten

mitra /'mitra/ *f*, miter; bishopric; archbishopric

mitrado /mi'traðo/ *a* mitred

mixto /'miksto/ *a* mixed, blended; hybrid; composite; mongrel. *m*, mixed train (carrying freight and passengers); sulphur match

mixtura /miks'tura/ *f*, mixture, blend; compound; mixture (medicine)

¡miz, miz! /miθ, miθ; mis, mis/ puss, puss!

moabita /moa'βita/ *mf* Moabite

mobiliario /moβi'liario/ *a* movable (goods). *m*, furniture

moblaje /mo'βlahe/ *m*, household goods and furniture

mocasín /moka'sin/ *m*, moccasin

mocedad /moθe'ðað; mose'ðað/ *f*, youth, adolescence; mischief, prank. *Fig. Inf.* **correr sus mocedades,** to sow one's wild oats

mochila /mo'tʃila/ *f*, knapsack; nosebag; military rations for a march

mocho /'motʃo/ *a* blunted, topless, lopped; *Inf.* shorn, cropped. *m*, butt, butt end

mochuelo /mo'tʃuelo/ *m*, owl; *Inf.* difficult job

moción /mo'θion; mo'sion/ *f*, motion, movement; impulse, tendency; divine inspiration; motion (of a debate)

moco /'moko/ *m*, mucus; candle drips; snuff of a candle. *Inf.* **caérsele el m.,** to be very simple, be easily deceived

mocoso /mo'koso/ **(-sa)** *a* running of the nose, sniffling; unimportant, insignificant —*n* coxcomb, stripling

moda /'moða/ *f*, fashion. **estar** *or* **ser de m.,** to be fashionable, be in fashion. **la última m.,** the latest fashion

modales /mo'ðales/ *m pl*, manners, behavior

modalidad /moðali'ðað/ *f*, form, nature; *Mus.* modality

modelado /moðe'laðo/ *m*, *Art.* modeling

modelar /moðe'lar/ *vt Art.* to model; —*vr* model oneself (on), copy

modelo /mo'ðelo/ *m*, example, pattern; model. *mf Art.* life model

módem *m*, modem

moderación /moðera'θion; moðerasion/ *f*, moderation; restraint, temperance, equability

moderado /moðe'raðo/ *a* moderate; restrained, temperate

moderador /moðera'ðor/ **(-ra)** *a* moderating —*n* moderator

moderantismo /moðeran'tismo/ *m*, moderate opinion; moderate political party

moderar /moðe'rar/ *vt* to moderate; temper, restrain; —*vr* regain one's self-control; behave with moderation

modernidad /moðerni'ðað/ *f*, modernity

modernismo /moðer'nismo/ *m*, modernism

modernista /moðer'nista/ *a* modernistic; modern. *mf* modernist

modernización /moðerniθa'θion; moðernisa'sion/ *f*, modernization

modernizar /moðerni'θar; moðerni'sar/ *vt* to modernize

moderno /mo'ðerno/ *a* modern. *m*, modern. **a la moderna,** in modern fashion

modestia /mo'ðestia/ *f*, modesty

modesto /mo'ðesto/ *a* modest

módico /'moðiko/ *a* moderate (of prices, etc.)

modificable /moðifi'kaβle/ *a* modifiable

modificación /moðifi'kaθion; moðifika'sion/ *f*, modification

modificador, modificante /moðifi'kaðor, moðifi'kante/ *a* modifying, moderating

modificar /moðifi'kar/ *vt* to modify; moderate

modismo /mo'ðismo/ *m*, idiom, idiomatic expression

modista /mo'ðista/ *mf* dressmaker; couturier; milliner

modo /'moðo/ *m*, mode, method, style; manner, way; moderation, restraint; civility, politeness (often *pl*); *Mus.* mode; *Gram.* mood. **m. de ser,** nature, temperament. **de m. que,** so that. **de ningún m.,** not at all, by no means. **de todos modos,** in any case

modorra /mo'ðorra/ *f*, deep sleep, stupor

modorro /mo'ðorro/ *a* drowsy, heavy

modoso /mo'ðoso/ *a* demure; well-behaved

modulación /moðula'θion; moðula'sion/ *f*, modulation

modulador /moðula'ðor/ **(-ra)** *a* modulative —*n* modulator, *m*, *Mus.* modulator

modular /moðu'lar/ *vt* and *vi* to modulate

mofa /'mofa/ *f*, mockery, ridicule, jeering

mofador /mofa'ðor/ **(-ra)** *a* jeering —*n* scoffer, mocker

mofarse /mo'farse/ *vr* (*with de*) to make fun of, jeer at

mofeta /mo'feta/ *f*, noxious gas; damp (gas); *Zool.* skunk

moflete /mo'flete/ *m*, *Inf.* plump cheek

mofletudo /mofle'tuðo/ *a* plump-cheeked

mogol /'mogol/ **(-la)** *a* and *n* Mongolian.

mogote /mo'gote/ *m*, hill; pyre, stack

mohicano /moi'kano/ *a* and *n* Mohican

mohín /mo'in/ *m*, grimace

mohína /mo'ina/ *f*, grudge, rancor; sullenness; sulkiness

mohíno /mo'ino/ *a* depressed, gloomy; sulky; black or black-nosed (of animals)

moho /'moo/ *m*, mold, fungoid growth; moldiness; moss. *Inf.* **no criar m.,** to be always on the move

mohoso /mo'oso/ *a* mossy; moldy

mojada /mo'haða/ *f,* wetting; *Inf.* stab; sop of bread
mojador /moha'ðor/ **(-ra)** *n* wetter. *m,* stamp moistener
mojar /mo'har/ *vt* to wet; moisten; *Inf.* stab, wound with a dagger; *—vi* take part in; meddle, interfere; *—vr* get wet
mojicón /mohi'kon/ *m,* kind of spongecake; *Inf.* slap in the face
mojiganga /mohi'gaŋga/ *f,* masquerade, mummer's show; farce; funny sight, figure of fun
mojigatería /mohigate'ria/ *f,* hypocrisy; sanctimoniousness; prudery
mojigato /mohi'gato/ **(-ta)** *a* hypocritical; sanctimonious; prudish *—n* hypocrite; bigot; prude
mojón /mo'hon/ *m,* boundary marker; milestone; heap. **m. kilométrico,** milestone
molar /mo'lar/ *a* molar
moldavo /mol'daβo/ **(-va)** *a* and *n* Moldavian
molde /'molde/ *m,* mold, matrix; *Fig.* model, pattern. **de m.,** printed; suitably, conveniently; perfectly. **letra de m.,** printed letters, print
moldeador /moldea'ðor/ **(-ra)** *n* molder
moldear /molde'ar/ *vt* to mold, cast
moldura /mol'dura/ *f,* molding
moldurar /moldu'rar/ *vt* to mold
molécula /mo'lekula/ *f,* molecule
molecular /moleku'lar/ *a* molecular
moler /mo'ler/ *vt irr* to grind, crush; tire, exhaust; ill-treat; pester, annoy. **m. a palos,** to beat black and blue *—Pres. Indic.* **muelo, mueles, muele, muelen.** *Pres. Subjunc.* **muela, muelas, muela, muelan**
molestia /mo'lestia/ *f,* inconvenience, trouble; annoyance; discomfort, pain; bore, nuisance. **Es una m.,** It's a nuisance
molesto /mo'lesto/ *a* inconvenient, troublesome; annoying; painful; uncomfortable; boring, tedious
moletón /mole'ton/ *m,* flannelet
molicie /mo'liθie; mo'lisie/ *f,* softness, smoothness; effeminacy, weakness
molienda /mo'lienda/ *f,* milling; grinding; mill; portion ground at one time; *Inf.* exhaustion, fatigue; *Inf.* nuisance
molificar /molifi'kar/ *vt* to mollify, appease
molimiento /moli'miento/ *m,* milling; grinding; exhaustion, fatigue
molinera /moli'nera/ *f,* (woman) miller; miller's wife
molinero /moli'nero/ *a* mill. *m,* miller
molinillo /moli'niʎo; moli'niyo/ *m,* hand mill, small grinder; mincing machine; beater. **m. de café,** coffee mill
molino /mo'lino/ *m,* mill; harum-scarum, rowdy; bore, tedious person; *Inf.* mouth. **m. de rueda de escalones,** treadmill. **m. de viento,** windmill
molleja /mo'ʎeha; mo'yeha/ *f,* gizzard
mollera /mo'ʎera; mo'yera/ *f,* crown of the head; brains, sense. *Inf.* **ser duro de m.,** to be obstinate; be stupid
molusco /mo'lusko/ *m,* mollusk
momentaneidad /momentanei'ðað/ *f,* momentariness
momentáneo /momen'taneo/ *a* momentary, brief; instantaneous, immediate
momento /mo'mento/ *m,* moment, minute; importance; *Mech.* moment. **al m.,** immediately. **a cada m.,** all the time; frequently. **por momentos,** continually; intermittently
momería /mome'ria/ *f,* mummery
momero /mo'mero/ **(-ra)** *n* mummer
momia /'momia/ *f,* mummy
momificación /momifika'θion; momifika'sion/ *f,* mummification
momificar /momifi'kar/ *vt* to mummify; *—vr* become mummified
mona /'mona/ *f,* female monkey; *Inf.* imitator; drinking bout; drunk. *Inf.* **Aunque la m. se vista de seda, m. se queda,** Breeding will tell. *Inf.* **ser la última m.,** to be of no account, be unimportant
monacal /mona'kal/ *a* monkish, monastic
monacillo /mona'θiʎo; mona'siyo/ *m, Eccl.* acolyte
monada /mo'naða/ *f,* mischievous prank; affected gesture or grimace; small, pretty thing; childish cleverness; flattery; rash act; *pl* monkey shines
monaguillo /mona'giʎo; mona'giyo/ *m, Eccl.* acolyte
monarca /mo'narka/ *mf* monarch
monarquía /monar'kia/ *f,* monarchy
monárquico /mo'narkiko/ **(-ca)** *a* monarchic *—n* monarchist
monarquismo /monar'kismo/ *m,* monarchism
monasterio /mona'sterio/ *m,* monastery; convent
monástico /mo'nastiko/ *a* monastic
monda /'monda/ *f,* skinning, peeling; *Agr.* pruning; cleansing
mondadientes /monda'ðientes/ *m,* toothpick
mondar /mon'dar/ *vt* to skin, peel; *Agr.* prune; cut the hair; cleanse; free of rubbish; *Inf.* deprive of possessions; *—vr* pick one's teeth
mondo /'mondo/ *a* simple, plain; bare; unadulterated, pure
moneda /mo'neða/ *f,* coin, piece of money; coinage; *Inf.* wealth; cash. **m. corriente,** currency. **m. metálica,** specie. **pagar en buena m.,** to give entire satisfaction. **pagar en la misma m.,** to pay back in the same coin, return like for like. *Inf.* **ser m. corriente,** to be usual or very frequent
monedero /mone'ðero/ *m,* coiner, minter; handbag; purse
monería /mone'ria/ *f,* mischievous trick; unimportant trifle; pretty thing; childish cleverness, pretty ways
monetario /mone'tario/ *a* monetary. *m,* collection of coins and medals
monetización /monetiθa'θion; monetisa'sion/ *f,* monetization
monigote /moni'gote/ *m, Inf.* boor; grotesque, puppet
monitor /moni'tor/ *m,* monitor
monitorio /moni'torio/ *a* monitory
monja /'monha/ *f,* nun; *pl* sparks
monje /'monhe/ *m,* monk
monjil /mon'hil/ *a* nun-like. *m,* nun's habit
mono /'mono/ *a Inf.* pretty, attractive; amusing, funny. *m,* monkey; person given to grimacing; rash youth; coverall. *Inf.* **estar de monos,** to be on bad terms
monocromo /mono'kromo/ *a* monochrome; monochromatic
monóculo /mo'nokulo/ *m,* monocle
monogamia /mono'gamia/ *f,* monogamy
monógamo /mo'nogamo/ *a* monogamous *—n* monogamist
monografía /monogra'fia/ *f,* monograph
monograma /mono'grama/ *m,* monogram
monolítico /mono'litiko/ *a* monolithic
monolito /mono'lito/ *m,* monolith
monólogo /mo'nologo/ *m,* monologue
monomanía /monoma'nia/ *f,* monomania
monomaníaco /monoma'niako/ **(-ca)** *n* monomaniac
monopatín /monopa'tin/ *m,* scooter
monoplano /mono'plano/ *m,* monoplane
monopolio /mono'polio/ *m,* monopoly
monopolista /monopo'lista/ *mf* monopolist
monopolizar /monopoli'θar; monopoli'sar/ *vt* to monopolize
monosilábico /monosi'laβiko/ *a* monosyllabic
monosílabo /mono'silaβo/ *m,* monosyllable
monoteísmo /monote'ismo/ *m,* monotheism
monoteísta /monote'ista/ *mf* monotheist
monotipia /mono'tipia/ *f,* monotype
monotonía /monoto'nia/ *f,* monotony; monotone
monótono /mo'notono/ *a* monotonous
monroísmo /monro'ismo/ *m,* Monroe doctrine
monseñor /monse'ɲor/ *m,* monsignor
monserga /mon'serga/ *f, Inf.* rigmarole; jargon
monstruo /'monstruo/ *m,* monster; freak, monstrosity; cruel person; hideous person or thing
monstruosidad /monstruosi'ðað/ *f,* monstrousness, monstrosity
monstruoso /mon'struoso/ *a* monstrous, abnormal; enormous; extraordinary; atrocious, outrageous
monta /'monta/ *f,* mounting a horse; total; *Mil.* mounting signal; breeding station (horses)

montacargas /monta'kargas/ *m,* hoist, lift; freight elevator
montador /monta'ðor/ *m,* mounter; mounting block
montadura /monta'ðura/ *f,* mounting; mount, setting (of jewels)
montaje /mon'tahe/ *m,* assembling, setting up (machines); presentation (of a book); (cinema) montage
montañés /monta'ɲes/ **(-esa)** *a* mountain —*n* mountain dweller; native of Santander
montano /mon'tano/ *a* hilly, mountainous
montante /mon'tante/ *m,* upright, stanchion; tent pole
montaña /mon'taɲa/ *f,* mountain; mountainous country. **montañas rusas,** roller coaster (at an amusement park)
montañés /mon'taɲes/ **(-esa)** *a* mountain —*n* mountain dweller; native of Santander
montañoso /monta'ɲoso/ *a* mountainous; hilly
montar /mon'tar/ *vi* to ascend, climb up, get on top; mount (a horse); ride (a horse); be important; —*vt* get on top of; ride (a horse); total, amount to; set up (apparatus, machinery); *Naut.* sail around, double; set, mount (gems); cock (firearms); fine for trespassing; wind (a clock); command (a ship); *Naut.* carry, be fitted with (guns, etc.). **m. a horcajadas en,** to mount astride; straddle. **montarse en cólera,** to fly into a rage
montaraz /monta'raθ; monta'ras/ *a* mountain-dwelling; wild, savage; rude, uncivilized, uncouth. *m,* gamekeeper, forester
montazgo /mon'taθgo; mon'tasgo/ *m,* toll payable for cattle moving from one province to another
monte /'monte/ *m,* mount, hill; woodland; obstacle, impediment. **m. de piedad,** pawnshop. **m. pío,** savings fund
montenegrino /montene'grino/ **(-na)** *a* and *n* Montenegrin
montera /mon'tera/ *f,* cap; glass roof
montería /monte'ria/ *f,* hunt, chase; art of hunting
montero /mon'tero/ **(-ra)** *n* hunter, huntsman
montés /mon'tes/ *a* wild, savage, untamed
montevideano /monteβiðe'ano/ **(-na)** *a* and *n* Montevidean
montículo /mon'tikulo/ *m,* mound, hill
montón /mon'ton/ *m,* heap, pile; *Inf.* abundance, lot. *Inf.* **a, de** *or* **en m.,** all jumbled up together. **a montones,** in abundance
montuoso /mon'tuoso/ *a* mountainous
montura /mon'tura/ *f,* riding animal, mount; horse trappings; setting up, mounting (artillery, etc.)
monumental /monumen'tal/ *a* monumental
monumento /monu'mento/ *m,* monument; document, record; tomb
monzón /mon'θon; mon'son/ *mf,* monsoon
moña /'moɲa/ *f,* doll; dressmaker's model; bow for the hair; bullfighter's black bow; baby's bonnet; *Inf.* drinking bout
moño /'moɲo/ *m,* bun, chignon; topknot (birds); bunch of ribbons; *pl* tawdry trimmings
moqueta /mo'keta/ *f,* moquette
moquete /mo'kete/ *m,* slap in the face
moquillo /mo'kiʎo; mo'kiyo/ *m,* distemper (of animals)
mora /'mora/ *f,* blackberry; mulberry; bramble; Moorish girl, Moorish woman
morada /mo'raða/ *f,* dwelling, abode; sojourn, stay
morado /mo'raðo/ *a* purple
morador /mora'ðor/ **(-ra)** *n* dweller; sojourner
moral /mo'ral/ *a* moral, ethical. *f,* morality, ethics; morale. *m,* blackberry bush
moraleja /mora'leha/ *f,* moral, lesson
moralidad /morali'ðað/ *f,* morality
moralista /mora'lista/ *mf* moralist
moralización /moraliθa'θion; moralisa'sion/ *f,* moralization
moralizador /moraliθa'ðor; moralisa'ðor/ **(-ra)** *a* moralizing —*n* moralizer
moralizar /morali'θar; morali'sar/ *vt* to reform, correct; —*vi* moralize
moratoria /mora'toria/ *f,* moratorium
moravo /mo'raβo/ **(-va)** *a* and *n* Moravian
morbidez /mor'βiðeθ; mor'βiðes/ *f, Art.* morbidezza; softness
mórbido /'morβiðo/ *a* morbid, diseased; *Art.* delicate (of flesh tones); soft
morbo /'morβo/ *m,* illness. **m. gálico,** syphilis
morboso /mor'βoso/ *a* ill; morbid, unhealthy
morcilla /mor'θiʎa; mor'siya/ *f, Cul.* black pudding; (*Inf. Theat.*) gag
morcillero /morθi'ʎero; morsi'yero/ **(-ra)** *n* seller of black puddings; (*Inf. Theat.*) actor who gags
mordacidad /morðaθi'ðað; morðasi'ðað/ *f,* corrosiveness; mordacity, sarcasm; *Cul.* piquancy
mordaz /mor'ðaθ; mor'ðas/ *a* corrosive; sarcastic, caustic, mordant; *Cul.* piquant
mordaza /mor'ðaθa; mor'ðasa/ *f,* gag
mordedor /morðe'ðor/ *a* biting; scandalmongering
mordedura /morðe'ðura/ *f,* bite, biting
morder /mor'ðer/ *vt irr* to bite; nibble, nip; seize, grasp; corrode, eat away; slander; etch —*Pres. Indic.* **muerdo, muerdes, muerde, muerden.** *Pres. Subjunc.* **muerda, muerdas, muerda, muerdan**
mordiente /mor'ðiente/ *m,* fixative (for dyeing); mordant —*a* mordant (of acid)
mordiscar /morðis'kar/ *vt* to nibble, bite gently; bite
mordisco /mor'ðisko/ *m,* nibble; nibbling; bite; biting; piece bitten off
morena /mo'rena/ *f,* moraine
moreno /mo'reno/ **(-na)** *a* dark brown; swarthy complexioned; dark (of people) —*n Inf.* negro, mulatto
morera /mo'rera/ *f,* mulberry bush
morería /more'ria/ *f,* Moorish quarter
morfina /mor'fina/ *f,* morphine
morfinómano /morfi'nomano/ **(-na)** *n* morphine addict
morfología /morfolo'hia/ *f,* morphology
morfológico /morfo'lohiko/ *a* morphological
morganático /morga'natiko/ *a* morganatic
moribundo /mori'βundo/ **(-da)** *a* moribund, dying —*n* dying person
morillo /mo'riʎo; mo'riyo/ *m,* andiron, fire-dog
morir /mo'rir/ *vi irr* to die; fade, wither; decline, decay; disappear; yearn (for); long (to); go out (lights, fire); —*vr* die; go numb (limbs); (*with por*) adore, be mad about. *Inf.* **m. vestido,** to die a violent death. **¡Muera!** Down with! *Past Part.* **muerto.** For other tenses see **dormir**
morisco /mo'risko/ **(-ca)** *a* Moorish —*n* Morisco, Moor converted to Christianity
morisma /mo'risma/ *f,* Mohammedanism; multitude of Moors
mormón /mor'mon/ **(-ona)** *n* Mormon
mormónico /mor'moniko/ *a* Mormon
mormonismo /mormo'nismo/ *m,* Mormonism
moro /'moro/ **(-ra)** *a* Moorish —*n* Moor; Mohammedan. *Inf.* **haber moros y cristianos,** to be the deuce of a row. *Inf.* **Hay moros en la costa,** The coast is not clear; There's trouble in the offing
morosidad /morosi'ðað/ *f,* slowness, delay; sluggishness, sloth
moroso /mo'roso/ *a* slow, dilatory; sluggish, lazy
morra /'morra/ *f,* crown of the head
morral /mo'rral/ *m,* nose-bag; knapsack; game-bag; *Inf.* lout
morriña /mo'rriɲa/ *f,* cattle plague, murrain; *Inf.* depression, blues; homesickness
morrión /mo'rrion/ *m,* morion (helmet)
morro /'morro/ *m,* anything round; hummock, hillock; round pebble; headland, cliff
morsa /'morsa/ *f,* walrus
mortaja /mor'taha/ *f,* shroud, winding sheet
mortal /mor'tal/ *a* mortal; fatal, deadly; on the point of death; great, tremendous; certain, sure. *mf* mortal
mortalidad /mortali'ðað/ *f,* humanity, human race; mortality, death-rate
mortandad /mortan'dað/ *f,* mortality, number of deaths
mortecino /morte'θino; morte'sino/ *a* dead from natural causes (animals); weak; fading; dull, dead (of eyes); flickering; on the point of death or extinction
mortero /mor'tero/ *m,* mortar (for building); *Mil.* mortar; pounding mortar

mortífero /mor'tifero/ *a* deadly, mortal
mortificación /mortifika'θion; mortifika'sion/ *f, Med.* gangrene; humiliation, wounding; mortification (of the flesh)
mortificar /mortifi'kar/ *vt Med.* to mortify; humiliate, wound, hurt; mortify (the flesh); *—vr* become gangrenous
mortuorio /mor'tuorio/ *a* mortuary. *m,* funeral, obsequies
mosaico /mo'saiko/ *a* and *m,* mosaic
mosca /'moska/ *f,* fly; *Inf.* nuisance; bore, pest; cash; *pl* sparks. *Inf.* **m. muerta,** underhanded person. *Inf.* **papar moscas,** to gape, be dumbfounded. *Inf.* **soltar la m.,** to give or spend money unwillingly
moscardón /moskar'ðon/ *m,* gadfly
moscatel /moska'tel/ *a* muscatel. *m,* muscatel (grapes and wine); *Inf.* pest, tedious person
moscovita /mosko'βita/ *a* and *mf* Muscovite
Moscú /mos'ku/ Moscow
mosquear /moske'ar/ *vt* to drive off flies; reply crossly; whip; *—vr* be exasperated; brush aside obstacles
mosquero /mos'kero/ *m,* flypaper
mosquete /mos'kete/ *m,* musket
mosquetería /moskete'ria/ *f,* musketry; (*Obs. Theat.*) male members of the audience who stood at the back of the pit
mosquetero /moske'tero/ *m,* musketeer; (Spanish theater of the sixteenth and seventeenth centuries) male member of the audience who stood at the back of the pit
mosquitero /moski'tero/ *m,* mosquito net
mosquito /mos'kito/ *m,* mosquito; midge, gnat; *Inf.* tippler, drunkard
mostacera /mosta'θera; mosta'sera/ *f,* mustard pot
mostacho /mos'tatʃo/ *m,* mustache, whiskers; *Inf.* smudge on the face
mostaza /mos'taθa; mos'tasa/ *f,* mustard plant or seed; *Cul.* mustard
mostela /mos'tela/ *f,* sheaf (of corn, etc.)
mosto /'mosto/ *m,* must, unfermented wine
mostrador /mostra'ðor/ **(-ra)** *n* one who shows, exhibitor. *m,* shop counter; face of a watch
mostrar /mos'trar/ *vt irr* to show; indicate, point out; demonstrate, prove; manifest, reveal; *—vr* show oneself, be (e.g. *Se mostró bondadoso,* He showed himself to be kind) *—Pres. Indic.* **muestro, muestras, muestra, muestran.** *Pres. Subjunc.* **muestre, muestres, muestre, muestren**
mostrenco /mos'trenko/ *a Inf.* stray, vagrant, homeless; *Inf.* dull, ignorant; *Inf.* fat, heavy
mota /'mota/ *f,* fault in cloth; mote, defect, fault; mound, hill; thread of cotton, speck of dust, etc.; fleck (of the sun, etc.); spot
mote /'mote/ *m,* maxim, saying; motto, device; catchword, slogan; nickname
motear /mote'ar/ *vt* to speckle, dot, variegate, spot
motejar /mote'har/ *vt* to nickname, call names, dub
motete /mo'tete/ *m,* motet
motín /mo'tin/ *m,* mutiny; riot
motivar /moti'βar/ *vt* to motivate, cause; explain one's reasons
motivo /mo'tiβo/ *a* motive. *m,* cause, motive; *Mus.* motif. **con m. de,** on account of, because of. **de m. propio,** of one's own free will
motocicleta /motoθi'kleta; motosi'kleta/ *f,* motorcycle
motociclista /motoθi'klista; motosi'klista/ *mf* motorcyclist
motor /mo'tor/ **(-ra)** *a* motive, driving. *m,* motor, engine *—n* (person) mover, motive force. **m. de combustión interna,** internal combustion engine. **m. de retroacción,** jet engine
motorista /moto'rista/ *mf* motorist, driver
movedizo /moβe'ðiθo; moβe'ðiso/ *a* movable; insecure, unsteady; shaky; changeable, vacillating
mover /mo'βer/ *vt irr* to move; operate, drive; sway; wag; persuade, induce; excite; move (to pity, etc.); (*with prep a*) cause; *—vi* sprout (plants); *—vr* move *—Pres. Indic.* **muevo, mueves, mueve, mueven.** *Pres. Subjunc.* **mueva, muevas, mueva, muevan**
movible /mo'βiβle/ *a* movable; insecure, shaky. *m,* motive, cause, incentive
movilidad /moβili'ðað/ *f,* mobility; changeableness, inconstancy
movilización /moβiliθa'θion; moβilisa'sion/ *f,* mobilization
movilizar /moβili'θar; moβili'sar/ *vt* to mobilize
movimiento /moβi'miento/ *m,* movement; perturbation, excitement; *Mus.* movement; *Lit.* fire, spirit; *Mech.* motion, movement. *Mil.* **m. envolvente,** encircling movement
moza /'moθa; 'mosa/ *f,* maid; girl; waitress. **m. de partido,** party girl, prostitute. **buena m.,** fine, upstanding young woman
mozalbete /moθal'βete; mosal'βete/ *m,* lad, stripling, boy
mozárabe /mo'θaraβe; mo'saraβe/ *a* Mozarabic. *mf* Mozarab
mozo /'moθo; 'moso/ *a* young, unmarried. *m,* boy, youth; bachelor; waiter; porter. **m. de cordel** *or* **m. de esquina,** street porter, message boy. **m. de estación,** railroad porter. **buen m.,** fine, upstanding young man
muaré /mua're/ *m,* moiré silk
muceta /mu'θeta; mu'seta/ *f, Educ.* hood, short cape (of a graduate's gown)
muchacha /mu'tʃatʃa/ *f,* girl, lass; female servant
muchachada /mutʃa'tʃaða/ *f,* childish prank
muchachez /mutʃa'tʃeθ; mutʃa'tʃes/ *f,* boyhood; girlhood
muchachil /mutʃa'tʃil/ *a* boyish; girlish
muchacho /mu'tʃatʃo/ *m,* boy, youth; male servant
muchedumbre /mutʃe'ðumbre/ *f,* abundance, plenty; crowd, multitude; mass, mob
muchísimo /mu'tʃisimo/ *a superl* very much *—adv* very great deal, very much
mucho /'mutʃo/ *a* much; plenty of; very; long (time); *pl* many, numerous *—adv* a great deal; much; very much; yes, certainly; frequently, often; very (e.g. *Me alegro m.,* I am very glad); to a great extent; long (time). **con m.,** by far, easily. **ni con m.,** nor anything like it, very far from it. **ni m. menos,** and much less. **por m. que,** however much
mucílago /mu'θilago; mu'silago/ *m,* mucilage, gum
mucosa /mu'kosa/ *f,* mucous membrane
mucosidad /mukosi'ðað/ *f,* mucosity
mucoso /mu'koso/ *a* mucous
muda /'muða/ *f,* change, transformation; change of clothes; molting season; molt, sloughing of skin (snakes, etc.); change of voice (in boys)
mudable /mu'ðaβle/ *a* changeable, inconstant
mudanza /mu'ðanθa; muðansa/ *f,* change; furniture removal; step, figure (in dancing); changeability, inconstancy
mudar /mu'ðar/ *vt* to change; alter, transform; exchange; remove; dismiss (from employment); molt; slough the skin (snakes, etc.); change the voice (boys); *—vr* alter one's behavior; change one's clothes; change one's residence; change one's expression; *Inf.* go away, depart
mudéjar /mu'ðehar/ *m, Archit.* style containing Moorish and Christian elements. *mf* Moor who remained in Spain under Christian rule
mudez /mu'ðeθ; mu'ðes/ *f,* dumbness; silence, muteness
mudo /'muðo/ *a* dumb; silent, mute, quiet
mueblaje /mue'βlahe/ *m,* household goods and furniture
mueble /'mueβle/ *m,* piece of furniture; furnishing
mueblería /mueβle'ria/ *f,* furniture store or factory
mueblista /mue'βlista/ *mf* furniture maker; furniture dealer
mueca /'mueka/ *f,* grimace
muela /'muela/ *f,* grindstone; molar (tooth); millstone; flat-topped hill. **m. del juicio,** wisdom tooth. **dolor de muelas,** toothache
muellaje /mue'ʎahe; mue'yahe/ *m,* wharfage, dock dues
muelle /'mueʎe; 'mueye/ *a* soft, smooth; voluptuous, sensuous; luxurious. *m,* spring (of a watch, etc.); wharf, quay; freight platform (railroad). **m. real,** mainspring (of a watch). **m. del volante,** hairspring.

muérdago /'muerðago/ *m,* mistletoe
muermo /'muermo/ *m,* glanders
muerte /'muerte/ *f,* death; destruction, annihilation; end, decline. *Inf.* **una m. chiquita,** a nervous shudder. **a m.,** to the death, with no quarter. **de m.,** implacably, inexorably (of hatred); very seriously (of being ill). **dar m.** (**a),** to kill. **estar a la m.,** to be on the point of death. **a cada m. de un obispo,** once in a blue moon
muerto /'muerto/ **(-ta)** *a* dead; slaked (lime); *Mech.* neutral; faded, dull (colors); languid, indifferent. **m.** is used in familiar speech as *past part* **matar** (e.g. *Le ha muerto,* He has killed him) —*n* corpse. *Inf.* **desenterrar los muertos,** to speak ill of the dead. *Inf.* **echarle a uno el m.,** to pass the buck. *Inf.* **estar m. por,** to be dying, yearning for. **ser el m.,** to be dummy (at cards)
muesca /'mueska/ *f,* notch, mortise, groove
muestra /'muestra/ *f,* shop sign; sample, specimen; pattern, model; demeanor; watch or clock face; sign, indication; poster, placard; *Mil.* muster roll. **hacer m.,** to show
muestrario /mues'trario/ *m,* sample book, collection of samples
mufla /'mufla/ *f,* muffler (of a furnace)
mugido /mu'hiðo/ *m,* mooing or lowing (of cattle)
mugir /mu'hir/ *vi* to low or moo (cattle); bellow, shout; rage (elements)
mugre /'mugre/ *f,* grease, grime, dirt
mugriento /mu'griento/ *a* grimy, greasy
muguete /mu'gete/ *m,* lily of the valley
mujer /mu'her/ *f,* woman; wife. **m. de la vida airada** *or* **m. del partido** *or* **m. pública,** prostitute. **m. de la luna,** man in the moon. **m. de su casa,** good housewife. **tomar m.,** to take a wife
mujeriego /muhe'riego/ *a* womanly, feminine; (of men) dissolute, given to philandering. **cabalgar a mujeriegas,** to ride sidesaddle
mujeril /muhe'ril/ *a* womanly, feminine
mula /'mula/ *f,* female mule; mule (heelless slipper). *Inf.* **Se me fue la m.,** My tongue ran away with me
muladar /mula'ðar/ *m,* refuse heap, junkpile, dunghill
mular /mu'lar/ *a* mule; mulish
mulatero /mula'tero/ *m,* mule hirer; muleteer
mulato /mu'lato/ **(-ta)** *a* and *n* mulatto
muleta /mu'leta/ *f,* crutch; bullfighter's red flag; support, prop
mullir /mu'ʎir; mu'yir/ *vt irr* to make soft, shake out (wool, down, etc.); *Fig.* prepare the way; *Agr.* hoe the roots (of vines, etc.) —*Pres. Part.* **mullendo.** *Preterite* **mulló, mulleron.** *Imperf. Subjunc.* **mullese,** etc.
mulo /'mulo/ *m,* mule
multa /'multa/ *f,* fine
multar /mul'tar/ *vt* to impose a fine on
multicolor /multiko'lor/ *a* multicolored
multiforme /multi'forme/ *a* multiform
multilátero /multi'latero/ *a* multilateral
multimillonario /multimiʎo'nario; multimiyo'nario/ **(-ia)** *a* and *n* multimillionaire
multiplicación /multiplika'θion; multiplika'sion/ *f,* multiplication
multiplicador /multiplika'ðor/ **(-ra)** *n* multiplier. *m, Math.* multiplier
multiplicando /multipli'kando/ *m,* multiplicand
multiplicar /multipli'kar/ **((se)** *vt* and *vr* to multiply; reproduce
multiplicidad /multipliθi'ðað; multiplisi'ðað/ *f,* multiplicity
múltiplo /'multiplo/ *a* and *m,* multiple
multisecular /multiseku'lar/ *a* age-old, many centuries old
multitud /multi'tuð/ *f,* multitude, great number; crowd; rabble, masses, mob
mundanal, mundano /munda'nal, mun'dano/ *a* worldly, mundane
mundanalidad /mundanali'ðað/ *f,* worldliness
mundial /mun'dial/ *a* world, worldwide
mundo /'mundo/ *m,* world, universe; human race; earth; human society; world (of letters, science, etc.); secular life; *Eccl.* vanities of the flesh; geographical globe. **echar al m.,** to give birth to; produce, bring forth. **el Nuevo M.,** the New World, America. *Inf.* **medio m.,** half the earth, a great crowd. *Inf.* **ponerse el m. por montera,** to treat the world as one's oyster. **ser hombre del m.,** to be a man of the world. *Inf.* **tener m.** *or* **mucho m.,** to be very experienced, know the world. **todo el m.,** everyone. **venir al m.,** to be born. **ver m.,** to travel, see the world
mundología /mundolo'hia/ *f,* worldliness, experience of the world
munición /muni'θion; muni'sion/ *f, Mil.* munition; small shot. *Mil.* **m. de boca,** fodder and food supplies
municionar /muniθio'nar; munisio'nar/ *vt* to munition, furnish with munitions
municionero /muniθio'nero; munisio'nero/ **(-ra)** *n* purveyor, supplier
municipal /muniθi'pal; munisi'pal/ *a* municipal. *m,* policeman
municipalidad /muniθipali'ðað; munisipali'ðað/ *f,* municipality
municipio /muni'θipio; muni'sipio/ *m,* municipality, town council
munificencia /munifi'θenθia; munifi'sensia/ *f,* munificence, generosity
munífico /mu'nifiko/ *a* munificent, generous
muñeca /mu'ɲeka/ *f, Anat.* wrist; doll; puppet; dressmaker's dummy; polishing pad; mannequin; boundary marker; *Inf.* flighty young woman
muñeco /mu'ɲeko/ *m,* boy doll; puppet; *Inf.* playboy
muñir /mu'ɲir/ *vt irr* to summon, convoke; arrange, dispose. See **mullir**
muñón /mu'ɲon/ *m, Surg.* stump of an amputated limb; *Mech.* gudgeon
mural /mu'ral/ *a* mural
muralla /mu'raʎa; mu'raya/ *f,* town wall; rampart, fortification
murar /mu'rar/ *vt* to surround with a wall, wall in
murciano /mur'θiano; mur'siano/ **(-na)** *a* and *n* Murcian
murciélago /mur'θielago; mur'sielago/ *m, Zool.* bat
murga /'murga/ *f,* band of street musicians
murmullo /mur'muʎo; mur'muyo/ *m,* whisper; whispering; rustling; purling, lapping, splashing; mumbling, muttering
murmuración /murmura'θion; murmura'sion/ *f,* slander, backbiting, gossip
murmurador /murmura'ðor/ **(-ra)** *a* gossiping, slanderous —*n* gossip, backbiter
murmurar /murmu'rar/ *vi* to rustle (leaves, etc.); purl, lap, splash (water); whisper; mumble, mutter; —*vi* and *vt Inf.* slander, backbite
murmurio /mur'murio/ *m,* rustling; lapping (of water); whispering; murmur; *Inf.* slander
muro /'muro/ *m,* wall; defensive wall, rampart
musa /'musa/ *f,* muse
musaraña /musa'raɲa/ *f, Zool.* shrew; any small animal; *Inf.* ridiculous effigy, guy. *Inf.* **mirar a las musarañas,** to be absent-minded
muscular /musku'lar/ *a* muscular
musculatura /muskula'tura/ *f,* musculature
músculo /'muskulo/ *m,* muscle; strength, brawn
musculoso /musku'loso/ *a* muscular; strong, brawny
muselina /muse'lina/ *f,* muslin
museo /mu'seo/ *m,* museum. **m. de pintura,** art gallery, picture gallery
musgo /'musgo/ *m,* moss
musgoso /mus'goso/ *a* mossy, moss-grown
música /'musika/ *f,* music; melody, harmony, musical performance; musical composition; group of musicians; sheet music. *Inf.* **m. celestial,** vain words, moonshine. *Inf.* **m. ratonera,** badly played music. *Inf.* **¡Vaya con su m. a otra parte!** Get out! Go to hell!
musical /musi'kal/ *a* musical
músico /'musiko/ **(-ca)** *a* music —*n* musician. **m. ambulante,** strolling musician. **m. mayor,** bandleader
musitar /musi'tar/ *vi* to mutter, mumble
muslo /'muslo/ *m,* thigh
mustio /'mustio/ *a* sad, disheartened, depressed; faded, withered
musulmán /musul'man/ **(-ana)** *a* and *n* Muslim

mutabilidad /mutaβili'ðað/ *f,* mutability, changeability

mutación /muta'θion; muta'sion/ *f,* change, mutation; sudden change in the weather; *Theat.* change of scene

mutilación /mutila'θion; mutila'sion/ *f,* mutilation; damage; defacement

mutilar /muti'lar/ *vt* to mutilate; spoil, deface, damage; cut short; reduce

mutis /'mutis/ *m, Theat.* exit. **hacer m.** *Theat.* to exit; keep quiet, say nothing

mutismo /mu'tismo/ *m,* mutism, dumbness; silence, speechlessness

mutualidad /mutuali'ðað/ *f,* reciprocity, mutuality, interdependence; principle of mutual aid; mutual aid society

mutualismo /mutua'lismo/ *m,* mutualism, organized mutual aid

mutualista /mutua'lista/ *mf* member of a mutual aid society

mutuante /mu'tuante/ *mf Com.* lender

mutuo /'mutuo/ *a* reciprocal, mutual, interdependent

muy /'mui/ *adv* very; very much; much. Used to form absolute superlative (e.g. *m. rápidamente,* very quickly). Can modify adjectives, nouns used adjectivally, adverbs, participles (e.g. *María es m. mujer,* Mary is very much a woman (very womanly)). **m. temprano,** very early. **M. señor mío,** Dear Sir (in letters)

N Ñ

naba /'naβa/ *f,* swede, turnip

nabar /na'βar/ *m,* turnip field

nabo /'naβo/ *m,* turnip; turnip root; any root stem; *Naut.* mast; stock (of a horse's tail)

nácar /'nakar/ *m,* mother-of-pearl

nacarado, nacáreo /naka'raðo, na'kareo/ *a* nacreous, mother-of-pearl

nacer /na'θer; na'ser/ *vi irr* to be born; rise (rivers, etc.); sprout; grow (plumage, fur, leaves, etc.); descend (lineage); appear (stars, etc.); originate; *Fig.* issue forth; appear suddenly; (*with prep a* or *para*) be destined for, have a natural leaning toward. **n. con pajitas de oro en la cuna,** to be born with a silver spoon in one's mouth —*vr* grow; sprout; *Sew.* split at the seams —*Pres. Indic.* **nazco, naces,** etc —*Pres. Subjunc.* **nazca,** etc.

nacido /na'θiðo; na'siðo/ *a* and *past part* born; suitable, fit. *m,* (gen. *pl*) the living and the dead. **bien n.,** noble, well-born; well-bred. **mal n.,** base-born; ill-bred

naciente /na'θiente; na'siente/ *a* growing; nascent. *m,* east

nacimiento /naθi'miento; nasi'miento/ *m,* birth; source (of rivers, etc.); birthplace; origin; lineage; *Astron.* rising; nativity crib, manger. **de n.,** from birth; by birth; born

nación /na'θion; na'sion/ *f,* nation; country; *Inf.* birth

nacional /naθio'nal; nasio'nal/ *a* national; native. *mf* citizen, national

nacionalidad /naθionali'ðað; nasionali'ðað/ *f,* nationality

nacionalismo /naθiona'lismo; nasiona'lismo/ *m,* nationalism

nacionalista /naθiona'lista; nasiona'lista/ *a* and *mf* nationalist

nacionalización /naθionaliθa'θion; nasionalisa'sion/ *f,* naturalization; nationalization; acclimatization

nacionalizar /naθionali'θar; nasionali'sar/ *vt* to naturalize; nationalize

nacionalsindicalismo /naθio,nalsindika'lismo; nasio,nalsindika'lismo/ *m,* national syndicalism

nacionalsocialismo /naθio,nalsoθia'lismo; nasio,nalsosia'lismo/ *m,* national socialism, nazism

nada /'naða/ *f,* void, nothingness —*pron indef* nothing —*adv* by no means. **casi n.,** very little, practically nothing. **¡De n.!** Not at all! Don't mention it! You're welcome! **No vale para n.,** He (it, she) is of no use

nadaderas /naða'ðeras/ *f pl,* water wings (for swimming)

nadador /naða'ðor/ **(-ra)** *n* swimmer —*a* swimming

nadar /na'ðar/ *vi* to swim; float; have an abundance (of); *Inf.* be too large (of garments, etc.). **n. y guardar la ropa,** *Fig.* to sit on the fence

nadería /naðe'ria/ *f,* trifle

nadie /'naðie/ *pron indef* no one. *m, Fig.* a nobody

nadir /na'ðir/ *m,* nadir

nado /'naðo/ *a* by swimming; afloat

nafta /'nafta/ *f,* naphtha

naftalina /nafta'lina/ *f,* naphthalene

naipe /'naipe/ *m,* playing card; pack of cards

naire /'naire/ *m,* elephant keeper or trainer

nalga /'nalga/ *f,* (gen. *pl*) buttock(s)

nana /'nana/ *f, Inf.* grandma; lullaby

nao /'nao/ *f,* ship

napoleónico /napole'oniko/ *a* Napoleonic

Nápoles /'napoles/ Naples

napolitano /napoli'tano/ **(-na)** *a* and *n* Neapolitan

naranja /na'ranha/ *f,* orange. **n. dulce,** blood orange. **n. mandarina,** tangerine. *Inf.* **media n.,** better half

naranjada /naran'haða/ *f,* orangeade

naranjal /naran'hal/ *m,* orange grove

naranjero /naran'hero/ **(-ra)** *n* orange seller

naranjo /na'ranho/ *m,* orange tree; *Inf.* lout, blockhead

narciso /nar'θiso; nar'siso/ *m,* narcissus; dandy, fop. **n. trompón,** daffodil

narcótico /nar'kotiko/ *a* and *m,* narcotic

narcotizar /narkoti'θar; narkoti'sar/ *vt* to narcotize

narcotraficante /narkotrafi'kante/ *mf* drug dealer

nardo /'narðo/ *m,* tuberose, spikenard, nard

narguile /nar'gile/ *m,* hookah, hubble-bubble, narghile

narigudo /nari'guðo/ *a* large-nosed; nose-shaped

nariz /na'riθ; na'ris/ *f,* nose; nostril; snout; nozzle; sense of smell; bouquet (of wine). **n. perfilada,** well-shaped nose. **n. respingona,** snub nose. *Inf.* **meter las narices,** to meddle, interfere

narración /narra'θion; narra'sion/ *f,* narration, account

narrador /narra'ðor/ **(-ra)** *a* narrative —*n* narrator

narrar /na'rrar/ *vt* to narrate, tell, relate

narrativa /narra'tiβa/ *f,* narrative; account; narrative skill

narrativo, narratorio /narra'tiβo, narra'torio/ *a* narrative

nata /'nata/ *f,* cream; *Fig.* the flower, elite; *pl* whipped cream with sugar

natación /nata'θion; nata'sion/ *f,* swimming. **n. a la marinera,** trudgen stroke

natal /na'tal/ *a* natal; native. *m,* birth; birthday

natalicio /nata'liθio; nata'lisio/ *a* natal —*a* and *m,* birthday

natalidad /natali'ðað/ *f,* birth rate

natatorio /nata'torio/ *a* swimming. *m,* swimming pool

natillas /na'tiʎas; na'tiyas/ *f pl,* custard

natividad /natiβi'ðað/ *f,* nativity; birth; Christmas

nativo /na'tiβo/ *a* indigenous; native; innate

nato /'nato/ *a* born; inherent; ex officio

natura /na'tura/ *f,* nature; *Mus.* major scale

natural /natu'ral/ *a* natural; native; indigenous; spontaneous; sincere, candid; physical; usual, ordinary; *Mus.* natural; unadulterated, pure; *Herald.* proper. *mf* native, citizen. *m,* temperament; disposition; instinct (of animals); natural inclination. **al n.,** naturally, without art. **del n.,** *Art.* from life

naturaleza /natura'leθa; natura'lesa/ *f,* nature; character; disposition; instinct; temperament; nationality, origin; naturalization; kind, class; constitution, physique. **n. humana,** humankind. **n. muerta,** *Art.* still life

naturalidad /naturali'ðað/ *f,* naturalness; nationality

naturalista /natura'lista/ *mf* naturalist

naturalización /naturaliθa'θion; naturalisa'sion/ *f,* naturalization; acclimatization

naturalizar /naturali'θar; naturali'sar/ *vt* to naturalize; acclimatize; —*vr* become naturalized; become acclimatized

naturalmente /natural'mente/ *adv* naturally; of course

naturismo /natu'rismo/ *m,* nature cure

naufragar /naufra'gar/ *vi* to be shipwrecked; fail, be unsuccessful

naufragio /nau'frahio/ *m,* shipwreck; disaster, loss

náufrago /'naufrago/ **(-ga)** *n* shipwrecked person. *m,* shark

náusea /'nausea/ *f,* nausea (*pl* more usual); repugnance

nauseabundo, nauseoso /nausea'βundo, nause'oso/ *a* nauseous; nauseating, repugnant

nauta /'nauta/ *mf* mariner

náutica /'nautika/ *f,* navigation; yachting; seamanship

náutico /'nautiko/ *a* nautical

navaja /na'βaha/ *f,* razor; clasp knife; boar tusk; sting; *Inf.* slanderous tongue. **n. de afeitar,** (shaving) razor

navajada /naβa'haða/ *f,* slash with a razor

navajero /naβa'hero/ *m,* razor case

naval /na'βal/ *a* naval

Navarra /na'βarra/ Navarre

navarro /na'βarro/ **(-ra)** *a* and *n* Navarrese

nave /'naβe/ *f*, ship; *Archit.* nave. **n. aérea,** airship. *Archit.* **n. lateral,** aisle. **n. principal,** *Archit.* nave

navegable /naβe'gaβle/ *a* navigable

navegación /naβega'θion; naβega'sion/ *f*, navigation; sea voyage

navegante /naβe'gante/ *a* voyaging; navigating. *m*, navigator

navegar /naβe'gar/ *vi* to navigate; sail; fly

navidad /naβi'ðað/ *f*, nativity; Christmas; *pl* Christmastime

naviero /na'βiero/ *a* shipping. *m*, ship owner

navío /na'βio/ *m*, warship; ship. **n. de transporte,** transport. **n. de tres puentes,** three-decker

náyade /'naiaðe/ *f*, naiad, water nymph

nazareno /naθa'reno; nasa'reno/ **(-na)** *a* and *n* Nazarene; Christian

Nazaret /naθa'ret; nasa'ret/ Nazareth

nazismo /na'θismo; na'sismo/ *m*, nazism

neblina /ne'βlina/ *f*, fog; mist

nebulosidad /neβulosi'ðað/ *f*, nebulousness; cloudiness

nebuloso /neβu'loso/ *a* foggy; misty; cloudy; somber, melancholy; confused, nebulous

necedad /neθe'ðað; nese'ðað/ *f*, silliness

necesario /neθe'sario; nese'sario/ *a* necessary; unavoidable

neceser /neθe'ser; nese'ser/ *m*, dressing case. *Sew.* **n. de costura,** workbox

necesidad /neθesi'ðað; nesesi'ðað/ *f*, necessity; poverty, want; shortage, need; emergency. **de n.,** necessarily

necesitado /neθesi'taðo; nesesi'taðo/ **(-da)** *a* needy, poor —*n* poor person

necesitar /neθesi'tar; nesesi'tar/ *vt* to necessitate; compel, oblige; —*vi* be necessary, need

necio /'neθio; 'nesio/ *a* stupid; senseless; unreasonable

necrología /nekrolo'hia/ *f*, necrology, obituary

necromancía /nekroman'θia; nekroman'sia/ *f*, necromancy

neerlandés /neerlan'des/ *a* Dutch

nefando /ne'fando/ *a* iniquitous

nefario /ne'fario/ *a* nefarious

nefasto /ne'fasto/ *a* disastrous, ill-omened

nefrítico /ne'fritiko/ *a* nephritic

nefritis /ne'fritis/ *f*, nephritis

negable /ne'gaβle/ *a* deniable

negación /nega'θion; nega'sion/ *f*, negation; privation; negative; nay; *Gram.* negative particle; *Law.* traverse

negado /ne'gaðo/ *a* inept, unfitted; stupid

negar /ne'gar/ *vt irr* to deny; refuse; prohibit; disclaim; dissemble; disown; *Law.* traverse; —*vr* refuse, avoid; decline (to receive visitors). See **acertar**

negativa /nega'tiβa/ *f*, denial; refusal; *Photo.* negative

negativo /nega'tiβo/ *a* negative

negligencia /negli'henθia; negli'hensia/ *f*, negligence; omission; carelessness; forgetfulness

negligente /negli'hente/ *a* negligent; careless; neglectful

negociable /nego'θiaβle; nego'siaβle/ *a* negotiable

negociación /negoθia'θion; negosia'sion/ *f*, negotiation; business affair, deal

negociado /nego'θiaðo; nego'siaðo/ *m*, department, section (of a ministry, etc.); business

negociante /nego'θiante; nego'siante/ *m*, businessman —*a* negotiating; trading

negociar /nego'θiar; nego'siar/ *vi* to trade, traffic; negotiate

negocio /ne'goθio; ne'gosio/ *m*, occupation; trade; business; employment; transaction; *pl* business affairs. **hombre de negocios,** businessman

negra /'negra/ *f*, black girl, black woman; *Inf.* honey, *West Hem.* sweetheart

negrecer /negre'θer; negre'ser/ *vi irr* to become black. See **conocer**

negrero /ne'grero/ **(-ra)** *n* slave trader

negro /'negro/ *a* black; dark; melancholy; disastrous; *Herald.* sable. *m*, black; black (color). **n. de humo,** lampblack

negrura /ne'grura/ *f*, blackness

negruzco /ne'gruθko; ne'grusko/ *a* blackish

nemotécnica /nemo'teknika/ *f*, mnemonics

nene /'nene/ **(-na)** *n Inf.* baby; darling

nenúfar /ne'nufar/ *m*, white water lily

neo /'neo/ *m*, neon

neocelandés /neoθelan'des; neoselan'des/ **(-esa)** *a* New Zealand —*n* New Zealander

neófito /ne'ofito/ **(-ta)** *n* neophyte

neoguineano /neogine'ano/ *a* New Guinean

neolítico /neo'litiko/ *a* neolithic

neologismo /neolo'hismo/ *m*, neologism

neoyorquino /neoior'kino/ **(-na)** *a* New York —*n* New Yorker

nepotismo /nepo'tismo/ *m*, nepotism

Neptuno /nep'tuno/ *m*, *Astron.* Neptune; *Poet.* sea

nereida /ne'reiða/ *f*, nereid, sea nymph

nervio /'nerβio/ *m*, nerve; sinew; *Bot.* vein; vigor; *Mus.* string. **n. ciático,** sciatic nerve

nervioso /ner'βioso/ *a* nervous; overwrought, agitated; vigorous; neural; sinewy; jerky (of style, etc.)

nervosidad /nerβosi'ðað/ *f*, nervousness; nervosity; flexibility (metals); jerkiness (of style, etc.); force, efficacy

nervudo /ner'βuðo/ *a* strong-nerved, vigorous

nesga /'nesga/ *f*, *Sew.* gore

neto /'neto/ *a* neat; clean; pure; *Com.* net. *m*, *Archit.* dado

neumático /neu'matiko/ *a* pneumatic. *m*, rubber tire

neumococo /neumo'koko/ *m*, pneumococcus

neurálgico /neu'ralhiko/ *a* neuralgic

neurastenia /neuras'tenia/ *f*, neurasthenia

neurasténico /neuras'teniko/ **(-ca)** *a* and *n* neurasthenic

neurología /neurolo'hia/ *f*, neurology

neurólogo /neu'rologo/ *m*, neurologist

neurópata /neu'ropata/ *mf* neuropath

neurosis /neu'rosis/ *f*, neurosis. **n. de guerra,** war neurosis; shell shock

neurótico /neu'rotiko/ **(-ca)** *a* and *n* neurotic

neutral /neu'tral/ *a* neutral; indifferent

neutralidad /neutrali'ðað/ *f*, neutrality; impartiality, indifference

neutralizar /neutrali'θar; neutrali'sar/ *vt* to neutralize; counteract, mitigate

neutro /'neutro/ *a* neuter; *Chem.* neutral; *Mech.* neuter; sexless

nevada /ne'βaða/ *f*, snowfall

nevar /ne'βar/ *vi irr impers* to snow —*Pres. Indic.* **nieva.** *Pres. Subjunc.* **nieve**

nevera /ne'βera/ *f*, refrigerator; icehouse

nevero /ne'βero/ *m*, ice-cream man; iceman

nevisca /ne'βiska/ *f*, light snowfall

nevoso /ne'βoso/ *a* snowy

nexo /'nekso/ *m*, nexus; connection, union

ni /ni/ *conjunc* neither, nor. **ni bien ni mal,** neither good nor bad. **ni siquiera,** not even. **¡Ni crea!, ¡Ni creas!** Nonsense!

niara /'niara/ *f*, haystack, rick

nicaragüeño /nikara'gueɲo/ **(-ña)** *a* and *n* Nicaraguan

nicho /'nitʃo/ *m*, niche; recess (in a wall)

nicotina /niko'tina/ *f*, nicotine

nidada /ni'ðaða/ *f*, nest full of eggs; brood, clutch

nidal /ni'ðal/ *m*, nest; nest egg; haunt; cause, foundation

nido /'niðo/ *m*, nest; den; hole; dwelling; haunt. **n. de ametralladoras,** *Mil.* pillbox

niebla /'nieβla/ *f*, fog; mist; cloud; mildew; haze

nieto /'nieto/ **(-ta)** *n* grandchild; descendant

nieve /'nieβe/ *f*, snow; whiteness. **deportes de n.,** winter sports

nigromancia /nigro'manθia; nigro'mansia/ *f*, necromancy

nigromante /nigro'mante/ *m*, necromancer

nihilismo /nii'lismo/ *m*, nihilism

nihilista /nii'lista/ *mf* nihilist

Nilo, el /'nilo, el/ the Nile

nimbo /'nimbo/ *m*, halo, nimbus

nimiedad /nimie'ðað/ *f,* prolixity; *Inf.* fussiness; fastidiousness, delicacy
nimio /'nimio/ *a* prolix; *Inf.* fussy; fastidious; *Inf.* parsimonious
ninfa /'ninfa/ *f,* nymph; *Ent.* chrysalis
ningún /niŋ'gun/ *a Abbr.* of **ninguno.** Used before *m, sing* nouns only. **De n. modo,** In no way! Certainly not!
Nínive /'niniβe/ Nineveh
niña /'niɲa/ *f,* girl. **n. del ojo,** pupil (of the eye). **n. de los ojos,** apple of one's eye, darling
niñada /ni'ɲaða/ *f,* childishness, foolish act
niñera /ni'ɲera/ *f,* nursemaid
niñería /niɲe'ria/ *f,* childish act; trifle; childishness, folly
niñez /ni'ɲeθ; ni'ɲes/ *f,* childhood; beginning, early days; *Fig.* cradle
niño /'niɲo/ **(-ña)** *a* childish; young; inexperienced; imprudent —*n* child; young or inexperienced person. **n. de la doctrina,** charity child. **n. terrible,** enfant terrible. **desde n.,** from childhood
nipón /ni'pon/ **(-ona)** *a* and *n* Japanese
níquel /'nikel/ *m, Chem.* nickel
niquelar /nike'lar/ *vt* to chrome-plate
nirvana /nir'βana/ *m,* nirvana
níspero /'nispero/ *m,* medlar tree; medlar
níspola /'nispola/ *f,* medlar
nitidez /niti'ðeθ; niti'ðes/ *f,* brightness, neatness, cleanliness
nítido /'nitiðo/ *a* bright, neat, clean (often *Poet.*)
nitrato /ni'trato/ *m,* nitrate
nítrico /'nitriko/ *a* nitric
nitrógeno /ni'troheno/ *m,* nitrogen
nivel /ni'βel/ *m,* level; levelness. **n. de albañil,** plummet. **n. de burbuja,** spirit level. **a n.,** on the level. **estar al n. de las circunstancias,** to rise to the occasion; save the day
nivelación /niβela'θion; niβela'sion/ *f,* leveling
nivelador /niβela'ðor/ **(-ra)** *a* leveling —*n* leveler
nivelar /niβe'lar/ *vt* to level; *Fig.* make equal
níveo /'niβeo/ *a* snowy; snow-white
Niza /'niθa; 'nisa/ Nice
no /no/ *adv* no; not. **no bien,** no sooner. **no sea que,** unless. **no tal,** no such thing
noble /'noβle/ *a* noble, illustrious; generous; outstanding, excellent; aristocratic. *mf* nobleman (-woman)
nobleza /no'βleθa; no'βlesa/ *f,* nobility
noche /'notʃe/ *f,* night; darkness; confusion, obscurity. *Inf.* **n. toledana,** restless night. **¡Buenas noches!** Good night! **de n.,** by night. **esta n.,** tonight
nochebuena /notʃe'βuena/ *f,* Christmas Eve
nochebueno /notʃe'βueno/ *m,* yule log; Christmas cake
nocherniego /notʃer'niego/ *a* night, nocturnal
noción /no'θion; no'sion/ *f,* notion, idea; *pl* elementary knowledge
nocividad /noθiβi'ðað; nosiβi'ðað/ *f,* noxiousness
nocivo /no'θiβo; no'siβo/ *a* noxious
nocturno /nok'turno/ *a* nocturnal; melancholy. *m, Mus.* nocturne
nodriza /no'ðriθa; no'ðrisa/ *f,* wet nurse
nogal /no'gal/ *m,* walnut tree; walnut wood
nómada /'nomaða/ *a* nomadic
nomadismo /noma'ðismo/ *m,* nomadism
nombradia /nom'βraðia/ *f,* renown
nombramiento /nombra'miento/ *m,* naming; appointment; nomination
nombrar /nom'βrar/ *vt* to name; nominate; appoint; mention (in dispatches, etc.)
nombre /'nombre/ *m,* name; title; reputation; proxy; *Gram.* noun; *Mil.* password. **n. de pila,** Christian name. **por n.,** called; by name. **Su n. anda puesto en el cuerno de la Luna,** He (she) is praised to the skies
nomenclatura /nomenkla'tura/ *f,* nomenclature
nómina /'nomina/ *f,* list, register; payroll; amulet
nominación /nomina'θion; nomina'sion/ *f,* nomination, appointment
nominador /nomina'ðor/ **(-ra)** *a* nominating —*n* nominator
nominal /nomi'nal/ *a* nominal
nominalismo /nomina'lismo/ *m,* nominalism
nominalista /nomina'lista/ *a* nominalistic. *mf* nominalist
nomo /'nomo/ *m,* gnome
non /non/ *a* odd (of numbers)
nonada /no'naða/ *f,* nothing, practically nothing
nonagenario /nonahe'nario/ **(-ia)** *a* and *n* nonagenarian
nonagésimo /nona'hesimo/ *a* ninetieth
nones /'nones/ *m, pl* certainly not, definitely not, nope
nopal /no'pal/ *m,* nopal, prickly pear tree
noque /'noke/ *m,* tanner's vat
noquear /noke'ar/ *vt* (*Boxing*) to knock out, K.O.
norabuena /nora'βuena/ *f,* congratulation
nordeste /nor'ðeste/ *m,* northeast
nórdico /'norðiko/ **(-ca)** *a* and *n* Nordic
noria /'noria/ *f,* water well; chain pump; *Inf.* hard, monotonous work
norma /'norma/ *f,* square (used by builders, etc.); *Fig.* norm, standard, model
normal /nor'mal/ *a* normal, usual; standard, average. *f,* normal school, teacher's college (also **escuela n.**)
normalidad /normali'ðað/ *f,* normality
normalista /norma'lista/ *mf* student at a teacher's college
normalización /normaliθa'θion; normalisa'sion/ *f,* normalization; standardization
normalizar /normali'θar; normali'sar/ *vt* to make normal; standardize
Normandía /norman'dia/ Normandy
normando /nor'mando/ **(-da)** *a* Norman —*n* Northman; Norman
nornordeste /nornor'ðeste/ *m,* northnortheast
nornorueste /norno'rueste/ *m,* northnorthwest
noroeste /noro'este/ *m,* northwest
norte /'norte/ *m,* north pole; north; north wind; polestar; *Fig.* guide
norteamericano /norteameri'kano/ **(-na)** *a* and *n* North American; (*U.S.A.*) American
norteño /nor'teɲo/ *a* northerly, northern
Noruega /no'ruega/ Norway
noruego /no'ruego/ **(-ga)** *a* and *n* Norwegian. *m,* Norwegian (language)
nos /nos/ *pers pron pl mf acc* and *dat* (direct and indirect object) of **nosotros,** us; to us (e.g. *Nos lo dio,* He gave it to us)
nosotros, nosotras /no'sotros, no'sotras/ *pers pron pl mf* we; us. Also used with preposition (e.g. *Lo hicieron por nosotros,* They did it for us)
nostalgia /nos'talhia/ *f,* nostalgia
nostálgico /nos'talhiko/ *a* nostalgic; melancholy; homesick
nóstico /'nostiko/ (**-ca**) *a* and *n* gnostic
nota /'nota/ *f,* mark, sign; annotation, comment; *Mus.* note; memorandum; *Com.* bill, account; criticism, imputation; mark (in exams); repute, renown; note (diplomatic)
notabilidad /notaβili'ðað/ *f,* notability
notable /no'taβle/ *a* notable, remarkable; outstanding, prominent; with distinction (examination mark). *m pl,* notabilities
notación /nota'θion; nota'sion/ *f,* (*Mus. Math.*) notation; annotation
notar /no'tar/ *vt* to mark, indicate; observe, notice; note down; annotate; dictate, read out; criticize, reproach; discredit
notaría /nota'ria/ *f,* profession of a notary; notary's office
notarial /nota'rial/ *a* notarial
notario /no'tario/ *m,* notary public
noticia /no'tiθia; no'tisia/ *f,* rudiment, elementary knowledge; information; news (gen. *pl*); *pl* knowledge. **atrasado de noticias,** *Fig.* behind the times
noticiar /noti'θiar; noti'siar/ *vt* to inform, give notice
noticiario /noti'θiario; noti'siario/ *m,* news bulletin, newsreel.
noticiero /noti'θiero; noti'siero/ *m,* newspaper
noticioso /noti'θioso; noti'sioso/ *a* informed; learned; newsy

notificación /notifika'θion; notifika'sion/ *f, Law.* notification. **n. de reclutamiento,** draft notice
notificar /notifi'kar/ *vt* to notify officially; inform; warn
noto /'noto/ *a* known. *m,* south wind
notoriedad /notorie'ðað/ *f,* notoriety, publicity; flagrancy; fame, renown
notorio /no'torio/ *a* well-known; notorious, obvious; flagrant
novatada /noβa'taða/ *f, Inf.* ragging (of a freshman); blunder
novato /no'βato/ **(-ta)** *a* new, inexperienced —*n* novice, beginner
novecientos /noβe'θientos; noβe'sientos/ *a* and *m,* nine hundred
novedad /noβe'ðað/ *f,* newness, novelty; change, alteration; latest news; surprise; *pl* novelties. **sin n.,** no change; all well (or as usual); safely, without incident
novel /no'βel/ *a* new; inexperienced
novela /no'βela/ *f,* novel; tale; falsehood. **n. caballista,** western, cowboy story. **n. por entregas,** serial (story)
novelero /noβe'lero/ **(-ra)** *a* fond of novelty and change; fond of novels; fickle —*n* newshound, gossip
novelesco /noβe'lesko/ *a* novelistic; imaginary
novelista /noβe'lista/ *mf* novelist
novelística /noβe'listika/ *f,* art of novel writing
novena /no'βena/ *f, Eccl.* novena, religious services spread over nine days
noveno /no'βeno/ *a* and *m,* ninth
noventa /no'βenta/ *a* and *m,* ninety; ninetieth
novia /'noβia/ *f,* bride; fiancée
noviazgo /no'βiaθgo; no'βiasgo/ *m,* engagement, betrothal
noviciado /noβi'θiaðo; noβi'siaðo/ *m,* novitiate; training, apprenticeship
novicio /no'βiθio; no'βisio/ **(-ia)** *n Eccl.* novice; beginner, apprentice; unassuming person
noviembre /no'βiembre/ *m,* November
novillada /noβi'ʎaða; noβi'yaða/ *f,* herd of young bulls; bullock baiting
novillo /no'βiʎo; no'βiyo/ *m,* bullock. **hacer novillos,** to play truant
novilunio /noβi'lunio/ *m,* new moon
novio /'noβio/ *m,* bridegroom; fiancé; novice, beginner
novísimo /no'βisimo/ *a superl* **nuevo** newest; latest, most recent
nubada /nu'βaða/ *f,* cloudburst, rainstorm; abundance, plenty
nubarrón /nuβa'rron/ *m,* dense, lowering cloud, storm cloud
nube /'nuβe/ *f,* cloud; *Fig.* screen, impediment. **n. de verano,** summer cloud; passing annoyance
nublado /nu'βlaðo/ *a* cloudy; overcast. *m,* storm cloud; menace, threat; multitude, crowd
nublarse /nu'βlarse/ *vr* to cloud over
nubloso /nu'βloso/ *a* cloudy; unfortunate, unhappy
nuca /'nuka/ *f,* nape
núcleo /'nukleo/ *m,* kernel; stone, pip (of fruit); nucleus; *Fig.* core, essence
nudillo /nu'ðiʎo; nu'ðiyo/ *m,* knuckle; *Mas.* plug
nudo /'nuðo/ *m,* knot; (*Bot. Med.*) node; joint; *Naut.* knot; *Fig.* bond, tie; *Fig.* crux, knotty point. **n. al revés,** granny knot. **n. de comunicaciones,** communication center. **n. de marino,** reef knot. **n. de tejedor,** sheet bend (knot). **n. en la garganta,** *Fig.* lump in the throat (from emotion)
nudoso /nu'ðoso/ *a* knotted, knotty; gnarled
nuera /'nuera/ *f,* daughter-in-law
nuestro, nuestra /'nuestro, 'nuestra/ *poss pron 1st pers pl mf* our; ours. **los nuestros,** our friends, supporters, party, profession, etc.
nueva /'nueβa/ *f,* news
Nueva Caledonia /'nueβa kale'ðonia/ New Caledonia
Nueva Escocia /'nueβa es'koθia; 'nueβa es'kosia/ Nova Scotia
Nueva Gales del Sur /'nueβa 'gales del sur/ New South Wales
Nueva Guinea /'nueβa gi'nea/ New Guinea
nuevamente /nueβa'mente/ *adv* again
Nueva Orleans /'nueβa orle'ans/ New Orleans
Nueva York /'nueβa york/ New York
Nueva Zelanda, Zelandia /'nueβa θe'landa, θe'landia; 'nueβa se'landa, se'landia/ New Zealand
nueve /'nueβe/ *a* nine; ninth. *m,* number nine; ninth (of the month) (e.g. *el nueve de marzo,* March 9th). **a las nueve,** at nine o'clock
nuevo /'nueβo/ *a* new; fresh; newly arrived; inexperienced; unused, scarcely worn. **de n.,** again. **¿Qué hay de n.?** What's the news? What's new?
nuez /nueθ; nues/ *f,* walnut; *Anat.* Adam's apple. **n. moscada,** nutmeg
nulidad /nuli'ðað/ *f,* nullity; incompetence, ineptitude; worthlessness
nulo /'nulo/ *a* null, void; incapable; worthless
numen /'numen/ *m,* divinity; inspiration
numeración /numera'θion; numera'sion/ *f,* calculation; numbering
numerador /numera'ðor/ *m,* numerator
numerar /nume'rar/ *vt* to number; enumerate; calculate
numerario /nume'rario/ *a* numerary. *m,* cash
numérico /nu'meriko/ *a* numerical
número /'numero/ *m,* number; figure; numeral; size (of gloves, etc.); quantity; issue, copy; rhythm; *Gram.* number; item (of a program); *pl Eccl.* Numbers. **n. del distrito postal,** ZIP code. **n. quebrado,** *Math.* fraction. **sin n.,** numberless
numeroso /nume'roso/ *a* numerous; harmonious
numismática /numis'matika/ *f,* numismatics
nunca /'nunka/ *adv* never. **n. jamás,** nevermore. **N. digas «De esta agua no beberé!»** Never say "Never!"
nuncio /'nunθio; 'nunsio/ *m,* messenger; papal nuncio; *Fig.* harbinger
nupcial /nup'θial; nup'sial/ *a* nuptial
nupcialidad /nupθiali'ðað; nupsiali'ðað/ *f,* marriage rate
nupcias /'nupθias; 'nupsias/ *f pl,* nuptials, marriage
nutria /'nutria/ *f,* otter, nutria
nutrición /nutri'θion; nutri'sion/ *f,* nourishment; nutrition
nutrido /nu'triðo/ *a* abundant; numerous
nutrimento /nutri'mento/ *m,* nutriment; nourishment; nutrition; *Fig.* food, encouragement
nutrir /nu'trir/ *vt* to nourish; encourage; *Fig.* fill
nutritivo /nutri'tiβo/ *a* nourishing, nutritive

O

o /o/ *f,* letter O —*conjunc* or, either. **o** becomes **u** before words beginning with **o** or **ho** (e.g. *gloria u honor*)
oasis /o'asis/ *m,* oasis; *Fig.* refuge, haven
obcecación /oβθeka'θion; oβseka'sion/ *f,* blindness; obstinacy; obsession
obcecar /oβθe'kar; oβse'kar/ *vt* to blind; obsess; *Fig.* dazzle; darken
obduración /oβðura'θion; oβðura'sion/ *f,* obstinacy, stubbornness, obduracy
obedecer /oβeðe'θer; oβeðe'ser/ *vt irr* to obey; *Fig.* respond; bend, yield (metals, etc.); —*vi* result (from), arise (from). See **conocer**
obedecimiento /oβeðeθi'miento; oβeðesi'miento/ *m,* **obediencia** *f,* obedience
obediente /oβe'ðiente/ *a* obedient; docile
obelisco /oβe'lisko/ *m,* obelisk
obertura /oβer'tura/ *f, Mus.* overture
obesidad /oβesi'ðað/ *f,* obesity
obeso /o'βeso/ *a* obese
óbice /'oβiθe; 'oβise/ *m,* obstacle, impediment
obispado /oβis'paðo/ *m,* bishopric
obispalía /oβispa'lia/ *f,* bishop's palace; bishopric
obispo /o'βispo/ *m,* bishop. **o. sufragáneo,** suffragan bishop
óbito /'oβito/ *m,* death, demise
obituario /oβi'tuario/ *m,* obituary; obituary column
objeción /oβhe'θion; oβhe'sion/ *f,* objection
objetar /oβhe'tar/ *vt* to object to, oppose
objetivar /oβheti'βar/ *vt* to view objectively
objetividad /oβhetiβi'ðað/ *f,* objectivity
objetivo /oβhe'tiβo/ *a* objective. *m, Opt.* eyepiece; object finder; aim, goal
objeto /oβ'heto/ *m,* object; subject, theme; purpose; aim, goal. **sin o.,** without object; aimlessly
oblea /o'βlea/ *f,* seal, wafer
oblicuidad /oβlikui'ðað/ *f,* obliqueness
oblicuo /o'βlikuo/ *a* slanting, oblique
obligación /oβliga'θion; oβliga'sion/ *f,* obligation; *Com.* bond; *Com.* debenture; *pl* responsibilities; *Com.* liabilities
obligacionista /oβligaθio'nista; oβligasio'nista/ *mf Com.* bond holder, debenture holder
obligado /oβli'gaðo/ *m,* contractor (to a borough, etc.); *Mus.* obbligato
obligar /oβli'gar/ *vt* to compel, oblige, constrain; lay under an obligation; *Law.* mortgage; —*vr* bind oneself, promise
obligatorio /oβliga'torio/ *a* obligatory
oblongo /o'βloŋgo/ *a* oblong
oboe /o'βoe/ *m,* oboe; oboe player, oboist
óbolo /'oβolo/ *m,* obol, ancient Greek coin
obra /'oβra/ *f,* work; anything made; literary, artistic, scientific production; structure, construction; repair, alteration (to buildings, etc.); means, influence, power; labor, or time spent; action, behavior. **o. de caridad,** charitable act. **o. maestra,** masterpiece. **obras públicas,** public works. **poner por o.,** to put into effect; to set to work on. **o. de,** about, approximately
obrar /o'βrar/ *vt* to work; make, do; execute, perform; affect; construct, build; —*vi* be, exist (things); act, behave. **o. mal,** to behave badly, do wrong
obrero /o'βrero/ **(-ra)** *a* working —*n* worker; *pl* workers
obscenidad /oβsθeni'ðað; oβsseni'ðað/ *f,* obscenity
obsceno /oβs'θeno; oβs'seno/ *a* obscene
obsequiar /oβse'kiar/ *vt* to entertain, be attentive (to); give presents (to); court, make love to. **Me obsequia con un reloj,** He is presenting me with a watch
obsequio /oβ'sekio/ *m,* attention; gift; deference. **en o. de,** as a tribute to
obsequioso /oβse'kioso/ *a* obliging, courteous, attentive
observable /oβser'βaβle/ *a* observable
observación /oβserβa'θion; oβserβa'sion/ *f,* observation; remark
observador /oβserβa'ðor/ **(-ra)** *a* observing —*n* observer
observancia /oβser'βanθia; oβser'βansia/ *f,* observance; respect, reverence
observar /oβser'βar/ *vt* to notice; inspect, examine; fulfill; remark; watch, spy upon; *Astron.* observe
observatorio /oβserβa'torio/ *m,* observatory
obsesión /oβse'sion/ *f,* obsession
obsesionar /oβsesio'nar/ *vt* to obsess
obseso /oβ'seso/ *a* obsessed
obsidiana /oβsi'ðiana/ *f,* obsidian
obsolecer /oβsole'θer; oβsole'ser/ *vi* to obsolesce, become obsolete
obsoleto /oβso'leto/ *a* obsolete
obstáculo /oβs'takulo/ *m,* impediment; obstacle
obstante, no /oβs'tante, no/ *adv* in spite of; nevertheless
obstar /oβs'tar/ *vi* to impede, hinder
obstetra /oβs'tetra/ *mf* obstetrician
obstetricia /oβste'triθia; oβste'trisia/ *f,* obstetrics
obstinación /oβstina'θion; oβstina'sion/ *f,* obstinacy
obstinado /oβsti'naðo/ *a* obstinate, stubborn
obstinarse /oβsti'narse/ *vr* (*with en*) to persist in, insist on, be stubborn about
obstinaz /oβsti'naθ; oβsti'nas/ *a* obstinate
obstrucción /oβstruk'θion; oβstruk'sion/ *f,* obstruction
obstruccionismo /oβstrukθio'nismo; oβstruksio'nismo/ *m,* obstructionism
obstruccionista /oβstrukθio'nista; oβstruksio'nista/ *mf* obstructionist
obstruir /oβs'truir/ *vt irr* to obstruct; block; hinder; —*vr* become choked or stopped up (pipes, etc.). See **huir**
obtención /oβten'θion; oβten'sion/ *f,* obtainment; attainment, realization
obtener /oβte'ner/ *vt irr* to obtain; attain; maintain, preserve. See **tener**
obturador /oβtura'ðor/ *m,* stopper; shutter (of a camera)
obturar /oβtu'rar/ *vt* to stopper, plug; block, obstruct
obtuso /oβ'tuso/ *a* blunt, dull; (*Geom.* and *Fig.*) obtuse
obús /o'βus/ *m,* howitzer; *Mil.* shell
obviar /oβ'βiar/ *vt* to obviate
obvio /'oββio/ *a* obvious, evident, apparent
oca /'oka/ *f,* goose
ocasión /oka'sion/ *f,* occasion; opportunity; motive, cause; danger, risk; *Inf.* **asir la o. por la melena,** to take time by the forelock. **de o.,** second-hand
ocasional /okasio'nal/ *a* chance, fortuitous; occasional
ocasionar /okasio'nar/ *vt* to cause, occasion; excite, provoke; risk, endanger
ocaso /o'kaso/ *m,* sunset; west; dusk; decadence, decline
occidental /okθiðen'tal; oksiðen'tal/ *a* Western
occidente /okθi'ðente; oksi'ðente/ *m,* West, Occident
occipital /okθipi'tal; oksipi'tal/ *a Anat.* occipital
occiso /ok'θiso; ok'siso/ *a* murdered; killed
oceánico /oθe'aniko; ose'aniko/ *a* oceanic
océano /o'θeano; o'seano/ *m,* ocean; immensity, abundance
oceanografía /oθeanogra'fia; oseanogra'fia/ *f,* oceanography
ocelote /oθe'lote; ose'lote/ *m,* ocelot
ochava /o'tʃaβa/ *f,* eighth; *Eccl.* octave
ochavo /o'tʃaβo/ *m, Obs.* small Spanish copper coin
ochenta /o'tʃenta/ *a* and *m,* eighty; eightieth
ochentón /otʃen'ton/ **(-ona)** *n* octogenarian
ocho /'otʃo/ *a* eight; eighth. *m,* figure eight; playing card with eight pips; eight; eighth day (of the month). **las o.,** eight o'clock

ochocientos /otʃo'θientos; otʃo'sientos/ *a* and *m*, eight hundred; eight-hundredth
ocio /'oθio; 'osio/ *m*, leisure, idleness; *pl* pastimes; leisure time
ociosidad /oθiosi'ðað; osiosi'ðað/ *f*, idleness, laziness; leisure
ocioso /o'θioso; o'sioso/ **(-sa)** *a* idle; useless, worthless; unprofitable, fruitless —*n* idle fellow
ocre /'okre/ *m*, ocher
octágono /ok'tagono/ *m*, octagon
octava /ok'taβa/ *f*, octave
octaviano /okta'βiano/ *a* Octavian
octavo /ok'taβo/ *a* eighth. *m*, eighth. **en o.,** in octavo
octeto /ok'teto/ *m*, octet
octogenario /oktohe'nario/ **(-ia)** *a* and *n* octogenarian
octogésimo /okto'hesimo/ *a* eightieth
octubre /ok'tuβre/ *m*, October
óctuple /'oktuple/ *a* octuple, eightfold
ocular /oku'lar/ *a* ocular. *m*, eyepiece
oculista /oku'lista/ *mf* oculist
ocultación /okulta'θion; okulta'sion/ *f*, hiding, concealment
ocultamente /okulta'mente/ *adv* secretly
ocultar /okul'tar/ *vt* to hide, conceal; disguise; keep secret
ocultismo /okul'tismo/ *m*, occultism
oculto /o'kulto/ *a* hidden; secret; occult. **en o.,** secretly, quietly
ocupación /okupa'θion; okupa'sion/ *f*, occupancy; occupation, pursuit; employment, office, trade
ocupado /oku'paðo/ *a* occupied; busy
ocupante /oku'pante/ *m*, occupant
ocupar /oku'par/ *vt* to take possession of; obtain or hold (job); occupy, fill; inhabit; employ; hinder, embarrass; hold the attention (of); —*vr* (*with en*) be engaged in, be occupied with; (*with con*) concentrate on (a business affair, etc.)
ocurrencia /oku'rrenθia; oku'rrensia/ *f*, occurrence, incident; bright idea; witty remark
ocurrir /oku'rrir/ *vi* to anticipate; happen, take place; occur, strike (ideas)
oda /'oða/ *f*, ode
odalisca /oða'liska/ *f*, odalisk
odiar /o'ðiar/ *vt* to hate
odio /'oðio/ *m*, hatred; malevolence
odioso /o'ðioso/ *a* hateful, odious
odisea /oði'sea/ *f*, odyssey
odontología /oðontolo'hia/ *f*, odontology
odontólogo /oðon'tologo/ *m*, odontologist
odorífero /oðo'rifero/ *a* odoriferous, fragrant
odre /'oðre/ *m*, goatskin, wineskin; *Inf.* wine bibber
oesnorueste /oesno'rueste/ *m*, westnorthwest
oessudueste /oessu'ðueste/ *m*, westsouthwest
oeste /o'este/ *m*, west
ofender /ofen'der/ *vt* to ill-treat, hurt; offend, insult; anger, annoy; —*vr* be offended
ofendido /ofen'diðo/ *a* offended; resentful
ofensa /o'fensa/ *f*, injury, harm; offense, crime
ofensiva /ofen'siβa/ *f*, *Mil.* offensive. **tomar la o.,** to take the offensive
ofensivo /ofen'siβo/ *a* offensive
ofensor /ofen'sor/ **(-ra)** *n* offender
oferta /o'ferta/ *f*, offer; gift; proposal; *Com.* tender. **o. y demanda,** supply and demand
ofertorio /ofer'torio/ *m*, *Eccl.* offertory
oficial /ofi'θial; ofi'sial/ *a* official. *m*, official; officer; clerk; executioner; worker
oficiala /ofi'θiala; ofi'siala/ *f*, trained female worker
oficialidad /ofiθiali'ðað; ofisiali'ðað/ *f*, officialdom; officers
oficiar /ofi'θiar; ofi'siar/ *vt Eccl.* to celebrate or serve (mass); communicate officially, inform; *Inf.* (*with de*) act as
oficina /ofi'θina; ofi'sina/ *f*, workshop; office; pharmaceutical laboratory; *pl* cellars, basement (of a house)
oficinesco /ofiθi'nesko; ofisi'nesko/ *a* bureaucratic, red-tape
oficinista /ofiθi'nista; ofisi'nista/ *mf* clerk, office employee, office worker
oficio /o'fiθio; o'fisio/ *m*, occupation, employment; office, function, capacity; craft; operation; trade, business; official communication; office, bureau; *Eccl.* office. **Santo O.,** Holy Office. *Fig.* **buenos oficios,** good offices
oficiosidad /ofiθiosi'ðað; ofisiosi'ðað/ *f*, diligence, conscientiousness; helpfulness, friendliness; officiousness
oficioso /ofi'θioso; ofi'sioso/ *a* conscientious; helpful, useful; officious; meddlesome; unofficial, informal
ofrecer /ofre'θer; ofre'ser/ *vt irr* to offer; present; exhibit; consecrate, dedicate; —*vr* occur, suggest itself; volunteer. **¿Qué se le ofrece?** What do you require? What would you like? See **conocer**
ofrecimiento /ofreθi'miento; ofresi'miento/ *m*, offer, offering
ofrenda /o'frenda/ *f*, *Eccl.* offering; gift, present
oftalmología /oftalmolo'hia/ *f*, ophthalmology
oftalmólogo /oftal'mologo/ *m*, oculist, ophthalmologist
ofuscación /ofuska'θion; ofuska'sion/ *f.* **ofuscamiento** *m*, obfuscation, dazzle, dimness of sight; mental confusion, bewilderment
ofuscar /ofus'kar/ *vt* to dazzle, daze; dim, obfuscate; confuse, bewilder
ogro /'ogro/ *m*, ogre
ohmio /'omio/ *m*, ohm
oídas, de /o'iðas, de/ *adv* by hearsay
oído /o'iðo/ *m*, sense of hearing; ear. **de o.,** by ear. **decir al o.,** to whisper in a person's ear. *Mus.* **duro de o.,** hard of hearing; having a bad ear (for music). **estar sordo de un o.,** to be deaf in one ear
oidor /oi'ðor/ *m*, hearer; judge, *Obs.* magistrate
oir /o'ir/ *vt irr* to hear; give ear to, listen; understand —*Pres. Part.* **oyendo.** *Pres. Indic.* **oigo, oyes, oye, oyen.** *Preterite* **oyó, oyeron.** *Pres. Subjunc.* **oiga,** etc. —*Imperf. Subjunc.* **oyese,** etc.
oíslo /o'islo/ *mf Inf.* better half
ojal /o'hal/ *m*, buttonhole; slit, hole
¡ojalá! /oha'la/ *interj* If only that were so! God grant!
ojeada /ohe'aða/ *f*, glance
ojear /ohe'ar/ *vt* to look at, stare at; bewitch; scare, startle
ojera /o'hera/ *f*, dark shadow (under the eye); eye bath
ojeriza /ohe'riθa; ohe'risa/ *f*, ill-will, spite
ojeroso /ohe'roso/ *a* having dark shadows under the eyes, wan, haggard
ojete /o'hete/ *m*, eyelet
ojinegro /ohi'negro/ *a* black-eyed
ojiva /o'hiβa/ *f*, ogive
ojo /'oho/ *m*, eye; hole; slit; socket; keyhole; eye (of a needle); span (of a bridge); core (of a corn); attention, care; mesh; spring, stream; well (of a staircase); *pl* darling. **¡Ojo!** Take care! **o. avizor,** sharp watch; lynx eye. **Ojos que no ven, corazón que no siente,** Out of sight, out of mind. **o. saltón,** prominent, bulging eye. **o. vivo,** bright eye. **a o. de buen cubero,** at a guess. **a ojos vistas,** visibly; patently
ola /'ola/ *f*, billow; wave (atmospheric)
ole /'ole/ *m*, Andalusian dance
¡olé! /o'le/ *interj* Bravo!
oleada /ole'aða/ *f*, big wave, breaker; swell (of the sea); *Fig.* surge (of a crowd)
oleaginoso /oleahi'noso/ *a* oleaginous
oleaje /ole'ahe/ *m*, swell, surge, billowing
olear /ole'ar/ *vt* to administer extreme unction
óleo /'oleo/ *m*, oil; *Eccl.* holy oil (gen. *pl*). **al ó.,** in oils
oleoducto /oleo'ðukto/ *m*, oil pipeline
oler /o'ler/ *vt irr* to smell; guess, discover; pry, smell out; —*vi* smell; (*with prep a*) smell of; smack of, be reminiscent of —*Pres. Indic.* **huelo, hueles, huele, huelen.** *Pres. Subjunc.* **huela, huelas, huela, huelan**
olfatear /olfate'ar/ *vt* to sniff, snuff, smell; *Inf.* pry into
olfativo, olfatorio /olfa'tiβo, olfa'torio/ *a* olfactory
olfato /ol'fato/ *m*, sense of smell; shrewdness
olfatorio /olfa'torio/ *a* olfactory
oliente /o'liente/ **(mal)** *a* evil-smelling

oligarquía /oligar'kia/ *f*, oligarchy
oligárquico /oli'garkiko/ *a* oligarchic
olímpico /o'limpiko/ *a* Olympic; Olympian
oliva /o'liβa/ *f*, olive tree; olive; barn owl; peace
olivar /oli'βar/ *m*, olive grove
olivo /o'liβo/ *m*, olive tree
olla /'oʎa; 'oya/ *f*, stew pot; Spanish stew; whirlpool. **o. podrida,** rich Spanish stew containing bacon, fowl, meat, vegetables, ham, etc. **las ollas de Egipto,** the fleshpots of Egypt
olmeda /ol'meða/ *f*, **olmedo** *m*, elm grove
olmo /'olmo/ *m*, elm tree
olor /o'lor/ *m*, odor, scent, smell; hope, promise; suspicion, hint; reputation. **o. de santidad,** odor of sanctity
oloroso /olo'roso/ *a* fragrant, perfumed
olvidadizo /olβiða'ðiθo; olβiða'ðiso/ *a* forgetful
olvidar /olβi'ðar/ **(se)** *vt* and *vr* to forget; neglect, desert. **Se me olvidó el libro,** I forgot the book. **Me olvidé de lo pasado,** I forgot the past
olvido /ol'βiðo/ *m*, forgetfulness; indifference, neglect; oblivion
ombligo /om'βligo/ *m*, navel; *Fig.* core, center
ominoso /omi'noso/ *a* ominous
omisión /omi'sion/ *f*, omission; carelessness, negligence; neglect
omiso /o'miso/ *a* omitted; remiss; careless. **hacer caso o. de,** to set aside, ignore
omitir /omi'tir/ *vt* to omit
ómnibus /'omniβus/ *m*, bus
omnímodo /om'nimoðo/ *a* all-embracing
omnipotencia /omnipo'tenθia; omnipo'tensia/ *f*, omnipotence
omnipotente /omnipo'tente/ *a* omnipotent, all-powerful
omnisciencia /omnis'θienθia; omnis'siensia/ *f*, omniscience
omniscio /om'nisθio; om'nissio/ *a* omniscient
omnívoro /om'niβoro/ *a* omnivorous
omoplato /omo'plato/ *m*, scapula, shoulder blade
once /'onθe; 'onse/ *a* eleven; eleventh. *m*, eleven; eleventh (of the month). **las o.,** eleven o'clock
onceno /on'θeno; on'seno/ *a* eleventh
onda /'onda/ *f*, wave; *Fig.* flicker (of flames); *Sew.* scallop; *Phys.* wave; ripple; *pl* waves (in hair). *Radio.* **o. corta,** short wave. **o. etérea,** ether wave. **o. sonora,** sound wave
ondeado /onde'aðo/ *a* undulating; wavy; scalloped
ondeante /onde'ante/ *a* waving; flowing
ondear /onde'ar/ *vi* to wave; ripple; undulate; roll (of the sea); float, flutter, stream; *Sew.* scallop; *—vr* swing, sway
ondeo /on'deo/ *m*, waving; undulation
ondina /on'dina/ *f*, undine, water sprite
ondulación /ondula'θion; ondula'sion/ *f*, undulation; wave; wriggling; twisting. **o. permanente,** permanent wave, perm
ondulado /ondu'laðo/ *a* wavy; undulating; scalloped
ondular /ondu'lar/ *vi* to writhe, squirm, wriggle; twist; coil; *—vt* wave (in hair)
oneroso /one'roso/ *a* onerous, heavy; troublesome
ónice /'oniθe; 'onise/ *m*, onyx
onomástico /ono'mastiko/ *a* onomastic. **día o.,** saint's day
onomatopeya /onomato'peia/ *f*, onomatopoeia
onza /'onθa; 'onsa/ *f*, ounce. **por onzas,** by ounces; sparingly
onzavo /on'θaβo; on'saβo/ *a* and *m*, eleventh
opacidad /opaθi'ðað; opasi'ðað/ *f*, opacity; obscurity; gloom
opaco /o'pako/ *a* opaque; dark; gloomy, sad
opalescente /opales'θente; opales'sente/ *a* opalescent
opalino /opa'lino/ *a* opaline
ópalo /'opalo/ *m*, opal
opción /op'θion; op'sion/ *f*, option; choice, selection; *Law.* option
ópera /'opera/ *f*, opera
operación /opera'θion; opera'sion/ *f*, *Surg.* operation; execution, performance; *Com.* transaction
operar /ope'rar/ *vt Surg.* to operate; *—vi* act, have an effect; operate, control; *Com.* transact
operario /ope'rario/ **(-ia)** *n* worker, hand; operator; mechanic
opereta /ope'reta/ *f*, operetta, light opera
opinar /opi'nar/ *vi* to have or form an opinion, think; judge, consider
opinión /opi'nion/ *f*, opinion, view; reputation
opio /'opio/ *m*, opium. **fumadero de o.,** opium den
opíparo /o'piparo/ *a* magnificent, sumptuous (banquets, etc.)
oponer /opo'ner/ *vt irr* to oppose; resist, withstand; protest against; *—vr* oppose; be contrary or hostile (to); face, be opposite; object (to), set oneself against; compete (in public exams.). See **poner**
oporto /o'porto/ *m*, port (wine)
oportunidad /oportuni'ðað/ *f*, opportunity, occasion
oportunismo /oportu'nismo/ *m*, opportunism
oportunista /oportu'nista/ *a* and *mf* opportunist
oportuno /opor'tuno/ *a* opportune, timely
oposición /oposi'θion; oposi'sion/ *f*, opposition; resistance; antagonism; public competitive exam for a post; (*Astron. Polit.*) opposition
opositor /oposi'tor/ **(-ra)** *n* opponent; competitor
opresión /opre'sion/ *f*, oppression; hardship; pressure. **o. de pecho,** difficulty in breathing
opresor /opre'sor/ **(-ra)** *a* oppressive *—n* oppressor
oprimir /opri'mir/ *vt* to oppress; treat harshly; press, crush; choke
oprobio /o'proβio/ *m*, opprobrium
optar /op'tar/ *vt* to take possession of; (*with por*) choose
óptica /'optika/ *f*, *Phys.* optics; peepshow
óptico /'optiko/ *a* optic, optical. *m*, optician
optimismo /opti'mismo/ *m*, optimism
optimista /opti'mista/ *mf* optimist *—a* optimistic
óptimo /'optimo/ *a superl* **bueno** best, optimal, optimum
opugnar /opug'nar/ *vt* to resist violently; *Mil.* assault, attack; impugn, challenge
opulencia /opu'lenθia; opu'lensia/ *f*, opulence, riches; excess, superabundance
opulento /opu'lento/ *a* opulent, rich
opúsculo /o'puskulo/ *m*, monograph, opuscule
oquedad /oke'ðað/ *f*, hollow, cavity; superficiality, banality
ora /'ora/ *adv* now
oración /ora'θion; ora'sion/ *f*, oration, speech; prayer; *Gram.* sentence
oráculo /o'rakulo/ *m*, oracle
orador /ora'ðor/ **(-ra)** *n* orator; speech maker. *m*, preacher
oral /o'ral/ *a* oral; verbal; buccal
orangután /oraŋgu'tan/ *m*, orangutan
orar /o'rar/ *vi* to harangue, make an oration; pray; *—vt* request, beg
orate /o'rate/ *mf* lunatic
oratoria /ora'toria/ *f*, oratory, eloquence
oratorio /ora'torio/ *a* oratorical. *m*, oratory, chapel; *Mus.* oratorio
orbe /'orβe/ *m*, sphere; orb; world
órbita /'orβita/ *f*, *Astron.* orbit; *Fig.* sphere; *Anat.* orbit, eye socket
Órcades, las /'orkaðes, las/ the Orkneys
ordalía /orða'lia/ *f*, (medieval hist.) ordeal
orden /'orðen/ *mf* order, mode of arrangement; succession, sequence; group; system; orderliness, neatness; coherence, plan; *Eccl.* order, brotherhood; (*Zool. Bot.*) group, class; *Archit.* order; *Math.* degree. *f*, precept, command; *Com.* order; *pl Eccl.* ordination. (*Mil. Naut.*) **o. de batalla,** battle array. **o. de caballería,** order of knighthood. **o. del día,** order of the day. *Eccl.* **dar órdenes,** to ordain. **en o.,** in order; with regard (to). **por su o.,** in its turn; successively
ordenación /orðena'θion; orðena'sion/ *f*, order, orderly arrangement, disposition; ordinance, precept; *Eccl.* ordination
ordenador /orðena'ðor/ *m Spain* computer
ordenamiento /orðena'miento/ *m*, ordaining; ordinance; edict

ordenancista /orðenan'θista; orðenan'sista/ *mf Mil.* martinet; disciplinarian

ordenanza /orðe'nanθa; orðe'nansa/ *f,* order, method; command, instruction; ordinance, regulation (gen. *pl*). *m, Mil.* orderly

ordenar /orðe'nar/ *vt* to put in order, arrange; command, give instructions to; decree; direct, regulate; *Eccl.* ordain; *—vr* (*with de*) *Eccl.* be ordained as

ordeñadero /orðeɲa'ðero/ *m,* milk pail

ordeñar /orðe'ɲar/ *vt* to milk

ordinal /orði'nal/ *a* ordinal. *m,* ordinal number

ordinariez /orðina'rieθ; orðina'ries/ *f,* rudeness, uncouthness; vulgarity

ordinario /orði'nario/ *a* ordinary, usual; vulgar, coarse, uncultured; rude; commonplace, average, mediocre. *m, Eccl.* ordinary; carrier; courier. **de o.,** usually, ordinarily

orear /ore'ar/ *vt* to ventilate; *—vr* dry; air; take the air

orégano /o'regano/ *m,* wild marjoram

oreja /o'reha/ *f,* external ear; lug; tab, flap; tongue (of a shoe). *Inf.* **con las orejas caídas,** down in the mouth, depressed

orejera /ore'hera/ *f,* earflap; mold board (of a plow)

orejudo /ore'huðo/ *a* large- or long-eared

oreo /o'reo/ *m,* zephyr; ventilation; airing

orfanato /orfa'nato/ *m,* orphanage, orphan asylum

orfandad /orfan'dað/ *f,* orphanhood; defenselessness, lack of protection

orfebre /or'feβre/ *mf* gold- or silversmith

orfebrería /orfeβre'ria/ *f,* gold- or silverwork

orfeón /orfe'on/ *m,* choral society

organdí /organ'di/ *m,* organdy

orgánico /or'ganiko/ *a* organic; harmonious; *Fig.* organized

organillero /organi'ʎero; organi'yero/ **(-ra)** *n* organ grinder

organillo /orga'niʎo; orga'niyo/ *m,* barrel organ

organismo /orga'nismo/ *m,* organism; organization, association

organista /orga'nista/ *mf* organist

organización /organiθa'θion; organisa'sion/ *f,* organization; order, arrangement

organizador /organiθa'ðor; organisa'ðor/ **(-ra)** *a* organizing *—n* organizer

organizar /organi'θar; organi'sar/ *vt* to organize; regulate; constitute

órgano /'organo/ *m, Mus.* organ; (*Anat. Bot.*) organ; means, agency. **o. de manubrio,** barrel organ

orgasmo /or'gasmo/ *m,* orgasm

orgía /or'hia/ *f,* orgy

orgullo /or'guʎo; or'guyo/ *m,* pride; arrogance

orgulloso /orgu'ʎoso; orgu'yoso/ *a* proud; haughty

orientación /orienta'θion; orienta'sion/ *f,* orientation; exposure, prospect; bearings

oriental /orien'tal/ *a* Oriental, Eastern. *mf* Oriental

orientalismo /orienta'lismo/ *m,* Orientalism

orientalista /orienta'lista/ *mf* Orientalist

orientar /orien'tar/ *vt* to orientate; *—vr* find one's bearings; familiarize oneself (with)

oriente /o'riente/ *m,* Orient, the East; luster (of pearls); youth, childhood; origin, source

orificio /ori'fiθio; ori'fisio/ *m,* orifice; hole

oriflama /ori'flama/ *f,* oriflamme; standard, flag

origen /o'rihen/ *m,* origin, source, root; stock, extraction; reason, genesis. **dar o. a,** to give rise to. **país de o.,** native land

original /orihi'nal/ *a* original; earliest, primitive; new, first-hand; novel, fresh; inventive, creative; eccentric; quaint. *m,* original manuscript; original; sitter (for portraits); eccentric

originalidad /orihinali'ðað/ *f,* originality

originar /orihi'nar/ *vt* to cause, originate; invent; *—vr* spring from, originate (in)

originario /orihi'nario/ *a* original, primary; primitive; native (of)

orilla /o'riʎa; o'riya/ *f,* limit, edge; hem, border; selvage; shore, margin; bank (of a river, etc.); sidewalk; brink, edge. **a la o.,** on the brink; nearly

orillar /ori'ʎar; ori'yar/ *vt* to settle, arrange, conclude; *—vi* reach the shore or bank; *Sew.* leave a hem; *Sew.* border; leave a selvage on cloth

orillo /o'riʎo; o'riyo/ *m,* selvage (of cloth)

orín /o'rin/ *m,* rust; *pl* urine

orinal /ori'nal/ *m,* chamber pot, urinal

orinar /ori'nar/ *vi* to urinate

oriundo /o'riundo/ *a* native (of); derived (from)

orla /'orla/ *f,* border, fringe; selvage (of cloth, garments); ornamental border (on diplomas, etc.)

orlar /or'lar/ *vt* to border; edge, trim

ornamentación /ornamenta'θion; ornamenta'sion/ *f,* ornamentation

ornamental /ornamen'tal/ *a* ornamental

ornamentar /ornamen'tar/ *vt* to ornament; embellish

ornamento /orna'mento/ *m,* ornament; decoration; gift, virtue, talent; *pl Eccl.* vestments

ornar /or'nar/ *vt* to ornament, adorn, embellish

ornato /or'nato/ *m,* decoration, ornament

ornitología /ornitolo'hia/ *f,* ornithology

ornitológico /ornito'lohiko/ *a* ornithological

ornitólogo /orni'tologo/ *m,* ornithologist

oro /'oro/ *m,* gold; gold coins or jewelery; *Fig.* riches; *pl* diamonds (cards). **o. batido,** gold leaf. **o. en polvo,** gold dust. *Fig.* **como un o.,** shining with cleanliness. **el as de oros,** the ace of diamonds

orondo /o'rondo/ *a* hollow; *Inf.* pompous; *Inf.* swollen, spongy

oropel /oro'pel/ *m,* brass foil; showy, cheap thing; trinket; tinsel

oropéndola /oro'pendola/ *f,* oriole

orquesta /or'kesta/ *f,* orchestra

orquestación /orkesta'θion; orkesta'sion/ *f,* orchestration

orquestal /orkes'tal/ *a* orchestral

orquestar /orkes'tar/ *vt* to orchestrate

orquídea /or'kiðea/ *f,* orchid

ortega /or'tega/ *f, Ornith.* grouse

ortiga /or'tiga/ *f, Bot.* nettle

orto /'orto/ *m,* rising (of sun, stars)

ortodoxia /orto'ðoksia/ *f,* orthodoxy

ortodoxo /orto'ðokso/ *a* orthodox

ortografía /ortogra'fia/ *f,* orthography

ortográfico /orto'grafiko/ *a* orthographical

ortopedia /orto'peðia/ *f,* orthopedics

ortopédico /orto'peðiko/ **(-ca)** *a* orthopedic *—n* orthopedist

ortopedista /ortope'ðista/ *mf* orthopedist

oruga /o'ruga/ *f,* caterpillar

orzuelo /or'θuelo; or'suelo/ *m, Med.* sty; trap (for wild animals)

os /os/ *pers pron 2nd pl mf dat* and *acc* of **vos** and **vosotros** you, to you

osa /'osa/ *f,* she-bear; *Astron.* **O. mayor,** Big Bear; **O. menor,** Little Bear

osadía /osa'ðia/ *f,* boldness, audacity

osado /o'saðo/ *a* daring, bold

osamenta /osa'menta/ *f,* skeleton; bones (of a skeleton)

osar /o'sar/ *vi* to dare; risk, venture

osario /o'sario/ *m,* charnel house, ossuary

oscilación /osθila'θion; ossila'sion/ *f,* oscillation

oscilante /osθi'lante; ossi'lante/ *a* oscillating

oscilar /osθi'lar; ossi'lar/ *vi* to oscillate, sway; hesitate, vacillate

ósculo /'oskulo/ *m,* kiss, osculation

oscurantismo /oskuran'tismo/ *m,* obscurantism

oscurantista /oskuran'tista/ *a* and *mf* obscurantist

oscurecer /oskure'θer; oskure'ser/ *vt irr* to darken; *Fig.* tarnish, dim, sully; confuse, bewilder; express obscurely; *Art.* shade; *—vr* grow dark; *—vr* cloud over (sky); *Inf.* disappear (things, gen. by theft). See **conocer**

oscuridad /oskuri'ðað/ *f,* darkness; gloom, blackness; humbleness; obscurity, abstruseness

oscuro /os'kuro/ *a* dark; humble, unknown; abstruse, involved; obscure; uncertain, dangerous. **a oscuras,** in the dark; ignorant

óseo /'oseo/ *a* osseous

osera /o'sera/ *f,* bear's den

osezno /o'seθno; o'sesno/ *m,* bear cub

osificación /osifika'θion; osifika'sion/ *f,* ossification

osificarse /osifi'karse/ *vr* to ossify
ósmosis /'osmosis/ *f,* osmosis
oso /'oso/ *m,* bear. **o. blanco,** polar bear
Ostende /os'tende/ Ostend
ostensible /osten'siβle/ *a* ostensible; obvious
ostensión /osten'sion/ *f,* show, display, manifestation
ostensivo /osten'siβo/ *a* ostensive
ostentación /ostenta'θion; ostenta'sion/ *f,* manifestation; ostentation
ostentar /osten'tar/ *vt* to exhibit, show; boast, show off
ostentoso /osten'toso/ *a* magnificent, showy, ostentatious
osteología /osteolo'hia/ *f,* osteology
osteópata /oste'opata/ *mf* osteopath
osteopatía /osteopa'tia/ *f,* osteopathy
ostra /'ostra/ *f,* oyster. **vivero de ostras,** oyster bed
ostracismo /ostra'θismo; ostra'sismo/ *m,* ostracism
otear /ote'ar/ *vt* to observe; look on at
otero /o'tero/ *m,* hill, height, eminence
otología /otolo'hia/ *f,* otology
otólogo /o'tologo/ *m,* otologist
otomana /oto'mana/ *f,* ottoman, couch
otomano /oto'mano/ *a* Ottoman
otoñal /oto'ɲal/ *a* autumnal, autumn, fall
otoño /o'toɲo/ *m,* autumn, fall
otorgamiento /otorga'miento/ *m,* granting; consent, approval; license, award
otorgar /otor'gar/ *vt* to grant; concede, approve; *Law.* grant, stipulate, execute
otro /'otro/ **(-ra)** *a* other, another —*n* another one
otrosí /otro'si/ *adv* besides, moreover
ovación /oβa'θion; oβa'sion/ *f,* ovation, triumph; applause
ovacionar /oβaθio'nar; oβasio'nar/ *vt* to applaud
oval /o'βal/ *a* oval
óvalo /'oβalo/ *m,* oval
ovario /o'βario/ *m,* ovary
oveja /o'βeha/ *f,* ewe
ovejuno /oβe'huno/ *a* relating to ewes or sheep, sheep-like
ovillar /oβi'ʎar; oβi'yar/ *vi* to wind thread into a ball; —*vr* curl up; huddle
ovillo /o'βiʎo; o'βiyo/ *m,* ball, bobbin (of thread); tangled heap (of things)
ovíparo /o'βiparo/ *a* oviparous
OVNI /'oβni/ *m,* UFO
ovulación /oβula'θion; oβula'sion/ *f,* ovulation
óvulo /'oβulo/ *m,* ovule
oxidación /oksiða'θion; oksiða'sion/ *f,* oxidation
oxidar /oksi'ðar/ *vt* oxidize; —*vr* become oxidized
óxido /'oksiðo/ *m,* oxide. **ó. de carbono,** carbon monoxide. **ó. de cinc,** zinc oxide
oxígeno /ok'siheno/ *m,* oxygen
oyente /o'iente/ *mf* hearer; *pl* audience
ozono /o'θono; o'sono/ *m,* ozone

P

pabellón /paβe'ʎon; paβe'yon/ *m,* pavilion; colors, flag; bell tent. **p. británico,** Union Jack. **p. de reposo,** rest home. **en p.,** stacked (of arms)
pábulo /'paβulo/ *m,* food; *Fig.* pabulum
pacedero /paθe'ðero; pase'ðero/ *a Agr.* grazing, meadow
pacer /pa'θer; pa'ser/ *vi irr Agr.* to graze; *—vt* nibble away; eat away. See **nacer**
paciencia /pa'θienθia; pa'siensia/ *f,* patience
paciente /pa'θiente; pa'siente/ *a* patient; long-suffering; complacent. *mf Med.* patient
pacienzudo /paθien'θuðo; pasien'suðo/ *a* extremely patient or long-suffering
pacificación /paθifika'θion; pasifika'sion/ *f,* pacification; serenity, peace of mind
pacificador /paθifika'ðor; pasifika'ðor/ **(-ra)** *a* peace making; pacifying *—n* peace maker
pacificar /paθifi'kar; pasifi'kar/ *vt* to pacify; *—vi* make peace; *—vr* grow quiet, become calm (sea, etc.)
pacífico /pa'θifiko; pa'sifiko/ *a* pacific, meek, mild; peace-loving, peaceful. **el Océano P.,** the Pacific Ocean
pacifismo /paθi'fismo; pasi'fismo/ *m,* pacifism
pacifista /paθi'fista; pasi'fista/ *a* and *mf* pacifist
pacotilla /pako'tiʎa; pako'tiya/ *f,* goods. *Inf.* **hacer su p.,** to make one's packet or fortune. **ser de p.,** to be poor stuff; be jerry-built (of houses)
pactar /pak'tar/ *vt* to stipulate, arrange; contract
pacto /'pakto/ *m,* agreement, contract; pact
padecer /paðe'θer; paðe'ser/ *vt irr* to suffer; feel keenly; experience, undergo; tolerate. **p. desnudez,** to go unclothed. **p. hambre,** to go hungry. See **conocer**
padecimiento /paðeθi'miento; paðesi'miento/ *m,* suffering
padrastro /pa'ðrastro/ *m,* stepfather; cruel father; *Fig.* impediment, obstacle; hangnail
padrazo /pa'ðraθo; pa'ðraso/ *m, Inf.* indulgent father
padre /'paðre/ *m,* father; stallion; head (of the family, etc.); *Eccl.* father; genesis, source; author, creator; *pl* parents; ancestors. **p. adoptivo,** foster father. **p. de familia,** paterfamilias. **P. Eterno,** Eternal Father. **p. nuestro,** Lord's Prayer. **P. Santo,** Holy Father, the Pope
padrear /paðre'ar/ *vi* to take after one's father; *Zool.* reproduce, breed
padrino /pa'ðrino/ *m,* godfather; sponsor; second (in duels, etc.); patron; best man
padrón /pa'ðron/ *m,* census; pattern, model; memorial stone
paella /pa'eʎa; pa'eya/ *f, Cul.* savory rice dish of shellfish, chicken, and meat
paga /'paga/ *f,* payment; amends, restitution; pay; payment of fine; reciprocity (in love, etc.)
pagadero /paga'ðero/ *a* payable. *m,* date and place when payment is due
pagador /paga'ðor/ **(-ra)** *n* payer. *m,* teller; wages clerk; paymaster
pagaduría /pagaðu'ria/ *f,* pay office
paganismo /paga'nismo/ *m,* paganism; heathenism
pagano /pa'gano/ **(-na)** *a* and *n* pagan; heathen
pagar /pa'gar/ *vt* to pay; make restitution, expiate; return, requite (love, etc.); *—vr* (*with de*) become fond of; be proud of. **p. adelantado,** to prepay. *Com.* **p. al contado,** to pay cash. **p. la casa,** to pay the rent (for one's residence)
pagaré /paga're/ *m, Com.* promissory note, I.O.U.
página /'pahina/ *f,* page (of a book); episode, occurrence
paginación /pahina'θion; pahina'sion/ *f,* pagination
paginar /pahi'nar/ *vt* to paginate
pago /'pago/ *m,* payment; recompense, reward; region of vineyards, olive groves, etc.
pagoda /pa'goða/ *f,* pagoda, temple; idol
paguro /pa'guro/ *m,* hermit crab
pailebote /paile'βote/ *m,* schooner
país /pa'is/ *m,* country, nation; region; *Art.* landscape. **del p.,** typical of the country of origin (gen. of food)
paisaje /pai'sahe/ *m,* countryside; landscape, scenery
paisajista, paisista /paisa'hista, pai'sista/ *mf* landscape painter
paisano /pai'sano/ **(-na)** *n* compatriot; peasant; civilian
Países Bajos, los /pa'ises 'bahos, los/ the Low Countries, the Netherlands
paja /'paha/ *f,* straw; chaff; trash; *Fig.* padding. **ver la p. en el ojo del vecino y no la viga en el nuestro,** to see the mote in our neighbor's eye and not the beam in our own
pajar /pa'har/ *m,* barn
pájara /'pahara/ *f,* hen (bird); kite (toy); *Inf.* jay; prostitute. **p. pinta,** game of forfeits
pajarear /pahare'ar/ *vt* to snare birds; loaf, idle about
pajarera /paha'rera/ *f,* aviary
pajarero /paha'rero/ *m,* bird catcher or seller *—a Inf.* frivolous, giddy; *Inf.* gaudy (colors)
pajarita /paha'rita/ *f,* bow tie
pájaro /'paharo/ *m,* bird. **p. bobo,** penguin. **p. carpintero,** woodpecker. *Fig. Inf.* **p. gordo,** big gun. **p. mosca,** hummingbird
pajarota /paha'rota/ *f, Inf.* canard, false report
paje /'pahe/ *m,* page; *Naut.* cabin boy
pajera /pa'hera/ *f,* hayloft
pajizo /pa'hiθo; pa'hiso/ *a* made of straw; covered or thatched with straw; strawcolored
pala /'pala/ *f,* paddle; blade (of an oar); shovel; spade; baker's peel (long-handled shovel); cutting edge of a spade, hoe, etc.; *Sports.* racket; vamp, upper (of a shoe); pelota or jai alai racket; tanner's knife; *Inf.* guile, cunning; cleverness, dexterity. **p. de hélice,** propeller blade. **p. para pescado,** fish server. *Inf.* **corta p.,** ignoramus; blockhead
palabra /pa'laβra/ *f,* word; power of speech; eloquence; offer, promise; *pl* magic formula, spell. **p. de clave,** code word. **p. de matrimonio,** promise of marriage. **p. de rey,** inviolable promise. **palabras cruzadas,** crossword puzzle. **bajo p. de,** under promise of. **cuatro palabras,** a few words; short conversation. **de p.,** verbally, by word of mouth. **dirigir la p. a,** to address, speak to. **faltar a su p.,** to break one's promise. **llevar la p.,** to be spokesperson. **medias palabras,** half-words; hint, insinuation. **su p. empeñada,** one's solemn word. **tener la p.,** to have the right to speak (in meetings, etc.) (e.g. *El señor Martínez tiene la p.,* Mr. Martinez has the floor)
palabrería /palaβre'ria/ *f,* verbosity, wordiness
palabrota /pala'βrota/ *f, Inf.* coarse language; long word
palaciego /pala'θiego; pala'siego/ **(-ga)** *a* pertaining to palaces; *Fig.* courtesan *—n* courtier
palacio /pa'laθio; pa'lasio/ *m,* palace; mansion
palada /pa'laða/ *f,* shovelful, spadeful; oar stroke
paladar /pala'ðar/ *m, Anat.* palate; taste; discernment, sensibility
paladear /palaðe'ar/ *vt* to taste with pleasure, savor; enjoy, relish
paladín /pala'ðin/ *m,* paladin
paladino /pala'ðino/ *a* public, clear, open
palafrén /pala'fren/ *m,* palfrey
palafrenero /palafre'nero/ *m,* groom; stablehand
palanca /pa'lanka/ *f, Mech.* lever; handle; bar; (high) diving board. **p. de arranque,** starting gear. **p. de cambio de velocidad,** gear-changing lever. **p. de mando,** control stick
palangana /palaŋ'gana/ *f,* washbasin
palanganero /palaŋga'nero/ *m,* washstand
palanqueta /palan'keta/ *f, dim* small lever; jimmy
palastro /pa'lastro/ *m,* sheet iron or steel
palatinado /palati'naðo/ *m,* Palatinate
palatino /pala'tino/ *a* palatine
palatizar /palati'θar; palati'sar/ *vt* to palatilize

palazón /pala'θon; pala'son/ *f*, woodwork
palco /'palko/ *m*, *Theat.* box; stand, raised platform, enclosure. **p. de platea,** orchestra
palenque /pa'lenke/ *m*, enclosure; stand; platform; palisade
paleografía /paleogra'fia/ *f*, paleography
paleógrafo /pale'ografo/ *m*, paleographer
paleolítico /paleo'litiko/ *a* paleolithic
paleología /paleolo'hia/ *f*, paleology
paleontología /paleontolo'hia/ *f*, paleontology
Palestina /pales'tina/ Palestine
palestra /pa'lestra/ *f*, tilt yard
paleta /pa'leta/ *f*, *dim* little shovel; trowel; *Art.* palette; fireplace shovel; mason's trowel; *Anat.* shoulder blade; blade (of a propeller, ventilator, etc.); *Chem.* spatula
paliación /palia'θion; palia'sion/ *f*, palliation; excuse
paliar /pa'liar/ *vt* to dissemble, excuse; palliate, mitigate
paliativo /palia'tiβo/ *a* palliative; extenuating
palidecer /paliðe'θer; paliðe'ser/ *vi irr* to turn pale. See **conocer**
palidez /pali'ðeθ; pali'ðes/ *f*, pallor, paleness
pálido /'paliðo/ *a* pale, pallid
paliducho /pali'ðutʃo/ *a* somewhat pale, palish; sallow
palillo /pa'liʎo; pa'liyo/ *m*, *dim* small stick; toothpick; bobbin (for lacemaking); drumstick; *Fig.* chatter; *pl* castanets
palimpsesto /palimp'sesto/ *m*, palimpsest
palinodia /pali'noðia/ *f*, *Lit.* palinode. **cantar la p.,** to eat one's words, recant
palio /'palio/ *m*, Greek mantle; cape; *Eccl.* pallium; canopy, awning
palique /pa'like/ *m*, *Inf.* chat. **estar de p.,** to be having a chat
paliquear /palike'ar/ *vi* to chat
paliza /pa'liθa; pa'lisa/ *f*, caning, beating
palizada /pali'θaða; pali'saða/ *f*, paling, fence; palisade, stockade. **p. de tablas,** hoarding
palma /'palma/ *f*, palm tree; palm leaf; date palm; palm (of the hand); hand; triumph. **llevarse la p.,** to bear away the palm; take the cake
palmada /pal'maða/ *f*, slap; *pl* hand-clapping
palmado /pal'maðo/ *a* web (of feet); palmy
palmar /pal'mar/ *a* palmaceous; palmar; clear, obvious. *m*, palm grove
palmatoria /palma'toria/ *f*, ferule, ruler; candlestick
palmear /palme'ar/ *vi* to clap hands
palmera /pal'mera/ *f*, palm tree
palmeta /pal'meta/ *f*, ferrule, ruler
palmetazo /palme'taθo; palme'taso/ *m*, slap on the hand with a ruler; *Fig.* slap in the face
Palmira /pal'mira/ Palmyra
palmo /'palmo/ *m*, span; hand's breadth. **p. a p.,** inch by inch, piecemeal
palmotear /palmote'ar/ *vt* to applaud; clap
palo /'palo/ *m*, stick; rod; pole; timber, wood; wooden log; *Naut.* mast; blow with a stick; execution by hanging; suit (of playing cards); fruit stalk; *Herald.* pale. **p. de Campeche,** logwood. **p. de hule,** rubber tree. **p. de rosa,** tulipwood. *Naut.* **p. mayor,** mainmast. *Naut.* **a p. seco,** under bare poles. **de tal p., tal astilla,** a chip off the old block; like father like son. **estar del mismo p.,** to be of the same mind, agree
paloma /pa'loma/ *f*, dove; pigeon; gentle person; *pl Naut.* white horses. **p. buchona,** pouter pigeon. **p. mensajera,** carrier pigeon. **p. torcaz,** wood pigeon
palomar /palo'mar/ *m*, dovecote; pigeon loft
palomero /palo'mero/ **(-ra)** *n* pigeon fancier; pigeon dealer
palomino /palo'mino/ *m*, young pigeon
palomo /pa'lomo/ *m*, male pigeon; wood pigeon
palotes /pa'lotes/ *m pl*, drumsticks; pothooks (in writing)
palpabilidad /palpaβili'ðað/ *f*, palpability
palpable /pal'paβle/ *a* palpable, tangible
palpación /palpa'θion; palpa'sion/ *f*, *Med.* palpation
palpar /pal'par/ *vt* to palpate, examine by touch; grope, walk by touch; *Fig.* see clearly
palpitación /palpita'θion; palpita'sion/ *f*, beating (of a heart); *Med.* palpitation; convulsive movement
palpitante /palpi'tante/ *a* palpitating; quivering; beating; (of a question) burning
palpitar /palpi'tar/ *vi* to beat (heart); throb, palpitate; shudder, move convulsively; *Fig.* manifest itself (passions, etc.)
palpo /'palpo/ *m*, palp, feeler
palúdico /pa'luðiko/ *a* marshy, swampy; malarial
paludismo /palu'ðismo/ *m*, malaria; paludism
palurdo /pa'lurðo/ **(-da)** *a Inf.* gross, rude, boorish —*n* boor
palustre /pa'lustre/ *m*, mason's trowel —*a* marshy, swampy
pamela /pa'mela/ *f*, wide-brimmed straw sailor (woman's hat)
pamema /pa'mema/ *f*, *Inf.* unimportant trifle; *Inf.* caress
pampa /'pampa/ *f*, pampa, treeless plain
pámpano /'pampano/ *m*, young vine shoot; vine leaf
pamplina /pam'plina/ *f*, *Inf.* nonsense, rubbish
pan /pan/ *m*, bread; loaf; *Cul.* piecrust; *Fig.* food; wheat; gold leaf; *pl* cereals. **p. ázimo,** unleavened bread. **p. de oro,** gold leaf. **llamar al p. p. y al vino vino,** to call a spade a spade. **venderse como p. bendito,** to sell like hot cakes
pana /'pana/ *f*, velveteen, velours
panacea /pana'θea; pana'sea/ *f*, panacea; cure-all
panadería /panaðe'ria/ *f*, bakery trade or shop; bakery
panadero /pana'ðero/ **(-ra)** *n* baker. *m pl*, Spanish dance
panadizo /pana'ðiθo; pana'ðiso/ *m*, *Med.* whitlow; *Inf.* ailing person, crock
panal /pa'nal/ *m*, honeycomb; wasp's nest
Panamá /pana'ma/ Panama
panameño /pana'meɲo/ **(-ña)** *a* and *n* Panamanian
panamericanismo /panamerika'nismo/ *m*, pan-Americanism
panarra /pa'narra/ *m*, *Inf.* simpleton
páncreas /'pankreas/ *m*, pancreas
pancreático /pankre'atiko/ *a* pancreatic
panda /'panda/ *f*, gallery of a cloister. *mf Zool.* panda
pandémico /pan'demiko/ *a* pandemic
pandemónium /pande'monium/ *m*, pandemonium
pandereta /pande'reta/ *f*, tambourine
pandero /pan'dero/ *m*, tambourine; *Inf.* windbag
pandilla /pan'diʎa; pan'diya/ *f*, league, group; gang (of burglars, etc.); party, crowd, band
pane /'pane/ *f*, breakdown
panecillo /pane'θiʎo; pane'siyo/ *m*, *dim* roll (of bread)
panegírico /pane'hiriko/ *a* and *m*, panegyric
panegirista /panehi'rista/ *mf* panegyrist; eulogizer
panel /pa'nel/ *m*, panel
panetela /pane'tela/ *f*, panada
pánfilo /'panfilo/ **(-la)** *a* sluggish, phlegmatic, slow-moving —*n* sluggard
panfleto /pan'fleto/ *m*, pamphlet
paniaguado /pania'guaðo/ *m*, servant; favorite, protégé
pánico /'paniko/ *a* and *m*, panic
panoja /pa'noha/ *f*, *Bot.* panicle; *Bot.* ear, beard, awn
panoli /pa'noli/ *a Inf.* doltish, stupid
panoplia /pa'noplia/ *f*, panoply; collection of arms
panorama /pano'rama/ *m*, panorama; view
panorámico /pano'ramiko/ *a* panoramic
pantalla /pan'taʎa; pan'taya/ *f*, lampshade; face screen; movie screen; shade, reflector
pantalón /panta'lon/ *m*, pant, trouser (gen. *pl*); knickers. **p. de corte,** striped trousers. **pantalones bombachos,** plus fours
pantano /pan'tano/ *m*, marsh, swamp; impediment; artificial pool
pantanoso /panta'noso/ *a* marshy, swampy; *Fig.* awkward, full of pitfalls
panteísmo /pante'ismo/ *m*, pantheism
panteísta /pante'ista/ *a* pantheistic. *mf* pantheist
panteón /pante'on/ *m*, pantheon
pantera /pan'tera/ *f*, panther
pantomima /panto'mima/ *f*, pantomime; mime

pantoque /pan'toke/ *m, Naut.* bilge
pantorrilla /panto'rriʎa; panto'rriya/ *f,* calf (of the leg)
pantuflo /pan'tuflo/ *m,* house slipper
panza /'panθa; 'pansa/ *f,* paunch, stomach; belly (of jugs, etc.). *Inf.* **un cielo de p. de burra,** a dark gray sky
panzudo /pan'θuðo; pan'suðo/ *a* paunchy
pañal /pa'ɲal/ *m,* diaper; shirttail; *pl* long clothes, swaddling clothes; infancy
pañería /paɲe'ria/ *f,* drapery stores; drapery
pañero /pa'ɲero/ **(-ra)** *n* draper
paño /'paɲo/ *m,* woolen material; cloth, fabric; drapery, hanging; tapestry; linen, bandage; tarnish or other mark; *Naut.* canvas; *Sew.* breadth, width (of cloth); panel (in a dress); floor cloth, duster; livid mark on the face; *pl* garments. **p. de lágrimas,** consoler, sympathizer. **p. mortuorio,** pall (on a coffin). **paños menores,** underwear. **p. verde,** gambling table. **al p.,** *Theat.* from the wings, from without. *Inf.* **poner el p. al púlpito,** to hold forth, spread oneself
pañoleta /paɲo'leta/ *f,* kerchief, triangular scarf; fichu
pañuelo /pa'ɲuelo/ *m,* kerchief; handkerchief
papa /'papa/ *m,* pope; *Inf.* papa, daddy. *f, Inf.* potato; stupid rumor; nonsense; *pl* pap; *Cul.* sop; food
papá /pa'pa/ *m, Inf.* papa, daddy
papada /pa'paða/ *f,* double chin; dewlap
papado /pa'paðo/ *m,* papacy
papagayo /papa'gaio/ *m,* parrot
papamoscas /papa'moskas/ *m, Ornith.* flycatcher; *Inf.* simpleton
papanatas /papa'natas/ *m, Inf.* simpleton
papar /pa'par/ *vt* to sip, take soft food; *Inf.* eat; neglect, be careless about
paparrucha /papa'rrutʃa/ *f, Inf.* stupid rumor; nonsense
papel /pa'pel/ *m,* paper; document; manuscript; *Theat.* role, part; pamphlet; sheet of paper; paper, monograph, essay; guise, role; *Theat.* character. **p. carbón, p. carbónico,** carbon paper. **p. celofán,** cellophane. **p. cuadriculado,** graph paper, cartridge paper. **p. de calcar,** carbon paper; tracing paper. **p. de escribir,** writing paper. **p. de estaño,** tinfoil. **p. de estraza,** brown paper. **p. de fumar,** cigarette paper. **p. de lija,** emery- or sandpaper. **p. de paja de arroz,** rice paper. **p. de seda,** tissue paper. **p. de tornasol,** litmus paper. **p. del estado,** government bonds. **p. higiénico,** toilet paper. **p. moneda,** paper money. **p. pintado,** wallpaper. **p. secante,** blotting paper. **p. sellado,** official stamped paper. **hacer buen (mal) p.,** to do well (badly). **hacer el p. (de),** *Theat.* to act the part (of); feign, pretend
papelear /papele'ar/ *vi* to turn over papers, search among them; *Inf.* cut a dash
papeleo /pape'leo/ *m,* bureacracy, red tape
papelera /pape'lera/ *f,* mass of papers; desk (for keeping papers)
papelería /papele'ria/ *f,* heap of papers; stationer's shop; stationery
papelero /pape'lero/ **(-ra)** *a* paper, stationery —*n* paper maker; stationer
papeleta /pape'leta/ *f,* slip or scrap of paper
papelista /pape'lista/ *mf* paper maker; stationer; paperhanger
papelucho /pape'lutʃo/ *m,* old or dirty piece of paper; trash, worthless writing; *Inf.* rag (newspaper)
papera /pa'pera/ *f,* mumps
papilla /pa'piʎa; pa'piya/ *f,* pap; guile, wiliness
papillote /papi'ʎote; papi'yote/ *m,* curl-paper
papiro /pa'piro/ *m,* papyrus
papista /pa'pista/ *a* and *mf* papist
papo /'papo/ *m,* dewlap; gizzard (of a bird); goiter. **p. de cardo,** thistledown
paquebote /pake'βote/ *m, Naut.* packet; mail boat; liner
paquete /pa'kete/ *m,* packet; parcel, package
paquidermo /paki'ðermo/ *m,* pachyderm
par /par/ *a* equal; alike; corresponding. *m,* pair, couple; team (of oxen, mules); peer (title); rafter (of a roof); *Mech.* torque, couple; *Elec.* cell. *f,* par. **a la p.,** jointly; simultaneously; *Com.* at par. **a pares,** two by two. **de p. en p.,** wide-open (doors, etc.). **sin p.,** peerless, excellent
para /'para/ *prep* in order to; for; to; for the sake of (e.g. *Lo hice p. ella,* I did it for her sake); enough to (gen. with *bastante,* etc.); in the direction of, toward; about to, on the point of (e.g. *Está p. salir,* He is on the point of going out). Expresses:
1. *Purpose* (e.g. *La educan p. bailarina,* They are bringing her up to be a dancer. *Lo dije p. ver lo que harías,* I said it to (in order to) see what you would do)
2. *Destination* (e.g. *Salió p. Londres,* He left for London)
3. *Use* (e.g. *seda p. medias,* silk for stockings. *un vaso p. flores,* a vase for flowers)
4. *An appointed time* (e.g. *Lo pagaré p. Navidad,* I will pay it at Christmas)
p. con, toward (a person) (e.g. *Ha obrado muy bien p. con mi hermano,* He has behaved very well toward my brother)
p. coneretar, to be exact, to wit
p. que, in order to, so that (e.g. *Lo puse en la mesa p. que lo vieses,* I put it on the table so that you would see it)
¿P. qué? Why? For what reason?
p. siempre, forever. **decir p. sí,** to say to oneself. **sin qué ni p. qué,** without rhyme or reason
parábola /pa'raβola/ *f,* parable; *Geom.* parabola
parabrisas /para'βrisas/ *m,* windshield
paracaídas /paraka'iðas/ *m,* parachute
paracaidista /parakai'ðista/ *mf* parachutist
parachoques /para'tʃokes/ *m, Auto.* bumper; buffer (railroad)
paráclito /pa'raklito/ *m,* Paraclete
parada /pa'raða/ *f,* stopping, halting; stop; stoppage, suspension; halt; *Mil.* review; interval, pause; cattle stall; dam; gambling stakes; parry (in fencing); relay (of horses). **p. de coches,** taxi rank. **p. de tranvía,** streetcar stop. **p. discrecional,** request stop (buses, etc.)
paradero /para'ðero/ *m,* railroad station; stopping place; end, conclusion; whereabouts
paradisíaco /paraði'siako/ *a* paradisaical
parado /pa'raðo/ *a* still; indolent, lazy; unoccupied, leisured; silent, reserved; timid; unemployed
paradoja /para'ðoha/ *f,* paradox
paradójico /para'ðohiko/ *a* paradoxical
parador /para'ðor/ *m,* inn, tavern, hostelry
parafina /para'fina/ *f,* paraffin
parafinar /parafi'nar/ *vt* to paraffin
parafrasear /parafrase'ar/ *vt* to paraphrase
paráfrasis /pa'rafrasis/ *f,* paraphrase
paraguas /pa'raguas/ *m,* umbrella
paraguayo /para'guayo/ **(-ya)** *a* and *n* Paraguayan
paragüería /parague'ria/ *f,* umbrella shop
paragüero /para'guero/ **(-ra)** *n* umbrella maker, umbrella seller. *m,* umbrella stand
paraíso /para'iso/ *m,* paradise; garden of Eden; heaven; (*Inf. Theat.*) gallery, gods
paraje /pa'rahe/ *m,* place, locality, spot; state, condition
paralela /para'lela/ *f, Mil.* parallel; *pl* parallel bars (for gymnastic exercises)
paralelismo /parale'lismo/ *m,* parallelism
paralelo /para'lelo/ *a* parallel; analogous; similar. *m,* parallel, similarity; *Geog.* parallel
paralelogramo /paralelo'gramo/ *m,* parallelogram
parálisis /pa'ralisis/ *f,* paralysis
paralítico /para'litiko/ **(-ca)** *a* and *n* paralytic
paralización /paraliθa'θion; paralisa'sion/ *f,* paralysis; cessation; *Com.* dullness, quietness
paralizar /parali'θar; parali'sar/ *vt* to paralyze; stop
paramento /para'mento/ *m,* ornament; trappings (of a horse); face (of a wall); facing (of a building). **paramentos sacerdotales,** liturgical vestments or ornaments
páramo /'paramo/ *m,* paramo, treeless plain; desert, wilderness
parangón /paraŋ'gon/ *m,* comparison; similarity
parangonar /paraŋgo'nar/ *vt* to compare
paraninfo /para'ninfo/ *m, Archit.* paranymph, university hall; best man (weddings); messenger of good

paranoico /para'noiko/ *m,* paranoiac
parapetarse /parape'tarse/ *vr* to shelter behind a parapet; take refuge behind
parapeto /para'peto/ *m,* parapet
parapoco /para'poko/ *mf Inf.* ninny, numskull
parar /pa'rar/ *vi* to stop, halt; end, finish; lodge; come into the hands of; *—vt* stop; detain; prepare; bet, stake; point (hunting dogs); parry (fencing); *—vr* halt; be interrupted **p. mientes en,** to notice; consider. **sin p.,** immediately, at once; without stopping
pararrayos /para'rraios/ *m,* lightning conductor
parasitario, parasítico /parasi'tario, para'sitiko/ *a* parasitic
parásito /pa'rasito/ *m,* parasite; *Fig.* sponger; *pl Radio.* interference *—a* parasitic
parasitología /parasitolo'hia/ *f,* parasitology
parasol /para'sol/ *m,* sunshade; *Bot.* umbel
paratifoidea /paratifoi'ðea/ *f,* paratyphoid
parca /'parka/ *f,* Fate; *Poet.* death. **las Parcas,** the Three Fates
parcela /par'θela; par'sela/ *f,* plot, parcel (of land); atom, particle
parche /'partʃe/ *m, Med.* plaster; *Auto.* patch; drum; drumhead, parchment of drum; patch, mend
parcial /par'θial; par'sial/ *a* partial, incomplete; biased, prejudiced; factional, party; participatory
parcialidad /parθiali'ðað; parsiali'ðað/ *f,* partiality, bias, prejudice; party, faction, group; intimacy, friendship
parco /'parko/ *a* scarce, scanty; temperate, moderate; frugal
¡pardiez! /par'ðieθ par'ðies/ *interj Inf.* By god!
pardo /'parðo/ *a* brown; gray, drab, dun-colored; cloudy, dark; husky (voices). *m,* leopard
pardusco /par'ðusko/ *a* grayish; fawn-colored
parear /pare'ar/ *vt* to pair, match; put in pairs; compare
parecer /pare'θer; pare'ser/ *vi irr* to appear; look, seem; turn up (be found) *—impers* believe, think (e.g. *me parece,* it seems to me, I think, my opinion is); *—vr* look alike, resemble one another. See **conocer**
parecer /pare'θer; pare'ser/ *m,* opinion, belief; appearance, looks
parecido /pare'θiðo; pare'siðo/ *a* (*with bien or mal*) good- or bad-looking. *m,* resemblance
pared /pa'reð/ *f,* wall; partition wall; side, face. **p. maestra,** main wall. **p. medianera,** party wall. **Las paredes oyen,** The walls have ears. *Inf.* **pegado a la p.,** confused, taken aback
pareja /pa'reha/ *f,* pair; dance partner; couple. **p. desparejada,** mismatched pair. **parejas mixtas,** mixed doubles (in tennis). **correr parejas** *or* **correr a las parejas,** to be equal; go together, happen simultaneously; be on a par
parejo /pa'reho/ *a* equal; similar; smooth, flat; even, regular
parentela /paren'tela/ *f,* relatives, kindred; parentage
parentesco /paren'tesko/ *m,* kinship; relationship; affinity; *Inf.* connection, link
paréntesis /pa'rentesis/ *m,* parenthesis; digression. **entre p.,** incidentally
paresa /pa'resa/ *f,* peeress
paria /'paria/ *mf* pariah; outcast
parida /pa'riða/ *a f,* newly delivered of a child
paridad /pari'ðað/ *f,* parity; analogy, similarity
pariente /pa'riente/ **(ta)** *n* relative, relation; *Inf.* husband (wife)
parihuela /pari'uela/ *f,* wheelbarrow; stretcher
parir /pa'rir/ *vt* to give birth to; *Fig.* bring forth; reveal, publish; *—vi* lay eggs
París /pa'ris/ Paris
parisiense /pari'siense/ *a* and *mf* Parisian
parla /'parla/ *f,* speech; loquaciousness, eloquence; verbiage
parlamentar /parlamen'tar/ *vi* to converse; discuss (contracts, etc.); *Mil.* parley
parlamentario /parlamen'tario/ *a* parliamentarian. *m,* member of parliament
parlamentarismo /parlamenta'rismo/ *m,* parliamentarianism
parlamento /parla'mento/ *m,* legislative assembly; parliament; discourse, speech; *Theat.* long speech; *Mil.* parley
parlanchín /parlan'tʃin/ *a Inf.* talkative, chattering, loquacious
parlar /par'lar/ *vt* and *vi* to speak freely or easily; chatter; reveal, speak indiscreetly; babble (of streams, etc.)
parlero /par'lero/ *a* talkative; gossiping, indiscreet; talking (birds); *Fig.* expressive (eyes, etc.); prattling, babbling (brook, etc.)
parlotear /parlote'ar/ *vi Inf.* to chatter, gossip
parloteo /parlo'teo/ *m,* chattering, gossip
parmesano /parme'sano/ **(-na)** *a* and *n* Parmesan
parnaso /par'naso/ *m,* Parnassus; anthology of verse
paro /'paro/ *m, Inf.* work stoppage; lockout; *Ornith.* tit. **p. forzoso,** unemployment
parodia /pa'roðia/ *f,* parody
parodiar /paro'ðiar/ *vt* to parody
parodista /paro'ðista/ *mf* parodist
parótida /pa'rotiða/ *f,* parotid gland; parotitis, mumps
parotiditis /paroti'ðitis/ *f,* parotitis, mumps
paroxismo /parok'sismo/ *m, Med.* paroxysm; frenzy, ecstasy, fit
parpadear /parpaðe'ar/ *vi* to blink
parpadeo /parpa'ðeo/ *m,* blinking
párpado /'parpaðo/ *m,* eyelid
parque /'parke/ *m,* park; depot, park; paddock, pen. **p. de atracciones,** pleasure ground. **p. de** (*or* **para**) **automóviles,** car park, parking lot
parquedad /parke'ðað/ *f,* scarcity; moderation, temperance; parsimony, frugality
parra /'parra/ *f,* vine. **hoja de p.,** *Fig.* fig leaf
párrafo /'parrafo/ *m,* paragraph; *Gram.* paragraph sign. **p. aparte,** new paragraph. **echar un p.,** to chat, gossip
parranda /pa'rranda/ *f, Inf.* binge; strolling band of musicians. **ir de p.,** to go on a binge
parricida /parri'θiða; parri'siða/ *mf* parricide (person)
parricidio /parri'θiðio; parri'siðio/ *m,* parricide (act)
parrilla /pa'rriʎa; pa'rriya/ *f, Cul.* griller, broiler; grill, gridiron; *Engin.* grate. *Cul.* **a la p.,** grilled
párroco /'parroko/ *m,* parish priest; parson
parroquia /pa'rrokia/ *f,* parish church; parish; clergy of a parish; clientele, customers
parroquial /parro'kial/ *a* parochial
parroquiano /parro'kiano/ **(-na)** *a* parochial *—n* parishioner; client, customer
parsi /'parsi/ *m,* Parsee; Parseeism
parsimonia /parsi'monia/ *f,* frugality, thrift; prudence, moderation
parsimonioso /parsimo'nioso/ *a* parsimonious
parte /'parte/ *f,* part; share; place; portion; side, faction; *Law.* party; *Theat.* part, role. *m,* communication, message; telegraph or telephone message; (*Mil. Nav.*) communiqué. *f pl,* parts, talents. **p. actora,** *Law.* prosecution. **p. de la oración,** part of speech. **partes litigantes,** *Law.* contending parties. **dar p.,** to notify; (*Mil. Naut.*) report; give a share (in a transaction). **de algún tiempo a esta p.,** for some time past. **de p. de,** in the name of, from. **en p.,** partly. **por todas partes,** on all sides, everywhere. **ser p. a** *or* **ser p. para que,** to contribute to. **tener de su p.** (**a**), to count on the favor of. **la quinta p.,** one-fifth, etc.
partear /parte'ar/ *vt* to assist in childbirth
partera /par'tera/ *f,* midwife
partero /par'tero/ *m,* accoucheur
partición /parti'θion; parti'sion/ *f,* partition, distribution; (*Aer. Naut.*) accommodation
participación /partiθipa'θion; partisipa'sion/ *f,* participation; notice, warning; announcement (of an engagement, etc.); *Com.* share
participante /partiθi'pante; partisi'pante/ *a* and *mf* participant
participar /partiθi'par; partisi'par/ *vi* to participate, take part (in), share; *—vt* inform; announce (an engagement, etc.)
partícipe /par'tiθipe; par'tisipe/ *a* sharing. *mf* participant
participio /parti'θipio; parti'sipio/ *m,* participle

partícula /par'tikula/ *f,* particle, grain; *Gram.* particle
particular /partiku'lar/ *a* private; peculiar; special, particular; unusual; individual. *mf* private individual. *m,* matter, subject. **en p.,** especially; privately
particularidad /partikulari'ðað/ *f,* individuality; specialty; rareness, unusualness; detail, circumstance; intimacy, friendship
particularizar /partikulari'θar; partikulari'sar/ *vt* to detail, particularize; single out, choose; *—vr* (*with en*) be characterized by
partida /par'tiða/ *f,* departure; entry, record (of birth, etc.); certificate (of marriage, etc.); *Com.* item; *Com.* lot, allowance; *Mil.* guerrilla; armed band; expedition, excursion; game (of cards, etc.); rubber (at bridge, etc.); *Inf.* conduct, behavior; place, locality; death. *Com.* **p. doble,** double entry. **Las siete Partidas,** code of Spanish laws compiled by Alfonso X (1252–84)
partidario /parti'ðario/ **(-ia)** *a* partisan *—n* adherent, disciple. *m,* partisan, guerrilla
partidarismo /partiða'rismo/ *m,* partisanship
partido /par'tiðo/ *m,* party, group, faction; profit; *Sports.* match; team; agreement, pact. **p. conservador,** *Polit.* conservative party. **p. obrero** *or* **p. laborista,** *Polit.* labor party. **buen p.,** *Fig.* good match, catch. **sacar p. de,** to take advantage of, make the most of. **tomar p.,** to enlist; join, become a supporter (of)
partidor /parti'ðor/ *m,* divider, apportioner; cleaver, chopper; hewer
partir /par'tir/ *vt* to divide; split; crack, break; separate; *Math.* divide; *—vi* go, depart; start (from). **p. como el rayo,** be off like a flash *—vr* disagree, become divided; leave, depart
partitura /parti'tura/ *f, Mus.* score
parto /'parto/ *m,* parturition, birth; newborn child; *Fig.* creation, offspring; important event
parturienta /partu'rienta/ *a f,* parturient
parva /'parβa/ *f,* light breakfast; threshed or unthreshed grain; heap, mass
parvedad /parβe'ðað/ *f,* smallness; scarcity; light breakfast (taken on fast days)
parvo /'parβo/ *a* little, small
párvulo /'parβulo/ **(-la)** *n* child *—a* small; innocent, simple; lowly, humble
pasa /'pasa/ *f,* raisin; *Naut.* channel; passage, flight (of birds). **p. de Corinto,** currant
pasacalle /pasa'kaʎe; pasa'kaye/ *m, Mus.* lively march
pasada /pa'saða/ *f,* passing, passage; money sufficient to live on; passage, corridor. **dar p.,** to let pass, put up with. *Inf.* **mala p.,** bad turn, dirty trick
pasadera /pasa'ðera/ *f,* steppingstone
pasadero /pasa'ðero/ *a* passable, traversable; fair (health); tolerable, passable. *m,* steppingstone
pasadizo /pasa'ðiθo; pasa'ðiso/ *m,* narrow corridor or passage; alley, narrow street; *Naut.* alleyway
pasado /pa'saðo/ *m,* past; *pl* ancestors. **Lo p., p.,** What's past is past. **p. de moda,** out of fashion, unfashionable
pasador /pasa'ðor/ *m,* bolt, fastener; *Mech.* pin, coupler; pin (of brooches, etc.); colander; *Naut.* marlin spike; shirt stud
pasajaretas /pasaha'retas/ *m,* bodkin
pasaje /pa'sahe/ *m,* passing; passage; fare; passage money; *Naut.* complement of passengers; channel, strait; (*Mus. Lit.*) passage; *Mus.* modulation, transition (of voice); voyage; passage; covered way; road
pasajero /pasa'hero/ **(-ra)** *a* crowded public (thoroughfare); transitory, fugitive; passing; temporary *—n* passenger
pasamanería /pasamane'ria/ *f,* passementerie work, industry or shop
pasamano /pasa'mano/ *m,* passementerie; banister, handrail; *Naut.* gangway
pasante /pa'sante/ *a Herald.* passant. *m,* student teacher; articled clerk; apprentice; student. **p. de pluma,** law clerk
pasaporte /pasa'porte/ *m,* passport; license, permission. **dar el p. (a),** *Inf.* to give the sack (to)
pasar /pa'sar/ *vt* to pass; carry, transport; cross over; send; go beyond, overstep; run through, pierce; upset; overtake; transfer; suffer, undergo; sieve; study; dry (grapes, etc.); smuggle; surpass; omit; swallow (food); approve; dissemble; transform; spend (time); *—vi* pass; be transferred; be infectious; have enough to live on; cease; last; die; pass away; pass (at cards); be transformed; be current (money); be salable (goods); (*with prep a + infin*) begin to; (*with por*) pass as; have a reputation as; visit; (*with sin*) do without *—impers* happen, occur *—vr* end; go over to another party; forget; go stale or bad; *Fig.* go too far, overstep the mark; permeate. **p. contrato,** to draw up a contract; sign a contract. **p. la voz,** to pass the word along. **p. por alto (de),** to omit, overlook. **p. de largo,** to go by without stopping. **pasarse de listo,** to be too clever. **¡No pases cuidado!** Don't worry!
pasarela /pasa'rela/ *f,* gangplank
pasatiempo /pasa'tiempo/ *m,* pastime, hobby, amusement
pasavante /pasa'βante/ *m, Naut.* safe conduct; navicert
pascua /'paskua/ *f,* Passover; Easter; Christmas; Twelfth Night; Pentecost; *pl* twelve days of Christmas. **P. florida,** Easter Sunday. **dar las pascuas,** to wish a merry Christmas. **¡Felices pascuas!** Merry Christmas!
pascual /pas'kual/ *a* paschal
pase /'pase/ *m,* pass (with the hands and in football, etc.); safe conduct; free pass; thrust (in fencing)
paseante /pase'ante/ *mf* stroller, promenader, passerby
pasear /pase'ar/ *vt* to take a walk; parade up and down, display; *—vi* take a walk; go for a drive; go for a ride (on horseback, etc.); stroll up and down; *—vr* touch upon lightly, pass over; loaf, be idle; drift; float
paseo /pa'seo/ *m,* walk, stroll; drive; outing, expedition; promenade; boulevard. **p. a caballo,** ride on horseback
pasiega /pa'siega/ *f,* wet nurse
pasillo /pa'siʎo; pa'siyo/ *m,* gallery; corridor; lobby; railway corridor; *Sew.* basting stitch
pasión /pa'sion/ *f,* suffering; passivity; passion; desire; *Eccl.* passion. **con p.,** passionately
pasional /pasio'nal/ *a* passionate; of passion
pasionaria /pasio'naria/ *f,* passionflower
pasiva /pa'siβa/ *f, Gram.* passive
pasividad /pasiβi'ðað/ *f,* passivity
pasivo /pa'siβo/ *a* passive; inactive; *Com.* sleeping (partner); *Gram.* passive. *m, Com.* liabilities
pasmar /pas'mar/ *vt* to freeze to death (plants); dumbfound, amaze, stun; chill; *—vr* be stunned or amazed
pasmo /'pasmo/ *m,* amazement, astonishment; wonder, marvel; *Med.* tetanus, lockjaw
pasmoso /pas'moso/ *a* astounding, amazing; wonderful
paso /'paso/ *a* dried (of fruit)
paso /'paso/ *m,* step; pace; passage, passing; way; footstep; progress, advancement; passage (in a book); *Sew.* tacking stitch; occurrence, event; *Theat.* short play; gait, walk; strait, channel; migratory flight (birds); *Mech.* pitch; event or scene from the Passion; armed combat; death; *pl* measures, steps *—adv* softly, in a low voice; gently. **p. a nivel,** level crossing. **p. a p.,** step by step. **p. doble,** quick march; Spanish dance. **p. volante,** (gymnastics) giant stride. **a cada p.,** at every step; often. **al p.,** without stopping; on the way, in passing. **ceder el p.,** to allow to pass. **de p.,** in passing; incidentally. **llevar el p.,** to keep in step. **marcar el p.,** to mark time. **salir al p. (a),** to waylay, confront; oppose. **seguir los pasos (a),** to follow; spy upon
pasquín /pas'kin/ *m,* **pasquinada** *f,* pasquinade, lampoon
pasta /'pasta/ *f, Cul.* dough; paste; pastry; piecrust; batter; *Cul.* noodle paste; paper pulp; board (bookbinding). **ser de buena p.,** to be good-natured
pastar /pas'tar/ *vt* to take to pasture; *—vi* graze, pasture
pastel /pas'tel/ *m,* cake; *Art.* pastel; pie; *Inf.* plot, se-

cret understanding; cheating (at cards); *Print.* pie; *Inf.* fat, stocky person
pastelear /pastele'ar/ *vi Inf.* to indulge in shady business (especially in politics)
pastelería /pastele'ria/ *f,* cake bakery; cake shop; confectioner's art; confectionery
pastelero /paste'lero/ **(-ra)** *n* confectioner, pastry cook; *Fig. Inf.* spineless person, jellyfish
pastelillo /paste'liʎo; paste'liyo/ *m, Cul.* turnover
pastelista /paste'lista/ *mf* pastelist
pastelón /paste'lon/ *m,* meat or game pie
pasteurización /pasteuriθa'θion; pasteurisa'sion/ *f,* pasteurization
pasteurizar /pasteuri'θar; pasteuri'sar/ *vt* to pasteurize
pastilla /pas'tiʎa; pas'tiya/ *f,* tablet, cake; lozenge; pastille, drop; tread (of a tire)
pasto /'pasto/ *m,* grazing land, pasture; fodder; *Fig.* fuel, food; spiritual food. **a p.,** in plenty, abundantly. **de p.,** of daily use
pastor /pas'tor/ **(-ra)** *n* shepherd. *m, Eccl.* pastor
pastoral /pasto'ral/ *a* rustic, country; *Eccl.* pastoral, *f,* pastoral poem; *Eccl.* pastoral letter
pastorear /pastore'ar/ *vt* to graze, put to grass; *Eccl.* have charge of souls
pastorela /pasto'rela/ *f,* pastoral
pastoreo /pasto'reo/ *m,* pasturage, grazing
pastoría /pasto'ria/ *f,* pastorate
pastoril /pasto'ril/ *a* shepherd, pastoral
pastoso /pas'toso/ *a* doughy; mealy; pasty; mellow
pata /'pata/ *f,* paw and leg (animals); foot (of table, etc.); duck; *Inf.* leg. **p. de gallo,** blunder; crow's-foot, wrinkle. **meter la p.,** to interfere, put one's foot in it. *Inf.* **tener mala p.,** to be unlucky
patada /pa'taða/ *f,* kick, stamp; *Inf.* step, pace
patagón /pata'gon/ **(-ona)** *a* and *n* Patagonian
patalear /patale'ar/ *vi* to stamp (with the feet)
pataleo /pata'leo/ *m,* kicking; stamping
pataleta /pata'leta/ *f, Inf.* convulsion; feigned hysterics
patán /pa'tan/ *m, Inf.* yokel; boor, churl
patanería /patane'ria/ *f, Inf.* boorishness, churlishness
patarata /pata'rata/ *f,* trash, useless thing; extravagant courtesy
patata /pa'tata/ *f,* potato
patatal, patatar /pata'tal, pata'tar/ *m,* potato patch
patatús /pata'tus/ *m, Inf.* petty worry; mishap; *Med.* stroke, fit
patear /pate'ar/ *vt Inf.* to stamp; *Fig.* walk on, treat badly; *—vi Inf.* stamp the feet; be furiously angry; (*Golf*) putt
patena /pa'tena/ *f,* engraved medal worn by country women; *Eccl.* paten
patentar /paten'tar/ *vt* to issue a patent; take out a patent, patent
patente /pa'tente/ *a* obvious, patent; *f,* patent; warrant, commission; letters patent. **p. de invención,** patent. **p. de sanidad,** clean bill of health
patentizar /patenti'θar; patenti'sar/ *vt* to make evident
paternidad /paterni'ðað/ *f,* paternity
paterno /pa'terno/ *a* paternal
patético /pa'tetiko/ *a* pitiable; pathetic, moving
patiabierto /patia'βierto/ *a Inf.* knock-kneed
patibulario /patiβu'lario/ *a* heartrending, harrowing
patíbulo /pa'tiβulo/ *m,* scaffold
paticojo /pati'koho/ *a Inf.* lame; wobbly; unsteady
patilla /pa'tiʎa; pa'tiya/ *f,* side whisker (gen. *pl*); *pl* old Nick, the Devil
patín /pa'tin/ *m,* skate; runner (of a sled); (*Aer.* and of vehicles) skid; *Mech.* shoe. **p. del diablo,** scooter. **p. de ruedas,** roller skate
patinador /patina'ðor/ **(-ra)** *n* skater
patinaje /pati'nahe/ *m,* skating; skidding (of planes and vehicles)
patinar /pati'nar/ *vi* to skate; slip, lose one's footing; skid (vehicles and planes)
patinazo /pati'naθo; pati'naso/ *m,* skid (of a vehicle)
patinete /pati'nete/ *m,* child's scooter
patio /'patio/ *m,* courtyard; *Theat.* pit
patitieso /pati'tieso/ *a Inf.* paralyzed in the hands or feet; open-mouthed, amazed; stiff, unbending, proud
patituerto /pati'tuerto/ *a* crooked-legged; pigeon-toed; *Inf.* lopsided
patizambo /pati'θambo; pati'sambo/ *a* knock-kneed
pato /'pato/ *m,* duck; *Inf.* **pagar el p.,** to be a scapegoat
patógeno /pa'toheno/ *a* pathogenic
patojo /pa'toho/ *a* waddling
patología /patolo'hia/ *f,* pathology
patológico /pato'lohiko/ *a* pathological
patólogo /pa'tologo/ *m,* pathologist
patoso /pa'toso/ *a Fig.* heavy, pedestrian, tedious
patraña /pa'traɲa/ *f,* nonsense, rubbish, fairy tale
patria /'patria/ *f,* motherland, native country; native place. **p. chica,** native region
patriarca /pa'triarka/ *m,* patriarch
patriarcado /patriar'kaðo/ *m,* patriarchy
patriarcal /patriar'kal/ *a* patriarchal
patricio /pa'triθio; pa'trisio/ **(-ia)** *a* and *n* patrician
patrimonio /patri'monio/ *m,* patrimony
patriota /pa'triota/ *mf* patriot
patriótico /pa'triotiko/ *a* patriotic
patriotismo /patrio'tismo/ *m,* patriotism
patrocinar /patroθi'nar; patrosi'nar/ *vt* to protect, defend; favor, sponsor; patronize
patrocinio /patro'θinio; patro'sinio/ *m,* protection, defense; sponsorship; patronage
patrón /pa'tron/ **(-ona)** *n* patron, sponsor; patron saint; landlord; employer. *m,* coxswain; *Naut.* master, skipper; pattern, model; standard. **p. de oro,** gold standard
patronato /patro'nato/ *m,* patronage, protection; employers' association; charitable foundation. **p. de turismo,** tourist bureau
patronímico /patro'nimiko/ *a* and *m,* patronymic
patrono /pa'trono/ **(-na)** *n* protector; sponsor; patron; patron saint; employer
patrulla /pa'truʎa; pa'truya/ *f, Mil.* patrol; group, band
patrullar /patru'ʎar; patru'yar/ *vi Mil.* patrol; march about
patudo /pa'tuðo/ *a Inf.* large-footed
paulatinamente /paulatina'mente/ *adv* slowly, by degrees
pauperismo /paupe'rismo/ *m,* destitution, pauperism
paupérrimo /pau'perrimo/ *a superl* **pobre** exceedingly poor
pausa /'pausa/ *f,* pause, interruption; delay; *Mus.* rest; *Mus.* pause. **a pausas,** intermittently
pausado /pau'saðo/ *a* deliberate, slow *—adv* slowly, deliberately
pausar /pau'sar/ *vi* to pause
pauta /'pauta/ *f,* standard, norm, design; *Fig.* guide, model
pavada /pa'βaða/ *f,* flock of turkeys
pavana /pa'βana/ *f,* pavane, stately dance
pavero /pa'βero/ **(-ra)** *a* vain; strutting *—n* turkey keeper or vendor. *m,* broad-brimmed Andalusian hat
pavimentación /paβimenta'θion; paβimenta'sion/ *f,* paving, flagging
pavimento /paβi'mento/ *m,* pavement
pavo /'paβo/ **(-va)** *n Ornith.* turkey. **p. real,** peacock. *Inf.* **pelar la pava,** to serenade, court
pavón /pa'βon/ *m, Ornith.* peacock; peacock butterfly; preservative paint (for steel, etc.); gunmetal
pavonear /paβone'ar/ *vi* to strut, peacock (also *vr*); *Inf.* hoodwink, dazzle
pavor /pa'βor/ *m,* terror, panic
pavoroso /paβo'roso/ *a* fearful, awesome, dreadful
payasada /paia'saða/ *f,* clowning, practical joke; clown's patter
payaso /pa'iaso/ *m,* clown
paz /paθ; pas/ *f,* peace; harmony, concord; peaceableness. **¡P. sea en esta casa!** Peace be upon this house! (salutation). **estar en p.,** to be at peace; be quits, be even. **poner** (*or* **meter**) **p.,** to make peace (between dissentients). **venir de p.,** to come with peaceful intentions
pazguato /paθ'guato; pas'guato/ **(-ta)** *n* simpleton, booby

pazpuerca /paθ'puerka; pas'puerka/ *f*, slattern
pe /pe/ *f*, name of the letter P. *Inf.* **de pe a pa,** from A to Z, from beginning to end
peaje /pe'ahe/ *m*, toll (on bridges, roads, etc.)
peatón /pea'ton/ *m*, pedestrian; walker; country postman
pebete /pe'βete/ *m*, joss stick; fuse; *Inf.* stench
peca /'peka/ *f*, mole, freckle
pecado /pe'kaðo/ *m*, sin; fault; excess; defect; *Inf.* the Devil. **p. capital,** mortal sin
pecador /peka'ðor/ *a* sinful. *m*, sinner. **¡P. de mí!** Poor me!
pecadora /peka'ðora/ *f*, sinner; *Inf.* prostitute
pecaminoso /pekami'noso/ *a* sinful
pecar /pe'kar/ *vi* to sin; trespass, transgress; (*with de) be too... (e.g. El libro peca de largo, The book is too long)*
peceño /pe'θeɲo; pe'seɲo/ *a* pitch-black (horses, etc.); tasting of pitch
pecera /pe'θera; pe'sera/ *f*, goldfish bowl; aquarium
pechera /pe'tʃera/ *f*, shirt front; chest protector; bib, tucker; shirt frill; *Inf.* bosom
pecho /'petʃo/ *m*, *Anat.* chest; breast; bosom; mind, conscience; courage, endurance; *Mus.* quality (of voice); incline, slope. **p. arriba,** uphill. **abrir su p. a** (*or* **con**), to unbosom oneself to. **dar el p. (a)**, to suckle. **de pechos,** leaning on. **echar el p. al agua,** *Fig.* to embark courageously upon. **tomar a pechos (una cosa),** to take (a thing) very seriously; take to heart
pechuga /pe'tʃuga/ *f*, breast (of a bird); *Inf.* breast, bosom; slope, incline
pecio /'peθio; 'pesio/ *m*, flotsam
pécora /'pekora/ *f*, sheep, head of sheep; wily woman, serpent
pecoso /pe'koso/ *a* freckled; spotted (with warts)
pecuario /pe'kuario/ *a Agr.* stock; cattle
peculiar /peku'liar/ *a* peculiar, individual
peculiaridad /pekuliari'ðað/ *f*, peculiarity
peculio /pe'kulio/ *m*, private money or property
pecunia /pe'kunia/ *f*, *Inf.* cash
pecuniario /peku'niario/ *a* pecuniary
pedagogía /peðago'hia/ *f*, education, pedagogy
pedagógico /peða'gohiko/ *a* educational, pedagogic
pedagogo /peða'gogo/ *m*, schoolmaster; educationalist; *Fig.* mentor
pedal /pe'ðal/ *m*, *Mech.* treadle, lever, *Mus.* pedal; *Mus.* sustained harmony. *Auto.* **p. de embrague,** clutch pedal
pedalear /peðale'ar/ *vi* to pedal
pedante /pe'ðante/ *a* pedantic. *mf* pedant
pedantería /peðante'ria/ *f*, pedantry
pedazo /pe'ðaθo; pe'ðaso/ *m*, bit, piece; lump; fragment, portion. *Inf.* **p. del alma, p. del corazón, p. de las entrañas,** loved one, dear one. **a pedazos** *or* **en pedazos,** in pieces, in bits. **hacer pedazos,** to break into fragments
pedernal /peðer'nal/ *m*, flint; anything very hard
pedestal /peðes'tal/ *m*, pedestal; base; stand; *Fig.* foundation
pedestre /pe'ðestre/ *a* pedestrian; dull, uninspired
pediatra /pe'ðiatra/ *mf* pediatrician
pedicuro /peði'kuro/ *m*, chiropodist
pedido /pe'ðiðo/ *m*, *Com.* order; request, petition
pedigüeño /peði'gueɲo/ *a* importunate, insistent
pedimento /peði'mento/ *m*, petition, demand; *Law.* claim; *Law.* motion
pedir /pe'ðir/ *vt irr* to ask, request; *Com.* order; demand; necessitate; desire; ask in marriage. **p. en juicio,** *Law.* to bring an action against. *Inf.* **pedírselo (a uno) el cuerpo,** to desire (something) ardently. **a p. de boca,** according to one's wish —*Pres. Part.* **pidiendo.** *Pres. Indic.* **pido, pides, pide, piden.** *Preterite* **pidió, pidieron.** *Pres. Subjunc.* **pida,** etc —*Imperf. Subjunc.* **pidiese,** etc.
pedo /'peðo/ *m*, fart
pedómetro /pe'ðometro/ *m*, pedometer
pedrada /pe'ðraða/ *f*, casting a stone; blow with a stone; innuendo
pedrea /pe'ðrea/ *f*, stone throwing; fight with stones; shower of hailstones
pedregal /peðre'gal/ *m*, stony ground
pedregoso /peðre'goso/ *a* stony
pedrera /pe'ðrera/ *f*, stone quarry
pedrería /peðre'ria/ *f*, precious stones
pedrisco /pe'ðrisko/ *m*, hailstone; shower of stones; pile of stones
pedrusco /pe'ðrusko/ *m*, *Inf.* rough, unpolished stone
pega /'pega/ *f*, sticking; cementing; joining; pitch; varnish; *Inf.* joke; beating; *Ornith.* magpie
pegadizo /pega'ðiθo; pega'ðiso/ *a* sticky, gummy, adhesive; detachable, removable; *Fig.* clinging, importunate (of people)
pegado /pe'gaðo/ *m*, sticking plaster; patch
pegajoso /pega'hoso/ *a* sticky, gluey; viscid; contagious, catching; *Inf.* oily, unctuous; *Fig. Inf.* cadging, sponging
pegar /pe'gar/ *vt* to stick; cement; join, fasten; press (against); infect with (diseases); hit, strike; give (a shout, jump, etc.); patch; —*vi* spread, catch (fire, etc.); *Fig.* make an impression, have influence; be opportune; —*vr Cul.* stick, burn; meddle; become enthusiastic about; take root in the mind. **p. un tiro (a),** to shoot
Pegaso /pe'gaso/ *m*, Pegasus
pegote /pe'gote/ *m*, sticking plaster; *Fig. Inf.* sponger; *Inf.* patch
peinado /pei'naðo/ *m*, hairdressing or style; headdress —*a Inf.* effeminate, overelegant (men); overcareful (style). **un p. al agua,** a finger wave
peinador /peina'ðor/ **(-ra)** *m*, peignoir, dressing gown —*n* hairdresser
peinadura /peina'ðura/ *f*, brushing or combing of hair; *pl* hair combings
peinar /pei'nar/ *vt* to comb, dress the hair; card (wool); cut away (rock)
peine /'peine/ *m*, comb; *Mech.* hackle, reed; instep; *Inf.* crafty person
peinería /peine'ria/ *f*, comb factory or shop
peinero /pei'nero/ *m*, comb manufacturer or seller
peineta /pei'neta/ *f*, high comb (for mantillas, etc.)
peladilla /pela'ðiʎa; pela'ðiya/ *f*, sugared almond; smooth, small pebble
pelado /pe'laðo/ *a* plucked; bare, unadorned; needy, poor; hairless; skinned; peeled; without shell; treeless
peladura /pela'ðura/ *f*, peeling; shelling; skinning; plucking (feathers)
pelafustán /pelafus'tan/ *m*, *Inf.* good-for-nothing, scamp
pelagatos /pela'gatos/ *m*, *Inf.* miserable wretch
pelágico /pe'lahiko/ *a* pelagian, oceanic
pelagra /pe'lagra/ *f*, pellagra
pelaje /pe'lahe/ *m*, fur, wool
pelamesa /pela'mesa/ *f*, brawl, fight; lock, tuft (of hair)
pelapatatas /pelapa'tatas/ *m*, potato peeler
pelar /pe'lar/ *vt* to tear out or cut the hair; pluck; skin; peel; shell; rob, fleece; —*vr* lose one's hair
peldaño /pel'daɲo/ *m*, step, stair, tread, rung
pelea /pe'lea/ *f*, battle; quarrel, dispute; fight (among animals); effort, exertion; *Fig.* struggle
peleador /pelea'ðor/ *a* fighting; quarrelsome, aggressive
pelear /pele'ar/ *vi* to fight; quarrel; struggle, strive. **p. como perro y gato,** to fight like cat and mouse —*vr* come to blows; fall out, become enemies
pelechar /pele'tʃar/ *vi* to get a new coat (of animals); grow new feathers (of birds); *Inf.* prosper, flourish, grow well
pelele /pe'lele/ *m*, effigy; *Inf.* nincompoop
peletería /pelete'ria/ *f*, furrier; fur shop
peletero /pele'tero/ *m*, furrier; skinner
peliagudo /pelia'guðo/ *a* long-haired (animals); *Inf.* complicated, difficult; wily, downy
pelícano /pe'likano/ *m*, pelican
pelicorto /peli'korto/ *a* short-haired
película /pe'likula/ *f*, film. **p. fotográfica,** roll of film. **p. sonora,** sound film
peligrar /peli'grar/ *vi* to be in danger
peligro /pe'ligro/ *m*, danger, peril. **correr p.** *or* **estar en p.,** to be in danger

peligroso /peli'groso/ *a* dangerous, perilous, risky
pelilargo /peli'largo/ *a* long-haired
pelirrojo /peli'rroho/ *a* red-haired
pelleja /pe'ʎeha; pe'yeha/ *f,* hide, skin (of animals); sheepskin
pellejo /pe'ʎeho; pe'yeho/ *m,* hide; pelt; skin; wineskin; *Inf.* drunkard; peel, skin (of fruit)
pelliza /pe'ʎiθa; pe'yisa/ *f,* fur or fur-trimmed coat
pellizcar /peʎiθ'kar; peyis'kar/ *vt* to pinch, tweak, nip; pilfer
pellizco /pe'ʎiθko; pe'yisko/ *m,* pinch, nip, tweak; pilfering, pinching; bit, pinch
pelmazo /pel'maθo; pel'maso/ *m,* squashed mass; *Inf.* idler, sluggard; *Inf.* bore
pelo /'pelo/ *m,* hair; down (on birds and fruit); fiber, filament; hair trigger (firearms); hairspring (watches); kiss (in billiards); nap (of cloth), grain (of wood); flaw (in gems); raw silk. **p. de camello,** camel's hair. **a p.,** in the nude; without a hat; opportunely. **en p.,** bareback (of horses). **hacerse el p.,** to do one's hair; have one's hair cut. *Inf.* **no tener p. de tonto,** to be smart, clever. *Inf.* **no tener pelos en la lengua,** to be outspoken. *Inf.* **tomar el p. (a),** to pull a person's leg. **venir a p.,** to be apposite; come opportunely
pelón /pe'lon/ *a* hairless; *Fig. Inf.* broke, fleeced
pelonería /pelone'ria/ *f, Inf.* poverty, misery
peloponense /pelopo'nense/ *a* and *mf* Peloponnesian
pelota /pe'lota/ *f,* ball; ball game. **p. base,** baseball. **p. vasca,** pelota. **en p.,** stark naked
pelotari /pelo'tari/ *m,* professional pelota player
pelotazo /pelo'taθo; pelo'taso/ *m,* knock or blow with a ball
pelotear /pelote'ar/ *vt* to audit accounts; *—vi* play ball; throw, cast; quarrel; argue
pelotera /pelo'tera/ *f, Inf.* brawl
pelotón /pelo'ton/ *m,* big ball; lump of hair; crowd, multitude; *Mil.* platoon. **p. de ejecución,** firing squad
peltre /'peltre/ *m,* pewter
peluca /pe'luka/ *f,* wig; periwig; *Inf.* scolding
peludo /pe'luðo/ *a* hairy. *m,* long-haired rug
peluquería /peluke'ria/ *f,* hairdressing establishment; hairdressing trade
peluquero /pelu'kero/ **(-ra)** *n* hairdresser; barber
peluquín /pelu'kin/ *m,* small wig
pelusa /pe'lusa/ *f,* down, soft hair; fluff, nap
pena /'pena/ *f,* punishment, penalty; grief; pain, suffering; difficulty, trouble; mourning veil; hardship; anxiety; embarrassment; tail feather. **p. capital** *or* **p. de la vida,** capital punishment. **a duras penas,** with great difficulty. **so p. de,** under penalty of. **valer** (*or* **merecer**) **la p.,** to be worth while
penable /pe'naβle/ *a* punishable
penacho /pe'natʃo/ *m,* topknot, crest (of birds); plume, panache; *Inf.* pride, arrogance
penado /pe'naðo/ **(-da)** *a* difficult, laborious; painful, troubled, afflicted *—n* convict
penal /pe'nal/ *a* penal; punitive
penalidad /penali'ðað/ *f,* trouble, labor, difficulty; *Law.* penalty
penar /pe'nar/ *vt* to penalize; punish; *—vi* suffer; undergo purgatorial pains; *—vr* suffer anguish. **p. por,** to long for
penca /'penka/ *f, Bot.* fleshy leaf; lash, strap, cat-o'-nine-tails
penco /'penko/ *m, Inf.* wretched nag
pendejo /pen'deho/ *m,* pubic hair; *Inf.* coward; jerk
pendencia /pen'denθia; pen'densia/ *f,* fight; quarrel
pendenciar /penden'θiar; penden'siar/ *vi* to fight; quarrel
pendenciero /penden'θiero; penden'siero/ *a* quarrelsome, aggressive
pender /pen'der/ *vi* to hang; depend; be pending
pendiente /pen'diente/ *a* pending; hanging; *Com.* outstanding. *m,* earring; pendant. *f,* slope, incline; gradient
péndola /'pendola/ *f,* feather, plume; quill pen; pendulum (of a clock)
pendolista /pendo'lista/ *mf* calligrapher
pendón /pen'don/ *m,* pennon, banner; *Bot.* shoot; *Inf.* lanky, slatternly woman; *pl* reins
péndulo /'pendulo/ *a* pendulous, hanging. *m,* pendulum
pene /'pene/ *m,* penis
penetrabilidad /penetraβili'ðað/ *f,* penetrability
penetración /penetra'θion; penetra'sion/ *f,* penetration; understanding, perspicuity; sagacity, shrewdness
penetrador /penetra'ðor/ *a* penetrating, perspicacious; sagacious, acute
penetrante /pene'trante/ *a* penetrating; deep; piercing (of sounds); acute, shrewd
penetrar /pene'trar/ *vt* to penetrate; permeate; master, comprehend; (*with en*) enter
penetrativo /penetra'tiβo/ *a* piercing
penicilina /peniθi'lina; penisi'lina/ *f,* penicillin
península /pe'ninsula/ *f,* peninsula. **la P.** the Iberian Peninsula
Península Ibérica, la /pe'ninsula i'βerika, la/ the Iberian Peninsula
penique /pe'nike/ *m,* penny
penitencia /peni'tenθia; peni'tensia/ *f,* penitence, repentance; penance
penitencial /peniten'θial; peniten'sial/ *a* penitential
penitenciaría /penitenθia'ria; penitensia'ria/ *f,* penitentiary
penitenciario /peniten'θiario; peniten'siario/ *a* penitentiary
penitente /peni'tente/ *a* penitent, repentant. *mf* penitent
penoso /pe'noso/ *a* laborious, difficult; grievous; painful; troublesome; *Inf.* foppish
pensado /pen'saðo/ *a* premeditated, deliberate. **de p.,** intentionally. **mal p.,** malicious, evil-minded
pensador /pensa'ðor/ *a* thinking; pensive. *m,* thinker
pensamiento /pensa'miento/ *m,* mind; thought; idea; suspicion, doubt; heartsease pansy; maxim; intention, project
pensar /pen'sar/ *vt irr* to think; purpose, intend; (*with en, sobre*) reflect upon; think about; *—vt* feed (animals). **p. entre sí, p. para consigo** *or* **p. para sí,** to think to oneself. See **acertar**
pensativo /pensa'tiβo/ *a* reflective, pensive
pensil /pen'sil/ *a* hanging. *m,* hanging garden; delightful garden
pensión /pen'sion/ *f,* pension, allowance; boarding house, private hotel; scholarship grant; cost of board; trouble, drudgery
pensionado /pensio'naðo/ **(-da)** *a* pensioned; retired *—n* scholarship holder. *m,* boarding school
pensionar /pensio'nar/ *vt* to pension, grant a pension to; charge a pension on
pensionista /pensio'nista/ *mf* pensioner; boarder
pentágono /pen'tagono/ *m,* pentagon *—a* pentagonal
pentagrama /penta'grama/ *or* **pentágrama** *m, Mus.* pentagram, stave
pentámetro /pen'tametro/ *m,* pentameter
Pentateuco /penta'teuko/ *m,* Pentateuch
Pentecostés /pentekos'tes/ *m,* Pentecost, Whitsuntide
penúltimo /pe'nultimo/ *a* next to the last, penultimate
penuria /pe'nuria/ *f,* scarcity; want, penury
peña /'peɲa/ *f,* crag, rock; boulder; group of friends; club. **ser una p.,** to be stony-hearted
peñasco /pe'ɲasko/ *m,* craggy peak
peñascoso /peɲas'koso/ *a* craggy, rocky
peñón /pe'ɲon/ *m,* rock; cliff; peak
peón /pe'on/ *m,* pedestrian; laborer; *South America* farmhand; top (toy); piece (chess, checkers); *Mech.* axle; infantryman. **p. caminero,** road mender. **p. de ajedrez,** pawn (in chess)
peonada /peo'naða/ *f,* day's manual labor; gang of laborers
peonía /peo'nia/ *f,* peony
peonza /pe'onθa; pe'onsa/ *f,* top; teetotum
peor /pe'or/ *a compar* **malo** worse *—adv compar* **mal,** worse *—a superl* **el (la, lo) peor; los (las) peores,** the worst. **p. que p.,** worse and worse. **tanto p.,** so much the worse
pepino /pe'pino/ *m,* cucumber plant; cucumber; *Fig.* pin, straw

pepita /pe'pita/ *f, Mineral.* nugget; pip, seed (of fruit)
peplo /'peplo/ *m,* Greek tunic, peplum
péptico /'peptiko/ *a* peptic
pequeñez /peke'ɲeθ; peke'ɲes/ *f,* littleness, smallness; pettiness; childhood; infancy; trifle, insignificant thing; meanness, baseness
pequeño /pe'keɲo/ *a* little, small; petty; very young; short, brief; humble, lowly
pera /'pera/ *f,* pear; goatee; *Fig.* plum, sinecure
peral /pe'ral/ *m,* pear tree; pearwood
perca /'perka/ *f, Ichth.* perch
percal /per'kal/ *m,* percale, calico
percalina /perka'lina/ *f,* percaline, binding cloth
percance /per'kanθe; per'kanse/ *m,* perquisite, attribute (gen. *pl*); disaster, mischance
percebe /per'θeβe; per'seβe/ *m,* (gen. *pl*) goose barnacle
percentaje /perθen'tahe; persen'tahe/ *m,* percentage
percepción /perθep'θion; persep'sion/ *f,* perception; idea, conception
perceptible /perθep'tiβle; persep'tiβle/ *a* perceptible
perceptivo /perθep'tiβo; persep'tiβo/ *a* perceptive
perceptor /perθep'tor; persep'tor/ **(-ra)** *a* perceptive —*n* observer
percha /'pertʃa/ *f,* stake, pole; coat hanger; perch (for birds); rack (for hay); hall stand, coat and hat stand, coatrack
perchero /per'tʃero/ *m,* hall stand; clothes rack; row of perches (for fowl, etc.)
percibir /perθi'βir; persi'βir/ *vt* to collect, draw, receive; perceive; understand, grasp
percibo /per'θiβo; per'siβo/ *m,* perceiving; collecting, drawing, receiving
percolador /perkola'ðor/ *m,* percolator (coffee)
percusión /perku'sion/ *f,* percussion; shock, vibration
percusor /perku'sor/ *m,* hammer (of a firearm)
percutir /perku'tir/ *vt* to percuss, strike
perdedor /perðe'ðor/ **(-ra)** *a* losing —*n* loser
perder /per'ðer/ *vt* to lose; throw away, squander; spoil, destroy; —*vi* fade (of colors); —*vr* lose one's way, be lost; be confused or perplexed; be shipwrecked; take to vice, become dissolute; be spoiled or destroyed; disappear; love madly. **p. la chaveta (por),** to go out of one's head (for), be wild (about). **p. la ocasión,** to let the chance slip. **p. los estribos,** to lose patience. **p. terreno,** to lose ground. **perderse de vista,** to be lost to sight. **echarse a p.,** to spoil, be damaged. See **entender**
perdición /perði'θion; perði'sion/ *f,* loss; perdition, ruin; damnation; depravity, viciousness
pérdida /'perðiða/ *f,* loss; waste. **p. cuantiosa,** heavy losses
perdidamente /perðiða'mente/ *adv* ardently, desperately; uselessly
perdigón /perði'gon/ *m,* young partridge; decoy partridge; hailstone, pellet, shot
perdigonada /perðigo'naða/ *f,* volley of hailstone; hailstone wound
perdiguero /perði'gero/ **(-ra)** *n* game dealer; setter, retriever
perdiz /per'ðiθ; per'ðis/ *f,* partridge. **p. blanca,** ptarmigan
perdón /per'ðon/ *m,* pardon, forgiveness; remission. **con p.,** with your permission; excuse me
perdonable /perðo'naβle/ *a* pardonable, excusable
perdonar /perðo'nar/ *vt* to pardon, forgive; remit, excuse; exempt; waste, lose; give up (a privilege)
perdonavidas /perðona'βiðas/ *m, Inf.* bully, braggart
perdulario /perðu'lario/ *a* careless, negligent; slovenly; vicious, depraved
perdurable /perðu'raβle/ *a* perpetual, everlasting; enduring, lasting
perdurar /perðu'rar/ *vi* to last, endure
perecedero /pereθe'ðero; perese'ðero/ *a* brief, fugitive, transient; perishable. *m, Inf.* poverty, want
perecer /pere'θer; pere'ser/ *vi irr* to end, finish; perish, die; suffer (damage, grief, etc.); be destitute; —*vr* (*with por*) long for, crave; desire ardently. See **conocer**
peregrinación /peregrina'θion; peregrina'sion/ *f,* journey, peregrination; pilgrimage
peregrinamente /peregrina'mente/ *adv* rarely, not often; beautifully, perfectly
peregrinar /peregri'nar/ *vi* to journey, travel; make a pilgrimage
peregrino /pere'grino/ **(-na)** *a* and *n* pilgrim —*a* migratory (birds); rare, unusual; extraordinary, strange; beautiful, perfect
perejil /pere'hil/ *m,* parsley; *Inf.* ornament or apparel (gen. *pl*); *pl* honors, titles
perengano /pereŋ'gano/ **(-na)** *n* so-and-so, such a one
perenne /pe'renne/ *a* incessant, constant; *Bot.* perennial
perennidad /perenni'ðað/ *f,* perpetuity
perentoriedad /perentorie'ðað/ *f,* peremptoriness; urgency
perentorio /peren'torio/ *a* peremptory; conclusive, decisive; urgent, pressing
pereza /pe'reθa; pe'resa/ *f,* laziness; languor, inertia; slowness, deliberateness
perezoso /pere'θoso; pere'soso/ *a* lazy; languid; slothful; slow, deliberate. *m, Zool.* sloth
perfección /perfek'θion; perfek'sion/ *f,* perfection; perfecting, perfect thing, virtue, grace
perfeccionamiento /perfekθiona'miento; perfeksiona'miento/ *m,* perfecting; progress, improvement
perfeccionar /perfekθio'nar; perfeksio'nar/ *vt* to perfect; complete
perfectamente /perfekta'mente/ *adv* perfectly; quite, entirely
perfecto /per'fekto/ *a* perfect; excellent, very good; complete; whole; *Gram.* perfect
perfidia /per'fiðia/ *f,* perfidy, treachery
pérfido /'perfiðo/ *a* perfidious, treacherous
perfil /per'fil/ *m,* ornament, decoration; outline, contour; profile; section (of metal); fine stroke (of letters); *pl* finishing touches; politeness, attention, courtesy. **de p.,** in profile; sideways
perfilado /perfi'laðo/ *a* long, elongated (of faces, etc.)
perfilar /perfi'lar/ *vt* to draw in profile; outline; —*vr* place oneself sideways, show one's profile; *Inf.* dress up, titivate
perforación /perfora'θion; perfora'sion/ *f,* perforation, boring; hole
perforador /perfora'ðor/ *a* perforating, boring. *m, Mech.* drill
perforar /perfo'rar/ *vt* to perforate, pierce; bore, drill, make a hole in
perfumador /perfuma'ðor/ **(-ra)** *a* perfuming —*n* perfumer. *m,* perfume burner
perfumar /perfu'mar/ *vt* to perfume; —*vi* give off perfume
perfume /per'fume/ *m,* perfume; scent, fragrance
perfumería /perfume'ria/ *f,* scent factory; perfumery; perfume shop
perfumista /perfu'mista/ *mf* perfumer
perfunctorio /perfunk'torio/ *a* perfunctory
pergamino /perga'mino/ *m,* parchment, vellum; document; diploma; *pl* aristocratic descent
pericardio /peri'karðio/ *m,* pericardium
pericia /pe'riθia; pe'risia/ *f,* expertness; skilled workmanship
pericial /peri'θial; peri'sial/ *a* expert, skillful
perico /pe'riko/ *m,* parakeet
periferia /peri'feria/ *f,* periphery
periférico /peri'feriko/ *a* peripheral
perifollos /peri'foʎos; peri'foyos/ *m pl, Inf.* frills, flounces, finery
perifrástico /peri'frastiko/ *a* periphrastic
perilla /pe'riʎa; pe'riya/ *f,* pear-shaped ornament; goatee; imperial. **p. de la oreja,** lobe of the ear. **venir de p.,** to be most opportune
perillán /peri'ʎan; peri'yan/ *m, Inf.* rascal, rogue
perímetro /pe'rimetro/ *m,* perimeter; precincts
perínclito /pe'rinklito/ *a* distinguished, illustrious; heroic
perineo /peri'neo/ *m,* perineum
perinola /peri'nola/ *f,* top, teetotum

periodicidad /perioðiθi'ðað; perioðisi'ðað/ *f*, periodicity
periódico /pe'rioðiko/ *a* periodic. *m*, newspaper; periodical publication
periodicucho /perioði'kutʃo/ *m*, rag (bad newspaper)
periodismo /perio'ðismo/ *m*, journalism
periodista /perio'ðista/ *mf* journalist
periodístico /perio'ðistiko/ *a* journalistic
período /pe'rioðo/ *m*, period; *Phys.* cycle; menstruation period; *Gram.* clause; age, era
periostio /pe'riostio/ *m*, periosteum
peripatético /peripa'tetiko/ *a* peripatetic
peripecia /peri'peθia; peri'pesia/ *f*, sudden change of fortune, vicissitude
peripuesto /peri'puesto/ *a Inf.* overelegant, spruce, too well-dressed; smart
periquete /peri'kete/ *m*, *Inf.* jiffy, trice
periquito /peri'kito/ *m*, parakeet; budgerigar
periscopio /peris'kopio/ *m*, periscope
perito /pe'rito/ **(-ta)** *a* expert; skillful, experienced —*n* expert
peritoneo /perito'neo/ *m*, peritoneum
perjudicador /perhuðika'ðor/ **(-ra)** *a* injurious, prejudicial —*n* injurer
perjudicar /perhuði'kar/ *vt* to harm, damage, injure; prejudice
perjudicial /perhuði'θial; perhuði'sial/ *a* injurious, noxious, harmful; prejudicial
perjuicio /per'huiθio; per'huisio/ *m*, injury, damage; harm; *Law.* prejudice
perjurador /perhura'ðor/ **(-ra)** *n* perjurer
perjurar /perhu'rar/ *vi* to perjure oneself, commit perjury; swear, curse
perjurio /per'hurio/ *m*, perjury
perjuro /per'huro/ **(-ra)** *a* perjured, forsworn —*n* perjurer
perla /'perla/ *f*, pearl; *Archit.* bead; *Fig.* treasure, jewel, dear. **de perlas,** excellent; exactly right
perlero /per'lero/ *a* pearl
perlesía /perle'sia/ *f*, paralysis; palsy
perlino /per'lino/ *a* pearly, pearl-colored
permanecer /permane'θer; permane'ser/ *vi irr* to stay, remain. **p. en posición de firme,** to stand at attention. See **conocer**
permanencia /perma'nenθia; perma'nensia/ *f*, stay, sojourn; permanence
permanente /perma'nente/ *a* permanent; lasting, enduring
permanganato /permaŋga'nato/ *m*, permanganate
permeabilidad /permeaβili'ðað/ *f*, permeability
permisible /permi'siβle/ *a* permissible, allowable
permisivo /permi'siβo/ *a* permissive
permiso /per'miso/ *m*, permission, leave; permit; (*Mil.* etc.) pass. **¡Con p.!** Excuse me!; Allow me!
permitir /permi'tir/ *vt* to permit, allow
permuta /per'muta/ *f*, exchange
permutación /permuta'θion; permuta'sion/ *f*, permutation, interchange
permutar /permu'tar/ *vt* to exchange
pernear /perne'ar/ *vi* to kick; *Inf.* bustle; fret, be impatient
pernetas, en /per'netas, en/ *adv* barelegged
perniciosidad /perniθiosi'ðað; pernisiosi'ðað/ *f*, perniciousness
pernicioso /perni'θioso; perni'sioso/ *a* pernicious
pernil /per'nil/ *m*, *Anat.* hock; ham; leg of pork; leg (of trousers)
pernio /'pernio/ *m*, hinge (of doors, windows)
perniquebrar /pernike'βrar/ *vt irr* to break the legs of. See **quebrar**
perno /'perno/ *m*, bolt, pin, spike
pernoctar /pernok'tar/ *vi* to spend the night (away from home)
pero /'pero/ *conjunc* but. *m*, *Inf.* defect; difficulty, snag
perogrullada /perogru'ʎaða; perogru'yaða/ *f*, *Inf.* truism
perol /pe'rol/ *m*, *Cul.* pan
peroné /pero'ne/ *m*, fibula
peroración /perora'θion; perora'sion/ *f*, peroration
perorar /pero'rar/ *vi* to make a speech; *Inf.* speak pompously; ask insistently
peróxido /pe'roksiðo/ *m*, peroxide
perpendicular /perpendiku'lar/ *a* perpendicular. *f*, perpendicular
perpetración /perpetra'θion; perpetra'sion/ *f*, perpetration
perpetrar /perpe'trar/ *vt* to perpetrate
perpetua /per'petua/ *f*, *Bot.* immortelle, everlasting
perpetuación /perpetua'θion; perpetua'sion/ *f*, perpetuation
perpetuar /perpe'tuar/ *vt* to perpetuate; —*vr* last, endure
perpetuidad /perpetui'ðað/ *f*, perpetuity
perpetuo /per'petuo/ *a* everlasting; lifelong
perplejidad /perplehi'ðað/ *f*, perplexity, bewilderment, doubt
perplejo /per'pleho/ *a* perplexed, bewildered, doubtful
perquirir /perki'rir/ *vt irr* to search carefully. See **adquirir**
perra /'perra/ *f*, bitch; *Inf.* sot, drunkard; tantrums. **p. chica,** five-cent coin. **p. gorda,** ten-cent coin
perrada /pe'rraða/ *f*, pack of dogs; *Inf.* dirty trick
perrengue /pe'rreŋgue/ *m*, *Inf.* short-tempered person
perrera /pe'rrera/ *f*, dog kennel; useless toil; *Inf.* tantrums
perrería /perre'ria/ *f*, pack of dogs; *Inf.* dirty trick; fit of anger
perrero /pe'rrero/ *m*, dog fancier; kennel worker
perro /'perro/ *m*, dog. **p. caliente** hot dog. **p. danés,** Great Dane. **p. de aguas,** poodle; spaniel. **p. de casta,** thoroughbred dog. **p. de lanas** poodle. **p. de muestra,** pointer. **p. de presa,** bulldog. **p. de San Bernardo,** St. Bernard (dog). **p. de Terranova,** Newfoundland (dog). **p. del hortelano,** dog in the manger. **p. dogo** bulldog. **p. esquimal** husky. **p. faldero,** lap dog. **p. lobo,** wolfhound. **p. pachón,** dachshund. **p. pastor alemán** *or* **p. policía,** German shepherd. **p. pequinés,** Pekingese. **p. perdiguero,** retriever. **p. pomerano,** spitz, Pomeranian (dog). **p. sabueso español,** spaniel. **p. zorrero,** foxhound. *Inf.* **A p. viejo no hay tus tus,** You can't fool an old dog. **vivir como perros y gatos,** *Inf.* to live like cat and dog
perruno /pe'rruno/ *a* dog, dog-like
persa /'persa/ *a* and *mf* Persian. *m*, Persian (language)
persecución /perseku'θion; perseku'sion/ *f*, pursuit; persecution; annoyance, importuning
perseguidor /persegi'ðor/ **(-ra)** *a* pursuing; tormenting —*n* pursuer; tormentor, persecutor
perseguimiento /persegi'miento/ *m*, pursuit
perseguir /perse'gir/ *vi irr* to pursue; persecute, torment; importune. See **seguir**
perseverancia /perseβe'ranθia; perseβe'ransia/ *f*, perseverance
perseverante /perseβe'rante/ *a* persevering; constant
perseverar /perseβe'rar/ *vi* to persevere; last, endure
persiana /per'siana/ *f*, Venetian blind; flowered silk material
pérsico /'persiko/ *a* Persian. *m*, peach tree; peach
persignar /persig'nar/ *vt* to sign; make the sign of the cross over; —*vr* cross oneself
persistencia /persis'tenθia; persis'tensia/ *f*, persistence
persistente /persis'tente/ *a* persistent
persistir /persis'tir/ *vi* to persist
persona /per'sona/ *f*, person; personage; character (in a play, etc.); (*Gram. Eccl.*) person. **de p. a p.,** in private, face to face
personaje /perso'nahe/ *m*, important person, personage; character (in a play, etc.)
personal /perso'nal/ *a* personal. *m*, staff, personnel
personalidad /personali'ðað/ *f*, personality
personalismo /persona'lismo/ *m*, personality; personal question
personalizar /personali'θar; personali'sar/ *vt* to become personal, be offensive
personalmente /personal'mente/ *adv* personally

personarse /perso'narse/ *vr* to present oneself, call, appear
personificación /personifika'θion; personifika'sion/ *f,* personification
personificar /personifi'kar/ *vt* to personify
perspectiva /perspek'tiβa/ *f,* perspective; view; outlook; aspect, appearance. **p. aérea,** bird's-eye view
perspicacia /perspi'kaθia; perspi'kasia/ *f,* perspicacity, shrewdness
perspicaz /perspi'kaθ; perspi'kas/ *a* perspicacious, clear-sighted
perspicuidad /perspikui'ðað/ *f,* perspicuity
perspicuo /pers'pikuo/ *a* lucid, clear
persuadir /persua'ðir/ *vt* to persuade
persuasible /persua'siβle/ *a* persuadable
persuasión /persua'sion/ *f,* persuasion; belief, conviction, opinion
persuasiva /persua'siβa/ *f,* persuasiveness
persuasivo /persua'siβo/ *a* persuasive
pertenecer /pertene'θer; pertene'ser/ *vi irr* to belong; relate, concern. See **conocer**
perteneciente /pertene'θiente; pertene'siente/ *a* belonging (to), pertaining (to)
pertenencia /perte'nenθia; perte'nensia/ *f,* ownership, proprietorship; property, accessory
pértiga /'pertiga/ *f,* long rod; pole. **salto de p.,** pole vaulting
pertinacia /perti'naθia; perti'nasia/ *f,* pertinacity, doggedness
pertinaz /perti'naθ; perti'nas/ *a* pertinacious, stubborn, dogged
pertinencia /perti'nenθia; perti'nensia/ *f,* relevance, appropriateness
pertinente /perti'nente/ *a* relevant, apposite; appropriate
pertrechar /pertre'tʃar/ *vt* to supply, equip; prepare, make ready
pertrechos /per'tretʃos/ *m pl, Mil.* armaments, stores; equipment, appliances
perturbación /perturβa'θion; perturβa'sion/ *f,* disturbance; agitation
perturbador /perturβa'ðor/ **(-ra)** *a* disturbing —*n* disturber; heckler
perturbar /pertur'βar/ *vt* to disturb; agitate
Perú /pe'ru/ Peru
peruano /pe'ruano/ **(-na)** *a* and *n* Peruvian
perversidad /perβersi'ðað/ *f,* wickedness, depravity
perversión /perβer'sion/ *f,* perversion; wickedness, evil
perversivo /perβer'siβo/ *a* perversive
perverso /per'βerso/ *a* wicked, iniquitous, depraved
pervertir /perβer'tir/ *vt irr* to pervert, corrupt; distort. See **sentir**
pesa /'pesa/ *f,* weight; clock weight; gymnast's weight. **pesas y medidas,** weights and measures
pesacartas /pesa'kartas/ *m,* letter scale, letter balance
pesada /pe'saða/ *f,* weighing
pesadez /pesa'ðeθ; pesa'ðes/ *f,* heaviness; obesity; tediousness, tiresomeness; slowness; fatigue
pesadilla /pesa'ðiʎa; pesa'ðiya/ *f,* nightmare
pesado /pe'saðo/ *a* heavy; obese; deep (of sleep); oppressive (of weather); slow; unwieldy; tedious; impertinent; dull, boring; offensive
pesadumbre /pesa'ðumbre/ *f,* heaviness; grief, sorrow; trouble, anxiety
pésame /'pesame/ *m,* expression of condolence. **dar el p.,** to present one's condolences
pesantez /pesan'teθ; pesan'tes/ *f,* weight, heaviness; seriousness, gravity
pesar /pe'sar/ *m,* grief, sorrow; remorse. **a p. de,** in spite of
pesar /pe'sar/ *vi* to weigh; be heavy; be important; grieve, cause regret (e.g. *Me pesa mucho,* I am very sorry); influence, affect; —*vt* weigh; consider. **Mal que me (te,** etc.) **pese...,** Much as I regret...
pesario /pe'sario/ *m,* pessary
pesaroso /pesa'roso/ *a* regretful, remorseful; sorrowful
pesca /'peska/ *f,* fishery; angling, fishing; catch of fish. **p. a la rastra,** trawling. **p. deportiva** sport fishing. **p. mayor,** deep-sea fishing
pescadería /peskaðe'ria/ *f,* fishery; fish store; fish market
pescadilla /peska'ðiʎa; peska'ðiya/ *f, Ichth.* whiting
pescado /pes'kaðo/ *m,* fish (out of the water); salt cod
pescador /peska'ðor/ **(-ra)** *n* fisherman; angler
pescante /pes'kante/ *m,* driving seat; coach box; jib (of a crane)
pescar /pes'kar/ *vt* to fish; *Inf.* catch in the act; acquire. **p. a la rastra,** to trawl
pescozón /pesko'θon; pesko'son/ *m,* slap on the neck or head
pescuezo /pes'kueθo; pes'kueso/ *m,* neck; throat; haughtiness, arrogance. **torcer el p.,** to wring the neck (of chickens, etc.)
pesebre /pe'seβre/ *m,* manger, stable; feeding trough
pésimamente /'pesimamente/ *adv* extremely badly
pesimismo /pesi'mismo/ *m,* pessimism
pesimista /pesi'mista/ *a* pessimistic. *mf* pessimist
pésimo /'pesimo/ *a superl* **malo** extremely bad
peso /'peso/ *m,* weighing; weight; heaviness; gravity; importance; influence; load; peso (coin); scale, balance. **p. bruto,** gross weight. **p. de joyería,** troy weight. **p. específico,** *Phys.* specific gravity. **p. pluma,** (*Boxing*) featherweight
pespunte /pes'punte/ *m,* backstitch
pesquera /pes'kera/ *f,* fishing ground, fishery
pesquería /peske'ria/ *f,* fishing, angling; fisherman's trade; fishing ground, fishery
pesquero /pes'kero/ *a* fishing (of boats, etc.)
pesquisa /pes'kisa/ *f,* investigation, examination; search
pesquisar /peski'sar/ *vt* to investigate, look into; search
pestaña /pes'taɲa/ *f,* eyelash; *Sew.* edging, fringe; ear, lug; *Naut.* fluke
pestañear /pestaɲe'ar/ *vi* to wink; blink; flutter the eyelashes
pestañeo /pesta'ɲeo/ *m,* winking; blinking
peste /'peste/ *f,* plague, pestilence; nauseous smell; epidemic; pest; vice; *pl* oaths, curses. **p. bubónica,** bubonic plague. **p. roja** syphilis. **p. de las abejas,** foul brood. **echar pestes,** to swear; fume
pestífero /pes'tifero/ *a* noxious
pestilencia /pesti'lenθia; pesti'lensia/ *f,* plague, pestilence
pestilente /pesti'lente/ *a* pestilential
pestillo /pes'tiʎo; pes'tiyo/ *m,* latch; lock bolt. **p. de golpe,** safety latch
petaca /pe'taka/ *f,* cigarette or cigar case; tobacco pouch
pétalo /'petalo/ *m,* petal
petardista /petar'ðista/ *mf* swindler, impostor
petardo /pe'tarðo/ *m,* detonator; torpedo; firecracker; fraud
petición /peti'θion; peti'sion/ *f,* petition, request
peticionario /petiθio'nario; petisio'nario/ **(-ia)** *n* petitioner —*a* petitionary
petimetra /peti'metra/ *f,* stylish and affected young woman
petimetre /peti'metre/ *m,* fop
petirrojo /peti'rroho/ *m,* robin
petitorio /peti'torio/ *a* petitionary. *m, Inf.* importunity
peto /'peto/ *m,* breastplate; front (of a shirt); bib
pétreo /'petreo/ *a* petrous
petrificación /petrifika'θion; petrifika'sion/ *f,* petrifaction
petrificar /petrifi'kar/ *vt* to petrify; —*vr* become petrified
petrografía /petrogra'fia/ *f,* petrology
petróleo /pe'troleo/ *m,* petroleum; oil, mineral oil. **p. bruto,** crude oil. **p. de lámpara,** kerosene
petrolero /petro'lero/ **(-ra)** *a* oil, petroleum —*n* petroleum seller; incendiarist. *m,* oil tanker
petrolífero /petro'lifero/ *a* oil-bearing
petroso /pe'troso/ *a* stony, rocky
petulancia /petu'lanθia; petu'lansia/ *f,* insolence; vanity
petulante /petu'lante/ *a* insolent; vain

pez /peθ; pes/ *m,* fish; *pl* Pisces. *f, Chem.* pitch. **p. sierra,** swordfish
pezón /pe'θon; pe'son/ *m, Bot.* stalk; nipple; axle pivot; point (of land, etc.)
pezonera /peθo'nera; peso'nera/ *f,* linchpin
pezuña /pe'θuɲa; pe'suɲa/ *f,* cloven hoof (of cows, pigs, etc.)
piada /'piaða/ *f,* chirping, twittering
piadoso /pia'ðoso/ *a* compassionate; kind, pitiful; pious, religious
piafar /pia'far/ *vi* to stamp, paw the ground (horses)
piamontés /piamon'tes/ **(-esa)** *a* and *n* Piedmontese
pianista /pia'nista/ *mf* piano maker; piano dealer; pianist
piano /'piano/ *m,* pianoforte. **p. de cola,** grand piano. **p. de media cola,** baby grand. **p. vertical,** upright piano
piante /'piante/ *a* chirping, twittering
piar /piar/ *vi* to chirp, twitter
piara /'piara/ *f,* herd of swine; pack (of horses, etc.)
pica /'pika/ *f, Mil.* pike; bullfighter's goad; pike soldier; stonecutter's hammer. **a p. seca,** in vain. **pasar por las picas,** to suffer hardship. **poner una p. en Flandes,** to triumph over great difficulties
picacho /pi'katʃo/ *m,* peak, summit
picada /pi'kaða/ *f,* prick; bite; peck; *Aer.* dive
picadero /pika'ðero/ *m,* riding school; paddock (of a racetrack)
picado /pi'kaðo/ *a Sew.* pinked. *m, Cul.* hash
picador /pika'ðor/ *m,* horse trainer; meat chopper; horseman armed with a goad (bullfights)
picadura /pika'ðura/ *f,* puncture; prick; sting; *Sew.* pinking; peck (of birds); cut tobacco; black tobacco; beginning of caries in teeth
picajoso /pika'hoso/ *a* hypersensitive, touchy, peevish
picamaderos /pikama'ðeros/ *m,* woodpecker
picante /pi'kante/ *a* piquant; mordant; hot, highly seasoned. *m,* mordancy; pungency
picapleitos /pika'pleitos/ *m, Inf.* shady lawyer, pettifogger
picaporte /pika'porte/ *m,* latch, door catch; door knocker
picar /pi'kar/ *vt* to prick; sting; peck; bite; chop fine; mince; nibble (of fishing); irritate (the skin); *Sew.* pink; burn (the tongue); eat (grapes); goad; spur; stipple (walls); stimulate, encourage; split, cleave; *Mil.* harass; vex; *Mus.* play staccato; *—vi* burn (of the sun); smart (of cuts, etc.); eat sparingly; *Auto.* knock; (*with en*) knock at (doors, etc.); *—vr* be moth-eaten; go rotten (fruit, etc.); grow choppy (of the sea); be piqued; boast
pícaramente /'pikaramente/ *adv* knavishly, cunningly
picardear /pikarðe'ar/ *vi* to play the rogue; behave mischievously
picardía /pikar'ðia/ *f,* knavery, roguery; mischievousness; practical joke; wantonness
picaresco /pika'resko/ *a* roguish, picaresque, knavish
pícaro /'pikaro/ **(-ra)** *a* knavish; base, vile; astute; mischievous *—n* rogue
picatoste /pika'toste/ *m,* kind of fritter
picaza /pi'kaθa; pi'kasa/ *f,* magpie
picazo /pi'kaθo; pi'kaso/ *m,* blow with a pike or anything pointed; peck, tap with a beak (of birds); sting
picazón /pika'θon; pika'son/ *f,* itch, irritation; annoyance
pícea /'piθea; 'pisea/ *f, Bot.* spruce
píceo /'piθeo; 'piseo/ *a* piscine, fish-like
pichel /pi'tʃel/ *m,* tankard
pichón /pi'tʃon/ **(-ona)** *m,* male pigeon *—n Inf.* darling
pico /'piko/ *m,* beak (of birds); peak; woodpecker; odd amount (e.g. *treinta y p.,* thirty-odd); sharp point; spout (of a jug, etc.); *Inf.* mouth; blarney, gab. **p. de cigüeña,** crane's-bill. **p. de oro,** silver-tongued orator
picor /pi'kor/ *m,* burning sensation in the mouth; smarting; itching, irritation
picoso /pi'koso/ *a* pitted, marked by smallpox
picota /pi'kota/ *f,* pillory; peak; spire
picotazo /piko'taθo; piko'taso/ *m,* peck; dab; sting, bite
picoteado /pikote'aðo/ *a* peaked, having points
picotear /pikote'ar/ *vt* to peck (of a bird); *—vi* toss the head (of horses); *Inf.* chatter senselessly; *—vr Inf.* slang each other
picotero /piko'tero/ *a Inf.* chattering, talkative; indiscreet
pictografía /piktogra'fia/ *f,* picture writing
pictórico /pik'toriko/ *a* pictorial
picudo /pi'kuðo/ *a* pointed, peaked; having a spout; *Inf.* chattering
pie /pie/ *m,* foot; stand, support; stem (of a glass, etc.); standard (of a lamp); *Bot.* trunk, stem; sapling; lees, sediment; *Theat.* cue; foot (measure); custom; (metrics) foot; motive, cause; pretext; (metrics) meter. **p. de cabra,** crowbar. **p. de imprenta,** printer's mark, printer's imprint. **p. de piña,** clubfoot. **p. de rey,** calliper. **p. palmado,** webfoot. **al p. de la letra,** punctiliously. *Inf.* **andar con pies de plomo,** to walk warily. **a p.,** on foot. **a p. firme,** without budging; steadfastly. *Inf.* **buscar tres pies al gato,** to look for something that isn't there; twist a person's words. **de a p.,** on foot. **en p. de guerra,** on a wartime footing. *Inf.* **poner pies en polvorosa,** to quit
piedad /pie'ðað/ *f,* piety; pity, compassion; *Art.* pietà
piedra /'pieðra/ *f,* stone; tablet; *Med.* gravel. **p. de amolar,** whetstone, grindstone. **p. angular,** cornerstone (also *Fig.*). **p. caliza,** limestone. **p. clave,** keystone. **p. de construcción,** building stone; child's block. **p. de toque,** touchstone, test. **p. filosofal,** philosopher's stone. **p. fundamental,** foundation stone. **p. miliaria,** milestone. **p. mortuoria,** tombstone. *Fig. Inf.* **no dejar p. sin remover,** to leave no stone unturned. **no dejar p. sobre p.,** to demolish, destroy completely
piel /piel/ *f,* skin; fur; hide; leather; peel (of some fruits); rind (of bacon). **p. de gallina,** *Fig.* goose flesh. **p. de rata,** horse blanket. **p. de Rusia,** Russian leather
piélago /'pielago/ *m,* high seas; sea, ocean; glut, superabundance
pienso /'pienso/ *m, Agr.* fodder
pierna /'pierna/ *f, Anat.* leg; *Mech.* shank; leg of a compass. *Inf.* **a p. suelta,** at one's ease. **en piernas,** barelegged
pietismo /pie'tismo/ *m,* pietism
pietista /pie'tista/ *a* pietistic. *mf* pietist
pieza /'pieθa; 'piesa/ *f,* portion; piece; component part; room; *Theat.* play; roll (of cloth); piece (in chess, etc.); coin; piece (of music). **p. de recambio** *or* **p. de repuesto,** spare part. **p. de recibo,** reception room. *Inf.* **quedarse en una p.,** to be struck dumb
pífano /'pifano/ *m,* fife; fife player, fifer
pigmentación /pigmenta'θion; pigmenta'sion/ *f,* pigmentation
pigmentario /pigmen'tario/ *a* pigmentary
pigmento /pig'mento/ *m,* pigment
pigmeo /pig'meo/ **(-ea)** *a* and *n* pygmy
pignoración /pignora'θion; pignora'sion/ *f,* hypothecation; pawning; mortgage
pignorar /pigno'rar/ *vt* to hypothecate; pawn; mortgage
pigre /'pigre/ *a* lazy; negligent, careless
pigricia /pi'griθia; pi'grisia/ *f,* laziness; negligence
pijama /pi'hama/ *m,* pajamas
pila /'pila/ *f,* trough, basin; heap, pile; *Elec.* battery; *Eccl.* parish; pier, pile; *Phys.* cell. **p. atómica,** atomic pile. **p. bautismal,** *Eccl.* font
pilar /pi'lar/ *m,* fountain basin; milestone; pillar
pilastra /pi'lastra/ *f,* pier, pile; pilaster
píldora /'pildora/ *f, Med.* pill; *Inf.* disagreeable news
pillador /piʎa'ðor; piya'ðor/ **(-ra)** *a* pillaging, plundering *—n* plunderer
pillaje /pi'ʎahe; pi'yahe/ *m,* pillaging, looting; robbery, theft
pillar /pi'ʎar; pi'yar/ *vt* to pillage; steal, rob; seize, snatch; *Inf.* surprise, find out (in a lie, etc.). **pillarse el dedo,** to get one's finger caught (in a door, etc.)
pillastre /pi'ʎastre; pi'yastre/ *m, Inf.* rogue, ragamuffin
pillear /piʎe'ar; piye'ar/ *vi Inf.* to lead a rogue's life

pillería /piʎe'ria; piye'ria/ *f, Inf.* gang of rogues; *Inf.* rogue's trick
pillo /'piʎo; 'piyo/ *m,* rogue, knave
pilón /pi'lon/ *m,* fountain basin; pestle; loaf sugar; pylon
pilongo /pi'loŋgo/ *a* thin, lean
píloro /'piloro/ *m,* pylorus
pilotaje /pilo'tahe/ *m,* pilotage; piling, pilework. **examen de p.,** flying test
pilotar /pilo'tar/ *vt* to pilot
pilote /pi'lote/ *m, Engin.* pile
pilotear /pilote'ar/ *vt* to pilot
piloto /pi'loto/ *m,* pilot; mate (in merchant ships). **p. de pruebas,** test pilot
pimentero /pimen'tero/ *m,* pepper plant; pepper shaker
pimentón /pimen'ton/ *m,* red pepper, cayenne
pimienta /pi'mienta/ *f,* pepper. **p. húngara,** paprika. *Inf.* **ser como una p.,** to be sharp as a needle
pimiento /pi'miento/ *m,* pimento; capsicum; red pepper; pepper plant. **p. de cornetilla,** chili pepper
pimpollo /pim'poʎo; pim'poyo/ *m,* sapling; sprout, shoot; rosebud
pina /'pina/ *f,* conical stone; felloe (of a wheel)
pinacoteca /pinako'teka/ *f,* art gallery, picture gallery
pináculo /pi'nakulo/ *m,* pinnacle, summit; climax, culmination; *Archit.* finial
pinar /pi'nar/ *m,* pinewood
pincarrasco /pinka'rrasko/ *m,* pin oak
pincel /pin'θel; pin'sel/ *m,* paintbrush; artist, painter; painting technique. **p. para las cejas,** eyebrow pencil
pincelada /pinθe'laða; pinse'laða/ *f,* brushstroke. **dar la última p.,** to add the finishing touch
pincelero /pinθe'lero; pinse'lero/ **(-ra)** *n* seller or maker of paintbrushes; brush box
pinchadura /pintʃa'ðura/ *f,* prick, puncture, piercing; sting; nipping, biting
pinchar /pin'tʃar/ *vt* to prick; puncture; pierce; sting; nip, bite. **no p. ni cortar,** to be ineffective (of persons)
pinchazo /pin'tʃaθo; pin'tʃaso/ *m,* prick; puncture; sting; incitement
pinche /'pintʃe/ *m,* scullion
pineda /pi'neða/ *f,* pinewood
pingajo /piŋ'gaho/ *m, Inf.* tatter, rag
pingajoso /piŋga'hoso/ *a Inf.* tattered, ragged
pingo /'piŋgo/ *m, Inf.* tatter, rag; *pl Inf.* cheap clothes
pingüe /'piŋgue/ *a* fat, greasy; fertile, rich
pingüino /piŋ'guino/ *m,* penguin
pino /'pino/ *a* steep. *m, Bot.* pine, deal; *Poet.* ship. **p. de tea,** pitch pine. **p. silvestre,** red fir
pinocha /pi'notʃa/ *f,* pine needle
pinta /'pinta/ *f,* spot; marking; mark; fleck; look, appearance; pint (measure); drop, drip; spot ball (in billiards)
pintamonas /pinta'monas/ *mf Inf.* dauber
pintar /pin'tar/ *vt* to paint; describe, picture; exaggerate; —*vi* show, manifest itself; —*vr* make up (one's face). *Inf.* **pintarse solo para,** to be very good at, excel at
pintiparado /pintipa'raðo/ *a* most similar, very alike; fitting, apposite
pintiparar /pintipa'rar/ *vt Inf.* to compare
pintor /pin'tor/ **(-ra)** *n* painter, artist. **p. callejero,** sidewalk artist, pavement artist. **p. de brocha gorda,** house painter
pintoresco /pinto'resko/ *a* picturesque, quaint, pretty
pintoresquismo /pintores'kismo/ *m,* picturesqueness
pintorrear /pintorre'ar/ *vt Inf.* to daub, paint badly
pintura /pin'tura/ *f,* painting; paint, pigment; picture, painting; description. **p. a la aguada,** watercolor painting. **p. al fresco,** fresco. **p. al látex,** latex paint. **p. al óleo,** oil painting. **p. al pastel,** pastel drawing
pinturería /pinture'ria/ *f,* paint store
pinturero /pintu'rero/ *a Inf.* affected, conceited; dandified, overdressed
pinza /'pinθa; 'pinsa/ *f,* clamp. **p. de la ropa,** clothes peg
pinzas /'pinθas; 'pinsas/ *f pl,* pincers; pliers; tweezers; forceps. **p. hemostáticas,** arterial forceps
pinzón /pin'θon; pin'son/ *m,* chaffinch
piña /'piɲa/ *f,* pineapple; cluster, knot (of people, etc.); pinecone
piñón /pi'ɲon/ *m,* pine nut; *Mech.* pinion, chain wheel
pío /'pio/ *a* pious; compassionate; good; piebald. *m,* chirping, cheep; *Inf.* longing
piojo /'pioho/ *m,* louse
piojoso /pio'hoso/ *a* lousy; avaricious, stingy
pionero /pio'nero/ *m,* pioneer
piorrea /pio'rrea/ *f,* pyorrhea
pipa /'pipa/ *f,* barrel, cask; tobacco pipe; pip (of fruits)
pipar /pi'par/ *vi* to smoke a pipe
pipeta /pi'peta/ *f,* pipette
pipiar /pi'piar/ *vi* to chirp, twitter
pique /'pike/ *m,* pique, resentment. **a p. de,** on the verge of, about to. **echar a p.,** *Naut.* to sink; destroy. **irse a p.,** to sink, founder
piquero /pi'kero/ *m,* pike soldier
piqueta /pi'keta/ *f,* pick, mattock; mason's hammer
piquete /pi'kete/ *m,* puncture, small wound; *Mil.* picket; pole, stake; small hole (in garments); picket (in strikes)
pira /'pira/ *f,* funeral pyre; bonfire
piragua /pi'ragua/ *f,* piragua, canoe
pirámide /pi'ramiðe/ *f,* pyramid
pirarse /pi'rarse/ *vr Inf.* to slip away
pirata /pi'rata/ *a* piratical *mf* pirate; savage, cruel person
piratear /pirate'ar/ *vi* to play the pirate
piratería /pirate'ria/ *f,* piracy; plunder, robbery
pirático /pi'ratiko/ *a* piratical
pirenaico, pirineo /pire'naiko, piri'neo/ *a* Pyrenean
pirético /pi'retiko/ *a* pyretic
piriforme /piri'forme/ *a* pear-shaped
Pirineos, los /piri'neos, los/ the Pyrenees
piromancia /piro'manθia; piro'mansia/ *f,* pyromancy
piropear /pirope'ar/ *vt Inf.* to pay compliments to
piropo /pi'ropo/ *m,* carbuncle; *Inf.* compliment. **echar piropos,** to pay compliments
pirotecnia /piro'teknia/ *f,* pyrotechnics
pirotécnico /piro'tekniko/ *a* pyrotechnical. *m,* pyrotechnist
pirrarse /pi'rrarse/ *vr Inf.* to desire ardently
pírrico /'pirriko/ *a* Pyrrhic
pirueta /pi'rueta/ *f,* pirouette, twirl
pisada /pi'saða/ *f,* treading, stepping; footprint, footstep; stepping on a person's foot. **seguir las pisadas de alguien,** *Fig.* to follow in someone's footsteps, imitate someone
pisano /pi'sano/ **(-na)** *a* and *n* Pisan
pisapapeles /pisapa'peles/ *m,* paperweight
pisar /pi'sar/ *vt* to tread upon; trample upon; crush; *Mus.* press (strings); trespass upon
pisaverde /pisa'βerðe/ *m, Inf.* fop, dandy
piscicultura /pisθikul'tura; pissikul'tura/ *f,* pisciculture, fish farming
piscina /pis'θina; pis'sina/ *f,* fishpond; swimming pool; *Eccl.* piscina
piscolabis /pisko'laβis/ *m, Inf.* snack, light meal
piso /'piso/ *m,* treading, trampling; story, floor; flooring; apartment. **p. bajo,** ground floor
pisón /pi'son/ *m,* rammer, ram
pisotear /pisote'ar/ *vt* to trample; crush under foot; tread on; step on; humiliate, treat inconsiderately
pisoteo /piso'teo/ *m,* trampling under foot; treading
pista /'pista/ *f,* track, trail (of animals); circus ring; racetrack, racecourse. **p. de patinar,** skating rink. **p. de vuelo,** *Aer.* landing field. *Inf.* **seguir la p. a,** to spy upon
pistacho /pis'tatʃo/ *m,* pistachio
pistar /pis'tar/ *vt* to pestle, pound
pistero /pis'tero/ *m,* feeding cup
pistilo /pis'tilo/ *m,* pistil
pistola /pis'tola/ *f,* pistol. **p. ametralladora,** machine gun.
pistolera /pisto'lera/ *f,* holster; pistol case
pistolero /pisto'lero/ *m,* gangster

pistoletazo /pistole'taθo; pistole'taso/ *m,* pistol shot; pistol wound
pistón /pis'ton/ *m, Mus.* piston; *Mil.* percussion cap; *Mech.* piston
pitada /pi'taða/ *f,* blast on a whistle, whistling; impertinence
pitagórico /pita'goriko/ **(-ca)** *a* and *n* Pythagorean
pitanza /pi'tanθa; pi'tansa/ *f,* alms, charity; *Inf.* daily food; pittance, scanty remuneration
pitar /pi'tar/ *vi* to play the whistle; *—vt* pay (debts); smoke; give alms to
pitido /pi'tiðo/ *m,* blast on a whistle; whistling (of birds)
pitillera /piti'ʎera; piti'yera/ *f,* cigarette case; female cigarette maker
pito /'pito/ *m,* whistle; *Mus.* fife. *Inf.* **Cuando pitos flautas, cuando flautas pitos,** It's always the unexpected that happens. *Inf.* **no valer un p.,** to be not worth a straw
pitoflero /pito'flero/ **(-ra)** *n* mediocre performer (gen. on a wind instrument); *Inf.* talebearer, gossip
pitón /pi'ton/ *m, Zool.* python; nascent horn (of goats, etc.); spout; protuberance; *Bot.* sprout
pitonisa /pito'nisa/ *f, Myth.* pythoness; witch, enchantress
pitorrearse /pitorre'arse/ *vr* to ridicule, mock
pituitario /pitui'tario/ *a* pituitary
pituso /pi'tuso/ *a* small and amusing (of children)
pivote /pi'βote/ *m,* pivot, swivel, gudgeon
piyama /pi'yama/ *m,* pajamas
pizarra /pi'θarra; pi'sarra/ *f,* slate; blackboard
pizarral /piθa'rral; pisa'rral/ *m.* **pizarrería** *f,* slate quarry
pizarrero /piθa'rrero; pisa'rrero/ *m,* slater
pizarrín /piθa'rrin; pisa'rrin/ *m,* slate pencil
pizca /'piθka; 'piska/ *f, Inf.* atom, speck, crumb; jot, whit. **¡Ni p.!** Not a scrap!
pizpireta /piθpi'reta; pispi'reta/ *a f, Inf.* coquettish; smart; dressed up
placa /'plaka/ *f,* plate, disk; *Art.* plaque; *Photo.* plate; star (insignia). **p. recordatorio,** commemorative plaque
placabilidad /plakaβili'ðað/ *f,* placability, appeasability
pláceme /'plaθeme; 'plaseme/ *m,* congratulation
placentero /plaθen'tero; plasen'tero/ *a* agreeable, pleasant
placer /pla'θer; pla'ser/ *vt irr* to please, give pleasure to, gratify. *m, Naut.* reef, sandbank; pleasure; wish, desire; permission, consent; entertainment, diversion. **a p.,** at one's convenience; at leisure *—Pres. Indic.* **plazco, places,** etc *—Preterite* **plugo, pluguieron.** *Pres. Subjunc.* **plazca,** etc *—Imperf. Subjunc.* **pluguiese,** etc.
placibilidad /plaθiβili'ðað; plasiβili'ðað/ *f,* agreeableness, pleasantness
placible /pla'θiβle; pla'siβle/ *a* agreeable, pleasant
placidez /plaθi'ðeθ; plasi'ðes/ *f,* placidity, calmness, serenity
plácido /'plaθiðo; 'plasiðo/ *a* placid, calm, serene
placiente /pla'θiente; pla'siente/ *a* pleasing, attractive
plácito /'plaθito; 'plasito/ *m,* decision, judgment, opinion
plafón /pla'fon/ *m,* ceiling light; *Archit.* panel
plaga /'plaga/ *f,* plague; disaster, calamity; epidemic; glut; pest; grief
plagar /pla'gar/ *vt* (*with de*) to infect with; *—vr* (*with de*) be covered with; be overrun by; be infested with
plagiar /pla'hiar/ *vt* to plagiarize, copy; kidnap, hold for ransom
plagiario /pla'hiario/ **(-ia)** *n* plagiarist
plagio /'plahio/ *m,* plagiary; kidnapping
plan /plan/ *m,* plan; scheme; plane. **p. quinquenal,** five-year plan
plana /'plana/ *f,* sheet, page; mason's trowel; plain. **p. mayor,** (*Mil. Nav.*) staff
planadora /plana'ðora/ *f,* steamroller
plancha /'plantʃa/ *f,* sheet, slab, plate; flatiron; horizontal suspension (in gymnastics); *Naut.* gangway, gangplank; *Inf.* howler
planchado /plan'tʃaðo/ *m,* ironing; ironing to be done or already finished
planchador /plantʃa'ðor/ **(-ra)** *n* ironer
planchar /plan'tʃar/ *vt* to iron, press with an iron
planchear /plantʃe'ar/ *vt* to plate (with metal)
planeador /planea'ðor/ *m, Aer.* glider
planear /plane'ar/ *vt* to plan out; make plans for; *—vi Aer.* glide
planeo /pla'neo/ *m, Aer.* glide
planeta /pla'neta/ *m,* planet
planetario /plane'tario/ *a* planetary. *m,* planetarium
planicie /pla'niθie; pla'nisie/ *f,* levelness, evenness; plain
plano /'plano/ *a* flat, level; plane. *m, Geom.* plane; plan, map; *Aer.* aileron, wing
planta /'planta/ *f, Bot.* plant; sole (of the foot); plantation; layout, plan; position of the feet (in dancing, fencing); scheme, project. **p. baja,** ground floor. **p. vivaz,** perennial plant. *Inf.* **buena p.,** good appearance
plantación /planta'θion; planta'sion/ *f,* planting; plantation, nursery
plantador /planta'ðor/ **(-ra)** *n* planter. *m, Agr.* dibble. *f.* **plantadora,** mechanical planter
plantar /plan'tar/ *vt* to plant; erect; place; found, set up; pose (a problem); raise (a question, etc.); *Inf.* leave in the lurch; *—vr* take up one's position; jib (of horses); oppose
planteamiento /plantea'miento/ *m,* execution; putting into practice; planning; statement (of problems)
plantel /plan'tel/ *m,* nursery garden; training school, nursery
plantilla /plan'tiʎa; plan'tiya/ *f,* young plant; insole (of shoes); *Mech.* template, jig
plantío /plan'tio/ *m,* plantation, afforestation; planting *—a* planted or ready for planting (ground)
plantón /plan'ton/ *m,* plant or sapling ready for transplanting; *Bot.* cutting; doorkeeper, porter. **dar un p.** (**a**), to keep (a person) waiting a long time
plañidera /plaɲi'ðera/ *f,* paid mourner
plañidero /plaɲi'ðero/ *a* mournful, piteous, anguished
plañido /pla'ɲiðo/ *m,* lament, weeping, wailing
plañir /pla'ɲir/ *vi* and *vt irr* to lament, wail, weep. See **tañer**
plasma /'plasma/ *m,* plasma
plasmar /plas'mar/ *vt* to mold, throw (pottery)
plástica /'plastika/ *f,* art of clay modeling; plastic
plasticidad /plastiθi'ðað; plastisi'ðað/ *f,* plasticity
plástico /'plastiko/ *a* plastic; flexible, malleable, soft
plata /'plata/ *f,* silver; silver (coins); money; white. **p. labrada,** silverware
plataforma /plata'forma/ *f,* platform; running board (of a train); *Rail.* turntable
plátano /'platano/ *m,* banana tree, banana; plantain; plane tree
platea /pla'tea/ *f, Theat.* pit. **butaca de p.,** pit stall
plateado /plate'aðo/ *a* silvered; silver-plated; silvery
plateador /platea'ðor/ *m,* plater
platear /plate'ar/ *vt* to electroplate, silver
platería /plate'ria/ *f,* silversmith's art or trade; silversmith's shop or workshop
platero /pla'tero/ *m,* silversmith; jeweler
plática /'platika/ *f,* conversation; exhortation, sermon; address, discourse
platicar /plati'kar/ *vt* and *vi* to converse (about)
platija /pla'tiha/ *f,* plaice
platillo /pla'tiʎo; pla'tiyo/ *m,* saucer; kitty (in card games); pan (of a scale); *pl* cymbals
platinado /plati'naðo/ *m,* plating
platino /pla'tino/ *m,* platinum
platívolo /pla'tiβolo/ *m,* flying saucer
plato /'plato/ *m,* plate; dish; *Cul.* course, dish; pan (of a scale). **p. sopero,** soup plate. **p. trinchero,** meat dish. *Inf.* **comer en un mismo p.,** to be on intimate terms. **nada entre dos platos,** much ado about nothing
platónico /pla'toniko/ *a* Platonic
platonismo /plato'nismo/ *m,* Platonism
plausibilidad /plausiβili'ðað/ *f,* plausibility
plausible /plau'siβle/ *a* plausible, reasonable

playa /'plaia/ *f,* beach, seashore, strand
plaza /'plaθa; 'plasa/ *f,* square (in a town, etc.); marketplace; fortified town; space; duration; employment, post.; *Com.* market. **p. de armas,** garrison town; military camp. **p. de toros,** bullring. **p. fuerte,** strong place, fortress. **sentar p.,** to enlist in the army
plazo /'plaθo; 'plaso/ *m,* term, duration; expiration of term, date of payment; installment. **a plazos,** *Com.* by installments, on the installment system
plazoleta /plaθo'leta; plaso'leta/ *f,* small square (in gardens, etc.)
pleamar /plea'mar/ *f, Naut.* high water
plebe /'pleβe/ *f,* common people; rabble, mob
plebeyo /ple'βeio/ **(-ya)** *a* plebeian —*n* commoner, plebeian
plebiscito /pleβis'θito; pleβis'sito/ *m,* plebiscite
plectro /'plektro/ *m,* plectrum
plegable /ple'gaβle/ *a* foldable
plegadera /plega'ðera/ *f,* folder; folding knife; paper folder
plegadizo /plega'ðiθo; plega'ðiso/ *a* folding; collapsible; jointed
plegado /ple'gaðo/ *m,* pleating; folding
plegador /plega'ðor/ *a* folding. *m,* folding machine
plegadura /plega'ðura/ *f,* folding, doubling; fold, pleat
plegar /ple'gar/ *vt irr* to fold; pleat; *Sew.* gather; —*vr* submit, give in. See **acertar**
plegaria /ple'garia/ *f,* fervent prayer
pleitear /pleite'ar/ *vt* to go to court about; indulge in litigation
pleitista /plei'tista/ *a* quarrelsome, litigious
pleito /'pleito/ *m,* action, lawsuit; dispute, quarrel; litigation. **p. de familia,** family squabble. **ver el p.,** *Law.* to try a case
plenamente /plena'mente/ *adv* fully, entirely
plenario /ple'nario/ *a* full, complete; *Law.* plenary
plenilunio /pleni'lunio/ *m,* full moon
plenipotencia /plenipo'tenθia; plenipo'tensia/ *f,* full powers (diplomatic, etc.)
plenipotenciario /plenipoten'θiario; plenipoten'siario/ *a* and *m,* plenipotentiary
plenitud /pleni'tuð/ *f,* fullness, completeness; plenitude, abundance
pleno /'pleno/ *a* full. *m,* general meeting
pleonasmo /pleo'nasmo/ *m, Gram.* pleonasm
pleonástico /pleo'nastiko/ *a* pleonastic
pleuresía /pleure'sia/ *f,* pleurisy
plexo /'plekso/ *m,* plexus
pléyades /'pleiaðes/ *f pl,* Pleiades
pliego /'pliego/ *m,* sheet (of paper); letter, packet of papers
pliegue /'pliege/ *m,* fold, pleat; *Sew.* gather
plinto /'plinto/ *m, Archit.* plinth (of a column); baseboard
plisar /pli'sar/ *vt* to pleat; fold
plomada /plo'maða/ *f,* plummet; sounding lead; plumb, lead
plomería /plome'ria/ *f,* plumbing; plumbing business; lead roofing
plomero /plo'mero/ *m,* plumber
plomizo /plo'miθo; plo'miso/ *a* lead-like; lead-colored, gray
plomo /'plomo/ *m,* lead (metal); plummet; bullet; *Inf.* bore, tedious person
pluma /'pluma/ *f,* feather; pen; plumage; quill; penmanship; writer; writing profession. **p. estilográfica,** fountain pen. **a vuela p.,** as the pen writes, written in a hurry
plumado /plu'maðo/ *a* feathered
plumaje /plu'mahe/ *m,* plumage, feathers; plume
plúmbeo /'plumbeo/ *a* plumbeous, leaden
plúmeo /'plumeo/ *a* feathered, plumed
plumero /plu'mero/ *m,* feather duster; plume, feather; plumage
plumón /plu'mon/ *m,* down; feather bed
plumoso /plu'moso/ *a* feathered
plural /plu'ral/ *a* and *m,* plural
pluralidad /plurali'ðað/ *f,* plurality; multitude, number
pluralizar /plurali'θar; plurali'sar/ *vt* to pluralize
plurilingüe /pluri'liŋgue/ *a* multilingual
pluscuamperfecto /pluskuamper'fekto/ *m,* pluperfect
plusmarquista /plusmar'kista/ *mf Sports.* recordholder
plutocracia /pluto'kraθia; pluto'krasia/ *f,* plutocracy
plutócrata /plu'tokrata/ *mf* plutocrat
plutocrático /pluto'kratiko/ *a* plutocratic
plutónico /plu'toniko/ *a Geol.* Plutonic
pluviómetro /plu'βiometro/ *m,* rain gauge
poblacho /po'βlatʃo/ *m,* miserable town or village
población /poβla'θion; poβla'sion/ *f,* peopling; population; town
poblado /po'βlaðo/ *m,* inhabited place; town; village
poblador /poβla'ðor/ **(-ra)** *a* populating —*n* colonist, settler
poblar /po'βlar/ *vt irr* to colonize; people, populate; breed fast; stock, supply; —*vr* put forth leaves (of trees). See **contar**
pobre /'poβre/ *a* poor; indigent, needy; mediocre; unfortunate; humble, meek. *mf* beggar, pauper, needy person. *Inf.* **ser p. de solemnidad,** to be down and out
pobrero /po'βrero/ *m, Eccl.* distributor of alms
pobretería /poβrete'ria/ *f,* poverty; needy people
pobretón /poβre'ton/ *a* extremely needy
pobreza /po'βreθa; po'βresa/ *f,* poverty, need; shortage; timidity; *Mineral.* baseness; poorness (of soil, etc.)
pocero /po'θero; po'sero/ *m,* well digger
pocilga /po'θilga; po'silga/ *f,* pigsty; *Inf.* filthy place
poción /po'θion; po'sion/ *f,* potion, drink; mixture, dose
poco /'poko/ *a* little, scanty; *pl* few. *m,* small amount, a little —*adv* little; shortly, in a little while. **p. a p.,** by degrees, little by little; slowly. **p. más o menos,** more or less, approximately. **por p.,** almost, nearly (always used with the present tense, e.g. *Por p. me caigo,* I almost fell). **tener en p. (a),** to have a poor opinion of; undervalue
poda /'poða/ *f, Agr.* pruning; pruning season
podadera /poða'ðera/ *f,* pruning knife
podar /po'ðar/ *vt Agr.* to prune, trim
poder /po'ðer/ *m,* power; authority, jurisdiction; *Law.* power of attorney; strength; ability; proxy; efficacy; possession; *pl* authority; power of attorney. **los poderes constituidos,** the established authorities; the powers that be. **p. de adquisición,** purchasing power. **casarse por poderes,** to be married by proxy
poder /po'ðer/ *vt irr* to be able to (e.g. *Podemos comprar estas naranjas,* We can (are able to) buy these oranges). **Dice que la calamidad podía haberse evitado,** He says that the disaster could have been averted). **p.** also expresses possibility (e.g. *Pueden haber ido a la ciudad,* They may have gone to the city. *¡Qué distinta pudo haber sido su vida!* How different his life might have been!) —*impers* be possible. **a más no p.,** of necessity, without being able to help it; to the utmost. **no p. con,** to be unable to control or manage. **no p. hacer más,** to have no alternative, have to; be unable to do more. **no p. menos de,** to be obliged to, have no alternative but. **no p. contener su emoción,** to be overcome with emotion. **no p. ver a,** to hate (persons) —*impers* **Puede que venga esta tarde,** He may come (perhaps he will come) this afternoon —*Pres. Part.* **pudiendo.** *Pres. Indic.* **puedo, puedes, puede, pueden.** *Fut.* **podré,** etc —*Condit.* **podría,** etc —*Preterite* **pude, pudiste,** etc —*Pres. Subjunc.* **pueda, puedas, pueda, puedan.** *Imperf. Subjunc.* **pudiese,** etc.
poderío /poðe'rio/ *m,* power, authority; sway, rule; dominion; wealth
poderoso /poðe'roso/ *a* powerful; opulent; effective, efficacious; mighty, magnificent
podredumbre /poðre'ðumbre/ *f,* decay; pus; *Fig.* canker, anguish
podredura, podrición /poðre'ðura, poðri'θion; poðre'ðura, poðri'sion/ *f,* putrefaction; decay
podrido /po'ðriðo/ *a* rotten; putrid; corrupt; decayed
podrir /po'ðrir/ *vt* See **pudrir**
poema /po'ema/ *m,* poem. **p. sinfónico,** tone poem
poesía /poe'sia/ *f,* poetry, verse; lyric, poem
poeta /po'eta/ *m,* poet

poetastro /poe'tastro/ *m,* poetaster
poética /po'etika/ *f,* poetics
poético /po'etiko/ *a* poetical
poetisa /poe'tisa/ *f,* poetess
poetizar /poeti'θar; poeti'sar/ *vi* to write verses; *—vt* poeticize
polaco /po'lako/ **(-ca)** *a* Polish *—n* Pole. *m,* Polish (language)
polainas /po'lainas/ *f pl,* leggings, puttees, gaiters
polar /po'lar/ *a* polar
polaridad /polari'ðað/ *f,* polarity; polarization
polarización /polariθa'θion; polarisa'sion/ *f,* polarization
polarizar /polari'θar; polari'sar/ *vt* to polarize
polca /'polka/ *f,* polka
polea /po'lea/ *f,* pulley; *Naut.* block
polémica /po'lemika/ *f,* polemic, controversy, dispute
polémico /po'lemiko/ *a* polemical
polemista /pole'mista/ *mf* disputant, controversialist
polen /'polen/ *m,* pollen
poliandria /po'liandria/ *f,* polyandry
polichinela /politʃi'nela/ *m,* Punchinello
policía /poli'θia; poli'sia/ *f,* police; government, polity, administration; civility, courtesy; cleanliness, tidiness. *m,* policeman. **p. urbana,** city police
policíaco /poli'θiako; poli'siako/ *a* police; detective
policromo /poli'kromo/ *a* polychrome
poliedro /po'lieðro/ *m,* polyhedron
polifacético /polifa'θetiko; polifa'setiko/ *a* many-sided
polifonía /polifo'nia/ *f,* polyphony
polifónico /poli'foniko/ *a* polyphonic
poligamia /poli'gamia/ *f,* polygamy
polígamo /po'ligamo/ **(-ma)** *a* polygamous *—n* polygamist
poligloto /poli'gloto/ **(-ta)** *n* polyglot. *f,* polyglot Bible
polígono /po'ligono/ *a* polygonal. *m,* polygon
polilla /po'liʎa; po'liya/ *f,* moth; moth grub; destroyer, ravager
polimorfismo /polimor'fismo/ *m, Chem.* polymorphism
polimorfo /poli'morfo/ *a* polymorphous
Polinesia /poli'nesia/ Polynesia
polinesio /poli'nesio/ **(-ia)** *a* and *n* Polynesian
polinización /poliniθa'θion; polinisa'sion/ *f,* pollination
poliomielitis /poliomie'litis/ *f,* poliomyelitis, polio
pólipo /'polipo/ *m, Zool.* polyp; octopus; *Med.* polyp
polisílabo /poli'silaβo/ *a* polysyllabic. *m,* polysyllable
polista /po'lista/ *mf* polo player
politécnico /poli'tekniko/ *a* polytechnic
politeísmo /polite'ismo/ *m,* polytheism
politeísta /polite'ista/ *a* polytheistic. *mf* polytheist
política /po'litika/ *f,* politics; civility, courtesy; diplomacy; tact; policy
politicastro /politi'kastro/ *m,* corrupt politician
político /po'litiko/ *a* political; civil, courteous; in-law, by marriage (relationships). *m,* politician
politiquear /politike'ar/ *vi Inf.* to dabble in politics, talk politics
politizarse /politi'θarse; politi'sarse/ *vr* to enter the political arena
póliza /'poliθa; 'polisa/ *f, Com.* policy; *Com.* draft; share certificate; revenue stamp; admission ticket; lampoon. **p. a prima fija,** fixed-premium policy. **p. de seguros,** insurance policy. **p. dotal,** endowment policy
polizón /poli'θon; poli'son/ *m,* loafer, tramp; stowaway; bustle (of a dress)
polla /'poʎa; 'poya/ *f,* pullet; *Inf.* flapper, young woman
pollada /po'ʎaða; po'yaða/ *f,* brood, hatch (especially of chickens)
pollastro /po'ʎastro; po'yastro/ **(-ra)** *n* pullet.
pollera /po'ʎera; po'yera/ *f,* female poultry breeder or seller; chicken coop; go-cart
pollería /poʎe'ria; poye'ria/ *f,* poultry market or shop
pollero /po'ʎero; po'yero/ *n* poultry breeder; poulterer. *m,* hen coop
pollino /po'ʎino; po'yino/ **(-na)** *n* young ass; donkey
pollo /'poʎo; 'poyo/ *m,* chicken; *Inf.* youth, stripling; *Fig. Inf.* downy bird. *Inf.* **p. pera,** young blood, lad. **sacar pollos,** to hatch chickens
polo /'polo/ *m,* pole (all meanings); *Fig.* support; popular Andalusian song; *Sports.* polo. **de p. a p.,** from pole to pole
polonés /polo'nes/ **(-esa)** *a* Polish *—n* Pole
polonesa /polo'nesa/ *f,* polonaise; short coat
Polonia /po'lonia/ Poland
poltrón /pol'tron/ *a* lazy, idle
poltronería /poltrone'ria/ *f,* idleness, laziness
polución /polu'θion; polu'sion/ *f, Med.* ejaculation
poluto /po'luto/ *a* filthy, unclean
Pólux /'poluks/ *m,* Pollux
polvareda /polβa'reða/ *f,* dust cloud; storm, agitation
polvera /pol'βera/ *f,* powder bowl; powder puff; powder compact
polvo /'polβo/ *m,* dust; powder; pinch (of snuff, etc.); *pl* face or dusting powder. **Se hizo como por polvos de la madre celestina,** It was done as if by magic. *Inf.* **limpio de p. y paja,** gratis, for nothing; net (of profit)
pólvora /'polβora/ *f,* gunpowder; bad temper. **p. de algodón,** guncotton.
polvorear /polβore'ar/ *vt* to powder, dust with powder
polvoriento /polβo'riento/ *a* dusty; powdery, covered with powder
polvorín /polβo'rin/ *m,* very fine powder; powder magazine; powder flask
polvoroso /polβo'roso/ *a* dusty; covered with powder
pomada /po'maða/ *f,* pomade; salve, ointment
pomar /po'mar/ *m,* orchard (especially an apple orchard)
pómez /'pomeθ; 'pomes/ *f,* pumice stone (**piedra p.**)
pomo /'pomo/ *m, Bot.* pome; pomander; nosegay; pommel, hilt (of a sword); handle; rose (of watering can)
pomología /pomolo'hia/ *f,* pomology, art of fruit growing
pompa /'pompa/ *f,* pomp, splendor; ceremonial procession; air bubble; peacock's outspread tail; *Naut.* pump; billowing of clothes in the wind
Pompeya /pom'peia/ Pompeii
pompeyano /pompe'iano/ *a* Pompeian
pomposidad /pomposi'ðað/ *f,* pomposity
pomposo /pom'poso/ *a* stately, ostentatious, magnificent; inflated, pompous; florid, bombastic
pómulo /'pomulo/ *m,* cheekbone
ponche /'pontʃe/ *m,* punch, toddy
ponchera /pon'tʃera/ *f,* punch bowl
poncho /'pontʃo/ *a* lazy, negligent. *m,* military cloak; poncho, cape
ponderación /pondera'θion; pondera'sion/ *f,* weighing; reflection, consideration; exaggeration
ponderador /pondera'ðor/ *a* reflective, deliberate; exaggerated
ponderar /ponde'rar/ *vt* to weigh; consider, ponder; exaggerate; overpraise
ponderosidad /ponderosi'ðað/ *f,* heaviness; ponderousness, dullness
ponderoso /ponde'roso/ *a* heavy; ponderous; circumspect
ponedero /pone'ðero/ *a* egg-laying (of hens). *m,* nest
ponencia /po'nenθia; po'nensia/ *f,* clause, section; office of referee or arbitrator; report, referendum
poner /po'ner/ *vt irr* to place, put; arrange; set (the table); bet, stake; appoint (to an office); call, name; lay (eggs); set down (in writing); calculate, count; suppose; leave to a person's judgment; risk; contribute; prepare; need, take; cause, inspire (emotions); make, cause; adapt; add; cause to become (angry, etc.); insult; praise; (*with prep a + infin*) begin to. **p. a contribución,** to lay under contribution, turn to account, utilize. **ponerle el cascabel al gato** *or* **el collar al gato,** to bell the cat. **p. los cuernos (a),** to cuckold. **p. al corriente,** to bring up to date, inform. **p. a prueba,** to test. **p. casa,** to set up house. *Inf.* **p. colorado a,** to make blush. **p. coto a,** to put a stop to, check. **p. en comparación,** to compare. **p. conato en,** to put a great deal of effort into. **p. en cotejo,** to

collate. **p. en limpio,** to make a fair copy (of). **p. en marcha,** to start, set in motion. **p. en práctica,** to put into effect. **p. por caso,** to take as an example (e.g. *Pongamos por caso...* For example,...). **p. por encima (de),** to prefer —*vr* to place oneself; become; put on (garments, etc.); dirty or stain oneself; set (of the sun, stars); oppose; deck oneself, dress oneself up; arrive; (*with prep a + infin*) begin to. **ponerse al corriente,** to bring oneself up to date. **ponerse bien,** to improve; get better (in health). **ponerse colorado,** to blush, flush. **p. una base racional a la fe,** to give faith a rational foundation. **p. los cimientos de,** lay the foundation of, lay the foundations for. **p. una conferencia,** to make a long-distance call —*Pres. Indic.* **pongo, pones,** etc —*Fut.* **pondré,** etc —*Condit.* **pondría,** etc —*Imperat.* **pon.** *Past Part.* **puesto.** *Preterite* **puse, pusiste,** etc —*Pres. Subjunc.* **ponga,** etc —*Imperf. Subjunc.* **pusiese,** etc.

ponientada /ponien'taða/ *f,* steady west wind

poniente /po'niente/ *m,* west; west wind

pontazgo /pon'taθgo; pon'tasgo/ *m,* bridge toll

pontear /ponte'ar/ *vt* to bridge; make bridges

pontificado /pontifi'kaðo/ *m,* pontificate, papacy

pontífice /pon'tifiθe; pon'tifise/ *m,* pontifex; pope, pontiff; archbishop; bishop

pontificial /pontifi'θial; pontifi'sial/ *a* and *m,* pontifical

pontificio /ponti'fiθio; ponti'fisio/ *a* pontifical

pontón /pon'ton/ *m, Mil.* pontoon; hulk used as a prison, hospital, store, etc.; wooden bridge

pontonero /ponto'nero/ *m,* pontonier, military engineer

ponzoña /pon'θoɲa; pon'soɲa/ *f,* poison, venom

ponzoñoso /ponθo'ɲoso; ponso'ɲoso/ *a* poisonous, venomous; noxious; harmful

popa /'popa/ *f, Naut.* stern, poop. **en p.,** abaft, astern, aft

popelina /pope'lina/ *f,* poplin

populachería /populatʃe'ria/ *f,* cheap popularity with the rabble

populachero /popula'tʃero/ *a* mob, vulgar

populacho /popu'latʃo/ *m,* mob, rabble

popular /popu'lar/ *a* popular

popularidad /populari'ðað/ *f,* popularity

popularizar /populari'θar; populari'sar/ *vt* to popularize; —*vr* grow popular

popularmente /popular'mente/ *adv* popularly

populoso /popu'loso/ *a* populous, crowded

popurrí /popu'rri/ *m, Cul.* stew; potpourri; miscellany

poquedad /poke'ðað/ *f,* paucity, scarcity; timidity, cowardice; trifle, mere nothing

poquísimo /po'kisimo/ *a superl* **poco** very little

poquito /po'kito/ *m,* very little

por /por/ *prep* for; by; through, along; during; because, as (e.g. *Lo desecharon p. viejo,* They threw it away because it was old); however (e.g. *p. bonito que sea,* however pretty it is); during; in order to (e.g. *Lo hice p. no ofenderla,* I did it in order not to offend her); toward, in favor of, for; for the sake of; on account of, by reason of (e.g. *No pudo venir p. estar enfermo,* He could not come on account of his illness); via, by (e.g. *p. correo aéreo,* by airmail); as for (e.g. *P. mí, lo rechazo,* As for me, I refuse it. *p. mi cuenta,* to my way of thinking; on my own); in exchange for (e.g. *Me vendió dos libros p. seis dólares,* He sold me two books for six dollars); in the name of; as a substitute for, instead of (e.g. *Hace mi trabajo p. mí,* He is doing my work for me), per. **Por** has several uses: 1. Introduces the agent after a passive (e.g. *La novela fue escrita p. él,* The novel was written by him). 2. Expresses movement through, along or about (e.g. *Andaban p. la calle,* They were walking along (or down) the street). 3. Denotes time at or during which an action occurs (e.g. *Ocurrió p. entonces un acontecimiento de importancia,* About that time an important event occurred). 4. Expresses rate or proportion (e.g. *seis por ciento,* six percent). 5. With certain verbs, means "to be' and expresses vague futurity (e.g. *El libro queda p. escribir,* The book remains to be written). **p. cortesía,** by courtesy, out of politeness. **p. cortesía de,** by courtesy of. **p. escrito,** in writing. **p. fas or p. nefas,** by fair means or foul; at any cost. **p. mucho que,** however great, however much; in spite of, notwithstanding. **¿P. qué?** Why? **p. si acaso,** in case, if by chance. **estar p.,** to be about to; be inclined to. **P. un clavo se pierde la herradura,** For want of a nail, the shoe was lost.

porcelana /porθe'lana; porse'lana/ *f,* porcelain, china; chinaware

porcentaje /porθen'tahe; porsen'tahe/ *m,* percentage

porche /'portʃe/ *m,* porch, portico

porcino /por'θino; por'sino/ *a* porcine. *m,* young pig; bruise

porción /por'θion; por'sion/ *f,* portion; *Com.* share; *Inf.* crowd; allowance, pittance

porcionista /porθio'nista; porsio'nista/ *mf* shareholder; sharer; boarding school student

porcuno /por'kuno/ *a* porcine, hoggish

pordiosear /porðiose'ar/ *vi* to ask alms, beg

pordioseo /porðio'seo/ *m,* asking alms, begging

pordiosero /porðio'sero/ **(-ra)** *a* begging —*n* beggar

porfía /por'fia/ *f,* obstinacy; importunity; tenacity. **a p.,** in competition

porfiadamente /porfiaða'mente/ *adv* obstinately

porfiado /por'fiaðo/ *a* obstinate, obdurate, persistent

porfiar /por'fiar/ *vi* to be obstinate, insist; persist

pórfido /'porfiðo/ *m,* porphyry

pormenor /porme'nor/ *m,* particular, detail (gen. *pl*); secondary matter

pormenorizar /pormenori'θar; pormenori'sar/ *vt* to describe in detail

pornografía /pornogra'fia/ *f,* pornography

pornográfico /porno'grafiko/ *a* pornographic, obscene

poro /'poro/ *m,* pore

porosidad /porosi'ðað/ *f,* porosity, permeability

poroso /po'roso/ *a* porous, leaky

porque /'porke/ *conjunc* because, for; in order that

porqué /por'ke/ *m,* reason, wherefore, why; *Inf.* money. **el cómo y el p.,** the why and the wherefore

porquería /porke'ria/ *f, Inf.* filth, nastiness; dirty trick; rudeness, gross act; trifle, thing of no account

porquerizo, porquero /porke'riθo, por'kero; porke'riso, por'kero/ *m,* swineherd

porra /'porra/ *f,* club, bludgeon; last player (in children's games); *Inf.* vanity, boastfulness; bore, tedious person

porrada /po'rraða/ *f,* blow with a club; buffet, knock, fall; *Inf.* folly; glut, abundance

porrazo /po'rraθo; po'rraso/ *m,* blow with a club; buffet, knock, fall

porrear /porre'ar/ *vi Inf.* to insist, harp on

porrería /porre'ria/ *f, Inf.* folly; obduracy, persistence

porreta /po'rreta/ *f,* green leaves of leeks, onions, and cereals. *Inf.* **en p.,** stark-naked

porrino /po'rrino/ *m,* seed of a leek; young leek plant

porrón /po'rron/ *m,* winebottle with a spout; earthenware jug

portaaviones /portaa'βiones/ *m,* aircraft carrier

portacartas /porta'kartas/ *m,* mailbag

portachuelo /porta'tʃuelo/ *m,* defile, narrow mountain pass

portada /por'taða/ *f,* front, facade; frontispiece, title page; portal, doorway

portado /por'taðo/ (**bien** *or* **mal**) *a* well- or ill-dressed or behaved

portador /porta'ðor/ **(-ra)** *n* carrier. *m, Com.* bearer; *Mech.* carrier

portaestandarte /ˌportaestan'darte/ *m,* standard-bearer

portafolio /porta'folio/ *m,* portfolio

portafusil /porta'fusil/ *m,* rifle sling

portal /por'tal/ *m,* entrance, porch; portico; city gate

portalámpara /porta'lampara/ *f,* lamp holder; *Elec.* socket

portalibros /porta'liβros/ *m,* bookstrap

portalón /porta'lon/ *m,* gangway

portamanteo /portaman'teo/ *m,* traveling bag

portamonedas /portamo'neðas/ *m,* pocketbook; handbag, purse

portanuevas /porta'nueβas/ *mf* bringer of news, newsmonger
portaobjetos /portaoβ'hetos/ *m*, stage (of a microscope)
portaplumas /porta'plumas/ *m*, pen holder
portar /por'tar/ *vt* to retrieve (of dogs); carry (arms); —*vr* behave (well or badly); bear oneself, act; be well, or ill (in health)
portátil /por'tatil/ *a* portable
portatostadas /portatos'taðas/ *m*, toast rack
portavoz /porta'βoθ; porta'βos/ *m*, megaphone; spokesman, mouthpiece
portazgo /por'taθgo; por'tasgo/ *m*, toll; tollbooth
portazguero /portaθ'gero; portas'gero/ *m*, toll collector
portazo /por'taθo; por'taso/ *m*, bang of the door; slamming the door in a person's face
porte /'porte/ *m*, transport; *Com.* carriage; postage; freight, transport cost; porterage; behavior, conduct; bearing, looks; capacity, volume; size, dimension; nobility (of descent); *Naut.* tonnage. **p. pagado,** charges prepaid
porteador /portea'ðor/ *m*, carrier; porter; carter
portear /porte'ar/ *vt* to carry, transport; —*vr* migrate (of birds)
portento /por'tento/ *m*, marvel, prodigy, portent
portentoso /porten'toso/ *a* marvelous, portentous
porteo /por'teo/ *m*, porterage, cartage
portería /porte'ria/ *f*, porter's lodge; porter's employment; *Sports.* goal
portero /por'tero/ **(-ra)** *n* doorman, doorkeeper; porter; concierge; janitor; *Sports.* goalkeeper. **p. eléctrico,** door buzzer
portezuela /porte'θuela; porte'suela/ *f*, *dim* small door; carriage door; pocket flap
pórtico /'portiko/ *m*, portico, piazza; porch; vestibule, hall
portillo /por'tiʎo; por'tiyo/ *m*, breach, opening; defile, narrow pass; *Fig.* loophole
portón /por'ton/ *m*, hall door, inner door
portorriqueño /portorri'keɲo/ **(-ña)** *a* and *n* Puerto Rican
portuario /por'tuario/ *a* dock, port
portugués /portu'ges/ **(-esa)** *a* and *n* Portuguese. *m*, Portuguese (language)
portuguesada /portuge'saða/ *f*, exaggeration
porvenir /porβe'nir/ *m*, future time
¡porvida! /por'βiða/ *interj* By the saints! By the Almighty!
pos /pos/ *prefix* after; behind. Also *adv* **en p.,** with the same meanings
posa /'posa/ *f*, tolling bell; *pl* buttocks
posada /po'saða/ *f*, dwelling; inn, tavern; lodging; hospitality
posaderas /posa'ðeras/ *f pl*, buttocks
posadero /posa'ðero/ **(-ra)** *n* innkeeper; boardinghouse keeper
posar /po'sar/ *vi* to lodge, live; rest; alight, perch; —*vt* set down (a burden); —*vr* settle (liquids); (*with en or sobre*) perch upon
posdata /pos'ðata/ *f*, P.S., postscript
pose /'pose/ *f*, *Photo.* time exposure; *Inf.* pose
poseedor /posee'ðor/ **(-ra)** *n* possessor, holder
poseer /pose'er/ *vt irr* to own, possess; know (a language, etc.); —*vr* restrain oneself. **estar poseído por,** to be possessed by (passion, etc.); be thoroughly convinced of. See **creer**
posesión /pose'sion/ *f*, ownership, occupancy; possession; property, territory (often *pl*)
posesionarse /posesio'narse/ *vr* to take possession; lay hold (of)
posesivo /pose'siβo/ *a* possessive
poseso /po'seso/ *a* possessed of an evil spirit
posesor /pose'sor/ **(-ra)** *n* owner, possessor
posfecha /pos'fetʃa/ *f*, postdate
posguerra /pos'gerra/ *f*, postwar period
posibilidad /posiβili'ðað/ *f*, possibility; probability; opportunity, means, chance; *pl* property, wealth
posibilitar /posiβili'tar/ *vt* to make possible, facilitate
posible /po'siβle/ *a* possible. *m pl*, property, personal wealth. **hacer lo p.** *or* **hacer todo lo p.,** to do everything possible; do one's best
posición /posi'θion; posi'sion/ *f*, placing; position; situation; status
positivamente /positiβa'mente/ *adv* positively, definitely
positivismo /positi'βismo/ *m*, positivism
positivista /positi'βista/ *a* positivistic. *mf* positivist
positivo /posi'tiβo/ *a* positive; certain, definite; (*Math. Elec.*) plus; true, real
pósito /'posito/ *m*, public granary; cooperative association
posma /'posma/ *f*, *Inf.* sluggishness, sloth
posmeridiano /posmeri'ðiano/ *a* and *m*, postmeridian
poso /'poso/ *m*, sediment; lees, dregs; repose, quietness
posponer /pospo'ner/ *vt irr* (*with prep a*) to place after; make subordinate to; value less than. See **poner**
posta /'posta/ *f*, post horse; stage, post; stake (cards)
postal /pos'tal/ *a* postal. *f*, postcard, postal card
poste /'poste/ *m*, post, stake
postema /pos'tema/ *f*, tumor, abscess; bore, tedious person
postergación /posterga'θion; posterga'sion/ *f*, delay; delaying; relegation; disregard of seniority (in promotion)
postergar /poster'gar/ *vt* to delay; disregard a senior claim to promotion
posteridad /posteri'ðað/ *f*, descendants; posterity
posterior /poste'rior/ *a* back, rear; hind; subsequent
posterioridad /posteriori'ðað/ *f*, posteriority
posteriormente /posterior'mente/ *adv* later, subsequently
postigo /pos'tigo/ *m*, secret door; grating, hatch; postern; shutter (of a window)
postillón /posti'ʎon; posti'yon/ *m*, postilion
postizo /pos'tiθo; pos'tiso/ *a* false, artificial, not natural. *m*, switch of false hair
postor /pos'tor/ *m*, bidder (at an auction)
postración /postra'θion; postra'sion/ *f*, prostration; exhaustion; depression, distress
postrar /pos'trar/ *vt* to cast down, demolish; prostrate, exhaust; —*vr* kneel down; be prostrated or exhausted
postre /'postre/ *a* last (in order). *m*, *Cul.* dessert. **a la p.,** at last, finally
postrero /pos'trero/ *a* last (in order); rearmost, hindmost
postrimeramente /postrimera'mente/ *adv* lastly, finally
postrimería /postrime'ria/ *f*, *Eccl.* last period of life
postulación /postula'θion; postula'sion/ *f*, entreaty, request
postulado /postu'laðo/ *m*, assumption; supposition; working hypothesis; *Geom.* postulate
postulante /postu'lante/ **(-ta)** *n* *Eccl.* postulant, applicant, candidate
postular /postu'lar/ *vt* to postulate
póstumo /'postumo/ *a* posthumous
postura /pos'tura/ *f*, posture, bearing; laying (of an egg); bid (at an auction); position; agreement, pact; bet, stake; planting; transplanted tree. **p. de vida,** way of life
potable /po'taβle/ *a* drinkable. **agua p.,** drinking water
potación /pota'θion; pota'sion/ *f*, potation, drink
potaje /po'tahe/ *m*, stew, potage; dried vegetables; mixed drink; hotchpotch
potasa /po'tasa/ *f*, potash
potasio /po'tasio/ *m*, potassium
pote /'pote/ *m*, pot; jar; flowerpot; *Cul.* cauldron; *Cul.* stew
potencia /po'tenθia; po'tensia/ *f*, power; potency; *Mech.* performance, capacity; strength, force; *Math.* power; rule, dominion
potencial /poten'θial; poten'sial/ *a* potential
potentado /poten'taðo/ *m*, potentate
potente /po'tente/ *a* potent; powerful; *Inf.* enormous
potestad /potes'tað/ *f*, authority, power; podesta,

Italian magistrate; potentate; *Math.* power; *pl* angelic powers
potestativo /potesta'tiβo/ *a Law.* facultative
potingue /po'tiŋgue/ *m, Inf.* brew; mixture; lotion; medicine; filthy place, pigsty
potra /'potra/ *f,* filly
potrada /po'traðа/ *f,* herd of colts
potrear /potre'ar/ *vt Inf.* to tease, annoy
potro /'potro/ *m,* colt, foal; rack (for torture); vaulting horse. **p. mesteño,** mustang
poyo /'poio/ *m,* stone seat
pozal /po'θal; po'sal/ *m,* pail, bucket
pozo /'poθo; 'poso/ *m,* well; shaft (in a mine). *Auto.* **p. colector,** crankcase
práctica /'praktika/ *f,* practice; custom, habit; method; exercise
practicabilidad /praktikaβili'ðað/ *f,* feasibility
practicable /prakti'kaβle/ *a* feasible, practicable
prácticamente /'praktikamente/ *adv* practically, in practice
practicante /prakti'kante/ *m,* medical practitioner; medical student; *Med.* intern; first-aid practitioner
practicar /prakti'kar/ *vt* to execute, perform; practice; make
práctico /'praktiko/ *a* practical; experienced, expert; workable. *m, Naut.* pilot
pradeño /pra'ðeɲo/ *a* meadow, prairie
pradera /pra'ðera/ *f,* meadow, field; lawn
pradería /praðe'ria/ *f,* meadowland, prairie
prado /'praðo/ *m,* meadow; grassland; field; lawn; walk (in cities)
Praga /'praga/ Prague
pragmatismo /pragma'tismo/ *m,* pragmatism
pragmatista /pragma'tista/ *a* pragmatic. *mf* pragmatist
pravedad /praβe'ðað/ *f,* wickedness, immorality, depravity
pravo /'praβo/ *a* wicked, immoral, depraved
pre /pre/ *m, Mil.* daily pay *—prep insep* pre-
preámbulo /pre'ambulo/ *m,* preamble, preface; importunate digression
prebenda /pre'βenda/ *f, Eccl.* prebend, benefice; *Inf.* sinecure
preboste /pre'βoste/ *m,* provost
precario /pre'kario/ *a* precarious, uncertain, insecure
precaución /prekau'θion; prekau'sion/ *f,* precaution, safeguard
precaucionarse /prekauθio'narse; prekausio'narse/ *vr* to take precautions, safeguard oneself
precautelar /prekaute'lar/ *vt* to forewarn; take precautions
precaver /preka'βer/ *vt* to prevent, avoid; *—vr* (*with de or contra*) guard against
precavido /preka'βiðo/ *a* cautious, forewarned
precedencia /preθe'ðenθia; prese'ðensia/ *f,* priority, precedence; superiority; preference, precedence
precedente /preθe'ðente; prese'ðente/ *a* preceding. *m,* antecedent; precedent
preceder /preθe'ðer; prese'ðer/ *vt* to precede; have precedence over, be superior to
preceptivo /preθep'tiβo; presep'tiβo/ *a* preceptive; didactic
precepto /pre'θepto; pre'septo/ *m,* precept; order, injunction; rule, commandment. **de p.,** obligatory
preceptor /preθep'tor; presep'tor/ **(-ra)** *n* teacher, instructor, tutor, preceptor
preces /'preθes; 'preses/ *f pl, Eccl.* prayers; entreaties
preciado /pre'θiaðo; pre'siaðo/ *a* excellent, esteemed, precious; boastful
preciar /pre'θiar; pre'siar/ *vt* to esteem, value; valuate, price; *—vr* boast
precintar /preθin'tar; presin'tar/ *vt* to seal; rope, string, tie up
precinto /pre'θinto; pre'sinto/ *m,* sealing; roping, tying up; strap
precio /'preθio; 'presio/ *m,* price, cost; recompense, reward; premium; rate; reputation, importance; esteem. **p. de tasa,** controlled price
preciosidad /preθiosi'ðað; presiosi'ðað/ *f,* preciousness; exquisiteness, fineness; richness; wittiness; *Inf.* loveliness, beauty; thing of beauty
precioso /pre'θioso; pre'sioso/ *a* precious; exquisite, fine, rare; rich; witty; *Inf.* lovely, delicious, attractive
precipicio /preθi'piθio; presi'pisio/ *m,* precipice; heavy fall; ruin, disaster
precipitación /preθipita'θion; presipita'sion/ *f,* precipitancy, haste; rashness; *Chem.* precipitation
precipitadamente /preθipitaða'mente; presipitaða'mente/ *adv* precipitately, in haste; rashly, foolishly
precipitado /preθipi'taðo; presipi'taðo/ *a* precipitate; rash, thoughtless. *m, Chem.* precipitate
precipitar /preθipi'tar; presipi'tar/ *vt* to precipitate, hurl headlong; hasten; *Chem.* precipitate; *—vr* hurl oneself headlong; hasten, rush
precipitoso /preθipi'toso; presipi'toso/ *a* precipitous; rash, heedless
precisamente /preθisa'mente; presisa'mente/ *adv* exactly, precisely, just; necessarily. **Y p. en aquel instante llegó,** And just at that moment he arrived
precisar /preθi'sar; presi'sar/ *vt* to fix, arrange; set forth, draw up, state; compel, force, oblige
precisión /preθi'sion; presi'sion/ *f,* accuracy, precision; necessity, conciseness, clarity; compulsion, obligation
preciso /pre'θiso; pre'siso/ *a* necessary, unavoidable; concise, clear; precise, exact
precitado /preθi'taðo; presi'taðo/ *a* aforementioned
preclaro /pre'klaro/ *a* illustrious, distinguished, celebrated
precocidad /prekoθi'ðað; prekosi'ðað/ *f,* precocity
precognición /prekogni'θion; prekogni'sion/ *f,* foreknowledge
preconcebido /prekonθe'βiðo; prekonse'βiðo/ *a* preconceived
preconcepto /prekon'θepto; prekon'septo/ *m,* preconceived idea, preconceived notion
preconizar /prekoni'θar; prekoni'sar/ *vt* to eulogize, praise publicly
preconocer /prekono'θer; prekono'ser/ *vt irr* to know beforehand; foresee. See **conocer**
precoz /pre'koθ; pre'kos/ *a* precocious
precursor /prekur'sor/ **(-ra)** *a* precursory; preceding, previous *—n* precursor
predecesor /preðeθe'sor; preðese'sor/ **(-ra)** *n* predecessor
predecir /preðe'θir; preðe'sir/ *vt irr* to foretell, prophesy. See **decir**
predestinación /preðestina'θion; preðestina'sion/ *f,* predestination
predestinado /preðesti'naðo/ **(-da)** *a* predestined; foreordained *—n* one of the predestined
predestinar /preðesti'nar/ *vt* to predestine, foreordain
predeterminación /preðetermina'θion; preðetermina'sion/ *f,* predetermination
predeterminar /preðetermi'nar/ *vt* to predetermine
prédica /'preðika/ *f, Inf.* (contemptuous) sermon
predicación /preðika'θion; preðika'sion/ *f,* preaching; homily, sermon
predicadera /preðika'ðera/ *f,* pulpit; *pl Inf.* talent for preaching
predicado /preði'kaðo/ *m,* (*Gram. Philos.*) predicate
predicador /preðika'ðor/ **(-ra)** *a* preaching *—n* preacher
predicamento /preðika'mento/ *m,* predicament; reputation
predicar /preði'kar/ *vt* to publish; manifest; preach; *—vi* overpraise; *Inf.* lecture, scold. **p. en el desierto,** to preach to the wind
predicción /preðik'θion; preðik'sion/ *f,* prediction, prophecy
predilección /preðilek'θion; preðilek'sion/ *f,* predilection, preference, partiality
predilecto /preði'lekto/ *a* favorite, preferred
predisponer /preðispo'ner/ *vt irr* to predispose. See **poner**
predisposición /preðisposi'θion; preðisposi'sion/ *f,* predisposition; tendency, prejudice
predominación /preðomina'θion; preðomina'sion/ *f,* predominance
predominante /preðomi'nante/ *a* predominant; prevailing

predominar /preðomi'nar/ *vi* and *vt* to predominate; prevail; tower above; overlook
predominio /preðo'minio/ *m,* predominance, ascendancy, preponderance
preeminencia /preemi'nenθia; preemi'nensia/ *f,* preeminence
preeminente /preemi'nente/ *a* preeminent
preexistencia /preeksis'tenθia; preeksis'tensia/ *f,* preexistence
preexistente /preeksis'tente/ *a* preexistent
preexistir /preeksis'tir/ *vi* to preexist, exist before
prefacio /pre'faθio; pre'fasio/ *m,* introduction, preface, prologue; *Eccl.* preface
prefecto /pre'fekto/ *m,* prefect
prefectura /prefek'tura/ *f,* prefecture
preferencia /prefe'renθia; prefe'rensia/ *f,* preference; superiority. **de p.,** preferred, favorite; preferably
preferente /prefe'rente/ *a* preferable; preferential; preferred (of stock)
preferible /prefe'riβle/ *a* preferable
preferir /prefe'rir/ *vt irr* to prefer; excel, exceed —*Pres. Part.* **prefiriendo.** *Pres. Indic.* **prefiero, prefieres, prefiere, prefieren.** *Preterite* **prefirió, prefirieron.** *Pres. Subjunc.* **prefiera, prefieras, prefiera, prefieran.** *Imperf. Subjunc.* **prefiriese,** etc.
prefijar /prefi'har/ *vt* to prefix
prefijo /pre'fiho/ *m,* prefix
prefinir /prefi'nir/ *vt* to fix a time limit for
prefulgente /preful'hente/ *a* brilliant, shining, resplendent
pregón /pre'gon/ *m,* public proclamation; marriage banns
pregonar /prego'nar/ *vt* to proclaim publicly; cry one's wares; publish abroad; eulogize, praise; proscribe, outlaw. **p. a los cuatro vientos,** *Inf.* to shout from the rooftops
pregonería /pregone'ria/ *f,* office of the town crier
pregonero /prego'nero/ *m,* town crier
preguerra /pre'gerra/ *f,* prewar period
pregunta /pre'gunta/ *f,* question; *Com.* inquiry; questionnaire, interrogation. *Inf.* **andar** (*or* **estar**) **a la cuarta p.,** to be very hard up, be on the rocks. **hacer una p.,** to ask a question
preguntador /pregunta'ðor/ **(-ra)** *a* questioning; inquisitive —*n* questioner; inquisitive person
preguntar /pregun'tar/ *vt* to question, ask; (*with por*) inquire for; —*vr* ask oneself, wonder
prehistoria /preis'toria/ *f,* prehistory
prehistórico /preis'toriko/ *a* prehistoric
prejuicio /pre'huiθio; pre'huisio/ *m,* prejudice
prejuzgar /prehuθ'gar; prehus'gar/ *vt* to prejudge, judge hastily
prelacía /prela'θia; prela'sia/ *f,* prelacy
prelación /prela'θion; prela'sion/ *f,* preference
prelado /pre'laðo/ *m,* prelate
preliminar /prelimi'nar/ *a* preliminary, prefatory. *m,* preliminary
preludiar /prelu'ðiar/ *vi* and *vt Mus.* to play a prelude (to); —*vt* prepare, initiate
preludio /pre'luðio/ *m,* introduction, prologue; *Mus.* prelude; *Mus.* overture
prematuro /prema'turo/ *a* premature, untimely; unseasonable; immature, unripe
premeditación /premeðita'θion; premeðita'sion/ *f,* premeditation
premeditar /premeði'tar/ *vt* to premeditate, plan in advance
premiador /premia'ðor/ **(-ra)** *a* rewarding —*n* rewarder
premiar /pre'miar/ *vt* to reward, requite
premio /'premio/ *m,* prize; reward; premium; *Com.* interest. **p. en metálico,** cash prize. *Inf.* **p. gordo,** first prize (in a lottery)
premioso /pre'mioso/ *a* tight; troublesome, annoying; stern, strict; slow-moving; burdensome, hard; labored (of speech or style)
premisa /pre'misa/ *f,* premise; sign, indication
premonitorio /premoni'torio/ *a* premonitory
premura /pre'mura/ *f,* urgency, haste
prenda /'prenda/ *f,* pledge; token, sign; jewel; article of clothing; talent, gift; loved one; *pl* game of forfeits
prendador /prenda'ðor/ **(-ra)** *n* pledger
prendamiento /prenda'miento/ *m,* pawning
prendar /pren'dar/ *vt* to pawn; charm, delight; —*vr* (*with de*) take a liking to
prender /pren'der/ *vt* to seize; arrest; capture, catch —*vi* take root (plants); catch fire; be infectious
prendería /prende'ria/ *f,* second-hand shop
prendero /pren'dero/ **(-ra)** *n* second-hand dealer
prendimiento /prendi'miento/ *m,* seizure, capture; arrest
prenombre /pre'nombre/ *m,* given name, praenomen
prensa /'prensa/ *f,* press; printing press; newspapers, the press. **dar a la p.,** to publish
prensado /pren'saðo/ *m,* **prensadura** *f,* pressing; flattening; squeezing
prensar /pren'sar/ *vt* to press; squeeze
prensil /pren'sil/ *a* prehensile
preñado /pre'ɲaðo/ *a* pregnant; bulging, sagging (walls, etc.); swollen. *m,* pregnancy
preñez /pre'ɲeθ; pre'ɲes/ *f,* pregnancy; suspense
preocupación /preokupa'θion; preokupa'sion/ *f,* anxiety, preoccupation; prejudice
preocupadamente /preokupaða'mente/ *adv* preoccupiedly, absentmindedly; with prejudice
preocupar /preoku'par/ *vt* to preoccupy; make anxious; bias, prejudice; —*vr* be anxious; be prejudiced
preordinar /preorði'nar/ *vt Eccl.* to predestine
preparación /prepara'θion; prepara'sion/ *f,* preparation; treatment; compound, specific
preparado /prepa'raðo/ *a* ready, prepared. *m,* preparation, patent food, etc.
preparar /prepa'rar/ *vt* to prepare; —*vr* prepare oneself; qualify
preparativo /prepara'tiβo/ *a* preparatory. *m,* preparation
preparatorio /prepara'torio/ *a* preparatory
preponderancia /preponde'ranθia; preponde'ransia/ *f,* preponderance
preponderante /preponde'rante/ *a* preponderant; dominant
preponderar /preponde'rar/ *vi* to preponderate; dominate; outweigh
preponer /prepo'ner/ *vt irr* to put before. See **poner**
preposición /preposi'θion; preposi'sion/ *f,* preposition
prepósito /pre'posito/ *m,* chairman, head, president; *Eccl.* provost
prepucio /pre'puθio; pre'pusio/ *m,* prepuce
prerrafaelista /prerrafae'lista/ *a* and *mf* Pre-Raphaelite
prerrogativa /prerroga'tiβa/ *f,* prerogative
presa /'presa/ *f,* hold, grasp; seizure, capture; booty; dam; lock (on rivers, canals); weir; ditch, trench; embankment; slice, bit. **hacer p.,** to seize; take advantage of (circumstances)
presagiar /presa'hiar/ *vt* to prophesy, presage, bode
presagio /pre'sahio/ *m,* presage, sign; presentiment, foreboding
présbita /'presβita/ *a* long-sighted, farsighted
presbiterado /presβite'raðo/ *m,* priesthood; holy orders
presbiteriano /presβite'riano/ **(-na)** *a* and *n* Presbyterian
presbítero /pres'βitero/ *m,* priest
presciencia /pres'θienθia; pres'siensia/ *f,* prescience, foresight
presciente /pres'θiente; pres'siente/ *a* prescient, farsighted
prescindible /presθin'diβle; pressin'diβle/ *a* nonessential, able to be dispensed with
prescindir /presθin'dir; pressin'dir/ *vi* (*with de*) to pass over, omit; do without. **Prescindiendo de esto...,** Leaving this aside....
prescribir /preskri'βir/ *vt* to prescribe, order
prescripción /preskrip'θion; preskrip'sion/ *f,* prescription
presea /pre'sea/ *f,* jewel, object of value
presencia /pre'senθia; pre'sensia/ *f,* presence, attendance; appearance, looks; ostentation. **p. de ánimo,** presence of mind

presenciar /presen'θiar; presen'siar/ *vt* to be present at; witness, behold
presentación /presenta'θion; presenta'sion/ *f,* presentation; introduction
presentar /presen'tar/ *vt* to show; present, make a gift of; introduce (persons); *—vr* occur; present oneself; offer one's services
presente /pre'sente/ *a* present. *m,* gift; present time. *Law.* **Por estas presentes...,** By these presents.... **tener p.,** to remember
presentimiento /presenti'miento/ *m,* presentiment, apprehension
presentir /presen'tir/ *vt irr* to have a presentiment of. See **sentir**
preservación /preserβa'θion; preserβa'sion/ *f,* preservation, protection, saving
preservar /preser'βar/ *vt* to preserve, protect, save
preservativo /preserβa'tiβo/ *a* preservative. *m,* preservative, safeguard, protection
presidencia /presi'ðenθia; presi'ðensia/ *f,* presidency; chairmanship; presidential seat or residence
presidencial /presiðen'θial; presiðen'sial/ *a* presidential
presidenta /presi'ðenta/ *f,* female president; president's wife, chairwoman
presidente /presi'ðente/ *m,* president; chairman; head, director; presiding judge
presidiar /presi'ðiar/ *vt* to garrison
presidiario /presi'ðiario/ *m,* convict
presidio /pre'siðio/ *m,* garrison; garrison town; fortress; penitentiary; imprisonment; *Law.* hard labor; assistance, protection
presidir /presi'ðir/ *vt* to preside over; act as chairperson for; influence, determine
presilla /pre'siʎa; pre'siya/ *f,* loop, shank, noose; press stud
presión /pre'sion/ *f,* pressure
preso /'preso/ **(-sa)** *n* prisoner, captive; convict
prestación /presta'θion; presta'sion/ *f,* lending, loan. **p. vecinal,** corvée
prestador /presta'ðor/ **(-ra)** *a* lending, loan *—n* lender
prestamente /presta'mente/ *adv* expeditiously, promptly
prestamista /presta'mista/ *mf* moneylender; pawnbroker
préstamo /'prestamo/ *m,* loan; lending. **casa de préstamos,** pawnshop
prestar /pres'tar/ *vt* to lend; assist; pay (attention); give; *—vi* be useful; give, expand; *—vr* be suitable; lend itself; offer oneself. **tomar prestado,** to borrow
prestatario /presta'tario/ **(-ia)** *n* money borrower, debtor
preste /'preste/ *m,* celebrant of high mass. **el p. Juan,** title of Prester John
presteza /pres'teθa; pres'tesa/ *f,* speed; promptness, dispatch
prestidigitación /prestiðihita'θion; prestiðihita'sion/ *f,* prestidigitation
prestidigitador /prestiðihita'ðor/ **(-ra)** *n* juggler, conjurer
prestigio /pres'tihio/ *m,* magic spell, sorcery; trick, illusion (of conjurers, etc.); influence, prestige
prestigioso /presti'hioso/ *a* illusory; influential
presto /'presto/ *a* quick, speedy; prompt, ready. *m,* pressure cooker *—adv* immediately; soon; quickly. **de p.,** speedily
presumido /presu'miðo/ *a* conceited, vain; presumptuous
presumir /presu'mir/ *vt* to suppose, presume; *—vi* be conceited
presunción /presun'θion; presun'sion/ *f,* supposition, presumption; vanity, presumptuousness
presuntivo /presun'tiβo/ *a* presumptive
presuntuosidad /presuntuosi'ðað/ *f,* presumptuousness
presuntuoso /presun'tuoso/ *a* presumptuous, vain
presuponer /presupo'ner/ *vt irr* to presuppose, assume; budget, estimate. See **poner**
presuposición /presuposi'θion; presuposi'sion/ *f,* presupposition
presupuesto /presu'puesto/ *m,* motive, reason; supposition, assumption; estimate; *Com.* tender; national budget
presuroso /presu'roso/ *a* swift, speedy
pretencioso /preten'θioso; preten'sioso/ *a* pretentious, vain
pretender /preten'der/ *vt* to seek, solicit; claim; apply for; attempt, try; woo, court
pretendiente /preten'diente/ **(-ta)** *n* pretender; candidate; petitioner; suitor
pretensión /preten'sion/ *f,* pretension; claim; *pl* ambitions
pretérito /pre'terito/ *a* past. *m,* preterite
pretextar /preteks'tar/ *vt* to allege as a pretext or excuse
pretexto /pre'teksto/ *m,* pretext, excuse
prevalecer /preβale'θer; preβale'ser/ *vi irr* to prevail; be dominant; take root (plants). See **conocer**
prevaleciente /preβale'θiente; preβale'siente/ *a* prevailing; prevalent
prevaricación /preβarika'θion; preβarika'sion/ *f,* prevarication
prevaricador /preβarika'ðor/ **(-ra)** *n* prevaricator
prevaricar /preβari'kar/ *vi* to prevaricate
prevención /preβen'θion; preβen'sion/ *f,* prevention; precaution; prejudice; police station; *Mil.* guard room; foresight, prevision; preparation. **de p.,** as a precaution
prevenido /preβe'niðo/ *a* prepared; cautious, forewarned
prevenir /preβe'nir/ *vt irr* to prepare; prevent, avoid; warn; prejudice; occur, happen; *Fig.* overcome (obstacles); *—vr* be ready; be forewarned. See **venir**
preventivo /preβen'tiβo/ *a* preventive
prever /pre'βer/ *vt irr* to foresee, forecast, anticipate. See **ver**
previamente /preβia'mente/ *adv* previously, in advance
previo /'preβio/ *a* previous, advance
previsión /preβi'sion/ *f,* forecast; foresight, prevision, prescience. **p. social,** social insurance
previsor /preβi'sor/ *a* farsighted, provident
prieto /'prieto/ *a* almost black, blackish; tight; mean, avaricious
prima /'prima/ *f, Eccl.* prime; *Com.* premium; female cousin
primacía /prima'θia; prima'sia/ *f,* supremacy, preeminence; primacy; primateship
primada /pri'maða/ *f, Inf.* act of sponging on, taking advantage of
primado /pri'maðo/ *m,* primate; primateship
primario /pri'mario/ *a* primary. *m,* professor who gives the first lecture of the day
primavera /prima'βera/ *f,* springtime; primrose; figured silk material; beautifully colored thing; youth; prime
primaveral /primaβe'ral/ *a* spring, spring-like
primeramente /primera'mente/ *adv* first; in the first place
primerizo /prime'riθo; prime'riso/ **(-za)** *n* novice; beginner; apprentice; firstborn
primero /pri'mero/ *a* first; former; excellent, first-rate *—adv* first; in the first place. **primera enseñanza,** primary education. **primera materia,** raw material. **primer plano,** *Art.* foreground. **primera cura,** first aid. **de buenas a primeras,** all at once, suddenly
primicia /pri'miθia; pri'misia/ *f,* first fruits; offering of first fruits; *pl* first effects
primitivo /primi'tiβo/ *a* original, early; primitive
primo /'primo/ **(-ma)** *a* first; excellent, fine *—n* cousin; *Inf.* simpleton; *Inf.* pigeon, dupe. **p. carnal,** first cousin. *Inf.* **hacer el p.,** to be a dupe. *Inf.* **ser prima hermana de,** to be the twin of (of things)
primogénito /primo'henito/ **(-ta)** *a* and *n* firstborn
primogenitura /primoheni'tura/ *f,* primogeniture
primor /pri'mor/ *m,* exquisite care; beauty, loveliness; thing of beauty
primoroso /primo'roso/ *a* beautiful; exquisitely done; dexterous, skillful
princesa /prin'θesa; prin'sesa/ *f,* princess

principado /prinθi'paðo; prinsi'paðo/ *m,* principality; princedom; superiority, preeminence

principal /prinθi'pal; prinsi'pal/ *a* chief, principal; illustrious; fundamental, first. *m,* head, principal (of a firm); *Com.* capital, principal; first floor

principalmente /prinθipal'mente; prinsipal'mente/ *adv* principally, chiefly

príncipe /'prinθipe; 'prinsipe/ *m,* leader; prince. **p. de Asturias,** prince of Asturias. **p. de la sangre,** prince of the blood royal

principesco /prinθi'pesko; prinsi'pesko/ *a* princely

principiante /prinθi'piante; prinsi'piante/ **(-ta)** *n* beginner, novice; apprentice

principiar /prinθi'piar; prinsi'piar/ *vt* to begin, commence

principio /prin'θipio; prin'sipio/ *m,* beginning; principle; genesis, origin; rudiment; axiom; constituent. **al p.,** at first. **a principios,** at the beginning (of the month, year, etc.). **en p.,** in principle

pringar /priŋ'gar/ *vt Cul.* to soak in fat; stain with grease; *Inf.* wound; take part in a business deal; slander; *—vr Inf.* appropriate, misuse (funds, etc.)

pringoso /priŋ'goso/ *a* greasy

pringue /'priŋgue/ *mf,* animal fat, lard; grease spot

prior /prior/ *m,* prior; parish priest

priora /'priora/ *f,* prioress

prioridad /priori'ðað/ *f,* priority

prisa /'prisa/ *f,* haste, speed; skirmish, foray. **a toda p.,** with all speed. **correr p.,** to be urgent. **dar p.,** to hasten, speed up. **darse** (*or* **estar de**) **p.,** to hurry

prisión /pri'sion/ *f,* prison, jail; seizure; captivity, imprisonment; *Fig.* bond; obstacle, shackle; *pl* fetters

prisma /'prisma/ *m,* prism

prismáticos /pris'matikos/ *m pl,* field glasses

prisonero /priso'nero/ **(-ra)** *n* prisoner; *Fig.* victim (of passion, etc.)

pristino /pris'tino/ *a* pristine

privación /priβa'θion; priβa'sion/ *f,* privation; lack, shortage; deprivation; degradation

privada /pri'βaða/ *f,* toilet, privy, water closet

privadamente /priβaða'mente/ *adv* privately; individually, separately

privado /pri'βaðo/ *a* private; individual, personal. *m,* favorite; confidant

privanza /pri'βanθa; pri'βansa/ *f,* court favor, intimacy of princes

privar /pri'βar/ *vt* to deprive; dismiss (from office); interdict, forbid; *—vi* prevail, be in favor; *—vr* swoon; deprive oneself

privilegiar /priβile'hiar/ *vt* to privilege; bestow a favor on

privilegio /priβi'lehio/ *m,* privilege; prerogative; concession; copyright; patent

pro /pro/ *mf* advantage, benefit. **el p. y el contra,** the pros and cons. **en p.,** in favor

proa /'proa/ *f,* prow, bow

probabilidad /proβaβili'ðað/ *f,* probability

probable /pro'βaβle/ *a* probable; likely; provable

probación /proβa'θion; proβa'sion/ *f,* proof, test; novitiate, probation

probado /pro'βaðo/ *a* tried, tested, proved

probar /pro'βar/ *vt irr* to prove; test; taste; try on (clothes); *—vi* suit; (*with prep a + infin*) try to. **p. fortuna,** to try one's luck *—Pres. Indic.* **pruebo, pruebas, prueba, prueban.** *Pres. Subjunc.* **pruebe, pruebes, prueben**

probatorio /proβa'torio/ *a* probationary

probidad /proβi'ðað/ *f,* probity, trustworthiness, honesty

problema /pro'βlema/ *m,* problem

problemático /proβle'matiko/ *a* problematical, uncertain

probo /'proβo/ *a* honest, trustworthy

procacidad /prokaθi'ðað; prokasi'ðað/ *f,* insolence, pertness

procaz /pro'kaθ; pro'kas/ *a* insolent, pert, brazen

procedencia /proθe'ðenθia; prose'ðensia/ *f,* origin, source; parentage, descent; port of sailing or call

procedente /proθe'ðente; prose'ðente/ *a* arriving or coming from

proceder /proθe'ðer; prose'ðer/ *vi* to proceed; behave; originate, arise; continue, go on; act. *Law.* **p. contra,** to proceed against (a person)

procedimiento /proθeði'miento; proseði'miento/ *m,* proceeding, advancement; procedure; legal practice; process

proceloso /proθe'loso; prose'loso/ *a* tempestuous

prócer /'proθer; 'proser/ *a* exalted, eminent; lofty. *m,* exalted personage

procesado /proθe'saðo; prose'saðo/ **(-da)** *n* defendant

procesamiento /proθesa'miento; prosesa'miento/ *m,* suing, suit; indictment. **p. de textos,** word processing.

procesar /proθe'sar; prose'sar/ *vt Law.* to proceed against, sue

procesión /proθe'sion; prose'sion/ *f,* proceeding, emanating; procession; *Inf.* train, string. **andar** (*or* **ir**) **por dentro la p.,** to feel keenly without betraying one's emotion

proceso /pro'θeso; pro'seso/ *m,* process; progress, advancement; lapse of time; lawsuit

proclama /pro'klama/ *f,* proclamation; announcement; publication of marriage banns

proclamación /proklama'θion; proklama'sion/ *f,* proclamation; acclaim, applause

proclamar /prokla'mar/ *vt* to proclaim; acclaim; publish abroad; reveal, show

proclividad /prokliβi'ðað/ *f,* proclivity, tendency

procomún /proko'mun/ *m,* social or public welfare

procreación /prokrea'θion; prokrea'sion/ *f,* procreation

procreador /prokrea'ðor/ **(-ra)** *a* procreative *—n* procreator

procrear /prokre'ar/ *vt* to procreate, beget, engender

procuración /prokura'θion; prokura'sion/ *f,* procurement; assiduity, care; *Law.* power of attorney; *Law.* attorneyship

procurador /prokura'ðor/ **(-ra)** *m,* proxy; *Law.* attorney; proctor *—n* procurer

procurar /proku'rar/ *vt* to try, attempt; procure, get; exercise the profession of a lawyer

prodigalidad /proðigali'ðað/ *f,* prodigality, lavishness; waste, extravagance

prodigar /proði'gar/ *vt* to waste, squander; lavish, bestow freely; *—vr* make oneself cheap

prodigio /pro'ðihio/ *m,* marvel, wonder; prodigy; monster; miracle

prodigiosidad /proðihiosi'ðað/ *f,* prodigiousness

prodigioso /proði'hioso/ *a* wonderful; prodigious; monstrous; miraculous

pródigo /'proðigo/ **(-ga)** *a* wasteful, extravagant; lavish, generous *—n* spendthrift, wastrel, prodigal

producción /proðuk'θion; proðuk'sion/ *f,* production; output, yield; generation (of heat, etc.); crop

producir /proðu'θir; proðu'sir/ *vt irr* to produce; generate; yield, give; cause, occasion; publish; *—vr* explain oneself; arise, appear, be produced. **p. efecto,** to have effect; take effect. See **conducir**

productividad /proðuktiβi'ðað/ *f,* productivity

productivo /proðuk'tiβo/ *a* productive; fertile; profitable

producto /pro'ðukto/ *m,* produce; product; profit; yield, gain; *Math.* product. *Chem.* **p. derivado,** by-product

productor /proðuk'tor/ **(-ra)** *a* productive *—n* producer

proemio /pro'emio/ *m,* prologue, preface, introduction

proeza /pro'eθa; pro'esa/ *f,* prowess, gallantry; skill

profanación /profana'θion; profana'sion/ *f,* profanation

profanador /profana'ðor/ **(-ra)** *n* profaner, transgressor

profanar /profa'nar/ *vt* to profane

profanidad /profani'ðað/ *f,* profanity

profano /pro'fano/ *a* profane; dissolute; pleasure-loving, worldly; immodest; lay, ignorant

profecía /profe'θia; profe'sia/ *f,* prophecy; *Eccl.* Book of the Prophets; opinion, view

proferir /profe'rir/ *vt irr* to utter, pronounce. See **herir**

profesar /profe'sar/ *vt* to exercise, practice (professions); *Eccl.* profess; believe in; teach
profesión /profe'sion/ *f,* profession; trade, occupation; avowal, admission
profesional /profesio'nal/ *a* professional
profesionalismo /profesiona'lismo/ *m,* professionalism
profeso /pro'feso/ **(-sa)** *a Eccl.* professed —*n* professed monk
profesor /profe'sor/ **(-ra)** *n* teacher; professor
profesorado /profeso'raðo/ *m,* teaching staff; teaching profession; professorship; professorate
profeta /pro'feta/ *m,* prophet; seer
profético /pro'fetiko/ *a* prophetic
profetisa /profe'tisa/ *f,* prophetess
profetizar /profeti'θar; profeti'sar/ *vt* to prophesy; imagine, suppose
proficiente /profi'θiente; profi'siente/ *a* proficient
profiláctico /profi'laktiko/ *a* and *m,* prophylactic
prófugo /'profugo/ **(-ga)** *a* and *n* fugitive from justice. *m, Mil.* one who evades military service
profundamente /profunda'mente/ *adv* profoundly; acutely, deeply
profundidad /profundi'ðað/ *f,* depth; profundity, obscurity; *Geom.* depth; concavity; intensity (of feeling); vastness (of knowledge, etc.)
profundizar /profundi'θar; profundi'sar/ *vt* to deepen; hollow out; *Fig.* go into deeply, fathom
profundo /pro'fundo/ *a* deep; low; *Fig.* intense, acute; abstruse, profound; *Fig.* vast, extensive; high. *m,* depth, profundity; *Poet.* ocean, the deep; *Poet.* hell
profuso /pro'fuso/ *a* profuse, abundant; extravagant, wasteful
progenie /pro'henie/ *f,* descendants
prognosis /prog'nosis/ *f,* prognosis; forecast
programa /pro'grama/ *m,* program; edict, public notice; plan, scheme; *Educ.* calendar; syllabus; timetable
progresar /progre'sar/ *vt* and *vi* to make progress; progress, advance
progresión /progre'sion/ *f,* progression; advancement, progress
progresista /progre'sista/ *a Polit.* progressive. *mf* progressive
progresivo /progre'siβo/ *a* progressive; advancing
progreso /pro'greso/ *m,* progress, advancement; growth; improvement, development
prohibente /proi'βente/ *a* prohibitory, prohibitive
prohibición /proiβi'θion; proiβi'sion/ *f,* forbidding, prohibition
prohibicionista /proiβiθio'nista; proiβisio'nista/ *mf* prohibitionist —*a* prohibitionist
prohibir /proi'βir/ *vt* to forbid, prohibit. **«Prohibido el paso,»** "No thoroughfare"
prohibitivo, prohibitorio /proiβi'tiβo, proiβi'torio/ *a* prohibitive
prohijador /proiha'ðor/ **(-ra)** *n* adopter (of a child)
prohijamiento /proiha'miento/ *m,* child adoption; fathering (of a bill, etc.)
prohijar /proi'har/ *vt* to adopt (children, ideas); *Fig.* father
prohombre /pro'ombre/ *m,* master of a guild; respected, wellliked man
prójimo /'prohimo/ *m,* fellow man, brother, neighbor.
prole /'prole/ *f,* progeny, young offspring
proletariado /proleta'riaðo/ *m,* proletariat
proletario /prole'tario/ *a* poor; common, vulgar. *m,* plebeian; pauper; proletarian
prolífico /pro'lifiko/ *a* prolific; abundant, fertile
prolijidad /prolihi'ðað/ *f,* verbosity, prolixity; nicety, scruple; importunity, tediousness
prolijo /pro'liho/ *a* verbose, prolix; fussy, fastidious; tedious, importunate
prologar /prolo'gar/ *vt* to prologue; provide with a preface
prólogo /'prologo/ *m,* preface; prologue; introduction
prolongación /proloŋga'θion; proloŋga'sion/ *f,* lengthening; prolongation, protraction; extension
prolongado /proloŋ'gaðo/ *a* prolonged; oblong, long
prolongar /proloŋ'gar/ *vt* to lengthen; *Geom.* produce; prolong, spin out
promediar /prome'ðiar/ *vt* to distribute or divide into two equal portions; average; —*vi* arbitrate; place oneself between two people; reach half-time
promedio /pro'meðio/ *m,* average; middle, center
promesa /pro'mesa/ *f,* promise; augury, favorable sign
prometedor /promete'ðor/ **(-ra)** *a* promising —*n* promiser
prometer /prome'ter/ *vt* to promise; attest, certify; —*vi* promise well, look hopeful; —*vr* devote oneself to service of God; anticipate confidently, expect; become engaged (marriage). *Inf.* **prometérselas muy felices,** to have high hopes
prometido /prome'tiðo/ **(-da)** *n* betrothed. *m,* promise
prometimiento /prometi'miento/ *m,* promise; promising
prominencia /promi'nenθia; promi'nensia/ *f,* prominence, protuberance; eminence, hill
prominente /promi'nente/ *a* prominent, protuberant; eminent, elevated
promiscuar /promis'kuar/ *vi* to eat meat and fish on fast days
promiscuidad /promiskui'ðað/ *f,* promiscuity; ambiguity
promiscuo /pro'miskuo/ *a* indiscriminate, haphazard, promiscuous; ambiguous
promisión /promi'sion/ *f,* promise
promisorio /promi'sorio/ *a* promissory
promoción /promo'θion; promo'sion/ *f,* promotion; batch, class, year (of recruits, students, etc.)
promontorio /promon'torio/ *m,* headland; promontory; cumbersome object
promotor /promo'tor/ **(-ra)** *a* promotive —*n* promoter; supporter
promover /promo'βer/ *vt irr* to promote, further, advance; promote (a person). **p. un proceso** (**a**), to bring a suit (against). See **mover**
promulgación /promulga'θion; promulga'sion/ *f,* promulgation
promulgar /promul'gar/ *vt* to publish officially, proclaim; promulgate. *Law.* **p. sentencia,** to pass judgment
pronombre /pro'nombre/ *m,* pronoun
pronosticación /pronostika'θion; pronostika'sion/ *f,* prognostication; presage
pronosticar /pronosti'kar/ *vt* to prognosticate, forecast; presage
pronóstico /pro'nostiko/ *m,* omen, prediction; almanac; prognosis; sign, indication. **p. del tiempo,** weather forecast
prontitud /pronti'tuð/ *f,* quickness, promptness; quick-wittedness; *Fig.* sharpness, liveliness; celerity, dispatch
pronto /'pronto/ *a* quick, speedy; prompt; ready, prepared. *m, Inf.* sudden decision —*adv* immediately; with all speed; soon. **de p.,** suddenly; without thinking. **por lo p.,** temporarily, provisionally
prontuario /pron'tuario/ *m,* compendium, handbook; summary
pronunciación /pronunθia'θion; pronunsia'sion/ *f,* pronunciation
pronunciamiento /pronunθia'miento; pronunsia'miento/ *m,* military uprising; political manifesto; *Law.* pronouncement of sentence
pronunciar /pronun'θiar; pronun'siar/ *vt* to pronounce, articulate; decide, determine; *Law.* pronounce judgment; give or make (a speech)
propagación /propaga'θion; propaga'sion/ *f,* propagation; dissemination; transmission
propagador /propaga'ðor/ *a* propagative. *m,* propagator
propaganda /propa'ganda/ *f,* propaganda organization; propaganda
propagandista /propagan'dista/ *mf* propagandist
propagar /propa'gar/ *vt* to reproduce; propagate, disseminate; —*vr* reproduce, multiply; propagate, spread
propalar /propa'lar/ *vt* to disseminate, spread abroad
propasarse /propa'sarse/ *vr* to go too far, forget oneself; overstep one's authority

propender /propen'der/ *vi* to be inclined, have a leaning toward
propensión /propen'sion/ *f*, propensity, inclination; tendency
propenso /pro'penso/ *a* inclined, disposed; liable
propiamente /propia'mente/ *adv* properly, suitably
propiciación /propiθia'θion; propisia'sion/ *f*, propitiation
propiciador /propiθia'ðor; propisia'ðor/ **(-ra)** *a* propitiatory —*n* propitiator
propiciar /propi'θiar; propi'siar/ *vt* to propitiate, appease
propiciatorio /propiθia'torio; propisia'torio/ *a* propitiatory
propicio /pro'piθio; pro'pisio/ *a* propitious, auspicious; kind, favorable
propiedad /propie'ðað/ *f*, estate, property; ownership; landed property; attribute, quality, property; *Art.* resemblance, naturalness
propietario /propie'tario/ **(-ia)** *a* proprietary —*n* proprietor, owner
propina /pro'pina/ *f*, gratuity, tip. *Inf.* **de p.,** in addition, extra
propinar /propi'nar/ *vt* to treat to a drink; administer (medicine); *Inf.* give (slaps, etc.)
propincuidad /propinkui'ðað/ *f*, propinquity, proximity
propincuo /pro'pinkuo/ *a* near, contiguous, adjacent
propio /'propio/ *a* own, one's own; typical, characteristic; individual, peculiar; suitable, apt; natural, real; same. *m*, messenger; *pl* public lands
proponente /propo'nente/ *a* proposing. *m*, proposer; *Com.* tenderer
proponer /propo'ner/ *vt irr* to propose, suggest; make a proposition; propose (for a post, office, etc.); *Math.* state; —*vr* intend, purpose. **proponerse para un empleo,** to apply for a post. See **poner**
proporción /propor'θion; propor'sion/ *f*, proportion; chance, opportunity; size; *Math.* proportion
proporcionado /proporθio'naðo; proporsio'naðo/ *a* fit, suitable; proportionate; symmetrical
proporcional /proporθio'nal; proporsio'nal/ *a* proportional
proporcionar /proporθio'nar; proporsio'nar/ *vt* to allot, proportion; supply, provide, give; adapt
proposición /proposi'θion; proposi'sion/ *f*, proposition; motion (in a debate)
propósito /pro'posito/ *m*, proposal; intention, aim; subject, question, matter. **a p.,** suitable, apropos; by the way, incidentally. **de p.,** with the intention, proposing. **fuera de p.,** irrelevant
propuesta /pro'puesta/ *f*, proposal, tender
propugnar /propug'nar/ *vt* to defend, protect
propulsar /propul'sar/ *vt* to repulse, throw back; propel, drive
propulsión /propul'sion/ *f*, repulse; propulsion
propulsor /propul'sor/ *a* driving, propelling. *m*, propeller
prorrata /pro'rrata/ *f*, quota, share, apportionment. **a p.,** in proportion
prorratear /prorrate'ar/ *vt* to apportion, distribute proportionately, prorate
prorrogación /prorroga'θion; prorroga'sion/ *f*, prorogation, adjournment; extension (of time); renewal (of a lease, etc.)
prorrogar /prorro'gar/ *vt* to extend, prolong; defer, suspend, prorogue; renew (leases, etc.)
prorrumpir /prorrum'pir/ *vt* (*with en*) to burst out; utter, give vent to, burst into
prosa /'prosa/ *f*, prose; prosaism, prosaic style; *Inf.* dull verbosity; monotony, tediousness
prosaico /pro'saiko/ *a* prosaic; prosy; monotonous, tedious; matter-of-fact
prosapia /pro'sapia/ *f*, family, lineage, descent
proscenio /pros'θenio; pros'senio/ *m*, proscenium
proscribir /proskri'βir/ *vt* to proscribe, outlaw; forbid, prohibit —*Past Part.* **proscrito**
proscripción /proskrip'θion; proskrip'sion/ *f*, proscription
proscrito /pros'krito/ **(-ta)** *n* outlaw, exile
prosecución /proseku'θion; proseku'sion/ *f*, prosecution, performance; pursuit
proseguir /prose'gir/ *vt irr* to continue, proceed with. See **pedir**
proselitismo /proseli'tismo/ *m*, proselytism
prosélito /pro'selito/ *m*, convert, proselyte
prosificar /prosifi'kar/ *vt* to turn verse into prose
prosista /pro'sista/ *mf* prose writer
prosodia /pro'soðia/ *f*, prosody
prospecto /pros'pekto/ *m*, prospectus
prosperar /prospe'rar/ *vt* to prosper; protect; —*vi* flourish, prosper
prosperidad /prosperi'ðað/ *f*, prosperity; wealth; success
próspero /'prospero/ *a* favorable, propitious, fortunate; prosperous
próstata /'prostata/ *f*, prostate
prostitución /prostitu'θion; prostitu'sion/ *f*, prostitution
prostituir /prosti'tuir/ *vt irr* to prostitute; —*vr* become a prostitute; sell oneself, debase oneself. See **huir**
prostituta /prosti'tuta/ *f*, prostitute
protagonista /protago'nista/ *mf* hero or heroine, principal character; leading figure, protagonist
protección /protek'θion; protek'sion/ *f*, protection, defense; favor, aid
proteccionismo /protekθio'nismo; proteksio'nismo/ *m*, protectionism
proteccionista /protekθio'nista; proteksio'nista/ *mf* protectionist
protector /protek'tor/ *a* protective. *m*, protector; guard
protectorado /protekto'raðo/ *m*, protectorate
protectriz /protek'triθ; protek'tris/ *f*, protectress
proteger /prote'her/ *vt* to protect, defend; favor, assist
protegido /prote'hiðo/ **(-da)** *n* protégé
proteico /pro'teiko/ *a* protean
proteína /prote'ina/ *f*, protein
protervia /pro'terβia/ *f*, depravity, perversity
protervo /pro'terβo/ *a* depraved, perverse
protesta, protestación /pro'testa, protesta'θion; pro'testa, protesta'sion/ *f*, protest; protestation, declaration
protestante /protes'tante/ *a* and *mf* Protestant
protestantismo /protestan'tismo/ *m*, Protestantism
protestar /protes'tar/ *vt* to declare, attest; (*with contra*) protest against; (*with de*) affirm vigorously
protesto /pro'testo/ *m*, *Com.* protest; objection
protocolizar /protokoli'θar; protokoli'sar/ *vt* to protocol, draw up
protocolo /proto'kolo/ *m*, protocol
protoplasma /proto'plasma/ *m*, protoplasm
prototipo /proto'tipo/ *m*, model, prototype
protuberancia /protuβe'ranθia; protuβe'ransia/ *f*, protuberance, projection, swelling
provecho /pro'βetʃo/ *m*, gain, benefit; profit; advantage; progress, proficiency. **¡Buen p.!** Enjoy your food! Enjoy your meal! **ser de p.,** to be advantageous or useful
provechoso /proβe'tʃoso/ *a* beneficial; profitable; advantageous; useful
provecto /pro'βekto/ *a* ancient, venerable; mature, experienced
proveedor /proβee'ðor/ **(-ra)** *n* provider; purveyor, supplier
proveer /proβe'er/ *vt irr* to provide; furnish; supply; confer (an honor or office); transact, arrange. **p. de,** to furnish or supply with; fit with. See **creer**
provenir /proβe'nir/ *vi irr* (*with de*) to originate in, proceed from. See **venir**
Provenza /pro'βenθa; pro'βensa/ Provence
provenzal /proβen'θal; proβen'sal/ *a* and *mf* Provençal. *m*, Provençal (language)
proverbio /pro'βerβio/ *m*, proverb; omen; *pl* Book of Proverbs
providencia /proβi'ðenθia; proβi'ðensia/ *f*, precaution, foresight; provision, furnishing; measure, preparation. **la Divina P.,** Providence
providencial /proβiðen'θial; proβiðen'sial/ *a* providential

próvido /'proβiðo/ *a* provident, thrifty, careful; kind, favorable

provincia /pro'βinθia; pro'βinsia/ *f,* province; *Fig.* sphere

provincial /proβin'θial; proβin'sial/ *a* provincial. *m, Eccl.* provincial

provincialismo /proβinθia'lismo; proβinsia'lismo/ *m,* provincialism

provinciano /proβin'θiano; proβin'siano/ **(-na)** *a* provincial —*n* provincial, rustic, countryman; native of Biscay

provisión /proβi'sion/ *f,* stock, store; provision; supply; food supply (gen. *pl*); catering; means, way

provisional /proβisio'nal/ *a* temporary, provisional

provisor /proβi'sor/ *m,* purveyor, supplier; *Eccl.* vicar general

provocación /proβoka'θion; proβoka'sion/ *f,* provocation

provocador /proβoka'ðor/ **(-ra)** *a* provocative —*n* provoker; instigator

provocar /proβo'kar/ *vt* to provoke; incite; irritate; help, assist; *Inf.* vomit

provocativo /proβoka'tiβo/ *a* provocative

próximamente /'proksimamente/ *adv* proximately; soon; approximately

proximidad /proksimi'ðað/ *f,* nearness, proximity (in time or space)

próximo /'proksimo/ *a* near, neighboring; next; not distant (of time)

proyección /proiek'θion; proiek'sion/ *f,* projection (all meanings)

proyectante /proiek'tante/ *a* projecting, jutting

proyectar /proiek'tar/ *vt* to throw, cast; plan, contrive; design; project; —*vr* jut out; be cast (a shadow, etc.)

proyectil /proyek'til/ *m,* projectile

proyectista /proiek'tista/ *mf* planner

proyecto /pro'iekto/ *a* placed in perspective. *m,* project, plan, scheme; planning; intention, idea

proyector /proiek'tor/ **(-ra)** *n* designer, planner. *m,* searchlight; spotlight; projector

prudencia /pru'ðenθia; pru'ðensia/ *f,* prudence, sagacity, caution; moderation

prudencial /pruðen'θial; pruðen'sial/ *a* prudent, discreet; safe

prudente /pru'ðente/ *a* prudent, cautious; provident

prueba /'prueβa/ *f,* proof; test; testing; trial; fitting (of garments); sample; taste; *Law.* evidence; (*Photo. Print.*) proof. *Law.* **p. de indicios** *or* **p. indiciaria,** circumstantial evidence. *Photo.* **p. negativa,** negative. *Com.* **a p.,** on approval; on trial; up to standard, perfect. **a p. de,** proof against (water, etc.). **poner a p.,** to put to the test, try out

prurito /pru'rito/ *m,* pruritus; desire, longing

Prusia /'prusia/ Prussia

ps- /ps-/ For words so beginning (e.g. *psicología, psiquiatría*), see spellings without **p**

púa /'pua/ *f,* prong; tooth (of a comb); quill (of a porcupine); *Agr.* graft; plectrum (for playing the mandolin, etc.); anxiety, grief; pine needle; *Inf.* crafty person

púber /'puβer/ *a* pubescent

pubertad /puβer'tað/ *f,* puberty

púbico /'puβiko/ *a* pubic

publicación /puβlika'θion; puβlika'sion/ *f,* publication; announcement, proclamation; revelation; publishing of marriage banns

publicador /puβlika'ðor/ **(-ra)** *a* publishing —*n* publisher; announcer

publicar /puβli'kar/ *vt* to publish; reveal; announce, proclaim; publish (marriage banns)

publicidad /puβliθi'ðað; puβlisi'ðað/ *f,* publicity; advertising, propaganda

publicista /puβli'θista; puβli'sista/ *mf* publicist; publicity agent

público /'puβliko/ *a* well-known, universal; common, general; public. *m,* public; audience; gathering, attendance. **dar al p.** *or* **sacar al p.,** to publish

pucherazo /putʃe'raθo; putʃe'raso/ *m, Inf.* electoral fraud, vote-fixing

puchero /pu'tʃero/ *m, Cul.* kind of stew; stew pot; *Inf.* daily food; puckering of the face preceding tears

pudendo /pu'ðendo/ *a* shameful, monstrous, obscene

pudicia /pu'ðiθia; pu'ðisia/ *f,* modesty; bashfulness; chastity

púdico /'puðiko/ *a* modest; bashful; chaste

pudiente /pu'ðiente/ *a* rich, wealthy; powerful

pudín /pu'ðin/ *m,* pudding

pudor /pu'ðor/ *m,* modesty; bashfulness, shyness

pudoroso /puðo'roso/ *a* modest; shy

pudrición /puðri'θion; puðri'sion/ *f,* putrefaction

pudrir /pu'ðrir/ *vt* to rot, putrefy; irritate, worry, provoke; —*vi* rot in the grave; —*vr* rot; be consumed with anxiety

puebla /'pueβla/ *f,* town; population; gardener's seed setting

pueblo /'pueβlo/ *m,* town; village, hamlet; people, population, inhabitants; common people; working classes; nation

puente /'puente/ *mf* bridge; *Mus.* bridge (of stringed instruments); *Naut.* bridge; crossbeam, transom. **p. colgante,** suspension bridge. **p. levadizo,** drawbridge. **hacer p. de plata** (**a**), to remove obstacles for, make plain sailing

puerca /'puerka/ *f,* sow; *Inf.* slattern; harridan, termagant

puerco /'puerko/ *m,* pig; wild boar —*a* filthy; rough, rude; low, mean. **p. espín** *or* **p. espino,** porcupine. **p. marino,** dolphin. **p. montés** *or* **p. salvaje,** wild boar

puericultura /puerikul'tura/ *f,* child care

pueril /pue'ril/ *a* childish, puerile; foolish, silly; trivial

puerilidad /puerili'ðað/ *f,* puerility; foolishness; triviality

puerro /'puerro/ *m,* leek

puerta /'puerta/ *f,* door; gate; goal (football, soccer, hockey); means, way. **p. batiente,** swinging door. **p. caediza,** trapdoor. **p. corrediza,** sliding door. **p. de servicio,** tradesman's entrance. **p. falsa** *or* **p. secreta,** secret door; side door. **p. trasera,** back door. **a p. cerrada,** in camera; in secret. *Inf.* **dar con la p. en las narices** (**de**), to slam the door in a person's face; offend, insult. **llamar a la p.,** to knock at the door; be on the verge of happening. **tomar la p.,** to depart, go away

puerto /'puerto/ *m,* harbor; port; defile, narrow pass; refuge, haven. **p. fluvial,** river port. **p. franco,** free port. **tomar p.,** to put into port; take refuge

pues /pues/ *conjunc* then; since, as; for, because; well —*adv* yes, certainly —*conjunc* **p. que,** since, as

puesta /'puesta/ *f, Astron.* setting, sinking; stake (in gambling). **p. al día,** aggiornamento, updating; modernization. **p. de largo,** coming of age; coming-out party. **p. del sol,** sunset

puesto /'puesto/ *m,* post, job; booth, stall; beat, pitch; place, position; state, condition; *Mil.* encampment, barracks; office, position. **p. de los testigos,** witness box. **p. de mando,** command, position of authority.

puesto /'puesto/ *a* (*with bien* or *mal*) well-or badly dressed —*conjunc* **p. que,** since, as; although

púgil /'puhil/ *mf* pugilist, boxer

pugilato /puhi'lato/ *m,* boxing; boxing match

pugilista /puhi'lista/ *mf* boxer

pugna /'pugna/ *f,* fight, struggle; rivalry, conflict

pugnante /pug'nante/ *a* hostile, conflicting, rival

pugnar /pug'nar/ *vi* to fight; quarrel; (*with con, contra*) struggle against, oppose; (*with por, para*) strive to

pugnaz /pug'naθ; pug'nas/ *a* pugnacious

puja /'puha/ *f,* outbidding (at an auction); higher bid; push, thrust

pujador /puha'ðor/ **(-ra)** *n* bidder or outbidder (at an auction)

pujante /pu'hante/ *a* strong, powerful, vigorous

pujanza /pu'hanθa; pu'hansa/ *f,* strength, vigor

pujar /pu'har/ *vt* to push on; bid or outbid (at an auction); —*vi* stutter; hesitate, falter; *Inf.* show signs of weeping

pujo /'puho/ *m,* irresistible impulse; desire; will; purpose, intention

pulchinela /pultʃi'nela/ *m,* Punchinello

pulcritud /pulkri'tuð/ *f*, beauty, loveliness, delicacy; fastidiousness, subtlety
pulcro /'pulkro/ *a* beautiful, lovely; delicate, fine; fastidious, subtle
pulga /'pulga/ *f*, flea; small top (toy). **el juego de la p.,** tiddlywinks. *Inf.* **tener malas pulgas,** to be irritable
pulgada /pul'gaða/ *f*, inch
pulgar /pul'gar/ *m*, thumb
pulgón /pul'gon/ *m*, aphid, greenfly
pulgoso /pul'goso/ *a* full of fleas
pulidez /puli'ðeθ; puli'ðes/ *f*, elegance, fineness; polish, smoothness; neatness
pulido /pu'liðo/ *a* elegant, fine; polished, smooth; neat
pulidor /puli'ðor/ *m*, polisher (machine)
pulimentar /pulimen'tar/ *vt* to polish, burnish
pulir /pu'lir/ *vt* to polish, burnish; give the finishing touch to; beautify, decorate; *Fig.* polish up, civilize; —*vr* beautify oneself; become polished and polite
pulla /'puʎa; 'puya/ *f*, lewd remark; strong hint; witty comment
pulmón /pul'mon/ *m*, lung
pulmonar /pulmo'nar/ *a* pulmonary
pulmonía /pulmo'nia/ *f*, pneumonia
pulpa /'pulpa/ *f*, fleshy part of fruit; *Anat.* pulp; wood pulp
pulpejo /pul'peho/ *m*, *Anat.* fleshy part, fat portion (of thumbs, etc.)
pulpería /pulpe'ria/ *f*, *West Hem.* grocery, grocery store, general store
púlpito /'pulpito/ *m*, pulpit
pulpo /'pulpo/ *m*, octopus. *Inf.* **poner como un p.,** to beat to a pulp
pulposo /pul'poso/ *a* pulpy, pulpous
pulquérrimo /pul'kerrimo/ *a superl* **pulcro** most lovely, most exquisite
pulsación /pulsa'θion; pulsa'sion/ *f*, pulsation; throb, beat
pulsar /pul'sar/ *vt* to touch, feel; take the pulse of; *Fig.* explore (a possibility); —*vi* beat (the heart, etc.)
pulsera /pul'sera/ *f*, bracelet; wrist bandage. **p. de pedida,** betrothal bracelet
pulso /'pulso/ *m*, pulse; steadiness of hand; tact, diplomacy, circumspection. **a p.,** freehand (drawing). **tomar a p.** (**una cosa),** to try a thing's weight. **tomar el p.** (**a),** to take a person's pulse
pulular /pulu'lar/ *vi* to pullulate, sprout; abound, be plentiful; swarm, teem; multiply (of insects)
pulverización /pulβeriθa'θion; pulβerisa'sion/ *f*, pulverization; atomization
pulverizador /pulβeriθa'ðor; pulβerisa'ðor/ *m*, atomizer, sprayer; scent spray
pulverizar /pulβeri'θar; pulβeri'sar/ *vt* to pulverize, grind, make into powder; atomize; spray
¡pum! /pum/ *interj* Bang! Thump!
pundonor /pundo'nor/ *m*, (**punto de honor**) point of honor, sense of honor
pundonoroso /pundono'roso/ *a* careful of one's honor; honorable, punctilious
pungir /pun'hir/ *vt* to prick, pierce; revive an old sorrow; *Fig.* wound, sting (passions)
punible /pu'niβle/ *a* punishable
púnico /'puniko/ *a* Punic
punitivo /puni'tiβo/ *a* punitive, punitory
punta /'punta/ *f*, sharp end, point; butt (of a cigarette); end, point, tip; cape, headland; trace, touch, suspicion; nib (of a pen); pointing (pointer dogs); *Herald.* point; *pl* point lace. **p. de París,** wire nail. **p. seca,** drypoint, engraving needle. **sacar p.,** to sharpen; *Inf.* twist (a remark)
puntación /punta'θion; punta'sion/ *f*, dotting, placing dots over (letters)
puntada /pun'taða/ *f*, *Sew.* stitch; innuendo, hint
puntal /pun'tal/ *m*, *Naut.* draft, depth; stanchion, prop, brace, pile; *Fig.* basis, foundation
puntapié /punta'pie/ *m*, kick
punteado /punte'aðo/ *m*, plucking the strings of a guitar, etc.; sewing
puntear /punte'ar/ *vt* to make dots; *Mus.* pluck the strings of; play the guitar; sew; *Art.* stipple; —*vi* *Naut.* tack
puntera /pun'tera/ *f*, mend in the toe of a stocking; toe cap; new piece on the toe of shoe; *Inf.* kick
puntería /punte'ria/ *f*, aiming (of a firearm); aim, sight (of a firearm); marksmanship
puntero /pun'tero/ *a* of a good aim, having a straight eye. *m*, pointer, wand; stonecutter's chisel
puntiagudo /puntia'guðo/ *a* pointed, sharp-pointed
puntilla /pun'tiʎa; pun'tiya/ *f*, narrow lace edging; headless nail, wire nail; brad, tack. **de puntillas,** on tiptoe
puntillismo /punti'ʎismo; punti'yismo/ *m*, pointillism
puntilloso /punti'ʎoso; punti'yoso/ *a* punctilious; overfastidious, fussy
punto /'punto/ *m* dot; point; pen nib; gun sight; *Sew.* stitch; dropped stitch, hole; weaving stitch, mesh; *Gram.* full stop, period; hole (in belts for adjustment); place, spot; point, mark; subject matter; *Mech.* cog; degree, extent; taxi stand; instant; infinitesimal amount; opportunity, chance; vacation, recess; aim, goal; point of honor. **p. de congelación,** freezing point. **p. de ebullición,** boiling point. **p. de fuga,** vanishing point. **p. de fusión,** melting point. **p. de partida,** starting point. **p. de vista,** point of view. **p. final,** *Gram.* period, full stop. **p. interrogante,** question mark. **p. menos,** a little less. **p. y coma,** semicolon. **p. cardinal,** cardinal point. **p. suspensivo,** *Gram.* ellipsis point, suspension point, leader, dot. **a p.,** in readiness; immediately. **en p.,** sharp, prompt (e.g. *a las seis en p.,* at six o'clock sharp)
puntoso /pun'toso/ *a* many-pointed
puntuación /puntua'θion; puntua'sion/ *f*, punctuation; *Sports.* score
puntual /pun'tual/ *a* punctual; punctilious; certain, indubitable; suitable, convenient
puntualidad /puntuali'ðað/ *f*, punctuality; punctiliousness; certainty; exactitude, accuracy
puntualizar /puntuali'θar; puntuali'sar/ *vt* to describe in detail; give the finishing touch to, perfect; impress on the mind
puntualmente /puntual'mente/ *adv* punctually; carefully, diligently; exactly
puntuar /pun'tuar/ *vt* to punctuate
punzada /pun'θaða; pun'saða/ *f*, prick, sting; puncture, piercing; sudden pain, twinge, stitch; *Fig.* anguish, pain
punzar /pun'θar; pun'sar/ *vt* to pierce, puncture; prick; punch, perforate; —*vi* revive, make itself felt (pain or sorrow)
punzón /pun'θon; pun'son/ *m*, awl; punch; die; engraver's burin
puñado /pu'ɲaðo/ *m*, handful; a few, some, a small quantity. **a puñados,** in handfuls; liberally, lavishly
puñal /pu'ɲal/ *m*, dagger
puñalada /puɲa'laða/ *f*, dagger thrust; stab, wound; *Fig.* unexpected blow (of fate). **p. por la espalda,** stab in the back
puñalero /puɲa'lero/ *m*, dagger maker or seller
puñetazo /puɲe'taθo; puɲe'taso/ *m*, blow with the fist
puño /'puɲo/ *m*, fist; handful; cuff (of a sleeve); wristband; handle, head, haft; hilt (of a sword); *pl* *Inf.* guts, courage. **p. de amura,** *Naut.* tack. **p. de un manillar,** handlebar grip. *Inf.* **meter en un p.,** to overawe. *Inf.* **ser como un p.,** to be tightfisted; be small (in stature)
pupila /pu'pila/ *f*, female child ward; *Anat.* pupil; *Inf.* cleverness, talent
pupilaje /pupi'lahe/ *m*, pupilage, minority; boarding house, guesthouse; boarding school; price of board residence; dependence, bondage
pupilo /pu'pilo/ **(-la)** *n* ward, minor; boarder; boarding school student
pupitre /pu'pitre/ *m*, desk, school desk
puramente /pura'mente/ *adv* purely; simply, solely; *Law.* unconditionally, without reservation
puré /pu're/ *m*, purée, thick soup
pureza /pu'reθa; pu'resa/ *f*, purity; perfection, excellence; chastity; disinterestedness, genuineness; clearness

purga /'purga/ *f*, laxative, purge; waste product
purgación /purga'θion; purga'sion/ *f*, purging; menstruation; gonorrhea
purgante /pur'gante/ *a* purgative. *m*, purge, cathartic
purgar /pur'gar/ *vt* to cleanse, purify; expiate, atone for; (*Med. Law.*) purge; suffer purgatorial pains; clarify, refine; —*vr* rid oneself, purge oneself
purgativo /purga'tiβo/ *a* purgative
purgatorio /purga'torio/ *m*, purgatory —*a* purgatorial
puridad /puri'ðað/ *f*, purity; secrecy, privacy. **en p.,** openly, without dissembling; secretly, in private
purificación /purifika'θion; purifika'sion/ *f*, purification; cleansing
purificador /purifika'ðor/ **(-ra)** *a* purifying; cleansing —*n* purifier; cleanser
purificar /purifi'kar/ *vt* to purify; cleanse; —*vr* be purified
purificatorio /purifika'torio/ *a* purificatory
Purísima /pu'risima/ **(la)** *f*, the Most Blessed Virgin
purista /pu'rista/ *mf* purist
puritanismo /purita'nismo/ *m*, Puritanism
puritano /puri'tano/ **(-na)** *a* puritanical —*n* Puritan
puro /'puro/ *a* pure; undiluted; unalloyed; unmixed; disinterested, honest; virgin; absolute, sheer; mere, simple. *m*, cigar. **de p.,** by sheer..., by dint of
púrpura /'purpura/ *f*, purple; *Poet.* blood; purpura; *Herald.* purpure; purple (cloth); dignity of an emperor, cardinal, consul
purpurear /purpure'ar/ *vi* to look like purple; be tinged with purple
purpúreo, purpurino /pur'pureo, purpu'rino/ *a* purple
purulencia /puru'lenθia; puru'lensia/ *f*, purulence
purulento /puru'lento/ *a* purulent
pus /pus/ *m*, pus, matter
pusilánime /pusi'lanime/ *a* pusillanimous, timid, cowardly
pusilanimidad /pusilanimi'ðað/ *f*, pusillanimity, timidity, cowardice
pústula /'pustula/ *f*, pustule
puta /'puta/ *f*, whore
putativo /puta'tiβo/ *a* putative
puto /'puto/ *m*, male prostitute
putrefacción /putrefak'θion; putrefak'sion/ *f*, putrefaction; rottenness, putrescence
putrefacto /putre'fakto/ *a* rotten, decayed
pútrido /'putriðo/ *a* putrid, rotten
puya /'puya/ *f*, goad
puyazo /pu'yaθo; pu'yaso/ *m*, prick with a goad

Q

que /ke/ *pron rel* all genders sing. and pl. who; which; that; whom; when (e.g. *Un poema en que habla de su juventud,* A poem in which he speaks of his youth. *El libro que tengo aquí,* The book (that) I have here. **No es oro todo lo que reluce,** All that glitters is not gold. **Un día que nos vimos,** One day when we met —*interr* **¿qué?** what? *interj* what a ------! what! how! (e.g. *¿Qué hay?* What's the matter? *¡Qué día más hermoso!* What a lovely day! *¿qué de...?* how many? *¿qué tal?* how? *Inf.* *¿Qué tal estás hoy?* How are you today? *¿qué tanto?* how much?) **¿a qué?** why? for what reason? (e.g. *¿A qué negarlo?* Why deny it?) —*conjunc* that (e.g. *Me dijo que vendría,* He said (that) he would come). Means "so that,' "that,' "for,' in commands (e.g. *Mandó que le trajesen el libro,* He ordered that they bring him the book (He ordered them to bring him the book)). Note that the translation of **que** is often omitted in English.
In compound tenses where the participle is placed first, **que** means "when' (e.g. *llegado que hube,* when I had arrived). In comparisons, **que** means "than' (e.g. *más joven que yo,* younger than I).
With subjunctives and expressing commands or wishes, **que** means "let' (e.g. *¡Que venga!* Let him come!) Preceding a subjunctive, **que** is generally translated by "to' (e.g. *Quiero, que venga or que llueva,* I want him to come *or* I want it to rain). Also means "may' (e.g. *¡Que lo pase bien!* May you enjoy yourself! (I hope you...)). **es** (**era**) **que,** the fact is (was) that... **que... que,** whether... or...

quebrada /ke'βraða/ *f,* mountain gorge; *Com.* bankruptcy

quebradizo /keβra'ðiθo; keβra'ðiso/ *a* brittle, fragile; ailing, infirm; delicate, frail

quebrado /ke'βraðo/ **(-da)** *m, Math.* fraction; —*n Com.* bankrupt —*a* rough, uneven (ground); *Med.* ruptured; bankrupt; ailing, broken-down

quebradura /keβra'ðura/ *f,* snap, breaking; gap, crevice; hernia

quebraja /ke'βraha/ *f,* split, crack; flaw (in wood, metal, etc.)

quebrantahuesos /keβranta'uesos/ *m,* sea eagle, osprey; *Inf.* bore, tedious person

quebrantamiento /keβranta'miento/ *m,* crushing; splitting, cleaving; fracture, rupture; profanation, desecration; burglary; violation, breaking, infringement; fatigue; *Law.* annulment; exhaustion

quebrantanueces /keβranta'nueθes; keβranta'nueses/ *m,* nutcrackers

quebrantaolas /keβranta'olas/ *m,* breakwater

quebrantar /keβran'tar/ *vt* to break, shatter; crush, pound; transgress, infringe; break out, force; tone down, soften; moderate, lessen; bore, exhaust; move to pity; *Inf.* break in (horses); profane; overcome (difficulties); assuage, placate; *Law.* revoke (wills); —*vr* be shaken or bruised, suffer from aftereffects

quebranto /ke'βranto/ *m,* breaking, shattering; crushing, pounding; infringement; breaking out (from prison); weakness, exhaustion; compassion, pity; loss, damage; pain, suffering

quebrar /ke'βrar/ *vt irr* to break, shatter; crush; impede, hinder; make pale (color, gen. of complexion); mitigate, moderate; bend, twist; overcome (difficulties); —*vi* break off (a friendship); weaken, give way; go bankrupt; —*vr Med.* suffer from hernia; be interrupted (of mountain ranges). **quebrarse los ojos,** to strain one's eyes —*Pres. Indic.* **quiebro, quiebras, quiebra, quiebran.** *Pres. Subjunc.* **quiebre, quiebres, quiebre, quiebren**

queche /'ketʃe/ *m,* ketch

queda /'keða/ *f,* curfew; curfew bell

quedada /ke'ðaða/ *f,* stay, sojourn

quedar /ke'ðar/ *vi* to stay, sojourn; remain; be left over; (*with por + infin.*) remain to be (e.g. *Queda por escribir,* It remains to be written); (*with por*) be won by or be knocked down to; be, remain in a place; end, cease; (*with en*) reach an agreement (e.g. *Quedamos en no ir,* We have decided not to go). **q. en esta alternativa...,** to face this alternative:... —*vr* remain; abate (wind); grow calm (sea); (*with con*) keep, retain possession of. **q. bien o mal,** to behave well or badly, come off well or badly (in business affairs, etc.). **quedarse muerto,** to be astounded

quedo /'keðo/ *a* still, motionless; quiet, tranquil —*adv* in a low voice; quietly, noiselessly. **de q.,** slowly, gradually —*interj* **¡Q.!** Quiet!

quehacer /kea'θer; kea'ser/ *m,* odd job; task; business (gen. *pl*)

queja /'keha/ *f,* lamentation, grief; complaint, grudge; quarrel

quejarse /ke'harse/ *vr* to lament; complain, grumble; *Law.* lodge an accusation (against)

quejido /ke'hiðo/ *m,* complaint, moan

quejoso /ke'hoso/ *a* querulous, complaining

quejumbre /ke'humbre/ *f,* complaint, whine; querulousness

quejumbroso /kehum'βroso/ *a* complaining, grumbling

quema /'kema/ *f,* burn; burning; fire, conflagration

quemadero /kema'ðero/ *a* burnable. *m,* stake (for burning people)

quemado /ke'maðo/ *m,* burned patch of forest; *Inf.* anything burned or burning

quemador /kema'ðor/ **(-ra)** *m,* jet, burner —*n* incendiary

quemadura /kema'ðura/ *f,* burn; scald; burning

quemajoso /kema'hoso/ *a* smarting, burning, pricking

quemar /ke'mar/ *vt* to burn; dry up, parch; scorch; tan, bronze; scald; throw away, sell at a loss; —*vi* burn, be excessively hot; —*vr* be very hot; be dried up with the heat; burn with (passions); *Inf.* be near the attainment of a desired end. **quemarse las cejas,** to burn the midnight oil, study too hard

quemazón /kema'θon; kema'son/ *f,* burning; conflagration; intense heat; *Inf.* smarting; *Inf.* hurtful remark; *Inf.* vexation, soreness

querella /ke'reʎa; ke'reya/ *f,* complaint; quarrel, fight

querellarse /kere'ʎarse; kere'yarse/ *vr* to complain; lament, bemoan; *Law.* lodge an accusation; *Law.* contest a will

querelloso /kere'ʎoso; kere'yoso/ *a* complaining, grumbling, querulous

querencia /ke'renθia; ke'rensia/ *f,* love, affection; homing instinct; lair; natural inclination or desire

querer /ke'rer/ *vt irr* to desire, wish; want, will; attempt, endeavor; (*with a*) love —*impers* be on the point of. **q. decir,** to mean. **¿Qué quiere decir esto?** What does this mean? **sin q.,** unintentionally. See **entender**

querer /ke'rer/ *m,* affection, love

querido /ke'riðo/ **(-da)** *n* lover; beloved; darling —*a* dear

querub, querube /ke'ruβ, ke'ruβe/ *Poet.* **querubín** *m,* cherub

querúbico /ke'ruβiko/ *a* cherubic

quesera /ke'sera/ *f,* dairymaid; dairy; cheese vat; cheese board; cheese dish

quesería /kese'ria/ *f,* dairy; cheese shop; season for making cheese

queso /'keso/ *m,* cheese. **q. de bola,** Dutch cheese. **q. rallado,** grated cheese

quetzal /ket'θal; ket'sal/ *m,* quetzal

quevedos /ke'βeðos/ *m pl,* glasses, eyeglasses; pince-nez

¡quia! /kia/ *interj Inf.* You don't say so!

quianti /'kianti/ *m,* chianti

quicial /ki'θial; ki'sial/ *m,* doorjamb

quicio /'kiθio; 'kisio/ *m,* threshold; hinge; *Mech.* bushing. **fuera de q.,** out of order; unhinged. **sacar de q.,** to displace (things); annoy, irritate; drive crazy

quiebra /'kieβra/ *f,* breach, crack; rut, fissure; loss; bankruptcy

quiebro /'kieβro/ *m,* twisting of the body, dodging; *Mus.* trill
quien /kien/ *rel pron mf pl* **quienes.** *interr* **quién, quiénes** who; whom; he (she, etc.) who, anyone who, whoever; which; whichever (e.g. *mis padres a quienes respeto,* my parents whom I respect. *Quien te quiere te hará llorar,* Whoever (he, those, who) love(s) you will make you weep. **¿Quién está a la puerta?** Who is at the door? **¿De quién es?** Whose is it? To whom does it belong?) —*indef pron* one (*pl* some)
quienquiera /kien'kiera/ *indef pron mf pl* **quienesquiera,** whosoever, whichever, whomsoever
quietación /kieta'θion; kieta'sion/ *f,* quieting, soothing
quietador /kieta'ðor/ **(-ra)** *a* tranquilizing, soothing —*n* soother
quietismo /kie'tismo/ *m,* quietism
quietista /kie'tista/ *mf* quietist —*a* quietistic
quieto /'kieto/ *a* quiet, still; peaceful, tranquil; virtuous, respectable
quietud /kie'tuð/ *f,* stillness, repose; peacefulness; rest, quietness
quif /kif/ *m,* hashish, marijuana
quijada /ki'haða/ *f,* jawbone, jaw; *Mech.* jaw
quijo /'kiho/ *m,* ore (gold or silver)
quijotada /kiho'taða/ *f,* quixotic action, quixotism
quijote /ki'hote/ *m,* cuisse; thigh guard; quixotic person
quijotería /kihote'ria/ *f,* **quijotismo** *m,* quixotism
quijotesco /kiho'tesko/ *a* quixotic
quilate /ki'late/ *m,* carat; degree of excellence (gen. *pl*). *Inf.* **por quilates,** in small bits, parsimoniously
quilla /'kiʎa; 'kiya/ *f, Naut.* keel; breastbone (of birds)
quillotrar /kiʎo'trar; kiyo'trar/ *vt Inf.* to encourage, incite; woo, make love to; consider; —*vr Inf.* fall in love; dress up; whine, complain
quillotro /ki'ʎotro; ki'yotro/ *m, Inf.* incentive; indication, sign; love affair; puzzle, knotty point; compliment; dressing up
quimera /ki'mera/ *f,* chimera; fancy, vision; quarrel, dispute
quimérico /ki'meriko/ *a* chimerical, fanciful
quimerista /kime'rista/ *mf* dreamer, visionary; quarreler, disputant
química /'kimika/ *f,* chemistry
químico /'kimiko/ *a* chemical. *m,* chemist. **productos químicos,** chemicals
quimono /ki'mono/ *m,* kimono
quina /'kina/ *f,* cinchona; quinine; *pl* Arms of Portugal. *Inf.* **tragar q.,** to suffer in patience, put up with
quinario /ki'nario/ *a* quinary
quincalla /kin'kaʎa; kin'kaya/ *f,* cheap jewelery; fancy goods
quincallería /kinkaʎe'ria; kinkaye'ria/ *f,* cheap jewelry shop; hardware factory or industry; cheap jewelry; fancy goods
quince /'kinθe; 'kinse/ *a* and *m,* fifteen; fifteenth
quinceañero /kinθea'ɲero; kinsea'ɲero/ *f,* sweet sixteen party, sweet sixteen (in Spanish-speaking areas, held at age fifteen)
quincena /kin'θena; kin'sena/ *f,* fortnight, two weeks; bimonthly pay; *Mus.* fifteenth
quincenal /kinθe'nal; kinse'nal/ *a* fortnightly; lasting a fortnight, lasting two weeks
quinceno /kin'θeno; kin'seno/ *a* fifteenth
quincuagenario /kinkuahe'nario/ *a* quinquagenarian
quincuagésimo /kinkua'hesimo/ *a* fiftieth
quindécimo /kin'deθimo; kin'desimo/ *a* fifteenth
quinientos /ki'nientos/ *a* five hundred; five-hundredth. *m,* five hundred
quinina /ki'nina/ *f,* quinine
quinqué /kin'ke/ *m,* oil lamp, student's lamp, table lamp; perspicuity, talent
quinquenio /kin'kenio/ *m,* period of five years, lustrum
quinta /'kinta/ *f,* country house; *Mus.* fifth; conscripting men into army by drawing lots; *Mil.* draft
quintaesencia /kintae'senθia; kintae'sensia/ *f,* quintessence
quintal /kin'tal/ *m,* hundredweight
quintar /kin'tar/ *vt* to draw one out of every five; draw lots for conscription into the army; —*vi* reach the fifth (day, etc., gen. of the moon)
quintería /kinte'ria/ *f,* farm
quintero /kin'tero/ *m,* farmer; farmworker
quinteto /kin'teto/ *m,* quintet
quintilla /kin'tiʎa; kin'tiya/ *f,* five-line stanza of eight syllables
Quintín, San. armarse /kin'tin, san ar'marse/ (*or* **haber**) **la de San Q.** to quarrel, make trouble; be a row
quinto /'kinto/ *a* fifth. *m,* one-fifth; *Mil.* conscript; duty of twenty percent; *Law.* fifth part of an estate. **quinta columna,** fifth column. **quinta esencia,** quintessence
quintuplicar /kintupli'kar/ *vt* to quintuplicate
quíntuplo /'kintuplo/ *a* fivefold, quintuple
quinzavo /kin'θaβo; kin'saβo/ *a* and *m,* fifteenth
quiñón /ki'ɲon/ *m,* share of land owned jointly, share of the profits
quiosco /'kiosko/ *m,* kiosk, stand; pavilion, pagoda. **q. de música,** bandstand
quiquiriquí /kikiri'ki/ *m,* cock-a-doodle-doo; *Fig. Inf.* cock of the walk
quiromancia /kiro'manθia; kiro'mansia/ *f,* chiromancy, palmistry
quiromántico /kiro'mantiko/ **(-ca)** *n* chiromancer, palmist
quirúrgico /ki'rurhiko/ *a* surgical
quirurgo /ki'rurgo/ *m,* surgeon
quisicosa /kisi'kosa/ *f, Inf.* riddle, puzzle, enigma
quisquilla /kis'kiʎa; kis'kiya/ *f,* trifle, quibble, scruple; prawn, shrimp
quisquilloso /kiski'ʎoso; kiski'yoso/ *a* quibbling, overscrupulous, fastidious; hypersensitive; irascible, touchy
quistarse /kis'tarse/ *vr* to make oneself well-liked or loved
quiste /'kiste/ *m, Med.* cyst
quita /'kita/ *f, Law.* discharge (of part of a debt)
quitaesmalte /kitaes'malte/ *m,* nail polish remover (for fingernails)
quitamanchas /kita'mantʃas/ *mf,* dry cleaner, clothes cleaner
quitamotas /kita'motas/ *mf Inf.* flatterer, adulator
quitanieve /kita'nieβe/ *m,* snowplow
quitanza /ki'tanθa; ki'tansa/ *f,* quittance; quietus
quitapesares /kitape'sares/ *m, Inf.* consolation, solace, comfort
quitar /ki'tar/ *vt* to remove; take off or away; clear (the table); rob, steal; prevent, impede; parry (in fencing); separate; redeem (pledges); forbid; annul, repeal (laws, etc.); free from (obligations); —*vr* shed, take off, remove; get rid of; leave, quit. **quitarse de encima (a),** to get rid of someone or something. **q. el polvo,** to dust. **de quita y pon,** detachable, removable; adjustable
quitasol /kita'sol/ *m,* parasol, sunshade
quitasueño /kita'sueɲo/ *m, Inf.* sleep banisher, anxiety
quite /'kite/ *m,* hindering, impeding; obstruction; parry (in fencing). **estar al q.,** to be ready to protect someone
quizá, quizás /ki'θa, ki'θas; ki'sa, ki'sas/ *adv* perhaps. **q. y sin q.,** without doubt, certainly

R

rabadán /rraβa'ðan/ *m*, head shepherd or herdsman
rabadilla /rraβa'ðiʎa; rraβa'ðiya/ *f*, rump, croup
rábano /'rraβano/ *m*, radish. **r. picante,** horseradish
rabel /rra'βel/ *m*, *Mus.* rebec; *Inf.* backside, seat
rabera /rra'βera/ *f*, tail-end; chaff, siftings
rabí /rra'βi/ *m*, rabbi
rabia /'rraβia/ *f*, rabies, hydrophobia; anger, fury. *Inf.* **tener r.** (**a),** to hate
rabiar /rra'βiar/ *vi* to suffer from hydrophobia; groan with pain; be furious; (*with por*) yearn for, desire. **a r.,** excessively
rabicorto /rraβi'korto/ *a* short-tailed
rabieta /rra'βieta/ *f*, *Inf.* tantrum
rabilargo /rraβi'largo/ *a* long-tailed
rabínico /rra'βiniko/ *a* rabbinical
rabinismo /rraβi'nismo/ *m*, rabbinism
rabino /rra'βino/ *m*, rabbi. **gran r.,** chief rabbi
rabioso /rra'βioso/ *a* rabid; furious, angry; vehement. **perro r.,** mad dog
rabo /'rraβo/ *m*, tail; *Bot.* stalk; *Inf.* train (of a dress); shank (of a button). **r. del ojo,** corner of the eye. *Fig. Inf.* **ir r. entre piernas,** to have one's tail between one's legs
rabón /rra'βon/ *a* tailless, docked; bobtailed
rabudo /rra'βuðo/ *a* big-tailed
racimo /rra'θimo; rra'simo/ *m*, bunch (of grapes or other fruits); cluster; raceme
racimoso /rraθi'moso; rrasi'moso/ *a* racemose
raciocinación /rraθioθina'θion; rrasiosina'sion/ *f*, ratiocination
raciocinar /rraθioθi'nar; rrasiosi'nar/ *vi* to reason
raciocinio /rraθio'θinio; rrasio'sinio/ *m*, reasoning; ratiocination; discourse, speech
ración /rra'θion; rra'sion/ *f*, ration; portion (in a restaurant); meal allowance; *Eccl.* prebendary. *Inf.* **r. de hambre,** starvation diet; pittance, starvation wages
racional /rraθio'nal; rrasio'nal/ *a* reasonable, logical; rational
racionalidad /rraθionali'ðað; rrasionali'ðað/ *f*, reasonableness; rationality
racionalismo /rraθiona'lismo; rrasiona'lismo/ *m*, rationalism
racionalista /rraθiona'lista; rrasiona'lista/ *a* and *mf* rationalist —*a* rationalistic
racionalización /rraθionaliθa'θion; rrasionalisa'sion/ *f*, rationalization
racionamiento /rraθiona'miento; rrasiona'miento/ *m*, rationing. *f.* **cartilla de r.,** ration book
racionar /rraθio'nar; rrasio'nar/ *vt* to ration
rada /'rraða/ *f*, bay, cove; *Naut.* road, roadstead
radar /rra'ðar/ *m*, radar
radiación /rraðia'θion; rraðia'sion/ *f*, radiation; *Radio.* broadcasting
radiactividad /rraðiaktiβi'ðað/ *f*, radioactivity
radiactivo /rraðiak'tiβo/ *a* radioactive
radiador /rraðia'ðor/ *m*, radiator (for heating); *Auto.* radiator
radial /rra'ðial/ *a* radial
radiante /rra'ðiante/ *a Phys.* radiating; brilliant, shining; *Fig.* beaming (with satisfaction)
radiar /rra'ðiar/ *vi Phys.* to radiate; —*vt* broadcast (by radio)
radical /rraði'kal/ *a* radical; fundamental; *Polit.* radical. *m*, *Gram.* root; (*Math. Chem.*) radical. *mf Polit.* radical
radicalismo /rraðika'lismo/ *m*, radicalism
radicar /rraði'kar/ **(se)** *vi* and *vr* to take root. **r. una solicitud,** file an application, submit an application —*vi* be (in a place)
radio /'rraðio/ *m*, (*Geom. Anat.*) radius; radium. *f*, radio
radioaficionado /rraðioafiθio'naðo; rraðioafisio'naðo/ **(-da)** *n* radio amateur; *Inf.* ham, wireless fan or enthusiast
radioaudición /rraðioauði'θion; rraðioauði'sion/ *f*, radio broadcast
radiocomunicación /rraðiokomunika'θion; rraðiokomunika'sion/ *f*, radio transmission
radiodifundir /rraðioðifun'dir/ *vt Radio.* to broadcast
radiodifusión, radioemisión /rraðioðifu'sion, rraðioemi'sion/ *f*, *Radio.* broadcast; broadcasting
radioemisora /rraðioemi'sora/ *f*, radio station
radioescucha /rraðioes'kutʃa/ *mf* radio listener
radiofotografía /rraðiofotogra'fia/ *f*, radiophotography; x-ray photograph. **tomar una r. de,** to x-ray
radiofrecuencia /rraðiofre'kuenθia; rraðiofre'kuensia/ *f*, radiofrequency
radiografía /rraðiogra'fia/ *f*, radiography
radiografiar /rraðiogra'fiar/ *vt* to x-ray, radiograph
radiografista /rraðiogra'fista/ *mf* radiographer
radiograma /rraðio'grama/ *m*, radiogram, cable
radiolocación /rraðioloka'θion; rraðioloka'sion/ *f*, radiolocation
radiología /rraðiolo'hia/ *f*, radiology
radiólogo /rra'ðiologo/ *mf* radiologist
radiometría /rraðiome'tria/ *f*, radiometry
radiómetro /rra'ðiometro/ *m*, radiometer
radiorreceptor /rraðiorreθep'tor; rraðiorresep'tor/ *m*, receiver, wireless set
radioscopia /rraðio'skopia/ *f*, radioscopy
radiotelefonía /rraðiotelefo'nia/ *f*, radiotelephony
radiotelegrafía /rraðiotelegra'fia/ *f*, radiotelegraphy
radiotelegrafiar /rraðiotelegra'fiar/ *vt* to radiotelegraph
radiotelegráfico /rraðiotele'grafiko/ *a* radiotelegraphic, wireless
radiotelegrafista /rraðiotelegra'fista/ *mf* wireless operator
radiotelegrama /rraðiotele'grama/ *m*, radiogram, radiotelegram
radioterapia /rraðiote'rapia/ *f*, radiotherapy, radiotherapeutics
radiotransmisor /rraðiotransmi'sor/ *m*, (radio) transmitter
radioyente /rraðio'yente/ *mf* radio listener
raedera /rrae'ðera/ *f*, scraper
raedor /rrae'ðor/ *a* scraping; abrasive
raedura /rrae'ðura/ *f*, scraping; rubbing; fraying
raer /rra'er/ *vt irr* to scrape; abrade; fray; *Fig.* extirpate. See **caer**
ráfaga /'rrafaga/ *f*, gust or blast of wind; light cloud; flash (of light)
rafe /'rrafe/ *m*, eaves
rafia /'rrafia/ *f*, raffia
raído /'rraiðo/ *a* frayed, threadbare; brazen, barefaced
raíz /rra'iθ; rra'is/ *f*, root. **r. amarga,** horseradish. **r. cuadrada** (**cúbica),** square (cubed) root. **r. pivotante,** tap root. **a r.,** close to the root, closely. **a r. de,** as a result of; after. **de r.,** from the root, entirely. **echar raíces,** to take root
raja /'rraha/ *f*, split, crack; chip, splinter (of wood); slice (of fruit, etc.)
rajá /rra'ha/ *m*, rajah
rajadura /rraha'ðura/ *f*, splitting; crack, split, crevice; *Geol.* break
rajar /rra'har/ *vt* to crack, split; slice; —*vi Inf.* boast; chatter; —*vr* crack, split; *Inf.* take back one's words
ralea /rra'lea/ *f*, kind, quality; (*Inf.* scornful) race, lineage
ralear /rrale'ar/ *vi* to grow thin (cloth, etc.); behave true to type (gen. in a bad sense)
rallador /rraʎa'ðor; rraya'ðor/ *m*, *Cul.* grater
rallar /rra'ʎar; rra'yar/ *vt Cul.* to grate; *Inf.* bother, annoy
rallo /'rraʎo; 'rrayo/ *m*, *Cul.* grater; rasp
ralo /'rralo/ *a* sparse, thin
rama /'rrama/ *f*, bough, branch; *Fig.* branch (of family). *Fig. Inf.* **andarse por las ramas,** to beat around the bush. **en r.,** *Com.* raw; unbound (of books)
ramaje /rra'mahe/ *m*, thickness of branches, denseness of foliage

ramal /rra'mal/ *m*, strand (of rope); halter; branch line (of a railroad); fork (of a road, etc.); ramification, division
ramalazo /rrama'laθo; rrama'laso/ *m*, blow with a rope; mark left by this; bruise
rambla /'rrambla/ *f*, bed, channel, course; avenue, boulevard (in Catalonia)
ramera /rra'mera/ *f*, whore
ramificación /rramifika'θion; rramifika'sion/ *f*, ramification; *Anat.* bifurcation
ramificarse /rramifi'karse/ *vr* to branch, fork; *Fig.* spread
ramillete /rrami'ʎete; rrami'yete/ *m*, bouquet; table centerpiece; *Bot.* cluster
ramo /'rramo/ *m*, *Bot.* branch; twig, spray; bouquet, bunch; wreath; *Fig.* branch (of learning, etc.); *Com.* line (of business); *Fig.* touch, slight attack. **Domingo de Ramos,** Palm Sunday
ramoso /rra'moso/ *a* branchy, thick with branches
rampa /'rrampa/ *f*, gradient, incline; *Mil.* ramp; launching site
ramplón /rram'plon/ *a* stout, heavy (of shoes); coarse; vulgar; bombastic
rana /'rrana/ *f*, frog. **r. de San Antonio,** tree frog
ranchero /rran'tʃero/ *m*, *Mil.* cook; small farmer; *West Hem.* rancher
rancho /'rrantʃo/ *m*, mess, rations; settlement, camp; hut, cabin; *Inf.* group, huddle; *West Hem.* ranch; *Naut.* gang. **hacer r.,** *Inf.* to make room
rancidez /rranθi'ðeθ; rransi'ðes/ *f*, rancidness; staleness; rankness; antiquity
ranciedad /rranθie'ðað; rransie'ðað/ *f*, rancidness; antiquity, oldness; mustiness
rancio /'rranθio; 'rransio/ *a* rancid, rank; mellow (of wine); ancient; traditional; musty
rango /'rraŋgo/ *m*, grade, class; range; (*Mil. Nav.* and social) rank; file, line
ranúnculo /rra'nunkulo/ *m*, buttercup
ranura /rra'nura/ *f*, groove; rabbet; slot, notch
rapacidad /rrapaθi'ðað; rrapasi'ðað/ *f*, rapacity, avidity, greed
rapador /rrapa'ðor/ *a* scraping. *m*, *Inf.* barber
rapapolvo /rrapa'polβo/ *m*, *Inf.* severe scolding, dressing-down
rapar /rra'par/ **(se)** *vt* and *vr* to shave; —*vt* crop, cut close (hair); *Inf.* steal, pinch
rapaz /rra'paθ; rra'pas/ *a* rapacious. *m*, young boy. **ave r.,** bird of prey
rapaza /rra'paθa; rra'pasa/ *f*, young girl
rape /'rrape/ *m*, *Inf.* hasty shave or haircut. **al r.,** close-cropped
rapé /rra'pe/ *m*, snuff
rapidez /rrapi'ðeθ; rrapi'ðes/ *f*, speed, swiftness, rapidity
rápido /'rrapiðo/ *a* quick, swift; express (trains). *m*, torrent, rapid; express train
rapiña /rra'piɲa/ *f*, robbery, plundering, sacking
rapiñar /rrapi'ɲar/ *vt Inf.* to steal, pinch
raposa /rra'posa/ *f*, vixen, fox; *Inf.* wily person
raposear /rrapose'ar/ *vi* to behave like a fox
raposo /rra'poso/ *m*, (male) fox
rapsodia /rrap'soðia/ *f*, rhapsody
raptar /rrap'tar/ *vt* to abduct; rob
rapto /'rrapto/ *m*, abduction, rape; snatching, seizing; ecstasy, trance; *Med.* loss of consciousness
raptor /rrap'tor/ *m*, kidnapper, abductor
raquero /rra'kero/ *a* pirate. *m*, wrecker; pickpocket, dock rat
raqueta /rra'keta/ *f*, racket (tennis, badminton, squash rackets); croupier's rake. **r. de nieve,** snowshoe
raquianestesia /rrakianes'tesia/ *f*, spinal anesthesia
raquídeo /rra'kiðeo/ *a* spinal
raquítico /rra'kitiko/ *a Med.* rachitic; small, minute; weak, feeble; rickety
raquitismo /rraki'tismo/ *m*, rickets
rarefacción /rrarefak'θion; rrarefak'sion/ *f*, rarefaction
rarefacer /rrarefa'θer; rrarefa'ser/ **(se)** *vt* and *vr irr* to rarefy. See **satisfacer**
rareza /rra'reθa; rra'resa/ *f*, rareness, unusualness; eccentricity, whim; oddity, curio
raridad /rrari'ðað/ *f*, rarity; thinness; scarcity
raro /'rraro/ *a* rare, unusual, uncommon; notable, outstanding; odd, eccentric, queer; rarefied (gases, etc.). **rara vez,** seldom. **lo r. de,** the strange thing about (e.g. *Lo r. del caso es...*, the strange thing about the case is...)
ras /rras/ *m*, level. **a r.,** flush (with), nearly touching
rasa /'rrasa/ *f*, worn place in cloth; clearing, glade
rasar /rra'sar/ *vt* to level with a strickle; graze, brush, touch lightly; —*vr* grow clear (of the sky, etc.)
rascacielos /rraska'θielos; rraska'sielos/ *m*, skyscraper
rascador /rraska'ðor/ *m*, scraper; ornamental hairpin
rascadura /rraska'ðura/ *f*, scraping; scratching
rascar /rras'kar/ *vt* to scratch; claw; scrape; twang (a guitar, etc.). *Inf.* **¡Que se rasque!** Let him put up with it! Let him lump it!
rascatripas /rraska'tripas/ *m*, *Inf.* caterwauler, squeaker (of violinists, etc.)
rascón /rras'kon/ *a* sour, tart
rasgadura /rrasga'ðura/ *f*, tearing; tear, rip, rent
rasgar /rras'gar/ **(se)** *vt* and *vr* to tear, rip; —*vt* strum the guitar
rasgo /'rrasgo/ *m*, flourish (of the pen); felicitous expression; characteristic, quality; *pl* features (of the face)
rasgón /rras'gon/ *m*, rip, tear
rasguear /rrasge'ar/ *vt* to strum, twang (the guitar); —*vi* write with a flourish
rasgueo /rras'geo/ *m*, flourish (on a guitar); scratch (of a pen)
rasguñar /rrasgu'ɲar/ *vt* to scratch, scrape; claw; *Art.* sketch
rasguño /rras'guɲo/ *m*, scratch; *Art.* sketch, outline
raso /'rraso/ *a* flat; free of obstacles; glossy; clear (sky, etc.); plain; undistinguished; backless (chairs). *m*, satin. **al r.,** in the open air
raspa /'rraspa/ *f*, *Bot.* beard (of cereals); fishbone; bunch of grapes; *Bot.* husk; scraper
raspador /rraspa'ðor/ *m*, eraser; scraper, rasp
raspadura /rraspa'ðura/ *f*, scraping; erasing; shavings, filings
raspar /rras'par/ *vt* to scrape; erase; rob, steal; burn, bite (wine, etc.)
rastra /'rrastra/ *f*, trace, sign; sled; string of onions, etc.; anything dragging; *Agr.* harrow; *Agr.* rake. **a la r.,** dragging; reluctantly. **pescar a la r.,** to trawl
rastreador /rrastrea'ðor/ *m*, *Naut.* minesweeper —*a* dragging
rastrear /rrastre'ar/ *vt* to trace, trail; drag, trawl; surmise, conjecture, investigate; —*vi Agr.* rake; fly low
rastreo /rras'treo/ *m*, dragging (of lakes, etc.)
rastrero /rras'trero/ *a* dragging, trailing; low-flying; servile, abject; *Bot.* creeping. *m*, slaughterhouse employee
rastrillador /rrastriʎa'ðor; rrastriya'ðor/ **(-ra)** *n* raker; hackler
rastrilladora /rrastriʎa'ðora; rrastriya'ðora/ *f*, mechanical harrow
rastrillaje /rrastri'ʎahe; rrastri'yahe/ *m*, raking
rastrillar /rrastri'ʎar; rrastri'yar/ *vt* to rake; dress, comb (flax)
rastrillo /rras'triʎo; rras'triyo/ *m*, *Agr.* rake; hackle; portcullis; *Agr.* rack
rastro /'rrastro/ *m*, *Agr.* rake; track, trail; wholesale meat market, slaughterhouse, trace, vestige; second-hand market (in Madrid)
rastrojo /rras'troho/ *m*, stubble; stubble field
rasura /rra'sura/ *f*, shaving
rasurar /rrasu'rar/ **(se)** *vt* and *vr* to shave
rata /'rrata/ *f*, rat. *m*, *Inf.* pickpocket. **r. almizclera,** muskrat. *Inf.* **más pobre que las ratas,** poorer than a church mouse
rataplán /rrata'plan/ *m*, rub-a-dub-dub, beating of a drum
ratear /rrate'ar/ *vt* to rebate pro rata; apportion; thieve on a small scale, filch; —*vi* crawl, creep
ratería /rrate'ria/ *f*, filching, petty theft, picking pockets; meanness, parsimony

ratero /rra'tero/ **(-ra)** *n* pilferer, petty thief, pickpocket
ratificación /rratifika'θion; rratifika'sion/ *f,* ratification
ratificador /rratifika'ðor/ **(-ra)** *n* ratifier
ratificar /rratifi'kar/ *vt* to ratify
ratificatorio /rratifika'torio/ *a* ratifying, confirmatory
rato /'rrato/ *m,* short interval of time, while. **buen (mal) r.,** pleasant (unpleasant) time. **r. perdido,** leisure moment. **a ratos,** sometimes, occasionally. **de r. en r.,** from time to time. **pasar el r.,** *Inf.* to while away the time
ratón /rra'ton/ **(-ona)** *n* mouse
ratonera /rrato'nera/ *f,* mousetrap; mousehole; mouse nest. *Fig.* **caer en la r.,** to fall into a trap
ratonero, ratonesco, ratonil /rrato'nero, rrato'nesko, rrato'nil/ *a* mousy
rauco /'rrauko/ *a Poet.* hoarse
raudal /rrau'ðal/ *m,* torrent, cascade; *Fig.* flood, abundance
raudo /'rrauðo/ *a* swift, rapid
ravioles /rra'βioles/ *m pl,* ravioli
raya /'rraya/ *f,* stripe, streak; limit, end; part (of the hair); boundary; *Gram.* dash; score (some games). *m, Ichth.* ray. **pasar de r.,** to go too far; misbehave
rayadillo /rraya'ðiʎo; rraya'ðiyo/ *m,* striped cotton
rayano /rra'yano/ *a* neighboring; border; almost identical, very similar
rayar /rra'yar/ *vt* to draw lines; streak; stripe; cross out; underline; rifle (a gun); —*vi* verge (on), border (on); appear (of dawn, daylight); excel; be similar. **Raya en los catorce años,** He is about fourteen
rayo /'rrayo/ *m, Phys.* beam, ray; thunderbolt; flash of lightning; spoke; quick-witted person; capable, energetic person; sudden pain; disaster, catastrophe. **r. de sol,** sunbeam. **r. catódico,** cathode ray. **r. x,** x-ray. *Fig.* **echar rayos,** to breathe forth fury
rayón /rra'yon/ *m,* rayon
raza /'rraθa; 'rrasa/ *f,* race; breed; lineage, family; kind, class; crack, crevice. **de r.,** purebred
razón /rra'θon; rra'son/ *f,* reason; reasoning; word, expression; speech, argument; motive, cause; order, method; justice, equity; right, authority; explanation; *Math.* ratio, proportion. **r. de estado,** raison d'état, reasons of state. *Com.* **r. social,** firm, trade name. **a r. de,** at a rate of. **dar la r. (a),** to agree with. **estar puesto en r.,** to stand to reason. **tener r.,** to be in the right
razonable /rraθo'naβle; rraso'naβle/ *a* reasonable; moderate
razonador /rraθona'ðor; rrasona'ðor/ **(-ra)** *n* reasoner
razonamiento /rraθona'miento; rrasona'miento/ *m,* reasoning
razonar /rraθo'nar; rraso'nar/ *vi* to reason; speak; —*vt* attest, confirm
razzia /'rraθθia; 'rrassia/ *f,* foray; pillaging, sacking; police raid
re /rre/ *m, Mus.* re, D
reabsorción /rreaβsor'θion; rreaβsor'sion/ *f,* reabsorption
reacción /rreak'θion; rreak'sion/ *f,* reaction. **r. de Bayardo,** quick reaction of someone always ready to help those in distress
reaccionar /rreakθio'nar; rreaksio'nar/ *vi* to react
reaccionario /rreakθio'nario; rreaksio'nario/ **(-ia)** *a* and *n* reactionary
reaccionarismo /rreakθiona'rismo; rreaksiona'rismo/ *m,* reactionism
reacio /rre'aθio; rre'asio/ *a* recalcitrant
reactivo /rreak'tiβo/ *m,* reagent —*a* reactive; reacting
readmisión /rreaðmi'sion/ *f,* readmission
readmitir /rreaðmi'tir/ *vt* to readmit
reajustar /rreahus'tar/ *vt* to readjust
real /rre'al/ *a* actual, real; kingly; royal; royalist; *Fig.* regal; *Inf.* fine, handsome. *m,* silver coin, real; *m pl,* encampment, camp. **alzar el r.,** *Mil.* to strike camp. **asentar el r.,** *Mil.* to encamp. **r. decreto,** royal decree. **sitio r.,** royal residence. **un r., sobre otro,** *Inf.* cash in full
realce /rre'alθe; rre'alse/ *m,* raised or embossed work; renown, glory; *Art.* high light
realeza /rrea'leθa; rrea'lesa/ *f,* royalty, royal majesty
realidad /rreali'ðað/ *f,* reality; sincerity, truth. **en r.,** in fact, actually
realismo /rrea'lismo/ *m,* realism; regalism; royalism
realista /rrea'lista/ *a* realistic; royalist. *mf* realist; royalist; regalist
realizable /rreali'θaβle; rreali'saβle/ *a* realizable; practicable
realización /rrealiθa'θion; rrealisa'sion/ *f,* realization; performance, execution
realizar /rreali'θar; rreali'sar/ *vt* to perform, execute, carry out; *Com.* realize. **r. beneficio,** to make a profit
realmente /rreal'mente/ *adv* really, truly; actually
realzar /rreal'θar; rreal'sar/ *vt* to heighten, raise; emboss; exalt; enhance; *Art.* intensify (colors, etc.)
reanimar /rreani'mar/ *vt* to reanimate; revive, restore, resuscitate; encourage
reanudación /rreanuða'θion; rreanuða'sion/ *f,* resumption, renewal
reanudar /rreanu'ðar/ *vt* to resume, continue
reaparecer /rreapare'θer; rreapare'ser/ *vi irr* to reappear. See **conocer**
reaparición /rreapari'θion; rreapari'sion/ *f,* reappearance
rearmamento /rrearma'mento/ *m,* rearmament
rearmar /rrear'mar/ *vi* to rearm
reasegurador /rreasegura'ðor/ *m,* underwriter
reasegurar /rreasegu'rar/ *vt* to reinsure, underwrite
reaseguro /rrease'guro/ *m,* reinsurance, underwriting
reasumir /rreasu'mir/ *vt* to reassume; resume
reasunción /rreasun'θion; rreasun'sion/ *f,* reassumption; resumption
reata /rre'ata/ *f,* string of horses or mules. **de r.,** in single file; *Inf.* blindly, unquestioningly; *Inf.* at once
rebaja /rre'βaha/ *f,* diminution; *Com.* discount, rebate; remission
rebajar /rreβa'har/ *vt* to lower; curtail, lessen; remit; *Com.* reduce in price; *Mech.* file; *Elec.* step down; humble, humiliate; —*vr* cringe, humble oneself
rebajo /rre'βaho/ *m,* reduction (in price, etc.); rabbet
rebanada /rreβa'naða/ *f,* slice, piece (of bread, etc.)
rebanar /rreβa'nar/ *vt* to cut into slices; split
rebaño /rre'βaɲo/ *m,* flock, drove, herd; *Eccl.* flock
rebasar /rreβa'sar/ *vt* to exceed, go beyond; *Mil.* bypass
rebate /rre'βate/ *m,* altercation, dispute, quarrel
rebatiña /rreβa'tiɲa/ *f,* grab; scrimmage. **andar a la r.,** to scuffle
rebatir /rreβa'tir/ *vt* to repulse, repel; fight again; fight hard; oppose, resist; *Com.* deduct; refuse, reject
rebato /rre'βato/ *m,* alarm, tocsin; *Mil.* surprise attack; panic, dismay
rebeca /rre'βeka/ *f,* cardigan, jersey
rebeco /rre'βeko/ *m, Zool.* chamois
rebelarse /rreβe'larse/ *vr* to mutiny, rebel; oppose, resist
rebelde /rre'βelde/ *a* mutinous, rebellious; wilful, disobedient; stubborn. *mf* rebel
rebeldía /rreβel'dia/ *f,* rebelliousness; willfulness; stubbornness; *Law.* nonappearance
rebelión /rreβe'lion/ *f,* insurrection, revolt
rebién /rre'βien/ *adv* very well, extremely well
rebisabuelo /rreβisa'βuelo/ **(-la)** *n.* See **tatarabuelo**
reblandecer /rreβlande'θer; rreβlande'ser/ *vt irr* to soften; —*vr* become soft. See **conocer**
reblandecimiento /rreβlandeθi'miento; rreβlandesi'miento/ *m,* softening; *Med.* flabbiness
reborde /rre'βorðe/ *m,* rim, edge; *Mech.* flange. **r. de acera,** curb
rebordear /rreβorðe'ar/ *vt* to flange
rebosar /rreβo'sar/ *vi* to overflow, run over; *Fig.* abound in; express one's feelings
rebotar /rreβo'tar/ *vi* to rebound; clinch (nails, etc.); refuse; —*vr* change color; *Inf.* be vexed
rebote /rre'βote/ *m,* rebounding; rebound
rebotica /rreβo'tika/ *f,* back room of a pharmacy; back of a shop
rebozar /rreβo'θar; rreβo'sar/ *vt* to muffle up; coat with batter
rebozo /rre'βoθo; rre'βoso/ *m,* muffling up, hiding

the face; head shawl; pretense, excuse. *Fig.* **sin r.,** openly
rebramo /rre'βramo/ *m,* barking of deer, stags, etc.
rebueno /rre'βueno/ *a Inf.* extremely good, fine
rebullicio /rreβu'ʎiθio; rreβu'yisio/ *m,* uproar, clamor
rebullir /rreβu'ʎir; rreβu'yir/ *vi* to stir, show signs of movement; *Fig.* swarm, seethe
rebusca /rre'βuska/ *f,* close search; gleaning; remains
rebuscado /rreβus'kaðo/ *a* affected, unnatural (of style)
rebuscar /rreβus'kar/ *vt* to search for; glean
rebuznar /rreβuθ'nar; rreβus'nar/ *vi* to bray
rebuzno /rre'βuθno; rre'βusno/ *m,* braying
recadero /rreka'ðero/ **(-ra)** *n* messenger, errand boy
recado /rre'kaðo/ *m,* message; greeting, note; gift, present; daily marketing; outfit, implements; precaution, safeguard
recaer /rreka'er/ *vi irr* to fall again; *Med.* relapse; lapse, backslide; devolve, fall upon. See **caer**
recaída /rreka'iða/ *f,* falling again; *Med.* relapse; lapse
recalar /rreka'lar/ *vt* to impregnate; *Naut.* call at (a port), come within sight of land
recalcada /rrekal'kaða/ *f,* pressing down, squeezing; emphasis; *Naut.* list
recalcar /rrekal'kar/ *vt* to press down; squeeze; pack tight; stress, emphasize; *—vi Naut.* list; *—vr Inf.* say over and over, savor one's words
recalcitrante /rrekalθi'trante; rrekalsi'trante/ *a* obdurate, recalcitrant
recalentador /rrekalenta'ðor/ *m, Mech.* superheater
recalentar /rrekalen'tar/ *vt irr* to overheat; superheat; reheat. See **sentar**
recamado /rreka'maðo/ *m,* raised embroidery
recámara /rre'kamara/ *f,* dressing room; explosives chamber; breech of a gun; *Inf.* caution
recambio /rre'kambio/ *m,* spare, spare part; *Com.* reexchange
recantación /rrekanta'θion; rrekanta'sion/ *f,* retraction, recantation
recapacitar /rrekapaθi'tar; rrekapasi'tar/ *vi* to search one's memory; think over
recapitulación /rrekapitula'θion; rrekapitula'sion/ *f,* summary, résumé
recapitular /rrekapitu'lar/ *vt* to recapitulate, summarize
recargar /rrekar'gar/ *vt* to recharge; load again; reaccuse; overcharge; overdress or overdecorate; *—vr Med.* become more feverish. **r. acumuladores,** to recharge batteries
recargo /rre'kargo/ *m,* charge; new load; *Law.* new accusation; overcharge, extra cost; *Med.* temperature increase
recatado /rreka'taðo/ *a* prudent, discreet, circumspect; modest, shy
recatar /rreka'tar/ *vt* to hide, conceal; *—vr* be prudent or cautious
recato /rre'kato/ *m,* caution, prudence; modesty, shyness, reserve
recauchutar /rrekautʃu'tar/ *vt* to retread (tires)
recaudación /rrekauða'θion; rrekauða'sion/ *f,* collecting; collection (of taxes, etc.); tax collector's office
recaudador /rrekauða'ðor/ *m,* tax collector
recaudar /rrekau'ðar/ *vt* to collect, recover (taxes, debts, etc.); deposit, place in custody
recaudo /rre'kauðo/ *m,* collecting; collection (of taxes, etc.); precaution, safeguard, *Law.* surety
recelar /rreθe'lar; rrese'lar/ *vt* to suspect, fear, mistrust; *—vr* (*with de*) be afraid or suspicious of
recelo /rre'θelo; rre'selo/ *m,* suspicion, mistrust, doubt, fear
receloso /rreθe'loso; rrese'loso/ *a* suspicious, distrustful, doubtful
recepción /rreθep'θion; rresep'sion/ *f,* receiving, reception; admission, acceptance; reception, party; *Law.* cross-examination
receptáculo /rreθep'takulo; rresep'takulo/ *m,* receptacle, container; *Fig.* refuge; *Bot.* receptacle
receptador /rreθepta'ðor; rresepta'ðor/ **(-ra)** *n* receiver (of stolen goods); accomplice
receptivo /rreθep'tiβo; rresep'tiβo/ *a* receptive
receptor /rreθep'tor; rresep'tor/ **(-ra)** *a* receiving *—n* recipient. *m, Elec.* receiver; wireless set. **r. de galena,** crystal set. **r. telefónico,** telephone receiver
receta /rre'θeta; rre'seta/ *f, Med.* prescription; *Cul.* recipe
recetar /rreθe'tar; rrese'tar/ *vt Med.* to prescribe; *Inf.* demand
rechapear /rretʃape'ar/ *vt* to replate
rechazar /rretʃa'θar; rretʃa'sar/ *vt* to repulse; resist; refuse; oppose, deny (the truth of); contradict
rechazo /rre'tʃaθo; rre'tʃaso/ *m,* recoil; rebound; refusal
rechinamiento, rechino /rretʃina'miento, rre'tʃino/ *m,* squeaking, creaking; gnashing (of teeth)
rechinar /rretʃi'nar/ *vi* to squeak, creak; gnash (teeth); chatter (teeth); do with a bad grace
rechoncho /rre'tʃontʃo/ *a* squat, stocky
reciamente /rreθia'mente; rresia'mente/ *adv* hard; strongly, firmly, vigorously
recibí /rreθi'βi; rresi'βi/ *m, Com.* receipt
recibidor /rreθiβi'ðor; rresiβi'ðor/ **(-ra)** *a* receiving *—n* recipient. *m,* reception room
recibimiento /rreθiβi'miento; rresiβi'miento/ *m,* reception; welcome, greeting; reception room, waiting room; hall, vestibule
recibir /rreθi'βir; rresi'βir/ *vt* to obtain, receive; support, bear; suffer, experience (attack, injury); approve; accept, receive; entertain; stand up to (attack); *—vr* (*with de*) graduate as, take office as
recibo /rre'θiβo; rre'siβo/ *m,* reception; *Com.* receipt; reception room, waiting room; hall, vestibule. *Com.* **acusar r.,** to acknowledge receipt
recidiva /rreθi'ðiβa; rresi'ðiβa/ *f, Med.* relapse
recién /rre'θien; rre'sien/ *adv* recently, newly. Shortened form of **reciente** before a past participle (e.g. *r. llegado,* newly arrived)
reciente /rre'θiente; rre'siente/ *a* recent; new; fresh
recinto /rre'θinto; rre'sinto/ *m,* precincts; neighborhood; premises, place
recio /'rreθio; 'rresio/ *a* strong; robust; bulky, thick; rough, uncouth; grievous, hard; severe (weather); impetuous, precipitate
recipiente /rreθi'piente; rresi'piente/ *a* receiving. *m,* receptacle, container, vessel
reciprocar /rreθipro'kar; rresipro'kar/ *vt* to reciprocate
reciprocidad /rreθiproθi'ðað; rresiprosi'ðað/ *f,* reciprocity; reciprocation
recíproco /rre'θiproko; rre'siproko/ *a* reciprocal
recitación /rreθita'θion; rresita'sion/ *f,* recitation
recitado /rreθi'taðo; rresi'taðo/ *m,* recitative
recitador /rreθita'ðor; rresita'ðor/ **(-ra)** *n* elocutionist, reciter
recitar /rreθi'tar; rresi'tar/ *vt* to recite, declaim
reclamación /rreklama'θion; rreklama'sion/ *f,* reclamation; objection, opposition; *Com.* claim
reclamar /rrekla'mar/ *vi* to oppose, object to; *Poet.* resound; *—vt* call repeatedly; *Com.* claim; decoy (birds)
reclamo /rre'klamo/ *m,* decoy bird; enticement, allurement; *Law.* reclamation; advertisement. **objeto de r.,** advertising sample. **venta de r.,** bargain sale
reclinación /rreklina'θion; rreklina'sion/ *f,* reclining; leaning
reclinatorio /rreklina'torio/ *m,* couch; prie-dieu
recluir /rre'kluir/ *vt irr* to immure, shut up; detain, arrest. See **huir**
reclusión /rreklu'sion/ *f,* confinement, seclusion; prison
recluso /rre'kluso/ **(-sa)** *n* recluse
recluta /rre'kluta/ *f,* recruiting. *mf Mil.* recruit
reclutador /rrekluta'ðor/ *m,* recruiting office
reclutamiento /rrekluta'miento/ *m,* recruiting
reclutar /rreklu'tar/ *vt* to enlist recruits, recruit
recobrar /rreko'βrar/ *vt* to recover, regain; *—vr* recuperate; regain consciousness
recobro /rre'koβro/ *m,* recovery; *Mech.* pick-up
recocer /rreko'θer; rreko'ser/ *vt irr* to reboil; recook; overboil; overcook; anneal (metals); *—vr Fig.* be tormented (by emotion), be all burned up. See **cocer**

recodo /rre'koðo/ *m*, bend, turn, loop
recogedor /rrekohe'ðor/ *a* sheltering. *m*, *Agr.* gleaner
recoger /rreko'her/ *vt* to gather, pick; pick up; retake; collect (letters from a mailbox, etc.); amass; shrink, narrow; keep; hoard; shelter; reap, pick; —*vr* withdraw, retire; go home; go to bed; retrench, economize; give oneself to meditation
recogida /rreko'hiða/ *f*, collection (of letters from a mailbox); withdrawal; retirement; harvest
recogido /rreko'hiðo/ *a* recluse; cloistered, confined
recogimiento /rrekohi'miento/ *m*, gathering, picking; collection, accumulation; seclusion; shelter; women's reformatory
recolección /rrekolek'θion; rrekolek'sion/ *f*, summary, résumé; harvest; collection (of taxes, etc.); *Eccl.* convent of a reformed order; mystic ecstasy
recoleto /rreko'leto/ *a Eccl.* reformed (of religious orders); recluse
recomendable /rrekomen'daβle/ *a* commendable, recommendable
recomendación /rrekomenda'θion; rrekomenda'sion/ *f*, recommendation (all meanings)
recomendar /rrekomen'dar/ *vt irr* to recommend (all meanings); entrust, commend —*Pres. Indic.* **recomiendo, recomiendas, recomienda, recomiendan.** *Pres. Subjunc.* **recomiende, recomiendes, recomiende, recomienden**
recompensa /rrekom'pensa/ *f*, compensation; recompense, reward
recompensar /rrekompen'sar/ *vt* to compensate; requite; reward, recompense
recomposición /rrekomposi'θion; rrekomposi'sion/ *f*, recomposition
recomprar /rrekom'prar/ *vt* to repurchase
reconcentrar /rrekonθen'trar; rrekonsen'trar/ *vt* to concentrate; dissemble; —*vr* withdraw into oneself, meditate
reconciliable /rrekonθi'liaβle; rrekonsi'liaβle/ *a* reconcilable
reconciliación /rrekonθilia'θion; rrekonsilia'sion/ *f*, reconciliation
reconciliador /rrekonθilia'ðor; rrekonsilia'ðor/ **(-ra)** *a* reconciliatory —*n* reconciler
reconciliar /rrekonθi'liar; rrekonsi'liar/ *vt* to reconcile; *Eccl.* reconsecrate; *Eccl.* hear a short confession; —*vr* become reconciled; *Eccl.* make an additional confession
recondicionar /rrekondiθio'nar; rrekondisio'nar/ *vt* to rebuild, overhaul, recondition
recóndito /rre'kondito/ *a* recondite
reconocer /rrekono'θer; rrekono'ser/ *vt irr* to examine, inspect; recognize; admit, acknowledge; own, confess; search; *Polit.* recognize; *Mil.* reconnoiter; (*with por*) adopt as (a son, etc.); recognize as; —*vr* be seen, show; acknowledge, confess; know oneself. **Bien se reconoce que no está aquí,** It's easy to see he's not here. See **conocer**
reconocido /rrekono'θiðo; rrekono'siðo/ *a* grateful
reconocimiento /rrekonoθi'miento; rrekonosi'miento/ *m*, examination, inspection; recognition; acknowledgement, admission; search; *Mil.* reconnoitering; adoption; gratitude
reconquista /rrekon'kista/ *f*, reconquest
reconquistar /rrekonkis'tar/ *vt* to reconquer; *Fig.* recover, win back
reconstitución /rrekonstitu'θion; rrekonstitu'sion/ *f*, reconstitution
reconstituir /rrekonsti'tuir/ *vt irr* to reconstitute. See **huir**
reconstituyente /rrekonstitu'yente/ *m*, *Med.* tonic
reconstrucción /rrekonstruk'θion; rrekonstruk'sion/ *f*, reconstruction
reconstruir /rrekons'truir/ *vt irr* to reconstruct, rebuild; recreate. See **huir**
reconvención /rrekomben'θion; rrekomben'sion/ *f*, rebuke, reproof; recrimination; *Law.* countercharge
reconversión /rrekomber'sion/ *f*, reconversion
recopilación /rrekopila'θion; rrekopila'sion/ *f*, summary, compendium; collection (of writings); digest (of laws)
recopilador /rrekopila'ðor/ *m*, compiler
recopilar /rrekopi'lar/ *vt* to compile, collect
recordar /rrekor'ðar/ *vt irr* to cause to remember, remind; remember; —*vi* remember; awake. See **acordar**
recordatorio /rrekorða'torio/ *m*, reminder —*a* commemorative (e.g. a plaque)
recorrer /rreko'rrer/ *vt* to travel over; pass through; wander around; examine, inspect; read hastily; overhaul, renovate
recorrido /rreko'rriðo/ *m*, journey, run; *Mech.* stroke; overhaul. **r. de despegue,** *Aer.* take-off run
recortado /rrekor'taðo/ *a Bot.* jagged, incised. *m*, paper cutout
recortar /rrekor'tar/ *vt* to clip, trim, pare; cut out; *Art.* outline; —*vr* stand out (against), be outlined (against)
recorte /rre'korte/ *m*, clipping, paring; cutting; cutout; *Art.* outline; *pl* snippets, clippings. **r. de periódico,** newspaper cutting, newspaper clipping
recostar /rrekos'tar/ *vt irr* (*with en or contra*) to lean, rest against; —*vr* (*with en or contra*) lean against, rest on; lean back; recline. See **contar**
recreación /rrekrea'θion; rrekrea'sion/ *f*, recreation, hobby
recrear /rrekre'ar/ *vt* to entertain, amuse; —*vr* amuse oneself; delight (in), enjoy
recreo /rre'kreo/ *m*, recreation, hobby; playtime, recess (in schools); place of amusement. **salón de r.,** recreation room
recriminación /rrekrimina'θion; rrekrimina'sion/ *f*, recrimination
recriminador /rrekrimina'ðor/ *a* recriminatory
recriminar /rrekrimi'nar/ *vt* to recriminate
recrudecer /rrekruðe'θer; rrekruðe'ser/ **(se)** *vi* and *vr irr* to recur, return. See **conocer**
recrudescencia /rrekruðes'θenθia; rrekruðes'sensia/ *f*, recrudescence, recurrence
rectángulo /rrek'taŋgulo/ *m*, rectangle —*a* rectangular
rectificable /rrektifi'kaβle/ *a* rectifiable
rectificación /rrektifika'θion; rrektifika'sion/ *f*, rectification; *Mech.* grinding
rectificador /rrektifika'ðor/ *m*, rectifier
rectificar /rrektifi'kar/ *vt* to rectify; *Mech.* grind; —*vr* mend one's ways; *Mil.* **r. el frente,** to straighten the line
rectilíneo /rrekti'lineo/ *a* rectilinear
rectitud /rrekti'tuð/ *f*, straightness; rectitude, integrity; exactness; righteousness
recto /'rrekto/ *a* straight; upright; erect; literal (meaning); just, fair; single-breasted (of coats); *m*, right angle; rectum
rector /rrek'tor/ **(-ra)** *n* director; principal, headmaster. *m*, *Eccl.* rector
rectorado /rrekto'raðo/ *m*, principalship, headmaster(mistress-) ship, directorship; *Eccl.* rectorship
rectoría /rrekto'ria/ *f*, rectorate, rectorship
recua /'rrekua/ *f*, drove of beasts of burden; *Inf.* string or line (of things)
recubrir /rreku'βrir/ *vt* to re-cover; coat; plate —*Past Part.* **recubierto**
recuento /rre'kuento/ *m*, calculation; recount; inventory
recuerdo /rre'kuerðo/ *m*, memory, remembrance; memento; *pl* greetings, regards
reculada /rreku'laða/ *f*, drawing back; recoil
recular /rreku'lar/ *vi* to recoil, draw back; *Inf.* go back on, give up
recuperable /rrekupe'raβle/ *a* recoverable, recuperable
recuperación /rrekupera'θion; rrekupera'sion/ *f*, recovery, recuperation; *Chem.* recovery
recurrente /rreku'rrente/ *a* recurrent
recurrir /rreku'rrir/ *vi* to recur; (*with prep a*) have recourse to; appeal to
recurso /rre'kurso/ *m*, recourse, resort; choice, option; reversion; petition; *Law.* appeal; *pl* means of livelihood; *Fig.* way out, last hope
recusar /rreku'sar/ *vt* to refuse; challenge the authority (of)
red /rreð/ *f*, net; network; hairnet; railing, grating; *Fig.* snare; system (of communications, etc.); *Fig.* combination (of events, etc.); *Elec.* mains. **r. de**

arrastre, trawl net. *Fig. Inf.* **caer en la r.,** to fall into the trap
redacción /rreðak'θion; rreðak'sion/ *f,* phrasing; editorial office; editing; editorial board
redactar /rreðak'tar/ *vt* to write, phrase; draw up; edit
redactor /rreðak'tor/ **(-ra)** *a* editorial —*n* editor
redada /rre'ðaða/ *f,* cast (of a fishing net); haul, catch
redecilla /rreðe'θiʎa; rreðe'siya/ *f, dim* small net; netting; hairnet
redención /rreðen'θion; rreðen'sion/ *f,* redemption; ransom; deliverance, salvation; redeeming, paying off (a mortgage, etc.)
redentor /rreðen'tor/ **(-ra)** *a* redeeming, redemptive —*n* redeemer
redificar /rreðifi'kar/ *vt* to rebuild
redifusión /rreðifu'sion/ *f, Radio.* relay
redil /rre'ðil/ *m,* sheepfold
redimible /rreði'miβle/ *a* redeemable
redimir /rreði'mir/ *vt* to ransom; redeem, buy back; pay off (a mortgage, etc.); deliver, free; *Eccl.* redeem
reditar /rreði'tar/ *vt* to reprint, reissue
rédito /'rreðito/ *m, Com.* income, revenue, interest, profit
redoblamiento /rreðoβla'miento/ *m,* redoubling; bending back (of nails, etc.); rolling (of a drum)
redoblar /rreðo'βlar/ *vt* to redouble; repeat; bend back (nails, etc.); —*vi* roll (a drum)
redoble /rre'ðoβle/ *m,* doubling; redoubling; repetition; roll (of a drum)
redoma /rre'ðoma/ *f,* flask, vial
redomado /rreðo'maðo/ *a* astute, crafty, sly; complete, perfect
redonda /rre'ðonda/ *f,* district; pasture ground; *Naut.* square sail; *Mus.* semibreve. **a la r.,** around
redondear /rreðonde'ar/ *vt* to make round; round; free (from debt, etc.); —*vr* acquire a fortune; clear oneself (of debts, etc.)
redondel /rreðon'del/ *m,* traffic circle, rotary, roundabout
redondez /rreðon'deθ; rreðon'des/ *f,* roundness
redondo /rre'ðondo/ *a* round; circular; unequivocal, plain. *m,* round, circle; *Inf.* cash
reducción /rreðuk'θion; rreðuk'sion/ *f,* reduction; *Mil.* defeat, conquest; decrease; *Com.* rebate; (*Math. Chem.*) reduction
reducible /rreðu'θiβle; rreðu'siβle/ *a* reducible
reducir /rreðu'θir; rreðu'sir/ *vt irr* to reduce; decrease, cut down; break up; *Art.* scale down; *Elec.* step down; subdue; (*Chem. Math. Surg.*) reduce; exchange; divide into small fragments; persuade; —*vr* be obliged to, have to; live moderately. See **conducir**
reducto /rre'ðukto/ *m, Mil.* redoubt (of fortifications)
redundancia /rreðun'danθia; rreðun'dansia/ *f,* redundance
redundante /rreðun'dante/ *a* redundant
redundar /rreðun'dar/ *vi* to overflow; be excessive or superfluous; (*with en*) redound to
reduplicación /rreðuplika'θion; rreðuplika'sion/ *f,* reduplication
reduplicar /rreðupli'kar/ *vt* to reduplicate
ree /rree/ For words so beginning (e.g. *reeditar, reexportar*), see spellings with one **e**
refacción /rrefak'θion; rrefak'sion/ *f,* refection, light meal; compensation, reparation
refajo /rre'faho/ *m,* skirt, underskirt
refección /rrefek'θion; rrefek'sion/ *f,* refection, light meal
refectorio /rrefek'torio/ *m,* refectory
referencia /rrefe'renθia; rrefe'rensia/ *f,* report, account; allusion; regard, relation; *Com.* reference (gen. *pl*); consideration
referente /rrefe'rente/ *a* concerning, related (to)
referir /rrefe'rir/ *vt irr* to narrate; describe; direct, guide; relate, refer, concern; —*vr* allude (to); refer (to); concern. See **sentir**
refinación /rrefina'θion; rrefina'sion/ *f,* refining
refinado /rrefi'naðo/ *a* refined; polished, cultured; crafty
refinador /rrefina'ðor/ *m,* refiner
refinamiento /rrefina'miento/ *m,* refinement, subtlety, care
refinar /rrefi'nar/ *vt* to refine, purify; polish, perfect
refinería /rrefine'ria/ *f,* refinery
reflector /rreflek'tor/ *a* reflecting. *m,* reflector; searchlight; shade (for lamps, etc.)
reflejar /rrefle'har/ *vi Phys.* to reflect; —*vt* consider; show, mirror; —*vr Fig.* be reflected, be seen
reflejo /rre'fleho/ *m,* reflection; image; glare —*a* reflex; considered, judicious
reflexión /rreflek'sion/ *f, Phys.* reflection; consideration, thought
reflexionar /rrefleksio'nar/ *vt* (*with en or sobre*) to consider, reflect upon
reflexivo /rreflek'siβo/ *a Phys.* reflective; thoughtful
reflorecer /rreflore'θer; rreflore'ser/ *vi irr* to flower again; return to favor (ideas, etc.). See **conocer**
reflujo /rre'fluho/ *m,* reflux, refluence; ebb tide
refocilar /rrefoθi'lar; rrefosi'lar/ *vt* to warm up, brace up; give pleasure to; —*vr* enjoy oneself
reforma /rre'forma/ *f,* reform; improvement; reformation; *Hist.* Reformation
reformación /rreforma'θion; rreforma'sion/ *f,* reform, improvement
reformador /rreforma'ðor/ **(-ra)** *a* reformatory, reforming —*n* reformer
reformar /rrefor'mar/ *vt* to remake; reshape; repair, mend, restore; improve, correct; *Eccl.* reform; reorganize; —*vr* mend one's ways, improve; control oneself
reformatorio /rreforma'torio/ *m,* reformatory —*a* reforming, reformatory
reformista /rrefor'mista/ *mf* reformist, reformer —*a* reformatory
reforzador /rreforθa'ðor; rreforsa'ðor/ *m, Photo.* reinforcing bath; *Elec.* booster
reforzamiento /rreforθa'miento; rreforsa'miento/ *m,* stiffening, reinforcing
reforzar /rrefor'θar; rrefor'sar/ *vt irr* to reinforce, strengthen, stiffen; encourage, inspirit. See **forzar**
refractar /rrefrak'tar/ *vt* to refract
refractario /rrefrak'tario/ *a* stubborn; (*Phys. Chem.*) refractory; unmanageable, unruly; fireproof
refrán /rre'fran/ *m,* proverb
refranero /rrefra'nero/ *m,* collection of proverbs
refregamiento /rrefrega'miento/ *m,* rubbing; scrubbing, scouring
refregar /rrefre'gar/ *vt irr* to rub; scrub, scour; *Fig. Inf.* rub in, insist on. See **cegar**
refrenamiento /rrefrena'miento/ *m,* curbing; control, restraint
refrenar /rrefre'nar/ *vt* to curb, check (horses); control, restrain
refrendar /rrefren'dar/ *vt* to countersign, endorse, legalize
refrescante /rrefres'kante/ *a* refreshing, cooling
refrescar /rrefres'kar/ *vt* to cool, chill; repeat; *Fig.* brush up, revise; —*vi* be rested or refreshed; grow cooler; take the air; freshen (wind); take a cool drink; —*vr* grow cooler; take the air; take a cool drink
refresco /rre'fresko/ *m,* refreshment; cool drink
refriega /rre'friega/ *f,* affray, scuffle, rough-and-tumble
refrigeración /rrefrihera'θion; rrefrihera'sion/ *f,* refrigeration
refrigerador /rrefrihera'ðor/ *m,* refrigerator
refrigerante /rrefrihe'rante/ *a* refrigerative; chilling; cooling. *m,* cooling chamber, cooler
refrigerar /rrefrihe'rar/ *vt* to chill; cool; freeze, refrigerate; refresh
refrigerio /rrefri'herio/ *m,* coolness; consolation; refreshment, food
refringente /rrefrin'hente/ *a Phys.* refringent
refuerzo /rre'fuerθo; rre'fuerso/ *m,* reinforcement, strengthening; aid, help
refugiado /rrefu'hiaðo/ **(-da)** *a* and *n* refugee
refugiar /rrefu'hiar/ *vt* to protect, shelter; —*vr* take refuge
refugio /rre'fuhio/ *m,* refuge, shelter, protection; traf-

fic island. **r. antiaéreo,** air raid shelter. **r. para peatones,** traffic island
refulgencia /rreful'henθia; rreful'hensia/ *f,* resplendence, splendor, brilliance
refulgente /rreful'hente/ *a* resplendent, refulgent, dazzling
refulgir /rreful'hir/ *vi* to shine, be dazzling
refundición /rrefundi'θion; rrefundi'sion/ *f,* recasting (of metals); adaptation; rehash, refurbishing
refundir /rrefun'dir/ *vt* to recast (metals); include, comprise; adapt; rehash, refurbish; *—vi Fig.* promote, contribute to
refunfuñador /rrefunfuɲa'ðor/ *a* grumbling, fuming
refunfuñar /rrefunfu'ɲar/ *vi* to grumble, growl, fume
refunfuño /rrefun'fuɲo/ *m,* grumble, fuming; snort
refutable /rrefu'taβle/ *a* refutable
refutación /rrefuta'θion; rrefuta'sion/ *f,* refutation
refutar /rrefu'tar/ *vt* to refute
regadera /rrega'ðera/ *f,* watering can; irrigation canal; sprinkler
regadío /rrega'ðio/ *m,* irrigated land; irrigation, watering *—a* irrigated
regajal, regajo /rrega'hal, rre'gaho/ *m,* pool, puddle; stream, brook
regalado /rrega'laðo/ *a* delicate, highly bred; luxurious, delightful
regalar /rrega'lar/ *vt* to make a gift of, give; caress, fondle; indulge, cherish; entertain, regale; *—vr* live in luxury
regalía /rrega'lia/ *f,* royal privilege; right, exemption; perquisite, emolument
regalismo /rrega'lismo/ *m,* regalism
regalista /rrega'lista/ *a* and *mf* regalist
regaliz /rrega'liθ; rrega'lis/ *m,* **regaliza** *f,* licorice
regalo /rre'galo/ *m,* gift, present; satisfaction, pleasure; entertainment, regalement; luxury, comfort
regalón /rrega'lon/ *a Inf.* pampered
regañadientes, a /rregaɲa'ðientes, a/ *adv* unwillingly, grumblingly
regañar /rrega'ɲar/ *vi* to snarl (dogs); crack (skin of fruits); grumble, mutter; *Inf.* quarrel; *—vt Inf.* scold
regaño /rre'gaɲo/ *m,* angry look or gesture; *Inf.* scolding
regañón /rrega'ɲon/ **(-ona)** *a Inf.* grumbling, complaining; scolding *—n Inf.* grumbler
regar /rre'gar/ *vt irr* to water, sprinkle with water; flow through, irrigate; spray; *Fig.* shower (with), strew. See **cegar**
regata /rre'gata/ *f,* regatta; small irrigation channel (for gardens, etc.)
regate /rre'gate/ *m,* twist of the body, sidestep; dribbling; (in soccer); *Inf.* dodging, evasion
regatear /rregate'ar/ *vt* to haggle over, beat down (prices); resell, retail; dribble (a ball); *Fig. Inf.* dodge, avoid; *—vi* bargain, haggle; *Naut.* take part in a regatta, race
regateo /rrega'teo/ *m,* haggling, bargaining
regatero /rrega'tero/ **(-ra)** *a* retail *—n* retailer
regatón /rrega'ton/ **(-ona)** *m,* ferrule, tip *—a* haggling, bargaining *—n* haggler; retailer
regatonear /rregatone'ar/ *vt* to resell at retail
regazo /rre'gaθo; rre'gaso/ *m,* lap, knees; *Fig.* heart, bosom
regencia /rre'henθia; rre'hensia/ *f,* regency
regeneración /rrehenera'θion; rrehenera'sion/ *f,* regeneration
regenerador /rrehenera'ðor/ **(-ra)** *n* regenerator *—a* regenerative, reforming
regenerar /rrehene'rar/ *vt* to regenerate, reform
regenta /rre'henta/ *f,* wife of the president of a court of session
regentar /rrehen'tar/ *vt* to fill temporarily (offices); rule, govern; manage, run (businesses)
regente /rre'hente/ *a* ruling. *mf* regent. *m,* president of a court of session; manager
regicida /rrehi'θiða; rrehi'siða/ *mf* regicide (person)
regicidio /rrehi'θiðio; rrehi'siðio/ *m,* regicide (act)
regidor /rrehi'ðor/ *a* ruling, governing. *m,* magistrate, alderman
régimen /'rrehimen/ *m,* administration, management; regime; (*Med. Gram.*) regimen; *Mech.* rating
regimentación /rrehimenta'θion; rrehimenta'sion/ *f,* regimentation
regimentar /rrehimen'tar/ *vt irr* to form into regiments; regiment *—Pres. Indic.* **regimiento, regimientas, regimienta, regimientan.** *Pres. Subjunc.* **regimiente, regimientes, regimiente, regimienten**
regimiento /rrehi'miento/ *m, Mil.* regiment; administration, rule
regio /'rrehio/ *a* royal; magnificent, regal
región /rre'hion/ *f,* region, country; area, tract, space. **r. industrial,** industrial area
regionalismo /rrehiona'lismo/ *m,* regionalism
regionalista /rrehiona'lista/ *mf* regionalist *—a* regional
regir /rre'hir/ *vt irr* to govern, rule; administer, conduct; *Gram.* govern; *—vi* be in force (laws, etc.); work, function; *Naut.* obey the helm. See **pedir**
registrador /rrehistra'ðor/ *a* recording. *m,* registrar, keeper of records; recorder. **caja (registradora),** (cash) register
registrar /rrehis'trar/ *vt* to examine, inspect; search; copy, record; mark the place (in a book); observe, note; (of thermometers, etc.) record, show; look on to (houses, etc.); *—vr* register (hotels, etc.)
registro /rre'histro/ *m,* search; registration, entry; record; recording; reading (of a thermometer, etc.); *Mech.* damper; registry; register (book); *Mus.* range, compass (voice); *Mus.* register (organ); (*Mech. Print.*) register; bookmark. **r. civil,** register of births, marriages, and deaths
regla /'rregla/ *f,* ruler, measuring stick; rule, principle, guide, precept; system, policy; *Med.* period; moderation; method, order. **r. de cálculo,** slide rule. **r. T,** T-square. **en r.,** in due form. **por r.,** general, generally, as a rule
reglamentación /rreglamenta'θion; rreglamenta'sion/ *f,* regulation; rules and regulations
reglamentar /rreglamen'tar/ *vt* to regulate
reglamento /rregla'mento/ *m,* bylaw; regulation, ordinance
reglar /rre'glar/ *vt* to rule (lines); regulate; govern; control; *—vr* restrain oneself, mend one's ways
regocijado /rregoθi'haðo; rregosi'haðo/ *a* merry, joyful, happy
regocijar /rregoθi'har; rregosi'har/ *vt* to cheer, delight; *—vr* enjoy oneself, rejoice
regocijo /rrego'θiho; rrego'siho/ *m,* happiness, joy; cheer, merriment
regordete /rregor'ðete/ *a Inf.* chubby
regresar /rregre'sar/ *vi* to return
regresión /rregre'sion/ *f,* return; retrogression; regression
regreso /rre'greso/ *m,* return
reguera /rre'gera/ *f,* irrigation channel, ditch
reguero /rre'gero/ *m,* trickle
regulación /rregula'θion; rregula'sion/ *f,* regulation; *Mech.* control, timing
regulador /rregula'ðor/ *m, Mech.* governor, regulator *—a* regulating, controlling
regular /rregu'lar/ *vt* to adjust, regulate; *Mech.* govern *—a* methodical, ordered; moderate; average, medium; (*Eccl. Mil. Geom. Gram.*) regular; so-so, not bad; probable. **por lo r.,** generally
regularidad /rregulari'ðað/ *f,* regularity
regularización /rregulariθa'θion; rregularisa'sion/ *f,* regularization; regulation
regularizar /rregulari'θar; rregulari'sar/ *vt* to regularize; regulate
regurgitar /rregurhi'tar/ *vi* to regurgitate
rehabilitación /rreaβilita'θion; rreaβilita'sion/ *f,* rehabilitation
rehabilitar /rreaβili'tar/ *vt* to rehabilitate; *—vr* rehabilitate oneself
rehacer /rrea'θer; rrea'ser/ *vt irr* to remake; repair, mend; *—vr* recover one's strength; control one's emotions; *Mil.* rally. See **hacer**
rehén /rre'en/ *m,* hostage (gen. *pl*); *Mil.* pledge, security
rehenchir /rreen'tʃir/ *vt irr* to restuff; refill, recharge. See **henchir**
reherir /rree'rir/ *vt irr* to repulse. See **herir**

rehilar /rrei'lar/ *vt* to spin too much or twist the yarn; —*vi* totter, stagger; whizz (arrows, etc.). See **prohibir**
rehuir /rre'uir/ *vt irr* to withdraw; avoid; reject. See **huir**
rehusar /rreu'sar/ *vt* to refuse, reject. See **desahuciar**
reimponer /rreimpo'ner/ *vt irr* to reimpose. See **poner**
reimportación /rreimporta'θion; rreimporta'sion/ *f*, reimportation
reimpresión /rreimpre'sion/ *f*, reprint
reimprimir /rreimpri'mir/ *vt* to reprint
reina /'rreina/ *f*, queen; queen (in chess); queen bee; peerless beauty, belle
reinado /rrei'naðo/ *m*, reign; heyday, fashion
reinante /rrei'nante/ *a* reigning; prevalent
reinar /rrei'nar/ *vi* to reign; influence; endure, prevail
reincidencia /rreinθi'ðenθia; rreinsi'ðensia/ *f*, relapse (into crime, etc.), recidivism
reincidente /rreinθi'ðente; rreinsi'ðente/ *mf* backslider
reincidir /rreinθi'ðir; rreinsi'ðir/ *vi* to relapse (into crime, etc.)
reincorporar /rreinkorpo'rar/ *vt* to reincorporate; —*vr* join again, become a member again
reingresar /rreiŋgre'sar/ *vi* to reenter
reingreso /rreiŋ'greso/ *m*, reentry
reino /'rreino/ *m*, kingdom
reinstalación /rreinstala'θion; rreinstala'sion/ *f*, reinstatement
reinstalar /rreinsta'lar/ *vt* to reinstate; —*vr* be reinstalled
reintegración /rreintegra'θion; rreintegra'sion/ *f*, reintegration
reintegrar /rreinte'grar/ *vt* to reintegrate; —*vr* be reinstated, recuperate, recover
reir /rre'ir/ *vi irr* to laugh; sneer, jeer; *Fig.* smile (nature); —*vt* laugh at; —*vr Inf.* (*with de*) scorn. **reírse a carcajadas,** to shout with laughter —*Pres. Part.* **riendo.** *Pres. Indic.* **río, ríes, ríe, ríen.** *Preterite* **rió, rieron.** *Pres. Subjunc.* **ría,** etc —*Imperf. Subjunc.* **riese,** etc.
reiteración /rreitera'θion; rreitera'sion/ *f*, reiteration, repetition
reiteradamente /rreiteraða'mente/ *adv* repeatedly, reiteratively
reiterar /rreite'rar/ *vt* to reiterate, repeat
reiterativo /rreitera'tiβo/ *a* reiterative
reivindicación /rreiβindika'θion; rreiβindika'sion/ *f*, *Law.* recovery
reivindicar /rreiβindi'kar/ *vt Law.* to recover
reja /'rreha/ *f*, colter, plowshare; plowing, tilling; grating, grille
rejado /rre'haðo/ *m*, railing, grating
rejilla /rre'hiʎa; rre'hiya/ *f*, grating; grille, lattice; luggage rack (in a train); cane (for chairs, seats, etc.); wire mesh; small brazier; *Elec.* grid; *Mech.* grate
rejuntar /rrehun'tar/ *vt* to point (a wall)
rejuvenecer /rrehuβene'θer; rrehuβene'ser/ *vt irr* to rejuvenate; *Fig.* revive; bring up to date; —*vi* and *vr* be rejuvenated, grow young again, rejuvenesce. See **conocer**
rejuvenecimiento /rrehuβeneθi'miento; rrehuβenesi'miento/ *m*, rejuvenation
relación /rrela'θion; rrela'sion/ *f*, relation; connection (of ideas); report, statement; narrative, account; *Math.* ratio; *Law.* brief; intercourse, association, dealings (gen. *pl*); list; analogy, relation. **tener relaciones con,** to have dealings with; be engaged or betrothed to; woo, court
relacionar /rrelaθio'nar; rrelasio'nar/ *vt* to recount, narrate, report; connect, relate; —*vr* be connected
relajación /rrelaha'θion; rrelaha'sion/ *f*, relaxation; recreation; laxity, dissoluteness
relajar /rrela'har/ *vt* to relax; recreate, amuse; make less rigorous; *Law.* remit; —*vr* become relaxed; be dissolute, lax, or vicious
relamer /rrela'mer/ *vt* to lick again; —*vr* lick one's lips; *Fig.* overpaint, make up too much; ooze satisfaction, brag
relamido /rrela'miðo/ *a* overdressed; affected
relámpago /rre'lampago/ *m*, lightning; flash, gleam; streak of lightning (of quick persons or things); flash of wit, witticism
relampaguear /rrelampage'ar/ *vi* to lighten (of lightning); flash, gleam
relapso /rre'lapso/ *a* relapsed, lapsed (into error, vice)
relatar /rrela'tar/ *vt* to relate, narrate, report
relatividad /rrelatiβi'ðað/ *f*, relativeness; *Phys.* relativity
relativo /rrela'tiβo/ *a* relevant, pertinent; relative, comparative; *Gram.* relative
relato /rre'lato/ *m*, narration, account, report
relator /rrela'tor/ **(-ra)** *a* narrating —*n* narrator. *m*, *Law.* reporter
relavar /rrela'βar/ *vt* to rewash, wash again
relección /rrelek'θion; rrelek'sion/ *f*, reelection
releer /rrele'er/ *vt irr* to reread; revise. See **creer**
relegación /rrelega'θion; rrelega'sion/ *f*, relegation
relegar /rrele'gar/ *vt* to banish; relegate, set aside
relegir /rrele'hir/ *vt irr* to reelect. See **elegir**
relente /rre'lente/ *m*, night dew, dampness; *Inf.* cheek, impudence
relevación /rreleβa'θion; rreleβa'sion/ *f*, *Art.* relief; release; remission, exemption
relevar /rrele'βar/ *vt Art.* to work in relief; emboss; relieve, free; dismiss; excuse, pardon; aid, succor; *Fig.* aggrandize; *Mil.* relieve; —*vi* carve in relief
relevo /rre'leβo/ *m*, relay; *Mil.* relief
relicario /rreli'kario/ *m*, reliquary
relieve /rre'lieβe/ *m*, *Art.* relief; *pl* leftovers, remains (of food). **alto r.,** high relief. **bajo r.,** low relief
religar /rreli'gar/ *vt* to retie, fasten again; fasten more securely; solder
religión /rreli'hion/ *f*, religion; creed, faith, philosophy; devotion, religious practice. **r. reformada,** Protestantism. **entrar en r.,** *Eccl.* to profess
religionario /rrelihio'nario/ *m*, Protestant
religiosidad /rrelihiosi'ðað/ *f*, religiosity; religiousness; conscientiousness, punctiliousness
religioso /rreli'hioso/ **(-sa)** *a* religious; punctilious, conscientious; moderate —*n* religious
relinchar /rrelin'tʃar/ *vi* to whinny, neigh
relincho /rre'lintʃo/ *m*, neigh, whinny
reliquia /rre'likia/ *f*, residue (gen. *pl*); *Eccl.* relic; vestige, remnant, memento; permanent disability or ailment
rellanar /rre'ʎanar; rre'yanar/ *vt* to make level again; —*vr* stretch oneself at full length
rellano /rre'ʎano; rre'yano/ *m*, landing (of a staircase); level stretch (of ground)
rellenar /rreʎe'nar; rreye'nar/ *vt* to refill, replenish; fill up; *Mas.* plug, point; *Cul.* stuff; *Inf.* cram with food (gen —*vr*)
relleno /rre'ʎeno; rre'yeno/ *m*, *Cul.* stuffing; replenishing; filling; *Fig.* padding (of speeches, etc.)
reloj /rre'loh/ *m*, clock; watch. **r. de arena,** hourglass. **r. de bolsillo,** watch. **r. de la muerte,** deathwatch beetle. **r. de péndulo,** grandfather clock. **r. de pulsera,** wristwatch. **r. de repetición,** repeater. **r. de sol** *or* **r. solar,** sundial
relojera /rrelo'hera/ *f*, clock stand; watch case
relojería /rrelohe'ria/ *f*, watch or clock making; jeweler, watch maker's shop
relojero /rrelo'hero/ **(-ra)** *n* watch maker, watch repairer
reluciente /rrelu'θiente; rrelu'siente/ *a* shining, sparkling; shiny
relucir /rrelu'θir; rrelu'sir/ *vi irr* to glitter, sparkle, gleam; *Fig.* shine, excel. See **lucir**
reluctante /rreluk'tante/ *a* unruly, refractory, disobedient
relumbrante /rrelum'βrante/ *a* resplendent, dazzling
relumbrar /rrelum'βrar/ *vi* to be resplendent, shine, glitter
remachar /rrema'tʃar/ *vt* to rivet; *Fig.* clinch
remache /rre'matʃe/ *m*, riveting; rivet
remanente /rrema'nente/ *m*, remains, residue
remanso /rre'manso/ *m*, backwater; stagnant water; sloth, dilatoriness
remar /rre'mar/ *vi* to row, paddle, scull; toil, strive

rematadamente /rremataðaˈmente/ *adv* completely, entirely, absolutely
rematado /rremaˈtaðo/ *a* beyond hope, extremely ill; utterly lost; *Law.* convicted
rematar /rremaˈtar/ *vt* to end, finish; finish off, kill; knock down at auction; *Sew.* finish; *—vi* end; *—vr* be ruined or spoiled
remate /rreˈmate/ *m,* end, conclusion; extremity; *Archit.* coping; *Archit.* terminal; highest bid; auction. **de r.,** utterly hopeless
rembarcar /rrembarˈkar/ *vt* to reembark, reship
rembarque /rremˈβarke/ *m,* reembarkation, reshipment
rembolsable /rrembolˈsaβle/ *a* repayable
rembolsar /rrembolˈsar/ *vt* to recover (money); refund, return (money)
rembolso /rremˈβolso/ *m,* repayment. **contra r.,** cash on delivery, C.O.D.
remedar /rremeˈðar/ *vt* to copy, imitate; mimic
remediador /rremeðiaˈðor/ **(-ra)** *a* remedying *—n* benefactor, helper
remediar /rremeˈðiar/ *vt* to remedy; aid, help; save from danger; prevent (trouble)
remedio /rreˈmeðio/ *m,* remedy; emendation, correction; help; refuge, protection; *Med.* remedy. **No hay más r.,** There's nothing else to do, It's the only way open. **no tener más r.,** to be unable to help (doing something), be obliged to
remedo /rreˈmeðo/ *m,* imitation; poor copy
remembranza /rrememˈβranθa; rrememˈβransa/ *f,* remembrance, memory
rememorar /rrememoˈrar/ *vt* to remember, recall to mind
remendar /rremenˈdar/ *vt irr* to mend, patch; darn; repair; correct. See **recomendar**
remendón /rremenˈdon/ **(-ona)** *n* cobbler; mender of old clothes
remero /rreˈmero/ **(-ra)** *n* oarsman, rower; sculler
remesa /rreˈmesa/ *f,* remittance; consignment, shipment
remesar /rremeˈsar/ **(se)** *vt* and *vr* to pluck out (hair); *—vt Com.* remit; consign
remiendo /rreˈmiendo/ *m, Sew.* patch; mend, darn; emendation; *Inf.* insignia of one of the Spanish military orders. **a remiendos,** *Inf.* piecemeal
remilgarse /rremilˈgarse/ *vr* to preen oneself, be overdressed
remilgo /rreˈmilgo/ *m,* affectation; mannerism; prudery, squeamishness
reminiscencia /rreminisˈθenθia; rreminisˈsensia/ *f,* reminiscence; memory, recollection
remirado /rremiˈraðo/ *a* wary, cautious, prudent, circumspect
remirar /rremiˈrar/ *vt* to revise, go over again; *—vr* take great care over; behold with pleasure
remisión /rremiˈsion/ *f,* sending; remission; pardon, forgiveness; foregoing, relinquishment; abatement, diminution; *Lit.* reference, allusion
remiso /rreˈmiso/ *a* timid, spiritless; languid, slow
remitente /rremiˈtente/ *mf* sender *—a* sending
remitir /rremiˈtir/ *vt* to remit, send; pardon, forgive; defer, postpone; abate, diminish; relinquish, forgo; *Lit.* refer; *—vr* remit, submit, consult; refer (to), cite
remo /ˈrremo/ *m,* oar, scull, paddle; arm or leg (of men or animals, gen. *pl*); wing (gen. *pl*); hard, continuous toil; galleys. **al r.,** by dint of rowing; *Inf.* struggling with hardships
remojar /rremoˈhar/ *vt* to soak, steep; celebrate by drinking
remojo /rreˈmoho/ *m,* soaking, steeping
remolacha /rremoˈlatʃa/ *f,* beet
remolcador /rremolkaˈðor/ *m, Naut.* tow, tug *—a Naut.* towing
remolcar /rremolˈkar/ *vt* (*Naut. Auto.*) to tow; *Fig.* press into service, use
remolinar /rremoliˈnar/ *vi* to spin, whirl, eddy; *—vr* throng, swarm
remolino /rremoˈlino/ *m,* whirlwind; eddy, swirl; whirlpool; crowd, throng, swarm; disturbance, riot
remolonear /rremoloneˈar/ *vi Inf.* to loiter, lag; avoid work; be lax or dilatory
remolque /rreˈmolke/ *m,* towage, towing; towline; barge; *Auto.* trailer. **a r.,** on tow
remonta /rreˈmonta/ *f,* resoling (of shoes); leather gusset (of riding breeches); *Mil.* remount
remontar /rremonˈtar/ *vt* to scare off (game); *Mil.* supply with fresh horses; resole (shoes); *Fig.* rise to great heights (of oratory, etc.); *—vr* soar (of birds); (*with prep a*) date from, go back to; originate in
remoquete /rremoˈkete/ *m,* blow with the fist; witticism; *Inf.* flirtation, courtship
rémora /ˈrremora/ *f, Ichth.* remora; delay, hindrance
remorder /rremorˈðer/ *vt irr* to bite again or repeatedly; *Fig.* gnaw, nag, cause uneasiness or remorse; *—vr* show one's feelings. See **morder**
remordimiento /rremorðiˈmiento/ *m,* remorse
remotamente /rremotaˈmente/ *adv* distantly, remotely; unlikely; vaguely, confusedly
remoto /rreˈmoto/ *a* distant, remote; unlikely, improbable
remover /rremoˈβer/ *vt irr* to remove, move; stir; turn over; dismiss, discharge. See **mover**
remozar /rremoˈθar; rremoˈsar/ *vt* to cause to appear young; freshen up, bring up to date; *—vr* look young
remplazar /rremplaˈθar; rremplaˈsar/ *vt* to replace; exchange, substitute; succeed, take the place of
remplazo /rremˈplaθo; rremˈplaso/ *m,* replacement; exchange, substitute; successor; *Mil.* replacement
remuda /rreˈmuða/ *f,* replacement, exchange
remudar /rremuˈðar/ *vt* to replace
remuneración /rremuneraˈθion; rremuneraˈsion/ *f,* remuneration; reward
remunerador /rremuneraˈðor/ **(-ra)** *a* remunerative, recompensing *—n* remunerator
remunerar /rremuneˈrar/ *vt* to recompense, reward
remusgar /rremusˈgar/ *vi* to suspect, imagine
renacentista /rrenaθenˈtista; rrenasenˈtista/ *a* renaissance
renacer /rrenaˈθer; rrenaˈser/ *vi irr* to be reborn. See **nacer**
renacimiento /rrenaθiˈmiento; rrenasiˈmiento/ *m,* rebirth; Renaissance
renacuajo /rrenaˈkuaho/ *m,* tadpole; *Mech.* frog; *Inf.* twerp
renano /rreˈnano/ *a* Rhenish
rencarcelar /rrenkarθeˈlar; rrenkarseˈlar/ *vt* to reimprison
rencarnación /rrenkarnaˈθion; rrenkarnaˈsion/ *f,* reincarnation
rencarnar /rrenkarˈnar/ **(se)** *vi* and *vr* to be reincarnated
rencilla /rrenˈθiʎa; rrenˈsiya/ *f,* grudge, grievance, resentment
rencilloso /rrenθiˈʎoso; rrensiˈyoso/ *a* peevish, easily offended, touchy
rencor /rrenˈkor/ *m,* rancor, spite, old grudge. **guardar r.,** to bear malice
rencoroso /rrenkoˈroso/ *a* rancorous, malicious, spiteful
rencuadernar /rrenkuaðerˈnar/ *vt* to rebind (books)
rencuentro /rrenˈkuentro/ *m,* collision; *Mil.* encounter, clash
rendición /rrendiˈθion; rrendiˈsion/ *f,* surrender; yield, profit
rendido /rrenˈdiðo/ *a* submissive, obsequious
rendija /rrenˈdiha/ *f,* crevice, cleft, crack, fissure
rendimiento /rrendiˈmiento/ *m,* weariness, fatigue; submissiveness, obsequiousness; yield, profit; *Mech.* efficiency
rendir /rrenˈdir/ *vt irr Mil.* to cause to surrender; defeat; overcome, conquer; give back, return; yield, provide; tire, exhaust; vomit; pay, render; *—vr* be exhausted, be worn out; surrender. *Mil.* **r. el puesto,** to retire from or give up a post. See **pedir**
renegado /rreneˈgaðo/ **(-da)** *n* renegade, apostate; turncoat; *Inf.* malignant person *—a* renegade
renegador /rrenegaˈðor/ **(-ra)** *n* blasphemer; foul-mouthed person
renegar /rreneˈgar/ *vt irr* to deny, disown; loathe, hate; *—vi* (*with de*) apostatize; blaspheme; *Inf.* curse. See **cegar**
renganchar /rreŋganˈtʃar/ **(se)** *vt* and *vr Mil.* to reenlist

renganche /rreŋ'gantʃe/ *m, Mil.* reenlistment
renglón /rreŋ'glon/ *m, Print.* line; *pl* writing, composition
reniego /rre'niego/ *m,* blasphemy; *Inf.* foul language, cursing
renitencia /rreni'tenθia; rreni'tensia/ *f,* repugnance
reno /'rreno/ *m,* reindeer
renombrado /rrenom'βraðo/ *a* illustrious, famous
renombre /rre'nombre/ *m,* surname; renown, reputation, fame
renovable /rreno'βaβle/ *a* renewable, replaceable
renovación /rrenoβa'θion; rrenoβa'sion/ *f,* replacement; renewal; renovation; transformation, reform
renovador /rrenoβa'ðor/ **(-ra)** *n* reformer; renovator —*a* renovating; reforming
renovar /rreno'βar/ *vt irr* to renew; renovate; replace; exchange; reiterate, repeat. See **contar**
renta /'rrenta/ *f,* yield, profit; income; revenue; government securities; rent; tax
rentar /rren'tar/ *vt* to yield, produce an income
rentero /rren'tero/ **(-ra)** *n* tenant farmer. *m,* one who farms out land
rentista /rren'tista/ *mf* financier; bondholder; person who lives on a private income, rentier
rentístico /rren'tistiko/ *a* revenue, financial
renuente /rre'nuente/ *a* refractory, willful
renuevo /rre'nueβo/ *m, Bot.* shoot; renewal
renuncia, renunciación /rre'nunθia, rrenunθia'θion; rre'nunsia, rrenunsia'sion/ *f,* renunciation; resignation; abandonment, relinquishment
renunciar /rrenun'θiar; rrenun'siar/ *vt* to renounce; refuse; scorn; abandon, relinquish; resign; revoke (at cards). **r. a,** to give up
renuncio /rre'nunθio; rre'nunsio/ *m,* revoke (cards); *Inf.* falsehood
reñidamente /rreɲiða'mente/ *adv* strongly, stubbornly, fiercely
reñir /rre'ɲir/ *vi irr* to quarrel, dispute; fight; be on bad terms, fall out; —*vt* scold; fight (battles, etc.). See **ceñir**
reo /'rreo/ *mf* criminal; offender, guilty party; *Law.* defendant
reojo /rre'oho/ *m,* (**mirar de**) to look out of the corner of the eye; *Fig.* look askance
reorganizador /rreorganiθa'ðor; rreorganisa'ðor/ **(-ra)** *a* reorganizing —*n* reorganizer
reorganizar /rreorgani'θar; rreorgani'sar/ *vt* to reorganize
reóstato /rre'ostato/ *m,* rheostat
repantigarse /rrepanti'garse/ *vr* to stretch out one's legs, make oneself comfortable
reparable /rrepa'raβle/ *a* remediable, reparable; worthy of note
reparación /rrepara'θion; rrepara'sion/ *f,* repair, mending; reparation, satisfaction; indemnity, compensation
reparada /rrepa'raða/ *f,* shying (of horses)
reparador /rrepara'ðor/ *a* repairing, mending; fault-finding; restoring; satisfying, compensating
reparar /rrepa'rar/ *vt* to repair; restore; consider; correct, remedy; atone for, expiate; indemnify; hold up, detain; protect, guard; (*with en*) notice; —*vi* halt, be detained; —*vr* control oneself
reparo /rre'paro/ *m,* repair; restoration; remedy; note, reflection; warning; doubt, scruple; guard, protection; parry (at fencing)
repartición /rreparti'θion; rreparti'sion/ *f,* distribution
repartidero /rreparti'ðero/ *a* distributable
repartidor /rreparti'ðor/ **(-ra)** *a* distributing —*n* distributor; tax assessor
repartimiento /rreparti'miento/ *m,* distribution, allotment; assessment
repartir /rrepar'tir/ *vt* to distribute; share out; allot; deal (cards); assess; *Com.* deliver
reparto /rre'parto/ *m,* distribution; assessment; delivery (of letters, etc.); *Theat.* cast; deal (at cards)
repasar /rrepa'sar/ *vt* to pass by again; peruse, reexamine; brush up, revise; skim, glance over; mend, repair (garments); edit, revise; hone
repaso /rre'paso/ *m,* second passage through; reexamination, perusal; revision, editing; brushing up, revision; repair, mending; *Inf.* dressing-down, scolding
repatriación /rrepatria'θion; rrepatria'sion/ *f,* repatriation
repatriado /rrepa'triaðo/ **(-da)** *n* repatriate
repatriar /rrepa'triar/ *vt* to repatriate; —*vi* and *vr* return to one's own country
repecho /rre'petʃo/ *m,* steep slope. **a r.,** uphill
repelar /rrepe'lar/ *vt* to pull by the hair; put through its paces (of a horse); clip, cut; remove, diminish
repeler /rrepe'ler/ *vt* to repel, throw back; reject, refute
repelo /rre'pelo/ *m,* anything against the grain; *Inf.* skirmish; reluctance, repugnance
repente /rre'pente/ *m, Inf.* sudden or unexpected movement. **de r.,** suddenly
repentino /rrepen'tino/ *a* sudden, unexpected
repentizar /rrepenti'θar; rrepenti'sar/ *vi Mus.* to sight-read
repercusión /rreperku'sion/ *f,* repercussion; vibration
repercutir /rreperku'tir/ *vi* to recoil, rebound; —*vr* reverberate; reecho; *Fig.* have repercussions; —*vt Med.* repel
repertorio /rreper'torio/ *m,* repertory
repesar /rrepe'sar/ *vt* to reweigh, weigh again
repetición /rrepeti'θion; rrepeti'sion/ *f,* repetition; *Art.* replica, copy; repeater (in clocks); recital
repetidamente /rrepetiða'mente/ *adv* repeatedly
repetidor /rrepeti'ðor/ *a* repeating
repetir /rrepe'tir/ *vt irr* to repeat, do over again; reiterate; *Art.* copy, make a replica of; recite. See **pedir**
repicar /rrepi'kar/ *vt* to chop, mince; peal (of bells); prick again; —*vr* pride oneself (on), boast
repique /rre'pike/ *m,* chopping, mincing; peal, pealing (of bells); disagreement, grievance
repisa /rre'pisa/ *f, Archit.* bracket; ledge; shelf. **r. de chimenea,** mantelpiece
replantar /rreplan'tar/ *vt* to replant; transplant
repleción /rreple'θion; rreple'sion/ *f,* repletion, satiety
replegar /rreple'gar/ *vt irr* to refold, fold many times; —*vr Mil.* retreat in good order. See **cegar**
repleto /rre'pleto/ *a* replete
réplica /'rreplika/ *f,* reply, answer; replica
replicar /rrepli'kar/ *vi* to contradict, dispute; answer, reply. **¡No me repliques!** *Inf.* Don't answer back!
repliegue /rre'pliege/ *m,* double fold, crease; doubling, folding; *Mil.* withdrawal
repoblación /rrepoβla'θion; rrepoβla'sion/ *f,* repeopling, repopulation
repoblar /rrepo'βlar/ *vt* to repeople, repopulate
repollo /rre'poʎo; rre'poyo/ *m,* white cabbage; heart (of lettuce, etc.)
reponer /rrepo'ner/ *vt irr* to replace; reinstate; restore; reply; —*vr* recover, regain (possessions); grow well again; grow calm. See **poner**
reportación /rreporta'θion; rreporta'sion/ *f,* serenity, moderation
reportaje /rrepor'tahe/ *m,* journalistic report
reportar /rrepor'tar/ *vt* to restrain, moderate; achieve, obtain; carry; bring; —*vr* control oneself
reporte /rre'porte/ *m,* report, news; rumor
reporterismo /rreporte'rismo/ *m,* newspaper reporting
reportero /rrepor'tero/ **(-ra)** *a* news, report —*n* reporter
reposado /rrepo'saðo/ *a* quiet, peaceful, tranquil
reposar /rrepo'sar/ *vi* to rest, repose oneself; sleep, doze; lie in the grave; settle (liquids); rest (on)
reposición /rreposi'θion; rreposi'sion/ *f,* replacement; restoration; renewal; recovery (of health); *Theat.* revival
repositorio /rreposi'torio/ *m,* repository
reposo /rre'poso/ *m,* rest, repose; peace, tranquility; sleep
repostería /rreposte'ria/ *f,* confectioner's shop; pantry; butler's pantry
repostero /rrepos'tero/ *m,* confectioner, pastry cook
repregunta /rrepre'gunta/ *f,* cross-examination
repreguntar /rrepregun'tar/ *vt* to cross-examine

reprender /rrepren'der/ *vt* to scold, reprimand, rebuke
reprensible /rrepren'siβle/ *a* reprehensible, censurable
reprensión /rrepren'sion/ *f,* scolding, reprimand, rebuke
represa /rre'presa/ *f,* damming, holding back (water); dam, lock; restraining, controlling
represalia /rrepre'salia/ *f,* reprisal (gen. *pl*); retaliation
represar /rrepre'sar/ *vt* to dam, harness (water); *Naut.* retake, recapture; *Fig.* restrain, control
representación /rrepresenta'θion; rrepresenta'sion/ *f,* representation; *Theat.* performance; authority; dignity; *Com.* agency; portrait, image; depiction, expression; petition
representador /rrepresenta'ðor/ *a* representative
representante /rrepresen'tante/ *a* representative. *mf* representative; actor; performer
representar /rrepresen'tar/ *vt* to represent; *Theat.* perform; depict, express; describe, portray; *—vr* imagine, picture to oneself
representativo /rrepresenta'tiβo/ *a* representative
represión /rrepre'sion/ *f,* repression; recapture
represivo /rrepre'siβo/ *a* repressive
reprimenda /rrepri'menda/ *f,* rebuke, reprimand
reprimir /rrepri'mir/ *vt* to repress, restrain, control; *—vr* restrain oneself
reprobación /rreproβa'θion; rreproβa'sion/ *f,* censure; reprobation
reprobar /rrepro'βar/ *vt irr* to reprove; censure; fail (in an exam). See **probar**
réprobo /'rreproβo/ **(-ba)** *n* reprobate
reprochar /rrepro'tʃar/ *vt* to reproach
reproche /rre'protʃe/ *m,* reproaching; rebuke, reproach
reproducción /rreproðuk'θion; rreproðuk'sion/ *f,* reproduction. **r. a gran escala,** large-scale model
reproducir /rreproðu'θir; rreproðu'sir/ *vt irr* to reproduce. See **conducir**
reproductor /rreproðuk'tor/ **(-ra)** *a* reproductive *—n* breeding animal
reps /rreps/ *m,* rep (fabric)
reptil /rrep'til/ *a* reptilian; crawling. *m,* reptile
república /rre'puβlika/ *f,* republic; state, commonwealth. **la r. de las letras,** the republic of letters
República Dominicana /rre'puβlika domini'kana/ Dominican Republic
República Malgache /rre'puβlika mal'gatʃe/ Republic of Madagascar
republicanismo /rrepuβlika'nismo/ *m,* republicanism
republicano /rrepuβli'kano/ **(-na)** *a* and *n* republican
repudiación /rrepuðia'θion; rrepuðia'sion/ *f,* repudiation
repudiar /rrepu'ðiar/ *vt* to cast off (a wife); repudiate, renounce
repuesto /rre'puesto/ *a* retired, hidden. *m,* stock, provision; serving table; pantry; stake (at cards, etc.). **de r.,** spare, extra
repugnancia /rrepug'nanθia; rrepug'nansia/ *f,* inconsistency, contradiction; aversion, dislike; reluctance; repugnance
repugnante /rrepug'nante/ *a* repugnant, loathsome
repugnar /rrepug'nar/ *vt* to contradict, be inconsistent with; hate, be averse to (e.g. *La idea me repugna,* I hate the idea)
repujado /rrepu'haðo/ *m,* repoussé work
repujar /rrepu'har/ *vt* to work in repoussé
repulir /rrepu'lir/ *vt* to repolish, reburnish; *—vt* and *vr* make up too much, overdress
repulsa /rre'pulsa/ *f,* snub, rebuff; rejection; repulse
repulsar /rrepul'sar/ *vt* to decline, reject; repulse; deny, refuse; rebuff
repulsión /rrepul'sion/ *f,* repulsion; rebuff; aversion, dislike
repulsivo /rrepul'siβo/ *a* repellent
repunta /rre'punta/ *f,* headland, cape; *Fig.* first sign; *Inf.* disgust; caprice; fight
reputación /rreputa'θion; rreputa'sion/ *f,* reputation
reputar /rrepu'tar/ *vt* to believe, consider (e.g. *Le reputo por honrado,* I believe him to be an honorable man); appreciate, esteem
requebrar /rreke'βrar/ *vt irr* to break into smaller pieces; make love to, woo; compliment, flatter. See **quebrar**
requemado /rreke'maðo/ *a* sunburned; brown
requemar /rreke'mar/ *vt* to burn again; overcook; dry up, parch (of plants, etc.); burn (the mouth) (of spicy foods, etc.); *—vr Fig.* suffer inwardly
requerimiento /rrekeri'miento/ *m,* requirement, demand; *Law.* summons
requerir /rreke'rir/ *vt irr* to inform, notify; examine; need, necessitate; require; summon; woo; persuade. See **sentir**
requesón /rreke'son/ *m,* cream cheese; curd
requetebién /rrekete'βien/ *adv Inf.* exceedingly well
requiebro /rre'kieβro/ *m,* compliment, expression of love; wooing, flirtation
requisa /rre'kisa/ *f,* inspection, visitation; *Mil.* requisitioning
requisar /rreki'sar/ *vt Mil.* to requisition
requisito /rreki'sito/ *m,* requisite
res /rres/ *f,* animal, beast; head of cattle
resabiar /rresa'βiar/ *vt* to make vicious, cause bad habits; *—vr* contract bad habits or vices; be discontented; relish
resabio /rre'saβio/ *m,* disagreeable aftertaste; bad habit, vice
resaca /rre'saka/ *f,* surf, undertow, surge; *Com.* redraft
resalado /rresa'laðo/ *a Inf.* very witty; most attractive
resaltar /rresal'tar/ *vi* to rebound; project, jut out; grow loose, fall out; *Fig.* stand out, be prominent
resalto /rre'salto/ *m,* rebound; projection
resarcir /rresar'θir; rresar'sir/ *vt* to compensate, indemnify
resbaladizo /rresβala'ðiθo; rresβala'ðiso/ *a* slippery; difficult, delicate (of a situation)
resbalar /rresβa'lar/ *vi* to slip; slide; skid; err, fall into sin
resbalón /rresβa'lon/ *m,* slip; slide; skid; temptation, error
rescatador /rreskata'ðor/ **(-ra)** *n* ransomer; rescuer
rescatar /rreska'tar/ *vt* to ransom; redeem, buy back; barter; free, rescue; *Fig.* redeem (time, etc.)
rescate /rres'kate/ *m,* ransom; redemption; barter; amount of ransom
rescindir /rresθin'dir; rressin'dir/ *vt* to annul, repeal, rescind
rescisión /rresθi'sion; rressi'sion/ *f,* annulment, abrogation
rescoldo /rres'koldo/ *m,* ember, cinder; scruple, qualm, doubt
resentimiento /rresenti'miento/ *m,* deterioration, impairment; animosity, resentment
resentirse /rresen'tirse/ *vr irr* to deteriorate, be impaired; be hurt or offended. See **sentir**
reseña /rre'seɲa/ *f, Mil.* review; short description; review (of a book)
reseñar /rrese'ɲar/ *vt Mil.* to review; describe briefly, outline
reserva /rre'serβa/ *f,* store, stock; exception, qualification; reticence; restraint, moderation; (*Eccl. Law.*) reservation; (*Mil. Naut.*) reserve. **sin r.,** frankly, without reserve
reservación /rreserβa'θion; rreserβa'sion/ *f,* reservation; scruple
reservado /rreser'βaðo/ *a* reserved, reticent; prudent, moderate; kept, reserved. *m,* reserved compartment; private apartment, private garden, etc.
reservar /rreser'βar/ *vt* to keep, hold; postpone; reserve (rooms, etc.); exempt; keep secret; withhold (information); *Eccl.* reserve; *—vr* await a better opportunity; be cautious
reservista /rreser'βista/ *a* (*Mil. Nav.*) reserved. *mf* reservist
resfriado /rres'friaðo/ *m, Med.* cold, chill
resfriar /rres'friar/ *vt* to chill; *Fig.* cool, moderate; *—vi* grow cold; *—vr* catch a cold; *Fig.* cool off (of love, etc.)
resguardar /rresguar'ðar/ *vt* to protect; shelter; *—vr*

take refuge; (*with de*) guard against; (*with con*) shelter by
resguardo /rres'guarðo/ *m*, protection, guard; *Com.* guarantee, security; *Com.* voucher; preservation; vigilance (to prevent smuggling, etc.); contraband guards
residencia /rresi'ðenθia; rresi'ðensia/ *f*, stay, residence; home, domicile; *Eccl.* residence
residencial /rresiðen'θial; rresiðen'sial/ *a* residential; resident, residentiary
residente /rresi'ðente/ *a* resident. *mf* inhabitant. *m*, resident, minister resident (diplomatic)
residir /rresi'ðir/ *vi* to live, inhabit; reside officially; be found, be, exist
residuo /rre'siðuo/ *m*, residuum, remainder; *Math.* remainder; *Chem.* residue
resignación /rresigna'θion; rresigna'sion/ *f*, resignation; fortitude, submission
resignar /rresig'nar/ *vt* to resign, relinquish; *—vr* submit, resign oneself
resina /rre'sina/ *f*, resin
resinoso /rresi'noso/ *a* resinous
resistencia /rresis'tenθia; rresis'tensia/ *f*, resistance, opposition; endurance; (*Phys. Mech. Psychol.*) resistance
resistente /rresis'tente/ *a* resistant; tough; hardy (of plants)
resistir /rresis'tir/ *vi* to resist, oppose; reject; *—vt* endure, bear; resist; *—vr* fight, resist
resma /'rresma/ *f*, ream (of paper)
resollar /rreso'ʎar; rreso'yar/ *vi irr* to breathe; pant. See **degollar**
resolución /rresolu'θion; rresolu'sion/ *f*, decision; boldness, daring; determination, resolution; decree
resoluto /rreso'luto/ *a* resolute, bold; brief, concise; able, expert
resolver /rresol'βer/ *vt irr* to determine, decide; summarize; solve; dissolve; analyze; (*Phys. Med.*) resolve; *—vr* decide, determine; be reduced to, become; *Med.* resolve *—Pres. Indic.* **resuelvo, resuelves, resuelve, resuelven.** *Past Part.* **resuelto.** *Pres. Subjunc.* **resuelva, resuelvas, resuelva, resuelvan**
resonancia /rreso'nanθia; rreso'nansia/ *f*, resonance, sonority, ring; fame, reputation
resonante /rreso'nante/ *a* resonant; resounding
resonar /rreso'nar/ *vi irr* to resound, echo. See **tronar**
resoplido, resoplo /rreso'pliðo, rre'soplo/ *m*, heavy breathing, pant, snort
resorber /rresor'βer/ *vt* to reabsorb
resorción /rresor'θion; rresor'sion/ *f*, reabsorption
resorte /rre'sorte/ *m*, *Mech.* spring; elasticity; *Fig.* means, instrument
respaldo /rres'paldo/ *m*, back (of chairs, etc.); reverse side (of a piece of paper)
respectivo /rrespek'tiβo/ *a* respective
respecto /rres'pekto/ *m*, relation, regard, reference. **con r. a,** *or* **r. a,** with regard to, with respect to, concerning
respetabilidad /rrespetaβili'ðað/ *f*, respectability; worthiness
respetable /rrespe'taβle/ *a* worthy of respect; respectable; *Fig.* considerable, large
respetar /rrespe'tar/ *vt* to respect, revere
respeto /rres'peto/ *m*, respect, honor; consideration, reason. **de r.,** spare, extra; special, ceremonial
respetuoso /rrespe'tuoso/ *a* venerable, worthy of honor; respectful, courteous
respingar /rrespiŋ'gar/ *vi* to flinch, wince, kick; *Inf.* be uneven, rise (hem of garments); *Inf.* do (a thing) grumblingly
respingo /rrespiŋ'go/ *m*, wincing; jerk, shake; *Inf.* gesture of reluctance or dislike
respirable /rrespi'raβle/ *a* breathable
respiración /rrespira'θion; rrespira'sion/ *f*, breathing, respiration; ventilation
respiradero /rrespira'ðero/ *m*, ventilator; air hole, vent; rest, breathing space
respirador /rrespira'ðor/ *a* breathing; respiratory. *m*, respirator
respirar /rrespi'rar/ *vi* to breathe; exhale, give off; take courage; have a breathing space, rest; *Inf.* speak. **sin r.,** continuously, without stopping for breath
respiratorio /rrespira'torio/ *a* respiratory
respiro /rres'piro/ *m*, breathing; breathing space, respite
resplandecer /rresplande'θer; rresplande'ser/ *vi irr* to glitter, gleam; shine, excel. See **conocer**
resplandeciente /rresplande'θiente; rresplande'siente/ *a* glittering, resplendent, shining
resplandor /rresplan'dor/ *m*, radiance, brilliance; glitter, gleam; majesty, splendor
responder /rrespon'der/ *vt* to reply; satisfy, answer; *—vi* reecho; requite, return; produce, provide; *Fig.* answer, have the desired effect; *Com.* (*with de*) answer for, guarantee; *Com.* correspond
respondón /rrespon'don/ *a Inf.* pert, impudent, cheeky, given to answering back
responsabilidad /rresponsaβili'ðað/ *f*, responsibility
responsable /rrespon'saβle/ *a* responsible
responso /rres'ponso/ *m*, *Eccl.* response, responsory
respuesta /rres'puesta/ *f*, answer, reply; response; refutation; repartee
resquebradura /rreskeβra'ðura/ *f*, fissure, crevice, crack
resquebrajarse /rreskeβra'harse/ *vr* to crack, split
resquemar /rreske'mar/ *vt* to bite, sting (of hot dishes)
resquicio /rres'kiθio; rres'kisio/ *m*, crack, chink, slit; opportunity
resta /'rresta/ *f*, *Math.* subtraction; *Math.* remainder
restablecer /rrestaβle'θer; rrestaβle'ser/ *vt irr* to reestablish; restore; *—vr* recover one's health; reestablish oneself. See **conocer**
restablecimiento /rrestaβleθi'miento; rrestaβlesi'miento/ *m*, reestablishment; restoration
restañar /rresta'ɲar/ *vt* to re-tin; staunch
restar /rres'tar/ *vt Math.* to subtract; deduct; return (a ball); *—vi* remain. **No me resta más que decir adiós,** It only remains for me to say good-by
restauración /rrestaura'θion; rrestaura'sion/ *f*, restoration; renovation
restaurador /rrestaura'ðor/ **(-ra)** *a* restorative *—n* restorer
restaurante /rrestau'rante/ *m*, restaurant
restaurantero /rrestauran'tero/ *m*, restaurant operator; restaurant owner; restaurateur
restaurar /rrestau'rar/ *vt* to recover, recuperate; renovate, repair; restore
restaurativo /rrestaura'tiβo/ *a* and *m*, restorative
restinga /rres'tiŋga/ *f*, sandbank, bar
restitución /rrestitu'θion; rrestitu'sion/ *f*, restitution
restituible /rresti'tuiβle/ *a* returnable, replaceable
restituir /rresti'tuir/ *vt irr* to return, give back; restore; reestablish; *—vr* return to one's place of departure. See **huir**
resto /'rresto/ *m*, rest, balance; *Math.* remainder; *pl* remains
restorán /rresto'ran/ *m*, restaurant
restricción /rrestrik'θion; rrestrik'sion/ *f*, limitation, restriction
restrictivo /rrestrik'tiβo/ *a* restrictive; restraining
restringir /rrestriŋ'gir/ *vt* to limit, restrict; contract
resucitar /rresuθi'tar; rresusi'tar/ *vt* to raise from the dead; *Fig. Inf.* revive; *—vi* resuscitate
resuello /rre'sueʎo; rre'sueyo/ *m*, breathing; panting, hard breathing
resuelto /rre'suelto/ *a* audacious, daring; resolute, capable
resulta /rre'sulta/ *f*, consequence, result; decision, resolution; vacant post. **de resultas de,** as the result of; in consequence of
resultado /rresul'taðo/ *m*, result, consequence, outcome
resultante /rresul'tante/ *a* resulting. *f*, *Mech.* resultant
resultar /rresul'tar/ *vi* to result, follow; turn out, happen; result (in); *Inf.* turn out well. **El vestido no me resulta,** The dress isn't a success on me
resumen /rre'sumen/ *m*, summary. **en r.,** in short
resumir /rresu'mir/ *vt* to summarize, abridge; sum up, recapitulate; *—vr* be contained, be included
resurgimiento /rresurhi'miento/ *m*, resurgence, revival

resurgir /rresur'hir/ *vi* to reappear, rise again, revive; resuscitate
resurrección /rresurrek'θion; rresurrek'sion/ *f,* resurrection
resurtir /rresur'tir/ *vi* to rebound
retablo /rre'taβlo/ *m, Archit.* altarpiece, retable; frieze; series of pictures
retaguardia /rreta'guarðia/ *f,* rear guard. **a r.,** in the rear. **picar la r.,** to harass the rear guard
retajar /rreta'har/ *vt* to cut in the round; circumcise
retal /rre'tal/ *m,* clipping, filing, shaving; remnant
retama /rre'tama/ *f, Bot.* broom. **r. común** *or* **r. de olor,** Spanish broom. **r. de escobas,** common broom
retar /rre'tar/ *vt* to challenge; *Inf.* reproach, accuse
retardación /rretarða'θion; rretarða'sion/ *f,* retardment
retardar /rretar'ðar/ *vt* to retard, delay
retardo /rre'tarðo/ *m,* delay, retardment
retazo /rre'taθo; rre'taso/ *m,* remnant, cutting; excerpt, fragment
retemblar /rretem'βlar/ *vi* to quiver, tremble constantly
retén /rre'ten/ *m,* stock, reserve, provision; *Mil.* reserve
retención /rreten'θion; rreten'sion/ *f,* retention
retener /rrete'ner/ *vt irr* to keep, retain; recollect, remember; keep back; *Law.* detain; deduct. See **tener**
retenidamente /rreteniða'mente/ *adv* retentively
retentiva /rreten'tiβa/ *f,* retentiveness, memory
retentivo /rreten'tiβo/ *a* retentive
reticencia /rreti'θenθia; rreti'sensia/ *f,* reticence
reticente /rreti'θente; rreti'sente/ *a* reticent
retículo /rre'tikulo/ *m,* reticulum, network; *Phys.* reticle
retina /rre'tina/ *f,* retina
retintín /rretin'tin/ *m,* ringing; tinkling; *Inf.* sarcastic tone
retiñir /rreti'ɲir/ *vi* to tinkle, clink; jingle
retirada /rreti'raða/ *f,* withdrawal; retirement; seclusion, refuge; *Mil.* retreat
retirado /rreti'raðo/ *a* remote, secluded; *Mil.* retired
retirar /rreti'rar/ *vt* to withdraw; remove; repel, throw back; hide, put aside; *—vr* withdraw; retire; *Mil.* retreat
retiro /rre'tiro/ *m,* withdrawal; removal; seclusion, privacy; *Mil.* retreat; retirement; *Eccl.* retreat. **dar el r. (a),** to place on the retired list
reto /'rreto/ *m,* challenge; threat
retocar /rreto'kar/ *vt* to touch again or repeatedly; *Photo.* retouch; restore (pictures); *Fig.* put the finishing touch to
retoñar /rreto'ɲar/ *vi* to sprout, shoot; *Fig.* revive, resuscitate
retoño /rre'toɲo/ *m,* sprout, shoot
retoque /rre'toke/ *m,* frequent touching; finishing touch; touch, slight attack
retorcer /rretor'θer; rretor'ser/ *vt irr* to twist; contort; confound with one's own argument; misconstrue, distort; *—vr* contort; writhe. See **torcer**
retórica /rre'torika/ *f,* rhetoric; *pl Inf.* quibbling
retórico /rre'toriko/ **(-ca)** *a* rhetorical *—n* rhetorician
retornar /rretor'nar/ *vt* to return, give back; turn, twist; turn back; *—vi* and *vr* return, go back
retorno /rre'torno/ *m,* return, going back; recompense, repayment; exchange; return journey
retorsión /rretor'sion/ *f,* twisting, writhing; *Fig.* misconstruction
retorta /rre'torta/ *f, Chem.* retort
retortijón /rretorti'hon/ *m,* twisting, curling. **r. de tripas,** stomachache
retozar /rreto'θar; rreto'sar/ *vi* to skip, frisk, frolic, gambol; romp; *Fig.* be aroused (passions)
retozón /rreto'θon; rreto'son/ *a* frolicsome
retracción /rretrak'θion; rretrak'sion/ *f,* drawing back, retraction
retractación /rretrakta'θion; rretrakta'sion/ *f,* retractation, recantation
retractar /rretrak'tar/ *vt* to retract, recant, withdraw
retráctil /rre'traktil/ *a* retractile
retraer /rretra'er/ *vt irr* to bring back again; dissuade; buy back, redeem; *—vr* take refuge; retire; withdraw; go into seclusion. See **traer**
retraído /rre'traiðo/ *a* fugitive, refugee; retired, solitary; timid, nervous, unsociable
retraimiento /rretrai'miento/ *m,* withdrawal; seclusion, privacy; refuge, asylum, sanctuary; timidity, unsociability
retrasar /rretra'sar/ *vt* to postpone, delay; turn back (the clock); *—vi* be slow (of clocks); *—vr* be behind time, be late; be backward (persons)
retraso /rre'traso/ *m,* lateness; delay, dilatoriness; loss of time (clocks); setting back (of the clock) (e.g. *El reloj lleva cinco minutos de r.,* The clock is five minutes slow)
retratar /rretra'tar/ *vt* to paint or draw the portrait of; portray, describe; photograph; copy, imitate
retratista /rretra'tista/ *mf* portrait painter; photographer; portrayer
retrato /rre'trato/ *m,* portrait; portrayal; *Fig.* image, likeness
retrechería /rretretʃe'ria/ *f, Inf.* craftiness, evasiveness
retreta /rre'treta/ *f, Mil.* retreat; tattoo
retrete /rre'trete/ *m,* toilet, water closet
retribución /rretriβu'θion; rretriβu'sion/ *f,* recompense, reward
retribuir /rretri'βuir/ *vt irr* to recompense, reward. See **huir**
retroactivo /rretroak'tiβo/ *a* retroactive
retroceder /rretroθe'ðer; rretrose'ðer/ *vi* to withdraw, move back, draw back; recede
retroceso /rretro'θeso; rretro'seso/ *m,* retrocedence, withdrawal; *Med.* retrogression
retrogradación /rretrograða'θion; rretrograða'sion/ *f,* retrogression
retrógrado /rretro'graðo/ *a* retrogressive, retrograde; *Polit.* reactionary
retronar /rretro'nar/ *vi irr* to bang, thunder, resound with noise. See **tronar**
retrospección /rretrospek'θion; rretrospek'sion/ *f,* retrospection
retrospectivo /rretrospek'tiβo/ *a* retrospective
retrotraer /rretrotra'er/ *vt irr* to antedate. See **traer**
retruécano /rre'truekano/ *m,* antithesis; play on words, pun
retumbante /rretum'βante/ *a* resounding; pompous, high-flown
retumbar /rretum'βar/ *vi* to resound, echo, reverberate; roll (of thunder); roar (of a cannon)
retumbo /rre'tumbo/ *m,* reverberation, echo; rumble; roll (of thunder); roar (of a cannon, etc.)
reuma /'rreuma/ *m,* rheumatism
reumático /rreu'matiko/ *a* rheumatic
reumatismo /rreuma'tismo/ *m,* rheumatism
reunión /rreu'nion/ *f,* reunion, union; meeting; assembly, gathering
reunir /rreu'nir/ *vt* to reunite; unite; join; gather, assemble; *—vr* meet, assemble; unite
revacunación /rreβakuna'θion; rreβakuna'sion/ *f,* revaccination
revacunar /rreβaku'nar/ *vt* to revaccinate
revalidación /rreβaliða'θion; rreβaliðasion/ *f,* ratification, confirmation
revalidar /rreβali'ðar/ *vt* to ratify, confirm; *—vr* pass a final examination
revejido /rreβe'hiðo/ *a* prematurely old
revelación /rreβela'θion; rreβela'sion/ *f,* revelation; *Photo.* developing
revelador /rreβela'ðor/ *a* revealing. *m, Photo.* developer
revelar /rreβe'lar/ *vt* to reveal; *Photo.* develop
revendedor /rreβende'ðor/ **(-ra)** *a* reselling, retail *—n* retailer
revender /rreβen'der/ *vt* to resell; retail (goods)
reventa /rre'βenta/ *f,* resale; retail
reventar /rreβen'tar/ *vi irr* to burst, explode; break in foam (waves); burst forth; *Fig.* burst (with impatience, etc.); *Inf.* explode (with anger, etc.); *—vt* break, crush; *Fig.* wear out, exhaust; *Inf.* irritate, vex; *—vr* burst; *Fig.* be exhausted. See **sentar**
reventón /rreβen'ton/ *a* bursting. *m,* explosion,

bursting; steep hill; hole, fix, difficulty; uphill work, heavy toil
rever /rre'βer/ *vt irr* to look at again, revise; *Law.* retry. See **ver**
reverberación /rreβerβera'θion; rreβerβera'sion/ *f,* reflection (of light); reverberation, resounding
reverberar /rreβerβe'rar/ *vi* to reflect; resound, reverberate
reverbero /rreβer'βero/ *m,* reverberation; reflector
reverdecer /rreβerðe'θer; rreβerðe'ser/ *vi irr* to grow green again; revive, acquire new vigor. See **conocer**
reverencia /rreβeren'θia; rreβeren'sia/ *f,* respect, veneration; bow; curtsy; *Eccl.* reverence (title)
reverencial /rreβeren'θial; rreβeren'sial/ *a* reverential, respectful
reverenciar /rreβeren'θiar; rreβeren'siar/ *vt* to revere; honor; respect
reverendo /rreβe'rendo/ *a* reverend; venerable; *Inf.* overprudent
reversibilidad /rreβersiβili'ðað/ *f,* reversibility
reversión /rreβer'sion/ *f,* reversion
reverso /rre'βerso/ *m,* wrong side, back; reverse side (of coins)
reverter /rreβer'ter/ *vi irr* to overflow. See **entender**
revertir /rreβer'tir/ *vi Law.* to revert
revés /rre'βes/ *m,* wrong side, back, reverse; cuff, slap; backhand (in ballgames); check, setback, reverse; disaster, misfortune. **al r.,** on the contrary; wrong side out. **de r.,** from left to right, counterclockwise
revesado /rreβe'saðo/ *a* complicated, difficult; willful
revestimiento /rreβesti'miento/ *m, Mas.* lining, coating
revestir /rreβes'tir/ *vt irr* to dress; *Mas.* coat, line; *Fig.* cover, clothe; *—vr* be dressed or dress oneself; *Fig.* be captivated (by an idea); become haughty or full of oneself; rise to the occasion, develop qualities necessary. See **pedir**
reviejo /rre'βieho/ *a* very old. *m,* dead branch (of trees)
revisar /rreβi'sar/ *vt* to revise; examine
revisión /rreβi'sion/ *f,* revision; reexamination; *Law.* retrial
revisor /rreβi'sor/ *a* revising, examining. *m,* reviser; ticket inspector
revista /rre'βista/ *f,* reexamination, revision; review, periodical; *Theat.* revue; reinspection; review (of a book, etc.); *Law.* new trial; *Mil.* review. **pasar r.,** to inspect; review
revistero /rreβis'tero/ **(-ra)** *n* reviewer, writer of reviews
revivificación /rreβiβifika'θion; rreβiβifika'sion/ *f,* revivification
revivificar /rreβiβifi'kar/ *vt* to revivify, revive
revivir /rreβi'βir/ *vi* to resuscitate; revive
revocación /rreβoka'θion; rreβoka'sion/ *f,* revocation, cancellation, annulment
revocar /rreβo'kar/ *vt* to revoke, annul; dissuade; repel, throw back; wash (walls); *Law.* discharge
revolcadero /rreβolka'ðero/ *m,* bathing place (of animals)
revolcar /rreβol'kar/ *vt irr* to knock down, trample underfoot; lay flat (in an argument); *—vr* wallow; dig one's heels in, be obstinate. See **volcar**
revolotear /rreβolote'ar/ *vi* to flutter, fly around; twirl; *—vt* hurl, toss
revoltillo /rreβol'tiʎo; rreβol'tiyo/ *m,* jumble, hodgepodge; confusion, tangle
revoltoso /rreβol'toso/ *a* rebellious, mischievous, willful; intricate
revolución /rreβolu'θion; rreβolu'sion/ *f,* turn, revolution; rebellion, uprising; revolution
revolucionar /rreβoluθio'nar; rreβolusio'nar/ *vt* to revolutionize
revolucionario /rreβoluθio'nario; rreβolusio'nario/ **(-ia)** *a* and *n* revolutionary
revolver /rreβol'βer/ *vt irr* to turn over; turn upside down; wrap up; revolve; stir; reflect upon, consider; upset, cause disharmony; search through, disorder (papers, etc.); *—vr* move from side to side; change (in the weather). See **resolver**
revólver /rre'βolβer/ *m,* revolver
revoque /rre'βoke/ *m, Mas.* washing, whitewash; plastering
revuelco /rre'βuelko/ *m,* wallowing
revuelo /rre'βuelo/ *m,* second flight (of birds); irregular course of flight; disturbance, upset
revuelta /rre'βuelta/ *f,* second turn or revolution; revolt, rebellion; quarrel, fight; turning point; change of direction, turn; change (of opinions, posts, etc.)
revueltamente /rreβuelta'mente/ *adv* in confusion, higgledy-piggledy
revulsión /rreβul'sion/ *f,* revulsion
rexaminación /rreksamina'θion; rreksamina'sion/ *f,* reexamination
rexaminar /rreksami'nar/ *vt* to reexamine
rexpedir /rrekspe'ðir/ *vt* to forward, send on
rexportación /rreksporta'θion; rreksporta'sion/ *f,* reexport
rexportar /rrekspor'tar/ *vt Com.* to reexport
rey /rrei/ *m,* king (in cards, chess); queen bee; *Inf.* swineherd; *Fig.* king, chief. *Herald.* **r. de armas,** king-of-arms. **reyes magos,** magi. **día de Reyes,** Twelfth Night. **servir al r.,** to fight for the king
reyerta /rre'yerta/ *f,* quarrel, row, rumpus
reyezuelo /rreye'θuelo; rreye'suelo/ *m,* kinglet, petty king; golden-crested wren
rezagar /rreθa'gar; rresa'gar/ *vt* to leave behind; postpone, delay; *—vr* lag behind, straggle
rezar /rre'θar; rre'sar/ *vt* to pray, say prayers; say mass; *Inf.* state, say; *—vi* pray; *Inf.* fume, grumble. **El edicto reza así,** The edict runs like this, The edict reads like this
rezo /'rreθo; 'rreso/ *m,* prayer; devotions
rezongar /rreθoŋ'gar; rresoŋ'gar/ *vi* to grouse, grumble
rezumar /rreθu'mar; rresu'mar/ **(se)** *vr* and *vi* to percolate, ooze through; *Inf.* leak out, be known
ría /'rria/ *f,* estuary, river mouth, firth
riachuelo /rria'tʃuelo/ *m,* rivulet, stream
riada /'rriaða/ *f,* flood. *Aer.* **r. de acero,** rain of flak
ribaldería /rriβalde'ria/ *f,* ribaldry
ribaldo /rri'βaldo/ *a* ribald. *m,* knave
ribazo /rri'βaθo; rri'βaso/ *m,* slope, incline
ribera /rri'βera/ *f,* bank, margin, shore, strand
ribereño /rriβe'reɲo/ **(-ña)** *a* and *n* riparian
ribero /rri'βero/ *m,* embankment, wall
ribete /rri'βete/ *m,* binding, border, trimming; stripe; increase, addition; dramatic touch, exaggeration; *pl* indications, signs
ribetear /rriβete'ar/ *vt Sew.* to bind, trim, edge
ricacho /rri'katʃo/ **(-cha)** *n Inf.* newly rich person, nouveau riche
ricahembra /rrika'embra/ *f,* lady; daughter or wife of a Spanish noble *Obs.*
ricamente /rrika'mente/ *adv* richly, opulently; beautifully, splendidly; luxuriously
ricino /rri'θino; rri'sino/ *m,* castor oil plant
rico /'rriko/ *a* wealthy, rich; abundant; magnificent, splendid; delicious. **r. como Creso,** rich as Croesus
ricohombre /rriko'ombre/ *m,* nobleman *Obs.*
ricura /rri'kura/ *f, Inf.* richness, wealth
ridiculez /rriðiku'leθ; rriðiku'les/ *f,* absurd action or remark; ridiculousness; affectation; folly
ridiculizar /rriðikuli'θar; rriðikuli'sar/ *vt* to ridicule, poke fun at
ridículo /rri'ðikulo/ *a* ridiculous, absurd; grotesque; preposterous, outrageous. *m,* reticule
riego /'rriego/ *m,* watering, spraying; irrigation
riel /'rriel/ *m,* ingot; rail (of a train or streetcar)
rielar /rrie'lar/ *vi* to glimmer, glisten; glitter; shimmer
rienda /'rrienda/ *f,* rein (gen. *pl*); restraint; *pl* administration, government. **a r. suelta,** swiftly; without restraint
riesgo /'rriesgo/ *m,* risk, danger
rifa /'rrifa/ *f,* raffle; quarrel, disagreement
rifar /rri'far/ *vt* to raffle; *—vi* quarrel, fall out
rifle /'rrifle/ *m,* rifle
rigidez /rrihi'ðeθ; rrihi'ðes/ *f,* stiffness; rigidity; harshness
rígido /'rrihiðo/ *a* stiff; rigid; inflexible; severe, harsh
rigodón /rrigo'ðon/ *m,* rigadoon

rigor /rri'gor/ *m,* severity, sternness; rigor; hardness; inflexibility; *Med.* rigor. **en r.,** strictly speaking. **ser de r.,** to be essential, be indispensable
rigorista /rrigo'rista/ *mf* martinet
riguroso /rrigu'roso/ *a* rigorous; harsh, cruel; austere, rigid; strict, exact, scrupulous
rijoso /rri'hoso/ *a* quarrelsome; lascivious
riksha /'rriksa/ *m,* rickshaw
rima /'rrima/ *f,* rhyme, rime; heap; *pl* lyrics
rimador /rrima'ðor/ **(-ra)** *a* rhyming, rimer *—n* rhymer, rimer
rimar /rri'mar/ *vi* to compose verses; *—vi* and *vt* rhyme, rime
rimbombo /rrim'βombo/ *m,* reverberation (of a sound)
rimero /rri'mero/ *m,* heap, pile
Rin, el /rrin, el/ the Rhine
rincón /rrin'kon/ *m,* corner, angle; retreat, hiding place; *Inf.* home, nest, nook
rinconada /rrinko'naða/ *f,* corner, angle
rinconera /rrinko'nera/ *f,* corner cupboard; corner table
ringlera /rriŋ'glera/ *f,* file, line, row
ringlero /rriŋ'glero/ *m,* guiding line for writing
ringorrangos /rriŋgo'rraŋgos/ *m pl, Inf.* exaggerated flourishes in writing; *Inf.* unnecessary frills or ornaments
rinoceronte /rrinoθe'ronte; rrinose'ronte/ *m,* rhinoceros
riñón /rri'ɲon/ *m,* kidney; *Fig.* center, heart; *pl Anat.* back
río /'rrio/ *m,* river; *Fig.* stream, flood
rioja /'rrioha/ *m,* red wine from Rioja
ripio /'rripio/ *m,* remains, rest; debris, rubbish; *Lit.* padding; verbiage, prolixity. **no perder r.,** to lose no occasion or opportunity
riqueza /rri'keθa; rri'kesa/ *f,* riches, wealth; abundance; richness, magnificence
risa /'rrisa/ *f,* laugh; laughter; cause of amusement, joke
risco /'rrisko/ *m,* crag
riscoso /rris'koso/ *a* craggy
risible /rri'siβle/ *a* laughable
risoles /rri'soies/ *m pl,* rissoles
risotada /rriso'taða/ *f,* loud laugh
ristra /'rristra/ *f,* string (of onions, etc.); file, line, row
risueño /rri'sueɲo/ *a* smiling; cheerful; pleasant, agreeable; favorable, hopeful
rítmico /'rritmiko/ *a* rhythmic
ritmo /'rritmo/ *m,* rhythm
rito /'rrito/ *m,* rite
ritualismo /rritua'lismo/ *m,* ritualism
ritualista /rritua'lista/ *mf* ritualist
rivalidad /rriβali'ðað/ *f,* rivalry, competition; hostility
rivalizar /rriβali'θar; rriβali'sar/ *vi* to compete, rival
rizado /rri'θaðo; rri'saðo/ *m,* curling; pleating, crimping; rippling, ruffling
rizar /rri'θar; rri'sar/ *vt* to curl (hair); ripple, ruffle (of water); pleat, crimp; *—vr* be naturally wavy (of hair)
rizo /'rriθo; 'rriso/ *m,* curl, ringlet; cut velvet. *Aer.* **hacer el r.,** to loop the loop; *Naut.* to take in reefs
rizoso /rri'θoso; rri'soso/ *a* naturally curly or wavy (hair)
ro, ro /rro, rro/ *m,* hushaby!
roano /rro'ano/ *a* roan (of horses)
robador /rroβa'ðor/ **(-ra)** *a* robbing *—n* robber, thief *m,* abductor
robar /rro'βar/ *vt* to rob; abduct; wash away, eat away (rivers, sea); remove honey from the hive; draw (in cards, dominoes); *Fig.* capture (love, etc.)
roblar /rro'βlar/ *vt* to reinforce, strengthen; clinch
roble /'rroβle/ *m,* oak tree; oak; *Fig.* bulwark, tower of strength
robledo /rro'βleðo/ *m,* oak grove
roblón /rro'βlon/ *m,* rivet
robo /'rroβo/ *m,* theft, robbery; booty
robustecer /rroβuste'θer; rroβuste'ser/ *vt irr* to strengthen. See **conocer**
robustez /rroβus'teθ; rroβus'tes/ *f,* strength, robustness
robusto /rro'βusto/ *a* vigorous, robust, hearty, strong
roca /'rroka/ *f,* rock; *Fig.* tower of strength
roce /'rroθe; 'rrose/ *m,* rubbing, brushing, touching, friction; social intercourse
rociada /rro'θiaða; rro'siaða/ *f,* dewing; sprinkling; dew-wet grass given as medicine to horses and mules; *Fig.* shower; general slander; harsh rebuke
rociar /rro'θiar; rro'siar/ *vi* to fall as dew; drizzle; *—vt* sprinkle, spray; *Fig.* shower (with)
rocín /rro'θin; rro'sin/ *m,* sorry nag; hack; *Inf.* ignoramus, boor
rocinante /rroθi'nante; rrosi'nante/ *m,* poor nag (alluding to Don Quixote's horse)
rocío /'rroθio; 'rrosio/ *m,* dew; dewdrop; drizzle, light shower; *Fig.* sprinkling, spray
rocoso /rro'koso/ *a* rocky
rodaballo /rroða'βaʎo; rroða'βayo/ *m,* turbot; *Inf.* crafty man
rodada /rro'ðaða/ *f,* wheel mark or track
rodado /rro'ðaðo/ *a* dappled (of horses)
rodaje /rro'ðahe/ *m,* wheeling; shooting (of a film)
rodante /rro'ðante/ *a* rolling
rodar /rro'ðar/ *vi* to roll; revolve, turn; run on wheels; wander, roam; be moved about; be plentiful, abound; happen successively; (*with por*) fall down, roll down
Rodas /'rroðas/ Rhodes
rodear /rroðe'ar/ *vi* to walk around; go by a roundabout way; *Fig.* beat around the bush; *—vt* encircle, surround; besiege; *West Hem.* round up (cattle)
rodela /rro'ðela/ *f,* round shield; buckler
rodeno /rro'ðeno/ *a* red (of rocks, earth, etc.)
rodeo /rro'ðeo/ *m,* encirclement; indirect and longer way; trick to evade pursuit; *West Hem.* rodeo, roundup; stockyard, cattle enclosure; *Fig.* beating around the bush; evasive reply
rodera /rro'ðera/ *f,* rail, track, line; cart rut or track
Rodesia /rro'ðesia/ Rhodesia
rodilla /rro'ðiʎa; rro'ðiya/ *f,* knee; floor cloth. **de rodillas,** on one's knees. **ponerse de rodillas,** *or* **hincar las rodillas,** to kneel down
rodillazo /rroði'ʎaθo; rroði'yaso/ *m,* push with the knee
rodillera /rroði'ʎera; rroði'yera/ *f,* kneecap, kneepad; mend at the knee of garments; bagginess of trouser knees
rodillo /rro'ðiʎo; rro'ðiyo/ *m,* roller; traction engine; *Print.* inking roller; garden roller. **r. de pastas,** *Cul.* rolling pin
rododendro /rroðo'ðendro/ *m,* rhododendron
rodrigón /rroðri'gon/ *m,* stake, prop (for plants); *Inf.* old retainer who serves as a ladies' escort
roedor /rroe'ðor/ *a* gnawing; *Fig.* nagging; biting *—a* and *m,* rodent
roedura /rroe'ðura/ *f,* biting, gnawing; corrosion
roer /rro'er/ *vt irr* to gnaw, nibble, eat; corrode, wear away; trouble, afflict *—Pres. Indic.* **roigo, roes,** etc *—Preterite* **royó, royeron.** *Imperf. Subjunc.* **royese,** etc.
rogación /rroga'θion; rroga'sion/ *f,* request, supplication, entreaty; *Eccl.* rogation
rogador /rroga'ðor/ **(-ra)** *a* requesting; beseeching *—n* suppliant
rogar /rro'gar/ *vt irr* to request; beseech, beg. See **contar**
rogativo /rroga'tiβo/ *a* supplicatory, petitioning
roído /rroi'ðo/ *a* gnawed, eaten; *Inf.* miserable, stingy
rojal /rro'hal/ *a* red (of soil, etc.). *m,* red earth
rojear /rrohe'ar/ *vi* to appear red; be reddish
rojete /rro'hete/ *m,* rouge
rojez /rro'heθ; rro'hes/ *f* ', redness
rojizo /rro'hiθo; rro'hiso/ *a* reddish
rojo /'rroho/ *a* red; fair; red-gold (of hair); *Polit.* radical, red
rol /rrol/ *m,* roll, list
roldana /rrol'dana/ *f,* pulley wheel
rollizo /rro'ʎiθo; rro'yiso/ *a* round; plump, sturdy. *m,* log
rollo /'rroʎo; 'rroyo/ *m,* roll; *Cul.* rolling pin; log;

town cross or pillar; anything rolled (paper, etc.); twist (of tobacco)

Roma /'rroma/ Rome

romance /rro'manθe; rro'manse/ *a* and *m,* romance (language). *m,* Spanish; ballad; romance of chivalry; *pl Fig.* fairy tales, excuses. **en buen r.,** *Fig.* in plain words

romancear /rromanθe'ar; rromanse'ar/ *vt* to translate from Latin into the spoken language; translate into Spanish; paraphrase the Spanish to assist translation

romancero /rroman'θero; rroman'sero/ **(-ra)** *n* balladeer. *m,* collection of ballads

romancista /rroman'θista; rroman'sista/ *mf* romancist

románico /rro'maniko/ *a Archit.* Romanesque

romanista /rroma'nista/ *mf* expert in Roman law or Romance languages and literature

romanizar /rromani'θar; rromani'sar/ *vt* to romanize; *—vr* become romanized

romano /rro'mano/ **(-na)** *a* and *n* Roman. **a la romana,** in the Roman way. **cabello a la romana,** *Inf.* bobbed hair

romanticismo /rromanti'θismo; rromanti'sismo/ *m,* romanticism

romántico /rro'mantiko/ **(-ca)** *a* romantic; emotional; fanciful *—n* romantic; romanticist

rombo /'rrombo/ *m,* rhombus

romería /rrome'ria/ *f,* pilgrimage; excursion, picnic (made on a saint's day)

romero /rro'mero/ **(-ra)** *m,* rosemary *—n* pilgrim

romo /'rromo/ *a* blunt, dull, unsharpened; flat (of noses)

rompecabezas /rrompeka'βeθas; rrompeka'βesas/ *m,* bludgeon; knuckleduster; *Inf.* teaser, puzzle, riddle; jigsaw puzzle

rompeimágenes /rrompei'mahenes/ *mf* iconoclast

rompeolas /rrompe'olas/ *m,* jetty, breakwater

romper /rrom'per/ *vt* to break; shatter, break into fragments; spoil, ruin; break up, plow; *Fig.* cut, divide (of water, etc.); *Fig.* end, break; interrupt; infringe, break; *—vi* break; break (of waves); sprout, flower; (*with prep a*) begin to. **Rompió a hablar,** He broke into speech *—Past Part.* **roto**

rompiente /rrom'piente/ *a* breaking. *m,* reef, shoal

rompimiento /rrompi'miento/ *m,* break, rupture; crack, split; breakage; infringement; plowing up; *Fig.* dividing (water, etc.); spoiling, ruining; opening (of buds, etc.)

ron /rron/ *m,* rum

roncar /rron'kar/ *vi* to snore; *Fig.* roar, howl (of the sea, wind, etc.); *Inf.* brag

roncear /rronθe'ar; rronse'ar/ *vi* to be dilatory or unwilling; *Inf.* flatter, cajole; *Naut.* lag behind, sail slowly

roncero /rron'θero; rron'sero/ *a* dilatory, slow; grumbling, complaining; cajoling, flattering

roncha /'rrontʃa/ *f,* wheal; bruise, bump; *Inf.* money lost through trickery; thin, round slice

ronco /'rronko/ *a* hoarse, husky

ronda /'rronda/ *f,* round, beat, patrol; serenading party; *Inf.* round (of drinks)

rondador /rronda'ðor/ *m,* watchman; roundsman; serenader; night wanderer

rondalla /rron'daʎa; rron'daya/ *f,* tale, fairy tale

rondar /rron'dar/ *vi* to patrol, police; walk the streets by night; serenade; *—vt* haunt; hover about; *Inf.* overcome (of sleep, etc.)

rondó /rron'do/ *m,* rondo

ronquear /rronke'ar/ *vi* to be hoarse

ronquera /rron'kera/ *f,* hoarseness

ronquido /rron'kiðo/ *m,* snore; hoarse sound

ronronear /rronrone'ar/ *vi* to purr (of cats)

ronzal /rron'θal; rron'sal/ *m,* halter

ronzar /rron'θar; rron'sar/ *vt* to munch, crack with the teeth

roña /'rroɲa/ *f,* mange (in sheep); grime, filth; mold; moral corruption; *Inf.* stinginess; *Inf.* trick, deception

roñería /rroɲe'ria/ *f, Inf.* meanness, stinginess

roñoso /rro'ɲoso/ *a* scabby; filthy; rusty; *Inf.* mean, stingy

ropa /'rropa/ *f,* fabric, material, stuff; clothes, wearing apparel; garment, outfit; robe (of office). **r. blanca,** underclothes; (domestic) linen. **r. hecha,** ready-made clothing. **r. talar,** long gown; cassock

ropaje /rro'pahe/ *m,* clothes, garments; vestments; drapery; *Fig.* form, outline

ropavejería /rropaβehe'ria/ *f,* old-clothes shop

ropavejero /rropaβe'hero/ **(-ra)** *n* old-clothes dealer

ropería /rrope'ria/ *f,* clothier's shop or trade; wardrobe; cloakroom

ropero /rro'pero/ **(-ra)** *n* clothier; keeper of the wardrobe. *m,* wardrobe; charitable organization

ropilla /rro'piʎa; rro'piya/ *f,* doublet

ropón /rro'pon/ *m,* a loose-fitting gown generally worn over clothes

roque /'rroke/ *m,* rook (in chess)

roqueño /rro'keɲo/ *a* rocky; hard as rock

roquete /rro'kete/ *m, Eccl.* rochet; barb of a lance

rorro /'rrorro/ *m, Inf.* infant, baby

rosa /'rrosa/ *f,* rose; anything rose-shaped; artificial rose; red spot on the body; *Archit.* rose window; *pl* rosettes. *m,* rose color. **r. de los vientos,** mariner's compass. **r. laurel,** oleander

rosado /rro'saðo/ *a* rose-colored; rose; rosé (wine)

rosal /rro'sal/ *m,* rose tree. **r. de tallo,** standard rose tree

rosaleda, rosalera /rrosa'leða, rrosa'lera/ *f,* rose garden

rosario /rro'sario/ *m,* rosary; *Fig.* string; chain pump; *Inf.* backbone

rosbif /rros'βif/ *m,* roast beef

rosca /'rroska/ *f,* screw and nut; *Cul.* twist (of bread or cake); spiral

roscado /rros'kaðo/ *a* twisted, spiral

rosear /rrose'ar/ *vi* to turn to rose, become rose-colored

Rosellón /rrose'ʎon; rrose'yon/ Rousillon

róseo /'rroseo/ *a* rose-colored

roseta /rro'seta/ *f, dim* small rose; rosette; rose of a watering can; rosette copper; *pl* toasted maize. **r. de fiebre,** rush of fever

rosetón /rrose'ton/ *m,* large rosette; *Archit.* rose window

rosicler /rrosi'kler/ *m,* rose-pink (first flush of dawn)

rosillo /rro'siʎo; rro'siyo/ *a* light red; roan (of horses)

rosmaro /rros'maro/ *m,* manatee, sea cow

roso /'rroso/ *a* bald, worn; red

rosquilla /rros'kiʎa; rros'kiya/ *f,* ring-shaped cake

rosquillero /rroski'ʎero; rroski'yero/ **(-ra)** *n* seller of rosquillas

rostrituerto /rrostri'tuerto/ *a Inf.* wry-faced (from sadness or anger)

rostro /'rrostro/ *m,* bird's beak; face, visage. **conocer de r.,** to know by sight. **dar en r.,** *Fig.* to throw in one's face

rota /'rrota/ *f, Mil.* defeat; *Eccl.* Rota; *Bot.* rattan

rotación /rrota'θion; rrota'sion/ *f,* rotation. **r. de cultivos,** rotation of crops

rotativa /rrota'tiβa/ *f,* rotary printing press

rotativo /rrota'tiβo/ *a* rotary

rotatorio /rrota'torio/ *a* rotatory

roto /'rroto/ *a* shabby, ragged; vicious, debauched

rotograbado /rrotogra'βaðo/ *m,* rotogravure

rotonda /rro'tonda/ *f,* rotunda

rótula /'rrotula/ *f,* rotula, patella

rotular /rrotu'lar/ *vt* to label; give a title or heading to

rótulo /'rrotulo/ *m,* title; poster, placard; label

rotundamente /rrotunda'mente/ *adv* tersely, roundly, plainly

rotundidad /rrotundi'ðað/ *f,* rotundity; roundness; finality (of words, etc.)

rotundo /rro'tundo/ *a* round; rotund; sonorous; final, plain (of words, etc.)

rotura /rro'tura/ *f,* breaking, shattering; plowing up; breakage; rupture

roturar /rrotu'rar/ *vt Agr.* to break up, plow up

roya /'rroya/ *f,* rust, mildew; tobacco

roza /'rroθa; 'rrosa/ *f, Agr.* clearing (of weeds, etc.);

ground ready for sowing. **de r. abierta,** open cast (of mining)

rozadura /rroθa'ðura; rrosa'ðura/ *f,* rubbing, friction; abrasion, chafing

rozagante /rroθa'gante; rrosa'gante/ *a* long and elaborate (dresses); upstanding; handsome; strapping, fine

rozamiento /rroθa'miento; rrosa'miento/ *m,* grazing, brushing, rubbing; discord, disharmony, disagreement; *Mech.* friction

rozar /rro'θar; rro'sar/ *vt Agr.* to clear of weeds; crop, nibble; scrape; brush against, touch; *—vi* brush, rub, touch; *—vr* have dealings with, know; stammer; be like, resemble

rúa /'rrua/ *f,* village street; highway

ruar /rru'ar/ *vi* to walk or ride through the streets; parade through the streets flirting with the ladies

rubeola /rruβe'ola/ *f,* rubella

rubí /rru'βi/ *m,* ruby; jewel (of a watch)

rubia /'rruβia/ *f, Bot.* madder; blonde (girl, woman)

rubicundez /rruβikun'deθ; rruβikun'des/ *f,* rubicundity, ruddiness, redness

rubicundo /rruβi'kundo/ *a* red-gold; ruddy-complexioned; reddish

rubio /'rruβio/ *a* red-gold, gold; fair, blond

rublo /'rruβlo/ *m,* ruble

rubor /rru'βor/ *m,* blush, flush; bashfulness

ruborizarse /rruβori'θarse; rruβori'sarse/ *vr* to blush; be shamefaced

ruboroso /rruβo'roso/ *a* shamefaced; blushing

rúbrica /'rruβrika/ *f,* rubric; personal mark, flourish added to one's signature

rubricar /rruβri'kar/ *vt* to sign and seal; sign with an X or other symbol; sign with a flourish

rubro /'rruβro/ *a* red

rucio /'rruθio; 'rrusio/ *a* fawn, light-gray (of animals); *Inf.* going gray, gray-haired

rudamente /rruða'mente/ *adv* rudely, abruptly, churlishly; roughly

rudeza /rru'ðeθa; rru'ðesa/ *f,* roughness; rudeness, uncouthness; stupidity

rudimentario /rruðimen'tario/ *a* rudimentary

rudimento /rruði'mento/ *m,* embryo; *pl* rudiments

rudo /'rruðo/ *a* rough; unfinished; uncouth, boorish, rude; stupid

rueca /'rrueka/ *f,* distaff (in spinning); spinning wheel; curve, twist

rueda /'rrueða/ *f,* wheel; group, circle; spread of a peacock's tail; roller, castor; round piece or slice; turn, chance; succession (of events); wheel (used for torture). **r. libre,** freewheeling. *Inf.* **hacer la r. (a),** to flatter, make a fuss of

ruedero /rrue'ðero/ *m,* wheelwright

ruedo /'rrueðo/ *m,* turning, rotation; circumference; lined hem of a cassock; circuit

ruego /'rruego/ *m,* request, entreaty

rufián /rru'fian/ *m,* ruffian; pimp

rufianesco /rrufia'nesko/ *a* ruffianly

rufo /'rrufo/ *a* fair; red-haired; curly-haired

rugido /rru'hiðo/ *m,* roaring, roar; creaking; gnashing; rumbling

rugir /rru'hir/ *vi* to roar; squeak, creak; gnash (the teeth)

ruibarbo /rrui'βarβo/ *m,* rhubarb

ruido /'rruiðo/ *m,* noise, din; disturbance; rumor. **hacer** (*or* **meter**) **r.,** to cause a sensation. *Inf.* **ser más el r. que las nueces,** to be much ado about nothing

ruidoso /rrui'ðoso/ *a* noisy; notable

ruin /rru'in/ *a* base, vile; despicable; mean; puny

ruina /'rruina/ *f,* ruin, downfall; financial ruin; fall, decline; *pl* ruins

ruinar /rrui'nar/ *vt* to ruin

ruindad /rruin'dað/ *f,* baseness; meanness; pettiness, unworthiness; mean trick, despicable action

ruinoso /rrui'noso/ *a* half-ruined; ruinous; useless, worthless

ruiseñor /rruise'ɲor/ *m,* nightingale

ruleta /rru'leta/ *f,* roulette

rumano /rru'mano/ **(-na)** *a* and *n* Romanian. *m,* Romanian (language)

rumbo /'rrumbo/ *m, Naut.* course, way, route; direction; *Inf.* swank. **con r. a,** headed for, in the direction of. **hacer r. a,** to sail for; make for

rumboso /rrum'βoso/ *a Inf.* pompous, dignified; open-handed, generous

rumia /'rrumia/ *f,* rumination; cud

rumiante /rru'miante/ *a* and *mf Zool.* ruminant *—a Inf.* reflective, meditative

rumiar /rru'miar/ *vt Zool.* to ruminate; *Inf.* reflect upon, chew on; *Inf.* fume, rage

rumor /rru'mor/ *m,* noise; rumor; murmur, babble; dull sound

runa /'rruna/ *f,* rune

rúnico /'rruniko/ *a* runic

runrunearse /rrunrune'arse/ *v impers* to be rumored

rupia /'rrupia/ *f,* rupee

ruptura /rrup'tura/ *f, Fig.* rupture; *Surg.* hernia

rural /rru'ral/ *a* rustic, rural

ruralmente /rrural'mente/ *adv* rurally

Rusia /'rrusia/ Russia

rusificar /rrusifi'kar/ *vt* to russianize

ruso /'rruso/ **(-sa)** *a* and *n* Russian. *m,* Russian (language)

rusticación /rrustika'θion; rrustika'sion/ *f,* rustication

rusticar /rrusti'kar/ *vi* to rusticate

rusticidad /rrustiθi'ðað; rrustisi'ðað/ *f,* rusticity; boorishness, coarseness

rústico /'rrustiko/ *a* rustic, country; boorish, uncouth. *m,* countryman; yokel; peasant. **en rústica,** in paper covers (of books)

ruta /'rruta/ *f,* route; *Fig.* way. **r. de evitación,** bypass, detour

ruteno /rru'teno/ **(-na)** *a* and *n* Ruthenian. *m,* Ruthenian (language)

rutilante /rruti'lante/ *a Poet.* sparkling, glowing

rutilar /rruti'lar/ *vi Poet.* to gleam, sparkle

rutina /rru'tina/ *f,* routine

rutinario /rruti'nario/ *a* routine

rutinero /rruti'nero/ **(-ra)** *a* routinistic *—n* routinist

S

sábado /'saβaðo/ *m,* Saturday; Jewish sabbath. **s. de gloria,** Easter Saturday
sábalo /'saβalo/ *m, Ichth.* shad
sabana /sa'βana/ *f,* savannah
sábana /'saβana/ *f,* bed sheet; altar cloth. *Inf.* **pegársele (a uno) las sábanas,** to be tied to the bed, get up late
sabandija /saβan'diha/ *f,* any unpleasant insect or reptile; *Fig.* vermin
sabanero /saβa'nero/ **(-ra)** *n* savannah dweller *—a* savannah
sabanilla /saβa'niʎa; saβa'niya/ *f,* small piece of linen (kerchief, towel, etc.); altar cloth
sabañón /saβa'ɲon/ *m,* chilblain
sabatario /saβa'tario/ *a* sabbatarian
sabático /sa'βatiko/ *a* sabbatical
sabatino /saβa'tino/ *a* Saturday, Sabbath
sabedor /saβe'ðor/ *a* aware; knowledgeable, knowing
sabelotodo /saβelo'toðo/ *mf Inf.* know-it-all
saber /sa'βer/ *m,* learning; wisdom
saber /sa'βer/ *vt irr* to know; be able to, know how; *—vi* know; be shrewd, be well aware of; (*with prep a*) taste of; be like or similar to. **s. al dedillo,** *Fig.* to have at one's fingertips. **a s.,** viz., namely. *Inf.* **no s. cuántas son cinco,** not to know how many beans make five. **no s. dónde meterse,** to be overcome by shame; have the jitters. **No sé cuántos,** I don't know how many. **No sé quién,** I don't know who (which person). **No sé qué,** I don't know what. **un no sé qué,** a certain something; a touch (of). **¡Quién sabe!** Who knows!; Time will tell *—Pres. Indic.* **sé, sabes,** etc *—Fut.* **sabré,** etc *—Condit.* **sabría,** etc *—Preterite* **supe,** etc *—Pres. Subjunc.* **sepa,** etc *—Imperf. Subjunc.* **supiese,** etc.
sabiamente /saβia'mente/ *adv* wisely, prudently
sabidillo /saβi'ðiʎo; saβi'ðiyo/ **(-lla)** *a* and *n Inf.* know-it-all
sabiduría /saβiðu'ria/ *f,* prudence, wisdom; erudition, learning; knowledge, awareness. **Libro de la S. de Salomón,** Book of Wisdom
sabiendas, a /sa'βiendas, a/ *adv* knowingly, consciously
sabihondo /sa'βiondo/ **(-da)** *n Inf.* know-it-all
sabino /sa'βino/ **(-na)** *a* and *n* Sabine *—a* roan (of horses)
sabio /'saβio/ **(-ia)** *a* wise; learned, erudite; prudent, sagacious; knowing (of animals); performing (of animals) *—n* wise person; scholar, erudite person
sablazo /sa'βlaθo; sa'βlaso/ *m,* saber thrust or wound; *Inf.* sponging, taking advantage of. **dar un s. (a),** *Inf.* to sponge on; touch for money
sable /'saβle/ *m,* saber; *Herald.* sable; *Inf.* talent for sponging on people *—a Herald.* sable
sablear /saβle'ar/ *vi Inf.* to touch for invitations, loans, etc.; cadge
sablista /sa'βlista/ *mf Inf.* sponger, cadger
saboneta /saβo'neta/ *f,* hunting case watch, hunter
sabor /sa'βor/ *m,* taste, flavor; impression, effect. **a s.,** to taste; at pleasure
saboreamiento /saβorea'miento/ *m,* savoring; relishing, enjoyment
saborear /saβore'ar/ *vt* to flavor, season; relish, savor; appreciate, enjoy; *—vr* relish, savor; enjoy
saboreo /saβo'reo/ *m,* tasting; savoring; relishing
sabotaje /saβo'tahe/ *m,* sabotage
saboteador /saβotea'ðor/ *m,* saboteur
Saboya /sa'βoya/ Savoy
saboyano /saβo'yano/ **(-na)** *a* and *n* Savoyard
sabroso /sa'βroso/ *a* tasty, savory, well-seasoned; delightful, delicious; *Inf.* piquant, racy
sabueso /sa'βueso/ *m,* cocker spaniel. **s. de artois,** hound
sabuloso /saβu'loso/ *a* sandy
saburra /sa'βurra/ *f,* fur (on the tongue)
saca /'saka/ *f,* drawing out, removing; export, transport, shipping; removal, extraction; legal copy (of a document). **estar de s.,** to be on sale; *Inf.* be marriageable (of women)
sacabocados /sakaβo'kaðos/ *m,* punch (tool); *Inf.* cinch, easy matter
sacabotas /saka'βotas/ *m,* bootjack
sacabrocas /saka'βrokas/ *m,* tack puller
sacabuche /saka'βutʃe/ *m, Mus.* sackbut; sackbut player; *Inf.* insignificant little man; *Naut.* hand pump
sacacorchos /saka'kortʃos/ *m,* corkscrew
sacacuartos /saka'kuartos/ *m, Inf.* catchpenny
sacada /sa'kaða/ *f,* territory cut off from a province
sacadineros /sakaði'neros/ *m, Inf.* catchpenny
sacamanchas /saka'mantʃas/ *mf.* See **quitamanchas**
sacamantas /saka'mantas/ *m, Inf.* tax collector
sacamiento /saka'miento/ *m,* removing, taking out
sacamuelas /saka'muelas/ *mf* dentist; charlatan, quack; *Inf.* windbag
sacapotras /saka'potras/ *m, Inf.* unskilled surgeon
sacar /sa'kar/ *vt* to draw out; extract; pull out; take out; remove; dispossess, turn out; free from, relieve; examine, investigate; extort (the truth); extract (sugar, etc.); win (prizes, games); copy; discover, find out; elect by ballot; obtain, achieve; exclude; show, exhibit; quote, mention; produce, invent; manufacture; note down; put forth; unsheath (swords); bowl (in cricket); serve (in tennis). **s. a bailar,** to invite to dance. **s. a luz,** to publish, print; reveal, bring out. **s. a paseo,** to take for a walk. **s. de pila,** to be a godfather or godmother to. **s. en claro** *or* **s. en limpio,** to copy; conclude, infer, gather. **sacarse en conclusión que...,** the conclusion is that...
sacarificar /sakarifi'kar/ *vt* to saccharify
sacarina /saka'rina/ *f,* saccharin
sacasillas /saka'siʎas; saka'siyas/ *m, Inf. Theat.* stagehand
sacerdocio /saθer'ðoθio; saser'ðosio/ *m,* priesthood
sacerdotal /saθerðo'tal; saserðo'tal/ *a* priestly
sacerdote /saθer'ðote; saser'ðote/ *m,* priest
sacerdotisa /saθerðo'tisa; saserðo'tisa/ *f,* priestess. **sumo s.,** high priestess
sachar /sa'tʃar/ *vt* to weed
sacho /'satʃo/ *m,* weeder
saciable /sa'θiaβle; sa'siaβle/ *a* satiable
saciar /sa'θiar; sa'siar/ *vt* to satisfy; satiate; *—vr* be satiated
saciedad /saθie'ðað; sasie'ðað/ *f,* satiety, surfeit
saco /'sako/ *m,* handbag; sack, bag; sackful; sack coat; *Biol.* sac; *Mil.* sack, plundering. **s. de noche,** dressing case, weekend case. *Inf.* **no echar en s. roto,** not to forget, to remember
sacramentalmente /sakramental'mente/ *adv* sacramentally; in confession
sacramentar /sakramen'tar/ *vt* to consecrate; administer the Blessed Sacrament; hide, conceal
sacramentario /sakramen'tario/ **(-ia)** *n* sacramentalist; sacramentarian
sacramento /sakra'mento/ *m,* sacrament; *Eccl.* Host; *Eccl.* mystery. **s. del altar,** Eucharist. **con todos los sacramentos,** with all the sacraments; done in order, complete with all formalities. **recibir los sacramentos,** to receive the last sacraments
sacratísimo /sakra'tisimo/ *a* most sacred
sacrificadero /sakrifika'ðero/ *m,* place of sacrifice
sacrificador /sakrifika'ðor/ **(-ra)** *a* sacrificing *—n* sacrificer
sacrificar /sakrifi'kar/ *vt* to sacrifice; slaughter; *—vr* consecrate oneself to God; sacrifice oneself; devote or dedicate oneself (to)
sacrificio /sakri'fiθio; sakri'fisio/ *m,* sacrifice; offering, dedication; surrendering, forgoing; compliance, submission. **s. del altar,** sacrifice of the mass
sacrilegio /sakri'lehio/ *m,* sacrilege
sacrílego /sa'krilego/ *a* sacrilegious
sacristán /sakris'tan/ *m,* sacristan; sexton; hoop (for dresses). *Inf.* **s. de amén,** yes-man. *Inf.* **ser gran s.,** to be very crafty

sacristana /sakris'tana/ *f*, wife of a sacristan or sexton; nun in charge of a convent sacristy
sacristanía /sakrista'nia/ *f*, office of a sacristan or sexton
sacristía /sakris'tia/ *f*, sacristy; vestry; office of a sacristan or sexton
sacro /'sakro/ *a* sacred; *Anat.* sacral
sacrosanto /sakro'santo/ *a* sacrosanct
sacudida /saku'ðiða/ *f*, shake, shaking; jerk, jar, jolt; twitch, pull; *Aer.* bump
sacudido /saku'ðiðo/ *a* unsociable; difficult, wayward; determined, bold
sacudidor /sakuði'ðor/ **(-ra)** *a* shaking; jerking —*n* shaker. *m*, carpet beater; duster
sacudidura /sakuði'ðura/ *f*, shaking (especially to remove dust); jerking
sacudimiento /sakuði'miento/ *m*, shake, shaking; jerk; twitch, pull; jolt
sacudir /saku'ðir/ *vt* to shake; flap, wave; jerk, twitch; beat, bang; shake off; —*vr* shake off, avoid
sadismo /sa'ðismo/ *m*, sadism
sadista /sa'ðista/ *mf* sadist
sadístico /sa'ðistiko/ *a* sadistic
saduceo /saðu'θeo; saðu'seo/ **(-ea)** *a* Sadducean —*n* Sadducee
saeta /sa'eta/ *f*, arrow, dart; clock hand, watch hand; magnetic needle; short sung expression of religious ecstasy; *Astron.* Sagitta
saetada /sae'taða/ *f*, **saetazo** *m*, arrow wound
saetera /sae'tera/ *f*, loophole; small window
saetero /sae'tero/ *a* arrow, arrow-like. *m*, archer, bowman
sáfico /'safiko/ *a* Sapphic
saga /'saga/ *f*, saga
sagacidad /sagaθi'ðað; sagasi'ðað/ *f*, sagacity
sagaz /sa'gaθ; sa'gas/ *a* sagacious, shrewd; farseeing; quick on the scent (dogs)
sagital /sahi'tal/ *a* arrow-shaped
sagitario /sahi'tario/ *m*, archer; *Astron.* Sagittarius
sagrado /sa'graðo/ *a* sacred; holy; sacrosanct, venerable; accursed, detestable. *m*, sanctuary, refuge; haven
sagrario /sa'grario/ *m*, sanctuary; sacrarium
sagú /sa'gu/ *m*, sago
Sáhara, el /'saara, el/ the Sahara
sahornarse /saor'narse/ *vr* to chafe, grow sore
sahorno /sa'orno/ *m*, chafing, abrasion
sahumado /sau'maðo/ *a* improved, rendered more excellent; perfumed; fumigated
sahumador /sauma'ðor/ *m*, perfumer; fumigating vessel
sahumar /sau'mar/ *vt* to perfume; fumigate. See **desahuciar**
sahumerio /sau'merio/ *m*, perfuming; fumigation; fume, smoke
saín /sa'in/ *m*, fat, grease; sardine oil (for lamps); grease spot (on clothes)
sainar /sai'nar/ *vt* to fatten up (animals)
sainete /sai'nete/ *m*, *Cul.* sauce; *Theat.* one-act parody or burlesque; farce; delicacy, tidbit; delicate taste (of food)
sainetero /saine'tero/ *m*, writer of sainetes
sainetesco /saine'tesko/ *a* pertaining to sainetes; burlesque, satirical
sajar /sa'har/ *vt Surg.* to scarify
sajón /sa'hon/ **(-ona)** *a* and *n* Saxon
Sajonia /sa'honia/ Saxony
sal /sal/ *f*, salt; wit; grace, gracefulness. **s. de cocina,** common kitchen salt. **s. de la Higuera,** Epsom salts. **s. gema,** rock salt. **s. marina,** sea salt. **sales inglesas,** smelling salts. *Inf.* **estar hecho de s.,** to be full of wit. *Inf.* **hacerse s. y agua,** to melt away, disappear (of riches, etc.)
sala /'sala/ *f*, drawing room; large room, hall; *Law.* courtroom; *Law.* bench; **s. de apelación,** court of appeal. **s. de hospital,** hospital ward. **s. de justicia,** court of justice. **s. de lectura,** reading room. *Law.* **guardar s.,** to respect the court
salacidad /salaθi'ðað; salasi'ðað/ *f*, lewdness, salaciousness
saladar /sala'ðar/ *m*, salt marsh
saladero /sala'ðero/ *m*, salting or curing place; *West Hem.* meat packing factory
saladillo /sala'ðiʎo; sala'ðiyo/ *m*, salt pork
salado /sa'laðo/ *a* salty, briny; brackish; witty; attractive, amusing
salador /sala'ðor/ **(-ra)** *a* salting, curing —*n* salter, curer. *m*, curing place
saladura /sala'ðura/ *f*, salting, curing
salamandra /sala'mandra/ *f*, salamander; fire sprite
salar /sa'lar/ *vt* to salt; season with salt; oversalt; cure, pickle (meat, etc.)
salario /sa'lario/ *m*, salary
salaz /sa'laθ; sa'las/ *a* lewd, lecherous
salazón /sala'θon; sala'son/ *f*, salting, curing; salt meat or fish trade
salazonero /salaθo'nero; salaso'nero/ *a* salting, curing
salchicha /sal'tʃitʃa/ *f*, sausage
salchichería /saltʃitʃe'ria/ *f*, sausage shop
salchichero /saltʃi'tʃero/ **(-ra)** *n* sausage maker, sausage seller
salchichón /saltʃi'tʃon/ *m*, *Cul.* salami, kind of sausage
saldar /sal'dar/ *vt Com.* to settle, pay in full; sell out cheap; balance
saldista /sal'dista/ *mf* remnant buyer
saldo /'saldo/ *m*, *Com.* balance; closing of an account; bargain sale. **s. acreedor,** credit balance. **s. deudor,** debit balance. **s. líquido,** net balance
salero /sa'lero/ *m*, saltshaker, saltcellar; salt storage warehouse; *Inf.* wit
saleta /sa'leta/ *f*, *dim* small hall; royal antechamber; court of appeal
salida /sa'liða/ *f*, going out; leaving; departure; sailing; exit, way out; projection, protrusion; *Fig.* escape, way out; outcome, result; witty remark; *Mil.* sally; *Com.* outlay, expense; *Com.* opening, sale, salability; environs, outskirts. **s. de dólares,** dollar drain. **s. de tono,** *Inf.* an impertinent remark. **dar s.,** *Com.* to enter on the credit side
salidero /sali'ðero/ *a* fond of going out; *m*, exit, way out
salidizo /sali'ðiθo; sali'ðiso/ *m*, *Archit.* projection —*a* projecting
saliente /sa'liente/ *a* outgoing; salient, projecting. *m*, east; projection; salient. **s. continental,** continental shelf
salina /sa'lina/ *f*, salt mine; saltworks
salinero /sali'nero/ *m*, salt merchant; salter; salt worker
salino /sa'lino/ *a* saline. *m*, *Med.* saline
salir /salir/ *vi irr* to go out; depart, leave; succeed in getting out; escape; appear (of the sun, etc.); sprout, show green; fade, come out (of stains); project, stand out; grow, develop; turn out, result; happen, take place; cost; sail; end (of seasons, time); lead off, start (some games); be published (books); do (well or badly), succeed or fail; appear, show oneself; be drawn, win (lottery tickets); balance, come out right (accounts); be elected; become; give up (posts); lead to (of streets, etc.); *Naut.* overtake; (*with prep a*) guarantee, be surety for; resemble, be like; (*with con*) utter, come out with; commit, do inopportunely; succeed in, achieve (e.g. *Salió con la suya,* He got his own way); (*with de*) originate in; break away from (traditions, conventions); get rid of; (*with por*) stand up for, protect; go surety for, guarantee —*vr* leak; boil over; overflow; (*with con*) achieve, get; (*with de*) *Fig.* break away from. *Theat.* **s. a la escena,** to enter, come on to the stage. **s. de,** to recover from (an illness). **no acabar de s. de,** to not be completely recovered from. **s. del apuro,** to get out of trouble. **s. de estampía,** to stampede (of animals). **s. pitando,** *Inf.* to get out in a hurry. **Esta idea no salió de Juan,** This wasn't John's idea. **salga lo que saliere,** *Inf.* come what may... —*Pres. Indic.* **salgo, sales,** etc —*Fut.* **saldré,** etc —*Condit.* **saldría,** etc —*Pres. Subjunc.* **salga,** etc.
salitral /sali'tral/ *a* nitrous. *m*, saltpeter bed
salitre /sa'litre/ *m*, saltpeter
salitrería /salitre'ria/ *f*, saltpeter works
salitrero /sali'trero/ *n* saltpeter worker or dealer

saliva /sa'liβa/ *f*, saliva. *Inf.* **tragar s.,** to put up with; be unable to speak through emotion
salivación /saliβa'θion; saliβa'sion/ *f*, salivation
salival /sali'βal/ *a* salivary
salivar /sali'βar/ *vi* to salivate; spit
sallar /sa'ʎar; sa'yar/ *vt* to weed
salmantino /salman'tino/ **(-na)** *a* and *n* Salamanca
salmear /salme'ar/ *vi* to intone psalms
salmista /sal'mista/ *mf* psalmist; psalmodist, psalm chanter
salmo /'salmo/ *m*, psalm
salmodia /sal'moðia/ *f*, psalmody; *Inf.* drone; psalter
salmodiar /salmo'ðiar/ *vi* to chant psalms; —*vt* drone
salmón /sal'mon/ *m*, salmon
salmonado /salmo'naðo/ *a* salmon-like
salmonera /salmo'nera/ *f*, salmon net
salmonete /salmo'nete/ *m*, red mullet
salmuera /sal'muera/ *f*, brine
salobre /sa'loβre/ *a* salt, salty; brackish
salobridad /saloβri'ðað/ *f*, saltiness
salomar /salo'mar/ *vi Naut.* to sing chanteys
salón /sa'lon/ *m*, drawing room; large room or hall; reception room; salon, reception, social gathering. **s. de muestras,** showroom
saloncillo /salon'θiʎo; salon'siyo/ *m*, *dim* small room; *Theat.* greenroom; rest room
salpicadura /salpika'ðura/ *f*, sprinkling, spattering, splashing
salpicar /salpi'kar/ *vt* to sprinkle, scatter; bespatter, splash
salpicón /salpi'kon/ *m*, *Cul.* kind of salmagundi; *Inf.* hodgepodge; spattering
salpimentar /salpimen'tar/ *vt irr* to season with pepper and salt; sprinkle; *Fig.* leaven, enliven (a speech, etc.). See **regimentar**
salpresar /salpre'sar/ *vt* to preserve in salt, salt
salpullido /salpu'ʎiðo; salpu'yiðo/ *m*, rash, skin eruption
salsa /'salsa/ *f*, sauce; gravy. **s. mahonesa** *or* **s. mayonesa,** mayonnaise sauce. **s. mayordoma,** sauce maître d'hôtel
salsera /sal'sera/ *f*, sauce boat, gravy boat
saltabanco /salta'βanko/ *m*, mountebank; street entertainer, juggler
saltabarrancos /saltaβa'rrankos/ *mf Inf.* madcap, harum-scarum
saltable /sal'taβle/ *a* jumpable
saltadero /salta'ðero/ *m*, jumping ground; fountain, jet
saltador /salta'ðor/ **(-ra)** *a* jumping —*n* jumper; acrobat. *m*, jump rope, skip rope
saltamontes /salta'montes/ *m*, grasshopper
saltaojos /salta'ohos/ *m*, peony
saltaparedes /saltapa'reðes/ *mf Inf.* madcap, romp
saltar /sal'tar/ *vi* to jump, leap, spring; prance; frisk, gambol; rebound; blow up; burst, break asunder; pop (of corks); fly off, come off (buttons, etc.); gush out, shoot up (liquids); break apart, be shattered; be obvious, stand out; come to mind, suggest itself; show anger; *Fig.* let slip, come out with (remarks); —*vt* leap or jump over; poke out (eyes); cover (the female); omit, pass over; blow up, explode. **s. a la cuerda,** to jump rope, play with a skip rope. **s. a la vista,** to be obvious, leap to the eye. **s. diciendo,** *Inf.* to come out with, say
saltarín /salta'rin/ **(-ina)** *a* dancing —*n* dancer
saltatriz /salta'triθ; salta'tris/ *f*, ballet dancer, female acrobat
saltatumbas /salta'tumbas/ *m*, (*Inf.* contemptuous) cleric who makes his living off funerals
salteador /saltea'ðor/ *m*, highwayman
salteamiento /saltea'miento/ *m*, highway robbery, holdup; assault, attack
saltear /salte'ar/ *vt* to hold up and rob; assault, attack; jump from one thing to another, do intermittently; forestall; surprise, amaze
salterio /sal'terio/ *m*, psaltery
saltimbanco, saltimbanqui /saltim'βanko, saltim'βanki/ *m*, *Inf.*. See **saltabanco**
salto /'salto/ *m*, jump, leap, bound; leapfrog (game); precipice, ravine; waterfall; assault; important promotion; omission (of words). **s. de agua,** waterfall. **s. de cama,** peignoir, bathrobe. **s. de campana,** overturning. *Inf.* **s. de mal año,** sudden improvement in circumstances. **s. de mata,** flight, escape. **s. mortal,** leap of death; somersault. **s. de pie,** spillway. **dar un s.,** to leap. **en un s.,** at one jump; swiftly
saltón /sal'ton/ *a* jumping, leaping; prominent (teeth, eyes). *m*, grasshopper
salubérrimo /salu'βerrimo/ *a superl* **salubre** most healthy
salubre /sa'luβre/ *a* salubrious, healthful
salubridad /saluβri'ðað/ *f*, healthfulness
salud /sa'luð/ *f*, health; salvation; welfare, well-being; *Eccl.* state of grace; *pl* civilities, greetings. **¡S. y pesetas!** Here's to your good health and prosperity! (on drinking). **gastar s.,** to enjoy good health. *Inf.* **vender** (*or* **verter**) **s.,** to look full of health
saludable /salu'ðaβle/ *a* healthy, wholesome
saludador /saluða'ðor/ **(-ra)** *a* greeting, saluting —*n* greeter. *m*, charlatan, quack
saludar /salu'ðar/ *vt* to greet, salute; hail (as king, etc.); send greetings to; bow; *Mil.* fire a salute
saludo /sa'luðo/ *m*, greeting, salutation; bow; (*Mil. Nav.*) salute
salutación /saluta'θion, saluta'sion/ *f*, greeting, salutation; Ave Maria
salutífero /salu'tifero/ *a* salubrious
salva /'salβa/ *f*, salutation, greeting; (*Mil. Nav.*) salvo, volley; salute (of guns); salver; ordeal (to establish innocence); solemn assurance, oath; sampling, tasting (of food, drink). **s. de veintiún cañonazos,** twenty-one–gun salute
salvación /salβa'θion; salβa'sion/ *f*, liberation, deliverance; salvation
salvado /sal'βaðo/ *m*, bran
salvador /salβa'ðor/ **(-ra)** *a* saving, redeeming —*n* deliverer. *m*, redeemer
salvadoreño /salβaðore'ɲo/ **(-ña)** *a* and *n* Salvadorean
salvaguardia /salβa'guarðia/ *m*, guard, watch. *f*, safeguard; protection, defense; safe conduct, passport
salvajada /salβa'haða/ *f*, savagery, brutal action
salvaje /sal'βahe/ *a* wild (plants, animals); rough, uncultivated; uncultured, uncivilized. *mf* savage
salvajismo /salβa'hismo/ *m*, savagery
salvamano, a /salβa'mano, a/ *adv* safely
salvamente /salβa'mente/ *adv* safely, securely
salvamento /salβa'mento/ *m*, salvation; deliverance, security, safety; place of safety; salvage
salvante /sal'βante/ *adv Inf.* except, save
salvar /sal'βar/ *vt* to save; *Eccl.* redeem; avoid (difficulty, danger); exclude, except; leap, jump; pass over, clear; *Law.* prove innocent; *Naut.* salve. **s. la diferencia,** to bridge the gap —*vi* taste, sample (food, drink); —*vr* be saved from danger; *Eccl.* be redeemed
salvavidas /salβa'βiðas/ *m*, life belt; safety belt; life preserver; traffic island
¡salve! /'salβe/ *interj Poet.* hail!; Hail Mary, Salve Regina
salvedad /salβe'ðað/ *f*, qualification, reservation
salvia /'salβia/ *f*, *Bot.* sage
salvilla /sal'βiʎa; sal'βiya/ *f*, salver
salvo /'salβo/ *a* safe, unharmed; excepting, omitting —*adv* except. **a s.,** safely, without harm. **a su s.,** to his (her, their) satisfaction; at his (her, etc.) pleasure. **dejar a s.,** to exclude, leave aside. **en s.,** in safety
salvoconducto /salβokon'dukto/ *m*, safe conduct, pass
samarita /sama'rita/ *a* and *mf* **samaritano** (**-na**) *a* and *n* Samaritan
sambenito /sambe'nito/ *m*, penitent's gown (Inquisition); disgrace, dishonor
Samotracia /samo'traθia; samo'trasia/ Samothrace
samotracio /samo'traθio; samo'trasio/ **(-ia)** *a* and *n* Samothracian
samoyedo /samo'yeðo/ **(-da)** *n* Samoyed
san /san/ *a Abbr.* of **santo.** Used before masculine singular names of saints except **Santos Tomás** (*or* **Tomé**)**, Domingo, Toribio**
sanable /sa'naβle/ *a* curable
sanador /sana'ðor/ **(-ra)** *a* healing, curing —*n* healer

sanalotodo /sanalo'toðo/ *m, Inf.* cure-all, universal remedy
sanar /sa'nar/ *vt* to cure, heal; *—vi* recover, get well; heal
sanatorio /sana'torio/ *m,* sanatorium; convalescent home
sanchopancesco /santʃopan'θesko; santʃopan'sesko/ *a* like or pertaining to Sancho Panza
sanción /san'θion; san'sion/ *f,* authorization, consent; sanction; penalty
sancionable /sanθio'naβle; sansio'naβle/ *a* sanctionable
sancionar /sanθio'nar; sansio'nar/ *vt* to authorize, approve; sanction
sancochar /sanko'tʃar/ *vt Cul.* to parboil, half-cook
sandalia /san'dalia/ *f,* sandal
sándalo /'sandalo/ *m,* sandalwood
sandez /san'deθ; san'des/ *f,* foolishness, stupidity; folly
sandía /san'dia/ *f,* watermelon
sandio /'sandio/ *a* foolish, inane
sandunga /san'duŋga/ *f, Inf.* attractiveness, winsomeness, grace
sandunguero /sanduŋ'guero/ *a Inf.* attractive, appealing, winsome
saneado /sane'aðo/ *a* unencumbered, nontaxable, free
saneamiento /sanea'miento/ *m,* guarantee, security; indemnity; stabilization (of currency); drainage
sanear /sane'ar/ *vt Com.* to guarantee, secure; indemnify; stabilize (currency); drain (land, etc.)
Sanedrín /sane'ðrin/ *m,* Sanhedrin
sangradera /saŋgra'ðera/ *f,* lancet; channel, sluice, drain
sangrador /saŋgra'ðor/ *m,* phlebotomist; outlet, drainage
sangradura /saŋgra'ðura/ *f,* inner bend of the arm; *Surg.* bleeding; draining off
sangrar /saŋ'grar/ *vt Surg.* to bleed; drain off; *Inf.* extort money, bleed; *Print.* indent; draw off resin (from pines, etc.); *—vi* bleed; *—vr* bleed; have oneself bled; run (of colors)
sangre /'saŋgre/ *f,* blood; lineage, family. **s. fría,** sang-froid. **a s. fría,** in cold blood, premeditated. **a s. y fuego,** by fire and sword, without quarter. *Inf.* **bullir la s.,** to have youthful blood in one's veins. **llevar en la s.,** *Fig.* to be in the blood. **subírsele la s. a la cabeza,** to grow excited. *Fig. Inf.* **tener s. de horchata,** to have milk and water in one's veins
sangría /saŋ'gria/ *f, Surg.* bloodletting; resin cut (on pines, etc.)
sangriento /saŋ'griento/ *a* bloody, bloodstained; bloodthirsty, cruel; mortal (insults, etc.); *Poet.* blood-colored
sangüesa /saŋ'guesa/ *f,* raspberry
sanguijuela /saŋgi'huela/ *f,* leech; *Fig. Inf.* sponger
sanguina /saŋ'gina/ *f,* red crayon drawing, sanguine
sanguinaria /saŋgi'naria/ *f,* bloodstone
sanguinario /saŋgi'nario/ *a* vengeful, bloody, cruel
sanguíneo /saŋ'gineo/ *a* blood; sanguineous; sanguine, fresh-complexioned; blood-colored
sanguinolento /saŋgino'lento/ *a.* See **sangriento**
sanidad /sani'ðað/ *f,* safety, security; healthiness; health department. **s. interior,** Public Health. **S. militar,** army medical corps
sanitario /sani'tario/ *a* sanitary, hygienic. *m, Mil.* medical officer
sano /'sano/ *a* healthy; safe, secure; healthful, wholesome; unhurt, unharmed; upright, honest; sincere; *Inf.* entire, undamaged; sane. **s. y salvo,** safe and sound. *Inf.* **cortar por lo s.,** to cut one's losses
sánscrito /'sanskrito/ *a* and *m,* Sanscrit
santa /'santa/ *f,* female saint
santabárbara /santa'βarβara/ *f, Nav.* magazine
santamente /santa'mente/ *adv* in a saintly manner; simply
santero /san'tero/ **(-ra)** *a* given to image worship *—n* accomplice (of a burglar); caretaker (of a hermitage); beggar
¡Santiago! /san'tiago/ *interj* St. James! (Spanish war cry). *m,* attack, assault
santiamén /santia'men/ *m, Inf.* trice, twinkling
santidad /santi'ðað/ *f,* sanctity; saintliness; godliness. **Su S.,** His Holiness
santificación /santifika'θion; santifika'sion/ *f,* sanctification
santificador /santifika'ðor/ **(-ra)** *a* sanctifying *—n* sanctifier
santificar /santifi'kar/ *vt* to sanctify, make holy; consecrate; dedicate; keep (feast days)
santiguada /santi'guaða/ *f,* crossing oneself; rough treatment, harsh reproof
santiguar /santi'guar/ *vt* to make the sign of the cross over; *Inf.* beat, rain blows on; *—vr* cross oneself; *Inf.* be dumbfounded
santísimo /san'tisimo/ *a superl* most saintly, most holy
santo /'santo/ *a* holy; saintly; saint (see **san**); consecrated; inviolate, sacred; *Inf.* simple, sincere, ingenuous. *m,* saint; image of a saint; saint's day, name day (of a person); *Mil.* password. **Santa Hermandad,** Holy Brotherhood (former name of the Spanish rural police force). **S. Oficio,** Holy Office, Inquisition. **S. y bueno,** Well and good, All right! *Inf.* **alzarse con el s. y la limosna,** to take the lot, make off with everything. **llegar y besar el s.,** to do in a trice. *Inf.* **No es s. de mi devoción,** I'm not very keen on him. *Inf.* **todo el s. día,** the whole blessed day
santón /san'ton/ *m,* dervish, santon. *Inf.* hypocrite, sham saint
santoral /santo'ral/ *m,* book of saints; calendar of saints; choir book
santuario /san'tuario/ *m,* sanctuary
santurrón /santu'rron/ **(-ona)** *a* sanctimonious; hypocritical; prudish *—n* hypocrite
santurronería /santurrone'ria/ *f,* sanctimoniousness
saña /'saɲa/ *f,* fury, blind rage; lust for revenge, cruelty
sañoso, sañudo /sa'ɲoso, sa'ɲuðo/ *a* furious, blind with rage; cruel
sapidez /sapi'ðeθ; sapi'ðes/ *f,* flavor, sapidity
sápido /'sapiðo/ *a* tasty, savory
sapiencia /sa'pienθia; sa'piensia/ *f,* wisdom; knowledge; erudition
sapino /sa'pino/ *m,* fir (tree)
sapo /'sapo/ *m,* toad
saque /'sake/ *m, Sports.* serve, service; service or bowling line; *Sports.* server; *Sports.* bowler; bowling (in cricket)
saqueador /sakea'ðor/ **(-ra)** *a* looting, pillaging *—n* pillager, plunderer
saquear /sake'ar/ *vt* to pillage, plunder, sack
saqueo /sa'keo/ *m,* plundering, pillage, sacking
saquilada /saki'laða/ *f,* small sackful (especially of grain)
sarampión /saram'pion/ *m,* measles
sarao /sa'rao/ *m,* soirée, evening party
sarasa /sa'rasa/ *m,* (*Inf.* and contemptuous) pansy, faggot
sarcasmo /sar'kasmo/ *m,* sarcasm
sarcástico /sar'kastiko/ *a* sarcastic
sarcia /'sarθia; 'sarsia/ *f,* load, cargo
sarcófago /sar'kofago/ *m,* sarcophagus
sarda /'sarða/ *f,* mackerel
sardana /sar'ðana/ *f,* traditional Catalonian dance
sardina /sar'ðina/ *f,* sardine. **s. arenque,** herring. **como sardinas en banasta,** *Fig.* packed like sardines
sardinal /sarði'nal/ *m,* sardine net
sardinero /sarði'nero/ **(-ra)** *a* sardine *—n* sardine seller or dealer. *m,* famous district of Santander
sardineta /sarði'neta/ *f,* sprat; small sardine; *Mil.* chevron
sardo /'sarðo/ **(-da)** *a* and *n* Sardinian
sardónico /sar'ðoniko/ *a* sardonic
sarga /'sarga/ *f,* (silk) serge; willow
sargenta /sar'henta/ *f,* sergeant's wife; *Inf.* mannish, overbearing woman
sargentear /sarhente'ar/ *vt* to be in charge as a sergeant; command, captain; *Inf.* boss
sargento /sar'hento/ *m,* sergeant
sarmentoso /sarmen'toso/ *a* vine-like; twining
sarmiento /sar'miento/ *m,* vine shoot

sarna /'sarna/ *f*, scabies. **s. perruna,** mange. **más viejo que la s.,** *Inf.* older than the plague
sarnoso /sar'noso/ *a* itchy; mangy
sarraceno /sarra'θeno; sarra'seno/ **(-na)** *a* Saracen —*n* Saracen; Moor
sarracina /sarra'θina; sarra'sina/ *f*, scuffle
sarrillo /sa'rriʎo; sa'rriyo/ *m*, death rattle, rale; arum lily
sarro /'sarro/ *m*, furry encrustation, scale; film; tartar (on teeth)
sarta /'sarta/ *f*, string, link (of pearls, etc.); file, line
sartén /sar'ten/ *f*, frying pan. **tener la s. por el mango,** *Inf.* to be top dog
sastra /'sastra/ *f*, female tailor; tailor's wife
sastre /'sastre/ *m*, tailor. **ser buen s.,** *Inf.* to be an expert (in)
sastrería /sastre'ria/ *f*, tailoring; tailor's shop
Satanás /sata'nas/ *m*, Satan; devil
satánico /sa'taniko/ *a* satanic
satélite /sa'telite/ *m*, satellite; follower, admirer, sycophant
satén /sa'ten/ *m*, sateen
satinar /sati'nar/ *vt* to calender; glaze; satin (paper)
sátira /'satira/ *f*, satire
satírico /sa'tiriko/ *a* satiric
satirizar /satiri'θar; satiri'sar/ *vi* to write satires; —*vt* satirize
sátiro /'satiro/ *m*, satyr; *Theat.* indecent play
satisfacción /satisfak'θion; satisfak'sion/ *f*, settlement, payment; atonement, expiation; satisfaction; gratification; amends; complacency, conceit; contentment; apology. **tomar s.,** to avenge oneself
satisfacer /satisfa'θer; satisfa'ser/ *vt irr* to pay, settle; atone for, expiate; gratify; quench; fulfill, observe; compensate, indemnify; discharge, meet; convince, persuade; allay, relieve; reward; explain; answer, satisfy; —*vr* avenge oneself; satisfy oneself —*Pres. Indic.* **satisfago, satisfaces,** etc —*Fut.* **satisfaré,** etc —*Condit.* **satisfaría,** etc —*Preterite* **satisfice,** etc —*Past Part.* **satisfecho.** *Pres. Subjunc.* **satisfaga,** etc —*Imperf. Subjunc.* **satisficiese,** etc.
satisfactorio /satisfak'torio/ *a* satisfactory
satisfecho /satis'fetʃo/ *a* self-satisfied, complacent; happy, contented
sátrapa /'satrapa/ *m*, satrap; *Inf.* cunning fellow
saturación /satura'θion; satura'sion/ *f*, saturation
saturar /satu'rar/ *vt* to satiate, fill; saturate
saturnino /satur'nino/ *a* saturnine, melancholy, morose
saturnismo /satur'nismo/ *m*, saturnism, lead poisoning
Saturno /sa'turno/ *m*, Saturn
sauce /'sauθe; 'sause/ *m*, willow. **s. llorón,** weeping willow
saúco /sa'uko/ *m*, elder tree
saurio /'saurio/ *a* and *m*, saurian
savia /'saβia/ *f*, sap; energy, zest
sáxeo /'sakseo/ *a* stone, stony
saxófono /sak'sofono/ *or* **saxofón** *m*, saxophone
saya /'saya/ *f*, skirt; long tunic
sayal /sa'yal/ *m*, thick woolen material
sayo /'sayo/ *m*, loose smock; *Inf.* any garment. **cortar un s.** (**a**), *Inf.* to gossip behind a person's back
sayón /sa'yon/ *m*, executioner; *Inf.* hideous-looking man
sazón /sa'θon; sa'son/ *f*, ripeness, maturity; season; perfection, excellence; opportunity; taste, flavor; seasoning. **a la s.,** at that time, then. **en s.,** in season; opportunely
sazonador /saθona'ðor; sasona'ðor/ **(-ra)** *a* seasoning —*n* seasoner
sazonar /saθo'nar; saso'nar/ *vt Cul.* to season; mature; —*vr* mature, ripen
se /se/ *object pron reflexive 3rd sing* and *pl mf* 1. Used as accusative (direct object) himself, herself, yourself, themselves, yourselves (e.g. *Juan se ha cortado,* John has cut himself). 2. Used as dative or indirect object to himself, at himself, herself, themselves, etc. (e.g. *María se mira al espejo,* Mary looks at herself in the mirror). Reciprocity is also expressed by reflexive (e.g. *No se hablan,* They do not speak to one another). When a direct object pron. (accusative) and an indirect object pron., both in the 3rd pers. (sing. or pl.), are used together, the indirect object pron. becomes **se** (instead of **le** or **les**) (e.g. *Se lo doy,* I give it to him). Many Spanish reflexive verbs have English equivalents that are not reflexive (e.g. *desayunarse,* to breakfast, *arrepentirse,* to repent, *quejarse,* to complain). Some intransitive (neuter) verbs have a modified meaning when used reflexively (e.g. *marcharse,* to go away, *dormirse,* to fall asleep). The passive may be formed by using **se** + 3rd pers. sing. of verb (e.g. *se dice,* it is said, people say). A number of impersonal phrases are also formed in this way (e.g. *«Se alquila,»* "To Let," *«Se vende,»* "For Sale"). The imperative is used in the same way (e.g. *Véase la página dos,* See page two)
sebáceo /se'βaθeo; se'βaseo/ *a* sebaceous
sebo /'seβo/ *m*, tallow; candle grease; fat, grease
seboso /se'βoso/ *a* tallowy; fat, greasy
seca /'seka/ *f*, drought; *Naut.* unsubmerged sandbank
secadero /seka'ðero/ *m*, drying place, drying room
secadora /seka'ðora/ *f*, dryer, drying machine, clothesdryer. **s. de cabello,** hairdryer
secafirmas /seka'firmas/ *m*, blotting pad
secamente /seka'mente/ *adv* tersely, brusquely, curtly; dryly
secamiento /seka'miento/ *m*, drying
secano /se'kano/ *m*, nonirrigated land; *Naut.* unsubmerged sandbank; anything very dry
secante /se'kante/ *a* drying —*a* and *f*, *Geom.* secant. **papel s.,** blotting paper
secar /se'kar/ *vt* to dry; desiccate; annoy, bore; —*vr* dry; dry up (of streams, etc.); wilt, fade (of plants); become parched; grow thin, become emaciated; be very thirsty; become hard-hearted
sección /sek'θion; sek'sion/ *f*, act of cutting; section, part, portion; *Geom. Mil.* section. **s. cónica,** conic section. **s. de amenidades,** entertainment section (of a newspaper). **s. de reserva,** *Mil.* reserve list
seccionar /sekθio'nar; seksio'nar/ *vt* to divide into sections, section
seccionario /sekθio'nario; seksio'nario/ *a* sectional
secesión /seθe'sion; sese'sion/ *f*, secession
secesionista /seθesio'nista; sesesio'nista/ *a* and *mf* secessionist
seco /'seko/ *a* dry; dried up, parched; faded, wilted; dead (plants); dried (fruits); thin, emaciated; unadorned; barren, arid; brusque, curt; severe, strict; indifferent, unenthusiastic; sharp (sounds); dry (wines). **a secas,** only; solely; simply, just. **en s.,** on dry land; curtly. *Inf.* **dejar s.** (**a**), to dumbfound, petrify
secreción /sekre'θion; sekre'sion/ *f*, segregation, separation; *Med.* secretion
secreta /se'kreta/ *f*, *Law.* secret trial or investigation; *Eccl.* secret(s); toilet, water closet
secretar /sekre'tar/ *vt Med.* to secrete
secretaría /sekreta'ria/ *f*, secretaryship; secretary's office, secretariat
secretario /sekre'tario/ **(-ia)** *n* secretary; amanuensis, clerk. *m*, actuary; registrar. **s. de asuntos exteriores** *or* **s. de asuntos extranjeros,** foreign secretary. **s. particular,** private secretary
secretear /sekrete'ar/ *vi Inf.* to whisper, have secrets
secreteo /sekre'teo/ *m*, *Inf.* whispering, exchanging of secrets
secreto /se'kreto/ *m*, secret; secrecy, silence; confidential information; mystery; secret drawer —*a* secret; private, confidential. **en s.,** in secret, confidentially. **s. a voces,** open secret
secta /'sekta/ *f*, sect
sectario /sek'tario/ **(-ia)** *a* and *n* sectarian —*n* fanatical believer
sectarismo /sekta'rismo/ *m*, sectarianism
sector /sek'tor/ *m*, sector
secuaz /se'kuaθ; se'kuas/ *mf* follower, disciple
secuela /se'kuela/ *f*, sequel, result
secuencia /se'kuenθia; se'kuensia/ *f*, *Eccl.* sequence; (cinema) sequence
secuestrador /sekuestra'ðor/ **(-ra)** *a* sequestrating —*n* sequestrator
secuestrar /sekues'trar/ *vt* to sequester; kidnap

secuestro /se'kuestro/ *m,* sequestration; kidnapping; *Surg.* sequestrum
secular /seku'lar/ *a* secular, lay; centennial; age-old, ancient; *Eccl.* secular
secularización /sekulariθa'θion; sekularisa'sion/ *f,* secularization
secularizar /sekulari'θar; sekulari'sar/ *vt* to secularize; —*vr* become secularized
secundar /sekun'dar/ *vt* to second, aid
secundario /sekun'dario/ *a* secondary; accessory, subordinate; *Geol.* mesozoic
sed /seð/ *f,* thirst; desire, yearning, appetite. **apagar** (*or* **matar) la s.,** to quench one's thirst. **tener s.,** to be thirsty
seda /'seða/ *f,* silk; bristle (boar, etc.). **s. cordelada,** twist silk. **s. ocal,** floss silk. **s. vegetal** *or* **s. artificial,** artificial silk. *Inf.* **como una s.,** as smooth as silk; sweet-tempered; achieved without any trouble
sedación /seða'θion; seða'sion/ *f,* calming, soothing
sedal /se'ðal/ *m,* fish line
sedar /se'ðar/ *vt* to soothe, calm
sedativo /seða'tiβo/ *a* and *m, Med.* sedative
sede /'seðe/ *f, Eccl.* see; bishop's throne; *Fig.* seat (of government, etc.); Holy See (also **Santa S.**)
sedentario /seðen'tario/ *a* sedentary
sedeño /se'ðeɲo/ *a* silky; silken, made of silk
sedería /seðe'ria/ *f,* silk goods; silks; silk shop
sedero /se'ðero/ **(-ra)** *a* silk —*n* silk weaver or worker; silk merchant
sedición /seði'θion; seði'sion/ *f,* sedition
sedicioso /seði'θioso; seði'sioso/ *a* seditious
sediento /se'ðiento/ *a* thirsty; parched, dry (land); eager (for), desirous (of)
sedimentación /seðimenta'θion; seðimenta'sion/ *f,* sedimentation
sedimentar /seðimen'tar/ *vt* to leave a sediment; —*vr* settle, form a sediment
sedimento /seði'mento/ *m,* sediment; dregs, lees; scale (on boilers)
sedoso /se'ðoso/ *a* silky, silk-like
seducción /seðuk'θion; seðuk'sion/ *f,* seduction; temptation, blandishment, wile; charm, allurement
seducir /seðu'θir; seðu'sir/ *vt irr* to seduce; tempt, lead astray; charm, attract; corrupt, bribe. See **conducir**
seductivo /seðuk'tiβo/ *a* tempting; seductive, charming
seductor /seðuk'tor/ **(-ra)** *a* tempting; charming —*n* seducer; charming person
sefardí /seˤar'ði/ *mf* Iberian Jew or Jewess; *pl* Sephardim —*a* Sephardic
segadera /sega'ðera/ *f,* sickle
segadero /sega'ðero/ *a* reapable, able to be reaped
segador /sega'ðor/ *m,* reaper, harvester
segadora /sega'ðora/ *f,* mowing machine, harvester; woman harvester
segar /se'gar/ *vt irr* to scythe, cut down; reap, harvest; mow. See **cegar**
seglar /seg'lar/ *a* secular, lay. *mf* layman
segmento /seg'mento/ *m,* segment; *Geom.* segment. **s. de émbolo,** piston ring
segoviano /sego'βiano/ **(-na)** *a* and *n* Segovian
segregación /segrega'θion; segrega'sion/ *f,* segregation
segregar /segre'gar/ *vt* to segregate, separate; *Med.* secrete
seguida /se'giða/ *f,* continuation, prolongation. **de s.,** continuously; immediately. **en s.,** at once, immediately
seguidamente /segiða'mente/ *adv* continuously; immediately
seguidilla /segi'ðiʎa; segi'ðiya/ *f,* popular Spanish tune and dance and verse sung to them; *Inf.* diarrhea
seguido /se'giðo/ *a* continuous, successive; direct, straight
seguidor /segi'ðor/ **(-ra)** *a* following —*n* follower, disciple
seguimiento /segi'miento/ *m,* following, pursuit; continuation, resumption
seguir /se'gir/ *vt irr* to follow; go after, pursue; prosecute, execute; continue, go on; accompany, go with; exercise (a profession); subscribe to, believe in; agree with; persecute; pester, annoy; imitate; *Law.* institute (a suit); handle, manage; —*vr* result, follow as a consequence; follow in order, happen by turn; originate —*Pres. Part.* **siguiendo.** *Pres. Indic.* **sigo, sigues, sigue, siguen.** *Pres. Subjunc.* **siga,** etc —*Imperf. Subjunc.* **siguiese**
según /se'gun/ *adv* according to; as. **s. parece,** as it seems. **s. y como,** as, according to
segunda /se'gunda/ *f, Mus.* second
segundar /segun'dar/ *vt* to repeat, do again; —*vi* be second, follow the first
segundero /segun'dero/ *a Agr.* of the second flowering or fruiting. *m,* second hand (of a watch)
segundo /se'gundo/ *a* second. *m,* second in command, deputy head; *Astron. Geom.* second. **segunda intención,** double meaning. **segunda velocidad,** *Auto.* second gear. **de segunda mano,** second-hand. **sin s.,** without peer or equal
segundogénito /segundo'henito/ **(-ta)** *a* and *n* secondborn
segundón /segun'don/ *m,* second son; any son but the eldest
segurador /segura'ðor/ *m,* surety, security (person)
seguramente /segura'mente/ *adv* securely, safely; surely, of course, naturally
seguridad /seguri'ðað/ *f,* security; safety; certainty; trustworthiness; *Com.* surety. **con toda s.,** with complete safety, surely, absolutely. **de s.,** *a* safety
seguro /se'guro/ *a* secure; safe; certain, sure; firm, fixed; reliable, trustworthy; unfailing. *m,* certainty; haven, place of safety; *Com.* insurance; permit; *Mech.* ratchet. **s. contra incendio, accidentes, robo,** fire, accident, burglary insurance. **s. sobre la vida,** life insurance. **de s.,** surely, certainly. **en s.,** in safety
seis /seis/ *a* six; sixth. *m,* six; sixth (of the month); playing card or domino with six spots. **Son las s.,** It is six o'clock
seiscientos /seis'θientos; seis'sientos/ *a* six hundred; six-hundredth. *m,* six hundred
selección /selek'θion; selek'sion/ *f,* selection, choice. **s. natural,** natural selection
seleccionar /selekθio'nar; seleksio'nar/ *vt* to select, choose
selectivo /selek'tiβo/ *a* selective
selecto /se'lekto/ *a* choice, select, excellent
sellador /seʎa'ðor; seya'ðor/ **(-ra)** *a* sealing, stamping —*n* sealer, stamper
selladura /seʎa'ðura; seya'ðura/ *f,* sealing, stamping
sellar /se'ʎar; se'yar/ *vt* to seal; stamp; end, conclude; close
sello /'seʎo; 'seyo/ *m,* seal; stamp. **s. fiscal,** stamp duty. **s. postal,** postage stamp
selva /'selβa/ *f,* forest, wood; jungle
Selva Negra, la /'selβa 'negra, la/ the Black Forest
selvático /sel'βatiko/ *a* sylvan, wood, forest; wild
selvoso /sel'βoso/ *a* wooded, sylvan
semafórico /sema'foriko/ *a* semaphoric
semáforo /se'maforo/ *m,* semaphore, traffic light.
semana /se'mana/ *f,* week; week's salary. **S. Mayor** *or* **S. Santa,** Holy Week. **entre s.,** during the week, on weekdays; weekdays
semanal /sema'nal/ *a* weekly; of a week's duration
semanario /sema'nario/ *a* weekly. *m,* weekly periodical
semanero /sema'nero/ *a* employed by the week
semántica /se'mantika/ *f,* semantics
semántico /se'mantiko/ *a* semantic
semblante /sem'βlante/ *m,* facial expression, countenance; face; appearance, look, aspect. **componer el s.,** to pull oneself together, straighten one's face. **mudar de s.,** to change color, change one's expression; alter (of circumstances)
semblanza /sem'βlanθa; sem'βlansa/ *f,* biographical sketch. **s. literaria,** short literary biography
sembradera /sembra'ðera/ *f,* sowing machine
sembradío /sembra'ðio/ *a Agr.* ready for sowing
sembrado /sem'βraðo/ *m,* sown land
sembrador /sembra'ðor/ **(-ra)** *a* sowing —*n* sower
sembradura /sembra'ðura/ *f, Agr.* sowing
sembrar /sem'βrar/ *vt irr Agr.* to sow; scatter, sprinkle; spread, disseminate. See **sentar**

semeja /se'meha/ *f,* resemblance, similarity; indication, sign (gen. *pl*)
semejante /seme'hante/ *a* like, similar; such a; *Math.* similar. *m,* similarity, imitation. *mf* fellow man
semejanza /seme'hanθa; seme'hansa/ *f,* similarity, likeness. **a s. de,** in the likeness of; like
semejar /seme'har/ **(se)** *vi* and *vr* to resemble
semen /'semen/ *m,* semen; *Bot.* seed
semental /semen'tal/ *a Agr.* seed; breeding (of male animals). *m,* stallion
sementar /semen'tar/ *vt Agr.* to sow
sementera /semen'tera/ *f, Agr.* sowing; sown land; seedbed; seedtime; *Fig.* hotbed, nursery, genesis
sementero /semen'tero/ *m,* seed bag; seed bed
semestral /semes'tral/ *a* biannual, half-yearly; lasting six months
semestre /se'mestre/ *a* biannual. *m,* half-year, period of six months; six months' salary; semester
semicircular /semiθirku'lar; semisirku'lar/ *a* semicircular
semicírculo /semi'θirkulo; semi'sirkulo/ *m,* semicircle
semidifunto /semiði'funto/ *a* half-dead
semidiós /semi'ðios/ *m,* demigod
semidiosa /semi'ðiosa/ *f,* demigoddess
semidormido /semiðor'miðo/ *a* half-asleep
semiesférico /semies'feriko/ *a* hemispherical
semilla /se'miʎa; se'miya/ *f, Bot.* seed; *Fig.* germ, genesis
semillero /semi'ʎero; semi'yero/ *m,* seedbed; nursery; *Fig.* hotbed, origin
semilunio /semi'lunio/ *m, Astron.* half-moon
seminario /semi'nario/ *m,* seedbed; nursery; genesis, origin; seminary; tutorial. **s. conciliar,** theological seminary
seminarista /semina'rista/ *mf* seminarist
semiótica /semi'otika/ *f, Med.* symptomatology; semiotics
semita /se'mita/ *mf* Semite —*a* Semitic
semítico /se'mitiko/ *a* Semitic
semitismo /semi'tismo/ *m,* Semitism
semitono /semi'tono/ *m, Mus.* semitone
semitransparente /semitranspa'rente/ *a* semitransparent
semivivo /semi'βiβo/ *a* half-alive
sémola /'semola/ *f,* semolina
sempiterna /sempi'terna/ *f,* everlasting flower; thick woolen material
sempiterno /sempi'terno/ *a* eternal
sen /sen/ *m,* senna
Sena, el /'sena, el/ the Seine
sena /'sena/ *f, Bot.* senna; six-spotted die
senado /se'naðo/ *m,* senate; senate house; any grave assembly
senador /sena'ðor/ *m,* senator
senaduría /sena'ðuria/ *f,* senatorship
senario /se'nario/ *a* senary
senatorio /sena'torio/ *a* senatorial
sencillez /senθi'ʎeθ; sensi'yes/ *f,* simplicity; naturalness; easiness; ingenuousness, candor
sencillo /sen'θiʎo; sen'siyo/ *a* simple; unmixed; natural; thin, light (fabric); easy; ingenuous, candid; unadorned, plain; single; sincere
senda /'senda/ *f,* path, footpath; way; means
senderear /sendere'ar/ *vt* to conduct along a path; make a pathway; —*vi* attain by tortuous means
sendero /sen'dero/ *m,* footpath, path
sendos, sendas /'sendos, 'sendas/ *a m,* and *f pl,* one each (e.g. *Les dio sendos lápices,* He gave them each a pencil)
senectud /senek'tuð/ *f,* old age
senegalés /senega'les/ **(-esa)** *a* and *n* Senegalese
senescal /senes'kal/ *m,* seneschal
senil /se'nil/ *a* senile
senilidad /senili'ðað/ *f,* senility
seno /'seno/ *m,* hollow; hole; concavity; bosom, breast; chest; uterus, womb; any internal cavity of the body; bay, cove; lap (of a woman); interior (of anything), heart; gulf; *Math.* sine; *Anat.* sinus
sensación /sensa'θion; sensa'sion/ *f,* sensation
sensacional /sensaθio'nal; sensasio'nal/ *a* sensational
sensacionalista /sensaθiona'lista; sensasiona'lista/ *a* sensationalist
sensatez /sensa'teθ; sensa'tes/ *f,* prudence, good sense
sensato /sen'sato/ *a* prudent, wise
sensibilidad /sensiβili'ðað/ *f,* sensibility
sensibilizar /sensiβili'θar; sensiβili'sar/ *vt Photo.* to sensitize
sensible /sen'siβle/ *a* sensible, sensitive; tender, feeling; perceptible; noticeable, definite; sensitive; sad, regrettable
sensiblemente /sensiβle'mente/ *adv* appreciably; perceptibly; painfully, sadly
sensiblería /sensiβle'ria/ *f,* sentimentality, sentimentalism
sensiblero /sensi'βlero/ *a* oversentimental
sensitiva /sensi'tiβa/ *f,* sensitive plant, mimosa
sensitivo /sensi'tiβo/ *a* sensuous; sensitive, sensible
sensorio /sen'sorio/ *a* sensory. *m,* sensorium
sensual /sen'sual/ *a* sensual; sensitive, sensible; carnal, voluptuous
sensualidad /sensuali'ðað/ *f,* sensuality; sensualism
sensualismo /sensua'lismo/ *m,* sensualism, *Philos.* sensationalism
sensualista /sensua'lista/ *mf Philos.* sensationalist; sensualist
sentadero /senta'ðero/ *m,* resting place, improvised seat
sentado /sen'taðo/ *a* prudent, circumspect
sentar /sen'tar/ *vt irr* to seat; —*vi Inf.* suit, agree with (e.g. *No me sienta este clima* (*este plato*), This climate (dish) doesn't suit me); fit, become; *Inf.* please, satisfy, be agreeable to; —*vr* sit down; *Inf.* leave a mark on the skin —*Pres. Ind.* **siento, sientas, sienta, sientan.** *Pres. Subjunc.* **siente, sientes, siente, sienten**
sentencia /sen'tenθia; sen'tensia/ *f,* opinion, belief; maxim; *Law.* verdict, sentence; decision, judgment. *Law.* **fulminar** (*or* **pronunciar) la s.,** to pass sentence
sentenciador /sentenθia'ðor; sentensia'ðor/ *a Law.* sentencing
sentenciar /senten'θiar; senten'siar/ *vt Law.* to sentence; *Inf.* destine, intend
sentencioso /senten'θioso; senten'sioso/ *a* sententious
sentidamente /sentiða'mente/ *adv* feelingly; sadly, regretfully
sentido /sen'tiðo/ *m,* sense (hearing, seeing, touch, smell, taste); understanding, sense; meaning, interpretation, signification; perception, discrimination; judgment; direction, way —*a* and *past part* felt; expressive; hypersensitive, touchy. **s. común,** common sense. **costar un s.,** *Fig. Inf.* to cost a fortune. **perder el s.,** to lose consciousness
sentimental /sentimen'tal/ *a* emotional; sentimental; romantic
sentimentalismo /sentimenta'lismo/ *m,* emotional quality; sentimentalism
sentimiento /senti'miento/ *m,* feeling, sentiment; sensation, impression; grief, sorrow. **Le acompaño a usted en su s.,** I sympathize with you in your sorrow (bereavement)
sentina /sen'tina/ *f,* well (of a ship); *Naut.* bilge; cesspool; sink of iniquity
sentir /sen'tir/ *vt irr* to feel, experience; hear; appreciate; grieve, regret; believe, consider; envisage, foresee; —*vi* complain; suffer; think or consider oneself; crack; feel, be; go rotten, decay (gen. with *estar* + *Past Part.*). *m,* view, opinion; feeling. **sin s.,** without feeling; without noticing —*Pres. Part.* **sintiendo.** *Pres. Indic.* **siento, sientes, siente, sienten.** *Preterite* **sintió, sintieron.** *Pres. Subjunc.* **sienta, sientas, sienta, sintamos, sintáis, sientan.** *Imperf. Subjunc.* **sintiese,** etc.
seña /'seɲa/ *f,* sign, mark; gesture; *Mil.* password; signal; *pl* address, domicile. **s. mortal,** definite or unmistakable sign. **dar señas,** to show signs, manifest. **hablar por señas,** to converse by signs
señal /se'ɲal/ *f,* mark, sign; boundary stone; landmark; scar; signal; trace, vestige; indication, symp-

tom, token; symbol, sign; image, representation; prodigy, marvel; deposit, advance payment. **s. de aterrizaje,** *Aer.* landing signal. **s. de niebla,** fog signal. **señales horarias,** *Radio.* time signal. **en s.,** as a sign, in proof of. **s. luminosa de la circulación,** traffic light, traffic robot

señaladamente /seɲalaða'mente/ *adv* especially, particularly, notably

señalado /seɲa'laðo/ *a* famous, distinguished; important, notable

señalador /seɲala'ðor/ *m, Argentina* bookmark

señalamiento /seɲala'miento/ *m,* marking; pointing out; appointment, designation

señalar /seɲa'lar/ *vt* to mark; indicate, point out; fix, arrange; wound; signal; stamp; appoint (to office); —*vr* excel

señero /se'ɲero/ *a* solitary, isolated

señor /se'ɲor/ *a Inf.* gentlemanly. *m,* owner, master; mister, esquire; **(S.)** the Lord; lord, sire. **s. de horca y cuchillo,** feudal lord, lord of life and death

señora /se'ɲora/ *f,* lady; owner, mistress; madam; wife. **s. de compañía,** chaperon; lady companion. **Nuestra S.,** Our Lady

señorear /seɲore'ar/ *vt* to control, run, manage; master; domineer; appropriate, seize; dominate, overlook; restrain (emotions); —*vr* behave with dignity

señoría /seɲo'ria/ *f,* lordship (title and person); lordship, jurisdiction; area, territory; control, restraint

señoría /seɲo'ria/ *f,* dignity, sedateness; self-control

señorial /seɲo'rial/ *a* manorial; noble, dignified, lordly

señoril /seɲo'ril/ *a* lordly, noble, aristocratic

señorío /seɲo'rio/ *m,* lordship; jurisdiction, dominion

señorita /seɲo'rita/ *f,* young lady; miss; *Inf.* mistress of the house

señorito /seɲo'rito/ *m,* young gentleman; *Inf.* master of the house; master (address); *Inf.* young man about town

señuelo /se'ɲuelo/ *m,* decoy; bait; allurement, attraction. **caer en el s.,** *Fig. Inf.* to fall into the trap

sepancuantos /sepan'kuantos/ *m, Inf.* scolding, rebuke; spanking

separación /separa'θion; separa'sion/ *f,* separation

separado /sepa'raðo/ *a* separate

separador /separa'ðor/ **(-ra)** *a* separating —*n* separator. *m,* filter. **s. de aceite,** oil filter

separar /sepa'rar/ *vt* to separate; divide; dismiss (from a post); lay aside; —*vr* retire, resign; separate

separatismo /separa'tismo/ *m,* separatism

separatista /separa'tista/ *a* and *mf* separatist

septeno /sep'teno/ *a.* See **séptimo**

septentrión /septen'trion/ *m, Astron.* Great Bear; north

septentrional /septentrio'nal/ *a* north; northern

septeto /sep'teto/ *m,* septet

septicemia /septi'θemia; septi'semia/ *f,* septicemia

séptico /'septiko/ *a* septic

septiembre /sep'tiembre/ *m,* September

septillo /sep'tiʎo; sep'tiyo/ *m, Mus.* septuplet

séptima /'septima/ *f, Mus.* seventh

séptimo /'septimo/ *a* and *m,* seventh

septuagenario /septuahe'nario/ **(-ia)** *a* and *n* septuagenarian

septuagésimo /septua'hesimo/ *a* seventieth; septuagesimal. *m,* seventieth

séptuplo /'septuplo/ *a* sevenfold

sepulcral /sepul'kral/ *a* sepulchral

sepulcro /se'pulkro/ *m,* sepulcher

sepultador /sepulta'ðor/ **(-ra)** *a* burying —*n* gravedigger; burier

sepultar /sepul'tar/ *vt* to inter, bury; hide, cover up

sepultura /sepul'tura/ *f,* interment; grave; tomb

sepulturero /sepultu'rero/ *m,* gravedigger

sequedad /seke'ðað/ *f,* dryness, barrenness; acerbity, sharpness

sequía /se'kia/ *f,* drought

séquito /'sekito/ *m,* following, suite, retinue; general approval, popularity

ser /ser/ *m,* essence, nature; being; existence, life. **El S. Supremo,** The Supreme Being, God

ser /ser/ *vi irr* to be (e.g. *El sombrero es azul,* The hat is blue). **Ser** may agree with either subject or complement, though when latter is *pl* the verb tends to be so too (e.g. *Son las once,* (*horas*), It is eleven o'clock. **Cien libras son poco dinero,** A hundred pounds is a small amount). If verbal complement is pers. pron., **ser** agrees with it both in number and person (e.g. *Son ellos,* It is they. *Soy yo,* It is I). In impers. phrases the pron. is not expressed (e.g. *Es difícil,* It is difficult. *Es sorprendente,* It is surprising). **ser** means to exist (e.g. *Pienso luego soy,* I think, therefore I am). **ser** (also **ser de** with nouns or obj. prons.) means to belong to, be the property of (e.g. *Este gato es mío,* This cat is mine. *El libro es de Juan,* The book belongs to John). Signifies to happen, occur (e.g. *¿Cómo fue eso?* How did that happen?). Means to be suitable or fitting (e.g. *Este vestido no es para una señora mayor,* This dress is not suitable for an elderly lady). Expresses price, to be worth (e.g. *¿A cuánto es la libra?* How much is it a pound?; How much is the pound (sterling) worth?). Means to be a member of, belong to (e.g. *Es de la Academia Española,* He is a member of the Spanish Academy). Means to be of use, be useful for (e.g. *Esta casa no es para una familia numerosa,* This house is no use for a large family). **Ser** expresses nationality (e.g. *Son francesas,* They are French. *Somos de Londres,* We are from London) —*Auxiliary verb* used to form passive tense (e.g. *Esta historia ha sido leída por muchos,* This story has been read by many. *Fueron mandados al Japón,* They were sent to Japan. *s. de ver,* to be worth seeing. *s. para poco,* to be of little use, amount to little. *s. testigo de,* to witness. *¡Cómo es eso!* How can that be! Surely not! *¡Cómo ha de s.!* How should it be!; One must resign oneself. *Érase una vez or que érase,* Once upon a time. *es a saber,* viz., that is to say. *un sí es no es,* a touch of, a suspicion of) —*Pres. Part.* **siendo.** *Pres. Indic.* **soy, eres, es, somos, sois, son.** *Fut.* **seré,** etc —*Condit.* **sería,** etc —*Preterite* **fui, fuiste, fue, fuimos, fuisteis, fueron.** *Imperf.* **era,** etc —*Past Part.* **sido.** *Pres. Subjunc.* **sea,** etc —*Imperf. Subjunc.* **fuese,** etc —*Imperat.* **sé**

sera /'sera/ *f,* large frail

seráfico /se'rafiko/ *a* seraphic

serafín /sera'fin/ *m,* seraphim

serbal /ser'βal/ *m,* service tree

serena /se'rena/ *f,* serenade; *Inf.* dew

serenar /sere'nar/ *vt* to calm; soothe; clear; —*vr* grow calm; clear up (weather); clear (liquids); be soothed or pacified

serenata /sere'nata/ *f,* serenade

serenidad /sereni'ðað/ *f,* serenity, composure, tranquility; Serene Highness (title)

sereno /se'reno/ *a* cloudless, fair; composed, serene. *m,* dew; night watchman

sericultor /serikul'tor/ *m,* silk cultivator, sericulturist

sericultura /serikul'tura/ *f,* silk culture

serie /'serie/ *f,* series, sequence, succession; *Math.* progression; (*Biol. Elec.*) series; break (in billiards)

seriedad /serie'ðað/ *f,* seriousness, earnestness; gravity; austerity; sternness; importance; sincerity; solemnity

serigrafía /serigra'fia/ *f,* silkscreen printing

serio /'serio/ *a* serious, earnest; grave; austere; stern; important; sincere, genuine; solemn. **en s.,** seriously

sermón /ser'mon/ *m,* sermon; scolding. **dar un s.,** to give a sermon; scold

sermonar /sermo'nar/ *vi* to preach

sermonear /sermone'ar/ *vi* to preach sermons; —*vt* scold

sermoneo /sermo'neo/ *m, Inf.* scolding

seroja /se'roha/ *f,* withered leaves; brushwood

serpear /serpe'ar/ *vi* to wind, twist; wriggle, squirm; coil

serpenteado /serpente'aðo/ *a* winding

serpentear /serpente'ar/ *vi* to wind, twist, meander; stagger along; wriggle; coil; *Aer.* yaw

serpenteo /serpen'teo/ *m,* winding, twisting; wriggling; coiling; *Aer.* yaw

serpentín /serpen'tin/ *m, Chem.* worm; coil (in industry); *Mineral.* serpentine

serpentina /serpen'tina/ *f, Mineral.* serpentine; paper streamer

serpentino /serpen'tino/ *a* serpentine; *Poet.* winding, sinuous
serpiente /ser'piente/ *f,* snake, serpent; Satan, the Devil; *Astron.* Serpent. **s. de anteojos,** cobra. **s. de cascabel,** rattlesnake
serpollo /ser'poʎo; ser'poyo/ *m, Bot.* shoot, new branch; sprout; sucker
serrado /se'rraðo/ *a* serrate
serrallo /se'rraʎo; se'rrayo/ *m,* harem, seraglio; brothel
serrana, serranilla /se'rrana; serra'niʎa, serra'niya/ *f,* pastoral poem
serranía /serra'nia/ *f,* mountainous territory
serrano /se'rrano/ **(-na)** *a* mountain, highland —*n* highlander, mountain dweller
serrucho /se'rrutʃo/ *m,* handsaw. **s. de calar,** fretsaw
Servia /'serβia/ Serbia
servible /ser'βiβle/ *a* serviceable; useful
servicial /serβi'θial; serβi'sial/ *a* useful, serviceable; obliging, obsequious
servicio /ser'βiθio; ser'βisio/ *m,* service; domestic service; cult, devotion; care, attendance; military service; set, service; department, section; present of money; cover (cutlery, etc., at table); domestic staff, servants. **s. informativo,** news service. **s. nocturno permanente,** all-night service. **hacer un flaco s. (a),** *Inf.* to do someone an ill turn. **prestar servicios,** to render service, serve
servidor /serβi'ðor/ **(-ra)** *n* servant, domestic; name by which one refers to oneself (e.g. *Un s. lo hará con mucho gusto,* I (your servant) will do it with much pleasure). *m,* wooer, lover; bowler (in cricket). **los servidores de una ametralladora,** the crew (of a gun). **Quedo de Vd. atento y seguro s.,** I remain your obedient servant (in letters), Yours faithfully
servidumbre /serβi'ðumbre/ *f,* serfdom; servitude; servants, domestic staff; obligation, duty; enslavement (by passions); right of way; use, service
servil /ser'βil/ *a* servile; humble
servilismo /serβi'lismo/ *m,* servility; abjectness; absolutism (Spanish history)
servilleta /serβi'ʎeta; serβi'yeta/ *f,* table napkin. **s. higiénica,** sanitary napkin
servilletero /serβiʎe'tero; serβiye'tero/ *m,* napkin ring
servio /'serβio/ **(-ia)** *a* and *n* Serbian
servir /ser'βir/ *vi irr* to be employed (by), be in the service (of); serve (as), perform the duties (of); be of use; wait (on), be subject to. *Mil.* serve in the armed forces; wait at table; be suitable or favorable; *Sports.* serve; perform a service; follow the lead (cards); (*with de*) act as, be a deputy for; be a substitute for; —*vt* serve; worship; do a favor to; woo, court; serve (food, drink); —*vr* be pleased or willing, deign; help oneself to (food); (*with de*) make use of. **no s. para nada,** to be good for nothing, be useless. **No sirves para tales cosas,** You are no good at this sort of thing. **Para s. a Vd,** At your service. **¡Sírvase de...!** (followed by infin.), Please! **s. de,** to serve as (e.g. *s. de base a,* to serve as a basis for). See **pedir**
sésamo /'sesamo/ *m,* sesame
sesenta /se'senta/ *a* and *m,* sixty; sixtieth
sesentavo /sesen'taβo/ *a* and *m,* sixtieth
sesentón /sesen'ton/ **(-ona)** *n Inf.* person of sixty
sesga /'sesga/ *f, Sew.* gore
sesgadamente /sesgaða'mente/ *adv* on the slant; askew; obliquely
sesgado /ses'gaðo/ *a* oblique, slanting
sesgar /ses'gar/ *vt Sew.* to cut on the bias; slant, slope; place askew, twist to one side
sesgo /'sesgo/ *a* slanting, oblique; serious-faced. *m,* slope, slant, obliquity; compromise, middle way. **al s.,** on the slant
sesión /se'sion/ *f,* session, meeting; conference, consultation; *Law.* sitting; term. **abrir la s.,** to open the meeting. **levantar la s.,** to adjourn the meeting
seso /'seso/ *m,* brain; prudence; *pl* brains. **perder el s.,** to go mad; *Fig.* lose one's head
sestear /seste'ar/ *vi* to take an afternoon nap; rest; settle
sesudez /sesu'ðeθ; sesu'ðes/ *f,* prudence, shrewdness
sesudo /se'suðo/ *a* sensible, prudent
seta /'seta/ *f,* mushroom. **s. venenosa,** poisonous toadstool
setal /se'tal/ *m,* mushroom bed, patch, or field
setecientos /sete'θientos; sete'sientos/ *a* and *m,* seven hundred; seven-hundredth
setenta /se'tenta/ *a* and *m,* seventy; seventieth
setentavo /seten'taβo/ *a* and *m,* seventieth
setentón /seten'ton/ **(-ona)** *n* septuagenarian
seter /'seter/ *m,* setter (dog)
setiembre /se'tiembre/ *m.* See **septiembre**
seto /'seto/ *m,* fence; hedge
seudo /'seuðo/ *a* pseudo
seudónimo /seu'ðonimo/ *m,* pseudonym
severamente /seβera'mente/ *adv* severely, harshly
severidad /seβeri'ðað/ *f,* severity; harshness; strictness, rigor; austerity, seriousness
severo /se'βero/ *a* severe; harsh; strict, rigid, scrupulous, exact; austere, serious
sevillanas /seβi'ʎanas; seβi'yanas/ *f pl,* Sevillian dance and its music
sevillano /seβi'ʎano; seβi'yano/ **(-na)** *a* and *n* of or from Seville, Sevillian
sexagenario /seksahe'nario/ **(-ia)** *n* sexagenarian
sexagésimo /seksa'hesimo/ *a* sixtieth
sexo /'sekso/ *m,* sex; (sexual) organ
sexología /seksolo'hia/ *f,* sexology
sexólogo /sek'sologo/ **(-ga)** *n* sexologist
sexta /'seksta/ *f, Eccl.* sext; *Mus.* sixth
sextante /seks'tante/ *m, Math.* sextant
sexteto /seks'teto/ *m,* sextet
sexto /'seksto/ *a* sixth
sextuplicación /sekstuplika'θion; sekstuplika'sion/ *f,* multiplication by six
sextuplicar /sekstupli'kar/ *vt* to multiply by six, sextuple
séxtuplo /'sekstuplo/ *a* sixfold
sexualidad /seksuali'ðað/ *f,* sexuality
si /si/ *m, Mus.* B, seventh note of the scale —*conjunc* if; whether; even if, although. In conditional clause, **si,** meaning if, is followed by indicative tense unless statement be contrary to fact (e.g. *Si pierdes el tren, volverás a casa,* If you miss your train you will return home, *but Si hubieran venido habríamos ido al campo,* If they had come (but they didn't) we would have gone to the country). **Si** is used at the beginning of a clause to make expressions of doubt, desire, or affirmation more emphatic (e.g. *¡Si lo sabrá él, con toda su experiencia!* Of course he knows it, with all his experience. *¿Si será falsa la noticia?* Can the news be false?) **Si** also means whether (e.g. *Me preguntaron si era médico o militar,* They asked me whether I was a doctor or a soldier). Sometimes means even if, although (e.g. *Si viniesen no lo harían,* Even if they came they would not do it. *como si,* as if. *por si acaso,* in case, in the event of. *si bien,* although.
sí /si/ *pers pron reflexive 3rd pers m,* and *f, sing* and *pl* himself, herself, itself, themselves. Always used with prep. (e.g. *para sí,* for himself, herself, etc. *de por sí,* separately, on its own. *decir para sí,* to say to oneself)
sí /si/ *adv* yes. **sí** *or* **sí que** is frequently used to emphasize a verb generally in contrast to a previous negative (e.g. *Ellos no lo harán, pero yo sí,* They won't do it but I will). Often translated by "did' (e.g. *No lo vi todo, pero lo que sí vi,* I didn't see it all, but what I did see...). *m,* assent; yes; consent. **dar el sí,** to say yes; agree; accept an offer of marriage
siamés /sia'mes/ **(-esa)** *a* and *n* Siamese. *m,* Thai (language)
sibarita /siβa'rita/ *a* sybaritic. *mf* sybarite
sibarítico /siβa'ritiko/ *a* sybaritic; sensual
sibaritismo /siβari'tismo/ *m,* sybaritism
siberiano /siβe'riano/ **(-na)** *a* and *n* Siberian
sibila /si'βila/ *f,* sibyl
sibilante /siβi'lante/ *a* sibilant
sibilino /siβi'lino/ *a* sibylline
sicario /si'kario/ *m,* paid assassin
Sicilia /si'θilia; si'silia/ Sicily
siciliano /siθi'liano; sisi'liano/ **(-na)** *a* and *n* Sicilian
sicoanálisis /sikoa'nalisis/ *m,* psychoanalysis
sicoanalista /sikoana'lista/ *mf* psychoanalyst

sicoanalizar /sikoanali'θar; sikoanali'sar/ *vt* to psychoanalyze
sicofanta, sicofante /siko'fanta, siko'fante/ *m,* sycophant
sicología /sikolo'hia/ *f,* psychology
sicológico /siko'lohiko/ *a* psychological
sicólogo /si'kologo/ **(-ga)** *n* psychologist
sicomoro /siko'moro/ *m,* sycamore
sicopático /siko'patiko/ *a* psychopathic
sicosis /si'kosis/ *f, Med.* psychosis
sicoterapia /sikote'rapia/ *f,* psychotherapy
SIDA /'siða/ *m,* AIDS
sideral, sidéreo /siðe'ral, si'ðereo/ *a* sidereal
sidra /'siðra/ *f,* cider
siega /'siega/ *f,* reaping, harvesting; harvest time; harvest, crop
siembra /'siembra/ *f, Agr.* sowing; seedtime; sown field
siempre /'siempre/ *adv* always. **s. que,** provided that; whenever. **para s.,** forever. **por s. jamás,** for always, for ever and ever
siempreviva /siempre'βiβa/ *f, Bot.* everlasting flower. **s. mayor,** houseleek
sien /sien/ *f, Anat.* temple
sierpe /'sierpe/ *f,* serpent, snake; anything that wriggles; kite (toy); *Bot.* sucker; hideous person
sierra /'sierra/ *f,* saw; ridge of mountains; sawfish; slope; hillside. **s. de cerrojero,** hacksaw. **s. de cinta,** handsaw
siervo /'sierβo/ **(-va)** *n* slave; servant; serf
siesta /'siesta/ *f,* noonday heat; afternoon nap
siete /'siete/ *a* seven; seventh. *m,* seven; seventh (days of the month); playing card with seven spots; number seven. **las s.,** seven o'clock. *Inf.* **más que s.,** more than somewhat, extremely
sietemesino /sieteme'sino/ **(-na)** *n* seven-month-old child; *Fig. Inf.* young cock
sífilis /'sifilis/ *f,* syphilis
sifilítico /sifi'litiko/ **(-ca)** *a* and *n* syphilitic
sifón /si'fon/ *m,* siphon; siphon bottle; soda water; *Mech.* trap
sigilar /sihi'lar/ *vt* to seal; hide, conceal
sigilo /si'hilo/ *m,* seal; secrecy, concealment; silence, reserve
sigiloso /sihi'loso/ *a* secret, silent
sigla /'sigla/ *f,* acronym
siglo /'siglo/ *m,* century; long time, age; social intercourse, society, world. **s. de oro,** golden age. **en** *or* **por los siglos de los siglos,** for ever and ever
signar /sig'nar/ *vt* to sign; make the sign of the cross over; *—vr* cross oneself
signatario /signa'tario/ **(-ia)** *a* and *n* signatory
signatura /signa'tura/ *f, Print.* signature; mark, sign; *Mus.* signature
significación /signifika'θion; signifika'sion/ *f,* **significado** *m,* meaning; importance, significance
significante /signifi'kante/ *a* significant
significar /signifi'kar/ *vt* to signify, indicate; mean; publish, make known; *—vi* represent, mean; be worth
significativo /signifika'tiβo/ *a* significant
signo /'signo/ *m,* sign, indication, token; sign, character; *Math.* symbol; sign of the zodiac; *Mus.* sign; *Med.* symptom; *Eccl.* gesture of benediction; destiny, fate
siguemepollo /sigeme'poʎo; sigeme'poyo/ *m, Inf.* streamer
siguiente /si'giente/ *a* following; next, subsequent. **el día s.,** the next day
sílaba /'silaβa/ *f,* syllable
silabario /sila'βario/ *m,* speller, spelling book
silabear /silaβe'ar/ *vi* and *vt* to pronounce by syllables, syllabize
silabeo /silaβe'o/ *m,* pronouncing syllable by syllable, syllabication
silábico /si'laβiko/ *a* syllabic
sílabo /'silaβo/ *m,* syllabus, list
silba /'silβa/ *f,* hissing (as a sign of disapproval)
silbador /silβa'ðor/ **(-ra)** *a* whistling; hissing *—n* whistler; one who hisses
silbar /sil'βar/ *vi* to whistle; whizz, rush through the air; *—vi* and *vt Theat.* hiss
silbato /sil'βato/ *m,* whistle; air hole
silbido, silbo /sil'βiðo, 'silβo/ *m,* whistle, whistling; hiss, hissing
silenciador /silenθia'ðor; silensia'ðor/ *m,* (*Auto.* firearms) silencer
silenciar /silen'θiar; silen'siar/ *vt* to silence; keep secret
silenciario /silen'θiario; silen'siario/ *a* vowed to perpetual silence
silencio /si'lenθio; si'lensio/ *m,* silence; noiselessness, quietness; omission, disregard; *Mus.* rest. **en s.,** in silence; quietly; uncomplainingly. **pasar en s. (una cosa),** to pass over (something) in silence, omit. **s. de muerte,** deathly silence
silencioso /silen'θioso; silen'sioso/ *a* silent; noiseless; tranquil, quiet. *m,* (*Auto.* firearms) silencer
silesio /si'lesio/ **(-ia)** *a* and *n* Silesian
sílfide /'silfiðe/ *f,* **silfo** *m,* sylph
silicato /sili'kato/ *m, Chem.* silicate
sílice /'siliθe; 'silise/ *f, Chem.* silica
silla /'siʎa; 'siya/ *f,* chair; riding saddle; *Mech.* rest, saddle; *Eccl.* see. **s. de manos,** sedan chair. **s. de montar,** riding saddle. **s. de posta,** post chaise. **s. de ruedas,** wheelchair. **s. de tijera,** deck chair; campstool. **s. giratoria,** swivel chair. **s. poltrona,** easy chair. *Inf.* **pegársele la s.,** to overstay one's welcome
sillar /si'ʎar; si'yar/ *m,* ashlar, quarry stone; horseback
sillería /siʎe'ria; siye'ria/ *f,* set of chairs; pew, choir stalls; chair factory; shop where chairs are sold; chair making; *Mas.* ashlar masonry
sillero /si'ʎero; si'yero/ **(-ra)** *n* chair maker or seller; saddler
silleta /si'ʎeta; si'yeta/ *f,* bedpan; fireman's lift
silletero /siʎe'tero; siye'tero/ *m,* runner, sedan chair carrier
sillín /si'ʎin; si'yin/ *m,* light riding saddle; seat, saddle (of bicycles, etc.)
sillón /si'ʎon; si'yon/ *m,* armchair; sidesaddle. **s.-cama,** reclining chair. **s. de mimbres,** cane chair
silo /'silo/ *m, Agr.* silo; dark cavern, dark cave
silogismo /silo'hismo/ *m,* syllogism
silogístico /silo'histiko/ *a* syllogistic
silueta /si'lueta/ *f,* silhouette; figure
silúrico /si'luriko/ *a* silurian
siluro /si'luro/ *m,* catfish; *Nav.* self-propelling torpedo
silva /'silβa/ *f,* literary miscellany; metrical form
silvestre /sil'βestre/ *a Bot.* wild; sylvan; uncultivated; savage
silvicultor /silβikul'tor/ *m,* forester
silvicultura /silβikul'tura/ *f,* forestry
sima /'sima/ *f,* abyss, chasm
simbiosis /sim'biosis/ *f,* symbiosis
simbólico /sim'boliko/ *a* symbolical
simbolismo /simbo'lismo/ *m,* symbolism
simbolista /simbo'lista/ *mf* symbolist
simbolización /simboliθa'θion; simbolisa'sion/ *f,* symbolization
simbolizar /simboli'θar; simboli'sar/ *vt* to symbolize, represent
símbolo /'simbolo/ *m,* symbol. **s. de la fe,** *Eccl.* Creed
simetría /sime'tria/ *f,* symmetry
simétrico /si'metriko/ *a* symmetric; symmetrical
simetrizar /simetri'θar; simetri'sar/ *vt* to make symmetrical
símico /'simiko/ *a* simian
simiente /si'miente/ *f,* seed; semen; germ, genesis, origin
simiesco /si'miesko/ *a* apish, ape-like
símil /'simil/ *a* similar. *m,* comparison; simile
similar /simi'lar/ *a* similar
similitud /simili'tuð/ *f,* similarity
simio /'simio/ **(-ia)** *n* ape
simón /si'mon/ *m,* horse cab; cabdriver
simonía /simo'nia/ *f,* simony
simpatía /simpa'tia/ *f,* liking, understanding, affection; fellow feeling; sympathy

simpático /sim'patiko/ *a* friendly, nice, decent, congenial; sympathetic. **gran s.,** *Anat.* sympathetic
simpatizar /simpati'θar; simpati'sar/ *vi* to get on well, be congenial
simple /'simple/ *a* simple; single, not double; insipid; easy; plain, unadorned; stupid, silly; pure, unmixed; easily deceived, simple; naïve, ingenuous; mere; mild, meek. *mf* simpleton; fool
simpleza /sim'pleθa; sim'plesa/ *f,* foolishness, stupidity; simplicity
simplicidad /simpliθi'ðað; simplisi'ðað/ *f,* simplicity; candor, ingenuousness
simplicísimo /simpli'θisimo; simpli'sisimo/ *a superl* most simple, exceedingly simple
simplificable /simplifi'kaβle/ *a* simplifiable
simplificación /simplifika'θion; simplifika'sion/ *f,* simplification, simplifying
simplificador /simplifika'ðor/ *a* simplifying
simplificar /simplifi'kar/ *vt* to simplify
simplista /sim'plista/ *mf* herbalist
simulación /simula'θion; simula'sion/ *f,* pretense, simulation
simulacro /simu'lakro/ *m,* image, simulacrum; vision, fancy; *Mil.* mock battle
simuladamente /simulaða'mente/ *adv* pretendedly
simulador /simula'ðor/ **(-ra)** *a* feigned —*n* dissembler
simular /simu'lar/ *vt* to feign, pretend
simultanear /simultane'ar/ *vt* to perform simultaneously
simultaneidad /simultanei'ðað/ *f,* simultaneousness
simultáneo /simul'taneo/ *a* simultaneous
simún /si'mun/ *m,* sandstorm
sin /sin/ *prep* without (e.g. *Lo hizo s. hablar,* He did it without speaking). **s. embargo,** nevertheless. **s. fin,** endless. **s. hilos,** radio, wireless
sinagoga /sina'goga/ *f,* synagogue
sinapismo /sina'pismo/ *m, Med.* mustard plaster; *Inf.* pest, bore
sincerarse /sinθe'rarse; sinse'rarse/ *vr* to justify oneself; vindicate one's actions
sinceridad /sinθeri'ðað; sinseri'ðað/ *f,* sincerity
sincero /sin'θero; sin'sero/ *a* sincere
síncopa /'sinkopa/ *f, Mus.* syncopation; *Gram.* syncope
sincopar /sinko'par/ *vt* to syncopate; abbreviate
síncope /'sinkope/ *m,* syncope
sincrónico /sin'kroniko/ *a* synchronous
sincronismo /sinkro'nismo/ *m,* synchronism
sincronizar /sinkroni'θar; sinkroni'sar/ *vt* to synchronize; *Radio.* tune in
sindéresis /sin'deresis/ *f,* discretion, good sense
sindicación /sindika'θion; sindika'sion/ *f,* syndication
sindicado /sindi'kaðo/ *m,* syndicate
sindical /sindi'kal/ *a* syndical
sindicalismo /sindika'lismo/ *m,* syndicalism, trade unionism
sindicalista /sindika'lista/ *mf* syndicalist, trade unionist —*a* syndicalistic, trade unionist
sindicar /sindi'kar/ *vt* to accuse, charge; censure; syndicate
sindicato /sindi'kato/ *m,* syndicate; trade union. **s. gremial,** trade union. **S. Internacional de Trabajadoras de la Aguja,** International Ladies' Garment Workers' Union
sindicatura /sindika'tura/ *f,* (official) receivership
síndico /'sindiko/ *m, Com.* receiver, trustee
síndrome /'sindrome/ *m,* syndrome
sinecura /sine'kura/ *f,* sinecure
sinergia /si'nerhia/ *f,* synergy
sinfín /sin'fin/ *m,* countless number
sinfonía /sinfo'nia/ *f,* symphony
sinfónico /sin'foniko/ *a* symphonic
sinfonista /sinfo'nista/ *mf* composer of symphonies, player in a symphony orchestra
sinfonola /sinfo'nola/ *f,* jukebox
Singapur /siŋga'pur/ Singapore
singladura /siŋgla'ðura/ *f, Naut.* day's sailing; nautical twenty-four hours (beginning at midday)
singlar /siŋ'glar/ *vi Naut.* to sail a given course
singular /siŋgu'lar/ *a* singular, single; individual; extraordinary, remarkable —*a* and *m, Gram.* singular
singularidad /siŋgulari'ðað/ *f,* individuality, peculiarity; strangeness, remarkableness; oddness, eccentricity
singularizar /siŋgulari'θar; siŋgulari'sar/ *vt* to particularize, single out; *Gram.* make singular, singularize; —*vr* distinguish oneself, stand out; be distinguished (by)
sinhueso /sin'ueso/ *f, Inf.* tongue (organ of speech)
sínico /'siniko/ *a* Chinese
siniestra /si'niestra/ *f,* left, lefthand
siniestro /si'niestro/ *a* left (side); vicious, perverse; sinister; unlucky. *m,* viciousness, depravity (gen. *pl*); shipwreck, sinking; disaster, catastrophe; *Com.* damage, loss
sinnúmero /sin'numero/ *m,* countless number
sino /'sino/ *m,* fate, destiny —*conjunc* but; except (e.g. *No lo hicieron ellos s. yo,* They didn't do it, I did. *no... s.,* not..., but); only (e.g. *No sólo lo dijo él s. ella,* Not only he said it, but she did too)
sínodo /'sinoðo/ *m,* (*Eccl. Astron.*) synod; council
sinología /sinolo'hia/ *f,* sinology
sinólogo /si'nologo/ *m,* sinologist
sinonimia /sino'nimia/ *f,* synonymy
sinónimo /si'nonimo/ *a* synonymous. *m,* synonym
sinopsis /si'nopsis/ *f,* synopsis
sinóptico /si'noptiko/ *a* synoptic
sinrazón /sinra'θon; sinra'son/ *f,* injustice, wrong
sinsabor /sinsa'βor/ *m,* unpleasantness, trouble; grief, anxiety
sintáctico /sin'taktiko/ *a* syntactic
sintaxis /sin'taksis/ *f,* syntax
síntesis /'sintesis/ *f,* synthesis
sintético /sin'tetiko/ *a* synthetic
sintetizar /sinteti'θar; sinteti'sar/ *vt* to synthesize
sintoísmo /sinto'ismo/ *m,* Shintoism
síntoma /'sintoma/ *m,* symptom
sintomático /sinto'matiko/ *a* symptomatic
sintomatología /sintomatolo'hia/ *f,* symptomatology
sintonización /sintoniθa'θion; sintonisa'sion/ *f, Radio.* tuning in
sintonizador /sintoniθa'ðor; sintonisa'ðor/ *m, Radio.* tuner
sintonizar /sintoni'θar; sintoni'sar/ *vt Radio.* to tune in
sinuosidad /sinuosi'ðað/ *f,* sinuosity
sinuoso /sin'uoso/ *a* sinuous, winding
sinvergüenza /simber'guenθa; simber'guensa/ *mf* rascal, knave, rogue
Sión /'sion/ Zion
sionismo /sio'nismo/ *m,* Zionism
sionista /sio'nista/ *a* and *mf* Zionist
siquiatra /si'kiatra/ *m,* psychiatrist
siquiatría /sikia'tria/ *f,* psychiatry
síquico /'sikiko/ *a* psychic
siquiera /si'kiera/ *conjunc* although, even if. **s.... s.,** whether... or —*adv* at least; even (e.g. *Hay que pedir mucho para tener s. la mitad,* One must ask a great deal to get even half). **ni s.,** not even (e.g. *No había nadie, ni s. un perro,* There was no one, not even a dog)
Siracusa /sira'kusa/ Syracuse
siracusano /siraku'sano/ **(-na)** *a* and *n* Syracusan
sirena /si'rena/ *f,* mermaid, siren; siren; foghorn
sirga /'sirga/ *f,* towline
sirgar /sir'gar/ *vt Naut.* to track, tow
Siria /'siria/ Syria
siríaco /si'riako/ **(-ca)** *a* and *n* Syriac
sirio /'sirio/ **(-ia)** *a* and *n* Syrian. *m,* Sirius
siroco /si'roko/ *m,* sirocco
sirte /'sirte/ *f,* sandbank, submerged rock
sirvienta /sir'βienta/ *f,* female servant
sirviente /sir'βiente/ *a* serving. *m,* servant
sisa /'sisa/ *f,* pilfering; *Sew.* dart. **s. dorada,** gold lacquer
sisador /sisa'ðor/ **(-ra)** *n* filcher, pilferer
sisar /si'sar/ *vt* to pilfer, filch, steal; *Sew.* take in, make darts in
sisear /sise'ar/ *vi* and *vt* to hiss (disapproval); sizzle
sísmico /'sismiko/ *a* seismic

sismógrafo /sis'mografo/ *m*, seismograph
sismología /sismolo'hia/ *f*, seismology
sismológico /sismo'lohiko/ *a* seismological
sismómetro /sis'mometro/ *m*, seismometer
sistema /sis'tema/ *m*, system. **s. ferroviario,** railroad system. **s. métrico,** metric system
sistemático /siste'matiko/ *a* systematic
sistematización /sistematiθa'θion; sistematisa'sion/ *f*, systematization
sistematizar /sistemati'θar; sistemati'sar/ *vt* to systematize
sístole /'sistole/ *f*, systole
sitiador /sitia'ðor/ *a* besieging. *m*, besieger
sitial /si'tial/ *m*, ceremonial chair
sitiar /si'tiar/ *vt Mil.* to lay siege to; surround, besiege
sitio /'sitio/ *m*, place, spot; room, space; site; locality; *Mil.* siege, blockade. **No hay s.,** There's no room
sito /'sito/ *past part* situated, located
situación /situa'θion; situa'sion/ *f*, situation; position; circumstances; condition, state; location
situado /si'tuaðo/ *past part* situated, placed. *m*, income, interest
situar /si'tuar/ *vt* to situate, locate, place; assign funds; *—vr* place oneself
smoking /'smokiŋg/ *m*, tuxedo, tux, dinner jacket
snobismo /sno'βismo/ *m*, snobbery
so /so/ *prep* under (used only with **color, pena, pretexto, capa**) (e.g. *so color de,* under the pretext of) *—interj* **¡So!** Whoa! (to horses)
soba /'soβa/ *f*, rubbing; kneading; massaging; drubbing, beating; handling, touching
sobacal /soβa'kal/ *a* underarm, axillary
sobaco /so'βako/ *m*, armpit; *Bot.* axil
sobajar /soβa'har/ *vt* to squeeze, press
sobaquera /soβa'kera/ *f*, *Sew.* armhole; dress shield
sobar /so'βar/ *vt* to rub; knead; massage; beat, thrash; handle, touch, paw (persons); soften
soberanear /soβerane'ar/ *vi* to tyrannize, domineer
soberanía /soβera'nia/ *f*, sovereignty; dominance, sway, rule; dignity, majesty
soberano /soβe'rano/ **(-na)** *a* sovereign; superb; regal, majestic *—n* ruler, lord. *m*, sovereign (coin)
soberbia /so'βerβia/ *f*, arrogance, haughtiness; conceit, presumption; ostentation, pomp; rage, anger
soberbio /so'βerβio/ *a* haughty, arrogant; conceited; superb, magnificent; lofty, soaring; spirited (of horses)
sobón /so'βon/ *a Inf.* overdemonstrative, mushy; *Inf.* lazy
sobordo /so'βorðo/ *m*, *Naut.* manifest, freight list
sobornación /soβorna'θion; soβorna'sion/ *f*, bribing; bribery
sobornador /soβorna'ðor/ **(-ra)** *a* bribing *—n* briber
sobornar /soβor'nar/ *vt* to bribe
soborno /so'βorno/ *m*, bribing; bribe; inducement
sobra /'soβra/ *f*, excess, surplus; insult, outrage; *pl* leftovers (from a meal); remains, residue; rubbish, trash. **de s.,** in abundance; in excess, surplus; unnecessary, superfluous; too well
sobradamente /soβraða'mente/ *adv* abundantly; in excess
sobrado /so'βraðo/ *a* excessive; brazen, bold; wealthy, rich. *m*, garret
sobrante /so'βrante/ *a* surplus, leftover, remaining. *m*, remainder, surplus, excess
sobrar /so'βrar/ *vt* to exceed; have too much of (e.g. *Me sobran mantas,* I have too many blankets); *—vi* be superfluous; remain, be left. *Inf.* **Aquí sobro yo,** I am in the way here, My presence is superfluous
sobrasada /soβra'saða/ *f*, spicy sausage
sobre /'soβre/ *prep* upon, on; above, over; concerning, about; apart from, besides; about (e.g. *s. las nueve,* at about nine o'clock) (indicates approximation); toward; after. *m*, envelope; address, superscription. **s. cero,** above freezing (Fahrenheit); above zero (Centigrade). **s. el nivel del mar,** above sea level. **s. manera,** excessively, extremely. **s. todo,** especially
sobreabundancia /soβreaβun'danθia; soβreaβun'dansia/ *f*, superabundance, excess
sobreabundante /soβreaβun'dante/ *a* superabundant
sobreabundar /soβreaβun'dar/ *vi* to be superabundant
sobreagudo /soβrea'guðo/ *a* and *m*, *Mus.* treble (pitch)
sobrealiento /soβrea'liento/ *m*, heavy, painful breathing
sobrealimentación /soβrealimenta'θion; soβrealimenta'sion/ *f*, overfeeding; *Auto.* supercharge
sobrealimentar /soβrealimen'tar/ *vt Auto.* to supercharge
sobreasar /soβrea'sar/ *vt* to roast or cook again
sobrecama /soβre'kama/ *f*, bedspread, quilt
sobrecarga /soβre'karga/ *f*, overload; rope, etc., for securing bales and packs; additional trouble or anxiety
sobrecargar /soβrekar'gar/ *vt* to overload; weigh down; *Sew.* oversew, fell
sobrecargo /soβre'kargo/ *m*, *Naut.* purser; flight attendant
sobrecarta /soβre'karta/ *f*, envelope (for a letter)
sobreceja /soβre'θeha; soβre'seha/ *f*, brow, lower forehead; frown
sobrecejo /soβre'θeho; soβre'seho/ *m*, frown
sobrecielo /soβre'θielo; soβre'sielo/ *m*, canopy
sobrecoger /soβreko'her/ *vt* to take by surprise; *—vr* be frightened or apprehensive
sobrecogimiento /soβrekohi'miento/ *m*, fright, apprehension
sobrecomida /soβreko'miða/ *f*, dessert
sobrecoser /soβreko'ser/ *vt Sew.* to oversew, whip
sobrecrecer /soβrekre'θer; soβrekre'ser/ *vi irr* to grow too much. See **conocer**
sobrecubierta /soβreku'βierta/ *f*, second lid or cover; dust jacket (of a book); *Naut.* upper deck
sobrecuello /soβre'kueʎo; soβre'kueyo/ *m*, overcollar; loose collar
sobredicho /soβre'ðitʃo/ *a* aforementioned, aforesaid
sobredorar /soβreðo'rar/ *vt* to gild (metals); make excuses for
sobreedificar /soβreeðifi'kar/ *vt* to build upon or above
sobreexcitar /soβreeksθi'tar; soβreekssi'tar/ *vt* to overexcite
sobrefaz /soβre'faθ; soβre'fas/ *f*, surface, exterior
sobreganar /soβrega'nar/ *vt* to make an excess profit
sobreguarda /soβre'guarða/ *m*, head guard; extra or second guard
sobreherido /soβree'riðo/ *a* lightly wounded
sobrehilar /soβrei'lar/ *vt* to oversew or overcast. See **prohibir**
sobrehumano /soβreu'mano/ *a* superhuman
sobrellenar /soβreʎe'nar; soβreye'nar/ *vt* to fill full
sobrellevar /soβreʎe'βar; soβreye'βar/ *vt* to help in the carrying of a burden; endure, bear; make excuses for, overlook; help
sobremesa /soβre'mesa/ *f*, tablecloth; after-dinner conversation. **de s.,** *Fig.* at the dinner table
sobrenadar /soβrena'ðar/ *vi* to float
sobrenatural /soβrenatu'ral/ *a* supernatural; extraordinary, singular
sobrenombre /soβre'nombre/ *m*, additional surname; nickname
sobrentender /soβrenten'der/ *vt irr* to take for granted, understand as a matter of course; *—vr* go without saying. See **entender**
sobrepaga /soβre'paga/ *f*, overpayment; extra pay
sobreparto /soβre'parto/ *m*, time after parturition; afterbirth
sobrepasar /soβrepa'sar/ *vt* to exceed; outdo, excel
sobrepelliz /soβrepe'ʎiθ; soβrepe'yis/ *f*, surplice
sobreponer /soβrepo'ner/ *vt irr* to place over; overlap; *—vr* rise above (circumstances); dominate (persons). See **poner**
sobreprecio /soβre'preθio; soβre'presio/ *m*, extra charge, rise in price
sobreproducción /soβreproðuk'θion; soβreproðuk'sion/ *f*, overproduction
sobrepuerta /soβre'puerta/ *f*, curtain pelmet; door curtain
sobrepujar /soβrepu'har/ *vt* to excel, surpass, outdo
sobrequilla /soβre'kiʎa; soβre'kiya/ *f*, keelson

sobrerrealismo /soβrerrea'lismo/ *m*, surrealism

sobrerrealista /soβrerrea'lista/ *a* and *mf* surrealist

sobresaliente /soβresa'liente/ *a* overhanging; projecting; distinctive, outstanding; excellent, remarkable. *m*, "excellent" (mark in examinations). *mf Theat.* understudy

sobresalir /soβresa'lir/ *vi irr* to overhang, project; stand out; be conspicuous or noticeable; excel; distinguish oneself. See **salir**

sobresaltar /soβresal'tar/ *vt* to assail, rush upon; startle, frighten suddenly; —*vi Art.* stand out, be striking; —*vr* be startled or frightened

sobresalto /soβre'salto/ *m*, sudden attack; unexpected shock; agitation; sudden fear. **de s.,** unexpectedly

sobresanar /soβresa'nar/ *vi* to heal superficially but not deeply; conceal, dissemble

sobrescribir /soβreskri'βir/ *vt* to label; address, superscribe —*Past Part.* **sobrescrito**

sobrescrito /soβres'krito/ *m*, address, superscription

sobresello /soβre'seʎo; soβre'seyo/ *m*, second seal

sobrestante /soβres'tante/ *m*, overseer; supervisor; foreman; inspector

sobresueldo /soβre'sueldo/ *m*, additional salary, bonus

sobresuelo /soβre'suelo/ *m*, second flooring

sobretarde /soβre'tarðe/ *f*, early evening, late afternoon

sobretodo /soβre'toðo/ *m*, overcoat

sobrevenida /soβreβe'niða/ *f*, sudden arrival

sobrevenir /soβreβe'nir/ *vi irr* occur, take place; supervene. See **venir**

sobrevidriera /soβreβi'ðriera/ *f*, storm window; wire-mesh window guard

sobrevienta /soβre'βienta/ *f*, gust of wind; fury, violence; shock, surprise. **a s.,** suddenly

sobreviviente /soβreβi'βiente/ *a* surviving. *mf* survivor

sobrevivir /soβreβi'βir/ *vi* to survive

sobriedad /soβrie'ðað/ *f*, sobriety, moderation

sobrina /so'βrina/ *f*, niece

sobrino /so'βrino/ *m*, nephew

sobrio /'soβrio/ *a* sober, moderate, temperate

socaliña /soka'liɲa/ *f*, cunning, craft

socaliñero /sokali'ɲero/ **(-ra)** *a* cunning —*n* trickster

socalzar /sokal'θar; sokal'sar/ *vt Mas.* to underpin

socapa /so'kapa/ *f*, blind, pretext. **a s.,** secretly; cautiously

socarra /so'karra/ *f*, scorching, singeing; craftiness

socarrón /soka'rron/ *a* cunning, deceitful; malicious, sly (of humor, etc.)

socarronería /sokarrone'ria/ *f*, cunning, craftiness; slyness (of humor, etc.); knavish action

socava /so'kaβa/ *f*, undermining; *Agr.* hoeing round tree roots

socavar /soka'βar/ *vt* to undermine

sociabilidad /soθiaβili'ðað; sosiaβili'ðað/ *f*, sociability

sociable /so'θiaβle; so'siaβle/ *a* sociable; social

social /so'θial; so'sial/ *a* social

socialdemócrata /soθialde'mokrata; sosialde'mokrata/ *a* and *mf* social democrat

socialismo /soθia'lismo; sosia'lismo/ *m*, socialism

socialista /soθia'lista; sosia'lista/ *mf* socialist —*a* socialistic

socialización /soθialiθa'θion; sosialisa'sion/ *f*, socialization

socializar /soθiali'θar; sosiali'sar/ *vt* to socialize

sociedad /soθie'ðað; sosie'ðað/ *f*, society; association; *Com.* partnership; *Com.* company. *Com.* **s. anónima,** incorporated company, limited company. **S. de las Naciones,** League of Nations. **s. de socorros mutuos,** mutual aid society. **s. en comandita,** private company

socio /'soθio; 'sosio/ **(-ia)** *n* associate, partner; member. **s. comanditario,** *Com.* silent partner

sociología /soθiolo'hia; sosiolo'hia/ *f*, sociology

sociológico /soθio'lohiko; sosio'lohiko/ *a* sociological

sociólogo /so'θiologo; so'siologo/ **(-ga)** *n* sociologist

socollada /soko'ʎaða; soko'yaða/ *f*, *Naut.* flapping (of sails); pitching (of a ship)

socolor /soko'lor/ *m*, pretext —*adv* (also **so c.**) under pretext

socorredor /sokorre'ðor/ **(-ra)** *a* aiding, succoring —*n* helper

socorrer /soko'rrer/ *vt* to aid, succor, assist; pay on account

socorrido /soko'rriðo/ *a* helpful, generous, prompt to assist; well-equipped, well-furnished; well-supplied

socorro /so'korro/ *m*, aid, help, assistance; payment on account; *Mil.* relief (provisions or arms)

socrático /so'kratiko/ *a* socratic

sodio /'soðio/ *m*, sodium

sodomía /soðo'mia/ *f*, sodomy

sodomita /soðo'mita/ *mf* sodomite —*a* sodomitic

soez /so'eθ; so'es/ *a* base, vile; vulgar

sofá /so'fa/ *m*, sofa, couch

sofaldar /sofal'dar/ *vt* to tuck up the skirts; disclose, reveal

sofisma /so'fisma/ *m*, sophism, fallacy

sofista /so'fista/ *a* sophistic. *mf* sophist, quibbler

sofistería /sofiste'ria/ *f*, sophistry

sofístico /so'fistiko/ *a* sophistic, fallacious

soflama /so'flama/ *f*, thin flame; glow; flush, blush; specious promise, deception

soflamar /sofla'mar/ *vt* to shame, make blush; promise with intent to deceive, swindle; —*vr Cul.* burn

sofocación /sofoka'θion; sofoka'sion/ *f*, suffocation, smothering; shame; anger

sofocador, sofocante /sofoka'ðor, sofo'kante/ *a* suffocating; stifling

sofocar /sofo'kar/ *vt* to suffocate, smother; extinguish; dominate, oppress; pester, importune; shame, make blush, make angry; agitate; —*vr* be ashamed; be angry

sofocleo /sofo'kleo/ *a* Sophoclean

sofoco /so'foko/ *m*, mortification, chagrin; shame; anger; suffocation, smothering; hot flush

sofreír /sofre'ir/ *vt irr* to fry lightly. See **reír**

sofrenada /sofre'naða/ *f*, sudden check, pulling up short (of horses); harsh scolding; moral restraint

sofrenar /sofre'nar/ *vt* to pull up, check suddenly (horses); scold harshly; restrain, repress (emotions)

soga /'soga/ *f*, rope; land measure (varies in length). *m*, *Inf.* rogue, knave

soguería /soge'ria/ *f*, rope making; rope walk; rope shop; ropes

soguero /so'gero/ *m*, rope maker or seller

soja /'soha/ *f*, soybean

sojuzgador /sohuθga'ðor; sohusga'ðor/ **(-ra)** *a* conquering, oppressive —*n* conqueror, oppressor

sojuzgar /sohuθ'gar; sohus'gar/ *vt* to conquer, oppress, subdue

sol /sol/ *m*, sun; sunlight; day; Peruvian coin; *Mus.* G, fifth note of the scale, sol. **de s. a s.,** from sunrise to sunset. **hacer s.,** to be sunny. **morir uno sin s. sin luz y sin moscas,** *Inf.* to die abandoned by all. **no dejar a s. ni a sombra,** *Inf.* to follow everywhere; pester constantly. **tomar el s.,** to bask in the sun

solado /so'laðo/ *m*, paving; tile floor

solador /sola'ðor/ *m*, tiler

solamente /sola'mente/ *adv* only; exclusively; merely, solely. **s. que,** only that; nothing but

solana /so'lana/ *f*, sunny corner; Solarium

solanera /sola'nera/ *f*, sunburn; sunny spot

solapa /so'lapa/ *f*, lapel; excuse, pretext. **de s.,** *Inf* secretly

solapado /sola'paðo/ *a* cunning, sly

solapar /sola'par/ *vt Sew.* to provide with lapels; *Sew.* cause to overlap; dissemble; —*vi Sew.* overlap

solapo /so'lapo/ *m*, lapel; *Inf.* slap, buffet. **a s.,** *Inf.* secretly, slyly

solar /so'lar/ *vt irr* to pave; sole (shoes). *m*, family seat, manor house; building site; lineage, family —*a* solar. See **colar**

solariego /sola'riego/ *a* memorial; of an old and noble family

solas, a /'solas, a/ *adv* alone, in private

solaz /so'laθ; so'las/ *m*, consolation; pleasure; relief, relaxation. **a s.,** enjoyably, pleasantly

solazar /sola'θar; sola'sar/ *vt* to solace, comfort; amuse, entertain; rest; *—vr* be comforted; find pleasure (in)
soldada /sol'daða/ *f,* salary, wages, emoluments; (*Nav. Mil.*) pay
soldadesca /solda'ðeska/ *f,* soldiering, military profession; troops. **a la s.,** in a soldier-like way
soldadesco /solda'ðesko/ *a* military, soldier
soldado /sol'daðo/ *m,* soldier; defender, partisan. **s. raso,** *Mil.* private
soldador /solda'ðor/ *m,* solderer, welder; soldering iron
soldadura /solda'ðura/ *f,* welding, soldering; correction, emendation
soldar /sol'dar/ *vt irr* to weld; mend by welding; correct, put right; *Mil.* wipe out, liquidate. See **contar**
solecismo /sole'θismo; sole'sismo/ *m,* solecism
soledad /sole'ðað/ *f,* solitude; loneliness; homesickness; *pl* melancholy Andalusian song and dance (also *f pl.* **soleares**)
solemne /so'lemne/ *a* solemn; magnificent; formal; serious, grave, important; pompous; *Inf.* downright, complete
solemnidad /solemni'ðað/ *f,* solemnity; magnificence; formality; gravity, seriousness; solemn ceremony; religious ceremony; legal formality
solemnización /solemniθa'θion; solemnisa'sion/ *f,* solemnization
solemnizar /solemni'θar; solemni'sar/ *vt* to solemnize, celebrate; extol
soler /so'ler/ *vi irr defective* to be in the habit, be used; happen frequently (e.g. *Solía hacerlo los lunes,* I generally did it on Mondays. *Suele llover mucho aquí,* It rains a great deal here). See **moler**
solercia /so'lerθia; so'lersia/ *f,* shrewdness, ability, astuteness
solevantado /soleβan'taðo/ *a* agitated; restless
solevantar /soleβan'tar/ *vt* to raise, push up; incite to rebellion. **s. con gatos,** *Mech.* to jack up
solfa /'solfa/ *f, Mus.* sol-fa
solfear /solfe'ar/ *vt Mus.* to sing in sol-fa; *Inf.* spank, buffet; *Inf.* scold
solfeo /sol'feo/ *m, Mus.* sol-fa; *Inf.* spanking, drubbing
solicitación /soliθita'θion; solisita'sion/ *f,* request; application; solicitation; wooing; search (for a post); attraction, inducement
solicitador /soliθita'ðor; solisita'ðor/ **(-ra)** *a* soliciting *—n* solicitor. *m,* agent; applicant
solicitante /soliθi'tante; solisi'tante/ *mf* applicant, candidate
solicitar /soliθi'tar; solisi'tar/ *vt* to solicit; request; apply for; make love to, court; seek (posts, etc.); try to, attempt to; manage (business affairs); *Phys.* attract; appeal to
solícito /so'liθito; so'lisito/ *a* solicitous; conscientious; careful
solicitud /soliθi'tuð; solisi'tuð/ *f,* diligence, conscientiousness; solicitude; request; application; appeal, entreaty; petition; *Com.* demand. **a s.,** on request
solidaridad /soliðari'ðað/ *f,* solidarity
solidario /soli'ðario/ *a Law.* jointly responsible or liable
solideo /soli'ðeo/ *m, Eccl.* small skullcap
solidez /soli'ðeθ; soli'ðes/ *f,* solidity; *Fig.* force, weight (of arguments, etc.)
solidificación /soliðifika'θion; soliðifika'sion/ *f,* solidification
solidificar /soliðifi'kar/ **(se)** *vt* and *vr* to solidify
sólido /'soliðo/ *a* compact, solid; thick; fast or lasting (of colors); indisputable, convincing. *m,* (*Geom. Phys.*) solid; solidus (ancient coin)
soliloquiar /solilo'kiar/ *vi Inf.* to soliloquize, talk to oneself
soliloquio /soli'lokio/ *m,* soliloquy
solio /'solio/ *m,* throne
solista /so'lista/ *mf* soloist
solitario /soli'tario/ **(-ia)** *a* abandoned, deserted; solitary; secluded; solitude-loving *—n* recluse. *m,* solitaire diamond; hermit; solitaire (card game). **hacer solitarios,** to play solitaire (card game)
sólito /'solito/ *a* accustomed, wonted; customary, habitual
soliviantar /soliβian'tar/ *vt* to rouse, incite, excite
soliviar /soli'βiar/ *vt* to help to lift up; *—vr* half get up, raise oneself
sollastre /so'ʎastre; so'yastre/ *m,* scullion; brazen rogue
sollozante /soʎo'θante; soyo'sante/ *a* sobbing
sollozar /soʎo'θar; soyo'sar/ *vi* to sob
sollozo /so'ʎoθo; so'yoso/ *m,* sob
solo /'solo/ *a* sole, only; alone; lonely; deserted, forsaken. *m,* solo performance; (cards) solo; solitaire (card game). **a solas,** alone; without help, unaided
sólo /'solo/ *or* **solo** *adv* only; merely, solely; exclusively
solomillo /solo'miʎo; solo'miyo/ *m,* sirloin; filet (of meat)
solsticio /sols'tiθio; sols'tisio/ *m,* solstice. **s. hiemal,** winter solstice. **s. vernal,** summer solstice
soltar /sol'tar/ *vt irr* to loosen; let go; disengage; untie; release; let drop; let out (a laugh, etc.); solve; *Inf.* utter; turn on (taps); set free; *—vr* work loose; grow skillful; (*with prep. a + infin.*) begin to do (something). See **contar**
soltera /sol'tera/ *f,* spinster
soltería /solte'ria/ *f,* bachelorhood; spinsterhood
soltero /sol'tero/ *a* unmarried, single. *m,* bachelor
solterón /solte'ron/ *m,* confirmed bachelor
solterona /solte'rona/ *f,* confirmed old maid
soltura /sol'tura/ *f,* loosening; untying; freedom from restraint; ease, independence; impudence; immorality, viciousness; facility of speech; *Law.* release
solubilidad /soluβili'ðað/ *f,* solubility
soluble /so'luβle/ *a* soluble, dissolvable; solvable
solución /solu'θion; solu'sion/ *f,* dissolution, loosening; (*Math. Chem.*) solution; answer, solution; payment, satisfaction; *Lit.* climax; conclusion, end (of negotiations)
solucionar /soluθio'nar; solusio'nar/ *vt* to solve, find a solution for
solvencia /sol'βenθia; sol'βensia/ *f, Com.* solvency
solventar /solβen'tar/ *vt* to pay or settle accounts; solve (problems, difficulties)
solvente /sol'βente/ *a Com.* solvent
somático /so'matiko/ *a* somatic, corporeal
somatología /somatolo'hia/ *f,* somatology
sombra /'sombra/ *f,* shadow; shade; darkness, dimness; specter, phantom; defense, refuge, protection; resemblance, likeness; defect; *Inf.* luck; gaiety, charm; trace, vestige; *Art.* shading, shadow. **sombras chinescas,** shadow show. **a la s.,** in the shade; *Inf.* in jail. **hacer s.,** to shade; *Fig.* stand in the light, be an obstacle; protect. **ni por s.,** by no means; without warning. **no tener s. de,** to have not a trace of.... **tener buena s.,** *Inf.* to be witty or amusing and agreeable. **tener mala s.,** *Inf.* to bring bad luck, exert an evil influence upon; be dull and disagreeable
sombrear /sombre'ar/ *vt* to shadow, shade; *Art.* shade; *—vi* begin to show (of mustaches, beards)
sombrerera /sombre'rera/ *f,* milliner; hatbox
sombrerería /sombrere'ria/ *f,* hat shop or trade; hat factory
sombrerero /sombre'rero/ *m,* hatter; hat manufacturer
sombrerete /sombre'rete/ *m, Mech.* bonnet, cap; cowl
sombrero /som'βrero/ *m,* hat; *Mech.* cap, cowl; sounding board; head (of mushrooms, toadstools). **s. calañés,** Andalusian hat. **s. chambergo,** broad-brimmed plumed hat. **s. de canal** *or* **teja,** shovel hat (worn by clergymen). **s. de copa,** top hat. **s. de jipijapa,** Panama hat. **s. de tres picos,** three-cornered hat, cocked hat. **s. flexible,** soft felt hat. **s. hongo,** bowler (hat)
sombría /som'βria/ *f,* shady spot
sombrilla /som'βriʎa; som'βriya/ *f,* sunshade
sombrío /som'βrio/ *a* dark; shadowy; overcast; *Art.* shaded; gloomy, melancholy
someramente /somera'mente/ *adv* superficially; briefly, summarily
somero /so'mero/ *a* superficial, shallow; summary, rudimentary, brief

someter /some'ter/ *vt* to put down, defeat; submit, place before; subject. **s. a votación,** to put to a vote —*vr* yield, surrender; (*with prep a*) undergo
sometimiento /someti'miento/ *m,* defeat; submission (to arbitration, etc.); subjection
somnambulismo /somnambu'lismo/ *m,* somnambulism, sleepwalking
somnámbulo /som'nambulo/ **(-la)** *a* somnambulistic —*n* somnambulist
somnífero /som'nifero/ *a* soporiferous
somnílocuo /som'nilokuo/ *a* somniloquous, sleep-talking
somnolencia /somno'lenθia; somno'lensia/ *f,* somnolence
son /son/ *m,* sound; rumor; reason, motive; means, way; guise, manner. **al s. de,** to the sound of; to the music of. **en s. de,** in the manner of, as, like, under pretext of
sonadera /sona'ðera/ *f,* nose blowing
sonado /so'naðo/ *a* famous; much admired or talked of. **hacer una que sea sonada,** *Inf.* to cause a great scandal; do something noteworthy
sonaja /so'naha/ *f,* metal jingles on a tambourine; baby's rattle
sonajero /sona'hero/ *m,* baby's rattle
sonar /so'nar/ *vi irr* to sound; be quoted, be mentioned; ring; *Inf.* be familiar, remember (e.g. *No me suena el nombre,* I don't remember the name); (*with prep a*) be reminiscent of; —*vt* sound; ring; play on; clink; —*vr* be rumored, be reported; blow one's nose —*Pres. Indic.* **sueno, suenas, suena, suenan.** *Pres. Subjunc.* **suene, suenes, suene, suenen**
sonata /so'nata/ *f,* sonata
sonda /'sonda/ *f, Naut.* taking of soundings, heaving the lead; sound, plummet, lead; dragrope; probe, sound
sondar /son'dar/ *vt Naut.* to take soundings; probe; *Inf.* sound, try to find out; bore, drill
sondeable /sonde'aβle/ *a* fathomable
sondeo /son'deo/ *m, Naut.* sounding; *Mineral.* drilling; probing
sonetear, sonetizar /sonete'ar, soneti'θar; sonete'ar, soneti'sar/ *vi* to write sonnets
sonetista /sone'tista/ *mf* sonneteer
soneto /so'neto/ *m,* sonnet
sonido /so'niðo/ *m,* sound; literal meaning; rumor, report
sonochar /sono'tʃar/ *vi* to keep watch in the early hours of the night
sonoridad /sonori'ðað/ *f,* sonorousness
sonoro /so'noro/ *a* sounding; resonant, loud; sonorous
sonreir, sonereírse /son'reir, sone'reirse/ *vi* and *vr irr* to smile; —*vi* look pleasant (landscape, etc.); look favorable (of circumstances). **sonreir tras la barba,** to laugh to oneself. See **reir**
sonriente /son'riente/ *a* smiling
sonrisa /son'risa/ *f,* smile
sonrojar /sonro'har/ *vt* to cause to blush; —*vr* blush
sonrosado /sonro'saðo/ *a* rosy, rose-colored, pink
sonrosar /sonro'sar/ *vt* to make rose-colored; —*vr* blush, flush
sonroseo /sonro'seo/ *m,* blush, flush
sonsaca /son'saka/ *f,* removal by stealth; pilfering; enticement; *Fig.* pumping (of a person for information)
sonsacar /sonsa'kar/ *vt* to remove by stealth; steal, pilfer; entice away; *Fig.* pump (a person for information), draw out
sonsonete /sonso'nete/ *m,* rhythmic tapping or drumming; monotonous sound (gen. unpleasant); sarcastic tone of voice
soñador /soɲa'ðor/ **(-ra)** *a* dreamy, sleepy —*n* dreamer
soñar /so'ɲar/ *vt* to dream; imagine, conjure up; (*with con*) dream of; (*with prep a*) fear (of persons)
soñoliento /soɲo'liento/ *a* sleepy, drowsy; soothing; slow, leisurely
¡Soo! /soo/ *interj* Whoa! (command to horses, etc.)
sopa /'sopa/ *f,* sop, piece of bread; soup. **s. boba,** beggar's portion; life of ease at others' expense. **andar a la s.,** to beg one's way. **hecho una s.,** *Inf.* wet through
sopapo /so'papo/ *m,* chuck under the chin; *Inf.* slap; valve
sopera /so'pera/ *f,* soup tureen
sopero /so'pero/ *m,* soup plate, soup bowl —*a* fond of soup
sopesar /sope'sar/ *vt* to try the weight of
sopetón /sope'ton/ *m,* blow, cuff. **de s.,** suddenly
soplada /so'plaða/ *f,* puff of wind
soplado /so'plaðo/ *a Inf.* overelegant; haughty, stiff. *m,* fissure, chasm
soplador /sopla'ðor/ **(-ra)** *a* instigatory. *m,* blower, fan —*n* instigator; blower
soplar /so'plar/ *vi* to blow; —*vt* blow; blow away; inflate, blow up; filch, steal; instigate, inspire; accuse; fan; prompt, help out; —*vr Inf.* eat and drink too much; *Inf.* be puffed up, grow haughty —*interj* **¡Sopla!** *Inf.* You don't say so!
soplete /so'plete/ *m,* blowpipe
soplo /'soplo/ *m,* blow; blowing; instant, trice; *Inf.* hint, tip; *Inf.* accusation; *Inf.* tale-bearer; puff, breath (of wind)
soplón /so'plon/ **(-ona)** *a Inf.* tale-bearing, backbiting —*n* tale-bearer. *m, Auto.* scavenger
soponcio /so'ponθio; so'ponsio/ *m, Inf.* fainting fit
sopor /so'por/ *m,* stupor; deep sleep
soporífero /sopo'rifero/ *a* soporiferous
soportable /sopor'taβle/ *a* bearable
soportador /soporta'ðor/ **(-ra)** *a* supporting —*n* supporter
soportal /sopor'tal/ *m,* portico
soportar /sopor'tar/ *vt* to bear; carry, support; put up with, tolerate
soporte /so'porte/ *m,* rest, support; *Mech.* bearing; *Mech.* bracket, support
sopuntar /sopun'tar/ *vt* to underline in dots
sor /sor/ *f, Eccl.* sister (used of nuns)
sorbedor /sorβe'ðor/ **(-ra)** *a* supping, sipping —*n* sipper
sorber /sor'βer/ *vt* to suck; imbibe; swallow; *Fig.* absorb eagerly (ideas); sip
sorbete /sor'βete/ *m,* sherbet, iced drink; French ice cream
sorbo /'sorβo/ *m,* sucking; imbibition; swallow; sip; mouthful, gulp
sordamente /sorða'mente/ *adv* secretly, quietly
sordera /sor'ðera/ *f,* deafness
sordidez /sorði'ðeθ; sorði'ðes/ *f,* sordidness
sórdido /'sorðiðo/ *a* dirty, squalid; mean, niggardly; sordid
sordina /sor'ðina/ *f, Mus.* sordine, mute; *Mus.* damper. **a la s.,** on the quiet, in secret
sordo /'sorðo/ *a* deaf; silent, quiet; dull, muted (of sounds); insensible, inanimate; obdurate, uncompliant. **a la sorda** *or* **a lo s.** *or* **a sordas,** in silence, quietly
sordomudez /sorðomu'ðeθ; sorðomu'ðes/ *f,* deaf-muteness, deaf-mutism
sordomudo /sorðo'muðo/ **(-da)** *a* and *n* deaf-mute
sorna /'sorna/ *f,* slowness, sluggishness; craftiness, guile, knavery; malice
sorprendente /sorpren'dente/ *a* surprising, amazing
sorprender /sorpren'der/ *vt* to surprise, amaze
sorpresa /sor'presa/ *f,* surprise; amazement; shock
sortear /sorte'ar/ *vt* to raffle; draw lots for; avoid artfully (difficulties, etc.); fight (bulls)
sorteo /sor'teo/ *m,* raffle; casting lots
sortero /sor'tero/ **(-ra)** *n* sorcerer; holder of a draw ticket
sortija /sor'tiha/ *f,* ring (for a finger); ring (for a curtain, etc.); curl
sortilegio /sorti'lehio/ *m,* sorcery, magic
sortílego /sor'tilego/ **(-ga)** *a* magic —*n* sorcerer, fortuneteller
sosa /'sosa/ *f,* sodium carbonate, soda ash. **s. cáustica,** sodiumhydroxide, caustic soda, soda
sosegado /sose'gaðo/ *a* tranquil, peaceful, calm
sosegador /sosega'ðor/ **(-ra)** *a* soothing, calming —*n* appeaser, soother
sosegar /sose'gar/ *vt irr* to soothe, quiet; reassure;

appease, moderate; *—vi* grow still; rest, sleep; *—vr* grow quiet; calm down, be appeased; grow still. See **cegar**
sosería /sose'ria/ *f,* insipidness; lack of wit, dullness; stupidity
sosia /'sosia/ *m,* double, exact likeness (of persons)
sosiego /so'siego/ *m,* calm; peace, tranquility
soslayar /sosla'yar/ *vt* to slant, place in an oblique position; *Fig.* go around (a difficulty)
soslayo /sos'layo/ *a* slanting. **al s.,** obliquely, on the slant; askance
soso /'soso/ *a* saltless, insipid; dull, uninteresting; heavy (of people)
sospecha /sos'petʃa/ *f,* suspicion
sospechar /sospe'tʃar/ *vt* and *vi* to suspect
sospechoso /sospe'tʃoso/ *a* suspicious. *m,* suspect
sostén /sos'ten/ *m,* support; *Mech.* stand, support; brassiere, bra, bustier; steadiness (of a ship)
sostenedor /sostene'ðor/ **(-ra)** *a* supporting *—n* supporter
sostener /soste'ner/ *vt irr* to support; defend, uphold; bear, tolerate; help, aid; maintain, support. **s. una conversación,** to carry on a conversation. See **tener**
sostenido /soste'niðo/ *a Mus.* sostenuto, sustained *—a* and *m, Mus.* sharp
sostenimiento /sosteni'miento/ *m,* support; defense; toleration, endurance; maintenance, sustenance
sota /'sota/ *f,* jack, knave (in cards); *Inf.* baggage, hussy. *m,* foreman, supervisor *—prep* deputy, substitute (e.g. *sotamontero,* deputy huntsman)
sotabanco /sota'βanko/ *m,* attic, garret
sotana /so'tana/ *f,* gown, cassock, robe
sótano /'sotano/ *m,* basement, cellar
sotavento /sota'βento/ *m,* leeward. **a s.,** on the lee
sotechado /sote'tʃaðo/ *m,* hut, shed
soterrar /sote'rrar/ *vt irr* to bury in the ground; hide, conceal. See **acertar**
sotileza /soti'leθa; soti'lesa/ *f,* fine cord for fishing (in Santander province)
soto /'soto/ *m,* thicket, grove, copse
soviético /so'βietiko/ *a* soviet
sovietismo /soβie'tismo/ *m,* sovietism
sovietizar /soβieti'θar; soβieti'sar/ *vt* to sovietize
sovoz, a /so'βoθ, a; so'βos, a/ *adv* in a low voice
su, sus /su, sus/ *poss pron 3rd pers mf sing* and *pl* his, her, its, one's, your, their
suasorio /sua'sorio/ *a* suasive, persuasive
suave /'suaβe/ *a* soft, smooth; sweet; pleasant, harmonious, quiet; slow, gentle; meek; delicate, subtle
suavidad /suaβi'ðað/ *f,* softness, smoothness; sweetness; pleasantness; quietness; gentleness; meekness; delicacy
suavizador /suaβiθa'ðor; suaβisa'ðor/ *a* softening, smoothing; soothing, quietening. *m,* razor strop
suavizar /suaβi'θar; suaβi'sar/ *vt* to soften; smooth; strop (a razor); moderate, temper; *Mech.* steady; quieten; ease
subalpino /suβal'pino/ *a* subalpine
subalternar /suβalter'nar/ *vt* to put down, subdue
subalterno /suβal'terno/ *a* subordinate. *m,* subordinate; *Mil.* subaltern
subarrendar /suβarren'dar/ *vt irr* to sublet. See **recomendar**
subarrendatario /suβarrenda'tario/ **(-ia)** *n* sublessee
subarriendo /suβa'rriendo/ *m,* sublease, sublet
subasta /su'βasta/ *f,* auction sale. **sacar a pública s.,** to sell by auction
subastar /suβas'tar/ *vt* to auction
subcentral /suβθen'tral; suβsen'tral/ *f,* substation
subclase /suβ'klase/ *f,* subclass
subcolector /suβkolek'tor/ *m,* assistant collector
subcomisión /suβkomi'sion/ *f,* subcommittee
subconsciencia /suβkons'θienθia; suβkons'siensia/ *f,* subconscious
subcutáneo /suβku'taneo/ *a* subcutaneous
subdelegar /suβðele'gar/ *vt* to subdelegate
subdirector /suβðirek'tor/ **(-ra)** *n* deputy, assistant director
súbdito /'suβðito/ **(-ta)** *a* dependent, subject *—n* subject (of a state)
subdividir /suβðiβi'ðir/ *vt* to subdivide
subdominante /suβðomi'nante/ *f, Mus.* subdominant
subgénero /suβ'henero/ *m,* subgenus
subgobernador /suβgoβerna'ðor/ *m,* deputy governor, lieutenant governor
subibaja /suβi'βaha/ *f,* seesaw, teetertotter
subida /su'βiða/ *f,* ascension, ascent; upgrade; rise; carrying up; raising (of a theater curtain)
subidero /suβi'ðero/ *m,* uphill road; mounting block; way up (to a higher level)
subido /su'βiðo/ *a* strong (of scents); deep (of colors); expensive, high-priced; best, finest
subidor /suβi'ðor/ *m,* porter, carrier; elevator
subintendente /suβinten'dente/ *m,* deputy or assistant intendant
subir /su'βir/ *vi* to ascend, climb, go up; mount; rise; *Com.* amount (to), reach; prosper, advance, be promoted; grow more acute (of illnesses); intensify; *Mus.* raise the pitch (of an instrument or voice); *—vt* ascend, climb; pick up, take up; raise up; place higher; build up, make taller; straighten up, place in a vertical position; increase, raise (in price or value); *—vr* ascend, climb. **s. a caballo,** to mount a horse. **subirse a la cabeza,** *Inf.* to go to one's head (of alcohol, etc.)
subitáneo /suβi'taneo/ *a* sudden
súbito /'suβito/ *a* unexpected, unforeseen; sudden; precipitate, impulsive *—adv* suddenly (also **de s.**)
subjefe /suβ'hefe/ *m,* deputy chief, second in command
subjetividad /suβhetiβi'ðað/ *f,* subjectivity
subjetivismo /suβheti'βismo/ *m,* subjectivism
subjetivo /suβhe'tiβo/ *a* subjective
subjuntivo /suβhun'tiβo/ *a* and *m,* subjunctive
sublevación /suβleβa'θion; suβleβa'sion/ *f,* **sublevamiento** *m,* rebellion, mutiny, uprising
sublevar /suβle'βar/ *vt* to rouse to rebellion; excite (indignation, etc.); *—vr* rebel
sublimación /suβlima'θion; suβlima'sion/ *f,* sublimation
sublimado /suβli'maðo/ *m, Chem.* sublimate
sublimar /suβli'mar/ *vt* to exalt, raise up; *Chem.* sublimate
sublime /su'βlime/ *a* sublime
sublimidad /suβlimi'ðað/ *f,* sublimity, majesty, nobility
submarino /suβma'rino/ *a* submarine. *m,* submarine. **s. de bolsillo** *or* **s. enano,** midget submarine
suboficial /suβofi'θial; suβofi'sial/ *m, Mil.* subaltern; *Nav.* petty officer
subordinación /suβorðina'θion; suβorðina'sion/ *f,* dependence, subordination
subordinado /suβorði'naðo/ **(-da)** *a* and *n* subordinate
subordinar /suβorði'nar/ *vt* to subordinate
subpolar /suβpo'lar/ *a* subpolar
subprefecto /suβpre'fekto/ *m,* subprefect
subproducto /suβpro'ðukto/ *m,* by-product
subrayar /suβra'yar/ *vt* to underline; emphasize
subrepción /suβrep'θion; suβrep'sion/ *f,* underhand dealing; *Law.* subreption
subrepticio /suβrep'tiθio; suβrep'tisio/ *a* surreptitious; clandestine
subrogación /suβroga'θion; suβroga'sion/ *f,* surrogation
subrogar /suβro'gar/ *vt Law.* to surrogate, elect as a substitute
subs /suβs/ -- For words so beginning not found here, see **sus-**
subsanar /suβsa'nar/ *vt* to make excuses for; remedy, put right; indemnify
subscriptor /suβskrip'tor/ **(-ra)** *n* subscriber
subsección /suβsek'θion; suβsek'sion/ *f,* subsection
subsecretaría /suβsekreta'ria/ *f,* assistant secretaryship; assistant secretary's office
subsecretario /suβsekre'tario/ **(-ia)** *n* assistant secretary
subsecuente /suβse'kuente/ *a* subsequent
subsidiario /suβsi'ðiario/ *a* subsidized; subsidiary
subsidio /suβ'siðio/ *m,* subsidy
subsiguiente /suβsi'giente/ *a* subsequent; next

subsistencia /suβsis'tenθia; suβsis'tensia/ *f,* permanence; stability; subsistence, maintenance; livelihood
subsistir /suβsis'tir/ *vi* to last, endure; subsist, live; make a livelihood
subsuelo /suβ'suelo/ *m,* subsoil, substratum
subteniente /suβte'niente/ *m, Mil.* second lieutenant
subterfugio /suβter'fuhio/ *m,* subterfuge, trick
subterráneo /suβte'rraneo/ *a* underground, subterranean. *m,* subterranean place
subtítulo /suβ'titulo/ *m,* subtitle; caption
subtropical /suβtropi'kal/ *a* subtropical
suburbano /suβur'βano/ **(-na)** *a* suburban —*n* suburbanite
suburbio /su'βurβio/ *m,* suburb
subvención /suββen'θion; suββen'sion/ *f,* subsidy, subvention, grant
subvencionar /suββenθio'nar; suββensio'nar/ *vt* to subsidize
subvenir /suββe'nir/ *vt irr* to help, succor; subsidize. See **venir**
subversivo /suββer'siβo/ *a* subversive
subvertir /suββer'tir/ *vt irr* to subvert, overturn, ruin. See **sentir**
subyugación /suβyuga'θion; suβyuga'sion/ *f,* subjugation
subyugador /suβyuga'ðor/ **(-ra)** *a* subjugating —*n* conqueror
subyugar /suβyu'gar/ *vt* to subjugate, overcome
succión /suk'θion; suk'sion/ *f,* suction
sucedáneo /suθe'ðaneo; suse'ðaneo/ *m, Med.* succedaneum
suceder /suθe'ðer; suse'ðer/ *vi* to follow, come after; inherit, succeed —*impers* happen, occur
sucedido /suθe'ðiðo; suse'ðiðo/ *m, Inf.* event, occurrence
sucesión /suθe'sion; suse'sion/ *f,* succession; series; offspring, descendants; *Law.* estate
sucesivo /suθe'siβo; suse'siβo/ *a* successive. **en lo s.,** in future
suceso /su'θeso; su'seso/ *m,* happening, occurrence; course (of time); outcome, result
sucesor /suθe'sor; suse'sor/ **(-ra)** *a* succeeding —*n* successor
suciedad /suθie'ðað; susie'ðað/ *f,* dirt; filth, nastiness; obscenity
sucinto /su'θinto; su'sinto/ *a* succinct, brief, concise
sucio /'suθio; 'susio/ *a* dirty, unclean; stained; easily soiled; *Fig.* sullied, spotted; obscene; dirty (of colors); *Fig.* tainted, infected. **jugar s.,** *Sports.* to play in an unsporting manner
suco /'suko/ *m,* juice
sucoso /su'koso/ *a* juicy
suculencia /suku'lenθia; suku'lensia/ *f,* succulence; juiciness
suculento /suku'lento/ *a* succulent; juicy
sucumbir /sukum'βir/ *vi* to yield, give in; die, succumb; lose a lawsuit
sucursal /sukur'sal/ *a* branch. *f, Com.* branch (of a firm)
sud /suð/ *m,* south (gen. **sur**). Used in combinations like **sudamericano**
sudadero /suða'ðero/ *m,* horse blanket; sudatorium, sweating bath
sudafricano /suðafri'kano/ **(-na)** *a* and *n* South African
sudamericano /suðameri'kano/ **(-na)** *a* and *n* South American
Sudán, el /su'ðan, el/ the Sudan
sudante /su'ðante/ *a* sweating, perspiring
sudar /su'ðar/ *vi* and *vt* to perspire, sweat; ooze; —*vi Inf.* toil; —*vt* bathe in sweat; *Inf.* give reluctantly. **s. frío,** to break out in a cold sweat. **s. la gota gorda,** *Fig. Inf.* to be in a stew
sudario /su'ðario/ *m,* shroud
sudeste /su'ðeste/ *m,* southeast; southeast wind
sudexpreso /suðeks'preso/ *m,* southern express
sudoeste /suðo'este/ *m,* southwest; southwest wind
sudor /su'ðor/ *m,* sweat, perspiration; toil; juice, moisture, sap, gum
sudoroso /suðo'roso/ *a* sweaty
sudsudeste /suðsu'ðeste/ *m,* southsoutheast
sudsudoeste /suðsuðo'este/ *m,* southsouthwest
Suecia /'sueθia; 'suesia/ Sweden
sueco /'sueko/ **(-ca)** *a* Swedish —*n* Swede. *m,* Swedish (language)
suegra /'suegra/ *f,* mother-in-law
suegro /'suegro/ *m,* father-in-law
suela /'suela/ *f,* sole (of a shoe); *Ichth.* sole; tanned leather; base. **no llegarle a uno a la s. del zapato,** *Inf.* to be not fit to hold a candle to.
sueldo /'sueldo/ *m,* salary, wages; *Obs.* Spanish coin. **a s.,** for a salary, salaried
suelo /'suelo/ *m,* ground, earth; soil; bottom, base; sediment, dregs; site, plot; floor; flooring; story; land, territory; hoof (of horses); earth, world; *pl* chaff of grain. **s. natal,** native land; **besar el s.,** *Inf.* to fall flat. **dar consigo en el s.,** to fall down. **dar en el s. con,** to throw down; damage, spoil. *Inf.* **estar** (**una cosa**) **por los suelos,** to be dirt cheap
suelta /'suelta/ *f,* loosening, unfastening; hobble (for horses); relay of oxen. **dar s. a,** to let loose, allow to go out for a time
suelto /'suelto/ *a* swift; competent, efficient; odd, separate; licentious; flowing, easy (style); loose, unbound. *m,* single copy (of a newspaper); loose change; newspaper paragraph
sueño /'sueɲo/ *m,* dream; sleep; drowsiness, desire for sleep; vision, fancy. **s. pesado,** deep sleep. **conciliar el s.,** to court sleep. **echar un s.,** *Inf.* to take a nap. **en sueños,** in a dream; while asleep. **entre sueños,** between sleeping and waking. **¡Ni por sueño!** *Inf.* Certainly not! I wouldn't dream of it!
suero /'suero/ *m,* serum. **s. de la leche,** whey
suerte /'suerte/ *f,* chance, luck; good luck; destiny, fate; condition, state; kind, species, sort; way, manner; bullfighter's maneuver; parcel of land. **de s. que,** so that; as a result. **echar suertes,** to draw lots. **tener buena s.,** to be lucky
sueste /'sueste/ *m,* southeast; sou'wester (cap)
suéter /'sueter/ *m,* sweater
suevo /'sueβo/ **(-va)** *a* and *n* Swabian
suficiencia /sufi'θienθia; sufi'siensia/ *f,* sufficiency; talent, aptitude; pedantry. **a s.,** enough
suficiente /sufi'θiente; sufi'siente/ *a* sufficient, enough; suitable
sufijo /su'fiho/ *m,* suffix
sufismo /su'fismo/ *m,* Sufism
sufragar /sufra'gar/ *vt* to assist, aid; favor; pay, defray
sufragio /su'frahio/ *m,* aid, assistance; *Eccl.* suffragium, pious offering; vote; suffrage
sufragista /sufra'hista/ *f,* suffragette
sufrible /su'friβle/ *a* bearable, endurable
sufrido /su'friðo/ *a* long-suffering, resigned; complaisant (of husbands); dirt-resistant (colors)
sufrimiento /sufri'miento/ *m,* suffering, pain; affliction; tolerance
sufrir /su'frir/ *vt* to suffer, undergo, experience; bear, endure; tolerate, put up with; allow, permit; resist, oppose; expiate; —*vi* suffer
sugerir /suhe'rir/ *vt irr* to suggest. See **sentir**
sugestión /suhes'tion/ *f,* suggestion
sugestionable /suhestio'naβle/ *a* easily influenced, open to suggestion
sugestionador /suhestiona'ðor/ *a* suggestive
sugestionar /suhestio'nar/ *vt* to suggest hypnotically; dominate, influence
sugestivo /suhes'tiβo/ *a* suggestive, stimulating
suicida /sui'θiða; sui'siða/ *a* suicidal, fatal. *mf* suicide (person)
suicidarse /suiθi'ðarse; suisi'ðarse/ *vr* to commit suicide
suicidio /sui'θiðio; sui'siðio/ *m,* suicide (act)
Suiza /'suiθa; 'suisa/ Switzerland
suiza /'suiθa; 'suisa/ *f,* row, rumpus, scrap
suizo /'suiθo; 'suiso/ **(-za)** *a* and *n* Swiss
sujeción /suhe'θion; suhe'sion/ *f,* subjection, domination; fastening, fixture; obedience, conformity
sujetador /suheta'ðor/ *m,* clamp; clip
sujetar /suhe'tar/ *vt* to fasten, fix; hold down; grasp, clutch; subdue; —*vr* (*with prep a*) conform to, obey. **s. con alfileres,** to pin up. **s. con tornillos,** to screw down

sujeto /su'heto/ *a* liable, subject. *m,* topic, subject; person, individual; *Gram. Philos.* subject
sulfatar /sulfa'tar/ *vt* to sulphate
sulfato /sul'fato/ *m,* sulphate
sulfurar /sulfu'rar/ *vt* to sulphurate; —*vr* grow irritated, become angry
sulfúrico /sul'furiko/ *a* sulphuric
sulfuro /sul'furo/ *m,* sulphide
sulfuroso /sulfu'roso/ *a* sulphurous
sultán /sul'tan/ *m,* sultan
sultana /sul'tana/ *f,* sultana
sultanía /sulta'nia/ *f,* sultanate
suma /'suma/ *f,* total; amount, sum; *Math.* addition; summary, digest; computation. **en s.,** in brief, in short, finally
sumador /suma'ðor/ **(-ra)** *n* summarizer; computator, adder
sumamente /suma'mente/ *adv* extremely, most
sumar /su'mar/ *vt* to sum up, summarize; *Math.* add up
sumaria /su'maria/ *f,* written indictment
sumariamente /sumaria'mente/ *adv* concisely, in brief; *Law.* summarily
sumario /su'mario/ *a* brief, concise, abridged; *Law.* summary. *m,* summary, résumé, digest
sumergible /sumer'hiβle/ *a* sinkable; submergible. *m,* submarine
sumergir /sumer'hir/ *vt* to dip, immerse; sink, submerge; *Fig.* overwhelm (with grief, etc.); —*vr* sink; dive; be submerged
sumersión /sumer'sion/ *f,* immersion, dive, submersion
sumidero /sumi'ðero/ *m,* cesspool; drain; sink; pit, gully
suministración /suministra'θion; suministra'sion/ *f.* See **suministro**
suministrador /suministra'ðor/ **(-ra)** *n* purveyor
suministrar /suminis'trar/ *vt* to purvey, supply, provide
suministro /sumi'nistro/ *m,* purveyance; provision; supply
sumir /su'mir/ *vt* to sink; submerge; *Eccl.* consummate; *Fig.* overwhelm (with grief, etc.); —*vr* fall in, become sunken (of cheeks, etc.); sink; be submerged
sumisión /sumi'sion/ *f,* submission, obedience; *Com.* estimate, tender
sumiso /su'miso/ *a* submissive, docile
sumista /su'mista/ *mf* quick reckoner, computator. *m,* condenser, summarizer, abridger
sumo /'sumo/ *a* supreme; high; tremendous, extraordinary. **a lo s.,** at the most; even if, although. **en s. grado,** in the highest degree
suntuosidad /suntuosi'ðað/ *f,* magnificence, luxury
suntuoso /sun'tuoso/ *a* magnificent, luxurious, sumptuous
supeditación /supeðita'θion; supeðita'sion/ *f,* subjection
supeditar /supeði'tar/ *vt* to oppress; overcome, conquer; subordinate
superabundancia /superaβun'danθia; superaβun'dansia/ *f,* superabundance, excess; glut
superabundante /superaβun'dante/ *a* superabundant, excessive
superádito /supe'raðito/ *a* superadded
superar /supe'rar/ *vt* to overcome, conquer; surpass; do better than
superávit /supe'raβit/ *m, Com.* balance, surplus
supercheria /supertʃe'ria/ *f,* trickery, guile
superchero /super'tʃero/ *a* guileful, wily
superconsciencia /superkons'θienθia; superkons'siensia/ *f,* higher consciousness
supereminencia /superemi'nenθia; superemi'nensia/ *f,* supereminence, greatest eminence
supereminente /superemi'nente/ *a* supereminent
superentender /superenten'der/ *vt irr* to supervise, superintend. See **entender**
supererogación /superceroga'θion; supereroga'sion/ *f,* supererogation
superestructura /superestruk'tura/ *f,* superstructure
superficial /superfi'θial; superfi'sial/ *a* surface, shallow; superficial, rudimentary; futile
superficialidad /superfiθiali'ðað; superfisiali'ðað/ *f,* superficiality; futility; shallowness
superficie /super'fiθie; super'fisie/ *f,* area; surface; outside, exterior. **s. de rodadura,** tire tread
superfino /super'fino/ *a* superfine
superfluidad /superflui'ðað/ *f,* superfluity
superfluo /su'perfluo/ *a* superfluous, redundant
superfortaleza volante /superforta'leθa bo'lante; superforta'lesa bo'lante/ *f, Aer.* superfortress
superhombre /super'ombre/ *m,* superman
superintendencia /superinten'denθia; superinten'densia/ *f,* supervision; superintendentship; higher administration
superintendente /superinten'dente/ *mf* superintendent; supervisor
superior /supe'rior/ *a* higher, upper; excellent, fine; superior; higher (education, etc.). *m,* head, director; superior
superiora /supe'riora/ *f,* mother superior
superioridad /superiori'ðað/ *f,* superiority
superlativo /superla'tiβo/ *a* and *m,* superlative
superno /su'perno/ *a* supreme
supernumerario /supernume'rario/ **(-ia)** *a* and *n* supernumerary
superposición /superposi'θion; superposi'sion/ *f,* superposition
superproducción /superproðuk'θion; superproðuk'sion/ *f,* overproduction; superproduction
superrealismo /superrea'lismo/ *m,* surrealism
superrealista /superrea'lista/ *a* surrealist
superstición /supersti'θion; supersti'sion/ *f,* superstition
supersticioso /supersti'θioso; supersti'sioso/ *a* superstitious
supervención /superβen'θion; superβen'sion/ *f, Law.* supervention
supervivencia /superβi'βenθia; superβi'βensia/ *f,* survival
superviviente /superβi'βiente/ *a* surviving. *mf* survivor
supino /su'pino/ *a* supine; foolish, stupid. *m, Gram.* supine
suplantación /suplanta'θion; suplanta'sion/ *f,* supplanting
suplantador /suplanta'ðor/ **(-ra)** *a* supplanting —*n* supplanter
suplantar /suplan'tar/ *vt* to forge, alter (documents); supplant
suplefaltas /suple'faltas/ *mf Inf.* scapegoat
suplementario /suplemen'tario/ *a* supplementary, additional
suplemento /suple'mento/ *m,* supplement; supply, supplying; newspaper supplement; *Geom.* supplement
suplente /su'plente/ *m,* substitute, proxy; *Fig.* makeweight
súplica /'suplika/ *f,* supplication, prayer; request
suplicación /suplika'θion; suplika'sion/ *f,* entreaty, supplication; *Law.* petition
suplicante /supli'kante/ *a* supplicatory; *Law.* petitioning. *mf* supplicator; *Law.* petitioner
suplicar /supli'kar/ *vt* to beg, supplicate; request; *Law.* appeal
suplicio /su'pliθio; su'plisio/ *m,* torment, torture; execution; place of torture or execution; affliction, anguish. **último s.,** capital punishment
suplir /su'plir/ *vt* to supply, furnish; substitute, take the place of; overlook, forgive
suponer /supo'ner/ *vt irr* to suppose, take for granted; simulate; comprise, include; —*vi* carry weight, wield authority. See **poner**
suposición /suposi'θion; suposi'sion/ *f,* supposition; conjecture, assumption; distinction, talent, importance; falsity, falsehood
supositorio /suposi'torio/ *m,* suppository
suprasensible /suprasen'siβle/ *a* supersensible
supremacía /suprema'θia; suprema'sia/ *f,* supremacy
supremo /su'premo/ *a* supreme; matchless, incomparable; last
supresión /supre'sion/ *f,* suppression; destruction, eradication; omission
suprimir /supri'mir/ *vt* to suppress; destroy, eradi-

cate; omit, leave out. **s. una calle al tráfico,** to close a street to traffic, ban traffic from a street

supuesto /su'puesto/ *a* supposed; so-called; reputed. *m,* supposition, hypothesis. **por s.,** presumably; doubtless

supuración /supura'θion; supura'sion/ *f,* suppuration

supurar /supu'rar/ *vi* to suppurate

suputar /supu'tar/ *vt* to calculate, compute

sur /sur/ *m,* south; south wind

surcador /surka'ðor/ *m,* plowman

surcar /sur'kar/ *vt* to plow furrows; furrow, line; cut, cleave (water, etc.)

surco /'surko/ *m,* furrow; wrinkle, line; groove, channel; rut

surgidero /surhi'ðero/ *m, Naut.* road, roadstead

surgir /sur'hir/ *vi* to spout, gush, spurt; *Naut.* anchor; appear, show itself; come forth, turn up

surrealismo /surrea'lismo/ *m,* surrealism

surrealista /surrea'lista/ *a* and *mf* surrealist

surtida /sur'tiða/ *f,* hidden exit; false door; *Naut.* slipway

surtidero /surti'ðero/ *m,* outlet, drain; jet, fountain

surtido /sur'tiðo/ *a* mixed, assorted. *m,* variety, assortment; stock, range. **de s.,** in everyday use

surtidor /surti'ðor/ **(-ra)** *n* purveyor, supplier. *m,* fountain, jet. **s. de gasolina,** gasoline pump, gas pump

surtimiento /surti'miento/ *m,* assortment; stock

surtir /sur'tir/ *vt* to provide, supply, furnish; *—vi* spurt, gush

surto /'surto/ *a* calm, reposeful; *Naut.* anchored

¡sus! /sus/ *interj* Come on! Hurry up!

susceptibilidad /susθeptiβili'ðað; susseptiβili'ðað/ *f,* susceptibility

susceptible /susθep'tiβle; sussep'tiβle/ *a* susceptible, open to; touchy, oversensitive

suscitar /susθi'tar; sussi'tar/ *vt* to cause, originate; provoke, incite; *—vr* arise, take place

suscribir /suskri'βir/ *vt* to sign; agree to; *—vr* subscribe, contribute; take out a subscription (to a periodical, etc.) *—Past Part.* **suscrito**

suscripción /suskrip'θion; suskrip'sion/ *f,* subscription; agreement, accession

susodicho /suso'ðitʃo/ *a* aforesaid

suspender /suspen'der/ *vt* to suspend, hang up; postpone, defer, stop; amaze, dumbfound; suspend (from employment); fail (an exam); adjourn (meetings); *—vr* rear (of horses)

suspensión /suspen'sion/ *f,* suspension; postponement, stoppage, deferment; amazement; failure (in an exam); adjournment (of a meeting); springs (of a car). *Com.* **s. de pagos,** suspension of payments. **con mala s.,** badly sprung (of a car)

suspensivo /suspen'siβo/ *a* suspensive

suspensivos /suspen'siβos/ *m, pl* suspension points, ellipsis points

suspenso /sus'penso/ *a* amazed, bewildered. *m,* failure slip (in an exam). **en s.,** in suspense

suspicacia /suspi'kaθia; suspi'kasia/ *f,* suspiciousness; mistrust, uneasiness

suspicaz /suspi'kaθ; suspi'kas/ *a* suspicious, mistrustful

suspirado /suspi'raðo/ *a* eagerly desired, longed for

suspirar /suspi'rar/ *vt* and *vi* to sigh. **s. por,** to long for

suspiro /sus'piro/ *m,* sigh; breath; glass whistle; *Mus.* brief pause, pause sign. **último s.,** *Inf.* last kick, end

suspirón /suspi'ron/ *a* given to sighing

sustancia /sus'tanθia; sus'tansia/ *f,* substance, juice, extract, essence; *Fig.* core, pith; *Fig.* meat; wealth, estate; worth, importance; nutritive part; *Inf.* common sense. *Anat.* **s. gris,** gray matter. **en s.,** in short

sustanciación /sustanθia'θion; sustansia'sion/ *f,* substantiation

sustancial /sustan'θial; sustan'sial/ *a* substantial, real; important, essential; nutritive; solid

sustanciar /sustan'θiar; sustan'siar/ *vt* to substantiate; summarize, extract, abridge

sustancioso /sustan'θioso; sustan'sioso/ *a* substantial; nutritive

sustantivo /sustan'tiβo/ *a* and *m, Gram.* substantive, noun

sustentable /susten'taβle/ *a* arguable, defensible

sustentación /sustenta'θion; sustenta'sion/ *f,* maintenance; defense

sustentar /susten'tar/ *vt* to sustain, keep; support, bear; nourish, feed; uphold, advocate. **s. un ciclo de conferencias,** to give a series of lectures

sustento /sus'tento/ *m,* maintenance, preservation; nourishment, sustenance, support

sustitución /sustitu'θion; sustitu'sion/ *f,* substitution

sustituible /susti'tuiβle/ *a* substitutive, replaceable

sustituir /susti'tuir/ *vt irr* to substitute. See **huir**

sustitutivo /sustitu'tiβo/ *a* substitutive

sustituto /susti'tuto/ **(-ta)** *n* substitute

susto /'susto/ *m,* fright, shock; apprehension. **dar un s. (a),** to scare

sustracción /sustrak'θion; sustrak'sion/ *f,* subtraction

sustraendo /sustra'endo/ *m, Math.* subtrahend

sustraer /sustra'er/ *vt irr* to remove, separate; rob, steal; *Math.* subtract; *—vr* depart, remove oneself; avoid. See **traer**

sustrato /sus'trato/ *m,* substratum

susurrador /susurra'ðor/ **(-ra)** *a* whispering; murmuring; rustling *—n* whisperer

susurrante /susu'rrante/ *a* whispering; murmuring; rustling

susurrar /susu'rrar/ *vi* to whisper; murmur; rustle; babble, purl, prattle (of water); *—vi* and *vr* be whispered abroad

susurro /su'surro/ *m,* whispering, whisper; murmur; rustle; lapping

sutil /'sutil/ *a* fine, thin; penetrating, subtle, keen

sutileza, sutilidad /suti'leθa, sutili'ðað; suti'lesa, sutili'ðað/ *f,* fineness, thinness; subtlety, penetration. **sutileza de manos,** dexterity; light-fingeredness; sleight of hand

sutilizaciones /sutiliθa'θiones; sutilisa'siones/ *f, pl* casuistry, hairsplitting, quibbling

sutilizar /sutili'θar; sutili'sar/ *vt* to make thin, refine; *Fig.* finish, perfect; *Fig.* split hairs, make subtle distinctions

sutura /su'tura/ *f,* suture

suyo, suya /'suyo, 'suya/ *m,* and *f, pl* **suyos, suyas,** *poss pron* and *a 3rd pers* his; hers; its; yours; theirs; of his, of hers, etc. (e.g. *Este libro es suyo,* This book is his (hers, yours, theirs). **Este libro es uno de los suyos,** This book is one of his (hers, etc.). (**suyo** is often used with def. art. **el, la,** etc.) **los suyos,** his (hers, yours, etc.) family, following, adherents, etc. **de suyo,** of its very nature, of itself; spontaneously. **salirse con la suya,** to get one's own way. *Inf.* **ver la suyo,** to see one's opportunity

T

tabacal /taβa'kal/ *m,* tobacco plantation
tabacalero /taβaka'lero/ **(-ra)** *a* tobacco —*n* tobacco merchant; tobacco planter
tabaco /ta'βako/ *m,* tobacco plant, tobacco leaf; tobacco; cigar. **t. de pipa,** pipe tobacco. **t. flojo,** mild tobacco. **t. rubio,** Virginia tobacco
tabalear /taβale'ar/ **(se)** *vt* and *vr* to rock, sway, swing; —*vi* drum with the fingers
tabaleo /taβa'leo/ *m,* swaying, rocking; drumming with the fingers
tabanco /ta'βanko/ *m,* market stall
tábano /'taβano/ *m, Ent.* horsefly
tabanque /ta'βanke/ *m,* potter's wheel
tabaque /ta'βake/ *m,* small osier basket (for fruit, sewing, etc.); large tack
tabaquera /taβa'kera/ *f,* tobacco jar, tobacco tin; bowl of pipe tobacco; tobacco pouch; snuffbox
tabaquería /taβake'ria/ *f,* tobacconist's shop
tabaquero /taβa'kero/ **(-ra)** *n* worker in a tobacco factory; tobacconist
tabaquismo /taβa'kismo/ *m,* nicotinism, nicotine poisoning
tabaquista /taβa'kista/ *mf* tobacco expert; heavy smoker
tabardillo /taβar'ðiʎo; taβarðiyo/ *m,* fever. **t. de tripas,** typhoid. **t. pintado,** typhus
tabardo /ta'βarðo/ *m,* tabard
taberna /ta'βerna/ *f,* public house, tavern
tabernáculo /taβer'nakulo/ *m,* tabernacle
tabernario /taβer'nario/ *a* public house, tavern; low, vulgar
tabernera /taβer'nera/ *f,* publican's wife; barmaid
tabernero /taβer'nero/ *m,* publican; barman, drawer
tabicar /taβi'kar/ *vt* to wall or board up; hide, cover up
tabique /ta'βike/ *m,* partition wall, inside wall; thin wall
tabla /'taβla/ *f,* plank of wood, board; *Metall.* plate; slab; flat side, face (of wood); *Sew.* box pleat; table (of contents, etc.); *Art.* panel; vegetable garden; butcher's slab; butcher's stall; *pl* tablets (for writing); (*Math.* etc.) tables; stalemate (chess, checkers); draw (in an election); *Theat.* boards, stage. **t. de armonía,** sounding board (of musical instruments). **t. de lavar,** washboard. **t. de materias,** table of contents. **t. de multiplicación,** multiplication table. **t. rasa,** clean sheet (of paper, etc.); complete ignorance. **T. Redonda,** Round Table (of King Arthur). **escapar** *or* **salvarse en una t.,** to have a narrow escape, escape in the nick of time
tablacho /ta'βlatʃo/ *m,* sluice gate. **echar el t.,** *Inf.* to interrupt the flow of someone's remarks
tablado /ta'βlaðo/ *m,* flooring; platform; *Theat.* stage; scaffold, gibbet. **sacar al t.,** to produce, put on the stage; to make known, publish
tablazón /taβla'θon; taβla'son/ *f,* planks, boards; flooring; *Naut.* deck planks or sheathing
tablear /taβle'ar/ *vt* to saw into planks; *Sew.* make box pleats in; hammer iron into sheets
tablero /ta'βlero/ *m,* board (of wood); paneling, boarding; slab; shop counter; board (checkers, chess). **t. de instrumentos,** dashboard; instrument panel
tableta /ta'βleta/ *f,* tablet; pastille, lozenge
tablilla /ta'βliʎa; ta'βliya/ *f,* small board; tablet; bulletin board, notice board
tablón /ta'βlon/ *m,* thick plank; wooden beam; *Inf.* drinking bout
tabú /ta'βu/ *m,* taboo
tabuco /ta'βuko/ *m,* miserable little room; hovel
taburete /taβu'rete/ *m,* stool; tabouret
tacañería /takaɲe'ria/ *f,* miserliness, niggardliness; craftiness
tacaño /ta'kaɲo/ *a* miserly, niggardly; crafty
tacha /'tatʃa/ *f,* imperfection, defect; spot, stain; fault; large tack. **poner t.,** to criticize, object to
tachable /ta'tʃaβle/ *a* censurable, blameworthy
tachar /ta'tʃar/ *vt* to criticize, blame; cross out, erase; charge, accuse
tacho de basura /'tatʃo de ba'sura/ *m, Argentina* garbage can
tachón /ta'tʃon/ *m,* round-headed ornamental nail; *Sew.* gold or silver studs, trimming; crossing out, erasure
tachonar /tatʃo'nar/ *vt* to stud with round-headed nails; *Sew.* trim with gold or silver studs or trimming
tachoso /ta'tʃoso/ *a* imperfect, defective, faulty; spotted, stained
tachuela /ta'tʃuela/ *f,* tack
tácito /'taθito; 'tasito/ *a* silent, unexpressed; tacit, implied
taciturnidad /taθiturni'ðað; tasiturni'ðað/ *f,* taciturnity; reserve; melancholy
taciturno /taθi'turno; tasi'turno/ *a* taciturn; reserved; dismal, gloomy, melancholy
taco /'tako/ *m,* stopper, plug; billiard cue; rammer; wad, wadding (in a gun); pop gun; taco (food); tear-off calendar; *Inf.* snack; obscenity, oath. **t. de papel,** writing tablet
tacón /ta'kon/ *m,* heel (of a shoe)
taconear /takone'ar/ *vi* to stamp with one's heels; walk heavily on one's heels; walk arrogantly
taconeo /tako'neo/ *m,* drumming or stamping of one's heels (gen. in dancing)
táctica /'taktika/ *f,* method, technique; *Mil.* tactics; policy, way, means
táctico /'taktiko/ *a* tactical. *m, Mil.* tactician
táctil /'taktil/ *a* tactile
tacto /'takto/ *m,* sense of touch; touch, feel; touching; skill; tact
tafetán /tafe'tan/ *m,* taffeta; *pl* flags, standards. **t. de heridas** *or* **t. inglés,** court plaster
tafilete /tafi'lete/ *m,* morocco leather
tahalí /taa'li/ *m,* sword shoulder belt
tahona /ta'ona/ *f,* horse mill; bakery; baker's shop
tahonero /tao'nero/ **(-ra)** *n* miller; baker
tahúr /ta'ur/ *m,* gambler; cardsharper
tahurería /taure'ria/ *f,* gambling den; gambling; cheating at cards
Tailandia /tai'landia/ Thailand
taimado /tai'maðo/ *a* knavish, crafty; obstinate, headstrong
taimería /taime'ria/ *f,* cunning, craftiness
taita /'taita/ *m,* daddy
taja /'taha/ *f,* cut, cutting; slice; washboard
tajada /ta'haða/ *f,* slice; strip, portion; steak, filet; *Inf.* cough; drinking bout; hoarseness
tajadera /taha'ðera/ *f,* cheese knife; chisel; *pl* sluice gate
tajado /ta'haðo/ *a* steep, sheer (of cliffs, etc.)
tajadura /taha'ðura/ *f,* cutting, dividing, dissection
tajamar /taha'mar/ *m,* cutwater; breakwater; raft
tajar /ta'har/ *vt* to cut, chop; sharpen, trim (quill pens)
tajea /ta'hea/ *f,* culvert; aqueduct; drain; watercourse
Tajo, el /'taho, el/ the Tagus
tajo /'taho/ *m,* cut, incision; task; cutting (in a mountain, etc.); cut, thrust (of sword); executioner's block; chopping board; washboard; steep cliff, precipice
tajón /ta'hon/ *m,* butcher block; chopping board
tal /tal/ *a pl* **tales,** such; said (e.g. *el t. Don Juan,* the said Don Juan). **tal** is always used before nouns and (except when meaning "the said") without def. art. **un t.,** a certain (e.g. *un t. hombre,* a certain man) —*pron* some, some people; someone; such a thing —*adv* so, thus. **t. para cual,** two of a kind, a well-matched pair; tit for tat. **con t. que,** *conjunc* on condition that, provided that. **No hay t.,** There is no such thing. *Inf.* **¿Qué t.?** How are you? What's the news? What's new?

tala /'tala/ *f*, felling or cutting down (of trees); cropping of grass (ruminants)
talabarte /tala'βarte/ *m*, sword belt
talabartería /talaβarte'ria/ *f*, saddlery
talabartero /talaβar'tero/ *m*, saddler
talador /tala'ðor/ **(-ra)** *a* felling, cutting; destructive —*n* feller, cutter; destroyer
taladrar /tala'ðrar/ *vt* to drill, bore, gouge holes; pierce, perforate; punch (a ticket); assail or hurt the ear (sounds); *Fig.* go into deeply (a subject)
taladro /ta'laðro/ *m*, drill, gimlet, gouge; drill hole, bore; puncher (for tickets, etc.)
tálamo /'talamo/ *m*, marriage bed; (*Bot. Anat.*) thalamus
talán /ta'lan/ *m*, peal, tolling (of a bell)
talanquera /talan'kera/ *f*, barricade; parapet, fence, wall; refuge, asylum; safety, security
talante /ta'lante/ *m*, mode of execution, technique; personal appearance, mien; disposition, temperament; wish, desire; aspect, appearance. **de buen** (**mal**) **t.,** willingly (unwillingly)
talar /ta'lar/ *a* full-length, long (of gowns, robes, etc.)
talar /ta'lar/ *vt* to fell, chop down (trees); ravage, lay waste; prune (gen. olive trees)
talco /'talko/ *m*, *Mineral.* talc; sequin, tinsel
talcualillo /talkua'liʎo; talkua'liyo/ *a Inf.* not too bad, fairly good; slightly better (of health)
taled /ta'leð/ *m*, prayer shawl, tales, tallit
talega /ta'lega/ *f*, sack, bag; sackful; money bag; *pl Inf.* cash wealth
talego /talego/ *m*, narrow sack; *Inf.* dumpy person
talento /ta'lento/ *m*, talent (Greek coin); talent, gift, quality; intelligence, understanding; cleverness
talentoso /talen'toso/ *a* talented
tálero /'talero/ *m*, thaler (old German coin)
talión /ta'lion/ *m*, (**ley de**) law of retaliation
talismán /talis'man/ *m*, talisman
talla /'taʎa; 'taya/ *f*, carving (especially wood); cutting (of gems); reward for apprehension of a criminal; ransom; stature, height, size; height measuring rod
tallado /ta'ʎaðo; ta'yaðo/ *a* **bien** (or **mal**), well (or badly) carved; well (or badly) proportioned, of a good (or bad) figure
tallado /ta'ʎaðo; ta'yaðo/ *m*, carving
tallador /taʎa'ðor; taya'ðor/ *m*, metal engraver; die sinker
tallar /ta'ʎar; ta'yar/ *vt Art.* to carve; engrave; cut (gems); value, estimate; measure height (of persons)
tallarín /taʎa'rin; taya'rin/ *m*, (gen. *pl*) *Cul.* noodle
talle /'taʎe; 'taye/ *m*, figure, physique; waist; fit (of clothes); appearance, aspect. *Inf.* **largo de t.,** long-waisted; long drawn out, overlong. **tener buen t.,** to have a good figure
tallecer /taʎe'θer; taye'ser/ *vi irr Bot.* to sprout, shoot. See **conocer**
taller /ta'ʎer; ta'yer/ *m*, workshop; factory; mill; workroom, atelier; industrial school; school of arts and crafts; studio
tallista /ta'ʎista; ta'yista/ *mf* engraver; wood carver; sculptor
tallo /'taʎo; 'tayo/ *m*, *Bot.* stalk; shoot; slice of preserved fruit; cabbage. **t. rastrero,** *Bot.* runner
talludo /ta'ʎuðo; ta'yuðo/ *a* long-stalked; lanky, overgrown; no longer young, aging (of women); habit-ridden
talmúdico /tal'muðiko/ *a* Talmudic
talón /ta'lon/ *m*, heel; heel (of a shoe); *Com.* counterfoil; luggage receipt; *Com.* sight draft; coupon; heel (of a violin bow). *Inf.* **apretar los talones,** to take to one's heels. *Inf.* **pisarle** (**a uno**) **los talones,** to follow on a person's heels; rival successfully
talonada /talo'naða/ *f*, dig in with the spurs
talonario /talo'nario/ *m*, stub book
tamaño /ta'maɲo/ *a compar* so big; so small (e.g. *La conocí tamaña,* I knew her when she was so high) (indicating her size with a gesture)); so great, so large (e.g. *tamaña empresa,* so great an undertaking). *m*, size
tamarindo /tama'rindo/ *m*, tamarind
tambaleante /tambale'ante/ *a* tottering, rickety; staggering
tambalear /tambale'ar/ **(se)** *vi* and *vr* to totter, sway, shake; reel, stagger
tambaleo /tamba'leo/ *m*, swaying; tottering; rocking; shaking; staggering, reeling
tambarillo /tamba'riʎo; tambariyo/ *m*, chest with an arched lid
también /tam'bien/ *adv* also, too; in addition, as well
tambor /tam'bor/ *m*, *Mus.* drum; drummer; embroidery frame; *Mech.* drum, cylinder; roaster (for coffee, chestnuts, etc.). **t. mayor,** drum major. **a t.** (*or* **con t.**) **batiente,** with drums beating; triumphantly, with colors flying
tamborear /tambore'ar/ *vi* to totter, sway; stagger, reel
tamboreo /tambo'reo/ *m*, tottering, swaying; staggering, reeling
tamboril /tambo'ril/ *m*, tabor
tamborilada /tambori'laða/ *f*, *Inf.* slap on the back or face; *Inf.* fall on the bottom
tamborilear /tamborile'ar/ *vi* to play the tabor; —*vt* eulogize, extol
tamborilero /tambori'lero/ *m*, tabor player
tamborín /tambo'rin/ *m*, tabor
Támesis, el /'tamesis, el/ the Thames
tamiz /ta'miθ; ta'mis/ *m*, sieve
tamizar /tami'θar; tami'sar/ *vt* to sieve
tamo /'tamo/ *m*, fluff; chaff
tampoco /tam'poko/ *adv* neither, not... either, nor... either; no more (e.g. *No lo ha hecho María t.*, Mary hasn't done it either)
tampón /tam'pon/ *m*, stamp moistener; *Surg.* tampon
tan /tan/ *adv Abbr.* **tanto** so, as. Used before adjectives and adverbs, excepting **más, mejor, menos, peor,** which need **tanto. t.... como,** as... as. **t. siquiera,** even (see **siquiera**). **t. sólo,** only, solely (e.g. *No vengo t. sólo para saludarte,* I do not come merely to greet you). **qué... t.,** what a... (e.g. *¡Qué día t. hermoso!* What a lovely day!)
tanda /'tanda/ *f*, turn; opportunity; task; shift, relay; game (of billiards); bad habit; collection, batch, group; round (of a game); (*Dance.*) set
tándem /'tandem/ *m*, tandem
tandeo /tan'deo/ *m*, allowance of irrigation water, turn for using water
Tangañica /taŋga'ɲika/ Tanganyika
tangente /tan'hente/ *a* and *f*, *Geom.* tangent
Tánger /'tanher/ Tangier
tangerino /tanhe'rino/ **(-na)** *a* and *n* of or from Tangier, Tangerine
tanque /'tanke/ *m*, *Mil.* tank; cistern, tank, reservoir; ladle, dipper
tanteador /tantea'ðor/ *m*, *Sports.* scorer, marker; scoreboard
tantear /tante'ar/ *vt* to measure, compare; consider fully; test, try out; *Fig.* probe, pump (persons); estimate roughly; *Art.* sketch, block in; —*vt* and *vi Sports.* keep the score of
tanteo /tan'teo/ *m*, measurement, comparison; test; rough estimate; *Sports.* score
tanto /'tanto/ *a* so much; as much; very great; as great; *pl* **tantos,** so many; as many (e.g. *Tienen tantas flores como nosotros,* They have as many flowers as we). In comparisons **tanto** is used before **más, mejor, menos, peor,** but generally **tan** is used before adjectives and adverbs (e.g. *¡Tanto peor!* So much the worse!) —*pron dem* that (e.g. *por lo t.*, therefore, on that account). *m*, so much, a certain amount; copy of a document; man, piece (in games); point (score in games); *Com.* rate (e.g. *el t. por ciento,* the percentage, the rate); *pl* approximation, odd (e.g. *Llegaron cien hombres y tantos,* A hundred-odd men arrived) —*adv* so much; as much; so, in such a way. **t.... como,** the same as, as much as. **t.... cuanto,** as much as. **t. más,** the more. **t. menos,** the less (e.g. *Cuanto más* (*menos*) **dinero tiene t. más** (**menos**) **quiere,** The more (less) money he has, the more (less) he wants). **t. más** (**menos**)... **cuanto que,** all the more (less)... because. **algún t.,** a certain amount, somewhat. **al t. de** (**una cosa**), aware of, acquainted with (a thing). **en t.** *or* **entre t.,** mean-

while. **las tantas,** *Inf.* late hour, wee hours. **No es para t.,** *Inf.* It's not as bad as that, there's no need to make such a fuss; he (she, it) isn't equal to it. **otro t.,** the same, as much; as much more. **un t.,** a bit, somewhat

tañedor /taɲe'ðor/ **(-ra)** *n Mus.* player

tañer /ta'ɲer/ *vt irr Mus.* to play; —*vi* sway, swing. **t. la occisa,** to sound the death (in hunting) —*Pres. Part.* **tañendo.** *Preterite* **tañó, tañeron.** *Imperf. Subjunc.* **tañese,** etc.

tañido /ta'ɲiðo/ *m,* tune, sound, note; toll, peal; ring

taoísmo /tao'ismo/ *m,* Taoism

taoísta /tao'ista/ *mf* Taoist

tapa /'tapa/ *f,* lid; cover; cover (of books)

tapaboca /tapa'βoka/ *m,* blow on the mouth; *f,* scarf, muffler; *Inf.* remark that silences someone

tapada /ta'paða/ *f,* veiled woman, one whose face is hidden

tapadera /tapa'ðera/ *f,* loose lid, top, cover

tapadero /tapa'ðero/ *m,* stopper

tapador /tapa'ðor/ **(-ra)** *a* covering —*n* coverer. *m,* stopper; lid; cover

tapagujeros /tapagu'heros/ *m, Inf.* unskilled mason or bricklayer; *Fig. Inf.* stopgap (person)

tapar /ta'par/ *vt* to cover; cover with a lid; muffle up, veil; hide, keep secret; close up, stop up

taparrabo /tapa'rraβo/ *m,* loincloth; swimming trunks

tapete /ta'pete/ *m,* rug; tablecover. *Inf.* **t. verde,** gaming table. *Fig.* **estar sobre el t.,** to be on the carpet, be under consideration

tapia /'tapia/ *f,* adobe; mud wall; fence. *Inf.* **más sordo que una t.,** as deaf as a post

tapiar /ta'piar/ *vt* to wall up; put a fence around, fence in

tapicería /tapiθe'ria; tapise'ria/ *f,* set of tapestries; tapestry work; art of tapestry making; upholstery; tapestry storehouse or shop

tapicero /tapi'θero; tapi'sero/ *m,* tapestry weaver or maker; upholsterer; carpet layer; furnisher

tapioca /ta'pioka/ *f,* tapioca

tapiz /ta'piθ; ta'pis/ *m,* tapestry; carpet

tapizar /tapi'θar; tapi'sar/ *vt* to cover with tapestry; cover, clothe; upholster; carpet; hang with tapestry; furnish with hangings or drapes

tapón /ta'pon/ *m,* stopper; cork (of a bottle); plug; *Surg.* tampon

taponar /tapo'nar/ *vt* to stopper, cork; plug; *Surg.* tampon; *Mil.* seal off

taponazo /tapo'naθo; tapo'naso/ *m,* pop (of a cork)

tapujarse /tapu'harse/ *vr* to wrap oneself up, muffle oneself

tapujo /ta'puho/ *m,* scarf, muffler, face covering; disguise; *Inf.* pretense, subterfuge

taquera /ta'kera/ *f,* rack (for billiard cues)

taquería /take'ria/ *f,* taco stand

taquigrafía /takigra'fia/ *f,* shorthand

taquigrafiar /takigra'fiar/ *vt* to write in shorthand

taquigráfico /taki'grafiko/ *a* shorthand

taquígrafo /ta'kigrafo/ **(-fa)** *n* shorthand writer, stenographer

taquilla /ta'kiʎa; ta'kiya/ *f,* booking office; box office; grille, window (in banks, etc.); rolltop desk, cupboard for papers; *Theat.* takings, cash

taquillero /taki'ʎero; taki'yero/ **(-ra)** *n* booking office clerk

tara /'tara/ *f,* tally stick; *Com.* tare

taracea /tara'θea; tara'sea/ *f,* inlaid work, marquetry

taracear /taraθe'ar; tarase'ar/ *vt* to inlay

tarambana /taram'bana/ *mf Inf.* madcap

tarantela /taran'tela/ *f,* tarantella

tarántula /ta'rantula/ *f,* tarantula

tararear /tarare'ar/ *vt* to hum a tune

tarareo /tara'reo/ *m,* humming, singing under one's breath

tarasca /ta'raska/ *f,* figure of a dragon (carried in Corpus Christi processions); *Inf.* hag, trollop

tarascada /taras'kaða/ *f,* bite, nip; *Inf.* insolent reply

tarascar /taras'kar/ *vt* to bite; wound with the teeth

tardanza /tar'ðanθa; tar'ðansa/ *f,* delay, tardiness; slowness

tardar /tar'ðar/ *vi* to delay; be tardy, arrive late; take a long time. **a más t.,** at the latest

tarde /'tarðe/ *f,* afternoon —*adv* late. **¡Buenas tardes!** Good afternoon! **de t. en t.,** from time to time, sometimes. **hacerse t.,** to grow late. **Más vale t. que nunca,** Better late than never

tardecer /tarðe'θer; tarðe'ser/ *vi impers irr* to grow dusk. See **conocer**

tardecica, tardecita /tarðe'θika, tarðe'θita; tarðe'sika, tarðe'sita/ *f,* dusk, late afternoon

tardíamente /tar'ðiamente/ *adv* late; too late

tardío /tar'ðio/ *a* late; backward; behind; slow, deliberate

tardo /'tarðo/ *a* slow, slothful, tardy; late; dilatory; stupid, slow-witted; badly spoken, inarticulate

tarea /ta'rea/ *f,* task, work

tarifa /ta'rifa/ *f,* price list; tariff

tarifar /tari'far/ *vt* to put a tariff on

tarima /ta'rima/ *f,* stand, raised platform

tarín barín /ta'rin ba'rin/ *adv Inf.* more or less, about

tarja /'tarha/ *f,* large shield; ancient coin; tally stick. *Inf.* **beber sobre t.,** to drink on credit

tarjar /tar'har/ *vt* to reckon by tally

tarjeta /tar'heta/ *f,* buckler, small shield; *Archit.* tablet bearing an inscription; title (of maps and charts); visiting card; invitation (card). **t. de visita,** visiting card. **t. postal,** postcard. **t. telefónica,** calling card (phone)

tarquín /tar'kin/ *m,* mud, mire

tárraga /'tarraga/ *f,* old Spanish dance

tarro /'tarro/ *m,* jar, pot

tarso /'tarso/ *m, Anat.* tarsus, ankle; *Zool.* hock; *Ornith.* shank

tarta /'tarta/ *f,* cake pan; cake; tart

tártago /'tartago/ *m,* spurge; *Inf.* misfortune, disappointment

tartajear /tartahe'ar/ *vi* to stammer; stutter

tartajeo /tarta'heo/ *m,* stammering; stutter

tartajoso /tarta'hoso/ **(-sa)** *a* stammering; stuttering —*n* stutterer

tartalear /tartale'ar/ *vi Inf.* to stagger, totter; be speechless, be dumbfounded

tartamudear /tartamuðe'ar/ *vi* to stammer, stutter

tartamudeo /tartamu'ðeo/ *m.* **tartamudez** *f,* stammering; stuttering

tartamudo /tarta'muðo/ **(-da)** *n* stammerer

tartán /tar'tan/ *m,* tartan

tartana /tar'tana/ *f, Naut.* tartan; covered two-wheeled carriage

tartáreo /tar'tareo/ *a Poet.* infernal, hellish

Tartaria /tar'taria/ Tartary

tártaro /'tartaro/ **(-ra)** *m,* cream of tartar; tartar (on teeth); *Poet.* hell, hades —*a* and *n* Tartar

tartufo /tar'tufo/ *m,* hypocrite

tarugo /ta'rugo/ *m,* thick wooden peg; stopper; wooden block

tasa /'tasa/ *f,* assessment, valuation; valuation certificate; fixed price; standard rate; measure, rule

tasación /tasa'θion; tasa'sion/ *f,* valuation; assessment

tasador /tasa'ðor/ *m,* public assessor; valuer

tasajo /ta'saho/ *m,* salt meat; piece of meat

tasar /ta'sar/ *vt* to value; price; fix remuneration; tax; regulate; rate; dole out sparingly

tasca /'taska/ *f,* gambling den; tavern

tascar /tas'kar/ *vt* to dress (hemp, etc.); graze, crop the grass

tasquera /tas'kera/ *f, Inf.* quarrel, row, rumpus

tasquil /tas'kil/ *m,* wood splinter, chip

tata /'tata/ *m, Inf. West Hem.* daddy

tatarabuela /tatara'βuela/ *f,* great-great-grandmother

tatarabuelo /tatara'βuelo/ *m,* great-great-grandfather

tataradeudo /tatara'ðeuðo/ **(-da)** *n* very old relative; ancestor

tataranieta /tatara'nieta/ *f,* great-great-granddaughter

tataranieto /tatara'nieto/ *m,* great-great-grandson

tatas, andar a /'tatas, an'dar a/ *vt* to walk on all fours

¡tate! /'tate/ *interj* Stop!; Be careful!; Go slowly!; Now I understand!, Of course!

tatuaje /ta'tuahe/ *m,* tattooing

tatuar /tatu'ar/ *vt* to tattoo

taumaturgia /tauma'turhia/ *f,* thaumaturgy, wonder-working

taumaturgo /tauma'turgo/ *m,* thaumaturge, magician

taurino /tau'rino/ *a* taurine; pertaining to bullfights

Tauro /'tauro/ *m,* Taurus

tauromaquia /tauro'makia/ *f,* bullfighting, tauromachy

tautología /tautolo'hia/ *f,* tautology

taxi /'taksi/ *m,* taxi

taxidermia /taksi'ðermia/ *f,* taxidermy

taxidermista /taksiðer'mista/ *mf* taxidermist

taxista /tak'sista/ *m,* taxi driver

taxonomía /taksono'mia/ *f,* taxonomy

taza /'taθa; 'tasa/ *f,* cup; cupful; basin (of a fountain)

tazar /ta'θar; ta'sar/ **(se)** *vt* and *vr* to fray (of cloth)

taz a taz /taθ a taθ; tas a tas/ *adv* in exchange, without payment; even

tazmía /taθ'mia; tas'mia/ *f,* tithe contribution; share of tithes; tithe register

tazón /ta'θon; ta'son/ *m,* large cup; bowl

te /te/ *f,* name of the letter T. *mf* dat. and acc. of *pers pron 2nd pers sing* thee; you; to thee, to you. Never used with a preposition

té /te/ *m,* tea

tea /tea/ *f,* torch; firebrand

teatral /tea'tral/ *a* theatrical

teatralidad /teatrali'ðað/ *f,* theatricality

teatro /te'atro/ *m,* theater; stage; dramatic works; dramatic art; drama, plays. **t. de variedades,** music hall. **t. por horas,** theater where short, one-act plays are staged hourly

tebano /te'βano/ **(-na), tebeo (-ea)** *a* and *n* Theban

Tebas /'teβas/ Thebes

teca /'teka/ *f,* teak

techado /te'tʃaðo/ *m,* ceiling; roof

techador /tetʃa'ðor/ *m,* roofer

techar /te'tʃar/ *vt* to roof

techo /'tetʃo/ *m,* roof; ceiling; dwelling, habitation

techumbre /te'tʃumbre/ *f,* ceiling; roof

tecla /'tekla/ *f,* key (of keyed instruments); typewriter, linotype, or calculating machine key; *Fig.* difficult or delicate point. *Inf.* **dar en la t.,** to hit on the right way of doing a thing

teclado /te'klaðo/ *m,* keyboard

tecleado /tekle'aðo/ *m, Mus.* fingering

teclear /tekle'ar/ *vi* to finger the keyboard; run one's fingers over the keyboard; *Inf.* drum or tap with the fingers; —*vt* tap (the keys, etc.); *Inf.* try out various schemes

tecleo /te'kleo/ *m,* fingering the keys; *Inf.* drumming with the fingers; scheme, means

técnica /'teknika/ *f,* technique

tecnicismo /tekni'θismo; tekni'sismo/ *m,* technical jargon; technicality, technical term

técnico /'tekniko/ *a* technical. *m,* technician

tecnicolor /tekniko'lor/ *m,* technicolor

tecnología /teknolo'hia/ *f,* technology

tecnológico /tekno'lohiko/ *a* technological

tecnólogo /tek'nologo/ *m,* technologist

tedero /te'ðero/ *m,* torch seller; torch holder

tedio /'teðio/ *m,* tedium, boredom, ennui

tedioso /te'ðioso/ *a* tedious, boring

tegumento /tegu'mento/ *m,* integument, tegument

teísmo /te'ismo/ *m,* theism

teísta /te'ista/ *a* theistic. *mf* theist

teja /'teha/ *f,* tile, slate. *Inf.* **de tejas abajo,** in the normal way; in the world of men. **de tejas arriba,** in a supernatural way; in heaven

tejadillo /teha'ðiʎo; teha'ðiyo/ *m,* roof (of a vehicle)

tejado /te'haðo/ *m,* roof

tejar /te'har/ *m,* tile works —*vt* to roof with tiles

tejavana /teha'βana/ *f,* penthouse, open shed

tejedor /tehe'ðor/ **(-ra)** *a* weaving; *Inf.* scheming —*n* weaver; *Inf.* schemer

tejedura /tehe'ðura/ *f,* weaving; fabric; texture

tejeduría /teheðu'ria/ *f,* art of weaving; weaving shed or mill

tejemaneje /tehema'nehe/ *m, Inf.* cleverness, knack

tejer /te'her/ *vt* to weave; plait; spin a cocoon; arrange, regulate; concoct, hatch (schemes); wind in and out (in dancing)

tejero /te'hero/ *m,* tile manufacturer

tejido /te'hiðo/ *m,* texture, weaving; textile; *Anat.* tissue; fabric, material

tejo /'teho/ *m,* quoit, discus; metal disk; yew tree

tejón /te'hon/ *m, Zool.* badger

tela /'tela/ *f,* fabric, material, cloth; membrane; film (on liquids); spiderweb, cobweb; inner skin (of fruit, vegetables); film over the eye; matter, subject; scheme, plot. **t. metálica,** wire gauze. **en t. de juicio,** under consideration, in doubt. **llegarle a uno a las telas del corazón,** to hurt deeply, cut to the quick

telar /te'lar/ *m,* loom, weaving machine; *Theat.* gridiron

telaraña /tela'raɲa/ *f,* cobweb; mere trifle, bagatelle. *Inf.* **mirar las telarañas,** to be absent-minded

telarañoso /telara'ɲoso/ *a* cobwebby

telecomunicación /telekomunika'θion; telekomunika'sion/ *f,* telecommunication

telefonear /telefone'ar/ *vt* to telephone, call

telefonía /telefo'nia/ *f,* telephony. **t. sin hilos,** wireless telephony, broadcasting

telefónico /tele'foniko/ *a* telephonic

telefonista /telefo'nista/ *mf* telephone operator

teléfono /te'lefono/ *m,* telephone. **t. automático,** dial telephone. **llamar por t.** (**a**), to telephone, call, ring up

telefundir /telefun'dir/ *vt* to telecast

telegrafía /telegra'fia/ *f,* telegraphy. **t. sin hilos,** wireless telegraphy

telegrafiar /telegra'fiar/ *vt* to telegraph

telegráfico /tele'grafiko/ *a* telegraphic

telegrafista /telegra'fista/ *mf* telegraph operator

telégrafo /te'legrafo/ *m,* telegraph. **t. sin hilos,** wireless telegraph. *Inf.* **hacer telégrafos,** to talk by signs

telegrama /tele'grama/ *m,* telegram

telemetría /teleme'tria/ *f,* telemetry

telémetro /te'lemetro/ *m,* telemeter, rangefinder

teleología /teleolo'hia/ *f,* teleology

telepatía /telepa'tia/ *f,* telepathy

telepático /tele'patiko/ *a* telepathic

telescópico /teles'kopiko/ *a* telescopic

telescopio /teles'kopio/ *m,* telescope

telespectador /telespekta'ðor/ *m,* TV viewer, member of the television audience

teletipo /tele'tipo/ *m,* teleprinter

televisión /teleβi'sion/ *f,* television

telilla /te'liʎa; te'liya/ *f,* film (on liquids); thin fabric

telón /te'lon/ *m, Theat.* curtain; drop scene. **t. contra incendios, t. de seguridad,** *Theat.* safety curtain. **t. de boca,** drop curtain. **t. de foro,** drop scene

tema /'tema/ *m,* theme, subject; *Mus.* motif, theme; thesis, argument. *f,* obstinacy; obsession, mania; hostility, grudge, rancor

temático /te'matiko/ *a* thematic; pigheaded, obstinate

temblador /tembla'ðor/ **(-ra)** *a* trembling, shaking —*n* Quaker

temblante /tem'blante/ *a* shaking; quivering. *m,* bracelet

temblar /tem'blar/ *vi irr* to tremble, shake; wave, quiver; shiver with fear. See **acertar**

temblequear, tembletear /tembleke'ar, temblete'ar/ *vi Inf.* tremble; shake with fear

temblón /tem'blon/ *a Inf.* trembling, shaking. *m, Inf.* aspen

temblor /tem'blor/ *m,* shake, trembling, shiver. **t. de tierra,** earthquake

tembloroso, tembloso /temblo'roso, tem'bloso/ *a* trembling, shaking, shivering, quivering

temedero /teme'ðero/ *a* fearsome, dread

temedor /teme'ðor/ **(-ra)** *a* fearful —*n* fearer, dreader

temer /te'mer/ *vt* to fear, dread; suspect, imagine; —*vi* be afraid

temerario /teme'rario/ *a* reckless, impetuous; thoughtless, hasty

temeridad /temeri'ðað/ *f,* recklessness, impetuosity, temerity; thoughtlessness; act of folly; rash judgment

temerón /teme'ron/ *a Inf.* swaggering, bombastic

temeroso /teme'roso/ *a* frightening, dread; fearful, timid; afraid, suspicious
temible /te'miβle/ *a* dread, awesome
temor /te'mor/ *m,* fear
temoso /te'moso/ *a* obstinate, headstrong
témpano /'tempano/ *m,* tabor; drumhead; block, flat piece; side of bacon. **t. de hielo,** iceberg, ice floe
temperación /tempera'θion; tempera'sion/ *f,* tempering
temperamento /tempera'mento/ *m,* temperament, nature; compromise, agreement
temperar /tempe'rar/ *vt* to temper
temperatura /tempera'tura/ *f,* temperature
temperie /tem'perie/ *f,* weather conditions
tempestad /tempes'tað/ *f,* storm
tempestividad /tempestiβi'ðað/ *f,* opportuneness, seasonableness
tempestivo /tempes'tiβo/ *a* opportune, seasonable
tempestuoso /tempes'tuoso/ *a* stormy
templa /'templa/ *f,* tempera; *pl Anat.* temples
templado /tem'plaðo/ *a* moderate; temperate (of regions); lukewarm; *Mus.* in tune; restrained (of style); *Inf.* brave, long-suffering. **estar bien** (*or* **mal**) **templado,** *Inf.* to be well (or badly) tuned (of musical instruments); be in a good (*or* bad) temper; be good-(*or* ill-) natured
templador /templa'ðor/ **(-ra)** *n* tuner. *m,* tuning key
templadura /templa'ðura/ *f,* tuning; tempering
templanza /tem'planθa; tem'plansa/ *f,* moderation; sobriety; mildness of climate
templar /tem'plar/ *vt* to tune; *Metall.* temper; moderate; warm; allay, appease; anneal; *Art.* harmonize, blend; *Naut.* trim the sails; *—vr* control oneself, be moderate; *—vi* grow warm
templario /tem'plario/ *m,* Knight Templar
temple /'temple/ *m,* weather conditions; temperature; temper (of metals, etc.); nature, disposition; bravery; mean, average; *Mus.* tuning. **al t.,** in tempera
templete /tem'plete/ *m, dim* shrine; niche (for statues); kiosk, pavilion
templo /'templo/ *m,* temple
temporada /tempo'raða/ *f,* space of time, season, while. **de t.,** seasonal; temporary. **estar de t.,** to be out of town, on holiday
temporal /tempo'ral/ *a* temporal; temporary; secular, lay; transient, fugitive. *m,* storm, tempest; rainy period; seasonal laborer
temporalidad /temporali'ðað/ *f,* secular character; temporality secular possession (gen. *pl*)
temporáneo, temporario /tempora'neo, tempo'rario/ *a* temporary, impermanent, fleeting
témporas /'temporas/ *f pl,* Ember days
temporejar /tempore'har/ *vt Naut.* to lie to in a storm
temporero /tempo'rero/ *a* temporary (of work)
temporizar /tempori'θar; tempori'sar/ *vi* to while away the time; temporize
tempranal /tempra'nal/ *a* early fruiting
tempranero /tempra'nero/ *a* early
temprano /tem'prano/ *a* early *—adv* in the early hours; prematurely, too soon
temulento /temu'lento/ *a* intoxicated, drunken
tenacear /tenaθe'ar; tenase'ar/ *vi* to insist, be obstinate
tenacidad /tenaθi'ðað; tenasi'ðað/ *f,* adhesiveness; resistance, toughness; obstinacy, tenacity
tenacillas /tena'θiʎas; tena'siyas/ *f pl, dim* small tongs; candle snuffers; sugar tongs; curling irons; tweezers
tenaz /te'naθ; te'nas/ *a* adhesive; hard, resistant, unyielding; tenacious, obstinate
tenaza /te'naθa; te'nasa/ *f,* claw (of a lobster, etc.); *pl* tongs; pincers; pliers; dental forceps
tenazada /tena'θaða; tena'saða/ *f,* seizing with tongs; strong bite, snap; rattle of tongs
tenazón /tena'θon; tena'son/ (**a** or **de**) *adv* without taking aim, wildly; unexpectedly
tenca /'tenka/ *f,* tench
tención /ten'θion; ten'sion/ *f,* retention, holding; grip
ten con ten /ten kon ten/ *m, Inf.* tact, diplomacy
tendal /ten'dal/ *m,* awning; sheet for catching olives
tendedero /tende'ðero/ *m,* drying ground
tendedura /tende'ðura/ *f,* laying out; stretching
tendencia /ten'denθia; tendensia/ *f,* tendency
tendencioso /tenden'θioso; tenden'sioso/ *a* tendentious, biased
tender /ten'der/ *vt irr* to hang out; unfold, spread out; extend, hold out; *Mas.* plaster; *—vi* tend, incline; *—vr* lie down at full length; place one's cards on the table; gallop hard (of horses). See **entender**
tendero /ten'dero/ **(-ra)** *n* shopkeeper; retailer. *m,* tent maker
tendido /ten'diðo/ *m,* row of seats in a bullfight arena; clothes hung out to dry; clear sky; *Mas.* plaster
tendón /ten'don/ *m,* tendon
tenducha /ten'dutʃa/ *f, Inf.* wretched little shop
tenebrosidad /teneβrosi'ðað/ *f,* gloom, darkness, obscurity
tenebroso /tene'βroso/ *a* dark, gloomy
tenedero /tene'ðero/ *m, Naut.* anchoring ground, anchorage
tenedor /tene'ðor/ *m,* table fork; possessor, retainer; *Com.* holder; payee. **t. de libros,** bookkeeper
teneduría /teneðu'ria/ *f,* employment of a bookkeeper. **t. de libros,** bookkeeping
tenencia /te'nenθia; te'nensia/ *f,* possession; tenancy, occupation; lieutenancy
tener /te'ner/ *vt irr* to have; hold; grasp; possess, own; uphold, maintain; contain; include; hold fast, grip; stop; keep (promises); lodge, accommodate; (*with en*) value, estimate (e.g. *Le tengo en poco,* I have a poor opinion of him); (*with para*) be of the opinion that (e.g. *tengo para mí,* my opinion is); (*with por*) believe, consider; *—vi* be wealthy; *—vr* steady oneself; hold on to; lean (on); rest (on); defend oneself; uphold; rely on; (*with por*) consider oneself as. **tener** is used to express: 1. *Age* (e.g. *¿Cuántos años tiene Vd?* How old are you?). 2. *Possession* (e.g. *Tenemos muchos sombreros,* We have a great many hats). 3. *Measurements* (e.g. *El cuarto tiene dieciocho metros de largo,* The room is eighteen meters long). Translated by "be' when describing some physical and mental states (e.g. *Tenemos miedo,* We are afraid. *Tengo sueño,* I am sleepy. *Tienen frío* (*calor*), They are cold (hot)). Used as *auxiliary verb* replacing **haber** in compound tenses of transitive verbs (e.g. *Tengo escritas las cartas,* I have written the letters). **t. a bien,** to think fit, please, judge convenient. **t. algo en cuenta a uno,** to hold something against someone. **t. a menos de hacer** (**una cosa**), to scorn to do (a thing). **t. cruda,** to have a hangover. **t. curiosidad por,** to be curious about. **t. curiosidad por que** + *subj* to be interested that. **t. en aprecio,** to appreciate, esteem, value. **t. en cuenta,** to bear in mind. **t. en menos** (**a**), to despise (a person). **t. gana,** to want, wish; feel disposed; have an appetite. **t. lugar,** to take place, occur. **t. muchas partes cruzadas,** to be well-traveled. **t. mucho colegio** to be well-educated. **t. muy en cuenta,** to certainly bear in mind. **t. poco colegio,** to have had little education. **t. presente,** to remember. **t. que,** to have to (e.g. *tengo que hacerlo,* I must do it). **t. que ver** (**con**), to have something to do (with), be related to. **no tenerlas todas consigo,** *Inf.* to have the jitters *—Pres. Ind.* **tengo, tienes, tiene, tenemos, tenéis, tienen.** *Preterite* **tuve,** etc *—Fut.* **tendré,** etc *—Condit.* **tendría,** etc *—Pres. Subjunc.* **tenga,** etc *—Imperf. Subjunc.* **tuviese,** etc.
tenguerengue, en /teŋgue'reŋgue, en/ *adv Inf.* rickety, insecure
tenia /'tenia/ *f,* tapeworm; *Archit.* fillet, narrow molding
teniente /te'niente/ *a* owning, holding; unripe (of fruit); *Inf.* slightly deaf; stingy, mean. *m,* deputy, substitute; *Mil.* first lieutenant, lieutenant. **t. coronel,** lieutenant colonel. **t. de navío,** naval lieutenant. **t. general,** *Mil.* lieutenant general. **t. general de aviación,** air marshal
tenis /'tenis/ *m,* tennis

tenor /te'nor/ *m,* import, contents (of a letter, etc.); constitution, composition; *Mus.* tenor
tenorio /te'norio/ *m,* rake, Don Juan, philanderer
tensar /ten'sar/ *vt* to tighten; tense
tensión /ten'sion/ *f,* tautness; tension; strain, stress; *Elec.* tension
tenso /'tenso/ *a* taut; tight; tense
tentación /tenta'θion; tenta'sion/ *f,* temptation; attraction, inducement
tentáculo /ten'takulo/ *m,* tentacle; feeler
tentadero /tenta'ðero/ *m,* yard for trying out young bulls for bullfighting
tentador /tenta'ðor/ **(-ra)** *a* tempting; attractive —*n* tempter. *m,* the Devil
tentalear /tentale'ar/ *vt* to examine by touch
tentar /ten'tar/ *vt irr* to touch, feel; examine by touch; incite, encourage; try, endeavor; test; tempt; *Surg.* probe. See **sentar**
tentativa /tenta'tiβa/ *f,* endeavor, attempt; preliminary exam (at some univs.)
tentativo /tenta'tiβo/ *a* tentative, experimental
tentemozo /tente'moθo; tente'moso/ *m,* support, prop; tumbler (toy)
tentempié /tentem'pie/ *m, Inf.* snack, bite
tenue /'tenue/ *a* thin; slender, delicate; trivial, worthless, insignificant; pale; faint
tenuidad /tenui'ðað/ *f,* slenderness; delicacy; triviality, insignificance; paleness; faintness
teñidura /teɲi'ðura/ *f,* dyeing, staining
teñir /te'ɲir/ *vt irr* to dye; *Art.* darken; color, tinge; —*vr* be dyed; be tinged or colored. See **ceñir**
teocracia /teo'kraθia; teo'krasia/ *f,* theocracy
teocrático /teo'kratiko/ *a* theocratic
teodolito /teoðo'lito/ *m,* theodolite
teologal /teolo'gal/ *a* theological
teología /teolo'hia/ *f,* theology, divinity
teológico /teo'lohiko/ *a* theological
teologizar /teolohi'θar; teolohi'sar/ *vi* to theologize
teólogo /te'ologo/ *a* theological. *m,* theologian, divine; student of theology
teorema /teo'rema/ *m,* theorem
teoría /teo'ria/ *f,* theory
teórica /te'orika/ *f,* theory
teórico /te'oriko/ *a* theoretical, speculative. *m,* theorist
teorizar /teori'θar; teori'sar/ *vt* to consider theoretically, theorize about
teoso /te'oso/ *a* resinous, gummy
teosofía /teoso'fia/ *f,* theosophy
teosófico /teo'sofiko/ *a* theosophical
teósofo /te'osofo/ *m,* theosophist
tepe /'tepe/ *m,* sod, cut turf
terapeuta /tera'peuta/ *mf* therapeutist
terapéutica /tera'peutika/ *f,* therapeutics
terapéutico /tera'peutiko/ *a* therapeutic
terapia /te'rapia/ *f,* therapy
teratología /teratolo'hia/ *f,* teratology
tercena /ter'θena; ter'sena/ *f,* warehouse for storing government monopoly goods (tobacco, etc.)
tercenista /terθe'nista; terse'nista/ *mf* person in charge of a tercena
tercer /ter'θer; ter'ser/ *a Abbr.* of **tercero** third. Used before *m, sing* nouns
tercera /ter'θera; ter'sera/ *f,* procuress; *Mus.* third
tercería /terθe'ria; terse'ria/ *f,* arbitration, mediation; temporary occupation of a fortress, etc.
tercero /ter'θero; ter'sero/ **(-ra)** *a* third; mediatory —*n* third; mediator. *m,* pimp; *Eccl.* tertiary; tithes collector; third person. **¡A la tercera va la vencida!** Third time lucky!
terceto /ter'θeto; ter'seto/ *m,* tercet, triplet
tercia /'terθia; 'tersia/ *f,* one-third; *Eccl.* tierce, third hour; storehouse for tithes. **tercias reales,** royal share of ecclesiastical tithes
terciana /ter'θiana; ter'siana/ *f,* tertian fever
terciar /ter'θiar; ter'siar/ *vt* to slant; sling sideways; divide into three; equalize weight (on beasts of burden); plow or dig for the third time; *Agr.* prune; —*vr* be opportune, come at the right time —*vi* mediate, arbitrate; make up a number (for cards, etc.); reach the third day (of the moon); take part, participate
terciario /ter'θiario; ter'siario/ *a* third, tertiary; *Geol.* tertiary. *m, Eccl.* tertiary
tercio /'terθio; 'tersio/ *a* third. *m,* one-third; *Mil.* infantry regiment; *Obs.,* body of foreign volunteers; fishermen's association; *pl* brawny limbs of a man. **hacer t.,** to take part in; make up the number of. **hacer buen** (*or* **mal**) **t. a alguien,** to do someone a good (or bad) turn
terciopelo /terθio'pelo; tersio'pelo/ *m,* velvet; velveteen
terco /'terko/ *a* pigheaded, obstinate; hard, tough
tergiversación /terhiβersa'θion; terhiβersa'sion/ *f,* tergiversation, vacillation
tergiversar /terhiβer'sar/ *vt* to tergiversate, shuffle, vacillate
termal /ter'mal/ *a* thermal
termas /'termas/ *f pl,* thermal springs, hot mineral baths; thermal
térmico /'termiko/ *a* thermic
terminable /termi'naβle/ *a* terminable
terminación /termina'θion; termina'sion/ *f,* conclusion, termination; end, finish; ending of a word; *Gram.* termination
terminador /termina'ðor/ **(-ra)** *a* concluding —*n* finisher
terminal /termi'nal/ *a* terminal; final. *m, Elec.* terminal. **t. de carga,** cargo terminal
terminante /termi'nante/ *a* conclusive, definite; categorical
terminar /termi'nar/ *vt* to end, conclude; complete; —*vr* and *vi* end
término /'termino/ *m,* limit, end; term, expression; boundary marker; district, suburb; space, period; state, condition; boundary; object, aim; appearance, demeanor, behavior (gen. *pl*); completion; *Mus.* tone; (*Math. Law. Logic.*) term. **t. medio,** *Math.* average; medium; compromise, middle way. **correr el t.,** to lapse (of time). **en primer t.,** *Art.* in the foreground. **medios términos,** evasions, excuses. **primer t.,** (cinema) closeup
terminología /terminolo'hia/ *f,* terminology
termita /ter'mita/ *f,* thermite. *m,* termite
termodinámica /termoði'namika/ *f,* thermodynamics
termoeléctrico /termoe'lektriko/ *a* thermoelectric
termómetro /ter'mometro/ *m,* thermometer
Termópilas /ter'mopilas/ Thermopylae
termos /'termos/ *m,* thermos, vacuum bottle
termoscopio /termos'kopio/ *m,* thermoscope
termostático /termos'tatiko/ *a* thermostatic
termóstato /ter'mostato/ *m,* thermostat
terna /'terna/ *f,* triad, trio; set of dice
ternario /ter'nario/ *a* ternal, ternary
terne /'terne/ *a Inf.* bullying, braggartly; persistent, obstinate; robust. *mf* bully
ternera /ter'nera/ *f,* female calf; veal
ternero /ter'nero/ *m,* male calf
terneza /ter'neθa; ter'nesa/ *f,* tenderness, kindness; softness; softheartedness; endearment, caress, compliment (gen. *pl*)
ternilla /ter'niʎa; ter'niya/ *f,* cartilage, gristle
ternísimo /ter'nisimo/ *a superl* **tierno** most tender
terno /'terno/ *m,* triad; suit of clothes, three-piece suit; oath, curse
ternura /ter'nura/ *f,* softness; softheartedness; tenderness, kindness, sweetness
terquedad, terquería, terqueza /terke'ðað, terke'ria, ter'keθa; ter'kesa/ *f,* obstinacy, obduracy
terracota /terra'kota/ *f,* terra cotta
terrado /te'rraðo/ *m,* flat roof
Terranova /terra'noβa/ Newfoundland
terraplén /terra'plen/ *m,* embankment; *Mil.* terreplein
terraplenar /terraple'nar/ *vt* to fill up with earth; fill in (a hollow); make into an embankment; terrace
terrateniente /terrate'niente/ *mf* landowner
terraza /te'rraθa; te'rrasa/ *f,* terrace; flat roof; flower border (of a garden)
terrazgo /te'rraθgo; te'rrasgo/ *m,* tillable land; rent for farming land
terregoso /terre'goso/ *a* lumpy, full of clods (of soil)
terremoto /terre'moto/ *m,* earthquake

terrenal /terre'nal/ *a* terrestrial
terreno /te'rreno/ *a* terrestrial. *m,* ground, land; *Fig.* sphere; region; soil; plot of land. **ganar t.,** *Fig.* to win ground, make progress. **medir el t.,** *Fig.* to feel one's way
térreo /'terreo/ *a* earthy
terrero /te'rrero/ *a* earthly; low-flying, almost touching the ground; humble. *m,* flat roof; pile or mound of earth; deposit of earth, alluvium; target; mineral refuse
terrestre /te'rrestre/ *a* terrestrial, earthly
terrezuela /terre'θuela; terre'suela/ *f,* poor soil
terribilidad /terriβili'ðað/ *f,* terribleness, horribleness; rudeness
terribilísimo /terriβi'lisimo/ *a superl* most terrible
terrible /te'rriβle/ *a* terrible, horrible; rude, unsociable, ill-humored; enormous, huge
terrífico /te'rrifiko/ *a* terrible, frightful
territorial /territo'rial/ *a* territorial
territorialidad /territoriali'ðað/ *f,* territoriality
territorio /terri'torio/ *m,* territory; jurisdiction. **t. bajo mandato,** mandated territory
terrizo /te'rriθo; te'rriso/ *a* earthen
terrón /te'rron/ *m,* clod (of earth); lump; *pl* lands, landed property. **t. de azúcar,** lump of sugar
terrorismo /terro'rismo/ *m,* terrorism
terrorista /terro'rista/ *mf* terrorist
terrosidad /terrosi'ðað/ *f,* earthiness
terroso /te'rroso/ *a* earthy; earthen
terruño /te'rruɲo/ *m,* plot of ground; native earth; country; soil
terso /'terso/ *a* smooth, shiny, glossy; *Lit.* elegant, polished (style)
tersura /ter'sura/ *f,* smoothness, glossiness; elegance (of style)
tertulia /ter'tulia/ *f,* regular social meeting (gen. in cafés); conversational group; party; part of Spanish cafés set apart for players of chess, etc. **hacer t.,** to meet for conversation
tertuliano /tertu'liano/ **(-na)** *n* **tertuliante,** *mf* **tertulio (-ia),** *n* member of a tertulia
terzuelo /ter'θuelo; ter'suelo/ *m,* third, third part
Tesalia /te'salia/ Thessaly
tesar /te'sar/ *vt Naut.* to make taut; *—vi* step backward, back (oxen)
tesela /te'sela/ *f,* tessera, square used in mosaic work
teselado /tese'laðo/ *a* tessellated
tesina /te'sina/ *f,* master's essay, thesis
tesis /'tesis/ *f,* thesis
teso /'teso/ *a* tight, taut, tense. *m,* hilltop; bulge, lump
tesón /te'son/ *m,* persistence, obstinacy, tenacity
tesonería /tesone'ria/ *f,* stubbornness, obstinacy
tesorería /tesore'ria/ *f,* treasury; treasuryship
tesorero /teso'rero/ **(-ra)** *n* treasurer
tesoro /te'soro/ *m,* treasure; public treasury; hoard; *Fig.* gem, excellent person; thesaurus. **t. de duende,** fairy gold
tespíades /tes'piaðes/ *f pl,* the muses
testa /'testa/ *f,* head; face, front; *Inf.* sense, acumen. **t. coronada,** crowned head
testación /testa'θion; testa'sion/ *f,* erasure, crossing out
testado /tes'taðo/ *a* testate
testador /testa'ðor/ **(-ra)** *n* testator
testaferro /testa'ferro/ *m, Fig.* figurehead, proxy
testamentar /testamen'tar/ *vt* to bequeath
testamentaria /testamen'taria/ *f,* execution of a will; *Law.* estate; executors' meeting
testamentario /testamen'tario/ *a* testamental, testamentary
testamento /testa'mento/ *m, Law.* will; testament. **Antiguo T.,** Old Testament. **ordenar** (*or* **otorgar**) **su t.,** to make one's will
testar /tes'tar/ *vi* to make a will; *—vt* erase, cross out
testarada /testa'raða/ *f,* a blow with the head; pigheadedness, stubbornness
testarrón /testa'rron/ *a Inf.* pigheaded
testarudez /testaru'ðeθ; testaru'ðes/ *f,* obstinacy, obduracy
testarudo /testa'ruðo/ *a* stubborn, obstinate
testera /tes'tera/ *f,* front, face; front seat (in a vehicle); upper half of an animal's face; tester, canopy
testículo /tes'tikulo/ *m,* testicle
testificación /testifika'θion; testifika'sion/ *f,* testification
testificar /testifi'kar/ *vt* to testify; affirm, assert; attest, prove
testigo /tes'tigo/ *mf* witness. *m,* proof, evidence. *Law.* **t. de cargo,** witness for the prosecution. *Law.* **t. de descargo,** witness for the defense. **t. de vista,** eyewitness. *Law.* **hacer testigos,** to bring forward witnesses
testimonial /testimo'nial/ *a* confirmatory, proven
testimoniar /testimo'niar/ *vt* to attest, confirm, bear witness to
testimoniero /testimo'niero/ **(-ra)** *a* slanderous; hypocritical *—n* slanderer, hypocrite
testimonio /testi'monio/ *m,* testimony, proof; slander; affidavit
testuz /tes'tuθ; tes'tus/ *m,* front of the head (of some animals); nape (of animals)
teta /'teta/ *f,* mammary gland, breast; teat, dug, udder. **dar la t.** (**a**), to suckle
tétano, tétanos /'tetano, 'tetanos/ *m,* tetanus
tetera /te'tera/ *f,* teapot; teakettle
tetilla /te'tiʎa; te'tiya/ *f, dim* rudimentary teat or nipple; nipple (of a nursing bottle)
tétrico /'tetriko/ *a* gloomy; somber
tetuaní /tetua'ni/ *a* and *mf* of or from Tetuan
teutón /teu'ton/ **(-ona)** *n* Teuton *—a* Teutonic
teutónico /teu'toniko/ *a* Teutonic
textil /teks'til/ *a* and *m,* textile
texto /'teksto/ *m,* text; quotation, citation; textbook
textorio /teks'torio/ *a* textile
textual /teks'tual/ *a* textual
textualista /tekstua'lista/ *mf* textualist
textura /teks'tura/ *f,* texture; weaving; structure (of a novel, etc.); animal structure
tez /teθ; tes/ *f,* complexion, skin
ti /ti/ *pers pron 2nd sing mf dat acc abl* thee, you. Always used with prep. (e.g. *por ti,* by thee (you))
tía /'tia/ *f,* aunt; *Inf.* wife, mother, dame; *Inf.* coarse creature. **t. abuela,** grandaunt, great-aunt. *Inf.* **quedarse para t.,** to be left an old maid
tiara /'tiara/ *f,* ancient Persian headdress; papal tiara; coronet; dignity and power of the papacy
tiberino /tiβe'rino/ *a* Tiberine
tibetano /tiβe'tano/ **(-na)** *a* and *n* Tibetan. *m,* Tibetan (language)
tibia /'tiβia/ *f,* flute; tibia
tibieza /ti'βieθa; ti'βiesa/ *f,* tepidity; indifference, lack of enthusiasm
tibio /'tiβio/ *a* tepid, warm; indifferent, unenthusiastic
tiburón /tiβu'ron/ *m,* shark
ticket /'tikket/ *m,* ticket; pass, membership card
tictac /tik'tak/ *m,* ticktock (of a clock)
tiempo /'tiempo/ *m,* time; season; epoch, period; chance, opportunity; leisure, free time; weather; *Mus.* tempo; *Gram.* tense; *Naut.* storm. **t. ha,** many years ago, long ago. **t. medio** *or* **medio t.,** *Sports.* halftime. **abrir el t.,** to clear up (of the weather). **ajustar los tiempos,** to fix the date (chronology). **a largo t.,** after a long time. **andando el t.,** in the course of time. **a su t.,** in due course, at the proper time. **a t.,** in time, at the right time. **a un t.,** simultaneously, at the same time. **cargarse el t.,** to cloud over (of the sky). **con t.,** in advance, with time; in time. **correr el t.,** to pass, move on (of time). **de t. en t.,** from time to time. **engañar** (*or* **entretener**) **el t.,** to kill time, while away the hours. *Inf.* **en t., de Maricastaña** *or* **del rey Perico,** long, long ago. **fuera de t.,** unseasonably, inopportunely; out of season. **ganar t.,** to gain time; *Inf.* hurry. **hacer t.,** to wait, cool one's heels; *Fig.* mark time. **perder el t.,** to waste time; misspend or lose time. **sentarse el t.,** to clear up (of the weather). **tomarse t.** (**para**), to postpone, take time for (or to)
tienda /'tienda/ *f,* tent; *Naut.* awning, canopy; shop, store. **t. de antigüedades,** antique shop. **t. de campaña,** bell tent, pavilion. **t. oxígena,** oxygen tent
tienta /'tienta/ *f,* astuteness; cleverness; *Surg.* probe;

trying out young bulls for the bullring. **a tientas,** by touch, gropingly

tientaparedes /tientapa'reðes/ *mf* one who gropes one's way

tiento /'tiento/ *m,* touching, feeling; touch, feel; blind person's cane; tightrope walker's pole; manual control, steady hand; caution, care, tact; *Mus.* preliminary flourish; *Inf.* slap buffet; tentacle. **a t.,** by touch; unsurely, gropingly

tierno /'tierno/ *a* soft; tender; kind; sweet; delicate; softhearted; fresh, recent; affectionate

tierra /'tierra/ *f,* world, planet; earth; soil; ground; cultivated ground, land; homeland, native land; region; district, territory. **t. adentro,** inland. **t. de batán,** fuller's earth. **t. de Promisión,** Promised Land. **t. de Siena,** sienna. **besar la t.,** *Inf.* to fall down. **dar en t. con,** to throw down; demolish. **echar en t.,** *Naut.* to put ashore, land. **echar por t.,** *Fig.* to overthrow, destroy. **echar t. a,** *Fig.* to bury, forget. *Inf.* **la t. de María Santísima,** Andalusia. **por t.,** overland. **saltar en t.,** to land, disembark. **venir** (*or* **venirse**) **a t.,** to fall down, topple over

Tierra Santa /'tierra 'santa/ Holy Land

tieso /'tieso/ *a* hard, rigid, stiff; healthy, robust; taut; spirited, courageous; obstinate, stiff-necked; distant, formal *—adv* firmly, strongly

tiesto /'tiesto/ *m,* flowerpot; broken piece of earthenware

tiesura /tie'sura/ *f,* hardness, rigidity, stiffness; physical fitness; courageousness; obstinacy; formality, stiffness

tifoidea /tifoi'ðea/ *f,* typhoid

tifón /ti'fon/ *m,* typhoon

tifus /'tifus/ *m,* typhus. **t. exantemático,** trench fever

tigre /'tigre/ *m,* tiger; ferocious person

tigresa /ti'gresa/ *f,* tigress

tigridia /ti'griðia/ *f,* tiger lily

tijera /ti'hera/ *f,* scissors (gen. *pl*); any scissor-shaped instrument; shears; drainage channel; carpenter's horse; scandalmonger, gossip

tijereta /tihe'reta/ *f,* vine tendril; earwig

tijeretada /tihere'taða/ *f,* cut or snip with scissors

tijeretear /tiherete'ar/ *vt* to cut with scissors; *Inf.* interfere arbitrarily

tijereteo /tihere'teo/ *m,* scissor cut; click of the scissors

tila /'tila/ *f,* lime tree or flower; linden tree or flower; infusion made of lime flowers

tildar /til'dar/ *vt* to cross out, erase; stigmatize; place a tilde over a letter

tilde /'tilde/ *mf,* bad reputation; tilde; *f,* jot, iota

tilín /ti'lin/ *m,* tinkle, peal (of a bell)

tillar /ti'ʎar; ti'yar/ *vt* to lay wood floors

tilo /'tilo/ *m,* lime tree

timador /tima'ðor/ **(-ra)** *n Inf.* swindler, sharper, cheat

timar /ti'mar/ *vt* to swindle, cheat, deceive; *—vr Inf.* exchange looks or winks

timba /'timba/ *f, Inf.* casino, gambling den; game of chance

timbal /tim'bal/ *m,* kettledrum

timbalero /timba'lero/ *m,* kettledrum player

timbrador /timbra'ðor/ *m,* stamper; stamping machine; rubber stamp

timbrar /tim'brar/ *vt* to stamp; place the crest over a coat of arms

timbre /'timbre/ *m,* postage stamp; heraldic crest; excise stamp; bell, push-button; *Mus.* timbre; noble deed; personal merit

timidez /timi'ðeθ; timi'ðes/ *f,* timidity, nervousness

tímido /'timiðo/ *a* timid, nervous

timo /'timo/ *m, Inf.* swindling, trick; thymus

timón /ti'mon/ *m, Naut.* helm; rudder; management, direction; stick of a rocket. **t. de dirección,** *Aer.* tailfin

timonear /timone'ar/ *vi Naut.* to steer

timonel, timonero /timo'nel, timo'nero/ *m,* helmsman, coxswain

timorato /timo'rato/ *a* godfearing; timid, vacillating

tímpano /'timpano/ *m, Anat.* eardrum, tympanum; *Mus.* kettledrum; *Archit.* tympanum; *Print.* tympan

tina /'tina/ *f,* vat; flour bin; large earthenware jar; wooden tub; bath

tinada /ti'naða/ *f,* woodpile; cow shed

tinaja /ti'naha/ *f,* large earthenware jar; jarful

tinajero /tina'hero/ *m,* seller of earthenware jars

tinelo /ti'nelo/ *m,* servants' hall

tinerfeño /tiner'feɲo/ **(-ña)** *a* and *n* of or from Tenerife

tinglado /tiŋ'glaðo/ *m,* overhanging roof; open shed; penthouse; intrigue

tiniebla /ti'nieβla/ *f,* gloom, darkness (gen. *pl*); *pl* profound ignorance; confusion of mind; *Eccl.* tenebrae

tino /'tino/ *m,* skilled sense of touch; good eye, accurate aim; judgment, shrewdness; vat. **sacar de t.** (**a**), to bewilder, confuse; irritate, exasperate. **sin t.,** without limit, excessively

tinta /'tinta/ *f,* color, tint; ink; staining, dyeing; dye, stain; *pl* shades, colors; *Art.* mixed colors ready for painting. **t. china,** India ink. **t. simpática,** invisible ink. **recargar las tintas,** *Fig.* to overpaint, lay the colors on too thick. *Inf.* **saber de buena t.** (**una cosa**), to learn (a thing) from a reliable source

tintar /tin'tar/ *vt* to dye; color, tinge, stain

tinte /'tinte/ *m,* dyeing, staining; color; dye; stain; dye house; pretext, disguise

tintero /tin'tero/ *m,* inkwell. *Inf.* **dejar** (*or* **quedársele a uno**) **en el t.,** to forget, omit (to say, write)

tintín /tin'tin/ *m,* ring, peal; clink; chink

tintinar /tinti'nar/ *vi* to ring, tinkle; clink; jingle

tintineo /tinti'neo/ *m,* ringing, tinkling; clinking; jingle

tintirintín /tintirin'tin/ *m,* bray of a trumpet

tinto /'tinto/ *a* red (of wine). *m,* red wine; dark red

tintorería /tintore'ria/ *f,* dyeing industry; dyeing and dry-cleaning shop

tintorero /tinto'rero/ **(-ra)** *n* dyer; dry cleaner

tintura /tin'tura/ *f,* dyeing, staining; color, tint; dye; stain; tincture; smattering, slight knowledge

tinturar /tintu'rar/ *vt* to dye; color, tinge, stain; give a superficial notion of

tiña /'tiɲa/ *f,* ringworm; *Inf.* meanness, stinginess

tiñoso /ti'ɲoso/ *a* mangy; afflicted with ringworm; *Inf.* mean, stingy

tiñuela /ti'ɲuela/ *f,* shipworm

tío /'tio/ *m,* uncle; gaffer; fellow, chap; fool; stepfather; father-in-law. **t. abuelo,** granduncle, great-uncle

tiovivo /tio'βiβo/ *m,* merry-go-round

tipiadora /tipia'ðora/ *f,* typewriter

típico /'tipiko/ *a* typical

tiple /'tiple/ *m,* soprano or treble voice. *mf* soprano

tipo /'tipo/ *m,* model, pattern; type; print, type; species, group (of animals, etc.); *Inf.* guy, chap

tipografía /tipogra'fia/ *f,* typography

tipográfico /tipo'grafiko/ *a* typographical

tipógrafo /ti'pografo/ *m,* typographer

típula /'tipula/ *f,* daddy-longlegs

tiquismiquis /tikis'mikis/ *m pl,* ridiculous scruples; affected courtesies *—a Inf.* faddy, fussy

tira /'tira/ *f,* strip, band, ribbon; stripe, rib. **t. cómica,** comic strip

tirabotas /tira'βotas/ *m,* buttonhook

tirabuzón /tiraβu'θon; tiraβu'son/ *m,* corkscrew; ringlet, curl; hair curler

tirada /ti'raða/ *f,* throwing; drawing, pulling; cast, throw; distance, space; *Print.* edition, issue; circulation (of a newspaper, etc.); stroke (in golf); lapse, interval (of time). **t. aparte,** reprint (of an article, etc.)

tiradero /tira'ðero/ *m,* shooting butt

tirado /ti'raðo/ *a Inf.* dirt-cheap. *m,* wire drawing

tirador /tira'ðor/ **(-ra)** *n* thrower, caster; drawer, puller; marksman. *m,* handle, knob; *Mech.* trigger; bell rope, bell pull; *Print.* pressman. **t. de bota,** boot tag. **t. de gomas,** catapult. **t. de oro,** gold wire drawer

tiralíneas /tira'lineas/ *m,* ruling pen

tiramiento /tira'miento/ *m,* pulling; stretching

tiramira /tira'mira/ *f,* long, narrow mountain range; long line of persons or things; distance

tiranía /tira'nia/ *f,* tyranny, despotism

tiranicida /tirani'θiða; tirani'siða/ *mf* tyrannicide (person)
tiranicidio /tirani'θiðio; tirani'siðio/ *m,* tyrannicide (act)
tiránico /ti'raniko/ *a* tyrannical
tiranización /tiraniθa'θion; tiranisa'sion/ *f,* tyranny, tyrannization
tiranizar /tirani'θar; tirani'sar/ *vt* to tyrannize over
tirano /ti'rano/ **(-na)** *a* tyrannous, tyrannical; *Fig.* overwhelming, dominating —*n* tyrant
tirante /ti'rante/ *a* taut; tense, strained. *m,* trace (of a harness); shoulderstrap; suspender (gen. *pl*); *Archit.* tie
tirantez /tiran'teθ; tiran'tes/ *f,* tautness; tension, strain; straight distance between two points. **estado de t.,** *Polit.* strained relations
tiranuelo /tira'nuelo/ *m,* petty tyrant
tirar /ti'rar/ *vt* to throw, cast; fling, aim, toss; throw down, overthrow; pull; draw; discharge, shoot; stretch, pull out; rule, draw (lines); squander, waste; *Print.* print; —*vi* attract; pull; (*with prep a*) turn to, turn in the direction of; incline, tend to; incline toward, have a tinge of (colors); try, aspire to; (*with de*) wield, unsheath, draw out (firearms, arms); —*vr* cast oneself, precipitate oneself; throw oneself on. *Inf.* **ir tirando,** to carry on, get along somehow
tirilla /ti'riʎa; ti'riya/ *f, Sew.* shirt neckband
tiritaña /tiri'taɲa/ *f,* thin silk material; *Inf.* mere nothing, trifle
tiritar /tiri'tar/ *vi* to shiver with cold
tiritón /tiri'ton/ *m,* shiver, shudder
Tiro /'tiro/ Tyre
tiro /'tiro/ *m,* throwing; throw, cast; toss, fling; try (in football); shooting; piece of artillery; report, shot (of a gun); discharge (firearms); shooting range or gallery; team (of horses); range (of firearms, etc.); hoisting cable; flight (of stairs); *Mineral.* shaft; *Inf.* trick; robbery, theft; innuendo, insinuation; grave harm or injury; *pl* sword belt. **t. de pichón,** pigeon shooting. **t. par,** four-in-hand. **a t.,** within firing range; within reach. **de tiros largos,** *Inf.* in full regalia
tirocinio /tiro'θinio; tiro'sinio/ *m,* apprenticeship
tiroideo /tiroi'ðeo/ *a* thyroid
tiroides /ti'roiðes/ *f,* thyroid gland
Tirol, el /ti'rol, el/ the Tyrol
tirón /ti'ron/ *m,* novice, beginner; pull, tug, heave. **de un t.,** with one tug; at one stroke, at one blow
tiroriro /tiro'riro/ *m, Inf.* sound of a wind instrument; *pl Inf.* wind instruments
tirotearse /tirote'arse/ *vr Mil.* to exchange fire; indulge in repartee
tiroteo /tiro'teo/ *m,* shooting, exchange of shots; crackle (of rifle fire)
Tirreno, el Mar /ti'rreno, el mar/ the Tyrrhenian Sea
tirria /'tirria/ *f, Inf.* hostility, grudge, dislike
tirulato /tiru'lato/ *a* dumbfounded, stupefied
tisana /ti'sana/ *f,* tisane
tísico /'tisiko/ **(-ca)** *a* tuberculous —*n* sufferer from tuberculosis, consumptive
tisis /'tisis/ *f,* tuberculosis
tisú /ti'su/ *m,* silver or gold tissue
titánico /ti'taniko/ *a* titanesque; colossal, huge
títere /'titere/ *m,* puppet; *Fig. Inf.* dummy, grotesque; *Inf.* fool; obsession, fixed idea; *pl Inf.* circus; Punch and Judy show. *Inf.* **echar los títeres a rodar,** to upset the whole show; quarrel, fall out with. *Inf.* **no dejar t. con cabeza,** to destroy entirely, smash up completely; leave no one
titerero /tite'rero/ **(-ra), titiritero (-ra),** *n* **titerista** *mf* puppet showman; acrobat; juggler
tití /ti'ti/ *m,* marmoset
titilación /titila'θion; titila'sion/ *f,* quiver, tremor; twinkling, winking, gleam
titilador, titilante /titila'ðor, titi'lante/ *a* quivering, trembling; twinkling
titilar /titi'lar/ *vi* to quiver, tremble; twinkle
titiritaina /titiri'taina/ *f, Inf.* muffled strains of musical instruments; merrymaking, uproar
titiritar /titiri'tar/ *vi* to tremble, shiver, shudder
titiritero /titiri'tero/ **(-ra)** *n* puppet master; acrobat
titubear /tituβe'ar/ *vi* to totter, sway, rock; stutter, stammer; toddle; hesitate, vacillate
titubeo /titu'βeo/ *m,* tottering, swaying; stuttering; hesitation
titulado /titu'laðo/ *m,* titled person; one who holds an academic title
titular /titu'lar/ *a* titular —*vt* to entitle, call; —*vi* obtain a title (of nobility); —*vr* style oneself, call oneself
título /'titulo/ *m,* title; heading; inscription; pretext, excuse; diploma, certificate; claim, right; noble title and its owner; section, clause; (univ.) degree; *Com.* stock certificate, bond; *Com.* title; caption; qualification, right, merit; basis of a claim or privilege; *pl Com.* securities, stocks. **t. de la columna,** *Print.* running title. **títulos de propiedad,** title deeds. **t. del reino,** title of nobility. **a t.,** under pretext
tiza /'tiθa; 'tisa/ *f,* chalk; whiting; calcined stag's antler
tiznar /tiθ'nar; tis'nar/ *vt* to make sooty; dirty, stain, begrime; *Fig.* sully, tarnish
tizne /'tiθne; 'tisne/ *m,* (sometimes *f*) soot; charcoal; stain (on one's honor, etc.); *Agr.* blight
tizón /ti'θon; ti'son/ *m,* firebrand; *Agr.* blight; *Fig.* stain (on one's honor, etc.)
tizona /ti'θona; ti'sona/ *f, Inf.* sword (by allusion to name of that of the Cid)
tizonear /tiθone'ar; tisone'ar/ *vi* to poke or rake the fire
toalla /to'aʎa; to'aya/ *f,* towel. **t. continua,** roller towel. **t. rusa,** Turkish towel
toallero /toa'ʎero; toa'yero/ *m,* towel rail
tobillera /toβi'ʎera; toβi'yera/ *f, Inf.* girl, flapper
tobillo /to'βiʎo; to'βiyo/ *m,* ankle
tobogán /toβo'gan/ *m,* toboggan; chute (in apartment buildings or amusement parks)
toca /'toka/ *f,* headdress; toque; wimple; coif
tocable /to'kaβle/ *a* touchable
tocado /to'kaðo/ *a Fig.* touched, half-crazy. *m,* headdress; coiffure, hairdressing
tocador /toka'ðor/ **(-ra)** *n Mus.* player. *m,* dressing table; kerchief; boudoir; cloakroom; dressing room; dressing case
tocamiento /toka'miento/ *m,* touching, feeling; touch; *Fig.* inspiration
tocante /to'kante/ *a* touching. **t. a,** concerning, with regard to
tocar /to'kar/ *vt* to touch, feel; *Mus.* play; knock, rap; summon; ring, peal; brush against; discover by experience; persuade, inspire; mention, touch upon; *Naut.* touch bottom; *Art.* retouch, touch up —*vi* belong; stop (at), touch at; be one's turn; concern, interest; be one's lot; adjoin, be near to; be opportune; be allied or closely related to; find the scent (of dogs). **t. en un puerto,** *Naut.* to touch at a port. **Ahora me toca a mí,** Now it's my turn. **Es un problema que me toca de cerca,** It is a problem that touches me very nearly. **a toca teja,** *Inf.* in ready cash
tocayo /to'kayo/ **(-ya)** *n* namesake
tochedad /totʃe'ðað/ *f,* boorishness, loutishness
tocho /'totʃo/ *a* boorish, loutish, countrified. *m,* iron bar
tocinería /toθine'ria; tosine'ria/ *f,* pork butcher's shop
tocinero /toθi'nero; tosi'nero/ *m,* pork butcher
tocino /to'θino; to'sino/ *m,* bacon; salt pork
tocología /tokolo'hia/ *f,* tokology, obstetrics
tocón /to'kon/ *m,* stump (of a tree or an amputated limb)
todavía /toða'βia/ *adv* still; even; nevertheless; yet. **No han venido t.,** They have not come yet. **Queda mucho que hacer t.,** There is still much to be done.
todo /'toðo/ *a* all; whole, entire; every, each. *m,* whole, entirety; whole word (in charades); all; *pl* all; everyone —*adv* wholly, entirely. **t. lo posible,** everything possible; all one can, one's best. **t. lo que,** all that which. **ante t.,** in the first place; especially, particularly. **así y t.,** nevertheless. **a t. esto,** in the meanwhile. **con t.** *or* **con t. esto** *or* **con t. y esto,** nevertheless, in spite of this. **del t.,** wholly, completely. **jugar el t. por el t.,** to risk everything on the outcome. **sobre t.,** especially. **y t.,** in addition, as

well. **Todos somos hijos de Adán y Eva, sino que nos diferencia la lana y la seda,** We are all equal, but some of us are more equal than others

todopoderoso /toðopoðe'roso/ *a* all-powerful, almighty. *m,* the Almighty, God

toga /'toga/ *f,* toga; robe, gown

toisón /toi'son/ *m,* fleece. **t. de oro,** Golden Fleece

Tokio /'tokio/ Tokyo

toldadura /tolda'ðura/ *f,* awning; canopy; hanging, curtain

toldillo /tol'diʎo; tol'diyo/ *m,* covered litter or sedan chair; *West Hem.* mosquito net

toldo /'toldo/ *m,* awning; canopy; pomp, show

tole /'tole/ *m,* outcry, uproar, tumult

toledano /tole'ðano/ **(-na)** *a* and *n* Toledan

tolerable /tole'raβle/ *a* bearable, tolerable

tolerancia /tole'ranθia; tole'ransia/ *f,* tolerance, forbearance; permission

tolerante /tole'rante/ *a* tolerant, broad-minded

tolerantismo /toleran'tismo/ *m,* religious toleration

tolerar /tole'rar/ *vt* to put up with, bear, tolerate; overlook, allow, forgive

tolla /'toʎa; 'toya/ *f,* marsh, bog

tollina /to'ʎina; to'yina/ *f, Inf.* spanking, whipping

tolmo /'tolmo/ *m,* tor

tolondro /to'londro/ *a* stupid, heedless, reckless. *m,* bump, bruise

tolonés /tolo'nes/ **(-esa)** *a* and *n* of or from Toulon

Tolosa /to'losa/ Toulouse

tolva /'tolβa/ *f,* chute (for grain, etc.)

toma /'toma/ *f,* taking; receiving; conquest, capture; dose (of medicine)

tomada /to'maða/ *f,* taking; take; capture

tomadero /toma'ðero/ *m,* handle, haft

tomadura /toma'ðura/ *f,* taking; receiving; dose (of medicine). *Inf.* **t. de pelo,** leg-pull, joke

tomar /to'mar/ *vt* to take; pick up; conquer; eat; drink; adopt, employ; contract (habits); engage (employees); rent; understand; steal; remove; buy; suffer; *Fig.* overcome (by laughter, sleep, etc.); choose; possess physically; *—vi* (*with por*) go in the direction of; *—vr* grow rusty; go moldy; (*with con*) quarrel with. **t. a chacota,** to take as a joke. **t. a pechos,** to take to heart. **t. el fresco,** to take the air. **tomarla con,** to contradict, oppose; bear a grudge. **t. la delantera,** to take the lead; excel, beat. **t. las de Villadiego,** *Inf.* to quit, show one's heels. **t. por su cuenta,** to undertake, take charge of; take upon oneself. **t. su desquite con,** to get even with. **Más vale un toma que dos te daré,** A little help is worth a lot of promises. **¡Toma!** *Inf.* Fancy! You don't say!; Of course! There's nothing new about that!

tomatal /toma'tal/ *m,* tomato bed, tomato patch

tomate /to'mate/ *m,* tomato; tomato plant; *Inf.* hole, potato (in stockings, etc.)

tomatera /toma'tera/ *f,* tomato plant

tomatero /toma'tero/ **(-ra)** *n* tomato seller

tómbola /'tombola/ *f,* raffle (gen. for charity); jumble sale

tomillo /to'miʎo; to'miyo/ *m,* thyme

tomo /'tomo/ *m,* volume, book; importance, worth

ton /ton/ *m, Abbr.* **tono. sin t. ni son,** *Inf.* without rhyme or reason

tonada /to'naða/ *f,* words of a song and its tune

tonadilla /tona'ðiʎa; tona'ðiya/ *f, dim* short song; comic song; *Theat.* musical interlude *Obs.*

tonadillero /tonaði'ʎero; tonaði'yero/ **(-ra)** *n* composer or singer of tonadillas

tonal /to'nal/ *a* tonal

tonalidad /tonali'ðað/ *f,* tonality

tonar /to'nar/ *vi Poet.* to thunder or lightning

tonel /to'nel/ *m,* barrel; cask; butt

tonelada /tone'laða/ *f,* ton

tonelería /tonele'ria/ *f,* cooperage; collection or stock of casks and barrels

tonelero /tone'lero/ *m,* cooper

tonga, tongada /'toŋga, toŋ'gaða/ *f,* layer, stratum; *Inf.* task

tónica /'tonika/ *f, Mus.* keynote

tónico /'toniko/ *a* tonic. *m, Med.* tonic; pick-me-up

tonificador, tonificante /tonifika'ðor, tonifi'kante/ *a* strengthening, invigorating tonic

tonillo /to'niʎo; to'niyo/ *m, dim* monotonous singsong voice; regional accent

tonina /to'nina/ *f,* tuna; dolphin

tono /'tono/ *m,* inflection, modulation; (*Mus. Med. Art.*) tone; pitch, resonance; energy, strength; style; manner, behavior; *Mus.* key; mode of speech. **bajar el t.,** *Fig. Inf.* to change one's tune. *Inf.* **darse t.,** to put on side, give oneself airs. **de buen** (**mal**) **t.,** in good (bad) taste

tonsila /ton'sila/ *f,* tonsil

tonsilitis /tonsi'litis/ *f,* tonsillitis

tonsura /ton'sura/ *f,* shearing; hair cutting; *Eccl.* tonsure

tonsurar /tonsu'rar/ *vt* to shear, clip; cut the hair off; *Eccl.* tonsure

tontaina /ton'taina/ *mf Inf.* ninny, fool

tontear /tonte'ar/ *vi* to behave foolishly; play the fool

tontería /tonte'ria/ *f,* foolishness, stupidity; piece of folly; trifle, bagatelle

tontillo /ton'tiʎo; ton'tiyo/ *m,* dress bustle; hoop (for dresses)

tontiloco /tonti'loko/ *a Inf.* crazy, daft

tontivano /tonti'βano/ *a* vain, conceited

tonto /'tonto/ **(-ta)** *a* silly, stupid, simple; foolish, absurd *—n* fool, idiot. *m,* short coat, stroller. **t. de capirote,** *Inf.* an utter fool. **a tontas y a locas,** without rhyme or reason, topsy-turvy. **volver t.** (**a**), *Fig. Inf.* to drive crazy

topacio /to'paθio; to'pasio/ *m,* topaz

topar /to'par/ *vt* (*with con*) to run into, collide with, hit; meet unexpectedly; come across, find; *—vi* butt (of horned animals); take a bet (in cards); consist in (of obstacles); meet with (difficulties); *Inf.* be successful

tope /'tope/ *m,* projection, part that juts out; obstacle, impediment; collision, bump; crux, difficult point; quarrel, fight; *Mech.* stop; *Naut.* masthead; *Rail.* buffer. **hasta el t.,** completely full, full to the brim

topera /to'pera/ *f,* molehill

topetada /tope'taða/ *f,* butt (of horned animals); *Inf.* knock, bang

topetar /tope'tar/ *vt* and *vi* to butt (of horned animals); *—vt* meet, run into

topetón /tope'ton/ *m,* butt; collision, impact, bump; blow on the head

tópico /'topiko/ *a* topical. *m,* topic, theme

topo /'topo/ *m, Zool.* mole; *Inf.* clumsy or shortsighted person; dolt, ninny

topografía /topogra'fia/ *f,* topography

topográfico /topo'grafiko/ *a* topographical

topógrafo /to'pografo/ *m,* topographer

toque /'toke/ *m,* touch, touching; pealing, ringing (of bells); crux, essence; test, proof; touchstone; *Metall.* assay; warning; *Inf.* tap (on the shoulder, etc.); *Art.* touch. **t. de luz,** *Art.* light (in a picture). **t. de obscuro,** *Art.* shade (in a picture). **t. de queda,** curfew. **t. de tambor,** beating of a drum. **dar un t. a,** *Inf.* to put to the test; pump (for information)

toquero /to'kero/ **(-ra)** *n* manufacturer of headdresses

toquetear /tokete'ar/ *vt* to keep touching, handle repeatedly

toquilla /to'kiʎa; to'kiya/ *f,* hatband, hat trimming; kerchief; small shawl

torácico /to'raθiko; to'rasiko/ *a* thoracic

toral /to'ral/ *a* principal, chief, main

tórax /'toraks/ *m,* thorax

torbellino /torβe'ʎino; torβe'yino/ *m,* whirlwind; spate of things; *Inf.* madcap

torcedero /torθe'ðero; torse'ðero/ *a* twisted, crooked

torcedor /torθe'ðor; torse'ðor/ *a* twisting. *m,* twister; cause of continual anxiety

torcedura /torθe'ðura; torse'ðura/ *f,* twisting; sprain, wrench

torcer /tor'θer; tor'ser/ *vt irr* to twist; bend; turn, bear (of roads, etc.); slant, slope, incline; misconstrue, pervert; dissuade; wrench, sprain (muscles); corrupt (justice). **t. el gesto,** to make a wry face *—vr* turn sour (of wine, milk); *Fig.* go astray; turn out

badly (of negotiations) —*Pres. Indic.* **tuerzo, tuerces,** etc —*Pres. Subjunc.* **tuerza, tuerzas, tuerza, tuerzan**
torcida /tor'θiða; tor'siða/ *f,* wick (of lamps, etc.)
torcido /tor'θiðo; tor'siðo/ *a* bent, crooked, sloping, inclined; curved; dishonest, tortuous. *m,* silk twist
torcijón /torθi'hon; torsi'hon/ *m,* stomachache
torcimiento /torθi'miento; torsi'miento/ *m,* twisting; twist, turn; circumlocution; digression
tordo /'torðo/ *a* piebald, black-and-white. *m, Ornith.* thrush. **t. de campanario** *or* **t. de Castilla,** starling
toreador /torea'ðor/ *m,* bullfighter
torear /tore'ar/ *vi* and *vt* to fight bulls; —*vt* ridicule; exasperate, provoke; *Inf.* string along, deceive
toreo /to'reo/ *m,* bullfighting
torera /to'rera/ *f,* bullfighter's jacket
torero /to'rero/ *a Inf.* bullfighting. *m,* bullfighter
torete /to'rete/ *m, dim* small bull; *Inf.* problem, difficult question; engrossing topic of conversation
toril /to'ril/ *m,* pen for fighting bulls
torio /'torio/ *m,* thorium
tormenta /tor'menta/ *f,* storm; misfortune, calamity; indignation, agitation
tormento /tor'mento/ *m,* torment; torture; pain; anxiety, anguish. **dar t. (a),** to torture; inflict pain (on)
tormentoso /tormen'toso/ *a* stormy, tempestuous; *Naut.* pitching, rolling
torna /'torna/ *f,* return; restitution; backwater
tornaboda /torna'βoða/ *f,* day after a wedding; rejoicings of this day
tornada /tor'naða/ *f,* return home; return visit, revisit; *Poet.* envoy
tornadizo /torna'ðiθo; torna'ðiso/ **(-za)** *a Inf.* changeable —*n* turncoat
tornamiento /torna'miento/ *m,* return; change, transformation
tornar /tor'nar/ *vt* to return, give back; change, transform; —*vi* return, go back; continue
tornasol /torna'sol/ *m,* sunflower; sheen, changing light; *Chem.* litmus
tornasolado /tornaso'laðo/ *a* shot (of silk, etc.)
tornasolar /tornaso'lar/ *vt* to look iridescent; change the color of, cause to appear variegated
tornátil /tor'natil/ *a* turned (in a lathe); inconstant, changeable; *Poet.* spinning, revolving
tornatrás /torna'tras/ *mf* half-caste
tornaviaje /torna'βiahe/ *m,* return journey
tornavoz /torna'βoθ; torna'βos/ *m,* soundboard, sounding board
torneador /tornea'ðor/ *m,* turner; jouster, fighter in a tournament
tornear /torne'ar/ *vt Sports.* to put a spin on (balls); turn in a lathe; —*vi* turn around, spin; fight in a tournament; turn over in the mind
torneo /tor'neo/ *m,* tournament
tornería /torne'ria/ *f,* turnery
tornero /tor'nero/ *m,* turner; lathe maker; convent messenger
tornillero /torni'ʎero; torni'yero/ *m,* (*Inf. Mil.*) deserter
tornillo /tor'niʎo; tor'niyo/ *m,* screw; (*Inf. Mil.*) desertion
torniquete /torni'kete/ *m,* turnstile; tourniquet. **dar t. (a),** to pervert, misinterpret (meanings)
torniscón /tornis'kon/ *m, Inf.* slap, buffet, blow; pinch
torno /'torno/ *m,* lathe; turntable (of a convent, etc.); turn, rotation; windlass; dumbwaiter; axletree; spinning wheel; bend, loop (in a river). **en t.,** round about, around; in exchange
toro /'toro/ *m,* bull; Taurus; *pl* bullfight. *Inf.* **t. corrido,** tough nut to crack, wise guy. *Inf.* **Ciertos son los toros,** So it's true (gen. of bad news)
toronja /to'ronha/ *f,* grapefruit
toroso /to'roso/ *a* strong, vigorous, robust
torpe /'torpe/ *a* heavy, slow, encumbered; torpid; clumsy, unskilled; stupid, dull-witted; obscene, indecent; base, infamous; ugly
torpedeamiento /torpeðea'miento/ *m,* torpedoing, sinking
torpedear /torpeðe'ar/ *vt* to torpedo
torpedeo /torpe'ðeo/ *m,* torpedoing
torpedero /torpe'ðero/ *m,* torpedo boat
torpedo /tor'peðo/ *m, Ichth.* torpedo fish, electric ray; torpedo; sports car. **t. automóvil,** self-propelling torpedo
torpeza /tor'peθa; tor'pesa/ *f,* slowness, heaviness; torpidity; stupidity; lack of skill, clumsiness; indecency; ugliness; baseness, infamy
tórpido /'torpiðo/ *a* torpid
torrar /to'rrar/ *vt* to toast, brown
torre /'torre/ *f,* tower; belfry, steeple; turret; rook (in chess); *Naut.* gun turret; stack, pile (of chairs, etc.); country house with a garden. **t. del tráfico,** traffic light. **t. de viento,** castle in the air, castle in Spain
torrefacción /torrefak'θion; torrefak'sion/ *f,* toasting (of coffee, etc.)
torrencial /torren'θial; torren'sial/ *a* torrential
torrente /to'rrente/ *m,* torrent; *Fig.* spate, rush; crowd
torreón /to'rreon/ *m,* large fortified tower
torrero /to'rrero/ *m,* lighthouse keeper; gardener
torreznero /torreθ'nero; torres'nero/ **(-ra)** *n Inf.* lazybones, idler
torrezno /to'rreθno; to'rresno/ *m,* rasher of bacon
tórrido /'torriðo/ *a* torrid
torsión /tor'sion/ *f,* twisting, torsion
torta /'torta/ *f,* cake; pastry, tart; *Inf.* slap. **t. de reyes,** traditional Twelfth Night cake
tortada /tor'taða/ *f,* meat pie, game pie
tortedad /torte'ðað/ *f,* twistedness, crookedness
tortera /tor'tera/ *f,* cake pan; baking dish; whorl (of a spindle)
tortícolis /tor'tikolis/ *m,* crick (in the neck)
tortilla /tor'tiʎa; tor'tiya/ *f,* omelet. **t. a la española,** potato omelet. **hacer t.,** to smash to atoms. **Se volvió la t.,** *Inf.* The tables are turned
tórtola /'tortola/ *f,* turtledove
tórtolo /'tortolo/ *m,* male turtledove; *Inf.* devoted lover
tortuga /tor'tuga/ *f,* turtle; tortoise. **a paso de t.,** at a snail's pace
tortuosidad /tortuosi'ðað/ *f,* tortuousness; winding; indirectness; deceitfulness
tortuoso /tor'tuoso/ *a* tortuous; winding; disingenuous, deceitful
tortura /tor'tura/ *f,* twistedness; torture, torment; anguish, grief. **una t. china,** excruciating torture
torturador /tortura'ðor/ *a* torturing, tormenting
torturar /tortu'rar/ *vt* to torture
torva /'torβa/ *f,* squall of rain or snow
torzal /tor'θal; tor'sal/ *m,* sewing silk; twist, plait
tos /tos/ *f,* cough. **t. ferina,** whooping cough
Toscana /tos'kana/ Tuscany
tosco /'tosko/ *a* rough, unpolished; coarse; boorish, uncouth
toser /to'ser/ *vi* to cough
tósigo /'tosigo/ *m,* poison, venom; anguish; affliction
tosigoso /tosi'goso/ *a* poisoned, venomous
tosquedad /toske'ðað/ *f,* roughness, lack of polish; coarseness; boorishness, uncouthness
tostada /tos'taða/ *f, Cul.* toast
tostadera /tosta'ðera/ *f,* toasting fork
tostado /tos'taðo/ *a* golden brown, tanned. *m,* roasting (of coffee, etc.)
tostador /tosta'ðor/ **(-ra)** *n* toaster (of peanuts, etc.). *m,* toaster (utensil); coffee or peanut roaster
tostadura /tosta'ðura/ *f,* toasting; roasting (of coffee, etc.)
tostón /tos'ton/ *m,* buttered toast; anything overtoasted; roast pig; *Inf.* nuisance, bore
total /to'tal/ *a* total, entire, whole; general. *m,* total —*adv* in short; so, therefore
totalidad /totali'ðað/ *f,* whole; aggregate, entirety
totalitario /totali'tario/ *a* totalitarian
tótem /'totem/ *m,* totem
totemismo /tote'mismo/ *m,* totemism
toxicidad /toksiθi'ðað; toksisi'ðað/ *f,* toxicity
tóxico /'toksiko/ *a* toxic. *m,* toxic substance
toxicología /toksikolo'hia/ *f,* toxicology
toxicológico /toksiko'lohiko/ *a* toxicological
toxicólogo /toksi'kologo/ *m,* toxicologist

toxina /tok'sina/ *f,* toxin
tozo /'toθo; 'toso/ *a* dwarfish, small
tozudez /toθu'ðeθ; tosu'ðes/ *f,* obstinacy
tozudo /to'θuðo; to'suðo/ *a* obstinate, obdurate
tozuelo /to'θuelo; to'suelo/ *m,* scruff, fat nape (of animals)
traba /'traβa/ *f,* setting (of a saw's teeth); tether (for horses); difficulty, obstacle; fastening; bond, tie; shackle; *Law.* distraint
trabacuenta /traβa'kuenta/ *f,* mistake in accounts; argument, difference of opinion
trabajado /traβa'haðo/ *a* and *past part* wrought; fashioned; labored, exhausted, weary
trabajador /traβaha'ðor/ **(-ra)** *a* working; conscientious —*n* worker
trabajar /traβa'har/ *vi* to work; function; stand the strain, resist (of machines, etc.); exert oneself, strive; toil, labor; operate, work; produce, yield (the earth fruits, etc.); —*vt* work; till, cultivate; exercise (a horse); worry, annoy, weary; operate, drive; —*vr* make every effort, work hard
trabajo /tra'βaho/ *m,* work; toil, labor; operation, working; difficulty, obstacle; literary work; hardship, trouble; process; *pl* poverty; hardship. **t. a destajo,** piecework. **t. al ralenti,** go slow tactics. **trabajos forzados** (*or* **forzosos**), *Law.* hard labor. **pasar trabajos,** to undergo hardships
trabajosamente /traβahosa'mente/ *adv* painstakingly
trabajoso /traβa'hoso/ *a* difficult, hard; ailing, delicate; needy; afflicted
trabalenguas /traβa'leŋguas/ *m, Inf.* tongue twister, jawbreaker
trabamiento /traβa'miento/ *m,* joining, fastening; uniting; initiation, commencement; shackling; hobbling (of horses)
trabar /tra'βar/ *vt* to join, unite, fasten; grasp, seize; set the teeth (of a saw); thicken; begin, initiate; hobble (of horses); reconcile, bring together, harmonize; shackle; *Law.* distrain; —*vr* speak with an impediment; stutter, hesitate. **t. amistad,** to make friends. **t. conversación,** to get into conversation. **Se me trabó la lengua,** I began to stutter
trabazón /traβa'θon; traβa'son/ *f,* join, union, fastening; connection; thickness, consistency
trabilla /tra'βiʎa; tra'βiya/ *f,* vest strap; dropped stitch (in knitting)
trabuca /tra'βuka/ *f,* squib, Chinese firecracker, riprap
trabucar /traβu'kar/ *vt* to turn upside down, upset; confuse, bewilder; mix up, confuse (news, etc.); pronounce or write incorrectly
trabucazo /traβu'kaθo; traβu'kaso/ *m,* shot or report of a blunderbuss; *Inf.* calamity, unexpected misfortune
trabuco /tra'βuko/ *m, Mil.* catapult; blunderbuss
trabuquete /traβu'kete/ *m,* catapult
tracamundana /trakamun'dana/ *f, Inf.* barter, exchange of trash; hubbub, uproar
tracción /trak'θion; trak'sion/ *f,* pulling; traction
Tracia /'traθia; 'trasia/ Thrace
tracoma /tra'koma/ *f,* trachoma
tracto /'trakto/ *m,* tract, area, expanse; lapse of time
tractor /trak'tor/ *m,* tractor. **t. de orugas,** caterpillar tractor
tractorista /trakto'rista/ *mf* driver of a tractor, tractor driver
tradición /traði'θion; traði'sion/ *f,* tradition
tradicional /traðiθio'nal; traðisio'nal/ *a* traditional
tradicionalismo /traðiθiona'lismo; traðisiona'lismo/ *m,* traditionalism
tradicionalista /traðiθiona'lista; traðisiona'lista/ *a* traditionalistic. *mf* traditionalist
traducción /traðuk'θion; traðuk'sion/ *f,* translation; interpretation, explanation
traducible /traðu'θiβle; traðu'siβle/ *a* translatable
traducir /traðu'θir; traðu'sir/ *vt irr* to translate; interpret, explain; express. See **conducir**
traductor /traðuk'tor/ **(-ra)** *n* translator; interpreter
traedizo /trae'ðiθo; trae'ðiso/ *a* portable, movable
traer /tra'er/ *vt irr* to bring; attract; cause, occasion; wear, have on; quote, cite (as proof); compel, force; persuade; conduct, lead (persons); be engaged in; —*vr* dress (well *or* badly). **t. consigo,** to bring with it; have or carry or bring with one. **t. entre manos,** to have on hand —*Pres. Indic.* **traigo, traes,** etc —*Pres. Part.* **trayendo.** *Preterite* **traje, trajiste,** etc —*Pres. Subjunc.* **traiga,** etc —*Imperf. Subjunc.* **trajese,** etc.
trafagador /trafaga'ðor/ *m,* dealer, trafficker, merchant
tráfago /'trafago/ *m,* traffic, trade; toil, drudgery
trafalmejas /trafal'mehas/ *a Inf.* rowdy, crazy, *mf Inf.* rowdy
traficante /trafi'kante/ *mf* dealer, merchant, trader
traficar /trafi'kar/ *vi* to trade; travel
tráfico /'trafiko/ *m,* traffic; trade, commerce
tragaderas /traga'ðeras/ *f pl,* throat, gullet. *Inf.* **tener buenas t.,** to be very credulous; be tolerant (of evil)
tragadero /traga'ðero/ *m,* throat, gullet; sink, drain; hole, plug
tragador /traga'ðor/ **(-ra)** *n* glutton, guzzler
tragahombres /traga'ombres/ *mf Inf.* braggart, bully
trágala /'tragala/ *m,* (**trágala tú, servilón**), title of Spanish Liberal song aimed at Absolutists; *Inf.* take that!
tragaleguas /traga'leguas/ *mf Inf.* fast walker
tragaluz /traga'luθ; traga'lus/ *m,* skylight; fan light
tragantón /tragan'ton/ **(-ona)** *a Inf.* guzzling, greedy —*n* glutton
tragantona /tragan'tona/ *f, Inf.* spread, large meal; swallowing with difficulty; *Fig. Inf.* hard pill to swallow
tragaperras /traga'perras/ *m, Inf.* vending machine, catchpenny
tragar /tra'gar/ *vt* to swallow; eat ravenously, devour; engulf, swallow up; believe, take in; tolerate, put up with; dissemble; consume, absorb
tragedia /tra'heðia/ *f,* tragedy
trágico /'trahiko/ **(-ca)** *a* tragic —*n* tragedian; writer of tragedies
tragicomedia /trahiko'meðia/ *f,* tragicomedy
tragicómico /trahi'komiko/ *a* tragicomic
trago /'trago/ *m,* swallow, gulp, draft; *Fig. Inf.* bitter pill. **a tragos,** *Inf.* little by little, slowly
tragón /tra'gon/ **(-ona)** *a Inf.* greedy, gluttonous —*n* glutton
tragonear /tragone'ar/ *vt Inf.* to devour, eat avidly
traición /trai'θion; trai'sion/ *f,* treason, treachery. **a t.,** treacherously
traicionar /traiθio'nar; traisio'nar/ *vt* to betray
traicionero /traiθio'nero; traisio'nero/ **(-ra)** *a* treacherous —*n* traitor
traída /tra'iða/ *f,* conduction. **t. de aguas,** water supply
traidor /trai'ðor/ **(-ra)** *a* treacherous —*n* traitor
traílla /tra'iʎa; tra'iya/ *f,* lead, leash (for animals)
traje /'trahe/ *m,* dress, apparel; outfit, costume; suit. **t. de americana,** lounge suit. **t. de ceremonia** *or* **t. de etiqueta,** full-dress uniform; evening dress (men). **t. de luces,** bullfighter's gala outfit. **t. de montar,** riding habit. **t. de noche,** evening dress (women). **t. paisano,** civilian dress; lounge suit
trajín /tra'hin/ *m,* carriage, transport; busyness, moving around; bustle; clatter
trajinar /trahi'nar/ *vt* to carry, transport; —*vi* be busy, go about one's business
tralla /'traʎa; 'traya/ *f,* rope, cord; lash (of a whip); whip
trama /'trama/ *f,* woof, texture (of cloth); twisted silk; intrigue, scheme; *Lit.* plot; olive flower
tramar /tra'mar/ *vt* to weave; prepare, hatch (plots); *Fig.* prepare the way for, —*vi* flower (of trees, especially olive)
tramitación /tramita'θion; tramita'sion/ *f,* transaction, conduct; procedure, method
tramitar /trami'tar/ *vt* to transact, conduct, settle
trámite /'tramite/ *m,* transit; negotiation, phase of a business deal; requirement, condition
tramo /'tramo/ *m,* plot of ground; flight of stairs, staircase; stretch, expanse, reach, tract
tramontana /tramon'tana/ *f,* north wind; arrogance, haughtiness
tramontano /tramon'tano/ *a* ultramontane, from beyond the mountains
tramontar /tramon'tar/ *vi* to cross the mountains;

sink behind the mountains (of the sun); *—vr* run away, escape
tramoya /tra'moya/ *f, Theat.* stage machinery; trick, deception, hoax
tramoyista /tramo'yista/ *mf* stage carpenter; stagehand; scene-shifter; trickster, impostor, swindler
trampa /'trampa/ *f,* trap, snare; trapdoor; flap of a shop counter; trouser fly; trick, swindle; overdue debt. *Fig. Inf.* **caer en la t.,** to fall into the trap. *Inf.* **coger en la t.,** to catch in a trap; catch in the act
trampal /tram'pal/ *m,* bog, marsh
trampantojo /trampan'toho/ *m, Inf.* optical illusion, swindle
trampeador /trampea'ðor/ *a Inf.* swindling *—n* trickster, swindler
trampear /trampe'ar/ *vi Inf.* to obtain money on false pretenses; struggle on (against illness, etc.); keep oneself alive, make shift; *—vt* defraud, swindle
trampolín /trampo'lin/ *m,* springboard; diving board; *Fig.* jumping-off place
tramposo /tram'poso/ **(-sa)** *n* debtor; cardsharper; swindler
tranca /'tranka/ *f,* thick stick, cudgel; bar (of a window, etc.)
trancada /tran'kaða/ *f,* stride
trancar /tran'kar/ *vt* to bar the door; *—vi Inf.* oppose, resist
trancazo /tran'kaθo; tran'kaso/ *m,* blow with a stick; influenza, flu
trance /'tranθe; 'transe/ *m,* crisis, difficult juncture; danger, peril. **t. de armas,** armed combat. **a todo t.,** at all costs, without hesitation
tranco /'tranko/ *m,* stride; threshold. *Inf.* **en dos trancos,** in a trice
tranquera /tran'kera/ *f,* stockade, palisade
tranquilar /tranki'lar/ *vt Com.* to check off
tranquilidad /trankili'ðað/ *f,* tranquility, peace, quietness; composure, serenity
tranquilizador /trankiliθa'ðor; trankilisa'ðor/ *a* tranquilizing, soothing
tranquilizar /trankili'θar; trankili'sar/ *vt* to calm, quiet; soothe
tranquilo /tran'kilo/ *a* tranquil, quiet, peaceful; serene, composed
transacción /transak'θion; transak'sion/ *f,* compromise, arrangement; transaction, negotiation, deal
transalpino /transal'pino/ *a* transalpine
transandino /transan'dino/ *a* transandean
transatlántico /transat'lantiko/ *a* transatlantic. *m,* (transatlantic) liner
transbordar /transβor'ðar/ *vt* to transship; transfer, remove goods from one vehicle to another
transbordo /trans'βorðo/ *m,* transshipment, transshipping; transfer, removal
transcendencia /transθen'denθia; transsen'densia/ *f* See **trascendencia**
transcendental /transθenden'tal; transsenden'tal/ *a.* See **trascendental**
transcribir /transkri'βir/ *vt* to transcribe; copy *—Past Part.* **transcrito**
transcripción /transkrip'θion; transkrip'sion/ *f,* transcription; copy, transcript
transcurrir /transku'rrir/ *vi* to elapse, pass (time)
transcurso /trans'kurso/ *m,* passage, lapse, course (of time)
transepto /tran'septo/ *m,* transept
transeúnte /tran'seunte/ *a* transient, temporary. *mf* passerby; visitor, sojourner
transferencia /transfe'renθia; transfe'rensia/ *f,* transfer (from one place to another); *Law.* conveyance, transference. **t. bancaria,** bank draft
transferidor /transferi'ðor/ **(-ra)** *a* transferring *—n* transferrer; *Law.* transferor
transferir /transfe'rir/ *vt irr* to transfer, move from one place to another; *Law.* convey (property, etc.); postpone. See **sentir**
transfiguración /transfigura'θion; transfigura'sion/ *f,* transfiguration
transfigurar /transfigu'rar/ *vt* to transfigure
transfijo /trans'fiho/ *a* transfixed
transfixión /transfik'sion/ *f,* transfixion
transformable /transfor'maβle/ *a* transformable
transformación /transforma'θion; transforma'sion/ *f,* transformation
transformador /transforma'ðor/ *a* transformative. *m, Elec.* transformer
transformar /transfor'mar/ *vt* to transform; reform (persons); *—vr* be transformed; reform, mend one's ways
transfregar /transfre'gar/ *vt irr* to rub, scrub. See **cegar**
transfretar /transfre'tar/ *vt Naut.* to cross the sea; *—vi* spread
tránsfuga /'transfuga/ *mf* **tránsfugo** *m,* fugitive; political turncoat
transfundir /transfun'dir/ *vt* to transfuse, pour from one vessel to another; imbue, transmit
transfusor /transfu'sor/ *a* transfusive
transgredir /transgre'ðir/ *vt* to transgress, infringe
transgresión /transgre'sion/ *f,* infringement, violation, transgression
transgresor /transgre'sor/ **(-ra)** *a* infringing *—n* transgressor, violator
transiberiano /transiβe'riano/ *a* trans-Siberian
transición /transi'θion; transi'sion/ *f,* transition, change
transido /tran'siðo/ *a* exhausted, worn-out, spent; niggardly, mean
transigencia /transi'henθia; transi'hensia/ *f,* tolerance, forbearance, indulgence
transigente /transi'hente/ *a* tolerant, forbearing
transigir /transi'hir/ *vi* to be tolerant; be broadminded *—vt* put up with, tolerate
transitable /transi'taβle/ *a* passable, traversable
transitar /transi'tar/ *vi* to cross, pass through; travel
transitivo /transi'tiβo/ *a* transitive
tránsito /'transito/ *m,* passage, crossing; transit; stopping place; transition, change; gallery of a cloister; *Eccl.* holy death. **de t.,** temporarily; in transit (of goods). **hacer tránsitos,** to break one's journey, stop
transitorio /transi'torio/ *a* transitory, fugitive, fleeting
translimitación /translimita'θion; translimita'sion/ *f,* trespass; bad behavior; armed intervention in a neighboring state
translimitar /translimi'tar/ *vt* to overstep the boundaries (of a state, etc.); overstep the limits (of decency, etc.)
translucidez /transluθi'ðeθ; translusi'ðes/ *f,* translucence, semitransparency
translúcido /trans'luθiðo; trans'lusiðo/ *a* translucent, semitransparent
transmarino /transma'rino/ *a* transmarine
transmigración /transmigra'θion; transmigra'sion/ *f,* transmigration
transmigrar /transmi'grar/ *vi* to migrate; transmigrate (of the soul)
transmisión /transmi'sion/ *f,* transmission. **t. del pensamiento,** thought transference
transmisor /transmi'sor/ *a* transmitting. *m, Elec.* transmitter, sender
transmitir /transmi'tir/ *vt* to transmit; *Mech.* drive
transmutable /transmu'taβle/ *a* transmutable
transmutación /transmuta'θion; transmuta'sion/ *f,* transmutation, transformation, change
transmutar /transmu'tar/ *vt* to transmute, transform, change
transmutativo /transmuta'tiβo/ *a* transmutative
transoceánico /transoθe'aniko; transose'aniko/ *a* transoceanic
transpacífico /transpa'θifiko; transpa'sifiko/ *a* transpacific
transparencia /transpa'renθia; transpa'rensia/ *f,* transparency; obviousness
transparentarse /transparen'tarse/ *vr* to be transparent; show through; *Fig.* reveal, give away (secrets)
transparente /transpa'rente/ *a* transparent; translucent; evident, obvious. *m,* windowshade, blind
transpiración /transpira'θion; transpira'sion/ *f,* transpiration; perspiration
transpirar /transpi'rar/ *vi* to perspire; transpire
transpirenaico /transpire'naiko/ *a* trans-Pyrenean

transponer /transpo'ner/ *vt irr* to move, transfer; transplant; transpose; *—vr* hide behind; sink behind the horizon (of the sun, stars); be half-asleep. See **poner**
transportable /transpor'taβle/ *a* transportable
transportación /transporta'θion; transporta'sion/ *f.* See **transporte**
transportador /transporta'ðor/ **(-ra)** *a* transport *—n* transporter. *m, Geom.* protractor
transportamiento /transporta'miento/ *m.* See **transporte**
transportar /transpor'tar/ *vt* to transport; *Mus.* transpose; carry; *—vr Fig.* be carried away by (anger, rapture)
transporte /trans'porte/ *m,* transport, carriage; cartage; *Naut.* transport; strong emotion, transport, ecstasy
transposición /transposi'θion; transposi'sion/ *f,* transposition
transpositivo /transposi'tiβo/ *a* transpositive
transubstanciación /transuβstanθia'θion; transuβstansia'sion/ *f,* transubstantiation
transubstanciar /transuβstan'θiar; transuβstan'siar/ *vt* to transubstantiate, transmute
transversal, transverso /transβer'sal, trans'βerso/ *a* transverse
tranvía /tram'bia/ *m,* street railway; streetcar. **t. de sangre,** horse-drawn streetcar.
tranviario /tram'biario/ *a* streetcar. *m,* streetcar employee
trapacear /trapaθe'ar; trapase'ar/ *vi* to cheat, swindle
trapacete /trapa'θete; trapa'sete/ *m, Com.* daybook
trapacista /trapa'θista; trapa'sista/ *mf* trickster, swindler, knave
trapajoso /trapa'hoso/ *a* ragged, shabby, tattered
trápala /'trapala/ *f,* noise, confusion, hubbub; noise of horse's hoofs, gallop; *Inf.* trick, swindle; prattling, babbling. *mf Inf.* babbler, prattler; trickster
trapalear /trapale'ar/ *vi* to walk noisily, tramp; *Inf.* chatter, babble
trapatiesta /trapa'tiesta/ *f, Inf.* brawl, row, quarrel
trapaza /tra'paθa; tra'pasa/ *f,* hoax, swindle
trapecio /tra'peθio; tra'pesio/ *m,* trapeze; *Geom.* trapezium, trapezoid
trapería /trape'ria/ *f,* old-clothes shop; old clothes, rags, trash, frippery
trapero /tra'pero/ **(-ra)** *n* old-clothes seller; rag merchant; ragpicker
trapezoide /trape'θoiðe; trape'soiðe/ *m,* trapezium, trapezoid
trapichear /trapitʃe'ar/ *vi Inf.* to make shift, endeavor
trapiento /tra'piento/ *a* ragged, shabby
trapillo /tra'piʎo; tra'piyo/ *m, Inf.* poverty-stricken lover; nest egg, savings. *Inf.* **de t.,** in a state of undress, in négligé
trapío /tra'pio/ *m, Inf.* spirit of a fighting bull; verve, dash, independent air (of women)
trapisonda /trapi'sonda/ *f, Inf.* uproar, brawl; hubbub, bustle; snare, fix
trapisondear /trapisonde'ar/ *vi Inf.* to be given to brawling; scheme, intrigue
trapisondista /trapison'dista/ *mf* brawler; schemer, trickster
trapo /'trapo/ *m,* rag; *Naut.* canvas; bullfighter's cape; *pl* garments, bits and pieces. *Inf.* **poner como un t. (a),** to dress down, scold. *Inf.* **soltar el t.,** to burst out crying or laughing
trapujo /tra'puho/ *m, Inf.* trick; subterfuge
traque /'trake/ *m,* report, bang (of a rocket, etc.); fuse (of a firework)
tráquea /'trakea/ *f,* trachea
traqueotomía /trakeoto'mia/ *f,* tracheotomy
traquetear /trakete'ar/ *vi* to crack, bang, go off with a report; rattle; jolt (of trains, etc.) *—vt* shake, stir; *Inf.* paw, handle too much
traqueteo /trake'teo/ *m,* banging (of fireworks); creaking; rattling; jolting (of trains, etc.)
traquido /tra'kiðo/ *m,* report (of a gun); crack (of a whip); creak
tras /tras/ *prep* after; behind; following, in pursuit of; trans- (in compounds). *m, Inf.* buttock; sound of a blow, bang, bump. **t. t.,** knocking (at a door); banging
trasalcoba /trasal'koβa/ *f,* dressing room
trasbarrás /trasβa'rras/ *m,* bang, bump, noise
trascendencia /trasθen'denθia; trassen'densia/ *f,* transcendence, excellence; consequence, result
trascendental /trasθenden'tal; trassenden'tal/ *a* transcendental; important, farreaching
trascender /trasθen'der; trassen'der/ *vi irr* to spread to, influence; become known, leak out; exhale a scent; *—vt* investigate, discover. See **entender**
trascocina /trasko'θina; trasko'sina/ *f,* back kitchen
trascolar /trasko'lar/ *vt irr* to filter, strain; cross over, traverse. See **colar**
trascordarse /traskor'ðarse/ *vr irr* to mix up, make a muddle of, forget. See **acordar**
trasechar /trase'tʃar/ *vt* to ambush, waylay
trasegar /trase'gar/ *vt irr* to upset, turn upside down; transfer, move from one place to another; empty, pour out, upset (liquids). See **cegar**
traseñalar /traseɲa'lar/ *vt* to re-mark, mark again
trasera /tra'sera/ *f,* rear, back, rear portion
trasero /tra'sero/ *a* rear, back. *m,* hindquarters, rump; buttocks, seat; *pl Inf.* ancestors
trasgo /'trasgo/ *m,* imp, sprite, puck
trashumante /trasu'mante/ *a* nomadic (of flocks)
trashumar /trasu'mar/ *vi* to go from winter to summer pasture (or vice versa) (of flocks)
trasiego /tra'siego/ *m,* emptying, pouring out, upsetting (of liquids); decanting (of wines)
traslación /trasla'θion; trasla'sion/ *f,* removal, transfer; alteration (of the date for a meeting); metaphor
trasladable /trasla'ðaβle/ *a* removable, movable, transferable
trasladar /trasla'ðar/ *vt* to remove, transfer; move from one place to another; alter (the date of a meeting); translate; copy, transcribe; *—vr* remove (from a place)
traslado /tras'laðo/ *m,* removal; transfer; transcription
traslapar /trasla'par/ *vt* to cover, overlap
traslapo /tras'lapo/ *m,* overlap, overlapping
traslucirse /traslu'θirse; traslu'sirse/ *vr irr* to be transparent or translucent; shine through; come out (of secrets); infer, gather. See **lucir**
traslumbramiento /traslumbra'miento/ *m,* dazzle, glare, brilliance
traslumbrar /traslum'βrar/ *vt* to dazzle; *—vr* flicker, glimmer; fade quickly, disappear
trasluz /tras'luθ; tras'lus/ *m,* reflected light. **al t.,** against the light
trasmañana /trasma'ɲana/ *adv* the day after tomorrow
trasmañanar /trasmaɲa'nar/ *vt* to put off from day to day
trasminar /trasmi'nar/ *vt* to undermine, excavate; *—vi* percolate, ooze; penetrate, spread
trasnochada /trasno'tʃaða/ *f,* previous night, last night; night's vigil; sleepless night; *Mil.* night attack
trasnochado /trasno'tʃaðo/ *a* stale, old; weary; hackneyed; drawn, pinched
trasnochador /trasnotʃa'ðor/ **(-ra)** *n* one who watches by night or stays up all night; *Inf.* night owl, reveler
trasnochar /trasno'tʃar/ *vi* to stay up all night; watch through the night; spend the night; *—vt* sleep on, leave for the following day
trasnoche, trasnocho /tras'notʃe, tras'notʃo/ *m, Inf.* night out; night vigil
trasoir /traso'ir/ *vt irr* to hear incorrectly, misunderstand. See **oir**
trasojado /traso'haðo/ *a* haggard, tired-eyed
trasoñar /traso'ɲar/ *vt irr* to imagine, mistake a dream for reality. See **contar**
traspalar /traspa'lar/ *vt* to fork (grain); shovel; transfer, move
trasparencia /traspa'renθia; traspa'rensia/ *f.* See **transparencia**
traspasar /traspa'sar/ *vt* to transfer, move; cross; *Law.* convey, make over to; pierce; transgress, flout; exceed one's authority; *Fig.* go too far; reexamine, go

over again; give intolerable pain (of illness, grief). **se traspasa,** to be disposed of (houses, etc.)
traspaso /tras'paso/ *m,* transport, transfer; *Law.* conveyance; property transferred; price agreed upon
traspié /tras'pie/ *m,* slip, catching of the foot, stumble; heel of the foot. **dar traspiés,** *Inf.* to blunder
trasplantación /trasplanta'θion; trasplanta'sion/ *f,* **trasplante** *m,* transplantation; emigration
trasplantar /trasplan'tar/ *vt Agr.* to transplant; *—vr* emigrate
trasplante /tras'plante/ *m,* planting out
traspuesta /tras'puesta/ *f,* transposition; back quarters; rear (of a house); back yard
traspunte /tras'punte/ *m, Theat.* prompter
traspuntín /traspun'tin/ *m, Auto.* folding seat
trasquilar /traski'lar/ *vt* to cut the hair unevenly; shear (sheep); *Inf.* cut down, diminish
trasquilón /traski'lon/ *m,* cropping (of hair); shearing; *Inf.* money stolen by pilfering
trastada /tras'taðа/ *f, Inf.* dirty trick, mean act
traste /'traste/ *m,* fret (of stringed instruments); tasting cup. **dar al t. con,** to spoil, upset, damage. *Inf.* **sin trastes,** topsy-turvy, without method
trastear /traste'ar/ *vt* to play well (on the mandolin, etc.); *Inf.* manage tactfully; *—vi* move around, change (furniture, etc.); discuss excitedly
trastejar /traste'har/ *vt* to repair the roof; renew slates; overhaul
trastienda /tras'tienda/ *f,* back of a shop; room behind a shop; *Inf.* wariness, caution
trasto /'trasto/ *m,* piece of furniture; (household) utensil; lumber, useless furniture; *Theat.* wing or set piece; *Inf.* useless person, ne'er-do-well; oddment, thing; *pl* implements, equipment
trastornable /trastor'naβle/ *a* easily overturned or upset; easily agitated
trastornar /trastor'nar/ *vt* to turn upside down; perturb, disturb; *Fig.* overpower (of scents, etc.); disorder, upset; dissuade; make mad; derange the mind
trastorno /tras'torno/ *m,* upset; perturbation, anxiety; disorder; mental derangement; confusion (of the senses)
trastrabillar /trastraβi'ʎar; trastraβi'yar/ *vi* to stumble, slip; totter, sway; hesitate; stutter, be tongue-tied
trastrás /tras'tras/ *m, Inf.* last but one (in games)
trastrocamiento /trastroka'miento/ *m,* alteration, change; disarrangement
trastrocar /trastro'kar/ *vt irr* to alter, change, disarrange; change the order of. See **contar**
trasudar /trasu'ðar/ *vt* to perspire
trasudor /trasu'ðor/ *m,* light perspiration
trasuntar /trasun'tar/ *vt* to copy, transcribe; summarize
trasunto /tra'sunto/ *m,* copy, transcript; imitation
trasver /tras'βer/ *vt irr* to see through or between, glimpse; see incorrectly. See **ver**
trasverter /trasβer'ter/ *vi irr* to overflow. See **entender**
trata /'trata/ *f,* slave trade. **t. de blancas,** white slave traffic
tratable /tra'taβle/ *a* easily accessible, sociable, unpretentious
tratadista /trata'ðista/ *mf* writer of a treatise; expert, writer on special subjects
tratado /tra'taðo/ *m,* pact, agreement; treaty; treatise
tratador /trata'ðor/ **(-ra)** *n* arbitrator
tratamiento /trata'miento/ *m,* treatment; courtesy title; address, style; *Med.* treatment; process. **t. de textos,** word processing
tratante /tra'tante/ *m,* merchant, dealer
tratar /tra'tar/ *vt* to handle, use; conduct, manage; have dealings with, meet, know (e.g. *Yo no le trato,* I don't know him); behave well or badly toward; care for, treat; discuss, deal with (e.g. *¿De qué trata el libro?* What is the book about?); propose, suggest; *Chem.* treat; (*with de*) address as, call; *—vi* have amorous relations; (*with de*) try to, endeavor to; (*with en*) trade in; *—vr* look after oneself, treat oneself; conduct oneself
trato /'trato/ *m,* use, handling; management; conduct, behavior; manner, demeanor; appellation, title; commerce, traffic; dealings, intercourse; treatment; agreement, arrangement. **t. colectivo,** collective bargaining
traumático /trau'matiko/ *a* traumatic
traumatismo /trauma'tismo/ *m,* traumatism
través /tra'βes/ *m,* slant, slope; mishap; (*Mil. Archit.*) traverse. **a t.** *or* **al t.,** across; through. **de t.,** athwart; through
travesaño /traβe'saɲo/ *m,* crossbar; bolster; rung (of a ladder); traverse
travesear /traβese'ar/ *vi* to run about, romp, be mischievous; lead a vicious life; speak wittily; move ceaselessly (of water, etc.)
travesía /traβe'sia/ *f,* crossing; traverse; crossroad; side road or street; distance, space; sea crossing; crosswise position; stretch of road within a town
travestido /traβes'tiðo/ *a* disguised, dressed up
travesura /traβe'sura/ *f,* romping, frolic; mischief; prank; quick-wittedness
traviesa /tra'βiesa/ *f,* sleeping car, sleeper (railroad); *Archit.* rafter; distance between two points
travieso /tra'βieso/ *a* transverse, crosswise; mischievous, willful; debauched; clever, subtle; ever-moving (of streams, etc.)
trayecto /tra'yekto/ *m,* run, distance, journey; stretch, expanse, tract; fare stage
trayectoria /trayek'toria/ *f,* trajectory; journey
traza /'traθa; 'trasa/ *f,* plan, design, draft; scheme, project; idea, proposal; aspect, appearance; means, manner. **Hombre pobre todo es trazas,** A poor man is full of schemes (for bettering himself)
trazado /tra'θaðo; tra'saðo/ *m,* designing, drawing; design, draft, model, plan; course, direction (of a canal, etc.)
trazador /traθa'ðor; trasa'ðor/ **(-ra)** *n* draftsman, designer; planner, schemer
trazar /tra'θar; tra'sar/ *vt* to plan, draft, design; make a drawing of; trace; describe; map out, arrange
trazo /'traθo; 'traso/ *m,* line, stroke; outline, contour, form, line; *Art.* fold in drapery; stroke of the pen
trebejar /treβe'har/ *vi* to frolic, skip, play
trebejo /tre'βeho/ *m,* chessman, chess piece; utensil, article (gen. *pl*); plaything
trébol /'treβol/ *m,* clover
trece /'treθe; 'trese/ *a* and *m,* thirteen, thirteenth. *m,* thirteenth (day of the month)
trecemesino /treθeme'sino; treseme'sino/ *a* thirteen months old
trecho /'tretʃo/ *m,* distance, space; interval (of time). **a trechos,** at intervals. **de t. en t.,** from time to time
trefe /'trefe/ *a* pliable, flexible; light; spurious (of coins)
tregua /'tregua/ *f,* truce, respite, rest. **dar treguas,** to afford relief, give a respite; give time
treinta /'treinta/ *a* and *m,* thirty; thirtieth. *m,* thirtieth (day of the month)
treintañal /treinta'ɲal/ *a* thirty years old
treintavo /trein'taβo/ *a* thirtieth
treintena /trein'tena/ *f,* thirtieth (part)
tremebundo /treme'βundo/ *a* fearsome, dread
tremedal /treme'ðal/ *m,* bog; quagmire
tremendo /tre'mendo/ *a* fearful, formidable; awesome; *Inf.* tremendous, enormous
trementina /tremen'tina/ *f,* turpentine
tremesino /treme'sino/ *a* three months old
tremolar /tremo'lar/ *vt* and *vi* to wave, fly (of banners); *Fig.* make a show of
tremolina /tremo'lina/ *f,* noise of the wind; *Inf.* hubbub, confusion
trémulo /'tremulo/ *a* trembling, tremulous
tren /tren/ *m,* supply, provision; outfit; equipment; pomp, show; railroad train; following, train. **t. ascendente,** up train (from coast to interior). *Inf.* **t. botijo,** excursion train. **t. con coches corridos,** corridor train. **t. correo,** mail train. **t. descendente,** down train (from interior to coast). **t. mixto,** train carrying passengers and freight. **t. ómnibus,** accommodation train, slow, stopping train. **t. rápido,** express
trencilla /tren'θiʎa; tren'siya/ *f,* braid, trimming
trencillar /trenθi'ʎar; trensi'yar/ *vt* to trim with braid, braid
treno /'treno/ *m,* threnody

Trento /'trento/ Trento
trenza /'trenθa; 'trensa/ *f,* plait, braid; plait of hair; bread twist. **en t.,** in plaits, plaited (of hair)
trenzadera /trenθa'ðera; trensa'ðera/ *f,* linen tape
trenzar /tren'θar; tren'sar/ *vt* to plait, braid; —*vi* curvet, prance
trepa /'trepa/ *f,* perforation, boring, piercing; climbing; creeping; *Inf.* half-somersault; grain, surface (of wood); craftiness, slyness; deception, fraud; beating, drubbing
trepador /trepa'ðor/ *a* climbing; crawling; *Bot.* creeping, climbing. *m,* climbing place
trepanación /trepana'θion; trepana'sion/ *f,* trepanning
trepanar /trepa'nar/ *vt* to trepan
trepante /tre'pante/ *a* creeping; *Bot.* twining, climbing
trepar /tre'par/ *vi* to climb, ascend; *Bot.* climb or creep; bore, perforate
trepatrepa /trepa'trepa/ *m,* jungle gym, monkey bars
trepidación /trepiða'θion; trepiða'sion/ *f,* trepidation, dread; vibration; jarring; shaking
trepidar /trepi'ðar/ *vi* to shiver, shudder; vibrate; shake; jar
trépido /'trepiðo/ *a* shuddering, shivering; vibrating
tres /tres/ *a* three; third. *m,* figure three; third (day of the month); three (of playing cards); trio. *Inf.* **como t. y dos son cinco,** as sure as two and two make four
trescientos /tres'θientos; tres'sientos/ *a* and *m,* three hundred; three-hundredth
tresillo /tre'siʎo; tre'siyo/ *m,* omber (card game); *Mus.* triplet
tresnal /tres'nal/ *m, Agr.* stook, cock, sheaf
treta /'treta/ *f,* scheme; trick, hoax; feint (in fencing)
trezavo /tre'θaβo; tre'saβo/ *a* thirteenth
tría /'tria/ *f,* selection, choice; worn place (in cloth)
triangulación /triaŋgula'θion; triaŋgula'sion/ *f,* triangulation
triángulo /tri'aŋgulo/ *a* triangular. *m,* (*Geom. Mus.*) triangle. **t. acutángulo,** acute triangle. **t. obtusángulo,** obtuse triangle. **t. rectángulo,** right-angled triangle
triar /triar/ *vt* to select, pick out; —*vi* fly in and out of the hive (of bees); —*vr* grow threadbare, become worn
tribu /'triβu/ *f,* tribe; species, family
tribulación /triβula'θion; triβula'sion/ *f,* tribulation, suffering
tribuna /tri'βuna/ *f,* tribune; platform, rostrum, pulpit; spectators' gallery; stand. **t. de la prensa,** press gallery. **t. del jurado,** jury box. **t. del órgano,** organ loft
tribunado /triβu'naðo/ *m,* tribunate
tribunal /triβu'nal/ *m,* law court; *Law.* bench; judgment seat; tribunal; board of examiners. **t. de menores,** children's court, juvenile court. *Naut.* **t. de presas,** prize court. **t. de primera instancia,** *Law.* petty sessions. **t. militar,** court-martial
tribuno /tri'βuno/ *m,* tribune; political speaker
tributar /triβu'tar/ *vt* to pay taxes; offer, render (thanks, homage, etc.)
tributario /triβu'tario/ **(-ia)** *a* tributary; tax-paying, contributive —*n* taxpayer. *m,* tributary (of a river)
tributo /tri'βuto/ *m,* contribution; tax; tribute, homage; census
tricenal /triθe'nal; trise'nal/ *a* of thirty years' duration; occurring every thirty years
tricentésimo /triθen'tesimo; trisen'tesimo/ *a* three-hundredth
triciclo /tri'θiklo; tri'siklo/ *m,* tricycle
tricolor /triko'lor/ *a* three-colored
tricorne /tri'korne/ *a Poet.* three-cornered, three-horned
tricornio /tri'kornio/ *a* three-cornered. *m,* three-cornered hat
tricotomía /trikoto'mia/ *f,* trichotomy, division into three
tricromía /trikro'mia/ *f,* three-color process
tridente /tri'ðente/ *a* tridentate, three-pronged. *m,* trident
tridentino /triðen'tino/ *a* Tridentine
trienal /trie'nal/ *a* triennial
trienio /'trienio/ *m,* space of three years
trifásico /tri'fasiko/ *a* three-phase
trifolio /tri'folio/ *m,* trefoil
trigal /tri'gal/ *m,* wheat field
trigésimo /tri'hesimo/ *a* thirtieth
trigo /'trigo/ *m,* wheat plant; ear of wheat; wheat field (gen. *pl*); wealth, money. **t. sarraceno,** buckwheat. **t. tremés** *or* **t. trechel** *or* **t. tremesino** *or* **t. de marzo,** summer wheat
trigonometría /trigonome'tria/ *f,* trigonometry
trigueño /tri'geɲo/ *a* brunette, dark
triguero /tri'gero/ *a* wheat; wheat-growing. *m,* grain sieve; grain merchant
trilátero /tri'latero/ *a* three-sided, trilateral
trilingüe /tri'liŋgue/ *a* trilingual
trilla /'triʎa; 'triya/ *f,* red mullet; *Agr.* harrow; threshing; threshing season
trillado /tri'ʎaðo; tri'yaðo/ *a* frequented, trodden, worn (of paths); hackneyed
trilladora /triʎa'ðora; triya'ðora/ *f,* threshing machine
trillar /tri'ʎar; tri'yar/ *vt* to thresh; *Inf.* frequent; ill-treat
trillo /'triʎo; 'triyo/ *m,* threshing machine; harrow
trillón /tri'ʎon; tri'yon/ *m,* trillion
trilogía /trilo'hia/ *f,* trilogy
trimestral /trimes'tral/ *a* quarterly; terminal (in schools, etc.)
trimestre /tri'mestre/ *a* quarterly; terminal. *m,* quarter, three months; term (in schools, etc.); quarterly payment; quarterly rent
trinado /tri'naðo/ *m, Mus.* trill; twittering, shrilling (of birds)
trinar /tri'nar/ *vi Mus.* to trill; twitter, shrill; *Inf.* get in a temper, be furious
trincapiñones /trinkapi'ɲones/ *m, Inf.* scatterbrained youth
trincar /trin'kar/ *vt* to fasten securely; tie tightly; pinion; *Naut.* lash, make fast; cut up, chop; *Inf.* tipple; —*vi Naut.* sail close to the wind
trincha /'trintʃa/ *f,* vest strap
trinchante /trin'tʃante/ *m,* table carver; carving fork; stonecutter's hammer
trinchar /trin'tʃar/ *vt* to carve (at table); *Inf.* decide, dispose
trinchera /trin'tʃera/ *f, Mil.* trench; cutting (for roads, etc.); trench coat
trinchero /trin'tʃero/ *m,* platter, trencher; serving table, side table
trineo /tri'neo/ *m,* sled, sledge, sleigh
trinidad /trini'ðað/ *f,* trinity
trinitaria /trini'taria/ *f, Bot.* heartsease
trinitario /trini'tario/ **(-ia)** *a* and *n Eccl.* Trinitarian
trino /'trino/ *a* triune; ternary. *m, Mus.* trill
trinomio /tri'nomio/ *m,* trinomial
trinquete /trin'kete/ *m, Naut.* mainmast; mainsail; *Sports.* rackets; *Mech.* ratchet
trinquis /'trinkis/ *m, Inf.* draft, drink
trío /'trio/ *m,* trio
tripa /'tripa/ *f,* entrail, gut; *Inf.* belly; inside (of some fruits). **hacer de tripas corazón,** *Inf.* to take heart, buck up. **revolver las tripas** (**a**), *Fig. Inf.* to make one sick
tripartición /triparti'θion; triparti'sion/ *f,* tripartition
tripartir /tripar'tir/ *vt* to divide into three
tripartito /tripar'tito/ *a* tripartite
triplicallos /tripli'kaʎos; tripli'kayos/ *m pl, Cul.* tripe
triple /'triple/ *a* triple; three-ply (of yarn)
triplicación /triplika'θion; triplika'sion/ *f,* trebling
triplicar /tripli'kar/ *vt* to treble
trípode /'tripoðe/ *m,* (sometimes *f*) three-legged stool or table; tripod; trivet
Trípoli /'tripoli/ Tripoli
tríptico /'triptiko/ *m,* triptych
triptongo /'triptoŋgo/ *m,* triphthong
tripulación /tripula'θion; tripula'sion/ *f,* crew (ships and aircraft)
tripulante /tripu'lante/ *m,* crew member
tripular /tripu'lar/ *vt* to provide with a crew, man; equip, furnish; serve in, work as the crew of

trique /'trike/ *m,* crack, creak. *Inf.* **a cada t.,** at every moment
triquiñuela /triki'ɲuela/ *f, Inf.* evasion, subterfuge
triquitraque /triki'trake/ *m,* tap, rap; crack; firework
tris /tris/ *m,* crack, noise of glass, etc., cracking; *Inf.* instant, trice. **estar en un t. (de),** to be on the verge (of), within an inch (of)
trisar /tri'sar/ *vt* to crack, break, splinter (of glass); —*vi* chirp, twitter (especially of swallows)
trisca /'triska/ *f,* cracking, crushing, crackling (of nuts, etc.); noise, tumult
triscar /tris'kar/ *vi* to make a noise with the feet; gambol, frolic; creak, crack; —*vt* blend, mingle; set the teeth of a saw
trisecar /trise'kar/ *vt* to trisect
trisección /trisek'θion; trisek'sion/ *f,* trisection
trisemanal /trisema'nal/ *a* three times weekly; every three weeks
trisílabo /tri'silaβo/ *a* trisyllabic
trismo /'trismo/ *m,* lockjaw, trismus
triste /'triste/ *a* unhappy, sorrowful; melancholy, gloomy; sad; piteous, unfortunate; useless, worthless
tristeza, tristura /tris'teθa, tris'tura; tris'tesa; *f,* unhappiness; melancholy, gloom; sadness; piteousness
tritón /tri'ton/ *m,* merman
triturar /tritu'rar/ *vt* to crumble, crush; chew; masticate; ill-treat, bruise; refute, contradict
triunfada /triun'faða/ *f,* trumping (at cards)
triunfador /triunfa'ðor/ **(-ra)** *a* triumphant —*n* victor
triunfal /triun'fal/ *a* triumphal
triunfante /triun'fante/ *a* triumphant
triunfar /triun'far/ *vi* to triumph; be victorious, win; trump (at cards); spend ostentatiously
triunfo /'triunfo/ *m,* triumph; victory; trump card; success; booty, spoils of war; conquest
triunvirato /triumbi'rato/ *m,* triumvirate
trivial /tri'βial/ *a* well-known, hackneyed; frequented, trodden; commonplace, mediocre; trivial, unimportant
trivialidad /triβiali'ðað/ *f,* banality, triteness; mediocrity; triviality
trivio /'triβio/ *m,* road junction
triza /'triθa; 'trisa/ *f,* fragment, bit; *Naut.* rope. **hacer trizas,** to smash to bits
trizar /tri'θar; tri'sar/ *vt* to smash up, destroy
trocable /tro'kaβle/ *a* exchangeable
trocada, a la /tro'kaða, a la/ *adv* contrariwise; in exchange
trocador /troka'ðor/ **(-ra)** *n* exchanger
trocar /tro'kar/ *vt irr* to exchange; vomit; distort, misconstrue, mistake; —*vr* change, alter one's behavior; change places with another; be transferred. See **contar**
trocear /troθe'ar; trose'ar/ *vt* to divide into pieces
trocha /'trotʃa/ *f,* short cut; trail, path, track
trochemoche, a /trotʃe'motʃe, a/ *adv Inf.* without rhyme or reason, pell-mell
trofeo /tro'feo/ *m,* trophy; victory; military booty
troglodita /troglo'ðita/ *a* and *mf* troglodyte. *m, Fig.* savage, barbarian. *mf* glutton
troglodítico /troglo'ðitiko/ *a* troglodytic
troj /troh/ *f,* granary
trojero /tro'hero/ *m,* granary keeper
trola /'trola/ *f, Inf.* lie, nonsense, hoax
trole /'trole/ *m,* trolley
trolebús /trole'βus/ *m,* trolley car
trolero /tro'lero/ *a Inf.* deceiving, lying
tromba /'tromba/ *f,* waterspout
trombón /trom'bon/ *m,* trombone; trombone player. **¡Trombones y platillos!** Great Scot!
trombosis /trom'bosis/ *f,* thrombosis
trompa /'trompa/ *f,* elephant's trunk; *Mus.* horn; proboscis (of insects); waterspout; humming top. **t. de Falopio,** fallopian tube
trompada /trom'paða/ *f, Inf.* bang, bump; blow, buffet, slap; collision
trompazo /trom'paθo; trom'paso/ *m,* heavy blow, knock, bang
trompear /trompe'ar/ *vi* to play with a top; —*vt* knock about
trompero /trom'pero/ *m,* top maker —*a* deceiving, swindling
trompeta /trom'peta/ *f,* trumpet; bugle. *m,* trumpeter; bugler; *Inf.* ninny. **t. de amor,** sunflower
trompetada /trompe'taða/ *f, Inf.* stupid remark, piece of nonsense
trompetazo /trompe'taθo; trompe'taso/ *m,* bray of a trumpet; bugle blast; *Inf.* stupid remark
trompetear /trompete'ar/ *vi Inf.* to play the trumpet or bugle
trompeteo /trompe'teo/ *m,* trumpeting, trumpet call; sound of the bugle
trompetería /trompete'ria/ *f,* collection of trumpets; metal organ pipes
trompetero /trompe'tero/ *m,* trumpet or bugle maker or player
trompetilla /trompe'tiʎa; trompe'tiya/ *f, dim* little trumpet; ear trumpet
trompicar /trompi'kar/ *vt* to make stumble, trip —*vi* stumble, trip up
trompicón /trompi'kon/ *m,* stumble
trompo /'trompo/ *m,* humming or spinning top; *Inf.* dolt, idiot
tronada /tro'naða/ *f,* thunderstorm
tronado /tro'naðo/ *a* worn-out; threadbare, old; poor, poverty-stricken; down at the heels
tronar /tro'nar/ *v impers irr* to thunder; —*vi* growl, roar (of guns); *Inf.* go bankrupt, be ruined; *Inf.* protest against, attack; (*with con*) quarrel with —*Pres. Indic.* **trueno, truenas, truena, truenan.** *Pres. Subjunc.* **truene, truenes, truene, truenen**
troncal /tron'kal/ *a* trunk; main, principal
tronchar /tron'tʃar/ *vt* to break off, lop off (branches)
troncho /'trontʃo/ *m, Bot.* stem, stalk, branch
tronco /'tronko/ *m, Anat. Bot.* trunk; main body or line (of communications); trunk line; common origin, stock; *Inf.* blockhead, dolt; callous person. *Fig.* **estar hecho un t.,** to lie like a log; sleep like a log
tronera /tro'nera/ *f, Naut.* porthole; embrasure; slit window; pocket of a billiards table. *mf Inf.* madcap, harumscarum
tronido /tro'niðo/ *m,* roll of thunder
trono /'trono/ *m,* throne; *Eccl.* tabernacle; shrine; kingly might; *pl* thrones, hierarchy of angels
tronzador /tronθa'ðor; tronsa'ðor/ *m,* two-handled saw
tronzar /tron'θar; tron'sar/ *vt* to smash, break into bits; *Sew.* pleat; exhaust, overtire
tropa /'tropa/ *f,* crowd (of people); troops, military; *Mil.* call to arms; *pl* army. **t. de línea,** regiment of the line. **tropas de asalto,** storm troopers. **tropas de refresco,** fresh troops. **en t.,** in a crowd; in groups
tropel /tro'pel/ *m,* rush, surge (of crowds, etc.); bustle, confusion; crowd, multitude; heap, jumble (of things). **en t.,** in a rush; in a crowd
tropelía /trope'lia/ *f,* rush, dash; violence; outrage
tropezar /trope'θar; trope'sar/ *vi irr* to stumble, slip; (*with con*) meet unexpectedly or accidentally come up against, be faced with (difficulties); quarrel with or oppose; fall into (bad habits). See **empezar**
tropezón /trope'θon; trope'son/ *m,* stumbling, slipping; stumbling block, obstacle. **a tropezones,** *Inf.* stumblingly; by fits and starts
tropical /tropi'kal/ *a* tropical
trópicos /'tropikos/ *m pl,* tropics
tropiezo /tro'pieθo; tro'pieso/ *m,* stumble; stumbling block, obstacle; hitch; impediment; slip, peccadillo, fault; difficulty, embarrassment; fight, skirmish; quarrel
tropismo /tro'pismo/ *m,* tropism
tropo /'tropo/ *m,* trope, figure of speech
troquel /tro'kel/ *m,* die, mold
trotaconventos /trotakom'bentos/ *f, Inf.* go-between, procuress
trotamundos /trota'mundos/ *m, Inf.* globetrotter
trotar /tro'tar/ *vi* to trot; *Inf.* hurry, get a move on
trote /'trote/ *m,* trot; toil, drudgery. **t. corto,** jog-trot. **al t.,** with all speed
trotón /tro'ton/ **(-ona)** *a* trotting. *m,* horse. *f,* chaperone
trova /'troβa/ *f,* verse; song, lay, ballad; love song

trovador /troβa'ðor/ **(-ra)** *m*, troubadour, minstrel —*n* poet
trovadoresco /troβaðo'resko/ *a* pertaining to minstrels, troubadour
trovar /tro'βar/ *vi* to compose verses; write ballads; misconstrue, misinterpret
Troya /'troia/ Troy
troyano /tro'iano/ **(-na)** *a* and *n* Trojan
trozo /'troθo; 'troso/ *m*, part, fragment; piece, portion; *Lit.* selection. **t. de abordaje,** *Nav.* landing party
trucha /'trutʃa/ *f*, trout. **t. asalmonada,** salmon trout
truchuela /tru'tʃuela/ *f*, small trout; salt cod
truco /'truko/ *m*, trick, deception
truculencia /truku'lenθia; truku'lensia/ *f*, harshness, cruelty, truculence
truculento /truku'lento/ *a* fierce, harsh, truculent
trueco /'trueko/ *m*, exchange. **a t. de,** in exchange for; on condition that
trueno /'trueno/ *m*, thunder; report, noise (of firearms); *Inf.* rake, scapegrace
trueque /'trueke/ *m*, exchange. **a.** (*or* **en**) **t.,** in exchange
trufa /'trufa/ *f*, *Bot.* truffle; nonsense, idle talk
trufar /tru'far/ *vt Cul.* to stuff with truffles; —*vi Inf.* lie, tell fibs
truhán /tru'an/ **(-ana)** *a* knavish, roguish, comic —*n* knave, rogue; clown, buffoon
truhanear /truane'ar/ *vi* to be a trickster, behave like a knave; play the clown
truhanería /truane'ria/ *f*, knavery, act of a rogue; clowning, buffoonery; collection of rogues
truhanesco /trua'nesko/ *a* knavish, scoundrelly; clownish
trujal /tru'hal/ *m*, oil or grape press; oil mill; vat for soap making
trujar /tru'har/ *vt* to partition off
trulla /'truʎa; 'truya/ *f*, uproar, tumult; crowd, throng
truncar /trun'kar/ *vt* to shorten, truncate; decapitate, mutilate; omit, cut out (words, etc.); curtail, abridge; mutilate, deform (texts, etc.)
truque /'truke/ *m*, card game; kind of hopscotch
trust /trust/ *m*, *Com.* trust
tú /tu/ *pers pron 2nd sing mf* thou, you. **tratar de t. (a),** to address familiarly; be on intimate terms with
tu /tu/ *poss pron mf* thy, your. Used only before nouns
tuberculina /tuβerku'lina/ *f*, tuberculin
tubérculo /tu'βerkulo/ *m*, (*Zool. Med.*) tubercle; *Bot.* tubercle, tuber
tuberculoso /tuβerku'loso/ *a* tubercular, tuberculous
tubería /tuβe'ria/ *f*, piping, tubing; pipe system; pipe factory
tuberosa /tuβe'rosa/ *f*, tuberose
tuberoso /tuβe'roso/ *a* tuberous
tubo /'tuβo/ *m*, pipe, tube; lamp chimney; flue; *Anat.* duct, canal. **t. acústico,** speaking tube. **t. de ensayo,** test tube. **t. de escape,** exhaust pipe. **t. lanzatorpedos,** torpedo tube. **t. termiónico,** *Radio.* thermionic valve
tubular /tuβu'lar/ *a* tubular
tucán /tu'kan/ *m*, toucan
tudesco /tu'ðesko/ *a* German
tueco /'tueko/ *m*, stump (of a tree); wormhole (in wood)
tuerca /'tuerka/ *f*, nut (of a screw)
tuerto /'tuerto/ *a* one-eyed. *m*, *Law.* tort; *pl* afterpains. **a t.,** unjustly
tueste /'tueste/ *m*, toasting
tuétano /'tuetano/ *m*, marrow. *Inf.* **hasta los tuétanos,** to the depths of one's being
tufillas /tu'fiʎas; tu'fiyas/ *mf Inf.* easily irritated person
tufo /'tufo/ *m*, strong smell, poisonous vapor; *Inf.* stink; side, airs, conceit (often *pl*); lock of hair over the ears
tugurio /tu'gurio/ *m*, shepherd's hut; miserable little room; *Inf.* haunt, low dive
tul /tul/ *m*, tulle
tulipa /tu'lipa/ *f*, small tulip; lampshade
tulipán /tuli'pan/ *m*, tulip
tullido /tu'ʎiðo; tu'yiðo/ *a* partially paralyzed; maimed, crippled
tullir /tu'ʎir; tu'yir/ *vt irr* to maim, cripple; paralyze; —*vr* become paralyzed; be crippled. See **mullir**
tumba /'tumba/ *f*, tomb; tumble, overbalancing; somersault; Catherine wheel
tumbar /tum'bar/ *vt* to knock down; kill, drop; *Inf.* overpower, overcome (of odors, wine) —*vi* fall down; *Naut.* run aground; —*vr Inf.* lie down, stretch oneself out
tumbo /'tumbo/ *m*, tumble, overbalancing; undulation (of ground); rise and fall of sea waves; imminent danger; book containing deeds and privileges of monasteries and churches
tumbón /tum'bon/ *a Inf.* crafty, sly; idle, lazy. *m*, trunk with an arched lid
tumefacción /tumefak'θion; tumefak'sion/ *f*, swelling
tumefacto, túmido /tume'fakto, 'tumiðo/ *a* swollen
tumor /tu'mor/ *m*, tumor
túmulo /'tumulo/ *m*, tumulus; catafalque; mound of earth
tumulto /tu'multo/ *m*, riot, uprising; tumult, commotion, disturbance
tumultuario, tumultuoso /tumul'tuario, tumul'tuoso/ *a* noisy, tumultuous, confused
tuna /'tuna/ *f*, prickly pear tree or fruit; vagrant life; strolling student musicians (playing to raise money for charity)
tunante /tu'nante/ *a* rascally, roguish. *mf* rascal, scoundrel
tunantuelo /tunan'tuelo/ **(-la)** *n Inf.* imp, little rascal
tunda /'tunda/ *f*, shearing of cloth; *Inf.* sound beating, hiding
tundear /tunde'ar/ *vt* to beat, drub, buffet
tundidora /tundi'ðora/ *f*, woman who shears cloth; cloth-shearing machine; lawn mower
tundir /tun'dir/ *vt* to shear (cloth); mow (grass); *Inf.* beat, wallop
tunecino /tune'θino; tune'sino/ **(-na)** *a* and *n* Tunisian
túnel /'tunel/ *m*, tunnel
Túnez /'tuneθ; 'tunes/ Tunis, Tunisia
tungsteno /tuŋgs'teno/ *m*, tungsten
túnica /'tunika/ *f*, tunic, chiton; tunicle; robe
Tunicia /tu'niθia; tu'nisia/ Tunisia
tuno /'tuno/ **(-na)** *a* knavish, rascally —*n* rascal, scoundrel
tupé /tu'pe/ *m*, forelock (of a horse); toupee; *Inf.* cheek, nerve
tupido /tu'piðo/ *a* thick, dense; obtuse, dull, stupid
tupir /tu'pir/ *vt* to thicken, make dense; press tightly; —*vr* stuff oneself with food or drink
turba /'turβa/ *f*, crowd, multitude; peat
turbación /turβa'θion; turβa'sion/ *f*, disturbance; upset; perturbation; bewilderment, confusion; embarrassment
turbador /turβa'ðor/ **(-ra)** *a* disturbing, upsetting —*n* disturber, upsetter
turbamulta /turβa'multa/ *f*, *Inf.* mob, rabble
turbante /tur'βante/ *a* upsetting, perturbing. *m*, turban
turbar /tur'βar/ *vt* to disturb, upset; make turbid, muddy; bewilder, confuse; embarrass
turbera /tur'βera/ *f*, peat bog
turbiedad /turβie'ðað/ *f*, muddiness (of liquids); obscurity
turbina /tur'βina/ *f*, turbine
turbio /'turβio/ *a* turbid, muddy; troublous; turbulent, disturbed; obscure, confused (style); indistinct, blurred, *m pl*, lees, sediment (of oil)
turbión /tur'βion/ *m*, brief storm, squall; *Fig.* shower, rush
turbulencia /turβu'lenθia; turβu'lensia/ *f*, turbidity, muddiness; turbulence, commotion; disturbance, confusion
turbulento /turβu'lento/ *a* muddy, turbid; turbulent, disturbed; confused
turca /'turka/ *f*, *Inf.* drinking bout
turco /'turko/ **(-ca)** *a* Turkish —*n* Turk. *m*, Turkish (language)

turgencia /tur'henθia; tur'hensia/ *f*, swelling, turgidity

turgente /tur'hente/ *a Med.* turgescent; *Poet.* turgid, prominent, swollen

Turingia /tu'rinhia/ Thuringia

turismo /tu'rismo/ *m*, touring, tourist industry. **coche de t.,** touring car

turista /tu'rista/ *mf* tourist

turno /'turno/ *m*, turn. **por t.,** in turn

turquesa /tur'kesa/ *f*, turquoise

turquesco /tur'kesko/ *a* Turkish

Turquía /tur'kia/ Turkey

turrón /tu'rron/ *m*, kind of nougat; almond paste; *Inf.* soft job, sinecure; civil service job

turulato /turu'lato/ *a Inf.* dumbfounded, speechless, inarticulate

¡tus! /tus/ *interj* word for calling dogs. **sin decir t. ni mus,** *Inf.* without saying anything

tutear /tute'ar/ *vt* to address as tú (instead of the formal usted); treat familiarly

tutela /tu'tela/ *f*, guardianship; tutelage; protection, defense

tuteo /tu'teo/ *m*, the use in speaking to a person of the familiar tú instead of the formal usted

tutor /tu'tor/ **(-ra)** *n* guardian. *m*, stake (for plants); protector, defender

tutoría /tuto'ria/ *f.* See **tutela**

tuyo, tuya, tuyos, tuyas /'tuyo, 'tuya, 'tuyos, 'tuyas/ *poss pron 2nd sing* and *pl mf* thine, yours. Used sometimes with def. art. (e.g. *Este sombrero es el tuyo,* This hat is yours)

U

u /u/ *f,* letter U *—conjunc* Used instead of **o** or before words beginning with **o** or **ho** (e.g. *fragante u oloroso*)
ubérrimo /u'βerrimo/ *a superl* most fruitful; very abundant
ubicación /uβika'θion; uβika'sion/ *f,* situation, position, location
ubicar /uβi'kar/ *vt* to place, situate; *—vi* and *vr* be situated
ubicuidad /uβikui'ðað/ *f,* ubiquity
ubicuo /u'βikuo/ *a* omnipresent; ubiquitous
ubre /'uβre/ *f,* udder
ucelele /uθe'lele; use'lele/ *m,* ukulele
Ucrania /u'krania/ Ukraine
ucranio /u'kranio/ **(-ia)** *a* and *n* Ukrainian
¡uf! /uf/ *interj* ugh!
ufanarse /ufa'narse/ *vr* to pride oneself, put on airs
ufa'nía /ufa'nia/ *f,* pride, conceit
ufano /u'fano/ *a* conceited, vain; satisfied, pleased; expeditious, masterly
ujier /u'hier/ *m,* usher
úlcera /'ulθera; 'ulsera/ *f,* ulcer
ulceración /ulθera'θion; ulsera'sion/ *f,* ulceration
ulcerar /ulθe'rar; ulse'rar/ **(se)** *vt* and *vr* to ulcerate
ulceroso /ulθe'roso; ulse'roso/ *a* ulcerous
ulterior /ulte'rior/ *a* farther, ulterior; subsequent
ulteriormente /ulterior'mente/ *adv* subsequently, later
ultimación /ultima'θion; ultima'sion/ *f,* ending, finishing
ultimar /ulti'mar/ *vt* to end, conclude
ultimátum /ulti'matum/ *m,* ultimatum
último /'ultimo/ *a* last; farthermost; ultimate; top; final, definitive; most valuable, best; latter; recent. **«Última Hora.»** "Stop Press." **a última hora,** *Fig.* at the eleventh hour. **en estos últimos años,** in recent years. **a últimos de mes,** towards the end of the month. **el ú. piso,** the top floor. **por ú.,** finally. *Inf.* **estar en las últimas,** to be at the end, be finishing
ultra /'ultra/, *adv* besides; (with words like *mar*) beyond; (as prefix) excessively
ultrajar /ultra'har/ *vt* to insult; scorn, despise
ultraje /ul'trahe/ *m,* insult, outrage
ultrajoso /ultra'hoso/ *a* offensive, insulting, abusive
ultramar /ultra'mar/ *m,* overseas, abroad
ultramarino /ultrama'rino/ *a* oversea; ultramarine. *m,* foreign produce (gen. *pl*)
ultramontano /ultramon'tano/ *a* ultramontane
ultrarrojo /ultra'rroho/ *a* infrared
ultratumba /ultra'tumba/ *adv* beyond the grave
ultravioleta /ultraβio'leta/ *a* ultraviolet
úlula /'ulula/ *f,* screech owl
ululación /ulula'θion; ulula'sion/ *f,* screech, howl; hoot of an owl
ulular /ulu'lar/ *vi* to howl, shriek, screech; hoot (of an owl)
ululato /ulu'lato/ *m,* ululation
umbilical /umbili'kal/ *a* umbilical
umbral /um'bral/ *m,* threshold; *Fig.* starting point; *Archit.* lintel. **atravesar** (*or* **pisar**) **los umbrales,** to cross the threshold
umbría /um'bria/ *f,* shady place
umbrío /um'brio/ *a* shady, dark
umbroso /um'broso/ *a* shady
un /un/ *Abbr.* of **uno, a,** one. Used before *m, sing f,* **una,** *indef art* a, an; a; one
unánime /u'nanime/ *a* unanimous
unanimidad /unanimi'ðað/ *f,* unanimity. **por u.,** unanimously
unción /un'θion; un'sion/ *f,* anointing; *Eccl.* Extreme Unction; unction, fervor
uncir /un'θir; un'sir/ *vt* to yoke
undécimo /un'deθimo; un'desimo/ *a* eleventh
undísono /un'disono/ *a Poet.* sounding, sonorous (waves, etc.)
undoso /un'doso/ *a* wavy, rippling
undulación /undula'θion; undula'sion/ *f,* undulation; *Phys.* wave
undular /undu'lar/ *vi* to undulate; wriggle; float, wave (flags, etc.)
undulatorio /undula'torio/ *a* undulatory
ungimiento /unhi'miento/ *m,* anointment
ungir /un'hir/ *vt* to anoint
ungüento /uŋ'guento/ *m,* ointment; lotion; *Fig.* balm, unguent
unicelular /uniθelu'lar; uniselu'lar/ *a* unicellular
único /'uniko/ *a* unique; sole, solitary, only. **Lo ú. que se puede hacer es...,** The only thing one can do is...
unicolor /uniko'lor/ *a* of one color
unicornio /uni'kornio/ *m,* unicorn
unidad /uni'ðað/ *f,* unity; unit; (*Math. Mil.*) unit. **u. de bagaje,** piece of baggage. (of drama) **u. de lugar,** unity of place. **u. de tiempo,** unity of time
unidamente /uniða'mente/ *adv* jointly; harmoniously
unificación /unifika'θion; unifika'sion/ *f,* unification
unificar /unifi'kar/ **(se)** *vt* and *vr* to unify, unite
uniformación /uniforma'θion; uniforma'sion/ *f,* standardization
uniformar /unifor'mar/ *vt* to make uniform, standardize; put into uniform; *—vr* become uniform
uniforme /uni'forme/ *a* uniform; same, similar. *m,* uniform
uniformidad /uniformi'ðað/ *f,* uniformity
unigénito /uni'henito/ *a* only-begotten. *m,* Christ
unilateral /unilate'ral/ *a* one-sided, unilateral
unión /u'nion/ *f,* union; correspondence, conformity; agreement; marriage; alliance, federation; composition, mixture; combination; proximity, nearness; (mystic) union
unionista /unio'nista/ *mf Polit.* unionist
Unión Soviética /u'nion so'βietika/ Soviet Union
unir /u'nir/ *vt* to unite, join; mix, combine; bind, fasten; connect, couple; bring together; marry; *Fig.* harmonize, conciliate; *—vr* join together, unite; be combined; marry; (*with prep a* or *con*) be near to; associate with
unísono /u'nisono/ *a* unisonant. **al u.,** in unison; unanimously
unitario /uni'tario/ **(-ia)** *a* and *n* Unitarian
universal /uniβer'sal/ *a* universal; well-informed; widespread
universalidad /uniβersali'ðað/ *f,* universality
universalizar /uniβersali'θar; uniβersali'sar/ *vt* to make universal, generalize
universidad /uniβersi'ðað/ *f,* university; universality; universe
universitario /uniβersi'tario/ *a* university
universo /uni'βerso/ *a* universal. *m,* universe
uno /'uno/ (*f,* **una**) *a* a, one; single, only; same; *pl* some; about, nearly. *m,* one (number). **Tiene unos doce años,** He is about twelve. **unas pocas manzanas,** a few apples *—pron* someone; one thing, same thing; *pl* some people. **No sabe uno qué creer,** One doesn't know what to believe. **Unos dicen que no, otros que sí,** Some (people) say no, others yes. **Juan no tiene libros y le voy a dar uno,** John has no books and I am going to give him one. **Todo es uno,** It's all the same. **u. a u.,** one by one. **u. que otro,** a few. **u. y otro,** both. **unos cuantos,** a few, some. **Es la una,** It is one o'clock
untar /un'tar/ *vt* to anoint; grease, oil; *Inf.* bribe; *—vr* smear oneself with grease or similar thing; *Fig. Inf.* line one's pockets. **u. el carro,** *Fig.* to grease the wheels
unto /'unto/ *m,* grease; animal fat; *Fig.* balm
untuoso /un'tuoso/ *a* fat, greasy
uña /'uɲa/ *f,* nail (of fingers or toes); hoof, trotter, claw; stinging tail of scorpion; thorn; stump of tree branch; *Naut.* fluke; *Fig. Inf.* light fingers (gen. *pl*). **afilarse las uñas,** to sharpen one's claws, prepare for

trouble. **comerse las uñas,** to bite one's nails. **caer en las uñas de,** to fall into the clutches of. **hincar la u.** (**en),** to stick the claws into; to defraud, overcharge. **ser u. y carne,** to be devoted friends
uñarada /uɲa'raða/ *f,* scratch with nails
uñero /u'ɲero/ *m,* ingrowing nail, ingrown nail
¡upa! /'upa/ *interj* Up you get! Up you go! Upsy daisy! (gen. to children)
Urales, los /u'rales, los/ the Urals
uranio /u'ranio/ *m,* uranium
urbanidad /urβani'ðað/ *f,* civility, good manners, urbanity
urbanismo /urβa'nismo/ *m,* town planning; housing scheme
urbanización /urβaniθa'θion; urβanisa'sion/ *f,* urbanization
urbanizar /urβani'θar; urβani'sar/ *vt* to civilize, polish; urbanize
urbano /ur'βano/ *a* urban, city; urbane
urbe /'urβe/ *f,* city, metropolis
urbícola /ur'βikola/ *mf* city dweller
urdemalas /urðe'malas/ *m,* schemer, intriguer
urdidera /urði'ðera/ *f,* warping-frame
urdimbre /ur'ðimbre/ *f,* warp; scheming, plotting
urdir /ur'ðir/ *vt* to warp; weave; scheme, intrigue
uréter /u'reter/ *m,* ureter
uretra /u'retra/ *f,* urethra
urgencia /ur'henθia; ur'hensia/ *f,* urgency; necessity; compulsion
urgente /ur'hente/ *a* urgent
urgir /ur'hir/ *vi* to be urgent; be valid, be in force (laws)
úrico /'uriko/ *a* uric
urinario /uri'nario/ *a* urinary. *m,* urinal
urna /'urna/ *f,* urn; ballot box; glass case
urraca /u'rraka/ *f,* magpie
uruguayo /uru'guayo/ **(-ya)** *a* and *n* Uruguayan
usado /u'saðo/ *a* worn out; accustomed, efficient. *Com.* **al u.,** in the usual form. **ropa usada,** second-hand clothing, worn clothing
usanza /u'sanθa; usansa/ *f,* custom, usage
usar /u'sar/ *vt* to use; wear, make use of; follow (trade, occupation); *—vi* be accustomed
uso /'uso/ *m,* use; custom; fashion; habit; wear and tear. **al u.,** according to custom. **al u. de,** in the manner of
usted /us'teð/ *mf* you *pl* **ustedes.** Often abbreviated to **Vd, V, Vds, VV** or **Ud, Uds**
usual /u'sual/ *a* usual; general, customary; sociable
usufructo /usu'frukto/ *m, Law.* usufruct; life-interest; profit
usura /u'sura/ *f,* usury; profiteering. **pagar con u.,** to pay back a thousandfold
usurario /usu'rario/ *a* usurious
usurear /usure'ar/ *vi* to lend or borrow with usury; profiteer, make excess profits
usurero /usu'rero/ **(-ra)** *n* usurer; profiteer
usurpación /usurpa'θion; usurpa'sion/ *f,* usurpation
usurpador /usurpa'ðor/ **(-ra)** *a* usurping *—n* usurper
usurpar /usur'par/ *vt* to usurp
utensilio /uten'silio/ *m,* utensil; tool, implement (gen. *pl*)
uterino /ute'rino/ *a* uterine
útero /'utero/ *m,* uterus
útil /'util/ *a* useful; profitable; *Law.* lawful (of days, etc.). *m,* usefuiness, profit; *pl* **útiles,** utensils, tools
utilidad /utili'ðað/ *f,* utility; usefulness; profit
utilitario /utili'tario/ *a* utilitarian
utilitarismo /utilita'rismo/ *m,* utilitarianism
utilizable /utili'θaβle; utilisaβle/ *a* utilizable
utilización /utiliθa'θion; utilisa'sion/ *f,* utilization
utilizar /utili'θar; utili'sar/ *vt* to utilize
utillaje /uti'ʎahe; uti'yahe/ *m,* machinery
utópico /u'topiko/ *a* Utopian
uva /'uβa/ *f,* grape. **u. espina,** kind of gooseberry. **u. moscatel,** muscatel grape. *Inf.* **hecho una u.,** dead-drunk
uvero /u'βero/ **(-ra)** *a* pertaining or relating to grapes, grape *—n* grape seller
uxoricidio /uksori'θiðio; uksori'siðio/ *m,* uxoricide (act)
uxorio /uk'sorio/ *a* uxorious

V

v /be/ *f,* letter V. **v doble** *or* **doble v,** letter W. **V** *or* **Vd, VV,** *Abbr.* **vuestra (s) merced (es),** *mf sing* and *pl* you

vaca /'baka/ *f,* cow. **v. de San Antón,** *Ent.* ladybug

vacación /baka'θion; baka'sion/ *f,* vacation, holiday (gen. *pl*); vacancy; act of vacating (employment). **vacaciones retribuídas,** paid vacation

vacada /ba'kaðа/ *f,* herd of cows

vacancia /ba'kanθia; ba'kansia/ *f,* vacancy

vacante /ba'kante/ *a* vacant. *f,* vacancy

vacar /ba'kar/ *vi* to be vacant; take a holiday; retire temporarily; (*with prep a*) dedicate oneself to, engage in

vaciadero /baθia'ðero; basia'ðero/ *m,* rubbish dump; sewer, drain

vaciado /ba'θiaðo; ba'siaðo/ *m,* plaster cast; *Archit.* excavation

vaciamiento /baθia'miento; basia'miento/ *m,* emptying; molding, casting; depletion

vaciar /ba'θiar; ba'siar/ *vt* to empty; drain, drink; mold, cast; *Archit.* excavate; hone; copy; *—vi* flow (into) (rivers); *—vr Inf.* blurt out

vaciedad /baθie'ðað; basie'ðað/ *f,* emptiness; foolishness, inanity

vacilación /baθila'θion; basila'sion/ *f,* swaying; tottering; staggering; hesitation, perplexity

vacilante /baθi'lante; basi'lante/ *a* swaying; tottering; staggering; hesitating, vacillating

vacilar /baθi'lar; basi'lar/ *vi* to sway; totter; stagger; flicker; hesitate

vacío /ba'θio; ba'sio/ *a* empty, void; fruitless, vain; unoccupied, vacant, deserted; imperfect; hollow, empty; conceited, immature. *m,* hollow; *Anat.* flank; vacancy; shortage; *Phys.* vacuum. **v. de aire,** airpocket. **de v.,** unloaded (carts, etc.). **en v.,** in vacuo. *Inf.* **hacer el v.** (**a**), to send to Coventry

vacuidad /bakui'ðað/ *f,* emptiness; vacuity

vacuna /ba'kuna/ *f,* cowpox; vaccine. **v. antivariolosa,** smallpox vaccine

vacunación /bakuna'θion; bakuna'sion/ *f,* vaccination

vacunar /baku'nar/ *vt* to vaccinate; inoculate

vacuno /ba'kuno/ *a* bovine

vacuo /'bakuo/ *a* empty; vacant. *m,* void; vacuum

vadeable /baðe'aβle/ *a* fordable (rivers, etc.); *Fig.* surmountable

vadear /baðe'ar/ *vt* to ford, wade; *Fig.* overcome (obstacles); *Fig.* sound, find out the opinion (of); *—vr* behave

vademécum /baðe'mekum/ *m,* vade mecum; school satchel

vado /'baðo/ *m,* ford; expedient, help

vagabundear /bagaβunde'ar/ *vi* to wander, roam, loiter

vagabundeo /bagaβun'deo/ *m,* vagabondage

vagabundo /baga'βundo/ **(-da)** *a* roving, wandering; vagrant *—n* tramp, vagabond

vagamundear /bagamunde'ar/ *vi.* See **vagabundear**

vagancia /ba'ganθia; ba'gansia/ *f,* vagrancy

vagar /ba'gar/ *m,* leisure; interval, pause *—vi* be idle or at leisure; wander, roam

vagido /ba'hiðo/ *m,* cry, wail (infants)

vagneriano /bagne'riano/ *a* Wagnerian

vago /'bago/ **(-ga)** *a* vagrant, idle; vague; *Art.* indefinite, blurred *—n* idler. *m,* tramp; loafer. **en v.,** unsuccessfully, vainly

vagón /ba'gon/ *m,* wagon; (railway) coach. **v. comedor,** dining car

vagoneta /bago'neta/ *f,* open truck (railways, mines, etc.)

vaguear /bage'ar/ *vi* to roam, wander; loaf

vaguedad /bage'ðað/ *f,* vagueness; vague remark

vaharada /baa'raða/ *f,* whiff, exhalation

vahído /ba'iðo/ *m,* vertigo

vaho /'bao/ *m,* vapor, fume

vaina /'baina/ *f,* scabbard; *Bot.* sheath, pod; case (scissors, etc.)

vainilla /bai'niʎa; bai'niya/ *f, Bot.* vanilla; *Sew.* drawn-thread work

vaivén /bai'βen/ *m,* swing, sway, seesaw; instability, fluctuation

vajilla /ba'hiʎa; ba'hiya/ *f,* china; dinner service

val /bal/ *m, Abbr.* **valle**

Valdepeñas /balde'peɲas/ *m,* red wine from Valdepeñas

vale /'bale/ *m, Com.* bond, I.O.U., promissory note; voucher; valediction

valedero /bale'ðero/ *a* valid, binding

valedor /bale'ðor/ **(-ra)** *n* protector, sponsor

valencia /ba'lenθia; ba'lensia/ *f,* valency

valenciano /balen'θiano; balen'siano/ **(-na)** *a* and *n* Valencian

valentía /balen'tia/ *f,* bravery; heroic deed; boast; (*Art, Lit.*) dash, imagination, fire; superhuman effort

valentón /balen'ton/ *a* boastful, blustering

valer /ba'ler/ *vt irr* to protect; defend; produce (income, etc.); cost; *—vi* be worth; deserve; have power or authority; be of importance or worth; be a protection; be current (money); be valid; *—vr* (*with de*) make use of. *m,* value, worth. **v. la pena,** to be worthwhile. **v. tanto como cualquiera,** to be as good as the next guy, be as good as the next fellow. **¡Válgame Dios!** Heavens! Bless me! **Más vale así,** It's better thus. **Vale más ser cola de león que cabeza de ratón.** Better a big frog in a small puddle than a small frog in a big puddle *—Pres. Indic.* **valgo, vales,** etc *—Fut.* **valdré,** etc *—Condit.* **valdría,** etc *—Pres. Subjunc.* **valga,** etc.

valeriana /bale'riana/ *f,* valerian

valeroso /bale'roso/ *a* active, energetic; courageous; powerful

valetudinario /baletuði'nario/ *a* valetudinarian

valía /ba'lia/ *f,* value, price; influence, worth; faction, party. **a las valías,** at the highest price

validación /baliða'θion; baliða'sion/ *f,* validation; force, soundness

validar /bali'ðar/ *vt* to make strong; validate

validez /bali'ðeθ; bali'ðes/ *f,* validity

valido /ba'liðo/ *a* favorite, esteemed. *m,* court favorite; prime minister

válido /'baliðo/ *a* firm, sound, valid; strong, robust

valiente /ba'liente/ *a* strong, robust; courageous; active; excellent; excessive, enormous (gen. *iron*); boastful

valija /ba'liha/ *f,* valise, suitcase, grip; mail bag; mail

valimiento /bali'miento/ *m,* value; favor; protection, influence

valioso /ba'lioso/ *a* valuable; powerful; wealthy

valisoletano /balisole'tano/ **(-na)** *a* and *n* of or from Valladolid

valla /'baʎa; 'baya/ *f,* barricade, paling; stockade; *Fig.* obstacle. **v. publicitaria,** billboard

vallado /ba'ʎaðo; ba'yaðo/ *m,* stockade; enclosure

valle /'baʎe; 'baye/ *m,* valley; vale; river-basin

valón /ba'lon/ *a* Walloon

valona /ba'lona/ *f,* Vandyke collar

valor /ba'lor/ *m,* worth, value; price; courage; validity; power; yield, income; insolence; *pl Com* securities

valoración /balora'θion; balora'sion/ *f,* valuation; appraisement

valorar /balo'rar/ *vt* to value; appraise

valorización /baloriθa'θion; balorisa'sion/ *f,* valuation

valquiria /bal'kiria/ *f,* Valkyrie

vals /bals/ *m,* waltz

valsar /bal'sar/ *vi* to waltz

valuación /balua'θion; balua'sion/ *f.* See **valoración**

valuar /balu'ar/ *vt* to value; appraise; assess

valva /'balβa/ *f, Zool.* valve

válvula /'balβula/ *f, Mech.* valve. *Auto.* **v. de cámara**

(**del neumático**), tire-valve. **v. de seguridad,** safety-valve
vampiro /bam'piro/ *m,* vampire; *Fig.* bloodsucker
vanagloria /bana'gloria/ *f,* vaingloriousness, conceit
vanagloriarse /banaglo'riarse/ *vr* to be conceited
vanaglorioso /banaglo'rioso/ **(-sa)** *a* conceited —*n* boaster
vanamente /bana'mente/ *adv* vainly; without foundation; superstitiously; arrogantly
vandálico /ban'daliko/ *a* Vandal
vandalismo /banda'lismo/ *m,* vandalism; destructiveness
vándalo /'bandalo/ **(-la)** *a* and *n* Vandal
vanguardia /baŋ'guarðia/ *f,* vanguard; *pl* outerworks. **a v.,** in the forefront
vanidad /bani'ðað/ *f,* vanity; ostentation; empty words; illusion. *Inf.* **ajar la v. de,** to take (a person) down a peg
vanidoso /bani'ðoso/ **(-sa)** *a* vain; ostentatious —*n* conceited person
vano /'bano/ *a* vain; hollow, empty; useless, ineffectual; unsubstantial, illusory. *m,* span (bridge). **v. único,** single span. **en v.,** uselessly, in vain
vapor /ba'por/ *m,* steam, vapor; fainting fit; steamboat; *pl* hysterics. **v. de ruedas, v. de paleta,** paddle steamer. **v. volandero,** tramp steamer. **al v.,** full steam ahead; *Inf.* with all speed
vaporable /bapo'raβle/ *a* vaporizable
vaporación /bapora'θion; bapora'sion/ *f,* evaporation
vaporización /baporiθa'θion; baporisa'sion/ *f,* vaporization
vaporizador /baporiθa'ðor; baporisa'ðor/ *m,* vaporizer; spray, sprayer
vaporizar /bapori'θar; bapori'sar/ *vt* to vaporize; spray
vaporoso /bapo'roso/ *a* vaporous; ethereal; gauzy
vapulación /bapula'θion; bapula'sion/ *f,* **vapulamiento** *m,* whipping
vapular /bapu'lar/ *vt* to whip
vapuleo /bapu'leo/ *m,* whipping, spanking
vaquería /bake'ria/ *f,* herd of cattle; dairy; dairy farm
vaquero /ba'kero/ **(-ra)** *n* cowboy; **vaqueros,** *m, pl* jeans
vaquilla /ba'kiʎa; ba'kiya/ *f,* heifer
vara /'bara/ *f,* staff; rod; wand (of authority); vara (nearly one yard); shaft (of cart). **v. de aforar,** water gauge
varada /ba'raða/ *f, Naut.* running aground
varadero /bara'ðero/ *m,* shipyard
varar /ba'rar/ *vi Naut.* to run aground; *Fig.* be held up (negotiations, etc.); —*vt Naut.* put in dry dock
varear /bare'ar/ *vt* to knock down (fruit from tree); beat (with a rod); measure with a rod; sell by the rod; —*vr* grow thin
variabilidad /bariaβili'ðað/ *f,* variableness
variable /ba'riaβle/ *a* variable; changeable, inconsistent
variación /baria'θion; baria'sion/ *f,* variation
variado /ba'riaðo/ *a* varied; variegated
variante /ba'riante/ *a* varying. *f,* variant; discrepancy
variar /ba'riar/ *vt* to vary; change; —*vi* change; be different
varice /ba'riθe; ba'rise/ *f,* varix
varicela /bari'θela; bari'sela/ *f,* chicken pox
varicoso /bari'koso/ *a* varicose
variedad /barie'ðað/ *f,* variety; change; inconstancy, instability; alteration; variation; *Biol.* variety
varilla /ba'riʎa; ba'riya/ *f, dim* rod; rib (fan, umbrella). **v. de virtudes,** conjurer's wand. *Mech.* **v. percusora,** tappet rod
vario /'bario/ *a* different, diverse; inconstant, changeable; variegated; *pl* some, a few
variopinto /bario'pinto/ *a* motley
varón /ba'ron/ *m,* male; man
varonil /baro'nil/ *a* male; manly
Varsovia /bar'soβia/ Warsaw
varsoviano /barso'βiano/ **(-na)** *a* and *n* of or from Warsaw
vasallaje /basa'ʎahe; basa'yahe/ *m,* vassalage; dependence; tribute money
vasallo /ba'saʎo; ba'sayo/ **(-lla)** *n* vassal —*a* vassal; dependent
vasco /'basko/ **(-ca), vascongado (-da)** *a* and *n* Basque
vascuence /bas'kuenθe; bas'kuense/ *m,* Basque (language); *Inf.* gibberish
vaselina /base'lina/ *f,* vaseline
vasija /ba'siha/ *f,* vessel, receptacle, jar
vaso /'baso/ *m,* receptacle; glass, tankard, mug; glassful; (*Naut. Anat. Bot.*) vessel; garden-urn; vase
vástago /'bastago/ *m,* stem, shoot; offspring, descendant; piston rod
vastedad /baste'ðað/ *f,* extensiveness, largeness, vastness
vasto /'basto/ *a* vast, extensive
vate /'bate/ *m,* bard; seer
vaticano /bati'kano/ *a* and *m,* Vatican
vaticinar /batiθi'nar; batisi'nar/ *vt* to prophesy, foretell
vaticinio /bati'θinio; bati'sinio/ *m,* prediction
vatímetro /ba'timetro/ *m,* water meter
vatio /'batio/ *m,* watt. **v. hora,** watt hour
ve /be/ *f,* name of the letter V. **v. doble** *or* **doble v.,** name of the letter W
vecinal /beθi'nal; besi'nal/ *a* neighboring
vecindad /beθin'dað; besin'dað/ *f,* neighborhood. **buena v.,** good neighborliness. **hacer mala v.,** to be a nuisance to one's neighbors
vecindario /beθin'dario; besin'dario/ *m,* neighborhood; population of a district
vecino /be'θino; be'sino/ **(-na)** *a* neighboring; near; similar —*n* neighbor; citizen; inhabitant
vector /bek'tor/ *m,* carrier (of disease)
veda /'beða/ *f,* close season; prohibition
vedamiento /beða'miento/ *m,* prohibition
vedar /be'ðar/ *vt* to forbid; prevent
vedija /be'ðiha/ *f,* tangled lock of hair; piece of matted wool; curl (of smoke)
veedor /bee'ðor/ **(-ra)** *a* prying —*n* busy-body. *m,* inspector; overseer
vega /'bega/ *f,* fertile lowland plain; meadow
vegada /be'gaða/ *f.* See **vez**
vegetable /behe'taβle/ *a* and *m,* vegetable
vegetación /beheta'θion; beheta'sion/ *f,* vegetation
vegetal /behe'tal/ *a* vegetal; plant. *m,* vegetable, plant
vegetar /behe'tar/ *vi* to flourish, grow (plants); *Fig.* vegetate
vegetarianismo /behetaria'nismo/ *m,* vegetarianism
vegetariano /beheta'riano/ **(-na)** *a* and *n* vegetarian
vegetativo /beheta'tiβo/ *a* vegetative
vehemencia /bee'menθia; bee'mensia/ *f,* vehemence
vehemente /bee'mente/ *a* vehement; vivid
vehículo /be'ikulo/ *m,* vehicle; means, instrument
veinte /'beinte/ *a* and *m,* twenty; twentieth
veintena /bein'tena/ *f,* a score
veinticinco /beinti'θinko; beinti'sinko/ *a* and *m,* twenty-five; twenty-fifth
veinticuatro /beinti'kuatro/ *a* and *m,* twenty-four; twenty-fourth
veintidós /beinti'ðos/ *a* and *m,* twenty-two; twenty-second
veintinueve /beinti'nueβe/ *a* and *m,* twenty-nine; twenty-ninth
veintiocho /bein'tiotʃo/ *a* and *m,* twenty-eight; twenty-eighth
veintiséis /beinti'seis/ *a* and *m,* twenty-six; twenty-sixth
veintisiete /beinti'siete/ *a* and *m,* twenty-seven; twenty-seventh
veintitrés /beinti'tres/ *a* and *m,* twenty-three; twenty-third
veintiuno /bein'tiuno/ *a* and *m,* twenty-one; twenty-first. Abbreviates to **veintiún** before a noun (even if one or more adjectives intervene)
vejación /beha'θion; beha'sion/ *f,* ill-treatment, persecution
vejamen /be'hamen/ *m,* irritation, provocation; taunt; lampoon
vejar /be'har/ *vt* to ill-treat, persecute; plague
vejatorio /beha'torio/ *a* vexing, annoying

vejete /be'hete/ *m, Inf.* silly old man
vejez /be'heθ; be'hes/ *f,* oldness; old age; platitude. **vejeces,** *pl* ailments of old age. *Inf.* **a la v., viruelas,** the older the madder
vejiga /be'higa/ *f,* bladder; blister. **v. natatoria,** float (of a fish)
vela /'bela/ *f,* vigil; watch; pilgrimage; sentinel, watchman; candle; *Naut.* sail; awning; night work, overtime. **v. de cangreja,** boom sail. **v. de mesana,** mizzen sail. **v. de trinquete,** foresail. **v. latina,** lateen sail. **a toda v.,** with all speed. **alzar velas,** to hoist sail. **en v.,** wakeful, without sleep. *Inf.* **estar entre dos velas,** to be tipsy
velación /bela'θion; bela'sion/ *f,* vigil; watch; marriage ceremony of veiling (gen. *pl*)
velada /be'laða/ *f,* vigil; watch; evening party
velado /be'laðo/ *a* veiled; dim; (of voice) thick, indistinct
velador /bela'ðor/ **(-ra)** *a* watchful; vigilant. *m,* candlestick; small round table *—n* watcher, guard
velar /be'lar/ *vi* to watch, be wakeful; work overtime or at night; *Eccl.* watch; *Fig.* (*with por*) watch over, defend; *—vt* veil; conceal; *Photo.* blur; (*with prep a*) wake (corpse); sit with (patient at night)
veleidad /belei'ðað/ *f,* velleity; fickleness
veleidoso /belei'ðoso/ *a* inconstant, changeable
velero /be'lero/ **(-ra)** *m,* sailing ship; sailmaker *—n* candlemaker
veleta /be'leta/ *f,* weathercock; float, quill (fishing). *mf* changeable person
vello /'beʎo; 'beyo/ *m,* down, soft hair
vellocino /beʎo'θino; beyo'sino/ *m,* wool; fleece
vellón /be'ʎon; be'yon/ *m,* fleece; copper and silver alloy formerly used in sense of "sterling"; *Obs.* copper coin
vellosidad /beʎosi'ðað; beyosi'ðað/ *f,* downiness, hairiness
velloso /be'ʎoso; be'yoso/ *a* downy, hairy
velludo /be'ʎuðo; be'yuðo/ *a* hairy, downy. *m,* plush, velvet
velo /'belo/ *m,* veil; curtain; *Eccl.* humeral veil; excuse, pretext; *Zool.* velum. **v. del paladar,** soft palate. **correr el v.,** to disclose a secret. **tomar el v.,** to take the veil, become a nun
velocidad /beloθi'ðað; belosi'ðað/ *f,* speed; *Mech.* velocity. *Aer.* **v. ascensional,** rate of climb. *Mech.* **v. del choque,** speed of impact. **en gran v.,** by passenger train. **en pequeña v.,** by goods train
velocípedo /belo'θipeðo; belo'sipeðo/ *m,* velocipede
velódromo /be'loðromo/ *m,* velodrome
velón /be'lon/ *m,* oil lamp
veloz /be'loθ; be'los/ *a* swift; quick-thinking or acting
vena /'bena/ *f,* (*Bot. Anat.*) vein; streak, veining (in wood or stone); *Mineral.* seam; underground spring; inspiration. **estar de v.,** to be in the mood; be inspired
venablo /be'naβlo/ *m,* javelin
venado /be'naðo/ *m,* venison; deer
venal /be'nal/ *a* venous; saleable; venal
venalidad /benali'ðað/ *f,* saleableness; venality
vencedor /benθe'ðor; bense'ðor/ **(-ra)** *a* conquering *—n* conqueror
vencer /ben'θer; ben'ser/ *vt* to conquer; defeat; overcome, rise above; outdo, excel; restrain, control (emotions); convince, persuade; *—vi* succeed, triumph; *Com.* fall due, mature; *Com.* expire; *—vr* control oneself; twist, incline
vencible /ben'θiβle; ben'siβle/ *a* conquerable; superable
vencimiento /benθi'miento; bensi'miento/ *m,* defeat; conquest, victory; bend, twist (of things); *Com.* expiration; *Com.* maturity (of a bill)
venda /'benda/ *f,* bandage; fillet. **tener una v. en los ojos,** to be blind (to the truth)
vendaje /ben'dahe/ *m,* bandage
vendar /ben'dar/ *vt* to bandage; *Fig.* blind (generally passions)
vendaval /benda'βal/ *m,* strong wind
vendedor /bende'ðor/ **(-ra)** *a* selling *—n* seller
vender /ben'der/ *vt* to sell; betray; *—vr* sell oneself; be sold; risk all (for someone); *Fig.* give away (secret); (*with por*) sell under false pretences. **v. al contado,** to sell for cash. **v. al por mayor,** to sell wholesale. **v. al por menor,** to sell retail. **venderse caro,** to be unsociable
vendí /ben'di/ *m, Com.* certificate of sale
vendible /ben'diβle/ *a* purchasable; saleable
vendimia /ben'dimia/ *f,* vintage; profit, fruits
vendimiador /bendimia'ðor/ **(-ra)** *n* vintager
vendimiar /bendi'miar/ *vt* to harvest the grapes; take advantage of; *Inf.* kill
Venecia /be'neθia; be'nesia/ Venice
veneciano /bene'θiano; bene'siano/ **(-na)** *a* and *n* Venetian
veneno /be'neno/ *m,* poison; venom; danger (to health or soul); evil passion
venenosidad /benenosi'ðað/ *f,* poisonousness
venenoso /bene'noso/ *a* poisonous, venomous
venera /be'nera/ *f,* scallop-shell (pilgrim's badge); badge, decoration
veneración /benera'θion; benera'sion/ *f,* respect, veneration
venerador /benera'ðor/ **(-ra)** *a* venerating *—n* venerator, respector
venerar /bene'rar/ *vt* to venerate; worship
venéreo /be'nereo/ *a* venereal
venero /be'nero/ *m,* spring of water; horary line on sundial; origin, genesis; *Mineral.* bed
venezolano /beneθo'lano; beneso'lano/ **(-na)** *a* and *n* Venezuelan
vengador /beŋga'ðor/ **(-ra)** *a* avenging *—n* avenger
venganza /beŋ'ganθa; beŋ'gansa/ *f,* revenge
vengar /beŋ'gar/ *vt* to avenge; *—vr* avenge oneself
vengativo /beŋga'tiβo/ *a* vindictive
venia /'benia/ *f,* pardon, forgiveness; permission; inclination of head (in greeting); *Law.* license issued to minors to manage their own estate
venial /be'nial/ *a* venial
venialidad /beniali'ðað/ *f,* veniality
venida /be'niða/ *f,* arrival, coming; return; attack (fencing); precipitancy
venidero /beni'ðero/ *a* future
venideros /beni'ðeros/ *m pl,* successors; posterity
venir /be'nir/ *vi irr* to come; arrive; turn up (at cards); fit, suit; consent, agree; *Agr.* grow; follow, come after, succeed; result, originate; occur (to the mind); feel, experience; (*with prep a + infin.*) happen finally, come to pass; (*with en*) decide, resolve; *—vr* ferment. **v. a menos,** to deteriorate, decline; come upon evil days. **v. a pelo,** to come opportunely, be just right. **v. a ser,** to become. **venirse abajo,** to fall, collapse. **¿A qué viene este viaje?** What is the purpose of this journey? **el mes que viene,** next month. **El vestido te viene muy ancho,** The dress is too wide for you. **Me vino la idea de marcharme,** It occurred to me to leave. **en lo por venir,** in the future *—Pres. Indic.* **vengo, vienes, viene, venimos, venís, vienen.** *Pres. Part.* **viniendo.** *Fut.* **vendré,** etc *—Condit.* **vendría,** etc *—Preterite* **vine, viniste, vino, vinimos, vinisteis, vinieron.** *Pres. Subjunc.* **venga,** etc *—Imperf. Subjunc.* **viniese,** etc.
venoso /be'noso/ *a* veined; venous
venta /'benta/ *f,* selling; sale; inn; *Inf.* wilderness; *pl Com.* turnover. **v. pública,** auction. **a la v.,** on sale. **la V. de la Mesilla,** the Gadsden Purchase
ventada /ben'taða/ *f,* gust of wind
ventaja /ben'taha/ *f,* advantage; profit
ventajoso /benta'hoso/ *a* advantageous
ventana /ben'tana/ *f,* window. **v. de guillotina,** sash window. **v. salediza,** bay window. **echar algo por la v.,** to waste a thing
ventanal /benta'nal/ *m,* large window
ventanilla /benta'niʎa; benta'niya/ *f,* small window (as in railway compartments); grill (ticket office, bank, etc.); nostril
ventarrón /benta'rron/ *m,* high wind
ventear /bente'ar/ *v impers* to blow (of the wind); *—vt* sniff air (animals); air, dry; investigate; *—vr* be spoiled by air (tobacco, etc.)
ventero /ben'tero/ **(-ra)** *n* innkeeper
ventilación /bentila'θion; bentila'sion/ *f,* ventilation; ventilator; current of air
ventilador /bentila'ðor/ *m,* ventilating fan; ventilator

ventilar /benti'lar/ *vt* to ventilate; shake, winnow; air; discuss
ventisca /ben'tiska/ *f*, snowstorm
ventiscar, ventisquear /bentis'kar, bentiske'ar/ *v impers* to snow with a high wind
ventisquero /bentis'kero/ *m*, glacier; snowfield, snowdrift; snowstorm
ventolera /bento'lera/ *f*, gust of wind; *Inf.* boastfulness; whim, caprice
ventor /ben'tor/ **(-ra)** *n* pointer (dog)
ventosa /ben'tosa/ *f*, vent (pipes, etc.); *Zool.* sucker; *Surg.* cupping glass
ventosidad /bentosi'ðað/ *f*, flatulence
ventoso /ben'toso/ *a* windy; flatulent
ventrículo /ben'trikulo/ *m*, ventricle
ventrílocuo /ben'trilokuo/ **(-ua)** *a* ventriloquial —*n* ventriloquist
ventriloquia /bentri'lokia/ *f*, ventriloquism
ventrudo /ben'truðo/ *a* big-bellied
ventura /ben'tura/ *f*, happiness; chance, hazard; risk, danger. **a la v.,** at a venture. **buena v.,** good luck. **por v.,** perhaps; by chance; fortunately
venturoso /bentu'roso/ *a* fortunate
Venus /'benus/ *m*, Venus. *f*, beautiful woman, beauty
ver /ber/ *vt irr* to see; witness, behold; visit; inspect, examine; consider; observe; know, understand; (*with de + infin.*) try to; —*vr* be seen; show oneself, appear; experience, find oneself; exchange visits; meet. **v. mundo,** to travel. **V. y creer,** Seeing is believing. **A mi v.,** In my opinion. **¡A v.!** Let's see!; Wait and see! **no tener nada que v. con,** to have no connection with, nothing to do with. **Veremos,** Time will tell. **Verse en la casa,** to be a stay-at-home. **Ya se ve,** Of course, Naturally —*Pres. Indic.* **veo, ves,** etc —*Imperf.* **veía,** etc —*Past Part.* **visto.** *Pres. Subjunc.* **vea,** etc —*Imperf. Subjunc.* **viese,** etc.
vera /'bera/ *f*, edge; border; shore. **a la v.,** on the edge, on the verge
veracidad /beraθi'ðað; berasi'ðað/ *f*, truthfulness, veracity
veranadero /berana'ðero/ *m*, summer pasture
veraneante /berane'ante/ *mf* summer resident, summer vacationist, holiday-maker
veranear /berane'ar/ *vi* to spend the summer
veraneo /bera'neo/ *m*, summer vacation, summer holidays, summering
veraniego /bera'niego/ *a* summer; light, unimportant
verano /be'rano/ *m*, summer; dry season *West Hem.*
veras /'beras/ *f pl*, reality, truth; fervor, earnestness. **de v.,** really; in earnest
veraz /be'raθ; be'ras/ *a* truthful, veracious
verbal /ber'βal/ *a* verbal; oral
verbena /ber'βena/ *f*, *Bot.* verbena, vervain; fair held on eve of a saint's day
verbigracia /berβi'graθia; berβi'grasia/ *adv* for instance. *m*, example
verbo /'berβo/ *m*, word; vow; *Gram.* verb. **v. activo** *or* **v. transitivo,** active or transitive verb. **v. auxiliar,** auxiliary verb. **v. intransitivo** *or* **v. neutro,** intransitive or neuter verb. **v. reflexivo** *or* **v. recíproco,** reflexive verb
verbosidad /berβosi'ðað/ *f*, verbosity
verboso /ber'βoso/ *a* verbose, prolix
verdad /ber'ðað/ *f*, truth, veracity; reality. **a la v.,** indeed; without doubt. **en v.,** in truth; indeed. **cantar cuatro verdades a alguien,** to tell someone a few home truths. **la pura v.,** the plain truth
verdadero /berða'ðero/ *a* true; real; sincere; truthful
verdal /ber'ðal/ *a* green. **ciruela v.,** greengage
verde /'berðe/ *a* green; unripe; fresh (vegetables); youthful; immature, undeveloped; obscene, dissolute. *m*, green (color); verdure, foliage
verdear /berðe'ar/ *vi* to look green; be greenish; grow green
verdecer /berðe'θer; berðe'ser/ *vi irr* to grow green, be verdant. See **conocer**
verdegay /berðe'gai/ *a* and *m*, bright green
verdemar /berðe'mar/ *a* and *m*, sea-green
verdín /ber'ðin/ *m*, verdure; mold; verdigris
verdinegro /berði'negro/ *a* dark green
verdor /ber'ðor/ *m*, verdure; greenness; strength; youth (also *pl*)
verdoso /ber'ðoso/ *a* greenish
verdugo /ber'ðugo/ *m*, hangman, executioner; wale, mark; shoot of tree; switch; whip; *Fig.* scourge; tyrant
verdulera /berðu'lera/ *f*, greengrocer; market woman; *Inf.* harridan
verdulería /berðule'ria/ *f*, greengrocer's shop
verdulero /berðu'lero/ *m*, greengrocer
verdura /ber'ðura/ *f*, verdure; green garden produce, vegetables (gen. *pl*); *Art.* foliage; obscenity
verecundo /bere'kundo/ *a* bashful
vereda /be'reða/ *f*, footpath; sheep track
veredicto /bere'ðikto/ *m*, *Law.* verdict; judgment, considered opinion
verga /'berga/ *f*, steel bow of crossbow; *Naut.* yard; *Inf.* penis
vergajo /ber'gaho/ *m*, rod (for punishment)
vergel /ber'hel/ *m*, orchard
vergonzoso /bergon'θoso; bergon'soso/ **(-sa)** *a* shameful; bashful, shamefaced —*n* shy person
vergüenza /ber'guenθa; ber'guensa/ *f*, shame; self-respect; bashfulness, timidity; shameful act; public punishment
vericueto /beri'kueto/ *m*, narrow, stony path
verídico /be'riðiko/ *a* veracious; true, exact
verificación /berifika'θion; berifika'sion/ *f*, verification, checking; *Law.* **v. de un testamento,** probate
verificador /berifika'ðor/ **(-ra)** *a* verifying, checking —*n* inspector, checker
verificar /berifi'kar/ *vt* to prove; verify; —*vr* take place, happen; check; come true. *Elec.* **v. las conexiones,** to check the connections
verisímil /beri'simil/ *a* credible, probable
verisimilitud /berisimili'tuð/ *f*, credibility
verismo /be'rismo/ *m*, realism; truthfulness
verja /'berha/ *f*, grating, grill; railing
vermífugo /ber'mifugo/ *a* and *m*, vermifuge
verminoso /bermi'noso/ *a* verminous
vermut /ber'mut/ *m*, vermouth
vernáculo /ber'nakulo/ *a* native, vernacular
vernal /ber'nal/ *a* vernal
veronés /bero'nes/ **(-esa)** *a* and *n* Veronese
verónica /be'ronika/ *f*, *Bot.* speedwell; veronica (bullfighting)
verosímil /bero'simil/ *a* credible, probable
verosimilitud /berosimili'tuð/ *f*, verisimilitude, probability
verraco /be'rrako/ *m*, boar
verruga /be'rruga/ *f*, *Med.* wart; *Inf.* bore; defect
versar /ber'sar/ *vi* to revolve; (*with sobre*) concern, deal with (book, etc.); —*vr* become versed (in)
versátil /ber'satil/ *a Zool.* versatile; changeable; fickle
versatilidad /bersatili'ðað/ *f*, *Zool.* versatility; changeableness; fickleness
versículo /ber'sikulo/ *m*, versicle; verse (of the Bible)
versificación /bersifika'θion; bersifika'sion/ *f*, versification
versificador /bersifika'ðor/ **(-ra)** *n* versifier
versificar /bersifi'kar/ *vi* to write verses; —*vt* put into verse, versify
versión /ber'sion/ *f*, translation; version; account
verso /'berso/ *m*, poetry, verse; stanza; line (of a poem). **v. suelto,** blank verse
vertebrado /berte'βraðo/ *a* and *m*, *Zool.* vertebrate
vertedor /berte'ðor/ *m*, drain, sewer; chute
verter /ber'ter/ *vt irr* to pour, spill; empty; translate; —*vi* flow. See **entender**
vertical /berti'kal/ *a* and *f*, vertical
verticalidad /bertikali'ðað/ *f*, verticality
vértice /'bertiθe; 'bertise/ *m*, vertex
vertiente /ber'tiente/ *a* emptying. *mf*, slope, incline; watershed
vertiginoso /bertihi'noso/ *a* giddy; vertiginous
vértigo /'bertigo/ *m*, giddiness, faintness
vesícula /be'sikula/ *f*, blister; (*Anat. Bot.*) vesicle
vespertino /besper'tino/ *a* evening
vestíbulo /bes'tiβulo/ *m*, hall, vestibule foyer
vestido /bes'tiðo/ *m*, dress; clothes
vestidura /besti'ðura/ *f*, garment; *pl* vestments

vestigio /bes'tihio/ *m*, footprint; trace, mark; remains; *Fig.* vestige

vestir /bes'tir/ *vt irr* to clothe, dress; adorn; embellish (ideas); *Fig.* disguise (truth); simulate, pretend; —*vi* be dressed; —*vr* dress oneself; *Fig.* be covered. See **pedir**

vestuario /bes'tuario/ *m*, clothing, dress; *Theat.* wardrobe or dressing room; *Eccl.* vestry; *Mil.* uniform

Vesubio /be'suβio/ Vesuvius

veta /'beta/ *f*, vein; stripe, rib (fabric)

veterano /bete'rano/ **(-na)** *a* and *n* veteran

veterinaria /beteri'naria/ *f*, veterinary science

veterinario /beteri'nario/ *a* veterinary. *m*, veterinary surgeon

veto /'beto/ *m*, veto; prohibition

vetustez /betus'teθ; betus'tes/ *f*, antiquity, oldness

vetusto /be'tusto/ *a* ancient, very old

vez /beθ; bes/ *f*, time, occasion; turn; *pl* proxy, deputy, substitute. **a la v.,** simultaneously. **alguna v.,** sometime. **a su v.,** in its (her, his, their) turn. **a veces,** sometimes. **de una v.,** at the one time. **de v. en cuando,** from time to time. **en v. de,** instead of. **hacer las veces de,** to be a substitute for. **otra v.,** again. **Su cuarto es dos veces más grande que éste,** His room is twice as large as this one

vía /'bia/ *f*, way; road; railway track or gauge; *Anat.* tract; (mystic) way; route; conduct; *pl* procedure. **v. ancha,** broad gauge (railway). **v. angosta,** narrow gauge. **v. de agua,** *Naut.* leak. *Law.* **v. ejecutiva,** seizure, attachment. **v. férrea,** railway. **v. láctea,** Milky Way. **v. muerta,** railway siding. **v. principal,** main line. **v. pública,** public thoroughfare. **v. romana,** Roman road. **v. secundaria,** *Rail.* side line. **por v. aérea,** by air, by airplane

viabilidad /biaβili'ðað/ *f*, viability

viable /'biaβle/ *a* viable; practicable; workable; passable

viaducto /bia'ðukto/ *m*, viaduct

viajante /bia'hante/ *mf* traveling salesman, commercial traveler

viajar /bia'har/ *vi* to travel, journey, voyage

viaje /'biahe/ *m*, journey; voyage; water-supply; travel journal; *Naut.* **v. de ensayo,** trial trip. **v. redondo,** circular tour. **¡Buen v.!** Have a good trip! Bon voyage!

viajero /bia'hero/ **(-ra)** *a* traveling —*n* traveler; passenger

vianda /'bianda/ *f*, viand, victual (gen. *pl*); meal

viático /'biatiko/ *m*, *Eccl.* viaticum; provisions for a journey

víbora /'biβora/ *f*, viper

viborezno /biβo'reθno; biβo'resno/ *m*, young viper

vibración /biβra'θion; biβra'sion/ *f*, vibration; jar, jolt; thrill

vibrante /bi'βrante/ *a* shaking; vibrant; thrilling

vibrar /bi'βrar/ *vt* to shake, oscillate; —*vi* vibrate; jar, jolt; quiver, thrill

vibratorio /biβra'torio/ *a* vibratory, vibrative

vicaría /bika'ria/ *f*, vicarage; vestry

vicario /bi'kario/ *a* vicarious. *m*, vicar; curate; deputy

vicealmirante /biθealmi'rante; bisealmi'rante/ *m*, vice-admiral

vicecanciller /biθekanθi'ʎer; bisekansi'yer/ *m*, vice-chancellor

vicecónsul /biθe'konsul; bise'konsul/ *m*, vice-consul

viceconsulado /biθekonsu'laðo; bisekonsu'laðo/ *m*, vice-consulate

vicepresidente /biθepresi'ðente; bisepresi'ðente/ **(-ta)** *n* vice president

vicesecretario /biθesekre'tario; bisesekre'tario/ **(-ia)** *n* assistant secretary

viciar /bi'θiar; bi'siar/ *vt* to corrupt; adulterate; forge; annul; interpret maliciously, misconstrue; —*vr* become vicious

vicio /'biθio; 'bisio/ *m*, vice; defect; error, fraud; bad habit; excess, exaggerated desire; viciousness (animals); overgrowth (plants); peevishness (children). **tener el v. de,** to have the bad habit of. **el v. del juego,** fondness for gambling

vicioso /bi'θioso; bi'sioso/ *a* vicious; vigorous, overgrown; abundant; *Inf.* spoiled (children)

vicisitud /biθisi'tuð; bisisi'tuð/ *f*, vicissitude

víctima /'biktima/ *f*, victim

¡víctor! /'biktor/ *interj* Victor!; Long live!; Hurrah!

victoria /bik'toria/ *f*, victory, triumph; victoria

victoriano /bikto'riano/ **(-na)** *a* and *n* Victorian

victorioso /bikto'rioso/ *a* victorious

vid /bið/ *f*, vine

vida /'biða/ *f*, life; livelihood; human being; biography; vivacity. **v. airada,** dissolute life. **la v. allende la muerte,** life after death. **de por v.,** for life. **darse buena v.,** to live comfortably; enjoy one's life. **dar mala v.,** to ill-treat. **en la v.,** in life; never. **ganarse la v.,** to make one's living

vidente /bi'ðente/ *m*, clairvoyant; seer

videocámara *f*, video camera, camcorder

videograbación /biðeograβa'θion; biðeograβa'sion/ *f*, videotape

vidriar /bi'ðriar/ *vt* to glaze (earthenware)

vidriera /bi'ðriera/ *f*, glass window (gen. stained or colored)

vidriero /bi'ðriero/ *m*, glazier —*a* made of glass

vidrio /'biðrio/ *m*, glass; anything made of glass; fragile thing; touchy person. **v. inastillable,** safety-glass. **v. jaspeado,** frosted glass. **v. pintado** *or* **v. de color,** stainedglass. **v. plano,** plate glass. **v. soplado,** blown glass

vidrioso /bi'ðrioso/ *a* brittle; slippery; fragile; hypersensitive; *Fig.* glazed (eyes)

vieja /'bieha/ *f*, old woman

viejo /'bieho/ *a* old; ancient; former; old-fashioned; worn out. *m*, old man

Viena /'biena/ Vienna

vienés /bie'nes/ **(-esa)** *a* and *n* Viennese

viento /'biento/ *m*, wind; scent (of game, etc.); guy (rope); upheaval; vanity. **v. en popa,** *Naut.* following wind; without a hitch, prosperously. **vientos alisios,** trade-winds. **v. terral,** land wind. **a los cuatro vientos,** in all directions. **contra v. y marea,** *Fig.* against all obstacles. **correr malos vientos,** to be unfavorable (of circumstances). **refrescar el v.,** to stiffen (of the breeze)

vientre /'bientre/ *m*, stomach; belly; vitals; *Law.* venter

viernes /'biernes/ *m*, Friday. **V. Santo,** Good Friday

viga /'biga/ *f*, beam, rafter; girder; joist; mill beam. **v. maestra,** main beam or girder

vigente /bi'hente/ *a* valid; in force (laws, customs)

vigésimo /bi'hesimo/ *a* twentieth

vigía /bi'hia/ *f*, watch tower; (gen. *m*) look-out, watch

vigilancia /bihi'lanθia; bihi'lansia/ *f*, watchfulness, vigilance; watch patrol

vigilante /bihi'lante/ *a* watchful. *m*, watcher; watchman. **v. escolar,** truant officer

vigilar /bihi'lar/ *vi* to watch over; supervise

vigilia /bi'hilia/ *f*, vigil; wakefulness; night study; *Eccl.* vigil, eve; wake; *Mil.* watch. **día de v.,** fast-day

vigor /bi'gor/ *m*, strength; activity; vigor, efficiency; validity

vigorizar /bigori'θar; bigori'sar/ *vt* to invigorate; exhilarate; encourage

vigorosidad /bigorosi'ðað/ *f*, vigorousness

vigoroso /bigo'roso/ *a* strong, vigorous

vihuela /bi'uela/ *f*, lute

vil /bil/ *a* vile, infamous; base; despicable; untrustworthy

vileza /bi'leθa; bi'lesa/ *f*, baseness; vileness, infamy

vilipendiar /bilipen'diar/ *vt* to revile

vilipendio /bili'pendio/ *m*, vilification; contempt

villa /'biʎa; 'biya/ *f*, villa; country house; town

villancico /biʎan'θiko; biyan'siko/ *m*, carol

villanesco /biʎa'nesko; biya'nesko/ *a* peasant; rustic, country

villanía /biʎa'nia; biya'nia/ *f*, humbleness of birth; vileness; villainy

villano /bi'ʎano; bi'yano/ **(-na)** *n* peasant —*a* rustic, country; boorish; base

vilo, en /'bilo, en/ *adv* hanging in the air; *Fig.* in suspense

vilorta /bi'lorta/ *f*, hoop; *Mech.* washer

vinagre /bi'nagre/ *m*, vinegar

vinagrera /bina'grera/ *f,* vinegar bottle; table cruet
vinagreta /bina'greta/ *f,* vinegar sauce
vinagroso /bina'groso/ *a* vinegary; *Inf.* bad-tempered, acid
vinatero /bina'tero/ **(-ra)** *n* wine merchant —*a* wine
vincapervinca /binkaper'βinka/ *f, Bot.* periwinkle
vinculación /binkula'θion; binkula'sion/ *f, Law.* entail
vincular /binku'lar/ *vt Law.* to entail; *Fig.* base; —*vr* perpetuate —*a Law.* entail
vínculo /'binkulo/ *m,* tie, bond; *Law.* entail
vindicación /bindika'θion; bindika'sion/ *f,* vindication; justification; excuse
vindicador /bindika'ðor/ **(-ra)** *n* vindicator —*a* vindicative
vindicar /bindi'kar/ *vt* to avenge; vindicate; justify; excuse
vindicativo /bindika'tiβo/ *a* avenging; vindicatory
vinícola /bi'nikola/ *a* wine-growing; wine
vinicultor /binikul'tor/ **(-ra)** *n* wine grower, viniculturalist
vinicultura /binikul'tura/ *f,* wine-growing, viniculture
vinificación /binifika'θion; binifika'sion/ *f,* vinification
vinillo /bi'niʎo; bi'niyo/ *m,* thin, weak wine
vino /'bino/ *m,* wine; fermented fruit juice. **v. de Oporto,** port wine. **v. generoso,** well-matured wine. **v. tinto,** red wine
vinosidad /binosi'ðað/ *f,* vinosity
vinoso /bi'noso/ *a* vinous; fond of wine
viña /'biɲa/ *f,* vineyard
viñador /biɲa'ðor/ *m,* vineyard-keeper; vine-cultivator
viñedo /bi'ɲeðo/ *m,* vineyard
viñeta /bi'ɲeta/ *f,* vignette
viola /'biola/ *f, Mus.* viola; *Bot.* viola, pansy. *mf* viola player
violación /biola'θion; biola'sion/ *f,* violation; infringement
violado /bio'laðo/ *a* violet
violador /biola'ðor/ **(-ra)** *n* violator. *m,* seducer
violar /bio'lar/ *vt* to violate; infringe; rape; spoil, harm
violencia /bio'lenθia; bio'lensia/ *f,* violence; outrage; rape
violentar /biolen'tar/ *vt* to force; falsify, misinterpret; force an entrance; —*vr* force oneself
violento /bio'lento/ *a* violent; repugnant; impetuous, hasty-tempered; unnatural, false; unreasonable
violeta /bio'leta/ *f, Bot.* violet. *m,* violet color. **v. de febrero,** snowdrop
violín /bio'lin/ *m,* violin
violinista /bioli'nista/ *mf* violinist
violón /bio'lon/ *m,* double-bass, bass viol; double-bass player
violoncelista /biolonθe'lista; biolonse'lista/ *mf* cellist
violoncelo /biolon'θelo; biolon'selo/ *m,* cello
viperino /bipe'rino/ *a* viperine; venomous, evil
vira /'bira/ *f,* welt (of a shoe); dart
viraje /bi'rahe/ *m, Auto.* change of direction; bend, turn
virar /bi'rar/ *vt Naut.* to put about; *Photo.* tone; —*vi Naut.* tack; *Auto.* change direction. **v. de bordo,** *Naut.* to lay off
virgen /bir'hen/ *mf* virgin. *f, Astron.* Virgo
virgiliano /birhi'liano/ *a* Virgilian
virginal /birhi'nal/ *a* virginal; pure, unspotted
virginidad /birhini'ðað/ *f,* virginity
virgulilla /birgu'liʎa; birgu'liya/ *f,* comma; cedilla; accent; apostrophe; fine line
viril /bi'ril/ *a* manly, virile. *m,* clear glass screen
virilidad /birili'ðað/ *f,* virility
virote /bi'rote/ *m,* arrow; shaft; *Inf.* young blood
virreina /bi'rreina/ *f,* vicereine
virreinato /birrei'nato/ *m,* viceroyship
virrey /bi'rrei/ *m,* viceroy
virtual /bir'tual/ *a* virtual; implicit
virtualidad /birtuali'ðað/ *f,* virtuality
virtualmente /birtual'mente/ *adv* virtually; tacitly
virtud /bir'tuð/ *f,* virtue; power; strength, courage; efficacy. **en v. de,** in virtue of
virtuosidad /birtuosi'ðað/ *f,* virtuosity
virtuoso /bir'tuoso/ *a* virtuous; powerful, efficacious. *m,* virtuoso, artist
viruela /bi'ruela/ *f,* smallpox (gen. *pl*)
virulencia /biru'lenθia; biru'lensia/ *f,* virulence
virulento /biru'lento/ *a* virulent
virus /'birus/ *m,* virus
viruta /bi'ruta/ *f,* wood-shaving
visaje /bi'sahe/ *m,* grimace
visar /bi'sar/ *vt* to visa; endorse
vis cómica /bis 'komika/ *f,* the comic spirit
viscosidad /biskosi'ðað/ *f,* viscosity
viscoso /bis'koso/ *a* viscous, sticky
visera /bi'sera/ *f,* visor; eye-shade; peak (of a cap)
visibilidad /bisiβili'ðað/ *f,* visibility
visigodo /bisi'goðo/ **(-da)** *a* Visigothic —*n* Visigoth
visigótico /bisi'gotiko/ *a* Visigothic
visillo /bi'siʎo; bi'siyo/ *m,* window-blind
visión /bi'sion/ *f,* seeing, sight; queer sight; vision; hallucination; *Inf.* scarecrow, sight
visionario /bisio'nario/ **(-ia)** *a* and *n* visionary
visir /bi'sir/ *m,* vizier. **gran v.,** grand vizier
visita /bi'sita/ *f,* visit; visitor; inspection. **v. de cumplido,** formal call. **v. de sanidad,** health inspection. **hacer una v.,** to pay a call
visitación /bisita'θion; bisita'sion/ *f,* visitation; visit
visitador /bisita'ðor/ **(-ra)** *n* regular visitor. *m,* inspector —*a* visiting; inspecting
visitar /bisi'tar/ *vt* to visit; inspect; *Med.* attend; *Eccl.* examine. **v. los monumentos,** to see the sights, go sightseeing
visiteo /bisi'teo/ *m,* receiving or paying of visits
vislumbrar /bislum'βrar/ *vt* to glimpse; surmise, conjecture
vislumbre /bis'lumbre/ *f,* glimmer, glimpse; surmise, glimmering (gen. *pl*); semblance, appearance
viso /'biso/ *m,* view point, elevation; glare; shimmer, gleam; colored slip under transparent dress; semblance. **de v.,** prominent (persons)
visón /bi'son/ *m,* mink
víspera /'bispera/ *f,* eve; *Eccl.* day before festival; prelude, preliminary *pl Eccl.* vespers. **en vísperas de,** on the eve of
vista /'bista/ *f,* vision, sight; view; eyes; eyesight; meeting, interview; *Law.* hearing (of a case); apparition; picture of a view; clear idea; connection (of things); proposition, intention; glance; *pl* window, door, skylight, opening for light. **v. corta,** short sight. **v. de lince,** sharp eyes. **a primera v.,** at first sight. **a v. de,** in sight of; in the presence of. **conocer de v.,** to know by sight. **dar una v.,** to take a look. **doble v.,** second sight; clairvoyance. **en v. de,** in view of, considering. **estar a la v.,** to be evident. *Inf.* **hacer la v. gorda,** to turn a blind eye. **¡Hasta la v.!** Good-bye! **perder de v.** (**a**), to lose sight of
vistazo /bis'taθo; bis'taso/ *m,* glance. **echar un v.,** to cast a glance
visto /'bisto/ *past part irr* **ver.** *Law.* whereas. **bien v.,** approved. **mal v.,** disapproved. **V. Bueno** (**V° B°**) Approved, Passed. **v. que,** since, inasmuch as
vistoso /bis'toso/ *a* showy, gaudy; beautiful
visual /bi'sual/ *a* visual
vital /bi'tal/ *a* vital; essential
vitalicio /bita'liθio; bita'lisio/ *a* lifelong. *m,* life-insurance
vitalidad /bitali'ðað/ *f,* vitality
vitalizar /bitali'θar; bitali'sar/ *vt* to vitalize
vitamina /bita'mina/ *f,* vitamin
vitando /bi'tando/ *a* odious; bad; vital
vitela /bi'tela/ *f,* vellum
vitícola /bi'tikola/ *a* viticultural. *mf* viticulturist
viticultura /bitikul'tura/ *f,* viticulture
¡vítor! /'bitor/ *interj* Victor!; Hurrah!; Long live!
vitorear /bitore'ar/ *vt* to cheer; applaud, acclaim
vítreo /'bitreo/ *a* glassy, vitreous
vitrificar /bitrifi'kar/ **(se)** *vt* and *vr* to vitrify
vitrina /bi'trina/ *f,* show-case; display cabinet
vitriólico /bi'trioliko/ *a* vitriolic
vitriolo /bi'triolo/ *m,* vitriol

vitualla /bi'tuaʎa; bi'tuaya/ *f,* (gen. *pl*) victuals, provisions
vituperable /bitupe'raβle/ *a* blameworthy, vituperable
vituperador /bitupera'ðor/ **(-ra)** *a* vituperative —*n* vituperator
vituperar /bitupe'rar/ *vt* to censure, blame, vituperate
vituperio /bitu'perio/ *m,* vituperation
viuda /'biuða/ *f,* widow
viudedad /biuðe'ðað/ *f,* widow's pension
viudez /biu'ðeθ; biu'ðes/ *f,* widowhood
viudita /biu'ðita/ *f,* young widow
viudo /'biuðo/ *m,* widower
¡viva! /'biβa/ *interj* Long live!; Hurrah!
vivacidad /biβaθi'ðað; biβasi'ðað/ *f,* vivacity, gaiety; ardor, warmth; brightness
vivamente /biβa'mente/ *adv* quickly, lively
vivandera /biβan'dera/ *f,* vivandiere
vivandero /biβan'dero/ *m,* sutler
vivaque /bi'βake/ *m,* bivouac
vivaquear /biβake'ar/ *vi* to bivouac
vivar /bi'βar/ *m,* warren; aquarium; breeding ground; well (of a fishing boat)
vivaracho /biβa'ratʃo/ *a Inf.* sprightly, cheery, lively
vivaz /bi'βaθ; bi'βas/ *a* vigorous; quick-witted; sprightly; *Bot.* perennial; vivid, bright
víveres /'biβeres/ *m pl,* provisions; *Mil.* stores
vivero /bi'βero/ *m, Bot.* nursery; vivarium; small marsh
viveza /bi'βeθa; bi'βesa/ *f,* quickness, briskness; vehemence; perspicuity; witticism; resemblance; brightness (eyes, colors); thoughtless word or act
vividero /biβi'ðero/ *a* habitable
vívido /bi'βiðo/ *a Poet.* vivid
vividor /biβi'ðor/ **(-ra)** *a* frugal, thrifty; dissolute —*n* liver; long-liver; libertine, rake
vivienda /bi'βienda/ *f,* dwelling
viviente /bi'βiente/ *a* living
vivificación /biβifika'θion; biβifika'sion/ *f,* vivification
vivificante /biβifi'kante/ *a* vivifying
vivificar /biβifi'kar/ *vt* to vivify; comfort
vivir /bi'βir/ *vi* to be alive, live; last, endure; (*with en*) inhabit. *m,* life. **¿Quién vive?** *Mil.* Who goes there? **v. a costillas ajenas,** to live at someone else's expense, live off someone else
vivisección /biβisek'θion; biβisek'sion/ *f,* vivisection
vivo /'biβo/ *a* alive; intense, strong; bright; *Mil.* active; subtle, ingenious; precipitate; *Fig.* lasting, enduring; diligent; hasty; persuasive, expressive. *m,* edge. **al v., a lo v.,** to the life; vividly
vizcaíno /biθ'kaino; bis'kaino/ **(-na)** *a* and *n* Biscayan
Vizcaya, el Golfo de /biθ'kaya, el 'golfo de; bis'kaya, el 'golfo de/ the Bay of Biscay
vizcondado /biθkon'daðo; biskon'daðo/ *m,* viscounty
vizconde /biθ'konde; bis'konde/ *m,* viscount
vizcondesa /biθkon'desa; biskon'desa/ *f,* viscountess
vocablo /bo'kaβlo/ *m,* word
vocabulario /bokaβu'lario/ *m,* vocabulary
vocación /boka'θion; boka'sion/ *f,* vocation; trade, profession
vocal /bo'kal/ *a* vocal; oral. *f, Gram.* vowel. *mf* voting member
vocalismo /boka'lismo/ *m,* vocalism, vowel system
vocalización /bokaliθa'θion; bokalisa'sion/ *f,* vocalization
vocalizar /bokali'θar; bokali'sar/ *vi* to vocalize
vocear /boθe'ar; bose'ar/ *vi* to cry out, shout; —*vt* proclaim; call for; acclaim
vocerío /boθe'rio; bose'rio/ *m,* shouting; clamor, outcry
vociferación /boθifera'θion; bosifera'sion/ *f,* vociferation, outcry
vociferar /boθife'rar; bosife'rar/ *vt* to boast (of); —*vi* shout, vociferate
vocinglería /boθiŋgle'ria; bosiŋgle'ria/ *f,* clamor; babble, chatter
vocinglero /boθiŋ'glero; bosiŋ'glero/ *a* vociferous; prattling, babbling
vodca /'boðka/ *m,* vodka
volada /bo'laða/ *f,* short flight. *Mech.* **v. de grúa,** jib
voladura /bola'ðura/ *f,* explosion; blasting
volandas (en), volandillas (en) /bo'landas, bolan'diʎas; bo'landas, bolan'diyas/ *adv* in the air, as though flying; *Inf.* in a trice
volante /bo'lante/ *a* flying; wandering, restless. *m,* frill, flounce; screen; fan (of a windmill); *Mech.* flywheel; *Mech.* balance wheel (watches); coiner's stamp mill; shuttle-cock. *Auto.* **v. de dirección,** steering-wheel
volantón /bolan'ton/ **(-ona)** *n* fledgling
volar /bo'lar/ *vi irr* to fly (birds, insects, aviation); float in the air; hurry; disappear suddenly; burst, explode; jut out (buttresses, etc.); cleave (air) (arrows, etc.); *Fig.* spread (rumors); —*vt* explode; blast; anger. See **contar**
volatería /bolate'ria/ *f,* fowling; fowls; poultry; flock of birds; *Fig.* crowd (of ideas)
volátil /bo'latil/ *a* volatile; inconstant
volatilizar /bolatili'θar; bolatili'sar/ *vt* to volatilize
volatinero /bolati'nero/ **(-ra)** *n* tight-rope walker, acrobat
volcán /bol'kan/ *m,* volcano; violent passion. **v. extinto,** extinct volcano
volcánico /bol'kaniko/ *a* volcanic
volcar /bol'kar/ *vt irr* to overturn, capsize; make dizzy; cause a change (of opinion); annoy; —*vi* overturn —*Pres. Indic.* **vuelco, vuelcas, vuelca, vuelcan.** *Preterite* **volqué, volcaste,** etc —*Pres. Subjunc.* **vuelque, vuelques, vuelque, vuelquen**
volear /bole'ar/ *vt* to strike in the air, volley; *Agr.* sow broadcast
voleo /bo'leo/ *m,* volley (tennis, etc.); high kick; straight punch
volframio /bol'framio/ *m,* wolfram, tungsten
volición /boli'θion; boli'sion/ *f,* volition
volquete /bol'kete/ *m,* tip-cart
voltaico /bol'taiko/ *a* voltaic
voltaje /bol'tahe/ *m,* voltage
voltario /bol'tario/ *a* versatile; capricious, headstrong
volteador /boltea'ðor/ **(-ra)** *n* acrobat
voltear /bolte'ar/ *vt* to whirl, turn; overturn; change place (of); *Archit.* construct an arch or vault; —*vi* revolve; tumble, twirl (acrobats)
volteo /bol'teo/ *m,* turning, revolution; whirl; overturning; twirling; *Elec.* voltage
voltereta /bolte'reta/ *f,* somersault
volteriano /bolte'riano/ *a* Voltairian
voltímetro /bol'timetro/ *m,* voltmeter
voltio /'boltio/ *m,* volt
volubilidad /boluβili'ðað/ *f,* inconstancy, fickleness
voluble /bo'luβle/ *a* easily turned; inconstant, changeable; *Bot.* twining
volumen /bo'lumen/ *m,* bulk, size; volume, book
volumétrico /bolu'metriko/ *a* volumetric
voluminoso /bolumi'noso/ *a* voluminous, bulky
voluntad /bolun'tað/ *f,* will, volition; wish; decree; free will; intention; affection; free choice; consent. **a v.,** at will; by choice. **de buena v.,** of good will; willingly, with pleasure. **de su propia v.,** of one's own free will. **mala v.,** hostility, ill-will
voluntario /bolun'tario/ **(-ia)** *a* voluntary; strong-willed —*n* volunteer
voluntarioso /bolunta'rioso/ *a* self-willed
voluptuosidad /boluptuosi'ðað/ *f,* voluptuousness
voluptuoso /bolup'tuoso/ *a* voluptuous
volver /bol'βer/ *vt irr* to turn; turn over; return; pay back; direct, aim; translate; restore; change, alter; close (doors, etc.); vomit; reflect, reverberate; —*vi* come back; continue (speech, etc.); bend, turn (roads); (*with prep a + infin.*) do something again (e.g. *v. a leer,* to read over again); (*with por + noun*) protect; —*vr* become; go sour; turn. **v. a las filas,** *Mil.* to reduce to the ranks. **v. en sí,** to regain consciousness. **v. la cabeza,** to turn one's head. **volverse atrás,** *Fig.* to back out. **volverse loco,** to go mad. See **resolver**
vomitar /bomi'tar/ *vt* to vomit; *Fig.* vomit forth; *Fig.* spit out (curses, etc.); *Inf.* burst into confidences
vomitivo /bomi'tiβo/ *a* and *m,* emetic

vómito /'bomito/ *m,* vomit
voracidad /boraθi'ðað; borasi'ðað/ *f,* voracity
vorágine /bo'rahine/ *f,* vortex, whirlpool
voraz /bo'raθ; bo'ras/ *a* voracious
vórtice /'bortiθe; 'bortise/ *m,* whirlpool; *Fig.* vortex
vortiginoso /bortihi'noso/ *a* vortical
vos /bos/ *pers pron 2nd pers sing* and *pl* you.
vosotros, vosotras /bo'sotros, bo'sotras/ *pers pron 2nd pers pl mf* you
votación /bota'θion; bota'sion/ *f,* voting
votador /bota'ðor/ **(-ra)** *n* voter; swearer
votar /bo'tar/ *vi* and *vt* to vote; make a vow; curse, swear. **v. una proposición de confianza,** to pass a vote of confidence
votivo /bo'tiβo/ *a* votive
voto /'boto/ *m,* vote; vow; voter; prayer; curse; desire; opinion. **v. de calidad,** casting vote. **v. de confianza,** vote of confidence
voz /boθ; bos/ *f,* voice; sound, noise; cry, shout (gen. *pl*); word; expression; *Mus.* singer or voice; *Gram.* mood; vote; rumor; instruction, order. **v. común,** general opinion. **a voces,** in a shout, loudly. **llevar la v. cantante,** *Inf.* to have the chief say
vuelco /'buelko/ *m,* overturning
vuelo /'buelo/ *m,* flight; wing; *Sew.* skirt-fullness; ruffle, frill; *Archit.* buttress. **v. a ciegas,** *Aer.* blind flying. **v. de distancia,** long-distance flight. **v. de patrulla,** patrol or reconnaissance flight. **v. de reconocimento,** reconnaissance flight. **v. nocturno,** *Aer.* night flying. **v. sin parar,** non-stop flight. **al v.,** on the wing; in passing; quickly. **alzar** (*or* **levantar**) **el v.,** to take flight
vuelta /'buelta/ *f,* revolution, turn; bend, curve; return; restitution; recompense; repetition; wrong side; beating; *Sew.* facing, cuff; change (money); conning (lessons, etc.); stroll, walk; change; vault, ceiling; *Sports.* round; *Mech.* **vueltas por minuto,** revolutions per minute. **a v. de correo,** by return mail, by return of post. **a la v.,** on returning; overleaf. **dar la v.,** to turn round, make a détour. **dar una v.,** to take a stroll. **dar vueltas,** to revolve; search (for); consider. **media v.,** half turn
vuestro, vuestra, vuestros, vuestras /'buestro, 'buestra, 'buestros, 'buestras/ *poss pron 2nd pl mf* your, yours
vulcanita /bulka'nita/ *f,* vulcanite
vulcanización /bulkaniθa'θion; bulkanisa'sion/ *f,* vulcanization
vulcanizar /bulkani'θar; bulkani'sar/ *vt* to vulcanize
vulgar /bul'gar/ *a* popular; general, common; vernacular; mediocre
vulgaridad /bulgari'ðað/ *f,* vulgarity
vulgarismo /bulga'rismo/ *m,* vulgarism
vulgarización /bulgariθa'θion; bulgarisa'sion/ *f,* vulgarization; popularization
vulgarizar /bulgari'θar; bulgari'sar/ *vt* to vulgarize; popularize; translate into the vernacular; *—vr* grow vulgar
vulgata /bul'gata/ *f,* Vulgate
vulgo /'bulgo/ *m,* mob
vulnerabilidad /bulneraβili'ðað/ *f,* vulnerability
vulnerable /bulne'raβle/ *a* vulnerable
vulpeja /bul'peha/ *f,* vixen
vulpino /bul'pino/ *a* vulpine; crafty

WXYZ

wagneriano /wagne'riano/ *a* Wagnerian
wáter /'water/ *m,* toilet, water-closet
whisky /'wiski/ *m,* whiskey
xenofobia /seno'foβia/ *f,* xenophobia, hatred of foreigners
xilófago /si'lofago/ *a* xylophagous, wood-boring. *m,* wood-borer
xilófono /si'lofono/ *m,* xylophone
xilografía /silogra'fia/ *f,* xylography
y /i/ *conjunc* and. See **e**
ya /ya/ *adv* already; formerly; soon; now; finally; immediately; well, yes, quite. Used of past, present and future time, and in various idiomatic ways. **Ha venido ya,** He has already come. **¡Ya caerá!** His time will come!, He will get his comeuppance! **Ya vendrá,** He will come soon. **¡Ya voy!** Coming! **¡Ya lo creo!** Of course!; I should think so! **¡Ya!** Quite!; I understand. **ya no,** no longer. **ya que,** since
yacente /ya'θente; ya'sente/ *a* recumbent, reclining (statues, etc.)
yacer /ya'θer; ya'ser/ *vi irr* to be lying at full length; lie (in the grave); be situated, be; lie (with), sleep (with); graze by night —*Pres. Indic.* **yazgo** *or* **yazco, yaces,** etc —*Pres. Subjunc.* **yazga** *or* **yazca,** etc.
yaciente /ya'θiente; ya'siente/ *a* recumbent
yacija /ya'θiha; ya'siha/ *f,* bed; couch; tomb
yacimiento /yaθi'miento; yasi'miento/ *m, Geol.* bed, deposit
yacio /'yaθio; 'yasio/ *m,* india-rubber tree
yak /yak/ *m,* yak
yámbico /'yambiko/ *a* and *m,* (metrics) iambic
yanqui /'yanki/ *a* and *mf contemptuous and offensive* North American (gen. U.S.A.)
yarda /'yarða/ *f,* yard (English measure)
yate /'yate/ *m, Naut.* yacht
ye /ye/ *f,* name of the letter Y
yegua /'yegua/ *f,* mare
yelmo /'yelmo/ *m,* helmet
yema /'yema/ *f,* bud; yolk (of egg); sweetmeat; *Fig.* best of anything. **y. del dedo,** finger-tip
yermo /'yermo/ *a* uninhabited, deserted; uncultivated. *m,* wilderness, desert
yerno /'yerno/ *m,* son-in-law
yerro /'yerro/ *m,* error; mistake; fault
yerto /'yerto/ *a* stiff, rigid
yesca /'yeska/ *f,* tinder; fuel, stimulus
yeso /'yeso/ *m,* gypsum, calcium sulphate; plaster; plaster cast
yídish /'yiðis/ *n* and *a* Yiddish
yo /yo/ *pers pron 1st sing mf* I. **el yo,** the ego
yodo /'yoðo/ *m,* iodine
yuca /'yuka/ *f,* yucca
yucateco /yuka'teko/ **(-ca)** *a* and *n* from or pertaining to Yucatan
yugo /'yugo/ *m,* yoke; nuptial tie; oppression; *Naut.* transom; *Fig.* **sacudir el y.,** to throw off the yoke
Yugo /'yugo/ **(e) slavia** Yugoslavia
yugo /'yugo/ **(e) slavo (-va)** *a* and *n* Yugoslav
yugular /yugu'lar/ *a Anat.* jugular. *m,* jugular vein
Yukón, el /yu'kon, el/ the Yukon
yunque /'yunke/ *m,* anvil; patient, undaunted person; hard worker; *Anat.* incus
yunta /'yunta/ *f,* yoke (of oxen, etc.)
yute /'yute/ *m,* jute fiber or fabric
yuxtaponer /yukstapo'ner/ *vt irr* to juxtapose. See **poner**
yuxtaposición /yukstaposi'θion; yukstaposi'sion/ *f,* juxtaposition
zabarcera /θaβar'θera; saβar'sera/ *f,* vegetable seller
zaborda /θa'βorða; sa'βorða/ *f,* **zabordamiento** *m, Naut.* grounding, stranding
zabordar /θaβor'ðar; saβor'ðar/ *vi Naut.* to run aground, strand
zacatín /θaka'tin; saka'tin/ *m,* street or square where clothes are sold
zafar /θa'far; sa'far/ *vt* to embellish, garnish, adorn; *Naut.* lighten (a ship); —*vr* escape, hide oneself; (*with de*) excuse oneself, avoid; get rid of
zafarrancho /θafa'rrantʃo; safa'rrantʃo/ *m, Naut.* clearing the decks; *Inf.* damage; *Inf.* scuffle
zafiedad /θafie'ðað; safie'ðað/ *f,* rudeness, ignorance, boorishness
zafio /'θafio; 'safio/ *a* rude, unlettered, boorish
zafiro /θa'firo; sa'firo/ *m,* sapphire
zafra /'θafra; 'safra/ *f,* olive oil container; sugar crop or factory; *Mineral.* waste
zaga /'θaga; 'saga/ *f,* rear. *m,* last player. **en z.,** behind. *Inf.* **no quedarse en z.,** not to be left behind; be not inferior
zagal /θa'gal; sa'gal/ *m,* youth; strong, handsome lad; young shepherd; full skirt
zagala /θa'gala; sa'gala/ *f,* maiden, girl; young shepherdess
zagual /θa'gual; sa'gual/ *m,* paddle
zaguán /θa'guan; sa'guan/ *m,* entrance hall; vestibule
zaguero /θa'gero; sa'gero/ *a* loitering, straggling. *m, Sports.* back
zahareño /θaa'reɲo; saa'reɲo/ *a* untamable, wild (birds); unsociable, disdainful
zaherimiento /θaeri'miento; saeri'miento/ *m,* upbraiding; nagging
zaherir /θae'rir; sae'rir/ *vt irr* to upbraid, reprehend; nag. See **herir**
zahína /θa'ina; sa'ina/ *f, Bot.* sorghum
zahón /θa'on; sa'on/ *m,* leather apron (worn by cowboys)
zahorí /θao'ri; sao'ri/ *m,* soothsayer; waterfinder; sagacious person
zahúrda /θa'urða; sa'urða/ *f,* pigsty
zaino /'θaino; 'saino/ *a* treacherous; vicious (horses); chestnut (horses); black (cows)
zalagarda /θala'garða; sala'garða/ *f,* ambush; skirmish; snare, trap; *Inf.* trick, ruse; *Inf.* mock battle
zalamería /θalame'ria; salame'ria/ *f,* adulation, flattery
zalamero /θala'mero; sala'mero/ **(-ra)** *a* wheedling, flattering —*n* flatterer
zalea /θa'lea; sa'lea/ *f,* sheepskin
zalear /θale'ar; sale'ar/ *vt* to shake; frighten away (dogs)
zalema /θa'lema; sa'lema/ *f,* salaam
zamacuco /θama'kuko; sama'kuko/ *m, Inf.* oaf, dolt; *Inf.* drinking bout
zamarra /θa'marra; sa'marra/ *f,* sheepskin jacket
zamarrear /θamarre'ar; samarre'ar/ *vt* to worry, shake (prey); *Fig. Inf.* beat up; *Inf.* floor, confound
zambo /'θambo; 'sambo/ *a* knock-kneed
zambomba /θam'βomba; sam'βomba/ *f,* rustic drum
zambra /'θambra; 'sambra/ *f,* Moorish festival; *Inf.* merrymaking; Moorish boat
zambuco /θam'βuko; sam'βuko/ *m, Inf.* concealment (especially of cards)
zambullida /θambu'ʎiða; sambu'yiða/ *f,* plunge, submersion; thrust (in fencing)
zambullir /θambu'ʎir; sambu'yir/ *vt* to plunge in water, submerge; —*vr* dive; hide oneself, cover oneself
zampar /θam'par; sam'par/ *vt* to conceal (one thing in another); eat greedily; (*with en*) arrive suddenly
zampatortas /θampa'tortas; sampa'tortas/ *mf Inf.* glutton
zampoña /θam'poɲa; sam'poɲa/ *f,* rustic flute; *Inf.* unimportant work
zanahoria /θana'oria; sana'oria/ *f,* carrot
zanca /'θanka; 'sanka/ *f,* long leg (birds); *Inf.* long thin leg; *Archit.* stringboard (of stairs)
zancada /θan'kaða; san'kaða/ *f,* swift stride
zancadilla /θanka'ðiʎa; sanka'ðiya/ *f,* trip (wrestling); *Inf.* trick, deceit. **echar la z.** (**a**)**,** to trip up
zancajear /θankahe'ar; sankahe'ar/ *vi* to stride about
zancajo /θan'kaho; san'kaho/ *m,* heel-bone; torn

heel (stocking, shoe); *Inf.* ill-shaped person. *Inf.* **no llegarle al z.,** to be immensely inferior to someone
zancajoso /θanka'hoso; sanka'hoso/ *a* flatfooted; slovenly
zanco /'θanko; 'sanko/ *m,* stilt. *Fig. Inf.* **andar** (*or* **estar) en zancos,** to have gone up in the world
zancudo /θan'kuðo; san'kuðo/ *a* long-legged
zangandungo /θaŋgan'duŋgo; saŋgan'duŋgo/ **(-ga)** *n Inf.* loafer
zanganear /θaŋgane'ar; saŋgane'ar/ *vi Inf.* to loaf
zángano /'θaŋgano; 'saŋgano/ *m, Ent.* drone; *Inf.* idler, parasite
zangolotear /θaŋgolote'ar; saŋgolote'ar/ *vt Inf.* to shake violently; *—vi* fuss about, bustle; *—vr* rattle (windows, etc.)
zangoloteo /θaŋgolo'teo; saŋgolo'teo/ *m,* shaking; rattling
zanguango /θaŋ'guaŋgo; saŋ'guaŋgo/ *m, Inf.* lazybones
zanja /'θanha; 'sanha/ *f,* trench, ditch; drain; furrow
zanjar /θan'har; san'har/ *vt* to excavate; *Fig.* remove (obstacles)
Zanzíbar /θan'θiβar; san'siβar/ Zanzibar
zapa /'θapa; 'sapa/ *f,* shovel, spade; *Mil.* sap; sandpaper
zapador /θapa'ðor; sapa'ðor/ *m, Mil.* sapper
zapapico /θapa'piko; sapa'piko/ *m,* pick-ax; mattock
zapaquilda /θapa'kilda; sapa'kilda/ *f, Inf.* she-cat
zapar /θa'par; sa'par/ *vi Mil.* to sap
zaparrastrar /θaparras'trar; saparras'trar/ *vi Inf.* to trail along the floor (dresses)
zapata /θa'pata; sa'pata/ *f,* half-boot; piece of leather used to stop creaking of a hinge; *Archit.* lintel; (*Naut. Mech.*) shoe
zapatazo /θapa'taθo; sapa'taso/ *m,* blow with a shoe; fall, thud; stamping (horses); flap (of sail)
zapateado /θapate'aðo; sapate'aðo/ *m,* dance in which rhythmic drumming of heels plays important part
zapatear /θapate'ar; sapate'ar/ *vt* to hit with a shoe; stamp feet; drum heels (in dancing); *Inf.* ill-treat; thump ground (rabbits); *—vi* stamp (horses); *Naut.* flap (sails); *—vr Fig.* stand one's ground
zapateo /θapa'teo; sapa'teo/ *m,* stamping; rhythmic drumming of heels
zapatera /θapa'tera; sapa'tera/ *f,* cobbler's wife; woman who makes or sells shoes
zapatería /θapate'ria; sapate'ria/ *f,* shoemaking; shoe shop
zapatero /θapa'tero; sapa'tero/ *m,* shoemaker; shoe seller. **z. remendón,** cobbler
zapateta /θapa'teta; sapa'teta/ *f,* caper, leap
zapatilla /θapa'tiʎa; sapa'tiya/ *f,* slipper; trotter, hoof
zapato /θa'pato; sa'pato/ *m,* shoe
¡zape! /'θape; 'sape/ *interj Inf.* shoo! Used for frightening away cats; exclamation of surprise or warning
zapear /θape'ar; sape'ar/ *vt* to scare away cats; *Inf.* frighten off
zaque /'θake; 'sake/ *m,* leather bottle, wineskin; *Inf.* drunkard, sot
zaquizamí /θakiθa'mi; sakisa'mi/ *m,* garret; dirty little house or room
zar /θar; sar/ *m,* tsar
zarabanda /θara'βanda; sara'βanda/ *f,* saraband; *Inf.* racket, row
zaragata /θara'gata; sara'gata/ *f, Inf.* fight, brawl
Zaragoza /θara'goθa; sara'gosa/ Saragossa
zaragozano /θarago'θano; sarago'sano/ **(-na)** *a* and *n* Saragossan
zaragüelles /θara'gueʎes; sara'gueyes/ *m, pl* wide pleated breeches
zaranda /θa'randa; sa'randa/ *f,* sieve, strainer, colander
zarandajas /θaran'dahas; saran'dahas/ *f, pl Inf.* odds and ends
zarandar /θaran'dar; saran'dar/ *vt* to sieve (grapes, grain); strain; *Inf.* pick out the best; *—vr Inf.* move quickly
zarandillo /θaran'diʎo; saran'diyo/ *m,* small sieve, strainer; *Inf.* a live wire, energetic person; Spanish dance
zaraza /θa'raθa; sa'rasa/ *f,* chintz
zarcillo /θar'θiʎo; sar'siyo/ *m,* earring; *Bot.* tendril; *Agr.* trowel
zarco /'θarko; 'sarko/ *a* light blue (generally eyes or water)
zarina /θa'rina; sa'rina/ *f,* tsarina
zarpa /'θarpa; 'sarpa/ *f, Naut.* weighing anchor; paw
zarpada /θar'paða; sar'paða/ *f,* blow with a paw
zarpar /θar'par; sar'par/ *vt* and *vi Naut.* to weigh anchor, sail
zarza /'θarθa; 'sarsa/ *f, Bot.* bramble, blackberry bush
zarzal /θar'θal; sar'sal/ *m,* bramble patch
zarzamora /θarθa'mora; sarsa'mora/ *f,* blackberry
zarzaparrilla /θarθapa'rriʎa; sarsapa'rriya/ *f,* sarsaparilla
zarzo /'θarθo; 'sarso/ *m,* hurdle; wattle
zarzoso /θar'θoso; sar'soso/ *a* brambly
zarzuela /θar'θuela; sar'suela/ *f,* comic opera; musical comedy
zarzuelista /θarθue'lista; sarsue'lista/ *mf* writer or composer of comic operas
¡zas! /θas; sas/ *m,* sound of a bang or blow
zascandil /θaskan'dil; saskan'dil/ *m, Inf.* busybody
zatara /θa'tara; sa'tara/ *f,* raft
zeda /'θeða; 'seða/ *f,* name of the letter Z
zedilla /θe'ðiʎa; se'ðiya/ *f,* cedilla
zenit /'θenit; 'senit/ *m.* See **cenit**
zepelín /θepe'lin; sepe'lin/ *m,* Zeppelin
zeta /'θeta; 'seta/ *f.* See **zeda**
zigzag /θig'θag; sig'sag/ *m,* zigzag
zigzaguear /θigθage'ar; sigsage'ar/ *vi* to zigzag
zinc /θink; sink/ *m,* zinc
zipizape /θipi'θape; sipi'sape/ *m, Inf.* row, quarrel
zoca /'θoka; 'soka/ *f,* square
zócalo /'θokalo; 'sokalo/ *m, Archit.* socle
zoclo /'θoklo; 'soklo/ *m,* clog, sabot
zoco /'θoko; 'soko/ *m,* square; market; clog, sabot
zodiaco /θo'ðiako; so'ðiako/ *m,* zodiac
zona /'θona; 'sona/ *f,* girdle, band; strip (of land); zone; *Med.* shingles. **z. de depresión,** air pocket. **z. templada,** temperate zone. **z. tórrida,** torrid zone
zonal /θo'nal; so'nal/ *a* zonal
zoología /θoolo'hia; soolo'hia/ *f,* zoology
zoológico /θoo'lohiko; soo'lohiko/ *a* zoological
zoólogo /θo'ologo; so'ologo/ *m,* zoologist
zopenco /θo'penko; so'penko/ *a Inf.* oafish
zopo /'θopo; 'sopo/ *a* maimed, deformed (hands, feet)
zoquete /θo'kete; so'kete/ *m,* block; dowel; hunk of bread; *Inf.* short, ugly man; *Inf.* dunderhead
zorcico /θor'θiko; sor'siko/ *m,* Basque song and dance
zorra /'θorra; 'sorra/ *f,* vixen; fox; *Inf.* cunning person; *Inf.* prostitute; *Inf.* drinking bout; truck, dray
zorrera /θo'rrera; so'rrera/ *f,* foxhole
zorrería /θorre'ria; sorre'ria/ *f,* foxiness; *Inf.* cunning
zorro /'θorro; 'sorro/ *m,* fox; fox-skin; *Inf.* knave
zóster /'θoster; 'soster/ *f, Med.* shingles
zote /'θote; 'sote/ *a* dull, ignorant
zozobra /θo'θoβra; so'soβra/ *f, Naut.* foundering, capsizing; anxiety
zozobrar /θoθo'βrar; soso'βrar/ *vi Naut.* to founder, sink; *Naut.* plunge, shiver; be anxious, vacillate
zueco /'θueko; 'sueko/ *m,* sabot, clog
zulú /θu'lu; su'lu/ *a* and *mf* Zulu
Zululandia /θulu'landia; sulu'landia/ Zululand
zumaque /θu'make, su'make/ *m, Bot.* sumach tree; *Inf.* wine
zumba /'θumba; 'sumba/ *f,* cow bell; jest
zumbar /θum'βar; sum'βar/ *vi* to buzz, hum; ring (of the ears); whizz; twang (of a guitar, etc.); *Fig. Inf.* be on the brink
zumbido /θum'βiðo; sum'βiðo/ *m,* buzzing, humming; ringing (in the ears); whizz; twanging (of a guitar, etc.); *Inf.* slap, blow
zumbón /θum'βon; sum'βon/ *a* waggish, jocose
zumo /'θumo; 'sumo/ *m,* sap; juice; profit, advantage
zumoso /θu'moso; su'moso/ *a* succulent, juicy
zupia /'θupia; 'supia/ *f,* wine lees; cloudy wine; *Fig.* dregs

zurcido /θur'θiðo; sur'siðo/ *m, Sew.* darn; mend
zurcidor /θurθi'ðor; sursi'ðor/ **(-ra)** *n* darner, mender. **z. de voluntades,** *humorous* pimp
zurcidura /θurθi'ðura; sursi'ðura/ *f,* darning; mending; darn
zurcir /θur'θir; sur'sir/ *vt* to darn; mend, repair; join; *Fig.* concoct, weave
zurdo /'θurðo; 'surðo/ *a* left-handed
zurra /'θurra; 'surra/ *f, Tan.* currying; *Inf.* spanking; *Inf.* quarrel
zurrador /θurra'ðor; surra'ðor/ *m, Tan.* currier, dresser
zurrapa /θu'rrapa; su'rrapa/ *f,* (gen. *pl*) sediment, lees, dregs
zurrar /θu'rrar; su'rrar/ *vt* to curry (leather); *Inf.* spank; *Inf.* dress down, scold
zurriagazo /θurria'gaθo; surria'gaso/ *m,* lash with a whip; *Fig.* blow of fate
zurriago /θu'rriago; su'rriago/ *m,* whip
zurribanda /θurri'βanda; surri'βanda/ *f, Inf.* whipping; fight, quarrel
zurriburri /θurri'βurri; surri'βurri/ *m, Inf.* ragamuffin; mob; uproar
zurrido /θu'rriðo; su'rriðo/ *m, Inf.* blow; dull noise
zurrir /θu'rrir; su'rrir/ *vi* to have a confused sound, hum, rattle
zurrón /θu'rron; su'rron/ *m,* shepherd's pouch; leather bag; *Bot.* husk
zutano /θu'tano; su'tano/ **(-na)** *n Inf.* so-and-so, such a one
Zuyderzee, el /θuiðer'θee, el; suiðer'see, el/ the Zuider Zee

English-Spanish Dictionary

a /ei/ *n* (letter) a, *f; Mus.* la, *m.* **symphony in A major,** sinfonía en la mayor, *f.* **A1,** de primera clase; de primera calidad, excelente

a, an /ə, ən; *when stressed* ei;, æn/ *indef art.* (one) un, *m;* una, *f;* (with weights, quantities) el, *m;* la, *f;* (with weeks, months, years, etc.) por, al, *m;* a la, *f.* The indef. art. is omitted in Spanish before nouns expressing nationality, profession, rank, and generally before a noun in apposition. It is omitted also before certain words such as **mil, ciento, otro, semejante, medio,** etc. Not translated in book titles, e.g., *A History of Spain,* Historia de España. *prep* a. In phrases such as *to go hunting,* ir a cazar. As prefix, see *abed, ashore,* etc. *Madrid, a Spanish city,* Madrid, ciudad de España. *three times a month,* tres veces al mes. *ten dollars an hour,* diez dólares por hora. *thirty miles an hour,* treinta millas por hora. *a certain Mrs. Brown,* una tal Sra. Brown. *a thousand soldiers,* mil soldados. *half an hour later,* media hora después

aback /ə'bæk/ *adv Naut.* en facha; *Fig.* sorprendido, desconcertado. **to take a.,** desconcertar, coger desprevenido (a)

abacus /'æbəkəs, ə'bækəs/ *n* ábaco, *m*

abaft /ə'bæft/ *adv Naut.* hacia la popa, en popa; atrás

abandon /ə'bændən/ *vt* abandonar; dejar; desertar, desamparar; renunciar; entregar. —*n* entusiasmo, fervor, *m;* naturalidad, *f.* **to a. oneself to,** (despair, vice, etc.) entregarse a

abandoned /ə'bændənd/ *a* entregado a los vicios, vicioso

abandonment /ə'bændənmənt/ *n* abandono, *m;* renunciación, *f;* deserción, *f*

abase /ə'beis/ *vt* humillar; degradar; abatir

abasement /ə'beismənt/ *n* humillación, degradación, *f;* abatimiento, *m*

abash /ə'bæʃ/ *vt* avergonzar; confundir, desconcertar

abashed /ə'bæʃt/ *a* avergonzado, confuso, consternado

abate /ə'beit/ *vt* disminuir, reducir; (a price) rebajar; (suppress) suprimir, abolir; (remit) condonar, remitir; (annul) anular; (moderate) moderar; (of pride, etc.) humillar; (of pain) aliviar. —*vi* disminuir; moderarse; (of the wind and *Fig.*) amainar; cesar; apaciguarse, calmarse

abatement /ə'beitmənt/ *n* disminución, *f;* reducción, *f;* mitigación, *f;* (of price) rebaja, *f;* supresión, *f;* remisión, *f;* (annulment) anulación, *f;* (of pride) humillación, *f;* (of the wind and of enthusiasm, etc.) amaine, *m;* (of pain, etc.) alivio, *m*

abattoir /'æbəˌtwɑr/ *n* matadero, *m*

abbey /'æbi/ *n* abadía, *f*

abbreviate /ə'briviˌeit/ *vt* abreviar; condensar, resumir

abbreviation /əˌbrivi'eiʃən/ *n* abreviación, *f;* resumen, *m,* condensación, *f;* (of a word) abreviatura, *f*

abdicate /'æbdɪˌkeit/ *vt* renunciar; (a throne) abdicar

abdication /ˌæbdɪ'keiʃən/ *n* renuncia, *f;* abdicación, *f*

abdomen /'æbdəmən/ *n* abdomen, *m*

abdominal /æb'dɒmən̩l/ *a* abdominal

abduct /æb'dʌkt/ *vt* raptar, secuestrar

abduction /æb'dʌkʃən/ *n* rapto, *m;* (*Anat., Philos.*) abducción, *f*

abductor /æb'dʌktər/ *n Anat.* abductor, *m;* raptor, *m*

aberration /ˌæbə'reiʃən/ *n* aberración (also *Astron., Phys., Biol.*), *f*

abet /ə'bɛt/ *vt* ayudar, apoyar, favorecer; incitar, alentar; (in bad sense) ser cómplice de

abetment /ə'bɛtmənt/ *n* ayuda, *f,* apoyo, *m;* instigación, *f*

abettor /ə'bɛtər/ *n* instigador (-ra); cómplice, *mf*

abeyance /ə'beiəns/ *n* suspensión, *f;* expectativa, esperanza, *f.* **in a.,** en suspenso; vacante; latente

abhor /æb'hɔr/ *vt* detestar, odiar, aborrecer; repugnar

abhorrence /æb'hɔrəns/ *n* detestación, *f,* odio, aborrecimiento, *m;* repugnancia, *f*

abhorrent /æb'hɔrənt/ *a* detestable, odioso, aborrecible; repugnante

abide /ə'baid/ *vi* morar, quedar. —*vt* aguardar; *Inf.* aguantar, sufrir. **to a. by,** atenerse a, cumplir; sostener

abiding /ə'baidɪŋ/ *a* permanente, constante, perenne

ability /ə'bɪlɪti/ *n* habilidad, facultad, *f,* poder, *m;* talento, *m,* capacidad, *f.* **to the best of my a.,** lo mejor que yo pueda

abject /'æbdʒɛkt/ *a* abyecto, miserable; despreciable, vil; servil

abjure /æb'dʒʊr/ *vt* abjurar; renunciar; retractar

ablaze /ə'bleiz/ *adv* en llamas, ardiendo. —*a* brillante; (with, of anger, etc.) dominado por

able /'eibəl/ *a* capaz (de); (clever) hábil; competente; en estado (de); *Law.* apto legalmente, capaz; bueno, excelente. **to be a. to,** poder; ser capaz de; (know how) saber. **a.-bodied,** fuerte, fornido. **a.-bodied seaman,** marinero práctico, *m*

abloom /ə'blum/ *adv* en flor

ablution /ə'bluʃən/ *n* ablución, *f*

ably /'eibli/ *adv* hábilmente; competentemente

abnegation /ˌæbnɪ'geiʃən/ *n* abnegación, *f*

abnormal /æb'nɔrməl/ *a* anormal; irregular

abnormality /ˌæbnɔr'mælɪti/ *n* anormalidad, *f;* irregularidad, *f*

abnormally /æb'nɔrməli/ *adv* anormalmente; demasiado

aboard /ə'bɔrd/ *adv* a bordo. —*prep* a bordo de. **to go a.,** embarcarse, ir a bordo. **All a.!** ¡Viajeros a bordo!; (a train) ¡Viajeros al tren!

abode /ə'boud/ *n* morada, habitación, *f;* residencia, *f;* (stay) estancia, *f*

abolish /ə'bɒlɪʃ/ *vt* abolir, suprimir, anular

abolition /ˌæbə'lɪʃən/ *n* abolición, supresión, *f;* anulación, *f*

abolitionism /ˌæbə'lɪʃəˌnɪzəm/ *n* abolicionismo, *m*

abolitionist /ˌæbə'lɪʃənɪst/ *n* abolicionista, *mf*

abominable /ə'bɒmənəbəl/ *a* abominable, aborrecible; repugnante, execrable; *Inf.* horrible

abominably /ə'bɒmənəbli/ *adv* abominablemente

abominate /ə'bɒməˌneit/ *vt* abominar, aborrecer, detestar

abomination /əˌbɒmə'neiʃən/ *n* abominación, *f;* aborrecimiento, *m;* horror, *m*

aboriginal /ˌæbə'rɪdʒən̩l/ *a* aborigen; primitivo

aborigines /ˌæbə'rɪdʒəˌniz/ *n pl* aborígenes, *m pl*

abort /ə'bɔrt/ *vi* abortar, malparir; *Fig.* malograrse

abortion /ə'bɔrʃən/ *n* aborto, *m; Fig.* fracaso, malogro, *m*

abortive /ə'bɔrtɪv/ *a* abortivo

abound /ə'baund/ *vi* abundar (en)

about /ə'baut/ *adv* (around) alrededor; (round about) a la redonda, en torno; (all over) por todas partes; (up and down) acá y acullá; por aquí, por ahí; en alguna parte; por aquí; (in circumference) en circunferencia; (almost) casi, aproximadamente; (by turns) por turnos, en rotación. —*prep* alrededor de; en torno; por; (near to) cerca de; (on one's person) sobre; (on the subject of) sobre; (concerning) acerca de; (over) por, a causa de; en; (of) de; (with time by the clock) a eso de, sobre; (towards) hacia; (engaged in) ocupado en; (on the point of) a punto de. **a. here,** por aquí. **a. nothing,** por nada. **a. supper time,** hacia la hora de cenar. **a. three o'clock,** a eso de las tres. **A. turn!** ¡Media vuelta! (a la izquierda or a la derecha). **He wandered a. the streets,** Vagaba por las calles. **somewhere a.,** en alguna parte. **to be a. to,** estar para, estar a punto de. **to bring a.,** ocasionar. **to come a.,** suceder. **to know a.,** saber de. **to set a.,** empezar, iniciar; (a person) acometer. **What are you thinking a.?** ¿En qué piensas?

above /ə'bʌv/ *adv* arriba; en lo alto; encima; (superior) superior; (earlier) antes; (higher up on a page, etc.) más arriba; (in heaven) en el cielo. —*prep* encima de; por encima de; sobre; (beyond) fuera de;

fuera del alcance de; (superior to) superior a; (more than) más de; (too proud to) demasiado orgulloso para; (too good to) demasiado bueno para; (in addition to) además de, en adición a; (with degrees of temperature) sobre. —*a* anterior; (with past participles) antes. **from a.,** desde arriba. **a. all,** sobre todo. **over and a.,** además de. **a. board,** *adv* abiertamente, con las cartas boca arriba. —*a* franco y abierto. **a. mentioned,** supradicho, susodicho, antes citado
abrasion /ə'breiʒən/ *n* abrasión, *f;* rozadura, *f; Geol.* denudación, *f*
abrasive /ə'breisɪv/ *a* abrasivo. —*n* substancia abrasiva, *f,* abrasivo, *m*
abreast /ə'brɛst/ *adv* de frente, al lado uno de otro; *Naut.* por el través. **to keep a. of the times,** mantenerse al dia. **to ride six a.,** cabalgar a seis de frente. **a. with,** al nivel de, a la altura de
abridge /ə'brɪdʒ/ *vt* abreviar; resumir, condensar, compendiar; disminuir; reducir
abridgment /ə'brɪdʒmənt/ *n* abreviación, *f;* resumen, *m,* sinopsis, *f;* disminución, *f;* reducción, *f*
abroad /ə'brɔd/ *adv* (out) fuera, afuera; (gone out) salido; ausente; (everywhere) en todas partes; (in foreign lands) en el extranjero. **to go a.,** salir de casa, echarse a la calle; ir al extranjero; (of rumors, etc.) propagarse, rumorearse
abrogation /ˌæbrə'geiʃən/ *n* abrogación, anulación, *f*
abrupt /ə'brʌpt/ *a* (precipitous) escarpado, precipitado, abrupto; (unexpected) repentino, inesperado; (of persons) brusco, descortés; (of style) seco
abruptly /ə'brʌptli/ *adv* bruscamente; repentinamente
abruptness /ə'brʌptnɪs/ *n* precipitación, *f;* brusquedad, *f*
abscess /'æbsɛs/ *n* absceso, *m*
abscond /æb'skɒnd/ *vi* evadirse; huir, escaparse; (with money) desfalcar
absence /'æbsəns/ *n* ausencia, *f;* alejamiento, *m;* (of mind) abstracción, *f,* ensimismamiento, *m;* (lack) falta, *f.* **leave of a.,** permiso para ausentarse, *m; Mil.* licencia, *f,* permiso, *m*
absent /*a* 'æbsənt; *v* æb'sɛnt/ *a* ausente; alejado (de); (in mind) abstraído, ensimismado, distraído. —*vt* ausentarse; alejarse. **the a.,** los ausentes. **a.-mindedness,** ensimismamiento, *m,* abstracción, *f*
absentee /ˌæbsən'ti/ *n* ausente, *mf*
absenteeism /ˌæbsən'tiɪzəm/ *n* absentismo, *m*
absently /'æbsəntli/ *adv* distraídamente
absinthe /'æbsɪnθ/ *n* ajenjo, *m*
absolute /'æbsəˌlut/ *a* absoluto; perfecto; puro; (unconditional) incondicional; (downright) categórico; completo; (true) verdadero; (unlimited) ilimitado. **the a.,** lo absoluto
absolutely /ˌæbsə'lutli/ *adv* absolutamente; enteramente, completamente; realmente, categóricamente
absolution /ˌæbsə'luʃən/ *n* (*Eccl. Law.*) absolución, *f*
absolutism /'æbsəluˌtɪzəm/ *n* absolutismo, despotismo, *m*
absolutist /'æbsəˌlutɪst/ *n* absolutista, *mf*
absolve /æb'zɒlv, -'sɒlv/ *vt* absolver; (free) exentar, eximir; librar; exculpar
absorb /æb'sɔrb, -'zɔrb/ *vt* absorber; (drink) beber; (use) gastar; (of shocks) amortiguar; (*Fig.* digest) asimilar; (engross) ocupar (el pensamiento, etc.). **to be absorbed in,** *Fig.* enfrascarse en, engolfarse en, estar entregado a
absorbent /æb'sɔrbənt, -'zɔr-/ *a* and *n* absorbente, *m.* **a. cotton,** algodón hidrófilo, *m*
absorbing /æb'sɔrbɪŋ, -'zɔr-/ *a* absorbente; *Fig.* sumamente interesante
absorption /æb'sɔrpʃən, -'zɔrp-/ *n* absorción, *f;* (*Fig.* digestion) asimilación, *f;* (engrossment) enfrascamiento, *m,* preocupación, abstracción, *f*
abstain /æb'stein/ *vi* abstenerse (de); evitar
abstemious /æb'stimiəs/ *a* abstemio, abstinente; sobrio; moderado
abstention /æb'stɛnʃən/ *n* abstención, *f;* abstinencia, *f;* privación, *f*
abstinence /'æbstənəns/ *n* abstinencia, *f.* **day of a.,** día de ayuno, *m*
abstinent /'æbstənənt/ *a* abstinente; sobrio
abstract /*a, v* æb'strækt, 'æbstrækt; *n* 'æbstrækt/ *a* abstracto. —*n* extracto, resumen, *m;* abstracción, *f.* —*vt* abstraer; separar; extraer; (précis) resumir; (steal) substraer. **in the a.,** en abstracto
abstracted /æb'stræktɪd/ *a* distraído, desatento, absorto, ensimismado
abstraction /æb'strækʃən/ *n* abstracción, *f;* (of mind) preocupación, desatención, *f;* (stealing) substracción, *f*
abstruse /æb'strus/ *a* abstruso, ininteligible; obscuro; recóndito
absurd /æb'sɜrd/ *a* absurdo, grotesco; ridículo, disparatado; cómico
absurdity /æb'sɜrdɪti/ *n* absurdidad, ridiculez, *f;* disparate, *m,* tontería, *f*
abundance /ə'bʌndəns/ *n* abundancia, copia, *f;* muchedumbre (de), multitud (de), *f;* riqueza, *f;* prosperidad, *f*
abundant /ə'bʌndənt/ *a* abundante, copioso; rico. **to be a. in,** abundar en
abundantly /ə'bʌndəntli/ *adv* en abundancia, abundantemente
abuse /*n* ə'byus; *v* ə'byuz/ *n* abuso, *m;* (bad language) insulto, *m,* injuria, *f.* —*vt* (ill-use) maltratar; (misuse) abusar (de); (revile) insultar, injuriar; (deceive) engañar
abuser /ə'byuzər/ *n* abusador (-ra); injuriador (-ra); (defamer) denigrante, *mf*
abusive /ə'byusɪv/ *a* abusivo; (scurrilous) insultante, injurioso, ofensivo
abusively /ə'byusɪvli/ *adv* insolentemente, ofensivamente
abut (on) /ə'bʌt/ *vi* lindar con; terminar en; estar adosado a
abysmal /ə'bɪzməl/ *a* abismal
abyss /ə'bɪs/ *n* abismo, *m,* sima, *f;* (hell) infierno, *m*
acacia /ə'keiʃə/ *n* acacia, *f*
academic /ˌækə'dɛmɪk/ *a* académico
academician /ˌækədə'mɪʃən/ *n* académico, miembro de la Academia, *m*
academy /ə'kædəmi/ *n* academia, *f;* conservatorio, *m;* (school) colegio, *m;* (of riding, etc.) escuela, *f.* **A. of Music,** Conservatorio de Música, *m*
accede /æk'sid/ *vi* (to a throne) ascender (al trono); tomar posesión (de); (join) hacerse miembro (de); aceptar; (agree) acceder (a), consentir (en), convenir (en)
accelerate /æk'sɛləˌreit/ *vt* acelerar; apresurar; (shorten) abreviar
acceleration /ækˌsɛlə'reiʃən/ *n* aceleración, *f*
accelerator /æk'sɛləˌreitər/ *n* (of a vehicle) acelerador, *m*
accent /'æksɛnt/ *n* acento (all meanings), *m.* —*vt* acentuar
accentuate /æk'sɛntʃuˌeit/ *vt* acentuar; dar énfasis a
accept /æk'sɛpt/ *vt* aceptar; (believe) creer; recibir; admitir; (welcome) acoger
acceptability /ækˌsɛptə'bɪlɪti/ *n* aceptabilidad, *f;* mérito, *m*
acceptable /æk'sɛptəbəl/ *a* aceptable; admisible; agradable; (welcome) bien acogido
acceptably /æk'sɛptəbli/ *adv* aceptablemente; agradablemente
acceptance /æk'sɛptəns/ *n* aceptación, *f.* **a. speech** discurso aceptatorio; (approval) aprobación, *f;* (welcome) buena acogida, *f; Com.* aceptación, *f*
access /'æksɛs/ *n* acceso, *m;* entrada, *f;* (way) camino, *m; Med.* ataque, *m;* (fit) transporte, *m;* (advance) avance, *m.* **easy of a.,** accesible; fácil de encontrar
accessibility /ækˌsɛsə'bɪlɪti/ *n* accesibilidad, *f*
accessible /æk'sɛsəbəl/ *a* accesible; asequible
accession /æk'sɛʃən/ *n* (to the throne, etc.) advenimiento, *m;* aumento, *m;* (acquisition) adición, *f;* adquisición, *f; Law.* accesión, *f*
accessory /æk'sɛsəri/ *a* accesorio; secundario; suplementario, adicional. —*n* accesorio, *m; Law.* cómplice, *mf.* **a. before the fact,** instigador (-ra). **a. after the fact,** encubridor (-ra)
accident /'æksɪdənt/ *n* accidente, *m;* (chance) casualidad, *f;* (mishap) contratiempo, *m.* **by a.,** por casualidad, accidentalmente. **a. insurance,** seguro contra accidentes, *m*

accidental /ˌæksɪˈdɛntl̩/ *a* accidental, casual, fortuito. —*n Mus.* accidente, *m*
accidentally /ˌæksɪˈdɛntl̩i/ *adv* accidentalmente; por casualidad; sin querer
acclaim /əˈkleim/ *vt* aclamar; proclamar; vitorear, aplaudir
acclamation /ˌækləˈmeiʃən/ *n* aclamación, *f;* aplauso, vítor, *m*
acclimatization /əˈklaimətəˌzeishən/ *n* aclimatación, *f*
acclimatize /əˈklaiməˌtaiz/ *vt* aclimatar
accolade /ˈækəˌleid/ *n* acolada, *f,* espaldarazo, *m*
accommodate /əˈkɒməˌdeit/ *vt* acomodar; ajustar; adaptar; (reconcile) reconciliar; (provide) proveer, proporcionar; (oblige) complacer; (fit) poner, instalar; (lodge) hospedar; (lend) prestar; (hold) tener espacio para, contener; (give a seat to) dar un sitio a. **to a. oneself to,** adaptarse a
accommodating /əˈkɒməˌdeitɪŋ/ *a* acomodadizo; (obliging) servicial
accommodation /əˌkɒməˈdeiʃən/ *n* acomodación, *f;* ajuste, *m;* adaptación, *f;* (arrangement) arreglo, *m;* (reconciliation) reconciliación, *f;* (lodging) alojamiento, *m;* (*Aer. Naut.*) partición, *f;* (space, room or seat) sitio, *m;* (loan) préstamo, *m.* **We found the accommodations good in this hotel,** Estuvimos muy bien en este hotel. **a. ladder,** escalera real, *f*
accompaniment /əˈkʌmpənɪmənt/ *n* acompañamiento, *m*
accompanist /əˈkʌmpənɪst/ *n* acompañante (-ta)
accompany /əˈkʌmpəni/ *vt* acompañar
accompanying /əˈkʌmpəniɪŋ/ *a* anexo *n* acompañamiento, *m*
accomplice /əˈkɒmplɪs/ *n* cómplice, comparte, *mf*
accomplish /əˈkɒmplɪʃ/ *vt* llevar a cabo, efectuar; terminar; (fulfil) cumplir; perfeccionar; (achieve) conseguir, lograr
accomplished /əˈkɒmplɪʃt/ *a* consumado; perfecto; culto; (talented) talentoso
accomplishment /əˈkɒmplɪʃmənt/ *n* efectuación, *f;* realización, *f,* logro, *m;* (fulfilment) cumplimiento, *m;* (gift) prenda, *f,* talento, *m;* *pl* **accomplishments,** partes, dotes, *f pl;* conocimientos, *m pl*
accord /əˈkɔrd/ *n* acuerdo, *m;* unión, *f;* consentimiento, *m;* concierto, *m,* concordia, *f;* voluntad, *f.* —*vt* otorgar, conceder. —*vi* estar de acuerdo (con); armonizar (con). **of one's own a.,** espontáneamente. **with one a.,** unánimemente
accordance /əˈkɔrdn̩s/ *n* acuerdo, *m,* conformidad, *f;* arreglo, *m.* **in a. with,** de acuerdo con, según, con arreglo a
according /əˈkɔrdɪŋ/ *adv* según, conforme. **a. as,** conforme a, a medida que. **a. to,** según
accordingly /əˈkɔrdɪŋli/ *adv* en consecuencia, por consiguiente; pues
accordion /əˈkɔrdiən/ *n* acordeón, *m.* **to a.-pleat,** *vt* plisar
accost /əˈkɔst/ *vt* abordar, acercarse a; dirigirse a, hablar
account /əˈkaunt/ *vt* (judge) considerar, creer, juzgar, tener por. —*vi* (for) explicar; (understand) comprender; (be responsible) responder de, dar razón de; justificar
account /əˈkaunt/ *n* (bill) cuenta, *f;* factura, *f;* (narrative) narración, relación, *f;* (description) descripción, *f;* historia, *f;* versión, *f;* (list) enumeración, *f;* (reason) motivo, *m,* causa, *f;* (importance) importancia, *f;* (weight) peso, *m;* (news) noticias, *f pl;* (advantage) provecho, *m,* ventaja, *f.* **by all accounts,** según lo que se oye, según voz pública. **current a.,** cuenta corriente, *f.* **outstanding a.,** cuenta pendiente, *f.* **on a.,** a cuenta. **on a. of,** a causa de, por motivo de. **on no a.,** de ninguna manera. **on that a.,** por lo tanto. **to be of no a.,** ser insignificante; ser de poca importancia; *Inf.* ser la última mona. **to give an a.,** contar, hacer una relación (de). **to give an a. of oneself,** explicarse. **to keep a.,** llevar la cuenta. **to settle accounts,** ajustar cuentas. **to take into a.,** considerar. **to turn to a.,** sacar provecho de. **a. book,** libro de cuentas, *m*
accountability /əˌkauntəˈbɪlɪti/ *n* responsabilidad, *f*
accountable /əˈkauntəbəl/ *a* responsable
accountancy /əˈkauntn̩si/ *n* contabilidad, *f*
accountant /əˈkauntn̩t/ *n* contador, *m.* **chartered a.,** contador autorizado, *m.* **accountant's office,** contaduría, *f*
accouterment /əˈkutərmənt/ *n* atavío, *m;* equipo, *m*
accredit /əˈkrɛdɪt/ *vt* acreditar
accretion /əˈkriʃən/ *n* acrecentamiento, aumento, *m;* *Law.* accesión, *f*
accrue /əˈkru/ *vi* resultar (de), proceder (de); originarse (en); aumentar
accumulate /əˈkyumyəˌleit/ *vt* acumular; amontonar, atesorar. —*vi* acumularse; aumentarse, crecer
accumulation /əˌkyumyəˈleiʃən/ *n* acumulación, *f;* amontonamiento, *m*
accumulative /əˈkyumyəˌleitɪv/ *a* acumulador; adquisitivo, ahorrador
accumulator /əˈkyumyəˌleitər/ *n Elec.* acumulador, *m*
accuracy /ˈækyərəsi/ *n* exactitud, corrección
accurate /ˈækyərɪt/ *a* exacto, correcto, fiel; (of persons) exacto, minucioso; (of apparatus) de precisión
accurately /ˈækyərɪtli/ *adv* con exactitud, correctamente; con precisión
accursed /əˈkɜrsɪd, əˈkɜrst/ *a* maldito.
accusation /ˌækyʊˈzeiʃən/ *n* acusación, *f.* **to lodge an a.,** querellarse ante el juez
accusatory /əˈkyuzəˌtɔri/ *a* acusatorio
accuse /əˈkyuz/ *vt* acusar
accused /əˈkyuzd/ *n Law.* acusado (-da)
accuser /əˈkyuzər/ *n* acusador (-ra)
accustom /əˈkʌstəm/ *vt* acostumbrar (a), habituar (a)
accustomed /əˈkʌstəmd/ *a* acostumbrado, usual; general; característico
ace /eis/ *n* as, *m;* *Fig.* pelo, *m.* **to be within an ace of,** estar a dos dedos de
acerbity /əˈsɜrbɪti/ *n* acerbidad, *f;* *Fig.* aspereza, *f;* severidad, *f;* sequedad, *f*
acetate /ˈæsɪˌteit/ *n* acetato, *m*
acetic /əˈsitɪk/ *a* acético
acetylene /əˈsɛtl̩ˌin/ *n* acetileno, *m.* **a. lamp,** lámpara de acetileno, *f*
ache /eik/ *n* dolor, *m;* pena, *f.* —*vi* doler. **My head aches,** Me duele la cabeza, Tengo dolor de cabeza
achievable /əˈtʃivəbəl/ *a* alcanzable, asequible; factible
achieve /əˈtʃiv/ *vt* conseguir, lograr; (reach) alcanzar; (obtain) obtener, ganar
achievement /əˈtʃivmənt/ *n* logro, *m,* realización, *f;* obtención, *f;* (deed) hazaña, *f;* (work) obra, *f;* (success) éxito, *m;* (discovery) descubrimiento, *m;* (victory) victoria, *f*
aching /ˈeikɪŋ/ *n* dolor, *m;* pena, angustia, *f.* —*a* doliente; afligido
achromatic /ˌeikrəˈmætɪk/ *a* acromático
achromic /eiˈkroumɪk/ *a* acrómico
acid /ˈæsɪd/ *a* and *n* ácido, *m.* **fatty a.,** ácido graso, *m*
acidify /əˈsɪdəˌfai/ *vt* acidificar
acidity /əˈsɪdɪti/ *n* acidez, *f*
acidosis /ˌæsɪˈdousɪs/ *n Med.* acidismo, *m*
acidulous /əˈsɪdʒələs/ *a* acídulo
acknowledge /ækˈnɒlɪdʒ/ *vt* reconocer; confesar; (reply to) contestar a; (appreciate) agradecer. **to a. receipt,** *Com.* acusar recibo
acknowledgment /ækˈnɒlɪdʒmənt/ *n* reconocimiento, *m;* confesión, *f;* (appreciation) agradecimiento, *m;* (reward) recompensa, *f;* (of a letter) acuse de recibo, *m*
acme /ˈækmi/ *n* cumbre, *f;* *Fig.* auge, apogeo, *m*
acne /ˈækni/ *n* acné, *m*
acolyte /ˈækəˌlait/ *n* acólito, monacillo (male) *m,* acólita, monacilla *f,* (female)
acorn /ˈeikɔrn/ *n* bellota, *f.* **a. cup,** capullo de bellota, *m.* **a.-shaped,** en forma de bellota, abellotado
acoustic /əˈkustɪk/ *a* acústico
acoustics /əˈkustɪks/ *n pl* acústica, *f*
acquaint /əˈkweint/ *vt* dar a conocer, comunicar, informar (de), dar parte (de); familiarizar (con). **to be acquainted with,** conocer; saber. **to make oneself acquainted with,** familiarizarse con; entablar amistad con
acquaintance /əˈkweintn̩s/ *n* conocimiento, *m;* (per-

son) conocido (-da); *pl* **acquaintances,** amistades, *f pl.* **to make their a.,** conocer (a), llegar a conocer (a)
acquiesce /ˌækwiˈɛs/ *vi* asentir (en), consentir (a)
acquiescence /ˌækwiˈɛsəns/ *n* acquiescencia, *f,* consentimiento, *m*
acquiescent /ˌækwiˈɛsənt/ *a* conforme; resignado
acquire /əˈkwaiᵊr/ *vt* adquirir, obtener; (diseases, habits) contraer; ganar; (learn) aprender
Acquired Immune Deficiency Syndrome /əˈkwaiᵊrd/ *n* el síndrome de Inmunodeficiencia Adquirida, *m*
acquirement /əˈkwaiᵊrmənt/ *n* adquisición, *f;* (learning) conocimiento, *m;* (talent) talento, *m*
acquirer /əˈkwaiᵊrər/ *n* adquisidor (-ra)
acquisition /ˌækwəˈzɪʃən/ *n* adquisición, *f*
acquisitive /əˈkwɪzɪtɪv/ *a* adquisitivo
acquit /əˈkwɪt/ *vt* (a debt) pagar; exonerar; *Law.* absolver; (a duty) cumplir. **to a. oneself well** (**badly**), portarse bien (mal); salir bien (mal)
acquittal /əˈkwɪtl̩/ *n* (of a debt) pago, *m; Law.* absolución, *f;* (of a duty) cumplimiento, *m*
acquittance /əˈkwɪtn̩s/ *n* descargo, *m;* quitanza, *f*
acre /ˈeikər/ *n* (measure) acre, *m; pl* **acres,** terrenos, campos, *m pl*
acreage /ˈeikərɪdʒ/ *n* acres, *m pl*
acrid /ˈækrɪd/ *a* acre
acrimonious /ˌækrəˈmouniəs/ *a* acrimonioso, áspero; mordaz, sarcástico
acrimony /ˈækrəˌmouni/ *n* acrimonia, acritud, *f;* sarcasmo, *m*
acrobat /ˈækrəˌbæt/ *n* acróbata, *mf*
acrobatic /ˌækrəˈbætɪk/ *a* acrobático
acrobatics /ˌækrəˈbætɪks/ *n pl* acrobacia, *f*
acronym /ˈækrənɪm/ *n* sigla, *f*
acropolis /əˈkrɒpəlɪs/ *n* acrópolis, *f*
across /əˈkrɔs/ *adv* a través, de través, transversalmente; (on the other side) al otro lado; de una parte a otra; (of the arms, etc.) cruzados, *m pl.* —*prep* a través de; al otro lado de; (upon) sobre; por. **He went a. the road,** Cruzó la calle. **to run a.,** correr por; tropezar con; dar con. **a. country,** a campo travieso. **a. the way,** en frente
acrostic /əˈkrɔstɪk/ *n* (poema) acróstico, *m, a* acróstico
act /ækt/ *n* acción, obra, *f,* hecho, *m;* acto, *m; Law.* ley, *f; Theat.* acto, *m.* **in the act,** en el acto. **in the act (of doing),** en acto de (hacer algo). **in the very act,** en flagrante. **the Acts of the Apostles,** los Actos de los Apóstoles. **act of God,** fuerza mayor, *f.* **act of indemnity,** bill de indemnidad, *m*
act /ækt/ *vt* (a play) representar, hacer; (a part) desempeñar, hacer (un papel); (pretend) simular, fingir. —*vi* obrar, actuar; (behave) portarse, conducirse; (function) funcionar; producir su efecto; (feign) fingir; (as a profession) ser actor. **to act as,** hacer de; cumplir las funciones de. **to act as a second,** (in a duel) apadrinar. **to act for,** representar; ser el representante de. **to act upon,** obrar sobre; afectar; influir en
acting /ˈæktɪŋ/ *n* (of a play) representación (de una comedia), *f;* (of an actor) interpretación (de un papel), *f;* (as a hobby) el hacer comedia; (dramatic art) arte dramática, *f.* —*a* interino, suplente; comanditario. **He is a. captain,** Está de capitán. **a. partner,** socio (-ia) comanditario (-ia)
action /ˈækʃən/ *n* acción, *f;* función, *f;* operación, *f;* (movement) movimiento, *m;* (effect) efecto, *m;* influencia, *f; Law.* proceso, *m; Mil.* batalla, acción, *f; Lit.* acción, *f.* **in a.,** en actividad; en operación; *Mil.* en el campo de batalla. **man of a.,** hombre de acción, *m.* **to be killed in a.,** morir en el campo de batalla. **to bring an a. against,** pedir en juicio, entablar un pleito contra. **to put into a.,** hacer funcionar; introducir. **to take a.,** tomar medidas (para). **to take a. against,** prevenirse contra; *Law.* proceder contra
actionable /ˈækʃənəbəl/ *a* procesable, punible
active /ˈæktɪv/ *a* activo; ágil; diligente; *Mil.* vivo; enérgico; *Gram.* activo. **to make a.,** activar, estimular
activity /ækˈtɪvɪti/ *n* actividad, *f*
actor /ˈæktər/ *n* actor, *m;* (in comedy) comediante, *m*
actress /ˈæktrɪs/ *n* actriz, *f;* (in comedy) comediante, *f*
actual /ˈæktʃuəl/ *a* actual, existente; real, verdadero
actuality /ˌæktʃuˈælɪti/ *n* realidad, *f*
actually /ˈæktʃuəli/ *adv* en efecto, realmente, en realidad
actuary /ˈæktʃuˌɛri/ *n* actuario de seguros, *m*
actuate /ˈæktʃuˌeit/ *vt* mover, animar, excitar
acumen /əˈkyumən/ *n* cacumen, *m,* agudeza, sagacidad, *f*
acute /əˈkyut/ *a* agudo; (shrewd) perspicaz; (of a situation) crítico. **a. accent,** acento agudo, *m.* **a.-angled,** acutángulo
acutely /əˈkyutli/ *adv* agudamente; (deeply) profundamente
acuteness /əˈkyutnɪs/ *n* agudeza, *f;* (shrewdness) perspicacia, penetración, *f*
ad /æd/ *n* anuncio, *m.* See **advertisement**
adage /ˈædɪdʒ/ *n* refrán, proverbio, decir, *m*
adagio /əˈdɑdʒou/ *n* adagio, *m*
Adam /ˈædəm/ *n* Adán, *m.* **Adam's apple,** nuez de la garganta, *f*
adamant /ˈædəmənt/ *a* firme, duro, inexorable
adamantine /ˌædəˈmæntin/ *a* adamantino
adapt /əˈdæpt/ *vt* adaptar; ajustar, acomodar; aplicar; (a play, etc.) refundir, arreglar; *Mus.* arreglar
adaptability /əˌdæptəˈbɪlɪti/ *n* adaptabilidad, *f*
adaptable /əˈdæptəbəl/ *a* adaptable
adaptation /ˌædəpˈteiʃən/ *n* adaptación, *f;* (of a play, etc.) refundición, *f;* (*Mus.* etc.) arreglo, *m*
adapter /əˈdæptər/ *n* (of a play, etc.) refundidor (-ra); *Elec.* enchufe de reducción, *m*
add /æd/ *vt* añadir; juntar; (up) sumar. **add insult to injury,** al mojado echarle agua, añadir a una ofensa otra mayor. **to add to,** añadir a; (increase) aumentar, acrecentar. **to add up,** sumar. **to add up to,** subir a; (mean) querer decir.
adder /ˈædər/ *n* víbora, serpiente, *f*
addict /ˈædɪkt/ *n* adicto (-ta).
addicted /əˈdɪktɪd/ *a* aficionado (a), amigo (de), dado (a); adicto (a)
addiction /əˈdɪkʃən/ *n* afición, propensión, *f;* adicción, *f*
addition /əˈdɪʃən/ *n* añadidura, *f; Math.* adición, suma, *f.* **in a.** (**to**), además (de), también
additional /əˈdɪʃənl̩/ *a* adicional
addled /ˈædl̩d/ *a* huero, podrido; *Fig.* confuso
address /*n* əˈdrɛs, ˈædrɛs; *v* əˈdrɛs/ *n* (on a letter) sobrescrito, *m;* (of a person) dirección, *f,* señas, *f pl;* (speech) discurso, *m;* (petition) memorial, *m,* petición, *f;* (dedication) dedicatoria, *f;* (invocation) invocación, *f;* (deportment) presencia, *f;* (tact) diplomacia, habilidad, *f; pl* **addresses,** corte, *f.* —*vt* (a ball) golpear; (a letter) dirigir, poner el sobrescrito a; (words, prayers) dirigir (a); hablar, hacer un discurso. **to a. oneself to a task,** dedicarse a (or entregarse a or emprender) una tarea. **to deliver an a.,** pronunciar un discurso. **to pay one's addresses to,** cortejar, hacer la corte (a), galantear
addressee /ˌædrɛˈsi/ *n* destinatario (-ia)
adduce /əˈdus/ *vt* aducir, alegar; aportar
Aden /ˈɑdn̩/ Adén *m*
adenoids /ˈædn̩ˌɔidz/ *n pl* amígdalas, *f pl*
adept /*a* əˈdɛpt; *n* ˈædɛpt/ *a* adepto, versado, consumado. —*n* adepto, *m*
adequacy /ˈædɪkwəsi/ *n* adecuación, *f;* suficiencia, *f;* competencia, *f*
adequate /ˈædɪkwɪt/ *a* adecuado; proporcionado; suficiente; competente; a la altura (de)
adequately /ˈædɪkwɪtli/ *adv* adecuadamente
adhere /ædˈhɪər/ *vi* adherirse; pegarse; ser fiel (a); persistir (en)
adherence /ædˈhɪərəns/ *n Fig.* adhesión, *f*
adherent /ædˈhɪərənt/ *n* partidario (-ia)
adhesion /ædˈhiʒən/ *n* adherencia, *f;* (to a party, etc.) adhesión, *f*
adhesive /ædˈhisɪv/ *a* adhesivo; (sticky) pegajoso. **a. tape,** esparadrapo, *m; Elec.* cinta aisladora adherente, *f*
adipose /ˈædəˌpous/ *a* adiposo
adjacent /əˈdʒeisənt/ *a* próximo, contiguo, adyacente, vecino
adjective /ˈædʒɪktɪv/ *n* adjetivo, *m*

adjoin /ə'dʒɔin/ *vt* estar contiguo a, lindar con; juntar. —*vi* colindar

adjoining /ə'dʒɔinɪŋ/ *a* vecino, de al lado, adyacente; cercano

adjourn /ə'dʒɜrn/ *vt* aplazar, diferir; (a meeting, etc.) suspender, levantar. —*vi* retirarse. **The debate was adjourned,** Se suspendió el debate. **to a. a meeting,** levantar la sesión

adjournment /ə'dʒɜrnmənt/ *n* aplazamiento, *m;* (of a meeting) suspensión (de la sesión), *f*

adjudicate /ə'dʒudɪˌkeit/ *vt* adjudicar; *Law.* declarar; juzgar. —*vi* ejercer las funciones del juez; fallar, dictar sentencia

adjudication /əˌdʒudɪ'keiʃən/ *n* adjudicación, *f; Law.* fallo, *m,* sentencia, *f;* (of bankruptcy) declaración (de quiebra), *f;* concesión, *f,* otorgamiento, *m*

adjudicator /ə'dʒudɪˌkeitər/ *n* adjudicador (-ra)

adjunct /'ædʒʌŋkt/ *n* atributo, *m;* accesorio, *m;* adjunto, *m; Gram.* adjunto, *m*

adjure /ə'dʒʊr/ *vt* conjurar; rogar encarecidamente

adjust /ə'dʒʌst/ *vt* ajustar; regular; arreglar; (correct) corregir; adaptar

adjustable /ə'dʒʌstəbəl/ *a* ajustable; regulable; desmontable; de quita y pon

adjustment /ə'dʒʌstmənt/ *n* ajuste, *m;* regulación, *f;* arreglo, *m;* (correction) corrección, *f;* adaptación, *f; Com.* prorrateo, *m*

adjutant /'ædʒətənt/ *n Mil.* ayudante, *m*

administer /æd'mɪnəstər/ *vt* administrar; (laws) aplicar; (blows, etc.) dar; (an office) ejercer; (govern) regir, gobernar; (provide) suministrar; (an oath) tomar; (justice) hacer; (the sacraments) administrar; (with to) contribuir a. **to a. an oath,** tomar juramento (a)

administration /ædˌmɪnə'streiʃən/ *n* administración, *f;* (government) gobierno, *m;* dirección, *f;* (of laws) aplicación, *f;* distribución, *f*

administrative /æd'mɪnəˌstreitɪv/ *a* administrativo; gubernativo

administrator /æd'mɪnəˌstreitər/ *n* administrador, *m*

administratrix /ædˌmɪnə'streitrɪks/ *n* administradora, *f*

admirable /'ædmərəbəl/ *a* admirable

admirably /'ædmərəbli/ *adv* admirablemente

admiral /'ædmərəl/ *n* almirante, *m.* **A. of the Fleet,** almirante supremo, *m.* **admiral's ship,** capitana, *f*

admiration /ˌædmə'reiʃən/ *n* admiración, *f*

admire /æd'maiᵊr/ *vt* sentir admiración por; (love) amar; (like) gustar; (respect) respetar

admirer /æd'maiᵊrər/ *n* admirador (-ra); (amateur) aficionado (-da), apasionado (-da); (partisan) satélite, *m;* (lover) enamorado, amante, *m*

admiring /æd'maiərɪŋ/ *a* admirativo, de admiración

admissible /æd'mɪsəbəl/ *a* admisible; aceptable; lícito, permitido

admission /æd'mɪʃən/ *n* admisión, *f;* recepción, *f;* entrada, *f;* confesión, *f,* reconocimiento, *m.* **No a.!** Entrada prohibida. **right of a.,** derecho de entrada, *m.* **A. free,** Entrada libre. **a. ticket,** entrada, *f*

admit /æd'mɪt/ *vt* admitir; recibir; dejar entrar; hacer entrar, introducir; (hold) contener; (concede) conceder; (acknowledge) reconocer, confesar. **to a. of,** permitir; sufrir

admittance /æd'mɪtn̩s/ *n* admisión, *f;* entrada, *f.* **No a.!** Prohibida la entrada. **to gain a.,** lograr entrar

admittedly /æd'mɪtɪdli/ *adv* según opinión general; sin duda

admonish /æd'mɒnɪʃ/ *vt* (advise) aconsejar; amonestar, advertir; (reprimand) reprender

admonition /ˌædmə'nɪʃən/ *n* amonestación, *f;* advertencia, *f;* admonición, *f*

admonitory /æd'mɒnɪˌtɔri/ *a* amonestador

ad nauseam /'æd nɔziəm/ *adv* hasta la saciedad

ado /ə'du/ *n* (noise) ruido, *m;* (trouble) trabajo, *m,* dificultad, *f;* (fuss) barahúnda, *f.* **much ado about nothing,** mucho ruido y pocas nueces, nada entre dos platos. **without more ado,** sin más ni más

adolescence /ˌædl̩'ɛsəns/ *n* adolescencia, *f*

adolescent /ˌædl̩'ɛsənt/ *a* and *n* adolescente, *mf*

adopt /ə'dɒpt/ *vt* adoptar

adopted /ə'dɒptɪd/ *a* adoptivo

adoption /ə'dɒpʃən/ *n* adopción, *f;* (choice) elección, *f*

adoptive /ə'dɒptɪv/ *a* adoptivo

adorable /ə'dɔrəbəl/ *a* adorable

adoration /ˌædə'reiʃən/ *n* adoración, *f.* **A. of the Magi,** Adoración de los Reyes, *f*

adore /ə'dɔr/ *vt* adorar

adorer /ə'dɔrər/ *n* adorador (-ra); amante, *m*

adoringly /ə'dɔrɪŋli/ *adv* con adoración

adorn /ə'dɔrn/ *vt* adornar, embellecer; (*Fig.* of persons) adornar con su presencia

adornment /ə'dɔrnmənt/ *n* adorno, *m;* ornamento, *m;* embellecimiento, *m*

adrenalin /ə'drɛnl̩ɪn/ *n* adrenalina, *f*

Adriatic, the /ˌeidri'ætɪk/ el (Mar) Adriático, *m*

adrift /ə'drɪft/ *a* and *adv* a merced de las olas; a la ventura. **to turn a.,** *Inf.* poner de patitas en la calle

adroit /ə'drɔit/ *a* hábil

adulate /'ædʒəˌleit/ *vt* adular

adulation /ˌædʒə'leiʃən/ *n* adulación, *f*

adulatory /'ædʒələˌtɔri/ *a* adulador

adult /ə'dʌlt/ *a* and *n* adulto (-ta)

adult education *n* educación de los adultos, *f*

adulterate /*v* ə'dʌltəˌreit; *a* ə'dʌltəˌreit; -tərɪt/ *vt* adulterar; falsificar; contaminar. —*a* adulterado; falsificado, impuro

adulteration /əˌdʌltə'reiʃən/ *n* adulteración, *f;* falsificación, *f;* impureza, *f;* contaminación, *f*

adulterer /ə'dʌltərər/ *n* adúltero, *m*

adulteress /ə'dʌltərɪs/ *n* adúltera, *f*

adulterous /ə'dʌltərəs/ *a* adúltero

adultery /ə'dʌltəri/ *n* adulterio, *m.* **to commit a.,** cometer adulterio, adulterar

advance /æd'væns/ *n* avance, *m;* (progress) progreso, adelantamiento, *m;* (improvement) mejora, *f;* (of shares) alza, *f;* (of price) subida, *f;* (loan) préstamo, *m;* (in rank) ascenso, *m; pl* **advances,** (overtures) avances, *m pl;* (proposals) propuestas, *f pl;* (of love) requerimientos amorosos, *m pl.* **in a.,** de antemano, con anticipación, con tiempo, previamente; (of money) por adelantado. **a. guard,** *Mil.* avanzada, *f.* **a. payment,** anticipo, *m,* paga por adelantado, *f*

advance /æd'væns/ *vt* avanzar; (suggest) sugerir, proponer; (encourage) fomentar; (a person) ascender; (improve) mejorar; (of events, dates) adelantar; (of prices, stocks) hacer subir; (money) anticipar; (of steps) tomar. —*vi* avanzar; (progress) progresar; (in rank, studies, etc.) adelantar; (of prices) subir

advanced /æd'vænst/ *a* avanzado; (developed) desarrollado; (mentally, of children) precoz; (course) superior. **a. research,** investigaciones superiores. **a. standing,** equivalencias, *f pl.* **a. views,** ideas avanzadas, *f pl*

advancement /æd'vænsmənt/ *n* adelantamiento, *m;* progreso, *m;* (encouragement) fomento, *m;* (in employment) promoción, *f;* prosperidad, *f*

advancing /æd'vænsɪŋ/ *a* que avanza; (of years) que pasan

advantage /æd'væntɪdʒ/ *n* ventaja, *f;* superioridad, *f;* (benefit) provecho, beneficio, *m;* interés, *m;* ocasión favorable, oportunidad, *f;* (tennis) ventaja, *f.* **to have the a. of,** tener la ventaja de. **to show to a.,** embellecer, realzar; aumentar la belleza (etc.) de. **to take a. of,** sacar ventaja de, aprovecharse de; (deceive) engañar. **to take a. of the slightest pretext,** asirse de un cabello

advantageous /ˌædvən'teidʒəs/ *a* ventajoso, provechoso. **to be a.,** ser de provecho

advent /'ædvɛnt/ *n* advenimiento, *m,* llegada, *f; Eccl.* Adviento, *m*

adventitious /ˌædvən'tɪʃəs/ *a* adventicio (all uses)

adventure /æd'vɛntʃər/ *n* aventura, *f;* riesgo, *m;* (chance) casualidad, *f; Com.* especulación, *f, vt* aventurar, arriesgar. —*vi* arriesgarse, osar

adventurer /æd'vɛntʃərər/ *n* aventurero, *m;* (one living by his wits) caballero de industria, *m;* (in commerce) especulador, *m*

adventuresome /æd'vɛntʃərsəm/ *a* de aventura

adventuress /æd'vɛntʃərɪs/ *n* aventurera, *f*

adventurous /æd'vɛntʃərəs/ *a* aventurero; osado, audaz; (dangerous) peligroso, arriesgado

adverb /'ædvɜrb/ *n* adverbio, *m*

adversary /'ædvərˌsɛri/ *n* adversario (-ia)

adverse /æd'vɜrs/ *a* adverso; hostil (a); malo; desfavorable; (opposite) opuesto
adversity /æd'vɜrsɪti/ *n* adversidad, *f*
advertise /'ædvər,taiz/ *vt* anunciar. —*vi* poner un anuncio; (oneself) llamar la atención
advertisement /,ædvər'taizmənt, æd'vɜrtɪsmənt/ *n* anuncio, *m;* (poster) cartel, *m;* (to attract attention) reclamo, *m.* **to put an a. in the paper,** poner un anuncio en el periódico. **a. hoarding,** cartelera, *f*
advertiser /'ædvər,taizər/ *n* anunciante, *mf*
advertising /'ædvər,taizɪŋ/ *n* anuncios, *m pl;* publicidad, propaganda, *f;* medios publicitarios, *m pl*
advice /æd'vais/ *n* consejo, *m;* (warning) advertencia, amonestación, *f;* (news) noticia, *f,* aviso, *m; Com.* comunicación, *f;* (belief) parecer, *m,* opinión, *f.* **piece of a.,** consejo, *m.* **to follow the a. of,** seguir los consejos de. **to give a.,** dar consejos
advisability /æd,vaizə'bɪlɪti/ *n* conveniencia, *f;* prudencia, *f*
advisable /æd'vaizəbəl/ *a* conveniente, aconsejable; prudente
advise /æd'vaiz/ *vt* aconsejar; (inform) avisar, informar
advised /æd'vaizd/ *a* avisado; premeditado. **ill-a.,** mal aconsejado; imprudente. **well-a.,** bien aconsejado; prudente
adviser /æd'vaizər/ *n* consejero (-ra)
advisory /æd'vaizəri/ *a* asesor, consultivo, consultativo
advocacy /'ædvəkəsi/ *n* defensa, *f;* apología, *f;* abogacía, intercesión, *f*
advocate /*n* 'ædvəkɪt; *v* -,keit/ *n Law.* abogado (-da); defensor (-ra); (champion) campeón, *m.* —*vt* abogar, defender; sostener, apoyar; recomendar
adze /ædz/ *n* azuela, *f*
Aegean, the /ə'dʒiən/ el (Mar) Egeo, *m*
aegis /'idʒɪs/ *n* égida, *f;* protección, *f*
aerated /'ɛə,reitɪd/ *a* aerado; (of lemonade, etc.) gaseoso. **a. waters,** aguas gaseosas, *f pl*
aeration /,ɛə'reiʃən/ *n* aeración, *f*
aerial /'ɛəriəl/ *a* aéreo, de aire; etéreo; fantástico. —*n* (radio) antena, *f.* **indoor a.,** antena interior, *f*
aerobics /ɛə'roubɪks/ *n* aerobismo *m*
aerodynamics /,ɛəroudai'næmɪks/ *n* aerodinámica, *f*
aeronaut /'ɛərə,nɔt/ *n* aeronauta, *mf*
aeronautical /,ɛərə'nɔtɪkəl/ *a* aeronáutico
aeronautics /,ɛərə'nɔtɪks/ *n* aeronáutica, *f*
afar /ə'fɑr/ *adv* a lo lejos, en la distancia. **from a.,** desde lejos
affability /,æfə'bɪlɪti/ *n* afabilidad, condescendencia, urbanidad, *f*
affable /'æfəbəl/ *a* afable, condescendiente
affably /'æfəbli/ *adv* afablemente
affair /ə'fɛər/ *n* asunto, *m,* cosa, *f;* cuestión, *f;* (business) negocio, *m;* (*Fam.* applied to a machine, carriage, etc.) artefacto, *m;* (of the heart) amorío, *m.* **a. of honour,** lance de honor, *m*
affect /ə'fɛkt/ *vt* afectar; influir; *Med.* atacar; (move) impresionar, conmover; enternecer; (harm) perjudicar; (frequent) frecuentar; (like) gustar de; (love) amar; (wear) vestir; (use) gastar, usar; (feign) aparentar; (boast) hacer alarde de
affectation /,æfɛk'teiʃən/ *n* afectación, *f*
affected /ə'fɛktɪd/ *a* afectado; influido; *Med.* atacado; (moved) conmovido, impresionado; enternecido; (inclined) dispuesto, inclinado; (artificial) artificioso; amanerado, afectado; (of style) rebuscado, artificial
affecting /ə'fɛktɪŋ/ *a* conmovedor, emocionante
affection /ə'fɛkʃən/ *n* afecto, cariño, *m;* amor, *m;* apego, *m;* simpatía, *f;* (emotion) emoción, *f,* sentimiento, *m; Med.* afección, enfermedad, *f*
affectionate /ə'fɛkʃənɪt/ *a* afectuoso, cariñoso; mimoso; (tender) tierno; expresivo
affectionately /ə'fɛkʃənɪtli/ *adv* afectuosamente. **Yours a.,** tu cariñoso..., tu..., que te quiere
affective /'æfɛktɪv/ *a* afectivo
affidavit /,æfɪ'deivɪt/ *n* declaración jurada, declaración jurídica *f,* atestiguación, *f*
affiliate /ə'fɪli,eit/ *vt* afiliar; adoptar; *Law.* imputar; *Law.* legitimar
affiliation /ə,fɪli'eiʃən/ *n* afiliación, *f;* adopción, *f;* legitimación de un hijo, *f*
affinity /ə'fɪnɪti/ *n* afinidad, *f*
affirm /ə'fɜrm/ *vt* afirmar, aseverar, declarar; confirmar. —*vi Law.* declarar ante un juez
affirmation /,æfər'meiʃən/ *n* afirmación, aserción, *f;* confirmación, *f; Law.* declaración, deposición, *f*
affirmative /ə'fɜrmətɪv/ *a* afirmativo. —*n* afirmativa, *f*
affix /*v* ə'fɪks; *n* 'æfɪks/ *vt* fijar; pegar; añadir; (seal, one's signature) poner. —*n Gram.* afijo, *m*
afflict /ə'flɪkt/ *vt* afligir, atormentar, aquejar
affliction /ə'flɪkʃən/ *n* aflicción, *f;* tribulación, pesadumbre, *f;* calamidad, *f;* miseria, *f;* (ailment) achaque, *m*
affluence /'æfluəns/ *n* afluencia, *f;* abundancia, *f;* riqueza, *f;* opulencia, *f*
affluent /'æfluənt/ *a* abundante; rico; opulento
afflux /'æflʌks/ *n* afluencia, *f; Med.* aflujo, *m*
afford /ə'fɔrd/ *vt* dar, proporcionar; producir; ofrecer; (bear) soportar; poder con; (financially) tener medios para; permitirse el lujo de; (be able) poder. **I could not a. to pay so much,** No puedo (podía) pagar tanto
afforest /ə'fɔrɪst/ *vt* convertir en bosque
afforestation /ə,fɔrə'steiʃən/ *n* conversión en bosque, *f;* plantación de un bosque, *f*
affray /ə'frei/ *n* riña, refriega, *f*
affront /ə'frʌnt/ *n* afrenta, *f,* insulto, agravio, *m.* —*vt* insultar, ultrajar, afrentar; (offend) ofender
Afghan /'æfgæn/ *a* and *n* afgano (-na)
Afghanistan /æf'gænə,stæn/ Afganistán, *m*
afield /ə'fild/ *adv* en el campo; lejos. **to go far a.,** ir muy lejos
afire /ə'faiər/ *adv* en fuego, en llamas; *Fig.* ardiendo
aflame /ə'fleim/ *adv* en llamas; *Fig.* encendido
afloat /ə'flout/ *adv* a flote; *Naut.* a bordo; (solvent) solvente; en circulación; (floating) flotante; (swamped) inundado; (in full swing) en marcha, en movimiento
afoot /ə'fʊt/ *adv* a pie; en marcha, en movimiento; en preparación. **to set a.,** iniciar, poner en marcha
aforementioned /ə'fɔr,mɛnʃənd/ *a* antedicho, ya mencionado
aforesaid /ə'fɔr,sɛd/ *a* consabido, dicho, susodicho
afraid /ə'freid/ *a* espantado; temeroso, miedoso. **I'm a. that...,** Me temo que.... **to be a.,** tener miedo. **to make a.,** dar miedo (a)
afresh /ə'frɛʃ/ *adv* de nuevo, otra vez
African /'æfrɪkən/ *a* and *n* africano (-na)
aft /æft/ *adv* en popa; a popa. **fore and aft,** de proa a popa
after /'æftər/ *prep* (of place) detrás de; (of time) después de; (behind) en pos de; (following) tras; (in spite of) a pesar de; (in consequence of) después de, a consecuencia de; (in accordance with) según; (in the style of) al estilo de, en imitación de. —*adv* (later) después, más tarde; (subsequently) después (que); (when) cuando. —*a* futuro, venidero. **day a. day,** día tras día. **on the day a.,** al día siguiente. **soon a.,** poco después. **to look a.,** cuidar de. **to go a.,** ir a buscar; seguir. **the day a. tomorrow,** pasado mañana. **What are you a.?** ¿Qué buscas? **a. all,** después de todo. **a. the manner of,** a la moda de, según la moda de; al estilo de. **a.-dinner conversation,** conversación de sobremesa, *f.* **a. glow,** resplandor crepuscular, reflejo del sol poniente en el cielo, *m.* **a. life,** vida futura, *f.* **a. pains,** dolores de sobreparto, *m pl.* **a. taste,** dejo, resabio, *m*
afterbirth /'æftər,bɜrθ/ *n* placenta, *f*
aftermath /'æftər,mæθ/ *n* consecuencias, *f pl,* resultado, *m*
afternoon /,æftər'nun/ *n* tarde, *f.* **Good a.!** ¡Buenas tardes! **a. nap,** siesta, *f.* **a. tea,** el té de las cinco
afterthought /'æftər,θɔt/ *n* reflexión tardía, *f;* segunda intención, *f.* **to have an a.,** pensar en segundo lugar
afterwards /'æftərwərdz/ *adv* después; más tarde
again /ə'gɛn/ *adv* (once more) otra vez, de neuvo; por segunda vez, dos veces; (on the other hand) por otra parte; (moreover) además; (likewise) también; (returned) de vuelta. Sometimes translated by prefix **re** in verbs. **as much a.,** otro tanto. **never a.,** nunca más. **not a.,** no más. **now and a.,** de vez en cuando.

to do a., volver a hacer, hacer de nuevo. **a. and a.,** repetidas veces
against /ə'gɛnst/ *prep* (facing) enfrente de; contra; (in preparation for) para; (contrary to) contrario a; (opposed to) opuesto a; (near) cerca de. **to be a.,** oponer; estar enfrente de. **a. the grain,** a contrapelo
agate /'ægɪt/ *n* ágata, *f;* heliotropo, *m*
age /eidʒ/ *n* edad, *f;* (generation) generación, *f;* (epoch) siglo, período, *m;* época, *f;* (old age) vejez, *f;* (majority) mayoría de edad, *f, vi* envejecer. **at any age,** a cualquier edad. **the golden age,** la edad de oro; (in literature, etc.) el siglo de oro. **from age to age,** por los siglos de los siglos. **to be of age,** ser mayor de edad. **to be under age,** ser menor de edad. **to come of age,** llegar a la mayoría de edad. **She is six years of age,** Ella tiene seis años. **age-old,** secular
aged /eidʒd; 'eidʒɪd/ *a* de la edad de; (old) anciano, viejo. **a girl a. four,** una niña de cuatro años
ageless /'eidʒlɪs/ *a* siempre joven; eterno
agency /'eidʒənsi/ *n* órgano, *m,* fuerza, *f;* acción, *f;* influencia, *f;* intervención, *f;* mediación, *f; Com.* agencia, *f.* **through the a. of,** por la mediación (or influencia) de
agenda /ə'dʒɛndə/ *n* agenda, *f*
agent /'eidʒənt/ *n* agente, *m; Com.* representante, *mf; Law.* apoderado (-da). **business a.,** agente de negocios, *m*
agglomerate /ə'glɒmə,reit/ *vt* and *vi* aglomerar(se)
agglomeration /ə,glɒmə'reiʃən/ *n* aglomeración, *f*
agglutinate /ə'glutn̩,eit/ *vt* and *vi* aglutinar(se)
aggrandize /ə'grændaiz/ *vt* engrandecer
aggrandizement /ə'grændɪzmənt/ *n* engrandecimiento, *m*
aggravate /'ægrə,veit/ *vt* agravar, hacer peor; intensificar; (annoy) irritar, exasperar
aggravating /'ægrə,veitɪŋ/ *a* agravante, agravador; (tiresome) molesto; (annoying) irritante. **a. circumstance,** circunstancia agravante, *f*
aggravation /,ægrə'veiʃən/ *n* agravación, *f,* intensificación, *f;* (annoyance)irritación, *f*
aggregate /'ægrɪgɪt, -,geit/ *a* total. —*n* agregado, conjunto, *m.* **in the a.,** en conjunto
aggression /ə'grɛʃən/ *n* agresión, *f*
aggressive /ə'grɛsɪv/ *a* agresivo
aggressiveness /ə'grɛsɪvnɪs/ *n* carácter agresivo, *m,* belicosidad, *f*
aggressor /ə'grɛsər/ *a* and *n* agresor (-ra)
aggrieved /ə'grivd/ *a* afligido; ofendido; lastimero
aghast /ə'gæst/ *a* horrorizado, espantado; (amazed) estupefacto
agile /'ædʒəl/ *a* ágil; ligero; vivo
agility /æ'dʒɪlɪti/ *n* agilidad, *f;* ligereza, *f*
agitate /'ædʒɪ,teit/ *vt* agitar; excitar; inquietar, perturbar; discutir. **to a. for,** luchar por; excitar la opinión pública en favor de
agitating /'ædʒɪ,teitɪŋ/ *a* agitador
agitation /,ædʒɪ'teiʃən/ *n* agitación, *f;* perturbación, *f;* discusión, *f*
agitator /'ædʒɪ,teitər/ *n* agitador (-ra); (apparatus) agitador, *m*
aglow /ə'glou/ *a* and *adv* brillante, fulgente; encendido
agnostic /æg'nɒstɪk/ *a* and *n* agnóstico (-ca)
agnosticism /æg'nɒstə,sɪzəm/ *n* agnosticismo, *m*
ago /ə'gou/ *adv* hace. **a short while ago,** hace poco. **How long ago?** ¿Cuánto tiempo hace? **long ago,** hace mucho. **many years ago,** hace muchos años. **I last saw him ten years ago,** La última vez que le vi fue hace diez años
agog /ə'gɒg/ *a* agitado; ansioso; excitado; impaciente; curioso. —*adv* con agitación; con ansia; con curiosidad
agonize /'ægə,naiz/ *vt* atormentar. —*vi* sufrir intensamente; retorcerse de dolor
agonizing /'ægə,naizɪŋ/ *a* (of pain) intenso, atormentador
agonizingly /'ægə,naizɪŋli/ *adv* dolorosamente
agony /'ægəni/ *n* agonía, *f;* angustia, *f;* paroxismo, *m.* **a. column,** columna de los suspiros, *f*
agrarian /ə'grɛəriən/ *a* agrario
agree /ə'gri/ *vi* estar de acuerdo. **Do you a. or disagree?** ¿Coincides o discrepas?; convenir (en); acordar; ponerse de acuerdo, entenderse; (suit) sentar bien, probar; (consent) consentir (en); *Gram.* concordar, (get on well) llevarse bien; (correspond) estar conforme (con). **to a. to,** convenir en, consentir en. **to a. with,** estar de acuerdo con, apoyar; dar la razón a; (suit) sentar bien; *Gram.* concordar
agreeable /ə'griəbəl/ *a* agradable; afable, amable; (pleasant) ameno, grato; conforme; dispuesto a (hacer algo); conveniente
agreeableness /ə'griəbəlnɪs/ *n* (of persons) afabilidad, amabilidad, *f;* amenidad, *f;* deleite, *m;* conformidad, *f*
agreeably /ə'griəbli/ *adv* agradablemente; de acuerdo (con), conforme (a)
agreed /ə'grid/ *a* convenido, acordado; (approved) aprobado. —*interj* ¡convenido! ¡de acuerdo!
agreement /ə'grimənt/ *n* acuerdo, *m;* pacto, *m;* acomodamiento, concierto, *m;* contrato, *m; Com.* convenio, *m;* conformidad, *f;* consentimiento, *m; Gram.* concordancia, *f.* **in a.,** conforme. **in a. with,** de acuerdo con; según. **to reach an a.,** ponerse de acuerdo
agricultural /,ægrɪ'kʌltʃərəl/ *a* agrícola. **a. engineer,** ingeniero agrónomo, *m.* **a. laborer,** labriego, *m.* **a. show,** exposición agrícola, *f*
agriculturalist /,ægrɪ'kʌltʃərəlɪst/ *n* agrícola, *mf*
agriculture /'ægrɪ,kʌltʃər/ *n* agricultura, *f*
agronomist /ə'grɒnəmɪst/ *n* agrónomo, *m*
agronomy /ə'grɒnəmi/ *n* agronomía, *f*
aground /ə'graund/ *adv Naut.* varado, encallado. **running a.,** varada, *f.* **to run a.,** varar
ague /'eigyu/ *n* fiebre intermitente, *f; Fig.* escalofrío, *m*
ah! /ɑ/ *interj* ¡ah! ¡ay!
aha! /ɑ'hɑ/ *interj* ¡ajá!
ahead /ə'hɛd/ *adv* delante; enfrente; al frente (de); a la cabeza (de); adelante; hacia delante; *Naut.* por la proa. **Go a.!** ¡Adelante! **It is straight a.,** Está directamente enfrente. **to go straight a.,** ir hacia delante; seguir (haciendo algo)
ahoy! /ə'hɔi/ *interj* ¡ah del barco!
aid /eid/ *n* ayuda, *f;* socorro, auxilio, *m;* subsidio, *m, vt* ayudar; socorrer, auxiliar. **in aid of,** pro, en beneficio de. **first aid,** primera cura, *f.* **first aid post,** puesto de socorro, *m.* **to come or go to the aid of,** acudir en defensa de
aide-de-camp /'eid də 'kæmp/ *n* edecán, *m*
AIDS /eidz/ *n* el SIDA, *m*
ail /eil/ *vt* afligir, doler; pasar. —*vi* estar indispuesto (or enfermo). **What ails you?** *Inf.* ¿Qué te pasa?
ailing /'eilɪŋ/ *a* enfermizo, enclenque, achacoso
ailment /'eilmənt/ *n* enfermedad, *f,* achaque, *m*
aim /eim/ *n* (of firearms) puntería, *f;* (mark) blanco, *m; Fig.* objeto, fin, *m; Fig.* intención, *f,* propósito, *m, vt* (a gun) apuntar; dirigir; (throw) lanzar; (a blow) asestar. —*vi* apuntar (a); (a remark at) decir por; aspirar (a); intentar, proponerse. **Is your remark aimed at me?** ¿Lo dices por mí? **to aim high,** apuntar alto; *Inf.* picar alto. **to miss one's aim,** errar el tiro. **to take aim,** apuntar. **with the aim of,** con objeto de, a fin de
aimless /'eimlɪs/ *a* **aimlessly,** *adv* sin objeto, a la ventura
air /ɛər/ *n* aire, *m,* (all meanings). **by air,** en avión; (of mail) por avión; (of goods) por vía aérea. **in the air,** al aire; al aire libre; (as though flying) en volandas. **in the open air,** al aire libre, al fresco, a la intemperie. **to be on the air,** *Radio.* hablar por radio. **to give oneself airs,** darse tono, tener humos. **to take the air,** tomar el fresco; despegar. **air balloon,** globo aerostático, *m;* (toy) globo, *m.* **air-base,** base aérea, *f.* **air-bed,** colchón de viento, *m.* **air-borne (to become),** levantar el vuelo, despegar. **air-brake,** *Mech.* freno neumático, *m.* **air-chamber,** cámara de aire, *f.* **air chief marshal,** general del ejército del aire, *m.* **air-cock,** válvula de escape de aire, *f.* **air commodore,** general de brigada de aviación, *m.* **air conditioning,** purificación de aire, *f.* **air-cooled,** enfriado por aire. **air crash,** accidente de avicación, *m.* **air cur-**

rent, corriente de aire, *f.* **air-cushion,** almohadilla neumática, *f.* **air-field,** campo de aviación, *m.* **air fleet,** flotilla aérea, *f.* **air force,** fuerza aérea, flota aérea, *f.* **air-gun,** escopeta de viento, *f.* **air-hole,** respiradero, *m.* **air-hostess,** azafata, *f.* **air-lift,** puente aéreo, *m.* **air-liner,** avión de pasajeros, *m.* **airline** linea aérea, aerolínea, *f.* **airmail,** correo aéreo, *m.* **by airmail,** por ayión. **air marshal,** teniente general de aviación, *m.* **air-pocket,** bolsa (or vacío, *m*) de aire, *f.* **air pollution** contaminación atmosférica, *f.* **air pump,** bomba neumática, *f.* **air raid,** bombardeo aéreo, *m.* **air-raid shelter,** refugio antiaéreo, *m.* **air-raid warning,** alarma aérea, *f.* **air-route,** vía aérea, *f.* **air-screw,** hélice de avión, *f.* **air-shaft,** respiradero de mina, *m.* **air shuttle,** puente aéreo, *m.* **air squadron,** escuadrilla aérea, *f.* **air stream,** chorro de aire, *m.* **air taxi,** avión taxi, *m.* **air-tight,** herméticamente cerrado. **air valve,** válvula de aire, *f.* **air vice-marshal,** general de división de aviación, *m*

air /ɛər/ *vt* airear, orear; secar al aire; ventilar; *Fig.* sacar a lucir, emitir; *Fig.* ostentar

aircraft /'ɛər,kræft/ *n* aparato, avión, *m.* **a. barrage,** cortina de fuego de artillería, *f.* **a.-carrier,** portaaviones, *m.* **a. factory,** fábrica de aeroplanos, *f*

airily /'ɛərəli/ *adv* ligeramente, sin preocuparse; alegremente

airiness /'ɛərinɪs/ *n* airosidad, *f;* ventilación, *f;* situación airosa, *f;* (lightness) ligereza, *f;* alegría, *f;* frivolidad, *f*

airing /'ɛərɪŋ/ *n* aireación, *f;* ventilación, *f;* secamiento, *m;* (walk) vuelta, *f,* paseo, *m.* **to take an a.,** dar una vuelta

airless /'ɛərlɪs/ *a* sin aire; falto de ventilación; sofocante

airman /'ɛərmən/ *n* aviador, *m*

airplane /'ɛər,plein/ *n* aeroplano, avión, *m.* **jet-propelled a.,** aeroplano de reacción, *m.* **model a.,** aeroplano en miniatura, *m*

airport /'ɛər,pɔrt/ *n* aeropuerto, *m*

airship /'ɛər,ʃɪp/ *n* aeronave, nave aérea, *f*

airsick /'ɛər,sɪk/ *a* mareado en el aire, mareado

airway /'ɛər,wei/ *n* vía aérea, *f*

airwoman /'ɛər,wʊmən/ *n* aviadora, *f*

airy /'ɛəri/ *a* aéreo; (breezy) airoso; ligero; vaporoso; alegre; (vain) vano; (flippant) frívolo

aisle /ail/ *n* nave lateral, ala, *f*

ajar /ə'dʒɑr/ *a* entreabierto, entornado. **to leave a.,** dejar entreabierto, entornar

akimbo /ə'kɪmbou/ *adv* en jarras. **with arms a.,** con los brazos en jarras

akin /ə'kɪn/ *a* consanguíneo, emparentado; análogo, relacionado; semejante

alabaster /'ælə,bæstər/ *n* alabastro, *m, a* alabastrino

alacrity /ə'lækrɪti/ *n* alacridad, *f*

alarm /ə'lɑrm/ *n* alarma, *f,* toque de alarma, *m;* (tocsin) rebato, *m;* sobresalto, *m,* alarma, *f.* —*vt* alarmar; *Mil.* dar la alarma (a); asustar. **to give the a.,** dar la alarma. **a. bell,** timbre de alarma, *m.* **a. clock,** despertador, *m.* **a. signal,** señal de alarma, *f*

alarming /ə'lɑrmɪŋ/ *a* alarmante

alarmingly /ə'larmɪŋli/ *adv* de un modo alarmante; espantosamente

alarmist /ə'lɑrmɪst/ *n* alarmista, *mf*

alas! /ə'læs/ *interj* ¡ay!

alb /ælb/ *n* alba, *f*

Albanian /æl'beiniən/ *a* and *n* albanés (-esa); (language) albanés, *m*

albatross /'ælbə,trɔs/ *n* albatros, *m*

albeit /ɔl'biɪt/ *conjunc* aunque, si bien; sin embargo

albinism /'ælbə,nɪzəm/ *n* albinismo, *m*

albino /æl'bainou/ *a* albino

album /'ælbəm/ *n* álbum, *m*

albumin /æl'byumən/ *n* albúmina, *f*

alchemist /'ælkəmɪst/ *n* alquimista, *m*

alchemy /'ælkəmi/ *n* alquimia, *f*

alcohol /'ælkə,hɔl/ *n* alcohol, *m.* **industrial a.,** alcohol desnaturalizado, *m.* **wood a.,** alcohol metílico, alcohol de madera, *m*

alcoholic /,ælkə'hɔlɪk/ *a* alcohólico

alcoholism /'ælkəhɔ,lɪzəm/ *n* alcoholismo, *m*

alcove /'ælkouv/ *n* alcoba, *f;* nicho, *m*

alder /'ɔldər/ *n* (tree and wood) aliso, *m*

alderman /'ɔldərmən/ *n* concejal, *m*

ale /eil/ *n* cerveza, *f.* **ale-house,** cervecería, *f*

alert /ə'lɜrt/ *a* alerto; vigilante; despierto; vivo. —*n* sirena, *f.* **to be on the a.,** estar sobre aviso; estar vigilante

alertly /ə'lɜrtli/ *adv* alertamente

alertness /ə'lɜrtnɪs/ *n* vigilancia, *f;* viveza, *f;* prontitud, *f*

Alexandria /,ælɪg'zændriə/ Alejandría, *f*

alga /'ælgə/ *n* alga, *f*

algebra /'ældʒəbrə/ *n* álgebra, *f*

algebraic /,ældʒə'breiɪk/ *a* algebraico

Algeria /æl'dʒɪəriə/ Argelia, *f*

Algerian /æl'dʒɪəriən/ *a* and *n* argelino (-na)

Algiers /æl'dʒɪərz/ Argel, *m*

alias /'eiliəs/ *adv* alias, por otro nombre. —*n* nombre falso, seudónimo, *m*

alibi /'ælə,bai/ *n Law.* coartada, *f.* **to prove an a.,** probar la coartada

alien /'eiliən/ *a* ajeno; (foreign) extranjero; extraño; contrario. —*n* extranjero (-ra). **a. to,** ajeno a; repugnante a. **Aliens Department,** Sección de Extranjeros, *f*

alienable /'eiliənəbəl/ *a* enajenable

alienate /'eiliə,neit/ *vt* alejar, hacer indiferente; (property) enajenar, traspasar

alienation /,eiliə'neiʃən/ *n* desvío, *m;* enajenación, *f;* traspaso, *m;* enajenación mental, *f*

alight /ə'lait/ *vi* apearse (de), bajar (de); desmontar (de); (of birds, etc.) posarse (sobre)

alight /ə'lait/ *a* encendido, iluminado; en llamas

align /ə'lain/ *vt* alinear

alignment /ə'lainmənt/ *n* alineación, *f*

alike /ə'laik/ *a* semejante; igual. —*adv* del mismo modo; igualmente

alimentary /,ælə'mɛntəri/ *a* nutritivo; alimenticio. **a. canal,** tubo digestivo, *m*

alimentation /,æləmɛn'teiʃən/ *n* alimentación, *f*

alimony /'ælə,mouni/ *n Law.* alimentos, *m pl,* pensión alimenticia, *f*

alive /ə'laiv/ *a* viviente; vivo; del mundo; (busy) animado, concurrido; (aware) sensible; (alert) lleno de vida, enérgico, despierto. **He is still a.,** Aún vive. **He is the best man a.,** Es el mejor hombre que existe, Es el mejor hombre del mundo. **half-a.,** semivivo. **while a.,** en vida. **a. to,** consciente de, sensible de. **a. with,** plagado de, lleno de

alkali /'ælkə,lai/ *n* álcali, *m*

alkaline /'ælkə,lain/ *a* alcalino

alkaloid /'ælkə,lɔid/ *n* alcaloide, *m*

all /ɔl/ *a* todo, *m;* toda, *f;* todos, *m pl*; todas, *f pl*; (in games) iguales. —*adv* enteramente, completamente; del todo; absolutamente. **after all,** después de todo; sin embargo. **at all,** nada; de ninguna manera; en absoluto. **fifteen all,** (tennis) quince iguales. **for good and all,** para siempre. **if that's all,** si no es más que eso. **in all,** en conjunto. **It is all one to me,** Me da igual. **not at all,** de ningún modo, nada de eso; nada; (never) jamás; (as a polite formula) No hay de qué. **once for all,** una vez por todas; por última vez. **That is all,** Eso es todo. **all along,** (of time) siempre, todo el tiempo; (of place) a lo largo de, de un extremo a otro de. **all but,** (almost) casi, por poco; (except) todo menos. **all joking aside,** fuera de burla. **all of them,** todos ellos, *m pl*; todas ellas, *f pl.* **All right!** ¡Bien! ¡Está bien! ¡Entendido! **all that,** todo eso; (as much as) cuanto. **all that which,** todo lo que. **all those who,** todos los que, *m pl*; todas las que, *f pl.* **all the more,** cuanto más. **all the same,** sin embargo, a pesar de todo. **all the worse,** tanto peor

all /ɔl/ *n* todo, *m;* todos, *m pl*; todas, *f pl*; (everyone, all men) todo el mundo. **to lose one's all,** perder todo lo que se tiene. **All is lost,** Todo se ha perdido. **all told,** en conjunto

all /ɔl/ (*in compounds*) **all-absorbing,** que todo lo absorbe; sumamente interesante. **all-bountiful,** de suma bondad. **all-conquering,** invicto. **all-consuming,** que todo lo consume; irresistible; ardiente. **all-enduring,** resignado a todo. **All Fools' Day,** Día de los Inocentes, *m,* (December 28). **all-fours,** a cuatro patas; a gatas. **to go on all fours,** andar a gatas. **All hail!** ¡Salud! ¡Bienvenido! **all-important,** sumamente importante. **all-in insurance,** seguro contra todo riesgo, *m.* **all-in wrestling,** lucha libre, *f.* **all-loving,** de un amor infinito. **all-merciful,** de una compasión infinita, sumamente misericordioso. **all-powerful,** omnipotente, todo poderoso. **all-round,** completo, cabal; universal. **an all-round athlete,** un atleta completo. **All Souls' Day,** Día de las Ánimas, Día de los difuntos, *m.* **all-wise,** omniscio

Allah /ˈælə/ *n* Alá, *m*

allay /əˈlei/ *vt* calmar; (relieve) aliviar; apaciguar

allaying /əˈleiɪŋ/ *n* alivio, *m;* apaciguamiento, *m*

allegation /ˌælɪˈgeiʃən/ *n* alegación, *f*

allege /əˈlɛdʒ/ *vt* afirmar, declarar; alegar

allegiance /əˈlidʒəns/ *n* lealtad, *f;* fidelidad, *f;* obediencia, *f*

allegorical /ˌælɪˈgɔrɪkəl/ *a* alegórico

allegory /ˈæləˌgɔri/ *n* alegoría, *f*

alleluia /ˌæləˈluyə/ *n* aleluya, *mf*

allergic /əˈlɜrdʒɪk/ *a* alérgico

allergist /ˈælərdʒɪst/ *n* alergólogo, *m*

allergy /ˈælərdʒi/ *n* alergia, *f*

alleviate /əˈliviˌeit/ *vt* aliviar

alleviation /əˌliviˈeiʃən/ *n* alivio, *m;* mitigación, *f*

alley /ˈæli/ *n* callejuela, *f,* callejón, *m;* avenida, *f;* (skittle a.) pista de bolos, *f.* **a.-way,** *Naut.* pasadizo, *m*

alliance /əˈlaiəns/ *n* alianza, *f;* parentesco, *m*

allied /ˈælaid/ *a* aliado; allegado

alligator /ˈælɪˌgeitər/ *n* caimán, *m.* **a. pear,** avocado, *m*

alliteration /əˌlɪtəˈreiʃən/ *n* aliteración, *f*

allocate /ˈæləˌkeit/ *vt* asignar, destinar; distribuir, repartir

allocation /ˌæləˈkeiʃən/ *n* asignación, *f;* distribución, *f,* repartimiento, *m*

allotment /əˈlɒtmənt/ *n* repartimiento, *m,* distribución, *f;* porción, *f;* lote, *m;* parcela de tierra, huerta, *f*

allow /əˈlau/ *vt* permitir; autorizar; dejar; tolerar, sufrir; (provide) dar; conceder, otorgar; (acknowledge) admitir; confesar; (discount) descontar; (a pension) hacer; deducir. **to a. for,** tener en cuenta; ser indulgente con; deducir; dejar (espacio, etc.) para

allowable /əˈlauəbəl/ *a* admisible, permisible; lícito, legítimo

allowance /əˈlauəns/ *n* ración, *f;* (discount) descuento, *m;* pensión, *f;* concesión, *f;* excusa, *f;* (subsidy) subsidio, *m;* (bonus) abono, *m;* (monthly) mesada, *f.* **to make a. for,** tener presente; hacer excusas para, ser indulgente con

alloy /*n* ˈælɔi, *v* əˈlɔi/ *n* aleación, *f;* liga, *f;* mezcla, *f.* —*vt* alear, ligar; mezclar

allspice /ˈɔlˌspais/ *n* guindilla de Indias, *f*

all-star game /ˈɔlˌstar/ *n* juego de estrellas, *m*

allude /əˈlud/ *vi* aludir (a), referirse (a)

allure /əˈlʊr/ *vt* convidar, provocar; atraer; seducir, fascinar

allurement /əˈlʊrmənt/ *n* (snare) añagaza, *f;* atracción, *f;* tentación, seducción, *f*

alluring /əˈlʊrɪŋ/ *a* atractivo, seductor, tentador; (promising) halagüeño

allusion /əˈluʒən/ *n* alusión, referencia, *f;* insinuación, *f*

allusive /əˈlusɪv/ *a* alusivo

ally /*n* ˈælai, *v* əˈlai/ *n* aliado (-da), allegado (-da); asociado (-da); (state) aliado, *m.* —*vt* unir. **to become allies,** aliarse

almanac /ˈɔlməˌnæk/ *n* almanaque, *m*

almighty /ɔlˈmaiti/ *a* omnipotente

almond /ˈɑmənd/ *n* almendra, *f;* (tree) almendro, *m.* **bitter a.,** almendra amarga, *f.* **green a.,** almendruco, *m.* **milk of almonds,** horchata de almendras, *f;* (for the hands) loción de almendras, *f.* **sugar a.,** almendra garapiñada, *f.* **a.-eyed,** con, or de, ojos rasgados. **a. paste,** pasta de almendras, *f.* **a.-shaped,** en forma de almendra, almendrado

almost /ˈɔlmoust/ *adv* casi; por poco

alms /ɑmz/ *n* limosna, *f.* **to ask a.,** pedir limosna, mendigar. **to give a.,** dar limosna. **a.-box,** cepillo de limosna, *m*

almsgiving /ˈɑmzˌgɪvɪŋ/ *n* caridad, *f*

aloe /ˈælou/ *n* áloe, *m; pl* **aloes,** *Med.* acíbar, *m*

aloft /əˈlɔft/ *adv* arriba, en alto

alone /əˈloun/ *a* solo; solitario. —*adv* a solas, sin compañía; solamente; únicamente. **to leave a.,** dejar solo; dejar en paz

along /əˈlɔŋ/ *adv* adelante; a lo largo; todo el tiempo. —*prep* a lo largo de; por; al lado (de); en compañía (de). **Come a.!** ¡Ven! **all a.,** todo el tiempo, desde el principio; a lo largo de. **a. with,** junto con; en compañía de

alongside /əˈlɔŋˈsaid/ *adv* al lado; *Naut.* al costado. —*prep* junto a, al lado de; *Naut.* al costado de. **to bring a.,** *Naut.* abarloar. **to come a.,** *Naut.* acostarse

aloof /əˈluf/ *adv* a distancia; lejos. —*a* altanero, esquivo; reservado. **to keep a.,** mantenerse alejado

aloofness /əˈlufnɪs/ *n* alejamiento, *m;* esquivez, *f;* reserva, *f*

aloud /əˈlaud/ *adv* en alta voz, alto

alpaca /ælˈpækə/ *n* alpaca, *f*

alphabet /ˈælfəˌbɛt/ *n* alfabeto, *m;* abecedario, *m*

alphabetical /ˌælfəˈbɛtɪkəl/ *a* alfabético

Alpine /ˈælpain/ *a* alpestre, alpino

Alps, the /ælps/ los Alpes, *m*

already /ɔlˈrɛdi/ *adv* ya; previamente

Alsace /ælˈsæs, -ˈseis/ Alsacia, *f*

Alsatian /ælˈseiʃən/ *a* and *n* alsaciano (-na†. **A. dog,** perro policía, perro pastor alemán, perro lobo, *m*

also /ˈɔlsou/ *adv* también, igualmente, además

altar /ˈɔltər/ *n* altar, *m.* **high a.,** altar mayor, *m.* **to lead a woman to the a.,** llevar a una mujer a la iglesia. **a.-cloth,** mantel del altar, *m.* **a.-piece,** retablo, *m.* **a.-rail,** mesa del altar, *f*

altar boy *n* acólito, monaguillo, *m*

altar girl *n* acólita, monaguilla, *f*

altar server *n* acólito, monaguillo, *m* (male), acólita, monaguilla, *f* (female)

alter /ˈɔltər/ *vt* cambiar; alterar; modificar; corregir; transformar; (clothes) arreglar. —*vi* cambiar

alterable /ˈɔltərəbəl/ *a* alterable

alteration /ˌɔltəˈreiʃən/ *n* cambio, *m,* alteración, *f;* modificación, *f;* correción, *f;* innovación, *f;* (to buildings, etc.) reforma, *f;* renovación, *f;* arreglo, *m*

altercation /ˌɔltərˈkeiʃən/ *n* altercación, *f*

alternate /*a* ˈɔltərnɪt; *v* -ˌneit/ *a* alternativo; (*Bot.* and of rhymes) alterno. —*vt* and *vi* alternar

alternately /ˈɔltərnɪtli/ *adv* alternativamente; por turno

alternating /ˈɔltərˌneitɪŋ/ *a* alternador. **a. current,** *Elec.* corriente alterna, *f*

alternation /ˌɔltərˈneiʃən/ *n* alternación, *f;* (of time) transcurso, *m;* turno, *m*

alternative /ɔlˈtɜrnətɪv/ *n* alternativa, *f, a* alternativo, alterno. **to have no a. but,** no poder menos de

alternatively /ɔlˈtɜrnətɪvli/ *adv* alternativamente

alternative medicine /ɔlˈtɜrnətɪv ˈmɛdəsɪn/ *n* medicina alternativa, *f*

alternator /ˈɔltərˌneitər/ *n Elec.* alternador, *m*

although /ɔlˈðou/ *conjunc* aunque, bien que; si bien; no obstante, a pesar de

altimeter /ælˈtɪmɪtər/ *n Aer.* altímetro, *m*

altitude /ˈæltɪˌtud/ *n* altitud, elevación, *f;* altura, *f*

alto /ˈæltou/ *n* (voice) contralto, *m;* (singer) contralto, *mf;* viola, *f*

altogether /ˌɔltəˈgɛðər/ *adv* completamente; del todo; en conjunto

altruism /ˈæltruˌɪzəm/ *n* altruísmo, *m*

altruist /ˈæltruɪst/ *n* altruista, *mf*

aluminum /əˈlumənəm/ *n* aluminio, *m*

aluminum foil *n* hoja de aluminio, *f*

always /ˈɔlweiz/ *adv* siempre

amalgam /əˈmælgəm/ *n* amalgama, *f;* mezcla, *f*

amalgamate /əˈmælgəˌmeit/ *vt* amalgamar; combinar, unir. —*vi* amalgamarse; combinarse, unirse

amalgamation /əˌmælgəˈmeiʃən/ *n* amalgamación, *f;* combinación, *f;* mezcla, *f*

amanuensis /əˌmænyuˈɛnsɪs/ *n* amanuense, *mf;* secretario (-ia)

amass /əˈmæs/ *vt* acumular, amontonar

amateur /ˈæməˌtʃʊr/ *a* and *n* aficionado (-da), (sports) no profesional. **a. theatricals,** función de aficionados, *f*

amateurish /'æmə,tʃʊrɪʃ/ *a* no profesional; de aficionado; superficial; (clumsy) torpe
amatory /'æmə,tɔri/ *a* amatorio
amaze /ə'meiz/ *vt* asombrar, sorprender; pasmar; confundir
amazed /ə'meizd/ *a* asombrado; sorprendido; admirado; asustado
amazement /ə'meizmənt/ *n* asombro, pasmo, *m;* sorpresa, *f;* (wonderment) admiración, *f;* estupor, *m*
amazing /ə'meizɪŋ/ *a* asombroso, pasmoso; sorprendente
amazingly /ə'meizɪŋli/ *adv* asombrosamente
Amazon /'æmə,zɒn/ *n* amazona, *f*
Amazon River, the el (Río de las) Amazonas, *m*
ambassador /æm'bæsədər/ *n* embajador, *m*
ambassadress /æm'bæsədrɪs/ *n* embajadora, *f*
amber /'æmbər/ *n* ámbar, *m, a* ambarino
ambergris /'æmbər,gris/ *n* ámbar gris, *m*
ambidextrous /,æmbɪ'dɛkstrəs/ *a* ambidextro
ambiguity /,æmbɪ'gyuɪti/ *n* ambigüedad, *f*
ambiguous /æm'bɪgyuəs/ *a* ambiguo, equivoco
ambition /æm'bɪʃən/ *n* ambición, *f*
ambitious /æm'bɪʃəs/ *a* ambicioso. **to be a. to,** ambicionar
amble /'æmbəl/ *n* (of a horse) paso de andadura, *m;* paso lento, *m.* —*vi* (of a horse) andar a paso de andadura; andar lentamente
ambulance /'æmbyələns/ *n* ambulancia, *f.* **a. corps,** cuerpo de sanidad, *m.* **a. man,** sanitario, *m*
ambulatory /'æmbyələ,tɔri/ *n* paseo, *m;* claustro, *m, a* ambulante
ambush /'æmbʊʃ/ *n* acecho, *m,* asechanza, *f; Mil.* emboscada, *f.* —*vt* acechar, asechar; *Mil.* emboscar; sorprender. **to be in a.,** emboscarse, estar en acecho
ameba /ə'mibə/ *n* amiba, *f*
amelioration /ə,milyə'reiʃən/ *n* mejora, *f*
amen /'ei'mɛn, 'ɑ'mɛn/ *n* amén, *m*
amenable /ə'minəbəl/ *a* sujeto (a); responsable; dócil; fácil de convencer, dispuesto a ser razonable; dispuesto a escuchar. **to make a. to reason,** hacer razonable
amend /ə'mɛnd/ *vt* enmendar; modificar. —*vi* reformarse
amendment /ə'mɛndmənt/ *n* enmienda, *f;* modificación, *f*
amends /ə'mɛndz/ *n pl* reparación, *f;* satisfacción, *f;* compensación, *f.* **to make a.,** dar satisfacción
amenity /ə'mɛnɪti/ *n* amenidad, *f*
America /ə'mɛrɪkə/ América, *f*
American /ə'mɛrɪkən/ *n* americano (-na); (U.S.A.) norteamericano (-na). —*a* americano, de América; norteamericano, de los Estados Unidos. **Central A.,** *a* and *n* centroamericano (-na). **A. bar,** bar americano, *m*
Americanism /ə'mɛrɪkə,nɪzəm/ *n* americanismo, *m*
Americanize /ə'mɛrɪkə,naiz/ *vt* americanizar
amethyst /'æməθɪst/ *n* amatista, *f*
amiability /,eimiə'bɪlɪti/ *n* amabilidad, afabilidad, cordialidad, *f*
amiable /'eimiəbəl/ *a* amable, afable, cordial
amiably /'eimiəbli/ *adv* amablemente, con afabilidad
amicable /'æmɪkəbəl/ *a* amigable, amistoso
amicably /'æmɪkəbli/ *adv* amigablemente
amice /'æmɪs/ *n* amito, *m*
amid, amidst /ə'mɪd; ə'mɪdst/ *prep* en medio de; entre; rodeado por
amidships /ə'mɪd,ʃɪps/ *adv* en el centro del buque, en medio del navío
amiss /ə'mɪs/ *adv* mal; de más; (ill) indispuesto, enfermo; (inopportunely) inoportunamente. —*a* malo. **It would not come a.,** No vendría mal. **to take a.,** llevar a mal
ammeter /'æm,mitər/ *n Elec.* amperímetro, *m*
ammonia /ə'mounyə/ *n* amoníaco, *m*
ammunition /,æmyə'nɪʃən/ *n* munición, *f.* **a. box,** cajón de municiones, *m*
amnesia /æm'niʒə/ *n* amnesia, *f*
amnesty /'æmnəsti/ *n* amnistía, *f.* **to concede an a. to,** amnistiar
amok /ə'mʌk/ **(to run a.)** atacar a ciegas
among /ə'mʌŋ/ *prep* en medio de; entre; con
amoral /ei'mɔrəl/ *a* amoral
amorality /,eimə'rælɪti/ *n* amoralidad, *f*
amorous /'æmərəs/ *a* amoroso; (tender) tierno
amorousness /'æmərəsnɪs/ *n* erotismo, *m;* galantería, *f*
amorphous /ə'mɔrfəs/ *a* amorfo
amortization /,æmərtə'zeiʃən/ *n* amorcización, *f*
amortize /'æmər,taiz/ *vt* amortizar
amount /ə'maunt/ *n* importe, *m,* suma, *f;* cantidad, *f, vi* (to) subir a, ascender a, llegar a; valer; reducirse a. **gross a.,** importe bruto, *m.* **net a.,** importe líquido, importe neto, *m.* **It amounts to the same thing, then.** Es igual entonces, Viene a ser lo mismo pues. **What he says amounts to this,** Lo que dice se reduce a esto
amperage /'æmpərɪdʒ/ *n* amperaje, *m*
ampere /'æmpɪər/ *n* amper, amperio, *m*
amphibian /æm'fɪbiən/ *n* anfibio, *m*
amphibious /æm'fɪbiəs/ *a* anfibio
amphitheater /'æmfə,θiətər/ *n* anfiteatro, *m*
amphora /'æmfərə/ *n* ánfora, *f*
ample /'æmpəl/ *a* amplio; abundante; extenso, vasto; (sufficient) bastante, suficiente
amplification /,æmpləfɪ'keiʃən/ *n* amplificación, *f*
amplifier /'æmplə,faiər/ *n* amplificador, *m*
amplify /'æmplə,fai/ *vt* amplificar; aumentar, ampliar
amplitude /'æmplɪ,tud/ *n* amplitud, *f;* abundancia, *f;* extensión, *f*
amply /'æmpli/ *adv* ampliamente; abundantemente; suficientemente
amputate /'æmpyʊ,teit/ *vt* amputar
amputation /,æmpyʊ'teiʃən/ *n* amputación, *f*
amulet /'æmyəlɪt/ *n* amuleto, *m*
amuse /ə'myuz/ *vt* divertir, entretener, distraer. **to a. oneself,** divertirse; pasarlo bien
amusement /ə'myuzmənt/ *n* diversión, *f,* entretenimiento, *m;* (hobby) pasatiempo, *m.* **a. park,** parque de atracciones, *m*
amusing /ə'myuzɪŋ/ *a* divertido, entretenido; (of people) salado
amusingly /ə'myuzɪŋli/ *adv* de un modo divertido, entretenidamente
an /ən/ See **a**
Anabaptist /,ænə'bæptɪst/ *n* anabaptista, *mf*
anachronism /ə'nækrə,nɪzəm/ *n* anacronismo, *m*
anachronistic /ə,nækrə'nɪstɪk/ *a* anacrónico
anagram /'ænə,græm/ *n* anagrama, *m*
analects /'ænḷ,ɛkts/ *n pl* analectas, *f pl*
analgesia /,ænḷ'dʒiziə/ *n* analgesia, *f*
analgesic /,ænḷ'dʒizɪk/ *a* and *n* analgésico, *m.*
analogous /ə'næləgəs/ *a* análogo
analogy /ə'nælədʒi/ *n* analogía, *f*
analysis /ə'næləsɪs/ *n* análisis, *m*
analyst /'ænḷɪst/ *n* analista, *mf*
analytical /,ænḷ'ɪtɪkəl/ *a* analítico
analyze /'ænḷ,aiz/ *vt* analizar
anaphora /ə'næfərə/ *n* anáfora, *f*
anarchic /æn'ɑrkɪk/ *a* anárquico
anarchism /'ænər,kɪzəm/ *n* anarquismo, *m*
anarchist /'ænərkɪst/ *n* anarquista, *mf*
anarchy /'ænərki/ *n* anarquía, *f*
anastigmatic /,ænəstɪg'mætɪk/ *a* anastigmático
anathema /ə'næθəmə/ *n* anatema, *mf*
anathematize /ə'næθəmə,taiz/ *vt* anatematizar
anatomic /,ænə'tɒmɪk/ *a* anatómico
anatomically /,ænə'tɒmɪkli/ *adv* anatómicamente; físicamente
anatomist /ə'nætəmɪst/ *n* anatomista, *mf*
anatomy /ə'nætəmi/ *n* anatomía, *f*
ancestor /'ænsɛstər/ *n* antepasado, abuelo, *m*
ancestral /æn'sɛstrəl/ *a* de sus antepasados; de familia; hereditario. **a. home,** casa solariega, *f*
ancestry /'ænsɛstri/ *n* antepasados, *m pl;* linaje, abolengo, *m;* estirpe, *f;* nacimiento, *m;* origen, *m*
anchor /'æŋkər/ *n* ancla, *f. Fig.* áncora, *f.* —*vt* sujetar con el ancla. —*vi* anclar, echar anclas, fondear. **at a.,** al ancla. **drag a.,** ancla flotante, ancla de arrastre, *f.* **sheet a.,** ancla de la esperanza, *f; Fig.* ancla de salvación, *f.* **to drop a.,** anclar. **to ride at a.,** estar al ancla. **to weigh a.,** levar el ancla

anchorage /ˈæŋkərɪdʒ/ *n* anclaje, *m;* ancladero, fondeadero, *m;* derechos de anclaje, *m pl*

anchorite /ˈæŋkəˌrait/ *n* anacoreta, *mf*

anchovy /ˈæntʃouvi/ *n* anchoa, *f,* boquerón, *m*

ancient /ˈeinʃənt/ *a* anciano; antiguo. —*n pl* **ancients,** los antiguos. **from a. times,** de antiguo. **most a.,** antiquísimo

and /ænd, ənd/ *conjunc* y; (before stressed i or hi) e; (after some verbs and before infin.) de, a; que; (with) con; (often not translated before infins.). **Better and better,** Mejor que mejor. **I shall try and do it,** Trataré de hacerlo. **to come and see,** venir a ver. **We shall try and speak to him,** Procuraremos hablar con él

Andalusia /ˌændl̩ˈuʒə/ Andalucía, *f*

Andalusian /ˌændl̩ˈuʒən/ *a* andaluz. —*n* andaluz (-za). **A. hat,** sombrero calañés, *m*

Andean /ˈændiən/ *a* andino

Andes, the /ˈændiz/ los Andes, *f*

andiron /ˈændˌaiᵊrn/ *n* morillo, *m*

Andorran /ænˈdɔrən/ *a* and *n* andorrano (-na)

androgynous /ænˈdrɒdʒənəs/ *a* andrógino

anecdotal /ˈænɪkˌdoutl̩/ *a* anecdótico

anecdote /ˈænɪkˌdout/ *n* anécdota, *f*

anemia /əˈnimiə/ *n* anemia, *f*

anemic /əˈnimɪk/ *a* anémico

anemometer /ˌænəˈmɒmɪtər/ *n* anemómetro, *m*

anemone /əˈnɛməˌni/ *n* anémona, anémone, *f*

aneroid /ˈænəˌrɔid/ *a* aneroide. —*n* barómetro aneroide, *m*

anesthesia /ˌænəsˈθiʒə/ *n* anestesia, *f*

anesthetic /ˌænəsˈθɛtɪk/ *a* and *n* acólito, monaguillo, *m*

anesthetist /əˈnɛsθɪtɪst/ *n* anestesiador (-ra)

anesthetize /əˈnɛsθɪˌtaiz/ *vt* anestesiar

aneurism /ˈænyəˌrɪzəm/ *n* aneurisma, *mf*

angel /ˈeindʒəl/ *n* ángel, *m*

angelic /ænˈdʒɛlɪk/ *a* angélico

angelica /ænˈdʒɛlɪkə/ *n* angélica, *f*

angelus /ˈændʒələs/ *n* ángelus, *m*

anger /ˈæŋgər/ *n* cólera, ira, *f,* enojo, *m, vt* enojar, encolerizar; hacer rabiar

angina /ænˈdʒainə/ *n* angina, *f.* **a. pectoris,** angina de pecho, *f*

angle /ˈæŋgəl/ *n* ángulo, *m;* rincón, *m;* esquina, *f;* (of a roof) caballette, *m; Fig.* punto de vista, *m, vi* pescar con caña. **at an a.,** a un lado. **a.-iron,** hierro angular, *m.* **to a. for,** pescar; *Fig.* procurar obtener

Angle /ˈæŋgəl/ *a* and *n* anglo (-la)

angler /ˈæŋglər/ *n* pescador (-ra) de caña

Anglican /ˈæŋglɪkən/ *a* and *n* anglicano (-na)

Anglicanism /ˈæŋlɪkəˌnɪzəm/ *n* anglicanismo, *m*

Anglicism /ˈæŋgləˌsɪzəm/ *n* anglicismo, inglesismo, *m*

Anglicize /ˈæŋgləˌsaiz/ *vt* inglesar

angling /ˈæŋglɪŋ/ *n* pesca con caña, *f*

Anglo- (in compounds) anglo-. **A.-American,** *a* and *n* angloamericano (-na). **A.-Indian,** *a* and *n* angloindio (-ia). **A.-Saxon,** *a* and *n* anglosajón (-ona); (language) anglosajón, *m*

anglomania /ˌæŋgləˈmeiniə/ *n* anglomanía, *f*

anglophile /ˈæŋgləˌfail/ *n* anglófilo (-la)

anglophobia /ˌæŋgləˈfoubiə/ *n* anglofobia, *f*

angora /æŋˈgɔrə/ *n* angora, *f.* **a. cat,** gato de angora, *m.* **a. rabbit,** conejo de angora, *m*

angrily /ˈæŋgrəli/ *adv* airadamente

angry /ˈæŋgri/ *a* (of persons) enfadado, enojado, airado; (of waves, etc.) furioso; *Med.* inflamado; (red) rojo; (scowling) ceñudo; (dark) obscuro. **to be a.,** estar enojado. **to grow a.,** enojarse, enfadarse; (of waves) encresparse; (of the sky) obscurecerse. **to make a.,** enojar

anguish /ˈæŋgwɪʃ/ *n* agonía, *f,* dolor, *m;* angustia, *f.* —*vt* angustiar

angular /ˈæŋgyələr/ *a* angular; (of features, etc.) anguloso

angularity /ˌæŋgyəˈlærɪti/ *n* angulosidad, *f*

anhydrous /ænˈhaidrəs/ *a* anhidro

aniline /ˈænl̩ɪn/ *n* anilina, *f*

animal /ˈænəməl/ *a* and *n* animal *m.* **a. fat,** grasa animal, *f.* **a. kingdom,** reino animal, *m.* **a. spirits,** *Philos.* espíritus animales, *m pl;* brío, *m,* energía, *f*

animalism /ˈænəməˌlɪzəm/ *n* animalidad, *f;* sensualidad, *f*

animate /*v* ˈænəˌmeit; *a* -mɪt/ *vt* animar; inspirar. —*a* animado; viviente

animated /ˈænəˌmeitɪd/ *a* animado; vivo, lleno de vida

animation /ˌænəˈmeiʃən/ *n* animación, *f;* vivacidad, *f;* calor, fuego, *m*

animism /ˈænəˌmɪzəm/ *n* animismo, *m*

animosity /ˌænəˈmɒsɪti/ *n* animosidad, hostilidad, *f*

aniseed /ˈænəˌsid/ *n* anís, *m*

anisette /ˌænəˈsɛt/ *n* (liqueur) anisete, *m*

ankle /ˈæŋkəl/ *n* tobillo, *m.* **a. bone,** hueso del tobillo, *m.* **a. sock,** calcetín corto, *m*

anklet /ˈæŋklɪt/ *n* brazalete para el tobillo, *m;* (support) tobillera, *f*

annals /ˈænl̩z/ *n pl* anales, *m pl*

anneal /əˈnil/ *vt* (metals) recocer; (glass) templar; (with oil) atemperar

annex /*v* əˈnɛks; ˈænɛks; *n* ˈænɛks/ *vt* unir, juntar; anexar. —*n* anexo, *m*

annexation /ˌænɪkˈseiʃən/ *n* anexión, *f*

annihilate /əˈnaiəˌleit/ *vt* aniquilar

annihilation /əˌnaiəˈleiʃən/ *n* aniquilación, *f*

anniversary /ˌænəˈvɜrsəri/ *a* and *n* aniversario, *m.*

annotate /ˈænəˌteit/ *vt* anotar, acotar, comentar, hacer anotaciones a

annotation /ˌænəˈteiʃən/ *n* anotación, *f;* nota, *f*

annotator /ˈænəˌteitər/ *n* anotador (-ra), comentador (-ra)

announce /əˈnauns/ *vt* proclamar; declarar; publicar; anunciar

announcement /əˈnaunsmənt/ *n* proclama, *f;* declaración, *f;* publicación, *f;* anuncio, *m;* (of a betrothal) participación, *f*

announcer /əˈnaunsər/ *n* anunciador (-ra); (radio or TV) locutor (-ra)

annoy /əˈnɔi/ *vt* exasperar, irritar, disgustar; molestar, incomodar

annoyance /əˈnɔiəns/ *n* disgusto, *m,* exasperación, *f;* molestia, *f,* fastidio, *m*

annoying /əˈnɔiɪŋ/ *a* enojoso, molesto, fastidioso

annual /ˈænyuəl/ *a* anual. —*n* anuario, *m;* calendario, *m;* planta anual, *f*

annually /ˈænyuəli/ *adv* anualmente, cada año

annuitant /əˈnuɪtn̩t/ *n* censualista, *mf*

annuity /əˈnuɪti/ *n* anualidad, pensión vitalicia, *f*

annul /əˈnʌl/ *vt* anular

annulment /əˈnʌlmənt/ *n* anulación, *f*

annunciation /əˌnʌnsiˈeiʃən/ *n* anunciación, *f.* **the A.,** la Anunciación

anodyne /ˈænəˌdain/ *a* and *n* anodino, *m*

anoint /əˈnɔint/ *vt* untar; (before death) olear; (a king, etc.) ungir

anointing /əˈnɔintɪŋ/ *n* unción, *f*

anomalous /əˈnɒmələs/ *a* anómalo

anomaly /əˈnɒməli/ *n* anomalía, *f*

anonymity /ˌænəˈnɪmɪti/ *n* anónimo, *m*

anonymous /əˈnɒnəməs/ *a* anónimo. **a. letter,** anónimo, *m*

anonymously /əˈnɒnəməsli/ *adv* anónimamente

another /əˈnʌðər/ *a* otro; (different) distinto. —*n* otro, *m;* otra, *f.* **For one thing... and for a.,** En primer lugar... y además (y por otra cosa). **one after a.,** uno después de otro. **They love one a.,** Ellos se aman. **They sent it from one to a.,** Lo mandaron de uno a otro

answer /ˈænsər, ˈɑn-/ *n* contestación, respuesta, *f;* (refutation) refutación, *f;* (pert reply) réplica, *f;* (solution) solución, *f; Math.* resultado, *m; Law.* contestación a la demanda, *f*

answer /ˈænsər, ˈɑn-/ *vt* responder, contestar; (a letter, etc.) contestar a; (refute) refutar; (reply pertly) replicar; (write) escribir; (return) devolver; (suit) servir; (a bell, etc.) acudir a; (the door) abrir. —*vi* contestar; (succeed) tener éxito; dar resultado. **to a. by return,** contestar a vuelta de correo, **to a. back,** replicar. **to a. for,** ser responsable por; ser responsable de; (speak for) hablar por; (guarantee) garantizar, responder de

answerable /ˈænsərəbəl/ *a* responsable; refutable;

(adequate) adecuado. **to make a. for,** hacer responsable de
answering machine *n* contestador telefónico, contestador, *m*
ant /ænt/ *n* hormiga, *f*. **ant-eater,** oso hormiguero, *m*. **ant-hill,** hormiguero, *m*
antagonism /æn'tægəˌnɪzəm/ *n* antagonismo, *m*, hostilidad, oposición, *f*
antagonist /æn'tægənɪst/ *n* antagonista, *mf*
antagonistic /ænˌtægə'nɪstɪk/ *a* antagónico, hostil
antagonize /æn'tægəˌnaiz/ *vt* contender; hacer hostil (a)
antarctic /ænt'ɑrktɪk/ *a* antártico. —*n* polo antártico, *m*
antecedent /ˌæntə'sidn̩t/ *a* and *n* antecedente, *m*.
antechamber /'æntiˌtʃeimbər/ *n* antecámara, antesala, *f*
antedate /'æntɪˌdeit/ *vt* antedatar; anticipar
antediluvian /ˌæntidɪ'luviən/ *a* antediluviano
antelope /'æntl̩ˌoup/ *n* antílope, *m*
antenna /æn'tɛnə/ *n* antena, *f*
anterior /æn'tɪəriər/ *a* anterior
anthem /'ænθəm/ *n* antífona, *f*
anthologist /æn'θɒlədʒɪst/ *n* antólogo, *m*
anthology /æn'θɒlədʒi/ *n* antología, floresta, *f*
anthracite /'ænθrəˌsait/ *n* antracita, *f*, carbón mineral, *m*
anthrax /'ænθræks/ *n* ántrax, *m*
anthropological /ˌænθrəpə'lɒdʒɪkəl/ *a* antropológico
anthropologist /ˌænθrə'pɒlədʒɪst/ *n* antropólogo, *m*
anthropology /ˌænθrə'pɒlədʒi/ *n* antropología, *f*
anti-aircraft /ˌænti'ɛərˌkræft, ˌæntai-/ *a* antiaéreo. **A.A. gun,** cañon antiaéreo, *m*
antibody /'æntɪˌbɒdi/ *n* anticuerpo, *m*
antic /'æntɪk/ *n* travesura, *f*
Antichrist /'æntiˌkraist/ *n* Anticristo, *m*
anticipate /æn'tɪsəˌpeit/ *vt* (foresee) prever; anticipar; adelantarse a; (hope) esperar; (frustrate) frustrar; (enjoy) disfrutar con anticipación de
anticipation /ænˌtɪsə'peiʃən/ *n* anticipación, *f;* adelantamiento, *m;* esperanza, expectación, *f*. **in a. of,** en espera de
anticipatory /æn'tɪsəpəˌtɔri/ *a* anticipador
anticlerical /ˌænti'klɛrɪkəl, ˌæntai-/ *a* anticlerical
anticlericalism /ˌænti'klɛrɪkəˌlɪzəm, ˌæntai-/ *n* anticlericalismo, *m*
anticlimax /ˌænti'klaimæks, ˌæntai-/ *n* anticlímax, *m*
antidote /'æntɪˌdout/ *n* antídoto, contraveneno, *m*
antifreeze /'æntɪˌfriz/ *n* anticongelante, *m*
Antilles, the /æn'tɪliz/ las Antillas, *f*
antimony /'æntəˌmouni/ *n* antimonio, *m*
antipathetic /ˌæntɪpə'θɛtɪk/ *a* antipático
antipathy /æn'tɪpəθi/ *n* antipatía, *f*
antipode /'æntɪˌpoud/ *n pl* antípodas, *mf pl*
antiquarian /ˌæntɪ'kwɛəriən/ *a* anticuario
antiquary /'æntɪˌkwɛri/ *n* anticuario, *m*
antiquated /'æntɪˌkweitɪd/ *a* anticuado
antique /æn'tik/ *a* antiguo. —*n* antigüedad, antigualla, *f*. **a. dealer,** anticuario, *m*. **a. shop,** tienda de antigüedades, *f*
antiquity /æn'tɪkwɪti/ *n* antigüedad, *f;* ancianidad, *f*
antireligious /ˌæntirɪ'lɪdʒəs, ˌæntai-/ *a* antirreligioso
antirepublican /ˌæntirɪ'pʌblɪkən/ *a* antirrepublicano
anti-Semitic /ˌæntisə'mɪtɪk, ˌæntai-/ *a* antisemita
anti-Semitism /ˌænti'sɛmɪˌtɪzəm, ˌæntai-/ *n* antisemitismo, *m*
antiseptic /ˌæntə'sɛptɪk/ *a* and *n* antiséptico, *m*
antisocial /ˌænti'souʃəl, ˌæntai-/ *a* antisocial
antithesis /æn'tɪθəsɪs/ *n* antítesis, *f*
antithetic /ˌæntɪ'θɛtɪk/ *a* antitético
antitoxin /ˌæntɪ'tɒksɪn/ *n* antitoxina, *f*
antler /'æntlər/ *n* asta, *f*
antonym /'æntənɪm/ *n* contrario, *m*
antrum /'æntrəm/ *n* antro, *m*
Antwerp /'æntwərp/ Amberes, *m*
anus /'einəs/ *n* ano, *m*
anvil /'ænvɪl/ *n* yunque, *m*, bigornia, *f*
anxiety /æŋ'zaiɪti/ *n* inquietud, intranquilidad, *f;* preocupación, *f;* ansiedad, *f;* curiosidad, *f;* impaciencia, *f;* (wish) deseo, afán, *m*
anxious /'æŋkʃəs, 'æŋʃəs/ *a* inquieto, intranquilo; preocupado; ansioso; impaciente; deseoso. **to be a.,** estar inquieto; apurarse. **to be a. to,** ansiar, tener deseos de. **to make a.,** preocupar, inquietar, intranquilizar
anxiously /'æŋkʃəsli, 'æŋʃəs-/ *adv* con inquietud; ansiosamente; impacientemente
any /'ɛni/ *a* cualquiera; (before the noun only) cualquier; (some) algún, *m;* alguna, *f;* (every) todo; (expressing condition or with interrogatives or negatives, following the noun) alguno, *m;* alguna, *f*, (is often not translated in a partitive sense, e.g. *Have you any butter?* ¿Tienes mantequilla?) —*pron* algo; (with the relevant noun) algún, etc.; lo, *m*, and *neut;* la, *f;* los, *m pl*; las, *f pl*. **He hasn't any pity,** No tiene piedad alguna. **at any rate,** de todos modos; por lo menos. **If there is any,** Si lo (la, etc.) hay. **in any case,** venga lo que venga. **not any,** ninguno, *m;* ninguna, *f*. **Whether any of them...,** Si alguno de ellos... **any further,** más lejos. **any longer,** más largo; (of time) más tiempo. **any more,** nada más; nunca más
anybody /'ɛniˌbɒdi/ *n* and *pron* (someone) alguien; cualquiera, *mf;* (everyone) todo el mundo; (with a negative) nadie; (of importance) persona de importancia, *f*. **hardly a.,** casi nadie
anyhow /'ɛniˌhau/ *adv* de cualquier modo; (with a negative) de ningún modo; de cualquier manera; (at least) por lo menos, en todo caso; (carelessly) sin cuidado
anyone /'ɛniˌwʌn/ *n*. See **anybody**
anything /'ɛniˌθɪŋ/ *n* algo, *m*, alguna cosa, *f;* (negative) nada; cualquier cosa, *f;* todo (lo que). **a. but,** todo menos
anyway /'ɛniˌwei/ *adv* de todos modos, con todo; venga lo que venga; (anyhow) de cualquier modo
anywhere /'ɛniˌwɛər/ *adv* en todas partes, dondequiera; en cualquier parte; (after a negative) en (or a) ninguna parte
A.O.B. (any other business) asuntos varios (on an agenda)
aorta /ei'ɔrtə/ *n* aorta, *f*
apart /ə'pɑrt/ *adv* aparte; a un lado; separadamente; separado (de); apartado (de). **a. from,** aparte de, dejando a un lado. **to keep a.,** mantener aislado; distinguir (entre). **to take a.,** desarmar. **wide a.,** muy distante
apartment /ə'pɑrtmənt/ *n* cuarto, *m*, habitación, *f;* (flat) piso, *m*
apathetic /ˌæpə'θɛtɪk/ *a* apático; indiferente
apathy /'æpəθi/ *n* apatía, *f;* indiferencia, *f*
ape /eip/ *n* simio, *m*
Apennines, the /'æpəˌnainz/ los Apeninos, *m*
aperitive /ə'pɛrɪtɪv/ *a* and *n* aperitivo, *m*.
aperture /'æpərtʃər/ *n* abertura, *f;* agujero, *m;* orificio, *m*
apex /'eipɛks/ *n* ápice, *m*
aphasia /ə'feiʒə/ *n* afasia, *f*
aphorism /'æfəˌrɪzəm/ *n* aforismo, *m*
aphrodisiac /ˌæfrə'diziˌæk/ *a* and *n* afrodisíaco, *m*
apiary /'eipiˌɛri/ *n* colmenar, *m*
apiece /ə'pis/ *adv* cada uno; por persona
apish /'eipɪʃ/ *a* simiesco, de simio; (affected) afectado; (foolish) tonto
aplomb /ə'plɒm/ *n* confianza en sí, *f*, aplomo, *m*
apocalypse /ə'pɒkəlɪps/ *n* Apocalipsis, *m*
apocalyptic /əˌpɒkə'lɪptɪk/ *a* apocalíptico
apocopate /ə'pɒkəˌpeit/ *vt* apocopar
Apocrypha /ə'pɒkrəfə/ *n* libros apócrifos, *m pl*
apocryphal /ə'pɒkrəfəl/ *a* apócrifo
apogee /'æpəˌdʒi/ *n* apogeo, *m*
apologetic /əˌpɒlə'dʒɛtɪk/ *a* apologético
apologist /ə'pɒlədʒɪst/ *n* apologista, *mf*
apologize /ə'pɒləˌdʒaiz/ *vi* presentar sus excusas; disculparse, excusarse; (regret) sentir
apology /ə'pɒlədʒi/ *n* excusa, disculpa, *f;* defensa, apología, *f;* (makeshift) substituto, *m*
apoplectic /ˌæpə'plɛktɪk/ *a* and *n* apoplético (-ca)
apoplexy /'æpəˌplɛksi/ *n* apoplegía, *f*
apostasy /ə'pɒstəsi/ *n* apostasía, *f*
apostate /ə'pɒsteit/ *n* apóstata, *mf*. renegado (-da)
apostatize /ə'pɒstəˌtaiz/ *vi* apostatar, renegar

apostle /ə'pɒsəl/ *n* apóstol, *m.* **Apostles' Creed,** el Credo de los Apóstoles

apostolic /ˌæpə'stɒlɪk/ *a* apostólico

apostrophe /ə'pɒstrəfi/ *n* apóstrofe, *mf;* (punctuation mark) apóstrofo, *m*

Apothecaries' weight peso de boticario, *m*

apothecary /ə'pɒθəˌkɛri/ *n* apotecario, *m*

apothegm /'æpəˌθɛm/ *n* apotegma, *m*

apotheosis /əˌpɒθi'ousɪs/ *n* apoteosis, *f*

appall /ə'pɔl/ *vt* horrorizar, espantar, aterrar

appalling /ə'pɔlɪŋ/ *a* espantoso, horrible

apparatus /ˌæpə'rætəs/ *n* aparato, *m;* máquina, *f;* instrumentos, *m pl*

apparel /ə'pærəl/ *n* ropa, *f;* vestiduras, *f pl*; ornamento, *m.* —*vt* vestir

apparent /ə'pærənt/ *a* aparente; visible; evidente, manifiesto; (of heirs) presunto. **to become a.,** manifestarse

apparently /ə'pærəntli/ *adv* al parecer, aparentemente

apparition /ˌæpə'rɪʃən/ *n* aparición, *f,* fantasma, espectro, *m*

appeal /ə'pil/ *n* súplica, *f;* llamamiento, *m;* (charm) atracción, *f,* encanto, *m; Law* apelación, alzada, *f.* —*vi* (to) suplicar (a); hacer llamamiento (a); poner por testigo (a); recurrir a; llamar la atención de; interesar (a); (attract) atraer, encantar; *Law.* apelar. **It doesn't a. to him,** No le atrae, No le gusta. **to allow an a.,** revocar una sentencia apelada. **without a.,** inapelable

appealing /ə'pilɪŋ/ *a* suplicante; atrayente

appealingly /ə'pilɪŋli/ *adv* de un modo suplicante

appear /ə'pɪər/ *vi* (of persons and things) aparecer; (seem) parecer; (before a judge) comparecer, presentarse (ante el juez); (of books) publicarse; (of lawyers) representar; (of the dawn) rayar; (of the sun, etc.) salir; (show itself) manifestarse. **to cause to a.,** hacer presentarse; (show) hacer ver; (prove) demonstrar, probar

appearance /ə'pɪərəns/ *n* aparición, *f;* (show, semblance or look, aspect) apariencia, *f;* presencia, *f;* aspecto, *m;* (in court of law) comparecencia, *f;* (of a book) publicación, *f;* (arrival) llegada, *f;* (view) perspectiva, *f;* (ghost) aparición, *f,* fantasma, *m.* **first a.,** (of an actor, etc.) debut, *m;* (of a play) estreno, *m.* **to all appearances,** según las apariencias. **to make one's first a.,** aparecer por primera vez; *Theat.* debutar. **Appearances are deceptive,** Las apariencias engañan

appease /ə'piz/ *vt* apaciguar, aplacar, pacificar; satisfacer

appeasement /ə'pizmənt/ *n* apaciguamiento, aplacamiento, *m,* pacificación, *f;* satisfacción, *f*

appellant /ə'pɛlənt/ *a* and *n Law.* apelante, *mf*

appellation /ˌæpə'leiʃən/ *n* nombre, *m;* título, *m*

append /ə'pɛnd/ *vt* añadir; (a seal) poner; (enclose) incluir, anexar

appendage /ə'pɛndɪdʒ/ *n* accesorio, *m;* (*Bot. Zool.*) apéndice, *m*

appendicitis /əˌpɛndə'saitɪs/ *n* apendicitis, *f*

appendix /ə'pɛndɪks/ *n* apéndice, *m*

appertain /ˌæpər'tein/ *vi* pertenecer (a)

appetite /'æpɪˌtait/ *n* apetito, *m; Fig.* hambre, *f;* deseo, *m.* **to have a bad a.,** no tener apetito, estar desganado. **to have a good a.,** tener buen apetito. **to whet the a.,** abrir el apetito

appetizer /'æpɪˌtaizər/ *n* aperitivo, *m*

appetizing /'æpɪˌtaizɪŋ/ *a* apetitoso

applaud /ə'plɔd/ *vt* and *vi* aplaudir; aclamar, ovacionar; celebrar

applause /ə'plɔz/ *n* aplauso, *m;* ovación, *f;* aprobación, alabanza, *f*

apple /'æpəl/ *n* manzana, *f.* **the a. of one's eye,** la niña de los ojos. **a. orchard,** manzanar, *m.* **a. sauce,** compota de manzanas, *f.* **a. tart,** pastel de manzanas, *m.* **a. tree,** manzano, *m*

appliance /ə'plaiəns/ *n* aparato, *m;* instrumento, *m;* utensilio, *m;* máquina, *f*

applicability /ˌæplɪkə'bɪlɪti/ *n* aplicabilidad, *f*

applicable /'æplɪkəbəl/ *a* aplicable

applicant /'æplɪkənt/ *n* candidato, *m;* aspirante, *m;* solicitante, *mf*

application /ˌæplɪ'keiʃən/ *n* aplicación, *f;* solicitud, *f;* petición, *f;* empleo, *m.* **on a.,** a solicitar

appliqué /ˌæplɪ'kei/ *a* aplicado. —*n* aplicación, *f*

apply /ə'plai/ *vt* aplicar; (use) emplear; (place) poner; (give) dar; (the brakes) frenar; *vi* ser aplicable; ser a propósito; dirigirse (a); acudir (a); (for a post) proponerse para. **a. for,** solicitar, pedir; (a post) proponerse para. **a. for admission (to...),** solicitar el ingreso (en...). **a. oneself to,** ponerse a; dedicarse a, consagrarse a

appoint /ə'pɔint/ *vt* (prescribe) prescribir, ordenar; señalar; asignar; (furnish) amueblar; equipar; (create) crear, establecer; (to a post) nombrar, designar; (manage) gobernar; organizar. **at the appointed hour,** a la hora señalada. **well-appointed,** bien amueblado; bien equipado

appointive /ə'pɔintɪv/ *a* por nombramiento

appointment /ə'pɔintmənt/ *n* (assignation) cita, *f;* (to a post) nombramiento, *m;* (post, office) cargo, *m;* creación, *f.* **By Royal A.,** Proveedor de la Real Casa. **to make an a. with,** citar

apportion /ə'pɔrʃən/ *vt* dividir; distribuir; prorratear; (taxes) derramar

apportionment /ə'pɔrʃənmənt/ *n* repartimiento, *m,* distribución, *f;* división, *f;* prorrateo, *m*

apposite /'æpəzɪt/ *a* a propósito, pertinente, oportuno; justo

appositeness /'æpəzɪtnɪs/ *n* pertinencia, oportunidad, *f*

appraisal /ə'preizəl/ *n* valoración, valuación, *f;* estimación, *f*

appraise /ə'preiz/ *vt* valorar, tasar; estimar

appreciable /ə'priʃiəbəl/ *a* apreciable, perceptible

appreciably /ə'priʃiəbli/ *adv* sensiblemente

appreciate /ə'priʃiˌeit/ *vt* (understand) darse cuenta de, comprender; estimar; apreciar; (distinguish) distinguir. —*vi* encarecer, aumentar en valor; (of shares) subir, estar en alza

appreciation /əˌpriʃi'eiʃən/ *n* (understanding) comprensión, *f;* apreciación, *f;* (recognition, etc.) aprecio, reconocimiento, *m;* (in value) aumento (en valor), *m;* subida de precio, *f*

appreciative /ə'priʃətɪv/ *a* apreciativo

appreciatively /ə'priʃətɪvli/ *adv* con aprecio

appreciator /ə'priʃieitər/ *n* apreciador (-ra)

apprehend /ˌæprɪ'hɛnd/ *vt* aprehender, prender; comprender, aprehender; (fear) temer

apprehension /ˌæprɪ'hɛnʃən/ *n* aprehensión, comprensión, *f;* (fear) aprensión, *f;* (seizure) aprehensión, presa, *f*

apprehensive /ˌæprɪ'hɛnsɪv/ *a* aprehensivo; (fearful) aprensivo

apprehensiveness /ˌæprɪ'hɛnsɪvnɪs/ *n* aprehensión, *f;* (fear) aprensión, *f,* temor, *m*

apprentice /ə'prɛntɪs/ *n* aprendiz (-za). **to bind a.,** poner de aprendiz

apprenticeship /ə'prɛntɪsˌʃɪp/ *n* aprendizaje, *m.* **to serve an a.,** hacer el aprendizaje

apprise /ə'praiz/ *vt* dar parte (de), informar (de)

approach /ə'proutʃ/ *vt* acercarse a; aproximarse a; (pull, etc. nearer) acercar, aproximar; (resemble) parecerse a, ser semejante a; (speak to) hablar con; entablar negociaciones con. —*vi* acercarse, aproximarse. —*n* acercamiento, *m;* (arrival) llegada, *f;* aproximación, *f;* (of night, etc.) avance, *m;* (entrance) entrada, *f;* avenida, *f;* vía, *f;* (step) paso, *m;* (to a subject) punto de vista (sobre), concepto (de), *m;* (introduction) introducción, *f; pl* **approaches,** (environs) alrededores, *m pl,* inmediaciones, *f pl;* (seas) mares, *m pl;* (overtures) avances, *m pl*

approachable /ə'proutʃəbəl/ *a* accesible

approaching /ə'proutʃɪŋ/ *a* venidero, próximo, cercano

approbation /ˌæprə'beiʃən/ *n* asentimiento, *m;* aprobación, *f*

appropriate /*a* ə'proupriɪt; *v* -ˌeit/ *a* apropiado; conveniente; *vt* adueñarse de, tomar posesión de, apropiar

appropriately /ə'proupriɪtli/ *adv* propiamente; convenientemente; justamente

appropriateness /ə'proupriɪtnɪs/ *n* conveniencia, *f;* justicia, *f*

appropriation /əˌproupri'eiʃən/ *n* apropiación, *f;* aplicación, *f;* empleo, *m*
approval /ə'pruvəl/ *n* aprobación, *f;* consentimiento, *m.* **on a.,** a prueba
approve /ə'pruv/ *vt* aprobar; confirmar; (sanction) autorizar, sancionar; ratificar; estar contento (de); (oneself) demostrarse. —*vi* aprobar
approved /ə'pruvd/ *a* aprobado; bien visto; (on documents) Visto Bueno (V° B°)
approximate /*a* ə'prɒksəmɪt; *v* -ˌmeit/ *a* aproximado. —*vt* acercar. —*vi* aproximarse (a)
approximately /ə'prɒksəmɪtli/ *adv* aproximadamente, poco más o menos
approximation /əˌprɒksə'meiʃən/ *n* aproximación, *f*
appurtenance /ə'pɜrtn̩əns/ *n* accesorio, *m,* pertenencia, *f*
apricot /'æprɪˌkɒt/ *n* albaricoque, *m.* **a. tree,** albaricoquero, *m*
April /'eiprəl/ *n* abril, *m, a* abrileño. **A. Fool's Day,** el 1° de abril; (in Spain) el Día de los Inocentes (December 28)
apron /'eiprən/ *n* delantal, *m;* (of artisans and freemasons) mandil, *m.* **to be tied to a mother's a.-strings,** estar cosido a las faldas de su madre. **a.-stage,** proscenio, *m.* **a.-string,** cinta del delantal, *f*
apse /æps/ *n* ábside, *mf*
apt /æpt/ *a* apto, listo; propenso (a), inclinado (a); expuesto (a); (suitable) apropiado, oportuno
aptitude /'æptɪˌtud/ *n* aptitud, disposición, facilidad, *f*
aptly /'æptli/ *adv* apropiadamente; justamente, bien
aquamarine /ˌækwəmə'rin/ *n* aguamarina, *f*
aquarelle /ˌækwə'rɛl/ *n* acuarela, *f*
aquarellist /ˌækwə'rɛlɪst/ *n* acuarelista, *mf*
aquarium /ə'kwɛəriəm/ *n* acuario, *m*
Aquarius /ə'kwɛəriəs/ *n* Acuario, *m*
aquatic /ə'kwætɪk/ *a* acuático
aquatint /'ækwəˌtɪnt/ *n* acuatinta, *f*
aqueduct /'ækwɪˌdʌkt/ *n* acueducto, *m*
aqueous /'ækwiəs/ *a* ácueo, acuoso
aquiline /'ækwəˌlain/ *a* aguileño
Arab /'ærəb/ *a* árabe. —*n* árabe, *mf*
arabesque /ˌærə'bɛsk/ *n* arabesco, *m*
Arabian /ə'reibiən/ *a* árabe, arábigo. **The A. Nights,** Las Mil y Una Noches
Arabic /'ærəbɪk/ *a* arábigo. —*n* (language) arábigo, árabe, *m*
Arabist /'ærəbɪst/ *n* arabista, *mf*
arable /'ærəbəl/ *a* cultivable, labrantío
Aragonese /ˌærəgə'niz/ *a* and *n* aragonés (-esa)
arbiter /'ɑrbɪtər/ *n* árbitro (-ra), arbitrador (-ra)
arbitrariness /'ɑrbɪˌtrɛrinɪs/ *n* arbitrariedad, *f*
arbitrary /'ɑrbɪˌtrɛri/ *a* arbitrario
arbitrate /'ɑrbɪˌtreit/ *vi* arbitrar, juzgar como árbitro; someter al arbitraje
arbitration /ˌɑrbɪ'treiʃən/ *n* arbitraje, *m*
arbitrator /'ɑrbɪˌtreitər/ See **arbiter**
arbor /'ɑrbər/ *n* glorieta, *f,* emparrado, *m*
arc /ɑrk/ *n* arco, *m.* **arc-light,** lámpara de arco, *f*
arcade /ɑr'keid/ *n* arcada, *f;* galería, *f;* pasaje, *m*
arch /ɑrtʃ/ *n* arco, *m;* (vault) bóveda, *f.* —*vt* abovedar; arquear; encorvar
arch /ɑrtʃ/ *a* (roguish) socarrón; (coy) coquetón
arch- /ɑrtʃ/ *prefix* archi-
archaic /ɑr'keiɪk/ *a* arcaico
archaism /'ɑrkiˌɪzəm/ *n* arcaísmo, *m*
archangel /'ɑrkˌeindʒəl/ *n* arcángel, *m*
archbishop /'ɑrtʃ'bɪʃəp/ *n* arzobispo, *m*
archenemy /'ɑrtʃ'ɛnəmi/ *n* mayor enemigo (-ga); Demonio, *m*
archeological /ˌɑrkiə'lɒdʒɪkəl/ *a* arqueológico
archeologist /ˌɑrki'ɒlədʒɪst/ *n* arqueólogo, *m*
archeology /ˌɑrki'ɒlədʒi/ *n* arqueología, *f*
archer /'ɑrtʃər/ *n* flechero, saltero, *m; Mil.* arquero, *m*
archery /'ɑrtʃəri/ *n* ballestería, *f*
archery range *n* campo de tiro con arco, *m*
archfiend /'ɑrtʃ'find/ *n* demonio, *m*
arching /'ɑrtʃɪŋ/ *n* arqueo, *m*
archipelago /ˌɑrkə'pɛləˌgou/ *n* archipiélago, *m*
architect /'ɑrkɪˌtɛkt/ *n* arquitecto, *m*
architectural /ˌɑrkɪ'tɛktʃərəl/ *n* arquitectónico
architecturally /ˌɑrkɪ'tɛktʃərəli/ *adv* arquitectónicamente; desde el punto de vista arquitectónico
architecture /'ɑrkɪˌtɛktʃər/ *n* arquitectura, *f*
archive /'ɑrkaiv/ *n* archivo, *m*
archivist /'ɑrkəvɪst/ *n* archivero, *m*
archness /'ɑrtʃnɪs/ *n* coquetería, *f;* malicia, *f*
archway /'ɑrtʃˌwei/ *n* arcada, *f,* pasaje abovedado, *m;* arco, *m*
arctic /'ɑrktɪk, 'ɑrtɪk/ *a* ártico; muy frío. **A. Circle,** Círculo ártico, *m*
ardent /'ɑrdn̩t/ *a* ardiente; apasionado, vehemente; fogoso
ardently /'ɑrdn̩tli/ *adv* ardientemente; con vehemencia, apasionadamente
ardor /'ɑrdər/ *n* ardor, *m*
arduous /'ɑrdʒuəs/ *a* arduo, difícil
arduousness /'ɑrdʒuəsnɪs/ *n* dificultad, arduidad, *f*
are /ɑr/ *pl* of present indicative of **be.** See **be. There are,** Hay
area /'ɛəriə/ *n* área, *f;* superficie, *f;* (extent) extensión, *f;* espacio, *m;* región, *f;* (of a house) patio, *m;* (of a concert hall, etc.) sala, *f*
area code *n* característica, *f,* (Chile), código territorial (Spain), prefijo (Spain), código interurbano, código (Argentina), *m*
arena /ə'rinə/ *n* arena, *f*
argent /'ɑrdʒənt/ *n Poet.* blancura, *f; Herald.* argén, *m*
Argentinian /ˌɑrdʒən'tɪniən/ *a* and *n* argentino (-na)
argonaut /'ɑrgəˌnɔt/ *n* (*Zool.* and *Myth.*) argonauta, *m*
argot /'ɑrgou, -gət/ *n* jerga, *f;* (thieves') germanía, *f*
arguable /'ɑrgyuəbəl/ *a* discutible
argue /'ɑrgyu/ *vt* discutir; persuadir; (prove) demostrar. —*vi* argüir, discutir; sostener. **to a. against,** hablar en contra de, oponer
arguing /'ɑrgyuɪŋ/ *n* razonamiento, *m;* argumentación, *f;* discusión, *f*
argument /'ɑrgyəmənt/ *n* argumento, *m*
argumentative /ˌɑrgyə'mɛntətɪv/ *a* argumentador; contencioso
arid /'ærɪd/ *a* árido, seco
aridity /ə'rɪdɪti/ *n* aridez, *f*
Aries /'ɛəriz/ *n* Aries, *m*
arise /ə'raiz/ *vi* levantarse; (appear) surgir, aparecer; ofrecerse, presentarse; (of sound) hacerse oír; provenir (de); proceder (de); (result) hacerse sentir; (rebel) sublevarse
aristocracy /ˌærə'stɒkrəsi/ *n* aristocracia, *f*
aristocrat /ə'rɪstəˌkræt/ *n* aristócrata, *mf*
aristocratic /əˌrɪstə'krætɪk/ *a* aristocrático
Aristotelian /ˌærəstə'tilyən/ *a* aristotélico
Aristotelianism /ˌærəstə'tilyənɪzəm/ *n* aristotelismo, *m*
arithmetic /ə'rɪθmətɪk/ *n* aritmética, *f*
arithmetical /ˌærɪθ'mɛtɪkəl/ *a* aritmético
ark /ɑrk/ *n* arca, *f.* **Noah's ark,** arca de Noé, *f.* **Ark of the Covenant,** arca de la alianza, *f*
arm /ɑrm/ *n* (*Anat. Geog. Mech.* of a chair, a cross, and *Fig.*) brazo, *m;* (lever) palanca, *f;* (of a tree) rama, *f,* brazo, *m;* (sleeve) manga, *f; Naut.* cabo de una verga, *m;* (weapon) arma, *f;* (of army, navy, etc.) ramo, *m pl.* **arms,** *Herald.* armas, *f pl,* escudo, *m.* **in arms,** en brazos; armado; en oposición. **To arms!** ¡A las armas! **to keep at arm's length,** guardar las distancias; tratar fríamente. **to lay down arms,** rendir las armas. **to present arms,** presentar las armas. **to receive with open arms,** recibir con los brazos abiertos. **to take up arms,** alzarse en armas, empuñar las armas. **under arms,** sobre las armas. **with folded arms,** con los brazos cruzados. **arm in arm,** del bracete, de bracero. **arm of the sea,** brazo de mar, *m.* **arm-rest,** brazo, *m*
arm /ɑrm/ *vt* armar; proveer (de); (*Fig.* fortify) fortificar. —*vi* armarse
armada /ɑr'mɑdə/ *n* armada, *f*
armament /'ɑrməmənt/ *n* armamento, *m*
armchair /'ɑrmˌtʃɛər/ *n* sillón, *m,* silla poltrona, *f*
armed /ɑrmd/ *a* armado
Armenian /ɑr'miniən/ *a* and *n* armenio (-ia); (language) armenio, *m*

armful /ˈɑrmˌfʊl/ *n* brazado, *m*
armhole /ˈɑrmˌhoul/ *n* sobaquera, *f*
arming /ˈɑrmɪŋ/ *n* armamento, *m*
armistice /ˈɑrməstɪs/ *n* armisticio, *m*
armless /ˈɑrmlɪs/ *a* sin brazos
armor /ˈɑrmər/ *n* armadura, *f;* (for ships, etc.) blindaje, *m.* —*vt* blindar, acorazar. **(to) a.-plate,** *vt* blindar. —*n* coraza, plancha blindada, *f*
armored /ˈɑrmərd/ *a* blindado, acorazado. **a. car,** carro blindado, *m.* **a. cruiser,** crucero acorazado, *m*
armory /ˈɑrməri/ *n* armería, *f*
army /ˈɑrmi/ *n* ejército, *m;* multitud, muchedumbre, *f.* **to be in the a.,** ser del ejército. **to go into the a.,** alistarse. **a. corps,** cuerpo del ejército, *m.* **a. estimates,** presupuesto del ejército, *m.* **a. list,** escalofón del ejército, *m.* **A. Medical Corps,** Sanidad Militar, *f.* **A. Supply Corps,** Cuerpo de Intendencia, *m*
aroma /əˈroumə/ *n* aroma, *m*
aromatic /ˌærəˈmætɪk/ *a* aromático
around /əˈraund/ *prep* alrededor de; por todas partes de; cerca de; (with words like corner) a la vuelta de. —*adv* alrededor; a la redonda, en torno; por todas partes; de un lado para otro
arouse /əˈrauz/ *vt* despertar; excitar. **a. (someone's) suspicions,** despertar las sospechas (de fulano)
arpeggio /ɑrˈpɛdʒiˌou/ *n* arpegio, *m*
arraign /əˈrein/ *vt* acusar; *Law.* procesar
arraignment /əˈreinmənt/ *n* acusación, *f; Law.* procesamiento, *m*
arrange /əˈreindʒ/ *vt* arregular; acomodar; poner en orden, clasificar; (place) colocar; (order) ordenar, disponer; (contrive) agenciar; organizar; preparar; *Mus.* adaptar; (of differences) concertar, ajustar. —*vi* convenir, concertarse; arreglar; hacer preparativos
arrangement /əˈreindʒmənt/ *n* arreglo, *m;* clasificación, *f;* disposición, *f;* (agreement) acuerdo, *m; Mus.* adaptación, *f; pl* **arrangements,** preparativos, *m pl*
array /əˈrei/ *n* (of troops) orden de batalla, *mf;* formación, *f;* colección, *f;* (dress) atavío, *m, vt* poner en orden de batalla; formar (las tropas, etc.); ataviar, adornar
arrears /əˈrɪərz/ *n pl* atrasos, *m pl.* **in a.,** atrasado
arrest /əˈrɛst/ *vt* detener, impedir; (the attention) atraer; (capture) arrestar, prender; (judgment) suspender. —*n* (stop) interrupción, parada, *f;* (hindrance) estorbo, *m;* (detention) arresto, *m,* detención, *f;* (of a judgment) suspensión, *f.* **under a.,** bajo arresto
arresting /əˈrɛstɪŋ/ *a* que llama la atención, notable, muy interesante; asombroso, chocador
arrival /əˈraivəl/ *n* llegada, venida, *f,* advenimiento, *m; Naut.* arribada, *f;* entrada, *f;* el, *m,* (la, *f*), que llega. **on a.,** al llegar, a la llegada. **the new arrivals,** los recién llegados
arrive /əˈraiv/ *vi* llegar; aparecer; (happen) suceder; *Naut.* arribar; entrar. **to a. at,** (a place or conclusion) llegar a
arrogance /ˈærəgəns/ *n* arrogancia altivez, soberbia, *f*
arrogant /ˈærəgənt/ *a* altivo, arrogante, soberbio
arrogate /ˈærəˌgeit/ *vt* arrogar
arrow /ˈærou/ *n* saeta, flecha, *f.* **a.-head,** punta de flecha, *f.* **a.-shaped,** en forma de flecha, sagital. **a. wound,** flechazo, saetazo, *m*
arsenal /ˈɑrsənl̩/ *n* arsenal, *m*
arsenic /ˈɑrsənɪk/ *n* arsénico, *m*
arson /ˈɑrsən/ *n* incendio premeditado, *m*
art /ɑrt/ *n* arte, *mf;* (cleverness) habilidad, *f;* (cunning) artificio, *m.* **Faculty of Arts,** Facultad de Letras, *f.* **fine arts,** bellas artes, *f pl.* **art exhibition,** exposición de pintuas, *f.* **art gallery,** museo de pinturas, *m.* **art school,** colegio de arte, *m*
arterial /ɑrˈtɪəriəl/ *a* arterial; (of roads) de primera clase. **a. forceps,** pinzas hemostáticas, *f pl*
artery /ˈɑrtəri/ *n* arteria, *f*
artesian /ɑrˈtiʒən/ *a* artesiano
artful /ˈɑrtfəl/ *a* habil, ingenioso; (crafty) astuto
artfully /ˈɑrtfəli/ *adv* ingeniosamente; con astucia
artfulness /ˈɑrtfəlnɪs/ *n* habilidad, ingeniosidad, *f;* astucia, maña, *f*
arthritic /ɑrˈθrɪtɪk/ *a* artrítico
arthritis /ɑrˈθraitɪs/ *n* artritis, *f*
artichoke /ˈɑrtɪˌtʃouk/ *n* alcachofa, *f.* **Jerusalem a.,** aguaturma, *f*
article /ˈɑrtɪkəl/ *n* artículo, *m;* (object) objeto, *m,* cosa, *f; pl* **articles,** escritura, *f;* contrato, *m;* estatutos, *m pl.* —*vt* escriturar; contratar. **leading a.,** artículo de fondo, *m.* **articles of apprenticeship,** contrato de aprendizaje, *m.* **articles of association,** estatutos de asociación, *m pl.* **articles of war,** código militar, *m*
articulate /*v* ɑrˈtɪkyəˌleit; *a* -lɪt/ *vt* articular; pronunciar, articular. —*vi* estar unido por articulación; articular. —*a* articulado; claro; expresivo
articulation /ɑrˌtɪkyəˈleiʃən/ *n* articulación, *f,* (all meanings)
artifice /ˈɑrtəfɪs/ *n* artificio, *m;* arte, *m,* or *f,* habilidad, *f*
artificer /ɑrˈtɪfəsər/ *n* artífice, *mf*
artificial /ˌɑrtəˈfɪʃəl/ *a* artificial; falso, fingido; afectado. **a. flowers,** flores de mano, *f pl.* **a. silk,** seda artificial, seda vegetal, *f*
artificial intelligence /ɑrtəˈfɪʃəl ɪnˈtɛlɪdʒəns/ *n* inteligencia artificial, *f*
artificiality /ˌɑrtəˌfɪʃiˈælɪti/ *n* artificialidad, *f;* falsedad, *f;* afectación, *f*
artificially /ˌɑrtəˈfɪʃəli/ *adv* artificialmente; con afectación
artillery /ɑrˈtɪləri/ *n* artillería, *f.* **field a.,** artillería volante (or ligera or montada), *f.* **a. practice,** ejercicio de cañón, *m*
artilleryman /ɑrˈtɪlərimən/ *n* artillero, *m*
artisan /ˈɑrtəzən/ *n* artesano (-na)
artist /ˈɑrtɪst/ *n* artista, *mf;* (painter) pintor (-ra)
artiste /ɑrˈtist/ *n* artista, *mf*
artistic /ɑrˈtɪstɪk/ *a* artístico
artistically /ɑrˈtɪstɪkli/ *adv* artísticamente
artistry /ˈɑrtɪstri/ *n* habilidad artística, *f,* arte, *mf*
artless /ˈɑrtlɪs/ *a* natural; sencillo, cándido, inocente
artlessly /ˈɑrtlɪsli/ *adv* con naturalidad; con inocencia
artlessness /ˈɑrtlɪsnɪs/ *n* naturalidad, *f;* sencillez, candidez, inocencia, *f*
art museum *n* museo de arte, *m*
Aryan /ˈɛəriən/ *a* ario
as /æz/ *adv conjunc rel pron* como; así como; (followed by infin.) de; (in comparisons) tan... como; (while) mientras; a medida que; (when) cuando, al (followed by infin.); (since) puesto que, visto que; (because) porque; (although) aunque; por; (according to) según; en; (in order that) para (que). **as a rule,** por regla general. **Once as he was walking,** Una vez mientras andaba. **as... as,** tan... como. **as far as,** hasta; en cuanto a. **as from,** desde. **as good as,** tan bueno como. **as if,** como si. **as it were,** por decirlo así, en cierto modo. **as many,** otros tantos (e.g. *six embassies in as many countries,* seis embajadas en otros tantos países). **as many as,** tanto... como; todos los que. **as soon as,** en cuanto, luego que, así que. **as soon as possible,** cuanto antes. **as sure as can be,** sin duda alguna. **as to,** en cuanto a. **as usual,** como de costumbre. **as well,** también. **as well as,** (besides) además de; tan bien como. **as yet,** todavía.
asbestos /æsˈbɛstəs/ *n* asbesto, amianto, *m*
ascend /əˈsɛnd/ *vt* and *vi* subir; (on, in) subir a; ascender; (rise) elevarse; (a river) remontar. **to a. the stairs,** subir las escaleras. **to a. the pulpit,** subir al púlpito. **to a. the throne,** subir al trono
ascendancy /əˈsɛndənsi/ *n* ascendiente, influjo, *m*
ascendant /əˈsɛndənt/ *n* elevación, *f.* —*a* ascendente; predominante. **to be in the a.,** *Fig.* ir en aumento; predominar
ascending /əˈsɛndɪŋ/ *a* ascendente
ascension /əˈsɛnʃən/ *n* subida, ascension, *f;* (of the throne) advenimiento (al trono), *m.* **The A.,** La Ascensión
ascent /əˈsɛnt/ *n* subida, *f,* ascenso, *m;* elevación, *f;* (slope) cuesta, pendiente, *f*
ascertain /ˌæsərˈtein/ *vt* averiguar, descubrir
ascertainable /ˌæsərˈteinəbəl/ *a* averiguable, descubrible
ascertainment /ˌæsərˈteinmənt/ *n* averiguación, *f*
ascetic /əˈsɛtɪk/ *a* ascético. —*n* asceta, *mf*
asceticism /əˈsɛtəˌsɪzəm/ *n* ascetismo, *m*
ascribable /əˈskraibəbəl/ *a* imputable, atribuible

ascribe /ə'skraib/ *vt* atribuir, adscribir, imputar
ascription /ə'skrɪpʃən/ *n* atribución, adscripción, *f*
asepsis /ə'sɛpsɪs/ *n* asepsia, *f*
aseptic /ə'sɛptɪk/ *a* aséptico
asexual /ei'sɛkʃuəl/ *a* asexual
ash /æʃ/ *n* ceniza, *f;* cenizas, *f pl;* (tree and wood) fresno, *m; pl* **ashes,** cenizas, *f pl;* restos mortales, *m pl.* **mountain ash,** serbal, *m.* **ash-bin,** basurero, *m.* **ash-coloured,** ceniciento. **ash grove,** fresneda, *f.* **ashtray,** cenicero, *m.* **Ash Wednesday,** miércoles de ceniza, *m*
ashamed /ə'ʃeimd/ *a* avergonzado. **to be a. of,** avergonzarse de. **to be a. of oneself,** avergonzarse, tener vergüenza de sí mismo
ashen /'æʃən/ *a* ceniciento; (of ash wood) de fresno; pálido como un muerto
ashlar /'æʃlər/ *n* sillar, *m*
ashore /ə'ʃɔr/ *adv* a tierra; en tierra. **to go** or **put a.,** desembarcar
Asia Minor /'eiʒə/ Asia Menor, *f*
Asiatic /ˌeiʒi'ætɪk/ *a* and *n* asiático (-ca)
aside /ə'said/ *adv* a un lado; aparte. —*n Theat.* aparte, *m.* **to set a.,** poner a un lado; (omit) dejar aparte; descontar; abandonar; (a judgment) anular. **to take a.,** llevar aparte
asinine /'æsəˌnain/ *a* asnal
ask /æsk/ *vt* (a question; enquire) preguntar; (request; demand) pedir; (beg) rogar; (invite) invitar. **to ask a question,** hacer una pregunta. **to ask about,** preguntar acerca de. **to ask after,** preguntar por. **to ask down,** invitar a bajar; invitar a visitar (a alguíen). **to ask for,** pedir; preguntar por. **ask for the moon,** pedir cotofas en el golfo. **to ask in,** invitar (a alguien) a entrar
askance /ə'skæns/ *adv* al (or de) soslayo, de reojo; con recelo
askew /ə'skyu/ *adv* oblicuamente; al lado; a un lado; sesgadamente
aslant /ə'slænt/ *prep* a través de
asleep /ə'slip/ *a* and *adv* dormido. **to be a.,** estar dormido. **to fall a.,** dormirse
asparagus /ə'spærəgəs/ *n* espárrago, *m.* **a. bed,** esparraguera, *f*
aspect /'æspɛkt/ *n* aspecto, *m;* vista, *f;* apariencia, *f,* semblante, *m.* **to have a southern a.,** dar (mirar) al sur
asperity /ə'spɛrɪti/ *n* aspereza, *f*
aspersion /ə'spɜrʒən/ *n Eccl.* aspersión, *f;* calumnia, *f;* insinuación, *f*
asphalt /'æsfɔlt/ *n* asfalto, *m, vt* asfaltar
asphyxia /æs'fɪksiə/ *n* asfixia, *f*
asphyxiate /æs'fɪksiˌeit/ *vt* asfixiar
asphyxiating /æs'fɪksiˌeitɪŋ/ *a* asfixiante
aspirant /'æspərənt/ *n* aspirante, candidato, *m*
aspirate /*v* 'æspəˌreit; *n* -pərɪt/ *vt* aspirar. —*n* letra aspirada, *f*
aspiration /ˌæspə'reiʃən/ *n* aspiración, ambición, *f;* deseo, anhelo, *m; Gram.* aspiración, *f*
aspire /ə'spaiər/ *vi* aspirar (a), pretender, ambicionar; alzarse
aspirin /'æspərɪn/ *n* aspirina, *f*
ass /æs/ *n* asno, *m*
assail /ə'seil/ *vt* atacar, acometer, arremeter
assailable /ə'seiləbəl/ *a* atacable
assailant /ə'seilənt/ *n* asaltador (-ra)
assassin /ə'sæsɪn/ *n* asesino, *mf*
assassinate /ə'sæsəˌneit/ *vt* asesinar
assassination /əˌsæsə'neiʃən/ *n* asesinato, *m*
assault /ə'sɔlt/ *n* asalto, *m;* acometida, embestida, *f; Fig.* ataque, *m.* —*vt* asaltar; acometer, embestir; atacar. **to take by a.,** tomar por asalto
assay /*n* 'æsei; *v* æ'sei/ *n* ensayo, *m, vt* ensayar, aquilatar
assayer /æ'seiər/ *n* ensayador, *m*
assaying /æ'seiɪŋ/ *n* ensaye, *m*
assemblage /ə'sɛmblɪdʒ/ *n* reunión, *f;* (of a machine) montaje, *m;* (of people) muchedumbre, *f,* concurso, *m;* (of things) colección, *f,* grupo, *m*
assemble /ə'sɛmbəl/ *vt* (persons) reunir, convocar; (things and persons) juntar; (a machine, etc.) armar, ensamblar. —*vi* reunirse, congregarse; acudir
assembly /ə'sɛmbli/ *n* asamblea, *f;* reunión, *f; Eccl.* concilio, *m.* **a. line,** cadena de montaje, línea de montaje, *f.* **a. room,** sala de reuniones, *f;* sala de baile, *f*
assent /ə'sɛnt/ *n* asentimiento, consentimiento, *m;* aprobación, *f;* (parliamentary, *Law.*) sanción, *f.* —*vi* asentir (a), consentir (en); aprobar
assert /ə'sɜrt/ *vt* mantener, defender; declarar, afirmar; hacer valer, reclamar. **to a. oneself,** imponerse, hacerse sentir; hacer valer sus derechos
assertion /ə'sɜrʃən/ *n* aserción, afirmación, *f;* defensa, *f;* reclamación, *f*
assertive /ə'sɜrtɪv/ *a* afirmativo; dogmático
assess /ə'sɛs/ *vt* tasar, valorar; fijar, señalar; repartir (contribuciones, etc.)
assessment /ə'sɛsmənt/ *n* tasación, *f;* fijación, *f;* repartimiento, *m*
assessor /ə'sɛsər/ *n Law.* asesor (-ra); (of taxes) repartidor (-ra); (valuer) tasador, *m.* **public a.,** tasador, *m*
asset /'æsɛt/ *n* ventaja, *f;* adquisición, *f;* cualidad, *f; pl* **assets,** fondos, *m pl; Com.* activo, *m,* créditos activos, *m pl*
assiduity /ˌæsɪ'dyuɪti/ *n* asiduidad, *f*
assiduous /ə'sɪdʒuəs/ *a* asiduo
assiduously /ə'sɪdʒuəsli/ *adv* asiduamente, con asiduidad
assign /ə'sain/ *vt Law.* ceder; señalar, asignar; (appoint) destinar; fijar; atribuir, imputar. —*n* cesionario (-ia)
assignation /ˌæsɪg'neiʃən/ *n* asignación, *f;* cita, *f; Law.* cesión, *f*
assignment /ə'sainmənt/ *n Law.* cesión, *f;* escritura de cesión, *f;* atribución, *f;* parte, porción, *f*
assimilable /ə'sɪmələbəl/ *a* asimilable
assimilate /ə'sɪməˌleit/ *vt* asimilar; incorporarse. —*vi* mezclarse
assimilation /əˌsɪmə'leiʃən/ *n* asimilación, *f;* incorporación, *f*
assimilative /ə'sɪmələtɪv/ *a* asimilativo
assist /ə'sɪst/ *vt* ayudar; auxiliar, socorrer; (uphold) apoyar; (further) promover, fomentar. —*vi* (be present) asistir (a)
assistance /ə'sɪstəns/ *n* ayuda, *f;* auxilio, socorro, *m;* apoyo, *m;* (furtherance) fomento, *m.* **public a.,** asistencia pública, *f*
assistant /ə'sɪstənt/ *n* ayudante, *m; Eccl.* asistente, *m;* (in a shop) dependiente (-ta); colaborador (-ra); (university) auxiliar, *m;* sub-. **a. secretary,** subsecretario (-ia). **a. secretaryship,** subsecretaría, *f*
associate /*n* ə'sousiɪt; *v* -siˌeit/ *n* asociado (-da); miembro, *m;* socio (-ia); compañero (-ra), amigo (-ga); colega, *m;* colaborador (-ra); (confederate) cómplice, *mf a* asociado; auxiliar. —*vt* asociar; unir, juntar. **to a. oneself with,** asociarse con; asociarse a. **to a. with,** frecuentar la compañía de, ir con
association /əˌsousi'eiʃən/ *n* asociación, *f;* unión, *f;* sociedad, *f;* compañía, corporación, *f;* (connection) relación, *f.* **a. football,** fútbol, *m*
assonance /'æsənəns/ *n* asonancia, *f*
assort /ə'sɔrt/ *vt* clasificar; mezclar
assorted /ə'sɔrtɪd/ *a* surtido, mezclado. **They are a well-a. pair,** Son una pareja bien avenida
assortment /ə'sɔrtmənt/ *n* clasificación, *f,* arreglo, *m;* surtido, *m,* mezcla, *f*
assuage /ə'sweidʒ/ *vt* mitigar; suavizar; calmar; aliviar
assume /ə'sum/ *vt* asumir; tomar; apropiarse; (wear) revestir; (suppose) suponer; poner por caso
assumed /ə'sumd/ *a* fingido, falso; supuesto
assumption /ə'sʌmpʃən/ *n* asunción, *f;* apropiación, arrogación, *f;* suposición, *f.* **Feast of the A.,** Fiesta de la Asunción, *f*
assurance /ə'ʃʊrəns/ *n* garantía, *f;* promesa, *f;* confianza, seguridad, *f;* (in a good sense) aplomo, *m,* naturalidad, *f;* (in a bad sense) presunción frescura, *f,* descaro, *m; Com.* seguro, *m*
assure /ə'ʃʊr/ *vt* asegurar
assured /ə'ʃʊrd/ *a* asegurado; seguro
assuredly /ə'ʃʊrɪdli/ *adv* seguramente
asterisk /'æstərɪsk/ *n* asterisco, *m*
astern /ə'stɜrn/ *adv* a popa; de popa; en popa; atrás
asthma /'æzmə/ *n* asma, *f*

asthmatic /æz'mætɪk/ *a* asmático
astigmatic /ˌæstɪg'mætɪk/ *a* astigmático
astigmatism /ə'stɪgməˌtɪzəm/ *n* astigmatismo, *m*
astir /ə'stɜr/ *adv* en movimiento; (out of bed) levantado; excitado
astonish /ə'stɒnɪʃ/ *vt* sorprender, asombrar
astonished /ə'stɒnɪʃt/ *a* atónito, estupefacto
astonishing /ə'stɒnɪʃɪŋ/ *a* sorprendente, asombroso
astonishment /ə'stɒnɪʃmənt/ *n* asombro, *m*, sorpresa, estupefacción, *f*
astound /ə'staund/ *vt* aturdir, pasmar. **to be astounded,** *Inf.* quedarse muerto
astounding /ə'staundɪŋ/ *a* asombroso
astray /ə'strei/ *adv* desviado, extraviado; por el mal camino. **to go a.,** errar el camino, perderse; *Fig.* descarriarse
astride /ə'straid/ *adv* a horcajadas. —*prep* a horcajadas sobre; a ambos lados de
astringent /ə'strɪndʒənt/ *a* astringente
astrologer /ə'strɒlədʒər/ *n* astrólogo (-ga)
astrological /ˌæstrə'lɒdʒɪkəl/ *a* astrológico
astrology /ə'strɒlədʒi/ *n* astrología, *f*
astronaut /'æstrəˌnɔt/ *n* astronauta, *mf*
astronomer /ə'strɒnəmər/ *n* astrónomo, *m*
astronomical /ˌæstrə'nɒmɪkəl/ *a* astronómico
astronomy /ə'strɒnəmi/ *n* astronomía, *f*
astrophysics /ˌæstrou'fɪzɪks/ *n* astrofísica, *f*
astute /ə'stut/ *a* astuto, sagaz; (with knave, etc.) redomado, pícaro
astuteness /ə'stutnɪs/ *n* astucia, sagacidad, *f*
asunder /ə'sʌndər/ *adv* en dos; separadamente; lejos uno de otro
asylum /ə'sailəm/ *n* asilo, *m;* (for the insane) manicomio, *m*
asymmetrical /ˌeisɪ'mɛtrɪkəl/ *a* asimétrico
asymmetry /ei'sɪmɪtri/ *n* asimetría, *f*
at /æt/ *prep* a; en casa de; en; de; con; por; (before) delante de. Sometimes forms part of verb, e.g. *to aim at,* apuntar. *to look at,* mirar. May be translated by using pres. part., e.g. *They were at play,* Estaban jugando. *at a bound,* de un salto. *at peace,* en paz. *at the doctor's,* en casa del médico. *at the crack of dawn,* al rayar el alba, al romper el alba. *at the head,* a la cabeza. *John is at Brighton,* Juan está en Brighton. *at first,* al principio. *at last,* por fin. *at no time,* jamás. *at once,* en seguida. *at most,* a lo más. *at all events,* en todo caso. *What is he getting at?* ¿Qué quiere saber? *at home,* en casa. *at-home day,* día de recibo, *m*
atavism /'ætəˌvɪzəm/ *n* atavismo, *m*
atavistic /ˌætə'vɪstɪk/ *a* atávico
atheism /'eiθiˌɪzəm/ *n* ateísmo, *m*
atheist /'eiθiɪst/ *n* ateo (-ea)
atheistic /ˌeiθi'ɪstɪk/ *a* ateo
Atheneum /ˌæθə'niəm/ *n* ateneo, *m*
Athenian /ə'θiniən/ *a* and *n* ateniense *mf*
Athens /'æθɪnz/ Atenas, *f*
athlete /'æθlit/ *n* atleta, *m*
athletic /æθ'lɛtɪk/ *a* atlético
athletics /æθ'lɛtɪks/ *n* atletismo, *m*
athwart /ə'θwɔrt/ *adv* de través. —*prep* al través de; contra
Atlantic /æt'læntɪk/ *a* and *n* atlántico *m.* **A. Charter,** Carta del Atlántico, *f.* **A. liner,** transatlántico, *m*
Atlantis /æt'læntɪs/ Atlántida, *f*
atlas /'ætləs/ *n* atlas, *m*
atmosphere /'ætməsˌfɪər/ *n* aire, *m;* atmósfera, *f; Fig.* ambiente, *m*
atmospheric /ˌætməs'fɛrɪk/ *a* atmosférico
atmospherics /ˌætməs'fɛrɪks/ *n pl* perturbaciones eléctricas atmosféricas, *f pl*
atoll /'ætɔl/ *n* atolón, *m*
atom /'ætəm/ *n* átomo, *m.* **splitting of the a.,** escisión del átomo, *f*
atomic /ə'tɒmɪk/ *a* atómico. **a. bomb,** bomba atómica, *f.* **a. pile,** pila atómica, *f.* **a. theory,** teoría atómica, *f*
atomize /'ætəˌmaiz/ *vt* pulverizar
atomizer /'ætəˌmaizər/ *n* pulverizador, *m*
atone /ə'toun/ *vi* (for) expiar
atonement /ə'tounmənt/ *n* expiación, *f*
atonic /ə'tɒnɪk, ei'tɒn-/ *a* átono, atónico
atrocious /ə'trouʃəs/ *a* atroz; horrible
atrocity /ə'trɒsɪti/ *n* atrocidad, *f*
atrophy /'ætrəfi/ *n* atrofia, *f, vi* atrofiarse
attach /ə'tætʃ/ *vt* (*Law.* of goods) embargar; (*Law.* of persons) arrestar; (fix) fijar; (tie) atar; (join) juntar; (stick) pegar; (connect) conectar; (hook) enganchar; (with a brooch, etc.) prender; (blame, etc.) imputar; (importance, etc.) dar, conceder; (assign) asignar; (attract) atraer; (enclose) adjuntar, incluir. —*vi* pertenecer (a), ser indivisible (de). **to a. oneself to,** pegarse a; adherirse a, asociarse con; acompañar; hacerse inseparable de
attaché /ætæ'ʃei/ *n* agregado, *m.* **a. case,** maletín, *m*
attachment /ə'tætʃmənt/ *n* (*Law.* of goods) embargo, *m,* vía ejecutiva, *f;* (*Law.* of persons) arresto, *m;* unión, *f;* conexión, *f;* (hooking) enganche, *m;* (with a brooch, etc.) prendimiento, *m;* (tying) atadura, *f;* (fixing) fijación, *f;* (affection) apego, cariño, *m;* (friendship) amistad, *f*
attack /ə'tæk/ *n* ataque, *m; Mil.* ofensiva, *f;* (access) acceso, *m.* —*vt* atacar
attacker /ə'tækər/ *n* atacador (-ra), asaltador (-ra)
attain /ə'tein/ *vt* alcanzar, conseguir, lograr. —*vi* llegar a; alcanzar
attainable /ə'teinəbəl/ *a* asequible, realizable; accesible
attainment /ə'teinmənt/ *n* consecución, obtención, *f;* logro, *m; pl* **attainments,** prendas, dotes, *f pl*
attempt /ə'tɛmpt/ *vt* (try) procurar, tratar de, intentar; ensayar; querer; *Law.* hacer una tentativa (de), atentar. —*n* tentativa, prueba, *f;* esfuerzo, ensayo, *m;* (criminal) atentado, *m,* tentativa, *f*
attend /ə'tɛnd/ *vi* prestar atención (a); escuchar; (look after) cuidar (de); (serve) servir; (accompany) acompañar; (await) esperar. —*vt* (be present) asistir (a); (of a doctor) visitar; (accompany) acompañar; (bring) acarrear, traer; (follow) seguir. **to be attended with,** traer consigo, acarrear
attendance /ə'tɛndəns/ *n* asistencia, presencia, *f;* (those present) público, *m,* concurrencia, *f;* servicio, *m;* (train) acompañamiento, *m; Med.* asistencia, *f,* tratamiento médico, *m.* **to be in a.,** acompañar (a)
attendant /ə'tɛndənt/ *a* que acompaña; que sigue; concomitante. —*n* criado (-da); (keeper) guardián (-ana); (nurse) enfermero (-ra); (in a cloakroom) guardarropa, *f;* (in a theater) acomodador (-ra); (on a train) mozo, *m;* (waiter) camarero, *m;* (at baths) bañero (-ra)
attention /ə'tɛnʃən; əˌtɛn'ʃʌn/ *n* atención, *f;* cuidado, *m.* **A.!** ¡Atención!; *Mil.* ¡Firmes! **to pay a.,** prestar atención. **to stand to a.,** cuadrarse, permanecer en posición de firmes
attentive /ə'tɛntɪv/ *a* atento; solícito; cortés, obsequioso
attentively /ə'tɛntɪvli/ *adv* con atención, atentamente; solícitamente
attentiveness /ə'tɛntɪvnɪs/ *n* cuidado, *m;* cortesía, *f*
attenuate /ə'tɛnyuˌeit/ *vt* atenuar
attenuating /ə'tɛnyuˌeitɪŋ/ *a* atenuante. **a. circumstance,** circunstancia atenuante, *f*
attenuation /əˌtɛnyu'eiʃən/ *n* atenuación, *f*
attest /ə'tɛst/ *vt* atestar. —*vi* atestiguar, deponer, dar fe
attestation /ˌætɛ'steiʃən/ *n* atestación, deposición, *f;* (certificate) certificado, *m,* fe, *f*
attic /'ætɪk/ *n* buhardilla, guardilla, *f,* desván, sotabanco, *m*
Attic /'ætɪk/ *a* ático
attire /ə'taiᵊr/ *n* atavío, *m;* (dress) traje, *m;* (finery) galas, *f pl, vt* ataviar, vestir; engalanar
attitude /'ætɪˌtud/ *n* actitud, *f;* postura, *f;* posición, *f*
attorney /ə'tɜrni/ *n* (solicitor) abogado (-da); (agent) apoderado (-da); (public) procurador, *m.* **power of a.,** poderes, *m pl* procuración, *f.* **A.-general,** fiscal, *m*
attract /ə'trækt/ *vt* atraer; (charm) seducir, cautivar, apetecer; (invite) convidar; (goodwill, etc.) captar
attraction /ə'trækʃən/ *n* atracción, *f;* atractivo, aliciente, encanto, *m*
attractive /ə'træktɪv/ *a* atrayente; atractivo, seductivo; apetecible; encantador
attractively /ə'træktɪvli/ *adv* atractivamente
attributable /ə'trɪbyʊtəbəl/ *a* imputable, atribuible

attribute /*v* ə'trɪbyut; *n* 'ætrəˌbyut/ *vt* atribuir (a), achacar (a), imputar (a). —*n* atributo, *m*

attribution /ˌætrə'byuʃən/ *n* atribución, imputación, *f;* atributo, *m*

attrition /ə'trɪʃən/ *n* atrición, *f*

auburn /'ɔbərn/ *a* castaño, rojizo

auction /'ɔkʃən/ *n* subasta, almoneda, *f;* venta pública, pública subasta, *f, vt* subastar. **to put up to a.,** sacar a pública subasta

auctioneer /ˌɔkʃə'nɪər/ *n* subastador (-ra)

audacious /ɔ'deiʃəs/ *a* atrevido, audaz, osado, temerario; (shameless) descarado, impudente

audaciously /ə'deiʃəsli/ *adv* osadamente; descaradamente

audacity /ɔ'dæsɪti/ *n* audacia, osadía, temeridad, *f,* atrevimiento, *m;* (shamelessness) descaro, *m,* desvergüenza, *f*

audibility /ˌɔdə'bɪlɪti/ *n* audibilidad, perceptibilidad, *f*

audible /'ɔdəbəl/ *a* audible, oíble

audibly /'ɔdəbli/ *adv* en forma audible, perceptiblemente, en alta voz

audience /'ɔdiəns/ *n* (interview and *Law.*) audiencia, *f;* oyentes, *m pl,* auditorio, público, *m.* **to give a.,** dar audiencia. **a. chamber,** sala de recepción, *f*

audiofrequency /'ɔdiouˌfrikwɛnsi/ *n* audiofrecuencia, *f*

audit /'ɔdɪt/ *vt* intervenir, examinar (cuentas). —*n* intervención, *f,* ajuste (de cuentas), *m*

audition /ɔ'dɪʃən/ *n* audición, *f*

auditor /'ɔdɪtər/ *n* (hearer) oyente, *mf;* interventor, contador, *m*

auditorium /ˌɔdɪ'tɔriəm/ *n* sala de espectáculos, *f*

auditory /'ɔdɪˌtɔri/ *a* auditivo, auditorio

Augean /ɔ'dʒiən/ *a* de Augeas; muy sucio

auger /'ɔgər/ *n* taladro, *m*

aught /ɔt/ *n* algo. **For a. I know,** Por lo que yo sepa

augment /ɔg'mɛnt/ *vt* aumentar, acrecentar. —*vi* aumentarse, acrecentarse

augmentation /ˌɔgmɛn'teiʃən/ *n* aumento, acrecentamiento, *m;* añadidura, *f*

augmentative /ɔg'mɛntətɪv/ *a* aumentativo

augur /'ɔgər/ *n* agorero (-ra). —*vt* and *vi* presagiar, anunciar; pronosticar, agorar

augury /'ɔgyəri/ *n* predicción, *f;* agüero, presagio, pronóstico, *m*

August /'ɔgəst/ *n* agosto, *m*

august /'ɔgəst/ *a* augusto

Augustan /ɔ'gʌstən/ *a* (of Roman emperor) augustal. **A. Age,** siglo de Augusto, *m*

Augustinian /ˌɔgə'stɪniən/ *a* and *n Eccl.* agustino (-na)

aunt /ænt, ɑnt/ *n* tía, *f.* **great-a.,** tía abuela, *f.* **A. Sally,** el pim, pam, pum

aura /'ɔrə/ *n* exhalación, *f;* influencia psíquica, *f; Med.* aura, *f*

aural /'ɔrəl/ *a* auricular. **a. surgeon,** otólogo, *m*

auricle /'ɔrɪkəl/ *n* (of the heart) aurícula, ala del corazón, *f;* oreja, *f,* pabellón de la oreja, *m*

aurora /ə'rɔrə/ *n* aurora, *f.* **a. borealis,** aurora boreal, *f*

auspice /'ɔspɪs/ *n* auspicio, *m*

auspicious /ɔ'spɪʃəs/ *a* propicio, favorable, feliz

auspiciously /ɔ'spɪʃəsli/ *adv* prósperamente, felizmente

auspiciousness /ɔ'spɪʃəsnɪs/ *n* buenos auspicios, *m pl;* felicidad, *f*

austere /ɔ'stɪər/ *a* severo, austero, adusto; ascético; (of style) desnudo

austerity /ɔ'stɛrɪti/ *n* austeridad, severidad, *f;* ascetismo, *m;* (of style) desnudez, *f*

Australian /ɔ'streilyən/ *a* and *n* australiano (-na)

Austrian /'ɔstriən/ *a* and *n* austríaco (-ca)

authentic /ɔ'θɛntɪk/ *a* auténtico

authenticate /ɔ'θɛntɪˌkeit/ *vt* autenticar

authentication /ɔˌθɛntɪ'keiʃən/ *n* autenticación, *f*

authenticity /ˌɔθɛn'tɪsɪti/ *n* autenticidad, *f*

author /'ɔθər/ *n* autor, *m*

authoress /'ɔθərɪs/ *n* autora, *f*

author index *n* índice de autores, *m*

authoritarian /əˌθɔrɪ'tɛəriən/ *a* autoritario

authoritative /ə'θɔrɪˌteitɪv/ *a* autoritario

authority /ə'θɔrɪti/ *n* autoridad, *f;* poder, *m.* **to have on the best a.,** tener de muy buena fuente

authorization /ˌɔθərə'zeiʃən/ *n* autorización, *f*

authorize /'ɔθəˌraiz/ *vt* autorizar

authorship /'ɔθərˌʃɪp/ *n* profesión de autor, *f;* paternidad (literaria), *f;* origen, *m*

autobiographical /ˌɔtəˌbaiə'græfɪkəl/ *a* autobiográfico

autobiography /ˌɔtəbai'ɒgrəfi/ *n* autobiografía, *f*

autocracy /ɔ'tɒkrəsi/ *n* autocracia, *f*

autocrat /'ɔtəˌkræt/ *n* autócrata, *mf*

autocratic /ˌɔtə'krætɪk/ *a* autocrático

autograph /'ɔtəˌgræf/ *n* autógrafo, *m*

autography /ɔ'tɒgrəfi/ *n* autografía, *f*

automatic /ˌɔtə'mætɪk/ *a* automático. **a. gate,** (at level crossings, etc.) barrera de golpe, *f.* **a. machine,** máquina automática, *f; Inf.* tragaperras, *m.* **a. pencil,** lapicero, *m*

automatically /ˌɔtə'mætɪkəli/ *adv* automáticamente

automatism /ɔ'tɒməˌtɪzəm/ *n* automatismo, *m*

automaton /ɔ'tɒməˌtɒn/ *n* autómata, *m*

automobile /ˌɔtəmə'bil/ *n* automóvil, *m*

autonomous /ɔ'tɒnəməs/ *a* autónomo

autonomy /ɔ'tɒnəmi/ *n* autonomía, *f*

autopsy /'ɔtɒpsi/ *n* autopsia, *f*

autosuggestion /ˌɔtousəg'dʒɛstʃən/ *n* autosugestión, *f*

autumn /'ɔtəm/ *n* otoño, *m*

autumnal /ɔ'tʌmnl̩/ *a* otoñal, de otoño

auxiliary /ɔg'zɪlyəri/ *a* auxiliar. —*n* auxiliador, *m*

avail /ə'veil/ *vi* servir; valer; importar. —*vt* aprovechar. **to a. oneself of,** valerse de, aprovecharse de. **to no a.,** en balde

availability /əˌveilə'bɪlɪti/ *n* utilidad, *f;* disponibilidad, *f;* provecho, *m;* (validity) validez, *f*

available /ə'veiləbəl/ *a* útil; disponible; aprovechable; válido

avalanche /'ævəˌlæntʃ/ *n* alud, lurte, *m*

avarice /'ævərɪs/ *n* avaricia, *f*

avaricious /ˌævə'rɪʃəs/ *a* avaro, avaricioso

ave /'ɑvei/ *interj* ¡ave! —*n* avemaría, *f;* despedida, *f*

avenge /ə'vɛndʒ/ *vt* vengar; vindicar. **to a. oneself for,** vengarse de

avenger /ə'vɛndʒər/ *n* vengador (-ra)

avenging /ə'vɛndʒɪŋ/ *a* vengador

avenue /'ævəˌnyu/ *n* avenida, *f*

aver /ə'vɜr/ *vt* afirmar, asegurar

average /'ævərɪdʒ/ *n* promedio, término medio, *m;* (marine insurance) avería, *f, a* de promedio; típico; corriente; normal. —*vt* hallar el término medio (de); prorratear, proporcionar; ser por término medio. **general a.,** (marine insurance) avería gruesa, *f.* **on the a.,** por término medio

averse /ə'vɜrs/ *a* opuesto (a); desinclinado (a); enemigo (de); repugnante. **to be a. to,** no gustar de; oponerse a; estar desinclinado a; ser enemigo de; repugnar

aversion /ə'vɜrʒən/ *n* aversión, *f;* repugnancia, *f*

avert /ə'vɜrt/ *vt* apartar; (avoid) evitar

aviary /'eiviˌɛri/ *n* avería, pajarera, *f*

aviation /ˌeivi'eiʃən/ *n* aviación, *f*

aviator /'eiviˌeitər/ *n* aviador (-ra)

avid /'ævɪd/ *a* ávido

avidity /ə'vɪdɪti/ *n* avidez, *f*

avidly /'ævɪdli/ *adv* ávidamente, con avidez

avocation /ˌævə'keiʃən/ *n* pasatiempo, *m,* distracción, *f;* ocupación, *f;* profesión, *f*

avoid /ə'vɔid/ *vt* evitar; (pursuit) evadir, eludir; guardarse (de), rehuir; *Law.* anular

avoidable /ə'vɔidəbəl/ *a* evitable, eludible

avoidance /ə'vɔidn̩s/ *n* evitación, *f*

avow /ə'vau/ *vt* confesar; declarar

avowal /ə'vauəl/ *n* confesión, admisión, *f*

avowedly /ə'vauɪdli/ *adv* por confesión propia

avuncular /ə'vʌŋkyələr/ *a* avuncular

await /ə'weit/ *vt* aguardar, esperar

awake /ə'weik/ *vt* despertar. —*vi* despertarse. —*a* despierto; vigilante; consciente (de); atento (a)

awakening /ə'weikənɪŋ/ *n* despertamiento, *m*

award /ə'wɔrd/ *n* sentencia, decisión, *f;* adjudicación, *f;* (prize) premio, *m.* —*vt* adjudicar; otorgar, conceder. **She was awarded a professorship in Greek,** Ganó unas oposiciones para una cátedra de griego

aware /ə'wɛər/ *a* consciente, sabedor. **to be well a. of,** saber muy bien. **to make a. of,** hacer saber

awash /ə'wɒʃ/ *adv* a flor de agua

away /ə'wei/ *adv* a distancia, a lo lejos, lejos; (absent) ausente; (out) fuera; (unceasingly) sin parar, continuamente; (wholly) completamente; (visibly) a ojos vistas. In verbs of motion **a.** is rendered by the reflexive, e.g. *to go a.*, marcharse. Sometimes not translated, e.g. *to take a.*, quitar. —*interj* ¡fuera de aquí! ¡márchese Vd.!; ¡vámonos! ¡adelante! *nine miles a.*, a nueve millas de distancia. *a. in the distance,* allá a lo lejos. *She sang a.*, Ella seguía cantando

awe /ɔ/ *n* temor reverente, *m;* horror, *m;* respeto, *m;* reverencia, *f, vt* intimidar, aterrar; infundir respeto (a). **to stand in awe of,** tener respeto (a), reverenciar

awesome /'ɔsəm/ *a* pavoroso, temible, aterrador; terrible; (august) augusto; (imposing) imponente

awestruck /'ɔ,strʌk/ *a* espantado, aterrado

awful /'ɔfəl/ *a* terrible, pavoroso; horrible; temible; atroz; *Inf.* enorme. **How a.!** *Inf.* ¡Qué barbaridad!

awfully /'ɔfəli, 'ɔfli/ *adv* terriblemente; horriblemente; *Inf.* muy

awfulness /'ɔfəlnɪs/ *n* lo terrible; lo horrible; atrocidad, *f;* (of a crime, etc.) enormidad, *f*

awkward /'ɔkwərd/ *a* difícil; peligroso; delicado; embarazoso; (of time, etc.) inconveniente, inoportuno; (of things) incómodo; (clumsy) torpe, desmañado; desagradable; (ungraceful) sin gracia. **the a. age,** la edad difícil

awkwardly /'ɔkwərdli/ *adv* torpemente; incómodamente; mal; con dificultad; sin gracia. **He is a. placed,** Se encuentra en una situación difícil

awkwardness /'ɔkwərdnɪs/ *n* dificultad, *f;* peligro, *m;* delicadeza, *f;* inconveniencia, inoportunidad, *f;* (clumsiness) torpeza, desmaña, *f;* (ungracefulness) falta de gracia, *f*

awl /ɔl/ *n* lezna, *f,* punzón, *m*

awning /'ɔnɪŋ/ *n* toldo, palio, *m; Naut.* toldilla, *f*

awry /ə'rai/ *adv* a un lado; oblicuamente; *Fig.* mal. —*a* torcido; *Fig.* descarriado

ax /æks/ *n* hacha, *f*

axiom /'æksiəm/ *n* axioma, *m*

axiomatic /,æksiə'mætɪk/ *a* axiomático

axis /'æksɪs/ *n* eje, *m; Zool.* axis, *m.* **A. power,** nacíon del Eje

axle /'æksəl/ *n* eje, *m;* peón, árbol (de una rueda), *m.* **back a.,** eje trasero, *m.* **differential a.,** eje diferencial, *m.* **front a.,** eje delantero, *m*

aye /ai/ *interj* sí. —*n* voto afirmativo, *m*

azalea /ə'zeilyə/ *n* azalea, *f*

Aztec /'æztɛk/ *a* and *n* azteca, *mf*

azure /'æʒər/ *n* azul celeste, *m*

B

b /bi/ *n* (letter) be, *f; Mus.* si, *m*

baa /bæ, bɑ/ *n* balido, be, *m*, *vi* balar, dar balidos

babble /ˈbæbəl/ *n* (chatter) charla, *f;* (of a child) gorjeo, *m;* (confused sound) vocinglería, barbulla, *f*, rumor, *m;* (of water) murmullo, susurro, *m.* —*vi* charlar; (of children) gorjearse; (incoherently) balbucir; (water) murmurar, susurrar; (a secret) descubrir

babbler /ˈbæblər/ *n* charlatán (-ana)

babbling /ˈbæblɪŋ/ *n* garrulería, locuacidad, *f;* (incoherent speech) balbuceo, *m.* (of water) murmullo, *m.* —*a* gárrulo, locuaz; balbuciente; murmurante

babel /ˈbæbəl/ *n* babel, *m*

baboon /bæˈbun; *esp. Brit.* bə-/ *n* babuino, *m*

baby /ˈbeibi/ *n* bebé, crío, *m;* niño (-ña) de pecho; *Fig.* gran bebé, *m;* niño mimado, *m*, *a* infantil. **b. blue,** azul claro, *m.* **b. doll,** muñeca bebé, *f.* **b. grand piano,** piano de media cola, *m*

baby carriage *n* coche de niños, *m*

baby-faced /ˈbeibi ˌfeist/ *a* con mejillas mofletudas

babyhood /ˈbeibiˌhʊd/ *n* infancia, niñez, *f*

babyish /ˈbeibiɪʃ/ *a* infantil, aniñado, pueril

Babylon /ˈbæbələn, -ˌlɒn/ babilonia, *f*

babysitter /ˈbeibiˌsɪtər/ *n* cuidaniños, *mf*

baccalaureate /ˌbækəˈlɔriɪt, -ˈlɒr-/ *n* bachillerato, *m*

baccarat /ˌbɑkəˈrɑ, ˌbækə-/ *n* bacará, *m*

bachelor /ˈbætʃələr/ *n* soltero, célibe, *m;* (of a university) licenciado, bachiller, *m;* (as a title) caballero, *m.* **confirmed b.,** solterón, *m.* **degree of b.,** licenciatura, *f.* **to receive the degree of b.,** licenciarse, bachillerarse

bachelorhood /ˈbætʃələrˌhʊd/ *n* soltería, *f*, celibato, *m*

bacillus /bəˈsɪləs/ *n* bacilo, *m*

back /bæk/ *n Anat.* espalda, *f;* (of an animal) lomo, espinazo, *m;* (reins, loins) riñones, *m pl;* (of chairs, sofas) respaldo, *m;* (of a book) lomo, *m;* (back, bottom) fondo, *m;* parte posterior, parte de atrás, *f;* (of a hand, brush and many other things) dorso, *m;* (of a coin) reverso, *m;* el otro lado de alguna cosa; (in football, hockey) defensa, *m; Theat.* foro, *m;* (of firearms) culata, *f;* (of a knife) canto, *m;* (upper portion) parte superior, *f.* —*a* posterior, trasero; de atrás; (remote) alejado, apartado; inferior; (overdue; past; out of date) atrasado; (earlier) anterior; *Anat.* dorsal. **at the b.,** detrás; en el fondo; en la última fila. **at the b. of one's mind,** por sus adentros, en el fondo del pensamiento. **behind one's b.,** a espaldas de uno, en ausencia de uno. **half-b.,** medio, *m.* **on one's b.,** boca arriba; a cuestas. **to see the b. of,** *Inf.* ver por última vez, desembarazarse de. **to turn one's b. on,** volver la espalda (a). **with one's b. to the engine,** de espaldas a la máquina. **b. to b.,** espalda con espalda

back /bæk/ *vt* empujar hacia atrás; (a vehicle) dar marcha atrás; hacer retroceder; (line) reforzar; (support) apoyar; (sign) endosar; (bind) forrar; (bet on) apostar a; (a sail) fachear. —*vi* retroceder; dar marchar atrás; (of the wind) girar; (with on to) dar sobre, dominar; (with down) abandonar (una pretensión, etc.). **to b. out,** salir, marcharse; volverse atrás; (retract) desdecirse

back /bæk/ *adv* detrás; atrás; otra vez, de nuevo; (returned) de vuelta; a alguna distancia; (at home) en casa. —*interj* ¡atrás! **A few weeks b.,** Hace unas semanas, Unas semanas atrás. **It stands b. from the road,** Está a alguna distancia del camino. **to go b. to,** (of families, etc.) remontar a. **to come b.,** regresar. **to come b. again,** regresar de nuevo, regresar por segunda vez

back axle *n* eje trasero, *m*

backbite /ˈbækˌbait/ *vt* cortar (a uno) un sayo, desollarle (a uno) vivo, murmurar de

backbiter /ˈbækˌbaitər/ *n* mala lengua, *f*, murmurador (-ra)

backbiting /ˈbækˌbaitɪŋ/ *n* murmuración, detracción, maledicencia, *f*, *a* murmurador, detractor

backbone /ˈbækˌboun/ *n* espinazo, *m*, columna vertebral, *f.* **to the b.,** hasta la médula

backchat /ˈbækˌtʃæt/ *n* dimes y diretes, *m pl;* insolencia, *f.* **to indulge in b.-c.,** andar en dimes y diretes

back door *n* puerta trasera, puerta de servicio, *f*

backed /bækt/ *a* (lined) forrado; (in compounds; of persons) de espalda; (of chairs) de respaldo

backer /ˈbækər/ *n* (better) apostador, *m;* protector (-ra, -triz)

backfire /ˈbækˌfaiər/ *n* contrafuego *m*, falsa explosión, *f*

backgammon /ˈbækˌgæmən/ *n* chaquete, *m*

back garden *n* jardín de atrás, *m*

background /ˈbækˌgraund/ *n* fondo, *m; Art.* último término, *m.* **in the b.,** en el fondo; *Art.* en último término; *Fig.* en las sombras; alejado, a distancia

backhand /ˈbækˌhænd/ *n Sports.* revés, *m*

backhanded /ˈbækˌhændɪd/ *a* de revés, dado con el revés de la mano; *Fig.* ambiguo, equívoco

backing /ˈbækɪŋ/ *n* forro, *m;* (lining) refuerzo, *m;* (of a vehicle) marcha atrás, *f;* retroceso, *m;* (betting) el apostar (a); (wagers) apuestas, *f pl;* (*Fig.* support) apoyo, *m*, ayuda, *f;* garantía, *f*

backlog /ˈbækˌlɔg/ *n Com.* rezago de pedidos, *m*

back number *n* (of a periodical) número atrasado, *m*

back pedal *vi* contrapedalear.

back premises *n* parte trasera (de una casa, etc.), *f*

backroom /ˈbækˈrum/ *n* cuarto interior, *m*, habitación trasera, *f.* **b. boy,** investigador ocupado en trabajos secretos para el gobierno, *m*

back seat *n* asiento trasero, *m;* fondo, *m.* **to take a b.-s.,** permanecer en el fondo, ceder el paso

back shop *n* trastienda, *f*

backside /ˈbækˌsaid/ *n* trasero, *m*, posaderas, nalgas, *f pl*

backslide /ˈbækˌslaid/ *vi* recaer, reincidir

backslider /ˈbækˌslaidər/ *n* (in religion or politics) apóstata, *mf;* reincidente, *mf*

backsliding /ˈbækˌslaidɪŋ/ *n* apostasía, *f;* reincidencia, *f*

backstage /ˈbækˈsteidʒ/ *n* foro, fondo del escenario, *m*, *adv* hacia el foro; detrás de bastidores

backstaircase /ˈbækˈstɛərˌkeis/ *n* escalera de servicio, *f;* escalera secreta, *f*

backstairs /ˈbækˈstɛərz/ *n* escalera de servicio, *f; Fig.* vías secretas, *f pl*, *a* de cocina; *Fig.* secreto

backstitch /ˈbækˌstɪtʃ/ *n Sew.* pespunte, *m*, *vt* and *vi* pespuntar

back street *n* calle secundaria, callejuela, *f; pl* **back streets,** barrios bajos, *m pl*

backstroke /ˈbækˌstrouk/ *n* reculada, *f; Sports.* revés, *m*

back tooth *n* muela, *f*

back view *n* vista de detrás, *f*

backward /ˈbækwərd/ *a* hacia atrás; vuelto hacia atrás; (in development) atrasado, poco avanzado; lento; negligente; (shy) modesto; (late) tardío; atrasado; retrógrado; (dull) torpe; retrospectivo. —*adv* hacia atrás; atrás; al revés; (of falling) de espaldas; (of time) al pasado. **to go b. and forward,** ir y venir. **b. and forward,** de acá para allá

backwardness /ˈbækwərdnɪs/ *n* atraso, *m;* lentitud, *f;* negligencia, *f;* modestia, *f;* (lateness) tardanza, *f;* atraso, *m;* (dullness) torpeza, *f;* falta de progreso, *f*

backwards /ˈbækwərdz/ *adv* See **backward**

backwash /ˈbækˌwɒʃ/ *n* agua de rechazo, *f*

backwater /ˈbækˌwɔtər/ *n* remanso, *m*

back wheel *n* rueda trasera, *f*, *vi* contrapedalear

backwoods /ˈbækˈwʊdz/ *n* monte, *m*, selva, *f*

back yard *n* corral, *m*

bacon /ˈbeikən/ *n* tocino, *m*

bacteria /bækˈtɪəriə/ *n* bacteria, *f*

bacterial /bækˈtɪəriəl/ *a* bacterial, bacteriano

bactericide /bækˈtɪərəˌsaid/ *n* bactericida, *m*

bacteriological /bækˌtɪəriəˈlɒdʒɪkəl/ *a* bacteriológico

bacteriologist /ˌbæktɪəriˈɒlədʒɪst/ *n* bacteriólogo, *m*

bacteriology /ˌbæktɪəri'ɒlədʒi/ *n* bacteriología, *f*

bad /bæd/ *a* malo; (wicked) perverso; (ill) enfermo, malo (with estar); (naughty; undutiful) malo (with ser); (of coins) falso; (of debts) incobrable; (rotten) podrido; (harmful) nocivo; (dangerous) peligroso; (of pains, a cold) fuerte; intenso; (of a shot) errado; (mistaken) equivocado; (unfortunate) desgraciado. —*n* el mal, lo malo; (persons) los malos. **extremely bad,** pésimo. **from bad to worse,** de mal en peor. **It's too bad!** ¡Esto es demasiado! **to go bad,** (fruit) macarse; (food) estropearse. **bad habit,** mala costumbre, *f*, vicio, *m*. **to have the bad habit of,** tener el vicio de. **bad temper,** malhumor, mal genio, *m*. **bad tempered,** malhumorado. **bad turn,** flaco servicio, *m*, mala pasada, *f*

badge /bædʒ/ *n* insignia, *f;* (decoration) condecoración, *f;* símbolo, emblema, *m;* (mark) marca, *f*

badger /'bædʒər/ *n* tejón, *m*, *vt* cansar, molestar

Bad Lands (of Nebraska and South Dakota) Tierras malas *f pl;* (of Argentina) la Travesía, *f*

badly /'bædli/ *adv* mal. **extremely b.,** pésimamente. **to want something b.,** necesitar algo con urgencia. **b. done,** mal hecho. **b. disposed,** malintencionado

badminton /'bædmɪntn̩/ *n* el juego del volante, *m*

badness /'bædnɪs/ *n* maldad, *f;* mala calidad, *f*, lo malo

bad-smelling /'bæd ˌsmɛlɪŋ/ *a* maloliente

baffle /'bæfəl/ *vt* desconcertar; (bewilder) tener perplejo (a); contrariar, frustrar; (obstruct) impedir; (avoid) evitar. **to b. description,** no haber palabras para describir

baffling /'bæflɪŋ/ *a* desconcertante; difícil; confuso; perturbador; (of people) enigmático

bag /bæg/ *n* saco, *m;* talega, *f;* (hand) bolsa, *f*, saco (de mano), *m;* (for tools) capacho, *m;* (for sewing) costurero, *m;* (of bagpipes) fuelle, *m;* (saddle) alforja, *f;* (briefcase) cartera, *f;* (suitcase) maleta, *f;* (under the eye) ojera, *f;* (game shot) caza, *f*. —*vt* entalegar; coger, cazar; matar; tomar. —*vi* (of garments) arrugarse. **to clear out bag and baggage,** liar el petate. **a bag of bones,** (person) un manojo de huesos. **bag wig,** peluquín, *m*

bagatelle /ˌbægə'tɛl/ *n* bagatela, friolera, *f;* (game) billar romano, *m*

bagful /'bægfʊl/ *n* saco, *m;* bolsa, *f*

baggage /'bægɪdʒ/ *n* equipaje, *m; Mil.* bagaje, *m;* (madcap) pícara, *f;* (jade) mujerzuela, *f*. **b. master,** (railway) factor, *m*. **b. car,** furgón de equipajes, *m*

baggage rack *n* (of automobile) portaequipajes, *m*

baggy /'bægi/ *a* (creased, of trousers) con rodilleras, arrugado; (wide) bombacho

bagpipe /'bæg,paip/ *n* gaita, *f*

bagpiper /'bæg,paipər/ *n* gaitero, *m*

bah /bɑ/ *interj* ¡bah!

Bahamas, the /bə'hɑməz/ las Islas Bahamas, las Islas Lucayas, *f*

bail /beil/ *n Law.* fianza, caución, *f;* (person) fiador (-ra); (cricket) travesaño, *m*, barra, *f*. —*vt Law.* poner en libertad bajo fianza; salir fiador (por); (a boat) achicar. **on b.,** en fiado. **to go b.,** dar fianza, fiar.

bailiff /'beilɪf/ *n Law.* agente ejecutivo, *m;* alguacil, *m;* mayordomo, *m;* capataz, *m*

bait /beit/ *n* cebo, *m;* anzuelo, *m;* (fodder) pienso, *m*, *vt* cebar; (feed) dar pienso (a); azuzar; atormentar; (attract) atraer

baiting /'beitɪŋ/ *n* cebadura, *f;* combate, *m;* tormenta, *f*

baize /beiz/ *n* bayeta, *f*. **green b.,** tapete verde, *m*

bake /beik/ *vt* cocer; hacer (pan, etc.). **I like to bake cakes,** Me gusta hacer pasteles; *Fig.* endurecer. —*vi* cocerse

bakelite /'beiklait/ *n* bakelita, *f*

baker /'beikər/ *n* panadero, hornero, *m*. **a baker's dozen,** la docena del fraile

bakery /'beikəri, 'beikri/ *n* panadería, *f*

baking /'beikɪŋ/ *n* cocimiento, *m*, cocción, *f;* (batch) hornada, *f;* el hacer (pan, etc.) *a Inf.* abrasador. **b.-dish,** tortera, *f*. **b.-powder,** levadura química, *f*

balance /'bæləns/ *n* balanza, *f;* equilibrio, *m; Com.* balance, saldo, *m;* (in a bank) saldo (a favor del cuentacorrentista), *m; Math.* resto, *m; Astron.* Libra, *f;* (pendulum) péndola, *f;* (counterweight) contrapeso, *m*. **credit b.,** saldo acreedor, *m*. **debit b.,** saldo deudor, *m*. **net b.,** saldo líquido, *m*. **to lose one's b.,** perder el equilibrio. **to strike a b.,** hacer balance. **b. of power,** equilibrio político, *m*. **b. of trade,** balanza de comercio, *f*. **b.-sheet,** balance, avanzo, *m*. **b. wheel,** (of watches) volante, *m*

balance /'bæləns/ *vt* balancear, abalanzar; contrapesar; (accounts) saldar; equilibrar; comparar; considerar, examinar. —*vi* balancearse; ser de igual peso; equilibrarse; (accounts) saldarse

balance of trade *n* balanza comercial, *f*

balancing /'bælənsɪŋ/ *n* balanceo, *m; Com.* balance, *m*. **b.-pole,** balancín, *m*

balconied /'bælkənid/ *a* con balcones, que tiene balcones

balcony /'bælkəni/ *n* balcón, *m;* galería, *f; Theat.* anfiteatro, *m*

bald /bɔld/ *a* calvo; (of style) seco, pobre; *Fig.* desnudo, árido, pelado; sin adorno; (simple) sencillo. **to grow b.,** ponerse calvo, encalvecer

balderdash /'bɔldər,dæʃ/ *n* galimatías, *m*, jerigonza, *f;* disparate, *m*

baldly /'bɔldli/ *adv* secamente; sencillamente

baldness /'bɔldnɪs/ *n* calvicie, *f;* (of style) sequedad, pobreza, *f;* (bareness) desnudez, aridez, *f*

bale /beil/ *n* (bundle) fardo, *m;* (of cotton, paper, etc.) bala, *f*

Balearic /ˌbæli'ærɪk/ *a* baleárico

Balearic Islands, the las Islas Baleares, *f*

baleful /'beilfəl/ *a* malicioso, siniestro, maligno

balefully /'beilfəli/ *adv* malignamente

balk /bɔk/ *n* obstáculo, *m;* (beam) viga, *f;* (billiards) cabaña, *f*. —*vt* frustrar; impedir. —*vi* resistirse, rehusar

Balkan /'bɔlkən/ *a* balcánico

Balkans, the los Balcanes, *m*

ball /bɔl/ *n* globo, *m*, esfera, *f;* (plaything) pelota, *f;* (as in billiards, cricket, croquet) bola, *f;* (in football, basket-ball) balón, *m;* (shot) bala, *f;* (of wool, etc.) ovillo, *m;* (of the eye) globo (del ojo), *m;* (of the thumb) yema (del pulgar), *f;* (of the foot) planta (del pie), *f;* (dance) baile, *m*. —*vi* apelotonarse. **red b.,** (in billiards) mingo, *m*. **to play b.,** jugar a la pelota. **to roll oneself into a b.,** aovillarse, hacerse un ovillo. **b.-and-socket joint,** articulación esférica, *f*. **b.-bearing,** cojinete de bolas, *m*

ballad /'bæləd/ *n* romance, *m;* (song) balada, *f*

balladmonger /'bæləd,mʌŋgər/ *n* coplero (-ra)

ballast /'bæləst/ *n* (*Naut.* and *Fig.*) lastre, *m; Rail.* balasto, *m*. —*vt* lastrar; llenar de balasto

ballerina /ˌbælə'rinə/ *n* bailarina, *f*

ballet /bæ'lei/ *n* baile ruso, ballet, *m;* baile, *m*. **b. master,** director de ballet, *m*

ballistics /bə'lɪstɪks/ *n* balística, *f*

balloon /bə'lun/ *n* globo aerostático, *m; Chem.* balón, *m;* (toy) globo, *m; Archit.* bola, *f*. **captive b.,** globo cautivo, *m*. **b. barrage,** cortina de globos de intercepción, *f*. **b.-tyre,** neumático balón, *m*

balloonist /bə'lunɪst/ *n* aeronauta, *mf*

ballot /'bælət/ *n* votación, *f;* papeleta para votar, cédu&;la de votación, *f*. —*vi* votar, balotar. **b. box,** urna electoral, *f*

ballpoint pen /'bɔl,pɔint/ *n* pluma esférica, *f*, birome, *m* (Argentina), punto-bola, *m* (Bolivia), esfero, *m* (Colombia)

ballroom /'bɔl,rum/ *n* salón de baile, *m;* salón de fiestas, *m*

ballroom dancing *n* baile de salón, *m*

balm /bɑm/ *n* bálsamo, *m; Fig.* ungüento, *m*

balminess /'bɑminɪs/ *n* fragancia, *f;* aroma, *m;* (gentleness) suavidad, *f*

balmy /'bɑmi/ *a* balsámico; fragante; aromático; (soft) suave; (soothing) calmante

balsam /'bɔlsəm/ *n* bálsamo, *m*

Baltic /'bɔltɪk/ *a* báltico

Baltic, the el (Mar) Báltico, *m*

baluster /'bæləstər/ *n* balaustre, *m*

balustrade /'bælə,streid/ *n* balaustrada, barandilla, *f*, antepecho, *m*

bamboo /bæm'bu/ *n* bambú, *m*

bamboozle /bæm'buzəl/ *vt* engatusar, embaucar

bamboozler /bæm'buzlər/ *n* embaucador (-ra)

bamboozling /bæm'buzlɪŋ/ *n* embaucamiento, engaño, *m*
ban /bæn/ *n* interdicción, *f;* prohibición, *f;* bando, *m.* —*vt* prohibir; proscribir
banal /bə'næl/ *a* banal, vulgar, trivial
banality /bə'nælɪti/ *n* banalidad, vulgaridad, trivialidad, *f*
banana /bə'nænə/ *n* (tree and fruit) plátano, *m;* (fruit) banana, *f.* **b. plantation,** platanar, *m*
band /bænd/ *n* lista, tira, *f;* zona, *f;* (black mourning) tira de gasa, *f;* (sash) faja, *f;* (ribbon) banda; cinta, *f;* (bandage) venda, *f; Mech.* correa, *f; Archit.* listón, *m; Mus.* banda, *f;* (group) pandilla, *f,* grupo, *m.* —*vt* congregar, reunir. —*vi* reunirse, asociarse. **b.-saw,** sierra de cinta, *f*
bandage /'bændɪdʒ/ *n* venda, *f,* vendaje, *m, vt* vendar, poner un vendaje en (limbs, etc. or persons)
bandaging /'bændɪdʒɪŋ/ *n* vendaje, *m*
banderol /'bændə,rɔl/ *n* banderola, *f*
bandit /'bændɪt/ *n* bandido, bandolero, *m*
bandmaster /'bænd,mæstər/ *n* músico mayor, *m;* director de orquesta, *m*
bandsman /'bændzmən/ *n* músico, *m*
bandstand /'bænd,stænd/ *n* quiosco de música, *m*
bandy /'bændi/ *vt* cambiar, trocar; pasar de uno a otro
bandy-legged /'bændi ,lɛgɪd/ *a* estevado zanquituerto
bane /bein/ *n* (poison) veneno, *m;* perdición, ruina, *f;* (nuisance) plaga, *f*
baneful /'beinfəl/ *a* pernicioso, funesto; dañino; maligno
banefully /'beinfəli/ *adv* funestamente; malignamente
bang /bæŋ/ *n* golpe, golpazo, *m;* (of an explosive, fire-arm) estallido, *m,* detonación, *f;* (of a firework) traque, *m;* (of a door) portazo, *m;* (with the fist) puñetazo, *m;* (noise) ruido, *m;* (fringe) flequillo, *m.* —*vt* golpear; (beat) sacudir; (throw) lanzar, arrojar con violencia; (a door, etc.) cerrar de golpe, cerrar con violencia. —*vi* golpear; estallar; (thunder) retronar; (in the wind) cencerrear. —*interj* ¡pum! ¡zas!
banging /'bæŋɪŋ/ *n* golpeadura, *f;* sacudidura, *f;* detonación, *f;* ruido, *m*
bangle /'bæŋgəl/ *n* (slave b.) esclava, *f;* pulsera, *f;* brazalete, *m;* (for ankles) ajorca, *f*
banish /'bænɪʃ/ *vt* desterrar; apartar; (from the mind) despedir, ahuyentar; (suppress) suprimir
banishment /'bænɪʃmənt/ *n* destierro, *m;* expulsión, *f;* relegación, *f;* (suppression) supresión, *f*
banister /'bænəstər/ *n* baranda, *f,* pasamano, *m*
banjo /'bændʒou/ *n* banjo, *m*
banjoist /'bændʒouɪst/ *n* tocador (-ra) de banjo
bank /bæŋk/ *n* (of rivers, etc.) ribera, orilla, *f,* margen, *m;* (of clouds) banda, capa, *f;* (of sand, fog, snow) banco, *m;* (embankment) terraplén, *m; Com.* banco, *m;* (gaming) banca, *f;* (for foreign exchange) casa de cambio, *f.* **b. account,** cuenta corriente, *f.* **b. book,** libreta de banco, *f.* **b. clerk,** empleado del banco, *m.* **b. holiday,** fiesta oficial, *f,* **b.-note,** billete de banco, *m.* **b. stock,** acciones de un banco, *f pl*
bank /bæŋk/ *vt* estancar, represar; amontonar; poner (dinero) en un banco, depositar en un banco. —*vi* tener cuenta corriente en un banco; (gaming) tener la banca; ser banquero; *Aer.* inclinarse al virar
banker /'bæŋkər/ *n* banquero, *m,* (also at cards); (money-changer) cambista, *mf*
banking /'bæŋkɪŋ/ *n Com.* banca, *f; Aer.* vuelo inclinado, *m, a Com.* bancario. **b. house,** casa de banca, *f*
bankrupt /'bæŋkrʌpt/ *a* insolvente, quebrado. —*n* quebrado (-da). **to go b.,** declararse en quiebra, hacer bancarrota
bankruptcy /'bæŋkrʌptsi/ *n* bancarrota, quiebra, *f; Fig.* pobreza, decadencia, *f.* **fraudulent b.,** quiebra fraudulenta, *f.* **b. court,** tribunal de quiebras, *m*
banner /'bænər/ *n* bandera, *f*
banns /bænz/ *n pl* amonestaciones, *f pl.* **to forbid the b.,** impedir las amonestaciones. **to publish the b.,** decir las amonestaciones
banquet /'bæŋkwɪt/ *n* banquete, *m, vt* and *vi* banquetear
banqueting /'bæŋkwɪtɪŋ/ *a* de banquetes. **b. hall,** sala de banquetes, *f*
bantam /'bæntəm/ *n* gallina enana, *f.* **b. weight,** (*Sports.*) *a* de peso gallo. —*n* peso gallo, *m*
banter /'bæntər/ *vt* and *vi* tomar el pelo (a). —*n* chistes, *m pl,* burlas, *f pl*
baptism /'bæptɪzəm/ *n* bautismo, *m; Fig.* bautizo, *m*
baptist /'bæptɪst/ *n* bautista, *m.* **St. John the B.,** San Juan Bautista
baptistry /'bæptəstri/ *n* baptisterio, bautisterio, *m*
baptize /bæp'taiz, 'bæptaiz/ *vt* bautizar
baptizing /bæp'taizɪŋ/ *n* bautizo, *m*
bar /bɑr/ *n* barra, *f;* (of chocolate, soap) pastilla, *f; Herald.* banda, *f;* (on a window) reja, *f;* (of a door) tranca, *f,* barrote, *m;* (bar lever) palanca, *f;* (of a balance) astil, *m; Mus.* barra, *f;* (in the sea, etc.) banco, alfaque, *m;* (barrier) barrera, *f;* (barrister's profession) foro, *m,* curia, *f; Fig.* tribunal, *m;* (in a court) barra, *f; Fig.* impedimento, *m;* (of light) rayo, *m;* (stripe) raya, *f;* (for refreshments) bar, *m;* mostrador del bar, *m.* —*vt* atrancar, abarrotar; impedir, obstruir; prohibir; exceptuar, excluir; (streak) rayar. **the b.,** el cuerpo de abogados. **to be called to the b.,** ser recibido como abogado en los tribunales. **b.-tender,** camarero del bar, *m*
bar association *n* colegio de abogados, *m*
barb /bɑrb/ *n* púa, *f;* (of an arrow, fish-hook, etc.) lengüeta, *f;* (of a lance) roquete, *m;* (of fish) barbilla, *f;* (of a feather) barba, *f;* (horse) caballo berberisco, *m.* —*vt* proveer de púas; armar de lengüetas
Barbados /bɑr'beidouz/ Isla de Barbados, *f*
barbarian /bɑr'bɛəriən/ *a* bárbaro, barbárico. —*n* bárbaro (-ra)
barbaric /bɑr'bærɪk/ *a* barbárico, salvaje
barbarism /'bɑrbə,rɪzəm/ *n* barbarismo, salvajismo, *m;* crueldad, *f;* (of style) barbarismo, *m*
barbarity /bɑr'bærɪti/ *n* barbaridad, ferocidad, *f*
barbarous /'bɑrbərəs/ *a* feroz, cruel, salvaje; inculto
barbarously /'bɑrbərəsli/ *adv* bárbaramente, cruelmente
barbarousness /'bɑrbərəsnɪs/ *n* barbaridad, *f;* crueldad, ferocidad, *f*
Barbary /'bɑrbəri/ Berbería, *f*
barbecue /'bɑrbɪ,kyu/ *n* barbacoa, *f*
barbed wire /'bɑrbd/ *n* alambre de púas, alambre espinoso, *m*
barber /'bɑrbər/ *n* barbero, *m.* **barber shop,** barbería, *f*
Barcelona /,bærsə'lounə/ (of or from) *a* and *n* barcelonés (-esa)
bard /bɑrd/ *n* bardo, vate, *m*
bare /bɛər/ *a* desnudo; descubierto; vacío; (mere) mero, solo; (worn) raído; pelado, raso; (unadorned) sencillo; (unsheathed) desnudo; (arid) árido; (curt) seco; (unprotected) desabrigado; pobre. —*vt* desnudar; descubrir; revelar. **He bared his head,** Se descubrió. **to lay b.,** dejar al desnudo; revelar
bareback /'bɛər,bæk/ *a* que monta en pelo. —*adv* en pelo
barefaced /'bɛər,feist/ *a* descarado, desvergonzado, cínico
barefoot /'bɛər,fʊt/ *a* descalzo
bareheaded /'bɛər,hɛdɪd/ *a* sin sombrero, descubierto
barelegged /'bɛər,lɛgɪd/ *a* en pernetas, en piernas
barely /'bɛərli/ *adv* apenas; escasamente; meramente, solamente
bareness /'bɛərnɪs/ *n* desnudez, *f;* desadorno, *m;* (aridity) aridez, *f;* pobreza, *f*
bargain /'bɑrgən/ *n* contrato, *m;* pacto, acuerdo, *m;* (purchase) ganga, *f.* —*vi* negociar; (haggle) regatear; (expect) esperar. **into the b.,** de añadidura, también. **It is a b.,** Es una ganga; Trato hecho. **to get the best of the b.,** salir ganando. **to strike a b.,** cerrar un trato. **b. counter,** sección de saldos, *f.* **b. sale,** venta de saldos, *f*
bargainer /'bɑrgənər/ *n* negociador (-ra); regatón (-ona)
bargaining /'bɑrgənɪŋ/ *n* negociación, gestión, *f;* (haggling) regateo, *m*
barge /bɑrdʒ/ *n* (for freight) barcaza, gabarra, *f;*

falúa, *f;* lancha, *f.* —*vi* (into) tropezar con; dar empujones
baritone /ˈbærɪˌtoun/ *n* barítono, *m*
barium /ˈbɛəriəm/ *n Chem.* bario, *m*
bark /bɑrk/ *n* (of a tree) corteza, *f;* (quinine) quina, *f;* (boat, *Poet.*) barca, *f; Naut.* buque de tres palos, *m;* (of a dog) ladrido, *m;* (of a fox) aullido, *m;* (of a gun) ruido, *m.* —*vi* (of a dog) ladrar; (of a fox) aullar; (of a gun) tronar
barking /ˈbɑrkɪŋ/ *n* ladrido, *m;* (of stags) rebramo, *m;* (of foxes) aullidos, *m pl;* (of guns) trueno, *m*
barley /ˈbɑrli/ *n* cebada, *f, a* de cebada. **pearl b.,** cebada perlada, *f.* **b.-bin,** cebadera, *f.* **b. dealer,** cebadero, *m.* **b. field,** cebadal, *m.* **b.-water,** hordiate, *m*
barm /bɑrm/ *n* (froth on beer) giste, *m;* (leaven) levadura, *f*
barmaid /ˈbɑrˌmeid/ *n* moza de bar, camarera, *f*
barn /bɑrn/ *n* pajar, granero, hórreo, *m.* **b.-owl,** lechuza, *f*
barnacle /ˈbɑrnəkəl/ *n* lapa, *f,* barnacla, *m*
barometer /bəˈrɒmɪtər/ *n* barómetro, *m*
barometric /ˌbærəˈmɛtrɪk/ *a* barométrico
baron /ˈbærən/ *n* barón, *m*
baroness /ˈbærənɪs/ *n* baronesa, *f*
Baron Munchausen /ˈbærən ˈmʊntʃˌhauzən/ el Baron de la Castaña
baroque /bəˈrouk/ *a* barroco. **the b.,** lo barroco
barrack /ˈbærək/ *n Mil.* cuartel, *m,* caserna, *f, vt* acuartelar
barrage /bəˈrɑʒ/ *n* presa de contención, *f; Mil.* cortina de fuego, *f;* (barrier) barrera, *f;* (of questions) lluvia, *f.* **b. balloon,** globo de intercepción, *m*
barrel /ˈbærəl/ *n* barril, *m;* tonel, *m,* cuba, *f;* (of a gun) cañón, *m; Mech.* cilindro, *m;* (of an animal) cuerpo, *m.* —*vt* embarrilar, entonelar. **b.-organ,** organillo, órgano de manubrio, *m*
barrelled /ˈbærəld/ *a* embarrilado; (of guns, generally in compounds) de... cañones. **double-b. gun,** escopeta de dos cañones, *f*
barren /ˈbærən/ *a* estéril; (of ground) árido; (fruitless) infructuoso
barrenness /ˈbærənˌnɪs/ *n* esterilidad, *f;* aridez, sequedad, *f;* (fruitlessness) inutilidad, *f*
barrens /ˈbærənz/ *n* yermo, *m sing,* yerma, *f sing*
barricade /ˈbærɪˌkeid/ *n* barricada, *f;* barrera, *f, vt* cerrar con barricadas; obstruir
barricading /ˈbærɪˌkeidɪŋ/ *n* el cerrar con barricadas; la defensa con barricadas (de)
barrier /ˈbæriər/ *n* barrera, *f;* impedimento, *m;* (for customs duties) portazgo, *m*
barring /ˈbɑrɪŋ/ *prep* salvo, excepto, con la excepción de, menos
barrister /ˈbærəstər/ *n* abogado (-da)
barrow /ˈbærou/ *n* carretón, *m;* carretilla, *f;* (tumulus) túmulo, *m*
barter /ˈbɑrtər/ *n* cambio, trueque, *m;* tráfico, *m, vt* and *vi* cambiar, trocar; traficar
barterer /ˈbɑrtərər/ *n* traficante, *mf*
basal /ˈbeisəl/ *a* básico, fundamental
basalt /bəˈsɔlt/ *n* basalto, *m*
base /beis/ *a* bajo, vil, ruin; soez; indigno; impuro; (of metals) de mala ley. —*n* base, *f;* fundamento, *m;* pie, *m; Archit.* pedestal, *m;* (*Mil. Chem. Geom.*) base, *f;* (of a vase) asiento, *m, vt* basar; fundar. **b. action,** bajeza, *f.* **b. line,** *Sports.* línea de base, *f.* **b. metal,** metal común, *m*
baseball /ˈbeisˌbɔl/ *n* pelota base, *f*
baseless /ˈbeislɪs/ *a* sin base; sin fundamento; insostenible
basely /ˈbeisli/ *adv* bajamente, vilmente
basement /ˈbeismənt/ *n* sótano, *m*
baseness /ˈbeisnɪs/ *n* bajeza, vileza, ruindad, *f*
bashful /ˈbæʃfəl/ *a* vergonzoso, ruboroso; tímido, corto; (unsociable) huraño, esquivo
bashfully /ˈbæʃfəli/ *adv* vergonzosamente; tímidamente
bashfulness /ˈbæʃfəlnɪs/ *n* vergüenza, *f,* rubor, *m;* encogimiento, *m,* timidez, cortedad, *f;* (unsociableness) huraňía, esquivez, *f*
basic /ˈbeisɪk/ *a* básico; fundamental
basic commodity *n* artículo básico, producto primario, *m*
basilica /bəˈsɪlɪkə/ *n* basílica, *f*
basilisk /ˈbæsəlɪsk/ *n* basilisco, *m*
basil (sweet) /ˈbæzəl, ˈbei-/ *n Bot.* albahaca, *f*
basin /ˈbeisən/ *n* vasija, *f;* (for washing) jofaina, *f;* (barber's) bacía, *f;* (of a fountain) taza, *f; Anat.* bacinete, *m;* (of a harbor) concha, *f;* (of a river) cuenca, *f* (in the earth) hoya, *f;* (dock) dársena, *f*
basis /ˈbeisɪs/ *n* base, *f;* fundamento, *m;* elemento principal, *m*
bask /bæsk/ *vi* calentarse; (in the sun) tomar el sol
basket /ˈbæskɪt/ *n* cesta, *f;* canasta, *f;* (frail) espuerta, *f.* **flat b.,** azafate, *m.* **large b.,** banasta, *f.* **b. with a lid,** excusabaraja, *f.* **b. ball,** baloncesto, *m.* **b. maker** or **dealer,** banastero, cestero, *m.* **b. work** or **shop** or **factory,** cestería, *f.* **b. work chair,** sillón de mimbres, *m*
basketful /ˈbæskɪtˌfʊl/ *n* cesta, cestada, *f*
Basle /bɑl/ Basilea, *f*
Basque /bæsk/ *a* and *n* vasco (-ca), vascongado (-da). —*n* (language) vascuence, *m*
Basque Provinces, the las Provincias Vascongadas
bas-relief /ˌbɑrɪˈlif, ˌbæs-/ *n* bajo relieve, *m*
bass /beis/ *n Mus.* bajo, *m;* (for tying) esparto, *m, a Mus.* bajo. **double b.,** contrabajo, *m.* **figured b.,** bajo cifrado, *m.* **b. clef,** clave de fa, *f.* **b. string,** bordón, *m.* **b. voice,** voz baja, *f*
bassinet /ˌbæsəˈnɛt/ *n* cochecito de niño, *m*
bassoon /bæˈsun/ *n Mus.* bajón, fagot, *m*
bassoonist /bæˈsunɪst/ *n* bajonista, fagotista, *mf*
bastard /ˈbæstərd/ *n* bastardo (-da), hijo (-ja) natural. —*a* bastardo, ilegítimo; espurio
baste /beist/ *vt Sew.* bastear, hilvanar, embastar; *Cul.* enlardar, lardear
basting /ˈbeistɪŋ/ *n Sew.* embaste, *m; Cul.* lardeamiento, *m.* **b. spoon,** cacillo, *m.* **b. stitch,** pasillo, *m*
bastion /ˈbæstʃən/ *n* bastión, baluarte, *m.* **to fortify with bastions,** abastionar
bastioned /ˈbæstʃənd/ *a* abastionado, con bastiones
bat /bæt/ *n Zool.* murciélago, *m;* (in cricket) paleta, *f;* (in table tennis) pala, *f.* —*vi* (cricket) golpear con la paleta. See **without**
batch /bætʃ/ *n* (of loaves, etc.) hornada, *f;* lote, *m;* (of recruits) promoción, *f*
bath /bæθ/ *n* baño, *m;* (room) cuarto de baño, *m;* (vat) bañador, *m;* (for swimming) piscina cubierta, *f;* (in the open air) piscina al aire libre, *f; Photo.* baño, *m,* solución, *f.* —*vt* bañar, lavar. **hot mineral baths,** termas, *f pl.* **Order of the B.,** Orden del Baño, *f.* **public baths,** casa de baños, *f.* **reinforcing b.,** *Photo.* reforzador, *m.* **to take a b.,** bañarse, tomar un baño. **b. -chair,** cochecillo de inválido, *m.* **b.-robe,** bata de baño, *f,* albornoz, *m.* **b. room,** cuarto de baño, *m.* **b. towel,** toalla del baño, *f.* **b. tub,** bañera, *f,* baño, *m*
bathe /beið/ *vt* bañar, lavar; (of light, etc.) bañar, envolver. —*vi* bañarse. —*n* baño, *m.* **to go for a b.,** ir a bañarse
bather /ˈbeiðər/ *n* bañista, *mf;* bañador (-ra)
bathing /ˈbeiðɪŋ/ *a* de baño; balneario, *n* baño, *m.* **b. cap,** gorro de baño, *m.* **b. dress,** traje de baño, *m.* **b. gown,** albornoz, *m,* bata de baño, *f.* **b. machine,** caseta de baños, *f.* **b.-pool,** piscina, *f.* **b.-resort,** estación balnearia, *f.* **b.-shoes,** calzado de baño, *m*
bathos /ˈbeiθɒs/ *n* paso de lo sublime a lo ridículo, *m;* anticlímax, *m*
batiste /bəˈtist/ *n;* batista, *f*
baton /bəˈtɒn/ *n* bastón de mando, *m; Mus.* batuta, *f;* (policeman's) porra, *f*
battalion /bəˈtælyən/ *n* batallón, *m*
batten /ˈbætn̩/ *vi* engordar (de); medrar, prosperar. **to b. down,** cerrar las escotillas
batter /ˈbætər/ *n Cul.* batido, *m;* pasta, *f; Sports.* lanzador, *m.* —*vt* apalear, golpear; (demolish) derribar, demoler; (with artillery) cañonear; batir. **to coat with b.,** rebozar. **to b. down,** derribar
battering ram /ˈbætərɪŋ/ *n* ariete, *m*
battery /ˈbætəri/ *n* (*Mil. Nav.*) batería, *f; Elec.* pila, batería, *f; Law.* agresión, *f.* **dry b.,** batería de pilas, *f.* **storage b.,** acumulador, *m.* **b. cell,** pila de batería eléctrica, *f*
battle /ˈbætl̩/ *n* batalla, *f;* pelea, *f,* combate, *m;*

(struggle) lucha, *f.* —*vi* batallar, pelear; luchar. **b.-array,** orden de batalla, *f.* **b.-axe,** hacha de combate, *f.* **b.-cruiser,** acorazado, *m.* **b.-field,** campo de batalla, *m.* **b.-front,** frente de combate, *m.* **b.-piece,** *Art.* batalla, *f.* **b.-ship,** buque de guerra, *m*

battledore (and shuttlecock) /'bætḷˌdɔr/ *n* raqueta (y volante), *f*

battlement /'bætḷmənt/ *n* almenaje, *m;* muralla almenada, *f*

bauble /'bɔbəl/ *n* (trifle) chuchería, fruslería, *f;* (fool's) cetro de bufón, *m*

bauxite /'bɔksait, 'bouzait/ *n* bauxita, *f*

Bavaria /bə'vɛəriə/ Baviera, *f*

Bavarian /bə'vɛəriən/ *a* and *n* bávaro (-ra)

bawdy /'bɔdi/ *a* obsceno, indecente, escabroso

bawl /bɔl/ *vi* chillar, vocear

bawling /'bɔlɪŋ/ *n* vocerío, *m,* chillidos, *m pl*

bay /bei/ *n Geog.* bahía, *f;* (small) abra, *f; Bot.* laurel, *m;* (horse) bayo, *m;* (howl) aullido, *m; Archit.* abertura, *f; Rail.* andén, *m.* —*a* (of horses) bayo, isabelino. —*vi* aullar. **at bay,** en jaque, acorralado. **sick-bay,** enfermería, *f.* **to keep at bay,** tener a distancia; tener alejado; entretener. **bay rum,** ron de malagueta, *m.* **bay window,** ventana salediza, *f*

baying /'beiɪŋ/ *n* aullido, *m*

bayonet /'beiənɛt/ *n* bayoneta, *f, vt* herir o matar con bayoneta. **fixed b.,** bayoneta calada, *f.* **b. charge,** carga de bayoneta, *f.* **b. thrust,** bayonetazo, *m*

Bayonne /ba'yɔn/ Bayona, *f*

bazaar /bə'zɑr/ *n* bazar, *m*

be /bi/ *vi* ser; (of position, place, state, temporariness) estar; (exist) existir; (in impersonal expressions) haber; (of expressions concerning the weather and time) hacer; (remain) quedar; (leave alone) dejar; (do) hacer; (of one's health) estar; (of feeling cold, hot, afraid, etc. and of years of one's age) tener; (live) vivir; (belong) ser (de), pertenecer (a); (matter, concern) importar (a); (happen) ocurrir, suceder; (find oneself) hallarse, encontrarse, estar; (arrive) llegar (a); (cost) costar; (be worth) valer; (celebrate, hold) celebrarse, tener lugar; (forming continuous tense with present participle active or passive) estar; (with past participle forming passive) ser (this construction is often replaced by reflexive form when no ambiguity is entailed); (with infinitive expressing duty, intention) haber de; (must) tener que. **He is a soldier (doctor, etc.),** Es soldado (médico, etc.). **He is on guard,** Está de guardia. **They were at the door (in the house, etc.),** Estaban a la puerta (en la casa, etc.). **I am writing a letter,** Estoy escribiendo una carta (but this form is often replaced by a simple tense, e.g. escribo...). **It remains to be written,** Queda por escribir. **What is to be done?** ¿Qué hay que hacer? **Woe is me!** ¡Ay de mí! **to be hot (cold),** (of things) estar caliente (frío); (of weather) hacer calor (frío); (of persons) tener calor (frío). **How is John? He is well,** ¿Cómo está Juan? Está bien de salud. **It is daylight,** Es de día. **It is cloudy,** Está nublado. **She is 10,** Tiene diez años. **They are afraid,** Tienen miedo. **I am to go there tomorrow,** He de ir allí mañana. **What is to be will be,** Lo que tiene que ser será. **If John were to come we could go into the country,** Si viniera Juan podríamos ir al campo. **Be that as it may,** Sea como sea. **It is seven years since we saw him,** Hace siete años que no le vemos. **We have been here for three years,** Hace tres años que estamos aquí, Llevamos tres años aquí. **There is** or **there are,** Hay. **There will be many people,** Habrá mucha gente. **There were many people,** Había mucha gente. **There are many people,** Hay mucha gente. **It is three miles to the next village,** Estamos a tres millas del pueblo próximo. **So be it!** Así sea. **Your pen is not to be seen,** Tu pluma no se ve. **It is to be hoped that...,** Se espera que...; ¡Ojalá que...! **The door is open,** La puerta está abierta. **The door was opened by Mary,** La puerta fue abierta por María. **He was accused of being a fascist,** Lo acusaron de fascista. **to be about to,** estar por; (of a more imminent action) estar para, estar a punto de. **to be in,** estar dentro; estar en casa. **to be off,** marcharse, irse. **Be off!** ¡Márchate! ¡Vete!; ¡Fuera! **to be out,** estar fuera; haber salido; no estar en casa; (of a light, etc.) estar apagado. **to be up,** estar levantado. **to be up to,** proyectar, traer entre manos; urdir, maquinar

beach /bitʃ/ *n* playa, *f;* costa, *f.* —*vt* (a boat) encallar en la costa. **b. shoes,** playeras, *f pl.* **b. suit,** vestido de playa, *m*

beach club *n* club de playa, *m*

beacon /'bikən/ *n* (lighthouse) faro, *m;* (buoy) baliza, *f,* fanal, *m;* (watch-tower) atalaya, *f; Fig.* guía, *f.* —*vt* iluminar. **b. fire,** almenara, *f*

bead /bid/ *n* cuenta, *f;* (of glass) abalorio, *m;* (drop) gota, *f; Archit.* perla, *f;* (bubble) burbuja, *f;* (foam) espuma, *f; pl* **beads,** rosario, *m, vt* adornar con abalorios. **to tell one's beads,** rezar el rosario. **b. work,** abalorio, *m*

beading /'bidɪŋ/ *n* abalorio, *m; Archit.* friso, listón, *m*

beadle /'bidḷ/ *n* bedel, *m*

beadleship /'bidəlˌʃɪp/ *n* bedelía, *f*

beagle /'bigəl/ *n* perro sabueso, *m*

beak /bik/ *n* pico, *m;* punta, *f; Naut.* espolón, *m.* **to tap with the b.,** picotear

beaked /'bikt/ *a* que tiene pico; (in compounds) de... pico

beaker /'bikər/ *n* copa, *f; Chem.* vaso de precipitado, *m*

beam /bim/ *n Archit.* madero, *m,* viga, *f;* (width of a ship) manga, *f;* (of a balance) palanca, *f;* (of a plough) cama, *f;* (of light) rayo, destello, *m; Phys.* rayo, *m;* (smile) sonrisa brillante, *f; pl* **beams,** (of a building) envigado, *m;* (of a ship) baos, *m pl.* **main b.,** *Archit.* viga maestra, *f.* **on her b.-ends,** de costado; *Fig.* arruinado; en la miseria. **b. feather,** astil, *m.* **b. of light,** rayo de luz, haz de luz, *m*

beam /bim/ *vt* lanzar, emitir; difundir. —*vi* brillar, fulgurar, destellar; estar radiante, estar rebosando de alegría

beaming /'bimɪŋ/ *a* brillante; radiante

bean /bin/ *n* haba, *f;* judía, alubia, *f;* (of coffee) grano, *m.* **broad b.,** haba, *f.* **French, haricot, kidney b.,** judía, *f.* **string b.,** judía verde, *f.* **b. field,** habar, *m*

bear /bɛər/ *n Zool.* oso, *m;* (she-bear) osa, *f;* (Stock Exchange) bajista, *mf.* **Great B.,** *Astron.* Osa Mayor, *f,* Septentrión, *m.* **Little B.,** *Astron.* Osa Menor, *f.* **polar b.,** oso blanco, *m.* **b.-cub,** osezno, *m.* **bear's den,** osera, *f.* **b.-garden,** patio de osos, *m; Inf.* merienda de negros, *f.* **b.-hunting,** caza de osos, *f.* **b.-like,** osuno. **b.-pit,** recinto de los osos, *m*

bear /bɛər/ *vt* and *vi* (carry) llevar; (show) ostentar; (company, etc.) hacer; (profess) profesar; (of spite, etc. and of relation) guardar; (have) tener; (fruit) dar; (give birth to) parir; (support) sostener; (endure) aguantar; (suffer) padecer, sufrir; (tolerate) tolerar, sufrir; (a strain, an operation, etc.) resistir; (lean on) apoyarse en; (experience) experimentar; (produce) producir, dar; (enjoy) disfrutar de; (use) usar; (impel) empujar; (occupy, hold) ocupar; (go) dirigirse. **It was suddenly borne in on them that...,** De pronto vieron claro que... **I cannot b. any more,** No puedo más. **We cannot b. him,** No le aguantamos, No le sufrimos. **His language won't b. repeating,** Su lenguaje no puede repetirse. **to bring to b.,** ejercer (presión, etc.). **to b. a grudge,** guardar rencor (a), tener ojeriza (a). **to b. arms,** llevar armas; servir en el ejército o la milicia. **to b. company,** hacer compañía (a), acompañar (a). **to b. in mind,** tener en cuenta, tener presente; acordarse de. **to b. oneself,** conducirse, portarse. **to b. to the right,** ir hacia la derecha. **to b. witness,** atestiguar. **to b. false witness,** levantar falso testimonio. **to b. away,** llevarse; ganar. **to b. down,** hundir; derribar; bajar. **to b. down on,** avanzar rápidamente hacia; correr hacia; *Naut.* arribar sobre; (attack) caer sobre. **to b. in,** llevar adentro. **to b. off,** llevarse; ganar; *Naut.* apartarse de la costa. **to b. on, upon,** apoyarse en; (refer to) referirse a. **to b. out,** llevar fuera; confirmar; apoyar; justificar. **to b. up,** llevar arriba; llevar a la cumbre (de); sostener; (recover) cobrar ánimo; (against) resistir; hacer frente a. **to b. with,** soportar; sufrir; aguantar; llevar con paciencia; ser indulgente con

bearable /ˈbɛərəbəl/ *a* soportable; aguantable; tolerable
beard /bɪərd/ *n* barba, *f;* (of cereals) raspa, arista, *f, vt* desafiar. **thick b.,** barba bien poblada, *f*
bearded /ˈbɪərdɪd/ *a* con barba, barbudo
beardless /ˈbɪərdlɪs/ *a* barbilampiño, desbarbado, imberbe, lampiño
bearer /ˈbɛərər/ *n* llevador (-ra), portador (-ra); (of a bier) andero, *m; Com.* dador, portador, *m.* **good b.,** *Agr.* árbol fructífero, *m.* **to b.,** *Com.* al portador
bearing /ˈbɛərɪŋ/ *n* porte, *m;* postura, *f;* presencia, *f;* conducta, *f;* aspecto, *m;* relación, *f;* (meaning) significación, *f; Naut.* demora, orientación, *f; Mech.* cojinete, soporte, *m;* (endurance) tolerancia, *f; pl* **bearings,** (way) camino, *m; Herald.* escudo de armas, *m.* **to get one's bearings,** orientarse; encontrar el camino. **to lose one's bearings,** desorientarse; perderse. **to have a b. on,** tener relación con; tener que ver con; influir en
bearish /ˈbɛərɪʃ/ *a* osuno; rudo, áspero
bearskin /ˈbɛərˌskɪn/ *n* piel de oso, *f;* birretina, *f*
beast /bist/ *n* animal, bruto, *m;* cuadrúpedo, *m;* (cattle) res, *f;* bestia, *f.* **wild b.,** fiera, *f.* **b. of burden,** acémila, bestia de carga, *f.* **b. of prey,** animal de rapiña, *m*
beastliness /ˈbistlinɪs/ *n* bestialidad, brutalidad, *f;* obscenidad, *f*
beastly /ˈbistli/ *a* bestial, brutal; obsceno; *Inf.* horrible
beat /bit/ *n* latido, *m,* pulsación, *f;* golpe, *m;* (of a drum) toque (de tambor), *m;* (of a clock) tictac, *m;* sonido repetido, *m;* vibración, *f*
beat /bit/ *vt* and *vi* batir; golpear; (thrash) pegar, dar una paliza (a); (to remove dust, etc.) sacudir; (shake) agitar; (the wings) aletear; (hunting) batir; (excel) exceder, superar; ganar; (defeat) vencer; (of the rain, etc.) azotar; (a drum) tocar; (of the sun) batir, dar (en); (throb) latir, palpitar, pulsar. **to b. about the bush,** andarse por las ramas. **to stop beating about the bush,** dejarse de historias. **to b. a retreat,** *Mil.* emprender la retirada; huir. **to b. black and blue,** moler a palos. **to b. hollow,** vencer completamente; ganar fácilmente; aventajar con mucho. **to b. it,** *Inf.* escaparse corriendo. **to b. time,** *Mus.* llevar el compás; triunfar sobre la vejez. **to b. to it,** *Inf.* tomar la delantera. **to b. against,** golpear contra; chocar contra. **to b. back,** rechazar; (sobs, etc.) ahogar; reprimir. **to b. down,** (prices) regatear; (of the sun) caer de plomo, caer de plano; reducir; suprimir; destruir. **to b. off,** rechazar; echar a un lado. **to b. out,** hacer salir; (metals) batir; (a tune) llevar el compás (de). **to b. up,** *Cul.* batir; (a mattress) mullir; asaltar; maltratar
beaten /ˈbitn̩/ *a* (of paths) trillado; (conquered) vencido; (of metals) batido; (dejected) deprimido; (trite) trivial, vulgar
beater /ˈbitər/ *n* batidor, *m;* (for carpets) sacudidor (de alfombras), *m; Cul.* batidor, *m*
beatific /ˌbiəˈtɪfɪk/ *a* beatífico
beatification /biˌætəfɪˈkeiʃən/ *n* beatificación, *f*
beatify /biˈætəˌfai/ *vt* beatificar
beating /ˈbitɪŋ/ *n* batimiento, *m;* vencimiento, *m;* (thrashing) paliza, *f;* (of the heart, etc.) palpitación, *f,* latido, *m;* (of metals) batida, *f;* (of a drum) rataplán, toque de tambor, *m;* (of waves) embate, *m;* (of wings) aleteo, aletazo, *m*
beatitude /biˈætɪˌtud/ *n* beatitud, *f*
beau /bou/ *n* galán, *m;* (fop) petimetre, *m*
beautiful /ˈbyutəfəl/ *a* bello, lindo, hermoso; magnífico; excelente; exquisito; elegante; encantador, delicioso
beautifully /ˈbyutəfəli/ *adv* bellamente; (richly) ricamente; admirablemente; magníficamente; elegantemente
beautify /ˈbyutəˌfai/ *vt* embellecer; hermosear; adornar. **to b. oneself,** arreglarse, ponerse elegante
beautifying /ˈbyutəfaiɪŋ/ *n* embellecimiento, *m;* adorno, *m*
beauty /ˈbyuti/ *n* belleza, hermosura, lindeza, *f;* magnificencia, *f;* excelencia, *f;* elegancia, *f;* encanto, *m;* (belle) beldad, Venus, *f.* **to lose one's b.,** desmejorarse, perder su hermosura. **b. contest,** concurso de belleza, *m.* **b. parlor,** salón de belleza, instituto de belleza, *m.* **b. sleep,** el primer sueño de la noche. **b. spot,** lunar, *m;* lunar postizo, *m;* (place) sitio hermoso, *m.* **b. treatment,** masaje facial, *m*
beaver /ˈbivər/ *n* castor, *m;* (hat) sombrero de copa, *m;* (of helmet) babera, *f*
because /bɪˈkɔz/ *conjunc* porque. **b. of,** debido a, a causa de
beckon /ˈbɛkən/ *vt* and *vi* hacer señas (a); llamar por señas, llamar con la mano
become /bɪˈkʌm/ *vi* volverse; llegar a ser, venir a ser; convertirse en; ponerse; hacerse; (befit) convenir; (suit) ir bien (a), favorecer. **He became red,** Se enrojeció. **The hat becomes you,** El sombrero te va bien. **He became king,** Llegó a ser rey. **What has b. of her?** ¿Qué es de ella?; (Where is she?) ¿Qué se ha hecho de ella? **b. binding,** adquirir carácter de compromiso
becoming /bɪˈkʌmɪŋ/ *a* propio; correcto; decoroso; (suitable) conveniente; (of dress) que favorece, que va bien. **This dress is b. to you,** Este vestido te favorece
becomingly /bɪˈkʌmɪŋli/ *adv* decorosamente
bed /bɛd/ *n* cama, *f,* lecho, *m;* (of sea) fondo, *m;* (of river) cauce, *m; Geol.* yacimiento, *m;* (in a garden) cuadro, macizo (de jardín), *m;* (of a machine) asiento, *m;* (of a building) cimiento, *m; Fig.* fundamento, *m,* base, *f, vt* (plants) plantar; (fix) fijar, poner. **double bed,** cama de matrimonio, *f.* **single bed,** cama de monja, *f.* **in bed,** en cama. **to be gone to bed,** haber ido a la cama. **to be in bed,** estar acostado. **to get into bed,** meterse en cama. **to get out of bed,** levantarse de la cama. **to go to bed,** acostarse, ir a la cama. **to make the beds,** hacer las camas. **to put to bed,** acostar. **to stay in bed,** quedarse en cama, guardar cama. **bed-bug,** chinche, *f.* **bed-clothes,** ropa de cama, *f.* **bed-cover,** cubrecama, colcha, *f.* **bed-head,** cabecera, *f.* **bed-pan,** silleta, *f.* **bed-sore,** úlcera de decúbito, *f*
bedaub, bedazzle /bɪˈdɔb; bɪˈdæzəl/. See **daub, dazzle**
bedchamber /ˈbɛdˌtʃeimbər/ *n* dormitorio, *m,* alcoba, *f*
bedded /ˈbɛdɪd/ *a* con... cama(s). **a double-b. room,** un cuarto con dos camas; un cuarto con cama de matrimonio
bedding /ˈbɛdɪŋ/ *n* ropa de cama, *f;* cama para el ganado, *f*
bedeck /bɪˈdɛk/ *vt* embellecer, adornar, engalanar
bedfellow /ˈbɛdˌfɛlou/ *n* compañero de almohada, compañero de cama
bedlam /ˈbɛdləm/ *n* belén, manicomio, *m; Fig.* babel, *m*
Bedouin /ˈbɛduɪn/ *a* and *n* beduino (-na)
bedraggled /bɪˈdrægəld/ *a* mojado y sucio
bedridden /ˈbɛdˌrɪdn̩/ *a* postrado en cama, inválido
bedrock /ˈbɛdˌrɒk/ *n* lecho de roca, *m; Fig.* principios fundamentales, fundamentos, *m pl*
bedroom /ˈbɛdˌrum/ *n* cuarto de dormir, dormitorio, *m,* habitación, *f*
bedside /ˈbɛdˌsaid/ *n* lado de cama, *m;* cabecera, *f.* **b. manner,** mano izquierda, diplomacia, *f.* **b.-table,** mesa de noche, *f*
bedspread /ˈbɛdˌsprɛd/ *n* colcha, cubrecama, sobrecama, *f*
bedstead /ˈbɛdˌstɛd/ *n* cama, *f*
bedtime /ˈbɛdˌtaim/ *n* hora de acostarse, *f*
bee /bi/ *n* abeja, *f;* (meeting) reunión, *f, a* abejuno. **queen bee,** rey, *m,* abeja maestra, *f.* **to have a bee in one's bonnet,** tener una manía (or idea fija). **to make a bee-line for,** ir directamente a. **bee-eater,** *Ornith.* abejaruco, *m.* **bee hive,** colmena, *f;* abejar, *m.* **bee-keeper,** apicultor (-ra), colmenero (-ra), abejero (-ra). **bee's wax,** cera de abeja, *f*
beech /bitʃ/ *n* haya, *f.* **plantation of b. trees,** hayal, *m.* **b.-nut,** hayuco, *m*
beef /bif/ *n* carne de vaca, *f;* (flesh) carne, *f;* (strength) fuerza, *f.* **roast b.,** rosbif, *m.* **b.-tea,** caldo, *m*
beefsteak /ˈbifˌsteik/ *n* biftec, bistec, *m*
beer /bɪər/ *n* cerveza, *f.* **b. barrel,** barril de cerveza,

m. **b.-house,** cervecería, *f.* **b. mug,** jarro para la cerveza, *m*

beery /'bɪəri/ *a* de cerveza; (tipsy) achispado

beet /bit/ *n* remolacha, *f.* **b. sugar,** azúcar de remolacha, *m*

beetle /'bitl̩/ *n* escarabajo, *m.* **b.-browed,** cejijunto

beetroot /'bit,rut/ *n* remolacha, *f*

befall /bɪ'fɔl/ *vi* acontecer, suceder, ocurrir. —*vt* ocurrir (a), acontecer (a)

befeathered /bɪ'fɛðərd/ *a* plumado; adornado con plumas

befit /bɪ'fɪt/ *vt* convenir (a), ser digno de

befitting /bɪ'fɪtɪŋ/ *a* conveniente, apropiado; digno; oportuno

before /bɪ'fɔr/ *adv* delante; al frente; (of time), antes, anteriormente; (of order) antes; (already) ya. —*prep* delante de; en frente de; (of time, order) ante; (in the presence of) ante, en presencia de; (rather than) antes de. **b. going,** antes de marcharse. **B. I did it,** Antes de que lo hiciera; Antes de hacerlo. **as never b.,** como nunca. **b. long,** en breve, dentro de poco. **b.-mentioned,** antes citado. **b. the mast,** al pie del mástil, e.g. *two years b. the mast,* dos años al pie del mástil.

beforehand /bɪ'fɔr,hænd/ *adv* previamente, de antemano

befoul /bɪ'faul/ *vt* ensuciar; *Fig.* manchar, difamar

befriend /bɪ'frɛnd/ *vt* proteger, ayudar, favorecer, amparar

beg /bɛg/ *vt* pedir, implorar, suplicar. —*vi* mendigar, pordiosear; vivir de limosna. **I beg to propose,** Me permito proponer; Tengo el gusto de proponer; (the health of) Brindo a la salud de. **I beg your pardon!** ¡Vd. dispense!; (when passing in front of anyone, etc.) Con permiso; (in conversation for repetition of a word) ¿Cómo? **to beg the question,** dar por sentado lo mismo que se trata de probar. **His conduct begs description,** No hay palabras para su comportamiento

beget /bɪ'gɛt/ *vt* procrear, engendrar; causar; suscitar

begetter /bɪ'gɛtər/ *n* procreador (-ra); creador (-ra)

begetting /bɪ'gɛtɪŋ/ *n* procreación, *f;* origen, *m,* causa, *f*

beggar /'bɛgər/ *n* mendigo (-ga), pordiosero (-ra). **beggars can't be choosers,** a falta de pan, se conforma con tortillas (Mexico); *vt* empobrecer; arruinar. **to b. description,** no haber palabras para describir

beggarliness /'bɛgərlinɪs/ *n* mendicidad, *f;* pobreza, *f*

beggarly /'bɛgərli/ *a* miserable, pobre

beggary /'bɛgəri/ *n* miseria, pobreza, *f*

begging /'bɛgɪŋ/ *a* mendicante, pordiosero. —*n* mendicidad, *f,* pordioseo, *m.* **to go b.,** andar mendigando. **b. letter,** carta pidiendo dinero, *f*

begin /bɪ'gɪn/ *vt* and *vi* empezar; comenzar; iniciar; (a conversation) entablar; (open) abrir; inaugurar; tener su principio; nacer. **to b. to,** empezar a; (start on) ponerse a; (with laughing, etc.) romper a. **to b. with,** empezar por; para empezar, en primer lugar

beginner /bɪ'gɪnər/ *n* principiante (-ta); (novice) novato (-ta); iniciador (-ra); autor (-ra)

beginning /bɪ'gɪnɪŋ/ *n* principio, comienzo, *m;* origen, *m.* **at the b.,** al principio; (of the month) a principios (de). **from the b. to the end,** desde el principio hasta el fin, *Inf.* de pe a pa. **in the b.,** al principio. **to make a b.,** comenzar, empezar

begone /bɪ'gɔn/ *interj* ¡fuera! ¡márchate! ¡vete!

begonia /bɪ'gounyə/ *n* begonia, *f*

begrudge /bɪ'grʌdʒ/ *vt* envidiar

beguile /bɪ'gail/ *vt* engañar; defraudar; (time) entretener; (charm) encantar, embelesar

beguilement /bɪ'gailmənt/ *n* engaño, *m;* (of time) entretenimiento, *m;* (charm) encanto, *m*

beguilingly /bɪ'gailɪŋli/ *adv* encantadoramente

behalf /bɪ'hæf/ *n* (preceded by on or upon) por; (from) de parte (de); a favor (de); en defensa (de)

behave /bɪ'heiv/ *vi* (oneself) conducirse, portarse; (act) obrar, proceder. **to b. badly,** portarse mal; obrar mal. **B.!** ¡Pórtate bien!

behavior /bɪ'heivyər/ *n* conducta, *f;* comportamiento, *m;* proceder, *m;* (manner) modales, *m pl*; *Biol.* reacción, *f*

behaviorism /bɪ'heivyə,rɪzəm/ *n Psychol.* behaviorismo, *m*

behead /bɪ'hɛd/ *vt* decapitar, descabezar

beheading /bɪ'hɛdɪŋ/ *n* decapitación, *f*

behest /bɪ'hɛst/ *n* precepto, mandato, *m*

behind /bɪ'haind/ *adv* detrás; por detrás; atrás; hacia atrás; en pos; (of time and order) después; (late and in arrears) con retraso; (old-fashioned) atrasado. —*prep* detrás de; por detrás de; inferior a; menos avanzado que. —*n Inf.* trasero, *m.* **from b.,** por detrás. **to be b. time,** retrasarse; llegar tarde. **b. the back of,** a espaldas de. **b. the scenes,** entre bastidores. **b. the times,** *Fig.* atrasado de noticias; pasado de moda. **the ideology b. the French Revolution,** la ideología que informó la Revolución Francesa.

behindhand /bɪ'haind,hænd/ *a* (out of date) atrasado; (late) tardío; *adv* con retraso

behold /bɪ'hould/ *vt* ver, mirar, contemplar; presenciar. —*interj* ¡he aquí! ¡mira!

beholden /bɪ'houldən/ *a* obligado, agradecido

beholder /bɪ'houldər/ *n* espectador (-ra). **the beholders,** los que lo presenciaban

beholding /bɪ'houldɪŋ/ *n* contemplación, vista, *f*

behoove /bɪ'houv/ *vt* incumbir, tocar, corresponder

beige /beiʒ/ *n* beige, color arena, *m*

being /'biɪŋ/ *n* existencia, *f;* operación, *f;* ser, *m;* (spirit) alma, *f,* espíritu, *m;* esencia, *f.* **human b.,** ser humano, *m,* alma viviente, *f.* **for the time b.,** por ahora, por el momento

bejewel /bɪ'dʒuəl/ *vt* enjoyar, adornar con joyas

belabor /bɪ'leibər/ *vt* apalear, golpear

belated /bɪ'leitɪd/ *a* tardío

belay /bɪ'lei/ *vt* amarrar

belch /bɛltʃ/ *n* eructo, *m;* detonación, *f;* (of a volcano) erupción, *f.* —*vi* eructar. —*vt* vomitar; (curses, etc.) escupir; despedir, arrojar

belching /'bɛltʃɪŋ/ *n* eructación, *f;* (of smoke, etc.) vómito, *m,* emisión, *f*

beleaguer /bɪ'ligər/ *vt* sitiar

belfry /'bɛlfri/ *n* campanario, *m*

Belgian /'bɛldʒən/ *a* and *n* belga, *mf*

Belgium /'bɛldʒəm/ Bélgica, *f*

Belgrade /'bɛlgreid/ Belgrado, *m*

belie /bɪ'lai/ *vt* desmentir, contradecir; defraudar

belief /bɪ'lif/ *n* creencia, *f;* fe, *f;* opinión, *f,* parecer, *m;* (trust) confianza, *f.* **in the b. that,** creyendo que, en la creencia de que

believable /bɪ'livəbəl/ *a* creíble

believe /bɪ'liv/ *vt* and *vi* creer; opinar, ser de la opinión, parecer (a uno); confiar, tener confianza. **I b. not,** Creo que no, Me parece que no. **I b. so,** Creo que sí, Me parece que sí. **to make (a person) b.,** hacer (a uno) creer. **to b. in,** creer en; confiar en, tener confianza en

believer /bɪ'livər/ *n* persona que cree, *f;* creyente, *mf*

belittle /bɪ'lɪtl̩/ *vt* achicar; conceder poca importancia a

bell /bɛl/ *n* campana, *f;* (hand-bell) campanilla, *f;* (small, round) cascabel, *m;* (on cows, etc.) cencerro, *m,* esquila, *f;* (electric, push, or bicycle) timbre, *m;* (jester's) cascabeles, *m pl*; (cry of stag) bramido, *m.* —*vt* poner un cascabel (a). —*vi* (stags) bramar, roncar. **To bear away the b.,** *Fig.* llevarse la palma. **to ring the b.,** tocar el timbre; agitar la campanilla. **to ring the bells,** tocar las campanas. **to b. the cat,** ponerle el cascabel al gato, ponerle el collar al gato. **b.-boy,** botones, mozo de hotel, *m.* **b.-clapper,** badajo, *m.* **b.-flower,** campanilla, *f.* **b.-founder,** campanero, *m.* **b.-mouthed,** abocinado. **b.-pull,** tirador de campanilla, *m.* **b.-ringer,** campanero, *m.* **b.-shaped,** campanudo. **b.-tent,** pabellón, *m.* **b. tower,** campanario, *m*

belladonna /,bɛlə'dɒnə/ *n* belladona, *f*

belle /bɛl/ *n* beldad, *f*

belles-lettres /bɛl 'lɛtrə/ *n pl* bellas letras, *f pl*

bellicose /'bɛlɪ,kous/ *a* belicoso, agresivo

bellicosity /,bɛlɪ'kɒsɪti/ *n* belicosidad, *f*

belligerency /bə'lɪdʒərənsi/ *n* beligerancia, *f*

belligerent /bə'lɪdʒərənt/ *a* beligerante; belicoso, guerrero. —*n* beligerante, *mf*

bellow /'bɛlou/ *n* (shout) grito, *m;* rugido, bramido, *m;* (of guns) trueno, *m.* —*vi* gritar, vociferar; rugir, bramar; tronar

bellowing /'bɛlouɪŋ/ *n.* See **bellow**

bellows /'bɛlouz/ *n* fuelle, *m*
belly /'bɛli/ *n* vientre, *m*, barriga, *f;* (of a jug, etc.) panza, *f;* estómago, *m;* (womb) seno, *m.* —*vt* hinchar. —*vi* hincharse
belong /bɪ'lɔŋ/ *vi* pertenecer (a); tocar (a), incumbir (a); (to a place) ser de; residir en
belongings /bɪ'lɔŋɪŋz/ *n pl* efectos, *m pl;* posesiones, *f pl;* (luggage) equipaje, *m*
beloved /bɪ'lʌvɪd/ *a* muy amado, muy querido. —*n* querido (-da)
below /bɪ'lou/ *adv* abajo; (under) debajo; (further on) más abajo; (in hell) en el infierno; (in this world) en este mundo, aquí abajo. —*prep* bajo; (underneath) debajo de; (after) después de; (unworthy of) indigno de; inferior a. **The valley lay b. us,** El valle se extendía a nuestros pies. **b. zero,** bajo cero
belt /bɛlt/ *n* cinturón, *m;* (of a horse) cincha, *f;* (corset) faja, *f; Geog.* zona, *f;* (of a machine) correa (de transmisión), *f*
beltway /'bɛlt,wei/ *n* anillo periférico, *m*
belvedere /'bɛlvɪ,dɪər/ *n* mirador, *m*
bemoan /bɪ'moun/ *vt* deplorar, lamentar
bemoaning /bɪ'mounɪŋ/ *n* lamentación, *f*
bemuse /bɪ'myuz/ *vt* confundir, desconcertar
bench /bɛntʃ/ *n* banco, *m;* (with a back) escaño, *m;* mesa de trabajo, *f;* (carpenter's, shoemaker's, in a boat, in parliament) banco, *m;* (judges) tribunal, *m*
bend /bɛnd/ *n* corvadura, curva, vuelta, *f;* (in a river, street) recodo, *m;* (on a road) codo viraje, *m;* (of the knee) corva, *f;* (in a pipe) codo, *m; Naut.* nudo, *m; Herald.* banda, *f.* **sheet b.,** (knot) nudo de tejedor, *m*
bend /bɛnd/ *vt* encorvar; doblegar; torcer; (the head) bajar; (the body) inclinar; (steps) dirigir, encaminar; (the mind) aplicarse, dedicarse. —*vi* encorvarse; doblegarse; torcerse; (arch) arquear; inclinarse. **to b. the knee,** arrodillarse. **on bended knee,** de rodillas. **to b. back,** *vt* redoblar. —*vi* redoblarse; inclinarse hacia atrás. **to b. down,** agacharse; inclinarse. **to b. forward,** inclinarse hacia delante. **to b. over,** inclinarse encima de
bendable /'bɛndəbəl/ *a* que puede doblarse; plegadizo; flexible
bending /'bɛndɪŋ/ *n* doblamiento, *m;* flexión, *f;* inclinación, *f.* —*a* doblado; inclinado
beneath /bɪ'niθ/ *adv* abajo; debajo; (at one's feet) a los pies de uno. —*prep* bajo; debajo de; al pie de; (unworthy, inferior) indigno. **He married b. him,** Se casó fuera de su clase
Benedictine /,bɛnɪ'dɪktɪn; -tin/ *a* benedictino. —*n* benedictino, *m;* (liqueur) benedictino, *m*
benediction /,bɛnɪ'dɪkʃən/ *n* bendición, *f;* gracia divina, merced, *f*
benefaction /'bɛnə,fækʃən/ *n* beneficiación, *f;* buena obra, *f;* beneficio, favor, *m*
benefactor /'bɛnə,fæktər/ *n* bienhechor, *m;* protector, *m;* patrono, *m;* fundador, *m*
benefactress /'bɛnə,fæktrɪs/ *n* bienhechora, *f;* protectora, *f;* patrona, *f;* fundadora, *f*
benefice /'bɛnəfɪs/ *n* beneficio eclesiástico, *m,* prebenda, *f*
beneficence /bə'nɛfəsəns/ *n* beneficiencia, caridad, *f,* buenas obras, *f pl*
beneficent /bə'nɛfəsənt/ *a* benéfico, caritativo
beneficial /,bɛnə'fɪʃəl/ *a* beneficioso; provechoso, útil
beneficiary /,bɛnə'fɪʃi,ɛri/ *n* beneficiado (-da), beneficiario (-ia)
benefit /'bɛnəfɪt/ *n* beneficio, bien, *m;* provecho, *m,* utilidad, *f;* (favor) favor, *m; Theat.* beneficio, *m;* (help) ayuda, *f,* servicio, *m.* —*vt* beneficiar; aprovechar; (improve) mejorar. —*vi* (with by) sacar provecho de; ganar. **for the b. of,** para; en pro de, a favor de. **b. society,** sociedad benéfica, *f*
benevolence /bə'nɛvələns/ *n* benevolencia, bondad, *f;* liberalidad, *f;* caridad, *f;* favor, *m*
benevolent /bə'nɛvələnt/ *a* benévolo; bondadoso; caritativo. **b. society,** sociedad de beneficencia, *f*
benevolently /bə'nɛvələntli/ *adv* benignamente, con benevolencia
Bengal /bɛn'gɔl/ Bengala, *f*
benighted /bɪ'naitɪd/ *a* sorprendido por la noche; *Fig.* ignorante
benign, benignant /bɪ'nain; bɪ'nɪgnənt/ *a* benigno
bent /bɛnt/ *n* talento, *m;* inclinación, afición, *f, a* torcido, encorvado; resuelto
benumb /bɪ'nʌm/ See **numb**
benzine /'bɛnzin/ *n* bencina, *f*
bequeath /bɪ'kwið/ *vt* legar, dejar (en el testamento); transmitir
bequest /bɪ'kwɛst/ *n* legado, *m*
Berber /'bɜrbər/ *a* and *n* bereber, *mf*
bereave /bɪ'riv/ *vt* privar (de), quitar; arrebatar; afligir. **the bereaved parents,** los padres afligidos
bereavement /bɪ'rivmənt/ *n* privación, *f;* (by death) pérdida, *f;* aflicción, *f*
bereft /bɪ'rɛft/ *a* privado (de); desamparado; indefenso. **utterly b.,** completamente solo
beret /bə'rei/ *n* boina, *f*
Berlin /bər'lɪn/ *a* and *n* (of or from) berlinés (-esa). —*n* (carriage) berlina, *f*
Bermudas, the /bər'myudəz/ *m* las Islas Bermudas
Bernard /bər'nɑrd/ *n* Bernardo, *m.* **St. B. dog,** perro de San Bernardo, *m*
Berne /bɜrn/ Berna, *f*
berry /'bɛri/ *n* baya, *f;* (of coffee, etc.) fruto, *m, vi* dar bayas; coger bayas
berth /bɜrθ/ *n* (bed) litera, *f;* (cabin) camarote, *m;* (anchorage) anclaje, fondeadero, *m;* (job) empleo, *m, vt* (a ship) fondear. **to give a wide b. to,** *Naut.* ponerse a resguardo de; apartarse mucho de; evitar
beseech /bɪ'sitʃ/ *vt* suplicar, rogar, implorar; (ask for) pedir con ahinco
beseeching /bɪ'sitʃɪŋ/ *a* suplicante, implorante. —*n* súplica, *f;* ruego, *m*
beseechingly /bɪ'sitʃɪŋli/ *adv* suplicantemente
beset /bɪ'sɛt/ *vt* atacar, acosar; aquejar, acosar, perseguir. **beset by personal misfortune,** acosado por las desgracias personales; (block) obstruir; (surround) rodear, cercar
besetting /bɪ'sɛtɪŋ/ *a* usual, frecuente; obsesionante
beside, besides /bɪ'said; bɪ'saidz/ *prep* al lado de; cerca de; (compared with) en comparación de, comparado con; (in addition) además de; aparte de; excepto. —*adv* además, también. **to be beside oneself,** estar fuera de sí
besiege /bɪ'sidʒ/ *vt* sitiar; (assail) asaltar, asediar; (surround) rodear; importunar
besieged /bɪ'sidʒd/ *n* sitiado (-da)
besieger /bɪ'sidʒər/ *n* sitiador, *m*
besieging /bɪ'sidʒɪŋ /*a* sitiador. —*n* sitio, asalto, *m;* asedio, *m,* importunación, *f*
besmear /bɪ'smɪər/ *vt* embadurnar, ensuciar
besotted /bɪ'sɒtɪd/ *a* estúpido; embrutecido; atontado
bespangled /bɪ'spæŋgəld/ *a* adornado con lentejuelas; brillante (con); (studded) salpicado (de)
bespatter /bɪ'spætər/ *vt* manchar; derramar; salpicar
bespeak /bɪ'spik/ *vt* reservar; (goods) encargar; (signify) demostrar, indicar, significar; *Poet.* hablar
besprinkle /bɪ'sprɪŋkəl/ *vt* rociar
best /bɛst/ *a superl* of **good** and **well,** mejor; el (la) mejor, *m, f.,* los (las) mejores, *m pl, f pl.* —*adv* mejor; el mejor; (most) más. **as b. I can,** como mejor pueda. **at the b.,** cuando más, en el mejor caso. **He did it for the b.,** Lo hizo con la mejor intención. **the b.,** lo mejor. **to be at one's b.,** brillar; lucirse. **to do one's b.,** hacer todo lo posible. **to get the b. of,** llevar la mejor parte de; triunfar de (or sobre). **to make the b. of,** sacar el mayor provecho de. **The next b. thing to do is...,** Lo mejor que queda ahora por hacer es... **b. man,** padrino de boda, *m.* **to be b. man to,** apadrinar, ser padrino de. **b. seller,** libro que se vende más, libro favorito, *m*
bestial /'bɛstʃəl/ *a* bestial
bestiality /,bɛstʃi'ælɪti/ *n* bestialidad, *f*
bestir (oneself) /bɪ'stɜr/ *vr* menearse, moverse; preocuparse; (hurry) darse prisa
bestow /bɪ'stou/ *vt* (place) poner; (with upon) conferir, conceder, otorgar; (a present) regalar
bestowal /bɪ'stouəl/ *n* puesta, *f;* otorgamiento, *m,* concesión, *f;* (of a present) regalo, *m,* dádiva, *f*
bestride /bɪ'straid/ *vt* montar a horcajadas en; poner una pierna en cada lado de; cruzar de un tranco
bestseller /'bɛst'sɛlər/ *n* campeón de venta, éxito editorial, triunfo de librería, *m*

bet /bɛt/ *n* apuesta, postura, *f*, *vi* apostar; (gamble) jugar. **What do you bet?** ¿Qué apuesta Vd.?
betake (oneself) /bɪ'teik/ *vr* acudir (a); darse (a); marcharse
bethink (oneself) /bɪ'θɪŋk/ *vr* pensar, reflexionar; (remember) recordar, hacer memoria; ocurrirse
Bethlehem /'bɛθlɪˌhɛm/ Belén, *m*
betimes /bɪ'taimz/ *adv* pronto; de buena hora, temprano; con tiempo
betoken /bɪ'toukən/ *vt* presagiar, prometer; indicar
betray /bɪ'trei/ *vt* traicionar; revelar, descubrir; (a woman) seducir; (show) dejar ver
betrayal /bɪ'treiəl/ *n* traición, *f;* (of confidence) abuso (de confianza), *m;* (of a woman) seducción, *f*
betrayer /bɪ'treiər/ *n* traidor (-ra)
betroth /bɪ'trouð/ *vt* desposar(se) con, prometer(se). **to be betrothed to,** estar desposado con
betrothal /bɪ'trouðəl/ *n* desposorio, *m*, esponsales, *m pl*; (duration) noviazgo, *m*
betrothed /bɪ'trouðd/ *n* desposado (-da), futuro (-ra)
better /'bɛtər/ *a compar* of **good,** mejor; superior. —*adv* mejor; más. —*vt* mejorar; exceder. —*n* apostador (-ra). **He has bettered himself,** Ha mejorado su situación. **It is b. to...,** Es mejor..., Vale más... (followed by infin.). **little b.,** poco mejor; algo mejor; poco más. **much b.,** mucho mejor. **our betters,** nuestros superiores. **so much the b.,** tanto mejor. **the b. to,** para mejor. **to be b.,** ser mejor; (of health) estar mejor. **to get b.,** mejorar. **to get the b. of,** triunfar sobre, vencer. **b. half,** *Inf.* media naranja, *f.* **b. off,** mejor situado, más acomodado
betterment /'bɛtərmənt/ *n* mejora, *f*, mejoramiento, *m;* adelantamiento, avance, *m*
betting /'bɛtɪŋ/ *n* apuesta, *f*
bettor /'bɛtər/ *n* apostador (-ra)
between /bɪ'twin/ *prep* entre; en medio de; de. **the break b. Mr. X and Mrs. Y,** el rompimiento del Sr. X y la Sra. Y. —*adv* en medio; entre los dos. **far b.,** a grandes intervalos. **b. now and then,** desde ahora hasta entonces. **b. one thing and another,** entre una cosa y otra. **b. ourselves,** entre nosotros
bevel /'bɛvəl/ *n* bisel, *m*, *vt* abiselar
beverage /'bɛvərɪdʒ/ *n* brebaje, *m*, bebida, *f*
bevy /'bɛvi/ *n* grupo, *m;* (of birds) bandada, *f;* (of roes) manada, *f*
bewail /bɪ'weil/ *vt* lamentar, llorar
bewailing /bɪ'weilɪŋ/ *n* lamentación, *f*
beware /bɪ'wɛər/ *vi* guardarse (de); cuidar (de); desconfiar (de). —*interj* ¡cuidado! ¡atención! **B. of imitations!** ¡Desconfiad de las imitaciones!
bewilder /bɪ'wɪldər/ *vt* aturdir, abobar; dejar perplejo (a); confundir
bewildered /bɪ'wɪldərd/ *a* aturdido, abobado; perplejo; confuso
bewildering /bɪ'wɪldərɪŋ/ *a* incomprensible; complicado
bewilderment /bɪ'wɪldərmənt/ *n* aturdimiento, *m;* perplejidad, *f;* confusión, *f*
bewitch /bɪ'wɪtʃ/ *vt* hechizar; fascinar, encantar
bewitching /bɪ'wɪtʃɪŋ/ *a* encantador, hechicero, fascinante. —*n* embrujamiento, encantamiento, *m*
bewitchingly /bɪ'wɪtʃɪŋli/ *adv* de un modo encantador
bewitchment /bɪ'wɪtʃmənt/ *n.* See **bewitching**
beyond /bi'ɒnd/ *prep* más allá de; más lejos que; (behind) tras, detrás de; (of time) después de; *Fig.* fuera del alcance de; (without) fuera de; (above) encima de; (not including) aparte. —*adv* más allá; más lejos; detrás. **b. doubt,** fuera de duda. **b. question,** indiscutible. **b. the sea,** allende el mar. **That is b. me,** Eso es demasiado para mí; Eso no está en mi mano; Eso está fuera de mi alcance. **the back of b.,** donde Cristo dio las tres voces, las quimbambas. **the B.,** la otra vida
Bhután /bu'tɑn/ Bután, *m*
bias /'baiəs/ *n* sesgo, bies, través, *m; Fig.* prejuicio, *m;* parcialidad, *f*, *vt* influir; predisponer. **to cut on the b.,** cortar al sesgo
biased /'baiəst/ *a* parcial; tendencioso
bib /bɪb/ *n* babero, *m;* pechera, *f*, *vi* beber mucho, empinar el codo
Bible /'baibəl/ *n* Biblia, *f*
biblical /'bɪblɪkəl/ *a* bíblico. **b. history,** historia sagrada, *f*
bibliographer /ˌbɪbli'ɒgrəfər/ *n* bibliógrafo (-fa)
bibliographical /ˌbɪbliə'græfɪkəl/ *a* bibliográfico
bibliography /ˌbɪbli'ɒgrəfi/ *n* bibliografía, *f*
bibliophile /'bɪbliəˌfail/ *n* bibliófilo, *m*
bibulous /'bɪbyələs/ *a* bebedor, borrachín
bicarbonate /bai'kɑrbənɪt/ *n* bicarbonato, *m*
bicentenary /ˌbaisɛn'tɛnəri/ *n* segundo centenario, *m*
biceps /'baisɛps/ *n* bíceps, *m*
bichloride /bai'klɔraid/ *n* bicloruro, *m*
bicker /'bɪkər/ *vi* disputar, altercar; (of stream, etc.) murmurar, susurrar; (of flame) bailar, centellear
bickering /'bɪkərɪŋ/ *n* altercado, argumento, *m*
bicycle /'baisɪkəl/ *n* bicicleta, *f*, *vi* andar en bicicleta, ir de bicicleta
bicycling /'baisɪklɪŋ/ *n* ciclismo, *m*
bicyclist /'baisɪklɪst/ *n* biciclista, *mf*
bid /bɪd/ *n* (at auction) postura, *f;* (bridge) puja, *f;* oferta, *f*, *vt* mandar, ordenar, invitar a; (at an auction) pujar, licitar. **to make a bid for,** (attempt) hacer un esfuerzo para; procurar. **to bid fair,** prometer; dar indicios de; dar esperanzas de. **to bid goodbye to,** decir adios (a), despedirse de. **to bid welcome,** dar la bienvenida (a)
biddable /'bɪdəbəl/ *a* obediente, dócil; manso
bidder /'bɪdər/ *n* postor, *m*, pujador (-ra). **the highest b.,** el mejor postor
bidding /'bɪdɪŋ/ *n* (order) orden, *f;* instrucción, *f;* invitación, *f;* (at an auction) postura, licitación, *f.* **to do a person's b.,** hacer lo que se le manda
bide /baid/ *vt* aguardar, esperar. **to b. by,** (fulfil) cumplir con
bidet /bi'dei/ *n* bidé, *m*
biennial /bai'ɛniəl/ *a* bianual, bienal
bier /bɪər/ *n* andas, *f pl*; féretro, ataúd, *m*
bifocal /bai'foukəl/ *a* bifocal
bifurcate /'baifərˌkeit/ *vt* and *vi* bifurcar(se)
bifurcation /ˌbaifər'keiʃən/ *n* bifurcación, *f*
big /bɪg/ *a* grande; grueso; (grown up) mayor; (tall) alto; voluminoso; (vast) extenso, vasto; (full) lleno (de); (with young) preñada; importante. **to talk big,** echarla de importante. **big-boned,** huesudo. **big-end,** *Auto.* biela, *f.* **big game,** caza mayor, *f.* **big gun,** *Inf.* pájaro gordo, *m*
bigamist /'bɪgəmɪst/ *n* bígamo (-ma)
bigamous /'bɪgəməs/ *a* bígamo
bigamy /'bɪgəmi/ *n* bigamia, *f*
bight /bait/ *n* (in a rope) vuelta (de un cabo), *f;* (bay) ensenada, *f*
bigness /'bɪgnɪs/ *n* grandor, *m;* gran tamaño, *m;* altura, *f;* (tallness of a person) gran talle, *m;* (vastness) extensión, *f;* importancia, *f*
bigot /'bɪgət/ *n* fanático (-ca)
bigoted /'bɪgətɪd/ *a* fanático, intolerante
bigotry /'bɪgətri/ *n* fanatismo, *m*, intolerancia, *f*
bikini /bɪ'kini/ *n* bikini, *m*
bilateral /bai'lætərəl/ *a* bilateral
bilberry /'bɪlˌbɛri/ *n* arándano, *m*
bile /bail/ *n* bilis, hiel, *f;* mal humor, *m*, cólera, *f*
bilge /bɪldʒ/ *n Naut.* pantoque, *m*, sentina, *f.* **b. water,** agua de pantoque, *f*
bilingual /bai'lɪŋgwəl/ *a* bilingüe
bilious /'bɪlyəs/ *a* bilioso
bill /bɪl/ *n* (parliamentary) proyecto de ley, *m; Law.* escrito, *m; Com.* cuenta, *f;* (poster) cartel, *m;* (program) programa, *m;* (cast) repertorio, *m;* (bank note) billete de banco, *m;* (of a bird) pico, *m;* (for pruning) podadera, *f.* **due b.,** *Com.* abonaré, *m.* **Post no bills!** Se prohíbe fijar carteles. **b. of exchange,** letra de cambio, *f.* **b. of fare,** lista de platos, *f; Fig.* programa, *m.* **b. of health,** patente de sanidad, *f.* **b. of lading,** conocimiento de embarque, *m.* **b. of rights,** declaración de derechos, *f.* **b. of sale,** contrato de venta, *m*, carta de venta, *f.* **b.-broker,** agente de bolsa, agente de cambio, *m.* **b.-poster,** fijador de carteles, cartelero, *m*
bill /bɪl/ *vt* anunciar; publicar; poner en el programa; fijar carteles en. **to b. and coo,** (doves) arrullar; *Inf.* besuquearse
billboard /'bɪlˌbɔrd/ *n* tablero publicitario, *m*

billed /bɪld/ *a* (in compounds) de pico

billet /'bɪlɪt/ *n* alojamiento, *m;* (of wood) pedazo (de leña), *m;* (job) empleo, destino, *m, vt* alojar (en or con)

billeting /'bɪlɪtɪŋ/ *n* alojamiento, *m.* **b. officer,** *Mil.* aposentador, *m;* oficial encargado de encontrar alojamiento, *m*

billiards /'bɪlyərdz/ *n pl* billar, *m.* **billiard ball,** bola de billar, *f.* **billiard cue,** taco, *m.* **billiard cushion,** baranda de la mesa de billar, *f.* **billiard marker,** marcador, *m.* **billiard match,** partida de billar, *f.* **billiard player,** jugador (-ra) de billar. **billiard room,** sala de billar, *f.* **billiard table,** mesa de billar, *f*

billing /'bɪlɪŋ/ *n* facturación, *f*

billion /'bɪlyən/ *n* billón, *m;* (U.S.A. and France) mil millones, *m pl*

billionth /'bɪlyənθ/ *a* billonésimo; (U.S.A. and France) milmillonésimo

bill of particulars *n* relación detallada, *f*

billow /'bɪlou/ *n* oleada, *f; Poet.* ola, *f; Fig.* onda, *f.* —*vi* hincharse, encresparse; ondular

billowy /'bɪloui/ *a* ondulante, ondeante

bimonthly /bai'mʌnθli/ *a* bimestral

bin /bɪn/ *n* hucha, *f;* arcón, *m;* recipiente, *m;* depósito, *m;* cajón, *m;* (for wine) estante, *m*

binary /'bainəri/ *a* binario

bind /baind/ *vt* atar; unir, ligar; amarrar; (in sheaves) agavillar; (bandage) vendar; sujetar; fijar; aprisionar; (a book) encuadernar; *Sew.* ribetear; (oblige) obligar; comprometer; (constipate) estreñir; contratar (como aprendiz). **I feel bound to,** Me siento obligado a. **to b. over,** obligar a comparecer ante el juez

binder /'baindər/ *n* encuadernador (-ra); *Agr.* agavilladora, *f*

binding /'baindɪŋ/ *a* válido, valedero; obligatorio; **become b.,** adquirir carácter de compromiso; *Med.* constrictivo. —*n* atadura, ligación, *f;* (of books) encuadernación, *f; Sew.* ribete, *m*

binge /bɪndʒ/ *n* parranda, juerga, *f.* **to go on the b.,** ir de parranda, ir de picos pardos, ir de juerga

binnacle /'bɪnəkəl/ *n Naut.* bitácora, *f*

binocular /bə'nɒkyələr/ *a* binocular. —*n pl* **binoculars,** binóculos, gemelos, *m pl*

binomial /bai'noumiəl/ *a* and *n* binomio *m.*

biochemist /ˌbaiou'kɛmɪst/ *n* bioquímico, *m*

biochemistry /ˌbaiou'kɛməstri/ *n* bioquímica, *f*

biodiversity /ˌbaioudɪ'vɜrsɪti/ *n* biodiversidad, *f*

biographer /bai'ɒgrəfər/ *n* biógrafo (-fa)

biographical /ˌbaiə'græfɪkəl/ *a* biográfico

biography /bai'ɒgrəfi/ *n* biografía, vida, *f*

biological /ˌbaiə'lɒdʒɪkəl/ *a* biológico

biologist /bai'ɒlədʒɪst/ *n* biólogo, *m*

biology /bai'ɒlədʒi/ *n* biología, *f*

bipartite /bai'pɑrtait/ *a* bipartido

biped /'baipɛd/ *n* bípedo, *m, a* bípedo, bípede

birch /bɜrtʃ/ *n Bot.* abedul, *m;* (rod) vara, *f.* —*a* de abedul. —*vt* pegar con una vara, dar una paliza (a)

bird /bɜrd/ *n* pájaro, *m;* ave, *f.* **Birds of a feather flock together,** Cada cual se arrima a su cada cual. **hen b.,** pájara, *f.* **b.-call,** voz del pájaro, *f,* canto del ave, *m.* **b. catcher or vendor,** pajarero, *m.* **bird's-eye view,** vista de pájaro, perspectiva aérea, *f.* **b.-fancier,** aficionado (-da) a las aves; criador (-ra) de pájaros. **b.-like,** como un pájaro; de pájaro. **b.-lime,** liga, *f.* **to go b.-nesting,** ir a coger nidos de pájaros. **b. of paradise,** ave del paraíso, *f.* **b. of passage,** ave de paso, *f.* **b. of prey,** ave rapaz, *f.* **b. seed,** alpiste, *m*

birth /bɜrθ/ *n* nacimiento, *m;* (act of) parto, *m;* origen, *m;* (childhood) infancia, *f;* (family) linaje, *m,* familia, *f; Fig.* creación, *f.* **from b.,** de nacimiento. **to give b. to,** dar a luz, echar al mundo, parir. **b. certificate,** partida de nacimiento, certificación de nacimiento, *f.* **b. control,** anticoncepcionismo, *m,* regulación de la fecundidad, *f.* **b.-mark,** antojos, *m pl.* **b.-place,** lugar de nacimiento, *m.* **b.-rate,** natalidad, *f*

birthday /'bɜrθˌdei/ *n* cumpleaños, *m*

birthright /'bɜrθˌrait/ *n* derecho de nacimiento, *m;* herencia, *f*

Biscayan /bɪs'keiən/ *a* and *n* vizcaíno (-na)

Biscay, the Bay of /bɪs'kei/ el Golfo de Vizcaya, *m*

biscuit /'bɪskɪt/ *n* galleta, *f;* bizcocho, *m.* **b. box or maker,** galletero, *m.* **b.-like,** abizcochado

bisect /bai'sɛkt/ *vt* dividir en dos partes iguales; *Geom.* bisecar

bisexual /bai'sɛkʃuəl/ *a* bisexual

bishop /'bɪʃəp/ *n* obispo, *m;* (in chess) alfil, *m.* **bishop's crozier,** báculo episcopal, cayado, *m*

bismuth /'bɪzməθ/ *n* bismuto, *m*

bison /'baisən/ *n* bisonte, *m*

bisque /bɪsk/ *n* porcelana blanca, *f,* bizcocho, *m*

bistoury /'bɪstəri/ *n* bisturí, *m*

bit /bɪt/ *n* pedazo, *m;* (of grass, etc.) brizna, *f;* (moment) instante, *m;* (quantity) cantidad, *f;* (of a drill) mecha, *f;* (part) parte, *f;* (passage) trozo, *m;* (horse's) bocado, *m; Inf.* miga, *f.* **a bit,** un tanto, algo, un poco. **in bits,** en pedazos. **Not a bit!** ¡Nada!; ¡Ni pizca!; ¡Claro que no! **bit by bit,** poco a poco, gradualmente. **to give someone a bit of one's mind,** contarle cuatro verdades. **to take the bit between one's teeth,** desbocarse; *Fig.* rebelarse. **Wait a bit!** ¡Espera un momento!

bitch /bɪtʃ/ *n* (female dog) perra, *f;* (fox) zorra, *f;* (wolf) loba, *f*

bite /bait/ *n* mordedura, *f;* mordisco, *m;* (mouthful, snack) bocado, *m;* (of fish and insects) picada, *f;* (hold) asimiento, *m;* (sting, pain) picadura, *f;* (pungency) resquemor, *m;* (offer) oferta, *f;* (*Fig.* mordancy) mordacidad, acritud, *f.* —*vt* and *vi* morder; (gnaw) roer; (of fish, insects) picar; (of hot dishes) resquemar; (of acids) corroer; (deceive) engañar, defraudar; (of wheels, etc.) agarrar; (hurt, wound) herir. **to b. one's tongue,** morderse la lengua. **to b. the dust,** caer al suelo

biting /'baitɪŋ/ *a* (stinging) picante; (mordant) mordaz, acre; (of winds, etc.) penetrante; satírico. —*n* mordedura, *f;* roedura, *f*

bitter /'bɪtər/ *a* amargo; (sour) agrio, ácido; (of winds) penetrante; (of cold) intenso; cruel. **to the b. end,** hasta la muerte; hasta el último extremo. **b.-sweet,** agridulce

bitterly /'bɪtərli/ *adv* amargamente; intensamente; cruelmente

bitterness /'bɪtərnɪs/ *n* amargura, *f;* (sourness) acidez, *f;* (of cold) intensidad, *f;* crueldad, *f*

bitters /'bɪtərz/ *n pl* (drink) bíter, *m,* angostura, *f*

bitumen /bai'tumən/ *n* betún, *m*

bituminous /bai'tumənəs/ *a* bituminoso, abetunado

bivalve /'baiˌvælv/ *n* bivalvo, *m*

bivouac /'bɪvuˌæk/ *n Mil.* vivaque, *m, vi* vivaquear

bizarre /bɪ'zɑr/ *a* raro, extravagante; grotesco

black /blæk/ *a* negro; obscuro; (sad) triste, melancólico; funesto; (wicked) malo, perverso; (sullen) malhumorado. —*n* (color) negro, *m;* (mourning) luto, *m;* (negro) negro, *m;* (negress) negra, *f;* (stain) mancha, *f;* (dirt) tizne, *m.* —*vt* ennegrecer; tiznar. **in b. and white,** por escrito. **to look on the b. side,** verlo todo negro. **b. art,** nigromancia, *f.* **b.-currant,** grosella negra, *f.* **b.-eyed,** ojinegro, con ojos negros. **b.-haired,** pelinegro, de pelo negro. **b.-lead,** plombagina, *f.* **b.-list,** lista negra, *f.* **b.-market,** estraperlo, mercado negro, *m.* **b.-marketeer,** estraperlista, *mf* **b.-out,** oscurecimiento, apagamiento, *m.* **b.-pudding,** morcilla, *f.* **b. sheep,** oveja negra, *f; Fig.* oveja descarriada, *f;* (of a family) garbanzo negro, *m.* **b.-water fever,** melanuria, *f*

blackberry /'blækˌbɛri/ *n* mora, zarzamora, *f;* (bush) zarza, *f,* moral, *m*

blackbird /'blækˌbɜrd/ *n* mirlo, *m*

blackboard /'blækˌbɔrd/ *n* encerado, *m,* pizarra, *f*

blacken /'blækən/ *vt* ennegrecer; tiznar; *Fig.* manchar, desacreditar. —*vi* ennegrecerse

black eye *n* ojo como un tomate, ojo morado, *m*

Black Forest, the la Selva Negra, *f*

blackguard /'blægɑrd/ *n* tipo de cuidado, perdido, *m*

blackhead /'blækˌhɛd/ *n* espinilla, *f*

blacking /'blækɪŋ/ *n* betún, *m*

blackish /'blækɪʃ/ *a* negruzco

blackmail /'blækˌmeil/ *n* chantaje, *m, vt* hacer víctima de un chantaje; arrancar dinero por chantaje (a)

blackmailer /'blækˌmeilər/ *n* chantajista, *mf*

blackness /'blæknɪs/ *n* negrura, *f;* obscuridad, *f;* (wickedness) maldad, perversidad, *f*

Black Sea, the el Mar Negro, *m*
blacksmith /'blæk,smɪθ/ *n* herrero, *m*. **blacksmith's forge,** herrería, *f*
bladder /'blædər/ *n Anat.* vejiga, *f;* ampolla, *f;* (of sea-plants) vesícula, *f;* (of fish) vejiga natatoria, *f*
blade /bleid/ *n* (leaf) hoja, *f;* (of grass, etc.) brizna, *f;* (of sharp instruments) hoja, *f;* (of oar) pala, *f;* (of propeller) paleta, ala, *f*
bladed /'bleidɪd/ *a* de... hojas. **a two-b. knife,** un cuchillo de dos hojas
blame /bleim/ *n* culpa, *f;* responsabilidad, *f;* censura, *f.* —*vt* culpar, echar la culpa (a); tachar, censurar, criticar; acusar. **You are to b. for this,** Vd. tiene la culpa de esto
blameless /'bleimlɪs/ *a* inculpable; inocente; intachable; elegante
blamelessness /'bleimlɪsnɪs/ *n* inculpabilidad, inocencia, *f;* elegancia, *f*
blameworthy /'bleim,wɜrði/ *a* culpable, digno de censura, vituperable
blanch /blæntʃ/ *vt Cul.* mondar; hacer palidecer. —*vi* palidecer, perder el color
blanching /'blæntʃɪŋ/ *n* palidecimiento, *m; Cul.* mondadura, *f*
blancmange /blə'mɑndʒ/ *n* manjar blanco, *m*
bland /blænd/ *a* afable, cortés; dulce, agradable
blandish /'blændɪʃ/ *vt* adular, halagar, acariciar
blandishment /'blændɪʃmənt/ *n* adulación, *f,* halago, *m,* caricia, *f*
blandness /'blændnɪs/ *n* afabilidad, urbanidad, *f;* dulzura, *f*
blank /blæŋk/ *a* en blanco; (empty) vacío; desocupado; pálido; (confused) confuso, desconcertado; (expressionless) sin expresión; (of verse) suelto; sin adorno. —*n* blanco, hueco, *m;* papel en blanco, *m;* laguna, *f.* **b. cartridge,** cartucho para salvas, cartucho de fogueo, *m.* **b. verse,** verso suelto, *m*
blanket /'blæŋkɪt/ *n* manta, frazada, *f;* (of a horse) sudadero *m; Fig.* capa, *f.* —*vt* cubrir con una manta. **to toss in a b.,** mantear. **wet b.,** aguafiestas, *mf.* **b. maker or seller,** mantero, *m.* **b. vote,** voto colectivo, *m*
blanketing /'blæŋkɪtɪŋ/ *n* manteamiento, *m*
blankly /'blæŋkli/ *adv* con indiferencia; sin comprender; (flatly) categóricamente
blankness /'blæŋknɪs/ *n* confusión, *f,* desconcierto, *m;* (emptiness) vaciedad, *f;* indiferencia, *f;* incomprensión, *f*
blare /blɛər/ *n* sonido de la trompeta o del clarín, *Poet.* clangor, *m;* (of a car horn) ruido, *m.* —*vi* sonar
blarney /'blɑrni/ *n* labia, *f.* —*vt* lisonjear
blaspheme /blæs'fim/ *vi* blasfemar. —*vt* renegar de, maldecir
blasphemer /blæs'fimər/ *n* blasfemador (-ra), blasfemo (-ma)
blasphemous /'blæsfəməs/ *a* blasfemo, blasfematorio
blasphemy /'blæsfəmi/ *n* blasfemia, *f*
blast /blæst/ *n* (of wind) ráfaga (de viento), *f;* (of a trumpet, etc.) trompetazo, son, *m;* (of a whistle) pitido, *m;* (draft) soplo, *m;* explosión, *f; Fig.* influencia maligna, *f.* —*vt* (rock) barrenar, hacer saltar; (wither) marchitar, secar; *Fig.* destruir; (curse) maldecir. **in full b.,** en plena marcha. **b.-furnace,** alto horno, horno de cuba, *m.* **b. hole,** barreno, *m*
blaster /'blæstər/ *n* barrenero, *m*
blasting /'blæstɪŋ/ *n* (of rock) voladura, *f;* (withering) marchitamiento, *m; Fig.* destrucción, ruina, *f;* (cursing) maldiciones, *f pl.* **a.** destructor; *Fig.* funesto. **b. charge,** carga explosiva, *f*
blatant /'bleitnt/ *a* ruidoso; agresivo; llamativo; (boastful) fanfarrón
blaze /bleiz/ *n* llama, *f;* fuego, *m;* conflagración, *f;* luz brillante, *f;* (of anger, etc.) acceso, *m.* —*vi* llamear, encenderse en llamas; brillar, resplandecer. **a b. of colour,** una masa de color. **Go to blazes!** ¡Vete al infierno!
blazon /'bleizən/ *n Herald.* blasón, *m; Fig.* proclamación, *f, vt* blasonar; adornar; proclamar
bleach /blitʃ/ *n* lejía, *f.* —*vt* blanquear; descolorar. —*vi* ponerse blanco; descolorarse
bleaching /'blitʃɪŋ/ *n* blanqueo, *m.* **b. powder,** hipoclorito de cal, *m*
bleak /blik/ *a* yermo, desierto; frío; expuesto; (sad) triste; severo
bleakness /'bliknɪs/ *n* situación expuesta, *f;* desnudez, *f;* frío, *m;* (sadness) tristeza, *f;* severidad, *f*
bleary-eyed /'blɪəri ,aid/ *a* legañoso, cegajoso
bleat /blit/ *n* balido, *m, vt* and *vi* balar, dar balidos
bleating /'blitɪŋ/ *a* balador, que bala. —*n* balido, *m*
bleed /blid/ *vi* sangrar, echar sangre; sufrir. —*vt* sangrar; arrancar dinero a
bleeding /'blidɪŋ/ *n* hemorragia, *f;* sangría, *f*
blemish /'blɛmɪʃ/ *n* imperfección, *f,* defecto, *m;* (on fruit) maca, *f;* (stain) mancha, *f;* deshonra, *f*
blend /blɛnd/ *n* mezcla, mixtura, *f;* combinación, *f;* fusión, *f.* —*vt* mezclar; combinar. —*vi* mezclarse; combinarse
blende /blɛnd/ *n Mineral.* blenda, *f*
blending /'blɛndɪŋ/ *n* mezcla, *f;* fusión, *f*
bless /blɛs/ *vt* bendecir; consagrar; (praise) alabar, glorificar; hacer feliz (a). **B. me!** ¡Válgame Dios!
blessed /'blɛsɪd/ *a* bendito; *Eccl.* beato, bienaventurado; (dear) querido; feliz; *Inf.* maldito
blessedness /'blɛsɪdnɪs/ *n* felicidad, *f;* bienaventuranza, *f*
blessing /'blɛsɪŋ/ *n* bendición, *f;* (grace) bendición de la mesa, *f;* (mercy) merced, gracia, *f;* favor, *m;* (good) bien, *m.* **He gave them his b.,** Les echó su bendición
Bless you! (to someone who has sneezed) ¡Jesús!
blight /blait/ *n Agr.* tizne, tizón, *m;* (of cereals) añublo, *m;* (mould) roña, *f;* (greenfly) pulgón, *m; Fig.* influencia maligna, *f;* (frustration) desengaño, *m;* (spoil-sport) aguafiestas, *mf vt* atizonar; anublar; (wither) marchitar, secar; *Fig.* frustrar, destruir; malograr
blind /blaind/ *a* ciego; (secret) secreto; (of a door, etc.) falso; (closed) cerrado, sin salida; (unaware) ignorante; sin apreciación (de). **to be b.,** ser ciego; *Fig.* tener una venda en los ojos. **to be b. in one eye,** ser tuerto. **to turn a b. eye,** hacer la vista gorda. **b. alley,** callejón sin salida, *m.* **b. as a bat,** más ciego que un topo. **b. flying,** *Aer.* vuelo a ciegas, *m.* **b. man,** ciego, hombre ciego, *m.* **b. obedience,** obediencia ciega, *f.* **b. side,** (of persons) lado débil, *m.* **b. woman,** ciega, mujer ciega, *f*
blind /blaind/ *vt* cegar; poner una venda en los ojos (de); (dazzle) deslumbrar; hacer cerrar los ojos a; hacer ignorar
blind /blaind/ *n* persiana, *f;* (Venetian) celosía, *f;* (deception) pretexto, *m;* velo, *m*
blindfold /'blaind,fould/ *vt* vendar los ojos (a); *Fig.* poner una venda en los ojos (de). —*a* and *adv* con los ojos vendados; a ciegas; con los ojos cerrados
blindly /'blaindli/ *adv* ciegamente; a ciegas; ignorantemente
blindman's buff /'blaind,mænz 'bʌf/ *n* gallina ciega, *f*
blindness /'blaindnɪs/ *n* ceguedad, *f;* ofuscación, *f;* ignorancia, *f*
blink /blɪŋk/ *n* parpadeo, *m,* guiñada, *f;* (of light) destello, *m;* reflejo, *m; vi* parpadear, pestañear; (of lights) destellar
blinkers /'blɪŋkərz/ *n pl* anteojeras, *f pl*
bliss /blɪs/ *n* felicidad, *f;* deleite, placer, *m; Eccl.* gloria, *f*
blissful /'blɪsfəl/ *a* feliz
blissfully /'blɪsfəli/ *adv* felizmente
blissfulness /'blɪsfəlnɪs/ *n.* See **bliss**
blister /'blɪstər/ *n Med.* vesícula, *f;* ampolla, *f,* (bubble) burbuja, *f.* —*vt* ampollar; *Fig.* herir
blithe /blaið/ *a* alegre
blithely /'blaiðli/ *adv* alegremente
blitheness /'blaiðnɪs/ *n* alegría, *f*
blitzkrieg /'blɪts,krig/ *n* blitzkrieg, *m,* guerra relámpago, *f*
blizzard /'blɪzərd/ *n* ventisca, nevasca, *f*
bloated /'bloutɪd/ *a* abotagado, hinchado; orgulloso; indecente
bloater /'bloutər/ *n* arenque ahumado, *m*
blob /blɒb/ *n* masa, *f;* mancha, *f;* gota, *f*
block /blɒk/ *n* bloque, *m;* (log) leño, *m; Naut.* polea, *f;* (for beheading and of a butcher) tajo, *m;* (for mounting) apeadero, *m;* (of shares, etc.) lote, *m;* (of

houses) manzana, *f;* (jam) atasco, *m;* (obstruction) obstrucción, *f;* (for hats) forma, *f.* **A chip off the old b.,** De tal palo tal astilla. **b. and tackle,** *Naut.* polea con aparejo. **b.-hook,** grapa, *f.* **b.-house,** *Mil.* blocao, *m*

block /blɒk/ *vt* bloquear; cerrar (el paso); (stop up) atarugar, atascar; (a wheel) calzar; (a bill, etc.) obstruir; (hats) poner en forma. **to b. the way,** cerrar el paso.

blockade /blɒ'keid/ *n* bloqueo, *m, vt* bloquear. **to run the b.,** violar el bloqueo

blockhead /'blɒk,hɛd/ *n* leño, zoquete, imbécil, *m*

blond(e) /blɒnd/ *a* (of hair) rubio; (of complexion) de tez blanca. *—n* hombre rubio, *m;* (woman) rubia, mujer rubia, *f.* **peroxide b.,** rubia oxigenada, *f.* **b. lace,** blondina, *f*

blood /blʌd/ *n* sangre, *f;* (relationship) parentesco, *m;* (family) linaje, *m,* prosapia, *f;* (life) vida, *f;* (sap) savia, *f;* jugo, *m;* (horse) caballo de pura raza, *m;* (dandy) galán, *m.* *—vt* sangrar. **bad b.,** mala sangre, *f;* odio, *m;* mala leche, *f.* **blue b.,** sangre azul, *f.* **in cold b.,** a sangre fría, *f.* **My b. is up,** Se me enciende la sangre. **My b. runs cold,** Se me hiela la sangre. **to be in the b.,** llevar en la sangre. **b.-bank,** banco de sangre, *m.* **b.-bath,** matanza, *f.* **b.-colored,** de color de sangre, sanguíneo. **b.-feud,** venganza de sangre, *f.* **b.-guilt,** culpabilidad de homicidio, *m.* **b.-heat,** calor de sangre, *m.* **b.-letting,** sangría, *f.* **b. orange,** naranja dulce, *f.* **b.-plasma,** plasma sanguíneo, *m.* **b.-poisoning,** septicemia, *f;* infección, *f.* **b.-pressure,** presión sanguínea, *f.* **b. purity,** limpieza de sangre, *f.* **b.-red,** rojo como la sangre. **b.-relation,** pariente (-ta) consanguíneo(a). **b.-relationship,** consanguinidad, *f.* **b.-stain,** mancha de sangre, *f.* **b.-stained,** ensangrentado, manchado de sangre. **b.-stone,** sanguinaria, *f.* **b.-sucker,** sanguijuela, *f; Fig.* vampiro, *m;* (usurer) avaro (-ra). **b.-vessel,** vaso sanguíneo, *m*

blooded /'blʌdɪd/ *a* de sangre...; de casta...

bloodhound /'blʌd,haund/ *n* sabueso, *m*

bloodily /'blʌdəli/ *adv* sangrientamente; cruentamente; con ferocidad, cruelmente

bloodiness /'blʌdinɪs/ *n* estado sangriento, *m;* crueldad, ferocidad, *f*

bloodless /'blʌdlɪs/ *a* exangüe; pálido; incruento; anémico; indiferente

bloodshed /'blʌd,ʃɛd/ *n* efusión de sangre, *f;* matanza, carnicería, *f*

bloodshot /'blʌd,ʃɒt/ *a* (of the eye) inyectado

bloodthirstiness /'blʌd,θɜrstinɪs/ *n* sed de sangre, *f*

bloodthirsty /'blʌd,θɜrsti/ *a* sanguinario, carnicero

bloody /'blʌdi/ *a* sangriento; (of battles) encarnizado; (cruel) sanguinario, cruel

bloom /blum/ *n* flor, *f;* florecimiento, *m;* (on fruit) flor, *f;* (prime) lozanía, *f;* (on the cheeks) color sano, *m.* *—vi* florecer. **in b.,** en flor

blooming /'blumɪŋ/ *a* florido; en flor; fresco; lozano; brillante

blossom /'blɒsəm/ *n* flor, *f.* *—vi* florecer. **to b. out into,** hacerse, llegar a ser; (wear) lucir; (buy) comprarse

blossomed /'blɒsəmd/ *a* con flores, de flores

blossoming /'blɒsəmɪŋ/ *n* floración, *f*

blot /blɒt/ *n* borrón, *m;* mancha, *f.* *—vt* manchar; (erase) tachar; (dry) secar. **to b. out,** borrar; destruir; secar con papel secante

blotch /blɒtʃ/ *n* (on the skin, or stain) mancha, *f*

blotter /'blɒtər/ *n Com.* libro borrador, *m;* teleta, *f*

blotting paper /'blɒtɪŋ/ *n* papel secante, *m*

blouse /blaus/ *n* blusa, *f*

blow /blou/ *n* golpe, *m;* bofetada, *f;* (with the fist) puñetazo, *m;* (with the elbow) codazo, *m;* (with a club) porrazo, *m;* (with a whip) latigazo, *m;* (blossoming) floración, *f;* (disaster) desastre, *m,* tragedia, *f.* **to come to blows,** venirse a las manos. **at a b.,** con un solo golpe; de una vez. **We are going for a b.,** Vamos a tomar el fresco. **b. below the belt,** golpe bajo, *m.* **b. in the air,** golpe en vago, *m.* **b. of fate,** latigazo de la fortuna, *m*

blow /blou/ *vi* (of wind) soplar (el viento), hacer viento, correr aire; (pant) jadear, echar resoplidos; (of fuses) fundirse. *—vt* (wind instruments) tocar; soplar; (inflate) inflar; (swell) hinchar. **to b. a kiss,** tirar un beso. **to b. one's nose,** sonarse las narices. **to b. away,** disipar; ahuyentar; llevar (el viento). **to b. down,** echar por tierra, derribar (el viento). **to b. in,** llevar adentro, hacer entrar (el viento); (windows, etc.) quebrar (el viento). **to b. off,** quitar (el viento). **to b. open,** abrir (el viento). **to b. out,** hacer salir (el viento); llevar afuera (el viento); (a light) matar de un soplo, apagar soplando. **to b. over,** pasar por (el viento); soplar por; disiparse; olvidarse. **to b. up,** (inflate) inflar; (the fire) avivar (el fuego); (explode) volar; (swell) hinchar

blowing /'blouɪŋ/ *n* soplo, *m;* violencia, *f;* (blossoming) florecimiento, *m.* **b. up,** voleo, *m;* explosión, *f*

blow-up /'blou ,ʌp/ *n* (photograph) fotografía ampliada, *f*

blowzy /'blauzi/ *a* desaliñado

blubber /'blʌbər/ *vi* gimotear; berrear. *—n* (of the whale) grasa de ballena, *f.* **b.-lip,** bezo, *m.* **b.-lipped,** bezudo

bludgeon /'blʌdʒən/ *n* cachiporra, porpa, *f;* garrote, *m;* estaca, *f.* *—vt* golpear con una porra, dar garrotazos (a)

blue /blu/ *a* azul; (with bruises) amoratado; (sad) deprimido, melancólico; (obscene) verde; (dark) sombrío; (traditionalist) conservador. *—n* azul, *m;* (sky) cielo, *m;* (for clothes) añil de lavandera, *m; pl* **blues,** melancolía, depresión, *f;* (homesickness) morriña, *f.* *—vt* (laundry) añilar. **to look b.,** parecer deprimido; (of prospects, etc.) ser poco halagüeño. **b. black,** azul negro, *m;* (of hair) azabache, *m.* **b.-bottle,** *Ent.* moscón, *m.* **b.-eyed,** con ojos azules. **b. gum,** eucalipto, *m.* **B. Peter,** bandera de salida, *f.* **b. print,** fotocopia, *f;* plan, *m*

bluebell /'blu,bɛl/ *n* campanilla, *f*

blueness /'blunɪs/ *n* color azul, *m*

bluestocking /'blu,stɒkɪŋ/ *n* marisabidilla, doctora, *f*

bluff /blʌf/ *a* (of cliffs, etc.) escarpado; (of persons) franco, campechano, brusco

bluffness /'blʌfnɪs/ *n* franqueza, brusquedad, *f*

bluish /'bluɪʃ/ *a* azulado

bluishness /'bluɪʃnɪs/ *n* color azulado, *m*

blunder /'blʌndər/ *n* desacierto, desatino, *m;* equivocación, *f;* (in a translation, etc.) falta, *f.* *—vi* tropezar (con); desacertar; equivocarse; *Inf.* meter la pata. *—vt* manejar mal; estropear

blunderer /'blʌndərər/ *n* desatinado (-da)

blundering /'blʌndərɪŋ/ *a* desacertado; equivocado; imprudente *n.* See **blunder**

blunt /blʌnt/ *a* romo, embotado; obtuso; (abrupt) brusco; franco; descortés; (plain) claro. *—vt* enromar, embotar; (the point) despuntar; *Fig.* hacer indiferente; (pain) mitigar

bluntly /'blʌntli/ *adv* sin filo; sin punta; bruscamente, francamente; claramente

bluntness /'blʌntnɪs/ *n* embotamiento, *m; Fig.* brusquedad, franqueza, *f;* claridad, *f*

blur /blɜr/ *n* borrón, *m;* mancha, *f;* imagen indistinta, *f.* *—vt* borrar; manchar; *Photo.* velar

blurred /blɜrd/ *a* borroso; indistinto; turbio

blurt (out) /blɜrt/ *vt* proferir bruscamente; revelar sin querer

blush /blʌʃ/ *n* rubor, *m;* rojo, *m.* *—vi* enrojecerse, ruborizarse, ponerse colorado; avergonzarse (por)

blushing /'blʌʃɪŋ/ *a* ruboroso; púdico

bluster /'blʌstər/ *vi* (of the wind) soplar con furia; (of waves) encresparse, embravecerse; (of persons) bravear, fanfarronear. *—n* furia, violencia, *f;* tumulto, *m;* fanfarronería, *f*

blustering /'blʌstərɪŋ/ *a* (of wind) violento, fuerte; (of waves) tumultuoso; (of people) fanfarrón, valentón

boar /bɔr/ *n* verraco, *m;* (wild) jabalí, *m*

board /bɔrd/ *n* tabla, *f;* (for notices) tablón, *m;* (b. residence) pensión, *f;* (table) mesa, *f;* (food) comida, *f;* (for chess, checkers) tablero, *m;* (sign) letrero, *m;* (of instruments) cuadro, *m;* (bookbinding) cartón, *m; Naut.* bordo, *m;* (committee) junta, dirección, *f;* tribunal, *m; pl* **boards** *Theat.* tablas, *f pl.* **above b.,** abiertamente, sin disimulo. **free on b.,** (f.o.b.) franco a bordo. **in boards,** (of books) encartonado. **managerial b.,** junta directiva, *f.* **on b.,** a bordo. **on the boards,** *Theat.* en las tablas. **to go on b.,** ir a bordo.

b. and lodging, pensión completa, casa y comida, *f.* **b. of directors,** consejo de administración, *m.* **b. of examiners,** tribunal de exámenes, *m.* **b. of trade,** junta de comercio, *f;* ministerio de comercio, *m*
board /bɔrd/ *vt* entablar, enmaderar; embarcar en; (*Nav.* a ship) abordar; (lodge) alojar, tomar a pensión
boarder /'bɔrdər/ *n* huésped (-da); (at school) pensionista, *mf* alumno (-na) interno (-na)
boarding /'bɔrdıŋ/ *n* entablado, *m;* (planking) tablazón, *f;* (of a ship) abordaje, *m;* (of a train) subida (al tren), *f.* **b.-house,** casa de huéspedes, pensión, *f.* **b.-school,** pensionado, *m*
boarding gate *n* puerta de embarque, *f*
boast /boust/ *n* jactancia, *f;* ostentación, *f;* (honor) gloria, *f.* —*vi* jactarse, vanagloriarse; alabarse; ostentar. **to b. about,** jactarse de; hacer gala de; gloriarse en
boaster /'boustər/ *n* vanaglorioso (-sa), jactancioso (-sa)
boastful /'boustfəl/ *a* vanaglorioso, jactancioso; ostentador
boastfully /'boustfəli/ *adv* con jactancia; con ostentación
boastfulness /'boustfəlnıs/ *n* vanagloria, jactancia, *f;* fanfarronería, *f;* ostentación, *f*
boasting /'boustıŋ/ *n* alardeo, *m;* fanfarronería, *f*
boat /bout/ *n* barco, *m;* bote, *m;* (in a fun fair) columpio, *m,* lancha, *f;* (for sauce or gravy) salsera, *f.* —*vi* ir en barco; (row) remar; navegar. **to b. down,** bajar en barco. **to b. up,** subir en barco. **b. building,** construcción de barcos, *f.* **b. club,** club náutico, *m.* **b. crew,** tripulación de un barco, *f.* **b.-hook,** bichero, garabato, *m.* **b.-house,** cobertizo de las lanchas, *m.* **b.-load,** barcada, *f.* **b.-race,** regata, *f.* **b.-scoop,** achicador, *m.* **b.-shaped,** en forma de barco. **b.-train,** tren que enlaza con un vapor, *m*
boating /'boutıŋ/ *n* pasear en bote, *m;* manejo de un bote, *m;* (rowing) remo, *m.* **b.-pole,** botador, *m*
boatman /'boutmən/ *n* barquero, *m*
boatswain /'bousən/ *n* contramaestre, *m.* **boatswain's mate,** segundo contramaestre, *m*
bob /bɒb/ *n* (curtsey) reverencia, *f;* (woman's hair) pelo a la romana, *m;* (of bells) toque (de campana), *m.* —*vi* saltar; moverse. —*vt* cortar corto. **long bob,** (hair) melena, *f.* **to bob up,** ponerse de pie; surgir. **to bob up and down,** subir y bajar; bailar. **bob-tail,** rabo corto, *m.* **bob-tailed,** rabón
Bob /bɒb/ (pet form of *Robert*) Beto (Mexico)
bobbin /'bɒbın/ *n* carrete, huso, *m;* (of wool, etc.) ovillo, *m;* (of looms, sewing machines) bobina, *f;* (in lace-making) bolillo, palillo, *m*
bobsled /'bɒbˌsled/ *n* trineo doble, *m*
bode /boud/ *vt* presagiar, prometer. **to b. ill,** prometer mal. **to b. well,** prometer bien
bodice /'bɒdıs/ *n* corpiño, *m*
bodied /'bɒdid/ *a* (in compounds) de cuerpo-
bodiless /'bɒdilıs/ *a* incorpóreo
bodily /'bɒdli/ *a* del cuerpo; físico; corpóreo; real; material; (of fear) de su persona. —*adv* corporalmente; en persona, personalmente; en conjunto, enteramente; en una pieza
boding /'boudıŋ/ *a* ominoso, amenazador. —*n* presagio, *m;* agüero, *m*
body /'bɒdi/ *n Anat.* cuerpo, *m;* (trunk) tronco, *m;* (corpse) cadáver, *m;* (of a vehicle) caja, *f;* (of a motor-car) carrocería, *f;* (of a ship) casco, *m;* (of a church) nave, *f;* (centre) centro, *m;* (of a book, persons, consistency and *Astron.*) cuerpo, *m;* (person) persona, *f;* corporación, *f;* grupo, *m;* (of an army) grueso (de ejercito), *m;* organismo, *m.* **in a b.,** en masa, juntos (juntas); en corporación. **to have enough to keep b. and soul together,** tener de que vivir. **b.-snatcher,** junta cadáveres *mf* ladrón de cadáveres, *m.* **b.-snatching,** robo de cadáveres, *m*
bodyguard /'bɒdiˌgɑrd/ *n* guardia de corps, *f;* guardia, *f;* (escort) escolta, *f*
body language *n* el lenguaje del cuerpo, *m*
bog /bɒg/ *n* pantano, marjal, *m,* marisma, *f*
bogey /'bougi; 'bʊgi/ *n* duende, *m;* (to frighten children) coco, *m;* (nightmare) pesadilla, *f*
boggy /'bɒgi/ *a* pantanoso, fangoso
bogus /'bougəs/ *a* postizo, falso
Bohemian /bou'himiən/ *a* and *n* bohemio (-ia)
boil /bɔil/ *vi* bullir, hervir; (cook) cocer. —*vt* hervir; cocer. —*n* ebullición, *f; Med.* divieso, *m.* **to b. away,** consumirse hirviendo; *Chem.* evaporar a seco. **to b. over,** rebosar
boiler /'bɔilər/ *n Cul.* marmita, olla, *f;* (of a furnace) caldera, *f.* **double-b.,** baño de María, *m.* **steam-b.,** caldera de vapor, *f.* **b.-maker,** calderero, *m.* **b. room,** cámara de la caldera, *f.* **b.-suit,** mono, *m*
boiling /'bɔilıŋ/ *n* ebullición, *f,* hervor, *m;* (cooking) cocción, *f, a* hirviente. **b. point,** punto de ebullición, *m*
boisterous /'bɔistərəs/ *a* (of persons) exuberante, impetuoso; (stormy) tempestuoso, borrascoso; violento
boisterously /'bɔistərəsli/ *adv* impetuosamente, ruidosamente; tempestuosamente; con violencia
boisterousness /'bɔistərəsnıs/ *n* exuberancia, impetuosidad, *f;* violencia, *f;* tempestuosidad, borrascosidad, *f*
bold /bould/ *a* intrépido, audaz; (determined) resuelto; (forward) atrevido; (showy) llamativo; (clear) claro. **b.-faced,** descarado, desvergonzado. **b.-faced type,** letra negra, *f*
boldly /'bouldli/ *adv* intrépidamente; descaradamente; resueltamente; claramente
boldness /'bouldnıs/ *n* intrepidez, valentía, *f;* resolución, *f;* (forwardness) osadia, *f,* descaro, atrevimiento, *m;* claridad, *f*
Bolivian /bou'lıviən/ *a* and *n* boliviano (-na)
Bolognese /ˌboulə'niz/ *a* and *n* boloñés (-esa)
Bolshevik /'boulʃəvık/ *a* and *n* bolchevique, *mf*
Bolshevism /'boulʃəˌvızəm/ *n* bolchevismo, *m*
Bolshevist /'boulʃəvıst/ *n* bolchevista, *mf*
bolster /'boulstər/ *n* travesaño, *m.* —*vt* apuntalar; *Fig.* apoyar
bolt /boult/ *n* pasador, cerrojo, *m;* (pin) perno, *m;* (knocker) aldaba, *f;* (roll) rollo, *m;* (flight) huida, *f;* (of a crossbow) flecha, *f;* (from the blue) rayo, *m.* —*adv* (upright) recto como una flecha; enhiesto; rígido. **b. and nut,** perno y tuerca, *m*
bolt /boult/ *vt* echar el cerrojo (a); empernar; (*Fam.* eat) zampar. —*vi* huir; (horses) desbocarse, dispararse; (plants) cerner. **to b. down,** cerrar con cerrojo. **to b. in,** entrar corriendo, entrar de repente. **to b. off,** marcharse corriendo. **to b. out,** *vi* salir de golpe. —*vt* cerrar fuera
bolus /'bouləs/ *n* bolo, *m*
bomb /bɒm/ *n* bomba, *f, vt* bombardear. **to be a b.-shell,** *Fig.* caer como una bomba. **b.-carrier,** portabombas, *m.* **b. crater,** bombazo, *m.* **b.-release,** (*Aer. Nav.*) lanzabombas, *m.* **b.-sight,** mira de avión de bombardeo, *f*
bombard /bɒm'bɑrd/ *vt* bombardear, bombear; *Fig.* llover (preguntas, etc.) sobre
bombardier /ˌbɒmbər'dıər/ *n* bombardero, *m*
bombardment /bɒm'bɑrdmənt/ *n* bombardeo, *m*
bombast /'bɒmbæst/ *n* ampulosidad, pomposidad, *f*
bombastic /bɒm'bæstık/ *a* bombástico, altisonante, pomposo
bomber /'bɒmər/ *n* avión de bombardeo, bombardero, *m.* **dive b.,** bombardero en picado, *m.* **heavy b.,** bombardero pesado, *m.* **light b.,** bombardero ligero, *m.* **b. command,** servicio de bombardero, *m*
bombproof /'bɒmˌpruf/ *a* a prueba de bomba
bonafide /'bounəˌfaid/ *a* fidedigno
bonbon /'bɒnˌbɒn/ *n* bombón, confite, dulce, *m.* **b. box,** bombonera, *f*
bond /bɒnd/ *n* lazo, vínculo, *m; Chem.* enlace, *m;* (financial) obligación, *f;* (security) fianza, *f;* (Customs) depósito, *m; pl* **bonds,** cadenas, *f pl, a* esclavo. **in b.,** en depósito. **bonds of interest,** intereses creados, *m pl.* **b.-holder,** obligacionista, *mf*
bondage /'bɒndıdʒ/ *n* esclavitud, *f;* servidumbre, *f;* cautiverio, *m;* prisión, *f*
bone /boun/ *n* hueso, *m;* (of fish) espina (de pez), *f;* (whale b.) ballena, *f; pl* **bones,** cuerpo, *m, vt* deshuesar; poner ballenas (a or en). **to be all skin and bones,** estar en los huesos. **to have a b. to pick with,** tener que arreglar las cuentas con. **b.-ash,** cendra, *f*

boned /bound/ *a* (in compounds) de huesos; deshuesado, sin hueso
boner /'bounər/ *n* gazapo, *m*, patochada, plancha, *f*
bonfire /'bɒn,faiᵊr/ *n* fogata, hoguera, *f*
Bonn /bɒn/ Bona, *f*
bonnet /'bɒnɪt/ *n* capota, *f;* (of babies) gorra, *f;* (of men) boina, *f;* (of chimney and of machines) sombrerete, *m*
bonny /'bɒni/ *a* sano; hermoso; (fat) gordo
bonus /'bounəs/ *n* paga extraordinaria, bonificación, *f;* sobresueldo, *m;* (of food, etc.) ración extraordinaria, *f*
bon vivant /bɔ̃ vi'vɑ̃/ *n* alegre, vividor, *m*
bon voyage /bɔ̃ vwa'yaʒ/ *interj* ¡buen viaje! ¡feliz viaje!
bony /'bouni/ *a* huesudo; (of fish-bones) lleno de espinas; óseo
booby /'bubi/ *n* pazguato, bobo, *m*. **b.-prize,** último premio, *m*. **b.-trap,** trampa, *f; Mil.* mina, *f*
book /bʊk/ *n* libro, *m;* volumen, tomo, *m;* (of an opera) libreto, *m*. —*vt* anotar en un libro; apuntar; (seats) tomar (localidades); (tickets) sacar (billetes); (of the issuing clerk) dar; (reserve) reservar; inscribir; consignar (a suspect); (engage) contratar; (invite) comprometer. **to turn the pages of a b.,** hojear un libro. **b.-ends,** sostén para libros, sujetalibros, *m*. **b.-keeper,** tenedor de libros, *m*. **b.-keeping,** teneduría de libros, *f*. **b.-maker,** apostador de profesión, *m*. **b. of reference,** libro de consulta, *m*. **b.-plate,** exlibris, *m*. **b.-post,** tarifa de impresos, *f*. **b.-shop,** librería, *f*. **b.-trade,** venta de libros, *f;* comercio de libros, *m*
bookbinder /'bʊk,baindər/ *n* encuadernador (-ra) de libros
bookbinding /'bʊk,baindɪŋ/ *n* encuadernación de libros, *f*
bookcase /'bʊk,keis/ *n* armario de libros, *m*
booking /'bʊkɪŋ/ *n* (of rooms, etc.) reservación, *f;* (of tickets) toma, *f; Com.* asiento, *m;* (engagement) contratación, *f*. **b.-clerk,** vendedor (-ra) de billetes. **b. -office,** despacho de billetes, *m;* taquilla, *f*
bookish /'bʊkɪʃ/ *a* aficionado a los libros; docto, erudito
bookishness /'bʊkɪʃnɪs/ *n* afición a los libros, *f;* erudición, *f*
bookmark /'bʊk,mɑrk/ *n* marcador, *m*
bookseller /'bʊk,sɛlər/ *n* librero, *m*
bookselling /'bʊk,sɛlɪŋ/ *n* venta de libros, *f;* comercio de libros, *m*
bookshelf /'bʊk,ʃɛlf/ *n* estante para libros, *m*
bookstall /'bʊk,stɔl/ *n* puesto de libros, *m*
bookstrap /'bʊk,stræp/ *n* portalibros, *m*
bookworm /'bʊk,wɜrm/ *n* polilla que roe los libros, *f; Fig.* ratón de biblioteca, *m*
boom /bum/ *n Naut.* botavara, *f;* (of a crane) aguilón, *m;* (noise) ruido, *m;* (of the sea) bramido, *m;* (thunder) trueno, *m;* (in a port) cadena de puerto, *f; Com.* actividad, *f;* (*Fig.* peak) auge, *m, vi* sonar; bramar; tronar; *Com.* subir; ser famoso. **b. sail,** vela de cangreja, *f*
boomerang /'bumə,ræŋ/ *n* bumerang, *m*
boon /bun/ *n* favor, *m*, merced, *f;* bien, *m*, ventaja, *f;* don, *m;* privilegio, *m, a* (of friends) intimo
boor /bʊr/ *n* monigote, patán, palurdo, *m*
boorish /'bʊrɪʃ/ *a* rudo, zafio, rústico, cerril
boorishness /'bʊrɪʃnɪs/ *n* zafiedad, patanería, tosquedad, *f*
boost /bust/ *vt Elec.* aumentar la fuerza de; *Inf.* empujar; subir; (advertise) dar bombo (a)
boot /but/ *n* bota, *f;* (of a car) compartimiento para equipaje, *m*. **button-boots,** botas de botones, *f pl*. **riding-boots,** botas de montar, *f pl*. **to b.,** además, de añadidura. **b.-maker,** zapatero, *m*. **b.-tag,** tirador de bota, *m*. **b.-tree,** horma de bota, *f*
bootblack /'but,blæk/ *n* limpiabotas, *m*
booted /'butɪd/ *a* con botas, calzado con botas; (in compounds) de botas...
bootee /bu'ti/ *n* botín, *m*
booth /buθ/ *n* puesto, *m*, barraca, *f*
bootlace /'but,leis/ *n* cordón para zapatos, *m*
bootlegger /'but,lɛgər/ *n* contrabandista de alcohol, *m*
boots /buts/ *n* mozo de hotel, botones, *m*
booty /'buti/ *n* botín, *m;* tesoro, *m*
booze /buz/ *vi* emborracharse. —*n* alcohol, *m;* borrachera, *f*
boozer /'buzər/ *n* borracho (-cha)
boracic /bə'ræsɪk/ *a* bórico. —*n* ácido bórico, *m*
borax /'bɔræks/ *n* bórax, *m*
Bordeaux /bɔr'dou/ *a* and *n* (of or from) bordelés (-esa). —*n* (wine) vino de Burdeos, *m*
bordello /bɔr'dɛlou/ *n* burdel, *m*
border /'bɔrdər/ *n* borde, *m;* (of a lake, etc.) orilla, *f;* (edge) margen, *m;* (of a diploma, etc.) orla, *f; Sew.* ribete, *m*, orla, *f;* (fringe) franja, *f;* (garden) arriate, *m;* (territory) frontera, *f;* límite, confín, *m*. —*vt Sew.* orlar, ribetear; ornar (de); (of land) lindar con. **to b. on,** (of land) tocar, lindar con; (approach) rayar en. **b. country,** región fronteriza, *f*
borderer /'bɔrdərər/ *n* habitante de una zona fronteriza, *m;* escocés (-esa) de la frontera con Inglaterra
borderland /'bɔrdər,lænd/ *n* zona fronteriza, *f;* lindes, *m pl*
borderline /'bɔrdər,lain/ *n* frontera, *f;* límite, *m;* margen, *m, a* fronterizo; lindero; (uncertain) dudoso, incierto
bore /bɔr/ *n* taladro, barreno, *m;* perforación, *f;* (hole) agujero, *m;* (of guns) calibre, *m;* (wave) oleada, *f;* (nuisance) fastidio, *m;* (dullness) aburrimiento, tedio, *m;* (person) pelmazo, *m*, machaca, *mf vt* taladrar, barrenar, horadar; perforar; hacer un agujero (en); (exhaust) aburrir; fastidiar. **It's a b.,** Es una lata. **to be bored,** aburrirse, fastidiarse
boredom /'bɔrdəm/ *n* aburrimiento, *m;* tedio, hastío, *m*
boric /'bɔrɪk/ *a* bórico
boring /'bɔrɪŋ/ *a* aburrido, pesado, tedioso; molesto, fastidioso. —*n* taladro, *m;* horadación, *f;* sondeo, *m;* perforación, *f*
born /bɔrn/ *a* nacido; (by birth) de nacimiento; (b. to be) destinado a; natural (de). **He was b. in 1870.** Nació en 1870. **to be b.,** nacer, venir al mundo. **to be b. again,** renacer, volver a nacer. **well-b.,** bien nacido. **b. with a silver spoon in one's mouth,** Nacido de pie, Nacido un domingo
-borne /-bɔrn/ trasmitido por... (e.g. *anthropod-b.*, trasmitido por los antrópodos)
borough /'bɜrou/ *n* burgo, *m;* villa, *f;* ciudad, *f*. **b. surveyor,** arquitecto municipal, *m*
borrow /'bɒrou/ *vt* pedir prestado; apropiarse, adoptar; copiar; (arithmetic) restar; (a book from a library) tomar prestado. **May I b. your pencil?** ¿Quieres prestarme tu lápiz?
borrower /'bɒrouər/ *n* el (la) que pide o toma prestado
borrowing /'bɒrouɪŋ/ *n* el pedir prestado, acto de pedir prestado, *m*
bosh /bɒʃ/ *n* patrañas, tonterías, *f pl*; palabrería, *f*
Bosnian /'bɒzniən/ *a* bosnio
bosom /'bʊzəm/ *n* pecho, *m;* (heart) corazón, *m;* (of the earth, etc.) seno, *m*. **b. friend,** amigo (-ga) del alma, amigo (-ga) íntimo (-ma)
Bosphorus, the /'bɒsfərəs/ el Bósforo, *m*
boss /bɒs/ *n* (of a shield) corcova saliente, *f;* tachón, *m; Archit.* pinjante, *m*. *Inf.* amo, *m;* jefe, *m*. —*vt* mandar; dominar. **political b.,** cacique, *m*
bossism /'bɒsɪzəm/ *n* caudillaje, *m*
bossy /'bɒsi/ *a* mandón, autoritario
botanical /bə'tænɪkəl/ *a* botánico. **b. garden,** jardín botánico, *m*
botanist /'bɒtn̩ɪst/ *n* botánico (-ca)
botany /'bɒtn̩i/ *n* botánica, *f*
botch /bɒtʃ/ *n* (clumsy work) chapucería, *f;* remiendo, *m*. —*vt* chapucear, chafallar; (patch) remendar
both /bouθ/ *a* and *pron* ambos, *m pl*; ambas, *f pl*; los dos, *m pl*; las dos, *f pl, adv* tan(to)... como; (and) y; a la vez, al mismo tiempo. **It appealed both to the young and the old,** Gustó tanto a los jóvenes como a los viejos. **b. of you,** ustedes dos, vosotros dos, vosotras dos. **b. pretty and useful,** bonito y útil a la vez
bother /'bɒðər/ *n* molestia, *f*, fastidio, *m;* (worry) preocupación, *f;* dificultad, *f;* (fuss) alboroto, *m*. —*vt* molestar, fastidiar; preocupar. —*vi* preocuparse

bottle /'bɒtl̩/ *n* botella, *f;* (smaller) frasco, *m;* (babies) biberón, *m;* (for water) cantimplora, *f, vt* embotellar, envasar, enfrascar. **to b. up,** (liquids, capital, armies, navies) embotellar; (feelings) refrenar. **to bring up on the b.,** criar con biberón. **b.-green,** verde botella, *m.* **b.-neck,** (in an industry) embotellado, *m;* (in traffic) atascadero, *m.* **b.-washer,** fregaplatos, *mf;* (machine) máquina para limpiar botellas, *f*
bottle cap *n* corchalata, *f*
bottled /'bɒtl̩d/ *a* en botella; (of fruit, vegetables) conservado
bottleful /'bɒtl̩ˌfʊl/ *n* botella, *f*
bottler /'bɒtl̩ər/ *n* embotellador (-ra)
bottling /'bɒtl̩ɪŋ/ *n* embotellado, *m;* envase, *m.* **b. outfit,** embotelladora, *f;* (for fruit, etc.) aparato para conservar frutas o legumbres, *m*
bottom /'bɒtəm/ *n* base, *f;* (deepest part) fondo, *m;* (last place) último lugar, *m;* fundamento, *m;* (of a chair) asiento, *m;* (of a page, table, mountain, etc.) pie, *m;* (posterior) culo, *m;* (of a river) lecho, *m;* (of the sea) fondo, *m;* (of a ship) casco, *m;* (of a skirt) orilla, *f;* (truth) realidad, verdad, *f;* (basis) origen, *m,* causa, *f.* **at b.,** en realidad. **at the b.,** en el fondo. **false b.,** fondo doble, fondo secreto, *m.* **to be at the b. of,** ocupar el último lugar en; ser el causante de. **to get to the b. of,** descubrir la verdad de; profundizar en, analizar. **to sink to the b.,** (of ships) irse a pique
bottomed /'bɒtəmd/ *a* (in compounds) de fondo...
bottomless /'bɒtəmlɪs/ *a* sin fondo; (of chairs, etc.) sin asiento; (unfathomable) insondable
boudoir /'budwɑr/ *n* tocador, gabinete de señora, *m*
bough /bau/ *n* rama, *f,* brazo (de un árbol) *m*
boulder /'bouldər/ *n* roca, peña, *f;* canto rodado, *m;* bloque de roca, *m*
boulevard /'bʊləˌvɑrd/ *n* bulevar, *m*
Boulogne /bʊ'loun/ Boloña, *f*
bounce /bauns/ *n* bote, rebote, *m;* salto, *m;* (boasting) fanfarronería, *f, vi* rebotar; saltar, brincar. —*vt* hacer botar o saltar
bouncing /'baunsɪŋ/ *a* (healthy) sano, robusto; vigoroso, fuerte
bound /baund/ *n* límite, *m;* (jump) salto, brinco, *m, vt* limitar, confinar. —*vi* saltar, brincar; (bounce) botar. **within bounds,** dentro del límite. **b. for,** con destino a; (of ships) con rumbo a
boundary /'baundəri/ *n* límite, lindero, término, *m;* frontera, *f;* raya, *f.* **b. stone,** mojón, *m*
bounden /'baundən/ *a* obligatorio, forzoso; indispensable
boundless /'baundlɪs/ *a* sin límites, infinito; inmenso
bounteous, bountiful /'bauntiəs; 'bauntɪfəl/ *a* dadivoso, generoso; bondadoso
bountifulness /'bauntɪfəlnɪs/ *n* munificencia, dadivosidad, generosidad, *f*
bounty /'baunti/ *n* generosidad, munificencia, *f;* don, *m;* (subsidy) subvención, *f*
bouquet /bou'kei, bu-/ *n* ramo, ramillete (de flores), *m;* perfume, *m;* (of wine) nariz, *f*
Bourbon /'bɜrbən; 'bʊrbən/ *a* borbónico. —*n* Borbón (-ona)
bourgeois /bʊr'ʒwɑ/ *a* and *n* burgués (-esa)
bourgeoisie /ˌbʊrʒwɑ'zi/ *n* burguesía, mesocracia, *f*
bout /baut/ *n* turno, *m;* (in fencing, boxing, wrestling) asalto, *m;* (of illness, coughing) ataque, *m;* (fight) lucha, *f,* combate, *m;* (of drinking) borrachera, *f*
bovine /'bouvaɪn/ *a* bovino, vacuno
bow /bou/ *n* (weapon) arco, *m;* (of a saddle) arzón (de silla), *m; Mus.* arco, *m;* (knot) lazo, *m;* (greeting) saludo, *m;* reverencia, inclinación, *f;* (of a boat) proa, *f.* **to tie a bow,** hacer un lazo. **bow and arrows,** arco y flechas, *m.* **bow-legged,** patizambo. **bow window,** ventana saliente, *f*
bow /bau/ *vi* inclinarse; hacer una reverencia, saludar; (remove the hat) descubrirse; *Fig.* inclinarse (ante); (submit) someterse (a), reconocer; agobiarse; *Mus.* manejar el arco. —*vt* (usher in) introducir en, conducir a; doblar; inclinar. **to bow down (to),** humillarse ante; obedecer; (worship) reverenciar, adorar. **to bow out,** despedir con una inclinación del cuerpo
bowel /'bauəl/ *n* intestino, *m; pl* **bowels,** *Fig.* seno, *m,* entrañas, *f pl*
bower /'bauər/ *n* (arbor) enramada, *f;* glorieta, *f;* (boudoir) tocador de señora, *m*
bowing /'bouɪŋ/ *n Mus.* arqueada, *f;* saludo, *m, a* (of acquaintance) superficial
bowl /boul/ *n* receptáculo, *m;* (of a fountain) taza, *f;* (of a pipe) cazoleta, *f;* (barber's) bacía, *f;* (for washing) jofaina, *f;* (for punch) ponchera, *f;* (goblet) copa, *f;* (for soup) escudilla, *f;* (for fruit) frutero, *m;* (of a spoon) paleta, *f;* (ball) boliche, *m.* —*vt* tirar; (in cricket) sacar; (a hoop) jugar con; (in ninepins) tumbar con una bola. **to b. along,** recorrer; ir en coche o carruaje (por). **to b. over,** *Fig.* dejar consternado (a), desconcertar
bowler /'boulər/ *n* (in cricket) servidor, *m;* (hat) sombrero hongo, *m;* (skittle player) jugador de bolos, *m*
bowling /'boulɪŋ/ *n* (in cricket) saque, *m;* (skittles) juego de bolos, *m;* juego de boliche, *m.* **b. alley,** bolera, pista de bolos, *f,* salón de boliche, *m.* **b.-green,** bolera en cesped, *f*
bowls /boulz/ *n* juego de boliche, *m*
bowsprit /'bausprɪt/ *n* bauprés, *m*
bowstring /'bouˌstrɪŋ/ *n* cuerda de arco, *f*
bow tie /bou/ *n* pajarita, *f*
bow-wow /'bau ˌwau/ *n* guau, *m*
box /bɒks/ *n* caja, *f;* (case) estuche, *m;* (luggage) baúl, *m,* maleta, *f;* (for a hat) sombrerera, *f; Bot.* boj, *m; Theat.* palco, *m;* (for a sentry, signalman, etc.) garita, casilla, *f;* (on a carriage) pescante, *m;* (blow) cachete, *m,* bofetada, *f;* (for a horse) vagón, *m.* **post office box,** apartado de correos, *m.* **box-kite,** cometa celular, *f.* **box-maker,** cajero, *m.* **box office,** taquilla, *f.* **box-pleat,** *Sew.* tabla, *f*
box /bɒks/ *vt* encajonar, meter en una caja. —*vi* boxear. **to box the ears of,** calentar las orejas de. **to box up,** encerrar
boxer /'bɒksər/ *n Sports.* boxeador, pugilista, *m*
boxing /'bɒksɪŋ/ *n* encajonamiento, *m;* envase, *m; Sports.* boxeo, pugilato, *m.* **B. Day,** Día de San Esteban, *m,* (A Spanish child receives its Christmas presents on the Día de Reyes (Twelfth Night).) **b.-gloves,** guantes de boxeo, *m pl.* **b.-ring,** cuadrilátero de boxeo, *m*
box-office success /'bɒks ˌɔfɪs/ *n* éxito de taquilla, *m*
boy /bɔi/ *n* muchacho, niño, rapaz, *m;* (older) chico, joven, *m.* **new boy,** nuevo alumno, *m.* **old boy,** (of a school) antiguo alumno, *m;* (*Fam.* address) chico. **small boy,** chiquillo, pequeño, crío, *m.* **b. doll,** muñeco, *m.* **boy scout,** muchacho explorador, *m*
boycott /'bɔikɒt/ *vt* boicotear. —*n* boicot, *m*
boyhood /'bɔihʊd/ *n* muchachez, mocedad, *f;* (childhood) niñez, *f*
boyish /'bɔiɪʃ/ *a* muchachil; pueril; de niñez
brace /breis/ *n* (prop) puntal, barrote, *m;* abrazadera, *f;* berbiquí, *m;* viento, tirante, *m;* freno (for the teeth), *m,* (pair) par, *m; pl* **braces,** tirantes, *m pl.* —*vt* apuntalar; asegurar; ensamblar; *Naut.* bracear; (trousers) tirar; *Fig.* fortalecer, refrescar
bracelet /'breislɪt/ *n* pulsera, *f,* brazalete, *m,* ajorca, *f*
bracing /'breisɪŋ/ *a* (of air, etc.) fortificante, tónico; estimulador
bracken /'brækən/ *n* helecho, *m*
bracket /'brækɪt/ *n* consola, *f; Archit.* repisa, *f;* soporte, *m;* (on furniture, etc.) cantonera, *f; Print.* paréntesis angular, *m;* (for a light) brazo (de alumbrado), *m.* —*vt Print.* poner entre paréntesis; juntar. **in brackets,** entre paréntesis. **They were bracketed equal,** Fueron juzgados iguales
brackish /'brækɪʃ/ *a* salobre
brag /bræg/ *vi* jactarse, fanfarronear. —*n* jactancia, *f.* **to b. about,** hacer alarde de
braggart /'brægərt/ *a* baladrón, jactancioso. —*n* jactancioso, fanfarrón, *m*
bragging /'brægɪŋ/ *n* jactancia, *f*
Brahmin /'brɑmɪn/ *n* brahmán, *m*
Brahminism /'brɑmɪˌnɪzəm/ *n* brahmanismo, *m*
braid /breid/ *n* trencilla, *f,* cordoncillo, *m;* (for trimming) galón, *m;* (plait) trenza, *f.* —*vt* (hair) trenzar; (trim) galonear; acordonar, trencillar
brain /brein/ *n* cerebro, *m;* entendimiento, *m,* inteli-

gencia, *f;* talento, *m;* (common sense) sentido común, *m; pl* **brains,** sesos, *m pl,* (animal and human); cacumen, *m.* —*vt* romper la crisma (a). **to blow one's brains out,** levantarse la tapa de los sesos. **to rack one's brains,** devanarse los sesos. **Brains Trust,** masa cefálica, *f;* consorcio de inteligencias, *m.* **b.-box,** cráneo, *m.* **b.-fever,** fiebre cerebal, *f.* **b.-storm,** crisis nerviosa, *f.* **b.-wave,** idea luminosa, *f.* **b.-work,** trabajo intelectual, *m*

brainchild /'breinˌtʃaild/ *n* engendro, *m*

brain drain *n* fuga de cerebros, *f*

brained /breind/ *a* de cabeza, de cerebro

brainless /'breinlɪs/ *a* sin seso; tonto

brainy /'breini/ *a* sesudo, inteligente, talentudo

braise /breiz/ *vt Cul.* asar

brake /breik/ *n* (of vehicles and *Fig.*) freno, *m;* (flax and hemp) caballete, *m;* (carriage) break, *m;* (thicket) matorral, *m.* —*vt* (vehicles) frenar; (hemp, etc.) rastrillar. **foot-b.,** freno de pedal, *m.* **hand-b.,** freno de mano, *m.* **to b. hard,** frenar de repente. **to release the b.,** quitar el freno

bramble /'bræmbəl/ *n* zarza, *f.* **b. patch,** breña, *f,* zarzal, *m*

brambly /'bræmbli/ *a* zarzoso

bran /bræn/ *n* salvado, *m*

branch /bræntʃ, brɑntʃ/ *n* (of a tree, a family) rama, *f;* (of flowers, of learning) ramo, *m;* (of a river) tributario, afluente, *m;* (of roads, railways) ramal, *m;* (of a firm) sucursal, dependencia, *f.* —*a* sucursal, dependiente; (of roads, railways) secundario. —*vi* echar ramas; bifurcarse, dividirse; ramificarse. **to b. off,** bifurcarse, ramificarse. **to b. out,** extenderse; emprender cosas nuevas

branched /bræntʃt/ *a* con ramas; *Bot.* ramoso; (of candlesticks) de... brazos

branchiness /'bræntʃinɪs/ *n* ramaje, *m,* frondosidad, *f*

branching /'bræntʃɪŋ/ *n* ramificación, *f;* división, *f.* **b. off,** bifurcación, *f*

brand /brænd/ *n* tizón, *m;* (torch) tea, *f;* (on cattle, etc.) hierro, *m;* (trademark) marca de fábrica, *f;* marca, *f;* (stigma) estigma, *m.* —*vt* marcar con el hierro, herrar; marcar; estigmatizar, tildar. **b.-new,** flamante

branding /'brændɪŋ/ *n* (of livestock) herradero, *m;* (of slaves, criminals) estigmatización, *f;* difamación, *f.* **b.-iron,** hierro de marcar, *m*

brandish /'brændɪʃ/ *vt* blandir

brandy /'brændi/ *n* coñac, *m*

brass /bræs/ *n* latón, *m; Mus.* metal, *m;* (tablet) placa conmemorativa, *f; Inf.* dinero, *m.* **the b.,** *Mus.* el metal. **b. band,** banda de instrumentos de viento, *f.* **b.-neck,** *Inf.* cara dura, *f.* **b. works** or **shop,** latonería, *f*

brassiere /brə'zɪər/ *n* sostén, *m*

brat /bræt/ *n* crío, *m*

bravado /brə'vɑdou/ *n* bravata, *f*

brave /breiv/ *a* valiente, animoso, intrépido; espléndido, magnífico; bizarro. —*n* valiente, *m.* —*vt* desafiar, provocar; arrostrar

bravely /'breivli/ *adv* valientemente; espléndidamente; bizarramente

bravery /'breivəri/ *n* valentía, *f,* valor, *m,* intrepidez, *f,* coraje, *m;* esplendidez, suntuosidad, *f;* bizarría, *f*

bravo /'brɑvou/ *n* bandido, *m;* asesino pagado, *m,* *interj* ¡bravo! ¡ole!

bravura /brə'vyʊrə/ *n* bravura, *f*

brawl /brɔl/ *n* camorra, reyerta, pelotera, *f.* —*vi* alborotar; (of streams) murmurar. **to start a b.,** armar camorra

brawler /'brɔlər/ *n* camorrista, *mf*

brawling /'brɔlɪŋ/ *n* alboroto, *m,* vocinglería, *f;* (of streams) murmullo, *m*

brawn /brɔn/ *n Cul.* embutido, *m;* músculo, *m;* (strength) fuerza, *f*

brawny /'brɔni/ *a* membrudo, musculoso, forzudo

bray /brei/ *n* rebuzno, *m;* (of trumpets) clangor, *m,* *vi* rebuznar; sonar

brazen /'breizən/ *a* de latón; (of voice) bronca; desvergonzado, descarado

brazier /'breiʒər/ *n* (fire) brasero, *m;* latonero, *m*

Brazil /brə'zɪl/ el Brasil, *m*

Brazilian /brə'zɪlyən/ *a* and *n* brasileño (-ña)

Brazil nut *n* nuez del Brasil, *f*

breach /britʃ/ *n* violación, contravención, *f;* (gap) abertura, *f; Mil.* brecha, *f.* —*vt Mil.* hacer brecha (en); (in a line of defence) hacer mella (en). **b. of confidence,** abuso de confianza, *m.* **b. of promise,** incumplimiento de la palabra de casamiento, *m.* **b. of the peace,** alteración del orden público, *f,* quebrantamiento de la paz, *m*

bread /brɛd/ *n* pan, *m.* **to earn one's b. and butter,** ganarse el pan. **brown b.,** pan moreno, *m.* **unleavened b.,** pan ázimo, *m.* **b. and butter,** pan con mantequilla, *m; Fig.* sustento diario, *m.* **b.-basket,** cesta de pan, *f; Inf.* estómago, *m.* **b.-bin,** caja del pan, *f.* **b.-crumb,** miga, *f;* migaja, *f.* **b.-knife,** cuchillo para cortar el pan, *m.* **b. poultice,** cataplasma de miga de pan, *f.* **b.-winner,** ganador (-ra) de pan, trabajador (-ra)

breadfruit tree /'brɛdˌfrut/ *n* árbol del pan, *m*

breadth /brɛdθ/ *n* anchura, *f;* latitud, *f;* liberalidad, *f; Sew.* ancho de una tela, *m*

breadthways /'brɛdθˌweiz/ *adv* a lo ancho

break /breik/ *n* rotura, *f;* (opening) abertura, *f; Geol.* rajadura, *f;* (fissure) grieta, *f;* solución de continuidad, *f;* interrupción, *f;* (billiards) serie, *f;* (change) cambio, *m;* (in a boy's voice) muda (de la voz), *f;* (blank) vacío, *m;* (in the market) baja, *f;* intervalo, *m;* descanso, *m;* pausa, *f;* (truce) tregua, *f;* (clearing) clara, *f; Mus.* quiebra (de la voz), *f;* (carriage) break, *m;* (*Fam.* folly) disparate, *m.* **with a b. in one's voice,** con voz entrecortada. **b. of day,** aurora, alba, *f.* **at the b. of day,** al despuntar el alba

break /breik/ *vt* romper; quebrar; quebrantar, fracturar; (breach) abrir brecha en; (in two) partir, dividir; (into pieces) hacer pedazos, despedazar; (into small pieces) desmenuzar; (into crumbs) desmigajar; (destroy) destrozar; (a blow) parar; (a law) infringir, violar; (the bank in gambling) quebrar; (a journey, etc.) interrumpir; (of a habit) desacostumbrar, hacer perder el vicio de; (a promise) no cumplir, faltar a; (a record) superar; (plow ground) roturar; (spoil) estropear; arruinar; *Com.* ir a la quiebra; (an official) degradar; (an animal) domar, amansar; (*Fig.* crush) subyugar; (betray) traicionar; (*Fig.* of silence, a spell, a lance, peace, the ranks) romper; (cushion) amortiguar; (lessen) mitigar; (disclose) revelar; *Elec.* interrumpir. **to b. one's promise,** faltar a su palabra. **to b. the ice,** *Fig.* romper el hielo. **to b. asunder,** romper en dos (partes); dividir. **to b. down,** derribar; echar abajo; destruir; (suppress) suprimir; subyugar; abolir; disolver. **to b. in,** (animals) domar, amaestrar; (persons) disciplinar; (new shoes) ahormar, romper. **to b. in two,** partir; dividir en dos; (split) hender. **to b. off,** separar, quitar; (a branch) desgajar; *Fig.* romper; interrumpir; cesar. **to b. open,** forzar, abrir a la fuerza. **to b. up,** hacer pedazos; (scatter) poner en fuga, dispersar; hacer levantar la sesión; (the ground) roturar; (parliament) disolver; (a ship) desguazar, deshacer (un buque)

break /breik/ *vi* romperse; quebrarse; quebrantarse; (of beads) desgranarse; (burst) reventar, estallar; (of abscesses) abrirse; (of a boy's voice) mudar; (*Fig.* and of clouds, etc.) romperse; desaparecer; (of the dawn) despuntar (el alba), amanecer; (sprout) brotar; (of a ball) torcerse; (of fine weather) terminar; (change) cambiar; (of a storm) estallar. **to b. loose,** desasirse; *Fig.* desencadenarse. **to b. away,** escaparse, fugarse; (from a habit) romper con, independizarse de (another country); disiparse. **to b. down,** (of machinery, cars) averiarse; (fail) frustrarse, malograrse; (weep) deshacerse en lágrimas; (lose one's grip) perder la confianza en sí; (in health) sufrir una crisis de salud. **The car broke down,** El auto tuvo una avería. **to b. in,** (of burglars) forzar la entrada; irrumpir (en), penetrar (en); exclamar. **to b. in on,** sorprender; entrar de sopetón; invadir; interrumpir; caer sobre; molestar. **to b. into,** (force) forzar; (utter) romper a, prorrumpir en; empezar (a); pasar de repente a; (of time, etc.) ocupar; hacer perder. **to b. off,** (of speech) interrumpirse; cesar; (detach) desprenderse, separarse; (of branches) desgajarse. **to b. out,** huir, escaparse; *Fig.* estallar; aparecer; declararse; (of fire) tomar fuego; derramarse; (of an eruption) salir. **to b. over,** derramarse por; bañar. **to b.**

through, abrirse paso (por); abrirse salida (por); atravesar; *Fig.* penetrar; (of the sun, etc.) romper (por). **to b. up,** (depart) separarse; (of meetings) levantarse la sesión; dispersarse; (smash) hacerse pedazos; disolverse; (of a school) cerrarse, empezar las vacaciones; (melt) fundir; desbandarse; (of a camp) levantar (el campo); (grow old) hacerse viejo; (be ill) estar agotado. **to b. with,** romper con; cesar; reñir con

breakable /'breikəbəl/ *a* quebradizo, frágil

breakage /'breikɪdʒ/ *n* rompimiento, quebrantamiento, *m;* cosa rota, *f;* fractura, *f*

breakdown /'breik,daun/ *n* accidente, *m;* (of a machine) avería, *f; Auto.* pane, *f;* (failure) fracaso, *m,* falta de éxito, *f;* deterioración, *f;* (in health) crisis de salud, *f.* **b. gang,** pelotón de reparaciones, *m*

breaker /'breikər/ *n* oleada, *f*

breakfast /'brɛkfəst/ *n* desayuno, *m.* —*vi* desayunar(se), tomar el desayuno. **to have a good b.,** desayunar bien. **b.-cup,** tazón, *m.* **b.-time,** hora del desayuno, *f*

breaking /'breikɪŋ/ *n* rompimiento, *m;* quebrantamiento, *m;* fractura, *f;* ruptura, *f;* (in two) división, *f;* (into pieces) despedazamiento, *m;* (into small pieces) desmenuzamiento, *m;* (destruction) destrozo, *m;* (of a blow) parada, *f;* (of a law, etc.) violación, *f;* (of one's word) no cumplimiento, *m;* (of a journey, of sleep, etc.) interrupción, *f;* (escape) escape, *m,* huida, *f;* (of an animal) domadura, *f;* (of a boy's voice) muda (de la voz), *f;* (of news) revelación, *f.* **b. down,** demolición, *f;* (of negotiations) suspensión, *f.* **b. in,** irrupción, *f;* (of an animal) domadura, *f;* (training) entrenamiento, *m.* **b. open,** forzamiento, *m;* quebranto, *m.* **b. out,** huida, *f,* escape, *m; Fig.* estallido, *m;* aparición, *f;* declaración, *f;* (scattering) derramamiento, *m;* (of a rash) erupción, *f.* **b. up,** dispersión, *f;* disolución, *f;* fin, *m;* ruina, *f;* (of a school) cierre, *m;* (change in weather) cambio, *m;* (of a meeting) levantamiento (de una sesión), *m;* (of the earth) roturación, *f*

breakneck /'breik,nɛk/ *a* rápido, veloz, precipitado

breakwater /'breik,wɔtər/ *n* malecón, rompeolas, *m*

bream /brɪm/ *n Ichth.* sargo, *m.* **sea-b.,** besugo, *m*

breast /brɛst/ *n* pecho, *m;* (of birds) pechuga, *f;* (of female animals) teta, mama, *f;* (heart) corazón, *m, vt* (the waves) cortar (las olas); luchar con; *Fig.* arrostrar, hacer frente a. **b.-bone,** esternón, *m.* **b. high,** alto hasta el pecho. **b.-pin,** alfiler de pecho, *m.* **b.-pocket,** bolsillo de pecho, *m.* **b.-stroke,** estilo pecho, *m*

breast cancer *n* el cáncer del seno, *m*

breasted /'brɛstɪd/ *a* de pecho...; de pechuga...; de tetas... **a double-b. jacket,** una chaqueta cruzada. **a single-b. jacket,** una chaqueta

breastwork /'brɛst,wɜrk/ *n Mil.* parapeto, *m*

breath /brɛθ/ *n* aliento, *m;* suspiro, *m;* (phonetics) aspiración, *f;* (breeze) soplo (de aire), *m;* (of scandal, etc.) murmurio, *m;* (fragrance) perfume, *m,* fragancia, *f;* (life) vida, *f.* **in a b.,** de un aliento. **in the same b.,** sin respirar. **out of b.,** sin aliento. **under one's b.,** por lo bajo, entre dientes. **to draw b.,** tomar aliento. **to get one's b. back,** cobrar aliento. **to hold one's b.,** contener el aliento. **to take one's b. away,** *Fig.* dejar consternado (a)

breathable /'briðəbəl/ *a* respirable

breathe /brið/ *vi* respirar; vivir; (of air, etc.) soplar; (take the air) tomar el fresco; (rest) tomar aliento. —*vt* respirar; exhalar; dar aire (a); (whisper) murmurar; (convey) expresar, revelar; (infuse) infundir. **to b. forth fury,** echar rayos. **to b. hard,** jadear. **to b. one's last,** exhalar el último suspiro. **to b. in,** inspirar

breathing /'briðɪŋ/ *n* respiración, *f;* (of the air, etc.) soplo, *m;* (phonetics) aspiración, *f.* —*a* que respira; viviente. **hard** or **heavy b.,** jadeo, resuello, resoplido, *m.* **b.-space,** *Fig.* respiro, *m*

breathless /'brɛθlɪs/ *a* jadeante, sin aliento; (dead) muerto; (sultry) sin un soplo de aire; intenso, profundo; (of haste) precipitado

breathlessly /'brɛθlɪsli/ *adv* anhelosamente; con expectación

breathlessness /'brɛθlɪsnɪs/ *n* falta de aliento, *f;* respiración difícil, *f;* (death) muerte, *f;* (of weather) falta de aire, *f*

bred /brɛd/ *a* criado. **ill (well) b.,** mal (bien) criado. **pure-b.,** de raza

breech /britʃ/ *n Anat.* trasero, *m;* (of fire-arms) recámara, *f*

breeches /'brɪtʃɪz/ *n* calzones, *m pl*; pantalones, *m pl.* **riding-b.,** pantalones de montar, *m pl.* **to wear the b.,** *Fig.* ponerse los calzones

breed /brid/ *n* casta, raza, *f;* tipo, *m;* clase, *f, vt* procrear; engendrar, crear; (bring up) educar; criar. —*vi* reproducirse; sacar cría; multiplicarse. **to b. in-and-in,** procrear sin mezclar razas

breeder /'bridər/ *n* criador (-ra); animal reproductor, *m*

breeding /'bridɪŋ/ *n* reproducción, *f;* cría, *f;* (upbringing) crianza, *f;* educación, *f;* instrucción, *f;* producción, *f;* creación, *f, a* de cría; (of male animals) semental; prolífico. **bad b.,** mala crianza, *f.* **good b.,** buena crianza, *f.* **cross b.,** cruzamiento de razas, *m.* **B. will out,** Aunque la mona se vista de seda, mona se queda. **b. farm,** criadero, *m*

breeze /briz/ *n* brisa, *f,* vientecillo, soplo de aire, *m;* (argument) altercación, *f,* argumento, *m;* (of coke) cisco de coque, *m.* **fresh b.,** brisa fresca, *f.* **light b.,** brisa floja, *f.* **strong b.,** viento fuerte, viento muy fresco, *m*

breezy /'brizi/ *a* con brisa, fresco; expuesto a la brisa; oreado; (of manner) animado, jovial

Bremen /'brɛmən, 'breimən/ Brema, *f*

brethren /'brɛðrɪn/ *n pl* hermanos, *m pl*

Breton /'brɛtn̩/ *a* and *n* bretón (-ona). —*n* (language) bretón, *m*

brevet /brə'vɛt/ *n Mil.* graduación honoraria, *f;* nombramiento honorario, *m.* —*vt Mil.* graduar

breviary /'brivi,ɛri/ *n* breviario, *m*

brevity /'brɛvɪti/ *n* brevedad, *f;* concisión, *f*

brew /bru/ *n* mezcla, *f;* brebaje, *m.* —*vt* hacer (cerveza, té, etc.); preparar, mezclar; *Fig.* urdir, tramar. —*vi* prepararse; urdirse; (storm) gestarse.

brewer /'bruər/ *n* cervecero (-ra)

brewery /'bruəri/ *n* cervecería, fábrica de cerveza, *f*

brewing /'bruɪŋ/ *n* elaboración de cerveza, *f*

briar /'braiər/ *n* (wild rose) rosal silvestre, *m;* (heather) brezo, *m.* **b. pipe,** pipa de brezo, *f*

bribable /'braibəbəl/ *a* sobornable

bribe /braib/ *n* soborno, cohecho, *m, vt* sobornar, cohechar. **to take bribes,** dejarse sobornar

briber /'braibər/ *n* cohechador (-ra)

bribery /'braibəri/ *n* soborno, *m*

brick /brɪk/ *n* ladrillo, *m;* (for children) piedra de construcción, *f;* bloque, *m; Inf.* buen chico, *m,* joya, *f, a* de ladrillo. —*vt* enladrillar. **b.-floor,** ladrillado, *m;* **b.-kiln,** horno de ladrillo, *m.* **b.-maker,** ladrillero, *m.* **b.-yard,** ladrillar, *m*

bricklayer /'brɪk,leiər/ *n* albañil, *m*

bricklaying /'brɪk,leiɪŋ/ *n* albañilería, *f*

brickwork /'brɪk,wɜrk/ *n* masonería, *f*

bridal /'braidl̩/ *a* nupcial; de la boda; de la novia. **b. bed,** tálamo, *m.* **b. cake,** torta de la boda, *f.* **b. shop,** tienda para novias, *f.* **b. shower,** despedida de soltera, despedida de soltería, *f.* **b. song,** epitalamio, *m.* **b. veil,** velo de la novia, velo nupcial, *m.* **b. wreath,** corona de azahar, *f*

bride /braid/ *n* novia, desposada, *f;* (after marriage) recién casada, *f*

bridegroom /'braid,grum/ *n* novio, *m;* (after marriage) recién casado, *m*

bridesmaid /'braidz,meid/ *n* madrina de boda, *f;* niña encargada de sostener la cola de la novia, *f*

bridge /brɪdʒ/ *n* (engineering, *Mus. Naut.*) puente, *m;* lomo (de la nariz), *m;* (game) bridge, *m, vt* construir un puente (sobre), pontear; (obstacles) salvar; evitar; (fill in) ocupar, llenar. **auction b.,** bridge por subasta, *m.* **contract b.,** bridge por contrato, *m.* **suspension-b.,** puente colgante, *m.* **b. toll,** pontazgo, *m*

bridgehead /'brɪdʒ,hɛd/ *n* cabeza de puente, *f*

bridle /'braidl̩/ *n* brida, *f;* freno, *m.* —*vt* embridar, enfrenar; *Fig.* reprimir. —*vi* (of horses) levantar la cabeza; (of persons) erguirse; hacer un gesto despreciativo. **snaffle b.,** bridón, *m.* **b. path,** camino de herradura, *m*

brief /brif/ *a* breve, corto; conciso; lacónico, seco; rápido; fugaz, pasajero. —*n* (papal) breve, *m; Law.* relación, *f;* escrito, *m.* —*vt* (a barrister) instruir. **to hold a b. for,** defender, abogar por. **b.-case,** portapapeles, *m;* cartera (grande), *f*

briefly /'brifli/ *adv* brevemente; en pocas palabras; sucintamente; (tersely) secamente

brier /'braiər/ *n* rosal silvestre, *m;* zarza, *f*

brigade /brɪ'geid/ *n Mil.* brigada, *f;* cuerpo, *m;* asociación, *f*

brigadier /ˌbrɪgə'dɪər/ *n* brigadier, *m*

brigand /'brɪgənd/ *n* bandolero, bandido, *m*

brigandage /'brɪgəndɪdʒ/ *n* bandolerismo, *m*

bright /brait/ *a* brillante, reluciente; vivo; cristalino; subido; claro; optimista; alegre; inteligente; (quick-witted) agudo; ilustre; (smiling) risueño; (of future, etc.) halagüeño. **to be as b. as a new pin,** estar como una ascua de oro. **b. blue,** azul subido, *m.* **b.-eyed,** con ojos vivos, con ojos chispeantes, ojialegre

brighten /'braitn̩/ *vt* hacer brillar; (polish) pulir; (make happy) alegrar; (improve) mejorar. —*vi* (of the weather) aclarar, despejarse (el cielo); sentirse más feliz; mejorar

brightly /'braitli/ *adv* brillantemente; alegremente

brightness /'braitnɪs/ *n* brillo, *m;* claridad, *f;* esplendor, *m;* (of colors) brillantez, *f;* vivacidad, *f;* inteligencia, *f;* agudeza de ingenio, *f*

Bright's disease /braits/ *n* enfermedad de Bright, glomerulonefritis, *f*

brilliance /'brɪlyəns/ *n* fulgor, brillo, *m,* refulgencia, *f;* esplendor, *m;* lustre, *m;* talento, *m;* brillantez, gloria, *f*

brilliant /'brɪlyənt/ *a* brillante. —*n* (gem) brillante, *m.* **to be b.,** (in conversation, etc.) brillar; (be clever) ser brillante

brilliantine /'brɪlyənˌtin/ *n* brillantina, *f*

brim /brɪm/ *n* (of a glass, etc.) borde, *m;* (of a hat) ala, *f;* margen, *m,* orilla, *f.* **to be full to the b.,** estar lleno hasta los bordes; *Fig.* rebosar. **eyes brimming with tears,** ojos arrasados de lágrimas

brimful /'brɪm'fʊl/ *a* hasta el borde (or los bordes); *Fig.* rebosante

brimless /'brɪmlɪs/ *a* (of hats) sin ala

brimmed /brɪmd/ *a* (of hats) con ala

brimstone /'brɪmˌstoun/ *n* azufre, *m*

brindled /'brɪndl̩d/ *a* atigrado, abigarrado

brine /brain/ *n* salmuera, *f;* mar, *m; Poet.* lágrimas, *f pl*

bring /brɪŋ/ *vt* traer; llevar; transportar; (take a person or drive a vehicle) conducir; *Fig.* acarrear, traer; causar, ocasionar; producir; crear; (induce) persuadir; hacer (ver, etc.); (be worth) valer; (sell for) vender por; *Law.* entablar (un pleito, etc.): (before a judge) hacer comparecer (ante); (present) presentar; (attract) atraer; (place) poner. **to b. home,** llevar a casa; *Fig.* hacer ver, hacer sentir; demostrar; (a crime) probar contra. **to b. near,** acercar. **to b. about,** efectuar, poner por obra; causar, ocasionar; (achieve) lograr, conseguir. **to b. again,** traer otra vez, llevar de nuevo. **to b. away,** llevarse. **to b. back,** devolver; traer; (of memories) recordar. **to b. down,** llevar abajo, bajar; (of persons) hacer bajar; (humble) humillar; hacer caer; (of prices) hacer bajar; arruinar; destruir. **to b. down the house,** *Theat.* hacer venirse el teatro abajo. **to b. forth,** (give birth to) dar a luz; producir; causar; sacar a luz. **to b. forward,** hacer adelantarse; empujar hacia adelante; *Fig.* avanzar; (allege) alegar; *Com.* llevar a nueva cuenta; presentar, producir. **brought forward,** *Com.* suma y sigue. **to b. in,** (things) llevar adentro; (persons) hacer entrar; introducir; aparecer con, presentarse con; (meals) servir; producir; declarar; (a verdict) dictar (sentencia de), fallar. **to b. into being,** poner en práctica; dar origen (a). **to b. off,** (a ship) poner a flote; (rescue) salvar, rescatar; (carry out) efectuar, poner en práctica; (achieve) conseguir, lograr. **B. me the glass off the table,** Tráeme el vaso que hay en la mesa. **to b. on,** causar, inducir; acarrear; iniciar. **He brought a book on to the stage,** Entró en escena llevando un libro (or con un libro). **to b. out,** sacar; poner afuera; (a person) hacer salir; publicar; (a play) poner en escena; sacar a luz; (an idea, jewels, etc.) sacar a relucir; revelar; demostrar; hacer aparecer; (a girl in society) poner de largo (a). **to b. over,** llevar al otro lado; hacer venir; traer; conducir; hacer cruzar; (convert) convertir. **to b. round,** traer; llevar; (from a swoon) sacar de un desmayo; curar; persuadir; conciliar. **to b. through,** hacer atravesar; llevar a través de; ayudar a salir (de un apuro); (an illness) curar de. **to b. to,** traer a; llevar a; (from a swoon) hacer volver en sí; *Naut.* ponerse a la capa. **He cannot b. himself to,** No puede persuadirse a. **to b. together,** reunir; (things) juntar, amontonar; reconciliar, poner en paz. **to b. under,** someter; sojuzgar; incluir. **to b. up,** llevar arriba, subir; (a person) hacer subir; hacer avanzar; (a price) hacer subir; ir (a); andar; (breed) criar; (educate) educar, criar; (in a discussion) hacer notar; vomitar. **to b. up the rear,** ir al fin (de); *Mil.* ir a la retaguardia. **well** (or **badly**) **brought up,** bien (o mal) educado. **to b. upon oneself,** buscarse, incurrir (en). **to b. up-to-date,** poner al día; refrescar; rejuvenecer

bringing /'brɪŋɪŋ/ *n* acción de llevar o traer, *f;* conducción, *f;* transporte, *m.* **b. forth,** producción, *f.* **b. in,** introducción, *f.* **b. out,** producción, *f;* publicación, *f;* (of a girl in society) puesta de largo, *f.* **b. under,** reducción, *f;* subyugación, *f.* **b. up,** educación, crianza, *f*

brink /brɪŋk/ *n* borde, margen, *m;* (of water) orilla, *f; Fig.* margen, *m.* **on the b.,** al margen; a la orilla. **to be on the b. of,** (doing something) estar para, estar a punto de

briny /'braini/ *a* salado

briquette /brɪ'kɛt/ *n* briqueta, *f,* aglomerado de carbón, *m*

brisk /brɪsk/ *a* activo; vivo; animado; rápido, acelerado; enérgico

brisket /'brɪskɪt/ *n* falda, *f*

briskly /'brɪskli/ *adv* vivamente; enérgicamente; aprisa

briskness /'brɪsknɪs/ *n* actividad, *f;* viveza, *f;* animación, *f;* rapidez, *f;* energía, *f*

brisling /'brɪzlɪŋ/ *n* sardina noruega

bristle /'brɪsəl/ *n* cerda, seda, *f, vi* erizarse

bristly /'brɪsli/ *a* erizado, cerdoso; espinoso; hirsuto

Bristol board /'brɪstl̩/ *n* cartulina, *f*

British /'brɪtɪʃ/ *a* británico. **the B.,** el pueblo británico; los ingleses

British Commonwealth, the la Mancomunidad Británica, *f*

Briton /'brɪtn̩/ *n* inglés (-esa). **ancient B.,** britano (-na)

Brittany /'brɪtn̩i/ Bretaña, *f*

brittle /'brɪtl̩/ *a* frágil, quebradizo, deleznable, friable

brittleness /'brɪtl̩nɪs/ *n* fragilidad, friabilidad, *f*

broach /broutʃ/ *n Cul.* espetón, asador, *m.* —*vt* espitar (un barril); abrir; *Fig.* introducir

broad /brɔd/ *a* ancho; grande; (extensive) vasto, extenso; **a b. confession,** una confesión amplia; (full) pleno; (of accents) marcado; (of words) lato; (clear) claro; (of the mind) liberal, tolerante; (of humor, etc.) grosero; (general) general, comprensivo. **in b. daylight,** en pleno día. **b.-brimmed,** de ala ancha. **b.-faced,** cariancho. **b.-minded,** tolerante, liberal, ancho de conciencia, abierto al mundo. **b.-mindedness,** tolerancia, liberalidad, *f.* **to be b.-minded,** ser tolerante, tener manga ancha. **b.-shouldered,** ancho de espaldas

broadcast /'brɔdˌkæst/ *n Agr.* siembra al vuelo, *f; Radio.* radiodifusión, radiotransmisión, emisión, *f, a* radiado. —*adv* por todas partes; extensamente. —*vt Agr.* sembrar a vuelo; *Radio.* radiodifundir, radiar, transmitir por radio; (news, etc.) diseminar

broadcaster /'brɔdˌkæstər/ *n* (lecturer) conferenciante, *mf;* radiodifusor (-ra); (announcer) locutor (-ra)

broadcasting /'brɔdˌkæstɪŋ/ *n* radiación, radiodifución, *f;* radio, *f.* **b.-station,** estación de radio, emisora, *f.* **b.-studio,** estudio de emisión, *m*

broaden /'brɔdn̩/ *vt* ampliar, ensanchar. —*vi* ampliarse, ensancharse

broad-leaved /'brɔdˌlivd/ *a* frondoso

broadly /'brɔdli/ *adv* anchamente; con marcado acento dialectal; de una manera general

broadness /'brɔdnɪs/ *n* anchura, *f;* extensión, vastedad, *f;* tolerancia, *f;* liberalidad, *f;* grosería, *f;* (of accent) acento marcado, *m*
broadside /'brɔd,said/ *n* (of a ship) costado, *m;* (of guns) andanada, *f; Fig.* batería, *f; Print.* cara de un pliego, *f.* **to be b. on,** dar el costado
brocade /brou'keid/ *a* and *n* brocado *m..* —*vt* decorar con brocado. **imitation b.,** brocatel, *m*
brocaded /brou'keidɪd/ *a* decorado con brocado; de brocado
broccoli /'brɒkəli/ *n* bróculi, brécol, *m*
brochure /brou'ʃʊr/ *n* folleto, *m*
brogue /broug/ *n* acento, *m;* acento irlandés, *m;* (shoe) zapato grueso, *m*
broil /brɔil/ *vt* emparrillar, asar. —*vi* asarse
broke /brouk/ *a* quebrado
broken /'broukən/ *a* roto; quebrado; (spiritless) abatido, desalentado; (infirm) agotado, debilitado; (ruined) arruinado; (of ground) desigual, escabroso; (of a language) chapucero; (spoilt) estropeado; imperfecto; incompleto; (loose) suelto; (of a horse, etc.) domado; (of the weather) variable; (of sleep) interrumpido; (of the heart, of shoes, etc.) roto; (of the voice, sobs, sighs) entrecortado; (of the voice through old age, etc.) cascada; (incoherent) incoherente. **b.-down,** (tired) rendido, agotado; arruinado; (not working) estropeado. **b.-hearted,** roto el corazón, angustiado. **b.-winged,** aliquebrado. **I speak broken Spanish,** Hablo el español chapuceramente
brokenly /'broukənli/ *adv* (of the voice) con voz entrecortada; a ratos; interrumpidamente
brokenness /'broukənnɪs/ *n* interrupción, *f;* (of the ground) desigualdad, *f;* (of speech) imperfección, *f*
broker /'broukər/ *n* corredor, *m;* (stock) corredor de bolsa, *m*
brokerage /'broukərɪdʒ/ *n* corretaje, *m*
bromide /'broumaid/ *n* bromuro, *m*
bromine /'broumin/ *n* bromo, *m*
bronchi /'brɒŋki/ *n pl* bronquios, *m pl*
bronchitis /brɒŋ'kaitɪs/ *n* bronquitis, *f*
broncopneumonia /'brɒŋkounʊ'mounyə/ *n* bronconeumonía, *f*
Brontosaurus /,brɒntə'sɔrəs/ *n* brontosauro, *m*
bronze /brɒnz/ *n* bronce, *m;* objeto de bronce, *m, a* de bronce. —*vt* broncear. **B. Age,** Edad de Bronce, *f*
brooch /broutʃ/ *n* broche, *m;* alfiler de pecho, *m*
brood /brud/ *n* (of birds) nidada, *f;* (of chickens) pollada, *f;* (other animals) cría, *f;* prole, *f, vi* empollar. **to b. over,** meditar sobre, rumiar; (of mountains, etc.) dominar
broody /'brudi/ *a* (of hens) clueca, *f*
brook /brʊk/ *n* arroyo, riachuelo, *m, vt* tolerar, sufrir, permitir
broom /brum/ *n* escoba, *f; Bot.* retama, *f;* hiniesta, *f.* **common b.,** retama de escobas, *f.* **Spanish b.,** retama común, retama de olor, hiniesta, *f.* **b.-handle,** palo de escoba, *m*
broomstick /'brum,stɪk/ *n* palo de escoba, *m*
broth /brɔθ/ *n* caldo, *m*
brothel /'brɒθəl/ *n* burdel, lupanar, *m,* casa de trato, *f*
brother /'brʌðər/ *n* hermano, *m;* (colleague) colega, *m; Inf.* compañero, *m.* **foster-b.,** hermano de leche, *m.* **half-b.,** medio hermano, *m.* **step-b.,** hermanastro, *m.* **b.-in-law,** hermano político, cuñado, *m.* **b.-officer,** compañero de promoción, *m*
brotherhood /'brʌðər,hʊd/ *n* fraternidad, *f; Eccl.* cofradía, *f;* hermandad, *f*
brotherliness /'brʌðərlinɪs/ *n* fraternidad, *f*
brotherly /'brʌðərli/ *a* fraterno
brow /brau/ *n* frente, *f;* ceja, *f;* (of a hill) cresta, cumbre, *f;* (edge) borde, *m.* **to knit one's b.,** fruncir el ceño
browbeat /'brau,bit/ *vt* intimidar, amenazar
browbeating /'brau,bitɪŋ/ *n* intimidación, *f*
brown /braun/ *a* castaño; (gallicism often used of shoes, etc.) marrón; pardo; (of complexion, eyes, hair) moreno; (dark brown) bruno; (blackish) negruzco; (toasted) tostado; (burnt) quemado. —*n* color moreno, *m;* color pardo, *m;* castaño, *m;* (from the sun) bronce, *m.* —*vt* (toast) tostar; (a person) volver moreno, broncear; (meat) asar. —*vi* tostarse; volverse moreno, broncearse; asarse. **b. bear,** oso pardo, *m.* **b. owl,** autillo, *m.* **b. paper,** papel de estraza, *m.* **b. study,** ensimismamiento, *m,* meditación, *f.* **b. sugar,** azúcar moreno (or quebrado), *m*
brownie /'brauni/ *n* duende benévolo, *m*
brownish /'braunɪʃ/ *a* morenucho; que tira a castaño o a bruno; parduzco; trigueño
brownness /'braunnɪs/ *n* color moreno, *m*
browse /brauz/ *vi* pacer; (through a publication) hojear (un libro)
browsing /'brauzɪŋ/ *n* apacentamiento, *m;* hojeo (de un libro), *m;* lectura, *f,* estudio, *m*
Bruges /'brudʒɪz/ Brujas, *f*
bruise /bruz/ *n* cardenal, *m;* abolladura, *f;* (in metal) bollo, *m;* (on fruit) maca, *f.* —*vt* acardenalar, magullar; abollar; (fruit) macar
bruising /'bruzɪŋ/ *n* magullamiento, *m;* (of metal) abolladura, *f;* (crushing) machacadura, *f;* (boxing) boxeo, pugilato, *m*
brunette /bru'nɛt/ *n* trigueña, morena, *f*
brunt /brʌnt/ *n* peso, *m;* golpe, *m;* choque, *m;* esfuerzo, *m.* **to bear the b.,** soportar el peso; sufrir el choque; *Inf.* pagar el pato
brush /brʌʃ/ *n* cepillo, *m;* (broom) escoba, *f;* (for whitewashing, etc.) brocha, *f;* (for painting) pincel, *m;* (of a fox) cola (de zorro), *f;* (undergrowth) breñal, matorral, *m;* (fight) escaramuza, *f;* (argument) altercación, *f.* **scrubbing-b.,** cepillo para fregar, *m.* **shoe-b.,** cepillo para limpiar los zapatos, *m.* **stroke of the b.,** brochada, *f;* pincelada, *f.* **whitewash-b.,** brochón, *m.* **b. maker** or **seller,** escobero (-ra); pincelero (-ra)
brush /brʌʃ/ *vt* cepillar; (sweep) barrer; frotar; (touch) rozar; (touch lightly) acariciar. **to b. against,** rozar, tocar. **to b. aside,** echar a un lado; *Fig.* no hacer caso de; ignorar. **to b. off,** sacudir(se); quitar(se); (sweep) barrer. **to b. up,** cepillar; (wool) cardar; (tidy) asear; (a subject) refrescar, repasar
brushing /'brʌʃɪŋ/ *n* acepilladura, *f;* (sweeping) barredura, *f;* (touching) roce, rozamiento, *m;* (of hair) peinadura, *f*
brushwood /'brʌʃ,wʊd/ *n* enjutos, *m pl,* chamarasca, *f;* matorral, *m*
brusque /brʌsk/ *a* brusco, seco
brusquely /'brʌskli/ *adv* secamente
brusqueness /'brʌsknɪs/ *n* brusquedad, *f*
Brussels /'brʌsəlz/ *a* bruselense; de Bruselas. **B. lace,** encaje de Bruselas, *m*
Brussels sprouts *n pl* bretones, *m pl*
brutal /'brutl̩/ *a* bestial, brutal; salvaje, inhumano
brutality /bru'tælɪti/ *n* brutalidad, bestialidad, *f;* barbaridad, ferocidad, *f*
brutalize /'brutl̩,aiz/ *vt* embrutecer
brutally /'brutl̩i/ *adv* brutalmente
brute /brut/ *n* bruto, animal, *m;* salvaje, bárbaro, *m.* **b. force,** la fuerza bruta
brutish /'brutɪʃ/ *a* bruto; sensual, bestial; grosero; salvaje; estúpido; ignorante. **to become b.,** embrutecerse
bubble /'bʌbəl/ *n* burbuja, *f;* borbollón, *m, vi* burbujear; borbollar, bullir, hervir
bubbling /'bʌbəlɪŋ/ *n* burbujeo, *m;* hervidero, *m;* (of brooks) murmullo, *m, a* burbujeante; hirviente; (of brooks) parlero; (of wine) espumoso, efervescente
bubonic /byu'bɒnɪk/ *a* bubónico. **b. plague,** peste bubónica, *f*
buccaneer /,bʌkə'nɪər/ *n* corsario, *m;* aventurero, *m*
Bucharest /'bukə,rɛst/ Bucarest, *m*
buck /bʌk/ *n Zool.* gamo, *m;* (male) macho, *m;* (fop) galán, petimetre, *m, vi* (of a horse) caracolear; fanfarronear. **to pass the b.,** *Inf.* echarle a uno el muerto. **b.-rabbit,** conejo, *m.* **to b. up,** hacer de tripas corazón
bucket /'bʌkɪt/ *n* cubo, balde, *m,* cubeta, *f*
buckle /'bʌkəl/ *n* hebilla, *f.* —*vt* enhebillar, abrochar con hebilla. —*vi* doblarse. **to b. to,** ponerse a hacer algo con ahinco
buckled /'bʌkəld/ *a* con hebillas
buckler /'bʌklər/ *n* broquel, *m,* rodela, tarjeta, *f*
buckram /'bʌkrəm/ *n* bocací, *m*
buckshot /'bʌk,ʃɒt/ *n* perdigón, *m*
buckskin /'bʌk,skɪn/ *n* ante, *m*

buckwheat /'bʌk,wit/ *n* alforfón, trigo sarraceno, *m*

bucolic /byu'kɒlɪk/ *a* bucólico, pastoril

bud /bʌd/ *n* brote, *m;* botón, capullo, *m;* (of vines) bollón, *m;* (of vegetables) gema, *f.* —*vi* brotar, germinar. —*vt* injertar de escudete

Buddhism /'budɪzəm/ *n* budismo, *m*

Buddhist /'budɪst/ *n* budista, *mf*

budding /'bʌdɪŋ/ *n* brotadura, *f;* (of roses, etc) injerto de escudete, *m; Fig.* germen, *m*

budge /bʌdʒ/ *vi* moverse, menearse. —*vt* mover

budgerigar /'bʌdʒəri,gɑr/ *n* periquito, *m*

budget /'bʌdʒɪt/ *n* presupuesto, *m;* (of news, etc.) colección, *f.* —*vi* presuponer

Buenos Aires /'bwei'nəs aiərɪz/ (of or from) *a* and *n* bonaerense, *mf*

buff /bʌf/ *n* color de ante, *m;* piel de ante, *f.* **b.-colored,** anteado

buffalo /'bʌfə,lou/ *n* búfalo, *f*

buffer /'bʌfər/ *n* (railway) parachoques, *m;* (of cars) amortiguador, *m.* **b. state,** estado tapón, *m*

buffet /bə'fei/ *n* bofetón, *m;* bofetada, *f;* bar, *m.* —*vt* abofetear; golpear; luchar con las olas

buffoon /bə'fun/ *n* bufón, *m*

buffoonery /bə'funəri/ *n* bufonería, *f*

bug /bʌg/ *n* chinche, *f*

bugbear /'bʌg,bɛər/ *n* pesadilla, *f*

bugle /'byugəl/ *n* corneta, trompeta, *f;* (bead) abalorio, *m.* **b. blast,** trompetazo, *m*

bugler /'byuglər/ *n* trompetero, *m*

build /bɪld/ *vt* edificar; (engines, ships, organs, etc.) construir; (a nest and *Fig.*) hacer; (have built) hacer, edificar; crear; formar; fundar. —*n* estructura, *f;* (of the body) hechura, *f;* talle, *m.* **to b. castles in Spain,** hacer castillos en el aire. **built-up area,** zona urbana, *f.* **to b. up,** construir, levantar; (block) tapar; (business, reputation) establecer, crear. **to b. upon,** *Fig.* contar con, confiar en; esperar de

builder /'bɪldər/ *n* constructor, *m;* maestro de obras, *m;* (laborer) albañil, *m;* creador (-ra), fundador (-ra); arquitecto, *m*

building /'bɪldɪŋ/ *n* edificación, *f;* construcción, *f;* edificio, *m;* fundación, *f;* creación, *f.* **b. contractor,** maestro de obras, *m.* **b. material,** material de construcción, *m.* **b. site,** solar, terreno, *m.* **b. timber,** madera de construcción, *f*

built-in /'bɪlt ,ɪn/ *a* empotrado. **b. closet,** armario empotrado, *m*

bulb /bʌlb/ *n Bot.* bulbo, *m;* (*Elec. Phys.*) bombilla, *f;* (of an oil lamp) cebolla, *f*

bulbous /'bʌlbəs/ *a* bulboso

Bulgarian /bʌl'gɛəriən/ *a* and *n* búlgaro (-ra)

bulge /bʌldʒ/ *n* bulto, *m;* hinchazón, *f;* protuberancia, *f; Mil.* bolsa (en el frente), *f.* —*vi* hincharse; estar lleno (de)

bulging /'bʌldʒɪŋ/ *a* lleno (de); con bultos; hinchado (de)

bulk /bʌlk/ *n* volumen, tamaño, *m;* bulto, *m;* (larger part) grueso, *m;* mayor parte, *f;* (of people) mayoría, *f;* (of a ship) capacidad, *f.* **in b.,** *Com.* en bruto, en grueso. **to b. large,** tener mucha importancia

bulkhead /'bʌlk,hɛd/ *n Naut.* mamparo, *m*

bulkiness /'bʌlkinɪs/ *n* abultamiento, *m;* volumen, tamaño, *m*

bulky /'bʌlki/ *a* voluminoso, grande, grueso

bull /bʊl/ *n* toro, *m; Astron.* Tauro, *m;* (of some animals) macho, *m;* (Stock Exchange) alcista, *mf;* (of the Pope) bula (del Papa), *f.* **a b. in a china shop,** un caballo loco en una cacharrería. **to fight bulls,** torear. **b.-calf,** ternero, *m.* **bull's eye,** blanco, *m;* acierto, *m.* **b. fight,** corrida de toros, *f.* **b. fighter's gala uniform,** traje de luces, *m.* **b.-ring,** plaza de toros, *f*

bulldog /'bʊl,dɔg/ *n* perro dogo, perro de presa, *m*

bulldozer /'bʊl,douzər/ *n* (excavator) tozodora, *f*

bullet /'bʊlɪt/ *n* bala, *f.* **spent b.,** bala fría, *f.* **stray b.,** bala perdida, *f.* **b.-proof,** a prueba de bala, blindado

bulletin /'bʊlɪtɪn/ *n* boletín, *m*

bulletin board *n* tablero de anuncios, tablero de avisos, tablón, *m*

bulletproof vest /'bʊlɪt,pruf/ *n* chaleco blindado, *m*

bullfighter /'bʊl,faitər/ *n* torero, *m* (on foot), toreador, *m* (on horseback)

bullfinch /'bʊl,fɪntʃ/ *n* pinzón real, *m*

bullion /'bʊlyən/ *n Com.* metálico, *m;* oro (or plata) en barras, *m, f.*

bullock /'bʊlək/ *n* becerro, *m;* buey, *m*

bullpen /'bʊl,pɛn/ *n* toril, *m* (bullfighting); calentador, *m* (baseball)

bully /'bʊli/ *n* valentón, perdonavidas, gallito, *m;* rufián, *m.* —*vt* intimidar; tratar mal. **b. beef,** vaca en lata, *f*

bulrush /'bʊl,rʌʃ/ *n* anea, *f*

bulwark /'bʊlwərk/ *n* baluarte, *m; Naut.* antepecho, *m*

bumblebee /'bʌmbəl,bi/ *n* abejorro, *m*

bump /bʌmp/ *n* golpe, *m;* ruido, *m;* choque, *m;* (bruise) chichón, *m,* roncha, *f; Aer.* sacudida, *f,* meneo, *m.* —*vi* (into, against) tropezar con; (along) saltar en. —*vt* chocar (contra)

bumper /'bʌmpər/ *n* copa llena hasta los bordes, *f,* vaso lleno, *m;* (of a car) parachoques, *m.* **a b. harvest,** una cosecha abundante

bumpkin /'bʌmpkɪn/ *n* patán, villano, *m*

bumptious /'bʌmpʃəs/ *a* fatuo, presuntuoso, presumido

bumptiousness /'bʌmpʃəsnɪs/ *n* fatuidad, presunción, *f*

bumpy /'bʌmpi/ *n* (of surface) desigual, escabroso; (of a vehicle) incómodo, con mala suspensión

bun /bʌn/ *n* buñuelo, bollo, *m;* (hair) moño, *m*

bunch /bʌntʃ/ *n* (of fruit) racimo, *m;* manojo, *m;* (of flowers) ramo, *m;* (tuft) penacho, *m;* (gang) pandilla, *f, vi* arracimarse; agruparse

bundle /'bʌndl̩/ *n* atado, lío, *m;* (of papers) legajo, *m;* (of sticks) haz, *m;* (sheaf) fajo, *m;* (package) paquete, *m;* fardo, hatillo, *m;* (roll) rollo, *m, vt* atar, liar; envolver; empaquetar; (stuff) meter, introducir. **to b. in,** meter dentro (de). **to b. out,** despachar sin ceremonia, poner de patitas en la calle

bung /bʌŋ/ *n* tapón, tarugo, *m, vt* atarugar

bungalow /'bʌŋgə,lou/ *n* casa de un solo piso, *f*

bungle /'bʌŋgəl/ *vt* estropear; hacer mal. —*n* equivocación, *f,* yerro, *m;* cosa (o obra) mal hecha, *f*

bungling /'bʌŋglɪŋ/ *a* chapucero, torpe

bunion /'bʌnyən/ *n* juanete (del pie), *m*

bunk /bʌŋk/ *n* litera, *f, vi Inf.* poner pies en polvorosa, pirarse

bunker /'bʌŋkər/ *n Naut.* pañol, *m;* (for coal) carbonera, *f;* (golf) hoya de arena, *f*

bunkum /'bʌŋkəm/ *n* patrañas, *f pl*

bunting /'bʌntɪŋ/ *n* gallardete, *m*

buoy /'bui/ *n* boya, baliza, *f, vt* boyar; abalizar; *Fig.* sostener. **light b.,** boya luminosa, *f*

buoyancy /'bɔiənsi/ *n* flotación, *f; Fig.* optimismo, *m,* alegría, *f*

buoyant /'bɔiənt/ *a* boyante; ligero

burden /'bɜrdn̩/ *n* carga, *f,* peso, *m;* (of a ship) tonelaje, *m,* capacidad, *f;* (of a song) estribillo, *m;* (gist) esencia, *f.* —*vt* cargar. **to be a b. on,** pesar sobre

burdensome /'bɜrdn̩səm/ *a* pesado, oneroso, gravoso; abrumador

burdensomeness /'bɜrdn̩səmnɪs/ *n* pesadez, *f;* agobio, *m*

bureau /'byʊrou/ *n* buró, secreter, *m;* escritorio, *m;* (office) dirección, oficina, *f;* departamento, *m*

bureaucracy /byʊ'rɒkrəsi/ *n* burocracia, *f*

bureaucrat /'byʊrə,kræt/ *n* burócrata, *mf; Inf.* mandarín, *m*

bureaucratic /,byʊrə'krætɪk/ *a* burocrático

burgher /'bɜrgər/ *n* ciudadano (-na), vecino (-na)

burglar /'bɜrglər/ *n* ladrón de casas, escalador, *m.* **cat b.,** gato, *m.* **b. alarm,** alarma contra ladrones, *f.* **b. insurance,** seguro contra robo, *m*

burglary /'bɜrgləri/ *n* robo nocturno de una casa, *m*

burgle /'bɜrgəl/ *vi* robar una casa de noche. —*vt* robar

burgomaster /'bɜrgə,mæstər/ *n* burgomaestre, *m*

Burgundian /bər'gʌndiən/ *a* and *n* borgoñón (-ona)

burgundy /'bɜrgəndi/ *n* vino de Borgoña, borgoña, *m*

burial /'bɛriəl/ *n* entierro, *m.* **b.-ground,** campo santo, cementerio, *m.* **b. service,** misa de difuntos, *f.* **b. society,** sociedad de entierros, *f*

burlap /'bɜrlæp/ *n* arpillera, *f*
burlesque /bər'lɛsk/ *a* burlesco. —*n* parodia. *f*. —*vt* parodiar
burliness /'bɜrlinɪs/ *n* corpulencia, *f*
burly /'bɜrli/ *a* corpulento, fornido
Burma /'bɜrmə/ Birmania, *f*
Burmese /bər'miz/ *a* and *n* birmano (-na)
burn /bɜrn/ *vt* quemar; calcinar; (bricks) cocer; cauterizar; (the tongue) picar; (dry up) secar; (the skin by sun or wind) tostar. —*vi* quemar; arder; *Fig.* abrasarse (en). **b. at the stake,** *vt* quemar en la hoguera. **to b. to ashes,** reducir a cenizas. **to b. away,** consumir(se). **to b. oneself,** quemarse. **to b. up,** quemar del todo, consumir. **to b. with,** *Fig.* abrasarse en
burn /bɜrn/ *n* quemadura, *f*; (stream) arroyo, *m*
burnable /'bɜrnəbəl/ *a* combustible
burner /'bɜrnər/ *n* quemador (-ra); mechero, *m*
burning /'bɜrnɪŋ/ *n* quema, *f*; incendio, *m*; fuego, *m*; (inflammation) inflamación, *f*; (pain) quemazón, *f*; abrasamiento, *m*. —*a* en llamas; ardiente; intenso; (notorious) notorio, escandaloso; abrasador; palpitante. **b. question,** cuestión palpitante, *f*
burnish /'bɜrnɪʃ/ *n* bruñido, *m*; lustre, brillo, *m*, *vt* bruñir; pulir, pulimentar, dar brillo a; (weapons) acicalar. —*vi* tomar lustre
burnisher /'bɜrnɪʃər/ *n* bruñidor, acicalador, *m*
burnishing /'bɜrnɪʃɪŋ/ *n* bruñido, *m*; pulimento, *m*; (of weapons) acicalado, *m*
burnoose /bər'nus/ *n* albornoz, *m*
burr /bɜr/ *n Bot.* cáliz de flor con espinas, *m*; *Mech.* rebaba, *f*; sonido fuerte de la erre, *m*
burrow /'bɜrou/ *n* madriguera, *f*, vivar, *m*; (for rabbits) conejera, *f*. —*vt* amadrigar; minar
bursar /'bɜrsər/ *n* tesorero, *m*; becario, *m*
bursary /'bɜrsəri/ *n* tesorería, *f*; beca, *f*
burst /bɜrst/ *n* estallido, *m*, explosión, *f*; (in a pipe) avería, *f*, (fit) acceso, *m*; transporte, *m*; (effort) esfuerzo, *m*; (expanse) extensión, *f*, panorama, *m*. **b. of applause,** salva de aplausos, *f*
burst /bɜrst/ *vi* estallar; reventar; quebrarse; romperse; (overflow) desbordar; (of seams) nacerse; derramarse (por); (into laughter) romper a; (into tears) deshacerse en. —*vt* quebrar; romper; hacer estallar. **to b. upon the view,** aparecer de pronto. **to b. into,** irrumpir en; (exclamations, etc.) prorrumpir en. **to b. into tears,** romper a llorar, deshacerse en lágrimas. **to b. open,** abrir con violencia; forzar
bursting /'bɜrstɪŋ/ *n* estallido, *m*; quebrantamiento, *m*; (overflowing) desbordamiento, *m*
bury /'bɛri/ *vt* enterrar, sepultar; sumergir; (hide) esconder, ocultar; (forget) echar tierra a
bus /bʌs/ *n* autobús, ómnibus, *Mexico* camión, *Caribbean* guagua, *m*. **double-decker bus,** ómnibus de dos pisos, *m*. **to travel by bus,** ir en autobús. **bus station,** estación de autobuses, *f*
busby /'bʌzbi/ *n* birretina, gorra de húsar, *f*
bush /bʊʃ/ *n* arbusto, matojo, *m*; (undergrowth) maleza, *f*; tierra virgen, *f*; *Mech.* manguito, *m*
bushel /'bʊʃəl/ *n* medida de áridos, *f*, (In England 8 gallons or 36.37 liters)
bushiness /'bʊʃinɪs/ *n* espesura, *f*; densidad, *f*
bushy /'bʊʃi/ *a* lleno de arbustos; denso; espeso; grueso; (eyebrows, etc.) poblado
busily /'bɪzəli/ *adv* diligentemente, solícitamente; afanosamente, laboriosamente. **He was b. occupied in...,** Estaba muy ocupado en...
business /'bɪznɪs/ *n* ocupación, *f*; quehaceres, *m pl*; (matter) asunto, *m*, cosa, *f*; empleo, oficio, *m*; *Com.* negocio(s), *m*, *pl*; casa comercial, *f*; (trade) comercio, *m*; (clients, connection) clientela, *f*; (right) derecho, *m*; *Theat.* juego escénico, *m*, pantomima, *f*. **He had no b. to do that,** No tenía derecho a hacer eso. **Mind your own b.!** ¡No te metas donde no te llaman! **on b.,** por negocios. **to be in b. for oneself,** tener negocios por su propia cuenta. **to mean b.,** hacer algo en serio; estar resuelto. **to send about his b.,** mandar a paseo (a). **to set up in b.,** establecer un negocio. **b. affairs,** negocios, *m pl*. **b. agent,** agente de negocios, *m*. **b. hours,** horas de trabajo, *f pl*. **b.-like,** formal, práctico, sistemático. **b. man,** hombre de negocios, negociante, *m*
business administration *n* administración de empresas, *f*
bust /bʌst/ *n Art.* busto, bulto, *m*; pecho, *m*. **b. bodice,** sostén, *m*
bustard /'bʌstərd/ *n* avutarda, *f*
bustle /'bʌsəl/ *n* actividad, animación, *f*; confusión, *f*; (of a dress) polizón, tontillo, *m*. —*vi* menearse, darse prisa. —*vt* dar prisa (a)
bustling /'bʌslɪŋ/ *a* activo; ocupado, atareado; animado; bullicioso, ruidoso
busy /'bɪzi/ *a* ocupado; atareado; activo, diligente; (of places) animado, bullicioso; (of streets) de gran circulación; (officious) entremetido. **to b. oneself,** ocuparse (en, con); dedicarse (a), entregarse (a); (interfere) entremeterse (con). **to be b.,** estar ocupado; estar atareado, tener mucho que hacer. **b.-body,** bullebulle, *mf*. entremetido (-da), chismoso (-sa)
busyness /'bɪzinɪs/ *n* ocupación, *f*; laboriosidad, *f*; actividad, *f*
but /bʌt/ *conjunc prep adv* pero; sino; (only) solamente; (except) menos; excepto; (almost) casi; que no; si no; (that) que; (nevertheless) sin embargo, empero, no obstante; (without) sin, sin que; (of time recently passed) no más que, tan recientemente. —*n* pero, *m*. **He cannot choose but go,** No puede hacer otra cosa que marcharse. **to do nothing but...,** hacer únicamente..., no hacer más que... **but for,** a no ser por. **but yesterday,** solamente ayer. **but then (or but yet),** pero
butcher /'bʊtʃər/ *n* carnicero, *m*. —*vt* matar reses; hacer una carnicería en. **butcher's boy,** mozo del carnicero, *m*. **butcher's shop,** carnicería, *f*
butchery /'bʊtʃəri/ *n* carnicería, *f*; matanza, *f*
butler /'bʌtlər/ *n* mayordomo, *m*. **butler's pantry,** despensa, repostería, *f*
butt /bʌt/ *n* (cask) tonel, *m*, pipa, *f*; (for water) barril, *m*; (of a cigarette, etc.) colilla, *f*; (of fire-arms) culata, *f*; (handle) mango, cabo, *m*; (billiards) mocho, *m*; (earthwork) terrero, *m*; (*Fig.* object) objeto (de), *m*; (of bulls, etc.) topetada, *f*; *pl* **butts,** campo de tiro, *m*; (target) blanco, *m*. —*vt* (toss) topar, acornear; (meet) tropezar (con). **to b. in,** *Inf.* entrometerse, meter baza; encajarse
butter /'bʌtər/ *n* mantequilla, *f*, *vt* untar con mantequilla. **b.-dish,** mantequera, *f*. **b.-fingers,** torpe, *m*. **b.-knife,** cuchillo para mantequilla, *m*. **b.-milk,** suero de mantequilla, *m*. **b.-print,** molde para mantequilla, *m*. **b.-sauce,** mantequilla fundida, *f*
buttercup /'bʌtər,kʌp/ *n* ranúnculo, botón de oro, *m*
butterfly /'bʌtər,flai/ *n* mariposa, *f*
butterscotch /'bʌtər,skɒtʃ/ *n* dulce de azúcar y mantequilla, *m*
buttery /'bʌtəri/ *n* despensa, *f*
buttocks /'bʌtəks/ *n pl* nalgas, posaderas, *f pl*
button /'bʌtn̩/ *n* botón, *m*; *pl* **buttons,** botones, paje, *m*. —*vt* abotonar, abrochar. —*vi* abotonarse, abrocharse. **to press the b.,** apretar el botón. **b.-hook,** abotonador, *m*
buttonhole /'bʌtn̩,houl/ *n* ojal, *m*; flor que se lleva en el ojal, *f*. —*vt Sew.* hacer ojales; (embroidery) hacer el festón; *Inf.* importunar
buttoning /'bʌtn̩ɪŋ/ *n* abrochamiento, *m*
buttress /'bʌtrɪs/ *n* estribo, macho, contrafuerte, *m*; *Fig.* apoyo, sostén, *m*. —*vt* afianzar, estribar; *Fig.* apoyar, sostener. **flying-b.,** arbotante, *m*
buxom /'bʌksəm/ *a* (of a woman) fresca, guapetona, frescachona
buxomness /'bʌksəmnɪs/ *n* frescura, *f*
buy /bai/ *vt* comprar; obtener; (achieve) lograr; (bribe) sobornar. **to buy on credit,** comprar al fiado. **to buy back,** comprar de nuevo; redimir; (ransom) rescatar. **to buy for,** (a price) comprar por; (purpose or destination) comprar para. **to buy in,** (at an auction) comprar por cuenta del dueño. **to buy off,** librarse de uno con dinero. **to buy out,** (of a business) comprar la parte de un socio. **to buy up,** comprar todo, acaparar
buyable /'baiəbəl/ *a* comprable, que se puede comprar
buyer /'baiər/ *n* comprador (-ra)
buying /'baiɪŋ/ *n* compra, *f*. **b. back,** rescate, *m*. **b. up,** acaparamiento, *m*

buying power *n* capacidad de compra, *f,* valor adquisitivo, *m*

buzz /bʌz/ *n* zumbido, *m;* (whisper) susurro, murmullo, *m;* (of a bell) sonido (del timbre), *m, vi* zumbar; susurrar

buzzer /ˈbʌzər/ *n* zumbadar, *m;* sirena, *f;* (bell) timbre, *m*

buzzing /ˈbʌzɪŋ/ *a* zumbador, que zumba, *n.* See **buzz**

by /bai/ *prep* por; de; en; a; con; (of place) cerca de, al lado de; (according to) según, de acuerdo con; (in front of, past) delante (de); (at the latest) antes de, al más tardar; (expressing agency) por; (by means of) mediante; (through, along) por; (upon) sobre; (for) para; (under) bajo. **He will be here by Wednesday,** Estará aquí para el miércoles; (not later than) Estará aquí antes del miércoles (or el miércoles al más tardar). **How did he come by it?** ¿Cómo llegó a su poder? **He will come by train,** Vendrá en tren. **I know her by sight,** La conozco de vista. **There are three children by the first marriage,** Hay tres niños del primer matrimonio. **He goes by the name of Pérez,** Se le conoce por (or bajo) el nombre de Pérez. **six feet by eight,** seis pies por ocho. **They called her by her name,** La llamaron por su nombre. **two by two,** dos por dos. **The picture was painted by Cézanne,** El cuadro fue pintado por Cézanne. **drop by drop,** gota a gota. **by a great deal,** con mucho. **by all means,** naturalmente; de todos modos; cueste lo que cueste. **by chance,** por ventura. **by day (night),** de día (noche). **by daylight,** a la luz del día. **by doing it,** con hacerlo. **by myself,** solo; sin ayuda. **"By Appointment"** «Cita Previa». **by chance or by mischance,** por ventura o por desdicha. **an hour away by car,** a una hora de automóvil. **music by Brahms,** música de Brahms. **pull by the hair,** tirar por el pelo. **take by the hand,** llevar de la mano.

by /bai/ *adv* (near) cerca; (before) delante; al lado; a un lado; aparte; (of time) pasado. **to put by,** (keep) guardar; (throw away) desechar; (accumulate) acumular; (put out of the way) arrinconar. **to pass by,** pasar; pasar delante (de). **by and by,** luego, pronto; más tarde. **by now,** ya, antes de ahora. **by the way,** entre paréntesis, a propósito; de paso; al lado del camino. **by-election,** elección parcial, *f.* **by-law,** reglamento, *m.* **by-pass,** ruta de evitación, *f,* desvío, *m;* (*Mech. Elec.*) derivación, *f.* —*vi* desviarse de; *Mil.* rebasar. **by-product,** derivado, *m; Chem.* producto derivado, *m; Fig.* consecuencia, *f;* resultado, *m*

bye /bai/ *n* (in cricket) meta, *f.* **by the bye,** a propósito, entre paréntesis

bygone /ˈbai,gɔn/ *a* pasado. **Let bygones be bygones,** Lo pasado pasado

byplay /ˈbai,plei/ *n* pantomima, *f,* gestos, *m pl; Theat.* juego escénico, *m,* escena muda, *f*

bystander /ˈbai,stændər/ *n* espectador (-ra); *pl* **bystanders,** los circunstantes

bystreet /ˈbai,strit/ *n* callejuela, *f;* calle pobre, *f*

byway /ˈbai,wei/ *n* camino desviado, *m; Fig.* senda indirecta, *f; pl* **byways,** andurriales, *m pl*

byword /ˈbai,wɜrd/ *n* proverbio, *m;* objeto de burla o escándalo, *m*

Byzantine /ˈbɪzən,tin/ *a* bizantino

Byzantine Empire, the el Imperio Bizantino, *m*

Byzantium /bɪˈzænʃiəm/ Bizancio, *m*

C

c /si/ *n* (letter) c, *f; Mus.* do, *m*
cab /kæb/ *n* (horse-drawn) simón, *m;* (taxi) coche de alquiler, *m;* (of a locomotive) cabina del conductor, *f.* **cab-rank,** punto de coches, *m*
cabala /ˈkæbələ/ *n* cábala, *f*
cabaret /ˌkæbəˈrei/ *n* cabaret, *m;* taberna, *f*
cabbage /ˈkæbɪdʒ/ *n* col, berza, *f.* **red c.,** lombarda, *f.* **c. butterfly,** mariposa de col, *f*
cabin /ˈkæbɪn/ *n* cabaña, choza, *f; Naut.* camarote, *m;* (railway) garita, *f; Aer.* cabina, *f.* **c. boy,** grumete, galopín, mozo de cámara, *m.* **c. trunk,** baúl mundo, *m*
cabinet /ˈkæbənɪt/ *n* (piece of furniture) vitrina, *f;* colección, exposición, *f; Polit.* gabinete, *m;* (of a radio) cónsola, *f.* **c.-maker,** ebanista, *m.* **c.-making,** ebanistería, *f.* **c. meeting,** consejo de ministros, *m.* **c. minister,** ministro, *m*
cable /ˈkeibəl/ *n* amarra, maroma, *f;* cable, *m;* cable(grama), *m, vt* cablegrafiar. **electric c.,** cable eléctrico, *m.* **overhead c.,** cable aéreo, *m*
cabman /ˈkæbmən/ *n* cochero de punto, simón, *m*
caboose /kəˈbus/ *n Naut.* cocina, *f*
cache /kæʃ/ *n* escondite, escondrijo, *m*
cackle /ˈkækəl/ *vi* (of a hen) cacarear; (of a goose) graznar; (of humans) chacharear. —*n* cacareo, *m;* graznido, *m;* cháchara, *f*
cacophony /kəˈkɒfəni/ *n* cacofonía, *f*
cactus /ˈkæktəs/ *n* cacto, *m*
cad /kæd/ *n* sinvergüenza, *m;* tipo de cuidado, *m*
cadaverous /kəˈdævərəs/ *a* cadavérico
caddish /ˈkædɪʃ/ *a* mal educado, grosero
caddy /ˈkædi/ *n* (for tea) cajita para té, *f;* (golf) cadi, *mf*
cadence /ˈkeidn̩s/ *n* cadencia, *f*
cadet /kəˈdɛt/ *n* hermano menor, *m; Mil.* cadete, *m*
cadge /kædʒ/ *vi* sablear. —*vt* dar un sablazo (a)
cadger /ˈkædʒər/ *n* sablista, *mf;* mendigo, *m;* (loafer) golfo, *m*
Cadiz /ˈkɑdis/ Cádiz, *m*
cadmium /ˈkædmiəm/ *n* cadmio, *m*
café /kæˈfei/ *n* café, *m*
cafeteria /ˌkæfɪˈtɪəriə/ *n* bar automático, *m*
caffeine /kæˈfin/ *n* cafeína, *f*
cage /keidʒ/ *n* (animal's, bird's) jaula, *f;* (of a lift) camarín, *m;* (for transporting miners) jaula, *f.* —*vt* enjaular; encerrar
Cain /kein/, **to raise** armar lo de Dios es Cristo
cairn /kɛərn/ *n* montón de piedras, *m*
Cairo /ˈkairou/ el Cairo, *m*
cajole /kəˈdʒoul/ *vt* lisonjear; engatusar, embromar; instar
cajolery /kəˈdʒouləri/ *n* zalamerías, *f pl;* marrullería, *f,* engatusamiento, *m*
cake /keik/ *n Cul.* pastel, *m,* torta, *f;* (of chocolate, etc.) pastilla, *f.* —*vt* and *vi* cuajar; formar costra; (with mud) enlodar. **to sell like hot cakes,** venderse como pan bendito. **to take the c.,** llevarse la palma. **c. of soap,** pastilla de jabón, *f.* **c.-shop,** pastelería, *f*
calamine /ˈkæləˌmain/ *n* calamina, *f*
calamitous /kəˈlæmɪtəs/ *a* calamitoso, desastroso
calamity /kəˈlæmɪti/ *n* calamidad, *f;* desastre, *m*
calash /kəˈlæʃ/ *n* (carriage) calesa, carretela, *f;* (hood) capota, *f*
calcium /ˈkælsiəm/ *n* calcio, *m*
calculate /ˈkælkyəˌleit/ *vt* calcular; adaptar. **to c. on,** contar con
calculated /ˈkælkyəˌleitɪd/ *a* premeditado. **to be c. to,** conducir a; ser a propósito para
calculatedly /ˈkælkyəˌleitɪdli/ *adv* calculadamente
calculating /ˈkælkyəˌleitɪŋ/ *n* cálculo, *m, a* calculador; (of persons) interesado; (shrewd) perspicaz; atento. **c. machine,** máquina de calcular, *f,* calculador, *m*
calculation /ˌkælkyəˈleiʃən/ *n* cálculo, *m;* calculación, *f*
calculus /ˈkælkyələs/ *n* cálculo, *m*
Calcutta /kælˈkʌtə/ Calcutta, *f*
calendar /ˈkæləndər/ *n* calendario, *m;* almanaque, *m;* (university, etc.) programa, *m*
calender /ˈkæləndər/ *n* calandria, *f, vt* calandrar, cilindrar
calf /kæf/ *n* becerro (-rra), ternero (-ra); (young of other animals) hijuelo, *m;* (of the leg) pantorrilla, *f;* (leather) cuero de becerro, *m;* piel, *f.* **calf's-foot,** pie de ternera, *m.* **c. love,** amor de muchachos, *m*
caliber /ˈkælɪbər/ *n* calibre, *m*
calibrate /ˈkæləˌbreit/ *vt* calibrar
calico /ˈkælɪˌkou/ *n* indiana, *f;* percal, *m.* **c.-printer,** fabricante de estampados, *m*
Californian /ˌkæləˈfɔrnyən/ *a* californio. —*n* californio (-ia)
caliph /ˈkeilɪf/ *n* califa, *m*
calk /kɔk/ See **caulk**
call /kɔl/ *n* llamada, *f;* (shout) grito, *m;* (of a bird) canto, *m;* (signal) señal, *f;* (visit) visita, *f;* (by a ship) escala, *f; Mil.* toque, *m;* (need) necesidad, *f;* (of religion, etc.) vocación, *f;* invitación, *f;* (demand) demanda, *f;* exigencia, *f.* **They came at my c.,** Acudieron a mi llamada. **c. to arms,** llamada, llamada a filas, *f.* **port of c.,** puerto de escala, *m.* **telephone c.,** llamada telefónica, *f.* **to pay a c.,** hacer una visita. **within c.,** al alcance de la voz. **c.-box,** cabina del teléfono, *f.* **c.-boy,** ayudante del traspunte, *m*
call /kɔl/ *vi* llamar; gritar, dar voces; (visit) visitar, hacer una visita (a); venir; (stop) parar; (of a ship) hacer escala. —*vt* llamar; (a meeting, etc.) convocar; (awaken) despertar, llamar; (say) decir; (appoint) nombrar; (at cards) declarar. **She is called Dorothy,** Se llama Dorotea. **Madrid calling!** ¡Aquí Radio Madrid! **Will you c. me at eight o'clock, please?** Haga el favor de despertarme (llamarme) a las ocho. **to c. at a port,** hacer escala en un puerto. **to c. a halt,** hacer alto. **to c. a strike,** declarar una huelga. **to c. names,** vituperar, injuriar. **to c. to account,** pedir cuentas (a). **to c. to arms,** tocar el arma; alarmar. **to c. to mind,** acordarse (de), recordar. **to c. to witness,** hacer testigo (de). **to c. back,** *vt* llamar; hacer volver; (unsay) desdecir. —*vi* (return) volver; venir a buscar; ir a buscar. **I called back for the parcel,** Volví a buscar el paquete. **to c. for,** pedir a gritos; llamar; (demand) pedir; exigir; (collect a person) pasar a buscar; (parcels, etc.) ir (or venir) a recoger. **He called for help,** Pidió socorro a gritos. **to c. forth,** producir; provocar; inspirar; revelar; (bring together) reunir. **to c. in,** hacer entrar; invitar; (a specialist, etc.) llamar; (worn coin) retirar de la circulación; recoger. **to c. in question,** poner en duda. **to c. off,** (dogs, etc.) llamar; (a strike) cancelar; parar; terminar; (a person) disuadir (de); (postpone) aplazar; suspender; (refrain) desistir (de). **to c. on,** (visit) hacer una visita (a), ir a ver, visitar; (of a doctor) visitar; (a person to do something) recurrir (a); (for a speech) invitar (a hablar); (invoke) invocar. **I shall now c. on Mr. Martínez,** Doy la palabra al señor Martínez. **to c. out,** *vt* hacer salir; provocar; inspirar; (challenge) desafiar, retar. —*vi* gritar. **c. the roll,** pasar lista. **to c. over,** (names) pasar lista (de). **to c. up,** hacer subir; (to the army) llamar a filas (a); (telephone) llamar por teléfono (a); (memories) evocar. **to c. upon.** See **to c. on**
caller /ˈkɔlər/ *n* visita, *f*
calligraphist /kəˈlɪgrəfɪst/ *n* calígrafo, *m*
calligraphy /kəˈlɪgrəfi/ *n* caligrafía, *f*
calling /ˈkɔlɪŋ/ *n* llamamiento, *m;* (occupation) profesión, *f;* empleo, *m;* vocación, *f;* (of a meeting) convocación, *f*
calling card /ˈkɔlɪŋ ˌkɑrd/ *n* (telephone) tarjeta telefónica, *f*
callipers /ˈkælɪpərz/ *n pl* compás de puntas, pie de rey, *m*
callisthenics /ˌkæləsˈθɛnɪks/ *n pl* calistenia, *f*
callosity /kəˈlɒsɪti/ *n* callosidad, *f*

callous /'kæləs/ *a* (of skin) calloso; *Fig.* insensible, duro, inhumano
callously /'kæləsli/ *adv* sin piedad
callousness /'kæləsnɪs/ *n* falta de piedad, inhumanidad, dureza, *f*
callow /'kælou/ *a* (of birds) implume; (inexperienced) bisoño, inexperto, novato
callus /'kæləs/ *n* callo, *m*
calm /kɑm/ *n* calma, *f;* paz, tranquilidad, *f;* sosiego, *m;* serenidad, *f.* —*a* (of the sea) en calma; tranquilo; sereno; sosegado. —*vt* calmar; tranquilizar; apaciguar. —*vi* calmarse; tranquilizarse; sosegarse. **dead c.,** calma chicha, *f*
calming /'kɑmɪŋ/ *a* calmante
calmly /'kɑmli/ *adv* tranquilamente, sosegadamente; con calma
calmness /'kɑmnɪs/ *n* calma, tranquilidad, *f;* ecuanimidad, serenidad, *f*
caloric /kə'lɔrɪk/ *a* calórico
calorie /'kæləri/ *n* caloría, *f*
calumniation /kəˌlʌmni'eiʃən/ *n* calumnia, *f*
calumniator /kə'lʌmniˌeitər/ *n* calumniador (-ra)
calumny /'kæləmni/ *n* calumnia, *f*
calvary /'kælvəri/ *n* calvario, *m*
calve /kæv/ *vi* (of a cow, etc.) parir
Calvinism /'kælvəˌnɪzəm/ *n* calvinismo, *m*
Calvinist /'kælvənɪst/ *n* calvinista, *mf*
Calvinistic /ˌkælvə'nɪstɪk/ *a* calvinista
calyx /'keilɪks/ *n* cáliz, *m*
cam /kæm/ *n Mech.* leva, *f.* **camshaft,** árbol de levas, *m*
camaraderie /ˌkɑmə'rɑdəri/ *n* compañerismo, *m*
camber /'kæmbər/ *n* comba(dura), *f*
cambric /'keimbrɪk/ *n* batista, *f*
camcorder /'kæmˌkɔrdər/ *n* videocámara, *f,* camcórder, *m*
camel /'kæməl/ *n* camello (-lla). **c.-driver,** camellero, *m.* **camel's hair,** pelo de camello, *m*
camellia /kə'milyə/ *n* camelia, *f*
cameo /'kæmiˌou/ *n* camafeo, *m*
camera /'kæmərə/ *n Photo.* máquina fotográfica, *f.* **folding c.,** máquina fotográfica plegable, *f.* **in c.,** a puerta cerrada. **c. obscura,** cámara obscura, *f*
Cameroons, the /ˌkæmə'runz/ el Camerón, los Camerones, *m*
camouflage /'kæməˌflɑʒ/ *n* camuflaje, *m, vt* camuflar
camp /kæmp/ *n* campamento, *m;* campo, *m; Fig.* vida de cuartel, *f;* (for school children, etc.) colonia, *f;* (party) partido, *m.* —*vi* acampar; vivir en tiendas de campaña. **to break c.,** levantar el campo. **c.-bed,** cama de campaña, *f.* **c.-stool,** silla de campaña, *f*
campaign /kæm'pein/ *n* campaña, *f.* —*vi* hacer una campaña
campaigner /kæm'peinər/ *n* veterano, *m;* propagandista, *mf*
campaigning /kæm'peinɪŋ/ *n* campañas, *f pl*
camphor /'kæmfər/ *n* alcanfor, *m*
camphorated /'kæmfəˌreitɪd/ *a* alcanforado
campus /'kæmpəs/ *n* recinto, *m* (Puerto Rico), ciudad universitaria, *f*
can /kæn/ *v aux* poder; (know how to) saber. **You can go to the village when you like,** Puedes ir al pueblo cuando quieras. **I cannot allow that,** No puedo permitir eso. **What can they mean?** ¿Qué quieren decir? **If only things could have been different!** ¡Si solamente las cosas hubiesen sido distintas! **Can you come to dinner on Saturday?** ¿Puede Vd. venir a cenar el sábado? **I can come later if you like,** Puedo (or Podría) venir más tarde si Vd. quiere. **Mary can** (knows how to) **play the piano,** María sabe tocar el piano **You can't have your cake and eat it too.** No hay rosa sin espinas
can /kæn/ *n* lata, *f;* (for carrying sandwiches, etc.) fiambrera, *f.* —*vt* conservar en latas. **canopener,** abrelatas, *m*
Canada /'kænədə/ el Canadá, *m*
Canadian /kə'neidiən/ *a* canadiense. —*n* canadiense, *mf*
canaille /kə'nai/ *n* gentualla, gentuza, *f*
canal /kə'næl/ *n* canal, *m*
canalization /ˌkænl̩ə'zeiʃən/ *n* canalización, *f*
canalize /'kænl̩ˌaiz/ *vt* canalizar
canary /kə'nɛəri/ *n* canario (-ia); color de canario, *m;* vino de Canarias, *m.* **roller c.,** canario de raza flauta, *m.* **c.-seed,** alpiste, *m*
Canary Islands, the /kə'nɛəri/ las Islas Canarias, *m*
cancel /'kænsəl/ *vt* cancelar; revocar; borrar; anular. **to c. out,** *Math.* anular
cancellation /ˌkænsə'leiʃən/ *n* cancelación, *f;* revocación, *f;* anulación, *f*
cancer /'kænsər/ *n Med.* cáncer, *m; Astron.* Cáncer, *m*
cancerous /'kænsərəs/ *a* canceroso. **to become c.,** cancerarse
candelabrum /ˌkændl̩'ɑbrəm/ *n* candelabro, *m*
candescent /kæn'dɛsənt/ *a* candente
candid /'kændɪd/ *a* franco; sincero. **If I am to be c.,** Si he de decir la verdad, Si he de ser franco
candidate /'kændɪˌdeit/ *n* candidato (-ta); aspirante, *m*
candidature /'kændɪdəˌtʃʊr/ *n* candidatura, *f*
candidly /'kændɪdli/ *adv* francamente; sinceramente
candidness /'kændɪdnɪs/ *n* franqueza, *f;* sinceridad, *f*
candied /'kændid/ *a* (of peel, etc.) almibarado, garapiñado
candle /'kændl̩/ *n* vela, candela, *f.* **wax c.,** cirio, *m.* **You cannot hold a c. to him,** No llegas a la suela de su zapato, Ni llegas a sus pies, Ni le llegas a los pies. **The game is not worth the c.,** La cosa no vale la pena. **to burn the c. at both ends,** consumir la vida. **c.-grease,** sebo, *m.* **c.-light,** luz de las velas, *f;* luz artificial, *f.* **c.-maker,** candelero, *m.* **c.-power,** *Elec.* potencia luminosa, bujía, *f.* **c.-snuffer,** apagavelas, matacandelas, *m*
Candlemas /'kændl̩məs/ *n* candelaria, *f*
candlestick /'kændl̩ˌstɪk/ *n* candelero, *m,* palmatoria, *f;* (processional) cirial, *m*
candor /'kændər/ *n* franqueza, *f;* sinceridad, *f;* candor, *m*
candy /'kændi/ *n* caramelo, bombón, *m, vt* garapiñar, almibarar
candytuft /'kændiˌtʌft/ *n* carraspique, *m*
cane /kein/ *n Bot.* caña, *f;* (for chair seats, etc.) rejilla, *f;* (walking stick) bastón, *m;* (for punishment) vara, *f.* —*vt* apalear, pegar. **sugar-c.,** caña de azúcar, *f.* **c.-break,** cañaveral, *m.* **c. chair,** sillón de mimbres, *m.* **c.-sugar,** azúcar de caña, *m.* **c.-syrup,** miel de caña, *f*
canine /'keinain/ *a* canino. —*n* (tooth) diente canino, *m*
caning /'keinɪŋ/ *n* paliza, *f*
canister /'kænəstər/ *n* bote, *m,* cajita, *f*
canker /'kæŋkər/ *n* úlcera, *f;* (in trees) cancro, *m; Fig.* cáncer, *m, vt* roer; *Fig.* corromper
canned /kænd/ *a* en lata
cannibal /'kænəbəl/ *n* caníbal, *mf* antropófago (-ga). —*a* caníbal, antropófago
cannibalism /'kænəbəˌlɪzəm/ *n* canibalismo, *m,* antropofagía, *f*
canning /'kænɪŋ/ *n* conservación en latas, *f.* **c. factory,** fábrica de conservas alimenticias, *f*
cannon /'kænən/ *n* (fire-arm) cañón, *m;* (billiards) carambola, *f, vi* carambolear. **to c. into,** chocar con. **c.-ball,** bala de cañón, *f.* **c.-shot,** cañonazo, *m*
cannonade /ˌkænə'neid/ *n* cañoneo, *m*
canny /'kæni/ *a* cuerdo, sagaz
canoe /kə'nu/ *n* canoa, *f;* piragua, *f, vi* ir en canoa
canoeist /kə'nuɪst/ *n* canoero (-ra)
canon /'kænən/ *n* (*Eccl. Mus. Print.*) canón, *m;* (dignitary) canónigo, *m;* (criterion) criterio, *m.* **c. law,** derecho canónico, *m*
canonical /kə'nɒnɪkəl/ *a* canónico
canonization /ˌkænənə'zeiʃən/ *n* canonización, *f*
canonize /'kænəˌnaiz/ *vt* canonizar
canopy /'kænəpi/ *n* dosel, toldo, *m;* palio, *m; Fig.* capa, bóveda, *f.* **the c. of heaven,** la capa (or bóveda) del cielo
cant /kænt/ *vt* inclinar; ladear. —*vi* inclinarse; (be a hypocrite) camandulear. —*n* (slope) inclinación, *f,* sesgo, desplomo, *m;* (hypocrisy) gazmoñería, *f*
Cantabrian /kæn'teibriən/ *a* cantábrico

cantankerous /kæn'tæŋkərəs/ *a* irritable, intratable, malhumorado
cantankerousness /kæn'tæŋkərəsnɪs/ *n* mal humor, *m*, irritabilidad, *f*
cantata /kən'tɑtə/ *n* cantata, *f*
canteen /kæn'tin/ *n* cantina, *f;* (water bottle) cantimplora, *f.* **c. of cutlery,** juego de cubiertos, *m*
canter /'kæntər/ *n* medio galope, *m*, *vi* andar a galope corto
Canterbury /'kæntərˌbɛri/ Cantórbery, Cantuaria, *f*
canticle /'kæntɪkəl/ *n* cántico, *m*
canting /'kæntɪŋ/ *a* hipócrita
canto /'kæntou/ *n* canto, *m*
canton /'kæntn̩/ *n* (province and *Herald.*) cantón, *m*, *vt* (of soldiers) acantonar
cantonment /kæn'tɒnmənt/ *n* acantonamiento, cantón, *m*
cantor /'kæntər/ *n Eccl.* chantre, *m*
canvas /'kænvəs/ *n* lona, *f; Art.* lienzo, *m; Naut.* vela, *f*, paño, *m*. **under c.,** en tiendas de campaña; (of ships) a toda vela
canvass /'kænvəs/ *vt* (votes, etc.) solicitar
canvasser /'kænvəsər/ *n* solicitador (-ra) (de votos, etc.)
canvassing /'kænvəsɪŋ/ *n* solicitación (de votos, etc.), *f*
canyon /'kænyən/ *n* cañón, *m*
canzonet /ˌkænzə'nɛt/ *n* chanzoneta, *f*
cap /kæp/ *n* gorra, *f;* (with a peak) montera, *f;* (type of military headgear with brim at front) quépis, *m;* (cardinal's) birrete, *m; Educ.* bonete, *m;* (pointed) caperuza, *f;* (woman's old-fashioned) cofia, *f;* (jester's) gorro de bufón, *m;* (on a bottle) cápsula, tapa, *f.* —*vt Educ.* conferir el grado (a). **cap and bells,** gorro de bufón, *m*. **cap and gown,** birrete y muceta, toga y birrete, toga y bonete. **to throw one's cap over the windmill,** echar la capa al toro. **to cap it all,** ser el colmo
capability /ˌkeipə'bɪlɪti/ *n* capacidad, *f;* aptitud, *f*
capable /'keipəbəl/ *a* capaz; competente; (of improvement) susceptible; (full of initiative) emprendedor
capably /'keipəbli/ *adv* competentemente
capacious /kə'peiʃəs/ *a* espacioso; grande; extenso
capaciousness /kə'peiʃəsnɪs/ *n* capacidad, *f;* amplitud, *f*
capacitate /kə'pæsɪˌteit/ *vt* capacitar
capacity /kə'pæsɪti/ *n* capacidad, *f;* calidad, *f;* aptitud, *f*. **in one's c. as,** en calidad de. **seating c.,** número de asientos, *m;* (in aircraft) número de plazas, *m*
caparison /kə'pærəsən/ *n* caparazón, *m*
cape /keip/ *n* (cloak) capa, *f;* (short) capotillo, *m*, capeta, *f;* (fur) cuello, *m; Geog.* cabo, promontorio, *m*. **c. coat,** capote, *m*
Cape Horn /'keip 'hɔrn/ Cabo de Hornos, *m*
caper /'keipər/ *vi* (gambol) brincar, saltar; cabriolar, corcovear; (play) juguetear. —*n* travesura, *f;* zapateta, *f;* cabriola, *f;* (whim) capricho, *m; Bot.* alcaparra, *f*. **to c. about,** dar saltos, brincar; juguetear
capillarity /ˌkæpə'lærɪti/ *n* capilaridad, *f*
capillary /'kæpəˌlɛri/ *a* capilar. —*n* vaso capilar, *m*
capital /'kæpɪtl̩/ *a* capital; mortal; de muerte; de vida; principal; (of letters) mayúscula; (very good) excelente. —*n* (city) capital, *f;* (letter) (letra) mayúscula, *f; Com.* capital, *m; Archit.* capitel, chapitel, *m*. **floating c.,** capital fluctuante, *m*. **idle c.,** fondos inactivos, *m pl*. **c. punishment,** pena de muerte, pena capital, pena de la vida, *f*. **C.!** ¡Estupendo! ¡Excelente! **to make c. out of,** aprovecharse de, sacar ventaja de
capitalism /'kæpɪtl̩ˌɪzəm/ *n* capitalismo, *m*
capitalist /'kæpɪtl̩ɪst/ *n* capitalista, *mf*
capitalistic /ˌkæpɪtl̩'ɪstɪk/ *a* capitalista
capitalization /ˌkæpɪtl̩ə'zeiʃən/ *n* capitalización, *f*
capitalize /'kæpɪtl̩ˌaiz/ *vt* capitalizar
capitally /'kæpɪtl̩i/ *adv* estupendamente
capitation /ˌkæpɪ'teiʃən/ *n* capitación, *f*
Capitol /'kæpɪtl̩/ *n* Capitolio, *m*
capitulate /kə'pɪtʃəˌleit/ *vi* capitular
capitulation /kəˌpɪtʃə'leiʃən/ *n* capitulación, *f*
capon /'keipɒn/ *n* capón, *m*
caprice /kə'pris/ *n* capricho, *m*
capricious /kə'prɪʃəs/ *a* caprichoso
capriciousness /kə'prɪʃəsnɪs/ *n* carácter inconstante, *m;* lo caprichoso
Capricorn /'kæprɪˌkɔrn/ *n* Capricornio, *m*
capsize /'kæpsaiz/ *vt Naut.* hacer zozobrar; volcar. —*vi Naut.* zozobrar; volcarse
capsizing /'kæpˌsaizɪŋ/ *n Naut.* zozobra, *f;* vuelco, *m*
capsule /'kæpsəl/ *n* (*Bot. Med. Chem. Zool.*) cápsula, *f*
captain /'kæptən/ *n* (*Mil. Nav. Aer.* and *Sports.*) capitán, *m*, *vt* capitanear. **to c. a team,** ser el capitán de un equipo. **group c.,** *Aer.* capitán de aviación, *m*
captaincy /'kæptənsi/ *n* capitanía, *f*
caption /'kæpʃən/ *n* (arrest) arresto, *m;* (heading) encabezamiento, título, pie, *m;* (cinema) subtítulo, *m*
captious /'kæpʃəs/ *a* capcioso, caviloso
captivate /'kæptəˌveit/ *vt* cautivar, seducir
captivating /'kæptəˌveitɪŋ/ *a* encantador, seductor
captive /'kæptɪv/ *a* cautivo, *n* cautivo (-va), prisionero (-ra), preso (-sa). **c. balloon,** globo cautivo, globo de observación, *m*
captivity /kæp'tɪvɪti/ *n* cautiverio, *m*
captor /'kæptər/ *n* el, *m*, (*f*, la) que hace prisionero (-ra)
capture /'kæptʃər/ *n* captura, *f;* presa, toma, *f; Law.* captura, *f*. —*vt* prender, capturar; tomar
Capuchin /'kæpyətʃɪn/ *a* capuchino. —*n* capuchino, *m*. **C. nun,** capuchina, *f*
car /kɑr/ *n* (chariot) carro, *m;* (tram) tranvía, *m;* (motor) automóvil, coche, *m;* (on a train) coche vagón, *m*. **sleeping car,** coche camas, *m*. **car park,** parque de automóviles, *m*
carabineer /ˌkɑrəbə'nɪər/ *n* carabinero, *m*
carafe /kə'ræf/ *n* garrafa, *f*
caramel /'kærəməl/ *n* caramelo, *m;* azúcar quemado, *m*
carapace /'kærəˌpeis/ *n* carapacho, *m*
carat /'kærət/ *n* quilate, *m*
caravan /'kærəˌvæn/ *n* caravana, *f;* coche de gitanos, *m;* coche habitación, *m*
caraway /'kærəˌwei/ *n* alcaravea, *f*
carbarn /'kɑrˌbɑrn/ *n* encierro, *m* (Mexico), cochera, cochera de tranvías, *f*, cobertizo, cobertizo para tranvías, *m*
carbide /'kɑrbaid/ *n* carburo, *m*
carbine /'kɑrbin/ *n* carabina, *f*
carbohydrate /ˌkɑrbou'haidreit/ *n* hidrato de carbono, *m*
carbolic /kɑr'bɒlɪk/ *a* carbólico. **c. acid,** ácido fénico, *m*
carbon /'kɑrbən/ *n* carbono, *m*. **c. copy,** copia en papel carbón, *f*. **c. dioxide,** anhídrido carbónico, *m*. **c. monoxide,** óxide de carbono, *m*. **c. paper,** papel carbón, papel de calcar, *m*
carbonate /'kɑrbəˌneit/ *n* carbonato, *m*
carbonated /'kɑrbəˌneitɪd/ *a* (beverage) carbónico (formal), con gas (informal)
carbonic /kɑr'bɒnɪk/ *a* carbónico
carbonization /ˌkɑrbənə'zeiʃən/ *n* carbonización, *f*
carbonize /'kɑrbəˌnaiz/ *vt* carbonizar
carboy /'kɑrbɔi/ *n* damajuana, garrafa, *f*
carbuncle /'kɑrbʌŋkəl/ *n Med.* carbunco, *m;* (stone) carbúnculo, *m*
carburetor /'kɑrbəˌreitər/ *n* carburador, *m*
carcass /'kɑrkəs/ *n* (animal) res muerta, *f;* (corpse) cadáver, *m;* (body) cuerpo, *m;* (of a ship) casco, *m*
carcinoma /ˌkɑrsə'noumə/ *n* carcinoma, *m*
card /kɑrd/ *n* (playing) naipe, *m;* (pasteboard) cartulina, *f;* (visiting, postal, etc.) tarjeta, *f;* (index) ficha, *f;* (for wool, etc.) carda, *f*. —*vt* (wool, etc.) cardar. **I still have a c. up my sleeve,** Me queda todavía un recurso. **to lay one's cards on the table,** poner las cartas boca arriba. **to play one's cards well,** *Fig.* jugar el lance. **admission c.,** billete de entrada, *m*. **post c.,** tarjeta postal, *f*. **visiting c.,** tarjeta de visita, *f*. **c.-case,** tarjetero, *m*. **c.-index,** fichero, *m*. —*vt* poner en el fichero. **c.-sharper,** fullero, *m*. **c.-table,** mesa de juego, *f*. **c. trick,** juego de manos con cartas, *m*
cardboard /'kɑrdˌbɔrd/ *n* cartón, *m*, *a* de cartón

cardiac /ˈkɑrdiˌæk/ *a* cardíaco

cardigan /ˈkɑrdɪgən/ *n* rebeca, chaqueta de punto, *f*

cardinal /ˈkɑrdn̩l/ *a* cardinal. —*n* cardenal, *m.* **c. number,** número cardinal, *m.* **c. points,** puntos cardinales, *m pl*

cardinalate /ˈkɑrdn̩lˌeit/ *n* cardenalato, *m*

carding /ˈkɑrdɪŋ/ *n* (of wool, etc.) cardadura, *f.* **c. machine,** carda mecánica, *f*

cardiogram /ˈkɑrdiəˌgræm/ *n* cardiograma, *m*

cardiograph /ˈkɑrdiəˌgræf/ *n* cardiógrafo, *m*

care /kɛər/ *n* cuidado, *m;* atención, *f;* inquietud, ansia, *f;* (charge) cargo, *m.* —*vi* preocuparse; tener interés; (suffer) sufrir. **I don't c.,** Me es igual; No me importa. **I don't c. a straw,** No se me da un bledo. **They don't c. for eggs,** No les gustan los huevos. **We don't c. what his opinion is,** Su opinión nos tiene sin cuidado (or no nos importa). **to c. for,** cuidar, mirar por; (love) querer (a); (like) gustar. **Take c.!** ¡Cuidado! ¡Ojo! **Take c. not to spoil it!** ¡Ten cuidado que no lo estropees! **Would you c. to...?** ¿Le gustaría...? ¿Tendría inconveniente en...? **c. of,** (on a letter, etc.) en casa de. **c.-free,** *a* libre de cuidados

careen /kəˈrin/ *vt* carenar. —*vi* dar a la banda

careening /kəˈrinɪŋ/ *n* carena, *f*

career /kəˈrɪər/ *n* carrera, *f;* curso, *m.* —*vi* correr a carrera tendida; galopar

careful /ˈkɛərfəl/ *a* cuidadoso (de); atento (a); prudente. **Be c.!** ¡Cuidado! **to be c.,** tener cuidado

carefully /ˈkɛərfəli/ *adv* con cuidado. **drive c.,** manejar con cuidado; cuidadosamente; prudentemente; atentamente

carefulness /ˈkɛərfəlnɪs/ *n* cuidado, *m;* atención, *f;* prudencia, *f*

careless /ˈkɛərlɪs/ *a* sin cuidado; indiferente (a); insensible (a); negligente; (of mistakes, etc.) de (or por) negligencia

carelessly /ˈkɛərlɪsli/ *adv* indiferentemente; negligentemente; descuidadamente

carelessness /ˈkɛərlɪsnɪs/ *n* indiferencia, *f;* negligencia, *f;* descuido, *m;* omisión, *f*

caress /kəˈrɛs/ *n* caricia, *f, vt* acariciar

caressing /kəˈrɛsɪŋ/ *a* acariciador

caretaker /ˈkɛərˌteikər/ *n* (of museums, etc.) guardián (-ana); (of flats, etc.) portero (-ra)

careworn /ˈkɛərˌwɔrn/ *a* devorado de inquietud, ansioso

cargo /ˈkɑrgou/ *n* cargamento, *m,* carga, *f.* **c.-boat,** barco de carga, *m*

Caribbean /ˌkærəˈbiən, kəˈrɪbi-/ *a* caribe

Caribbean Sea, the el Mar Caribe, *m*

caricature /ˈkærɪkətʃər/ *n* caricatura, *f, vt* caricaturizar

caricaturist /ˈkærɪkəˌtʃʊrɪst/ *n* caricaturista, *mf*

caries /ˈkɛəriz/ *n* caries, *f*

carious /ˈkɛəriəs/ *a* cariado. **to become c.,** cariarse

Carmelite /ˈkɑrməˌlait/ *a* carmelita. —*n* carmelita, *mf*

carmine /ˈkɑrmɪn/ *n* carmín, *m, a* de carmín

carnage /ˈkɑrnɪdʒ/ *n* carnicería, *f*

carnal /ˈkɑrnl̩/ *a* carnal; sensual

carnality /kɑrˈnælɪti/ *n* carnalidad, *f*

carnally /ˈkɑrnl̩i/ *adv* carnalmente

carnation /kɑrˈneiʃən/ *n* clavel, *m*

carnival /ˈkɑrnəvəl/ *n* carnaval, *m, a* de carnaval, carnavalesco

carnivore /ˈkɑrnəˌvɔr/ *n* carnívoro, *m*

carnivorous /kɑrˈnɪvərəs/ *a* carnívoro

carol /ˈkærəl/ *n* villancico, *m;* canto, *m.* —*vi* cantar alegremente; (of birds) trinar, gorjear

Carolingian /ˌkærəˈlɪndʒiən/ *a* carolingio

carotid /kəˈrɒtɪd/ *n* carótida, *f*

carousal /kəˈrauzəl/ *n* borrachera, *f;* holgorio, *m,* jarana, *f*

carouse /kəˈrauz/ *vi* emborracharse. —*n* borrachera, orgía, *f*

carp /kɑrp/ *n* carpa, *f, vi* criticar, censurar

Carpathian Mountains, the /kɑrˈpeiθiən/ los Montes Carpotes, *m*

carpel /ˈkɑrpəl/ *n* carpelo, *m*

carpenter /ˈkɑrpəntər/ *n* carpintero, *m, vi* carpintear. **carpenter's bench,** banco de carpintero, *m.* **carpenter's shop,** carpintería, *f*

carpentry /ˈkɑrpəntri/ *n* carpintería, *f*

carpet /ˈkɑrpɪt/ *n* alfombra, *f; Fig.* tapete, *m.* —*vt* cubrir de una alfombra, alfombrar; entapizar. **to be on the c.,** estar sobre el tapete. **c.-beater,** sacudidor de alfombras, *m.* **c. merchant,** alfombrista, *m.* **c. slippers,** zapatillas de fieltro, *f pl.* **c.-sweeper,** aspirador de polvo, *m*

carpeting /ˈkɑrpɪtɪŋ/ *n* alfombrado, *m*

carping /ˈkɑrpɪŋ/ *a* capcioso, criticón

carriage /ˈkærɪdʒ/ *n* (carrying) transporte, porte, *m;* (deportment) porte, continente, *m,* presencia, *f;* (vehicle) carruaje, *m;* carroza, *f;* coche, *m;* (railway) departamento, *m;* (chassis) chasis, bastidor, *m;* (of a typewriter, etc.) carro, *m.* **hackney c.,** coche de plaza, *m.* **c. and pair,** carroza de dos caballos, *f.* **c. door,** portezuela, *f.* **c.-forward,** porte debido. **c.-free,** franco de porte. **c.-paid,** porte pagado

carrier /ˈkæriər/ *n* el, *m,* (*f,* la) que lleva; portador (-ra); *Com.* mensajero, *m;* (on a car, bicycle) portaequipajes, *m;* (of a disease) vector, *m;* (aircraft) porta-aviones, *m.* **c.-pigeon,** paloma mensajera, *f*

carrion /ˈkæriən/ *n* carroña, *f.* **c.-crow,** chova, *f*

carrot /ˈkærət/ *n* zanahoria, *f*

carry /ˈkæri/ *vt* llevar; transportar; traer; conducir; (*Mil.* of arms) portar; (have with one) tener consigo; (an enemy position) tomar, ganar; (a motion) aprobar; (oneself) portarse; (one's point, etc.) ganar; (in the mind) retener; (conviction) convencer; (involve) implicar; (influence) influir; (send) despachar, enviar; (contain) incluir, comprender. —*vi* (of the voice, etc.) alcanzar, llegar. **The noise of the guns carried a long way,** El ruido de los cañones se oía desde muy lejos. **to fetch and c.,** traer y llevar. **to c. all before one,** vencer todos los obstáculos. **to c. into effect,** poner en efecto. **to c. one's audience with one,** captar (or cautivar) su auditorio. **to c. oneself well,** tener buena presencia. **to c. on one's back,** llevar a cuestas. **to c. the day,** quedar victorioso, quedar señor del campo. **to c. weight,** *Fig.* ser de peso. **to c. along,** llevar; (drag) arrastrar; conducir; acarrear. **to c. away,** llevar; llevarse, llevar consigo; (kidnap) robar, secuestrar; (of emotions) dominar; (by enthusiasm) entusiasmar; (inspire) inspirar. **to c. forward,** llevar a cabo; avanzar; fomentar; (bookkeeping) pasar a cuenta nueva. **to c. off,** (things) llevarse; (persons) llevar consigo (a); (abduct or steal) robar; (kill) matar; (a prize) ganar. **to c. (a thing) off well,** llevar la mejor parte, salir vencedor. **to c. on,** *vt* (a discussion, etc.) seguir, continuar. **c. on a conversation,** llevar una conversación; mantener; (a business, etc.) tener; dirigir. —*vi* ir tirando; seguir trabajando. **to c. out,** realizar, llevar a cabo; hacer, ejecutar, efectuar; (a promise) cumplir. **to c. through,** llevar a cabo

carrying /ˈkæriɪŋ/ *n* transporte, *m;* (of a motion) adopción, *f*

cart /kɑrt/ *n* carro, *m.* —*vt* acarrear; llevar. **c.-horse,** caballo de tiro, *m.* **c.-load,** carretada, *f,* carro, *m.* **c.-wheel,** rueda de carro, *f;* (somersault) voltereta, *f*

cartage /ˈkɑrtɪdʒ/ *n* carretaje, transporte, porte, *m*

carte blanche /ˈkɑrt ˈblɑntʃ/ *n* carta blanca, *f*

cartel /kɑrˈtɛl/ *n* cartel, *m*

carter /ˈkɑrtər/ *n* carretero, *m*

Cartesian /kɑrˈtiʒən/ *a* cartesiano. —*n* cartesiano (-na)

Carthage /ˈkɑrθɪdʒ/ Cartago, *m*

Carthaginian /ˌkɑrθəˈdʒɪniən/ *a* cartaginés. —*n* cartaginés (-esa)

Carthusian /kɑrˈθuʒən/ *a* cartujano. **C. monk,** cartujo, *m*

cartilage /ˈkɑrtl̩ɪdʒ/ *n* cartílago, *m*

cartilaginous /ˌkɑrtl̩ˈædʒənəs/ *a* cartilaginoso

cartographer /kɑrˈtɒgrəfər/ *n* cartógrafo, *m*

cartography /kɑrˈtɒgrəfi/ *n* cartografía, *f*

cartomancy /ˈkɑrtəmənsi/ *n* cartomancia, *f*

carton /ˈkɑrtn̩/ *n* caja de cartón, *f*

cartoon /kɑrˈtun/ *n* (design for tapestry, etc.) cartón, *m;* caricatura, *f*

cartoonist /kɑrˈtunɪst/ *n* caricaturista, *mf*

cartridge /ˈkɑrtrɪdʒ/ *n* cartucho, *m.* **blank c.,** cartucho sin bala, *m.* **c.-belt,** cartuchera, canana, *f.* **c.-case,** cápsula de proyectil, *f*

carve /kɑrv/ *vt* tallar, labrar; grabar; cortar; (meat, etc.) trinchar; (a career, etc.) hacer, forjarse

carver /'kɑrvər/ *n* tallador, *m;* (at table) trinchador, *m;* (implement) trinchante, *m*
carving /'kɑrvɪŋ/ *n* talla, *f;* (design) tallado, *m.* **c.-knife,** trinchante, *m*
cascade /kæs'keid/ *n* cascada, catarata, *f,* salto de agua, *m; Fig.* chorro, *m.* —*vi* chorrear
case /keis/ *n* caso, *m; Law.* proceso, *m,* causa, *f; Gram.* caso, *m; Med.* caso, *m;* enfermo (-ma); (box) caja, *f;* (for scissors, etc.) vaina, *f;* (for a cushion, etc.) funda, *f;* (for jewels, manicure implements, etc.) estuche, *m;* (of a piano, watch and *Print.*) caja, *f;* (for documents) carpeta, *f;* (glass) vitrina, *f;* (for a book) sobrecubierta, *f;* (dressing) neceser, *m.* —*vt* cubrir; forrar; resguardar. **packing-c.,** caja de embalaje, *f.* **c. of goods,** caja de mercancías, *f;* bulto, *m.* **in any c.,** en todo caso; venga lo que venga. **in c.,** por si acaso. **in c. of emergency,** en caso de urgencia. **in such a c.,** en tal caso. **in the c. of,** en el caso de; respecto a. **lower c.,** *Print.* caja baja, *f.* **upper c.,** *Print.* caja alta, *f.* **c.-hardened,** (of iron) templado; *Fig.* endurecido, indiferente
case closed! ¡asunto concluido!
casement window /'keismənt/ *n* ventana, *f*
cash /kæʃ/ *n* efectivo, metálico, *m;* dinero contante, *m; Inf.* dinero, *m; Com.* caja, *f.* —*vt* cobrar; pagar, hacer efectivo. **hard or ready c.,** dinero contante, *m.* **to pay c.,** pagar al contado. **c. on delivery,** (C.O.D.) contra reembolso. **c. on hand,** efectivo en caja, *m.* **c.-book,** libro de caja, *m.* **c.-box,** caja, *f.* **c.-desk,** caja, *f.* **c. down,** pago al contado, *m.* **c. prize,** premio en metálico, *m.* **c.-register,** caja registradora, *f*
cashew /'kæʃu/ *n* anacardo, *m*
cashier /kæ'ʃɪər/ *n* cajero (-ra). —*vt* degradar. **cashier's desk,** caja, *f*
cash machine *n* cajero automático, *m*
cashmere /'kæʒmɪər/ *n* cachemira, *f*
casino /kə'sinou/ *n* casino, *m*
cask /kæsk/ *n* pipa, barrica, *f,* tonel, *m;* cuba, *f*
casket /'kæskɪt/ *n* cajita, arquilla, *f,* cofrecito, *m*
Caspian /'kæspiən/ *a* caspio
Caspian Sea, the el (Mar) Caspio, *m*
casserole /'kæsə,roul/ *n* cacerola, *f*
cassock /'kæsək/ *n* sotana, *f*
cast /kæst/ *vt* arrojar, tirar; (in fishing, the anchor, dice, darts, lots, a net, glances, blame, etc.) echar; (skin) mudar; (lose) perder; (a shadow, etc.) proyectar; (a vote) dar; (mold) vaciar; (accounts) echar, calcular; (a horoscope) hacer; (the parts in a play) repartir; (an actor for a part) dar el papel de; (metals) colar, fundir. **the shadow c. by the wall,** la sombra proyectada por el muro. **to c. anchor,** echar anclas, anclar. **to c. in one's lot with,** compartir la suerte de. **to c. something in a person's teeth,** echar en cara (a). **to c. lots,** echar suertes. **to c. about,** meditar, considerar; imaginar; (devise) inventar. **to c. aside,** desechar; poner a un lado; abandonar. **to c. away,** tirar lejos; desechar; (money) derrochar, malgastar. **to be c. away,** *Naut.* naufragar. **to c. down,** (overthrow) derribar, destruir; (eyes) bajar; (depress) desanimar, deprimir; (humiliate) humillar. **to be c. down,** estar deprimido. **c. iron,** *n* hierro colado, hierro fundido, *m.* **c.-iron,** *a* de hierro colado; *Fig.* inflexible. **to c. off,** quitarse; desechar; (a wife) repudiar; (desert) abandonar; (free oneself) librarse (de). **c.-off,** *n* desecho, *m.* **c.-off clothing,** ropa de desecho, *f.* **to c. out,** echar fuera; hacer salir; excluir. **to c. up,** echar; vomitar; (a sum) sumar; (something at a person) reprochar
cast /kæst/ *n* (of dice, fishing-line) echada, *f;* (of a net) redada, *f;* (worm) molde, *m;* (of a play) reparto, *m;* (of mind) inclinación, *f;* (in the eye) defecto en la mirada, *m;* (of colour) matiz, tinte, *m.* **c. of features,** facciones, *f pl,* fisonomía, *f.* **plaster c.,** vaciado, *m*
castanets /,kæstə'nɛts/ *n pl* castañuelas, *f pl*
castaway /'kæstə,wei/ *n* náufrago (-ga); *Fig.* perdido (-da)
caste /kæst/ *n* casta, *f;* clase social, *f.* **to lose c.,** desprestigiarse
castigate /'kæstɪ,geit/ *vt* castigar
Castile /kæ'stil/ Castilla, *f*
Castilian /kæ'stɪlyən/ *a* castellano. —*n* castellano (-na); (language) castellano, *m*
casting /'kæstɪŋ/ *n* lanzamiento, *m;* (of metals) fundición, colada, *f;* obra de fundición, *f.* **c.-net,** esparavel, *m.* **c.-vote,** voto de calidad, *m*
castle /'kæsəl/ *n* castillo, *m;* (in chess) torre, *f,* roque, *m.* **to build castles in Spain,** hacer castillos en el aire
castor /'kæstər/ *n Zool.* castor, *m;* (for sugar) azucarero, *m;* (cruet) convoy, *m;* (on chairs, etc.) ruedecilla, roldana, *f.* **c.-oil,** aceite de ricino, *m.* **c.-sugar,** azúcar en polvo, *m*
castrate /'kæstreit/ *vt* castrar, capar
castration /kæs'treiʃən/ *n* castración, capadura, *f*
casual /'kæʒuəl/ *a* fortuito, accidental; ligero, superficial; *Inf.* despreocupado. **c. worker,** jornalero, *m*
casually /'kæʒuəli/ *adv* por casualidad; de paso; negligentemente
casualness /'kæʒuəlnɪs/ *n Inf.* negligencia, despreocupación, *f*
casualty /'kæʒuəlti/ *n* víctima, *f;* herido, *m; Mil.* baja, *f; pl* **casualties,** heridos, *m pl;* muertos, *m pl.* **c.-list,** lista de víctimas, *f; Mil.* lista de bajas, *f*
casuist /'kæʒuɪst/ *n* casuista, *mf*
casuistry /'kæʒuəstri/ *n* casuística, *f*
cat /kæt/ *n* gato (-ta). **She is an old cat,** Ella es una vieja chismosa. **to be like a cat on hot bricks,** estar como en brasas, **to let the cat out of the bag,** tirar de la manta. **to lead a cat-and-dog life,** vivir como perros y gatos. **cat's-cradle,** (game) cunas, *f pl.* **cat's paw,** (person) hombre de paja, *m; Naut.* bocanada de viento, *f.* **cat o' nine tails,** gato de siete colas, *m,* penca, *f.* **catwhisker,** *Radio.* detector, *m*
cataclysm /'kætə,klɪzəm/ *n* cataclismo, *m*
catacombs /'kætə,koumz/ *n pl* catacumbas, *f pl*
catafalque /'kætə,fɔk/ *n* catafalco, *m*
Catalan /'kætḷ,æn/ *a* catalán (-ana). —*n* catalán; (language) catalán, *m*
catalepsy /'kætḷ,ɛpsi/ *n* catalepsia, *f*
catalogue /'kætḷ,ɔg/ *n* catálogo, *m, vt* catalogar
Catalonia /,kætḷ'ouniə/ Cataluña, *f*
catalysis /kə'tæləsɪs/ *n* catálisis, *f*
cat-and-mouse /'kæt ṇ 'maus/ *n* el juego de ratón, *m*
catapult /'kætə,pʌlt/ *n Mil.* catapulta, *f; Aer.* catapulta (para lanzar aviones), *f;* (toy) tirador de gomas, *m.* —*vt* tirar con una catapulta (or con un tirador de gomas); (throw) lanzar
cataract /'kætə,rækt/ *n* catarata, cascada, *f,* salto de agua, *m;* (of the eye) catarata, *f*
catarrh /kə'tɑr/ *n* catarro, *m;* constipado, resfriado, *m*
catastrophe /kə'tæstrəfi/ *n* catástrofe, *f,* desastre, *m;* (in drama) desenlace, *m*
catastrophic /,kætəs'trɒfɪk/ *a* catastrófico
catcall /'kæt,kɔl/ *n* silbido, *m*
catch /kætʃ/ *vt* coger; agarrar, asir; (capture) prender, haber; (a disease) contraer; (habit) tomar; (on a hook, etc.) enganchar; (surprise) sorprender; (understand) comprender; (hear) oír; (with blows, etc.) dar. —*vi* (of a lock) encajarse; (become entangled) engancharse; (of a fire) encenderse. **to c. a glimpse of,** ver por un instante (a); alcanzar a ver, entrever. **to c. at,** asir; agarrarse (a); echar mano de; procurar asir; alargar la mano hacia; (an idea, etc.) adoptar con entusiasmo. **to c. on,** (be popular) tener éxito; (understand) comprender. **to c. out,** coger en el acto; coger en un error; *Sports.* coger. **to c. up,** coger; interrumpir. **to c. up with,** (a person) alcanzar; (news) ponerse al corriente de
catch /kætʃ/ *n* presa, *f;* (of fish) redada, pesca, *f;* (of a window, etc.) cerradura, *f;* (latch) pestillo, *m;* (trick) trampa, *f; Mus.* canon, *m.* **a good c.,** (matrimonial) un buen partido. **to have a c. in one's voice,** hablar con voz entrecortada. **c.-as-c.-can,** lucha libre, *f*
catching /'kætʃɪŋ/ *a* contagioso
catchment /'kætʃmənt/ *n* desagüe, *m*
catchword /'kætʃ,wɜrd/ *n* reclamo, *m;* (theater cue) pie, apunte, *m;* (slogan) mote, *m*
catchy /'kætʃi/ *a* atractivo. **It's a c. tune,** Es una canción que se pega
catechism /'kætɪ,kɪzəm/ *n* catequismo, *m*
categorical /,kætɪ'gɔrɪkəl/ *a* categórico
category /'kætɪ,gɔri/ *n* categoría, *f*
cater /'keitər/ *vi* proveer, abastecer. **to c. for all tastes,** atender a todos los gustos

caterer /'keitərər/ *n* despensero (-ra)

catering /'keitərɪŋ/ *n* provisión, *f*

caterpillar /'kætəˌpɪlər/ *n* oruga, *f*. **c. tractor,** tractor de orugas, *m*

caterwaul /'kætərˌwɔl/ *vi* (of a cat) maullar

caterwauler /'kætərˌwɔlər/ *n* (violinist, etc.) rascatripas, *m*

caterwauling /'kætərˌwɔlɪŋ/ *n* maullidos, *m pl*; música ratonera, *f*

catfish /'kætˌfɪʃ/ *n* siluro, *m*

catgut /'kætˌgʌt/ *n Surg.* catgut, *m; Mus.* cuerda, *f*

catharsis /kə'θɑrsɪs/ *n Med.* purga, *f; Fig.* catarsis, *f*

cathedral /kə'θidrəl/ *n* catedral, *f*

Catherine wheel /'kæθrɪn/ *n Archit.* rosa, *f;* (firework) rueda de Santa Catalina, *f;* (somersault) tumba, *f*

catheter /'kæθɪtər/ *n* catéter, *m*

cathode /'kæθoud/ *n* cátodo, *m*. **c. rays,** rayos catódicos, *m pl*. **c. ray tube,** tubo de rayos catódicos, *m*

cathodic /kæ'θɒdɪk/ *a* catódico

catholic /'kæθəlɪk/ *a* católico

Catholicism /kə'θɒləˌsɪzəm/ *n* catolicismo, *m*

catkin /'kætkɪn/ *n* amento, *m*. **male c.,** amento macho, *m*

catlike /'kætˌlaik/ *a* de gato; gatuno

cattle /'kætl̩/ *n* ganado vacuno, *m;* ganado, *m;* animales, *m pl*. **c.-dealer,** ganadero, *m*. **c.-lifter,** hurtador de ganado, *m*. **c.-pen,** corral, *m*. **c.-raiser,** criador de ganado, *m*. **c.-raising,** ganadería, *f*. **c.-ranch,** hacienda de ganado, estancia, *f*. **c.-show,** exposición de ganado, *f*. **c.-truck,** vagón de ferrocarril para ganado, *m*

cattle rustler *n* abigeo, cuatrero, ladrón de ganado, *m*

cattle rustling *n* abigeato, *m*

catty /'kæti/ *a* gatuno; malicioso, chismoso

Caucasian /kɔ'keiʒən/ *a* and *n* caucáseo (-ea)

Caucasus, the /'kɔkəsəs/ el Cáucaso

cauldron /'kɔldrən/ *n* caldera, *f*

cauliflower /'kɔləˌflauər/ *n* coliflor, *f*

caulk /kɔk/ *vt* calafatear

caulker /'kɔkər/ *n* calafate, *m*

caulking /'kɔkɪŋ/ *n* calafateado, *m*. **c. iron,** calador, *m*

causality /kɔ'zælɪti/ *n* causalidad, *f*

causative /'kɔzətɪv/ *a* causante

cause /kɔz/ *n* causa, *f;* (reason) motivo, *m*, razón, *f;* (lawsuit) proceso, *m*. —*vt* causar; ocasionar, suscitar; (oblige) hacer, obligar (a). **final c.,** *Philos.* causa final, *f*. **to have good c. for,** tener buen motivo para

causeway /'kɔzˌwei/ *n* dique, *m;* acera, *f*

caustic /'kɔstɪk/ *a* cáustico; *Fig.* mordaz. **c. soda,** sosa cáustica, *f*

caustically /'kɔstɪkli/ *adv* mordazmente, con sarcasmo

causticity /kɔ'stɪsɪti/ *n* causticidad, *f*

cauterization /ˌkɔtərə'zeiʃən/ *n* cauterización, *f*

cauterize /'kɔtəˌraiz/ *vt* cauterizar

cautery /'kɔtəri/ *n* cauterio, *m*

caution /'kɔʃən/ *n* prudencia, cautela, *f;* (warning) amonestación, *f;* aviso, *m*. —*vt* amonestar. **to proceed with c.,** ir con prudencia; ir despacio

"Caution" /'kɔʃən/ (road sign) «Precaución»

cautionary /'kɔʃəˌnɛri/ *a* (of tales) de escarmiento

cautious /'kɔʃəs/ *a* cauteloso, cauto; prudente, circunspecto

cautiously /'kɔʃəsli/ *adv* cautamente; prudentemente. **to go c.,** *Inf.* ir con pies de plomo

cavalcade /ˌkævəl'keid/ *n* cabalgata, *f*

cavalier /ˌkævə'lɪər/ *n* jinete, *m;* caballero, *m;* galán, *m*, *a* arrogante, altanero

cavalry /'kævəlri/ *n* caballería, *f*. **c.-man,** jinete, soldado de a caballo, *m*

cave /keiv/ *n* cueva, caverna, *f*. **to c. in,** hundirse; desplomarse; *Fig.* rendirse. **c.-man,** hombre cavernícola, *m*

cavern /'kævərn/ *n* caverna, *f*

cavernous /'kævərnəs/ *a* cavernoso

caviar /'kæviˌɑr/ *n* caviar, *m*

cavil /'kævəl/ *vi* cavilar

cavity /'kævɪti/ *n* cavidad, *f;* hoyo, *m;* hueco, *m;* (in a lung) caverna, *f*

cavy /'keivi/ *n* cobayo (-ya), conejillo (-lla) de las Indias

caw /kɔ/ *n* graznido, *m*, *vi* graznar, grajear

cawing /'kɔɪŋ/ *n* graznidos, *m pl*

cayenne /kai'ɛn/ *n* pimentón, *m*

cease /sis/ *vi* cesar (de), dejar de; parar. —*vt* cesar de; parar de; (payments, etc.) suspender; discontinuar. **C. fire!** ¡Cesar fuego!

ceaseless /'sislɪs/ *a* incesante,continuo, sin cesar

ceaselessly /'sislɪsli/ *adv* sin cesar, incesantemente

ceasing /'sisɪŋ/ *n* cesación, *f*. **without c.,** sin cesar

cedar /'sidər/ *n* (tree and wood) cedro, *m*. **red c.,** cedro dulce, *m*

cede /sid/ *vt* ceder, traspasar; (admit) conceder

cedilla /sɪ'dɪlə/ *n* zedilla, *f*

ceiling /'silɪŋ/ *n* techo, *m; Aer.* altura máxima, *f*. **c. price,** máximo precio, *m*

celebrant /'sɛləbrənt/ *n Eccl.* celebrante, *m*

celebrate /'sɛləˌbreit/ *vt* celebrar; solemnizar. **Their marriage was celebrated in the autumn,** Su casamiento se solemnizó en el otoño

celebrated /'sɛləˌbreitɪd/ *a* célebre, famoso

celebration /ˌsɛlə'breiʃən/ *n* celebración, *f;* festividad, *f*

celebrity /sə'lɛbrɪti/ *n* celebridad, *f*

celerity /sə'lɛrɪti/ *n* celeridad, *f*

celery /'sɛləri/ *n* apio, *m*

celestial /sə'lɛstʃəl/ *a* celestial

celibacy /'sɛləbəsi/ *n* celibato, *m*

celibate /'sɛləbɪt/ *a* célibe. —*n* célibe, *mf*

cell /sɛl/ *n* celda, *f;* (*Bot. Biol.*) célula, *f;* (bees, wasps) celdilla, *f; Elec.* elemento, *m*

cellar /'sɛlər/ *n* sótano, *m;* (wine) bodega, *f*

cellist /'tʃɛlɪst/ *n* violoncelista, *mf*

cello /'tʃɛlou/ *n* violoncelo, *m*

cellophane /'sɛləˌfein/ *n* (papel) celofán, *m*

cellular /'sɛlyələr/ *a* celular, celuloso

cellular phone /'sɛlyələr 'foun/ *n* móvil, *m*, celular, *m* (WH)

cellule /'sɛlyul/ *n* célula, *f*

celluloid /'sɛlyəˌlɔid/ *n* celuloide, *f*

cellulose /'sɛlyəˌlous/ *n* celulosa, *f*

Celt /kɛlt, sɛlt/ *n* celta, *mf*

Celtiberian /ˌkɛltə'bɪəriən, ˌsɛl-/ *a* celtibérico

Celtic /'kɛltɪk, 'sɛl-/ *a* celta

cement /sɪ'mɛnt/ *n* cemento, *m*, *vt* cementar

cemetery /'sɛmɪˌtɛri/ *n* cementerio, *m*

cenotaph /'sɛnəˌtæf/ *n* cenotafio, *m*

cense /sɛns/ *vt* incensar

censer /'sɛnsər/ *n* incensario, *m*

censor /'sɛnsər/ *n* censor, *m*, *vt* censurar. **banned by the c.,** prohibido por la censura

censorious /sɛn'sɔriəs/ *a* severo; crítico

censoriousness /sɛn'sɔriəsnɪs/ *n* severidad, propensión a censurar, *f*

censorship /'sɛnsərˌʃɪp/ *n* censura, *f*

censure /'sɛnʃər/ *vt* censurar, culpar, criticar

census /'sɛnsəs/ *n* censo, *m*. **to take the c.,** formar el censo, levantar el censo, tomar el censo, empadronar

census-taking /'sɛnsəs ˌteikɪŋ/ *n* la formación del censo, la formación de los censos, *f*, el levantamiento del censo, el levantamientos de los censos, *m*

cent /sɛnt/ *n* (coin) centavo, *m*. **per c.,** por ciento. **not to have a c., not to have a c. to one's name,** no tener donde caer muerto

centaur /'sɛntɔr/ *n* centauro, *m*

centenarian /ˌsɛntn̩'ɛəriən/ *a* and *n* centenario (-ia)

centenary /sɛn'tɛnɛri/ *n* centenario, *m*, *a* centenario

center /'sɛntər/ *n* centro, *m;* medio, *m*. —*a* central; centro. —*vt* centrar; concentrar (en). **nervous centers,** centros nerviosos, *m pl*. **c.-forward,** *Sports.* delantero centro, *m*. **c.-half,** *Sports.* medio centro, *m*. **c. of gravity,** centro de gravedad, *m*. **c.-piece,** centro, *m*

centerfold /'sɛntərˌfould/ *n* páginas centrales, *f pl*

centigrade /'sɛntɪˌgreid/ *a* centígrado

centigram /'sɛntɪˌgræm/ *n* centigramo, *m*

centiliter /'sɛntl̩ˌitər/ *n* centilitro, *m*

centime /'sɑntim/ *n* céntimo, *m*

centimeter /'sɛntəˌmitər/ *n* centímetro, *m*. **cubic c.,** centímetro cúbico, *m*

centipede /ˈsɛntəˌpid/ *n* ciempiés, *m*
central /ˈsɛntrəl/ *a* central; céntrico. **The house is very c.,** La casa es muy céntrica. **C. American,** *a* and *n* centroamericano (-na). **c. depot,** central, *f.* **c. heating,** calefacción central, *f*
centralism /ˈsɛntrəˌlɪzəm/ *n* centralismo, *m*
centralist /ˈsɛntrəlɪst/ *n* centralista, *mf*
centralization /ˌsɛntrələˈzeiʃən/ *n* centralización, *f*
centralize /ˈsɛntrəˌlaiz/ *vt* centralizar
centrally /ˈsɛntrəli/ *adv* centralmente; céntricamente
centric /ˈsɛntrɪk/ *a* céntrico; central
centrifugal /sɛnˈtrɪfyəgəl/ *a* centrífugo
centripetal /sɛnˈtrɪpɪtl̩/ *a* centrípeto
centumvir /ˈsɛntəmˌvɪər/ *n* centunviro, *m*
centuple /sɛnˈtupəl/ *a* céntuplo
centuplicate /sɛnˈtuplɪˌkeit/ *vt* centuplicar
centurion /sɛnˈtyʊriən/ *n* centurión, *m*
century /ˈsɛntʃəri/ *n* siglo, *m,* centuria, *f*
ceramic /səˈræmɪk/ *a* cerámico
ceramics /səˈræmɪks/ *n* cerámica, *f*
Cerberus /ˈsɜrbərəs/ *n* Cancerbero, *m*
cereal /ˈsɪəriəl/ *a* cereal. —*n* cereal, *m*
cerebellum /ˌsɛrəˈbɛləm/ *n* cerebelo, *m*
cerebral /səˈribrəl/ *a* cerebral
cerebrospinal /səˌribrouˈspainl̩/ *a* cerebroespinal
cerebrum /səˈribrəm/ *n* cerebro, *m*
ceremonial /ˌsɛrəˈmouniəl/ *a* ceremonial; de ceremonia. —*n* ceremonial, *m*
ceremonially /ˌsɛrəˈmouniəli/ *adv* ceremonialmente; con ceremonia
ceremonious /ˌsɛrəˈmouniəs/ *a* ceremonioso
ceremoniously /ˌsɛrəˈmouniəsli/ *adv* ceremoniosamente
ceremoniousness /ˌsɛrəˈmouniəsnɪs/ *n* ceremonia, formalidad, *f*
ceremony /ˈsɛrəˌmouni/ *n* ceremonia, *f.* **to stand on c.,** gastar cumplidos. **without c.,** sin cumplidos
cerise /səˈris/ *a* de color cereza
certain /ˈsɜrtn̩/ *a* (sure) seguro; cierto; (unerring) certero. **a c. man,** cierto hombre. **I am c. that...,** Estoy seguro de que... **to know for c.,** saber con toda seguridad, saber a ciencia cierta. **to make c. of,** asegurarse de
certainly /ˈsɜrtn̩li/ *adv* seguramente; ciertamente; (as a reply) sin duda; naturalmente. **c. not,** no, por cierto; claro que no
certainty /ˈsɜrtn̩ti/ *n* certidumbre, *f;* seguridad, *f;* convicción, *f.* **of a c.,** seguramente
certificate /*n* sərˈtɪfɪkɪt; *v* -ˌkeit/ *n* certificado, *m;* fe, *f;* partida, *f; Com.* bono, título, *m;* diploma, *m.* —*vt* certificar. **birth c.,** partida de nacimiento, *f.* **death c.,** partida de defunción, *f.* **marriage c.,** partida de casamiento, *f*
certificated /sərˈtɪfɪˌkeitɪd/ *a* (of teachers, etc.) con título
certify /ˈsɜrtəˌfai/ *vt* certificar; atestiguar; declarar
certitude /ˈsɜrtɪˌtyud/ *n* certeza, certidumbre, *f*
cerulean /səˈruliən/ *a* cerúleo
Cervantine /sərˈvæntin/ *a* cervantino
cervix /ˈsɜrvɪks/ *n Anat.* cerviz, *f*
Cesarean /səˈzɛəriən/ *a* cesáreo
cessation /sɛˈseiʃən/ *n* cesación, *f*
cession /ˈsɛʃən/ *n* cesión, *f*
cessionary /ˈsɛʃənɛri/ *n* cesionario (-ia)
cesspool /ˈsɛsˌpul/ *n* sumidero, *m*
cetacean /sɪˈteiʃən/ *a* cetáceo. —*n* cetáceo, *m*
Ceylon /sɪˈlɒn/ Ceilán, *m*
cf. cfr.
chafe /tʃeif/ *vt* (rub) frotar; (make sore) escocer, rozar. —*vi* raerse, desgastarse; escocerse; *Fig.* impacientarse; *Fig.* irritarse, enojarse
chaff /tʃæf/ *n* (of grain) ahechadura, *f;* (in a general sense and *Fig.*) paja, *f;* tomadura de pelo, burla, *f.* —*vt* (a person) tomar el pelo (a), burlarse de
chaffinch /ˈtʃæfɪntʃ/ *n* pinzón, *m*
chafing /ˈtʃeifɪŋ/ *n* frotación, *f;* (soreness) excoriación, *f; Fig.* impaciencia, *f.* **c.-dish,** escalfador, *m*
chagrin /ʃəˈgrɪn/ *n* mortificación, decepción, *f,* disgusto, *m, vt* mortificar
chain /tʃein/ *n* cadena, *f, vt* encadenar. **c. of mountains,** cadena de montañas, cordillera, *f.* **c.-gang,** cadena de presidiarios, *f.* **c.-mail,** cota de malla, *f.* **c.-stitch,** cadeneta, *f.* **c.-stores,** empresa con sucursales, *f.* **in chains,** cargado de cadenas (e.g., *prisoners in chains,* prisioneros cargados de cadenas)
chair /tʃɛər/ *n* silla, *f; Educ.* cátedra, *f;* (of a meeting) presidencia, *f.* —*vt* llevar en hombros (a). **C.!** ¡Orden! **easy-c.,** (silla) poltrona, *f.* **to be in the c.,** ocupar la presidencia; presidir. **to take a c.,** sentarse, tomar asiento. **to take the c.,** presidir. **swivel-c.,** silla giratoria, *f.* **wheel-c.,** silla de ruedas, *f.* **c.-back,** respaldo de una silla, *m*
chairman /ˈtʃɛərmən/ *n* presidente (-ta). **to act as c.,** presidir
chairmanship /ˈtʃɛərmənˌʃɪp/ *n* presidencia, *f*
chaise longue /ˈʃeiz ˈlɔŋ/ *n* meridiana, tumbona, *f*
Chaldea /kælˈdiə/ Caldea, *f*
Chaldean /kælˈdiən/ *a* caldeo
chalet /ʃæˈlei/ *n* chalet, *m*
chalice /ˈtʃælɪs/ *n* cáliz, *m*
chalk /tʃɔk/ *n* creta, *f;* (for writing, etc.) tiza, *f,* yeso, *m.* —*vt* marcar con tiza; dibujar con tiza. **to c. up,** apuntar. **not by a long c.,** no con mucho
chalky /ˈtʃɔki/ *a* cretáceo; cubierto de yeso; (of the complexion) pálido
challenge /ˈtʃælɪndʒ/ *n* provocación, *f;* (of a sentry) quién vive, *m;* (to a duel, etc.) desafío, reto, *m; Law.* recusación, *f;* concurso, *m.* —*vt* (of a sentry) dar el quién vive (a); desafiar; provocar; *Law.* recusar
challenger /ˈtʃælɪndʒər/ *n* desafiador (-ra)
challenging /ˈtʃælɪndʒɪŋ/ *a* desafiador, provocador
chamber /ˈtʃeimbər/ *n* cuarto, *m;* sala, *f;* (bed-) dormitorio, *m,* alcoba, *f;* cámara, *f; Mech.* cilindro, *m;* (in a gun) cámara, *f.* **c. concert,** concierto de música de cámara, *m.* **c.-maid,** camarera, *f.* **c. music,** música de cámara, *f.* **c. of commerce,** cámara de comercio, *f.* **c.-pot,** orinal, *m*
chamberlain /ˈtʃeimbərlɪn/ *n* camarero, *m.* **court c.,** chambelán, *m.* **Lord C.,** camarero mayor, *m*
chameleon /kəˈmiliən/ *n* camaleón, *m*
chamfer /ˈtʃæmfər/ *n* chaflán, bisel, *m*
chamois /ˈʃæmi/ *n* gamuza, *f,* rebeco, *m.* **c. leather,** piel de gamuza, *f*
chamomile /ˈkæməˌmail/ *n* camomila, manzanilla, *f*
champ /tʃæmp/ *vt* mascar; morder. —*vi Fig.* impacientarse
champagne /ʃæmˈpein/ *n* (vino de) champaña, *m*
champion /ˈtʃæmpiən/ *n* campeón, *m;* defensor (-ra)
championship /ˈtʃæmpiənˌʃɪp/ *n* campeonato, *m;* (of a cause) defensa, *f*
chance /tʃæns/ *n* casualidad, *f;* suerte, fortuna, *f;* posibilidad, *f;* probabilidad, *f;* esperanza, *f;* (opportunity) ocasión, oportunidad, *f.* —*a* fortuito; accidental. —*vi impers* suceder, acontecer. —*vt Inf.* arriesgar; probar. **by c.,** por casualidad; por ventura. **if by c.,** si acaso. **If it chances that...,** Si sucede que; Si a mano viene que... **The chances are that...,** Las probabilidades son que... **There is no c.,** No hay posibilidad; No hay esperanza. **to let the c. slip,** perder la ocasión. **to take a c.,** aventurarse, arriesgarse. **to c. to do,** hacer algo por casualidad. **to c. upon,** encontrar por casualidad.
chancel /ˈtʃænsəl/ *n* antealtar, entrecoro, *m*
chancellery /ˈtʃænsələri/ *n* cancillería, *f*
chancellor /ˈtʃænsələr/ *n* canciller, *m; Educ.* cancelario, *m.* **C. of the Exchequer,** Ministro de Hacienda, *m*
chancellorship /ˈtʃænsələrʃɪp/ *n* cancillería, *f*
chancery /ˈtʃænsəri, ˈtʃɑn-/ *n* chancillería, *f;* (papal) cancelaría, *f*
chandelier /ˌʃændl̩ˈɪər/ *n* araña de luces, *f*
chandler /ˈtʃændlər/ *n* velero, *m*
change /tʃeindʒ/ *vt* cambiar; transformar; modificar; (clothes) mudarse (de); (one thing for another) trocar; sustituir (por). —*vi* cambiar; (clothes) mudarse. **All c.!** ¡Cambio de tren! **to c. a check,** cambiar un cheque. **to c. color,** cambiar de color; (of persons) mudar de color. **to c. countenance,** demudarse. **to c. front,** *Fig.* cambiar de frente. **to c. hands,** (of shops, etc.) cambiar de dueño. **to c. one's clothes,** cambiar de ropa, mudarse de ropa. **to c. one's mind,** cambiar de opinión. **to c. one's tune,** cambiar de tono. **to c.**

the subject, cambiar de conversación. **to c. trains,** cambiar de trenes

change /tʃeindʒ/ *n* cambio, *m;* transformación, *f;* modificación, *f;* variedad, *f;* (of clothes, feathers) muda, *f;* (*Theat.* of scene) mutación, *f;* (money) cambio, *m;* (small coins) suelto, *m;* (stock) bolsa, *f;* lonja, *f;* vicisitud, *f;* (of bells) toque (de campanas), *m.* **for a c.,** para cambiar, como un cambio; para variar. **small c.,** suelto, *m,* moneda suelta, *f.* **c. for the better,** cambio para mejor, *m.* **c. for the worse,** cambio para peor, *m.* **c. of clothes,** cambio de ropa, *m;* **c. of front,** *Fig.* cambio de frente, *m.* **c. of heart,** cambio de sentimientos, *m;* conversión, *f.* **c. of life,** menopausia, *f.* **c.-over,** cambio, *m*

changeability /ˌtʃeindʒəˈbɪlɪti/ *n* mutabilidad, *f;* inconstancia, volubilidad, *f*

changeable /ˈtʃeindʒəbəl/ *a* voluble; variable; cambiable

changeless /ˈtʃeindʒlɪs/ *a* immutable; constante

changeling /ˈtʃeindʒlɪŋ/ *n* niño (-ña) cambiado (-da) por otro

changing /ˈtʃeindʃɪŋ/ *a* cambiante. **c.-room,** vestuario, *m*

channel /ˈtʃænl̩/ *n* (of a river, etc.) cauce, *m;* canal, *m,* (irrigation) acequia, *f,* (strait) estrecho, *m; Fig.* conducto, *m;* (furrow) surco, *m,* estría, *f;* (of information, etc.) medio, *m.* —*vt* acanalar; (furrow) surcar; (conduct) encauzar

chant /tʃænt/ *n* canto llano, *m;* salmo, *m.* —*vt* salmodiar; cantar; recitar

chantey /ˈʃænti/ *n* saloma, *f*

chaos /ˈkeiɒs/ *n* caos, *m*

chaotic /keiˈɒtɪk/ *a* caótico, desordenado

chaotically /keiˈɒtɪkli/ *adv* en desorden

chap /tʃæp/ *vt* agrietar. —*vi* agrietarse. —*n Inf.* chico, *m*

chapbook /ˈtʃæpˌbʊk/ *n* librito de cordel, *m*

chapel /ˈtʃæpəl/ *n* capilla, *f;* templo disidente, *m*

chaperon /ˈʃæpəˌroun/ *n* dama de compañía, señora de compañía, dueña, *f, vt* acompañar

chaplain /ˈtʃæplɪn/ *n* capellán, *m*

chaplaincy /ˈtʃæplɪnsi/ *n* capellanía, *f*

chaplet /ˈtʃæplɪt/ *n* guirnalda, *f;* rosario, *m;* (necklace) collar, *m*

chapter /ˈtʃæptər/ *n* (in a book) capítulo, *m; Eccl.* cabildo, capítulo, *m.* **a c. of accidents,** una serie de desgracias. **c. house,** sala capitular, *f*

char /tʃɑr/ *vt* (a house, etc.) fregar, hacer la limpieza de; (of fire) carbonizar. —*n Inf.* fregona, asistenta, *f*

character /ˈkærɪktər/ *n* carácter, *m;* (of a play) personaje, *m;* (role) papel, *m;* (eccentric) tipo, *m.* **Gothic characters,** caracteres góticos, *m pl.* **in c.,** característico; apropiado. **in the c. of,** en el papel de. **out of c.,** nada característico; no apropiado. **principal c.,** protagonista, *mf.* **c. actor,** actor de carácter, *m.* **c. actress,** actriz de carácter

characteristic /ˌkærɪktəˈrɪstɪk/ *a* característico, típico. —*n* característica, peculiaridad, *f,* rasgo, *m*

characterization /ˌkærɪktərəˈzeiʃən/ *n* caracterización, *f*

characterize /ˈkærɪktəˌraiz/ *vt* caracterizar

characterless /ˈkærɪktərlɪs/ *a* sin carácter; insípido, soso

charade /ʃəˈreid/ *n* charada, *f*

charcoal /ˈtʃɑrˌkoul/ *n* carbón de leña, *m;* (for blacking the face, etc.) tizne, *m; Art.* carboncillo, *m.* **c. burner,** carbonera, *f.* **c. crayon,** carboncillo, *m.* **c. drawing,** dibujo al carbón, *m*

charge /tʃɑrdʒ/ *vt* cargar; (enjoin) encargar; (accuse) acusar (de); (with price) cobrar; (with a mission, etc.) encomendar, confiar; *Mil.* acometer, atacar. —*vi Mil.* atacar; (a price) cobrar, pedir. **How much do you c.?** ¿Cuánto cobra Vd.? **to c. with a crime,** acusar de un crimen

charge /tʃɑrdʒ/ *n* (load) carga, *f;* (price) precio, *m;* gasto, *m;* (on an estate, etc.) derechos, *m pl*; (task) encargo, *m;* (office or responsibility) cargo, *m;* (guardianship) tutela, *f;* (care) cuidado, *m;* exhortación, *f; Law.* acusación, *f; Mil.* ataque, *m.* **He is in c. of...,** Está encargado de...; Es responsable de... **The diamonds are in the c. of...,** Los diamantes están a cargo de. **depth c.,** carga de profundidad, *f.* **extra c.,** gasto suplementario, *m;* (on a train) suplemento, *m.* **free of c.,** gratis. **c. for admittance,** entrada, *f.* **to bring a c. against,** acusar de. **to give (someone) in c.,** entregar (una persona) a la policía. **to take c. of,** encargarse de

chargé d'affaires /ʃarˈʒei dəˈfɛər/ *n* encargado de negocios, *m*

charger /ˈtʃɑrdʒər/ *n* caballo de guerra, corcel, *m*

chariness /ˈtʃɛərinɪs/ *n* cautela, *f*

chariot /ˈtʃæriət/ *n* carro, *m*

charioteer /ˌtʃæriəˈtɪər/ *n* auriga, *m*

charitable /ˈtʃærɪtəbəl/ *a* caritativo; benéfico

charitableness /ˈtʃærɪtəbəlnɪs/ *n* caridad, *f*

charity /ˈtʃærɪti/ *n* caridad, *f;* beneficencia, *f;* (alms) limosna, *f.* **c. child,** niño (-ña) de la doctrina

charlatan /ˈʃɑrlətn̩/ *n* charlatán (-ana); (quack) curandero, *m*

charlatanism /ˈʃarlətn̩ˌɪzəm/ *n* charlatanismo, *m;* curanderismo, *m*

charm /tʃɑrm/ *n* hechizo, *m;* ensalmo, *m;* (amulet) amuleto, *m;* (trinket) dije, *m;* (general sense) encanto, atractivo, *m.* —*vt* encantar, hechizar, fascinar

charming /ˈtʃɑrmɪŋ/ *a* encantador; atractivo, seductor, fascinador

charm school *n* academia de buenos modales, *f*

chart /tʃɑrt/ *n Naut.* carta de marear, *f;* (graph) gráfica, *f.* —*vt* poner en una carta

charter /ˈtʃɑrtər/ *n* carta, *f;* (of a city, etc.) fuero, *m;* cédula, *f.* —*vt* (a ship) fletar; (hire) alquilar. **royal c.,** cédula real, *f*

Chartism /ˈtʃɑrtɪzəm/ *n* el cartismo, *m*

chartist /ˈtʃɑrtɪst/ *n* cartista, *mf*

charwoman /ˈtʃɑrˌwʊmən/ *n* fregona, asistenta; mujer de hacer faenas, *f*

chary /ˈtʃɛəri/ *a* cauteloso; desinclinado; frugal

chase /tʃeis/ *n* caza, *f;* seguimiento, *m.* —*vt* cazar; dar caza (a); perseguir; (drive off) ahuyentar; *Fig.* disipar, hacer desaparecer; (engrave) cincelar. **to give c. to,** dar caza (a). **to go on a wild goose c.,** buscar pan de trastrigo

chasm /ˈkæzəm/ *n* sima, *f,* precipicio, *m; Fig.* abismo, *m*

chassis /ˈtʃæsi/ *n* chasis, *m*

chaste /tʃeist/ *a* casto

chasten /ˈtʃeisən/ *vt* castigar; corregir; humillar, mortificar

chastened /ˈtʃeisənd/ *a* sumiso, dócil

chastise /tʃæsˈtaiz/ *vt* castigar

chastisement /tʃæsˈtaizmənt/ *n* castigo, *m*

chastity /ˈtʃæstɪti/ *n* castidad, *f*

chat /tʃæt/ *vi* charlar, conversar. —*n* conversación, charla, *f.* **They are having a c.,** Están charlando, Están de palique

chattels /ˈtʃætəlz/ *n pl* bienes muebles, efectos, *m pl*

chatter /ˈtʃætər/ *vi* charlar; hablar por los codos, chacharear; (of water) murmurar; (of birds) piar; (of monkeys, etc.) chillar; (of teeth) rechinar; (of a person's teeth) dar diente con diente. —*n* charla, *f;* cháchara, parla, *f;* (of water) murmurio, *m;* (of birds) gorjeo, *m;* (of monkeys, etc.) chillidos, *m pl*

chatterbox /ˈtʃætˌər bɒks/ *n* badajo, *m,* cotorra, *f*

chatterer /ˈtʃætərər/ *n* hablador (-ra)

chattering /ˈtʃætərɪŋ/ *n* charla, cháchara, *f;* (of teeth) rechinamiento, *m, a* gárrulo, chacharero, locuaz

chauffeur /ˈʃoufər/ *n* chófer, *m*

chauvinism /ˈʃouvəˌnɪzəm/ *n* chauvinismo, *m*

cheap /tʃip/ *a* barato; (of works of art) cursi. —*adv* barato. **dirt c.,** baratísimo. **to be dirt c.,** estar por los suelos. **to hold** (something) **c.,** tener en poco, estimar en poco

cheapen /ˈtʃipən/ *vt* disminuir el valor de; reducir el precio de

cheaply /ˈtʃipli/ *adv* barato; a bajo precio

cheapness /ˈtʃipnɪs/ *n* baratura, *f;* precio módico, *m;* mal gusto, *m,* vulgaridad, *f*

cheat /tʃit/ *n* engaño, fraude, *m,* estafa, *f;* (person) fullero (-ra), trampista, *mf* embustero (-ra). —*vt* engañar; defraudar; (at cards) hacer trampas. **He cheated me out of my property,** Me defraudó de mi propiedad

cheating /ˈtʃitɪŋ/ *n* engaño, *m;* fraude, *m;* (at cards) fullerías, *f pl*
check /tʃɛk/ *n* (chess) jaque, *m;* revés, *m;* impedimento, *m;* contratiempo, *m;* (of a bridle) cama, *f;* (control) freno, *m;* control, *m;* (checking) verificación, *f;* (ticket) papeleta, *f;* (counterfoil) talón, *m;* (square) cuadro, *m;* (bill) cuenta, *f;* (bank) cheque, *m.* —*vt* (chess) jaquear; (hamper) refrenar; detener; contrarrestar; (test) verificar. —*vi* detenerse. **to c. off,** marcar. **to c. oneself,** detenerse; contenerse. **to c. up,** comprobar. **crossed c.,** cheque cruzado, *m.* **c. book,** libro de cheques, *m*
checked /tʃɛkt/ *a* (cloth) a cuadros
checker /ˈtʃɛkər/ *vt* escaquear; (variegate) motear, salpicar; diversificar. **a checkered career,** una vida accidentada
checkers /ˈtʃɛkərz/ *n. pl.* damas, *f.*
checking /ˈtʃɛkɪŋ/ *n* represión, *f;* control, *m;* verificación, *f;* comprobación, *f*
checkmate /ˈtʃɛkˌmeit/ *n* mate, jaque, mate, *m.* —*vt* dar mate (a); (plans, etc.) frustrar
checks and balances *n pl* frenos y contrapesos, *m pl*
cheek /tʃik/ *n* mejilla, *f; Inf.* descaro, *m;* insolencia, *f.* **They have plenty of c.,** Tienen mucha cara dura. **c. by jowl,** cara a cara; al lado de. **c.-bone,** pómulo, *m*
cheekiness /ˈtʃikinɪs/ *n* cara dura, insolencia, *f*
cheeky /ˈtʃiki/ *a* insolente, descarado; (pert) respondón
cheep /tʃip/ *n* pío, *m, vi* piar
cheer /tʃɪər/ *n* alegría, *f,* regocijo, *m;* vítor, *m;* aplauso, *m.* —*vt* animar; alegrar, regocijar; vitorear, aplaudir. **to be of good c.,** estar alegre; ser feliz. **C. up!** ¡Ánimo! **to c. up,** animarse, cobrar ánimo
cheerful /ˈtʃɪərfəl/ *a* alegre; jovial; de buen humor. **It is a c. room,** Es un cuarto alegre
cheerfully /ˈtʃɪərfəli/ *adv* alegremente; (willingly) con mucho gusto, de buena gana
cheerfulness /ˈtʃɪərfəlnɪs/ *n* alegría, *f;* jovialidad, *f;* buen humor, *m*
cheering /ˈtʃɪərɪŋ/ *n* vítores, *m pl,* aclamaciones, *f pl, a* animador
cheerleader /ˈtʃɪərˌlidər/ *n* porro, *m*
cheerless /ˈtʃɪərlɪs/ *a* triste; sin alegría; (dank) obscuro, lóbrego
cheese /tʃiz/ *n* queso, *m.* **cream c.,** queso de nata, *m.* **grated c.,** queso rallado, *m.* **c.-dish,** quesera, *f.* **c.-mite,** cresa, *f.* **c.-paring,** *n* corteza de queso, *f.* —*a Inf.* tacaño. **c.-vat,** quesera, *f*
cheesy /ˈtʃizi/ *a* caseoso
chemical /ˈkɛmɪkəl/ *a* químico. **c. warfare,** defensa química, *f*
chemicals /ˈkɛmɪkəlz/ *n pl* productos químicos, *m pl*
chemise /ʃəˈmiz/ *n* camisa (de mujer), *f*
chemist /ˈkɛmɪst/ *n* químico, *m.* **chemist's shop,** farmacia, *f;* droguería, *f*
chemistry /ˈkɛməstri/ *n* química, *f*
chenille /ʃəˈnil/ *n* felpilla, *f*
cherish /ˈtʃɛrɪʃ/ *vt* amar, querer; (a hope, etc.) abrigar, acariciar
cherry /ˈtʃɛri/ *n* (fruit) cereza, *f;* (tree and wood) cerezo, *m.* **c. brandy,** aguardiente de cerezas, *m.* **c. orchard,** cerezal, *m*
cherub /ˈtʃɛrəb/ *n* querub(e), querubín, *m*
cherubic /tʃəˈrubɪk/ *a* querúbico
chess /tʃɛs/ *n* ajedrez, *m.* **c.-board,** tablero de ajedrez, *m*
chessman /ˈtʃɛsˌmæn/ *n* pieza de ajedrez, *f*
chest /tʃɛst/ *n* arca, *f,* cofre, *m;* cajón, *m; Anat.* pecho, *m.* **to throw out one's c.,** inflar el pecho. **c.-expander,** extensor, *m.* **c. of drawers,** cómoda, *f*
chested /ˈtʃɛstɪd/ *a* (in compounds) de pecho...
chestnut /ˈtʃɛsˌnʌt/ *n* (tree) castaño, *m;* (fruit) castaña, *f;* (color) castaño, color castaño, *m;* (horse) caballo castaño, *m;* (joke) chiste del tiempo de Maricastaña, *m, a* castaño. **horse-c. tree,** castaño de Indias, *m*
chevron /ˈʃɛvrən/ *n Herald.* cabrio, *m;* (*Mil.* etc.) sardineta, *f*
chew /tʃu/ *vt* mascar, mascullar; (ponder) masticar
chewing /ˈtʃuɪŋ/ *n* masticación, *f.* **c.-gum,** chicle, *m*
chianti /kiˈanti/ *n* (wine) quianti, *m*
chiaroscuro /kiˌɑrəˈskyʊrou/ *n* claroscuro, *m*
chic /ʃik/ *n* chic, *m,* elegancia, *f*
chicanery /ʃɪˈkeinəri/ *n* sofistería, *f*
chicken /ˈtʃɪkən/ *n* pollo, *m.* **c.-hearted,** medroso, cobarde, timorato. **c.-pox,** varicela, *f*
chickenwire /ˈtʃɪkənˌwaiᵊr/ *n* alambrillo, *m*
chickpea /ˈtʃɪkˌpi/ *n* garbanzo, *m*
chickweed /ˈtʃɪkˌwid/ *n* pamplina, *f*
chicory /ˈtʃɪkəri/ *n* achicoria, *f*
chide /tʃaid/ *vt* reprender, reñir
chidingly /ˈtʃaidɪŋli/ *adv* en tono de reprensión
chief /tʃif/ *n* jefe, *m, a* principal; primero; en jefe; mayor. **c.-of-staff,** jefe de estado mayor, *m*
chiefly /ˈtʃifli/ *adv* principalmente; sobre todo
chieftain /ˈtʃiftən/ *n* caudillo, *m;* (of a clan) cabeza, jefe, *m*
chiffon /ʃɪˈfɒn/ *n* chifón, *m,* gasa, *f*
chiffonier /ˌʃɪfəˈnɪər/ *n* cómoda, *f*
chignon /ˈʃinyɒn/ *n* moño, *m*
chilblain /ˈtʃɪlblein/ *n* sabañón, *m*
child /tʃaild/ *n* niño (-ña); hijo (-ja). **from a c.,** desde niño, desde la niñez. **with c.,** encinta, embarazada. **How many children do you have?** ¿Cuántos hijos tiene Vd.? **child's play,** juegos infantiles, *m pl; Fig.* niñerías, *f pl.* **c. welfare,** puericultura, *f*
childbirth /ˈtʃaildˌbɜrθ/ *n* parto, *m*
childhood /ˈtʃaildhʊd/ *n* niñez, infancia, *f.* **from his c.,** desde su niñez, desde niño
childish /ˈtʃaildɪʃ/ *a* de niño; aniñado; pueril; fútil. **to grow c.,** chochear
childishly /ˈtʃaildɪʃli/ *adv* como un niño
childishness /ˈtʃaildɪʃnɪs/ *n* puerilidad, *f;* futilidad, *f*
child labor *n* trabajo de menores, trabajo infantil, *m*
childless /ˈtʃaildlɪs/ *a* sin hijos; sin niños
childlike /ˈtʃaildˌlaik/ *a* de niño, aniñado; pueril
children /ˈtʃɪldrən/ See **child**
Chilean /ˈtʃɪliən/ *a* and *n* chileno (-na)
chili /ˈtʃɪli/ *n* chile, pimento de cornetilla, *m*
chill /tʃɪl/ *n* frío, *m;* (of fear, etc.) estremecimiento, *m;* (illness) resfriado, *m;* (unfriendliness) frialdad, frigidez, *f, a* frío; (unfriendly) frígido. —*vt* enfriar; helar; (with fear, etc.) dar escalofríos (de); (discourage) desalentar. —*vi* tener frío; tener escalofríos. **to take the c. off,** templar, calentar un poco
chilliness /ˈtʃɪlinɪs/ *n* frío, *m;* (unfriendliness) frialdad, frigidez, *f*
chilly /ˈtʃɪli/ *a* frío; (sensitive to cold) friolero; (of politeness, etc.) glacial, frígido
chime /tʃaim/ *n* juego de campanas, *m;* repique, campaneo, *m;* armonía, *f.* —*vi* (of bells) repicar; *Fig.* armonizar. **to c. the hour,** dar la hora
chimera /kɪˈmɪərə/ *n* quimera, *f*
chimerical /kɪˈmɛrɪkəl/ *a* quimérico
chimney /ˈtʃɪmni/ *n* chimenea, *f;* (of a lamp) tubo (de lámpara), *m.* **c.-corner,** rincón de chimenea, *m.* **c.-pot,** sombrerete de chimenea, *m.* **c.-stack,** chimenea, *f.* **c.-sweep,** limpiador de chimeneas, deshollinador, *m*
chimpanzee /ˌtʃɪmpænˈzi, tʃɪmˈpænzi/ *n* chimpancé, *m*
chin /tʃɪn/ *n* barbilla, barba, *f,* mentón, *m.* **c.-rest,** mentonera, *f.* **c.-strap,** barboquejo, *m;* venda para la barbilla, *f*
china /ˈtʃainə/ *n* china, porcelana, *f;* loza, *f.* —*a* de porcelana; de loza. **c. cabinet,** chinero, *m*
chinchilla /tʃɪnˈtʃɪlə/ *n* (animal and fur) chinchilla, *f*
Chinese /tʃaiˈniz/ *a* and *n* chino (-na); (language) chino, *m.* **C. lantern,** farolillo de papel, *m.* **C. white,** óxido blanco de cinc, *m*
chink /tʃɪŋk/ *n* resquicio, *m,* grieta, hendidura, *f;* (clink) retintín, tintineo, *m.* —*vi* tintinar
chintz /tʃɪnts/ *n* zaraza, *f*
chip /tʃɪp/ *n* astilla, *f;* (counter) ficha, *f.* —*vt* picar; cincelar. **a c. off the old block,** de tal palo tal astilla. **c. potatoes,** patatas fritas, *f pl*
chiromancy /ˈkairəˌmænsi/ *n* quiromancia, *f*
chiropodist /kɪˈrɒpədɪst/ *n* pedicuro, *m,* callista, *mf*
chiropody /kɪˈrɒpədi/ *n* pedicura, *f*
chiropractor /ˈkairəˌpræktər/ *n* quiropráctico, *m*
chirp /tʃɜrp/ *vi* piar, gorjear. —*n* pío, gorjeo, *m*
chirping /ˈtʃɜrpɪŋ/ *n* pïada, *f, a* gárrulo, piante

chisel /'tʃɪzəl/ *n* escoplo, cincel, *m*, *vt* cincelar. **cold c.,** cortafrío, *m*

chitchat /'tʃɪt,tʃæt/ *n* charla, *f*

chitterlings /'tʃɪtlɪnz/ *n* asadura, *f*

chivalrous /'ʃɪvəlrəs/ *a* caballeroso

chivalry /'ʃɪvəlri/ *n* caballería, *f;* caballerosidad, *f.* **novel of c.,** novela de caballería, *f*

chive /tʃaiv/ *n Bot.* cebollana, *f*, cebollino, *m*

chloral /'klɔrəl/ *n* cloral, *m*

chlorate /'klɔreit/ *n* clorato, *m*

chloride /'klɔraid/ *n* cloruro, *m*

chlorine /'klɔrin/ *n* cloro, *m*

chloroform /'klɔrə,fɔrm/ *n* cloroformo, *m*, *vt* cloroformizar

chlorophyll /'klɔrəfɪl/ *n* clorófila, *f*

chock-full /'tʃɒk 'fʊl/ *a* lleno de bote en bote

chocolate /'tʃɔkəlɪt/ *n* chocolate, *m*, *a* de chocolate. **thick drinking-c.,** chocolate a la española, *m.* **thin drinking-c.,** chocolate a la francesa, *m.* **c. shop,** chocolatería, *f*

choice /tʃɔis/ *n* selección, *f;* preferencia, *f;* elección, *f;* opción, *f;* alternativa, *f;* lo más escogido. —*a* escogido, selecto; excelente. **for c.,** con preferencia

choir /kwaiᵊr/ *n* coro, *m.* **c.-boy,** niño del coro, *m.* **c.-master,** maestro de capilla, *m*

choke /tʃouk/ *vi* ahogarse; atragantarse; obstruirse. —*vt* ahogar; estrangular. **to c. with laughter,** ahogarse de risa. **to c. back,** (words) tragar. **to c. off,** (a person) disuadir (de); quitarse de encima(a). **to c. up,** obstruir, cerrar, obturar; (hide) cubrir, tapar

choking /'tʃoukɪŋ/ *a* asfixiante, sofocante. —*n* ahogamiento, *m*, sofocación, *f*

cholera /'kɒlərə/ *n* cólera, *m*

choleric /'kɒlərɪk/ *a* colérico

cholesterol /kə'lɛstə,roul/ *n* colesterina, *f*

choline /'koulin/ *n* colina, *f*

choose /tʃuz/ *vt* escoger; elegir; optar por; (wish) querer, gustar. **They will do it when they c.,** Lo harán cuando les parezca bien. **If you c.,** Si Vd. quiere; Si Vd. gusta. **He was chosen as Mayor,** Fue elegido alcalde. **There is nothing to c. between them,** No hay diferencia entre ellos; Tanto vale el uno como el otro. **You cannot c. but love her,** No puedes menos de quererla

choosing /'tʃuzɪŋ/ *n* selección, *f;* (for an office, etc.) elección, *f*

chop /tʃɒp/ *vt* cortar; (mince) picar; (split) hender, partir. —*n* (meat) chuleta, *f;* (jaw) quijada, *f.* **to c. about, round,** (of the wind) girar, virar. **to c. down,** (trees) talar. **to c. off,** separar; cortar; tajar. **to c. up,** cortar en pedazos

chopper /'tʃɒpər/ *n* hacha, *f*

choppy /'tʃɒpi/ *a* picado, agitado

chopstick /'tʃɒp,stɪk/ *n* palillo chino, *m*

choragus /kə'reigəs/ *n* corega, corego, *m*

choral /'kɔrəl/ *a* coral

chord /kɔrd/ *n* cuerda, *f; Mus.* acorde, *m;* **the right c.,** *Fig.* la cuerda sensible

choreographer /,kɔri'ɒgrəfər/ *n* coreógrafo, *m*

choreographic /,kɔriə'græfɪk/ *a* coreográfico

choreography /,kɔri'ɒgrəfi, ,kour-/ *n* coreografía, *f*

chorister /'kɔrəstər/ *n* corista, *m*

chorus /'kɔrəs/ *n* coro, *m;* (in revues) comparsa, *f*, acompañamiento, *m;* (of a song) refrán, *m.* **to sing in c.,** cantar a coro. **c. girl,** corista, *f*

chosen /'tʃouzən/ *a* escogido; elegido. **the c.,** los elegidos

chrestomathy /krɛs'tɒməθi/ *n* crestomatía, *f*

Christ /kraist/ *n* Cristo, Jesucristo, *m*

christen /'krɪsən/ *vt* bautizar

Christendom /'krɪsəndəm/ *n* cristianismo, *m*, cristiandad, *f*

christening /'krɪsənɪŋ/ *n* bautizo, *m*, *a* bautismal, de bautizo

Christian /'krɪstʃən/ *a* cristiano. —*n* cristiano (-na). **C. name,** nombre de pila, *m*

Christianity /,krɪstʃi'ænɪti/ *n* cristianismo, *m*

Christmas /'krɪsməs/ *n* Navidad, *f.* **A Merry C.!** ¡Felices Pascuas (de Navidad)! **Father C.,** Padre Noel, *m;* (Sp. equivalent) Los Reyes Magos. **C. box,** regalo de Navidad, *m.* **C. card,** felicitación de Navidad, *f.* **C. carol,** villancico de Navidad, *m.* **C. Day,** día de Navidad, *m.* **C. Eve,** Nochebuena, *f.* **C.-tide,** Navidades, *f pl.* **C. tree,** árbol de Navidad, *m*

Christopher Columbus /'krɪstəfər kə'lʌmbəs/ Cristóbal Colón, *m*

chromate /'kroumeit/ *n* cromato, *m*

chromatic /krou'mætɪk/ *a* cromático

chrome /kroum/ *n* cromo, *m.* **c. yellow,** amarillo de cromo, *m*

chromic /'kroumɪk/ *a* crómico

chromium /'kroumiəm/ *n* cromo, *m.* **c.-plated,** cromado

chromosome /'kroumə,soum/ *n* cromosoma, *m*

chronic /'krɒnɪk/ *a* crónico; inveterado

chronicle /'krɒnɪkəl/ *n* crónica, *f*, *vt* narrar

chronicler /'krɒnɪklər/ *n* cronista, *mf*

chronological /,krɒnl'ɒdʒɪkəl/ *a* cronológico. **in c. order,** por orden cronológico

chronology /krə'nɒlədʒi/ *n* cronología, *f*

chronometer /krə'nɒmɪtər/ *n* cronómetro, *m*

chrysalis /'krɪsəlɪs/ *n* crisálida, *f*

chrysanthemum /krɪ'sænθəməm/ *n* crisantemo, *m*

chubbiness /'tʃʌbinɪs/ *n* gordura, *f*

chubby /'tʃʌbi/ *a* regordete, gordito. **c.-cheeked,** mofletudo

chuck /tʃʌk/ *vt* (throw) lanzar, arrojar; (discontinue) abandonar, dejar. —*n* (in a lathe) mandril, *m.* **to c. under the chin,** acariciar la barbilla (a). **to c. away,** derrochar; malgastar, perder. **to c. out,** echar, poner en la calle

chuckle /'tʃʌkəl/ *vi* reír entre dientes. —*n* risa ahogada, *f;* risita, *f*

chum /tʃʌm/ *n* compinche, camarada, *mf.* **to c. up with,** ser camarada de

chunk /tʃʌŋk/ *n* pedazo, trozo, *m*

church /tʃɜrtʃ/ *n* iglesia, *f;* (Protestant) templo, *m*, *vt* (a woman) purificar. **poor as a c. mouse,** más pobre que las ratas. **the C. of England,** la iglesia anglicana. **to go to c.,** ir a misa; ir al templo. **c. music,** música sagrada, *f*

churchyard /'tʃɜrtʃ,yɑrd/ *n* cementerio, *m*

churl /tʃɜrl/ *n* patán, *m*

churlish /'tʃɜrlɪʃ/ *a* grosero, cazurro; (mean) tacaño, ruin

churn /tʃɜrn/ *n* mantequera, *f.* —*vt* (cream) batir; *Fig.* azotar, agitar

chute /ʃut/ *n* (for grain, etc.) manga de tolva, *f;* vertedor, *m;* (in flats and fun fairs) tobogán, deslizadero, *m*

ciborium /sɪ'bɔriəm/ *n* (chalice) copón, *m;* (tabernacle) sagrario, *m; Archit.* ciborio, *m*

cicada /sɪ'keidə/ *n* cigarra, *f*

cicatrice /'sɪkətrɪs/ *n* cicatriz, *f*

cicatrization /,sɪkətrə'zeiʃən/ *n* cicatrización, *f*

cicatrize /'sɪkə,traiz/ *vt* cicatrizar. —*vi* cicatrizarse

cider /'saidər/ *n* sidra, *f*

cigar /sɪ'gɑr/ *n* cigarro, *m.* **c.-box,** cigarrera, *f.* **c.-case,** petaca, cigarrera, *f.* **c.-cutter,** corta-puros, *m*

cigarette /,sɪgə'rɛt/ *n* cigarrillo, pitillo, *m.* **c.-butt,** colilla, *f.* **c.-case,** pitillera, *f.* **c.-holder,** boquilla, *f.* **c.-lighter,** encendedor de cigarrillos, *m.* **c.-paper,** papel de fumar, *m*

cinch /sɪntʃ/ *n* (of a saddle) cincha, *f; Inf.* ganga, *f; Inf.* seguridad, *f.* **c.-strap,** látigo, *m*

cinchona /sɪŋ'kounə/ *n* quina, cinchona, *f*

cinder /'sɪndər/ *n* ceniza, *f;* carbonilla, *f.* **red-hot c.,** rescoldo, *m.* **c.-track,** pista de ceniza, *f*

cinema /'sɪnəmə/ *n* cine, cinematógrafo, *m*

cinematographic /,sɪnə,mætə'græfɪk/ *a* cinematográfico

cinematography /,sɪnəmə'tɒgrəfi/ *n* cinematografía, *f*

cinemogul /,sɪnə'mougəl/ *n* magnate del cine, *mf*

cinnamon /'sɪnəmən/ *n* (spice) canela, *f;* (tree) canelo, *m;* color de canela, *m*

cipher /'saifər/ *n Math.* cero, *m; Fig.* nulidad, *f;* (code) cifra, *f;* monograma, *m.* **to be a mere c.,** ser un cero

Circassian /sər'kæʃən/ *a* circasiano. —*n* circasiano (-na)

circle /'sɜrkəl/ *n* círculo, *m;* (revolution) vuelta, *f;*

(group) grupo; *m;* (club, etc.) centro, *m;* (cycle) ciclo, *m.* —*vt* dar vueltas alrededor de; rodear; ceñir; (on an application, examination, etc.) encerrar en un círculo. —*vi* dar vueltas; (aircraft) volar en círculo; (of a hawk, etc.) cernerse. **dress-c.,** *Theat.* anfiteatro, *m.* **the family c.,** el círculo de la familia. **to come full c.,** dar la vuelta. **upper c.,** *Theat.* segundo piso, *m.* **vicious c.,** círculo vicioso, *m*

circlet /'sɜrklɪt/ *n* (of flowers, etc.) corona, *f;* (ring) anillo, *m*

circuit /'sɜrkɪt/ *n* circuito, *m;* (tour) gira, *f;* (revolution) vuelta, *f;* (radius) radio, *m.* **short c.,** corto circuito, *m.* **c.-breaker,** corta-circuitos, *m*

circuit court of appeals *n* tribunal colegial de circuito, *m*

circuitous /sər'kyuɪtəs/ *a* indirecto; tortuoso

circuitously /sər'kyuɪtəsli/ *adv* indirectamente

circular /'sɜrkyələr/ *a* circular; redondo. —*n* carta circular, *f;* circular, *f.* **c. tour,** viaje redondo, *m*

circularize /'sɜrkyələ,raiz/ *vt* enviar circulares (a)

circulate /'sɜrkyə,leit/ *vi* circular. —*vt* hacer circular; poner en circulación; (news, etc.) divulgar, diseminar

circulating library /'sɜrkyə,leitɪŋ/ *n* biblioteca por subscripción, *f*

circulation /,sɜrkyə'leiʃən/ *n* circulación, *f;* (of a newspaper, etc.) tirada, circulación, *f.* **c. of the blood,** circulación de la sangre, *f*

circulatory /'sɜrkyələ,tɔri/ *a* circulatorio

circumcise /'sɜrkəm,saiz/ *vt* circuncidar

circumcised /'sɜrkəm,saizd/ *a* circunciso

circumcision /,sɜrkəm'sɪʒən/ *n* circuncisión, *f*

circumference /sər'kʌmfərəns/ *n* circunferencia, *f*

circumflex /'sɜrkəm,flɛks/ *a* circunflejo. **c. accent,** acento circunflejo, *m,* (informal) capucha, *f*

circumlocution /,sɜrkəmlou'kyuʃən/ *n* circumlocución, *f*

circumnavigate /,sɜrkəm'nævɪ,geit/ *vt* circunnavegar

circumnavigation /'sɜrkəm,nævə'geiʃən/ *n* circunnavegación, *f*

circumscribe /'sɜrkəm,skraib/ *vt* circunscribir; *Fig.* limitar

circumscribed /'sɜrkəm,skraibd/ *a* circunscripto; *Fig.* limitado

circumscription /,sɜrkəm'skrɪpʃən/ *n* circunscripción, *f; Fig.* limitación, restricción, *f*

circumspect /'sɜrkəm,spɛkt/ *a* circunspecto; discreto, correcto; prudente

circumspection /,sɜrkəm'spɛkʃən/ *n* circunspección, *f;* prudencia, *f*

circumspectly /'sɜrkəm,spɛktli/ *adv* con circunspección; prudentemente

circumstance /'sɜrkəm,stæns/ *n* circunstancia, *f;* detalle, *m.* **aggravating c.,** circunstancia agravante, *f.* **attenuating c.,** circunstancia atenuante, *f.* **in the circumstances,** en las circunstancias. **in easy circumstances,** en buena posición, acomodado. **Do you know what his circumstances are?** ¿Sabes cuál es su situación económica? **under the circumstances,** bajo las circunstancias

circumstantial /,sɜrkəm'stænʃəl/ *a* circunstancial; detallado. **c. evidence,** prueba de indicios, *f*

circumvent /,sɜrkəm'vɛnt/ *vt* frustrar; impedir

circumvention /,sɜrkəm'vɛnʃən/ *n* frustración, *f*

circumvolution /,sɜrkəmvə'luʃən/ *n* circunvolución, *f*

circus /'sɜrkəs/ *n* circo, *m;* plaza redonda, *f;* (traffic) redondel, *m*

cirrhosis /sɪ'rousɪs/ *n* cirrosis, *f*

cirrus /'sɪrəs/ *n* (all meanings) cirro, *m*

cistern /'sɪstərn/ *n* tanque, *m;* cisterna, *f,* aljibe, *m*

citadel /'sɪtədl̩/ *n* ciudadela, *f*

citation /sai'teiʃən/ *n Law.* citación, *f;* cita, *f*

citation dictionary *n* diccionario de autoridades, *m*

cite /sait/ *vt* citar

citizen /'sɪtəzən/ *n* ciudadano (-na); vecino (-na); natural, *mf.* **fellow c.,** conciudadano, *m;* compatriota, *mf*

citizenship /'sɪtəzən,ʃɪp/ *n* ciudadanía, *f*

citrate /'sɪtreit/ *n* citrato, *m*

citric /'sɪtrɪk/ *a* cítrico

citrine /'sɪtrin/ *a* cetrino

citron /'sɪtrən/ *n* (fruit) cidra, *f;* (tree) cidro, *m*

city /'sɪti/ *n* ciudad, *f, a* municipal

city-state /'sɪti,steit/ *n* ciudad-estado, *f,* (plural: ciudades-estado)

civet /'sɪvɪt/ *n* algalia, *f*

civic /'sɪvɪk/ *a* cívico; municipal

civics /'sɪvɪks/ *n* civismo, *m*

civil /'sɪvəl/ *a* civil; doméstico; (polite) cortés, atento; (obliging) servicial. **C. Aeronautics Board,** Dirección general de aeronáutica civil, *f.* **c. defense,** defensa pasiva, *f.* **c. engineer,** ingeniero de caminos, canales y puertos, *m.* **C. Service,** cuerpo de empleados del Estado, *m*

civilian /sɪ'vɪlyən/ *a* civil. —*n* ciudadano (-na). **c. dress,** traje paisano, *m*

civility /sɪ'vɪlɪti/ *n* civilidad, cortesía, *f*

civilization /,sɪvələ'zeiʃən/ *n* civilización, *f*

civilize /'sɪvə,laiz/ *vt* civilizar

civilized /'sɪvə,laizd/ *a* civilizado

civilizing /'sɪvə,laizɪŋ/ *a* civilizador

civilly /'sɪvəli/ *adv* civilmente, cortésmente

clack /klæk/ *n* golpeo, ruido sordo, *m*

clad /klæd/ *a* vestido

claim /kleim/ *vt* reclamar; pretender exigir; *Law.* demandar; (assert) afirmar. —*vi Law.* pedir en juicio. —*n* reclamación, *f;* pretensión, *f; Law.* demanda, *f;* (in a gold-field, etc.) concesión, *f;* (right) derecho, *m.* **to lay c. to,** pretender a; exigir. **to put in a c. for,** reclamar

claimant /'kleimənt/ *n Law.* demandante, *mf;* pretendiente (-ta); *Com.* acreedor (-ra)

clairvoyance /klɛər'vɔiəns/ *n* doble vista, *f*

clairvoyant /klɛər'vɔiənt/ *n* vidente, *m*

clam /klæm/ *n* almeja, chirla, *f*

clamber /'klæmbər/ *vi* trepar, encaramarse. —*n* subida difícil, *f*

clamminess /'klæminɪs/ *n* viscosidad, humedad, *f*

clammy /'klæmi/ *a* viscoso; húmedo, mojado

clamor /'klæmər/ *n* clamor, estruendo, *m;* gritería, vocería, *f.* —*vi* gritar, vociferar. **to c. against,** protestar contra. **to c. for,** pedir a voces

clamorous /'klæmərəs/ *a* clamoroso, ruidoso, estrepitoso

clamp /klæmp/ *n* grapa, *f;* abrazadera, *f;* tornillo, *m;* (pile) montón, *m.* —*vt* empalmar; sujetar, lañar

clan /klæn/ *n* clan, *m;* familia, *f;* partido, grupo, *m*

clandestine /klæn'dɛstɪn/ *a* clandestino, furtivo

clandestinely /klæn'dɛstɪnli/ *adv* en secreto, clandestinamente

clang /klæŋ/ *vi* sonar; (of a gate, etc.) rechinar. —*vt* hacer sonar. —*n* sonido metálico, *m;* estruendo, *m*

clank /klæŋk/ *vi* dar un ruido metálico; crujir. —*vt* hacer sonar; (glasses) hacer chocar. —*n* ruido metálico, *m;* el crujir

clannish /'klænɪʃ/ *a* exclusivista

clansman /'klænzmən/ *n* miembro de un clan, *m*

clap /klæp/ *vt* (hands) batir; (spurs, etc.) poner rápidamente; (one's hat on) encasquetarse (el sombrero); (shut) cerrar apresuradamente. —*vi* aplaudir. —*n* (of the hands) palmada, *f;* (of thunder) trueno, *m;* (noise) ruido, *m.* **to c. eyes on,** echar la vista encima de. **to c. someone on the back,** dar una palmada en la espalda (a). **to c. the hands,** batir las palmas

clapper /'klæpər/ *n* (of a bell) badajo, *m*

clapping /'klæpɪŋ/ *n* aplausos, *m pl*

claque /klæk/ *n* claque, *f*

claret /'klærɪt/ *n* clarete, *m*

clarification /,klærəfə'keiʃən/ *n* clarificación, *f;* elucidación, *f*

clarify /'klærə,fai/ *vt* clarificar; elucidar, aclarar

clarinet /,klærə'nɛt/ *n* clarinete, *m*

clarinettist /,klærə'nɛtɪst/ *n* clarinete, *m*

clarion /'klæriən/ *n* clarín, *m*

clarity /'klærɪti/ *n* claridad, *f;* lucidez, *f*

clash /klæʃ/ *vi* chocar; encontrarse; (of events) coincidir; (of opinions, etc.) oponerse, estar en desacuerdo; (of colors) desentonar, chocar. —*n* estruendo, fragor, *m;* choque, *m; Mil.* encuentro, *m;* (of opinions, etc.) desacuerdo, *m;* disputa, *f*

clasp /klæsp/ *vt* (a brooch, etc.) abrochar, enganchar; (embrace) abrazar; (of plants, etc.) ceñir. —*n* (brooch) broche, *m;* (of a belt) hebilla, *f;* (of a necklace, handbag, book) cierre, *m;* (for the hair) pasador, *m.* **to c. someone in one's arms,** tomar en los brazos (a), abrazar. **c.-knife,** navaja, *f*

class /klæs/ *n* clase, *f;* (kind) especie, *f;* (of exhibits, etc.) categoría, *f.* —*vt* clasificar. **in a c. by itself,** único en su línea. **the lower classes,** las clases bajas. **the middle classes,** la clase media. **the upper classes,** la clase alta. **c.-mate,** condiscípulo (-la). **c.-room,** sala de clase, *f,* salón de clase, *f.* **c. war,** lucha de clases, *f*

classic /'klæsɪk/ *a* clásico. —*n* clásico, *m*

classical /'klæsɪkəl/ *a* clásico

classicism /'klæsə,sɪzəm/ *n* clasicismo, *m*

classicist /'klæsəsɪst/ *a* and *n* clasicista, *mf*

classifiable /'klæsə,faiəbəl/ *a* clasificable

classification /,klæsəfɪ'keiʃən/ *n* clasificación, *f*

classified /'klæsə,faid/ *a* (secreto) reservado, secreto; (advertisement) por palabras

classified advertisement *n* anuncio por palabras, *m*

classify /'klæsə,fai/ *vt* clasificar

clatter /'klætər/ *vi* hacer ruido; (knock) golpear; (of loose horseshoes) chacolotear. —*vt* hacer ruido con; chocar (una cosa contra otra). —*n* ruido, *m;* (hammering) martilleo, *m;* (of horseshoes) chacoloteo, *m;* (of a crowd) estruendo, *m,* bulla, *f.* **John clattered along the street,** Los pasos de Juan resonaban por la calle

clause /klɔz/ *n Gram.* cláusula, *f; Law.* condición, estipulación, cláusula, *f*

claustrophobia /,klɔstrə'foubiə/ *n* claustrofobia, *f*

clavichord /'klævɪ,kɔrd/ *n* clavicordio, *m*

clavicle /'klævɪkəl/ *n* clavícula, *f*

claw /klɔ/ *n* garra, *f;* (of a lobster, etc.) tenaza, *f;* (hook) garfio, gancho, *m.* —*vt* arañar, clavar las uñas en; (tear) desgarrar. **c.-hammer,** martillo de orejas, *m*

clay /klei/ *n* arcilla, *f;* barro, *m;* (pipe) pipa de barro, *f.* **c.-pit,** barrizal, *m*

clayey /'kleii/ *a* arcilloso

clean /klin/ *a* limpio; puro, casto. —*adv* limpio; completamente; exactamente. **to make a c. sweep (of),** no dejar títere con cabeza. **to make a c. breast of,** confesar sin tormento, no quedarse con nada en el pecho. **to show a c. pair of heels,** tomar las de Villadiego. **c. bill of health,** patente de sanidad, *m.* **c.-cut,** bien definido; claro. **c.-limbed,** bien proporcionado, gallardo. **c.-shaven,** lampiño; sin barba, bien afeitado

clean /klin/ *vt* limpiar; (streets) barrer; (a floor) fregar; (dryclean) lavar al seco. **to c. one's hands (teeth),** limpiarse las manos (los dientes). **to c. up,** limpiar; (tidy) asear; poner en orden

cleaner /'klinər/ *n* limpiador (-ra); (charwoman) fregona, *f;* (stain remover) sacamanchas, *m;* (drycleaner, person) tintorero (-ra)

cleaning /'klinɪŋ/ *n* limpieza, *f, a* de limpiar. **dry-c.,** lavado al seco, *m.* **c. rag,** trapo de limpiar, *m*

cleanliness /'klɛnlinɪs/ *n* limpieza, *f;* aseo, *m*

cleanness /'klinnɪs/ *n* limpieza, *f;* aseo, *m;* pureza, *f*

cleanse /klɛnz/ *vt* limpiar; lavar; purgar; purificar

cleansing /'klɛnzɪŋ/ *n* limpieza, *f;* lavamiento, *m;* purgación, *f;* purificación, *f*

clear /klɪər/ *a* claro; (of the sky) sereno, despejado; transparente; (free (from)) libre (de); (open) abierto; (of profit, etc.) neto; (of thoughts, etc.) lúcido; (apparent) evidente; explícito; (of images) distinto; absoluto; (whole) entero, completo. **c. majority,** mayoría absoluta, *f.* **c. profit,** beneficio neto, *m.* **c.-cut,** bien definido. **c.-headed,** perspicaz; inteligente. **c.-sighted,** clarividente

clear /klɪər/ *vt* aclarar; despejar; limpiar; librar (de); quitar; (one's throat) carraspear; (*Com.* stock) liquidar; (of a charge) absolver; (one's character) vindicar; (avoid, miss) evitar; (jump) salvar, saltar; (a court, etc.) desocupar; (a debt) satisfacer; (an account) saldar; (a mortgage) cancelar; (win) ganar; hacer un beneficio de; (through customs) despachar en la aduana. —*vi* (of sky, etc.) serenarse; escampar; (of wine, etc.) aclararse; despacharse en la aduana. **to c. the table,** levantar la mesa, levantar los manteles. **to c. the way,** abrir calle; *Fig.* abrir paso. **to c. away,** *vt* quitar; disipar. —*vi* disiparse. **to c. off,** *vt* (finish) terminar; (debts) pagar; (discharge) despedir. —*vi* (of rain) despejarse, escampar; marcharse. **to c. out,** *vt* limpiar; (a drain, etc.) desatascar; vaciar; echar. —*vi* marcharse, escabullirse. **C. out!** ¡Fuera! **c. the decks,** hacer zafarrancho. **c. the decks for action,** hacer zafarrancho. **to c. up,** *vt* poner en orden; (a mystery, etc.) aclarar, resolver, *vi* (of weather) serenarse, escampar, despejarse

clearance /'klɪərəns/ *n* (of trees, etc.) desmonte, *m;* eliminación, *f;* expulsión, *f; Mech.* espacio muerto, *m;* despacho de aduana, *m.* **to make a c. of,** deshacerse de. **c. sale,** liquidación, venta de saldos, *f*

clearing /'klɪərɪŋ/ *n* (in a wood) claro, *m;* desmonte, *m;* (*Com.* of goods) liquidación, *f;* (of one's character) vindicación, *f.* **c.-house,** casa de compensación, *f*

clearly /'klɪərli/ *adv* claramente

clearness /'klɪərnɪs/ *n* claridad, *f*

cleavage /'klivɪdʒ/ *n* hendimiento, *m;* (in views, etc.) escisión, *f*

cleave /kliv/ *vt* partir; abrir; (air, water, etc.) surcar, hender. —*vi* partirse; (stick) pegarse, adherirse

cleaver /'klivər/ *n* partidor, *m;* hacha, *f*

clef /klɛf/ *n* clave, *f.* **treble c.,** clave de sol, *f*

cleft /klɛft/ *n* hendedura, fisura, rendija, abertura, *f.* **c.-palate,** paladar hendido, *m*

clematis /'klɛmətɪs/ *n* clemátide, *f*

clemency /'klɛmənsi/ *n* (of weather) benignidad, *f;* (of character, etc.) clemencia, *f*

clement /'klɛmənt/ *a* (of weather) benigno; (of character, etc.) clemente, benévolo

clench /klɛntʃ/ *vt* agarrar; (teeth, etc.) apretar; (a bargain) cerrar, concluir

clergy /'klɜrdʒi/ *n* clero, *m,* clérigos, *m pl*

clergyman /'klɜrdʒimən/ *n* clérigo, *m*

cleric /'klɛrɪk/ *n* eclesiástico, *m*

clerical /'klɛrɪkəl/ *a* clerical; de oficina. **c. error,** error de oficina, *m.* **c. work,** trabajo de oficina, *m*

clericalism /'klɛrɪkə,lɪzəm/ *n* clericalismo, *m*

clerk /klɜrk/ *n* (clergyman) clérigo, *m;* (in an office) oficinista, escribiente, *m;* oficial, *m;* secretario, *m*

clerkship /'klɜrkʃɪp/ *n* puesto de oficinista, *m;* escribanía, *f;* secretaría, *f*

clever /'klɛvər/ *a* listo, inteligente; ingenioso; hábil; (dexterous) diestro

cleverly /'klɛvərli/ *adv* hábilmente; diestramente, con destreza

cleverness /'klɛvərnɪs/ *n* talento, *m;* inteligencia, *f;* habilidad, *f;* (dexterity) destreza, *f*

cliché /kli'ʃei/ *n* frase hecha, frase de cajón, *f*

click /klɪk/ *vi* (of the tongue) dar un chasquido; (of a bolt, etc.) cerrarse a golpe; hacer tictac. —*vt* (one's tongue) chascar; (a bolt, etc.) cerrar a golpe. —*n* golpe seco, *m;* tictac, *m;* (of the tongue) chasquido, *m.* **to c. one's heels together,** hacer chocar los talones

client /'klaiənt/ *n* cliente, *mf;* (customer) parroquiano (-na)

clientele /,klaiən'tɛl/ *n* clientela, *f*

cliff /klɪf/ *n* acantilado, *m,* roca, escarpa, *f*

cliff dweller *n* hombre de la roca, hombre de las rocas, *m,* mujer de la roca, mujer de las rocas, *f*

climate /'klaimɪt/ *n* clima, *m*

climatic /klai'mætɪk/ *a* climático

climatology /,klaimə'tɒlədʒi/ *n* climatología, *f*

climax /'klaimæks/ *n* culminación, *f;* (rhetoric) clímax, *m;* gradación, *f;* punto más alto, apogeo, cenit, *m;* (of a play, etc.) desenlace, *m*

climb /klaim/ *vt* and *vi* trepar; escalar; montar; subir; ascender. **rate of c.,** *Aer.* velocidad ascensional, *f.* **to c. down,** bajar; *Fig.* echar el pie atrás. **to c. over,** (obstacles) salvar. **to c. up,** encaramarse por; subir por; montar

climber /'klaimər/ *n* alpinista, *mf;* (plant) trepadera, enredadera, *f;* (social) arribista, *mf*

clime /klaim/ *n* clima, *m*

clinch /klɪntʃ/ *vt* (nails, etc.) remachar, rebotar; (a bargain, etc.) cerrar; (an argument, etc.) remachar. —*n* (wrestling) cuerpo a cuerpo, *m*

cling /klɪŋ/ *vi* pegarse (a); agarrarse (a); (of scents) pegarse; (follow) seguir. **They clung together for an instant,** Quedaron abrazados un instante

clinging /'klɪŋɪŋ/ *a* tenaz; (of plants, etc.) trepador; (of persons) manso, dócil. **to be a c. vine,** *Inf.* ser una malva

clinic /'klınık/ *n* clínica, *f*
clinical /'klınıkəl/ *a* clínico. **c. thermometer,** termómetro clínico, *m*
clink /klıŋk/ *vi* retiñir; (of glasses) chocarse. —*vt* hacer sonar; (glasses) chocar. —*n* retintín, *m;* (of a hammer) martilleo, *m;* sonido metálico, *m;* (of glasses) choque, *m*
clip /klıp/ *vt* (grasp) agarrar; (sheep, etc.) esquilar; (trim) recortar, cercenar; (prune) podar; (a ticket) taladrar. —*n* pinza, *f;* (paper-clip) sujetapapeles, *m; Mech.* grapa, escarpia, *f;* (for ornament) sujetador, *m.* **to c. a person's wings,** *Fig.* cortar (or quebrar) las alas (a)
clipper /'klıpər/ *n* (person) esquilador (-ra); (*Naut.* and *Aer.*) clíper, *m; pl* **clippers,** tenazas de cortar, *f pl;* (for pruning) podaderas, *f pl;* (punch) taladro, *m*
clipping /'klıpıŋ/ *n* (of sheep, etc.) esquileo, *m;* (of a newspaper, etc.) recorte, *m*
clique /klik/ *n* camarilla, *f*
cliquish /'klikıʃ/ *a* exclusivista
cloak /klouk/ *n* capa, *f;* manto, *m; Fig.* velo, *m.* —*vt* encapotar; embozar; (conceal) ocultar, encubrir. **c. and sword play,** comedia de capa y espada, *f.* **c.-room,** guardarropa, *m;* (ladies') tocador, *m;* (on a station) consigna, *f*
clock /klɒk/ *n* reloj, *m;* (of a stocking) cuadrado, *m.* **It is six o'clock,** Son las seis. **c.-face,** esfera de reloj, *f.* **c.-maker,** relojero, *m.* **c.-making,** relojería, *f.* **c.-work,** aparato de relojería, *m.* **to go like c.-work,** ir como un reloj. **c.-work train,** tren de cuerda, *m*
clockwise /'klɒk,waiz/ *a* and *adv* en el sentido de las agujas del reloj; de derecha a izquierda
clod /klɒd/ *n* (of earth) terrón, *m;* (corpse) tierra, *f;* (person) zoquete, *m.* **c.-hopper,** patán, *m*
clog /klɒg/ *n* (shoe) zueco, zoclo, *m;* (obstacle) estorbo, obstáculo, *m.* —*vt* embarazar; estorbar, impedir; (block) obturar, cerrar; *Fig.* paralizar
cloister /'klɔistər/ *n* claustro, *m;* convento, *m.* —*vt* enclaustrar
cloistered /'klɔistərd/ *a* enclaustrado; retirado, aislado
cloistered nun *n* monja de claustro, *f*
close /klous/ *a* estrecho; (of a prisoner) incomunicado; (reticent) reservado; (niggardly) tacaño, avaro; (scarce) escaso; (of friends) íntimo; (equal) igual; (lacking space) apretado; (dense) denso; (thick) tupido; compacto; (of a copy, etc.) fiel, exacto; (thorough) concienzudo; (careful) cuidadoso; (attentive) atento; (to the roots) a raíz; (of shaving) bueno; (of weather) pesado, sofocante; (of rooms) mal ventilado. **at c. quarters,** de cerca. **It is c. to eight o'clock,** Son casi las ocho. **to press c.,** perseguir de cerca; fatigar. **c. at hand, c. by,** cerca; al lado; a mano. **c.-cropped,** (of hair) al rape. **c. fight,** lucha igualada, *f.* **c.-fisted,** tacaño, apretado. **c.-fitting,** ajustado, ceñido al cuerpo; pequeño. **c. season,** veda, *f.* **c.-up,** *n* (cinema) primer plano, *m*
close /klouz/ *n* (end) fin, *m,* conclusión, *f;* (of day) caída, *f; Mus.* cadencia, *f;* (enclosure) cercado, *m;* (square) plazoleta, *f;* (alley) callejón, *m;* (of a cathedral) patio, *m.* **at the c. of day,** a la caída de la tarde. **to bring to a c.,** terminar; llevar a cabo. **to draw to a c.,** tocar a su fin; estar terminando
close /klouz/ *vt* cerrar; (end) concluir, terminar; poner fin a. —*vi* cerrar(se); (of a wound) cicatrizarse, cerrarse; (end) terminar(se), acabar, concluir. **to c. the ranks,** cerrar filas. **to c. about,** (surround) rodear, cercar; (envelop) envolver. **to c. down,** *vt* cerrar. —*vi* cerrar; *Radio.* cerrarse. **to c. in,** (surround) cercar; (of night) cerrar; caer; (envelop) envolver; (of length of days) acortarse. **to c. in on,** cercar. **to c. round,** envolver; (of water) tragar. **to c. up,** *vt* cerrar; cerrar completamente; obstruir. —*vi* (of persons) acercarse; (of a wound) cicatrizarse; cerrarse
closed /klouzd/ *a* cerrado. **"Road C.,"** Paso Cerrado. **to have a c. mind,** ser cerrado de mollera; sufrir de estrechez de miras
closely /'klousli/ *adv* estrechamente; de cerca; (carefully) cuidadosamente; (exactly) exactamente; (attentively) con atención, atentamente
closeness /'klousnıs/ *n* estrechez, *f;* densidad, *f;* (nearness) proximidad, *f;* (of a copy, etc.) fidelidad, exactitud, *f;* (stuffiness), falta de aire, *f;* (of friendship) intimidad, *f;* (stinginess) tacañería, *f;* (reserve) reserva.
closet /'klɒzıt/ *n* camarín, *m;* (cupboard) alacena, *f;* (water) excusado, *m*
closing /'klouzıŋ/ *n* cerramiento, *m;* (of an account) saldo, *m.* **c. time,** cierre, *m,* hora de cerrar, *f*
closure /'klouʒər/ *n* conclusión, *f; Polit.* clausura, *f*
clot /klɒt/ *n* coágulo, grumo, *m.* —*vt* coagular. —*vi* coagularse, cuajarse
cloth /klɔθ/ *n* tela, *f;* paño, *m;* (table) mantel, *m;* (clergy) clero, *m.* **She cleaned the books with a c.,** Ella limpió los libros con un paño. **in c.,** (of books) en tela
clothe /klouð/ *vt* vestir; cubrir; (with authority, etc.) revestir. **to c. oneself,** vestirse
clothes /klouz/ *n pl* vestidos, *m pl,* ropa, *f.* **a suit of c.,** un traje. **old c. shop,** ropavejería, *f.* **c.-basket,** cesta de la colada, *f.* **c.-brush,** cepillo para ropa, *m.* **c.-hanger,** percha, *f.* **c.-horse,** enjugador, *m.* **c.-line,** cuerda de la ropa, *f.* **c.-peg,** pinza de la ropa, *f.* **c.-prop,** palo para sostener la cuerda de la colada, *m*
clothier /'klouðiər/ *n* ropero, *m.* **clothier's shop,** ropería, *f*
clothing /'klouðıŋ/ *n* vestidos, *m pl,* ropa, *f.* **article of c.,** prenda de vestir, *f*
clotted /'klɒtıd/ *a* grumoso
cloud /klaud/ *n* nube, *f.* —*vt* anublar, oscurecer; empañar; (blot out) borrar. —*vi* anublarse. **to be under a c.,** estar bajo sospecha. **summer c.,** nube de verano, *f.* **storm-c.,** nubarrón, *m.* **c.-burst,** nubada, *f,* chaparrón, *m.* **c.-capped,** coronado de nubes
cloudiness /'klaudinıs/ *n* nebulosidad, *f;* obscuridad, *f;* (of liquids) turbiedad, *f*
cloudless /'klaudlıs/ *a* sin nubes, despejado; sereno, claro
cloudy /'klaudi/ *a* nublado, nubloso; obscuro; (of liquids) turbio
clove /klouv/ *n* clavo de especia, *m;* (of garlic) diente de ajo, *m.* **c.-tree,** clavero, *m*
cloven /'klouvən/ *a* hendido. **to show the c. hoof,** enseñar la oreja. **c. hoof,** pezuña, *f*
clover /'klouvər/ *n* trébol, *m.* **to be in c.,** nadar en la abundancia
clown /klaun/ *n* patán, *m;* bufón, tonto, *m;* (in a circus) payaso, *m.* —*vi* hacer el tonto, hacer el payaso
clowning /'klaunıŋ/ *n* payasada, *f*
clownish /'klaunıʃ/ *a* grosero; palurdo, zafio; bufón
cloy /klɔi/ *vt* empalagar
cloying /'klɔiıŋ/ *a* empalagoso
club /klʌb/ *n* porra, cachiporra, clava, *f;* (gymnastic) maza, *f;* (hockey) bastón de hockey, *m;* (golf) palo de golf, *m;* (in cards) basto, *m;* (social) club, *m.* —*vt* golpear. **to c. together,** asociarse, unirse. **We clubbed together to buy him a present,** Entre todos le compramos un regalo. **c.-house,** club, *m*
clubfoot /'klʌb,fʊt/ *n* pie calcáneo, pie contrahecho, pie de piña, pie equino, pie talo, pie zambo, *m*
clubman /'klʌb,mæn/ *n* miembro de un club, *m*
cluck /klʌk/ *vi* cloquear. —*n* cloqueo, *m*
clucking /'klʌkıŋ/ *n* cloqueo, *m*
clue /klu/ *n* indicio, *m;* (to a problem) clave, *f;* (of a crossword) indicación, *f;* idea, *f*
clump /klʌmp/ *n* bloque, pedazo, *m;* (of trees) grupo, *m;* (of feet) ruido, *m*
clumsily /'klʌmzəli/ *adv* torpemente; pesadamente
clumsiness /'klʌmzinıs/ *n* torpeza, *f;* falta de maña, *f;* pesadez, *f*
clumsy /'klʌmzi/ *a* torpe; desmañado; chapucero, sin arte; (lumbering) pesado; (in shape) disforme
cluster /'klʌstər/ *n* (of currants, etc.) racimo, *m;* (of flowers) ramillete, *m;* grupo, *m.* —*vi* arracimarse; agruparse. **They clustered round him,** Se agrupaban a su alrededor
clutch /klʌtʃ/ *vt* agarrar; sujetar, apretar. —*n Mech.* embrague, *m;* (of eggs) nidada, *f; Fig.* garras, *f pl.* **to fall into the clutches of,** caer en las garras de. **to make a c. at,** procurar agarrar. **to throw in the c.,** *Mech.* embragar. **to throw out the c.,** *Mech.* desembragar. **c. pedal,** pedal de embrague, *m*
clutter /'klʌtər/ *n* desorden, *m,* confusión, *f, vt* desordenar

coach /koutʃ/ *n* carroza, *f;* charabán, *m; Rail.* vagón, coche, *m;* (hackney) coche de alquiler, *m; Sports.* entrenador, *m;* (tutor) profesor particular, *m.* —*vt Sports.* entrenar; (teach) preparar, dar lecciones particulares (a). **through c.,** coche directo, *m.* **c.-box,** pescante, *m.* **c.-house,** cochera, *f*
coaching /ˈkoutʃɪŋ/ *n Sports.* entrenamiento, *m;* lecciones particulares, *f pl*
coachman /ˈkoutʃmən/ *n* cochero, *m*
coagulate /kouˈægyəˌleit/ *vi* coagularse. —*vt* coagular, cuajar
coagulation /kouˌægyəˈleiʃən/ *n* coagulación, *f*
coal /koul/ *n* carbón, *m;* pedazo de carbón, *m;* (burning) brasa, *f.* —*vi* carbonear, hacer carbón. —*vt* proveer de carbón; carbonear. **to carry coals to Newcastle,** llevar leña al monte, elevar aqua al mar. **to haul a person over the coals,** reprender a alguien. **c.-barge,** (barco) carbonero, *m.* **c.-black,** negro como el azabache. **c.-cellar, house,** carbonera, *f.* **c.-dust,** cisco, *m.* **c.-field,** yacimiento de carbón, *m.* **c.-gas,** gas de hulla, *m.* **c.-heaver,** cargador de carbón, *m.* **c.-merchant,** carbonero, *m.* **c.-mine,** mina de carbón, *f.* **c.-miner,** minero de carbón, *m.* **c.-scuttle,** carbonera, *f.* **c.-tar,** alquitrán mineral, *m*
coalesce /ˌkouəˈlɛs/ *vi* fundirse; unirse; incorporarse
coalescence /ˌkouəˈlɛsəns/ *n* fusión, *f;* unión, *f;* incorporación, *f*
coalition /ˌkouəˈlɪʃən/ *n* coalición, *f*
coarse /kɔrs/ *a* (in texture) basto, burdo; tosco; (gross) grosero; vulgar. **c.-grained,** de fibra gruesa; (of persons) vulgar, poco fino
coarsen /ˈkɔrsən/ *vt* (of persons) embrutecer. —*vi* embrutecerse; (of the skin) curtirse
coarseness /ˈkɔrsnɪs/ *n* basteza, *f;* tosquedad, *f;* (of persons) grosería, indelicadeza, *f;* vulgaridad, *f*
coast /koust/ *n* costa, *f;* litoral, *m.* —*vi* costear; deslizarse en un tobogán; dejar muerto el motor. **The c. is not clear,** Hay moros en la costa. **c.-guard,** guardacostas, *m.* **c.-line,** litoral, *m*
coastal /ˈkoustḷ/ *a* costanero, costero. **c. defences,** defensas costeras, *f pl*
coaster /ˈkoustər/ *n Naut.* barco costanero, barco de cabotaje, *m*
coasting /ˈkoustɪŋ/ *n Naut.* cabotaje, *m*
coat /kout/ *n* abrigo, *m;* gabán, *m;* chaqueta, *f;* (animal's) capa, *f;* (of paint) mano, *f.* —*vt* recubrir; (with paint, etc.) dar una mano de. **fur c.,** abrigo de pieles, *m.* **sports c.,** Americana sport, *f.* **c. of arms,** escudo de armas, *m.* **c. of mail,** cota de malla, *f.* **c.-hanger,** percha, *f*
coating /ˈkoutɪŋ/ *n* (of paint, etc.) capa, mano, *f*
co-author /ˌkouˈɔθər/ *n* coautor, *m*
coax /kouks/ *vt* instar; halagar; persuadir (a)
coaxing /ˈkouksɪŋ/ *n* ruegos, *m pl*; mimos, *m pl,* caricias, *f pl*; persuasión, *f.* —*a* mimoso, zalamero; persuasivo
cob /kɒb/ *n* (horse) jaca, *f;* (lump) pedazo, *m;* (swan) cisne macho, *m*
cobalt /ˈkoubɔlt/ *n* cobalto, *m.* **c. blue,** azul cobalto, *m*
cobble /ˈkɒbəl/ *n* (stone) guijarro, *m, vt* (with stones) empedrar con guijarros; (shoes) remendar
cobbler /ˈkɒblər/ *n* zapatero remendón, *m.* **cobbler's last,** horma, *f.* **cobbler's wax,** cerote, *m*
cobblestone /ˈkɒbəlˌstoun/ *n* guijarro, *m,* piedra, *f*
cobelligerent /ˌkoubəˈlɪdʒərənt/ *n* cobeligerante, *mf*
cobra /ˈkoubrə/ *n* cobra, serpiente de anteojos, *f*
cobweb /ˈkɒbˌwɛb/ *n* telaraña, *f*
cobwebby /ˈkɒbˌwɛbi/ *a* cubierto de telarañas; transparente; de gasa
cocaine /kouˈkein/ *n* cocaína, *f*
coccyx /ˈkɒksɪks/ *n* cóccix, *m, Inf.* rabadilla, *f*
cochlea /ˈkɒkliə/ *n* caracol (del oído), *m*
cock /kɒk/ *n* gallo, *m;* (male) macho, *m;* (tap) grifo, *m,* espita, *f;* (of a gun) martillo, *m;* (weather-vane) veleta, *f;* (of hay) montón, *m.* —*vt* (a gun) amartillar; (a hat) ladear; (raise) erguir, enderezar. **a cocked hat,** un sombrero de tres picos. **at half c.,** (of a gun) desamartillada *f.*. **He cocked his head,** Erguió la cabeza. **The dog cocked its ears,** El perro aguzó las orejas. **to c. one's eye at,** lanzar una mirada (a). **c.-a-doodle-doo,** quiquiriquí, *m.* **c.-a-hoop,** triunfante, jubiloso; arrogante. **c.-crow,** canto del gallo, *m.* **c.-fight,** riña de gallos, *f.* **c.-of-the-walk,** gallito, *m.* **c.-sure,** pagado de sí mismo; completamente convencido
cockerel /ˈkɒkərəl/ *n* gallo joven, gallito, *m*
cocker spaniel /ˌkɒkər ˈspænyəl/ *n* cóquer, *m*
cockle /ˈkɒkəl/ *n* (bivalve) bucarda, *f.* —*vi* arrugarse; (warp) torcerse; doblarse. **c.-shell,** (pilgrims') concha, *f;* (boat) cascarón de nuez, *m*
cockpit /ˈkɒkˌpɪt/ *n* gallería, *f; Aer.* casilla del piloto, *f; Fig.* arena, *f*
cockroach /ˈkɒkˌroutʃ/ *n* cucaracha, *f*
cockscomb /ˈkɒksˌkoum/ *n* cresta de gallo, *f*
cocktail /ˈkɒkˌteil/ *n* (drink) cótel, coctel, *m.* **to shake a c.,** mezclar un coctel. **c. party,** coctel *m.* **c. shaker,** cotelera, *f*
cocky /ˈkɒki/ *a* fatuo, presuntuoso
cocoa /ˈkoukou/ *n* cacao, *m*
coconut /ˈkoukəˌnʌt/ *n* coco, *m; Inf.* cabeza, *f.* **c. milk,** agua de coco, *f.* **c. shy,** pim, pam, pum, *m.* **c. tree,** cocotero, *m*
cocoon /kəˈkun/ *n* capullo, *m*
cod /kɒd/ *n* bacalao, *m.* **cod-liver oil,** aceite de hígado de bacalao, *m*
coddle /ˈkɒdḷ/ *vt* criar con mimo, mimar, consentir
code /koud/ *n* código, *m;* clave, *f;* (secret) cifra, *f.* —*vt* poner en cifra. **signal c.,** *Naut.* código de señales, *m.* **c. word,** palabra de clave, *f*
codeine /ˈkoudin/ *n* codeína, *f*
codex /ˈkoudɛks/ *n* códice, *m*
codicil /ˈkɒdəsəl/ *n* codicilio, *m*
codification /ˌkɒdəfɪˈkeiʃən/ *n* codificación, *f*
codify /ˈkɒdəˌfai/ *vt* codificar
coeducation /ˌkouɛdʒʊˈkeiʃən/ *n* coeducación, *f*
coefficient /ˌkouəˈfɪʃənt/ *n* coeficiente, *m*
coequality /ˌkouɪˈkwɒlɪti/ *n* coigualdad, *f*
coerce /kouˈɜrs/ *vt* forzar, obligar; constreñir
coercion /kouˈɜrʃən/ *n* coerción, coacción, *f*
coercive /kouˈɜrsɪv/ *a* coercitivo, coactivo
coeval /kouˈivəl/ *a* coevo
coexist /ˌkouɪgˈzɪst/ *vi* coexistir
coexistence /ˌkouɪgˈzɪstəns/ *n* coexistencia, *f*
coffee /ˈkɔfi/ *n* café, *m.* **black c.,** café solo, *m.* **white c.,** café con leche, *m.* **c.-bean,** grano de café, *m.* **c.-cup,** taza para café, *f.* **c.-house,** café, *m.* **c.-mill,** molinillo de café, *m.* **c.-plantation,** cafetal, *m.* **c.-pot,** cafetera, *f.* **c.-set,** juego de café, *m.* **c.-tree,** cafeto, *m*
coffer /ˈkɔfər/ *n* cofre, *m;* arca, caja, *f*
coffin /ˈkɔfɪn/ *n* ataúd, féretro, *m;* caja, *f*
cog /kɒg/ *n Mech.* diente (de rueda), *m*
cogency /ˈkoudʒənsi/ *n* fuerza, *f*
cogent /ˈkoudʒənt/ *a* convincente, fuerte; urgente
cogitate /ˈkɒdʒɪˌteit/ *vi* pensar, considerar, meditar
cogitation /ˌkɒdʒɪˈteiʃən/ *n* reflexión, meditación, consideración, *f*
cognac /ˈkounyæk/ *n* coñac, *m*
cognate /ˈkɒgneit/ *a* (of stock) consanguíneo; afín; análogo; semejante
cognition /kɒgˈnɪʃən/ *n* cognición, *f*
cognitive /ˈkɒgnɪtɪv/ *a* cognoscitivo
cognizance /ˈkɒgnəzəns/ *n* conocimiento, *m;* jurisdicción, *f*
cogwheel /ˈkɒgˌwil/ *n* rueda dentada, *f*
cohabit /kouˈhæbɪt/ *vi* cohabitar
cohabitation /kouˌhæbɪˈteiʃən/ *n* cohabitación, *f*
coheir /kouˈɛər/ *n* coheredero, *m*
coheiress /kouˈɛərɪs/ *n* coheredera, *f*
cohere /kouˈhɪər/ *vi* pegarse, adherirse; unirse
coherent /kouˈhɪərənt/ *a* coherente; consecuente
cohesion /kouˈhiʒən/ *n* cohesión, *f;* coherencia, *f*
cohort /ˈkouhɔrt/ *n* cohorte, *f*
coif /kwɑf/ *n* cofia, *f;* toca, *f*
coiffure /kwɑˈfyʊr/ *n* peinado, *m;* tocado, *m*
coil /kɔil/ *vt* arrollar; (*Naut.* of ropes) adujar. —*vi* arrollarse; enroscarse; serpentear. —*n* rollo, *m;* (of a serpent and ropes) anillo, *m;* (of hair) trenza, *f; Elec.* carrete, *m.* **coil of smoke,** nube de humo, *f.* **to c. up,** hacerse un ovillo
coiling /ˈkɔilɪŋ/ *n* arrollamiento, *m;* serpenteo, *m*
coin /kɔin/ *n* moneda, *f; Inf.* dinero, *m.* —*vt* acuñar;

(a new word) inventar. **to pay back in the same c.,** pagar en la misma moneda
coinage /'kɔinɪdʒ/ *n* acuñación, *f;* moneda, *f;* sistema monetario, *m;* invención, *f;* (new word) neologismo, *m*
coincide /ˌkouɪn'said/ *vi* coincidir (con); estar conforme, estar de acuerdo
coincidence /kou'ɪnsɪdəns/ *n* coincidencia, *f;* (chance) casualidad, *f*
coiner /'kɔinər/ *n* acuñador de moneda, *m;* monedero falso, *m;* (of phrases, etc.) inventor, *m*
coitus /'kouɪtəs/ *n* coito, *m*
coke /kouk/ *n* (carbón de) coque, *m*
colander /'kɒləndər/ *n* colador, *m*
cold /kould/ *a* frío. —*n* frío, *m; Med.* catarro, constipado, *m.* **I am c.,** Tengo frío. **It is c.,** Está frío; (weather) Hace frío. **to catch a c.,** acatarrarse, resfriarse. **to grow c.,** enfriarse; (of the weather) empezar a hacer frío. **in c. blood,** a sangre fría. **c.-blooded,** (fishes, etc.) de sangre fría; (chilly, of persons) friolero; (pitiless) insensible, sin piedad; (of actions) a sangre fría, premeditado. **c.-chisel,** cortafrío, *m.* **c. cream,** crema (para el cutis), *f.* **c.-hearted,** seco, insensible. **c.-shoulder,** *n* frialdad, *f.* —*vt* tratar con frialdad (a). **c.-storage,** conservación refrigerada, *f*
coldly /'kouldli/ *adv* fríamente
coldness /'kouldnɪs/ *n* frío, *m;* (of one's reception, etc.) frialdad, *f;* (of heart) inhumanidad, *f*
coleopterous /ˌkouli'ɒptərəs/ *a* coleóptero
colic /'kɒlɪk/ *n* cólico, *m*
coliseum /ˌkɒlɪ'siəm/ *n* coliseo, *m*
colitis /kə'laitɪs/ *n* colitis, *f*
collaborate /kə'læbəˌreit/ *vi* colaborar (con)
collaboration /kəˌlæbə'reiʃən/ *n* colaboración, *f*
collaborationist /kəˌlæbə'reiʃənɪst/ *n* colaboracionista, *mf*
collaborator /kə'læbəˌreitər/ *n* colaborador (-ra); (quisling) colaboracionista, *mf*
collapse /kə'læps/ *n* derrumbamiento, *m;* desplome, *m; Med.* colapso, *m;* (of buildings and *Fig.*) hundimiento, *m;* (of plans) frustración, *f;* (failure) fracaso, *m.* —*vi* derrumbarse; (of buildings, etc.) hundirse, venirse abajo; (of persons, fall) desplomarse; *Med.* sufrir colapso; (of plans, etc.) frustrarse, venirse abajo. **George came to us after the c. of France,** Jorge vino a quedarse con nosotros después del hundimiento de Francia
collapsible /kə'læpsəbəl/ *a* plegable
collar /'kɒlər/ *n* (of a garment and of fur) cuello, *m;* (of a dog, etc., and necklace) collar, *m.* —*vt* (seize) agarrar. **detachable c.,** cuello suelto, *m.* **high c.,** alzacuello, *m.* **c.-bone,** clavícula, *f*
collate /kou'leit/ *vt* cotejar; (to a benefice) colacionar
collateral /kə'lætərəl/ *a* colateral
collation /kə'leiʃən/ *n* colación, *f*
colleague /'kɒlig/ *n* colega, *m;* compañero (-ra)
collect /'kɒlɛkt/ *vt* (assemble) reunir; (catch) coger; acumular; (call for) pasar a buscar, ir (or venir) a buscar; (pick up) recoger; (taxes, etc.) recaudar; coleccionar; (one's strength, etc. and debts, etc.) cobrar; (letters) recoger. —*vi* reunirse, congregarse; acumularse. —*n Eccl.* colecta, *f.* **to c. oneself,** reponerse
collected /kə'lɛktɪd/ *a* (of persons) seguro de sí.
collection /kə'lɛkʃən/ *n* reunión, *f;* (of data, etc.) acumulación, *f;* (of pictures, stamps, etc.) colección, *f;* (of a debt, etc.) cobranza, *f;* (of taxes, etc.) recaudación, *f;* (from a mail box) recogida, *f;* (of laws, etc.) compilación, *f; Eccl.* ofertorio, *m;* (of donations) colecta, *f*
collection agency *n* agencia de cobros de cuentas, *f*
collective /kə'lɛktɪv/ *a* colectivo. **c. bargaining,** regateo colectivo, trato colectivo, *m*
collectivism /kə'lɛktəˌvɪzəm/ *n* colectivismo, *m*
collector /kə'lɛktər/ *n* (of pictures, etc.) coleccionador (-ra), coleccionista, *mf;* cobrador, *m; Elec.* colector, *m*
college /'kɒlɪdʒ/ *n* colegio, *m;* escuela, *f;* universidad, *f.* **C. of Cardinals,** Colegio de Cardenales, *m*
collegiate /kə'lidʒɪt/ *a* colegial, colegiado. **c. church,** iglesia colegial, *f*
collide /kə'laid/ *vi* chocar (contra), topar (con); estar en conflicto (con). **c. head-on,** chocar frontalmente
collie /'kɒli/ *n* perro de pastor escocés, *m*
collier /'kɒlyər/ *n* minero de carbón, *m;* (barco) carbonero, *m*
collision /kə'lɪʒən/ *n* choque, *m,* colisión, *f;* (of interests, etc.) antagonismo, conflicto, *m.* **to come into c. with,** chocar con
colloid /'kɒlɔid/ *a* coloide. —*n* coloide, *m*
colloquial /kə'loukwiəl/ *a* familiar
colloquialism /kə'loukwiəˌlɪzəm/ *n* expresión familiar, *f*
colloquially /kə'loukwiəli/ *adv* en lenguaje familiar; familiarmente
colloquy /'kɒləkwi/ *n* coloquio, *m*
collusion /kə'luʒən/ *n* colusión, *f.* **to be in c.,** *Law.* coludir; conspirar, estar de manga
Cologne /kə'loun/ Colonia, *f*
Colombia /kə'lʌmbiə/ Colombia, *f*
Colombian /kə'lʌmbiən/ *a* colombiano. —*n* colombiano (-na)
colon /'koulən/ *n Anat.* colon, *m;* (punctuation) dos puntos, *m pl*
colonel /'kɜrnḷ/ *n* coronel, *m*
colonial /kə'louniəl/ *a* colonial. —*n* habitante de las colonias, *m.* **C. Office,** Ministerio de Asuntos Coloniales, *m*
colonist /'kɒlənɪst/ *n* colono, *m;* colonizador (-ra)
colonization /ˌkɒlənə'zeiʃən/ *n* colonización, *f*
colonize /'kɒləˌnaiz/ *vt* colonizar. —*vi* establecerse en una colonia
colonizer /'kɒləˌnaizər/ *n* colonizador (-ra)
colonizing /'kɒləˌnaizɪŋ/ *n* colonización, *f, a* colonizador
colonnade /ˌkɒlə'neid/ *n* columnata, *f*
colony /'kɒləni/ *n* colonia, *f*
color /'kʌlər/ *n* color, *m;* colorido, *m;* tinta, *f;* materia colorante, *f; pl* **colors,** insignia, *f;* bandera, *f,* estandarte, *m; Naut.* pabellón, *m.* —*vt* colorar; pintar; iluminar; (influence) influir, afectar. —*vi* colorarse; ruborizarse; encenderse. **fast c.,** color estable, color sólido, *m.* **regimental colors,** bandera del regimiento, *f.* **with colors flying,** con tambor batiente, a banderas desplegadas. **to be off c.,** estar malucho, estar indispuesto. **to change c.,** (of persons) mudar de color, mudar de semblante. **to give c. to,** (a story, etc.) hacer verosímil. **to lay the colors on too thick,** recargar las tintas. **to pass with flying colors,** salir triunfante. **under c. of,** so color de, a pretexto de. **c.-blind,** daltoniano. **c.-blindness,** daltonismo, *m*
Colorado beetle /ˌkɒlə'rɑdou/ *n* escarabajo de la patata, *m*
colored /'kʌlərd/ *a* colorado; de color
colorimeter /ˌkʌlə'rɪmɪtər/ *n* colorímetro, *m*
coloring /'kʌlərɪŋ/ *n* (substance) colorante, *m;* (act of) coloración, *f; Art.* colorido, *m;* (of complexion) colores, *m pl*
colorist /'kʌlərɪst/ *n* colorista, *mf*
colorless /'kʌlərlɪs/ *a* sin color, incoloro; *Fig.* insípido
colossal /kə'lɒsəl/ *a* colosal, gigantesco; enorme; *Inf.* estupendo
colossus /kə'lɒsəs/ *n* coloso, *m*
colt /koult/ *n* potro, *m;* (boy) muchacho alegre, *m*
colter /'koultər/ *n* reja, reja del arado, *f*
colt's-foot *n Bot.* fárfara, *f*
columbine /'kɒləmˌbain/ *n Bot.* aguileña, *f;* (in pantomime) Colombina, *f*
column /'kɒləm/ *n* columna, *f.* **Fifth c.,** quinta columna, *f*
columned /'kɒləmd/ *a* con columnas
columnist /'kɒləmnɪst/ *n* periodista, *m*
coma /'koumə/ *n* coma, *m*
comatose /'kɒməˌtous/ *a* comatoso
comb /koum/ *n* peine, *m;* (for flax) carda, *f;* (curry) almohaza, *f;* (of cock) cresta, carúncula, *f;* (of a wave) cima, cresta, *f;* (honey) panal, *m, vt* (hair) peinar; (flax) rastrillar, cardar. **c. and brush,** cepillo y peine. **high c.,** peineta, *f.* **to c. one's hair,** peinarse
combat /*v* kəm'bæt; *n* 'kɒmbæt/ *vt* luchar contra, combatir, resistir. —*vi* combatir, pelear. —*n* combate, *m;* lucha, batalla, *f.* **in single c.,** cuerpo a cuerpo

combatant /kəm'bætn̩t/ *n* combatiente, *m*, *a* combatiente

combative /kəm'bætɪv/ *a* belicoso, pugnaz

combination /ˌkɒmbə'neiʃən/ *n* combinación, *f;* mezcla, *f;* unión, *f;* asociación, *f; pl* **combinations.** camisa pantalón, *f.* **c. lock,** cerradura de combinación, *f*

combine / *v* kəm'bain; *n* 'kɒmbain/ *vt* combinar; reunir, juntar; *Chem.* combinar. —*vi* combinarse; asociarse (con); *Com.* fusionarse. —*n* asociación, *f; Com.* monopolio, *m*

combings /'koumɪŋz/ *n pl* peinaduras, *f pl*

combustible /kəm'bʌstəbəl/ *a* combustible. —*n* combustible, *m*

combustion /kəm'bʌstʃən/ *n* combustión, *f.* **rapid c.,** combustión rápida, *f.* **spontaneous c.,** combustión espontánea, *f*

come /kʌm/ *vi* venir; llegar; avanzar; acercarse; (happen) suceder, acontecer; (result) resultar; (find oneself) encontrarse, hallarse; (become) llegar a ser; (begin to) ponerse (a), empezar (a). **Coming!** ¡Voy! ¡Allá voy! **C., c.!** ¡Vamos! ¡No es para tanto! ¡Ánimo! **I am ready whatever comes,** Estoy preparado venga lo que venga. **He comes of a good family,** Es (Viene) de buena familia. **I came to know him well,** Llegué a conocerle bien. **I don't know what came over me,** No sé lo que me pasó. **When I came to consider it,** Cuando me puse a considerarlo. **The bill comes to six thousand pesetas,** La cuenta sale a seis mil pesetas. **He comes up before the judge tomorrow,** Ha de comparecer ante el juez mañana. **What you say comes to this,** Lo que dice Vd. se reduce a esto. **What is the world coming to?** ¿A dónde va parar el mundo? **It does not c. within my scope,** No está dentro de mi alcance. **to c. apart,** deshacerse; romperse; dividirse. **to c. home to,** *Fig.* impresionar mucho, tocar en lo más íntimo; hacer comprender (a). **to c. into bloom,** empezar a tener flores, florecer. **to c. into one's head,** venir a las mientes. **to c. into the world,** venir al mundo. **to c. near,** acercarse; aproximarse, estar próximo. **to c. next,** venir después; suceder luego. **to c. to an end,** terminar, acabarse. **to c. to blows,** venir a las manos. **to c. to grief,** salir mal parado; (of schemes, etc.) malograrse. **to c. to hand,** venir a mano; (of letters) llegar a las manos (de). **to c. to life,** despertar; animarse; resucitarse. **to c. to nothing,** frustrarse; no quedar en nada. **to c. to pass,** suceder; realizarse. **to c. to terms,** ponerse de acuerdo. **to c. true,** cumplirse, verificarse. **to c. about,** suceder, acontecer, tener lugar; (of the wind) girar. **to c. across,** dar con, encontrar por casualidad; tropezar con. **to c. after,** (a situation) solicitar; (follow) seguir (a); venir más tarde (que); (succeed) suceder. **to c. again,** volver. **to c. along,** caminar (por); andar (por); (arrive) llegar. **C. along!** ¡Ven! ¡Vamos! ¡Andamos! **to c. at,** alcanzar; (attack) embestir, atacar; (gain) obtener, adquirir. **to c. away,** irse, marcharse; (break) deshacerse. **to c. back,** volver. **c.-back,** *n Inf.* respuesta, *f;* contraataque, *m.* **to c. before,** llegar antes; preceder (a). **to c. between,** interponerse (entre), intervenir. **to c. by,** pasar por, pasar junto a; (acquire) obtener, adquirir; (achieve) conseguir. **to c. down,** bajar, descender; (in the world) venir a menos; (be demolished) demolerse; (collapse) derrumbarse, hundirse; (of prices) bajar; (of traditions, etc.) llegar e.g. *This work has c. down to us in two fifteenth-century manuscripts* Esta obra nos ha llegado en dos manuscritos del siglo quince; (fall) caer. **c.-down,** *n* caída, *f;* frustración, *f;* desengaño, *m;* desprestigio, *m;* pérdida de posición, *f.* **to c. down on a person,** cantar la cartilla (a). **to c. forward,** avanzar, adelantarse; (offer) ofrecerse; presentarse. **to c. in,** entrar; (of money) ingresar; (of trains, etc.) llegar; (of the tide) crecer; (of the new year) empezar; (of fashion) ponerse de moda; (be useful) servir (para). **C. in!** ¡Adelante! ¡Pase Vd.! **to c. into,** (a scheme) asociarse con; (property) heredar; (the mind) presentarse a la imaginación, ocurrirse (a). **to c. off,** (happen) tener lugar; realizarse, efectuarse; (be successful) tener éxito; (break off) separarse (de); romperse. **to c. off well,** tener éxito; (of persons) salir bien. **c. off the press,** salir de prensas. **to c. on,** avanzar; (of actors) salir a la escena; (progress) hacer progresos; (develop) desarrollarse; (of pain, etc.) acometer (a); (arrive) llegar; (of a lawsuit) verse. **C. on!** ¡Vamos! ¡En marcha! **to c. out,** salir; (of stars) nacer; (of buds, etc.) brotar; (of the moon, etc.) asomarse; (of stains) borrarse, salir; (of a book) ver la luz, publicarse; (of secrets) divulgarse, saberse; (of a girl, in society) ponerse de largo; (on strike) declararse en huelga; (of fashions, etc.) aparecer. **to c. out with,** (a remark) soltar; (oaths, etc.) prorrumpir (en); (disclose) revelar, hacer público. **to c. round,** (to see someone) venir a ver (a); (coax) engatusar; (after a faint, etc.) volver en sí; (after illness) reponerse; (to another's point of view) aceptar, compartir. **to c. through,** pasar por; (trials, etc.) subir; salir de; (of liquids) salirse. **to c. to,** volver en sí. **to c. together,** reunirse, juntarse; venir juntos; unirse. **to c. under,** venir (or estar) bajo la jurisdicción de; (the influence of) estar dominado por; (figure among) figurar entre, estar comprendido en. **to c. up,** subir; (of sun, moon) salir; (of plants) brotar; (of problems, etc.) surgir; (in conversation) discutirse; (before a court) comparecer. **to c. up to,** (equal) igualar, ser igual (a); rivalizar con; (in height) llegar hasta. **He came up to them in the street,** Les abordó (or se les acercó) en la calle. **We have c. up against many difficulties,** Hemos tropezado con muchas dificultades. **This novel does not c. up to his last,** Esta última novela no es tan buena como la anterior. **The party did not c. up to their expectations,** La reunión no fue tan divertida como esperaban. **to c. up with,** (a person) alcanzar (a). **to c. upon,** encontrar, hallar; tropezar con; encontrar por casualidad. **to c. upon evil days,** venir a menos

comedian /kə'midiən/ *n* actor cómico, comediante, *m*

comedy /'kɒmɪdi/ *n* comedia, *f.* **c. of manners,** comedia de costumbres, *f*

comeliness /'kʌmlinɪs/ *n* hermosura, *f*

comely /'kʌmli/ *a* hermoso

comer /'kʌmər/ *n* el, *m,* (*f,* la) que viene. **all comers,** todo el mundo. **first c.,** primer (-ra) venido (-da)

comet /'kɒmɪt/ *n* cometa, *m*

comfort /'kʌmfərt/ *vt* consolar, confortar; (encourage) animar; (reassure) alegrar. —*n* consuelo, *m;* satisfacción, *f;* comodidad, *f;* bienestar, *m.* **He lives in great c.,** Vive con mucha comodidad. **c.-loving,** comodón

comfortable /'kʌmftəbəl/ *a* cómodo; (with income) suficiente; (consoling) consolador. **to make oneself c.,** ponerse cómodo

comfortably /'kʌmftəbli/ *adv* cómodamente; suficientemente; fácilmente; con facilidad; (well) bien. **He is c. off,** Está bien de dinero

comforter /'kʌmfərtər/ *n* consolador (-ra); (baby's) chupador, *m;* (scarf) bufanda, *f*

comforting /'kʌmfərtɪŋ/ *a* consolador

comfortless /'kʌmfərtlɪs/ *a* incómodo, sin comodidad; desconsolador; (of persons) inconsolable, desconsolado

comic /'kɒmɪk/ *a* cómico; bufo; satírico. —*n* cómico, *m; pl* **comics,** (printed) historietas cómicas, *f pl.* **c. opera,** ópera cómicas, *f.* **c. paper,** periódico satírico, *m*

comical /'kɒmɪkəl/ *a* cómico; divertido, gracioso

coming /'kʌmɪŋ/ *a* (with year, etc.) próximo, que viene; (promising) de porvenir; (approaching) que se acerca. —*n* venida, *f;* llegada, *f;* advenimiento, *m.* **c.-out party,** puesta de largo, *f.* **comings and goings,** entradas y salidas, *f pl*

comma /'kɒmə/ *n* coma, *f.* **inverted commas,** comillas, *f pl*

command /kə'mænd/ *vt* mandar, ordenar; (silence, respect, etc.) imponer; (an army, fleet, etc.) comandar; capitanear; (one's emotions) dominar; (have at one's disposal) disponer de; (a military position, view) dominar; (sympathy, etc.) despertar, merecer; (of price) venderse por. —*vi* mandar. —*n* orden, *f;* (*Mil. Nav.*) mando, *m;* (of an army, etc.) comandancia, *f;* (of one's emotions, etc.) dominio, *m;* (of a military position, etc.) dominación, *f;* disposición, *f.* **By Royal C.,** Por Real Orden; (of shops, etc.) Proveedor

de la Real Casa. **The house commands lovely views of the mountains,** La casa tiene hermosas vistas de las montañas. **word of c.,** orden, *f.* **Yours to c.,** A la disposición de Vd.
commandant /ˌkɒmənˈdænt/ *n* comandante, *m*
commandeer /ˌkɒmənˈdɪər/ *vt* (conscript) reclutar; *Mil.* requisar; expropiar
commander /kəˈmændər/ *n Mil.* comandante, *m; Nav.* capitán de fragata, *m;* (of order of Knighthood) comendador, *m.* **c.-in-chief,** generalísimo, *m.* **C. of the Faithful,** Comendador de los creyentes, *m*
commanding /kəˈmændɪŋ/ *a Mil.* comandante; imponente; (of manner) imperioso; dominante. **c. officer,** comandante en jefe, *m*
commandment /kəˈmændmənt/ *n* precepto, mandamiento, *m.* **the Ten Commandments,** los diez mandamientos
commando /kəˈmændou/ *n Mil.* comando, *m*
commemorate /kəˈmɛməˌreit/ *vt* conmemorar
commemoration /kəˌmɛməˈreiʃən/ *n* conmemoración, *f*
commemorative /kəˈmɛməˌreitɪv/ *a* conmemorativo
commence /kəˈmɛns/ *vt* comenzar, empezar, principiar. *—vi* comenzar. **He commenced to eat,** Empezó a comer
commencement /kəˈmɛnsmənt/ *n* principio, comienzo, *m*
commend /kəˈmɛnd/ *vt* (entrust) encomendar; recomendar; alabar
commendable /kəˈmɛndəbəl/ *a* loable; recomendable
commendation /ˌkɒmənˈdeiʃən/ *n* aprobación, alabanza, *f,* aplauso, *m*
commendatory /kəˈmɛndəˌtɔri/ *a* (of letters) comendatorio
commensurable /kəˈmɛnsərəbəl/ *a* conmensurable
commensurate /kəˈmɛnsərɪt/ *a* proporcionado (a); conforme (a)
comment /ˈkɒmɛnt/ *n* observación, *f;* (on a work) comento, *m;* explicación, nota, *f.* *—vi* hacer una observación (sobre); (a work) comentar, anotar. **to c. unfavorably on,** criticar
commentary /ˈkɒmənˌtɛri/ *n* comentario, *m;* (on a person, etc.) comentos, *m pl,* observaciones, *f pl*
commentator /ˈkɒmənˌteitər/ *n* comentador (-ra); (of a work) comentarista, *mf*
commerce /ˈkɒmərs/ *n* comercio, *m;* negocios, *m pl;* (social) trato, *m*
commercial /kəˈmɜrʃəl/ *a* comercial; mercantil. **c. traveler,** viajante, *mf*
commercialism /kəˈmɜrʃəˌlɪzəm/ *n* mercantilismo, *m*
commercialize /kəˈmɜrʃəˌlaiz/ *vt* hacer objeto de comercio
commercially /kəˈmɜrʃəli/ *adv* comercialmente
commingle /kəˈmɪŋgəl/ *vt* mezclar. *—vi* mezclarse
commiserate /kəˈmɪzəˌreit/ *vi* compadecerse (de), apiadarse (de)
commiseration /kəˌmɪzəˈreiʃən/ *n* conmiseración, compasión, *f*
commissariat /ˌkɒməˈsɛəriət/ *n* comisaría, *f; Inf.* despensa, *f*
commissary /ˈkɒməˌsɛri/ *n* comisario, *m*
commission /kəˈmɪʃən/ *n* comisión, *f; Mil.* graduación de oficial, *f.* *—vt* comisionar; (a ship) poner en servicio activo, armar; (appoint) nombrar. **in c.,** en servicio, activo. **out of c.,** (of ships) inutilizado; inservible. **c. agent,** comisionista, *mf* **to gain one's c.,** *Mil.* graduarse de oficial. **to put out of c.,** retirar del servicio; poner fuera de combate; estropear
commissionaire /kəˌmɪʃəˈnɛər/ *n* portero, *m*
commissioned /kəˈmɪʃənd/ *a* comisionado. **c. officer,** oficial, *m*
commissioner /kəˈmɪʃənər/ *n* comisario, *m.* **High C.,** alto comisario, *m.* **c. for oaths,** notario, *m.* **c. of police,** jefe de policía, *m*
commit /kəˈmɪt/ *vt* entregar (a); (a crime) cometer; (to prison) encarcelar; (for trial) remitir. **to c. oneself,** comprometerse. **to c. to memory,** aprender de memoria. **to c. to writing,** poner por escrito
commitment /kəˈmɪtmənt/ *n* (financial, etc.) obligación, responsabilidad, *f;* compromiso, *m*
committal /kəˈmɪtl̩/ *n* (of an offence) comisión, *f;* (placing, entrusting) entrega, *f;* (to prison) encarcelamiento, *m;* (legal procedure) auto de prisión, *m*
committee /kəˈmɪti/ *n* comité, *m;* comisión, junta, *f;* consejo, *m.* **They decided in c.,** Tomaron la resolución en comité. **c. of management,** consejo de administración, *m*
commodious /kəˈmoudiəs/ *a* espacioso, grande
commodiousness /kəˈmoudiəsnɪs/ *n* espaciosidad, *f*
commodity /kəˈmɒdɪti/ *n* artículo, *m,* mercancía, *f*
commodore /ˈkɒməˌdɔr/ *n Nav.* jefe de escuadra, *m;* comodoro, *m*
common /ˈkɒmən/ *a* común; general, corriente; universal; vulgar; (disparaging) cursi; (elementary) elemental. *—n* pastos comunes, *m pl.* **He is not a c. man,** No es un hombre cualquiera; No es un hombre vulgar. **in c.,** en común. **the c. man,** el hombre medio. **the c. people,** el pueblo. **c. sense,** sentido común, *m.* **c. soldier,** soldado raso, *m.* **c. speech,** lenguaje vulgar, *m.* **c. usage,** uso corriente, *m*
commoner /ˈkɒmənər/ *n* plebeyo (-ya)
commonly /ˈkɒmənli/ *adv* comúnmente, por lo general
commonness /ˈkɒmənnɪs/ *n* frecuencia, *f;* vulgaridad, *f*
commonplace /ˈkɒmənˌpleis/ *n* lugar común, *m;* trivialidad, *f.* *—a* trivial
commons /ˈkɒmənz/ *n* el pueblo; (House of) Cámara de los Comunes, *f;* (food) provisiones, *f pl.* **to be on short c.,** comer mal, estar mal alimentado
Commonwealth /ˈkɒmənˌwɛlθ/ *n* estado, *m;* república, *f;* comunidad (de naciones), *f;* mancomunidad, *f.* **the Commonwealth of Puerto Rico,** el Estado Libre Asociado de Puerto Rico, *m*
commotion /kəˈmouʃən/ *n* confusión, *f;* conmoción, perturbación, *f;* tumulto, *m*
communal /kəˈmyunl̩/ *a* comunal
commune /ˈkɒmyun/ *n* comuna, *f;* comunión, *f, vi* conversar (con). **to c. with oneself,** hablar consigo
communicable /kəˈmyunɪkəbəl/ *a* comunicable
communicant /kəˈmyunɪkənt/ *n Eccl.* comulgante, *mf;* (of information) informante, *mf*
communicate /kəˈmyunɪˌkeit/ *vt* comunicar; (diseases) transmitir. *—vi* comunicarse (con); *Eccl.* comulgar
communication /kəˌmyunɪˈkeiʃən/ *n* comunicación, *f.* **lines of c.,** comunicaciones, *f pl.* **to get into c. with,** ponerse en comunicación con. **c.-cord,** (in a railway carriage) timbre de alarma, *m*
communicative /kəˈmyunɪˌkeitɪv/ *a* comunicativo; expansivo
communicativeness /kəˈmyunɪˌkeitɪvnɪs/ *n* carácter expansivo, *m;* locuacidad, *f*
communion /kəˈmyunyən/ *n* comunión, *f.* **Holy c.,** comunión, *f.* **to take c.,** comulgar. **c. card,** cédula de comunión, *f.* **c. cup,** cáliz, *f.* **c. table,** sagrada mesa, *f;* altar, *m*
communiqué /kəˌmyunɪˈkei/ *n* comunicación, parte, *f.* **to issue a c.,** dar parte
communism /ˈkɒmyəˌnɪzəm/ *n* comunismo, *m*
communist /ˈkɒmyənɪst/ *n* comunista, *mf a* comunista
community /kəˈmyunɪti/ *n* comunidad, *f.* **the c.,** la nación; el público. **c. center,** centro social, *m*
commutation /ˌkɒmyəˈteiʃən/ *n* conmutación, *f;* reducción, *f*
commute /kəˈmyut/ *vt* conmutar; reducir
compact / *n* ˈkɒmpækt; *v* kəmˈpækt/ *n* (pact) acuerdo, pacto, *m;* (powder) polvorera, *f.* *—a* compacto; firme; sólido; apretado, cerrado; (of persons) bien hecho; (of style) conciso, sucinto
compact disc /ˈkɒmpækt ˈdɪsk/ *n* disco compacto, *m*
compactness /kəmˈpæktnɪs/ *n* compacidad, *f;* (of style) concisión, *f*
companion /kəmˈpænyən/ *n* compañero (-ra); camarada, *mf;* (of an Order) caballero, *m,* (or dama, *f*). *—vt* acompañar. **lady c.,** señora de compañía, *f.* **c.-hatch,** cubierta de escotilla, *f.* **c.-ladder,** escala de toldilla, *f*
companionable /kəmˈpænyənəbəl/ *a* sociable, amistoso
companionably /kəmˈpænyənəbli/ *adv* sociablemente, amistosamente

companionship /kəm'pænyən,ʃɪp/ *n* compañía, *f;* compañerismo, *m*
company /'kʌmpəni/ *n* (*Com. Mil.* etc.) compañía, *f;* (ship's) tripulación, *f.* **I will keep you c.,** Te haré compañía. **to part c. with,** separarse de. **Present c. excepted!** ¡Mejorando lo presente! **They are not very good c.,** No son muy divertidos
company store *n* tienda de raya, *f* (Mexico)
comparable /'kɒmpərəbəl/ *a* comparable
comparably /'kɒmpərəbli/ *adv* comparablemente
comparative /kəm'pærətɪv/ *a* comparativo; relativo
comparatively /kəm'pærətɪvli/ *adv* comparativamente; relativamente
compare /kəm'pɛər/ *vt* comparar. —*vi* compararse; poder compararse. ser comparable. **beyond c.,** sin comparación; sin igual. **to c. favorably with,** no perder por comparación con. **to c. notes,** cambiar impresiones
comparison /kəm'pærəsən/ *n* comparación, *f.* **in c. with,** comparado con
compartment /kəm'pɑrtmənt/ *n* compartimiento, *m; Rail.* departamento, *m*
compass /'kʌmpəs/ *n* circuito, *m;* límites, *m pl;* alcance, *m;* (of a voice) gama, *f; Naut.* brújula, *f; pl* **compasses,** compás, *m.* —*vt* (achieve) conseguir; (plan) idear, **mariner's c.,** compás de mar. *m,* rosa de los vientos, *f.* **pocket c.,** brújula de bolsillo, *f.* **to c. about,** cercar, rodear
compassion /kəm'pæʃən/ *n* compasión, *f.* **to have c. on,** apiadarse de, compadecerse de
compassionate /kəm'pæʃənɪt/ *a* compasivo, piadoso. **c. leave,** permiso, *m*
compassionately /kəm'pæʃənɪtli/ *adv* compasivamente, con piedad
compatibility /kəm,pætə'bɪlɪti/ *n* compatibilidad, *f*
compatible /kəm'pætəbəl/ *a* compatible, conciliable
compatriot /kəm'peitriət/ *n* compatriota, *mf*
compel /kəm'pɛl/ *vt* obligar (a), forzar (a); exigir; imponer. **His attitude compels respect,** Su actitud impone el respeto
compelling /kəm'pɛlɪŋ/ *a* compulsivo
compendious /kəm'pɛndiəs/ *a* compendioso, sucinto
compendium /kəm'pɛndiəm/ *n* compendio, *m;* resumen, *m*
compensate /'kɒmpən,seit/ *vt* compensar; (reward) recompensar; (for loss, etc.) indemnizar. **to c. for,** compensar; indemnizar contra
compensation /,kɒmpən'seiʃən/ *n* compensación, *f;* (reward) recompensa, *f;* (for loss, etc.) indemnización, *f*
compensatory /kəm'pɛnsə,tɔri/ *a* compensatorio
compete /kəm'pit/ *vi* competir (con); rivalizar; ser rivales; (in a competition) concurrir
competence /'kɒmpɪtəns/ *n* aptitud, *f;* capacidad, *f;* competencia, *f*
competent /'kɒmpɪtənt/ *a* competente; capaz
competently /'kɒmpɪtəntli/ *adv* competentemente
competition /,kɒmpɪ'tɪʃən/ *n* competencia, competición, rivalidad, *f;* emulación, *f;* (contest, etc.) concurso, *m.* **spirit of c.,** espíritu de competencia, *m*
competitive /kəm'pɛtɪtɪv/ *a* competidor; de competición. **c. examination,** oposición, *f*
competitor /kəm'pɛtɪtər/ *n* competidor (-ra)
compilation /,kɒmpə'leiʃən/ *n* compilación, *f*
compile /kəm'pail/ *vt* compilar
compiler /kəm'pailər/ *n* compilador (-ra)
complacence /kəm'pleisəns/ *n* complacencia, satisfacción, *f,* contento de sí mismo, *m*
complacent /kəm'pleisənt/ *a* satisfecho; pagado de sí mismo
complacently /kəm'pleisəntli/ *adv* con satisfacción
complain /kəm'plein/ *vi* quejarse; lamentarse; *Law.* querellarse. **He complains about everything,** Se queja de todo
complainant /kəm'pleinənt/ *n Law.* demandante, *mf*
complaint /kəm'pleint/ *n* queja, *f;* lamento, *m; Law.* demanda, *f;* (illness) enfermedad, *f.* **to lodge a c. (against),** quejarse (de)
complaisance /kəm'pleisəns/ *n* afabilidad, cortesía, *f*
complaisant /kəm'pleisənt/ *a* complaciente, cortés, afable; (of husbands) consentido, sufrido
complement / *n* 'kɒmpləmənt; *v* -,mɛnt/ *n* complemento, *m;* total, número completo, *m.* —*vt* completar
complementary /,kɒmplə'mɛntəri/ *a* complementario
complete /kəm'plit/ *a* entero; completo; perfecto; acabado. —*vt* completar; acabar; (happiness, etc.) coronar, poner el último toque (a); (years) cumplir; (forms) llenar
completely /kəm'plitli/ *adv* completamente, enteramente
completeness /kəm'plitnɪs/ *n* entereza, *f;* totalidad, *f*
completion /kəm'pliʃən/ *n* terminación, *f,* fin, *m*
complex / *a* kəm'plɛks; *n* 'kɒmplɛks/ *a* complejo. —*n* complejo, *m.* **inferiority c.,** complejo de inferioridad, *m*
complexion /kəm'plɛkʃən/ *n* tez, *f,* cutis, *m; Fig.* carácter, *m*
complexity /kəm'plɛksɪti/ *n* complejidad, *f*
compliance /kəm'plaiəns/ *n* condescendencia, *f;* (subservience) sumisión, *f;* obediencia, *f.* **in c. with,** de acuerdo con, en conformidad con
compliant /kəm'plaiənt/ *a* condescendiente; sumiso, dócil; obediente
complicate /'kɒmplɪ,keit/ *vt* complicar
complicated /'kɒmplɪ,keitɪd/ *a* complejo; complicado; enredado
complication /,kɒmplɪ'keiʃən/ *n* complicación, *f*
complicity /kəm'plɪsɪti/ *n* complicidad, *f.* **c. in a crime,** complicidad en un crimen
compliment / *n* 'kɒmpləmənt; *v* -,mɛnt/ *n* cumplido, *m,* cortesía, *f;* requiebro, *Inf.* piropo, *m;* favor, *m;* honor, *m;* (greeting) saludo, *m;* (congratulation) felicitación, *f.* —*vt* cumplimentar; requebrar; (flatter) adular, lisonjear; (congratulate) felicitar. **They did him the c. of reading his book,** Le hicieron el honor de leer su libro. **to pay compliments,** hacer cumplidos; *Inf.* echar piropos
complimentary /,kɒmplə'mɛntəri/ *a* lisonjero; galante. **c. ticket,** billete gratuito, *m*
comply /kəm'plai/ *vi* (with) cumplir, obedecer; conformarse (con); consentir
component /kəm'pounənt/ *a* componente. —*n* componente, *m*
comport /kəm'pɔrt/ *vt* **(oneself),** comportarse
comportment /kəm'pɔrtmənt/ *n* comportamiento, *m,* conducta, *f*
compose /kəm'pouz/ *vt* (all meanings) componer. **to c. oneself,** serenarse, calmarse. **to c. one's features,** componer el semblante
composed /kəm'pouzd/ *a* sereno, tranquilo, sosegado
composer /kəm'pouzər/ *n* compositor (-ra)
composite /kəm'pɒzɪt/ *a* compuesto; mixto. —*n* compuesto, *m; Bot.* planta compuesta, *f*
composition /,kɒmpə'zɪʃən/ *n* (all meanings) composición, *f*
compositor /kəm'pɒzɪtər/ *n Print.* cajista, *mf*
composure /kəm'pouʒər/ *n* tranquilidad, serenidad, calma, *f;* sangre fría, *f,* aplomo, *m*
compote /'kɒmpout/ *n* compota, *f*
compound /'kɒmpaund/ *vt* mezclar, componer; concertar. —*a* compuesto. —*n* compuesto, *m;* mixtura, *f.* **c. interest,** interés compuesto, *m*
comprehend /,kɒmprɪ'hɛnd/ *vt* comprender
comprehensible /,kɒmprɪ'hɛnsəbəl/ *a* comprensible
comprehensibly /,kɒmprɪ'hɛnsəbli/ *adv* comprensiblemente
comprehension /,kɒmprɪ'hɛnʃən/ *n* comprensión, *f*
comprehensive /,kɒmprɪ'hɛnsɪv/ *a* comprensivo
comprehensiveness /,kɒmprɪ'hɛnsɪvnɪs/ *n* alcance, *m,* extensión, *f*
compress / *v* kəm'prɛs; *n* 'kɒmprɛs/ *vt* comprimir; condensar; reducir, abreviar. —*n* compresa, *f*
compression /kəm'prɛʃən/ *n* compresión, *f*
compressor /kəm'prɛsər/ *n* compresor, *m*
comprise /kəm'praiz/ *vt* comprender, abarcar, incluir
compromise /'kɒmprə,maiz/ *n* compromiso, *m,* transacción, *f;* componenda, *f.* —*vt* (settle) componer, arreglar; (jeopardize) arriesgar; comprometer. —*vi* transigir. **to c. oneself,** comprometerse
compromising /'kɒmprə,maizɪŋ/ *a* comprometedor

compulsion /kəm'pʌlʃən/ *n* compulsión, fuerza, *f.* **under c.,** a la fuerza
compulsory /kəm'pʌlsəri/ *a* obligatorio. **c. measures,** medidas obligatorias, *f pl.* **c. powers,** poderes absolutos, *m pl*
compunction /kəm'pʌŋkʃən/ *n* compunción, *f,* remordimiento, *m;* escrúpulo, *m.* **without c.,** sin escrúpulo
computable /kəm'pyutəbəl/ *a* calculable
computation /ˌkɒmpyʊ'teiʃən/ *n* computación, *f,* cómputo, *m*
compute /kəm'pyut/ *vt* computar, calcular.
computer /kəm'pyutər/ *m* computador, *m* (Western Hemisphere), ordenador, *m* (Spain)
computer center *n* centro calculador, centro de computación, *m*
comrade /'kɒmræd/ *n* camarada, *mf* compañero (-ra)
comradeship /'kɒmrædˌʃɪp/ *n* compañerismo, *m*
con /kɒn/ *vt* estudiar; leer con atención; *Naut.* gobernar (el buque)
concatenation /kɒnˌkætn̩'eiʃən/ *n* concatenación, *f*
concave /kɒn'keiv/ *a* cóncavo
conceal /kən'sil/ *vt* esconder, ocultar; (the truth, etc.) encubrir, callar; disimular
concealed /kən'sild/ *a* oculto; escondido; disimulado. **c. lighting,** iluminación indirecta, *f.* **c. turning,** (on a road) viraje oculto, *m*
concealment /kən'silmənt/ *n* ocultación, *f;* encubrimiento, *m;* (place of) escondite, *m;* secreto, *m*
concede /kən'sid/ *vt* conceder
conceit /kən'sit/ *n* presunción, vanidad, fatuidad, *f,* envanecimiento, *m.* **to have a good c. of oneself,** estar pagado de sí mismo
conceited /kən'sitɪd/ *a* presumido, fatuo, vanidoso
conceivable /kən'sivəbəl/ *a* concebible, imaginable
conceivably /kən'sivəbli/ *adv* posiblemente
conceive /kən'siv/ *vt* concebir; (affection, etc.) tomar; (an idea, etc.) formar; (plan) formular, idear. *—vi* concebir; (understand) comprender; (suppose) imaginar, suponer
concentrate /'kɒnsənˌtreit/ *vt* concentrar. *—vi* concentrarse; (on, upon) dedicarse (a), entregarse (a); prestar atención (a), concentrar atención (en)
concentrated /'kɒnsənˌtreitɪd/ *a* concentrado
concentration /ˌkɒnsən'treiʃən/ *n* concentración, *f.* **c. camp,** campo de concentración, *m*
concentric /kən'sɛntrɪk/ *a* concéntrico
concept /'kɒnsɛpt/ *n* concepto, *m*
conception /kən'sɛpʃən/ *n* concepción, *f;* conocimiento, *m;* idea, *f,* concepto, *m.* **to have not the remotest c. of,** no tener la menor idea de
conceptualism /kən'sɛptʃuəˌlɪzəm/ *n* conceptualismo, *m*
concern /kən'sɜrn/ *vt* tocar, tener que vercon, importar, concernir; interesar; referirse (a); tratar (de); (trouble) preocupar, inquietar; (take part in) ocuparse (de or con). *—n* asunto, *m,* cosa, *f;* (share) interés, *m;* (anxiety) inquietud, *f;* solicitud, *f;* (business) casa comercial, firma, *f.* **as concerns...,** en cuanto a..., respecto a... **It concerns the date of the next meeting,** Es cuestión de la fecha de la próxima reunión. **It is no c. of yours,** No tiene nada que ver contigo. **The book is concerned with the adventures of two boys,** El libro trata de las aventuras de dos muchachos
concerned /kən'sɜrnd/ *a* ocupado (en); afectado; (in a crime) implicado (en); (troubled) preocupado; inquieto, agitado
concerning /kən'sɜrnɪŋ/ *prep* tocante a, con respecto a, referente a, sobre
concert /'kɒnsɜrt/ *n* acuerdo, concierto, *m,* armonía, *f; Mus.* concierto, *m, vt* concertar, acordar. **in c. with,** de acuerdo con. **c. hall,** sala de conciertos, *f*
concerted /kən'sɜrtɪd/ *a* concertado
concertina /ˌkɒnsər'tinə/ *n* concertina, *f*
concerto /kən'tʃɛrtou/ *n* concierto, *m*
concession /kən'sɛʃən/ *n* concesión, *f;* privilegio, *m*
concessionaire /kənˌsɛʃə'nɛər/ *n* concesionario, *m*
concierge /ˌkɒnsi'ɛərʒ/ *n* conserje, *m*
conciliate /kən'sɪliˌeit/ *vt* conciliar
conciliation /kənˌsɪli'eiʃən/ *n* conciliación, *f*
conciliatory /kən'sɪliəˌtɔri/ *a* conciliador
concise /kən'sais/ *a* conciso, breve, sucinto
concisely /kən'saisli/ *adv* concisamente
concision /kən'sɪʒən/ *n* concisión, *f*
conclave /'kɒnkleiv/ *n* conciliábulo, *m;* (of cardinals) conclave, *m*
conclude /kən'klud/ *vt* concluir. *—vi* concluirse
conclusion /kən'kluʒən/ *n* conclusión, *f.* **in c.,** en conclusión, para terminar. **to come to the c. that...,** concluir que...
conclusive /kən'klusɪv/ *a* conclusivo, concluyente, decisivo
conclusively /kən'klusɪvli/ *adv* concluyentemente
conclusiveness /kən'klusɪvnɪs/ *n* carácter decisivo, *m,* lo concluyente
concoct /kɒn'kɒkt/ *vt* confeccionar; inventar
concoction /kɒn'kɒkʃən/ *n* confección, *f;* mezcla, *f;* invención, *f;* (of a plot) maquinación, *f*
concomitant /kɒn'kɒmɪtənt/ *a* concomitante. *—n* concomitante, *m*
concord /'kɒnkɔrd/ *n* concordia, buena inteligencia, armonía, *f;* (*Mus. Gram.*) concordancia, *f;* (of sounds) armonía, *f*
concordance /kɒn'kɔrdns/ *n* concordia, armonía, *f;* (book) concordancias, *f pl*
concordat /kɒn'kɔrdæt/ *n* concordato, *m*
concourse /'kɒnkɔrs/ *n* concurrencia, muchedumbre, *f*
concrete /'kɒnkrit/ *a* concreto; de hormigón. *—n* hormigón, *m.* *—vt* concretar; cubrir de hormigón. **reinforced c.,** hormigón armado, *m*
concretion /kɒn'kriʃən/ *n* concreción, *f*
concubine /'kɒŋkyəˌbain/ *n* concubina, manceba, *f*
concur /kən'kɜr/ *vi* coincidir, concurrir; estar de acuerdo, convenir (en)
concurrence /kən'kɜrəns/ *n* (agreement) acuerdo, consentimiento, *m,* aprobación, *f*
concurrent /kən'kɜrənt/ *a* concurrente; unánime; coincidente
concurrently /kən'kɜrəntli/ *adv* concurrentemente
concussion /kən'kʌʃən/ *n* concusión, *f; Med.* concusión cerebral, *f*
condemn /kən'dɛm/ *vt* condenar; censurar, culpar; (forfeit) confiscar. **condemned cell,** celda de los condenados a muerte, *f*
condemnation /ˌkɒndɛm'neiʃən/ *n* condenación, *f;* censura, *f*
condensation /ˌkɒndɛn'seiʃən/ *n* condensación, *f*
condense /kən'dɛns/ *vt* condensar. *—vi* condensarse
condenser /kən'dɛnsər/ *n* (*Elec. Mech. Chem.*) condensador, *m*
condescend /ˌkɒndə'sɛnd/ *vi* dignarse; (in a bad sense) consentir (en); (with affability) condescender
condescending /ˌkɒndə'sɛndɪŋ/ *a* condescendiente
condescendingly /ˌkɒndə'sɛndɪŋli/ *adv* con condescendencia
condescension /ˌkɒndə'sɛnʃən/ *n* condescendencia, *f;* afabilidad, *f*
condign /kən'dain/ *a* condigno
condiment /'kɒndəmənt/ *n* condimento, *m*
condition /kən'dɪʃən/ *n* condición, *f;* estado, *m; pl* **conditions,** condiciones, *f pl;* circunstancias, *f pl.* **on c. that,** con tal que; siempre que, dado que. **to be in no c. to,** no estar en condiciones de. **to change one's c.,** cambiar de estado. **to keep oneself in c.,** mantenerse en buena forma
conditional /kən'dɪʃənl̩/ *a* condicional. **to be c. on,** depender de
conditionally /kən'dɪʃənl̩i/ *adv* condicionalmente
conditioned /kən'dɪʃənd/ *a* acondicionado. **c. reflex,** reflejo acondicionado, *m*
condole /kən'doul/ *vi* condolerse (de); (on a bereavement) dar el pésame
condolence /kən'douləns/ *n* condolencia, *f.* **to present one's condolences,** dar el pésame
condom /'kɒndəm/ *n* condón, *m*
condone /kən'doun/ *vt* condonar, perdonar
conduce /kən'dus/ *vi* contribuir, conducir
conducive /kən'dusɪv/ *a* que contribuye, conducente; favorable
conduct /*n* 'kɒndʌkt; *v* kən'dʌkt/ *n* conducta, *f.* *—vt* conducir; guiar; *Mus.* dirigir; (oneself) portarse, con-

ducirse; *Phys.* conducir. *—vi Mus.* dirigir (una orquesta, etc.); *Phys.* ser conductor. **conducted tour,** excursión acompañada, *f;* viaje acompañado, *m*
conduction /kən'dʌkʃən/ *n* conducción, *f*
conductive /kən'dʌktɪv/ *a* conductivo
conductivity /ˌkɒndʌk'tɪvɪti/ *n* conductibilidad, *f*
conductor /kən'dʌktər/ *n* (guide) guía, *mf;* (of an orchestra) director, *m;* (on a tram, etc.) cobrador, *m; Phys.* conductor, *m*
conduit /'kɒnduɪt/ *n* conducto, *m;* cañería, *f;* canal, *m*
cone /koun/ *n* (*Bot. Geom.* etc.) cono, *m*
confabulation /kənˌfæbyə'leiʃən/ *n* confabulación, *f*
confection /kən'fɛkʃən/ *n* confección, *f, vt* confeccionar
confectioner /kən'fɛkʃənər/ *n* confitero (-ra); pastelero (-ra)
confectionery /kən'fɛkʃəˌnɛri/ *n* confitería, pastelería, repostería, *f*
confederate / *a, n* kən'fɛdərɪt; *v* -'fɛdəˌreit/ *a* confederado; aliado. *—n* confederado, *m;* (in crime) cómplice, *mf.* *—vt* confederar. *—vi* confederarse; aliarse
confederation /kənˌfɛdə'reiʃən/ *n* confederación, *f*
confer /kən'fɜr/ *vt* conceder, conferir; (an honor, etc.) otorgar, investir (con). *—vi* consultar (con); deliberar, considerar
conference /'kɒnfərəns/ *n* conferencia, consulta, *f;* conversación, *f*
conferment /kən'fɜrmənt/ *n* otorgamiento, *m;* concesión, *f*
confess /kən'fɛs/ *vt* confesar, reconocer; *Inf.* admitir; (of a priest) confesar; (of a penitent) confesarse. *—vi* hacer una confesión; (one's sins) confesarse. **I c. that I was surprised,** No puedo negar que me sorprendió
confessed /kən'fɛst/ *a* confesado, declarado
confession /kən'fɛʃən/ *n* confesión, *f;* reconocimiento, *m;* declaración, *f;* religión, *f;* (creed) credo, *m.* **to go to c.,** confesarse. **to hear a c.,** confesar (a)
confessional /kən'fɛʃənḷ/ *n* confesionario, *m*
confessor /kən'fɛsər/ *n* confesor, *m*
confetti /kən'fɛti/ *n pl* confeti, papel picado *m,* serpentina, *f*
confidant /'kɒnfɪˌdænt/ *n* confidente, *m*
confidante /ˌkɒnfɪ'dænt/ *n* confidenta, *f*
confide /kən'faid/ *vi* confiar (a or en). *—vt* confiar
confidence /'kɒnfɪdəns/ *n* confianza, *f;* seguridad, *f;* (revelation) confidencia, *f.* **in c.,** en confianza. **over-c.,** presunción, *f.* **to have c. in,** tener confianza en. **c. man,** caballero de industria, estafador, *m.* **c. trick,** timo, *m*
confident /'kɒnfɪdənt/ *a* confiado; seguro; (conceited) presumido
confidential /ˌkɒnfɪ'dɛnʃəl/ *a* confidencial; de confianza. **c. clerk,** empleado (-da) de confianza. **c. letter,** carta confidencial, *f*
confidentially /ˌkɒnfɪ'dɛnʃəli/ *adv* en confianza, confidencialmente
confidently /'kɒnfɪdəntli/ *adv* confiadamente
confiding /kən'faidɪŋ/ *a* confiado
confidingly /kən'faidɪŋli/ *adv* con confianza
configuration /kənˌfɪgyə'reiʃən/ *n* configuración, *f*
confine /kən'fain/ *vt* limitar; (imprison) encerrar. **confined space,** espacio limitado, *m.* **to be confined,** (of a woman) estar de parto, parir. **to be confined to one's room,** no poder dejar su cuarto. **to c. oneself to,** limitarse a
confinement /kən'fainmənt/ *n* encierro, *m,* prisión, *f;* reclusión, *f;* (of a woman) parto, *m.* **to suffer solitary c.,** estar incomunicado
confines /'kɒnfainz/ *n pl* límites, *m pl*; confines, *m pl*; fronteras, *f pl*
confirm /kən'fɜrm/ *vt* confirmar; corroborar; *Eccl.* confirmar
confirmation /ˌkɒnfər'meiʃən/ *n* confirmación, *f;* (of a treaty) ratificación, *f; Eccl.* confirmación, *f*
confirmatory /kən'fɜrməˌtɔri/ *a* confirmatorio
confirmed /kən'fɜrmd/ *a* inveterado
confiscate /'kɒnfəˌskeit/ *vt* confiscar
confiscation /ˌkɒnfə'skeiʃən/ *n* confiscación, *f*
conflagration /ˌkɒnflə'greiʃən/ *n* conflagración, *f,* incendio, *m*
conflict / *n* 'kɒnflɪkt; *v* kən'flɪkt/ *n* conflicto, *m;* lucha, *f.* *—vi* estar opuesto (a), estar en contradicción (con)
conflicting /kən'flɪktɪŋ/ *a* opuesto; incompatible; (of evidence) contradictorio
confluence /'kɒnfluəns/ *n* confluencia, *f*
conform /kən'fɔrm/ *vt* ajustar, conformar. *—vi* ajustarse (a), amoldarse (a); conformarse (a); adaptarse (a)
conformation /ˌkɒnfɔr'meiʃən/ *n* conformación, *f*
conformity /kən'fɔrmɪti/ *n* conformidad, *f.* **in c. with,** en conformidad con, con arreglo a
confound /kɒn'faund/ *vt* confundir. **C. it!** ¡Demonio!
confounded /kɒn'faundɪd/ *a* perplejo; *Inf.* maldito
confraternity /ˌkɒnfrə'tɜrnɪti/ *n* cofradía, hermandad, *f*
confront /kən'frʌnt/ *vt* hacer frente (a), afrontar; salir al paso; confrontar
Confucianism /kən'fyuʃəˌnɪzəm/ *n* el confucianismo, *m*
confuse /kən'fyuz/ *vt* turbar, aturdir; confundir (con); (the issue) obscurecer; (disconcert) desconcertar, dejar confuso (a); dejar perplejo (a). **You have confused one thing with another,** Has confundido una cosa con otra. **My mind was confused,** Mis ideas eran confusas; Tenía la cabeza trastornada
confused /kən'fyuzd/ *a* confuso
confusing /kən'fyuzɪŋ/ *a* turbador; desconcertante. **It is all very c.,** Todo ello es muy difícil de comprender
confusion /kən'fyuʒən/ *n* confusión, *f.* **covered with c.,** confuso, avergonzado. **to be in c.,** estar confuso; estar en desorden
confute /kən'fyut/ *vt* (a person) confundir; (by evidence) refutar, confutar
congeal /kən'dʒil/ *vt* congelar; (blood) coagular. *—vi* congelarse, helarse; coagularse
congealment /kən'dʒilmənt/ *n* congelación, *f;* (of blood) coagulación, *f*
congenial /kən'dʒinyəl/ *a* (of persons) simpático; propicio, favorable; agradable
congenital /kən'dʒɛnɪtḷ/ *a* congénito
congest /kən'dʒɛst/ *vt* atestar; amontonar; *Med.* congestionar
congested /kən'dʒɛstɪd/ *a Med.* congestionado; (of places) atestado de gente; de mayor población; concurrido. **c. area,** área de mayor densidad de población, *f*
congestion /kən'dʒɛstʃən/ *n Med.* congestión, *f;* densidad del tráfico, *f;* mayor densidad de población, *f*
conglomerate /kən'glɒmərɪt/ *a* conglomerado. *—n* conglomerado, *m*
conglomeration /kənˌglɒmə'reiʃən/ *n* conglomeración, *f*
congratulate /kən'grætʃəˌleit/ *vt* felicitar, dar la enhorabuena (a); congratular
congratulation /kənˌgrætʃə'leiʃən/ *n* felicitación, enhorabuena, *f;* congratulación, *f*
congratulatory /kən'grætʃələˌtɔri/ *a* de felicitación, congratulatorio
congregate /'kɒŋgrɪˌgeit/ *vi* congregarse, reunirse, juntarse
congregation /ˌkɒŋgrɪ'geiʃən/ *n* congregación, *f;* asamblea, reunión, *f;* (in a church) fieles, *m pl*; (parishioners) feligreses, *m pl*
congress /'kɒŋgrɪs/ *n* congreso, *m.* **C.-man,** miembro del Congreso, *m*
conical /'kɒnɪkəl/ *a* cónico
conifer /'kounəfər/ *n* conífera, *f*
coniferous /kou'nɪfərəs/ *a* conífero
conjectural /kən'dʒɛktʃərəl/ *a* conjetural
conjecture /kən'dʒɛktʃər/ *n* conjetura, *f, vt* conjeturar
conjoint /kən'dʒɔint/ *a* asociado, conjunto
conjointly /kən'dʒɔintli/ *adv* juntamente, en común
conjugal /'kɒndʒəgəl/ *a* conyugal
conjugate /'kɒndʒəˌgeit/ *vt* conjugar. *—vi* conjugarse
conjugation /ˌkɒndʒə'geiʃən/ *n* conjugación, *f*
conjunction /kən'dʒʌŋkʃən/ *n* conjunción, *f.* **in c. with,** de acuerdo con

conjunctive /kən'dʒʌŋktɪv/ *a* conjuntivo. *—n* conjunción, *f*
conjunctivitis /kən,dʒʌŋktə'vaitɪs/ *n* conjuntivitis, *f*
conjure /'kɒndʒər/ *vt* (implore) rogar, suplicar. *—vi* (juggle) hacer juegos de manos. **a name to c. with,** un nombre todopoderoso. **to c. up,** (spirits) conjurar; *Fig.* evocar
conjurer, conjuror /'kɒndʒərər/ *n* (magician) nigromante, *m;* prestidigitador, *m.* **conjuror's wand,** varilla de virtudes, *f*
conjuring /'kɒndʒərɪŋ/ *n* prestidigitación, *f,* juegos de manos, *m pl.* **c. trick,** juego de manos, *m.* **c. up,** evocación, *f*
connect /kə'nɛkt/ *vt* juntar, unir; (relate) relacionar; asociar; (*Elec.* and *Mech.*) conectar. *—vi* juntarse, unirse; relacionarse; asociarse; (of events) encadenarse; (of trains) enlazar. **This train connects with the Madrid express,** Este tren enlaza con el expreso de Madrid. **They are connected with the Borgia family,** Están emparentados con los Borgia, Son parientes de los Borgia
connected /kə'nɛktɪd/ *a* conexo; (coherent) coherente; relacionado; asociado; (in a crime) implicado; (by marriage, etc.) emparentado
connectedly /kə'nɛktɪdli/ *adv* coherentemente
connecting /kə'nɛktɪŋ/ *a* que une; (*Mech.* and *Elec.*) conectivo; (of doors, etc.) comunicante. **c.-link,** *Mech.* varilla de conexión, *f; Fig.* lazo, *m.* **c.-rod,** biela, *f*
connection /kə'nɛkʃən/ *n* conexión, *f;* unión, *f;* (of ideas) relación, *f;* (junction) empalme, *m;* (of trains, boats) enlace, *m;* (intimacy) intimidad, *f;* (relative) pariente, *m;* (of a firm, etc.) clientela, *f; Elec.* conexión, *f.* **in c. with,** con referencia a; en asociación con. **in this c.,** respecto a esto
conning tower /'kɒnɪŋ/ *n* torre de mando, *f*
connivance /kə'naivəns/ *n* consentimiento, *m;* complicidad, *f*
connive (at) /kə'naiv/ *vi* hacer la vista gorda, ser cómplice (en)
connotation /,kɒnə'teiʃən/ *n* connotación, *f*
connote /kə'nout/ *vt* connotar
connubial /kə'nubiəl/ *a* conyugal
conquer /'kɒŋkər/ *vt* conquistar; vencer. *—vi* triunfar
conquering /'kɒŋkərɪŋ/ *a* conquistador, vencedor; triunfante, victorioso
conqueror /'kɒŋkərər/ *n* conquistador, *m;* vencedor, *m*
conquest /'kɒnkwɛst/ *n* conquista, *f.* **to make a c. of,** conquistar
consanguineous /,kɒnsæŋ'gwɪniəs/ *a* consanguíneo
consanguinity /,kɒnsæŋ'gwɪnɪti/ *n* consanguinidad, *f*
conscience /'kɒnʃəns/ *n* conciencia, *f.* **in all c.,** en verdad. **with a clear c.,** con la conciencia limpia. **c.-stricken,** lleno de remordimientos
conscienceless /'kɒnʃənslɪs/ *a* desalmado, falto de conciencia
conscientious /,kɒnʃi'ɛnʃəs/ *a* concienzudo; diligente. **c. objector,** objetor de conciencia, *m*
conscientiously /,kɒnʃi'ɛnʃəsli/ *adv* concienzudamente
conscientiousness /,kɒnʃi'ɛnʃəsnɪs/ *n* conciencia, diligencia, *f;* rectitud, *f*
conscious /'kɒnʃəs/ *a* consciente. *—n Psychol.* consciente, *m.* **to become c.,** (after unconsciousness) volver en sí. **to become c. of,** darse cuenta de
consciously /'kɒnʃəsli/ *adv* conscientemente, a sabiendas
consciousness /'kɒnʃəsnɪs/ *n* conciencia, *f;* conocimiento, sentido, *m.* **to lose c.,** perder el conocimiento, perder el sentido. **to recover c.,** recobrar el sentido, volver en sí
conscript / *n* 'kɒnskrɪpt; *v* kən'skrɪpt/ *n* conscripto, *m, a* conscripto. *—vt* reclutar
conscription /kən'skrɪpʃən/ *n* conscripción, *f*
consecrate /'kɒnsɪ,kreit/ *vt* consagrar; bendecir
consecration /,kɒnsɪ'kreiʃən/ *n* consagración, *f;* dedicación, *f*
consecutive /kən'sɛkyətɪv/ *a* consecutivo
consecutively /kən'sɛkyətɪvli/ *adv* consecutivamente
consensus /kən'sɛnsəs/ *n* consenso, *m,* unanimidad, *f.* **c. of opinion,** opinión general, *f*
consent /kən'sɛnt/ *vi* consentir. *—n* consentimiento, *m;* permiso, *m,* aquiescencia, *f.* **by common c.,** de común acuerdo
consequence /'kɒnsɪ,kwɛns/ *n* consecuencia, *f;* resultado, *m;* importancia, *f,* **in c.,** por consiguiente. **in c. of,** de resultas de. **of no c.,** sin importancia
consequences /'kɒnsɪ,kwɛnsɪz/ *n* (game) cartas rusas, *f pl*
consequent /'kɒnsɪ,kwɛnt/ *a* consecuente, consiguiente
consequential /,kɒnsɪ'kwɛnʃəl/ *a* consecuente; (of persons) fatuo, engreído
consequently /'kɒnsɪ,kwɛntli/ *adv* por consiguiente, en consecuencia
conservation /,kɒnsər'veiʃən/ *n* conservación, *f.* **c. of energy,** conservación de energía, *f*
conservatism /kən'sɜrvə,tɪzəm/ *n* conservadurismo, *m*
conservative /kən'sɜrvətɪv/ *a* preservativo; conservador. *—n* conservador (-ra). **c. party,** partido conservador, *m*
conservatoire /kən,sɜrvə'twɑr/ *n* conservatorio de música, *m*
conservatory /kən'sɜrvə,tɔri/ *n* invernáculo, invernadero, *m*
conserve /kən'sɜrv/ *vt* conservar
consider /kən'sɪdər/ *vt* considerar, pensar meditar; tomar en cuenta; examinar; (deem) juzgar; (believe) creer, estar convencido de (que); (of persons) considerar. **all things considered,** considerando todos los puntos, después de considerarlo todo
considerable /kən'sɪdərəbəl/ *a* considerable
considerably /kən'sɪdərəbli/ *adv* considerablemente
considerate /kən'sɪdərɪt/ *a* considerado, solícito
considerately /kən'sɪdərɪtli/ *adv* con consideración, solícitamente
consideration /kən,sɪdə'reiʃən/ *n* consideración, *f;* reflexión, deliberación, *f;* remuneración, *f.* **out of c. for,** en consideración de; por consideración a. **to take into c.,** tomar en cuenta, tomar en consideración
considered /kən'sɪdərd/ *a* considerado
considering /kən'sɪdərɪŋ/ *prep* en consideración de, considerando, en vista de
consign /kən'sain/ *vt* consignar; *Fig.* enviar. **to c. to oblivion,** sepultar en el olvido
consignee /,kɒnsai'ni/ *n* consignatorio, *m*
consignment /kən'sainmənt/ *n* consignación, *f;* envío, *m*
consignor /kən'sainər/ *n* consignador, *m*
consist /kən'sɪst/ *vi* consistir (en); ser compatible (con). **to c. of,** componerse de, consistir de
consistence, consistency /kən'sɪstəns; kən'sɪstənsi/ *n* consistencia, *f;* compatibilidad, *f;* lógica, *f;* (of persons) consecuencia, *f*
consistent /kən'sɪstənt/ *a* compatible; lógico; (of persons) consecuente
consistently /kən'sɪstəntli/ *adv* conformemente (a); consecuentemente
consolation /,kɒnsə'leiʃən/ *n* consuelo, *m,* consolación, *f*
console /'kɒnsoul/ *vt* consolar; confortar. *—n Archit.* cartela, *f.* **c. table,** consola, *f*
consolidate /kən'sɒlɪ,deit/ *vt* consolidar. *—vi* consolidarse
consolidation /kən,sɒlɪ'deiʃən/ *n* consolidación, *f*
consoling /kən'soulɪŋ/ *a* consolador; confortador
consols /'kɒnsɒlz, kən'sɒlz/ *n pl* (títulos) consolidados, *m pl*
consonance /'kɒnsənəns/ *n* consonancia, *f*
consonant /'kɒnsənənt/ *a* consonante
consort / *n* 'kɒnsɔrt, *v* kən'sɔrt/ *n* consorte, *mf.* **to c. with,** frecuentar la compañía de; ir con; acompañar (a). **prince c.,** príncipe consorte, *m*
conspicuous /kən'spɪkyuəs/ *a* conspicuo; prominente; notable. **to be c.,** destacarse; llamar la atención. **to make oneself c.,** ponerse en evidencia, llamar la atención
conspicuously /kən'spɪkyuəsli/ *adv* visiblemente; muy en evidencia
conspiracy /kən'spɪrəsi/ *n* conspiración, *f;* complot, *m*
conspirator /kən'spɪrətər/ *n* conspirador (-ra)
conspire /kən'spaiᵊr/ *vi* conspirar

constable /ˈkɒnstəbəl/ *n* agente de policía, *m;* (historical) condestable, *m.* **chief c.,** jefe de policía, *m*
constabulary /kənˈstæbyəˌlɛri/ *n* policía, *f*
constancy /ˈkɒnstənsi/ *n* constancia, *f*
constant /ˈkɒnstənt/ *a* constante; incesante. —*n* constante, *m*
Constantinople /ˌkɒnstæntn̩ˈoupəl/ Constantinopla, *f*
constantly /ˈkɒnstəntli/ *adv* constantemente
constellation /ˌkɒnstəˈleiʃən/ *n* constelación, *f*
consternation /ˌkɒnstərˈneiʃən/ *n* consternación, *f;* espanto, terror, *m*
constipate /ˈkɒnstəˌpeit/ *vt* estreñir
constipation /ˌkɒnstəˈpeiʃən/ *n* estreñimiento, *m,* constipación de vientre, *f*
constituency /kənˈstɪtʃuənsi/ *n* distrito electoral, *m*
constituent /kənˈstɪtʃuənt/ *a* constituyente. —*n* constituyente, *m;* componente, *m;* elector (-ra)
constitute /ˈkɒnstɪˌtut/ *vt* constituir; nombrar; autorizar
constitution /ˌkɒnstɪˈtuʃən/ *n* constitución, *f*
constitutional /ˌkɒnstɪˈtuʃənl̩/ *a* constitucional
constitutionally /ˌkɒnstɪˈtuʃənl̩i/ *adv* constitucionalmente
constrain /kənˈstrein/ *vt* obligar, forzar. **I felt constrained to help them,** Me sentí obligado a ayudarles
constrained /kənˈstreind/ *a* (of smiles, etc.) forzado; (of silences) violento; (of persons) avergonzado
constraint /kənˈstreint/ *n* fuerza, compulsión, *f;* (of atmosphere) tensión, *f;* (reserve) reserva, *f;* vergüenza, *f*
constrict /kənˈstrɪkt/ *vt* apretar, estrechar
constriction /kənˈstrɪkʃən/ *n* constricción, *f*
construct /kənˈstrʌkt/ *vt* edificar; construir
construction /kənˈstrʌkʃən/ *n* construcción, *f;* interpretación, *f.* **to put a wrong c. on,** interpretar mal
constructional /kənˈstrʌkʃənl̩/ *a* construccional
constructive /kənˈstrʌktɪv/ *a* constructor
constructor /kənˈstrʌktər/ *n* constructor, *m*
construe /kənˈstru/ *vt* construir; (translate) traducir; *Fig.* interpretar
consul /ˈkɒnsəl/ *n* cónsul, *m*
consular /ˈkɒnsələr/ *a* consular
consular fees *n pl* derechos consulares, *m pl*
consulate /ˈkɒnsəlɪt/ *n* consulado, *m.* **c. general,** consulado general, *m*
consult /kənˈsʌlt/ *vt* consultar. —*vi* consultar (con), aconsejarse (con)
consultant /kənˈsʌltənt/ *n* (*Med.* and other uses) especialista, *m*
consultation /ˌkɒnsəlˈteiʃən/ *n* consulta, *f*
consultative /kənˈsʌltətɪv/ *a* consultativo
consulting /kənˈsʌltɪŋ/ *a* consultor. **c. hours,** horas de consulta, *f pl.* **c. rooms,** consultorio, *m*
consume /kənˈsum/ *vt* consumir; (eat) comerse, tragarse. —*vi* consumirse. **to be consumed by envy,** estar consumido por la envidia. **to be consumed by thirst,** estar muerto de sed
consumer /kənˈsumər/ *n* consumidor (-ra)
consummate / *a* ˈkɒnsəmɪt; *v* -ˌmeit/ *a* consumido, perfecto. —*vt* consumar
consummation /ˌkɒnsəˈmeiʃən/ *n* consumación, *f*
consumption /kənˈsʌmpʃən/ *n* consumo, *m;* gasto, *m; Med.* tuberculosis, *f.* **fuel c.,** consumo de combustible, *m*
consumptive /kənˈsʌmptɪv/ *a* destructivo; *Med.* tísico, hético. —*n* tísico (-ca)
contact /ˈkɒntækt/ *n* contacto, *m, vt* ponerse en contacto con. **to be in c. with,** estar en contacto con
contagion /kənˈteidʒən/ *n* contagio, *m*
contagious /kənˈteidʒəs/ *a* contagioso
contain /kənˈtein/ *vt* contener; incluir; *Geom.* encerrar; (arithmetic) ser divisible por; (oneself) dominarse. **I could not c. myself,** No pude dominarme
container /kənˈteinər/ *n* recipiente, *m;* envase, *m;* (box) caja, *f*
contaminate /kənˈtæməˌneit/ *vt* contaminar; corromper
contamination /kənˌtæməˈneiʃən/ *n* contaminación, *f*
contemplate /ˈkɒntəmˌpleit/ *vt* contemplar; meditar, considerar; (plan) tener intención de, pensar, proponerse
contemplation /ˌkɒntəmˈpleiʃən/ *n* contemplación, *f;* meditación, *f;* expectación, esperanza, *f;* (plan) proyecto, *m.* **to have something in c.,** proyectar algo
contemplative /kənˈtɛmplətɪv/ *a* contemplativo
contemplatively *adv* contemplativamente; atentamente
contemporaneous /kənˌtɛmpəˈreiniəs/ *a* contemporáneo
contemporary /kənˈtɛmpəˌrɛri/ *a* contemporáneo; (of persons) coetáneo; (of events, etc.) actual. —*n* contemporáneo (-ea)
contempt /kənˈtɛmpt/ *n* desprecio, menosprecio, *m;* desdén, *m.* **c. of court,** falta de respeto a la sala, *f*
contemptible /kənˈtɛmptəbəl/ *a* menospreciable, despreciable; vil
contemptibly /kənˈtɛmptəbli/ *adv* vilmente
contempt of court *n* rebeldía a la corte, *f*
contempt of law *n* rebeldía a la ley, *f*
contemptuous /kənˈtɛmptʃuəs/ *a* desdeñoso; despectivo; de desprecio. **to be c. of,** desdeñar; menospreciar, tener en poco (a)
contemptuously /kənˈtɛmptʃuəsli/ *adv* con desprecio, desdeñosamente
contend /kənˈtɛnd/ *vi* contender; (affirm) sostener, mantener. **He contended that...,** Sostuvo que...; **contending party,** *Law.* parte litigante, *f*
content / *n* ˈkɒntɛnt; *a, v* kənˈtɛnt/ *n* contenido, *m;* capacidad, *f;* (emotion) contento, *m;* satisfacción, *f.* —*a* contento; satisfecho (de). —*vt* contentar; satisfacer. **to one's heart's c.,** a pedir de boca; a gusto de uno; cuanto quisiera
contented /kənˈtɛntɪd/ *a* satisfecho, contento
contentedly /kənˈtɛntɪdli/ *adv* con satisfacción, contentamente
contention /kənˈtɛnʃən/ *n* disputa, controversia, discusión, *f;* argumento, *m,* opinión, *f*
contentious /kənˈtɛnʃəs/ *a* contencioso
contentment /kənˈtɛntmənt/ *n* contentamiento, *m;* contento, *m*
contest / *v* kənˈtɛst; *n* ˈkɒntɛst/ *vt* disputar; (a suit) defender; (a match, an election, etc.) disputar. —*n* disputa, *f;* combate, *m,* lucha, *f;* (competition) concurso, *m*
contestant /kənˈtɛstənt/ *n* contendiente, *mf*
context /ˈkɒntɛkst/ *n* contexto, *m*
contiguity /ˌkɒntɪˈgyuɪti/ *n* contigüidad, *f*
contiguous /kənˈtɪgyuəs/ *a* contiguo, lindero, adyacente
continence /ˈkɒntn̩əns/ *n* continencia, *f*
continent /ˈkɒntn̩ənt/ *a* continente. —*n* continente, *m*
continental /ˌkɒntn̩ˈɛntl̩/ *a* continental
continental shelf *n* plataforma continental, *f*
contingency /kənˈtɪndʒənsi/ *n* contingencia, *f*
contingent /kənˈtɪndʒənt/ *a* contingente. —*n Mil.* contingente, *m.* **to be c. on,** (of events) depender de
continual /kənˈtɪnyuəl/ *a* continuo
continually /kənˈtɪnyuəli/ *adv* continuamente
continuance /kənˈtɪnyuəns/ *n* continuación, *f*
continuation /kənˌtɪnyuˈeiʃən/ *n* continuación, *f;* prolongación, *f*
continue /kənˈtɪnyu/ *vi* continuar; seguir; prolongarse; durar. —*vt* continuar; seguir; proseguir; perpetuar; (in an office) retener. **to be continued,** se continuará, continuará, seguirá
continuer /kənˈtɪnyuər/ *n* continuador (-ra)
continuity /ˌkɒntn̩ˈuɪti/ *n* continuidad, *f*
continuous /kənˈtɪnyuəs/ *a* continuo. **c. performance,** sesión continua, *f*
continuously /kənˈtɪnyuəsli/ *adv* de continuo, continuamente
contort /kənˈtɔrt/ *vt* retorcer
contortion /kənˈtɔrʃən/ *n* contorsión, *f*
contortionist /kənˈtɔrʃənɪst/ *n* contorsionista, *m*
contour /ˈkɒntʊr/ *n* contorno, *m;* curva de nivel, *f.* **c. map,** mapa con curvas de nivel, *m*
contraband /ˈkɒntrəˌbænd/ *n* contrabando, *m*
contrabandist /ˈkɒntrəˌbændɪst/ *n* contrabandista, *mf*
contrabass /ˈkɒntrəˌbeis/ *n* contrabajo, *m*
contraception /ˌkɒntrəˈsɛpʃən/ *n* anticoncepción, *f*
contraceptive /ˌkɒntrəˈsɛptɪv/ *n* anticonceptivo, *m*

contract /*n* 'kɒntrækt; *v* kən'trækt/ *n* pacto, *m;* (*Com.* and *Law.*) contrato, *m;* (betrothal) esponsales, *m pl;* (marriage) capitulaciones, *f pl;* (cards) "Bridge," *m.* —*vt* contraer; (acquire) adquirir, contraer; (a marriage, etc.) contraer; (be betrothed to) desposarse con; (by formal contract) contratar; pactar. —*vi* (shrink) contraerse, encogerse; comprometerse por contrato. **breach of c.,** no cumplimiento de contrato, *m.* **c. party,** (of matrimony) contrayente, *mf*

contractile /kən'træktḷ/ *a* contráctil

contraction /kən'trækʃən/ *n* contracción, *f* (act or process); forma contracta, *f* (like *isn't* or *can't*)

contractor /'kɒntræktər/ *n* contratista, *mf*

contradict /ˌkɒntrə'dɪkt/ *vt* contradecir; desmentir

contradiction /ˌkɒntrə'dɪkʃən/ *n* contradicción, *f;* negación, *f*

contradictory /ˌkɒntrə'dɪktəri/ *a* contradictorio; opuesto (a), contrario (a)

contralto /kən'træltou/ *n* (voice) contralto, *m;* (woman) contralto, *f*

contraption /kən'træpʃən/ *n Inf.* artefacto, *m*

contrapuntal /ˌkɒntrə'pʌntḷ/ *a Mus.* de contrapunto

contrariness /'kɒntrɛrinɪs/ *n Inf.* testarudez, terquedad, *f*

contrariwise /'kɒntrɛriˌwaiz/ *adv* al contrario; al revés

contrary /'kɒntrɛri/ *a* contrario; opuesto (a); desfavorable, poco propicio; (of persons) difícil, terco. —*n* contraria, *f;* (logic) contrario, *m, adv* en contra, contrariamente. **on the c.,** al contrario. **to be c.,** (of persons) llevar la contraria

contrast /*n* 'kɒntræst; *v* kən'træst/ *n* contraste, *m.* —*vt* contrastar (con). —*vi* contrastar (con), hacer contraste (con)

contravene /ˌkɒntrə'vin/ *vt* contravenir; atacar, oponerse (a)

contravention /ˌkɒntrə'vɛnʃən/ *n* contravención, *f*

contribute /kən'trɪbyut/ *vt* contribuir; (an article) escribir

contribution /ˌkɒntrə'byuʃən/ *n* contribución, *f;* (to a review, etc.) artículo, *m*

contributor /kən'trɪbyətər/ *n* contribuyente, *mf;* (to a journal) colaborador (-ra)

contributory /kən'trɪbyəˌtɔri/ *a* contribuyente

contrite /kən'trait/ *a* penitente, arrepentido, contrito

contritely /kən'traitli/ *adv* contritamente

contrition /kən'trɪʃən/ *n* contrición, penitencia, *f,* arrepentimiento, *m*

contrivance /kən'traivəns/ *n* invención, *f;* (scheme) treta, idea, estratagema, *f;* (machine) aparato, mecanismo, artefacto, *m*

contrive /kən'traiv/ *vt* inventar; idear, proyectar. —*vi* (succeed in) lograr, conseguir; (manage) arreglárselas

control /kən'troul/ *n* autoridad, *f;* dominio, *m;* gobierno, *m;* dirección, *f;* regulación, *f;* (restraint) freno, *m;* (*Biol.* and *Spirit.*) control, *m;* (of a vehicle) conducción, *f;* manejo, *m,* manipulación, *f; pl* **controls,** *Mech.* mando, *m.* —*vt* dirigir, regir; regular; usar, manejar, manipular; controlar; (dominate) dominar; (curb) refrenar, reprimir; (command) mandar. **He lost c. of the car,** Perdió el mando (or control) del automóvil. **out of c.,** fuera de mando, fuera de control. **remote c.,** mando a distancia, *m.* **to c. oneself,** dominarse, contenerse. **to lose c. of oneself,** no lograr dominarse, perder el control. **c. stick,** *Aer.* palanca de mando, *f.* **c. tower,** *Aer.* torre de mando, *f*

controller /kən'troulər/ *n* interventor, *m;* (device) regulador, *m*

controlling /kən'troulɪŋ/ *n* See **control.** *a* regulador

controversial /ˌkɒntrə'vɜrʃəl/ *a* debatible, discutible

controversy /'kɒntrəˌvɜrsi/ *n* controversia, *f;* argumento, *m;* altercación, disputa, *f*

contumacious /ˌkɒntʊ'meiʃəs/ *a* contumaz

contumacy /'kɒntʊməsi/ *n* contumacia, *f*

contumely /'kɒntʊməli/ *n* contumelia, *f*

contusion /kən'tuʒən/ *n* herida contusa, *f*

conundrum /kə'nʌndrəm/ *n* acertijo, rompecabezas, *m;* problema, *m*

convalesce /ˌkɒnvə'lɛs/ *vi* convalecer, estar convaleciente

convalescence /ˌkɒnvə'lɛsəns/ *n* convalecencia, *f*

convalescent /ˌkɒnvə'lɛsənt/ *a* convaleciente. —*n* convaleciente, *mf.* **c. home,** casa de convalecencia, *f*

convene /kən'vin/ *vt* (a meeting) convocar; (person) citar. —*vi* reunirse

convenience /kən'vinyəns/ *n* conveniencia, *f;* (comfort) comodidad, *f;* utilidad, *f;* (advantage) ventaja, *f;* (public) retretes, *m pl.* **at one's c.,** cuando le sea conveniente a uno. **to make a c. of,** abusar de. **with all modern conveniences,** con todo el confort moderno

convenient /kən'vinyənt/ *a* conveniente; apropiado; cómodo. **I shall make it c. to see him at 6 p.m.,** Arreglaré mis asuntos para verle a las seis

conveniently /kən'vinyəntli/ *adv* cómodamente; oportunamente; sin inconveniente

convent /'kɒnvɛnt/ *n* convento, *m*

convention /kən'vɛnʃən/ *n* convención, *f*

conventional /kən'vɛnʃənḷ/ *a* convencional

conventual /kən'vɛntʃuəl/ *a* conventual. —*n* conventual, *m*

converge /kən'vɜrdʒ/ *vi* convergir

convergence /kən'vɜrdʒəns/ *n* convergencia, *f*

convergent /kən'vɜrdʒənt/ *a* convergente

conversance /kən'vɜrsəns/ *n* familiaridad, *f,* conocimiento, *m*

conversant /kən'vɜrsənt/ *a* familiar, versado, conocedor. **c. with,** versado en

conversation /ˌkɒnvər'seiʃən/ *n* conversación, *f.* **to engage in c. with,** entablar conversación con

conversational /ˌkɒnvər'seiʃənḷ/ *a* de conversación; (talkative) locuaz

conversationally /ˌkɒnvər'seiʃənḷi/ *adv* en tono familiar; familiarmente; en conversación

converse /kən'vɜrs/ *vi* conversar. **to c. by signs,** hablar por señas

conversely /kən'vɜrsli/ *adv* recíprocamente

conversion /kən'vɜrʒən/ *n* conversión, *f*

convert /*v* kən'vɜrt; *n* 'kɒnvɜrt/ *vt* convertir; transformar. —*n* converso (-sa). **to become a c.,** convertirse

convertible /kən'vɜrtəbəl/ *a* convertible; transformable

convex /*a* kɒn'vɛks; *n* 'kɒnvɛks/ *a* convexo

convey /kən'vei/ *vt* transportar; conducir, llevar; (a meaning, etc.) comunicar, dar a entender; expresar; *Law.* traspasar

conveyance /kən'veiəns/ *n* transporte, *m;* conducción, *f;* medio de transporte, *m;* vehículo, *m;* carruaje, *m;* (of property) traspaso, *m;* (document) escritura de traspaso, *f.* **public c.,** coche de alquiler, *m;* ómnibus, *m*

convict /*n* 'kɒnvɪkt; *v* kən'vɪkt/ *n* convicto, *m;* presidiario, *m.* —*vt Law.* condenar; culpar. **c. settlement,** colonia penal, *f*

conviction /kən'vɪkʃən/ *n* (of a prisoner) condenación, *f;* (belief) convencimiento, *m,* convicción, *f*

convince /kən'vɪns/ *vt* convencer

convincing /kən'vɪnsɪŋ/ *a* convincente

convivial /kən'vɪviəl/ *a* convivial

conviviality /kənˌvɪvi'ælɪti/ *n* jovialidad, *f*

convocation /ˌkɒnvə'keiʃən/ *n* convocación, *f*

convoke /kən'vouk/ *vt* convocar

convolution /ˌkɒnvə'luʃən/ *n* circunvolución, *f;* espira, *f*

convoy /'kɒnvɔi/ *vt* convoyar, escoltar. —*n* convoy, *m.* **to sail in a c.,** navegar en convoy

convulse /kən'vʌls/ *vt* agitar; sacudir; estremecer. **to be convulsed with laughter,** desternillarse de risa, morirse de risa

convulsion /kən'vʌlʃən/ *n* convulsión, *f;* conmoción, *f*

convulsive /kən'vʌlsɪv/ *a* convulsivo

coo /ku/ *vi* arrullar; (of infants) gorjearse. —*n* arrullo, *m*

cooing /'kuɪŋ/ *n* arrullo, *m*

cook /kʊk/ *n* cocinero (-ra). —*vt* guisar, cocer, cocinar; (falsify) falsear

cooker /'kʊkər/ *n* cocina, *f.* **gas c.,** cocina de gas, *f*

cookery /'kʊkəri/ *n* cocina, *f.* **c.-book,** libro de cocina, *m*

cooking /'kʊkɪŋ/ *n* arte de guisar, *m,* or *f;* cocina, *f;*

(of accounts, etc.) falsificación, *f.* **c. range,** cocina económica, *f.* **c.-stove,** cocina, *f.* **c. utensils,** batería de cocina, *f*

cool /kul/ *a* fresco; bastante frío; (not ardent and of receptions, etc.) frío; (calm) sereno, imperturbable. —*n* fresco, *m.* —*vi* enfriarse; (of love, etc.) resfriarse; (of the weather) refrescar; (of persons) refrescarse. —*vt* refrescar; enfriar. **to grow cooler,** (of weather) refrescarse; (of persons) tener menos calor. **It is c.,** Hace fresco. **to be as c. as a cucumber,** tener sangre fría. **c. drink,** bebida fría, *f.* **c.-headed,** sereno, imperturbable

coolie /'kuli/ *n* culí, *m*

cooling /'kulɪŋ/ *n* enfriamiento, *m, a* refrescante

coolly /'kuli/ *adv* frescamente; fríamente, con frialdad; imperturbablemente; (impudently) descaradamente

coolness /'kulnɪs/ *n* frescura, *f;* (of a welcome, etc.) frialdad, *f;* (sangfroid) sangre fría, serenidad, *f;* aplomo, *m*

coop /kup/ *n* gallinero, *m;* caponera, *f, vt* enjaular; encerrar. **to keep** (someone) **cooped up,** tener encerrado (a)

cooper /'kupər/ *n* tonelero, barrilero, *m, vt* hacer barriles

cooperate /kou'ɒpəˌreit/ *vi* cooperar; colaborar

cooperation /kouˌɒpə'reiʃən/ *n* cooperación, *f*

cooperative /kou'ɒpərətɪv/ *a* cooperativo. **c. society,** cooperativa, *f*

coopt /kou'ɒpt/ *vt* elegir por votación

coordinate /*v* kou'ɔrdṇˌeit; *n, a* kou'ɔrdṇɪt/ *vt* coordinar. —*n Math.* coordenada, *f.* —*a* coordenado

coordination /kouˌɔrdṇ'eiʃən/ *n* coordinación, *f*

coot /kut/ *n* fúlica, *f*

cop /kɒp/ *n* (police officer) chapa (Ecuador), polizonte, *mf*

copartner /kou'pɑrtnər/ *n* copartícipe, *mf;* socio (-ia)

cope /koup/ *n Eccl.* capa, *f;* (of heaven) dosel, *m,* bóveda, *f.* **to c. with,** contender con; (a difficulty) hacer cara a, arrostrar

copeck /'koupɛk/ *n* copec, *m*

Copenhagen /ˌkoupən'heigən, -'hɑgən/ Copenhague, *m*

Copernican /kou'pɜrnɪkən/ *a* copernicano

copier /'kɒpiər/ *n* copiador (-ra)

coping /'koupɪŋ/ *n Archit.* albardilla, *f.* **c.-stone,** teja cumbrera, *f; Fig.* coronamiento, *m*

copious /'koupiəs/ *a* copioso, abundante

copiously /'koupiəsli/ *adv* en abundancia

copiousness /'koupiəsnɪs/ *n* abundancia, *f*

copper /'kɒpər/ *n* cobre, *m;* (coin) calderilla, *f;* (vessel) caldera, *f.* —*a* de cobre. **c.-colored,** cobrizo. **c.-smith,** calderero, *m.* **c.-sulphate,** sulfato de cobre, *m*

copperplate /'kɒpərˌpleit/ *n* lámina de cobre, *f;* grabado en cobre, *m*

coppery /'kɒpəri/ *a* cobrizo

coppice /'kɒpɪs/ *n* soto, bosquecillo, *m.* **c. with standards,** monte medio, *m*

coproprietor /ˌkouprə'praiɪtər/ *n* copropietario, *m*

copse /kɒps/ *n* arboleda, *f,* bosquecillo, *m*

Coptic /'kɒptɪk/ *a* cóptico, copto. —*n* (language) copto, cóptico, *m*

copulate /'kɒpyəˌleit/ *vi* copularse

copulation /ˌkɒpyə'leiʃən/ *n* cópula, *f*

copy /'kɒpi/ *n* copia, *f;* (of a book) ejemplar, *m;* (of a paper) número, *m;* manuscrito, *m;* (subject-matter) material, *m.* —*vt* copiar; imitar; tomar como modelo (a). **rough c.,** borrador, *m.* **c.-book,** cuaderno de escritura, *m*

copy editor *n* redactor de textos, *m*

copying /'kɒpiɪŋ/ *n* imitación, *f;* transcripción, *f.* **c. ink,** tinta de copiar, *f*

copyist /'kɒpiɪst/ *n* copiador (-ra); (plagiarist) copiante, *mf*

copyright /'kɒpiˌrait/ *n* derechos de autor, *m pl*; propiedad literaria, *f.* —*a* protegido por los derechos de autor. —*vt* registrar como propiedad literaria. **C. reserved,** Derechos reservados, Queda hecho el depósito que marca la ley

copywriter /'kɒpiˌraitər/ *n* escritor de anuncios, *m*

coquet /kou'kɛt/ *vi* coquetear; *Fig.* jugar (con)

coquetry /'koukɪtri/ *n* coquetería, *f*

coquette /kou'kɛt/ *n* coqueta, *f*

coquettish /kou'kɛtɪʃ/ *a* coquetón; atractivo

coral /'kɔrəl/ *n* coral, *m;* (polyp) coralina, *f.* —*a* de coral, coralino. **white c.,** madrépora, *f.* **c. beads,** corales, *m pl.* **c.-island,** atalón, *m.* **c.-reef,** escollo de coral, *m.* **c. snake,** coral, *f*

corbel /'kɔrbəl/ *n Archit.* ménsula, *f*

cord /kɔrd/ *n* cuerda, *f;* cordel, *m;* cordón, *m.* —*vt* encordelar. **spinal c.,** médula espinal, *f.* **umbilical c.,** cordón umbilical, *m*

cordial /'kɔrdʒəl/ *a* cordial; sincero, fervoroso. —*n* cordial, *m*

cordiality /kɔr'dʒælɪti/ *n* cordialidad, *f*

cordon /'kɔrdṇ/ *n* cordón, *m;* cinto, *m.* **to c. off,** acordonar

Cordova /'kɔrdəvə/ Córdoba, *f*

cordovan /'kɔrdəvən/ *a* cordobés. —*n* (leather) cordobán, *m*

corduroy /'kɔrdəˌrɔi/ *n* pana de cordoncillo, *f*

core /kɔr/ *n* (of a fruit) corazón, *m;* (of a rope) alma, *f,* centro, *m;* (of an abscess) foco, *m;* (of a corn) ojo, *m; Fig.* núcleo, *m;* esencia, *f;* lo esencial

coreligionist /ˌkourɪ'lɪdʒənɪst/ *n* correligionario (-ia)

corespondent /ˌkourɪ'spɒndənt/ *n* cómplice en un caso de divorcio, *mf*

Corinth /'kɔrɪnθ/ Corinto, *m*

Corinthian /kə'rɪnθiən/ *a* corintio. —*n* corintio (-ia)

cork /kɔrk/ *n* corcho, *m;* (of a bottle) tapón, *m, a* de corcho. —*vt* tapar con corcho, taponar; (wine) encorchar; (the face) tiznar con corcho quemado. **pop of a c.,** taponazo, *m.* **to draw a c.,** descorchar. **c.-jacket,** chaleco salvavidas, *m.* **c. tree,** alcornoque, *m*

corkscrew /'kɔrkˌskru/ *n* sacacorchos, *m*

cormorant /'kɔrmərənt/ *n* cormorán, *m*

corn /kɔrn/ *n* grano, cereal, *m;* (wheat) trigo, *m;* (maize) maíz, *m;* (single seed) grano, *m;* (on the foot, etc.) callo, *m.* **Indian c.,** maíz, *m.* **c. cure,** callicida, *m.* **c.-exchange,** bolsa de granos, *f.* **c.-field,** campo de trigo, *m.* **c.-flower,** aciano, *m*

cornea /'kɔrniə/ *n* córnea, *f*

corner /'kɔrnər/ *n* ángulo, *m;* (of a street or building) esquina, *f;* (of a room) rincón, *m; Auto.* viraje, *m; Com.* monopolio, *m;* (of the eye) rabo, *m;* (Assoc. football) "corner," *m.* —*vt* arrinconar; acorralar; *Com.* acaparar. **the four corners of the earth,** las cinco partes del mundo. **a tight c.,** un lance apretado, un apuro. **to drive into a c.,** *Fig.* poner entre la espada y la pared. **to look out of the c. of the eye,** mirar de reojo. **to turn the c.,** doblar la esquina; *Fig.* pasar la crisis. **c.-cupboard,** rinconera, *f.* **c. seat,** asiento del rincón, *m.* **c.-stone,** piedra angular, *f.*

cornered /'kɔrnərd/ *a* (of a person) acorralado, en aprieto; (of hats) de... picos. **three-c. hat,** sombrero de tres picos, *m*

cornet /kɔr'nɛt/ *n* (musical instrument) corneta, *f; Mil.* corneta, *m;* (paper) cucurucho, *m.* **c. player,** cornetín, *m*

cornflour /'kɔrnˌflauər/ *n* harina de maíz, *f*

cornice /'kɔrnɪs/ *n* cornisa, *f*

Cornish /'kɔrnɪʃ/ *a* de Cornualles

cornucopia /ˌkɔrnə'koupiə/ *n* cornucopia, *f*

corollary /'kɔrəˌlɛri/ *n* corolario, *m*

corona /kə'rounə/ *n* (*Astron. Archit.*) corona, *f*

coronation /ˌkɔrə'neiʃən/ *n* coronación, *f*

coroner /'kɔrənər/ *n* juez de guardia, *mf,* médico forense, *m*

coronet /ˌkɔrə'nɛt/ *n* (of a peer, etc.) corona, *f;* tiara, *f;* guirnalda, *f*

corporal /'kɔrpərəl/ *a* corporal, *n Mil.* cabo, *m;* (altar-cloth) corporal, *m.* **c. punishment,** castigo corporal, *m*

corporate /'kɔrpərɪt/ *a* corporativo

corporation /ˌkɔrpə'reiʃən/ *n* corporación, *f;* concejo, cabildo municipal, *m;* (*Com.* U.S.A.) sociedad anónima, *f*

corporeal /kɔr'pɔriəl/ *a* corpóreo

corps /kɔr/ *n* cuerpo, *m*

corpse /kɔrps/ *n* cadáver, *m*

corpulence /'kɔrpyələns/ *n* gordura, obesidad, *f*

corpulent /'kɔrpyələnt/ *a* corpulento, grueso, gordo

corpus /'kɔrpəs/ *n* cuerpo, *m.* **C. Christi,** Corpus, *m.* **c. delicti,** cuerpo del delito, *m*
corpuscle /'kɔrpəsəl/ *n* corpúsculo, *m*
correct /kə'rɛkt/ *a* correcto; exacto, justo. —*vt* corregir; rectificar; amonestar, reprender
correction /kə'rɛkʃən/ *n* corrección, *f;* rectificación, *f*
corrective /kə'rɛktɪv/ *a* correctivo. —*n* correctivo, *m*
correctness /kə'rɛktnɪs/ *n* corrección, *f;* exactitud, *f;* justicia, *f*
correlate /'kɔrəˌleit/ *vt* poner en correlación. —*vi* tener correlación
correlation /ˌkɔrə'leiʃən/ *n* correlación, *f*
correspond /ˌkɔrə'spɒnd/ *vi* corresponder (a); (by letter) escribirse, corresponderse
correspondence /ˌkɔrə'spɒndəns/ *n* correspondencia, *f; Com.* correo, *m.* **c. course,** curso por correspondencia, *m*
correspondent /ˌkɔrə'spɒndənt/ *n* correspondiente, *mf;* (*Com.* and journalist) corresponsal, *mf.* **special c.,** corresponsal extraordinario, *m*
corresponding /ˌkɔrə'spɒndɪŋ/ *a* correspondiente. **c. member,** miembro correspondiente, *m*
corridor /'kɔrɪdər/ *n* corredor, pasillo, *m;* (railway) pasillo, *m; Polit.* corredor, *m.* **c. train,** tren con coches corridos, *m*
corroborate /kə'rɒbəˌreit/ *vt* corroborar, confirmar
corroboration /kəˌrɒbə'reiʃən/ *n* corroboración, confirmación, *f*
corroborative /kə'rɒbəˌreitɪv/ *a* corroborativo, confirmatorio
corrode /kə'roud/ *vt* corroer, morder; *Fig.* roer
corrosion /kə'rouʒən/ *n* corrosión, *f*
corrosive /kə'rousɪv/ *a* corrosivo; mordaz
corrugate /'kɔrəˌgeit/ *vt* arrugar. —*vi* arrugarse
corrugated /'kɔrəˌgeitɪd/ *a* arrugado; ondulado. **c. iron,** chapa canaleta, *f*
corrugation /ˌkɔrə'geiʃən/ *n* corrugación, *f,* arrugamiento, *m*
corrupt /kə'rʌpt/ *a* corrompido; vicioso, desmoralizado. —*vt* corromper. —*vi* corromperse
corrupter /kə'rʌptər/ *n* corruptor (-ra)
corruption /kə'rʌpʃən/ *n* corrupción, *f*
corsage /kɔr'sɑʒ/ *n* corpiño, *m*
corset /'kɔrsɪt/ *n* corsé, *m, vt* encorsetar. **c. shop,** corsetería, *f*
Corsica /'kɔrsɪkə/ Córcega, *f*
Corsican /'kɔrsɪkən/ *a* corso. —*n* corso (-sa)
cortege /kɔr'tɛʒ/ *n* séquito, acompañamiento, *m;* desfile, *m*
cortex /'kɔrtɛks/ *n Bot. Anat.* corteza, *f*
cortisone /'kɔrtəˌzoun/ *n* (drug) cortisona, *f*
Corunna /kə'runyə/ La Coruña, *f*
coruscation /ˌkɔrə'skeiʃən/ *n* brillo, *m*
corvette /kɔr'vɛt/ *n* corbeta, *f*
cosignatory /kou'sɪgnəˌtɔri/ *n* cosignatario (-ia)
cosine /'kousain/ *n* coseno, *m*
cosiness /'kouzinɪs/ *n* comodidad, *f*
cosmetic /kɒz'mɛtɪk/ *a* cosmético. —*n* afeite, cosmético, *m*
cosmic /'kɒzmɪk/ *a* cósmico
cosmographer /kɒz'mɒgrəfər/ *n* cosmógrafo, *m*
cosmography /kɒz'mɒgrəfi/ *n* cosmografía, *f*
cosmopolitan /ˌkɒzmə'pɒlɪtn̩/ *a* cosmopolita. —*n* cosmopolita, *mf*
cosmopolitanism /ˌkɒzmə'pɒlɪtn̩ˌɪzəm/ *n* cosmopolitismo, *m*
cosmos /'kɒzməs/ *n* cosmos, universo, *m*
Cossack /'kɒsæk/ *a* cosaco. —*n* cosaco (-ca)
cosset /'kɒsɪt/ *vt* mimar, consentir
cost /kɔst/ *vi* costar. —*n* costa, *f,* coste, precio, *m; Fig.* costa, *f; pl* **costs,** *Law.* costas, *f pl.* **at all costs,** cueste lo que cueste, a toda costa. **to my c.,** a mi costa. **c. of living,** coste de la vida, *m.* **to c. a fortune,** costar un sentido
Costa Rican /ˌkɒstə'rikən/ *a* costarriqueño. —*n* costarriqueño (-ña)
coster /'kɔstər/ *n* vendedor (-ra) ambulante
costliness /'kɔstlinɪs/ *n* alto precio, *m;* suntuosidad, *f*
costly /'kɔstli/ *a* costoso; suntuoso, magnífico
costume /'kɒstum/ *n* traje, *m;* (fancy-dress) disfraz, *m;* (tailored) traje sastre, *m;* **"Costume,"** (among credits in films and plays) «Vestuario»
costumier /ˌkɒstu'mɪər/ *n* modista, *mf;* sastre, *m*
cot /kɒt/ *n* (hut) choza, cabaña, *f;* (child's) camita, *f*
coterie /'koutəri/ *n* círculo, grupo, *m;* (clique) camarilla, *f*
cotillion /kə'tɪlyən/ *n* cotillón, *m*
cottage /'kɒtɪdʒ/ *n* cabaña, choza, *f;* casita, *f,* hotelito, *m;* torre, villa, *f*
cotter /'kɒtər/ *n* chaveta, llave, *f*
cotton /'kɒtn̩/ *n* algodón, *m, a* de algodón. **I don't c. to the idea at all,** No me gusta nada la idea; La idea no me seduce. **sewing-c.,** hilo de coser, *m.* **c. goods,** géneros de algodón, *m pl.* **c. mill,** hilandería de algodón, algodonería, *f.* **c. plantation,** algodonal, *m.* **c.-seed oil,** aceite de semilla de algodón, *m.* **c.-spinner,** hilandero (-ra) de algodón. **c.-wool,** algodón en rama, *m.* **c.-yarn,** hilo de algodón, *m*
cottony /'kɒtn̩i/ *a* algodonoso
couch /kautʃ/ *n* sofá, canapé, *m;* (bed) lecho, *m;* (lair) cama, *f.* —*vt* (lay down) acostar, echar; (a lance) enristrar; (express) expresar, redactar. —*vi* acostarse; (crouch) agacharse; estar en acecho
cough /kɔf/ *vi* toser. —*n* tos, *f.* **to c. up,** escupir, expectorar. **c.-drop,** pastilla para la tos, *f*
coughing /'kɔfɪŋ/ *n* tos, *f*
could /kʊd/. See **can**
council /'kaunsəl/ *n* consejo, *m;* junta, *f; Eccl.* concilio, *m.* **Privy C.,** consejo privado, *m.* **C. of the Realm,** Concejo del Reino, *m.* **to hold c.,** celebrar un consejo; aconsejarse (con); consultarse. **town c.,** ayuntamiento, *m.* **c. chamber,** sala consistorial, *f;* sala de actos, *f.* **c. houses,** casas baratas, *f pl.* **c. of war,** consejo de guerra, *m*
councilor /'kaunsələr/ *n* concejal, *m;* miembro de la junta, *m*
counsel /'kaunsəl/ *n* consultación, *f;* deliberación, *f;* consejo, *m; Law.* abogado, *m.* —*vt* aconsejar. **a c. of perfection,** un ideal imposible. **to keep one's own c.,** no decir nada, callarse, guardar silencio. **to take c. with,** consultar (a), aconsejarse con
counselor /'kaunsələr/ *n* consejero, *m.* **c. of state,** consejero de estado, *m*
count /kaunt/ *vt* contar; calcular; (consider) creer, considerar. —*vi* contar. —*n* cuenta, *f;* (of votes) escrutinio, *m; Law.* capítulo, *m.* **John simply doesn't c.,** Juan no cuenta para nada. **Erudition alone counts for very little,** La mera erudición sirve para muy poco. **to keep c. of,** tener cuenta de. **to lose c. of,** perder cuenta de. **to c. on,** contar con; (doing something) esperar. **to c. up,** contar
count /kaunt/ *n* (title) conde, *m*
countenance /'kauntn̩əns/ *n* semblante, *m;* expresión de la cara, *f;* aspecto, *m;* (favor) apoyo, *m,* ayuda, *f.* —*vt* autorizar, aprobar; apoyar, ayudar. **to put (a person) out of c.,** desconcertar (a)
counter /'kauntər/ *n* (in a bank) contador, *m;* (in a shop) mostrador, *m;* (in games) ficha, *f, adv* contra, al contrario; al revés. —*a* opuesto (a), contrario (a). —*vt* parar; contestar. **to run c. to my inclinations,** oponerse a mis deseos. **to c. with the left,** (boxing) contestar con la izquierda. **c.-attack,** contraataque, *m.* **c.-attraction,** atracción contraria, *f.* **c.-offensive,** contraofensiva, *f.* **c.-reformation,** contrarreforma, *f.* **c.-revolution,** contrarevolución, *f*
counteract /ˌkauntər'ækt/ *vt* neutralizar; frustrar
counterbalance /'kauntərˌbæləns/ *n* contrapeso, *m, vt* contrabalancear; compensar, igualar
counterblast /'kauntərˌblæst/ *n* denunciación, *f;* respuesta, *f*
countercharge /'kauntərˌtʃɑrdʒ/ *n* recriminación, *f.* —*vt* recriminar; *Law.* reconvenir
counterfeit /'kauntərˌfɪt/ *a* falso, espurio; fingido. —*n* falsificación, *f;* imitación, *f;* moneda falsa, *f;* (person) impostor (-ra). —*vt* imitar; (pretend) fingir; (coins, handwriting, etc.) falsificar
counterfeiter /'kauntərˌfɪtər/ *n* falsario (-ia)
counterfoil /'kauntərˌfɔil/ *n* talón, *m*
countermand /*v* ˌkauntər'mænd; *n* 'kauntərˌmænd/ *vt* contramandar; (an order) revocar, cancelar. —*n* contraorden, *f;* revocación, *f*
countermarch /'kauntərˌmɑrtʃ/ *n* contramarcha, *f*

countermeasure /ˈkauntərˌmɛʒər/ *n* contramedida, *f*
counterpane /ˈkauntərˌpein/ *n* sobrecama, colcha, *f*
counterpart /ˈkauntərˌpɑrt/ *n* contraparte, *f;* (of a document) duplicado, *m*
counterplot /ˈkauntərˌplɒt/ *n* contratreta, *f*
counterpoint /ˈkauntərˌpɔint/ *n Mus.* contrapunto, *m*
counterpoise /ˈkauntərˌpɔiz/ *n* contrapeso, *m;* equilibrio, *m, vt* contrabalancear, contrapesar
countersign /ˈkauntərˌsain/ *n* contraseña, *f, vt* refrendar
countess /ˈkauntɪs/ *n* condesa, *f*
counting /ˈkauntɪŋ/ *n* cuenta, *f;* numeración, *f;* (of votes) escrutinio, *m.* **c.-house,** contaduría, *f*
countless /ˈkauntlɪs/ *a* innumerable. **a c. number,** un sinfín, un sinnúmero
countrified /ˈkʌntrəˌfaid/ *a* rústico, campesino
country /ˈkʌntri/ *n* país, *m;* (fatherland) patria, *f;* región, campiña, tierra, *f;* (as opposed to town) campo, *m.* —*a* del campo; campesino, campestre, rústico. **He lives in the c.,** Vive en el campo. **c. club,** club campestre, *m.* **c. cousin,** provinciano (-na). **c.-dance,** baile campestre, *m.* **c. gentleman,** hacendado, *m.* **c. girl,** campesina, *f;* aldeana, *f.* **c.-house,** finca, *f;* casa de campo, *f.* **c. life,** vida del campo, *f.* **c.-seat,** finca, *f*
countryman /ˈkʌntrimən/ *n* campesino, *m;* hombre del campo, *m;* compatriota, *m*
countryside /ˈkʌntriˌsaid/ *n* campo, *m;* campiña, *f*
countrywoman /ˈkʌntriˌwʊmən/ *n* campesina, *f;* compatriota, *f*
county /ˈkaunti/ *n* condado, *m;* provincia, *f.* **c. council,** diputación provincial, *f.* **c. town,** cabeza de partido, *f;* ciudad provincial, *f*
county seat *n* cabecera municipal, cabeza de partido, *f*
coup /ku/ *n* golpe, *m.* **c. d'état,** golpe de estado, *m*
coupe /kup/ *n* cupé, *m*
couple /ˈkʌpəl/ *n* par, *m;* (in a dance, etc.) pareja, *f.* —*vt* enganchar, acoplar; (in marriage) casar; (animals) aparear; (ideas) asociar; (names) juntar. **the young (married) c.,** el matrimonio joven
couplet /ˈkʌplɪt/ *n* copla, *f*
coupling /ˈkʌplɪŋ/ *n* enganche, acoplamiento, *m;* (of railway carriages) enganche, *m;* (of ideas) asociación, *f*
coupon /ˈkupɒn/ *n* talón, *m;* cupón, *m*
courage /ˈkɜrɪdʒ/ *n* valor, *m.* **C.!** ¡Ánimo! **to muster up c.,** cobrar ánimo
courageous /kəˈreidʒəs/ *a* valiente
courageously /kəˈreidʒəsli/ *adv* valientemente
courier /ˈkɜriər/ *n* correo, *m,* estafeta, *f;* (guide) guía, *m;* (newspaper) estafeta, *f*
course /kɔrs/ *n* curso, *m;* (of time) transcurso, *m;* (of events) marcha, *f;* (of a river, etc.) cauce, *m;* (of stars) carrera, *f,* curso, *m;* (of a ship) derrota, *f,* rumbo, *m;* (way) camino, *m,* ruta, *f;* (of conduct) línea de conducta, *f;* actitud, *f;* (of study) curso, *m;* (of a meal) plato, *m;* (of an illness) desarrollo, *m; Med.* tratamiento, *m.* **He took it as a matter of c.,** Lo tomó sin darle importancia. **in due c.,** a su tiempo debido. **in the c. of time,** andando el tiempo, en el transcurso de los años. **of c.,** claro está; naturalmente. **Are you coming tomorrow? Of c.!** ¿Vienes mañana? ¡Ya lo creo! **the best c. to take,** lo mejor que se puede hacer, el mejor plantamiento, *m*
course /kɔrs/ *vt* cazar, perseguir; *Poet.* correr por, cruzar. —*vi* (of blood, etc.) correr; cazar
court /kɔrt/ *n* (yard) patio, *m;* (tennis) campo de tenis, *m;* (fives, racquets) cancha, *f;* (royal) corte, *f;* (of justice) tribunal, *m;* (following) séquito, acompañamiento, *m.* —*vt* hacer la corte (a); cortejar, pretender; solicitar; (sleep) conciliar. **to pay c. to,** (a woman) galantear, pretender; (a person) hacer la rueda (a). **to respect the c.,** *Law.* guardar sala. **c. of appeal,** sala de apelación, *f.* **c. of justice,** sala de justicia, *f;* tribunal de justicia, *m.* **supreme c.,** tribunal supremo, *m.* **c.-card,** figura, *f.* **c.-dress,** traje de corte, *m.* **c. house,** palacio de justicia, *m.* **c. jester,** bufón, *m.* **c.-martial,** tribunal militar, *m.* **c.-plaster,** tafetán inglés, tafetán de heridas, *m.* **c.-room,** sala de justicia, *f*
courteous /ˈkɜrtiəs/ *a* cortés
courteousness /ˈkɜrtiəsnɪs/ *n* cortesía, *f*
courtesan /ˈkɔrtəzən/ *n* cortesana, *f*
courtesy /ˈkɜrtəsi/ *n* cortesía, *f;* favor, *m,* merced, *f;* permiso, *m*
courtier /ˈkɔrtiər/ *n* cortesano, palaciego, *m*
courtliness /ˈkɔrtlinɪs/ *n* cortesía, urbanidad, *f;* dignidad, *f;* elegancia, *f*
courtly /ˈkɔrtli/ *a* cortés, galante; digno; elegante
courtship /ˈkɔrtʃɪp/ *n* noviazgo, *m;* galanteo, *m*
courtyard /ˈkɔrtˌyɑrd/ *n* patio, *m*
cousin /ˈkʌzən/ *n* primo (-ma). **first c.,** primo (-ma) carnal. **second c.,** primo (-ma) segundo (-da)
cove /kouv/ *n* cala, abra, ensenada, *f*
covenant /ˈkʌvənənt/ *n* contrato, *m;* estipulación, *f;* pacto, *m;* alianza, *f.* —*vt* prometer; estipular
Coventry, to send to, /ˈkʌvəntri/ hacer el vacío (a)
cover /ˈkʌvər/ *vt* cubrir; abrigar; (dissemble) disimular; (a distance) recorrer; (comprise) comprender, abarcar; (with confusion, etc.) llenar (de); (with a revolver, etc.) amenazar (con); (an overdraft, etc.) garantizar; (of stallions) cubrir; (of a hen and eggs) empollar; (a story, journalism) investigar. —*n* cubierta, *f;* (for a chair, umbrella, etc.) funda, *f;* (of a saucepan, jar, etc.) tapa, *f;* (dish-cover) tapadera, *f;* (of a book) cubierta, tapa, *f;* (of a letter) sobre, *m;* (shelter) abrigo, *m;* protección, *f;* (undergrowth) maleza, *f; Fig.* velo, manto, *m;* (pretence) pretexto, *m; Com.* garantía, *f.* **outer c.,** (of tire) cubierta de neumático, *f.* **to c. oneself with glory,** cubrirse de gloria. **to c. up,** cubrir completamente; (with clothes) arropar; (wrap up) envolver. **to c. with a revolver,** amenazar con un revólver. **to read a book from c. to c.,** leer un libro del principio al fin. **to take c.,** refugiarse, tomar abrigo. **under c.,** bajo tejado; al abrigo
cover charge *n* consumo mínimo, precio del cubierto, *m*
covering /ˈkʌvərɪŋ/ *n* cubrimiento, *m;* cubierta, *f;* envoltura, *f;* capa, *f,* abrigo, *m.* **c. letter,** carta adjunta, *f*
coverlet /ˈkʌvərlɪt/ *n* colcha, sobrecama, *f*
covert /*a* ˈkouvərt; *n* ˈkʌvərt/ *a* oculto; furtivo. —*n* guardia *f*
covertly /ˈkouvərtli/ *adv* secretamente, furtivamente
covet /ˈkʌvɪt/ *vt* codiciar; ambicionar, suspirar por
covetous /ˈkʌvɪtəs/ *a* codicioso; ávido; ambicioso
covetously /ˈkʌvɪtəsli/ *adv* codiciosamente; ávidamente
covetousness /ˈkʌvɪtəsnɪs/ *n* codicia, avaricia, *f;* avidez, *f;* ambición, *f*
cow /kau/ *vt* intimidar, acobardar
cow /kau/ *n* vaca, *f;* (of other animals) hembra, *f.* **c.-bell,** cencerro, *m,* zumba, *f.* **c.-catcher,** *Auto.* salvavidas, *m.* **c.-hide,** cuero, cuero de vaca, zurriago, *m;* penca, *f.* **c.-house,** establo, *m,* boyera, *f.* **c.-pox,** vacuna, *f*
coward /ˈkauərd/ *n* cobarde, *m, a* cobarde
cowardice /ˈkauərdɪs/ *n* cobardía, *f*
cowardly /ˈkauərdli/ *a* cobarde
cowboy /ˈkauˌbɔi/ *n* vaquero, *m;* gaucho, "cowboy," *m*
cower /ˈkauər/ *vi* no saber dónde meterse; temblar, acobardarse
cowherd /ˈkauˌhɜrd/ *n* vaquero, boyero, *m*
cowl /kaul/ *n* capucha, *f;* (of a chimney) sombrerete, *m*
cowlike /ˈkauˌlaik/ *a* de vaca; bovino
coworker /ˈkouˌwɜrkər, kouˈwɜr-/ *n* colaborador (-ra)
cowshed /ˈkauˌʃɛd/ *n* establo, *m*
cowslip /ˈkauslɪp/ *n* prímula, *f*
cox /kɒks/ *n* timonel, *m*
coxcomb /ˈkɒksˌkoum/ *n* (of a jester) gorra de bufón, *f;* mequetrefe, *m*
coxswain /ˈkɒksən/ *n* patrón, *m;* (of a rowboat) timonel, *m*
coy /kɔi/ *a* modoso, tímido; coquetón
coyly /ˈkɔili/ *adv* tímidamente; con coquetería
coyness *n* timidez, modestia, *f;* coquetería, *f*
cozy /ˈkouzi/ *a* cómodo; agradable; caliente. **You are very c. here,** Estás muy bien aquí
crab /kræb/ *n* (sea) cangrejo de mar, cámbaro, *m;* (river) cangrejo, *m; Astron.* Cáncer, *m.* —*vt* (thwart)

frustrar. **hermit c.,** cangrejo ermitaño, *m.* **c.-apple,** manzana silvestre, *f.* **c.-louse,** ladilla, *f*
crabbed /'kræbɪd/ *a* áspero, hosco, desabrido, arisco; (of handwriting) apretado, metido
crack /kræk/ *vt* hender; quebrantar, romper; (nuts) cascar; (a whip and fingers) chasquear; (a bottle of wine) abrir. *—vi* (of earth, skin, etc.) agrietarse; romperse, quebrarse; (of the voice) romper; (of the male voice) mudar. *—n* hendedura, rendija, *f;* quebraja, *f;* (of a whip) chasquido, *m;* (of a rifle) estallido, *m;* (blow) golpe, garrotazo, *m, a* excelente, de primera categoría; estupendo. **to c. a joke,** decir un chiste. **to c. up,** *vt* dar bombo (a), alabar. *—vi* (in health) quebrantarse; (airplane) cuartearse, estrellarse. **c.-brained,** chiflado; estúpido, loco
cracked /krækt/ *a* grietado; (of a bell, etc.) hendido; (of the voice) cascada; (of a person) chiflado
cracker /'krækər/ *n* (firework) petardo, *m;* buscapiés, *m*
crackle /'krækəl/ *vi* (of burning wood, etc.) crepitar; (rustle) crujir; (of rifle fire) tirotear. *—n* crepitación, *f;* crujido, *m;* (of rifle fire) tiroteo, *m*
crackling /'kræklɪŋ/ *n.* See crackle; *Cul.* chicharrón, *m*
Cracow /'krækau/ Cracovia, *f*
cradle /'kreidl̩/ *n* cuña, *f; Fig.* niñez, infancia, *f;* (for a limb) arco de protección, *m;* (for winebottle) cesta, *f.* *—vt* mecer. **c.-song,** canción de cuna, *f*
craft /kræft/ *n* (guile) astucia, *f;* (skill) habilidad, *f;* arte, *mf;* (occupation) oficio manual, *m;* profesión, *f;* (guild) gremio, *m;* (boat) barco, *m,* embarcación, *f*
craftily /'kræftl̩i/ *adv* astutamente
craftiness /'kræftinɪs/ *n* astucia, *f*
craftsman /'kræftsmən/ *n* artífice, *m;* arte sano, *m;* artista, *m*
craftsmanship /'kræftsmən,ʃɪp/ *n* arte, *m,* or *f;* habilidad, *f;* artificio, *m*
crafty /'kræfti/ *a* astuto, taimado
crag /kræg/ *n* peña, *f,* risco, despeñadero, *m*
cragginess /'kræginɪs/ *n* escabrosidad, aspereza, fragosidad, *f*
craggy /'krægi/ *a* escabroso, escarpado, peñascoso, riscoso
cram /kræm/ *vt* henchir; atestar; (one's mouth) llenar (de); (poultry) cebar; (a pupil) preparar para un examen; (a subject) empollar. *—vi* (with food) atracarse. **The room was crammed with people,** La sala estaba atestada de gente
cramp /kræmp/ *n Med.* calambre, *m;* (numbness) entumecimiento, *m;* (rivet) grapa, *f.* *—vt* dar calambre (a); (numb) entumecer; (fasten) lañar; (*Fig.* hamper) estorbar. **to c. someone's style,** cortar los vuelos (a). **writer's c.,** calambre del escribiente, *m*
cramped /kræmpt/ *a* (of space) apretado, estrecho; (of writing) menuda
cranberry /'kræn,bɛri/ *n* arándano, *m*
crane /krein/ *n Ornith.* grulla, *f;* (machine) grúa, *f.* **jib c.,** grúa de pescante, *f.* **travelling c.,** grúa móvil, *f.* **to c. one's neck,** estirar el cuello. **crane's bill,** pico de cigüeña, *m*
cranium /'kreiniəm/ *n* cráneo, *m*
crank /kræŋk/ *n* (handle) manivela, *f;* (person) maniático (-ca). *—vt* poner en marcha (un motor) con la manivela
crankiness /'kræŋkinɪs/ *n* (crossness) irritabilidad, *f,* mal humor, *m;* (eccentricity) excentricidad, *f*
cranky /'kræŋki/ *a* (cross) irritable, malhumorado; (eccentric) chiflado, maniático, excéntrico
cranny /'kræni/ *n* hendedura, grieta, *f*
crape /kreip/ *n* crespón, *m*
crash /kræʃ/ *vi* caer estrepitosamente; romperse; estallarse; (of aircraft, cars) estrellarse; *Fig.* hundirse, arruinarse. *—n* estrépito, estruendo, *m;* estallido, *m;* (of aircraft) accidente de aviación, *m;* (car) accidente, *m,* (or choque, *m*) de automóviles; (financial) ruina, *f; Fig.* hundimiento, *m.* **to c. into,** estrellarse contra, chocar con. **c. helmet,** casco, *m.* **c.-landing,** aterrizaje violento, *m*
crass /kræs/ *a* craso
crassness /'kræsnɪs/ *n* estupidez, *f*
crate /kreit/ *n* (box) caja de embalaje, *f;* (basket) canasto, *m,* banasta, *f*
crater /'kreitər/ *n* cráter, *m*
cravat /krə'væt/ *n* corbata, *f*
crave /kreiv/ *vt* suplicar, implorar. **to c. for,** perecer por, suspirar por, anhelar
craven /'kreivən/ *a* cobarde, pusilánime. *—n* poltrón, cobarde, *m*
craving /'kreivɪŋ/ *n* deseo vehemente, *m,* sed, *f*
crawfish /'krɔ,fɪʃ/ *n* cangrejo de río, *m;* cigala, *f*
crawl /krɔl/ *vi* arrastrarse; andar a gatas; andar a paso de tortuga; (abase oneself) humillarse; (be full of) abundar (en). *—n* paso de tortuga, *m;* (swimming) arrastne *m*
crayfish /'krei,fɪʃ/ *n* cangrejo de río, *m;* cigala, *f*
crayon /'kreiɒn/ *n* carbón, *m;* pastel, *m;* (pencil) lápiz de color, *m.* *—vt* dibujar con pastel, etc. **c. drawing,** dibujo al carbón, *m*
craze /kreiz/ *vt* enloquecer, volver loco (a). *—n* manía, *f,* capricho, entusiasmo, *m;* (fashion) moda, *f*
crazily /'kreizəli/ *adv* locamente
craziness /'kreizinɪs/ *n* locura, *f*
crazy /'kreizi/ *a* loco; chiflado; (of structure) dilapidado. **He is c. about music,** Está loco por la música. **to be completely c.,** (of persons) ser un loco de atar; ser completamente loco. **to drive c.,** volver loco (a)
creak /krik/ *vi* (of shoes, chairs, etc.) crujir; (of gates, etc.) rechinar, chirriar. *—n* crujido, *m;* chirrido, *m*
creaking /'krikɪŋ/ *n.* See **creak**
creaky /'kriki/ *a* crujiente, que cruje; chirriador
cream /krim/ *n* crema, *f;* nata, *f; Fig.* flor, nata, *f.* *—a* de nata. **whipped c.,** nata batida, *f.* **c. cake,** pastel de nata, *m.* **c.-cheese,** queso de nata, *m.* **c.-colored,** de color crema. **c.-jug,** jarro para crema, *m.* **c. of tartar,** cremor, tártaro, *m*
creamery /'krimәri/ *n* lechería, *f*
creamy /'krimi/ *a* cremoso
crease /kris/ *n* (wrinkle) arruga, *f;* (fold) pliegue, *m;* (in trousers) raya, *f;* (in cricket) línea de la meta, *f.* *—vt* (wrinkle) arrugar; (fold) plegar; (trousers) poner la raya en. *—vi* arrugarse
create /kri'eit/ *vt* crear; (appoint) nombrar; (produce) suscitar, producir
creation /kri'eiʃən/ *n* creación, *f;* establecimiento, *m;* (appointment) nombramiento, *m*
creative /kri'eitɪv/ *a* creador; de la creación
creativeness /kri'eitɪvnɪs/ *n* facultad creativa, inventiva, *f*
creator /kri'eitər/ *n* creador (-ra)
creature /'kritʃər/ *n* criatura, *f;* animal, *m.* **c. comforts,** bienestar material, *m*
crèche /krɛʃ/ *n* casa cuna, *f*
credence /'kridns/ *n* crédito, *m,* fe, creencia, *f; Eccl.* credencia, *f.* **to give c. to,** dar crédito (a), creer
credentials /krɪ'dɛnʃəlz/ *n pl* credenciales, *f pl*
credibility /,krɛdə'bɪlɪti/ *n* credibilidad, verosimilitud, *f*
credible /'krɛdəbəl/ *a* creíble, verosímil; (of persons) digno de confianza
credibly /'krɛdəbli/ *adv* creíblemente
credit /'krɛdɪt/ *n* crédito, *m;* reputación, *f;* honor, *m;* (*Com.* and banking) crédito, *m;* (in bookkeeping) data, *f.* *—vt* dar fe (a), dar crédito (a); creer; atribuir; (bookkeeping) acreditar. **It does them c.,** Les hace honor. **on c.,** a crédito, al fiado. **open c.,** *Com.* letra abierta, *f.* **to give on c.,** dar fiado. **c. balance,** haber, *m*
creditable /'krɛdɪtəbəl/ *a* loable, honroso, digno de alabanza
creditably /'krɛdɪtəbli/ *adv* honrosamente
creditor /'krɛdɪtər/ *n* acreedor (-ra); (bookkeeping) haber, *m*
credulity /krə'dulɪti/ *n* credulidad, *f*
credulous /'krɛdʒələs/ *a* crédulo
credulously /'krɛdʒələsli/ *adv* con credulidad, crédulamente
creed /krid/ *n* credo, *m*
creek /krik/ *n* caleta, abra, *f*
creel /kril/ *n* (for fish) cesta de pescador, *f*
creep /krip/ *vi* arrastrarse; (of plants and birds) trepar; (of infants) andar a gatas; (totter) hacer pinitos; (slip) deslizarse; (cringe) lisonjear, rebajarse; (of one's flesh) sentir hormigueo. **to c. about on tiptoe,**

andar de puntillas. **to c. into a person's favor,** insinuarse en el favor de. **to c. in,** entrar sin ser notado (en); deslizarse en. **to c. on,** (of time) avanzar lentamente; (of old age, etc.) acercarse insensiblemente. **to c. out,** salir sin hacer ruido; escurrirse. **to c. up,** trepar por; subir a gatas

creeper /'kripər/ *n Bot.* enredadera, *f; Ornith.* trepador, *m; Zool.* reptil, *m*

creeping /'kripɪŋ/ *a Bot.* trepante; *Zool.* trepador; (servile) rastrero

cremate /'krimeit/ *vt* incinerar

cremation /krɪ'meiʃən/ *n* cremación, *f*

crematorium /ˌkrimə'tɔriəm/ *n* crematorio, *m;* horno de incineración, *m,* inhumadora, *f*

creole /'krioul/ *a* criollo. —*n* criollo (-lla)

creolize /'kriəˌlaiz/ *vt* acriollar

crescent /'krɛsənt/ *n* media luna, *f; Herald.* creciente, *m;* calle en forma de semicírculo, *f.* —*a* en forma de media luna; *Poet.* creciente

cress /krɛs/ *n Bot.* berro, *m*

crest /krɛst/ *n* (of a cock, etc.) cresta, *f;* (plume) penacho, *m;* (of a helmet) cimera, *f;* (of a hill) cumbre, cima, *f;* (of a wave) cresta, *f.* **family c.,** blasón, escudo, *m*

crestfallen /'krɛstˌfɔlən/ *a* cabizbajo, cariacontecido

cretan /'kritn̩/ *a* cretense. —*n* cretense, *mf*

Crete /krit/ Creta, *f*

cretin /'kritn̩/ *n* cretino (-na)

cretinism /'kritn̩ˌɪzəm/ *n* cretinismo, *m*

crevasse /krə'væs/ *n* grieta en un ventisquero, *f*

crevice /'krɛvɪs/ *n* intersticio, *m,* rendija, grieta, *f*

crew /kru/ *n* (of ships, boats, aircraft) tripulación, *f;* (of a gun) servidores de una ametralladora, *m pl;* (gang) pandilla, cuadrilla, *f*

crib /krɪb/ *n* pesebre, *m;* (child's) camita de niño, *f;* (plagiary) plagio, *m.* —*vt* (plagiarize) plagiar; (steal) hurtar

crick /krɪk/ *n* (in the neck) tortícolis, *m*

cricket /'krɪkɪt/ *n Ent.* grillo, *m;* (game) cricquet, *m.* **c. ball,** pelota de cricquet, *f.* **c. bat,** paleta de cricquet, *f.* **c. ground,** campo de cricquet, *m.* **c. match,** partido de cricquet, *m*

cricketer /'krɪkɪtər/ *n* jugador de cricquet, *m*

crier /'kraiər/ *n* (town) pregonero, *m*

crime /kraim/ *n* crimen, *m;* ofensa, *f,* delito, *m*

Crimean War, the /krai'miən/ la guerra de Crimea, la guerra de Oriente, *f*

Crimea, the /krai'miə/ la Crimea, *f*

criminal /'krɪmənl̩/ *a* criminal. —*n* criminal, *m;* reo, *mf* **C. Investigation Department,** (nearest equivalent) policía secreta, *f.* **c. laws,** código penal, *m*

criminally /'krɪmənl̩i/ *adv* criminalmente

criminologist /ˌkrɪmə'nɒlədʒɪst/ *n* criminalista, *m*

criminology /ˌkrɪmə'nɒlədʒi/ *n* criminología, *f*

crimp /krɪmp/ *vt* (hair) rizar

crimson /'krɪmzən, -sən/ *n* carmesí, *m.* —*a* de carmesí. —*vt* teñir de carmesí. —*vi* enrojecerse

cringe /krɪndʒ/ *vi* temblar; asustarse, acobardarse; inclinarse (ante)

cringing /'krɪndʒɪŋ/ *a* servil, humilde; adulador

crinkle /'krɪŋkəl/ *vi* arrugarse; rizarse. —*vt* arrugar. —*n* arruga, *f*

crinoline /'krɪnl̩ɪn/ *n* crinolina, *f,* miriñaque, guardainfante, *m*

cripple /'krɪpəl/ *n* tullido (-da); cojo (-ja). —*vt* lisiar, tullir, estropear; *Fig.* paralizar

crisis /'kraisɪs/ *n* crisis, *f*

crisp /krɪsp/ *a* (of hair and of leaves) crespo; (fresh) fresco; (stiff) tieso; (of style) nervioso, vigoroso; (of manner) decidido; (of repartee) chispeante; (of tone) incisivo

crisscross /'krɪsˌkrɔs/ *vt* (a body of water or land) surcar

criterion /krai'tɪəriən/ *n* criterio, *m*

critic /'krɪtɪk/ *n* crítico, *m;* censor, *m*

critical /'krɪtɪkəl/ *a* crítico

criticism /'krɪtəˌsɪzəm/ *n* crítica, *f*

criticize /'krɪtəˌsaiz/ *vt* criticar; censurar

critique /krɪ'tik/ *n* crítica, *f*

croak /krouk/ *vi* (of frogs) croar; (of ravens) graznar; (of persons) lamentarse, gruñir

croaking /'kroukɪŋ/ *n* canto de la rana, *m;* graznido, *m*

Croat /'krouæt/ *a* croata. —*n* croata, *mf*

Croatia /krou'eiʃə/ Crocia, *f*

crochet /krou'ʃei/ *n* ganchillo, *m, vi* hacer ganchillo. —*vt* hacer (algo) de ganchillo. **c. hook,** aguja de gancho, *f,* ganchillo, *m.* **c. work,** croché, ganchillo, *m*

crockery /'krɒkəri/ *n* loza, *f,* cacharros, *m pl.* **c. store,** cacharrería, *f*

crocodile /'krɒkəˌdail/ *n* cocodrilo, *m.* **c. tears,** lágrimas de cocodrilo, *f pl*

crocus /'kroukəs/ *n* azafrán, *m*

croft /krɔft/ *n* campillo, *m;* (farm) heredad, *f*

crofter /'krɔftər/ *n* colono, *m*

crone /kroun/ *n* bruja, *f*

crony /'krouni/ *n* compinche, *mf*

crook /krʊk/ *n* curva, *f;* (staff) cayado, *m;* (swindler) caballero de industria, estafador, *m, vt* doblar, encorvar

crooked /'krʊkɪd/ *a* curvo; encorvado; torcido; ladeado; (deformed) contrahecho; (of paths, etc.) tortuoso; (dishonest) torcido, tortuoso

crookedly /'krʊkɪdli/ *adv* torcidamente; de través

crookedness /'krʊkɪdnɪs/ *n* encorvadura, *f;* tortuosidad, *f;* sinuosidad, *f*

croon /krun/ *vt* and *vi* canturrear; cantar

crooner /'krunər/ *n* cantante, *mf*

crop /krɒp/ *n* (of birds) buche, *m;* (whip) látigo, *m,* fusta, *f;* (handle) mango, *m;* (harvest) cosecha, *f;* (of the hair) cortadura, *f.* —*vt* cortar; (nibble) rozar; (hair) rapar. **Eton c.,** pelo a la garçonne, *m.* **to c. up,** aparecer, surgir

crop rotation *n* la rotación de cultivos, *f*

croquet /krou'kei/ *n* juego de la argolla, juego de croquet, *m*

croquette /krou'kɛt/ *n Cul.* croqueta, *f*

crosier /'krouʒər/ *n* báculo, cayado del obispo, *m*

cross /krɔs/ *n* cruz, *f; Biol.* cruzamiento, *m;* (*Sew.* bias) bies, *m.* **in the shape of a c.,** en cruz. **the Red C.,** la Cruz Roja. **c.-bearer,** *Eccl.* crucero, *m*

cross /krɔs/ *vt* cruzar; atravesar; pasar por; (a check and animals) cruzar; (thwart) contrariar. **It did not c. my mind,** No se me ocurrió. **Our letters must have crossed,** Nuestras cartas deben haberse cruzado. **to c. oneself,** *Eccl.* persignarse. **to c. out,** tachar, rayar. **to c. over,** *vt* atravesar, cruzar. —*vi* ir al otro lado

cross /krɔs/ *a* transversal; cruzado; oblicuo; (contrary) opuesto (a); (bad-tempered) malhumorado. **c.-breed,** *a* mestizo, atravesado. **c.-country,** *a* a campo travieso. **c.-examination,** *Law.* repregunta, *f,* contrainterrogatorio, *m.* **c.-examine,** *vt Law.* repreguntar; interrogar. **c.-eyed,** bizco. **c.-fire,** *Mil.* fuego cruzado, *m sing* fuegos cruzados, *m pl; Fig.* tiroteo, *m.* **c.-grained,** (of wood) vetisesgado; (of persons) áspero, intratable, desabrido. **c.-legged,** con las piernas cruzadas. **c.-purpose,** despropósito, *m.* **at c.-purposes,** a despropósito. **c.-question,** *vt Law.* repreguntar; interrogar. **c. reference,** contrarreferencia, *f.* **c. section,** sección transversal, *f.* **c.-stitch,** punto cruzado, *m.* **c.-word puzzle,** crucigrama, *m*

crossbar /'krɔsˌbɑr/ *n* travesaño, *m*

crossbeam /'krɔsˌbim/ *n* viga transversal, *f*

crossbench /'krɔsˌbɛntʃ/ *a* atravesado

crossbred /'krɔsˌbrɛd/ *a* cruzado, mestizo; híbrido

crossbreed /'krɔsˌbrid/ *n* mestizo (-za); híbrido, *m*

crossing /'krɔsɪŋ/ *n* cruzamiento, *m;* (of the sea) travesía, *f;* (intersection) cruce, *m;* paso, *m.* **level c.,** paso a nivel, *m.* **pedestrian c.,** paso para peatones, *m.* **c.-sweeper,** barrendero, *m*

crossly /'krɔsli/ *adv* con mal humor, con displicencia, irritablemente

crossness /'krɔsnɪs/ *n* irritabilidad, *f,* mal humor, *m*

crossroad /'krɔsˌroud/ *n* travesía, *f;* cruce, *m; pl* **crossroads,** cruce, cruce de caminos, *m sing* encrucijada, *f sing*

crosswise /'krɔsˌwaiz/ *adv* en cruz; a través

crotch /krɒtʃ/ *n* (of a tree) bifurcación, *f; Anat.* horcajadura, *f;* (of breeches) entrepiernas, *f pl*

crotchet /'krɒtʃɪt/ *n Mus.* semínima, *f;* (fad) capricho, *m;* extravagancia, excentricidad, *f*

crotchety /'krɒtʃɪti/ *a* caprichoso; raro, excéntrico; difícil

crouch /krautʃ/ *vi* acurrucarse, agacharse, acuclillarse
croup /krup/ *n* (disease) crup, garrotillo, *m;* (of a horse) grupa, anca, *f*
croupier /'krupiər/ *n* coime, crupié, *m*
crow /krou/ *n Ornith.* cuervo, *m; Ornith.* grajo, *m;* (of a cock) canto del gallo, cacareo, *m;* (of an infant) gorjeo, *m.* —*vi* (of a cock) cantar, cacarear; (of an infant) gorjearse. **as the c. flies,** en línea recta. **to c. over,** gallear, cantar victoria. **crow's-foot,** pata de gallo, *f.* **crow's-nest,** *Naut.* gavias, *f pl*
crowbar /'krouˌbɑr/ *n* alzaprima, palanca, *f*
crowd /kraud/ *n* multitud, muchedumbre, *f;* concurso, *m;* vulgo, *m;* (majority) mayoría, *f; Theat.* acompañamiento, *m.* —*vi* reunirse, congregarse; agolparse, remolinarse, apiñarse. —*vt* (fill) llenar; atestar. **in a c.,** en tropel. **So many ideas crowded in on me,** Se me ocurrieron tantas ideas a la vez. **to follow the c.,** seguir la multitud; *Fig.* ir con la mayoría. **to c. in,** entrar en tropel. **to c. round,** cercar, agruparse alrededor de. **to c. together,** apiñarse. **to c. up,** subir en masa, subir en tropel
crowded /'kraudɪd/ *a* lleno; atestado, apiñado; (weighed down) agobiado; (of hours, etc.) lleno
crowing /'krouɪŋ/ *n* cacareo, canto del gallo, *m;* (of an infant) gorjeos, *m pl;* (boasting) jactancia, *f*
crown /kraun/ *n* corona, *f;* (of the head) coronilla, corona, *f;* (of a hat) copa, *f; Archit.* coronamiento, *m.* —*vt* coronar. **c. prince,** príncipe heredero, *m*
crowning /'kraunɪŋ/ *n* coronamiento, *m; Archit.* remate, *m, a* final; supremo
crozier /'krouʒər/ *n.* See **crosier**
crucial /'kruʃəl/ *a* decisivo, crítico; difícil
crucible /'krusəbəl/ *n* crisol, *m*
crucifix /'krusəfɪks/ *n* crucifijo, *m*
crucifixion /ˌkrusə'fɪkʃən/ *n* crucifixión, *f*
cruciform /'krusəˌfɔrm/ *a* cruciforme
crucify /'krusəˌfai/ *vt* crucificar
crude /krud/ *a* crudo; (of colors) chillón, llamativo; (uncivilized) cerril, inculto; (vulgar) cursi; (of truth, etc.) desnudo
crudity /'krudɪti/ *n* crudeza, *f*
cruel /'kruəl/ *a* cruel
cruelty /'kruəlti/ *n* crueldad, *f*
cruet /'kruɪt/ *n* ánfora, vinagrera, *f;* (stand) angarillas, *f pl,* convoy, *m*
cruise /kruz/ *vi* cruzar, navegar; (of cars) correr. —*n* viaje por mar, *m*
cruiser /'kruzər/ *n* crucero, *m*
crumb /krʌm/ *n* miga, *f;* (spongy part of bread) migaja, *f.* —*vt* (bread) desmigajar; desmenuzar. **c. brush,** recogemigas, *m*
crumble /'krʌmbəl/ *vt* desmigajar, desmenuzar. —*vi* desmoronarse, desmigajarse; *Fig.* hundirse, derrumbarse; *Fig.* desaparecer
crumbling /'krʌmblɪŋ/ *n* (of buildings, etc.) desmoronamiento, *m; Fig.* destrucción, *f*
crumple /'krʌmpəl/ *vt* arrugar, ajar. —*vi* arrugarse. **to c. up,** *vt* (crush) estrujar; (persons) dejar aplastado. —*vi* (collapse) hundirse, derrumbarse; (of persons) desplomarse; (despair) desalentarse
crunch /krʌntʃ/ *vt* mascar; hacer crujir. —*vi* crujir
crupper /'krʌpər/ *n* baticola, *f*
crusade /kru'seid/ *n* cruzada, *f*
crusader /kru'seidər/ *n* cruzado, *m*
crush /krʌʃ/ *vt* aplastar; (to powder) moler, triturar; (grapes, etc.) exprimir; (crease) arrugar; (opposition, etc.) vencer; (annihilate) aniquilar, destruir; (abash) humillar, confundir; (hope, etc.) matar; (of sorrow, etc.) agobiar. **We all crushed into his diningroom,** Fuimos en tropel a su comedor. **to c. up,** machacar, moler; (paper, etc.) estrujar
crushing /'krʌʃɪŋ/ *a* (of defeats and replies) aplastante; (of sorrow, etc.) abrumador
crust /krʌst/ *n* (of bread, pie) corteza, *f;* (scab) costra, *f;* (of the earth, snow) capa, *f.* —*vt* encostrar. —*vi* encostrarse. **c. of bread,** mendrugo de pan, *m*
crustacean /krʌ'steiʃən/ *a* crustáceo. —*n* crustáceo, *m*
crustily /'krʌstḷi/ *adv* irritablemente, malhumoradamente
crustiness /'krʌstinɪs/ *n* mal humor, *m,* aspereza, *f*
crusty /'krʌsti/ *a* costroso; (of persons) malhumorado, irritable; áspero
crutch /krʌtʃ/ *n* muleta, *f;* (fork) horquilla, *f;* (crotch) horcajadura, *f*
crux /krʌks/ *n* problema, *m;* (knotty point) nudo, *m*
cry /krai/ *vi* (weep) llorar; (shout) gritar; (exclaim) exclamar. —*vt* (one's wares) pregonar. —*n* grito, *m.* **to cry for help,** pedir socorro a voces. **to cry to high heaven,** poner el grito en el cielo. **to cry one's eyes out,** llorar a mares. **to cry down,** desacreditar. **to cry off,** desdecirse; volverse atrás. **to cry out,** *vt* gritar. —*vi* dar gritos; gritar; *Fig.* clamar. **cry-baby,** niño (-ña) llorón (-ona)
crying /'kraiɪŋ/ *a* urgente; notorio. —*n* gritos, *m pl;* (weeping) llanto, *m,* lamentaciones, *f pl;* (tears) lágrimas, *f pl*
crypt /krɪpt/ *n* cripta, *f*
cryptic /'krɪptɪk/ *a* secreto, oculto
cryptography /krɪp'tɒgrəfi/ *n* criptografía, *f*
crystal /'krɪstḷ/ *n* cristal, *m.* **c. set,** *Radio.* receptor de galena, *m*
crystal ball *n* bola de cristal, esfera de cristal, *f*
crystalline /'krɪstḷɪn/ *a* cristalino
crystallization /ˌkrɪstḷə'zeiʃən/ *n* cristalización, *f*
crystallize /'krɪstḷˌaiz/ *vt* and *vi* cristalizar
crystallography /ˌkrɪstḷ'ɒgrəfi/ *n* cristalografía, *f*
cub /kʌb/ *n* cachorro (-rra)
Cuban /'kyubən/ *a* cubano. —*n* cubano (-na)
cubbyhole /'kʌbiˌhoul/ *n* refugio, *m;* garita, *f;* cuarto pequeño, *m;* chiribitil, *m*
cube /'kyub/ *n* cubo, *m;* (of sugar) terrón, *m.* —*vt* cubicar. **c. root,** raíz cúbica, *f*
cubic /'kyubɪk/ *a* cúbico
cubicle /'kyubɪkəl/ *n* cubículo, *m*
cubism /'kyubɪzəm/ *n* cubismo, *m*
cubist /'kyubɪst/ *n* cubista, *mf*
cubit /'kyubɪt/ *n* codo, *m*
cuckold /'kʌkəld/ *n* cornudo, *m*
cuckoo /'kuku/ *n* cuclillo, *m;* (cry) cucú, *m.* **c.-clock,** reloj de cuclillo, *m*
cucumber /'kyukʌmbər/ *n* cohombro *m*
cud /kʌd/ *n* rumia, *f.* **to chew the cud,** rumiar
cuddle /'kʌdḷ/ *vt* abrazar. —*n* abrazo, *m.* **to c. up together,** estar abrazados
cudgel /'kʌdʒəl/ *n* porra, estaca, tranca, *f, vt* aporrear, apalear. **to c. one's brains,** devanarse los sesos. **to take up the cudgels for,** salir en defensa de
cue /kyu/ *n Theat.* pie, *m;* (lead) táctica, *f;* (hint) indicación, *f;* (of hair) coleta, *f;* (billiard) taco (de billar), *m.* **to take one's cue from,** tomar como modelo (a); seguir el ejemplo de
cuff /kʌf/ *vt* abofetear. —*n* (blow) bofetón, *m;* (of sleeve) puño, *m,* bocamanga, valenciana, *f.* **c.-links,** gemelos, *m pl*
cuisine /kwɪ'zin/ *n* cocina, *f*
cul-de-sac /'kʌldə'sæk/ *n* callejón sin salida, *m*
culinary /'kyuləˌnɛri/ *a* culinario
cullender /'kʌləndər/ *n* colador, *m*
culminate /'kʌlməˌneit/ *vi* culminar (en), terminar (en). **culminating point,** punto culminante, *m*
culmination /ˌkʌlmə'neiʃən/ *n* culminación, *f; Fig.* apogeo, punto culminante, *m*
culpability /ˌkʌlpə'bɪlɪti/ *n* culpabilidad, *f*
culpable /'kʌlpəbəl/ *a* culpable
culpably /'kʌlpəbli/ *adv* culpablemente
culprit /'kʌlprɪt/ *n* culpado (-da)
cult /kʌlt/ *n* culto, *m*
cultivable /'kʌltəvəbəl/ *a* cultivable, labradero
cultivate /'kʌltəˌveit/ *vt* cultivar
cultivated /'kʌltəˌveitɪd/ *a* cultivado; (of persons) culto, fino
cultivation /ˌkʌltə'veiʃən/ *n* cultivación, *f;* (of the land) cultivo, *m;* (of persons, etc.) cultura, *f*
cultivator /'kʌltəˌveitər/ *n* cultivador (-ra); (machine) cultivador, *m*
cultural /'kʌltʃərəl/ *a* cultural
culture /'kʌltʃər/ *n* cultura, *f;* (bacteriology) cultivo, *m, vt* (bacteriology) cultivar
cultured /'kʌltʃərd/ *a* culto
culvert /'kʌlvərt/ *n* alcantarilla, *f*
cumbersome /'kʌmbərsəm/ *a* pesado; incómodo

cumulative /'kyumyələtɪv/ *a* cumulativo

cumulus /'kyumyələs/ *n* cúmulo, *m*

cuneiform /kyu'niəˌfɔrm/ *a* cuneiforme

cunning /'kʌnɪŋ/ *a* astuto, taimado. —*n* (skill) habilidad, *f;* astucia, *f*

cup /kʌp/ *n* taza, *f;* (*Eccl.* and *Bot.*) cáliz, *m; Sports.* copa, *f;* (hollow) hoyo, *m,* hondonada, *f.* **c.-final,** *Sports.* final de la copa, *m.* **c.-tie,** *Sports.* partido eliminatorio, *m*

cup-and-ball /'kʌpən'bɔl/ *n* boliche, *m*

cupboard /'kʌbərd/ *n* armario, *m;* (in the wall) alacena, *f.* **c. love,** amor interesado, *m*

cupful /'kʌpfʊl/ *n* taza, *f*

cupidity /kyu'pɪdɪti/ *n* avaricia, codicia, *f*

cup of sorrow *n* ramito de amargura, *m*

cupola /'kyupələ/ *n* cúpula, *f*

cur /kɜr/ *n* perro mestizo, *m;* canalla, *m*

curable /'kyʊrəbəl/ *a* curable

curableness /'kyʊrəbəlnɪs/ *n* curabilidad, *f*

curative /'kyʊrətɪv/ *a* curativo, terapéutico

curator /kyʊ'reitər/ *n* (of a museum) director, *m;* (Scots law) curador, *m*

curb /kɜrb/ *n* (of a bridle) barbada, *f; Fig.* freno, *m;* (stone) bordillo, *m,* guarnición, *f.* —*vt* (a horse) enfrenar; *Fig.* refrenar, reprimir; (limit) limitar

curd /kɜrd/ *n* requesón, *m;* cuajada, *f*

curdle /'kɜrdl̩/ *vi* coagularse; (of blood) helarse. —*vt* coagular; (blood) helar

cure /kyʊr/ *n* cura, *f; Eccl.* curato, *m.* —*vt* curar; (salt) salar; *Fig.* remediar. **to take a c.,** tomar una cura. **c.-all,** panacea, *f.* **c. of souls,** cura de almas, *f*

curer /'kyʊrər/ *n* (of fish, etc.) salador, *m;* (of evils, etc.) remediador, *m*

curfew /'kɜrfyu/ *n* toque de queda, *m*

curia /'kyʊriə/ *n Eccl.* curia, *f*

curing /'kyʊrɪŋ/ *n* curación, *f;* (salting) saladura, *f*

curio /'kyʊriˌou/ *n* curiosidad, antigüedad, *f*

curiosity /ˌkyʊri'ɒsɪti/ *n* curiosidad, *f*

curious /'kyʊriəs/ *a* (all meanings) curioso

curiously /'kyʊriəsli/ *adv* curiosamente

curl /kɜrl/ *n* (of hair) rizo, bucle, *m;* (of smoke) penacho, *m.* —*vt* rizar. —*vi* rizarse; *Sports.* jugar al curling. **in c.,** rizado. **to c. one's lip,** hacer una mueca de desdén. **to c. up,** *vt* arrollar; *Fig.* dejar fuera de combate (a). —*vi* hacerse un ovillo, enroscarse; (of leaves) abarquillarse; *Fig.* desplomarse; desanimarse. **c.-paper,** papillote, *m*

curlew /'kɜrlu/ *n Ornith.* zarapito, *m*

curling /'kɜrlɪŋ/ *n* (game) curling, *m, a* rizado. **c.-tongs,** encrespador, *m*

curly /'kɜrli/ *a* rizado, crespo

curmudgeon /kər'mʌdʒən/ *n* erizo, misántropo, cara de viernes, *m*

currant /'kɜrənt/ *n* (dry) pasa de Corinto, *f;* (fresh) grosella, *f.* **black c.,** grosella negra, *f;* (bush) grosellero negro, *m.* **c.-bush,** grosellero, *m*

currency /'kɜrənsi/ *n* uso corriente, *m;* moneda corriente, *f,* dinero, *m;* dinero en circulación, *m;* valor corriente, *m;* estimación, *f*

current /'kɜrənt/ *a* corriente; presente, de actualidad; (of money) en circulación. —*n* (of water, etc., *Fig. Elec.*) corriente, *f.* **alternating c.,** *Elec.* corriente alterna, *f.* **direct c.,** *Elec.* corriente continua, *f.* **the c. number of a magazine,** el último número de una revista. **c. events,** actualidades, *f pl*

currently /'kɜrəntli/ *adv* corrientemente, generalmente

curricle /'kɜrɪkəl/ *n* carriola, *f*

curriculum /kə'rɪkyələm/ *n* plan de estudios, *m;* curso, *m*

curriculum vitae /'vaiti/ *n* hoja de vida, *f*

curry /'kɜri/ *vt* (leather) zurrar; (a horse) almohazar; *Cul.* condimentar con cari. **to c. favor with,** insinuarse en el favor de. **c.-comb,** almohaza, *f*

curse /kɜrs/ *n* maldición, *f;* blasfemia, *f;* (ruin) azote, castigo, *m.* —*vt* maldecir; (afflict) castigar. —*vi* blasfemar, echar pestes

cursed /'kɜrsɪd, kɜrst/ *a* maldito; abominable, odioso

cursing /'kɜrsɪŋ/ *n* maldición, *f;* blasfemias, *f pl*

cursive /'kɜrsɪv/ *a* cursivo

cursorily /'kɜrsərəli/ *adv* rápidamente; de prisa; superficialmente

cursory /'kɜrsəri/ *a* rápido; apresurado; superficial

curt /kɜrt/ *a* seco, brusco; corto

curtail /kər'teil/ *vt* abreviar; reducir; disminuir

curtailment /kər'teilmənt/ *n* abreviación, *f;* reducción, *f;* disminución, *f*

curtain /'kɜrtn̩/ *n* cortina, *f; Theat.* telón, *m.* —*vt* poner cortinas (a) **drop c.,** telón de boca, *m.* **iron c.,** *Polit.* telón de acero, *m.* **to c. off,** separar por cortinas. **c.-lecture,** reprimenda conyugal, *f.* **c.-raiser,** entremés, *m.* **c.-ring,** anilla, *f*

curtly /'kɜrtli/ *adv* secamente, bruscamente

curtness /'kɜrtnɪs/ *n* brusquedad, sequedad, *f*

curtsey /'kɜrtsi/ *n* reverencia, cortesía, *f, vi* hacer una reverencia

curvature /'kɜrvətʃər/ *n* curvatura, *f*

curve /kɜrv/ *n* curva, *f; Mech.* codo, *m;* (*Auto.* of a road) viraje, *m.* —*vt* encorvar, torcer. —*vi* encorvarse, torcerse; (of a road) hacer un viraje.

curved /kɜrvd/ *a* curvo

curvet /'kɜrvɪt/ *n* corveta, cabriola, *f, vi* corvetear, corcovear, cabriolar

curvilinear /ˌkɜrvə'lɪniər/ *a* curvilíneo

cushion /'kʊʃən/ *n* almohada, *f;* cojín, *m;* (billiards) banda, *f;* (of fingers, etc.) pulpejo, *m.* —*vt* proveer de almohadas; (a shock) amortiguar; suavizar

custard /'kʌstərd/ *n* flan, *m,* natillas, *f pl*

custodian /kʌ'stoudiən/ *n* custodio, *m;* guardián, *m;* (of a museum, etc.) director, *m*

custody /'kʌstədi/ *n* custodia, *f;* guarda, *f;* prisión, *f.* **in safe c.,** en lugar seguro. **to take** (a person) **into c.,** arrestar

custom /'kʌstəm/ *n* costumbre, *f;* uso, *m; Com.* parroquia, clientela, *f;* (sales) ventas, *f pl*; *pl* **Customs,** aduana, *f.* **to go through the Customs,** pasar por la aduana. **Customs duty,** derechos de aduana, *m pl.* **Customs officer,** aduanero, *m.* **c.-house,** aduana, *f*

customarily /ˌkʌstə'mɛrəli/ *adv* habitualmente, por lo general

customary /'kʌstəˌmɛri/ *a* acostumbrado, usual, habitual

customer /'kʌstəmər/ *n* cliente, *mf* parroquiano (-na). **He is a queer c.,** Es un tipo raro

customs barrier *n* barrera aduanera, barrera arancelaria, *f*

cut /kʌt/ *vt* cortar; (diamonds) tallar; (hay, etc.) segar; (carve) labrar, tallar; (engrave) grabar; (a lecture, etc.) no asistir a; (cards) destajar, cortar; (*Fig.* wound) herir; (reduce) reducir; abreviar; (teeth) echar; (of lines) cruzar. —*vi* cortar; cortar bien; (*Fam.* go) marcharse a prisa y corriendo. **I must get my hair cut,** He de hacerme cortar el pelo. **That cuts both ways,** Es una arma de dos filos. **His opinion cuts no ice,** Su opinión no cuenta. **Mary cut him dead,** María hizo como si no le reconociera. **to cut a caper,** dar saltos; hacer cabriolas. **to cut a person short,** echar el tablacho (a). **to cut and run,** poner los pies en polvorosa. **to cut for deal,** (cards) cortar para ver quién da las cartas. **to cut short,** (a career) terminar. **to cut to the quick,** herir en lo más vivo. **to cut across,** cortar al través; (fields, etc.) atravesar; tomar por un atajo. **to cut away,** *vt* quitar. —*vi Inf.* poner pies en polvorosa. **to cut down,** derribar; (by the sword) acuchillar; (by death, etc.) segar, malograr; (expenses, etc.) reducir; (abbreviate) cortar, abreviar. **to cut off,** cortar, separar; amputar; (on a telephone) cortar la comunicación; (gas, water, etc.) cortar; (supply of food, etc.) interrumpir; (of death) llevarse. **to cut off with a shilling,** desheredar (a). **to cut out,** (dresses, etc.) cortar; (oust) suplantar. **He is not cut out for medicine,** No tiene la disposición para la medicina. **to cut up,** trinchar, cortar en pequeños trozos; (afflict) entristecer, afligir. **to cut up rough,** *Inf.* ponerse furioso

cut /kʌt/ *a* cortado. **well-cut features,** facciones regulares, *f pl.* **cut and dried opinion,** opinión hecha, idea fija, *f;* ideas cerradas, *f pl.* **cut glass,** cristal tallado, *m*

cut /kʌt/ *n* corte, *m;* (with a whip) latigazo, *m;* (with a sword) cuchillada, *f;* (with a sharp instrument) tajo, *m;* cortadura, *f;* (in prices, etc.) reducción, *f;* (engraving) grabado, *m;* clisé, *m;* (of cards) corte, *m.* **short cut,** atajo, *m.* **the cut of a coat,** el corte de un abrigo. **to give** (someone) **the cut direct,** pasar cerca de (una persona) sin saludarle. **cut-out,** *n* (paper) recortado, *m; Elec.* cortacircuitos, *m.* **cut-throat,** *n* asesino, *m*

cutaneous /kyu'teiniəs/ *a* cutáneo

cute /kyut/ *a* cuco, listo; mono

cuteness /'kyutnɪs/ *n* cuquería, inteligencia, *f;* monería, *f*

cuticle /'kyutɪkəl/ *n* cutícula, *f*

cutler /'kʌtlər/ *n* cuchillero, *m*

cutlery /'kʌtləri/ *n* cuchillería, *f*

cutlet /'kʌtlɪt/ *n* chuleta, *f*

cutter /'kʌtər/ *n* cortador, *m; Naut.* cúter, *m;* escampavía, *f*

cutting /'kʌtɪŋ/ *n* corte, *m;* (of diamonds) talla, *f;* (in a mountain, etc.) tajo, *m; Agr.* plantón, *m;* (of cloth) retazo, *m;* (newspaper) recorte, *m.* —*a* cortante; (of remarks) mordaz. **newspaper c.,** recorte de periódico. **c. down,** (of trees) tala, *f;* reducción, *f*

cuttingly /'kʌtɪŋli/ *adv* mordazmente, con malicia.

cuttlefish /'kʌtl̩,fɪʃ/ *n* jibia, *f*

cyanide /'saiə,naid/ *n* cianuro, *m*

cyberspace /'saibər,speis/ *n* ciberespacio, *m*

cycle /'saikəl/ *n* ciclo, *m;* período, *m;* (bicycle) bicicleta, *f.* —*vi* ir en bicicleta

cyclic /'saiklɪk/ *a* cíclico

cycling /'saiklɪŋ/ *n* ciclismo, *m*

cyclist /'saiklɪst/ *n* ciclista, *mf*

cyclone /'saikloun/ *n* ciclón, *m*

Cyclopean /,saiklə'piən/ *a* ciclópeo

Cyclopean task *n* obra ciclopéa, *f*

cygnet /'sɪgnɪt/ *n* pollo del cisne, *m*

cylinder /'sɪlɪndər/ *n* cilindro, *m; Mech.* tambor, *m.* **c. head,** culata, *f*

cylindrical /sɪ'lɪndrɪkəl/ *a* cilíndrico

cymbal /'sɪmbəl/ *n* címbalo, platillo, *m*

cymbalist /'sɪmbəlɪst/ *n* cimbalero (-ra)

cynic /'sɪnɪk/ *n* cínico, *m*

cynical /'sɪnɪkəl/ *a* cínico

cynicism /'sɪnə,sɪzəm/ *n* cinismo, *m*

cynosure /'sainə,ʃʊr/ *n Astron.* Osa Menor, *f;* blanco, *m*

cypress /'saiprəs/ *n* (tree and wood) ciprés, *m.* **c. grove,** cipresal, *m*

Cypriot /'sɪpriət/ *a* chipriota. —*n* chipriota, *mf*

Cyprus /'saiprəs/ Isla de Chipre, *f*

cyst /sɪst/ *n* quiste, *m*

cystic /'sɪstɪk/ *a* cístico

Czech /tʃɛk/ *a* checo. —*n* checo (-ca); (language) checo, *m*

Czechoslovak /'tʃɛkə'slouvæk/ *n* checoslovaco (-ca)

Czechoslovakia /,tʃɛkəslə'vɑkiə/ Czechoslovaquia, *f*

Czechoslovakian /,tʃɛkəslə'vɑkiən/ *a* checoslovaco

D

d /di/ *n* (letter) de, *f; Mus.* re, *m*
dab /dæb/ *vt* golpear suavemente, tocar; (sponge) esponjar; (moisten) mojar. —*n* golpecito, golpe blando, *m;* (small piece) pedazo pequeño, *m;* (blob) borrón, *m;* (peck) picotazo, *m; Inf.* experto (-ta). **to dab at one's eyes,** secarse los ojos
dabble /'dæbəl/ *vt* mojar (en). —*vi* chapotear; (engage in) entretenerse en; (meddle in) meterse en; (speculate in) especular en. **to d. in politics,** meterse en política
dabbler /'dæblər/ *n* aficionado (-da)
dace /deis/ *n* dardo, albur, *m*
dachshund /'dɑks,hʊnt/ *n* perro pachón, *m*
daddy /'dædi/ *n* papaíto, *m.* **d.-longlegs,** típula, *f*
dado /'deidou/ *n Archit.* dado, neto, *m;* friso, *m*
daffodil /'dæfədɪl/ *n* narciso trompón, *m*
daft /dæft/ *a* bobo, tonto, chiflado; loco
dagger /'dægər/ *n* daga, *f,* puñal, *m; Print.* cruz, *f.* **to be at daggers drawn,** estar a matar. **to look daggers (at),** lanzar miradas de odio (hacia), mirar echando chispas. **d. thrust,** puñalada, *f*
daguerreotype /də'gɛərə,taip/ *n* daguerrotipo, *m*
dahlia /'dælyə/ *n* dalia, *f*
daily /'deili/ *a* diario, de todos los días; cotidiano. —*adv* diariamente, cada día, todos los días; cotidianamente. —*n* (paper) diario, *m.* **d. bread,** pan cotidiano, pan de cada día, *m.* **d. help,** (person) asistenta, *f.* **d. pay,** jornal, *m; Mil.* pre, *m*
daintily /'deintḷi/ *adv* delicadamente; elegantemente; con primor
daintiness /'deintinɪs/ *n* delicadeza, *f;* elegancia, *f;* (beauty) primor, *m*
dainty /'deinti/ *a* delicado; elegante; primoroso, exquisito; (fastidious) melindroso, difícil. —*n* bocado exquisito, *m,* golosina, *f*
dairy /'dɛəri/ *n* lechería, *f.* **d. cattle,** vacas lecheras, *f pl.* **d.-farm,** granja, *f.* **d.-farmer,** granjero (-ra). **d.-farming,** industria lechera, *f*
dairymaid /'dɛəri,meid/ *n* lechera, *f*
dairyman /'dɛərimən/ *n* lechero, *m*
dais /'deiɪs/ *n* estrado, *m*
daisy /'deizi/ *n* margarita, *f*
dale /deil/ *n* valle, *m*
dalliance /'dæliəns/ *n* (delay) tardanza, *f;* (play) jugueteo, *m;* diversiones, *f pl;* (caresses) caricias, *f pl,* abrazos, *m pl*
dally /'dæli/ *vi* tardar, perder el tiempo; entretenerse, divertirse; (make love) holgar (con); (with an idea) entretenerse con, jugar con
Dalmatian /dæl'meiʃən/ *a* dalmático, dálmata. —*n* dálmata, *mf.* **D. dog,** perro dálmata, *m*
dalmatic /dæl'mætɪk/ *n* dalmática, *f*
daltonism /'dɔltṇ,ɪzəm/ *n* daltonismo, *m*
dam /dæm/ *n* (of animals) madre, *f;* (of a river, etc.) presa, *f,* embalse, *m;* (mole) dique, *m;* pared de retención, *f.* —*vt* represar, embalsar; cerrar; (restrain) contener, reprimir
damage /'dæmɪdʒ/ *n* daño, perjuicio, *m;* mal, *m;* avería, *f;* pérdida, *f;* (*Fam.* price) precio, *m; pl* **damages,** *Law.* daños y perjuicios, *m pl.* —*vt* dañar, perjudicar; estropear; deteriorar; (reputation, etc.) comprometer
damageable /'dæmɪdʒəbəl/ *a* que puede ser dañado, frágil
damaging /'dæmɪdʒɪŋ/ *a* perjudicial; comprometedor
damascene /'dæməsin/ *vt* damasquinar
Damascus /də'mæskəs/ Damasio, *m*
damask /'dæməsk/ *n* (cloth) damasco, *m;* (steel) acero damasquino, *m.* —*a* de damasco; damasquino. —*vt* (metals) damasquinar; (cloth) adamascar. **d.-like,** adamascado. **d. rose,** rosa de Damasco, *f*
dame /deim/ *n* dama, señora, *f; Inf.* madre, *f;* (schoolmistress) amiga, *f.* **to attend a d. school,** ir a la amiga
damming /'dæmɪŋ/ *n* embalse, *m,* represa, *f;* retención, *f;* represión, *f*
damn /dæm/ *vt* condenar al infierno; maldecir; vituperar. **D. it!** ¡Maldito sea!
damnable /'dæmnəbəl/ *a* detestable, infame; *Inf.* horrible
damnably /'dæmnəbli/ *adv* abominablemente; *Inf.* horriblemente
damnation /dæm'neiʃən/ *n* condenación, perdición, *f;* maldición, *f;* vituperación, *f*
damned /dæmd/ *a* condenado; maldito; detestable, odioso
damning /'dæmɪŋ/ *a* que condena; irresistible
damp /dæmp/ *a* húmedo. —*n* humedad, *f;* (mist) niebla, *f;* exhalación, *f;* (gas) mofeta, *f; Fig.* tristeza, depresión, *f.* —*vt* humedecer, mojar; apagar, amortiguar; (depress) deprimir, entristecer; (stifle) ahogar; (lessen) moderar; (trouble) turbar. **d.-proof,** impermeable
damper /'dæmpər/ *n* (of a chimney) registro de humos, *m;* (of a piano) batiente, *m;* (for stamps) mojador, *m;* (gloom) depresión, tristeza, *f;* (restraint) freno, *m*
dampish /'dæmpɪʃ/ *a* algo húmedo
dampness /'dæmpnɪs/ *n* humedad, *f*
damsel /'dæmzəl/ *n* chica, muchacha, *f;* damisela, *f*
damson /'dæmzən/ *n* ciruela damascena, *f.* **d. tree,** ciruelo damasceno, *m*
dance /dæns/ *n* danza, *f;* baile, *m.* —*vi* bailar, danzar; saltar, brincar. —*vt* bailar; hacer saltar. **to d. attendance on,** servir humildemente; hacer la rueda (a). **to lead someone a d.,** hacer bailar. **d. band,** orquestina, *f;* orquesta de jazz, *f.* **d. floor,** pista de baile, *f.* **d. hall,** salón de baile, *m.* **d. music,** música bailable, *f.* **d.-number,** (in a theater) bailable, *m.* **d. of death,** danza de la muerte, *f*
dancer /'dænsər/ *n* bailarín (-ina); danzador (-ra), bailador (-ra); *pl* **dancers,** (partners) parejas de baile, *f pl*
dancing /'dænsɪŋ/ *n* baile, *m,* danza, *f.* **d.-girl,** bailarina, *f;* (Indian) bayadera, *f.* **d.-master,** maestro de baile, *m.* **d. school,** academia de baile, *f.* **d. slipper,** zapatilla de baile, *f*
dandelion /'dændḷ,aiən/ *n* diente de león, *m*
dandle /'dændḷ/ *vt* mecer, hacer saltar sobre las rodillas, hacer bailar
dandruff /'dændrəf/ *n* caspa, *f*
dandy /'dændi/ *n* dandi, petimetre, barbilindo, *m*
Dane /dein/ *n* danés (-esa). **Great D.,** perro danés, *m*
danger /'deindʒər/ *n* peligro, *m;* riesgo, *m.* **out of d.,** fuera de peligro. **to be in d.,** correr peligro, peligrar, estar en peligro
dangerous /'deindʒərəs/ *a* peligroso; arriesgado; nocivo
dangerously /'deindʒərəsli/ *adv* peligrosamente
dangerousness /'deindʒərəsnɪs/ *n* peligro, *m*
dangle /'dæŋgəl/ *vi* colgar, pender. —*vt* dejar colgar; oscilar; (show) mostrar
Danish /'deinɪʃ/ *a* danés, de Dinamarca. —*n* (language) danés, *m*
dank /dæŋk/ *a* húmedo
dankness /'dæŋknɪs/ *n* humedad, *f*
Danube, the /'dænyub/ el (Río) Danubio, *m*
dapper /'dæpər/ *a* apuesto, aseado; activo, vivaz
dapple /'dæpəl/ *vt* motear, salpicar, manchar. **d.-grey,** *a* rucio
dappled /'dæpəld/ *a* (of horses) rodado, empedrado
Dardanelles, the /,dɑrdṇ'ɛlz/ los Dardanelos, *m*
dare /dɛər/ *vi* atreverse, osar. —*vt* arriesgar; desafiar, provocar; hacer frente a, arrostrar. —*n* reto, *m.* **I d. say!** ¡Ya lo creo! ¡No lo dudo! **I d. say that...,** No me sorprendería que...; Supongo que... **d.-devil,** calavera, *m;* atrevido (-da), valeroso (-sa)
daring /'dɛərɪŋ/ *a* intrépido, audaz; atrevido; (dangerous) arriesgado, peligroso. —*n* audacia, osadia, *f,* atrevimiento, *m;* peligro, *m*
daringly /'dɛərɪŋli/ *adv* atrevidamente
dark /dɑrk/ *a* oscuro; (of complexion, etc.) moreno;

negro; lóbrego; (of colours) oscuro; misterioso; enigmático; secreto, escondido; (sad) funesto, triste; (evil) malo, malévolo; (ignorant) ignorante, supersticioso. —*n* oscuridad, *f;* (shade) sombra, *f;* ignorancia, *f.* **after d.,** *a* nocturno. —*adv* después del anochecer. **in the d.,** a oscuras; de noche; *Fig.* **be in the d.,** quedarse en la luna. **to become d.,** oscurecerse; (cloud over) anublarse; (become night) anochecer. **to keep d.,** *vt* tener secreto. —*vi* esconderse. **d. ages,** los siglos de la ignorancia y de la superstición. **d.-eyed,** de ojos negros, ojinegro. **d. horse,** caballo desconocido, *m; Polit.* batacazo, *m.* **d. lantern,** linterna sorda, *f.* **d. room,** cuarto oscuro, *m; Photo.* laboratorio fotográfico, *m;* (optics) cámara oscura, *f*

darken /ˈdɑrkən/ *vt* obscurecer; sombrear; (of color) hacer más oscuro; (sadden) entristecer. —*vi* obscurecerse; (of the sky) anublarse; (of the face with emotion) inmutarse.

darkening /ˈdɑrkənɪŋ/ *n* oscurecimiento, *m*

darkly /ˈdɑrkli/ *adv* oscuramente; misteriosamente; con malevolencia; secretamente; (archaic) indistintamente

darkness /ˈdɑrknɪs/ *n* oscuridad, *f,* tinieblas, *f pl;* sombra, *f;* (of color) oscuro, *m;* (of the complexion) color moreno, *m;* (of eyes, hair) negrura, *f;* (night) noche, *f;* (ignorance) ignorancia, *f;* (privacy) secreto, *m.* **Prince of d.,** el príncipe de las tinieblas

darling /ˈdɑrlɪŋ/ *a* querido, amado; (greatest) mayor. —*n* querido (-da); (favorite) el predilecto, la predilecta, el favorito, la favorita. **My d.!** ¡Amor mío! ¡Vida mía! ¡Pichoncito mío!

darn /dɑrn/ *vt* zurcir, remendar. —*n* zurcido, remiendo, *m*

darner /ˈdɑrnər/ *n* zurcidor (-ra); (implement) huevo de zurcir, *m*

darning /ˈdɑrnɪŋ/ *n* zurcidura, *f;* zurcido, recosido, *m.* **d.-needle,** aguja de zurcir, *f.* **d. wool,** lana de zurcir, *f*

dart /dɑrt/ *n* dardo, *m;* movimiento rápido, *m;* avance rápido, *m; Sew.* sisa, *f.* —*vi* lanzarse, abalanzarse (sobre); volar; correr, avanzar rápidamente. —*vt* lanzar, arrojar; dirigir. **to make darts in,** *Sew.* sisar

Darwinian /dɑrˈwɪniən/ *a* darviniano. —*n* darvinista, *mf*

Darwinism /ˈdɑrwəˌnɪzəm/ *n* darvinismo, *m*

dash /dæʃ/ *n* (spirit) fogosidad, *f,* brío, *m;* energía, *f;* (impact) choque, golpe, *m;* (mixture) mezcla, *f;* (of a liquid) gota, *f;* (of the pen) rasgo, *m;* (attack) ataque, *m;* avance rápido, *m;* (a little) algo, un poco (de); *Gram.* raya, *f;* (show) ostentación, *f.* **He made a d. for the door,** Se precipitó a la puerta, Corrió hacia la puerta. **to cut a d.,** hacer gran papel. **d.-board,** tablero de instrumentos, *m*

dash /dæʃ/ *vt* arrojar con violencia; (break) quebrar, estrellar; (sprinkle) rociar (con), salpicar (con); (mix) mezclar; (knock) golpear; (disappoint) frustrar, destruir; (confound) confundir; (depress) desanimar. —*vi* (rush) precipitarse; quebrarse, estrellarse; chocar (contra); (of waves) romperse. **to d. to pieces,** hacer añicos, estrellar. **to d. along,** avanzar rápidamente; correr. **to d. away,** *vi* marcharse apresuradamente. —*vt* apartar bruscamente. **to d. down,** *vi* bajar aprisa. —*vt* derribar; (overturn) volcar; (throw) tirar. **to d. off,** *vi* marcharse rápidamente. —*vt* hacer apresuradamente; (a letter, etc.) escribir de prisa; (sketch) bosquejar rápidamente. **to d. out,** *vi* salir precipitadamente, lanzarse a la calle. —*vt* (erase) borrar; hacer saltar. **to d. through,** atravesar rápidamente; hacer de prisa. **to d. up,** llegar a prisa; (sprout) saltar

dashing /ˈdæʃɪŋ/ *a* valiente; (spirited) fogoso, gallardo; majo, brillante. —*n* choque, *m;* (breaking) quebrantamiento, *m;* (of the waves) embate, *m*

dastardly /ˈdæstərdli/ *a* cobarde

data /ˈdeitə/ *n pl* datos, *m pl*

database /ˈdeitəˌbeis/ *n* base de datos, *f*

data processing *n* elaboración electrónica de datos, *f,* recuento de datos, *m*

date /deit/ *n* fecha, *f;* (period) época, *f;* (term) plazo, *m;* (duration) duración, *f;* (appointment) cita, *f; Bot.* dátil, *m.* —*vt* fechar, datar; poner fecha a; asignar. —*vi* datar (de), remontar (a). **out of d.,** anticuado; pasado de moda; (of persons) atrasado de noticias. **to be up to d.,** ser nuevo; ser de última moda; (of persons) estar al día. **to bring up to d.,** renovar; (of persons) poner al corriente. **to fix the d.,** señalar el día; (chronologically) ajustar los tiempos. **to d.,** hasta la fecha. **under d. (of),** con fecha (de). **up to d.,** hasta hoy, hasta ahora. **What is the d.?** ¿Qué fecha es? ¿A cómo estamos hoy? ¿A cuántos estamos hoy? **d. palm,** datilera, *f*

date of expiry *n* fecha de caducidad, *f*

daub /dɔb/ *vt* barrar, embadurnar; manchar, ensuciar; untar; (paint) pintorrear. —*n* embadurnamiento, *m;* (picture) aleluya, *f*

dauber /ˈdɔbər/ *n* chafalmejas, pintamonas, *mf* pintor (-ra) de brocha gorda

daughter /ˈdɔtər/ *n* hija, *f.* **adopted d.,** hija adoptiva, *f.* **little d.,** hijuela, *f.* **d.-in-law,** nuera, *f*

daughterly /ˈdɔtərli/ *a* de hija

daunt /dɔnt, dɑnt/ *vt* intimidar, acobardar; dar miedo (a), espantar; (dishearten) desanimar

dauntless /ˈdɔntlɪs/ *a* impávido, intrépido

dauphin /ˈdɔfɪn/ *n* delfín, *m*

dawdle /ˈdɔdl̩/ *vi* perder el tiempo; haraganear, gandulear

dawdler /ˈdɔdlər/ *n* gandul (-la)

dawdling /ˈdɔdlɪŋ/ *a* perezoso, lento

dawn /dɔn/ *n* alba, madrugada, primera luz, *f; Fig.* aurora, *f.* —*vi* amanecer, alborear, romper el día; (appear) mostrarse, asomar. **at d.,** a primera luz, al amanecer, de madrugada, al alba. **It had not dawned on me,** No me había ocurrido

day /dei/ *n* día, *m;* luz del día, *f;* (day's work) jornada, *f;* (battle) batalla, *f;* (victory) victoria, *f; pl* **days,** (time) tiempos, *m pl,* época, *f;* (life) vida, *f;* (years) años, *m pl, a* diario. **all day long,** durante todo el día. **any day,** cualquier día. **by day,** de día. **by the day,** al día. **every day,** todos los días, cada día. **every other day,** un día sí y otro no, cada dos días. **from this day forward,** desde hoy en adelante. **from day to day,** de día en día. **Good day!** ¡Buenos días! **in these days,** en estos días. **in olden days,** en la antigüedad; *Inf.* en tiempos de Maricastaña. **in the days of,** en los tiempos de; durante los años de; durante la vida de. **next day,** el día siguiente. **(on) the next day,** al día siguiente, al otro día. **one of these days,** un día de éstos. **some fine day,** el mejor día, de un día a otro. **the day after tomorrow,** pasado mañana. **the day before yesterday,** anteayer. **the day before,** la víspera. **to win the day,** ganar el día, salir victorioso. **day after day,** cada día, día tras día. **day by day,** día por día. **day in, day out,** sin cesar, día tras día. **day-book,** *Com.* libro diario, *m.* **day's holiday,** día de asueto, *m;* día libre, *m.* **day laborer,** jornalero, *m.* **day nursery,** guardería de niños, *f.* **day-pupil,** alumno (-na) externo (-na). **day-school,** externado, *m.* **day shift,** turno de día, *m.* **day-star,** lucero del alba, *m.* **day ticket,** billete de excursión, *m*

daybreak /ˈdeiˌbreik/ *n* alba, *f,* amanecer, *m.* **at d.,** al romper el día, al amanecer

daydream /ˈdeiˌdrim/ *n* ensueño, *m;* ilusión, *f;* fantasía, visión, *f.* —*vi Lit.* soñar despierto, dejar volar sus pensamientos; *Fig.* hacerse ilusiones

daydreamer /ˈdeiˌdrimər/ *n* soñador (-ra); visionario (-ia)

daylight /ˈdeiˌlait/ *n* luz del día, *f,* día, *m;* (contrasted with artificial light) luz natural, *f.* **in broad d.,** a plena calle, a plena luz, en plena luz del día. **It's d. robbery!** ¡Es un desuello! **d.-saving,** hora de verano, *f*

daytime /ˈdeiˌtaim/ *n* día, *m.* **in the d.,** durante el día

daze /deiz/ *vt* aturdir, confundir; (dazzle) deslumbrar. —*n* aturdimiento, *m,* confusión, *f;* perplejidad, *f*

dazzle /ˈdæzəl/ *vt* (camouflage) disfrazar; deslumbrar, ofuscar. —*n* deslumbramiento, *m;* brillo, *m,* refulgencia, *f*

dazzling /ˈdæzlɪŋ/ *a* deslumbrador; brillante

deacon /ˈdikən/ *n* diácono, *m*

deaconess /ˈdikənɪs/ *n* diaconisa, *f*

dead /dɛd/ *a* and *past part* muerto; inanimado; (withered) marchito; (deep) profundo; (unconscious) inerte; inmóvil; insensible; (numb) entumecido;

(complete) absoluto, completo; (sure) certero, excelente; (useless) inútil; (of color and human character) apagado; sin espíritu; inactivo; (of eyes) mortecino; (of sound) sordo, opaco; (of villages, etc.) desierto, despoblado; (quiet) silencioso; (empty) vacío; (monotonous) monótono; (of fire) apagado; (with weight, language) muerto; *Elec.* interrumpido; *Law.* muerto civilmente. —*adv* completamente, enteramente; del todo; directamente; exactamente; profundamente. **the d.,** los muertos. **in the d. of night,** en las altas horas de la noche. **to be d.,** estar muerto; haber muerto. **to be d. against,** estar completamente opuesto a. **to drop d.,** caer muerto; morir de repente. **to go d. slow,** ir muy lentamente. **to rise from the d.,** resucitar. **to sham d.,** hacer la mortecina, fingirse muerto. **to speak ill of the d.,** hablar mal de los muertos; *Inf.* desenterrar los muertos. **d. ball,** pelota fuera de juego, *f.* **d.-beat,** muerto de cansancio. **d. body,** cadáver, cuerpo muerto, *m.* **d. calm,** calma profunda, *f; Naut.* calma chicha, *f.* **d. certainty,** seguridad completa, *f.* **d.-drunk,** hecho una uva. **d. end,** callejón sin salida, *m.* **d. heat,** empate, *m.* **d. language,** lengua muerta, *f.* **d.-letter,** letra muerta, *f;* carta devuelta o no reclamada, *f.* **d.-lock,** punto muerto, *m.* **to reach a d.-lock,** llegar a un punto muerto. **d. march,** marcha fúnebre, *f.* **d. season,** temporada de calma, *f.* **d. set,** empeñado (en). **d. shot,** (person) tirador (-ra) certero (-ra) (shot) tiro certero, *m.* **d. silence,** silencio profundo, *m.* **d. stop,** parada en seco, *f.* **d. tired,** rendido. **d. weight,** peso muerto, *m.* **d. wood,** leña seca, *f;* material inútil, *m*

deaden /ˈdɛdn̩/ *vt* amortiguar; (of pain) calmar; (remove) quitar; (of colours) apagar

deadening /ˈdɛdn̩ɪŋ/ *n* amortiguamiento, *m*

deadliness /ˈdɛdlinɪs/ *n* carácter mortal, *m;* implacabilidad, *f*

deadly /ˈdɛdli/ *a* mortal; implacable; *Inf.* insoportable. —*adv* mortalmente. **He was d. pale,** Estaba pálido como un muerto. **the seven d. sins,** los siete pecados mortales. **d. nightshade,** belladona, *f*

deadness /ˈdɛdnɪs/ *n* falta de vida, *f;* inercia, *f;* marchitez, *f;* (numbness) entumecimiento, *m;* desanimación, *f;* parálisis, *f*

Dead Sea Scrolls, the los rollos del mar Muerto, *m pl*

Dead Sea, the el mar Muerto, *m*

deaf /dɛf/ *a* sordo. **d. people,** los sordos. **to be d.,** ser sordo; padecer sordera. **to be as d. as a post,** ser más sordo que una tapia. **to become d.,** ensordecer, volverse sordo. **to fall on d. ears,** caer en saco roto. **to turn a d. ear,** hacerse el sordo. **d. aid,** audífono, *m.* **d.-and-dumb,** sordomudo. **d.-and-dumb alphabet,** alfabeto manual, abecedario manual, *m.* **d.-mute,** sordomudo (-da). **d.-mutism,** sordomudez, *f*

deafen /ˈdɛfən/ *vt* asordar, ensordecer

deafening /ˈdɛfənɪŋ/ *a* ensordecedor

deafly /ˈdɛfli/ *adv* sordamente

deafness /ˈdɛfnɪs/ *n* sordera, *f*

deal /dil/ *n* (transaction) negocio, trato, *m;* (at cards) reparto, *m;* (wood) pino, *m;* (plank) tablón de pino, *m.* **a d., a great d.,** mucho. **a very great d.,** muchísimo. **to conclude a d.,** cerrar un trato

deal /dil/ *vt* repartir; (a blow) asestar, dar; (cards) dar; (justice) dispensar. **to d. a blow at,** asestar un golpe; *Fig.* herir (en); *Fig.* destruir de un golpe. **to d. in,** comerciar en, traficar en; ocuparse en; meterse en. **to d. out,** dispensar. **to d. with,** (buy from) comprar de; tener relaciones con, tratar; entenderse con; portarse con; (of affairs) ocuparse en, arreglar, dirigir; (contend) luchar con; (discuss) discutir, tratar de; (of books) versar sobre

dealer /ˈdilər/ *n* traficante, *mf* mercader, *m;* (at cards) el que da las cartas

dealing /ˈdilɪŋ/ *n* conducta, *f;* proceder, *m;* trato, *m;* tráfico, *m; pl* **dealings,** relaciones, *f pl;* transacciones, *f pl*

dean /din/ *n Eccl.* deán, *m; Educ.* decano, *m*

dear /dɪər/ *a* (beloved) querido, amado; (charming) encantador, simpático; (in letters) estimado, querido; (favorite) predilecto; (expensive) caro. —*n* querido (-da); persona querida, *f,* bien amado (-da). —*adv* caro. **Oh d.!** ¡Dios mío! ¡Ay!

dearly /ˈdɪərli/ *adv* tiernamente, entrañablemente; caro

dearness /ˈdɪərnɪs/ *n* cariño, afecto, *m,* ternura, *f;* (of price) precio alto, *m*

dearth /dɜrθ/ *n* carestía, *f;* (of news, etc.) escasez, *f*

death /dɛθ/ *n* muerte, *f;* (*Law.* and in announcements) fallecimiento, *m,* defunción, *f.* **to be at death's door,** estar a la muerte. **to put to d.,** ajusticiar. **to the d.,** a muerte. **untimely d.,** muerte repentina, *f;* malogro, *m.* **death's head,** calavera, *f.* **d. certificate,** partida de defunción, *f.* **d.-duties,** derechos de herencia, *m pl.* **d.-like,** cadavérico. **d.-mask,** mascarilla, *f.* **d. penalty,** pena de muerte, *f.* **d.-rate,** mortalidad, *f.* **d.-rattle,** sarrillo, *m.* **d.-trap,** lugar peligroso, *m; Fig.* trampa, *f.* **d.-warrant,** sentencia de muerte, *f.* **d.-watch bettle,** reloj de la muerte, *m*

deathbed /ˈdɛθˌbɛd/ *n* lecho mortuorio, lecho de muerte, *m.* **on one's d.,** en su lecho de muerte

deathblow /ˈdɛθˌblou/ *n* golpe mortal, *m*

deathless /ˈdɛθlɪs/ *a* inmortal, eterno

deathly /ˈdɛθli/ *a* mortal

death toll *n* (of a bell) doble, toque de difuntos, *m;* (casualties) número de muertos, saldo de muertos, *m*

debacle /dəˈbɑkəl/ *n Fig.* ruina, *f*

debar /dɪˈbɑr/ *vt* excluir, privar

debase /dɪˈbeis/ *vt* degradar, humillar, envilecer; (the coinage) alterar (la moneda)

debasement /dɪˈbeismənt/ *n* degradación, humillación, *f,* envilecimiento, *m;* (of the coinage) alteración (de la moneda), *f*

debasing /dɪˈbeisɪŋ/ *a* degradante, humillante

debatable /dɪˈbeitəbəl/ *a* discutible

debate /dɪˈbeit/ *n* debate, *m;* discusión, *f;* disputa, *f.* —*vt* and *vi* debatir; discutir; disputar; considerar

debater /dɪˈbeitər/ *n* discutidor (-ra); orador (-ra).

debating /dɪˈbeitɪŋ/ *n* discusión, *f;* argumentación, *f*

debauch /dɪˈbɔtʃ/ *vt* corromper, pervertir; (a woman) seducir, violar. —*n* libertinaje, *m;* borrachera, *f*

debauched /dɪˈbɔtʃt/ *a* vicioso, licencioso

debauchee /ˌdɛbɔˈtʃi, -ˈʃi/ *n* libertino, vicioso, *m*

debauchery /dɪˈbɔtʃəri/ *n* libertinaje, mal vivir, *m,* viciosidad, licencia, *f*

debenture /dɪˈbɛntʃər/ *n* obligación, *f.* **d. holder,** obligacionista, *mf*

debilitate /dɪˈbɪlɪˌteit/ *vt* debilitar

debilitating /dɪˈbɪlɪˌteitɪŋ/ *a* debilitante

debilitation /dɪˌbɪlɪˈteiʃən/ *n* debilitación, *f*

debility /dɪˈbɪlɪti/ *n* debilidad, *f*

debit /ˈdɛbɪt/ *n* débito, cargo, *m;* saldo deudor, *m;* "debe" de una cuenta, *m.* —*vt* adeudar. **d. and credit,** el cargo y la data. **d. balance,** saldo deudor, *m*

debonair /ˌdɛbəˈnɛər/ *a* gallardo, gentil, donairoso; alegre

debonairly /ˌdɛbəˈnɛərli/ *adv* gallardamente; alegremente

débris /deiˈbri/ *n* escombros, desechos, *m pl;* ruinas, *f pl; Geol.* despojos, *m pl*

debt /dɛt/ *n* deuda, *f.* **a bad d.,** una deuda incobrable. **to be in the d. of,** ser en cargo a; deber dinero a; *Fig.* sentirse bajo una obligación. **to get into d.,** adeudarse, contraer deudas

debtor /ˈdɛtər/ *n* deudor (-ra); *Com.* debe, *m*

debunk /dɪˈbʌŋk/ *vt* demoler

debut /deiˈbyu/ *n* (of a debutante) puesta de largo, *f;* (of a play, etc.) estreno, *m.* **to make one's d.,** ponerse de largo, presentarse en sociedad

debutante /ˈdɛbyʊˌtɑnt/ *n* debutante, *f*

decade /ˈdɛkeid/ *n* década, *f,* decenio, *m;* (of the rosary) decena, *f*

decadence /ˈdɛkədəns/ *n* decadencia, *f*

decadent /ˈdɛkədənt/ *a* decadente

decagram /ˈdɛkəˌgræm/ *n* decagramo, *m*

decaliter /ˈdɛkəˌlitər/ *n* decalitro, *m*

decalogue /ˈdɛkəˌlɔg/ *n* decálogo, *m*

decameter /ˈdɛkəˌmitər/ *n* decámetro, *m*

decamp /dɪˈkæmp/ *vi Mil.* decampar; escaparse, fugarse

decant /dɪˈkænt/ *vt* decantar

decanter /dɪˈkæntər/ *n* garrafa, *f*

decapitate /dɪˈkæpɪˌteit/ *vt* decapitar, descabezar

decapitation /dɪˌkæpɪ'teiʃən/ *n* decapitación, *f*
decarbonization /dɪˌkɑrbənə'zeiʃən/ *n* descarburación, *f*
decarbonize /di'kɑrbəˌnaiz/ *vt* descarbonizar
decay /dɪ'kei/ *vi* (rot) pudrirse; degenerar; marchitarse; (of teeth) cariarse; (crumble) desmoronarse, caer en ruinas; decaer, declinar; (come down in the world) venir a menos, arruinarse. —*n* pudrición, putrefacción, *f;* (of teeth) caries, *f;* (withering) marchitez, *f;* degeneración, *f;* desmoronamiento, *m;* ruina, *f;* (oldness) vejez, *f;* decadencia, declinación, *f;* (fall) caída, *f*
decease /dɪ'sis/ *n* fallecimiento, *m,* defunción, *f, vi* fallecer
deceased /dɪ'sist/ *n* finado (-da), difunto (-ta). —*a* difunto
deceit /dɪ'sit/ *n* engaño, fraude, *m;* duplicidad, *f*
deceitful /dɪ'sitfəl/ *a* engañoso, falso; embustero, mentiroso; ilusorio
deceitfully /dɪ'sitfəli/ *adv* engañosamente
deceitfulness /dɪ'sitfəlnɪs/ *n* falsedad, duplicidad, *f*
deceivable /dɪ'sivəbəl/ *a* fácil a engañar, engañadizo
deceive /dɪ'siv/ *vt* engañar; (disappoint) decepcionar, desilusionar; frustrar. **If my memory does not d. me,** Si la memoria no me engaña, Si mal no me acuerdo
deceiver /dɪ'sivər/ *n* engañador (-ra); seductor, *m*
deceiving /dɪ'sivɪŋ/ *a* engañador
December /dɪ'sɛmbər/ *n* diciembre, *m*
decency /'disənsi/ *n* decoro, *m,* decencia, *f;* pudor, *m,* modestia, *f;* conveniencias, *f pl; Inf.* bondad, *f;* (manners) cortesía, *f,* buenos modales, *m pl*
decennial /dɪ'sɛniəl/ *a* decenal
decent /'disənt/ *a* decente; decoroso, honesto; púdico; (likable) simpático; (of things) bastante bueno; (honorable) honrado
decently /'disəntli/ *adv* decentemente
decentralization /diˌsɛntrələ'zeiʃən/ *n* descentralización, *f*
decentralize /di'sɛntrəˌlaiz/ *vt* descentralizar
deception /dɪ'sɛpʃən/ *n* engaño, *m;* ilusión, *f*
deceptive /dɪ'sɛptɪv/ *a* engañoso, mentiroso, ilusorio
deceptively /dɪ'sɛptɪvli/ *adv* engañosamente
decide /dɪ'said/ *vt* decidir; *Law.* determinar. —*vi* decidir, resolver; acordar, quedar en; juzgar; *Law.* dictar sentencia, fallar
decided /dɪ'saidɪd/ *a* decidido; (downright) categórico, inequívoco; resuelto; positivo; definitivo
decidedly /dɪ'saidɪdli/ *adv* decididamente; categóricamente; definitivamente
deciduous /dɪ'sɪdʒuəs/ *a Bot.* caedizo
decigram /'dɛsɪˌgræm/ *n* decigramo, *m*
decimal /'dɛsəməl/ *a* decimal. **d. fraction,** fracción decimal, *f.* **d. point,** punto decimal, *m.* **d. system,** sistema métrico, *m*
decimate /'dɛsəˌmeit/ *vt* diezmar
decimation /ˌdɛsə'meiʃən/ *n* gran mortandad, *f;* matanza, *f*
decimeter /'dɛsəˌmitər/ *n* decímetro, *m*
decipher /dɪ'saifər/ *vt* descifrar; deletrear
decipherable /dɪ'saifərəbəl/ *a* descifrable
decipherer /dɪ'saifərər/ *n* descifrador, *m*
decipherment /dɪ'saifərmənt/ *n* el descifrar; deletreo, *m*
decision /dɪ'sɪʒən/ *n* decisión, determinación, *f; Law.* sentencia, *f,* fallo, *m;* (agreement) acuerdo, *m;* (of character) firmeza, resolución, *f*
decisive /dɪ'saisɪv/ *a* decísivo; terminante, conclusivo; crítico
decisively /dɪ'saisɪvli/ *adv* decisivamente
decisiveness /dɪ'saisɪvnɪs/ *n* carácter decisivo, *m;* firmeza, resolución, *f;* decisión, *f*
deck /dɛk/ *n* cubierta, *f;* (of cards) baraja (de naipes), *f.* —*vt* adornar, ataviar; decorar. **between decks,** entrecubiertas, *f pl.* **lower d.,** cubierta, *f.* **promenade d.,** cubierta de paseo, *f.* **upper d.,** cubierta superior, *f.* **d.-cabin,** camarote de cubierta, *m.* **d.-chair,** silla de cubierta, silla de tijera, silla extensible, *f.* **d.-hand,** marinero, estibador, *m*
decked /dɛkt/ *a* ornado, ataviado; engalanado; *Naut.* de... puentes
declaim /dɪ'kleim/ *vt* recitar. —*vi* perorar, declamar
declamation /ˌdɛklə'meiʃən/ *n* declamación, *f*
declamatory /dɪ'klæməˌtɔri/ *a* declamatorio
declaration /ˌdɛklə'reiʃən/ *n* declaración, *f;* manifiesto, *m;* proclamación, *f*
declarative /dɪ'klærətɪv/ *a* declaratorio, declarativo
declare /dɪ'klɛər/ *vt* declarar; proclamar; afirmar; manifestar; confesar. —*vi* declarar; *Law.* deponer, testificar. **to d. war (on)** declarar la guerra (a)
declaredly /dɪ'klɛərɪdli/ *adv* declaradamente, explícitamente, abiertamente
declension /dɪ'klɛnʃən/ *n* declinación, *f*
declination /ˌdɛklə'neiʃən/ *n* declinación, *f*
decline /dɪ'klain/ *n* declinación, decadencia, *f;* disminución, *f;* debilitación, *f;* (of the day) caída, *f;* (of stocks, shares) depresión, *f;* (illness) consunción, *f;* (*Fig.* setting) ocaso, *m, vi* declinar; inclinarse; decaer; disminuir; debilitarse; (refuse) negarse (a). —*vt* (refuse) rechazar, rehusar; *Gram.* declinar; (avoid) evitar
declining /dɪ'klainɪŋ/ *a* declinante. **in one's d. years,** en sus últimos años
declivity /dɪ'klɪvɪti/ *n* cuesta, pendiente, *f,* declive, *m*
declutch /di'klʌtʃ/ *vi* desembragar
decoction /dɪ'kɒkʃən/ *n* decocción, *f*
decode /di'koud/ *vt* descifrar
decoder /di'koudər/ *n* descifrador, *m*
décolletee /ˌdeikɒlə'tei/ *a* escotado
decoloration /dɪˌkʌlə'reiʃən/ *n* decoloración, *f*
decompose /ˌdikəm'pouz/ *vt* descomponer. —*vi* descomponerse
decomposition /dɪˌkɒmpə'zɪʃən/ *n* descomposición, *f*
decompressor /ˌdikəm'prɛsər/ *n* decompresor, *m*
decontaminate /ˌdikən'tæməˌneit/ *vt* descontaminar
decontamination /ˌdikənˌtæmə'neiʃən/ *n* descontaminación, *f*
decontrol /ˌdikən'troul/ *vt* suprimir las restricciones sobre
decorate /'dɛkəˌreit/ *vt* adornar (con), embellecer; (by painting, etc.) decorar, pintar; (honor) investir (con), condecorar
decoration /ˌdɛkə'reiʃən/ *n* decoración, *f; Theat.* decorado, *m;* (honor) condecoración, *f;* ornamento, *m*
decorative /'dɛkərətɪv/ *a* decorativo
decorator /'dɛkəˌreitər/ *n* decorador, *m;* (interior) adornista, *m*
decorous /'dɛkərəs/ *a* decoroso, decente; correcto
decorum /dɪ'kɔrəm/ *n* decoro, *m;* corrección, *f*
decoy /*n* 'dikɔi; *v* dɪ'kɔi/ *n* señuelo, *m;* añagaza, *f;* (trap) lazo, *m,* trampa, *f; Fig.* añagaza, *f.* —*vt* (birds) reclamar, atraer con señuelo; *Fig.* tentar (con), seducir (con). **d. bird,** pájaro de reclamo, *m*
decrease /*n* 'dikris; *v* dɪ'kris/ *n* disminución, *f;* baja, *f;* reducción, *f;* (of the moon, waters) mengua, *f, vi* decrecer, disminuir; bajar; menguar. —*vt* disminuir; reducir
decreasingly /dɪ'krisɪŋli/ *adv* de menos en menos
decree /dɪ'kri/ *n* decreto, *m;* edicto, *m.* —*vi* and *vt* decretar, mandar
decrepit /dɪ'krɛpɪt/ *a* decrépito
decry /dɪ'krai/ *vt* desacreditar, rebajar
dedicate /*v* 'dɛdɪˌkeit; *a* -kɪt/ *vt* dedicar; consagrar; destinar; aplicar; (a book, etc.) dedicar. **to d. oneself to,** dedicarse a, consagrarse a, entregarse a
dedication /ˌdɛdɪ'keiʃən/ *n* dedicación, *f;* consagración, *f;* (of a book, etc.) dedicatoria, *f*
dedicatory /'dɛdɪkəˌtɔri/ *a* dedicatorio
deduce /dɪ'dus/ *vt* derivar; deducir, inferir
deduct /dɪ'dʌkt/ *vt* deducir; descontar
deduction /dɪ'dʌkʃən/ *n* deducción, *f;* descuento, *m*
deductive /dɪ'dʌktɪv/ *a* deductivo
deed /did/ *n* acción, *f;* hecho, acto, *m;* hazaña, *f;* (reality) realidad, *f; Law.* escritura, *f; Law.* contrato, *m.* **d. of gift,** escritura de donación, *f*
deem /dim/ *vt* juzgar, creer, estimar
deep /dip/ *a* profundo; (wide) ancho; (low) bajo; (thick) espeso; (of colours) subido; (of sounds) grave, profundo; (immersed (in)) absorto (en); (of the mind) penetrante; (secret) secreto; (intense) intenso, hondo; (cunning) astuto, artero; (dark) oscuro; (of mourning) riguroso. —*n Poet.* piélago, mar, *m;*

profundidad, *f;* abismo, *m, adv* profundamente; a una gran profundidad. **to be in d. waters,** *Fig.* estar con el agua al cuello. **to be three feet d.,** tener tres pies de profundidad. **to be d. in,** estar absorto en; (of debt) estar cargado de. **three d.,** tres de fondo. **d. into the night,** hasta las altas horas de la noche. **d.-felt,** hondamente sentido. **d. mourning,** luto riguroso, *m.* **d.-rooted,** arraigado. **d.-sea fishing,** pesca mayor, *f.* **d.-sea lead,** escandallo, *m.* **d.-seated,** intimo, profundo; arraigado. **d.-set,** hundido

deepen /'dipən/ *vt* profundizar, ahondar; (broaden) ensanchar; (intensify) intensificar; (increase) aumentar; (of colors) aumentar el tono de, intensificar. *—vi* hacerse más profundo, hacerse más hondo; intensificarse; aumentarse; (of sound) hacerse más grave

deeply /'dipli/ *adv* profundamente; intensamente; fuertemente

deepness /'dipnɪs/ *n* (cunning) astucia, *f;* see **depth**

deer /dɪər/ *n* ciervo (-va), venado, *m, a* cervuno. **d.-hound,** galgo de cazar venados, *m.* **d.-skin,** piel de venado, *f.* **d.-stalking,** caza del ciervo, *f*

deface /dɪ'feis/ *vt* desfigurar, mutilar; estropear; (erase) borrar

defacement /dɪ'feismənt/ *n* desfiguración, mutilación, *f;* afeamiento, *m;* borradura, *f*

defamation /ˌdɛfə'meiʃən/ *n* difamación, denigración, *f*

defamatory /dɪ'fæməˌtɔri/ *a* difamatorio, denigrante

defame /dɪ'feim/ *vt* difamar, denigrar, calumniar

default /dɪ'fɔlt/ *n* omisión, *f,* descuido, *m;* falta, *f;* ausencia, *f; Law.* rebeldía, *f.* *—vi* dejar de cumplir; faltar; no pagar. *—vt Law.* condenar en rebeldía. **in d. of,** en la ausencia de

defaulter /dɪ'fɔltər/ *n* el, *m,* (*f,* la) que no cumple sus obligaciones; delincuente, *mf;* desfalcador (-ra); *Law.* rebelde, *mf*

defeat /dɪ'fit/ *vt* vencer, derrotar; frustrar; (reject) rechazar; (elude) evitar; *Fig.* vencer, triunfar sobre. *—n* derrota, *f;* vencimiento, *m;* frustración, *f;* rechazamiento, *m.* **to d. one's own ends,** defraudar sus intenciones

defeatism /dɪ'fitɪzəm/ *n* derrotismo, *m*

defeatist /dɪ'fitɪst/ *n* derrotista, *mf*

defecate /'dɛfɪˌkeit/ *vt* defecar

defecation /ˌdɛfɪ'keiʃən/ *n* defecación, *f*

defect /*n* 'difɛkt, dɪ'fɛkt; *v* dɪ'fɛkt/ *n* defecto, *m;* imperfección, *f;* falta, *f*

defection /dɪ'fɛkʃən/ *n* defección, *f;* deserción, *f;* (from a religion) apostasía, *f*

defective /dɪ'fɛktɪv/ *a* defectuoso; *Gram.* defectivo; falto; imperfecto; (mentally) anormal. *—n* persona anormal, *f,* anormal, *m*

defectiveness /dɪ'fɛktɪvnɪs/ *n* imperfección, *f;* deficiencia, *f;* defecto, *m*

defend /dɪ'fɛnd/ *vt* defender; proteger; preservar; sostener; (a thesis) sustentar

defendant /dɪ'fɛndənt/ *n Law.* acusado (-da), procesado (-da), demandado (-da)

defender /dɪ'fɛndər/ *n* defensor (-ra); (of a thesis) sustentante, *mf*

defense /dɪ'fɛns/ *n* defensa, *f;* justificación, *f; pl* **defenses,** defensas, *f pl;* obras de fortificación, *f pl.* **for the d.,** (of witnesses) de descargo; (of counsel) para la defensa. **in d. of,** en defensa de. **in one's own d.,** en su propia defensa. **d. in depth,** *Mil.* defensa en fondo, *f*

defenseless /dɪ'fɛnslɪs/ *a* indefenso, sin defensa

defenselessness /dɪ'fɛnslɪsnɪs/ *n* incapacidad de defenderse, *f;* debilidad, *f,* desvalimiento, *m*

defensible /dɪ'fɛnsəbəl/ *a* defendible; justificable

defensive /dɪ'fɛnsɪv/ *a* defensivo. *—n* defensiva, *f.* **to be on the d.,** estar a la defensiva

defensively /dɪ'fɛnsɪvli/ *adv* defensivamente

defer /dɪ'fɜr/ *vt* (postpone) diferir, aplazar; suspender. *—vi* (yield) deferir, ceder; (delay) tardar, aguardar. **deferred payment,** pago a plazos, *m*

deference /'dɛfərəns/ *n* deferencia, *f,* respeto, *m;* consideración, *f*

deferential /ˌdɛfə'rɛnʃəl/ *a* deferente, respetuoso

deferment /dɪ'fɜrmənt/ *n* aplazamiento, *m;* suspensión, *f*

defiance /dɪ'faiəns/ *n* desafío, *m;* provocación, *f;* oposición, *f;* insolencia, *f.* **in d. of,** en contra de

defiant /dɪ'faiənt/ *a* provocativo; insolente

defiantly /dɪ'faiəntli/ *adv* de un aire provocativo; insolentemente

deficiency /dɪ'fɪʃənsi/ *n* falta, deficiencia, *f;* imperfección, *f;* defecto, *m;* omisión, *f;* (scarcity) carestía, *f;* (in accounts) déficit, *m*

deficient /dɪ'fɪʃənt/ *a* deficiente; falto, incompleto; imperfecto; pobre; defectuoso; (not clever at) débil (en); (mentally) anormal. **to be d. in,** carecer de; ser pobre en

deficit /'dɛfəsɪt/ *n* déficit, *m;* descubierto, *m*

defile /dɪ'fail/ *n* desfiladero, *m.* *—vt* contaminar; profanar; manchar; deshonrar. *—vi Mil.* desfilar

defilement /dɪ'failmənt/ *n* contaminación, *f;* corrupción, *f;* profanación, *f*

definable /dɪ'fainəbəl/ *a* definible

define /dɪ'fain/ *vt* definir; (throw into relief) destacar; fijar; *Law.* determinar

definite /'dɛfənɪt/ *a* definido; positivo; categórico; exacto; concreto. **d. article,** artículo definido, *m*

definitely /'dɛfənɪtli/ *adv* positivamente; claramente. **definitely not!** ¡definitivamente no!

definiteness /'dɛfənɪtnɪs/ *n* carácter definido, *m;* exactitud, *f;* lo categórico

definition /ˌdɛfə'nɪʃən/ *n* definición, *f*

definitive /dɪ'fɪnɪtɪv/ *a* definitivo

deflate /dɪ'fleit/ *vt* desinflar. *—vi* desinflarse, deshincharse

deflation /dɪ'fleiʃən/ *n* desinflación, *f*

deflect /dɪ'flɛkt/ *vt* desviar; apartar. *—vi* desviarse; apartarse

deflection /dɪ'flɛkʃən/ *n* desviación, *f;* apartamiento, *m*

defloration /ˌdɛflə'reiʃən/ *n* desfloración, *f*

deflower /dɪ'flauər/ *vt* desflorar

deforestation /dɪˌfɔrɪ'steiʃən/ *n* desforestación, desmontadura, despoblación forestal, *f*

deform /dɪ'fɔrm/ *vt* deformar, desfigurar; afear

deformation /ˌdifɔr'meiʃən/ *n* deformación, *f*

deformed /dɪ'fɔrmd/ *a* deformado; contrahecho

deformity /dɪ'fɔrmɪti/ *n* deformidad, *f*

defraud /dɪ'frɔd/ *vt* defraudar

defrauder /dɪ'frɔdər/ *n* defraudador (-ra)

defrauding /dɪ'frɔdɪŋ/ *n* defraudación, *f*

defray /dɪ'frei/ *vt* sufragar, costear, pagar

defrayal /dɪ'freiəl/ *n* pago, *m*

defrost /dɪ'frɔst/ *vt* deshelar

deft /dɛft/ *a* diestro; hábil

deftly /'dɛftli/ *adv* con destreza; hábilmente

deftness /'dɛftnɪs/ *n* destreza, *f;* habilidad, *f*

defunct /dɪ'fʌŋkt/ *a* and *n* difunto (-ta)

defy /dɪ'fai/ *vt* desafiar; (face) arrostrar; (violate) contravenir

degeneracy /dɪ'dʒɛnərəsi/ *n* degeneración, *f;* depravación, degradación, *f*

degenerate /*a, n* dɪ'dʒɛnərɪt; *v* -ˌreit/ *a* and *n* degenerado (-da). *—vi* degenerar

degeneration /dɪˌdʒɛnə'reiʃən/ *n* degeneración, *f*

degradation /ˌdɛgrɪ'deiʃən/ *n* degradación, *f;* abyección, *f*

degrade /dɪ'greid/ *vt* degradar; envilecer, deshonrar

degrading /dɪ'greidɪŋ/ *a* degradante

degree /dɪ'gri/ *n* grado, *m;* punto, *m;* clase social, *f.* **by degrees,** poco a poco, gradualmente, **five degrees below zero,** cinco grados bajo cero. **in the highest d.,** en sumo grado, en grado superlativo. **to a certain d.,** hasta cierto punto. **to receive a d.,** graduarse

degree-granting institution /dɪ'gri ˌgræntɪŋ/ *n* plantel habilitado para expedir títulos, *m*

dehydrate /di'haidreit/ *vt* deshidratar

dehydration /ˌdihai'dreiʃən/ *n* deshidratación, *f*

de-ice /di'ais/ *vt* deshelar

deicide /'diəˌsaid/ *n* (act) deicidio, *m;* (person) deicida, *mf*

deification /ˌdiəfɪ'keiʃən/ *n* deificación, *f*

deify /'diəˌfai/ *vt* deificar, endiosar

deign /dein/ *vi* dignarse. *—vt* conceder

deism /'diɪzəm/ *n* deísmo, *m*

deist /'diɪst/ *n* deísta, *mf*

deity /ˈdiɪti/ *n* deidad, divinidad, *f;* dios, *m*
dejected /dɪˈdʒɛktɪd/ *a* abatido, desanimado, deprimido
dejectedly /dɪˈdʒɛktɪdli/ *adv* tristemente, abatidamente
dejection /dɪˈdʒɛkʃən/ *n* abatimiento, desaliento, *m,* melancolía, *f*
delay /dɪˈlei/ *n* retraso, *m,* dilación, tardanza, demora, *f.* —*vt* retrasar, demorar; (a person) entretener; (postpone) aplazar; (obstruct) impedir. —*vi* tardar; entretenerse. **without more d.,** sin más tardar
delectable /dɪˈlɛktəbəl/ *a* deleitoso, delicioso
delectably /dɪˈlɛktəbli/ *adv* deliciosamente
delectation /ˌdilɛkˈteiʃən/ *n* delectación, *f,* deleite, *m*
delegacy /ˈdɛlɪgəsi/ *n* delegación, *f*
delegate /*n* ˈdɛlɪgɪt; *v* -ˌgeit/ *n* delegado (-da). —*vt* delegar, diputar
delegation /ˌdɛlɪˈgeiʃən/ *n* delegación, *f*
delete /dɪˈlit/ *vt* suprimir, borrar
deleterious /ˌdɛlɪˈtɪəriəs/ *a* deletéreo
deletion /dɪˈliʃən/ *n* supresión, borradura, *f*
deliberate /*a* dɪˈlɪbərɪt; *v* -əˌreit/ *a* premeditado, intencionado; (slow) pausado, lento. —*vi* and *vt* deliberar, discurrir, considerar
deliberately /dɪˈlɪbərɪtli/ *adv* (intentionally) con premeditación, a sabiendas; (slowly) pausadamente, lentamente
deliberation /dɪˌlɪbəˈreiʃən/ *n* reflexión, deliberación, consideración, *f;* (slowness) lentitud, pausa, *f*
deliberative /dɪˈlɪbərətɪv/ *a* deliberativo, de liberante
delicacy /ˈdɛlɪkəsi/ *n* delicadeza, *f;* fragilidad, *f;* suavidad, *f;* sensibilidad, *f;* escrupulosidad, *f;* (of health) debilidad, delicadez, *f;* (difficulty) dificultad, *f;* (food) manjar exquisito, *m,* golosina, *f*
delicate /ˈdɛlɪkɪt/ *a* delicado; fino; frágil; suave; exquisito; delicado (de salud); (of situations) difícil
delicatessen /ˌdɛlɪkəˈtɛsən/ *n* (store) fiambrería, *f*
delicious /dɪˈlɪʃəs/ *a* delicioso
deliciously /dɪˈlɪʃəsli/ *adv* deliciosamente
deliciousness /dɪˈlɪʃəsnɪs/ *n* deleite, *m,* lo delicioso; excelencia, *f;* delicias, *f pl*
delict /dɪˈlɪkt/ *n* delito, *m*
delictive /dɪˈlɪktɪv/ *a* delictivo
delight /dɪˈlait/ *n* deleite, regocijo, *m;* encanto, *m,* delicia, *f;* placer, gozo, *m.* —*vt* deleitar, encantar; halagar. —*vi* deleitarse, complacerse. **to be delighted with,** estar encantado con. **to d. in,** deleitarse en, complacerse en; tomar placer en
delightful /dɪˈlaitfəl/ *a* delicioso, precioso, encantador
delightfully /dɪˈlaitfəli/ *adv* deliciosamente
delimit /dɪˈlɪmɪt/ *vt* delimitar
delimitation /dɪˌlɪmɪˈteiʃən/ *n* delimitación, *f*
delineate /dɪˈlɪniˌeit/ *vt* delinear, diseñar; *Fig.* pintar, describir
delineation /dɪˌlɪniˈeiʃən/ *n* delineación, *f;* retrato, *m; Fig.* descripción, *f*
delineator /dɪˈlɪnieitər/ *n* diseñador, *m*
delinquency /dɪˈlɪŋkwənsi/ *n* delincuencia, *f;* criminalidad, *f;* culpa, *f;* delito, *m*
delinquent /dɪˈlɪŋkwənt/ *a* delincuente. —*n* delincuente, *mf*
deliquescence /ˌdɛlɪˈkwɛsəns/ *n* delicuescencia, *f*
deliquescent /ˌdɛlɪˈkwɛsənt/ *a* delicuescente
delirious /dɪˈlɪəriəs/ *a* delirante; desvariado; *Inf.* loco. **to be d.,** delirar, desvariar
delirium /dɪˈlɪəriəm/ *n* delirio, desvarío, *m.* **d. tremens,** delirium tremens, *m*
deliver /dɪˈlɪvər/ *vt* librar (de); salvar (de); (distribute) repartir; (hand over) entregar; (recite) recitar, decir; (a speech) pronunciar; comunicar; (send) despachar, expedir; (a blow) asestar; (give) dar; (bring) traer; (battle, a lecture) dar; (a woman, of a doctor) asistir en el parto (a); (a child) traer al mundo; (a judgment) pronunciar. **to be delivered (of a child),** dar a luz. **to d. oneself up,** entregarse. **delivered free,** porte pagado.
deliverance /dɪˈlɪvərəns/ *n* libramiento, rescate, *m;* redención, salvación, *f;* (of a judgment) pronuncia, *f*
deliverer /dɪˈlɪvərər/ *n* libertador (-ra); salvador (-ra); (distributor) repartidor (-ra); entregador (-ra)
delivery /dɪˈlɪvəri/ *n* (distribution) reparto, *m,* distribución, *f;* entrega, *f; Law.* cesión, *f;* (of a judgment) pronuncia, *f;* (of a speech) pronunciación, *f;* (manner of speaking) declamación, *f;* dicción, *f;* (of a child) parto, *m.* **on d.,** al entregarse. **The letter came by the first d.,** La carta llegó en el primer reparto. **d. man,** mozo de reparto, *m.* **d. note,** nota de entrega, *f.* **d. van,** camión de reparto, *m*
delivery truck *n* camioneta de reparto, furgoneta, *f,* sedán de reparto, *m*
dell /dɛl/ *n* hondonada, *f;* pequeño valle, *m*
delouse /diˈlaus/ *vt* despiojar, espulgar
Delphi /ˈdɛlfai/ Delfos, *m*
delta /ˈdɛltə/ *n* (Greek letter) delta, *f;* (of a river) delta, *m*
delude /dɪˈlud/ *vt* engañar; ilusionar. **to d. oneself,** engañarse
deluded /dɪˈludɪd/ *a* iluso, engañado, ciego
deluge /ˈdɛlyudʒ/ *n* diluvio, *m.* —*vt* diluviar; inundar (con)
delusion /dɪˈluʒən/ *n* engaño, *m,* ceguedad, *f;* error, *m;* ilusión, *f*
delve /dɛlv/ *vt* and *vi* cavar; *Fig.* ahondar (en), penetrar (en), investigar
demagogic /ˌdɛməˈgɒdʒɪk/ *a* demagógico
demagogue /ˈdɛməˌgɒg/ *n* demagogo (-ga)
demagogy /ˈdɛməˌgoudʒi/ *n* demagogia, *f*
demand /dɪˈmænd/ *n* exigencia, *f; Com.* demanda, *f;* petición, *f; Polit. Econ.* consumo, *m.* —*vt* exigir; requerir; pedir; (claim) reclamar. **in d.,** en demanda. **on d.,** al solicitarse. **to be in d.,** ser popular. **d. note,** apremio, *m*
demanding /dɪˈmændɪŋ/ *a* exigente
demarcate /dɪˈmɑrkeit/ *vt* demarcar
demarcation /ˌdimɑrˈkeiʃən/ *n* demarcación, *f*
demean (oneself) /dɪˈmin/ *vr* degradarse, rebajarse
demeanor /dɪˈminər/ *n* conducta, *f;* continente, porte, aire, *m;* (manners) modales, *m pl*
demented /dɪˈmɛntɪd/ *a* demente, loco
demerit /dɪˈmɛrɪt/ *n* demérito, *m*
demi- *prefix* semi; casi. **d.-tasse,** taza cafetera, jícara, *f*
demigod /ˈdɛmiˌgɒd/ *n* semidios, *m*
demigoddess /ˈdɛmiˌgɒdɪs/ *n* semidiosa, *f*
demijohn /ˈdɛmɪˌdʒɒn/ *n* damajuana, *f*
demilitarize /diˈmɪlɪtəˌraiz/ *vt* desmilitarizar
demise /dɪˈmaiz/ *n Law.* traslación de dominio, *f;* sucesión de la corona, *f;* (death) óbito, fallecimiento, *m*
demisemiquaver /ˌdɛmiˈsɛmiˌkweivər/ *n* fusa, *f*
demobilization /diˌmoubələˈzeiʃən/ *n* desmovilización, *f*
demobilize /diˈmoubəˌlaiz/ *vt* desmovilizar
democracy /dɪˈmɒkrəsi/ *n* democracia, *f*
democrat /ˈdɛməˌkræt/ *n* demócrata, *mf*
democratic /ˌdɛməˈkrætɪk/ *a* democrático. **to make d.,** democratizar
demolish /dɪˈmɒlɪʃ/ *vt* demoler, derribar; *Fig.* destruir; (eat) engullir, devorar
demolisher /dɪˈmɒlɪʃər/ *n* demoledor, *m; Fig.* destructor (-ra)
demolition /ˌdɛməˈlɪʃən/ *n* demolición, *f;* derribo, *m,* *a* demoledor; de demolición. **d. squad,** pelotón de demolición, *m*
demon /ˈdimən/ *n* demonio, diablo, *m*
demonetization /diˌmɒnɪtəˈzeiʃən/ *n* desmonetización, *f*
demonetize /diˈmɒnɪˌtaiz/ *vt* desmonetizar
demoniacal /ˌdiməˈnaiɪkəl/ *a* demoníaco
demonology /ˌdiməˈnɒlədʒi/ *n* demonología, *f*
demonstrable /dɪˈmɒnstrəbəl, ˈdɛmən-/ *a* demostrable
demonstrably /dɪˈmɒnstrəbli/ *adv* demostrablemente
demonstrate /ˈdɛmənˌstreit/ *vt* demostrar; mostrar, probar. —*vi* hacer una demostración
demonstration /ˌdɛmənˈstreiʃən/ *n* demostración, *f;* manifestación, *f*
demonstrative /dəˈmɒnstrətɪv/ *a* demostrativo; (of persons) expresivo, mimoso. **d. pronoun,** pronombre demostrativo, *m*
demonstrator /ˈdɛmənˌstreitər/ *n* demostrador (-ra)

demoralization /dɪˌmɔrələ'zeiʃən/ *n* desmoralización, *f*
demoralize /dɪ'mɔrəˌlaiz, -'mɒr-/ *vt* desmoralizar
demoralizing /dɪ'mɔrəˌlaizɪŋ/ *a* desmoralizador
demur /dɪ'mɜr/ *vi* dudar, vacilar; objetar, protestar; poner dificultades. —*n* objeción, protesta, *f*
demure /dɪ'myʊr/ *a* serio, modoso recatado; púdico; de una coquetería disimulada
demurely /dɪ'myʊrli/ *adv* modestamente; con recato; con coquetería disimulada
demureness /dɪ'myʊrnɪs/ *n* seriedad, *f*, recato, *m;* modestia fingida, coquetería disimulada, *f*
demy /də'mai/ *n* papel marquilla, *m;* becario de Magdalen College, Oxford, *m*
den /dɛn/ *n* madriguera, guardia, *f;* (of thieves) cueva, *f;* (in a zoo) cercado, recinto, *m;* (study) gabinete, *m;* (squalid room) cuartucho, *m*
denaturalization /diˌnætʃərələ'zeiʃən/ *n* desnaturalización, *f*
denaturalize /di'nætʃərəˌlaiz/ *vt* desnaturalizar
denial /dɪ'naiəl/ *n* negación, *f;* rechazo, *m;* contradicción, *f;* negativa, *f*
denizen /'dɛnəzən/ *n* habitante, *m;* ciudadano (-na)
Denmark /'dɛnmark/ Dinamarca, *f*
denominate /dɪ'nɒməˌneit/ *vt* denominar, nombrar
denomination /dɪˌnɒmə'neiʃən/ *n* denominación, *f;* secta, *f;* clase, *f*
denominational /dɪˌnɒmə'neiʃənl/ *a* sectario
denominator /dɪ'nɒməˌneitər/ *n Math.* denominador, *m*
denote /dɪ'nout/ *vt* denotar, indicar; significar
dénouement /ˌdeinu'mɑ̃/ *n* desenlace, desenredo, *m;* solución, *f*
denounce /dɪ'nauns/ *vt* denunciar; delatar, acusar
denouncer /dɪ'naunsər/ *n* denunciante, *mf* delator (-ra)
dense /dɛns/ *a* denso; espeso, compacto; tupido; impenetrable; *Inf.* estúpido
densely /'dɛnsli/ *adv* densamente; espesamente. **d. populated,** con gran densidad de población
density /'dɛnsɪti/ *n* densidad, *f;* espesor, *m;* consistencia, *f; Inf.* estupidez, *f*
dent /dɛnt/ *n* mella, *f;* (in metal) abolladura, *f*, *vt* mellar; abollar
dental /'dɛntl/ *a* dental. —*n* letra dental, *f.* **d. forceps,** gatillo, *m.* **d. mechanic,** mecánico dentista, *m.* **d. surgeon,** odontólogo, *m*
dental floss *n* seda dental, *f*
dentifrice /'dɛntəfrɪs/ *n* dentífrico, *m*
dentist /'dɛntɪst/ *n* dentista, *mf;* odontólogo, *m*
dentistry /'dɛntəstri/ *n* odontología, *f*
dentition /dɛn'tɪʃən/ *n* dentición, *f*
denture /'dɛntʃər/ *n* dentadura, *f*
denudation /ˌdinu'deiʃən/ *n* denudación, *f*
denude /dɪ'nud/ *vt* denudar, despojar, privar (de)
denunciation /dɪˌnʌnsi'eiʃən/ *n* denuncia, *f;* acusación, delación, *f*
denunciatory /dɪ'nʌnsiəˌtɔri/ *a* denunciatorio
Denver boot /'dɛnvər/ *n* cepo, *m*
deny /dɪ'nai/ *vt* negar; desmentir; rehusar; rechazar; renegar (de); (give up) renunciar, sacrificar. **to d. oneself,** privarse (de); sacrificar; negarse
deodorant /di'oudərənt/ *a* and *n* desodorante *m.*
deodorize /di'oudəˌraiz/ *vt* desinfectar, destruir el olor de
depart /dɪ'pɑrt/ *vi* marcharse, irse, partir; (of trains, etc., and meaning go out) salir; (deviate) desviarse (de), apartarse (de); (go away) alejarse; (leave) dejar; (disappear) desaparecer; (alter) cambiar; (die) morir
departed /dɪ'pɑrtɪd/ *a* (past) pasado; desaparecido; (dead) difunto, muerto. —*n* difunto (-ta)
department /dɪ'pɑrtmənt/ *n* departamento, *m;* sección, *f;* (of learning) ramo, *m;* (in France) distrito administrativo, *m.* **d. store,** grandes tiendas, *f pl*, (Argentina), grandes almacenes, *m pl*
departmental /dɪˌpɑrt'mɛntl/ *a* departamental
departure /dɪ'pɑrtʃər/ *n* partida, ida, *f;* (going out, and of trains, etc.) salida, *f;* (deviation) desviación, el apartarse. **d. from the rules,** el apartarse de las reglas), *f;* (disappearance) desaparición, *f;* (change) cambio, *m;* (giving up) renuncia, *f;* (death) muerte, *f.* **to take one's d.,** marcharse
depend /dɪ'pɛnd/ *vi* depender. **to d. on,** depender de; (rest on) apoyarse en; (count on) contar con; (trust) fiarse de; tener confianza en, estar seguro de. **That depends!** ¡Eso depende!
dependable /dɪ'pɛndəbəl/ *a* digno de confianza; seguro
dependence, dependency /dɪ'pɛndəns; dɪ'pɛndənsi/ *n* dependencia, *f;* subordinación, *f;* (trust) confianza, *f*
dependent /dɪ'pɛndənt/ *a* dependiente; subordinado; condicional. —*n* dependiente, *m.* **to be d. on,** depender de
depict /dɪ'pɪkt/ *vt* representar; pintar; dibujar; *Fig.* describir, retratar
depiction /dɪ'pɪkʃən/ *n* representación, *f;* pintura, *f;* dibujo, *m; Fig.* descripción, *f*
depilate /'dɛpəˌleit/ *vt* depilar
depilation /ˌdɛpə'leiʃən/ *n* depilación, *f*
depilatory /dɪ'pɪləˌtɔri, -ˌtouri/ *a* and *n* depilatorio *m.*
deplete /dɪ'plit/ *vt* agotar; disipar
depletion /dɪ'pliʃən/ *n* agotamiento, *m*
deplorable /dɪ'plɔrəbəl/ *a* lamentable, deplorable
deplorably /dɪ'plɔrəbli/ *adv* lamentablemente
deplore /dɪ'plɔr/ *vt* deplorar, lamentar
deploy /dɪ'plɔi/ *vt* desplegar. —*vi* desplegarse. —*n* despliegue, *m*
deployment /dɪ'plɔimənt/ *n* despliegue, *m*
deponent /dɪ'pounənt/ *n Law.* declarante, deponente, *mf a* deponente. **d. verb,** verbo deponente, *m*
depopulate /di'pɒpyəˌleit/ *vt* despoblar
depopulation /diˌpɒpyə'leiʃən/ *n* despoblación, *f*
deport /dɪ'pɔrt/ *vt* deportar
deportation /ˌdipɔr'teiʃən/ *n* deportación, *f*
deportment /dɪ'pɔrtmənt/ *n* comportamiento, *m;* porte, aire, *m;* conducta, *f*
depose /dɪ'pouz/ *vt* destronar; (give evidence) testificar, declarar
deposit /dɪ'pɒzɪt/ *n* depósito, *m; Geol.* yacimiento, filón, *m;* sedimento, *m.* —*vt* depositar. **to leave a d.,** dejar un depósito. **d. account,** cuenta corriente, *f*
deposition /ˌdɛpə'zɪʃən/ *n* deposición, *f; Law.* testimonio, *m*, declaración, *f;* (from the Cross) descendimiento, *m*, (de la Cruz)
depositor /dɪ'pɒzɪtər/ *n* depositador (-ra)
depository /dɪ'pɒzɪˌtɔri/ *n* depositaría, *f*, almacén, *m;* (of knowledge, etc.) pozo, *m*
depot /'dipou/ *n* almacén, *m;* (military headquarters) depósito, *m;* (for army vehicles, etc.) parque, *m;* (for buses, etc.) estación, *f*
depravation /ˌdɛprə'veiʃən/ *n* depravación, *f*
depraved /dɪ'preivd/ *a* depravado, perverso, vicioso
depravity /dɪ'prævɪti/ *n* corrupción, maldad, perversión, *f*
deprecate /'dɛprɪˌkeit/ *vt* desaprobar, criticar; lamentar, deplorar
deprecatingly /'dɛprɪˌkeitɪŋli/ *adv* con desaprobación, críticamente
deprecation /ˌdɛprɪ'keiʃən/ *n* deprecación, *f;* desaprobación, crítica, *f*
deprecatory /'dɛprɪkəˌtɔri/ *a* deprecativo; de desaprobación, de crítica
depreciate /dɪ'priʃiˌeit/ *vt* depreciar, rebajar; *Fig.* tener en poco, menospreciar. —*vi* depreciarse, deteriorarse; bajar de precio
depreciatingly /dɪ'priʃiˌeitɪŋli/ *adv* con desprecio
depreciation /dɪˌpriʃi'eiʃən/ *n* (in value) amortización, depreciación, *f; Fig.* desprecio, *m*
depreciatory /dɪ'priʃiəˌtɔri/ *a Fig.* despectivo, despreciativo
depredation /ˌdɛprə'deiʃən/ *n* depredación, *f*
depress /dɪ'prɛs/ *vt* deprimir; (weaken) debilitar; (humble) humillar; (dispirit) abatir, entristecer; (trade) desanimar, paralizar
depressed /dɪ'prɛst/ *a* deprimido, desalentado, melancólico, triste; (of an area) necesitado
depressing /dɪ'prɛsɪŋ/ *a* melancólico, triste; pesimista
depressingly /dɪ'prɛsɪŋli/ *adv* con tristeza; con pesimismo

depression /dɪ'prɛʃən/ *n* depresión, *f;* (hollow) hoyo, *m;* (sadness) desaliento, abatimiento, *m,* melancolía, *f;* (in prices) baja, *f;* (in trade) desanimación, parálisis, *f; Astron.* depresión, *f*
deprivation /ˌdɛprə'veiʃən/ *n* privación, *f;* pérdida, *f*
deprive /dɪ'praiv/ *vt* privar (de), despojar (de); defraudar (de); *Eccl.* destituir (de)
depth /dɛpθ/ *n* profundidad, *f;* (thickness) espesor, *m;* fondo, *m;* (of night, winter, the country) medio, *m;* (of sound) gravedad, *f;* (of colour, feeling) intensidad, *f;* (abstruseness) dificultad, *f;* (sagacity) sagacidad, *f; pl* **depths,** profundidades, *f pl*; abismo, *m;* lo más hondo; lo más íntimo. **to be 4 feet in d.,** tener cuatro pies de profundidad. **to the depths of one's being,** hasta lo más íntimo de su ser; hasta los tuétanos. **d. charge,** carga de profundidad, *f*
deputation /ˌdɛpyə'teiʃən/ *n* deputación, delegación, *f*
deputize (for) /'dɛpyəˌtaiz/ *vi* desempeñar las funciones de, substituir
deputy /'dɛpyəti/ *n* (substitute) lugarteniente, *m;* (agent) representante, *m;* apoderado, *m;* (parliamentary) diputado, *m;* (in compounds) sub, vice. **d.-governor,** subgobernador, *m.* **d.-head,** subjefe, *m;* (of a school) subdirector (-ra)
derail /di'reil/ *vt* (hacer) descarrilar
derailment /di'reilmənt/ *n* descarrilamiento, *m*
derange /dɪ'reindʒ/ *vt* desordenar; desorganizar; turbar; (mentally) trastornar, hacer perder el juicio (a)
derangement /dɪ'reindʒmənt/ *n* desorden, *m;* turbación, *f;* (mental) trastorno, *m,* locura, *f*
derby /'dɜrbi/ *n* carrera del Derby, *f;* (hat) sombrero hongo, *m*
deregulate /di'rɛgyəˌleit/ *vt* desregular
deregulation /diˌrɛgyə'leiʃən/ *n* desregulación, *f*
derelict /'dɛrəlɪkt/ *a* abandonado, derrelicto. —*n* derrelicto, *m*
dereliction /ˌdɛrə'lɪkʃən/ *n* abandono, *m;* omisión, negligencia, *f;* descuido, *m*
deride /dɪ'raid/ *vt* burlarse de, mofarse de; ridiculizar
derision /dɪ'rɪʒən/ *n* irrisión, *f,* menosprecio, *m*
derisive /dɪ'raisɪv/ *a* irrisorio; irónico
derisively /dɪ'raisɪvli/ *adv* irrisoriamente; con ironía, irónicamente
derivation /ˌdɛrə'veiʃən/ *n* derivación, *f*
derivative /dɪ'rɪvətɪv/ *a* derivativo. —*n* derivado, *m*
derive /dɪ'raiv/ *vt* derivar; obtener; extraer; *Fig.* sacar, hallar. —*vi* (from) derivar de; proceder de; remontar a
dermatitis /ˌdɜrmə'taitɪs/ *n* dermatitis, *f*
dermatologist /ˌdɜrmə'tɒlədʒɪst/ *n* dermatólogo, *m*
dermatology /ˌdɜrmə'tɒlədʒi/ *n* dermatología, *f*
derogatory /dɪ'rɒgəˌtɔri/ *a* despectivo, despreciativo; deshonroso
derrick /'dɛrɪk/ *n* grúa, machina, *f;* abanico, *m*
descant /*n* 'dɛskænt; *v* dɛs'kænt/ *n Mus.* discante, *m.* —*vi Mus.* discantar; discurrir (sobre), disertar (sobre)
descend /dɪ'sɛnd/ *vi* descender, bajar; (be inherited) pasar a; (fall) caer; (of the sun) ponerse. —*vt* bajar. **to d. from,** descender de. **to d. to,** (lower oneself) rebajarse; (consider) venir a, considerar. **to d. upon,** caer sobre; (arrive unexpectedly) llegar inesperadamente, invadir
descendant /dɪ'sɛndənt/ *n* descendiente, *mf; pl* **descendants,** descendencia, *f*
descent /dɪ'sɛnt/ *n* descenso, *m;* bajada, *f;* (slope) pendiente, cuesta, *f,* (attack) invasión, *f,* ataque, *m;* (lineage) descendencia, alcurnia, procedencia, *f;* (inheritance) herencia, *f;* transmisión, *f.* **D. from the Cross,** Descendimiento de la Cruz, *m*
describable /dɪ'skraibəbəl/ *a* descriptible
describe /dɪ'skraib/ *vt* describir; pintar
description /dɪ'skrɪpʃən/ *n* descripción, *f*
descriptive /dɪ'skrɪptɪv/ *a* descriptivo
descry /dɪ'skrai/ *vt* divisar, descubrir; *Poet.* ver
Desdemona /ˌdɛzdə'mounə/ Desdémona, *f*
desecrate /'dɛsɪˌkreit/ *vt* profanar
desecration /ˌdɛsɪ'kreiʃən/ *n* profanación, *f*
desert /dɪ'zɜrt/ *vt* abandonar; dejar; (*Mil.* etc.) desertar. —*vi* desertar
desert /'dɛzərt/ *n* desierto, *m*
desert /dɪ'zɜrt/ *n* (merit) mérito, *m* **to receive one's deserts,** llevar su merecido
deserted /dɪ'zɜrtɪd/ *a* abandonado; desierto; solitario; inhabitado, despoblado
deserter /dɪ'zɜrtər/ *n* desertor, *m*
desertion /dɪ'zɜrʃən/ *n* abandono, *m,* deserción, *f;* (*Mil.* etc.) deserción, *f*
deserve /dɪ'zɜrv/ *vt* and *vi* merecer
deservedly /dɪ'zɜrvɪdli/ *adv* merecidamente
deserving /dɪ'zɜrvɪŋ/ *a* merecedor; meritorio. **to be d. of,** merecer
desiccate /'dɛsɪˌkeit/ *vt* desecar. —*vi* desecarse
design /dɪ'zain/ *n* proyecto, *m;* plan, *m;* intención, *f,* propósito, *m;* objeto, *m;* modelo, *m;* (pattern) diseño, dibujo, *m;* arte del dibujo, *mf vt* idear; proyectar; (destine) destinar, dedicar; diseñar, dibujar, delinear; planear. **by d.,** expresamente, intencionalmente
designate /*v* 'dɛzɪgˌneit; *a* -nɪt/ *vt* señalar; designar; (appoint) nombrar. —*a* electo
designation /ˌdɛzɪg'neiʃən/ *n* designación, *f;* nombramiento, *m*
designedly /dɪ'zainɪdli/ *adv* de propósito
designer /dɪ'zainər/ *n* inventor (-ra), autor (-ra); delineador (-ra); dibujante, *mf;* (of public works, etc.) proyectista, *mf*
designing /dɪ'zainɪŋ/ *a* intrigante, astuto
desirability /dɪˌzaiᵊrə'bɪlɪti/ *n* lo deseable; conveniencia, *f;* ventaja, *f*
desirable /dɪ'zaiᵊrəbəl/ *a* deseable; conveniente; ventajoso; agradable; apetecible
desire /dɪ'zaiᵊr/ *vt* desear; querer; ansiar, ambicionar; (request) rogar, pedir; (order) mandar. —*n* deseo, *m;* ansia, aspiración, *f;* ambición, *f;* impulso, *m;* (will) voluntad, *f.* **to d. ardently,** perecerse por; suspirar por
desirous /dɪ'zaiᵊrəs/ *a* deseoso (de); ambicioso (de); ansioso (de); impaciente (a); curioso (de)
desist /dɪ'sɪst/ *vi* desistir; dejar (de)
desk /dɛsk/ *n* pupitre, *m;* escritorio, buró, *m;* mesa de trabajo, *f;* (cashier's) caja, *f;* (teacher's, lecturer's; pulpit) cátedra, *f*
desolate /*a* 'dɛsəlɪt; *v* -ˌleit/ *a* solitario; desierto; deshabitado; abandonado; arruinado; árido; (afflicted) desolado, angustiado. —*vt* desolar; despoblar
desolation /ˌdɛsə'leiʃən/ *n* desolación, *f;* aflicción, angustia, *f,* desconsuelo, *m*
despair /dɪ'spɛər/ *n* desesperación, *f, vi* perder toda esperanza. **His life is despaired of,** Se ha perdido la esperanza de salvarle (la vida). **to be in d.,** estar desesperado
despairing /dɪ'spɛərɪŋ/ *a* desesperado
despairingly /dɪ'spɛərɪŋli/ *adv* sin esperanza
desperate /'dɛspərɪt/ *a* desesperado; sin esperanza; irremediable; furioso; violento; (dangerous) arriesgado, peligroso; terrible
desperately /'dɛspərɪtli/ *adv* desesperadamente; furiosamente; terriblemente
desperation /ˌdɛspə'reiʃən/ *n* desesperación, *f;* furia, violencia, *f*
despicable /'dɛspɪkəbəl/ *a* vil, despreciable; insignificante
despise /dɪ'spaiz/ *vt* despreciar; desdeñar
despiser /dɪ'spaizər/ *n* menospreciador (-ra)
despite /dɪ'spait/ *prep* a pesar de
despoil /dɪ'spɔil/ *vt* despojar, desnudar
despoiler /dɪ'spɔilər/ *n* despojador (-ra)
despoliation /dɪˌspouli'eiʃən/ *n* despojo, *m*
despondency /dɪ'spɒndənsi/ *n* abatimiento, desaliento, *m,* desesperación, *f*
despondent /dɪ'spɒndənt/ *a* abatido, desanimado, deprimido
despondently /dɪ'spɒndəntli/ *adv* con desaliento
despot /'dɛspət/ *n* déspota, *m*
despotic /dɛs'pɒtɪk/ *a* despótico
despotism /'dɛspəˌtɪzəm/ *n* despotismo, *m*
dessert /dɪ'zɜrt/ *n* postre, *m, a* de postre. **d. plate,** plato para postre, *m.* **d.-spoon,** cuchara de postre, *f*
destination /ˌdɛstə'neiʃən/ *n* destinación, *f*
destine /'dɛstɪn/ *vt* destinar; dedicar; predestinar
destiny /'dɛstəni/ *n* destino, *m*
destitute /'dɛstɪˌtut/ *a* indigente, menesteroso; des-

nudo (de); privado (de); desprovisto (de), falto (de); desamparado
destitution /ˌdɛstɪ'tuʃən/ *n* destitución, indigencia, miseria, *f;* privación, falta, *f;* desamparo, *m*
destroy /dɪ'strɔi/ *vt* destruir; demoler; deshacer; (kill) matar; exterminar; (finish) acabar con
destroyer /dɪ'strɔiər/ *n* destructor (-ra); *Nav.* destructor, cazatorpedero, *m*
destructible /dɪ'strʌktəbəl/ *a* destructible, destruible
destruction /dɪ'strʌkʃən/ *n* destrucción, *f;* demolición, *f;* ruina, *f;* pérdida, *f;* muerte, *f;* exterminio, *m;* perdición, *f*
destructive /dɪ'strʌktɪv/ *a* destructivo, destructor; (of animals) dañino. **d. animal,** animal dañino, *m,* alimaña, *f*
destructiveness /dɪ'strʌktɪvnɪs/ *n* destructividad, *f;* instinto destructor, *m*
desultory /'dɛsəlˌtɔri/ *a* inconexo; sin método, descosido; irregular
detach /dɪ'tætʃ/ *vt* separar, desprender; (unstick) despegar; *Mil.* destacar
detachable /dɪ'tætʃəbəl/ *a* separable, de quita y pon
detached /dɪ'tætʃt/ *a* suelto, separado; (*Fig.* with outlook, etc.) imparcial; indiferente, despegado. **d. house,** hotelito, *m*
detachment /dɪ'tætʃmənt/ *n* separación, *f; Mil.* destacamento, *m;* (*Fig.* of mind) imparcialidad, *f;* independencia (de espíritu, etc.), *f;* indiferencia, *f*
detail /dɪ'teil/ *n* detalle, *m;* pormenor, *m,* particularidad, *f;* circunstancia, *f; Mil.* destacamento, *m.* —*vt* detallar; particularizar, referir con pormenores; *Mil.* destacar. **in d.,** detalladamente; al por menor; *Inf.* ce por be. **to go into details,** entrar en detalles
detain /dɪ'tein/ *vt* detener; (arrest) arrestar, prender; (withhold) retener; (prevent) impedir
detect /dɪ'tɛkt/ *vt* descubrir; averiguar; (discern) discernir, percibir; *Elec.* detectar
detectable /dɪ'tɛktəbəl/ *a* perceptible
detection /dɪ'tɛkʃən/ *n* descubrimiento, *m;* averiguación, *f;* percepción, *f*
detective /dɪ'tɛktɪv/ *n* detective, *m, a* de detectives, policíaco. **d. novel,** novela policíaca, *f*
detector /dɪ'tɛktər/ *n* descubridor, *m; Elec.* detector, *m; Mech.* indicador, *m*
detention /dɪ'tɛnʃən/ *n* detención, *f;* (arrest) arresto, *m;* (confinement) encierro, *m*
deter /dɪ'tɜr/ *vt* desanimar, desalentar; acobardar; (dissuade) disuadir; (prevent) impedir
detergent /dɪ'tɜrdʒənt/ *a* detersorio. —*n* detersorio, *m*
deteriorate /dɪ'tɪəriəˌreit/ *vt* deteriorar. —*vi* deteriorarse; empeorar
deterioration /dɪˌtɪəriə'reiʃən/ *n* deterioración, *f;* empeoramiento, *m*
determinable /dɪ'tɜrmənəbəl/ *a* determinable
determination /dɪˌtɜrmə'neiʃən/ *n* determinación, *f;* definición, *f;* resolución, decisión, *f; Law.* fallo, *m; Med.* congestión, *f*
determine /dɪ'tɜrmɪn/ *vt* determinar; definir; decidir, resolver; concluir; (fix) señalar; *Law.* sentenciar. —*vi* resolverse, decidirse; (insist (on)) empeñarse en, insistir en
determined /dɪ'tɜrmɪnd/ *a* determinado; resuelto, decidido; (of price) fijo
determining /dɪ'tɜrmənɪŋ/ *a* determinante
determinism /dɪ'tɜrməˌnɪzəm/ *n* determinismo, *m*
deterministic /dɪˌtɜrmə'nɪstɪk/ *a* determinista
deterrent /dɪ'tɜrənt/ *a* disuasivo. —*n* freno, *m.* **to act as a d.,** servir como un freno
deterrent capability *n* poder de disuasión, *m*
detest /dɪ'tɛst/ *vt* detestar, abominar, aborrecer
detestable /dɪ'tɛstəbəl/ *a* detestable, aborrecible, abominable
detestation /ˌditɛ'steiʃən/ *n* detestación, abominación, *f,* aborrecimiento, *m*
dethrone /di'θroun/ *vt* destronar
detonate /'dɛtn̩ˌeit/ *vt* hacer detonar. —*vi* detonar, estallar
detonation /ˌdɛtn̩'eiʃən/ *n* detonación, *f*
detonator /'dɛtn̩ˌeitər/ *n* detonador, *m;* señal detonante, *f*
detour /'ditʊr/ *n* rodeo, *m;* desvío, *m,* desviación, *f*
detract /dɪ'trækt/ *vt* quitar; (diminish) disminuir; (slander) detraer, denigrar
detraction /dɪ'trækʃən/ *n* detracción, denigración, *f*
detractor /dɪ'træktər/ *n* detractor (-ra); infamador (-ra)
detriment /'dɛtrəmənt/ *n* detrimento, *m;* perjuicio, *m;* daño, *m*
detrimental /ˌdɛtrə'mɛntl̩/ *a* perjudicial
deuce /dus/ *n* (dice, cards) dos, *m;* (tennis) "dos," *m.* **The d.!** ¡Diantre! **to be the d. of a row,** haber moros y cristianos. **D. take it!** ¡Demonios!
Deuteronomy /ˌdutə'rɒnəmi/ *n* Deuteronomio, *m*
devaluation /diˌvælyu'eiʃən/ *n* desvalorización, *f*
devalue /di'vælyu/ *vt* rebajar el valor de
devastate /'dɛvəˌsteit/ *vt* devastar, asolar
devastation /ˌdɛvə'steiʃən/ *n* devastación, *f*
develop /dɪ'vɛləp/ *vt* desarrollar; (make progress) avanzar, fomentar; perfeccionar; *Photo.* revelar. —*vi* desarrollarse; crecer; avanzar, progresar; evolucionar
developer /dɪ'vɛləpər/ *n Photo.* revelador, *m*
development /dɪ'vɛləpmənt/ *n* desarrollo, *m;* evolución, *f;* progreso, avance, *m;* (encouragement) fomento, *m;* (event) acontecimiento, suceso, *m;* (product) producto, *m;* (working) explotación, *f; Photo.* revelación, *f*
deviate /'diviˌeit/ *vi* desviarse (de); (disagree) disentir (de)
deviation /ˌdivi'eiʃən/ *n* desviación, *f*
device /dɪ'vais/ *n* (contrivance) aparato, artefacto, mecanismo, *m;* (invention) invento, *m;* (trick) expediente, artificio, *m;* (scheme) proyecto, *m;* (design) dibujo, emblema, *m;* (motto) divisa, leyenda, *f; pl* **devices,** placeres, caprichos, *m pl*
devil /'dɛvəl/ *n* diablo, Satanás, *m;* demonio, *m;* (printer's) aprendiz de impresor, *m.* **Go to the d.!** ¡Vete enhoramala! **He is a poor d.,** Es un pobre diablo. **little d.,** diablillo, *m.* **The devil's abroad,** Anda el diablo suelto. **The d. take it!** ¡Lléveselo el diablo! **to play the d. with,** arruinar por completo. **What the d.!** ¡Qué diablos! **d.-possessed,** endemoniado
devilish /'dɛvəlɪʃ/ *a* diabólico, demoníaco; infernal
devilry /'dɛvəlri/ *n* diablura, *f;* magia, *f;* demonología, *f;* (wickedness) maldad, *f;* crueldad, *f*
devious /'diviəs/ *a* desviado; tortuoso
deviousness /'diviəsnɪs/ *n* tortuosidad, *f*
devise /dɪ'vaiz/ *vt* idear, inventar; fabricar; *Law.* legar
deviser /dɪ'vaizər/ *n* inventor (-ra)
devitalize /di'vaitl̩ˌaiz/ *vt* restar vitalidad, privar de vitalidad
devoid /dɪ'vɔid/ *a* desprovisto (de), privado (de); libre (de), exento (de)
devolve /dɪ'vɒlv/ *vt* traspasar, transmitir. —*vi* (on, upon) incumbir (a), corresponder (a), tocar (a)
devote /dɪ'vout/ *vt* dedicar; consagrar. **to d. oneself to,** darse a, dedicarse a; consagrarse a
devoted /dɪ'voutɪd/ *a* fervoroso, apasionado; (faithful) fiel, leal
devotedly /dɪ'voutɪdli/ *adv* con devoción
devotee /ˌdɛvə'ti/ *n* devoto (-ta), admirador (-ra); aficionado (-da)
devotion /dɪ'vouʃən/ *n* devoción, *f;* dedicación, *f;* (zeal) celo, *m;* afición, *f;* (loyalty) lealtad, *f; pl* **devotions,** rezos, *m pl,* oraciones, *f pl*
devotional /dɪ'vouʃənl̩/ *a* devoto, religioso, de devoción. **devotional literature,** literatura de devoción, *f*
devour /dɪ'vaur/ *vt* devorar; consumir
devourer /dɪ'vaurər/ *n* devorador (-ra)
devouring /dɪ'vaurɪŋ/ *a* devorador; absorbente
devout /dɪ'vaut/ *a* devoto, piadoso, practicante (e.g., *a d. Catholic,* un católico practicante)
devoutly /dɪ'vautli/ *adv* piadosamente
devoutness /dɪ'vautnɪs/ *n* piedad, devoción, *f*
dew /du/ *n* rocío, sereno, relente, *m; Fig.* rocío, *m, vt* rociar; humedecer; (refresh) refrescar. **d.-drop,** aljófar, *m,* gota de rocío, *f*
dewlap /'duˌlæp/ *n* papada, *f,* papo, *m*
dewy /'dui/ *a* rociado, lleno de rocío; húmedo; (of eyes) lustroso
dexterity /dɛk'stɛrɪti/ *n* destreza, *f*

dextrine /'dɛkstrın/ *n* dextrina, *f*
dextrose /'dɛkstrous/ *n* dextrosa, glucosa, *f*
dextrous /'dɛkstrəs/ *a* diestro; hábil, listo
diabetes /ˌdaiə'bitıs/ *n* diabetes, *f*
diabetic /ˌdaiə'bɛtık/ *a* diabético
diabolical /ˌdaiə'bɒlıkəl/ *a* diabólico
diadem /'daiəˌdɛm/ *n* diadema, *f*
diagnose /'daiəgˌnous/ *vt* diagnosticar
diagnosis /ˌdaiəg'nousıs/ *n* diagnóstico, *m*, diagnosis, *f*
diagnostician /ˌdaiəgnɒ'stıʃən/ *n* diagnóstico, *m*
diagonal /dai'ægənl/ *n* diagonal, *f*
diagram /'daiəˌgræm/ *n* diagrama, *m;* esquema, *f;* gráfico, *m*
diagrammatic /ˌdaiəgrə'mætık/ *a* esquemático
dial /'daiəl/ *n* (sundial) reloj de sol, *m;* (of clocks, gas-meter) esfera, *f;* (of machines) indicador, *m;* (of a wireless set) cuadrante graduado, *m;* (of a telephone) marcador, disco, *m.* —*vt* (a telephone number) marcar. **d. telephone,** teléfono automático, *m*
dialect /'daiəˌlɛkt/ *n* dialecto, *m,* habla, *f, a* dialectal
dialectic /ˌdaiə'lɛktık/ *a* dialéctico
dialectics /ˌdaiə'lɛktıks/ *n* dialéctica, *f*
dialogue /'daiəˌlɔg/ *n* diálogo, *m.* **to hold a d.,** dialogar
dialysis /dai'æləsıs/ *n* diálisis, *f*
diameter /dai'æmıtər/ *n* diámetro, *m*
diametrical /ˌdaiə'mɛtrıkəl/ *a* diametral
diamond /'daimənd/ *n* diamante, *m;* brillante, *m;* (tool) cortavidrios, *m;* (cards) oros (de baraja), *m pl.* **rough d.,** diamante bruto, *m.* **d.-bearing,** diamantífero. **d. cutter,** diamantista, *mf* **d. cutting,** talla de diamantes, *f.* **d. edition,** edición diamante, *f.* **d.-like,** adiamantado. **d. wedding,** bodas de diamante, *f pl*
diapason /ˌdaiə'peizən/ *n* diapasón, *m*
diaper /'daipər/ *n* lienzo adamascado, *m;* (baby's) pañal, *m;* (woman's) servilleta higiénica, *f*
diaphanous /dai'æfənəs/ *a* diáfano, transparente
diaphragm /'daiəˌfræm/ *n* diafragma, *m*
diarist /'daiərıst/ *n* diarista, *mf*
diarrhea /ˌdaiə'riə/ *n* diarrea, *f*
diary /'daiəri/ *n* diario, *m*
diastase /'daiəˌsteis/ *n* diastasa, *f*
diastole /dai'æstl/ *n* diástole, *f*
diatribe /'daiəˌtraib/ *n* diatriba, denunciación violenta, *f*
dibble /'dıbəl/ *n* plantador, *m, vt* and *vi* plantar con plantador
dice /dais/ *n pl* dados, *m pl.* **to load the d.,** cargar los dados
dicky /'dıki/ *n* (front) pechera postiza, *f;* (seat) trasera, *f;* (apron) delantal, *m.* **d. seat,** *Inf.* ahí te pudras, *m*
dictaphone /'dıktəˌfoun/ *n* dictáfono, *m*
dictate /'dıkteit/ *vt* dictar; mandar. —*n* (order) dictamen, *m; Fig.* dictado, *m*
dictation /dık'teiʃən/ *n* dictado, *m.* **to write from d.,** escribir al dictado
dictator /'dıkteitər/ *n* dictador, *m*
dictatorial /ˌdıktə'tɔriəl/ *a* dictatorial, dictatorio, imperioso
dictatorship /dık'teitərˌʃıp/ *n* dictadura, *f*
diction /'dıkʃən/ *n* dicción, *f*
dictionary /'dıkʃəˌnɛri/ *n* diccionario, *m*
dictum /'dıktəm/ *n* dictamen, *m;* (saying) sentencia, *f; Law.* fallo, *m*
didactic /dai'dæktık/ *a* didáctico
die /dai/ *vi* morir; fallecer, finar; (wither) marchitarse; (disappear) desvanecerse, desaparecer; (of light) palidecer; extinguirse; (end) cesar; (desire) ansiar, perecerse (por). **Never say die!** ¡Mientras hay vida, hay esperanza! **to die early,** morir temprano; malograrse. **to die a violent death,** tener una muerte violenta, *Inf.* morir vestido. **to die from natural causes,** morir por causas naturales; *Inf.* morir en la cama. **to die hard,** luchar contra la muerte; tardar en morir; tardar en desaparecer. **to die of a broken heart,** morir con el corazón destrozado, morir de pena. **to die away,** desaparecer gradualmente; extinguirse poco a poco; dejar de oírse poco a poco; cesar; pasar. **to die down,** extinguirse gradualmente; palidecer; dejar de oírse; desaparecer; (of the wind) amainar; perder su fuerza. **to die out,** desaparecer; olvidarse; dejar de existir; pasarse de moda
die /dai/ *n* dado, *m; Fig.* suerte, *f;* (stamp) cuño, troquel, *m; Archit.* cubo, *m.* **The die is cast,** La suerte está echada. **die-sinker,** grabador en hueco, *m*
diehard /'daiˌhɑrd/ *n* valiente, *m;* tradicionalista empedernido, *m;* partidario (-ia) entusiasta
Dieppe /di'ɛp/ Diepa, *f*
dieresis /dai'ɛrəsıs/ *n* diéresis, crema, *f*
diesel /'dizəl, -səl/ *a* Diesel. **d. engine,** motor Diesel, *m*
diet /'daiıt/ *n* dieta, *f,* régimen dietario, *m;* (assembly) dieta, *f.* —*vi* estar a dieta, hacer régimen
dietetic /ˌdaiı'tɛtık/ *a* dietético
dietetics /ˌdaiı'tɛtıks/ *n* dietética, *f*
dietician /ˌdaiı'tıʃən/ *n* dietista, *mf*
differ /'dıfər/ *vi* diferenciarse; (contradict) contradecir; (disagree) no estar de acuerdo; disentir
difference /'dıfərəns/ *n* diferencia, *f;* disparidad, *f;* contraste, *m;* (of opinion) disensión, *f;* controversia, disputa, *f.* **to make no d.,** no hacer diferencia alguna; no afectar; dar lo mismo, no importar
different /'dıfərənt/ *a* distinto; diferente; vario, diverso
differential /ˌdıfə'rɛnʃəl/ *a* diferencial. **d. calculus,** cálculo diferencial, *m*
differentiate /ˌdıfə'rɛnʃiˌeit/ *vt* diferenciar, distinguir. —*vi* diferenciarse, distinguirse
differentiation /ˌdıfəˌrɛnʃi'eiʃən/ *n* diferenciación, *f*
differently /'dıfərəntli/ *adv* diferentemente
difficult /'dıfıˌkʌlt/ *a* difícil. **to make d.,** dificultar
difficulty /'dıfıˌkʌlti/ *n* dificultad, *f.* **d. in breathing,** opresión de pecho, *f*
diffidence /'dıfıdəns/ *n* modestia, timidez, *f;* huraňía, *f;* falta de confianza en sí mismo, *f*
diffident /'dıfıdənt/ *a* modesto, tímido; huraño; sin confianza en sí mismo
diffidently /'dıfıdəntli/ *adv* tímidamente; vergonzosamente
diffract /dı'frækt/ *vt* difractar
diffraction /dı'frækʃən/ *n* difracción, *f*
diffractive /dı'fræktıv/ *a* difrangente
diffuse /*v* dı'fyuz; *a* -'fyus/ *vt* difundir. —*a* difuso; (long-winded) prolijo
diffuseness /dı'fyusnıs/ *n* difusión, *f;* prolijidad, *f*
diffusion /dı'fyuʒən/ *n* difusión, *f;* esparcimiento, *m;* diseminación, *f*
diffusive /dı'fyusıv/ *a* difusivo
dig /dıg/ *vt* and *vi* cavar; excavar; (of animals) escarbar; (mine) zapar, minar; (into a subject) ahondar (en); (with the spurs) aguijonear, dar con las espuelas; (poke) clavar. **to dig in,** enterrarse; *Mil.* abrir trincheras; *Inf.* arreglarse las cosas. **to dig out,** excavar; sacar cavando, sacar con azadón; extraer. **to dig up,** desenterrar; descubrir
digest /*v* dı'dʒɛst, dai-; *n* 'daidʒɛst/ *vt* clasificar; codificar; (food, also *chem.* and *Fig.* tolerate and think over) digerir; (of knowledge and territory) asimilar. —*vi* digerir. —*n* compendio, resumen, *m; Law.* digesto, *m;* recopilación, *f.* **This food is easy to d.,** Este alimento es fácil de digerir; Este alimento es muy ligero
digestibility /dıˌdʒɛstə'bılıti, dai-/ *n* digestibilidad, *f*
digestible /dı'dʒɛstəbəl, dai-/ *a* digerible, digestible
digestion /dı'dʒɛstʃən, dai-/ *n* digestión, *f;* (of ideas) asimilación, *f; Chem.* digestión, *f*
digestive /dı'dʒɛstıv, dai-/ *a* digestivo
digger /'dıgər/ *n* cavador (-ra)
digging /'dıgıŋ/ *n* cavadura, *f;* excavación, *f; pl* **diggings,** minas, *f pl*; excavaciones, *f pl*; *Inf.* alojamiento, *m,* posada, *f*
digit /'dıdʒıt/ *n* dígito, *m*
digital /'dıdʒıtl/ *a* digital, dígito
digitalin /ˌdıdʒı'tælın/ *n* digitalina, *f*
digitalis /ˌdıdʒı'tælıs/ *n* digital, *f*
dignified /'dıgnəˌfaid/ *a* serio, grave; majestuoso; (worthy) digno; solemne; altivo; noble
dignify /'dıgnəˌfai/ *vt* dignificar, honrar; exaltar; dar dignidad (a); ennoblecer
dignitary /'dıgnıˌtɛri/ *n* dignatario, *m;* dignidad, *f*

dignity /'dɪgnɪti/ *n* dignidad, *f;* (rank) rango, *m;* (post) cargo, puesto, *m;* (honor) honra, *f;* (stateliness) majestad, *f;* mesura, seriedad, *f;* (haughtiness) altivez, *f;* (nobility) nobleza, *f.* **to stand on one's d.,** darse importancia
digress /dɪ'grɛs, dai-/ *vi* divagar
digression /dɪ'grɛʃən, dai-/ *n* digresión, divagación, *f*
dike /daik/ *n* dique, *m;* (ditch) acequia, *f;* canal, *m;* (embankment) zanja, *f, vt* represar
dilapidated /dɪ'læpɪˌdeitɪd/ *a* arruinado, destartalado; (of fortune) dilapidado; (of persons, families) venido a menos; (shabby) raído
dilapidation /dɪˌlæpə'deiʃən/ *n* deterioración, *f;* ruina, *f,* estado ruinoso, *m*
dilatation /ˌdɪlə'teiʃən/ *n* dilatación, *f;* ensanche, *m*
dilate /dai'leit/ *vt* dilatar; ensanchar. —*vi* dilatarse. **to d. upon,** extenderse sobre, dilatarse en
dilator /dai'leitər/ *n* dilatador, *m*
dilatoriness /'dɪlətɔrinɪs/ *n* tardanza, *f;* (slowness) lentitud, *f*
dilatory /'dɪləˌtɔri/ *a* dilatorio, tardo; (slow) lento
dilemma /dɪ'lɛmə/ *n* dilema, *m*
dilettante /'dɪlɪˌtɑnt/ *n* diletante, *m;* aficionado (-da)
dilettantism /'dɪlɪtɑnˌtɪzəm/ *n* diletantismo, *m*
diligence /'dɪlɪdʒəns/ *n* diligencia, *f;* asiduidad, *f;* (care) cuidado, *m;* (coach) diligencia, *f*
diligent /'dɪlɪdʒənt/ *a* diligente, asiduo, aplicado, industrioso; (painstaking) concienzudo
dilute /dɪ'lut, dai-/ *vt* diluir; *Fig.* adulterar. —*a* diluido
dilution /dɪ'luʃən, dai-/ *n* dilución, *f; Fig.* adulteración, *f*
diluvian /dɪ'luviən/ *a* diluviano
dim /dɪm/ *a* (of light) apagado, débil, tenue; (of sight) turbio; (dark) sombrío, oscuro; (blurred, etc.) empañado; indistinto, confuso. —*vt* obscurecer; empañar; (dazzle) ofuscar; (eclipse) eclipsar; reducir la intensidad (de una luz); (of memories) borrar. **dim intelligence,** de brumoso seso
dimension /dɪ'mɛnʃən/ *n* dimensión, *f;* (size) tamaño, *m;* (scope) extensión, *f,* alcance, *m*
dimensional /dɪ'mɛnʃənl/ *a* dimensional
diminish /dɪ'mɪnɪʃ/ *vt* disminuir; reducir; debilitar, atenuar. —*vi* disminuir; reducirse; debilitarse, atenuarse
diminishing /dɪ'mɪnɪʃɪŋ/ *a* menguante
diminution /ˌdɪmə'nuʃən/ *n* disminución, *f;* reducción, *f;* atenuación, *f*
diminutive /dɪ'mɪnyətɪv/ *a* diminutivo. —*n* diminutivo, *m*
diminutiveness /dɪ'mɪnyətɪvnɪs/ *n* pequeñez, *f*
dimly /'dɪmli/ *adv* obscuramente; vagamente; indistintamente. **dimly lit,** apenas alumbrado
dimness /'dɪmnɪs/ *n* oscuridad, *f;* deslustre, *m;* (of light) tenuidad (de la luz), *f;* confusión, *f*
dimple /'dɪmpəl/ *n* hoyuelo, *m*
dimpled /'dɪmpəld/ *a* con hoyuelos, que tiene hoyuelos
din /dɪn/ *n* estrépito, estruendo, ruido, *m;* algarabía, barahúnda, *f, vt* ensordecer
dine /dain/ *vi* (in the evening) cenar; (at midday) comer. —*vt* convidar a cenar or a comer. **to d. out,** cenar or comer fuera
diner /'dainər/ *n* (on a train) coche comedor, coche restaurante, *m;* cenador, *m;* comedor, *m*
ding-dong /'dɪŋˌdɔŋ/ *n* tintín, *m*
dinghy /'dɪŋgi/ *n* lancha, *f;* canoa, *f,* bote, *m.* **rubber d.,** canoa de goma, *f*
dinginess /'dɪndʒinɪs/ *n* deslustre, *m;* suciedad, *f;* oscuridad, *f;* (of a person) desaseo, *m*
dingy /'dɪndʒi/ *a* deslucido, empañado; sucio; oscuro; (of persons) desaseado
dining car /'dainɪŋ/ *n* coche comedor, vagón restaurante, *m*
dining room *n* comedor, *m;* refectorio, *m*
dining table *n* mesa del comedor, *f*
dinner /'dɪnər/ *n* (in the evening) cena, *f;* (at midday) comida, *f.* **over the d. table,** de sobremesa. **d.-jacket,** smoking, *m.* **d. party,** cena, *f.* **d. plate,** plato, *m.* **d. roll,** panecillo, *m.* **d. service,** vajilla, *f*
dinosaur /'dainəˌsɔr/ *n* dinosauro, *m*
dint /dɪnt/ **(by d. of)** a fuerza de, a costa de
diocesan /dai'ɒsəsən/ *a* diocesano
diocese /'daiəsɪs/ *n* diócesis, *f*
Dionysus Thrax /ˌdaiə'naisəs 'θræks/ Dionisio el Tracio, *m*
dioxide /dai'ɒksaid, -sɪd/ *n* dióxido, *m*
dip /dɪp/ *n* inmersión, *f;* baño, *m;* (in the ground) declive, *m;* (in the road) columpio, *m,* depresión, *f;* (slope) pendiente, *f;* (candle) vela de sebo, *f;* (of the horizon) depresión (del horizonte), *f;* (of the needle) inclinación (de la aguja), *f.* —*vt* sumergir; bañar; (put) poner. —*vi* inclinarse hacia abajo. **to dip into a book,** hojear un libro. **to dip the colors,** saludar con la bandera. **to dip the headlights,** bajar los faros
diphtheria /dɪf'θɪəriə/ *n* difteria, *f*
diphthong /'dɪfθɔŋ/ *n* diptongo, *m*
diploma /dɪ'ploumə/ *n* diploma, *m*
diplomacy /dɪ'ploumәsi/ *n* diplomacia, *f;* tacto, *m*
diploma mill *n* fábrica de títulos académicos, *f*
diplomat /'dɪpləˌmæt/ *n* diplomático, *m*
diplomatic /ˌdɪplə'mætɪk/ *a* diplomático. **d. bag,** valija diplomática, *f.* **d. corps,** cuerpo diplomático, *m*
diplomatically /ˌdɪplə'mætɪkəli/ *adv* diplomáticamente
dipper /'dɪpər/ *n* (ladle) cazo, *m; Astron.* Osa Mayor, *f*
dipsomania /ˌdɪpsə'meiniə/ *n* dipsomanía, *f*
dipsomaniac /ˌdɪpsə'meiniæk/ *n* dipsómano (-na)
diptych /'dɪptɪk/ *n* diptica, *f*
dire /daiər/ *a* espantoso, horrible; cruel; funesto
direct /dɪ'rɛkt, dai-/ *a* directo; claro, inequívoco; (of descent) recto; (of electric current) continuo; exacto. —*adv* directamente. —*vt* dirigir; (command) ordenar, encargar; dar instrucciones. **d. action,** acción directa, *f.* **d. current,** corriente continua, *f.* **d. line,** línea directa, *f;* (of descent) línea recta, *f.* **d. object,** acusativo, *m.* **d. speech,** oración directa, *f*
direct dialing *n* discado directo, *m*
direction /dɪ'rɛkʃən, 'dai-/ *n* dirección, *f;* rumbo, *m;* instrucción, *f;* (on a letter) sobrescrito, *m;* señas, *f pl.* **in the d. of,** en la dirección de; hacia; *Naut.* con rumbo a. **in all directions,** por todas partes; a los cuatro vientos. **to go in the d. of,** ir en la dirección de; tomar por. **Directions for use,** Direcciones para el uso. **d. indicator, d. signal,** (on car) indicador de dirección, *m*
directive /dɪ'rɛktɪv, dai-/ *a* directivo, director
directly /dɪ'rɛktli, dai-/ *adv* directamente; inmediatamente, en seguida
directness /dɪ'rɛktnɪs, dai-/ *n* derechura, *f*
director /dɪ'rɛktər, dai-/ *n* director (-triz, -ora), **managing d.,** director gerente, *m*
directorate /dɪ'rɛktərɪt, dai-/ *n* directorio, *m,* junta directiva, *f;* cargo de director, *m*
directory /dɪ'rɛktəri, dai-/ *n* directorio, *m,* guía, *f.* **telephone d.,** guía de teléfonos, *f*
dirge /dɜrdʒ/ *n* endecha, *f,* lamento, *m;* canto fúnebre, *m*
dirigible /'dɪrɪdʒəbəl/ *n* dirigible, *m*
dirt /dɜrt/ *n* mugre, suciedad, *f;* (mud) lodo, *m;* (earth) tierra, *f;* (dust) polvo, *m; Fig.* inmundicia, *f.* **d.-cheap,** sumamente barato. **to be d. cheap,** (of goods) estar por los suelos. **d.-track,** pista de ceniza, *f.* **d.-track racing,** carreras en pista de ceniza, *f pl*
dirtiness /'dɜrtinɪs/ *n* suicedad, *f;* (untidiness) desaseo, *m;* sordidez, *f;* (meanness) bajeza, *f*
dirty /'dɜrti/ *a* sucio; (untidy) desaseado; (muddy) enlodado; (dusty) polvoriento; (of weather) borrascoso; (sordid) sórdido; (base, mean) vil; (indecent) indecente, verde, obsceno. —*vt* ensuciar. **d. trick,** mala pasada, *f*
disability /ˌdɪsə'bɪlɪti/ *n* incapacidad, *f;* impotencia, *f;* desventaja, *f*
disable /dɪs'eibəl/ *vt* (cripple) estropear, tullir; hacer incapaz (de), incapacitar; imposibilitar; (destroy) destruir; *Law.* incapacitar legalmente
disabled /dɪs'eibəld/ *a* inválido; impedido, lisiado; (in the hand) manco; incapacitado; (of ships, etc.) fuera de servicio, estropeado. **d. soldier,** inválido, *m*
disablement /dɪs'eibəlmənt/ *n* (physical) invalidez, *f;* inhabilitación, *f; Law.* impedimento, *m*

disabuse /ˌdɪsə'byuz/ *vt* desengañar, sacar de un error
disadvantage /ˌdɪsəd'væntɪdʒ/ *n* desventaja, *f.* **to be under the d. of,** sufrir la desventaja de
disadvantaged /ˌdɪsəd'væntɪdʒd/ *a* (financially) de escasos recursos
disadvantageous /dɪsˌædvən'teidʒəs/ *a* desventajoso
disaffected /ˌdɪsə'fɛktɪd/ *a* desafecto
disaffection /ˌdɪsə'fɛkʃən/ *n* desafecto, descontento, *m*
disagree /ˌdɪsə'gri/ *vi* no estar de acuerdo; diferir; (quarrel) reñir; (not share the opinion of) no estar de la opinión (de); (of food, etc.) sentar mal; no probar. **The meat disagreed with me,** La carne me sentó mal
disagreeable /ˌdɪsə'griəbəl/ *a* desagradable; repugnante; (of persons) antipático, displicente
disagreeableness /ˌdɪsə'griəbəlnɪs/ *n* lo desagradable; (of persons) displicencia, *f*
disagreeably /ˌdɪsə'griəbli/ *adv* desagradablemente; con displicencia
disagreement /ˌdɪsə'grimənt/ *n* desacuerdo, *m;* diferencia, *f;* desavenencia, *f;* discordia, *f;* (quarrel) riña, disputa, *f;* discrepancia, *f*
disallow /ˌdɪsə'lau/ *vt* negar; rechazar
disappear /ˌdɪsə'pɪər/ *vi* desaparecer. **to cause to d.,** hacer desaparecer
disappearance /ˌdɪsə'pɪərəns/ *n* desaparición, *f*
disappoint /ˌdɪsə'pɔint/ *vt* desilusionar; frustrar; (hopes) defraudar; (deprive) privar de; (annoy) contrariar; (break a promise) faltar (a la palabra)
disappointedly /ˌdɪsə'pɔintɪdli/ *adv* con desilusión, con desengaño
disappointing /ˌdɪsə'pɔintɪŋ/ *a* desengañador; pobre; triste; poco halagüeño
disappointment /ˌdɪsə'pɔintmənt/ *n* desengaño, *m,* decepción, *f;* frustración, *f;* desilusión, *f;* (vexation) contrariedad, *f;* contratiempo, *m.* **to suffer a d.,** sufrir un desengaño; *Inf.* llevarse un chasco
disapproval /ˌdɪsə'pruvəl/ *n* desaprobación, *f*
disapprove /ˌdɪsə'pruv/ *vt* desaprobar
disapproving /ˌdɪsə'pruvɪŋ/ *a* de desaprobación, severo
disapprovingly /ˌdɪsə'pruvɪŋli/ *adv* con desaprobación
disarm /dɪs'ɑrm/ *vt* desarmar. —*vi* desarmarse; deponer las armas
disarmament /dɪs'ɑrməmənt/ *n* desarme, *m*
disarrange /ˌdɪsə'reindʒ/ *vt* desarreglar; descomponer, desajustar; (hair) despeinar
disarrangement /ˌdɪsə'reindʒmənt/ *n* desarreglo, *m;* desajuste, *m;* desorden, *m*
disarray /ˌdɪsə'rei/ *n* desorden, desarreglo, *m;* confusión, *f.* —*vt* desordenar, desarreglar
disarticulate /ˌdɪsɑr'tɪkyəˌleit/ *vt* desarticular
disarticulation /ˌdɪsɑrˌtɪkyə'leiʃən/ *n* desarticulación, *f*
disaster /dɪ'zæstər/ *n* desastre, *m;* catástrofe, *m;* infortunio, *m*
disastrous /dɪ'zæstrəs/ *a* desastroso; funesto, trágico
disastrously /dɪ'zæstrəsli/ *adv* desastrosamente
disastrousness /dɪ'zæstrəsnɪs/ *n* carácter desastroso, *m*
disavow /ˌdɪsə'vau/ *vt* repudiar; retractar
disavowal /ˌdɪsə'vauəl/ *n* repudiación, *f*
disband /dɪs'bænd/ *vt* licenciar. —*vi* desbandarse, dispersarse
disbelief /ˌdɪsbɪ'lif/ *n* incredulidad, *f;* desconfianza, *f*
disbelieve /ˌdɪsbɪ'liv/ *vt* and *vi* descreer, no creer; desconfiar (de)
disburse /dɪs'bɜrs/ *vt* desembolsar, pagar
disbursement /dɪs'bɜrsmənt/ *n* desembolso, *m*
disc /dɪsk/ *n* disco, *m*
discard /*v* dɪ'skɑrd; *n* 'dɪskɑrd/ *vt* desechar, arrinconar; despedir; (at cards) descartar. —*n* (at cards) descarte, *m*
discern /dɪ'sɜrn/ *vt* discernir, distinguir, percibir
discerner /dɪ'sɜrnər/ *n* discernidor (-ra)
discernible /dɪ'sɜrnəbəl/ *a* distinguible, perceptible
discerning /dɪ'sɜrnɪŋ/ *a* perspicaz, discernidor
discernment /dɪ'sɜrnmənt/ *n* discernimiento, *m*
discharge /*v* dɪs'tʃɑrdʒ/ *vt* descargar; (a gun) disparar, tirar; (an arrow) lanzar; *Elec.* descargar; emitir; (dismiss) destituir, despedir; arrojar; *Mil.* licenciar; (exempt) dispensar (de); (exonerate) absolver, exonerar; (free) dar libertad (a); (from hospital) dar de baja (a); *Law.* revocar; (perform) cumplir, ejecutar; (pay) pagar, saldar; (of an abscess, etc.) supurar.
discharge /*n* 'dɪstʃɑrdʒ/ *n* (of firearms) disparo, tiro, *m;* (of artillery) descarga, *f;* (of goods, cargo) descargue, *m; Elec.* descarga, *f;* (from a wound, etc.) pus, *m,* supuración, *f;* (from the intestine) flujo, *m;* (of a debt) pago, m.; *Com.* descargo, *m;* (receipt) carta de pago, quitanza, *f; Mil.* licencia absoluta, *f;* (dismissal) despedida, destitución, *f;* (exoneration) exoneración, *f;* (freeing) liberación, *f;* (from hospital) baja, *f;* (performance) cumplimiento, *m;* ejecución, *f*
disciple /dɪ'saipəl/ *n* discípulo (-la)
disciplinarian /ˌdɪsəplə'nɛəriən/ *n* disciplinario (-ia)
disciplinary /'dɪsəpləˌnɛri/ *a* disciplinario
discipline /'dɪsəplɪn/ *n* disciplina, *f, vt* disciplinar
disclaim /dɪs'kleim/ *vt* renunciar (a); (repudiate) rechazar, repudiar
disclaimer /dɪs'kleimər/ *n Law.* renunciación, *f;* repudiación, *f*
disclose /dɪ'sklouz/ *vt* descubrir, revelar
disclosure /dɪ'sklouʒər/ *n* descubrimiento, *m,* revelación, *f*
discolor /dɪs'kʌlər/ *vt* descolorar. —*vi* descolorarse
discoloration /dɪsˌkʌlə'reiʃən/ *n* descoloramiento, *m*
discomfit /dɪs'kʌmfɪt/ *vt* desconcertar
discomfiture /dɪs'kʌmfɪtʃər/ *n* desconcierto, *m*
discomfort /dɪs'kʌmfərt/ *n* falta de comodidades, *f;* incomodidad, *f;* malestar, *m;* molestia, *f;* inquietud, *f;* dolor, *m*
discomposure /ˌdɪskəm'pouʒər/ *n* confusión, agitación, inquietud, *f*
disconcert /ˌdɪskən'sɜrt/ *vt* desconcertar, turbar; (of plans, etc.) frustrar
disconnect /ˌdɪskə'nɛkt/ *vt* separar; (of railway engines, etc.) desacoplar; desconectar; (of electric plugs) desenchufar
disconnected /ˌdɪskə'nɛktɪd/ *a* inconexo; incoherente, deshilvanado
disconnectedness /ˌdɪskə'nɛktɪdnɪs/ *n* inconexión, *f;* incoherencia, *f*
disconsolate /dɪs'kɒnsəlɪt/ *a* desconsolado, triste
disconsolately /dɪs'kɒnsəlɪtli/ *adv* desconsoladamente, tristemente
disconsolateness /dɪs'kɒnsəlɪtnɪs/ *n* desconsuelo, *m*
discontent /ˌdɪskən'tɛnt/ *n* descontento, disgusto, *m, vt* descontentar, desagradar
discontented /ˌdɪskən'tɛntɪd/ *a* descontentadizo, descontento, disgustado
discontinuance /ˌdɪskən'tɪnyuəns/ *n* descontinuación, cesación, *f;* interrupción, *f*
discontinue /ˌdɪskən'tɪnyu/ *vt* descontinuar; cesar; interrumpir; (of payments, etc.) suspender. —*vi* cesar
discontinuous /ˌdɪskən'tɪnyuəs/ *a* descontinuo; interrumpido; intermitente
discord /'dɪskɔrd/ *n* discordia, *f; Mus.* disonancia, *f,* desentono, *m*
discordant /dɪs'kɔrdənt/ *a* discorde, poco armonioso; incongruo; *Mus.* disonante, desentonado. **to be d.,** discordar; ser incongruo; *Mus.* disonar
discount /'dɪskaunt; *v also* dɪs'kaunt/ *n* descuento, *m;* rebaja, *f.* —*vt* descontar; rebajar; balancear; (disconsider) desechar. **at a d.,** al descuento; bajo la par; fácil de obtener; superfluo; *Fig.* en disfavor, en descrédito. **rate of d.,** tipo de descuento, *m.* **d. for cash,** descuento por venta al contado, *m*
discourage /dɪ'skɜrɪdʒ/ *vt* desalentar, desanimar; oponerse a; disuadir; frustrar
discouragement /dɪ'skɜrɪdʒmənt/ *n* desaliento, *m;* desaprobación, oposición, *f;* disuasión, *f;* (obstacle) estorbo, *m*
discouraging /dɪ'skɜrɪdʒɪŋ/ *a* poco animador, que ofrece pocas esperanzas; (with prospect, etc.) nada halagüeño
discourse /*n* 'dɪskɔrs; *v* dɪs'kɔrs/ *n* discurso, *m;* plática, *f;* (treatise) disertación, *f.* —*vi* (converse) platicar, conversar; (with on, upon) disertar sobre, discurrir sobre; tratar de

discourteous /dɪs'kɜrtiəs/ *a* descortés, desconsiderado
discourtesy /dɪs'kɜrtəsi/ *n* descortesía, *f*
discover /dɪ'skʌvər/ *vt* descubrir; (see) ver; (realize) darse cuenta de; (show) manifestar; revelar
discoverable /dɪ'skʌvərəbəl/ *a* que se puede descubrir; averiguable; distinguible, perceptible
discoverer /dɪ'skʌvərər/ *n* descubridor (-ra); revelador (-ra)
discovery /dɪ'skʌvəri/ *n* descubrimiento, *m;* revelación, *f*
discredit /dɪs'krɛdɪt/ *n* descrédito, *m;* des honra, *f;* duda, *f.* —*vt* dudar (de), no creer (en); desacreditar; deshonrar
discreditable /dɪs'krɛdɪtəbəl/ *a* deshonroso, ignominioso, vergonzoso
discreet /dɪ'skrit/ *a* discreto; prudente, circunspecto
discreetly /dɪ'skritli/ *adv* discretamente; prudentemente
discrepancy /dɪ'skrɛpənsi/ *n* discrepancia, diferencia, *f;* contradicción, *f*
discrepant /dɪ'skrɛpənt/ *a* discrepante; contradictorio, inconsistente
discretion /dɪ'skrɛʃən/ *n* discreción, *f;* prudencia, circunspección, *f;* juicio, *m;* voluntad, *f.* **at d.,** a discreción. **at one's own d.,** a voluntad (de uno). **years of d.,** edad de discreción, *f*
discriminate /dɪ'skrɪm,əneit/ *vi* distinguir (entre); hacer una distinción (en favor de or en perjuicio de). —*vt* distinguir
discriminating /dɪ'skrɪmə,neitɪŋ/ *a* discerniente, que sabe distinguir, juicioso; culto; diferencial
discrimination /dɪ,skrɪmə'neiʃən/ *n* discernimiento, *m;* gusto, *m;* distinción, *f;* discriminación, *f*
discursive /dɪ'skɜrsɪv/ *a* discursivo; digresivo
discus /'dɪskəs/ *n* disco, *m.* **d. thrower,** discóbolo, *m*
discuss /dɪ'skʌs/ *vt* discutir; hablar de; debatir; (deal with) tratar; (*Fam.* a dish) probar; (a bottle of wine) vaciar
discussion /dɪ'skʌʃən/ *n* discusión, *f;* debate, *m*
disdain /dɪs'dein/ *n* desdén, *m;* altivez, *f.* —*vt* desdeñar, desairar, despreciar. **to d. to,** desdeñarse de
disdainful /dɪs'deinfəl/ *a* desdeñoso; altivo
disdainfully /dɪs'deinfəli/ *adv* desdeñosamente
disease /dɪ'ziz/ *n* enfermedad, *f; Fig.* mal, *m.* **infectious d.,** enfermedad contagiosa, *f*
diseased /dɪ'zizd/ *a* enfermo; (of fruit, etc.) malo
disembark /,dɪsɛm'bɑrk/ *vt* and *vi* desembarcar
disembarkation /dɪs,ɛmbɑr'keiʃən/ *n* desembarque, *m; Mil.* desembarco (de tropas), *m*
disembodied /,dɪsɛm'bɒdid/ *a* incorpóreo
disembowel /,dɪsɛm'bauəl/ *vt* desentrañar, destripar
disenchant /,dɪsɛn'tʃænt/ *vt* desencantar; deschechizar; desilusionar
disenchantment /,dɪsɛn'tʃæntmənt/ *n* desencanto, *m;* desilusión, *f*
disengage /,dɪsɛn'geidʒ/ *vt* desasir; soltar; (gears) desembragar; (uncouple) desacoplar; (free) librar
disengaged /,dɪsɛn'geidʒd/ *a* (free) libre
disentangle /,dɪsɛn'tæŋgəl/ *vt* (undo) desatar, desanudar; separar; (of threads, etc., and *Fig.*) desenredar, desenmarañar. —*vi* desenredarse
disentanglement /,dɪsɛn'tæŋgəlmənt/ *n* desatadura, *f;* separación, *f;* desenredo, *m*
disestablish /,dɪsɪ'stæblɪʃ/ *vt* separar (la Iglesia del Estado)
disestablishment /,dɪsɪ'stæblɪʃmənt/ *n* separación (de la Iglesia del Estado), *f*
disfavor /dɪs'feivər/ *n* disfavor, *m;* (disapproval) desaprobación, *f.* —*vt* desaprobar
disfigure /dɪs'fɪgyər/ *vt* desfigurar, afear; deformar; (mar) estropear
disfigurement /dɪs'fɪgyərmənt/ *n* desfiguración, *f;* deformidad, *f;* defecto, *m*
disfranchise /dɪs'fræntʃaiz/ *vt* privar de los derechos civiles (a)
disfranchisement /dɪs'fræntʃaizmənt/ *n* privación de los derechos civiles, privación del derecho de votar, *f*
disgorge /dɪs'gɔrdʒ/ *vt* and *vi* vomitar; (of a river) desembocar (en); hacer restitución (de lo robado)
disgrace /dɪs'greis/ *n* vergüenza, ignominia, *f;* deshonra, *f;* (insult) afrenta, *f;* (scandal) escándalo, *m;* disfavor, *m.* —*vt* deshonrar; despedir con ignominia. **in d.,** fuera de favor; desacreditado; (of children and animals) castigado
disgraceful /dɪs'greisfəl/ *a* deshonroso; ignominioso; escandaloso
disgracefully /dɪs'greisfəli/ *adv* escandalosamente
disgracefulness /dɪs'greisfəlnɪs/ *n* ignominia, vergüenza, *f;* deshonra, *f*
disgruntled /dɪs'grʌntld/ *a* refunfuñador, enfurruñado, malhumorado
disguise /dɪs'gaiz/ *n* disfraz, *m;* (mask) máscara, *f.* —*vt* disfrazar; cubrir, tapar; (*Fig.* conceal) ocultar. **in d.,** disfrazado
disgust /dɪs'gʌst/ *n* repugnancia, aversión, *f;* aborrecimiento, *m;* asco, *m.* —*vt* repugnar, inspirar aversión; disgustar; dar asco (a)
disgusted /dɪs'gʌstɪd/ *a* asqueado; disgustado; furioso; (bored) aburrido
disgusting /dɪs'gʌstɪŋ/ *a* repugnante; odioso, horrible; asqueroso
dish /dɪʃ/ *n* (for meat, vegetables, fruit, etc.) fuente, *f;* (food) plato, *m; pl* **dishes,** platos, *m pl,* vajilla, *f.* —*vt* servir; *Inf.* frustrar. **cooked d.,** guiso, *m.* **special d. for today,** plato del día, *m.* **to wash the dishes,** fregar los platos. **d.-cloth,** (for washing) fregador, *m;* (for drying) paño de los platos, *m.* **d.-cover,** cubreplatos, *m.* **d.-rack,** escurre-platos, *m.* **d.-washer,** lavaplatos, lavavajillas, *m.* **d.-water,** agua de lavar los platos, *f*
disharmony /dɪs'hɑrməni/ *n* falta de armonía, *f;* (disagreement) discordia, desavenencia, *f;* incongruencia, *f; Mus.* disonancia, *f*
dishearten /dɪs'hɑrtn/ *vt* desalentar, desanimar; desesperar; disuadir (de)
disheveled /dɪ'ʃɛvəld/ *a* despeinado, desgreñado; (untidy) desaseado
dishonest /dɪs'ɒnɪst/ *a* falto de honradez, tramposo; fraudulento; falso, desleal
dishonestly /dɪs'ɒnɪstli/ *adv* de mala fe, sin honradez; fraudulentamente; deslealmente
dishonesty /dɪs'ɒnəsti/ *n* falta de honradez, falta de integridad, *f;* fraude, *m;* falsedad, deslealtad, *f*
dishonor /dɪs'ɒnər/ *n* deshonra, *f, vt* deshonrar; *Com.* no pagar, o no aceptar, un giro
dishonorable /dɪs'ɒnərəbəl/ *a* deshonroso
dishonorer /dɪs'ɒnərər/ *n* deshonrador (-ra); profanador (-ra)
disillusion /,dɪsɪ'luʒən/ *vt* desengañar, desilusionar
disillusionment /,dɪsɪ'luʒənmənt/ *n* desilusión, *f,* desengaño, desencanto, *m*
disinclination /dɪs,ɪnklə'neiʃən/ *n* aversión, *f*
disincline /,dɪsɪn'klain/ *vt* desinclinar
disinfect /,dɪsɪn'fɛkt/ *vt* desinfectar
disinfectant /,dɪsɪn'fɛktənt/ *a* and *n* desinfectante *m.*
disinfection /,dɪsɪn'fɛkʃən/ *n* desinfección, *f*
disingenuous /,dɪsɪn'dʒɛnyuəs/ *a* tortuoso, doble, falso, insincero
disinherit /,dɪsɪn'hɛrɪt/ *vt* desheredar
disinheritance /,dɪsɪn'hɛrɪtəns/ *n* desheredación, *f*
disintegrate /dɪs'ɪntə,greit/ *vt* despedazar, disgregar. —*vi* disgregarse; desmoronarse
disintegration /dɪs,ɪntə'greiʃən/ *n* disgregración, *f;* disolución, *f;* desmoronamiento, *m*
disinter /,dɪsɪn'tɜr/ *vt* desenterrar
disinterested /dɪs'ɪntə,rɛstɪd, -trɪstɪd/ *a* desinteresado
disinterestedness /dɪs'ɪntə,rɛstɪdnɪs, -trɪstɪd-/ *n* desinterés, *m*
disinterment /,dɪsɪn'tɜrmənt/ *n* desenterramiento, *m*
disjointed /dɪs'dʒɔintɪd/ *a* dislocado; desarticulado; incoherente, inconexo; (of a speech, etc.) descosido
disjointedness /dɪs'dʒɔintɪdnɪs/ *n* descoyuntamiento, desencajamiento, *m;* incoherencia, *f*
disk /dɪsk/ *n* disco, *m*
dislike /dɪs'laik/ *n* aversión, *f;* antipatía, *f;* (hostility) animosidad, *f.* —*vt* desagradar, no gustar; repugnar. **I d. the house,** No me gusta la casa. **I d. them,** No me gustan
dislocate /'dɪslou,keit/ *vt* dislocar, descoyuntar; *Fig.* interrumpir
dislocation /,dɪslou'keiʃən/ *n* dislocación, *f,* descoyuntamiento, *m; Fig.* interrupción, *f*

dislodge /dɪs'lɒdʒ/ *vt* desalojar
dislodgement /dɪs'lɒdʒmənt/ *n* desalojamiento, *m*
disloyal /dɪs'lɔiəl/ *a* desleal, infiel, falso
disloyalty /dɪs'lɔiəlti/ *n* deslealtad, infidelidad, falsedad, *f*
dismal /'dɪzməl/ *a* lóbrego, sombrío; lúgubre; funesto; triste
dismantle /dɪs'mæntl̩/ *vt* (a ship or fort) desmantelar; (a machine) desmontar; (a house, etc.) desamueblar
dismantling /dɪs'mæntl̩ɪŋ/ *n* desmantelamiento, *m*
dismay /dɪs'mei/ *n* desmayo, desaliento, *m;* consternación, *f;* espanto, terror, *m.* —*vt* desanimar; consternar; espantar, horrorizar
dismember /dɪs'mɛmbər/ *vt* desmembrar
dismemberment /dɪs'mɛmbərmənt/ *n* desmembración, *f*
dismiss /dɪs'mɪs/ *vt* (from a job) despedir (de); (from an official position) destituir (de); (bid good-bye to) despedirse de; (after military parade) dar la orden de romper filas; (thoughts) apartar de sí; ahuyentar; (discard) desechar, descartar; (omit) pasar por alto de; (disregard) rechazar; (a parliament, etc.) disolver; (a law case) absolver de la instancia. **to d. in a few words,** tratar someramente; hablar brevemente de
dismissal /dɪs'mɪsəl/ *n* despedida, *f;* (from an official post) destitución, *f;* apartamiento, *m;* (discard) descarte, *m;* (of a parliament, etc.) disolución, *f*
dismount /*v* dɪs'maunt; *n also* 'dɪs,maunt/ *vi* apearse, desmontar, echar pie a tierra; bajar. —*vt* desmontar; (dismantle) desarmar
disobedience /,dɪsə'bidiəns/ *n* desobediencia, *f*
disobedient /,dɪsə'bidiənt/ *a* desobediente
disobey /,dɪsə'bei/ *vt* and *vi* desobedecer
disobliging /,dɪsə'blaidʒɪŋ/ *a* poco servicial
disobligingly /,dɪsə'blaidʒɪŋli/ *adv* descortésmente
disorder /dɪs'ɔrdər/ *n* desorden, *m;* confusión, *f;* (unrest) perturbación del orden público, *f,* motín, *m;* (disease) enfermedad, *f;* (mental) enajenación mental, *f;* trastorno, *m.* —*vt* desordenar, desarreglar; (of health) perjudicar; (the mind) trastornar. **in d.,** en desorden, desarreglado; (helter-skelter) atropelladamente
disordered /dɪs'ɔrdərd/ *a* en desorden; irregular, desordenado; (of the mind and bodily organs) trastornado; (ill) enfermo; (confused) confuso
disorganization /dɪs,ɔrgənə'zeiʃən/ *n* desorganización, *f*
disorganize /dɪs'ɔrgə,naiz/ *vt* desorganizar
disorganizing /dɪs'ɔrgə,naizɪŋ/ *a* desorganizador
disorientate /dɪs'ɔriən,teit/ *vt* desorientar
disorientation /dɪs,ɔriən'teiʃən/ *n* desorientación, *f*
disown /dɪs'oun/ *vt* repudiar; negar; renegar de
disparage /dɪ'spærɪdʒ/ *vt* menospreciar; desacreditar; denigrar; (spoil) perjudicar; (scorn) despreciar
disparagement /dɪ'spærɪdʒmənt/ *n* menosprecio, *m;* denigración, *f;* desprecio, *m*
disparagingly /dɪ'spærɪdʒɪŋli/ *adv* con desprecio
disparity /dɪ'spærɪti/ *n* disparidad, *f*
dispassionate /dɪs'pæʃənɪt/ *a* desapasionado, sereno; imparcial; moderado
dispassionately /dɪs'pæʃənɪtli/ *adv* con imparcialidad; serenamente; con moderación
dispatch /dɪ'spætʃ/ *n* despacho, *m; Com.* envío, *m;* (message) mensaje, *m;* (communiqué) parte, *f;* (cable) telegrama, *m;* (promptness) prontitud, presteza, *f;* (execution) ejecución, muerte, *f.* —*vt* despachar; enviar, remitir; (*Fam.* kill) despachar. **d.-case,** cartera, *f.* **d.-rider,** mensajero motociclista, *m*
dispel /dɪ'spɛl/ *vt* disipar
dispensable /dɪ'spɛnsəbəl/ *a* dispensable
dispensary /dɪ'spɛnsəri/ *n* dispensario, *m*
dispensation /,dɪspən'seiʃən/ *n* dispensación, *f;* (of the Pope, etc.) dispensa, *f;* (decree) ley, *f,* decreto, *m;* (of justice) administración, *f*
dispense /dɪ'spɛns/ *vt* dispensar; (of justice) administrar. **to d. with,** pasar sin, prescindir de
dispenser /dɪ'spɛnsər/ *n* dispensador (-ra); administrador (-ra)
dispersal /dɪ'spɜrsəl/ *n* dispersión, *f;* disipación, *f;* esparcimiento, *m*
disperse /dɪ'spɜrs/ *vt* dispersar; disipar; esparcir. —*vi* dispersarse disiparse
dispirited /dɪ'spɪrɪtɪd/ *a* abatido, desanimado, deprimido; lánguido
dispiritedly /dɪ'spɪrɪtɪdli/ *adv* desanimadamente, con desaliento; lánguidamente
displace /dɪs'pleis/ *vt* desalojar; cambiar de situación; (of liquids) desplazar; (oust) quitar el puesto (a), destituir
displacement /dɪs'pleismənt/ *n* desalojamiento, *m;* cambio de situación, *m;* (of liquid) desplazamiento, *m;* (from a post) destitución, *f*
display /dɪ'splei/ *n* exhibición, *f;* ostentación, *f;* presentación, *f;* (development) desarrollo, *m;* manifestación, *f;* (naval or military) maniobras, *f pl;* espectáculo, *m;* (pomp) pompa, *f;* fausto, *m.* —*vt* exhibir; mostrar, manifestar; ostentar; (unfold) desplegar, extender; (develop) desarrollar. **d. cabinet,** vitrina, *f*
displease /dɪs'pliz/ *vt* desagradar; ofender; enojar
displeasing /dɪs'plizɪŋ/ *a* desagradable
displeasure /dɪs'plɛʒər/ *n* desagrado, *m;* disgusto, *m;* disfavor, *m;* indignación, *f;* enojo, *m;* (grief) angustia, *f*
disport /dɪ'spɔrt/ *vi* (**oneself**), divertirse, entretenerse, recrearse; retozar, jugar
disposal /dɪ'spouzəl/ *n* disposición, *f;* (transfer) cesión, enajenación, *f;* (sale) venta, *f;* (gift) donación, *f.* **I am at your d.,** Estoy a la disposición de Vd. **the d. of the troops,** la disposición de las tropas
dispose /dɪ'spouz/ *vt* disponer; inclinar. —*vi* disponer. **to d. of,** disponer de; (finish) terminar, concluir; (get rid of) deshacerse de; (give away) regalar; (sell) vender; (transfer) ceder; (of houses, etc.) traspasar; (kill) matar; (send) enviar; (use) servirse de; (refute) refutar. **"To be disposed of,"** (a business, etc.) «Se traspasa»
disposed /dɪ'spouzd/ *a* (in compounds) intencionado, dispuesto. **well-d.,** bien intencionado
disposition /,dɪspə'zɪʃən/ *n* disposición, *f;* (temperament) naturaleza, índole, *f,* temperamento, carácter, *m;* (humor) humor, *m*
dispossess /,dɪspə'zɛs/ *vt* desposeer (de); privar (de); desahuciar
dispossession /,dɪspə'zɛʃən/ *n* desposeimiento, *m;* desahúcio, *m*
disproportion /,dɪsprə'pɔrʃən/ *n* desproporción, *f*
disproportionate /,dɪsprə'pɔrʃənɪt/ *a* desproporcionado
disproportionately /,dɪsprə'pɔrʃənɪtli/ *adv* desproporcionadamente
disprovable /dɪs'pruvəbəl/ *a* refutable
disprove /dɪs'pruv/ *vt* refutar
disputable /dɪ'spyutəbəl/ *a* disputable; discutible
disputant /dɪ'spyutənt/ *n* disputador (-ra)
dispute /dɪ'spyut/ *n* disputa, controversia, *f;* altercación, *f;* discusión, *f;* debate, *m.* —*vt* and *vi* disputar. **beyond d.,** *a* incontestable. —*adv* incontestablemente; fuera de duda
disqualification /dɪs,kwɒləfɪ'keiʃən/ *n* incapacidad, *f;* inhabilitación, *f;* impedimento, *m; Sports.* descalificación, *f*
disqualify /dɪs'kwɒlə,fai/ *vt* incapacitar; inhabilitar; *Sports.* descalificar
disquiet /dɪs'kwaiɪt/ *n* desasosiego, *m;* intranquilidad, inquietud, agitación, *f.* —*vt* desasosegar, intranquilizar, perturbar, agitar
disquieting /dɪs'kwaiɪtɪŋ/ *a* intranquilizador, perturbador
disquisition /,dɪskwə'zɪʃən/ *n* disquisición, *f*
disregard /,dɪsrɪ'gɑrd/ *n* indiferencia, *f,* omisión, *f,* descuido, *m;* (scorn) desdén, *m.* —*vt* no hacer caso de, desatender; omitir; desconocer; descuidar; despreciar
disregardful /,dɪsrɪ'gɑrdfəl/ *a* indiferente; negligente; desatento; desdeñoso
disrepair /,dɪsrɪ'pɛər/ *n* deterioro, mal estado, *m*
disreputable /dɪs'rɛpyətəbəl/ *a* de mala fama; (shameful) vergonzoso, vil; (compromising) comprometedor; de mal aspecto, horrible; ruin
disreputably /dɪs'rɛpyətəbli/ *adv* ruinmente; vergonzosamente
disrepute /,dɪsrɪ'pyut/ *n* disfavor, *m;* mala fama, *f;* deshonra, *f;* descrédito, *m.* **to come into d.,** caer en disfavor; perder su reputación

disrespect /ˌdɪsrɪ'spɛkt/ *n* falta de respeto, *f;* irreverencia, *f*
disrespectful /ˌdɪsrɪ'spɛktfəl/ *a* irrespetuoso, irreverente
disrobe /dɪs'roub/ *vt* desnudar. —*vi* desnudarse
disrupt /dɪs'rʌpt/ *vt* quebrar; desorganizar; interrumpir; separar
disruption /dɪs'rʌpʃən/ *n* quebrantamiento, *m;* desorganización, *f;* interrupción, *f;* separación, *f*
dissatisfaction /ˌdɪssætɪs'fækʃən/ *n* descontento, desagrado, disgusto, *m*
dissatisfied /dɪs'sætɪsˌfaid/ *a* descontentado, malcontento, no satisfecho
dissect /dɪ'sɛkt/ *vt* disecar; *Fig.* analizar
dissecting table *n* mesa de disección, *f*
dissection /dɪ'sɛkʃən/ *n* disección, *f;* análisis, *m*
dissector /dɪ'sɛktər/ *n* disector, *m; Fig.* analizador (-ra)
dissemble /dɪ'sɛmbəl/ *vt* and *vi* disimular, fingir
dissembler /dɪ'sɛmblər/ *n* hipócrita, *mf;* disimulador (-ra)
disseminate /dɪ'sɛməˌneit/ *vt* diseminar; propagar, sembrar
dissemination /dɪˌsɛmə'neiʃən/ *n* diseminación, *f;* propagación, *f*
dissension /dɪ'sɛnʃən/ *n* disensión, *f;* disidencia, *f*
dissent /dɪ'sɛnt/ *n* disentimiento, *m, vi* disentir, disidir
dissenter /dɪ'sɛntər/ *n* disidente, *mf*
dissentient /dɪ'sɛnʃənt/ *a* disidente, divergente. **without one d. voice,** unánimemente
dissertation /ˌdɪsər'teiʃən/ *n* disertación, *f*
disservice /dɪs'sɜrvɪs/ *n* deservicio, *m*
dissimilar /dɪ'sɪmələr/ *a* disímil, desemejante, diferente
dissimilarity /dɪˌsɪmə'lærɪti/ *n* desemejanza, diferencia, disparidad, *f*
dissimulation /dɪˌsɪmyə'leiʃən/ *n* disimulación, *f,* disimulo, *m*
dissipate /'dɪsəˌpeit/ *vt* disipar; dispersar; (waste) derrochar, desperdiciar. —*vi* disiparse; dispersarse; (vanish) desvanecerse; (of persons) ser disoluto
dissipated /'dɪsəˌpeitɪd/ *a* (of persons) disipado, disoluto, vicioso
dissipation /ˌdɪsə'peiʃən/ *n* disipación, *f;* (waste) derroche, *m;* libertinaje, *m*
dissociate /dɪ'souʃiˌeit/ *vt* disociar
dissociation /dɪˌsousi'eiʃən/ *n* disociación, *f*
dissoluble /dɪ'sɒlyəbəl/ *a* disoluble
dissolute /'dɪsəˌlut/ *a* disoluto, vicioso, licencioso
dissoluteness /'dɪsəˌlutnɪs/ *n* disolución, inmoralidad, *f*
dissolution /ˌdɪsə'luʃən/ *n* disolución, *f;* separación, *f;* muerte, *f*
dissolvable /dɪ'zɒlvəbəl/ *a* soluble
dissolve /dɪ'zɒlv/ *vt* disolver; derretir; (of parliament) prorrogar; (a marriage, etc.) anular; *Fig.* disipar. —*vi* disolverse; derretirse; (vanish) desvanecerse, disiparse, evaporarse. **to d. into tears,** deshacerse en lágrimas
dissolvent /dɪ'zɒlvənt/ *a* disolutivo. —*n* disolvente, *m*
dissonance /'dɪsənəns/ *n* disonancia, *f; Fig.* discordia, falta de armonía, *f*
dissonant /'dɪsənənt/ *n* disonancia, *f, a* disonante
dissuade /dɪ'sweid/ *vt* disuadir (de), apartar (de)
dissuasion /dɪ'sweiʒən/ *n* disuasión, *f*
distaff /'dɪstæf/ *n* rueca, *f*
distance /'dɪstəns/ *n* distancia, *f;* lontananza, *f;* lejanía, *f;* trecho, *m;* (of time) intervalo, *m;* (difference) diferencia, *f.* **at a d.,** a alguna distancia; lejos; (from afar) desde lejos. **from a d.,** desde (or de) lejos. **in the d.,** a lo lejos, en lontananza. **to keep at a d.,** mantener lejos; guardar las distancias (con). **to keep one's d.,** mantenerse a distancia; no intimarse, guardar las distancias. **What is the d. from London to Madrid?** ¿Qué distancia hay desde Londres a Madrid?
distant /'dɪstənt/ *a* distante; lejano; remoto; (of manner) frío, reservado; (slight) ligero; (of references, etc.) indirecto. **He is a d. relation,** Es un pariente lejano. **They are always rather d. with her,** La tratan siempre con bastante frialdad
distantly /'dɪstəntli/ *adv* a distancia; a lo lejos; desde lejos; remotamente; (of manner) con frialdad; (slightly) ligeramente
distaste /dɪs'teist/ *n* aversión, repugnancia, *f;* disgusto, hastío, *m*
distasteful /dɪs'teistfəl/ *a* desagradable
distemper /dɪs'tɛmpər/ *n* enfermedad, *f;* (in animals) moquillo, *m; Fig.* mal, *m;* (for walls) pintura al temple, *f.* —*vt* desordenar, perturbar; (walls) pintar al temple
distend /dɪ'stɛnd/ *vt* ensanchar; dilatar; inflar, henchir; *Med.* distender. —*vi* ensancharse, etc.
distension /dɪs'tɛnʃən/ *n* dilatación, *f;* inflación, *f;* henchimíento, *m; Med.* distensión, *f*
distill /dɪ'stɪl/ *vt* destilar; extraer. —*vi* destilar; exudar
distillation /ˌdɪstḷ'eiʃən/ *n* destilación, *f;* extracción, *f;* exudación, *f*
distiller /dɪ'stɪlər/ *n* destilador (-ra)
distillery /dɪ'stɪləri/ *n* destilería, *f,* destilatorio, *m*
distinct /dɪ'stɪŋkt/ *a* distinto; diferente; claro; notable, evidente
distinction /dɪ'stɪŋkʃən/ *n* distinción, *f*
distinctive /dɪ'stɪŋktɪv/ *a* distintivo; característico
distinctive feature *n Ling.* rasgo pertinente, *m*
distinctly /dɪ'stɪŋktli/ *adv* claramente; distintamente
distinctness /dɪ'stɪŋktnɪs/ *n* claridad, *f;* distinción, *f;* carácter distintivo, *m*
distinguish /dɪ'stɪŋgwɪʃ/ *vt* distinguir; discernir; caracterizar; (honor) honrar. —*vi* distinguir, diferenciar
distinguishable /dɪ'stɪŋgwɪʃəbəl/ *a* distinguible; perceptible, discernible
distinguished /dɪ'stɪŋgwɪʃt/ *a* distinguido; eminente; famoso, ilustre, egregio
distinguishing /dɪ'stɪŋgwɪʃɪŋ/ *a* distintivo
distort /dɪ'stɔrt/ *vt* (twist) torcer; deformar; falsear; pervertir
distorting mirror *n* (at fairs) espejo de la risa, *m;* espejo deformador, *m*
distortion /dɪ'stɔrʃən/ *n* deformación, *f;* torcimiento, *m;* contorsión, *f;* perversión, *f; Radio.* deformación, *f*
distract /dɪ'strækt/ *vt* distraer; interrumpir; perturbar; (turn aside) desviar, apartar; (madden) enloquecer, volver loco (a)
distracted /dɪ'stræktɪd/ *a* aturdido; demente, loco
distractedly /dɪ'stræktɪdli/ *adv* locamente; perdidamente
distraction /dɪ'strækʃən/ *n* distracción, *f;* (amusement) diversion, *f,* pasatiempo, *m;* (bewilderment) confusión, *f,* aturdimiento, *m;* (madness) locura, *f;* frenesí, *m.* **to drive to d.,** trastornar, sacar de quicio.
distrain /dɪ'strein/ *vi* embargar
distraint /dɪ'streint/ *n* embargo, *m*
distraught /dɪ'strɔt/ *a* aturdido; desesperado; enloquecido
distress /dɪ'strɛs/ *n* dolor, *m,* aflicción, *f;* pena, *f;* miseria, penuria, *f;* (exhaustion) fatiga, *f,* cansancio, *m;* (pain) dolor, *m;* (misfortune) desdicha, *f;* apuro, *m;* (danger) peligro, *m; Law.* embargo, *m.* —*vt* afligir, dar pena (a), llenar de angustia; cansar, fatigar; (pain) doler
distressed /dɪ'strɛst/ *a* afligido; necesitado, pobre
distressing /dɪ'strɛsɪŋ/ *a* congojoso, doloroso, penoso
distributable /dɪ'strɪbyʊtəbəl/ *a* repartible
distribute /dɪ'strɪbyut/ *vt* (of justice, etc.) administrar; distribuir; repartir
distribution /ˌdɪstrə'byuʃən/ *n* (of justice) administración, *f;* distribución, *f;* reparto, *m*
distributive /dɪ'strɪbyətɪv/ *a* distributivo
distributor /dɪ'strɪbyətər/ *n* distribuidor (-ra); repartidor (-ra). **d. of false money,** expendedor (-ra) de moneda falsa
district /'dɪstrɪkt/ *n* distrito, *m;* comarca, *f;* (of a town) barrio, *m;* (judicial) partido judicial, *m;* jurisdicción, *f;* región, zona, *f*
distrust /dɪs'trʌst/ *n* desconfianza, *f;* recelo, *m,* sospecha, *f.* —*vt* desconfiar de, sospechar
distrustful /dɪs'trʌstfəl/ *a* desconfiado, receloso, suspicaz

distrustfully /dɪs'trʌstfəli/ *adv* desconfiadamente, con recelo
disturb /dɪ'stɜrb/ *vt* perturbar; interrumpir; incomodar; (make anxious) inquietar; (alter) cambiar; (disarrange) desordenar, desarreglar. **to d. the peace,** perturbar el orden público
disturbance /dɪ'stɜrbəns/ *n* perturbación, *f;* disturbio, *m,* conmoción, *f;* incomodidad, *f;* agitación, *f;* confusión, *f;* tumulto, *m;* desorden, *m; Radio.* parásitos, *m pl*
disturber /dɪ'stɜrbər/ *n* perturbador (-ra)
disturbing /dɪ'stɜrbɪŋ/ *a* perturbador; inquietador; conmovedor, impresionante, emocionante
disunion /dɪs'yunyən/ *n* desunión, *f;* discordia, *f*
disunite /ˌdɪsyu'nait/ *vt* desunir; separar, dividir. *—vi* separarse
disuse /*n* dɪs'yus; *v* -'yuz/ *n* desuso, *m.* *—vt* desusar; desacostumbrar. **to fall into d.,** caer en desuso
ditch /dɪtʃ/ *n* zanja, *f;* (for defense, etc.) foso, *m;* (irrigation) acequia, *f.* *—vt* zanjar; abarrancar. **to die in the last d.,** morir en la brecha
ditto /'dɪtou/ *adv* ídem; también
ditty /'dɪti/ *n* canción, cantinela, *f*
diuretic /ˌdaiə'rɛtɪk/ *a* diurético
divan /dɪ'væn/ *n* diván, *m*
dive /daiv/ *n* buceo, *m; Aer.* picada, *f, vi* bucear; sumergirse (en); *Aer.* volar en picado; penetrar (en); (into a book) enfrascarse en. **to d. out,** salir precipitadamente. **to d.-bomb,** bombardear en picado. **d.-bomber,** avión en picado, *m.* **d.-bombing,** bombardeo en picado, *m*
diver /'daivər/ *n* buceador, *m;* buzo, *m;* (bird) somorgujo, *m*
diverge /dɪ'vɜrdʒ/ *vi* divergir
divergence /dɪ'vɜrdʒəns/ *n* divergencia, *f*
divergent /dɪ'vɜrdʒənt/ *a* divergente
diverse /dɪ'vɜrs/ *a* diverso, vario
diversify /dɪ'vɜrsəˌfai/ *vt* diversificar
diversion /dɪ'vɜrʒən/ *n* diversión, *f;* entretenimiento, *m,* recreación, *f;* pasatiempo, *m;* placer, *m; Mil.* diversión, *f*
diversity /dɪ'vɜrsɪti/ *n* diversidad, variedad, *f*
divert /dɪ'vɜrt/ *vt* desviar; (amuse) divertir, entretener
diverting /dɪ'vɜrtɪŋ/ *a* divertido, entretenido
divide /dɪ'vaid/ *vt* dividir; partir; separar; (cut) cortar; (share) repartir, distribuir; (hair) hacer la raya (del pelo); (of voting) provocar una votación. *—vi* dividirse; separarse; (of roads, etc.) bifurcarse; (of voting) votar. **divided skirt,** *n* falda pantalón, *f*
dividend /'dɪvɪˌdɛnd/ *n* dividendo, *m.* **d. warrant,** cupón de dividendo, *m*
dividers /dɪ'vaidərz/ *n pl* compás de puntas, *m*
dividing /dɪ'vaidɪŋ/ *a* divisorio, divisor
divination /ˌdɪvə'neiʃən/ *n* adivinación, *f*
divine /dɪ'vain/ *a* divino; sublime; *Inf.* estupendo. *—n* teólogo, *m.* *—vt* (foretell) vaticinar, pronosticar; presentir; (guess) adivinar
diving /'daivɪŋ/ *n* buceo, *m; Aer.* picado, *m.* **d.-bell,** campana de bucear, *f.* **d.-board,** (low) trampolín, *m;* (high) palanca, *f.* **d.-suit,** escafandra, *f*
divining rod /dɪ'vainɪŋ/ *n* vara divinatoria, *f*
divinity /dɪ'vɪnɪti/ *n* divinidad, *f;* teología, *f*
divisibility /dɪˌvɪzə'bɪlɪti/ *n* divisibilidad, *f*
divisible /dɪ'vɪzəbəl/ *a* divisible
division /dɪ'vɪʒən/ *n* división, *f;* separación, *f;* (distribution) repartimiento, *m;* (*Mil. Math.*) división, *f;* sección, *f;* grupo, *m;* (voting) votación, *f;* (discord) discordia, desunión, *f.* **without a d.,** por unanimidad, sin votar
divisor /dɪ'vaizər/ *n Math.* divisor, *m*
divorce /dɪ'vɔrs/ *n* divorcio, *m.* *—vt* divorciarse de; *Fig.* divorciar, separar. **to file a petition of d.,** poner una petición de divorcio
divorcee /dɪvɔr'sei/ *n* (wife) divorciada, *f;* (husband) divorciado, *m*
divulge /dɪ'vʌldʒ/ *vt* divulgar, revelar
dizzily /'dɪzəli/ *adv* vertiginosamente
dizziness /'dɪzinɪs/ *n* vértigo, *m;* mareo, *m;* (bewilderment) aturdimiento, *m,* confusión, *f*
dizzy /'dɪzi/ *a* vertiginoso; mareado; confuso, perplejo, aturdido
do /du/ *vt* hacer; ejecutar; (one's duty, etc.) cumplir con; concluir; (cause) causar; (homage) rendir; (commit) cometer; (arrange) arreglar; (cook) cocer, guisar; (roast) asar; (*Fam.* cheat) engañar; (suit) convenir; (suffice) bastar; (act) hacer el papel (de); (*Fam.* treat) tratar (bien o mal); (learn) aprender; (exhaust) agotar; (walk) andar; (travel, journey) recorrer; (translate) traducir; (prepare) preparar. *—vi* hacer; (behave) conducirse; (of health) estar (bien o mal); (act) obrar; (get on) ir; (be suitable, suit) convenir; (suffice) bastar; (of plants) florecer; (cook) cocerse; (last) durar. **Don't!** ¡No lo hagas! ¡Quieto! ¡Calla! **How do you do?** ¿Cómo está Vd.? ¡Buenos días! **Have done!** ¡Acaba de una vez! **It will do you good,** Te conviene; Te hará bien; Te sentará bien. **It will do you no harm,** No te perjudicará; No te hará daño. **I could do with one,** Me gustaría (tener) uno; (of drinks) Me bebería uno con mucho gusto. **That will do,** Eso basta; Se puede servirse de eso; Está bien así; (leave it alone) ¡Déjate de eso! (be quiet!) ¡No digas más! ¡Cállate! **That won't do,** Eso no es bastante; Eso no sirve; Eso no se hace así; Eso no se hace. **That will never do,** Eso no servirá; Eso no puede ser. **This will do,** (when buying an article) Me quedaré con éste; Me serviré de esto; Esto basta; Esto será suficiente; (is all right) Está bien así. **Thy will be done!** ¡Hágase tu voluntad! **to be doing,** estar haciendo; estar ocupado en (or con) hacer; (of food) estar cocinando. **to be done for,** estar perdido; estar muerto. **to do better,** hacer mejor (que); (mend one's ways) enmendarse, corregirse; (improve) mejorar, hacer progresos; (in health) encontrarse mejor. **to do nothing,** no hacer nada. **to do reverence,** rendir homenaje; inclinarse. **to do to death,** matar; asesinar; ejecutar. **to do violence to,** *Fig.* hacer fuerza a. **to do well,** hacer bien; obrar bien; (be successful) tener éxito; hacer buena impresión; (prosperous) tener una buena posición. **to do wonders,** hacer maravillas. **to have done with,** renunciar (a); dejar de usar; dejar de hacer, cesar; concluir, terminar; no tener más que ver con; (forsake) abandonar; (a person) romper con. **to have nothing to do,** no tener nada que hacer. **to have nothing to do with,** no tener nada que ver con; (of people) no tratar; (end a friendship) romper su amistad con, dejar de ver. **well done,** bien hecho; (of food) bien guisado; (of meat) bien asado. **What is to be done?** ¿Qué hay que hacer? ¿Qué se puede hacer? **What is to do?** ¿Qué pasa? ¿Qué hay? **When he had done speaking,** Cuando hubo terminado de hablar. **to do again,** hacer de nuevo, volver a hacer, rehacer; repetir. **He will not do it again,** No lo hará más. **to do away with,** quitar; eliminar; suprimir; hacer desaparecer; poner fin a; hacer cesar; destruir; matar. **to do by,** tratar (a), portarse con. **to do for,** arruinar; matar; (suffice) bastar para; ser a propósito para, servir para; (look after) cuidar; (as a housekeeper) dirigir la casa para. **to do out,** (a room) limpiar. **to do out of,** quitar; privar de; (steal) robar. **to do up,** (tie) atar; (fold) enrollar, plegar; envolver; (parcel) empaquetar; (arrange) arreglar; decorar; poner en orden; poner como nuevo; (iron) planchar; (launder) lavar y planchar; (tire) fatigar. **to do with,** (of people) tratar; (of things) tener que ver con; (put up with) poder con; poder sufrir. **to do without,** prescindir de; pasarse sin
do /du/ as an auxiliary verb is not translated in Spanish, e.g. *I do believe,* creo. *Do not do that,* no hagas eso. *I did not know,* no sabía. When it is used for emphasis, *do* is translated by *sí, ciertamente, claro* and similar words, e.g.: *She did not know, but he did,* Ella no lo sabía pero él sí. *You do paint well,* Pintas muy bien por cierto. *Do come this time,* No dejes de venir esta vez.
docile /'dɒsəl/ *a* dócil
docility /dɒ'sɪlɪti/ *n* docilidad, *f*
dock /dɒk/ *n* dique, *m,* dársena, *f;* (wharf) muelle, *m;* (in a law court) banquillo de los acusados, *m; Bot.* romaza, *f.* *—vt* (a tail) descolar; cortar, cercenar; reducir; (money) descontar; (a ship) poner en dique. *—vi* entrar en dársena, entrar en dique, entrar en

muelle. **dry-d.,** dique seco, *m.* **floating-d.,** dique flotante, *m.* **d.-dues,** muellaje, *m.* **d. rat,** (thief) raquero, *m*
docker /'dɒkər/ *n* estibador, descargador del muelle, *m*
docket /'dɒkɪt/ *n* (bundle) legajo, *m;* extracto, *m;* minuta, *f;* (label) etiqueta, *f,* marbete, *m*
dockyard /'dɒkˌyɑrd/ *n* arsenal, astillero, *m*
doctor /'dɒktər/ *n* doctor (-ra); (medical practitioner) médico (-ca), asistir; (repair) reparar, componer; adulterar; mezclar drogas con; falsificar. —*vi* ejercer la medicina. **family d.,** médico de cabecera, *m.* **to graduate as a d.,** doctorarse. **d. of divinity, laws, medicine,** doctor (-ra) en teología, en derecho, en medicina, *m*
doctoral /'dɒktərəl/ *a* doctoral
doctorate /'dɒktərɪt/ *n* doctorado, *m*
doctrinaire /'dɒktrə'nɛər/ *a* and *n* doctrinario (-ia)
doctrinal /'dɒktrənl̩/ *a* doctrinal
doctrine /'dɒktrɪn/ *n* doctrina, *f*
document /*n* 'dɒkyəmənt; *v* -ˌmɛnt/ *n* documento, *m.* —*vt* documentar; probar con documentos. **d.-case,** carpeta, *f*
documentary /ˌdɒkyə'mɛntəri/ *a* documental; escrito, auténtico. **d. film,** película documental, *f*
documentation /ˌdɒkyəmɛn'teiʃən/ *n* documentación, *f*
Dodecanese, the /ˌdɒdɪkə'niz/ el Dodecaneso, *m*
dodge /dɒdʒ/ *n* esguince, regate, *m;* evasiva, *f;* (trick) estratagema, *m,* maniobra, *f;* artefacto, *m.* —*vt* esquivar, evadir
doe /dou/ *n* gama, *f.* **doe rabbit,** coneja, *f*
doer /'duər/ *n* hacedor (-ra); autor (-ra)
doeskin /'douˌskɪn/ *n* ante, *m,* piel de gama, *f*
doff /dɒf/ *vt* quitar; (of hats, etc.) quitarse; desnudarse de
dog /dɔg/ *n* perro, *m;* (male) macho, *m;* (andiron) morillo, *m; Astron.* Can Mayor (or Menor), Sirio, *m.* —*vt* perseguir; seguir los pasos de; espiar. **You can't deceive an old dog,** A perro viejo no hay tus tus. **to go to the dogs,** ir a las carreras de galgos; *Fig.* ir cuesta abajo. **mongrel dog,** perro mestizo, *m.* **thoroughbred dog,** perro de raza pura, *m.* **dog-collar,** collar de perro, *m; Eccl.* alzacuello, *m.* **dog-days,** días caniculares, *m pl,* canícula, *f.* **dog-eared** (of books) con las puntas de las hojas dobladas. **dog-fight,** lucha de perros, *f;* combate aéreo, *m.* **dog-fish,** lija, *f,* cazón, *m.* **dog in the manger,** el perro del hortelano. **dog-kennel,** perrera, *f.* **dog-latin,** bajo latín, *m.* **dog license,** matrícula de perros, *f.* **dog-racing,** carrera de galgos, *f.* **dog-rose,** escaramujo, *m.* **dog show,** exposición canina, *f.* **dog-tooth,** *Archit.* diente de perro, *m.* **dog-vane,** *Naut.* cataviento, *m*
doge /doudʒ/ *n* dux, *m*
dogged /'dɔgɪd/ *a* persistente, tenaz, pertinaz, obstinado
doggedly /'dɔgɪdli/ *adv* tenazmente
doggedness /'dɔgɪdnɪs/ *n* pertinacia, tenacidad, terquedad, persistencia, *f*
doggerel /'dɔgərəl/ *n* malos versos, *m pl*; aleluyas, coplas de ciego, *f pl, a* malo, irregular
dogma /'dɔgmə/ *n* dogma, *m*
dogmatic /dɔg'mætɪk/ *a* dogmático
dogmatize /'dɔgməˌtaiz/ *vt* and *vi* dogmatizar; mostrarse dogmático
doh /dou/ *n Mus.* do, *m*
doily /'dɔili/ *n* carpeta, *f,* pañito de adorno, *m*
doings /'duɪŋz/ *n pl* acciones, *f pl*; (deeds) hechos, *m pl*; (behavior) conducta, *f;* (happenings) acontecimientos, *m pl*; (works) obras, *f pl*; (things) cosas, *f pl*
doldrums /'douldrəmz/ *n pl* calmas ecuatoriales, *f pl*
dole /doul/ *n* limosna, *f;* porción, *f.* **to d. out,** repartir; distribuir en porciones pequeñas; racionar; dar contra la voluntad de uno.
doleful /'doulfəl/ *a* triste, lúgubre, melancólico; doloroso
dolefulness /'doulfəlnɪs/ *n* tristeza, melancolía, *f;* dolor, *m*
doll /dɒl/ *n* muñeca, *f*
dollar /'dɒlər/ *n* dólar, *m*
dolly /'dɒli/ *n* muñeca, *f;* (for clothes) moza, *f.* **d.-tub,** cubo para la colada, *m*
dolman /'doulmən/ *n* dormán, *m*
dolphin /'dɒlfɪn/ *n* delfín, *m*
dolt /doult/ *n* cabeza de alcornoque, *mf,* zamacuco, *m*
domain /dou'mein/ *n* territorio, *m;* heredad, posesión, propiedad, *f;* (empire) dominio, *m*
dome /doum/ *n* cúpula, *f;* bóveda, *f;* (palace) palacio, *m*
domestic /də'mɛstɪk/ *a* doméstico; familiar; (home-loving) casero; (of animals) doméstico; (national) interior, nacional. —*n* doméstico, sirviente, *m;* criada, *f.* **d. economy,** economía doméstica, *f*
domesticate /də'mɛstɪˌkeit/ *vt* domesticar
domesticated /də'mɛstɪˌkeitɪd/ *a* (of animals) domesticado; (of persons) casero
domestication /dəˌmɛstɪ'keiʃən/ *n* domesticación, *f*
domesticity /ˌdoumɛ'stɪsɪti/ *n* domesticidad, *f*
domicile /'dɒməˌsail/ *n* domicilio, *m, vt* domiciliar
domiciliary /ˌdɒmə'sɪliˌɛri/ *a* domiciliario
dominant /'dɒmənənt/ *a* dominante; imperante. —*n Mus.* dominante, *f.* **to be d.,** prevalecer
dominate /'dɒməˌneit/ *vt* and *vi* dominar
domination /ˌdɒmə'neiʃən/ *n* dominación, *f*
domineer /ˌdɒmə'nɪər/ *vi* dominar, tiranizar. **to d. over,** mandar en
domineering /ˌdɒmə'nɪərɪŋ/ *a* dominante, mandón, tiránico
Dominican /də'mɪnɪkən/ *a* dominicano. —*n* dominicano, *m*
Dominican Republic, the la República Dominicana, *f*
dominion /də'mɪnyən/ *n* dominio, *m;* autoridad, soberanía, *f;* imperio, *m; pl* **dominions,** *Eccl.* dominaciones, *f pl*
Dominions, the /də'mɪnyənz/ los Dominios, *m*
domino /'dɒməˌnou/ *n* dominó, *m.* **to go d.,** nacer domino
don /dɒn/ *n* (Spanish and Italian title) don, *m;* señor, *m.* —*vt* ponerse, vestirse
donation /dou'neiʃən/ *n* donación, dádiva, *f;* contribución, *f*
done /dʌn/ *a* and *past part* hecho; (of food) cocido; (roasted) asado; (tired) rendido; (*Fam.* deceived) engañado. **Well d.!** ¡Bien hecho! **d. for,** arruinado; muerto; perdido; vencido; (spoilt) estropeado
donkey /'dɒŋki/ *n* borrico (-ca), burro (-rra). **d.-engine,** máquina auxiliar, *f*
donor /'dounər/ *n* donador (-ra); dador (-ra)
doodle /'dudl̩/ *v* borrajear, garabatear, hacer garabatos
doom /dum/ *n* condena, *f;* (fate) suerte, *f;* (judgment) destino, *m;* ruina, *f;* juicio, *m.* —*vt* sentenciar; condenar
doomsday /'dumzˌdei/ *n* día del juicio final, *m*
door /dɔr/ *n* puerta, *f;* entrada, *f.* **front d.,** puerta de entrada, *f.* **next d.,** la casa vecina; la puerta de al lado, la puerta vecina. **next d. neighbor,** vecino (-na) de al lado. **out of doors,** al aire libre; en la calle. **to knock at the d.,** llamar a la puerta. **to slam the d. in a person's face,** dar con la puerta en las narices de alguien. **d.-bell,** timbre (non-electric, campanilla, *f*) de llamada, *m.* **d.-jamb,** quicial, *m.* **d. keeper,** portero, *m.* **d.-knob,** tirador, *m.* **d.-knocker,** manija, *f;* picaporte, *m,* aldaba, *f.* **d.-plate,** placa, *f.* **d.-shutter,** cierre metálico, *m.* **d.-step,** peldaño de la puerta, *m;* umbral, *m.* **d.-way,** portal, *m*
dope /doup/ *n* drogas, *f pl,* narcóticos, *m pl*; (news) información, *f.* **d. fiend,** morfinómano (-na)
dope-pusher /'doup ˌpʊʃər/ *n* narcotraficante, *mf*
Doric /'dɔrɪk/ *a* dórico
dormant /'dɔrmənt/ *a* durmiente; latente; secreto; inactivo. **to go d.,** dormirse
dormer window /'dɔrmər/ *n* lumbrera, *f*
dormitory /'dɔrmɪˌtɔri/ *n* dormitorio, *m*
dormouse /'dɔrˌmaus/ *n* lirón, *m*
dorsal /'dɔrsəl/ *a* dorsal
dorsum /'dɔrsəm/ *n* dorso, *m*
dory /'dɔri/ *n* (fish) dorado, *m*
dose, dosage /dous; 'dousɪdʒ/ *n*; dosis, *f*
dossier /'dɒsiˌei/ *n* documentación, *f*
dot /dɒt/ *n* punto, *m; Mus.* puntillo, *m; pl* **dots,** *Gram.* puntos suspensivos, *m pl.* —*vt* poner punto (a

una letra); (scatter) salpicar. **on the dot,** (of time) en punto. **to dot one's i's,** poner los puntos sobre las íes
dotage /'doutɪdʒ/ *n* senectud, chochera, *f*
dotard /'doutərd/ *n* viejo chocho, *m;* vieja chocha, *f; Inf.* carcamal, *m*
dote /dout/ *vi* chochear. **to d. on,** adorar en, idolatrar
doting /'doutɪŋ/ *a* chocho
double /'dʌbəl/ *a* and *adv* doble; dos veces; (in a pair) en par; en dos; doblemente; (deceitful) doble, de dos caras, falso; ambiguo. —*n* doble, *m;* duplicado, *m; Theat.* contrafigura, *f; pl* **doubles,** (tennis) dobles, *m pl,* juego doble, *m.* —*vt* doblar; duplicar; (fold) doblegar; (the fist) cerrar (el puño); (*Theat.* and *Naut.*) doblar. —*vi* doblarse; (dodge) volverse atrás, hacer un rodeo, dar una vuelta; esquivarse. **to d. up,** *vt* envolver; arrollar; (a person) doblar. —*vi* doblegarse; arrollarse; (collapse) desplomarse. **at the d.,** corriendo. **He was doubled up with pain,** El dolor le hacía retorcerse. **mixed doubles,** parejas mixtas, *f pl;* dobles mixtos, *m pl.* **double two,** (telephone) dos dos. **with a d. meaning,** con segunda intención. **d.-barrelled,** de dos cañones. **d.-bass,** contrabajo, *m.* **d. bed,** cama de matrimonio, *f.* **d.-bedded,** con cama de matrimonio; con dos camas. **d. -breasted,** cruzado. **d.-chin,** papada, *f.* **d.-dealing,** duplicidad, *f.* **d.-edged,** de doble filo. **d.-entry,** *Com.* partida doble, *f.* **d.-faced,** de dos caras. **d.-jointed,** con articulaciones dobles
double-spaced /'dʌbəl 'speist/ *a* a doble espacio, a dos espacios
doublet /'dʌblɪt/ *n* (garment) jubón, justillo, *m;* pareja, *f,* par, *m*
doubling /'dʌblɪŋ/ *n* doblamiento, *m;* doblez, plegadura, *f;* duplicación, *f;* (dodging) evasiva, *f,* esguince, *m*
doubloon /dʌ'blun/ *n* doblón, *m*
doubly /'dʌbli/ *adv* doblemente; con duplicidad
doubt /daut/ *n* duda, *f;* incertidumbre, *f;* sospecha, *f.* —*vt* and *vi* dudar; sospechar; titubear, hesitar; temer. **beyond all d.,** fuera de duda. **no d.,** sin duda. **There is no d. that,** No hay duda de que, No cabe duda de que. **When in d....,** En caso de duda...
doubter /'dautər/ *n* incrédulo (-la)
doubtful /'dautfəl/ *a* dudoso; incierto; perplejo; ambiguo; (of places) sospechoso
doubtfully /'dautfəli/ *adv* dudosamente; inciertamente; irresolutamente; ambiguamente
doubtfulness /'dautfəlnɪs/ *n* duda, incertidumbre, *f;* ambigüedad, *f*
doubtless /'dautlɪs/ *adv* sin duda, por supuesto; probablemente
douche /duʃ/ *n* ducha, *f, vt* duchar
dough /dou/ *n* pasta, masa, *f;* (money) lana, *f*
dour /dʊr/ *a* huraño, adusto, austero
dourly /'dʊrli/ *adv* severamente
douse /daus/ *vt* zambullir; (a sail) recoger; *Inf.* apagar
dove /duv/ *n* paloma, *f.* **d.-cote,** palomar, *m*
Dover /'douvər/ Dóver, *m*
dovetail /'dʌvˌteil/ *n* cola de milano, *f, vt* machihembrar, empalmar; *Fig.* encajar
dowager /'dauədʒər/ *n* viuda, *f;* matrona, *f.* **d. countess,** condesa viuda, *f*
dowager empress *n* emperatriz viuda, *f*
dowdiness /'daudinɪs/ *n* desaliño, desaseo, *m;* falta de elegancia, *f*
dowdy /'daudi/ *a* desaliñado, desaseado, poco elegante. —*n* mujer poco elegante, *f*
dowel /'dauəl/ *n* espiga, clavija, *f,* zoquete, *m, vt* enclavijar
down /daun/ *n* (of a bird) plumón, *m;* (on a peach, etc.) pelusilla, *f;* (hair) vello, *m;* (before the beard) bozo, *m;* (of a thistle, etc.) vilano, *m.* **ups and downs,** vicisitudes, *f pl*
down /daun/ *a* pendiente; (of trains, etc.) descendente. —*adv* abajo; hacia abajo; (lowered) bajado; (of the eyes) bajos; (on the ground) en tierra, por tierra; (stretched out) tendido a lo largo; (depressed) triste, abatido; (ill) enfermo; (fallen) caído; (of the wind) cesado; (closed) cerrado; (exhausted) agotado; *Com.* al contado; (of temperature) más bajo. —*prep* abajo de; abajo; en la dirección de; (along) a lo largo de; por. **"Down"** (on elevators) «Para bajar». —*interj* ¡Abajo!; ¡A tierra! **He went d. the hill,** Bajaba la colina. **He is d. now,** Ha bajado ahora; Está abajo ahora; Está derribado ahora. **The sun has gone d.,** Se ha puesto el sol. **His stock has gone d.,** *Fig. Inf.* Ha caído en disfavor. **Prices have come d.,** Los precios han bajado. **Their numbers have gone d.,** Sus números han disminuido. **to be d. and out,** estar completamente arruinado, ser pobre de solemnidad. **to boil d.,** reducir hirviendo. **to come d. in the world,** venir a menos. **while I was going d. the river,** mientras iba río abajo, mientras bajaba al río. **d. below,** allá abajo; abajo; en el piso de abajo. **D. on your knees!** ¡De rodillas! **d. to,** hasta. **d. spout,** tubo de bajada, *m.* **D. with!** ¡Abajo! ¡Muera! **d.-stream,** agua abajo. **d. train,** tren descendente, *m*
down /daun/ *vt* derribar; vencer. **to d. tools,** declararse en huelga
downcast /'daunˌkæst/ *a* bajo; cabizbajo, deprimido, abatido
downfall /'daunˌfɔl/ *n* caída, *f;* derrumbamiento, *m;* (failure) fracaso, *m;* (*Fig.* ruin) decadencia, ruina, *f*
downhearted /'daun'hɑrtɪd/ *a* descorazonado, alicaído, desalentado
downhill / *adv* 'daun'hɪl; *a* 'daunˌhɪl/ *adv* cuesta abajo, hacia abajo. —*a* en declive, inclinado. **to go d.,** ir cuesta abajo
downiness /'dauninɪs/ *n* vellosidad, *f*
downpour /'daunˌpɔr/ *n* chubasco (Mexico), aguacero, chaparrón, *m*
downright /'daunˌrait/ *a* franco, sincero; categórico, terminante; absoluto. —*adv* muy; completamente
downstairs /'daun'stɛərz/ *adv* escalera abajo; al piso de abajo; en el piso bajo; abajo. —*a* del piso de abajo. —*n* planta baja, *f;* piso de abajo, *m.* **to go d.,** bajar la escalera; ir al piso de abajo
downtrodden /'daunˌtrɒdn̩/ *a* oprimido, esclavizado
downward /'daunwərd/ *a* descendente; inclinado. —*adv* hacia abajo
downy /'dauni/ *a* velloso; (*Fam.* of persons) con más conchas que un galápago
dowry /'dauri/ *n* dote, *mf.* **to give as a d.,** dotar
dowse /dauz/ *vt.* See **douse**
doze /douz/ *vi* dormitar. —*n* sueño ligero, *m*
dozen /'dʌzən/ *n* docena, *f*
drab /dræb/ *a* pardo, parduzco, grisáceo; *Fig.* gris, monótono. —*n* (slut) pazpuerca, *f;* (prostitute) ramera, *f*
drachma /'drækmə/ *n* dracma, *f*
draft /dræft/ *n* (act of drawing) tiro, *m;* (of liquid) trago, *m;* (of a ship) calado, *m;* (of air) corriente de aire, *f; Com.* giro, *m,* letra de cambio, *f;* (for the army, navy) conscripción, leva, *f;* (outline) bosquejo, *m;* proyecto, *m;* borrador, *m.* —*vt* (recruit) reclutar; (outline) bosquejar, delinear; (draw up) redactar; proyectar. **on d.,** (of beer, etc.) por vaso. **d. horse,** caballo de tiro, *m.*
draft card *n* cartilla (Mexico), libreta de enrolamiento (Argentina), *m*
draft dodger *n* emboscado, prófugo, *m*
drafting /'dræftɪŋ/ *n* (*Mil. Nav.*) reclutamiento, *m;* (of a bill, etc.) redacción, *f;* (wording) términos, *m pl*
draftsman /'dræftsmən/ *n* dibujante, *m;* delineante, *m;* redactor, *m*
drag /dræg/ *n* (for dredging) draga, *f;* (harrow) rastrillo, *m;* (break) freno, *m;* (obstacle) estorbo, *m; Aer.* sonda, *f.* —*vt* arrastrar; (fishing nets) rastrear; (harrow) rastrillar. —*vi* (of the anchor) garrar; arrastrarse por el suelo; (of time) pasar lentamente; ir más despacio (que); (of interest) decaer, disminuir. **d.-hook,** garfio, *m.* **d.-net,** brancada, *f*
dragging /'drægɪŋ/ *n* arrastre, *m;* (of lakes, etc.) rastreo, *m, a* rastrero; cansado
draggled /'drægəld/ *a* mojado y sucio
dragon /'drægən/ *n* dragón, *m.* **d.-fly,** libélula, *f,* caballito del diablo, *m*
dragoon /drə'gun/ *n Mil.* dragón, *m, vt* someter a una disciplina rigurosa; obligar a la fuerza (a)
drain /drein/ *n* desaguadero, *m;* (sewer) cloaca, alcantarilla, *f;* sumidero, *m; Agr.* acequia, *f.* —*vt* desaguar; sanear; (lakes, etc.) desangrar; secar;

(bail) achicar; (empty and drink) vaciar; (swallow) tragar; (*Fig.* of sorrow, etc.) apurar; (despoil) despojar; (deprive) privar (de); (impoverish) empobrecer; (exhaust) agotar. —*vi* desaguarse; vaciarse; (with off) escurrirse. **to be well drained,** tener buen drenaje. **to d. the sump,** vaciar la culata. **to d. away,** vaciar. **d.-pipe,** tubo de desagüe, *m*

drainage /'dreinɪdʒ/ *n* (of land) drenaje, *m;* desagüe, *m;* (of wounds) drenaje, *m;* (sewage) aguas del alcantarillado, *f pl.* **main d.,** drenaje municipal, *m*

draining /'dreinɪŋ/ *a* de desagüe; de drenaje. **d.-board,** escurridor, *m*

drake /dreik/ *n* ánade macho, *m*

dram /dræm/ *n* dracma, *f;* (of liquor) trago, *m*

drama /'drɑmə, 'dræmə/ *n* drama, *m*

dramatic /drə'mætɪk/ *a* dramático

dramatically /drə'mætɪkli/ *adv* dramáticamente

dramatis personae /'dræmətɪs pər'souni/ *n pl* personajes, *m pl*

dramatist /'dræmətɪst, 'drɑmə-/ *n* dramaturgo, *m*

dramatization /ˌdræmətə'zeiʃən, ˌdrɑmə-/ *n* versión escénica, *f;* descripción dramática, *f;* (of emotions) dramatización, *f*

dramatize /'dræməˌtaiz, 'drɑmə-/ *vt* dramatizar

drape /dreip/ *vt* colgar, cubrir; vestir

draper /'dreipər/ *n* pañero (-ra)

drapery /'dreipəri/ *n* colgaduras, *f pl*; ropaje, *m,* ropas, *f pl*; pañería, *f*

drastic /'dræstɪk/ *a* drástico; enérgico, fuerte; **a drastic measure,** una medida avanzada, *f*

draw /drɔ/ *vt* tirar; arrastrar; traer; (pluck) arrancar; (attract) atraer; (extract) extraer; sacar; hacer salir; (unsheath) desenvainar; (a bow-string) tender; (cards, dominoes) tomar, robar; (threads) deshilar; (disembowel) destripar; (a check, etc.) girar, librar; (of a ship) calar; (of lines) hacer (rayas); (curtains) correr; (to draw curtains back) descorrer; (salary, money) cobrar, percibir; (obtain) obtener; (persuade) persuadir, inducir; (inhale) respirar; (a sigh) dar; (win) ganar; (a conclusion) deducir, inferir; (a distinction) hacer formular; *Sports.* empatar; (a number, etc.) sortear; (suck) chupar; (tighten) estirar; (lengthen) alargar; (comfort, etc.) tomar; (inspiration) inspirarse en; (obtain money) procurarse (recursos); (withdraw funds) retirar; (write) escribir; (draw) dibujar; (trace) trazar; (provoke) provocar. **to be drawn,** (of tickets in a lottery and cards) salir. **to d. lots,** echar suertes. **to d. water,** sacar agua. **to d. along,** arrastrar; conducir. **to d. aside,** tomar a un lado, tomar aparte; quitar de en medio, poner a un lado; (curtains) descorrer. **to d. away,** (remove) quitar; (a person) llevarse (a); apartar. **to d. back,** hacer recular; hacer retirarse; hacer volverse atrás; (curtains) descorrer. **to d. down,** hacer bajar; tirar a lo largo de (or por); bajar; (attract) atraer. **to d. forth,** hacer salir; hacer avanzar; tirar hacia adelante; conducir; (develop) desarrollar; sacar; hacer aparecer; (comment, etc.) suscitar. **to d. in,** tirar hacia adentro; sacar; acercar; atraer. **to d. off,** sacar; retirar; quitar; (water from pipes, etc.) vaciar; *Print.* tirar; (turn aside) desviar. **to d. on,** (of apparel) ponerse; (boots) calzarse; (occasion) ocasionar. **to d. out,** sacar fuera; hacer salir; tirar (de); (extract) extraer; (trace) trazar; (a person) hacer hablar. **to d. over,** poner encima de; arrastrar por; hacer acercarse (a), tirar hacia; atraer; persuadir. **d. prestige (from),** cobrar prestigio (de). **to d. round,** poner alrededor de. **to d. together,** reunir; acercar. **to d. up,** tirar hacia arriba; subir; sacar; extraer; (raise) levantar, alzar; (bring) traer; (bring near) acercar; (order) ordenar; *Mil.* formar; (a document) redactar; formular. **to d. oneself up,** erguirse

draw /drɔ/ *vi* tirar; (shrink) encogerse; (wrinkle) arrugarse; (of chimneys, etc.) tirar; (a picture) dibujar; *Sports.* empatar; (move) moverse; avanzar, adelantarse; (of a ship) calar; (a sword) desnudar (la espada); (lots) echar suertes; (attract people) atraer gente; *Com.* girar. **to d. aside,** ponerse a un lado; retirarse. **to d. back,** retroceder, recular; retirarse; vacilar. **to d. in,** retirarse; (of days) hacerse corto; (of dusk) caer. **to d. off,** alejarse; apartarse, retirarse. **to d. on,** (approach) acercarse; avanzar; *Com.* girar contra; inspirarse en. **to d. out,** hacerse largo; (of a vehicle) ponerse en marcha, empezar a andar. **to d. round,** ponerse alrededor; reunirse alrededor. **to d. together,** reunirse. **to d. up,** parar.

draw /drɔ/ *n* tirada, *f;* (of lotteries) sorteo, *m; Sports.* empate, *m;* atracción, *f;* (*Fig.* feeler) tanteo, *m.* **to be a big d.,** ser una gran atracción

drawback /'drɔˌbæk/ *n* desventaja, *f,* inconveniente, *m*

drawbridge /'drɔˌbrɪdʒ/ *n* puente levadizo, *m*

drawee /drɔ'i/ *n Com.* girado, *m*

drawer /'drɔər *for* ; drɔr *for* / *n* tirador (-ra); (of water) aguador (-ra); extractor (-ra); (in a public-house) mozo de taberna, *m;* (designer) diseñador, *m;* (sketcher) dibujante, *mf; Com.* girador, *m;* (receptacle) cajón, *m; pl* **drawers,** (men's) calzoncillos, *m pl*; (women's) pantalones, *m pl*

drawing /'drɔɪŋ/ *n* (pulling) tiro, *m;* atracción, *f;* (extraction) extracción, *f;* saca, *f;* (in raffles, etc. and of lots) sorteo, *m;* (of money) percibo, *m; Com.* giro, *m;* (sketch) dibujo, *m;* (plan) esquema, *f.* **free-hand d.,** dibujo a pulso, *m.* **d. from life,** dibujo del natural, *m.* **d.-board,** tablero de dibujo, *m.* **d.-paper,** papel para dibujar, *m.* **d.-pin,** chinche, *f.* **d.-room,** salón, *m*

drawl /drɔl/ *vi* hablar arrastrando las palabras

drawn /drɔn/ *past part* See **draw.** *a* (tired) ojeroso, con ojeras, con un aspecto de cansancio; (with pain) desencajado. **long d. out,** demasiado largo. **d. sword,** espada desnuda, *f.* **d.-thread work,** deshilados, *m pl*

dray /drei/ *n* carro, *m.* **d.-horse,** caballo de tiro, *m*

dread /drɛd/ *n* pavor, temor, terror, espanto, *m;* trepidación, *f,* miedo, *m.* —*a* temible, espantoso, terrible; augusto. —*vt* temer. —*vi* tener miedo, temer. **in d. of,** con miedo de, con terror de

dreader /'drɛdər/ *n* el, *m,* (*f,* la) que teme, temedor (-ra)

dreadful /'drɛdfəl/ *a* terrible, pavoroso, espantoso, horroroso; formidable; augusto

dreadfully /'drɛdfəli/ *adv* terriblemente, horriblemente

dreadfulness /'drɛdfəlnɪs/ *n* horror, *m*

dreadnought /'drɛdˌnɔt/ *n* acorazado de línea, *m*

dream /drim/ *n* sueño, *m;* ilusión, *f;* ensueño, *m;* fantasía, *f.* —*vt* and *vi* soñar; imaginar. **He dreamed away the hours,** Pasaba las horas soñando. **I wouldn't d. of it!** ¡Ni por sueño! **in a d.,** en sueños; (waking) como en sueños; mecánicamente. **Sweet dreams!** ¡Duerme bien! **to d. of,** soñar con

dreamer /'drimər/ *n* soñador (-ra); visionario (-ia)

dreamily /'driməli/ *adv* como en sueños; soñolientamente; vagamente

dreaming /'drimɪŋ/ *n* sueños, *m pl*

dreamland /'drimˌlænd/ *n* reino de los sueños, *m*

dreamy /'drimi/ *a* soñador; soñoliento; fantástico; (empty) vació

dreariness /'drɪərinɪs/ *n* tristeza, *f;* melancolía, *f;* lobreguez, *f*

dreary /'drɪəri/ *a* triste; melancólico; lóbrego

dredge /drɛdʒ/ *vt* dragar; (with sugar, etc.) espolvorear

dredger /'drɛdʒər/ *n* draga, *f;* (for sugar) azucarera, *f;* (for flour) harinero, *m*

dredging /'drɛdʒɪŋ/ *n* dragado, *m;* (sprinkling) salpicadura, *f.* **d. bucket,** cangilón, *m*

dregs /drɛgz/ *n pl* heces, *f pl,* posos, *m pl.* **to drain to the d.,** vaciar hasta las heces

drench /drɛntʃ/ *vt* mojar, calar. **He is drenched to the skin,** Está calado hasta los huesos

Dresden /'drɛzdən/ *n* Dresde, *f.* **D. china,** loza de Dresde, *f*

dress /drɛs/ *vt* (with clothes) vestir; (arrange) arreglar; (the hair) peinar(se); (a wound) curar; (hides); adobar; (cloth) aprestar; (flax) rastrillar; (stone) labrar; (wood) desbastar; (prune) podar; (a garden) cultivar; (manure) abonar; *Cul.* aderezar; preparar; (season) condimentar; (a table) poner; (adorn) ataviar, adornar; revestir; (a dead body) amortajar. —*vi* vestirse; ataviarse; (of troops) alinearse. **all dressed up and nowhere to go,** compuesta y sin novio. **dressed up to the nines,** vestido de veinticinco alfileres. **Left (Right) d.!** ¡A la izquierda (A la derecha) alinearse! **to d. down,** (scold) poner como un trapo (a), dar una calada (a). **to d. up,** *vt* ataviar; (disguise) disfrazar. —*vi* ponerse muy elegante; disfrazarse

dress /drɛs/ *n* (in general) el vestir; (clothes) ropa, *f;* (frock) vestido, traje, *m;* (uniform) uniforme, *m;* (*Fig.* covering) hábitos, *m pl;* (appearance) aspecto, *m;* forma, *f.* **full d.,** (uniform) uniforme de gala, *m;* (civilian, man's) traje de etiqueta, *m;* (woman's) traje de gala, *m.* **morning d.,** (man's) traje de paisano, *m;* (woman's) vestido de todos los dias, *m;* (man's formal dress) chaqué, *m.* **ready-made d.,** traje hecho, *m.* **d. allowance,** alfileres, *m pl.* **d.-circle,** anfiteatro, *m.* **d.-coat,** frac, *m.* **d. protector,** sobaquera, *f.* **d. rehearsal,** ensayo general, *m.* **d. shirt,** camisa de pechera dura, *f.* **d. suit,** (with white tie) traje de frac, *m;* (with black tie) smoking, *m.* **d. sword,** espada de gala, *f.* **d. tie,** corbata de smoking (or de frac), *f*

dresser /ˈdrɛsər/ *n* el que adereza; (of wounds) practicante (de hospital), *m;* (valet) ayuda de cámara, *m;* (maid) doncella, *f;* (of skins) adobador de pieles, *m;* (furniture) aparador, *m;* (in the kitchen) armario de la cocina, *m*

dressing /ˈdrɛsɪŋ/ *n* el vestir(se); aderezamiento, *m;* (for cloth) apresto, *m;* (of leather) adobo, *m;* (of wood) desbaste, *m;* (of stone) labrado, *m;* (manuring) estercoladura, *f;* (sauce) salsa, *f;* (seasoning) condimentación, *f;* (of a wound) cura, *f;* (bandage) apósito, *m,* vendaje, *m.* **d.-case,** neceser, saco de noche, *m.* **d.-down,** *Inf.* rapapolvo, *m.* **d.-gown,** (woman's) salto de cama, quimono, *m;* (man's) batín, *m.* **d.-jacket,** chambra, *f,* peinador, *m.* **d.-room,** *Theat.* camarín, *m;* (in a house) trasalcoba, recámara, *f.* **d.-station,** puesto de socorro, *m.* **d.-table,** tocador, *m,* mesa de tocador, *f*

dressmaker /ˈdrɛsˌmeikər/ *n* modista, *mf*

dressmaking /ˈdrɛsˌmeikɪŋ/ *n* confección de vestidos, *f;* arte de la modista, *mf*

dribble /ˈdrɪbəl/ *vi* gotear; (slaver) babear. —*vt* (in football) regatear. —*n* (in football) regate, *m*

dried /draid/ *a* seco; (of fruit) paso. **d. up,** (withered) marchito; (of people) enjuto. **d. fish,** cecial, *m.* **d. meat,** cecina, *f*

drift /drɪft/ *n* (in a ship or airplane's course) deriva, *f;* (of a current) velocidad, *f;* (tendency) tendencia, *f;* (meaning) significación, *f;* (heap) montón, *m;* (aim) objeto, propósito, fin, *m;* *Mineral.* galería, *f;* (of dust, etc.) nube, *f;* (shower) lluvia, *f;* (impulsion) impulso, *m;* violencia, *f.* —*vi* flotar, ir arrastrado por la corriente; amontonarse; *Naut.* derivar; *Aer.* abatir. —*vt* llevar; amontonar. **drifts of sand,** arena movediza, *f.* **to d. into,** (war, etc.) entrar sin querer en; (habits) dar en la flor de; (a room, etc.) deslizarse en. **d.-wood,** madera de deriva, *f*

drill /drɪl/ *n* (instrument) taladro, perforador, *m,* barrena, *f;* ejercicio, *m,* educación física, *f;* *Mil.* instrucción militar, *f;* (cloth) dril, *m;* *Agr.* sembradora mecánica, *f;* (for seeds) hilera, *f;* (discipline) disciplina, *f;* (teaching) instrucción, *f.* —*vt* taladrar, barrenar; enseñar el ejercicio (a); enseñar la instrucción; disciplinar; (seed) sembrar en hileras. —*vi* hacer el ejercicio; hacer la instrucción militar. **d. ground,** (in a barracks) patio de un cuartel, *m;* (in a school) patio de recreo, *m.* **d.-sergeant,** sargento instructor, *m*

drilling /ˈdrɪlɪŋ/ *n* (boring) perforación, *f,* barrenamiento, *m;* (of seeds) sembradura en hileras, *f;* ejercicios, *m pl;* (maneuvers) maniobras, *f pl*

drink /drɪŋk/ *n* bebida, *f;* (glass of wine, etc.) copita, *f;* (of water, etc.) vaso, *m.* —*vt* beber; tomar; (empty) vaciar. —*vi* beber. **to d. the health of,** beber a la salud de, brindar por. **to give someone a d.,** dar a beber. **Would you like a d.?** ¿Quieres tomar algo? **to d. in,** absorber. **to d. off, up,** beber de un trago

drinkable /ˈdrɪŋkəbəl/ *a* potable, bebedero

drinker /ˈdrɪŋkər/ *n* bebedor (-ra)

drinking /ˈdrɪŋkɪŋ/ *n* acción de beber, *f;* el beber, *m;* (alcoholism) bebida, *f.* —*a* que bebe; aficionado a la bebida; (of things) para beber; (drinkable) potable; (tavern) de taberna. **d.-fountain,** fuente pública para beber agua, *f.* **d. place,** bebedero, *m;* bar, *m.* **d.-song,** canción de taberna, *f.* **d.-trough,** abrevadero, *m;* **d.-water,** agua potable, *f*

drip /drɪp/ *vi* and *vt* chorrear, gotear; caer gota a gota; escurrir; destilar; chorrear. —*n* goteo, *m;* gota, *f;* *Archit.* goterón, *m*

dripping /ˈdrɪpɪŋ/ *n* goteo, *m;* chorreo, *m;* (fat) grasa, *f,* *a* que gotea; mojado; que chorrea agua. **d.-pan,** grasera, *f*

drive /draiv/ *vt* empujar; arrojar; conducir; (grouse, etc.) batir; (a ball) golpear; (a nail, etc.) clavar; (oblige) compeler, forzar a; (a horse, plough, etc.) manejar; (*Mech.* work) mover; (cause to work, of machines) hacer funcionar; (a tunnel, etc.) abrir, construir; (a bargain, etc.) hacer; (cause) impulsar, hacer; (mad, etc.) volver. —*vi* lanzarse; (of rain) azotar; (a vehicle) conducir; (in a vehicle) ir en (coche, etc.). **to let d. at,** (aim) asestar. **to d. a wedge,** hacer mella. **to d. home an argument,** convencer; hacer convincente. **What is he driving at?** ¿Qué se propone?; ¿Qué quiere?; ¿Qué quiere decir con sus indirectas? ¿A dónde quiere llegar con esto? **to d. along,** ir en coche o carruaje por; pasearse en coche o carruaje; conducir un auto, etc., por. **to d. away,** *vt* echar; (chase) cazar; (flies, etc.) sacudirse, espantar; (care, etc.) ahuyentar; (of persons) apartar, alejar. —*vi* (depart) marcharse (en coche, etc.). **to d. back,** *vt* rechazar; (a ball) devolver. —*vi* volver (en auto, etc.); (arrive) llegar. **to d. down,** hacer bajar; arrojar hacia abajo; (in a vehicle) bajar (por). **to d. in, into,** *vt* hacer entrar; (of teeth, etc.) hincar; (nails) clavar; *Fig.* introducir. —*vt* entrar (en coche, carruaje); llegar (en coche, etc.). **to d. off,** See **away. to d. off the stage,** hacer dejar la escena, silbar. **to d. on,** *vt* empujar; hacer avanzar; (attack) atacar. —*vi* seguir su marcha; seguir avanzando; emprender la marcha. **to d. out,** *vt* expulsar; hacer salir; (chase) cazar. —*vi* salir (en coche, etc.). **to d. up,** *vi* illegar (en coche, etc.); parar. **to d. up to,** avanzar hasta, llegar hasta; conducir (el coche, etc.) hasta

drive /draiv/ *n* paseo (en coche, etc.), *m;* (avenue) avenida, *f;* (distance) trayecto, *m;* (journey) viaje, *m;* *Mech.* acción, *f;* conducción, *f;* *m;* *Mil.* ataque, *m;* (of a person) energía, *f;* campaña vigorosa, *f;* impulso, *m.* **left (right) hand d.,** conducción a la izquierda (derecha). **to take a d.,** dar un paseo en (auto, etc.). **to take for a d.,** llevar a paseo en (auto, etc.)

drive-in /ˈdraivˌɪn/ *n* autocine, autocinema, *m*

drivel /ˈdrɪvəl/ *n* vaciedades, patrañas, *f pl,* disparates, *m pl,* *vi* decir disparates, chochear

driver /ˈdraivər/ *n* conductor (-ra); chófer, *m;* (of an engine) maquinista, *m;* (of a cart) carretero, *m;* (of a coach, carriage) cochero, *m;* (of cattle, etc.) ganadero, *m;* (golf) conductor, *m*

"Driveway" «Vado Permante», «Paso de Carruajes»

driving /ˈdraivɪŋ/ *n* conducción, *f;* modo de conducir, *m;* paseo (en coche, etc.), *m;* impulsión, *f.* —*a* de conducir; de chófer; para choferes; motor; propulsor; impulsor; de transmisión; *Fig.* impulsor; (violent) violento, impetuoso. **to go d.,** ir de paseo (en auto o carruaje). **d. license,** carnet de chófer, *m.* **d. mirror,** espejo retrovisor, *m.* **d. seat,** asiento del conductor, *m;* (of an old-fashioned coach, etc.) pescante, *m.* **d.-shaft,** *Mech.* árbol motor, *m.* **d. test,** examen para choferes, *m.* **d.-wheel,** volante, *m;* rueda motriz, *f.* **d.-whip,** látigo, *m*

drizzle /ˈdrɪzəl/ *n* llovizna, *f,* *vi* lloviznar

droll /droul/ *a* chusco, gracioso. —*n* bufón, *m*

dromedary /ˈdrɒmɪˌdɛri/ *n* dromedario, *m*

drone /droun/ *n* abejón, *m;* *Fig.* zángano, *m;* (hum) zumbido, *m;* (of a song, voice) salmodia, *f,* *vt* and *vi* (hum) zumbar; (of a song, voice) salmodiar; (idle) zanganear

droning /ˈdrounɪŋ/ *a* zumbador; confuso

droop /drup/ *vi* inclinarse; colgar; caer; (wither) marchitarse; (fade) consumirse; (pine) desanimarse. —*vt* bajar; dejar caer. —*n* caída, *f;* inclinación, *f*

drooping /ˈdrupɪŋ/ *a* caído; debilitado; lánguido; (of ears) gacho; (depressed) alicaído, deprimido

drop /drɒp/ *n* gota, *f;* (tear) lágrima, *f;* (for the ear) pendiente, *m;* (sweet) pastilla, *f;* (of a chandelier) almendra, *f;* (fall) caída, *f;* (in price, etc.) baja, *f;*

(slope) pendiente, cuesta, *f.* **by drops,** a gotas. **d. bottle,** frasco cuentagotas, *m.* **d.-curtain,** telón de boca, *m.* **d.-hammer,** martinete, *m.* **d.-head coupé,** cupé descapotable, *m.* **d.-scene,** telón de foro, *m*
drop /drɒp/ *vt* verter a gotas; destilar; (sprinkle) salpicar, rociar; dejar caer; soltar; (lower) bajar; (of clothes, etc.) desprenderse de, quitar; (lose) perder; (a letter in a mailbox) echar; (leave) dejar; (give up) renunciar (a); desistir (de); abandonar; (kill) tumbar; (a hint) soltar; (a curtsey) hacer. —*vi* gotear, caer en gotas, destilar; (descend) bajar, descender; caer muerto; caer desmayado; (sleep) dormirse; (fall) caer; (of the wind) amainar; (of prices, temperature) bajar. **to let the matter d.,** poner fin a una cuestión. **to d. a line,** poner unas líneas. **to d. anchor,** anclar. **to d. behind,** quedarse atrás. **to d. down,** caer (a tierra). **to d. in,** entrar al pasar. **d. in on somebody,** pasarse por casa de fulano, pasarse por el despacho de (etc.). **to d. off,** separarse (de); disminuir; (sleep) quedar dormido; (die) morir de repente. **to d. out,** separarse; (from a race, etc.) retirarse (de); quedarse atrás; desaparecer; ausentarse, apartarse; (decrease) disminuir; decaer. **He has dropped out of my life,** Le he perdido de vista. **to d. through,** caer por; frustrarse; no dar resultado
dropping /ˈdrɒpɪŋ/ *n* gotera, *f;* gotas, *f pl;* (fall) caída, *f; pl* **droppings** (of a candle) moco, *m;* (dung) cagadas, *f pl.* **Constant d. wears away the stone,** La gotera cava la piedra
dropsy /ˈdrɒpsi/ *n* hidropesía, *f*
dross /drɔs/ *n* escoria, *f;* (rubbish) basura, *f*
drought /draut/ *n* aridez, *f;* (thirst) sed, *f;* (dry season) sequía, *f*
drove /drouv/ *n* manada, *f,* hato, *m;* (of sheep) rebaño, *m;* (crowd) muchedumbre, *f*
drown /draun/ *vi* ahogarse. —*vt* ahogar; sumergir; inundar; (*Fig.* of cries, sorrow, etc.) ahogar
drowning /ˈdraunɪŋ/ *n* ahogamiento, *m;* sumersión, *f;* inundación, *f.* —*a* que se ahoga
drowse /drauz/ *vi* adormecerse
drowsily /ˈdrauzəli/ *adv* soñolientamente
drowsiness /ˈdrauzinɪs/ *n* somnolencia, *f;* sueño, *m;* (laziness) indolencia, pereza, *f*
drowsy /ˈdrauzi/ *a* soñoliento; adormecedor, soporífero; (heavy) amodorrado. **to grow d.,** adormecerse. **to make d.,** adormecer
drubbing /ˈdrʌbɪŋ/ *n* tunda, zurra, felpa, *f*
drudgery /ˈdrʌdʒəri/ *n* trabajo arduo, *m,* faena monótona, *f*
drug /drʌg/ *n* droga, *f;* medicamento, *m;* narcótico, *m.* —*vt* mezclar con drogas; administrar drogas (a); narcotizar. —*vi* tomar drogas. **d. trade,** comercio de drogas, *m.* **d. traffic,** contrabando de drogas, narcotráfico *m*
drug addict *n* toxicómano, *m*
drug addiction *n* toxicomanía, *f*
druggist /ˈdrʌgɪst/ *n* droguero (-ra)
druid /ˈdruɪd/ *n* druida, *m*
drum /drʌm/ *n* tambor, *m;* (of the ear) tímpano (del oído), *m;* (cylinder) cilindro, *m;* (box) caja, *f; Archit.* cuerpo de columna, *m.* **bass d.,** bombo, *m.* **with drums beating,** con tambor batiente. **d.-head,** parche (del tambor), *m.* **d.-head service,** misa de campaña, *f.* **d.-major,** tambor mayor, *m*
drum /drʌm/ *vt* and *vi* tocar el tambor; (with the fingers) tabalear, teclear; (with the heels) zapatear; (into a person's head) machacar. **to d. out,** *Mil.* expulsar a tambor batiente
drummer /ˈdrʌmər/ *n* tambor, *m*
drumming /ˈdrʌmɪŋ/ *n* ruido del tambor, *m;* (of the heels) taconeo, *m;* (of the fingers) tabaleo, tecleo, *m*
drumstick /ˈdrʌmˌstɪk/ *n* palillo (de tambor), *m*
drunk /drʌŋk/ *a* borracho, ebrio. —*n* borracho, *m.* **to be d.,** estar borracho. **to get d.,** emborracharse; *Inf.* pillar un lobo. **to make d.,** emborrachar
drunkard /ˈdrʌŋkərd/ *n* borracho (-cha)
drunken /ˈdrʌŋkən/ *a* borracho, ebrio
drunkenness /ˈdrʌŋkənnɪs/ *n* embriaguez, borrachera, ebriedad, *f*
dry /drai/ *vi* secarse. —*vt* secar; desaguar; (wipe) enjugar. **to dry one's tears,** enjugarse las lágrimas; *Fig.* secarse las lágrimas. **to dry up,** secarse; (of persons) acecinarse; (with old age) apergaminarse; (of ideas, etc.) agotarse; (be quiet) callarse
dry /drai/ *a* seco; árido; estéril; (thirsty) sediento; (of wine) seco; (U.S.A.) prohibicionista; (squeezed) exprimido; (of toast) sin mantequilla; (*Fig.* chilly) aburrido; (sarcastic) sarcástico; (of humour) agudo. **on dry land,** en seco. **dry battery,** pila seca, *f.* **to dry-clean,** lavar al seco. **dry-cleaner,** tintorero (-ra). **dry-cleaning,** lavado al seco, *m.* **dry-cleaning shop,** tintorería, *f.* **dry goods,** lencería, *f.* **dry land,** tierra firme, *f.* **dry measure,** medida para áridos, *f.* **dry-nurse,** ama seca, *f.* **dry-point,** punta seca, *f.* **dry-rot,** carcoma, *f.* **dry-shod,** con los pies secos
drying /ˈdraiɪŋ/ *n* secamiento, *m;* desecación, *f, a* secante; seco; para secar. **d. ground,** tendedero, *m.* **d. machine,** secadora, *f;* (for the hair) secadora de cabello, *f.* **d. room,** secadero, *m*
dryly /ˈdraili/ *adv* secamente
dryness /ˈdrainɪs/ *n* sequedad, *f;* aridez, *f;* (of humour) agudeza, *f*
dual /ˈduəl/ *a* doble; *Gram.* dual. **d. control,** mandos gemelos, *m pl.* **d. personality,** conciencia doble, *f*
dualism /ˈduəˌlɪzəm/ *n* dualismo, *m*
duality /duˈælɪti/ *n* dualidad, *f*
dub /dʌb/ *vt* (a knight) armar caballero; (call) apellidar; (nickname) motejar, apodar
dubbing /ˈdʌbɪŋ/ *n* (of films) doblaje, *m*
dubious /ˈdubiəs/ *a* dudoso, incierto; indeciso; problemático; ambiguo
dubiously /ˈdubiəsli/ *adv* dudosamente
dubiousness /ˈdubiəsnɪs/ *n* carácter dudoso, *m;* incertidumbre, *f;* ambigüedad, *f*
Dublin /ˈdʌblɪn/ Dublín, *f*
Dubliner /ˈdʌblənər/ *n* dublinés (-esa)
ducat /ˈdʌkət/ *n* ducado, *m*
duchess /ˈdʌtʃɪs/ *n* duquesa, *f*
duchy /ˈdʌtʃi/ *n* ducado, *m*
duck /dʌk/ *n* pato (-ta), ánade, *mf; Sports.* cero, *m;* (darling) vida mía, querida, *f;* (jerk) agachada, *f;* (under the water) chapuz, *m;* (material) dril, *m; Mil.* auto anfibio, *m; pl* **ducks,** pantalones de dril, *m pl.* —*vi* agacharse; (under water) chapuzarse. —*vt* zabullir, sumergir; bajar, inclinar
ducking /ˈdʌkɪŋ/ *n* chapuz, *m.* **d.-stool,** silla de chapuzar, *f*
duckling /ˈdʌklɪŋ/ *n* anadino (-na)
duct /dʌkt/ *n* conducto, canal, *m; Bot.* tubo, *m*
ductile /ˈdʌktl̩/ *a* dúctil
ductility /dʌkˈtɪlɪti/ *n* ductilidad, *f*
ductless /ˈdʌktlɪs/ *a* sin tubos
due /du/ *a* debido; (payable) pagadero; (fallen due) vencido; (fitting) propio; (expected) esperado. —*n* impuesto, *m;* derecho, *m.* **in due form,** en regla. **in its due time,** a su tiempo debido. **to fall due,** vencerse. **due bill,** *Com.* abonaré, *m.* **due west,** poniente derecho, *m*
duel /ˈduəl/ *n* duelo, lance de honor, *m; Fig.* lucha, *f.* **to fight a d.,** batirse en duelo
dueling /ˈduəlɪŋ/ *n* el (batirse en) duelo
duelist /ˈduəlɪst/ *n* duelista, *m*
duenna /duˈɛnə/ *n* dueña, *f*
duet /duˈɛt/ *n* dúo, *m*
duettist /duˈɛtɪst/ *n* duetista, *mf*
duffer /ˈdʌfər/ *n* estúpido (-da); ganso, *m;* (at games, etc.) maleta, *m*
dug /dʌg/ *n* teta, *f*
dugout /ˈdʌgˌaut/ *n* trinchera, *f*
duke /duk/ *n* duque, *m*
dukedom /ˈdukdəm/ *n* ducado, *m*
dulcet /ˈdʌlsɪt/ *a* dulce
dulcimer /ˈdʌlsəmər/ *n* dulcémele, *m*
dull /dʌl/ *a* (stupid) lerdo, estúpido, obtuso; (boring, tedious) aburrido; (of pain, sounds) sordo; (of colors and eyes) apagado; (of light, beams, etc.) sombrío; (not polished) mate; (pale) pálido; (insipid) insípido, insulso; (of people) soso, poco interesante; (dreary, sad) triste; (gray) gris; (of mirrors, etc.) empañado; (of weather) anublado; (of hearing) duro; (slow) lento; lánguido; insensible; (blunt) romo; *Com.* encalmado, inactivo. **to find life d.,** encontrar la vida aburrida. **d. of hearing,** duro de oído, algo sordo. **d.**

pain, dolor sordo, *m.* **d. season,** temporada de calma, *f.* **d.-eyed,** con ojos apagados. **d.-witted,** lerdo
dull /dʌl/ *vt* (make stupid) entontecer; (lessen) mitigar; (weaken) debilitar; (pain) calmar, aliviar; (sadden) entristecer; (blunt) embotar; (spoil) estropear; (a mirror, etc.) empañar; (a polished surface) hacer mate, deslustrar; (of enthusiasm, etc.) enfriar; (tire) fatigar; (obstruct) impedir
dullness /ˈdʌlnɪs/ *n* (stupidity) estupidez, *f;* (boredom) aburrimiento, *m;* (heaviness) pesadez, *f;* (drowsiness) somnolencia, *f;* (insipidity) insipidez, insulsez, *f;* (of literary style) prosaísmo, *m;* (of persons) sosería, *f;* (of a surface) deslustre, *m;* (laziness) pereza, languidez, *f;* (slowness) lentitud, *f;* (tiredness) cansancio, *m;* (sadness) tristeza, *f;* (bluntness) embotamiento, *m;* (of hearing) dureza, *f; Com.* desanimación, *f*
dully /ˈdʌli/ *adv* (stupidly) estúpidamente; sin comprender; (insipidly) insípidamente; (not brightly) sin brillo; (slowly) lentamente; (sadly) tristemente; (tiredly) con cansancio; (of sound) sordamente
duly /ˈduli/ *adv* debidamente; puntualmente
dumb /dʌm/ *a* mudo; callado; silencioso; *Inf.* tonto, estúpido. **to become d.,** enmudecer. **to strike d.,** dejar sin habla. **d.-bell,** barra con pesas, *f.* **d. show,** pantomima, *f.* **d. waiter,** bufete, *m*
dumbfound /dʌmˈfaund/ *vt* dejar sin habla; confundir; pasmar
dumbness /ˈdʌmnɪs/ *n* mudez, *f,* mutismo, *m;* silencio, *m*
dummy /ˈdʌmi/ *n* (tailor's, etc.) maniquí, *m;* (puppet) títere, *m;* cabeza para pelucas, *f;* (figurehead) hombre de paja, testaferro, *m;* (baby's) chupador, *m;* (at cards) el muerto. —*a* fingido. **to be d.,** (at cards) ser el muerto
dump /dʌmp/ *n* depósito, *m;* vaciadero, *m.* —*vt* depositar; (goods on a market) inundar (con)
dumping /ˈdʌmpɪŋ/ *n* depósito, *m;* vaciamiento, *m;* (of goods on a market) inundación, *f.* **"D. prohibited,"** «Se prohibe arrojar la basura»
dumps /dʌmps/ *n* murria, *f*
dun /dʌn/ *vt* apremiar, importunar
dunce /dʌns/ *n* asno, bobo, zoquete, *m.* **dunce's cap,** coroza, *f*
dun-colored /ˈdʌnˌkʌlərd/ *a* pardo
dunderhead /ˈdʌndərˌhɛd/ *n* cabeza de alcornoque, zoquete, *m*
dune /dun/ *n* duna, *f*
dung /dʌŋ/ *n* estiércol, *m;* (of rabbits, mice, deer, sheep, goats) cagarruta, *f;* (of cows) boñiga, *f;* (of hens) gallinaza, *f.* **d.-cart,** carro de basura, *m*
dungarees /ˌdʌŋgəˈriz/ *n* mono, *m,* pantalones-vaquero, *m pl*
dungeon /ˈdʌndʒən/ *n* mazmorra, *f,* calabozo, *m*
dunghill /ˈdʌŋˌhɪl/ *n* muladar, *m*
Dunkirk /ˈdʌnkɜrk/ Dunquerque, *m*
duodenum /ˌduəˈdinəm/ *n* duodeno, *m*
dupe /dup/ *n* víctima, *f;* tonto (-ta). —*vt* embelecar, engañar. **to be a d.,** *Inf.* hacer el primo
duplicate /*a, n* ˈduplɪkɪt, ˈdyu-; *v* -ˌkeit/ *a* duplicado, doble. —*n* duplicado, *m;* copia, *f.* —*vt* duplicar
duplication /ˌduplɪˈkeiʃən/ *n* duplicación, *f*
duplicator /ˈduplɪˌkeitər/ *n* copiador, *m*
duplicity /duˈplɪsɪti/ *n* duplicidad, *f*
durability /ˌdʊrəˈbɪlɪti/ *n* duración, *f.* **This is a cloth of great d.,** Este es un paño que dura mucho, Este es un paño muy duradero
durable /ˈdʊrəbəl/ *a* duradero
duration /dʊˈreiʃən/ *n* duración, *f*
duress /dʊˈrɛs/ *n* compulsión, *f;* (prison) prisión, *f*
during /ˈdʊrɪŋ/ *prep* durante
dusk /dʌsk/ *n* atardecer, anochecer, *m;* (twilight) crepúsculo, *m;* (darkness) oscuridad, *f.* **at d.,** al atardecer, a la caída de la tarde
dusky /ˈdʌski/ *a* (swarthy) moreno; (black) negro; (dim, dark) oscuro; (of colors) sucio
dust /dʌst/ *n* polvo, *m;* (cloud of dust) polvareda, *f;* (ashes) cenizas, *f pl;* (of coal) cisco, *m;* (sweepings) barreduras, *f pl;* (of grain) tamo, *m.* —*vt* desempolvar, quitar (or sacudir) el polvo de; (cover with dust) polvorear; (scatter) salpicar; (sweep) barrer; (clean) limpiar. **d.-bin,** basurero, *m.* **d.-cart,** carro de la basura, *m.* **d. cloud,** polvareda, *f.* **d. jacket,** (books) sobrecubierta, *f.* **d.-pan,** recogedor de basura, *m.* **d.-sheet,** guardapolvo, *m.* **d. storm,** vendaval de polvo, *m*
duster /ˈdʌstər/ *n* el, *m,* que quita el polvo; paño (para quitar el polvo), *m;* (of feathers) plumero, *m*
dustiness /ˈdʌstinɪs/ *n* empolvoramiento, *m;* estado polvoriento, *m*
dusting /ˈdʌstɪŋ/ *n* limpieza, *f;* (sweeping) barredura, *f;* (powder) polvos antisépticos, *m pl*
dusty /ˈdʌsti/ *a* polvoriento, polvoroso, empolvado; del color del polvo; (of colours) sucio. **It is very d.,** Hay mucho polvo. **to get d.,** llenarse (or cubrirse) de polvo
Dutch /dʌtʃ/ *a* holandés. **the D.,** los holandeses. **double D.,** griego, galimatías, *m.* **D. cheese,** queso de bola, *m.* **D. courage,** coraje falso, *m.* **D. woman,** holandesa, *f*
Dutchman /ˈdʌtʃmən/ *n* holandés, *m*
dutiable /ˈdutiəbəl/ *a* sujeto a derechos de aduana
dutiful /ˈdutəfəl/ *a* que cumple con sus deberes; obediente, sumiso; respetuoso; excelente, muy bueno
dutifully /ˈdutəfəli/ *adv* obedientemente; respetuosamente
dutifulness /ˈdutəfəlnɪs/ *n* obediencia, docilidad, *f;* respeto, *m*
duty /ˈduti/ *n* deber, *m;* obligación, *f;* (greetings) respetos, *m pl*; (charge, burden) carga, *f;* (tax) derecho, impuesto, *m; Mil.* servicio, *m;* (guard) guardia, *f.* **off d.,** libre. **on d.,** de servicio. **to be on sentry d.,** estar de guardia. **to do d. as,** servir como. **to do one's d.,** hacer (or cumplir con) su deber. **to pay d. on,** pagar derechos de aduana sobre. **d.-free,** franco de derechos
dwarf /dwɔrf/ *a* enano. —*n* enano (-na). —*vt* impedir el crecimiento de; empequeñecer
dwarfish /ˈdwɔrfɪʃ/ *a* enano
dwell /dwɛl/ *vi* vivir, habitar; (with on, upon) (think about) meditar sobre, pensar en; (deal with) tratar de; hablar largamente de; (insist on) insister en; apoyarse en, hacer hincapié en; (pause over) detenerse en
dweller /ˈdwɛlər/ *n* habitante, *mf;* (more poetic) morador (-ra)
dwelling /ˈdwɛlɪŋ/ *n* vivienda, *f;* (abode) morada, habitación, *f;* residencia, *f;* casa, *f;* (domicile) domicilio, *m.* **d.-house,** casa, *f*
dwindle /ˈdwɪndl̩/ *vi* disminuirse; consumirse; (decay) decaer; (degenerate) degenerar. **to d. to,** reducirse a
dwindling /ˈdwɪndl̩ɪŋ/ *n* disminución, *f*
dye /dai/ *vt* teñir, colorar. —*vi* teñirse. —*n* tinte, *m;* (colour) color, *m.* **fast dye,** tinte estable, *m.* **dye-house,** tintorería, *f.* **dye-stuff,** materia colorante, *f.* **dye-works,** tintorería, *f*
dyed-in-the-wool /ˈdaid ən ðə ˈwʊl/ *a* de pies a cabeza
dyeing /ˈdaiɪŋ/ *n* teñidura, tintura, *f;* (as a trade) tintorería, *f.* **d. and dry-cleaning shop,** tintorería, *f*
dyer /ˈdaiər/ *n* tintorero (-ra)
dyestuff /ˈdaiˌstʌf/ *n* materia colorante, materia de tinte, materia tintórea, *f*
dying /ˈdaiɪŋ/ *a* moribundo, agonizante; de la muerte; (of light) mortecino; (last) último; supremo; (languishing) lánguido; (deathbed) hecho en su lecho mortuorio. **to be d.,** estar agonizando; (of light) fenecer. **to be d. for,** estar muerto por
dynamic /daiˈnæmɪk/ *a* dinámico
dynamics /daiˈnæmɪks/ *n* dinámica, *f*
dynamite /ˈdainəˌmait/ *n* dinamita, *f*
dynamo /ˈdainəˌmou/ *n* dinamo, *f*
dynastic /daiˈnæstɪk/ *a* dinástico
dynasty /ˈdainəsti/ *n* dinastía, *f*
dysentery /ˈdɪsənˌtɛri/ *n* disentería, *f*
dyspepsia /dɪsˈpɛpʃə/ *n* dispepsia, *f*
dyspeptic /dɪsˈpɛptɪk/ *a* dispéptico. —*n* dispéptico (-ca)

E

e /i/ *n* (letter) e, *f; Mus.* mi, *m*

each /itʃ/ *a* cada (invariable), todo. —*pron* cada uno, *m;* cada una, *f.* **e. of them,** cada uno de ellos. **They help e. other,** Se ayudan mutuamente, Se ayudan entre sí. **to love e. other,** amarse

eager /ˈigər/ *a* impaciente; ansioso, deseoso; ambicioso

eagerly /ˈigərli/ *adv* con impaciencia; con ansia; ambiciosamente

eagerness /ˈigərnɪs/ *n* impaciencia, *f;* ansia, *f,* deseo, *m;* (promptness) alacridad, *f;* (zeal) fervor, *m*

eagle /ˈigəl/ *n* águila, *f.* **royal e.,** águila caudal, águila real, *f.* **e.-eyed,** con ojos de lince, de ojo avizor. **have the eyes of an e.,** tener ojos de lince, tener vista de lince

ear /ɪər/ *n* (outer ear) oreja, *f;* (inner ear and sense of hearing) oído, *m; Bot.* espiga, panoja, *f.* **to begin to show the ear,** (grain) espigar. **to be all ears,** ser todo oídos. **to give ear,** dar oído. **to have a good ear,** tener buen oído. **to play by ear,** tocar de oído. **to turn a deaf ear,** hacerse el sordo. **ear-ache,** dolor de oídos, *m.* **ear-drum,** tímpano (del oído), *m.* **ear-flap,** orejera, *f.* **ear-phone, ear-piece,** auricular, *m.* **ear-piercing,** penetrante, agudo. **ear-shot,** alcance del oído, *m.* **to be within ear-shot,** estar al alcance del oído. **ear-trumpet,** trompetilla, *f.* **ear wax,** cerilla, *f*

eared /ɪərd/ *a* con orejas; de orejas; *Bot.* con espigas

earl /ɜrl/ *n* conde, *m*

earldom /ˈɜrldəm/ *n* condado, *m*

earlier, earliest /ˈɜrliər; ˈɜrliɪst/ *a compar* and *superl* más temprano; más primitivo; más antiguo; (first, of time) primero. —*adv* más temprano; más pronto; antes

earliness /ˈɜrlinɪs/ *n* lo temprano; antigüedad, *f,* lo primitivo; (precocity) precocidad, *f.* **The e. of his arrival,** Su llegada de buena hora

early /ˈɜrli/ *a* temprano; primitivo; (of fruit, etc.) temprano, adelantado; (movement) primero (e.g. *early Romanticism,* el primer romanticismo); (person) de la primera época (e.g. *the early Cervantes,* Cervantes de la primera época); (work) un primer (e.g. *an early work of Unamuno's,* una primera obra de Unamuno); (advanced) avanzado; (precocious) precoz; (first, of time) primero; (in the morning) matutino; (near) próximo; cercano; (premature) prematuro; (of child's age) tierno; joven. **in the e. hours,** en las primeras horas; en las altas horas (de la noche). **e. age,** edad temprana, tierna edad, *f.* **e.-fruiting,** *Agr.* tempranal. **e. riser,** madrugador (-ra). **e.-rising,** *a* madrugador. **e. years,** primeros años, años de la niñez, *m pl*

early /ˈɜrli/ *adv* temprano; al principio (de); en los primeros días (de); desde los primeros días (de); (in the month, year) a principios (de); (in time) a tiempo; (in the day) de buena hora; (soon) pronto; (among the first) entre los primeros (de). **as e. as possible,** lo más temprano posible; lo más pronto posible. **to be e.,** llegar antes de tiempo; llegar de buena hora. **to get up e.,** madrugar. **to go to bed e.,** acostarse temprano. **too e.,** demasiado temprano. **e. in the morning,** de madrugada

earmark /ˈɪər,mɑrk/ *vt* marcar; *Fig.* destinar, reservar

earn /ɜrn/ *vt* ganar; obtener, adquirir; (deserve) merecer

earnable /ˈɜrnəbəl/ *a* ganabie

earnest /ˈɜrnɪst/ *a* serio; fervoroso; diligente; sincero. **to be in e. about something,** tomarlo en serio; ser sincero (en). **e. money,** arras, *f pl*

earnestly /ˈɜrnɪstli/ *adv* seriamente; fervorosamente; con diligencia; sinceramente, de buena fe

earnestness /ˈɜrnɪstnɪs/ *n* seriedad, *f;* fervor, celo, *m;* diligencia, *f;* sinceridad, buena fe, *f*

earnings /ˈɜrnɪŋz/ *n pl Com.* ingresos, *m pl*; (salary) salario, *m;* estipendio, *m;* (of a workman) jornal, *m*

earring /ˈɪər,rɪŋ/ *n* pendiente, arete, *m*

earth /ɜrθ/ *n* tierra, *f;* (of a badger, etc.) madriguera, *f; Radio.* tierra, *f.* —*vt* cubrir con tierra; *Radio.* conectar con tierra. **clod of e.,** terrón, *m.* **half the e.,** *Inf.* medio mundo, *m.* **on e.,** en este mundo, sobre la tierra

earthen /ˈɜrθən/ *a* terrizo, terroso; (of mud) de barro

earthenware /ˈɜrθən,wɛər/ *n* alfar, *m,* —*a* de loza, de barro

earthiness /ˈɜrθinɪs/ *n* terrosidad, *f*

earthly /ˈɜrθli/ *a* terrestre, terrenal; de la tierra; (fleshly) carnal; (worldly) mundano; material. **There is not an e. chance,** No hay la más mínima posibilidad

earthquake /ˈɜrθ,kweik/ *n* terremoto, temblor de tierra, *m*

earth tremor movimiento sísmico, *m*

earthwork /ˈɜrθ,wɜrk/ *n* terraplén, *m*

earthworm /ˈɜrθ,wɜrm/ *n* gusano de tierra, *m*

earthy /ˈɜrθi/ *a* térreo, terroso

earwig /ˈɪər,wɪg/ *n* tijereta, *f*

ease /iz/ *n* bienestar, *m;* tranquilidad, *f;* descanso, *m;* (leisure) ocio, *m;* (comfortableness) comodidad, *f;* (freedom from embarrassment) naturalidad, *f,* desembarazo, desenfado, *m;* (from pain) alivio, *m;* (simplicity) facilidad, *f.* —*vt* (widen) ensanchar; aflojar; (pain) aliviar; (lighten) aligerar; (moderate) moderar; (soften) suavizar; (free) librar; (one's mind) tranquilizar. **in my moments of e.,** en mis ocios, en mis momentos de ocio. **Stand at e.!** *Mil.* ¡En su lugar descansen! **to be at e.,** estar a sus anchas; encontrarse bien; comportarse con toda naturalidad. **with e.,** fácilmente. **to e. off,** *vt* (*Naut.* cables, sails) arriar. —*vi* sentirse menos, cesar

easel /ˈizəl/ *n* caballete (de pintor) *m*

easily /ˈizəli/ *adv* fácilmente. **The engine runs e.,** El motor marcha bien

easiness /ˈizinɪs/ *n* facilidad, *f;* sencillez, *f;* (of manner) desembarazo, *m,* naturalidad, *f*

east /ist/ *n* este, *m;* oriente, *m,* (of countries) Oriente, *m;* Levante, *m.* —*a* del este; del oriente; (of countries) de Oriente, oriental; levantino. **e. North e.,** estenordeste, *m.* **e. South e.,** estesudeste, *m.* **e. wind,** viento del este, *m*

Easter /ˈistər/ *n* Pascua de Resurrección, *f.* **E. egg,** huevo de Pascua, *m.* **E. Saturday,** sábado de gloria, *m.* **E. Sunday,** domingo de Pascua, *m*

easterly /ˈistərli/ *a* del este; al este. —*adv* hacia el este

eastern /ˈistərn/ *a* del este; de Oriente; oriental. —*n* oriental, *mf*

easternmost /ˈistərn,moust/ *a* situado más al este

East Indies Indias Orientales, *f pl*

eastward /ˈistwərd/ *adv* hacia el este, hacia oriente

easy /ˈizi/ *a* fácil; sencillo; (comfortable) cómodo; (free from pain) aliviado; *Com.* flojo; (well-off) acomodado, holgado; (calm) tranquilo; tolerante; natural; afable, condescendiente; (of virtue, women) fácil. —*adv* con calma; despacio. **I must make myself e. about,** he de tranquilizarme sobre. **Stand e.!** ¡En su lugar descansen! **to take it e.,** tomarlo con calma. **e.-chair,** (silla) poltrona, *f.* **easy come, easy go,** lo que por agua, agua (Mexico and Colombia), los dineros del sacristán cantando vienen y cantando se van (Spain). **e.-going,** acomodadizo; indolente, (morally) de manga ancha; (casual) descuidado

eat /it/ *vt* comer; (meals, soup, refreshments) tomar; (with a good, bad appetite) hacer; consumir; (corrode) corroer; desgastar. —*vi* comer; (*Fam.* of food) ser de buen (or mal) comer. **to eat one's breakfast (lunch),** tomar el desayuno, desayunar (almorzar). **to eat one's words,** retractarse. **to eat away,** comer; consumir; corroer. **to eat into,** (of chemicals) morder; (a fortune) consumir; gastar. **eat out of s. b.'s hand,** comer de la mano de fulano, comer en la mano de fulano. **to eat up,** devorar (also *Fig.*)

eatable /ˈitəbəl/ *a* comestible, comedero. —*n pl* **eatables,** comestibles, *m pl*

eater /'itər/ *n* el, *m,* (*f,* la) que come
eating /'itɪŋ/ *n* el comer; comida, *f.* **e. and drinking,** el comer y beber. **e.-house,** casa de comidas, *f*
eau de cologne /'ou də kə'loun/ *n* agua de Colonia, *f*
eaves /ivz/ *n* rafe, alero, *m.* **under the e.,** debajo del alero
eavesdrop /'ivz,drɒp/ *vi* escuchar a las puertas; fisgonear, espiar
eavesdropper /'ivz,drɒpər/ *n* fisgón (-ona)
eavesdropping /'ivz,drɒpɪŋ/ *n* fisgoneo, *m*
ebb /ɛb/ *n* (of the tide) reflujo, *m;* menguante, *f; Fig.* declinación, *f; Fig.* decadencia, *f;* (of life) vejez, *f.* —*vi* (of tide) menguar; declinar; decaer. **to ebb and flow,** fluir y refluir. **to ebb away from,** dejar; dejar aislado. **ebb-tide,** marea menguante, *f*
ebonite /'ɛbə,nait/ *n* ebonita, *f*
ebony /'ɛbəni/ *n* ébano, *m*
ebullience /ɪ'bʌlyəns/ *n* efervescencia, exuberancia, *f*
ebullient /ɪ'bʌlyənt/ *a* efervescente, exuberante
ebullition /,ɛbə'lɪʃən/ *n* (boiling) ebullición, *f,* hervor, *m; Fig.* efervescencia, *f,* estallido, *m*
eccentric /ɪk'sɛntrɪk/ *a Geom.* excéntrico; raro, original; extravagante, excéntrico. —*n* persona excéntrica, *f,* original, *m*
eccentrically /ɪk'sɛntrɪkəli/ *adv* excéntricamente
eccentricity /,ɛksən'trɪsɪti/ *n Geom.* excentricidad, *f;* rareza, extravagancia, excentricidad, *f*
Ecclesiastes /ɪ,klizi'æstiz/ *n* Eclesiastés, *m*
ecclesiastic /ɪ,klizi'æstɪk/ *a* eclesiástico. —*n* eclesiástico, clérigo, *m*
ecclesiastically /ɪ,klizi'æstɪkəli/ *adv* eclesiásticamente
echo /'ɛkou/ *n* eco, *m;* reverberación, resonancia, *f.* —*vt* repercutir; *Fig.* repetir. —*vi* resonar, retumbar, reverberar
echoing /'ɛkouɪŋ/ *a* retumbante. —*n* eco, *m*
eclectic /ɪ'klɛktɪk/ *a* and *n* ecléctico (-ca)
eclecticism /ɪ'klɛktə,sɪzəm/ *n* eclecticismo, *m*
eclipse /ɪ'klɪps/ *n Astron.* eclipse, *m, vt* eclipsar, hacer eclipse a. **to be in e.,** estar en eclipse
ecliptic /ɪ'klɪptɪk/ *n Astron.* eclíptica, *f, a* eclíptico
eclogue /'ɛklɔg/ *n* égloga, *f*
economic /,ɛkə'nɒmɪk, ,ikə-/ *a* económico
economical /,ɛkə'nɒmɪkəl, ,ikə-/ *a* económico
economics /,ɛkə'nɒmɪks, ,ikə-/ *n* economía política, *f*
economist /ɪ'kɒnəmɪst/ *n* economista, *mf*
economize /ɪ'kɒnə,maiz/ *vt* economizar, ahorrar. —*vi* hacer economías
economy /ɪ'kɒnəmi/ *n* economía, *f.* **domestic e.,** economía doméstica, *f.* **political e.,** economía política, *f*
ecstasy /'ɛkstəsi/ *n* éxtasis, arrebato, *m;* transporte, *m.* **to be in e.,** estar en éxtasis
ecstatic /ɛk'stætɪk/ *a* extático
Ecuador /'ɛkwə,dɔr/ el Ecuador
Ecuadorian /,ɛkwə'dɔriən/ *a* and *n* ecuatoriano (-na)
ecumenical /'ɛkyʊ'mɛnɪkəl/ *a* ecuménico
eczema /'ɛksəmə/ *n* eczema, *f*
eddy /'ɛdi/ *n* remolino, *m, vi* remolinar; *Fig.* remolinear
edelweiss /'eidl̩,wais/ *n* inmortal de las nieves, *f*
edema /ɪ'dimə/ *n Med.* edema, *m*
Eden /'idn̩/ *n* Edén, *m*
edge /ɛdʒ/ *n* (of sharp instruments) filo, *m;* (of a skate) cuchilla, *f;* margen, *mf;* (shore) orilla, *f;* (of two surfaces) arista, *f;* (of books) borde, *m;* (of a coin) canto, *m;* (of a chair, a precipice, a forest, a curb, etc.) borde, *m;* (extreme) extremidad, *f.* **on e.,** de canto; *Fig.* ansioso. **to be on e.,** *Fig.* tener los nervios en punta. **to set on e.,** poner de canto; (of teeth) dar dentera
edge /ɛdʒ/ *vt* (sharpen) afilar; *Sew.* ribetear; orlar; poner un borde (a); (cut) cortar. **to e. away,** escurrirse. **to e. into,** *vt* insinuarse. —*vi* deslizarse en. **to e. out,** salir poco a poco
edged /ɛdʒd/ *a* afilado, cortante; (in compounds) de... filos; (bordered) bordeado; (of books) de bordes...
edgeways /'ɛdʒweiz/ *adv* de lado; de canto. **He couldn't get a word in e.,** No pudo meter baza en la conversación
edging /'ɛdʒɪŋ/ *n* borde, *m;* ribete, *m*
edibility /,ɛdə'bɪlɪti/ *n* el ser comestible
edible /'ɛdəbəl/ *a* comestible
edict /'idɪkt/ *n* edicto, *m*
edification /,ɛdəfɪ'keiʃən/ *n* edificación, *f*
edifice /'ɛdəfɪs/ *n* edificio, *m*
edify /'ɛdə,fai/ *vt* edificar
edifying /'ɛdə,faiɪŋ/ *a* edificante, edificador, de edificación
Edinburgh /'ɛdn̩,bɜrə/ Edinburgo, *m*
edit /'ɛdɪt/ *vt* editar; (a newspaper, journal) ser director de; (prepare for press) redactar; (correct) corregir
editing /'ɛdɪtɪŋ/ *n* trabajo editorial, *m;* redacción, *f;* dirección, *f;* corrección, *f*
edition /ɪ'dɪʃən/ *n* edición, *f; Print.* tirada, *f.* **first e.,** edición príncipe, *f.* **miniature e.,** edición diamante, *f*
editor /'ɛdɪtər/ *n* (of a book) editor (-ra); (of a newspaper, journal) director (-ra)
editorial /,ɛdɪ'tɔriəl/ *a* de redacción; editorial. —*n* editorial, artículo de fondo, *m.* **e. staff,** redacción, *f*
editorial board consejo de redacción, *m*
editorship /'ɛdɪtər,ʃɪp/ *n* dirección (de un periódico, de una revista), *f*
educability /,ɛdʒəkə'bɪlɪti/ *n* educabilidad, *f*
educable /'ɛdʒʊkəbəl/ *a* educable
educate /'ɛdʒʊ,keit/ *vt* educar; formar; (accustom) acostumbrar
educated /'ɛdʒʊ,keitɪd/ *a* culto
education /,ɛdʒʊ'keiʃən/ *n* educación, *f;* enseñanza, *f;* pedagogía, *f.* **chair of e.,** cátedra de pedagogía, *f.* **early e.,** primeras letras, *f pl.* **higher e.,** enseñanza superior, *f*
educational /,ɛdʒʊ'keiʃənl̩/ *a* educativo; pedagógico; instructivo
educationalist /,ɛdʒə'keiʃənl̩ɪst/ *n* pedagogo, *m*
educative /'ɛdʒʊ,keitɪv/ *a* educativo
educator /'ɛdʒʊ,keitər/ *n* educador (-ra)
educe /ɪ'dus/ *vt* educir; deducir; *Chem.* extraer
eduction /ɪ'dʌkʃən/ *n* educción, *f*
Edwardian /ɛd'wɔrdiən/ *a* and *n* eduardiano (-na)
eel /il/ *n* anguila, *f.* **electric eel,** gimnoto, *m.* **eel-basket,** nasa para anguilas, *f*
eerie /'ɪəri/ *a* misterioso, fantástico; sobrenatural; lúgubre
eerily /'ɪərəli/ *adv* fantásticamente; de modo sobrenatural
eeriness /'ɪərinɪs/ *n* ambiente de misterio, *m;* efecto misterioso, *m*
efface /ɪ'feis/ *vt* borrar, destruir; quitar. **to e. oneself,** retirarse; permanecer en el fondo
effacement /ɪ'feismənt/ *n* borradura, *f*
effect /ɪ'fɛkt/ *n* efecto, *m;* impresión, *f;* (result) resultado, *m,* consecuencia, *f,* (meaning) substancia, *f,* significado, *m; pl* **effects,** efectos, bienes, *m pl.* —*vt* efectuar; producir. **in e.,** en efecto, efectivamente. **of no e.,** inútil. **striving after e.,** efectismo, *m.* **to feel the effects of,** sentir los efectos de; padecer las consecuencias de. **to put into e.,** poner en práctica; hacer efectivo. **to take e.,** producir efecto; ponerse en vigor
effective /ɪ'fɛktɪv/ *a* eficaz; (striking) de mucho efecto, poderoso, vistoso. **to make e.,** llevar a efecto
effectively /ɪ'fɛktɪvli/ *adv* eficazmente; (strikingly) con gran efecto; efectivamente, en efecto
effectiveness /ɪ'fɛktɪvnɪs/ *n* eficacia, *f;* efecto, *m*
effectuate /ɪ'fɛktʃu,eit/ *vt* efectuar
effeminacy /ɪ'fɛmənəsi/ *n* afeminación, *f*
effeminate /ɪ'fɛmənɪt/ *a* afeminado, adamado. **to make e.,** afeminar
efferent /'ɛfərənt/ *a* eferente
effervesce /,ɛfər'vɛs/ *vi* estar efervescente, hervir
effervescence /,ɛfər'vɛsəns/ *n* efervescencia, *f*
effervescent /,ɛfər'vɛsənt/ *a* efervescente
effete /ɪ'fit/ *a* gastado; estéril; decadente
effeteness /ɪ'fitnɪs/ *n* decadencia, *f;* esterilidad, *f*
efficacious /,ɛfɪ'keiʃəs/ *a* eficaz
efficacy /'ɛfɪkəsi/ *n* eficacia, *f*
efficiency /ɪ'fɪʃənsi/ *n* eficiencia, *f;* buen estado, *m;* habilidad, *f; Mech.* rendimiento, *m*
efficient /ɪ'fɪʃənt/ *a* (e.g. medicine) eficaz; eficiente; (person) competente, capaz

efficiently /ɪ'fɪʃəntli/ *adv* eficientemente; eficazmente; competentemente
effigy /'ɛfɪdʒi/ *n* efigie, imagen, *f*
efflorescence /ˌɛflə'rɛsəns/ *n Chem.* eflorescencia, *f; Bot.* florescencia, *f*
effluvium /ɪ'fluviəm/ *n* efluvio, *m*
effort /'ɛfərt/ *n* esfuerzo, *m.* **to make an e.,** hacer un esfuerzo. **make every effort to,** hacer lo posible por + *Inf.*; empeñar sus máximos esfuerzos en el sentido de + *Inf.*
effortless /'ɛfərtlɪs/ *a* sin esfuerzo
effrontery /ɪ'frʌntəri/ *n* descaro, *m,* insolencia, *f*
effulgence /ɪ'fʌldʒəns/ *n* esplendor, fulgor, *m*
effulgent /ɪ'fʌldʒənt/ *a* fulgente, resplandeciente
effusion /ɪ'fyuʒən/ *n* efusión, *f*
effusive /ɪ'fyusɪv/ *a* efusivo, expansivo
egg /ɛg/ *n* huevo, *m.* **to egg on,** incitar (a). **boiled egg,** huevo cocido, *m.* **fried egg,** huevo frito, *m.* **hard egg,** huevo duro, *m.* **poached egg,** huevo escalfado, *m.* **scrambled egg,** huevos revueltos, *m pl.* **soft egg,** huevo pasado por agua, *m.* **to lay eggs,** poner huevos. **to put all one's eggs in one basket,** *Fig.* poner toda la carne en el asador. **egg-cup,** huevera, *f.* **egg dealer,** vendedor (-ra) de huevos. **egg flip,** huevo batido con ron, *m.* **eggplant,** berenjena, *f.* **egg-shaped,** aovado. **egg-shell,** cascarón, *m,* cáscara de huevo, *f.* **egg-shell china,** loza muy fina, *f.* **egg-spoon,** cucharita para comer huevos, *f.* **egg-whisk,** batidor de huevos, *m*
ego /'igou/ *n* yo
egoism /'igouˌɪzəm/ *n* egoísmo, *m*
egoist /'igouɪst/ *n* egoísta, *mf*
egoistic /ˌigou'ɪstɪk/ *a* egoísta
egoistically /ˌigou'ɪstɪkəli/ *adv* egoístamente
egotism /'igəˌtɪzəm/ *n* egotismo, *m,* egolatría, *f*
egotist /'igətɪst/ *n* egotista, *mf*
egotistic /ˌigə'tɪstɪk/ *a* egotista
egregious /ɪ'gridʒəs/ *a* notorio
egress /'igrɛs/ *n* salida, *f*
Egypt /'idʒɪpt/ Egipto, *m*
Egyptian /ɪ'dʒɪpʃən/ *a* egipcio. —*n* egipcio (-ia); cigarrillo egipcio, *m*
Egyptologist /ˌidʒɪp'tɒlədʒɪst/ *n* egiptólogo (-ga)
Egyptology /ˌidʒɪp'tɒlədʒi/ *n* egiptología, *f*
eh? /ei/ *interj* ¿eh? ¿qué?
eider /'aidər/ *n Ornith.* pato de flojel, *m*
eiderdown /'aidərˌdaun/ edredón, *m*
eight /eit/ *a* and *n* ocho *m.* **He is e. years old,** Tiene ocho años. **It is e. o'clock,** Son las ocho. **e.-day clock,** reloj con cuerda para ocho dias, *m.* **e. hundred,** *a* and *n* ochocientos *m..* **e.-syllabled,** octosilábico
eighteen /'ei'tin/ *a* and *n* diez y ocho, *m.*
eighteenth /'ei'tinθ/ *a* décimoctavo; (of the month) (el) diez y ocho, dieciocho; (of monarchs) diez y ocho. —*n* décimoctava parte, *f.* **Louis the E.,** Luis diez y ocho
eightfold /'eitˌfould/ *a* óctuple
eighth /eitθ, eiθ/ *a* octavo, *m;* (of the month) (el) ocho; (of monarchs) octavo. —*n* octavo, *m*
eighthly /'eitθli/ *adv* en octavo lugar
eightieth /'eitiɪθ/ *a* octogésimo
eighty /'eiti/ *a* and *n* ochenta, *m.*
either /'iðər/ *a* and *pron* uno u otro, cualquiera de los dos; ambos (-as). —*conjunc* o (becomes **u** before words beginning with **o** or **ho**). —*adv* tampoco. **I do not like e.,** No me gusta ni el uno ni el otro (ni la una ni la otra). **e.... or,** o... o
ejaculate /ɪ'dʒækyəˌleit/ *vt* exclamar, lanzar; *Med.* eyacular
ejaculation /ɪˌdʒækyə'leiʃən/ *n* exclamación, *f; Med.* eyaculación, *f*
ejaculatory /ɪ'dʒækyələˌtɔri/ *a* jaculatorio
eject /ɪ'dʒɛkt/ *vt* echar, expulsar; *Law.* desahuciar; (emit) despedir, emitir
ejection /ɪ'dʒɛkʃən/ *n* echamiento, *m,* expulsión, *f; Law.* desahúcio, *m;* (emission) emisión, *f*
eke /ik/ (out) *vt* aumentar, añadir a
elaborate /*a* ɪ'læbərɪt; *v* -əˌreit/ *a* elaborado; primoroso; elegante; complicado; (detailed) detallado; (of meals) de muchos platos; (of courtesy, etc.) estudiado. —*vt* elaborar; amplificar
elaborately /ɪ'læbərɪtli/ *adv* primorosamente; elegantemente; complicadamente; con muchos detalles
elaborateness /ɪ'læbərɪtnɪs/ *n* primor, *m;* elegancia, *f;* complicación, *f;* (care) cuidado, *m;* minuciosidad, *f*
elaboration /ɪˌlæbə'reiʃən/ *n* elaboración, *f*
elapse /ɪ'læps/ *vi* transcurrir, andar, pasar
elastic /ɪ'læstɪk/ *a* elástico. —*n* elástico, *m.* **e. band,** anillo de goma, *m;* cinta de goma, *f.* **e. girdle,** faja elástica, *f*
elasticity /ɪlæ'stɪsɪti/ *n* elasticidad, *f*
elate /ɪ'leit/ *vt* alegrar; animar
elatedly /ɪ'leitɪdli/ *adv* alegremente; triunfalmente
elation /ɪ'leiʃən/ *n* alegría, *f,* júbilo, *m;* triunfo, *m*
elbow /'ɛlbou/ *n* codo, *m;* ángulo, *m;* (of a chair) brazo, *m.* —*vt* codear, dar codazos (a). **at one's e.,** a la mano. **nudge with the e.,** codazo, *m.* **to be out at e.,** enseñar los codos, tener los codos raídos; ser harapiento. **to e. one's way,** abrirse paso a codazos. **e.-chair,** silla de brazos, *f.* **e.-grease,** jugo de muñeca, *m.* **e.-piece** or **patch,** codera, *f.* **e. room,** libertad de movimiento, *f*
elder /'ɛldər/ *a compar* mayor. —*n* persona mayor, *f;* señor mayor, *m;* (among Jews and in early Christian Church) anciano, *m; Bot.* saúco, *m*
elderly /'ɛldərli/ *a* mayor
eldest /'ɛldɪst/ *a superl* old (el, la, etc.) mayor. **e. daughter,** hija mayor, *f.* **e. son,** hijo mayor, *m*
elect /ɪ'lɛkt/ *vt* elegir. —*a* elegido; predestinado. —*n* electo, *m;* elegido, *m*
election /ɪ'lɛkʃən/ *n Theol.* predestinación, *f;* elección, *f.* **by-e.,** elección parcial, *f*
electioneer /ɪˌlɛkʃə'nɪər/ *vi* solicitar votos; distribuir propaganda electoral
electioneering /ɪˌlɛkʃə'nɪərɪŋ/ *n* solicitación de votos, *f;* propaganda electoral, *f*
elective /ɪ'lɛktɪv/ *a* electivo. —*n* (subject at school) materia optativa, *f*
elector /ɪ'lɛktər/ *n* elector (-ra); (prince) elector, *m*
electoral /ɪ'lɛktərəl/ *a* electoral. **e. register,** lista electoral, *f*
electoral college colegio de compromisarios, *m*
electorate /ɪ'lɛktərɪt/ *n* electorado, *m*
electric, electrical /ɪ'lɛktrɪk; ɪ'lɛktrɪkəl/ *a* eléctrico; *Fig.* vivo, instantáneo. **e. arc,** arco voltaico, *m.* **e. engineer,** ingeniero electricista, *m.* **electric fan,** (Spain) ventilador, (Western Hemisphere) ventilador eléctrico, *m.* **e. fire,** estufa eléctrica, *f.* **e. immersion heater,** calentador de agua eléctrico, *m.* **e. light,** luz eléctrica, *f.* **e. pad,** alfombrilla eléctrica, *f.* **e. shock,** conmoción eléctrica, *f.* **e. washing-machine,** lavadora eléctrica, *f.* **e. wire** or **cable,** conductor eléctrico, *m*
electrically /ɪ'lɛktrɪkəli/ *adv* por electricidad
electrician /ɪlɛk'trɪʃən/ *n* electricista, *mf*
electricity /ɪlɛk'trɪsɪti/ *n* electricidad, *f*
electrification /ɪˌlɛktrəfɪ'keiʃən/ *n* electrificación, *f*
electrify /ɪ'lɛktrəˌfai/ *vt* electrificar; *Fig.* electrizar
electro- *prefix* (in compounds) electro. **e.-chemistry,** electroquímica, *f.* **e.-dynamics,** electrodinámica, *f.* **e.-magnet,** electroimán, *m.* **e.-magnetic,** electromagnético. **e.-plate,** *vt* galvanizar, platear. —*n* artículo galvanizado, *m.* **e.-therapy,** electroterapia, *f*
electrocute /ɪ'lɛktrəˌkyut/ *vt* electrocutar
electrocution /ɪˌlɛktrə'kyuʃən/ *n* electrocución, *f*
electrode /ɪ'lɛktroud/ *n* electrodo, *m*
electrolysis /ɪlɛk'trɒləsɪs/ *n* electrólisis, *f*
electrolyte /ɪ'lɛktrəˌlait/ *n* electrólito, *m*
electrolyze /ɪ'lɛktrəˌlaiz/ *vt* electrolizar
electrometer /ɪlɛk'trɒmɪtər/ *n* electrómetro, *m*
electromotive /ɪˌlɛktrə'moutɪv/ *a* electromotriz. **e. force,** fuerza electromotriz, *f*
electron /ɪ'lɛktrɒn/ *n* electrón, *m*
electroscope /ɪ'lɛktrəˌskoup/ *n* electroscopio, *m*
elegance /'ɛlɪgəns/ *n* elegancia, *f*
elegant /'ɛlɪgənt/ *a* elegante; bello
elegantly /'ɛlɪgəntli/ *adv* elegantemente, con elegancia
elegiac /ˌɛlɪ'dʒaiək/ *a* elegíaco
elegy /'ɛlɪdʒi/ *n* elegía, *f*
element /'ɛləmənt/ *n* elemento, *m;* factor, *m;* in-

gradiente, *m; Elec.* par, elemento, *m; Chem. Phys.* cuerpo simple, *m; pl* **elements,** rudimentos, *m pl,* nociones, *f pl;* (weather) intemperie, *f;* (Eucharist) el pan y el vino. **to be in one's e.,** estar en su elemento

elemental /ˌɛlə'mɛntl̩/ *a* elemental; rudimentario, lo elemental

elementariness /ˌɛlə'mɛntərinɪs/ *n* el carácter, elemental

elementary /ˌɛlə'mɛntəri/ *a* elemental; rudimentario; primario. **e. education,** enseñanza primaria, *f*

elephant /'ɛləfənt/ *n* elefante (-ta). **e. keeper** or **trainer,** naire, *m*

elephantiasis /ˌɛləfən'taiəsɪs/ *n* elefantíasis, *f*

elephantine /ˌɛlə'fæntin/ *a* elefantino

elevate /'ɛləˌveit/ *vt* (the Host) alzar; elevar; (the eyes, the voice) levantar; (honor) enaltecer

elevated /'ɛləˌveitɪd/ *a* noble, elevado, sublime; edificante; (drunk) achispado

elevation /ˌɛlə'veiʃən/ *n* elevación, *f;* enaltecimiento, *m;* (of style, thought) nobleza, sublimidad, *f;* (hill) eminencia, altura, *f*

elevator /'ɛləˌveitər/ *n* (lift) ascensor, *m;* (for grain, etc.) montacargas, *m*

elevator shaft caja, *f,* hueco pozo, *m*

eleven /ɪ'lɛvən/ *a* once. —*n* once, *m.* **It is e. o'clock,** Son las once

eleventh /ɪ'lɛvənθ/ *a* onceno, undécimo; (of month) (el) once; (of monarchs) once. —*n* onzavo, *m;* undécima parte, *f.* **at the e. hour,** *Fig.* a última hora. **Louis the E.,** Luis once (XI)

elf /ɛlf/ *n* elfo, duende, *m;* (child) trasgo, *m;* (dwarf) enano, *m*

elfin /'ɛlfɪn/ *a* de duendes; de hada

elicit /ɪ'lɪsɪt/ *vt* sacar; hacer contestar; hacer confesar; descubrir

elicitation /ɪˌlɪsɪ'tɛiʃən/ *n* descubrimiento, *m*

elide /ɪ'laid/ *vt* elidir

eligibility /ˌɛlɪdʒə'bɪlɪti/ *n* elegibilidad, *f*

eligible /'ɛlɪdʒəbəl/ *a* elegible; deseable

eliminate /ɪ'lɪməˌneit/ *vt* eliminar; quitar

elimination /ɪˌlɪmə'neiʃən/ *n* eliminación, *f*

eliminatory /ɪ'lɪmənəˌtɔri/ *a* eliminador

elision /ɪ'lɪʒən/ *n* elisión, *f*

elite /ɪ'lit/ *n* nata, flor, *f*

elixir /ɪ'lɪksər/ *n* elixir, *m*

Elizabethan /ɪˌlɪzə'biθən/ *a* de la época de la Reina Isabel I de Inglaterra

elk /ɛlk/ *n* ante, *m*

ell /ɛl/ *n* (measure) ana, *f*

ellipse /ɪ'lɪps/ *n Geom.* elipse, *f;* óvalo, *m*

ellipsis /ɪ'lɪpsɪs/ *n Gram.* elipsis, *f*

elliptic /ɪ'lɪptɪk/ *a Geom. Gram.* elíptico

elm /ɛlm/ *n* olmo, *m.* **e. grove,** olmeda, *f*

elocution /ˌɛlə'kyuʃən/ *n* elocución, *f;* (art of elocution) declamación, *f*

elocutionist /ˌɛlə'kyuʃənɪst/ *n* recitador (-ra), declamador (-ra)

elongate /ɪ'lɔŋgeit/ *vt* alargar; extender. —*vi* alargarse; extenderse. —*a* alargado; (of face) perfilado

elongation /ɪlɔŋ'geiʃən/ *n* alargamiento, *m;* prolongación, *f;* extensión, *f*

elope /ɪ'loup/ *vi* evadirse, huir; fugarse (con un amante)

elopement /ɪ'loupmənt/ *n* fuga, *f*

eloquence /'ɛləkwəns/ *n* elocuencia, *f*

eloquent /'ɛləkwənt/ *a* elocuente

eloquently /'ɛləkwəntli/ *adv* elocuentemente

else /ɛls/ *adv* (besides) más; (instead) otra cosa, más; (otherwise) si no, de otro modo. **anyone e.,** (cualquier) otra persona; alguien más. **Anything e.?** ¿Algo más? **everyone e.,** todos los demás. **everything e.,** todo lo demás. **nobody e.,** ningún otro, nadie más. **nothing e.,** nada más. **or e.,** o bien, de otro modo; si no. **someone e.,** otra persona, otro. **somewhere e.,** en otra parte. **There's nothing e. to do,** No hay nada más que hacer; No hay más remedio

elsewhere /'ɛlsˌwɛər/ *adv* a, or en, otra parte

elucidate /ɪ'lusɪˌdeit/ *vt* elucidar, aclarar

elucidation /ɪˌlusɪ'deiʃən/ *n* elucidación, aclaración, *f*

elucidatory /ɪ'lusɪdəˌtɔri/ *a* aclaratorio

elude /ɪ'lud/ *vt* eludir, evitar

elusive /ɪ'lusɪv/ *a* (of persons) esquivo; fugaz; difícil de comprender

elusiveness /ɪ'lusɪvnɪs/ *n* esquivez, *f;* fugacidad, *f*

Elysian /ɪ'lɪʒən/ *a* elíseo. **E. Fields,** campos elíseos, *m pl*

Elysium /ɪ'lɪʒiəm/ *n* elíseo, *m*

emaciate /ɪ'meiʃiˌeit/ *vt* extenuar, demacrar, enflaquecer

emaciated /ɪ'meiʃiˌeitɪd/ *a* extenuado, demacrado. **to become e.,** demacrarse

emaciation /ɪˌmeiʃi'eiʃən/ *n* demacración, emaciación, *f; Med.* depauperación, *f*

e-mail /'iˌmeil/ *n* correo electrónico, *m*

emanate /'ɛməˌneit/ *vi* emanar (de), proceder (de)

emanation /ˌɛmə'neiʃən/ *n* emanación, *f;* exhalación, *f*

emancipate /ɪ'mænsəˌpeit/ *vt* emancipar

emancipated /ɪ'mænsəˌpeitɪd/ *a* emancipado

emancipation /ɪˌmænsə'peiʃən/ *n* emancipación, *f*

emancipator /ɪ'mænsəˌpeitər/ *n* emancipador (-ra), libertador (-ra)

emancipatory /ɪ'mænsəpəˌtɔri/ *a* emancipador

emasculate /*a* ɪ'mæskyəlɪt; *v* -ˌleit/ *a* afeminado. —*vt* emascular; *Fig.* afeminar; mutilar

emasculation /ɪˌmæskyə'leiʃən/ *n* emasculación, *f*

embalm /ɛm'bɑm/ *vt* embalsamar; *Fig.* conservar el recuerdo de; perfumar

embalmer /ɛm'bɑmər/ *n* embalsamador, *m*

embalmment /ɛm'bɑmmənt/ *n* embalsamamiento, *m*

embankment /ɛm'bæŋkmənt/ *n* declive, *m;* ribera, *f;* terraplén, *m;* dique, *m;* (quay) muelle, *m*

embargo /ɛm'bɑrgou/ *n* embargo, *m, vt* embargar. **to put an e. on,** embargar. **to remove an e.,** sacar de embargo

embark /ɛm'bɑrk/ *vi* embarcarse; lanzarse (a). —*vt* embarcar

embarkation /ˌɛmbɑr'keiʃən/ *n* (of persons) embarcación, *f;* (of goods) embarque, *m*

embarrass /ɛm'bærəs/ *vt* impedir; (financially) apurar; (perplex) tener perplejo; (worry) preocupar; (confuse) desconcertar, turbar; (annoy) molestar

embarrassed /ɛm'bærəst/ *a* turbado

embarrassing /ɛm'bærəsɪŋ/ *a* embarazoso; desconcertante; molesto

embarrassingly /ɛm'bærəsɪŋli/ *adv* de un modo desconcertante; demasiado

embarrassment /ɛm'bærəsmənt/ *n* impedimento, *m;* (financial) apuro, *m;* (obligation) compromiso, *m;* (perplexity) perplejidad, *f;* (worry) preocupación, *f;* (confusion) turbación, *f*

embassy /'ɛmbəsi/ *n* embajada, *f*

embattled /ɛm'bætl̩d/ *a* en orden de batalla; *Herald.* almenado

embed /ɛm'bɛd/ *vt* empotrar, enclavar; fijar

embellish /ɛm'bɛlɪʃ/ *vt* embellecer; adornar

embellishment /ɛm'bɛlɪʃmənt/ *n* embellecimiento, *m;* adorno, *m*

ember /'ɛmbər/ *n* rescoldo, *m.* **E. days,** témporas, *f pl*

embezzle /ɛm'bɛzəl/ *vt* desfalcar

embezzlement /ɛm'bɛzəlmənt/ *n* desfalco, *m*

embezzler /ɛm'bɛzlər/ *n* desfalcador (-ra)

embitter /ɛm'bɪtər/ *vt Fig.* amargar; envenenar

embittering /ɛm'bɪtərɪŋ/ *a* amargo

embitterment /ɛm'bɪtərmənt/ *n* amargura, *f*

emblazon /ɛm'bleizən/ *vt* blasonar; *Fig.* ensalzar

emblem /'ɛmbləm/ *n* emblema, *m*

emblematic /ˌɛmblə'mætɪk/ *a* emblemático

embodiment /ɛm'bɒdimənt/ *n* incarnación, *f;* expresión, *f;* personificación, *f;* símbolo, *m;* síntesis, *f*

embody /ɛm'bɒdi/ *vt* encarnar; expresar; personificar; incorporar; contener; formular; sintetizar. **to be embodied in,** quedar plasmado en

embolden /ɛm'bouldən/ *vt* animar, dar valor (a)

embolism /'ɛmbəˌlɪzəm/ *n Med.* embolia, *f*

emboss /ɛm'bɔs/ *vt* repujar, abollonar; estampar en relieve

embossment /ɛm'bɔsmənt/ *n* abolladura, *f;* relieve, *m*

embrace /ɛm'breis/ *n* abrazo, *m.* —*vt* abrazar, dar un abrazo (a); (*Fig*.. seize) aprovechar; (accept) aceptar; adoptar; (engage in) dedicarse a; (comprise) incluir, abarcar; (comprehend) comprender. **They embraced,** Se abrazaron

embroider /ɛm'brɔidər/ *vt* bordar; embellecer; (a tale, etc.) exagerar; *vi* hacer bordado

embroiderer /ɛm'brɔidərər/ *n* bordador (-ra)

embroidery /ɛm'brɔidəri, -dri/ *n* bordado, *m;* labor, *f.* **e.-frame,** bastidor, *m.* **e. silk,** hilo de bordar, *m*

embroil /ɛm'brɔil/ *vt* enredar, embrollar; desordenar

embryo /'ɛmbri,ou/ *n* embrión, *m; Fig.* germen, *m.* —*a* embrionario

embryology /,ɛmbri'ɒlədʒi/ *n* embriología, *f*

embryonic /,ɛmbri'ɒnɪk/ *a* embrionario

emend /ɪ'mɛnd/ *vt* enmendar; corregir

emendation /,imən'deiʃən/ *n* enmienda, *f;* corrección, *f*

emerald /'ɛmərəld/ *n* esmeralda, *f, a* de color de esmeralda. **e. green,** verde esmeralda, *m*

emerge /ɪ'mɜrdʒ/ *vt* emerger; surgir; *Fig.* salir; aparecer

emergence /ɪ'mɜrdʒəns/ *n* emergencia, *f;* salida, *f;* aparición, *f*

emergency /ɪ'mɜrdʒənsi/ *n* urgencia, *f;* necesidad, *f;* emergencia, *f;* aprieto, *m.* **e. exit,** salida de urgencia, *f.* **e. port,** *Naut.* puerto de arribada, *m*

emergent /ɪ'mɜrdʒənt/ *a* emergente; que sale; naciente

emery /'ɛməri/ *n* esmeril, *m.* **to polish with e.,** esmerilar. **e.-paper,** papel de lija, *m*

emetic /ɪ'mɛtɪk/ *a* and *n* emético, vomitivo, *m.*

emigrant /'ɛmɪgrənt/ *a* emigrante. —*n* emigrante, *mf* emigrado, *m*

emigrate /'ɛmɪ,greit/ *vi* emigrar; *Inf.* trasladarse

emigration /,ɛmə'greiʃən/ *n* emigración, *f.* **e. officer,** oficial de emigración, *m*

eminence /'ɛmənəns/ *n* (hill) elevación, prominencia, *f;* eminencia (also as title), *f;* distinción, *f*

eminent /'ɛmənənt/ *a* distinguido, eminente; famoso, ilustre; notable; conspicuo

eminently /'ɛmənəntli/ *adv* eminentemente

emir /ə'mɪər/ *n* amir, *m*

emissary /'ɛmə,sɛri/ *n* emisario (-ia); embajador (-ra); agente, *m*

emission /ɪ'mɪʃən/ *n* emisión, *f*

emit /ɪ'mɪt/ *vt* despedir; exhalar; emitir

emollient /ɪ'mɒlyənt/ *a* emoliente, lenitivo. —*n* emoliente, *m*

emolument /ɪ'mɒlyəmənt/ *n* emolumento, *m*

emotion /ɪ'mouʃən/ *n* emoción, *f.* **to cause e.,** emocionar

emotional /ɪ'mouʃənḷ/ *a* emocional, sentimental; emocionante

emotionalism /ɪ'mouʃənḷ'ɪzəm/ *n* sentimentalismo, *m*

emotionalize /ɪ'mouʃənḷ,aiz/ *vt* considerar bajo un punto de vista sentimental

emotionally /ɪ'mouʃənḷi/ *adv* con emoción, sentimentalmente

emotionless /ɪ'mouʃənlɪs/ *a* sin emoción

emotive /ɪ'moutɪv/ *a* emotivo

emperor /'ɛmpərər/ *n* emperador, *m*

emphasis (on) /'ɛmfəsɪs/ *n* énfasis (en), *mf;* insistencia especial (en), especial atención (a), *f;* accentuación, *f*

emphasize /'ɛmfə,saiz/ *vt* subrayar, dar énfasis a, poner de relieve, hacer resaltar, dar importancia a; acentuar; insistir en, hacer hincapié (en)

emphatic /ɛm'fætɪk/ *a* enfático

emphatically /ɛm'fætɪkəli/ *adv* con énfasis

empire /'ɛmpaiᵊr/ *n* imperio, *m*

empiric /ɛm'pɪrɪk/ *a* empírico

empiricism /ɛm'pɪrə,sɪzəm/ *n* empirismo, *m*

employ /ɛm'plɔi/ *n* empleo, *m;* servicio, *m.* —*vt* emplear; ocupar; tomar; servirse de, usar. **How do you e. yourself?** ¿Cómo te ocupas? ¿Cómo pasas el tiempo?

employable /ɛm'plɔiəbəl/ *a* empleable; utilizable

employee /ɛm'plɔii/ *n* empleado (-da)

employer /ɛm'plɔiər/ *n* el, *m,* (*f,* la) que emplea; dueño (-ña), amo (-a); patrón (-ona)

employment /ɛm'plɔimənt/ *n* empleo, *m;* uso, *m;* ocupación, *f;* aprovechamiento, *m;* (post) puesto, cargo, *m;* (situation) colocación, *f.* **e. exchange,** bolsa de trabajo, *f*

emporium /ɛm'pɔriəm/ *n* emporio, *m;* (store) almacén, *m*

empower /ɛm'pauər/ *vt* autorizar; permitir; ayudar (a); dar el poder (para)

empress /'ɛmprɪs/ *n* emperatriz, *f*

emptiness /'ɛmptinɪs/ *n* vaciedad, *f;* futilidad, *f;* vacuidad, *f;* (verbosity) palabrería, *f*

empty /'ɛmpti/ *a* vacío; (of a house, etc.) deshabitado, desocupado; (deserted) desierto; (vain) vano, inútil; frívolo; (hungry) hambriento. —*n* envase vacío, *m.* —*vt* vaciar; descargar. —*vi* vaciarse; (river, etc.) desembocar, venir a morir en. **e.-handed,** con las manos vacías. **e.-headed,** casquivano

emptying /'ɛmptiɪŋ/ *n* vaciamiento, *m;* abandono, *m; pl* **emptyings,** heces de la cerveza, *f pl*

emu /'imyu/ *n* emu, *m*

emulate /'ɛmyə,leit/ *vt* emular

emulation /,ɛmyə'leiʃən/ *n* emulación, *f*

emulative /'ɛmyə,leitɪv/ *a* emulador

emulsify /ɪ'mʌlsɪfai/ *vt* emulsionar

emulsion /ɪ'mʌlʃən/ *n* emulsión, *f*

emulsive /ɪ'mʌlsɪv/ *a* emulsivo

enable /ɛn'eibəl/ *vt* (to) hacer capaz (de); ayudar (a); autorizar (para); permitir (de)

enact /ɛn'ækt/ *vt Law.* promulgar; decretar; (a part) hacer, desempeñar (un papel); (a play) representar; (happen) ocurrir, tener lugar

enaction /ɛn'ækʃən/ *n Law.* promulgación, *f*

enamel /ɪ'næməl/ *n* esmalte, *m, vt* esmaltar

enameler /ɪ'næmələr/ *n* esmaltador (-ra)

enameling /ɪ'næməlɪŋ/ *n* esmaltadura, *f*

enamor /ɪ'næmər/ *vt* enamorar. **to be enamored of,** estar enamorado de; estar aficionado a

encamp /ɛn'kæmp/ *vt* and *vi* acampar

encampment /ɛn'kæmpmənt/ *n* campamento, *m*

encase /ɛn'keis/ *vt* encajar; encerrar; (line) forrar

encasement /ɛn'keismənt/ *n* encaje, *m;* encierro, *m*

encephalitis /ɛn,sɛfə'laitɪs/ *n* encefalitis, *f.* **e. lethargica,** encefalitis letárgica, *f*

enchant /ɛn'tʃænt/ *vt* encantar, hechizar; fascinar, embelesar, deleitar

enchanter /ɛn'tʃæntər/ *n* encantador, *m*

enchanting /ɛn'tʃæntɪŋ/ *a* encantador, fascinador

enchantment /ɛn'tʃæntmənt/ *n* encantamiento, *m;* fascinación, *f,* encanto, deleite, *m*

enchantress /ɛn'tʃæntrɪs/ *n* bruja, *f; Fig.* mujer seductora, *f*

encircle /ɛn'sɜrkəl/ *vt* cercar; rodear; dar la vuelta (a)

enclose /ɛn'klouz/ *vt* cercar; meter dentro de; encerrar; (with a letter, etc.) incluir, adjuntar

enclosed /ɛn'klouzd/ *a* (of letters) adjunto

enclosure /ɛn'klouʒər/ *n* cercamiento, *m;* cercado, *m;* recinto, *m;* (wall) tapia, cerca, *f;* (with a letter) contenido adjunto, *m*

encomium /ɛn'koumiəm/ *n* encomio, *m*

encompass /ɛn'kʌmpəs/ *vt* cercar, rodear

encore /'ɑŋkɔr/ *n* repetición, *f, interj* ¡bis!

encounter /ɛn'kauntər/ *n* encuentro, *m;* combate, *m;* conflicto, *m;* lucha, *f.* —*vt* encontrar; atacar; tropezar con

encourage /ɛn'kɜrɪdʒ/ *vt* animar; alentar; estimular; incitar; ayudar; (approve) aprobar; (foster) fomentar

encouragement /ɛn'kɜrɪdʒmənt/ *n* ánimos, *m pl*; estímulo, incentivo, *m;* ayuda, *f;* (approval) aprobación, *f;* (promotion) fomento, *m*

encourager /ɛn'kɜrɪdʒər/ *n* instigador (-ra); ayudador (-ra); aprobador (-ra); fomentador (-ra)

encouraging /ɛn'kɜrɪdʒɪŋ/ *a* alentador; estimulante; fomentador; (favorable) halagüeño, favorable

encouragingly /ɛn'kɜrɪdʒɪŋli/ *adv* de un modo alentador; con aprobación

encroach /ɛn'kroutʃ/ *vi* usurpar; abusar (de); invadir; robar; (of sea, river) hurtar

encroaching /ɛn'kroutʃɪŋ/ *a* usurpador; invadiente

encroachment /ɛn'kroutʃmənt/ *n* usurpación, *f;* abuso, *m;* invasión, *f*

encrust /ɛn'krʌst/ *vt* encostrar; incrustar

encumber /ɛn'kʌmbər/ *vt* impedir, estorbar; llenar; (burden) cargar; (mortgage) hipotecar; (overwhelm) agobiar
encumbrance /ɛn'kʌmbrəns/ *n* impedimento, estorbo, *m;* gravamen, *m;* carga, *f;* (mortgage) hipoteca, *f*
encyclical /ɛn'sɪklɪkəl/ *n* encíclica, *f*
encyclopedia /ɛn,saiklə'pidiə/ *n* enciclopedia, *f*
encyclopedic /ɛn,saiklə'pidɪk/ *a* enciclopédico
encyclopedist /ɛn,saiklə'pidɪst/ *n* enciclopedista, *m*
end /ɛnd/ *n* fin, *m;* extremidad, *f;* extremo, *m;* conclusión, *f;* (point) punta, *f;* cabo, *m;* (district) barrio, *m;* cabeza, *f;* (death) muerte, *f;* (aim) objeto, intento, *m;* (purpose) propósito, *m;* (issue) resultado, *m;* (bit) fragmento, pedazo, *m;* (of a word) terminación, *f.* —*vi* terminar; acabar; concluir; cesar; (in) terminar en; resultar en; (with) terminar con. —*vt* terminar; acabar, dar fin a. **at an end,** terminado. **at the end,** al cabo (de); al extremo (de). **end of quotation,** fin de cita, final de la cita, *m.* **from end to end,** de un extremo a otro; de un cabo a otro. **in the end,** por fin, finalmente. **on end,** de pie, de cabeza, derecho; de punta; (of hair) erizado. **no end of,** un sinnúmero de. **to make both ends meet,** pasar con lo que se tiene. **to make an end of,** acabar con. **to put an end to,** poner fin a. **to the end that,** a fin de que, para que; con objeto de. **toward the end of,** (months, years, etc.) a fines de, a últimos de; hacia el fin de. **two hours on end,** dos horas seguidas. **endpaper,** guarda, *f*
endanger /ɛn'deindʒər/ *vt* arriesgar, poner en peligro
endear /ɛn'dɪər/ *vt* hacer querer
endearing /ɛn'dɪərɪŋ/ *a* que inspira cariño; atrayente; cariñoso
endearment /ɛn'dɪərmənt/ *n* cariño, amor, *m;* caricia, terneza, *f;* palabra de cariño, *f*
endeavor /ɛn'dɛvər/ *vi* procurar, intentar, hacer un esfuerzo. —*n* esfuerzo, *m,* tentativa, *f*
endemic /ɛn'dɛmɪk/ *a Med.* endémico
ending /'ɛndɪŋ/ *n* fin, *m;* conclusión, *f; Gram.* terminación, *f;* cesación, *f;* (climax) desenlace, *m*
endive /'ɛndaiv/ *n Bot.* escarola, *f*
endless /'ɛndlɪs/ *a* eterno; inacabable; infinito; sin fin; interminable; incesante
endlessly /'ɛndlɪsli/ *adv* sin fin; incesantemente; sin parar
endlessness /'ɛndlɪsnɪs/ *n* eternidad, *f;* infinidad, *f;* continuidad, *f*
endocrine /'ɛndəkrɪn/ *a* endocrino. —*n* secreción interna, *f*
endocrinology /,ɛndoukrə'nɒlədʒi/ *n* endocrinología, *f*
end-of-season /'ɛnd əv 'sizən/ *a* por final de temporada (e.g., *end-of-season reductions,* rebajos por final de temporada, *m pl. end-of-season sale,* liquidación por final de temporada, *f*)
endogenous /ɛn'dɒdʒənəs/ *a* endógeno
endorse /ɛn'dɔrs/ *vt Com.* endosar; garantizar; (uphold) apoyar; confirmar
endorsee /ɛndɔr'si/ *n* endosatario (-ia)
endorsement /ɛn'dɔrsmənt/ *n Com.* endoso, *m;* aval, *m,* garantía, *f;* corroboración, confirmación, *f*
endorser /ɛn'dɔrsər/ *n Com.* endosante, *m*
endow /ɛn'dau/ *vt* dotar; fundar; crear
endowment /ɛn'daumənt/ *n* dotación, *f;* fundación, *f;* creación, *f;* (mental) inteligencia, *f;* cualidad, *f,* don, *m.* **e. policy,** póliza dotal, *f*
endurable /ɛn'dʊrəbəl/ *a* sufrible, soportable; tolerable
endurance /ɛn'dʊrəns/ *n* aguante, *m;* resistencia, *f;* sufrimiento, *m;* tolerancia, *f;* paciencia, *f;* (lastingness) duración, continuación, *f.* **beyond e.,** intolerable, inaguantable. **e. test,** prueba de resistencia, *f*
endure /ɛn'dʊr/ *vt* soportar; tolerar, aguantar; sufrir; resistir. —*vi* sufrir; (last) durar, continuar
enduring /ɛn'dʊrɪŋ/ *a* permanente, perdurable; continuo; constante
enduringness /ɛn'dʊrɪŋnɪs/ *n* (lastingness) permanencia, *f;* paciencia, *f;* aguante, *m*
enema /'ɛnəmə/ *n* lavativa, enema, *f*
enemy /'ɛnəmi/ *n* enemigo (-ga); adversario (-ia); (in war) enemigo, *m.* —*a* del enemigo, enemigo. **to be one's own e.,** ser enemigo de sí mismo. **to become an e. of,** enemistarse con; hacerse enemigo de, volverse hostil a
energetic /,ɛnər'dʒɛtɪk/ *a* enérgico
energy /'ɛnərdʒi/ *n* energía, fuerza, *f,* vigor, *m*
enervate / *v* 'ɛnər,veit; *a* 'ɪnɜrvɪt/ *vt* enervar; debilitar. —*a* enervado
enervation /,ɛnər'veiʃən/ *n* enervación, *f;* debilitación, *f*
enfeeble /ɛn'fibəl/ *vt* debilitar
enfeeblement /ɛn'fibəlmənt/ *n* debilitación, *f,* desfallecimiento, *m*
enfold /ɛn'fould/ *vt* envolver; abrazar
enforce /ɛn'fɔrs/ *vt* (a law) poner en vigor; (impose) imponer a la fuerza; hacer cumplir; conseguir por fuerza; (demonstrate) demostrar
enforcement /ɛn'fɔrsmənt/ *n* (of a law) ejecución (de una ley), *f;* imposición a la fuerza, *f;* observación forzosa, *f*
enfranchise /ɛn'fræntʃaiz/ *vt* emancipar; conceder derechos civiles (a)
enfranchisement /ɛn'fræntʃaizmənt/ *n* emancipación, *f;* concesión de derechos civiles, *f*
engage /ɛn'geidʒ/ *vt* empeñar; contratar; tomar en alquiler; tomar a su servicio; (seats, etc.) reservar; (occupy) ocupar; (attention) atraer; (in) aplicarse a, dedicarse a; *Mil.* combatir con, librar batalla con; atacar; (of wheels) endentar con. —*vi* obligarse; dedicarse (a); tomar parte (en); (bet) apostar; *Mil.* librar batalla; (fight) venir a las manos. **to be engaged in,** traer entre manos, ocuparse en. **to become engaged,** prometerse. **Number engaged!** (telephone) ¡Están comunicando!
engaged /ɛn'geidʒd/ *a* ocupado; (betrothed) prometido; reservado
engagement /ɛn'geidʒmənt/ *n* obligación, *f;* compromiso, *m;* (date) cita, *f;* (betrothal) palabra de casamiento, *f;* (battle) combate, *m,* batalla, *f.* **I have an e. at two o'clock.** Tengo una cita a las dos
engagement gift regalo de esponsales, *m*
engaging /ɛn'geidʒɪŋ/ *a* simpático, atractivo
engagingly /ɛn'geidzɪŋli/ *adv* de un modo encantador
engender /ɛn'dʒɛndər/ *vt Fig.* engendrar; excitar
engine /'ɛndʒən/ *n* máquina, *f;* motor, *m;* (locomotive) locomotora, *f;* (pump) bomba, *f.* **to sit with one's back to the e.,** estar sentado de espaldas a la máquina (or locomotora). **e. builder,** constructor de máquinas, *m.* **e. driver,** maquinista, *mf.* **e. room,** cuarto de máquinas, *m.* **e. works,** taller de maquinaria, *m*
engineer /,ɛndʒə'nɪər/ *n* ingeniero, *m;* mecánico, *m.* —*vt Fig.* gestionar, arreglar. **civil e.,** ingeniero de caminos, canales y puertos, *m.* **Royal Engineers,** Cuerpo de Ingenieros, *m*
engineering /,ɛndʒə'nɪərɪŋ/ *n* ingeniería, *f; Fig.* manejo, *m.* —*a* de ingeniería
England /'ɪŋglənd/ Inglaterra, *f*
English /'ɪŋglɪʃ/ *a* inglés. —*n* (language) inglés, *m.* **in E. fashion,** a la inglesa. **to speak E.,** hablar inglés. **to speak plain E.,** hablar sin rodeos; hablar en cristiano. **E. Church,** iglesia anglicana, *f.* **E.-teacher,** maestro (-ra) de inglés. **English-translator,** traductor al inglés, *m*
English Channel, the el Canal de la Mancha
Englishman /'ɪŋglɪʃmən/ *n* inglés, *m*
Englishwoman /'ɪŋglɪʃ,wʊmən/ *n* inglesa, *f*
engrain /ɛn'grein/ *vt* inculcar
engrave /ɛn'greiv/ *vt* grabar; esculpir, cincelar; *Fig.* grabar
engraver /ɛn'greivər/ *n* grabador (-ra); (tool) cincel, *m*
engraving /ɛn'greivɪŋ/ *n* grabadura, *f;* (picture) grabado, *m.* **e. needle,** punta seca, *f*
engross /ɛn'grous/ *vt* (a document) poner en limpio; redactar; (absorb) absorber
engrossing /ɛn'grousɪŋ/ *a* absorbente
engulf /ɛn'gʌlf/ *vt* hundir, sumir, sumergir
enhance /ɛn'hæns/ *vt* realzar; intensificar; aumentar; mejorar
enhancement /ɛn'hænsmənt/ *n* realce, *m;* intensificación, *f;* aumento, *m;* mejoría, *f*

enigma /ə'nɪgmə/ *n* enigma, *m*
enigmatic /ˌɛnɪg'mætɪk/ *a* enigmático
enjoin /ɛn'dʒɔin/ *vt* imponer; ordenar, mandar; encargar
enjoy /ɛn'dʒɔi/ *vt* disfrutar; gustar de; gozar de; poseer, tener. **to e. oneself,** recrearse, regocijarse; (amuse oneself) divertirse; entretenerse; pasarlo bien. **Did you e. yourself?** ¿Lo pasaste bien?
enjoyable /ɛn'dʒɔiəbəl/ *a* agradable; divertido, entretenido
enjoyableness /ɛn'dʒɔiəbəlnɪs/ *n* lo agradable; lo divertido
enjoyably /ɛn'dʒɔiəbli/ *adv* de un modo muy agradable
enjoyer /ɛn'dʒɔiər/ *n* el, *m*, (*f*, la) que disfruta; poseedor (-ra); (amateur) aficionado (-da)
enjoyment /ɛn'dʒɔimənt/ *n* posesión, *f;* goce, disfruto, *m;* (pleasure) placer, *m;* aprovechamiento, *m;* utilización, *f;* (satisfaction) satisfacción, *f*
enlarge /ɛn'lɑrdʒ/ *vt* agrandar; aumentar; ensanchar; extender; *Photo.* ampliar; dilatar; (the mind, etc.) ensanchar. —*vi* agrandarse; ensancharse; aumentarse; extenderse. **an enlarged heart,** dilatación del corazón, *f.* **to e. upon,** tratar detalladamente, explayarse en
enlargement /ɛn'lɑrdʒmənt/ *n* engrandecimiento, *m;* ensanchamiento, *m; Photo.* ampliación, *f; Med.* dilatación, *f;* aumento, *m;* amplificación, *f;* (of a town, etc.) ensanche, *m*
enlarger /ɛn'lɑrdʒər/ *n Photo.* ampliadora, *f*
enlighten /ɛn'laitn̩/ *vt* iluminar; aclarar; informar
enlightened /ɛn'laitn̩d/ *a* culto; ilustrado; inteligente
enlightening /ɛn'laitn̩ɪŋ/ *a* instructivo
enlightenment /ɛn'laitn̩mənt/ *n* ilustración, *f;* cultura, civilización, *f*
enlist /ɛn'lɪst/ *vt Mil.* reclutar; alistar; obtener, conseguir. —*vi Mil.* sentar plaza, sentar plaza de soldado; engancharse; alistarse
enlistment /ɛn'lɪstmənt/ *n Mil.* enganche, *m;* reclutamiento, *m;* alistamiento, *m*
enliven /ɛn'laivən/ *vt* animar; avivar; alegrar
enmity /'ɛnmɪti/ *n* enemistad, enemiga, hostilidad, *f*
ennoble /ɛn'noubəl/ *vt* ennoblecer; ilustrar
ennui /ɑn'wi/ *n* tedio, *m;* aburrimiento, *m*
enormity /ɪ'nɔrmɪti/ *n* enormidad, *f;* gravedad, *f;* atrocidad, *f*
enormous /ɪ'nɔrməs/ *a* enorme, colosal
enormously /ɪ'nɔrməsli/ *adv* enormemente
enormousness /ɪ'nɔrməsnɪs/ *n* enormidad, *f*
enough /ɪ'nʌf/ *a* bastante, suficiente. —*n* lo bastante, lo suficiente. —*adv* bastante; suficientemente. —*interj* ¡bastante! ¡basta! **to be e.,** ser suficiente; bastar. **two are enough,** con dos tenemos bastante, con dos tengo bastante
enquire /ɛn'kwaiᵊr/. See **inquire**
enrage /ɛn'reidʒ/ *vt* enfurecer, hacer furioso; *Inf.* hacer rabiar
enraged /ɛn'reidʒd/ *a* furioso
enrapture /ɛn'ræptʃər/ *vt* entusiasmar, extasiar; (intoxicate) embriagar; (charm) encantar, deleitar
enrich /ɛn'rɪtʃ/ *vt* enriquecer; (adorn) adornar, embellecer; (the land) fertilizar
enrichment /ɛn'rɪtʃmənt/ *n* enriquecimiento, *m;* embellecimiento, *m;* (of the land) abono, *m*
enroll /ɛn'roul/ *vt* alistar; matricular; inscribir; (perpetuate) inmortalizar
enrollment /ɛn'roulmənt/ *n* alistamiento, *m;* inscripción, *f*
ensconce /ɛn'skɒns/ *vt* acomodar, colocar; ocultar
ensemble /ɑn'sɑmbəl/ *n* conjunto, *m*
enshrine /ɛn'ʃrain/ *vt* poner en sagrario; guardar con cuidado; *Fig.* guardar como una reliquia
enshroud /ɛn'ʃraud/ *vt* amortajar; envolver; esconder
ensign /'ɛnsən/ *n* (badge) insignia, *f;* (flag) enseña, bandera, *f;* pabellón, *m;* bandera de popa, *f; Mil.* alférez, *m;* (U.S.A. navy) subteniente, *m*
enslave /ɛn'sleiv/ *vt* esclavizar; *Fig.* dominar
enslavement /ɛn'sleivmənt/ *n* esclavitud, *f*
ensue /ɛn'su/ *vt* conseguir. —*vi* resultar; suceder, sobrevenir
ensuing /ɛn'suɪŋ/ *a* (next) próximo; (resulting) resultante
ensure /ɛn'ʃʊr/ *vt* asegurar; estar seguro de que; garantizar
entail /ɛn'teil/ *vt* traer consigo, acarrear; *Law.* vincular; *n Law.* vinculación, *f;* herencia, *f*
entangle /ɛn'tæŋgəl/ *vt* enredar; coger; *Fig.* embrollar
entanglement /ɛn'tæŋgəlmənt/ *n* enredo, *m;* complicación, *f;* intriga, *f;* (*Mil.* of wire) alambrada, *f*
entangling /ɛn'tæŋglɪŋ/ *a* enmarañador (e.g., *entangling alliances,* alianzas enmarañadoras, *f pl*)
enter /'ɛntər/ *vt* entrar en; penetrar; (of thoughts) ocurrirse; (join) ingresar en; entrar en; (become a member of) hacerse miembro de; (enroll) alistarse; (a university) matricularse; (inscribe) inscribir, poner en la lista; (note) anotar, apuntar; (a protest) hacer constar; (make) hacer; formular. —*vi* entrar; *Theat.* salir (a la escena); penetrar; *Com.* anotarse. **to e. for,** *vt* inscribir. —*vi* inscribirse, tomar parte en. **to e. into,** entrar en; formar parte de; (conversation) entablar (conversación); (negotiations) iniciar; considerar; (another's emotion) acompañar en; (an agreement, etc.) hacer; (sign) firmar; (bind oneself) obligarse a, comprometerse a, tomar parte en; (undertake) emprender; empezar; adoptar. **to e. up,** anotar; poner en la lista; registrar. **to e. upon,** comenzar, emprender; tomar posesión de; encargarse de, asumir; inaugurar, dar principio a
enteric /ɛn'tɛrɪk/ *a* entérico
enteritis /ˌɛntə'raitɪs/ *n* enteritis, *f*
enterprise /'ɛntərˌpraiz/ *n* empresa, *f;* aventura, *f;* (spirit) iniciativa, *f,* empuje, *m*
enterprising /'ɛntərˌpraizɪŋ/ *a* emprendedor, acometedor; de mucha iniciativa
entertain /ˌɛntər'tein/ *vt* (an idea, etc.) acariciar, abrigar; considerar; (as a guest) agasajar, obsequiar; recibir en casa; (amuse) divertir, entretener. —*vi* ser hospitalario; tener invitados en casa; dar fiestas
entertaining /ˌɛntər'teinɪŋ/ *a* entretenido, divertido
entertainingly /ˌɛntər'teinɪŋli/ *adv* entretenidamente; (witty) graciosamente
entertainment /ˌɛntər'teinmənt/ *n* convite, *m;* fiesta, *f;* reunión, *f;* banquete, *m;* (hospitality) hospitalidad, *f;* (amusement) diversión, *f,* entretenimiento, *m;* espectáculo, *m;* función, *f;* concierto, *m*
enthrall /ɛn'θrɔl/ *vt* seducir, atraer, encantar; absorber, captar la atención
enthralling /ɛn'θrɔlɪŋ/ *a* absorbente; atrayente, halagüeño
enthrallment /ɛn'θrɔlmənt/ *n* absorción, *f;* atracción, *f*
enthrone /ɛn'θroun/ *vt* entronizar
enthronement /ɛn'θrounmənt/ *n* entronización, *f*
enthusiasm /ɛn'θuziˌæzəm/ *n* entusiasmo, *m*
enthusiast /ɛn'θuziˌæst, -ɪst/ *n* entusiasta, *mf*
enthusiastic /ɛnˌθuzi'æstɪk/ *a* entusiasta. **to make e.,** entusiasmar. **to be e.,** entusiasmarse
enthusiastically /ɛnˌθuzi'æstɪkəli/ *adv* con entusiasmo
entice /ɛn'tais/ *vt* tentar, inducir; atraer, seducir
enticement /ɛn'taismənt/ *n* tentación, *f;* atractivo, *m*
enticing /ɛn'taisɪŋ/ *a* seduciente, atrayente; halagüeño
entire /ɛn'taiᵊr/ *a* entero; completo; intacto; absoluto; perfecto; íntegro; total
entirely /ɛn'taiᵊrli/ *adv* enteramente; completamente; integralmente; totalmente
entirety /ɛn'taiᵊrti/ *n* totalidad, *f;* integridad, *f;* todo, *m*
entitle /ɛn'taitl̩/ *vt* (designate) intitular; dar derecho (a); autorizar. **to be entitled to,** tener derecho a
entity /'ɛntɪti/ *n* entidad, *f;* ente, ser, *m*
entombment /ɛn'tummənt/ *n* sepultura, *f,* entierro, *m*
entomological /ˌɛntəmə'lɒdʒɪkəl/ *a* entomológico
entomologist /ˌɛntə'mɒlədʒɪst/ *n* entomólogo, *m*
entomology /ˌɛntə'mɒlədʒi/ *n* entomología, *f*
entourage /ˌɑntʊ'rɑʒ/ *n* séquito, *m;* (environment) medio ambiente, *m*
entr'acte /ɑn'trækt/ *n* entreacto, *m*

entrails /'ɛntreilz/ *n* entrañas, tripas, *f pl,* intestinos, *m pl*
entrain /ɛn'trein/ *vi* tomar el tren, subir al tren
entrance /ɛn'trəns/ *n* entrada, *f; Theat.* salida (a la escena), *f;* (into a profession, etc.) ingreso, *m;* alistamiento, *m;* (beginning) principio, *m;* (door) puerta, *f;* (porch) portal, *m;* (of a cave) boca, *f.* **e. fee,** cuota de entrada, *f.* **e. hall,** zaguán, *m.* **e. money,** entrada, *f*
entrance /ɛn'træns/ *vt Fig.* encantar, fascinar; ecstasiar
entrancing /ɛn'trænsɪŋ/ *a* encantador
entreat /ɛn'trit/ *vt* suplicar, implorar, rogar
entreating /ɛn'tritɪŋ/ *a* suplicante, implorante
entreatingly /ɛn'tritɪŋli/ *adv* de un modo suplicante; insistentemente
entreaty /ɛn'triti/ *n* súplica, instancia, *f,* ruego, *m*
entree /'ɑntrei/ *n* entrada, *f*
entrench /ɛn'trɛntʃ/ *vt* atrincherar
entrenchment /ɛn'trɛntʃmənt/ *n* atrincheramiento, *m; Mil.* parapeto, *m;* (encroachment) invasión, *f*
entresol /'ɛntər,sɒl/ *n* entresuelo, *m*
entrust /ɛn'trʌst/ *vt* confiar a (or en), encomendar a; encargar
entry /'ɛntri/ *n* entrada, *f;* (passage) callejuela, *f;* (note) inscripción, apuntación, *f; Com.* partida, *f;* (registration) registro, *m.* **double e.,** *Com.* partida doble, *f.* **single e.,** *Com.* partida simple, *f*
entwine /ɛn'twain/ *vt* entrelazar, entretejer
enumerate /ɪ'numə,reit/ *vt* enumerar
enumeration /ɪ,numə'reiʃən/ *n* enumeración, *f*
enumerative /ɪ'numə,reitɪv/ *a* enumerativo
enunciate /ɪ'nʌnsi,eit/ *vt* enunciar; articular
enunciation /ɪ,nʌnsi'eiʃən/ *n* enunciación, *f;* articulación, *f*
envelop /ɛn'vɛləp/ *vt* envolver, cubrir
envelope /'ɛnvə,loup/ *n* sobre, *m*
envelopment /ɛn'vɛləpmənt/ *n* envolvimiento, *m;* cubierta, *f*
enviable /'ɛnviəbəl/ *a* envidiable
envious /'ɛnviəs/ *a* envidioso. **an e. look,** una mirada de envidia
enviously /'ɛnviəsli/ *adv* con envidia
environment /ɛn'vairənmənt/ *n* medio ambiente, *m*
environs /ɛn'vairənz/ *n* inmediaciones, *f pl,* alrededores, *m pl*
envisage /ɛn'vɪzɪdʒ/ *vt* hacer frente a; contemplar; imaginar
envoy /'ɛnvɔi/ *n* enviado, *m;* mensajero (-ra)
envy /'ɛnvi/ *n* envidia, *f, vt* envidiar
enzyme /'ɛnzaim/ *n* fermento, *m,* enzima, *f*
eon /'iən/ *n* eón, *m*
epaulette /'ɛpə,lɛt/ *n* hombrera, *f*
ephemeral /ɪ'fɛmərəl/ *a* efímero; *Fig.* fugaz, pasajero
Ephesus /'ɛfəsəs/ Efiso, *m*
Ephraim /'ifriəm/ Efraín, *m*
Ephraimite /'ifriə,mait/ *n* and *a* efraíta, *mf*
epic /'ɛpɪk/ *a* épico. —*n* epopeya, *f*
epicenter /'ɛpə,sɛntər/ *n* epicentro, *m*
epicure /'ɛpɪ,kyʊr/ *n* epicúreo (-ea)
epicurean /,ɛpɪkyʊ'riən/ *a* epicúreo
Epicureanism /,ɛpɪkyʊ'riə,nɪzəm/ *n* epicureísmo, *m*
epidemic /,ɛpɪ'dɛmɪk/ *n* epidemia, *f;* plaga, *f, a* epidémico
epidermis /,ɛpɪ'dɜrmɪs/ *n* epidermis, *f*
epiglottis /,ɛpɪ'glɒtɪs/ *n* epiglotis, *f*
epigram /'ɛpɪ,græm/ *n* epigrama, *m*
epigrammatic /,ɛpɪgrə'mætɪk/ *a* epigramático
epigraph /'ɛpɪ,græf/ *n* epígrafe, *m*
epigraphy /ɪ'pɪgrəfi/ *n* epigrafía, *f*
epilepsy /'ɛpə,lɛpsi/ *n* epilepsia, alferecía, *f*
epileptic /,ɛpə'lɛptɪk/ *a* and *n* epiléptico (-ca). **e. fit,** ataque epiléptico, *m.* **e. aura,** aura epiléptica, *f*
epilogue /'ɛpə,lɔg/ *n* epílogo, *m*
epiphany /ɪ'pɪfəni/ *n* epifanía, *f*
Epirus /ɪ'pairəs/ Epiro, *m*
episcopacy /ɪ'pɪskəpəsi/ *n* episcopado, *m*
episcopal /ɪ'pɪskəpəl/ *a* episcopal
episcopalianism /ɪ,pɪskə'peilyə,nɪzəm/ *n* episcopalismo, *m*
episode /'ɛpə,soud/ *n* suceso, incidente, *m; Lit.* episodio, *m*
episodic /,ɛpə'sɒdɪk/ *a* episódico
epistle /ɪ'pɪsəl/ *n* epístola, *f*
epistolary /ɪ'pɪstl,ɛri/ *a* epistolar
epitaph /'ɛpɪ,tæf/ *n* epitafio, *m*
epithet /'ɛpə,θɛt/ *n* epíteto, *m*
epitome /ɪ'pɪtəmi/ *n* epítome, *m*
epitomize /ɪ'pɪtə,maiz/ *vt* resumir, abreviar
epoch /'ɛpək/ *n* época, edad, *f*
epode /'ɛpoud/ *n* épodo, *m*
Epsom salts /'ɛpsəm/ *n* sal de la Higuera, *f*
equability /,ɛkwə'bɪlɪti/ *n* igualdad (de ánimo), ecuanimidad, *f;* uniformidad, *f*
equable /'ɛkwəbəl/ *a* igual, ecuánime; uniforme
equably /'ɛkwəbli/ *adv* con ecuanimidad; igualmente; uniformemente
equal /'ikwəl/ *a* igual; uniforme; imparcial; equitativo, justo. —*n* igual, *mf.* —*vt* ser igual a; equivaler a; igualar; *Sports.* empatar. **to be e. to,** (of persons) ser capaz de; servir para; atreverse a; (circumstances) estar al nivel de; sentirse con fuerzas para. **without e.,** sin igual; (of beauty, etc.) sin par. **e. sign,** *Math.* igual, *m*
equality /ɪ'kwɒlɪti/ *n* igualdad, *f;* uniformidad, *f*
equalization /,ikwələ'zeiʃən/ *n* igualación, *f*
equalize /'ikwə,laiz/ *vt* igualar
equalizing /'ikwə,laizɪŋ/ *a* igualador; compensador
equally /'ikwəli/ *adv* igualmente; imparcialmente
equanimity /,ikwə'nɪmɪti/ *n* ecuanimidad, *f*
equation /ɪ'kweiʒən/ *n* ecuación, *f*
equator /ɪ'kweitər/ *n* ecuador, *m*
equatorial /,ikwə'tɔriəl/ *a* ecuatorial
equerry /'ɛkwəri/ *n* caballerizo del rey, *m*
equestrian /ɪ'kwɛstriən/ *a* ecuestre
equiangular /,ikwi'æŋgyələr/ *a* equiángulo
equidistance /,ikwɪ'dɪstəns/ *n* equidistancia, *f*
equidistant /,ikwɪ'dɪstənt/ *a* equidistante
equilateral /,ikwə'lætərəl/ *a* equilátero
equilibrist /ɪ'kwɪləbrɪst/ *n* equilibrista, *mf*
equilibrium /,ikwə'lɪbriəm/ *n* equilibrio, *m*
equine /'ikwain/ *a* equino; hípico; de caballo
equinoctial /,ikwə'nɒkʃəl/ *a* equinoccial. **e. gale,** tempestad equinoccial, *f*
equinox /'ikwə,nɒks/ *n* equinoccio, *m*
equip /ɪ'kwɪp/ *vt* proveer; pertrechar; equipar
equipage /'ɛkwəpɪdʒ/ *n* (train) séquito, tren, *m;* (carriage) carruaje, *m*
equipment /ɪ'kwɪpmənt/ *n* habilitación, *f;* equipo, *m;* pertrechos, *m pl;* material, *m;* aparatos, *m pl;* armamento, *m*
equitable /'ɛkwɪtəbəl/ *a* equitativo, justo
equitableness /'ɛkwɪtəbəlnɪs/ *n* equidad, justicia, *f*
equitably /'ɛkwɪtəbli/ *adv* equitativamente, con justicia
equity /'ɛkwɪti/ *n* equidad, *f;* imparcialidad, justicia, *f*
equivalence /ɪ'kwɪvələns/ *n* equivalencia, *f*
equivalent /ɪ'kwɪvələnt/ *a* and *n* equivalente, *m.* **to be e. to,** equivaler a
equivocal /ɪ'kwɪvəkəl/ *a* equívoco, ambiguo
equivocally /ɪ'kwɪvəkəli/ *adv* equivocadamente
equivocate /ɪ'kwɪvə,keit/ *vi* usar frases equívocas, emplear equívocos, tergiversar
equivocation /ɪ,kwɪvə'keiʃən/ *n* equívoco, *m*
era /'ɪərə, 'ɛrə/ *n* época, era, *f*
eradiation /ɪ,reidi'eiʃən/ *n* irradiación, *f*
eradicable /ɪ'rædɪkəbəl/ *a* erradicable
eradicate /ɪ'rædɪ,keit/ *vt* erradicar; destruir, extirpar; suprimir
eradication /ɪ,rædɪ'keiʃən/ *n* erradicación, *f;* destrucción, *f;* supresión, *f*
erasable /ɪ'reisəbəl/ *a* borrable
erase /ɪ'reis/ *vt* borrar; tachar
eraser /ɪ'reisər/ *n* goma de borrar, *f.* **ink e.,** goma para tinta, *f*
erasure /ɪ'reiʃər/ *n* borradura, *f;* tachón, *m*
ere /ɛər/ *conjunc* antes de (que), antes de. —*prep* antes de
erect /ɪ'rɛkt/ *a* (upright) derecho; erguido; vertical; (uplifted) levantado; (standing) de pie; (firm) firme,

resuelto; (alert) vigilante. —*vt* (build) edificar, construir; instalar; (raise) alzar; convertir

erectile /ɪ'rɛktḷ/ *a* eréctil

erection /ɪ'rɛkʃən/ *n* erección, *f;* construcción, edificación, *f;* (building) edificio, *m;* (structure) estructura, *f;* instalación, *f;* (assembling) montaje, *m*

erectly /ɪ'rɛktli/ *adv* derecho

erectness /ɪ'rɛktnɪs/ *n* derechura, *f*

erg /ɜrg/ *n Phys.* ergio, *m*

ermine /'ɜrmɪn/ *n* armiño, *m, a* de armiño

erode /ɪ'roud/ *vt* corroer; comer; *Geol.* denudar

erosion /ɪ'rouʒən/ *n* erosión, *f*

erotic /ɪ'rɒtɪk/ *a* erótico

err /ɜr, ɛr/ *vi* desviarse; errar; desacertar; pecar

errand /'ɛrənd/ *n* mensaje, recado, *m;* encargo, *m;* misión, *f.* **e.-boy,** mandadero, mensajero, motril, mozo, recadero, *m*

errant /'ɛrənt/ *a* errante; (of knights) andante

erratic /ɪ'rætɪk/ *a* (of conduct) excéntrico, irresponsable; (of thoughts, etc.) errante; *Med.* errático

erratum /ɪ'rɑtəm/ *n* errata, *f*

erring /'ɛrɪŋ/ *a* extraviado; pecaminoso

erroneous /ə'rouniəs/ *a* erróneo; falso; injusto

erroneously /ə'rouniəsli/ *adv* erróneamente; falsamente; injustamente

erroneousness /ə'rouniəsnɪs/ *n* falsedad, *f*

error /'ɛrər/ *n* error, *m;* equivocación, *f,* desacierto, *m;* (sin) pecado, *m.* **in e.,** por equivocación

erudite /'ɛryʊˌdait/ *a* erudito; sabio

erudition /ˌɛryʊ'dɪʃən/ *n* erudición, *f*

erupt /ɪ'rʌpt/ *vi* entrar en erupción, estar en erupción; *Fig.* salir con fuerza

eruption /ɪ'rʌpʃən/ *n* erupción, *f*

erysipelas /ˌɛrə'sɪpələs/ *n* erisipela, *f*

escalade /ˌɛskə'leid/ *n* escalada, *f, vt* escalar

escalator /'ɛskəˌleitər/ *n* escalera automática, escalera eléctrica, escalera mecánica, escalera móvil, escalera rodante, *f*

escapable /ɪ'skeipəbəl/ *a* evitable, eludible

escapade /'ɛskəˌpeid/ *n* escapada, *f;* aventura, *f*

escape /ɪ'skeip/ *n* huida, fuga, *f;* evasión, evitación, *f;* (leak) escape, *m; Fig.* salida, *f.* —*vt* eludir, evitar; (of cries, groans, etc.) dar, salir de. —*vi* huir, fugarse, escapar; (slip away) escurrirse; librarse; salvarse; (leak) escaparse. **His name escapes me,** Se me escapa (or se me olvida) su nombre. **to e. notice,** pasar inadvertido. **to have a narrow e.,** salvarse en una tabla. **to e. from,** escaparse de; librarse de; huir de

escape clause *n* cláusula de salvaguardia, *f*

escaping /ɪ'skeipɪŋ/ *a* fugitivo

escarpment /ɪ'skɑrpmənt/ *n* escarpa, *f*

eschew /ɛs'tʃu/ *vt* evitar

eschewal /ɛs'tʃuəl/ *n* evitación, *f*

escort /*n* 'ɛskɔrt; *v* ɪ'skɔrt/ *n Mil.* escolta, *f;* (of ships) convoy, *m;* acompañamiento, *m;* acompañante, *m.* —*vt Mil.* escoltar; (of ships) convoyar; acompañar

escritoire /ˌɛskrɪ'twɑr/ *n* escritorio, *m*

escudo /ɛ'skudou/ *n* escudo, *m*

escutcheon /ɪ'skʌtʃən/ *n* escudo, blasón, *m*

Eskimo /'ɛskəˌmou/ *a* and *n* esquimal *mf*

esoteric /ˌɛsə'tɛrɪk/ *a* esotérico

esparto /ɪ'spɑrtou/ *n* esparto, *m*

especial /ɪ'spɛʃəl/ *a* especial; particular

especially /ɪ'spɛʃəli/ *adv* especialmente; ante todo; en particular

Esperantist /ˌɛspə'rɑntɪst/ *n* esperantista, *mf*

Esperanto /ˌɛspə'rɑntou/ *n* esperanto, *m*

espionage /'ɛspiəˌnɑʒ/ *n* espionaje, *m*

esplanade /'ɛspləˌnɑd/ *n Mil.* explanada, *f;* bulevar, paseo, *m*

espousal /ɪ'spauzəl/ *n* desposorio, *m; Fig.* adhesión (a una causa), *f*

espouse /ɪ'spauz/ *vt* desposar; (a cause) abrazar; defender

espy /ɪ'spai/ *vt* divisar, ver, observar

esquire /'ɛskwaiər/ *n* escudero, *m;* (landowner) hacendado, *m;* (as a title) don (before given name)

essay /'ɛsei; *v* ɛ'sei/ *n* tentativa, *f; Lit.* ensayo, *m, vt* probar; procurar; (on an examination) tema, *m.* **essay question,** tema, *m*

essayist /'ɛseiɪst/ *n* ensayista, *mf*

essence /'ɛsəns/ *n* esencia, *f*

essential /ə'sɛntʃəl/ *a* esencial; indispensable, imprescindible; intrínseco. —*n* artículo de primera necesidad, *m;* elemento necesario, *m*

essentially /ə'sɛntʃəli/ *adv* esencialmente

establish /ɪ'stæblɪʃ/ *vt* establecer; fundar; crear; erigir; (constitute) constituir; (order) disponer; (prove) demostrar, probar; (take root, settle) arraigarse

established /ɪ'stæblɪʃt/ *a* establecido; arraigado; (proved) demostrado; bien conocido; (author) consagrado; (of churches) oficial

establishment /ɪ'stæblɪʃmənt/ *n* establecimiento, *m;* fundación, *f;* creación, *f;* institución, *f;* (building) erección, *f;* arraigo, *m;* (house) casa, *f;* (church) iglesia oficial, *f;* demostración, *f;* reconocimiento, *m*

estate /ɪ'steit/ *n* estado, *m;* clase, *f;* condición, *f;* (land) propiedad, finca, *f;* fortuna, *f;* (inheritance) heredad, *f,* patrimonio, *m; Law.* bienes, *m pl.* **personal e.,** bienes muebles, *m pl;* fortuna personal, *f.* **third e.,** estado llano, *m.* **e. agent,** agente de fincas, *m;* agente de casas, *m*

esteem /ɪ'stim/ *n* estima, *f,* aprecio, *m;* consideración, *f, vt* estimar, apreciar; creer, juzgar

ester /'ɛstər/ *n Chem.* éster, *m*

esthete /'ɛsθit/ *n* estético, *m*

esthetic /ɛs'θɛtɪk/ *a* estético

esthetically /ɛs'θɛtɪkli/ *adv* estéticamente

esthetics /ɛs'θɛtɪks/ *n* estética, *f*

estimable /'ɛstəməbəl/ *a* apreciable, estimable

estimableness /'ɛstəməbəlnɪs/ *n* estimabilidad, *f*

estimate /*n* 'ɛstəˌmɪt; *v* -ˌmeit/ *n* estimación, tasa, *f;* cálculos, *m pl;* apreciación, *f;* opinión, *f; pl* **estimates,** presupuesto, *m.* —*vt* (value) avalorar, tasar; calcular, computar; considerar. —*vi* hacer un presupuesto

estimation /ˌɛstə'meiʃən/ *n* opinión, *f;* cálculo, cómputo, *m;* (esteem) aprecio, *m,* estima, *f*

Estonian /ɛ'stouniən/ *a* and *n* estonio (-ia); (language) estonio, *m*

estrange /ɪ'streindʒ/ *vt* enajenar; ofender

estrangement /ɪ'streindʒmənt/ *n* enajenación, alienación, *f*

estuary /'ɛstʃuˌɛri/ *n* estuario, *m,* ría, *f*

etcetera /ɛt'sɛtərə/ etcétera. (Used as noun, *f*)

etch /ɛtʃ/ *vt* grabar al agua fuerte

etcher /'ɛtʃər/ *n* grabador (-ra) al agua fuerte

etching /'ɛtʃɪŋ/ *n* aguafuerte, *f;* grabado al agua fuerte, *m.* **e. needle,** punta seca, aguja de grabador, *f*

eternal /ɪ'tɜrnḷ/ *a* eterno; incesante. —*n* (E.) el Eterno

eternally /ɪ'tɜrnḷi/ *adv* eternamente

eternity /ɪ'tɜrnɪti/ *n* eternidad, *f*

eternize /ɪ'tɜrnaiz/ *vt* eternizar

ether /'iθər/ *n* éter, *m*

ethereal /ɪ'θɪəriəl/ *a* etéreo; vaporoso, aéreo

etheric /ɪ'θɛrɪk/ *a* etéreo

etherize /'iθəˌraiz/ *vt* eterizar

ethical /'ɛθɪkəl/ *a* ético, moral; *n* droga de ordenanza, *f*

ethics /'ɛθɪks/ *n* ética, *f;* (filosofía) moral, *f*

Ethiopia /ˌiθi'oupiə/ Etiopia, *f*

ethnic /'ɛθnɪk/ *a* étnico

ethnographic /ˌɛθnou'græfɪk/ *a* etnográfico

ethnography /ɛθ'nɒgrəfi/ *n* etnografía, *f*

ethnologist /ɛθ'nɒlədʒɪst/ *n* etnólogo, *m*

ethnology /ɛθ'nɒlədʒi/ *n* etnología, *f*

ethyl /'ɛθəl/ *n Chem.* etilo, *m*

ethylene /'ɛθəˌlin/ *n Chem.* etileno, *m*

etiquette /'ɛtɪkɪt/ *n* etiqueta, *f*

Etna, Mount /'ɛtnə/ el Etna

Eton coat /'itṇ/ *n* chaquetilla, *f*

Eton collar *n* cuello de colegial, *m*

Eton crop *n* pelo a la garçonne, *m*

Etruscan /ɪ'trʌskən/ *a* and *n* etrusco (-ca)

etymological /ˌɛtəmə'lɒdʒɪkəl/ *a* etimológico

etymologist /ˌɛtə'mɒlədʒɪst/ *n* etimólogo, *m,* etimologista, *mf*

etymology /ˌɛtə'mɒlədʒi/ *n* etimología, *f*

eucalyptus /ˌyukə'lɪptəs/ *n* eucalipto, *m*

Eucharist /'yukərɪst/ *n* Eucaristía, *f*

eucharistic /ˌyukəˈrɪstɪk/ *a* eucarístico
Euclidean /yuˈklɪdiən/ *a* euclídeo
eugenic /yuˈdʒɛnɪk/ *a* eugenésico
eugenics /yuˈdʒɛnɪks/ *n* eugenesia, *f*
eulogist /ˈyulədʒɪst/ *n* elogiador (-ra), loador (-ra)
eulogistic /ˌyuləˈdʒɪstɪk/ *a* elogiador
eulogize /ˈyuləˌdʒaiz/ *vt* elogiar, alabar, encomiar
eulogy /ˈyulədʒi/ *n* elogio, encomio, *m;* alabanza, *f;* panegírico, *m*
eunuch /ˈyunək/ *n* eunuco, *m*
euphemism /ˈyufəˌmɪzəm/ *n* eufemismo, *m*
euphonious /yuˈfouniəs/ *a* eufónico
euphony /ˈyufəni/ *n* eufonía, *f*
euphuistic /ˌyufyuˈɪstɪk/ *a* alambicado, gongorino
Eurasian /yʊˈreiʒən/ *a* and *n* eurasio (-ia)
eurhythmic /yʊˈrɪðmɪk/ *a* eurítmico
eurhythmics /yʊˈrɪðmɪks/ *n* euritmia, *f*
European /ˌyʊrəˈpiən/ *a* and *n* europeo (-ea)
europeanize /ˌyʊrəˈpiəˌnaiz/ *vt* europeanizar
euthanasia /ˌyuθəˈneiʒə, -ʒiə, -ziə/ *n* eutanasia, *f*
evacuate /ɪˈvækyuˌeit/ *vt* evacuar
evacuation /ɪˌvækyuˈeiʃən/ *n* evacuación, *f*
evade /ɪˈveid/ *vt* evadir, eludir; evitar, esquivar; rehuir
evaluate /ɪˈvælyuˌeit/ *vt* evaluar, estimar; calcular
evaluation /ɪˌvælyuˈeiʃən/ *n* evaluación, estimación, *f*
evanescent /ˌɛvəˈnɛsənt/ *a* transitorio, fugaz, pasajero
evangelical /ˌivænˈdʒɛlɪkəl/ *a* evangélico
evangelicalism /ˌivænˈdʒɛlɪkəˌlɪzəm/ *n* evangelismo, *m*
evangelist /ɪˈvændʒəlɪst/ *n* evangelista, *m*
evangelize /ɪˈvændʒəˌlaiz/ *vt* evangelizar
evaporate /ɪˈvæpəˌreit/ *vi* evaporarse; desvanecerse. —*vt* evaporar
evaporation /ɪˌvæpəˈreiʃən/ *n* evaporación, *f;* desvanecimiento, *m*
evaporative /ɪˈvæpəˌreitɪv/ *a* evaporatorio
evasion /ɪˈveiʒən/ *n* (escape) fuga, *f;* evasión, *f;* evasiva, *f,* efugio, *m*
evasive /ɪˈveisɪv/ *a* evasivo, ambiguo
evasively /ɪˈveisɪvli/ *adv* evasivamente
evasiveness /ɪˈveisɪvnɪs/ *n* carácter evasivo, *m*
eve /iv/ *n* víspera, *f; Eccl.* vigilia, *f.* **on the eve of,** la víspera de; *Fig.* en vísperas de
even /ˈivən/ *a* (flat) llano; (smooth) liso; igual; (level with) al mismo nivel (de); uniforme; (of numbers) par; (approximate, of sums) redondo; rítmico; invariable, constante; (of temper) apacible; (just) imparcial; (monotonous) monótono, igual; (paid) pagado; (*Com.* of date) mismo. **to get e. with,** pagar en la misma moneda, vengarse de
even /ˈivən/ *adv* siquiera; aun; hasta; (also) también. **not e.,** ni siquiera. **e. as,** así como, del mismo modo que. **e. if,** aun cuando, si bien. **e. now,** aun ahora; ahora mismo. **e. so,** aun así; (nevertheless) sin embargo. **e. though,** aunque; suponiendo que
even /ˈivən/ *vt* igualar; (level) allanar, nivelar; (accounts) desquitar; compensar; hacer uniforme
evening /ˈivnɪŋ/ *n* tarde, *f,* atardecer, *m;* noche, *f; Fig.* fin, *m, a* vespertino, de la tarde. **Good e.!** ¡Buenas tardes! ¡Buenas noches! **in the e.,** al atardecer. **tomorrow e.,** mañana por la tarde. **yesterday e.,** ayer por la tarde. **e. class,** clase nocturna, *f.* **e. dress,** (women) traje de noche, *m;* (men) traje de etiqueta, *m.* **e. meal,** cena, *f.* **e. paper,** periódico (or diario) de la noche, *m.* **evening primrose,** hierba del asno, onagra, *f.* **e. star,** estrella vespertina, estrella de la tarde, *f;* (Venus) lucero de la tarde, *m*
evenly /ˈivənli/ *adv* igualmente; (on a level) a nivel; uniformemente; imparcialmente; (of speech) con suavidad
evenness /ˈivənnɪs/ *n* igualdad, *f;* (smoothness) lisura, *f;* uniformidad, *f;* imparcialidad, *f;* (of temper) ecuanimidad, serenidad, *f*
evensong /ˈivənˌsɔŋ/ *n* vísperas, *f pl*
event /ɪˈvɛnt/ *n* incidente, suceso, acontecimiento, *m;* (result) consecuencia, *f;* resultado, *m;* caso, *m;* (athletics) prueba, *f;* (race) carrera, *f.* **at all events,** de todas maneras. **in such an e.,** en tal caso. **in the e. of,** en el caso de
eventful /ɪˈvɛntfəl/ *a* lleno de acontecimientos; accidentado; memorable
eventual /ɪˈvɛntʃuəl/ *a* eventual; final, último
eventuality /ɪˌvɛntʃuˈælɪti/ *n* eventualidad, *f*
eventually /ɪˈvɛntʃuəli/ *adv* a la larga, al fin
ever /ˈɛvər/ *adv* siempre; (at any time) jamás; alguna vez; nunca; (even) siquiera; (very) muy; (in any way) en modo alguno. **As fast as e. he can,** Lo más aprisa que pueda. **Be it e. so big,** Por grande que sea. **Did you e.!** ¡Habráse visto! ¡Qué cosa! **for e.,** para siempre. **for e. and e.,** para siempre jamás; (mostly ecclesiastical) por los siglos de los siglos; eternamente. **He is e. so nice,** Es muy simpático. **Hardly e.,** casi nunca. **I don't think I have e. been there,** No creo que haya estado nunca allí. **if e.,** si alguna vez; (rarely) raramente. **nor... e.,** ni nunca. **not... e.,** nunca. **e. after,** desde entonces; (afterward) después. **e. and anon,** de vez en cuando. **e. so little,** siquiera un poco; muy poco
evergreen /ˈɛvərˌgrin/ *a* siempre verde. —*n* planta vivaz, *f.* **e. oak,** encina, *f*
everlasting /ˌɛvərˈlæstɪŋ/ *a* eterno, perpetuo; (of colors) estable; incesante. **e. flower,** perpetua, *f*
evermore /ˌɛvərˈmɔr/ *adv* eternamente
every /ˈɛvri/ *a* todo; cada (invariable); todos los, *m pl;* todas las, *f pl.* **e. day,** todos los días, cada día. **e. now and then,** de cuando en cuando. **e. other day,** cada dos días
everybody /ˈɛvriˌbɒdi, -ˌbʌdi/ *n* todo el mundo, *m;* todos, *m pl;* todas, *f pl;* cada uno, *m;* cada una, *f*
everyday /ˈɛvriˌdei/ *a* diario, cotidiano; corriente, de cada día, usual
everything /ˈɛvriˌθɪŋ/ *n* todo, *m;* (e. that, which) todo lo (que). **e. possible,** todo lo posible
everywhere /ˈɛvriˌwɛər/ *adv* por todas partes
evict /ɪˈvɪkt/ *vt* desahuciar; expulsar
eviction /ɪˈvɪkʃən/ *n* evicción, *f,* desahúcio, *m;* expulsión, *f*
evidence /ˈɛvɪdəns/ *n Law.* testimonio, *m,* deposición, *f;* indicios, *m pl;* evidencia, *f;* prueba, *f;* hecho, *m, vt* patentizar, probar. **to give e.,** dar testimonio, deponer
evident /ˈɛvɪdənt/ *a* evidente, patente, manifiesto; claro. **to be e.,** ser patente, estar a la vista
evidently /ˈɛvɪdəntli/ *adv* evidentemente; claramente
evil /ˈivəl/ *a* malo; malvado, perverso; de maldad; (unfortunate) aciago; de infortunio; (of spirits) diabólico, malo. —*n* mal, *m;* maldad, perversidad, *f;* (misfortune) desgracia, *f.* **the E. one,** el Malo. **e.-doer,** malhechor (-ra). **e. eye,** mal de ojo, aojo, *m.* **e.-minded,** mal pensado; malintencionado. **e.-speaking,** maledicencia, calumnia, *f.* **e. spirit,** demonio, espíritu malo, *m*
evince /ɪˈvɪns/ *vt* evidenciar; mostrar
eviscerate /ɪˈvɪsəˌreit/ *vt* destripar, desentrañar
evocation /ˌɛvəˈkeiʃən/ *n* evocación, *f*
evocative /ɪˈvɒkətɪv/ *a* evocador
evoke /ɪˈvouk/ *vt* evocar
evolution /ˌɛvəˈluʃən/ *n* evolución, *f;* desarrollo, *m;* (*Nav. Mil.*) maniobra, *f; Math.* extracción de una raíz, *f;* (revolution) revolución, vuelta, *f*
evolutionism /ˌɛvəˈluʃəˌnɪzəm/ *n* evolucionismo, *m*
evolutive /ˌɛvəˈlutɪv/ *a* evolutivo
evolve /ɪˈvɒlv/ *vi* evolucionar; desarrollarse. —*vt* producir por evolución; desarrollar; pensar
ewe /yu/ *n* oveja, *f.* **ewe lamb,** cordera, *f*
ewer /ˈyuər/ *n* aguamanil, *m*
exacerbate /ɪgˈzæsərˌbeit/ *vt* exacerbar; agravar, empeorar
exacerbation /ɪgˌzæsərˈbeiʃən/ *n* exacerbación, *f;* agravación, *f*
exact /ɪgˈzækt/ *a* exacto; fiel; metódico; estricto. —*vt* exigir
exacting /ɪgˈzæktɪŋ/ *a* exigente; severo, estricto; (hard) agotador, arduo
exaction /ɪgˈzækʃən/ *n* exigencia, *f;* extorsión, exacción, *f*
exactly /ɪgˈzæktli/ *adv* exactamente; precisamente
exactness /ɪgˈzæktnɪs/ *n* exactitud, *f*
exaggerate /ɪgˈzædʒəˌreit/ *vt* exagerar; acentuar. —*vi* exagerar
exaggerated /ɪgˈzædʒəˌreitɪd/ *a* exagerado

exaggeration /ɪg,zædʒə'reiʃən/ *n* exageración, *f*
exaggerator /ɪg'zædʒə,reitər/ *n* exagerador (-ra)
exalt /ɪg'zɔlt/ *vt* exaltar; enaltecer, elevar; (praise) glorificar, magnificar; (intensify) realzar; intensificar
exaltation /,ɛgzɔl'teiʃən/ *n* exaltación, elevación, *f;* alegría, *f,* júbilo, *m;* (ecstasy) éxtasis, arrobamiento, *m;* (of the Cross) exaltación, *f*
exalted /ɪg'zɔltɪd/ *a* exaltado, eminente
exaltedness /ɪg'zɔltɪdnɪs/ *n* exaltación, *f*
examination /ɪg,zæmə'neiʃən/ *n* examen, *m;* inspección, *f;* investigación, *f;* *Law.* interrogatorio, *m;* prueba, *f.* **to sit an e.,** examinarse. **written e.,** prueba escrita, *f*
examine /ɪg'zæmɪn/ *vt* examinar; inspeccionar; investigar; *Law.* interrogar; (search) reconocer; (by touch) tentar; observar; analizar. **to e. into,** examinar; considerar detenidamente; ahondar en
examinee /ɪg,zæmə'ni/ *n* examinando (-da)
examiner /ɪg'zæmɪnər/ *n* examinador (-ra); inspector (-ra)
examinership /ɪg'zæmɪnər,ʃɪp/ *n* cargo de examinador, *m*
examining /ɪg'zæmɪnɪŋ/ *a* que examina; de examen; *Law.* interrogante
example /ɪg'zæmpəl/ *n* ejemplo, *m;* ilustración, *f;* (parallel) ejemplar, *m;* (warning) escarmiento, *m.* **for e.,** por ejemplo. **to set an e.,** dar ejemplo, dar el ejemplo.
exasperate /ɪg'zæspə,reit/ *vt* exasperar, irritar; (increase) aumentar; (worsen) agravar
exasperating /ɪg'zæspə,reitɪŋ/ *a* exasperante, irritante, provocador
exasperation /ɪg,zæspə'reiʃən/ *n* exasperación, irritación, *f;* (worsening) agravación, *f;* enojo, *m*
excavate /'ɛkskə,veit/ *vt* excavar; (hollow) vaciar
excavation /,ɛkskə'veiʃən/ *n* excavación, *f;* *Archit.* vaciado, *m*
excavator /'ɛkskə,veitər/ *n* excavador (-ra); (machine) excavadora, *f*
exceed /ɪk'sid/ *vt* exceder; (excel) superar, aventajar; (one's hopes, etc.) sobrepujar. —*vi* excederse. **e. all expectations,** exceder a toda ponderación. **to e. one's rights,** abusar de sus derechos, ir demasiado lejos
exceedingly /ɪk'sidɪŋli/ *adv* sumamente, extremadamente; sobre manera
excel /ɪk'sɛl/ *vt* aventajar, superar; vencer. —*vi* sobresalir; distinguirse, señalarse; ser superior
excellence /'ɛksələns/ *n* excelencia, *f;* superioridad, *f;* perfección, *f;* mérito, *m;* buena calidad, *f*
excellency /'ɛksələnsi/ *n* (title) Excelencia, *f.* **Your E.,** Su Excelencia
excellent /'ɛksələnt/ *a* excelente; superior; perfecto; magnífico; (in examinations) sobresaliente
excellently /'ɛksələntli/ *adv* excelentemente; perfectamente; magníficamente
except /ɪk'sɛpt/ *vt* exceptuar; omitir
except, excepting /ɪk'sɛpt; ɪk'sɛptɪŋ/ *prep* excepto, con excepción de; exceptuando; menos; salvo; fuera de. —*conjunc* a menos que. **except for,** si no fuese por; con excepción de; fuera de
exception /ɪk'sɛpʃən/ *n* excepción, *f;* objeción, protesta, *f.* **to make an e.,** hacer una excepción. **to take e. to,** protestar contra; tachar, criticar; desaprobar
exceptional /ɪk'sɛpʃənl̩/ *a* excepcional
excerpt /*n* 'ɛksɜrpt; *v* ɪk'sɜrpt/ *n* excerpta, *f,* extracto, *m.* ——*vt* extraer
excess /ɪk'sɛs, 'ɛksɛs/ *n* exceso, *m;* superabundancia, *f,* demasía, *f;* *Com.* superávit, *m.* **in e.,** en exceso, de sobra. **in e. of,** en exceso de; arriba de. **to e.,** excesivamente, demasiado. **e. fare,** suplemento, *m.* **e. luggage,** exceso de equipaje, *m;* (overweight) exceso de peso, *m*
excessive /ɪk'sɛsɪv/ *a* excesivo; superabundante; inmoderado, desmesurado; exagerado
excessively /ɪk'sɛsɪvli/ *adv* excesivamente; exageradamente
excessiveness /ɪk'sɛsɪvnɪs/ *n* exceso, *m;* superabundancia, *f;* exageración, *f*
exchange /ɪks'tʃeindʒ/ *n* cambio, trueque, *m;* (of prisoners) canje, *m;* (financial) cambio, *m;* (building) bolsa, lonja, *f;* (telephone) oficina central de teléfonos, *f.* —*vt* cambiar (for, por); trocar; (replace) reemplazar; (prisoners) canjear; (of blows) darse; (pass from, into) pasar de... a. —*vi* hacer un cambio. **in e. for,** en cambio de, a trueque de; por. **to e. greetings,** saludarse; cambiar saludos. **They exchanged looks,** Se miraron. **What is the rate of e.?** ¿Cuál es el tipo de cambio? **e. of prisoners,** canje de prisioneros, *m*
exchangeable /ɪks'tʃeindʒəbəl/ *a* cambiable; trocable
exchequer /'ɛkstʃɛkər/ *n* (public finance) Hacienda pública, *f;* tesorería, *f;* (funds) fondos, *m pl.* **Chancellor of the E.,** Ministro de Hacienda, *m*
excise /*n* 'ɛksaiz; *v* ɪk'saiz/ *n* contribución indirecta, *f;* (customs and e.) Aduana, *f.* —*vt* (cut) cortar, extirpar; imponer una contribución indirecta. **e. duty,** derecho de aduana, *m*
excise tax arbitrios, *m pl*
excision /ɛk'sɪʒən/ *n* excisión, *f;* extirpación, *f*
excitability /ɪk,saitə'bɪlɪti/ *n* excitabilidad, *f*
excitable /ɪk'saitəbəl/ *a* excitable
excitation /,ɛksai'teiʃən/ *n* excitación, *f*
excite /ɪk'sait/ *vt* emocionar; conmover; agitar; excitar; suscitar, provocar; incitar, instigar; (attention, interest) despertar; estimular. **to become excited,** emocionarse; exaltarse; (annoyed) acalorarse; (upset) agitarse
excitedly /ɪk'saitɪdli/ *adv* con emoción; acaloradamente; agitadamente
excitement /ɪk'saitmənt/ *n* conmoción, *f;* agitación, *f;* (annoyance) acaloramiento, *m;* emoción, *f;* estímulo, *m;* instigación, *f,* fomento, *m;* (amusement) placer, *m*
exciting /ɪk'saitɪŋ/ *a* emocionante; conmovedor; agitador; muy interesante
exclaim /ɪk'skleim/ *vt* and *vi* exclamar. **to e. against,** clamar contra
exclamation /,ɛksklə'meiʃən/ *n* exclamación, *f.* **e. mark,** punto de exclamación, *m*
exclamatory /ɪk'sklæmə,tɔri/ *a* exclamatorio
exclude /ɪk'sklud/ *vt* excluir; exceptuar; evitar; (refuse) rechazar
exclusion /ɪk'skluʒən/ *n* exclusión, *f;* exceptuación, *f;* eliminación, *f*
exclusive /ɪk'sklusɪv/ *a* exclusivo; (snobbish) exclusivista. **e. of,** no incluido; aparte de
exclusively /ɪk'sklusɪvli/ *adv* exclusivamente; únicamente
exclusiveness /ɪk'sklusɪvnɪs/ *n* carácter exclusivo, *m*
exclusivism /ɪk'sklusə,vɪzəm/ *n* exclusivismo, *m*
exclusivist /ɪk'sklusəvɪst/ *n* exclusivista, *mf*
excommunicate /*v* ,ɛkskə'myunɪ,keit; -kɪt/ *vt* excomulgar. —*a* excomulgado
excommunication /,ɛkskə,myunɪ'keiʃən/ *n* excomunión, *f*
excrement /'ɛkskrəmənt/ *n* excremento, *m*
excrescence /ɪk'skrɛsəns/ *n* excrecencia, *f*
excrescent /ɪk'skrɛsənt/ *a* que forma excrecencia; superfluo
excrete /ɪk'skrit/ *vt* excretar
excretion /ɪk'skriʃən/ *n* excreción, *f*
excretory /'ɛkskrɪ,tɔri/ *a* excretorio
excruciating /ɪk'skruʃi,eitɪŋ/ *a* atormentador, angustioso; (of pain) agudísimo
excursion /ɪk'skɜrʒən/ *n* excursión, *f;* expedición, *f;* (digression) digresión, *f.* **e. ticket,** billete de excursión, *m.* **e. train,** tren de excursionistas, *m*
excursionist /ɪk'skɜrʒənɪst/ *n* excursionista, *mf;* turista, *mf*
excusable /ɪk'skyuzəbəl/ *a* disculpable, excusable
excusably /ɪk'skyuzəbli/ *adv* excusablemente
excuse /ɪk'skyus/ *n* excusa, *f;* disculpa, *f;* pretexto, *m;* justificación, defensa, *f.* **to give as an e.,** pretextar
excuse /ɪk'skyuz/ *vt* disculpar, excusar; dispensar (de); librar (de); (forgive) perdonar; (defend) justificar, defender; (minimize) paiar; (oneself) disculparse. **E. me!** ¡Con permiso!; ¡Perdone Vd.!; ¡Dispense Vd.!
execrable /'ɛksɪkrəbəl/ *a* execrable, abominable
execrate /'ɛksɪ,kreit/ *vt* execrar, abominar. —*vi* maldecir
execration /,ɛksɪ'kreiʃən/ *n* execración, abominación, *f;* maldición, *f*
execute /'ɛksɪ,kyut/ *vt* (perform) ejecutar, poner en

efecto, realizar; (*Art. Mus.*) ejecutar; (part in a play) hacer, desempeñar; (fulfil) cumplir; *Law.* otorgar (un documento); (kill) ajusticiar
execution /ˌɛksɪ'kyuʃən/ *n* efectuación, realización, *f;* (*Art., Mus.*) ejecución, *f;* (of part in a play) desempeño (de un papel), *m;* (fulfilment) cumplimiento, *m;* *Law.* otorgamiento (de un documento), *m;* (killing) suplicio, *m,* ejecución de la pena de muerte, *f;* (*Law.* seizure) ejecución, *f*
executioner /ˌɛksɪ'kyuʃənər/ *n* verdugo, *m*
executive /ɪg'zɛkyətɪv/ *a* ejecutivo; administrativo. —*n* poder ejecutivo, *m*
executor /ɪg'zɛkyətər/ *n* administrador testamentario, *m*
executorship /ɪg'zɛkyətərˌʃɪp/ *n* ejecutoría, *f*
executrix /ɪg'zɛkyətrɪks/ *n* administradora testamentaria, *f*
exegesis /ˌɛksɪ'dʒisɪs/ *n* exégesis, *f*
exegetical /ˌɛksɪ'dʒɛtɪkəl/ *a* exegético
exemplary /ɪg'zɛmpləri/ *a* ejemplar
exemplification /ɪgˌzɛmpləfɪ'keiʃən/ *n* ejemplificación, ilustración, demostración, *f*
exemplify /ɪg'zɛmpləˌfai/ *vt* ejemplificar; ilustrar, demostrar
exempt /ɪg'zɛmpt/ *vt* exentar, eximir; librar; dispensar, excusar. —*a* exento; libre; excusado; inmune
exemption /ɪg'zɛmpʃən/ *n* exención, *f;* libertad, *f;* inmunidad, *f*
exercise /'ɛksərˌsaiz/ *n* ejercicio, *m;* uso, *m;* (essay) ensayo, *m; pl* **exercises,** (on land or sea) maniobras, *f pl.* —*vt* ejercer; usar, emplear; (train) ejercitar, entrenar; adiestrar; pasear, dar un paseo; (worry) preocupar. —*vi* hacer ejercicio; ejercitarse; adiestrarse. **spiritual exercises,** ejercicios espirituales, *m pl.* **to take e. in the open air,** tomar ejercicio al aire libre. **to write an e.,** escribir un ejercicio. **e. book,** cuaderno de ejercicios, *m*
exert /ɪg'zɜrt/ *vt* hacer uso de, emplear, ejercer, poner en juego; (deploy) desplegar. **to e. oneself,** hacer un esfuerzo (para); esforzarse (de); trabajar mucho; tratar (de); apurarse, tomarse mucha molestia; preocuparse
exertion /ɪg'zɜrʃən/ *n* esfuerzo, *m;* uso, *m;* (exercise) ejercicio, *m;* (good offices) diligencias, gestiones, *f pl;* buenos oficios, *m pl*
exhalation /ˌɛkshə'leiʃən/ *n* exhalación, *f;* efluvio, *m;* vapor, *m;* humo, *m*
exhale /ɛks'heil/ *vt* exhalar; emitir, despedir. —*vi* evaporarse; disiparse
exhaust /ɪg'zɔst/ *vt* agotar; (empty) vaciar; (end) acabar; apurar; consumir; (tire) rendir, cansar mucho; (weaken) debilitar; (a subject) tratar detalladamente. —*n Mech.* escape, *m;* emisión de vapor, *f;* vapor de escape, *m.* **e. pipe,** tubo de escape, *m*
exhaustible /ɪg'zɔstəbəl/ *a* agotable
exhausting /ɪg'zɔstɪŋ/ *a* cansado, agotador
exhaustion /ɪg'zɔstʃən/ *n* agotamiento, *m;* rendimiento, cansancio, *m;* lasitud, *f;* postración, *f*
exhaustive /ɪg'zɔstɪv/ *a* completo; minucioso
exhaustively /ɪg'zɔstɪvli/ *adv* detenidamente; detalladamente; minuciosamente
exhaustiveness /ɪg'zɔstɪvnɪs/ *n* lo completo; minuciosidad, *f*
exhibit /ɪg'zɪbɪt/ *vt* exhibir; manifestar, ostentar; revelar, descubrir; presentar. —*vi* exhibir, ser expositor. —*n* objeto exhibido, *m;* *Law.* prueba, *f*
exhibition /ˌɛksə'bɪʃən/ *n* exposición, *f;* (performance) función, *f;* espectáculo, *m;* exhibición, *f;* (showing) manifestación, *f;* (grant) bolsa de estudio, beca, *f*
exhibitionism /ˌɛksə'bɪʃəˌnɪzəm/ *n* exhibicionismo, *m*
exhibitionist /ˌɛksə'bɪʃənɪst/ *n* exhibicionista, *mf*
exhibitor /ɪg'zɪbɪtər/ *n* expositor (-ra)
exhilarate /ɪg'zɪləˌreit/ *vt* alegrar, alborozar
exhilarating /ɪg'zɪləˌreitɪŋ/ *a* alegre; estimulador; vigorizador, tonificante
exhilaration /ɪgˌzɪlə'reiʃən/ *n* alegría, *f,* alborozo, regocijo, *m*
exhort /ɪg'zɔrt/ *vt* and *vi* exhortar
exhortation /ˌɛgzɔr'teiʃən/ *n* exhortación, *f*
exhumation /ˌɛkshyu'meiʃən/ *n* exhumación, *f*
exhume /ɪg'zum/ *vt* exhumar
exigence /'ɛksɪdʒəns/ *n* exigencia, *f;* urgencia, *f;* (need) necesidad, *f*
exigent /'ɛksɪdʒənt/ *a* exigente; urgente
exiguous /ɪg'zɪgyuəs/ *a* exiguo
exiguousness /ɪg'zɪgyuəsnɪs/ *n* exigüidad, *f*
exile /'ɛgzail/ *n* destierro, *m;* (person) desterrado (-da). —*vt* desterrar
exist /ɪg'zɪst/ *vi* existir
existence /ɪg'zɪstəns/ *n* existencia, *f;* (being) ser, *m;* (life) vida, *f.* **to bring into e.,** causar; producir
existentialism /ˌɛgzɪ'stɛnʃəˌlɪzəm/ *n* existencialismo, *m*
existing /ɪg'zɪstɪŋ/ *a* existente
exit /'ɛgzɪt, 'ɛksɪt/ *n* salida, *f;* partida, *f;* (death) muerte, *f;* *Theat.* mutis, *m.* —*vi Theat.* hacer mutis. **to make one's e.,** salir; marcharse; irse; morir; *Theat.* hacer mutis
exodus /'ɛksədəs/ *n* éxodo, *m;* salida, *f;* emigración, *f;* (Old Testament) Éxodo, *m*
exonerate /ɪg'zɒnəˌreit/ *vt* exonerar
exoneration /ɪgˌzɒnə'reiʃən/ *n* exoneración, *f*
exorbitance /ɪg'zɔrbɪtəns/ *n* exorbitancia, *f*
exorbitant /ɪg'zɔrbɪtənt/ *a* exorbitante
exorcism /'ɛksɔrˌsɪzəm/ *n* exorcismo, *m*
exorcist /'ɛksɔrsɪst/ *n* exorcista, *m*
exorcize /'ɛksərˌsaiz/ *vt* exorcizar, conjurar
exotic /ɪg'zɒtɪk/ *a* exótico. —*n* planta exótica, *f;* *Fig.* flor de estufa, *f*
expand /ɪk'spænd/ *vt* extender; abrir; (wings, etc.) desplegar; (the chest, etc.) expandir; dilatar; (amplify) ampliar; (an edition) ampliar, aumentar; (develop) desarrollar; *Fig.* ensanchar; (increase) aumentar. —*vi* dilatarse; hincharse; abrirse; extenderse; *Fig.* ensancharse; (increase) aumentarse
expanse /ɪk'spæns/ *n* extensión, *f*
expansibility /ɪkˌspænsə'bɪlɪti/ *n Phys.* expansibilidad, *f;* dilatabilidad, *f*
expansible /ɪk'spænsəbəl/ *a Phys.* expansible; dilatable
expansion /ɪk'spænʃən/ *n* expansión, *f;* extensión, *f;* dilatación, *f;* (amplification) ampliación, *f;* (development) desarrollo, *m;* *Fig.* ensanchamiento, *m;* (increase) aumento, *m*
expansionism /ɪk'spænʃəˌnɪzəm/ *n* expansionismo, *m*
expansive /ɪk'spænsɪv/ *a* expansivo; (of persons) efusivo, expresivo, comunicativo, afable
expansiveness /ɪk'spænsɪvnɪs/ *n* expansibilidad, *f;* (of persons) afabilidad, *f*
expatiate /ɪk'speiʃiˌeit/ **(upon)** *vi* extenderse en
expatiation /ɪkˌspeiʃi'eiʃən/ *n* discurso, *m;* digresión, *f*
expatriation /ɛksˌpeitri'eiʃən/ *n* expatriación, *f*
expect /ɪk'spɛkt/ *vt* esperar; (await) aguardar; (suppose) suponer; (demand) exigir; (count on) contar con. —*vi* creer
expectance /ɪk'spɛktəns/ *n* expectación, *f;* esperanza, *f*
expectant /ɪk'spɛktənt/ *a* expectante; (hopeful) esperanzudo; (pregnant) embarazada
expectantly /ɪk'spɛktəntli/ *adv* con expectación
expectation /ˌɛkspɛk'teiʃən/ *n* expectación, *f;* (hope) esperanza, expectativa, *f;* probabilidad, *f*
expectorate /ɪk'spɛktəˌreit/ *vt* expectorar. —*vi* escupir
expectoration /ɪkˌspɛktə'reiʃən/ *n* expectoración, *f*
expedience /ɪk'spidiəns/ *n* conveniencia, *f;* oportunidad, *f;* aptitud, *f;* (self-interest) egoísmo, *m*
expedient /ɪk'spidiənt/ *a* conveniente; oportuno; apto; prudente; político. —*n* expediente, recurso, medio, *m*
expedite /'ɛkspɪˌdait/ *vt* acelerar; facilitar; (send off) despachar
expedition /ˌɛkspɪ'dɪʃən/ *n* expedición, *f;* (haste) celeridad, diligencia, *f*
expeditionary /ˌɛkspɪ'dɪʃəˌnɛri/ *a* expedicionario. **e. force,** fuerza expedicionaria, *f*
expeditious /ˌɛkspɪ'dɪʃəs/ *a* expedito, pronto
expeditiously /ˌɛkspɪ'dɪʃəsli/ *adv* expeditamente, prontamente
expeditiousness /ˌɛkspɪ'dɪʃəsnɪs/ *n* prontitud, *f*

expel /ɪk'spɛl/ *vt* expeler, expulsar; echar, arrojar; despedir
expend /ɪk'spɛnd/ *vt* gastar, expender; (time) perder
expenditure /ɪk'spɛndɪtʃər/ *n* gasto, desembolso, *m;* (of time) pérdida, *f*
expense /ɪk'spɛns/ *n* gasto, *m;* pérdida, *f;* costa, *f; pl* **expenses,** expensas, *f pl,* gastos, *m pl.* **at the e. of,** a costa de. **to be put to great e.,** tener que gastar mucho. **to pay one's expenses,** pagar sus gastos
expensive /ɪk'spɛnsɪv/ *a* costoso; caro
expensively /ɪk'spɛnsɪvli/ *adv* costosamente
expensiveness /ɪk'spɛnsɪvnɪs/ *n* lo costoso; costa, *f*
experience /ɪk'spɪəriəns/ *n* experiencia, *f.* —*vt* experimentar; sentir; sufrir. **by e.,** por experiencia
experienced /ɪk'spɪəriənst/ *a* experimentado; experto; hábil; (lived) vivido
experiment /*n* ɪk'spɛrəmənt; *v* -ˌmɛnt/ *n* experimento, *m;* prueba, *f;* ensayo, *m,* tentativa, *f.* —*vi* experimentar; hacer una prueba
experimental /ɪkˌspɛrə'mɛntḷ/ *a* experimental; tentativo
experimentally /ɪkˌspɛrə'mɛntḷi/ *adv* experimentalmente; por experiencia
expert /'ɛkspɜrt/ *a* experto; perito; hábil; (finished) acabado. —*n* experto, *m,* especialista, *mf*
expertly /'ɛkspɜrtli/ *adv* expertamente; hábilmente
expertness /'ɛkspɜrtnɪs/ *n* pericia, *f;* maestría, *f;* habilidad, *f;* (knowledge) conocimiento, *m*
expiable /'ɛkspiəbəl/ *a* que se puede expiar
expiate /'ɛkspiˌeit/ *vt* expiar; reparar
expiation /ˌɛkspi'eiʃən/ *n* expiación, *f*
expiatory /'ɛkspiəˌtɔri/ *a* expiatorio
expiration /ˌɛkspə'reiʃən/ *n* (breathing out) espiración, *f;* (ending) expiración, *f;* terminación, *f; Com.* vencimiento, *m;* (death) muerte, *f*
expiration date fecha de caducidad, *f*
expire /ɪk'spaiᵊr/ *vi* (exhale) espirar; (die) morir, dar el último suspiro; (of fire, light) extinguirse; (end) expirar; terminar; *Com.* vencer
expiry /ɪk'spaiᵊri/ *n* terminación, *f;* expiración, *f; Com.* vencimiento, *m*
explain /ɪk'splein/ *vt* explicar; aclarar; demostrar; exponer; (justify) justificar, defender. —*vi* explicarse. **to e. away,** explicar; justificar
explainable /ɪk'spleinəbəl/ *a* explicable
explanation /ˌɛksplə'neiʃən/ *n* explicación, *f;* aclaración, *f*
explanatory /ɪk'splænəˌtɔri/ *a* explicativo; aclaratorio
expletive /'ɛksplɪtɪv/ *a* expletivo. —*n* interjección, *f*
explicable /'ɛksplɪkəbəl/ *a* explicable
explicit /ɪk'splɪsɪt/ *a* explícito
explode /ɪk'sploud/ *vi* estallar; detonar; reventar. —*vt* hacer estallar; (a mine) hacer saltar; (a belief, etc.) hacer abandonar; desechar
exploit /ɪk'splɔit/ *n* hazaña, proeza, *f;* aventura, *f.* —*vt* explotar
exploitation /ˌɛksplɔi'teiʃən/ *n* explotación, *f*
exploiter /ɪk'splɔitər/ *n* explotador (-ra)
exploration /ˌɛksplə'reiʃən/ *n* exploración, *f*
exploratory /ɪk'splɔrəˌtɔri/ *a* exploratorio
explore /ɪk'splɔr/ *vt* explorar; examinar; averiguar; investigar; (*Med. Surg.*) explorar
explorer /ɪk'splɔrər/ *n* explorador (-ra)
explosion /ɪk'splouʒən/ *n* explosión, *f;* estallido, *m,* detonación, *f*
explosive /ɪk'splousɪv/ *a* and *n* explosivo, *m.* **high e.,** explosivo violento, *m.* **explosives chamber,** recámara, *f*
explosiveness /ɪk'splousɪvnɪs/ *n* propiedad explosiva, *f;* lo explosivo; violencia, *f*
exponent /ɪk'spounənt/ *a* and *n* exponente, *mf*
export /*n* 'ɛkspɔrt; *v* ɪk'spɔrt/ *n* exportación, *f.* —*vt* exportar. **e. license,** permiso de exportación, *m.* **e. trade,** comercio de exportación, *m*
exportation /ˌɛkspɔr'teiʃən/ *n* exportación, *f*
exporter /ɪk'spɔrtər/ *n* exportador (-ra)
expose /ɪk'spouz/ *vt* exponer; arriesgar; (exhibit) exhibir, (unmask) desenmascarar; descubrir; revelar; *Photo.* exponer; (ridicule) ridiculizar
exposed /ɪk'spouzd/ *a* descubierto; no abrigado; expuesto, peligroso
exposition /ˌɛkspə'zɪʃən/ *n* explicación, interpretación, *f;* declaración, *f;* (exhibition) exposición, *f*
expostulate /ɪk'spɒstʃəˌleit/ *vi* protestar, **to e. with,** reprochar; reconvenir
expostulation /ɪkˌspɒstʃə'leiʃən/ *n* protesta, *f;* reconvención, *f*
exposure /ɪk'spouʒər/ *n* exposición, *f;* (aspect) orientación, *f;* (scandal) revelación, *f,* escándalo, *m;* peligro, *m;* exposición al frío or al calor, *f*
expound /ɪk'spaund/ *vt* exponer, explicar; comentar
expounder /ɪk'spaundər/ *n* intérprete, *mf;* comentador (-ra)
express /ɪk'sprɛs/ *a* (clear) categórico, explícito, claro; expreso; (exact) exacto; (quick) rápido. —*n* (messenger, post) expreso, *m;* (train) (tren) expreso, (tren) rápido, *m;* (goods) exprés, *m.* —*vt* expresar; (a letter, etc.) mandar por expreso
expressible /ɪk'sprɛsəbəl/ *a* decible
expression /ɪk'sprɛʃən/ *n* expresión, *f*
expressionless /ɪk'sprɛʃənlɪs/ *a* sin expresión
expressive /ɪk'sprɛsɪv/ *a* expresivo; que expresa
expropriate /ɛks'proupriˌeit/ *vt* expropiar
expropriation /ɛksˌproupri'eiʃən/ *n* expropiación, *f*
expulsion /ɪk'spʌlʃən/ *n* expulsión, *f*
expunge /ɪk'spʌndʒ/ *vt* borrar, testar, omitir
expunging /ɪk'spʌndʒɪŋ/ *n* borradura, *f;* testación, *f;* omisión, *f*
expurgate /'ɛkspərˌgeit/ *vt* expurgar
expurgation /ˌɛkspər'geiʃən/ *n* expurgación, *f*
expurgator /'ɛkspərˌgeitər/ *n* expurgador, *m*
expurgatory /ɪk'spɜrgəˌtɔri/ *a* expurgatorio
exquisite /ɪk'skwɪzɪt/ *a* exquisito, precioso, primoroso; excelente; (acute) agudo, intenso; (keen) vivo. —*n* elegante, petimetre, *m*
exquisitely /ɪk'skwɪzɪtli/ *adv* primorosamente, pulcramente; a la perfección
exquisiteness /ɪk'skwɪzɪtnɪs/ *n* primor. *m;* pulcritud, perfección, *f;* excelencia, *f;* (of pain) intensidad, *f;* (keenness) viveza, *f*
ex-serviceman /'ɛks's3rvɪsmən/ *n* excombatiente, antiguo soldado, *m*
extant /'ɛkstənt/ *a* estante; existente; viviente
extempore /ɪk'stɛmpəri/ *a* improvisado
extemporize /ɪk'stɛmpəˌraiz/ *vt* and *vi* improvisar
extend /ɪk'stɛnd/ *vt* extender; (hold out) tender, alargar; (lengthen) prolongar; (a period of time) prorrogar, diferir; (make larger) ensanchar; (increase) aumentar; dilatar; ampliar; (offer) ofrecer; *vi* extenderse; dilatarse; continuar; (give) dar de sí, estirarse; (last) prolongarse, durar; (become known) propagarse
extensible /ɪk'stɛnsəbəl/ *a* extensible
extension /ɪk'stɛnʃən/ *n* extensión, *f;* expansión, *f;* (increase) aumento, *m;* prolongación, *f;* ampliación, *f; Com.* prórroga, *f;* (telephone number) extensión, *f,* interno, *m*
extension cord *n* cordón de extensión, *m;* ladrón *m,* (Mexico; slang)
extensive /ɪk'stɛnsɪv/ *a* extenso, ancho, vasto; grande, considerable; (comprehensive) comprensivo
extensively /ɪk'stɛnsɪvli/ *adv* extensamente; generalmente
extensiveness /ɪk'stɛnsɪvnɪs/ *n* extensión, *f;* amplitud, *f*
extensor /ɪk'stɛnsər, -sɔr/ *n Anat.* extensor, *m*
extent /ɪk'stɛnt/ *n* extensión, *f;* (degree) punto, *m;* (limit) límite, *m.* **to a great e.,** en gran parte; considerablemente. **to some e.,** hasta cierto punto. **to the full e.,** en toda su extensión; completamente. **to what e.?** ¿hasta qué punto?
extenuate /ɪk'stɛnyuˌeit/ *vt* atenuar, desminuir, mitigar, paliar
extenuating /ɪk'stɛnyuˌeitɪŋ/ *a* atenuante
extenuation /ɪkˌstɛnyu'eiʃən/ *n* atenuación, mitigación, *f*
exterior /ɪk'stɪəriər/ *a* exterior, externo; de fuera; (foreign) extranjero. —*n* exterior, *m;* aspecto, *m;* forma, *f*
exterminate /ɪk'stɜrməˌneit/ *vt* exterminar
extermination /ɪkˌstɜrmə'neiʃən/ *n* exterminio, *m*
exterminator /ɪk'stɜrməˌneitər/ *n* exterminador (-ra)

exterminatory /ɪk'stɜrmənəˌtɔri/ *a* exterminador
external /ɪk'stɜrnḷ/ *a* externo, exterior; (foreign) extranjero. —*n pl* **externals,** apariencias, *f pl*; aspecto exterior, *m;* comportamiento, *m*
externally /ɪk'stɜrnḷi/ *adv* exteriormente
exterritorial /ˌɛkstɛrɪ'tɔriəl/ *a* extraterritorial
exterritoriality /ˌɛkstɛrɪtɔri'ælɪti/ *n* extraterritorialidad, *f*
extinct /ɪk'stɪŋkt/ *a* extinto; (of light, fire) extinguido; suprimido
extinction /ɪk'stɪŋkʃən/ *n* extinción, *f*
extinguish /ɪk'stɪŋgwɪʃ/ *vt* extinguir; apagar; *Fig.* eclipsar
extinguishable /ɪk'stɪŋgwɪʃəbəl/ *a* apagable
extinguisher /ɪk'stɪŋgwɪʃər/ *n* apagador (-ra); (for fires) extintor, *m;* (snuffer) matacandelas, *m*
extinguishment /ɪk'stɪŋgwɪʃmənt/ *n* apagamiento, *m;* extinción, *f;* abolición, *f;* (destruction) aniquilamiento, *m*
extirpate /'ɛkstərˌpeit/ *vt* extirpar
extirpation /ˌɛkstər'peiʃən/ *n* extirpación, *f*
extol /ɪk'stoul/ *vt* elogiar, encomiar, alabar; cantar
extoller /ɪk'stoulər/ *n* alabador (-ra)
extort /ɪk'stɔrt/ *vt* arrancar, sacar por fuerza; exigir por amenazas
extortion /ɪk'stɔrʃən/ *n* extorsión, *f;* exacción, *f*
extortionate /ɪk'stɔrʃənɪt/ *a* injusto; opresivo; (of price) exorbitante, excesivo
extra /'ɛkstrə/ *a* and *adv* adicional; extraordinario; suplementario; (spare) de repuesto. —*prefix* (in compounds) extra. —*n* extra, *m;* suplemento, *m;* (of a paper) hoja extraordinaria, *f;* (actor) supernumerario (-ia). **e. charge,** gasto suplementario, *m;* (on the railway, etc.) suplemento, *m.* **e.-mural,** *a* de extramuros.
extract /*v* ɪk'strækt; *n* 'ɛkstrækt/ *vt* sacar; (*Chem. Math.*) extraer; extractar; (obtain) obtener. —*n Chem.* extracto, *m;* (excerpt) cita, *f*
extraction /ɪk'strækʃən/ *n* saca, *f;* extracción, *f;* obtención, *f*
extradite /'ɛkstrəˌdait/ *vt* entregar por extradición
extradition /ˌɛkstrə'dɪʃən/ *n* extradición, *f*
extraneous /ɪk'streiniəs/ *a* extraño; (irrelevant) ajeno (a)
extraordinarily /ɪkˌstrɔrdṇ'ɛrəli/ *adv* extraordinariamente, singularmente
extraordinariness /ɪk'strɔrdṇˌɛrinɪs/ *n* lo extraordinario; singularidad, *f;* (queerness) rareza, *f*
extraordinary /ɪk'strɔrdṇˌɛri/ *a* extraordinario; singular; (queer) raro, excéntrico; (incredible) increíble
extravagance /ɪk'strævəgəns/ *n* (in spending) prodigalidad, *f,* derroche, *m;* (of dress, speech) extravagancia, *f;* (foolishness) disparate, *m;* (luxury) lujo, *m*
extravagant /ɪk'strævəgənt/ *a* extravagante; (queer) extraño, raro; (wasteful) pródigo; (of persons) gastador, manirroto; (of price) exorbitante; excesivo
extravagantly /ɪk'strævəgəntli/ *adv* extravagantemente; de un modo extraño; pródigamente; profusamente; excesivamente
extreme /ɪk'strim/ *a* extremo. —*n* extremo, *m.* **in e.,** extremamente, en extremo, en sumo grado. **to carry to extremes,** llevar a extremos; **E. Unction,** Extremaunción, *f*
extremely /ɪk'strimli/ *adv* sumamente; *Inf.* muy
extremism /ɪk'striˌmɪzəm/ *n* extremismo, *m*
extremist /ɪk'strimɪst/ *a* and *n* extremista, *mf*
extremity /ɪk'strɛmɪti/ *n* extremidad, *f;* (point) punta, *f;* necesidad, *f; pl* **extremities,** *Anat.* extremidades, *f pl*; (measures) medidas extremas, *f pl*
extricate /'ɛkstrɪˌkeit/ *vt* desenredar; librar; sacar
extrication /ˌɛkstrɪ'keiʃən/ *n* liberación, *f*
extrinsic /ɪk'strɪnsɪk/ *a* extrínseco
extrovert /'ɛkstrəˌvɜrt/ *n Psychol.* extravertido, *m*
exuberance /ɪg'zubərəns/ *n* exuberancia, *f*
exuberant /ɪg'zubərənt/ *a* exuberante
exudation /ˌɛksyʊ'deiʃən/ *n* exudación, *f*
exude /ɪg'zud/ *vt* exudar; rezumar; sudar. —*vi* exudar; rezumarse
exult /ɪg'zʌlt/ *vi* exultar; alegrarse
exultant /ɪg'zʌltṇt/ *a* exultante, triunfante
exultantly /ɪg'zʌltṇtli/ *adv* con exultación; triunfalmente
exultation /ˌɛgzʌl'teiʃən/ *n* exultación, *f;* triunfo, *m*
eye /ai/ *n* ojo, *m;* (sight) vista, *f;* (look) mirada, *f;* atención, *f;* (opinion) opinión, *f,* juicio, *m;* (of a needle, of cheese) ojo, *m;* (of a hook) corcheta, *f; Bot.* yema, *f;* (of a potato) grillo, *m.* —*vt* ojear; fijar los ojos en; examinar, mirar detenidamente. **bright eyes,** ojos vivos, *m pl.* **prominent eyes,** ojos saltones, *m pl.* **He couldn't keep his eyes off Mary,** Se le fueron los ojos tras María. **as far as the eye can reach,** hasta donde alcanza la vista. **before one's eyes,** a la vista de uno, ante los ojos de uno. **in my (etc.) eyes,** *Fig.* según creo yo, en mi opinión. **in the twinkling of an eye,** en un abrir y cerrar de ojos. **with an eye to,** pensando en. **with my own eyes,** con mis propios ojos. **with the naked eye,** con la simple vista. **to keep an eye on,** vigilar. **to make eyes at,** guiñar el ojo; mirar con ojos de enamorado. **to have one's eyes opened,** *Fig.* caérsele la venda. **eye-bath,** ojera, *f.* **eye-opener,** revelación, sorpresa, *f.* **eye-pencil,** pincel para las cejas, *m.* **eye-piece,** objetivo, ocular, *m.* **eye-shade,** visera, *f.* **eye-tooth,** colmillo, *m.* **eye-witness,** testigo ocular, testigo de vista, testigo presencial, *mf*
eyeball /'aiˌbɔl/ *n* globo ocular, *m*
eyebrow /'aiˌbrau/ *n* ceja, *f*
eye care atención de la vista, *f*
eyed /aid/ *a* que tiene ojos; (in compounds) de ojos..., con ojos...; con los ojos; (of a needle) con el ojo... **She is a blue-eyed child,** Es una niña de ojos azules
eyeglass /'aiˌglæs/ *n* lente, *m*
eyelash /'aiˌlæʃ/ *n* pestaña, *f*
eyeless /'ailɪs/ *a* sin ojos
eyelet /'ailɪt/ *n* ojete, *m*
eyelid /'aiˌlɪd/ *n* párpado, *m*
eyesight /'aiˌsait/ *n* vista, *f*
eyewash /'aiˌwɒʃ/ *n* colirio, *m; Inf.* camelo, *m.* **That's all e.!** ¡Eso es un camelo!
eyrie /'ɛəri/ *n* nido (of any bird of prey), nido de águila (eagle's) *m*

F

f /ɛf/ *n* (letter) efe, *f;* *Mus.* fa, *m.* **f sharp,** fa sostenido, *m*

fa /fɑ/ *n Mus.* fa, *m*

fable /ˈfeibəl/ *n* fábula, leyenda, historia, *f,* apólogo, cuento, *m;* (untruth) invención, mentira, *f*

fabled /ˈfeibəld/ *a* celebrado, famoso

fabric /ˈfæbrɪk/ *n* obra, fábrica, *f;* estructura, construcción, *f;* (making) manufactura, *f;* (cloth) tejido, paño, *m;* textura, *f*

fabricate /ˈfæbrɪˌkeit/ *vt* fabricar, construir; (invent) fingir, inventar

fabrication /ˌfæbrɪˈkeiʃən/ *n* fabricación, manufactura, *f;* construcción, *f;* (lie) invención, ficción, *f*

fabulist /ˈfæbyəlɪst/ *n* fabulista, *mf*

fabulous /ˈfæbyələs/ *a* fabuloso

fabulousness /ˈfæbyələsnɪs/ *n* fabulosidad, *f*

façade /fəˈsɑd/ *n* fachada, frente, *f*

face /feis/ *n* superficie, *f;* (of persons) cara, *f,* rostro, *m;* (look) semblante, aire, *m;* (of coins) anverso, *m;* (grimace) mueca, *f,* gesto, *m;* (dial) esfera, *f;* (of gems) faceta, *f;* (of a wall) paramento, *m;* (front) fachada, frente, *f;* (effrontery) cara dura, *f,* descaro, *m.* **in the f. of,** ante; en presencia de. *Mil.* **Left f.!** ¡Izquierda! **on the f. of it,** juzgando por las apariencias. **to bring f. to f.,** confrontar (con). **to laugh in a person's f.,** reírse a la cara (de). **to make a f.,** hacer muecas. **to my f.,** en mi cara, en mis barbas. **to put a good f. on,** *Fig.* poner (or hacer) buena cara a. **to set one's f. against,** oponerse resueltamente a. **to straighten one's f.,** componer el semblante. **to throw in one's f.,** *Fig.* dar en rostro, dar en cara. **to wash one's f.,** lavarse la cara. **f. card,** figura (de la baraja), *f.* **f.-cloth,** paño para lavar la cara, *m.* **f. downward,** boca abajo. **f. lift,** operación estética facial, *f.* **f. of the waters,** faz de las aguas, *f.* **f. powder,** polvos de arroz, *m pl.* **f. to f.,** cara a cara, de persona a persona; frente a frente. **f. value,** significado literal, *m;* *Com.* valor nominal, *m*

face /feis/ *vt* mirar hacia; confrontar, hacer cara (a); (of buildings, etc.) mirar a, caer a (or hacia); *Fig.* arrostrar, enfrentarse con; *Sew.* guarnecer, aforrar. —*vi* estar orientado. **to f. the facts,** enfrentarse con la
realidad. **to f. the music,** *Fig.* arrostrar las consecuencias. **to f. about,** volver la espalda; *Mil.* dar una vuelta, cambiar de frente. **to f. up to,** *Fig.* hacer cara a

faced /feist/ *a* con cara..., de cara...; *Sew.* forrado (de). **to be two-f.,** *Fig.* ser de dos haces

facer /ˈfeisər/ *n* puñetazo en la cara, *m;* *Fig.* dificultad insuperable, *f,* problema muy grande, *m*

facet /ˈfæsɪt/ *n* faceta, *f*

facetious /fəˈsiʃəs/ *a* chancero, chistoso, jocoso

facetiousness /fəˈsiʃəsnɪs/ *n* jocosidad, festividad, *f*

facial /ˈfeiʃəl/ *a* facial. **f. expression,** expresión de la cara, *f,* semblante, *m*

facile /ˈfæsɪl/ *a* (frivolous) ligero (e.g., a deduction or inference)

facilitate /fəˈsɪlɪˌteit/ *vt* facilitar

facilitation /fəˌsɪlɪˈteiʃən/ *n* facilitación, *f*

facility /fəˈsɪlɪti/ *n* facilidad, *f;* habilidad, destreza, *f*

facing /ˈfeisɪŋ/ *n Sew.* vuelta, *f;* (of a building) paramento, *m;* (of lumber) chapa *f;* encaramiento, *m*

facsimile /fækˈsɪməli/ *n* facsímile, *m*

fact /fækt/ *n* (event) hecho, suceso, *m;* (datum) dato, *m;* realidad, verdad, *f.* **as a matter of f.,** en realidad. **in f.,** en efecto, en realidad. **I know as a f.,** Tengo por cierto. **The f. is...,** La verdad es (que)... **the f. that,** el hecho de que

fact-finding /ˈfækt ˌfaindɪŋ/ informador (e.g. *send s.b. on a fact-finding mission,* enviar a fulano en misión informadora)

faction /ˈfækʃən/ *n* facción, *f,* partido, bando, *m;* (tumult) alboroto, *m*

factional /ˈfækʃənl̩/ *a* partidario

factious /ˈfækʃəs/ *a* faccioso, sedicioso

factiousness /ˈfækʃəsnɪs/ *n* espíritu de facción, *m;* rebeldía, *f*

factitious /fækˈtɪʃəs/ *a* falso; artificial

factor /ˈfæktər/ *n* (fact) factor, elemento, *m;* consideración, *f;* *Math.* factor, *m;* *Com.* agente, factor, *m*

factory /ˈfæktəri/ *n* fábrica, manufactura, *f;* taller, *m.* **F. Act,** ley de trabajadores industriales, *f.* **f. hand,** operario (-ia)

factotum /fækˈtoutəm/ *n* factótum, *m*

factual /ˈfæktʃuəl/ *a* basado en hechos, objetivo

faculty /ˈfækəlti/ *n* facultad, *f;* (talent) habilidad, *f,* talento, *m;* (university division) facultad, *f;* (teachers as a group) claustro de profesores, claustro, profesorado, *m;* (authorization) privilegio, *m,* autoridad, *f*

fad /fæd/ *n* capricho, *m,* chifladura, *f,* dengue, *m*

faddiness /ˈfædinɪs/ *n* manías, *f pl,* excentricidad, *f*

faddist /ˈfædɪst/ *n* chiflado (-da)

faddy /ˈfædi/ *a* caprichoso, dengoso, difícil, excéntrico

fade /feid/ *vi* (of plants) marchitarse, secarse; (of color) palidecer, descolorarse; (vanish) disiparse, desaparecer; (of persons) desmejorarse; (of stains) salir. —*vt* descolorar. **to f. away,** desvanecer; (of persons) consumirse. **f.-out,** *n* (cinema) desaparecimiento gradual, *m*

faded /ˈfeidɪd/ *a* (of plants) seco, marchito, mustio; (of colors) descolorado, pálido; (of people) desmejorado

fadeless /ˈfeidlɪs/ *a* de colores resistentes; eterno, no olvidado; siempre joven

fading /ˈfeidɪŋ/ *a* que palidece; (of flowers) medio marchito; (of light) mortecino, pálido; decadente. —*n* desaparecimiento, *m,* marchitez, *f;* decadencia, *f*

fag /fæg/ *n Inf.* pitillo, *m.* **f.-end,** fin, *m;* restos, *m pl,* sobras, *f pl;* (of a cigarette) colilla, *f;* (*offensive*) maricón. —*vi* trabajar mucho. —*vt* fatigar mucho; hacer trabajar.

faggot /ˈfægət/ *n* haz (or gavilla) de leña, *f*

faience /faiˈɑns/ *n* fayenza, *f*

fail /feil/ *vi* faltar; fracasar, malograrse; no tener éxito, salir mal; (of strength) decaer, acabarse; (be short of) carecer (de); *Com.* hacer bancarrota, suspender pagos. —*vt* abandonar; (disappoint) decepcionar, engañar; (in exams) suspender. **Do not f. to see her,** No dejes de verla. **He failed to do his duty,** Faltó a su deber

fail /feil/ *n* **without f.,** sin falta

failing /ˈfeilɪŋ/ *n* falta, *f;* (shortcoming) vicio, flaco, *m,* debilidad, *f;* malogro, fracaso, *m;* decadencia, *f*

failure /ˈfeilyər/ *n* fracaso, *m;* falta de éxito, *f;* (in exams) suspensión, *f;* (of power) no funcionamiento, *m;* omisión, *f,* descuido, *m;* *Com.* quiebra, bancarrota, *f;* (decay) decadencia, *f.* **on f. of,** al fracasar; bajo pena de

fain /fein/ *a* deseoso, muy contento. **He was f. to...,** Se sintió obligado a...; Quería

faint /feint/ *a* débil; (dim) indistinto, vago, borroso; (of colors) pálido, desmayado; (weak) lánguido, desfallecido; (slight) superficial, rudimentario. —*vi* perder el sentido, desmayarse. —*n* desmayo, *m.* **to be f. with hunger,** estar muerto de hambre. **to cause to f.,** hacer desmayar. **f.-hearted,** pusilánime, medroso. **f.-heartedness,** pusilanimidad, *f*

faintly /ˈfeintli/ *adv* débilmente; en voz débil; indistintamente

faintness /ˈfeintnɪs/ *n* languidez, debilidad, *f;* (swoon) desmayo, *m;* lo indistinto; lo borroso.

fair /fɛər/ *n* feria, *f;* (sale) mercado, *m;* (exhibition) exposición, *f*

fair /fɛər/ *a* (beautiful) hermoso, lindo, bello; (of hair) rubio; (of skin) blanco; (clear, fresh) limpio, claro; (good) bueno; (favorable) favorable, propicio, próspero; (of weather) despejado, sereno; (just) imparcial; (straightforward) honrado, recto, justo; (passable) regular, mediano; (of writing) legible; (proper) conveniente. —*adv* honradamente; (politely) cortésmente; exactamente. **by f. means,** por medios honrados. **It's not f.!** ¡No hay derecho! **to become f.,** (of weather) serenarse. **to give a f. trial,** juzgar imparcialmente; dar una buena oportunidad; *Law.* procesar imparcialmente. **to make a f. copy,** poner en limpio. **f.-haired,** de pelo rubio, rubio. **f. one,** una beldad, *f.* **f. play,** *Sports.* juego limpio, *m;* proceder leal, *m.* **f.-skinned,** de tez blanca, rubio. **f.-weather,** buen tiempo, *m,* bonanza, *f.* **f.-weather friends,** amigos de los días prósperos, *m pl*

fairing /'fɛərɪŋ/ *n Brit* regalo de feria, *m.* **to give fairings,** feriar

fairly /'fɛərli/ *adv* (justly) con imparcialidad; (moderately) bastante; totalmente, enteramente. **f. good,** bastante bueno; regular

fairness /'fɛərnɪs/ *n* belleza, hermosura, *f;* (of skin) blancura, *f;* (justness) imparcialidad, *f;* (reasonableness) justicia, equidad, *f;* (of hair) color rubio, oro, *m*

fairway /'fɛərˌwei/ *n Naut.* canalizo, paso, *m;* (golf) terreno sin obstáculos, *m*

fairy /'fɛəri/ *n* hada, *f,* duende, *m.* —*a* de hada, de duendes; *Fig.* delicado. **f.-gold,** tesoro de duendes, *m;* **f.-light,** lucecillo, *m;* luminaria, *f.* **f.-like,** aduendado, como una hada. **f.-ring,** círculo mágico, *m.* **f.-tale,** cuento de hadas, *m;* patraña, *f,* cuento de viejas, *m*

fairyland /'fɛəriˌlænd/ *n* país de las hadas, *m*

faith /feiθ/ *n* fe, *f;* confianza, *f;* (doctrine) creencia, religión, filosofía, *f;* (honor) palabra, *f.* **in good f.,** de buena fe. **to break f.,** faltar a la palabra dada. **f.-healing,** curanderismo, *m*

faithful /'feiθfəl/ *a* fiel, leal; (accurate) exacto; (trustworthy) veraz. **the f.,** los creyentes

faithfully /'feiθfəli/ *adv* fielmente, lealmente; (accurately) con exactitud. **Yours f.,** Queda de Vd. su att. s.s.

faithfulness /'feiθfəlnɪs/ *n* fidelidad, lealtad, *f;* (accuracy) exactitud, *f*

faithless /'feiθlɪs/ *a* infiel, desleal, pérfido.

faithlessness /'feiθlɪsnɪs/ *n* infidelidad, deslealtad, traición, *f*

fake /feik/ *vt* imitar, falsificar. —*n* imitación, falsificación, *f.* **to f. up,** inventar

Falangist /fei'lɑndʒɪst/ *a* and *n* falangista *mf*

falcon /'fɔlkən/ *n* halcón, *m.* **f. gentle,** *Ornith.* neblí, *m*

falconer /'fɔlkənər/ *n* halconero, *m*

falconry /'fɔlkənri/ *n* cetrería, *f*

fall /fɔl/ *n* caída, *f;* (of temperature, mercury) baja, *f;* (of water) salto de agua, *m,* catarata, cascada, *f;* (in value) depreciación, *f;* (in price and Stock Exchange) baja, *f;* (descent) bajada, *f;* (autumn) otoño, *m;* (declivity) declinación, *f,* declive, desnivel, *m;* (ruin) ruina, *f;* destrucción, *f;* (of night, etc.) caída (de la noche), *f;* (of snow) nevada, *f;* (of rain) golpe, *m;* (*Theat.* of curtain) caída, bajada, *f;* (surrender) capitulación, rendición, *f;* (of earth) desprendimiento de tierras, *m;* (of the tide) reflujo, *m*

fall /fɔl/ *vi* caer; (of mercury, temperature) bajar; (collapse) desplomarse, hundirse, derrumbarse; (die) caer muerto; (descend) descender; (*Theat.* of the curtain) bajar, caer; (of a river into the sea, etc.) desembocar, desaguar; (of hair, draperies) caer; (decrease) disminuir; (of spirits) ponerse triste, sentirse deprimido; (sin) caer; (come upon) sobrevenir; (of dusk, etc.) caer, llegar; (strike, touch) tocar; (as a share) tocar en suerte; (as a duty, responsibility) tocar, corresponder; (of seasons) caer en; (of words from the lips) caer de (los labios); (say) decir, pronunciar palabras; (of exclamations) escaparse; (become) venir a ser; (happen) suceder; (be) ser. **fallen upon evil days,** venido a menos. **His face fell,** Puso una cara de desengaño. **Christmas falls on a Thursday this year,** Navidad cae en jueves este año. **to let f.,** dejar caer. **to f. a-** (followed by verb) empezar a. **He fell a-crying,** Empezó a llorar. **to f. again,** volver a caer, recaer. **to f. among,** caer entre. **to f. astern,** quedarse atrás. **to f. away,** (leave) abandonar, dejar; (grow thin) enflaquecer; marchitarse; (crumble) desmoronarse. **to f. back,** retroceder, volver hacia atrás. **to f. back upon,** recurrir a; *Mil.* replegarse hacia. **to f. backward,** caer de espaldas, caer hacia atrás. **to f. behind,** quedarse atrás. **to f. down,** venirse a tierra; venirse abajo, dar consigo en el suelo, caer. **to f. due,** vencer. **to f. flat,** caer de bruces; (be unsuccessful) no tener éxito. **to f. in,** caer en; (collapse) desplomarse; *Mil.* alinearse; (expire) vencer. **to f. into,** caer en. **to f. in with,** tropezar con; reunirse con, juntarse con; (agree) convenir en; **to f. off,** caer de; (of leaves, etc.) desprenderse de, separarse de; (abandon) abandonar; (diminish) disminuir. **to f. on,** caer de (e.g. *to f. on one's back,* caer de espaldas); (of seasons) caer en; (attack) echarse encima de, atacar. **to f. out,** (of a window, etc.) caer por; (happen) acontecer, suceder; (quarrel) pelearse, reñir; *Mil.* romper filas. **to f. out with,** reñir con. **to f. over,** volcar, caer; (stumble) tropezar con. **to f. short,** faltar; carecer, ser deficiente; (fail) malograrse, no llegar a sus expectaciones; (of shooting) errar el tiro. **to f. through,** caer por; (fail) malograrse, fracasar. **to f. to,** empezar a, ponerse a; (be incumbent on) tocar a, corresponder a; (attack) atacar. **to f. under,** caer debajo; caer bajo; sucumbir, perecer; (incur) incurrir en, merecer. **to f. upon,** (attack) caer sobre, acometer; acaecer, tener lugar; (be incumbent) tocar a

fallacious /fə'leiʃəs/ *a* falaz, engañoso, ilusorio

fallaciousness /fə'leiʃəsnɪs/ *n* falacia, *f,* engaño, *m*

fallacy /'fæləsi/ *n* error, *m,* ilusión, *f*

fallen /'fɔlən/ *a* caído; arruinado; degradado. **f. angel,** ángel caído, *m.* **f. woman,** perdida, mujer caída, *f*

fallibility /ˌfælə'bɪlɪti/ *n* falibilidad, *f*

fallible /'fæləbəl/ *a* falible

falling /'fɔlɪŋ/ *a* que cae, cayente. —*n* caída, *f;* (of mercury, temperature) baja, *f;* (crumbling) desmoronamiento, *m;* (collapse) hundimiento, derrumbamiento, *m;* (of tide) reflujo, *m;* (of waterlevel) bajada, *f;* (in value) depreciación, *f;* (of prices and Stock Exchange) baja, *f;* (diminishment) disminución, *f;* (in level of earth) declinación, *f;* (*Com.* expiry) vencimiento, *m;* (*Theat.* of curtain) bajada, caída, *f.* **f. away,** (crumbling) desmoronamiento, *m;* desprendimiento de tierras, *m;* (desertion) deserción, *f,* abandono, *m.* **f. back,** retirada, *f,* retroceso, *m.* **f. down,** caída, *f;* derrumbamiento, *m.* **f. due,** vencimiento, *m.* **f. in,** hundimiento, *m;* (crumbling) desmoronamiento, *m.* **f. off,** caída de, *f;* (disappearance) desaparición, *f;* (diminution) disminución, *f;* (deterioration) deterioración, *f.* **f. out,** caída por, *f;* disensión, *f.* **f. short,** falta, *f;* carácter inferior, *m;* frustración, *f.* **f. star,** estrella fugaz, *f*

fallout /'fɔlˌaut/ caída radiactiva, llovizna radiactiva, precipitación radiactiva, *f*

fallow /'fælou/ *a* (of color) leonado; *Agr.* barbechado; descuidado. —*n* barbecho, *m.* —*vt* barbechar. **to leave f.,** dejar en barbecho. **f. deer,** corzo (-za)

false /fɔls/ *a* incorrecto, erróneo, equivocado; falso; (unfounded) infundado; (disloyal) infiel, traidor, desleal; (not real) postizo; artificial; de imitación; *Mus.* desafinado; (pretended) fingido; engañoso, mentiroso. **to play a person f.,** traicionar (a). **f. bottom,** fondo doble, *m;* **f. claim,** pretensión infundada, *f.* **f. door,** surtida, *f.* **f.-hearted,** pérfido, desleal. **f. teeth,** dientes postizos, *m pl,* dentadura postiza, *f*

falsehood /'fɔlshʊd/ *n* mentira, *f*

falseness /'fɔlsnɪs/ *n* falsedad, *f;* (disloyalty) duplicidad, perfidia, traición, *f*

falsetto /fɔl'sɛtou/ *n* falsete, *m,* voz de cabeza, *f*

falsification /ˌfɔlsəfɪ'keiʃən/ *n* falsificación, *f;* (of texts) corrupción, *f*

falsifier /'fɔlsəfaiər/ *n* falsificador (-ra)

falsify /'fɔlsəfai/ *vt* falsear, falsificar; (disappoint) defraudar, frustrar, contrariar

falter /'fɔltər/ *vi* (physically) titubear; (of speech) balbucir, tartamudear; (of action) vacilar. **to f. out,** balbucir; hablar con voz entrecortada; decir con vacilación

faltering /'fɔltərɪŋ/ *a* titubeante; (of speech) entrecortado; vacilante. —*n* temblor, *m;* vacilación, *f*

falteringly /'fɔltərɪŋli/ *adv* (of speech) balbuciente, en una voz temblorosa; con dificultad, vacilantemente

fame /feim/ *n* fama, *f;* reputación, *f;* (renown) celebridad, *f,* renombre, *m.* **of ill f.,** de mala fama

famed /feimd/ *a* reputado; renombrado, célebre, famoso

familiar /fə'mılyər/ *a* íntimo, familiar; afable, amistoso; (ill-bred) insolente, demasiado familiar; (usual) corriente, usual, común; conocido. *—n* amigo (-ga) íntimo (-ma); *Eccl.* familiar, *m;* demonio familiar, *m.* **to be f. with,** (a subject) estar versado en, conocer muy bien; (a person) tratar con familiaridad. **to become f. with,** acostumbrarse a; familiarizarse con; (a person) hacerse íntimo de

familiarity /fə,mıli'ærıti/ *n* intimidad, familiaridad, confianza, *f;* (friendliness) afabilidad, *f;* (over-familiarity) insolencia, demasiada familiaridad, *f;* (with a subject) conocimiento (de), *m,* experiencia (de), *f*

familiarize /fə'mılyə,raiz/ *vt* familiarizar, acostumbrar, habituar. *—vr* familiarizarse

familiarly /fə'mılyərli/ *adv* familiarmente; amistosamente

family /'fæməli/ *n* familia, *f;* (lineage) linaje, abolengo, *m;* (*Bot. Zool.*) familia, *f;* (of languages) grupo, *m.* *—a* de familia; familiar; casero. **f. doctor,** médico de cabecera, *m.* **f. life,** vida de familia, *f;* hogar, *m.* **f. man,** padre de familia, *m.* **f. name,** apellido, *m.* **f. seat,** casa solar, *f.* **f. tree,** árbol genealógico, *m*

family quarrel disputa de familia, *f*

famine /'fæmın/ *n* hambre, *f;* carestía, escasez, *f*

famish /'fæmıʃ/ *vt* matar de hambre. *—vi* morirse de hambre

famished /'fæmıʃt/ *a* hambriento

famous /'feiməs/ *a* famoso, célebre, renombrado; insigne, distinguido; *Inf.* excelente

famously /'feiməsli/ *adv Inf.* muy bien, excelentemente

fan /fæn/ *n* abanico, *m; Agr.* aventador, *m; Mech.* ventilador, *m;* (on a windmill) volante, *m;* (amateur) aficionado (-da); (admirer) admirador (-ra); *Archit.* abanico, *m.* *—vt* abanicar; *Agr.* aventar; ventilar. **fan oneself,** hacerse viento. **tap with a f.,** abanicazo, golpecito con el abanico, *m.* **f.-belt,** *Mech.* correa de transmisión del ventilador, *f.* **f.-light,** tragaluz, *m.* **f. maker** or **seller,** abaniquero (-ra). **f.-shaped,** en abanico, abanicado, en forma de abanico

fanatic /fə'nætık/ *a* and *n* fanático (-ca)

fanaticism /fə'nætə,sızəm/ *n* fanatismo, *m*

fanaticize /fə'nætə,saiz/ *vt* fanatizar

fancied /'fænsid/ *a* imaginario

fancier /'fænsiər/ *n* aficionado (-da); (of animals) criador (-ra)

fanciful /'fænsıfəl/ *a* romántico, caprichoso; fantástico

fancifulness /'fænsıfəlnıs/ *n* extravagancia, *f;* romanticismo, *m*

fancy /'fænsi/ *n* fantasía, imaginación, *f;* (idea) idea, *f,* ensueño, *m;* (caprice) capricho, antojo, *m;* (liking) afecto, cariño, *m;* gusto, *m,* afición, *f;* (wish) deseo, *m;* (fantasy) quimera, *f,* *a* imaginario; elegante, ornado; *Com.* de capricho, de fantasía; fantástico, extravagante. *—vt* imaginar, figurarse; (like) gustar de; aficionarse a; antojarse. **I have a f. for...,** Se me antoja.... **Just f.!** ¡Toma! ¡Quia! ¡Parece mentira! **to take a f. to,** (things) tomar afición a; (people) tomar cariño (a). **f.-dress,** disfraz, *m.* **f.-dress ball,** baile de trajes, *m*

fancy goods *n pl* artículos suntuarios *m pl*

fane /fein/ *n* templo, *m*

fanfare /'fænfɛər/ *n* tocata de trompetas, *f*

fang /fæŋ/ *n* colmillo, *m;* raíz de un diente, *f*

fanged /fæŋd/ *a* que tiene colmillos; (of teeth) acolmillado

fangless /'fæŋlıs/ *a* sin colmillos

fanner /'fænər/ *n* abanicador (-ra); *Agr.* aventador, *m*

fanning /'fænıŋ/ *n* abaniqueo, *m; Agr.* avienta, *f*

fantastic /fæn'tæstık/ *a* fantástico; extravagante

fantastically /fæn'tæstıkəli/ *adv* fantásticamente; extravagantemente

fantasy /'fæntəsi/ *n* imaginación, *f;* fantasía, quimera, visión, *f;* creación imaginativa, *f*

far /fɑr/ *adv* lejos; a lo lejos; (much, greatly) mucho, en alto grado; (very) muy; (mostly) en gran parte. *—a* lejano, distante; (farther) ulterior. **as far as,** tan lejos como; (up to, until) hasta; en cuanto, por lo que, según que. (e.g. *As far as we know,* Por lo que nosotros sepamos. *As far as we are concerned,* En cuanto a nosotros toca). **by far,** con mucho. **from far and near,** de todas partes. **from far off,** desde lejos. **He read far into the night,** Leyó hasta las altas horas de la noche. **how far?** ¿a qué distancia?; (to what extent) ¿hasta qué punto? ¿hasta dónde? **How far is it to...?** ¿Qué distancia hay a...? **in so far as,** en tanto que. **on the far side,** al lado opuesto; al otro extremo. **so far,** tan lejos; (till now) hasta ahora. **to go far,** ir lejos. **far away,** *a* distante, remoto, lejano; *Fig.* abstraído. *—adv* muy lejos. **far beyond,** mucho más allá. **far-fetched,** increíble, improbable. **far-off,** *a* distante. *—adv* a lo lejos, en lontananza. **far-reaching,** de gran alcance. **far-sighted,** sagaz, presciente, previsor. **far-sightedness,** sagacidad, previsión, *f*

farce /fɑrs/ *n* farsa, *f.* *—vt Cul.* embutir, rellenar

farcical /'fɑrsıkəl/ *a* burlesco, cómico, sainetesco; absurdo, grotesco, ridiculo

fare /fɛər/ *n* (price) pasaje, precio del billete, *m;* (traveler) viajero (-ra), pasajero (-ra); (food) comida, *f.* *—vi* pasarlo (e.g. *to f. well,* pasarlo bien). **bill of f.,** menú, *m.* **full f.,** billete entero, *m.* **f. stage,** trayecto, *m*

farewell /,fɛər'wɛl/ *n* despedida, *f,* adiós, *m.* *—a* de despedida. *—interj* ¡adiós! ¡quede Vd. con Dios! **to bid f. to,** despedirse de

farewell address *n* discurso de despedida *m*

farflung /'fɑr'flʌŋ/ de gran alcance, extenso, vasto; (empire) dilatado

farina /fə'rinə/ *n* harina (de cereales), *f; Chem.* fécula, *f,* almidón, *m; Bot.* polen, *m*

farm /fɑrm/ *n* granja, hacienda, quintería, finca, chacra, *f,* cortijo, *m.* *—vt* cultivar, labrar (la tierra); (taxes) arrendar. *—vi* ser granjero. **to f. out,** (taxes) dar en arriendo. **f. girl,** labradora, *f.* **f. house,** alquería, casa de labranza, granja, *f.* **f. laborer,** labriego, peón, *m.* **f. yard,** corral de una granja, *m*

farmer /'fɑrmər/ *n* granjero, hacendado, quintero, *m,* agrícola, *mf;* (small) colono, labrador, *m;* (of taxes) arrendatario, *m*

farmhand /'fɑrm,hænd/ gañán, mozo, mozo de granja, peón *m*

farming /'fɑrmıŋ/ *n* labranza, *f,* cultivo, *m;* agricultura, labor agrícola, *f;* (of taxes) arriendo, *m.* *—a* de labranza, labradoril; agrícola

faro /'fɛərou/ *n* (card game) faraón, *m*

farouche /fə'ruʃ/ *a* huraño, esquivo

farrago /fə'rɑgou/ *n* fárrago, *m,* mezcla, *f*

farrier /'færiər/ *n* herrador, *m*

farther /'fɑrðər/ *adv* más lejos; (beyond) más adelante; (besides) además. *—a* ulterior; más distante. **at the f. end,** al otro extremo; en el fondo. **f. on,** más adelante; más allá

farthest /'fɑrðıst/ *adv* más lejos. *—a* más lejano, más distante; extremo

farthing /'fɑrðıŋ/ *n* cuarto, *m; Fig.* ardite, maravedí, *m.* **He hasn't a brass f.,** No tiene dos maravedís

fasces /'fæsiz/ *n pl* fasces, *f pl*

fascicle /'fæsıkəl/ *n Bot.* hacecillo, *m*

fascinate /'fæsə,neit/ *vt* fascinar; encantar, hechizar, seducir

fascinating /'fæsə,neitıŋ/ *a* fascinador; encantador, seduciente

fascination /,fæsə'neiʃən/ *n* fascinación, *f;* encanto, hechizo, *m*

Fascism /'fæʃ,ızəm/ *n* fascismo, *m*

Fascist /'fæʃıst/ *a* and *n* fascista *mf*

fashion /'fæʃən/ *n* (form) forma, hechura, *f;* (way) modo, *m;* (custom) costumbre, *f,* uso, *m;* (vogue) moda, *f;* (high life) alta sociedad, *f;* (tone) buen tono, *m.* *—vt* hacer, labrar; inventar. **in Spanish f.,** a la española, al uso de España. **the latest f.,** la última moda. **to be in f.,** estar de moda. **to go out of f.,** dejar de ser de moda, perder la popularidad. **f. book,** revista de modas, *f.* **f. plate,** figurín, *m*

fashionable /'fæʃənəbəl/ *a* de moda; elegante; de

buen tono. **to be f.,** estar en boga, ser de moda. **f. world,** mundo elegante, mundo de sociedad, *m*
fashionableness /'fæʃənəbəlnɪs/ *n* buen tono, *m;* elegancia, *f*
fashionably /'fæʃənəbli/ *adv* a la moda, elegantemente
fashion show desfile de modas, *m,* exhibición de modas, *f*
fast /fæst/ *a* (firm) firme; (secure) seguro; (strong) fuerte; (fixed) fijo; (closed) cerrado; (of boats) amarrado; (tight) apretado; (of colors) estable; (of trains) rápido; (of sleep) profundo; (of friends) leal, seguro; (quick) rápido, veloz; (of a watch) adelantado; (dissipated) disoluto. —*adv* firmemente, seguramente; (quickly) rápidamente; (of sleep) profundamente; (tightly) estrechamente, apretadamente; (of rain) (llover) a cántaros; (ceaselessly) continuamente; (often) frecuentemente; (entirely) completamente. **to be f.,** (clocks) adelantar. **to make f.,** *Naut.* amarrar, trincar. **f. asleep,** profundamente dormido. **f. color,** color estable, color sólido, *m*
fast /fæst/ *n* ayuno, *m, vi* ayunar. **to break one's f.,** romper el ayuno. **f.-day,** día de ayuno, día de vigilia, *m*
fasten /'fæsən/ *vt* (tie) atar; (fix) fijar; sujetar; (stick) pegar; (a door) cerrar; (bolt) echar el cerrojo; *Naut.* trincar; (together) juntar, unir; (with buttons, hooks, etc.) abrochar; (on, upon) fijar en; *Fig.* imputar (a). —*vi* fijarse; pegarse; (upon) agarrarse a, asir. **to f. one's eyes on,** fijar los ojos en. **to f. up,** cerrar; atar; (nail) clavar
fastener /'fæsənər/ *n* (bolt) pasador, *m;* (for bags, jewelery, etc.) cierre, *m;* (buckle) hebilla, *f;* (of a coat, etc.) tiador, *m;* (of a book, file) sujetador, *m;* (lock) cerrojo, *m.* **paper-f.,** sujetador de papeles, *m.* **patent-f.,** botón automático, *m*
fastening /'fæsənɪŋ/ *n* atadura, *f;* sujeción, *f,* afianzamiento, *m;* (together) union, *f;* (of a garment) brochadura, *f;* (of a handbag) cierre, *m*
fastidious /fæ'stɪdiəs/ *a* dengoso, melindroso, desdeñoso; (sensitive) sensitivo, delicado; (critical) discerniente, crítico
fastidiously /fæs'tɪdiəsli/ *adv* melindrosamente
fastidiousness /fæs'tɪdiəsnɪs/ *n* dengues, melindres, *m pl,* nimiedad, *f,* desdén, *m;* sensibilidad, delicadeza, *f;* sentido crítico, *m*
fasting /'fæstɪŋ/ *n* ayuno, *m.* —*a* and *part* de ayuno; en ayunas
fastness /'fæstnɪs/ *n* firmeza, solidez, *f;* (stronghold) fortaleza, *f;* (retreat) refugio, *m;* (speed) velocidad, rapidez, *f;* (dissipation) disipación, *f,* libertinaje, *m*
fat /fæt/ *a* (stout) gordo, grueso; mantecoso, graso, seboso; (greasy) grasiento; (rich) fértil, pingüe; (productive) lucrativo. —*n* (stoutness) gordura, *f;* (for cooking) manteca, *f;* (lard) lardo, *m;* (of animal or meat) grasa, *f;* sebo, saín, *m; Fig.* riqueza, *f; Fig.* fertilidad, *f.* **to grow fat,** engordarse, ponerse grueso
fatal /'feitl̩/ *a* fatal, mortal; funesto
fatalism /'feitl̩ˌɪzəm/ *n* fatalismo, *m*
fatalist /'feitl̩ɪst/ *n* fatalista, *mf*
fatalistic /ˌfeitl̩'ɪstɪk/ *a* fatalista
fatality /fei'tælɪti/ *n* fatalidad, *f;* infortunio, *m,* calamidad, *f;* muerte, *f*
fatally /'feitl̩i/ *adv* mortalmente, fatalmente; inevitablemente
fate /feit/ *n* destino, sino, hado, *m,* providencia, *f;* fortuna, suerte, *f;* destrucción, ruina, *f;* muerte, *f.* **the Three Fates,** las Parcas
fated /'feitɪd/ *a* fatal, destinado; predestinado
fateful /'feitfəl/ *a* decisivo, fatal; aciago, ominoso
father /'fɑðər/ *n* padre, *m.* —*vt* prohijar, adoptar; (on or upon) atribuir (a), imputar (a). **Eternal F.,** Padre Eterno, *m.* **Holy F.,** Padre Santo, *m.* **indulgent f.,** padre indulgente, padrazo, *m.* **Like f. like son,** De tal palo tal astilla. **f. confessor,** *Eccl.* director espiritual, *m.* **f.-in-law,** suegro, *m*
fatherhood /'fɑðərˌhʊd/ *n* paternidad, *f*
fatherland /'fɑðərˌlænd/ *n* patria, madre patria, *f*
fatherless /'fɑðərlɪs/ *a* sin padre, huérfano de padre
fatherliness /'fɑðərlinɪs/ *n* amor paternal, *m;* sentimiento paternal, *m*
fatherly /'fɑðərli/ *a* paternal, de padre
fathom /'fæðəm/ *n Naut.* braza, *f.* —*vt* sondear; *Fig.* profundizar, tantear; (a mystery) desentrañar
fathomless /'fæðəmlɪs/ *a* insondable; *Fig.* incomprensible, impenetrable
fatigue /fə'tig/ *n* fatiga, *f,* cansancio, *m; Mil.* faena, *f; Mech.* pérdida de resistencia, *f.* —*vt* fatigar, cansar. **to be fatigued,** estar cansado, cansarse, fatigarse. **f. party,** *Mil.* pelotón de castigo, *m*
fatiguing /fə'tigɪŋ/ *a* fatigoso
fatness /'fætnɪs/ *n* (stoutness) gordura, carnosidad, *f;* grasa, *f,* gordo, *m;* (richness) fertilidad, *f;* lo lucrativo
fatten /'fætn̩/ *vt* engordar; (animals) cebar, sainar; (land) abonar, fertilizar. —*vi* ponerse grueso, echar carnes
fatty /'fæti/ *a* untoso, grasiento; *Chem.* graso. **f. acid,** ácido graso, *m.* **f. degeneration,** degeneración grasienta, *f*
fatuity /fə'tuɪti/ *n* fatuidad, necedad, *f*
fatuous /'fætʃuəs/ *a* fatuo, necio, lelo
faucet /'fɔsɪt/ *n* canilla, llave, *f,* grifo, *m*
fault /fɔlt/ *n* defecto, *m,* imperfección, *f;* (blame) culpa, *f;* (mistake) falta, *f,* error, *m;* (in cloth) canilla, barra, *f; Geol.* falla, quiebra, *f; Elec.* avería, *f; Sports.* falta, *f, vi Sports.* cometer una falta. **to a f.,** excesivamente. **to be at f.,** (to blame) tener la culpa; (mistaken) estar equivocado; (puzzled) estar perplejo; (of dogs) perder el rastro. **to find f.,** tachar, culpar, criticar. **Whose f. is it?** ¿Quién tiene la culpa?
faultfinder /'fɔltˌfaindər/ *n* criticón (-ona)
faultiness /'fɔltinɪs/ *n* defectuosidad, imperfección, *f*
faultless /'fɔltlɪs/ *a* sin faltas; perfecto, sin tacha; impecable
faulty /'fɔlti/ *a* defectuoso, imperfecto
faun /fɔn/ *n* fauno, *m*
fauna /'fɔnə/ *n* fauna, *f*
favor /'feivər/ *n* favor, *m;* (protection) amistad, protección, *f,* amparo, *m;* (permission) permiso, *m,* licencia, *f;* (kindness) merced, gracia, *f;* (gift) obsequio, *m;* (favoritism) favoritismo, *m,* preferencia, *f;* (benefit) beneficio, *m;* (badge) colores, *m pl; Com.* grata, atenta, *f.* —*vt* favorecer, apoyar; mirar con favor, mostrar parcialidad (hacia); (suit) favorecer; (be advantageous) ser propicio (a); (contribute to) contribuir a, ayudar; (resemble) parecerse (a). **Circumstances f. the idea,** Las circunstancias son propicias a la idea, Las circunstancias militan en pro de la idea. **I f. the teaching of modern languages,** Soy partidario de la enseñanza de lenguas vivas. **in f. of,** a favor de, en pro de. **in the f. of,** en el favor de. **out of f.,** fuera de favor; (not fashionable) fuera de moda. **to count on the f. of,** tener de su parte (a), contar con el apoyo de. **to do a f.,** hacer un favor. **to enjoy the f. of,** gozar del favor de. **to fall out of f.,** caer en desgracia; (go out of fashion) pasar de moda. **to grow in f.,** aumentar en favor
favorable /'feivərəbəl/ *a* favorable; propicio, próspero
favorableness /'feivərəbəlnɪs/ *n* lo favorable; lo propicio; benignidad, benevolencia, *f*
favorably /'feivərəbli/ *adv* favorablemente
favored /'feivərd/ *a* favorecido; predilecto; (in compounds) parecido, encarado
favoring /'feivərɪŋ/ *a* favorecedor, propicio
favorite /'feivərɪt/ *a* favorito; predilecto, preferido. —*n* favorito (-ta). **court f.,** valido, privado, *m;* (mistress) querida (de un rey), *f;* (lover) amante (de una reina), *m.* **to be a f.,** ser favorito
favoritism /'feivərɪˌtɪzəm/ *n* favoritismo, *m*
fawn /fɔn/ *n Zool.* cervato, *m;* (color) color de cervato, color de ante, *m.* —*a* de color de cervato, anteado, pardo; (of animals) rucio, pardo. —*vt* and *vi* parir la cierva. —*vi* acariciar; (on, upon) adular, lisonjear
fawning /'fɔnɪŋ/ *n* adulación, *f, a* adulador, lisonjero
fear /fɪər/ *n* miedo, temor, *m;* (apprehension) ansiedad, aprensión, *f,* recelo, *m;* (respect) veneración, *f.* —*vt* temer; recelar; (respect) reverenciar. —*vi* tener miedo; estar receloso, estar con cuidado. **for f. of,** por miedo de. **for f. that,** por temor de que, por miedo de que. **from f.,** por miedo. **There is no f. of...,** No hay miedo de (que)...
fearer /'fɪərər/ *n* temedor (-ra), el (la) que teme

fearful /'fɪərfəl/ *a* miedoso, aprensivo, receloso; (cowardly) tímido, pusilánime; (terrible) horrible, espantoso, pavoroso; *Inf.* tremendo, enorme
fearfully /'fɪərfəli/ *adv* con miedo; tímidamente; (terribly) horriblemente; *Inf.* enormemente
fearfulness /'fɪərfəlnɪs/ *n* temor, miedo, *m;* (horribleness) lo horrible
fearless /'fɪərlɪs/ *a* sin miedo, intrépido, audaz
fearlessness /'fɪərlɪsnɪs/ *n* intrepidez, valentía, *f*
fearsome /'fɪərsəm/ *a* temible, horrible, espantoso
feasibility /ˌfizə'bɪlɪti/ *n* practicabilidad, posibilidad, *f*
feasible /'fizəbəl/ *a* factible, hacedero, practicable, ejecutable
feast /fist/ *n Eccl.* fiesta, *f;* banquete, *m; Fig.* abundancia, *f, vi* regalarse. —*vt* festejar, agasajar; (delight) recrear, deleitar. **immovable f.,** *Eccl.* fiesta fija, *f.* **movable f.,** fiesta movible, *f.* **f. day,** día de fiesta, *m,* festividad *f*
feasting /'fistɪŋ/ *n* banquetes, *m pl;* fiestas, *f pl*
feat /fit/ *n* hazaña, proeza, *f,* hecho, *m*
feather /'fɛðər/ *n* pluma, *f;* (of the tail) pena, *f; pl* **feathers,** plumaje, *m;* plumas, *f pl.* —*vt* emplumar; adornar con plumas; (rowing) poner casi horizontal la pala del remo. **to f. one's nest,** *Inf.* hacer su agosto. **f. bed,** plumón, colchón de plumas, *m.* **f.-brained,** casquivano, alocado, aturdido. **f.-duster,** plumero, *m.* **f.-stitch,** *Sew.* diente de perro, *m.* **f. weight,** (boxing) peso pluma, *m*
feathered /'fɛðərd/ *a* plumado, plumoso; adornado con plumas; (winged) alado
feathery /'fɛðəri/ *a* plumoso; como plumas
feature /'fitʃər/ *n* rasgo, *m,* característica, *f;* (cinema) número de programa, *m; pl* **features** (of the face) facciones, *f pl.* —*vt* dar importancia (a); (cinema) presentar. **f. film,** documentaria, *f*
febrile /'fibrəl/ *a* febril
February /'fɛbruˌɛri, 'fɛbyu-/ *n* febrero, *m*
fecal /'fikəl/ *a* fecal
feces /'fisiz/ *n* heces, *f pl;* excremento, *m*
fecund /'fikʌnd/ *a* fecundo, fértil
fecundate /'fikənˌdeit/ *vt* fecundar
fecundity /fɪ'kʌndɪti/ *n* fecundidad, fertilidad, *f*
federal /'fɛdərəl/ *a* federal, federalista
federalism /'fɛdərəˌlɪzəm/ *n* federalismo, *m*
federalist /'fɛdərəlɪst/ *n* federalista, federal, *mf*
federate /*v* 'fɛdəˌreit; -ərɪt/ *vt* confederar. —*vi* confederarse. —*a* confederado
federation /ˌfɛdə'reiʃən/ *n* confederación, federación, *f;* liga, unión, asociación, *f*
federative /'fɛdəˌreitɪv/ *a* federativo
fee /fi/ *n* (feudal law) feudo, *m;* (homage) homenaje, *m;* (duty) derecho, *m;* (professional) honorario, estipendio, *m;* (to a servant) gratificación, *f;* (entrance, university, etc.) cuota, *f;* (payment) paga, *f*
feeble /'fibəl/ *a* débil; lánguido; enfermizo; (of light, etc.) tenue; *Fig.* flojo. **to grow f.,** debilitarse; disminuir. **f.-minded,** anormal
feebleness /'fibəlnɪs/ *n* debilidad, *f; Fig.* flojedad, *f*
feebly /'fibli/ *adv* débilmente; lánguidamente
feed /fid/ *n* alimento, *m;* (meal) comida, *f;* (of animals) pienso, forraje, *m; Mech.* alimentación, *f.* —*vt* alimentar; dar de comer (a); (animals) cebar; *Mech.* alimentar; mantener; *Fig.* nutrir. —*vi* comer, alimentarse; (graze) pastar. **to be fed up,** *Inf.* estar hasta la coronilla, estar harto. **to f. on,** alimentarse de; *Fig.* nutrirse de. **f. pipe,** tubo de alimentación, *m*
feedback /'fidˌbæk/ retrocomunicación, *f*
feeder /'fidər/ *n* el, *m,* (*f,* la) que da de comer a; (eater) comedor (-ra); (of a river) tributario, afluente, *m;* (bib) babero, *m; Mech.* alimentador, *m;* (cup for invalids) pistero, *m*
feeding /'fidɪŋ/ *n* alimentación, *f, a* alimenticio, de alimentación. **f.-bottle,** biberón, *m.* **f.-cup,** pistero, *m.* **f.-trough,** pesebre, *m*
feel /fil/ *n* (touch) tacto, *m;* (feeling) sensación, *f;* (instinct) instinto, *m,* percepción innata, *f*
feel /fil/ *vt* (touch) tocar, tentar, palpar; (experience) sentir, experimentar; (understand) comprender; (believe) creer; (be conscious of) estar consciente de; (the pulse) tomar; examinar. —*vi* sentir, ser sensible; sentirse, encontrarse; (to the touch) ser... al tacto, estar. **How do you f.?** ¿Cómo se siente Vd.? **I f. cold,** Tengo frío. **I f. for you,** Lo siento en el alma; Estoy muy consciente de ello. **I f. strongly that...,** Estoy convencido de que... **I f. that it is a difficult question,** Me parece una cuestión difícil. **It feels like rain,** Creo que va a llover. **to f. at home,** sentirse a sus anchas, sentirse como en su casa. **to f. hungry (thirsty),** tener hambre (sed). **to f. one's way,** andar a tientas; *Fig.* medir el terreno. **to f. soft,** ser blando al tacto. **to make itself felt,** hacerse sentir. **Your hands f. cold,** Tus manos están frías
feeler /'filər/ *n* (of insects) palpo, *m,* antena, *f;* tentáculo, *m; Fig.* tentativa, *f,* balón de ensayo, *m*
feeling /'filɪŋ/ *n* (touch) tacto, *m;* (sensation) sensación, *f;* (sentiment) sentimiento, *m;* emoción, *f;* (premonition) corazonada, intuición, premonición, *f;* (tenderness) ternura, *f;* (perception) sensibilidad, percepción, *f;* (passion) pasión, *f;* (belief) opinión, *f,* sentir, *m.* —*a* sensible; tierno; (compassionate) compasivo; apasionado; (moving) conmovedor
feelingly /'filɪŋli/ *adv* con emoción; (strongly) enérgicamente, vivamente; (understandingly) comprensivamente
feign /fein/ *vt* fingir; (invent) inventar, imaginar; simular; (allege) pretextar; (dissemble) disimular. *vi* disimular
feint /feint/ *n* artificio, engaño, *m;* (in fencing) treta, finta, *f.* —*vi* hacer finta
feldspar /'fɛldˌspɑr/ *n Mineral.* feldespato, *m*
felicitate /fɪ'lɪsɪˌteit/ *vt* felicitar, congratular, dar el parabién (a)
felicitation /fɪˌlɪsɪ'teiʃən/ *n* felicitación, *f,* parabién, *m*
felicitous /fɪ'lɪsɪtəs/ *a* feliz, dichoso, afortunado; (of phrases, etc.) feliz, acertado; oportuno
felicity /fɪ'lɪsɪti/ *n* felicidad, dicha, *f*
feline /'filain/ *a* felino, gatuno, de gato. —*n* felino, *m*
fell /fɛl/ *n* (skin) piel, *f;* (upland) altura, cuesta de montaña, *f.* —*a* cruel, feroz; (unhappy) aciago, funesto. —*vt* talar, cortar; (knock down) derribar; *Sew.* sobrecoser
feller /'fɛlər/ *n* talador, leñador, *m*
felling /'fɛlɪŋ/ *n* corta, tala, *f*
fellow /'fɛlou/ *n* compañero (-ra); (equal) igual, *mf;* (in crime) cómplice, *mf;* (man) hombre, *m;* (boy, youth) chico, *m;* (colleague) colega, *m;* (of a society) miembro, *m;* (of a pair of objects) pareja, *f; Inf.* tipo, chico, *m.* **He's a good f.,** Es un buen chico. **How are you, old f.?** ¡Hombre! ¿Cómo estás? **f.-citizen,** conciudadano (-na). **f.-countryman,** compatriota, *m;* paisano (-na). **f.-creature,** semejante, *mf* **f.-feeling,** simpatía, comprensión mutua, *f.* **f.-member,** compañero (-ra); colega, *m.* **f.-passenger,** compañero (-ra) de viaje. **f.-prisoner,** compañero (-ra) de prisión. **f.-student,** condiscípulo (-la). **f.-worker,** compañero (-ra) de trabajo; (collaborator) colaborador (-ra); (colleague) colega, *m*
fellowship /'fɛlouˌʃɪp/ *n* coparticipación, *f;* (companionship) compañerismo, *m;* (brotherhood) comunidad, confraternidad, *f;* (society) asociación, *f;* (grant) beca, *f;* (of a university) colegiatura, *f*
felon /'fɛlən/ *n* reo, criminal, *mf;* felón (-ona); malvado (-da); (swelling) panadizo, *m*
felonious /fə'louniəs/ *a* criminal; pérfido, traidor
felony /'fɛləni/ *n* felonía, *f*
felt /fɛlt/ *n* fieltro, *m.* **a f. hat,** un sombrero de fieltro
female /'fimeil/ *n* hembra, *f, a* femenino. (**f.** is often rendered in Sp. by the feminine ending of the noun, e.g. *a f. cat,* una gata; *a f. friend,* una amiga.) **This is a f. animal,** Este animal es una hembra. **f. screw,** hembra de tornillo, tuerca, *f*
feminine /'fɛmənɪn/ *a* femenino; mujeril, afeminado. **in the f. gender,** en el género femenino
feminism /'fɛməˌnɪzəm/ *n* feminismo, *m*
feminist /'fɛmənɪst/ *n* feminista, *mf*
feministic /ˌfɛmə'nɪstɪk/ *a* feminista
femur /'fimər/ *n Anat.* fémur, *m*
fen /fɛn/ *n* marjal, pantano, *m*
fence /fɛns/ *n* cerca, *f;* (of stakes) estacada, palizada, *f;* (hedge) seto, *m;* (fencing) esgrima, *f; Mech.* guía, *f; Inf.* comprador (-ra) de efectos robados. —*vi* esgrimir; *Fig.* defenderse; *Inf.* recibir efectos robados. —*vt* cercar; estacar; *Fig.* defender; proteger. **to sit on the f.,** *Fig.* estar a ver venir

fencer /'fɛnsər/ *n* esgrimidor, *m*
fencesitter /'fɛns,sɪtər/ bailarín de la cuerda flaja, *m*
fencing /'fɛnsɪŋ/ *n* esgrima, *f;* palizada, empalizada, *f.* **f. mask,** careta, *f.* **f. master,** maestro de esgrima, maestro de armas, *m.* **f. match,** asalto de esgrima, *m*
fend /fɛnd/ **(off)** *vt* parar; defenderse de, guardarse de. —*vi* (for) mantener, cuidar de. **to f. for oneself,** ganarse la vida; defenderse
fender /'fɛndər/ *n* (round hearth) guardafuegos, *m; Naut.* espolón, *m,* defensas, *f pl; Auto.* parachoques, *m*
fennel /'fɛnl̩/ *n Bot.* hinojo, *m*
ferment /*n* 'fɜrmɛnt; *v* fər'mɛnt/ *n* fermento, *m;* fermentación, *f; Fig.* agitación, conmoción, efervescencia *f.* —*vt* hacer fermentar; *Fig.* agitar, excitar. —*vi* fermentar, estar en fermentación; *Fig.* hervirse, agitarse, excitarse
fermentation /,fɜrmɛn'teiʃən/ *n* fermentación, *f*
fern /fɜrn/ *n* helecho, *m*
ferny /'fɜrni/ *a* cubierto de helechos
ferocious /fə'rouʃəs/ *a* feroz, bravo, salvaje
ferocity /fə'rɒsɪti/ *n* ferocidad, braveza, fiereza, *f*
ferreous /'fɛriəs/ *a* férreo
ferret /'fɛrɪt/ *n Zool.* hurón (-ona); **to f. out,** cazar con hurones; (discover) husmear, descubrir
Ferris wheel /'fɛrɪs/ *n* estrella giratoria, gran rueda, novia, rueda de feria, *f*
ferroconcrete /,fɛrou'kɒnkrit/ *n* hormigón armado, *m*
ferrous /'fɛrəs/ *a* ferroso
ferruginous /fə'rudʒənəs/ *a* ferruginoso; aherrumbrado, rojizo
ferrule /'fɛrəl/ *n* herrete, regatón, *m,* contera, *f;* garrucha de tornillos, *f*
ferry /'fɛri/ *n* barca de transporte, *f;* barca de pasaje, *f,* transbordador, *m.* —*vt* transportar de una a otra orilla, llevar en barca. —*vi* cruzar un río en barca. **ferry across** *vt* transbordar. **F.-Command,** servicio de entrega y transporte de aeroplanos, *m*
ferryman /'fɛrimən/ *n* barquero, *m*
fertile /'fɜrtl̩/ *a* fértil, fecundo; (rich) pingüe; *Fig.* prolífico, abundante
Fertile Crescent, the el Creciente Fértil *m*
fertility /fər'tɪlɪti/ *n* fertilidad, fecundidad, *f*
fertilization /,fɜrtl̩ə'zeiʃən/ *n Biol.* fecundación, *f; Agr.* fertilización, *f,* abono, *m*
fertilize /'fɜrtl̩,aiz/ *vt Biol.* fecundar; *Agr.* fertilizar, abonar
fertilizer /'fɜrtl̩,aizər/ *n* abono, *m*
ferule /'fɛrəl/ *n* palmatoria, palmeta, férula, *f*
fervent /'fɜrvənt/ *a* ardiente; fervoroso, intenso; (enthusiastic) entusiasta, apasionado
fervently /'fɜrvəntli/ *adv* con fervor, con vehemencia
fervor /'fɜrvər/ *n* ardor, fervor, *m,* pasión, *f;* (enthusiasm) entusiasmo, celo, *m;* vehemencia, *f*
festal /'fɛstl̩/ *a* de fiesta; alegre, festivo, regocijado
fester /'fɛstər/ *vi* ulcerarse, enconarse; *Fig.* inflamarse, amargarse. —*vt* ulcerar
festival /'fɛstəvəl/ *a* de fiesta. —*n* festividad, *f; Eccl.* fiesta, *f;* (musical, etc.) festival, *m*
festive /'fɛstɪv/ *a* de fiesta; festivo, alegre
festivity /fɛ'stɪvɪti/ *n* festividad, fiesta, *f;* (merriment) alegría, *f,* júbilo, *m*
festoon /fɛ'stun/ *n* festón, *m,* guirnalda, *f.* —*vt* festonear
festschrift /'fɛst,ʃrɪft/ *n* libro de homenaje, libro jubilar, *m*
fetal /'fitl̩/ *a* fetal
fetch /fɛtʃ/ *vt* traer; ir a buscar; ir por; llevar; (conduct) conducir; (of tears) hacer derramar lágrimas, hacer saltársele las lágrimas; (blood) hacer correr la sangre; (produce, draw) sacar; (a blow, a sigh) dar; (acquire) conseguir; (charm) fascinar; (of price) venderse por. **to go and f.,** ir a buscar. **to f. and carry,** *vt* (news) divulgar, publicar. —*vi* estar ocupado en oficios humildes, trajinar. **to f. away,** llevarse; ir a buscar; venir a buscar. **to f. back,** devolver; (of persons) traer (a casa, etc.); traer otra vez. **to f. down,** bajar, llevar abajo; hacer bajar. **to f. in,** hacer entrar; (place inside) poner adentro; (persons and things) llevar adentro. **to f. out,** hacer salir; (bring out things) sacar; (put out) poner afuera; (an idea, etc.) sacar a relucir. **to f. up,** (a parcel, etc.) subir; (a person) hacer subir; llevar arriba
fete /feit/ *n* fiesta, *f*
fetid /'fɛtɪd/ *a* fétido, hediondo
fetidness /'fɛtɪdnɪs/ *n* fetidez, *f,* hedor, *m*
fetish /'fɛtɪʃ/ *n* fetiche, *m*
fetishism /'fɛtɪ,ʃɪzəm/ *n* fetichismo, *m*
fetter /'fɛtər/ *n* grillete, *m; pl* **fetters,** grillos, *m pl,* cadenas, *f pl;* prisión, cárcel, *f.* —*vt* encadenar, atar
fettle /'fɛtl̩/ *n* condición, *f,* estado, *m*
fetus /'fitəs/ *n* feto, *m*
feud /fyud/ *n* enemistad, riña, *f;* (feudal law) feudo, *m*
feudal /'fyudl̩/ *a* feudal. **f. lord,** señor feudal, señor de horca y cuchillo, *m*
feudalism /'fyudl̩,ɪzəm/ *n* feudalismo, *m*
feudatory /'fyudə,tɔri/ *a* and *n* feudatario (-ia)
fever /'fivər/ *n* fiebre, *f;* calentura, *f;* (enthusiasm) pasión, afición, *f.* **to be in a f.,** tener fiebre; (agitated) estar muy agitado. **to be in a f. to,** estar muy impaciente de. **puerperal f.,** fiebre puerperal, *f.* **tertian f.,** fiebre terciana, *f.* **yellow f.,** fiebre amarilla, *f*
feverish /'fivərɪʃ/ *a* febril; *Fig.* ardiente, febril, vehemente. **to grow f.,** empezar a tener fiebre, acalenturarse
feverishness /'fivərɪʃnɪs/ *n* calentura, *f;* (impatience) impaciencia, *f*
few /fyu/ *a* and *n* pocos, *m pl;* pocas, *f pl;* algunos, *m pl;* algunas, *f pl;* (few in number) número pequeño (de), *m.* **a good f.,** bastantes, *mf pl.* **not a f.,** no pocos, *m pl,* (pocas, *f pl*). **the f.,** la minoría, *f.* **f. and far between,** raramente, en raras ocasiones; pocos y contados
fewer /'fyuər/ *a compar* menos. **The f. the better,** Cuantos menos mejor
fewest /'fyuɪst/ *a superl* (el) menos, *m;* el menor número (de), *m;* (el) menos posible de, *m*
fewness /'fyunɪs/ *n* corto número, *m*
fez /fɛz/ *n* fez, *m*
fiancé(e) /,fiɑn'sei/ *n* novio (-ia); desposado (-da), prometido (-da)
fiasco /fi'æskou/ *n* fiasco, mal éxito, fracaso, malogro, *m*
fiat /'fiɑt/ *n* fiat, mandato, *m,* orden, *f*
fib /fɪb/ *n* mentirilla, *f, vt* decir mentirillas, mentir
fibber /'fɪbər/ *n* embustero (-ra), mentiroso (-sa)
fiber /'faibər/ *n* fibra, *f;* filamento, *m,* hebra, *f;* (of grass, etc.) brizna, *f; Fig.* naturaleza, *f*
fibroid /'faibrɔid/ *a* fibroso. —*n* fibroma, *m*
fibrous /'faibrəs/ *a* fibroso
fibula /'fɪbyələ/ *n Anat.* peroné, *m*
fichu /'fɪʃu/ *n* pañoleta, *f,* fichú, *m*
fickle /'fɪkəl/ *a* inconstante; mudable; (of persons) liviano, ligero, voluble
fickleness /'fɪkəlnɪs/ *n* inconstancia, *f;* mudanza, *f;* liviandad, ligereza, veleidad, volubilidad, *f*
fiction /'fɪkʃən/ *n* ficción, *f;* invención, *f;* literatura narrativa, *f;* novelas, *f pl.* **legal f.,** ficción legal, ficción de derecho, *f*
fictitious /fɪk'tɪʃəs/ *a* ficticio; imaginario; fingido
fictitiousness /fɪk'tɪʃəsnɪs/ *n* carácter ficticio, *m;* falsedad, *f*
fiddle /'fɪdl̩/ *n* violín, *m.* —*vt* tocar... en el violín. —*vi* tocar el violín; (fidget) jugar; perder el tiempo. **to play second f.,** tocar el segundo violín; *Fig.* ser plato de segunda mesa
fiddler /'fɪdlər/ *n* violinista, *mf*
fiddling /'fɪdlɪŋ/ *a* insignificante, trivial, frívolo
fidelity /fɪ'dɛlɪti/ *n* fidelidad, *f*
fidget /'fɪdʒɪt/ *vi* estar nervioso, estar inquieto; impacientarse; trajinar; (with) jugar con. —*vt* molestar; impacientar
fidgetiness /'fɪdʒɪtinɪs/ *n* inquietud, nerviosidad, *f*
fidgety /'fɪdʒɪti/ *a* inquieto, nervioso. **to be f.,** tener hormiguillo
fiduciary /fɪ'duʃi,ɛri/ *a* fiduciario. —*n* fideicomisario (-ia)
fief /fif/ *n* feudo, *m*
field /fild/ *n* campo, *m;* (meadow) prado, *m,* pradera, *f;* (sown field) sembrado, *m;* (*Phys. Herald.*) campo, *m;* (of ice) banco, *m; Mineral.* yacimiento, *m;*

(background) fondo, *m;* (campaign) campaña, *f;* (battle) batalla, lucha, *f;* (space) espacio, *m;* (of knowledge, etc.) especialidad, esfera, *f;* (hunting) caza, *f;* *Sports.* campo, *m;* (competitors) todos los competidores en una carrera, etc.; (horses in a race) el campo. —*a* campal, pradeño; de campo; de los campos. —*vt Sports.* parar y devolver la pelota. **in the f.,** *Mil.* en el campo de batalla, en campaña. **magnetic f.,** campo magnético, *m.* **to take the f.,** entrar en campaña. **f.-artillery,** artillería ligera, artillería montada, *f.* **f.-day,** (holiday) día de asueto, *m;* (day out) día en el campo, *m; Mil.* día de maniobras, *m.* **f.-glasses,** anteojos, gemelos, *m pl.* **f.-hospital,** hospital de sangre, *m;* ambulancia fija, *f.* **f.-kitchen,** cocina de campaña, *f.* **f.-marshal,** capitán general de ejército, *m.* **f.-mouse,** ratón silvestre, *m.* **f. of battle,** campo de batalla, *m.* **f. of vision,** campo visual, *m.* **f.-telegraph,** telégrafo de campaña, *m*

fielder /'fildər/ *n* (baseball) jardinero (-ra)

field work prácticas de campo, *f pl*

fiend /find/ *n* diablo, demonio, *m;* malvado (-da); (addict) adicto (-ta). **morphia f.,** morfinónamo (-ma)

fiendish /'findɪʃ/ *a* diabólico, infernal; malvado, cruel, malévolo

fiendishness /'findɪʃnɪs/ *n* perversidad, crueldad, *f*

fierce /fɪərs/ *a* salvaje, feroz, cruel; (of the elements) violento, furioso; (intense) intenso, vehemente

fiercely /'fɪərsli/ *adv* ferozmente; violentamente, con furia; intensamente, con vehemencia

fierceness /'fɪərsnɪs/ *n* ferocidad, fiereza, *f;* violencia, furia, *f;* intensidad, vehemencia, *f*

fieriness /'faiərinɪs/ *n* ardor, *m;* (flames) las llamas, *f pl*; (redness) rojez, *f;* (irritability) ferocidad, irritabilidad, *f;* (vehemence) pasión, vehemencia, *f;* (of horses) fogosidad, *f*

fiery /'faiəri/ *a* ardiente; (red) rojo; (irritable) feroz, colérico, irritable; (vehement) apasionado, vehemente; (of horses) fogoso

fife /faif/ *n Mus.* pífano, pito, *m*

fifteen /'fɪf'tin/ *a* and *n* quince *m.*; (of age) quince años, *m pl*

fifteenth /'fɪf'tinθ/ *a* and *n* décimoquinto *m.*; (part) quinzavo, *m,* décimoquinta parte, *f;* (of the month) (el) quince, *m;* (of monarchs) quince; *Mus.* quincena, *f*

fifth /fɪfθ/ *a* quinto; (of monarchs) quinto; (of the month) (el) cinco. —*n* quinto, *m;* (part) quinto, *m,* quinta parte, *f; Mus.* quinta, *f,* **Charles V,** Carlos quinto. **f. column,** quinta columna, *f*

fifthly /'fɪfθli/ *adv* en quinto lugar

fiftieth /'fɪftiɪθ/ *a* quincuagésimo; (part) quincuagésima parte, *f,* cincuentavo, *m*

fifty /'fɪfti/ *a* and *n* cincuenta *m.*; (of age) cincuenta años, *m pl*

fiftyfold /'fɪfti,fould/ *a* and *adv* cincuenta veces

fig /fɪg/ *n* higo, *m;* (tree) higuera, *f; Fig.* bledo, ardite, *m.* **green fig,** higo, *m,* breva, *f.* **I don't care a fig,** No se me da un higo. **to be not worth a fig,** no valer un ardite. **fig-leaf,** hoja de higuera, *f; Fig.* hoja de parra, *f*

fight /fait/ *n* lucha, pelea, *f,* combate, *m;* batalla, *f;* (struggle) lucha, *f;* (quarrel) riña, pelea, *f;* (conflict) conflicto, *m;* (valor) coraje, brío, *m.* **hand-to-hand** *f,* cachetina, *f.* **in fair f.,** en buena lid. **to have a f.,** tener una pelea. **to show f.,** mostrarse agresivo

fight /fait/ *vt* luchar contra, batirse con; (a battle) dar (batalla); (oppose) oponer; (defend) defender, pelear por; hacer batirse. —*vi* luchar, batirse, pelear; (with words) disputar; (struggle) luchar; (make war) hacer la guerra; (in a tournament) tornear. **to f. one's way,** abrirse paso con las armas. **to f. against,** luchar contra. **to f. off,** librarse de; sacudirse. **to f. with,** luchar con; pelear con; reñir con

fighter /'faitər/ *n* luchador (-ra); combatiente, *m;* guerrero, *m;* duelista, *m;* (boxer) boxeador, *m; Aer.* (avión de) caza, *m.* **night f.,** *Aer.* (avión de) caza nocturno, *m.* **f.-bomber,** *Aer.* caza bombardero, *m.* **F. Command,** *Aer.* servicio de aviones de caza, *m*

fighting /'faitɪŋ/ *n* lucha, *f,* combate, *m;* el pelear; (boxing) boxeo, *m, a* combatiente; (bellicose) agresivo, belicoso. **f.-man,** combatiente, guerrero, *m*

figment /'fɪgmənt/ *n* ficción, invención, *f*

figurative /'fɪgyərətɪv/ *a* figurado, metafórico; figurativo; simbólico

figuratively /'fɪgyərətɪvli/ *adv* en sentido figurativo; metafóricamente

figure /'fɪgyər/ *n* figura, *f;* forma, *f;* (statue) estatua, figura, *f;* (of a person) silueta, *f;* talle, *m;* (number) cifra, *f,* número, *m;* (quantity) cantidad, *f;* (price) precio, *m; Geom. Gram. Dance.* (skating) figura, *f;* (appearance) presencia, *f,* aire, *m;* (picture) imagen, *m;* (on fabric) diseño, *m; Mus.* cifra, *f; pl* **figures,** aritmética, *f,* matemáticas, *f pl.* —*vt* figurar; (imagine) figurarse, imaginar; *Mus.* cifrar. —*vi* figurar, hacer un papel; (calculate) calcular, hacer cuentas. **to f. out,** calcular; (a problem, etc.) resolver. **a fine f. of a woman,** *Inf.* una real hembra. **lay f.,** maniquí, *m.* **to be good at figures,** estar fuerte en matemáticas. **to cut a f.,** *Fig.* hacer figura. **to have a good f.,** tener buen talle. **f. of speech,** figura retórica, figura de dicción *f;* (manner of speaking) metáfora *f.* **f. dance,** baile de figuras, *m,* contradanza, *f.* **f.-head,** *Naut.* mascarón, *m,* (or figura, *f*) de proa; *Fig.* figura decorativa, *f*

figured /'fɪgyərd/ *a* estampado, con diseños, labrado

figurine /,fɪgyə'rin/ *n* figurilla, *f*

filament /'fɪləmənt/ *n* filamento, *m;* hebra, *f*

filamentous /,fɪlə'mɛntəs/ *a* filamentoso, fibroso

filbert /'fɪlbərt/ *n* avellana, *f;* (tree) avellano, *m*

filch /fɪltʃ/ *vt* sisar, ratear

filching /'fɪltʃɪŋ/ *n* sisa, *f*

file /fail/ *n* (line) fila, hilera, sarta, línea, *f; Mil.* fila, *f;* (tool) lima, *f;* (rasp) escofina, *f;* (list) lista, *f,* catálogo, *m;* (for documents) carpeta, *f,* cartapacio, *m;* (bundle of papers) legajo, *m;* (for bills, letters, etc.) clasificador, *m;* archivo, *m;* (in an archives) expediente *m.* **in a f.,** en fila; en cola

file /fail/ *vt* hacer marchar en fila; (smooth) limar; (literary work) pulir; (classify) clasificar; (note particulars) fichar; (keep) guardar; (a petition, etc.) presentar, registrar. —*vi* marchar en fila. **to f. in,** entrar en fila. **to f. off,** desfilar. **to file a brief,** presentar un escrito. **to f. letters,** clasificar correspondencia. **to f. past,** *Mil.* desfilar

filial /'fɪliəl/ *a* filial

filiation /,fɪli'eiʃən/ *n* filiación, *f*

filibuster /'fɪlə,bʌstər/ *n* filibustero, pirata, *m*

filigree /'fɪlə,gri/ *n* filigrana, *f, a* afiligranado

filing /'failɪŋ/ *n* (with a tool) limadura, *f;* clasificación, *f;* (of a petition, etc.) presentación, *f,* registro, *m; pl* **filings,** limaduras, *f pl,* retales, *m pl.* **f.-cabinet,** fichero, *m.* **f.-card,** ficha, *f*

fill /fɪl/ *vt* llenar; (stuff) rellenar; (appoint to a post) proveer; (occupy a post) desempeñar; (imbue) henchir; (saturate) saturar; (occupy) ocupar; (a tooth) empastar; (fulfil) cumplir; (charge, fuel) cargar; (with food) hartar. —*vi* llenarse. **fill an order,** servir un pedido. **fill a prescription,** surtir una receta. **to f. the chair,** ocupar la presidencia; (university) ocupar la cátedra. **to f. the place of,** ocupar el lugar de; substituir; suplir. **It will be difficult to find someone to f. his place,** Será difícil de encontrar uno que haga lo que hizo él. **to f. to the brim,** llenar hasta los bordes. **to f. in, f. out,** (a form) llenar (or completar) (una hoja); (insert) insertar, añadir; (a hollow) terraplenar. **to f. out,** *vt* hinchar. —*vi* hincharse; echar carnes; (of the face) redondearse. **to f. up,** colmar, llenar hasta los bordes; (an office) proveer; (block) macizar; (a form) completar, llenar

fillet /'fɪlɪt/ *n* venda, cinta, *f;* (of meat or fish) filete, *m;* (of meat) solomillo, *m; Archit.* filete, *m.* *vt* atar con una venda o cinta; *Cul.* cortar en filetes

filling /'fɪlɪŋ/ *n* envase, *m;* (swelling) henchimiento, *m;* (of a tooth) empastadura, *f;* (in or up, of forms, etc.) llenar, *m.* **f. station,** depósito de gasolina, *m*

fillip /'fɪləp/ *n* capirotazo, *m;* (stimulus) estímulo, *m;* (trifle) bagatela, *f.* —*vt* and *vi* dar un capirotazo (a); *vt* estimular, incitar

filly /'fɪli/ *n* jaca, potra, *f*

film /fɪlm/ *n* (on liquids) tela, *f;* membrana, *f;* (coating) capa ligera, *f;* (on eyes) tela, *f;* (cinema) película, cinta, *f; Photo.* película, *f; Fig.* velo, *m;* nube, *f, vi* cubrirse de un velo, etc. —*vt* cubrir de un velo, etc.; filmar, fotografiar para el cine. **roll f.,**

película fotográfica, *f.* **silent f.,** película muda, *f.* **talking f.,** película sonora, *f.* **to shoot a f.,** hacer una película. **to take part in a f.,** actuar, or tomar parte, en una película. **f. pack,** película en paquetes *f.* **f. star,** estrella de la pantalla (or del cine), *f*

film industry industria fílmica, *f*

filminess /ˈfɪlmɪnɪs/ *n* transparencia, diafanidad, *f*

filmy /ˈfɪlmi/ *a* transparente, diáfano

filter /ˈfɪltər/ *n* filtro, *m.* —*vt* filtrar. —*vi* infiltrarse; (*Fig.* of news) trascender, divulgarse. **f.-bed,** filtro, *m.* **f.-paper,** papel filtro, *m*

filth /fɪlθ/ *n* inmundicia, suciedad, *f; Fig.* corrupción, *f; Fig.* obscenidad, *f*

filthiness /ˈfɪlθinɪs/ *n* suciedad, *f;* escualidez, *f; Fig.* asquerosidad, *f; Fig.* obscenidad, *f*

filthy /ˈfɪlθi/ *a* inmundo, sucio; escuálido; *Fig.* asqueroso; *Fig.* obsceno

filtrate /ˈfɪltreit/ *n* filtrado, *m, vt* filtrar

filtration /fɪlˈtreiʃən/ *n* filtración, *f*

fin /fɪn/ *n* (of fish) aleta, ala, *f;* (of whale) barba, *f; Aer.* aleta, *f*

final /ˈfainḷ/ *a* último, final; (conclusive) conclusivo, decisivo, terminante. —*n Sports.* finales, *m pl; Educ.* último examen, *m.* **f. blow,** *Fig.* golpe decisivo, *m.* **f. cause,** *Philos.* causa final, *f*

finale /fɪˈnæli/ *n* final, *m*

finalist /ˈfainḷɪst/ *n Sports.* finalista, *mf*

finality /faiˈnælɪti/ *n* finalidad, *f;* (decision) determinación, resolución, decisión, *f*

finally /ˈfainḷi/ *adv* por fin, finalmente, por último, a la postre; (irrevocably) irrevocablemente

finance /ˈfainæns/ *n* hacienda pública, *f,* asuntos económicos, *m pl;* finanzas, *f pl.* —*vt* financiar

financial /fɪˈnænʃəl/ *a* financiero, monetario. **f. year,** año económico, *m*

financially /fɪˈnænʃəli/ *adv* del punto de vista financiero

financier /ˌfɪnənˈsɪər, ˌfainən-/ *n* financiero, *m*

find /faind/ *vt* encontrar, hallar; (discover) descubrir, dar con; (invent) inventar, crear; (supply) facilitar, proporcionar; (provide) proveer; (instruct) instruir; *Law.* declarar. —*vi Law.* fallar, dar sentencia. —*n* hallazgo, *m;* descubrimiento, *m.* **I found him out a long time ago,** *Fig.* Hace tiempo que me di cuenta de cómo era él. **I found it possible to go out,** Me fue posible salir. **The judge found them guilty,** El juez les declaró culpables. **to f. a verdict,** *Law.* dar sentencia, fallar. **to f. one's way,** encontrar el camino. **to f. oneself,** hallarse, verse, encontrarse. **to f. out,** averiguar, descubrir. **to f. out about,** informarse sobre (or de)

finder /ˈfaindər/ *n* hallador (-ra); (inventor) inventor (-ra), descubridor (-ra); (telescope, camera) buscador, *m*

finding /ˈfaindɪŋ/ *n* hallazgo, *m;* (discovery) descubrimiento, *m; Law.* fallo, *m,* sentencia, *f*

fine /fain/ *n* multa, *f;* (end) fin, *m.* **in f.,** en fin, en resumen

fine /fain/ *vt* multar, cargar una multa de

fine /fain/ *a* (thin) delgado; (sharp) agudo; (delicate) fino, delicado; (minute) menudo; (refined) refinado, puro; (healthy) saludable; (of weather) bueno; magnífico; (beautiful) hermoso, lindo; excelente; (perfect) perfecto; (good) bueno; elegante; (showy) ostentoso, vistoso; (handsome) guapo; (subtle) sutil; (acute) agudo; (noble) noble; (eminent, accomplished) distinguido, eminente; (polished) pulido; (affected) afectado; (clear) claro; (transparent) transparente, diáfano. —*adv* muy bien. **a f. upstanding young man,** un buen mozo. **a f. upstanding young woman,** una real moza. **He's a f. fellow,** (ironically) Es una buena pieza. **That is all very f. but...,** Todo eso está muy bien pero.... **to become f.,** (weather) mejorar

finely /ˈfainli/ *adv* finamente; menudamente; elegantemente; (ironically) lindamente

fineness /ˈfainnɪs/ *n* (thinness) delgadez, *f;* (excellence) excelencia, *f;* delicadeza, *f;* (softness) suavidad, *f;* elegancia, *f;* (subtlety) sutileza, *f;* (acuteness) agudeza, *f;* (perfection) perfección, *f;* (nobility) nobleza, *f;* (beauty) hermosura, *f*

finery /ˈfainəri/ *n* galas, *f pl,* atavíos magníficos, *m pl;* adornos, *m pl;* primor, *m,* belleza, *f*

finesse /fɪˈnɛs/ *n* sutileza, diplomacia, *f;* estratagema, artificio, *m;* (cunning) astucia, *f, vi* valerse de estratagemas y artificios

finger /ˈfɪŋgər/ *n* dedo, *m;* (of a clock, etc.) manecilla, *f;* (measurement) dedada, *f; Fig.* mano, *f.* —*vt* manosear, tocar; (soil) ensuciar con los dedos; (steal) sisar; (*Mus.* a keyed instrument) teclear, (a stringed instrument) tocar. **first f.,** dedo índice, *m.* **fourth f.,** dedo anular, *m.* **little f.,** dedo meñique, *m.* **second f.,** dedo de en medio, dedo del corazón, *m.* **to burn one's fingers,** quemarse los dedos; *Fig.* cogerse los dedos. **to have at one's f.-tips,** *Fig.* saber al dedillo. **f.-board,** (of piano) teclado, *m;* (of stringed instruments) diapasón, *m.* **f.-bowl,** lavadedos, lavafrutas, *m.* **finger's breadth,** dedo, *m.* **f.-mark,** huella digital, *f.* **f.-nail,** uña del dedo, *f.* **f.-print,** impresión digital, *f.* **f.-stall,** dedil, *m.* **f.-tip,** punta del dedo, yema del dedo, *f.* **f.-wave,** peinado al agua, *m*

fingered /ˈfɪŋgərd/ *a* (in compounds) con dedos, que tiene los dedos...

fingering /ˈfɪŋgərɪŋ/ *n* (touching) manoseo, *m; Mus.* digitación, *f;* (*Mus.* the keys) tecleo, *m;* (wool) estambre, *m*

finial /ˈfɪniəl/ *n* pináculo, *m*

finicky /ˈfɪnɪki/ *a* (of persons) dengoso, remilgado; (of things) nimio

finish /ˈfɪnɪʃ/ *n* fin, *m,* conclusión, terminación, *f;* (final touch) última mano, *f;* perfección, *f;* (of an article) acabado, *m; Sports.* llegada, (*horse race*) meta, *f.* —*vt* terminar, acabar, concluir; llevar a cabo, poner fin a; (perfect) perfeccionar; (put finishing touch to) dar la última mano a; (kill) matar; (exhaust) agotar, rendir; (overcome) vencer. —*vi* acabar; concluirse. **to f. off,** acabar, terminar; (kill) matar, acabar con; (destroy) destruir. **to f. up,** acabar; (eat) comer; (drink) beber

finishable /ˈfɪnɪʃəbəl/ *a* acabable

finished /ˈfɪnɪʃt/ *a* acabado, terminado, completo; perfecto; (careful) cuidadoso

finished goods *n pl* bienes terminados, *m pl*

finisher /ˈfɪnɪʃər/ *n* terminador (-ra), acabador (-ra); pulidor (-ra); (final blow) golpe de gracia, *m*

finishing /ˈfɪnɪʃɪŋ/ *a* concluyente. —*n* terminación, *f,* fin, *m;* perfección, *f;* (last touch) última mano, *f.* **to put the f. touch,** dar la última pincelada

finite /ˈfainait/ *a* finito

Finland /ˈfɪnlənd/ Finlandia, *f*

Finn /fɪn/ *n* finlandés (-esa)

Finnish /ˈfɪnɪʃ/ *a* finlandés. —*n* (language) finlandés, *m*

fir /fɜr/ *n* abeto, sapino, pino, *m.* **red fir,** pino silvestre, *m.* **fir-cone,** piña de abeto, *f.* **fir grove,** abetal, *m*

fire /faiᵊr/ *n* fuego, *m;* (conflagration) incendio, *m;* (on the hearth) lumbre, *f,* fuego, *m; Fig.* ardor, *m,* pasión, *f;* (shooting) fuego, tiro, *m.* **by f. and sword,** a sangre y fuego. **by the f.,** cerca del fuego; (in a house) al lado de la chimenea. **long-range f.,** *Mil.* fuego de largo alcance, *m.* **short-range f.,** *Mil.* fuego de corto alcance, *m.* **on f.,** en fuego, ardiendo, en llamas; *Fig.* impaciente; *Fig.* lleno de pasión. **to be between two fires,** *Fig.* estar entre dos aguas. **to make a f.,** encender un fuego. **to miss f.,** no dar en el blanco, errar el tiro. **to open f.,** *Mil.* hacer una descarga. **to set on f.,** prender fuego a, incendiar. **to take f.,** encenderse. **under f.,** bajo fuego. **f.-alarm,** alarma de incendios, *f.* **f.-arm,** arma de fuego, *f.* **f.-box,** hogar, *m.* **f.-brand,** tea, *f.* **f.-brigade,** cuerpo de bomberos, *m.* **f.-damp,** aire detonante, grisú, *m,* mofeta, *f.* **f.-dog,** morillo, *m.* **f.-drill,** (firefighters') instrucción de bomberos, *f,* (others') simulacro de incendio, *m.* **f.-engine,** autobomba, bomba, de incendios, *f.* **f.-escape,** escalera de incendios, *f.* **f.-extinguisher,** apagador de incendio, extintor, matafuego, *m.* **f.-guard,** vigilante de incendios, *m;* alambrera, *f.* **f.-hose,** manguera de incendios, *f.* **f.-insurance,** seguro contra incendios, *m.* **f.-irons,** badil *m.* y tenazas *f pl.* **f.-lighter,** encendedor, *m.* **f.-screen,** pantalla, *f.* **f.-ship,** brulote, *m.* **f.-shovel,** badil, *m,* paleta, *f.* **f.-spotter,** vigilante de incendios, *m.* **f.-sprite,** salamandra, *f.* **f.-watching,** servicio de vigilancia de incendios, *m*

fire /faiᵊr/ *vt* incendiar, prender (or pegar) fuego a; quemar; (bricks) cocer; (fire-arms) disparar; (cauterize) cauterizar; (*Fig.* stimulate) estimular, excitar; (inspire) inspirar; (*Inf.* of questions) disparar; (*Inf.* sack) despedir. —*vi* encenderse; (shoot) hacer fuego, disparar (un tiro); (*Inf.* away) disparar; (up) enojarse. **to f. a salute,** disparar un saludo. *Mil.* **F.!** ¡Fuego!

fire department *n* parque de bomberos, servicis de bomberos, servicio de incendios, parque de bombas (Puerto Rico), *m*

firefly /ˈfaiᵊrˌflai/ *n* cocuyo, *m*

fireman /ˈfaiᵊrmən/ *n* bombero, *m;* (of an engine, etc.) fogonero, *m.* **fireman's lift,** silleta, *f*

fireplace /ˈfaiᵊrˌpleis/ *n* chimenea francesa, chimenea, *f;* (hearth) hogar, *m*

fireproof /ˈfaiᵊrˌpruf/ *a* a prueba de incendios; incombustible

firer /ˈfaiᵊrər/ *n* disparador, *m*

firewood /ˈfaiᵊrˌwʊd/ *n* leña, *f.* **f. dealer,** leñador (-ra), vendedor (-ra) de leña

firework /ˈfaiᵊrˌwɜrk/ *n* fuego artificial, *m*

firing /ˈfaiᵊrɪŋ/ *n* (of fire-arms) disparo, *m;* (burning) incendio, *m,* quema, *f;* (of bricks, etc.) cocimiento, *m;* (of pottery) cocción, *f;* (cauterization) cauterización, *f;* (fuel) combustible, *m;* (*Inf.* sacking) despedida, *f.* **within f. range,** a tiro. **f.-line,** línea de fuego, *f.* **f.-oven,** (pottery) horno alfarero, *m.* **f.-squad,** pelotón de ejecución, *m*

firm /fɜrm/ *a* firme; (strong) fuerte; (secure) seguro; sólido; (resolute) inflexible, resoluto; severo; (steady) constante; (persistent) tenaz. —*n Com.* casa (de comercio), empresa, *f;* razón social, *f*

firmament /ˈfɜrməmənt/ *n* firmamento, *m*

firmly /ˈfɜrmli/ *adv* firmemente; inflexiblemente; constantemente

firmness /ˈfɜrmnɪs/ *n* firmeza, *f;* solidez, *f;* inflexibilidad, resolución, *f;* severidad, *f;* constancia, *f;* tenacidad, *f*

first /fɜrst/ *a* primero (primer before *m sing* nouns); (of monarchs) primero; (of dates) (el) primero. —*n* primero, *m;* (beginning) principio, *m.* —*adv* primero, en primer lugar; (before, of time) antes; (for the first time) por primera vez; (at the beginning) al principio; (ahead) adelante. **at f.,** al principio. **from the very f.,** desde el primer momento. **to appear for the f. time,** aparecer (or presentarse) por primera vez; *Theat.* debutar. **to go f.,** ir delante de todos, ir a la cabeza; ir adelante. **f. and foremost,** en primer lugar; ante todo. **f.-aid,** primera cura, *f.* **f.-aid post,** casa de socorro, *f.* **f.-aider,** practicante, *m.* **f.-born,** *a* and *n* primogénito (-ta). **f.-class,** *a* de primera clase; *Fig.* excelente. **f.-cousin,** primo (-ma) carnal, primo (-ma) hermano (-na). **f. edition,** edición príncipe, *f.* **f. floor,** primer piso, *m.* **f. fruits,** frutos primerizos, *m pl; Fig.* primicias, *f pl.* **f.-hand,** *a* original, de primera mano. **f. letters,** primeras letras, *f pl.* **f. night,** *Theat.* estreno, *m.* **f. of all,** primero, ante todo. **f.-rate,** *a* de primera clase

firstly /ˈfɜrstli/ *adv* en primer lugar, primero

firth /fɜrθ/ *n* ría, *f*

fiscal /ˈfɪskəl/ *a* and *n* fiscal *m..* **f. year,** año económico, *m*

fish /fɪʃ/ *n* pez, *m;* (out of the water) pescado, *m; Inf.* tipo, indivíduo, *m.* —*vt* pescar; (out) sacar. —*vi* pescar; *Fig.* buscar. **fried f.,** pescado frito, *m.* **He is a queer f.,** Es un tipo muy raro. **to be neither f. nor fowl,** no ser ni carne ni pescado. **to feel like a f. out of water,** sentirse fuera de su ambiente. **to f. in troubled waters,** A río revuelto ganancia de pescadores. **f.-eating,** *a* ictiófago. **f.-fork,** tenedor de pescado, *m.* **f.-glue,** cola de pescado, *f.* **f.-hook,** anzuelo, *m.* **f.-knife,** cuchillo de pescado, *m.* **f.-like,** de pez; como un pez, parecido a un pez. **f. roe,** hueva, *f.* **f.-server,** pala para pescado, *f*

fishbone /ˈfɪʃˌboun/ *n* espina de pescado, raspa de pescado, *f*

fisherman /ˈfɪʃərmən/ *n* pescador, *m*

fishery /ˈfɪʃəri/ *n* pesquería, *f*

fishing /ˈfɪʃɪŋ/ *n* pesca, *f, a* de pescar. **to go f.,** ir de pesca. **f.-boat,** bote de pesca, *m.* **f.-floats,** levas, *f pl.* **f.-line,** sedal, *m.* **f.-net,** red de pesca, *f.* **f.-reel,** carretel, carrete, *m.* **f.-rod,** caña de pescar, *f.* **f.-tackle,** aparejo de pesca, *m.* **f. village,** pueblo de pescadores, *m*

fishmeal /ˈfɪʃˌmil/ harina de pescado, *f*

fishmonger /ˈfɪʃˌmʌŋgər/ *n* pescadero (-ra).

fishmonger's shop pescadería, *f*

fishpond /ˈfɪʃˌpɒnd/ *n* vivero, *m,* piscina, *f*

fishwife /ˈfɪʃˌwaif/ *n* pescadora, *f*

fishy /ˈfɪʃi/ *a* de pescado; (of eyes, etc.) de pez, como un pez; (in smell) que huele a pescado; *Inf.* sospechoso; (of stories) inverosímil

fissure /ˈfɪʃər/ *n* grieta, hendidura, rendija, *f;* (*Anat. Geol.*) fisura, *f*

fissured /ˈfɪʃərd/ *a* hendido

fist /fɪst/ *n* puño, *m; Print.* manecilla, *f;* (handwriting) letra, *f.* **with clenched fists,** a puño cerrado

fisticuff /ˈfɪstɪˌkʌf/ *n* puñetazo, *m; pl* **fisticuffs,** agarrada, riña, *f*

fit /fɪt/ *n* espasmo, paroxismo, *m;* ataque, *m;* (impulse) acceso, arranque, *m;* (whim) capricho, *m;* (of a garment) corte, *m;* (adjustment) ajuste, encaje, *m.* **by fits and starts,** a tropezones, espasmódicamente

fit /fɪt/ *a* a propósito (para), bueno (para); (opportune) oportuno; (proper) conveniente; apto; (decent) decente; (worthy) digno; (ready) preparado, listo; (adequate) adecuado; (capable) capaz, en estado (de); (appropriate) apropiado; (just) justo. **It is not in a fit state to be used,** No está en condiciones para usarse. **to be not fit for,** no servir para; (through ill-health) no tener bastante salud para. **to think fit,** creer (or juzgar) conveniente. **fit for use,** usable. **fit to eat,** comestible

fit /fɪt/ *vt* ajustar, acomodar, encajar; adaptar (a); (furnish) proveer (de), surtir (con); (of tailor, dressmaker) entallar, probar; (of shoemaker) calzar; (of garments, shoes) ir (bien o mal); (prepare) preparar; (go with) ser apropiado (a); (adapt itself to) adaptarse a. —*vi* ajustarse, acomodarse, encajarse; adaptarse; (clothes) ir (bien o mal). **to fit in,** *vt* encajar; incluir. —*vi* encajarse; caber; adaptarse. **to fit out,** equipar; proveer (de); preparar. **to fit up,** montar, instalar; proveer (de). **to fit with,** proveer de

fitful /ˈfɪtfəl/ *a* intermitente; espasmódico; caprichoso

fitfully /ˈfɪtfəli/ *adv* por intervalos, a ratos; caprichosamente

fitly /ˈfɪtli/ *adv* adecuadamente; justamente; apropiadamente

fitment /ˈfɪtmənt/ *n* equipo, *m;* instalación, *f;* (of bookcase, etc.) sección, *f;* (furniture) pieza, *f,* mueble, *m*

fitness /ˈfɪtnɪs/ *n* conveniencia, *f;* aptitud, capacidad, *f;* oportunidad, *f;* salud, *f;* (good health) vigor, *m*

fitted /ˈfɪtɪd/ *a* (of clothes) ajustado

fitter /ˈfɪtər/ *n* ajustador, *m;* (mechanic) armador, mecánico, *m;* (tailoring) cortador, *m;* (dressmaking) probador (-ra)

fitting /ˈfɪtɪŋ/ *n* encaje, ajuste, *m;* adaptación, *f;* (of a garment) prueba, *f;* (size) medida, *f;* (installation) instalación, *f;* **pl. fittings,** guarniciones, *f pl;* instalaciones, *f pl;* accesorios, *m pl.* —*a* conveniente, justo; apropiado; adecuado; (worthy) digno; (of coats, etc.) ajustado. **f. room,** cuarto de pruebas, *m.* **f. in,** encaje, *m.* **f. out,** equipo, *m.* **f. up,** arreglo, *m;* (of machines) montaje, *m;* (of a house) mueblaje, *m*

five /faiv/ *a* and *n* cinco *m.;* (of the clock) las cinco, *f pl;* (of age) cinco años, *m pl.* **to be f.,** tener cinco años. **f. feet deep,** de cinco pies de profundidad. **f. feet high,** cinco pies de altura. **f.-finger exercises,** ejercicios de piano, *m pl.* **F.-Year Plan,** Plan Quinquenal, *m*

fivefold /ˈfaivˌfould/ *a* quíntuplo

fix /fɪks/ *n* aprieto, apuro, *m;* callejón sin salida, *m.* —*vt* fijar; sujetar, afianzar; (bayonets) calar; (with nails) clavar; (*Photo., Chem., Med.*) fijar; (decide) establecer; (a date) señalar; (eyes, attention) clavar; (on the mind) grabar, estampar; (one's hopes) poner; (base) basar, fundar; (*Inf.* put right) arreglar, componer. —*vi* fijarse; establecerse; determinarse. **to get in a fix,** hacerse un lío. **to fix a price,** fijar un precio. **to fix on, upon,** elegir, escoger; decidir, determinar. **to fix up,** arreglar; decidir; organizar; (differences) olvidar (sus disensiones)

fixation /fɪk'seiʃən/ *n* obsesión, idea fija, *f;* (scientific) fijación, *f*
fixative /'fɪksətɪv/ *n* (*Med., Photo.*) fijador, *m;* (dyeing) mordiente, *m.* —*a* que fija
fixed /fɪkst/ *a* fijo; inmóvil; permanente; (of ideas) inflexible. **f. bayonet,** bayoneta calada, *f.* **f. price,** precio fijo, *m.* **f. star,** estrella fija, *f*
fixedly /'fɪksɪdli/ *adv* fijamente; resueltamente; firmemente
fixing /'fɪksɪŋ/ *n* fijación, *f;* afianzamiento, *m;* arreglo, *m;* (of a date) señalamiento, *m.* **f. bath,** *Photo.* baño fijador, *m*
fixity /'fɪksɪti/ *n* permanencia, *f;* inmovilidad, *f;* invariabilidad, *f;* firmeza, *f*
fixture /'fɪkstʃər/ *n* instalación, *f;* accesorio fijo, *m; Sports.* partido, *m; Inf.* permanencia, *f.* **f. card,** *Sports.* calendario deportivo, *m*
fizz /fɪz/ *n* espuma, *f;* chisporroteo, *m. Inf.* champaña, *m.* —*vi* (liquids) espumear; (sputter) chisporrotear
fizzle /'fɪzəl/ *n* (failure) fiasco, fracaso, *m.* —*vi* chisporrotear; (out) apagarse; (fail) fracasar, no tener éxito
fjord /fyɔrd/ *n* fiordo, *m*
flabbergast /'flæbər,gæst/ *vt* dejar con la boca abierta, dejar de una pieza
flabbiness, flaccidity /'flæbinɪs; flæk'sɪdɪti/ *n* flaccidez, flojedad, *f; Med.* reblandecimiento, *m;* (of character) debilidad, flaqueza del ánimo, *f*
flabby, flaccid /'flæbi; 'flæksɪd/ *a* fláccido, flojo; *Fig.* débil
flag /flæg/ *n* bandera, *f;* pabellón, estandarte, *m;* (small) banderola, *f;* (iris) (yellow) cala, *f,* (purple) lirio cárdeno, *m;* (stone) losa, *f.* **to dip the f.,** saludar con la bandera. **to hoist the f.,** izar la bandera. **to strike the f.,** bajar la bandera; (in defeat) rendir la bandera. **f. bearer,** portaestandarte, abanderado, *m.* **f.-day,** día de la banderita, *m;* (in U.S.A.) día de la bandera, *m.* **f.-officer,** almirante, *m;* vicealmirante, *m;* jefe de escuadra, *m.* **f. of truce,** bandera blanca, bandera de paz, *f*
flag /flæg/ *vi* flaquear, debilitarse; languidecer; (wither) marchitarse; decaer, disminuir. —*vt* adornar con banderas; (signal) hacer señales con una bandera; (for a race, etc.) marcar con banderas; (with stones) enlosar, embaldosar.
flagellant /'flædʒələnt/ *n* flagelante, *m*
flagellate /'flædʒə,leit/ *vt* flagelar
flagellation /,flædʒə'leiʃən/ *n* flagelación, *f*
flageolet /,flædʒə'lɛt/ *n Mus.* caramillo, *m,* chirimía, *f.* **f. player,** chirimía, *m*
flagging /'flægɪŋ/ *n* pavimentación, *f;* (floor) enlosado, *m.* —*a* lánguido, flojo
flagon /'flægən/ *n* frasco, *m;* botella, *f*
flagrancy /'fleigrənsi/ *n* escándalo, *m,* notoriedad, *f*
flagrant /'fleigrənt/ *a* escandaloso, notorio
flagship /'flæg,ʃɪp/ *n* capitana, *f*
flagstaff /'flæg,stæf/ *n* asta de bandera, *f*
flagstone /'flæg,stoun/ *n* losa, lancha, *f*
flail /fleil/ *n* mayal, *m*
flair /flɛər/ *n* instinto natural, *m,* comprensión innata, *f;* habilidad natural, *f*
flak /flæk/ *n* cortina (or barrera) antiaérea, *f*
flake /fleik/ *n* escama, *f;* laminilla, hojuela, *f;* (of snow) copo, *m;* (of fire) chispa, *f.* —*vt* cubrir con escamas, etc.; exfoliar; (crumble) hacer migas de, desmigajar. —*vi* escamarse; (off) exfoliarse; caer en copos
flaky /'fleiki/ *a* escamoso; en laminillas; (of pastry) hojaldrado. **f. pastry,** hojaldre, *f*
flamboyance /flæm'bɔiəns/ *n* extravagancia, *f, Lit.* ampulosidad, *f*
flamboyant /flæm'bɔiənt/ *a Archit.* flamígero; extravagante, llamativo, rimbombante; (of style) ampuloso. **f. gothic,** gótico florido, *m*
flame /fleim/ *n* llama, *f; Fig.* fuego, *m. Inf.* amorío, *m, vi* flamear, llamear; arder, abrasarse; (shine) brillar; (up, *Fig.*) inflamarse; acalorarse. **f.-colored,** de color de llama, anaranjado. **f.-thrower,** lanzallamas, *m*
flaming /'fleimɪŋ/ *a* llameante; abrasador; (of colors) llamativo, chillón; (of feelings) ardiente, fervoroso, apasionado
flamingo /flə'mɪŋgou/ *n Ornith.* flamenco, *m*
Flanders /'flændərz/ flandes, *m*
flange /flændʒ/ *n Mech.* reborde, *m, vt* rebordear
flank /flæŋk/ *n* (of animal) ijada, *f;* (human) costado, *m;* (of hill, etc.) lado, *m,* falda, *f; Mil.* flanco, *m.* —*a* (*Mil. Nav.*) por el flanco. —*vt* lindar con, estar contiguo a; (*Mil., Nav.*) flanquear. —*vi* estar al lado de; tocar a, lindar con.
flannel /'flænl̩/ *n* franela, *f, a* de franela
flannelette /,flænl̩'ɛt/ *n* moletón, *m*
flap /flæp/ *n* golpe, *m;* (of a sail) zapatazo, *m,* sacudida, *f;* (of a pocket) cartera, tapa, *f;* (of skin) colgajo, *m;* (of a shoe, etc.) oreja, *f;* (of a shirt, etc.) falda, *f;* (of a hat) ala, *f;* (of trousers) bragueta, *f;* (rever) solapa, *f;* (of a counter) trampa, *f;* (of a table) hoja plegadiza, *f;* (of the wings) aletazo, *m;* (of w.c.) tapa, *f.* —*vt* sacudir, golpear, batir; agitar; (the tail) menear. —*vi* agitarse; (of wings) aletear; (of sails) zapatear, sacudirse; colgar. **f.-eared,** de orejas grandes y gachas
flapjack /'flæp,dʒæk/ *n Cul.* torta de sartén, *f;* (for powder) polvorera, *f*
flapper /'flæpər/ *n Inf.* polla, tobillera, chica "topolino," *f*
flapping /'flæpɪŋ/ *n* batimiento, *m;* (waving) ondulación, *f;* (of sails) zapatazo, *m;* (of wings) aleteo, *m*
flare /flɛər/ *n* fulgor, *m,* llama, *f;* hacha, *f; Aer.* cohete de señales, *m; Sew.* vuelo, *m.* —*vi* relampaguear, fulgurar; brillar; (of a lamp) llamear; (up) encolerizarse, salirse de tino; (of epidemic) declararse; (war, etc.) desencadenarse
flash /flæʃ/ *n* relámpago, centelleo, *m,* ráfaga de luz, *f;* brillo, *m;* (from a gun) fuego, fogonazo, *m;* (of wit, genius) rasgo, *m;* (of joy, etc.) acceso, *m.* —*vi* relampaguear, fulgurar, centellear; brillar; cruzar rápidamente, pasar como un relámpago. —*vt* hacer relampaguear; hacer brillar; (a look, etc.) dar; lanzar; (light) encender; (powder) quemar; transmitir señales por heliógrafo; *Inf.* sacar a relucir, enseñar. **shoulder-f.,** *Mil.* emblema, *m.* **to be gone like a f.,** desaparecer como un relámpago. **to f. out,** brillar, centellear. **f. of lightning,** relámpago, rayo, *m.* **f. of wit,** agudeza, *f,* rasgo de ingenio, *m*
flashback /'flæʃ,bæk/ *n* episodio intercalado, *m,* retrospección, *f*
flashily /'flæʃəli/ *adv* llamativamente, con mal gusto
flashing /'flæʃɪŋ/ *n* centelleo, *m,* llamarada, *f.* —*a* centellador, relampagueante; brillante; chispeante
flashlight /'flæʃ,lait/ *n* luz de magnesio, *f;* (torch) lamparilla eléctrica, *f,* rayo, *m* (Mexico); **f. photograph,** magnesio, *m*
flashy /'flæʃi/ *a* llamativo, de mal gusto, charro; frívolo, superficial
flask /flæsk/ *n* frasco, *m,* redoma, botella, *f;* (for powder) frasco, *m;* (vacuum) termos, *m*
flat /flæt/ *a* llano; (smooth) liso; (lying) tendido, tumbado; (flattened) aplastado; (destroyed) arrasado; (stretched out) extendido; (of nose, face) chato, romo; (of tire) desinflado; (uniform) uniforme; (depressed) desanimado; (uninteresting) monótono; (boring) aburrido; *Com.* paralizado; (downright) categórico; absoluto; (net) neto; *Mus.* bemol; (of boats) de fondo plano. —*adv* See **flatly.** *n* planicie, *f;* (of a sword) hoja, *f;* (of the hand) palma, *f;* (land) llanura, *f;* (apartment) piso, *m; Mus.* bemol, *m.* **to fall f.,** caer de bruces; *Fig.* no tener éxito. **to make f.,** allanar. **to sing f.,** desafinar. **f. boat,** barco de fondo plano, *m.* **f.-footed,** de pies achatados; *Fig.* pedestre. **f.-iron,** plancha, *f.* **f. roof,** azotea, *f*
flatly /'flætli/ *adv* de plano; a nivel; (plainly) llanamente, netamente; (dully) indiferentemente; (categorically) categóricamente
flatness /'flætnɪs/ *n* planicie, *f;* llanura, *f;* (smoothness) lisura, *f;* (evenness) igualdad, *f;* (uninterestingness) insulsez, insipidez, *f;* aburrimiento, *m;* (depression) desaliento, abatimiento, *m*
flatten /'flætn̩/ *vt* aplanar, allanar; aplastar; (smooth) alisar; (even) igualar; (destroy) derribar, arrasar, destruir; (dismay) desconcertar; (out) extender. —*vi* aplanarse, allanarse; aplastarse

flattening /'flætn̩ıŋ/ *n* achatamiento, *m*, allanamiento, *m;* aplastamiento, *m;* igualación, *f*
flatter /'flætər/ *vt* adular, lisonjear, halagar; (of a dress, photograph, etc.) favorecer, (please the senses) regalar, deleitar; (oneself) felicitarse
flatterer /'flætərər/ *n* adulador (-ra), lisonjero (-ra)
flattering /'flætərıŋ/ *a* adulador, lisonjero; (promising) halagüeño; favoreciente; deleitoso
flattery /'flætəri/ *n* adulación, *f*
flat tire llanta desinflada, *f*
flatulence /'flætʃələns/ *n* flatulencia, *f*
flatulent /'flætʃələnt/ *a* flatulento
flaunt /flɔnt/ *vi* (flutter) ondear; pavonearse. *—vt* desplegar; ostentar, sacar a relucir; enseñar
flaunting /'flɔntıŋ/ *n* ostentación, *f;* alarde, *m. —a* ostentoso; magnífico; (fluttering) ondeante
flautist /'flɔtıst/ *n* flautista, *mf*
flavor /'fleivər/ *n* sabor, gusto, *m; Cul.* condimento, *m; Fig.* dejo, *m. —vt Cul.* sazonar, condimentar; dar un gusto (de), hacer saborear (a); *Fig.* dar un dejo (de)
flavored /'fleivərd/ *a* (in compounds) de sabor...; sazonado; que tiene sabor de...
flavoring /'fleivərın/ *n Cul.* condimento, *m; Fig.* sabor, dejo, *m*
flavorless /'fleivərlıs/ *a* insípido, soso, sin sabor
flaw /flɔ/ *n* desperfecto, *m*, imperfección, *f;* (crack) grieta, hendedura, *f;* (in wood, metals) quebraja, *f;* (in gems) pelo, *m;* (in fruit) maca, *f;* (in cloth) gabarro, *m; Fig.* defecto, error, *m;* (wind) ráfaga de viento, *f*
flawless /'flɔlıs/ *a* sin defecto; perfecto; impecable
flawlessness /'flɔlısnıs/ *n* perfección, *f;* impecabilidad, *f*
flax /flæks/ *n* lino, *m.* **to dress f.,** rastrillar lino. **f.-comb,** rastrillo, *m.* **f. field,** linar, *m*
flaxen /'flæksən/ *a* de lino; (fair) rubio, blondo. **f.-haired,** de pelo rubio
flay /flei/ *vt* desollar; (criticize) despellejar
flaying /'fleiıŋ/ *n* desuello, *m*, desolladura, *f*
flea /fli/ *n* pulga, *f.* **f. bite,** picada de pulga, *f*
fleck /flɛk/ *n* pinta, mancha, *f*, lunar, *m;* (of sun) mota, *f;* (speck) partícula, *f;* (freckle) peca, *f. —vt* abigarrar; manchar; (dapple) salpicar, motear
fledged /flɛdʒd/ *a* emplumecido, plumado; alado; *Fig.* maduro
fledgling /'flɛdʒlıŋ/ *n* volantón, *m; Fig.* niño (-ña); *Fig.* novato (-ta)
flee /fli/ *vi* huir, fugarse, escapar; (vanish) desaparecer; (avoid) evitar, huir de. *—vt* abandonar
fleece /flis/ *n* vellón, *m;* lana, *f;* toisón, *m. —vt* esquilar; *Fig. Inf.* pelar. **Order of the Golden F.,** Orden del Toisón de Oro, *f*
fleecy /'flisi/ *a* lanudo, lanar; (white) blanquecino; (of clouds) borreguero. **f. clouds,** borregos, *m pl*
fleet /flit/ *n* (navy) armada, *f;* escuadra, flota, *f; Fig.* serie, *f*, *a* alado, rápido, veloz. **F. Air Arm,** Aviación Naval, *f.* **f.-footed,** ligero de pies
fleeting /'flitıŋ/ *a* fugaz, momentáneo, efímero, pasajero
Flemish /'flɛmıʃ/ *a* flamenco. *—n* (language) flamenco, *m*
flesh /flɛʃ/ *n* carne, *f;* (mankind) género humano, *m*, humanidad, *f;* (of fruit) pulpa, *f.* **a man of f. and blood,** un hombre de carne y hueso. **of one's own f. and blood,** de la misma sangre de uno. **to make one's f. creep,** dar carne de gallina (a). **f.-coloured,** encarnado, de color de carne. **f.-eating,** carnívoro. **f. wound,** herida superficial, *f*
fleshiness /'flɛʃinıs/ *n* carnosidad, gordura, *f*
fleshpot /'flɛʃˌpɒt/ *n* marmita, *f; Fig.* olla, *f.* **the fleshpots of Egypt,** las ollas de Egipto
fleshy /'flɛʃi/ *a* carnoso, grueso; (of fruit) pulposo; suculento
fleur-de-lis /ˌflɜrdl̩'i/ *n* flor de lis, *f*
flex /flɛks/ *n Elec.* flexible, *m*, *vt* doblar. *—vi* doblarse
flexibility /ˌflɛksə'bılıti/ *n* flexibilidad, *f;* (of style) plasticidad, *f;* docilidad, *f*
flexible /'flɛksəbəl/ *a* flexible; dúctil, maleable; (of style) plástico; of) voice) quebradizo; adaptable; dócil
flexion /'flɛkʃən/ *n* flexión, *f; Gram.* inflexión, *f; Gram.* flexión, *f*
flexor /'flɛksər/ *n Anat.* músculo flexor, *m*
flick /flık/ *n* golpecito, toque, *m;* (of the finger) capirotazo, *m; Inf.* cine, *m*, *vt* dar un golpecito a; dar ligeramente con un látigo; sacudir. **flick one's wrist** hacer girar la muñeca **to f. over the pages of,** hojear
flicker /'flıkər/ *n* estremecimiento, temblor, *m;* fluctuación, *f;* (of bird) aleteo, *m;* (of flame) onda (de una llama), *f;* (of eyelashes) pestañeo, *m;* (of a smile) indicio, *f*, *vi* agitarse; (of flags) ondear; vacilar
flickering /'flıkərıŋ/ *a* tenue; vacilante
flier /'flaiər/ *n* volador (-ra); aviador (-ra); piloto, *m;* fugitivo (-va)
flight /flait/ *n* vuelo, *m;* (of bird of prey) colada, *f;* (flock of birds) bandada, *f;* (migration) migración, *f;* (of time) transcurso, *m;* (of imagination, etc.) arranque, *m;* (volley) lluvia, *f;* (of aeroplanes) escuadrilla (de aviones), *f;* (of stairs) tramo, tiro, *m;* (staircase) escalera, *f;* (of locks on canal, etc.) ramal, *m;* (escape) huida, fuga, *f.* **long-distance f.,** *Aer.* vuelo de distancia, *m.* **non-stop f.,** *Aer.* vuelo sin parar, *m.* **reconnaissance f.,** *Aer.* vuelo de reconocimiento, vuelo de patrulla, *m.* **test f.,** *Aer.* vuelo de pruebas, *m.* **to put to f.,** ahuyentar, poner en fuga. **to take f.,** alzar el vuelo. **f.-lieutenant,** teniente aviador, *m.* **f.-sergeant,** sargento aviador, *m*
flight attendant sobrecarbo *mf*
flightiness /'flaitinıs/ *n* frivolidad, veleidad, ligereza, *f*
flighty /'flaiti/ *a* frívolo, inconstante, veleidoso
flimsiness /'flımzinıs/ *n* falta de solidez, endeblez, *f;* fragilidad, *f;* (of arguments) futilidad, *f*
flimsy /'flımzi/ *a* endeble; frágil; fútil, insubstancial
flinch /flıntʃ/ *vi* echarse atrás, retirarse (ante); vacilar, titubear. **without flinching,** sin vacilar; sin quejarse
fling /flıŋ/ *vt* arrojar, echar, tirar; lanzar; (scatter) derramar; (oneself) echarse; (oneself upon) echarse encima; *Fig.* confiar en. *—vi* lanzarse; marcharse precipitadamente; saltar. *—n* tiro, *m;* (of dice, etc.) echada, *f;* (gibe) sarcasmo, *m*, burla, chufleta, *f;* (of horse) respingo, brinco, *m;* baile escocés, *m.* **in full f.,** en plena operación; en progreso. **to have one's f.,** darse un verde, correrla. **to f. away,** *vt* desechar; (waste) desperdiciar, malgastar, perder. *—vi* marcharse enfadado; marcharse rápidamente. **to f. back,** (a ball) devolver; (the head) echar atrás. **to f. down,** tirar al suelo; arrojar; derribar. **to f. off,** *vt* rechazar; apartar; (a garment, etc.) quitar. *—vi* marcharse sin más ni más. **to f. oneself down,** tumbarse, echarse; despeñarse (por). **to f. oneself headlong,** despeñarse. **to f. open,** abrir violentamente, abrir de repente. **to f. out,** *vt* echar a la fuerza; (a hand) alargar, extender. *—vi* salir apresuradamente. **to f. over,** (upset) volcar; arrojar por; abandonar. **to f. up,** lanzar al aire; levantar, erguir; renunciar (a), abandonar; dejar
flint /flınt/ *n* pedernal, *m;* (for producing fire) piedra de encendedor, *f*
flinty /'flınti/ *a* pedernalino; *Fig.* endurecido
flippancy /'flıpənsi/ *n* levedad, ligereza, *f;* frivolidad, *f;* impertinencia, *f*
flippant /'flıpənt/ *a* poco serio, ligero; frívolo; impertinente
flipper /'flıpər/ *n* aleta, *f*
flirt /flɜrt/ *n* (man) coquetón, castigador, *m;* (woman) coqueta, castigadora, *f. —vt* (shake) sacudir; (move) agitar; (wave) menear. *—vi* flirtear, coquetear; (toy with) jugar con; divertirse con
flirtation /flɜr'teiʃən/ *n* flirteo, amorío, *m*
flirtatious /flɜr'teiʃəs/ *a* (of men) galanteador, castigador; (of women) coqueta
flit /flıt/ *vi* revolotear, mariposear; (move silently) deslizarse, pasar silenciosamente; (depart) irse, marcharse; mudarse por los aires. **to f. about,** ir y venir silenciosamente. **to f. past,** pasar como una sombra
flitch /flıtʃ/ *n* (of bacon) hoja de tocino, *f*
float /flout/ *n* masa flotante, *f;* (raft) balsa, *f; Mech.* flotador, *m;* (of fishing rod or net) corcho, *m;* (of fish) vejiga natatoria, *f;* (for swimming) nadadera, calabaza, *f;* (for tableaux) carroza, *f; pl* **floats,** *Theat.*

candilejas, *f pl.* —*vi* flotar; (flags, hair, etc.) ondear; (wander) vagar; *Naut.* boyar. —*vt* poner a flote; hacer flotar; (a grounded ship) desencallar; (*Com.* a company) fundar; (a loan, etc.) emitir, poner en circulación; (launch a ship) botar; (flood) inundar

floating /ˈfloutɪŋ/ *n* flotación, *f,* flote, *m; Com.* fundación (de una compañía), *f;* (of a loan) emisión, *f;* (of a ship) botadura, *f.* —*a* flotante; boyante; *Com.* en circulación, flotante; fluctuante, variable. **f. capital,** capital fluctuante, *m.* **f. debt,** deuda flotante, *f.* **f. dock,** dique flotante, *m.* **f. light,** buque faro, *m.* **f. population,** población flotante, *f.* **f. rib,** costilla flotante, *f*

flock /flɒk/ *n* rebaño, *m,* manada, *f;* (of birds) bandada, *f; Fig.* grey, *f;* (crowd) multitud, muchedumbre, *f;* (parishioners) congregación, *f;* (of wool or cotton) vedija (de lana or de algodón), *f; pl* **flocks,** (for stuffing) borra, *f.* —*vi* concurrirse, reunirse, congregarse; ir en tropel, acudir; (birds) volar en bandada. **f.-bed,** colchón de borra, *m*

floe /flou/ *n* banco de hielo, *m*

flog /flɒg/ *vt* azotar; castigar

flogging /ˈflɒgɪŋ/ *n* azotamiento, vapuleo, *m*

flood /flʌd/ *n* inundación, *f;* (Bible) diluvio, *m;* (of the tide) flujo, *m; Fig.* torrente, *m;* (abundance) copia, abundancia, *f;* (fit) paroxismo, *m.* —*vt* inundar; sumergir; (of tears) mojar. —*vi* desbordar. **f. lighting,** iluminación intensiva, *f*

floodgate /ˈflʌdˌgeit/ *n* compuerta (de esclusa), *f*

flooding /ˈflʌdɪŋ/ *n* inundación, *f;* desbordamiento, *m; Med.* hemorragia uterina, *f*

floodtide /ˈflʌdˌtaid/ *n* marea creciente, *f*

floor /flɔr/ *n* suelo, piso, *m;* (wooden) entarimado, *m;* (story) piso, *m;* (of a cart) cama, *f; Agr.* era, *f.* —*vt* entablar; echar al suelo, derribar; *Fig.* desconcertar, confundir. **on the f.,** en el suelo. **on the ground f.,** en el piso bajo. **to take the f.,** *Fig.* tener la palabra. **f.-polisher,** lustrador de piso, *m*

flooring /ˈflɔrɪŋ/ *n* tablado, *m,* tablazón, *f;* piso, *m*

flop /flɒp/ *n* golpe, *m;* ruido sordo, *m;* (splash) chapoteo, *m; Inf.* fiasco, *m.* —*vi* dejarse caer

flora /ˈflɔrə/ *n* flora, *f*

floral /ˈflɔrəl/ *a* floral. **f. games,** juegos florales, *m pl*

Florence /ˈflɔrəns/ Florencia, *f*

Florentine /ˈflɔrənˌtin/ *a* and *n* florentino (-na)

florescence /flɔˈrɛsəns/ *n* florescencia, *f*

florid /ˈflɔrɪd/ *a* florido; demasiado ornado, cursi, llamativo; (of complexion) rubicundo

floridness /ˈflɔrɪdnɪs/ *n* floridez, *f,* estilo florido, *m;* demasiada ornamentación, vulgaridad, *f,* mal gusto, *m;* (of complexion) rubicundez, *f*

florin /ˈflɔrɪn/ *n* florín, *m*

florist /ˈflɔrɪst/ *n* florista, *mf*

floss /flɔs/ *n* seda floja, filoseda, *f;* (of maize) penacho, *m;* (of a cocoon) cadarzo, *m.* **f. silk,** seda floja, *f*

flotilla /flouˈtɪlə/ *n* flotilla, *f*

flotsam /ˈflɒtsəm/ *n* pecio, *m*

flounce /flauns/ *n* volante, *m, vi* saltar de impaciencia. **to f. out,** salir airadamente

flounder /ˈflaundər/ *n* (nearest equivalent) *Ichth.* platija, *f;* tumbo, *m.* —*vi* tropezar; revolcarse; andar dificultosamente

flour /flauᵊr/ *n* harina, *f, vt* enharinar. **f.-bin,** tina, *f,* harinero, *m.* **f. merchant,** harinero, *m*

flourish /ˈflɜrɪʃ/ *n* movimiento, *m;* gesto, saludo, *m;* (of a pen) plumada, *f;* (on the guitar, in fencing) floreo, *m;* preludio, *m;* (fanfare) tocata (de trompetas), *f;* (of a signature) rúbrica, *f;* (in rhetoric) floreo, *m.* —*vi* (of plants) vegetar; (prosper) prosperar, medrar; florecer; (of the guitar, in fencing) florear; *Mus.* preludiar; (with a pen) hacer plumadas (or rasgos de pluma); (of a signature) firmar con rúbrica; (sound a fanfare) hacer una tocata (de trompetas). —*vt* agitar en el aire, blandir

flourishing /ˈflɜrɪʃɪŋ/ *a* (of plants) lozano; floreciente; (prosperous) próspero; (happy) feliz

flourmill /ˈflauᵊrˌmɪl/ *n* molino de harina, *m,* fábrica de harina, *f,* molina harinero, *m*

floury /ˈflauᵊri, ˈflauəri/ *a* harinoso

flout /flaut/ *vt* burlarse de; despreciar, no hacer caso de

flow /flou/ *n* flujo, *m;* corriente, *f;* chorro, *m;* (of water) caudal, *m;* (output) producción total, cantidad, *f;* (of the tide) flujo (de la marea), *m;* (of words) facilidad, *f.* —*vi* fluir, manar; correr; (of the tide) crecer (la marea); (pass) pasar, correr; (result) resultar (de), provenir (de); (of hair, drapery) caer, ondular; (abound) abundar (en). **to f. away,** escaparse, salir. **to f. back,** refluir. **to f. down,** descender, fluir hacia abajo; (of tears) correr por. **to f. from,** dimanar de; manar de; *Fig.* provenir de. **to f. in,** llegar en abundancia. **to f. into,** (rivers) desaguar en, desembocar en. **to f. over,** derramarse por. **to f. through,** fluir por; atravesar; (water) regar. **to f. together,** (rivers) confluir

flower /ˈflauər/ *n* flor, *f;* (best) flor y nata, crema, *f.* —*vi* florecer. **in f.,** en flor. **No flowers by request,** (for a funeral) No flores por deseo del finado. **f.-bud,** capullo, *m.* **f.-garden,** jardín, *m.* **f. girl,** florista, vendedora de flores, *f.* **f. market,** mercado de flores, *m.* **f.-piece,** florero, *m.* **f. pot,** tiesto, *m,* maceta, *f.* **f. show,** exposición de flores, *f.* **f. vase,** florero, *m*

flowerbed /ˈflauərˌbɛd/ *n* cuadro, macizo, *m*

flower car coche portacoronas, *m*

flowered /ˈflauərd/ *a* (in compounds) con flores; con dibujos de flores

floweriness /ˈflauərinɪs/ *n* abundancia de flores, *f;* (of style) floridez, *f,* estilo florido, *m*

flowering /ˈflauərɪŋ/ *n* florecimiento, *m.* —*a* floreciente; con flores; (of shrubs) de adorno. **f. season,** época de la floración, *f*

flowery /ˈflauəri/ *a* florido

flowing /ˈflouɪŋ/ *n* flujo, *m;* derrame, *m.* —*a* fluente, corriente; (of tide) creciente; (waving) ondeante; suelto; (of style) flúido

flow of capital corriente de capital, *f*

fluctuate /ˈflʌktʃuˌeit/ *vi* fluctuar, vacilar; variar

fluctuating /ˈflʌktʃuˌeitɪŋ/ *a* fluctuante, vacilante; variable; (hesitating) irresoluto, dudoso

fluctuation /ˌflʌktʃuˈeiʃən/ *n* fluctuación, *f;* cambio, *m,* variación, *f;* (hesitancy) indecisión, vacilación, *f*

flue /flu/ *n* (of a chimney) cañón, *m;* (of a boiler) tubo, *m*

fluency /ˈfluənsi/ *n* fluidez, *f*

fluent /ˈfluənt/ *a* flúido; fácil

fluently /ˈfluəntli/ *adv* corrientemente, con facilidad, de corrido

fluff /flʌf/ *n* borra, pelusa, *f,* tamo, *m*

fluffy /ˈflʌfi/ *a* velloso; (feathered) plumoso; (woolly) lanudo; (of hair) encrespado

fluid /ˈfluɪd/ *n* flúido, líquido, *m, a* flúido

fluidity /fluˈɪdɪti/ *n* fluidez, *f*

fluke /fluk/ *n* (in billiards) chiripa, *f; Naut.* uña, *f; Inf.* carambola, chiripa, chambonada, *f.* **by a f.,** de carambola, por suerte. **f.-worm,** duela del hígado, *f*

flunkey /ˈflʌŋki/ *n* lacayo, *m; Fig.* adulador, *m*

fluorescence /flʊˈrɛsəns/ *n* fluorescencia, *f*

fluorescent /flʊˈrɛsənt/ *a* fluorescente

fluorine /ˈflʊrin/ *n Chem.* flúor, *m*

fluorite /ˈflʊrait/ *n* fluorita, *f*

flurry /ˈflɜri/ *n* (of wind) ráfaga, *f;* (squall) chubasco, *m;* agitación, *f;* conmoción, *f.* —*vt* agitar

flush /flʌʃ/ *n* rubor, *m;* (in the sky) arrebol, rojo, color de rosa, *m;* emoción, *f,* acceso, *m;* sensación, *f;* (at cards) flux, *m;* vigor, *m;* (flowering) floración, *f;* abundancia, *f;* (of youth, etc.) frescura, *f.* —*a* (level) igual, parejo; abundante; (generous) pródigo, liberal; (rich) adinerado. —*vi* ruborizarse, enrojecerse, ponerse colorado; (flood) inundarse, llenarse (de agua, etc.); (of sky) arrebolarse. —*vt* inundar, limpiar con un chorro de agua, etc., lavar; (of blood) circular por; (redden) enrojecer; (make blush) hacer ruborizarse; (exhilarate) excitar, animar; (inflame) inflamar, encender; (make level) igualar, nivelar. **f. with,** a ras de

flushing /ˈflʌʃɪŋ/ *n* rojez, *f;* (cleansing) limpieza, lavadura, *f;* (flooding) inundación, *f*

fluster /ˈflʌstər/ *n* agitación, confusión, *f,* aturdimiento, *m.* —*vt* agitar, poner nervioso (a), aturdir; (oneself) preocuparse. —*vi* agitarse; estar nervioso, estar perplejo; (with drink) estar entre dos velas

flute /flut/ *n* flauta, *f; Archit.* estría, *f;* (organ-stop) flautado, *m.* —*vi* tocar la flauta, flautear; tener la voz flauteada. —*vt* tocar (una pieza) en la flauta; (groove) encanutar, acanalar, estriar. **f. player,** flautista, *mf*

fluted /ˈflutɪd/ *a* (grooved) acanalado

fluting /ˈflutɪŋ/ *n Mus.* son de la flauta, *m;* (of birds) trinado, *m; Archit.* estría, *f; Sew.* rizado, *m*

flutter /ˈflʌtər/ *n* (of wings) aleteo, *m;* (of leaves, etc.) murmurio, *m;* (of eyelashes) pestañeo, *m;* (of flags, etc.) ondeo, *m,* ondulación, *f;* (excitement) agitación, *f;* (stir) sensación, *f;* (gamble) jugada, *f.* —*vi* (of birds) aletear; revolotear; (of butterflies) mariposear; (of flags) ondear; palpitar; (of persons) estar agitado. —*vt* agitar; (the eyelashes) pestañear; (agitate) agitar, alarmar

fluttering /ˈflʌtərɪŋ/ *n* mariposeo, *m;* revoloteo, *m;* (of birds) aleteo, *m;* (of leaves, etc.) murmurio, *m;* (of flags, etc.) ondeo, *m,* ondulación, *f;* (of eyelashes) pestañeo, *m*

fluvial /ˈfluviəl/ *a* fluvial

flux /flʌks/ *n* flujo, *m*

fly /flai/ *n* (insect) mosca, *f;* (on a fishhook) mosca artificial, *f;* (carriage) calesín, *m;* (of breeches) bragueta, *f; Theat.* bambalina, *f;* (of a tent) toldo, *m;* (flight) vuelo, *m;* (of a flag) vuelo, *m.* **fly-blown,** manchado por las moscas. **fly by night,** trasnochador (-ra). **fly-catcher,** *Ornith.* papamoscas, *m;* matamoscas, *m.* **fly-fishing,** pesca con moscas artificiales, *f.* **fly-leaf,** guarda (de un libro), *f.* **fly-paper,** papel matamoscas, *m.* **fly-swatter,** matamoscas, *m.* **fly-wheel,** *Mech.* volante, *m*

fly /flai/ *vi* volar; (flutter) ondear; (jump) saltar; (rush) lanzarse, precipitarse; (pass away) pasar volando, volar; (run off) marcharse a todo correr; (escape) huir, escapar; (seek refuge) refugiarse; (to the head, of intoxicants) subirse; (vanish) desaparecer. —*vt* hacer volar; hacer ondear, enarbolar; (an airplane) pilotar, dirigir; (flee from) huir de; evitar. **to let fly (at),** descargar, tirar; *Fig.* saltar la sinhueso. **to fly about,** volar en torno de; revolotear. **to fly at,** lanzarse sobre; acometer, asaltar. **to fly away,** emprender el vuelo. **to fly back,** volar hacia el punto de partida; (of doors, etc.) abrir, *or* cerrar, de repente. **to fly down,** volar abajo. **to fly in,** volar dentro de; volar adentro; (of airplanes) llegar (el avión). **to fly in pieces,** hacerse pedazos. **to fly into a rage,** montarse en cólera. **to fly low,** rastrear; *Aer.* volar a poca altura. **to fly off,** emprender el vuelo; (hasten) marcharse volando; (of buttons, etc.) saltar (de), separarse (de). **to fly open,** abrirse de repente. **to fly over,** volar por, volar por encima de. **to fly upwards,** volar hacia arriba; subir

flying /ˈflaiɪŋ/ *n* vuelo, *m.* —*a* volante, volador; que vuela; de volar; volátil; (hasty) rápido; (flowing) ondeante, ondulante. **to shoot f.,** tirar al vuelo. **with f. colors,** con banderas desplegadas, triunfante. **f.-boat,** hidroavión, *m.* **f.-buttress,** botarel, arbotante, *m.* **f.-column,** *Mil.* cuerpo volante, *m.* **f.-fish,** (pez) volador, *m.* **f.-fortress,** *Aer.* fortaleza volante, *f.* **f.-officer,** oficial de aviación, *m.* **f.-sickness,** mal de altura, *m.* **f.-squad,** escuadra ligera, *f.* **f.-test,** *Aer.* examen de pilotaje, *m*

foal /foul/ *n* potro (-ra). —*vi* and *vt* parir una yegua

foam /foum/ *n* espuma, *f.* —*vi* espumar; (of horses, etc.) echar espumarajos. **to f. and froth,** (of the sea) hervir. **f. at the mouth,** echar espuma por la boca.

foam rubber *n* caucho esponjoso, *m,* espuma de caucho, *f,* espuma sintética, *f*

foamy /ˈfoumi/ *a* espumoso

fob /fɒb/ *n* bolsillo del reloj, *m;* faltriquera pequeña, *f.* —*vt* (off) engañar con

focal /ˈfoukəl/ *a* focal

focus /ˈfoukəs/ *n* foco, *m;* centro, *m.* —*vt* enfocar; concentrar. —*vi* convergir. **in f.,** en foco

fodder /ˈfɒdər/ *n Agr.* pienso, forraje, *m.* —*vt* dar forraje (a)

foe /fou/ *n* enemigo, *m*

fog /fɒg/ *n* neblina, niebla, *f; Fig.* confusión, *f; Fig.* perplejidad, *f, vt* obscurecer; *Photo.* velar; *Fig.* ofuscar. —*vi* hacerse nebuloso; *Photo.* velarse. **fog-signal,** señal de niebla, *f*

fogbound /ˈfɒgˌbaund/ *a* rodeado de niebla; detenido por la niebla

fogey /ˈfougi/ *n* obscurantista, *m.* **He is an old f.,** Es un señor chapado a la antigua

fogginess /ˈfɒginɪs/ *n* oscuridad, neblina, *f*

foggy /ˈfɒgi/ *a* nebuloso; *Photo.* velado. **It is f.,** Hay niebla

foghorn /ˈfɒgˌhɔrn/ *n* sirena, *f;* bocina, *f*

foible /ˈfɔibəl/ *n* flaco, *m,* debilidad, *f*

foil /fɔil/ *n* (sword) florete, *m;* (coat) hoja, *f;* (of a mirror) azogado, *m.* —*vt* frustrar. **f. a plot,** desbaratar un complot. **She makes a good f. for her sister's beauty,** Hace resaltar la belleza de su hermana

foiling /ˈfɔilɪŋ/ *n* frustración, *f*

foist /fɔist/ *vt* imponer; insertar, incluir; engañar (con)

fold /fould/ *n* doblez, *f,* pliegue, *m;* arruga, *f; Sew.* cogido, *m;* (for sheep) redil, aprisco, *m; Fig.* iglesia, congregación de los fieles, *f;* (in compounds) vez, *f.* —*vt* doblar, plegar, doblegar; (the arms) cruzar (los brazos); (embrace) abrazar; (wrap) envolver; (clasp) entrelazar; (sheep) meter en redil, encerrar. —*vi* doblarse, plegarse; cerrarse

folder /ˈfouldər/ *n* doblador (-ra); plegadera, *f*

folding /ˈfouldɪŋ/ *n* plegadura, *f,* doblamiento, *m;* (of sheep) encerramiento, *m, a* plegadizo. **f.-door,** puerta plegadiza, *f.* **f.-machine,** plegador, *m.* **f.-seat,** *Auto.* traspuntín, *m.* **f.-table,** mesa de tijeras, *f;* mesa plegadiza, *f*

foliage /ˈfouliɪdʒ/ *n* follaje, *m,* frondas, *f pl.* **thick f.,** frondosidad, *f*

folio /ˈfouliˌou/ *n* folio, *m;* (a volume) infolio, *m.* —*a* de infolio. —*vt* foliar

folk /fouk/ *n* (nation) pueblo, *m,* nación, *f;* gente, *f; pl* **folks,** *Inf.* familia, *f;* parientes, *m pl.* **f.-dance,** danza popular, *f*

folklore /ˈfoukˌlɔr/ *n* folclore, *m,* tradiciones folclóricas, *f pl*

folklorist /ˈfoukˌlɔrɪst/ *n* folclorista, *mf*

folksong /ˈfoukˌsɔŋ/ *n* canción popular, *f;* romance, *m;* copla, *f*

folktale /ˈfoukˌteil/ *n* conseja, *f,* cuento popular, *m*

follicle /ˈfɒlɪkəl/ *n* (*Anat., Bot.*) folículo, *m*

follow /ˈfɒlou/ *vt* seguir; (pursue) perseguir; (hunt) cazar; (adopt) adoptar; (understand) comprender; (notice) observar. —*vi* ir, *or* venir, detrás; (of time) venir después; (gen. impers.) seguir, resultar; seguirse. **as follows,** como sigue. **I shall f. your advice,** Seguiré tus consejos. **to f. on the heels of,** *Fig.* pisar los talones (a). **to f. suit,** (at cards) asistir, jugar el mismo palo; *Fig.* imitar. **to f. up,** proseguir; continuar; (pursue) perseguir; (enhance) reforzar. **f.-me-lads,** *Inf.* siguemepollo, *m*

follower /ˈfɒlouər/ *n* seguidor (-ra); adherente, secuaz, *mf;* (imitator) imitador (-ra); (lover) novio, *m; pl* **followers,** acompañamiento, séquito, *m*

following /ˈfɒlouɪŋ/ *n* séquito, acompañamiento, *m,* comitiva, *f;* partidarios, *m pl,* adherentes, *mf pl.* —*a* siguiente; próximo. **f. wind,** viento en popa, *m*

folly /ˈfɒli/ *n* locura, extravagancia, absurdidad, tontería, *f,* disparate, *m*

foment /fouˈmɛnt/ *vt* (poultice) fomentar; provocar, incitar, instigar; (assist) fomentar, proteger, promover

fomentation /ˌfoumɛnˈteiʃən/ *n Med.* fomentación, *f;* provocación, instigación, *f;* fomento, *m,* protección, *f*

fomenter /ˈfoumɛntər/ *n* fomentador (-ra), instigador (-ra)

fond /fɒnd/ *a* (credulous) vano, crédulo, vacío; (doting) demasiado indulgente; (loving) cariñoso, tierno, afectuoso; (addicted to) aficionado a, adicto a, amigo de. **to be f. of,** (things) tener afición a, estar aficionado de; (people) tener cariño (a). **to grow f. of,** (things) aficionarse a; (people) tomar cariño (a)

fondle /ˈfɒndl̩/ *vt* mimar, acariciar; jugar (con.)

fondly /ˈfɒndli/ *adv* (vainly) vanamente, sin razón; cariñosamente, tiernamente

fondness /ˈfɒndnɪs/ *n* cariño, afecto, *m;* (for things) afición, inclinación, *f;* gusto, *m*

font /fɒnt/ *n* pila bautismal, *f; Poet.* fuente, *f; Print.* fundición, *f*

food /fud/ *n* alimento, *m;* comida, *f,* el comer; (of animals) pasto, *m; Fig.* pábulo, *m;* materia, *f.* **She gave him f.** Le dio de comer. **You have given me f. for thought,** Me has dado en qué pensar. **f.-card,**

cartilla de racionamiento, **food, clothing, and shelter** comida, abrigo y vivienda, *f.* **F. Ministry,** Ministerio de Alimentación, *m.* **f. value,** valor nutritivo, *m.*
food poisoning, intoxicación alimenticia, *f*

foodstuffs /'fud,stʌfs/ *n pl* comestibles, víveres, *m pl*

fool /ful/ *n* tonto (-ta), mentecato (-ta), majadero (ra) necio (-ia); (jester) bufón, *m;* (butt of jest) hazmerreír, *m;* víctima, *f; Cul.* compota de frutas con crema, *f, vi* tontear, hacer tonterías. *—vt* poner en ridículo (a); (deceive) engañar, embaucar; (with) jugar con. **to make a f. of oneself,** ponerse en ridículo. **to f. about,** *vi* perder el tiempo, vagabundear. **to f. away,** malgastar, malbaratar. **fool's bauble,** cetro de bufón, *m.* **fool's cap,** gorro de bufón, *m*

foolhardiness /'ful,hɑrdinɪs/ *n* temeridad, *f*

foolhardy /'ful,hɑrdi/ *a* temerario, atrevido

fooling /'fulɪŋ/ *n* payasada, bufonada, *f;* (deceiving) engaño, *m,* burla, *f*

foolish /'fulɪʃ/ *a* imprudente; estúpido, tonto; ridículo, absurdo; imbécil

foolishly /'fulɪʃli/ *adv* imprudentemente; tontamente; imbécilmente

foolishness *n* /'fulɪʃnɪs/ imprudencia, *f;* estupidez, tontería, *f,* disparate, *m;* ridiculez, *f;* imbecilidad, *f*

foolproof /'ful,pruf/ *a* (of utensils, etc.) con garantía absoluta

foolscap /'fulz,kæp/ *n* (nearest equivalent) papel de barba, *m*

fool's gold *n* pirita amarilla, *f,* sulfuro de hierro *m*

foot /fʊt/ *n* pie, *m;* (of animals, furniture) pata, *f;* (of bed, sofa, grave, ladder, page, etc.) pie, *m;* (hoof) pezuña, *f;* (metric unit and measure) pie, *m; Mil.* infantería, *f;* (base) base, *f;* (step) paso, *m.* *—a Mil.* de a pie; a pie. *—vi* ir a pie; venir a pie; bailar. *—vt* hollar; (account) pagar (una cuenta); (stockings) poner pie (a). **on f.,** a pie; (of soldiers) de a pie; (in progress) en marcha. **to go on f.,** ir a pie, andar. **to put one's best f. forward,** apretar el paso; *Fig.* hacer de su mejor. **to put one's f. down,** poner pies en pared, pararle fulano el alto. **to put one's f. in it,** meter la pata. **to rise to one's feet,** ponerse de pie. **to set f. on,** pisar, hollar. **to set on f.,** poner en pie; *Fig.* poner en marcha. **to trample under f.,** pisotear. **f.-and-mouth disease,** glosopeda, *f.* **f.-brake,** freno de pedal, *m.* **f.-pump,** fuelle de pie, *m.* **f.-rule,** (nearest equivalent) doble decímetro, *m.* **f.-soldier,** soldado de a pie, infante, *m*

football /'fʊt,bɔl/ *n* (game) fútbol, *m;* (ball) pelota de fútbol, *f.* **f. field,** campo de fútbol, *m.* **f. match,** partida de fútbol, *f.* **f. pools,** apuestas de fútbol, *f pl;* (in Spain) apuestas benéficas de fútbol, *f pl*

footballer /'fʊt,bɔlər/ *n* fútbolista, *m*

footbath /'fʊt,bæθ/ *n* baño de pies, *m*

footbridge /'fʊt,brɪdʒ/ *n* puente para peatones, *m*

footed /'fʊtɪd/ *a* con pies; de pies...; de patas...

footfall /'fʊt,fɔl/ *n* pisada, *f,* paso, *m*

foothills /'fʊt,hɪlz/ *n pl* faldas de la montaña, *f pl*

foothold /'fʊt,hould/ *n* hincapié, *m;* posición establecida, *f*

footing /'fʊtɪŋ/ *n* hincapié, *m;* posición firme, *f;* condiciones, *f pl;* relaciones, *f pl.* **on a peacetime f.,** en pie de paz. **to be on an equal f.,** estar en pie de igualdad, estar en iguales condiciones. **to miss one's f.,** resbalar

footlights /'fʊt,laits/ *n pl* canilejas, candilejas, *f pl.* **to get across the f.,** hacer contacto con el público

footman /'fʊtmən/ *n* lacayo, *m*

footnote /'fʊt,nout/ *n* llamada a pie de página, nota a pie de página, *f*

footpath /'fʊt,pæθ/ *n* senda, vereda, *f,* sendero, *m*

footprint /'fʊt,prɪnt/ *n* huella, pisada, *f,* vestigio, *m*

footsore /'fʊt,sɔr/ *a* con los pies lastimados

footstep /'fʊt,stɛp/ *n* paso, *m;* (trace) pisada, huella, *f.* **to follow in the footsteps of,** *Fig.* seguir las pisadas de

footstool /'fʊt,stul/ *n* escabel, banquito, *m*

footwarmer /'fʊt,wɔrmər/ *n* calientapiés, *m*

footwear /'fʊt,wɛər/ *n* calzado, *m*

fop /fɒp/ *n* petimetre, *m*

foppery /'fɒpəri/ *n* afectación en el vestir, *f;* vanidad, *f*

foppish /'fɒpɪʃ/ *a* presumido, afectado; elegante

for /fɔr; *unstressed* fər/ *prep* (expressing exchange, price or penalty of, instead of, in support or favor of, on account of) por; (expressing destination, purpose, result) para; (during) durante, por; (for the sake of) para; (because of) a causa de; (in spite of) a pesar de; (as) como; (with) de; (in favor of) en favor de; (in election campaign) con (e.g., "Ecuadorians for Martínez!" ¡Ecuatorianos con Martínez!) (toward) hacia; (that) que, para que (with *subjunc*); a, (before) antes de; (searching for) en busca de; (bound for) con rumbo a; (regarding) en cuanto a; (until) hasta. What's for dinner? ¿Qué hay de comida? **center for...** centro de... (e.g., *Center for Applied Linguistics,* Centro de Lingüística Aplicada). **He is in business for himself,** Tiene negocios por su propia cuenta. **It is raining too hard for you to go there,** Llueve demasiado para que vayas allí. **It is not for him to decide,** No le toca a él decidirlo. **Were it not for...,** Si no fuese por... **She has not been to see me for a week,** Hace una semana que no viene a verme. **It is impossible for them to go out,** Les es imposible salir. **but for all that,** pero con todo. **for ever,** por (or para) siempre. **for fear that,** por miedo de que. **for myself,** en cuanto a mí, personalmente. **for the present,** por ahora. **for what reason?** ¿para qué? ¿por cuál motivo? **for brevity's sake, for the sake of brevity,** por causa de la brevedad

for /fɔr; *unstressed* fər/ *conjunc* porque; visto que, pues, puesto que, en efecto, ya que

forage /'fɔrɪdʒ/ *n* forraje, *m.* *—vt* and *vi* forrajear. **to f. for,** buscar. **f. cap,** gorra de cuartel, *f*

forager /'fɔrɪdʒər/ *n* forrajeador, *m*

foraging /'fɔrɪdʒɪŋ/ *n* forraje, *m*

forasmuch as /,fɔrəz'mʌtʃ ,æz/ *conjunc* puesto que, como que, ya que

foray /'fɔrei/ *n* correría, cabalgada, *f;* saqueo, *m*

forbear /'fɔr,bɛər/ *vt* and *vi* dejar (de), guardarse (de); abstenerse de; evitar; reprimirse (de); rehusarse (de); (cease) cesar (de); (be patient) ser paciente; ser tolerante

forbearance /fɔr'bɛərəns/ *n* abstención, *f;* tolerancia, transigencia, *f;* indulgencia, *f;* paciencia, *f*

forbearing /fɔr'bɛərɪŋ/ *a* tolerance, transigente; generoso, magnánimo; paciente

forbid /fər'bɪd/ *vt* prohibir, defender (de); impedir. **I f. you to do it,** Te prohibo hacerlo. **The game is forbidden,** El juego está prohibido. **They have forbidden me to...,** Me han defendido de... **Heaven f.!** ¡Dios no lo quiera!

forbidden /fər'bɪdn̩/ *a* prohibido; ilícito. **f. fruit,** fruto prohibido, *m*

forbidding /fər'bɪdɪŋ/ *a* repugnante, horrible; antipático, desagradable; (dismal) lúgubre; (threatening) amenazador. *—n* prohibición, *f*

force /fɔrs/ *n* fuerza, *f;* violencia, *f;* vigor, *m;* (efficacy) eficacia, *f;* (validity) validez, *f;* (power) poder, *m;* (motive) motivo, *m,* razón, *f;* (weight) peso, *m,* importancia, *f;* (police) policía, *f; pl* **forces,** *Mil.* fuerzas, tropas, *f pl.* **by main f.,** por fuerza mayor. **in f.,** vigente, en vigor. **to be in f.,** estar vigente

force /fɔrs/ *vt* forzar; (compel) obligar, constreñir, precisar; (ravish) violar; *Cul.* rellenar; (impose) imponer; (plants) forzar; (the pace) apresurar; (cause) hacer; (a lock, etc.) forzar. **to f. oneself into,** entrar a la fuerza en; (a garment) ponerse con dificultad; imponerse a la fuerza. **to f. oneself to,** esforzarse a. **to f. the pace,** forzar el paso. **to f. away,** ahuyentar. **to f. back,** hacer retroceder; rechazar; (a sigh, etc.) ahogar. **to f. down,** hacer bajar, obligar a bajar; (make swallow) hacer tragar; (of airplanes) hacer tomar tierra. **to f. in,** introducir a la fuerza; obligar a entrar. **to f. into,** meter a la fuerza; obligar a entrar (en). **to f. on, upon,** imponer. **to f. open,** abrir a la fuerza; (a lock) romper, forzar. **to f. out,** hacer salir; empujar hacia fuera; (words) pronunciar con dificultad. **to f. up,** obligar a subir; hacer subir; hacer vomitar

forced /fɔrst/ *a* forzado; forzoso; afectado. **f. landing,** *Aer.* aterrizaje forzoso, *m.* **f. march,** *Mil.* marcha forzada, *f*

forceful /'fɔrsfəl/ *a* See **forcible**

forcemeat /ˈfɔrsˌmit/ *n* picadillo, *m;* relleno, *m.* **f. ball,** albóndiga, *f*
forceps /ˈfɔrsəps/ *n pl* fórceps, *m pl*; pinzas, *f pl.* **arterial f.,** pinzas hemostáticas, *f pl*
forcible /ˈfɔrsəbəl/ *a* fuerte; a la fuerza; violento; enérgico, vigoroso; poderoso; *Lit.* vívido, gráfico, vehemente. **f. feeding,** alimentación forzosa, *f*
forcibleness /ˈfɔrsəbəlnɪs/ *n* fuerza, *f;* vigor, *m,* energía, *f;* vehemencia, *f*
forcibly /ˈfɔrsəbli/ *adv* a la fuerza
forcing /ˈfɔrsɪŋ/ *n* forzamiento, *m;* compulsión, *f.* **f. frame,** semillero, *m,* especie de invernadero, *f*
ford /fɔrd/ *n* esguazo, vado, *m.* —*vt* esguazar, vadear
fordable /ˈfɔrdəbəl/ *a* esguazable, vadeable
fore /fɔr/ *a* delantero; *Naut.* de proa. —*adv* delante; *Naut.* de proa. **f.-and-aft,** *Naut.* de popa a proa.
forearm /fɔrˈɑrm/ *n* antebrazo, *m.* —*vt* armar de antemano; preparar
forebear /ˈfɔrˌbɛər/ *n* antecesor, *m,* ascendiente, *mf*
forebode /fɔrˈboud/ *vt* presagiar, augurar, anunciar; presentir
foreboding /fɔrˈboudɪŋ/ *n* presagio, augurio, *m;* presentimiento, *m,* corazonada, *f*
forecast /ˈfɔrˌkæst/ *n* pronóstico, *m;* proyecto, plan, *m, vt* pronosticar, proyectar. **weather f.,** pronóstico del tiempo, *m*
forecastle /ˈfouksəl/ *n Naut.* castillo de proa, *m*
foreclose /fɔrˈklouz/ *vt* excluir; impedir; vender por orden judicial; anticipar el resultado de; decidir de antemano
foreclosure /fɔrˈklouʒər/ *n* venta por orden judicial, *f;* juicio hipotecario, *m*
foredoom /fɔrˈdum/ *vt* predestinar
forefather /ˈfɔrˌfɑðər/ *n* antepasado, antecesor, *m*
forefinger /ˈfɔrˌfɪŋgər/ *n* índice, dedo índice, *m*
forefoot /ˈfɔrˌfʊt/ *n* pata delantera, *f*
forefront /ˈfɔrˌfrʌnt/ *n* delantera, primera línea, *f;* frente, *m;* vanguardia, *f.* **in the f.,** en la vanguardia; en el frente
foregoing /fɔrˈgouɪŋ/ *a* precedente, anterior
foregone /fɔrˈgɔn/ *a* decidido de antemano; previsto
foreground /ˈfɔrˌgraund/ *n* primer plano, primer término, frente, *m.* **in the f.,** *Art.* en primer término
forehand /ˈfɔrˌhænd/ *a* derecho. **f. stroke,** golpe derecho, *m*
forehead /ˈfɔrɪd/ *n* frente, *f*
foreign /ˈfɔrɪn/ *a* extranjero; extraño; exótico; exterior; (alien) ajeno. **f. affairs,** asuntos extranjeros, *m pl.* **f. body,** cuerpo extraño, *m.* **f. debt,** deuda exterior, *f.* **F. Legion,** tercio extranjero, *m.* **F. Office,** Ministerio de Relaciones Extranjeras, *m.* **f. parts,** extranjero, *m.* **f. policy,** política internacional, *f.* **F. Secretary,** Secretario de Asuntos Extranjeros, Secretario de Asuntos Exteriores, Ministro de Relaciones Extranjeras, *m.* **f. trade,** comercio con el extranjero, *m*
foreigner /ˈfɔrənər/ *n* extranjero (-ra)
foreignness /ˈfɔrənnɪs/ *n* extranjerismo, *m;* (strangeness) extrañeza, *f;* lo exótico
foreknowledge /ˈfɔrˌnɒlɪdʒ/ *n* presciencia, precognición, *f*
foreland /ˈfɔrˌlænd/ *n* promontorio, cabo, *m*
foreleg /ˈfɔrˌlɛg/ *n* pata delantera, *f*
forelock /ˈfɔrˌlɒk/ *n* guedeja, vedeja, *f;* (of a horse) copete, tupé, *m.* **to take time by the f.,** asir la ocasión por la melena
foreman /ˈfɔrmən/ *n* (of jury) presidente (del jurado), *m;* (of a farm) mayoral, *m;* (in a works) capataz, *m*
foremost /ˈfɔrˌmoust/ *a* delantero; de primera fila; más importante. —*adv* en primer lugar; en primera fila
forensic /fəˈrɛnsɪk/ *a* forense, legal. **f. medicine,** medicina legal, *f*
foreordained /ˌfɔrɔrˈdeind/ *a* predestinado
forerunner /ˈfɔrˌrʌnər/ *n* precursor (-ra), predecessor (-ra); (presage) anuncio, presagio, *m*
foresee /fɔrˈsi/ *vt* prever, anticipar
foreseeing /fɔrˈsiɪŋ/ *a* presciente, sagaz
foreseer /fɔrˈsiər/ *n* previsor (-ra)
foreshadow /fɔrˈʃædou/ *vt* anunciar, prefigurar; simbolizar; hacer sentir.
foreshorten /fɔrˈʃɔrtn̩/ *vt Art.* escorzar
foreshortening /fɔrˈʃɔrtn̩ɪŋ/ *n Art.* escorzo, *m*
foresight /ˈfɔrˌsait/ *n* presciencia, *f;* previsión, prudencia, *f;* (of gun) punto de mira, *m;* (optical) croquis de nivel, *m*
forest /ˈfɔrɪst/ *n* bosque, *m,* selva, *f.* —*vt* arbolar
forestall /fɔrˈstɔl/ *vt* anticipar, saltear; prevenir; *Com.* acaparar
forestalling /fɔrˈstɔlɪŋ/ *n* anticipación, *f*
forestation /ˌfɔrəˈsteiʃən/ *n* repoblación forestal, *f*
forester /ˈfɔrəstər/ *n* silvicultor, guardamonte, ingeniero forestal, *m;* habitante de los bosques, *m*
forest fire incendio forestal, *m*
forestry /ˈfɔrəstri/ *n* silvicultura, *f*
foresworn /fɔrˈswɔrn/ *a* perjuro
foretaste /*n* ˈfɔrˌteist; *v* fɔrˈteist/ *n* muestra, *f;* presagio, *m.* —*vt* gustar con anticipación
foretell /fɔrˈtɛl/ *vt* predecir, profetizar; anunciar, presagiar
foreteller /fɔrˈtɛlər/ *n* profeta, *m;* presagio, *m*
foretelling /fɔrˈtɛlɪŋ/ *n* profecía, predicción, *f*
forethought /ˈfɔrˌθɔt/ *n* presciencia, previsión, *f;* prevención, *f*
forewarn /fɔrˈwɔrn/ *vt* prevenir
forewarning /fɔrˈwɔrnɪŋ/ *n* presagio, *m*
forewoman /ˈfɔrˌwʊmən/ *n* encargada, *f;* primera oficiala, *f*
foreword /ˈfɔrˌwɜrd/ *n* prefacio, *m,* introducción, *f*
forfeit /ˈfɔrfɪt/ *n* pérdida, *f;* (fine) multa, *f;* (in games) prenda, *f;* (of rights, goods, etc.) confiscación, *f.* —*a* confiscado. —*vt* perder; perder el derecho o el título de
forfeiture /ˈfɔrfɪtʃər/ *n* pérdida, *f;* confiscación, *f;* secuestro, *m*
forge /fɔrdʒ/ *n* fragua, *f;* (smithy) herrería, *f.* —*vt* and *vi* fraguar, forjar; (fabricate) inventar, fabricar; falsificar; (advance) avanzar lentamente. **to f. ahead,** abrirse camino; avanzar
forged /fɔrdʒd/ *a* (of iron) forjado; (of checks, etc.) falso, falsificado
forger /ˈfɔrdʒər/ *n* falsificador (-ra), falsario (-ia); (creator) artífice, *mf*
forgery /ˈfɔrdʒəri/ *n* falsificación, *f*
forget /fərˈgɛt/ *vt* olvidar; descuidar. —*vi* olvidarse. **to f. about,** olvidarse de, desacordarse de. **to f. oneself,** olvidarse de sí mismo; propasarse; (in anger) perder los estribos
forgetful /fərˈgɛtfəl/ *a* olvidadizo; descuidado, negligente
forgetfulness /fərˈgɛtfəlnɪs/ *n* olvido, *m;* descuido, *m;* falta de memoria, *f*
forget-me-not /fərˈgɛtmiˌnɒt/ *n Bot.* miosota nomeolvides, *f*
forging /ˈfɔrdʒɪŋ/ *n* fraguado, *m;* falsificación, *f*
forgivable /fərˈgɪvəbəl/ *a* perdonable, excusable
forgive /fərˈgɪv/ *vt* perdonar, disculpar, condonar; (debts) remitir
forgiveness /fərˈgɪvnɪs/ *n* perdón, *m;* condonación, *f;* (remission) remisión, *f*
forgiving /fərˈgɪvɪŋ/ *a* misericordioso, clemente, dispuesto a perdonar
forgo /fɔrˈgou/ *vt* renunciar, sacrificar, privarse de; abandonar, ceder
forgoing /fɔrˈgouɪŋ/ *n* renunciación, *f,* sacrificio, *m;* cesión, *f*
"For Immediate Occupancy" «De Ocupación Inmediata»
fork /fɔrk/ *n Agr.* horca, horquilla, *f;* (table fork) tenedor, *m;* bifurcación, *f;* (of rivers) confluencia, *f;* (of branches) horcadura, *f;* (of legs) horcajadura, *f;* (for supporting trees, etc.) horca, *f; Mus.* diapasón normal, *m.* —*vt* hacinar con horca. —*vi* bifurcarse; ramificarse
forked /fɔrkt/ *a* bifurcado, hendido, ahorquillado. **f. lightning,** relámpago, *m.* **f. tail,** cola hendida, *f*
forlorn /fɔrˈlɔrn/ *a* abandonado, desamparado, desesperado. **f. hope,** aventura desesperada, *f*
forlornness /fɔrˈlɔrnnɪs/ *n* desamparo, *m,* miseria, *f;* desolación, *f,* desconsuelo, *m*
form /fɔrm/ *n* forma, *f;* figura, *f;* (shadowy) bulto, *m;* (formality) formalidad, *f;* ceremonia, *f; Eccl.* rito,

m; método, *m;* regla, *f;* (in a school) clase, *f;* (lair) cama, *f;* (seat) banco, *m;* (system) sistema, *m;* (ghost) espectro, *m;* aparición, *f;* (to fill up) documento, *m;* hoja, *f;* (state) condición, *f; Lit.* construcción, forma, *f.* **It is a matter of f.,** Es una pura formalidad. **in due f.,** en debida forma, en regla. **in the usual f.,** *Com.* al usado. **It is not good f.,** No es de buena educación

form /fɔrm/ *vt* formar; (a habit) contraer; (an idea) hacerse (una idea). *—vi* formarse. **to f. fours,** *Mil.* formar a cuatro

formal /ˈfɔrməl/ *a* esencial; formal; ceremonioso, solemne; (of person) etiquetero, formalista. **f. call,** visita de cumplido, *f*

formaldehyde /fɔrˈmældəˌhaid/ *n* formaldehído. *m*

formalism /ˈfɔrməˌlɪzəm/ *n* formalismo, *m*

formality /fɔrˈmælɪti/ *n* formalidad, *f;* ceremonia, solemnidad, *f*

formally /ˈfɔrməli/ *adv* formalmente

format /ˈfɔrmæt/ *n* formato, *m*

formation /fɔrˈmeiʃən/ *n* formación, *f;* disposición, *f,* arreglo, *m;* organización, *f;* (*Mil., Geol.*) formación, *f*

formative /ˈfɔrmətɪv/ *a* formativo

former /ˈfɔrmər/ *a* primero; antiguo; anterior; pasado. **in f. times,** antes, antiguamente. **the f.,** ése, aquél, *m;* ésa, aquélla, *f;* aquéllos, *m pl;* aquéllas, *f pl*

former /ˈfɔrmər/ *n* formador (-ra); creador (-ra), autor (-ra)

formerly /ˈfɔrmərli/ *adv* antiguamente, antes

formidable /ˈfɔrmɪdəbəl/ *a* formidable; terrible, espantoso

formless /ˈfɔrmlɪs/ *a* informe

formlessness /ˈfɔrmlɪsnɪs/ *n* falta de forma, *f*

formula /ˈfɔrmyələ/ *n* fórmula, *f.* **standard f.,** (*Math. ,Chem.*) fórmula clásica, *f*

formulate /ˈfɔrmyəˌleit/ *vt* formular

fornicate /ˈfɔrnɪˌkeit/ *vi* fornicar

fornication /ˌfɔrnɪˈkeiʃən/ *n* fornicación, *f*

fornicator /ˈfɔrnɪˌkeitər/ *n* fornicador (-ra)

forsake /fɔrˈseik/ *vt* dejar, desertar; abandonar, desamparar; separarse de; (of birds, the nest) aborrecer; (one's faith) renegar de

forsaker /fɔrˈseikər/ *n* el, *m,* (la, *f*) que abandona; desertor, *m;* renegado (-da)

"For Sale" «Se Vende»

forsooth /fɔrˈsuθ/ *adv* ciertamente, claro está

forswear /fɔrˈswɛər/ *vt* abjurar; renunciar a. **to f. oneself,** perjurarse

forswearing /fɔrˈswɛərɪŋ/ *n* abjuración, *f;* renuncia, *f;* perjurio, *m*

fort /fɔrt/ *n* fortaleza, *f,* fuerte, *m*

forte /ˈfɔrtei/ *n* fuerte, *m.* *—a Mus.* fuerte

forth /fɔrθ/ *adv* (on) adelante, hacia adelante; (out) fuera; (in time) en adelante, en lo consecutivo; (show) a la vista. **and so f.,** y así en lo sucesivo; etcétera

forthcoming /ˈfɔrθˈkʌmɪŋ/ *a* próximo; futuro; en preparación

forthwith /ˌfɔrθˈwɪθ/ *adv* en seguida, sin tardanza

fortieth /ˈfɔrtiɪθ/ *a* cuadragésimo; cuarenta. *—n* cuarentavo, *m*

fortifiable /ˈfɔrtəˌfaiəbəl/ *a* fortificable

fortification /ˌfɔrtəfɪˈkeiʃən/ *n* fortificación, *f*

fortify /ˈfɔrtəˌfai/ *vt* fortificar; fortalecer; confirmar; *Fig.* proveer (de)

fortitude /ˈfɔrtɪˌtud/ *n* aguante, *m,* fortaleza, *f,* estoicismo, *m*

fortnight /ˈfɔrtˌnait/ *n* quince días, *m pl,* dos semanas, *f pl;* quincena, *f.* **a f. ago,** hace quince días. **a f. tomorrow,** mañana en quince. **in a f.,** dentro de quince días; al cabo de quince días. **once a f.,** cada quince días

fortnightly /ˈfɔrtˌnaitli/ *a* quincenal. *—adv* cada dos semanas, dos veces al mes. *—n* revista quincenal, *f*

fortress /ˈfɔrtrɪs/ *n* fortaleza, plaza fuerte, *f*

fortuitous /fɔrˈtuɪtəs/ *a* fortuito, accidental

fortuitously /fɔrˈtuɪtəsli/ *adv* accidentalmente

fortuity /fɔrˈtuɪti/ *n* casualidad, *f;* accidente, *m*

fortunate /ˈfɔrtʃənɪt/ *a* dichoso, feliz; afortunado; próspero. **to be f.,** (of persons) tener suerte

fortunately /ˈfɔrtʃənɪtli/ *adv* afortunadamente, por dicha, felizmente

fortune /ˈfɔrtʃən/ *n* suerte, fortuna, *f,* destino, *m;* (money) caudal, *m,* fortuna, *f;* bienes, *m pl;* buena ventura, *f.* **good f.,** buena fortuna, dicha, *f.* **ill f.,** mala suerte, *f.* **to cost a f.,** costar un sentido. **to make one's f.,** enriquecerse; *Inf.* hacer su pacotilla. **to tell fortunes,** echar las cartas. **f. hunter,** buscador de dotes, cazador de dotes, cazador de fortunas, aventurero, *m.* **f.-teller,** adivinadora, *f;* echadora de cartas, *f.* **f.-telling,** buenaventura, *f*

forty /ˈfɔrti/ *a* and *n* cuarenta, *m.* **He is turned f.,** Ha cumplido los cuarenta. **person of f.,** cuarentón (-ona). **She is f.,** Tiene cuarenta años

forum /ˈfɔrəm/ *n* foro, tribuna *f,* (e.g., *to serve as a forum for discussion,* servir de tribuna de discusión)

forward /ˈfɔrwərd/ *a* avanzado; adelantado; (of position) delantero; (ready) preparado; (eager) pronto, listo, impaciente; activo, emprendedor; (of persons, fruit, etc.) precoz; (pert) insolente, desenvuelto, atrevido. *—adv* adelante; hacia adelante; (of time) en adelante; (farther on) más allá; hacia el frente; en primera linea. *—vt* ayudar, promover; adelantar; (letters) hacer seguir; *Com.* expedir, remitir; (a parcel) despachar; (hasten) apresurar; (plants) hacer crecer. *—n Sports.* delantero, *m.* **center-f.,** *Sports.* delantero centro, *m.* **from this time f.,** de hoy en adelante. **Please f.,** ¡Haga seguir! **putting f. of the clock,** el adelanto de la hora. **to carry f.,** *Com.* pasar a cuenta nueva. **to go f.,** adelantarse; estar en marcha, estar en preparación. **f. line,** *Sports.* delantera, *f.* **F.!** ¡Adelante!

forwarder /ˈfɔrwərdər/ *n* promotor (-ra); *Com.* remitente, *m*

forwarding /ˈfɔrwərdɪŋ/ *n* fomento, *m,* promoción, *f; Com.* expedición, *f,* envío, *m*

forwardness /ˈfɔrwərdnɪs/ *n* progreso, adelantamiento, *m;* (haste) apresuramiento, *m;* (of persons, fruit, etc.) precocidad, *f;* (pertness) desenvoltura, insolencia, frescura, *f,* descaro, *m;* (eagerness) impaciencia, *f*

fosse /fɒs/ *n* foso, *m*

fossil /ˈfɒsəl/ *a* and *n* fósil, *m.*

fossilization /ˌfɒsələˈzeiʃən/ *n* fosilización, *f*

fossilize /ˈfɒsəˌlaiz/ *vt* fosilizar; petrificar. *—vi* fosilizarse

foster /ˈfɔstər/ *vt* provocar, promover, suscitar; (favor) favorecer, ser propicio a. **f.-brother,** hermano de leche, *m.* **f.-child,** hijo (-ja) de leche. **f.-father,** padre adoptivo, *m.* **f.-mother,** ama de leche, *f.* **f.-sister,** hermana de leche, *f*

foul /faul/ *a* sucio, asqueroso, puerco; (evil-smelling) hediondo, fétido; (of air) viciado; impuro; (language) ofensivo; (coarse) indecente, obsceno; (harmful) nocivo, dañino; (wicked) malvado; infame; vil; (unfair) injusto; *Sports.* sucio; (ugly) feo; (entangled) enredado; (with corrections) lleno de erratas; (choked) atascado; (of weather) borrascoso, tempestuoso; malo, desagradable; (repulsive) repugnante. *—n Sports.* juego sucio, *m.* *—vt* ensuciar; *Naut.* chocar, abordar; (block) atascar; (the anchor) enredar; (dishonor) deshonrar. *—vi* atascarse; (anchor) enredarse; *Naut.* chocar. **to fall f. of,** *Naut.* abordar (un buque); *Fig.* habérselas con. **by fair means or f.,** a las buenas o a las malas. **f. breath,** aliento fétido, aliento corrompido, *m.* **f. brood,** peste de las abejas, *f.* **f. language,** palabras ofensivas, *f pl;* lenguaje obsceno, *m.* **f. play,** juego sucio, *m.* **f. weather,** mal tiempo, tiempo borrascoso, *m*

found /faund/ *vt* fundar; (metal, glass) fundir; (create, etc.) establecer

foundation /faunˈdeiʃən/ *n* fundación, *f;* establecimiento, *m;* creación, *f; Archit.* cimiento, embasamiento, *m;* (basis) base, *f;* (cause) causa, *f,* origen, principio, *m;* (endowment) dotación, *f; Sew.* refuerzo, *m.* **to lay the f.,** poner las fundaciones. **f. stone,** piedra angular, *f; Fig.* primera piedra, *f.* **to lay the f. stone,** poner la piedra angular

founder /ˈfaundər/ *n* fundador (-ra); (of metals) fundidor, *m.* *—vt* (a ship) hacer zozobrar. *—vi* zozobrar, irse a pique; *Fig.* fracasar

foundering /ˈfaundərɪŋ/ *n Naut.* zozobra, *f*

founding /'faundɪŋ/ *n* fundación, *f;* establecimiento, *m;* (of metals) fundición, *f*
foundling /'faundlɪŋ/ *n* hijo (-ja) de la cuna, expósito (-ta). **f. hospital** or **home,** casa de cuna, casa de expósitos, inclusa, *f*
foundry /'faundri/ *n* fundición, *f*
fountain /'fauntn̩/ *n* fuente, *f;* (spring) manantial, *m;* (jet) chorro, *m;* (artificial) fuente, *f,* surtidero, *m;* (source) origen, principio, *m.* **f.-head,** fuente, *f.* **Fountain of Youth,** Fuente de la juventud, Fuente de Juvencio, *f.* **f. pen,** pluma estilográfica, *f*
four /fɔr/ *a* and *n* cuatro, *m.* **It is f. o'clock,** Son las cuatro. **She is f.,** Tiene cuatro años. **on all fours,** a gatas. **f.-course,** (of meals) de cuatro platos. **f.-engined,** cuadrimotor. **f.-engined plane,** cuadrimotor, *m.* **f.-footed,** cuadrúpedo. **f.-horse,** de cuatro caballos. **f. hundred,** cuatrocientos. **f.-inhand,** tiro par, *m.* **f.-part,** (of a song) a cuatro voces. **f.-wheel brakes,** freno en las cuatro ruedas, *m*
fourfold /'fɔr,fould/ *a* cuádruple
fourposter /'fɔr'poustər/ *n* cama de matrimonio, *f*
fourscore /'fɔr'skɔr/ *a* and *n* ochenta, *m.*
foursome /'fɔrsəm/ *n* partido de cuatro personas, *m*
fourteen /'fɔr'tin/ *a* and *n* catorce, *m.* **He is f.,** Tiene catorce años
fourteenth /'fɔr'tinθ/ *a* and *n* décimocuarto *m.*; (of the month) (el) catorce, *m;* (of monarchs) catorce. **April f.,** El 14 (catorce) de abril
fourth /fɔrθ/ *a* cuarto; (of the month) el cuatro; (of monarchs) cuarto. —*n* (fourth part) cuarta parte, *f; Mus.* cuarta, *f.* **f. dimension,** cuarta dimensión, *f.* **f. term,** (U.S.A. *Polit.*) cuarto mandato, *m*
fourthly /'fɔrθli/ *adv* en cuarto lugar
fowl /faul/ *n* gallo. *m;* gallina, *f;* (chicken) pollo, *m;* (bird) ave, *f;* (barndoor f.) ave de corral, *f.* —*vi* cazar aves. **f.-house or run,** gallinero, *m*
fox /fɒks/ *n* zorro, *m;* (vixen) zorra, raposa, *f; Fig.* zorro, taimado, *m.* —*vi* disimular. —*vt* (books) descolorar. **f.-brush,** cola de raposa, *f.* **f.-earth,** zorrera, *f.* **f.-hunting,** caza de zorras, *f.* **f. terrier,** fox-térrier, *m*
foxglove /'fɒks,glʌv/ *n* digital, dedalera, *f*
foxhound /'fɒks,haund/ *n* perro zorrero, *m*
foxiness /'fɒksinɪs/ *n* zorrería, astucia, *f*
foxtrot /'fɒks,trɒt/ *n* foxtrot, *m*
foxy /'fɒksi/ *a* de zorro; zorrero, astuto
foyer /'fɔiər/ *n* foyer, salón de descanso, *m*
fraction /'frækʃən/ *n Math.* fracción, *f,* número quebrado, *m;* pequeña parte, *f;* fragmento, *m.* **improper f.,** *Math.* fracción impropia, *f.* **proper f.,** *Math.* fracción propia, *f*
fractional /'frækʃənl̩/ *a* fraccionario
fractious /'frækʃəs/ *a* malhumorado, enojadizo
fractiousness /'frækʃəsnɪs/ *n* mal humor, *m*
fracture /'fræktʃər/ *n Surg.* fractura, *f.* —*vt* fracturar. **compound f.,** fractura conminuta, *f*
fragile /'frædʒəl/ *a* frágil, quebradizo; (of persons) delicado
fragility /frə'dʒɪlɪti/ *n* fragilidad, *f*
fragment /'frægmənt/ *n* fragmento, *m;* trozo, pedazo, *m.* **to break into fragments,** hacer pedazos, hacer añicos
fragmentary /'frægmən,tɛri/ *a* fragmentario
fragrance /'freigrəns/ *n* fragancia, *f,* buen olor, perfume, aroma, *m*
fragrant /'freigrənt/ *a* fragante, oloroso. **to make f.,** perfumar
frail /freil/ *a* frágil, quebradizo; débil, endeble. —*n* capacho, *m,* espuerta, *f*
frailty /'freilti/ *n* fragilidad, *f;* debilidad, *f*
frame /freim/ *n* constitución, *f;* sistema, *m;* organización, *f;* (of the body) figura, *f,* talle, *m;* (of window, picture) marco, *m;* (of machine, building) armadura, *f;* (of a bicycle) cuadro (de bicicleta), *m; Agr.* cajonera, *f;* (embroidery) bastidor (para bordar), *m;* (skeleton) esqueleto, *m; Lit.* composición, construcción, *f;* (of spectacles) armadura, *f;* (of mind) disposición (de ánimo), *f;* humor, *m.* —*vt* formar; construir; arreglar; ajustar; (a picture) enmarcar; componer, hacer; (draw up) redactar; (think up) idear, inventar; (words) articular, pronunciar. **f. a constitution,** elaborar una constitución
framer /'freimər/ *n* fabricante de marcos, *m;* autor (-ra), creador (-ra), inventor (-ra)
framework /'freim,wɜrk/ *n* armadura, armazón, *f,* esqueleto, *m;* organización, *f;* (basis) base, *f*
franc /fræŋk/ *n* (coin) franco, *m*
France /fræns/ Francia, *f*
Franche-Comté /frɑ̃ʃ kɔ̃'tei/ Franco-Condado, *m*
franchise /'fræntʃaiz/ *n* (exemption) franquicia, *f;* privilegio, *m;* (vote) derecho de sufragio, *m;* (citizenship) derecho político, *m*
Franciscan /fræn'sɪskən/ *a* and *n* franciscano (-na)
Franco- (in compounds) franco-... —*a* (referring to General Franco) franquista
Francophile /'fræŋkə,fail/ *a* and *n* afrancesado (-da)
Frank /fræŋk/ *n* franco (-ca), galo (-la)
frank /fræŋk, frɑŋk/ *a* franco, cándido, sincero; abierto. —*vt* franquear
frankincense /'fræŋkɪn,sɛns/ *n* incienso, *m*
frankly /'fræŋkli/ *adv* francamente; sinceramente; cara a cara; sin rodeos, claramente; abiertamente. **to speak f.,** hablar claro, hablar sin rodeos
frankness /'fræŋknɪs/ *n* franqueza, *f;* sinceridad, *f,* candor, *m*
frantic /'fræntɪk/ *a* frenético, furioso, loco. **He drives me f.,** Me vuelve loco
fraternal /frə'tɜrnl̩/ *a* fraterno, fraternal
fraternity /frə'tɜrnɪti/ *n* fraternidad, hermandad, *f*
fraternization /,frætərnə'zeiʃən/ *n* fraternización, *f*
fraternize /'frætər,naiz/ *vi* fraternizar
fratricidal /,frætrɪ'saidl̩/ *a* fratricida
fratricide /'frætrɪ,said/ *n* (person) fratricida, *mf;* (action) fratricidio, *m*
fraud /frɔd/ *n* fraude, *m;* engaño, embuste, *m;* (person) farsante, *m,* embustero (-ra)
fraudulence /'frɔdʒələns/ *n* fraudulencia, fraude, *f*
fraudulent /'frɔdʒələnt/ *a* fraudulento
fraught /frɔt/ *a* (with) cargado de; lleno de, preñado de
fray /frei/ *n* refriega, riña, *f;* combate, *m,* batalla, *f;* (rubbing) raedura, *f.* —*vt* raer, tazar. —*vi* tazarse, deshilarse
frayed /freid/ *a* raído
fraying /'freiɪŋ/ *n* raedura, deshiladura, *f*
freak /frik/ *n* monstruo, *m;* fenómeno, *m;* (whim) capricho, *m*
freakish /'frikɪʃ/ *a* monstruoso; caprichoso; extravagante; raro, singular
freakishness /'frikɪʃnɪs/ *n* carácter caprichoso, *m;* extravagancia, *f;* rareza, extrañeza, *f*
freckle /'frɛkəl/ *n* peca, *f.* —*vi* tener pecas; salir pecas (a la cara, etc.)
freckled /'frɛkəld/ *a* pecoso, con pecas
free /fri/ *a* (in most senses) libre; independiente; emancipado; desembarazado; abierto; limpio (de); franco; (voluntary) voluntario; (self-governing) autónomo, independiente; accesible; (disengaged) desocupado; (vacant) vacío; (exempt) exento (de); (immune) immune (de); ajeno; gratuito; (loose) suelto; (generous) generoso, liberal; (vicious) disoluto, licencioso; (bold) atrevido; (impudent) insolente, demasiado familiar. —*adv* gratis, gratuitamente. **There are two f. seats in the train,** Hay dos asientos libres en el tren. **to get f.,** libertarse. **to make f. with,** tomarse libertades con; usar como si fuera suyo. **to set f.,** poner en libertad. **f. agent,** libre albedrió, *m.* **f. and easy,** familiar, sin ceremonia. **f. gift,** *Com.* objeto de reclamo, *m.* **f.-hand drawing,** dibujo a pulso, *m.* **f. kick,** *Sports.* golpe franco, *m.* **f. love,** amor libre, *m.* **f. play,** rienda suelta, *f; Mech.* holgura, *f.* **f. port,** puerto franco, *m.* **f. speech,** libertad de palabra, *f.* **f. thought,** libre pensamiento, *m.* **f. ticket,** *Theat.* billete de favor, *m.* **f. trade,** *a* librecambista. —*n* librecambio, *m.* **f. trader,** librecambista, *mf.* **f. verse,** verso libre, verso suelto, *m.* **f.-wheeling,** desenfrenado, libre. **f. will,** propia voluntad, *f;* (theology) libre albedrío, *m*
free /fri/ *vt* libertar, poner en libertad (a); librar (de); (slave) salvar; emancipar; exentar; (of obstacles, difficulties) desembarazar; **to f. from,** libertar de; librar de; (clean) limpiar de
freebooter /'fri,butər/ *n* pirata, filibustero, *m*
freeborn /'fri,bɔrn/ *a* nacido libre, libre por herencia

freedman /'fridmən/ *n* liberto, *m*
freedom /'fridəm/ *n* libertad, *f;* independencia, *f;* exención, *f;* inmunidad, *f;* soltura, facilidad, *f,* franqueza, *f;* (over-familiarity) insolencia, *f;* (boldness) audacia, intrepidez, *f;* (of customs) licencia, *f.* **to receive the f. of a city,** ser recibido como ciudadano de honor. **f. of speech,** libertad de palabra, *f.* **f. of the press,** libertad de la prensa, *f.* **f. of worship,** libertad de cultos, *f*
freehold /'fri,hould/ *n* feudo franco, *m*
freeing /'friıŋ/ *n* liberación, *f;* emancipación, *f;* salvación, *f;* (from obstruction) desembarazo, *m;* limpieza, *f*
freelance /'fri,læns/ *n Mil.* soldado libre, *m; Polit.* independiente, *m;* aventurero (-ra). **f. journalist,** periodista libre, *m*
freely /'frili/ *adv* libremente; francamente; generosamente; sin reserva
freeman /'frimən/ *n* hombre libre, *m;* (of a city) ciudadano de honor, *m*
freemason /'fri,meisən/ *n* francmasón, *m.* **freemason's lodge,** logia masónica, *f*
freemasonry /'fri,meisənri/ *n* francmasonería, masonería, *f*
freethinker /'fri'θıŋkər/ *n* librepensador (-ra)
freeze /friz/ *vt* helar; (meat, etc.) congelar; *Fig.* helar. —*vi* helarse; congelarse; (*impers,* of the weather) helar. **to f. to death,** morir de frío
freezing /'frizıŋ/ *n* hielo, *m;* congelación, *f.* —*a* glacial; congelante, frigorífico. **f. mixture,** mezcla frigorífica, *f.* **f. of assets,** bloqueo de los depósitos bancarios, *m.* **f.-point,** punto de congelación, *m.* **above f.-point,** sobre cero. **below f.-point,** bajo cero
freight /freit/ *n* flete, *m;* porte, *m.* —*vt* fletar
freighter /'freitər/ *n* fletador, *m;* (ship) buque de carga, *m*
French /frɛntʃ/ *a* francés. —*n* (language) francés, *m;* (people) los franceses, *m pl.* **in F. fashion,** a la francesa. **to take F. leave,** despedirse a la inglesa. **What is the F. for "hat"?** ¿Cómo se dice «sombrero» en francés? **F. spoken,** Se habla francés. **F. bean,** judía, *f.* **F. chalk,** jabón de sastre, *m.* **F. horn,** trompa, *f.* **F. lesson,** lección de francés, *f.* **F. marigold,** flor del estudiante, *f.* **F. polish,** barniz de muebles, *m.* **F. poodle,** perro (-rra) de aguas. **F. roll,** panecillo, *m.* **F. window,** puerta ventana, *f*
Frenchify /'frɛntʃə,fai/ *vt* afrancesar
Frenchman /'frɛntʃmən/ *n* francés, *m.* **a young F.,** un joven francés
Frenchwoman /'frɛntʃ,wʊmən/ *n* francesa, mujer francesa, *f.* **a young F.,** una joven francesa, una muchacha francesa, *f*
frenzied /'frɛnzid/ *a* frenético
frenzy /'frɛnzi/ *n* frenesí, delirio, paroxismo, *m*
frequency /'frikwənsi/ *n* frecuencia, *f.* **high f.,** alta frecuencia, *f.* **low f.,** baja frecuencia, *f*
frequent /'frikwənt; *v* frı'kwɛnt/ *a* frecuente; (usual) común, corriente. —*vt* frecuentar
frequentation /,frikwən'teiʃən/ *n* frecuentación, *f*
frequenter /'frikwəntər/ *n* frecuentador (-ra)
frequently /'frikwəntli/ *adv* frecuentemente, con frecuencia, muchas veces; comúnmente
fresco /'frɛskou/ *n Art.* fresco, *m,* pintura al fresco, *f.* —*vt* pintar al fresco
fresh /frɛʃ/ *a* fresco; nuevo; reciente; (newly arrived) recién llegado; (inexperienced) inexperto, bisoño; (of water, not salt) dulce; puro; (healthy) sano; (brisk) vigoroso, enérgico; (vivid) vivo, vívido; (bright) brillante; (cheeky) fresco. —*adv* neuvamente, recién (with past participle). **He came to us f. from school,** Vino a nosotros recién salido de su colegio. **We are going to take the f. air,** Vamos a tomar el fresco. **The milk is not f.,** La leche no está fresca. **f.-complexioned,** de buenos colores. **f. news,** noticias nuevas, *f pl.* **f. troops,** tropas nuevas, *f pl,* (reinforcements) tropas de refuerzo, *f pl.* **f. water,** agua fresca, *f;* (not salt) agua dulce, *f.* **f. wind,** viento fresco, *m*
freshen /'frɛʃən/ *vt* refrescar; (remove salt) desalar. —*vi* (wind) refrescar. **to f. up,** renovar; refrescar; (of dress, etc.) arreglar
freshly /'frɛʃli/ *adv* nuevamente; recientemente
freshness /'frɛʃnıs/ *n* frescura, *f;* (newness) novedad, *f;* (vividness, brightness) intensidad, *f;* pureza, *f;* (beauty) lozanía, hermosura, *f;* (cheek) frescura, *f,* descaro, *m*
freshwater /'frɛʃ,wɔtər/ *n* agua dulce, *f.* **f. sailor,** marinero de agua dulce, *m*
fret /frɛt/ *n* agitación, *f;* ansiedad, preocupación, *f; Archit.* greca, *f;* (of stringed instrument) traste, *m.* —*vt* roer; (of a horse) bocezar; (corrode) desgastar, corroer; (of the wind, etc.) rizar; (worry) tener preocupado (a); irritar, enojar; (lose) perder; (oneself) apurarse, consumirse; *Archit.* calar. —*vi* torturarse, preocuparse, inquietarse; (complain) quejarse; (mourn) lamentarse, estar triste
fretful /'frɛtfəl/ *a* mal humorado, mohíno, quejoso, irritable
fretfully /'frɛtfəli/ *adv* irritablemente, con mal humor
fretwork /'frɛt,wɜrk/ *n* calado, *m*
Freudian /'frɔidiən/ *a* freudiano
friar /'fraiər/ *n* fraile, *m.* **Black f.,** dominicano, *m.* **Gray f.,** franciscano, *m.* **White f.,** carmelita, *m.* **f.-like,** frailesco
friction /'frıkʃən/ *n* frote, frotamiento, roce, *m; Phys.* rozamiento, *m;* fricción, *f.* **to give a f.,** friccionar, dar fricciones (a). **f. gearing,** engranaje de fricción, *m.* **f. glove,** guante de fricciones, *m*
Friday /'fraidei/ *n* viernes, *m.* **Good F.,** Viernes Santo, *m*
fried /fraid/ *a* frito. **f. egg,** huevo frito, *m*
friend /frɛnd/ *n* amigo (-ga); (acquaintance) conocido (-da); (Quaker) cuáquero (-ra); (follower) adherente, *m;* partidario (-ia); (ally) aliado (-da); *pl* **friends,** amistades, *f pl*; amigos, *m pl.* **a f. of yours,** un amigo tuyo, uno de tus amigos. **to make friends,** hacer amigos; (become friends) hacerse amigos; (after a quarrel) hacer las paces. **Friends!** (to sentinel) ¡Gente de paz!
friendless /'frɛndlıs/ *a* sin amigos; desamparado
friendliness /'frɛndlinıs/ *n* amabilidad, afabilidad, cordialidad, amigabilidad, *f*
friendly /'frɛndli/ *a* amistoso, amigable, amigo; afable, acogedor, simpático; propicio, favorable. **to be f. with,** ser amigo de. **f. society,** sociedad de socorros, *f*
friendship /'frɛndʃıp/ *n* amistad, intimidad, *f*
Friesland /'frizlənd/ Frisia, *f*
frieze /friz/ *n* friso, *m;* (cloth) frisa, jerga, *f*
frigate /'frıgıt/ *n Nav.* fragata, *f*
fright /frait/ *n* terror, susto, *m;* (guy) espantajo, *m.* —*vt* asustar. **to have a f.,** tener un susto. **to take f.,** asustarse
frighten /'fraitn̩/ *vt* espantar, dar un susto (a), alarmar, asustar; horrorizar; (overawe) acobardar. **to be frightened out of one's wits,** estar muerto de miedo. **to f. away,** ahuyentar, espantar
frightened /'fraitn̩d/ *a* miedoso, tímido, medroso, nervioso
frightening /'fraitn̩ıŋ/ *a* que da miedo; alarmante, amedrentador; horrible
frightful /'fraitfəl/ *a* horrible, espantoso, horroroso; *Inf.* tremendo, enorme
frightfully /'fraitfəli/ *adv* horrorosamente; *Inf.* enormemente
frigid /'frıdʒıd/ *a* frío; helado; *Med.* impotente
frigidity /frı'dʒıdıti/ *n* frialdad, frigidez, *f; Med.* impotencia, *f*
frigidly /'frıdʒıdli/ *adv* fríamente
frill /frıl/ *n Sew.* volante, *m;* (jabot) chorrera, *f;* (round a bird's neck) collarín de plumas, *m;* (of paper) frunce, *m.* —*vt* alechugar; fruncir
fringe /frındʒ/ *n* fleco, *m,* franja, *f;* (of hair) flequillo, *m;* (edge) borde, *m,* margen, *mf.* —*vt* guarnecer con fleco, franjar; adornar; (grow by) crecer al margen (de)
Frisian /'frıʒən/ *a* and *n* frisón (-ona); (language) frisón, *m*
frisk /frısk/ *vi* retozar, brincar
friskiness /'frıskinıs/ *n* viveza, agilidad, *f*
frisky /'frıski/ *a* retozón, juguetón
fritter /'frıtər/ *n Cul.* fruta de sartén, *f.* —*vt* (away) malgastar, desperdiciar; perder
frivolity /frı'vɒlıti/ *n* frivolidad, ligereza, *f;* futilidad, *f*

frivolous /'frɪvələs/ *a* frívolo, ligero, liviano; (futile) trivial, fútil

frizz /frɪz/ *vt* (cloth) frisar; (hair) rizar

frizzy /'frɪzi/ *a* (of hair) crespo, rizado

fro /frou/ *adv* hacia atrás. **movement to and fro,** vaivén, *m.* **to and fro,** de un lado a otro. **to go to and fro,** ir y venir

frock /frɒk/ *n* vestido, *m;* (of a monk) hábito, *m;* (of priest) sotana, *f.* **f.-coat,** levita, *f*

frog /frɒg/ *n* rana, *f.* **to have a f. in the throat,** padecer carraspera

frolic /'frɒlɪk/ *n* (play) juego, *m;* (mischief) travesura, *f;* (folly) locura, extravagancia, *f;* (joke) chanza, *f;* (amusement) diversión, *f;* (wild party) holgorio, *m,* parranda, *f.* —*vi* retozar, juguetear; divertirse

frolicsome /'frɒlɪksəm/ *a* retozón, juguetón

from /frʌm, frɒm; *unstressed* frəm/ *prep* de; desde; (according to) según; (in the name of, on behalf of) de parte de; (through, by) por; (beginning on) a contar de; (with) con; **F.** (on envelope) Remite, Remitente. **He is coming here f. the dentist's,** Vendrá aquí desde casa del dentista. **Give him this message f. me,** Dale este recado de mi parte. **Judging f. his appearance,** Juzgando por su apariencia. **prices f. five hundred pesetas upward,** precios desde quinientos pesetas en adelante. **f. what I hear,** según mi información, según lo que oigo. **f. above,** desde arriba. **f. among,** de entre. **f. afar,** de lejos, desde lejos. **f. time to time,** de cuando en cuando, de vez en cuando

frond /frɒnd/ *n Bot.* fronda, *f*

front /frʌnt/ *n* frente, *f;* cara, *f; Mil.* frente, *m;* (battle line) línea de combate, *f;* (of a building) fachada, *f;* (of shirt) pechera, *f;* (at the seaside) playa, *f;* (promenade) paseo de la playa, *m;* (forefront) primera línea, *f;* (forepart) parte delantera, *f; Theat.* auditorio, *m;* (organization) organización de fachada, *f;* (impudence) descaro, *m, a* delantero; anterior; de frente; primero. —*adv* hacia delante. —*vi* mirar a, dar a; hacer frente a. **in f.,** en frente. **in f. of,** en frente de; (in the presence of) delante de, en la presencia de. **to face f.,** hacer frente. **to put on a bold f.,** hacer de tripas corazón. **f. door,** puerta de entrada, puerta principal, *f.* **f. line,** *Mil.* línea del frente, *f;* primera línea, *f.* **f. seat,** (at an entertainment, etc.) delantera, *f.* **f. organization** organización de fachada *f.* **f. tooth,** diente incisivo, *m.* **f. view,** vista de frente, *f;* vista de cerca, *f*

frontage /'frʌntɪdʒ/ *n* (of a building) fachada, *f;* (site) terreno de... metros de fachada, *m*

frontal /'frʌntl̩/ *a Mil.* de frente; *Anat.* frontal

frontier /frʌn'tɪər/ *n* frontera, *f; Fig.* límite, *m.* —*a* fronterizo

frontispiece /'frʌntɪsˌpis/ *n* (of a building) frontispicio, *m,* fachada, *f;* (of a book) portada, *f*

frontless /'frʌntlɪs/ *a* sin frente

frost /frɔst/ *n* escarcha, *f;* helada, *f.* —*vt* helar; *Cul.* escarchar; (glass) deslustrar; *Fig.* escarchar. —*vi* helar. **f.-bitten,** helado

frostbite /'frɔstˌbait/ *n* efectos del frío, *m pl*

frosted /'frɔstɪd/ *a* escarchado; helado; (of glass) deslustrado, opaco; *Cul.* escarchado

frostily /'frɔstəli/ *adv Fig.* glacialmente, con frialdad.

frostiness /'frɔstinɪs/ *n;* frío glacial, *m*

frosting /'frɔstɪŋ/ *n* escarcha, *f;* (of glass) deslustre, *m; Cul.* cobertura, escarcha, *f*

frosty /'frɔsti/ *a* helado; de hielo; (of hair) canoso; *Fig.* glacial, frío. **It was f. last night,** Anoche heló

froth /frɔθ/ *n* espuma, *f; Fig.* frivolidad, vanidad, *f, vi* espumar, hacer espuma; echar espuma. —*vt* hacer espumar; hacer echar espuma

frothiness /'frɔθinɪs/ *n* espumosidad, *f; Fig.* frivolidad, superficialidad, vaciedad, *f*

frothy /'frɔθi/ *a* espumoso, espumajoso; *Fig.* frívolo, superficial

frown /fraun/ *n* ceño, *m;* cara de juez, expresión severa, *f;* desaprobación, *f;* (of fortune) revés, golpe, *m.* —*vi* fruncir el ceño. **to f. at, on, upon,** mirar con desaprobación, ver con malos ojos; ser enemigo de; desaprobar

frowning /'fraunɪŋ/ *a* ceñudo; severo; amenazador

frowningly /'fraunɪŋli/ *adv* severamente

frowsiness /'frauzinɪs/ *n* mal olor, *m;* (dirtiness) suciedad, *f;* (untidiness) desaliño, desaseo, *m*

frowsy /'frauzi/ *a* fétido, mal oliente; mal ventilado; (dirty) sucio; (untidy) desaliñado, desaseado

frozen /'frouzən/ *a* helado; cubierto de hielo; congelado; (*Geog.* and *Fig.*) glacial. **to be f. up,** estar helado. **f. meat,** carne congelada, *f*

frugal /'frugəl/ *a* económico; frugal; sobrio

frugality /fru'gælɪti/ *n* economía, *f;* frugalidad, sobriedad, *f*

fruit /frut/ *n* (in general sense) fruto, *m;* (off a tree or bush) fruta, *f; Fig.* fruto, *m;* resultado, *m,* consecuencia, *f.* —*vi* frutar, dar fruto. **bottled f.,** fruta en almíbar, *f.* **candied f.,** fruta azucarada, *f.* **dried f.,** fruta seca, *f.* **first fruits,** primicias, *f pl.* **soft f.,** frutas blandas, *f pl.* **stone f.,** fruta de hueso, *f.* **f.-bearing,** frutal. **f.-cake,** pastel de fruta, *m.* **f.-dish,** frutero, *m.* **f. farming,** fruticultura, *f.* **f.-knife,** cuchillo de postres, *m.* **f. shop,** frutería, *f.* **f. tree,** frutal, *m*

fruiterer /'frutərər/ *n* frutero (-ra)

fruitful /'frutfəl/ *a* fructuoso, fértil; prolífico, fecundo; provechoso

fruitfulness /'frutfəlnɪs/ *n* fertilidad, *f;* fecundidad, *f;* provecho, *m*

fruition /fru'ɪʃən/ *n* fruición, *f*

fruitless /'frutlɪs/ *a* infructuoso, estéril; inútil

fruitlessness /'frutlɪsnɪs/ *n* infructuosidad, esterilidad, *f;* inutilidad, *f*

fruity /'fruti/ *a* de fruta; (wines) vinoso; (of voice) melodioso

frump /frʌmp/ *n* estantigua, *f*

frumpish /'frʌmpɪʃ/ *a* estrafalario; fuera de moda

frustrate /'frʌstreit/ *vt* frustrar; defraudar; malograr; destruir; anular

frustration /frʌ'streiʃən/ *n* frustración, *f;* defraudación, *f;* malogro, *m;* destrucción, *f;* desengaño, *m*

fry /frai/ *n Cul.* fritada, *f, vt* freír. —*vi* freírse. **small fry,** *Inf.* gente menuda, *f*

frying /'fraiɪŋ/ *n* fritura, *f,* el freír. **to fall out of the f.-pan into the fire,** ir de mal en peor, andar de zocos en colodros, ir de Guatemala en Guatapeor. **f.-pan,** sartén, *f*

fuchsia /'fyuʃə/ *n Bot.* fuscia, *f*

fuddle /'fʌdl̩/ *vt* atontar, aturdir; embriagar, emborrachar

fudge /fʌdʒ/ *n* patraña, tontería, *f,* disparate, *m.* —*interj* ¡qué disparate! ¡qué va!

fuel /'fyuəl/ *n* combustible, *m; Fig.* cebo, pábulo, *m.* —*vt* cebar, echar combustible en. —*vi* tomar combustible. **to add f. to the flame,** echar leña al fuego. **f. consumption,** consumo de combustible, *m.* **f.-oil,** aceite combustible, aceite de quemar, *m.* **f.-tank,** depósito de combustible, *m*

fueling /'fyuəlɪŋ/ *n* aprovisionamiento de combustible, *m*

fugitive /'fyudʒɪtɪv/ *a* fugitivo; pasajero, perecedero; transitorio, efímero, fugaz. —*n* fugitivo (-va); (from justice) prófugo (-ga); *Mil.* desertor, *m;* (refugee) refugiado (-da)

fugue /fyug/ *n Mus.* fuga, *f*

fulcrum /'fʊlkrəm/ *n Mech.* fulcro, *m*

fulfill /fʊl'fɪl/ *vt* cumplir; (satisfy) satisfacer; (observe) observar; guardar. **to be fulfilled,** cumplirse, realizarse

fulfillment /fʊl'fɪlmənt/ *n* cumplimiento, *m;* desempeño, ejercicio, *m;* (satisfaction) satisfacción, realización, *f;* (observance) observancia, *f*

full /fʊl/ *a* lleno; colmado; todo; pleno; (crowded) atestado; (replete) harto, abundante, (intent on) preocupado con, pensando en; (loose) amplio; (plentiful) copioso; (occupied) ocupado; completo; (resonant) sonoro; (mature) maduro; puro; perfecto; (satiated) saciado (de); (of the moon, sails) lleno; (weighed down) agobiado, abrumado; (detailed) detallado; (with uniform, etc.) de gala; (with years, etc.) cumplido. —*n* colmo, *m;* totalidad, *f.* —*adv* muy; completamente, totalmente. **f. many a flower,** muchas flores. **at f. gallop,** a galope tendido. **at f. speed,** a todo correr; a toda velocidad. **His hands are f.,** Sus manos están llenas. **The moon was at the f.,** La luna estaba llena. **in f.,** por completo; sin abreviaciones; integralmente. **in f. swing,** en plena actividad. **in f.**

vigor, en pleno vigor. **to the f.,** completamente; hasta la última gota; a la perfección. **to be f. to the brim,** estar lleno hasta el tope. **f.-blooded,** sanguíneo; de pura raza; *Fig.* viril, vigoroso; *Fig.* apasionado. **f.-blown,** en plena flor, abierto. **f. dress,** *a* de gala. —*n* traje de etiqueta, traje de ceremonia, *m.* **f.-face,** de cara. **f.-flavored,** (wine) abocado. **f.-grown,** adulto; completamente desarrollado. **f.-length,** de cuerpo entero. **f. moon,** luna llena, *f;* plenilunio, *m.* **f. name,** nombre y apellidos, *m.* **f. powers,** plenos poderes, *m pl.* **f. scale,** tamaño natural, *m.* **f. scope,** carta blanca, *f;* toda clase de facilidades. **f. steam ahead,** a todo vapor. **f. stop,** *Gram.* punto final, *m*

full /fʊl/ *vt* (cloth) abatanar

full-color /'fʊl 'kʌlər/ *a* a todo color. **full-color plates,** láminas a todo color

fuller /'fʊlər/ *n* batanero, *m.* **fuller's earth,** tierra de batán, galactita, *f*

fulling /'fʊlɪŋ/ *n* abatanadura, *f.* **f.-mill,** batán, *m*

fullness /'fʊlnɪs/ *n* abundancia, *f;* plenitud, *f;* (repletion) hartura, *f;* (of clothes) amplitud, *f;* (stoutness) gordura, *f;* (swelling) hinchazón, *f.* **She wrote with great f. of all that she had seen,** Describía muy detalladamente todo lo que había visto. **in the f. of time,** andando el tiempo

full-page /'fʊl 'peidʒ/ *a* a toda plana. **full-page advertisement,** anuncio a toda plana.

full-time /'fʊl 'taim/ *a* de tiempo completo

fully /'fʊli/ *adv* plenamente; enteramente. **It is f. six years since...,** Hace seis años bien cumplidos que... **It is f. 9 o'clock,** Son las nueve bien sonadas. **f. dressed,** completamente vestido

fulminant /'fʌlmənənt/ *a Med.* fulminante

fulminate /'fʌlmə,neit/ *n Chem.* fulminato, *m.* —*vi* estallar; fulminar. —*vt* volar; fulminar

fulminous /'fʌlmənəs/ *a* fulmíneo, fulminoso

fulsome /'fʊlsəm/ *a* servil; insincero, hipócrita; asqueroso, repugnante

fumble /'fʌmbəl/ *vi* (grope) ir a tientas; procurar hacer algo; chapucear (con); (for a word) titubear

fumbling /'fʌmblɪŋ/ *n* hesitación, *f;* tacto incierto, *m.* —*a* incierto; vacilante

fumblingly /'fʌmblɪŋli/ *adv* de manera incierta; a tientas

fume /fyum/ *n* vaho, humo, gas, *m;* emanación, *f;* mal olor, *m,* fetidez, *f; Fig.* vapor, *m;* (state of mind) agitación, *f;* frenesí, *m.* —*vi* humear; refunfuñar, echar pestes

fumigate /'fyumɪ,geit/ *vt* fumigar; sahumar, perfumar; desinfectar

fumigation /,fyumə'geiʃən/ *n* fumigación, *f;* sahumerio, *m*

fumigator /'fyumɪ,geitər/ *n* fumigador (-ra); (apparatus) fumigador, *m*

fumigatory /'fyuməgə,tɔri/ *a* fumigatorio

fuming /'fyumɪŋ/ *n* refunfuño, *m.* —*a* refunfuñador

fumy /'fyumi/ *a* humoso

fun /fʌn/ *n* diversión, *f,* entretenimiento, *m;* (joke) chanza, broma, *f.* **for fun,** para divertirse; en chanza. **in fun,** de burlas. **to have fun,** divertirse. **to poke fun at,** burlarse de, mofarse de, ridiculizar

funambulist /fyu'næmbyəlɪst/ *n* funámbulo (-la)

function /'fʌŋkʃən/ *n* función, *f.* —*vi* funcionar

functional /'fʌŋkʃənl̩/ *a* funcional

functionary /'fʌŋkʃə,nɛri/ *n* funcionario, *m.* —*a* funcional

functioning /'fʌŋkʃənɪŋ/ *n* funcionamiento, *m*

fund /fʌnd/ *n* fondo, *m; pl* **funds,** fondos, *m pl; Inf.* dinero, *m.* **public funds,** fondos públicos, *m pl.* **sinking f.,** fondo de amortización, *m*

fundamental /,fʌndə'mɛntl̩/ *a* fundamental, básico; esencial. —*n* fundamento, *m*

fundamentally /,fʌndə'mɛntl̩i/ *adv* fundamentalmente, básicamente; esencialmente

funeral /'fyunərəl/ *a* funeral, fúnebre, funerario. —*n* funerales, *m pl;* entierro, *m.* **to attend the f. (of),** asistir a los funerales (de). **f. feast,** banquetes fúnebres, *m pl.* **f. director, f. furnisher,** director de pompas fúnebres, *m.* **f. procession,** cortejo fúnebre, *m.* **f. pyre,** pira funeraria, *f.* **f. service,** misa de difuntos, *f*

funereal /fyu'nɪəriəl/ *a* fúnebre, lúgubre

fungicide /'fʌndʒə,said/ *n* anticriptógamo, *m*

fungous /'fʌŋgəs/ *a* fungoso

fungus /'fʌŋgəs/ *n* hongo, *m*

funicular /fyu'nɪkyələr/ *a* funicular. **f. railway,** ferrocarril funicular, *m*

funnel /'fʌnl̩/ *n Chem.* embudo, *m; Naut.* chimenea, *f;* (of a chimney) cañón (de chimenea), *m.* **f.-shaped,** en forma de embudo

funnlly /'fʌnl̩i/ *adv* de un modo raro

funniness /'fʌninɪs/ *n* lo divertido; rareza, extrañeza, *f*

funny /'fʌni/ *a* cómico, gracioso; divertido; (strange) extraño, raro; (mysterious) misterioso. **It struck me as f.,** (amused me) Me hizo gracia; (seemed strange) Me pareció raro. **f.-bone,** hueso de la alegría, *m*

fur /fɜr/ *n* piel, *f;* depósito, sarro, *m;* (on tongue) saburra, *f.* —*a* hecho de pieles. —*vt* forrar, or adornar, or cubrir, con pieles; depositar sarro sobre; (the tongue) ensuciarse la lengua. —*vi* estar forrado, or adornado, or cubierto, con pieles; formarse incrustaciones; (of the tongue) tener la lengua sucia. **fur cap,** gorra de pieles, *f.* **fur cape,** cuello de piel, *m;* capa de pieles, *f.* **fur trade,** peletería, *f*

furbish /'fɜrbɪʃ/ *vt* pulir; renovar; limpiar

furious /'fyʊriəs/ *a* furioso. **to become f.,** ponerse furioso, enfurecerse

furiously /'fyʊriəsli/ *adv* furiosamente, con furia

furiousness /'fyʊriəsnɪs/ *n* furia, *f*

furl /fɜrl/ *vt* plegar; enrollar; *Naut.* aferrar

furlong /'fɜrlɔŋ/ *n* estadio, *m*

furlough /'fɜrlou/ *n Mil.* permiso, *m.* —*vt* conceder un permiso (a). **on f.,** de permiso

furnace /'fɜrnɪs/ *n* horno, *m;* (of steam boiler) fogón, *m;* (for central heating) caldera de calefacción central, *f;* (for smelting) cubilote, *m*

furnish /'fɜrnɪʃ/ *vt* proveer (de), equipar (de), suplir (de); amueblar; (an opportunity) proporcionar; producir

furnished /'fɜrnɪʃt/ *a* amueblado, con muebles. **f. house,** casa amueblada, *f*

furnisher /'fɜrnɪʃər/ *n* decorador, *m;* proveedor (-ra)

furnishing /'fɜrnɪʃɪŋ/ *n* provisión, *f,* equipo, *m; pl* **furnishings,** accesorios, *m pl;* mobiliario, mueblaje, *m*

furniture /'fɜrnɪtʃər/ *n* mobiliario, mueblaje, *m;* ajuar, equipo, *m;* avíos, *m pl; Naut.* aparejo, *m.* **a piece of f.,** un mueble. **to empty of f.,** desamueblar, quitar los muebles (de). **f. dealer** or **maker,** mueblista, *mf.* **f. factory,** mueblería, *f.* **f. polish,** crema para muebles, *f.* **f. mover,** transportador de muebles, *m;* (packer) embalador, *m.* **f. repository,** guardamuebles, *m.* **f. van,** carro de mudanzas, *m*

furor /'fyʊrɔr/ *n* furor, *m*

furred /fɜrd/ *a* forrado or cubierto or adornado de piel; (of the tongue) sucia

furrier /'fɜriər/ *n* peletero, *m.* **furrier's shop,** peletería, *f*

furrow /'fɜrou/ *n* surco, *m;* muesca, *f; Archit.* estría, *f;* (wrinkle) arruga, *f.* —*vt* surcar

furry /'fɜri/ *a* cubierto de piel; parecido a una piel; hecho de pieles

further /'fɜrðər/ *a* ulterior, más distante; (other) otro; opuesto; adicional, más. —*adv* más lejos; más allá; además; también; por añadidura. —*vt* promover, fomentar; ayudar. **on the f. side,** al otro lado. **till f. orders,** hasta nueva orden. **f. on,** más adelante; más allá

furtherance /'fɜrðərəns/ *n* fomento, *m,* promoción, *f;* progreso, avance, *m*

furthermore /'fɜrðər,mɔr/ *adv* además, por añadidura

furthest /'fɜrðɪst/ *a* (el, la, lo) más lejano or más distante; extremo. —*adv* más lejos

furtive /'fɜrtɪv/ *a* furtivo

furtively /'fɜrtɪvli/ *adv* furtivamente, a hurtadillas. **to look at f.,** mirar de reojo

fury /'fyʊri/ *n* furor, enfurecimiento, *m,* rabia, *f;* violencia, *f;* frenesí, arrebato, *m;* furia, *f.* **like a f.,** hecho una furia. **to breathe forth f.,** echar rayos

fuse /fyuz/ *n* (of explosives) espoleta, mecha, *f; Elec.* fusible, *m.* —*vt* (metals) fundir; fusionar, mezclar. —*vi* (metals) fundirse; mezclarse. **safety-f.,** espoleta de seguridad, *f.* **time-f.,** espoleta de tiempo, *f.* **to**

blow a f., fundir un fusible. **f. box,** caja de fusibles, *f.* **f. wire,** fusible, *m*
fuselage /'fyusə,lɑʒ/ *n Aer.* fuselaje, *m*
fusible /'fyuzəbəl/ *a* fusible
fusillade /'fyusə,lɑd/ *n* descarga cerrada, *f*
fusion /'fyuʒən/ *n* fusión, *f;* unión, *f;* (melting) fundición, *f*
fuss /fʌs/ *n* agitación, *f;* (bustle) conmoción, bulla, *f;* bullicio, *m.* —*vi* agitarse, preocuparse. —*vt* poner nervioso. **There's no need to make such a f.,** No es para tanto. **to make a f. of,** (a person) hacer la rueda (a), ser muy atento (a); (spoil) mimar mucho (a). **to f. about,** andar de acá para allá
fussily /'fʌsəli/ *adv* nerviosamente; de un aire importante
fussy /'fʌsi/ *a* meticuloso, nimio; nervioso; (of style) florido, hinchado; (of dress) demasiado adornado
fustigate /'fʌstɪ,geit/ *vt* fustigar
fusty /'fʌsti/ *a* (moldy) mohoso; mal ventilado; mal oliente; (of views, etc.) pasado de moda
futile /'fyutl̩/ *a* fútil, superficial, frívolo; inútil
futility /fyu'tɪlɪti/ *n* futilidad, superficialidad, frivolidad, *f;* (action) tontería, estupidez, *f*
future /'fyutʃər/ *a* futuro, venidero. —*n* futuro, porvenir, *m.* **in the f.,** en adelante, en lo venidero, en lo sucesivo. **for f. reference,** para información futura. **f. perfect tense,** *Gram.* futuro perfecto, *m.* **f. tense,** *Gram.* futuro, *m*
futurism /'fyutʃə,rɪzəm/ *n* futurismo, *m*
futurist /'fyutʃərɪst/ *n* futurista, *mf*
futuristic /,fyutʃə'rɪstɪk/ *a* futurístico
fuzz /fʌz/ *n* tamo, *m,* pelusa, *f.* **f.-ball,** *Bot.* bejín, *m*
fuzzy /'fʌzi/ *a* crespo rizado; velloso

G

g /dʒi/ *n* (letter) ge, *f; Mus.* sol, *m.* **G clef,** clave de sol, *f*
gab /gæb/ *n Inf.* labia, *f.* **to have the gift of the gab,** tener mucha labia
gabardine /'gæbər,din/ *n* gabardina, *f*
gabble /'gæbəl/ *vi* chacharear, garlar; hablar indistintamente; (of goose and some birds) graznar. —*vt* decir indistintamente; decir rápidamente; (a language) chapurrear; mascullar. —*n* cháchara, *f;* vocerío, *m;* (of goose and some birds) graznido, *m*
gabbler /'gæblər/ *n* charlatán (-ana), chacharero (-ra)
gabbling /'gæblıŋ/ *n* See **gabble**
gable /'geibəl/ *n Archit.* gablete, hastial, *m.* **g. end,** alero, *m*
gad /gæd/ *vi* corretear, callejear. **to gad about,** correr por todos lados; divertirse.
gadabout /'gædə,baut/ *n* azotacalles, *mf;* gandul (-la), vagabundo (-da)
gadding /'gædıŋ/ *a* callejero; vagabundo. —*n* vagancia, *f;* vida errante, *f;* gandulería, *f*
gadfly /'gæd,flai/ *n Ent.* tábano, *m; Inf.* moscardón, *m*
gadget /'gædʒıt/ *n* accesorio, *m;* aparato, *m;* chuchería, *f*
Gadsden Purchase /'gædzdən/ la Venta de la Meseta, *f*
Gael /geil/ *n* escocés (-esa) del norte; celta, *mf*
Gaelic /'geilık/ *a* gaélico. —*n* gaélico, *m*
gaff /gæf/ *n* (hook) garfio, *m; Naut.* pico de cangrejo, *m; Theat.* teatrucho, *m*
gaffer /'gæfər/ *n* viejo, tío, abuelo, *m*
gag /gæg/ *n* mordaza, *f; Theat.* morcilla, *f.* —*vt* amordazar; *Fig.* hacer callar. —*vi Theat.* meter morcillas
gage /geidʒ/ *n* prenda, fianza, *f;* (symbol of challenge) guante, *m;* (challenge) desafío, *m.* See **gauge**
gagging /'gægıŋ/ *n* amordazamiento, *m*
gaggle /'gægəl/ *n* (cry) graznido, *m;* (of geese) manada (de ocas), *f.* —*vi* graznar; cacarear
gaiety /'geiıti/ *n* alegría, *f;* animación, vivacidad, *f;* (entertainment) diversión, festividad, *f*
gaily /'geili/ *adv* alegremente
gain /gein/ *n* ganancia, *f;* provecho, beneficio, *m;* (increase) aumento, *m;* (riches) riqueza, *f.* —*vt* ganar; (acquire) conseguir; adquirir; obtener; conquistar, captar; (friends) hacerse; (reach) llegar a, alcanzar. —*vi* ganar; (improve) mejorar; (of a watch) adelantarse. **What have they gained by going to Canada?** ¿Qué han logrado con marcharse al Canadá? **to g. ground,** *Fig.* ganar terreno. **to g. momentum** adquirir velocidad **to g. time,** ganar tiempo. **to g. on, upon,** acercarse a; (overtake) alcanzar; (outstrip) dejar atrás, pasar; (of sea) invadir; (of habits) imponerse
gainful /'geinfəl/ *a* ganancioso, lucrativo; ventajoso
gainfully /'geinfəli/ *adv* ventajosamente; lucrativamente
gainsay /'gein,sei/ *vt* contradecir; oponer; negar
gainsaying /'gein,seiıŋ/ *n* contradicción, *f;* oposición, *f;* negación, *f*
gait /geit/ *n* porte, andar, *m;* paso, *m,* andadura, *f*
galter /'geltər/ *n* polaina, *f;* (spat) botín, *m*
gala /'geilə/ *n* gala, fiesta, *f.* **g.-day.** día de fiesta, *m.* **g.-dress,** traje de gala, *m*
galaxy /'gæləksi/ *n Astron.* vía láctea, *f; Fig.* constelación, *f;* grupo brillante, *m*
gale /geil/ *n* vendaval, ventarrón, *m;* (storm) temporal, *m;* tempestad, *f*
Galician /gə'lıʃən/ *a* and *n* gallego (-ga).
Galilean /,gælə'leiən/ *a* and *n* galileo (-ea)
Galilee /'gælə,li/ Galilea, *f*
gall /gɔl/ *n* (on horses) matadura, *f;* (abrasion) rozadura, *f;* hiel, bilis, *f; Fig.* hiel, amargura, *f;* rencor, *m;* (American slang) descaro, *m,* impertinencia, *f; Bot.* agalla, *f.* —*vt* rozar; *Fig.* mortificar, herir. **g.-apple,** agalla, *f.* **g.-bladder,** vejiga de la hiel, *f.* **g.-stone,** cálculo hepático, *m*
gallant /'gælənt, gə'lænt, -'lɑnt/ *a* hermoso; (imposing) imponente, majestuoso; (brave) valiente, gallardo, valeroso, intrépido; (chivalrous) caballeroso; noble; (attentive to ladies, or amorous) galante. —*n* galán, *m.* —*vt* galantear, cortejar
gallantly /'gæləntli/ *adv* (bravely) valientemente; caballerosamente; cortésmente; galantemente
gallantry /'gæləntri/ *n* (bravery) valentía, *f,* valor, *m;* heroísmo, *m,* proeza, *f;* (chivalry) caballerosidad, *f;* (toward women, or amorousness) galantería, *f*
galleon /'gæliən/ *n* galeón, *m*
gallery /'gæləri/ *n* galería, *f;* pasillo, *m;* (of a cloister) tránsito, *m;* (cloister) claustro, *m;* (for spectators) tribuna, *f; Theat.* paraíso, gallinero, *m;* (theater audience) galería, *f;* (of portraits, etc.) galería, colección, *f;* (*Mineral., Mil.*) galería, *f;* (building) museo, *m.* **art g.,** museo de pinturas, *m*
galley /'gæli/ *n* (*Naut., Print.*) galera, *f;* (kitchen) cocina, *f;* (rowboat) falúa de capitán, *f.* **to condemn to the galleys,** echar a galeras. **wooden g.,** *Print.* galerín, *m.* **g.-proof,** galerada, *f.* **g.-slave,** galeote, *m*
Gallic /'gælık/ *a* gálico, galicano; francés
gallicism /'gælısızəm/ *n* galicismo, *m*
galling /'gɔlıŋ/ *a Fig.* irritante; mortificante
gallivant /'gælə,vænt/ *vi* callejear, corretear; divertirse; ir de parranda
gallon /'gælən/ *n* galón, *m*
galloon /gə'lun/ *n* galón, *m,* trencilla, *f*
gallop /'gæləp/ *n* galope, *m.* —*vi* galopar; ir aprisa. —*vt* hacer galopar, **at full g.,** a rienda suelta, a galope tendido. **to g. back,** volver a galope. **to g. down,** bajar a galope. **to g. off,** marcharse galopando; alejarse corriendo. **to g. past,** desfilar a galope ante. **to g. through,** cruzar a galope. **to g. up,** *vt* subir a galope. —*vi* llegar a galope
gallopade /,gælə'peid/ *n* (dance) galop, *m*
galloping /'gæləpıŋ/ *n* galope, *m;* galopada, *f.* —*a* que va a galope; *Med.* galopante. **g. consumption,** tisis galopante, *f*
gallows /'gælouz/ *n* patíbulo, *m,* horca, *f;* (framework) montante, *m.* **g.-bird,** criminal digno de la horca, *m*
galop /'gæləp/ *n* galop, *m*
galore /gə'lɔr/ *adv* a granel, en abundancia (e.g. *sunshine galore,* sol a granel)
galosh /gə'lɒʃ/ *n* chanclo, *m*
galvanic /gæl'vænık/ *a Elec.* galvánico; espasmódico
galvanism /'gælvə,nızəm/ *n Elec.* galvanismo, *m*
galvanize /'gælvə,naiz/ *vt* galvanizar
gambit /'gæmbıt/ *n* (chess) gambito, *m; Fig.* táctica, *f*
gamble /'gæmbəl/ *n* juego de azar, *m;* jugada, *f;* aventura, *f; Com.* especulación, *f.* —*vi* jugar por dinero; especular; (with) *Fig.* aventurar, arriesgar. **to g. on the Stock Exchange,** jugar en la bolsa. **to g. away,** perder al juego
gambler /'gæmblər/ *n* jugador (-ra)
gambling /'gæmblıŋ/ *n* juego, *m.* —*a* jugador; de juego. **g.-den,** casa de juego, *f,* garito, *m*
gambol /'gæmbəl/ *n* salto, brinco, retozo, *m;* cabriola, *f;* juego, *m.* —*vi* saltar, brincar, retozar; juguetear
game /geim/ *n* juego, *m;* (match) partido, *m;* (jest) chanza, *f;* (trick) trampa, *f;* (birds, hares, etc.) caza menor, *f;* (tigers, lions, etc.) caza mayor, *f;* (flesh of game) caza, *f; pl* **games,** deportes, *m pl.* —*a* de caza; (courageous) valiente, animoso, brioso; resuelto. —*vi* jugar por dinero. **He is g. for anything,** Se atreve a todo. **big g. hunting,** caza mayor, *f.* **head of g.,** pieza de caza, *f.* **It is a g. at which two can play,** Donde las dan las toman. **The g. is not worth the candle,** La cosa no vale la pena. **The g. is up,** *Fig.* El proyecto se ha frustrado. **to make g. of,** (things) burlarse de; (persons) tomar el pelo a; mofarse de. **to**

play the g., *Fig.* jugar limpio. **to g. away,** perder al juego. **g. of cards,** juego de naipes, *m.* **g. of chance,** juego de azar, *m.* **g.-bag,** morral, *m.* **g. drive,** batida de caza, *f.* **g.-laws,** leyes de caza, *f pl.* **g.-licence,** licencia de caza, *f.* **g.-pie,** tortada, *f.* **g. preserve,** coto de caza, *m*

gamekeeper /ˈgeimˌkipər/ *n* guardabosque, *m*

gamely /ˈgeimli/ *adv* valientemente

gameness /ˈgeimnɪs/ *n* valentía, resolución, fortaleza, *f*

gamete /ˈgæmit/ *n* gameto, *m*

gaming /ˈgeimɪŋ/ *n* juego, *m, a* de juego. **g.-house,** garito, *m.* **g.-table,** mesa de juego, *f; Fig.* juego, *m*

gammon /ˈgæmən/ *n* (of bacon) jamón, *m.* —*vt* curar (jamón)

gamut /ˈgæmət/ *n* gama, *f*

gander /ˈgændər/ *n* ganso, *m*

gang /gæŋ/ *n* cuadrilla, pandilla, *f;* (squad) pelotón, *m;* (of workers) brigada, cuadrilla, *f;* group, *m.* **g.-plank,** plancha, *f*

ganglion /ˈgæŋgliən/ *n* ganglio, *m; Fig.* centro, *m*

gangrene /ˈgæŋgrin/ *n* gangrena, *f.* —*vt* gangrenar. —*vi* gangrenarse

gangrenous /ˈgæŋgrɪnəs/ *a* gangrenoso

gangster /ˈgæŋstər/ *n* pistolero, gangster, *m*

gangway /ˈgæŋˌwei/ *n* pasillo, *m; Naut.* plancha, *f,* pasamano, *m;* (opening in ship's side) portalón, *m.* **midship g.,** crujía, *f*

gap /gæp/ *n* brecha, *f;* abertura, *f;* (hole) boquete, *m;* (pass) desfiladero, paso, *m;* (ravine) hondonada, barranca, *f;* (blank) laguna, *f,* vacío, *m;* (crack) intersticio, *m,* hendedura, *f,* resquicio, *m.* **to fill a gap,** llenar un boquete; llenar un vacío

gape /geip/ *vi* estar con la boca abierta, papar moscas. **to g. at,** mirar con la boca abierta

gaping /ˈgeipɪŋ/ *n* huelgo, *m;* abertura, *f, a* que bosteza; boquiabierto; abierto

garage /gəˈrɑʒ/ *n* garaje, *m.* —*vt* poner (un coche, etc.) en un garaje. **g. owner,** garajista, *mf*

garb /gɑrb/ *n* traje, vestido, *m;* uniforme, *m; Herald.* espiga, *f.* —*vt* vestir, ataviar

garbage /ˈgɑrbɪdʒ/ *n* basura, inmundicia, *f*

garbage can basurero, tarro de la basura, *m*

garble /ˈgɑrbəl/ *vt* falsear, mutilar, pervertir

garden /ˈgɑrdn̩/ *n* jardín, *m;* huerto, *m;* (fertile region) huerta, *f.* —*a* de jardín. —*vi* trabajar en el jardín, cultivar un huerto. **g. city,** ciudad jardín, *f.* **g.-frame,** semillero, *m.* **g. mold,** tierra vegetal, *f.* **g.-party,** fiesta de jardín, *f.* **g.-plot,** parterre, *m.* **g. produce,** hortalizas, legumbres, *f pl.* **g. roller,** rodillo, *m.* **g.-seat,** banco de jardín, *m.* **g. urn,** jarrón, *m*

gardener /ˈgɑrdnər/ *n* jardinero, *m*

gardenia /gɑrˈdinyə/ *n* gardenia, *f,* jazmín de la India, *m*

gardening /ˈgɑrdn̩ɪŋ/ *n* jardinería, *f;* horticultura, *f.* —*a* de jardinería

gargantuan /gɑrˈgæntʃuən/ *a* gargantuesco; tremendo, enorme

gargle /ˈgɑrgəl/ *n* (liquid) gargarismo, *m;* gárgaras, *f pl.* —*vi* hacer gárgaras, gargarizar

gargling /ˈgɑrglɪŋ/ *n* gargarismo, *m*

gargoyle /ˈgɑrgɔil/ *n* gárgola, *f*

garish /ˈgɛərɪʃ/ *a* cursi, llamativo, charro, chillón

garishness /ˈgɛərɪʃnɪs/ *n* cursería, ostentación, *f,* lo llamativo

garland /ˈgɑrlənd/ *n* guirnalda, *f;* corona, *f;* (anthology) florilegio, *m; Archit.* festón, *m.* —*vt* enguirnaldar

garlic /ˈgɑrlɪk/ *n* ajo, *m*

garment /ˈgɑrmənt/ *n* prenda de vestir, *f;* traje, vestido, *m; Fig.* vestidura, *f;* (*Fig.* cloak) capa, *f*

garner /ˈgɑrnər/ *n* granero, *m;* tesoro, *m;* colección, *f.* —*vt* atesorar, guardar

garnet /ˈgɑrnɪt/ *n* granate, *m*

garnish /ˈgɑrnɪʃ/ *n Cul.* aderezo, *m;* adorno, *m.* —*vt Cul.* aderezar; embellecer, adornar

garnishing /ˈgɑrnɪʃɪŋ/ *n.* See **garnish**

garret /ˈgærɪt/ *n* guardilla, buhardilla, *f,* desván, *m*

garrison /ˈgærəsən/ *n* guarnición, *f,* presidio, *m.* —*vt* guarnecer, presidiar. **g. town,** plaza de armas, *f*

garrote /gəˈrɒt/ *n* garrote, *m.* —*vt* agarrotar, dar garrote (a)

garrulity /gəˈrulɪti/ *n* garrulidad, locuacidad, charlatanería, *f*

garrulous /ˈgærələs/ *a* gárrulo, locuaz, charlatán

garter /ˈgɑrtər/ *n* liga, *f;* (G.) Jarretera, *f, vt* atar con liga; investir con la Jarretera. **Order of the G.,** Orden de la Jarretera, *f*

gas /gæs/ *n* gas, *m; Fig. Inf.* palabrería, *f;* (petrol) bencina, *f, a* de gas; con gas; para gases. —*vt* asfixiar con gas; *Mil.* atacar con gas; saturar de gas. **gas attack,** ataque con gases asfixiantes, *m.* **gas-bag,** bolsa de gas, *f; Inf.* charlatán (-ana). **gas-burner,** mechero de gas, *m.* **gas-chamber,** cámara de gas, *f.* **gas detector,** detector de gases, *m.* **gas-fire,** estufa de gas, *f.* **gas-fitter,** gasista, *m.* **gas-fittings,** lámparas de gas, *f pl.* **gas-light,** luz de gas, *f;* mechero de gas, *m.* **gas-main,** cañería maestra de gas, *f.* **gas-man,** gasista, *m.* **gas-mantle,** camiseta incandescente, *f.* **gas-mask,** máscara para gases, *f.* **gas-meter,** contador de gas, *m.* **gas-pipes,** cañerías (or tuberías) de gas, *f pl.* **gas-ring,** fogón de gas, *m.* **gas-shell,** obús de gases asfixiantes, *m.* **gas-stove,** cocina de gas, *f.* **gas warfare,** guerra química, *f.* **gas-works,** fábrica de gas, *f*

Gascon /ˈgæskən/ *a* and *n* gascón (-ona)

Gascony /ˈgæskəni/ Gascuña, *f*

gaseous /ˈgæsiəs/ *a* gaseoso

gash /gæʃ/ *n* cuchillada, *f;* herida extensa, *f.* —*vt* acuchillar; herir extensamente

gasket /ˈgæskɪt/ *n* aro de empaquetadura, *m*

gasoline /ˌgæsəˈlin/ *n* gasolina, *f*

gasp /gæsp/ *n* boqueada, *f.* —*vi* boquear. **to be at the last g.,** estar agonizando. **to g. for breath,** luchar por respirar. **to g. out,** decir anhelante, decir con voz entrecortada

gastric /ˈgæstrɪk/ *a* gástrico

gastritis /gæˈstraitɪs/ *n* gastritis, *f*

gastronome /ˈgæstrəˌnoum/ *n* gastrónomo (-ma)

gastronomic /ˌgæstrəˈnɑmɪk/ *a* gastronómico

gastronomy /gæˈstrɒnəmi/ *n* gastronomía, *f*

gate /geit/ *n* puerta, *f;* cancela, verja, *f;* entrada, *f;* (of a lock, etc.) compuerta, *f;* (across a road, etc.) barrera, *f;* (money) entrada, *f; Fig.* puerta, *f.* **automatic g.,** (at level crossings, etc.) barrera de golpe, *f.* **to g.-crash,** asistir sin invitación. **g.-keeper,** portero, *m;* guardabarrera, *mf* **g.-money,** entrada, *f.* **g.-post,** soporte de la puerta, *m*

gateway /ˈgeitˌwei/ *n* entrada, *f;* puerta, *f;* paso, *m;* vestíbulo, *m; Fig.* puerta, *f*

gather /ˈgæðər/ *vt* (assemble) reunir; (amass) acumular, amontonar; (acquire) obtener, adquirir; hacer una colección (de); cobrar; (harvest) cosechar, recolectar; (pick up) recoger; (pluck) coger; (infer) sacar en limpio, aprender; *Sew.* fruncir; (the brows) fruncir (el ceño). —*vi* reunirse, congregarse; amontonarse; (threaten) amenazar; (sadden) amargar; (*Fig.* hover over) cernerse (sobre); (increase) aumentar, crecer; (be covered) cubrirse; (fester) supurar. —*n Sew.* frunce, pliegue, *m.* **to g. breath,** tomar aliento. **to g. speed,** ganar velocidad. **to g. strength,** cobrar fuerzas. **I g. from Mary that they are going abroad,** Según lo que me ha dicho María, van al extranjero. **to g. in,** juntar; reunir; (harvest) cosechar; coger. **to g. together,** *vt* reunir. —*vi* reunirse. **to g. up,** recoger; coger; tomar; (one's limbs) encoger. **to g. up the threads,** *Fig.* recoger los hilos.

gatherer /ˈgæðərər/ *n* cogedor, colector, *m;* (harvester) segador, *m;* (of grapes) vendimiador (-ra); (of taxes) recaudador, *m*

gathering /ˈgæðərɪŋ/ *n* cogedura, *f;* (fruit, etc.) recolección, *f;* (of taxes) recaudación, *f;* amontonamiento, *m;* colección, *f; Med.* absceso, *m; Sew.* fruncimiento, *m;* (assembly) reunión, asamblea, *f;* (crowd) concurrencia, muchedumbre, *f*

gathers /ˈgæðərz/ *n Sew.* fruncidos, pliegues, *m pl*

gauche /gouʃ/ *a* torpe, huraño

gaudily /ˈgɔdəli/ *adv* ostentosamente; brillantemente

gaudiness /ˈgɔdinɪs/ *n* ostentación, *f;* brillantez, *f*

gaudy /ˈgɔdi/ *a* llamativo, vistoso, brillante, ostentoso

gauge /geidʒ/ *n* (of gun) calibre, *m;* (railway) entrevía, *f;* (for measuring) indicator, *m;* regla de medir, *f; Naut.* calado, *m; Fig.* medida, *f;* (test) indicación, *f;* (model) norma, *f.* —*vt* calibrar; medir; estimar; (ship's capacity) arquear; (judge) juzgar; (size

up) tomar la medida (de); *Fig.* interpretar; *Sew.* fruncir; (liquor) aforar. **broad (narrow) g. railway,** ferrocarril de vía ancha (estrecha), *m.* **pressure g.,** manómetro, *m.* **water g.,** indicador del nivel de agua, *m*
gauging /'geidʒɪŋ/ *n* medida, *f;* (of ship's capacity) arqueo, *m;* (of liquor) aforamiento, *m; Fig.* apreciación, *f;* interpretación, *f*
Gaul /gɔl/ Galia, *f*
gaunt /gɔnt/ *a* anguloso, huesudo, desvaído; (of houses, etc.) lúgubre
gauntlet /'gɔntlɪt/ *n* guante de manopla, *m;* (part of armor) manopla, *f,* guantelete, *m.* **to throw down the g.,** echar el guante, desafiar
gauntness /'gɔntnɪs/ *n* angulosidad, flaqueza, *f*
gauze /gɔz/ *n* gasa, *f;* (mist) bruma, *f.* **wire-g.,** tela metálica, *f*
gauziness /'gɔzinɪs/ *n* diafanidad, *f*
gauzy /'gɔzi/ *a* diáfano; de gasa
gavotte /gə'vɒt/ *n* gavota, *f*
gawkiness /'gɔkinɪs/ *n* torpeza, desmaña, *f*
gawky /'gɔki/ *a* anguloso, desgarbado, torpe
gay /gei/ *a* alegre; festivo, animado; ligero de cascos, disipado; homosexual; (of colors) brillante, llamativo
Gaza Strip /'gɑzə/ la franja de Gaza, *f*
gaze /geiz/ *n* mirada, *f;* mirada fija, *f.* —*vi* mirar; mirar fijamente, contemplar
gazelle /gə'zɛl/ *n* gacel (-la)
gazer /'geizər/ *n* espectador (-ra)
gazette /gə'zɛt/ *n* gaceta, *f.* —*vt* publicar en la gaceta.
gazing /'geizɪŋ/ *n* contemplación, *f, a* contemplador; que presencia, que asiste a
gear /gɪər/ *n* (apparel) atavíos, *m pl;* (harness) guarniciones, *f pl,* arneses, *m pl;* (tackle) utensilios, *m pl,* herramientas, *f pl; Naut.* aparejo, *m; Mech.* engranaje, *m;* juego, *m,* marcha, *f.* —*vt* aparejar, enjaezar; *Mech.* poner en marcha, hacer funcionar. —*vi Mech.* engranar, endentar. **low g.,** pimera velocidad, *f.* **neutral g.,** punto muerto, *m.* **reverse g.,** marcha atrás, *f.* **second g.,** segunda velocidad, *f.* **three-speed g.,** cambio de marchas de tres velocidades, *m.* **top g.,** tercera (or cuarta--according to gear-box) velocidad, *f.* **to change g.,** cambiar de marcha, cambiar de velocidad. **to throw out of g.,** *Fig.* desquiciar. **g.-box,** caja de velocidades, *f.* **g.-changing,** cambio de velocidad, *m.* **g.-changing lever,** palanca de cambio de velocidad, palanca de cambio de marchas, *f*
gearing /'gɪərɪŋ/ *n* engranaje, *m*
gee up /dʒi/ *interj* ¡arre!
gehenna /gɪ'hɛnə/ *n* gehena, *m*
geisha /'geiʃə/ *n* geisha, *f*
gelatin /'dʒɛlətn̩/ *n* gelatina, *f.* **cooking g.,** gelatina seca, *f*
gelatinous /dʒə'lætn̩əs/ *a* gelatinoso
geld /gɛld/ *vt* capar, castrar
gelder /'gɛldər/ *n* castrador, *m*
gelding /'gɛldɪŋ/ *n* castración, capadura, *f;* caballo castrado, *m;* animal castrado, *m*
gelid /'dʒɛlɪd/ *a* gélido, helado; *Fig.* frío, frígido
gem /dʒɛm/ *n* piedra preciosa, *f;* joya, alhaja, *f; Fig.* joya, *f.* —*vt* adornar con piedras preciosos; enjoyar
Gemini /'dʒɛmə,nai/ *n* (los) Gemelos
gender /'dʒɛndər/ *n Gram.* género, *m;* sexo, *m*
gene /dʒin/ *n Biol.* gene, *m*
genealogical /,dʒiniə'lɒdʒɪkəl/ *a* genealógico. **g. tree,** árbol genealógico, *m*
genealogist /,dʒini'ɒlədʒɪst/ *n* genealogista, *mf*
genealogy /,dʒini'ɒlədʒi/ *n* genealogía, *f*
general /'dʒɛnərəl/ *a* general; universal; común; corriente; (usual) acostumbrado, usual; del público, público. —*n* lo general; (*Mil., Eccl.*) general, *m; Inf.* criada para todo, *f.* **in g.,** por lo general, en general, generalmente. **to become g.,** generalizarse. **to make g.,** generalizar, hacer general. **g. average,** (marine insurance) avería gruesa, *f.* **g. election,** elección general, *f.* **g. meeting,** pleno, mitin general, *m.* **g. opinion,** voz común, opinión general, *f.* **G. Post Office,** Oficina Central de Correos, *f.* **g. practitioner,** médico (-ca) general. **g. public,** público, *m.* **the general reader** el lector de tipo general *m*
generalissimo /,dʒɛnərə'lɪsə,mou/ *n* generalísimo, *m*
generality /,dʒɛnə'rælɪti/ *n* generalidad, *f*
generalization /,dʒɛnərələ'zeiʃən/ *n* generalización, *f*
generalize /'dʒɛnərə,laiz/ *vt* and *vi* generalizar
generally /'dʒɛnərəli/ *adv* en general, por regla general, por lo general, generalmente; comúnmente, por lo común
generalship /'dʒɛnərəl,ʃɪp/ *n Mil.* generalato, *m;* (strategy) táctica, estrategia, *f;* dirección, jefatura, *f*
generate /'dʒɛnə,reit/ *vt* (beget) engendrar, procrear; (*Phys., Chem.*) generar; *Fig.* producir, crear
generation /,dʒɛnə'reiʃən/ *n* procreación, *f;* generación, *f; Fig.* producción, creación, *f.* **the younger g.,** los jóvenes
generative /'dʒɛnərətɪv/ *a* generador
generator /'dʒɛnə,reitər/ *n Mech.* generador, *m;* dínamo, *f*
generic /dʒə'nɛrɪk/ *a* genérico
generosity /,dʒɛnə'rɒsɪti/ *n* generosidad, *f;* liberalidad, *f*
generous /'dʒɛnərəs/ *a* generoso; liberal, dadivoso; magnánimo; (plentiful) abundante; (of wines) generoso
generously /'dʒɛnərəsli/ *adv* generosamente; abundantemente
genesis /'dʒɛnəsɪs/ *n* principio, origen, *m;* (G.) Génesis, *m*
genetic /dʒə'nɛtɪk/ *a* genético
genetics /dʒə'nɛtɪks/ *n* genética, *f*
Geneva /dʒə'nivə/ Ginebra *f*
Genevan /dʒə'nivən/ *a* and *n* ginebrés (-esa), ginebrino (-na)
genial /'dʒinyəl/ *a* (of climate) agradable, bueno; (of persons) afable, bondadoso; de buen humor, bonachón
geniality /,dʒini'ælɪti/ *n* afabilidad, bondad, *f;* buen humor, *m*
genially /'dʒinyəli/ *adv* afablemente
genie /'dʒini/ *n* genio, *m*
genital /'dʒɛnɪtl̩/ *a* genital, sexual. —*n pl* **genitals,** genitales, *m pl*
genitive /'dʒɛnɪtɪv/ *a* and *n Gram.* genitivo *m.*
genius /'dʒinyəs/ *n* genio, *m;* carácter, *m,* índole, *f;* ingenio, *m; Inf.* talento, *m*
Genoa /'dʒɛnouə/ Genova, *f*
Genoese /,dʒɛnou'iz/ *a* and *n* genovés (-esa)
genre /'ʒɑnrə/ *n* género, *m.* **g. painting,** cuadro de género, *m*
genteel /dʒɛn'til/ *a* fino; (affected) remilgado, melindroso; de buen tono; de buena educación
gentile /'dʒɛntail/ *a* and *n* gentil *mf*
gentility /dʒɛn'tɪlɪti/ *n* aristocracia, *f;* respetabilidad, *f*
gentle /'dʒɛntl̩/ *a* noble, bien nacido, de buena familia; amable; suave; ligero; dulce; (docile) manso, dócil; (affectionate) cariñoso; bondadoso; sufrido, paciente; cortés; pacífico, tolerante. **He was a man of g. birth,** Era un hombre bien nacido. **"G. reader,"** «Querido lector»
gentlefolk /'dʒɛntl̩,fouk/ *n pl* gente de bien, gente fina, *f;* gente de buena familia, *f*
gentleman /'dʒɛntl̩mən/ *n* caballero, señor, *m;* gentilhombre, *m.* **Ladies and gentlemen,** Señoras y caballeros, Señores. **young g.,** señorito, *m.* **to be a perfect g.,** ser un caballero perfecto. **g.-inwaiting,** gentilhombre de la cámara, *m*
gentlemanliness /'dʒɛntl̩mənlinɪs/ *n* caballerosidad, *f*
gentlemanly /'dʒɛntl̩mənli/ *a* caballeroso
gentleness /'dʒɛntl̩nɪs/ *n* amabilidad, *f;* suavidad, *f;* dulzura, *f;* mansedumbre, docilidad, *f;* bondad, *f;* paciencia, *f;* cortesía, *f;* tolerancia, *f*
gentlewoman /'dʒɛntl̩,wʊmən/ *n* dama, *f;* dama de servicio, *f*
gently /'dʒɛntli/ *adv* suavemente; dulcemente; silenciosamente, sin ruido; (slowly) despacio, poco a poco. **g. born,** bien nacido
gentry /'dʒɛntri/ *n* pequeña aristocracia, alta clase media, *f;* (disparaging) gentle, *f*
genuflect /'dʒɛnyʊ,flɛkt/ *vi* doblar la rodilla
genuflection /,dʒɛnyə'flɛkʃən/ *n* genuflexión, *f*
genuine /'dʒɛnyuɪn/ *a* puro; genuino; verdadero; real; sincero; auténtico

genuinely /'dʒɛnyuɪnli/ *adv* genuinamente; verdaderamente; realmente; sinceramente
genuineness /'dʒɛnyuɪnnɪs/ *n* pureza, *f;* autenticidad, *f;* verdad, *f;* sinceridad, *f*
genus /'dʒinəs/ *n* género, *m*
geodesic /ˌdʒiə'dɛsɪk/ *a* geodésico
geodesy /dʒi'ɒdəsi/ *n* geodesia, *f*
geographer /dʒi'ɒgrəfər/ *n* geógrafo, *m*
geographical /ˌdʒiə'græfɪkəl/ *a* geográfico
geographically /ˌdʒiə'græfɪkəli/ *adv* geográficamente; desde el punto de vista geográfico
geography /dʒi'ɒgrəfi/ *n* geografía, *f*
geological /ˌdʒiə'lɒdʒɪkəl/ *a* geológico
geologically /ˌdʒiə'lɒdʒɪkəli/ *adv* geológicamente; desde el punto de vista geológico
geologist /dʒi'ɒlədʒɪst/ *n* geólogo, *m*
geologize /dʒi'ɒləˌdʒaiz/ *vi* estudiar la geología. *—vt* estudiar desde un punto de vista geológico
geology /dʒi'ɒlədʒi/ *n* geología, *f*
geometric /ˌdʒiə'mɛtrɪk/ *a* geométrico
geometry /dʒi'ɒmɪtri/ *n* geometría, *f*
geophysics /ˌdʒiou'fɪzɪks/ *n* geofísica, *f*
Georgian /'dʒɔrdʒən/ *a Geog.* georgiano; del principio del siglo diez y nueve
georgic /'dʒɔrdʒɪk/ *n* geórgica, *f*
geotropism /dʒi'ɒtrəˌpɪzəm/ *n* geotropismo, *m*
geranium /dʒə'reiniəm/ *n* geranio, *m*
germ /dʒɜrm/ *n* embrión, germen, *m;* microbio, bacilo, *m; Fig.* germen, *m.* **g.-cell,** célula germinal, *f*
German /'dʒɜrmən/ *a* alemán; germánico. *—n* alemán (-ana); (language) alemán, *m;* germano (-na), germánico (-ca). **Sudeten G.,** alemán (-ana) sudete. **G. measles,** rubeola, *f.* **G. silver** alpaca, *f,* melchor *m,* plata alemana *f*
germander /dʒər'mændər/ *n Bot.* camedrio, *m*
germane /dʒər'mein/ *a* pertinente (a), a propósito (a)
Germanic /dʒər'mænɪk/ *a* germánico. *—n* (language) germánico, *m*
Germanization /ˌdʒɜrmənɪ'zeiʃən/ *n* germanización, *f*
Germanize /'dʒɜrməˌnaiz/ *vt* germanizar. *—vi* germanizarse
Germanophile /dʒər'mænəˌfail/ *n* germanófilo (-la)
Germany /'dʒɜrməni/ Alemania, *f*
germicidal /ˌdʒɜrmə'saidl̩/ *a* bactericida
germicide /'dʒɜrməˌsaid/ *n* desinfectante, *m*
germinal /'dʒɜrmənl̩/ *a* germinal. *—n* (G.) germinal, *m*
germinate /'dʒɜrməˌneit/ *vi* germinar, brotar. *—vt* hacer germinar
germination /ˌdʒɜrmə'neiʃən/ *n* germinación, *f*
germinative /'dʒɜrməˌneitɪv/ *a* germinativo
gerund /'dʒɛrənd/ *n* gerundio, *m*
gerundive /dʒə'rʌndɪv/ *n* gerundio adjetivado, *m*
Gestapo /gə'stɑpou/ *n* Gestapo, *f*
gestation /dʒɛ'steiʃən/ *n* gestación, *f*
gesticulate /dʒɛ'stɪkyəˌleit/ *vi* gesticular, hacer gestos; accionar. *—vt* expresar por gestos
gesticulation /dʒɛˌstɪkyə'leiʃən/ *n* gesticulación, *f*
gesticulatory /dʒɛ'stɪkyələˌtɔri/ *a* gesticular
gesture /'dʒɛstʃər/ *n* movimiento, *m;* gesticulación, *f;* (of the face) gesto, *m,* mueca, *f;* ademán, *m,* acción, *f.* *—vi* gesticular. *—vt* decir por gestos; acompañar con gestos
get /gɛt/ *vt* (obtain) obtener; (acquire) adquirir; (buy) comprar; (take) tomar; (receive) recibir; (gain, win) ganar; (hit) acertar, dar; (place) poner; (achieve) alcanzar, lograr; (make) hacer; (call) llamar; (understand) comprender; (catch) coger; (procreate) procrear, engendrar; (induce) persuadir; (invite) convidar, invitar; (cause) hacer; (with have and past part.) tener; (with have and past part. followed by infin.) tener que; (followed by noun and past part.) hacer; (fetch) buscar, ir a buscar; (order) mandar, disponer; (procure) procurar; (bring) traer; (money) hacer; (a reputation, etc.) hacerse; (a prize, an advantage) llevar; (learn) aprender; (be) ser. *—vi* (become) hacerse; ponerse; venir a ser; (old) envejecerse; (angry) montar (en cólera), enojarse; (arrive) llegar a; (attain) alcanzar; (accomplish) conseguir, lograr; (drunk) emborracharse; (hurt) hacerse daño; (wet) mojarse; (cool) enfriarse; (money) hacer (dinero); (of health) ponerse; (find oneself) hallarse, encontrarse; (late) hacerse (tarde); (dark) empezar a caer (la noche), empezar a caer (la noche), empezar a oscurecer; (put oneself) meterse; (grow, be) estar; (on to or on top of) montar sobre, subir a. **He has got run over,** Ha sido atropellado. **It gets on my nerves,** Se me pone los nervios en punta. **Let's get it over!** ¡Vamos a concluir de una vez! **How do you get on with her?** ¿Cómo te va con ella? **She must be getting on for twenty,** Tendrá alrededor de veinte años. **to get a suit made,** mandar hacerse un traje. **to get better,** (in health) mejorar de salud; hacer progresos adelantar. **to get dark,** obscurecer. **to get into conversation with,** trabar conversación con. **to get into bad company,** frecuentar malas compañías. **to get into the habit of,** acostumbrarse a. **to get married,** casarse. **to get near,** acercarse. **to get one's own way,** salir con la suya. **to get oneself up as,** disfrazarse de. **to get out in a hurry,** salir apresuradamente; marcharse rápidamente, *Inf.* salir pitando. **to get out of the way,** quitarse de en medio, apartarse. **to get rid of,** desembarazarse de, librarse de; salir de; perder. **to have got,** poseer; tener; padecer. **Get on!** ¡Adelante!; (to a horse) ¡Arre!; (continue) ¡Sigue! **Get out!** ¡Fuera! ¡Largo de aquí! ¡Sal! **Get up!** ¡Levántate!; (to a horse) ¡Arre! **to get about,** moverse mucho; andar mucho; (attend to business affairs) ir a sus negocios; (travel) viajar; (get up from sick bed) levantarse; (go out) salir; (be known) saberse, divulgarse, hacerse público. **to get above,** subir a un nivel más alto (de). **to get across,** *vi* cruzar, atravesar. *—vt* hacer cruzar. **to get along,** *vi* (depart) marcharse; (continue) seguir, vivir; (manage) ir, ir tirando. *—vt* llevar; traer; hacer andar por. **How are you getting along?** ¿Cómo le va? **I am getting along all right, thank you,** Voy tirando, gracias. **to get along without,** pasarse sin. **to get at,** (remove) sacar; (find) encontrar; (reach) llegar a; alcanzar; (discover) descubrir; (allude to) aludir a; (understand) comprender. **to get away,** *vi* dejar (un lugar); marcharse, irse; (escape) escaparse. *—vt* ayudar a marcharse; ayudar a escaparse. **to get away with,** llevarse, marcharse con; *Inf.* salir con la suya. **to get back,** *vi* regresar, volver; (get home) volver a casa; (be back) estar de vuelta. *—vt* (recover) recobrar; (receive) recibir; (find again) hallar de nuevo. **to get down,** *vi* bajar, descender. *—vt* bajar; (take off a hook) descolgar; (swallow) tragar; (note) anotar; escribir. **to get down on all fours,** ponerse en cuatro patas. **to get down to,** ponerse a (estudiar, trabajar, etc.). **to get in,** *vi* entrar en; lograr entrar en; (slip in) colarse en; (of political party) entrar en el poder; (of a club) hacerse socio de; (return) regresar; (home) volver a casa; (find oneself) hallarse, estar; (a habit) adquirir. *—vt* hacer entrar en; (a club, etc.) hacer socio de; (a word) decir. **to get into.** See **to get in. to get off,** *vt* apearse de; bajar de; (send) enviar; (from punishment) librar; (bid goodbye) despedirse de; (remove) quitar, sacar. *—vi* apearse; bajar; (from punishment) librarse; (leave) ponerse en camino, marcharse. **to get on,** *vi* (wear) tener puesto; (progress) hacer progresos, adelantar; (prosper) medrar, prosperar; (succeed) tener éxito; avanzar; seguir el camino; (agree) avenirse. *—vt* (push) empujar; (place) poner; (cause) hacer; (clothes) ponerse; (mount) subir a. **to get open,** abrir. **to get out,** *vt* hacer salir; sacar; (publish) publicar; divulgar. *—vi* salir; escapar; **to get out of a jam,** salir de un paso; (descend) bajar (de). **to get over,** (cross) atravesar, cruzar; (an illness, grief, etc.) reponerse, reponerse de; (excuse) perdonar; (surmount) superar; (ground) recorrer. **to get round,** (a person) persuadir; (surround) rodear; (avoid) evitar; (difficulties) superar, vencer. **to get through,** pasar por; (time) pasar, entretener; (money) gastar; (finish) terminar, acabar; (pierce or enter) penetrar; (communicate) comunicar (con); (difficulties) vencer; (an exam) aprobar. **to get to,** llegar a; encontrar; (begin) empezar. **to get together,** *vt* reunir, juntar. *—vi* reunirse, juntarse. **to get under,** ponerse debajo de; (control) dominar. **to get up,** *vt* (raise) alzar, levantar; (carry up things) subir; hacer subir; organizar;

preparar; (learn) aprender; (linen) blanquear, colar; (ascend) subir; hacer; (dress) ataviar; (steam) generar; (a play) ensayar, poner en escena. *—vi* levantarse; (on a horse) montar a caballo; (of the wind) refrescarse; (of the fire) avivarse; (of the sea) embravecerse. **to get up to,** llegar a; alcanzar

get-at-able /ˈgɛt ˌæt əbəl/ *a* accesible

getting /ˈgɛtɪŋ/ *n* adquisición, *f;* (of money) ganancia, *f.* **g. up,** preparación, *f;* organización, *f;* (of a play) representación (de una comedia), puesta en escena, *f*

get-up /ˈgɛt ˌʌp/ *n* atavío, *m;* (of a book, etc.) aspecto, *m*

gewgaw /ˈgyugɔ/ *n* chuchería, *f*

geyser /ˈgaizər/ *n* géiser, *m;* (for heating water) calentador (de agua), *m*

ghastliness /ˈgæstlinɪs/ *n* horror, *m;* palidez mortal, *f;* aspecto miserable, *m;* (boringness) tedio, aburrimiento, *m;* lo desagradable

ghastly /ˈgæstli/ *a* horrible; de una palidez mortal; cadavérico; (boring) aburrido; muy desagradable

gherkin /ˈgɜrkɪn/ *n* cohombrillo, *m*

ghetto /ˈgɛtou/ *n* gueto *m*

ghost /goust/ *n* fantasma, espectro, aparecido, *m;* (spirit) alma, *f,* espíritu, *m;* (shadow) sombra. *f;* (writer) mercenario, *m.* **Holy G.,** Espíritu Santo, *m.* **to give up the g.,** entregar el alma; perder la esperanza, desesperarse. **to look like a g.,** parecer un fantasma

ghostliness /ˈgoustlinɪs/ *n* espiritualidad, *f;* lo misterioso; palidez, *f;* tenuidad, *f*

ghostly /ˈgoustli/ *a* espiritual; espectral; misterioso; pálido; vaporoso, tenue; indistinto

ghost town *n* pueblo-fantasma, *m*

ghost word *n* palabra-fantasma, *f*

ghoul /gul/ *n* vampiro, *m*

ghoulish /ˈgulɪʃ/ *a* insano; cruel; sádico

giant /ˈdʒaiənt/ *n* gigante, *m; Fig.* coloso, *m, a* gigantesco; de gigantes; de los gigantes. **g.-killer,** matador de gigantes, *m.* **g.-stride,** (gymnastics) paso volante, *m*

giantess /ˈdʒaiəntɪs/ *n* giganta, *f*

gibber /ˈdʒɪbər/ *vi* hablar incoherentemente, hablar entre dientes; farfullar, hablar atropelladamente; decir disparates

gibberish /ˈdʒɪbərɪʃ/ *n* galimatías, *m;* jerigonza, *f,* griego, *m*

gibbet /ˈdʒɪbɪt/ *n* horca, *f,* patíbulo, *m.* **to die on the g.,** morir ahorcado

gibbon /ˈgɪbən/ *n Zool.* gibón, *m*

gibe /dʒaib/ *n* improperio, escarnio, *m,* burla, mofa, *f.* *—vi* criticar. **to g. at,** burlarse de, ridiculizar, mofarse de

gibing /ˈdʒaibɪŋ/ *a* burlón, mofador. *—n* mofas, burlas, *f pl*

gibingly /ˈdʒaibɪŋli/ *adv* burlonamente, con sorna

giblets /ˈdʒɪblɪts/ *n* menudillos, *m pl*

giddily /ˈgɪdl̩i/ *adv* vertiginosamente; frívolamente, atolondradamente

giddiness /ˈgɪdinɪs/ *n* vértigo, *m;* atolondramiento, *m;* inconstancia, *f;* frivolidad, ligereza de cascos, *f*

giddy /ˈgɪdi/ *a* vertiginoso; mareado; atolondrado, casquivano, frívolo; inconstante. **She felt very g.,** Se sintió muy mareada. **to make g.,** dar vértigo (a), marear

gift /gɪft/ *n* regalo, *m,* dádiva, *f;* (quality) don, talento, *m;* prenda, *f;* poder, *m; Law.* donación, *f;* (offering) ofrenda, oblación, *f.* *—vt* dotar. **deed of g.,** *Law.* escritura de donación, *f.* **in the g. of,** en el poder de, en las manos de. **I wouldn't have it as a g.,** No lo tomaría ni regalado. **Never look a g. horse in the mouth,** A caballo regalado no se le mira el diente. **g. of tongues,** don de las lenguas, genio de las lenguas, *m*

gifted /ˈgɪftɪd/ *a* talentoso

gig /gɪg/ *n* (carriage) carrocín, *m;* (boat) falúa, lancha, *f;* (for wool) máquina de cardar paño, *f;* (harpoon) arpón, *m*

gigantic /dʒaiˈgæntɪk/ *a* gigantesco; colosal, enorme

giggle /ˈgɪgəl/ *vi* reírse sin motivo; reírse disimuladamente. *—n* risa disimulada, *f*

giggling /ˈgɪglɪŋ/ *n* risa estúpida, *f;* risa nerviosa, *f*

gigolo /ˈdʒɪgəˌlou/ *n* gigolo, mantenido, jinetero (Cuba), *m*

gild /gɪld/ *vt* dorar; (metals) sobredorar; embellecer. **to g. the pill,** dorar la píldora

gilder /ˈgɪldər/ *n* dorador, *m*

gilding /ˈgɪldɪŋ/ *n* dorado, *m,* doradura, *f;* embellecimiento, *m*

Gileadite /ˈgɪliəˌdait/ *n* and *a* galaadita, *mf*

gill /gɪl/ *n* (of fish) agalla, branquia, *f;* (ravine) barranco, *m;*

gill /dʒɪl/ *n* (measure) cierta medida de líquidos, *f,* ($\frac{1}{8}$ litro)

gilt /gɪlt/ *n* dorado, *m;* pan de oro, *m;* relumbrón, *m; Fig.* encanto, *m, a* dorado, áureo. **g.-edged,** (of books) con los bordes dorados. **g.-edged security,** papel del Estado, *m;* valores de toda confianza, *m pl*

gimcrack /ˈdʒɪmˌkræk/ *n* chuchería, *f.* *—a* de baratillo, cursi; mal hecho

gimlet /ˈgɪmlɪt/ *n* barrena, *f,* taladro, *m*

gin /dʒɪn/ *n* (drink) ginebra, *f;* (snare) trampa, *f.* *—vt* (snare) coger con trampa. **g. block,** *Mech.* garrucha, *f*

ginger /ˈdʒɪndʒər/ *n* jengibre, *m; Inf.* energía, *f,* brío, *m, a* rojo. *—vt* sazonar con jengibre; *Inf.* animar, estimular. **g.-beer,** gaseosa, *f*

gingerly /ˈdʒɪndʒərli/ *adv* con gran cuidado; delicadamente

gingham /ˈgɪŋəm/ *n* guinga, *f*

gingivitis /ˌdʒɪndʒəˈvaitɪs/ *n* gingivitis, *f*

gipsy /ˈdʒɪpsi/ *n.* See **gypsy**

giraffe /dʒəˈræf/ *n* jirafa, *f*

gird /gɜrd/ *vt* ceñir; (invest) investir; (surround) cercar, rodear; (put on) revestir. **to g. oneself for the fray,** prepararse para la lucha

girder /ˈgɜrdər/ *n* viga, jácena, *f.* **main g.,** viga maestra, *f*

girdle /ˈgɜrdl̩/ *n* (belt) cinturón, *m;* (corset) faja, *f;* circunferencia, *f;* zona, *f.* *—vt* ceñir; *Fig.* cercar, rodear

girl /gɜrl/ *n* niña, *f;* chica, muchacha, *f;* (maidservant) criada, muchacha, *f;* (young lady) señorita, *f.* **a young g.,** una jovencita; (a little older) una joven. **old g.,** (of a school) antigua alumna, *f; Inf.* vieja, *f;* (*Inf.* affectionate) chica, *f.* **g. friend,** amiguita, *f.* **g. guide, girl scout,** exploradora, *f.* **girls' school,** colegio de niñas, colegio de señoritas, *m*

girlhood /ˈgɜrlhʊd/ *n* niñez, *f;* juventud, *f*

girlish /ˈgɜrlɪʃ/ *a* de niña, de muchacha; (of boys) afeminado; joven

girth /gɜrθ/ *n* (of horse, etc.) cincha, *f;* circunferencia, *f;* (of person) talle, *m;* (obesity) corpulencia, obesidad, *f*

gist /dʒɪst/ *n* esencia, substancia, *f,* importe, *m*

give /gɪv/ *vt* dar; (a present) regalar; (infect) contagiar; (impart) comunicar; (grant) otorgar; (allow, concede) conceder; (assign) asignar, señalar; (appoint) nombrar; (a toast) brindar (a la salud de); (a party, ball, etc.) dar; (a bill) presentar; (wish) desear; (punish) castigar; (pay) pagar; (hand over) entregar; (names at baptism) imponer; (produce) producir; dar; (cause) causar; (of judicial sentences) condenar a; (evoke) proporcionar; (provoke) provocar; (devote) dedicar, consagrar; (sacrifice) sacrificar; (evidence, an account, orders, a lesson, a performance, a concert) dar; (a cry, shout) lanzar, proferir; (a laugh) soltar; (describe) describir; (paint) pintar; (write) escribir; (offer) ofrecer; (show) mostrar; (transmit) transmitir; (heed, pain) hacer, (a speech) pronunciar, hacer; (award, adjudge) adjudicar; (ear) prestar (oído (a)). *—vi* dar; ser dadivoso, mostrarse generoso; (give in) ceder; (be elastic) dar de sí; ablandarse; (collapse) hundirse. **G. them my best wishes!** ¡Dales mis mejores recuerdos! **G. us a song!** ¡Cántanos algo! **I can g. him a lift in my car,** Puedo ofrecerle un asiento en mi auto. **I g. you my word,** Os doy mi palabra. **to g. a good account of oneself,** defenderse bien; hacer bien; salir bien. **to g. a person a piece of one's mind,** contarle cuatro verdades. **to g. chase,** dar caza (a). **to g. it to a person,** poner a uno como nuevo; reprender; (beat) pegar, dar de palos. **to g. of itself,** dar de sí. **to g. rise to,** dar lugar a, ocasionar, causar. **to g. way,** no poder resistir; (break) romperse;

(yield) ceder; (collapse) hundirse; (retreat) retroceder. **to g. way to,** (retreat before) retirarse ante; (abandon oneself to) entregarse a, abandonarse a. **to g. away,** enajenar; dar; regalar; (sell cheaply) vender a un precio muy bajo; (get rid of) deshacerse de; (sacrifice) sacrificar; (a secret) revelar; (betray) traicionar; (expose) descubrir; (tell) contar; (a bride) conducir al altar. **He gave himself away,** Reveló su pensamiento sin querer. **to g. back,** *vt* devolver; restituir. —*vi* retirarse, cejar. **to g. forth,** divulgar, publicar; (scatter) derramar; (emit) emitir, despedir; (smoke, rays) echar. **to g. in,** *vt* entregar; presentar. —*vi* darse por vencido. **to g. in to,** (agree with) asentir en, consentir en; rendirse ante. **Mary always gives in to George,** María hace siempre lo que Jorge quiere. **to g. off,** (of odors, etc.) emitir, exhalar, despedir. **to g. out,** *vt* (distribute) distribuir, repartir; (allocate) asignar; (publish) publicar; (announce) anunciar; (reveal) divulgar; (allege) afirmar, hacer saber; (emit) emitir. —*vi* (be exhausted) agotarse; (end) acabarse; (be lacking) faltar. **to g. over,** *vt* entregar; (transfer) traspasar; cesar de. —*vi* cesar. **to g. up,** entregar; ceder; (renounce) renunciar (a); (sacrifice) sacrificar; (abandon) abandonar; (cease) dejar de, (as lost) dar por perdido; (of a patient) desahuciar; (a post) dimitir de; (return) devolver, restituir; (a problem) renunciar (a resolver un problema); (lose hope) perder la esperanza; (give in) darse por vencido. **I had given you up,** (didn't expect you), Creí que no ibas a venir. **to g. oneself up to,** entregarse a; dedicarse a; *Mil.* rendirse a. **to g. up one's seat,** ceder su sitio (or asiento). **to g. upon,** (overlook) dar sobre

give /gɪv/ *n* elasticidad, *f;* el dar de sí; (concession) concesión, *f.* **g. and take,** concesiones mutuas, *f pl.* **g. away,** *Inf.* revelación indiscreta, *f*

given /ˈgɪvən/ *a* dado; especificado; convenido; (with to) dado a, adicto a. **in a g. time,** en un tiempo dado. **g. that,** dado que

giver /ˈgɪvər/ *n* dador (-ra); donador (-ra)

gizzard /ˈgɪzərd/ *n* molleja, *f.* **It sticks in my g.,** *Inf.* No lo puedo tragar

glacial /ˈgleiʃəl/ *a* glacial

glacier /ˈgleiʃər/ *n* glaciar, *m*

glad /glæd/ *a* feliz, alegre; contento, satisfecho; *Inf.* elegante. **to be g.,** alegrarse, estar contento; estar satisfecho. **to give the g. eye,** hacer ojos

gladden /ˈglædn̩/ *vt* alegrar, regocijar

glade /gleid/ *n* claro, *m;* rasa, *f*

gladiator /ˈglædiˌeitər/ *n* gladiador, *m*

gladiatorial /ˌglædiəˈtɔriəl/ *a* gladiatorio

gladiolus /ˌglædiˈouləs/ *n Bot.* gladíolo, gladio, *m;* espadaña, *f*

gladly /ˈglædli/ *adv* alegremente; con mucho gusto, gustoso, de buena gana

gladness /ˈglædnɪs/ *n* alegría, felicidad, *f,* contento, *m;* placer, *m*

glamorous /ˈglæmərəs/ *a* exótico; garboso

glamour /ˈglæmər/ *n* encanto, *m,* fascinación, *f;* garbo, *m.* **g. girl,** belleza exótica, *f*

glance /glæns/ *n* (of a projectile) desviación, *f;* (of light) vislumbre, *m;* relumbrón, centelleo, *m;* (look) vistazo, *m,* ojeada, *f;* mirada, *f, vi* desviarse; relumbrar, centellear, brillar; (with at) ojear, echar un vistazo a, lanzar miradas a; (a book) hojear; mirar; mirar de reojo; *Fig.* indicar brevemente. **at a g.,** con un vistazo; en seguida. **at the first g.,** a primera vista. **to g. off,** desviarse (al chocar). **to g. over,** repasar, echar un vistazo a, (a book) hojear

glancing /ˈglænsɪŋ/ *a* (of a blow) que roza

gland /glænd/ *n* (*Anat., Bot.*) glándula, *f;* (in the neck) ganglio, *m.* **to have swollen glands,** tener inflamación de los ganglios

glandular /ˈglændʒələr/ *a* glandular

glare /glɛər/ *n* brillo, fulgor, *m;* luminosidad, *f;* reflejo, *m;* (look) mirada feroz, *f.* —*vi* relumbrar, centellear; (stare) mirar con ferocidad, mirar fijamente

glaring /ˈglɛərɪŋ/ *a* deslumbrante, brillante; (of colors) chillón, llamativo; (of looks) de mirada feroz; (flagrant) notorio, evidente

glaringly /ˈglɛərɪŋli/ *adv* brillantemente; con mirada feroz; notoriamente

glass /glæs/ *n* vidrio, *m;* cristal, *m;* (glassware) artículos de vidrio, *m pl;* cristalería, *f;* (for drinking) vaso, *m,* copa, *f;* (pane) cristal, *m;* (mirror) espejo, *m;* (telescope) telescopio, *m;* catalejo, *m;* (barometer) barómetro, *m;* (hour-glass) reloj de arena, *m;* (of a watch) vidrio (de reloj), *m; pl* **glasses,** (binoculars) anteojos, *m pl;* (spectacles) gafas, lentes, *m pl;* (opera glasses) gemelos de teatro, *m pl, a* de vidrio; de cristal. —*vt* vidriar. **John wears glasses,** Juan lleva gafas. **The g. is falling (rising),** El barómetro baja (sube). **to clink glasses,** trincar las copas. **to look in the g.,** mirarse en el espejo. **clear g.,** vidrio trasparente, *m.* **cut g.,** cristal tallado, *m.* **frosted g.,** vidrio jaspeado, *m.* **plate-g.,** vidrio plano, *m;* **safety g.,** vidrio inastillable, *m.* **stained g.,** vidrio de color, vidrio pintado, *m.* **under g.,** bajo vidrio; en invernáculo. **g. bead,** abalorio, *m;* cuenta de vidrio, *f.* **g.-blower,** soplador de vidrio, *m.* **g.-blowing,** el soplar de vidrio. **g. case,** escaparate, *m.* **g.-cloth,** paño para vasos, *m.* **g. eye,** ojo de cristal, *m.* **g. paper,** papel de vidrio, *m.* **g. roof,** techo de cristal, *m.* **g. window,** vidriera, *f*

glasscutter /ˈglæsˌkʌtər/ *n* cortador de vidrio, *m*

glassful /ˈglæsfʊl/ *n* contenido de un vaso, *m;* vaso, vaso lleno, *m,* copa, *f*

glasshouse /ˈglæsˌhaus/ *n* fábrica de vidrio, *f;* vidriería, *f;* invernáculo, invernadero, *m,* estufa, *f*

glassware /ˈglæsˌwɛər/ *n* cristalería, *f*

glassy /ˈglæsi/ *a* vitreo; (of eyes) vidrioso; *Fig.* cristalino; (smooth) liso, raso

glaucous /ˈglɔkəs/ *a* de color verdemar; *Bot.* glauco

glaze /gleiz/ *n* barniz, *m:* lustre, brillo, *m.* —*vt* poner vidrios (a); vidriar; barnizar; (paper, leather, etc.) satinar. —*vi* (of eyes) vidriarse, ponerse vidrioso

glazier /ˈgleiʒər/ *n* vidriero, *m*

glazing /ˈgleizɪŋ/ *n* vidriado, *m;* barnizado, *m;* satinado, *m;* (material) barniz, *m*

gleam /glim/ *n* rayo, destello, *m;* (of color) viso, *m,* mancha, *f; Fig.* rayo, *m;* (in the eye) chispa, *f.* —*vi* relucir, centellear, resplandecer; brillar; reflejar la luz; *Fig.* brillar. **g. of hope,** rayo de esperanza, *m*

gleaming /ˈglimɪŋ/ *a* reluciente, centelleante; brillante. —*n* see **gleam**

glean /glin/ *vt* espigar, rebuscar; recoger. —*vi* espigar

gleaner /ˈglinər/ *n* espigador, *m;* recogedor (-ra)

gleaning /ˈglinɪŋ/ *n* espigueo, *m;* rebusca, recolección, *f; pl* **gleanings,** fragmentos, *m pl*

glee /gli/ *n* alegría, *f,* júbilo, alborozo, *m; Mus.* canción para voces solas, *f*

gleeful /ˈglifəl/ *a* alegre, jubiloso, gozoso

gleefully /ˈglifəli/ *adv* alegremente, con júbilo

glen /glɛn/ *n* cañada, *f,* cañón, *m,* hondonada, *f*

glib /glɪb/ *a* locuaz, voluble; (easy) fácil

glibness /ˈglɪbnɪs/ *n* locuacidad, volubilidad, *f;* (easiness) facilidad, *f*

glide /glaid/ *n* deslizamiento, *m; Aer.* planeo, *m.* —*vi* deslizarse; resbalar; *Aer.* planear. **to g. away,** escurrirse; desaparecer silenciosamente

glider /ˈglaidər/ *n Aer.* deslizador, planeador, *m*

gliding /ˈglaidɪŋ/ *n Aer.* vuelo sin motor, *m*

glimmer /ˈglɪmər/ *n* luz trémula, luz débil, *f,* tenue resplandor, *m;* vislumbre, *m.* —*vi* brillar con luz trémula, rielar *Fig.*; tener vislumbres (de)

glimpse /glɪmps/ *n* vistazo, *m;* vislumbre, *m;* indicio, *m;* impresión, *f;* vista, *f.* —*vt* entrever, divisar; tener una vista (de); ver por un instante; vislumbrar

glint /glɪnt/ *n* tenue resplandor, *m;* lustre, *m;* centelleo, *m;* reflejo, *m;* (in the eye) chispa, *f.* —*vi* relucir, destellar, rutilar; reflejar

glisten /ˈglɪsən/ *vi* brillar, relucir

glistening /ˈglɪsənɪŋ/ *a* coruscante; brillante, reluciente

glitter /ˈglɪtər/ *n* brillo, resplandor, *m,* rutilación, *f.* —*vi* brillar, resplandecer, relucir; rutilar. **All that glitters is not gold,** Todo lo que reluce no es oro

glittering /ˈglɪtərɪŋ/ *a* reluciente, resplandeciente; *Fig.* brillante

gloat (over) /glout/ *vi* recrearse en, gozarse en, deleitarse en

globe /gloub/ *n* globo, *m;* esfera, *f;* (for fish) pecera, *f;* (for gas, electric light) globo, *m.* **geographical g.,** globo terrestre, *m.* **g.-trotter,** trotamundos, *m*

globular /'glɒbyələr/ *a* globular, esférico
globule /'glɒbyul/ *n* glóbulo, *m*
globulous /'glɒbyələs/ *a* globuloso
gloom /glum/ *n* obscuridad, *f;* lobreguez, *f,* tinieblas, *f pl; Fig.* melancolía, tristeza, *f;* taciturnidad, *f.* —*vi Fig.* ponerse melancólico; ser taciturno
gloomily /'glumǝli/ *adv* obscuramente; *Fig.* tristemente; taciturnamente
gloomy /'glumi/ *a* obscuro; sombrío, lóbrego; melancólico, triste; taciturno; (of prospects, etc.) poco halagüeño, nada atrayente
glorification /,glɔrəfɪ'keiʃən/ *n* glorificación, *f*
glorify /'glɔrə,fai/ *vt* glorificar; exaltar; alabar
glorious /'glɔriəs/ *a* glorioso; espléndido, magnífico; insigne; *Inf.* estupendo
glory /'glɔri/ *n* gloria, *f;* esplendor, *m,* magnificencia, *f; Art.* gloria, *f.* —*vi* recrearse, gozarse; glorificarse, jactarse. **to be in one's g.,** estar en la gloria. **to g. in,** hacer gala de, glorificarse en
gloss /glɒs/ *n* (sheen) lustre, brillo, *m; Fig.* apariencia, *f;* (note) glose, *m;* (excuse) disculpa, *f.* —*vt* pulir; glosar. **to g. over,** (faults) disculpar, excusar
glossary /'glɒsəri/ *n* glosario, *m*
glossiness /'glɒsinɪs/ *n* lustre, *m,* tersura, *f;* brillo, *m*
glossy /'glɒsi/ *a* lustroso, terso; brillante; (of hair) liso
glottal stop /'glɒtl̩/ *n* choque glótica, golpe de glotis, *m*
glottis /'glɒtɪs/ *n Anat.* glotis, *f*
glove /glʌv/ *n* guante. **evening gloves,** guantes largos, *m pl.* **to be hand in g. with,** juntar diestra con diestra. **to fit like a g.,** sentar como un guante. **to put on one's gloves,** ponerse los guantes. **g. shop,** guantería, *f.* **g.-stretcher,** ensanchador (or abridor) de guantes, *m*
glove compartment gaveta, guantera, *f,* guantero, portaguantes *m*
glove-compartment light luz de portaguantes, *f*
glover /'glʌvər/ *n* guantero (-ra)
glow /glou/ *n* incandescencia, *f;* claridad, *f;* luz difusa, *f;* (heat) calor, *m;* (of color) intensidad, *f;* color vivo, *m;* (enthusiasm) ardor, entusiasmo, *m;* (redness) rojez, *f;* (in the sky) arrebol, *m;* (of pleasure, etc.) sentimiento de placer, *m;* sensación de bienestar, *f.* —*vi* estar incandescente; arder; abrasarse; sentir entusiasmo; mostrarse rojo; experimentar un sentimiento de placer o una sensación de bienestar. **to g. with health,** estar rebosando de salud. **g.-worm,** luciérnaga, *f*
glower /'glauər/ *n* ceño, *m;* mirada amenazadora, *f.* —*vi* poner cara de pocos amigos, mirar airadamente; tener los ojos puestos (en)
glowing /'glouɪŋ/ *a* candente, incandescente; ardiente; entusiasta; satisfecho; intenso; (bright) vivo; (red) encendido; (with health) rebosante de salud. —*n* see **glow**
glowingly /'glouɪŋli/ *adv* encendidamente; *Fig.* con entusiasmo
glucose /'glukous/ *n* glucosa, *f*
glue /glu/ *n* engrudo, *m,* cola, *f.* —*vt* encolar, engrudar; pegar; *Fig.* fijar, poner. **He kept his eyes glued on them,** Tenía los ojos fijados (or pegados) en ellos. **g.-pot,** pote de cola, *m*
gluey /'glui/ *a* gomoso; pegajoso, viscoso
glueyness /'gluinɪs/ *n* viscosidad, *f*
gluing /'gluɪŋ/ *n* encoladura, *f*
glum /glʌm/ *a* deprimido, taciturno, sombrío
glumly /'glʌmli/ *adv* taciturnamente
glut /glʌt/ *n* superabundancia, *f,* exceso, *m.* —*vt* (satiate) hartar; *Fig.* saciar; (the market) inundar
gluteal /'glutiəl/ *a* glúteo
glutinous /'glutn̩əs/ *a* glutinoso, pegajoso, viscoso
glutton /'glʌtn̩/ *n* glotón (-ona); *Fig.* ávido (-da)
gluttonous /'glʌtn̩əs/ *a* glotón, comilón
gluttony /'glʌtn̩i/ *n* glotonería, gula, *f*
glycerin /'glɪsərɪn/ *n* glicerina, *f*
gnarled /nɑrld/ *a* nudoso; (of human beings) curtido
gnash /næʃ/ *vt* rechinar, crujir (los dientes)
gnashing /'næʃɪŋ/ *n* rechinamiento (de dientes), *m*
gnat /næt/ *n* mosquito, *m*
gnaw /nɔ/ *vt* roer; morder; (of wood by worms) carcomer; *Fig.* roer
gnawing /'nɔɪŋ/ *n* roedura, *f;* mordedura, *f, a* roedor; mordedor
gnome /noum/ *n* nomo, *m*
gnostic /'nɒstɪk/ *a* and *n* nóstico (-ca)
gnosticism /'nɒstɪsɪzəm/ *n* nosticismo, *m*
go /gou/ *vi* ir; (depart) irse, marcharse; (go toward) dirigirse a, encaminarse a; (lead to, of roads, etc.) conducir a, ir a; (vanish) desaparecer; (leave) dejar, salir de; (lose) perder; (pass) pasar; (of time) transcurrir, pasar; (be removed) quitarse; (be prohibited) prohibirse; (fall) caer; (collapse) hundirse; (be torn off) desprenderse; desgajarse; *Mech.* funcionar, trabajar, andar; (sound) sonar; (of the heart) palpitar, latir; (follow) seguir; (gesture) hacer un gesto; (be stated) decirse, afirmarse; (live) vivir; (wear) llevar; (turn out) salir, resultar; (improve) mejorar; (prosper) prosperar; (turn, become) ponerse; volverse; (to sleep) dormirse; (into a faint) desmayarse; (decay) echarse a perder, estropearse; (turn sour) agriarse; (become, adopt views, etc.) hacerse; (be sold) venderse; (be decided); decidirse, ser decidido; (have) tener; (by will) pasar; (belong) pertenecer; (receive) recibir; (have its place) estar; (put) ponerse; (going plus infin.) ir a; (die) morir, irse; (do a journey, a given distance) hacer; (a pace, step) dar; (take) tomar; (escape) escaparse, (contribute) contribuir (a); (harmonize) armonizar (con); (be current) ser válido; (be) ser; (of a document, etc., run) rezar, decir; (attend) asistir a; (be broken) estar roto; (be worn) estar raído; (be granted) darse, otorgarse. **It's gone five,** Ya dieron las cinco. **It's time to be going,** Es hora de marcharse. **Let's go!** ¡Vamos! **These two colours go well together,** Estos colores armonizan bien. **Well, how goes it?** Bueno, ¿qué tal? ¿Cómo te va? **Who goes there?** *Mil.* ¿Quién va? **to go and fetch,** ir a buscar. **to let go,** soltar; dejar ir. **to go one's way,** seguir su camino. **to go wrong,** salir mal, fracasar; (sin) descarriarse. **"Go!"** (traffic sign) «¡Siga!» **Go on!** ¡Adelante!; (continue) ¡Siga!; *Inf.* ¡Qué va! **to go about,** dar la vuelta a; rodear; recorrer; (undertake) emprender, hacer; intentar; (of news, etc.) circular; *Naut.* virar de bordo. **Go about your business!** ¡Métete en lo que to importa! **to go abroad,** ir al extranjero; salir a la calle; publicarse, divulgarse. **to go across,** cruzar, atravesar; pasar. **to go after,** andar tras; seguir; (seek) ir a buscar; (persecute) perseguir. **to go again,** ir de nuevo; (be present) asistir otra vez; volver. **to go against,** ir contra; militar contra; oponerse a; ser desfavorable a. **to go ahead,** adelantar, avanzar; progresar; prosperar; (lead) ir a la cabeza (de), conducir; *Naut.* marchar hacia adelante. **to go along,** andar por; recorrer; (depart) irse, marcharse. **go apartment-hunting,** ir en busca de piso. **to go along with,** acompañar (a). **to go aside,** quitarse de en medio; apartarse, retirarse. **to go astray,** perderse; extraviarse, descarriarse. **to go at,** atacar, acometer; (undertake) emprender; empezar a. **to go at it again,** *Inf.* volver a la carga. **to go away,** irse, marcharse; ausentarse; alejarse; desaparecer. **to go away with,** marcharse con; (an object) llevarse. **to go back,** volver; (retreat) retroceder, volverse atrás; (in history) remontarse a. **to go back on,** (a promise, etc.) faltar a; (retract) retractarse; (betray) traicionar. **to go backwards,** retroceder, cejar; desandar lo andado; *Fig.* deteriorar, empeorar. **to go backwards and forwards,** ir y venir; oscilar. **to go before,** (lead) ir a la cabeza de, conducir; anteceder; proceder; (a judge, etc.) comparecer ante. **to go behind,** ir detrás de; esconderse detrás de; seguir; (evidence, etc.) mirar más allá de. **to go between,** ponerse entre; interponerse; (as a mediator) mediar; (insert) intercalarse; (travel) ir entre; llevar cartas entre, ser mensajero de. **to go beyond,** ir más allá; exceder. **to go by,** pasar por; pasar cerca de, pasar junto a; ir por; (of time) transcurrir, pasar; (follow) seguir; guiarse por, atenerse a; (judge by) juzgar por; (a name) pasar por; tomar el nombre de. **to go down,** bajar, descender; (of the sun) ponerse; (sink) hundirse; sumergirse; (fall) caer; (be remembered) ser recordado; (believe) tragar; ser creído. **to go down again,** bajar de nuevo; volver a

caer. **go Dutch,** ir a escote, ir a la gringa, ir a la par, ir a limón. **to go far,** ir lejos; influir mucho (en); impresionar mucho; (contribute) contribuir (a). **to go for,** (seek) ir en busca de; procurar tener; (attack) echarse encima de, atacar. **to go for a ride (by car, bicycle, on horseback),** dar un paseo (en coche, en bicicleta, a caballo). **to go forth,** salir; publicarse. **to go forward,** adelantar, avanzar; progresar; continuar; (happen) tener lugar. **to go from,** dejar, abandonar; separarse de, apartarse de; marcharse de. **to go in,** entrar en; (a railway carriage, etc.) subir a; (compete) concurrir. **to go in again,** volver a entrar en, entrar de nuevo en. **to go in and out,** entrar y salir; ir y venir. **to go in for,** entrar a buscar; dedicarse a, entregarse a; (buy) comprarse; tomar parte en; (an examination) tomar (un examen); (for a competition) entrar en (un concurso); (try) ensayar; arriesgar. **to go into,** entrar en; examinar; investigar; ocuparse con. **to go near,** acercarse a. **to go off,** marcharse; (explode) estallar; (of fire-arms) disparse; (of the voice, etc.) perder (la voz, etc.); (run away) huir, fugarse. **to go off badly,** salir mal, fracasar, no tener éxito. **to go off well,** salir bien, tener éxito. **to go on,** subirse a; continuar; durar; avanzar; proseguir su marcha, progresar, prosperar; *Theat.* entrar en escena; (of clothes) ponerse; (rely on) apoyarse en. **Don't go on like that,** No seas así, No te pongas así. **This glove will not go on me,** No puedo ponerme este guante. **to be gone on a person,** *Inf.* estar loco por. **I went on to say...,** Después dije; Continuando mi discurso dije... **It was going on for six o'clock when...** Serían alrededor de las seis cuando... **He is going on for fifty,** Raya en los cincuenta años. **to go on foot,** ir a pie. **to go on with,** continuar con; empezar. **to go out,** salir; (descend) bajar; (of fires, lights) extinguirse, apagarse; (of fashion, etc.) pasar (de); (the tide) menguar; (retire) retirarse; (in society) frecuentar la alta sociedad; (die) morir; (arouse) excitar. **to go out of fashion,** pasar de moda. **to go out of one's way (to),** dejar su camino (para); (lose oneself) perder el camino, extraviarse; (take trouble) desvivirse (por), tomarse molestia (para). **to go over,** cruzar; pasar por encima; (to another party or to the other side) pasarse a; (read) repasar; examinar. **to go past,** pasar; pasar en frente de. **to go round,** dar la vuelta a; (revolve) girar: (surround) rodear; (of news, etc.) divulgarse; (be enough) ser suficiente para todos. **to go through,** ir por, pasar por; recorrer; (pierce) penetrar, atravesar; (examine) examinar; (suffer) padecer, sufrir; (experience) experimentar; (live) vivir; (of time) pasar; (of money) malgastar, derrochar. **to go through with,** llevar a cabo; terminar. **to go to,** ir a, encaminarse a; (a person) acercarse a, dirigirse a; (help, be useful) servir para; (be meant for) destinarse a; (rise of price) subir a; (find) encontrar; (of a bid) subir una apuesta hasta. **to go to war,** declarar la guerra. **to go together,** ir juntos (juntas). **to go toward,** encaminarse hacia; ir hacia; (help) ayudar a. **to go under,** pasar por debajo de; (sink) hundirse; (fail) fracasar; (be bankrupt) arruinarse, declarare en quiebra; (the name of) hacerse pasar por. **to go up,** subir; ir arriba; (a tree) trepar; (a ladder, etc.) subir; (a river) ir río arriba; (to town) ir a; (explode) estallar. **to go up and down,** subir y bajar; oscilar; ir de una parte a otra. **to go upon,** subirse a; (rely on) apoyarse en; obrar según; emprender. **to go upstairs,** ir arriba; (to another story, as in a flat) subir al otro piso; subir la escalera. **to go up to,** acercarse a; (of a bid) subir una apuesta hasta. **to go with,** acompañar; (agree with) estar de acuerdo con; (of principles) seguir, ser fiel a; (harmonize) armonizar con; (be suitable to) ir bien con; convenir a; (*Inf.* get along) ir. **to go without,** marcharse sin; (lack) pasarse sin. **It goes without saying that...,** Huelga decir que **Where are you going with this?** (What do you mean?) ¿A dónde quieres llegar con esto?

go /gou/ *n* (fashion) moda, boga, *f;* (happening) suceso, *m;* (fix) apuro, *m;* (energy) energía, *f,* empuje, brío, *m;* (turn) turno, *m;* (attempt) tentativa, *f;* (action) movimiento, *m,* acción, *f;* (bargain) acuerdo, *m.* **It's a go!** (agreed) ¡Trato hecho! ¡Acordado! ¡Entendidos! ¡Entendidas! **It is all the go,** Hace furor, Es la gran moda. **It is no go,** No puede ser, Es imposible. **Now it's my go,** Ahora me toca a mí, Ahora es mi turno. **on the go,** en movimiento; entre manos; ocupado. **to have a go,** probar suerte; procurar, tratar de; tener un turno

goad /goud/ *n* garrocha, aguijada, *f,* aguijón, *m; Fig.* acicate, estímulo, *m.* —*vt* aguijar, picar; *Fig.* incitar, estimular, empujar. **prick with a g.,** aguijonazo, *m*

go-ahead /'gou əˌhɛd/ *a* emprendedor: progresivo

goal /goul/ *n* (posts in football, etc.) meta, portería, *f;* (score) gol, *m;* (in racing) meta, *f;* (destination) destinación, *f; Fig.* ambición, *f;* (purpose, objective) fin, objeto, *m.* **to score a g.,** marcar un gol. **g.-keeper,** guardameta, *m,* portero (-ra). **g.-post,** palo de la portería, *m*

goat /gout/ *n* cabra, *f; Astron.* capricornio, *m.* **he-g.,** cabrón, *m.* **young g.,** cabrito, *m,* chivo (-va). **g.-herd,** cabrero, *m.* **g. skin,** piel de cabra, *f;* (wineskin) odre, *m*

goatee /gou'ti/ *n* pera, perilla, *f*

goatish /'goutɪʃ/ *a* cabruno; de cabra; lascivo

gobble /'gɒbəl/ *vt* and *vi* engullir, tragar. —*vi* (of turkey) gluglutear. —*n* glugluteo, *m,* voz del pavo, *f*

gobbler /'gɒblər/ *n* engullidor (-ra), tragón (-ona); *Inf.* pavo, *m*

go-between /'gou bɪˌtwin/ *n* trotaconventos, *f;* alcahuete, *m;* (mediator) medianero (-ra)

goblet /'gɒblɪt/ *n* copa, *f*

goblin /'gɒblɪn/ *n* trasgo, duende, *m*

go-by, to give the /'gou ˌbai/ evitar; pasar por alto de; omitir

go-cart /'gou ˌkɑrt/ *n* andaderas, *f pl;* pollera, *f;* cochecito de niño, *m*

god /gɒd/ *n* dios, *m; pl* **gods,** dioses, *m pl;* (in a theater) público del paraíso, *m;* paraíso, *m.* **By God!** ¡Vive Dios! **For God's sake,** ¡Por el amor de Dios!; ¡Por Dios! **Please God,** ¡Plegue a Dios! **Thank God!** ¡Gracias a Dios! **God Bless You!** (to someone who has sneezed) ¡Jesús! **God forbid!** ¡No lo quiera Dios! **God grant it!** ¡Dios lo quiera! **God keep you!** ¡Dios le guarde! ¡Vaya Vd. con Dios! **God willing,** Dios mediante. **My father, God rest his soul, was...,** Mi padre, que Dios perdone, era...

godchild /'gɒdˌtʃaild/ *n* ahijado (-da)

goddaughter /'gɒdˌdɔtər/ *n* ahijada, *f*

goddess /'gɒdɪs/ *n* diosa, *f; Poet.* dea, *f*

godfather /'gɒdˌfɑðər/ *n* padrino, *m.* **to be a g. to,** ser padrino de, sacar de pila (a)

godfearing /'gɒdˌfɪərɪŋ/ *a* timorato, temeroso de Dios; religioso

godforsaken /'gɒdfərˌseikən/ *a* dejado de la mano de Dios; (of places) remoto, solitario

Godhead /'gɒdˌhɛd/ *n* divinidad, *f*

godless /'gɒdlɪs/ *a* impío, irreligioso; sin Dios

godlessness /'gɒdlɪsnɪs/ *n* impiedad, irreligiosidad, *f*

godlike /'gɒdˌlaik/ *a* divino

godliness /'gɒdlinɪs/ *n* piedad, *f;* santidad, *f*

godling /'gɒdlɪŋ/ diosecillo, *m*

godly /'gɒdli/ *a* devoto, piadoso, religioso

godmother /'gɒdˌmʌðər/ *n* madrina, *f.* **fairy g.,** hada madrina, *f.* **to be a g. to,** ser madrina de

godparent /'gɒdˌpɛərənt/ *n* padrino, *m;* madrina, *f pl.* **godparents,** padrinos, *m pl*

godsend /'gɒdˌsɛnd/ *n* bien, *m;* buena suerte, *f;* fortuna, *f*

go-getter /'gou ˌgɛtər/ *n* buscavidas, *mf*

goggle /'gɒgəl/ *n* mirada fija, *f; pl* **goggles,** anteojos, *m pl,* gafas, *f pl;* (of a horse) anteojeras, *f pl.* —*vi* mirar fijamente; salirse a uno los ojos de la cabeza. **g.-eyed,** de ojos saltones. **g.-eyes,** ojos saltones, *m pl*

going /'gouɪŋ/ *n* ida, *f;* (departure) partida, marcha, *f;* salida, *f;* (pace) paso, *m;* (speed) velocidad, *f.* **It was heavy g.,** El avance era lento; El progreso era lento; (of parties, etc.) Era aburrido. **The g. was difficult on those mountainous roads,** El conducir (or el ir or el andar) era difícil en aquellos caminos de montaña. **g. back,** vuelta, *f,* regreso, *m.* **g. down,** bajada, *f,* descenso, *m;* (of the sun, etc.) puesta, *f.* **g. forward,** avance, *m;* progreso, *m.* **g. in,** entrada, *f.* **g. in and out,** idas y venidas, *f pl.* **g. out,** salida, *f;* (of a fire, light) apagamiento, *m*

going /'gouɪŋ/ *a* and *pres part* que va, yendo; que

funciona. **G., g., gone** (at an auction) A la una, a las dos, a las tres. **goings-on,** (tricks) trapujos, *m pl;* (conduct) conducta, *f.* **g. concern,** empresa próspera, *f.* **g. to,** con destino a
going-away present /'gouɪŋ ə,wei/ *n* regalo de despedida, *m*
goiter /'gɔitər/ *n* bocio, *m*
gold /gould/ *n* oro, *m;* color de oro, *m.* —*a* de oro; áureo. **All that glitters is not g.,** No es oro todo lo que reluce. **cloth of g.,** tela de oro, *f.* **dull g.,** oro mate, *m.* **light g.,** oro pálido, *m.* **old g.,** oro viejo, *m.* **g.-beater,** batidor de oro, *m.* **g.-digger,** minero de oro, *m;* (woman) aventurera, *f.* **g. dust,** oro en polvo, *m.* **g.-fever,** fiebre de oro, *f.* **g. lace,** galón de oro, *m.* **g. lacquer,** sisa dorada, *f.* **g. leaf,** pan de oro, oro batido, *m.* **g.-mine,** mina de oro, *f.* **g. piece,** moneda de oro, *f.* **g. plate,** vajilla de oro, *f.* **g. standard,** patrón oro, *m.* **g.-thread,** hilo de oro, *m.* **g.-yielding,** *a* aurífero
golden /'gouldən/ *a* de oro; dorado; áureo; amarillo; *Fig.* feliz; excelente. **to become g.,** dorarse. **g. age,** edad de oro, *f.* **g.-crested wren,** abadejo, *m.* **g. hair,** cabellos dorados (or de oro), *m pl.* **G. Legend,** leyenda áurea, *f.* **g. mean,** justo medio, *m.* **g. rose,** rosa de oro, *f.* **g. rule,** regla áurea, *f.* **g. syrup,** jarabe de arce, *m.* **g. voice,** voz de oro, *f.* **g. wedding,** bodas de oro, *f pl*
goldfinch /'gould,fɪntʃ/ *n* jilguero, *m*
goldfish /'gould,fɪʃ/ *n* carpa dorada, *f.* **g. bowl,** pecera, *f*
goldrush /'gould,rʌʃ/ carrera de oro, *f*
goldsmith /'gould,smɪθ/ *n* orfebre, oribe, orífice, *m*
golf /gɒlf/ *n* golf, *m.* **g.-club,** (stick) palo de golf, *m;* (organization) club de golf, *m.* **g.-course,** campo de golf, *m*
golfer /'gɒlfər/ *n* jugador (-ra) de golf
gonad /'gounæd/ *n* gonada, *f*
gondola /'gɒndḷə/ *n* góndola, *f*
gondolier /,gɒndḷ'ɪər/ *n* gondolero, *m*
gone /gɔn/ *a* and *past part* ido; (lost) perdido; (ruined) arruinado; (dead) muerto; (past) pasado; (disappeared) desaparecido; (fainted) desmayado; (suppressed) suprimido; (pregnant) encinta; (drunk) borracho; (ended) terminado; (exhausted) agotado; (ill) enfermo. **far g.,** avanzado; (in years) de edad avanzada; (of illness) cerca de la muerte, muy enfermo; (in love) loco de amor; (drunk) muy borracho. **It is all g.,** No hay más. **It is g. seven o'clock,** Son las siete y pico, Son las siete ya
gong /gɔŋ/ *n* gong, *m;* (Chinese) batintín, *m*
gonorrhea /,gɒnə'riə/ *n* gonorrea, *f*
good /gʊd/ *a* bueno (before *m sing* nouns) buen; agradable; afortunado; (appropriate) apropiado, oportuno; (beneficial) provechoso, ventajoso; (wholesome) sano, saludable; (suitable) apto; (useful) útil; (kind) bondadoso; (much) mucho; (obliging) amable; (virtuous) virtuoso; (skilled) experto; (fresh) fresco; (genuine) genuino, legítimo; verdadero. —*adv* bien. —*interj* ¡bueno! ¡bien! **a g. deal,** mucho. **a g. many,** bastantes. **a g. turn,** un favor. **a g. way,** (distance) un buen trecho; mucho. **a g. while,** un buen rato. **as g. as,** tan bueno como. **Be so g. as to...!** Haga el favor de, Tenga Vd. la bondad de (followed by infin.). **fairly g.,** *a* bastante bueno. —*adv* bastante bien. **I'm g. for another five miles,** Tengo fuerzas para cinco millas más. **It was g. of you to do it,** Vd. fue muy amable de hacerlo, Vd. tuvo mucha bondad de hacerlo. **to be no g. at this sort of thing,** no servir para tales cosas. **to have a g. time,** pasarlo bien. **to make g.,** reparar; indemnizar; (accomplish) llevar a cabo, poner en práctica; justificar; (a promise) cumplir. **very g.,** *a* muy bueno. —*adv* muy bien. **g.-feeling,** buena voluntad, *f.* **g.-fellowship,** compañerismo, *m;* buena compañía, *f.* **g.-for-nothing,** *n* papanatas, badulaque, *m.* **to be g.-for-nothing,** no servir para nada. **g. luck,** buena suerte, *f.* **g. manners,** buenos modales, *m pl;* buena crianza, educación, *f.* **g. nature,** buen natural, *m;* buen humor, *m.* **g.-natured,** de buen natural; de buen humor, bonachón. **g. offices,** buenos oficios, *m pl.* **g.-tempered,** de buen humor
good /gʊd/ *n* bien, *m;* provecho, *m;* utilidad, *f; pl* **goods.** See separate entry. **I am saying this for your g.,** Lo digo para tu bien. **Much g. may it do you!** ¡Buen provecho te haga! **for g. and all,** para siempre jamás. **It is no g.,** Es inútil; No vale la pena. **the g.,** el bien; (people) los buenos. **They have gone for g.,** Se han marchado para no volver. **to do one g.,** hacer bien a uno; mejorar; ser provechoso (a uno); (suit) sentar bien (a uno). **What is the g. of...?** ¿Para qué sirve...?; ¿Qué vale...? **g. and evil,** el bien y el mal
good-bye /,gʊd 'bai/ *interj* ¡adiós! —*n* adiós, *m,* despedida, *f.* **to bid g.-b.,** decir adiós. **G.-b. for the present!** ¡Hasta la vista! ¡Hasta luego! **G.-b. until tomorrow, then,** Hasta mañana pues, adiós, Hasta mañana entonces
goodness /'gʊdnɪs/ *n* bondad, *f;* (of quality) buena calidad, *f;* (of persons) amabilidad, benevolencia, *f;* (essence) esencia, substancia, *f;* bien, *m:* excelencia, *f; interj* ¡Jesús! ¡Dios mío! **For g. sake!** ¡Por Dios! **I wish to g. that,** ¡Ojalá que...!
goods /gʊdz/ *n pl* bienes, efectos, *m pl;* artículos, *m pl; Com.* mercancías, *f pl,* géneros, *m pl.* **by g.-train,** en pequeña velocidad. **stolen g.,** objetos robados, *m pl.* **g. lift,** montacargas, *m.* **g. office,** depósito de mercancías, *m.* **g. station,** estación de carga, *f.* **g.-train,** tren de mercancías, *m.* **g. van,** furgón, *m.* **g. wagon,** vagon de mercancías, *m*
good-smelling /'gʊd ,smɛlɪŋ/ *a* oloroso
goodwill /'gʊd'wɪl/ *n* benevolencia, *f;* buena voluntad, *f;* (of a business) clientela, *f*
goose /gus/ *n* oca, *f,* ganso (-sa); plancha de sastre, *f.* —*a* de oca. **g.-flesh,** *Fig.* carne de gallina, *f.* **g. girl,** ansarera, *f.* **g.-step,** paso de oca, *m*
gooseberry /'gus,bɛri/ *n* uva espina, *f*
Gordian /'gɔrdiən/ *a* gordiano. **G. knot,** nudo gordiano, *m*
gore /gɔr/ *n* sangre, *f; Sew.* sesga, nesga, *f.* —*vt* acornear; desgarrar; herir (con arma blanca)
gorge /gɔrdʒ/ *n* (valley) cañón, barranco, *m;* (heavy meal) comilona, *f,* atracón, *m.* —*vt* engullir, tragar. —*vi* hartarse, atracarse
gorgeous /'gɔrdʒəs/ *a* magnífico; espléndido, suntuoso; *Inf.* maravilloso, estupendo
gorgeously /'gɔrdʒəsli/ *adv* magníficamente
gorgeousness /'gɔrdʒəsnɪs/ *n* magnificencia, *f;* suntuosidad, *f,* esplendor, *m*
gorilla /gə'rɪlə/ *n* gorila, *m*
gormandize /'gɔrmən,daiz/ *vi* glotonear
gormandizer /'gɔrmən,daizər/ *n* glotón (-ona)
gorse /gɔrs/ *n* tojo, *m,* aulaga, *f*
gory /'gɔri/ *a* ensangrentado; sangriento
gosh /gɒʃ/ *interj* ¡caray! ¡caramba!
goshawk /'gɒs,hɔk/ *n Ornith.* azor, *m*
gosling /'gɒzlɪŋ/ *n* ansarino, *m*
gospel /'gɒspəl/ *n* evangelio, *m;* doctrina, *f.* **The G. according to St. Mark,** El Evangelio según San Marcos. **to believe as g. truth,** creer como si fuese el evangelio. **to preach the G.,** predicar el evangelio
gossamer /'gɒsəmər/ *n* hilo de araña, *m,* red de araña, telaraña, *f;* (filmy material) gasa, *f;* hilo finísimo, *m, a* de gasa; sutil, delgado, fino
gossip /'gɒsəp/ *n* murmurador (-ra), chismoso (-sa), hablador (-ra); (scandal) chisme, *m;* habladuría, murmuración, *f;* (obsolete, of a woman) comadre, *f;* (talk) charla, *f.* —*vi* charlar, conversar; (in bad sense) murmurar, chismear; criticar. **to g. about,** charlar de; poner lenguas en, cortar un sayo (a); hablar mal de. **g. column,** gacetilla, *f*
gossiping /'gɒsəpɪŋ/ *a* charlatán, hablador; chismoso, murmurador. —*n* See **gossip**
Goth /gɒθ/ *n* godo (-da); bárbaro (-ra)
Gothic /'gɒθɪk/ *a Art.* gótico; (of race) godo; bárbaro. —*n* (language) gótico, *m;* arquitectura gótica, *f.* **G. characters,** letra gótica, *f*
gouge /gaudʒ/ *n* gubia, *f.* —*vt* escoplear. **to g. out,** vaciar; sacar
gourd /gɔrd/ *n* calabaza, *f*
gourmand /gʊr'mɑnd/ *n* glotón, *m*
gourmet /gʊr'mei/ *n* gastrónomo, *m*
gout /gaut/ *n Med.* gota, *f*
gouty /'gauti/ *a* gotoso
govern /'gʌvərn/ *vt* gobernar; regir; (guide) guiar;

dominar; domar, refrenar; *Gram.* regir; (regulate) regular
governable /'gʌvərnəbəl/ *a* gobernable; manejable; dócil
governess /'gʌvərnɪs/ *n* institutriz, *f;* (in a school) maestra, *f*
governing /'gʌvərnɪŋ/ *a* gubernante; director; (with principle, etc.) directivo. —*n* See **government**
government /'gʌvərnmənt, -ərmənt/ *n* gobierno, *m;* dirección, *f;* autoridad, *f.* **g. bond,** bono del gobierno, *m.* **g. house,** palacio del gobernador, *m.* **g. office,** oficina del gobierno, *f.* **g. stock,** papel del Estado, *m*
governmental /ˌgʌvərn'mɛntl̩, ˌgʌvər-/ *a* gubernamental, gubernativo
Government Printing Office Talleres Gráficos de la Nación, *m pl*
governor /'gʌvərnər/ *n* gobernador (-ra); vocal de la junta de gobierno, *mf;* (of a prison) director (-ra) (de una prisión); *Mech.* regulador, *m.* **g.-general,** gobernador general, *m*
governorship /'gʌvərnərˌʃɪp/ *n* gobierno, *m;* dirección, *f*
gown /gaun/ *n* toga, *f;* (cassock) sotana, *f;* (dressing-g.) bata, *f;* (for sleeping) camisa de noche, *f;* (bathing-wrap) albornoz, *m;* (dress) vestido, traje, *m*
Goyesque /gɔi'ɛsk/ *a* goyesco
grab /græb/ *n* asimiento, *m,* presa, *f; Mech.* gancho, *m.* —*vt* arrebatar, asir, agarrar; *Fig.* alzarse con, tomar
grabber /'græbər/ *n* cogedor (-ra); codicioso (-sa)
grace /greis/ *n* elegancia, *f;* simetría, armonía, *f;* gracia, gentileza, *f,* donaire, *m;* encanto, *m;* (goodness) bondad, *f;* gracia, *f;* merced, *f,* favor, *m;* (period of time) plazo, *m;* (privilege) privilegio, *m; Theol.* gracia divina, *f;* (at table) bendición de la mesa, *f;* (as a title) excelentísimo, (to an archbishop) ilustrísimo. —*vt* adornar; favorecer; honrar. **airs and graces,** humos, *m pl.* **the Three Graces,** las Gracias. **three days' g.,** plazo de tres dias, *m.* **to get into a person's good graces,** congraciarse con; caer en gracia con. **to say g.,** bendecir la mesa. **with a bad g.,** a regañadientes. **with a good g.,** de buena gana. **g.-note,** *Mus.* nota de adorno, *f*
graceful /'greisfəl/ *a* airoso, gentil, gracioso; elegante; bonito
gracefully /'greisfəli/ *adv* airosamente, gentilmente; con gracia; elegantemente
gracefulness /'greisfəlnɪs/. See **grace**
graceless /'greislɪs/ *a* réprobo; dejado de la mano de Dios; sin gracia
gracious /'greiʃəs/ *a* (merciful) piadoso, clemente; (urbane) afable, condescendiente, agradable. **Good g.!** ¡Vamos!, ¡Dios mío!
graciously /'greiʃəsli/ *adv* afablemente; con benevolencia. **to be g. pleased,** tener a bien
graciousness /'greiʃəsnɪs/ *n* amabilidad, afabilidad, condescendencia, *f*
gradate /'greideit/ *vt* graduar; *Art.* degradar
gradation /grei'deiʃən/ *n* graduación, *f; Mus.* gradación, *f;* paso gradual, *m;* serie, *f*
grade /greid/ *n* grado, *m;* (quality) calidad, clase, *f;* (in a school) clase, *f;* (gradient) pendiente, *f,* declive, *m.* —*vt* graduar, clasificar; (cattle breeding) cruzar. **down g.,** cuesta abajo. **up g.,** cuesta arriba. **highest g.,** *n* primera clase, *f.* —*a* de primera clase; de calidad excelente
gradient /'greidiənt/ *n* declive, *m.* cuesta, pendiente, *f*
gradual /'grædʒuəl/ *a* gradual. —*n Eccl.* gradual, *m*
gradually /'grædʒuəli/ *adv* gradualmente; poco a poco
graduate / *n, a* 'grædʒuɪt; *v* -ˌeit/ *n* licenciado (-da). —*a* graduado. —*vt* graduar. —*vi* graduarse; (as a doctor) doctorarse. **to g. as,** recibirse de
graduation /ˌgrædʒu'eiʃən/ *n* graduación, *f*
graft /græft/ *n Bot.* injerto, *m; Surg.* injerto de piel, *m;* (swindle) estafa, *f;* (bribery) soborno, *m.* —*vt Bot.* injertar; *Surg.* injertar un trozo de piel; *Fig.* injerir
grafting /'græftɪŋ/ *n Bot.* injerto, *m; Surg.* injerto de piel, *m; Fig.* inserción, *f*
grain /grein/ *n* (corn) grano, *m;* (cereal) cereal, *m,* or *f;* (seed, weight) grano, *m;* (trace) pizca, *f;* (of wood, etc.) hila, *m,* fibra, hebra, veta, *f;* (of leather) flor, *f;* (texture) textura, *f.* —*vt* granear; granular; (wood, marble, etc.) vetear. **against the g.,** a contrapelo. **g. lands,** mieses, *f pl*
gram /græm/ *n* gramo, *m*
grammar /'græmər/ *n* gramática, *f.* **g. school,** instituto de segunda enseñanza, *m*
grammarian /grə'mɛəriən/ *n* gramático, *m*
grammatical /grə'mætɪkəl/ *a* gramático
grammatically /grə'mætɪkəli/ *adv* gramaticalmente, como la gramática lo quiere. (e.g., *She now speaks Catalan g.,* Ahora habla el catalán como la gramática lo quiere)
grammaticalness /grə'mætɪkəlnɪs/ *n* corrección gramatical, *f*
gramophone /'græməˌfoun/ *n* gramófono, *m.*
granary /'greinəri/ *n* granero, hórreo, *m,* troj, *f.* **g. keeper,** trojero, *m*
grand /grænd/ *a* magnífico, soberbio; imponente; (of dress) espléndido, vistoso; (of people) distinguido, importante; aristocrático; (proud) orgulloso; (of style) elevado, sublime; (morally) noble; augusto; (main) principal; (full) completo; *Inf.* estupendo, magnífico; (with duke, etc.) gran. —*n* piano de cola, *m.* **g.-aunt,** tía abuela, *f.* **g. cross,** gran cruz, *f.* **g. duchess,** gran duquesa, *f.* **g. duke,** gran duque, *m.* **g. lodge,** (of freemasons) Gran Oriente, *m.* **g. master,** gran maestre, *m.* **g.-nephew,** resobrino, *m.* **g.-niece,** resobrina, *f.* **g. opera,** ópera, *f.* **g. piano,** piano de cola, *m.* **g.-stand,** tribuna, *f.* **g.-uncle,** tío abuelo, *m.* **g. vizier,** gran visir, *m*
grandchild /'grænˌtʃaild/ *n* nieto (-ta). **great-g.,** bisnieto (-ta). **great-great-g.,** tataranieto (-ta)
granddaughter /'grænˌdɔtər/ *n* nieta, *f.* **great-g.,** bisnieta, *f.* **great-great-g.,** tataranieta, *f*
grandee /græn'di/ *n* grande (de España, grande de Portugal), *m*
grandeur /'grændʒər/ *n* magnificencia, *f;* grandiosidad, *f;* magnitud, grandeza, *f;* (pomp) pompa, *f,* fausto, *m*
grandfather /'grænˌfɑðər/ *n* abuelo, *m.* **great-g.,** bisabuelo, *m.* **great-great-g.,** tatarabuelo, *m*
grandfatherly /'grænˌfɑðərli/ *a* de abuelo
grandfather's clock reloj de péndulo, *m*
grandiloquence /græn'dɪləkwəns/ *n* grandilocuencia, *f*
grandiloquent /græn'dɪləkwənt/ *a* grandílocuo
grandiose /'grændiˌous/ *a* grandioso, sublime; impresionante; imponente; (in a bad sense) extravagante: (of style) bombástico, hinchado
grand jury *n* jurado de acusación, jurado de jucio, *m*
grandmother /'grænˌmʌðər/ *n* abuela, *f.* **great-g.,** bisabuela, *f.* **great-great-g.,** tatarabuela, *f*
grandness /'grændnɪs/ *n* magnificencia, *f;* aristocracia, *f;* (pride) orgullo, *m;* grandiosidad, *f;* (of style) sublimidad, *f;* (of character) nobleza, *f*
grandparent /'grænˌpɛərənt/ *n* abuelo, *m;* abuela, *f; pl* **grandparents,** abuelos, *m pl.* **great-grandparents,** bisabuelos, *m pl.* **great-great-grandparents,** tatarabuelos, *m pl*
grandson /'grænˌsʌn/ *n* nieto, *m.* **great-g.,** bisnieto, *m.* **great-great-g.,** tataranieto, *m*
grange /greindʒ/ *n* granja, *f;* casa de campo, *f*
granite /'grænɪt/ *n* granito, *m*
granny /'græni/ *n* abuelita, nana, *f;* abuela, *f.* **g. knot,** nudo al revés, *m*
grant /grænt/ *n* concesión, *f;* otorgamiento, *m;* donación, *f;* privilegio, *m;* (for study) beca, bolsa de estudio, *f;* (transfer) traspaso, *m,* cesión, *f.* —*vt* conceder; (bestow) otorgar, dar; donar; (agree to) acceder a, asentir en; permitir; (transfer) traspasar; (assume) suponer. **to g. a degree,** expedir un título. **to g. a motion,** dar por entrada a una moción. **to take for granted,** descontar; dar por hecho, dar por sentado. **God g. it!** ¡Dios lo quiera! **granted that,** dado que
grantee /græn'ti/ *n* cesionario (-ia), adjudicatorio (-ia)
grantor /'græntər/ *n* cesionista, *mf;* otorgador (-ra)
granulated /'grænyəˌleitɪd/ *a* granulado
granule /'grænyul/ *n* gránulo, *m*
granulous /'grænyələs/ *a* granuloso
grape /greip/ *n* uva, *f.* **bunch of grapes,** racimo de

uvas, *m.* **muscatel g.,** uva moscatel, *f.* **sour grapes,** uvas agrias, *f pl;* (phrase) ¡están verdes! **g.-fruit,** toronja, *f.* **g. gatherer,** vendimiador (-ra). **g. harvest,** vendimia, *f.* **g. juice,** mosto, *m.* **g.-shot,** metralla, *f.* **g. stone,** granuja, *f.* **g.-sugar,** glucosa, *f.* **g.-vine,** vid, parra, *f*

graph /græf/ *n* gráfica, *f;* diagrama, *m*

graphic /ˈgræfɪk/ *a* gráfico

graphite /ˈgræfait/ *n* grafito, *m*

graphology /græˈfɒlədʒi/ *n* grafología, *f*

grapple /ˈgræpəl/ *n Naut.* rezón, arpeo, *m;* lucha a brazo partido, *f.* —*vt Naut.* aferrar; asir, agarrar. —*vi Naut.* aferrarse. **to g. with,** luchar a brazo partido (con); *Fig.* luchar con

grappling /ˈgræplɪŋ/ *n Naut.* aferramiento, *m;* lucha cuerpo a cuerpo, *f;* (with a problem) lucha con, *f*

grasp /græsp/ *n* agarro, *m;* (reach) alcance, *m;* (of a hand) apretón, *m;* (power) garras, *f pl,* poder, *m;* (understanding) comprensión, *f;* inteligencia, capacidad intelectual, *f.* —*vt* agarrar, asir; empuñar; abrazar; *Fig.* comprender, alcanzar; (a hand) estrechar. —*vi* agarrarse. **within one's g.,** al alcance de uno. **to g. at,** asirse de

grasping /ˈgræspɪŋ/ *n* asimiento, *m;* (understanding) comprensión, *f, a* codicioso, tacaño, mezquino

graspingness /ˈgræspɪŋnɪs/ *n* codicia, *f*

grass /græs/ *n* hierba, *f;* (pasture) pasto, herbaje, *m;* (sward) césped, *m.* —*vt* cubrir de hierba; sembrar de hierba; apacentar. **to hear the g. grow,** sentir crecer la hierba. **to let the g. grow,** *Fig.* dejar crecer la hierba. **to turn out to g.,** echar al pasto. **g.-blade,** brizna de hierba, *f.* **g.-green,** *a* and *n* verde como la hierba *m..* **g.-grown,** cubierto de hierba. **g.-land,** pradera, *f.* **g.-snake,** culebra *f.* **g. widow,** mujer cuyo marido está ausente

grasshopper /ˈgræsˌhɒpər/ *n* saltamontes, *m.* **grasshopper's chirp,** chirrido (del saltamontes), *m*

grassy /ˈgræsi/ *a* parecido a la hierba, como la hierba; cubierto de hierba; de hierba

grate /greit/ *n* parrilla, *f;* (grating) reja, *f.* —*vt* raspar, raer; *Cul.* rallar; (make a noise) hacer rechinar. —*vi* rozar; rechinar, chirriar. **to g. on, upon,** (of sounds) irritar, molestar; chocar con. **to g. on the ear,** herir el oído

grateful /ˈgreitfəl/ *a* agradecido, reconocido; (pleasant) agradable, grato

gratefully /ˈgreitfəli/ *adv* agradecidamente; gratamente

gratefulness /ˈgreitfəlnɪs/ *n* agradecimiento, *m,* gratitud, *f;* (pleasantness) agrado, *m*

grater /ˈgreitər/ *n Cul.* rallador, *m*

gratification /ˌgrætəfɪˈkeiʃən/ *n* satisfacción, *f;* (pleasure) placer, gusto, *m*

gratified /ˈgrætəˌfaid/ *a* satisfecho, contento

gratify /ˈgrætəˌfai/ *vt* satisfacer; (please) gratificar, agradar

gratifying /ˈgrætəˌfaiɪŋ/ *a* satisfactorio, agradable

grating /ˈgreitɪŋ/ *n* reja, *f;* rejilla, *f; Naut.* jareta, *f;* (optics) retículo, *m;* (sound) rechinamiento, chirrido, *m.* —*a* rechinante, chirriador; áspero

gratis /ˈgrætɪs/ *a* and *adv* gratis

gratitude /ˈgrætɪˌtud/ *n* agradecimiento, *m,* gratitud, *f*

gratuitous /grəˈtuɪtəs/ *a* gratuito

gratuitousness /grəˈtuɪtəsnɪs/ *n* gratuidad, *f*

gratuity /grəˈtuɪti/ *n* gratificación, propina, *f*

grave /greiv/ *n* (hole) sepultura, fosa, *f;* (monument) tumba, *f,* sepulcro, *m; Fig.* muerte, *f.* **g.-digger,** enterrador, sepulturero, *m*

grave /*a* greiv; *n* grɒv/ *a* grave; importante; serio; sobrio; (anxious) preocupado; (of accent) grave. —*n* (grave accent) acento grave, *m*

gravel /ˈgrævəl/ *n* grava, *f;* cascajo, casquijo, *m; Med.* arenillas, *f pl,* cálculo, *m*

gravely /ˈgreivli/ *adv* gravemente; seriamente

Graves' disease /greivz/ *n* bocio exoftálmico, *m*

gravestone /ˈgreivˌstoun/ *n* lápida mortuoria, *f*

graveyard /ˈgreivˌyɑrd/ *n* camposanto, cementerio, *m*

gravitate /ˈgrævɪˌteit/ *vi* gravitar; tender

gravitation /ˌgrævɪˈteiʃən/ *n* gravitación, *f;* tendencia, *f*

gravitational /ˌgrævɪˈteiʃənl̩/ *a* de gravitación, gravitacional, gravitatorio

gravitational pull *n* atracción gravitatoria, *f*

gravity /ˈgrævɪti/ *n Phys.* gravedad, *f;* seriedad, *f;* solemnidad, *f;* gravedad, *f;* (weight) peso, *m;* importancia, *f;* (enormity) enormidad, *f;* (danger) peligro, *m.* **center of g.,** centro de gravedad, *m.* **law of g.,** ley de la gravedad, *f.* **specific g.,** peso específico, *m*

gravy /ˈgreivi/ *n* salsa, *f;* jugo (de la carne), *m.* **g.-boat,** salsera, *f*

gray /grei/ *a* gris; (of animals) rucio. —*n* color gris, gris, *m;* caballo gris, *m.* **His hair is turning g.,** El pelo se le vuelve gris. **g.-haired,** de pelo gris. **g. matter,** materia gris, *f;* cacumen, *m.* **g. mullet,** *Ichth.* mújol, *m.* **g. squirrel,** gris, *m.* **g. wolf,** lobo gris, *m*

grayish /ˈgreiɪʃ/ *a* grisáceo, agrisado; (of hair) entrecano

grayness /ˈgreinɪs/ *n* color gris, gris, *m; Fig.* monotonía, *f*

graze /greiz/ *n* abrasión, *f;* (brush) roce, *m, vi* pacer, apacentarse. —*vt* pastorear, apacentar; (brush) rozar

grazing /ˈgreizɪŋ/ *n Agr.* apacentamiento, pastoreo, *m;* (brushing) rozadura, *f.* —*a* que pace, herbívoro; (of land) pacedero. **g. land,** pasto, *m*

grease /gris/ *n* grasa, *f;* (dirt) mugre, *f;* (of a candle) sebo, *m,* cera, *f.* —*vt* engrasar; manchar con grasa; *Fig. Inf.* untar. **to g. the wheels,** *Fig.* untar el carro. **g.-box,** *Mech.* caja de sebo, *f.* **g.-gun,** engrasador de compresión, *m.* **g.-paint,** afeites de actor (or de actriz), *m pl.* **g.-proof paper,** papel impermeable, *m.* **g. spot,** lámpara, mancha de grasa, *f,* saín, *m*

greaser /ˈgrisər/ *n* engrasador, *m*

greasiness /ˈgrisinɪs/ *n* graseza, *f;* lo aceitoso; untuosidad, *f*

greasing /ˈgrisɪŋ/ *n* engrasado, *m*

greasy /ˈgrisi/ *a* grasiento; (oily) aceitoso; (grubby) mugriento, bisunto; *Fig.* lisonjero. **g. pole,** cucaña, *f*

great /greit/ *a* gran; grande; enorme; vasto; (much) mucho; (famous) famoso, ilustre; noble, sublime; (intimate) íntimo; importante; principal; poderoso; magnífico, impresionante; *Inf.* famoso, estupendo; (of time) largo; (clever) fuerte. **Alexander the G.,** Alejandro Magno. **the G. Mogul,** el Gran Mogul. **a g. deal,** mucho. **a g. man,** un grande hombre, un hombre famoso. **a g. many,** muchos (muchas). **He lived to a g. age,** Vivió hasta una edad avanzada. **so g.,** tan grande, tamaño. **the g.,** los grandes hombres. **g. on,** aficionado a. **g.-aunt,** tía abuela, *f.* **g.-grandchild,** etc. See **grandchild,** etc. **g.-hearted,** valeroso; magnánimo, generoso. **g. power,** gran poder, *m.* **G. War,** Gran Guerra, *f.* **the Great Schism,** el Gran Cisma, *m*

greater /ˈgreitər/ *a* comp. of **great,** mayor; más grande. **to make g.,** agrandar. **G. London,** el Gran Londres, *m*

greatest /ˈgreitɪst/ *a* sup. of **great,** más grande; mayor; máximo; más famoso; sumo

greatly /ˈgreitli/ *adv* mucho; con mucho; (very) muy; noblemente

greatness /ˈgreitnɪs/ *n* grandeza, *f;* grandiosidad, *f;* extensión, vastedad, *f;* importancia, *f;* poder, *m;* majestad, *f;* esplendor, *m;* (intensity) intensidad, *f;* (enormity) enormidad, *f*

Grecian /ˈgriʃən/ *a* griego

Greco- *prefix* (in compounds) greco-, greco

Greece /gris/ Grecia, *f*

greed /grid/ *n* (cupidity) codicia, rapacidad, avaricia, *f;* avidez, ansia, *f;* (of food) gula, glotonería, *f*

greedily /ˈgridəli/ *adv* codiciosamente; con avidez; (of eating) vorazmente

greedy /ˈgridi/ *a* (for food) glotón; codicioso; ambicioso; ávido; deseoso

Greek /grik/ *a* and *n* griego (-ga); (language) griego, *m.* **It's all G. to me,** Para mí es como si fuese en latín, Me es chino. **G. tunic,** peplo, *m*

green /grin/ *a* verde; (inexpert) inexperto, bisoño; (recent) nuevo, reciente; (fresh) fresco; (of complexion) pálido, descolorido; (flowery) floreciente; (vigorous) lozano; (young) joven; (unripe) verde; (credulous) crédulo; (raw) crudo; (of wood, vegetables) verde. —*n* verde, color verde, *m;* (vegetables) verdura, *f;* (meadow) prado, *m;* (turf) césped, *m;* (grass) hierba, *f;* (bowling) campo de juego, *m.* —*vt* teñir (or pintar) de verde. **bright g.,** *n* verdegay,

verde claro, *m.* **dark g.,** *n* verdinegro, *m.* **light g.,** *n* verde pálido, *m.* **to grow** or **look g.,** verdear. **g.-eyed,** de ojos verdes. **g. peas,** guisantes, *m pl.* **g. table,** tapete verde, *m*
greenery /'grinəri/ *n* follaje, *m;* verdura, *f*
greengrocer /'grin,grousər/ *n* verdulero (-ra)
greengrocery /'grin,grousəri/ *n* verduleria, *f*
greenhorn /'grin,hɔrn/ *n* bisoño (-ña); papanatas, *m*
greenhouse /'grin,haus/ *n* invernáculo, invernadero, *m*
greenish /'griniʃ/ *a* verdoso. **g.-yellow,** cetrino
Greenland /'grinlənd/ Groenlandia, *f*
Greenlander /'grinləndər/ *n* groenlandés (-esa)
greenness /'grinnɪs/ *a* lo verde; verdor, *m,* verdura, *f;* (inexperience) falta de experiencia, *f;* (vigor) vigor, *m,* lozanía, *f;* (newness) novedad, *f;* (of wood, fruit) falta de madurez, *f*
greenroom /'grin,rum/ *n Theat.* saloncillo, *m*
greenstuff /'grin,stʌf/ *n* hortalizas, legumbres, *f pl*
greet /grit/ *vt* saludar; recibir; (express pleasure) dar la bienvenida (a)
greeting /'gritɪŋ/ *n* salutación, *f,* saludo, *m;* recepción, *f;* (welcome) bienvenida, *f; pl* **greetings,** recuerdos, *m pl*
gregarious /grɪ'gɛəriəs/ *a* gregario
gregariousness /grɪ'gɛəriəsnɪs/ *n* gregarismo, *m*
Gregorian /grɪ'gɔriən/ *a* gregoriano
grenade /grɪ'neid/ *n* granada, bomba, *f.* **hand-g.,** bomba de mano, *f*
grey /grei/ See **gray**
greyhound /'grei,haund/ *n* galgo, lebrel, *m.* **g. bitch,** galga, *f;* **g. racing,** carreras de galgos, *f pl*
grid /grɪd/ *n* (of electric power) red, *f;* rejilla, *f;* (for water, etc.) alcantarilla, *f*
gridiron /'grɪd,aiərn/ *n Cul.* parrilla, *f;* (of electric power) red, *f; Theat.* telar, *m*
grief /grif/ *n* angustia, pena, aflicción, *f;* dolor, suplicio, *m.* **to come to g.,** pasarlo mal, tener un desastre
grievance /'grivəns/ *n* injusticia, *f;* motivo de queja, *m*
grieve /griv/ *vt* entristecer, afligir, angustiar; atormentar. *—vi* entristecerse, afligirse, acongojarse. **to g. for,** lamentar: echar de menos
grievous /'grivəs/ *a* (heavy) oneroso, gravoso; opresivo; doloroso, penoso; lamentable; cruel. **g. error,** error lamentable
grievousness /'grivəsnɪs/ *n* (weight) peso, *m;* carácter opresivo, *m;* dolor, *m,* aflicción, *f;* enormidad, *f;* crueldad, *f*
griffin /'grɪfɪn/ *n* grifo, *m;* (*Fig.* chaperon) carabina, *f;* (dog) grifón, *m*
grill /grɪl/ *n Cul.* parrilla, *f;* (grating) rejilla, *f;* (before a window) reja, *f;* (food) asado a la parrilla, *m.* *—vt Cul.* asar a la parrilla; (burn) quemar; (question) interrogar; (torture) torturar. *—vi Cul.* asarse a la parrilla; (be burnt) quemarse. **g.-room,** parrilla, *f*
grille /grɪl/ *n* reja, *f;* rejilla, *f;* (screen) verja, *f*
grilled /grɪld/ *a Cul.* a la parrilla; con rejilla
griller /'grɪlər/ *n Cul.* parrilla, *f*
grim /grɪm/ *a* (fierce) feroz, salvaje; (severe) severo, ceñudo, adusto; inflexible; (frightful) horrible
grimace /'grɪməs/ *n* mueca, *f,* gesto, mohín, visaje, *m, vi* hacer muecas
grime /graim/ *n* mugre, *f;* suciedad, *f.* **to cover with g.,** enmugrecer
grimly /'grɪmli/ *adv* severamente; sin sonreír; inflexiblemente; (without retreating) sin cejar; (frightfully) horriblemente; de un modo espantoso
grimness /'grɪmnɪs/ *n* (ferocity) ferocidad, *f;* (severity) severidad, *f;* inflexibilidad, *f;* (frightfulness) horror, *m,* lo espantoso
grimy /'graimi/ *a* mugriento, sucio
grin /grɪn/ *n* sonrisa grande, *f;* sonrisa burlona, *f;* (grimace) mueca, *f.* *—vi* sonreír mostrando los dientes; sonreír bonachonamente; sonreír de un modo burlón
grind /graind/ *vt* (to powder) pulverizar; moler; (break up) quebrantar; (oppress) agobiar, oprimir; (sharpen) afilar, amolar; (a barrel-organ) tocar (un manubrio); (the teeth) crujir, rechinar (los dientes); (into) reducir a; (*Inf.* teach) empollar. *—vi* moler; *Fig. Inf.* trabajar laboriosamente. *—n Fig. Inf.* trabajo pesado, *m; n Fig. Inf.* estudiantón, *m*
grinder /'graindər/ *n* (of scissors, etc.) afilador, *m;* (of an organ) organillero; (mill-stone) piedra de moler, *f;* (molar) muela, *f*
grinding /'graindɪŋ/ *a* (tedious) cansado, aburrido; opresivo; (of pain) incesante. *—n* pulverización, *f;* amoladura, *f;* (of grain) molienda, *f;* (polishing) pulimento, bruñido, *m;* (oppression) opresión, *f;* (of teeth) rechinamiento, *m*
grindstone /'graind,stoun/ *n* amoladera, afiladera, piedra de amolar, *f.* **to have one's nose to the g.,** batir el yunque
grinning /'grɪnɪŋ/ *a* sonriente; riente; (mocking) burlón
grip /grɪp/ *n* asimiento, agarro, *m;* (claws, clutches) garras, *f pl;* (hand) mano, *f;* (of shaking hands) apretón de manos, *m;* (of a weapon, etc.) empuñadura, *f;* (reach) alcance, *m;* (understanding) comprensión, *f;* (control) dominio, *m;* (bag) portamanteo, *m;* maleta, *f.* *—vt* asir, agarrar; (of wheels) agarrarse; *Mech.* morder; (a sword, etc.) empuñar; (pinch) pellizcar; (surround) cercar; (understand) comprender; (press; to grip the hand and *Fig.* the heart) apretar; (fill) llenar; (the attention) atraer, llamar; (sway, hold) dominar
gripe /graip/ *n* (*Inf.* pain) retortijón (de tripas), *m*
grisly /'grɪzli/ *a* espantoso; repugnante
grist /grɪst/ *n* molienda, *f.* **Everything is g. to their mill,** Sacan partido de todo
gristle /'grɪsəl/ *n* cartílago, *m,* ternilla, *f*
gristly /'grɪsli/ *a* cartilaginoso
grit /grɪt/ *n* cascajo, *m;* polvo, *m; Fig.* firmeza (de carácter), *f;* (courage) valor, *m;* (endurance) aguante, *m*
gritty /'grɪti/ *a* arenoso, arenisco
grizzled /'grɪzəld/ *a* (of hair, etc.) gris; canoso; grisáceo
grizzly bear /'grɪzli/ *n* oso (-sa) pardo (-da)
groan /groun/ *n* gemido, *m.* *—vi* gemir; (creak) crujir. **to g. out,** decir (or contar) entre gemidos. **to g. under,** sufrir bajo, gemir bajo; (of weight) crujir bajo
groaning /'grounɪŋ/ *n* gemidos, *m pl.* *—a* que gime, gemidor; (under a weight) crujiente
grocer /'grousər/ *n* abacero (-ra) vendedor (-ra) de comestibles. **grocer's shop,** tienda de comestibles, bodega, *f*
grocery /'grousəri/ *n* tienda de comestibles, tienda de ultramarinos, abarrotería, lonja, bodega, *f,* negocio de comestibles, *m; pl* **groceries,** provisiones, *f pl,* comestibles, *m pl*
grog /grɒg/ *n* grog, *m*
groin /grɔin/ *n Anat.* ingle, *f*
groom /grum/ *n* (in a royal household) gentilhombre, *m;* lacayo, *m;* mozo de caballos, *m;* (of a bride) novio, *m.* *—vt* (a horse) cuidar; (oneself) arreglarse. **She is always well groomed,** Está siempre muy bien arreglada
groomsman /'grumzmən/ *n* padrino de boda, *m*
groove /gruv/ *n* ranura, muesca, *f;* estría, *f;* surco, *m; Fig.* rutina, *f.* *—vt* entallar; estriar
grooved /gruvd/ *a* con ranura; estriado
grope /group/ *vi* andar a tientas; (with for) buscar a tientas; procurar, encontrar, buscar. **to g. one's way toward,** avanzar a tientas hacia; *Fig.* avanzar poco a poco hacia
gropingly /'groupɪŋli/ *adv* a tientas; irresolutamente
gross /grous/ *n Com.* gruesa, *f;* totalidad, *f, a* grueso; denso, espeso; (unrefined) grosero, (great) grande; (crass) craso; total; *Com.* bruto; (tremendous) enorme. **in g.,** en grueso. **g. amount,** total, *m; Com.* importe bruto, *m.* **g. weight,** peso bruto, *m*
grossly /'grousli/ *adv* groseramente; (much) enormemente
grossness /'grousnɪs/ *n* gordura, *f;* (vulgarity) grosería, *f;* obscenidad, *f;* (enormity) enormidad, *f*
grotesque /grou'tɛsk/ *a* grotesco; extravagante, estrambótico; ridiculo. *—n* grotesco, *m*
grotesqueness /grou'tɛsknɪs/ *n* lo grotesco; ridiculez, *f*
grotto /'grɒtou/ *n* gruta, *f*
ground /graund/ *n* suelo, *m;* (of water and *Naut.*)

fondo, *m;* (earth) tierra, *f; Fig.* terreno, *m;* (strata) capa, *f; Sports.* campo, *m;* (parade) plaza (de armas), *f;* (background) fondo, *m;* (basis) base, *f,* fundamento, *m;* (reason) causa, *f;* motivo, *m;* (excuse) pretexto, *m; pl* **grounds,** jardines, *m pl,* parque, *m;* (sediment) sedimento, *m,* heces, *f pl;* (reason) causa, *f.* —*vi Naut.* varar, encallar. —*vt* poner en tierra; *Naut.* hacer varar; *Elec.* conectar con tierra; (base) fundar (en), basar (en); (teach) enseñar los rudimentos (de). —*a* molido; en polvo; (of floors, stories) bajo; (of glass) deslustrado; *Bot.* terrestre. **common g.,** tierra comunal, *f; Fig.* tierra común, *f.* **He is on his own g.,** Está en terreno propio. **It fell to the g.,** Cayó al suelo; *Fig.* Fracasó. **It is on the g.,** Está en el suelo. **It suits me to the g.,** Me viene de perilla. **to break fresh g.,** *Fig.* tratar problemas nuevos. **to be well grounded in,** conocer bien los elementos (or rudimentos) de. **to cover g.,** cubrir terreno; recorrer; (in discussion) tocar muchos puntos. **to cut the g. from beneath one's feet,** hacer perder la iniciativa (a). **to give g.,** retroceder; perder terreno. **to raze to the g.,** echar por tierra, arrasar. **to stand one's g.,** resistir el ataque; no darse por vencido; *Fig.* mantenerse firme, mantenerse en sus trece. **to win g.,** ganar terreno. **g. coffee,** café molido, *m.* **g.-color,** (of paint) primera capa, *f;* (color de) fondo, *m;* **g.-floor,** piso bajo, *m.* **g. glass,** vidrio deslustrado, *m.* **g.-ivy,** hiedra terrestre, *f.* **g. nut,** cacahuete, *m.* **g.-plan,** *Archit.* planta, *f.* **g.-rent,** censo, *m.* **g.-sheet,** tela impermeable, *f;* **g. staff,** *Aer.* personal del aeropuerto, *m.* **g.-swell,** mar de fondo, *m*

grounded /'graundɪd/ *a* fundado. **The airplanes are g.,** Los aviones están sin volar. **His suspicions are well g.,** Tiene motivos para sus sospechas

grounding /'graundɪŋ/ *n Naut.* encalladura, *f;* (teaching) instrucción en los rudimentos, *f*

groundless /'graundlɪs/ *a* sin fundamento, inmotivado, sin causa, sin motivo

groundwork /'graund,wɜrk/ *n* fundamento, *m;* base, *f;* principio, *m*

group /grup/ *n* grupo, *m.* —*vt* agrupar. —*vi* agruparse. **g. captain,** coronel de aviación, *m*

grouping /'grupɪŋ/ *n* agrupación, *f*

grouse /graus/ *n Ornith.* ortega, *f.* —*vi* rezongar, refunfuñar

grove /grouv/ *n* soto, boscaje, *m;* arboleda, *f*

grovel /'grɒvəl/ *vi* arrastrarse; *Fig.* humillarse

groveling /'grɒvəlɪŋ/ *a Fig.* servil; ruin

grow /grou/ *vi* crecer; (increase) aumentar; (become) hacerse; empezar a; llegar a; (turn) volverse, ponerse; (flourish) progresar, adelantar; (develop) desarrollarse; (extend) extenderse. —*vt* cultivar; dejar crecer. **I grew to fear it,** Llegué a temerlo. **to g. cold,** ponerse frío; enfriarse; (of weather) empezar a hacer frío. **to g. fat,** engordar. **to g. hard,** ponerse duro; *Fig.* endurecerse. **to g. hot,** ponerse caliente; calentarse; (of weather) empezar a hacer calor. **to g. like Topsy,** crecer a la buena de Dios. **to g. old,** envejecer. **to g. tall,** crecer mucho; ser alto. **to g. again,** crecer de nuevo. **to g. into,** hacerse, llegar a ser; venir a ser. **to g. out of,** brotar de; originarse en; (a habit) desacostumbrarse poco a poco. **He is growing out of his clothes,** La ropa se le hace pequeña. **to g. up,** (of persons) hacerse hombre (mujer); desarrollarse; (of a custom, etc.) imponerse. **to g. on, upon,** crecer sobre; llegar a dominar; (make think) hacer creer, empezar a pensar; (of a habit) arraigar en

grower /'grouər/ *n* cultivador (-ra)

growing /'grouɪŋ/ *n* crecimiento, *m;* desarrollo, *m;* (increase) aumento, *m;* (of flowers, etc.) cultivación, *f,* *a* creciente

growing pains *n pl* crisis de desarrollo, *f*

growl /graul/ *n* gruñido, *m;* reverberación, *f;* trueno, *m.* —*vi* gruñir; (of guns) tronar; (of thunder) reverberar. **to g. out,** decir gruñendo

grown /groun/ *a* crecido; maduro; adulto. **a g. up,** una persona mayor. **to be full-g.,** estar completamente desarrollado; haber llegado a la madurez. **g. over with,** cubierto de

growth /grouθ/ *n* crecimiento, *m;* (development) desarrollo, *m;* (progress) progreso, adelanto, *m;* (increase) aumento, *m;* (cultivation) cultivo, *m;* (vegetation) vegetación, *f; Med.* tumor, *m.* **He has a week's g. on his chin,** Tiene una barba de una semana

grub /grʌb/ *n* larva, *f,* gusano, *m.* —*vt* (with up, out) desarraigar; cavar; desmalezar; *Fig. Inf.* buscar

grubbiness /'grʌbinɪs/ *n* suciedad, *f;* (untidiness) desaliño, *m*

grubby /'grʌbi/ *a* lleno de gusanos; sucio; bisunto; desaliñado

grudge /grʌdʒ/ *n* motivo de rencor, *m;* rencor, resentimiento, *m,* ojeriza, *f;* mala voluntad, *f;* aversión, *f.* —*vt* envidiar. **to bear a g.,** tener ojeriza

grudging /'grʌdʒɪŋ/ *a* (niggardly) mezquino; envidioso; poco generoso; de mala gana; nada afable

grudgingly /'grʌdʒɪŋli/ *adv* de mala gana, contra su voluntad; con rencor; a regañadientes

gruel /'gruəl/ *n* gachas, *f pl*

gruesome /'grusəm/ *a* pavoroso, horrible; macabro

gruff /grʌf/ *a* (of the voice) bronco, grave, áspero; (of manner) brusco, malhumorado

gruffly /'grʌfli/ *adv* en una voz bronca (or áspera); bruscamente, con impaciencia, malhumoradamente

gruffness /'grʌfnɪs/ *n* aspereza, bronquedad, *f;* brusquedad, sequedad, impaciencia, *f,* mal humor, *m*

grumble /'grʌmbəl/ *n* ruido sordo, trueno, *m;* estruendo, *m;* (complaint) refunfuño, rezongo, *m.* —*vi* tronar; refunfuñar, rezongar; hablar entre dientes; quejarse; protestar (contra). —*vt* decir refunfuñando

grumbler /'grʌmblər/ *n* murmurador (-ra), refunfuñador (-ra)

grumbling /'grʌmblɪŋ/ *a* gruñón, refunfuñador; regañón; descontento. —*n* See **grumble**

grumblingly /'grʌmblɪŋli/ *adv* a regañadientes, refunfuñando

grumpiness /'grʌmpinɪs/ *n* mal humor, *m,* irritabilidad, *f*

grumpy /'grʌmpi/ *a* malhumorado, irritable

grunt /grʌnt/ *n* gruñido, *m.* —*vi* gruñir

grunting /'grʌntɪŋ/ *a* gruñidor

guarantee /,gærən'ti/ *n Law.* persona de quien otra sale fiadora, *f;* garantía, *f;* abono, *m.* —*vt* garantizar; responder de; abonar; (assure) asegurar, acreditar

guarantor /'gærən,tɔr/ *n* garante, *mf*

guard /gɑrd/ *n* (watchfulness) vigilancia, *f;* (in fencing) guardia, *f;* (of a sword) guarnición, *f;* (sentry) centinela, *m;* (soldier) guardia, *m;* (body of soldiers) guardia, *f;* (escort) escolta, *f;* (keeper) guardián, *m;* (protection) protección, defensa, *f;* (of a train) jefe de tren, *m.* —*vt* guardar; proteger, defender; vigilar; (escort) escoltar. **to g. against,** guardarse de. **the changing of the g.,** el relevo de la guardia. **to be on g.,** *Mil.* estar de guardia; (in fencing) estar en guardia. **to be on one's g.,** estar prevenido, estar alerta. **to be off one's g.,** estar desprevenido. **to mount g.,** *Mil.* montar la guardia; vigilar. **guard's van,** furgón de equipajes, *m.* **g.-house,** cuerpo de guardia, *m;* prisión militar, *f*

guarded /'gɑrdɪd/ *a* (reticent) reservado, circunspecto, prudente, discreto

guardedly /'gɑrdɪdli/ *adv* prudentemente, con circunspección, discretamente

guardian /'gɑrdiən/ *n* protector (-ra); guardián (-ana); *Law.* tutor, *m.* —*a* que guarda; tutelar. **g. angel,** ángel de la guarda, ángel custodio, *m;* deidad tutelar, *f*

guardianship /'gɑrdiən,ʃɪp/ *n* protección, *f;* patronato, *m; Law.* curaduría, tutela, *f*

guardsman /'gɑrdzmən/ *n* guardia, *m*

Guatemalan /,gwɑtə'mɑlən/ *a* and *n* guatemalteco (-ca)

guava /'gwɑvə/ *n Bot.* guayaba, *f*

Guernsey /'gɜrnzi/ Guenesy, *m*

guerrilla /gə'rɪlə/ *n* guerrilla, *f;* (soldier) guerrillero, *m.* —*a* de guerrilla. **g. warfare,** guerra de guerrillas, *f*

guess /gɛs/ *n* adivinación, *f;* estimación, *f;* conjetura, *f;* sospecha, *f.* —*vt* and *vi* adivinar; conjeturar; sospechar; imaginar; (suppose) suponer, creer; calcular. **to g. at,** formar una opinión sobre; imaginar. **a rough g.,** estimación aproximada, *f.* **at a g.,** a poco más o menos, a ojo de buen cubero. **g.-work,** conjeturas, suposiciones, *f pl*

guest /gɛst/ *n* (at a meal) convidado (-da), invitado

(-da); (at a hotel, etc.) cliente (-da); *Biol.* parásito, *m.* **g.-room,** alcoba de respeto, alcoba de honor, alcoba de huéspedes, *f,* cuarto de amigos, cuarto para invitados, *m*

guffaw /gʌ'fɔ/ *n* carcajada, *f.* —*vi* reírse a carcajadas, soltar el trapo

Guiana /gi'ænə/ Guayana, *f*

guidance /'gaidn̩s/ *n* dirección, *f;* gobierno, *m;* (advice) consejos, *m pl;* inspiración, *f*

guide /gaid/ *n* (person) guía, *mf;* (girl g.) exploradora, *f;* (book and *Fig.*) guía, *f;* mentor, *m;* modelo, *m;* (inspiration) norte, *m; Mech.* guía, *f.* —*vt* guiar; conducir; encaminar; dirigir; (govern) gobernar. **g.-book,** guía (de turistas), *f.* **g.-post,** poste indicador, *m*

guided tour /'gaidɪd/ *n* visita explicada, visita programada, *f*

guideline /'gaid,lain/ *Lit.* falsarregla, falsilla, *f; Fig.* pauta, *f*

guiding /'gaidɪŋ/ *a* que guía; directivo; decisivo. —*n* See **guidance**

guild /gɪld/ *n* gremio, *m.* —*a* gremial. **g. member,** gremial, *m*

guilder /'gɪldər/ *n* (coin) florín holandés, *m*

guile /gail/ *n* astucia, superchería, maña, *f*

guileful /'gailfəl/ *a* astuto

guileless /'gaillɪs/ *a* cándido, sin malicia, inocente

guilelessly /'gaillɪsli/ *adv* inocentemente

guilelessness /'gaillɪsnɪs/ *n* inocencia, candidez, *f*

guillotine /'gɪlə,tin/ *n* guillotina, *f.* —*vt* guillotinar

guilt /gɪlt/ *n* culpabilidad, *f;* crimen, *m;* (sin) pecado, *m*

guilt complex complejo de culpa, *m*

guiltily /'gɪltəli/ *adv* culpablemente; como si fuese culpable

guiltless /'gɪltlɪs/ *a* libre de culpa, inocente; puro; ignorante

guilty /'gɪlti/ *a* culpable; delincuente; criminal. **to find g.,** encontrar culpable. **to plead g.,** confesarse culpable. **g. party,** culpable, *m*

Guinea /'gɪni/ Guinea, *f*

guinea /'gɪni/ *n* guinea, *f.* **g.-fowl,** gallina de Guinea, *f.* **g.-pig,** conejillo de Indias, cobayo, *m*

guise /gaiz/ *n* manera, guisa, *f;* (garb) traje, *m;* máscara, *f; Fig.* pretexto, *m.* **under the g. of,** bajo el pretexto de; bajo la apariencia de

guitar /gɪ'tɑr/ *n* guitarra, *f*

guitarist /gɪ'tɑrɪst/ *n* guitarrista, *mf*

gulf /gʌlf/ *n* golfo, *m;* abismo, *m*

Gulf Stream, the la Corriente del Golfo

gull /gʌl/ *n Ornith.* gaviota, *f;* (dupe) primo, *m.* —*vt* engañar, timar, defraudar

gullet /'gʌlɪt/ *n* esófago, *m;* garganta, *f*

gullibility /,gʌlə'bɪlɪti/ *n* credulidad, *f*

gullible /'gʌləbəl/ *a* crédulo

gully /'gʌli/ *n* hondonada, barranca, *f;* (gutter) arroyo, *m*

gulp /gʌlp/ *n* trago, sorbo, *m.* —*vt* engullir, tragar; (repress) ahogar; (believe) tragar. **to g. up,** vomitar

gum /gʌm/ *n* (of the mouth) encía, *f;* goma, *f.* —*vt* engomar; pegar con goma. **gum arabic,** goma arábiga, *f.* **gum boots,** botas de goma, *f.* **gum-resin,** gomorresina, *f.* **gum starch,** aderezo, *m.* **gum tree,** eucalipto, *m*

gumminess /'gʌminɪs/ *n* gomosidad, *f*

gummy /'gʌmi/ *a* gomoso

gumption /'gʌmpʃən/ *n* sentido común, seso, *m*

gun /gʌn/ *n* arma de fuego, *f;* (handgun) fusil, *m;* (sporting g.) escopeta, *f;* (pistol) pistola, *f,* revólver, *m;* (cannon) cañón, *m;* (firing) cañonazo, *m.* **big gun,** *Inf.* pájaro gordo, *m.* **heavy gun,** cañón de grueso calibre, *m.* **gun-barrel,** cañón de escopeta, *m.* **gun-carriage,** cureña, *f.* **gun-cotton,** pólvora de algodón, *f.* **gun-fire,** cañonazos, *m pl,* fuego, *m.* **gun-metal,** bronce de cañón, *m;* pavón, *m.* **gun-room,** armería, *f;* (on a ship) polvorín, *m.* **gun-running,** contrabanda de armas, *f.* **gun-turret,** torre, *f.* **gun wound,** balazo, *m*

gunboat /'gʌn,bout/ *n* cañonero, *m,* lancha bombardera, *f*

gunflint /'gʌn,flɪnt/ *n* piedra de escopeta, *f*

gunman /'gʌnmən/ *n* escopetero, armero, *m;* bandido armado, *m;* gángster, apache, *m*

gunner /'gʌnər/ *n* artillero, *m;* escopetero, *m*

gun permit *n* licencia de armas, *f,* permiso de armas, *m*

gunpowder /'gʌn,paudər/ *n* pólvora, *f*

gunshot /'gʌn,ʃɒt/ *n* escopetazo, *m;* tiro de fusil, *m*

gunsmith /'gʌn,smɪθ/ *n* escopetero, armero, *m*

gunwale /'gʌnl̩/ *n Naut.* regala, borda, *f*

gurgle /'gɜrgəl/ *n* murmullo, murmurio, gorgoteo, *m;* gluglú, *m;* (of a baby) gorjeo, *m.* —*vi* murmurar; hacer gluglú; (of babies) gorjear

gurgling /'gɜrglɪŋ/ *a* murmurante; (of babies) gorjeador. —*n* See **gurgle**

gush /gʌʃ/ *n* chorro, *m;* (of words) torrente, *m;* (of emotion) efusión, *f.* —*vi* chorrear, borbotar; surtir, surgir. **to g. out,** saltar, brotar a borbotones, salir a borbollones, salira borbotones. **to g. over,** *Fig.* hablar con efusión de

gushing /'gʌʃɪŋ/ *a* hirviente; (of people) efusivo, extremoso, empalagoso

gusset /'gʌsɪt/ *n Sew.* escudete, *m*

gust /gʌst/ *n* (of wind) ráfaga, bocanada (de aire), *f; Fig.* arrebato, acceso, *m*

gusto /'gʌstou/ *n* brío, *m;* entusiasmo, *m*

gusty /'gʌsti/ *a* borrascoso

gut /gʌt/ *n* intestino, *m,* tripa, *f;* (catgut) cuerda de tripa, *f; Naut.* estrecho, *m; pl* **guts,** tripas, *f pl;* (content) meollo, *m,* substancia, *f;* (stamina) aguante, espíritu, *m.* —*vt* (of fish, etc.) destripar; (plunder) saquear; destruir por completo; quemar completamente

gutta-percha /'gʌtə 'pɜrtʃə/ *n* gutapercha, *f*

gutter /'gʌtər/ *n* canal, *m;* (of a street) arroyo (de la calle), *m;* (ditch) zanja, *f; Fig.* hampa, *f.* —*vt* surcar. —*vi* gotear; (of a candle) cerotear, gotear la cera. **g. spout,** canalón, *m*

guttersnipe /'gʌtər,snaip/ *n* golfillo, *m,* niño (-ña) del hampa

guttural /'gʌtərəl/ *a* gutural. —*n* letra gutural, *f*

guy /gai/ *n* (rope) viento, *m; Naut.* guía, *f;* (effigy) mamarracho, *m;* (scarecrow) espantajo, *m, vt* sujetar con vientos o guías; burlarse de

guzzle /'gʌzəl/ *vt* tragar, engullir. —*vi* atracarse, engullir; emborracharse. —*n* comilón, *m;* borrachera, *f*

guzzler /'gʌzlər/ *n* tragador (-ra); borracho (-cha)

gymnasium /dʒɪm'nɑziəm/ *n* gimnasio, *m*

gymnast /'dʒɪmnæst/ *n* gimnasta, *mf*

gymnastic /dʒɪm'næstɪk/ *a* gimnástico. **g. rings,** anillas, *f pl*

gymnastics /dʒɪm'næstɪks/ *n* gimnasia, *f*

gynecological /,gainɪkə'lɒdʒɪkəl/ *a* ginecológico

gynecologist /,gainɪ'kɒlədʒɪst/ *n* ginecólogo (-ga)

gynecology /,gainɪ'kɒlədʒi/ *n* ginecología, *f*

gypsum /'dʒɪpsəm/ *n* yeso, *m*

gypsy /'dʒɪpsi/ *n* gitano (-na). —*a* gitano, gitanesco; (music) flamenco

gyrate /'dʒaireit/ *vi* girar, rodar

gyration /dʒai'reiʃən/ *n* giro, *m,* vuelta, *f*

gyratory /'dʒairə,tɔri/ *a* giratorio

gyro-compass /'dʒairou ,kʌmpəs/ *n* brújula giroscópica, *f*

gyroscope /'dʒairə,skoup/ *n Phys.* giroscopio, *m*

H

h /eitʃ/ *n* (letter) hache, *f*
ha /hɑ/ *interj* ¡ah!
haberdasher /ˈhæbərˌdæʃər/ *n* mercero, *m*
haberdashery /ˈhæbərˌdæʃəri/ *n* mercería, *f*
habiliment /həˈbɪləmənt/ *n* vestidura, *f*; *pl* **habiliments,** indumentaria, *f*
habilitate /həˈbɪlɪˌteit/ *vt* habilitar
habilitation /həˌbɪlɪˈteiʃən/ *n* habilitación, *f*
habit /ˈhæbɪt/ *n* costumbre, *f*, hábito, *m*; (temperament) temperamento, carácter, *m*; (use) uso, *m*; (of body) complexión, constitución, *f*; *Eccl.* hábito, *m*. **to be in the h. of,** soler, acostumbrar, estar acostumbrado a. **to have bad habits,** estar malacostumbrado. **to have the bad h. of,** tener el vicio (or la mala costumbre) de. **to contract the h. of,** contraer la costumbre de. **h. maker,** sastre de trajes de montar, *m*
habitable /ˈhæbɪtəbəl/ *a* habitable, vividero
habitat /ˈhæbɪˌtæt/ *n* (*Bot.*, *Zool.*) medio, *m*, habitación, *f*
habitation /ˌhæbɪˈteiʃən/ *n* habitación, *f*
habit-forming /ˈhæbɪtˌfɔrmɪŋ/ *a* enviciador, que crea vicio
habitual /həˈbɪtʃuəl/ *a* habitual, acostumbrado, usual; constante; común
habitually /həˈbɪtʃuəli/ *adv* habitualmente; constantemente; comúnmente
habituate /həˈbɪtʃuˌeit/ *vt* habituar, acostumbrar
habituation /həˌbɪtʃuˈeiʃən/ *n* habituación, *f*
habitué /həˈbɪtʃuˌei/ *n* parroquiano (-na); veterano (-na)
hack /hæk/ *n* caballo de alquiler, *m*; rocín, jaco, *m*; (writer) escritor mercenario, *m*. —*vt* acuchillar; tajar, cortar. —*vi* cortar. **to h. to pieces,** cortar en pedazos; pasar a cuchillo
hacking /ˈhækɪŋ/ *a* (of coughs) seco
hackle /ˈhækəl/ *n* (for flax, hemp) rastrillo, *m*
hackney carriage /ˈhækni/ *n* coche de plaza, coche de alquiler, *m*
hackneyed /ˈhæknid/ *a* gastado, trillado, muy usado, repetido, resobado
hacksaw /ˈhækˌsɔ/ *n* sierra de cerrajero, sierra para metal, *f*
hackwork /ˈhækˌwɜrk/ *n* trabajo de rutina, *m*
haddock /ˈhædək/ *n* merlango, *m*, pescadilla, *f*
Hades /ˈheidiz/ *n* Hades, *m*; *Inf.* el infierno, *m*
haft /hæft/ *n* mango, tomadero, *m*, manija, *f*; puño, *m*
hag /hæg, hɑg/ *n* bruja, *f*
haggard /ˈhægərd/ *a* ojeroso, trasnochado, trasojado
haggardly /ˈhægərdli/ *adv* ansiosamente
haggardness /ˈhægərdnɪs/ *n* aspecto ojeroso, *m*
haggle /ˈhægəl/ *vi* regatear; vacilar
haggling /ˈhæglɪŋ/ *n* regateo, *m*, *a* regatón
hagiographer /ˌhægiˈɒgrəfər/ *n* hagiógrafo, *m*
hagiography /ˌhægiˈɒgrəfi/ *n* hagiografía, *f*
Hague, The /heig/ La Haya
ha, ha! /ˈhɑ ˈhɑ/ *interj* ¡ja, ja!
hail /heil/ *n* (salutation) saludo, *m*; (shout) grito, *m*; aclamación, *f*; (frozen rain) granizo, *m*; (of blows) lluvia, *f*. —*interj* ¡salve! —*vt* saludar; llamar; aclamar; *Fig.* lanzar, echar. —*vi* (hailstones) granizar; (blows, etc.) llover. **to h. from,** proceder de, ser natural de. **within h.,** al habla. **H. Mary,** Salve Regina, Avemaría, *f*
hailstone /ˈheilˌstoun/ *n* granizo, pedrisco, *m*
hailstorm /ˈheilˌstɔrm/ *n* granizada, *f*
hair /hɛər/ *n* (single h.) cabello, *m*; (*Zool. Bot.*) pelo, *m*; (of horse's mane) crin, *f*; (head of h.) cabellera, mata de pelo, *f*, pelo, *m*; (superfluous) vello, *m*; (fiber) fibra, *f*, filamento, *m*; (on the pen) raspa, *f*, pelo, *m*; *Fig.* pelo, *m*. **lock of h.,** bucle, rizo, *m*; mecha, *f*. **to dress one's h.,** peinarse. **to have one's h. cut,** hacerse cortar el pelo. **to part the h.,** hacer(se) la raya del pelo. **to put up one's h.,** hacerse el moño; (to "come out") ponerse de largo. **to tear one's h.,** mesarse los cabellos. **h. combings,** peinaduras, *f pl*. **h.-curler,** tirabuzón, *m*. **h. dryer,** secadora de cabello, *f*. **h. dye,** tinte para el pelo, *m*. **h.-net,** redecilla, *f*. **h.-oil,** brillantina, *f*. **h.-raising,** horripilante, espeluznante. **h.-ribbon,** cinta para el pelo, *f*. **h.-shirt,** cilicio, *m*. **h. slide,** pasador, *m*. **h.-splitting,** sofistería, argucia, *f*; mez quinas argucias, quis quillas, *f pl*. **h.-spring,** muelle del volante, *m*. **h.-switch,** añadido, *m*. **h.-trigger,** pelo de una pistola, *m*
hairbrush /ˈhɛərˌbrʌʃ/ *n* cepillo para el cabello, *m*
hairdresser /ˈhɛərˌdrɛsər/ *n* peluquero (-ra), peinadora, *f*
hairdressing /ˈhɛərˌdrɛsɪŋ/ *n* peinado, *m*. **h. establishment** or **trade,** peluquería, *f*
haired /hɛərd/ *a* peludo, con pelo; (in compounds) de pelo...
hairiness /ˈhɛərinɪs/ *n* vellosidad, *f*
hairless /ˈhɛərlɪs/ *a* sin pelo; calvo
hairlike /ˈhɛərˌlaik/ *a* filiforme
hairpin /ˈhɛərˌpɪn/ *n* horquilla, *f*. **h. bend,** viraje en horquilla, *m*
hairsbreadth /ˈhɛərzˌbrɛdθ/ *n* pelo, *m*. **to have a h. escape,** escapar por un pelo.
hairy /ˈhɛəri/ *a* peludo; velloso; *Bot.* hirsuto
Haiti /ˈheiti/ Haití, *m*
Haitian /ˈheiʃən/ *a* and *n* haitiano (-na)
hake /heik/ *n* merluza, *f*
halcyon /ˈhælsiən/ *n* alción, martín pescador, *m*. —*a Fig.* feliz, sereno, tranquilo
hale /heil/ *a* fuerte, sano, robusto. —*vt* hacer comparecer
half /hæf/ *n* mitad, *f*; (school term) trimestre, *m*. —*a* medio; semi. —*adv* a medias; mitad; (almost) casi; insuficientemente; imperfectamente. **I don't h. like it,** No me gusta nada. **It is h.-past two,** Son las dos y media. **an hour and a h.,** una hora y media. **better h.,** *Inf.* media naranja, cara mitad, *f*. **by halves,** a medias. **in h.,** en dos mitades. **one h.,** la mitad. **to go halves,** ir a medias. **to h. close,** entornar. **to h. open,** entreabrir. **h. a bottle,** media botella, *f*. **h. a crown,** media corona, *f*. **h.-alive,** semivivo. **h. an hour,** media hora, *f*. **h.-and-h.,** mitad y mitad; en partes iguales. **h.-asleep,** semidormido, medio dormido. **h.-awake,** medio despierto, entre duerme y vela. **h.-back,** *Sports.* medio, *m*. **h.-baked,** medio cocido, crudo; *Fig.* poco maduro. **h.-binding,** encuadernación en media pasta, *f*. **h.-breed,** *a* mestizo. —*n* cruce, *m*. **h.-brother,** hermanastro, hermano de padre, hermano de madre, *m*. **h.-caste,** mestizo. **h. circle,** semicírculo, *m*. **h.-closed,** entreabierto; medio cerrado. **h.-dead,** medio muerto; más muerto que vivo. **h.-done,** hecho a medias, sin acabar. **h.-dozen,** media docena, *f*. **h.-dressed,** medio desnudo. **h. fare,** medio billete, *m*. **h.-full,** medio lleno. **h.-hearted,** débil, poco eficaz, lánguido; indiferente, sin entusiasmo. **h.-heartedness,** debilidad, *f*; indiferencia, *f*. **h.-holiday,** media fiesta, *f*. **h.-hourly,** cada media hora. **h.-length,** (portrait) de medio cuerpo. **h.-length coat,** abrigo de tres cuartos, *m*. **h.-light,** media luz, *f*. **h.-mast,** a media asta. **h.-measure,** medida poco eficaz, *f*. **h.-moon,** *n* media luna, *f*; *Astron.* semilunio, *m*; (of a nail) blanco (de la uña), *m*. **h.-mourning,** medio luto, *m*. **h.-pay,** media paga, *f*. **h.-price,** a mitad de precio. **h.-seas-over,** *Inf.* entre dos velas. **h.-sister,** hermanastra, hermana de padre, hermana de madre, *f*. **h.-time,** *Sports.* media parte, *f*, medio tiempo, *m*. **h.-tone,** de medio tono. **h.-tone illustration,** fotograbado a media tinta, *m*. **h.-truth,** verdad a medias, *f*. **h.-turn,** media vuelta, *f*. **h.-way,** a medio camino; medio. **h.-witted,** medio loco, tonto, imbécil. **h.-year,** medio año, *m*. **h.-yearly,** semestral
halfpenny /ˈheipəni/ *n* medio penique, *m*; *Inf.* perra gorda, *f*
half title anteportada, falsa portada, portadilla, preportada, *f*
halibut /ˈhæləbət/ *n* halibut, *m*; (genus) hipogloso, *m*
halitosis /ˌhælɪˈtousɪs/ *n* halitosis, *f*
hall /hɔl/ *n* (mansion) mansión, casa de campo, *f*,

caserón, *m;* (public building) edificio, *m,* casa (de); (town h.) casa del ayuntamiento, *f;* (room) sala, *f;* (entrance) vestíbulo, *m;* (dining room) comedor, *m;* (of residence for students) residencia, *f.* **h. door,** portón, *m,* puerta del vestíbulo, *f.* **h. porter,** conserje, *m.* **h.-stand,** perchero, *m*

hallelujah /ˌhælə'luyə/ *n* aleluya, *f*

hallmark /'hɔlˌmɑrk/ *n* marca de ley, *f; Fig.* señal, *f;* indicio, *m.* —*vt* poner la marca de ley sobre; *Fig.* sellar

halloo /hə'lu/ *vt* (hounds) azuzar; perseguir dando voces; (call) llamar

hallow /'hælou/ *vt* santificar; reverenciar; (consecrate) consagrar

Halloween /ˌhælə'win/ *n* la víspera de Todos los Santos, *f*

hallucination /həˌlusə'neiʃən/ *n* alucinación, ilusión, *f;* visión, *f;* fantasma, *m*

hallucinatory /hə'lusənəˌtɔri/ *a* alucinador

halo /'heilou/ *n* halo, nimbo, *m*

halogen /'hælədʒən/ *n Chem.* halógeno, *m*

halt /hɔlt/ *n Mil.* alto, *m;* cesación, *f;* interrupción, *f;* (on a railway) apeadero, *m;* (for trams, buses) parada, *f.* —*vt* parar, detener. —*vi* pararse, detenerse; *Mil.* hacer alto; cesar; interrumpirse; (in speech) titubear; (of verse) estar cojo; (doubt) dudar; (limp) cojear. **H.!** *Mil.* ¡Alto!

halter /'hɔltər/ *n* ronzal, cabestro, *m;* (for hanging) dogal, *m.* —*vt* encabestrar, cabestrar

halting /'hɔltɪŋ/ *n* parada, *f;* interrupción, *f.* —*a* (of gait) cojo; incierto; vacilante; (of speech) titubeante

halve /hæv/ *vt* partir (or dividir) en dos mitades

ham /hæm/ *n* jamón, *m; Anat.* pernil, *m;* (radio-operator) radioaficionado, *m*

Hamburg /'hæmbɜrg/ Hamburgo, *m*

hamlet /'hæmlɪt/ *n* aldea, *f,* pueblecito, *m*

hammer /'hæmər/ *n* martillo, *m;* (stone cutter's) maceta, *f;* (mason's) piqueta, *f;* (of fire-arms) percusor, *m;* (of piano) macillo, *m.* —*vt* amartillar, martillar, batir. **to throw the h.,** lanzar el martillo. **under the h.,** en subasta, al remate. **h. blow,** martillazo, *m*

hammering /'hæmərɪŋ/ *n* martilleo, martillazo, *m.* **by h.,** a martillo

hammock /'hæmək/ *n* hamaca, *f; Naut.* coy, *m*

hamper /'hæmpər/ *n* banasta, canasta, *f,* cesto grande, *m.* —*vt* estorbar, dificultar, impedir; *Fig.* embarazar

hamster /'hæmstər/ *n Zool.* hámster, *m,* marmota de Alemania, rata del trigo, *f*

hand /hænd/ *n* mano, *f;* (of animal) pata, mano, *f;* (worker) operario (-ia); obrero (-ra); (skill) habilidad, *f;* (side) mano, *f,* lado, *m;* (measure) palmo, *m;* (of a clock) manecilla, *f;* (of instruments) aguja, *f;* (applause) aplauso, *m;* (power) poder, *m;* las manos; (at cards) mano, *f;* (card player) jugador, *m;* (signature) firma, *f;* (handwriting) letra, escritura, *f;* (influence) influencia, parte, mano, *f.* **old h.,** veterano; perro viejo. **at h.,** a mano, al lado, cerca. **have at hand,** tener a la mano. **at the hands of,** de manos de. **by h.,** a mano; (on the bottle) con biberón. **from h. to h.,** de mano a mano. **in h.,** entre manos; (of money) de contado. **in the hands of,** *Fig.* en el poder de. **"Hands wanted,"** «Se desean trabajadores.» **h. over h.,** mano sobre mano. **hand's breadth,** palmo, *m.* **Hands off!** ¡Fuera las manos! **Hands up!** ¡Manos arriba! **lost with all hands,** (of a ship) perdido con toda su tripulación. **off one's hands,** despachado; (of a daughter) casada. **on all hands,** por todas partes. **on h.,** entre manos; (of goods) existente; (present) presente. **on one's hands,** a cargo de uno. **on the one h.,** por un lado; a un lado. **on the other h.,** por otra parte; en cambio. **out of h.,** luego, inmediatamente; revoltoso. **to come to h.,** venir a mano; (of letters) llegar a las manos (de). **to get one's h. in,** ejercitarse. **to have a h. in,** tener parte en; intervenir en. **to have no h. in,** no tener arte ni parte en. **to have on h.,** traer entre manos. **to have the upper h.,** tener la sartén por el mango, llevar la ventaja. **to hold one's h.,** abstenerse; detenerse. **to hold hands,** cogerse de las manos. **to lay hands on,** tocar; poner mano en; echar manos a. **to set one's h. to,** emprender; (sign) firmar. **to shake hands,** estrechar la mano. **to stretch out one's hands,** tender las manos. **to take one's hands off,** no tocar. **with folded hands,** mano sobre mano. **with his hands behind his back,** con las manos en la espalda. **h.-in-h.,** cogidos (cogidas) de las manos. **h.-lever,** manija, *f.* **h.-loom,** telar de mano, *m.* **h. luggage,** equipaje de mano, *m.* **h.-made,** hecho a mano. **h.-mill,** molinillo, *m.* **h.-pump,** *n Naut.* sacabuche, *m.* **h. rail,** pasamano, *m,* baranda, balustrada, *f.* **h.-sewn,** cosido a mano. **h.-to-h.,** de mano en mano; (of a fight) a brazo partido, cuerpo a cuerpo. **h.-to-h. fight,** cachetina, *f.* **h.-to-mouth,** precario. **to live from h.-to-mouth,** vivir de día en día

hand /hænd/ *vt* dar; entregar; alargar. **to h. down,** bajar; (a person) ayudar a bajar; transmitir. **to h. in,** entregar; (a person) ayudar a entrar; (one's resignation) dimitir; (send) mandar, enviar. **to h. on,** transmitir. **to h. out,** *vt* distribuir; (a person) ayudar a salir; (from a vehicle) ayudar a bajar. —*vi Inf.* pagar. **to h. over,** *vt* entregar. —*vi Mil.* traspasar los poderes (a). **to h. round,** pasar de mano en mano; pasar; ofrecer. **to h. up,** subir; (a person) ayudar a subir

handbag /'hændˌbæg/ *n* bolso, saco, monedero, *m*

handbill /'hændˌbɪl/ *n* anuncio, *m*

handbook /'hændˌbʊk/ *n* manual, compendio, tratado, *m;* anuario, *m;* (guide) guía, *f*

handcart /'hændˌkɑrt/ *n* carretilla de mano, *f,* carretón, *m*

handcuff /'hændˌkʌf/ *n* esposa, *f,* grillo, *m,* (gen. —*pl*). —*vt* poner las esposas (a), maniatar

handed /'hændɪd/ *a* (in compounds) que tiene manos; de manos...; con las manos... **four-h.,** *Sports.* de cuatro personas. **one-h.,** manco

handful /'hændfʊl/ *n* puño, puñado, manojo, *m.* **to be a h.,** *Inf.* tener el diablo en el cuerpo. **in handfuls,** a manojos

handgrip /'hændˌgrɪp/ *n* apretón de manos, *m*

handicap /'hændiˌkæp/ *n* desventaja, *f;* obstáculo, *m; Sports.* handicap, *m;* ventaja, *f.* —*vt Fig.* perjudicar, impedir, dificultar. **the handicapped,** los lisiados, *m pl*

handicraft /'hændiˌkræft/ *n* mano de obra, *f;* (skill) destreza manual, *f,*

handiwork /'hændiˌwɜrk/ *n* mano de obra, *f;* trabajo manual, *m;* obra, *f;* (deed) acción, *f,* hecho, *m*

handkerchief /'hæŋkərtʃɪf/ *n* pañuelo, *m*

handle /'hændl̩/ *n* mango, puño, *m;* (lever) palanca, *f;* (of baskets, dishes, jugs) asa, *f;* (of doors, windows, drawers) pomo, *m,* (of a car door) picaporte *m;* (to one's name) designación, *f;* título, *m;* (excuse) pretexto, *m.* —*vt* (touch) tocar; manejar, manipular; (treat) tratar; **h. with kid gloves,** tratar con guantes de seda; (deal in) comerciar en; tomar; (paw) manosear; (direct) dirigir; (control) gobernar; (pilot) pilotar; (a theme) explicar, tratar de. **h.-bar,** manillar, *m.* **h.-bar grip,** puño de un manillar, *m*

handless /'hændlɪs/ *a* sin manos; manco; *Fig.* torpe

handling /'hændlɪŋ/ *n* manejo, *m;* manipulación, *f;* (treatment) trato, *m,* relaciones (con), *f pl;* (thumbing) manosco, *m;* interpretación, *f; Art.* tratamiento, *m,* técnica, *f*

handmaid /'hændˌmeid/ *n* sirvienta, criada, *f; Fig.* mayordomo, *m*

handsaw /'hændˌsɔ/ *n* sierra de mano, *f,* serrucho, *m*

handsbreadth /'hændzˌbrɛdθ/ *n* palmo, *m*

handshake /'hændˌʃeik/ *n* apretón de manos, *m*

handsome /'hænsəm/ *a* (generous) generoso; magnánimo; considerable; hermoso, bello; elegante; (of people) guapo, distinguido; excelente; (flattering) halagüeño. **He was a very h. man,** Era un hombre muy guapo

handsomely /'hænsəmli/ *adv* generosamente; con magnanimidad; elegantemente; bien

handsomeness /'hænsəmnɪs/ *n* generosidad, *f;* magnanimidad, *f;* hermosura, *f;* elegancia, *f;* distinción, *f*

handspring /'hændˌsprɪŋ/ *n* voltereta sobre las manos, *f*

handwork /'hændˌwɜrk/ *n* obra hecha a mano, *f,* trabajo a mano, *m;* (needlework) labor de aguja, *f*

handworked /'hændˌwɜrkt/ *a* hecho a mano; (embroidered) bordado

handwriting /'hændˌraitɪŋ/ *n* caligrafía, letra, escritura, *f.* **the h. on the wall,** la mano que escribía en la pared, *f*

handy /'hændi/ *a* (of persons) diestro, mañoso, hábil; (of things) conveniente; útil; (near) cercano, a mano. —*adv* cerca. **h.-man,** hombre de muchos oficios, *m;* factótum, *m*

hang /hæŋ/ *vt* colgar; suspender; (execute) ahorcar; (the head) bajar; dejar caer; (upholster) entapizar; (with wallpaper) empapelar; (drape) poner colgaduras en; (place) poner; (cover) cubrir. —*vi* colgar, pender; estar suspendido; (be executed) ser ahorcado; (of garments) caer. —*n* (of garments) caída, *f;* (of a machine) mecanismo, *m;* (meaning) sentido, *m,* significación, *f.* **to h. by a thread,** pender de un hilo. **to h. in the balance,** estar en la balanza. **to h. fire,** estar (una cosa) en suspenso. **to h. loose,** caer suelto; (clothes) venir ancho. **to h. about,** (surround) rodear, pegarse a; (frequent) frecuentar; (haunt) rondar; (be imminent) ser inminente, amenazar; (embrace) abrazar. **to h. back,** retroceder; quedarse atrás; *Fig.* vacilar, titubear. **to h. down,** colgar, pender; estar caído; caerse. **to h. on,** seguir agarrado (a); apoyarse en; *Fig.* persistir; (a person's words) estar pendiente de, beber; (remain) quedarse. **to h. out,** *vt* tender. —*vi* (lean out) asomarse (por); (*Inf.* live) habitar. **to h. over,** colgar por encima; (brood) cernerse sobre; (lean over) inclinarse sobre; quedarse cerca de; (overhang) sobresalir; (overarch) abovedar; (threaten) amenazar. **to h. together,** (of persons) permanecer unidos; (of things) tener cohesión; (be consistent) ser lógico, ser consistente. **to h. up,** colgar; suspender; *Fig.* dejar pendiente, interrumpir. **to h. upon,** apoyarse en; (a person's words) beber las palabras de uno

hangar /'hæŋər/ *n* cobertizo; *Aer.* hangar, *m*

hanger /'hæŋər/ *n* colgadero, *m;* percha *f.* **h.-on,** parásito, *m;* dependiente, *m*

hanging /'hæŋıŋ/ *n* colgamiento, *m;* (killing) ahorcamiento, *m; pl* **hangings,** colgaduras, *f pl,* cortinajes, *m pl.* —*a* pendiente colgante; péndulo; (of gardens) pensil. **It's not a h. matter,** No es una cuestión de vida y muerte. **h. bridge,** puente colgante, *m.* **h. committee,** junta (de una exposición,) *f.* **h. lamp,** lámpara de techo, *f*

hangman /'hæŋmən/ *n* verdugo, *m*

hangnail /'hæŋˌneil/ *n* padrastro, *m*

hangover /'hæŋˌouvər/ *n* (after drinking) resaca, cruda (Mexico), *f*

hank /hæŋk/ *n* madeja, *f*

hanker /'hæŋkər/ *vi* (with after) ansiar, ambicionar; (with for) anhelar, suspirar por, desear con vehemencia

hankering /'hæŋkərıŋ/ *n* ambición, *f;* deseo vehemente, *m*

hanky-panky /'hæŋki 'pæŋki/ *n* superchería, *f;* engaño, *m*

hap /hæp/ *n* casualidad, suerte, *f;* suceso fortuito, *m*

haphazard /*n* 'hæpˌhæzərd; *a* hæp'hæzərd/ *n* casualidad, *f.* —*a* fortuito, casual

hapless /'hæplıs/ *a* desgraciado, desdichado

haplessness /'hæplısnıs/ *n* desgracia, desdicha, *f*

happen /'hæpən/ *vi* suceder, acontecer, ocurrir, pasar; (to be found, be) hallarse por casualidad; (take place) tener lugar, verificarse; (arise) sobrevenir. **Do you know what has happened to...?** ¿Sabes qué se ha hecho de...? **as if nothing had happened,** como si no hubiese pasado nada. **He turned up as if nothing had happened,** Se presentó como si tal cosa. **How did it h.?** ¿Cómo fue esto? **If they h. to see you,** Si acaso te vean. **I happened to be in London,** Me hallaba por casualidad en Londres. **It won't h. again,** No volverá a suceder. **whatever happens,** venga lo que venga

happening /'hæpənıŋ/ *n* suceso, acontecimiento, hecho, *m,* ocurrencia, *f*

happily /'hæpəli/ *adv* felizmente; por suerte

happiness /'hæpinıs/ *n* felicidad, dicha, *f;* alegría, *f,* regocijo, *m*

happy /'hæpi/ *a* (lucky) afortunado; (felicitous) feliz, oportuno; feliz, dichoso; alegre, regocijado. **to be h.,** estar contento, ser feliz. **to be h. about,** alegrarse de. **to make h.,** hacer feliz, alegrar. **h.-go-lucky,** irresponsable, descuidado

harangue /hə'ræŋ/ *n* arenga, *f.* —*vt* arengar. —*vi* pronunciar una arenga

harass /hə'ræs/ *vt* hostigar, acosar; atormentar; preocupar; *Mil.* picar. **to h. the rear-guard,** picar la retaguardia

harbinger /'hɑrbındʒər/ *n Fig.* precursor, heraldo, *m;* presagio, anuncio, *m.* —*vt* anunciar, presagiar

harbor /'hɑrbər/ *n* puerto, *m;* (bay) bahía, *f;* (haven) asilo, refugio, *m.* —*vt* dar refugio (a), albergar, acoger; (cherish) abrigar, acariciar; (conceal) esconder. **inner h.,** puerto, *m.* **outer h.,** rada del puerto, *f.* **to put into h.,** entrar en el puerto. **h. bar,** barra del puerto, *f.* **h.-dues,** derechos de puerto, *m pl.* **h.-master,** capitán de puerto, contramaestre de puerto, *m*

harborer /'hɑrbərər/ *n* amparador (-ra), protector (-ra); (criminal) encubridor (-ra)

hard /hɑrd/ *a* duro; (firm) firme; difícil; laborioso, agotador; violento; poderoso; arduo; fuerte, recio; vigoroso, robusto; insensible, inflexible; cruel; (of weather) inclemente, severo; (unjust) injusto, opresivo; (stiff) tieso; (of water) cruda; (of wood) brava. —*adv* duro; duramente; con ahínco; con fuerza; de firme; difícilmente; (of gazing) fijamente; severamente; (firmly) firmemente; vigorosamente; (of raining) a cántaros, mucho; (quickly) rápidamente; excesivamente; (much) mucho; (of bearing misfortune) a pechos; (attentively) atentamente; (heavily) pesadamente; (badly) mal; (closely) de cerca, inmediatamente. **It was a h. blow,** Fue un golpe recio. **to be h. put to,** encontrar difícil. **to go h.,** endurecerse. **to go h. with,** irle mal a uno. **to have a h. time,** pasar apuros, pasarlo mal. **to look h. at,** mirar atentamente, examinar detenidamente; mirar fijamente. **to be a h. drinker,** ser un bebedor empedernido. **h. and fast rule,** regla inalterable, *f.* **h.-bitten,** de carácter duro. **a h.-boiled egg,** un huevo duro. **h. breathing,** resuello, *m.* **h. by,** muy cerca. **h. cash,** efectivo, *m.* **h.-earned,** difícilmente conseguido; ganado con el sudor de la frente. **h.-featured,** de facciones duras. **h.-fisted,** tacaño. **h.-fought,** arduo, reñido. **h.-headed,** práctico, perspicaz. **h.-hearted,** duro de corazón, insensible. **h.-heartedness,** insensibilidad, *f.* **h. labor,** *Law.* trabajos forzados, *m pl,* presidio, *m.* **h.-mouthed,** (of horses) boquiduro. **h. of hearing,** duro de oído. **h.-up,** apurado. **to be very h.-up,** ser muy pobre; *Inf.* estar a la cuarta pregunta. **h.-wearing,** duradero; sufrido. **h.-won,** See **h.-earned. h.-working,** trabajador, hacendoso, diligente

harden /'hɑrdn̩/ *vt* endurecer; (metal) templar; robustecer; (to war) aguerrir; (make callous) hacer insensible. —*vi* endurecerse; hacerse duro; templarse; robustecerse; (of shares) entonarse

hardening /'hɑrdn̩ıŋ/ *n* endurecimiento, *m;* (of metal) temple, *m.* **h. of the arteries,** arteriosclerosis, *f*

hardiness /'hɑrdinıs/ *n* vigor, *m,* fuerza, robustez, *f;* audacia, *f*

hardly /'hɑrdli/ *adv* duramente; difícilmente; (badly) mal; severamente; (scarcely) apenas, casi. **h. ever,** casi nunca

hardness /'hɑrdnıs/ *n* dureza, *f;* severidad, *f;* inhumanidad, insensibilidad, *f;* (stiffness) tiesura, *f;* (difficulty) dificultad, *f;* (of water) crudeza, *f;* (of hearing) dureza de oído, *f*

hardship /'hɑrdʃıp/ *n* penas, *f pl,* trabajos, *m pl;* infortunio, *m,* desdicha, *f;* (suffering) sufrimiento, *m;* (affliction) aflicción, *f;* (privation) privación, *f.* **to undergo h.,** pasar trabajos

hardware /'hɑrdˌwɛər/ *n* ferretería, *f*

hardwood /'hɑrdˌwʊd/ *n* madera brava, *f*

hardy /'hɑrdi/ *a* audaz, intrépido; (strong) fuerte, robusto; *Bot.* resistente

hare /hɛər/ *n* liebre, *f.* **young h.,** lebrato, *m.* **h. and hounds,** rally paper, *m,* caza de papelitos, *f.* **h.-brained,** casquivano, atronado, con cabeza de chorlito. **hare's foot,** mano de gato, *f.* **h.-lip,** labio leporino, *m.* **h.-lipped,** labihendido

harebell /'hɛərˌbɛl/ *n* campanilla, campánula, *f*

harem /'hɛərəm/ *n* harén, serrallo, *m*

haricot /ˈhærəˌkou/ *n* (green bean) judía, *f;* (dried bean) alubia, *f*

hark /hɑrk/ *vt* escuchar; oír. **to h. back,** volver al punto de partida; volver a la misma canción

harlequin /ˈhɑrləkwɪn/ *n* arlequín, *m*

harlequinade /ˌhɑrləkwɪˈneid/ *n* arlequinada, *f*

harlot /ˈhɑrlət/ *n* ramera, prostituta, meretriz, *f*

harlotry /ˈhɑrlətri/ *n* prostitución, *f*

harm /hɑrm/ *n* mal, *m;* daño, *m;* perjuicio, *m;* (danger) peligro, *m;* (detriment) menoscabo, *m;* (misfortune) desgracia, *f, vt* hacer mal (a); dañar, hacer daño (a); perjudicar. **And there's no h. in that,** Y en eso no hay mal. **to keep out of harm's way,** evitar el peligro; guardarse del mal

harmful /ˈhɑrmfəl/ *a* malo; dañino, perjudicial, nocivo; (dangerous) peligroso. **to be h.,** (of food, etc.) hacer mal (a); (of pests) ser dañino; (of behavior, etc.) perjudicar

harmfulness /ˈhɑrmfəlnɪs/ *n* lo malo; perniciosidad, *f;* daño, *m;* peligro, *m*

harmless /ˈhɑrmlɪs/ *a* innocuo; inofensivo; inocente

harmlessness /ˈhɑrmlɪsnɪs/ *n* innocuidad, *f;* inocencia, *f*

harmonic /hɑrˈmɒnɪk/ *n* (*Phys. Math.*) harmónica, *f; Mus.* armonico, *m, a Mus.* armónico

harmonica /hɑrˈmɒnɪkə/ *n* armónica, *f*

harmonics /hɑrˈmɒnɪks/ *n* armonía, *f;* (tones) armónicos, *m pl*

harmonious /hɑrˈmouniəs/ *a* armonioso

harmoniously /hɑrˈmouniəsli/ *adv* armoniosamente; *Fig.* en armonía

harmoniousness /hɑrˈmouniəsnɪs/ *n* armonía, *f*

harmonium /hɑrˈmouniəm/ *n* armonio, *m*

harmonization /ˌhɑrmənɪˈzeiʃən/ *n* armonización, *f*

harmonize /ˈhɑrməˌnaiz/ *vt* armonizar. *—vi* armonizarse, estar en armonía

harmony /ˈhɑrməni/ *n* armonía, *f; Fig.* paz, *f,* buenas relaciones, *f pl;* música, *f.* **to live in h.,** vivir en paz

harness /ˈhɑrnɪs/ *n* guarniciones, *f pl,* jaeces, *m pl;* (armor) arnés, *m.* *—vt* enjaezar; (yoke) enganchar; (water) represar. **to die in h.,** *Fig.* morir en la brecha. **h. maker,** guarnicionero, *m.* **h. room,** guadarnés, *m*

harp /hɑrp/ *n* arpa, *f.* **to h. on,** volver a la misma canción, volver a repetir

harpist /ˈhɑrpɪst/ *n* arpista, *mf*

harpoon /hɑrˈpun/ *n* arpón, *m.* *—vt* arponear

harpooner /hɑrˈpunər/ *n* arponero, *m*

harpsichord /ˈhɑrpsɪˌkɔrd/ *n* arpicordio, *m*

harpy /ˈhɑrpi/ *n* arpía, *f*

harridan /ˈhærədn̩/ *n* bruja, *f*

harrow /ˈhærou/ *n Agr.* rastra, *f,* escarificador, *m.* *—vt Agr.* escarificar; *Fig.* lastimar, atormentar

harrowing /ˈhærouɪŋ/ *a* patibulario, conmovedor, atormentador, angustioso

harry /ˈhæri/ *vt* devastar, asolar; (persons) robar; perseguir; (worry) atormentar; (annoy) molestar

harsh /hɑrʃ/ *a* áspero; (of voice) ronco; (of sound) discordante; (of colors) áspero; duro; chillón; severo, duro; (of features) duro; (of taste) ácido, acerbo

harshly /ˈhɑrʃli/ *adv* severamente

harshness /ˈhɑrʃnɪs/ *n* (roughness) aspereza, *f;* (of voice) ronquedad, aspereza, *f;* (of sound) disonancia, *f;* (of colors) aspereza, *f;* severidad, *f;* dureza, *f;* (of taste) acidez, *f*

hart /hɑrt/ *n* ciervo, *m*

harum-scarum /ˈhɛərəm ˈskɛərəm/ *n* tronera, saltabarrancos, *mf* molino, *m, a* irresponsable

harvest /ˈhɑrvɪst/ *n* cosecha, siega, *f;* recolección, *f; Fig.* producto, fruto, *m.* *—vt* cosechar; recoger. **h. festival,** fiesta de la cosecha, *f*

harvester /ˈhɑrvəstər/ *n* segador, *m,* cosechero (-ra); (machine) segadora, *f*

hash /hæʃ/ *n Cul.* picado, *m.* *—vt Cul.* picar

hashish /ˈhæʃiʃ/ *n* hachich, hachís, quif, *m*

hasp /hæsp/ *n* pasador, *m;* sujetador, *m*

hassock /ˈhæsək/ *n* cojín, *m*

haste /heist/ *n* prisa, rapidez, *f;* precipitación, *f;* urgencia, *f.* *—vt* dar prisa (a); acelerar; precipitar. *—vi* darse prisa; acelerarse; precipitarse. **in h.,** de prisa, aprisa. **to be in h.,** estar de prisa, llevar prisa. **in great h.,** muy aprisa, aprisa y corriendo, precipitadamente; con mucha prisa. **More h. less speed,** (Spanish equivalent. Words said by Charles III of Spain to his valet) ¡Vísteme despacio que voy de prisa!

hasten /ˈheisən/ *vt* acelerar, apresurar; precipitar. *—vi* darse prisa, apresurarse; moverse con rapidez; correr. **to h. one's steps,** apretar el paso. **to h. away,** marcharse rápidamente. **to h. back,** regresar apresuradamente. **to h. down,** bajar rápidamente. **to h. on,** seguir el camino sin descansar; seguir rápidamente. **to h. out,** salir rápidamente. **to h. towards,** ir rápidamente hacia; correr hacia. **to h. up,** subir aprisa, correr hacia arriba; darse prisa

hastily /ˈheistl̩i/ *adv* de prisa, rápidamente; con precipitación, precipitadamente; (angrily) impacientemente, airadamente; (thoughtlessly) sin reflexión

hastiness /ˈheistinɪs/ *n* rapidez, *f;* precipitación, *f;* (anger) impaciencia, irritación, *f*

hasty /ˈheisti/ *a* rápido, apresurado; precipitado; (superficial) superficial, ligero; (ill-considered) desconsiderado, imprudente; (angry) impaciente, irritable; violento, apasionado

hat /hæt/ *n* sombrero, *m.* **to pass round the h.,** pasar el platillo. **Andalusian h.,** sombrero calañés, *m.* **bowler h.,** sombrero hongo, *m.* **broad brimmed h.,** sombrero chambergo, *m.* **Panama h.,** sombrero de jipijapa, *m.* **picture h.,** pamela, *f.* **shovel h.,** sombrero de teja, *m.* **soft felt h.,** sombrero flexible, *m.* **straw h.,** sombrero de paja, *m.* **three-cornered h.,** sombrero de tres picos, *m.* **top-h.,** sombrero de copa, *m.* **h. shop** or **trade,** sombrerería, *f*

hatband /ˈhætˌbænd/ *n* cinta de sombrero, *f,* cintillo, *m*

hatblock /ˈhætˌblɒk/ *n* formillón, *f*

hatbox /ˈhætˌbɒks/ *n* sombrerera, *f*

hatbrush /ˈhætˌbrʌʃ/ *n* cepillo para sombreros, *m*

hatch /hætʃ/ *n* (wicket) compuerta, *f;* (trap-door) puerta caediza, *f; Naut.* escotilla, *f;* compuerta de esclusa, *f;* (of chickens) pollada, *f;* (of birds) nidada, *f.* *—vt* (birds) empollar; incubar, encobar; *Fig.* tramar, urdir. *—vi* empollarse, salir del cascarón; incubarse; *Fig.* madurarse. **to h. a plot,** urdir un complot, conspirar. **to h. chickens,** sacar pollos

hatchet /ˈhætʃɪt/ *n* hacha pequeña, *f,* machado, *m.* **to bury the h.,** hacer la paz. **h.-faced,** de cara de cuchillo

hatching /ˈhætʃɪŋ/ *n* incubación, *f;* (of a plot) maquinación, *f*

hatchway /ˈhætʃˌwei/ *n Naut.* escotilla, *f*

hate /heit/ *n* odio, aborrecimiento, *m,* aversión, *f;* abominación, *f.* *—vt* odiar, aborrecer, detestar; repugnar; saber mal, sentir. **I h. to trouble you,** Me sabe mal molestarle, Siento mucho molestarle. **to h. the sight of,** *Inf.* no poder ver (a)

hateful /ˈheitfəl/ *a* odioso, aborrecible; repugnante

hatefulness /ˈheitfəlnɪs/ *n* odiosidad, *f,* lo odioso; maldad, *f*

hater /ˈheitər/ *n* aborrecedor (-ra). **to be a good h.,** saber odiar

hatful /ˈhætfəl/ *n* un sombrero lleno (de)

hatless /ˈhætlɪs/ *a* sin sombrero, descubierto

hatpin /ˈhætˌpɪn/ *n* horquilla de sombrero, *f*

hatred /ˈheitrɪd/ *n* odio, aborrecimiento, *m,* detestación, *f;* aversión, enemistad, *f*

hatstand /ˈhætˌstænd/ *n* perchera, *f*

hatter /ˈhætər/ *n* sombrerero, *m.* **as mad as a h.,** loco como una cabra

haughtiness /ˈhɔtinɪs/ *n* altanería, arrogancia, altivez, soberbia, *f,* orgullo, *m*

haughty /ˈhɔti/ *a* altanero, arrogante, altivo, orgulloso

haul /hɔl/ *n* (pull) tirón, *m;* (of fish) redada, *f;* (booty) botín, *m.* *—vt* arrastrar, tirar de; *Naut.* halar. **to h. at, upon,** (ropes, etc.) aflojar, soltar, arriar. **to h. down,** (flags, sails) arriar

haulage /ˈhɔlɪdʒ/ *n* transporte, acarreo, *m;* coste de transporte, *m.* **h. contractor,** contratista de transporte, *m*

haunch /hɔntʃ/ *n* anca, culata, *f;* (of meat) pierna, *f.* **h.-bone,** hueso ilíaco, *m*

haunt /hɔnt/ *n* punto de reunión, lugar frecuentado (por), *m;* (lair) cubil, nido, *m,* guarida, *f.* *—vt* frecuentar; rondar; (of ideas) perseguir; (of ghosts) aparecer, visitar. **It is a h. of thieves,** Es una cueva de ladrones

haunted /ˈhɔntɪd/ *a* (by spirits) encantado

haunter /ˈhɔntər/ *n* frecuentador (-ra); (ghost) fantasma, espectro, *m*

haunting /ˈhɔntɪŋ/ *n* frecuentación, *f;* aparición de un espectro, *f.* —*a* persistente

hautboy /ˈhoubɔi, ˈoubɔi/ *n* oboe, *m*

hauteur /houˈtɜr/ *n* altivez, *f*

Havana /həˈvænə/ la Habana, *f.* —*n* (cigar) habano, *m.* (native) habanero (-ra), habano (-na)

have /hæv; *unstressed* həv, əv/ *vt* tener; poseer; (suffer) padecer; (spend) pasar; (eat or drink) tomar; (eat) comer; (a cigarette) fumar; (a bath, etc.) tomar; (a walk, a ride) dar; (cause to be done) mandar (hacer), hacer (hacer); (deceive) engañar; (defeat) vencer; (catch) coger; (say) decir; (allow) permitir; (tolerate) tolerar, sufrir; (obtain) lograr, conseguir; (wish) querer; (know) saber; (realize) realizar; (buy) comprar; (acquire) adquirir. As an auxiliary verb, haber (e.g. *I h. done it,* Lo he hecho, etc.). **As fate would h. it,** Según quiso la suerte. **Do you h. to go?** ¿Tiene Vd. que marcharse? **H. him come here,** Hazle venir aquí. **I h. been had,** Me han engañado. **I h. a good mind to...,** Tengo ganas de... **I had all my books stolen,** Me robaron todos los libros. **You had better go,** Es mejor que te vayas. **I had rather,** Preferiría, Me gustaría más bien. **I h. had a suit made,** Mandé hacerme un traje, Hice hacerme un traje. **I would not h. had it otherwise,** No lo hubiese querido de otra manera. **I will not h. it,** No lo quiero; No quiero tomarlo; (object) No lo permitiré. **If we had known,** Si lo hubiésemos sabido. **It has to do with the sun,** Está relacionado con el sol, Tiene que ver con el sol. **Have a good trip!** ¡Buen viaje!, ¡Feliz viaje! **What are you going to h.?** ¿Qué quiere Vd. tomar? **Will you h. some jam?** ¿Quiere Vd. mermelada? **to h. breakfast,** desayunar. **to h. dinner, supper,** cenar. **to h. lunch,** almorzar. **to h. for tea,** invitar a tomar el té; (of food) merendar. **to h. tea,** tomar el té. **to h. it out with,** habérselas con. **to h. just,** acabar de. **I h. just done it,** Acabo de hacerlo. **to h. on hand,** traer entre manos. **to h. one's eye on,** no perder de vista (a), vigilar. **to h. one's tail between one's legs,** ir rabo entre piernas. **to h. to,** tener que; deber. **It has to be so,** Tiene que ser así. **to h. too much of,** sobrar, tener demasiado de. **He has too much time,** Le sobra tiempo. **to h. about one,** tener (or llevar) consigo. **to h. back,** aceptar; recibir. **to h. down,** hacer bajar. **She had her hair down,** El pelo le caía por las espaldas. **to h. in,** hacer entrar. **to h. on,** vestir, llevar puesto; (engagements) tener (compromisos). **to h. out,** hacer salir; llevar a paseo; llevar fuera; (have removed) hacerse sacar; quitar. **to h. up,** (persons) hacer subir; (things) subir; *Law.* llevar a (ante) los tribunales. **to h. with one,** tener consigo. **I h. her with me,** La tengo conmigo, Ella me acompaña

haven /ˈheivən/ *n* puerto, *m,* abra, *f; Fig.* oasis, abrigo, refugio, *m*

haversack /ˈhævərˌsæk/ *n* mochila, *f,* morral, *m*

havoc /ˈhævək/ *n* destrucción, ruina, *f; Fig.* estrago, *m.* **to wreak h. among,** destruir; *Fig.* hacer estragos entre (or en)

Hawaii /həˈwaii/ Hawai, *m*

Hawaiian /həˈwaiən/ *a* and *n* hawaiano; *n* (language) hawaiano, *m*

hawk /hɔk/ *n* halcón, *m;* gavilán, milano, *m.* —*vi* cazar con halcón. —*vt* vender mercancías por las calles; *Fig.* difundir. **h.-eyed,** de ojos de lince. **h.-nosed,** de nariz aguileña

hawker /ˈhɔkər/ *n* halconero, *m;* (vendor) buhonero, *m,* vendedor (-ra) ambulante

hawking /ˈhɔkɪŋ/ *n* caza con halcones, cetrería, *f;* (expectorating) gargajeo, *m;* (selling) buhonería, *f*

hawser /ˈhɔzər/ *n* maroma, *f,* calabrote, *m*

hawthorn /ˈhɔˌθɔrn/ *n* espino, *m.* **white h.,** espino blanco, *m*

hay /hei/ *n* heno, *m.* **to make hay while the sun shines,** hacer su agosto. **hay fever,** fiebre del heno, *f.* **hay-fork,** horca, *f*

hayloft /ˈheiˌlɔft/ *n* henil, *m*

haymaker /ˈheiˌmeikər/ *n* segador (-ra); (machine) segadora, *f*

haymaking /ˈheiˌmeikɪŋ/ *n* recolección del heno, *f*

haystack /ˈheiˌstæk/ *n* almiar, *m,* niara, *f*

hazard /ˈhæzərd/ *n* azar, *m,* suerte, *f;* riesgo, peligro, *m;* (game) juego de azar, *m.* —*vt* arriesgar, aventurar. **at all hazards,** a todo riesgo

hazardous /ˈhæzərdəs/ *a* azaroso, arriesgado, peligroso

haze /heiz/ *n* bruma, *f;* confusión, *f*

hazel /ˈheizəl/ *n* avellano, *m.* **h.-nut,** avellana, *f*

hazy /ˈheizi/ *a* brumoso, calinoso; confuso

he /hi/ *pers pron* él. —*n* (of humans) varón, *m;* (of animals) macho, *m.* **he who,** el que, quien. **he-goat,** macho cabrío, *m.* **he-man,** todo un hombre, hombre cabal, *m*

head /hɛd/ *vt* golpear con la cabeza; encabezar; (lead) capitanear; (direct) dirigir, guiar; (wine) cabecear. —*vi* estar a la cabeza de; dirigirse a. **headed for,** con rumbo a, en dirección a. **to h. off,** interceptar; desviar; *Fig.* distraer

head /hɛd/ *n Anat.* cabeza, *f;* (upper portion) parte superior, *f;* (of a coin) cara, *f;* (hair) cabellera, *f;* (individual) persona, *f;* (of cattle) res, *f;* (of a mountain) cumbre, *f;* (of a ladder) último peldaño, *m;* (of toadstools) sombrero, *m;* (of trees) copa, *f;* (of a stick) puño, *m;* (of a cylinder) culata, *f;* (of a river, etc.) manantial, origen, *m;* (of a bed) cabecera, *f;* (of nails, pins) cabeza, *f;* (froth) espuma, *f;* (flower) flor, *f;* (leaves) hojas, *f pl;* (first place) primer puesto, *m;* (of game, fish) pieza, *f;* (of a page, column) cabeza, *f;* (cape) cabo, *m;* (of an arrow, dart, lance) punta, *f;* (front) frente, *m;* (leader) jefe, cabeza, *m;* (chief) director (-ra), superior (-ra); presidente (-ta); (of a school) director (-ra); (of a cask) fondo, *m; Mech.* cabezal, *m;* (of an ax) filo, *m;* (of a bridge) cabeza, *f;* (of a jetty, pier) punta, *f;* (of a ship) proa, *f;* (of a flower) cabezuela, *f;* (of asparagus) punta, *f;* (of a table) cabeza, *f;* (of the family) jefe, cabeza, *m;* (seat of honor) cabecera, *f;* (title) título, *m;* (aspect) punto de vista, *m;* (division) capítulo, *m;* (management, direction) dirección, *f;* (talent) talento, *m,* cabeza, *f;* (intelligence) inteligencia, *f.* —*a* principal; primero; en jefe. **at the h. of,** a la cabeza de. **crowned h.,** testa coronada, *f.* **from h. to foot,** de pies a cabeza; de hito en hito; de arriba abajo. **He took it into his h. to...,** Se le ocurrió de... **This story has neither h. nor tail,** Este cuento no tiene pies ni cabeza. **with h. held high,** con la frente levantada. **to come to a h.,** llegar a la crisis; llegar al punto decisivo. **to get an idea out of a person's h.,** quitar una idea a uno de la cabeza. **to keep one's h.,** *Fig.* conservar la sangre fría, no perder la cabeza. **to lose one's h.,** *Fig.* perder la cabeza. **to put into a person's h.,** *Fig.* meter (a uno) en la cabeza. **to run one's h. against,** golpear la cabeza contra. **h. first,** de cabeza. **h. of cattle,** res, *f.* **h. office,** central, *f.* **h. of hair,** cabellera, *f;* mata de pelo, *f.* **h.-on,** de cabeza. **h.-on collision,** choque de frente, *m.* **h. opening,** (of a garment) cabezón, *m.* **heads or tails,** cara o cruz, águila o sol (Mexico). **h. over heels,** de patas arriba. **h. over heels in love,** calado hasta los huesos. **h.-dress,** tocado, *m;* peinado, *m;* sombrero, *m.* **h. voice,** voz de cabeza, *f.* **h. waiter,** encargado de comedor, jefe de camareros, *m*

headache /ˈhɛdˌeik/ *n* dolor de cabeza, *m; Fig.* quebradero de cabeza, *m*

headboard /ˈhɛdˌbɔrd/ *n* cabecera de una cama, *f*

headed /ˈhɛdɪd/ *a* con cabeza...; que tiene la cabeza...; de cabeza...; (of an article) intitulado. **large h.,** cabezudo

header /ˈhɛdər/ *n* caída de cabeza, *f;* salto de cabeza, *m*

headgear /ˈhɛdˌgɪər/ *n* tocado, *m;* sombrero, gorro, *m*

head-hunting /ˈhɛdˌhʌntɪŋ/ *n* la caza de cabezas, *f*

heading /ˈhɛdɪŋ/ *n Naut.* el poner la proa en dirección (a); el guiar en dirección (a); (of a book, etc.) título, encabezamiento, *m;* (soccer) golpe de cabeza, *m.* **to come under the h. of,** estar incluido entre; clasificarse bajo

headland /ˈhɛdlənd/ *n* cabo, promontorio, *m*
headless /ˈhɛdlɪs/ *a* sin cabeza
headlight /ˈhɛdˌlait/ *n Auto.* faro, *m;* (*Rail. Naut.*) farol, *m.* **to dip the headlights,** bajar los faros. **to switch on the headlights,** encender los faros (or los faroles)
headline /ˈhɛdˌlain/ *n* (of a newspaper) titular, *m;* (to a chapter) título de la columna, *m*
headlong /ˈhɛdˌlɔŋ/ *a* precipitado; despeñado. —*adv* de cabeza; precipitadamente. **to fall h.,** caer de cabeza
headman /ˈhɛdˈmæn/ *n* cacique, cabecilla, *m;* (foreman) capataz, contramaestre, *m*
headmaster /ˈhɛdˈmæstər/ *n* director de colegio, rector, *m*
headmistress /ˈhɛdˈmɪstrɪs/ *n* directora de colegio, rectora, *f*
head nurse enfermero-jefe, *m*
head-on collision /ˈhɛd ˌɒn/ *n* choque frontal, *m*
headphones /ˈhɛdˌfounz/ *n pl* auriculares, *m pl*
headquarters /ˈhɛdˌkwɔrtərz/ *n Mil.* cuartel general, *m;* oficina central, *f;* jefatura, *f;* centro, *m*
headrest /ˈhɛdˌrɛst/ *n* respaldo, *m;* apoyo para la cabeza, *m*
headstone /ˈhɛdˌstoun/ *n* piedra mortuoria, *f*
headstrong /ˈhɛdˌstrɔŋ/ *a* impetuoso, terco, testarudo
headway /ˈhɛdˌwei/ *n* marcha, *f; Fig.* progreso, avance, *m.* **to make h.,** avanzar; *Fig.* hacer progresos; *Fig.* prosperar
headwind /ˈhɛdˌwɪnd/ *n* viento en contra, *m*
heady /ˈhɛdi/ *a* apasionado, violento; impetuoso, precipitado; (obstinate) terco; (of alcohol) encabezado; *Fig.* embriagador
heal /hil/ *vt* curar, sanar; (flesh) cicatrizar. —*vi* curar, sanar; cicatrizarse; (superficially) sobresanar
healable /ˈhiləbəl/ *a* curable
healer /ˈhilər/ *n* sanador (-ra), curador (-ra); curandero, *m*
healing /ˈhilɪŋ/ *a* curador, sanador; médico. —*n* curación, *f;* cura, *f,* remedio, *m*
health /hɛlθ/ *n* salud, *f;* higiene, sanidad, *f.* **Here's to your very good h.!** ¡Salud y pesetas! **He is in good h.,** Disfruta de buena salud. **to drink a person's h.,** beber a la salud de. **to enjoy good h.,** gozar de buena salud. **to look full of h.,** vender salud. **h.-giving,** saludable. **h. inspection,** visita de sanidad, *f.* **h. officer,** inspector de sanidad, *m.* **h. resort,** balneario, *m*
healthiness /ˈhɛlθinɪs/ *n* buena salud, *f;* sanidad, salubridad, *f*
healthy /ˈhɛlθi/ *a* sano; con buena salud; (healthful) saludable. **to be h.,** tener buena salud
heap /hip/ *n* montón, *m;* rima, pila, *f,* acervo, *m;* (of people) muchedumbre, *f,* tropel, *m.* —*vt* amontonar; apilar; colmar. **in heaps,** a montones. **We have heaps of time,** Nos sobra tiempo, Tenemos tiempo de sobra. **to h. together,** juntar, mezclar. **to h. up, upon,** colmar; amontonar; *Agr.* hacinar; *Fig.* acumular
hear /hɪər/ *vt* oír; (listen) escuchar; (attend) asistir a; (give audience) dar audiencia (a); (a lawsuit) ver (un pleito); (speak) hablar; (be aware of, feel) sentir. —*vi* oír; tener noticias; (learn) enterarse de; (allow) permitir. **H.! H.!** ¡Muy bien! ¡Bravo! **I have heard it said that...** He oído decir que... **Let me h. from you!** ¡Mándame noticias tuyas! **They were never heard of again,** No se volvió a saber de ellos, No se supo más de ellos. **to h. about,** oír de; (know) saber de, tener noticias de; recibir información sobre. **to h. from,** ser informado por; tener noticias de: recibir carta de. **to h. of,** enterarse de, saber; recibir información sobre; (allow) permitir
hearer /ˈhɪərər/ *n* oyente, *mf*
hearing /ˈhɪərɪŋ/ *n* (sense of) oído, *m;* alcance del oído, *m;* presencia, *f;* audición, *f; Law.* vista (de una causa) *f.* **It was said in my h.,** Fue dicho en mi presencia. **out of h.,** fuera del alcance del oído. **within h.,** al alcance del oído. **have a h. problem,** ser parcialmente sordo
hearing aid acústica, aparato auditivo, aparato acústico, audífono, *m*
hearsay /ˈhɪərˌsei/ *n* fama, *f,* rumor, *m.* **by h.,** de oídas
hearse /hɜrs/ *n* coche fúnebre, *m*
heart /hɑrt/ *n* corazón, *m;* (feelings) entrañas, *f pl;* (of the earth, etc.) seno, corazón, *m;* (of lettuce, etc.) cogollo, repollo, *m;* (suit in cards) copas, *f pl; Bot.* médula, *f;* (soul) alma, *f;* (courage) valor, *m;* ánimo, *m.* **at h.,** en el fondo, esencialmente. **by h.,** de memoria. **from the h.,** con toda sinceridad, de todo corazón. **He is a man after my own h.,** Es un hombre de los que me gustan. **I have no h. to do it,** No tengo valor de hacerlo. **in the h. of the country,** en medio del campo. **to break one's h.,** partirse el corazón. **to have one's h. in one's mouth,** tener el alma en un hilo, estar muerto de miedo. **to have no h.,** *Fig.* no tener entrañas. **to lose h.,** desanimarse, descorazonarse. **to set one's h. on,** poner el corazón en. **to take h.,** cobrar ánimo; *Inf.* hacer de tripas corazón. **to take to h.,** tomar a pechos. **to wear one's h. on one's sleeve,** tener el corazón en la mano. **with all my h.,** con toda el alma. **h.-ache,** angustia, pena, *f;* **h.-beat,** latido del corazón, *m.* **h.-breaker,** (woman) coqueta, *f;* (man) ladrón de corazones, *m.* **h. disease,** enfermedad del corazón, enfermedad cardíaca, *f.* **h. failure,** colapso cardíaco, *m.* **h. rending,** desgarrador, angustioso. **h.-searching,** examen de conciencia, *m.* **h.-shaped,** acorazonado, en forma de corazón. **h.-strings,** fibras del corazón, *f pl.* **h.-to-h. talk,** conversación íntima, *f.* **h.-whole,** libre de afectos
heartbreaking /ˈhɑrtˌbreikɪŋ/ *a* desgarrador, angustioso, doloroso, lastimoso
heartbroken /ˈhɑrtˌbroukən/ *a* acongojado, afligido, transido de dolor
heartburn /ˈhɑrtˌbɜrn/ *n* acidez del estómago, acedia, pirosis, rescoldera, *f*
heartburning /ˈhɑrtˌbɜrnɪŋ/ *n* rencor, *m,* animosidad, envidia, *f*
hearted /ˈhɑrtɪd/ *a* de corazón... que tiene el corazón... **kind-h.,** de buen corazón, bondadoso
hearten /ˈhɑrtn̩/ *vt* alentar, animar
heartfelt /ˈhɑrtˌfɛlt/ *a* hondo; de todo corazón, sincero; más expresivo
hearth /hɑrθ/ *n* hogar, *m;* chimenea, *f; Fig.* hogar, *m*
heartily /ˈhɑrtl̩i/ *adv* cordialmente; sinceramente; enérgicamente; con entusiasmo; (of eating) con buen apetito; (very) muy, completamente. **I am h. sick of it all,** *Inf.* Estoy harto hasta los dientes
heartiness /ˈhɑrtinɪs/ *n* cordialidad, *f;* sinceridad, *f;* energía, *f,* vigor, *m;* vehemencia, *f;* entusiasmo, *m;* (of appetite) buen diente, buen apetito, *m*
heartless /ˈhɑrtlɪs/ *a* sin corazón, sin piedad, despiadado, inhumano, cruel
heartlessness /ˈhɑrtlɪsnɪs/ *n* falta de corazón, inhumanidad, crueldad, *f*
hearty /ˈhɑrti/ *a* cordial; sincero; enérgico; vigoroso; robusto; (frank) campechano; (of appetite) voraz; bueno; (big) grande
heat /hit/ *n* calor, *m;* (in animals) celo, *m;* (of an action) calor, *m; Fig.* vehemencia, fogosidad, *f; Fig.* fuego, *m;* (passion) ardor, *m,* pasión, *f;* (of a race) carrera eliminatoria, *f.* —*vt* calentar; (excite) conmover, acalorar, excitar; (annoy) irritar. —*vi* calentarse. **dead h.,** empate, *m.* **in h.,** en celo. **in the h. of the moment,** en el calor del momento. **to become heated,** *Fig.* acalorarse, exaltarse. **white h.,** candencia, incandescencia, *f.* **h. lightning,** fucilazo, *m.* **h. spot,** pápula, *f;* terminación sensible, *f.* **h. stroke,** insolación, *f.* **h. wave,** onda de calor, *f*
heated /ˈhitɪd/ *a* calentado; caliente; excitado; apasionado
heatedly /ˈhitɪdli/ *adv* con vehemencia, con pasión
heater /ˈhitər/ *n* calentador, *m;* calorífero, *m;* (stove) estufa, *f;* (for plates) calientaplatos, *m.* **water-h.,** calentador de agua, *m*
heath /hiθ/ *n* brezal, *m;* yermo, páramo, *m; Bot.* brezo, *m*
heathen /ˈhiðən/ *n* pagano (-na); idólatra, *mf;* ateo (-ea), descreído (-da). —*a* pagano; ateo; bárbaro
heathenism /ˈhiðəˌnɪzəm/ *n* paganismo, *m;* idolatría, *f;* ateísmo, *m*
heather /ˈhɛðər/ *n* brezo, *m*

heating /ˈhitɪŋ/ *n* calefacción, *f*, *a* calentador; (of drinks) fortificante. **central h.,** calefacción central, *f*
heave /hiv/ *vt* alzar, levantar; *Naut.* izar; (the anchor, etc.) virar; (throw) arrojar, lanzar; elevar; (extract) extraer; (emit) dar, exhalar. —*vi* subir y bajar; palpitar; agitarse. —*n* tirón, *m;* (of the sea) vaivén, *m.* **to h. in sight,** aparecer, surgir. **to h. out sail,** *Naut.* desenvergar. **to h. the lead,** *Naut.* escandallar. **to h. to,** *Naut.* estarse a la capa
heaven /ˈhɛvən/ *n* cielo, *m;* firmamento, *m;* paraíso, *m.* **Heavens!** ¡Cielos! ¡Por Dios! **Thank H.!** ¡Gracias a Dios! **h.-born,** celeste. **h.-sent,** *Fig.* providencial
heavenliness /ˈhɛvənlinɪs/ *n* carácter celestial, *m;* delicia, *f*
heavenly /ˈhɛvənli/ *a* celeste, celestial; divino; *Fig.* delicioso. **h. body,** astro, *m*
heavily /ˈhɛvəli/ *adv* pesadamente; torpemente; penosamente; (slowly) lentamente; severamente; excesivamente; (of sighing) hondamente; (sadly) tristemente; (of rain, etc.) reciamente, fuertemente; (of wind) con violencia. **He fell h.,** Cayó de plomo. **to lie h. upon,** pesar mucho sobre. **to rain h.,** llover mucho, diluviar
heaviness /ˈhɛvinɪs/ *n* peso, *m;* (lethargy) torpor, letargo, *m;* sueño, *m,* languidez, *f;* (clumsiness) torpeza, *f;* (severity) severidad, *f;* importancia, responsabilidad, *f;* dificultad, *f;* (gravity) gravedad, *f;* tristeza, melancolía, *f;* (boredom) sosería, insulsez, *f;* (of style) monotonía, ponderosidad, *f*
heaving /ˈhivɪŋ/ *n* levantamiento, *m;* (of the anchor, etc.) virada, *f;* (of the sea) vaivén, *m;* (of the breast) palpitación, *f*
heavy /ˈhɛvi/ *a* pesado; torpe; sin gracia; (slow) lento; (thick) grueso; (strong) fuerte; (hard) duro; grave; difícil; oneroso; responsable, importante; (oppresive) opresivo; penoso; grande; (sad) triste, melancólico; (of the sky) anublado; (of food) indigesto; (tedious) aburrido, soso; (pompous) pomposo; (of roads) malo; (of scents) fuerte, penetrante; (of sleep, weather) pesado; (weary) rendido; (charged with) cargado de; (of a meal) grande, abundante; (violent) violento; (of a cold, etc.) malo; (drowsy) soñoliento; (torpid) tórpido; (of rain, snow, hail) fuerte, recio; (of firing) intenso; (of sighs) profundo; (of soil) recio, de mucha miga; (*Phys. Chem.*) pesado. **to be h.,** pesar mucho. **How h. are you?** ¿Cuánto pesa Vd.? **h.-armed,** pesado; armado hasta los dientes. **h.-eyed,** con ojeras. **h. guns,** artillería pesada, *f.* **h.-handed,** de manos torpes; *Fig.* tiránico, opresivo. **h.-hearted,** triste, apesadumbrado. **h. industry,** la gran industria, la industria pesada, *f.* **h.-laden,** muy cargado. **h. losses,** *Mil.* pérdidas cuantiosas, *f pl.* **h.weight,** *Sports.* peso pesado, *m*
Hebraic /hɪˈbreiɪk/ *a* hebraico, hebreo, judaico
Hebraism /ˈhibreiˌɪzəm/ *n* judaísmo, hebraísmo, *m*
Hebraist /ˈhibreiɪst/ *n* hebraísta, *m*
Hebrew /ˈhibru/ *n* hebreo (-ea), judío (-ía): (language) hebreo, *m*
Hebrides, the /ˈhɛbrɪdiz/ las Hébridas
hecatomb /ˈhɛkəˌtoum/ *n* hecatombe, *f*
heckle /ˈhɛkəl/ *vt Fig.* interrumpir, importunar con preguntas
heckler /ˈhɛklər/ *n* perturbador (-ra)
heckling /ˈhɛklɪŋ/ *n* interrupción, *f*
hectare /ˈhɛktɛər/ *n* hectárea, *f*
hectic /ˈhɛktɪk/ *a* (consumptive) hético; (feverish) febril; *Fig. Inf.* agitado
hectogram /ˈhɛktəˌgræm/ *n* hectogramo, *m*
hectoliter /ˈhɛktəˌlitər/ *n* hectolitro, *m*
hector /ˈhɛktər/ *vt* intimidar, amenazar
hectoring /ˈhɛktərɪŋ/ *a* imperioso; amenazador
hectowatt /ˈhɛktəˌwɑt/ *n Elec.* hectovatio, *m*
hedge /hɛdʒ/ *n* seto, *m;* barrera, *f.* —*vt* cercar con un seto; rodear. —*vi Fig.* titubear, vacilar. **h.-hopping,** *Aer.* vuelo a ras de tierra, *m.* **h.-sparrow,** acentor de bosque, *m*
hedgehog /ˈhɛdʒˌhɒg/ *n* erizo, *m.* **h. position,** *Mil.* puesto fuerte, *m*
hedonism /ˈhidn̩ˌɪzəm/ *n* hedonismo, *m*
hedonist /ˈhidn̩ɪst/ *n* hedonista, *mf*
heed /hid/ *n* atención, *f,* cuidado, *m.* —*vt* atender; observar, considerar; escuchar. —*vi* hacer caso
heedful /ˈhidfəl/ *a* atento; cuidadoso
heedless /ˈhidlɪs/ *a* desatento; descuidado, negligente; distraído
heedlessly /ˈhidlɪsli/ *adv* sin hacer caso; negligentemente; distraídamente
heedlessness /ˈhidlɪsnɪs/ *n* desatención, distracción, *f;* descuido, *m;* negligencia, *f;* inconsideración, *f*
heel /hil/ *n Anat.* talón, calcañar, *m;* (of shoe) tacón, *m;* (of a violin, etc., bow) talón, *m;* (remains) restos, *m pl.* —*vt* poner tacón a; poner talón a; *Naut.* hacer zozobrar. —*vi Naut.* zozobrar. **rubber h.,** tacón de goma, *m.* **She let him cool his heels for half an hour,** le dio un plantón de media hora. **to follow on a person's heels,** pisarle (a uno) los talones. **to be down at h.,** (of shoes) estar gastados los tacones; estar desaseado. **to take to one's heels,** apretar a correr, poner pies en polvorosa. **to turn on one's h.,** dar media vuelta. **h.-bone,** zancajo, *m.* **h.-piece,** talón, *m*
heeltap /ˈhilˌtæp/ *n* tapa de tacón, *f;* escurridura, *f*
heft /hɛft/ *vt* sopesar, tomar al peso
hegemony /hɪˈdʒɛməni/ *n* hegemonía, *f*
heifer /ˈhɛfər/ *n* ternera, vaquilla, *f*
heigh /hei/ *interj* (calling attention) ¡oye! ¡ioiga! **h. -ho!** ¡ay!
height /hait/ *n* altura, *f;* elevación, *f;* altitud, *f;* (stature) estatura, *f;* (high ground) cerro, *m,* colina, *f;* (sublimity) sublimidad, excelencia, *f;* colmo, *m;* (zenith) auge, *m,* cumbre, *f*
heighten /ˈhaitn̩/ *vt* hacer más alto; (enhance) realzar; (exaggerate) exagerar; (perfect) perfeccionar; (intensify) intensificar
heightening /ˈhaitn̩ɪŋ/ *n* elevación, *f;* (enhancement) realce, *m;* (exaggeration) exageración, *f;* (perfection) perfección, *f;* (intensification) intensificación, *f*
heinous /ˈheinəs/ *a* atroz, nefando, horrible.
heinousness /ˈheinəsnɪs/ *n* atrocidad, enormidad, *f*
heir /ɛər/ *n* heredero, *m.* **h. apparent,** heredero aparente, *m.* **h.-at-law,** heredero forzoso, *m.* **h. presumptive,** presunto heredero, *m*
heiress /ˈɛərɪs/ *n* heredera, *f*
heirloom /ˈɛərˌlum/ *n* reliquia de familia, *f; Fig.* herencia, *f*
helicopter /ˈhɛlɪˌkɒptər/ *n* helicóptero, *m*
helium /ˈhiliəm/ *n Chem.* helio, *m*
helix /ˈhilɪks/ *n Geom.* hélice, *m;* (*Archit. Geom.*) espira, *f*
hell /hɛl/ *n* infierno, *m.* **h.-fire,** fuego del infierno, *m,* llamas del infierno, *f pl*
Hellenic /hɛˈlɛnɪk/ *a* helénico
Hellenism /ˈhɛləˌnɪzəm/ *n* helenismo, *m*
Hellenist /ˈhɛlənɪst/ *n* helenista, *mf*
Hellenistic /ˌhɛləˈnɪstɪk/ *a* helenístico
Hellenize /ˈhɛləˌnaiz/ *vt* helenizar
hellish /ˈhɛlɪʃ/ *a* infernal; *Inf.* horrible, detestable
hello /hɛˈlou/ *interj* ¡hola!; (on telephoning someone) ¡oiga! ¡alo!; (answering telephone) ¡diga! ¡alo!
helm /hɛlm/ *n* caña del timón, *f;* timón, gobernalle, *m.* **to obey the h.,** obedecer el timón. **to take the h.,** gobernar el timón; ponerse a pilotar
helmet /ˈhɛlmɪt/ *n* casco, *m;* (in olden days) yelmo, capacete, *m;* (sun) casco colonial, *m*
helminthic /hɛlˈmɪnθɪk/ *a* helmíntico, vermífugo
helmsman /ˈhɛlmzmən/ *n* timonero, *m*
help /hɛlp/ *n* ayuda, *f;* auxilio, socorro, *m;* (protection) favor, *m,* protección, *f;* (remedy) remedio, *m;* (cooperation) cooperación, *f,* concurso, *m;* (domestic) criada, *f.* **A little h. is worth a lot of sympathy,** Más vale un toma que dos te daré. **There's no h. for it,** No hay más remedio. **to call for h.,** pedir socorro a gritos. **without h.,** a solas, sin la ayuda de nadie
help /hɛlp/ *vt* ayudar; socorrer, auxiliar; (favor) favorecer; (mitigate) aliviar; (contribute to) contribuir a, facilitar; (avoid) evitar. —*vi* ayudar. **He cannot h. worrying,** No puede menos de preocuparse. **God h. you!** ¡Dios te ampare! **So h. me God!** ¡Así Dios me salve! **to h. one another,** ayudarse mutuamente, ayudarse los unos a los otros. **to h. oneself,** (to food) servirse. **to h. down, off,** ayudar a bajar; ayudar a apearse. **to h. in,** ayudar a entrar. **to h. along, forward, on,** avanzar, fomentar, promover; contribuir a. **Shall I h. you on with the dress?** ¿Quieres que te

ayude a ponerte el vestido? **to h. out,** ayudar a salir; (from a vehicle) ayudar a bajar; (of a difficulty, etc.) sacar; suplir la falta de; ayudar. **to h. over,** ayudar a cruzar; (a difficulty) ayudar a salir (de un apuro); ayudar a vencer (un obstáculo, etc.); (a period) ayudar a pasar. **to h. to,** contribuir a, ayudar en; (food) servir. **to h. up,** ayudar a subir; ayudar a levantarse, levantar

helper /'hɛlpər/ *n* auxiliador (-ra); asistente (-ta); (protector) favorecedor (-ra); bienhechor (-ra); (colleague) colega, *m;* (co-worker) colaborador (-ra). **He thanked all his helpers,** Dio las gracias a todos los que le habían ayudado

helpful /'hɛlpfəl/ *a* útil, provechoso; (obliging) servicial, atento; (favorable) favorable; (healthy) saludable

helpfulness /'hɛlpfəlnɪs/ *n* utilidad, *f;* bondad, *f*

helping /'hɛlpɪŋ/ *n* ayuda, *f;* (of food) porción, ración, *f,* plato, *m.* **Won't you have a second h.?** ¿No quiere usted servirse más (or otra vez)? ¿No quiere usted repetir? **to lend a h. hand (to),** prestar ayuda (a)

helpless /'hɛlplɪs/ *a* desamparado, abandonado; (through infirmity) imposibilitado; impotente, sin fuerzas (para); (shiftless) incompetente, inútil

helplessness /'hɛlplɪsnɪs/ *n* desamparo, *m;* invalidez, debilidad, *f;* impotencia, *f;* incompetencia, *f*

helpmeet /'hɛlp,mit/ *n* compañero (-ra) perfecto (-ta); esposa, *f*

helter-skelter /'hɛltər 'skɛltər/ *adv* atropelladamente; en desorden. —*n* barahunda, *f*

hem /hɛm/ *n Sew.* dobladillo, filete, *m,* bastilla, *f;* (edge) orilla, *f.* —*interj* ¡ejem! —*vt* hacer dobladillo en, dobladillar. —*vi* (cough) fingir toser. **false hem,** *Sew.* dobladillo falso, *m.* **running hem,** *Sew.* jareta, *f.* **to hem and haw,** tartamudear; vacilar. **to hem in,** cercar, sitiar

hemisphere /'hɛmɪ,sfɪər/ *n* hemisferio, *m*

hemispherical /,hɛmɪ'sfɛrɪkəl/ *a* hemisférico, semiesférico

hemlock /'hɛm,lɒk/ *n Bot.* cicuta, *f*

hemoglobin /'himə,gloubɪn/ *n Chem.* hemoglobina, *f*

hemophilia /,himə'fɪliə/ *n Med.* hemofilia, *f*

hemorrhage /'hɛmərɪdʒ/ *n* hemorragia, *f,* flujo de sangre, *m*

hemorrhoids /'hɛmə,rɔidz/ *n pl Med.* hemorroides, *f*

hemp /hɛmp/ *n* cáñamo, *m.* **h. cloth,** lienzo, *m.* **h.-seed,** cañamón, *m*

hemstitch /'hɛm,stɪtʃ/ *n* vainica, *f.* —*vt* hacer vainica en

hen /hɛn/ *n* gallina, *f;* (female bird) hembra, *f.* **the hen pheasant,** la hembra del faisán. **hen bird,** pájara, *f.* **hen-coop** or **house,** gallinero, *m.* **hen party,** *Inf.* reunión de mujeres, *f.* **hen-roost,** nidal, ponedero, *m*

hence /hɛns/ *adv* (of place) de aquí; (of time) de ahora, de aquí a, al cabo de, en; (therefore) por eso, por lo tanto, por consiguiente. —*interj* ¡fuera! ¡fuera de aquí! **I shall come to see you a month h.,** Vendré a verte en un mes (or al cabo de un mes). **ten years h.,** de aquí a diez años. **h. the fact that...,** de aquí que.... **H. it happens that...,** Por eso sucede que...

henceforth /,hɛns'fɔrθ/ *adv* desde aquí en adelante, de hoy en adelante

henchman /'hɛntʃmən/ *n* escudero, *m;* satélite, secuaz, *m*

henna /'hɛnə/ *n* alheña, *f*

henpecked /'hɛn,pɛkt/ *a* gobernado por su mujer, que se deja mandar por su mujer

her /hɜr, *unstressed* hər, ər/ *pers pron direct object* la; (with prepositions) ella. —*pers pron indirect object* le, a ella. —*poss a* su, *mf;* sus, *mf pl,* de ella. **I saw her on Wednesday,** La vi el miércoles. **The message is for her,** El recado es para ella. **It is her book,** Es su libro, Es el libro de ella

herald /'hɛrəld/ *n* heraldo, *m;* presagio, anuncio, *m.* —*vt* proclamar; anunciar, presagiar

heraldic /hɛ'rældɪk/ *a* heráldico

heraldry /'hɛrəldri/ *n* heráldica, *f*

herb /ɜrb; *esp. Brit.* hɜrb/ *n* hierba, *f*

herbaceous /hɜr'beiʃəs, ɜr-/ *a* herbáceo

herbage /'ɜrbɪdʒ, 'hɜr-/ *n* herbaje, *m;* pasto, *m*

herbal /'ɜrbəl, 'hɜr-/ *a* herbario. —*n* herbolaria, *f*

herbalist /'hɜrbəlɪst, 'ɜr-/ *n* herbario, *m,* simplista, *mf*

herbarium /hɜr'bɛəriəm, ɜr-/ *n* herbario, *m*

herbivorous /hɜr'bɪvərəs, ɜr-/ *a* herbívoro

herby /'ɜrbi, 'hɜr-/ *a* herbáceo

Herculean /,hɜrkyə'liən/ *a* hercúleo

herd /hɜrd/ *n* manada, *f;* (of cattle) hato, *m;* (race) raza, *f;* (*Fig.* contemptuous) populacho, *m,* masa, *f.* —*vt* reunir en manadas; reunir en hatos; (sheep) reunir en rebaños; guiar las manadas, etc. —*vi* ir en manadas, hatos o rebaños; asociarse, reunirse. **h.-instinct,** instinto gregario, *m;* instinto de las masas, *m*

herdsman /'hɜrdzmən/ *n* ganadero, pastor, manadero, *m;* (head herdsman) rabadán, *m*

here /hɪər/ *adv* aquí; (at roll-call) ¡presente!; acá; an este punto; ahora. —*n* presente, *m.* **And h. he looked at me,** Y a este punto me miró. **Come h.!** ¡Ven acá! **in h.,** aquí dentro. **h. below,** aquí abajo, en la tierra. **h. and there,** aquí y allá. **h., there and everywhere,** en todas partes. **H. I am,** Heme aquí. **h. is...,** he aquí.... **H. they are,** Aquí los tienes, Aquí están. **Here's to you!** (on drinking) ¡Salud y pesetas! ¡A tu salud!

hereabouts /'hɪərə,bauts/ *adv* por aquí cerca

hereafter /hɪər'æftər/ *adv* en lo futuro; desde ahora; en adelante. —*n* futuro, *m.* **the H.,** la otra vida

hereat /hɪər'æt/ *adv* en esto

hereby /hɪər'bai/ *adv* por esto, por las presentes

hereditarily /hə,rɛdɪ'tɛrəli/ *adv* hereditariamente, por herencia

hereditary /hə'rɛdɪ,tɛri/ *a* hereditario

heredity /hə'rɛdɪti/ *n* herencia, *f*

herein /hɪər'ɪn/ *adv* en esto; aquí dentro; incluso

hereinafter /,hɪərɪn'æftər/ *adv* después, más abajo, más adelante, en adelante, en lo sucesivo

hereinbefore /,hɪərɪnbɪ'fɔr/ *adv* en la anterior, en lo arriba citado, en lo antes mencianado, en lo precedente.

hereof /hɪər'ʌv/ *adv* de esto

heresy /'hɛrəsi/ *n* herejía, *f*

heretic /'hɛrɪtɪk/ *n* hereje, *mf*

heretical /hə'rɛtɪkəl/ *a* herético

hereunder /hɪər'ʌndər/ *adv* abajo

hereupon /,hɪərə'pɒn/ *adv* en esto, en seguida

herewith /hɪər'wɪθ/ *adv* junto con esto, con esto; ahora, en esta ocasión

heritage /'hɛrɪtɪdʒ/ *n* herencia, *f*

hermaphrodite /hɜr'mæfrə,dait/ *a* and *n* hermafrodita, *mf*

hermetic /hɜr'mɛtɪk/ *a* hermético

hermit /'hɜrmɪt/ *n* ermitaño, *m.* **h. crab,** paguro, cangrejo ermitaño, *m*

hernia /'hɜrniə/ *n* hernia, *f*

hero /'hɪərou/ *n* héroe, *m.* **h.-worship,** culto a los héroes, *m*

heroic /hɪ'rouɪk/ *a* heroico, épico

heroin /'hɛrouɪn/ *n Chem.* heroína, *f*

heroine /'hɛrouɪn/ *n* heroína, *f*

heroism /'hɛrou,ɪzəm/ *n* heroísmo, *m*

heron /'hɛrən/ *n* garza, *f*

herpes /'hɜrpiz/ *n pl* herpes, *mf pl*

herring /'hɛrɪŋ/ *n* arenque, *m*

hers /hɜrz/ *poss pron 3rd sing* (el) suyo, *m;* (la) suya, *f;* (los) suyos, *m pl;* (las) suyas, *f pl;* de ella. **This book is h.,** Este libro es suyo, Este libro es de ella. **This book is h., not mine,** Este libro es el suyo no el mío. **a sister of h.,** una de sus hermanas, una hermana suya

herself /hər'sɛlf/ *pron* sí misma, sí; ella misma; (with reflexive verb) se. **She has done it by h.,** Lo ha hecho por sí misma. **She h. told me so,** Ella misma me lo dijo. **She is by h.,** Está a solas, Está sola

hesitancy /'hɛzɪtənsi/. See **hesitation**

hesitant /'hɛzɪtənt/ *a* indeciso, vacilante, irresoluto. **to be h.,** mostrarse irresoluto

hesitate /'hɛzɪ,teit/ *vi* vacilar, dudar; titubear. **I do not h. to say...,** No vacilo en decir... **He hesitated over his reply,** Tardaba en dar su respuesta

hesitatingly /'hɛzɪ,teitɪŋli/ *adv* irresolutamente; titubeando

hesitation /,hɛzɪ'teiʃən/ *n* vacilación, hesitación, *f;*

irresolución, indecisión, *f;* (reluctance) aversión, repugnancia, *f;* titubeo, *m*
heterodox /ˈhɛtərəˌdɒks/ *a* heterodoxo
heterodoxy /ˈhɛtərəˌdɒksi/ *n* heterodoxia, *f*
heterogeneity /ˌhɛtəroudʒəˈniɪti/ *n* heterogeneidad, *f*
heterogeneous /ˌhɛtərəˈdʒiniəs/ *a* heterogéneo
hew /hyu/ *vt* cortar, tajar; (trees) talar; (a career, etc.) hacerse
hewer /ˈhyuər/ *n* partidor, talador, *m*
hexagon /ˈhɛksəˌgɒn/ *n* hexágono, *m*
hey /hei/ *interj* ¡he! ¡oye!
heyday /ˈheiˌdei/ *n* apogeo, colmo, *m;* buenos tiempos, *m pl;* reinado, *m;* pleno vigor, *m*
hi /hai/ *interj* ¡oye! ¡hola!
hiatus /haiˈeitəs/ *n* hiato, *m;* laguna, *f,* vacío, *m*
hibernate /ˈhaibərˌneit/ *vi* invernar
hibernation /ˌhaibərˈneiʃən/ *n* invernada, *f*
hibiscus /haiˈbɪskəs/ *n Bot.* hibisco, *m*
hiccup /ˈhɪkʌp/ *n* hipo, *m.* —*vi* hipar. —*vt* decir con hipo
hidden /ˈhɪdn̩/ *a* escondido, secreto, oculto
hide /haid/ *n* piel, *f;* pellejo, cuero, *m*
hide /haid/ *vt* esconder, ocultar; (cover) cubrir, tapar; (dissemble) disimular; (meaning) obscurecer. —*vi* esconderse; ocultarse; refugiarse. **to h. from each other,** esconderse el uno del otro. **h.-and-seek,** escondite, dormirlas, *m*
hidebound /ˈhaidˌbaund/ *a Fig.* muy conservador, reaccionario, de ideas muy tradicionales
hideous /ˈhɪdiəs/ *a* horrible, repulsivo, horroroso; repugnante, odioso
hideously /ˈhɪdiəsli/ *adv* horriblemente. **to be h. ugly,** (of people) ser más feo que Picio
hideousness /ˈhɪdiəsnɪs/ *n* fealdad, horribilidad, *f;* repugnancia, *f*
hiding /ˈhaidɪŋ/ *n* ocultación, *f;* encubrimiento, *m;* refugio, *m; Inf.* paliza, tunda, *f.* **h.-place,** escondite, escondrijo, *m*
hie /hai/ *vi* apresurarse, ir a prisa
hierarch /ˈhaiəˌrɑrk/ *n* jerarca, *m*
hierarchical /ˌhaiəˈrɑrkɪkəl/ *a* jerárquico
hierarchy /ˈhaiəˌrɑrki/ *n* jerarquía, *f*
hieroglyph /ˈhaiərəˌglɪf/ *n* jeroglífico, *m*
higgledy-piggledy /ˈhɪgəldi ˈpɪgəldi/ *adv* revueltamente, en confusión; en montón, en desorden
high /hai/ *a* alto; elevado; (with altar, Mass, street, festival) mayor; grande; eminente; aristocrático; (of shooting) fijante; (of quality) superior; excelente; (haughty) orgulloso; (solemn) solemne; (good) bueno; noble; supremo; sumo; (of price) subido; *Mus.* agudo; (of the sea) tempestuoso, borrascoso; (of wind and explosives) violento, fuerte; (of polish) brillante; (with speed) grande; (with tension, frequency) alto; (with number, etc.) importante, grande; (with colors) subido; (of food) pasado; (angry) enojado, airado; (of cheek bones) saliente, prominente; (well-seasoned) picante; (flattering) lisonjero. —*adv* alto; hacia arriba; arriba; (deeply) profundamente; fuertemente; con violencia; (of price) a un precio elevado; (luxuriously) lujosamente; *Mus.* agudo. **a room 12 ft. h.,** un cuarto de doce pies de altura. **I knew her when she was so h.,** La conocí tamaña. **It is h. time he came,** Ya es hora de que viniese. **on h.,** en alto, arriba; en los cielos. **h. altar,** altar mayor, *m.* **h. and dry,** en la playa, varado; *Fig.* en seco. **h. and low,** de arriba abajo; por todas partes. **h.-born,** aristocrático, de alta alcurnia. **h.-bred,** (of people) de buena familia; (of animals) de buena raza. **h.-class,** de buena clase; de alta calidad. **h. collar,** alzacuello, *m.* **h. colored,** de colores vivos; *Fig.* exagerado. **h. command,** (*Mil. Nav.*) alto mando, *m.* **h. court,** tribunal supremo, *m.* **h. day,** día festivo, *m.* **h. explosive,** explosivo violento, *m.* **h.-flown,** hinchado, retumbante, altisonante. **h. frequency,** alta frecuencia, *f.* **h.-handed,** arbitrario, dominador, despótico. **h.-heeled,** *a* de tacón alto. **h. jump,** salto de altura, *m.* **h. land,** tierras altas, *f pl;* eminencia, *f.* **h. light,** *Art.* realce, *m;* acontecimiento de más interés, *m;* momento culminante, *m.* **h. mass,** misa mayor, *f.* **h.-minded,** de nobles pensamientos; arrogante. **h.-necked,** con cuello alto. **h.-pitched,** de tono alto, agudo. **h.-powered,** de alta potencia. **h.-powered car,** coche de muchos caballos, *m.* **h. precision,** suma precisión, *f.* **h. pressure,** *n* alta presión, *f; Fig.* urgencia, *f; n* de alta presión; *Fig.* urgente. **h.-priced,** caro. **h. priest,** sumo pontífice, sumo sacerdote, alto sacerdote, *m.* **h. relief,** alto relieve, *m.* **h. road,** carretera mayor, *f.* **h. school,** instituto de segunda enseñanza, instituto, colegio, liceo, *m;* colegio, liceo, instituto, *m,* escuela secundaria, secundaria, *f.* **h. sea,** marejada, *f.* **h. seas,** alta mar, *f.* **h.-seasoned,** picante. **h. society,** alta sociedad, *f.* **h.-sounding,** altisonante, bombástico. **h.-speed,** de alta velocidad. **h.-spirited,** brioso; alegre. **h.-strung,** nervioso, excitable, sensitivo. **h. tension,** alta tensión, *f.* **h. tide,** marea alta, *f.* **h.-toned,** *Mus.* agudo; *Inf.* de alto copete; aristocrático. **h. treason,** alta traición, *f.* **h. water,** marea alta, pleamar, *f.* **h.-water mark,** límite de la marea, *m; Fig.* colmo, *m;* apogeo, *m*
highbrow /ˈhaiˌbrau/ *a* and *n* intelectual, *mf*
high-ceilinged /ˈhai ˈsilɪŋd/ *a* alto de techo
higher /ˈhaiər/ *a compar* of **high,** más alto; más elevado; superior. **on a h. plane,** en un nivel más alto. **h. education,** enseñanza superior, *f.* **h. mathematics,** la alta matemática, *f.* **h. criticism,** la alta crítica. **h. up,** más arriba. **h. up the river,** río arriba
highest /ˈhaiɪst/ *a superl* of **high,** el más alto; la más alta; los más altos; las más altas; sumo, supremo; excelente. **h. common factor,** *Math.* máximo común divisor, *m.* **h. references,** (of cook, gardener, etc.) informes inmejorables, *m pl; Com.* referencias excelentes, *f pl*
highland /ˈhailənd/ *n* altiplanicie, *f;* montañas, *f pl,* distrito montañoso, *m.* —*a* montañoso
highlander /ˈhailəndər/ *n* montanés (-esa); escocés (-esa) del norte
highlight /ˈhaiˌlait/ *vt* dar relieve a, destacar
highly /ˈhaili/ *adv* altamente; mucho; muy; extremadamente; grandemente; bien; favorablemente; con lisonja, lisonjeramente. **h. seasoned,** picante. **h. strung,** nervioso, excitable
highness /ˈhainɪs/ *n* altura, *f;* elevación, *f;* excelencia, *f;* nobleza, *f;* (title) Alteza, *f.* **His Royal H., Her Royal Highness,** Su Alteza Real
high-ranking /ˈhai ˈræŋkɪŋ/ *a* de alta jerarquía, de alto rango
highway /ˈhaiˌwei/ *n* camino real, *m,* carretera, *f.* **h. code,** código de la via pública (or de la circulación), *m.* **h. robbery,** salteamiento de caminos, atraco, *m*
highwayman /ˈhaiˌweimən/ *n* salteador de caminos, *m*
highways and byways /ˈhaiˌweiz ən ˈbaiˌweiz/ caminos y veredas
hike /haik/ *vi* ir de excursión. —*n* marcha con equipo, *f*
hiker /ˈhaikər/ *n* excursionista, *mf*
hiking /ˈhaikɪŋ/ *n* excursionismo, *m;* marcha con equipo, *f*
hilarious /hɪˈlɛəriəs/ *a* alegre
hilarity /hɪˈlærɪti/ *n* hilaridad, *f*
hill /hɪl/ *n* colina, *f,* cerro, otero, *m;* monte, *m,* montaña, *f;* (pile) montón, *m.* **h.-side,** falda de montaña, ladera de una colina, *f.* **h.-top,** cumbre de una colina, *f*
hilliness /ˈhɪlinɪs/ *n* montuosidad, *f,* lo montañoso
hillman /ˈhɪlˌmæn/ *n* montañés, *m*
hillock /ˈhɪlək/ *n* altozano, montículo, collado, *m*
hilly /ˈhɪli/ *a* montañoso
hilt /hɪlt/ *n* puño, *m,* empuñadura, *f*
him /hɪm/ *pron 3rd sing direct object* le, lo; (with prep.) él; *indirect object* le, a él; (with a direct obj. in 3rd person) se. **I gave him the magazine,** Le di la revista. **I gave it to him,** Se lo di a él. **This is for him,** Esto es para él
Himalayan /ˌhɪməˈleiən/ *a* himalayo
Himalayas, the /ˌhɪməˈleiəz/ los Himalayas, *m pl*
himself /hɪmˈsɛlf/ *pron* sí, sí mismo; él mismo; (reflexive) se. **He did it by h.,** Lo hizo por sí mismo. For more examples see **herself**
hind /haind/ *n* corza, cierva, *f.* —*a* trasero, posterior. **h.-quarters,** cuarto trasero, *m;* (of a horse) ancas, *f pl*
hinder /ˈhɪndər/ *a* trasero, posterior
hinder /ˈhɪndər/ *vt* impedir, estorbar; embarazar, di-

ficultar; interrumpir. —*vi* ser un obstáculo; formar un obstáculo

hinderer /ˈhɪndərər/ *n* estorbador (-ra); interruptor (-ra)

hindmost /ˈhaindˌmoust/ *a* posterior, postrero, último

hindrance /ˈhɪndrəns/ *n* obstáculo, estorbo, impedimento, *m;* perjuicio, *m;* interrupción, *f*

Hindu /ˈhɪndu/ *a* hindú, *mf*

Hinduism /ˈhɪnduˌɪzəm/ *n* indoísmo, *m*

Hindustani /ˌhɪndʊˈstɑni/ *a* indostanés. —*n* (language) indostani, *m*

hinge /hɪndʒ/ *n* gozne, pernio, *m,* bisagra, *f;* articulación, *f; Fig.* eje, *m.* —*vi* moverse (or abrirse) sobre goznes; *Fig.* depender (de). —*vt* engoznar

hinged /hɪndʒd/ *a* con goznes

hint /hɪnt/ *n* indirecta, insinuación, sugestión, *f;* (advice) consejo, *m.* —*vt* dar a entender, decir con medias palabras, insinuar, sugerir. —*vi* insinuar. **to take the h.,** darse por aludido

hinterland /ˈhɪntərˌlænd/ *n* interior (de un país), *m*

hip /hɪp/ *n Anat.* cadera, *f; Bot.* fruto del rosal silvestre, *m.* **h.-bath,** baño de asiento, *m.* **h.-bone,** hueso ilíaco, *m.* **h.-joint,** articulación de la cadera, *f.* **h.-pocket,** faltriquera, *f*

hipped /hɪpt/ *a* de caderas

hippodrome /ˈhɪpəˌdroum/ *n* hipódromo, *m*

hippopotamus /ˌhɪpəˈpɒtəməs/ *n* hipopótamo, *m*

hire /haiᵊr/ *n* alquiler, arriendo, *m;* salario, *m.* —*vt* alquilar, arrendar; tomar en arriendo; (person) contratar; tomar a su servicio. **to h. out,** alquilar. **for** or **on h.,** de alquiler. **h.-purchase,** compra a plazos, *f*

hireling /ˈhaiᵊrlɪŋ/ *n* mercenario, *m*

hirer /ˈhaiᵊrər/ *n* alquilador (-ra), arrendador (-ra)

hirsute /ˈhɜrsut/ *a* hirsuto. **non-h.** *Bot.* lampiño

his /hɪz; *unstressed* ɪz/ *poss pron 3rd sing* (el) suyo, *m;* (la) suya, *f;* (los) suyos, *m pl*; (las) suyas, *f pl*; de él. —*poss a* su, *mf;* sus, *mf pl*; de él. **his handkerchiefs,** sus pañuelos. **his mother,** su madre, la madre de él. **a sister of his,** una de sus hermanas, una hermana suya. See **hers** for more examples.

Hispanism /ˈhɪspəˌnɪzəm/ *n* hispanismo, *m*

Hispanist /ˈhɪspənɪst/ *n* hispanista, *mf*

hispanize /ˈhɪspəˌnaiz/ *vt* españolizar

Hispano-American /hɪsˈpænou əˈmɛrɪkən/ *a* hispano-americano

hiss /hɪs/ *n* silbido, *m;* (sputter) chisporroteo, *m.* —*vi* silbar

hissing /ˈhɪsɪŋ/ *n* silbido, *m;* chisporroteo, *m.* —*a* silbante

hist /hɪst/ *interj* ¡chist!

histologist /hɪsˈtɒlədʒɪst/ *n* histólogo, *m*

histology /hɪˈstɒlədʒi/ *n* histología, *f*

historian /hɪˈstɔriən/ *n* historiador (-ra)

historic /hɪˈstɔrɪk/ *a* histórico

historical /hɪˈstɔrɪkəl/ *a* histórico. **h. truth,** verdad histórica, *f*

historically /hɪsˈtɔrɪkəli/ *adv* históricamente

historiographer /hɪˌstɔriˈɒgrəfər/ *n* historiógrafo, *m*

historiography /hɪˌstɔriˈɒgrəfi/ *n* historiografía, *f*

history /ˈhɪstəri/ *n* historia, *f.* **Biblical h.,** historia sagrada, *f.* **natural h.,** historia natural, *f*

histrionic /ˌhɪstriˈɒnɪk/ *a* histriónico

hit /hɪt/ *n* golpe, *m; Aer.* impacto, *m;* (success) éxito, *m;* (piece of luck) buena suerte, *f;* (satire) sátira, *f.* —*vt* golpear; (buffet) abofetear, pegar; (find) dar con, tropezar con; (attain) acertar; (guess) adivinar; (attract) atraer; (deal) lanzar, dar; (wound) herir, hacer daño (a). **The sun hits me right in the eyes,** El sol me da en la cabeza. **direct hit,** *Aer.* impacto de lleno, *m.* **lucky hit,** acierto, *m.* **to hit a straight left,** (boxing) lanzar un directo con la izquierda. **to hit the mark,** dar en el blanco; *Fig.* dar en el clavo. **hit or miss,** acierto o error. **to hit against,** dar contra, estrellar contra. **to hit back,** defenderse; devolver golpe por golpe. **to hit off,** imitar; (a likeness) coger. **to hit out,** abofetear; *Fig.* atacar; golpear (la pelota) fuera. **to hit upon,** dar con; tropezar con; encontrar por casualidad; (remember) acordarse de

hitch /hɪtʃ/ *n* (jerk) sacudida, *f;* nudo fácil de soltar, *m; Fig.* obstáculo, *m; Fig.* dificultad, *f.* **give s.b. a hitch,** levantar a fulano. —*vt* sacudir; (a chair, etc.) arrastrar, empujar; amarrar, enganchar; atar. —*vi* (along a seat, etc.) correrse (en); (get entangled) enredarse, cogerse; (rub) rascarse. **without a h.,** sin dificultad alguna, viento en popa; (smoothly) a pedir de boca. **to h. up,** sacudir, dar una sacudida (a)

hitchhike /ˈhɪtʃˌhaik/ *vi* ir a dedo (Argentina), pedir aventón (Mexico), pedir botella (Cuba), hacer autostop, ir por autostop (Spain)

hither /ˈhɪðər/ *adv* acá, hacia acá; *a* citerior, más cercano. **h. and thither,** acá y aculla allá

hitherto /ˈhɪðərˌtu/ *adv* hasta ahora, hasta el presente

Hitlerian /hɪtˈlɛəriən/ *a* hitleriano, nacista

Hitlerism /ˈhɪtləˌrɪzəm/ *n* hitlerismo, nacismo, *m*

Hittite /ˈhɪtaiᵗ/ *a* and *n* heteo (-ea)

hive /haiv/ *n* (for bees) colmena, *f;* (swarm) enjambre, *m; Fig.* centro, *m.* —*vt* (bees) enjambrar. **h. of industry,** centro de industria

hoard /hɔrd/ *n* acumulación, *f;* provisión, *f;* tesoro, *m.* —*vt* acumular, amasar, amontonar; guardar

hoarder /ˈhɔrdər/ *n* acaparador (-ra)

hoarding /ˈhɔrdɪŋ/ *n* amontonamiento, *m;* acaparamiento, *m;* (fence) empalizada, cerca, *f;* palizada de tablas, *f*

hoarfrost /ˈhɔrˌfrɔst/ *n* escarcha, helada blanca, *f*

hoariness /ˈhɔrinɪs/ *n* (of the hair) canicie, *f;* blancura, *f;* (antiquity) vejez, vetustez, *f*

hoarse /hɔrs/ *a* ronco; discordante. **to be h.,** tener la voz ronca. **to grow h.,** enronquecerse

hoarsely /ˈhɔrsli/ *adv* roncamente

hoarseness /ˈhɔrsnɪs/ *n* ronquera, *f; Inf.* carraspera, *f*

hoary /ˈhɔri/ *a* (of the hair) canoso; blanco; (old) vetusto, antiguo, viejo

hoax /houks/ *n* estafa, *f,* engaño, *m;* broma pesada, *f;* burla, *f.* —*vt* estafar, engañar; burlar

hoaxer /ˈhouksər/ *n* burlador (-ra); estafador (-ra)

hob /hɒb/ *n* repisa interior del hogar, *f*

hobble /ˈhɒbəl/ *n* (gait) cojera, *f;* traba, maniota, *f.* —*vi* cojear. —*vt* manear. **h. skirt,** falda muy estrecha, *f*

hobby /ˈhɒbi/ *n* pasatiempo, *m,* recreación, *f;* manía, afición, *f.* **h.-horse,** caballo de cartón, *m; Fig.* caballo de batalla, *m*

hobgoblin /ˈhɒbˌgɒblɪn/ *n* trasgo, duende, *m*

hobnail /ˈhɒbˌneil/ *n* clavo de herradura, clavo de botas, *m*

hobnailed /ˈhɒbˌneild/ *a* (of boots) con clavos

hobnob /ˈhɒbˌnɒb/ *vi* codearse, tratar con familiaridad

hock /hɒk/ *n Anat.* pernil, *m;* (wine) vino del Rin, *m*

hockey /ˈhɒki/ *n* chueca, *m.* **h. ball,** bola, pelota de chueca, *f.* **h. stick,** bastón de chueca, *m*

hocus-pocus /ˈhoukəs ˈpoukəs/ *n* juego de pasa pasa, *m;* engaño, *m,* treta, *f*

hod /hɒd/ *n* cuezo, *m*

hodgepodge /ˈhɒdʒˌpɒdʒ/ See **hotchpotch**

hoe /hou/ *n* azadón, *m.* —*vt* azadonar; sachar

hoeing /ˈhouɪŋ/ *n* cavadura con azadón, *f;* sachadura, *f*

hoer /ˈhouər/ *n* azadonero, *m*

hog /hɔg/ *n* cerdo, puerco, *m.* **to go the whole hog,** ir al extremo. **hogskin,** piel de cerdo, *f*

hoggish /ˈhɔgɪʃ/ *a* porcuno; (greedy) comilón, tragón; (selfish) egoísta

hoist /hɔist/ *n* levantamiento, *m;* (lift) montacargas, *m;* (winch) cabria, *f;* (crane) grúa, *f.* —*vt* levantar, alzar; (flags) enarbolar; suspender; *Naut.* izar

hoity-toity /ˈhɔiti ˈtɔiti/ *a* picajoso, quisquilloso; presuntuoso

hold /hould/ *n* asimiento, agarro, *m,* presa, *f;* asidero, *m; Fig.* autoridad, *f,* poder, *m; Fig.* comprensión, *f;* (of a ship) cala, bodega, *f.* **to loose one's h.,** aflojar su presa. **to lose one's h.,** perder su presa. **to seize h. of,** asirse de, echar mano de. **h.-all,** funda, *f.* **h.-up,** (robbery) atraco, robo a mano armada, *m;* (in traffic) atasco (or obstáculo) en el tráfico, *m;* (in work) parada, cesación (de trabajo), *f*

hold /hould/ *vt* tener; asir, agarrar; coger; retener; (embrace) abrazar; (a post) ocupar; (a meeting, etc.) celebrar; (bear weight of) aguantar, soportar; (own) poseer; *Mil.* ocupar, defender; (contain) contener; (have in store) reservar; tener capacidad para; (retain) retener; (believe) creer, sostener; (consider) opinar, tener para (mí, etc.); juzgar; (restrain) detener; contener; (of attention, etc.) mantener; (maneuvers) hacer; (observe) guardar. *—vi* resistir, aguantar; (be valid) ser válido; regir; (apply) aplicarse; (last) continuar, seguir. *—interj* ¡tente! ¡para! **The room won't h. more,** En este cuarto no caben más. **They h. him in great respect,** Le tienen mucho respeto. **The theory does not h. water,** La teoría es falsa, La teoría no es lógica. **to h. one's own,** defenderse, mantenerse en sus trece. **to h. one's breath,** contener la respiración. **to h. one's tongue,** callarse. **to h. sway,** mandar; reinar. **to h. tightly,** agarrar fuertemente; (clasp) estrechar. **H. the line!** (telephone) ¡Aguarde un momento! **to h. back,** *vt* detener; contener; retener; esconder; abstenerse de entregar. *—vi* quedarse atrás; vacilar, dudar; tardar en. **to h. by,** seguir; basarse en, apoyarse en. **to h. down,** sujetar; (oppress) oprimir. **to h. fast,** *vt* sujetar fuertemente. *—vi* mantenerse firme; *Fig.* estar agarrado (a). **to h. forth,** *vt* ofrecer; expresar. *—vi* hacer un discurso, perorar. **to h. in,** *vt* contener; retener. *—vi* contenerse. **to h. off,** *vt* apartar, alejar. *—vi* apartarse, alejarse, mantenerse alejado. **to h. on,** seguir, persistir en; aguantar. **to h. out,** *vt* alargar, extender; ofrecer. *—vi* aguantar; durar, resistir. **to h. over,** tener suspendido sobre; (postpone) aplazar; *Fig.* amenazar con. **to h. to,** agarrarse a; atenerse a. **to h. together,** *vt* unir; juntar. *—vi* mantenerse juntos. **to h. up,** *vt* (display) mostrar, enseñar; levantar; sostener, soportar; (rob) atracar, saltear; (delay) atrasar; (stop) interrumpir, parar. *—vi* mantenerse en pie; (of weather) seguir bueno. **The train has been held up by fog,** El tren viene con retraso a causa de la niebla

holder /ˈhouldər/ *n* el *m*, (*f*, la) que tiene; poseedor (-ra); *Com.* tenedor (-ra); inquilino (-na); propietario (-ia); (support) soporte, *m;* mango, *m;* asa, *f;* (in compounds) porta...

holding /ˈhouldɪŋ/ *n* tención, *f;* posesión, *f;* propiedad, *f;* (leasing) arrendamiento, *m;* (celebration) solemnización, *f;* (of a meeting) el celebrar, el tener; *pl* **holdings,** *Com.* valores habidos, *m pl*

holding company *n* compañía de cartera, *f*

hole /houl/ *n* hoyo, *m;* boquete, *m;* agujero, *m;* cavidad, *f;* (hollow) depresión, *f,* hueco, *m;* orificio, *m;* (tear) roto, desgarro, *m;* (eyelet) punto, *m;* (in cheese) ojo, *m;* (in stocking) rotura, *f,* punto, *m;* (lair) madriguera, *f;* (nest) nido, *m;* (golf) hoyo, *m;* (fix) aprieto, *m.* *—vt* agujerear; excavar; (bore) taladrar; *Sports.* meter la pelota (en). **to h. out,** (golf) meter la pelota en el hoyo. **h.-and-corner,** *a Inf.* bajo mano, secreto

hole-puncher /ˈhoul ˌpʌntʃər/ *n* agujereadora, *f*

holiday /ˈhɒlɪˌdei/ *n* día feriado, *m;* día de fiesta, día festivo, *m;* vacación, *f.* *—a* festivo, alegre; de vacación; de vacaciones; de excursión; (summer) veraniego. **day's h.,** día de asueto, *m.* **to take a h.,** tomar una vacación; hacer fiesta. **h. camp,** colonia veraniega, *f.* **h.-maker,** excursionista, turista, *mf;* (in the summer) veraneante, *mf* **holidays with pay,** vacaciones retribuidas, *f pl*

holiness /ˈhoulinɪs/ *n* santidad, *f*

Holland /ˈhɒlənd/ Holanda, *f*

holland /ˈhɒlənd/ *n* lienzo crudo. *—a* holandés. **H. gin,** ginebra holandesa, *f*

hollow /ˈhɒlou/ *a* hueco; cóncavo; (empty) vacío; (of eyes, etc.) hundido; (of sound) sordo; (of a cough) cavernoso; (echoing) retumbante, (*Fig.* unreal) vacío, falso; insincero. *—adv* vacío; *Inf.* completamente. *—n* hueco, *m;* concavidad, *f;* (hole) hoyo, *m;* cavidad, *f;* (valley) hondanada, *f,* barranco, *m;* (groove) ranura, *f;* (depression) depresión, *f;* (in the back) curvadura, *f.* *—vt* excavar, ahuecar; vaciar. **h.-cheeked,** con las mejillas hundidas. **h.-eyed,** con los ojos hundidos, de ojos hundidos

hollowness /ˈhɒlounɪs/ *n* concavidad, *f;* (falseness) falsedad, *f;* insinceridad, *f*

holly /ˈhɒli/ *n* acebo, agrifolio, *m*

holocaust /ˈhɒləˌkɔst/ *n* holocausto, *m*

holograph /ˈhɒləˌgræf/ *n* hológrafo, *m*

holster /ˈhoulstər/ *n* pistolera, *f*

holy /ˈhouli/ *a* santo; sagrado; (blessed) bendito. **most h.,** *a* santísimo. **to make h.,** santificar. **H. Father,** Padre Santo, el Papa, *m.* **H. Ghost,** Espíritu Santo, *m.* **H. Office,** Santo Oficio, *m,* Inquisición, *f.* **H. Orders,** órdenes sagradas, *f pl.* **h. places,** santos lugares, *m pl.* **H. Scripture,** Sagrada Escritura, *f.* **H. See,** Cátedra de San Pedro, *f.* **h. water,** agua bendita, *f.* **H. Souls,** las Ánimas Benditas. **h. water stoup,** acetre, *m.* **H. Week,** Semana Santa, *f*

Holy Land, the la Tierra Santa, *f.*

homage /ˈhɒmɪdʒ/ *n* homenaje, *m;* culto, *m;* reverencia, *f.* **to pay h.,** rendir homenaje

home /houm/ *n* casa, *f;* hogar, *m;* domicilio, *m,* residencia, *f;* (institution) asilo, *m;* (haven) refugio, *m;* (habitation) morada, *f;* (country of origin) país de origen, *m;* (native land) patria, *f;* (environment) ambiente natural, *m; Sports.* meta, *f.* *—a* casero, doméstico; nativo; nacional, del país; indígena. *—adv* a casa, hacia casa; (in one's country) en su patria; (returned) de vuelta; (of the feelings) al corazón, al alma; (to the limit) al límite. **at h.,** en casa; *Fig.* en su elemento; (of games) en campo propio; de recibo. **at-h. day,** día de recibo, *m.* **He shot the bolt h.,** Echó el cerrojo. **one's long h.,** su última morada. **to be at h.,** estar en casa; estar de recibo. **to be away from h.,** estar fuera de casa; estar ausente. **to bring h.,** traer (or llevar) a casa; hacer ver; convencer; llegar al alma; (a crime) probar (contra). **to go h.,** volver a casa; volver a la patria; (be effective) hacer su efecto; (move) herir en lo más vivo. **to make oneself at h.,** ponerse a sus anchas, sentirse como en casa de uno. **Please make yourself at home!** ¡Ha tomado posesión de su casa! **to strike h.,** dar en el blanco; herir; (hit) golpear; herir en lo más vivo; hacerse sentir. **h. affairs,** asuntos domésticos, *m pl,* (Ministry of) Gobernación, *f.* **h.-bred,** criado en el país. **h.-brewed,** fermentado en el país; fermentado en casa. **h.-coming,** regreso al hogar, *m.* **h. counties,** condados alrededor de Londres, *m pl.* **H. Defense,** defensa nacional, *f.* **h. farm,** residencia del propietario de una finca, *f.* **h. for the aged,** asilo de ancianos, *m.* **h. front,** frente doméstico, *m.* **H. Guard,** milicia nacional, *f.* **h. life,** vida de familia, *f.* **h.-made** casero, de fabricación casera, hecho en casa. **H. Office,** Ministerio de Gobernación, *m.* **H. Rule,** autonomía, *f.* **H. Secretary,** Ministro de Gobernación, *m.* **h. stretch,** último trecho (de una carrera), *m.* **h. truth,** verdad, *Inf.* fresca, *f.* **to tell someone a few h. truths,** contarle cuatro verdades

homeless /ˈhoumlɪs/ *a* sin casa; sin hogar. **the h.,** los sin techo

homeliness /ˈhoumlinɪs/ *n* comodidad, *f;* sencillez, *f;* (ugliness) fealdad, *f*

homely /ˈhoumli/ *a* doméstico; familiar; (unpretentious) sencillo; llano; (ugly) feo; desabrido

homemaker /ˈhoumˌmeikər/ *n* ama de casa, *f*

homeopath /ˈhoumiəˌpæθ/ *n* homeópata, *mf*

homeopathic /ˌhoumiəˈpæθɪk/ *a* homeópata

homeopathy /ˌhoumiˈɒpəθi/ *n* homeopatía, *f*

Homeric /houˈmɛrɪk/ *a* homérico

homesick /ˈhoumˌsɪk/ *a* nostálgico. **to be h.,** tener morriña

homesickness /ˈhoumˌsɪknɪs/ *n* nostalgia, añoranza, morriña, *f*

homespun /ˈhoumˌspʌn/ *a* tejido en casa; hecho en casa; basto, grueso

homestead /ˈhoumstɛd/ *n* hacienda, *f;* casa solariega, *f;* casa, *f*

homeward /ˈhoumwərd/ *adv* hacia casa, en dirección al hogar; de vuelta; hacia la patria. **h.-bound,** en dirección a casa; (of ships) con rumbo al puerto de origen; (of other traffic) de vuelta

homicidal /ˌhɒməˈsaidl̩/ *a* homicida

homicide /ˈhɒməˌsaid/ *n* (act) homicidio, *m;* (person) homicida, *mf*

homily /ˈhɒməli/ *n Eccl.* homilía, *f;* sermón, *m*

homing pigeon /ˈhoumɪŋ/ *n* palomo (-ma) mensajero (-ra)

homogeneity /ˌhoumədʒəˈniɪti/ *n* homogeneidad, *f*

homogeneous /ˌhouməˈdʒiniəs/ *a* homogéneo

homologous /həˈmɒləgəs/ *a* homólogo

homonym /ˈhɒmənɪm/ *n* homónimo, *m*

homonymous /həˈmɒnəməs/ *a* homónimo

homosexual /ˌhouməˈsɛkʃuəl/ *a* and *n* homosexual, *mf*

Honduran /hɒnˈdurən/ *a* and *n* hondureño (-ña)

hone /houn/ *n* piedra de afilar, *f.* —*vt* afilar, vaciar

honest /ˈɒnɪst/ *a* honrado; decente, honesto; (chaste) casto; (loyal) sincero, leal; (frank) franco; imparcial. **an h. man,** un hombre de buena fe, un hombre honrado, un hombre decente

honesty /ˈɒnəsti/ *n* honradez, *f;* honestidad, *f;* (chastity) castidad, *f;* sinceridad, *f;* rectitud, imparcialidad, *f*

honey /ˈhʌni/ *n* miel, *f.* **h.-bee,** abeja obrera, *f.* **h.-colored,** melado. **h.-pot,** jarro de miel, *m.* **h.-tongued,** melifluo; de pico de oro

honeycomb /ˈhʌniˌkoum/ *n* panal, *m*

honeycombed /ˈhʌniˌkoumd/ *a* apanalado

honeydew /ˈhʌniˌdu/ *n* mielada, *f; Fig.* ambrosia, *f*

honeyed /ˈhʌnid/ *a* de miel; *Fig.* meloso, adulador

honeymoon /ˈhʌniˌmun/ *n* luna de miel, *f;* viaje de novios, viaje nupcial, *m.* —*vi* hacer un viaje nupcial

honeysuckle /ˈhʌniˌsʌkəl/ *n* madreselva, *f*

honor /ˈɒnər/ *n* honor, *m;* honra, *f;* honradez, rectitud, integridad, *f; pl* **honors,** honores, *m pl;* condecoraciones, *f pl;* (last h.) honras, pompas fúnebres, *f pl.* —*vt* honrar; (God) glorificar; (decorate) condecorar, laurear; (respect) respetar; reverenciar; *Com.* aceptar; (a toast) beber. **On my h.,** A fe mía. **point of h.,** punto de honor, pundonor, *m.* **word of h.,** palabra de honor, *f.* **Your H.,** (to a judge) Excelentísimo Señor Juez

honorable /ˈɒnərəbəl/ *a* honorable; glorioso; digno; ilustre; (sensitive of honor) pundonoroso

honorable mention *n* accésit, *m*

honorableness /ˈɒnərəbəlnɪs/ *n* honradez, *f*

honorably /ˈɒnərəbli/ *adv* honorablemente; dignamente

honorarium /ˌɒnəˈrɛəriəm/ *n* honorario, *m*

honorary /ˈɒnəˌrɛri/ *a* honorario, honorífico. **h. member,** socio (-ia) honorario (-ia). **h. mention,** mención honorífica, *f*

hood /hʊd/ *n* capucha, caperuza, *f;* (folding, of vehicles) capota, cubierta, cubierta del motor *f;* (of a carriage) caparazón, fuelle, *m;* (of a car) capó, *m,* (university) muceta, *f;* (of a fireplace) campana (de hogar), *f;* (cowl of chimney) sombrerete (de chimenea), *m.* —*vt* cubrir con capucha; cubrir; (the eyes) ocultar, cubrir, velar

hooded /ˈhʊdɪd/ *a* con capucha

hoodwink /ˈhʊdˌwɪŋk/ *vt* vendar (los ojos); *Fig.* engañar, embaucar, burlar

hoof /hʊf/ *n* casco, *m;* (cloven) pezuña, *f*

hoofed /hʊft/ *a* ungulado

hoof it ir a golpe de calcetín

hook /hʊk/ *n* gancho, garfio, *m;* (boat-) bichero, *m;* (fish-) anzuelo, *m;* (on a dress) corchete, *m;* (hanger) colgadero, *m;* (claw) garra, *f.* —*vt* enganchar; (a dress) abrochar; (fish) pescar, coger; (nab) atrapar, pescar. **by h. or by crook,** a tuertas o a derechas. **left h.,** (boxing) izquierdo, *m.* **right h.,** (boxing) derecho, *m.* **to catch oneself on a h.,** engancharse. **h. and eye,** los corchetes. **h.-nosed,** con nariz de gancho, con nariz aguileña. **h.-up,** *Radio.* circuito, *m;* transmisión en circuito, *f*

hooked /hʊkt/ *a* con ganchos; corvo, ganchoso

hooking /ˈhʊkɪŋ/ *n* enganche, *m;* (of a dress) abrochamiento, *m;* (of fish and *Inf.*) pesca, *f*

hookworm /ˈhʊkˌwɜrm/ *n* anquilostoma, *m*

hooligan /ˈhulɪgən/ *n* rufián, *m*

hooliganism /ˈhulɪgəˌnɪzəm/ *n* rufianería, *f*

hoop /hup/ *n* aro, arco, *m;* (of a skirt) miriñaque, *m;* (croquet) argolla, *f;* (toy) aro, *m;* círculo, *m.* —*vt* poner aros a; *Fig.* rodear

hoot /hut/ *n* (of owls) ululación, *f,* grito, *m;* (whistle) silbido, *m;* ruido, clamor, *m.* —*vi* (of owls) ulular, gritar; silbar; *Auto.* avisar con la bocina. **to h. off the stage,** hacer abandonar la escena. **to h. down,** silbar

hooter /ˈhutər/ *n* sirena, *f; Auto.* bocina, *f;* (whistle) pito, *m*

hooting /ˈhutɪŋ/ *n* See **hoot**

hop /hɒp/ *n* salto, brinco, *m; Bot.* lúpulo, *m; Bot.* flores de oblón, *f pl;* (dance) baile, *m.* —*vi* saltar con un pie; andar dando brincos; saltar; (limp) cojear; recoger lúpulo; (of plant) dar lúpulo. —*vt* saltar. **hop-garden,** huerto de lúpulo, *m.* **hop-kiln,** horno para secar lúpulo, *m.* **hop-picker,** recolector (-ra) de lúpulo. **hop-picking,** recolección de lúpulos, *f*

hope /houp/ *n* esperanza, *f;* (faith) confianza, *f;* (expectation) anticipación, expectación, *f;* (probability) probabilidad, *f;* (illusion) ilusión, *f;* sueño, *m.* —*vi* esperar. **to live in h. that,** vivir con la esperanza de que. **to lose h.,** desesperarse. **to h. against h.,** esperar sin motivo, esperar lo imposible. **to h. for,** desear. **to h. in,** confiar en

hopeful /ˈhoupfəl/ *a* lleno de esperanzas, confiado; optimista; (*Fig.*) risueño. —*n Inf.* la esperanza de la casa. **to look h.,** *Fig.* prometer bien

hopefully /ˈhoupfəli/ *adv* con esperanza

hopefulness /ˈhoupfəlnɪs/ *n* optimismo, *m; Fig.* aspecto prometedor, *m*

hopeless /ˈhouplɪs/ *a* desesperado, sin esperanza; irremediable; (of situations) imposible; (of disease) incurable. **to be h.,** (lose hope) desesperarse; (have no remedy) ser irremediable; (of disease) no tener cura. **to make h.,** hacer perder la esperanza, desesperar; dejar sin remedio; (a situation) hacer imposible; (an illness) hacer imposible de curar

hopelessly /ˈhouplɪsli/ *adv* sin esperanza; sin remedio; imposiblemente; incurablemente

hopelessness /ˈhouplɪsnɪs/ *n* desesperación, *f;* (of an illness) imposibilidad de curar, *f;* lo irremediable; imposibilidad, *f*

hopscotch /ˈhɒpˌskɒtʃ/ *n* infernáculo, *m,* rayuela, *f*

horal, horary /ˈhɔrəl; ˈhɔrəri/ *a* horario

horde /hɔrd/ *n* horda, *f*

horizon /həˈraizən/ *n* horizonte, *m*

horizontal /ˌhɔrəˈzɒntl̩/ *a* horizontal. **h. suspension,** (gymnastics) plancha, *f*

horizontality /ˌhɔrəzɒnˈtælɪti/ *n* horizontalidad, *f*

horizontally /ˌhɔrəˈzɒntl̩i/ *adv* horizontalmente

hormone /ˈhɔrmoun/ *n* hormona, *f*

horn /hɔrn/ *n* (of bull, etc.) cuerno, *m;* (antler) asta, *f;* (of an insect) antena, *f;* (of a snail) tentáculo, *m; Mus.* cuerno, *m;* trompa, *f;* (of motor and phonograph) bocina, *f;* (of moon) cuerno (de la luna), *m.* **article made of h.,** objeto de cuerno, *m.* **on the horns of a dilemma,** entre la espada y la pared. **h. of plenty,** cuerno de abundancia, *m;* cornucopia, *f.* **h.-rimmed spectacles,** anteojos de concha, *m pl.* **h. thrust,** cornada, *f*

horned /hɔrnd/ *a* cornudo; (antlered) enastado

hornet /ˈhɔrnɪt/ *n* avispón, abejón, *m*

horny /ˈhɔrni/ *a* córneo; calloso; duro. **h.-handed,** con manos callosas

horoscope /ˈhɔrəˌskoup/ *n* horóscopo, *m*

horrible /ˈhɔrəbəl/ *a* horrible, repugnante, espantoso; (of price) enorme; *Inf.* horrible

horribleness /ˈhɔrəbəlnɪs/ *n* horribilidad, *f,* horror, *m,* lo espantoso

horribly /ˈhɔrəbli/ *adv* horriblemente

horrid /ˈhɔrɪd/ *a* horroroso; desagradable

horridness /ˈhɔrɪdnɪs/ *n* horror, *m;* lo desagradable

horrific /hɔˈrɪfɪk/ *a* horrífico, horrendo

horrify /ˈhɔrəˌfai/ *vt* horrorizar; escandalizar

horrifying /ˈhɔrəˌfaiɪŋ/ *a* horroroso, horripilante

horror /ˈhɔrər/ *n* horror, *m.* **h.-stricken,** horrorizado

hors d'œuvres /ɔrˈdɜrvz/ *n pl* entremeses, *m pl*

horse /hɔrs/ *n* caballo, *m;* (cavalry) caballería, *f;* (frame) caballete, *m;* (gymnastics and as punishment) potro, *m.* —*a* caballar, caballuno. —*vt* montar a caballo. **pack of horses,** caballada, *f.* **to ride a h.,** cabalgar, montar a caballo. **H. Artillery,** artillería montada, *f.* **h. blanket,** manta para caballos, *f;* sudadero, *m.* **h.-block,** montador, *m.* **h.-box,** vagón para caballos, *m.* **h.-breaker,** domador de caballos, *m.* **h.-cab,** simón, *m.* **h.-chestnut,** castaña pilonga, *f.* **h.-chestnut flower,** candela, *f.* **h.-collar,** collera, *f.* **h.-dealer,** chalán, *m.* **h.-doctor,** veterinario, *m.* **h.-flesh,** carne de caballo, *f.* **h.-fly,** tábano, *m.* **H. Guards,** guardias montadas, *f pl.* **h.-latitudes,** calmas de Cáncer, *f pl.* **h.-laugh,** carcajada, *f.* **h.-master,** maestro de equitación, *m.* **h. meat,** carne de caballo, *f.* **h. pistol,** pistola de arzón, *f.* **h.-play,** payasada, *f.* **h.-power,** caballo de vapor, *m;* potencia, *f.* **a twelve-**

h.p. car, un coche de doce caballos. **h.-race,** carrera de caballos, *f.* **h.-radish,** rábano picante, raíz amarga, *m.* **h.-sense,** sentido común, *m,* gramática parda, *f.* **h. show,** exposición de caballos, feria equina *f;* concurso de caballos, *m.* **h.-trainer,** entrenador de caballos, *m.* **h. tram,** tranvía de sangre, *m.* **h. trappings,** monturas, *f pl*

horseback /'hɔrs,bæk/ *n* lomo de caballo, *m.* **on h.,** a caballo. **to ride on h.,** ir a caballo

horseman /'hɔrsmən/ *n* jinete, cabalgador, *m*

horsemanship /'hɔrsmən,ʃɪp/ *n* equitación, *f,* manejo del caballo, *m*

horseshoe /'hɔrs,ʃu/ *n* herradura, *f.* **h. arch,** arco de herradura, arco morisco, *m*

horsewhip /'hɔrs,wɪp/ *n* látigo, *m.* —*vt* zurriagar, pegar con látigo

horsewoman /'hɔrs,wʊmən/ *n* amazona, *f*

horsey /'hɔrsi/ *a* de caballo; aficionado a caballos; grosero

horticultural /,hɔrtɪ'kʌltʃərəl/ *a* horticultural. **h. show,** exposición de flores, *f*

horticulturalist /,hɔrtɪ'kʌltʃərɪst/ *n* horticultor (-ra)

horticulture /'hɔrtɪ,kʌltʃər/ *n* horticultura, *f*

hosanna /hou'zænə/ *n* hosanna, *m*

hose /houz/ *n* (tube) manga, *f;* (breeches) calzón, *m;* (stockings) medias, *f pl;* (socks) calcetines, *m pl.* **h. man,** manguero, *m.* **h.-pipe,** manga de riego, manguera, *f*

hosier /'houʒər/ *n* calcetero (-ra)

hosiery /'houʒəri/ *n* calcetería, *f.* **h. trade,** calcetería, *f*

hospice /'hɒspɪs/ *n* hospicio, *m;* asilo, refugio, *m*

hospitable /'hɒspɪtəbəl/ *a* hospitalario

hospitableness /'hɒspɪtəbəlnɪs/ *n* hospitalidad, *f*

hospitably /'hɒspɪtəbəli/ *adv* hospitalariamente

hospital /'hɒspɪtl̩/ *n* hospital, *m;* (school) colegio, *m.* **h. nurse,** enfermera, *f.* **h. ship,** buque hospital, *m*

hospital bed cama hospitalaria, *f*

hospitality /,hɒspɪ'tælɪti/ *n* hospitalidad, *f*

host /houst/ *n* huésped, convidador, (of radio or tv program) presentador, *m;* (at an inn) patrón, mesonero, *m;* (army) ejército, *m;* (crowd) multitud, muchedumbre, *f; Eccl.* hostia, *f; pl* **hosts,** huestes, *f pl.* **h.-plant,** planta huésped, *f*

hostage /'hɒstɪdʒ/ *n* rehén, *m; Fig.* prenda, *f*

host country *n* (of an organization) país-sede, *m*

hostel /'hɒstl̩/ *n* hostería, *f;* club, *m;* residencia de estudiantes, *f*

hostelry /'hɒstl̩ri/ *n* hospedería, *f;* parador, mesón, *m*

hostess /'houstɪs/ *n* ama de la casa, *f;* la que recibe a los invitados; la que convída; (of an inn) patrona, mesonera, *f*

hostile /'hɒstl̩/ *a* enemigo; hostil, contrario (a); (of circumstances, etc.) desfavorable

hostility /hɒ'stɪlɪti/ *n* enemistad, *f,* antagonismo, *m,* mala voluntad, *f;* hostilidad, guerra, *f.* **suspension of hostilities,** suspensión de hostilidades, *f*

hot /hɒt/ *a* caliente; (of a day, etc.) caluroso; (piquant) picante; ardiente; vehemente, impetuoso; violento; impaciente; colérico; entusiasta; lleno de deseo; *Art.* intenso; (great) grande, mucho; (vigorous) enérgico. **You are getting very hot now,** *Inf.* (in a game, etc.) Te estás quemando. **It is hot,** Está caliente; (of weather) Hace calor. **to grow hot,** calentarse; *Fig.* acalorarse; (of weather) empezar a hacer calor. **to make hot,** calentar; dar calor (a); *Inf.* dar vergüenza. **hot-blooded,** de sangre caliente; apasionado; colérico. **hot-foot,** aprisa, apresuradamente. **hot-headed,** impetuoso. **hot-plate,** *Elec.* calientaplatos, *m.* **hot springs,** termas, *f pl.* **hot-tempered,** colérico, irascible. **hot water,** agua caliente, *f.* **hot-water bottle,** bolsa de goma, *f.* **hot-water pipes,** las cañerías del agua caliente

hotbed /'hɒt,bɛd/ *n* semillero, vivero, *m; Fig.* semillero, foco, *m*

hotchpotch /'hɒtʃ,pɒtʃ/ *n* potaje, *m; Fig.* mezcolanza, *f,* fárrago, *m*

hotel /hou'tɛl/ *n* hotel, *m.* **h.-keeper,** hotelero (-ra)

hothead /'hɒt,hɛd/ *n* exaltado (-da), fanático (-ca)

hothouse /'hɒt,haus/ *n* invernáculo, *m,* estufa, *f.* **h. plant,** *Fig.* planta de estufa, *f*

hotly /'hɒtli/ *adv* calurosamente; con vehemencia; coléricamente

hough /hɒk/ *n Zool.* pernil, *m;* (in man) corva, *f*

hound /haund/ *n* perro de caza, sabueso de artois, *m;* perro, *m; Inf.* canalla, *m.* —*vt* cazar con perros; *Fig.* perseguir; *Fig.* incitar. **master of hounds,** montero, *m.* **pack of hounds,** jauría, *f*

hour /auᵊr/ *n* hora, *f;* momento, *m;* ocasión, oportunidad, *f pl.* **hours,** horas, *f pl.* **after hours,** fuera de horas. **at the eleventh h.,** en el último minuto. **by the h.,** por horas; horas enteras. **small hours,** altas horas de la noche, *Inf.* las tantas, *f pl.* **to keep late hours,** acostarse tarde. **to strike the h.,** dar la hora. **h.-glass,** reloj de arena, *m.* **h.-hand,** horario, *m.* **h. of death,** hora suprema, hora de la muerte, *f*

hourly /'auᵊrli/ *a* cada hora; por hora; continuo. —*adv* a cada hora; de un momento a otro

house /*n* haus; *v* hauz/ *n* casa, *f;* (home) hogar, *m;* (lineage) familia, *f,* abolengo, *m;* (*Theat.*) sala, *f,* teatro, *m; Com.* casa comercial, *f;* (takings) entrada, *f;* (audience) público, *m;* (of Lords, Commons) cámara, *f;* (college) colegio, *m;* (parliament) parlamento, *m;* (building) edificio, *m.* —*a* de casa; de la casa; doméstico. —*vt* dar vivienda (a); alojar, recibir (or tener) en casa de uno; (store) poner, guardar. **The cottage will not h. them all,** No habrá bastante lugar para todos ellos en la cabaña, No cabrán todos en la cabaña. **country-h.,** finca, *f;* casa de campo, *f.* **full h.,** casa llena, *f; Theat.* lleno, *m.* **to bring down the h.,** *Theat.* hacer venirse el teatro abajo. **to keep h.,** llevar la casa; ser ama de casa. **to keep open h.,** tener mesa puesta, ser hospitalario. **to set up h.,** poner casa. **h. of cards,** castillo de naipes, *m.* **H. of Commons,** Cámara de los Comunes, *f.* **H. of Lords,** Cámara de los Lores, *f.* **h.-agent,** agente de casas, *m.* **h.-boat,** barco-habitación, *m,* casa flotante, *f.* **h.-dog,** perro de guardia, *m;* perro de casa, *m.* **h.-fly,** mosca doméstica, *f.* **h. furnisher,** mueblista, *mf.* **h. painter,** pintor de brocha gorda, *m.* **h. party,** reunión en una casa de campo, *f.* **h.-physician,** médico (-ca) interno (-na). **h. porter,** portero, *m.* **h. property,** propiedad inmueble, *f.* **h.-room,** capacidad de una casa, *f.* **h. slipper,** zapatilla, *f,* pantuflo, *m.* **h.-surgeon,** cirujano interno, *m.* **h.-to-h.,** de casa en casa. **h.-warming,** reunión para colgar la cremallera, *f*

housebreaker /'haus,breikər/ *n* ladrón de casas, *m*

housebreaking /'haus,breikɪŋ/ *n* robo de una casa, *m*

houseful /'hausfʊl/ *n* casa, *f*

house furnishings *n pl* artefactos para el hogar, accesorios caseros, aparatos electrodomésticos, *m pl*

household /'haus,hould/ *n* casa, *f;* familia, *f;* hogar, *m.* —*a* de la casa; doméstico; del hogar. **to be a h. word,** andar en lenguas. **h. accounts,** cuentas de la casa, *f pl.* **h. duties,** labores de la casa, *f pl.* **h. gods,** penates, *m pl.* **h. goods,** ajuar, mobiliario, *m.* **h. management,** gobierno de la casa, *m*

householder /'haus,houldər/ *n* padre de familia, *m;* dueño (-ña) (or inquilino (-na)) de una casa

housekeeper /'haus,kipər/ *n* ama de llaves, *f;* mujer de su casa, *f*

housekeeping /'haus,kipɪŋ/ *n* gobierno de la casa, *m;* economía doméstica, *f.* —*a* doméstico. **to set up h.,** poner casa

housemaid /'haus,meid/ *n* camarera, sirvienta, *f.* **housemaid's knee,** rodilla de fregona, *f*

house of ill repute *n* burdel, *m,* casa de citas, casa de zorras, casa pública, *f;* lupanar, *m*

housetops /'haus,tɒps/ *n* tejado, *m;* (flat roof) azotea, *f.* **to shout from the h.,** pregonar a los cuatro vientos

housewife /'haus,waif/ *n* madre de familia, mujer de su casa, *f;* (sewing-bag) neceser de costura, *m*

housewifely /'haus,waifli/ *a* propio de una mujer de su casa; doméstico; (of a woman) hacendosa

housewifery /'haus,waifəri/ *n* economía doméstica, *f*

housing /'hauzɪŋ/ *n* provisión de vivienda, *f;* (storage) almacenaje, *m;* alojamiento, *m; Inf.* casa, vivienda, *f.* **h. scheme,** urbanización, *f.* **h. shortage,** crisis de vivienda, *f,* déficit habitacional, *m*

hovel /'hʌvəl/ *n* casucha, *f*

hover /'hʌvər/ *vi* revolotear; (of hawks, etc.)

cernerse; estar suspendido; rondar; seguir de cerca, estar al lado (de); *Fig.* vacilar, dudar

hovering /ˈhʌvərɪŋ/ *n* revoloteo, *m;* (of birds of prey) calada, *f; Fig.* vacilación, *f.* —*a* revolante, que revolotea; que se cierne (sobre); (menacing) que amenaza, inminente

how /hau/ *adv* cómo; (by what means, in what manner) de qué modo; (at what price) a qué precio; qué; cuánto. —*n* el cómo. **to know how,** saber. **For how long?** ¿Por cuánto tiempo? **How are you?** ¿Cómo está Vd.? *Inf.* ¿Qué tal? **How do you do!** ¡Mucho gusto (en conocerlo/conocerla/conocerlos/conocerlas)! **How old are you?** ¿Qué edad tiene Vd.? **How beautiful!** ¡Qué hermoso! **How big!** ¡Cuán grande! **How early?** ¿Cuán temprano?; ¿Cuándo a más tardar? **How far?** ¿A qué distancia? ¿Hasta qué punto? ¿Hasta dónde? **How fast?** ¿A qué velocidad? **How few!** ¡Qué pocos! **How little!** ¡Qué pequeño!; ¡Qué poco! **How long?** ¿Cuánto tiempo? **How many?** ¿Cuántos? *m pl*; ¿Cuántas? *f pl.* **How much is it?** ¿Cuánto vale? **How much cloth do you want?** ¿Cuánta tela quieres? **How often?** ¿Cuán a menudo? ¿Cuántas veces? **How would you like to go for a walk?** ¿Te gustaría pasearte? **How are you going to Lisbon?** ¿En qué vas a Lisboa?

however /hauˈɛvər/ *adv* como quiera (que) (followed by subjunctive); por más que (followed by subjunctive); por... que (followed by subjunctive). —*conjunc* (nevertheless) sin embargo, no obstante. **h. good it is,** por bueno que sea. **h. he does it,** como quiera que lo haga. **h. it may be,** sea como sea. **h. much,** por mucho que

howl /haul/ *n* aullido, *m;* (groan) gemido, *m;* (cry) grito, *m;* (roar) rugido, bramido, *m;* lamento, *m.* —*vi* aullar; gemir; gritar; rugir, bramar. —*vt* chillar. **Each time he opened his mouth he was howled down,** Cada vez que abrió la boca se armó una bronca

howler /ˈhaulər/ *n* aullador (-ra); *Zool.* mono (-na) chillón (-ona); (blunder) coladura, plancha, *f*

howling /ˈhaulɪŋ/ *a* aullante; gemidor; (crying) que llora; bramante, rugiente. —*n* los aullidos; (groaning) el gemir, los gemidos; (crying) los gritos; (weeping) el lloro; (roaring) los bramidos, el rugir; los lamentos

hub /hʌb/ *n* (of a wheel) cubo (de rueda) *m; Fig.* centro, *m.* **hub cap,** tapa de cubo, *f*

hubbub /ˈhʌbʌb/ *n* algarada, barahúnda, *f*

huckster /ˈhʌkstər/ *n* revendedor (-ra). —*vi* revender; (haggle) regatear

huddle /ˈhʌdl/ *n* (heap) montón, *m;* colección, *f;* (group) corrillo, grupo, *m;* (mixture) mezcla, *f.* —*vt* arrebujar, amontonar; acurrucar, arrebujar; (throw on) echarse. —*vi* amontonarse; apiñarse; acurrucarse, arrebujarse

hue /hyu/ *n* color, *m;* matiz, tono, *m;* (of opinion) matiz, *m;* (clamor) clamor, *m,* gritería, *f.* **hue and cry,** alarma, *f*

huff /hʌf/ *n* acceso de cólera, *m*

huffily /ˈhʌfəli/ *adv* malhumoradamente; petulantemente

huffiness /ˈhʌfinɪs/ *n* mal humor, *m;* petulancia, *f;* arrogancia, *f*

hug /hʌg/ *n* abrazo, *m.* —*vt* abrazar, apretujar; *Fig.* acariciar; *Naut.* navegar muy cerca de. **to hug oneself,** *Fig.* congratularse

huge /hyudʒ/ *a* enorme, inmenso; gigante; vasto

hugely /ˈhyudʒli/ *adv* inmensamente, enormemente

hugeness /ˈhyudʒnɪs/ *n* inmensidad, enormidad, *f;* vastedad, *f*

Huguenot /ˈhyugəˌnɒt/ *a* and *n* hugonote (-ta)

hulk /hʌlk/ *n* barco viejo, *m;* pontón, *m*

hulking /ˈhʌlkɪŋ/ *a* pesado, desgarbado

hull /hʌl/ *n Naut.* casco (de un buque), *m;* (shell) cáscara, *f;* (pod) vaina, *f, vt* mondar

hullabaloo /ˈhʌləbəˌlu/ *n* alboroto, tumulto, *m;* vocerío, *m*

hullo /həˈlou/ *interj* See **hallo**

hum /hʌm/ *n* zumbido, *m;* ruido confuso, *m.* —*vi* (sing) canturrear; zumbar; (confused sound) zurrir; (hesitate) vacilar. —*vt* (a tune) tararear

human /ˈhyumən/ *a* humano. **the h. touch,** el don de gentes. **h. being,** ser humano, hombre, *m*

humane /hyuˈmein/ *a* humanitario, humano

humanely /hyuˈmeinli/ *adv* humanitariamente

humaneness /hyuˈmeinnɪs/ *n* humanidad, *f*

humanism /ˈhyuməˌnɪzəm/ *n* humanismo, *m*

humanist /ˈhyumənɪst/ *n* humanista, *mf*

humanistic /ˌhyuməˈnɪstɪk/ *a* humanista

humanitarian /hyuˌmænɪˈtɛəriən/ *a* humanitario

humanitarianism /hyuˌmænɪˈtɛəriəˌnɪzəm/ *n* humanitarismo, *m*

humanity /hyuˈmænɪti/ *n* humanidad, *f;* raza humana, *f.* **the humanities,** las humanidades

humanize /ˈhyuməˌnaiz/ *vt* humanizar; (milk) maternizar. —*vi* humanizarse

humanly /ˈhyumənli/ *adv* humanamente

humble /ˈhʌmbəl/ *a* humilde; modesto; (cringing) servil; sumiso; pobre. —*vt* humillar; mortificar. **to h. oneself,** humillarse

humbleness /ˈhʌmbəlnɪs/ *n* humildad, *f;* modestia, *f;* (abjectness) servilismo, *m;* sumisión, *f;* pobreza, *f;* (of birth, etc.) obscuridad, *f*

humbling /ˈhʌmblɪŋ/ *n* humillación, *f;* mortificación, *f*

humbly /ˈhʌmbli/ *adv* humildemente; modestamente; servilmente

humbug /ˈhʌmˌbʌg/ *n* (fraud) embuste, engaño, *m;* (nonsense) disparate, *m,* tontería, *f;* mentira, *f,* (person) farsante, charlatán, *m;* (sweetmeat) caramelo de menta, *m.* —*vt* engañar, embaucar; burlarse de

humdrum /ˈhʌmˌdrʌm/ *a* monótono; aburrido

humeral /ˈhyumərəl/ *a* humeral. —*n Eccl.* velo humeral, *m*

humerus /ˈhyumərəs/ *n Anat.* húmero, *m*

humid /ˈhyumɪd/ *a* húmedo

humidity /hyuˈmɪdɪti/ *n* humedad, *f*

humiliate /hyuˈmɪliˌeit/ *vt* humillar, mortificar. **to h. oneself,** humillarse

humiliating /hyuˈmɪliˌeitɪŋ/ *a* humillante; degradante

humiliation /hyuˌmɪliˈeiʃən/ *n* humillación, mortificación, *f;* degradación, *f*

humility /hyuˈmɪlɪti/ *n* humildad, *f;* modestia, *f*

humming /ˈhʌmɪŋ/ *n* zumbido, *m;* (of a tune) tarareo, *m.* —*a* zumbador. **h.-bird,** pájaro mosca, colibrí, *m.* **h.-top,** trompa, *f*

humor /ˈhyumər/ *n* humor, *m;* humorismo, *m;* (temperament) disposición, *f,* carácter, *m;* (whim) capricho, *m.* —*vt* seguir el humor (a), complacer; satisfacer, consentir en; (a lock, etc.) manejar. **in a good (bad) h.,** de buen (mal) humor. **I am not in the h. to...** No estoy de humor para... **sense of h.,** sentido de humor, *m*

humored /ˈhyumərd/ *a* (in compounds) de humor... **good-h.,** de buen humor. **ill-h.,** malhumorado, de mal humor

humoresque /ˌhyuməˈrɛsk/ *n Mus.* capricho musical, *m*

humorist /ˈhyumərɪst/ *n* humorista, *mf*

humorless /ˈhyumərlɪs/ *a* sin sentido humorístico, sin sentido de humor

humorous /ˈhyumərəs/ *a* humorístico; cómico, risible

humorously /ˈhyumərəsli/ *adv* humorísticamente; cómicamente

humorousness /ˈhyumərəsnɪs/ *n* humorismo, *m;* lo cómico

hump /hʌmp/ *n* joroba, giba, *f;* (hillock) montecillo, *m; Inf.* depresión, *f*

humpback /ˈhʌmpˌbæk/ *n* giba, joroba, *f;* (person) jorobado (-da), giboso (-sa)

humpbacked /ˈhʌmpˌbækt/ *a* jorobado, giboso, corcovado

humph /*an inarticulate expression resembling a snort or grunt; spelling pron.* hʌmf/ *interj* ¡qué va!; ¡patrañas!

humus /ˈhyuməs/ *n* humus, mantillo, *m*

hunchback /ˈhʌntʃˌbæk/ *n* joroba, giba, *f;* (person) jorobado (-da), corcovado (-da), giboso (-sa)

hunchbacked /ˈhʌntʃˌbækt/ *a* jorobado, giboso, corcovado

hundred /ˈhʌndrɪd/ *n* ciento, *m;* centenar, *m,* centena, *f.* —*a* ciento; (before nouns and adjectives, excluding numerals, with the exception of mil and millón) cien. **a h. thousand,** cien mil. **one h. and one,** ciento uno. **by the h.,** a centenares. **hundreds of people,** centenares de personas, *m pl.* **h.-millionth,** *a*

and *n* cienmillonésimo *m*. **h.-thousandth,** *a* and *n* cienmilésimo *m*.
hundredfold /'hʌndrɪd,fould/ *adv* cien veces. —*n* céntuplo, *m*
hundredth /'hʌndrɪdθ/ *a* centésimo, céntimo. —*n* centésimo, *m*, centésima parte, *f*
hundredweight /'hʌndrɪd,weit/ *n* quintal, *m*
Hungarian /hʌŋ'gɛəriən/ *a* and *n* húngaro (-ra); (language) húngaro, *m*
Hungary /'hʌŋgəri/ Hungría, *f*
hunger /'hʌŋgər/ *n* hambre, *f;* apetito, *m;* (craving) deseo, *m*, ansia, *f*. —*vi* estar hambriento, tener hambre. **to h. for,** desear, ansiar. **h.-strike,** huelga de hambre, *f*
hungrily /'hʌŋgrəli/ *adv* hambrientamente, con hambre; ansiosamente
hungry /'hʌŋgri/ *a* hambriento; (of land) pobre; (anxious) deseoso. **to be h.,** tener hambre. **to make h.,** dar hambre
hunk /hʌŋk/ *n* rebanada, *f*, pedazo, *m*
hunt /hʌnt/ *n* caza, cacería, montería, *f;* grupo de cazadores, *m;* (search) busca, *f;* (pursuit) persecución, *f*. —*vt* cazar; cazar a caballo; (search) buscar; rebuscar, explorar; (pursue) perseguir. **to h. down,** perseguir. **to h. for,** buscar. **to h. out,** buscar; descubrir, desenterrar
hunter /'hʌntər/ *n* cazador, *m;* caballo de caza, *m;* (watch) saboneta, *f*
hunting /'hʌntɪŋ/ *n* caza, *f;* caza a caballo, *f;* persecución, *f*. —*a* cazador, de caza. **to go h.,** ir a cazar. **h.-box,** pabellón de caza, *m*. **h.-cap,** gorra de montar, *f*. **h.-crop,** látigo para cazar, *m*. **h.-ground,** coto de caza, terreno de caza, *m*. **h.-horn,** cuerno de caza, *m*, corneta de monte, *f*. **h. party,** partido de caza, *m*, cacería, *f*
hunting lodge *n* pabellón *m*
huntress /'hʌntrɪs/ *n* cazadora, *f*
huntsman /'hʌntsmən/ *n* cazador, montero, *m*
huntsmanship /'hʌntsmən,ʃɪp/ *n* montería, arte de cazar, *f*
hurdle /'hɜrdl̩/ *n* valla, *f;* zarzo, *m*. **h.-race,** carrera de obstáculos, *f;* carrera de vallas, *f*
hurdy-gurdy /'hɜrdi'gɜrdi/ *n* organillo, *m*
hurl /hɜrl/ *vt* lanzar, tirar, arrojar, echar. **to h. oneself,** lanzarse. **to h. oneself against,** arrojarse a (or contra). **to h. oneself upon,** abalanzarse sobre
hurly-burly /'hɜrli'bɜrli/ *n* alboroto, tumulto, *m*
hurrah /hə'rɑ/ *interj* ¡hurra! ¡viva! —*n* vítor, *m*. **H. for...!** ¡Viva...!, ¡Vivan...! **to shout h.,** vitorear
hurricane /'hɜrɪ,kein/ *n* huracán, *m*. **h.-lamp,** lámpara sorda, *f*
hurried /'hɜrid/ *a* apresurado, precipitado; hecho a prisa; superficial
hurriedly /'hɜridli/ *adv* apresuradamente, precipitadamente, con prisa; superficialmente; (of writing) a vuela pluma
hurry /'hɜri/ *n* prisa, *f;* precipitación, *f;* urgencia, *f;* confusión, *f;* alboroto, *m*. **in a h.,** aprisa. **in a great h.,** aprisa y corriendo. **to be in a h.,** llevar prisa, estar de prisa. **There is no h.,** No corre prisa, No hay prisa
hurry /'hɜri/ *vt* apresurar, dar prisa (a); llevar aprisa; hacer andar aprisa; enviar apresuradamente; precipitar; acelerar. —*vi* darse prisa; apresurarse. **to h. after,** correr detrás de, seguir apresuradamente. **to h. away,** *vi* marcharse aprisa, marcharse corriendo; huir; salir precipitadamente. —*vt* hacer marcharse aprisa; llevar con prisa. **to h. back,** *vi* volver aprisa, apresurarse a volver. —*vt* hacer volver aprisa. **to h. in,** *vi* entrar aprisa, entrar corriendo. —*vt* hacer entrar aprisa. **to h. off.** See **to h. away. to h. on,** *vi* apresurarse. —*vt* apresurar, precipitar. **to h. out,** salir rápidamente. **to h. over,** hacer rápidamente; concluir aprisa; despachar rápidamente; (travel over) atravesar aprisa; pasar rápidamente por. **to h. toward,** llevar rápidamente hacia; arrastrar hacia; impeler hacia. **to h. up,** *vi* darse prisa. —*vt* apresurar, precipitar; estimular
hurt /hɜrt/ *n* herida, *f;* (harm) daño, mal, *m;* perjuicio, *m*. —*vt* (wound) herir; (cause pain) doler; hacer daño (a); hacer mal (a); (damage) perjudicar, estropear; (offend) ofender; (the feelings) mortificar, lastimar, herir. —*vi* doler; hacer mal; perjudicarse, estropearse. **I haven't h. myself,** No me he hecho daño. **Does it still h. you?** ¿Te duele todavía? **to h. deeply,** *Fig.* herir en el alma. **to h. a person's feelings,** herirle (a uno) el amor propio, lastimar, ofender
hurtful /'hɜrtfəl/ *a* nocivo, dañino; injurioso, pernicioso
hurtfulness /'hɜrtfəlnɪs/ *n* nocividad, *f;* perniciosidad, *f*
hurtle /'hɜrtl̩/ *vt* lanzar. —*vi* lanzarse; volar; caer
husband /'hʌzbənd/ *n* esposo, marido, *m*. —*vt* economizar, ahorrar. **h. and wife,** los esposos, los cónyuges
husbandry /'hʌzbəndri/ *n* labor de los campos, agricultura, *f;* (thrift) frugalidad, parsimonia, *f*
hush /hʌʃ/ *n* silencio, *m*, tranquilidad, *f*. —*interj* ¡chitón! ¡calla! ¡silencio! —*vt* silenciar, hacer callar, imponer silencio (a); (a baby) adormecer; *Fig.* sosegar, calmar. —*vi* callarse, enmudecer. **to h. up,** mantener secreto, ocultar. **h.-h.,** secreto. **h. money,** soborno, chantaje, *m*
hushaby /'hʌʃə,bai/ *interj* ¡duerme!
husk /hʌsk/ *n* (of grain) cascabillo, *m;* zurrón, *m;* cáscara, *f;* (of chestnut) erizo, *m*
huskily /'hʌskəli/ *adv* roncamente
huskiness /'hʌskinɪs/ *n* ronquera, *f; Inf.* robustez, *f*
husky /'hʌski/ *a* (of voice) ronco; *Bot.* cascarudo; (Eskimo) esquimal; *Inf.* robusto, fuerte. —*n* perro esquimal, *m*
hussy /'hʌsi/ *n* pícara, bribona, *f*
hustle /'hʌsəl/ *vt* empujar, codear; *Fig.* precipitar; *Inf.* acelerar. —*vi* codearse; andarse de prisa
hut /hʌt/ *n* choza, cabaña, barraca, *f*
hutch /hʌtʃ/ *n* (chest) arca, *f*, cofre, *m;* (cage) jaula, *f;* (for rabbits) conejera, *f;* (for rats) ratonera, *f; Inf.* choza, *f*
hutment /'hʌtmənt/ *n* campamento de chozas, *m*
hyacinth /'haiəsɪnθ/ *n* jacinto, *m*
hybrid /'haibrɪd/ *a* híbrido; mestizo, mixto. —*n* híbrido, *m*
hybridism /'haibrɪ,dɪzəm/ *n* hibridismo, *m*
hybridization /,haibrɪdə'zeiʃən/ *n* hibridación, *f*
hybridize /'haibrɪ,daiz/ *vt* cruzar. —*vi* producir (or generar) híbridos
hydrangea /hai'dreindʒə/ *n Bot.* hortensia, *f*
hydrant /'haidrənt/ *n* boca de riego, *f*
hydrate /'haidreit/ *n Chem.* hidrato, *m*. —*vt* hidratar
hydration /hai'dreiʃən/ *n* hidratación, *f*
hydraulic /hai'drɔlɪk/ *a* hidráulico. **h. engineering,** hidrotecnia, *f*
hydraulics /hai'drɔlɪks/ *n* hidráulica, *f*
hydrocarbon /,haidrə'kɑrbən/ *n Chem.* hidrocarburo, *m*
hydrochloric /,haidrɔ'klɔrɪk/ *a* clorhídrico. **h. acid,** ácido clorhídrico, *m*
hydrogen /'haidrədʒən/ *n* hidrógeno, *m*. **h. peroxide,** agua oxigenada, *f*
hydrogenation /,haidrədʒə'neiʃən/ *n* hidrogenación, *f*
hydrogenize /'haidrədʒə,naiz/ *vt* hidrogenizar
hydrolysis /hai'drɒləsɪs/ *n* hidrólisis, *f*
hydromel /'haidrə,mɛl/ *n* aguamiel, *f*, hidromel, *m*
hydropathic /,haidrə'pæθɪk/ *a* hidropático. **h. establishment,** balneario, *m*
hydrophobia /,haidrə'foubiə/ *n* hidrofobia, rabia, *f*
hydrophobic /,haidrə'foubɪk/ *a* hidrofóbico, rabioso
hydroplane /'haidrə,plein/ *n* hidroplano, *m*
hydrotherapic /,haidrouθə'ræpɪk/ *a* hidroterápico
hydrotherapy /,haidrə'θɛrəpi/ *n* hidroterapia, *f*
hyena /hai'inə/ *n* hiena, *f*
hygiene /'haidʒin/ *n* higiene, *f*. **personal h.,** higiene privada, *f*
hygienic /,haidʒi'ɛnɪk/ *a* higiénico
hymen /'haimən/ *n Anat.* himen, *m;* himeneo, *m*
hymeneal /,haimə'niəl/ *a* nupcial
hymn /hɪm/ *n* himno, *m*. **h.-book,** himnario, *m*
hyperbole /hai'pɜrbəli/ *n* hipérbole, *f*
hyperbolical /,haipər'bɒlɪkəl/ *a* hiperbólico
hypercorrection /,haipərkə'rɛkʃən/ *n* seudocultismo, supercultismo, *m*, ultracorrección, *f*

hypercritic /ˌhaipər'krɪtɪk/ *n* hipercrítico, *m*
hypercritical /ˌhaipər'krɪtɪkəl/ *a* hipercrítico, criticón
hypersensitive /ˌhaipər'sɛnsɪtɪv/ *a* vidrioso, quisquilloso
hypertrophy /hai'pɜrtrəfi/ *n* hipertrofia, *f.* —*vi* hipertrofiarse
hyphen /'haifən/ *n* guión, *m*
hypnosis /hɪp'nousɪs/ *n* hipnosis, *f*
hypnotic /hɪp'nɒtɪk/ *a* hipnótico. —*n* (person) hipnótico (-ca); (drug) hipnótico, narcótico, *m*
hypnotism /'hɪpnəˌtɪzəm/ *n* hipnotismo, *m*
hypnotist /'hɪpnətɪst/ *n* hipnotizador (-ra)
hypnotization /ˌhɪpnətə'zeiʃən/ *n* hipnotización, *f*
hypnotize /'hɪpnəˌtaiz/ *vt* hipnotizar
hypo /'haipou/ *n* (sodium hyposulphite) hiposulfito sólido, *m*
hypochondria /ˌhaipə'kɒndriə/ *n* hipocondria, *f*
hypochondriac /ˌhaipə'kɒndriˌæk/ *n* hipocondríaco (-ca)
hypochondriacal /ˌhaipoukən'draiəkəl/ *a* hipocondríaco
hypocrisy /hɪ'pɒkrəsi/ *n* hipocresía, *f;* mojigatería, gazmoñería, *f*
hypocrite /'hɪpəkrɪt/ *n* hipócrita, *mf;* mojigato (-ta). **to be a h.,** ser hipócrita
hypocritical /ˌhɪpə'krɪtɪkəl/ *a* hipócrita; mojigato, gazmoño
hypocritically /ˌhɪpə'krɪtɪkəli/ *adv* hipócritamente, con hipocresía
hypodermic /ˌhaipə'dɜrmɪk/ *a* hipodérmico. **h. syringe,** jeringa de inyecciones, *f*
hypotenuse /hai'pɒtn̩ˌus/ *n Geom.* hipotenusa, *f*
hypothesis /hai'pɒθəsɪs/ *n* hipótesis, *f*
hypothetical /ˌhaipə'θɛtɪkəl/ *a* hipotético
hysterectomy /ˌhɪstə'rɛktəmi/ *n Surg.* histerectomía, *f*
hysteria /hɪ'stɛriə/ *n Med.* histerismo, *m;* histeria, *f,* ataque de nervios, *m*
hysterical /hɪ'stɛrɪkəl/ *a* histérico. **to become h.,** tener un ataque de nervios. **hysterics,** *n pl* ataque de nervios, *m*

I

i /ai/ *n* (letter) i. —*1st pers pron* yo. **It is I,** Soy yo. Normally omitted, the verb alone being used except when **yo** is needed for emphasis, e.g. *Hablo a María,* I speak to Mary, *but Yo toco el violín, pero Juan toca el piano,* I play the violin, but *John* plays the piano
Iago /i'ɑgou/ Yago, *m*
Iberian /ai'bɪəriən/ *a* ibero, ibérico. —*n* ibero (-ra)
Iberian Peninsula, the la Peninsula Ibérica
ibex /'aibɛks/ *n Zool.* íbice, *m*
ice /ais/ *n* hielo, *m;* (ice cream) helado, *m.* —*vt* helar; cubrir de hielo; congelar, cuajar; (a cake, etc.) garapiñar, escarchar, alcorzar. **to ice up,** (*Aer., Auto.*) helarse. **to be as cold as ice,** *Inf.* estar hecho un hielo. **His words cut no ice,** Sus palabras ni pinchan ni cortan. **ice-age,** edad del hielo, *f.* **ice-ax,** piolet, *m.* **ice-box,** nevera, *f.* **ice-cream,** helado, mantecado, *m.* **ice-cream cone,** cucurucho de helado, *m.* **ice-cream freezer,** heladora, *f.* **ice-cream vendor,** mantequero (-ra). **ice-field,** campo de hielo, *m.* **ice-floe,** témpano de hielo flotante, *m.* **ice hockey,** hockey sobre patines, *m.* **ice-pack,** bolsa para hielo, *f.* **ice-skates,** patines de cuchilla, *m pl.* **ice water,** agua helada, *f*
iceberg /'aisbɜrg/ *n* iceberg, témpano de hielo, banco de hielo, *m*
icebound /'ais,baund/ *a* aprisionado por el hielo; atascado en el hielo; (of roads, etc.) helado
iced /aist/ *a* helado; congelado, cuajado; (cakes) garapiñado, escarchado; (of drinks) con hielo. **i. drink,** sorbete, *m*
Iceland /'aislənd/ Islandia, *f*
Icelander /'ais,lændər/ *n* islandés (-esa)
icelandic /ais'lændɪk/ *a* islandes, islándico. —*n* (language) islandés, *m*
icicle /'aisɪkəl/ *n* carámbano, canelón, cerrión, *m*
icily /'aisəli/ *adv* fríamente; *Fig.* frígidamente, con indiferencia, con frialdad
iciness /'aisinɪs/ *n* frialdad, frigidez, *f; Fig.* indiferencia, frigidez, *f*
icing /'aisɪŋ/ *n* helada, *f,* hielo, *m;* (on a cake, etc.) alcorza, capa de azúcar, *f*
icon /'aikɒn/ *n* icono, *m*
iconoclast /ai'kɒnə,klæst/ *n* iconoclasta, *mf*
iconoclastic /ai,kɒnə'klæstɪk/ *a* iconoclasta
iconography /,aikə'nɒgrəfi/ *n* iconografía, *f*
iconology /,aikə'nɒlədʒi/ *n* iconología, *f*
icy /'aisi/ *a* helado; glacial, frío; *Med.* álgido; *Fig.* indiferente, desabrido; *Poet.* frígido, gélido
idea /ai'diə/ *n* idea, *f,* concepto, *m;* (opinion) juicio, *m,* opinión, *f;* (notion) impresión, noción, *f;* (plan) proyecto, plan, designio, *m.* **to form an i. of,** hacerse una idea de, formar un concepto de. **to have an i. of,** tener una idea de; tener nociones de. **An i. struck me,** Se me ocurrió una idea. **full of ideas,** preñado (or lleno) de ideas. **I had no i. that...** No tenía la menor idea de que... No sabía que... **What an i.!** ¡Qué idea!
ideal /ai'diəl/ *a* ideal; excelente, perfecto; (utopian) utópico; (imaginary) imaginario, irreal, ficticio. —*n* ideal, *m;* modelo, prototipo, *m*
idealism /ai'diə,lɪzəm/ *n* idealismo, *m*
idealist /ai'diəlɪst/ *n* idealista, *mf*
idealistic /ai,diə'lɪstɪk/ *a* idealista
idealization /ai,diəlɪ'zeiʃən/ *n* idealización, *f*
idealize /ai'diə,laiz/ *vt* idealizar
ideally /ai'diəli/ *adv* idealmente
ideation /,aidi'eiʃən/ *n Philos.* ideación, *f*
idem /'aidɛm/ *adv* ídem
identical /ai'dɛntɪkəl/ *a* idéntico, mismo, igual; muy parecido, semejante
identically /ai'dɛntɪkəli/ *adv* idénticamente
identifiable /ai,dɛntɪ'faiəbəl/ *a* identificable
identification /ai,dɛntəfɪ'keiʃən/ *n* identificación, *f.* **i. number,** placa de identidad, *f*
identify /ai'dɛntə,fai/ *vt* identificar. **to i. oneself with,** identificarse con
identity /ai'dɛntɪti/ *n* identidad, *f.* **i. card,** cédula personal, *f;* carnet de identidad, *m.* **i. disc,** disco de identidad, *m*
ideogram /'ɪdiə,græm/ *n* ideograma, *m*
ideography /,ɪdi'ɒgrəfi/ *n* ideografía, *f*
ideological /,aidiə'lɒdʒɪkəl/ *a* ideológico
ideologist /,aidi'ɒlədʒɪst/ *n* ideólogo (-ga)
ideology /,aidi'ɒlədʒi/ *n* ideología, *f*
Ides /aidz/ *n pl* idus, *m pl*
idiocy /'ɪdiəsi/ *n* idiotez, imbecilidad, *f;* (foolishness) necedad, tontería, sandez, *f*
idiom /'ɪdiəm/ *n* idiotismo, *m;* modismo, *m,* locución, *f;* (language) habla, *f;* lenguaje, *m*
idiomatic /,ɪdiə'mætɪk/ *a* idiomático
idiopathy /,ɪdi'ɒpəθi/ *n Med.* idiopatía, *f*
idiosyncrasy /,ɪdiə'sɪŋkrəsi/ *n* idiosincrasia, *f*
idiosyncratic /,ɪdiousɪn'krætɪk/ *a* idiosincrásico
idiot /'ɪdiət/ *n* idiota, imbécil, *mf;* (fool) necio (-ia), tonto (-ta), mentecato (-ta)
idiotic /,ɪdi'ɒtɪk/ *a* idiota, imbécil; (foolish) necio, tonto, sandío
idle /'aidḷ/ *a* desocupado; indolente, ocioso; (unemployed) cesante, sin empleo; (lazy) perezoso, holgazán; (of machines) parado, inactivo; (useless) vano, inútil, sin efecto; (false) falso, mentiroso, infundado; (stupid) fútil, frívolo. —*vi* holgar, estar ocioso; holgazanear, haraganear, gandulear. **to i. away,** malgastar, perder. **to i. away the time,** pasar el rato, matar el tiempo. **i. efforts,** vanos esfuerzos, *m pl.* **i. fancies,** ilusiones, fantasías, *f pl,* sueños, *m pl.* **i. hours,** horas desocupadas, *f pl,* ratos perdidos, *m pl.* **i. question,** pregunta ociosa, *f.* **i. tale,** cuento de viejas, *m.* **i. threat,** reto vacuo, *m*
idleness /'aidḷnɪs/ *n* ociosidad, indolencia, inacción, *f;* pereza, holgazanería, gandulería, *f;* (uselessness) inutilidad, futilidad, *f*
idler /'aidlər/ *n* ocioso (-sa); haragán (-ana); perezoso (-sa), holgazán (-ana), gandul (-la)
idly /'aidli/ *adv* ociosamente, perezosamente; (uselessly) vanamente
idol /'aidḷ/ *n* ídolo, *m.* **a popular i.,** el ídolo de las masas, *m*
idolater /ai'dɒlətər/ *n* idólatra, *mf;* (admirer) amante, *mf* esclavo (-va), admirador (-ra)
idolatrous /ai'dɒlətrəs/ *a* idólatra, idolátrico
idolatrously /ai'dɒlətrəsli/ *adv* idolatradamente, con idolatría
idolatry /ai'dɒlətri/ *n* idolatría, *f;* (devotion) adoración, pasión, *f*
idolization /,aidḷə'zeiʃən/ *n* idolatría, *f*
idolize /'aidḷ,aiz/ *vt* idolatrar, adorar
idyll /'aidḷ/ *n* idilio, *m*
idyllic /ai'dɪlɪk/ *a* idílico
if /ɪf/ *conjunc* si; (even if) aunque, aun cuando; (whenever) cuando, en caso de que; (whether) si. **as if,** como si (foll. by subjunc.). **If he comes, we shall tell him,** Si viene se lo diremos. **If he had not killed the tiger, she would be dead,** Si él no hubiera matado al tigre, ella estaría muerta. **If ever there was one,** Si alguna vez lo hubiera. **if necessary,** si fuese necesario. **if not,** si no, si no es que (e.g., *Poet and philosopher are twins, if not one and the same,* Poeta y filósofo son hermanos gemelos, si no es que la misma cosa). **If only!** ¡Ojalá que! (foll. by subjunc.)
igloo /'ɪglu/ *n* iglú, *m*
igneous /'ɪgniəs/ *a* ígneo
ignite /ɪg'nait/ *vt* encender, pegar fuego (a), incendiar. —*vi* prender fuego, incen&;diarse; arder
ignition /ɪg'nɪʃən/ *n* ignición, *f; Auto.* encendido, *m.* **i. coil,** *Auto.* carrete de inducción del encendido, *m.* **i. key,** *Auto.* llave del contacto, *f*
ignoble /ɪg'noubəl/ *a* innoble, vil, indigno
ignobly /ɪg'noubli/ *adv* bajamente, vilmente
ignominious /,ɪgnə'mɪniəs/ *a* ignominioso
ignominiously /,ɪgnə'mɪniəsli/ *adv* ignominiosamente
ignominy /'ɪgnə,mɪni/ *n* ignominia, deshonra, afrenta, *f*

ignoramus /ˌɪgnə'reiməs/ *n* ignorante, *mf*

ignorance /'ɪgnərəns/ *n* ignorancia, *f;* (unawareness) desconocimiento, *m.* **to plead i.,** pretender ignorancia

ignorant /'ɪgnərənt/ *a* ignorante; inculto. **He is an i. fellow,** Es un ignorante. **to be i. of,** no saber, ignorar. **to be very i.,** ser muy ignorante, *Inf.* ser muy burro

ignorantly /'ɪgnərəntli/ *adv* ignorantemente, por ignorancia; neciamente

ignore /ɪg'nɔr/ *vt* no hacer caso de, desatender; (omit) pasar por alto de; *Law.* rechazar; (pretend not to recognize) hacer semblante de no reconocer; (not recognize) no reconocer

iguana /ɪ'gwɑnə/ *n Zool.* iguana, *f*

ileac /'ɪliæk/ *a Anat.* ilíaco

ileum /'ɪliəm/ *n Anat.* íleon, *m*

Iliad /'ɪliəd/ *n* Ilíada, *f*

ilium /'ɪliəm/ *n Anat.* ilion, *m*

ill /ɪl/ *n* mal, *m.* —*a* (sick) enfermo, malo; (bad) malo; (unfortunate) desdichado, funesto. —*adv* mal. **to be ill,** estar malo. **to be taken ill,** caer enfermo. **ill-advised,** mal aconsejado; desacertado, imprudente. **ill-advisedly,** imprudentemente. **ill at ease,** incómodo. **ill-bred,** mal criado, mal educado, mal nacido. **ill-breeding,** mala crianza, mala educacion, *f.* **ill-disposed,** malintencionado. **ill fame,** mala fama, *f.* **ill-fated,** malhadado, malaventurado, aciago, fatal. **ill-favored,** mal parecido, feúcho. **ill-feeling,** hostilidad, *f,* rencor, *m.* **ill-gotten,** maladquirido. **ill-humor,** mal humor, *m.* **ill-humored,** de mal humor, malhumorado. **ill-luck,** desdicha, mala suerte, malaventura, *f;* infortunio, *m.* **ill-mannered,** mal educado. **ill-natured,** malévolo, perverso. **ill-naturedly,** malignamente. **ill-omened,** nefasto. **ill-spent,** malgastado, perdido. **ill-spoken,** mal hablado. **ill-suited,** malavenido. **ill-timed,** inoportuno, intempestivo. **ill-treat,** maltratar, malparar, tratar mal. **ill-treated,** que ha sido tratado mal; maltrecho. **ill-treatment,** maltratamiento, *m,* crueldad, *f.* **ill-turn,** mala jugada, *f.* **to do an ill-turn,** hacer un flaco servicio. **ill will,** mala voluntad, *f;* rencor, *m,* ojeriza, *f.* **to bear a person ill will,** guardarle rencor

illegal /ɪ'ligəl/ *a* ilegal; indebido, ilícito

illegality /ˌɪli'gælɪti/ *n* ilegalidad, *f*

illegally /ɪ'ligəli/ *adv* ilegalmente

illegibility /ɪˌlɛdʒə'bɪlɪti/ *n* ilegibilidad, *f*

illegible /ɪ'lɛdʒəbəl/ *a* ilegible, indescrifrable

illegibly /ɪ'lɛdʒəbli/ *adv* de un modo ilegible

illegitimacy /ˌɪlɪ'dʒɪtəməsi/ *n* ilegitimidad, *f;* falsedad, *f*

illegitimate /ˌɪlɪ'dʒɪtəmɪt/ *a* ilegítimo, bastardo; falso; ilícito, desautorizado

illegitimately /ˌɪlɪ'dʒɪtəmɪtli/ *adv* ilegítimamente

illiberal /ɪ'lɪbərəl/ *a* iliberal; intolerante, estrecho de miras; (mean) avaro, tacaño, ruin

illiberality /ɪˌlɪbə'rælɪti/ *n* iliberalidad, *f;* intolerancia, *f;* (avarice) tacañería, avaricia, ruindad, *f*

illiberally /ɪ'lɪbərəli/ *adv* avariciosamente, ruinmente

illicit /ɪ'lɪsɪt/ *a* ilícito, indebido, ilegal

illicitly /ɪ'lɪsɪtli/ *adv* ilícitamente, ilegalmente

illicitness /ɪ'lɪsɪtnɪs/ *n* ilicitud, ilegalidad, *f*

illimitable /ɪ'lɪmɪtəbəl/ *a* ilimitado, sin límites, infinito

illiteracy /ɪ'lɪtərəsi/ *n* analfabetismo, *m*

illiterate /ɪ'lɪtərɪt/ *a* and *n* analfabeto (-ta), iliterato (-ta)

illness /'ɪlnɪs/ *n* enfermedad, dolencia, *f,* mal, *m*

illogical /ɪ'lɒdʒɪkəl/ *a* ilógico; absurdo, irracional

illogicality /ɪˌlɒdʒɪ'kælɪti/ *n* falta de lógica, *f;* absurdo, *m,* irracionalidad, *f*

illuminant /ɪ'lumənənt/ *a* iluminador, alumbrador

illuminate /ɪ'luməˌneit/ *vt* iluminar, alumbrar; *Art.* iluminar; (explain) aclarar, ilustrar

illuminated /ɪ'luməˌneitɪd/ *a* iluminado, encendido; *Art.* iluminado. **i. sign,** letrero luminoso, *m*

illuminati /ɪˌlumə'nɑti/ *n pl* secta de los alumbrados, *f*

illuminating /ɪ'luməˌneitɪŋ/ *a* iluminador; (explanatory) aclaratorio. —*n Art.* iluminación, *f*

illumination /ɪˌlumə'neiʃən/ *n* iluminación, *f,* alumbrado, *m;* (for decoration) luminaria, *f; Art.* iluminación, *f; Fig.* inspiración, *f*

illuminator /ɪ'luməˌneitər/ *n Art.* iluminador (-ra)

illumine /ɪ'lumɪn/ *vt* encender, alumbrar; *Fig.* inspirar

illusion /ɪ'luʒən/ *n* ilusión, *f,* engaño, *m;* (dream) esperanza, ilusión, *f,* ensueño, *m.* **to harbor illusions,** tener ilusiones

illusive /ɪ'lusɪv/ *a* ilusivo, engañoso, falso

illusively /ɪ'lusɪvli/ *adv* falsamente, aparentemente

illusoriness /ɪ'lusərinɪs/ *n* ilusión, falsedad, *f,* engaño, *m*

illusory /ɪ'lusəri/ *a* ilusorio, deceptivo, falso, irreal

illustrate /'ɪləˌstreit/ *vt* ilustrar, aclarar, explicar, elucidar; *Art.* ilustrar; (prove) probar, demostrar

illustration /ˌɪlə'streiʃən/ *n* ejemplo, *m;* ilustración, *f; Art.* grabado, *m;* estampa, *f;* (explanation) elucidación, aclaración, *f*

illustrative /ɪ'lʌstrətɪv/ *a* ilustrativo, ilustrador, explicativo, aclaratorio

illustrator /'ɪləˌstreitər/ *n* ilustrador (-ra), grabador (-ra)

illustrious /ɪ'lʌstriəs/ *a* ilustre, famoso, renombrado, distinguido

illustriously /ɪ'lʌstriəsli/ *adv* ilustremente, noblemente

illustriousness /ɪ'lʌstriəsnɪs/ *n* eminencia, *f,* renombre, *m,* grandeza, *f*

image /'ɪmɪdʒ/ *n* (optics) imagen, *f;* efigie, imagen, *f;* (religious) imagen, estatua, *f; Art.* figura, *f;* (metaphor) metáfora, expresión, *f;* (of a person) retrato, *m.* **to be the i. of,** ser el retrato de. **sharp i.,** imagen nítida, *f.* **i. breaker,** iconoclasta, *mf.* **i. vendor,** vendedor (-ra) de imágenes

imagery /'ɪmɪdʒri/ *n Art.* imaginería, *f;* (style) metáforas, *f pl*

imaginable /ɪ'mædʒənəbəl/ *a* imaginable

imaginary /ɪ'mædʒəˌnɛri/ *a* imaginario; fantástico, de ensueño

imagination /ɪˌmædʒə'neiʃən/ *n* imaginación, *f;* imaginativa, fantasía, inventiva, *f,* ingenio, *m*

imaginative /ɪ'mædʒənətɪv/ *a* imaginativo; fantástico

imagine /ɪ'mædʒɪn/ *vt* imaginar, concebir; idear, proyectar, inventar; figurarse, suponer. **Just i.!** ¡Imagínese usted!

imam /ɪ'mɑm/ *n* imán, *m*

imbecile /'ɪmbəsɪl/ *a* imbécil; (foolish) necio, estúpido, tonto. —*n* imbécil, *mf;* (fool) necio (-ia), tonto (-ta), estúpido (-da)

imbecility /ˌɪmbə'sɪlɪti/ *n* imbecilidad, *f;* (folly) necedad, sandez, *f*

imbibe /ɪm'baib/ *vt* embeber, absorber; (drink) sorber, chupar; empaparse de

imbibing /ɪm'baibɪŋ/ *n* imbibición, absorción, *f*

imbricate /'ɪmbrɪkɪt/ *a* (*Zool. Bot.*) imbricado

imbroglio /ɪm'broulyou/ *n* embrollo, lío, *m*

imbue /ɪm'byu/ *vt* imbuir, calar, empapar; teñir. **to i. with,** infundir de

imitable /'ɪmɪtəbəl/ *a* imitable

imitate /'ɪmɪˌteit/ *vt* imitar; copiar, reproducir; (counterfeit) contrahacer

imitation /ˌɪmɪ'teiʃən/ *n* imitación, *f;* copia, *f;* remedo, traslado, *m.* —*a* imitado; falso, artificial

imitative /'ɪmɪˌteitɪv/ *a* imitativo; imitador

imitativeness /'ɪmɪˌteitɪvnɪs/ *n* facultad imitativa (or de imitacion), *f*

imitator /'ɪmɪˌteitər/ *n* imitador (-ra); contrahacedor (-ra), falsificador (-ra)

immaculate /ɪ'mækyəlɪt/ *a* inmaculado, puro; (of dress) elegante. **I. Conception,** la Purísima Concepción

immaculately /ɪ'mækyəlɪtli/ *adv* inmaculadamente; elegantemente

immaculateness /ɪ'mækyəlɪtnɪs/ *n* pureza, *f;* (of dress) elegancia, *f*

immanence /'ɪmənəns/ *n* inmanencia, inherencia, *f*

immanent /'ɪmənənt/ *a* inmanente; inherente

immaterial /ˌɪmə'tɪəriəl/ *a* inmaterial, incorpóreo; sin importancia. **It is i. to me,** Me es indiferente, No me importa, Me da lo mismo, Me da igual

immateriality /ˌɪməˌtɪəri'ælɪti/ *n* inmaterialidad, *f*

immature /ˌɪmə'tʃʊr/ *a* inmaturo; precoz; (of fruit) verde

immaturity /ˌɪmə'tʃʊrɪti/ *n* falta de madurez, *f;* precocidad, *f*
immeasurability /ɪˌmɛʒərə'bɪlɪti/ *n* inmensurabilidad, inmensidad, *f*
immeasurable /ɪ'mɛʒərəbəl/ *a* inmensurable, inmenso, imponderable
immeasurably /ɪ'mɛʒərəbli/ *adv* inmensamente, enormemente
immediate /ɪ'midiɪt/ *a* (of place) inmediato, cercano, contiguo; (of time) próximo, inmediato, directo; (of action) inmediato, perentorio; (on letters) urgente. **to take i. action,** tomar acción inmediata
immediately /ɪ'midiɪtli/ *adv* (of place) próximamente, contiguamente; (of time) luego, seguidamente, en el acto, ahora mismo, enseguida; directamente; (as soon as) así que
immemorial /ˌɪmə'mɔriəl/ *a* inmemorial, inmemorable
immemorially /ˌɪmə'mɔriəli/ *adv* desde tiempo inmemorial
immense /ɪ'mɛns/ *a* inmenso, enorme; vasto, extenso; infinito
immensely /ɪ'mɛnsli/ *adv* inmensamente, enormemente
immensity /ɪ'mɛnsɪti/ *n* inmensidad, *f;* extensión, vastedad, *f*
immerse /ɪ'mɜrs/ *vt* sumergir, hundir en, zambullir; bautizar por sumersión. *Fig.* **to be immersed in,** estar absorto en
immersion /ɪ'mɜrʒən/ *n* sumersion, *f,* hundimiento, *m; Astron.* inmersión, *f*
immigrant /'ɪmɪgrənt/ *a* and *n* inmigrante, *mf*
immigrate /'ɪmɪˌgreit/ *vi* inmigrar
immigration /ˌɪmɪ'greiʃən/ *n* inmigración, *f*
imminence /'ɪmənəns/ *n* inminencia, *f*
imminent /'ɪmənənt/ *a* inminente
immobile /ɪ'moubəl/ *a* inmóvil, inmoble; impasible, imperturbable
immobility /ˌɪmou'bɪlɪti/ *n* inmovilidad, *f;* impasibilidad, imperturbabilidad, *f*
immobilization /ɪˌmoubələ'zeiʃən/ *n* inmovilización, *f*
immobilize /ɪ'moubəˌlaiz/ *vt* inmovilizar
immoderate /ɪ'mɒdərɪt/ *a* inmoderado, excesivo, indebido
immoderately /ɪ'mɒdərɪtli/ *adv* inmoderadamente, excesivamente
immoderateness /ɪ'mɒdərɪtnɪs/ *n* inmoderación, *f,* exceso, *m*
immodest /ɪ'mɒdɪst/ *a* inmodesto; indecente, deshonesto; (pert) atrevido, descarado
immodestly /ɪ'mɒdɪstli/ *adv* impúdicamente, inmodestamente
immodesty /ɪ'mɒdɪsti/ *n* inmodestia, impudicia, *f;* deshonestidad, licencia, *f;* (forwardness) descaro, atrevimiento, *m*
immolate /'ɪməˌleit/ *vt* inmolar, sacrificar
immolation /ˌɪmə'leiʃən/ *n* inmolación, *f,* sacrificio, *m*
immolator /'ɪməˌleitər/ *n* inmolador (-ra)
immoral /ɪ'mɔrəl/ *a* inmoral; licencioso, vicioso; incontinente
immorality /ˌɪmə'rælɪti/ *n* inmoralidad, *f*
immortal /ɪ'mɔrtḷ/ *a* inmortal; perenne, eterno, imperecedero. —*n* inmortal, *mf*
immortality /ˌɪmɔr'tælɪti/ *n* inmortalidad, *f;* fama inmortal, *f*
immortalize /ɪ'mɔrtḷˌaiz/ *vt* inmortalizar, perpetuar
immortally /ɪ'mɔrtḷi/ *adv* inmortalmente, eternamente, para siempre
immovability /ɪˌmuvə'bɪlɪti/ *n* inamovibilidad, inmovilidad, *f;* (of purpose) inflexibilidad, tenacidad, constancia, *f*
immovable /ɪ'muvəbəl/ *a* inmoble, fijo, inmóvil; (of purpose) inconmovible, inalterable, constante. —*n pl.* **immovables** *Law.* bienes inmuebles, *m pl. Eccl.* **i. feast,** fiesta fija, *f*
immovably /ɪ'muvəbli/ *adv* inmóvilmente, fijamente
immune /ɪ'myun/ *a* inmune, libre; *Med.* inmune. **i. from,** exento de; libre de
immunity /ɪ'myunɪti/ *n* inmunidad, libertad, *f;* exención, *f; Med.* inmunidad, *f*
immunization /ɪˌmyunə'zeiʃən/ *n Med.* inmunización, *f*
immunize /'ɪmyəˌnaiz/ *vt* inmunizar
immure /ɪ'myʊr/ *vt* emparedar, recluir, encerrar
immutability /ɪˌmyutə'bɪlɪti/ *n* inmutabilidad, inalterabilidad, *f*
immutable /ɪ'myutəbəl/ *a* inmutable, inalterable, constante
immutably /ɪ'myutəbli/ *adv* inmutablemente
imp /ɪmp/ *n* trasgo, diablillo, duende, *m;* (child) picaruelo (-la)
impact /'ɪmpækt/ *n* impacto, *m,* impacción, *f;* choque, *m,* colisión, *f*
impair /ɪm'pɛər/ *vt* perjudicar, echar a perder, deteriorar, empeorar, desmejorar. **to be impaired,** deteriorarse, perjudicarse
impairment /ɪm'pɛərmənt/ *n* deterioración, perjuicio, empeoramiento, *m*
impale /ɪm'peil/ *vt* (punishment) empalar; (with a sword) atravesar, espetar
impalement /ɪm'peilmənt/ *n* (punishment) empalamiento, *m;* atravesamiento, *m,* transfixión, *f*
impalpability /ɪmˌpælpə'bɪlɪti/ *n* impalpabilidad, intangibilidad, *f*
impalpable /ɪm'pælpəbəl/ *a* impalpable, intangible; incorpóreo
impart /ɪm'pɑrt/ *vt* comunicar, dar parte (de); conferir
impartial /ɪm'pɑrʃəl/ *a* imparcial, ecuánime
impartiality /ɪmˌpɑrʃi'ælɪti/ *n* imparcialidad, ecuanimidad, entereza, *f,* desinterés, *m*
impartially /ɪm'pɑrʃəli/ *adv* imparcialmente, con desinterés
impassability /ɪmˌpæsə'bɪlɪti/ *n* impracticabilidad, *f*
impassable /ɪm'pæsəbəl/ *a* intransitable, impracticable; (of water) invadeable
impasse /'ɪmpæs/ *n* callejón sin salida, *m*
impassibility /ɪmˌpæsə'bɪlɪti/ *n* impasibilidad, imperturbabilidad, indiferencia, *f*
impassible /ɪm'pæsəbəl/ *a* impasible, insensible; indiferente, imperturbable
impassion /ɪm'pæʃən/ *vt* apasionar, conmover
impassioned /ɪm'pæʃənd/ *a* apasionado, vehemente, ardiente
impassive /ɪm'pæsɪv/ *a* impasible, insensible; indiferente, imperturbable; apático
impassively /ɪm'pæsɪvli/ *adv* indiferentemente
impassivity /ˌɪmpæ'sɪvɪti/ *n* impasibilidad, *f;* indiferencia, *f;* apatía, *f*
impatience /ɪm'peiʃəns/ *n* impaciencia, *f*
impatient /ɪm'peiʃənt/ *a* impaciente; intolerante. **to make i.,** impacientar. **to grow i.,** impacientarse, perder la paciencia. **to grow i. at,** impacientarse ante. **to grow i. to,** impacientarse a or por. **to grow i. under,** impacientarse bajo
impatiently /ɪm'peiʃəntli/ *adv* con impaciencia, impacientemente
impeach /ɪm'pitʃ/ *vt Law.* denunciar, delatar, acusar, hacer juicio político (Argentina); censurar, criticar, tachar
impeachable /ɪm'pitʃəbəl/ *a Law.* delatable, denunciable, acusable; censurable
impeacher /ɪm'pitʃər/ *n* acusador (-ra), denunciador (-ra), delator (-ra)
impeachment /ɪm'pitʃmənt/ *n Law.* acusación, denuncia, *f;* reproche, *m,* queja, *f*
impeccability /ɪmˌpɛkə'bɪlɪti/ *n* (perfection) impecabilidad, perfección, *f;* elegancia, *f*
impeccable /ɪm'pɛkəbəl/ *a* impecable, intachable, perfecto; elegante
impeccably /ɪm'pɛkəbli/ *adv* perfectamente; elegantemente
impecuniosity /ˌɪmpəˌkyuni'ɒsɪti/ *n* indigencia, pobreza, *f*
impecunious /ˌɪmpə'kyuniəs/ *a* indigente, pobre
impede /ɪm'pid/ *vt* impedir, obstruir, estorbar; *Fig.* dificultar, embarazar
impediment /ɪm'pɛdəmənt/ *n* obstáculo, estorbo, *m; Fig.* dificultad, *f; Law.* impedimento, *m.* **to have an i. in one's speech,** tener una dificultad en el hablar
impel /ɪm'pɛl/ *vt* impulsar, impeler; *Fig.* estimular,

obligar, mover, constreñir. **I felt impelled (to),** Me sentí obligado (a)
impend /ɪm'pɛnd/ *vi* ser inminente, amenazar
impending /ɪm'pɛndɪŋ/ *a* inminente, pendiente
impenetrability /ɪm,pɛnɪtrə'bɪlɪti/ *n* impenetrabilidad, *f; Fig.* enigma, secreto, misterio, *m*
impenetrable /ɪm'pɛnɪtrəbəl/ *a* impenetrable; intransitable; denso, espeso; *Fig.* enigmático, insondable, secreto
impenetrably /ɪm,pɛnɪtrə'bɪlɪti/ *adv* impenetrablemente, densamente
impenitence /ɪm'pɛnɪtəns/ *n* impenitencia, *f*
impenitent /ɪm'pɛnɪtənt/ *a* impenitente, incorregible
impenitently /ɪm'pɛnɪtəntli/ *adv* sin penitencia
imperative /ɪm'pɛrətɪv/ *a* imperioso, perentorio; *Gram.* imperativo; (necessary) esencial, urgente. —*n* mandato, *m,* orden, *f; Gram.* imperativo, *m.* **in the i.,** en el imperativo
imperatively /ɪm'pɛrətɪvli/ *adv* imperativamente
imperativeness /ɪm'pɛrətɪvnɪs/ *n* perentoriedad, *f;* urgencia, importancia, *f*
imperceptible /,ɪmpər'sɛptəbəl/ *a* imperceptible, insensible
imperceptibly /,ɪmpər'sɛptəbli/ *adv* imperceptiblemente
imperceptive /,ɪmpər'sɛptɪv/ *a* insensible
imperfect /ɪm'pɜrfɪkt/ *a* imperfecto; incompleto, defectuoso. —*a* and *n Gram.* imperfecto *m*
imperfection /,ɪmpər'fɛkʃən/ *n* imperfección, *f;* defecto, desperfecto, *m;* falta, tacha, *f*
imperfectly /ɪm'pɜrfɪktli/ *adv* imperfectamente
imperial /ɪm'pɪəriəl/ *a* imperial, imperatorio. —*n* (beard) pera, *f.* **i. preference,** preferencia dentro del Imperio, *f*
imperial /ɪm'pɪəriəl/ *vt* arriesgar, poner en peligro, aventurar
imperialism /ɪm'pɪəriə,lɪzəm/ *n* imperialismo, *m*
imperialist /ɪm'pɪəriəlɪst/ *n* imperialista, *mf*
imperialistic /ɪm,pɪəriə'lɪstɪk/ *a* imperialista
imperious /ɪm'pɪəriəs/ *a* imperioso, altivo, arrogante; (pressing) urgente, apremiante
imperiously /ɪm'pɪəriəsli/ *adv* imperiosamente, con arrogancia
imperiousness /ɪm'pɪəriəsnɪs/ *n* autoridad, arrogancia, altivez, *f;* necesidad, urgencia, *f,* apremio, *m*
imperishability /ɪm,pɛrɪʃə'bɪlɪti/ *n* (immortality) inmortalidad, perennidad, *f*
imperishable /ɪm'pɛrɪʃəbəl/ *a* imperecedero, inmarchitable, perenne, eterno
impermanence /ɪm'pɜrmənəns/ *n* inestabilidad, interinidad, *f;* brevedad, fugacidad, *f*
impermanent /ɪm'pɜrmənənt/ *a* interino, no permanente
impermeability /ɪm,pɜrmiə'bɪlɪti/ *n* impermeabilidad, *f*
impermeable /ɪm'pɜrmiəbəl/ *a* impermeable
impersonal /ɪm'pɜrsənl̩/ *a* impersonal, objetivo; *Gram.* impersonal
impersonality /ɪm,pɜrsə'nælɪti/ *n* objetividad, *f*
impersonally /ɪm'pɜrsənl̩i/ *adv* impersonalmente
impersonate /ɪm'pɜrsə,neit/ *vt* personificar, simbolizar; *Theat.* representar
impersonation /ɪm,pɜrsə'neiʃən/ *n* personificación, simbolización, *f; Theat.* representación, *f*
impertinence /ɪm'pɜrtn̩əns/ *n* impertinencia, majadería, insolencia, *f;* inoportunidad, *f;* despropósito, *m*
impertinent /ɪm'pɜrtn̩ənt/ *a* impertinente, insolente; (unseasonable) intempestivo, inoportuno; (irrelevant) fuera de propósito
impertinently /ɪm'pɜrtn̩əntli/ *adv* con insolencia, impertinentemente
imperturbability /,ɪmpərtɜrbə'bɪlɪti/ *n* imperturbabilidad, serenidad, impasibilidad, *f;* impavidez, *f*
imperturbable /,ɪmpər'tɜrbəbəl/ *a* imperturbable, impasible, sereno; impávido
imperturbably /,ɪmpər'tɜrbəbli/ *adv* con serenidad, imperturbablemente
impervious /ɪm'pɜrviəs/ *a* impermeable, impenetrable; *Fig.* insensible. **He is i. to arguments,** No hace caso de argumentos
imperviousness /ɪm'pɜrviəsnɪs/ *n* impermeabilidad, impenetrabilidad, *f; Fig.* insensibilidad, *f*
impetigo /,ɪmpɪ'taigou/ *n Med.* impétigo, *m*
impetuosity /ɪm,pɛtʃu'ɒsɪti/ *n* impetuosidad, temeridad, irreflexión, *f*
impetuous /ɪm'pɛtʃuəs/ *a* impetuoso, temerario, irreflexivo; violento, vehemente
impetuously /ɪm'pɛtʃuəsli/ *adv* impetuosamente; con vehemencia
impetus /'ɪmpɪtəs/ *n Mech.* ímpetu, *m,* impulsión, *f; Fig.* incentivo, estímulo, impulso, *m*
impiety /ɪm'paiɪti/ *n* impiedad, irreligión, irreligiosidad, *f*
impinge (upon) /ɪm'pɪndʒ/ *vi* chocar con, tropezar con
impious /'ɪmpiəs/ *a* impío, irreligioso, sacrílego; (wicked) malvado, perverso, malo
impish /'ɪmpɪʃ/ *a* travieso, revoltoso, enredador
implacability /ɪm,plækə'bɪlɪti/ *n* implacabilidad, *f*
implacable /ɪm'plækəbəl/ *a* implacable, inexorable, inflexible, riguroso
implacably /ɪm'plækəbli/ *adv* implacablemente
implant /ɪm'plænt/ *vt Fig.* implantar, inculcar, instilar
implantation /,ɪmplæn'teiʃən/ *n Fig.* implantación, instilación, inculcación, *f*
implement /*n* 'ɪmpləmənt; *v also* -,mɛnt/ *n* instrumento, utensilio, *m,* herramienta, *f;* (of war) elemento, *m.* —*vt* cumplir, hacer efectivo; llevar a cabo
implicate /'ɪmplɪ,keit/ *vt* enredar, envolver; (imply) implicar, contener, llevar en sí; (in a crime) comprometer. **to be implicated in a crime,** estar implicado en un crimen.
implication /,ɪmplɪ'keiʃən/ *n* implicación, inferencia, repercusión, sugestión, *f;* (in a crime) complicidad, *f*
implicit /ɪm'plɪsɪt/ *a* implícito, virtual, tácito; (absolute) ciego, absoluto, implícito. **with i. faith,** con fe ciega
implicitness /ɪm'plɪsɪtnɪs/ *n* carácter implícito, *m,* lo implícito
implied /ɪm'plaid/ *a* tácito, implícito
implore /ɪm'plɔr/ *vt* implorar, suplicar
imploring /ɪm'plɔrɪŋ/ *a* suplicante, implorante
imploringly /ɪm'plɔrɪŋli/ *adv* con encarecimiento, a súplica, de un modo suplicante
imply /ɪm'plai/ *vt* implicar, indicar, presuponer; (mean) querer decir, significar; (hint) insinuar, sugerir
impolicy /ɪm'pɒləsi/ *n* indiscreción, imprudencia, impolítica, *f*
impolite /,ɪmpə'lait/ *a* descortés, mal educado
impolitely /,ɪmpə'laitli/ *adv* con descortesía
impoliteness /,ɪmpə'laitnɪs/ *n* descortesía, falta de urbanidad, *f*
impolitic /ɪm'pɒlɪtɪk/ *a* impolítico
imponderability /ɪm,pɒndərə'bɪlɪti/ *n* imponderabilidad, *f*
imponderable /ɪm'pɒndərəbəl/ *a* imponderable
import /*v* ɪm'pɔrt; *a, n* 'ɪmpɔrt/ *vt Com.* importar; (mean) significar, querer decir. —*a Com.* importado, de importación. —*n Com.* importación, *f;* (meaning) significado, sentido, *m;* (value) importe, valor, *m;* (contents) contenido, tenor, *m;* importancia, *f.* **i. duty,** derechos de importación derechos de entrada, *m pl,* gravamen a la importación, *m.* **i. licence,** permiso de importación, *m.* **i. trade,** negocios de importación, *m pl*
importable /ɪm'pɔrtəbəl/ *a* importable, que se puede importar
importance /ɪm'pɔrtn̩s/ *n* importancia, *f;* valor, alcance, *m,* magnitud, *f;* consideración, eminencia, *f.* **to be fully conscious of one's i.,** tener plena conciencia de su importancia
important /ɪm'pɔrtn̩t/ *a* importante; distinguido; presuntuoso, vanidoso. **to be i.,** importar, ser importante. **i. person,** personaje, *m,* persona importante, *f*
importantly /ɪm'pɔrtn̩tli/ *adv* importantemente, con importancia
importation /,ɪmpɔr'teiʃən/ *n* importación, *f; Com.* introducción (or importación) de géneros extranjeros, *f*
importer /ɪm'pɔrtər/ *n* importador (-ra)

importunate /ɪm'pɔrtʃənɪt/ *a* (of a demand) insistente, importuno; (of persons) impertinente, pesado
importunately /ɪm'pɔrtʃənɪtli/ *adv* importunadamente
importune /ˌɪmpɔr'tun/ *vt* importunar, asediar, perseguir
importuning /ˌɪmpɔr'tunɪŋ/ *n* persecución, importunación, *f*
importunity /ˌɪmpɔr'tunɪti/ *n* importunidad, insistencia, impertinencia, *f*
impose /ɪm'pouz/ *vt* (on, upon) imponer, infligir, cargar; *Print.* imponer. —*vi* (on, upon) (deceive) engañar, embaucar
imposing /ɪm'pouzɪŋ/ *a* imponente, impresionante; (of persons) majestuoso, importante
imposition /ˌɪmpə'zɪʃən/ *n* imposición, *f;* (burden) impuesto, tributo, *m,* carga, *f;* (*Print., etc.*) imposición, *f;* (trick) fraude, engaño, *m,* decepción, *f*
impossibility /ɪmˌpɒsə'bɪlɪti/ *n* imposibilidad, *f*
impossible /ɪm'pɒsəbəl/ *a* imposible. **Nothing is i.,** No hay nada imposible, *Inf.* De menos nos hizo Dios. **to do the i.,** hacer lo imposible
impost /'ɪmpoust/ *n* impuesto, *m,* contribución, gabela, *f*
impostor /ɪm'pɒstər/ *n* impostor (-ra), bribón (-ona), embustero (-ra)
imposture /ɪm'pɒstʃər/ *n* impostura, *f,* engaño, fraude, *m*
impotence /'ɪmpətəns/ *n* impotencia, *f*
impotent /'ɪmpətənt/ *a* impotente
impound /ɪm'paund/ *vt* acorralar; (water) embalsar; (goods) confiscar
impoverish /ɪm'pɒvərɪʃ/ *vt* empobrecer, depauperar, arruinar; (health) debilitar; (land) agotar
impoverished /ɪm'pɒvərɪʃt/ *a* indigente, necesitado; (of land) agotado
impoverishment /ɪm'pɒvərɪʃmənt/ *n* empobrecimiento, *m,* ruina, *f;* (of land) agotamiento, *m*
impracticability /ɪmˌpræktɪkə'bɪlɪti/ *n* impracticabilidad, imposibilidad, *f*
impracticable /ɪm'præktɪkəbəl/ *a* impracticable, no factible, imposible
imprecation /ˌɪmprɪ'keiʃən/ *n* imprecación, maldición, *f*
imprecatory /'ɪmprɪkəˌtɔri/ *a* imprecatorio, maldiciente
impregnable /ɪm'prɛgnəbəl/ *a* inexpugnable, inconquistable
impregnate /ɪm'prɛgneit/ *vt* impregnar, empapar; *Biol.* fecundar. **to become impregnated,** impregnarse
impregnation /ˌɪmprɛg'neiʃən/ *n* impregnación, *f;* *Biol.* fecundación, fertilización, *f;* *Fig.* inculcación, *f*
impresario /ˌɪmprə'sɑriˌou/ *n* empresario, *m*
imprescriptible /ˌɪmprə'skrɪptəbəl/ *a* imprescriptible, inalienable
impress /*v* ɪm'prɛs; *n* 'ɪmprɛs/ *vt* imprimir; (on the mind) impresionar; inculcar, imbuir; (with respect) imponer; *Mil.* reclutar; (of goods) confiscar. —*n* impresión, marca, señal, huella, *f*
impression /ɪm'prɛʃən/ *n* impresión, *f;* marca, señal, huella, *f;* *Print.* impresión, *f;* efecto, *m;* idea, noción, *f.* **He has the i. that they do not like him,** Sospecha que no les es simpático. **to be under the i.,** tener la impresión
impressionability /ɪmˌprɛʃənə'bɪlɪti/ *n* susceptibilidad, sensibilidad, *f*
impressionable /ɪm'prɛʃənəbəl/ *a* susceptible, impresionable, sensitivo
impressionism /ɪm'prɛʃəˌnɪzəm/ *n* impresionismo, *m*
impressionist /ɪm'prɛʃənɪst/ *n* impresionista, *mf*
impressionistic /ɪmˌprɛʃə'nɪstɪk/ *a* impresionista
impressive /ɪm'prɛsɪv/ *a* impresionante; emocionante; imponente, majestuoso; enfático
impressively /ɪm'prɛsɪvli/ *adv* solemnemente, de modo impresionante; enfáticamente
impressiveness /ɪm'prɛsɪvnɪs/ *n* efecto impresionante, *m;* grandiosidad, pompa, *f;* majestuosidad, *f;* fuerza, *f*
imprint /*n* 'ɪmprɪnt; *v* ɪm'prɪnt/ *n* impresión, señal, marca, huella, *f;* *Print.* pie de imprenta, *m.* —*vt* imprimir; (on the mind) grabar, fijar
imprison /ɪm'prɪzən/ *vt* encerrar, encarcelar, aprisionar
imprisonment /ɪm'prɪzənmənt/ *n* encarcelación, prisión, *f,* encierro, *m*
improbability /ɪmˌprɒbə'bɪlɪti/ *n* improbabilidad, *f;* inverosimilitud, *f*
improbable /ɪm'prɒbəbəl/ *a* improbable; inverosímil
improbity /ɪm'proubɪti/ *n* improbidad, *f*
impromptu /ɪm'prɒmptu/ *a* indeliberado, impremeditado, espontáneo. —*adv* de improviso, in promptu. —*n* improvisación, *f*
improper /ɪm'prɒpər/ *a* impropio, inadecuado; incorrecto; indebido; indecente, indecoroso. **i. fraction,** *Math.* quebrado impropio, *m*
improperly /ɪm'prɒpərli/ *adv* impropiamente, incorrectamente; indecorosamente
impropriety /ˌɪmprə'praiɪti/ *n* inconveniencia, *f;* incorrección, *f;* (style) impropiedad, *f;* falta de decoro, *f*
improvable /ɪm'pruvəbəl/ *a* mejorable, perfectible
improve /ɪm'pruv/ *vt* mejorar; perfecionar; (beautify) embellecer, hermosear; (land) bonificar; *Lit.* corregir, enmendar; (cultivate) cultivar; (increase) aumentar; (an opportunity) aprovechar; (strengthen) fortificar; (business) sacar provecho de, explotar. —*vi* mejorar; perfeccionarse; (progress) hacer progresos, progresar, adelantarse; *Com.* subir; (become beautiful) hacerse hermoso, embellecerse; (increase) aumentarse. **to i. upon,** mejorar, perfeccionar; pulir
improvement /ɪm'pruvmənt/ *n* mejora, *f;* perfeccionamiento, *m;* aumento, *m;* adelantamiento, progreso, *m;* (in health) mejoría, *f;* embellecimiento, *m;* cultivación, *f;* (of land) abono, *m*
improver /ɪm'pruvər/ *n* aprendiz (-za)
improvidence /ɪm'prɒvɪdəns/ *n* imprevisión, *f;* improvidencia, *f*
improvident /ɪm'prɒvɪdənt/ *a* impróvido, desprevenido
improvidently /ɪm'prɒvɪdəntli/ *adv* impróvidamente
improvisation /ɪmˌprɒvə'zeiʃən/ *n* improvisación, *f*
improvise /'ɪmprəˌvaiz/ *vt* improvisar
improviser /'ɪmprəˌvaizər/ *n* improvisador (-ra)
imprudence /ɪm'prudn̩s/ *n* imprudencia, *f;* desacierto, *m,* indiscreción, *f*
imprudent /ɪm'prudn̩t/ *a* imprudente; desacertado, indiscreto, mal avisado, irreflexivo
imprudently /ɪm'prudn̩tli/ *adv* imprudentemente; sin pensar
impudence /'ɪmpyədəns/ *n* impudencia, *f,* descaro, *m,* insolencia, desvergüenza, *f,* atrevimiento, *m*
impudent /'ɪmpyədənt/ *a* impudente, descarado, insolente, desvergonzado, atrevido
impudently /'ɪmpyədəntli/ *adv* descaradamente, con insolencia
impugn /ɪm'pyun/ *vt* impugnar, contradecir, atacar
impugnable /ɪm'pyunəbəl/ *a* impugnable, atacable
impugnment /ɪm'pyunmənt/ *n* impugnación, *f*
impulse /'ɪmpʌls/ *n* ímpetu, *m,* impulsión, *f;* impulso, estímulo, *m;* incitación, instigación, *f;* motivo, *m;* (fit) arranque, arrebato, acceso, *m*
impulsion /ɪm'pʌlʃən/ *n* ímpetu, *m,* impulsión, *f;* empuje, *m,* arranque, *m*
impulsive /ɪm'pʌlsɪv/ *a* impelente; irreflexivo, impulsivo
impulsively /ɪm'pʌlsɪvli/ *adv* por impulso
impulsiveness /ɪm'pʌlsɪvnɪs/ *n* irreflexión, *f;* carácter impulsivo, *m*
impunity /ɪm'pyunɪti/ *n* impunidad, *f.* **with i.,** impunemente
impure /ɪm'pyʊr/ *a* impuro; adulterado, mezclado; (indecent) deshonesto, indecente; (dirty) turbio, sucio
impurity /ɪm'pyʊrɪti/ *n* impureza, *f;* adulteración, mezcla, *f;* deshonestidad, liviandad, *f;* suciedad, turbiedad, *f*
imputable /ɪm'pyutəbəl/ *a* imputable, atribuible
imputation /ˌɪmpyʊ'teiʃən/ *n* imputación, atribución, *f;* (in a bad sense) acusación, *f,* reproche, *m*
impute /ɪm'pyut/ *vt* imputar, achacar, atribuir; acusar, reprochar
imputer /ɪm'pyutər/ *n* imputador (-ra); recriminador (-ra), acusador (-ra)
in /ɪn/ *prep* en; a; (of duration) durante, mientras; (with) con; (through) por; dentro de; (under) bajo;

(following a superlative) de; (of specified time) dentro de, de aquí a; (with afternoon, etc.) por; (out of) sobre. **course in medieval Catalan literature,** curso de literatura catalana medioeval. **dressed in black,** vestido de negro. **in London,** en Londres. **in the morning,** por la mañana; (in the course of) durante la mañana. **in time,** a tiempo; dentro de algún tiempo. **in a week,** dentro de una semana. **in the best way,** del mejor modo. **in writing,** por escrito. **in anger,** con enojo. **in one's hand,** en la mano. **in addition to,** además de, a más de. **in case,** por si acaso, en caso de que. **in order to,** a fin de, para (foll. by infin.). **in order that,** para que (foll. by subjunc.). **in so far as,** en cuanto. **in spite of,** a pesar de. **in the distance,** a lo lejos, en lontananza. **in the meantime,** entre tanto. **in the middle of,** en el medio de; a la mitad de. **in the style of,** al modo de; a la manera [illegible]

in /ɪn/ *adv* adentro, dentro; (at home) en casa; (of sun) escondido; (of fire) alumbrado; (in power) en el poder; (of harvest) cosechado; (of boats) entrado (with haber); (of trains) llegado (with haber). **to be in,** estar dentro; haber llegado; estar en casa. **to be in for,** estar expuesto a, correr el riesgo de. **to be in with a person,** ser muy amigo de, estar muy metido con. **Come in!** ¡Adelante!; ¡Pase usted! **ins and outs,** sinuosidades, *f pl;* (of river) meandros, *m pl;* (of an affair) pormenores, detalles, *m pl.* **in less time than you can say Jack Robinson,** en menos de Jesús, en un credo, en menos que canta un gallo, en menos que se persigna un cura loco. **in the middle of nowhere,** donde Cristo dio las tres voces, (Western Hemisphere) donde el diablo perdió el poncho.

in /ɪn/ *a* interno. **in-law** (of relations) político. **in-patient,** enfermo (-ma) de hospital

inability /ˌɪnəˈbɪlɪti/ *n* incapacidad, inhabilidad, ineptitud, incompetencia, *f;* impotencia, *f*

inaccessibility /ˌɪnəkˌsɛsəˈbɪlɪti/ *n* inaccesibilidad, *f*

inaccessible /ˌɪnəkˈsɛsəbəl/ *a* inaccesible

inaccuracy /ɪnˈækyərəsi/ *n* inexactitud, incorrección, *f*

inaccurate /ɪnˈækyərɪt/ *a* inexacto, incorrecto

inaccurately /ɪnˈækyərɪtli/ *adv* inexactamente, erróneamente

inaction /ɪnˈækʃən/ *n* inacción, *f*

inactive /ɪnˈæktɪv/ *a* inactivo, pasivo; (of things) inerte; (lazy) perezoso, indolente; (machinery) parado; (motionless) inmóvil; (at leisure) desocupado, sin empleo

inactivity /ˌɪnækˈtɪvɪti/ *n* inactividad, pasividad, *f;* (of things) inercia, *f;* pereza, indolencia, *f;* (of machinery) paro, *m;* inmovilidad, *f;* (leisure) desocupación, *f*

inadaptable /ˌɪnəˈdæptəbəl/ *a* inadaptable, no adaptable

inadequacy /ɪnˈædɪkwəsi/ *n* insuficiencia, escasez, *f;* imperfección, *f,* defecto, *m*

inadequate /ɪnˈædɪkwɪt/ *a* inadecuado, insuficiente, escaso; imperfecto, defectuoso

inadequately /ɪnˈædɪkwɪtli/ *adv* inadecuadamente

inadmissible /ˌɪnədˈmɪsəbəl/ *a* inadmisible, no admisible

inadvertence /ˌɪnədˈvɜrtn̩s/ *n* inadvertencia, *f;* equivocación, *f,* descuido, *m*

inadvertent /ˌɪnədˈvɜrtn̩t/ *a* inadvertido, accidental, casual; negligente

inadvertently /ˌɪnədˈvɜrtn̩tli/ *adv* inadvertidamente, sin querer

inalienability /ɪnˌeilyənəˈbɪlɪti/ *n* inalienabilidad, *f*

inalienable /ɪnˈeilyənəbəl/ *a* inajenable, inalienable

inalterability /ɪnˌɔltərəˈbɪlɪti/ *n* inalterabilidad, *f*

inalterable /ɪnˈɔltərəbəl/ *a* inalterable

inalterably /ɪnˈɔltərəbli/ *adv* inalterablemente, sin alteración

inane /ɪˈnein/ *a* lelo, fatuo, vacío, necio

inanimate /ɪnˈænəmɪt/ *a* (of matter) inanimado; sin vida, exánime, muerto

inanition /ˌɪnəˈnɪʃən/ *n* inanición, *f*

inanity /ɪˈnænɪti/ *n* vacuidad, fatuidad, necedad, *f*

inappeasable /ˌɪnəˈpizəbəl/ *a* implacable, riguroso

inapplicability /ɪnˌæplɪkəˈbɪlɪti/ *n* no aplicabilidad, *f*

inapplicable /ɪnˈæplɪkəbəl/ *a* inaplicable

inapposite /ɪnˈæpəzɪt/ *a* fuera de propósito, no pertinente, inoportuno

inappreciable /ˌɪnəˈpriʃiəbəl/ *a* inapreciable, imperceptible

inappreciation /ˌɪnəpriʃiˈeiʃən/ *n* falta de apreciación, *f*

inappreciative /ˌɪnəˈpriʃiətɪv/ *a* desagradecido, ingrato. **i. of,** insensible a, indiferente a

inapproachable /ˌɪnəˈproutʃəbəl/ *a* inaccesible, huraño, adusto

inappropriate /ˌɪnəˈproupriɪt/ *a* impropio, inconveniente, inadecuado, incongruente; inoportuno

inappropriately /ˌɪnəˈproupriɪtli/ *adv* impropiamente; inoportunamente

inappropriateness /ˌɪnəˈproupriɪtnɪs/ *n* impropiedad, inconveniencia, incongruencia, *f;* inoportunidad, *f*

inapt /ɪnˈæpt/ *a* inepto, inhábil; impropio

inaptitude /ɪnˈæptɪˌtud/ *n* ineptitud, inhabilidad, *f;* impropiedad, *f*

inarticulate /ˌɪnɑrˈtɪkyəlɪt/ *a* (of speech) inarticulado; (reticent) inexpresivo, reservado; indistinto; *Anat.* inarticulado

inarticulately /ˌɪnɑrˈtɪkyəlɪtli/ *adv* indistintamente, de un modo inarticulado

inarticulateness /ˌɪnɑrˈtɪkyəlɪtnɪs/ *n* tartamudez, *f;* inexpresión, reserva, *f;* silencio, *m*

inartistic /ˌɪnɑrˈtɪstɪk/ *a* antiartístico, antiestético

inartistically /ˌɪnɑrˈtɪstɪkli/ *adv* sin gusto (estético)

inasmuch (as) /ˌɪnəzˈmʌtʃ/ *adv* puesto que, visto que, dado que

inattention /ˌɪnəˈtɛnʃən/ *n* desatención, inaplicación, abstracción, *f;* falta de solicitud, *f*

inattentive /ˌɪnəˈtɛntɪv/ *a* desatento, distraído; poco solícito, no atento

inattentively /ˌɪnəˈtɛntɪvli/ *adv* sin atención, distraídamente

inaudibility /ɪnˌɔdəˈbɪlɪti/ *n* imposibilidad de oír, *f*

inaudible /ɪnˈɔdəbəl/ *a* inaudible, no audible, ininteligible

inaudibly /ɪnˈɔdəbli/ *adv* indistintamente, de modo inaudible

inaugurate /ɪnˈɔgyəˌreit/ *vt* inaugurar; (open) estrenar, abrir, dedicar; (install) investir, instalar; (initiate) originar, iniciar, dar lugar (a)

inauguration /ɪnˌɔgyəˈreiʃən/ *n* inauguración, *f;* (opening) estreno, *m,* apertura, *f;* (investiture) instalación, investidura, *f*

inauspicious /ˌɪnɔˈspɪʃəs/ *a* poco propicio, desfavorable; ominoso, triste, infeliz

inauspiciously /ˌɪnɔˈspɪʃəsli/ *adv* en condiciones desfavorables, desfavorablemente; infelizmente, bajo malos auspicios

inauspiciousness /ˌɪnɔˈspɪʃəsnɪs/ *n* condiciones desfavorables, *f pl;* infelicidad, *f;* malos auspicios, *m pl*

inborn /ˈɪnˈbɔrn/ *a* innato, instintivo, inherente

inbred /ˈɪnˈbrɛd/ *a* innato, inherente, instintivo

Inca /ˈɪŋkə/ *a* incaico, de los incas. —*n* inca, *m*

incalculability /ɪnˌkælkyələˈbɪlɪti/ *n* imposibilidad de calcular, *f;* (of persons) volubilidad, veleidad, *f;* infinidad, immensidad, *f*

incalculable /ɪnˈkælkyələbəl/ *a* incalculable, innumerable; (of persons) voluble, veleidoso, caprichoso; infinito, immenso

incalculably /ɪnˈkælkyələbli/ *adv* enormemente, infinitamente; caprichosamente

incandescence /ˌɪnkənˈdɛsəns/ *n* incandescencia, candencia, *f*

incandescent /ˌɪnkənˈdɛsənt/ *a* incandescente, candente. **i. light,** luz incandescente, *f.* **to make i.,** encandecer

incantation /ˌɪnkænˈteiʃən/ *n* hechizo, *m,* encantación, *f,* ensalmo, *m*

incapability /ɪnˌkeipəˈbɪlɪti/ *n* incapacidad, *f;* inhabilidad, ineptitud, incompetencia, *f*

incapable /ɪnˈkeipəbəl/ *a* incapaz; inhábil, incompetente; (physically) imposibilitado

incapacitate /ˌɪnkəˈpæsɪˌteit/ *vt* imposibilitar, incapacitar, inutilizar; (disqualify) inhabilitar, incapacitar

incapacitation /ˌɪnkəˌpæsɪˈteiʃən/ *n* inhabilitación, *f*

incapacity /ˌɪnkəˈpæsɪti/ *n* incapacidad, inhabilidad, *f*

incarcerate /ɪnˈkɑrsəˌreit/ *vt* encarcelar

incarceration /ɪnˌkɑrsəˈreiʃən/ *n* encarcelación, prisión, *f*

incarnate /*a* ɪn'kɑrnɪt; *v* -neit/ *a* encarnado. *—vt* encarnar
incarnation /ˌɪnkɑr'neiʃən/ *n* encarnación, *f*
incautious /ɪn'kɔʃəs/ *a* incauto, imprudente
incautiously /ɪn'kɔʃəsli/ *adv* incautamente
incautiousness /ɪn'kɔʃəsnɪs/ *n* imprudencia, negligencia, falta de cautela, *f*
incendiary /ɪn'sɛndiˌɛri/ *a* incendiario. **i. bomb,** incendiaria, *f*
incense /ɪn'sɛns/ *n* incienso, *m; Fig.* adulación, *f.* *—vt Eccl.* incensar; (annoy) irritar, exasperar, enojar. **i. burner,** incensario, *m*
incentive /ɪn'sɛntɪv/ *n* incentivo, estímulo, motivo, *m.* *—a* estimulador, incitativo
inception /ɪn'sɛpʃən/ *n* comienzo, principio, *m;* inauguración, *f*
incertitude /ɪn'sɜrtɪˌtud/ *n* incertidumbre, *f*
incessant /ɪn'sɛsənt/ *a* incesante, continuo, constante
incessantly /ɪn'sɛsəntli/ *adv* incesantemente, sin cesar
incest /'ɪnsɛst/ *n* incesto, *m*
incestuous /ɪn'sɛstʃuəs/ *a* incestuoso
inch /ɪntʃ/ *n* pulgada, *f.* **every i. a man,** hombre hecho y derecho. **Not an i.!** ¡Ni pizca! **within an i. of,** a dos dedos de. **i. by i.,** palmo a palmo, paso a paso. **i. tape,** cinta métrica, *f*
inchoate /ɪn'kouɪt/ *a* rudimentario; imperfecto, incompleto
incidence /'ɪnsɪdəns/ *n* incidencia, *f*
incident /'ɪnsɪdənt/ *a* propio, característico, incidental. *—n* incidente, acontecimiento, *m,* ocurrencia, *f*
incidental /ˌɪnsɪ'dɛntl/ *a* incidente, incidental; accidental, accesorio, no esencial. **i. expense,** gasto imprevisto, *m*
incidentally /ˌɪnsɪ'dɛntli/ *adv* (secondarily) incidentalmente; (by the way) de propósito
incident of navigation *n* accidente de navegación, *m*
incinerate /ɪn'sɪnəˌreit/ *vt* incinerar
incineration /ɪnˌsɪnə'reiʃən/ *n* incineración, cremación, *f*
incinerator /ɪn'sɪnəˌreitər/ *n* incinerador, *m*
incipient /ɪn'sɪpiənt/ *a* incipiente, naciente, rudimentario
incise /ɪn'saiz/ *vt* cortar; *Art.* grabar, tajar
incision /ɪn'sɪʒən/ *n* incisión, *f;* corte, tajo, *m; Med.* abscisión, *f*
incisive /ɪn'saisɪv/ *a* (of mind) agudo, penetrante; (of words) mordaz, incisivo, punzante
incisively /ɪn'saisɪvli/ *adv* en pocas palabras; mordazmente, incisivamente
incisiveness /ɪn'saisɪvnɪs/ *n* (of mind) agudeza, penetración, *f;* (of words) mordacidad, *f,* sarcasmo, *m*
incisor /ɪn'saizər/ *n* diente incisivo, *m*
incite /ɪn'sait/ *vt* incitar, estimular, animar; provocar, tentar. **to i. to,** mover a, incitar a
incitement /ɪn'saitmənt/ *n* incitación, instigación, *f;* estímulo, *m;* tentación, *f;* aliciente, *m*
incivility /ˌɪnsə'vɪlɪti/ *n* incivilidad, descortesía, *f*
inclemency /ɪn'klɛmənsi/ *n* inclemencia, *f,* rigor, *m*
inclement /ɪn'klɛmənt/ *a* inclemente, riguroso, borrascoso
inclination /ˌɪnklə'neiʃən/ *n* inclinación, *f;* (slope) declive, *m,* pendiente, cuesta, *f;* (tendency) propensión, tendencia, *f;* (liking) afición, *f;* amor, *m;* (bow) reverencia, *f; Geom.* inclinación, *f*
incline /*v* ɪn'klain; *n* 'ɪnklain/ *vt* inclinar, torcer; doblar; (cause) inclinar (a), hacer. *—vi* inclinarse, torcerse; (tend) tender, propender, inclinarse; (colors) tirar (a). *—n* declive, *m,* pendiente, cuesta, inclinación, *f.* **I am inclined to believe it,** Me inclino a creerlo. **I am inclined to do it,** Estoy por hacerlo, Creo que lo haré
inclined /ɪn'klaind/ *a* torcido, inclinado, doblado; *Fig.* propenso, adicto. **i. plane,** plano inclinado, *m*
include /ɪn'klud/ *vt* incluir, contener, encerrar; comprender, abrazar
including /ɪn'kludɪŋ/ *present part* incluso, inclusive. **not i.,** no comprendido
inclusion /ɪn'kluʒən/ *n* inclusión, *f*
inclusive /ɪn'klusɪv/ *a* inclusivo. **January 2 to January 12 i.,** del 2 al 12 de enero, ambos inclusivos. **not i. of,** sin contar, exclusivo de. **i. of,** que incluye. **i. terms,** todo incluido, todos los gastos incluidos
incognito /ˌɪnkɒg'nitou/ *a* and *adv* and *n* incógnito, *m.*
incoherence /ˌɪnkou'hɪərəns/ *n* incoherencia, inconsecuencia, *f*
incoherent /ˌɪnkou'hɪərənt/ *a* incoherente, inconexo, inconsecuente. **an i. piece of writing,** un escrito sin pies ni cabeza
incoherently /ˌɪnkou'hɪərəntli/ *adv* con incoherencia
incombustibility /ˌɪnkəmˌbʌstə'bɪlɪti/ *n* incombustibilidad, *f*
incombustible /ˌɪnkəm'bʌstəbəl/ *a* incombustible
income /'ɪnkʌm/ *n* renta, *f,* ingreso, *m; Com.* rédito, *m.* **i.-tax,** impuesto de utilidades, *m.* **i.-tax commissioners,** inspectores de impuestos de utilidades, *m pl.* **i.-tax return,** declaración de utilidades, *f*
incoming /'ɪnˌkʌmɪŋ/ *a* entrante; nuevo. *—n* entrada, llegada, *f.* *—n pl* **incomings,** ingresos, *m pl*
incommensurability /ˌɪnkəˌmɛnsərə'bɪlɪti/ *n* inconmensurabilidad, *f*
incommensurable /ˌɪnkə'mɛnsərəbəl/ *a* inconmensurable, no conmensurable
incommensurate /ˌɪnkə'mɛnsərɪt/ *a* desproporcionado, desmedido
incommode /ˌɪnkə'moud/ *vt* incomodar, molestar, fastidiar
incommodious /ˌɪnkə'moudiəs/ *a* estrecho; incómodo, inconveniente
incommodiousness /ˌɪnkə'moudiəsnɪs/ *n* estrechez, *f;* incomodidad, *f*
incommunicable /ˌɪnkə'myunɪkəbəl/ *a* incommunicable, indecible, inexplicable
incommunicative /ˌɪnkə'myunɪkətɪv/ *a* insociable, intratable, adusto, huraño
incomparable /ɪn'kɒmpərəbəl/ *a* incomparable; sin par, sin igual, excelente
incomparableness /ɪn'kɒmpərəbəlnɪs/ *n* excelencia, perfección, *f*
incomparably /ɪn'kɒmpərəbli/ *adv* incomparablemente, con mucho
incompatibility /ˌɪnkəmˌpætə'bɪlɪti/ *n* incompatibilidad, *f*
incompatible /ˌɪnkəm'pætəbəl/ *a* incompatible
incompetence /ɪn'kɒmpɪtəns/ *n* incompetencia, ineptitud, inhabilidad, *f; Law.* incapacidad, *f*
incompetent /ɪn'kɒmpɪtənt/ *a* incompetente, incapaz, inepto, inhábil; *Law.* incapaz
incompetently /ɪn'kɒmpɪtəntli/ *adv* inhábilmente
incomplete /ˌɪnkəm'plit/ *a* incompleto; imperfecto, defectuoso; (unfinished) sin terminar, inacabado, inconcluso. **incomplete sentence,** frase que queda colgando, *f*
incompletely /ˌɪnkəm'plitli/ *adv* incompletamente; imperfectamente
incompleteness /ˌɪnkəm'plitnɪs/ *n* estado incompleto, *m;* imperfección, *f;* inconclusión, *f*
incomprehensibility /ˌɪnkɒmprɪˌhɛnsə'bɪlɪti/ *n* incomprensibilidad, *f*
incomprehensible /ˌɪnkɒmprɪ'hɛnsəbəl/ *a* incomprensible
incomprehension /ˌɪnkɒmprɪ'hɛnʃən/ *n* incomprensión, falta de comprensión, *f*
inconceivable /ˌɪnkən'sivəbəl/ *a* inconcebible, inimaginable
inconclusive /ˌɪnkən'klusɪv/ *a* inconcluyente, cuestionable, dudoso, no convincente
inconclusiveness /ˌɪnkən'klusɪvnɪs/ *n* carácter inconcluso, *m,* falta de conclusiones, *f*
incongruity /ˌɪnkən'gruɪti/ *n* incongruencia, desproporción, disonancia, *f*
incongruous /ɪn'kɒŋgruəs/ *a* incongruente, incongruo; chocante, desproporcionado, disonante
incongruously /ɪn'kɒŋgruəsli/ *adv* incongruentemente, incongruamente
inconsequence /ɪn'kɒnsɪˌkwɛns/ *n* inconsecuencia, *f*
inconsequent, inconsequential /ɪn'kɒnsɪˌkwɛnt; ɪnˌkɒnsɪ'kwɛnʃəl/ *a* inconsecuente, ilógico; inconsistente
inconsiderable /ˌɪnkən'sɪdərəbəl/ *a* insignificante
inconsiderate /ˌɪnkən'sɪdərɪt/ *a* desconsiderado, irreflexivo, irrespetuoso

inconsiderately /ˌɪnkənˈsɪdərɪtli/ *adv* sin consideración, desconsideradamente
inconsiderateness /ˌɪnkənˈsɪdərɪtnɪs/ *n* desconsideración, falta de respeto, *f*
inconsistency /ˌɪnkənˈsɪstənsi/ *n* inconsistencia, inconsecuencia, incompatibilidad, contradicción, anomalía, *f*
inconsistent /ˌɪnkənˈsɪstənt/ *a* inconsistente, inconsiguiente, incompatible, contradictorio, anómalo
inconsistently /ˌɪnkənˈsɪstəntli/ *adv* contradictoriamente
inconsolable /ˌɪnkənˈsouləbəl/ *a* inconsolable, desconsolado. **to be i.,** estar inconsolable, (*Inf.* of a woman) estar hecha una Magdalena
inconsolably /ˌɪnkənˈsouləbli/ *adv* desconsoladamente
inconspicuous /ˌɪnkənˈspɪkyuəs/ *a* que no llama la atención; insignificante, humilde, modesto
inconspicuously /ˌɪnkənˈspɪkyuəsli/ *adv* humildemente, modestamente
inconspicuousness /ˌɪnkənˈspɪkyuəsnɪs/ *n* modestia, humildad, *f*
inconstancy /ɪnˈkɒnstənsi/ *n* inconstancia, movilidad, *f;* mudanza, veleidad, *f*
inconstant /ɪnˈkɒnstənt/ *a* inconstante, mudable, variable; veleidoso, volátil, voluble
incontestable /ˌɪnkənˈtɛstəbəl/ *a* incontestable, evidente, indisputable
incontinence /ɪnˈkɒntn̩əns/ *n* incontinencia, *f*
incontinent /ɪnˈkɒntn̩ənt/ *a* incontinente
incontrollable /ˌɪnkənˈtrouləbəl/ *a* ingobernable, indomable
incontrovertible /ˌɪnkɒntrəˈvɜrtəbəl/ *a* incontrovertible, incontrastable
inconvenience /ˌɪnkənˈvinyəns/ *n* incomodidad, inconveniencia, *f;* (of time) inoportunidad, *f.* —*vt* incomodar, causar inconvenientes (a)
inconvenient /ˌɪnkənˈvinyənt/ *a* incómodo, inconveniente, molesto, embarazoso; (of time) inoportuno. **at an i. time,** a deshora
inconveniently /ˌɪnkənˈvinyəntli/ *adv* incómodamente; (of time) inoportunamente
incorporate /*v* ɪnˈkɔrpəˌreit; *a* -pərɪt/ *vt* incorporar, agregar; comprender, incluir, encerrar. —*vi* asociarse, incorporarse. —*a* incorpóreo, inmaterial; incorporado, asociado
incorporation /ɪnˌkɔrpəˈreiʃən/ *n* incorporación, agregación, *f;* asociación, *f*
incorporeal /ˌɪnkɔrˈpɔriəl/ *a* incorpóreo, inmaterial
incorporeity /ɪnˌkɔrpəˈriɪti/ *n* incorporeidad, inmaterialidad, *f*
incorrect /ˌɪnkəˈrɛkt/ *a* incorrecto; inexacto, erróneo, falso
incorrectness /ˌɪnkəˈrɛktnɪs/ *n* incorrección, *f*
incorrigibility /ɪnˌkɔrɪdʒəˈbɪlɪti/ *n* incorregibilidad, *f*
incorrigible /ɪnˈkɔrɪdʒəbəl/ *a* incorregible, empecatado
incorrigibly /ɪnˈkɔrɪdʒəbli/ *adv* incorregiblemente, obstinadamente
incorrupt /ˌɪnkəˈrʌpt/ *a* incorrupto; recto, honrado
incorruptibility /ˌɪnkəˌrʌptəˈbɪlɪti/ *n* incorruptibilidad, *f;* honradez, probidad, *f*
incorruptible /ˌɪnkəˈrʌptəbəl/ *a* incorrupto; honrado, incorruptible
incorruption /ˌɪnkəˈrʌpʃən/ *n* incorrupción, *f*
increase /*v* ɪnˈkris; *n* ˈɪnkris/ *vt* aumentar, acrecentar; (in numbers) multiplicar; (extend) ampliar, extender; (of price) encarecer, aumentar. —*vi* aumentar, crecer; multiplicarse; extenderse; encarecerse, aumentar. —*n* aumento, crecimiento, *m;* multiplicación, *f;* (in price) encarecimiento, *m,* alza, *f;* (of water) crecida, *f;* (of moon) creciente, *f.* **It is on the i.,** Va en aumento. **to i. and multiply,** crecer y multiplicar
increasingly /ɪnˈkrisɪŋli/ *adv* más y más; en creciente, en aumento
incredibility /ɪnˌkrɛdəˈbɪlɪti/ *n* incredibilidad, *f*
incredible /ɪnˈkrɛdəbəl/ *a* increíble; fabuloso, extraordinario. **It seems i.,** Es increíble, *Inf.* Parece mentira
incredibly /ɪnˈkrɛdəbli/ *adv* increíblemente
incredulity /ˌɪnkrɪˈdulɪti/ *n* incredulidad, *f,* escepticismo, *m*
incredulous /ɪnˈkrɛdʒələs/ *a* incrédulo, escéptico
incredulously /ɪnˈkrɛdʒələsli/ *adv* con incredulidad, escépticamente
increment /ˈɪnkrəmənt/ *n* aumento, incremento, *m;* adición, añadidura, *f; Math.* incremento, *m.* **unearned i.,** plusvalía, mayor valía, *f*
incriminate /ɪnˈkrɪməˌneit/ *vt* incriminar
incriminating /ɪnˈkrɪməˌneitɪŋ/ *a* incriminante, acriminador
incrust /ɪnˈkrʌst/ *vt* incrustar, encostrar
incrustation /ˌɪnkrʌˈsteiʃən/ *n* incrustación, *f;* (scab) costra, *f*
incubate /ˈɪnkyəˌbeit/ *vt* empollar; *Med.* incubar
incubation /ˌɪnkyəˈbeiʃən/ *n* empolladura, incubación, *f; Med.* incubación, *f*
incubator /ˈɪnkyəˌbeitər/ *n* incubadora, *f*
incubus /ˈɪnkyəbəs/ *n* íncubo, *m;* (burden) carga, *f*
inculcate /ɪnˈkʌlkeit/ *vt* inculcar, implantar, instilar
inculcation /ˌɪnkʌlˈkeiʃən/ *n* inculcación, implantación, instilación, *f*
incumbency /ɪnˈkʌmbənsi/ *n* posesión, duración de, posesión, duración (de cualquier puesto), *f*
incumbent /ɪnˈkʌmbənt/ *a* obligatorio. —*n Eccl.* beneficiado, *m.* **to be i. on,** incumbir a, ser de su obligación
incur /ɪnˈkɜr/ *vi* incurrir (en), incidir (en). **to i. an obligation,** contraer una obligación
incurability /ɪnˌkyʊrəˈbɪlɪti/ *n* incurabilidad, *f*
incurable /ɪnˈkyʊrəbəl/ *a* incurable, insanable; *Fig.* sin solución, irremediable. —*n* incurable, *mf*
incurably /ɪnˈkyʊrəbli/ *adv* incurablemente, irremediablemente
incurious /ɪnˈkyʊriəs/ *a* indiferente, sin interés; incurioso, negligente, descuidado
incursion /ɪnˈkɜrʒən/ *n* incursión, invasión, irrupción, *f,* acometimiento, *m*
indebted /ɪnˈdɛtɪd/ *a* empeñado, adeudado; (obliged) reconocido
indebtedness /ɪnˈdɛtɪdnɪs/ *n* deuda, *f;* (gratitude) obligación, *f;* agradecimiento, *m*
indecency /ɪnˈdisənsi/ *n* indecencia, *f*
indecent /ɪnˈdisənt/ *a* indecente; obsceno, deshonesto
indecently /ɪnˈdisəntli/ *adv* torpemente, indecentemente
indecision /ˌɪndɪˈsɪʒən/ *n* indecisión, vacilación, irresolución, *f*
indecisive /ˌɪndɪˈsaisɪv/ *a* indeciso, irresoluto, vacilante
indeclinable /ˌɪndɪˈklainəbəl/ *a* indeclinable
indecorous /ɪnˈdɛkərəs/ *a* indecoroso, indecente, indigno
indecorum /ˌɪndɪˈkɔrəm/ *n* indecoro, *m,* indecencia, *f;* incorrección, *f*
indeed /ɪnˈdid/ *adv* en efecto, de veras, a la verdad, realmente, por cierto, claro está. —*interr* ¿de veras? ¿es posible? **I shall be very glad i.,** Estaré contento de veras. **It is i. an excellent book,** Es en efecto un libro excelente. **There are differences i. between this house and the other,** Hay diferencias, claro está, entre esta casa y la otra
indefatigability /ˌɪndɪˌfætɪgəˈbɪlɪti/ *n* resistencia, *f,* aguante, *m,* tenacidad, *f*
indefatigable /ˌɪndɪˈfætɪgəbəl/ *a* incansable, infatigable, resistente
indefatigably /ˌɪndɪˈfætɪgəbli/ *adv* infatigablemente
indefensible /ˌɪndɪˈfɛnsəbəl/ *a* indefendible, insostenible
indefinable /ˌɪndɪˈfainəbəl/ *a* indefinible
indefinite /ɪnˈdɛfənɪt/ *a* indefinido, incierto; (delicate) sutil, delicado; *Gram.* indefinido; (vague) vago. *Gram.* **i. article,** artículo indefinido, *m*
indefinitely /ɪnˈdɛfənɪtli/ *adv* indefinidamente
indefiniteness /ɪnˈdɛfənɪtnɪs/ *n* lo indefinido, el carácter indefinido, *m;* vaguedad, *f*
indelibility /ɪnˌdɛləˈbɪlɪti/ *n* resistencia, *f,* lo indeleble; *Fig.* duración, tenacidad, *f*
indelible /ɪnˈdɛləbəl/ *a* indeleble, imborrable; *Fig.* inolvidable
indelibly /ɪnˈdɛləbli/ *adv* indeleblemente

indelicacy /ɪn'dɛlɪkəsi/ *n* falta de buen gusto, grosería, *f;* (tactlessness) indiscreción, falta de tacto, *f*
indelicate /ɪn'dɛlɪkɪt/ *a* grosero, descortés; indecoroso, inmodesto; (tactless) inoportuno, indiscreto
indemnification /ɪn,dɛmnəfɪ'keiʃən/ *n* indemnización, compensación, *f*
indemnify /ɪn'dɛmnə,fai/ *vt* indemnizar, compensar
indemnity /ɪn'dɛmnɪti/ *n* indemnización, reparación, *f*
indent /ɪn'dɛnt/ *vt* endentar, mellar; *Print.* sangrar
indentation /,ɪndɛn'teiʃən/ *n* impresión, depresión, *f;* corte, *m,* mella, *f;* línea quebrada, *f,* zigzag, *m*
indenture /ɪn'dɛntʃər/ *n* escritura, *f,* instrumento, *m.* —*vt* escriturar
independence /,ɪndɪ'pɛndəns/ *n* independencia, libertad, *f;* (autonomy) autonomía, *f.* **I. Day,** Fiesta de la Independencia, *f.* **i. movement,** movimiento en favor de la independencia, *m*
independent /,ɪndɪ'pɛndənt/ *a* independiente; libre; (autonomous) autónomo; **i. of,** libre de; aparte de. **a person of i. means,** una persona acomodada
independently /,ɪndɪ'pɛndəntli/ *adv* independientemente
indescribability /,ɪndɪ,skraibə'bɪlɪti/ *n* imposibilidad de describir, *f,* lo indescriptible
indescribable /,ɪndɪ'skraibəbəl/ *a* indescriptible; indefinible, indecible, inexplicable; incalificable
indestructibility /,ɪndɪ,strʌktə'bɪlɪti/ *n* indestructibilidad, *f*
indestructible /,ɪndɪ'strʌktəbəl/ *a* indestructible
indeterminable /,ɪndɪ'tɜrmənəbəl/ *a* indeterminable
indeterminate /,ɪndɪ'tɜrmənɪt/ *a* indeterminado, indefinido, vago; *Math.* indeterminado
indetermination /,ɪndɪ,tɜrmə'neiʃən/ *n* irresolución, indecisión, duda, vacilación, *f*
index /'ɪndɛks/ *n* (forefinger) dedo índice, *m;* (of book) tabla de materias, *f,* indice, *m;* (on instruments) manecilla, aguja, *f; Math.* índice, *m;* (sign) señal, indicación, *f.* —*vt* poner índice (a); poner en el índice. **i. card,** ficha, *f.* **I. expurgatorius,** Índice expurgatorio, *m*
India /'ɪndiə/ *n* la India, *f.* **I. paper,** papel de China, *m.* **i.-rubber,** *Bot.* caucho, *m;* (eraser) goma de borrar, *f.* **i.-rubber tree,** yacio, *m*
Indian /'ɪndiən/ *a* and *n* indio (-ia). **I. chief,** cacique, *m.* **I. club,** maza, *f.* **I. corn,** maíz, *m.* **I. ink,** tinta china, *f.* **I. summer,** veranillo, veranillo de San Martín, *m*
Indian Ocean, the el Océano Indico, *m*
indicate /'ɪndɪ,keit/ *vt* indicar, señalar; (show) denotar, mostrar, anunciar
indication /,ɪndɪ'keiʃən/ *n* indicación, *f;* señal, *f,* indicio, síntoma, *m;* prueba, *f*
indicative /ɪn'dɪkətɪv/ *a* indicador, indicativo, demostrativo; *Gram.* indicativo. —*n Gram.* indicativo, *m.* **to be i. of,** indicar, señalar
indicator /'ɪndɪ,keitər/ *n* indicador, señalador, *m*
indict /ɪn'dait/ *vt* acusar; *Law.* demandar, enjuiciar
indictable /ɪn'daitəbəl/ *a* procesable, denunciable, enjuiciable
indictment /ɪn'daitmənt/ *n* acusación, *f; Law.* procesamiento, *m*
indifference /ɪn'dɪfərəns/ *n* indiferencia, apatía, *f,* desinterés, desapego, *m;* imparcialidad, neutralidad, *f;* (coldness) frialdad, tibieza, *f*
indifferent /ɪn'dɪfərənt/ *a* indiferente, apático; imparcial, neutral; frío; (ordinary) regular, ordinario, ni bien ni mal
indifferently /ɪn'dɪfərəntli/ *adv* con indiferencia; imparcialmente; friamente
indigence /'ɪndɪdʒəns/ *n* indigencia, necesidad, penuria, *f*
indigenous /ɪn'dɪdʒənəs/ *a* indígena, nativo, natural
indigent /'ɪndɪdʒənt/ *a* indigente, necesitado, menesteroso
indigestible /,ɪndɪ'dʒɛstəbəl/ *a* indigesto
indigestion /,ɪndɪ'dʒɛstʃən/ *n* indigestión, *f; Fig.* empacho, ahíto, *m*
indignant /ɪn'dɪgnənt/ *a* indignado. **to make i.,** indignar
indignantly /ɪn'dɪgnəntli/ *adv* con indignación
indignation /,ɪndɪg'neiʃən/ *n* indignación, cólera, *f*
indignity /ɪn'dɪgnɪti/ *n* indignidad, *f;* ultraje, *m*
indigo /'ɪndɪ,gou/ *n* añil, índigo, *m*
indirect /,ɪndə'rɛkt/ *a* indirecto; oblicuo; tortuoso; *Gram.* **i. case,** caso oblicuo, *m*
indirectness /,ɪndə'rɛktnɪs/ *n* (of route) rodeo, *m,* desviación, *f;* oblicuidad, *f;* (falsity) tortuosidad, *f*
indiscernible /,ɪndɪ'sɜrnəbəl/ *a* imperceptible
indiscipline /ɪn'dɪsəplɪn/ *n* indisciplina, falta de disciplina, *f*
indiscreet /,ɪndɪ'skrit/ *a* indiscreto, imprudente, impolítico
indiscreetly /,ɪndɪ'skritli/ *adv* indiscretamente
indiscretion /,ɪndɪ'skrɛʃən/ *n* indiscreción, imprudencia, *f;* (slip) desliz, *m*
indiscriminate /,ɪndɪ'skrɪmənɪt/ *a* general, universal; indistinto, promiscuo
indiscriminately /,ɪndɪ'skrɪmənɪtli/ *adv* promiscuamente
indiscrimination /,ɪndɪ,skrɪmə'neiʃən/ *n* universalidad, indistinción, *f*
indispensability /,ɪndɪ,spɛnsə'bɪlɪti/ *n* indispensabilidad, precisión, necesidad, *f*
indispensable /,ɪndɪ'spɛnsəbəl/ *a* imprescindible, indispensable, insustituible
indispensably /,ɪndɪ'spɛnsəbli/ *adv* forzosamente, indispensablemente
indispose /,ɪndɪ'spouz/ *vt* indisponer. **to be indisposed,** estar indispuesto, indisponerse
indisposed /,ɪndɪ'spouzd/ *a* indispuesto, enfermo, destemplado; (reluctant) maldispuesto
indisposition /,ɪndɪspə'zɪʃən/ *n* indisposición, enfermedad, *f*
indisputability /,ɪndɪ,spyutə'bɪlɪti/ *n* verdad manifiesta, certeza, evidencia, *f*
indisputable /,ɪndɪ'spyutəbəl/ *a* innegable, incontestable; irrefutable, evidente
indisputably /,ɪndɪ'spyutəbli/ *adv* indisputablemente
indissolubility /,ɪndɪ,sɒlyə'bɪlɪti/ *n* indisolubilidad, *f*
indissoluble /,ɪndɪ'sɒlyəbəl/ *a* indisoluble
indistinct /,ɪndɪ'stɪŋkt/ *a* indistinto; indeterminado, confuso, vago
indistinctly /,ɪndɪ'stɪŋktli/ *adv* indistintamente; confusamente, vagamente
indistinctness /,ɪndɪ'stɪŋktnɪs/ *n* incertidumbre, vaguedad, indistinción, indeterminación, *f*
indistinguishable /,ɪndɪ'stɪŋgwɪʃəbəl/ *a* indistinguible
individual /,ɪndə'vɪdʒuəl/ *a* (single) solo, único; individual, individuo, particular, propio; personal. —*n* individuo, *m,* particular, *mf*
individualism /,ɪndə'vɪdʒuə,lɪzəm/ *n* individualismo, *m*
individualist /,ɪndə'vɪdʒuəlɪst/ *n* individualist, *mf*
individualistic /,ɪndə,vɪdʒuə'lɪstɪk/ *a* individualista
individuality /,ɪndə,vɪdʒu'ælɪti/ *n* individualidad, personalidad, *f;* carácter, *m,* naturaleza, *f*
individualize /,ɪndə'vɪdʒuə,laiz/ *vt* particularizar, individuar
individually /,ɪndə'vɪdʒuəli/ *adv* individualmente, particularmente
indivisibility /,ɪndə,vɪzə'bɪlɪti/ *n* indivisibilidad, *f*
indivisible /,ɪndə'vɪzəbəl/ *a* incompartible, impartible, indivisible
indivisibly /,ɪndə'vɪzəbli/ *adv* indivisiblemente
Indo (in compounds) indo. **I.-Chinese,** *a* and *n* indochino (-na). **I.-European,** indoeuropeo. **I.-Germanic,** indogermánico
indocile /ɪn'dɒsɪl/ *a* indócil, desobediente, rebelde
indocility /,ɪndɒ'sɪlɪti/ *n* indocilidad, desobediencia, falta de docilidad, *f*
indolence /'ɪndḷəns/ *n* indolencia, pereza, desidia, *f*
indolent /'ɪndḷənt/ *a* indolente, perezoso, holgazán; *Med.* indoloro
indolently /'ɪndḷəntli/ *adv* perezosamente
indomitable /ɪn'dɒmɪtəbəl/ *a* indomable, indómito
indoor /'ɪn,dɔr/ *a* de casa; de puertas adentro, interno. **i. swimming pool,** piscina bajo techo, *f.* **i. tennis,** tenis en pistas cubiertas, tenis bajo techo, *m*
indoors /ɪn'dɔrz/ *adv* en casa; adentro, bajo techo
indorsee /ɪndɔr'si/ *n* endosatario (-ia)
indubitable /ɪn'dubɪtəbəl/ *a* indudable

indubitably /ɪn'dubɪtəbli/ *adv* indudablemente, sin duda
induce /ɪn'dus/ *vt* inducir, mover; instigar, incitar; producir, ocasionar; *Elec.* inducir. **Nothing would i. me to do it,** Nada me induciría a hacerlo
inducement /ɪn'dusmənt/ *n* incitamento, *m;* estímulo, *m;* aliciente, atractivo, *m;* tentación, *f*
induct /ɪn'dʌkt/ *vt* instalar; introducir, iniciar
induction /ɪn'dʌkʃən/ *n* instalación, *f;* iniciación, introducción, *f; Phys.* inducción, *f.* **i. coil,** carrete de inducción, *m*
inductive /ɪn'dʌktɪv/ *a* (of reasoning) inductivo; *Phys.* inductor
indulge /ɪn'dʌldʒ/ *vt* (children) consentir, mimar; (a desire) satisfacer, dar rienda suelta a; (with a gift) agasajar (con), dar gusto (con). **to i. in,** *vt* consentir en. —*vi* entregarse a, permitirse, gustar de
indulgence /ɪn'dʌldʒəns/ *n* (of children) mimo, cariño excesivo, *m;* (of a desire) propensión (a), afición (a), *f;* (toward others) tolerancia, transigencia, *f; Eccl.* indulgencia, *f*
indulgent /ɪn'dʌldʒənt/ *a* indulgente; tolerante, transigente
indult /ɪn'dʌlt/ *n Eccl.* indulto, *m*
industrial /ɪn'dʌstriəl/ *a* industrial. **i. alcohol,** alcohol desnaturalizado, *m.* **i. school,** escuela de artes y oficios, *f, Com.* **i. shares,** valores industriales, *m pl*
industrialism /ɪn'dʌstriə,lɪzəm/ *n* industrialismo, *m*
industrialist /ɪn'dʌstriəlɪst/ *n* industrial, *m*
industrialization /ɪn,dʌstriəlɪ'zeiʃən/ *n* industrialización, *f*
industrialize /ɪn'dʌstriə,laiz/ *vt* industrializar
industrious /ɪn'dʌstriəs/ *a* industrioso, aplicado, diligente
industriously /ɪn'dʌstriəsli/ *adv* industriosamente, diligentemente
industriousness /ɪn'dʌstriəsnɪs/ *n* industria, laboriosidad, *f*
industry /'ɪndəstri/ *n* diligencia, aplicación, *f;* (work) trabajo, *m,* labor, *f; Com.* industria, *f*
inebriate /*a, n* ɪ'nibriɪt; *v* -bri,eit/ *a* borracho, ebrio. —*n* borracho (-cha). —*vt* embriagar, emborrachar
inebriation /ɪ,nibri'eiʃən/ *n* embriaguez, borrachera, *f*
inedible /ɪn'ɛdəbəl/ *a* incomible, no comestible
inedited /ɪn'ɛdɪtɪd/ *a* inédito
ineffable /ɪn'ɛfəbəl/ *a* indecible, inefable
ineffaceable /,ɪnɪ'feisəbəl/ *a* imborrable, indeleble
ineffective /,ɪnɪ'fɛktɪv/ *a* ineficaz; vano, fútil. **to be i.,** (of persons) no pinchar ni cortar. **to prove i.,** quedar sin efecto; no tener influencia
ineffectiveness /,ɪnɪ'fɛktɪvnɪs/ *n* ineficacia, *f;* futilidad, *f*
inefficiency /,ɪnɪ'fɪʃənsi/ *n* ineficacia, incompetencia, ineptitud, *f*
inefficient /,ɪnɪ'fɪʃənt/ *a* ineficaz, incapaz
inefficiently /,ɪnɪ'fɪʃəntli/ *adv* ineficazmente
inelastic /,ɪnɪ'læstɪk/ *a* inelástico
inelegance /ɪn'ɛlɪgəns/ *n* inelegancia, fealdad, vulgaridad, *f*
inelegant /ɪn'ɛlɪgənt/ *a* inelegante, ordinario, de mal gusto
inelegantly /ɪn'ɛlɪgəntli/ *adv* sin elegancia
ineligibility /ɪn,ɛlɪdʒə'bɪlɪti/ *n* ineligibilidad, *f*
ineligible /ɪn'ɛlɪdʒəbəl/ *a* inelegible
inept /ɪn'ɛpt/ *a* inepto, inoportuno; absurdo, ridículo; (of persons) incompetente, ineficaz
ineptitude /ɪn'ɛptɪ,tud/ *n* ineptitud, *f;* necedad, *f;* (of persons) incapacidad, incompetencia, *f*
ineptly /ɪn'ɛptli/ *adv* ineptamente, neciamente
inequality /,ɪnɪ'kwɒlɪti/ *n* desigualdad, desemejanza, disparidad, *f;* (of surface) escabrosidad, aspereza, *f; Fig.* injusticia, *f;* (of opportunity) diferencia, *f*
inequitable /ɪn'ɛkwɪtəbəl/ *a* desigual, injusto
inequity /ɪn'ɛkwɪti/ *n* injusticia, desigualdad, *f*
ineradicable /,ɪnɪ'rædɪkəbəl/ *a* indeleble, imborrable
ineradicably /,ɪnɪ'rædɪkəbli/ *adv* indeleblemente
inert /ɪn'ɜrt/ *a* inerte, inactivo, pasivo; ocioso, flojo, perezoso
inertia /ɪn'ɜrʃə/ *n* inercia, inacción, *f;* abulia, pereza, *f; Phys.* inercia, *f*
inertly /ɪn'ɜrtli/ *adv* indolentemente, sin mover, pasivamente
inescapable /,ɪnə'skeipəbəl/ *a* ineludible, inevitable
inessential /,ɪnɪ'sɛnʃəl/ *a* no esencial
inestimable /ɪn'ɛstəməbəl/ *a* inestimable
inevitability /ɪn,ɛvɪtə'bɪlɪti/ *n* fatalidad, necesidad, *f;* lo inevitable
inevitable /ɪn'ɛvɪtəbəl/ *a* inevitable, necesario, fatal, forzoso, ineludible
inevitably /ɪn'ɛvɪtəbli/ *adv* inevitablemente, necesariamente, forzosamente
inexact /,ɪnɪg'zækt/ *a* inexacto, incorrecto
inexactitude /,ɪnɪg'zæktɪ,tud/ *n* inexactitud, *f*
inexcusable /,ɪnɪk'skyuzəbəl/ *a* imperdonable, inexcusable, irremisible
inexcusableness /,ɪnɪk'skyuzəbəlnɪs/ *n* enormidad, *f;* lo inexcusable
inexcusably /,ɪnɪk'skyuzəbli/ *adv* inexcusablemente
inexhaustible /,ɪnɪg'zɔstəbəl/ *a* inagotable, inexhausto
inexorability /ɪn,ɛksərə'bɪlɪti/ *n* inflexibilidad, inexorabilidad, *f*
inexorable /ɪn'ɛksərəbəl/ *a* inexorable, inflexible, duro
inexorably /ɪn'ɛksərəbli/ *adv* inexorablemente, implacablemente
inexpediency /,ɪnɪk'spidiənsi/ *n* inoportunidad, inconveniencia, imprudencia, *f*
inexpedient /,ɪnɪk'spidiənt/ *a* inoportuno; inconveniente; impolítico, imprudente. **to deem i.,** creer inoportuno
inexpensive /,ɪnɪk'spɛnsɪv/ *a* poco costoso, barato
inexpensiveness /,ɪnɪk'spɛnsɪvnɪs/ *n* baratura, *f,* bajo precio, *m*
inexperience /,ɪnɪk'spɪəriəns/ *n* inexperiencia, falta de experiencia, *f*
inexperienced /,ɪnɪk'spɪəriənst/ *a* inexperto, novato
inexpert /ɪn'ɛkspɜrt/ *a* inexperto, imperito
inexpertly /ɪn'ɛkspərtli/ *adv* sin habilidad
inexpertness /ɪn'ɛkspərtnɪs/ *n* impericia, torpeza, *f*
inexpiable /ɪn'ɛkspiəbəl/ *a* inexpiable
inexplicable /ɪn'ɛksplɪkəbəl/ *a* inexplicable
inexplicit /,ɪnɪk'splɪsɪt/ *a* no explícito
inexplosive /,ɪnɪk'splousɪv/ *a* inexplosible
inexpressible /,ɪnɪk'sprɛsəbəl/ *a* inexplicable, indecible, inefable
inexpressive /,ɪnɪk'sprɛsɪv/ *a* inexpresivo; (of persons) reservado, callado, poco expresivo, retraído
inexpressiveness /,ɪnɪk'sprɛsɪvnɪs/ *n* falta de expresión, *f;* (of persons) reserva, *f,* silencio, retraimiento, *m*
inexpugnable /,ɪnɪk'spʌgnəbəl/ *a* inexpugnable
inextinguishable /,ɪnɪk'stɪŋgwɪʃəbəl/ *a* inapagable, inextinguible
inextricable /ɪn'ɛkstrɪkəbəl/ *a* inextricable, intrincado, enmarañado
inextricably /ɪn'ɛkstrɪkəbli/ *adv* intrincadamente
infallibility /ɪn,fælə'bɪlɪti/ *n* infalibilidad, *f*
infallible /ɪn'fæləbəl/ *a* infalible
infamous /'ɪnfəməs/ *a* infame, torpe, vil, ignominioso; odioso, repugnante
infamously /'ɪnfəməsli/ *adv* infamemente
infamy /'ɪnfəmi/ *n* infamia, torpeza, vileza, ignominia, *f;* deshonra, *f*
infancy /'ɪnfənsi/ *n* infancia, niñez, *f; Law.* minoridad, *f*
infant /'ɪnfənt/ *n* criatura, *f;* crío (-ía), niño (-ña); *Law.* menor, *mf* **i. school,** escuela de párvulos, *f*
infanticidal /ɪn,fæntə'saidl/ *a* infanticida
infanticide /ɪn'fæntə,said/ *n* (act) infanticidio, *m;* (person) infanticida, *mf*
infantile /'ɪnfən,tail/ *a* infantil. **i. paralysis,** parálisis infantil, *f*
infantry /'ɪnfəntri/ *n Mil.* infantería, *f*
infantryman /'ɪnfəntrimən/ *n Mil.* infante, peón, *m*
infatuate /ɪn'fætʃu,eit/ *vt* infatuar, embobar
infatuation /ɪn,fætʃu'eiʃən/ *n* infatuación, *f,* encaprichamiento, *m*
infect /ɪn'fɛkt/ *vt* infectar, contagiar; *Fig.* pegar, influir; (*Fig.* in a bad sense) corromper, pervertir, inficionar. **to become infected,** infectarse

infected /ɪn'fɛktɪd/ *a* infecto
infection /ɪn'fɛkʃən/ *n* infección, *f,* contagio, *m; Fig.* influencia, *f;* (*Fig.* in a bad sense) corrupción, perversión, *f*
infectious /ɪn'fɛkʃəs/ *a* infeccioso, contagioso; (*Fig.* in a bad sense) corruptor; *Fig.* contagioso
infectiousness /ɪn'fɛkʃəsnɪs/ *n* contagiosidad, *f*
infelicitous /ˌɪnfə'lɪsɪtəs/ *a* poco apropiado, desacertado
infelicity /ˌɪnfə'lɪsɪti/ *n* infelicidad, desdicha, *f,* infortunio, *m;* desacierto, *m,* inoportunidad, *f*
infer /ɪn'fɜr/ *vt* inferir, concluir, educir, deducir, implicar
inferable /ɪn'fɜrəbəl/ *a* deducible, demostrable
inference /'ɪnfərəns/ *n* inferencia, deducción, conclusión, *f*
inferential /ˌɪnfə'rɛnʃəl/ *a* ilativo, deductivo
inferior /ɪn'fɪəriər/ *a* inferior; (in rank) subordinado, subalterno; (of position) secundario. —*n* inferior, *mf* subordinado (-da). **to be not i.,** no ser inferior, *Inf.* no quedarse en zaga
inferiority /ɪnˌfɪəri'ɔrɪti/ *n* inferioridad, *f.* **i. complex,** complejo de inferioridad, *m*
infernal /ɪn'fɜrnl̩/ *a* infernal; *Poet.* inferno, tartáreo
infernally /ɪn'fɜrnli/ *adv* infernalmente
inferno /ɪn'fɜrnou/ *n* infierno, *m*
infertile /ɪn'fɜrtl̩/ *a* infértil, infecundo, estéril
infertility /ˌɪnfər'tɪlɪti/ *n* infertilidad, infecundidad, esterilidad, *f*
infest /ɪn'fɛst/ *vt* infestar. **to be infested with,** plagarse de
infestation /ˌɪnfɛs'teiʃən/ *n* infestación, *f*
infidel /'ɪnfɪdl̩/ *n* infiel, gentil, *mf* pagano (-na); (atheist) descreído (-da), ateo (-ea). —*a* pagano; infiel, descreído, ateo
infidelity /ˌɪnfɪ'dɛlɪti/ *n* infidelidad, alevosía, perfidia, *f*
infiltrate /ɪn'fɪltreit/ *vt* infiltrar. —*vi* infiltrarse
infiltration /ˌɪnfɪl'treiʃən/ *n* infiltración, *f*
infinite /'ɪnfənɪt/ *a* infinito, ilimitado; inmenso, enorme; (of number) innumerable, infinito. —*n* infinito, *m*
infinitely /'ɪnfənɪtli/ *adv* infinitamente
infinitesimal /ˌɪnfɪnɪ'tɛsəməl/ *a* infinitesimal. **i. calculus,** cálculo infinitesimal, *m*
infinitive /ɪn'fɪnɪtɪv/ *a* and *n Gram.* infinitivo, *m.*
infinitude, infinity /ɪn'fɪnɪtud; ɪn'fɪnɪti/ *n* infinidad, infinitud, *f;* (extent) inmensidad, *f;* (of number) sinfín, *m; Math.* infinito, *m*
infirm /ɪn'fɜrm/ *a* achacoso, enfermizo, enclenque; (shaky) inestable, inseguro; (of purpose) irresoluto, vacilante
infirmary /ɪn'fɜrməri/ *n* enfermería, *f,* hospital, *m*
infirmity /ɪn'fɜrmɪti/ *n* achaque, *m,* enfermedad, dolencia, *f;* (fault) flaqueza, falta, *f*
inflame /ɪn'fleim/ *vt* encender; (excite) acalorar, irritar, provocar; *Med.* inflamar. —*vi* encenderse, arder; acalorarse, irritarse; *Med.* inflamarse
inflammability /ɪnˌflæmə'bɪlɪti/ *n* inflamabilidad, *f*
inflammable /ɪn'flæməbəl/ *a* inflamable
inflammation /ˌɪnflə'meiʃən/ *n* inflamación, *f*
inflammatory /ɪn'flæməˌtɔri/ *a* inflamador; *Med.* inflamatorio
inflate /ɪn'fleit/ *vt* inflar, hinchar; (with pride) engreír, ensoberbecer
inflation /ɪn'fleiʃən/ *n* inflación, hinchazón, *f; Com.* inflación, *f*
inflationism /ɪn'fleiʃəˌnɪzəm/ *n* inflacionismo, *m*
inflator /ɪn'fleitər/ *n Mech.* bomba para inflar, *f*
inflect /ɪn'flɛkt/ *vt* torcer; (voice) modular; *Gram.* conjugar, declinar
inflection /ɪn'flɛkʃən/ *n* dobladura, *f;* (of voice) tono, acento, *m,* modulación, *f; Gram.* conjugación, declinación, *f*
inflexibility /ɪnˌflɛksə'bɪlɪti/ *n* inflexibilidad, dureza, rigidez, *f*
inflexible /ɪn'flɛksəbəl/ *a* inflexible, rígido; *Fig.* inexorable, inalterable
inflexibly /ɪn'flɛksəbli/ *adv* inflexiblemente
inflict /ɪn'flɪkt/ *vt* infligir, imponer
infliction /ɪn'flɪkʃən/ *n* imposición, *f;* castigo, *m*
inflorescence /ˌɪnflɔ'rɛsəns/ *n Bot.* inflorescencia, *f*
inflow /'ɪnˌflou/ *n* afluencia, *f,* flujo, *m*
influence /'ɪnfluəns/ *n* influencia, *f,* influjo, *m;* ascendiente, *m;* (importance) influencia, importancia, *f.* —*vt* influir, afectar; persuadir, inducir. **to have i. over,** (a person) tener ascendiente sobre. *Law.* **undue i.,** influencia indebida, *f*
influential /ˌɪnflu'ɛnʃəl/ *a* influyente; (of person) prestigioso, importante
influenza /ˌɪnflu'ɛnzə/ *n Med.* gripe, *f,* trancazo, *m*
influx /'ɪnˌflʌks/ *n* influjo, *m;* (of rivers) desembocadura, afluencia, *f*
inform /ɪn'fɔrm/ *vt* (fill) infundir, llenar; (tell) informar, enterar, advertir; instruir; (with about) poner al corriente de, participar. —*vi* (with against) delatar (a), denunciar. **to i. oneself,** informarse, enterarse. **to be informed about,** estar al corriente de
informal /ɪn'fɔrməl/ *a* irregular; sin ceremonia, de confianza; (meeting) no oficial, extraoficial
informality /ˌɪnfɔr'mælɪti/ *n* irregularidad, *f;* falta de ceremonia, sencillez, *f;* intimidad, *f*
informally /ɪn'fɔrməli/ *adv* sin ceremonia
informant /ɪn'fɔrmənt/ *n* informante, *mf;* informador (-ra)
information /ˌɪnfər'meiʃən/ *n* información, instrucción, *f;* noticia, *f,* aviso, *m; Law.* denuncia, delación, *f.* **piece of i.,** información, *f.* **i. bureau,** oficina de información, *f*
informative /ɪn'fɔrmətɪv/ *a* informativo
informer /ɪn'fɔrmər/ *n* delator (-ra), denunciador (-ra)
infraction /ɪn'frækʃən/ *n* contravención, infracción, transgresión, *f*
infrared /ˌɪnfrə'rɛd/ *a Phys.* infrarrojo, ultrarrojo
infrequency /ɪn'frikwənsi/ *n* infrecuencia, rareza, irregularidad, *f*
infrequent /ɪn'frikwənt/ *a* infrecuente, raro, irregular
infrequently /ɪn'frikwəntli/ *adv* rara vez, infrecuentemente
infringe /ɪn'frɪndʒ/ *vt* infringir, violar, contravenir, quebrantar
infringement /ɪn'frɪndʒmənt/ *n* contravención, violación, infracción, *f*
infringer /ɪn'frɪndʒər/ *n* infractor (-ra), contraventor (-ra), violador (-ra), transgresor (-ra)
infuriate /ɪn'fyʊriˌeit/ *vt* enfurecer, enloquecer, enojar. **to be infuriated,** estar furioso
infuse /ɪn'fyuz/ *vt* vaciar, infiltrar; *Fig.* infundir, inculcar, instilar
infusible /ɪn'fyuzəbəl/ *a* infundible
infusion /ɪn'fyuʒən/ *n* infusión, *f; Fig.* instilación, inculcación, *f*
ingathering /ɪn'gæðərɪŋ/ *n* cosecha, recolección, *f*
ingenious /ɪn'dʒinyəs/ *a* ingenioso; mañoso, hábil
ingeniously /ɪn'dʒinyəsli/ *adv* ingeniosamente, hábilmente
ingenuity /ˌɪndʒə'nuɪti/ *n* ingeniosidad, inventiva, listeza, habilidad, *f*
ingenuous /ɪn'dʒɛnyuəs/ *a* ingenuo, franco, sincero, cándido, sencillo, inocente
ingenuousness /ɪn'dʒɛnyuəsnɪs/ *n* ingenuidad, franqueza, sinceridad, *f;* candor, *m*
ingest /ɪn'dʒɛst/ *vt* ingerir
ingestion /ɪn'dʒɛstʃən/ *n* ingestión, *f*
inglorious /ɪn'glɔriəs/ *a* vergonzoso, ignominioso, deshonroso; desconocido, obscuro
ingloriously /ɪn'glɔriəsli/ *adv* vergonzosamente, ignominiosamente; obscuramente
ingloriousness /ɪn'glɔriəsnɪs/ *n* deshonra, ignominia, *f;* obscuridad, *f*
ingoing /'ɪnˌgouɪŋ/ *a* entrante, que entra. —*n* ingreso, *m,* entrada, *f; Com.* **i. and outgoing,** entradas y salidas, *f pl*
ingot /'ɪŋgət/ *n* pepita, *f,* lingote, *m;* (of any metal) barra, *f*
ingrained /ɪn'greind, 'ɪnˌgreind/ *a* innato, natural
ingratiate /ɪn'greiʃiˌeit/ *vt* (oneself with) congraciarse con, captarse la buena voluntad de, insinuarse en el favor de
ingratiating /ɪn'greiʃiˌeitɪŋ/ *a* obsequioso

ingratitude /ɪn'grætɪˌtud/ *n* ingratitud, *f,* desagradecimiento, *m*

ingredient /ɪn'gridiənt/ *n* ingrediente, *m*

ingress /'ɪngrɛs/ *n* ingreso, *m;* derecho de entrada, *m*

ingrowing /'ɪnˌgrouɪŋ/ *a* que crece hacia adentro. **i. nail,** uñero, *m*

inhabit /ɪn'hæbɪt/ *vt* habitar, ocupar, vivir en, residir en

inhabitable /ɪn'hæbɪtəbəl/ *a* habitable, vividero

inhabitant /ɪn'hæbɪtənt/ *n* habitante, residente, *m;* vecino (-na)

inhabited /ɪn'hæbɪtɪd/ *a* habitado, poblado

inhalation /ˌɪnhə'leiʃən/ *n* inspiración, *f; Med.* inhalación, *f*

inhale /ɪn'heil/ *vt* aspirar; *Med.* inhalar

inharmonious /ˌɪnhɑr'mouniəs/ *a Mus.* disonante, inarmónico; desavenido, discorde, desconforme. **to be i.,** disonar; (of people) llevarse mal

inhere /ɪn'hɪər/ *vi* ser inherente; pertenecer (a), residir (en)

inherence /ɪn'hɪərəns/ *n* inherencia, *f*

inherent /ɪn'hɪərənt/ *a* inherente; innato, intrínseco, natural

inherently /ɪn'hɪərəntli/ *adv* intrínsecamente

inherit /ɪn'hɛrɪt/ *vt* heredar

inheritance /ɪn'hɛrɪtəns/ *n* herencia, *f;* patrimonio, abolengo, *m*

inheritor /ɪn'hɛrɪtər/ *n* heredero (-ra)

inhibit /ɪn'hɪbɪt/ *vt* inhibir, impedir; *Eccl.* prohibir. **be inhibited, became inhibited,** cohibirse

inhibition /ˌɪnɪ'bɪʃən/ *n* inhibición, *f*

inhibitory /ɪn'hɪbɪˌtɔri/ *a* inhibitorio

inhospitable /ɪn'hɒspɪtəbəl/ *a* inhospitalario

inhospitably /ɪn'hɒspɪtəbli/ *adv* desabridamente

inhospitality /ˌɪnhɒspɪ'tælɪti/ *n* inhospitalidad, *f*

inhuman /ɪn'hyumən/ *a* inhumano; cruel, bárbaro

inhumanity /ˌɪnhyu'mænɪti/ *n* inhumanidad, crueldad, *f*

inhumanly /ɪn'hyumənli/ *adv* inhumanamente, cruelmente

inhume /ɪn'hyum/ *vt* inhumar, sepultar

inimical /ɪ'nɪmɪkəl/ *a* enemigo, hostil, opuesto, contrario

inimically /ɪ'nɪmɪkəli/ *adv* hostilmente

inimitable /ɪ'nɪmɪtəbəl/ *a* inimitable

inimitably /ɪ'nɪmɪtəbli/ *adv* inimitablemente

iniquitous /ɪ'nɪkwɪtəs/ *a* inicuo, malvado, perverso, nefando; *Inf.* diabólico

iniquity /ɪ'nɪkwɪti/ *n* iniquidad, maldad, injusticia, *f*

initial /ɪ'nɪʃəl/ *a* inicial. —*n* inicial, letra inicial, *f.* —*vt* firmar con las iniciales

initially /ɪ'nɪʃəli/ *adv* al principio, en primer lugar

initiate /*a* ɪ'nɪʃiɪt; *v* ɪ'nɪʃiˌeit/ *a* iniciado. —*vt* iniciar, poner en pie, empezar, entablar; (a person) admitir

initiation /ɪˌnɪʃi'eiʃən/ *n* principio, *m;* (of a person) iniciación, admisión, *f*

initiative /ɪ'nɪʃiətɪv/ *n* iniciativa, *f.* **to take the i.,** tomar la iniciative

initiator /ɪ'nɪʃiˌeitər/ *n* iniciador (-ra)

inject /ɪn'dʒɛkt/ *vt* inyectar

injection /ɪn'dʒɛkʃən/ *n* inyección, *f.* **i. syringe,** jeringa de inyecciones, *f*

injudicious /ˌɪndʒu'dɪʃəs/ *a* imprudente, indiscreto

injudiciously /ˌɪndʒu'dɪʃəsli/ *adv* imprudentemente

injudiciousness /ˌɪndʒu'dɪʃəsnɪs/ *n* imprudencia, indiscreción, *f*

injunction /ɪn'dʒʌŋkʃən/ *n* precepto, mandato, *m; Law.* embargo, *m*

injure /'ɪndʒər/ *vt* perjudicar, dañar; menoscabar, deteriorar; (hurt) lastimar, lisiar. **to i. oneself,** hacerse daño

injured /'ɪndʒərd/ *a* (physically) lisiado; (morally) ofendido

injurer /'ɪndʒərər/ *n* perjudicador (-ra)

injurious /ɪn'dʒʊriəs/ *a* dañoso, perjudicial, malo; ofensivo, injurioso

injuriously /ɪn'dʒʊriəsli/ *adv* perjudicialmente

injury /'ɪndʒəri/ *n* perjuicio, daño, *m;* (physical) lesión, *f;* (insult) agravio, insulto, *m*

injustice /ɪn'dʒʌstɪs/ *n* injusticia, desigualdad, *f.* **You do him an i.,** Le juzgas mal

ink /ɪŋk/ *n* tinta, *f.* —*vt* entintar. **copying-ink,** tinta de copiar, *f.* **marking-ink,** tinta indeleble, *f.* **printer's ink,** tinta de imprenta, *f.* **ink-stand** or **ink-well,** tintero, *m*

inker /'ɪŋkər/ *n Print.* rodillo, *m*

inkling /'ɪŋklɪŋ/ *n* sospecha, noción, *f*

inky /'ɪŋki/ *a* manchado de tinta. **i. black,** negro como el betún

inland /'ɪnlænd/ *n* el interior de un país, *a* interior, mediterráneo; del país, regional. —*adv* tierra adentro. **to go i.,** internarse en un país. **I. Revenue,** delegación de contribuciones, *f.* **i. town,** ciudad del interior, *f*

inlay /'ɪnˌlei/ *vt* taracear, ataracear, embutir; incrustar. —*n* taracea, *f,* embutido, *m*

inlet /'ɪnlɛt/ *n* entrada, admisión, *f; Geog.* ensenada, *f.* **i. valve,** válvula de admisión, *f*

inmate /'ɪnˌmeit/ *n* residente, habitante, *m;* (of hospital) paciente, *mf;* enfermo (-ma); (of prison) prisionero

inmost /'ɪnmoust/. See **innermost**

inn /ɪn/ *n* posada, fonda, venta, *f,* mesón, *m.* **Inns of Court,** Colegio de Abogados, *m*

innate /ɪ'neit/ *a* innato, inherente, instintivo, nativo

innately /ɪ'neitli/ *adv* naturalmente, instintivamente

innavigable /ɪ'nævɪgəbəl/ *a* innavegable

inner /'ɪnər/ *a* interior, interno. **i. tube** *Auto.* cámara de neumatico, cámara de aire, *f*

innermost /'ɪnərˌmoust/ *a* más adentro; *Fig.* más íntimo, más hondo

innings /'ɪnɪŋz/ *n* (sport) turno, *m*

innkeeper /'ɪnˌkipər/ *n* fondista, *mf;* tabernero (-ra), mesonero (-ra), posadero (-ra)

innocence /'ɪnəsəns/ *n* inocencia, *f;* pureza, *f;* (guilelessness) simplicidad, *f,* candor, *m*

innocent /'ɪnəsənt/ *a* inocente, puro; (guiltless) inocente, inculpable; (foolish) simple, tonto, candoroso, inocentón; (harmless) innocuo. —*n* inocente, *mf* **Holy Innocents,** Santos Inocentes, *m pl*

innocuous /ɪ'nɒkyuəs/ *a* innocuo, inofensivo

innocuousness /ɪ'nɒkyuəsnɪs/ *n* inocuidad, *f*

innovate /'ɪnəˌveit/ *vt* innovar

innovation /ˌɪnə'veiʃən/ *n* innovación, *f*

innovator /'ɪnəˌveitər/ *n* innovador (-ra)

innuendo /ˌɪnyu'ɛndou/ *n* indirecta, insinuación, *f*

innumerable /ɪ'numərəbəl/ *a* innumerable, incalculable. **i. things,** un sinfín de cosas

inobservance /ˌɪnəb'zɜrvəns/ *n* inobservancia, *f,* incumplimiento, *m*

inoculate /ɪ'nɒkyəˌleit/ *vt* inocular

inoculation /ɪˌnɒkyə'leiʃən/ *n* inoculación, *f*

inoculator /ɪ'nɒkyəˌleitər/ *n* inoculador, *m*

inodorous /ɪn'oudərəs/ *a* inodoro

inoffensive /ˌɪnə'fɛnsɪv/ *a* inofensivo, innocuo; (of people) pacífico, apacible, manso

inoffensively /ˌɪnə'fɛnsɪvli/ *adv* inofensivamente

inoffensiveness /ˌɪnə'fɛnsɪvnɪs/ *n* inocuidad, *f;* (of people) mansedumbre, *f*

inoperable /ɪn'ɒpərəbəl/ *a* inoperable

inoperative /ɪn'ɒpərətɪv/ *a* ineficaz, impracticable, inútil

inopportune /ɪnˌɒpər'tun/ *a* inoportuno, intempestivo, inconveniente

inopportunely /ɪnˌɒpər'tunli/ *adv* inoportunamente, a destiempo

inopportuneness /ɪnˌɒpər'tunnɪs/ *n* inoportunidad, inconveniencia, *f*

inordinate /ɪn'ɔrdn̩ɪt/ *a* desordenado, excesivo

inordinately /ɪn'ɔrdn̩ɪtli/ *adv* desmedidamente

inorganic /ˌɪnɔr'gænɪk/ *a* inorgánico

inoxidizable /ɪn'ɒksɪˌdaizəbəl/ *a* inoxidable

input /'ɪnˌpʊt/ *n* capacidad instalada, *f,* insumo, *m*

inquest /'ɪnkwɛst/ *n Law.* indagación, investigación, *f*

inquietude /ɪn'kwaiɪˌtud/ *n* inquietud, *f,* desasosiego, *m,* agitación, preocupación, *f*

inquire /ɪn'kwaiᵊr/ *vt* and *vi* preguntar, averiguar, indagar. **to i. about,** (persons) preguntar por; (things) hacer preguntas sobre. **to i. into,** investigar, examinar, averiguar. **to i. of,** preguntar a. **"I. within,"** «Se dan informaciones»

inquirer /ɪn'kwaiᵊrər/ *n* indagador (-ra), inquiridor (-ra)
inquiring /ɪn'kwaiᵊrɪŋ/ *a* indagador, inquiridor
inquiringly /ɪn'kwaiᵊrɪŋli/ *adv* interrogativamente
inquiry /ɪn'kwaiᵊri/ *n* interrogación, pregunta, *f;* indagación, pesquisa, investigación, *f;* examen, *m.* **i. office,** oficina de informaciones, *f.* **on i.,** al preguntar
inquisition /ˌɪnkwə'zɪʃən/ *n* investigación, indagación, *f;* inquisición, *f.* **Holy I.,** Santo Oficio, *m,* Inquisición, *f*
inquisitive /ɪn'kwɪzɪtɪv/ *a* curioso, inquiridor; preguntador, impertinente, mirón
inquisitively /ɪn'kwɪzɪtɪvli/ *adv* con curiosidad, impertinentemente
inquisitiveness /ɪn'kwɪzɪtɪvnɪs/ *n* curiosidad, *f;* impertinencia, *f*
Inquisitor /ɪn'kwɪzɪtər/ *n Eccl.* inquisidor, *m*
inquisitorial /ɪnˌkwɪzɪ'tɔriəl/ *a* inquisitorial, inquisidor
inroad /'ɪnˌroud/ *n* incursión, *f*
insalubrious /ˌɪnsə'lubriəs/ *a* malsano, insalubre
insane /ɪn'sein/ *a* loco, demente, insano; (senseless) insensato, ridículo. **to become i.,** enloquecer, volverse loco, perder la razón. **to drive i.,** volver a uno el juicio, enloquecer, trastornar. **i. person,** demente, *mf.* loco (-ca)
insanely /ɪn'seinli/ *adv* locamente
insanitary /ɪn'sænɪˌtɛri/ *a* antihigiénico, malsano
insanity /ɪn'sænɪti/ *n* demencia, locura, *f;* enloquecimiento, *m;* (folly) insensatez, ridiculez, *f*
insatiability /ɪnˌseiʃə'bɪlɪti/ *n* insaciabilidad, *f*
insatiable /ɪn'seiʃəbəl/ *a* insaciable
insatiably /ɪn'seiʃəbli/ *adv* insaciablemente
inscribe /ɪn'skraib/ *vt* inscribir
inscription /ɪn'skrɪpʃən/ *n* inscripción, *f;* letrero, *m;* (of a book) dedicatoria, *f; Com.* inscripción, anotación, *f,* asiento, *m*
inscrutability /ɪnˌskrutə'bɪlɪti/ *n* enigma, misterio, *m;* incomprensibilidad, *f*
inscrutable /ɪn'skrutəbəl/ *a* enigmático, insondable, incomprensible, inescrutable
inscrutably /ɪn'skrutəbli/ *adv* incomprensiblemente, enigmáticamente
insect /'ɪnsɛkt/ *n* insecto, *m.* **i. powder,** polvos insecticidas, *m pl*
insecticide /ɪn'sɛktəˌsaid/ *a* and *n* insecticida *m.*
insecure /ˌɪnsɪ'kyʊr/ *a* inseguro, precario
insecurely /ˌɪnsɪ'kyʊrli/ *adv* inseguramente
insecurity /ˌɪnsɪ'kyʊrɪti/ *n* inseguridad, *f;* incertidumbre, inestabilidad, *f*
inseminate /ɪn'sɛməˌneit/ *vt Fig.* implantar; *Med.* fecundar
insemination /ɪnˌsɛmə'neiʃən/ *n Fig.* implantación, *f; Med.* fecundación, *f*
insensate /ɪn'sɛnseit/ *a* (unfeeling) insensible, insensitivo; (stupid) insensato, sin sentido, necio
insensibility /ɪnˌsɛnsə'bɪlɪti/ *n* insensibilidad, inconsciencia, *f;* (stupor) sopor, letargo, *m;* impasibilidad, indiferencia, *f*
insensible /ɪn'sɛnsəbəl/ *a* insensible, inconsciente; indiferente, impasible, duro de corazón; (scarcely noticeable) imperceptible. **to make i.,** (to sensations) hacer indiferente (a); insensibilizar
insensibly /ɪn'sɛnsəbli/ *adv* insensiblemente, imperceptiblemente
insensitive /ɪn'sɛnsɪtɪv/ *a* insensible, insensitivo; (person) hecho un tronco, hecho un leño
insensitiveness /ɪn'sɛnsɪtɪvnɪs/ *n* insensibilidad, *f*
insentient /ɪn'sɛnʃiənt/ *a* insensible
inseparability /ɪnˌsɛpərə'bɪlɪti/ *n* inseparabilidad, *f*
inseparable /ɪn'sɛpərəbəl/ *a* inseparable
inseparably /ɪn'sɛpərəbli/ *adv* inseparablemente
insert /ɪn'sɜrt/ *vt* insertar, intercalar; (introduce) meter dentro, introducir, encajar; (in a newspaper) publicar
insertion /ɪn'sɜrʃən/ *n* inserción, intercalación, *f;* (introduction) introducción, *f;* metimiento, encaje, *m; Sew.* entredós, *m;* (in a newspaper) publicación, *f*
inshore /'ɪn'ʃɔr/ *a* cercano a la orilla. —*adv* cerca de la orilla. **i. fishing,** pesca de arrastre, *f*
inside /ˌɪn'said/ *a* interior, interno. —*adv* adentro, dentro. —*n* interior, *m;* (contents) contenido, *m;* (lining) forro, *m;* (*Inf.* stomach) entrañas, *f pl.* **to turn i. out,** volver al revés. **to walk on the i. of the pavement,** andar a la derecha de la acera. **from the i.,** desde el interior; por dentro. **on the i.,** por dentro, en el interior. **i. information,** información confidencial, *f.* **i. out,** al revés, de dentro afuera
insidious /ɪn'sɪdiəs/ *a* insidioso, enganoso, traidor
insidiously /ɪn'sɪdiəsli/ *adv* insidiosamente
insidiousness /ɪn'sɪdiəsnɪs/ *n* insidia, *f;* engaño, *m,* traición, *f*
insight /'ɪnˌsait/ *n* percepción, perspicacia, intuición, *f.* atisbo, *m*
insignia /ɪn'sɪgniə/ *n pl* insignias, *f pl*
insignificance /ˌɪnsɪg'nɪfɪkəns/ *n* insignificancia, futilidad, pequeñez, *f*
insignificant /ˌɪnsɪg'nɪfɪkənt/ *a* insignificante; fútil, trivial
insincere /ˌɪnsɪn'sɪər/ *a* insincero, hipócrita, falso
insincerely /ˌɪnsɪn'sɪərli/ *adv* falsamente, hipócritamente
insincerity /ˌɪnsɪn'sɛrɪti/ *n* insinceridad, hipocresía, falsedad, falta de sinceridad, doblez, *f*
insinuate /ɪn'sɪnyuˌeit/ *vt* insinuar, introducir; (hint) soltar una indirecta, sugerir; (oneself) insinuarse, introducirse con habilidad
insinuation /ɪnˌsɪnyu'eiʃən/ *n* insinuación, introducción, *f;* (hint) indirecta, *f*
insipid /ɪn'sɪpɪd/ *a* insípido, insulso; (dull) soso
insipidity /ˌɪnsə'pɪdɪti/ *n* insipidez, insulsez, *f,* desabor, *m;* (dullness) sosería, *f*
insist /ɪn'sɪst/ *vi* insistir; persistir, obstinarse. **to i. on,** insistir en; obstinarse en, hacer hincapié en, aferrarse en (or a)
insistence /ɪn'sɪstəns/ *n* insistencia, *f;* obstinación, pertinacia, *f*
insistent /ɪn'sɪstənt/ *a* insistente; porfiado, obstinaz
insistently /ɪn'sɪstəntli/ *adv* con insistencia; porfiadamente
insobriety /ˌɪnsə'braiɪti/ *n* falta de sobriedad, *f;* embriaguez, ebriedad, *f*
insole /'ɪnˌsoul/ *n* (of shoes) plantilla, *f*
insolence /'ɪnsələns/ *n* insolencia, altanería, majadería, frescura, *f,* atrevimiento, descaro, *m*
insolent /'ɪnsələnt/ *a* insolente, arrogante, atrevido, descarado, desmesurado, fresco
insolently /'ɪnsələntli/ *adv* insolentemente, con descaro
insolubility /ɪnˌsɒlyə'bɪlɪti/ *n* insolubilidad, *f*
insoluble /ɪn'sɒlyəbəl/ *a* insoluble
insolvency /ɪn'sɒlvənsi/ *n* in olvencia, *f*
insolvent /ɪn'sɒlvənt/ *a* insolvente
insomnia /ɪn'sɒmniə/ *n* insomnio, *m*
insomuch /ˌɪnsə'mʌtʃ/ *adv* (gen. with as or that) de modo (que), así (que), de suerte (que)
inspect /ɪn'spɛkt/ *vt* examinar, investigar, inspeccionar; (officially) registrar, reconocer
inspection /ɪn'spɛkʃən/ *n* inspección, investigación, *f;* examen, *m;* (official) reconocimiento, registro, *m*
inspector /ɪn'spɛktər/ *n* inspector, *m,* veedor, interventor, *m*
inspectorate /ɪn'spɛktərɪt/ *n* inspectorado, *m;* cargo de inspector, *m*
inspiration /ˌɪnspə'reiʃən/ *n* (of breath) inspiración, aspiración, *f;* numen, *m,* inspiración, vena, *f.* **to find i. in,** inspirarse en.
inspire /ɪn'spaiᵊr/ *vt* (inhale) aspirar, inspirar; (stimulate) animar, alentar, iluminar; (suggest) sugerir, inspirar; infundir. **to i. enthusiasm,** entusiasmar. **to i. hope,** dar esperanza, esperanzar
inspired /ɪn'spaiᵊrd/ *a* inspirado, intuitivo, iluminado; (of genius) genial
inspirer /ɪn'spaiᵊrər/ *n* inspirador (-ra)
inspiring /ɪn'spaiᵊrɪŋ/ *a* alentador, animador; inspirador
inspirit /ɪn'spɪrɪt/ *vt* alentar, inspirar, estimular, animar
inspiriting /ɪn'spɪrɪtɪŋ/ *a* alentador, estimulador
instability /ˌɪnstə'bɪlɪti/ *n* inestabilidad, mutabilidad, inconstancia, *f*

install /ɪn'stɔl/ *vt* (all meanings) instalar. **to i. oneself,** instalarse, establecerse
installation /ˌɪnstə'leiʃən/ *n* (all meanings) instalación, *f*
installment /ɪn'stɔlmənt/ *n* (of a story) entrega, *f; Com.* plazo, *m,* cuota, *f.* **by installments,** *Com.* a plazos. **i. plan,** pago a plazos, pago por cuotas, *m*
instance /'ɪnstəns/ *n* ejemplo, caso, *m;* (request) solicitación, *f,* ruego, *m; Law.* instancia, *f.* —*vt* citar como ejemplo, mencionar; demostrar, probar. **for i.,** por ejemplo, verbigracia. **in that i....,** en el caso... **in the first i.,** en primer lugar, primero
instant /'ɪnstənt/ *a* immediato, urgente; *Com.* corriente, actual. —*n* instante, momento, *m; Inf.* tris, santiamén, *m. Com.* **the 2nd i.,** el 2° (segundo) del corriente. **this i.,** (immediately) en seguida
instantaneous /ˌɪnstən'teiniəs/ *a* instantáneo. *Photo.* **i. exposure,** instantánea, *f*
instantaneously /ˌɪnstən'teiniəsli/ *adv* instantáneamente
instantaneousness /ˌɪnstən'teiniəsnɪs/ *n* instantaneidad, *f*
instantly /'ɪnstəntli/ *adv* en seguida, al instante, inmediatamente
instead /ɪn'stɛd/ *adv* en cambio; (with of) en vez de, en lugar de
instep /'ɪnˌstɛp/ *n* empeine, *m*
instigate /'ɪnstɪˌgeit/ *vt* instigar, incitar, aguijar, animar, provocar; fomentar
instigating /'ɪnstɪˌgeitɪŋ/ *a* instigador, provocador, fomentador
instigation /ˌɪnstɪ'geiʃən/ *n* instigación, incitación, *f;* estímulo, *m*
instigator /'ɪnstɪˌgeitər/ *n* instigador (-ra), provocador (-ra), fomentador (-ra)
instill /ɪn'stɪl/ *vt* instilar; (ideas) inculcar, infundir
instillment /ɪn'stɪlmənt/ *n* inculcación, implantación, insinuación, *f*
instinct /ɪn'stɪŋkt/ *n* instinto, *m.* **i. with,** imbuido de, lleno de. **by i.,** por instinto, movido por instinto
instinctive /ɪn'stɪŋktɪv/ *a* instintivo, espontáneo
instinctively /ɪn'stɪŋktɪvli/ *adv* por instinto
institute /'ɪnstɪˌtut/ *vt* instituir, fundar, establecer; (an inquiry) iniciar, empezar. —*n* instituto, *m; pl* **institutes,** *Law.* instituta, *f*
institution /ˌɪnstɪ'tuʃən/ *n* (creation) fundación, creación, *f;* institución, *f,* instituto, *m;* (beginning) comienzo, *m,* iniciación, *f;* (charitable) asilo, *m;* (custom) uso, *m,* costumbre, tradición, *f*
institutional /ˌɪnstɪ'tuʃənl̩/ *a* institucional
instruct /ɪn'strʌkt/ *vt* (teach) instruir, enseñar; (order) mandar, dar orden (a)
instruction /ɪn'strʌkʃən/ *n* (teaching) instrucción, enseñanza, *f; pl* **instructions,** (orders) instrucciones, *f pl* orden, *f,* mandato, *m*
instructive /ɪn'strʌktɪv/ *a* instructivo, instructor, informativo
instructively /ɪn'strʌktɪvli/ *adv* instructivamente
instructiveness /ɪn'strʌktɪvnɪs/ *n* el carácter informativo, lo instructivo
instructor /ɪn'strʌktər/ *n* instructor, preceptor, *m*
instrument /'ɪnstrəmənt/ *n* instrumento, *m;* (tool) herramienta, *f,* utensilio, aparato, *m;* (agent) órgano, agente, medio, *m; Law.* instrumento, *m,* escritura, *f.* —*vt Mus.* instrumentar. **percussion i.,** instrumento de percusión, *m.* **scientific i.,** instrumento científico, *m.* **stringed i.,** instrumento de cuerda, *m.* **wind i.,** instrumento de viento, *m*
instrumental /ˌɪnstrə'mɛntl̩/ *a* instrumental; influyente. **to be i. in,** contribuir a
instrumentalist /ˌɪnstrə'mɛntl̩ɪst/ *n Mus.* instrumentista, *m*
instrumentality /ˌɪnstrəmɛn'tælɪti/ *n* mediación, intervención, agencia, *f,* buenos oficios, *m pl*
instrumentation /ˌɪnstrəmɛn'teiʃən/ *n Mus.* instrumentación, *f;* mediación, *f*
insubordinate /ˌɪnsə'bɔrdn̩ɪt/ *a* insubordinado, rebelde, desobediente, refractario
insubordination /ˌɪnsəˌbɔrdn̩'eiʃən/ *n* insubordinación, rebeldía, desobediencia, *f*
insubstantial /ˌɪnsəb'stænʃəl/ *a* irreal; insubstancial
insubstantiality /ˌɪnsəbˌstænʃi'ælɪti/ *n* irrealidad, *f;* insubstancialidad, *f*
insufferable /ɪn'sʌfərəbəl/. See **intolerable**
insufficiency /ˌɪnsə'fɪʃənsi/ *n* insuficiencia, falta, carestía, *f*
insufficient /ˌɪnsə'fɪʃənt/ *a* insuficiente, falto. **"I. Postage,"** «Falta de franqueo»
insufficiently /ˌɪnsə'fɪʃəntli/ *adv* insuficientemente
insular /'ɪnsələr/ *a* isleño, insular; (narrow-minded) intolerante, iliberal
insularity /ˌɪnsə'lɛərɪti/ *n* carácter isleño, *m;* (narrow-mindedness) iliberalidad, intolerancia, *f*
insulate /'ɪnsəˌleit/ *vt* aislar
insulating /'ɪnsəˌleitɪng/ *a* aislador. **i. tape,** *Elec.* cinta aisladora, *f*
insulation /ˌɪnsə'leiʃən/ *n* aislamiento, *m*
insulator /'ɪnsəˌleitər/ *n Elec.* aislador, *m*
insulin /'ɪnsəlɪn/ *n Med.* insulina, *f*
insult /*n.* 'ɪnsʌlt; *v.* ɪn'sʌlt/ *n* insulto, agravio, ultraje, *m,* afrenta, ofensa, *f.* —*vt* insultar, ofender, afrentar. **He was insulted,** Fue insultado; Se mostró ofendido
insulter /ɪn'sʌltər/ *n* insultador (-ra)
insulting /ɪn'sʌltɪŋ/ *a* insultante, injurioso, ofensivo. **He was very i. to them,** Les insultó, Les trató con menosprecio
insultingly /ɪn'sʌltɪŋli/ *adv* con insolencia, ofensivamente
insuperability /ɪnˌsupərə'bɪlɪti/ *n* dificultades insuperables, *f pl,* imposibilidad, *f,* lo insuperable
insuperable /ɪn'supərəbəl/ *a* insuperable, invencible
insuperably /ɪn'supərəbli/ *adv* invenciblemente
insupportable /ˌɪnsə'pɔrtəbəl/ *a* insoportable, inaguantable, intolerable, insufrible
insupportably /ˌɪnsə'pɔrtəbli/ *adv* insufriblemente, insoportablemente
insurable /ɪn'ʃʊrəbəl/ *a* asegurable
insurance /ɪn'ʃʊrəns/ *n* aseguramiento, *m; Com.* seguro, *m;* aseguración, *f.* **accident i.,** seguro contra accidentes, *m.* **fire-i.,** seguro contra incendio, *m.* **life i.,** seguro sobre la vida, *m.* **maritime i.,** seguro marítimo, *m.* **National I. Act,** Ley del Seguro Nacional Obligatorio, *f.* **i. broker,** corredor de seguros, *m.* **i. company,** compañía de seguros, *f.* **i. policy,** póliza de seguros, *f.* **i. premium,** prima de seguros, *f*
insure /ɪn'ʃʊr, -'ʃɜr/ *vt Com.* asegurar. **to i. oneself,** asegurarse. **the insured,** (person) el asegurado
insurer /ɪn'ʃʊrər/ *n* asegurador (-ra)
insurgent /ɪn'sɜrdʒənt/ *a* insurgente, rebelde; (of sea) invasor. —*n* rebelde, *mf* insurrecto (-ta)
insurmountable /ˌɪnsər'mauntəbəl/ *a* insalvable, insuperable, invencible, intransitable
insurrection /ˌɪnsə'rɛkʃən/ *n* insurrección, sublevación, *f,* levantamiento, *m*
insurrectionary /ˌɪnsə'rɛkʃəˌnɛri/ *a* rebelde, amotinado, insurgente
insusceptible /ˌɪnsə'sɛptəbəl/ *a* no susceptible, indiferente, insensible
intact /ɪn'tækt/ *a* intacto, íntegro, indemne
intake /'ɪnˌteik/ *n* (of a stocking) menguado, *m; Mech.* aspiración, *f;* válvula de admisión, *f; Aer.* admisión, toma, *f;* orificio de entrada, *m*
intangibility /ɪnˌtændʒə'bɪlɪti/ *n* intangibilidad, *f*
intangible /ɪn'tændʒəbəl/ *a* intangible; incomprensible
integer /'ɪntɪdʒər/ *n Math.* número entero, *m*
integral /'ɪntɪgrəl/ *a* íntegro, intrínseco, inherente; *Math.* entero. —*n Math.* integral, *f.* **i. calculus,** cálculo integral, *m*
integrate /'ɪntɪˌgreit/ *vt* integrar, completar; formar en un todo; *Math.* integrar
integrity /ɪn'tɛgrɪti/ *n* integridad, honradez, rectitud, entereza, *f*
intellect /'ɪntl̩ˌɛkt/ *n* intelecto, entendimiento, *m*
intellectual /ˌɪntl̩'ɛktʃuəl/ *a* intelectual, mental. —*n* intelectual
intellectualism /ˌɪntl̩'ɛktʃuəˌlɪzəm/ *n* intelectualismo, *m,* intelectualidad, *f*
intellectually /ˌɪntl̩'ɛktʃuəli/ *adv* intelectualmente, mentalmente
intelligence /ɪn'tɛlɪdʒəns/ *n* inteligencia, comprensión, mente, *f;* (quickness of mind) agudeza, perspi-

cacia, *f;* (news) noticia, *f,* conocimiento, informe, *m.* **the latest i.,** las últimas noticias. **i. quotient,** cociente de inteligencia, *m.* **I. Service,** Inteligencia, *f;* policía secreta, *f.* **i. test,** prueba de inteligencia, *f*
intelligent /ɪn'tɛlɪdʒənt/ *a* inteligente
intelligentsia /ɪn,tɛlɪ'dʒɛntsiə/ *n* clase intelectual, intelectualidad, *f, Inf.* masa cefálica, *f*
intelligibility /ɪn,tɛlɪdʒə'bɪlɪti/ *n* comprensibilidad, inteligibilidad, *f*
intelligible /ɪn'tɛlɪdʒəbəl/ *a* inteligible, comprensible
intelligibly /ɪn'tɛlɪdʒəbəl/ *adv* inteligiblemente
intemperance /ɪn'tɛmpərəns/ *n* intemperancia, inmoderación, *f;* exceso en la bebida, *m*
intemperate /ɪn'tɛmpərɪt/ *a* intemperante, destemplado, descomedido; inmoderado; bebedor en exceso
intemperately /ɪn'tɛmpərɪtli/ *adv* inmoderadamente
intend /ɪn'tɛnd/ *vt* intentar, proponerse, pensar; destinar, dedicar; (mean) querer decir. **to be intended,** estar destinado; tener por fin; querer decir
intendant /ɪn'tɛndənt/ *n* intendente, *m*
intended /ɪn'tɛndɪd/ *a* pensado, deseado. *—n Inf.* novio (-ia), futuro (-ra), prometido (-da)
intense /ɪn'tɛns/ *a* intenso, vivo, fuerte; (of emotions) profundo, hondo, vehemente; (of colors) subido, intenso; (great) extremado, sumo, muy grande
intensification /ɪn,tɛnsəfɪ'keiʃən/ *n* intensificación, *f;* aumento, *m*
intensify /ɪn'tɛnsə,fai/ *vt* intensar, intensificar; aumentar
intensity /ɪn'tɛnsɪti/ *n* intensidad, fuerza, *f;* (of emotions) profundidad, vehemencia, violencia, *f;* (of colors) intensidad, *f*
intensive /ɪn'tɛnsɪv/ *a* intensivo
intensive-care unit /ɪn'tɛnsɪv'kɛər/ *n* sala de terapia intensiva, unidad de cuidades intensivos, unidad de vigilancia intensiva, *f*
intent /ɪn'tɛnt/ *n* intento, propósito, deseo, *m. —a* atento; (absorbed) absorto, interesado; (on doing) resuelto a, decidido a. **to all intents and purposes,** en efecto, en realidad. **to be i. on,** (reading, etc.) estar absorto en, entregarse a. **with i. to defraud,** con el propósito deliberado de defraudar
intention /ɪn'tɛnʃən/ *n* intención, voluntad, *f,* propósito, pensamiento, proyecto, *m*
intentional /ɪn'tɛnʃənḷ/ *a* intencional, deliberado, premeditado
intentionally /ɪn'tɛnʃənḷi/ *adv* a propósito, intencionalmente, de pensado
intentioned /ɪn'tɛnʃənd/ *a* intencionado
intently /ɪn'tɛntli/ *adv* atentamente
inter /ɪn'tɜr/ *vt* enterrar, sepultar
inter- *prefix* inter, entre. **i.-allied,** interaliado, de los aliados. **i.-denominational,** intersectario. **i.-university,** interuniversitario. **i.-urban,** interurbano
interaction /,ɪntər'ækʃən/ *n* interacción, acción recíproca, acción mutua, *f*
intercalate /ɪn'tɜrkə,leit/ *vt* intercalar, interpolar
intercede /,ɪntər'sid/ *vi* interceder, mediar. **to i. for,** hablar por
intercept /,ɪntər'sɛpt/ *vt* interceptar, detener; entrecoger, atajar
interception /,ɪntər'sɛpʃən/ *n* interceptación, detención, *f*
intercession /,ɪntər'sɛʃən/ *n* mediación, intercesión, *f*
intercessor /,ɪntər'sɛsər/ *n* intercesor (-ra), mediador (-ra)
interchange /*n.* 'ɪntər,tʃeindʒ; *v.* ,ɪntər'tʃɛndʒ/ *n* intercambio, *m;* (of goods) comercio, tráfico, *m. —vt* cambiar, trocar; alternar
interchangeable /,ɪntər'tʃeindʒəbəl/ *a* intercambiable
intercom /'ɪntər,kɒm/ *n* teléfono interior, *m*
intercommunicate /,ɪntərkə'myunɪ,keit/ *vi* comunicarse
intercommunication /,ɪntərkə,myunɪ'keiʃən/ *n* comunicación mutua, *f;* comercio, *m*
intercostal /,ɪntər'kɒstḷ/ *a Anat.* intercostal
intercourse /'ɪntər,kɔrs/ *n* (social) trato, *m,* relaciones, *f pl; Com.* comercio, tráfico, *m;* (of ideas) intercambio, *m;* (sexual) coito, trato sexual, *m*
interdependence /,ɪntərdɪ'pɛndənt/ *n* dependencia mutua, mutualidad, *f*
interdependent /,ɪntərdɪ'pɛndənt/ *a* mutuo
interdict /*n* 'ɪntər,dɪkt; *v* ,ɪntər'dɪkt/ *n* interdicto, veto, *m,* prohibición, *f; Eccl.* entredicho, *m. —vt* interdecir, prohibir, privar; *Eccl.* poner entredicho
interdiction /,ɪntər'dɪkʃən/ *n* interdicción, prohibición, *f*
interest /'ɪntərɪst/ *n* interés, *m;* provecho, *m; Com.* premio, rédito, interés, *m;* (in a firm) participación, *f;* (curiosity) interés, *m;* curiosidad, *f;* simpatía, *f;* (influence) influencia, *f. —n pl* **interests,** (commercial undertakings) empresas, *f pl,* intereses, negocios, *m pl. —vt* interesar. **to be interested in,** interesarse en, (on behalf of) por. **to be in one's own i.,** ser en provecho de uno, ser en su propio interés. **to bear eight per cent. i.,** dar interés del ocho por ciento. **to pay with i.,** pagar con creces. **to put out at i.,** dar a interés. **in the interests of,** en interés de. **compound i.,** interés compuesto, *m.* **simple i.,** interés sencillo, *m.* **vested interests,** intereses creados, *m pl*
interesting /'ɪntərəstɪŋ/ *a* interesante, curioso, atractivo
interestingly /'ɪntərəstɪŋli/ *adv* amenamente, de modo interesante
interfere /,ɪntər'fɪər/ *vi* intervenir, meterse, entremeterse, mezclarse; *Inf.* mangonear, meter las narices; (with) meterse con; (impede) estorbar, impedir
interference /,ɪntər'fɪərəns/ *n* intervención, *f,* entrometimiento, *m;* (obstacle) estorbo, obstáculo, *m; Phys.* interferencia, *f; Radio.* parásitos, *m pl*
interfering /,ɪntər'fɪərɪŋ/ *a* entremetido, oficioso; *Inf.* mangoneador
interim /'ɪntərəm/ *n* ínterin, intermedio, *m. —a* interino, provisional. **in the i.,** entre tanto, en el ínterin. *Com.* **i. dividend,** dividendo interino, *m*
interior /ɪn'tɪəriər/ *a* interior, interno; doméstico. *—n* interior, *m*
interject /,ɪntər'dʒɛkt/ *vt* interponer
interjection /,ɪntər'dʒɛkʃən/ *n* exclamación, interjección, *f;* interposición, *f*
interlace /,ɪntər'leis/ *vt* entrelazar, entretejer
interleave /,ɪntər'liv/ *vt* interfoliar, interpaginar
interline /'ɪntər,lain/ *vt* entrerrenglonar, interlinear
interlinear /,ɪntər'lɪniər/ *a* interlineal
interlineation /,ɪntər,lɪni'eiʃən/ *n* interlineación, *f*
interlining /'ɪntər,lainɪŋ/ *n* entretela, *f*
interlock /,ɪntər'lɒk/ *vt* (of wheels, etc.). endentar; trabar; cerrar. *—vi* endentarse; entrelazarse, unirse; cerrar
interlocutor /,ɪntər'lɒkyətər/ *n* interlocutor (-ra)
interloper /'ɪntər,loupər/ *n* intruso (-sa); *Com.* intérlope, *m*
interloping /,ɪntər'loupɪŋ/ *a* intérlope
interlude /'ɪntər,lud/ *n* intervalo, intermedio, *m; Mus.* interludio, *m; Theat.* entremés, *m*
intermarriage /,ɪntər'mærɪdʒ/ *n* casamiento entre parientes próximos, entre razas distintas, o entre grupos étnicos distintos, *m*
intermarry /,ɪntər'mæri/ *vi* contraer matrimonio entre parientes próximos, entre personas de razas distintas, o entre grupos étnicos distintos
intermediary /,ɪntər'midi,ɛri/ *a* and *n* intermediario (-ia)
intermediate /,ɪntər'midi,eit/ *a* intermedio, medio, medianero. *—n* sustancia intermedia, *f. —vi* intervenir, mediar
interment /ɪn'tɜrmənt/ *n* entierro, *m*
intermezzo /,ɪntər'mɛtsou/ *n Theat.* intermedio, *m; Mus.* intermezzo, *m*
interminable 'ɪn'tɜrmənəbəl/ *a* interminable, inacabable
interminably /ɪn'tɜrmənəbli/ *adv* interminablemente, sin fin, sin cesar
intermingle /,ɪntər'mɪŋgəl/ *vt* entremezclar, entreverar. *—vi* mezclarse
intermission /,ɪntər'mɪʃən/ *n* intermisión, interrupción, pausa, *f; Theat.* entreacto, *m.* **without i.,** sin pausa, sin tregua
intermittence /,ɪntər'mɪtṇs/ *n* intermitencia, alternación, *f*
intermittent /,ɪntər'mɪtṇt/ *a* intermitente, discontinuo; (of fever) intermitente
intermittently /,ɪntər'mɪtṇtli/ *adv* a intervalos, a ratos, a pausas

intern /ɪn'tɜrn/ *n Med.* practicante de hospital *m*, interno (-na), interno de hospital, alumno interno, *m*. —*vt* confinar, encerrar

internal /ɪn'tɜrnḷ/ *a* interno, interior; (of affairs) doméstico, civil; intrínseco; íntimo. **i.-combustion engine,** motor de combustión interna, *m*

internally /ɪn'tɜrnḷi/ *adv* interiormente

international /ˌɪntər'næʃənḷ/ *a* internacional. —*n Sports.* un partido internacional. **i. law,** derecho internacional, *m*

internationalism /ˌɪntər'næʃənḷˌɪzəm/ *n* internacionalismo, *m*

internationalist /ˌɪntər'næʃənḷɪst/ *n* internacionalista, *mf*

internationalization /ˌɪntərˌnæʃənḷə'zeiʃən/ *n* internacionalización, *f*

internationalize /ˌɪntər'næʃənḷˌaiz/ *vt* hacer internacional, poner bajo un control internacional

internecine /ˌɪntər'nisin/ *a* sanguinario, feroz

internee /ˌɪntɜr'ni/ *n* internado (-da)

Internet, the /'ɪntərˌnɛt/ *n* el Internet, *m*

internment /ɪn'tɜrnmənt/ *n* internamiento, *m*. **i. camp,** campo de internamiento, *m*

interoceanic /ˌɪntərˌouʃi'ænɪk/ *a* interoceánico

interpolate /ɪn'tɜrpəˌleit/ *vt* interpolar, intercalar, interponer

interpolation /ɪnˌtɜrpə'leiʃən/ *n* interpolación, inserción, añadidura, *f*

interpolator /ɪn'tɜrpəˌleitər/ *n* interpolador (-ra)

interpose /ˌɪntər'pouz/ *vt* interponer; (a remark) interpolar. —*vi* interponerse, intervenir; (interfere) entrometerse; interrumpir

interposition /ˌɪntərpə'zɪʃən/ *n* interposición, *f;* entrometimiento, *m*

interpret /ɪn'tɜrprɪt/ *vt* interpretar; (translate) traducir; (explain) explicar, descifrar. —*vi* interpretar.

interpretation /ɪnˌtɜrprɪ'teiʃən/ *n* interpretación, *f;* (translation) traducción, *f;* (explanation) explicación, *f*

interpretative /ɪn'tɜrprɪˌteitɪv/ *a* interpretativo, interpretador

interpreter /ɪn'tɜrprɪtər/ *n* intérprete, *mf*

interregnum /ˌɪntər'rɛgnəm/ *n* interregno, *m*

interrelation /ˌɪntərrɪ'leiʃən/ *n* relación mutua, *f*

interrogate /ɪn'tɛrəˌgeit/ *vt* interrogar, examinar, preguntar

interrogating /ɪn'tɛrəˌgeitɪŋ/ *a* interrogante

interrogation /ɪnˌtɛrə'geiʃən/ *n* interrogación, *f*, examen, *m;* pregunta, *f*. **mark of i.,** punto de interrogación, *m*

interrogative /ˌɪntə'rɒgətɪv/ *a* interrogativo. —*n* palabra interrogativa, *f*

interrogatively /ˌɪntə'rɒgətɪvli/ *adv* interrogativamente

interrogator /ɪn'tɛrə'getər/ *n* examinador (-ra), interrogador (-ra)

interrogatory /ˌɪntə'rɒgəˌtɔri/ *a* interrogativo. —*n* interrogatorio, *m*

interrupt /ˌɪntə'rʌpt/ *vt* interrumpir

interruptedly /ˌɪntə'rʌptɪdli/ *adv* interrumpidamente

interrupter /ˌɪntə'rʌptər/ *n* interruptor (-ra); *Elec.* interruptor, *m*

interruption /ˌɪntə'rʌpʃən/ *n* interrupción, *f*

intersect /ˌɪntər'sɛkt/ *vt* cruzar. —*vi* cruzarse, intersecarse

intersection /ˌɪntər'sɛkʃən/ *n* intersección, *f;* cruce, *m,* (of streets) bocacalle, *f*

intersperse /ˌɪntər'spɜrs/ *vt* diseminar, esparcir; interpolar, entremezclar

interstice /ɪn'tɜrstɪs/ *n* intervalo, intermedio, *m;* (chink) intersticio, *m,* hendedura, *f*

intertwine /ˌɪntər'twain/ *vt* entretejer, entrelazar. —*vi* entrelazarse

interval /'ɪntərvəl/ *n* intervalo, intermedio, *m,* pausa, *f; Theat.* entreacto, *m,* intermisión, *f;* (in schools) recreo, *m*. **at intervals,** a trechos, de vez en cuando. **lucid i.,** intervalo claro, intervalo lúcido, *m*

intervene /ˌɪntər'vin/ *vi* intervenir, tomar parte (en), mediar; (occur) sobrevenir, acaecer; *Law.* interponerse

intervening /ˌɪntər'vinɪŋ/ *a* intermedio; interventor

intervention /ˌɪntər'vɛnʃən/ *n* intervención, mediación, *f*

interventionist /ˌɪntər'vɛnʃənɪst/ *n Polit.* partidario (-ia) de la intervención

interview /'ɪntərˌvyu/ *n* entrevista, *f,* interviev, *m*. —*vt* entrevistarse con

interviewer /'ɪntərˌvyuər/ *n* interrogador (-ra); (reporter) reportero, periodista, *m*

interweave /ˌɪntər'wiv/ *vt* entretejer, entrelazar

interweaving /ˌɪntər'wivɪŋ/ *n* entretejimiento, *m*

intestacy /ɪn'tɛstəsi/ *n* ausencia de un testamento, *f*

intestate /ɪn'tɛsteit/ *a* and *n* intestado (-da)

intestinal /ɪn'tɛstənḷ/ *a* intestinal, intestino. **i. worm,** lombriz intestinal, *f*

intestine /ɪn'tɛstɪn/ *n* intestino, *m*. **large i.,** intestino grueso, *m*. **small i.,** intestino delgado, *m*

intimacy /'ɪntəməsi/ *n* intimidad, *f,* familiaridad, *f;* (of nobility and others) privanza, *f*

intimate /'ɪntəmɪt/ *a* íntimo; (of relations) entrañable, estrecho; intrínseco, esencial; (of knowledge) profundo, completo, detallado. —*n* amigo (-ga) de confianza. —*vt* intimar, dar a entender, indicar. **to become i.,** intimarse. **to be on i. terms with,** tratar de tú (a), ser amigo íntimo de

intimately /'ɪntəmɪtli/ *adv* íntimamente, al fondo

intimation /ˌɪntə'meiʃən/ *n* intimación, indicación, *f;* (hint) insinuación, indirecta, *f*

intimidate /ɪn'tɪmɪˌdeit/ *vt* intimidar, aterrar, infundir miedo (a), espantar, acobardar, amedrentar

intimidation /ɪnˌtɪmɪ'deiʃən/ *n* intimidación, *f*

intimidatory /ɪn'tɪmɪdəˌtɔri/ *a* aterrador, amenazador

into /'ɪntu; *unstressed* -tʊ, -tə/ *prep* en; a, al, a la; dentro, adentro; (of transforming, forming, etc.) en. **Throw it i. the fire,** Échalo al (or en el) fuego. **She went i. the house,** Entró en la casa. **to look i.,** mirar dentro de; mirar hacia el interior (de); investigar

intolerable /ɪn'tɒlərəbəl/ *a* intolerable, insufrible, inaguantable, insoportable, inllevable

intolerableness /ɪn'tɒlərəbəlnɪs/ *n* intolerabilidad, *f*

intolerably /ɪn'tɒlərəbli/ *adv* intolerablemente, insufriblemente

intolerance /ɪn'tɒlərəns/ *n* intolerancia, intransigencia, *f*

intolerant /ɪn'tɒlərənt/ *a* intolerante, intransigente; *Med.* intolerante

intonation /ˌɪntou'neiʃən/ *n* entonación, *f*

intone /ɪn'toun/ *vt* entonar; *Eccl.* salmodiar

intoxicant /ɪn'tɒksɪkənt/ *a* embriagador. —*n* bebida alcohólica, *f*

intoxicate /ɪn'tɒksɪˌkeit/ *vt* emborrachar, embriagar; *Med.* intoxicar, envenenar; (excite) embriagar, embelesar

intoxicated /ɪn'tɒksɪˌkeitɪd/ *a* borracho; (excited) ebrio, embriagado; *Med.* intoxicado

intoxicating /ɪn'tɒksɪˌkeitɪŋ/ *a* embriagador

intoxication /ɪnˌtɒksɪ'keiʃən/ *n* borrachera, embriaguez, *f; Med.* intoxicación, *f,* envenenamiento, *m;* (excitement) entusiasmo, *m,* ebriedad, *f*

intractability /ɪnˌtræktə'bɪlɪti/ *n* insociabilidad, hurañería, *f*

intractable /ɪn'træktəbəl/ *a* intratable, insociable, huraño

intramural /ˌɪntrə'myʊrəl/ *adv* intramuros

intransigence /ɪn'trænsɪdʒəns/ *n* intransigencia, intolerancia, *f*

intransigent /ɪn'trænsɪdʒənt/ *a* intransigente, intolerante

intransitive /ɪn'trænsɪtɪv/ *a* intransitivo, neutro

intrauterine /ˌɪntrə'yutərɪn/ *a Med.* intrauterino

intravenous /ˌɪntrə'vinəs/ *a Med.* intravenoso

intrepid /ɪn'trɛpɪd/ *a* intrépido, osado, audaz

intrepidity /ɪntrə'pɪdɪti/ *n* intrepidez, osadía, audacia, *f*

intrepidly /ɪn'trɛpɪdli/ *adv* intrépidamente, audazmente

intricacy /'ɪntrɪkəsi/ *n* intrincación, complejidad, *f*

intricate /'ɪntrɪkɪt/ *a* intrincado, complejo

intricately /'ɪntrɪkɪtli/ *adv* intrincadamente

intrigue /ɪn'trig; *n. also* 'ɪntrig/ *n* intriga, maquinación, *f,* enredo, *m;* (amorous) lío, *m*. —*vi* intrigar, en-

redar; (amorous) tener un lío. —*vt* (interest) atraer, interesar; (with) intrigar con
intriguer /ɪn'trigər/ *n* intrigante, *mf.* urdemalas, *m,* enredador (-ra)
intriguing /ɪn'trigɪŋ/ *a* enredador; (attractive) atrayente, interesante, seductor
intrinsic /ɪn'trɪnsɪk/ *a* intrínseco, innato, inherente, esencial
intrinsically /ɪn'trɪnsɪkli/ *adv* intrínsecamente, esencialmente
introduce /ˌɪntrə'dus/ *vt* introducir; hacer entrar; insertar, injerir; (a person) presentar; poner de moda, introducir; (a bill) presentar; (a person to a thing) llamar la atención sobre. **Permit me to i. my friend,** Permítame que le presente mi amigo
introduction /ˌɪntrə'dʌkʃən/ *n* introducción, *f;* (of a book) prefacio, prólogo, *m,* advertencia, *f;* (of a person) presentación, *f;* inserción, *f*
introductory /ˌɪntrə'dʌktəri/ *a* introductor, preliminar, preparatorio
intromission /ˌɪntrə'mɪʃən/ *n* intromisión, *f*
introspection /ˌɪntrə'spɛkʃən/ *n* introspección, *f*
introspective /ˌɪntrə'spɛktɪv/ *a* introspectivo
introversion /ˌɪntrə'vɜrʒən/ *n Psychol.* introversión *f*
introvert /'ɪntrəˌvɜrt/ *a* and *n Psychol.* introverso (-sa)
intrude /ɪn'trud/ *vt* introducir, imponer. —*vi* entremeterse, inmiscuirse. **Do I i.?** ¿Estorbo?
intruder /ɪn'trudər/ *n* intruso (-sa)
intrusion /ɪn'truʒən/ *n* intrusión, *f; Geol.* intromisión, *f*
intrusive /ɪn'trusɪv/ *a* intruso
intuition /ˌɪntu'ɪʃən/ *n* intuición, *f.* **to know by i.,** intuir, saber por intuición
intuitive /ɪn'tuɪtɪv/ *a* intuitivo
inundate /'ɪnənˌdeit/ *vt* inundar, anegar; *Fig.* abrumar
inundation /ˌɪnən'deiʃən/ *n* inundación, anegación, *f; Fig.* diluvio, *m,* abundancia, *f*
inure /ɪn'yʊr/ *vt* endurecer, habituar
inurement /ɪn'yʊrmənt/ *n* habituación, *f*
invade /ɪn'veid/ *vt* invadir, irrumpir, asaltar; *Med.* invadir
invader /ɪn'veidər/ *n* invasor (-ra), acometedor (-ra), agresor (-ra)
invading /ɪn'veidɪŋ/ *a* invasor, irruptor
invalid /ɪn'vælɪd/ *a* inválido, nulo. **to become i.,** caducar
invalid /'ɪnvəlɪd/ *n* inválido (-da), enfermo (-ma). **to become an i.,** quedarse inválido. **to i. out of the army,** licenciar por invalidez. **i. carriage,** cochecillo de inválido, *m*
invalidate /ɪn'vælɪˌdeit/ *vt* invalidar, anular
invalidation /ɪnˌvælɪ'deiʃən/ *n* invalidación, *f*
invalidity /ˌɪnvə'lɪdɪti/ *n* invalidez, nulidad, *f*
invaluable /ɪn'vælyuəbəl/ *n* inestimable
invariability /ɪnˌvɛəriə'bɪlɪti/ *n* invariabilidad, invariación, inalterabilidad, inmutabilidad, *f*
invariable /ɪn'vɛəriəbəl/ *a* invariable, inmutable, inalterable
invariably /ɪn'vɛəriəbli/ *adv* invariablemente, inmutablemente
invariant /ɪn'vɛəriənt/ *n Math.* invariante, *m*
invasion /ɪn'veiʒən/ *n* invasión, irrupción, *f; Med.* invasión, *f*
invective /ɪn'vɛktɪv/ *n* invectiva, diatriba, *f*
inveigh (against) /ɪn'vei/ *vi* desencadenarse (contra), prorrumpir en invectivas (contra)
inveigle /ɪn'veigəl/ *vt* seducir, engatusar, persuadir
inveiglement /ɪn'veigəlmənt/ *n* seducción, persuasión, *f*
invent /ɪn'vɛnt/ *vt* inventar, descubrir, originar; (a falsehood) fingir; (create) idear, componer
invention /ɪn'vɛnʃən/ *n* invención, *f,* invento, descubrimiento, *m;* (imagination) ingeniosidad, inventiva, *f;* (falsehood) ficción, mentira, *f;* (finding) invención, *f,* hallazgo, *m*
inventive /ɪn'vɛntɪv/ *a* inventor, inventivo; ingenioso, despejado
inventiveness /ɪn'vɛntɪvnɪs/ *n* inventiva, *f*
inventor /ɪn'vɛntər/ *n* inventor (-ra), autor (-ra)
inventory /'ɪnvənˌtɔri/ *n* inventario, *m;* descripción, *f.* —*vt* inventariar
inverse /ɪn'vɜrs/ *a* inverso. **i. proportion,** razón inversa, *f*
inversely /ɪn'vɜrsli/ *adv* inversamente, a la inversa
inversion /ɪn'vɜrʒən/ *n* inversión, *f,* trastrocamiento, *m; Gram.* hipérbaton, *m*
invert /ɪn'vɜrt/ *vt* invertir, trastornar, trastrocar. **inverted commas,** comilla, *f*
invertebrate /ɪn'vɜrtəbrɪt/ *a* and *n* invertebrado *m.*
invest /ɪn'vɛst/ *vt Com.* invertir; *Mil.* sitiar, cercar; (foll. by with) poner, cubrir con; (of qualities) conferir, otorgar, dar. —*vi* (with in) poner dinero en, echar caudal en; *Inf.* comprar
investigable /ɪn'vɛstɪgəbəl/ *a* averiguable
investigate /ɪn'vɛstɪˌgeit/ *vt* investigar, estudiar; examinar, averiguar; explorar
investigation /ɪnˌvɛstɪ'geiʃən/ *n* investigación, *f,* estudio, *m;* examen, *m,* averiguación, *f;* encuesta, pesquisa, *f*
investigator /ɪn'vɛstɪˌgeitər/ *n* investigador (-ra); averiguador (-ra)
investigatory /ɪn'vɛtɪgəˌtɔri/ *a* investigador
investiture /ɪn'vɛstɪtʃər/ *n* investidura, instalación, *f*
investment /ɪn'vɛstmənt/ *n* (*Com.* of money) inversión, *f,* empleo, *m; Mil.* cerco, *m;* (investiture) instalación, *f; pl* **investments,** *Com.* acciones, *f pl,* fondos, *m pl*
investor /ɪn'vɛstər/ *n* inversionista, *m;* accionista, *mf*
inveteracy /ɪn'vɛtərəsi/ *n* antigüedad, *f,* lo arraigado
inveterate /ɪn'vɛtərɪt/ *a* inveterado, antiguo, arraigado, incurable
invidious /ɪn'vɪdiəs/ *a* odioso, repugnante, injusto
invidiousness /ɪn'vɪdiəsnɪs/ *n* injusticia, *f,* lo odioso
invigorate /ɪn'vɪgəˌreit/ *vt* vigorizar, dar fuerza (a), avivar
invigorating /ɪn'vɪgəˌreitɪŋ/ *a* fortaleciente, fortificador, vigorizador
invincibility /ɪnˌvɪnsə'bɪlɪti/ *n* invencibilidad, *f*
invincible /ɪn'vɪnsəbəl/ *a* invencible, indomable; *Fig.* insuperable
inviolability /ɪnˌvaiələ'bɪlɪti/ *n* inviolabilidad, *f*
inviolable /ɪn'vaiələbəl/ *a* inviolable
inviolate /ɪn'vaiəlɪt/ *a* inviolado
invisibility /ɪnˌvɪzə'bɪlɪti/ *n* invisibilidad, *f*
invisible /ɪn'vɪzəbəl/ *a* invisible. **i. ink,** tinta simpática, *f.* **i. mending,** zurcido invisible, *m*
invitation /ˌɪnvɪ'teiʃən/ *n* invitación, *f;* convite, *m;* (card) tarjeta de invitación, *f*
invite /ɪn'vait/ *vt* invitar, convidar; (request) pedir, rogar; (of things) incitar, tentar.
inviting /ɪn'vaitɪŋ/ *a* atrayente, incitante; (of food) apetitoso; (of looks) provocativo
invocation /ˌɪnvə'keiʃən/ *n* invocación, *f*
invocatory /ɪn'vɒkətɔri/ *a* invocatorio, invocador
invoice /'ɪnvɔis/ *n Com.* factura, *f.* —*vt* facturar. **pro-forma i.,** factura simulada, *f.* **shipping i.,** factura de expedición, *f.* **i. book,** libro de facturas, *m*
invoke /ɪn'vouk/ *vt* invocar; suplicar, implorar; (*laws*) acogerse (a)
involuntarily /ɪnˌvɒlən'tɛərəli/ *adv* sin querer, involuntariamente
involuntariness /ɪn'vɒlənˌtɛrinɪs/ *n* involuntariedad, *f*
involuntary /ɪn'vɒlənˌtɛri/ *a* involuntario; instintivo, inconsciente
involve /ɪn'vɒlv/ *vt* (entangle) enredar, embrollar, enmarañar; (implicate) comprometer; (imply) implicar, ocasionar, suponer, traer consigo
involved /ɪn'vɒlvd/ *a* complejo, intrincado; (of style) confuso, obscuro
invulnerability /ɪnˌvʌlnərə'bɪlɪti/ *n* invulnerabilidad, *f*
invulnerable /ɪn'vʌlnərəbəl/ *a* invulnerable
inward /'ɪnwərd/ *a* interior, interno; íntimo, espiritual. —*adv* adentro
inwardly /'ɪnwərdli/ *adv* interiormente; para sí, entre sí
inwards /'ɪnw'ərdz/ *adv* hacia dentro; adentro
iodine /'aiəˌdain/ *n* yodo, *m.* **i. poisoning,** yodismo, *m*

ion /'aiən/ *n Chem.* ion, *m*

Ionian /ai'ouniən/ *a* and *n* jónico (-ca)

Ionic /ai'ɒnɪk/ *a* jónico. **i. foot** *Poet.* jónico, *m*

iota /ai'outə/ *n* (letter) iota, *f;* jota, pizca, *f,* ápice, *m.* **not an i.,** ni pizca

I.O.U. *n Com.* abonaré, *m*

ipecacuanha /ˌɪpɪˌkækyə'wanyˈə/ *n* ipecacuana, *f*

Iranian /ɪ'reiniən/ *a* and *n* iranio (-ia)

Iraq /ɪ'ræk/ Irak, *m*

irascibility /ɪˌræsə'bɪlɪti/ *n* irascibilidad, iracundia, irritabilidad, *f*

irascible /ɪ'ræsəbəl/ *a* irascible, iracundo, irritable

irate /ai'reit/ *a* airado, colérico, enojado

ire /aiᵊr/ *n* ira, cólera, furia, *f*

Ireland /'aiᵊrlənd/ Irlanda, *f*

iridescence /ˌɪrɪ'dɛsəns/ *n* iridiscencia, *f*

iridescent /ˌɪrɪ'dɛsənt/ *a* iridiscente. **to look i.,** irisar, tornasolarse

iridium /ɪ'rɪdiəm/ *n Chem.* iridio, *m*

iris /'airɪs/ *n Anat.* iris, *m; Bot.* irídea, *f*

Irish /'airɪʃ/ *a* and *n* irlandés (-esa). **the I.,** los irlandeses

Irish Sea Mar de Irlanda, *f*

irksome /'ɜrksəm/ *a* fastidioso, tedioso, aburrido

irksomeness /'ɜrksəmnis/ *n* tedio, fastidio, aburrimiento, *m*

iron /'aiərn/ *n* hierro, *m;* (for clothes) plancha, *f;* (tool) utensilio, *m,* herramienta, *f;* (golf) hierro, *m; pl* **irons,** grillos, *m pl,* cadenas, *f pl.* —*a* de hierro, férreo; *Fig.* duro, severo. —*vt* (linen) planchar; (with out) allanar. **to have too many irons in the fire,** tener demasiados asuntos entre manos. **to put in irons,** echar grillos (a). **to strike while the i. is hot,** A hierro caliente batir de repente. **cast-i.,** hierro colado, *m.* **scrap i.,** hierro viejo, *m.* **sheet i.,** hierro en planchas, *m.* **wrought i.,** hierro dulce, *m.* **i. age,** edad de hierro, *f.* **i.-foundry,** fundición de hierro, *f.* **i. lung,** *Med.* pulmón de hierro, pulmón de acero, *m.* **i.-mold,** mancha de orín, *f.* **i. smelting furnace,** alto horno, *m.* **i. tonic,** *Med.* reconstituyente ferruginoso, *m.* **i. will,** voluntad de hierro, *f*

ironclad /*a* 'aiərn'klæd; *n* -ˌklæd/ *a* blindado, acorazado. —*n* buque de guerra blindado, acorazado, *m*

ironer /'aiərnər/ *n* planchador (-ra)

ironical /ai'rɒnɪkəl/ *a* irónico

ironically /ai'rɒnɪkli/ *adv* con ironía, irónicamente

ironing /'aiərnɪŋ/ *n* planchado, *m;* ropa por planchar, *f.* —*a* de planchar. **i. board,** tabla de planchar, *f*

ironist /'airənɪst/ *n* ironista, *mf*

ironmonger /'aiərnˌmʌŋgər/ *n* ferretero (-ra). **ironmonger's shop,** ferretería, *f*

ironmongery /'aiərnˌmʌŋgəri/ *n* ferretería, quincallería, *f*

iron sulphide sulfuro de hierro, *m*

ironwork /'aiərnˌwɜrk/ *n* herraje, *m;* obra de hierro, *f*

ironworks /'aiərnˌwɜrks/ *n* herrería, *f*

irony /'airəni/ *n* ironía, *f.* —*a* (like iron) ferrugiento

Iroquois /'ɪrəˌkwɔi/ *a* and *n* iroqués (-esa)

irradiate /ɪ'reidiˌeit/ *vt* irradiar; *Fig.* iluminar, aclarar

irradiation /ɪˌreidi'eiʃən/ *n* irradiación, *f; Fig.* iluminación, *f*

irrational /ɪ'ræʃənl̩/ *a* ilógico, ridículo, irracional

irrationality /ɪˌræʃə'nælɪti/ *n* irracionalidad, *f*

irreclaimable /ˌɪrɪ'kleiməbəl/ *a* irrecuperable, irredimible, (of land) inservible, improductivo, irreformable

irreconcilable /ɪ'rɛkənˌsailəbəl/ *a* irreconciliable

irreconcilably /ɪ'rɛkənˌsailəbli/ *adv* irremediablemente

irrecoverable /ˌɪrɪ'kʌvərəbəl/ *a* irrecuperable, incobrable

irredeemable /ˌɪrɪ'diməbəl/ *a* irredimible, perdido. **i. government loan,** deuda perpetua, *f*

irredeemably /ˌɪrɪ'diməbli/ *adv* perdidamente

irreducible /ˌɪrɪ'dusəbəl/ *a* irreducible

irrefutability /ɪˌrɛfyətə'bɪlɪti/ *n* verdad, *f*

irrefutable /ɪ'rɛfyətəbəl/ *a* irrefutable, indisputable, innegable, irrebatible

irregular /ɪ'rɛgyələr/ *a* irregular; anormal; (of shape) disforme; desordenado; *Gram.* irregular; (of surface) desigual, escabroso

irregularity /ɪˌrɛgyə'lærɪti/ *n* irregularidad, *f;* anormalidad, *f;* (of shape) desproporción, irregularidad, *f;* (of surface) escabrosidad, desigualdad, *f;* exceso, *m,* demasía, *f*

irrelevance /ɪ'rɛləvəns/ *n* inconexión, *f;* inoportunidad, *f;* futilidad, poca importancia, *f;* (stupidity) desatino, *m,* impertinencia, *f*

irrelevant /ɪ'rɛləvənt/ *a* inaplicable, fuera de propósito; inoportuno; sin importancia, fútil; (stupid) impertinente

irreligion /ˌɪrɪ'lɪdʒən/ *n* irreligión, impiedad, *f*

irreligious /ˌɪrɪ'lɪdʒəs/ *a* irreligioso, impío

irremediable /ˌɪrɪ'midiəbəl/ *a* irremediable, irreparable

irremediably /ˌɪrɪ'midiəbli/ *adv* sin remedio, irremediablemente

irreparable /ɪ'rɛpərəbəl/ *a* irreparable

irreplaceable /ˌɪrɪ'pleisəbəl/ *a* irreemplazable

irrepressible /ˌɪrɪ'prɛsəbəl/ *a* incontrolable, indomable

irreproachable /ˌɪrɪ'proutʃəbəl/ *a* irreprochable, intachable

irresistible /ˌɪrɪ'zɪstəbəl/ *a* irresistible

irresistibleness /ˌɪrɪ'zɪstəbəlnɪs/ *n* superioridad, *f*

irresolute /ɪ'rɛzəˌlut/ *a* irresoluto, indeciso, vacilante

irresoluteness /ɪ'rɛzəˌlutnɪs/ *n* irresolución, indecisión, *f*

irrespective /ˌɪrɪ'spɛktɪv/ *a* (with of) independiente de, aparte de, sin distinción de

irresponsibility /ˌɪrɪˌspɒnsə'bɪlɪti;/ *n* irresponsabilidad, *f*

irresponsible /ˌɪrɪ'spɒnsəbəl/ *a* irresponsable

irretrievable /ˌɪrɪ'trivəbəl/ *a* irrecuperable

irretrievably /ˌɪrɪ'trivəbli/ *adv* irreparablemente, sin remedio

irreverence /ɪ'rɛvərəns/ *n* irreverencia, *f*

irreverent /ɪ'rɛvərənt/ *a* irreverente, irrespetuoso

irrevocability /ɪˌrɛvəkə'bɪlɪti/ *n* irrevocabilidad, *f*

irrevocable /ɪ'rɛvəkəbəl/ *a* irrevocable; inquebrantable

irrigable /'ɪrɪgəbəl/ *a* regadío

irrigate /'ɪrɪˌgeit/ *vt Agr.* poner en regadío, regar; *Med.* irrigar

irrigation /ˌɪrɪ'geiʃən/ *n Agr.* riego, *m; Med.* irrigación, *f.* **i. channel,** cacera, acequia, *f,* canal de riego, *m*

irritability /ˌɪrɪtə'bɪlɪti/ *n* irritabilidad, iracundia, *f*

irritable /'ɪrɪtəbəl/ *a* irritable, irascible, iracundo

irritably /'ɪrɪtəbli/ *adv* con irritación, airadamente

irritant /'ɪrɪtn̩t/ *a* irritante, irritador. —*n* irritador, *m; Med.* medicamento irritante, *m*

irritate /'ɪrɪˌteit/ *vt* provocar, estimular; irritar, molestar, exasperar; *Med.* irritar

irritating /'ɪrɪˌteitɪŋ/ *a* irritador, irritante

irritatingly /'ɪrɪˌteitɪŋli/ *adv* de un modo irritante

irritation /ˌɪrɪ'teiʃən/ *n* irritación, *f,* enojo, *m; Physiol.* picazón, *f,* picor, *m*

irruption /ɪ'rʌpʃən/ *n* irrupción, invasión, *f*

isinglass /'aizənˌglæs/ *n* cola de pescado, *f*

Islamic /ɪs'læmɪk/ *a* islámico

Islamism /ɪs'lɑmɪzəm/ *n* islamismo, *m*

Islamite /ɪs'læmait/ *a* and *n* islamita *mf*

island /'ailənd/ *n* isla, *f, a* isleño

islander /'ailəndər/ *n* isleño (-ña)

islet /'ailɪt/ *n* isleta, *f;* isolote, *m*

isobaric /ˌaisə'bærɪk/ *a* isobárico

isolate /*v.* 'aisəˌleit/ *vt* aislar, apartar

isolated /'aisəˌleitɪd/ *a* aislado, apartado, solitario; único, solo

isolation /ˌaisə'leiʃən/ *n* aislamiento, apartamiento, *m,* soledad, *f*

isolationism /ˌaisə'leiʃəˌnɪzəm/ *n Polit.* aislacionismo, aislamientismo, *m*

isolationist /ˌaisə'leiʃənɪst/ *a* and *n Polit.* aislacionista, aislamientista, *mf*

isomerism /ai'sɒməˌrɪzəm/ *n Chem.* isomería, *f*

isometric /ˌaisə'mɛtrɪk/ *a* isométrico

isosceles /ai'sɒsəˌliz/ *a* isósceles

isotope /'aisəˌtoup/ *n* isotope, isotopo, *m*

Israelite /'ɪzriəˌlait/ *a* and *n* israelita *mf*

issue /'ɪʃu/ *n* salida, *f;* (result) resultado, *m,* consecuencia, *f;* (of a periodical) número, *m; Print.* edición, tirada, *f;* (offspring) prole, sucesión, *f;* (of notes, bonds) emisión, *f; Med.* flujo, *m;* cuestión, *f,* problema, *m.* —*vi* salir, fluir, manar; nacer, originarse; resultar, terminarse. —*vt* (an order) expedir, emitir, dictar; publicar, dar a luz; (of notes, bonds) poner en circulación, librar. **at i.,** en disputa, en cuestión. **to join i.,** llevar la contraria, oponer

isthmian /ˈɪsmiən/ *a* ístmico

isthmus /ˈɪsməs/ *n* istmo, *m*

it /ɪt/ *pron* (as subject) él, *m;* ella, *f;* (gen. omitted with all verbs in Sp.); (as object) lo, *m;* la, *f;* (as indirect object) le (se with an object in 3rd pers.); (meaning that thing, that affair) eso, ello. Sometimes omitted in other cases, e.g. *He has thought it necessary to stay at home,* Ha creído necesario de quedarse en casa. *We heard it said that...,* Oímos decir que... *to make it perfectly clear that...,* dejar bien claro que... —*n* (slang) garbo, aquél, *m;* atractivos, *m pl.* **Is it not so?** ¿No es así? **That is it,** Eso es. **It's me,** Soy yo

Italian /ɪˈtælyən/ *a* and *n* italiano (-na) (language) italiano, *m. Art.* **I. School,** escuela italiana, *f*

italic /ɪˈtælɪk/ *a* (of Italy) itálico; *Print.* itálico, bastardillo. —*n* letra bastardilla, bastardilla, letra itálica, *f.* **italics mine,** el subrayado es mío, los subrayados son míos

italicize /ɪˈtæləˌsaiz/ *vt* imprimir en bastardilla; dar énfasis (a)

Italy /ˈɪtl̩i/ Italia, *f*

itch /ɪtʃ/ *n* sarna, *f; Fig.* picazón, *f;* prurito, capricho, *m.* —*vi* picar; *Fig.* sentir picazón; (with to) rabiar por, suspirar por.

itching /ˈɪtʃɪŋ/ *n* picazón, *f,* picor, *m.* —*a* sarnoso, picante; *Med.* pruriginoso. **to have an i. palm,** *Fig.* ser de la virgen del puño

item /*n* ˈaitəm; *adv* ˈaitɛm/ *n* ítem, artículo, *m; Com.* partida, *f;* punto, detalle, *m;* (of a program) número, *m;* asunto, *m.* —*adv* ítem

iterative /ˈɪtəˌreitɪv/ *a* iterativo

Ithaca /ˈɪθəkə/ Ítaca, *f*

itinerant /aiˈtɪnərənt/ *a* nómada, errante

itinerary /aiˈtɪnəˈrɛri/ *n* itinerario, *m,* ruta, *f*

its /ɪts/ *poss a* su (with pl. obj.) sus. **a book and its pages,** un libro y sus páginas.

itself /ɪtˈsɛlf/ *pron* él mismo, *m;* ella misma, *f;* (with prep.) sí; (with reflex. verb) se; (with noun) el mismo, la misma; (meaning alone) solo. **in i.,** en sí

ivied /ˈaivid/ *a* cubierto de hiedra

ivory /ˈaivəri/ *n* marfil, *m.* —*a* ebúrneo, de marfil, marfileño. **vegetable i.,** marfil vegetal, *m.* **i. carving,** talla de marfil, *f*

ivory tower *n* torre de marfil, *f*

ivory-tower /ˈaivəri ˈtauər/ *a* de torre de marfil

ivy /ˈaivi/ *n* hiedra, *f*

J

j /dʒei/ *n* (letter) jota, *f*

jab /dʒæb/ *vt* (with a hypodermic needle, etc.) pinchar; introducir (en); clavar (con); (scrape) hurgar; (place) poner. —*n* pinchazo, *m;* golpe, *m.* **He jabbed his pistol in my ribs,** Me puso la pistola en las costillas

jabber /'dʒæbər/ *vt* and *vi* chapurrear; (of monkeys) chillar

jabbering /'dʒæbərıŋ/ *n* chapurreo, *m;* (of monkeys) chillidos, *m pl*

Jack /dʒæk/ *n* Juan, *m;* (man) hombre, *m;* (sailor) marinero, *m;* (in cards) sota, *f;* (for raising weights) gato, *m;* (of a spit) torno, *m;* (of some animals) macho, *m;* (bowls) boliche, *m.* —*vt* (with up) solevantar con gatos. **Union J.,** pabellón británico, *m.* **j.-boot,** bota de montar, *f.* **J.-in-office,** mandarín, funcionario impertinente, *m.* **J.-in-the-box,** faca, *f.* **j.-knife,** navaja, *f.* **J. of all trades,** hombre de muchos oficios, *m.* **jack of all trades, master of none,** aprendiz de todo, oficial de nada. **j.-rabbit,** liebre americana, *f.* **J.-tar,** marinero, *m*

jackal /'dʒækəl/ *n* chacal, adive, *m*

jackanapes /'dʒækə,neips/ *n* impertinente, *m;* mequetrefe, *m*

jackass /'dʒæk,æs/ *n* asno, *m;* (fool) tonto, asno, *m.* **laughing j.,** martín pescador, *m*

jacket /'dʒækıt/ *n* chaqueta, *f;* americana, *f;* (for boilers, etc.) camisa, *f;* (of a book) forro, *m,* sobrecubierta, *f.* **strait j.,** camisa de fuerza, *f*

jacks /dʒæks/ *n* (game) matatenas, *f pl,* cantillos, *m pl*

jade /dʒeid/ *n Mineral.* jade, *m;* (horse) rocín, *m;* (woman) mala pécora, *f;* (saucy wench) mozuela, picaruela, *f*

jaded /'dʒeidıd/ *a* fatigado, agotado, rendido; (of the palate) saciado

jagged /dʒægıd/ *a* dentado

jaguar /'dʒægwɑr/ *n* jaguar, *m*

jail /dʒeil/ cárcel, prisión, *f;* encierro, *m.* —*vt* encarcelar. —*a* carcelario, carcelero.

jailbird /'dʒeil,bɜrd/ malhechor; presidiario, *m*

jailer /'dʒeilər/ *n* carcelero (-ra)

jalopy /dʒə'lɒpi/ carcacho, *m,* (Mexico), cafetera rusa, *f,* (Spain)

jalousie /'dʒælə,si/ *n* celosía, *f*

jam /dʒæm/ *vt* (ram) apretar; apiñar; estrujar; (a machine) atascar; (radio) causar interferencia (a); (preserve) hacer confitura de. —*vi* atascarse. —*n* (of people) agolpamiento, *m;* (traffic) atasco, *m;* (preserve) confitura, mermelada, compota, *f.* **He jammed his hat on,** Se encasquetó el sombrero. **She suddenly jammed down on the brakes,** Frenó de repente. **jam-dish,** compotera, *f.* **jam-jar,** pote para confitura, *m*

Jamaican /dʒə'meikən/ *a* jamaicano, *n* jamaicano (-na)

jamboree /,dʒæmbə'ri/ campamento, *m*

jamming /'dʒæmıŋ/ *n Radio.* interferencias, *f pl*

jangle /'dʒæŋgəl/ *vi* cencerrear; chocar; rechinar. —*n* cencerreo, *m,* choque, *m,* rechinamiento, *m*

janissary /'dʒænə,sɛri/ *n* jenízaro, *m*

janitor /'dʒænıtər/ *n* portero, *m;* (in a university, etc.) bedel, *m*

Jansenist /'dʒænsənıst/ *a* and *n* jansenista, *mf*

January /'dʒænyu,ɛri/ *n* enero, *m*

Japan /dʒə'pæn/ el Japón, *m*

japan /dʒə'pæn/ *n* charol, *m.* —*vt* charolar

Japanese /,dʒæpə'niz/ *a* japonés. —*n* japonés (-esa); (language) japonés, *m*

jar /dʒɑr/ *n* chirrido, *m;* choque, *m;* sacudida, *f;* vibración, trepidación, *f;* (quarrel) riña, *f;* (receptacle) jarra, *f;* (for tobacco, honey, cosmetics, etc.) pote, *m;* (Leyden) botella (de Leyden), *f.* —*vi* chirriar; vibrar, trepidar; chocar; (of sounds) ser discorde; (of colors) chillar. —*vt* sacudir; hacer vibrar. **It jarred on my nerves,** Me atacaba los nervios. **It gave me a nasty jar,** *Fig.* Me hizo una impresión desagradable. **on the jar,** entreabierto

jardiniere /,dʒɑrdn̩'ıər/ *n* jardinera, *f*

jargon /'dʒɑrgən/ *n* jerga, jerigonza, *f;* monserga, *f;* (technical) lenguaje especial, *m*

jarring /'dʒarıŋ/ *a* discorde, disonante; en conflicto, opuesto; (to the nerves) que ataca a los nervios

jasmine /'dʒæzmın/ *n* jazmín, *m.* **yellow j.,** jazmín amarillo, *m*

jasper /'dʒæspər/ *n Mineral.* jaspe, *m*

jaundice /'dʒɔndıs/ *n* ictericia, *f*

jaundiced /'dʒɔndıst/ *a* envidioso; desengañado, desilusionado

jaunt /dʒɔnt/ *n* excursión, *f, vi* ir de excursión

jauntily /'dʒɔntl̩i/ *adv* airosamente, con garbo

jauntiness /'ʒɔntinıs/ *n* garbo, *m,* gentileza, ligereza, *f*

jaunty /'dʒɔnti/ *a* garboso, airoso

Javanese /,dʒævə'niz/ *a* javanés. —*n* javanés (-esa)

javelin /'dʒævlın/ *n* jabalina, *f.* **j. throwing,** lanzamiento de la jabalina, *m*

jaw /dʒɔ/ *n* quijada, *f;* maxilar, *m; pl* **jaws,** boca, *f;* (of death, etc.) garras, *f pl; Mech.* quijada, *f;* (narrow entrance) boca, abertura, *f.* **jaw-bone,** mandíbula, *f; Anat.* hueso maxilar, *m*

jay /dʒei/ *n* arrendajo, *m*

jazz /dʒæz/ *n* jazz, *m.* —*vi* bailar el jazz. **j. band,** orquesta de jazz, *f*

jealous /'dʒɛləs/ *a* celoso; envidioso. **to be j. of,** tener celos de. **to make j.,** dar celos (a)

jealously /'dʒɛləsli/ *adv* celosamente

jealousy /'dʒɛləsi/ *n* celos, *m pl*

jeans /dʒinz/ *n* vaqueros, *m pl*

jeep /dʒip/ *n Mil.* yip, *m*

jeer /dʒıər/ *n* burla, mofa, *f;* insulto, *m, vi* burlarse; (with at) mofarse de

jeerer /'dʒıərər/ *n* mofador (-ra)

jeering /'dʒıərıŋ/ *a* mofador. —*n* burlas, *f pl;* insultos, *m pl*

jeeringly /'dʒıərıŋli/ *adv* burlonamente

jellied /'dʒɛlid/ *a* en gelatina

jelly /'dʒɛli/ *n* jalea, *f;* gelatina, *f, vi* solidificarse. **j.-bag,** manga, *f.* **j.-fish,** aguamala, aguaviva, malagna, medusa, *f*

jeopardize /'dʒɛpər,daiz/ *vt* arriesgar, poner en juego; comprometer

jeopardy /'dʒɛpərdi/ *n* peligro, *m*

jeremiad /,dʒɛrə'maiəd/ *n* jeremiada, *f*

jerk /dʒɜrk/ *n* sacudida, *f.* —*vt* sacudir, dar una sacudida (a); lanzar bruscamente; (pull) tirar de; (push) empujar. —*vi* moverse a sacudidas. **I jerked myself free,** Me libré de una sacudida

jerkily /'dʒɜrkəli/ *adv* con sacudidas; espasmódicamente; nerviosamente

jerkin /'dʒɜrkın/ *n* justillo, *m*

jerky /'dʒɜrki/ *a* espasmódico; nervioso (also of style)

jerry-built /'dʒɛri,bılt/ *a* mal construido, de pacotilla

jersey /'dʒɜrzi/ *n* jersey, *m.* —*a* de jersey; de Jersey. **football j.,** camiseta de fútbol, *f,* jersey de fútbol, *m.* **J. cow,** vaca jerseysa, *f*

Jerusalem /dʒı'rusələm/ Jerusalén, *m*

jest /dʒɛst/ *n* broma, chanza, *f;* (joke) chiste, *m;* (laughingstock) hazmerreír, *m.* —*vi* bromear; burlarse (de). **in j.,** en broma, de guasa

jester /'dʒɛstər/ *n* burlón (-ona); (practical joker, etc.) bromista, *mf;* (at a royal court) bufón, *m*

jesting /'dʒɛstıŋ/ *n* bromas, *f pl;* chistes, *m pl;* burlas, *f pl.* —*a* de broma; burlón

jestingly /'dʒɛstıŋli/ *adv* en broma

Jesuit /'dʒɛʒuıt/ *n* Jesuita, *m*

Jesuitical /,dʒɛʒu'ıtıkəl/ *a* jesuítico

jet /dʒɛt/ *n Mineral.* azabache, *m;* (stream) chorro, *m;* (pipe) surtidero, *m;* (burner) mechero, *m, vi* chorrear. **jet-black,** negro como el azabache, de azabache. **jet-propelled engine,** motor de retroacción, *m.* **jet-propelled plane,** aeroplano de reacción, *m*

jetsam /'dʒɛtsəm/ *n* echazón, *f; Fig.* víctima, *f*
jettison /'dʒɛtəsən/ *n* echazón, *f.* —*vt* echar (mercancías) al mar; *Fig.* librarse de, abandonar
jetty /'dʒɛti/ *n* dique, malecón, *m;* (landing pier) embarcadero, muelle, *m*
Jew /dʒu/ *n* judío, *m.* **Jew's harp,** birimbao, *m*
jewel /'dʒuəl/ *n* joya, alhaja, *f;* (of a watch) rubí, *m; Fig.* alhaja, *f.* —*vt* enjoyar, adornar con piedras preciosas. **j.-box, -case,** joyero, *m*
jeweled /'dʒuəld/ *a* adornado con piedras preciosas, enjoyado; (of a watch) con rubíes
jeweler /'dʒuələr/ *n* joyero (-ra). **jeweler's shop,** joyería, *f*
jewelry /'dʒuəlri/ *n* joyas, *f pl;* artículos de joyería, *m pl*
Jewess /'dʒuɪs/ *n* judía, *f*
Jewish /'dʒuɪʃ/ *a* judío
Jewry /'dʒuri/ *n* judería, *f*
jib /dʒɪb/ *n Naut.* foque, *m.* —*vi* (of a horse) plantarse; (refuse) rehusar. **to jib at,** vacilar en; mostrarse desinclinado. **jib-boom,** *Naut.* botalón de foque, *m*
jiffy /'dʒɪfi/ *n* instante, credo, *m.* **in a j.,** en un decir Jesús, en un credo, en un santiamén
jig /dʒɪg/ *n* (dance) jiga, *f.* —*vi* bailar una jiga; bailar, agitarse, sacudirse. —*vt* agitar, sacudir; (sieve) cribar
jigger /'dʒɪgər/ *n Naut.* cangreja de mesana, *f;* aparejo de mano, *m;* jigger, *m*
jigsaw puzzle /'dʒɪg,sɔ/ *n* rompecabezas, *m*
jilt /dʒɪlt/ *vt* dar calabazas (a)
jingle /'dʒɪŋgəl/ *n* tintineo, *m;* ruido, *m;* verso, *m;* estribillo, *m.* —*vi* tintinar; sonar; rimar
jingoism /'dʒɪŋgou,ɪzəm/ *n* jingoísmo, *m*
jitters, to have the /'dʒɪtərz/ no tenerlas todas consigo, no saber dónde meterse
job /dʒɒb/ *n* tarea, *f;* trabajo, *m;* empleo, *m;* (affair) asunto, *m;* (thing) cosa, *f;* (unscrupulous transaction) intriga, *f.* **It is a good (bad) job that...,** Es una buena (mala) cosa que... **He has done a good job,** Ha hecho un buen trabajo. **He has lost his job,** Ha perdido su empleo, Le han declarado cesante. **odd-job man,** factótum, *m.* **job-lot,** colección miscelánea, *f; Com.* saldo de mercancías, *m*
jobber /'dʒɒbər/ *n* (workman) destajista, *m;* (in stocks) agiotista, *m; Com.* corredor, *m*
jobless /'dʒɒblɪs/ *a* sin trabajo
jockey /'dʒɒki/ *n* jockey, *m.* —*vt* engañar; (with into) persuadir, hacer; (with out of) quitar, robar. **j. cap,** gorra de jockey, *f.* **J. Club,** jockey-club, *m*
jocose /dʒou'kous/ *a* jocoso, gracioso, guasón
jocosity /dʒou'kɒsɪti/ *n* jocosidad, *f*
jocular /'dʒɒkyələr/ *a* gracioso, alegre; chistoso, zumbón
jocularity /,dʒɒkyə'lærɪti/ *n* alegría, jocosidad, *f*
jocularly /'dʒɒkyələrli/ *adv* en broma; alegremente
jocund /'dʒɒkənd/ *a* alegre, jovial; jocundo
jocundity /dʒou'kʌndɪti/ *n* alegría, *f;* jocundidad, *f*
jog /dʒɒg/ *vt* empujar; (the memory) refrescar. —*vi* ir despacio; andar a trote corto. —*n* empujón, *m.* **He jogged me with his elbow,** Me dio con el codo. **jog-trot,** trote corto, *m*
joie de vivre /ʒwadᵊ'vivrᵊ/ *n* goce de vivir, arregosto de vivir, *m*
join /dʒɔin/ *vt* juntar; unir; añadir; (railway lines) empalmar; juntarse con; (meet) encontrarse (con); reunirse (con); (a club, etc.) hacerse miembro (de); (share) acompañar; (regiments, ships) volver (a). —*vi* juntarse; unirse; asociarse. —*n* unión, *f;* (railway) empalme, *m;* (roads) bifurcación, *f.* **At what time will you j. me?** ¿A qué hora me vendrás a buscar? **He has joined his ship,** Ha vuelto a su buque. **Will you j. me in a drink?** ¿Me quieres acompañar en una bebida? **to j. battle,** librar batalla. **to j. forces,** combinar; *Inf.* juntar meriendas. **to j. in,** tomar parte en, participar en. **to j. together,** *vt* unir, juntar. —*vi* juntarse; asociarse. **to j. up,** alistarse
joiner /'dʒɔinər/ *n* carpintero, ensamblador, *m,*
joinery /'dʒɔinəri/ *n* ensambladuría, *f;* carpintería, *f*
joining /'dʒɔinɪŋ/ *n* juntura, conjunción, *f;* (etc.) ensambladura, *f; Fig.* unión, *f*
joint /dʒɔint/ *n* juntura, junta, *f; Anat.* coyuntura, articulación, *f;* (knuckle) nudillo, *m;* (of meat) cuarto, *m;* (hinge) bisagra, *f; Bot.* nudo, *m,* *a* unido; combinado; colectivo; mixto; mutuo; (in compounds) co. —*vt* juntar; (meat) descuartizar. **out of j.,** dislocado; (of the times) fuera de compás. **j. account,** cuenta corriente mutua, *f.* **j.-heir,** coheredero, *m.* **j. stock company,** compañía por acciones, sociedad anónima, *f*
jointed /'dʒɔintɪd/ *a* articulado; (foldable) plegadizo
jointly /'dʒɔintli/ *adv* juntamente, en común, colectivamente
joist /dʒɔist/ *n* sopanda, viga, *f*
joke /dʒouk/ *n* chiste, *m;* burla, broma, *f.* —*vi* bromear, chancearse. —*vt* burlarse (de). **Can he take a j.?** ¿Sabe aguantar una broma? **practical j.,** broma pesada, *f.* **to play a j.,** gastar una broma, hacer una burla
joker /'dʒoukər/ *n* bromista, *mf;* (in cards) comodín, *m*
joking /'dʒoukɪŋ/ *n* chistes, *m pl,* bromas, *f pl.* —*a* chistoso; cómico
jokingly /'dʒoukɪŋli/ *adv* en broma, de guasa
jollification /,dʒɒləfɪ'keiʃən/ *n* regocijo, *m;* festividades, fiestas, *f pl*
jollity /'dʒɒlɪti/ *n* alegría, *f,* regocijo, *m*
jolly /'dʒɒli/ *a* alegre, jovial; (tipsy) achispado; (amusing) divertido; (nice) agradable. —*adv* muy. **He is a j. good fellow,** Es un hombre estupendo. **I am j. glad,** Estoy contentísimo, Me alegro mucho
jolt /dʒoult/ *n* sacudida, *f.* —*vt* sacudir. —*vi* (of a vehicle) traquetear
jolting /'dʒoultɪŋ/ *n* sacudidas, *f pl,* sacudimiento, *m;* (of a vehicle) traqueteo, *m*
jongleur /'dʒɒŋglər/ *n* juglar, *m*
jonquil /'dʒɒŋkwɪl/ *n Bot.* junquillo, *m*
Jordan /'dʒɔrdn̩/ Jordania, *f*
joss /dʒɒs/ *n* ídolo chino, *m.* **j.-stick,** pebete, *m*
jostle /'dʒɒsəl/ *vt* empujar, empellar. —*vi* dar empujones, codear
jot /dʒɒt/ *n* jota, pizca, *f.* —*vt* (down) apuntar. **not a jot,** ni jota, ni pizca. **to be not worth a jot,** no valer un comino
jotter /'dʒɒtər/ *n* taco para notas, *m;* (exercise book) cuaderno, *m*
jotting /'dʒɒtɪŋ/ *n* apunte, *m;* observación, *f*
journal /'dʒɜrnl̩/ *n* (diary) diario, *m;* (ship's) diario de navegación, *m;* (newspaper) periódico, *m;* (review) revista, *f*
journalese /,dʒɜrnl̩'iz/ *n* lenguaje periodistico, *m*
journalism /'dʒɜrnl̩,ɪzəm/ *n* periodismo, *m*
journalist /'dʒɜrnl̩ɪst/ *n* periodista, *mf*
journalistic /,dʒɜrnl̩'ɪstɪk/ *a* periodistico
journey /'dʒɜrni/ *n* viaje, *m;* expedición, *f;* trayecto, *m;* camino, *m.* —*vi* viajar. **j. by sea,** viaje por mar. **Pleasant j.!** ¡Buen viaje! ¡Feliz viaje! **outward j.,** viaje de ida, *m.* **return j.,** viaje de regreso, *m*
Jove /dʒouv/ *n* Júpiter, *m.* **By J.!** ¡Pardiez! ¡Caramba!
jovial /'dʒouviəl/ *a* jovial
joviality /,dʒouvi'ælɪti/ *n* jovialidad, *f*
jowl /dʒaul/ *n* (cheek) carrillo, *m;* (of cattle, etc.) papada, *f;* (jaw) quijada, *f*
joy /dʒɔi/ *n* alegría, *f;* felicidad, *f;* deleite, placer, *m, vi* alegrarse. **I wish you joy,** Te deseo la felicidad. **joy-ride,** excursión en coche, *f;* vuelo en avión, *m.* **joy-stick,** (of an airplane) palanca de gobierno, *f*
joyful /'dʒɔifəl/ *a* alegre
joyfulness /'dʒɔifəlnɪs/ *n* alegría, *f*
joyless /'dʒɔilɪs/ *a* sin alegría, triste
joylessness /'dʒɔilɪsnɪs/ *n* falta de alegría, tristeza, *f*
joyous /'dʒɔiəs/. See **joyful**
jubilant /'dʒubələnt/ *a* jubiloso; triunfante
jubilantly /'dʒubələntli/ *adv* con júbilo, alegremente; triunfalmente
jubilation /,dʒubə'leiʃən/ *n* júbilo, *m,* alegría, *f;* ruido triunfal, *m*
jubilee /'dʒubə,li/ *n* jubileo, *m*
jubilee volume *n* libro de homenaje, libro jubilar, *m*
Judaic /dʒu'deiɪk/ *a* judaico
Judaism /'dʒudi,ɪzəm/ *n* judaísmo, *m*
Judas /'dʒudəs/ *n* (traitor and hole) judas, *m*
Judezmo /dʒu'dɛzmou/ el judesmo, *m*
judge /dʒʌdʒ/ *n* juez, *m;* (connoisseur) conocedor

(-ra) (de); (umpire) arbitrio, *m.* —*vt* juzgar; considerar, tener por. —*vi* servir como juez; juzgar. **judging by,** a juzgar por. **to be a good j. of,** ser buen juez de. **to j. for oneself,** formar su propia opinión

judgment /'dʒʌdʒmənt/ *n Law.* fallo, *m;* sentencia, *f;* juicio, *m;* (understanding) entendimiento, discernimiento, *m;* (opinion) opinión, *f,* parecer, *m.* **In my j...,** Según mi parecer,... Según creo yo... **Last J.,** Juicio Final, *m.* **to pass j. on,** *Law.* pronunciar sentencia (en or sobre); dictaminar sobre; juzgar. **to sit in j. on,** ser juez de; juzgar. **j.-day,** Día del Juicio, *m.* **j.-seat,** tribunal, *m*

judicature /'dʒudɪˌkeitʃər/ *n* judicatura, *f;* (court) juzgado, *m*

judicial /dʒu'dɪʃəl/ *a* judicial; legal; (of the mind) juicioso. **j. inquiry,** investigación judicial, *f.* **j. separation,** separación legal, *f*

judiciary /dʒu'dɪʃiˌɛri/ *a* judicial. —*n* judicatura, *f*

judicious /dʒu'dɪʃəs/ *a* juicioso, prudente.

judiciously /dʒu'dɪʃəsli/ *adv* prudentemente, juiciosamente

judiciousness /dʒu'dɪʃəsnɪs/ *n* juicio, *m,* prudencia, sensatez, *f*

judo /'dʒudou/ *n* yudo, *m*

judoka /'dʒudouˌka/ *n* yudoca, *mf*

jug /dʒʌg/ *n* jarro, *m;* cántaro, *m;* pote, *m.* —*vt Cul.* estofar. —*vi* (of nightingale) trinar, cantar. **jugged hare,** *n* liebre en estofado, *f*

juggle /'dʒʌgəl/ *vi* hacer juegos malabares. **to j. out of,** (money, etc.) quitar con engaño, estafar. **to j. with,** *Fig.* (facts, etc.) tergiversar, falsificar; (person) engañar

juggler /'dʒʌglər/ *n* malabarista, *mf;* (deceiver) estafador (-ra)

jugglery /dʒʌgləri/ *n* prestidigitación, *f;* juegos malabares, *m pl;* (imposture) engaño, *m,* estafa, *f;* trampas, *f pl*

jugular /'dʒʌgyələr/ *a Anat.* yugular. **j. vein,** yugular, *m*

juice /dʒus/ *n* jugo, *m; Fig.* zumo, *m.* **digestive j.,** jugo digestivo, *m*

juiciness /'dʒusinɪs/ *n* jugosidad, *f;* suculencia, *f*

juicy /'dʒusi/ *a* jugoso; suculento

jujube /'dʒudʒub/ *n* pastilla, *f*

jukebox /'dʒukˌbɒks/ *n* tocadiscos, vitrola, sinfonola, *f*

July /dʒu'lai/ *n* julio, *m*

jumble /'dʒʌmbəl/ *vt* mezclar, confundir. —*n* mezcla confusa, colección miscelánea, confusión, *f.* **j. sale,** tómbola, *f*

jump /dʒʌmp/ *n* salto, *m;* (in prices, etc.) aumento, *m.* **at one j.,** de un salto. **high j.,** salto de altura, *m.* **long j.,** salto de longitud, *m.* **to be on the j.,** *Inf.* estar nervioso, tener los nervios en punta

jump /dʒʌmp/ *vi* saltar; dar un salto; brincar; (of tea-cups, etc.) bailar; (throb) pulsar. —*vt* saltar; hacer saltar; (a child) brincar; (omit) pasar por alto de, omitir. **The train jumped the rails,** El tren se descarriló. **to j. out of bed,** saltar de la cama. **to j. to the conclusion that...,** darse prisa a concluir que... **to j. about,** dar saltos, brincar; revolverse, moverse de un lado para otro. **to j. at,** saltar sobre; precipitarse sobre, abalanzarse hacia; (an offer) apresurarse a aceptar; (seize) coger con entusiasmo. **to j. down,** bajar de un salto. **to j. over,** saltar, saltar por encima de. **to j. up,** saltar; (on to a horse, etc.) montar rápidamente; levantarse apresuradamente. **to j. with,** (agree) convenir en, estar conforme con

jumper /'dʒʌmpər/ *n* saltador (-ra); (sailor's) blusa, *f* jersey, sweater, *m*

jumpiness /'dʒʌmpinɪs/ *n* nerviosidad, *f*

jumping /'dʒʌmpɪŋ/ *n* saltos, *m pl.* —*a* saltador. **j.-off place,** base avanzada, *f; Fig.* trampolín, *m.* **j.-pole,** pértiga, *f*

jumpy /'dʒʌmpi/ *a* nervioso, agitado

junction /'dʒʌŋkʃən/ *n* unión, *f;* (of roads) bifurcación, *f;* (railway) empalme, *m;* (connection) conexión, *f*

juncture /'dʒʌŋktʃər/ *n* coyuntura, *f;* momento, *m;* crisis, *f,* momento crítico, *m;* (joint) junta, *f*

June /dʒun/ *n* junio, *m*

jungle /'dʒʌŋgəl/ *n* selva, *f.* **j.-fever,** fiebre de los grandes bosques, *f*

junior /'dʒunyər/ *a* joven; hijo; más joven; menos antiguo; subordinado, segundo. —*n* joven, *mf* **Carmen is my j. by three years,** Carmen es tres años más joven que yo. **James Thomson, Jr.,** James Thomson, hijo. **the j. school,** los pequeños. **j. partner,** socio menor, *m*

juniper /'dʒunəpər/ *n Bot.* enebro, *m*

junk /dʒʌŋk/ *n* trastos viejos, *m pl;* (nonsense) patrañas, *f pl; Naut.* junco, *m;* (salt meat) tasajo, *m.* **j.-shop,** tienda de trastos viejos, *f*

junk bond bono-basura, *m*

junketing /'dʒʌŋkɪtɪŋ/ *n* festividades, *f pl*

juridical /dʒʊ'rɪdɪkəl/ *a* jurídico

jurisconsult /ˌdʒʊrɪskən'sʌlt/ *n* jurisconsulto, *m*

jurisdiction /ˌdʒʊrɪs'dɪkʃən/ *n* jurisdicción, *f;* competencia, *f*

jurisprudence /ˌdʒʊrɪs'prudns/ *n* jurisprudencia, *f*

jurist /'dʒʊrɪst/ *n* jurista, legista, *mf*

juror /'dʒʊrər/ *n* (miembro del) jurado, *m*

jury /'dʒʊri/ *n* jurado, *m.* **to be on the j.,** formar parte del jurado. **j.-box,** tribuna del jurado, *f*

juryman /'dʒʊrimən/ *n* miembro del jurado, *m*

just /dʒʌst/ *a* justo; justiciero; exacto; fiel. **Peter the J.,** Pedro el justiciero

just /dʒʌst/ *adv* justamente, exactamente; precisamente; (scarcely) apenas; (almost) casi; (entirely) completamente; (simply) meramente, solamente, tan sólo; (newly) recién (followed by past part.), recientemente. **He only j. missed being run over,** Por poco le atropellan. **It is j. near,** Está muy cerca. **It is j. the same to me,** Me es completamente igual. **J. as he was leaving,** Cuando estaba a punto de marcharse, En el momento de marcharse. **Just as you arrive in Spain, you must...** Nada más llegar a España, tienes que... **That's j. it!** ¡Eso es! ¡Exactamente! **to have j.,** acabar de. **They have j. dined,** Acaban de cenar. **J. as you wish,** Como Vd. quiera. **j. at that moment,** precisamente en aquel momento. **j. by,** muy cerca; al lado. **j. now,** ahora mismo; hace poco; pronto, dentro de poco. **j. yet,** todavía. **They will not come j. yet,** No vendrán todavía. **Just looking** (browser to shopkeeper) Estoy viendo, Estamos viendo

justice /'dʒʌstɪs/ *n* justicia, *f;* (judge) juez, *m;* (magistrate) juez municipal, *m.* **to bring to j.,** llevar ante el juez (a). **to do j. to,** (a person) hacer justicia (a); (a meal) hacer honor (a). **to do oneself j.,** quedar bien

justifiable /'dʒʌstəˌfaiəbəl/ *a* justificable

justifiably /'dʒʌstəˌfaiəbli/ *adv* con justicia, justificadamente

justification /ˌdʒʌstəfɪ'keiʃən/ *n* justificación, *f*

justify /'dʒʌstəˌfai/ *vt* justificar, vindicar; (excuse) disculpar; *Print.* justificar. **to be justified (in),** tener derecho (a), tener motivo (para), tener razón (en)

justly /'dʒʌstli/ *adv* justamente; con justicia; con derecho; con razón; exactamente; debidamente

justness /'dʒstnɪs/ *n* justicia, *f;* exactitud, *f*

jute /dʒut/ *n* yute, *m*

jut (out) /dʒʌt/ *vi* salir, proyectar; sobresalir

juvenile /'dʒuvənl̩/ *a* juvenil; de la juventud; para la juventud; joven; de niños; para niños. —*n* joven, *mf.* **j. court,** tribunal de menores, *m.* **j. lead,** *Theat.* galancete, galán joven, *m.* **j. offender,** delincuente infantil, *m*

juxtapose /'dʒʌkstəˌpouz/ *vt* yuxtaponer

juxtaposition /ˌdʒʌkstəpə'zɪʃən/ *n* yuxtaposición, *f*

K

k /kei/ *n* (letter) ka, *f*
kaiser /ˈkaizər/ *n* káiser, emperador, *m.* **the K.** el emperador alemán, *m*
kaleidoscope /kəˈlaidəˌskoup/ *n* calidoscopio, *m*
kaleidoscopic /kəˌlaidəˈskɒpɪk/ *a* calidoscópico
kangaroo /ˌkæŋgəˈru/ *n* canguro, *m*
kaolin /ˈkeiəlɪn/ *n* caolín, *m*
kapok /ˈkeipɒk/ *n* miraguano, *m*
keel /kil/ *n* quilla, *f.* —*vt* carenar. **to k. over,** volcar; caer; *Naut.* zozobrar
keelson /ˈkɛlsən/ *n* sobrequilla, *f*
keen /kin/ *a* (of edges) afilado; agudo; penetrante; vivo; sutil; ardiente; celoso, entusiasta; mordaz; (desirous) ansioso; (of appetite) grande, bueno. **He is a k. tennis player,** Es tenista entusiasta. **Joan has a very k. ear,** Juana tiene un oído muy agudo. **I'm not very k. on apples,** No me gustan mucho las manzanas
keenly /ˈkinli/ *adv* agudamente; vivamente; (of feeling) hondamente; (of looking) atentamente
keenness /ˈkinnɪs/ *n* (of a blade) afiladura, *f;* agudeza, *f;* viveza, *f;* sutileza, *f;* perspicacia, *f;* (enthusiasm) entusiasmo, *m,* afición, *f;* (desire) ansia, *f*
keep /kip/ *vt* guardar; tener; que darse con; retener; conservar; mantener; (a shop, hotel, etc.) dirigir, tener; (a school) ser director de; (a promise, etc.) cumplir; (the law, etc.) observar, guardar; (celebrate) solemnizar; (a secret) guardar; (books, accounts, a house, in step) llevar; (sheep, etc., one's bed) guardar; (a city, etc.) defender; (domestic animals, cars, etc.) tener; (lodge) alojar; (detain) detener; (reserve) reservar; (cause) hacer. **They had kept this room for me,** Me habían reservado este cuarto. **Dorothy has kept the blue dress,** Dorotea se ha quedado con el vestido azul. **The government could not k. order,** El gobierno no sabía mantener el orden. **I did not know how to k. their attention,** No sabía retener su atención. **Carmen kept quiet,** Carmen guardó silencio, Carmen se calló. **Can you k. a secret?** ¿Sabes guardar un secreto? **to k. an appointment,** acudir a una cita. **to k. in repair,** conservar en buen estado. **to k. someone from doing something,** evitar que uno haga algo. **to k. someone waiting,** hacer que espere uno. **to k. something from someone,** ocultar algo de uno. **We were kept at it night and day,** Nos hacían trabajar día y noche. **I always k. it by me,** Lo tengo siempre a mi lado (or conmigo). **to k. away,** alejar; mantener a distancia; no dejar venir. **to k. back,** (a crowd, etc.) detener; cortar el paso (a); no dejar avanzar; (retain) guardar, retener; reservar; (tears, words) reprimir, contener; (evidence, etc.) callar, suprimir. **to k. down,** no dejar subir (a); sujetar; (a nation, etc.) oprimir, subyugar; (emotions) dominar; (prices, expenses) mantener bajo; (check) moderar, reprimir. **to k. in,** (feelings) contener; reprimir; (the house) hacer quedarse en casa, no dejar salir; (imprison) encerrar; (school) hacer quedar en la escuela (a). **to k. off,** alejar; tener a distancia (a); cerrar el paso (a), no dejar avanzar; no andar sobre; no tocar; (a subject) no tratar de, no discutir, no tocar. **K. your hands off!** ¡No toques! **to k. on,** guardar; retener; (eyes) fijar en, poner en. **to k. out,** no dejar entrar; excluir. **It is difficult to k. him out of trouble,** Es difícil de evitar que se meta en líos. **to k. to,** seguir; limitarse a; adherirse a; **K. to the Left,** «Tome su izquierda», **K. to the right,** «Tome su derecha»; (a path, etc.) seguir por; (one's bed) guardar; (fulfil) cumplir; (oblige) hacer, obligar. **to k. under,** subyugar, oprimir; dominar; controlar. **to k. up,** mantener; (appearances) guardar; conservar; persistir en; (prices) sostener; (in good repair) conservar en buen estado; (go on doing) continuar. **He kept me up late last night,** Anoche me entretuvo hasta muy tarde; Ayer me hizo trasnochar; Anoche me hizo velar. **to k. one's end up,** volver por sí, hacerse fuerte. **to k. up one's spirits,** no desanimarse
keep /kip/ *vi* quedar; (be) estar; (continue) seguir, continuar; mantenerse; (at home, etc.) quedarse, permanecer; (be accustomed) acostumbrar, soler; (persist) perseverar; (of food) conservarse fresco. **How is he keeping?** ¿Cómo está? **to k. in with someone,** cultivar a alguien. **to k. up with the times,** mantenerse al corriente. **to k. at,** seguir; persistir; perseverar; (pester) importunar. **John keeps at it,** Juan trabaja sin descansar. **to k. away,** mantenerse apartado; mantenerse a distancia; no acudir. **to k. back,** hacerse a un lado, apartarse, alejarse. **to k. down,** quedarse tumbado; seguir acurrucado; no levantarse; esconderse. **to k. from,** (doing something) guardarse de. **to k. off,** mantenerse a distancia. **If the storm keeps off,** Si no estalla una tempestad. **If the rain keeps off,** Si no empieza a llover, Si no hay lluvia. **to k. on,** continuar; seguir. **to k. straight on,** seguir derecho. **I'm tired, but I still k. on,** Estoy cansado, pero sigo trabajando. **to k. out,** quedarse fuera. **to k. out of,** (quarrels, trouble, etc.) no meterse en, evitar. **to k. out of sight,** no dejarse ver, no mostrarse, mantenerse oculto. **to k. together,** quedarse juntos; reunirse
keep /kip/ *n* (of a castle) mazmorra, *f;* (maintenance) subsistencia, *f;* comida, *f.* **for keeps,** para siempre jamás
keeper /ˈkipər/ *n* guarda, *mf;* (in a park, zoo, of a lunatic) guardián, *m;* (of a museum, etc.) director, *m;* (of animals) criador (-ra); (gamekeeper) guardabosque, *m;* (of a boardinghouse, shop, etc.) dueño (-ña); (of accounts, books) tenedor, *m.* **Am I my brother's k.?** ¿Soy yo responsable por mi hermano?
keeping /ˈkipɪŋ/ *n* guarda, *f;* conservación, *f;* protección, *f;* (of a rule) observación, *f;* (of an anniversary, etc.) celebración, *f;* (of a person) mantenimiento, *m.* **in k. with,** en armonía con; de acuerdo con. **out of k. with,** en desacuerdo con. **to be in safe k.,** estar en buenas manos; estar en un lugar seguro. **k. back,** retención, *f*
keepsake /ˈkipˌseik/ *n* recuerdo, *m*
keg /kɛg/ *n* barrilete, *m*
ken /kɛn/ *n* alcance de la vista, *m;* vista, *f;* comprensión, *f*
Kennedy Round /ˈkɛnɪdi/, **the** la serie Kénnedy, *f*
kennel /ˈkɛnl̩/ *n* (of a dog) perrera, *f;* (of hounds) jauría, *f;* (dwelling) cuchitril, *m;* (gutter) arroyo, *m.* **k. man,** perrero, *m*
kepi /ˈkeipi/ *n* quepis, *m*
Kepler /ˈkɛplər/ Keplero
kerchief /ˈkɜrtʃɪf/ *n* pañuelo, *m;* pañoleta, *f.* **brightly-colored k.,** pañuelo de hierbas, *m*
kernel /ˈkɜrnl̩/ *n* almendra, semilla, *f; Fig.* meollo, *m,* esencia, *f*
kerosene /ˈkɛrəˌsin/ *n* petróleo de lámpara, *m;* kerosén, *m*
ketchup /ˈkɛtʃəp/ *n* salsa de tomate y setas, *f*
kettle /ˈkɛtl̩/ *n* caldero, *m.* **pretty k. of fish,** olla de grillos, *f.* **k.-drum,** timbal, *m.* **k.-drum player,** timbalero, *m*
key /ki/ *n* llave, *f;* (*Fig. Archit. Mus.*) clave, *f;* (tone) tono, *m;* (of a piano, typewriter, etc.) tecla, *f; Mech.* chaveta, *f;* (of a wind instrument) pistón, *m;* (winged fruit) sámara, *f; Elec.* conmutador, *m.* **major (minor) key,** tono mayor (menor), *m.* **latch-key,** llave de la puerta, *f;* (Yale) llavín, *m.* **master key,** llave maestra, *f.* **skeleton key,** ganzúa, *f.* **He is all keyed up,** Tiene los nervios en punta. **key industry,** industria clave, *f.* **key man,** hombre indispensable, *m.* **key point,** punto estratégico, *m.* **key-ring,** llavero, *m.* **key signature,** *Mus.* clave, *f.* **key word,** palabra clave, *f*
keyboard /ˈkiˌbɔrd/ *n* teclado, *m*
keyhole /ˈkiˌhoul/ *n* ojo de la cerradura, *m.* **through the k.,** por el ojo de la cerradura
keynote /ˈkiˌnout/ *n Mus.* tónica, *f; Fig.* piedra clave, idea fundamental, *f*
keystone /ˈkiˌstoun/ *n* piedra clave, *f*
khaki /ˈkæki/ *n* caqui, *m*

kick /kɪk/ *vt* dar un puntapié (a); golpear; (a goal) chutar. —*vi* (of horses, etc.) dar coces, cocear; (of guns) recular. **to k. one's heels,** hacer tiempo. **to kick the bucket,** palmarla. **to k. up a row,** hacer un ruido de mil diablos; (quarrel) armar camorra. **to k. about,** dar patadas (a). **to k. away,** quitar con el pie; lanzar con el pie. **to k. off,** quitar con el pie; lanzar; sacudirse. **k.-off,** *n* golpe de salida, puntapié inicial, saque, *m.* **to k. out,** echar a puntapiés

kick /kɪk/ *n* puntapié, *m;* golpe, *m;* coz, *f;* (of guns) culatazo, *m.* **free k.,** golpe franco, *m*

kicking /'kɪkɪŋ/ *n* coces, *f pl*; acoceamiento, *m;* pataleo, *m;* golpeamiento, *m*

kid /kɪd/ *n* cabrito, *m,* chivo (-va); carne de cabrito, *f;* (leather) cabritilla, *f; Inf.* crío, *m.* **kid gloves,** guantes de cabritilla, *m pl*

kidnap /'kɪdnæp/ *vt* secuestrar

kidnapper /'kɪdnæpər/ *n* secuestrador (-ra); ladrón (-ona) de niños

kidnapping /'kɪdnæpɪŋ/ *n* secuestro, *m*

kidney /'kɪdni/ *n* riñón, *m; Fig.* especie, índole, *f.* **k.-bean,** (plant) judía, *f;* (fruit) habichuela, judía, *f,* fréjol, *m*

Kidron /'kidrən/ Cedrón, *m*

kill /kɪl/ *vt* matar; destruir; suprimir. **to k. off,** exterminar. **to k. time,** entretener el tiempo, pasarse las horas muertas. **to k. two birds with one stone,** matar dos pájaros de un tiro. **k.-joy,** aguafiestas, *mf*

killer /'kɪlər/ *n* matador (-ra); (murderer) asesino, *mf*

killing /'kɪlɪŋ/ *n* matanza, *f;* (murder) asesinato, *m.* —*a* matador; destructivo; (comic) cómico; ridículo, absurdo; (ravishing) irresistible

kiln /kɪl/ *n* horno de cerámica, horno, *m*

kilo /'kilou/ *n* kilo, *m*

kilocycle /'kɪlə,saikəl/ *n Elec.* kilociclo, *m*

kilogram /'kɪlə,græm/ *n* kilogramo, *m*

kiloliter /'kɪlə,litər/ *n* kilolitro, *m*

kilometer /kɪ'lɒmɪtər/ *n* kilómetro, *m*

kilometric /,kɪlə'mɛtrɪk/ *a* kilométrico

kilowatt /'kɪlə,wɒt/ *n Elec.* kilovatio, *m*

kilt /kɪlt/ *n* enagüillas, *f pl*

kimono /kə'mounə/ *n* quimono, *m*

kin /kɪn/ *n* parientes, *m pl*; familia, *f;* clase, especie, *f.* **the next of kin,** los parientes próximos, la familia

kind /kaind/ *n* género, *m,* clase, *f;* especie, *f; Inf.* tipo, *m.* **He is a queer k. of person,** Es un tipo muy raro. **What k. of cloth is it?** ¿Qué clase de tela es? **Nothing of the k!** ¡Nada de eso! **payment in k.,** pago en especie, *m*

kind /kaind/ *a* bondadoso, bueno; cariñoso, tierno; amable; favorable, propicio. **Will you be so k. as to...** Tenga Vd. la bondad de... **With k. regards,** Con un saludo afectuoso. **You have been very k. to her,** Vd. ha sido muy bueno para ella. **k.-hearted,** bondadoso. **k.-heartedness,** bondad, benevolencia, *f*

kindergarten /'kɪndər,gɑrtn̩/ *n* jardín de la infancia, kindergarten, *m*

kindle /'kɪndl̩/ *vt* encender; hacer arder; *Fig.* avivar. —*vi* prender, empezar a arder; encenderse; *Fig.* inflamarse

kindliness /'kaindlinɪs/ *n* bondad, *f*

kindling /'kɪndlɪŋ/ *n* encendimiento (del fuego), *m;* (wood) leña menuda, *f*

kindly /'kaindli/ *a* bondadoso; bueno; benévolo; propicio; favorable; (of climate) benigno. —*adv* con bondad, bondadosamente; fácilmente. **K. sit down,** Haga el favor de sentarse

kindness /'kaindnɪs/ *n* bondad, *f;* benevolencia, *f;* amabilidad, *f;* cariño, *m;* favor, *m,* atención, *f*

kindred /'kɪndrɪd/ *n* parentesco, *m;* parientes, *m pl*; familia, *f;* afinidad, *f,* *a* emparentado; hermano

king /kɪŋ/ *n* (ruler, important person, chess, cards) rey, *m;* (in draughts) dama, *f.* **king's evil,** escrófula, *f.* **k.-bolt,** perno real, *m.* **k.-craft,** arte de reinar, *m,* or *f.* **k.-cup,** *Bot.* botón de oro, *m.* **K.-of-Arms,** rey de armas, *m.* **k.-post,** pendolón, *m*

kingdom /'kɪŋdəm/ *n* reino, *m.* **animal k.,** reino animal, *m*

kingfisher /'kɪŋ,fɪʃər/ *n* martín pescador, alción, *m*

kink /kɪŋk/ *n* nudo, *m;* pliegue, *m;* (curl) rizo, *m; Fig.* peculiaridad, *f*

kinsfolk /'kɪnz,fouk/ *n* parientes, *m pl,* familia, *f*

kinship /'kɪnʃɪp/ *n* parentesco, *m;* afinidad, *f*

kinsman /'kɪnzmən/ *n* pariente, deudo, *m*

kinswoman /'kɪnz,wʊmən/ *n* parienta, *f*

kiosk /'kiɒsk/ *n* quiosco, *m*

kipper /'kɪpər/ *n* arenque ahumado, *m.* —*vt* ahumar

kiss /kɪs/ *n* beso, *m;* (in billiards) pelo, *m.* —*vt* besar; dar un beso (a); (of billiard balls) tocar. **to k. each other,** besarse. **k.-curl,** rizo de la sien, *m,* sortijilla, *f*

kit /kɪt/ *n* (tub) cubo, *m;* (for tools, etc.) cajita, caja, *f;* (soldier's) equipo, *m.* **kit-bag,** mochila, *f*

kitchen /'kɪtʃən/ *n* cocina, *f.* **k.-boy,** pinche (de cocina), *m.* **k.-garden,** huerta, *f.* **k.-maid,** fregona, *f.* **k.-range,** cocina económica, *f.* **k.-sink,** fregadero, *m.* **k.-stove,** horno de cocina, *m.* **k. utensils,** batería de cocina, *f*

kitchenette /,kɪtʃə'nɛt/ *n* cocinilla, *f*

kite /kait/ *n Ornith.* milano, *m;* cometa, pájara, *f.* **to fly a k.,** hacer volar una cometa. **box-k.,** cometa celular, *f*

kith and kin /kɪθ/ *n pl* parientes y amigos, *m pl*

kitten /'kɪtn̩/ *n* gatito (-ta). —*vi* (of a cat) parir

kittenish /'kɪtn̩ɪʃ/ *a* de gatito; juguetón

kitty /'kɪti/ *n* michito, *m;* (in card games) platillo, *m*

kleptomania /,klɛptə'meiniə/ *n* cleptomanía, *f*

kleptomaniac /,klɛptə'meiniæk/ *a* cleptómano. —*n* cleptómano (-na)

knack /næk/ *n* destreza, *f;* talento, *m;* (trick) truco, *m*

knapsack /'næp,sæk/ *n* mochila, *f; Mil.* alforja, *f*

knave /neiv/ *n* bellaco, truhán, tunante, *m;* (at cards) sota, *f*

knavery /'neivəri/ *n* bellaquería, truhanería, *f*

knavish /'neivɪʃ/ *a* de bribón; taimado, truhanesco

knead /nid/ *vt* amasar; (massage) sobar; *Fig.* formar

kneading /'nidɪŋ/ *n* amasijo, *m;* (massaging) soba, *f.* **k.-trough,** amasadera artesa *f*

knee /ni/ *n* rodilla, *f; Fig.* ángulo, codillo, *m.* **on bended k.,** de hinojos. **on one's knees,** de rodillas, arrodillado. **to go down on one's knees,** arrodillarse, ponerse de rodillas. **k.-breeches,** calzón corto, *m;* calzón ceñido, *m;* (Elizabethan) gregüescos, *m pl.* **k.-cap,** rótula, *f.* **k.-deep,** hasta las rodillas. **k.-joint,** articulación de la rodilla, *f; Mech.* junta de codillo, *f.* **k.-pad,** rodillera, *f*

kneel (down) /nil/ *vi* arrodillarse, hincarse de rodillas, ponerse de rodillas

kneeling /'nilɪŋ/ *a* arrodillado, de rodillas

knell /nɛl/ *n* toque de difuntos, tañido fúnebre, *m;* toque de campanas, *m; Fig.* muerte, *f.* —*vi* tocar a muerto. —*vt Fig.* anunciar, presagiar

knickerbockers /'nɪkər,bɒkərz/ *n pl* bragas, *f pl*; calzón corto, *m;* (women's) pantalones, *m pl*

knickknack /'nɪk,næk/ *n* chuchería, *f*

knife /naif/ *n* cuchillo, *m.* **to have one's k. in someone,** tener enemiga (a), querer mal (a). **war to the k.,** guerra a muerte, *f.* **k.-edge,** filo de cuchillo, *m;* fiel de soporte, *m.* **k. grinder,** amolador, *m.* **k.-handle,** mango de cuchillo, *m.* **k. thrust,** cuchillada, *f*

knife, fork, and spoon cuchara, tenedor, y cuchillo

knight /nait/ *n* caballero, *m;* (chess) caballo, *m.* —*vt* armar caballero, calzar la espuela; (in modern usage) dar el título de caballero. **untried k.,** caballero novel, *m.* **k. commander,** comendador, *m.* **k.-errant,** caballero andante, *m.* **k.-errantry,** caballería andante, *f.* **Knight of Labor,** Caballero del Trabajo *m.* **K. of the rueful countenance,** el caballero de la triste figura

knighthood /'naithʊd/ *n* caballería, *f;* (in modern usage) título de caballero, *m*

knightly /'naitli/ *a* caballeresco; de caballero; de caballería

knit /nɪt/ *vt* and *vi* hacer calceta, hacer media; juntar, ligar; unir. **Isabel is knitting me a jumper,** Isabel me hace un jersey de punto de media. **to k. one's brows,** fruncir el ceño

knitted /'nɪtɪd/ *a* de punto. **k. goods,** géneros de punto, *m pl*

knitter /'nɪtər/ *n* calcetero (-ra); (machine) máquina de hacer calceta, *f*

knitting /'nɪtɪŋ/ *n* acción de hacer calceta, *f;* trabajo de punto, *m,* labor de calceta, *f;* unión, *f.* **k.-machine,** máquina de hacer calceta, *f.* **k.-needle,** aguja de media, aguja de hacer calceta, *f*

knob /nɒb/ *n* protuberancia, *f;* (of a door, etc.) perilla, borlita, *f;* (ornamental) bellota, *f;* (of sugar) terrón, *m;* (of a stick) puño, *m*

knock /nɒk/ *n* golpe, *m;* choque, *m;* (with a knocker) aldabada, *f*

knock /nɒk/ *vt* golpear; chocar (contra). —*vi* llamar a la puerta; (of an engine) picar. **to k. one's head against,** chocar con la cabeza contra, dar con la cabeza contra. **to k. about,** *vt* pegar; aporrear. —*vi* viajar; vagar, rodar; callejear. **to k. against,** golpear contra; chocar contra. **to k. down,** derribar; (of vehicles) atropellar; (houses, etc.) demoler; (an argument, etc.) destruir; (a tender, etc.) rebajar; (of an auctioneer) rematar al mejor postor. **to k. in,** (nails, etc.) clavar. **to k. into one another,** toparse. **to k. off,** hacer caer; sacudir; quitar; (from price) descontar; (from speed, etc.) reducir; (finish) terminar pronto; (runs in cricket) hacer. **to k. out,** (remove) quitar; (boxing) dejar fuera de combate, noquear; (*Fig.* stun) atontar; (an idea, etc.) bosquejar. **to k. over,** volcar. **to k. up,** hacer saltar; (call) llamar; (runs at cricket) hacer; (tire) agotar, rendir; (building) construir toscamente. **to k. up against,** chocar contra; tropezar con. **k.-kneed,** *a* patiabierto. **k.-out,** "knock-out," *m*

knocker /'nɒkər/ *n* (on a door) aldaba, *f.* **k.-up,** despertador, *m*

knocking /'nɒkɪŋ/ *n* golpes, *m pl,* golpeo, *m;* (with a knocker) aldabeo, *m.* **k. over,** vuelco, *m;* (by a vehicle) atropello, *m*

knoll /noul/ *n* altillo, otero, *m*

knot /nɒt/ *n* nudo, *m;* (bow) lazo, *m;* (of hair) moño, *m; Naut.* nudo, *m,* milla náutica, *f;* (of people) corrillo, grupo, *m;* (on timber) nudo, *m.* —*vt* anudar. —*vi* hacer nudos; enmarañarse. **to tie a k.,** hacer un nudo

knotted /'nɒtɪd/ *a* nudoso

knotty /'nɒti/ *a* nudoso; *Fig.* intrincado, difícil, complicado. **a k. problem,** problema espinoso

know /nou/ *vt* conocer; saber; (understand) comprender; (recognize) reconocer. **I k. her very well by sight,** La conozco muy bien de vista. **John knows Latin,** Juan sabe latín. **How can I k.?** ¿Cómo lo voy a saber yo? **I knew you at once,** Te reconocí en seguida. **They always k. best,** Siempre tienen razón. **Did you k. about Philip?** ¿Has oído lo de Felipe? **to be in the k.,** estar bien informado, saber de buena tinta. **to get to k.,** (a person) llegar a conocer, trabar amistad con. **to make known,** dar a conocer; manifestar. **Who knows?** ¿Quién sabe? **to k. by heart,** saber de coro. **to k. how,** (to do something) saber. **to k. oneself,** conocerse a sí mismo. **k.-it-all,** sabelotodo, *mf,* marisabidilla, *f*

knowing /'nouɪŋ/ *a* inteligente; malicioso; (of animals) sabio. **There is no k.,** No hay modo de saberlo. **worth k.,** digno de saberse

knowingly /'nouɪŋli/ *adv* a sabiendas, de intento; conscientemente; (cleverly) hábilmente; (with look, etc.) de un aire malicioso

knowledge /'nɒlɪdʒ/ *n* conocimiento, *m.* **To the best of my k. the book does not exist,** El libro no existe que yo sepa. **He has a thorough k. of...,** Conoce a fondo... **lack of k.,** ignorancia, *f.* **He did it without my k.,** Lo hizo sin que lo supiera yo. **It is a matter of common k. that...** Es notorio que...

knowledgeable /'nɒlɪdʒəbəl/ *a* sabedor

known /noun/ *a* conocido

knuckle /'nʌkəl/ *n* (of a finger) nudillo, *m,* articulación del dedo, *f;* (of meat) jarrete, *m.* **He knuckled down to his work,** Se puso a trabajar con ahínco. **to k. under,** someterse. **k.-duster,** rompecabezas, *m*

kopeck /'koupɛk/ *n* copec, *f*

Koran /kə'rɑn/ *n* Corán, Alcorán, *m*

Korea /kə'riə/ Corea, *f*

kosher /'kouʃər/ *a* cosher; (slang) genuino

kowtow /'kau'tau/ *vi* saludar humildemente; *Fig.* bajar la cerviz

Kremlin /'krɛmlɪn/ *n* Kremlín, *m*

kudos /'kudouz/ *n* prestigio, *m,* gloria, *f*

Kurdish /'kɜrdɪʃ/ *a* curdo

kyrie eleison /'kɪəri,ei ɛ'leiə,sɔn/ *n* kirieleisón, *m*

L

l /ɛl/ *n* (letter) ele, *f*
la /lɑ/ *n Mus.* la, *m*
label /ˈleibəl/ *n* etiqueta, (on a garment), rótula, *m,* (on a can), *f;* (on a museum specimen, etc.) letrero, *m; Fig.* calificación, *f.* —*vt* poner etiqueta en; marcar, rotular; *Fig.* calificar, designar, clasificar
labial /ˈleibiəl/ *a* labial. —*n* letra labial, *f*
labor /ˈleibər/ *n* trabajo, *m;* labor, *f;* fatiga, pena, *f;* clase obrera, *f;* (manual workers) mano de obra, *f;* (effort) esfuerzo, *m;* (of childbirth) dolores de parto, *m pl.* —*vi* trabajar; (strive) esforzarse, afanarse; (struggle) forcejar, luchar; (try) procurar, tratar de; avanzar con dificultad; (in childbirth) estar de parto. —*vt* elaborar; pulir, perfeccionar. **to l. under,** sufrir; tener que luchar contra. **hard l.,** trabajo arduo, *m; Law.* trabajos forzosos, *m pl,* presidio, *m.* **Ministry of L.,** Ministerio de Trabajo, *m.* **to be in l.,** estar de parto. **to l. in vain,** trabajar en balde, arar en el mar. **to l. under a delusion,** estar en el error, estar equivocado. **L. Exchange,** Bolsa de Trabajo, *f.* **l. leader,** dirigente sindical, *m.* **L. party,** partido laborista, partido obrero, *m.* **l. question,** cuestión obrera, *f;* (domestic) problema del servicio, *m.* **l.-saving,** *a* que ahorra trabajo. **l. union,** sindicato, *m*
laboratory /ˈlæbrəˌtɔri/ *n* laboratorio, *m*
labored /ˈleibərd/ *a* (of style) premioso, artificial; forzado; (of breathing) fatigoso; (slow) torpe, lento
laborer /ˈleibərər/ *n* obrero, *m;* (on the land) labrador, labriego, *m;* (on the roads, etc.) peón, *m;* (by the day) jornalero, *m*
laborious /ləˈbɔriəs/ *a* laborioso; arduo, difícil, penoso
laboriously /ləˈbɔriəsli/ *adv* laboriosamente; con dificultad, penosamente
laboriousness /ləˈbɔriəsnɪs/ *n* laboriosidad, *f;* dificultad, *f*
Labrador dog /ˈlæbrəˌdɔr/ *n* perro de Labrador, *m*
labyrinth /ˈlæbərɪnθ/ *n* laberinto, *m*
labyrinthine /ˌlæbəˈrɪnθɪn/ *a* laberíntico; intrincado
lace /leis/ *n* (of shoes, corsets, etc.) cordón, *m;* (tape) cinta, *f;* encaje, *m;* (narrow, for trimming) puntilla, *f;* (of gold or silver) galón, *m.* —*vt* and *vi* (shoes, etc.) atarse los cordones; (trim) guarnecer con encajes, etc.; *Fig.* ornar; (a drink) echar (coñac, etc.) en. **blond l.,** blonda, *f.* **gold l.,** galón de oro, *m.* **point l.,** encaje de aguja, *m.* **l. curtain,** cortina de encaje, *f;* (of net) visillo, *m.* **l. maker** or **seller,** encajera, *f.* **l. making,** obra de encaje, *f.* **l.-pillow,** almohadilla para encajes, *f.* **l. shoes,** zapatos con cordones, *m pl*
lacerate /ˈlæsəˌreit/ *vt* lacerar
laceration /ˌlæsəˈreiʃən/ *n* laceración, *f*
lachrymal /ˈlækrəməl/ *a* lagrimal, lacrimal
lachrymose /ˈlækrəˌmous/ *a* lacrimoso
lack /læk/ *n* falta, *f.* **l. of evidence,** falta de pruebas, *f;* carestía, escasez, *f;* (absence) ausencia, *f;* (need) necesidad, *f.* —*vt* carecer de; no tener; necesitar. —*vi* hacer falta; necesitarse. **to l. confidence in oneself,** no tener confianza en sí mismo, carecer de confianza en sí mismo. **l.-luster,** (of eyes) apagado, mortecino. **l. of evidence,** falta de pruebas, *f*
lackadaisical /ˌlækəˈdeizɪkəl/ *a* lánguido; indiferente; (dreamy) ensimismado, distraído
lackey /ˈlæki/ *n* lacayo, *m*
laconic /ləˈkɒnɪk/ *a* lacónico
lacquer /ˈlækər/ *n* laca, *f, vt* dar laca (a), barnizar con laca. **gold l.,** sisa dorada, *f.* **l. work,** laca, *f*
lacquering /ˈlækərɪŋ/ *n* barnizado de laca, *m;* laca, capa de barniz de laca, *f*
lactate /ˈlækteit/ *n* lactato, *m, vi* lactar
lactation /lækˈteiʃən/ *n* lactancia, *f*
lacteal /ˈlæktiəl/ *a* lácteo
lactic /ˈlæktɪk/ *a* láctico
lactose /ˈlæktous/ *n* lactosa, *f*
lacuna /ləˈkyunə/ *n* laguna, *f*
lacy /ˈleisi/ *a* de encaje; parecido a encaje; *Fig.* transparente, etéreo
lad /læd/ *n* muchacho, joven, mozalbete, *m;* zagal, *m;* (stable, etc.) mozo, *m.* **He's some l.!** ¡Qué tío que es! **l. of the village,** chulo, *m*
ladder /ˈlædər/ *n* escalera de mano, *f; Naut.* escala, *f;* (in a stocking, etc.) carrera, *f.* **companion l.,** escala de toldilla, *f.* **to l. one's stocking,** escurrirse un punto de las medias
Ladies and gentlemen /ˈleidiz/ *n pl* Señoras y señores, Señoras y caballeros. **ladies' man,** hombre de salón, Perico entre ellas, mujeriego, *m*
lading /ˈleidɪŋ/ *n* flete, *m,* carga, *f*
ladle /ˈleidl̩/ *n* cucharón, cazo, *m.* —*vt* servir con cucharón; (a boat) achicar; *Inf.* distribuir, repartir
lady /ˈleidi/ *n* dama, *f;* señora, *f;* (English title) milady, *f;* (woman) mujer, *f.* **to be a l.,** ser una señora. **leading l.,** *Theat.* dama primera, *f.* **Our L.,** Nuestra Señora. **young l.,** señorita, *f; Inf.* novia, *f.* **lady's maid,** doncella, *f.* **l. of the house,** señora de la casa, *f.* **l. bug,** *Ent.* catalina mariquita, vaca de San Antonio, *f.* **L. Chapel,** capilla de la Virgen, *f.* **L. Day,** día de la Anunciación (de Nuestra Señora), *m.* **l.-help,** asistenta, *f.* **l.-in-waiting,** dama de servicio, *f.* **l.-killer,** ladrón de corazones, castigador, tenorio, *m.* **l.-love,** querida, amada, *f.* **l. mayoress,** alcaldesa, *f*
ladylike /ˈleidiˌlaik/ *a* de dama; elegante; distinguido; bien educado; delicado; (of men) afeminado
ladyship /ˈleidiˌʃɪp/ *n* señoría, *f.* **Your L.,** Su Señoría
lag /læg/ *vt* recubrir; aislar. —*vi* retrasarse; quedarse atrás; ir (or andar) despacio; rezagarse; *Naut.* roncear. —*n* retraso, *m; Mech.* retardación de movimiento, *f*
laggard /ˈlægərd/ *n* holgazán (-ana), haragán (-ana)
lagoon /ləˈgun/ *n* laguna, *f*
laid /leid/ *past part* of verb **to lay. l. up,** (ill) enfermo; *Naut.* inactivo; (of cars, etc.) fuera de circulación
lair /lɛər/ *n* cubil, *m;* guarida, madriguera, *f*
laity /ˈleiɪti/ *n* legos, *m pl*
lake /leik/ *n* lago, *m;* (pigment) laca, *f.* **small l.,** laguna, *f.* **l. dwelling,** vivienda palustre, *f*
lama /ˈlɑmə/ *n* lama, *m*
lamb /læm/ *n* cordero (-ra). —*vi* parir corderos. **lamb's wool,** lana de cordero. *f*
lambent /ˈlæmbənt/ *a* ondulante, vacilante; centelleante
lamblike /ˈlæmˌlaik/ *a* manso como un cordero; inocente
lambskin /ˈlæmˌskɪn/ *n* corderina, piel de cordero, *f*
lame /leim/ *a* estropeado, lisiado; (in the feet) cojo; (of meter) que cojea, malo; (of arguments) poco convincente; frívolo, flojo. —*vt* lisiar; hacer cojo. **l. excuse,** pretexto frívolo. **to be l.,** (in the feet) (permanently) ser cojo; (temporarily) estar cojo
lamely /ˈleimli/ *adv* cojeando, con cojera; *Fig.* sin convicción; mal
lameness /ˈleimnɪs/ *n* cojera, *f;* falta de convicción, *f*
lament /ləˈmɛnt/ *n* lamento, *m;* queja, lamentación, *f.* —*vi* lamentarse; quejarse. —*vt* lamentar, deplorar, llorar
lamentable /ləˈmɛntəbəl/ *a* lamentable, deplorable; lastimero
lamentation /ˌlæmənˈteiʃən/ *n* lamentación, *f,* lamento, *m.* **Book of Lamentations,** Libro de los lamentos, *m*
lamenting /ləˈmɛntɪŋ/ *n* lamentación, *f*
lamina /ˈlæmənə/ *n* lámina, *f*
laminate /ˈlæməˌneit/ *a* laminado, laminar. —*vt* laminar
lamp /læmp/ *n* lámpara, *f;* (on vehicles, trains, ships and in the street) farol, *m;* luz, *f;* (oil) candil, *m,* lámpara de aceite, *f.* **safety-l.,** lámpara de seguridad, lámpara de los mineros, *f.* **street l.,** farol (de las calles), *m.* **l.-black,** negro de humo, *m.* **l.-chimney,** tubo de una lámpara, *m.* **l. factory** or **shop,** lamparería, *f.* **l.-holder,** portalámpara, *f.* **l.-lighter,**

farolero, lamparero, *m.* **l.-post,** farola, *f.* **l.-shade,** pantalla (de lámpara,) *f.* **l. stand,** pie de lámpara, *m*
lamplight /'læmp,lait/ *n* luz de la lámpara, *f;* luz artificial, *f.* **in the l.,** a la luz de la lámpara; en luz artificial
lampoon /læm'pun/ *n* pasquinada, *f,* pasquín, *m, vt* pasquinar, satirizar
lampooner /læm'punər/ *n* escritor (-ra) de pasquinadas, libelista, *m*
lamprey /'læmpri/ *n* lamprea, *f*
lance /læns/ *n* lanza, *f;* (soldier) lancero, *m.* —*vt* alancear; *Med.* lancinar. **l. in rest,** lanza en ristre, *f.* **l. thrust,** lanzada, *f.* **l.-corporal,** soldado de primera clase, *m*
lancer /'lænsər/ *n Mil.* lancero, *m; pl* lancers, (dance and music) lanceros, *m pl*
lancet /'lænsɪt/ *n* apostemero, *m,* lanceta, *f.* **l. arch,** arco puntiagudo, *m*
land /lænd/ *n* tierra, *f;* terreno, *m;* (country) país, *m;* (region) región, *f;* territorio, *m;* (estate) bienes raíces, *m pl,* tierras, fincas, *f pl.* —*vt* desembarcar; echar en tierra; (*Fig.* place) poner; *Inf.* dejar plantado (con); (obtain) obtener; (a fish) sacar del agua; (a blow) dar (un golpe); (leave) dejar. —*vi* desembarcar; saltar en tierra; (of a plane) aterrizar; (arrive) llegar; (fall) caer. **cultivated l.,** tierras cultivadas, *f pl.* **dry l.,** (not sea) tierra firme, *f.* **native l.,** patria, *f;* suelo natal, *m.* **on l.,** en tierra. **to see how the l. lies,** *Fig.* tantear el terreno. **l. of milk and honey,** jauja, *f,* paraíso, *m.* **l. of promise,** tierra de promisión, *f.* **l. agent,** procurador de fincas, *m.* **l. breeze,** brisa de tierra, *f.* **l. forces,** fuerzas terrestres, *f pl.* **l. law,** leyes agrarias, *f pl.* **l.-locked,** cercado de tierra, mediterráneo **l.-lubber,** marinero de agua dulce, *m.* **l. mine,** mina terrestre, *f.* **l. surveying,** agrimensura, *f.* **l. surveyor,** agrimensor, *m.* **l. tax,** contribución territorial, *f*
landau /'lændɔ/ *n* landó, *m*
landed /'lændɪd/ *a* hacendado. **l. gentry,** hacendados, terratenientes, *m pl.* **l. property,** bienes raíces, *m pl*
landfall /'lænd,fɔl/ *n* derrumbamiento de tierras, *m*
landing /'lændɪŋ/ *n* desembarque, desembarco, *m;* (landing place) desembarcadero, *m; Aer.* aterrizaje, *m;* (of steps) descanso, rellano, *m,* mesa, mesilla, *f.* **forced l.,** aterrizaje forzoso, *m.* **l. certificate,** *Com.* tornaguía, *f.* **l. craft,** barcaza de desembarco, *f.* **l. field,** campo de aterrizaje, *m,* pista de vuelo, *f.* **l.-net,** salabardo, *m.* **l. party,** trozo de abordaje, *m.* **l. signal,** *Aer.* señal de aterrizaje, *f.* **l.-stage,** desembarcadero, *m;* (jetty) atracadero, *m*
landlady /'lænd,leidi/ *n* patrona, huéspeda, *f*
landlord /'lænd,lɔrd/ *n* (of houses, land) propietario, *m;* hotelero, patrón, *m*
landmark /'lænd,mɑrk/ *n* (of a hill or mountain) punto destacado, *m;* lugar conocido, *m;* característica, *f; Fig.* monumento, *m*
landmass /'lænd,mæs/ *n* unidad territorial, *f*
landowner /'lænd,ounər/ *n* hacendado, terrateniente, *m*
landscape /'lænd,skeip/ *n* paisaje, *m;* perspectiva, *f.* **l. gardener,** arquitecto de jardines, *m.* **l. painter,** paisajista, *mf*
landslide /'lænd,slaid/ *n* desprendimiento de tierras, *m; Fig.* cambio brusco de la opinión pública, *m*
landward /'lændwərd/ *adv* hacia tierra
lane /lein/ *n* vereda, senda, *f;* (of traffic) carril, *m,* (Argentina, Spain), línea, *f*
language /'læŋgwɪdʒ/ *n* lenguaje, *m,* lengua, *f,* idioma, *m.* **modern l.,** lengua viva, *f.* **strong l.,** palabras mayores, *f pl*
languid /'læŋgwɪd/ *a* lánguido
languidness /'læŋgwɪdnɪs/ *n* languidez, *f*
languish /'læŋgwɪʃ/ *vi* languidecer
languishing /'læŋgwɪʃɪŋ/ *a* lánguido; amoroso, sentimental
languishingly /'læŋgwɪʃɪŋli/ *adv* lánguidamente; amorosamente
languor /'læŋgər/ *n* languidez, *f*
languorous /'læŋgərəs/ *a* lánguido
languorously /'læŋgərəsli/ *adv* con langor
lank /læŋk/ *a* flaco, descarnado, alto y delgado; (of hair) lacio
lankiness /'læŋkinɪs/ *n* flacura, *f*
lanky /'læŋki/ *a* larguirucho, descarnado
lanolin /'lænḷɪn/ *n* lanolina, *f*
lantern /'læntərn/ *n* linterna, *f;* (*Naut.* and of a lighthouse) farol, *m; Archit.* linterna, *f;* (small) farolillo, *m.* **dark l.,** linterna sorda, *f.* **magic l.,** linterna mágica, *f.* **l.-jawed,** carilargo. **l. maker,** farolero, *m.* **l. slide,** diapositiva, *f*
lap /læp/ *n* regazo, *m;* falda, *f;* (knees) rodillas, *f pl;* (lick) lamedura, *f;* (of water) murmurio, susurro, *m;* (in a race) vuelta, *f;* (stage) etapa, *f.* —*vt* (wrap) envolver; (cover) cubrir; (fold) plegar; (lick) lamer; (swallow) tragar. —*vi* (overlap) traslaparse; estar replegado; (lick) lamer; (of water) murmurar, susurrar, besar. **l.-dog,** perro de faldas, perro faldero, *m*
lapel /lə'pɛl/ *n* solapa, *f*
lapidary /'læpɪ,dɛri/ *a* lapidario
lapidate /'læpɪ,deit/ *vt* lapidar
lapis lazuli /'læp'ɪs læzʊli/ *n* lapislázuli, *m*
Lapland /'læp,lænd/ Laponia, *f*
Laplander /'læp,lændər/ *n* lapón (-ona)
lapping /'læpɪŋ/ *n* (licking) lamedura, *f;* (of water) murmurio, susurro, chapaleteo, *m*
lapse /læps/ *n* lapso, *m;* (fault) desliz, *m,* falta, *f;* (of time) transcurso, intervalo, *m;* (fall) caída, *f;* (*Law.* termination) caducidad, *f.* **lapse (into),** *vi* caer (en), recaer (en), reincidir (en); volver a, caer de nuevo (en); (*Law.* cease) caducar; (*Law.* pass to) pasar (a); dejar de existir, desaparecer. **after the l. of three days,** después de tres días, al cabo de tres días. **with the l. of years,** en el transcurso de los años
larboard /'lɑr,bɔrd/ *n* babor, *m, a* de babor
larceny /'lɑrsəni/ *n* latrocinio, *m*
lard /lɑrd/ *n* manteca, *f;* lardo, *m.* —*vt Cul.* lardear, mechar; *Fig.* sembrar (con), adornar (con)
larder /'lɑrdər/ *n* despensa, *f*
large /lɑrdʒ/ *a* grande; grueso; amplio; vasto, extenso; (wide) ancho; considerable; (in number) numeroso; (main, chief) principal; liberal; magnánimo. **at l.,** en libertad, suelto. **on the l. side,** algo grande. **l.-headed,** cabezudo. **l.-hearted,** que tiene un gran corazón, magnánimo. **l. mouth,** boca grande, boca rasgada, *f.* **l.-nosed,** narigudo. **l. scale,** en gran escala. **l.-sized,** de gran tamaño. **l.-toothed,** dentudo, que tiene dientes grandes. **l. type,** letras grandes, *f pl*
largely /'lɑrdʒli/ *adv* grandemente; en gran manera; en so mayor parte, considerablemente; muy; ampliamente; liberalmente; extensamente
largeness /'lɑrdʒnɪs/ *n* gran tamaño, *m;* (of persons) gran talle, *m;* amplitud, *f;* vastedad, extensión, *f;* (width) anchura, *f;* liberalidad, *f;* (generosity) magnanimidad, *f;* grandeza de ánimo, *f*
larger /'lɑrdʒər/ *a compar* más grande, etc. See **large.** **to grow l.,** crecer, aumentarse. **to make l.,** hacer más grande; aumentar
largesse /lɑr'dʒɛs/ *n* liberalidad, *f*
largo /'lɑrgou/ *n* and *adv Mus.* largo, *m*
lariat /'læriət/ *n* lazo, *m*
lark /lɑrk/ *n* alondra, *f;* (spree) juerga, *f;* (joke) risa, *f.* **to rise with the l.,** levantarse con las gallinas
larva /'lɑrvə/ *n* larva, *f*
laryngeal /lə'rɪndʒiəl/ *a* laríngeo
laryngitis /,lærən'dʒaitɪs/ *n* laringitis, *f*
larynx /'lærɪŋks/ *n* laringe, *f*
lascivious /lə'sɪviəs/ *a* lascivo, lujurioso
lasciviousness /lə'sɪviəsnɪs/ *n* lujuria, lascivia, *f*
lash /læʃ/ *n* (thong) tralla, *f;* (whip) látigo, *m;* (blow) latigazo, *m,* azote, *m,* (of the eye) pestaña, *f.* —*vt* dar latigazos (a); azotar; (of waves) romper contra; (of hail, rain) azotar; (excite) provocar; (the tail) agitar (la cola); (scold) fustigar; (fasten) sujetar, atar; *Naut.* trincar. **to l. out,** (of horses, etc.) dar coces; (in words) prorrumpir (en)
lashing /'læʃɪŋ/ *n* (whipping) azotamiento, *m;* (tying) ligadura, atadura, *f;* amarradura, *f*
lass /læs/ *n* muchacha, chica, mozuela, *f;* zagala, *f;* niña, *f*
lassitude /'læsɪ,tud/ *n* lasitud, *f*
lasso /'læsou/ *n* lazo, *m,* mangana, *f, vt* lazar, manganear
last /læst/ *vi* durar; subsistir, conservarse; continuar
last /læst/ *a* último; (with month, week, etc.) pasado;

(supreme) extremo, (el) mayor. —*adv* al fin; finalmente; por último; después de todos; por última vez; la última vez. —*n* el, *m,* (*f,* la) último (-ma); los últimos, *m pl,* (*f pl,* las últimas); (end) fin, *m;* (for shoes) horma, *f.* **at l.,** en fin; por fin, a la postre. **at the l. moment,** a última hora. **I have not been there these l. five years,** Hace cinco años que no voy allá. **John spoke l.,** Juan habló el último. **She came at l.,** Por fin llegó. **to the l.,** hasta el fin. **l. but one,** penúltimo (-ma). **l. hope,** última esperanza, *f;* último recurso, *m.* **l. kick,** *Inf.* último suspiro, *m.* **l. night,** anoche. **l. week,** la semana pasada

lasting /ˈlæstɪŋ/ *a* permanente, perdurable; duradero; constante; (of colours) sólido

lastingness /ˈlæstɪŋnɪs/ *n* permanencia, *f;* duración, *f*

lastly /ˈlæstli/ *adv* en conclusión, por fin, finalmente, por último

latch /lætʃ/ *n* pestillo, *m, vt* cerrar con pestillo. **l.-key,** llave de la puerta, *f;* (Yale) llavín, *m*

late /leit/ *a* tarde; tardío; (advanced) avanzado; (last) último; reciente; (dead) difunto; (former) antiguo, ex...; (new) nuevo. —*adv* tarde. **Better l. than never,** Más vale tarde que nunca. **Helen arrived l.,** Elena llegó tarde. **The train arrived five minutes l.,** El tren llegó con cinco minutos de retraso. **He keeps l. hours,** Se acuesta muy tarde, Se acuesta a las altas horas de la noche (*Inf.* a las tantas). **of l.,** últimamente. **to grow l.,** hacerse tarde. **l.-eighteenth-century poetry,** la poesía de fines del siglo diez y ocho; llorado, malogrado (e.g. *the l. Mrs. Smith,* la llorada Sra. Smith, la malograda Sra. Smith);

lateen /læˈtin/ *a* latino. **l. sail,** vela latina, *f*

lately /ˈleitli/ *adv* recientemente; últimamente, hace poco

latency /ˈleitn̩si/ *n* estado latente, *m*

lateness /ˈleitnɪs/ *n* lo tarde; lo avanzado; retraso, *m.* **the l. of the hour,** la hora avanzada

latent /ˈleitn̩t/ *a* latente

later /ˈleitər/ *a* más tarde; posterior; más reciente. —*adv* más tarde; (afterwards) luego, después; posteriormente. **sooner or l.,** tarde o temprano. **l. on,** más tarde

lateral /ˈlætərəl/ *a* lateral, ladero

late registration *n* matrícula tardía, *f*

latest /ˈleitɪst/ *a* and *adv superl* último; más reciente, etc. See **late. at the l.,** a lo más tarde, a más tardar. **l. fashion,** última moda, *f.* **l. news,** últimas noticias, *f pl*; novedad, *f*

latex /ˈleitɛks/ *n* (*Bot. Chem.*) látex, *m*

lath /læθ/ *n* listón, *m.* **to be as thin as a l.,** no tener más que el pellejo, estar en los huesos

lathe /leið/ *n* torno, *m*

lather /ˈlæðər/ *n* espuma de jabón, *f,* jabonaduras, *f pl*; (of sweat) espuma, *f.* —*vt* enjabonar; *Inf.* zurrar. —*vi* hacer espuma

lathering /ˈlæðərɪŋ/ *n* jabonadura, *f; Inf.* tunda, zurra, *f*

Latin /ˈlætn̩/ *n* latín, *m, a* latino. **Low L.,** bajo latín, *m.* **L.-American,** *a* latinoamericano. —*n* latinoamericano (-na)

Latinism /ˈlætn̩ˌɪzəm/ *n* latinismo, *m*

Latinist /ˈlætn̩ɪst/ *n* latinista, *mf*

latitude /ˈlætɪˌtud/ *n* latitud, *f;* libertad, *f*

latitudinal /ˌlætɪˈtudn̩l/ *a* latitudinal

latrine /ləˈtrin/ *n* letrina, *f*

latter /ˈlætər/ *a* más reciente; último, posterior; moderno. **the l.,** éste, *m;* ésta, *f;* esto, *neut;* éstos, *m pl*; éstas, *f pl.* **the l. half,** la segunda mitad. **toward the l. end of the year,** hacia fines del año. **L.-Day Saint,** santo de los últimos días *m,* santa de los últimos días, *f*

latterly /ˈlætərli/ *adv* recientemente, últimamente; en los últimos tiempos; hacia el fin

lattice /ˈlætɪs/ *n* rejilla, *f;* celosía, reja, *f.* —*vt* poner celosía (a); entrelazar. **l.-work,** enrejado, *m*

latticed /ˈlætɪst/ *a* (of windows, etc.) con reja

Latvia /ˈlætviə/ Latvia, Letonia, *f*

Latvian /ˈlætviən/ *a* latvio. —*n* latvio (-ia)

laud /lɔd/ *n* alabanza, *f; pl.* **lauds,** *Eccl.* laudes, *f pl.* —*vt* alabar, elogiar

laudability /ˌlɔdəˈbɪlɪti/ *n* mérito, *m,* lo meritorio

laudable /ˈlɔdəbəl/ *a* loable, meritorio

laudably /ˈlɔdəbli/ *adv* laudablemente

laudatory /ˈlɔdəˌtɔri/ *a* laudatorio

laugh /læf/ *n* risa, *f;* carcajada, *f.* —*vi* reír; (smile) sonreír; reírse. **loud l.,** risa estrepitosa, *f.* **to l. in a person's face,** reírsele a uno en las barbas. **to l. loudly,** reírse a carcajadas. **to l. to oneself,** reírse interiormente. **to l. to scorn,** poner en ridículo. **to l. at,** reírse de; burlarse de, ridiculizar

laughable /ˈlæfəbəl/ *a* risible, irrisible, ridículo, absurdo

laughing /ˈlæfɪŋ/ *a* risueño, alegre; (absurd) risible, *n* risa, *f.* **to burst out l.,** reírse a carcajadas. **l.-gas,** gas hilarante, *m.* **l.-stock,** hazmerreír, *m*

laughingly /ˈlæfɪŋli/ *adv* riendo

laughter /ˈlæftər/ *n* risa, *f;* (in a report) risas, *f pl.* **burst of l.,** carcajada, *f.* **to burst into l.,** soltar el trapo, reírse a carcajadas, desternillarse de risa

launch /lɔntʃ/ *n* botadura (de un buque), *f;* lancha, *f;* bote, *m;* canoa, *f.* —*vt* (throw) lanzar; (a blow) asestar; (a vessel) botar, echar al agua; (begin) iniciar, dar principio a; (make) hacer. **to l. an offensive,** *Mil.* emprender una ofensiva. **to l. into,** arrojarse en; entregarse a. **motor l.,** canoa automóvil, *f.* **steam l.,** bote de vapor, *m*

launching /ˈlɔntʃɪŋ/ *n* botadura (de un buque), *f;* (throwing) lanzamiento, *m;* (beginning) iniciación, *f;* inauguración, *f;* (of a loan, etc.) emisión, *f.* **l. site,** rampa, *f*

launder /ˈlɔndər/ *vt* lavar y planchar (ropa)

laundress /ˈlɔndrɪs/ *n* lavandera, *f*

laundromat /ˈlɔndrəˌmæt/ *n* lavandería automática, *f*

laundry /ˈlɔndri/ *n* lavadero, *m,* lavandería, *f;* (washing) colada, *f; Inf.* ropa lavada or ropa para lavar, *f.* **l. -man,** lavandero, *m*

laureate /ˈlɔriɪt/ *a* laureado. —*n* poeta laureado, *m*

laurel /ˈlɔrəl/ *n* laurel, cerezo, *m, a* láureo. **to crown with l.,** laurear. **l. wreath,** lauréola, *f*

Lausanne /louˈzæn/ Lausana, Losana, *f*

lava /ˈlɑvə/ *n* lava, *f*

lavabo /ləˈveibou/ *n* lavabo, *m; Eccl.* lavatorio, *m*

lavatory /ˈlævəˌtɔri/ *n* lavabo, *m;* retrete, excusado, *m*

lave /leiv/ *vt* bañar

lavender /ˈlævəndər/ *n* espliego, *m,* lavanda, *f.* **l.-water,** agua de lavanda, *f*

lavish /ˈlævɪʃ/ *a* pródigo; profuso, abundante. —*vt* prodigar

lavishly /ˈlævɪʃli/ *adv* pródigamente; en profusión

lavishness /ˈlævɪʃnɪs/ *n* prodigalidad, *f;* profusión, abundancia, *f*

law /lɔ/ *n* ley, *f;* derecho, *m;* jurisprudencia, *f;* código de leyes, *m.* **according to law,** según derecho. **canon law,** derecho civil, *m.* **constitutional law,** derecho político, *m.* **criminal law,** derecho penal, *m.* **in law,** por derecho, de acuerdo con la ley; desde el punto de vista legal. **international law,** derecho internacional, *m.* **maritime law,** código marítimo, *m.* **sumptuary law,** ley suntuaria, *f.* **to be the law,** ser la ley. **to go to law,** pleitear (sobre). **to sue at law,** pedir en juicio, poner pleito. **to take the law into one's own hands,** tomar la ley por su propia mano. **law-abiding,** observante de la ley; amigo del orden. **law-breaker,** transgresor (-ra). **law court,** tribunal de justicia, *m;* palacio de justicia, *m.* **law of nature,** ley natural, *f.* **law report,** revista de tribunales, *f.* **law school,** escuela de derecho, *f.* **law student,** estudiante de derecho, *mf*

lawful /ˈlɔfəl/ *a* legítimo; legal; lícito; válido

lawfully /ˈlɔfəli/ *adv* legalmente; legítimamente, lícitamente

lawfulness /ˈlɔfəlnɪs/ *n* legalidad, *f;* legitimidad, *f*

lawgiver /ˈlɔˌgɪvər/ *n* legislador (-ra)

lawless /ˈlɔlɪs/ *a* ilegal; desordenado; ingobernable, rebelde

lawlessness /ˈlɔlɪsnɪs/ *n* ilegalidad, *f;* desorden, *m;* rebeldía, *f*

lawn /lɔn/ *n* césped, prado, *m;* (cloth) estopilla, *f.* **l.-mower,** cortacésped *m,* tundidora de césped, *f,* máquina segadora del césped, *f.* **l.-tennis,** tenis (en pista de hierba), *m*

lawsuit /ˈlɔˌsut/ *n* pleito, litigio, *m,* causa, acción, *f*

lawyer /ˈlɔyər/ *n* abogado (-da). **lawyer's office** or **practice,** bufete, *m*
lax /læks/ *a* laxo; indisciplinado; vago; descuidado
laxative /ˈlæksətɪv/ *n* laxante, *m*, purga, *f*, *a* laxativo
laxity /ˈlæksɪti/ *n* laxitud, *f;* descuido, *m;* indiferencia, *f*
lay /lei/ *a* laico, seglar, lego; profano. —*n* poema, *m*, trova, *f;* romance, *m;* (song) canción, *f*. **the lay of the land,** la configuración del terreno. **lay brother,** confeso, monigote, *m*. **lay figure,** maniquí, *m*. **lay sister,** (hermana) lega, *f*
lay /lei/ *vt* and *vi* poner; colocar; dejar; (strike) tumbar; (demolish) derribar; (the dust) matar; (pipes, etc.) instalar; (hands on) asentar (la mano en); (deposit) depositar; (beat down corn, etc.) encamar, abatir; (eggs, keel) poner; (the table) cubrir, poner; (stretch) extender(se); (bury) depositar en el sepulcro; (a bet) hacer; (wager) apostar; (an accusation) acusar; (the wind, etc.) sosegar, amainar; (a ghost) exorcizar; (impute) atribuir, imputar; (impose) imponer; (prepare) prepara; (make) hacer; (open) abrir; (blame, etc.) echar; (claim) reclamar; (reveal) revelar. **Don't lay the blame on me!** ¡No me eches la culpa! **We laid our plans,** Hicimos nuestros planes; Hicimos nuestros preparativos. **to lay siege to,** asediar. **to lay the colors on too thick,** *Fig.* recargar las tintas. **to lay the foundations,** abrir los cimientos; *Fig.* crear, establecer; fundar. **to lay about one,** dar garrotazos de ciego. **to lay aside,** poner a un lado; arrinconar; (save) ahorrar; (cast away) desechar; abandonar; (reserve) reservar; (a person) apartar de sí; (incapacitate) incapacitar. **lay something at somebody's feet,** embutir algo en el guante de fulano. **to lay before,** mostrar; presentar; poner a la vista; revelar. **to lay by,** See **to lay aside. to lay down,** acostar; depositar; (a burden) posar; (arms) rendir; (one's life); entregar; (give up) renunciar (a); (sketchout) trazar, dibujar; (plan) proyectar; (keep) guardar; (as a principle) establecer, sentar; (the law) dictar. **to lay oneself down,** echarse, tumbarse. **to lay in,** (a stock) proveerse de, hacer provisión de; (hoard) ahorrar; (buy) compara. **to lay off,** *Naut.* virar de bordo; *Inf.* quitarse de encima. **to lay on,** *vt* colocar sobre; (thrash) pegar; (blows) descargar; (paint, etc.) dar; (water, etc.) instalar; (impose) imponer; (exaggerate) exagerar. —*vi* atacar. **to lay open,** abrir; descubrir, revelar; manifestar; exponer. **to lay oneself open to attack,** exponerse a ser atacado. **to lay out,** poner; arreglar; (the dead) amortajar; (one's money) invertir, emplear; (at interest) poner a rédito; (plan) planear; (knock down) derribar. **to lay oneself out to,** esforzarse a; tomarse la molestia de. **to lay over,** cubrir; sobreponer; extender sobre. **to lay to,** *vi Naut.* estar a la capa. **to lay up,** guardar, acumular, atesorar; poner a un lado; (a ship) desarmar; (a car) poner fuera de circulación; (a person) obligar a guardar cama, incapacitar
layer /ˈleiər/ *n* capa, *f;* *Geol.* estrato, *m;* *Mineral.* manto, *m;* (bird) gallina (pata, etc.) ponedera, *f;* (one who bets) apostador (-ra); *Agr.* acodo, *m*. —*vt* (of plants) acodar
layette /leiˈɛt/ *n* canastilla, *f*
laying /ˈleiɪŋ/ *n* colocación, *f;* puesta, *f;* (of an egg) postura, *f*. **l. down,** depósito, *m;* conservación, *f;* (explanation) exposición, *f*. **l. on of hands,** imposición de manos, *f*. **l. out,** tendedura, *f;* (of money) empleo, *m;* inversión, *f;* (arrangement) arreglo, *m*
layman /ˈleimən/ *n* seglar, *mf;* profano (-na)
layout /ˈleiˌaut/ *n* plan, *m;* diagramación, disposición, *f;* distribución, *f;* esquema, *m*
laze /leiz/ *vi* holgazanear, gandulear, no hacer nada; encontrarse a sus anchas
lazily /ˈleizəli/ *adv* perezosamente; indolentemente; lentamente
laziness /ˈleizinɪs/ *n* pereza, holgazanería, *f;* indolencia, *f;* lentitud, *f*
lazy /ˈleizi/ *a* perezoso, holgazán; indolente. **l.-bones,** gandul (-la)
lead /lɛd/ *n* (metal) plomo, *m;* (in a pencil) mina, *f;* (plummet) sonda, *f;* *Print.* interlínea, *f;* *pl* **leads,** (roofs) tejados, *m pl*. —*vt* emplomar; guarnecer con plomo; *Print.* interlinear. **black-l.,** grafito, *m*. **deep-sea l.,** *Naut.* escandallo, *m*. **white l.,** albayalde, *m*. **to heave the l.,** echar el escandallo, sondar. **l.-colored,** de color de plomo, plomizo. **l. mine,** mina de plomo, *f*. **l. poisoning,** saturnismo, *m*
lead /lid/ *n* delantera, *f;* primer lugar, *m;* dirección, *f*, mando, *m;* (suggestion) indicación, *f;* (influence) influencia, *f;* (dog's) traílla, *f;* *Theat.* protagonista, *mf;* *Theat.* papel principal, *m;* (at cards) mano, *f*
lead /lid/ *vt* and *vi* (conduct) conducir, llevar; guiar; (induce) mover, persuadir, inducir; inclinar; (cause) hacer, causar; (captain) capitanear, encabezar; dirigir; (channel) encauzar; (with life) llevar; (give) dar; (head) ir a la cabeza de; *Mil.* mandar; (at cards) salir; (at games) jugar en primer lugar; tomar la delantera; *Fig.* superar a los demás; (of roads) conducir. **to take the l.,** ir delante; ir a la cabeza, tomar la delantera; tomar la iniciativa. **to l. one to think,** hacer pensar. **to l. the way,** mostrar el camino; ir adelante. **to l. along,** llevar (por la mano, etc.), conducir; conducir por; guiar. **to l. astray,** descarriar; desviar (de), seducir (de). **to l. away,** conducir (a otra parte); llevarse (a). **to l. back,** conducir de nuevo; hacer volver. **This path leads back to the village,** Por esta senda se vuelve al pueblo. **to l. in, into,** conducir a (or ante); introducir en, hacer entrar en; invitar a entrar en; (of rooms) comunicarse con; (sin, etc.) inducir a. **to l. off,** *vi* ir adelante; (begin) empezar; (of rooms) comunicarse con. —*vt* hacer marcharse, llevarse (a). **to l. on,** *vt* conducir; guiar; hacer pensar en; (make talk) dar cuerda (a). —*vi* ir a la cabeza; tomar la delantera. **to l. out,** conducir afuera; (to dance) sacar. **to l. to,** conducir a; desembocar en, salir a; (cause) dar lugar a, causar; (make) hacer; (incline) inclinar. **This street leads to the square,** Por esta calle se va a la plaza, Esta calle conduce a la plaza. **to l. up to,** conducir a; (in conversation, etc.) preparar el terreno para; preparar; tener lugar antes de, ocurrir antes de
leaden /ˈlɛdn̩/ *a* hecho de plomo, plúmbeo; (of skies, etc.) plomizo, de color de plomo, aplomado. **l.-footed,** pesado; lento
leader /ˈlidər/ *n* conductor (-ra); guía, *mf;* jefe (-fa); general, *m;* director (-ra); (in a journal) artículo de fondo, *m;* (of an orchestra) primer violín, *m*. **follow-the-l.,** (game) juego de seguir la fila, *m*
leadership /ˈlidərˌʃɪp/ *n* dirección, *f;* jefatura, *f;* *Mil.* mando, *m*
lead-in /ˈlid ˌɪn/ *a Radio.* de entrada. —*n Radio.* conductor de entrada, *m*
leading /ˈlɛdɪŋ/ *n* (leadwork) emplomadura, *f*
leading /ˈlidɪŋ/ *n* (guidance) dirección, *f*. —*a* principal; primero; importante; eminente. **l. article,** artículo de fondo, *m;* editorial, *m*. **l. card,** primer naipe, *m*. **l. counsel,** abogado (-da) principal. **l. lady,** *Theat.* dama primera, primera actriz, *f;* (cinema) estrella (de la pantalla), *f*. **l. man,** *Theat.* primer galán, *m*. **l. question,** pregunta que sugiere la respuesta, *f;* cuestión importante, *f*. **l. strings,** andadores, *m pl;* *Fig.* tutelaje, *m*
leaf /lif/ *n* (*Bot.* and of a page, door, window, table, screen, etc.) hoja, *f;* (petal) pétalo, *m*, *vi* echar hojas. **gold l.,** pan de oro, *m*. **to turn over a new l.,** volver la hoja, hacer libro nuevo, hacer vida nueva. **to turn over the leaves of a book,** hojear (un libro). **l.-bud,** yema, *f*. **l.-mold,** abono verde, *m*. **l. tobacco,** tabaco en hoja, *m*
leafiness /ˈlifinɪs/ *n* frondosidad, *f*
leafless /ˈliflɪs/ *a* sin hojas
leaflet /ˈliflɪt/ *n* hojuela, *f;* (pamphlet) folleto, *m*
leafy /ˈlifi/ *a* frondoso
league /lig/ *n* (measure) legua, *f;* liga, federación, sociedad, *f;* (football) liga, *f*. —*vt* aliar; asociar. —*vi* aliarse; asociarse, confederarse. **to be in l.,** *Inf.* estar de manga. **L. of Nations,** Sociedad de las Naciones, *f*
leak /lik/ *n* (hole) agujero, *m*, grieta, *f;* *Naut.* vía de agua, *f;* (of gas, liquids, etc.) escape, *m;* (in a roof, etc.) gotera, *f;* *Elec.* resistencia de escape, *f*. —*vi* *Naut.* hacer agua; (gas, liquids, etc.) escaparse, salirse; (drip) gotear. **to l. out,** (of news, etc.) trascender, saberse. **to spring a l.,** aparecer una vía de agua, hacer agua

leakage /ˈlikɪdʒ/ *n* (of gas, liquids) escape, *m*, fuga, *f;* derrame, *m;* pérdida, *f;* (of information) revelación, *f*

leaky /ˈliki/ *a Naut.* que hace agua; agujereado; poroso; que tiene goteras

lean /lin/ *a* magro, seco, enjuto, delgado; (of meat) magro; *Fig.* pobre, estéril. —*n* carne magra, *f*, magro, *m.* **to grow l.,** enflaquecer

lean /lin/ *vi* inclinarse; apoyarse (en). —*vt* apoyar (en); dejar arrimado (en). **to l. out of the window,** asomarse a la ventana. **to l. against,** apoyarse en, recostarse en (or contra). **to l. back,** echarse hacia atrás; recostarse. **to l. over,** inclinarse. **to l. upon,** apoyarse en; descansar sobre

leaning /ˈlinɪŋ/ *n* inclinación, tendencia, *f;* predilección, afición, *f*

leanness /ˈlinnɪs/ *n* magrura, flaqueza, *f;* (of meat) magrez, *f; Fig.* pobreza, *f*

leap /lip/ *n* salto, *m;* brinco, *m;* (caper) zapateta, *f; Fig.* salto, *m.* —*vi* saltar, dar un salto; brincar. —*vt* saltar; hacer saltar. **at one l.,** en un salto. **by leaps and bounds,** en saltos. **My heart leaped,** Mi corazón dio un salto. **to l. to the conclusion that...,** saltar a la conclusión de que... **to l. to the eye,** saltar a la vista. **l. frog,** salto, salto de la muerte, *m*, pídola *f.* **l. year,** año bisiesto, *m*, salta cabrillas, *f pl*

leaping /ˈlipɪŋ/ *a* saltador. —*n* saltos, *m pl*

learn /lɜrn/ *vt* and *vi* aprender; instruirse; enterarse de. **to l. by heart,** aprender de memoria. **to l. from a reliable source,** saber de buena tinta. **to l. from experience,** aprender por experiencia

learned /ˈlɜrnɪd/ *a* sabio, docto; erudito; (of professions) liberal; versado (en), entendido (en). **a l. society,** una sociedad erudita

learner /ˈlɜrnər/ *n* aprendedor (-ra)

learning /ˈlɜrnɪŋ/ *n* saber, *m;* conocimientos, *m pl;* erudición, *f;* estudio, *m;* (literature) literatura, *f*

lease /lis/ *n* arrendamiento, arriendo, *m;* contrato de arrendamiento, *m.* —*vt* dar en arriendo, arrendar. **on l.,** en arriendo. **to take a new l. on life,** recobrar su vigor. **Lend L. Act,** ley de préstamo y arriendo, *f*

leasehold /ˈlisˌhould/ *n* censo, *m*, *a* censatario

leaseholder /ˈlisˌhouldər/ *n* concesionario, *m;* arrendatario (-ia)

leash /liʃ/ *n* (of a dog) traílla, *f*

least /list/ *a superl* **little,** mínimo; el (la, etc.) menor; más pequeño. —*adv* menos. —*n* lo menos. **at l.,** siquiera; por lo menos, al menos. **at the very l.,** a lo menos. **not in the l.,** de ninguna manera, nada. **to say the l. of,** sin exagerar, para no decir más

leather /ˈlɛðər/ *n* cuero, *m;* piel, *f*, *a* de cuero; de piel. **patent l.,** charol, *m.* **Spanish l.,** cordobán, *m.* **tanned l.,** curtido, *m.* **l. apron,** mandil, *m.* **l. bag,** saco de cuero, *m.* **l. bottle,** bota, *f.* **l. breeches,** pantalón de montar, *m.* **l. jerkin,** coleto, *m.* **l. shield,** adarga, *f.* **l. strap,** correa, *f.* **l. trade,** comercio en cueros, *m*

leatherette /ˌlɛðəˈrɛt/ *n* cartón cuero, *m*

leathery /ˈlɛðəri/ *a* de cuero; (of the skin) curtido por la intemperie; (tough) correoso

leave /liv/ *n* (permission) permiso, *m;* (*Mil.* etc.) licencia, *f;* (farewell) despedida, *f.* —*vt* and *vi* dejar; abandonar; salir (de), quitar, marcharse (de); (as surety) empeñar; (by will) legar, mandar; (an employment) darse de baja (de), dejar; (give into the keeping of) entregar; (bid farewell) despedirse (de). **By your l.,** Con permiso de Vd. (Vds.). Con la venia de Vd. (Vds.) **on l.,** de permiso. **l.-taking,** despedidas, *f pl.* **to be left,** quedar. **to be left over,** quedar; sobrar. **Two from four leaves two,** De cuatro a dos van dos. **to take French l.,** despedirse a la inglesa. **to take l. of,** despedirse de. **to take one's l.,** marcharse; despedirse. **to l. a deep impression,** *Fig.* impresionar mucho; quedar grabado (en). **to l. undone,** dejar de hacer, no hacer; dejar sin terminar. **to l. about,** *vt* dejar por todas partes. —*vi* (of time) marcharse a eso de... **to l. ajar,** entreabrir, entornar. **to l. alone,** dejar a solas; dejar en paz; no molestar, no meterse con. **to l. aside,** omitir; prescindir de; olvidar. **to l. behind,** dejar atrás; olvidar. **l. much to be desired,** tener mucho que desear. **to l. off,** *vt* dejar de; abandonar; (garments) no ponerse, quitarse. —*vi* terminar. **to l. out,** dejar fuera; dejar a un lado, descontar; omitir; pasar por; (be silent about) callar; suprimir. **to l. to,** dejar para; dejar hacer

leaven /ˈlɛvən/ *n* levadura, *f*, fermento, *m*, *vt* fermentar; (*Fig.* permeate) penetrar (en), infiltrar en, imbuir; (a speech) salpimentar (con)

leaving /ˈlivɪŋ/ *n* salida, partida, marcha, *f; pl* **leavings,** sobras, *f pl;* desechos, *m pl*

Lebanon /ˈlɛbənən/ el Líbano, *m*

lecherous /ˈlɛtʃərəs/ *a* lascivo, lujurioso

lechery /ˈlɛtʃəri/ *n* lascivia, lujuria, *f*

lectern /ˈlɛktərn/ *n* atril, *m;* (in a church) facistol, *m*

lecture /ˈlɛktʃər/ *n* conferencia, *f;* (in a university) lección, clase, *f;* discurso, *m;* (*Inf.* scolding) sermoneo, *m.* —*vi* dar una conferencia; (in a university) dar clase. —*vt* (*Inf.* scold) predicar, sermonear. **l. room,** sala de conferencias, *f;* (in a university) sala de clase, aula, *f*

lecturer /ˈlɛktʃərər/ *n* conferenciante, *mf;* (in a university) auxiliar, *m;* (professor) catedrático (-ca), profesor (-ra)

lectureship /ˈlɛktʃərˌʃɪp/ *n* auxiliaría, *f*

ledge /lɛdʒ/ *n* borde, *m;* capa, *f;* (of a window) alféizar, *m;* (shelf) anaquel, *m*

ledger /ˈlɛdʒɛr/ *n* libro mayor, *m*

lee /li/ *n Naut.* sotavento, *m*, *a* a sotavento

leech /litʃ/ *n* sanguijuela, *f*

leek /lik/ *n* puerro, *m*

leer /lɪər/ *vi* mirar de soslayo; guiñar el ojo; mirar con los ojos llenos de deseo. —*n* mirada de soslayo, *f;* mirada de lascivia, *f*

lees /liz/ *n pl* heces, *f pl;* sedimento, *m*

leeward /ˈliwərd/ *n* sotavento, *m.* **on the l. side,** a sotavento

leeway /ˈliˌwei/ *n Naut.* deriva, *f; Fig.* amplitud, margen de holgura, márgenes de maniobra, *f pl*

left /lɛft/ *past part* dejado, etc. See **leave.** *a* izquierdo. —*adv* a la izquierda; hacia la izquierda. —*n* izquierda, *f.* **on the l.,** a la izquierda. **the L.,** *Polit.* las izquierdas. **the Left Bank** (**of Paris**) la Ribera izquierda, la Orilla izquierda **L. face!** ¡Izquierda! **l.-hand,** mano izquierda, *f;* izquierda, *f.* **l.-hand drive,** conducción a la izquierda, *f.* **l.-handed,** zurdo. **l. luggage office,** consigna, *f.* **l.-overs,** sobras, *f pl,* desperdicios, *m pl*

leg /lɛg/ *n* pierna, *f;* (of animals, birds, furniture) pata, *f;* (of a triangle) cateto, *m;* (of a pair of compasses, trousers, lamb, veal) pierna, *f;* (of boots, stockings) caña, *f;* (of pork) pernil, *m;* (support) pie, *m;* (stage) etapa, *f.* **to be on one's last legs,** estar en las últimas; estar acabándose; estar sin recursos. **to pull a person's leg,** tomar el pelo (a). **leg-pull,** tomadura de pelo, *f.* **leg-of-mutton sleeve,** manga de pernil, *f*

legacy /ˈlɛgəsi/ *n* legado, *m*, manda, *f;* herencia, *f*

legal /ˈligəl/ *a* legal; de derecho; jurídico; (lawful, permissible) legítimo, lícito; (of a lawyer) de abogado. **l. expenses,** litisexpensas, *f pl.* **l. inquiry,** investigación jurídica, *f*

legality /liˈgælɪti/ *n* legalidad, *f*

legalization /ˌligələˈzeiʃən/ *n* legalización, *f*

legalize /ˈligəˌlaiz/ *vt* legalizar; autorizar, legitimar

legally /ˈligəli/ *adv* según la ley; según derecho; legalmente

legal tender *n* moneda de curso liberatorio, *f*

legate /ˈlɛgɪt/ *n* legado, *m.* **papal l.,** legado papal, *m*

legatee /ˌlɛgəˈti/ *n* legatario (-ia)

legation /lɪˈgeiʃən/ *n* legación, *f*

legend /ˈlɛdʒənd/ *n* leyenda, *f*

legendary /ˈlɛdʒənˌdɛri/ *a* legendario

legerdemain /ˌlɛdʒərdəˈmein/ *n* juegos de manos, *m pl*

legged /ˈlɛgɪd/ *a* con piernas; de piernas...; de patas... **a three-l. stool,** un taburete de tres patas. **long l.,** zancudo

leggings /ˈlɛgɪŋz/ *n pl* polainas, *f pl*

legibility /ˌlɛdʒəˈbɪlɪti/ *n* legibilidad, *f*

legible /ˈlɛdʒəbəl/ *a* legible

legion /ˈlidʒən/ *n* legión, *f.* **L. of Honor,** Legión de Honor, *f*

legionary /ˈlidʒəˌnɛri/ *a* legionario. —*n* legionario, *m*

legislate /ˈlɛdʒɪsˌleit/ *vt* legislar

legislation /ˌlɛdʒɪsˈleiʃən/ *n* legislación, *f*

legislative /ˈlɛdʒɪsˌleitɪv/ *a* legislativo, legislador
legislator /ˈlɛdʒɪsˌleitər/ *n* legislador (-ra)
legislature /ˈlɛdʒɪsˌleitʃər/ *n* legislatura, *f*
legitimacy /lɪˈdʒɪtəməsi/ *n* legitimidad, *f;* justicia, *f*
legitimate /lɪˈdʒɪtəmɪt/ *a* legítimo; justo
legitimation /lɪˌdʒɪtəˈmeiʃən/ *n* legitimación, *f*
leguminous /lɪˈgyumənəs/ *a* leguminoso
leisure /ˈliʒər/ *n* ocio, *m,* desocupación, *f;* tiempo libre, *m.* **at one's l.,** con sosiego, despacio. **You can do it at your l.,** Puedes hacerlo cuando tengas tiempo. **to be at l.,** estar desocupado, no tener nada que hacer. **l. moments,** ratos perdidos, momentos de ocio, *m pl*
leisured /ˈliʒərd/ *a* desocupado, libre; sin ocupación; (wealthy) acomodado
leisurely /ˈliʒərli/ *a* pausado, lento, deliberado; tardo
lemon /ˈlɛmən/ *n* limón, *m;* (tree) limonero, *m, a* limonado, de color de limón; hecho o sazonado con limón. **l. drop,** pastilla de limón, *f.* **l.-grove,** limonar, *m.* **l.-squash,** limonada natural, *f.* **l.-squeezer,** exprime limones, *m,* exprimidera, *f*
lemonade /ˌlɛməˈneid/ *n* limonada, *f.* **l. powder,** limonada seca, *f*
lemur /ˈlimər/ *n* lemur, *m*
lend /lɛnd/ *vt* prestar. **to l. an ear to,** prestar atención a. **It does not l. itself to...,** No se presta a... **to l. a hand,** echar una mano, dar una mano
lender /ˈlɛndər/ *n* el, *m,* (*f,* la) que presta; prestador (-ra); (of money) prestamista, *mf; Com.* mutuante, *mf*
lending /ˈlɛndɪŋ/ *n* prestación, *f,* préstamo, *m.* **l.-library,** biblioteca circulante, *f*
length /lɛŋkθ/ *n* largo, *m;* longitud, *f;* (of fabric) corte, *m;* (of a ship) eslora, *f;* (in racing) largo, *m;* distancia, *f;* (in time) duración, *f;* alcance, *m.* **at l.,** por fin, finalmente; (in full) extensamente, largamente. **by a l.,** por un largo. **full-l.,** de cuerpo entero. **three feet in l.,** tres pies de largo. **to go the l. of...,** llegar al extremo de...
lengthen /ˈlɛŋkθən/ *vt* alargar; prolongar; extender. —*vi* alargarse; prolongarse; extenderse; (of days) crecer
lengthening /ˈlɛŋkθənɪŋ/ *n* alargamiento, *m;* prolongación, *f;* crecimiento, *m*
lengthily /ˈlɛŋkθəli/ *adv* largamente
lengthiness /ˈlɛŋkθinɪs/ *n* largueza, *f;* prolijidad, *f*
lengthy /ˈlɛŋkθi/ *a* largo; demasiado largo, larguísimo; (of speech) prolijo; verboso
leniency /ˈliniənsi/ *n* lenidad, *f;* indulgencia, *f*
lenient /ˈliniənt/ *a* indulgente; poco severo
leniently /ˈliniəntli/ *adv* con indulgencia
Leningrad /ˈlɛnɪnˌgræd/ Leningrado, *m*
lenitive /ˈlɛnɪtɪv/ *a* lenitivo. —*n* lenitivo, *m*
lens /lɛnz/ *n* lente, *m;* (of the eye) cristalino, *m*
Lent /lɛnt/ *n* Cuaresma, *f*
Lenten /ˈlɛntn̩/ *a* de Cuaresma, cuaresmal
lentil /ˈlɛntɪl/ *n* lenteja, *f*
lentitude /ˈlɛntɪˌtud/ *n* lentitud, *f*
Leo /ˈliou/ *n* León, *m*
leonine /ˈliəˌnain/ *a* leonino
leopard /ˈlɛpərd/ *n* leopardo, *m*
leper /ˈlɛpər/ *n* leproso (-sa). **l. colony,** colonia de leprosos, *f*
leprosy /ˈlɛprəsi/ *n* lepra, *f*
leprous /ˈlɛprəs/ *a* leproso
lesbian /ˈlɛzbiən/ *a* and *n* lesbiana
lesion /ˈliʒən/ *n* lesión, *f*
less /lɛs/ *a* menor; más pequeño; menos; inferior. —*adv* menos; sin. **l. than,** menos de (que). **more or l.,** poco más o menos. **no l.,** nada menos. **none the l.,** sin embargo. **to grow l.,** disminuir. **l. and l.,** cada vez menos
lessee /lɛˈsi/ *n* arrendatario (-ia); inquilino (-na)
lessen /ˈlɛsən/ *vi* disminuir; reducirse. —*vt* disminuir; reducir; (lower) rebajar; (disparage) menospreciar
lessening /ˈlɛsənɪŋ/ *n* disminución, *f;* reducción, *f*
lesser /ˈlɛsər/ *a compar* menor; más pequeño. See **little**
lesson /ˈlɛsən/ *n* lección, *f.* **to give a l.,** dar lección, dar clase; *Fig.* dar una lección (a). **to hear a l.,** tomar la lección
lessor /ˈlɛsɔr/ *n* arrendador (-ra)
lest /lɛst/ *conjunc* para que no; por miedo de (que), no sea que. **I did not do it l. they should not like it,** No lo hice por miedo de que no les gustase
let /lɛt/ *vt* dejar, permitir; (lease) arrendar. —*vi* alquilarse, ser alquilado. **Let** as an expression of the imperative is rendered in Spanish by the subjunctive or the imperative, e.g. *Let them go!* ¡Que se vayan! ¡Déjalos marchar! *He let them go,* Les dejó marchar. *to let fall,* dejar caer. *to let go,* dejar marchar; soltar; poner en libertad (a). **to let loose,** dar suelta a; *Fig.* desencadenar. **to let one know,** hacer saber, comunicar. **to let the cat out of the bag,** tirar de la manta. **to let th chance slip,** perder la ocasión. **to let alone,** (a thing) no tocar; (a person) dejar en paz, dejar tranquilo; (an affair) no meterse (en or con); (omit) no mencionar, omitir toda mención de. **to let down,** bajar; (by a rope) descolgar; (hair, etc.) dejar caer; (a dress, etc.) alargar; *Naut.* calar; (disappoint) dejar plantado. **to let in,** dejar entrar; hacer entrar; invitar a entrar; recibir; (insert) insertar. **to let into,** (initiate) iniciar en, admitir en; (a secret) revelar. Other meanings, see **to let in. to let off,** dejar salir; dejar en libertad; exonerar; perdonar; (a gun) disparar; (fireworks, etc.) hacer estallar. **to let out,** dejar salir; poner en libertad; (from a house) acompañar a la puerta; abrir la puerta; *Sew.* ensanchar; (hire) alquilar; (the fire, etc.) dejar extinguirse. **to let up,** dejar subir; (decrease) disminuir; (end) terminar
let /lɛt/ *n* estorbo, impedimento, obstáculo, *m.* **without let or hindrance,** sin estorbo ni obstáculo
lethal /ˈliθəl/ *a* letal. **l. weapon,** instrumento de muerte, *m*
lethargic /ləˈθɑrdʒɪk/ *a* aletargado; letárgico
lethargy /ˈlɛθərdʒi/ *n* letargo, *m; Med.* letargía, *f*
letter /ˈlɛtər/ *n* (of the alphabet) letra, *f;* (epistle) carta, *f; Print.* carácter, *m;* (lessor) arrendador (-ra); *pl* **letters,** letras, *f pl*; (correspondence) correo, *m;* correspondencia, *f.* —*vt* inscribir; imprimir. **capital l.,** letra mayúscula, *f.* **first letters,** *Fig.* primeras letras, *f pl.* **registered l.,** carta certificada, *f,* certificado, *m.* **small l.,** letra minúscula, *f.* **the l. of the law,** la ley escrita. **to be l.-perfect,** saber de memoria. **to the l.,** *Fig.* a la letra. **letters patent,** patente, *f;* título de privilegio, *m.* **l.-balance,** pesacartas, *m.* **l.-book,** *Com.* libro copiador, *m.* **l.-box,** buzón de correos, *m.* **l.-card,** tarjeta postal del gobierno, *f.* **l. of credit,** carta de crédito, *f.* **l. of introduction,** carta de presentación, *f.* **l.-writer,** escritor (-ra) de cartas
lettered /ˈlɛtərd/ *a* culto, instruido; (printed) impreso
lettering /ˈlɛtərɪŋ/ *n* inscripción, *f;* letrero, rótulo, *m*
letterpress /ˈlɛtərˌprɛs/ *n* imprenta, *f;* (not illustrations) texto, *m*
letting /ˈlɛtɪŋ/ *n* (hiring) arrendamiento, *m*
lettuce /ˈlɛtɪs/ *n* lechuga, *f.* **l. plant,** lechuguino, *m.* **l. seller,** lechuguero (-ra)
Leuven /ˈluvən/ Lovaina, *f*
Levantine /ˈlɛvənˌtain/ *a* and *n* levantino (-na)
Levant, the /lɪˈvænt/ el Levante, *m*
levee /ˈlɛvi/ *n* besamanos, *m,* recepción, *f*
level /ˈlɛvəl/ *n* nivel, *m;* ras, *m,* flor, *f;* llano, *m;* (plain) llanura, *f;* (instrument) nivel, *m, a* llano; igual; al nivel (de); uniforme; imparcial. —*adv* a nivel; igualmente. —*vt* nivelar; igualar; allanar; (a blow) asestar; (a gun) apuntar; (raze) arrasar, derribar; adaptar; hacer uniforme. **on the l.,** a nivel; *Fig.* de buena fe. **spirit l.,** nivel de burbuja, *m.* **to make l. again,** rellanar. **l. country,** campaña, llanura, *f.* **l. with the ground,** a ras de la tierra. **l. with the water,** a flor de agua. **l. crossing,** paso a nivel, *m.* **l.-headed,** sensato, cuerdo. **l. stretch,** rellano, *m;* llanura, *f*
leveler /ˈlɛvələr/ *n* nivelador (-ra)
leveling /ˈlɛvəlɪŋ/ *a* nivelador; de nivelación; igualador. —*n* nivelación, *f;* allanamiento, *m;* (to the ground) arrasamiento, *m;* igualación, *f*
levelness /ˈlɛvəlnɪs/ *n* nivel, *m;* planicie, *f;* igualdad, *f*
lever /ˈlɛvər/ *n* palanca, *f;* (handle) manivela, *f;* escape de reloj, *m;* (excuse) pretexto, *m;* (means) modo, *m.* —*vt* sopalancar. **control l.,** *Aer.* palanca de mando, *f.* **hand-l.,** palanca de mano, *f*

leverage /ˈlɛvərɪdʒ/ *n* sistema de palancas, *m;* acción de palanca, *f; Fig.* influencia, fuerza, *f,* poder, *m*
Leviathan /lɪˈvaiəθən/ *n* leviatán, *m*
levitation /ˌlɛvɪˈteiʃən/ *n* levitación, *f*
Levite /ˈlivait/ *n* levita, *m*
Levitical /lɪˈvɪtɪkəl/ *a* levítico
Leviticus /lɪˈvɪtɪkəs/ *n* Levítico, *m*
levity /ˈlɛvɪti/ *n* levedad, frivolidad, ligereza, *f*
levy /ˈlɛvi/ *n* exacción (de tributos), *f;* impuesto, *m;* (of a fine) imposición, *f; Mil.* leva, *f.* —*vt* (taxes) exigir; (a fine) imponer; (troops) reclutar, enganchar
levying /ˈlɛviɪŋ/ *n* (of a tax) exacción (de tributos), *f;* (of a fine) imposición, *f;* (of troops) leva, *f*
lewd /lud/ *a* lascivo, lujurioso, impúdico
lewdness /ˈludnɪs/ *n* lascivia, lujuria, impudicia, *f*
lexicographer /ˌlɛksɪˈkɒgrəfər/ *n* lexicógrafo, *m*
lexicography /ˌlɛksɪˈkɒgrəfi/ *n* lexicografía, *f*
lexicon /ˈlɛksɪˌkɒn/ *n* léxico, *m*
liability /ˌlaiəˈbɪlɪti/ *n* responsabilidad, obligación, *f;* tendencia, *f;* riesgo, *m; pl* **liabilities,** obligaciones, *f pl; Com.* pasivo, *m*
liable /ˈlaiəbəl/ *a* responsable; propenso (a); expuesto (a); sujeto (a)
liaison /liˈeizən/ *n* lío, *m;* coordinación, *f.* **l. officer,** oficial de coordinación, *m*
liar /ˈlaiər/ *n* mentiroso (-sa)
libation /laiˈbeiʃən/ *n* libación, *f*
libel /ˈlaibəl/ *n* libelo, *m;* difamación, *f, vt* difamar, calumniar
libeler /ˈlaibələr/ *n* libelista, *mf* difamador (-ra)
libelous /ˈlaibələs/ *a* difamatorio
liberal /ˈlɪbərəl/ *a* liberal; generoso; abundante. —*n* liberal, *mf* **l. profession,** carrera liberal, *f.* **l.-minded,** tolerante. **l.-mindedness,** tolerancia, *f*
liberalism /ˈlɪbərəˌlɪzəm/ *n* liberalismo, *m*
liberality /ˌlɪbəˈrælɪti/ *n* liberalidad, *f;* generosidad, *f*
liberalize /ˈlɪbərəˌlaiz/ *vt* liberalizar
liberate /ˈlɪbəˌreit/ *vt* (a prisoner) poner en libertad; librar (de); (a gas, etc.) dejar escapar
liberation /ˌlɪbəˈreiʃən/ *n* liberación, *f;* (of a captive) redención, *f;* (of a slave) manumisión, *f*
liberator /ˈlɪbəˌreitər/ *n* libertador (-ra)
libertinage /ˈlɪbərˌtinɪdʒ/ *n* libertinaje, *m*
libertine /ˈlɪbərˌtin/ *n* libertino, *m*
libertinism /ˈlɪbərtiˌnɪzəm/ *n* libertinaje, *m*
liberty /ˈlɪbərti/ *n* libertad, *f;* (familiarity) familiaridad, *f;* (right) privilegio, *m,* prerrogativa, *f;* (leave) permiso, *m.* **at l.,** en libertad; desocupado, libre. **I have taken the l. of giving them your name,** Me he tomado la libertad de darles su nombre. **to set at l.,** poner en libertad (a). **to take liberties with,** tratar con familiaridad; (a text) tergiversar. **l. of speech,** libertad de palabra, libertad de expresión, *f.* **l. of thought,** libertad de pensamiento, *f*
libidinous /lɪˈbɪdn̩əs/ *a* libidinoso
Libra /ˈlibrə/ *n* Libra, *f*
librarian /laiˈbrɛəriən/ *n* bibliotecario (-ia)
librarianship /laiˈbrɛəriənˌʃɪp/ *n* carrera *f,* or empleo *m,* de bibliotecario
library /ˈlaiˌbrɛri/ *n* biblioteca, *f;* (book shop) librería, *f.* **l. catalog,** catálogo de la biblioteca, *m*
librettist /lɪˈbrɛtɪst/ *n* libretista, *mf*
libretto /lɪˈbrɛtou/ *n* libreto, *m*
Libya /ˈlɪbiə/ Libia, *f*
Libyan /ˈlɪbiən/ *a* and *n* libio (-ia)
license /ˈlaisəns/ *n* licencia, *f,* permiso, *m;* autorización, *f;* (driving) carnet de chófer, permiso de conducción, *m;* (of a car) permiso de circulación, *m;* (for a wireless, etc.) licencia, *f;* (marriage) licencia de casamiento, *f;* (excess) libertinaje, desenfreno, *m.* **import l.,** permiso de importación, *m.* **poetic l.,** licencia poética, *f.* **l. number,** (of a car) número de matriculación, *m.* —*vt* licenciar; autorizar; (a car) sacar la licencia del automóvil
licensee /ˌlaisənˈsi/ *n* concesionario (-ia)
licentiate /laiˈsɛnʃiɪt/ *n* licenciado (-da)
licentious /laiˈsɛnʃəs/ *a* licencioso, disoluto
licentiousness /laiˈsɛnʃəsnɪs/ *n* libertinaje, *m,* disipación, *f*
lichen /ˈlaikən/ *n* liquen, *m*
licit /ˈlɪsɪt/ *a* lícito
lick /lɪk/ *vt* lamer; (of waves) besar; (of flames) bailar; (thrash) azotar; (defeat) vencer. **to l. one's lips,** relamerse los labios, chuparse los dedos. **to l. the dust,** morder el polvo
licking /ˈlɪkɪŋ/ *n* lamedura, *f;* (beating) paliza, tunda, *f;* (defeat) derrota, *f*
licorice /ˈlɪkərɪʃ, ˈlɪkrɪʃ, ˈlɪkərɪs/ *n* regaliz, *m*
lid /lɪd/ *n* cobertera, *f;* tapa, *f;* (of the eye) párpado, *m*
lie /lai/ *n* mentira, *f;* invención, falsedad, *f;* mentís, *m, vi* mentir. **to give the lie to,** desmentir, dar el mentís. **to lie barefacedly,** mentir por la mitad de la barba. **white lie,** mentira oficiosa, *f*
lie /lai/ *vi* estar tumbado, estar echado; estar recostado; descansar, reposar; (in the grave) yacer; (be) estar; (be situated) hallarse, estar situado; (stretch) extenderse; (sleep) dormir; (depend) depender; (consist) consistir, estribar; (as an obligation) incumbir. **Here lies...,** Aquí descansa..., Aquí yace... **It does not lie in my power,** No depende de mí. **to let lie,** dejar; dejar en paz. **to lie at anchor,** estar anclado. **to lie fallow,** estar en barbecho; *Fig.* descansar. **to lie about,** estar esparcido por todas partes; estar en desorden. **to lie along,** estar tendido a lo largo de; *Naut.* dar a la banda. **to lie back,** recostarse; apoyarse (en). **to lie by,** estar acostado al lado de; (of things, places) estar cerca (de); descansar. **to lie down,** tenderse, tumbarse, echarse, acostarse; reposar. **Lie down!** (to a dog) ¡Echate! **to lie down under,** tenderse bajo; (an insult) tragar, sufrir. **to lie in,** consistir en; depender de; (of childbirth) estar de parto. **to lie open,** estar abierto; estar expuesto (a); estar al descubierto, estar a la vista. **to lie over,** (be postponed) quedar aplazado. **to lie to,** *Naut.* estarse a la capa, ponerse en facha. **to lie under,** estar bajo, hallarse bajo; estar bajo el peso de; (be exposed to) estar expuesto a. **to lie with,** dormir con; (concern) tocar (a); corresponder (a)
lie /lai/ *n* configuración, *f;* disposición, *f;* posición, *f.* **the lie of the land,** la configuración del terreno
lieu /lu/ *n* lugar, *m.* **in l. of,** en lugar de, en vez de
lieutenant /luˈtɛnənt/ *n* teniente, lugarteniente, *m;* (naval) alférez, *m.* **first l.,** (in the army) primer teniente, teniente, *m;* (in the navy) alférez de navío, *m.* **naval l.,** teniente de navío, *m.* **second l.,** (in the army) segundo teniente, *m;* (in the navy) alférez de fragata, *m.* **l.-colonel,** teniente coronel, *m.* **l.-commander,** capitán de fragata, *m.* **l.-general,** teniente general, *m.* **l.-governor,** subgobernador, *m*
life /laif/ *n* vida, *f;* (being) ser, *m;* (society) mundo, *m,* sociedad, *f;* (vitality) vitalidad, *f;* vigor, *m, a* de vida; (of annuities, etc.) vitalicio; (life-saving) de salvamento. **for l.,** de por vida. **from l.,** del natural. **high l.,** gran mundo, *m,* alta sociedad, *f.* **low l.,** vida del hampa, vida de los barrios bajos, *f.* **to the l.,** al vivo. **to lay down one's l.,** entregar la vida. **to take one's l. in one's hands,** jugarse la vida. **l. annuity,** fondo vitalicio, *m.* **l.-belt,** (cinturón) salvavidas, *m.* **l.-blood,** sangre vital, *f; Fig.* nervio, *m;* vigor, *m.* **l.-boat,** (on a ship) bote salvavidas, *m;* (on the coast) lancha de salvamento, *f.* **l.-boat station,** estación de salvamento, *f.* **l.-giving,** vivificante, que da vida; tonificante. **l.-guard,** (soldier) guardia militar, *f;* Guardia de Corps, *f,* (at beach or swimming pool) guardavivas, *mf.* **l.-insurance,** seguro sobre la vida, *m.* **l.-interest,** usufructo, *m.* **l.-jacket,** chaleco salvavidas, *m.* **l.-like,** natural. **l.-line,** cable de salvamento, *m.* **l.-saving,** *a* de salvamento; curativo. **l.-saving apparatus,** aparato salvavidas, *m.* **l.-sized,** de tamaño natural
life cycle *n* ciclo vital, *m*
life imprisonment *n* reclusión perpetua, *f*
life jacket *n* chaleco salvavidas, *f*
lifeless /ˈlaiflɪs/ *a* sin vida, muerto; inanimado; *Fig.* desanimado
lifelong /ˈlaifˌlɔŋ/ *a* de toda la vida
lifetime /ˈlaifˌtaim/ *n* vida, *f*
lift /lɪft/ *n* esfuerzo para levantar, *m;* acción de levantar, *f;* alza, *f;* (blow) golpe, *m;* (help) ayuda, *f;* (elevator) ascensor, *m;* (for goods) montacargas, *m; pl* **lifts,** *Naut.* balancines, *m pl.* **to give a l. to,** (help)

ayudar; (hitchhiker etc.) dar un aventón. **l. attendant,** ascensorista, *mf*

lift /lɪft/ *vt* levantar; alzar, elevar; (pick up) coger; (one's hat) quitarse; (steal) hurtar; exaltar. —*vi* (of mist) disiparse; desaparecer. **to l. the elbow,** empinar el codo. **to l. down,** quitar (de); (a person) bajar en brazos. **to l. up,** alzar; erguir, levantar; levantar en brazos

lifting /ˈlɪftɪŋ/ *n* acción de levantar, *f;* levantamiento, alzamiento, *m*

ligament /ˈlɪgəmənt/ *n* ligamento, *m*

ligature /ˈlɪgətʃər/ *n* (*Surg. Mus.*) ligadura, *f*

light /lait/ *a* (not dark) claro, con mucha luz, bañado de luz; (of colors) claro; (not heavy, and of sleep, food, troops, movements) ligero; (of reading) de entretenimiento; (irresponsible) frívolo; (easy) fácil; (slight) leve; (of hair) rubio; (happy) alegre; (fickle) inconstante, liviano; (of complexion) blanco. —*adv* ligero. **to be l.,** no pesar mucho; estar de día. **to grow l.,** (dawn) clarear; iluminarse. **to make l. of,** no tomar en serio; no preocuparse de; (suffering) sufrir sin quejarse. **l.-colored,** (de color) claro. **l.-fingeredness,** sutileza de manos, *f.* **l.-footed,** ligero de pies. **l.-haired,** de pelo rubio. **l.-headed,** casquivano, ligero de cascos; delirante. **l.-headedness,** ligereza de cascos, frivolidad, *f;* delirio, *m.* **l.-hearted,** alegre (de corazón). **l.-heartedness,** alegría, *f.* **l. horse,** *Mil.* caballería ligera, *f.* **l. troops,** tropas ligeras, *f pl.* **l.-weight,** *n* (*boxing*) peso ligero, *m, a* de peso ligero

light /lait/ *n* luz., *f;* (day) día, *m;* (match) cerilla, *f;* (of a cigarette, etc.) fuego, *m;* (of a window) cristal, vidrio, *m;* (point of view) punto de vista, *m;* (in a picture) toque de luz, *m; pl* **lights,** (offal) bofes, *m pl.* **against the l.,** al trasluz. **by the l. of,** a la luz de; según. **half-l.,** media luz, *f.* **high light** (**s**), *Art.* claros, *m pl; Fig.* momento culminante, *m;* acontecimiento de más interés, *m.* **to come to l.,** descubrirse. **to put a l. to the fire,** encender el fuego. **l.-year,** año de luz, *m*

light /lait/ *vt* (a lamp, fire, etc.) encender; iluminar. —*vi* encenderse; iluminarse; *Fig.* animarse; brillar. **to l. upon,** encontrar por casualidad; tropezar con

lighten /ˈlaitn̩/ *vt* (illuminate) iluminar; (of weight) aligerar; (cheer) alegrar; (mitigate) aliviar. —*vi* (grow light) clarear; (of lightning) relampaguear; (become less heavy) disminuir de peso, aligerarse; volverse más alegre

lightening /ˈlaitn̩ɪŋ/ *n* aligeramiento, *m;* (easing) alivio, *m;* luz, *f*

lighter /ˈlaitər/ *n* (boat) lancha, barcaza, gabarra, *f;* (device) encendedor, *m.* **pocket l.,** encendedor de bolsillo, *m.* **l. man,** gabarrero, *m*

light-fingered *a* ligero de manos

lighthouse /ˈlaitˌhaus/ *n* faro, *m.* **l.-keeper,** guardafaro, *m*

lighting /ˈlaitɪŋ/ *n* iluminación, *f;* alumbrado, *m.* **flood l.,** iluminación intensiva, *f.* **l.-up time,** hora de encender los faros, *f*

lightly /ˈlaitli/ *adv* ligeramente; fácilmente; (slightly) levemente; ágilmente; sin seriedad. **l. wounded,** levemente herido

lightness /ˈlaitnɪs/ *n* ligereza, *f;* poco peso, *m;* agilidad, *f;* (brightness) claridad, *f;* (inconstancy) liviandad, inconstancia, *f;* frivolidad, *f*

lightning /ˈlaitnɪŋ/ *n* relámpago, rayo, *m.* **as quick as l.,** como un relámpago. **to be struck by l.,** ser herido por un relámpago. **l.-rod,** pararrayos, *m*

lightship /ˈlaitˌʃɪp/ *n* buque faro, *m*

ligneous /ˈlɪgniəs/ *a* leñoso

lignite /ˈlɪgnait/ *n* lignito, *m*

likable /ˈlaikəbəl/ *a* simpático

like /laik/ *a* semejante; parecido; igual, mismo; (characteristic) típico, característico; (likely) probable; (equivalent) equivalente. —*adv* como; igual (que); del mismo modo (que). —*n* semejante, igual, *mf;* tal cosa, *f;* cosas semejantes, *f pl.* **Don't speak to me l. that,** No me hables así. **He was l. a fury,** Estaba hecho una furia. **They are very l. each other,** Se parecen mucho. **to be l.,** parecerse (a), semejar. **to look l.,** parecer ser (que); tener el aspecto de; (of persons) parecerse (a). **to return l. for l.,** pagar en la misma moneda

like /laik/ *vt* gustar, agradar; estar aficionado (a), gustar de; (wish) querer. **As you l.,** Como te parezca bien, Como quieras. **If you l.,** Si quieres. **James likes painting,** Jaime está aficionado a la pintura. **Judith does not l. the north of England,** A Judit no le gusta el norte de Inglaterra. **I don't l. to do it,** No me gusta hacerlo. **I should l. him to go to Madrid,** Me gustaría que fuese a Madrid

likelihood /ˈlaikliˌhʊd/ *n* posibilidad, *f;* probabilidad, *f*

likely /ˈlaikli/ *a* probable; verosímil, creíble, plausible; posible; (suitable) satisfactorio, apropiado; (handsome) bien parecido. —*adv* probablemente. **They are not l. to come,** No es probable que vengan

liken /ˈlaikən/ *vt* comparar

likeness /ˈlaiknɪs/ *n* parecido, *m,* semejanza, *f;* (portrait) retrato, *m*

likewise /ˈlaikˌwaiz/ *adv* igualmente, asimismo, también. —*conjunc* además

liking /ˈlaikɪŋ/ *n* (for persons) simpatía, *f,* cariño, *m;* (for things) gusto, *m,* afición, *f;* (appreciation) aprecio, *m.* **I have a l. for old cities,** Me gustan (or me atraen) las viejas ciudades. **to take a l. to,** (things) aficionarse a; (persons) prendarse de, tomar cariño (a)

lilac /ˈlailək/ *n* lila, *f.* **l. color,** color de lila, *m*

Lilliputian /ˌlɪlɪˈpyuʃən/ *a* liliputiense. —*n* liliputiense, *mf*

lilt /lɪlt/ *n* canción, *f;* ritmo, *m;* armonía, *f*

lily /ˈlɪli/ *n* lirio, *m,* azucena, *f;* (of France) flor de lis, *f.* **l. of the valley,** lirio de los valles, muguete, *m.* **l.-white,** blanco como la azucena

limb /lɪm/ *n Anat.* miembro, *m;* (of a tree) rama, *f*

limbless /ˈlɪmlɪs/ *a* mutilado

limbo /ˈlɪmbou/ *n* limbo, *m*

lime /laim/ *n Chem.* cal, *f;* (for catching birds) liga, hisca, *f;* (linden tree) tilo, *m;* (tree like a lemon) limero, *m;* (fruit) lima, *f.* —*vt* (whiten) encalar; *Agr.* abonar con cal. **slaked l.,** cal muerta, *f.* **l.-flower,** flor del tilo, tila, *f;* flor del limero, *f.* **l.-juice,** jugo de lima, *m.* **l.-kiln,** calera, *f.* **l.-pit,** pozo de cal, *m*

limelight /ˈlaimˌlait/ *n* luz de calcio, *f; Fig.* centro de atención, *m;* publicidad, *f.* **to be in the l.,** ser el centro de atención, estar a la vista (de público)

limestone /ˈlaimˌstoun/ *n* piedra caliza, *f.* **l. deposit,** calar, *m*

limit /ˈlɪmɪt/ *n* límite, *m;* confín, *m;* linde, *m,* or *f;* limitación, *f, vt* limitar; fijar; (restrict) restringir. **This is the l.!** ¡Este es el colmo! ¡No faltaba más!

limitation /ˌlɪmɪˈteiʃən/ *n* limitación, *f;* restricción, *f*

limitative /ˈlɪmɪˌteitɪv/ *a* restrictivo, limitativo

limited /ˈlɪmɪtɪd/ *a* limitado; restringido; escaso; (of persons) de cortos alcances; *Com.* anónimo. **l. company,** sociedad anónima, *f*

limited monarchy *n* monarquía moderada, *f*

limiting adjective /ˈlɪmɪtɪŋ/ *n* adjetivo determinativo, *m*

limitless /ˈlɪmɪtlɪs/ *a* sin límites; ilimitado, inmenso

limousine /ˈlɪməˌzin/ *n* limousina, *f,* coche cerrado, *m*

limp /lɪmp/ *a* flojo; débil; fláccido; lánguido. —*n* cojera, *f.* —*vi* cojear. **to l. off,** marcharse cojeando. **to l. up,** acercarse cojeando; subir cojeando

limpid /ˈlɪmpɪd/ *a* límpido, cristalino, puro

limpidity /lɪmˈpɪdɪti/ *n* limpidez, *f*

limping /ˈlɪmpɪŋ/ *a* cojo

limply /ˈlɪmpli/ *adv* flojamente; débilmente; lánguidamente

limpness /ˈlɪmpnɪs/ *n* flojedad, *f;* debilidad, *f;* languidez, *f*

linchpin /ˈlɪntʃˌpɪn/ *n* pezonera, *f*

linden /ˈlɪndən/ *n* tilo, *m*

line /lain/ *vt* (furrow) surcar; (troops, etc.) poner en fila; alinear; (clothes, nests, etc.) forrar; (building) revestir; (one's pocket) llenar. —*vi* estar en línea, alinearse

line /lain/ *n* (most meanings) línea, *f;* (cord) cuerda, *f; Naut.* cordel, *m;* (fishing) sedal, *m;* (railway) vía, *f;* (wrinkle) surco, *m;* arruga, *f;* (row) hilera, ringlera, fila, *f;* (of verse) verso, *m; Print.* renglón, *m;* (of business) ramo, *m;* profesión, *f;* (interest) especialidad, *f.* **bowling** or **serving l.,** línea de saque, *f;* **hard lines,** mala suerte, *f;* apuro, *m,* situación difícil, *f.* **in a l.,** en fila; en cola. **in direct l.,** (of descent) en línea recta. **It is not in my l.,** No es una especialidad mía; No es uno de mis intereses. **on the lines of,** conforme a; parecido a. **to cross the l.,** (equator) pasar la línea; (railway) cruzar la vía. **to drop a l.,** escribir unas líneas, poner unas líneas. **to read between the lines,** leer entre líneas. **l.-drawing,** dibujo de líneas, *m.* **l. of battle,** línea de batalla, *f*

lineage /'lɪnɪdʒ/ *n* linaje, *m,* familia, raza, *f*

lineal /'lɪniəl/ *a* lineal

lineament /'lɪniəmənt/ *n* lineamento, *m;* (of the face) facciones, *f pl*

linear /'lɪniər/ *a* lineal. **l. equation,** ecuación de primer grado, *f*

lined /laind/ *a* rayado, con líneas; (of the face) surcado, arrugado; (of gloves, etc.) forrado. **lined paper,** papel rayado, *m*

linen /'lɪnən/ *n* lino, *m; Inf.* ropa blanca, *f; a* de lino. **clean l.,** ropa limpia, *f.* **dirty l.,** ropa sucia, *f;* ropa para lavar, *f.* **table-l.,** mantelería, *f.* **l. cupboard,** armario para ropa blanca, *m.* **l. draper,** lencero (-ra). **l.-draper's shop,** lencería, *f.* **l. room,** lencería, *f.* **l. tape,** trenzadera, *f.* **l. thread,** hilo de lino, *m*

liner /'lainər/ *n* (ship) transatlántico, *m;* buque de vapor, *m; Aer.* avión de pasaje, *m*

linesman /'lainzmən/ *n* soldado de línea, *m; Sports.* juez de línea, *m*

ling /lɪŋ/ *n Bot.* brezo, *m; Ichth.* especie de abadejo, *f*

linger /'lɪŋgər/ *vi* (remain) quedarse; tardar en marcharse; ir lentamente; hacer algo despacio

lingerie /ˌlɑnʒə'rei/ *n* ropa blanca, *f*

lingering /'lɪŋgərɪŋ/ *a* lento; largo, prolongado; melancólico, triste

lingeringly /'lɪŋgərɪŋli/ *adv* lentamente; largamente; melancólicamente

linguist /'lɪŋgwɪst/ *n* lingüista, *mf*

linguistic /lɪŋ'gwɪstɪk/ *a* lingüístico

linguistics /lɪŋ'gwɪstɪks/ *n* lingüística, *f*

liniment /'lɪnəmənt/ *n* linimento, *m*

lining /'lainɪŋ/ *n* (of a garment, etc.) forro, *m;* (building) revestimiento, *m*

link /lɪŋk/ *n* (in a chain) eslabón, *m;* (of beads) sarta, *f; Fig.* enlace, *m,* cadena, *f;* conexión, *f; Mech.* corredera, *f;* (torch) hacha de viento, *f.* —*vt* enlazar, unir; *Fig.* encadenar. **missing l.,** *Fig.* estabón perdido, *m.* **to l. arms,** cogerse del brazo

linking /'lɪŋkɪŋ/ *n* encadenamiento, *m; Fig.* conexión, *f*

links /lɪŋks/ *n pl* campo de golf, *m*

linoleum /lɪ'nouliəm/ *n* linóleo, *m*

linotype /'lainəˌtaip/ *n* linotipia, *f*

linseed /'lɪnˌsid/ *n* linaza, *f.* **l. cake,** bagazo, *m.* **l.-oil,** aceite de linaza, *m*

lint /lɪnt/ *n Med.* hilas, *f pl;* (fluff) borra, *f*

lintel /'lɪntl̩/ *n* dintel, *m;* (threshold) umbral, *m*

lion /'laiən/ *n* león, *m; Fig.* celebridad, *f.* **l. cage** or **den,** leonera, *f.* **l.-hearted,** valeroso. **l.-hunter,** cazador (-ra) de leones. **l.-keeper,** leonero (-ra). **lion's mane,** melena, *f.* **l.-tamer,** domador (-ra) de leones

lioness /'laiənɪs/ *n* leona, *f*

lionize /'laiəˌnaiz/ *vt* dar bombo (a), hacer la rueda (a), tratar como una celebridad (a)

lion's share *n* parte del león, tajada del león, *f*

lip /lɪp/ *n* labio, *m;* (of a vessel) pico, *m;* (of a crater) borde, *m; Fig.* boca, *f.* **to open one's lips,** abrir la boca. **to smack one's lips,** chuparse los dedos. **lip reading,** lectura labial, *f.* **lip-service,** amor fingido, *m;* promesas hipócritas, *f pl.* **lip stick,** lápiz para los labios, *m*

lipped /lɪpt/ *a* (in compounds) con labios..., que tiene labios; (of vessels in compounds) con... picos

liquefaction /ˌlɪkwə'fækʃən/ *n* licuefacción, *f*

liquefiable /'lɪkwəˌfaiəbəl/ *a* liquidable

liquefy /'lɪkwəˌfai/ *vt* liquidar. —*vi* liquidarse

liqueur /lɪ'kɜr/ *n* licor, *m.* **l.-glass,** copita de licor, *f.* **l.-set,** licorera, *f*

liquid /'lɪkwɪd/ *n* líquido, *m, a* líquido; límpido. **l. air,** aire líquido, *m.* **l. measure,** medida para líquidos, *f*

liquidate /'lɪkwɪˌdeit/ *vt* liquidar; saldar (cuentas); *Mil.* soldar

liquidation /ˌlɪkwɪ'deiʃən/ *n* liquidación, *f*

liquidness /'lɪkwɪdnɪs/ *n* liquidez, *f;* fluidez, *f*

liquor /'lɪkər/ *n* licor, *m.* **l. shop,** aguardentería, *f.* **l. traffic,** negocio de vinos y licores, *m;* contrabando, *m*

lira /'lɪərə/ *n* lira, *f*

Lisbon /'lɪzbən/ Lisboa, *f*

lisp /lɪsp/ *n* ceceo, *m;* balbuceo, *m, vi* cecear; balbucir

lisping /'lɪspɪŋ/ *a* ceceoso; balbuciente. —*n* ceceo, *m;* (of a child, etc.) balbuceo, *m*

lissome /'lɪsəm/ *a* flexible; ágil

list /lɪst/ *n* lista, *f;* catálogo, *m;* matrícula, *f; Naut.* recalcada, *f;* inclinación, *f;* (tournament) liza, *f.* —*vt* hacer una lista de; catalogar; matricular, inscribir. —*vi Naut.* recalcar; inclinarse a un lado. **to enter the lists,** entrar en liza. **l. of wines,** lista de vinos, *f*

listen /'lɪsən/ *vi* escuchar; (attend) attender. **Don't you want to l. to the music?** ¿No quieres escuchar la música? **to l. in,** (to the radio) escuchar la radio; (eavesdrop) escuchar a hurtadillas

listener /'lɪsənər/ *n* oyente, *mf;* (to radio) radiooyente, *mf*

listless /'lɪstlɪs/ *a* lánguido, apático, indiferente

listlessly /'lɪstlɪsli/ *adv* lánguidamente, indiferentemente

listlessness /'lɪstlɪsnɪs/ *n* apatía, languidez, indiferencia, inercia, *f*

litany /'lɪtn̩i/ *n* letanía, *f*

liter /'litər/ *n* litro, *m*

literal /'lɪtərəl/ *a* literal. **l.-minded,** sin imaginación

literalness /'lɪtərəlnɪs/ *n* literalidad, *f*

literary /'lɪtəˌrɛri/ *a* literario

literary executor *n* depositario de la obra literaria, *m*

literate /'lɪtərɪt/ *a* and *n* literato (-ta)

literature /'lɪtərətʃər/ *n* literatura, *f*

lithe /laið/ *a* flexible; sinuoso y delgado; ágil

litheness /'laiðnɪs/ *n* flexibilidad, *f;* sinuosidad, *f;* delgadez, *f;* agilidad, *f*

lithograph /'lɪθəˌgræf/ *n* litografía, *f, vt* litografiar

lithographer /lɪ'ðɒgrəfər/ *n* litógrafo, *m*

lithographic /ˌlɪðə'græfɪk/ *a* litográfico

lithography /lɪ'θɒgrəfi/ *n* litografía, *f*

Lithuania /ˌlɪθu'einiə/ Lituania, *f*

Lithuanian /ˌlɪθu'einiən/ *a* lituano, *n* lituano (-na); (language) lituano, *m*

litigant /'lɪtɪgənt/ *n* litigante, *mf*

litigate /'lɪtɪˌgeit/ *vi* and *vt* litigar, pleitear

litigation /ˌlɪtɪ'geiʃən/ *n* litigación, *f*

litigious /lɪ'tɪdʒəs/ *a* litigioso

litmus /'lɪtməs/ *n* tornasol, *m.* **l. paper,** papel de tornasol, *m*

litter /'lɪtər/ *n* litera, *f;* (stretcher) camilla, *f;* (bed) lecho, *m;* cama de paja, *f;* (brood) camada, cría, *f;* (rubbish) cosas en desorden, *f pl;* (papers) papeletas, *f pl;* (untidiness) desarreglo, desorden, *m,* confusión, *f, vt* poner en desorden

little /'lɪtl̩/ *a* pequeño; poco; (scanty) escaso; insignificante; bajo, mezquino. —*adv* poco. **a l.,** un poco (de); un tanto. **in l.,** en pequeño. **not a l.,** no poco; bastante. **l. by l.,** poco a poco. **l. or no,** poco o nada. **however l.,** por pequeño que. **as l. as possible,** lo menos posible. **to make l. of,** no dar importancia a; sacar poco en claro de, no comprender bien; no hacer caso de; (persons) acoger mal. **l. by l.,** poco a poco. **l. finger,** dedo meñique, *m.* **l. one,** pequeñuela, *f,* pequeñito, *m*

littleness /'lɪtl̩nɪs/ *n* pequeñez, *f;* poquedad, *f;* mezquindad, *f;* trivialidad, *f*

littoral /'lɪtərəl/ *a* and *n* litoral, *m*

liturgical /lɪ'tɜrdʒɪkəl/ *a* litúrgico. **l. calendar,** calendario litúrgico, *m*

liturgical vestment *n* paramento litúrgico, *m*

liturgy /'lɪtərdʒi/ *n* liturgia, *f*

live /laiv/ *a* vivo, viviente; (alight) encendido; (of a wire, etc.) cargado de electricidad. **l. cartridge,** cartucho con bala, *m.* **l. coal,** ascua, *f.* **l.-stock,**

ganadería, *f.* **l. wire,** conductor eléctrico, *m; Fig.* fuerza viva, *f*

live /laiv/ *vi* vivir; residir, habitar; (of ships) mantenerse a flote; salvarse; subsistir. —*vt* (one's life) llevar, pasar. **Long l.!** ¡Viva! **to have enough to l. on,** tener de que vivir. **to l. together,** convivir. **to l. again,** volver a vivir. **to l. at,** vivir en, habitar. **to l. down,** sobrevivir a; (a fault) lograr borrar. **to l. on,** vivir de. **to l. up to,** vivir con arreglo a, vivir en conformidad con; estar al nivel de, merecer. **to l. up to one's income,** vivir al día, gastarse toda la renta

live broadcast *n* emisión en directo, *f*

livelihood /'laivli,hʊd/ *n* vida, subsistencia, *f.* **to make a l.,** ganarse la vida

liveliness /'laivlinɪs/ *n* vivacidad, vida, *f;* animación, *f;* alegría, *f*

livelong /'lɪv,lɔŋ/ *a* entero, todo; eterno. **all the l. day,** todo el santo día

lively /'laivli/ *a* vivo; vivaracho; brioso, enérgico; alegre; bullicioso; animado; (fresh) fresco; (of colors) brilliante; intenso

liver /'lɪvər/ *n* vividor (-ra), el, *m,* (*f,* la) que vive; habitante, *m; Anat.* hígado, *m.* **l. cancer,** cáncer del hígado, *m.* **l. complaint,** mal de hígado, *m.* **l. extract,** extracto de hígado, *m*

livery /'lɪvəri/ *n* librea, *f;* uniforme, *m; Poet.* vestiduras, *f pl.* **l. stables,** pensión de caballos, *f;* cochería de alquiler, *f*

livid /'lɪvɪd/ *a* lívido; cárdeno, amoratado

lividness /'lɪvɪdnɪs/ *n* lividez, *f*

living /'lɪvɪŋ/ *a* viviente; vivo, vital. —*n* vida, *f;* modo de vivir, *m;* beneficio eclesiástico, *m.* **the l.,** los vivos. **to make one's l.,** ganarse la vida. **l. memory,** memoria de personas vivientes, memoria de los que aún viven, *f.* **l.-room,** sala de estar, *f.* **l. soul,** ser viviente; *Inf.* bicho viviente, *m.* **l. wage,** jornal básico, *m*

lizard /'lɪzərd/ *n* lagarto (-ta). **giant l.,** dragón, *m.* **wall l.,** lagartija, *f.* **l. hole,** lagartera, *f*

llama /'lɑmə/ *n* llama, *f*

load /loud/ *n* carga, *f;* peso, *m;* (cart) carretada, *f; Elec.* carga, *f;* (quantity) cantidad, *f.* —*vt* cargar (con); (with honors) llenar (de); (*Fig.* weigh down) agobiar (con); (a stick with lead) emplomar; (*Elec.* and of dice) cargar; (wine) mezclar vino con un narcótico. **to be loaded with fruit,** estar cargado de fruta. **to l. oneself with,** cargarse de. **to l. the dice,** cargar los dados. **to l. again,** recargar

loader /'loudər/ *n* cargador, *m*

loading /'loudɪŋ/ *n* carga, *f.* **l. depot,** cargadero, *m*

loaf /louf/ *n* pan, *m;* (French) barra de pan, *f.* —*vi* golfear, vagabundear, gandulear. **l. sugar,** azúcar de pilón, *m*

loafer /'loufər/ *n* vago (-ga); azotacalles, *mf;* gandul (-la); golfo (-fa)

loafing /'loufɪŋ/ *n* gandulería, *f,* vagabundeo, *m*

loam /loum/ *n* marga, *f*

loamy /'loumi/ *a* margoso

loan /loun/ *n* empréstito, *m;* (lending) prestación, *f;* préstamo, *m.* —*vt* prestar. **l. fund,** caja de empréstitos, *f.* **l. company office,** casa de préstamos, *f*

loath /louθ/ *a* desinclinado, poco dispuesto

loathe /louð/ *vt* abominar, detestar, odiar, aborrecer; repugnar

loather /'louðər/ *n* el, *m,* (*f,* la) que odia; aborrecedor (-ra)

loathing /'louðɪŋ/ *n* aborrecimiento, odio, *m;* repugnancia, aversión, *f*

loathsome /'louðsəm/ *a* odioso, aborrecible; asqueroso; repugnante

loathsomeness /'louðsəmnɪs/ *n* carácter repugnante, *m;* asquerosidad, *f*

lobby /'lɒbi/ *n* pasillo, *m;* antecámara, *f;* (in a hotel, house) vestíbulo, recibidor, *m;* (waiting-room) sala de espera, *f;* (in Parliament) sala de los pasos perdidos, *f.* —*vt* and *vi* cabildear

lobe /loub/ *n Bot.* lobo, *m;* (*Anat. Archit.*) lóbulo, *m*

lobster /'lɒbstər/ *n* langosta, *f;* bogavante, *m.* **l.-pot,** cambín, *m,* nasa, *f*

local /'loukəl/ *a* local; de la localidad. **l. anesthetic,** anestésico local, *m.* **l. color,** color local, *m*

locale /lou'kæl/ *n* local, *m*

locality /lou'kælɪti/ *n* localidad, *f;* situación, *f*

localization /,loukələ'zeiʃən/ *n* localización, *f*

localize /'loukə,laiz/ *vt* localizar

locate /'loukeit/ *vt* situar; colocar; localizar. **to be located,** situarse; hallarse

location /lou'keiʃən/ *n* colocación, *f;* emplazamiento, *m;* localidad, *f;* situación, posición, *f*

loch /lɒk/ *n* lago, *m*

lock /lɒk/ *n* cerradura (of a door, including a vehicle) *f;* (of a gun) cerrojo, *m;* (in wrestling) llave, *f;* (on rivers, canals) presa, *f;* (at a dock) esclusa, *f;* (of hair) mechón, *m,* guedeja, *f;* (ringlet) bucle, *m; pl* **locks,** (hair) cabellos, *m pl,* pelo, *m.* **spring l.,** cerradura de golpe, *f.* **to put a l. on,** poner cerradura a. **under l. and key,** bajo cuatro llaves. **l.-jaw,** trismo, *m.* **l. keeper,** esclusero, *m.* **l.-out strike,** huelga patronal, *f*

lock /lɒk/ *vt* cerrar con llave; *Fig.* encerrar; (embrace) abrazar estrechamente; (of wheels, etc.) trabar; (twine) entrelazar. —*vi* cerrarse con llave. **to l. in,** cerrar con llave; encerrar. **to l. out,** cerrar la puerta (a); dejar en la calle (a). **to l. up,** encerrar; (imprison) encarcelar

locker /'lɒkər/ *n* (drawer) cajón, *m;* (cupboard) armario, *m; Naut.* cajonada, *f*

locket /'lɒkɪt/ *n* guardapelo, *m;* medallón, *m*

locksmith /'lɒk,smɪθ/ *n* cerrajero, *m.* **locksmith's trade,** cerrajería, *f*

locomotion /,loukə'mouʃən/ *n* locomoción, *f*

locomotive /,loukə'moutɪv/ *a* locomotor. —*n* locomotora, *f*

locum tenens /'loukəm 'tinɛnz/ *n* interino (-na)

locust /'loukəst/ *n* langosta migratoria, *f*

locution /lou'kyuʃən/ *n* locución, *f*

lode /loud/ *n* filón, *m*

lodestar /'loud,stɑr/ *n* estrella polar, *f; Fig.* norte, *m*

lodge /lɒdʒ/ *n* casita, garita, *f;* casa de guarda, *f;* (freemason's) logia, *f;* (porter's) portería, *f, vi* hospedarse, alojarse, vivir, parar; penetrar; entrar (en); fijarse (en). —*vt* hospedar, alojar; albergar; (a blow) asestar; (a complaint) hacer, dar; (money, etc.) depositar. **to l. an accusation against,** querellarse contra, quejarse de. **l.-keeper,** conserje, *m*

lodger /'lɒdʒər/ *n* huésped (-eda)

lodging /'lɒdʒɪŋ/ *n* hospedaje, alojamiento, *m;* (inn) posada, *f;* residencia, *f;* casa, *f.* **l.-house,** casa de huéspedes, *f*

loft /lɔft/ *n* desván, sotabanco, *m;* pajar, *m*

loftily /'lɔftḷi/ *adv* en alto; (proudly) con arrogancia, con altanería

loftiness /'lɔftinɪs/ *n* altura, *f;* sublimidad, *f;* nobleza, *f;* dignidad, *f;* (haughtiness) altanería, soberbia, *f*

lofty /'lɔfti/ *a* alto; sublime; noble; eminente; (haughty) altanero, soberbio

log /lɔg/ *n* madero, tronco, *m;* palo, *m;* leño, *m; Naut.,* diario de a bardo *m,* barquilla, *f.* **to lie like a log,** estar hecho un tronco. **log-book,** *Naut.* cuaderno de bitácora, *m.* **log-cabin,** cabañas de troncos, *m.* **log-wood,** palo campeche, *m*

logarithm /'lɔgə,rɪðəm/ *n* logaritmo, *m*

logarithmic /,lɔgə'rɪðmɪk/ *a* logarítmico

logic /'lɒdʒɪk/ *n* lógica, *f*

logical /'lɒdʒɪkəl/ *a* lógico

logician /lou'dʒɪʃən/ *n* lógico (-ca)

loin /lɔin/ *n* ijar, *m;* (of meat) falda, *f; pl* **loins,** lomos, riñones *m pl.* **to gird up one's loins,** *Fig.* arremangarse los faldones. **l.-cloth,** taparrabo, *m*

loiter /'lɔitər/ *vi* vagabundear, vagar, errar; haraganear; rezagarse

loiterer /'lɔitərər/ *n* haragán (-ana); vago (-ga); rezagado (-da)

loll /lɒl/ *vi* recostarse (en), apoyarse (en). —*vt* (the tongue) sacar

Lombardy-Venetia /'lɒmbərdi və'niʃə/ Lombardo-Véneto, *m*

London /'lʌndən/ Londres, *m*

Londoner /'lʌndənər/ *n* londinense, *mf*

lone /loun/. See **lonely**

loneliness /'lounlinɪs/ *n* soledad, *f;* aislamiento, *m*

lonely /'lounli/ *a* solitario; solo; aislado, remoto; desierto

lonesome /'lounsəm/ *a* solo, solitario

long /lɔŋ/ *a* largo; prolongado; de largo; (extensive) extenso; (big) grande; (much) mucho. **a l. time,** mucho tiempo. **It is five feet l.,** Tiene cinco pies de largo. **l.-armed,** que tiene los brazos largos. **l.-boat,** falúa, *f.* **l. clothes,** (infant's) mantillas, *f pl.* **l.-distance call,** conferencia telefónica, *f.* **l.-distance race,** carrera de fondo, *f.* **l.-eared,** de orejas largas. **l.-faced,** de cara larga, carilargo. **l.-forgotten,** olvidado hace mucho tiempo. **l.-haired,** que tiene el pelo largo. **l.-headed,** dolicocéfalo; *Fig.* astuto, sagaz. **l.-legged,** zanquilargo, zancudo. **l.-lived,** que vive hasta una edad avanzada; longevo; duradero. **l.-lost,** perdido hace mucho tiempo. **l.-sighted,** présbita; previsor; sagaz. **l.-standing,** viejo, de muchos años. **l.-suffering,** sufrido, paciente. **l.-tailed,** de cola larga. **l.-waisted,** de talle largo. **l.-winded,** prolijo

long /lɔŋ/ *adv* mucho tiempo; mucho; durante mucho tiempo. **as l. as,** mientras (que). **before l.,** dentro de poco. **the l. and the short of it,** en resumidas cuentas. **How l. has she been here?** ¿Cuánto tiempo hace que está aquí? **not l. before,** poco tiempo antes. **l. ago,** tiempo ha, muchos años ha

long /lɔŋ/ *vi* anhelar, suspirar (por), desear con vehemencia

longanimity /ˌlɒŋgə'nɪmɪti/ *n* longanimidad, *f*

longer /'lɔŋgər/ *a compar* más largo. —*adv compar* más tiempo. **How much l. must we wait?** ¿Cuánto tiempo más hemos de esperar? **He can no l. walk as he used,** Ya no puede andar como antes

longevity /lɒn'dʒɛvɪti/ *n* longevidad, *f*

longing /'lɔŋɪŋ/ *a* anheloso, ansioso; de envidia. —*n* anhelo, *m,* ansia, *f;* deseo vehemente, *m;* envidia, *f*

longingly /'lɔŋɪŋli/ *adv* con ansia; impacientemente; con envidia

longish /'lɔŋɪʃ/ *a* algo largo

longitude /'lɒndʒɪˌtud/ *n* longitud, *f*

longitudinal /ˌlɒndʒɪ'tudn̩l/ *a* longitudinal

long take *n Cinema.* toma larga, *f*

loofah /'lufə/ *n* esponja vegetal, *f*

look /lʊk/ *n* mirada, *f;* (glance) vistazo, *m,* ojeada, *f;* (air) semblante, aire, porte, *m;* (appearance) aspecto, *m;* apariencia, *f.* **good looks,** buen parecer, *m;* guapeza, *f.* **the new l.,** la nueva línea, la nueva silueta, la nueva moda. **to be on the l.-out,** andar a la mira

look /lʊk/ *vi* and *vt* mirar; considerar, contemplar; (appear, seem) parecer; tener aire (de); tener aspecto (de); hacer el efecto (de); (show oneself) mostrarse; (of buildings, etc.) caer (a), dar (a); mirar (a).; (seem to be) revelar (e.g., *You don't l. thirty,* No revelas treinta años) **to l. alike,** parecerse. **to l. hopeful,** *Fig.* prometer bien. **to l. out of the corner of the eye,** mirar de reojo. **to l. (a person) up and down,** mirar de hito en hito. **to l. about one,** mirar a su alrededor; observar. **to l. after,** tener la mirada puesta en, mirar; (care for) cuidar; (watch) vigilar; mirar por. **to l. at,** mirar; considerar; examinar. **He looked at his watch,** Miró su reloj. **He looked at her,** La miró. **to l. away,** desviar los ojos, apartar la mirada. **to l. back,** mirar hacia atrás, volver la cabeza; (in thought) pensar en el pasado. **to l. down,** bajar los ojos; mirar el suelo; mirar hacia abajo. **to l. down upon,** dominar, mirar a; (scorn) despreciar; mirar de arriba para abajo. **to l. for,** buscar; buscar con los ojos; (await) aguardar; (expect) esperar. **to l. forward,** mirar hacia el porvenir; pensar en el futuro; esperar con ilusión. **to l. in,** entrar por un instante, hacer una visita corta. **to l. into,** mirar dentro de; mirar hacia el interior de; estudiar, investigar. **to l. on,** *vt* mirar; considerar; (of buildings, etc.) dar a. —*vi* ser espectador. **to l. on to,** dar a, mirar a. **to l. out,** *vi* (be careful) tener cuidado; (look through) mirar por; asomarse a. —*vt* (search) buscar; (find) hallar; (choose) escoger, elegir. **L. out!** ¡Atención! ¡Ojo! **to l. out for,** buscar; (await) aguardar, esperar; (be careful) tener cuidado con. **to l. out of,** mirar por; asomarse a. **to l. over,** mirar bien; (persons) mirar de hito en hito; examinar; visitar; (a house) inspeccionar; (a book) hojear; mirar superficialmente. **to l. round,** *vt* (a place) visitar. —*vi* volver la cabeza, volverse; mirar hacia atrás. **to l. round for,** buscar con los ojos; buscar por todas partes. **to l. through,** mirar por; mirar a través de; examinar; (search) registrar; (understand) registrar. **to l. to,** (be careful of) tener cuidado de; (attend to) atender a; (care for) cuidar de; (count on) contar con; (resort to) acudir a; (await) esperar. **to l. toward,** mirar hacia, mirar en la dirección de; caer a. **to l. up,** *vi* mirar hacia arriba; (aspire) aspirar; (improve) mejorar. —*vt* visitar, ir (or venir) a ver; (turn up) buscar; averiguar. **to l. upon,** mirar. Other meanings see to l. on. **They l. upon her as their daughter,** La miran como una hija suya. **to l. up to,** *Fig.* respetar

looked-for /'lʊkt ˌfɔr/ *a* esperado; deseado

looking /'lʊkɪŋ/ *a* (in compounds) de... aspecto, de... apariencia. **dirty-l.,** de aspecto sucio. **l.-glass,** espejo, *m*

lookout /'lʊkˌaut/ vigilancia, observación, *f;* (view) vista, *f,* panorama, *m;* (viewpoint) miradero, *m; Mil.* atalaya, *m; Naut.* gaviero, *m;* (*Fig.* prospect) perspectiva, *f*

loom /lum/ *n* telar, *m, vi* asomar, aparecer

loop /lup/ *n* (turn) vuelta, *f;* (in rivers, etc.) recodo, *m,* curva, *f;* (fold) pliegue, *m;* bucle, *m;* (fastening) fiador, *m,* presilla, *f; Aer.* rizo, *m;* (knot) nudo corredizo, *m.* **to l. the l.,** *Aer.* hacer el rizo, hacer rizos. **l.-line,** empalme de ferrocarril, *m*

loophole /'lupˌhoul/ *n* saetera, aspillera, *f; Fig.* escapatoria, *f;* pretexto, *m,* excusa, *f*

loose /lus/ *a* suelto; (free) libre; (slack) flojo; (of garments) holgado; (untied) desatado; (unfastened) desprendido; movible; (unchained) desencadenado; en libertad; (of the bowels) suelto (de vientre); (pendulous) colgante; (of a nail, tooth, etc.) inseguro; poco firme; que se mueve; (of knots, etc.) flojo; (of the mind, etc.) incoherente, ilógico; poco exacto; (of style, etc.) vago, impreciso; (of conduct) disoluto, vicioso; (careless) negligente, descuidado. —*vt* (untie) desatar; desprender; soltar; aflojar; (of a priest) absolver; *Fig.* desencadenar. **to break l.,** desprenderse; soltarse; libertarse; escapar; *Fig.* desencadenarse. **to let l.,** desatar; aflojar; poner en libertad; soltar; *Fig.* desencadenar; (interject) lanzar. **to turn l.,** poner en libertad; dar salida (a); echar de casa, poner en la calle. **to work l.,** desprenderse; aflojarse; desvencijarse. **l.-box,** caballeriza, *f.* **l. change,** suelto, *m.* **l.-leaf notebook,** libreta de hojas sueltas, *f*

loosely /'lusli/ *adv* flojamente; sueltamente; (vaguely) vagamente; incorrectamente; incoherentemente; (carelessly) negligentemente; (viciously) disolutamente

loosen /'lusən/ *vt* (untie) desatar; aflojar; soltar; desasir; (the tongue) desatar; *Fig.* hacer menos riguroso, ablandar

looseness /'lusnɪs/ *n* flojedad, *f;* (of clothing) holgura, *f;* soltura, *f;* relajación, *f;* (of the bowels) diarrea, *f;* (viciousness) licencia, *f,* libertinaje, *m;* (vagueness) vaguedad, *f;* incoherencia, *f*

loosening /'lusənɪŋ/ *n* desprendimiento, *m;* desasimiento, *m;* aflojamiento, *m*

loot /lut/ *n* botín, *m, vt* saquear

looter /'lutər/ *n* saqueador (-ra)

looting /'lutɪŋ/ *n* saqueo, pillaje, *m, a* saqueador

lop /lɒp/ *vt* mochar; podar; destroncar; cortar de un golpe. —*a* (of ears) gacho. **to lop off the ends,** cercenar. **to lop off the top,** desmochar. **lop-sided,** desproporcionado; desequilibrado

lopping /'lɒpɪŋ/ *n* desmoche, *m;* poda, *f*

loquacious /lou'kweiʃəs/ *a* locuaz, gárrulo

loquacity /lou'kwæsɪti/ *n* locuacidad, garrulidad, *f*

lord /lɔrd/ *n* señor, *m;* (husband) esposo, *m;* (English title) lord, *m,* (*pl* lores); (Christ) Señor, *m.* **feudal l.,** señor de horca y cuchillo, *m.* **my l.,** milord. **my lords,** milores. **Our L.,** Nuestro Señor. **the Lord's Prayer,** el Padrenuestro. **to l. it over,** mandar como señor, mandar a la baqueta. **L. Chamberlain,** camarero mayor, *m.* **L. Chancellor,** gran canciller, *m.* **L. Chief Justice,** presidente del tribunal supremo, *m.* **L.-Lieutenant,** virrey, *m.* **L. Mayor,** alcalde, *m.* **L. Privy Seal,** guardasellos del rey, *m*

lordliness /'lɔrdlinɪs/ *n* suntuosidad, *f;* liberalidad, munificencia, *f;* dignidad, *f;* (haughtiness) altivez, arrogancia, *f*

lordly /'lɔrdli/ *a* señorial, señoril; altivo, arrogante

lordship /ˈlɔrdʃɪp/ *n* señoría, *f;* señorío, poder, *m.* **his l.,** su señoría
lore /lɔr/ *n* saber, *m;* erudición, *f;* tradiciones, *f pl*
lorgnette /lɔrnˈyɛt/ *n* impertinentes, *m pl*
lorry /ˈlɔri/ *n* camión, *m;* carro, *m*
lose /luz/ *vt* perder; hacer perder, quitar; (forget) olvidar. —*vi* perder; (of clocks) atrasar. **to be lost in thought,** estar ensimismado, estar absorto. **to l. oneself (in)** perderse (en); abstraerse (en); entregarse (a). **to l. one's footing,** resbalar. **to l. one's way,** extraviarse, perder el camino. **to l. one's self-control,** perder el tino. **to l. one's head,** perder la cabeza. **to l. ground,** perder terreno. **to l. one's voice,** perder la voz. **to l. patience,** perder la paciencia, perder los estribos
loser /ˈluzər/ *n* perdedor (-ra)
losing /ˈluzɪŋ/ *a* perdedor. —*n* pérdida, *f*
loss /lɔs/ *n* pérdida, *f.* **at a l.,** *Com.* con pérdida; perplejo, dudoso. **heavy losses,** *Mil.* pérdidas cuantiosas, *f pl.* **We are at a l. for words...,** No tenemos palabras para...
lot /lɒt/ *n* suerte, *f;* fortuna, *f;* lote, *m;* parte, porción, cuota, *f;* (for building) solar, *m.* **a lot of people,** muchas personas. **Our lot would have been very different,** Nuestra suerte hubiera sido muy distinta, Otro gallo nos cantara. **to draw lots,** echar suertes, sortear. **to take the lot,** *Inf.* alzarse con el santo y la limosna
lotion /ˈlouʃən/ *n* loción, *f*
lottery /ˈlɒtəri/ *n* lotería, *f.* **l. ticket,** billete de la lotería, *m*
lotus /ˈloutəs/ *n* loto, *m.* **l.-eating,** lotofagía, *f; Fig.* indolencia, pereza, *f*
loud /laud/ *a* fuerte; (noisy) ruidoso, estrepitoso; alto; (gaudy) chillón, llamativo, cursi. —*adv* ruidosamente. **l.-speaker,** *Radio.* altavoz, altoparlante, *m*
loudly /ˈlaudli/ *adv* en alta voz; fuertemente; ruidosamente, con estrépito
loudness /ˈlaudnɪs/ *n* (noise) ruido, *m;* sonoridad, *f;* (force) fuerza, *f;* (of colors, etc.) mal gusto, *m,* vulgaridad, *f*
lounge /laundʒ/ *n* sala de estar, *f;* salón, *m, vi* reclinarse, ponerse a sus anchas; apoyarse (en); gandulear; vagar. **l. chair,** poltrona, *f.* **l.-lizard,** *Inf.* pollo pera, *m.* **l.-suit,** traje americano, *m*
lounger /ˈlaundʒər/ *n* holgazán (-ana); golfo (-fa), azotacalles, *mf*
louse /laus/ *n* piojo, *m*
lousy /ˈlauzi/ *a* piojoso
lout /laut/ *n* patán, zamacuco, *m*
loutish /ˈlautɪʃ/ *a* rústico
lovable /ˈlʌvəbəl/ *a* amable; simpático
lovableness /ˈlʌvəbəlnɪs/ *n* amabilidad, *f*
love /lʌv/ *n* amor, *m;* (friendship) amistad, *f;* (enthusiasm, liking) afición, *f;* (in tennis) cero, *m, vt* querer, amar; gustar mucho; tener afición (a). —*vi* estar enamorado. **I should l. to dine with you,** Me gustaría mucho cenar con Vds. **to be in l. with,** estar enamorado de. **to fall in l. with,** enamorarse de. **They l. each other,** Se quieren. **to make l. to,** hacer el amor (a), galantear. **l. affair,** amorío, lance de amor, *m.* **l.-bird,** periquito, *m.* **l.-letter,** carta amatoria, carta de amor, *f.* **l.-making,** galanteo, *m.* **l.-philtre,** filtro, *m.* **l.-song,** canción de amor, *f.* **l.-story,** historia de amor, *f.* **l.-token,** prenda de amor, *f*
loveless /ˈlʌvlɪs/ *a* sin amor
loveliness /ˈlʌvlinɪs/ *n* hermosura, belleza, *f;* encanto, *m;* amabilidad, *f*
lovely /ˈlʌvli/ *a* hermoso, bello; delicioso; amable; *Inf.* estupendo
lover /ˈlʌvər/ *n* amante, *mf;* aficionado (-da)
lovesick /ˈlʌvˌsɪk/ *a* enfermo de amor, enamorado
loving /ˈlʌvɪŋ/ *a* amoroso; cariñoso; (friendly) amistoso; de amor
low /lou/ *a* bajo; de poca altura; (of dresses, etc.) escotado; (of musical notes) grave; (soft) suave; (feeble) débil; (depressed) deprimido, triste, abatido; (plain) sencillo; (of a fever) lento; (of a bow) profundo; pequeño; inferior; humilde; (ill) enfermo; (vile) vil, ruin; obsceno, escabroso. —*adv* bajo; cerca de la tierra; en voz baja; (cheaply) barato, a bajo precio. **in a low voice,** en voz baja, paso. **to lay low,** (kill) tumbar; (knock down) derribar; incapacitar. **to lie low,** descansar; estar muerto; esconderse, agacharse; callar. **to run low,** escasear. **low-born,** de humilde cuna. **low-brow,** nada intelectual. **low comedy,** farsa, *f.* **low flying,** *n* bajo vuelo, *m, a* que vuela bajo; terrero, rastrero; que vuela a ras de tierra. **low frequency,** baja frecuencia, *f.* **low Latin,** bajo latín, *m.* **Low Mass,** misa rezada, *f.* **low neck,** escote, *m.* **low-necked,** escotado. **low-pitched,** grave. **low-spirited,** deprimido. **Low Sunday,** domingo de Cuasimodo, *m.* **low tension,** baja tensión, *f.* **low trick,** mala pasada, *f.* **low water,** marea baja, bajamar, *f;* (of rivers) estiaje, *m*
low /lou/ *vi* berrear, mugir. —*n* berrido, mugido, *m*
low-ceiling /ˈlou ˈsilɪŋ/ *a* bajo de techo.
Low Countries, the Los Países Bajos, *m*
lower /ˈlouər/ *vt* bajar; descolgar; disminuir; (price) rebajar; (a boat, sails) arriar. —*vi* (of persons) fruncir el ceño, mostrarse malhumorado; (of the sky) encapotarse, cargarse; (menace) amenazar. **to l. a boat,** arriar un bote. **to l. oneself,** (by a rope, etc.) descolgarse. **to l. the flag,** abatir la bandera
lower /ˈlouər/ *a compar* más bajo; menos alto; bajo; inferior. **l. classes,** clase obrera, *f,* clases bajas, *f pl.* **l. down,** más abajo. **L. House,** Cámara de los Comunes, *f;* cámara baja, *f.* **l. jaw,** mandibula inferior, *f.* **l. storey,** piso bajo, *m;* piso de abajo, *m*
lowering /ˈlouərɪŋ/ *n* abajamiento, *m;* descenso, *m;* (of prices) baja, *f;* (of a boat) arriada, *f;* (of the flag) abatimiento, *m, a* (of persons) ceñudo; (of the sky) anublado, encapotado; (threatening) amenazador
lowest /ˈlouɪst/ *a superl* el (la, etc.) más bajo; el (la, etc.) más profundo; ínfimo
lowing /ˈlauɪŋ/ *n* berrido, mugido, *m*
lowland /ˈloulənd/ *n* tierra baja, *f.* **the Lowlands,** las tierras bajas de Escocia
lowliness /ˈloulinɪs/ *n* humildad, *f;* modestia, *f*
lowly /ˈlouli/ *a* humilde
lowness /ˈlounɪs/ *n* poca altura, *f;* situación poco elevada, *f;* pequeñez, *f;* (of musical notes) gravedad, *f;* (softness) suavidad, *f;* (feebleness) debilidad, *f;* (sadness) tristeza, *f,* abatimiento, *m;* (of price) baratura, *f;* inferioridad, *f;* humildad, *f;* (vileness) bajeza, *f;* obscenidad, *f*
loyal /ˈlɔiəl/ *a* leal, fiel
loyalist /ˈlɔiəlɪst/ *n* realista, *mf;* defensor (-ra) del gobierno legítimo
loyalty /ˈlɔiəlti/ *n* lealtad, fidelidad, *f*
loyalty oath *n* (approximate equivalent) certificado de adhesión, *m*
lozenge /ˈlɒzɪndʒ/ *n* pastilla, *f*
lubricant /ˈlubrɪkənt/ *a* and *n* lubricante *m*
lubricate /ˈlubrɪˌkeit/ *vt* lubricar, engrasar
lubricating oil *n* aceite lubricante, *m*
lubrication /ˌlubrɪˈkeiʃən/ *n* lubricación, *f,* engrasado, *m*
lubricator /ˈlubrɪˌkeitər/ *n* lubricador, *m;* engrasador, *m*
Lucerne /luˈsɜrn/ Lucerna, *f*
lucid /ˈlusɪd/ *a* lúcido; claro
lucidity /luˈsɪdɪti/ *n* lucidez, *f;* claridad, *f*
lucidly /ˈlusɪdli/ *adv* claramente
luck /lʌk/ *n* destino, azar, *m;* (good) buenaventura, suerte, *f.* **to bring bad l.,** traer mala suerte. **to try one's l.,** probar fortuna
luckily /ˈlʌkəli/ *adv* por fortuna, afortunadamente, felizmente
luckless /ˈlʌklɪs/ *a* desdichado
lucky /ˈlʌki/ *a* afortunado; dichoso, venturoso; feliz. **to be l.,** tener buena suerte
lucrative /ˈlukrətɪv/ *a* lucrativo
lucre /ˈlukər/ *n* lucro, *m*
lucubration /ˌlukyʊˈbreiʃən/ *n* lucubración, *f*
ludicrous /ˈludɪkrəs/ *a* absurdo, risible, ridiculo
ludicrousness /ˈludɪkrəsnɪs/ *n* ridiculez, *f*
lug /lʌg/ *n* tirón, *m;* (ear and projection) oreja, *f, vt* tirar (de); arrastrar. **to lug about,** arrastrar (por); llevar con dificultad. **to lug in,** arrastrar adentro; introducir; hacer entrar. **to lug out,** arrastrar afuera; hacer salir
luggage /ˈlʌgɪdʒ/ *n* equipaje, *m.* **excess l.,** exceso de

equipaje, *m.* **piece of l.,** bulto, *m.* **to register one's l.,** facturar el equipaje. **l. carrier,** (on buses, etc.) baca, *f;* (on a car) portaequipajes, *m.* **l. porter,** mozo de equipajes, *m.* **l. rack,** (on a car) portaequipajes, *m;* (in a train) rejilla para el equipaje, *f.* **l. receipt,** talón de equipaje, *m.* **l. room,** consigna, *f.* **l. van,** furgón de equipajes, *m*

lugubrious /lʊ'gubriəs/ *a* lúgubre

lukewarm /'luk'wɔrm/ *a* tibio, templado; *Fig.* indiferente, frío

lukewarmness /'luk'wɔrmnɪs/ *n* tibieza, *f; Fig.* indiferencia, frialdad, *f*

lull /lʌl/ *n* momento de calma, *m;* tregua, *f;* silencio, *m, vt* (a child) arrullar, adormecer; (soothe) sosegar, calmar; disminuir, mitigar

lullaby /'lʌlə,bai/ *n* canción de cuna, *f*

lumbago /lʌm'beigou/ *n* lumbago, *m*

lumbar /'lʌmbər/ *a* lumbar

lumber /'lʌmbər/ *n* (wood) maderas de sierra, *f pl;* (rubbish) trastos viejos, *m pl.* —*vt* amontonar trastos viejos; obstruir. —*vi* andar pesadamente; avanzar ruidosamente, avanzar con ruido sordo. **l.-jack,** maderero, ganchero, *m.* **l.-room,** leonera, *f.* **l.-yard,** maderería, *f,* depósito de maderas, *m*

lumbering /'lʌmbərɪŋ/ *a* pesado

luminary /'lumə,nɛri/ *n* lumbrera, *f*

luminosity /,lumə'nɒsɪti/ *n* luminosidad, *f*

luminous /'lumənəs/ *a* luminoso

lump /lʌmp/ *n* masa, *f;* bulto, *m;* pedazo, *m;* (of sugar) terrón *m;* (swelling) hinchazón, *f;* protuberancia, *f.* —*vt* amontonar. **to l. together,** mezclar; incluir. **in the l.,** en la masa; en grueso. **Let him l. it!** ¡Que se rasque! **l. in one's throat,** nudo en la garganta, *m.* **l. of sugar,** terrón de azúcar, *m.* **l. sum,** cantidad gruesa, *f*

lumpishness /'lʌmpɪʃnɪs/ *n* hobachonería, *f*

lunacy /'lunəsi/ *n* locura, *f*

lunar /'lunər/ *a* lunar

lunatic /'lunətɪk/ *n* loco (-ca); demente, *mf a* de locos; loco. **l. asylum,** manicomio, *m*

lunch, luncheon /lʌntʃ; 'lʌntʃən;/ *n* almuerzo, *m;* (snack) merienda, *f.* —*vi* almorzar. **l. basket** or **pail,** fiambrera, *f*

lunette /lu'nɛt/ *n* (*Archit. Mil.*) luneta, *f*

lung /lʌŋ/ *n* pulmón, *m*

lunge /lʌndʒ/ *n* (fencing) estocada, *f;* embestida, *f, vi* dar una estocada; abalanzarse sobre

lurch /lɜrtʃ/ *n* sacudida, *f; Naut.* guiñada, *f;* tambaleo, *m;* movimiento brusco, *m.* —*vi Naut.* guiñar; tambalearse; andar haciendo eses. **to leave in the l.,** dejar plantado

lure /lʊr/ *n* añagaza, *f;* reclamo, *m;* aliciente, atractivo, *m;* seducción, *f.* —*vt* atraer, tentar

lurid /'lʊrɪd/ *a* misterioso, fantástico; cárdeno; ominoso; funesto, triste; (orange) anaranjado; (vicissitudinous) accidentado

lurk /lɜrk/ *vi* acechar, espiar; esconderse

lurking /'lɜrkɪŋ/ *a* (in ambush) en acecho; (of fear, etc.) vago

luscious /'lʌʃəs/ *a* delicioso; suculento; meloso; atractivo, apetitoso; sensual

lusciousness /'lʌʃəsnɪs/ *n* suculencia, *f;* melosidad, *f;* atractivo, *m;* sensualidad, *f*

lush /lʌʃ/ *a* jugoso; fresco y lozano; maduro

lust /lʌst/ *n* lujuria, lascivia, *f;* codicia, *f;* deseo, *m.* **l. for revenge,** deseo de venganza, *m*

luster /'lʌstər/ *n* lustre, brillo, *m;* brillantez, *f*

lusterless /'lʌstərlɪs/ *a* sin brillo; mate, deslustrado; (of eyes) apagado

lustful /'lʌstfəl/ *a* lujurioso, lúbrico, lascivo

lustrous /'lʌstrəs/ *a* lustroso

lusty /'lʌsti/ *a* vigoroso, fuerte, lozano

lute /lut/ *n* laúd, *m,* vihuela, *f.* **l.-player,** vihuelista, *mf*

Lutheran /'luθərən/ *a* luterano. —*n* luterano (-na)

Lutheranism /'luθərə,nɪzəm/ *n* luteranismo, *m*

luxation /lʌk'seiʃən/ *n* luxación, *f*

Luxembourg /'lʌksəm,bɜrg/ Luxemburgo, *m*

luxuriance /lʌg'ʒʊriəns/ *n* lozanía, *f;* exuberancia, superabundancia, *f*

luxuriant /lʌg'ʒʊriənt/ *a* lozano; fértil; exuberante

luxuriate /lʌg'ʒʊri,eit/ *vi* crecer con exuberancia; complacerse (en); disfrutar (de), gozar (de)

luxurious /lʌg'ʒʊriəs/ *a* lujoso

luxuriously /lʌg'ʒʊriəsli/ *adv* lujosamente, con lujo

luxury /'lʌkʃəri/ *n* lujo, *m.* **l. goods,** artículos de lujo, *m pl*

lyceum /lai'siəm/ *n* liceo, *m*

lye /lai/ *n* lejía, *f*

lying /'laiɪŋ/ *a* (recumbent) recostado; (untrue) mentiroso, falso. —*n* mentiras, *f pl.* **l.-in,** parto, *m*

lymph /lɪmf/ *n* linfa, *f;* vacuna, *f*

lymphatic /lɪm'fætɪk/ *a* linfático; flemático

lynch /lɪntʃ/ *vt* linchar

lynching /'lɪntʃɪŋ/ *n* linchamiento, *m*

lynx /lɪŋks/ *n* lince, *m.* **l.-eyed,** de ojos de lince

lyre /laiᵊr/ *n* lira, *f.* **l.-bird,** pájaro lira, *m*

lyric /'lɪrɪk/ *n* poesía lírica, *f;* poema lírico, *m;* letra (de una canción,) *f*

lyrical /'lɪrɪkəl/ *a* lírico

lyricism /'lɪrə,sɪzəm/ *n* lirismo, *m*

M

m /ɛm/ *n* (letter) eme, *f*
ma'am /mæm/ *n* señora, *f*
macabre /mə'kɑbrə/ *a* macabro
macadam /mə'kædəm/ *n* macadán, *m*, *a* de macadán
macadamize /mə'kædəˌmaiz/ *vt* macadanizar
macaroni /ˌmækə'rouni/ *n* macarrones, *m pl*
macaronic /ˌmækə'rɒnɪk/ *a* macarrónico
macaroon /ˌmækə'run/ *n* macarrón de almendras, *m*
Macassar oil /mə'kæsər/ *n* aceite de Macasar, *m*
macaw /mə'kɔ/ *n* macagua, *f*, guacamayo, *m*
mace /meis/ *n* maza, *f*; *Cul.* macis, *f*. **m.-bearer,** macero, *m*
Macedonian /ˌmæsɪ'douniən/ *a* macedón, macedonio. —*n* macedonio (-ia)
macerate /'mæsəˌreit/ *vt* macerar. —*vi* macerarse
Machiavellian /ˌmækiə'vɛliən/ *a* maquiavélico
Machiavellism /ˌmækiə'vɛlɪzəm/ *n* maquiavelismo, *m*
machination /ˌmækə'neiʃən/ *n* maquinación, *f*
machine /mə'ʃin/ *n* máquina, *f*; mecanismo, *m*; aparato, *m*; instrumento, *m*; organización, *f*, *vt* trabajar a máquina; *Sew.* coser a máquina. **m.-gun,** *n* ametralladora, *f*. —*vt* ametrallar. **m.-gun carrier,** portametralladoras, *m*. **m.-gunner,** ametrallador, *m*. **m.-made,** hecho a máquina. **m.-oil,** aceite de motores, *m*. **m.-shop,** taller de maquinaria, *m*. **m.-tool,** máquina herramienta, *f*
machinery /mə'ʃinəri/ *n* maquinaria, *f*; mecanismo, *m*; organización, *f*; sistema, *m*
machinist /mə'ʃinɪst/ *n* maquinista, *mf*; *Sew.* costurera a máquina, *f*
mackerel /'mækərəl/ *n* caballa, *f*. **m. sky,** cielo aborregado, *m*
mackintosh /'mækɪnˌtɒʃ/ *n* impermeable, *m*
macrocosm /'mækrəˌkɒzəm/ *n* macrocosmo, *m*
mad /mæd/ *a* loco; fuera de sí; (of a dog, etc.) rabioso; furioso. **as mad as a hatter,** loco como una cabra. **to drive mad,** volver loco (a). **to go mad,** volverse loco, enloquecer, perder el seso. **mad with joy (pain),** loco de alegría (dolor). **mad dog,** perro rabioso, *m*
madam /'mædəm/ *n* señora, *f*; (French form) madama, *f*. **Yes, m.,** Sí señora
madcap /'mædˌkæp/ *n* locuelo (-la), *f*, botarate, *m*; tarambana, *mf*
madden /'mædn̩/ *vt* enloquecer; enfurecer, exasperar
maddening /'mædn̩ɪŋ/ *a* exasperante, irritador
madder /'mædər/ *n Bot.* rubia, *f*
made /meid/ *past part* and *a* hecho; formado. **self-m. man,** un hombre hecho y derecho. **m.-to-measure,** hecho a la medida. **m.-up,** compuesto; (of clothes) confeccionado, ya hecho; (of the face) pintado; (ficticious) inventado, ficticio; artificial
Madeira /mə'dɪərə/ *n* vino de Madera, *m*, *a* de Madera
madhouse /'mædˌhaus/ *n* casa de locos, *f*, manicomio, *m*
madly /'mædli/ *adv* locamente; furiosamente
madman /'mædˌmæn/ *n* loco, *m*
madness /'mædnɪs/ *n* locura, *f*; (of a dog, etc.) rabia, *f*; furia, *f*
Madonna /mə'dɒnə/ *n* Madona, *f*
madrigal /'mædrɪgəl/ *n* madrigal, *m*
Madrilenian /ˌmædrə'liniən/ *a* madrileño, matritense. —*n* madrileño (-ña)
madwoman /'mædˌwʊmən/ *n* loca, *f*
Maecenas /mi'sinəs/ *n* mecenas, *m*
maelstrom /'meilstrəm/ *n* remolino, vórtice, *m*
magazine /ˌmægə'zin/ *n* (store) almacén, *m*; (for explosives) polvorín, *m*, santabárbara, *f*; (periodical) revista, *f*. **m. rifle,** rifle de repetición, *m*
Magdalene /'mægdəˌlin/ *n* magdalena, *f*
magenta /mə'dʒɛntə/ *n* color magenta, *m*
maggot /'mægət/ *n* gusano, *m*, cresa, *f*; *Fig.* manía, *f*, capricho, *m*
maggoty /'mægəti/ *a* gusanoso
magic /'mædʒɪk/ *n* magia, *f*; mágica, *f*; *Fig.* encanto, *m*, *a* mágico. **as if by m.,** por ensalmo. **m. lantern,** linterna mágica, *f*
magically /'mædʒɪkli/ *adv* por encanto
magician /mə'dʒɪʃən/ *n* mago, mágico, brujo, *m*; (conjurer) jugador de manos, *m*
magisterial /ˌmædʒə'stɪəriəl/ *a* magistral
magistracy /'mædʒəstrəsi/ *n* magistratura, *f*
magistrate /'mædʒəˌstreit/ *n* magistrado, *m*; juez municipal, *m*
Magi, the /'meidʒai/ *n pl* los reyes magos
Magna Carta /'mægnə 'kartə/ *n* Carta Magna, *f*
magnanimity /ˌmægnə'nɪmɪti/ *n* magnanimidad, generosidad, *f*
magnanimous /mæg'nænəməs/ *a* magnánimo, generoso
magnanimously /mæg'nænəməsli/ *adv* magnánimamente
magnate /'mægneit/ *n* magnate, *m*
magnesia /mæg'niʒə/ *n* magnesia, *f*
magnesium /mæg'niziəm/ *n* magnesio, *m*. **m. light,** luz de magnesio, *f*
magnet /'mægnɪt/ *n* imán, *m*
magnetic /mæg'nɛtɪk/ *a* magnético; *Fig.* atractivo. **m. field,** campo magnético, *m*. **m. needle,** brújula, *f*
magnetics /mæg'nɛtɪks/ *n* la ciencia del magnetismo, *f*
magnetism /'mægnɪˌtɪzəm/ *n* magnetismo, *m*
magnetization /ˌmægɪtɪ'zeiʃən/ *n* imanación, magnetización, *f*
magnetize /'mægnɪˌtaiz/ *vt* magnetizar, imanar; (hypnotize) magnetizar; *Fig.* atraer
magnification /ˌmægnəfɪ'keiʃən/ *n* (by a lens, etc.) aumento, *m*; exageración, *f*
magnificence /mæg'nɪfəsəns/ *n* magnificencia, *f*
magnificent /mæg'nɪfəsənt/ *a* magnífico
magnify /'mægnəˌfai/ *vt* (by lens) aumentar; exagerar; (praise) magnificar
magnifying /'mægnəˌfaiɪŋ/ *a* de aumento, vidrio de aumento. **m. glass,** lente de aumento, *m*
magniloquence /mæg'nɪləkwəns/ *n* grandilocuencia, *f*
magniloquent /mæg'nɪləkwənt/ *a* grandílocuo
magnitude /'mægnɪˌtud/ *n* magnitud, *f*
magnolia /mæg'noulyə/ *n* magnolia, *f*
magnum /'mægnəm/ *n* botella de dos litros, *f*
magpie /'mægˌpai/ *n* marica, picaza, *f*
maharajah /ˌmahə'radʒə/ *n* maharajá, *m*
mahogany /mə'hɒgəni/ *n* caoba, *f*, *a* de caoba
maid /meid/ *n* doncella, muchacha, *f*; virgen, *f*; soltera, *f*; (servant) criada, *f*; (daily) asistenta, *f*. **old m.,** solterona, *f*. **m.-of-all-work,** criada para todo, *f*. **m.-of-honor,** dama de honor, *f*
maiden /'meidn̩/ *n* doncella, joven, soltera, *f*; virgen, *f*; zagala, *f*. —*a* de soltera; soltera *f*; virginal; (of speeches, voyages, etc.) primero. **m. lady,** dama soltera, *f*. **m.-name,** apellido de soltera, *m*. **m. speech,** primer discurso, *m*
maidenhood /'meidn̩ˌhʊd/ *n* doncellez, virginidad, *f*
maidenly /'meidn̩li/ *a* virginal; modesto, modoso; tímido
maidservant /'meidˌsɜrvənt/ *n* criada, sirvienta, *f*
mail /meil/ *n* mala, *f*, (bag) valija, *f*, correo, *m*; correspondencia, *f*; (armour) cota de malla, *f*. —*vt* mandar por correo; armar con cota de malla. **coat of m.,** cota de malla, *f*. **royal m.,** malla real, *f*. **m.-bag,** valija de correo, *f*; portacartas, *m*. **m.-boat,** buque correo, *m*. **m.-cart,** ambulancia de correos, *f*. **m.-clad,** vestido de cota de malla; armado. **m.-coach,** coche correo, *m*, diligencia, *f*. **m.-order,** pedido postal, *m*. **m.-order business,** negocio de ventas por correo, *m*. **m.-plane,** avión postal, *m*. **m. service,** servicio de correos, *m*. **m. steamer,** vapor correo, *m*. **m. train,** tren correo, *m*. **m. van,** (on a train) furgón postal, *m*
mailed /meild/ *a* de malla; armado. **m. fist,** *Fig.* puño de hierro, *m*
maim /meim/ *vt* mancar; mutilar, tullir; estropear

maimed /meimd/ *a* manco; tullido, mutilado
main /mein/ *a* mayor; principal; más importante, esencial; maestro. —*n* (mainland) continente, *m;* (sea) océano, *m;* (pipe) cañería maestra, *f.* **by m. force,** por fuerza mayor. **in the m.,** en general, generalmente; en su mayoría. **m. beam,** viga maestra, *f.* **m. body,** (of a building) ala principal, *f;* (of a church) cuerpo (de iglesia), *m;* (of an army) cuerpo (del ejército), *m;* mayor parte, mayoría, *f.* **m. line,** línea principal, *f.* **m. mast,** palo mayor, *m.* **m. thing,** cosa principal, *f,* lo más importante. **m. wall,** pared maestra, *f*
mainland /ˈmeinˌlænd/ *n* continente, *m;* tierra firme, *f*
mainly /ˈmeinli/ *adv* principalmente; en su mayoría; generalmente
mainsail /ˈmeinˌseil/ *n* vela mayor, *f*
mainspring /ˈmeinˌsprɪŋ/ *n* (of a watch) muelle real, *m;* motivo principal, *m;* origen, *m*
mainstay /ˈmeinˌstei/ *n* estay mayor, *m; Fig.* sostén principal, *m*
maintain /meinˈtein/ *vt* mantener; sostener; tener; guardar; afirmar
maintainable /meinˈteinəbəl/ *a* sostenible; defendible
maintenance /ˈmeintənəns/ *n* mantenimiento, *m;* manutención, *f,* sustento, *m;* conservación, *f,* subsistencia, *f*
maize /meiz/ *n* maíz, *m.* **m. field,** maizal, *m*
majestic /məˈdʒɛstɪk/ *a* majestuoso
majesty /ˈmædʒəsti/ *n* majestad, *f;* majestuosidad, *f.* **His** or **Her M.,** Su Majestad
majolica /məˈdʒɒlɪkə/ *n* mayólica, *f*
major /ˈmeidʒər/ *a* mayor; principal. —*n* mayor de edad, *m; Mil.* comandante. **anthropology major,** alumno con la especialidad en antropología *m.* **m.-domo,** mayordomo, *m.* **m.-general,** general de división, *m.* **m. road,** carretera, *f;* ruta de prioridad, *f.* **m. scale,** escala mayor, *f*
Majorca /məˈdʒɔrkə/ Mallorca, *f*
majority /məˈdʒɔrɪti/ *n* mayoría, *f;* mayor número, *m;* generalidad, *f.* **to have attained one's m.,** ser mayor de edad
make /meik/ *vt* hacer; crear, formar; (manufacture) fabricar, confeccionar; construir; (produce) producir; causar; (prepare) preparar; (a bed, a fire, a remark, poetry, friends, enemies, war, a curtsey) hacer; (earn, win) ganar; (a speech) pronunciar; (compel) obligar (a), forzar (a); inclinar (a); (arrive at) alcanzar, llegar (a); (calculate) calcular; (arrange) arreglar; deducir; (be) ser; (equal) ser igual a; (think) creer; (appoint as) constituir (en), hacer; (behave) portarse (como). —*vi* (begin) ir (a), empezar (a); (make as though) hacer (como si); (of the tide) crecer; contribuir (a); tender (a). **He made as if to go,** Hizo como si de marchara. **to m. as though...,** aparentar, fingir. **It made me ill,** Me hizo sentir mal. **They have made it up,** Han hecho las paces. **They m. a great deal of money,** Hacen (or ganan) mucho dinero. **You cannot m. me believe it,** No puedes hacerme creerlo. **He is making himself ridiculous,** Se está poniendo en ridículo. **to m. ready,** preparar. **to m. the tea,** hacer el té; preparar el té. **Two and two m. four,** Dos y dos son cuatro. **to m. oneself known,** darse a conocer. **to m. one of...,** ser uno de... **to m. after,** seguir; correr detrás de. **to m. again,** hacer de nuevo, rehacer. **to m. away with,** quitar; suprimir; destruir; (kill) matar; (squander) derrochar; (steal) llevarse; hurtar. **to m. away with oneself,** quitarse la vida, suicidarse. **to m. for,** encaminarse a, dirigirse a; (attack) abalanzarse sobre, atacar; (tend to) contribuir a, tender a. **to m. off,** marcharse corriendo, largarse; huir, escaparse. **to m. out,** (discern) distinguir; descifrar; (understand) comprender; (prove) probar, justificar; (draw up) redactar; (fill in a form) completar, llenar; (a check, etc.) extender; (an account) hacer; (get on, succeed or otherwise) ir (with bien or mal); (convey) dar la impresión de que; sugerir. **I cannot m. it out,** No lo puedo comprender. **How did you m. out** (get on)? ¿Cómo te fue? **to m. over,** hacer de nuevo, rehacer; (transfer) ceder, traspasar. **to m. up,** hacer; acabar; concluir; (clothes) confeccionar; fabricar; (the face) pintarse, maquillarse; (the fire) echar carbón, etc. a; *Print.* compaginar; (invent) inventar; (lies) fabricar; (compose) formar; (package) empaquetar; reparar; indemnizar; compensar; (an account) ajustar; preparar; arreglar; (conciliate) conciliar; enumerar; *Theat.* caracterizarse. **to m. up for,** reemplazar; compensar; (lost time, etc.) recobrar. **to m. up to,** compensar; indemnizar; (flatter) adular, halagar; procurar congraciarse con, procurar obtener el favor de; (court) galantear (con). **m. an impression (on),** dejar(le a fulano) una impresión
make /meik/ *n* forma, *f;* hechura, *f;* estructura, *f;* confección, *f;* manufactura, *f;* producto, *m;* (trade name) marca, *f;* (character) carácter, temperamento, *m.* **m.-believe,** *n* artificio, pretexto, *m, a* fingido, *vi* fingir. **land of m.-believe,** reino de los sueños, *m.* **m. -up,** (for the face, etc.) maquillaje, *m; Theat.* caracterización, *f; Print.* imposición, *f;* (whole) conjunto, *m;* (character) carácter, modo de ser, *m*
maker /ˈmeikər/ *n* creador, *m;* autor (-ra); artífice, *mf;* (manufacturer) fabricante, *m;* constructor, *m;* (of clothes, etc.) confeccionador (-ra); (worker) obrero (-ra)
makeshift /ˈmeikˌʃɪft/ *n* expediente, *m, a* provisional
makeweight /ˈmeikˌweit/ *n* añadidura (de peso), *f,* contrapeso, *m; Fig.* suplente, *m*
making /ˈmeikɪŋ/ *n* creación, *f;* hechura, *f;* (manufacture) fabricación, *f;* construcción, *f;* (of clothes, etc.) confección, *f;* formación, *f;* preparación, *f;* estructura, *f;* composición, *f; pl* **makings,** (profits) ganancias, *f pl;* (elements) elementos, *m pl;* germen, *m;* rasgos esenciales, *m pl,* características, *f.* —*pl* **m.-up,** (of clothes) confección, *f; Print.* ajuste, *m;* (of the face) maquillaje, *m;* (invention) invención, *f;* fabricación, *f*
Malachite /ˈmæləˌkait/ *n* malaquita, *f*
maladjustment /ˌmæləˈdʒʌstmənt/ *n* mal ajuste, *m;* inadaptación, *f*
maladministration /ˌmælədˌmɪnəˈstrɛiˈʃən/ *n* desgobierno, *m,* mala administración, *f;* (of funds) malversación, *f*
maladroit /ˌmæləˈdrɔit/ *a* torpe
maladroitness /ˌmæləˈdrɔitnɪs/ *n* torpeza, *f*
malady /ˈmælədi/ *n* enfermedad, *f;* mal, *m*
Malaga /ˈmæləgə/ *n* vino de Málaga, *m*
malaria /məˈlɛəriə/ *n* paludismo, *m*
malarial /məˈlɛəriəl/ *a* palúdico. **m. fever,** fiebre palúdica, *f*
Malaya /məˈleiə/ Malasia, *f,* Archipiélago Malayo, *m*
Malayan /məˈleiən/ *a* malayo. —*n* malayo (-ya)
malcontent /ˌmælkənˈtɛnt/ *n* malcontento (-ta). —*a* descontento
Maldives /ˈmɔldivz/ Maldivas, *f pl*
male /meil/ *a* macho; masculino. —*n* macho, *m;* varón, *m.* **m. child,** niño, *m;* niño varón, *m;* (son) hijo varón, *m.* **m. flower,** flor masculina, *f.* **m. issue,** sucesión masculina, *f.* **m. nurse,** enfermero, *m.* **m. sex,** sexo masculino, *m*
malediction /ˌmælɪˈdɪkʃən/ *n* maldición, *f*
malefactor /ˈmæləˌfæktər/ *n* malhechor (-ra)
malefic /məˈlɛfɪk/ *a* maléfico
malevolence /məˈlɛvələns/ *n* malevolencia, *f*
malevolent /məˈlɛvələnt/ *a* malévolo, maligno
malformation /ˌmælfɔrˈmeiʃən/ *n* formación anormal, deformidad, deformación congénita, *f*
malice /mælɪs/ *n* malicia, *f; Law.* alevosía, *f.* **to bear m.,** guardar rencor
malicious /məˈlɪʃəs/ *a* malicioso; maligno, rencoroso
maliciousness /məˈlɪʃəsnɪs/ *n* malicia, mala intención, *f*
malign /məˈlain/ *vt* calumniar, difamar. —*a* maligno; malévolo
malignancy /məˈlɪgnənsi/ *n* malignidad, *f;* malevolencia, *f*
malignant /məˈlɪgnənt/ *a* maligno; malévolo; *Med.* maligno
malinger /məˈlɪŋgər/ *vi* fingirse enfermo
malingerer /məˈlɪŋgərər/ *n* enfermo (-ma) fingido (-da)
malingering /məˈlɪŋgərɪŋ/ *n* enfermedad fingida, *f*
mallard /ˈmælərd/ *n* pato (-ta), silvestre
malleability /ˌmæliəˈbɪlɪti/ *n* maleabilidad, *f*

malleable /'mæliəbəl/ *a* maleable

mallet /'mælɪt/ *n* mazo, *m;* (in croquet) pala, *f,* mazo, *m;* (in polo) maza (de polo), *f*

mallow /'mælou/ *n* malva, *f*

malmsey /'mɑmzi/ *n* (wine) malvasía, *f*

malnutrition /ˌmælnu'trɪʃən/ *n* desnutrición, alimentación deficiente, *f*

malodorous /mæl'oudərəs/ *a* de mal olor, hediondo, fétido

malpractice /mæl'præktɪs/ *n* (wrongdoing) maleficencia, *f;* (by a doctor) tratamiento equivocado, perjudicial o ilegal, *m;* (malversation) malversación, *f;* inmoralidad, *f*

malt /mɔlt/ *n* malta, *m.* —*vt* preparar el malta. **m.-house,** fábrica de malta, *f.* **m. vinegar,** vinagre de malta, *m*

malted milk /'mɔltɪd/ *n* leche malteada, *f*

Maltese /mɔl'tiz/ *a* maltés. —*n* maltés (-esa). **M. cat,** gato maltés, *m.* **M. cross,** cruz de Malta, *f.* **M. dog,** perro maltés, *m*

Malthusian /mæl'θuʒən/ *a* maltusiano

Malthusianism /mæl'θuʒəˌnɪzəm/ *n* maltusianismo, *m*

maltose /'mɔltous/ *n* maltosa, *f*

maltreat /mæl'trit/ *vt* maltratar

maltreatment /mæl'tritmənt/ *n* maltrato, *m,*

malt shop *n* café-nevería, *m*

mamma /'mæmə *for 1;* 'mamə *for 2*/ *n Anat.* mama, *f;* (mother) mamá, *f*

mammal /'mæməl/ *n* mamífero, *m*

mammalian /mə'meiliən/ *a* mamífero

mammary /'mæməri/ *a* mamario. **m. gland,** mama, teta, *f*

mammon /'mæmən/ *n* becerro de oro, *m*

mammoth /'mæməθ/ *n* mamut, *m, a* gigantesco, enorme

man /mæn/ *n* hombre, *m;* varón, *m;* persona, *f;* (servant) criado, *m;* (workman) obrero, *m;* (soldier) soldado, *m;* (sailor) marinero, *m;* (humanity) raza humana, *f;* (husband) marido, *m;* (chess) peón, *m;* (checkers) dama, *f;* (a ship) buque, *m.* **no man,** nadie; ningún hombre. **young man,** joven, *m.* **to a man,** como un solo hombre. **to come to man's estate,** llegar a la edad viril. **Man overboard!** ¡Hombre al agua! **man and wife,** marido y mujer, *m,* cónyuges, esposos, *m pl.* **man about town,** hombre de mundo, señorito, *m.* **man-at-arms,** hombre de armas, *m.* **man-eater,** caníbal, *mf;* tigre, *m.* **man-eating,** *a* antropófago. **man hater,** misántropo, *m;* mujer que odia a los hombres, *f.* **man-hole,** pozo, *m.* **man-hunter,** caníbal, *mf;* (woman) castigadora, *f.* **man in charge,** encargado, *m.* **man in the moon,** mujer de la luna, *f.* **man in the street,** hombre de la calle, hombre medio, *m.* **man of letters,** hombre de letras, literato, *m;* **man of straw,** bausán, *m;* (figure-head) testaferro, *m.* **man of the world,** hombre del mundo, *m.* **man of war,** buque de guerra, *m.* **man-power,** mano de obra, *f,* brazos, *m pl,* (e.g. *lack of man-power,* falta de brazos, *f*). **man servant,** criado, *m*

man /mæn/ *vt* armar; *Mil.* poner guarnición (a); ocupar; *Naut.* tripular; dirigir; *Fig.* fortificar

manacle /'mænəkəl/ *n* manilla, *f; pl* **manacles,** esposas, *f pl;* grillos, *m pl.* —*vt* poner esposas (a)

manage /'mænɪdʒ/ *vt* manejar; (animals) domar; dirigir; gobernar; administrar; (arrange) agenciar, arreglar; (work) explotar; (do) hacer; (eat) comer. —*vi* arreglárselas (para); (get along) ir tirando; (know how) saber hacer; (succeed in) lograr; (do) hacer

manageability /ˌmænɪdʒə'bɪlɪti/ *n* lo manejable; flexibilidad, *f;* (of animals, persons) docilidad, mansedumbre, *f*

manageable /'mænɪdʒəbəl/ *a* manejable; flexible; (of persons, animals) dócil

management /'mænɪdʒmənt/ *n* manejo, *m;* dirección, *f;* gobierno, *m;* administración, *f;* arreglo, *m;* (working) explotación, *f; Com.* gerencia, *f; Theat.* empresa, *f;* conducta, *f;* (economy) economía, *f;* (skill) habilidad, *f;* prudencia, *f.* **the m.,** la dirección, el cuerpo de directores. **domestic m.,** economía doméstica, *f*

manager /'mænɪdʒər/ *n* director, *m;* administrador, *m;* jefe, *m; Theat.* empresario, *m; Com.* gerente, *m;* regente, *m.* **She is not much of a m.,** No es muy mujer de su casa. **manager's office,** dirección, *f*

managerial /ˌmænɪ'dʒɪəriəl/ *a* directivo; administrativo. **m. board,** junta directiva, *f*

managership /'mænɪdʒərˌʃɪp/ *n* puesto de director, *m;* jefatura, *f*

managing /'mænɪdʒɪŋ/ *a* directivo; (officious) mandón, dominante; (niggardly) tacaño

manatee /'mænəˌti/ *n* manatí, *m*

Manchurian /mæn'tʃʊriən/ *a* manchuriano. —*n* manchuriano (-na)

mandarin /'mændərɪn/ *n* mandarín, *m;* (language) mandarina, *f.* **m. orange,** mandarina, *f*

mandate /'mændeit/ *n* mandato, *m.* **mandated territory,** territorios bajo mandato, *m pl*

mandatory /'mændəˌtɔri/ *a* obligatorio

mandible /'mændəbəl/ *n* mandíbula, *f*

mandolin /'mændl̩ɪn/ *n* bandolín, *m,* bandurria, *f*

mandrake /'mændreik, -drɪk/ *n* mandrágora, *f*

mandrill /'mændrɪl/ *n* mandril, *m*

mane /mein/ *n* melena, *f;* (of a horse) crines, *f pl*

maned /meind/ *a* (in compounds) con melena...; con crines...

maneuver /mə'nuvər/ *n* maniobra, *f.* —*vi* maniobrar, hacer maniobras. —*vt* hacer maniobrar; manipular

maneuvering /mə'nuvərɪŋ/ *n* maniobras, *f pl;* maquinaciones, intrigas, *f pl*

manfully /'mænfəli/ *adv* valientemente; vigorosamente

manganate /'mæŋgəneit/ *n* manganato, *m*

manganese /'mæŋgəˌnis, -ˌniz/ *n* manganeso, *m*

mange /meindʒ/ *n* sarna, *f;* (in sheep) roña, *f*

manger /'meindʒər/ *n* pesebre, *m*

manginess /'meindʒinɪs/ *n* estado sarnoso, *m*

mangle /'mæŋgəl/ *n* (for clothes) exprimidor de la ropa, *m.* —*vt* pasar por el exprimidor; (mutilate) mutilar, lacerar, magullar; (a text) mutilar

mangling /'mæŋglɪŋ/ *n* (mutilation) mutilación, laceración, *f*

mango /'mæŋgou/ *n* mango, *m*

mangy /'meindʒi/ *a* sarnoso

manhandle /'mænˌhændl̩/ *vt* maltratar

manhood /'mænhʊd/ *n* virilidad, *f;* edad viril, *f;* masculinidad, *f;* los hombres; (manliness) hombradía, *f,* valor, *m*

mania /'meiniə/ *n* manía, *f;* obsesión, *f;* capricho, *m,* chifladura, *f*

maniac /'meiniˌæk/ *n* maníaco (-ca). —*a* maníaco, maniático

manicure /'mænɪˌkyʊr/ *n* manicura, *f.* —*vt* arreglar las uñas. **m.-set,** estuche de manicura, *m*

manicurist /'mænɪˌkyʊrɪst/ *n* manicuro (-ra)

manifest /'mænəˌfɛst/ *n Naut.* manifiesto, *m.* —*vt* mostrar; hacer patente, probar; manifestarse. —*vi* publicar un manifiesto; (of spirits) manifestarse. —*a* manifiesto, evidente, claro, patente. **to make m.,** poner de manifiesto

manifestation /ˌmænəfə'steiʃən/ *n* manifestación, *f*

manifestly /'mænəˌfɛstli/ *adv* evidentemente, manifiestamente

manifesto /ˌmænə'fɛstou/ *n* manifiesto, *m*

manifold /'mænəˌfould/ *a* múltiple; numeroso; diverso, vario

manikin /'mænɪkɪn/ *n* enano, *m;* muñeco, *m; Art.* maniquí, *m*

Manilla /mə'nɪlə/ *n* Manila, *f;* cigarro filipino, *m.* **M. hemp,** cáñamo de Manila, *m*

maniple /'mænəpəl/ *n* manípulo, *m*

manipulate /mə'nɪpyəˌleit/ *vt* manipular

manipulation /məˌnɪpyə'leiʃən/ *n* manipulación, *f*

manipulative /mə'nɪpyəˌleitɪv/ *a* manipulador

mankind /'mæn'kaind/ *n* humanidad, raza humana, *f,* género humano, *m*

manlike /'mænˌlaik/ *a* de hombre, masculino; varonil; (of a woman) hombruno

manliness /'mænlinɪs/ *n* masculinidad, hombradía, *f;* virilidad, *f;* valor, *m;* (of a woman) aire hombruno, *m*

manly /'mænli/ *a* masculino, de hombre; varonil, viril; valiente; fuerte. **to be very m.,** ser muy hombre, ser todo un hombre

manna /'mænə/ *n* maná, *m*

mannequin /'mænɪkɪn/ *n* manequín, modelo, *f*. **m. parade,** exposición de modelos, *f*

manner /'mænər/ *n* manera, *f*, modo, *m;* aire, porte, *m;* conducta, *f;* (style) estilo, *m;* (sort) clase, *f; Gram.* modo, *m; pl* **manners,** modales, *m pl,* crianza, educación, *f;* (customs) costumbres, *f pl*. **after the m. of,** en (or según) el estilo de. **in a m. of speaking,** en cierto modo, para decirlo así. **in this m.,** de este modo. **to have bad (good) manners,** tener malos (buenos) modales, ser mal (bien) criado. **the novel of manners,** la novela de costumbres

mannered /'mænərd/ *a* amanerado; (in compounds)... educado, de... modales; de costumbres... **well-m.,** bien educado, de buenos modales

mannerism /'mænəˌrɪzəm/ *n* amaneramiento, *m;* afectación, *f; Theat.* latiguillo, *m*. **to acquire mannerisms,** amanerarse

mannerliness /'mænərlinɪs/ *n* cortesía, buena educación, urbanidad, *f*

mannerly /'mænərli/ *a* cortés, bien educado, atento

mannish /'mænɪʃ/ *a* (of a woman) hombruno; de hombre, masculino

manor /'mænər/ *n* feudo, *m;* finca, hacienda, *f;* casa solariega, *f;* señorío, *m*

manorial /mə'nɔriəl/ *a* señorial

mansion /'mænʃən/ *n* mansión, *f;* casa solariega, *f;* hotel, *m*. **m.-house,** casa solariega, *f;* residencia del alcalde de Londres, *f*

manslaughter /'mænˌslɔtər/ *n* homicidio, *m; Law.* homicidio sin premeditación, *m*

mantelpiece /'mæntl̩ˌpis/ *n* repisa de chimenea, *f*

mantilla /mæn'tɪlə/ *n* mantilla, *f*

mantle /'mæntl̩/ *n* capa, *f*, manto, *m; Fig.* cobertura, *f;* (gas) camiseta, *f*, manguito, *mf; Zool.* manto, *m*. —*vt* cubrir; envolver; ocultar. —*vi* extenderse; (of blushes) inundar, subirse (a las mejillas)

Mantuan /'mæntʃuən/ *a* mantuano

manual /'mænyuəl/ *a* manual. —*n* manual, *m; Mus.* teclado de órgano, *m*. **m. work,** trabajo manual, *m*

manufactory /ˌmænyə'fæktəri/ *n* fábrica, *f*, taller, *m*

manufacture /ˌmænyə'fæktʃər/ *n* fabricación, *f;* manufactura, *f*. —*vt* manufacturar, fabricar

manufacturer /ˌmænyə'fæktʃərər/ *n* fabricante, industrial, *m*. **manufacturer's price,** precio de fábrica, *m*

manufacturing /ˌmænyə'fæktʃərɪŋ/ *a* manufacturero, fabril. —*n* fabricación, *f*

manure /mə'nʊr/ *n* estiércol, abono, *m*. —*vt* estercolar, abonar. **m. heap,** estercolero, *m*

manuring /mə'nʊrɪŋ/ *n* estercoladura, *f*

manuscript /'mænyəˌskrɪpt/ *n* manuscrito, *m*, *a* manuscrito

Manx /mæŋks/ *a* manés

many /'mɛni/ *a* muchos (-as); numeroso; diversos (-as); varios (-as). —*n* muchos (-as); la mayoría; las masas; muchedumbre, multitud, *f*. **a great m.,** muchísimos, *m pl,* muchísimas, *f pl*; un gran número. **as m. as...,** tantos como... **How m. are there?** ¿Cuántos hay? ¿Cuántas hay? **m. a time,** muchas veces. **three too m.,** tres de más. **for m. long years,** por largos años. **m.-colored,** multicolor. **m.-headed,** con muchas cabezas. **m.-sided,** multilátero; polifacético; complicado

Maori /'mauri/ *n* maorí, *m*, (*pl* maoríes)

map /mæp/ *n* mapa, *m;* plano, *m;* (chart) carta, *f*. —*vt* hacer un mapa (or plano) de. **to map out,** *Surv.* apear; trazar; (plan) proyectar. **ordnance map,** mapa del estado mayor, *m*. **map of the world,** mapamundi, mapa del mundo, *m*. **map-making,** cartografía, *f*

maple /'meipəl/ *n* (tree) arce, *m;* (wood) madera de arce, *f*. **m.-syrup,** jarabe de arce, *m*

mapping /'mæpɪŋ/ *n* cartografía, *f*

mar /mɑr/ *vt* estropear; desfigurar; (happiness) destruir, aguar; frustrar

marabou /'mærəˌbu/ *n* marabú, *m*

maraschino /ˌmærə'skinou/ *n* marrasquino, *m*. **m. cherry,** cerezas en marrasquino, *f pl*

maraud /mə'rɔd/ *vi* merodear

marauder /mə'rɔdər/ *n* merodeador, *m*

marauding /mə'rɔdɪŋ/ *a* merodeador, *n* merodeo, *m*

marble /'mɑrbəl/ *n* mármol, *m;* (for playing with) canica, *f*, *a* de marmol, marmóreo; *Fig.* insensible; (of paper, etc.) jaspeado. —*vt* jaspear. **m. cutter,** marmolista, *m*. **m. works,** marmolería, *f*

marbled /'mɑrbəld/ *a* jaspeado

March /mɑrtʃ/ *n* marzo, *m*. **as mad as a M. hare,** loco como una cabra, loco de atar

march /mɑrtʃ/ *n* marcha, *f;* (step) paso, *m; Fig.* marcha, *f*, progreso, *m*. **forced m.,** marcha forzada, *f*. **quick m.,** paso doble, *m*. **to steal a m. on,** tomar la delantera (a), ganar por la mano (a). **to strike up a m.,** batir la marcha. **m.-past,** desfile, *m*

march /mɑrtʃ/ *vi* marchar; (of properties) lindar (con). —*vt* hacer marchar, poner en marcha (a). **to m. back,** *vi* regresar (or volver) a pie. —*vt* hacer volver a pie. **to m. in,** entrar (a pie) en. **to m. off,** marcharse. **to m. on,** seguir marchando; seguir adelante; avanzar. **to m. past,** desfilar ante

marching /'mɑrtʃɪŋ/ *n* marcha, *f*. —*a* en marcha; de marcha. **to receive one's m. orders,** recibir la orden de marchar; *Inf.* ser despedido. **m. order,** orden de marcha, *m*. **m. song,** canción de marcha, *f*

marchioness /'mɑrʃənɪs/ *n* marquesa, *f*

mardi gras /'mɑrdi ˌgrɑ/ *n* martes de carnaval, *m*

mare /mɛər/ *n* yegua, *f*

margarine /'mɑrdʒərɪn/ *n* margarina, *f*

margin /'mɑrdʒɪn/ *n* borde, lado, *m*, orilla, *f;* (of a page) margen, *mf;* reserva, *f;* sobrante, *m*. **in the m.,** al margen

marginal /'mɑrdʒənl̩/ *a* marginal. **m. note,** acotación, nota marginal, *f*

marigold /'mærɪˌgould/ *n* caléndula, maravilla, *f*

marine /mə'rin/ *a* marino, de mar; marítimo; naval. —*n* (fleet) marina, *f;* (soldier) soldado de marina, *m*. **Tell that to the marines!** ¡Cuéntaselo a tu tía! **mercantile m.,** marina mercante, *f*. **m. forces,** infantería de marina, *f*. **m. insurance,** seguro marítimo, *m*

mariner /'mærənər/ *n* marinero, marino, *m*. **mariner's compass,** aguja de marear, brújula, *f*

marionette /ˌmæriə'nɛt/ *n* marioneta, *f*, títere, *m*

marital /'mærɪtl̩/ *a* marital

maritime /'mærɪˌtaim/ *a* marítimo

mark /mɑrk/ *n* marca, *f;* señal, *f;* mancha, *f;* impresión, *f;* (target) blanco, *m;* (standard) norma, *f;* (level) nivel, *m;* (distinction) importancia, distinción, *f;* (in examinations) nota, *f;* calificación, *f;* (signature) cruz, *f;* (coin) marco, *m*. —*vt* marcar; señalar; (price) poner precio (a); (notice) observar, darse cuenta (de); (characterize) caracterizar. **trade-m.,** marca de fábrica, *f*. **to be beside the m.,** no dar en el blanco; errar el tiro; *Fig.* no tener nada que ver con; equivocarse. **to hit the m.,** dar en el blanco; *Fig.* dar en el clavo. **to make one's m.,** firmar con una cruz; distinguirse. **to m. time,** marcar el paso; *Fig.* hacer tiempo. **to m. down,** (a person) señalar; escoger; (in price) rebajar. **to m. out,** marcar; trazar; definir; (erase) borrar; (a person) escoger; destinar **m. somebody absent,** ponerle a fulano su ausencia. **m. somebody present,** ponerle a fulano su asistencia.

Mark /mɑrk/ *n* Marcos. **the Gospel according to St. M.,** el Evangelio de San Marcos

marked /mɑrkt/ *a* marcado; señalado; notable; acentuado; particular, especial. **He speaks with a m. Galician accent,** Habla con marcado acento gallego

markedly /'mɑrkɪdli/ *adv* marcadamente; notablemente; especialmente, particularmente

marker /'mɑrkər/ *n* (billiards) marcador, *m;* (football, etc.) tanteador, *m*

market /'mɑrkɪt/ *n* mercado, *m;* tráfico, *m;* venta, *f;* (price) precio, *m;* (shop) bazar, emporio, *m*. —*vt* and *vi* comprar en un mercado; vender en un mercado. **black m.,** mercado negro, estraperlo, *m*. **open m.,** mercado al aire libre, *m; Fig.* mercado libre, *m*. **m. day,** día de mercado, *m*. **m. garden,** huerto, *m*, huerta, *f*. **m. gardener,** hortelano, *m*. **m.-place,** plaza de mercado, *f; Fig.* mercado, *m*. **m. price,** precio corriente, *m*. **m. stall,** tabanco, puesto de mercado, *m*. **m.-woman,** verdulera, *f*

marketable /'mɑrkɪtəbəl/ *a* comerciable, vendible; corriente

marketing /'mɑrkɪtɪŋ/ *n* venta, *f;* compra en un mercado, *f;* mercado, *m*. **to go m.,** ir al mercado

marking /ˈmɑrkɪŋ/ *n* marca, *f;* (spot on animals, etc.) pinta, *f.* **m.-ink,** tinta de marcar, *f.* **m.-iron,** ferrete, hierro de marcar, *m*
marksman /ˈmɑrksmən/ *n* tirador (-ra)
marksmanship /ˈmarksmən,ʃɪp/ *n* puntería, *f*
marl /mɑrl/ *n* marga, *f*
marlinespike /ˈmɑrlɪn,spaik/ *n* pasador, *m*
marmalade /ˈmɑrmə,leid/ *n* mermelada de naranjas amargas, *f*
marmoset /ˈmɑrmə,zɛt/ *n* tití, *m*
marmot /ˈmɑrmət/ *n* *Zool.* marmota, *f*
maroon /məˈrun/ *n* (color) marrón, *m;* (slave) cimarrón (-ona); (firework) petardo, *m.* —*a* de marrón. —*vt* abandonar, dejar
marquee /mɑrˈki/ *n* marquesina, *f*
marquetrie /ˈmarkɪtri/ *n* marquetería, *f*
marquis /ˈmɑrkwɪs/ *n* marqués, *m*
marriage /ˈmærɪdʒ/ *n* matrimonio, *m;* unión, *f;* (wedding) boda, *f,* casamiento, *m.* **by m.,** (of relationship) político. **She is an aunt by m.,** tía política. **m. articles,** capitulaciones (matrimoniales), *f pl.* **m. contract,** contrato matrimonial, *m.* **m. license,** licencia de casamiento, *f.* **m. portion,** dote, *mf.* **m. rate,** nupcialidad, *f.* **m. register,** acta matrimonial, *f.* **m. song,** epitalamio, *m*
marriageable /ˈmærɪdʒəbəl/ *a* casadero
married /ˈmærid/ *past part* and *a* casado; matrimonial, conyugal. **newly-m. couple,** los recién casados. **to get m. to,** casarse con. **m. couple,** matrimonio, *m,* cónyuges, *m pl.* **m. life,** vida conyugal, *f*
married name *n* nombre de casada, *f*
marrow /ˈmærou/ *n* tuétano, *m,* médula, *f; Fig.* meollo, *m.* **to the m. of one's bones,** hasta los tuétanos.
marrowbone /ˈmærou,boun/ *n* hueso medular, *m.* **on one's marrowbones,** de rodillas
marry /ˈmæri/ *vt* casarse con, contraer matrimonio con; casar; (of a priest) unir en matrimonio; *Fig.* juntar, unir. —*vi* casarse. **to m. again,** volver a casarse
Marseillaise /,mɑrseiˈɛz/ *n* marsellesa, *f*
Marseilles /mɑrˈsei/ Marsella, *f*
marsh /mɑrʃ/ *n* marjal, pantano, *m.* **m.-mallow,** *Bot.* malvavisco, *m.* **m. marigold,** calta, *f*
marshal /ˈmɑrʃəl/ *n* mariscal, *m, vt* poner en orden, arreglar; dirigir. **field-m.,** capitán general de ejército, *m*
marshaling /ˈmarʃəlɪŋ/ *n* ordenación, *f;* dirección, *f.* **m.-yard,** (railway) apartadero ferroviario, *m*
marshy /ˈmarʃi/ *a* pantanoso
mart /mɑrt/ *n* *Poet.* plaza de mercado, *f;* mercado, *m;* emporio, *m;* (auction rooms) martillo, *m*
marten /ˈmɑrtn̩/ *n* marta, *f*
martial /ˈmɑrʃəl/ *a* militar; marcial, belicoso. **m. array,** orden de batalla, *m.* **m. law,** derecho militar, *m;* estado de guerra, *m.* **m. spirit,** marcialidad, *f,* espíritu belicoso, *m*
martially /ˈmarʃəli/ *adv* militarmente; marcialmente
Martian /ˈmɑrʃən/ *a* marciano
martinet /,mɑrtn̩ˈɛt/ *n* *Mil.* ordenancista, *m;* rigorista, *mf*
Martinique /,mɑrtn̩ˈik/ Martinica, *f*
Martinmas /ˈmɑrtn̩məs/ *n* día de San Martín, *m*
martyr /ˈmɑrtər/ *n* mártir, *mf vt* martirizar
martyrdom /ˈmɑrtərdəm/ *n* martirio, *m*
martyrize /ˈmɑrtə,raiz/ *vt* martirizar
marvel /ˈmɑrvəl/ *n* maravilla, *f.* **to m. at,** maravillarse de, admirarse de
marvelous /ˈmɑrvələs/ *a* maravilloso
marvelousness /ˈmɑrvələsnɪs/ *n* maravilla, *f,* carácter maravilloso, *m,* lo maravilloso
Marxism /ˈmɑrksɪzəm/ *n* marxismo, *m*
Marxist /ˈmɑrksɪst/ *a* and *n* marxista, *mf*
marzipan /ˈmɑrzə,pæn/ *n* mazapán, *m*
mascot /ˈmæskɒt/ *n* mascota, *f*
masculine /ˈmæskyəlɪn/ *a* masculino; varonil, macho; de hombre; (of a woman) hombruno. —*n* masculino, *m*
masculinity /,mæskyəˈlɪnɪti/ *n* masculinidad, *f*
mash /mæʃ/ *n* mezcla, *f;* amasijo, *m;* pasta, *f,* puré, *m.* —*vt* mezclar; amasar. **mashed potatoes,** puré de patatas (de papas), *m*
mask /mæsk/ *n* máscara, *f;* antifaz, *m;* (death) mascarilla, *f;* (person) máscara, *mf.* —*vt* enmascarar; *Fig.* encubrir, disimular. —*vi* ponerse una máscara; disfrazarse. **masked ball,** *n* baile de máscaras, *m*
masker /ˈmæskər/ *n* máscara, *mf*
masochism /ˈmæsə,kɪzəm/ *n* masoquismo, *m*
mason /ˈmeisən/ *n* albañil, *m;* (freemason) francmasón, masón, *m*
masonic /məˈsɒnɪk/ *a* masónico. **m. lodge,** logia de francmasones, *f*
masonry /ˈmeisənri/ *n* (trade) albañilería, *f;* mampostería, *f*
masque /mæsk/ *n* mascarada, *f*
masquerade /,mæskəˈreid/ *n* mascarada, *f*
masquerader /,mæskəˈreidər/ *n* máscara, *mf*
mass /mæs/ *n* misa, *f.* **to hear m.,** oír misa. **to say m.,** celebrar misa. **high m.,** misa mayor, *f.* **low m.,** misa rezada, *f.* **m. book,** libro de misa, *m*
mass /mæs/ *n* masa, *f;* (shape) bulto, *m;* (heap) montón, *m;* (great number) muchedumbre, *f;* (cloud of steam, etc.) nube, *f.* —*vt* amasar; *Mil.* concentrar. —*vi* congregarse en masa. **in a m.,** en masa; en conjunto. **the m. (of)...,** la mayoría (de)... **the masses,** las masas, el vulgo, el pueblo. **m. formation,** columna cerrada, *f.* **m.-meeting,** mitin, mitin popular, *m.* **m.-production,** fabricación en serie, *f*
massacre /ˈmæsəkər/ *n* matanza, carnicería, *f, vt* hacer una carnicería (de)
massage /məˈsɑʒ/ *n* masaje, *m;* (friction) fricción, *f.* —*vt* dar un masaje (a)
masseur, masseuse /məˈsɜr; məˈsus/ *n* masajista, *mf*
massive /ˈmæsɪv/ *a* macizo; sólido
massively /ˈmæsɪvli/ *adv* macizamente; sólidamente
massiveness /ˈmæsɪvnɪs/ *n* macicez, *f;* solidez, *f*
mast /mæst/ *n* *Naut.* palo, árbol, *m;* (for wireless) mástil, *m;* poste, *m;* (beech) hayuco, *m;* (oak) bellota, *f.* —*vt Naut.* arbolar. **at half-m.,** a media asta. **m.-head,** calcés, tope, *m*
masted /ˈmæstɪd/ *a* arbolado; (in compounds) de... palos
master /ˈmæstər/ *n* (of the house, etc.) señor, amo, *m;* maestro, *m; Naut.* patrón, *m;* (owner) dueño, *m;* (teacher) profesor, maestro, *m;* (young master and as address) señorito, *m;* director, *m;* jefe, *m;* (expert) perito, *m;* (of a military order) maestre, *m, a* maestro; superior. —*vt* dominar; ser maestro en; dominar, conocer a fondo. **This picture is by an old m.,** Este cuadro es de un gran maestro antiguo. **to be m. of oneself,** ser dueño de sí. **to be one's own m.,** ser dueño de sí mismo; trabajar por su propia cuenta; ser independiente; estar libre. **m. builder,** maestro de obras, *m.* **m. hand,** mano maestra, *f.* **M. of Arts,** maestro (-tra) en artes. **M. of Ceremonies,** maestro de ceremonias, *m.* **M. of Foxhounds,** cazador mayor, *m.* **M. of the Horse,** caballerizo mayor del rey, *m.* **M. of the Rolls,** archivero mayor, *m.* **m.-key,** llave maestra, *f.* **m. mind,** águila, *f,* ingenio, *m.* **m. stroke,** golpe maestro, *m*
masterful /ˈmæstərfəl/ *a* imperioso, dominante; autoritario, arbitrario
masterfulness /ˈmæstərfəlnɪs/ *n* imperiosidad, *f;* arbitrariedad, *f*
masterless /ˈmæstərlɪs/ *a* sin amo
masterliness /ˈmæstərlinɪs/ *n* maestría, *f;* excelencia, *f;* perfección, *f*
masterly /ˈmæstərli/ *a* maestro; excelente; perfecto. **m. performance,** obra maestra, *f; Theat.* representación perfecta, *f;* ejecución excelente, *f*
masterpiece /ˈmæstər,pis/ *n* obra maestra, *f*
master plan *n* plan regulador, *m*
masterstroke /ˈmæstər,strouk/ *n* golpe magistral, golpe de maestro, *m*
mastery /ˈmæstəri/ *n* dominio, *m;* autoridad, *f;* poder, *m;* ventaja, *f;* superioridad, maestría, *f;* conocimiento profundo, *m.* **to gain the m. of,** hacerse el señor de; llegar a dominar
mastic /ˈmæstɪk/ *n* masilla, almáciga, *f*
masticate /ˈmæstɪ,keit/ *vt* masticar, mascar
mastication /,mæstɪˈkeiʃən/ *n* masticación, *f*
mastiff /ˈmæstɪf/ *n* mastín, alano, *m*
mastodon /ˈmæstə,dɒn/ *n* mastodonte, *m*

mastoid /'mæstɔid/ *a* mastoides. —*n* apófisis mastoides, *f*

masturbate /'mæstər,beit/ *vi* masturbarse

masturbation /,mæstər'beiʃən/ *n* masturbación, *f*

mat /mæt/ *n* esterilla, *f;* alfombrilla, *f;* (on the table) tapete individual, *m.* —*vt* (tangle) enmarañar, desgreñar. —*vi* enmarañarse

match /mætʃ/ *n Sports.* partido, *m;* (wrestling, boxing) lucha, *f;* (fencing) asalto, *m;* (race) carrera, *f;* (contest) concurso, *m;* (equal) igual, *mf;* (pair) pareja, *f;* compañero (-ra); (marriage) boda, *f,* casamiento, *m;* (for lighting) cerilla, *f,* fósforo, *m;* (for guns) mecha, *f.* —*vt* competir con; (equal) igualar; ser igual (a); hacer juego con; emparejar, aparear; armonizar. —*vi* ser igual; hacer juego; armonizarse. **good m.,** *Inf.* buen partido, *m.* **as thin as a m.,** más delgado que una cerilla. **to meet one's m.,** dar con la horma de su zapato. **to play a m.,** jugar un partido. **m.-box,** cajita de cerillas, fosforera, *f.* **m.-seller,** fosforero (-ra)

matchless /'mætʃlɪs/ *a* incomparable, sin igual, sin par

matchwood /'mætʃ,wʊd/ *n* madera para cerillas, *f*

mate /meit/ *n* compañero, camarada, *m;* (spouse) compañero (-ra); pareja, *f,* (on merchant ships) piloto, *m;* (assistant) ayudante, *m;* (at chess) mate, *m.* —*vt* (marry) casar, desposar; (animals, birds) aparear, acoplar; (chess) dar jaque mate (a). —*vi* casarse; aparearse, acoplarse

maté /'mɑtei/ maté, té del Paraguay, *m*

materfamilias /,meitərfə'mɪliəs/ *n* madre de familia, *f*

material /mə'tɪəriəl/ *a* material; importante, esencial; considerable; sensible, notable; grave. —*n* material, *m;* materia, *f;* (fabric) tela, *f;* tejido, *m.* **raw materials,** materias primas, *f pl.* **writing materials,** utensilios de escritorio, *m pl*; papel de escribir, *m*

materialism /mə'tɪəriə,lɪzəm/ *n* materialismo, *m*

materialist /mə'tɪəriəlɪst/ *n* materialista, *mf*

materialistic /mə,tɪəriə'lɪstɪk/ *a* materialista

materiality /mə,tɪəri'ælɪti/ *n* materialidad, *f;* importancia, *f*

materialization /mə,tɪəriəlɪ'zeiʃən/ *n* materialización, *f*

materialize /mə'tɪəriə,laiz/ *vt* materializar

maternal /mə'tɜrnl̩/ *a* materno, maternal. **m. grandparents,** abuelos maternos, *m pl*

maternity /mə'tɜrnɪti/ *n* maternidad, *f.* **m. center,** centro de maternidad, *m.* **m. hospital,** casa de maternidad, *f*

mathematical /,mæθə'mætɪkəl/ *a* matemático

mathematician /,mæθəmə'tɪʃən/ *n* matemático, *m*

mathematics /,mæθə'mætɪks/ *n pl*; matemáticas, *f pl.* **applied m.,** matemáticas prácticas, *f pl.* **higher m.,** matemáticas superiores, *f pl.* **pure m.,** matemáticas teóricas, *f pl*

matinee /,mætn̩'ei/ *n* función de tarde, *f*

mating /'meitɪŋ/ *n* (of animals) apareamiento, acoplamiento, *m;* unión, *f;* casamiento, *m*

matins /'mætn̩z/ *n pl Eccl.* maitines, *m pl*

matriarch /'meitri,ɑrk/ *n* matriarca, *f*

matriarchal /,meitri'ɑrkəl/ *a* matriarcal

matriarchy /'meitri,ɑrki/ *n* matriarcado, *m*

matricide /'mætrɪ,said/ *n* (crime) matricidio, *m;* (person) matricida, *mf*

matriculate /mə'trɪkyə,leit/ *vt* matricular. —*vi* matricularse

matriculation /mə,trɪkyə'leiʃən/ *n* matriculación, *f*

matrimonial /,mætrə'mouniəl/ *a* matrimonial, de matrimonio; marital. **m. agency,** agencia de matrimonios, *f*

matrimony /'mætrə,mouni/ *n* matrimonio, *m*

matrix /'meitrɪks/ *n* matriz, *f*

matron /'meitrən/ *n* matrona, mujer casada, madre de familia, *f;* (of a hospital) matrona, *f;* (of a school) ama de llaves, *f;* directora, *f.* **m. of honor,** (at a wedding) madrina, *f*

matronly /'meitrənli/ *a* de matrona, matronal; respetable; serio

matte /mæt/ *a* mate

matted /'mætɪd/ *a* enmarañado, enredado

matter /'mætər/ *n* materia, *f;* substancia, *f;* caso, *m;* cuestión, *f;* asunto, *m;* causa, *f;* (distance) distancia, *f;* (amount) cantidad, *f;* (duration) espacio de tiempo, *m;* (importance) importancia, *f; Med.* pus, *m; pl* **matters,** asuntos, *m pl,* etc.; situación, *f.* **as if nothing were the m.,** como si no hubiese pasado nada. **for that m.,** en cuanto a eso. **grey m.,** substancia gris, *f.* **in the m. of,** en el caso de. **It is a m. of taste,** Es cuestión de gusto. **printed m.,** impresos, *m pl.* **What is the m.?** ¿Qué pasa? ¿Qué hay? **What is the m. with him?** ¿Qué tiene? ¿Qué le pasa? **m.-of-course,** cosa natural, *f.* **m.-of-fact,** práctico; sin imaginación; positivista. **m. of fact,** *n* hecho positivo, *m,* realidad, *f.* **As a m. of fact...,** En realidad..., El caso es que... **m. of form,** cuestión de fórmula, *f;* pura formalidad, *f*

matter /'mætər/ *vi* importar; (discharge) supurar. **What does it m.?** ¿Qué importa? **It doesn't m.,** Es igual, No importa, Da lo mismo

Matterhorn /'mætər,hɔrn/, **the** el Matterhorn, *m*

matting /'mætɪŋ/ *n* estera, *f*

mattress /'mætrɪs/ *n* colchón, *m.* **spring-m.,** colchón de muelles, *m.* **m.-maker,** colchonero, *m*

mature /mə'tʃʊr/ *a* maduro; *Com.* vencido. —*vt* madurar. —*vi* madurarse; *Com.* vencer

maturity /mə'tʃʊrɪti/ *n* madurez, *f;* edad madura, *f;* (*Com.* of a bill) vencimiento, *m*

matutinal /mə'tutn̩l/ *a* matutino

maudlin /'mɔdlɪn/ *a* sensiblero; lacrimoso; (tipsy) calamocano

maul /mɔl/ *vt* maltratar; herir

maundy /'mɔndi/ *n* lavatorio, *m.* **M. Thursday,** Jueves Santo, *m*

Mauritius /mɔ'rɪʃəs/ Mauricio, *m,* Isla de Francia, *f*

mausoleum /,mɔsə'liəm/ *n* mausoleo, *m*

mauve /mouv/ *n* color purpúreo delicado, color de malva, *m, a* de color de malva

maw /mɔ/ *n* (of a ruminant) cuajar, *m;* (of a bird) buche, *m; Fig.* abismo, *m*

mawkish /'mɔkɪʃ/ *a* insípido, insulso; sensiblero; asqueroso

mawkishness /'mɔkɪʃnɪs/ *n* insipidez, insulsez, *f;* sensiblería, *f;* asquerosidad, *f*

maxilla /mæk'sɪlə/ *n* hueso maxilar, maxilar, *m*

maxillary /'mæksə,lɛri/ *a* maxilar

maxim /'mæksɪm/ *n* máxima, *f*

maximum /'mæksəməm/ *a* máximo. —*n* máximo, *m*

may /mei/ *v aux* poder; ser posible; (expressing wish, hope) ojalá que..., Dios quiera que..., or the present subjunctive may be used, e.g. *May you live many years!* ¡(qué) Viva Vd. muchos años! (to denote uncertainty, the future tense of the verb is often used, e.g. *You may perhaps remember the date,* Vd. quizás se acordará de la fecha. *Who may he be?* ¿Quién será?) **May God grant it!** ¡(que) Dios lo quiera! **It may be that...,** Puede ser que..., Es posible que..., Quizás... **He may come on Saturday,** Es posible que venga el sábado; Puede venir el sábado. **May I come in?** ¿Puedo entrar? ¿Se puede entrar? **May I come and see you?** ¿Me das permiso para hacerte una visita? ¿Me dejas venir a verte? **May I go then?** ¿Puedo irme pues? ¿Tengo permiso para marcharme entonces?

May /mei/ *n* mayo, *m; Fig.* abril, *m; Bot.* espina blanca, *f.* **May Day,** primero de mayo, *m.* **mayflower,** flor del cuclillo, *f.* **mayfly,** cachipolla, *f.* **May queen,** maya, *f*

maybe /'meibi/ *adv* quizás, tal vez

mayonnaise /,meiə'neiz/ *n* mayonesa, *f.* **m. sauce,** salsa mayonesa, *f*

mayor /'meiər/ *n* alcalde, *m*

mayoral /'meiərəl/ *a* de alcalde

mayoress /'meiərɪs/ *n* alcaldesa, *f*

maypole /'mei,poul/ *n* mayo, *m.* **m. dance,** danza de cintas, *f*

maze /meiz/ *n* laberinto, *m; Fig.* perplejidad, *f.* —*vt* dejar perplejo, aturdir

mazurka /mə'zɜrkə/ *n* mazurca, *f*

me /mi/ *pron* me; (after a preposition only) mí. **They sent it for me,** Lo mandaron para mí. **Dear me!** ¡Ay de mí!

meadow /'mɛdou/ *n* prado, *m,* pradera, *f.* **m.-sweet,** reina de los prados, *f*

meager /'migər/ *a* magro, enjuto, flaco; (scanty) exiguo, escaso, insuficiente; pobre; *Fig.* árido
meagerly /'migərli/ *adv* pobremente
meagerness /'migərnıs/ *n* exigüidad, escasez, *f;* pobreza, *f; Fig.* aridez, *f*
meal /mil/ *n* comida, *f;* (flour) harina, *f.* **to have a good m.,** comer bien. **test m.,** *Med.* comida de prueba, *f.* **m.-time,** hora de comida, *f*
mealy /'mili/ *a* harinoso; (of the complexion) pastoso
mean /min/ *a* (middle) medianero; (average) mediano; (humble) humilde; pobre; inferior; bajo, vil, ruin; (avaricious) tacaño, mezquino. **m.-spirited,** vil, de alma ruin
mean /min/ *n* medio, *m;* medianía, *f; pl* **means,** medio, *m;* expediente, *m;* medios, *m pl;* (financial) recursos, *m pl;* modo, *m,* manera, *f.* **by all means,** por todos los medios; (certainly) ¡ya lo creo! ¡no faltaba más! ¡naturalmente! **by means of,** mediante, por medio de; con la ayuda de. **by no means,** de ningún modo; nada. **by some means,** de algún modo, de alguna manera
mean /min/ *vt* destinar (para); pretender, proponerse; intentar, pensar; querer decir, significar; importar; (wish) querer; (concern, speak about) tratarse (de). *—vi* tener el propósito, tener la intención. **I did not m. to do it,** Lo hice sin querer. **What does this word m.?** ¿Qué significa esta palabra? **What do you m. by that?** ¿Qué quieres decir con eso? **This portrait is meant to be Joan,** Este retrato quiere ser Juana. **What do they m. to do?** ¿Qué piensan (or se proponen) hacer? **Do you really m. it?** ¿Lo dices en serio? **Charles always means well,** Carlos siempre tiene buenas intenciones
meander /mi'ændər/ *n* meandro, serpenteo, *m;* camino tortuoso, *m, vi* serpentear; errar, vagar; (in talk) divagar
meandering /mi'ændərıŋ/ *n* meandros, *m pl,* serpenteo, *m;* (in talk) divagaciones, *f pl, a* serpentino, tortuoso
meaning /'minıŋ/ *n* intención, voluntad, *f;* significación, *f,* significado, *m;* (of words) acepción, *f;* (sense) sentido, *m;* (thought) pensamiento, *m.* *—a* significante. **double m.,** doble intención, *f.* **He gave me a m. look,** Me miró con intención. **What is the m. of it?** ¿Qué significa? ¿Qué quiere decir?
meaningful /'minıŋfəl/ *a* significante
meaningless /'minıŋlıs/ *a* sin sentido; insensato; insignificante
meaningly /'minıŋli/ *adv* significativamente; con intención
meanness /'minnıs/ *n* pobreza, *f;* inferioridad, *f;* mediocridad, *f;* bajeza, ruindad, *f;* (stinginess) mezquindad, tacañería, *f*
meantime, meanwhile /'min,taim; 'min,wail/ *n* ínterin, *m, adv* entre tanto, mientras tanto, a todo esto. **in the m.,** mientras tanto, en el ínterin
measles /'mizəlz/ *n* sarampión, *m.* **German m.,** rubéola, *f*
measurable /'mɛʒərəbəl/ *a* mensurable
measure /'mɛʒər/ *n* medida, *f;* capacidad, *f;* (for measuring) regla, *f;* número, *m;* proporción, *f;* (limit) límite, *m;* (*Fig.* step) medida, *f;* (metre) metro, *m; Mus.* compás, *m;* (degree) grado, *m;* manera, *f;* (parliamentary) proyecto (de ley), *m.* *—vt* medir; proporcionar, distribuir; (water) aforar; (land) apear; (height of persons) tallar; (for clothes) tomar las medidas (a); (judge) juzgar; (test) probar; (*Poet.* traverse) recorrer. **a suit made to m.,** un traje hecho a medida. **in great m.,** en gran manera, en alto grado. **in some m.,** hasta cierto punto. **to m. one's length,** caer tendido. **to take a person's m.,** *Fig.* tomar las medidas (a). **to m. up to,** *Fig.* estar al nivel de, ser igual a
measured /'mɛʒərd/ *a* mesurado, moderado; uniforme; limitado. **to walk with m. tread,** andar a pasos contados
measurement /'mɛʒərmənt/ *n* medición, *f;* medida, *f;* dimensión, *f*
meat /mit/ *n* carne, *f;* (food) alimento, *m;* (meal) comida, *f; Fig.* substancia, *f.* **to sit at m.,** estar a la mesa. **cold meats,** fiambres, *m pl.* **m.-ball,** albóndiga, *f.* **m.-chopper,** picador, *m.* **m.-dish,** fuente, *f.* **m.-eater,** comedor (-ra) de carne. **m. extract,** carne concentrada, *f.* **m.-market,** carnicería, *f.* **m.-pie,** pastel de carne, *m.* **m.-safe,** fresquera, *f*
meaty /'miti/ *a* carnoso; *Fig.* substancial
Mecca /'mɛkə/ la Meca, *f*
mechanic /mə'kænık/ *n* mecánico, *m*
mechanical /mə'kænıkəl/ *a* mecánico; maquinal
mechanically /mə'kænıkli/ *adv* mecánicamente; maquinalmente
mechanical pencil *n* lapicero, *m*
mechanics /mə'kænıks/ *n* mecánica, *f*
mechanism /'mɛkə,nızəm/ *n* mecanismo, *m;* (philosophy) mecanicismo, *m*
mechanize /'mɛkə,naiz/ *vt* convertir en máquina; (gen. *Mil.*) mecanizar; motorizar
medal /'mɛdl̩/ *n* medalla, *f*
medallion /mə'dælyən/ *n* medallón, *m*
medallist /'mɛdl̩ıst/ *n* grabador de medallas, *m;* el, *m,* (*f,* la) que recibe una medalla
meddle /'mɛdl̩/ *vi* tocar; meterse (con or en); entremeterse, inmiscuirse; intrigar
meddler /'mɛdlər/ *n* entremetido (-da); intrigante, *mf*
meddlesome /'mɛdl̩səm/ *a* entremetido; oficioso; impertinente; enredador, intrigante. **to be very m.,** meterse en todo
meddlesomeness /'mɛdl̩səmnıs/ *n* entremetimiento, *m;* oficiosidad, *f;* impertinencia, *f;* intrigas, *f pl*
median /'midiən/ *a* del medio
mediate / *v* 'midi,eit; *a* -ıt/ *vi* intervenir, mediar, arbitrar; abogar (por). *—a* medio; interpuesto
media /'midiə/, **the** los medios informativos, *m pl*
mediation /,midi'eiʃən/ *n* mediación, intervención, *f;* intercesión, *f;* interposición, *f*
mediator /'midi,eitər/ *n* mediador (-ra); arbitrador, *m;* intercesor (-ra)
mediatory /'midiə,tɔri/ *a* de mediador; intercesor
medical /'mɛdıkəl/ *a* médico; de medicina; de médico. *—n Inf.* estudiante de medicina, *m.* **Army M. Service,** Servicio de Sanidad Militar, *m.* **m. books,** libros de medicina, *m pl.* **m. examination,** examen médico, *m,* exploración médica, *f.* **m. jurisprudence,** medicina legal, *f.* **m. knowledge,** conocimientos médicos, *m pl.* **m. practitioner,** médico (-ca). **m. school,** escuela de medicina, *f*
medicament /mə'dıkəmənt/ *n* medicamento, *m*
medicate /'mɛdı,keit/ *vt* medicar; medicinar
medicated /'mɛdı,keitıd/ *a* medicado
medication /,mɛdı'keiʃən/ *n* medicación, *f*
medicinal /mə'dısənl̩/ *a* medicinal
medicine /'mɛdəsın/ *n* medicina, *f;* medicamento, *m;* (charm) ensalmo, hechizo, *m.* **patent m.,** específico farmacéutico, *m.* **m. ball,** balón medical, *m.* **m. chest,** botiquín, *m.* **m. man,** hechizador, *m*
medico- *prefix* médico-. **m.-legal,** médicolegal
medieval /,midi'ivəl/ *a* medieval
medievalism /,midi'ivə,lızəm/ *n* afición a la edad media, *f;* espíritu medieval, *m*
mediocre /,midi'oukər/ *a* mediocre
mediocrity /,midi'ɒkrıti/ *n* mediocridad, *f;* medianía, *f*
meditate /'mɛdı,teit/ *vt* idear, proyectar, meditar. *—vi* meditar, reflexionar; pensar, intentar
meditation /,mɛdı'teiʃən/ *n* meditación, *f*
meditative /'mɛdı,teitıv/ *a* meditabundo, contemplativo; de meditación
meditatively /'mɛdı,teitıvli/ *adv* reflexivamente
Mediterranean /,mɛdıtə'reiniən/ *a* mediterráneo. *—n* Mar Mediterráneo, *m*
medium /'midiəm/ *n* medio, *m;* (cooking) término medio, a medio cocer, a medio asar, *m;* (environment) medio ambiente, *m;* (agency) intermediario, *m;* (spiritualism) médium, *m; Art.* medio, *m, a* mediano; regular; mediocre. **through the m. of,** por medio de. **m.-sized,** de tamaño regular
medlar /'mɛdlər/ *n* (fruit) níspola, *f;* (tree) níspero, *m*
medley /'mɛdli/ *n* mezcla, *f;* miscelánea, *f, a* mezclado, mixto
medulla /mə'dʌlə/ *n* medula, *f*
meek /mik/ *a* dulce, manso; humilde; modesto; pacífico

meekly /'mikli/ *adv* mansamente; humildemente; modestamente

meekness /'miknɪs/ *n* mansedumbre, *f;* humildad, *f;* modestia, *f*

meet /mit/ *vt* encontrar; encontrarse con; tropezar con; (by arrangement) reunirse con; (make the acquaintance of) conocer (a); (satisfy) satisfacer; cumplir (con); (a bill) pagar, saldar; (refute) refutar; (fight) batirse (con); (confront) hacer frente (a). —*vi* juntarse; encontrarse; reunirse; verse; (of rivers) confluir. —*n* montería, *f,* *a* conveniente. **I shall m. you at the station,** Te esperaré en la estación. **Until we m. again!** ¡Hasta la vista! **to go to m.,** ir al encuentro de. **to m. half-way,** encontrar a la mitad del camino; partir la diferencia con; hacer concesiones (a). **to m. the eye,** saltar a la vista. **to m. with,** encontrar; experimentar; sufrir

meeting /'mitɪŋ/ *n* encuentro, *m;* reunión, *f;* (interview) entrevista, *f;* (of rivers, etc.) confluencia, *f;* (public, etc.) mitin, *m;* (council) concilio, *m;* concurso, *m;* (race) concurso de carreras de caballos, *m.* **creditors' m.,** concurso de acreedores, *m.* **m.-house,** templo de los Cuáqueros, *m.* **m.-place,** lugar de reunión, *m;* lugar de cita, *m;* centro, *m.* **to adjourn the m.,** levantar la sesión. **to call a m.,** convocar una sesión. **to open the m.,** abrir la sesión

megalomania /ˌmɛgəlou'meiniə/ *n* megalomanía, monomanía de grandezas, *f*

megalomaniac /ˌmɛgəlou'meiniæk/ *n* megalómano (-na)

megaphone /'mɛgəˌfoun/ *n* megáfono, portavoz, *m*

Meknès /mɛk'nɛs/ Mequínez, *f*

melancholia /ˌmɛlən'kouliə/ *n* melancolía, *f*

melancholy /'mɛlənˌkɒli/ *a* melancólico. —*n* melancolía, *f*

mellifluence /mə'lɪfluəns/ *n* melifluidad, *f*

mellifluous /mə'lɪfluəs/ *a* melifluo; dulce

mellow /'mɛlou/ *a* maduro; dulce; (of wine) rancio; blando; suave; (of sound) melodioso; (slang) alegre; (tipsy) entre dos luces. —*vt* madurar; ablandar; suavizar. —*vi* madurarse

mellowing /'mɛlouɪŋ/ *n* maduración, *f*

mellowness /'mɛlounɪs/ *n* madurez, *f;* dulzura, *f;* (of wine) ranciedad, *f;* blandura, *f;* suavidad, *f;* melodia, *f*

melodic /mə'lɒdɪk/ *a* melódico

melodious /mə'loudiəs/ *a* melodioso

melodiously /mə'loudiəsli/ *adv* melodiosamente

melodiousness /mə'loudiəsnɪs/ *n* melodía, *f*

melodrama /'mɛləˌdrɑmə/ *n* melodrama, *m*

melodramatic /ˌmɛlədrə'mætɪk/ *a* melodramático

melody /'mɛlədi/ *n* melodía, *f*

melon /'mɛlən/ *n* melón, *m;* sandía, *f.* **slice of m.,** raja de melón, *f.* **m. bed,** sandiar, *m.* **m.-shaped,** amelonado

melt /mɛlt/ *vi* derretirse; deshacerse; disolverse; evaporarse; desaparecer; (of money, etc.) hacerse sal y agua; (relent) enternecerse, ablandarse. —*vt* fundir; (snow, etc.) derretir; (*Fig.* soften) ablandar. **He melted away,** *Inf.* Se escurrió. **to m. into tears,** deshacerse en lágrimas. **to m. down,** fundir

melting /'mɛltɪŋ/ *a* fundente; (forgiving) indulgente; (tender) de ternura; lánguido; dulce. —*n* fusión, *f;* derretimiento, *m.* **m. point,** punto de fusión, *m.* **m. pot,** *Metall.* crisol, *m;* *Fig.* caldera de razas, *f, m*

member /'mɛmbər/ *n* miembro, *m;* (of a club, etc.) socio (-ia). **M. of Parliament,** diputado a Cortes, *m*

membership /'mɛmbərˌʃɪp/ *n* calidad de miembro, socio(-ia), número de miembros (*or* socios), *m,* composición, integración, *f*

membrane /'mɛmbrein/ *n* membrana, *f*

membranous /'mɛmbrənəs/ *a* membranoso

memento /mə'mɛntou/ *n* recuerdo, *m*

memoir /'mɛmwɑr/ *n* memoria, *f*

memorable /'mɛmərəbəl/ *a* memorable

memorably /'mɛmərəbli/ *adv* memorablemente

memorandum /ˌmɛmə'rændəm/ *n* memorándum, *m*

memorial /mə'mɔriəl/ *a* conmemorativo. —*n* monumento conmemorativo, *m;* memorial, *m*

memorize /'mɛməˌraiz/ *vt* aprender de memoria

memory /'mɛməri/ *n* memoria, *f;* recuerdo, *m.* **from m.,** de memoria. **If my m. does not deceive me,** Si mal no me acuerdo. **in m. of,** en conmemoración de; en recuerdo de

memory span *n* retentiva memorística, *f*

menace /'mɛnɪs/ *n* amenaza, *f, vt* amenazar

menacing /'mɛnəsɪŋ/ *a* amenazador

menacingly /'mɛnəsɪŋli/ *adv* con amenazas

menagerie /mə'nædʒəri/ *n* colección de fieras, *f;* casa de fieras, *f*

mend /mɛnd/ *vt* remendar; componer; reparar; (darn) zurcir; (rectify) remediar; reformar; enmendar; (a fire) echar carbón (or leña, etc.) a; (one's pace) avivar. —*vi* (in health and of the weather) mejorar. —*n* remiendo, *m;* (darn) zurcido, *m.* **to be on the m.,** ir mejorando. **to m. one's ways,** reformarse, enmendarse

mendacious /mɛn'deiʃəs/ *a* mendaz

mendacity /mɛn'dæsɪti/ *n* mendacidad, *f*

Mendelism /'mɛndḷˌɪzəm/ *n* mendelismo, *m*

mender /'mɛndər/ *n* componedor (-ra); (darner) zurcidor (-ra); reparador (-ra); (cobbler and tailor) remendón, *m*

mendicancy /'mɛndɪkənsi/ *n* mendicidad, *f*

mendicant /'mɛndɪkənt/ *a* mendicante. —*n* mendicante, *mf.* **m. friar,** fraile mendicante, *m*

mending /'mɛndɪŋ/ *n* compostura, *f;* reparación, *f;* (darning) zurcidura, *f;* ropa por zurcir, *f*

menial /'miniəl/ *a* doméstico; servil; bajo, ruin. —*n* criado (-da); lacayo, *m*

meningeal /ˌmɛnɪn'dʒiəl/ *a* meningeo

meningitis /ˌmɛnɪn'dʒaitɪs/ *n* meningitis, *f*

menopause /'mɛnəˌpɔz/ *n* menopausia, *f*

menses /'mɛnsiz/ *n* menstruación, *f*

menstrual /'mɛnstruəl/ *a* menstrual

menstruate /'mɛnstruˌeit/ *vi* menstruar

menstruation /ˌmɛnstru'eiʃən/ *n* menstruación, *f,*

mental /'mɛntḷ/ *a* mental; intelectual. **m. derangement,** enajenación mental, *f.* **m. hospital,** manicomio, *m*

mentality /mɛn'tælɪti/ *n* mentalidad, *f*

mentally /'mɛntḷi/ *adv* mentalmente. **m. deficient,** anormal

menthol /'mɛnθɔl/ *n* mentol, *m*

mention /'mɛnʃən/ *n* mención, *f;* alusión, *f.* —*vt* hacer mención (de), mencionar, mentar, hablar (de); aludir (a); (quote) citar; (in dispatches) nombrar. **Don't m. it!** (keep silent) ¡No digas nada!; (you're welcome) ¡No hay de que!

mentor /'mɛntɔr/ *n* mentor, *m*

menu /'mɛnyu/ *n* menú, *m;* lista de platos, *f*

meow /mi'au/ *vi* maullar. —*n* maullido, *m*

Mephistophelean /ˌmɛfəstə'filiən/ *a* mefistofélico

mephitic /mə'fɪtɪk/ *a* mefítico

mercantile /'mɜrkənˌtil/ *a* mercantil; mercante. **m. law,** derecho mercantil, *m.* **m. marine,** marina mercante, *f*

mercantilism /'mɜrkəntɪˌlɪzəm/ *n* mercantilismo, *m*

mercenariness /'mɜrsəˌnɛrinɪs/ *n* lo mercenario

mercenary /'mɜrsəˌnɛri/ *a* mercenario. —*n* (soldier) mercenario, *m*

mercer /'mɜrsər/ *n* mercero, *m*

mercerize /'mɜrsəˌraiz/ *vt* mercerizar

mercery /'mɜrsəri/ *n* mercería, *f*

merchandise /'mɜrtʃənˌdaiz/ *n* mercancía, *f*

merchant /'mɜrtʃənt/ *n* traficante (en), *mf,* negociante (en), *m;* comerciante, *mf* mercader, *m.* —*a* mercante. **The M. of Venice,** El Mercader de Venecia. **m. navy, service,** marina mercante, *f.* **m. ship,** buque mercante, *m*

merchantman /'mɜrtʃəntmən/ *n* buque mercante, *m*

merciful /'mɜrsɪfəl/ *a* misericordioso, piadoso; compasivo; clemente; indulgente

mercifully /'mɜrsɪfəli/ *adv* misericordiosamente; compasivamente; con indulgencia

mercifulness /'mɜrsɪfəlnɪs/ *n* misericordia, *f;* compasión, *f;* indulgencia, *f*

merciless /'mɜrsɪlɪs/ *a* despiadado, inhumano

mercilessly /'mɜrsɪlɪsli/ *adv* sin piedad

mercilessness /'mɜrsɪlɪsnɪs/ *n* inhumanidad, *f;* falta de compasión, *f*

mercurial /mər'kyʊriəl/ *a* mercurial; (changeable) volátil; (lively) vivo

mercury /ˈmɜrkyəri/ *n* mercurio, *m;* (*Astron.* and *Myth.*) Mercurio, *m.* **Mercury's wand,** caduceo, *m*
mercy /ˈmɜrsi/ *n* misericordia, *f;* compasión, *f;* clemencia, *f;* indulgencia, *f;* merced, *f.* **at the m. of the elements,** a la intemperie. **to be at the m. of,** estar a la merced de
mere /mɪər/ *a* mero; simple; no más que, solo. —*n* lago, *m*
merely /ˈmɪərli/ *adv* meramente, solamente; simplemente, sencillamente
meretricious /ˌmɛrɪˈtrɪʃəs/ *a* (archaic) meretricio; (flashy) de oropel; llamativo, charro
meretriciousness /ˌmɛrɪˈtrɪʃəsnɪs/ *n* mal gusto, *m*
merge /mɜrdʒ/ *vt* fundir; *Com.* fusionar; mezclar. —*vi* fundirse; *Com.* fusionarse; mezclarse
merger /ˈmɜrdʒər/ *n* combinación, *f;* *Com.* fusión, *f*
meridian /məˈrɪdiən/ *n* (*Geog. Astron.*) meridiano, *m;* (noon) mediodía, *m;* (peak) apogeo, *m*
meringue /məˈræŋ/ *n* merengue, *m*
merino /məˈrinou/ *a* de merino; merino. —*n* (fabric and sheep) merino, *m*
merit /ˈmɛrɪt/ *n* mérito, *m, vt* merecer, ser digno de
meritorious /ˌmɛrɪˈtɔriəs/ *a* meritorio
meritoriously /ˌmɛrɪˈtɔriəsli/ *adv* merecidamente
meritoriousness /ˌmɛrɪˈtɔriəsnɪs/ *n* mérito, *m*
merlon /ˈmɜrlən/ *n* merlón, *m,* almena, *f*
mermaid /ˈmɜrˌmeid/ *n* sirena, *f*
merrily /ˈmɛrɪli/ *adv* alegremente
merriment /ˈmɛrɪmənt/ *n* alegría, *f;* júbilo, *m;* regocijo, *m;* diversión, *f;* juego, *m*
merriness /ˈmɛrinɪs/ *n* alegría, *f;* regocijo, *m;* *Inf.* ebriedad, *f*
merry /ˈmɛri/ *a* alegre; jovial; feliz; regocijado, divertido; (tipsy) calamocano. **to make m.,** divertirse. **to make m. over,** reírse de. **M. Christmas!** ¡Felices Navidades! **m.-andrew,** bufón, *m.* **m.-go-round,** caballitos, *m pl,* tiovivo, *m.* **m.-making,** festividades, fiestas, *f pl*
meseta *n* meseta, *f*
mesh /mɛʃ/ *n* malla, *f;* *Mech.* engranaje, *m;* (network) red, *f;* (snare) lazo, *m.* —*vt* coger con red; *Mech.* endentar
mesmerism /ˈmɛzməˌrɪzəm/ *n* mesmerismo, *m*
mesmerize /ˈmɛzməˌraiz/ *vt* hipnotizar
mess /mɛs/ *n* (of food) plato de comida, *m;* porción, ración, *f;* rancho, *m;* (mixture) mezcla, *f;* (disorder) desorden, *m;* suciedad, *f;* (failure) fracaso, *m.* —*vt* (dirty) ensuciar; desordenar; (mismanage) echar a perder. **to be in a m.,** *Inf.* estar aviado. **to get in a m.,** *Inf.* hacerse un lío. **to make a m. of,** ensuciar; desordenar; (spoil) echarlo todo a rodar
message /ˈmɛsɪdʒ/ *n* mensaje, *m;* recado, *m;* (telegraphic) parte, *m.* **I have to take a m.,** Tengo que hacer un recado
messenger /ˈmɛsəndʒər/ *n* mensajero (-ra); (of telegrams) repartidor, *m;* heraldo, *m;* anuncio, *m*
Messiah /mɪˈsaiə/ *n* Mesías, *m*
Messianic /ˌmɛsiˈænɪk/ *a* mesiánico
messrs. /ˈmɛsərz/ *n pl* (abbreviation) sres. (from señores), *m pl*
metabolism /məˈtæbəˌlɪzəm/ *n* metabolismo, *m*
metabolize /məˈtæbəˌlaiz/ *vt* metabolizar
metal /ˈmɛtl̩/ *n* metal, *m;* vidrio en fusión, *m;* (road) grava, *f;* *Herald.* metal, *m;* (mettle) temple, temperamento, *m;* brío, fuego, *m;* *pl* metals, (of a railway) rieles, *m pl.* **m. engraver,** grabador en metal, *m.* **m. polish,** limpiametales, *m.* **m. shavings,** cizallas, *f pl.* **m. work,** metalistería, *f.* **m. worker,** metalario, *m*
metallic /məˈtælɪk/ *a* metálico
metalliferous /ˌmɛtl̩ˈɪfərəs/ *a* metalífero
metalloid /ˈmɛtl̩ˌɔid/ *n* metaloide, *m*
metallurgic /ˌmɛtl̩ˈɜrdʒɪk/ *a* metalúrgico
metallurgist /ˈmɛtl̩ˌɜrdʒɪst/ *n* metalúrgico, *m*
metallurgy /ˈmɛtl̩ˌɜrdʒi/ *n* metalurgia, *f*
metamorphosis /ˌmɛtəˈmɔrfəsɪs/ *n* metamorfosis, *f*
metaphor /ˈmɛtəˌfɔr/ *n* metáfora, *f*
metaphorical /ˌmɛtəˈfɔrɪkəl/ *a* metafórico
metaphysical /ˌmɛtəˈfɪzɪkəl/ *a* metafísico
metaphysician /ˌmɛtəfəˈzɪʃən/ *n* metafísico, *m*
metaphysics /ˌmɛtəˈfɪzɪks/ *n* metafísica, *f*
metathesis /məˈtæθəsɪs/ *n* metátesis, *f*
mete /mit/ *vt* repartir, distribuir
metempsychosis /məˌtɛmsəˈkousɪs/ *n* metempsicosis, *f*
meteor /ˈmitiər/ *n* meteoro, *m*
meteoric /ˌmitiˈɔrɪk/ *a* meteórico
meteorite /ˈmitiəˌrait/ *n* meteorito, *m*
meteorological /ˌmitiərəˈlɒdʒɪkəl/ *a* meteorológico
meteorologist /ˌmitiəˈrɒlədʒɪst/ *n* meteorologista, *mf*
meteorology /ˌmitiəˈrɒlədʒi/ *n* meteorología, *f*
meter /ˈmitər/ *n* (for gas, etc.) contador, *m;* (verse and measure) metro, *m*
methane /ˈmɛθein/ *n* metano, *m*
method /ˈmɛθəd/ *n* método, *m;* técnica, *f;* táctica, *f*
methodical /məˈθɒdɪkəl/ *a* metódico; ordenado, sistemático
Methodism /ˈmɛθəˌdɪzəm/ *n* metodismo, *m*
Methodist /ˈmɛθədɪst/ *n* metodista, *mf*
methyl /ˈmɛθəl/ *n* metilo, *m.* **m. alcohol,** alcohol metílico, *m*
methylated spirit /ˈmɛθəˌleitɪd/ *n* alcohol desnaturalizado, *m*
meticulous /məˈtɪkyələs/ *a* meticuloso; minucioso
meticulously /məˈtɪkyələsli/ *adv* con meticulosidad
meticulousness /məˈtɪkyələsnɪs/ *n* meticulosidad, *f;* minuciosidad, *f*
metric /ˈmɛtrɪk/ *a* métrico. **m. system,** sistema métrico, *m*
metrics /ˈmɛtrɪks/ *n* métrica, *f*
metronome /ˈmɛtrəˌnoum/ *n* metrónomo, *m*
metropolis /mɪˈtrɒpəlɪs/ *n* metrópoli, *f;* capital, *f*
metropolitan /ˌmɛtrəˈpɒlɪtn̩/ *a* metropolitano; de la capital. —*n Eccl.* metropolitano, *m*
mettle /ˈmɛtl̩/ *n* temple, temperamento, *m;* fuego, brío, *m;* valor, *m.* **You have put him on his m.,** Le has picado en el amor propio
mew /myu/ *n* (gull) gaviota, *f;* (of a cat) maullido, *m;* (of sea-birds) alarido, *m.* —*vi* (of a cat) maullar; (of sea-birds) dar alaridos. **to mew up,** encerrar
mews /myuz/ *n* establos, *m pl,* caballeriza, *f*
Mexican /ˈmɛksɪkən/ *a* mejicano. —*n* mejicano (-na)
Mexico /ˈmɛksɪˌkou/ Méjico, *m*
mezzanine /ˈmɛzəˌnin/ *n* entresuelo, *m*
mezzo soprano /ˈmɛtsou səˈprænou/ *n* mezzosoprano
mi /mi/ *n Mus.* mi, *m*
miaow /miˈau/ *n* miau, *m, vi* maullar
miasma /maiˈæzmə/ *n* miasma, *m*
miasmatic /ˌmaiəzˈmætɪk/ *a* miasmático
mica /ˈmaikə/ *n* mica, *f*
microbe /ˈmaikroub/ *n* microbio, *m*
microbial /maiˈkroubiəl/ *a* microbiano
microbiologist /ˌmaikroubaiˈɒlədʒɪst/ *n* microbiólogo, *m*
microbiology /ˌmaikroubaiˈɒlədʒi/ *n* microbiología, *f*
microcosm /ˈmaikrəˌkɒzəm/ *n* microcosmo, *m*
microphone /ˈmaikrəˌfoun/ *n* micrófono, *m*
microscope /ˈmaikrəˌskoup/ *n* microscopio, *m*
microscopic /ˌmaikrəˈskɒpɪk/ *a* microscópico
microwave /ˈmaikrouˌweiv/ *n* microonda, *f*
mid /mɪd/ *a* medio. —*prep* entre; en medio de; a mediados de. **from mid May to August,** desde mediados de mayo hasta agosto. **a mid-fourteenth century castle,** un castillo de mediados del siglo catorce. **in mid air,** en medio del aire. **in mid channel,** en medio del canal. **in mid winter,** en medio del invierno
midday /ˈmɪdˈdei/ *n* mediodía, *m, a* del mediodía, meridional. **at m.,** a mediodía
midden /ˈmɪdn̩/ *n* muladar, *m*
middle /ˈmɪdl̩/ *a* medio; en medio de; del centro; intermedio; (average) mediano. —*n* medio, *m;* mitad, *f;* centro, *m;* (waist) cintura, *f.* **in the m. of,** en medio de. **in the m. of nowhere,** donde Cristo dio las tres voces. **toward the m. of the month,** a mediados del mes. **m. age,** edad madura, *f.* **m.-aged,** de edad madura, de cierta edad. **M. Ages,** edad media, *f.* **m. class,** clase media, burguesía, *f, a* de la clase media, burgués. **m. distance,** término medio, *m.* **m. ear,** oído medio, *m.* **m. finger,** dedo de en medio (or del corazón), *m.* **m. way,** *Fig.* término medio, *m.* **m. weight,** peso medio, *m*

Middle East, the el Oriente Medio, el Levante, *m*
middleman /'mɪdḷˌmæn/ *n* agente de negocios, *m;* (retailer) revendedor, *m;* intermediario, *m*
middling /'mɪdlɪŋ/ *a* mediano; mediocre; regular, así, así
midge /mɪdʒ/ *n* mosquito, *m,* mosca de agua, *f*
midget /'mɪdʒɪt/ *n* enano (-na). **m. submarine,** submarino de bolsillo, *m*
midnight /'mɪdˌnait/ *n* medianoche, *f.* —*a* de medianoche; nocturno. **at m.,** a medianoche. **to burn the m. oil,** quemarse las cejas. **m. mass,** misa del gallo, *f*
midriff /'mɪdrɪf/ *n* diafragma, *m*
midship /'mɪdˌʃɪp/ *a* maestro. —*n* medio del buque, *m.* **m. beam,** bao maestro, *m.* **m. gangway,** crujía, *f*
midshipman /'mɪdˌʃɪpmən/ *n* guardiamarina, *m*
midst /mɪdst/ *n* medio, *m;* seno, *m, prep* entre. **in the m. of,** en medio de. **There is a traitor in our m.,** Hay un traidor entre nosotros (or en nuestra compañía)
midstream, /'mɪd'strim/ *n* **in m.** *m.* en medio de la corriente
midsummer /'mɪd'sʌmər/ *n* pleno verano, *m;* solsticio estival, *m;* fiesta de San Juan, *f.* **A M. Night's Dream,** El Sueño de la Noche de San Juan
midway /*adv, a* 'mɪd'wei, *n* -ˌwei/ *a* and *adv* situado a medio camino; a medio camino, a la mitad del camino; entre. —*n* mitad del camino, *f;* medio, *m.* **m. between...,** equidistante de..., entre
midwife /'mɪdˌwaif/ *n* comadrona, partera, *f*
midwifery /mɪd'wɪfəri/ *n* obstetricia, *f*
midwinter /*n.* 'mɪd'wɪntər, -ˌwɪn-; *a* -ˌwɪn-/ *n* medio del invierno, *m*
mien /min/ *n* aire, *m;* porte, semblante, *m*
might /mait/ *vi* poder. **It m. or m. not be true,** Podría o no podría ser verdad. **How happy Mary m. have been!** ¡Qué feliz pudo haber sido María! **I thought that you m. have seen him in the theater,** Creí que pudieras haberle visto en el teatro. **That I m....!** ¡Que yo pudiese...! **This m. have been avoided if...** Esto podía haberse evitado si...
might /mait/ *n* fuerza, *f;* poder, *m.* **with m. and main,** con todas sus fuerzas
mightily /'maitḷi/ *adv* fuertemente; poderosamente; *Inf.* muchísimo, sumamente
mightiness /'maitinɪs/ *n* fuerza, *f;* poder, *m;* grandeza, *f*
mighty /'maiti/ *a* fuerte, vigoroso; poderoso; grande; *Inf.* enorme; (proud) arrogante. —*adv Inf.* enormemente, muy
migraine /'maigrein/ *n* migraña, jaqueca, *f*
migrant /'maigrənt/ *a* migratorio, de paso. —*n* ave migratoria, ave de paso, *f*
migrate /'maigreit/ *vi* emigrar
migration /mai'greiʃən/ *n* migración, *f*
migratory /'maigrəˌtɔri/ *a* migratorio, de paso; (of people) nómada, pasajero
migratory worker *n* trabajador golondrino, *m*
Milanese /ˌmɪlə'niz/ *a* milanés. —*n* milanés (-esa)
milch /mɪltʃ/ *a f,* (of cows) lechera
mild /maild/ *a* apacible, pacífico; manso; dulce; suave; (of the weather) blando; *Med.* benigno; (light) leve; (of drinks) ligero; (weak) débil
mildew /'mɪlˌdu/ *n* mildiu, añublo, *m;* moho, *m.* —*vt* anublar; enmohecer. —*vi* anublarse; enmohecerse
mildly /'maildli/ *adv* suavemente; dulcemente; con indulgencia
mildness /'maildnɪs/ *n* apacibilidad, *f;* mansedumbre, *f;* suavidad, *f;* (of weather) blandura, *f;* dulzura, *f;* indulgencia, *f;* (weakness) debilidad, *f*
mile /mail/ *n* milla, *f*
mileage /'mailɪdʒ/ *n* distancia en millas, *f;* kilometraje, *m*
milestone /'mailˌstoun/ *n* hito, *m,* piedra miliaria, *f;* mojón kilométrico, *m*
milfoil /'mɪlˌfɔil/ *n* milenrama, *f*
militancy /'mɪlɪtənsi/ *n* carácter militante, *m;* belicosidad, *f*
militant /'mɪlɪtənt/ *a* militante, combatiente; belicoso; agresivo. —*n* combatiente, *mf*
militarily /ˌmɪlɪ'tɛrəli/ *adv* militarmente
militariness /'mɪlɪˌtɛrinɪs/ *n* lo militar, el carácter militar
militarism /'mɪlɪtəˌrɪzəm/ *n* militarismo, *m*
militarist /'mɪlɪtərɪst/ *n* militarista, *mf*
militaristic /ˌmɪlɪtə'rɪstɪk/ *a* militarista
militarization /ˌmɪlɪtərɪ'zeiʃən/ *n* militarización, *f*
militarize /'mɪlɪtəˌraiz/ *vt* militarizar
military /'mɪlɪˌtɛri/ *a* militar; de guerra. **the m.,** los militares. **m. academy,** colegio militar, *m.* **m. camp,** campo militar, *m.* **m. law,** código militar, *m.* **m. man,** militar, *m.* **m. police,** policía militar, *f.* **m. service,** servicio militar, *m*
militate /'mɪlɪˌteit/ **(against)** *vi* militar contra
militia /mɪ'lɪʃə/ *n* milicia, *f*
militiaman /mɪ'lɪʃəmən/ *n* miliciano, *m*
milk /mɪlk/ *n* leche, *f.* —*a* de leche; lácteo. —*vt* ordeñar. —*vi* dar leche. **to have m. and water in one's veins,** tener sangre de horchata. **condensed m.,** leche condensada, leche en lata, *f.* **m.-can,** lechera, *f.* **m.-cart,** carro de la leche, *m.* **m. chocolate,** chocolate con leche, *m.* **m. of magnesia,** leche de magnesia, *f.* **m.-pail,** ordeñadero, *m.* **m.-tooth,** diente de leche, *m.* **m.-white,** blanco como la leche
milkiness /'mɪlkinɪs/ *n* lactescencia, *f;* carácter lechoso, *m;* (whiteness) blancura, *f*
milking /'mɪlkɪŋ/ *n* ordeño, *m.* **m.-machine,** máquina ordeñadora, *f.* **m.-stool,** taburete, banquillo, *m*
milkmaid /'mɪlkˌmeid/ *n* lechera, *f*
milkman /'mɪlkˌmæn/ *n* lechero, *m*
milksop /'mɪlkˌsɒp/ *n* marica, *m*
milky /'mɪlki/ *a* lechero; de leche; lechoso, como leche; *Astron.* lácteo. **the Milky Way** la Vía láctea *f*
mill /mɪl/ *n* molino, *m;* (for coffee, etc.) molinillo, *m;* (factory) fábrica, *f;* taller, *m;* (textile) hilandería, *f;* fábrica de tejidos, *f;* (fight) riña a puñetazos, *f;* pugilato, *m.* —*vt* (grind) moler; (coins) acordonar; (cloth) abatanar; (chocolate) batir. **cotton m.,** hilandería de algodón, *f.* **hand-m.,** molinillo, *m.* **paper-m.,** fábrica de papel, *f.* **saw-m.,** serrería, *f.* **spinning m.,** hilandería, *f.* **water m.,** molino de agua, *m.* **m.-course,** saetín, canal de molino, *m.* **m.-dam,** esclusa de molino, *f.* **m.-hand,** obrero (-ra). **m.-pond,** cubo, *m.* **m.-race,** caz, *m.* **m.-wheel,** rueda de molino, *f*
millennial /mɪl'lɛniəl/ *a* milenario
millennium /mɪ'lɛniəm/ *n* milenario, *m*
miller /'mɪlər/ *n* molinero, *m.* **miller's wife,** molinera
millet /'mɪlɪt/ *n* mijo, *m*
milligram /'mɪlɪˌgræm/ *n* miligramo, *m*
milliliter /'mɪləˌlitər/ *n* mililitro, *m*
millimeter /'mɪləˌmitər/ *n* milímetro, *m*
milliner /'mɪlənər/ *n* sombrerero (-ra), modista, *mf* **milliner's shop,** sombrerería, tienda de modista, *f*
millinery /'mɪləˌnɛri/ *n* sombreros, *m pl*; modas, *f pl*; tienda de modista, *f*
milling /'mɪlɪŋ/ *n* molienda, *f;* acuñación, *f;* (edge of coin) cordoncillo, *m.* **m. machine,** fresadora, *f*
million /'mɪlyən/ *n* millón, *m.* **the m.,** las masas
millionaire /ˌmɪlyə'nɛər/ *a* millonario. —*n* millonario, *m*
millionairess /ˌmɪlyə'nɛərɪs/ *n* millonaria, *f*
millionth /'mɪlyənθ/ *a* millonésimo
millstone /'mɪlˌstoun/ *n* piedra de moler, muela, *f*
mime /maim/ *n* (Greek farce and actor) mimo, *m;* (mimicry) mímica, *f;* pantomima, *f.* —*vi* hacer en pantomima
mimetic /mɪ'mɛtɪk/ *a* mímico, imitativo
mimic /'mɪmɪk/ *a* mímico; (pretended) fingido. —*n* imitador (-ra). —*vt* imitar, contrahacer; *Biol.* imitar, adaptarse a
mimicry /'mɪmɪkri/ *n* mímica, imitación, *f; Biol.* mimetismo, *m*
minaret /ˌmɪnə'rɛt/ *n* minarete, *m;* (of a mosque) alminar, *m*
minatory /'mɪnəˌtɔri, -ˌtouri/ *a* amenazador
mince /mɪns/ *vt* desmenuzar; (meat) picar; (words) medir (las palabras). —*vi* andar con pasos menuditos; andar o moverse con afectación; hacer remilgos. **m.-meat,** carne picada, *f;* (sweet) conserva de fruta y especias, *f*
mincing /'mɪnsɪŋ/ *a* afectado. —*n* acción de picar carne, *f.* **m. machine,** máquina de picar carne, *f*

mincingly /ˈmɪnsɪŋli/ *adv* con afectación; con pasos menuditos
mind /maind/ *n* inteligencia, *f;* espíritu ánimo, *m;* imaginación, *f;* alma, *f;* (memory) memoria, *f,* recuerdo, *m;* (understanding) entendimiento, *m;* (genius) ingenio, *m;* (cast of mind) mentalidad, *f;* (opinion) opinión, *f;* (liking) gusto, *m;* (thoughts) pensamiento, *m;* (intention) propósito, *m,* intención, *f;* (tendency) propensión, inclinación, *f.* **I have a good m. to go away,** Por poco me marcho; Tengo ganas de marcharme. **I have changed my m.,** He cambiado de opinión. **out of m.,** olvidado. **I shall give him a piece of my m.,** Le diré cuatro verdades. **It had quite gone out of my m.,** Lo había olvidado completamente. **I can see it in my mind's eye,** Está presente a mi imaginación. **I shall bear it in m.,** Lo tendré en cuenta. **I thought in my own m. that...,** Pensé por mis adentros que... **We are both of the same m.,** Ambos somos de la misma opinión. **to be out of one's m.,** estar fuera de juicio. **to call to m.,** acordarse de. **to have something on one's m.,** estar preocupado. **to make up one's m.** (**to**), resolverse (a), decidirse (a), determinar; animarse (a). **m.-reader,** adivinador (-ra) del pensamiento
mind /maind/ *vt* (remember) recordar, no olvidar; (heed) atender a; hacer caso de; tener cuidado de; (fear) tener miedo de; (obey) obedecer; preocuparse de; (object to) molestar; importar; (care for) cuidar. —*vi* tener cuidado; molestar; (feel) sentir; (fear) tener miedo; (be the same thing) ser igual. **Do you m. being quiet a moment?** ¿Quieres hacer el favor de callarte un momento? **Do you m. if I smoke?** ¿Le molesta si fumo? **They don't m.,** No les importa, Les da igual. **Never m.!** ¡No se moleste!; ¡No se preocupe!; ¡No importa! ¡Vaya! **M. what you are doing!** ¡Cuidado con lo que haces! **M. your own business!** ¡No te metas donde no te llaman!
minded /ˈmaindɪd/ *a* dispuesto, inclinado; de... pensamientos; de... disposición
mindful /ˈmaindfəl/ *a* atento (a), cuidadoso (de); que se acuerda (de)
mine /main/ *a poss* mío, *m,* (mía, *f;* míos, *m pl;* mías, *f pl*); el mío, *m,* (la mía, *f;* lo mío, *neut;* los míos, *m pl*; las mías, *f pl*); mi (*pl* mis). **a friend of m.,** un amigo mío; uno de mis amigos
mine /main/ *n* mina, *f.* —*vt* minar; extraer; sembrar minas en, colocar minas en. —*vi* minar; hacer una mina; dedicarse a la minería. **drifting m.,** mina a la deriva, *f.* **land m.,** mina terrestre, *f.* **magnetic m.,** mina magnética, *f.* **to lay mines,** colocar (or sembrar) minas. **m.-sweeper,** dragaminas, buque barreminas, *m*
minefield /ˈmainˌfild/ *n* campo de minas, *m;* barrera de minas, *f*
minelayer /ˈmainˌleiər/ *n* barca plantaminas, *f,* barco siembraminas, lanzaminas, *m*
miner /ˈmainər/ *n* minero, *m; Mil.* zapador minador, *m*
mineral /ˈmɪnərəl/ *n* mineral, *m, a* mineral. **m. baths,** baños, *m pl.* **m. water,** agua mineral, *f;* gaseosa, *f*
mineralogical /ˌmɪnərəˈlɒdʒɪkəl/ *a* mineralógico
mineralogist /ˌmɪnəˈrɒlədʒɪst/ *n* mineralogista, *m*
mineralogy /ˌmɪnəˈrɒlədʒi/ *n* mineralogía, *f*
mingle /ˈmɪŋgəl/ *vt* mezclar; confundir. —*vi* mezclarse; confundirse
mingling /ˈmɪŋglɪŋ/ *n* mezcla, *f*
miniature /ˈmɪniətʃər/ *n* miniatura, *f.* —*a* en miniatura. **m. edition,** edición diamante, *f*
miniature golf *n* minigolf, *m*
miniaturist /ˈmɪniətʃərɪst/ *n* miniaturista, *mf*
minimize /ˈmɪnəˌmaiz/ *vt* aminorar, reducir al mínimo; mitigar; (underrate) tener en menos, despreciar
minimum /ˈmɪnəməm/ *n* mínimo, *m, a* mínimo
mining /ˈmainɪŋ/ *n* minería, *f, a* minero; de mina; de minas; de minero. **m. engineer,** ingeniero de minas, *m*
minion /ˈmɪnyən/ *n* favorito (-ta); satélite, *m; Print.* miñona, *f*
minister /ˈmɪnəstər/ *n* ministro, *m.* —*vi* servir; suministrar, proveer de; (contribute) contribuir (a). **m. of health,** ministro de sanidad, *m.* **m. of war,** ministro de la guerra, *m*
ministerial /ˌmɪnəˈstɪəriəl/ *a* ministerial
ministration /ˌmɪnəˈstreiʃən/ *n Eccl.* ministerio, *m;* servicio, *m;* agencia, *f*
ministry /ˈmɪnəstri/ *n* ministerio, *m.* **m. of food,** Ministerio de Abastecimientos, *m*
mink /mɪŋk/ *n* visón, *m*
minnow /ˈmɪnou/ *n* pez pequeño de agua dulce, *m*
minor /ˈmainər/ *a* menor. —*n* menor de edad, *m;* (logic) menor, *f; Mus.* tono menor, *m; Eccl.* menor, *m.* **to be a m.,** ser menor de edad. **m. key,** tono menor, *m.* **m. orders,** *Eccl.* órdenes menores, *f pl.* **m. scale,** escala menor, *f*
Minorca /mɪˈnɔrkə/ Menorca, *f*
minority /mɪˈnɔrɪti/ *n* minoría, *f;* (of age) minoridad, *f.* **in the m.,** en la minoría
minster /ˈmɪnstər/ *n* catedral, *f;* monasterio, *m*
minstrel /ˈmɪnstrəl/ *n* trovador, juglar, *m;* músico, *m;* cantante, *m*
minstrelsy /ˈmɪnstrəlsi/ *n* música, *f;* canto, *m;* arte del trovador, *m,* or *f;* gaya ciencia, *f*
mint /mɪnt/ *n Bot.* menta, hierbabuena, *f;* casa de moneda, casa de la moneda, ceca, *f; Fig.* mina, *f;* (source) origen, *m.* —*vt* (money) acuñar; *Fig.* inventar, *a* (postage stamp) en estado nuevo
minter /ˈmɪntər/ *n* acuñador, *m; Fig.* inventor (-ra)
minting /ˈmɪntɪŋ/ *n* (of coins) acuñación, *f; Fig.* invención, *f*
minuet /ˌmɪnyuˈɛt/ *n* minué, *m*
minus /ˈmainəs/ *a* menos; negativo; desprovisto de; sin. —*n* signo menos, *m;* cantidad negativa, *f*
minute /maiˈnut/ *a* menudo, diminuto; insignificante; minucioso
minute /ˈmɪnɪt/ *n* minuto, *m;* momento, *m;* instante, *m;* (note) minuta, *f; pl* **minutes,** actas, *f pl.* **in a m.,** en un instante. **m.-book,** libro de actas, minutario, *m.* **m.-hand,** minutero, *m*
minutely /maiˈnutli/ *adv* minuciosamente; en detalle; exactamente
minuteness /maiˈnutnɪs/ *n* suma pequeñez, *f;* minuciosidad, *f*
minx /mɪŋks/ *n* picaruela, *f;* coqueta, *f*
miracle /ˈmɪrəkəl/ *n* milagro, *m.* **m.-monger,** milagrero (-ra). **m. play,** milagro, *m*
miraculous /mɪˈrækyələs/ *a* milagroso
miraculously /mɪˈrækyələsli/ *adv* milagrosamente, por milagro
miraculousness /mɪˈrækyələsnɪs/ *n* carácter milagroso, *m,* lo milagroso
mirage /mɪˈrɑʒ/ *n* espejismo, *m*
mire /maiᵊr/ *n* fango, lodo, *m;* (miry place) lodazal, *m*
mirror /ˈmɪrər/ *n* espejo, *m.* —*vt* reflejar. **to look in the m.,** mirarse al espejo. **full-length m.,** espejo de cuerpo entero, *m.* **small m.,** espejuelo, *m*
mirth /mɜrθ/ *n* alegría, *f,* júbilo, *m;* risa, *f;* hilaridad, *f*
mirthful /ˈmɛrθfəl/ *a* alegre
mirthless /ˈmɛrθlɪs/ *a* sin alegría, triste
miry /ˈmaiᵊri/ *a* lodoso, fangoso, cenagoso
misadventure /ˌmɪsədˈvɛntʃər/ *n* desgracia, *f;* accidente, *m*
misanthrope /ˈmɪsənˌθroup/ *n* misántropo, *m*
misanthropic /ˌmɪsənˈθrɒpɪk/ *a* misantrópico
misanthropy /mɪsˈænθrəpi/ *n* misantropía, *f*
misapplication /ˌmɪsæplɪˈkeiʃən/ *n* mala aplicación, *f;* mal uso, *m;* abuso, *m*
misapply /ˌmɪsəˈplai/ *vt* aplicar mal; hacer mal uso de; abusar de
misapprehend /ˌmɪsæprɪˈhɛnd/ *vt* comprender mal; equivocarse sobre
misapprehension /ˌmɪsæprəˈhɛnʃən/ *n* concepto erróneo, *m;* equivocación, *f,* error, *m*
misappropriate /ˌmɪsəˈproupriˌeit/ *vt* malversar
misappropriation /ˌmɪsəproupriˈeiʃən/ *n* malversación, *f*
misbehave /ˌmɪsbɪˈheiv/ *vi* portarse mal; (of a child) ser malo
misbehavior /ˌmɪsbɪˈheivyər/ *n* mala conducta, *f*

miscalculate /mɪs'kælkyəleit/ *vt* calcular mal; engañarse (sobre)

miscalculation /ˌmɪskælkyə'leiʃən/ *n* mal cálculo, error, *m;* desacierto, *m*

miscall /mɪs'kɔl/ *vt* mal nombrar; llamar equivocadamente; (abuse) insultar

miscarriage /mɪs'kærɪdʒ/ *n Med.* aborto, *m;* (failure) malogro, fracaso, *m;* (of goods) extravío, *m*

miscarriage of justice *n* yerro en la administración de la justicia, *m*

miscarry /mɪs'kæri/ *vi Med.* abortar, malparir; (fail) malograrse, frustrarse; (of goods) extraviarse

miscellaneous /ˌmɪsə'leiniəs/ *a* misceláneo; vario, diverso

miscellany /'mɪsəˌleini/ *n* miscelánea, *f*

mischance /mɪs'tʃæns/ *n* mala suerte, *f;* infortunio, *m,* desgracia, *f;* accidente, *m*

mischief /'mɪstʃɪf/ *n* daño, *m;* mal, *m;* (wilfulness) travesura, *f;* (person) diablillo, *m.* **m.-maker,** enredador (-ra), chismoso (-sa); alborotador, *m;* malicioso (-sa). **m.-making,** *a* enredador; chismoso; malicioso; alborotador

mischievous /'mɪstʃəvəs/ *a* dañino, perjudicial, malo; malicioso; chismoso; (wilful) travieso; juguetón; (of glances, etc.) malicioso

mischievously /'mɪstʃəvəsli/ *adv* maliciosamente; con (or por) travesura

mischievousness /'mɪstʃəvəsnɪs/ *n* mal, *m;* malicia, *f;* maleficencia, *f;* travesura, *f*

misconceive /ˌmɪskən'siv/ *vt* formar un concepto erróneo de; concebir mal, juzgar mal

misconception /ˌmɪskən'sɛpʃən/ *n* concepto erróneo, *m,* idea falsa, *f;* error, *m,* equivocación, *f;* engaño, *m*

misconduct / *n* mɪs'kɒndʌkt; *v* ˌmɪskən'dʌkt/ *n* mala conducta, *f.* **to m. oneself,** portarse mal

misconstruction /ˌmɪskən'strʌkʃən/ *n* mala interpretación, *f;* falsa interpretación, *f;* tergiversación, *f;* mala traducción, *f*

misconstrue /ˌmɪskən'stru/ *vt* interpretar mal; entender mal; tergiversar; traducir mal

miscount / *v* mɪs'kaunt; *n* 'mɪsˌkaunt/ *vt* contar mal, equivocarse en la cuenta de; calcular mal. —*n* error, *m;* yerro de cuenta, *m*

miscreant /'mɪskriənt/ *n* malandrín, *m;* bribón, *m,* *a* vil, malandrín

misdeed /mɪs'did/ *n* delito, malhecho, crimen, *m*

misdemeanor /ˌmɪsdɪ'minər/ *n* mala conducta, *f; Law.* delito, *m;* ofensa, *f,* malhecho, *m*

misdirect /ˌmɪsdɪ'rɛkt/ *vt* informar mal (acerca del camino); (a letter) dirigir mal, poner unas señas incorrectas en

miser /'maizər/ *n* avaro (-ra)

miserable /'mɪzərəbəl/ *a* infeliz, desgraciado; miserable; despreciable; sin valor

miserably /'mɪzərəbli/ *adv* miserablemente

miserliness /'maizərlinɪs/ *n* avaricia, tacañería, *f*

miserly /'maizərli/ *a* avaro, tacaño

misery /'mɪzəri/ *n* miseria, *f;* sufrimiento, *m;* dolor, tormento, *m*

misfire /mɪs'fɪᵊr/ *vi* no dar fuego; (of a motor-car, etc.) hacer falsas explosiones, errar el encendido

misfit /mɪs'fɪt; 'mɪsˌfɪt *for person*/ *n* traje que no cae bien, *m;* zapato que no va bien, *m;* (person) inadaptado, *m*

misfortune /mɪs'fɔrtʃən/ *n* infortunio, *m,* mala suerte, adversidad, *f;* desdicha, desgracia, *f;* mal, *m*

misgive /mɪs'gɪv/ *vt* hacer temer; llenar de duda; hacer recelar; hacer presentir

misgiving /mɪs'gɪvɪŋ/ *n* temor, *m;* duda, *f;* recelo, *m,* presentimiento, *m*

misgovern /mɪs'gʌvərn/ *vt* gobernar mal; administrar mal; dirigir mal

misgovernment /mɪs'gʌvərnmənt/ *n* desgobierno, *m;* mala administración, *f*

misguided /mɪs'gaidɪd/ *a* mal dirigido; extraviado; engañado; (blind) ciego

misguidedly /mɪs'gaidɪdli/ *adv* equivocadamente

mishap /'mɪshæp/ *n* desgracia, *f;* contratiempo, accidente, *m.* **to have a m.,** sufrir una desgracia; tener un accidente

misinform /ˌmɪsɪn'fɔrm/ *vt* informar mal; dar informes erróneos (a)

misinformation /ˌmɪsɪnfər'meiʃən/ *n* noticia falsa, *f;* información errónea, *f*

misinterpret /ˌmɪsɪn'tɜrprɪt/ *vt* interpretar mal; entender mal; torcer; tergiversar; traducir mal

misinterpretation /ˌmɪsɪnˌtɜrprɪ'teiʃən/ *n* mala interpretación, *f;* interpretación falsa, *f;* tergiversación, *f;* mala traducción, *f*

misjudge /mɪs'dʒʌdʒ/ *vt* juzgar mal; equivocarse (en or sobre); tener una idea falsa de

misjudgment /mɪs'dʒʌdʒmənt/ *n* juicio errado, *m;* idea falsa, *f;* juicio injusto, *m*

mislay /mɪs'lei/ *vt* extraviar, perder

mislead /mɪs'lid/ *vt* extraviar; llevar a conclusiones erróneas, despistar; engañar

misleading /mɪs'lidɪŋ/ *a* de falsas apariencias; erróneo, falso; engañoso

mismanage /mɪs'mænɪdʒ/ *vt* administrar mal; dirigir mal; echar a perder

mismanagement /mɪs'mænɪdʒmənt/ *n* mala administración, *f;* desgobierno, *m*

misname /mɪs'neim/ *vt* mal nombrar; llamar equivocadamente

misnomer /mɪs'noumər/ *n* nombre equivocado, *m;* nombre inapropiado, *m*

misogynist /mɪ'sɒdʒənɪst/ *n* misógino, *m*

misogyny /mɪ'sɒdʒəni/ *n* misoginia, *f*

misplace /mɪs'pleis/ *vt* colocar mal; poner fuera de lugar

misplaced /mɪs'pleist/ *a* mal puesto; inoportuno; equivocado

misprint /*n.* 'mɪsˌprɪnt; *v.* mɪs'prɪnt/ *n* error de imprenta, *m,* errata, *f, vt* imprimir con erratas

mispronounce /ˌmɪsprə'nouns/ *vt* pronunciar mal

mispronunciation /ˌmɪsprənʌnsi'eiʃən/ *n* mala pronunciación, *f*

misquotation *n* cita errónea, *f*

misquote /mɪs'kwout/ *vt* citar mal, citar erróneamente

misrepresent /ˌmɪsrɛprɪ'zɛnt/ *vt* desfigurar; tergiversar; falsificar

misrepresentation /mɪsˌrɛprɪzɛn'teiʃən/ *n* desfiguración, *f;* tergiversación, *f;* falsificación, *f*

misrule /mɪs'rul/ *vt* gobernar mal. —*n* mal gobierno, desgobierno, *m;* confusión, *f*

miss /mɪs/ *n* señorita, *f*

miss /mɪs/ *vt* (one's aim) errar (el tiro, etc.); no acertar (a); (let fall) dejar caer; (lose a train, the post, etc., one's footing, an opportunity, etc.) perder; (fall short of) dejar de; no ver; no notar; pasar por alto de; omitir; echar de menos; notar la falta de; no encontrar. —*vi* errar; (fail) salir mal, fracasar. **I m. you,** Te echo de menos. **to be missing,** faltar; estar ausente; haberse marchado; haber desaparecido. **to m. one's mark,** errar el blanco. **to m. out,** omitir, pasar por alto de. **She doesn't miss a beat,** (fig.) No se le escapa nada

missal /'mɪsəl/ *n* misal, *m*

misshapen /mɪs'ʃeipən/ *a* deforme

missile /'mɪsəl/ *n* arma arrojadiza, *f;* proyectil, *m*

missing /'mɪsɪŋ/ *a* que falta; perdido; ausente; *Mil.* desaparecido

mission /'mɪʃən/ *n* misión, *f*

missionary /'mɪʃəˌnɛri/ *n* misionero, *m*

missionize /'mɪʃəˌnaiz/ *vi* misionar

missis /'mɪsəz/ *n* señora, *f; Inf.* mujer, *f*

Mississippi /ˌmɪsə'sɪpi/ el Misisipí, *m*

missive /'mɪsɪv/ *n* misiva, *f*

Missouri /mɪ'zʊri/ el Misuri, *m*

misspend /mɪs'spɛnd/ *vt* malgastar; desperdiciar; perder

mist /mɪst/ *n* bruma, neblina, *f;* vapor, *m;* (drizzle) llovizna, *f; Fig.* nube, *f.* —*vt* anublar, empañar. —*vi* lloviznar

mistakable /mɪ'steikəbəl/ *a* confundible

mistake /mɪ'steik/ *vt* comprender mal; equivocarse sobre; errar; (with for) confundir con, equivocarse con. —*n* equivocación, *f;* error, *m;* inadvertencia, *f;* (in an exercise, etc.) falta, *f.* **And no m.!** *Inf.* Sin duda alguna. **by m.,** por equivocación; (involuntarily) sin querer. **If I am not mistaken,** Si no me engaño, Si no estoy equivocado. **to make a m.,** equivocarse

mistaken /mɪ'steikən/ *a* (of persons and things) equivocado; (of things) erróneo; incorrecto
mistakenly *adv* equivocadamente; injustamente, falsamente
mister /'mɪstər/ *n* señor, *m*
mistily /'mɪstəli/ *adv* a través de la neblina; obscuramente; indistintamente, vagamente
mistimed /mɪs'taimd/ *a* intempestivo; inoportuno
mistiness /'mɪstinɪs/ *n* neblina, bruma, *f;* vaporosidad, *f;* obscuridad, *f*
mistletoe /'mɪsəl,tou/ *n* muérdago, *m*
mistranslate /,mɪstrænz'leit/ *vt* traducir mal; interpretar mal
mistranslation /,mɪstrænz'leiʃən/ *n* mala traducción, *f;* traducción inexacta, *f*
mistress /'mɪstrɪs/ *n* señora, *f;* maestra, *f;* (fiancée) prometida, *f;* (beloved) amada, dulce dueña, *f;* (concubine) amiga, querida, *f.* **M. (Mrs.) Gómez,** Sra Gómez. **m. of the robes,** camarera mayor, *f*
mistrust /mɪs'trʌst/ *vt* desconfiar de, no tener confianza en; dudar de. —*n* desconfianza, *f;* recelo, *m,* suspicacia, *f;* aprensión, *f*
mistrustful /mɪs'trʌstfəl/ *a* desconfiado; receloso, suspicaz. **to be m. of,** recelarse de
misty /'mɪsti/ *a* brumoso, nebuloso; vaporoso; (of the eyes) anublado; (of windows, etc.) empañado
misunderstand /,mɪsʌndər'stænd/ *vt* comprender mal; tomar en sentido erróneo; interpretar mal
misunderstanding /,mɪsʌndər'stændɪŋ/ *n* concepto erróneo, error, *m;* equivocación, *f;* (disagreement) desavenencia, *f*
misuse /*n* mɪs'yus; *v* -'yuz/ *vt* emplear mal; abusar de; (funds) malversar; (ill-treat) tratar mal. —*n* abuso, *m;* (of funds) malversación, *f*
mite /mait/ *n* (coin) ardite, *m;* (trifle) pizca, *f;* óbolo, *m; Ent.* ácaro, *m*
miter /'maitər/ *n* mitra, *f;* inglete, *m, vt* cortar ingletes en
mitigate /'mɪtɪ,geit/ *vt* (pain) aliviar; mitigar; suavizar
mitigation /,mɪtɪ'geiʃən/ *n* (of pain) alivio, *m;* mitigación, *f*
mitten /'mɪtn̩/ *n* mitón, *m*
mix /mɪks/ *vt* mezclar; (salad) aderezar; (concrete, etc.) amasar; combinar, unir; (sociably) alternar (con); (confuse) confundir. —*vi* mezclarse; frecuentar la compañía (de); frecuentar; (get on well) llevarse bien
mixed /mɪkst/ *a* mezclado; vario, surtido; mixto; (confused) confuso. **m. doubles,** parejas mixtas, *f pl.* **m. up,** (in disorder) revuelto; confuso. **m. up with,** implicado en; asociado con
mixer /'mɪksər/ *n* mezclador, *m;* (person) mezclador (-ra); *Inf.* persona sociable, *f.* **electric m.,** mezclador eléctrico, *m*
mixture /'mɪkstʃər/ *n* mezcla, *f;* (medicine) poción, medicina, *f*
mizzen /'mɪzən/ *n* mesana, *f.* **m.-mast,** palo de mesana, *m.* **m.-sail,** vela de mesana, *f.* **m.-topsail,** sobremesana, *f*
mnemonics /nɪ'mɒnɪks/ *n* mnemotecnia, *f*
Moabite /'mouə,bait/ *n* moabita, *mf*
moan /moun/ *vt* lamentar; llorar. —*vi* gemir; quejarse, lamentarse. —*n* gemido, *m;* lamento, *m;* quejido, *m*
moaning /'mounɪŋ/ *n* gemidos, *m pl*
moat /mout/ *n* foso, *m*
mob /mɒb/ *n* (crowd) muchedumbre, multitud, *f;* (rabble) populacho, *m,* gentuza, *f.* —*vt* atropellar; atacar. **mob-cap,** cofia, *f*
mobile /'moubil/ *a* móvil; ambulante; (fickle) voluble. **m. canteen,** cantina ambulante, *f*
mobility /mou'bɪlɪti/ *n* movilidad, *f*
mobilization /,moubələ'zeiʃən/ *n* movilización, *f*
mobilize /'moubə,laiz/ *vt* movilizar. —*vi* movilizarse
moccasin /'mɒkəsɪn, -zən/ *n* mocasín, *m*
mocha /'moukə/ *n* café de Moca, *m*
mock /mɒk/ *vt* ridiculizar; burlarse (de), mofarse (de); (cause to fail) frustrar; (mimic) imitar; (delude) engañar. —*vi* mofarse, burlarse, reírse. —*a* cómico, burlesco; falso; fingido; imitado. **to make a m. of,** poner en ridículo; hacer absurdo; burlarse de. **m.-heroic,** heroico-cómico. **m.-orange,** *Bot.* jeringuilla, *f.* **m.-turtle soup,** sopa hecha con cabeza de ternera a imitación de tortuga, *f*
mocker *n* mofador (-ra); el, *m,* (*f,* la) que se burla de
mockery /'mɒkəri/ *n* mofa, burla, *f;* ridículo, *m;* ilusión, apariencia, *f.* **to make a m. of,** mofarse de; hacer ridículo
mocking /'mɒkɪŋ/ *a* burlón. **m. bird,** pájaro burlón, *m*
mockingly /'mɒkɪŋli/ *adv* burlonamente
modality /mou'dælɪti/ *n* modalidad, *f*
mode /moud/ *n* modo, *m;* manera, *f;* (fashion) moda, *f;* uso, *m,* costumbre, *f*
model /'mɒdl̩/ *n* modelo, *m;* (artist's) modelo vivo, *m, a* modelo; en miniatura. —*vt* modelar; moldear; formar; hacer; planear. **m. display,** (hats, etc.) exposición de modelos, *f.* **m. railway,** ferrocarril en miniatura, *m*
modeler /'mɒdl̩ər/ *n* modelador (-ra); disenador, *m*
modeling /'mɒdl̩ɪŋ/ *n* modelado, *m;* modelo, *m.* **m. wax,** cera para moldear, *f*
modem /'moudəm, -dɛm/ *n* módem, *m*
moderate /*a, n.* 'mɒdərɪt *v.* -ə,reit/ *a* moderado; (of prices, etc.) módico; (fair, medium) regular, mediano; razonable; mediocre. —*n* moderado, *m.* —*vt* moderar; modificar; calmar. —*vi* moderarse; calmarse
moderately /'mɒdərɪtli/ *adv* moderadamente; módicamente; medianamente; bastante; razonablemente; mediocremente
moderation /,mɒdə'reiʃən/ *n* moderación, *f.* **in m.,** en moderación
moderator /'mɒdə,reitər/ *n* moderador, *m;* (Church of Scotland) presidente, *m; Educ.* examinador, *m; Educ.* inspector de exámenes, *m.* **m. lamp,** lámpara de regulador, *f*
modern /'mɒdərn/ *a* moderno. —*n* modernista, *mf.* **in the m. way,** a la moderna. **m. language,** lengua viva, *f*
modernism /'mɒdər,nɪzəm/ *n* modernismo, *m*
modernist /'mɒdərnɪst/ *n* modernista, *mf*
modernistic /,mɒdər'nɪstɪk/ *a* modernista
modernity /mɒ'dɜrnɪti/ *n* modernidad, *f*
modernization /,mɒdərnə'zeiʃən/ *n* modernización, *f*
modernize /'mɒdər,naiz/ *vt* modernizar
modernness /'mɒdərnnɪs/ *n* modernidad, *f*
modest /'mɒdɪst/ *a* modesto; (of a woman) púdico
modesty /'mɒdəsti/ *n* modestia, *f;* (of a woman) pudor, *m*
modicum /'mɒdɪkəm/ *n* porción pequeña, *f;* poco, *m*
modifiable *a* modificable
modification /,mɒdəfɪ'keiʃən/ *n* modificación, *f*
modify /'mɒdə,fai/ *vt* modificar. **It has been much modified,** Se ha modificado mucho; Se han hecho muchas modificaciones
modifying *a* modificante, modificador
modish /'moudɪʃ/ *a* de moda en boga; elegante
modishness /'moudɪʃnɪs/ *n* elegancia, *f*
modiste /mou'dist/ *n* modista, *mf*
modulate /'mɒdʒə,leit/ *vt* and *vi* modular
modulation /,mɒdʒə'leiʃən/ *n* modulación, *f*
modus vivendi /'moudəs vɪ'vɛndi, -dai/ *n* modo de conveniencia, *m*
Mogul /'mougəl/ *a* mogol. —*n* mogol (-la). **the Great M.,** el Gran Mogol
Mohammedan /mʊ'hæmɪdn̩, mou-/ *a* mahometano, agareno
Mohammedanism /mʊ'hæmɪdn̩,ɪzəm, mou-/ *n* mahometismo, *m*
Mohican /mou'hikən/ *n* mohican, *m*
moiety /'mɔiɪti/ *n* mitad, *f*
moiré /mwɑ'rei, mɔ-/ *n* muaré, *m*
moist /mɔist/ *a* húmedo
moisten /'mɔisən/ *vt* humedecer, mojar
moisture /'mɔistʃər/ *n* humedad, *f*
molar /'moulər/ *n* muela, *f, a* molar
molasses /mə'læsɪz/ *n pl* melaza, *f*
mold /mould/ *n* (fungus) moho, *m;* (humus) mantillo, *m;* (iron-mould) mancha de orín, *f;* (matrix) molde, *m,* matriz, *f; Cul.* cubilete, *m; Naut.* gálibo, *m;* (for jelly, etc.) molde, *m; Archit.* moldura, *f;*

(temperament) temple, *m,* disposición, *f.* —*vt* moldear; (cast) vaciar; moldurar; *Naut.* galibar; *Fig.* amoldar, formar; *Agr.* cubrir con mantillo. **to m. oneself on,** modelarse sobre. **m.-board,** (of a plough) orejera, *f*

Moldavian /moul'deiviən/ *a* moldavo. —*n* moldavo (-va)

molder /'mouldər/ *n* moldeador, *m; Fig.* amolador (-ra); creador (-ra). —*vi* desmoronarse, convertirse en polvo; *Fig.* decaer, desmoronarse; vegetar

moldiness /'mouldinɪs/ *n* moho, *m*

molding /'mouldɪŋ/ *n* amoldamiento, *m;* vaciado, *m; Archit.* moldura, *f; Fig.* formación,

moldy /'mouldi/ *a* mohoso, enmohecido; *Fig.* anticuado

mole /'moulei/ *n* (animal) topo, *m;* (spot) lunar, *m;* (breakwater) dique, malecón, *m;* muelle, *m*

molecular /mə'lɛkyələr/ *a* molecular

molecule /'mɒlɪˌkyul/ *n* molécula, *f*

molehill /'moulˌhɪl/ *n* topera, *f*

moleskin /'moulˌskɪn/ *n* piel de topo, *f*

molest /mə'lɛst/ *vt* molestar; perseguir, importunar; faltar al respeto (a)

molestation /ˌmoulə'steiʃən/ *n* importunidad, persecución, *f;* molestia, incomodidad, *f*

mollification /ˌmɒləfɪ'keiʃən/ *n* apaciguamiento, *m;* mitigación, *f*

mollify /'mɒləˌfai/ *vt* apaciguar, calmar; mitigar

mollusk /'mɒləsk/ *n* molusco, *m*

mollycoddle /'mɒliˌkɒdl̩/ *n* alfeñique, mírame y no me toques, *m;* niño (-ña), mimado (-da)

Moloch /'moulɒk/ *n* Moloc, *m*

molt /moult/ *vi* mudar, *n* muda, *f*

molten /'moultn̩/ *a* fundido; derretido

Moluccas, the /mə'lukəz/ las Malucas, *f pl*

moment /'moumənt/ *n* momento, *m;* instante *m;* (importance) importancia, *f.* **at this m.,** en este momento. **Do it this m.!** ¡Hazlo al instante (or en seguida)!

momentarily /ˌmoumən'tɛərəli, 'moumənˌtɛr-/ *adv* momentáneamente; cada momento

momentariness /'moumənˌtɛrinɪs/ *n* momentaneidad, *f*

momentary /'moumənˌtɛri/ *a* momentáneo

momentous /mou'mɛntəs/ *a* de suma importancia; crítico; grave

momentousness /mou'mɛntəsnɪs/ *n* importancia, *f;* gravedad, *f*

momentum /mou'mɛntəm/ *n* momento, *m,* velocidad adquirida *f; Fig.* ímpetu, *m.* **to gather m.,** cobrar velocidad, acelerar

monarch /'mɒnərk/ *n* monarca, *m*

monarchic /mə'narkɪk/ *a* monárquico

monarchism /'mɒnərˌkɪzəm/ *n* monarquismo, *m*

monarchist *n* monárquico (-ca)

monarchy /'mɒnərki/ *n* monarquía, *f*

monastery /'mɒnəˌstɛri/ *n* monasterio, *m*

monastic /mə'næstɪk/ *a* monástico. **m. life,** vida de clausura, *f*

monasticism *n* vida monástica, *f*

Monday /'mʌndei, -di/ *n* lunes, *m*

monetary /'mɒnɪˌtɛri/ *a* monetario

monetization *n* monetización, *f*

money /'mʌni/ *n* dinero, *m;* (coin) moneda, *f;* sistema monetario, *m.* **paper m.,** papel moneda, *m.* **ready m.,** dinero contante, *m.* **to make m.,** ganar (or hacer) dinero; enriquecerse. **M. talks,** Poderoso caballero es Don Dinero. **m.-bag,** talega, *f;* (person) ricacho (-cha). **m.-bags,** riqueza, *f.* **m.-box,** alcancía, hucha, *f.* **m.-changer,** cambista, *mf* **m.-lender,** prestamista, *mf* **m.-making,** *n* el hacer dinero; prosperidad, ganancia, *f.* —*a* lucrativo. **m.-order,** giro postal, *m*

moneyed /'mʌnid/ *a* adinerado; acomodado

Mongolian /mɒŋ'gouliən/ *a* mogol. —*n* mogol (-la); (language) mogol, *m*

mongoose /'mɒŋˌgus/ *n* mangosta, *f*

mongrel /'mʌŋgrəl/ *a* mestizo, atravesado. —*n* perro mestizo, *m;* (in contempt) mestizo. *m*

monitor /'mɒnɪtər/ *n* monitor, *m*

monitory /'mɒnɪˌtɔri/ *a* monitorio. —*n Eccl.* monitorio, *m*

monk /mʌŋk/ *n* monje, *m.* **to become a m.,** hacerse monje, tomar el hábito. **monk's-hood,** acónito, *m*

monkey /'mʌŋki/ *n* mono (-na); (imp) diablillo, *m;* (of a pile-driver) pilón de martinete, *m;* (in glass-making) crisol, *m.* **to m. with,** meterse con; entremeterse. **m. nut,** cacahuete, *m.* **m.-puzzle,** (tree) - araucaria, *f.* **m. tricks,** monadas, travesuras, diabluras, *f pl.* **m.-wrench,** llave inglesa, *f*

monkish /'mʌŋkɪʃ/ *a* monacal, de monje; monástico

monochromatic /ˌmɒnəkrou'mætɪk/ *a* monocromo

monochrome /'mɒnəˌkroum/ *n* monocromo, *m*

monocle /'mɒnəkəl/ *n* monóculo, *m*

monogamist /mə'nɒgəmɪst/ *n* monógamo (-ma)

monogamous /mə'nɒgəməs/ *a* monógamo

monogamy /mə'nɒgəmi/ *n* monogamia, *f*

monogram /'mɒnəˌgræm/ *n* monograma, *m*

monograph /'mɒnəˌgræf/ *n* monografía, *f,* opúsculo, *m*

monolith /'mɒnəlɪθ/ *n* monolito, *m*

monolithic /ˌmɒnə'lɪθɪk/ *a* monolítico

monologue /'mɒnəˌlɔg/ *n* monólogo, *m*

monomania /ˌmɒnə'meiniə/ *n* monomanía, *f*

monomaniac /ˌmɒnə'meiniˌæk/ *n* monomaníaco (-ca)

monomial /mou'noumiəl/ *n* monomio, *m, a* de un solo término

monoplane /'mɒnəˌplein/ *n* monoplano, *m*

monopolist /mə'nɒpəlɪst/ *n* monopolista, *mf;* acaparador (-ra)

monopolization /məˌnɒpələ'zeiʃən/ *n* monopolio, *m*

monopolize /mə'nɒpəˌlaiz/ *vt* monopolizar

monopoly /mə'nɒpəli/ *n* monopolio, *m*

monotheism /'mɒnəθiˌɪzəm/ *n* monoteísmo, *m*

monotheist /'mɒnəˌθiɪst/ *n* monoteísta, *mf*

monotone /'mɒnəˌtoun/ *n* monotonía, *f*

monotonous /mə'nɒtn̩əs/ *a* monótono

monotony /mə'nɒtn̩i/ *n* monotonía, *f*

monoxide /mɒn'ɒksaid/ *n* monóxido, *m*

Monroe doctrine /mən'rou/ *n* monroísmo, *m*

monsignor /mɒn'sinyər/ *n* monseñor, *m*

monsoon /mɒn'sun/ *n* monzón, *mf*

monster /'mɒnstər/ *n* monstruo, *m*

monstrance /'mɒnstrəns/ *n* custodia, *f*

monstrosity /mɒn'strɒsɪti/ *n* monstruosidad, *f*

monstrous /'mɒnstrəs/ *a* monstruoso; horrible, atroz; enorme

montage /mɒn'tɑʒ/ *n* montaje, *m*

month /mʌnθ/ *n* mes, *m.* **He arrived a m. ago,** Llegó hace un mes

monthly /'mʌnθli/ *a* mensual. —*adv* mensualmente, cada mes. —*n* revista (or publicación) mensual, *f; pl* **monthlies,** menstruación, regla, *f.* **m. salary** or **payment,** mensualidad, *f*

monument /'mɒnyəmənt/ *n* monumento, *m*

monumental /ˌmɒnyə'mɛntl̩/ *a* monumental

moo /mu/ *vi* (of cattle) mugir. —*n* mugido, *m*

mood /mud/ *n* humor, *m;* espíritu, *m; Gram.* modo, *m*

moodily /'mudl̩i/ *adv* taciturnamente; tristemente, pensativamente

moodiness /'mudinɪs/ *n* mal humor, *m,* taciturnidad, *f;* melancolía, tristeza, *f*

moody /'mudi/ *a* taciturno, de mal humor; triste, melancólico, pensativo

mooing /'muɪŋ/ *n* (of cattle) mugido, *m*

moon /mun/ *n* luna, *f,* satélite, *m,* mes lunar, *m,* luz de la luna, *f.* **full m.,** plenilunio, *m;* luna llena, *f.* **new m.,** novilunio, *m,* luna nueva, *f*

moonbeam /'munˌbim/ *n* rayo de luna, *m*

moonless /'munlɪs/ *a* sin luna

moonlight /'munˌlait/ *n* luz de la luna, *f.* **in the m.,** a la luz de la luna. **to do a m. flit,** *Inf.* mudarse por el aire

moonlighting /'munˌlaitɪŋ/ *n* el pluriempleo, *m*

moonlit /'munˌlɪt/ *a* iluminado por la luna. **moonlit night,** noche de luna, *f*

moonshine /'munˌʃain/ *n* claridad de la luna, *f; Fig.* música celestial, ilusión, *f*

moonstone /'munˌstoun/ *n* adularia, *f*

moonstruck /'mun,strʌk/ *a* lunático
Moor /mʊr/ *n* moro (-ra)
moor /mʊr/ *n* páramo, brezal, *m;* (marsh) pantano, *m;* (for game) coto, *m.* —*vt* amarrar, aferrar; afirmar con anclas o cables. **m.-hen,** polla de agua, *f*
mooring /'mʊrɪŋ/ *n* amarre, *m.* **m.-mast,** *Aer.* poste de amarre, *m*
moorings /'mʊrɪŋz/ *n pl* amarradero, *m*
Moorish /'mʊrɪʃ/ *a* moro; árabe. **M. architecture,** arquitectura árabe, *f.* **M. girl,** mora, *f*
moorland /'mʊrlənd/ *n* páramo, brezal, *m*
moose /mus/ *n* anta, *f*
moot /mut/ *n* junta, *f;* ayuntamiento, *m.* —*a* discutible. —*vt* (bring up) suscitar; (discuss) discutir, debatir
mop /mɒp/ *n* (implement) trapeador, *m* (Ecuador), escoba con fleco, *f;* (of hair) mata (de pelo), *f.* —*vt* trapear (Ecuador); (dry) enjugar, secar. **to mop up,** *Inf.* limpiar; *Mil.* acabar con (el enemigo)
mope /moup/ *vi* replace by tristear. **to m. about,** vagar tristemente
moquette /mou'kɛt/ *n* moqueta, *f*
moraine /mə'rein/ *n* morena, *f*
moral /'mɔrəl/ *a* moral; (chaste) casto, virtuoso; honrado. —*n* (maxim) moraleja, *f; pl* **morals,** moralidad, *f;* ética, *f;* moral, *f;* (conduct) costumbres, *f pl.* **m. philosophy,** filosofía moral, *f.* **m. support,** apoyo moral, *m.* **m. tale,** apólogo, *m*
morale /mə'ræl/ *n* moral, *f*
moralist /'mɔrəlɪst/ *n* moralista, *m*
morality /mə'rælɪti/ *n* moralidad, *f;* virtud, *f;* castidad, *f.* **m. play,** moralidad, *f,* drama alegórico, *m*
moralization /,mɔrələ'zeiʃən/ *n* moralización, *f*
moralize /'mɔrə,laiz/ *vt* and *vi* moralizar
moralizer /'mɔrə,laizər/ *n* moralizador (-ra)
moralizing /'mɔrə,laizɪŋ/ *a* moralizador
morally /'mɔrəli/ *adv* moralmente
morals /'mɔrəlz/. See **moral**
morass /mə'ræs/ *n* marisma, ciénaga, *f*
moratorium /,mɔrə'tɔriəm/ *n* moratoria, *f*
Moravian /mɔ'reiviən/ *a* moravo. —*n* moravo (-va)
morbid /'mɔrbɪd/ *a* mórbido, mórboso; (of the mind, etc.) insano
morbidezza /,mɔrbɪ'dɛtsə/ *n* (*Art.* and *Lit.*) morbidez, *f*
morbidity /mɔr'bɪdɪti/ *n* morbidez, *f*
mordacity /mɔr'dæsɪti/ *n* mordacidad, *f*
mordant /'mɔrdn̩t/ *a* mordaz; (of acid) mordiente. —*n* mordiente, *m*
more /mɔr/ *a* and *adv* más. **The m. he earns, the less he saves,** Cuanto más gana, menos ahorra. **the m. the better,** cuanto más, tanto mejor. **without m. ado,** sin más ni más; sin decir nada. **Would you like some m.?** ¿Quiere Vd. más? (of food) ¿Quiere Vd. repetir? **no m.,** no más; (never) nunca más; (finished) se acabó. **once m.,** otra vez, una vez más. **m. and m.,** cada vez más, más y más. **m. or less,** más o menos; (about) poco más o menos
moreover /mɔr'ouvər/ *adv* además, también; por otra parte
morganatic /,mɔrgə'nætɪk/ *a* morganático
morgue /mɔrg/ *n* depósito de cadáveres, *m*
moribund /'mɔrə,bʌnd/ *a* moribundo
Mormon /'mɔrmən/ *a* mormónico. —*n* mormón (-ona)
Mormonism /'mɔrmə,nɪzəm/ *n* mormonismo, *m*
morning /'mɔrnɪŋ/ *n* mañana, *f, a* matutino, de la mañana. **Good m.!** ¡Buenos días! **the next m.,** la mañana siguiente. **very early in the m.,** muy de mañana. **m. coat,** chaqué, *m.* **m. dew,** rocío de la mañana, *m.* **m. paper,** periódico de la mañana, *m.* **m. star,** lucero del alba, *m.* **m. suit,** chaqué, *m*
Moroccan /mə'rɒkən/ *a* marroquí, marrueco. —*n* marrueco (-ca), marroquí, *mf*
Morocco /mə'rɒkou/ Marruecos, *m*
morocco /mə'rɒkou/ *n* (leather) marroquí, tafilete, *m*
morose /mə'rous/ *a* sombrío, taciturno, malhumorado
morosely /mə'rousli/ *adv* taciturnamente
moroseness /mə'rousnɪs/ *n* taciturnidad, *f;* mal humor, *m*
morphine /'mɔrfin/ *n* morfina, *f.* **m. addict,** morfinómano (-na)
morrow /'mɔrou/ *n* mañana, *f;* día siguiente, *m*
Morse code /mɔrs/ *n* la clave telegráfica de Morse, *f,* el alfabeto de Morse, *m*
morsel /'mɔrsəl/ *n* pedazo, *m;* (mouthful) bocado, *m*
mortal /'mɔrtl̩/ *a* mortal. —*n* mortal, *mf.* **m. sin,** pecado mortal, pecado capital, *m*
mortality /mɔr'tælɪti/ *n* mortalidad, *f*
mortally wounded /'mɔrtl̩i/ *adv* herido de muerte
mortar /'mɔrtər/ *n* (for building) argamasa, *f;* (for mixing and *Mil.*) mortero, *m.* **m. and pestle,** mortero y majador, *m.* **m.-board,** (in building) cuezo, *m;* (academic cap) birrete, *m*
mortgage /'mɔrgɪdʒ/ *n* hipoteca, *f.* —*vt* hipotecar. —*a* hipotecario. **to pay off a m.,** redimir una hipoteca
mortgageable /'mɔrgɪdʒəbəl/ *a* hipotecable
mortgaged debt /'mɔrgɪdʒd/ *n* deuda garantizada con una hipoteca, *f*
mortgagee /,mɔrgə'dʒi/ *n* acreedor (-ra) hipotecario (-ia)
mortgagor /'mɔrgədʒər/ *n* deudor (-ra) hipotecario (-ia)
mortification /,mɔrtəfɪ'keiʃən/ *n* mortificación, *f;* humillación, *f; Med.* gangrena, *f*
mortify /'mɔrtə,fai/ *vt* mortificar; humillar. —*vi Med.* gangrenarse
mortifying /'mɔrtə,faiɪŋ/ *a* humillante
mortise /'mɔrtɪs/ *n* muesca, *f.* —*vt* hacer muescas (en); ensamblar
mortuary /'mɔrtʃu,ɛri/ *a* mortuorio. —*n* depósito de cadáveres, *m*
Mosaic /mou'zeiɪk/ *a* mosaico
mosaic /mou'zeiɪk/ *n* mosaico, *m*
Moscow /'mɒskou,-kau/ Moscú, *m*
mosque /mɒsk/ *n* mezquita, *f*
mosquito /mə'skitou/ *n* mosquito, *m.* **m. net,** mosquitero, *m*
moss /mɔs/ *n* musgo, *m;* moho, *m;* (swamp) marjal, *m*
mossgrown /'mɔs,groun/ *a* musgoso, cubierto de musgo; *Fig.* anticuado
mossiness /'mɔsinɪs/ *n* estado musgoso, *m*
mossy /'mɔsi/ *a* musgoso
most /moust/ *a* el (la, los, etc.) más; la mayor parte de; la mayoría de; (el, etc.) mayor. —*adv* más; el (la, etc.) más; (extremely) sumamente; (very) muy; (before adjectives sometimes expressed by superlative, e.g. *m. reverend,* reverendísimo, *m. holy,* santísimo, etc.). —*n* (highest price) el mayor precio; la mayor parte; el mayor número; lo más. **m. of all,** sobre todo. **m. people**, la mayoría de la gente. **at the m.,** a lo más, a lo sumo. **for the m. part,** en su mayor parte; casi todos; generalmente, casi siempre. **to make the m. of,** sacar el mayor partido posible de; aprovechar bien; exagerar
mostly /'moustli/ *adv* principalmente; en su mayoría; en su mayor parte; casi siempre; en general, generalmente
mote /mout/ *n* átomo, *m;* mota, *f.* **to see the m. in our neighbor's eye and not the beam in our own,** ver la paja en el ojo del vecino y no la viga en el nuestro
motet /mou'tɛt/ *n* motete, *m*
moth /mɔθ/ *n* mariposa nocturna, *f;* polilla, *f.* **m.ball,** bola de naftalina, *f.* **m.-eaten,** apolillado
mother /'mʌðər/ *n* madre, *f;* madre de familia, *f;* (of alcoholic beverages) madre, *f.* —*vt* cuidar como una madre (a); servir de madre (a); (animals) ahijar. **M. Church,** madre iglesia, *f;* iglesia metropolitana, *f.* **m.-in-law,** suegra, *f.* **m. land,** (madre) patria, *f.* **m.-of-pearl,** *n* madreperla, *f,* nácar, *m.* —*a* nacarado, nacáreo. **M. Superior,** (madre) superiora, *f.* **m. tongue,** lengua materna, *f*
motherhood /'mʌðər,hʊd/ *n* maternidad, *f*
motherless /'mʌðərlɪs/ *a* huérfano de madre, sin madre
motherlike *a* de madre, como una madre
motherliness /'mʌðərlinɪs/ *n* cariño maternal, *m*
motherly /'mʌðərli/ *a* maternal

motif /mou'tif/ *n* motivo, *m;* tema, *m; Sew.* adorno, *m*

motion /'mouʃən/ *n* movimiento, *m; Mech.* marcha, operación, *f;* mecanismo, *m;* (sign) seña, señal, *f;* (gesture) ademán, gesto, *m;* (carriage) aire, porte, *m;* (of the bowels) movimiento del vientre, *m,* deyección, *f;* (will) voluntad, *f,* deseo, *m;* (proposal in an assembly or debate) proposición, moción, *f; Law.* pedimento, *m.* —*vt* hacer una señal (a). —*vi* hacer señas. **to set in m.,** poner en marcha. **m. picture,** fotografía cinematográfica, película, *f.* **m.-picture theater,** cine, *m*

motionless /'mouʃənlıs/ *a* inmóvil

motivate /'moutə,veit/ *vt* motivar

motive /'moutıv/ *n* motivo, *m.* —*a* **motor** motivo. **with no m.,** sin motivo. **m. power,** fuerza motriz, *f*

motley /'mɒtli/ *a* abigarrado, multicolor; (mixed) diverso, vario. —*n* traje de colores, *m,* botarga, *f*

motor /'moutər/ *n* motor, *m;* automóvil, *m, a* motor; movido por motor; con motor; (traveling) de viaje. —*vi* ir en automóvil. —*vt* llevar en automóvil (a). **m. boat,** lancha automóvil, *f.* **m.bus,** autobús, ómnibus, *m.* **m.car,** automóvil, *m.* **m.-coach,** autobús, *m.* **m. cycle,** motocicleta, *f.* **m.cyclist,** motociclista, *mf* **m.-launch,** canoa automóvil, *f.* **m.oil,** aceite para motores, *m.* **m.-road,** autopista, *f.* **m.-rug,** manta de viaje, *f.* **m.-scooter,** bicicleta con motor, *f.* **m.-spirit,** bencina, *f*

motoring /'moutərıŋ/ *n* automovilismo, *m*

motorist /'moutərıst/ *n* automovilista, motorista, *mf*

mottled /'mɒtl̩d/ *a* abigarrado; (of marble, etc.) jaspeado, esquizado; manchado (con), con manchas (de); pintado (con)

motto /'mɒtou/ *n Herald.* divisa, *f;* mote, *m;* (in a book, etc.) lema, *m*

mound /maund/ *n* montón, *m;* (knoll) altozano, *m;* (for defence) baluarte, *m;* (for burial) túmulo, *m*

mount /maunt/ *n* (hill, and in palmistry) monte, *m;* (for riding) caballería, *f;* montadura, *f;* (for a picture) borde, *m.* —*vt* subir; (machines, etc.) montar; (jewels) engastar; (a picture) poner un borde a; (a play) poner en escena; poner a caballo; proveer de caballo. —*vi* montar; subir; (increase) aumentar. **to m. a horse,** subir a caballo, montar. **to m. guard,** *Mil.* montar la guardia. **to m. the throne,** subir al trono

mountain /'mauntn̩/ *n* montaña, *f;* (mound) montón, *m.* —*a* de montaña(s); montañés; alpino, alpestre. **to make a m. out of a molehill,** convertir un grano de arena en una montaña. hacer de una pulga un camello, hacer de una pulga un elefante. **m.-chain,** cadena de montañas, *f.* **m. dweller,** montañés (-esa). **m. railway,** ferrocárril de cremallera, *m.* **m.-side,** falda de una montaña, *f*

mountaineer /,mauntn̩'ıər/ *n* (inhabitant) montañés (-esa); (climber) alpinista, *mf.* —*vi* hacer alpinismo

mountaineering /,mauntn̩'ıərıŋ/ *n* alpinismo, *m*

mountainous /'mauntn̩əs/ *a* montañoso; (huge) enorme

mountebank /'mauntə,bæŋk/ *n* saltabanco, *m;* charlatán, *m*

mounting /'mauntıŋ/ *n* (ascent) subida, *f;* ascensión, *f;* (of machinery, etc.) armadura, *f;* montadura, *f;* (of a precious stone) engaste, *m.* **m.-block,** subidero, *m*

mourn /mɔrn/ *vi* afligirse, lamentarse; (wear mourning) estar de luto. —*vt* llorar; lamentar; llevar luto por

mourner /'mɔrnər/ *n* lamentador (-ra); (paid) plañidera, *f;* el, *m,* (*f,* la) que acompaña al féretro

mournful /'mɔrnfəl/ *a* triste, acongojado; funesto, lúgubre; fúnebre; lamentable

mournfully /'mɔrnfəli/ *adv* tristemente

mournfulness /'mɔrnfəlnıs/ *n* tristeza, *f;* melancolía, aflicción, *f,* pesar, *m*

mourning /'mɔrnıŋ/ *n* aflicción, *f;* lamentación, *f;* luto, *m.* **deep m.,** luto riguroso, *m.* **half m.,** medio luto, *m.* **to be in m.,** estar de luto. **to be in m. for,** llevar luto por. **to come out of m.,** dejar el luto. **m.-band,** (on the hat) tira de gasa, *f;* (on the arm) brazal de luto, *m.* **m.-coach,** coche fúnebre, *m*

mouse /*n.* maus; *v.* mauz/ *n* ratón (-na); *Naut.* barrilete, *m.* —*vi* cazar ratones. **m.-coloured,** de color de rata. **m.-hole, m.-trap,** ratonera, *f*

mouser /'mauzər/ *n* gato ratonero, *m*

mousing /'mausıŋ/ *n* caza de ratones, *f*

moustache /'mʌstæʃ, mə'stæʃ/ *n* bigote, mostacho, *m*

mousy /'mausi/ *a* ratonesco, ratonil

mouth /*n.* mauθ; *v.* mauð/ *n* (*Anat.* human being, of a bottle, cave) boca, *f;* entrada, *f;* (of a river) desembocadura, *f;* (of a channel) embocadero, *m;* (of a wind-instrument) boquilla, *f.* —*vt* pronunciar con afectación; (chew) mascar. —*vi* clamar a gritos, vociferar. **down in the m.,** *Inf.* con las orejas caídas. **It makes my m. water,** Se me hace la boca agua. **large m.,** boca rasgada, *f.* **m.-gag,** abrebocas, *m.* **m.-organ,** armónica, *f.* **m.-wash,** antiséptico bucal, *m* (Argentina), enjuague, *m*

mouthed /mauðd, mauθt/ *a* que tiene boca...; de boca... **open-m.,** boquiabierto

mouthful /'mauθ,fʊl/ *n* bocado, *m;* (of smoke, air) bocanada, *f*

mouthpiece /'mauθ,pis/ *n* (of wind-instruments, tobacco-pipe, waterpipe) boquilla, *f;* (of a wineskin) brocal, *m;* (spokesman) portavoz, *m;* intérprete, *mf*

movable /'muvəbəl/ *a* movible; (of goods) mobiliario. **m. feast,** fiesta movible, *f*

movables /'muvəbəlz/ *n pl* bienes muebles, efectos, *m pl*

movable type *n* tipos sueltos, *m pl*

move /muv/ *n* movimiento, *m;* (of household effects) mudanza, *f;* (motion) marcha, *f;* (in a game) jugada, *f;* (*Fig.* step) paso, *m;* (device) maniobra, *f.* **Whose m. is it?** ¿A quién le toca jugar? **to be on the m.,** estar en movimiento; estar de viaje. **to be always on the m.,** *Inf.* parecer una lanzadera

move /muv/ *vt* mover; poner en marcha; (furniture) trasladar; cambiar de lugar; (stir) remover; (shake) agitar, hacer temblar; (transport) transportar; (a piece in chess, etc.) jugar; (pull) arrancar; (impel) impulsar; (incline) inclinar, disponer; (affect emotionally) conmover, emocionar, enternecer; impresionar. —*vi* moverse; ponerse en marcha; (walk) andar; ir; avanzar; (a step forward, etc.) dar; (move house) trasladarse; (act) entrar en acción; (in games) hacer una jugada; (progress) progresar; (shake) agitarse, temblar; removerse; (propose in an assembly) hacer una proposición; (in a court of law) hacer un pedimento; (grow) crecer. **to m. about,** pasearse; ir y venir; (of traffic) circular; (remove) trasladarse; (stir, tremble) agitarse. **to m. along,** caminar por; avanzar por. **to m. aside,** *vt* apartar; poner a un lado; (curtains) descorrer. —*vi* ponerse a un lado; quitarse de en medio. **to m. away,** *vt* alejar. —*vi* alejarse; marcharse; trasladarse; mudar de casa. **to m. back,** retroceder, volver hacia atrás. **to m. down,** bajar, descender. **to m. forward,** adelantarse; avanzar; progresar. **to m. in,** entrar (en); tomar posesión de una casa. **to m. off,** *vt* quitar. —*vi* marcharse; ponerse en marcha; alejarse, apartarse. **to m. on,** avanzar; ponerse en marcha; circular; (of time) pasar, correr. **to m. out,** *vt* sacar, quitar. —*vi* salir; (from a house) mudarse, abandonar (una casa, etc.). **to m. round,** dar vueltas, girar; (turn round) volverse. **to m. to,** (make) hacer, animar (a); causar. **to m. up,** *vt* montar, subir. —*vi* montar; avanzar

movement /'muvmənt/ *n* movimiento, *m; Mech.* mecanismo, *m;* (Stock Exchange) actividad, *f.* **encircling m.,** *Mil.* movimiento envolvente, *m*

mover /'muvər/ *n* motor, *m;* móvil, *m;* promotor (-ra); (of a motion, proposer) autor (-ra) de una moción

movie /'muvi/ *n Inf.* cine, *m.* **m. camera,** máquina de impresionar, *f.* **m. star,** estrella de la pantalla, *f*

moving /'muvıŋ/ *a* móvil; motor; (affecting) emocionante, conmovedor; impresionante; patético. —*n* movimiento, *m;* traslado, *m;* cambio de domicilio, *m.* **m. picture,** fotografía cinematográfica, *f.* **m. staircase,** escalera móvil, *f*

movingly /'muvıŋli/ *adv* con emoción; patéticamente

mow /mou/ *vt* segar.

mowing /'mouıŋ/ *n* siega, *f.* **m.-machine,** segadora, *f*

Mr. /'mıstər/ See **mister**

Mrs. /'mısəz/ See **mistress**

much /mʌtʃ/ *a* mucho. —*adv* mucho; (by far) con mucho; (with past part.) muy; (pretty nearly) casi, más o menos. **m. of a size,** más o menos del mismo tamaño. **I was m. angered,** Estuve muy enfadado. **as m. as,** tanto como. **as m. more,** otro tanto. **How m. is it?** ¿Cuánto es? ¿Cuánto cuesta? **however m....,** por mucho que... **not m.,** no mucho. **not to think m. of,** tener en poco (a). **so m. so that,** tanto que. **too m.,** demasiado. **to make m. of,** dar grande importancia a; (a person) apreciar, querer; agasajar; (a child) mimar, acariciar
mucilage /'myusəlɪdʒ/ *n* mucílago, *m*
muck /mʌk/ *n* (dung) estiércol, *m;* (filth) porquería, inmundicia, *f;* suciedad, *f;* (rubbish, of a literary work, etc.) porquería, *n.* **to m. up,** ensuciar; (spoil) estropear por completo
mucky /'mʌki/ *a* muy sucio; puerco; asqueroso, repugnante
mucosity /mu'kɒsɪti/ *n* mucosidad, *f*
mucous /'myukəs/ *a* mucoso. **m. membrane,** mucosa, *f*
mucus /'myukəs/ *n* mucosidad, *f;* (from the nose) moco, *m*
mud /mʌd/ *n* lodo, barro, fango, *m.* **to stick in the mud,** (of a ship, etc.) embarrancarse. **mudbath,** baño de barro, *m.* **mud wall,** tapia, *f*
muddiness /'mʌdinɪs/ *n* estado fangoso, *m;* (of liquids) turbiedad, *f;* suciedad, *f*
muddle /'mʌdl̩/ *vt* (bewilder) dejar perplejo, aturdir; (intoxicate) emborrachar; (stupefy) entontecer; (spoil) estropear; embarullar, dejar en desorden; hacer un lío de. —*n* desorden, *m;* confusión, *f;* lío, embrollo, *m.* **in a m.,** en desorden; en confusión. **to make a m.,** armar un lío. **to m. away,** derrochar sin ton ni son
muddled /'mʌdl̩d/ *a* desordenado; confuso; estúpido; torpe; (drunk) borracho
muddy /'mʌdi/ *a* fangoso, lodoso, barroso; cubierto de lodo; (of liquids, etc.) turbio; (of the complexion) cetrino. —*vt* enlodar, cubrir de lodo; ensuciar; (liquids) enturbiar
mudguard /'mʌdˌgɑrd/ *n* guardabarro, *m*
muezzin /myu'ɛzɪn, mu-/ *n* almuecín, almuédano, *m*
muff /mʌf/ *n* manguito, *m;* (for a car radiator) cubierta para radiador, *f;* (*Inf.* at games, etc.) maleta, *m.* —*vt* dejar escapar (una pelota); (an opportunity) perder
muffin /'mʌfɪn/ *n* mollete, *m*
muffle /'mʌfəl/ *vt* embozar, arrebozar; envolver; encubrir, ocultar, tapar; (stifle sound of) apagar; (oars, bells) envolver con tela para no hacer ruido; *Fig.* ahogar. **to m. oneself up,** embozarse
muffled /'mʌfəld/ *a* (of sound) sordo; confuso; apagado. **m. drum,** tambor enlutado, *m*
muffler /'mʌflər/ *n* bufanda, tapaboca, *f;* (furnace) mufla, *f;* (of a car radiator) cubierta para radiador, *f;* (silencer) silencioso, *m*
mufti /'mʌfti/ *n* mufti, *m*
mug /mʌg/ *n* vaso, *m;* (tankard) pichel, tarro, *m;* (face) jeta, *f;* (dupe) primo, *m;* (at games, etc.) maleta, *m*
mulatto /mə'lætou/ *a* mulato. —*n* mulato (-ta). **m.-like,** amulatado
mulberry /'mʌlˌbɛri/ *n* (fruit) mora, *f;* (bush) morera, *f.* **m. plantation,** moreral, *m*
mule /myul/ *n* mulo (-la); (slipper) mula, chinela, *f;* (spinning-jenny) huso mecánico, *m*
mulish /'myulɪʃ/ *a* mular; terco como una mula
mulishness /'myulɪʃnɪs/ *n* terquedad de mula, *f*
mullet /'mʌlɪt/ *n* (red) salmonete, *m,* trilla, *f;* (grey) mújol, *m*
multicolored /'mʌltiˌkʌlərd/ *a* multicolor
multifarious /ˌmʌltə'fɛəriəs/ *a* numeroso, mucho; diverso, vario
multiform /'mʌltəˌfɔrm/ *a* multiforme
multilateral /ˌmʌltɪ'lætərəl/ *a* multilátero
multimillionaire /ˌmʌltɪ'mɪlyəˌnɛər/ *a* archimillonario, multimillonario, *n* multimillonario, *m*
multiple /'mʌltəpəl/ *a* múltiple, múltiplo. —*n* múltiplo, *m*
multiple-choice question *n* pregunta optativa, *f*
multiplicand /ˌmʌltəplɪ'kænd/ *n* multiplicando, *m*
multiplication /ˌmʌltəplɪ'keiʃən/ *n* multiplicación, *f.* **m. table,** tabla de multiplicación, *f*
multiplicity /ˌmʌltə'plɪsɪti/ *n* multiplicidad, *f*
multiplier /'mʌltəˌplaiər/ *n Math.* multiplicador, *m;* máquina de multiplicar, *f*
multiply /'mʌltəpli/ *vt* multiplicar. —*vi* multiplicarse
multitude /'mʌltɪˌtud/ *n* multitud, *f.* **the m.,** las masas
multitudinous /ˌmʌltɪ'tudn̩əs/ *a* muy numeroso
mumble /'mʌmbəl/ *vi* and *vt* musitar, hablar entre dientes; refunfuñar; (chew) mascullar
mummer /'mʌmər/ *n* momero (-ra); máscara, *mf*
mummery /'mʌməri/ *n* momería, *f;* mascarada, *f*
mummification /ˌmʌməfɪ'keiʃən/ *n* momificación, *f*
mummify /'mʌməˌfai/ *vt* momificar. —*vi* momificarse
mummy /'mʌmi/ *n* momia, *f;* carne de momia, *f;* (*Inf.* mother) mama, *f.* **m. case,** sarcófago, *m*
mumps /mʌmps/ *n pl* parotiditis, papera, *f*
munch /mʌntʃ/ *vt* masticar, mascullar, mascar
mundane /mʌn'dein/ *a* mundano
municipal /myu'nɪsəpəl/ *a* municipal. **m. charter,** fuero municipal, *m.* **m. government,** gobierno municipal, *m*
municipality /myuˌnɪsə'pælɪti/ *n* municipio, *m*
munificence /myu'nɪfəsəns/ *n* munificencia, *f*
munificent /myu'nɪfəsənt/ *a* munífico, generoso
munition /myu'nɪʃən/ *n* munición, *f.* —*vt* municionar. **m. dump,** depósito de municiones, *m.* **m. factory,** fábrica de municiones, *f.* **m. worker,** obrero (-ra) de una fábrica de municiones
mural /'myʊrəl/ *a* mural. —*n* pintura mural, *f*
murder /'mɜrdər/ *n* asesinato, *m.* —*vt* asesinar; dar muerte (a), matar; (a work, etc.) degollar. **He was murdered,** Fue asesinado. **willful m.,** homicidio premeditado, *m*
murderer /'mɜrdərər/ *n* asesino, *m*
murderess /'mɜrdərɪs/ *n* asesina, *f*
murderous /'mɜrdərəs/ *a* homicida; cruel, sanguinario; fatal; imposible, intolerable
murderously /'mɜrdərəsli/ *adv* con intento de asesinar; (with look) con ojos asesinos; cruelmente
murkiness /'mɜrkinɪs/ *n* obscuridad, lobreguez, *f,* tinieblas, *f pl*
murky /'mɜrki/ *a* lóbrego, negro, obscuro; (of one's past, etc.) negro, accidentado
murmur /'mɜrmər/ *n* murmullo, *m;* rumor, *m;* susurro, *m;* (grumble) murmurio, *m.* —*vi* murmurar, susurrar; (complain) murmurar, quejarse. —*vt* murmurar, decir en voz baja
murmuring /'mɜrmərɪŋ/ *n* murmurio, *m, a* que murmura, susurrante
muscatel /ˌmʌskə'tɛl/ *a* moscatel. —*n* moscatel, *m.* **m. grape,** uva moscatel, *f*
muscle /'mʌsəl/ *n* músculo, *m*
Muscovite /'mʌskəˌvait/ *a* moscovita. —*n* moscovita, *mf*
muscular /'mʌskyələr/ *a* muscular, musculoso; (brawny) membrudo, fornido. **m. pains,** (in the legs, etc.) agujetas, *f pl*
muscularity /ˌmʌskyə'lærɪti/ *n* fuerza muscular, *f*
musculature /'mʌskyələtʃər/ *n* musculatura, *f*
Muse /myuz/ *n* musa, *f*
muse /myuz/ *n* meditación, *f.* —*vi* meditar, reflexionar, rumiar; mirar las musarañas, estar distraído. **to m. on,** meditar en (or sobre)
museum /myu'ziəm/ *n* museo, *m*
museum of arms *n* museo de armas, *m,* aploteca, *f*
mushroom /'mʌʃrum/ *n* seta, *f.* —*a* de setas; de forma de seta; (upstart) advenedizo; (ephemeral) efímero, de un día. **m.-bed,** setal, *m.* **m.-spawn,** esporas de setas, *f pl*
music /'myuzɪk/ *n* música, *f;* armonía, *f;* melodía, *f.* —*a* de música. **to set to m.,** poner en música. **m.-hall,** teatro de variedades, *m;* salón de conciertos, *m.* **m. master,** profesor de música, *m.* **m. publisher,** editor de obras musicales, *m.* **m. stand,** atril, *m;* tablado para una orquesta, *m.* **m. stool,** taburete de piano, *m*
musical /'myuzɪkəl/ *a* musical; de música; armonioso, melodioso. **She is very m.,** Es muy aficionada a la música; Tiene mucho talento para la mú-

sica. **m.-box,** caja de música, *f.* **m. comedy,** zarzuela, *f.* **m. instrument,** instrumento de música, *m*
musical chairs *n* escobas, *f pl,* el juego de sillas, *m sing*
musically /'myuzɪkli/ *adv* musicalmente; melodiosamente
musician /myu'zɪʃən/ *n* músico (-ca)
musing /'myuzɪŋ/ *n* meditación, *f;* ensueños, *m pl, a* pensativo, meditabundo
musingly /'myuzɪŋli/ *adv* reflexivamente
musk /mʌsk/ *n* (substance) almizcle, *m;* perfume de almizcle, *m.* —*a* de almizcle; almizclero; (of scents) almizcleño. **m.-deer,** almizclero, *m.* **m.-rat,** rata almizclera, *f*
musket /'mʌskɪt/ *n* mosquete, *m*
musketeer /ˌmʌskɪ'tɪər/ *n* mosquetero, *m*
Muslim /'mʌzlɪm/ *a* musulmán, mahometano. —*n* musulmán (-ana)
muslin /'mʌzlɪn/ *n* muselina, *f, a* de muselina
mussel /'mʌsəl/ *n* mejillón, *m.* **m.-bed,** criadero de mejillones, *m*
must /mʌst/ *vi* haber de; tener que; deber; (expressing probability) deber de, ser. **This question m. be settled without delay,** Esta cuestión debe ser resuelta sin demora. **You m. do it at once,** Tienes que hacerlo en seguida. **I m. have seen him in the street sometime,** Debo haberle visto en la calle alguna vez. **One m. eat to live,** Se ha de comer para vivir. **Well, go if you m.,** Bueno, vete si no hay más remedio. **It m. be a difficult decision for him,** Debe ser una decisión difícil para él. **It m. have been about twelve o'clock when...,** Serían las doce cuando...
must /mʌst/ *n* mosto, zumo de la uva, *m;* (mould) moho, *m*
mustang /'mʌstæŋ/ *n* potro mesteño, *m*
mustard /'mʌstərd/ *n* mostaza, *f.* **m. gas,** iperita, *f.* **m. plaster,** sinapismo, *m.* **m. pot,** mostacera, *f.* **m. spoon,** cucharita para la mostaza, *f*
muster /'mʌstər/ *n* lista, *f,* rol, *m;* revista, *f;* reunión, *f, vt* pasar lista (de); pasar revista (a); reunir. —*vi* juntarse, reunirse. **to m. out,** (from the army) dar de baja (a). **to m. up sufficient courage,** cobrar ánimos suficientes. **to pass m.,** pasar revista; ser aceptado. **m.-roll,** *Mil.* muestra, *f; Naut.* rol de la tripulación, *m*
mustiness /'mʌstinɪs/ *n* moho, *m;* ranciedad, *f;* (of a room, etc.) olor de humedad, *m*
musty /'mʌsti/ *a* mohoso; rancio; que huele a humedad. **to go m.,** enmohecerse
mutability /ˌmyutə'bɪlɪti/ *n* mutabilidad, *f;* inconstancia, inestabilidad, *f*
mutable /'myutəbəl/ *a* mudable; inconstante, inestable
mutation /myu'teiʃən/ *n* mutación, *f*
mute /myut/ *a* mudo; silencioso. —*n* mudo (-da); *Mus.* sordina, *f;* (phonetics) letra muda, *f.* **deaf m.,** sordomudo (-da)
muted /'myutɪd/ *a* (of sounds) sordo, apagado
mutely /'myutli/ *adv* mudamente; en silencio
muteness /'myutnɪs/ *n* mudez, *f;* silencio, *m*
mutilate /'myutḷˌeit/ *vt* mutilar; estropear
mutilation /ˌmyutḷ'eiʃən/ *n* mutilación, *f*
mutineer /ˌmyutṇ'ɪər/ *n* amotinador, rebelde, *m*
mutinous /'myutṇəs/ *a* amotinado; rebelde, sedicioso; turbulento
mutiny /'myutṇi/ *n* motín, *m;* sublevación, insurrección, *f, vi* amotinarse, sublevarse
mutt /mʌt/ *n* chucho, *m*
mutter /'mʌtər/ *vt* and *vi* murmurar, musitar; mascullar, decir (or hablar) entre dientes; gruñir, refunfuñar; (of thunder, etc.) tronar, retumbar. —*n* murmurio, *m;* rumor, *m;* retumbo, *m*
mutton /'mʌtṇ/ *n* carnero, *m, a* de carnero. **m.-chop,** chuleta, *f*
mutual /'myutʃuəl/ *a* mutuo, recíproco; común. **by m. consent,** de común acuerdo. **m. aid society,** sociedad de socorros mutuos, *f.* **m. insurance company,** sociedad de seguros mutuos, *f*
mutual fund *n* fondo de inversiones rentables, *m*
mutualism /'myutʃuəˌlɪzəm/ *n* mutualismo, *m*
mutuality /ˌmyutʃu'ælɪti/ *n* mutualidad, *f*
mutually /'myutʃuəli/ *adv* mutuamente, recíprocamente
muzzle /'mʌzəl/ *n* (snout) hocico, *m;* (for a dog) bozal, *m;* (of a gun) boca, *f.* —*vt* abozalar, poner un bozal (a); (*Fig.* gag) amordazar, imponer silencio (a)
muzzling /'mʌzlɪŋ/ *n* acción de abozalar, *f;* (*Fig.* gagging) amordazamiento, *m*
my /mai/ *a poss* mi, *mf;* mis, *mf pl* **my relatives,** mis parientes. **My goodness!** ¡Dios mío!
myelitis /ˌmaiə'laitɪs/ *n* mielitis, *f*
myopia /mai'oupiə/ *n* miopía, *f*
myopic /mai'ɒpɪk/ *a* miope
myriad /'mɪriəd/ *n* miríada, *f*
myrmidon /'mɜrmɪˌdɒn/ *n* rufián, *m;* asesino, *m;* secuaz, *m*
myrrh /mɜr/ *n* mirra, *f*
myrtle /'mɜrtḷ/ *n* mirto, arrayán, *m*
myself /mai'sɛlf/ *pron* yo mismo; (as a reflexive with a preposition) mí; (with a reflexive verb) me. **I m. sent it,** yo mismo (-ma) lo mandé
mysterious /mɪ'stɪəriəs/ *a* misterioso
mysteriousness /mɪ'stɪəriəsnɪs/ *n* misterio, *m,* lo misterioso
mystery /'mɪstəri/ *n* misterio, *m.* **m. play,** (religious) misterio, drama litúrgico, *m;* (thriller) comedia de detectives, *f.* **m. story,** novela policíaca, *f;* novela de aventuras, *f*
mystic /'mɪstɪk/ *a* místico
mysticism /'mɪstəˌsɪzəm/ *n* misticismo, *m*
mystification /ˌmɪstəfɪ'keiʃən/ *n* mistificación, *f*
mystify /'mɪstəˌfai/ *vt* mistificar
myth /mɪθ/ *n* mito, *m*
mythical /'mɪθɪkəl/ *a* mítico
mythologist /mɪ'θɒlədʒɪst/ *n* mitólogo, *m*
mythology /mɪ'θɒlədʒi/ *n* mitología, *f*

N

n /ɛn/ *n* (letter) ene, *f*
nab /næb/ *vt Inf.* atrapar, apresar, agazapar
nabob /'neibɒb/ *n* nabab, *m;* ricacho, *m*
nacre /'neikər/ *n* nácar, *m,* madreperla, *f*
nadir /'neidər/ *n* nadir, *m*
nag /næg/ *n* jaca, *f;* (wretched hack) rocín, jamelgo, penco, *m.* —*vt* zaherir, echar en cara, regañar; (of one's conscience) remorder. —*vi* criticar, regañar
nagging /'nægɪŋ/ *n* zaherimiento, *m.* —*a* zaheridor, criticón; (pain) continuo, incesante, constante
naiad /'neiæd/ *n Myth.* náyade, *f*
nail /neil/ *vt* clavar, enclavar; (for ornament) clavetear, tachonar, adornar con clavos. —*n* uña, *f; Mech.* clavo, *m;* (animal's) garra, *f.* **to n. down,** sujetar (or cerrar) con clavos. **to n. to (on to),** clavar en. **to n. together,** fijar con clavos. *Inf.* **on the n.,** en el acto, en seguida. *Inf.* **to hit the n. on the head,** dar en el clavo. **brass-headed n.,** tachón, *m.* **French n.,** punta de París, *f.* **headless n.,** puntilla, *f.* **hob-n.,** clavo de herradura, *m.* **hook n.,** gancho, *m.* **round-headed n.,** bellota, *f.* **n.-brush,** cepillo para las (or de) uñas, *m.* **n.-file,** lima para las uñas, *f.* **n. head,** cabeza de un clavo, *f.* **n.-puller,** sacaclavos, arrancaclavos, botador, *m.* **n.-scissors,** tijeras para las uñas, *f pl.* **n. trade,** ferretería, *f.* **n. varnish,** barniz para las uñas, *m*
nailed /neild/ *a* adornado con clavos, claveteado
nailer /'neilər/ *n* fabricante de clavos, chapucero, *m*
nailing /'neilɪŋ/ *n* enclavación, *f*
naive /nɑ'iv/ *a* ingenuo, candoroso, espontáneo
naively /na'ivli/ *adv* ingenuamente, espontáneamente
naiveté /nɑiv'tei, -ˌivə'tei, -'ivtei, -'ivə-/ *n* ingenuidad, naturalidad, franqueza, *f;* candor, *m*
naked /'neikɪd/ *a* desnudo, nudo; desabrigado, indefenso, desamparado; (birds) implume; calvo; (truth) simple, sencillo, puro; evidente, patente. **stark n.,** en cueros vivos, tal como le parió su madre. **with the n. sword,** con la espada desnuda. **n. eye,** simple vista, *f.* **n. light,** llama descubierta, *f*
nakedly /'neikɪdli/ *adv* nudamente; desabrigadamente; abiertamente, claramente
nakedness /'neikɪdnɪs/ *n* desnudez, *f; Fig.* desabrigo, *m,* aridez, *f; Fig.* claridad, *f.* **the truth in all its n.,** la verdad desnuda
namby-pamby /'næmbi'pæmbi/ *a* soso, insípido, ñoño
name /neim/ *n* nombre, *m;* título, *m;* fama, opinión, *f;* renombre, crédito, *m;* autoridad, *f;* apodo, mal nombre, *m.* —*vt* nombrar, llamar, imponer el nombre de, apellidar; mencionar, señalar; (appoint) designar, elegir; (ships) bautizar. **by n.,** por nombre. **Christian n.,** nombre de pila, *m.* **in his n.,** en nombre de él, en nombre suyo; de parte de él. **in n. only,** nada más que en nombre. **to be named,** llamarse. **to call** (a person) **names,** poner como un trapo (a). **to go under the n. of,** vivir bajo el nombre de. **to have a good n.,** tener buena fama. **What is her n.?** ¿Cómo se llama? **n. day,** santo, *m.* **n. plate,** (machinery) placa de fábrica, *f;* (streets) rótulo, *m;* (professional) placa profesional, *f*
nameless /'neimlɪs/ *a* anónimo; desconocido; (inexpressible) vago, indecible
namely /'neimli/ *adv* a saber, es decir
namesake /'neimˌseik/ *n* tocayo (-ya)
naming /'neimɪŋ/ *n* bautizo, *m;* nombramiento, *m;* designación, *f*
nannygoat /'næniˌgout/ *n* cabra, *f*
nap /næp/ *n* (cloth) pelusa, *f,* pelo, tamo, *m;* (plants) vello, *m,* pelusilla, *f;* (sleep) siesta, *f,* sueño, *m;* (cards) napolitana, *f.* **to take a nap,** *vi* dormitar, echar un sueño, echar una siesta. **to take an afternoon nap,** dormir la siesta. **to be caught napping,** estar desprevenido
nape /neip/ *n* nuca, *f,* cogote, *m;* (animal's) testuz, *m,*
naphtha /'næfθə, 'næp-/ *n Chem.* nafta, *f.* **wood n.,** alcohol metílico, *m*
naphthalene /'næfθəˌlin, 'næp-/ *n Chem.* naftalina, *f*
napkin /'næpkɪn/ *n* (table) servilleta, *f;* (babies') pañal, *m.* **n.-ring,** servilletero, *m*
Naples /'neipəlz/ Nápoles, *m*
Napoleonic /nəˌpouli'ɒnɪk/ *a* napoleónico
narcissism /'nɑrsəˌsɪzɛm/ *n* narcisismo, *m*
narcissus /nɑr'sɪsəs/ *n* narciso, *m*
narcosis /nɑr'kousɪs/ *n Med.* narcosis, *f*
narcotic /nɑr'kɒtɪk/ *a Med.* narcótico, calmante, soporífero. —*n Med.* narcótico, *m,* opiata, *f*
nard /nɑrd/ *n Bot.* nardo, *m,* tuberosa, *f*
narrate /'næreit/ *vt* narrar, contar; referir, relatar
narration /næ'reiʃən/ *n* narración, narrativa; relación, descripción, *f,* relato, *m*
narrative /'nærətɪv/ *a* narrador, narrativo, narratorio. —*n* narrativa, *f;* descripción, *f*
narrator /'næreitər/ *n* narrador (-ra), relator (-ra), descriptor (-ra)
narrow /'nærou/ *vt* estrechar, angostar; reducir, limitar. —*vi* reducirse, hacerse más estrecho; (eyes) entornarse; (knitting) menguar. —*a* estrecho, angosto; limitado, restringido, reducido, corto; (avaricious) ruin, avaro, mezquino; (ideas) intolerante, intransigente. **"Narrow Road,"** «Camino Estrecho». —*n pl* **narrows,** *Naut.* estrecho, *m;* desfiladero, paso estrecho, *m.* **to have a n. escape,** escapar en una tabla. **n.-brimmed** (hats), de ala estrecha. **n. circumstances,** estrechez, escasez de medios, *f.* **n.-gauge railway,** ferrocarril de vía estrecha (or de vía angosta), *m.* **n. life,** vida de horizontes estrechos, *f.* **n. majority,** escasa mayoría, *f.* **n.-minded,** cerrado al mundo, intolerante, intransigente. **n.-mindedness,** intolerancia, intransigencia, estrechez de miras, *f*
narrowing /'nærouɪŋ/ *n* estrechez, *f,* estrechamiento, *m;* reducción, limitación, *f;* (in knitting) menguado, *m*
narrowly /'nærouli/ *adv* estrechamente; por poco, con dificultad; atentamente, cuidadosamente. **I n. escaped being run over,** Por poco me atropellan
narrowness /'nærounɪs/ *n* estrechez, angostura, *f;* (of means) pobreza, miseria, *f;* (of ideas) intolerancia, intransigencia, *f*
nasal /'neizəl/ *a* nasal, gangoso. —*n* letra nasal, *f*
nasalize /'neizəˌlaiz/ *vt* nasalizar
nasally /'neizəli/ *adv* nasalmente. **to speak n.,** hablar por las narices, ganguear
nascent /'næsənt, 'neisənt/ *a* naciente
nastily /'næstəli/ *adv* suciamente; ofensivamente, de un modo insultante; maliciosamente, con malignidad
nastiness /'næstinɪs/ *n* suciedad, inmundicia, porquería, *f;* (indecency) obscenidad, indecencia, *f;* (rudeness) insolencia, impertinencia, grosería, *f;* (difficulty) dificultad, *f,* lo malo
nasturtium /nə'stɜrʃəm/ *n* mastuerzo, *m,* capuchina, *f*
nasty /'næsti/ *a* nauseabundo, repugnante; asqueroso, inmundo, sucio; (obscene) indecente, obsceno; desagradable, malo; (malicious) rencoroso, malicioso; violento; malévolo, amenazador; peligroso; difícil. *Fig.* **to be in a n. mess,** tener el agua al cuello. **to turn n.,** *Inf.* ponerse desagradable
natal /'neitl̩/ *a* natal, natalicio, de nacimiento, nativo
nation /'neiʃən/ *n* nación, *f,* estado, país, *m;* (people) pueblo, *m*
national /'næʃənl̩/ *a* nacional; público; patriótico. —*n* nacional, *mf.* **n. anthem,** himno nacional, *m.* **n. debt,** deuda pública, *f.* **n. schools,** escuelas públicas, *f pl.* **n. socialism,** nacionalsocialismo, *m.* **n. socialist,** *a* and *n* nacionalsocialista *mf.* **n. syndicalism,** *Polit.* nacionalsindicalismo, *m.* **n. syndicalist,** *a* and *n Polit.* nacionalsindicalista, *mf*
nationalism /'næʃənl̩ˌɪzəm/ *n* nacionalismo, patriotismo, *m*
nationalist /'næʃənl̩ɪst/ *a* and *n* nacionalista, *mf*
nationality /ˌnæʃ ə'nælɪti/ *n* nacionalidad, *f;* nación, *f*

nationalization /ˌnæʃənl̩əˈzeiʃən/ *n* nacionalización, *f*
nationalize /ˈnæʃənl̩ˌaiz, ˈnæʃnəˌlaiz/ *vt* nacionalizar
National Labor Relations Board *n* Junta Nacional de Relaciones Laborales
nationally /ˈnæʃənl̩i/ *adv* nacionalmente, como nación; del punto de vista nacional
native /ˈneitɪv/ *a* (of a place) nativo, natal, oriundo; indígena; nacional, típico, del país; (vocabulary) patrimonial (as opposed to borrowed vocabulary); (of genius) natural, innato, instintivo; *Mineral.* nativo; (language) vernáculo. —*n* nacional, *mf;* natural, *mf;* ciudadano (-na) indígena, aborigen (gen. pl.), *mf;* producto nacional, *m.* **He is a n. of Madrid,** Nació en Madrid, Es natural de Madrid, Es madrileño. **native informant,** sujeto, *m.* **n. land,** patria, tierra, *f.* **n. place,** lugar natal, *m.* **n. region,** patria chica, *f.* **n. soil,** terruño, *m.* **n. tongue,** lengua materna, *f*
nativity /nəˈtɪvɪti/ *n* navidad, natividad, *f;* (manger) nacimiento, *m*
natty /ˈnæti/ *a Inf.* chulo, majo; coquetón
natural /ˈnætʃərəl/ *a* natural; (wild) virgen, salvaje; nativo; (of products) crudo; normal; (usual) acostumbrado, corriente, natural; (of likeness) fiel, verdadero; (illegitimate) ilegítimo, bastardo; (of qualities) innato, instintivo; físico; característico, propio; (of people) inafectado, sencillo, genuino; *Mus.* natural. —*n Mus.* becuadro, *m; Mus.* nota natural, *f;* imbécil, *mf* **n. features,** geografía física, *f.* **n. history,** historia natural, *f.* **n. philosophy,** filosofía natural, *f.* **n. science,** ciencias naturales, *f pl.* **n. selection,** selección natural, *f.* **n. state,** estado virgen, *m*
natural child *n* hijo ilegítimo, *m*
natural daughter *n* hija ilegítima, *f*
naturalism /ˈnætʃərəˌlɪzəm/ *n* naturalismo, *m*
naturalist /ˈnætʃərəlɪst/ *n* (*Lit.* and *Science.*) naturalista, *mf*
naturalistic /ˌnætʃərəˈlɪstɪk/ *a* naturalista
naturalization /ˌnætʃərələˈzeiʃən/ *n* naturalización, *f;* aclimatación, *f.* **n. papers,** carta de naturaleza, *f*
naturalize /ˈnætʃərəˌlaiz/ *vt* naturalizar; aclimatar. **to become naturalized,** naturalizarse
naturally /ˈnætʃərəli/ *adv* naturalmente, por naturaleza; normalmente; sin afectación; instintivamente, por instinto; (without art) al natural
naturalness /ˌnætʃərəlnɪs/ *n* naturalidad, *f;* sencillez, desenvoltura, *f;* desembarazo, *m*
nature /ˈneitʃər/ *n* naturaleza, *f;* (of people) carácter, fondo, temperamento, genio, natural, modo de ser, *m;* (kind) género, *m,* especie, *f;* (essence) condición, esencia, cualidad, *f, Art.* **from n.,** del natural. **good n.,** bondad natural, afabilidad, *f.* **ill n.,** mala índole, *f.* **nature cure,** naturismo, *m.* **n. curist,** naturista, *mf.* **n. study,** historia natural, *f.* **n. worship,** panteísmo, culto de la naturaleza, *m*
natured /ˈneitʃərd/ *a* de carácter, de índole, con un modo de ser, de condición
naught /nɔt/ *n* nada, *f;* cero, *m.* —*a* inútil, sin valor. **all for n.,** todo en balde. **to come to n.,** malograrse. **to set at n.,** tener en menos; despreciar
naughtily /ˈnɔtl̩i/ *adv* traviesamente; con picardía, con malicia
naughtiness /ˈnɔtinɪs/ *n* travesura, picardía, mala conducta, *f;* malicia, *f*
naughty /ˈnɔti/ *a* travieso, pícaro, revoltoso, malo; salado, escabroso, verde (stories, etc.). **to be n.,** (children) ser malo
nausea /ˈnɔziə, -ʒə/ *n* náusea, *f,* bascas, *f pl,* mareo, *m; Fig.* asco, *m;* repugnancia, *f*
nauseate /ˈnɔziˌeit, -ʒi-/ *vt* dar náuseas; *Fig.* repugnar, dar asco
nauseating /ˈnɔziˌeitɪŋ, -ʒi-/ *a* repugnante, horrible; asqueroso
nauseous /ˈnɔʃəs/ *a* nauseabundo, asqueroso; *Fig.* repugnante
nauseousness /ˈnəʃəsnɪs/ *n* náusea, asquerosidad, *f; Fig.* repugnancia, *f,* asco, *m*
nautical /ˈnɔtɪkəl/ *a* náutico, marítimo. **n. day, twenty-four hours,** singladura, *f*
nautilus /ˈnɔtl̩əs/ *n Zool.* argonauta, nautilo, *m*
naval /ˈneivəl/ *a* naval; de marina, marítimo. **n. base,** base naval, *f.* **n. engagement,** batalla naval, *f.* **n. hospital,** hospital de marina, *m.* **n. law,** código naval, *m.* **n. officer,** oficial de marina, *m.* **n. power,** poder marítimo, *m.* **n. reservist,** marinero de reserva, *m.* **n. yard,** arsenal, *m*
Navarre /nəˈvɑr/ Navarra, *f*
Navarrese /ˌnævəˈriz/ *a* and *n* navarro (-rra)
nave /neiv/ *n Archit.* nave, *f;* (of wheels) cubo, *m*
navel /ˈneivəl/ *n* ombligo, *m.* **n. string,** cordón umbilical, *m*
navigability /ˌnævɪgəˈbɪlɪti/ *n* navegación, practicabilidad de navegar, *f*
navigable /ˈnævɪgəbəl/ *a* navegable, practicable
navigate /ˈnævɪˌgeit/ *vt* navegar, marear, dirigir (un buque); *Fig.* conducir, guiar. —*vi* navegar
navigation /ˌnævɪˈgeiʃən/ *n* navegación, *f;* (science of) náutica, marina, *f.* **n. company,** empresa naviera, *f.* **n. laws,** derecho marítimo, *m.* **n. lights,** luces de navegación, *f pl*
navigator /ˈnævɪˌgeitər/ *n* navegador, navegante, *m;* piloto, *m*
navvy /ˈnævi/ *n* peón, bracero, jornalero, *m; Mech.* máquina, excavadora, *f.* **road n.,** peón caminero, *m.* **to work like a n.,** estar hecho un azacán, sudar la gota gorda
navy /ˈneivi/ *n* marina, *f;* armada, *f;* (color) azul marino, *m.* **n. board,** consejo de la armada, *m.* **n. department** ministerio de marina, *m.* **n. estimates,** presupuesto de marina, *m.* **n. list,** escalafón de marina, *m*
nay /nei/ *adv* no; al contrario, más bien, mejor dicho. —*n* negativa, *f,* voto contrario, *m*
Nazarene /ˌnæzəˈrin/ *a* and *n* nazareno (-na)
Nazareth /ˈnæzərəθ/ Nazaret, *m*
Nazi /ˈnɑtsi/ *a* and *n* nacionalsocialista, naci, *mf*
Nazism /ˈnatsɪzəm/ *n* nacismo, *m*
n.d. (no date) *s.f.* (sin fecha)
Neapolitan /ˌniəˈpɒlɪtn̩/ *a* and *n* neapolitano (-na)
near /nɪər/ *vi* acercarse, aproximarse. —*a* cercano, immediato, contiguo; (of time) inminente, próximo; (relationship) cercano, consanguíneo; (of friends) íntimo, entrañable; (mean) tacaño, avariento
near /nɪər/ *prep* cerca de, junto a; hacia, en la dirección de; (of time) cerca de, casi. —*adv* cerca; (time) cerca, próximamente. **to be n. to,** estar cerca de. **to bring n.,** acercar, aproximar. **It was a n. thing,** Escapamos por un pelo. **n. at hand,** a la mano; (time) cerca, inminente. **n.-by,** *a* cercano, inmediato. —*adv* cerca. **n. side,** (of vehicles) lado de la acera, *m.* **n.-sighted,** corto de vista, miope. **n.-sightedness,** miopía, cortedad de vista, *f*
nearest /ˈnɪərɪst/ *a compar* and *superl* más cercano, más cerca; más corto. **the n. way,** el camino más corto, el camino directo
nearly /ˈnɪərli/ *adv* casi; cerca de, aproximadamente; estrechamente; íntimamente. **It touches me n.,** Me toca de cerca, Es de sumo interés para mí. **They n. killed me,** Por poco me matan. **to be n.,** (of age) frisar en, rayar en
nearness /ˈnɪərnɪs/ *n* (of place) cercanía, proximidad, contigüidad, *f;* (of time) inminencia, proximidad, *f;* (relationship) consanguinidad, *f;* (avarice) avaricia, tacañería, *f;* (dearness) intimidad, amistad estrecha, *f*
neat /nit/ *a Zool.* vacuno; elegante, sencillo, de buen gusto; (of the body) bien hecho, airoso, esbelto; (clean) limpio, aseado; (of handwriting) legible, bien proporcionado; pulido, esmerado, acabado; hábil, astuto, diestro; (of liquor, spirits) puro, solo. **to make a n. job of,** hacer (algo) bien
neatly /ˈnitli/ *adv* sencillamente, con elegancia, con primor; con aseo, limpiamente; bien (proporcionado); diestramente, hábilmente
neatness /ˈnitnɪs/ *n* aseo, *m,* limpieza, *f;* elegancia, sencillez, *f;* buen gusto, *m;* destreza, habilidad, *f;* (aptness) pertinencia, *f*
nebula /ˈnɛbyələ/ *n Astron.* nebulosa, *f*
nebulosity /ˌnɛbyəˈlɒsɪti/ *n* nebulosidad, *f; Astron.* nebulosa, *f;* vaguedad, imprecisión, *f*
nebulous /ˈnɛbyələs/ *a* nebuloso; vago, impreciso, confuso
necessarily /ˌnɛsəˈsɛərəli/ *adv* necesariamente; inevitablemente, sin duda
necessary /ˈnɛsəˌsɛri/ *a* necesario, inevitable; imprescindible, preciso, indispensable, esencial; obligatorio,

debido, forzoso. —*n* requisito esencial, *m.* **if n.,** en caso de necesidad; si fuera necesario. **to be n.,** hacer falta; necesitarse

necessitate /nə'sɛsɪˌteit/ *vt* necesitar, exigir, requerir, obligar

necessitous /nə'sɛsɪtəs/ *a* pobre, indigente, miserable, necesitado

necessity /nə'sɛsɪti/ *n* necesidad, *f;* menester, *m,* (e.g., *an indispensable n.*, un menester imprescindible); consecuencia, *f,* resultado, efecto, *m;* inevitabilidad, fatalidad, *f;* (poverty) indigencia, pobreza, *f.* **Fire and clothing are necessities,** El fuego y el vestir son cosas necesarias. **from n.,** por necesidad. **in case of n.,** si fuese necesario, en caso de necesidad. **of n.,** de necesidad, sin remedio. **physical necessities,** menesteres físicos, *m pl.* **prime n.,** artículo de primera necesidad, *m.* **to be under the n. of,** tener que, tener la necesidad de

Necessity is the mother of invention La necesidad es una gran inventora, La necesidad aguza el ingenio

neck /nɛk/ *n* cuello, *m,* garganta, *f;* (of bottles) gollete, cuello, *m;* (of animals) pescuezo, *m; Geog.* istmo, *m,* lengua de tierra, *f;* (of musical instruments) clavijero, mástil, *m; Sew.* escote, *m.* **low-necked,** (of dresses) escotado. **She fell on his n.,** Se colgó de su cuello. **He won by a n.,** Ganó por un cuello; *Fig.* Ganó por un tris. **to break anyone's n.,** romperle el pescuezo. **to wring the n. of,** torcer el pescuezo (a). **n. and n.,** parejos. **n. or nothing,** todo o nada, perdiz o no comerla. **n. stock,** alzacuello, *m*

neckband /'nɛkˌbænd/ *n* tirilla de camisa, *f*

necklace /'nɛklɪs/ *n* collar, *m*

necklet /'nɛklɪt/ *n* collar, *m;* (of fur) cuello, *m*

necktie /'nɛkˌtai/ *n* corbata, *f*

necrological /ˌnɛkrə'lɒdʒɪkəl/ *a* necrológico

necrology /nə'krɒlədʒi/ *n* necrología, *f*

necropolis /nə'krɒpəlɪs/ *n* necrópolis, *f*

nectar /'nɛktər/ *n* néctar, *m*

nectarine /ˌnɛktə'rin/ *n Bot.* variedad de melocotón, *f*

need /nid/ *vt* necesitar, haber menester, requerir, exigir. —*vi* ser necesario, hacer falta, carecer; haber (de). **N. I obey?** ¿He de obedecer? **You need to write carefully,** Hay que escribir con cuidado. **The work n. not be done for tomorrow,** No es preciso hacer el trabajo para mañana

need /nid/ *n* necesidad, *f;* cosa necesaria, *f;* falta; (poverty) indigencia, pobreza, *f;* urgencia, *f;* (shortage) escasez, carestía, *f.* **in case of n.,** en caso de necesidad, en caso de urgencia. **I have n. of two more books,** Me hacen falta dos libros más

needful /'nidfəl/ *a* necesario, preciso; indispensable, esencial. **the n.,** lo necesario

needfulness /'nidfəlnɪs/ *n* necesidad, falta, *f*

neediness /'nidinɪs/ *n* pobreza, penuria, miseria, estrechez, *f*

needle /'nidḷ/ *n Sew.* aguja, *f;* (of compass) brújula, aguja imanada, *f;* (monument) obelisco, *m;* (of scales) field, *m,* lengüeta, *f;* (of phonograph) pría, *f,* (of measuring instruments) índice, *m; Med.* aguja de inyecciones, *f. Inf.* **to be as sharp as a n.,** no tener pelo de tonto. **pack n.,** aguja espartera, *f.* **n.-case,** alfiletero, agujero, *m.* **n. maker,** fabricante de agujas, *m.* **n.-shaped,** en forma de aguja, acicular

needle and thread hilo y aguja

needless /'nidlɪs/ *a* innecesario, supérfluo. **n. to say,** claro está que..., huelga decir que...

needlessly /'nidlɪsli/ *adv* innecesariamente, inútilmente; en vano, de balde

needlessness /'nidlɪsnɪs/ *n* superfluidad, *f,* lo innecesario

needlewoman /'nidḷˌwʊmən/ *n* (professional) cosedora, *f;* costurera, *f.* **She is a good n.,** Cose bien (or es una buena cosedora)

needlework /'nidḷˌwɜrk/ *n* labor de aguja, labor blanca, costura, *f;* bordado, *m.* **to do n.,** hacer costura

needs /nidz/ *adv* necesariamente, sin remedio *n pl* necesidades, *f pl.* **if n. must,** si hace falta. **N. must when the devil drives,** A la fuerza ahorcan

needy /'nidi/ *a* necesitado, menesteroso, corto de medios, pobre, apurado

ne'er-do-well /'nɛərduˌwɛl/ *n* calavera, perdido, *m.* **to be a n.,** ser de mala madera

nefarious /nɪ'fɛəriəs/ *a* nefario, vil, nefando

nefariously /nɪ'fɛəriəsli/ *adv* vilmente, nefariamente

negation /nɪ'geiʃən/ *n* negación, *f*

negative /'nɛgətɪv/ *vt* negar, denegar; votar en contra (de), oponerse (a); (prevent) impedir, imposibilitar. —*a* negativo. —*n* negativa, negación, *f;* repulsa, denegación, *f; Photo.* negativo, *m,* prueba negativa, *f; Elec.* electricidad negativa, *f.* **to reply in the n.,** dar una respuesta negativa

negativeness /'nɛgətɪvnɪs/ *n* el carácter negativo, *m*

neglect /nɪ'glɛkt/ *vt* descuidar, desatender; abandonar, dejar; (ignore) despreciar, no hacer caso (de); omitir, olvidar. —*n* descuido, *m,* desatención, *f;* inobservancia, *f;* abandono, olvido, *m;* desdén, *m,* frialdad, *f.* **to fall into n.,** caer en desuso. **to n. one's obligations,** descuidar sus obligaciones

neglectful /nɪ'glɛktfəl/ *a* negligente, descuidado, omiso

negligee /ˌnɛglɪ'ʒei/ *n* salto de cama, quimono, *m,* bata, *f*

negligence /'nɛglɪdʒəns/ *n* negligencia, *f,* descuido, *m;* flojedad, pereza, *f;* (of dress) desaliño, *m*

negligent /'nɛglɪdʒənt/ *a* negligente, descuidado; remiso, flojo, perezoso

negligently /'nɛglɪdʒəntli/ *adv* negligentemente; con indiferencia

negligible /'nɛglɪdʒəbəl/ *a* insignificante, escaso, insuficiente; sin importancia, desdeñable

negotiable /nɪ'gouʃiəbəl, -ʃəbəl/ *a* negociable; (of a road) practicable, transitable

negotiate /nɪ'gouʃiˌeit/ *vt* gestionar, agenciar, tratar; (a bend) tomar; (an obstacle) salvar, franquear; *vi* negociar. **to n. a bill of exchange,** descontar una letra de cambio. **to n. for a contract,** tratar un contrato

negotiation /nɪˌgouʃi'eiʃən/ *n* negociación, *f; Com.* gestión, transacción, *f;* (of a bend) toma, *f;* (of an obstacle) salto, *m*

negotiator /nɪ'gouʃiˌeitər/ *n* negociador (-ra)

neigh /nei/ *vi* relinchar. —*n* relincho, relinchido, *m*

neighbor /'neibər/ *n* vecino (-na); (biblical) prójimo (-ma)

neighborhood /'neibərˌhʊd/ *n* vecindad, *f,* vecindario, *m;* cercanía, *f,* afueras, *f pl,* alrededores, *m pl; a* de barrio (e.g. *neighborhood moviehouse,* cine del barrio)

neighboring /'neibərɪŋ/ *a* vecino; cercano, inmediato, adyacente

neighborliness /'neibərlinɪs/ *n* buena vecindad, *f*

neighborly /'neibərli/ *a* amistoso, sociable, bondadoso. **to be n.,** ser de buena vecindad.

neither /'niðər, 'nai-/ *a* ningún; ninguno de los dos, e.g. *N. explanation is right,* Ninguna de las dos explicaciones es correcta. —*conjunc* ni, tampoco, e.g. *N. Mary nor John,* Ni María ni Juan. *N. will he give it to her,* Tampoco se lo dará. —*pron* ni uno ni otro, ninguno, e.g. *N. of them heard it,* Ni uno ni otro lo oyó.

nemesis /'nɛməsɪs/ *n* némesis, *f;* justicia, *f*

neo- *prefix* neo. **neo-Catholic,** *a* and *n* neo-católico (-ca). **neo-Platonic,** neoplatónico. **neo-Platonism,** neoplatonismo, *m*

neolithic /ˌniə'lɪθɪk/ *a* neolítico

neologism /ni'ɒləˌdʒɪzəm/ *n* neologismo, *m*

neon /'niɒn/ *n Chem.* neón, *m*

neon sign anuncio luminoso, *m*

neophyte /'niəˌfait/ *n* neófito (-ta); aspirante, *mf*

nephew /'nɛfyu/ *n* sobrino, *m*

nephritis /nə'fraitɪs/ *n Med.* nefritis, *f*

nepotism /'nɛpəˌtɪzəm/ *n* nepotismo, *m*

nerve /nɜrv/ *n* (*Anat. Bot.*) nervio, *m;* valor, ánimo, *m;* vitalidad, *f; Inf.* descaro, *m,* desvergüenza, frescura, *f.* —*vt* animar, alentar, envalentonar; esforzar; dar fuerza (a). —*vi* animarse, esforzarse (a). **My nerves are all on edge,** Se me crispan los nervios. **n.-cell,** neurona, *f.* **to lose one's n.,** perder la cabeza; perder los nervios. **to strain every n.,** hacer un esfuerzo supremo. **n. center,** centro nervioso, *m.* **n.-racking,** espantoso, horripilante. **n. strain,** tensión nerviosa, *f*

nerveless /ˈnɜrvlɪs/ *a* sin nervio; enervado
nerviness /ˈnɜrvinɪs/ *n* nervosidad, *f*
nervous /ˈnɜrvəs/ *a* nervioso, asustadizo, tímido; agitado, excitado; (of style) vigoroso. **n. breakdown,** crisis nerviosa, *f.* **n. system,** sistema nervioso, *m*
nervously /ˈnɜrvəsli/ *adv* nerviosamente; tímidamente
nervousness /ˈnɜrvəsnɪs/ *n* nervosidad, timidez, *f;* agitación, *f;* (of style) vigor, *m;* energía, *f*
nervy /ˈnɜrvi/ *a* nervioso
nest /nɛst/ *vi* anidar, hacerse un nido. —*n* (bird's) nido, *m;* (animal's) madriguera, *f;* (of drawers) juego, *m,* serie, *f;* (of thieves) cueva, guarida, *f; Inf.* casita, *f,* hogar, *m.* **to feather one's n.,** hacer su agosto. **n.-egg,** *Fig.* nidal, *m.* **n. of eggs,** nidada de huevos, *f*
nestle /ˈnɛsəl/ *vt* apoyar. —*vi* apiñarse, hacerse un ovillo. **to n. up to a person,** apretarse contra
nestling /ˈnɛstlɪŋ/ *n* pichón, pollo, *m;* pajarito, *m*
net /nɛt/ *vt* coger con redes; obtener, coger; cubrir con redes. —*vi* hacer redes. —*n* red, *f;* (mesh) malla, *f;* (fabric) tul, *m.* **net making,** manufactura de redes, *f*
net /nɛt/ *a Com.* líquido, neto, limpio; (of fabric) de tul. **net amount,** importe líquido, importe neto, *m.* **net balance,** saldo líquido, *m.* **net cost,** precio neto, *m.* **net profit,** beneficio neto (or líquido), *m*
nether /ˈnɛðər/ *a* inferior, bajero, más bajo. **n. regions,** infierno, *m*
Netherland /ˈnɛðərlənd/ *a* neerlandés, holandés
Netherlander /ˈnɛðərˌlændər/ *n* neerlandés (-esa), holandés (-esa)
Netherlands, the /ˈnɛðərləndz/ los Países Bajos *m pl*
nethermost /ˈnɛðərˌmoust/ *a* lo más bajo, ínfimo, más hondo
netting /ˈnɛtɪŋ/ *n* red, (obra de) malla, *f; Naut.* jareta, *f;* manufactura de redes, *f;* pesca con redes, *f.* **wire-n.,** tela metálica, malla de alambre, *f*
nettle /ˈnɛtl̩/ *vt* picar; *Fig.* irritar, picar, fastidiar, disgustar. —*n* ortiga, *f.* **n.-rash,** urticaria, *f*
network /ˈnɛtˌwɜrk/ *n* red, malla, randa, *f;* (of communications) sistema, *m,* red, *f*
neuralgia /nʊˈrældʒə/ *n* neuralgia, *f*
neuralgic /nʊˈrældʒɪk/ *a* neurálgico
neurasthenia /ˌnʊrəsˈθiniə/ *n* neurastenia, *f*
neurasthenic /ˌnʊrəsˈθɛnɪk/ *a* and *n* neurasténico (-ca)
neuritis /nʊˈraitɪs/ *n* neuritis, *f*
neurologist /nʊˈrɒlədʒɪst/ *n* neurólogo, *m*
neurology /nʊˈrɒlədʒi/ *n* neurología, *f*
neuropath /ˈnʊrəˌpæθ/ *n* neurópata, *m*
neuropathic /ˌnʊrəˈpæθɪk/ *a* neuropático
neurosis /nʊˈrousɪs/ *n* neurosis, *f*
neurosurgeon /ˈnʊrouˌsɜrdʒən/ *n* neurocirujano, *m*
neurotic /nʊˈrɒtɪk/ *a* and *n* neurótico (-ca)
neuter /ˈnutər/ *a* neutro; (of verbs) intransitivo; (*Zool. Bot.*) sin sexo
neutral /ˈnutrəl/ *a* neutral; (*Chem. Mech.*) neutro; (of colors) indeciso, indeterminado; (of persons) imparcial, indiferente. —*n* neutral, *mf Mech.* **to go into n.,** pasar a marcha neutra
neutrality /nuˈtrælɪti/ *n* neutralidad, *f;* indiferencia, *f;* imparcialidad, *f*
neutralization /ˈnutrələˈzeiʃən/ *n* neutralización, *f*
neutralize /ˈnutrəˌlaiz/ *vt* neutralizar
never /ˈnɛvər/ *adv* nunca, jamás; de ningún modo, no; ni aun, ni siquiera. **Better late than n.,** Más vale tarde que nunca. **Never look a gift horse in the mouth,** A caballo regalado no se le mira el diente. **Were the hour n. so late,** Por más tarde que fuese la hora. **n. again,** nunca jamás. **n. a one,** ni siquiera uno. **n. a whit,** ni pizca. **N. mind!** ¡No importa! ¡No te preocupes! ¡No hagas caso! **n.-ceasing,** continuo, incesante. **n.-ending,** inacabable, eterno, sin fin. **n.-failing,** infalible. **n.-to-be-forgotten,** inolvidable
nevermore /ˌnɛvərˈmɔr/ *adv* nunca jamás
nevertheless /ˌnɛvərðəˈlɛs/ *adv* sin embargo, no obstante, con todo
new /nu/ *a* nuevo; novel, fresco; distinto, diferente; moderno; (inexperienced) novato, no habituado; reciente. —*adv* (in compounds) recién. **as good as new,** como nuevo. **brand-new,** flamante, nuevecito. **new-born,** recién nacido. **new-comer,** recién llegado (-da). **new-fashioned,** de última moda. **new-found,** recién hallado. **new-laid egg,** huevo fresco, *m.* **new moon,** luna nueva, *f,* novilunio, *m.* **new rich,** ricacho (-cha); indio, *m.* **new student,** alumno de nuevo ingreso. **New Testament,** Nuevo Testamento, *m.* **New World,** Nuevo Mundo, *m.* **New York (er),** *a* and *n* neoyorquino (-na). **New Zealand (er),** *a* and *n* neozelandés (-esa)
newel /ˈnuəl/ *n* (of stair) alma, *f,* árbol, nabo, *m.* **n.-post,** pilarote (de escalera), *m*
newest /ˈnuɪst/ *a superl* novísimo; más reciente
Newfoundland /ˈnufənlənd/ Terranova, *f.* **N. dog,** perro de Terranova, *m*
New Guinea /ˈgɪni/ Nueva Guinea, *f*
newish /ˈnuɪʃ/ *a* bastante nuevo
newly /ˈnuli/ *adv* nuevamente; hace poco, recientemente. The abb. form **recién** is used only with past part, e.g. *the n. painted door,* la puerta recién pintada. *the n.-weds,* los desposados, los recién casados
newness /ˈnunɪs/ *n* novedad, *f;* inexperiencia, falta de práctica, *f;* innovación, *f*
New Orleans /ˈɔrliənz, ɔrˈlinz/ Nueva Orleans, *f*
news /nuz/ *n pl* noticias, *f pl*; nueva, *f;* reporte, aviso, *m;* novedad, *f.* **No n. is good n.,** Falta de noticias, buena señal. **piece of n.,** noticia, *f.* **What's the n.?** ¿Qué hay de nuevo? **n. agency,** agencia de noticias, agencia periodística, *f.* **n.-agent,** agente de la prensa, *m;* vendedor (-ra) de periódicos. **n. bulletin,** *Radio.* boletín de noticias, *m. Inf.* **n.-hound,** gacetillero (-ra). **n. item,** noticia de actualidad, *f.* **n.-print,** papel para periódicos, *m.* **n.-room,** gabinete de lectura, *m.* **n. reel,** película noticiera, revista cinematográfica, *f,* noticiario cinematográfico, noticiero *m,* actualidades, *f pl.* **n.-stand,** puesto de periódicos, quiosco de periódicos, *m.* **n. theater,** cine de actualidades, *m*
newscast /ˈnuzˌkæst/ *n* noticiario, *m*
newsletter circular /ˈnuzˌlɛtər/ noticiera, relación de sucesos, *f*
New South Wales La Nueva Gales del Sur, *f*
newspaper /ˈnuzˌpeipər/ *n* periódico, diario, noticiero, *m.* **n. clipping, n. cutting,** recorte de periódico, *m.* **n. paragraph,** suelto, *m.* **n. reporter,** reportero (-ra); periodista, *mf* **n. reporting,** reporterismo, *m.* **n. serial,** folletín, *m,* novela por entregas, *f.* **n. vendor,** vendedor (-ra) de periódicos, *n*
news report *n* reportaje, *m*
newsy /ˈnuzi/ *a Inf.* lleno de noticias, noticioso
newt /nut/ *n* tritón, *m*
Newtonian /nuˈtouniən/ *a* neutoniano
New York /yɔrk/ Nueva York, *f*
New Zealand /ˈzilənd/ Nueva Zelandia, *f*
next /nɛkst/ *a* (of place) siguiente, vecino, contiguo; (of time) próximo, siguiente. **on the n. page,** en la página siguiente. **the n. day,** el día siguiente. **the n.-door house,** la casa vecina. **the n. life,** la otra vida. **n. month (yesar),** el mes (año) próximo (or que viene). **n. time,** otra vez, la próxima vez
next /nɛkst/ *adv* (of time) luego, en seguida; (of place) inmediatamente después. **I come n.,** Ahora me toca a mí. **It is n. to a certainty that...,** Es casi seguro que... **the n. best,** el segundo. **the n. of kin,** los pariente más cercarro, *m,* parientes más cercanos, *m pl.* **to wear n. to the skin,** llevar sobre la piel. **n. to,** al lado de, junto a; primero después de; casi. **n. to nothing,** casi nada, muy poco. **What n.?** ¿Qué más?; ¿Y ahora qué?
nib /nɪb/ *n* punto, tajo (de una pluma), *m*
nibble /ˈnɪbəl/ *vt* mordiscar, mordisquear, roer; (horses) rozar; (fish) picar; *Fig.* considerar, tantear; *vi* picar. —*n* mordisco, *m;* roedura, *f*
Nicaraguan /ˌnɪkəˈragwən/ *a* and *n* nicaragüeño (-ña)
Nice /nis/ Niza, *f*
nice /nais/ *a* escrupuloso, minucioso, exacto; (of persons) simpático, afable, amable; fino; (of things) agradable, bonito; bueno; sutil, delicado; (*Inf. Ironic.*) bonito. **a n. point,** un punto delicado. **a n. view,** una vista agradable (or bonita). **n.-looking,** guapo. **n. people,** gente fina, *f;* gente simpática, *f*
nicely /ˈnaisli/ *adv* muy bien; con elegancia; primorosamente; con amabilidad, gentilmente; agradablemente
Nicene /naiˈsin/ *a* niceno

niceness /'naisnɪs/ *n* exactitud, minuciosidad, *f;* (of persons) bondad, amabilidad, *f;* amenidad, hermosura, *f;* lo bonito; sutileza, *f;* refinamiento, *m*

nicety /'naisɪti/ *n* exactitud, *f;* sutileza, *f,* refinamiento, *m.* **niceties,** *n pl* detalles, *m pl.* **to a n.,** con la mayor precisión; a la perfección

niche /nɪtʃ/ *n* nicho, templete, *m;* (vaulted) hornacina, *f, Fig.* **to find a n. for oneself,** encontrarse una buena posición; situarse

nick /nɪk/ *vt* cortar en muescas, mellar, tarjar. *—n* mella, muesca, *f.* **in the n. of time,** en el momento oportuno, a tiempo

nickel /'nɪkəl/ *n* níquel, *m; Com.* moneda de níquel, *f.* **n.-plated,** niquelado

nickname /'nɪk,neim/ *vt* apodar, motejar, apellidar. *—n* apodo, sobrenombre, mote, mal nombre, *m*

nicotine /'nɪkə,tin/ *n* nicotina, *f*

nicotinism /'nɪkəti,nɪzəm/ *n* nicotismo, *m*

nictitating membrane /'nɪktɪ,teitɪŋ/ *n Anat.* membrana nictitante, *f*

niece /nis/ *n* sobrina, *f*

niggardliness /'nɪgərdlinɪs/ *n* tacañería, avaricia, parsimonia, mezquindad, *f*

niggardly /'nɪgərdli/ *a* tacaño, avaricioso, mezquino, ruin, miserable

niggling /'nɪglɪŋ/ *a* nimio, meticuloso; escrupuloso, minucioso

nigh. /nai/ See **near**

night /nait/ *n* noche, *f; Fig.* oscuridad, *f,* tinieblas, *f pl.* **all n.,** toda la noche, la noche entera. **all n. service,** servicio nocturno permanente, *m.* **at** or **by n.,** de noche. **every n.,** todas las noches, cada noche. **Good n.!** ¡Buenas noches! **last n.,** ayer por la noche, anoche, la noche pasada. **restless n.,** noche mala, noche toledana, *f.* **the n. before last,** anteayer por la noche, *m.* **to-n.,** esta noche. **tomorrow n.,** mañana por la noche. **to be n.,** ser de noche. **to spend the n.,** pernoctar, pasar la noche. **n.-bird,** pájaro nocturno, *m; Inf.* trasnochador (-ra). **n.-blindness,** nictalopia, *f.* **n.-cap,** gorro de dormir, *m.* **n. clothes,** traje de dormir, *m.* **n. club,** cabaré *m.* **n. dew,** relente, sereno, *m.* **n. flying,** vuelo nocturno, *m.* **n.-jar,** *Ornith.* chotacabras, *m.* **n.-light,** mariposa, lamparilla, *f.* **n. mail,** último correo, *m;* tren correo de la noche, *m.* **n. school,** escuela nocturna, *f.* **n. shift,** turno de noche, *m.* **n. watch,** ronda de noche, *f; Naut.* sonochada, *f.* **n. watchman,** (in the street) sereno, *m;* (of a building) vigilante nocturno, *m*

nightfall /'nait,fɔl/ *n* anochecer, crepúsculo, atardecer, *m*

nightgown /'nait,gaun/ *n* camisa de noche, *f*

nightingale /'naitṇ,geil, 'naitɪŋ-/ *n* ruiseñor, *m*

nightly /'naitli/ *a* de noche; nocturno, nocturnal. *—adv* todas las noches, cada noche

nightmare /'nait,mɛər/ *n* pesadilla, *f*

nightmarish /'nait,mɛərɪʃ/ *a* de pesadilla, horrible

nightshade /'nait,ʃeid/ *n Bot.* hierba mora, *f,* solano, *m*

nihilism /'naiə,lɪzəm, 'ni-/ *n* nihilismo, *m*

nihilist /'naiəlɪst, 'ni-/ *n* nihilista, *mf*

Nile, the /nail/ el Nilo, *m*

nimble /'nɪmbəl/ *a* ágil, activo; vivo, listo. **n.-fingered,** ligero de dedos. **n.-witted,** despierto, vivo

nimbleness /'nɪmbəlnɪs/ *n* agilidad, actividad, *f;* viveza, habilidad, *f*

nimbly /'nɪmbli/ *adv* ágilmente, ligeramente

nimbus /'nɪmbəs/ *n* nimbo, *m,* aureola, *f*

nincompoop /'nɪnkəm,pup, 'nɪŋ-/ *n* papirote, *m,* papanatas, *mf* tonto (-ta)

nine /nain/ *a* and *n* nueve, *m.* **He is n.,** Tiene nueve años. **the N.,** las nueve Musas. **n. o'clock,** las nueve. **to be dressed up to the nines,** estar hecho un brazo de mar

ninefold /*a* 'nain,fould; *adv.* 'nain'fould/ *a* and *adv* nueve veces

ninepins /'nain,pɪnz/ *n* juego de bolos, *m*

nineteen /'nain'tin/ *a* and *n* diez y nueve, diecinueve *m*

nineteenth /'nain'tinθ/ *a* décimonono. *—n* (of month) el diez y nueve; (of monarchs) diez y nueve. **the n. century,** el siglo diez y nueve

ninetieth /'naintiəθ/ *a* nonagésimo, noventa

ninety /'nainti/ *a* and *n* noventa *m.* **n.-one,** noventa y uno. **n.-two,** noventa y dos. **the n.-first chapter,** el capítulo noventa y uno

ninny /'nɪni/ *n* parapoco, chancleta, *mf;* mentecato (-ta)

ninth /nainθ/ *a* noveno, nono. *—n* nueve, *m;* (of the month) el nueve (of sovereigns) nono. **one n.,** un noveno

ninthly /'nainθli/ *adv* en noveno (or nono) lugar

nip /nɪp/ *vt* pellizcar, pinchar; mordiscar, morder; (wither) marchitar; (freeze) helar; (run) correr. *—vi* pinchar; picar (el viento). *—n* pellizco, pinchazo, *m;* mordisco, *m;* (of spirits) trago, *m;* copita, *f;* (in the air) viento frío, hielo, *m.* **to nip in,** colarse dentro, deslizarse en. **to nip off,** pirarse, mudarse. *Fig.* **to nip in the bud,** cortar en flor

nippers /'nɪpərz/ *pl* alicates, *m pl*; tenacillas, pinzas, *f pl*

nipping /'nɪpɪŋ/ *n* pinchadura, *f;* mordedura, *f.* *—a* punzante; helado, glacial, mordiente. **n. off,** (of a point) despuntadura, *f*

nipple /'nɪpəl/ *n* pezón, *m;* pezón artificial, *m*

nit /nɪt/ *n Ent.* liendre, *f*

niter /'naitər/ *n* salitre, *m*

nitrate /'naitreit/ *n Chem.* nitrato, *m*

nitric /'naitrɪk/ *a* nítrico

nitrite /'naitrait/ *n Chem.* nitrito, *m*

nitro- *prefix Chem.* nitro. **n.-cellulose,** algodón pólvora, *m.* **n.-glycerine,** nitroglicerina, *f*

nitrogen /'naitrədʒən/ *n Chem.* nitrógeno, *m*

nitrous /'naitrəs/ *a* nitroso, salitral

no /nou/ *a* ningún, ninguno, ninguna, e.g. *by no means,* de ningún modo. *No* is often not translated in Sp., e.g. *I have no time,* No tengo tiempo. *—adv* no. *—n* voto negativo, no, *m. to be of no account,* no tener importancia; no significar nada. *to be no good for,* no servir para. *to be of no use,* ser inútil. *to have no connection with,* no tener nada que ver con. *for no reason,* sin motivo alguno. *"No Admittance,"* «Entrada Prohibida.» *no, indeed,* Cierto que no. *no-man's land,* tierra de nadie, *f. no more,* no más. *No more of this!* ¡No hablemos más de eso! *no one,* nadie, ninguno. *no sooner,* no bien, tan pronto (como). **no such thing,** no tal. **"No Thoroughfare,"** «Prohibido el Paso.» **whether or not,** sea o no sea

Noah's Ark /'nouəz/ *n* arca de Noé, *f*

nobility /nou'bɪlɪti/ *n* nobleza, *f;* (of rank) aristocracia, nobleza, *f;* (of conduct) caballerosidad, hidalguía, generosidad, bondad, *f;* (grandeur) grandeza, sublimidad, *f.* **the higher n.,** los nobles de primera clase

noble /'noubəl/ *a* noble; (in rank) aristocrático, noble, linajudo; (of conduct) caballeroso, generoso; (of buildings) sublime, magnífico. *—n* noble, *m,* aristócrata, *mf* **to make n.,** ennoblecer. **n.-mindedness,** generosidad, grandeza de alma, *f.* **n. title,** título de nobleza, título del reino, *m*

noblewoman /'noubəl,wʊmən/ *n* dama noble, mujer noble, aristócrata, *f*

nobly /'noubli/ *adv* noblemente, generosamente. **n. born,** noble de nacimiento

nobody /'nou,bɒdi/ *n* nadie, ninguno. **There was n. there,** No había nadie allí. *Inf.* **a n.,** un (una) cualquiera, una persona insignificante. **n. else,** nadie más, ningún otro

nocturnal /nɒk'tɜrnḷ/ *a* nocturno, nocherniego, nocturnal

nocturne /'nɒktɜrn/ *n Mus.* nocturno, *m*

nod /nɒd/ *vt* inclinar la cabeza; hacer una señal (or señas) con la cabeza; *vi* dar cabezadas; cabecear; (of trees) mecerse, inclinarse; inclinar la cabeza. *—n* señal (or seña) con la cabeza, *f;* inclinación de la cabeza, *f;* cabeceo, *m,* cabezada, *f.* **A nod is as good as a wink,** A buen entendedor pocas palabras. **He nodded to me as he passed,** Me saludó con la cabeza al pasar. **He signed to me with a nod,** Me hizo una señal con la cabeza

nodding /'nɒdɪŋ/ *a* que cabecea; *Bot.* colgante, inclinado; temblante. *—n* cabeceo, *m;* saludo con la cabeza, *m*

noddle /'nɒdḷ/ *n* mollera, *f*

node /noud/ *n* (*Bot. Med.*) nudo, *m*

nodule /'nɒdʒul/ *n* nódulo, *m;* nudillo, *m*

noise /nɔiz/ *n* ruido, son, *m;* tumulto, clamor, estruendo, alboroto, *m.* **to make a n.,** hacer ruido. **to n. abroad,** divulgar, publicar
noiseless /ˈnɔizlɪs/ *a* silencioso, callado, sin ruido
noiselessness /ˈnɔizlɪsnɪs/ *n* silencio, *m,* falta de ruido, *f*
noisily /ˈnɔizəli/ *adv* ruidosamente
noisiness /ˈnɔizinɪs/ *n* ruido, estrépito, tumulto, clamor, *m;* (of voices) gritería, *f*
noisome /ˈnɔisəm/ *a* ofensivo; fétido, apestoso
noisy /ˈnɔizi/ *a* ruidoso; estruendoso; estrepitoso, clamoroso
nomad /ˈnoumæd/ *a* nómada, errante; (of flocks) trashumante. —*n* nómada, *mf*
nomadism /ˈnoumædɪzəm/ *n* nomadismo, *m*
nomenclature /ˈnoumənˌkleitʃər/ *n* nomenclatura, *f*
nominal /ˈnɒmənl̩/ *a* nominal; titular; insignificante, de poca importancia. **the n. head,** el director en nombre
nominalism /ˈnɒmənl̩ˌɪzəm/ *n* nominalismo, *m*
nominalist /ˈnɒmənl̩ɪst/ *a* and *n* nominalista *mf*
nominally /ˈnɒmənl̩i/ *adv* nominalmente, en nombre
nominate /ˈnɒməˌneit/ *vt* nombrar, designar, elegir; fijar, señalar
nominating /ˈnɒməˌneitɪŋ/ *a* nominador
nomination /ˌnɒməˈneiʃən/ *n* nombramiento, *m,* nominación, *f;* señalamiento, *m*
nominator /ˈnɒməˌneitər/ *n* nominador (-ra)
nominee /ˌnɒməˈni/ *n* nómino propuesto, *m*
non /nɒn/ *adv* non; des-; in-; falta de. **non-acceptance,** rechazo, *m.* **non-acquaintance,** ignorancia, *f.* **non-admission,** no admisión, *f;* denegación, *f,* rechazo, *m.* **non-aggression,** no agresión, *f.* **non-alcoholic,** no alcohólico. **non-appearance,** ausencia, *f; Law.* no comparecencia, contumacia, *f.* **non-arrival,** ausencia, *f;* falta de recibo, *f.* **non-attendance,** falta de asistencia, ausencia, *f.* **non-carbonated,** sin gas. **non-combatant,** no combatiente. **non-commissioned officer,** oficial subalterno, *m.* **non-committal,** evasivo, equívoco, ambiguo. **non-compliance,** falta de obediencia, *f.* **non-concurrence,** falta de acuerdo, *f.* **non-conducting,** no conductivo. **non-conductor,** mal conductor, *m; Elec.* aislador, *m.* **non-contagious,** no contagioso. **non-cooperation,** *Polit.* resistencia pasiva, *f;* no cooperación, *f.* **non-delivery,** falta de entrega, *f.* **non-essential,** no esencial, prescindible. **non-execution,** no cumplimiento, *m.* **non-existence,** no existencia, *f.* **non-existent,** inexistente, no existente. **non-intervention,** no intervención, *f.* **non-manufacturing,** no industrial. **non-member,** visitante, *mf* **non-observance,** incumplimiento, *m;* violación, *f.* **non-payment,** falta de pago, *f.* **non-performance,** falta de ejecución, *f.* **non-poisonous,** no venenoso, innocuo. **non-resistance,** falta de resistencia, *f;* obediencia pasiva, *f.* **non-skid,** antideslizante, antirresbaladizo. **non-smoking,** que no fuma; (of a railway compartment, etc.) para no fumadores. **non-stop,** continuo, incesante; directo, sin parar; *Aer.* sin escalas
nonagenarian /ˌnɒnədʒəˈnɛəriən/ *a* and *n* nonagenario (-ia)
non-aligned /ˌnɒn əˈlaind/ *a* no abanderado
non-alignment /ˌnɒn əˈlainmənt/ *n* no abanderamiento *m*
nonce word /nɒns/ *n* palabra ocasional, *f*
nonchalance /ˌnɒnʃəˈlɑns/ *n* aplomo, *m,* indiferencia, frialdad, calma, *f*
nonchalant /ˌnɒnʃəˈlɑnt/ *a* indiferente, frío, impasible
nonchalantly /ˌnɒnʃəˈlantli/ *adv* con indiferencia
nonconformist /ˌnɒnkənˈfɔrmɪst/ *a* and *n* disidente *mf; a* inconforme, *n,* inconformista, *mf*
nonconformity /ˌnɒnkənˈfɔrmɪti/ *n* disidencia, *f*
nondescript /ˌnɒndɪˈskrɪpt/ *a* indeterminado, indefinido, indeciso, mediocre
none /nʌn/ *pron* nadie, ninguno; nada. —*a* and *n* ninguno (-na). —*adv* no; de ningún modo, de ninguna manera. **I have n.,** No lo tengo, No tengo ninguno. **We have n. of your things,** No tenemos ninguna de tus cosas. **I was n. the worse,** No me hallaba peor. **N. can read his account with pleasure,** Nadie puede leer su narración con gusto. **n. the less,** no menos; sin embargo
nonentity /nɒnˈɛntɪti/ *n* persona sin importancia, medianía, *f,* cero, *m*
nones /nounz/ *n pl Eccl.* nona, *f;* (Roman Calendar) nonas, *f pl,*
nonplussed /nɒnˈplʌst/ *a* cortado, perplejo, confuso
non-profit /nɒn ˈprɒfɪt/ *a* sin fines de lucro, sin fines lucrativos
non-self-governing /ˈnɒn sɛlfˈgʌvərnɪŋ/ *a* no autónomo
nonsense /ˈnɒnsɛns/ *n* disparate, despropósito, desatino, *m,* absurdidad, *f; Inf.* galimatías, *m;* pamplina, patraña, *f.* **to talk n.,** hablar sin ton ni son. **N.!** ¡A otro perro con este hueso! ¡Patrañas!
nonsensical /nɒnˈsɛnsɪkəl/ *a* absurdo, ridículo, disparatado
noodle /ˈnudl̩/ *n Cul.* tallarín, *m; Inf.* mentecato (-ta), bobo (-ba)
nook /nʊk/ *n* escondrijo, lugar retirado, rincón, *m*
noon /nun/ *n* mediodía, *m; Fig.* punto culminante, apogeo, *m, a* de mediodía, meridional. **at n.,** a mediodía
noose /nus/ *vt* coger con lazos. —*n* lazo corredizo, dogal, *m*
nopal /ˈnoupəl/ *n Bot.* nopal, *m*
No Parking «Se Prohibe Estacionar,» «Se Prohibe Estacionarse»
nor /nɔr; *unstressed* nər/ *conjunc* ni, no, tampoco. **He removed neither his coat nor his hat,** No se quitó ni el gabán ni el sombrero. **Nor was this the first time,** Y no fue ésta la primera vez. **Nor I,** Ni yo tampoco
Nordic /ˈnɔrdɪk/ *a* and *n* nórdico (-ca)
norm /nɔrm/ *n* modelo, *m,* norma, regla, pauta, *f;* (of size) marca, *f;* (*Bot. Zool.*) tipo, *m*
normal /ˈnɔrməl/ *a* normal; común, natural, corriente, regular; *Math.* perpendicular, normal. —*n* condición normal, *f,* estado normal, *m; Math.* normal, *f.* **to become n.,** normalizarse, hacerse normal. **to make n.,** normalizar. **n. school,** escuela normal, *f*
normality /nɔrˈmælɪti/ *n* normalidad, *f*
normalization /ˌnɔrmələˈzeiʃən/ *n* normalización, *f*
normalize /ˈnɔrməˌlaiz/ *vt* normalizar
normally /ˈnɔrməli/ *adv* normalmente
Norman /ˈnɔrmən/ *a* and *n* normando (-da)
Normandy /ˈnɔrməndi/ Normandía, *f*
Norse /nɔrs/ *n* noruego (language), *m, a* escandinavo
Norseman /ˈnɔrsmən/ *n* normando, viking (*pl* -os), hombre del norte, *m*
north /nɔrθ/ *n* norte, *m.* —*a* del norte, septentrional. **n. by west,** norte, cuarta noroeste. **n. of the city,** al norte de la ciudad. **N.-American,** *a* and *n* norteamericano (-na). **n.-east,** *a* and *n* nordeste *m.* **n.-easter,** viento del nordeste, *m.* **n.-easterly,** del nordeste (winds). **n.-eastern,** del nordeste (places). **n.-eastward,** hacia el nordeste. **n.-n.-east,** nornordeste, *m.* **n.-n.-west,** nornorueste, *m.* **n.-polar,** ártico. **N. Star,** estrella del norte, estrella polar, *f.* **n.-west,** noroeste, *m.* **n.-wester,** viento del noroeste, *m.* **n.-westerly,** del noroeste (winds). **n.-westerly gale,** temporal del noroeste, *m.* **n.-western,** del noroeste; situado al noroeste. **n.-westwards,** hacia el noroeste. **n. wind,** el viento del norte, el cierzo
North America, Norteamérica, América del Norte, *f*
northern /ˈnɔrðərn/ *a* del norte, septentrional, norteño; (of races) nórdico. **N. Cross,** crucero, *m.* **n. lights,** aurora boreal, *f*
northerner /ˈnɔrðərnər/ *n* hombre del norte, *m,* habitante del norte, *mf*
northernmost /ˈnɔrðərnˌmoust/ *a superl* al extremo norte, más septentrional
northwards /ˈnɔrθwərdz/ *adv* hacia el norte
Norway /ˈnɔrwei/ Noruega, *f*
Norwegian /nɔrˈwidʒən/ *a* and *n* noruego (-ga); (language) noruego, *m*
nose /nouz/ *n* nariz, *f;* (of animals) hocico, *m;* (sense of smell) olfato, *m;* (of ships) proa, *f;* (of jug) pico, *m,* boca, *f;* (projecting piece) cuerno, *m,* nariz, *f;* (of airplane) cabeza, *f, vt* acariciar con la nariz; avanzar lentamente. —*vi* husmear, olfatear. **to n. into,** *Inf.* meter las narices, poner baza. **to n. out,** descubrir, averiguar. **to bleed at the n.,** echar sangre

por las narices. **to blow one's n.,** sonar (or limpiarse) las narices. **to keep one's n. to the grindstone,** estar sobre el yunque, batir el cobre. *Fig.* **to lead by the n.,** tener a uno agarrado por las narices. **to pay through the n.,** costar un ojo de la cara. **to speak through the n.,** ganguear. **to turn up one's n.,** *Fig.* hacer gestos (a), volver la cara. **flat n.,** nariz chata, *f.* **snub n.,** nariz respingona, *f.* **well-shaped n.,** nariz perfilada, *f.* **under one's n.,** bajo las narices de uno. **n.-bag,** cebadera, mochila, *f;* morral, *m.* **n.-bleeding,** *Med.* epistaxis, *f;* hemorragia de las narices, *f.* **n.-dive,** *Aer.* descenso de cabeza, picado, *m.* —*vi* picar. **n.-piece,** (of microscope) ocular, *m.* **n.-ring,** (of a bull, etc.) narigón, *m*

-nosed *a* de nariz..., con la nariz...

nosegay /ˈnouzˌgei/ *n* ramillete, *m*

nosey Parker /ˈnouzi ˈpɑrkər/ *n Inf.* mequetrefe, *m;* cócora, *mf*

No Smoking «Prohibido Fumar», Se Prohibe Fumar

nostalgia /nɒˈstældʒə/ *n* nostalgia, añoranza, *f*

nostalgic /nɒˈstældʒɪk/ *a* nostálgico

nostril /ˈnɒstrəl/ *n* ventana de la nariz, *f, n pl* **nostrils,** narices, *f pl*

nostrum /ˈnɒstrəm/ *n* panacea, *f,* curalotodo, *m;* medicina patentada, *f*

not /nɒt/ *adv* no; sin; ni, ni siquiera. **Is it not true? We think not,** ¿No es verdad? No lo creemos. **You have seen Mary, have you not?** Vd. ha visto a María, ¿verdad? **not caring whether he came or not,** sin preocuparse de que viniese o no. **not that he will come,** no es decir que venga. **not at all,** de ningún modo; (courtesy) ¡de nada! **not even,** ni siquiera. **not guilty,** no culpable. **not one,** ni uno. **not so much as,** no tanto como; ni siquiera. **It is not so much that, as it is...** No es tanto eso, cuanto que... **not to say,** por no decir

notability /ˌnoutəˈbɪlɪti/ *n* notabilidad, *f;* (person) notable, *mf* persona de importancia, *f*

notable /ˈnoutəbəl/ *a* notable, señalado, memorable; digno de atención. —*n* persona eminente, *f,* notable, *mf*

notably /ˈnoutəbli/ *adv* notablemente, señaladamente

notary /ˈnoutəri/ *n* notario, escribano, *m*

notation /nouˈteiʃən/ *n* notación, *f*

notch /nɒtʃ/ *vt* cortar muescas (en); mellar, ranurar, entallar. —*n* muesca, mella, ranura, entalladura, *f*

note /nout/ *vt* notar, observar; anotar, apuntar; advertir, hacerse cuenta de. —*n Mus.* nota, *f;* son, acento, *m;* (letter) recado, billete, *m;* anotación, glosa, *f;* apuntación, *f,* apunte, *m,* nota, *f;* (importance) importancia, distinción, *f; Com.* vale, abonaré, *m;* (sign) marca, señal, *f.* **to n. down,** anotar. **worthy of note,** digno de atención. **n.-book,** libro de apuntes, cuaderno, *m,* libreta, *f.* **n.-case,** cartera, *f, Com.* **n. of hand,** pagaré, *m.* **n.-paper,** papel de escribir, *m.* **n.-taker,** apuntador (-ra)

noted /ˈnoutɪd/ *a* célebre, famoso, ilustre, eminente, insigne

noteworthy /ˈnoutˌwɜrði/ *a* digno de nota, notable, digno de atención

nothing /ˈnʌθɪŋ/ *n* nada, *f;* la nada; cero, *m.* —*adv* en nada. **to come to n.,** anonadarse, fracasar. **to do n.,** no hacer nada. **to do n. but,** no hacer más que. **to have n. to do with,** no tener nada que ver con; *Inf.* no tener arte ni parte en. **There is n. else to do,** No hay nada más que hacer; No hay más remedio. **There is n. to fear,** No hay de que tener miedo. **We could make n. of the book,** No llegamos a comprender el libro. **for n.,** de balde, en vano; gratis. **next to n.,** casi nada. **n. else or more,** nada más. **n. like,** ni con mucho. **n. much,** poca cosa. **n. new,** nada nuevo. **n. similar,** nada semejante. **n. to speak of,** poca cosa

nothingness /ˈnʌθɪŋnɪs/ *n* nada, *f*

notice /ˈnoutɪs/ *vt* observar, reparar en, darse cuenta (de), marcar, caer en la cuenta (de), fijarse (en). —*n* observación, atención, *f;* aviso, *m,* notificación, *f;* anuncio, *m;* (term) plazo, *m;* (review) crítica, *f.* **at short n.,** a corto aviso. **until further n.,** hasta nuevo aviso (or orden). **to attract n.,** atraer la atención. **I hadn't noticed,** No me había fijado. **to be beneath one's n.,** no merecer su atención. **to be under n.,** estar dimitido. **to bring to the n. of,** dar noticia de. **to escape n.,** pasar desapercibido. **to give n.,** hacer saber, informar; (of employer) despedir (a); (of employee) dimitir, dar la dimisión. **to take n. of,** notar, darse cuenta de; hacer caso, atender (a). **n. board,** letrero, tablero de anuncios, *m.* **n. to quit,** desahúcio, *m*

noticeable /ˈnoutɪsəbəl/ *a* perceptible, evidente; digno de observación, notable

noticeably /ˈnoutɪsəbli/ *adv* perceptiblemente; notablemente

notifiable /ˌnoutəˈfaiəbəl/ *a* declarable, notificable

notification /ˌnoutəfɪˈkeiʃən/ *n* notificación, intimación, advertencia, *f,* aviso, *m*

notify /ˈnoutəˌfai/ *vt* notificar, comunicar, avisar, intimar, hacer saber

notion /ˈnouʃən/ *n* noción, idea, *f,* concepto, *m;* (view) opinión, *f,* parecer, *m;* (novelty) novedad, *f;* artículo de fantasía, *m.* **I have a n. that...,** Tengo la idea de que..., Sospecho que... **I haven't a n.,** No tengo idea

No Tipping «No Se Admiten Propinas»

notoriety /ˌnoutəˈraiɪti/ *n* notoriedad, publicidad, *f;* escándalo, *m;* persona notoria, *f*

notorious /nouˈtɔriəs/ *a* notorio, famoso, conocido; escandaloso, sensacional

notoriously /nouˈtɔriəsli/ *adv* notoriamente

notwithstanding /ˌnɒtwɪðˈstændɪŋ/ *prep* a pesar de. —*adv* sin embargo, no obstante. —*conjunc* aunque, bien que, por más que

nougat /ˈnugət/ *n* turrón, *m*

nought /nɔt/ *n Math.* cero, *m;* nada, *f*

noun /naun/ *n* substantivo, nombre, *m*

nourish /ˈnɜrɪʃ/ *vt* sustentar, alimentar, nutrir; *Fig.* fomentar, favorecer

nourishing /ˈnɜrɪʃɪŋ/ *a* nutritivo, alimenticio, nutricio

nourishment /ˈnɜrɪʃmənt/ *n* nutrición, *f;* sustento, *m;* alimento, *m; Fig.* fomento, pasto, *m*

Nova Scotia /ˈnouvə ˈskouʃə/ Nueva Escocia, *f*

novel /ˈnɒvəl/ *a* nuevo, original, inacostumbrado. —*n* novela, *f.* **n. of roguery,** novela picaresca, *f*

novelette /ˌnɒvəˈlɛt/ *n* novela corta, *f*

novelist /ˈnɒvəlɪst/ *n* novelista, *mf*

novelty /ˈnɒvəlti/ *n* novedad, *f;* innovación, *f;* cambio, *m*

November /nouˈvɛmbər/ *n* noviembre, *m*

novice /ˈnɒvɪs/ *n Eccl.* novicio (-ia); comenzante, principiante, *mf,* aspirante, *m*

novocain /ˈnouvəˌkein/ *n Med.* novocaína, *f*

now /nau/ *adv* ahora, actualmente, al presente, a la fecha; en seguida, ahora, inmediatamente; poco ha, hace poco; pues bien. —*interj* ¡A ver! ¡Vamos! —*conjunc* pero, mas. —*n* presente, *m,* actualidad, *f.* **before now,** antes, en otras ocasiones, ya, previamente. **just now,** ahora mismo, hace poco. **now... now,** ya... ya; sucesivamente, en turno. **now and then,** de vez en cuando, de tarde en tarde. **now that,** ya que, ahora que, dado que. **until now,** hasta el presente, hasta aquí, hasta ahora

nowadays /ˈnauəˌdeiz/ *adv* hoy en día, actualmente, en nuestros días

nowhere /ˈnouˌwɛər/ *adv* en ninguna parte. **in the middle of n.,** donde Cristo dio las tres voces. **n. else,** en ninguna otra parte. *Inf.* **n. near,** ni con mucho; muy lejos (de)

nowise /ˈnouˌwaiz/ *adv* de ningún modo, en modo alguno, de ninguna manera

noxious /ˈnɒkʃəs/ *a* dañoso, nocivo; pestífero

noxiousness /ˈnɒkʃəsnɪs/ *n* nocividad, *f*

nozzle /ˈnɒzəl/ *n* (of a hose-pipe) boquilla, *f; Mech.* gollete, *m;* tubo de salida, *m,* tobera, *f;* inyector, *m*

n.p. (no place) s.l. (sin lugar)

nuance /ˈnuɑns/ *n* matiz, *m,* gradación, sombra, *f*

nubile /ˈnubɪl, -bail/ *a* núbil

nuclear /ˈnukliər/ *a* nuclear

nucleus /ˈnukliəs/ *n* núcleo, *m;* centro, foco, *m*

nude /nud/ *a* desnudo, nudo

nudge /nʌdʒ/ *vt* dar un codazo (a). —*n* codazo, *m*

nudism /ˈnudɪzəm/ *n* nudismo, *m*

nudist /ˈnudɪst/ *n* nudista, *mf*

nudity /ˈnudɪti/ *n* desnudez, *f*

nugget /ˈnʌgɪt/ *n Mineral.* pepita, *f*

nuisance /ˈnusəns/ *n* molestia, incomodidad, *f,* fastidio, *m; Inf.* tostón, *m,* lata, *f.* **to make a n. of oneself,** meterse donde no le llaman, ser un pelmazo. **What a n.!** ¡Qué lata! ¡Qué fastidio!

null /nʌl/ *a* nulo, inválido, sin fuerza legal. **n. and void,** nulo, írrito

nullification /ˌnʌləfɪˈkeiʃən/ *n* anulación, invalidación, *f*

nullity /ˈnʌlɪti/ *n* nulidad, *f*

numb /nʌm/ *vt* entumecer, entorpecer. —*a* entumecido; torpe, dormido; paralizado; *Fig.* insensible, pasmado. **n. with cold,** entumecido de frío

number /ˈnʌmbər/ *vt* numerar, contar; poner número (a); (pages of a book) foliar; ascender a. —*n* número, *m;* (figure) cifra, *f;* (crowd) multitud, muchedumbre, *f;* cantidad, *f;* (of a periodical) ejemplar, *m; Gram.* número, *m; pl* versos, *m pl.* **Numbers,** (Bible) Números, *m pl;* **to be numbered among,** figurar entre. **among the n. of,** entre la muchedumbre de. **a n. of,** varios, muchos, una cantidad de. **in great n.,** en gran número; en su mayoría. **6 Peace Street,** Calle de la Paz N° (número) 6. **one of their n.,** uno entre ellos. **n. board,** (racing) indicador, *m.* **n. plate,** *Auto.* chapa de identidad, placa de número, *f*

numbering /ˈnʌmbərɪŋ/ *n* numeración, *f*

numberless /ˈnʌmbərlɪs/ *a* innumerable, sin número, sin fin, infinito

numbness /ˈnʌmnɪs/ *n* entumecimiento, entorpecimiento, *m; Fig.* insensibilidad, *f*

numeral /ˈnumərəl/ *a* numeral. —*n* número, *m,* cifra, *f; Gram.* nombre o adjetivo numeral, *m*

numerator /ˈnuməˌreitər/ *n* numerador

numerical /nuˈmɛrɪkəl/ *a* numérico

numerous /ˈnumərəs/ *a* numeroso; nutrido, grande; muchos (-as)

numerousness /ˈnumərəsnɪs/ *n* numerosidad, multitud, muchedumbre, *f*

numismatic /ˌnumɪzˈmætɪk/ *a* numismático. —*n pl* **numismatics,** numismática, *f*

numismatist /nuˈmɪzmətɪst/ *n* numismático, *m*

numskull /ˈnʌmˌskʌl/ *n* zote, topo, *m*

nun /nun/ *n* monja, religiosa, *f.* **to become a nun,** profesar, tomar el hábito, meterse monja

nuncio /ˈnʌnʃiˌou/ *n* nuncio, *m.* **acting n.,** pronuncio, *m*

nunnery /ˈnʌnəri/ *n* convento de monjas, *m*

nuptial /ˈnʌpʃəl/ *a* nupcial. —*n pl* **nuptials,** nupcias, *f pl,* enlace, *m.* **n. mass,** *Eccl.* misa de velaciones, *f.* **n. song,** epitalamio, *m*

nurse /nɜrs/ *vt* criar; dar de mamar (a), amamantar; (the sick) cuidar, asistir; (fondle) acariciar, mecer; *Fig.* fomentar, promover. —*vi* trabajar como enfermera. —*n* (of the sick) enfermera, *f;* (wet) nodriza, ama de leche, *f;* (children's) niñera, *f; Fig.* fomentador, *m.* **male n.,** enfermero, *m*

nursery /ˈnɜrsəri/ *n Agr.* plantel, vivero semillero, criadero, *m;* (children's room) cuarto de los niños, *m; Fig.* sementera, *f;* semillero, *m.* **n. governess,** aya, *f.* **n. rhyme,** canción infantil, *f*

nurseryman /ˈnɜrsərimən/ *n* horticultor, *m;* jardinero, *m*

nursing /ˈnɜrsɪŋ/ *n* lactancia, crianza, *f;* (of the sick) asistencia, *f,* cuido, *m.* **n. home,** clínica, *f.* **n. mother,** madre lactante, *f*

nurture /ˈnɜrtʃər/ *vt* alimentar; criar, educar. —*n* nutrición, alimentación, *f;* crianza, educación, *f*

nut /nʌt/ *vi* coger nueces. —*n Bot.* nuez, *f; Mech.* tuerca, hembra de tornillo, *f, Inf.* **to be a tough nut to crack,** ser un tío de cuidado. **to crack nuts,** cascar nueces. **to go nutting,** coger nueces. **cashew nut,** anacardo, *m.* **loose nut,** *Mech.* tuerca aflojada, *f.* **nut-brown,** castaño. **nut tree,** nogal, *m*

nutcrackers /ˈnʌtˌkrækərz/ *n pl* cascanueces, quebrantanueces, *m*

nutmeg /ˈnʌtmɛg/ *n* nuez moscada, nuez de especia, *f*

nutria /ˈnutriə/ *n Zool.* nutria, *f*

nutriment /ˈnutrəmənt/ *n* nutrimento, alimento, *m*

nutrition /nuˈtrɪʃən/ *n* nutrición, alimentación, *f*

nutritious, nutritive /nuˈtrɪʃəs; ˈnutrɪtɪv/ *a* nutritivo, alimenticio, alible

nutshell /ˈnʌtˌʃɛl/ *n* cáscara de nuez, *f.* **to put in a n.,** decir en resumidas cuentas, decir en forma apastillada

nutty /ˈnʌti/ *a* de nuez

nuzzle /ˈnʌzəl/ *vt* acariciar con la nariz

nylon /ˈnailɒn/ *n* nilón, nylon, *m.* **n. stockings,** medias de cristal (or de nilón), *f pl*

nymph /nɪmf/ *n* ninfa, *f; Ent.* crisálida, *f.* **n.-like,** como una ninfa; de ninfa

nymphomania /ˌnɪmfəˈmeiniə/ *n* ninfomanía, *f,* furor uterino, *m*

O

o /ou/ *n* (letter) o, *f*, *interj* ¡o! **O that...!** ¡Ojalá que!
oaf /ouf/ *n* zoquete, zamacuco, *m*
oafish /'oufɪʃ/ *a* lerdo, torpe
oafishness /'oufɪʃnɪs/ *n* torpeza, estupidez, *f*
oak /ouk/ *n* (tree and wood) roble, *m*, *a* de roble. **carved oak,** roble tallado, *m*. **holm-oak,** encina, *f*. **oak-apple,** agalla, *f*. **oak grove,** robledo, *m*
oakum /'oukəm/ *n* estopa, *f*
oar /ɔr/ *n* remo, *m*. **to lie on the oars,** cesar de remar. **to pull at the oars,** bogar, remar. **to put in one's oar,** *Inf.* meter baza. **to ship the oars,** armar los remos. **to unship the oars,** desarmar los remos. **oar-stroke,** palada, *f*
oarsman /'ɔrzmən/ *n* remero, bogador, *m*
oarsmanship /'ɔrzmən,ʃɪp/ *n* arte de remar, *m*, or *f*
oasis /ou'eisɪs/ *n* oasis, *m*
OAS (Organization of American States) OEA (Organización de los Estados Americanos)
oast /oust/ *n* horno para secar el lúpulo, *m*
oat /out/ *n Bot.* avena, *f*. **wild oat,** avena silvestre, *f*. **to sow one's wild oats,** correrla, andarse a la flor del berro. **oat field,** avenal, *m*
oath /ouθ/ *n* juramento, *m;* (curse) blasfemia, *f*, reniego, *m*. **on o.,** bajo juramento. **to break an o.,** violar el juramento. **to put on o.,** tomar juramento, hacer prestar juramento. **to take an o.,** prestar (or hacer) juramento. **to take the o. of allegiance,** jurar la bandera
oatmeal /'out,mil/ *n* harina de avena, *f*
obduracy /'ɒbdʊrəsi/ *n* obduración, obstinación, terquedad, *f*
obdurate /'ɒbdʊrɪt/ *a* obstinado, terco, porfiado. **He is o. to our requests,** Es sordo a nuestros ruegos
obedience /ou'bidiəns/ *n* obediencia, sumisión, docilidad, *f*. **blind o.,** obediencia ciega, *f*. **in o. to,** conforme a, de acuerdo con
obedient /ou'bidiənt/ *a* obediente, sumiso, dócil. **to be o. to,** ser obediente (a), obedecer (a)
obediently /ou'bidiəntli/ *adv* obedientemente, dócilmente. **Yours o.,** Su atento servidor (su att. s.)
obeisance /ou'beisəns, ou'bi-/ *n* reverencia, cortesía, *f*, saludo, *m;* (homage) homenaje, *m*
obelisk /'ɒbəlɪsk/ *n* obelisco, *m*
obese /ou'bis/ *a* obeso, corpulento, grueso, gordo
obesity /ou'bisɪti/ *n* obesidad, gordura, corpulencia, *f*
obey /ou'bei/ *vt* and *vi* obedecer. —*vt* (carry out) cumplir, observar. **to be obeyed,** ser obedecido
obfuscate /'ɒbfə,skeit/ *vt* ofuscar, cegar
obfuscation /,ɒbfə'skeiʃən/ *n* ofuscamiento, *m*, confusión, *f*
obituary /ou'bɪtʃu,ɛri/ *a* mortuorio, necrológico. —*n* obituario, *m*, necrología, *f*. **o. column,** (in newspaper) sección necrológica, *f*. **o. notice,** esquela de defunción, *f*
object /*n.* 'ɒbdʒɪkt; *v.* əb'dʒɛkt/ *n* objeto, artículo, *m*, cosa, *f;* (purpose) propósito, intento, *m;* (aim) fin, término, *m; Gram.* complemento, *m; Inf.* individuo, *m*. —*vt* objetar, poner reparos (a). —*vi* oponerse, poner objeciones. **I o. to that remark,** Protesto contra esa observación. **If you don't o.,** Si Vd. no tiene inconveniente. **o. finder,** objetivo, *m*. **o. lesson,** lección de cosas, *f;* lección práctica, *f*
objection /əb'dʒɛkʃən/ *n* objeción, protesta, *f*, reparo, *m;* (obstacle) dificultad, *f*, inconveniente, *m*. **to have no o.,** no tener inconveniente. **to raise an o.,** hacer constar una protesta, poner una objeción
objectionable /əb'dʒɛkʃənəbəl/ *a* censurable, reprensible; desagradable, molesto
objective /əb'dʒɛktɪv/ *a* objetivo; *Gram.* acusativo. —*n* objeto, propósito, *m;* destinación, *f; Mil.* objetivo, *m, Gram.* **o. case,** caso acusativo, *m*,
objectivism /əb'dʒɛktə,vɪzəm/ *n Philos.* objetivismo, *m*
objectivity /,ɒbdʒɪk'tɪvɪti/ *n* objetividad, *f*
objector /ɒb'dʒɛktər/ *n* objetante, *mf*, impugnador (-ra). **conscientious o.,** (dissident) el, *m*, (*f*, la) que protesta contra; (pacifist) pacifista, *mf*
oblation /ɒ'bleiʃən/ *n* oblación, ofrenda, *f*
obligation /,ɒblɪ'geiʃən/ *n* obligación, *f;* deber, *m*, precisión, *f;* compromiso, *m*. **of o.,** de deber; de precepto. **to be under an o.,** estar bajo una obligación; deber un favor. **to place under an o.,** poner bajo una obligación
obligatory /ə'blɪgə,tɔri/ *a* obligatorio, forzoso
oblige /ə'blaidʒ/ *vt* (insist on) obligar, hacer, forzar; (gratify) hacer un favor (a), complacer. **He obliged me with a match,** Me hizo el favor de una cerilla. **They are much obliged to you,** Le están muy reconocidos. **Much obliged!** ¡Se agradece!
obliging /ə'blaidʒɪŋ/ *a* atento, condescendiente, complaciente, servicial
obligingly /ə'blaidʒɪŋli/ *adv* cortésmente
obligingness /ə'blaidʒɪŋnɪs/ *n* cortesía, amabilidad, bondad, *f*
oblique /ə'blik/ *a* oblicuo, sesgado; (indirect) indirecto, evasivo; *Gram.* oblicuo
obliquely /ə'blikli/ *adv* oblicuamente, al sesgo, sesgadamente; indirectamente. **to place o.,** poner al sesgo
obliquity /ə'blɪkwɪti/ *n* oblicuidad, *f*, sesgo, *m;* (of conduct, etc.) tortuosidad, *f*
obliterate /ə'blɪtə,reit/ *vt* borrar; destruir, aniquilar. **to be obliterated,** borrarse; quedar destruido
obliteration /ə,blɪtə'reiʃən/ *n* testación, *f;* destrucción, *f*. **o. raid,** bombardeo de saturación, *m*
oblivion /ə'blɪviən/ *n* olvido, *m*. **to cast into o.,** echar al olvido
oblivious /ə'blɪviəs/ *a* olvidadizo, descuidago
oblong /'ɒb,lɔŋ/ *a* oblongo, cuadrilongo, rectangular. —*n* rectángulo, cuadrilongo, *m*
obloquy /'ɒbləkwi/ *n* infamia, maledicencia, deshonra, *f*
obnoxious /əb'nɒkʃəs/ *a* odioso, ofensivo, aborrecible
obnoxiously /əb'nɒkʃəsli/ *adv* odiosamente
obnoxiousness /əb'nɒkʃəsnɪs/ *n* odiosidad, *f*
oboe /'oubou/ *n Mus.* oboe, *m*. **o. player,** oboe, *m*
obol /'ɒbəl/ *n* óbolo, *m*
obscene /əb'sin/ *a* indecente, obsceno, escabroso
obscenely /əb'sinli/ *adv* obscenamente, escabrosamente
obscenity /əb'sɛnɪti/ *n* indecencia, obscenidad, *f*
obscurantism /əb'skyʊrən,tɪzəm/ *n* obscurantismo, *m*
obscurantist /əb'skyʊrəntɪst/ *a* and *n* obscurantista *mf*
obscure /əb'skyʊr/ *a* (indistinct) obscuro, indistinto; (dark) lóbrego, tenebroso; (remote) retirado, apartado; (puzzling) confuso; (unknown) desconocido; humilde; (difficult to understand) abstruso, obscuro; (vague) vago. —*vt* obscurecer; (hide) esconder; (eclipse) eclipsar. **to o. the issue,** hacer perder de vista el problema
obscurely /əb'skyʊrli/ *adv* obscuramente; humildemente, retiradamente; confusamente; vagamente
obscurity /əb'skyʊrɪti/ *n* (darkness) obscuridad, lobreguez, *f;* (difficulty of meaning) ambigüedad, confusión, vaguedad, *f;* humildad, *f*
obsequies /'ɒbsɪkwiz/ *n pl* exequias, *f pl*, ritos fúnebres, *m pl*
obsequious /əb'sikwiəs/ *a* servil, empalagoso, zalamero
obsequiously /əb'sikwiəsli/ *adv* servilmente
obsequiousness /əb'sikwiəsnɪs/ *n* servilismo, *m*, sumisión, *f*
observable /əb'zɜrvəbəl/ *a* observable, perceptible, visible; notable
observably /əb'zɜrvəbli/ *adv* notablemente
observance /əb'zɜrvəns/ *n* observancia, *f*, cumplimiento, *m;* práctica, costumbre, *f;* (religious) rito, *m*
observant /əb'zɜrvənt/ *a* observador; obediente, atento. **o. of,** observador de; atento a
observation /,ɒbzɜr'veiʃən/ *n* observación, *f*, exa-

men, escrutinio, *m;* (experience) experiencia, *f;* (remark) advertencia, *f,* comento, *m.* **to escape o.,** no ser advertido. **o. car.,** vagón-mirador, *m,* **o. post,** puesto de observación, *m*

observatory /əb'zɜrvəˌtɔri/ *n* observatorio, *m*

observe /əb'zɜrv/ *vt* (laws) cumplir; (holy days, etc.) guardar; (notice) observar, mirar, notar, ver, reparar en; (remark) decir, advertir; (examine) vigilar, atisbar, examinar; *Astron.* observar. —*vi* ser observador. **to o. silence,** guardar silencio

observer /əb'zɜrvər/ *n* observador (-ra)

obsess /əb'sɛs/ *vt* obsesionar, obcecar

obsessed /əb'sɛst/ *a* obseso

obsession /əb'sɛʃən/ *n* obsesión, obcecación, idea fija, manía, *f*

obsidian /əb'sɪdiən/ *n Mineral.* obsidiana, *f*

obsolescent /ˌɒbsə'lɛsənt/ *a* que se hace antiguo, que cae en desuso

obsolete /ˌɒbsə'lit/ *a* obsoleto, anticuado; *Biol.* rudimentario, atrofiado

obstacle /'ɒbstəkəl/ *n* obstáculo, impedimento, *m;* dificultad, *f,* inconveniente, *m.* **to put obstacles in the way of,** *Fig.* dificultar, hacer difícil. **o. race,** carrera de obstáculos, *f*

obstetric /əb'stɛtrɪk/ *a* obstétrico

obstetrician /ˌɒbstɪ'trɪʃən/ *n* obstétrico (-ea), médico (-ca) partero (-ra)

obstetrics /əb'stɛtrɪks/ *n* obstetricia, tocología, *f*

obstinacy /'ɒbstənəsi/ *n* obstinación, terquedad, tenacidad, porfía, *f,* tesón, *m;* persistencia, *f*

obstinate /'ɒbstənɪt/ *a* terco, porfiado, obstinado, tenaz; refractario; persistente, pertinaz. **to be o.,** ser terco; porfiar. **to be o. about,** obstinarse en.

obstinately /'ɒbstənɪtli/ *adv* tercamente

obstreperous /əb'strɛpərəs/ *a* turbulento, ruidoso

obstruct /əb'strʌkt/ *vt* obstruir: impedir; cerrar; (thwart) estorbar; (hinder) dificultar, embarazar; (the traffic) obstruir, atascar. —*vi* estorbar. **to become obstructed,** obstruirse, cerrarse

obstruction /əb'strʌkʃən/ *n* obstrucción, *f;* estorbo, obstáculo, *m.* **to cause a street o.,** obstruir el tráfico

obstructionism /əb'strʌkʃəˌnɪzəm/ *n* obstruccionismo, *m*

obstructionist /əb'strʌkʃənɪst/ *n* obstruccionista, *mf*

obstructive /əb'strʌktɪv/ *a* estorbador, obstructor

obtain /əb'tein/ *vt* obtener, conseguir, lograr; recibir; (by threats) arrancar. —*vi* estar en boga, estar en vigor, predominar. **to o. on false pretences,** conseguir por engaño

obtainable /əb'teinəbəl/ *a* asequible, alcanzable. **easily o.,** fácil a obtener

obtainer /əb'teinər/ *n* conseguidor (-ra), adquisidor (-ra)

obtainment /əb'teinmənt/ *n* obtención, *f,* logro, *m*

obtrude /əb'trud/ *vt* imponer

obtrusion /əb'truʒən/ *n* imposición, *f;* importunidad, *f*

obtrusive /əb'trusɪv/ *a* importuno; entremetido; pretencioso

obtrusiveness /əb'trusɪvnɪs/ *n* importunidad, *f;* entremetimiento, *m*

obtuse /əb'tus/ *a* (blunt) obtuso, romo; (stupid) estúpido, torpe, lerdo. **o. angle,** obtusángulo, *m*

obtuseness /əb'tusnɪs/ *n* (bluntness) embotamiento, *m;* (stupidity) estupidez, torpeza, *f*

obverse / *a.* ɒb'vɜrs; *n.* 'ɒbvɜrs/ *a* del anverso. —*n* anverso, *m*

obviate /'ɒbviˌeit/ *vt* obviar, evitar

obvious /'ɒbviəs/ *a* evidente, manifiesto, patente, obvio, aparente, transparente; poco sutil

obviously /'ɒbviəsli/ *adv* evidentemente, patentemente

obviousness /'ɒbviəsnɪs/ *n* evidencia, transparencia, *f*

occasion /ə'keiʒən/ *n* ocasión, *f;* oportunidad, *f,* momento oportuno, tiempo propicio, *m;* (reason) motivo, origen, *m,* causa, razón, *f;* (need) necesidad, *f.* —*vt* ocasionar, causar, producir. **as o. demands,** cuando las circunstancias lo exigen, en caso necesario. **for the o.,** para la ocasión. **on one o.,** una vez. **on the o. of,** en la ocasión de. **on that o.,** en tal ocasión, en aquella ocasión. **He has given me no o. to say so,** No me ha dado motivos de decirlo. **There is no o. for it,** No hay necesidad para ello. **to have o. to,** haber de, tener que, necesitar. **to lose no o.,** no perder ripio (or oportunidad). **to rise to the o.,** estar al nivel de las circunstancias. **to take this o.,** aprovechar esta oportunidad

occasional /ə'keiʒənl̩/ *a* (occurring at times) de vez en cuando, intermitente; poco frecuente, infrecuente; (of verse) de ocasión. **o. table,** mesilla, *f*

occasionally /ə'keiʒənl̩i/ *adv* de vez en cuando

occiput /'ɒksəˌpʌt/ *n Anat.* occipucio, *m*

occlude /ə'klud/ *vt* obstruir, cerrar; *Med.* ocluir; *Chem.* absorber

occlusion /ə'kluʒən/ *n* cerramiento, *m; Med.* oclusión, *f; Chem.* absorción de gases, *f*

occlusive /ə'klusɪv/ *a* oclusivo

occult /ə'kʌlt/ *a* oculto, escondido, misterioso; mágico. **o. sciences,** creencias ocultas, *f pl*

occultation /ˌɒkʌl'teiʃən/ *n Astron.* ocultación, *f,* eclipse, *m*

occultism /ə'kʌltɪzəm/ *n* ocultismo, *m*

occultist /ə'kʌltɪst/ *n* ocultista, *mf*

occupancy /'ɒkyəpənsi/ *n* ocupación, posesión, *f;* (tenancy) tenencia, *f*

occupant /'ɒkyəpənt/ *n* habitante, *mf;* ocupante, *mf;* (tenant) inquilino (-na)

occupation /ˌɒkyə'peiʃən/ *n* ocupación *f;* (tenure) inquilinato, *m,* tenencia, *f;* (work) trabajo, quehacer, *m,* labor, *f;* (employment) empleo, oficio, *m;* profesión, *f*

occupational /ˌɒkyə'peiʃənl̩/ *a* de oficio. **o. disease,** enfermedad profesional, *f*

occupier /'ɒkyəˌpaiər/ *n* ocupante, *mf,* inquilino (-na)

occupy /'ɒkyəˌpai/ *vt* ocupar; (live in) vivir en, habitar; (time) emplear, pasar; (take over) apoderarse de, ocupar. **to o. oneself in** or **with,** ocuparse en, ocuparse con. **to be occupied in** or **with,** estar ocupado con, ocuparse en

occur /ə'kɜr/ *vi* (happen) suceder, tener lugar, acaecer; (exist) encontrarse, existir; (of ideas) ocurrirse, venirse. **to o. to one's mind,** venírsele a las mientes. **to o. again,** volver a suceder, ocurrir de nuevo. **An idea occurred to her,** Se le ocurrió una idea

occurrence /ə'kɜrəns/ *n* ocurrencia, *f;* incidente, suceso, acontecimiento, *m.* **to be of frequent o.,** ocurrir con frecuencia, acontecer a menudo

ocean /'ouʃən/ *n* océano, *m; Fig.* mar, abundancia, *f.* **o.-going vessel,** buque de alta mar, *m*

Oceania /ˌouʃi'æniə/ el Mundo Novísmo, *m*

oceanic /ˌouʃi'ænɪk/ *a* oceánico

oceanography /ˌouʃə'nɒgrəfi/ *n* oceanografía, *f*

ocelot /'ɒsəˌlɒt/ *n Zool.* ocelote, *m*

ocher /'oukər/ *n* ocre, *m*

octagon /'ɒktəˌgɒn/ *n* octágono, *m*

octagonal /ɒk'tægənl̩/ *a* octagonal

octave /'ɒktɪv/ *n* (*Eccl.* metrics, *Mus.*) octava, *f*

octavo /ɒk'teivou, -'tɑ-/ *n Print.* libro, etc. en octavo (8°), *m.* **in o.,** en octavo. **large o.,** octavo mayor, *m.* **small o.,** octavo menor, *m*

octet /ɒk'tɛt/ *n Mus.* octeto, *m*

October /ɒk'toubər/ *n* octubre, *m,* 2 October 1996, el segundo (2°) de octubre de mil novecientos noventa y seis

octogenarian /ˌɒktədʒə'nɛəriən/ *a* and *n* octogenario (-ia)

octopus /'ɒktəpəs/ *n* pulpo, *m*

ocular /'ɒkyələr/ *a* ocular, visual. —*n* ocular, *m*

oculist /'ɒkyəlɪst/ *n* oculista, *mf*

odd /ɒd/ *a* (of numbers) impar; (of volumes, etc.) suelto; (strange) raro, curioso, extraño, extravagante; (casual) casual, accidental; (extra) y pico, y tantos, sobrante; (of gloves, etc.) sin pareja. **at odd moments,** en momentos de ocio. **at odd times,** de vez en cuando. **thirty odd,** treinta y pico. **odd number,** número impare, *m.* **odd or even,** pares o impares. **odd trick,** (at cards) una baza más

oddity /'ɒdɪti/ *n* excentricidad, rareza, extravagancia, *f;* (person) ente singular, *m;* (curio) objeto curioso, *m,* antigüedad, *f*

oddly /'ɒdli/ *adv* singularmente

oddment /'ɒdmənt/ *n* bagatela, baratija, *f*

oddness /'ɒdnɪs/ *n* singularidad, rareza, extravagancia, *f*

odds /ɒdz/ *n pl* diferencia, desigualdad, *f;* (superiority) ventaja, superioridad, *f;* (quarrel) disputa, riña, *f.* **The o. are that...,** Lo más probable es que... **to fight against dreadful o.,** luchar contra fuerzas muy superiores. **o. and ends,** (remains) sobras y picos, *f pl;* (trifles) ñaques, *m pl,* chucherías, *f pl*
Odessa /ou'dɛsə/ Odesa, *f*
odious /'oudiəs/ *a* odioso, detestable, aborrecible, repugnante
odiousness /'oudiəsnɪs/ *n* odiosidad, *f*
odium /'oudiəm/ *n* odio, *m*
odor /'oudər/ *n* olor, *m,* (fragrance) perfume, aroma, *m,* fragancia, *f; Fig.* sospecha, *f.* **in bad o.,** *Fig.* en disfavor. **o. of sanctity,** olor de santidad, *m*
odoriferous /ˌoudə'rɪfərəs/ *a* odorífero; (perfumed) oloroso, perfumado
odorless /'oudərlɪs/ *a* inodoro
odorous /'oudərəs/ *a* fragante, oloroso
odyssey /'ɒdəsi/ *n* odisea, *f*
Oedipus complex /'ɛdəpəs/ *n* complejo de Edipo, *m*
of /əv/ *prep* de. **of** has many idiomatic translations which are given as far as possible under the heading of the word concerned. It is also not translated. **I robbed him of his reward,** Le robé su recompensa. **I was thinking of you,** Pensaba en tí. **It was very good of you to...,** Vd. ha tenido mucha bondad de... **Your naming of the child Mary,** El que Vd. haya dado el nombre de María al niño. **29th of Sept., 1936,** el 29 de septiembre de 1936. **Of course!** ¡Claro está! ¡Ya lo creo! ¡Naturalmente! **of late,** últimamente. **of the** (before *m, sing*) del; (before *f, sing*) de la; (before *m pl*) de los; (before *f pl*) de las. **to dream of,** soñar con. **to smell of,** oler a tener olor de. **to taste of, etc.,** saber a, tener gusto de.
off /ɔf/ *prep* de; fuera de; cerca de; desde; *Naut.* a la altura de. **from off,** de. **Take your gloves off the table!** ¡Quítate los guantes de la mesa! **The wheel was off the car,** La rueda se había desprendido del coche. **to be off duty,** no estar de servicio; *Mil.* no estar de guardia. **to lunch off cold meat,** almorzar de carne fría. **off one's head,** chiflado
off /ɔf/ *a* (contrasted with near) de la derecha, derecho; (unlikely) improbable, remoto. —*adv* (with intransitive verbs of motion) se (e.g. *He has gone off,* Se ha marchado); (contrasted with on) de (e.g. *He has fallen off the horse,* Ha caído del caballo); (of place at a distance) lejos, a distancia de; (of time) generally a verb is used (e.g. *The wedding is three months off,* Faltan tres meses para la boda); (completely) enteramente. **Off** is often not translated in Sp. (e.g. *to put off,* aplazar, *to cut off,* cortar). **day off,** día libre, día de asueto, *m.* **How far off is the house from here? The house is five miles off.** ¿Cuántas millas está la casa de aquí? La casa está a cinco millas de aquí. **His hat is off,** Está sin sombrero, Se ha quitado el sombrero. **The cover is off,** La cubierta está quitada. **The party is off,** Se ha anulado la reunión. **6% off,** un descuento de seis por ciento. —*interj* **Off with you!** ¡Márchate! ¡Fuera! **off and on,** de vez en cuando, espasmódicamente. **off color,** (ill) malucho; (of jokes) verde. **off season,** estación muerta, *f.* **off-shore,** a vista de tierra. **off-stage,** entre bastidores
offal /'ɔfəl/ *n* (butchers') menudencias, *f pl,* asadura, *f,* menudos, despojos, *m pl;* desperdicio, *m*
offend /ə'fɛnd/ *vt* ofender; agraviar, insultar; herir; desagradar, disgustar; *vi* ofender, pecar. **to be offended,** resentirse, insultarse. **This offends my sense of justice,** Esto ofende mi sentimiento de justicia. **to o. against,** pecar contra; violar
offender /ə'fɛndər/ *n* delincuente, *mf;* agraviador (-ra), pecador (-ra), transgresor (-ra). **old o.,** *Law.* criminal inveterado, *m*
offense /ə'fɛns/ *n* ofensa, transgresión, violación, *f;* pecado, *m; Law.* delito, crimen, *m;* (insult) agravio, *m,* afrenta, *f.* **the first o.,** el primer delito, *m.* **fresh o.,** nuevo delito, *m.* **political o.,** crimen político, *m.* **technical o.,** *Law.* cuasidelito, *m.* **to commit an o. against,** ofender contra. **to take o.,** resentirse, darse por ofendido
offensive /ə'fɛnsɪv/ *a* ofensivo, desagradable, repugnante; (insulting) injurioso, agraviador, agresivo. —*n Mil.* ofensiva, *f.* **to take the o.,** tomar la ofensiva
offensiveness /ə'fensɪvnɪs/ *n* lo desagradable; (insult) ofensa, *f;* lo injurioso
offer /'ɔfər/ *n* oferta, *f;* ofrecimiento, *m;* (of help) promesa, *f;* proposición, *f; Com.* oferta, *f.* —*vt* ofrecer; prometer; (opportunities, etc.) deparar, brindar; tributar. —*vi* ofrecerse, ocurrir, surgir. **to o. up,** ofrecer; inmolar, sacrificar. **He did not offer to go,** No hizo ademán de marcharse. **to o. resistance,** oponer resistencia. **o. of marriage,** oferta de matrimonio, *f*
offerer /'ɔfərər/ *n* ofrecedor (-ra)
offering /'ɔfərɪŋ/ *n* ofrecimiento, *m; Eccl.* ofrenda, oblación, *f,* sacrificio, *m;* regalo, don, *m,* dádiva, *f*
offhand /'ɔf'hænd/ *a* sin preparación, de repente; (casual) casual, despreocupado; (discourteous) brusco, descortés
offhandedly /'ɔf'hændɪdli/ *adv* sin preparación, espontáneamente; negligentemente; bruscamente
office /'ɔfɪs/ *n* oficina, *m;* (post) cargo, puesto, destino, *m;* (state department) ministerio, *m;* (of a Cabinet minister) cartera, *f;* (room) oficina, *f;* despacho, escritorio, *m;* (of a newspaper) redacción, *f;* (lawyer's) bufete, *m;* departamento, *m; Eccl.* oficio, *m pl.* **offices,** negocio, *m;* oficinas, *f pl;* (prayers) rezos, *m pl; Eccl.* oficios, *m pl.* **domestic offices,** dependencias, *f pl.* **good offices,** *Fig.* buenos oficios, *m pl.* **head o.,** casa central, oficina principal, *f.* **private o.,** despacho particular, *m.* **to be in o.,** estar en el poder. **o.-bearer,** miembro de la junta, *m;* funcionario, *m.* **o. -boy,** mozo de oficina, *m.* **o. employee,** oficinista, *mf.* **o. hours,** horas de oficina, *f pl;* (professions) horas de consulta, *f pl.* **o.-seeker,** aspirante, *m;* pretendiente, *m.* **o. work,** trabajo de oficina, *m*
officer /'ɔfəsər/ *n* oficial, funcionario, *m;* (police) agente de policía, *m;* (of the Church) dignatario, *m;* (*Mil. Nav. Aer.*) oficial, *m.* —*vt* mandar. **commissioned o.,** oficial, *m.* **non-commissioned o.,** oficial subalterno, *m.* **to be well officered,** tener buena oficialidad. **Officers' Training Corps,** Escuela de Oficiales, *f*
office worker *n* oficinista, *mf*
official /ə'fɪʃəl/ *a* oficial; autorizado; ceremonioso, grave. —*n* funcionario, *m;* oficial público, *m.* **high o.,** funcionario importante. *m.* **o. mourning,** duelo oficial, *m.* **o. receiver,** fiscal de quiebras, *m*
officialdom /ə'fɪʃəldəm/ *n* funcionarismo, *m;* círculos oficiales, *m pl*
officiant /ə'fɪʃiənt/ *n* oficiante, *m*
officiate /ə'fɪʃiˌeit/ *vi* celebrar; oficiar, funcionar
officiating /ə'fɪʃiˌeitɪŋ/ *a* oficiante; celebrante. **o. priest,** sacerdote oficiante, celebrante, *m*
officious /ə'fɪʃəs/ *a* oficioso, entremetido
officiousness /ə'fɪʃəsnɪs/ *n* oficiosidad, *f*
offing /'ɔfɪŋ/ *n Naut.* mar afuera, *m.* **in the o.,** cerca
off season fuera de temporada
offset /*n.* 'ɔfˌsɛt; *v.* ˌɔf'sɛt/ *n* compensación, *f, vt* compensar, neutralizar
offshoot /'ɔfˌʃut/ *n* renuevo, vástago, *m*
offside /'ɔf'said/ *a* (of a car) del lado derecho (or izquierda); *Sports.* fuera de juego
offspring /'ɔfˌsprɪŋ/ *n* vástago, *m;* descendiente, *mf;* prole, *f;* hijos, *m pl*
often /'ɔfən/ *adv* a menudo, mucho, con frecuencia, frecuentemente, muchas veces. **as o. as,** tan a menudo como, siempre que. **as o. as not,** no pocas veces. **How o.?** ¿Cuántas veces? **It is not o. that...,** No ocurre con frecuencia que... **so o.,** tantas veces, con frecuencia. **Do you go there o.?** ¿Va Vd. allí con frecuencia (or frecuentemente)? **Not o.,** Voy rara vez allá
ogival /'oudʒaivəl/ *a Archit.* ojival
ogive /'oudʒaiv/ *n Archit.* ojiva, *f*
ogle /'ougəl/ *vt* and *vi* comer(se) con los ojos (a), ojear, guiñar el ojo (a). —*n* ojeada, *f,* guiño, *m*
ogling /'ouglɪŋ/ *n* guiño, *m,* ojeada, *f*
ogre /'ougər/ *n* ogro, *m*
oh! /ou/ *interj* ¡o! **O no!** ¡Ca! ¡Claro que no!
ohm /oum/ *n Elec.* ohmio, *m*
oil /ɔil/ *n* aceite, *m;* petróleo, *m;* óleo, *m.* —*vt* aceitar, engrasar; olear, ungir, untar; (bribe) sobornar, untar la mano; *Fig.* suavizar. —*a* aceitero; petrolero. **to pour oil on troubled waters,** echar

aceite sobre aguas turbulentas. **to strike oil,** encontrar un pozo de petróleo; *Fig.* encontrar un filón. **crude oil,** petróleo bruto, *m.* **heavy oil,** aceite pesado, *m.* **thin oil,** aceite ligero, *m.* *Art.* **in oils,** al óleo. **oil-bearing,** petrolífero. **oil-box,** engrasador, *m.* **oil-burner,** quemador de petróleo, *m.* **oil-can,** aceitera, *f.* **oil-colors,** pinturas al óleo, *f pl.* **oil field,** yacimiento petrolífero, campo de petróleo, *m.* **oil-filter,** separador de aceite, *m.* **oil-gauge,** nivel de aceite, *m.* **oil lamp,** velón, candil, quinqué, *m.* **oil of turpentine,** aceite de trementina, aguarrás, *m.* esencia de trementina, *f.* **oil-painting,** pintura al óleo, *f.* **oil pipeline,** oleoducto, *m.* **oil shop,** aceitería, *f.* **oil-silk,** encerado, *m.* **oil stove,** estufa de petróleo, *f.* **oil tanker,** *Naut.* petrolero, *m.* **oil-well,** pozo de petróleo, *m*

oilcake /'ɔil,keik/ *n* bagazo, *m*

oilcloth /'ɔil,klɔθ/ *n* hule, *m;* linóleo, *m*

oiler /'ɔilər/ *n* (can) aceitera, *f; Naut.* petrolero, *m;* lubricador, *m*

oiliness /'ɔilinɪs/ *n* oleaginosidad, untuosidad, *f*

oiling /'ɔilɪŋ/ *n* engrasado, *m*

oil seed *n* semilla oleaginosa, *f*

oilskin /'ɔil,skɪn/ *n* encerado, *m*

oily /'ɔili/ *a* aceitoso, grasiento

ointment /'ɔintmənt/ *n* ungüento, *m,* pomada, *f*

old /ould/ *a* viejo; antiguo, anciano; (of wines, etc.) añejo; (worn out) usado, gastado; (inveterate) arraigado, inveterado. **How old are you?** ¿Cuántos años tiene usted? **to be sixteen years old,** tener dieciséis años. **He is old enough to know his own mind,** Tiene bastante edad para saber lo que quiere. **to grow old,** envejecer. **to remain an old maid,** quedar soltera; *Inf.* quedarse para vestir imágenes. **of old,** antiguamente. **prematurely old,** revejido averiado. **old age,** vejez, senectud, *f.* **old bachelor,** solterón, *m.* **old clothes,** ropa vieja (or usada), ropa de segunda mano, *f.* **old-clothes dealer,** ropavejero (-ra). **old-clothes shop,** ropavejería, *f.* **old-established,** viejo. **old-fashioned,** pasado de moda, viejo; (of people) chapado a la antigua. **old lady,** anciana, dama vieja, *f.* **old-looking,** de aspecto viejo, avejentado. **old maid,** solterona, *f.* **old-maidish,** remilgado. **old man,** viejo, *m; Theat.* barba, *m.* **old salt,** lobo de mar, *m.* **Old Testament,** Antiguo Testamento, *m.* **old wives' tale,** cuento de viejas, *m.* **old woman,** vieja, *f.* **Old World,** Viejo Mundo, mundo antiguo, *m*

old-age home /'ould 'eidʒ/ *n* asilo de ancianos, *m*

olden /'ouldən/ *a* antiguo. **o. days,** días pasados, *m pl*

older /'ouldər/ *a compar* más viejo, mayor. **The older the madder,** A la vejez viruelas

old hat *n* viejo conocido

oldish /'ouldɪʃ/ *a* bastante viejo, de cierta edad

oldness /'ouldnɪs/ *n* antigüedad, ancianidad, edad, *f*

oleaginous /,ouli'ædʒənəs/ *a* oleaginoso

oleander /'ouli,ændər/ *n Bot.* adelfa, *f,* baladre, *m*

olfactory /ɒl'fæktəri/ *a* olfatorio, olfativo

oligarchic /,ɒlɪ'gɑrkɪk/ *a* oligárquico

oligarchy /'ɒlɪ,gɑrki/ *n* oligarquía, *f*

olive /'ɒlɪv/ *n* (tree) olivo, *m;* (fruit) aceituna, oliva, *f,* *a* aceitunado. **wild o. tree,** acebuche, *m.* **o.-complexioned,** con tez aceitunada. **o. green,** verde oliva, *m.* **o. grove,** olivar, *m.* **o. oil,** aceite de oliva, *m*

olympiad /ə'lɪmpi,æd/ *n* olimpíada, *f*

olympian /ə'lɪmpiən/ *a* olímpico

olympic /ə'lɪmpɪk/ *a* olímpico. **o. games,** juegos olímpicos, *m pl*

olympus /ə'lɪmpəs/ *n* olimpo, *m*

omasum /ou'meisəm/ *n Zool.* librillo, libro, *m*

omber /'ɒmbər/ *n* tresillo, hombre, *m*

omega /ou'migə, ou'mei-/ *n* omega, *f*

omelet /'ɒmlɪt/ *n* tortilla, *f.* **sweet o.,** tortilla dulce, *f*

omen /'oumən/ *n* pronóstico, presagio, agüero, *m, vt* agorar, anunciar

ominous /'ɒmənəs/ *a* ominoso, azaroso, siniestro, amenazante

ominously /'ɒmənəsli/ *adv* ominosamente, con amenazas

omission /ou'mɪʃən/ *n* omisión, *f;* olvido, descuido, *m;* supresión, *f*

omit /ou'mɪt/ *vt* omitir; olvidar, descuidar; (suppress) suprimir, excluir, callar, dejar a un lado

omitting /ou'mɪtɪŋ/ *pres part* salvo, excepto

omnibus /'ɒmnə,bʌs/ *n* ómnibus, autobús, *m.* **o. conductor,** cobrador de autobús, *m.* **o. driver,** conductor de autobús, *m.* **o. route,** trayecto de autobús, *m.* **o. service,** servicio de autobuses, *m.* **o. volume,** volumen de obras coleccionadas, *m*

omnipotence /ɒm'nɪpətəns/ *n* omnipotencia, *f*

omnipotent /ɒm'nɪpətənt/ *a* omnipotente, todopoderoso

omnipresence /,ɒmnə'prɛzəns/ *n* omnipresencia, ubicuidad, *f*

omnipresent /,ɒmnə'prɛzənt/ *a* ubicuo

omniscience /ɒm'nɪʃəns/ *n* omnisciencia, *f*

omniscient /ɒm'nɪʃənt/ *a* omniscio, omnisciente

omnivorous /ɒm'nɪvərəs/ *a* omnívoro

on /ɒn/ *prep* (upon) sobre, en, encima de; (concerning) de, acerca de, sobre; (against) contra; (after) después; (according to) según; (with gerund) en; (with infin.) al; (at) a; (connected with, employed in) de; (by means of) por, mediante; (near to) cerca de, sobre; (into) en. Untranslated before days of week, dates of month or time of day (e.g. *on Monday,* el lunes. *on Friday afternoons,* los viernes por la tarde). **She has a bracelet on her wrist,** Tiene una pulsera en la muñeca. **He will retire on a good income,** Se jubilará con una buena renta. **on my uncle's death,** después de la muerte (or a la muerte) de mi tío, al morir. **On seeing them, he stopped,** Al verles se paró. **on leave,** con licencia, en uso de licencia. **on the next page,** en la página siguiente. **on this occasion,** en esta ocasión. **on the other hand,** en cambio. **on second thoughts,** luego de pensarlo bien. **on the way,** en camino. **on one side,** a un lado. **on the left,** a la izquierda. **on time,** a tiempo. **on my honor,** bajo palabra de honor. **on pain of death,** so pena de muerte, bajo pena de muerte. **on an average,** por término medio. **on his part,** por su parte. **on and after,** desde, a partir de. **on credit,** de fiado. **on fire,** ardiendo, en llamas. **on foot,** a pie. **on purpose,** a propósito; con intención. **on,** *adv* puesto (e.g. *She has her gloves on,* Tiene los guantes puestos); (forward) adelante, hacia adelante; (continue, with a verb) seguir, continuar (e.g. *He went on talking,* Siguió hablando). Often **on** is included in Sp. verb (e.g. *The new play is on,* Se ha estrenado la nueva comedia. *The fight is on,* Ya ha empezado la lucha). **On!** *interj* ¡Adelante! **and so on,** y así sucesivamente. **to have on,** llevar puesto. **on and off,** de vez en cuando. **on and on,** sin cesar

onanism /'ounə,nɪzəm/ *n* onanismo, *m*

once /wʌns/ *adv* una vez; (formerly) en otro tiempo, antiguamente; *conjunc* si (e.g. *O. you give him the opportunity,* Si le das la oportunidad). **all at o.,** todo junto, a un mismo tiempo; simultáneamente; (suddenly) súbitamente, de repente. **at o.,** en seguida, inmediatamente. **for o.,** por una vez. **more than o.,** más de una vez. **not o.,** ni siquiera una vez. **o. before,** una vez antes. **o. and for all,** una vez para siempre; por última vez. **o. in a while,** de vez en cuando. **o. more,** otra vez. **o. or twice,** una vez o dos, algunas veces. **o. too often,** una vez demasiado. **O. upon a time,** En tiempos pasados, En tiempos de Maricastaña; (as beginning of a story) Érase una vez, Había una vez, Hubo una vez

once in a blue moon a cada muerte de un obispo

one /wʌn/ *a* un, uno, una; (first) primero; (single) único, solo; (indifferent) igual, indiferente; (some, certain) algún, cierto, un (e.g. *one day,* cierto día). —*n* uno; (hour) la una; (of age) un año. Often not translated in Sp. (e.g. *I shall take the blue one,* Tomaré el azul). —*pron* se; uno. **one's,** su, de uno (e.g. *one's work,* el trabajo de uno). **I for one do not think so,** Yo por uno no lo creo. **It is all one,** Es igual, No hace diferencia alguna. **only one,** un solo. **that one,** ése, *m,* ésa, *f,* eso, *neut.* **this one,** éste, *m,* ésta, *f,* esto, *neut.* **these ones,** éstos, etc. **those ones,** ésos, etc. **the one,** el (que), *m,* la (que), *f.* **with one accord,** unánimemente. **one and all,** todos. **one an-**

other, se, uno a otro, mutuamente. **one by one,** uno a uno. **one day,** un día; un día de éstos, algún día. **one-eyed,** tuerto. **one-handed,** manco. **one-sided,** parcial. **one-way street,** calle de dirección única, *f.* **one-way traffic,** tráfico en una sola dirección, *m*

oneiric /ou'nairɪk/ *a* onírico

oneness /'wʌnnɪs/ *n* unidad, *f*

onerous /'ɒnərəs/ *a* oneroso, pesado, molesto, gravoso

onerousness /'ɒnərəsnɪs/ *n* pesadez, molestia, dificultad, inconveniencia, *f*

one-seater /'wʌn 'sitər/ *n* avión de una plaza, *m*

oneself /wʌn'sɛlf/ *pron* se, uno mismo (una misma); (after prep.) sí mismo, si. **It must be done by o.,** Uno mismo ha de hacerlo

onion /'ʌnyən/ *n* cebolla, *f.* **string of onions,** ristra de cebollas, *f.* **young o.,** babosa, *f.* **o. bed,** cebollar, *m.* **o. seed,** cebollino, *m.* **o. seller,** cebollero (-ra)

on-line /'ɒn'lain, 'ɔn-/ *a* conectado, en línea

onlooker /'ɒn,lʊkər/ *n* espectado (-ra), observador (-ra); testigo, *mf*

only /'ounli/ *a* único, solo. —*adv* únicamente, sólo; no... más (que), tan sólo; con la excepción de, salvo. —*conjunc* pero, salvo (que), si no fuera (que). **I shall o. give you three,** No te daré más de tres. **The o. thing one can do,** Lo único que se puede hacer. **I o. wished to see her,** Quería verla nada más. **if o.,** ¡ojalá (que)! **not o....,** no sólo... **o.-begotten,** *a* unigénito. **o. child,** hijo (-ja) único (-ca)

onomatopoeia /,ɒnə,mætə'piə/ *n* onomatopeya, *f*

onomatopoeic /,ɒnə,mætə'piɪk/ *a* onomatopéyico

onrush /'ɒn,rʌʃ/ *n* asalto, ataque, acometimiento, *m,* acometida, embestida, *f;* (of water, etc.) acceso, *m;* torrente, *m,* corriente, *f*

onset /'ɒn,sɛt/ *n* ataque, *m,* acometida, *f;* (beginning) principio, *m.* **at the first o.,** al primer ímpetu

onslaught /'ɒn,slɔt/ *n* asalto, ataque, *m*

ontology /ɒn'tɒlədʒi/ *n Philos.* ontología, *f*

onus /'ounəs/ *n* responsabilidad, *f.* **o. of proof,** obligación de probar, *f*

onward /'ɒnwərd/ *a* progresivo. —*adv* adelante, hacia adelante; (as a command) ¡Adelante!

onyx /'ɒnɪks/ *n Mineral.* ónice, *m*

ooze /uz/ *n* légamo, limo, fango, *m,* lama, *f.* —*vi* exudar, rezumarse; manar; *vt* sudar. **to o. satisfaction,** caérsele (a uno) la baba. **to o. away,** (of money, etc.) desaparecer, volar. **to o. out,** (news) divulgarse

oozing /'uzɪŋ/ *a* fangoso, legamoso, lamoso

opacity /ou'pæsɪti/ *n* opacidad, *f*

opal /'oupəl/ *n* ópalo, *m*

opalescence /,oupə'lɛsəns/ *n* opalescencia, *f*

opalescent /,oupə'lɛsənt/ *a* opalescente, iridiscente

opaline /'oupəlɪn/ *a* opalino

opaque /ou'peik/ *a* opaco

opaqueness /ou'peiknɪs/ *n* opacidad, *f*

op. cit. /'ɒp' sɪt/ (opere citato) obra cit. (obra citada)

open /'oupən/ *vt* abrir; (a package) desempaquetar, desenvolver; (remove lid) destapar; (unfold) desplegar; (inaugurate) inaugurar; iniciar, empezar; establecer; (an abscess) cortar; (with arms, heart, eyes) abrir; (with mind, thought) descubrir, revelar; (make accessible) franquear, hacer accesible; (tear) romper; *vi* abrirse; empezar, comenzar; (of a view, etc.) aparecer, extenderse; inaugurarse; (of a career, etc.) prepararse. **to o. fire against,** abrir el fuego contra. **to o. into,** comunicar con, salir a. **to o. into each other,** (of rooms) comunicarse. **to o. on,** mirar a, dar a, caer a. **to o. out,** *vt* abrir; desplegar; revelar. —*vi* extenderse; revelarse. **to o. the eyes of,** *Fig.* desengañar, desilusionar. **to o. up,** abrir; explorar, hacer accessible; revelar; *Fig. Inf.* desabrocharse. **to o. with** or **by,** empezar con

open /'oupən/ *a* abierto; descubierto; expuesto; (unfenced) descercado; (not private) público; libre; (unfolded) desplegado, extendido; (persuasible) receptivo; no resuelto, pendiente; (frank) franco, candoroso; (with sea) alto; (liberal) generoso, hospitalario; sin prejuicios; *Com.* abierto, pendiente; sin defensa; (of weather) despejado; (of a letter) sin sellar; (without a lid) destapado; (well-known) manifiesto, bien conocido. —*n* aire libre, *m.* **in the o.,** al descubierto. **in the o. air,** al aire libre, al raso, a cielo abierto. **to break o.,** forzar. **to cut o.,** abrir de un tajo, cortar. **to leave o.,** dejar abierto. **wide o.,** muy abierto; (of doors) de par en par. **o. boat,** barco descubierto, *m.* **o. car,** coche abierto, *m.* **o. carriage,** carruaje descubierto, *m.* **o. cast,** *Mineral.* roza abierta, *f.* **o.-eyed,** con los ojos abiertos. **o.-handed,** generoso, dadivoso. **o. letter,** carta abierta, *f.* **o.-minded,** imparcial. **o.-mouthed,** con la boca abierta, boquiabierto. **o. question,** cuestión por decidir, cuestión discutible, *f.* **o. secret,** secreto a voces, *m.* **o. sea,** alta mar, *f.* **o. town,** ciudad abierta, *f.* **o. tram-car,** jardinera, *f.* **o. truck,** vagoneta, *f.* **o.-work,** *Sew.* calado, enrejado, *m*

opener /'oupənər/ *n* abridor, *m*

opening /'oupənɪŋ/ *n* abertura, brecha, *f;* orificio, *m;* inauguración, apertura, *f;* principio, *m;* (chance) oportunidad, *f;* (employment) puesto, *m.* **o. price,** *Com.* (on Exchange) precio de apertura, *m,* primer curso *m*

openly /'oupənli/ *adv* abiertamente, francamente; públicamente

openness /'oupənnɪs/ *n* situación expuesta, *f;* espaciosidad, *f;* franqueza, *f,* candor, *m;* imparcialidad, *f*

opera /'ɒpərə/ *n* ópera, *f.* **comic o.,** zarzuela, *f.* **o.-cloak,** abrigo de noche, *m.* **o.-glasses,** gemelos de teatro, *m pl.* **o.-hat,** clac, *m.* **o.-house,** teatro de la ópera, *m.* **o. singer,** cantante de ópera, operista, *mf*

operate /'ɒpə,reit/ *vi* funcionar, trabajar; obrar; (with on, upon) producir efecto sobre; influir; *Surg.* operar; (on Exchange) especular, jugar a la bolsa; *vt* hacer funcionar, manejar; mover, impulsar; dirigir

operatic /,ɒpə'rætɪk/ *a* de ópera, operístico

operating /'ɒpə,reitɪŋ/ *a* (of surgeons) operante; de operación. **o. table,** mesa de operaciones, *f.* **o. theater,** anfiteatro, *m;* sala de operaciones, *f*

operation /,ɒpə'reiʃən/ *n* funcionamiento, *m,* acción, *f; Surg.* intervención quirúrgica, operación, *f;* (*Mil. Naut.*) maniobra, *f;* manipulación, *f.* **to come into o.,** ponerse en práctica; hacerse efectivo. **to continue in o.,** (**laws**) seguir en vigor. **to perform an o.,** *Surg.* operar, praticar una intervención quirúrgica; hacer una maniobra. **to put into o.,** poner en práctica

operative /'ɒpərətɪv/ *a* operativo, activo. —*n* operario (-ia), obrero (-ra). **to become o.,** tener efecto

operator /'ɒpə,reitər/ *n* operario (-ia); (telephone) telefonista, *mf;* (machines, engines) maquinista, *mf; Surg.* operador, *m*

operetta /,ɒpə'rɛtə/ *n* opereta, *f*

ophthalmologist /,ɒfθəl'mɒlədʒɪst/ *n* oftalmólogo, *m*

ophthalmology /,ɒfθəl'mɒlədʒi/ *n* oftalmología, *f*

opiate /'oupiɪt/ *n* opiata, *f,* narcótico, *m, a* opiado

opine /ou'pain/ *vi* and *vt* opinar, creer

opinion /ə'pɪnyən/ *n* opinión, *f,* parecer, juicio, *m;* concepto, *m,* idea, *f.* **in my o.,** según mi parecer. **to be of the o. that,** ser de la opinión que, opinar que. **to be of the same o.,** estar de acuerdo, concurrir. **public o.,** opinión (or voz) pública, *f*

opinionated /ə'pɪnyə,neitɪd/ *a* terco, obstinado

opium /'oupiəm/ *n* opio, *m.* **o. addict,** opiónamo (-ma). **o. den,** fumadero de opio, *m.* **o. eater,** mascador de opio, opiófago, *m.* **o. smoker,** fumador (-ra) de opio

Oporto /ou'pɔrtou/ Oporto, Porto, *m*

opponent /ə'pounənt/ *n* antagonista, *mf,* enemigo (-ga); contrario (-ia), adversario (-ia), competidor (-ra)

opportune /,ɒpər'tun/ *a* oportuno, tempestivo, conveniente, a propósito. **to be o.,** venir al caso. **o. moment,** momento oportuno, *m;* hora propicia, *f*

opportunely /,ɒpər'tunli/ *adv* oportunamente. **to come o.,** venir a pelo

opportuneness /,ɒpər'tunnɪs/ *n* oportunidad, tempestividad, conveniencia, *f*

opportunism /,ɒpər'tunɪzəm/ *n* oportunismo, *m*

opportunist /,ɒpər'tunɪst/ *n* oportunista, *mf*

opportunity /,ɒpər'tunɪti/ *n* oportunidad, ocasión, posibilidad, *f.* **to give an o. for,** dar margen para. **to open new opportunities,** abrir nuevos horizontes. **to take the o.,** tomar la oportunidad

opposable /ə'pouzəbəl/ *a* oponible

oppose /ə'pouz/ *vt* (counterbalance) oponer, contrarrestar; combatir; hacer frente (a), contrariar, pugnar contra, oponerse (a)
opposed (to) /ə'pouzd/ *a* opuesto a, enemigo de, contra
opposing /ə'pouzɪŋ/ *a* opuesto; enemigo, contrario
opposite /'ɒpəzɪt/ *a* (facing) de cara a, frente a, del otro lado de; opuesto; (antagonistic) contrario, antagónico; otro, diferente. —*n* contraria, *f,* lo opuesto; antagonista, *mf;* adversario (-ia). **the o. sex,** el otro sexo. **o. leaves,** *Bot.* hojas opuestas, *f pl.* **o. to,** frente a; distinto de
opposition /ˌɒpə'zɪʃən/ *n* oposición, *f;* (obstacle) estorbo, impedimento, *m,* dificultad, *f;* resistencia, hostilidad, *f;* (*Astron. Polit.*) oposición, *f;* (difference) contraste, *m,* diferencia, *f.* —*a* de la oposición. **in o.,** en oposición; *Polit.* en la oposición. **to be in o.,** estar en oposición; *Polit.* ser de la oposición, estar en la oposición
oppress /ə'prɛs/ *vt* oprimir, tiranizar, sojuzgar, apremiar; (of moral causes) abrumar, agobiar, desanimar; (of heat, etc.) ahogar
oppression /ə'prɛʃən/ *n* opresión, tiranía, crueldad, *f;* (moral) agobio, sufrimiento, *m,* ansia, *f;* (difficulty in breathing) sofocación, *f,* ahogo, *m*
oppressive /ə'prɛsɪv/ *a* opresivo, tiránico, cruel; (taxes, etc.) gravoso; (of heat) sofocante, asfixiante; agobiador, abrumador
oppressor /ə'prɛsər/ *n* opresor (-ra), sojuzgador (-ra), tirano (-na)
opprobrious /ə'proubriəs/ *a* oprobioso, vituperioso; infame
opprobrium /ə'proubriəm/ *n* oprobio, *m,* ignominia, *f*
opt /ɒpt/ *vi* optar, escoger, elegir
optic, optical *a* óptico. **o. illusion,** ilusión óptica, *f;* engaño a la vista, trampantojo, *m.* **o. nerve,** nervio óptico, *m*
optician /ɒp'tɪʃən/ *n* óptico, *m*
optics /'ɒptɪks/ *n* óptica, *f*
optimism /'ɒptəˌmɪzəm/ *n* optimismo, *m*
optimist /'ɒptəmɪst/ *n* optimista, *mf*
optimistic /ˌɒptə'mɪstɪk/ *a* optimista
optimum /'ɒptəməm/ *n* lo óptimo; (used as adjective) óptimo
option /'ɒpʃən/ *n* opción, *f,* (all meanings)
optional /'ɒpʃənl̩/ *a* discrecional, facultativo
opulence /'ɒpyələns/ *n* opulencia, riqueza, magnificencia, *f;* (abundance) abundancia, copia, *f*
opulent /'ɒpyələnt/ *a* opulento, rico, acaudalado; abundante
opus /'oupəs/ *n* obra, composición, *f*
opuscule /ou'pʌskyul/ *n* opúsculo, *m*
or /ɔr/ *conjunc* o; (before a word beginning with o or ho) u; (negative) ni. —*n Herald.* oro, *m.* **an hour or so,** una hora más o menos, alrededor de una hora. **either... or,** o... o. **or else,** o bien. **whether... or,** que... que, siquiera... siquiera, ya... ya. **without... or,** sin... ni
oracle /'ɔrəkəl/ *n* oráculo, *m*
oracular /ɔ'rækyələr/ *a* profético, vatídico; ambiguo, misterioso, sibilino; dogmático, magistral
oral /'ɔrəl/ *a* verbal, hablado; *Anat.* oral, bucal
oral cavity *n* cavidad bucal, *f*
orange /'ɔrɪndʒ/ *n* (tree) naranjo, *m;* (fruit) naranja, *f;* **bitter o.,** naranja amarga, *f.* **blood o.,** naranja dulce, *f.* **tangerine o.,** naranja mandarina, *f.* **o. blossom,** azahar, *m.* **o. color,** color de naranja, *m.* **o.-colored,** de color de naranja, anaranjado. **o.-flower water,** agua de azahar, *f.* **o. grove,** naranjal, *m.* **o. grower** (or **seller**), naranjero (-ra). **o. peel,** piel de naranja, *f.* **o.-stick,** (for nails) limpiauñas, *m*
orangeade /ˌɔrɪndʒ'eid/ *n* naranjada, *f;* (mineral water) gaseosa, *f*
orangery /'ɔrɪndʒri/ *n* naranjal, *m*
orangutan /ɔ'ræŋʊˌtæn/ *n Zool.* orangután, *m*
oration /ɔ'reiʃən/ *n* oración, declamación, *f,* discurso, *m*
orator /'ɔrətər/ *n* orador (-ra), declamador (-ra)
oratorical /ˌɔrə'tɔrɪkəl/ *a* oratorio, declamatorio, retórico
oratorio /ˌɔrə'tɔriˌou/ *n Mus.* oratorio, *m*
oratory /'ɔrəˌtɔri/ *n* oratoria, elocuencia, *f; Eccl.* oratorio, *m,* capilla, *f*
orb /ɔrb/ *n* orbe, *m;* esfera, *f,* globo, *m;* astro, *m; Poet.* ojo, *m*
orbit /'ɔrbɪt/ *n Astron.* órbita, *f; Anat.* órbita, cuenca del ojo, *f*
orbital /'ɔrbɪtl̩/ *a Anat.* orbital
orchard /'ɔrtʃərd/ *n* huerto, vergel, *m;* (especially of apples) pomar, *m*
orchestra /'ɔrkəstrə/ *n* orquesta, *f.* **with full o.,** con gran orquesta. *Theat.* **o. seat, o. stall,** butaca de platea, *f*
orchestral /ɔr'kɛstrəl/ *a* orquestal, instrumental
orchestrate /'ɔrkəˌstreit/ *vt* orquestar, instrumentar
orchestration /ˌɔrkə'streiʃən/ *n* orquestración, instrumentación, *f*
orchid /'ɔrkɪd/ *n* orquídea, *f*
orchitis /ɔr'kaitɪs/ *n Med.* orquitis, *f*
ordain /ɔr'dein/ *vt* mandar, disponer, decretar; *Eccl.* ordenar. **to be ordained as,** *Eccl.* ordenarse de
ordeal /ɔr'dil/ *n Hist.* ordalías, *f pl;* prueba severa, *f*
order /'ɔrdər/ *n* (most meanings) orden, *m;* (command) precepto, mandamiento, decreto, *m;* orden, *f;* (rule) regla, *f;* (for money) libranza postal, *f;* (for goods) pedido, encargo, *m;* (arrangement) método, arreglo, *m,* clasificación, *f;* (condition) estado, *m; Archit.* estilo, *m;* (*Zool. Bot.*) orden, *m;* (sort) clase, especie, *f;* (rank) clase social, *f; Eccl.* orden, *f;* (badge) condecoración, insignia, *f;* (association) sociedad, asociación, compañía, *f;* (to view a house, etc.) permiso, *m;* (series) serie, *f.* **in good o.,** en buen estado; arreglado. **in o.,** (alphabetical, etc.) en orden; arreglado; (parliamentary) en regla. **in o. that,** para que, a fin de que. **in o. to,** a fin de, para. **out of o.,** estropeado, descompuesto; (on a notice) No funciona; (parliamentary) fuera del orden del dia. **till further o.,** hasta nueva orden. **to o.,** *Com.* por encargo especial. **to give an o.,** dar una orden; *Com.* poner un pedido. **to go out of o.,** descomponerse. **to keep in o.,** mantener en orden. **to put in o.,** poner en orden, ordenar. **O.!** ¡Orden! orden real, *f.* **o. of knighthood,** orden de caballería, *f.* **o. of the day,** orden del día, *f.* reglamento, *m*
order /'ɔrdər/ *vt* disponer; arreglar; (command) mandar, ordenar; (request) rogar, pedir; (direct) dirigir, gobernar; *Com.* encargar, cometer; (a meal, a taxi) encargar. **I ordered them to do it,** Les mandé hacerlo. **to o. about,** mandar. **to o. back,** hacer volver, mandar que vuelva. **to o. down,** hacer bajar, pedir (a uno) que baje. **to o. in,** mandar entrar. **to o. off,** despedir, decir (a uno) que se vaya. **to o. out,** mandar salir; (the troops) hacer salir la tropa; echar. **to o. up,** mandar subir, hacer subir
orderliness /'ɔrdərlinɪs/ *n* orden, aseo, método, *m;* limpieza, *f;* buena conducta, formalidad, *f;* buena administración, *f*
orderly /'ɔrdərli/ *a* bien arreglado, metódico; aseado, en orden; (of behaviour) formal, bien disciplinado. —*n Mil.* ordenanza, *m;* ayudante de hospital *m*
ordinal /'ɔrdn̩əl/ *a* and *n* ordinal *m*
ordinance /'ɔrdn̩əns/ *n* ordenanza, *f,* reglamento, *m; Archit.* ordenación, *f; Eccl.* rito, *m*
ordinarily /ˌɔrdn̩'ɛərəli/ *adv* de ordinario, ordinariamente, comúnmente
ordinary /'ɔrdn̩ˌɛri/ *a* (usual) corriente, común, usual, ordinario, normal; (average) mediano, mediocre; (somewhat vulgar) ordinario, vulgar. —*n Eccl.* ordinario, *m.* **out of the o.,** excepcional; poco común. **o. seaman,** marinero, *m.* **o. share,** *Com.* acción ordinaria, *f*
ordination /ˌɔrdn̩'eiʃən/ *n Eccl.* ordenación, *f*
ordnance /'ɔrdnəns/ *n* artillería, *f,* cañones, *m pl;* pertrechos de guerra, *m pl.* **o. survey map,** mapa del estado mayor, *m.* **o. survey number,** acotación, *f*
ore /ɔr/ *n Mineral.* mena, *f,* quijo, *m*
organ /'ɔrgən/ *n* (all meanings) órgano, *m.* **barrel-o.,** organillo, órgano de manubrio, *m.* **o.-blower,** entonador (-ra). **o.-grinder,** organillero (-ra). **o.-loft,** tribuna del órgano, *f.* **o.-pipe,** cañón de órgano, *m.* **o.-stop,** registro de órgano, *m*
organdy *n* organdí, *m*

organic /ɔr'gænɪk/ *a* orgánico. **o. chemistry,** química orgánica, *f*
organism /'ɔrgə,nɪzəm/ *n* organismo, *m*
organist /'ɔrgənɪst/ *n* organista, *mf*
organization /,ɔrgənə'zeiʃən/ *n* organización, *f;* grupo, *m,* asociación, sociedad, *f;* organismo, *m*
organize /'ɔrgə,naiz/ *vt* organizar; arreglar. *—vi* organizarse; asociarse, constituirse
organizer /'ɔrgə,naizər/ *n* organizador (-ra)
organizing /'ɔrgə,naizɪŋ/ *a* organizador
orgasm /'ɔrgæzəm/ *n Med.* orgasmo, *m*
orgiastic /,ɔrdʒi'æstɪk/ *a* orgiástico
orgy /'ɔrdʒi/ *n* orgía, *f*
oriel /'ɔriəl/ *n Archit.* mirador, *m*
orient /'ɔriənt/ *a Poet.* naciente, oriental. *—n* Oriente, Este, *m.* **pearl of fine o.,** perla de hermoso oriente, *f*
oriental /,ɔri'ɛntl̩/ *a* and *n* oriental, *mf*
orientalism /,ɔri'ɛntl̩ɪzəm/ *n* orientalismo, *m*
orientalist /,ɔri'ɛntl̩ɪst/ *n* orientalista, *mf*
orientate /'ɔriən,teit/ *vt* orientar; dirigir, guiar. *—vi* mirar (or caer) hacia el este; orientarse
orientation /,ɔriən'teiʃən/ *n* orientación, *f*
orifice /'ɔrəfɪs/ *n* orificio, *m;* abertura, boca, *f*
origin /'ɔrɪdʒɪn/ *n* origen, génesis, *m;* raíz, causa, *f;* principio, comienzo, *m;* (extraction) descendencia, procedencia, familia, *f,* nacimiento, *m*
original /ə'rɪdʒənl̩/ *a* original; primitivo, primero; ingenioso. *—n* original, *m;* prototipo, modelo, *m.* **o. sin,** pecado original, *m*
originality /ə,rɪdʒə'nælɪti/ *n* originalidad, *f*
originally /ə'rɪdʒənl̩i/ *adv* originalmente; al principio; antiguamente
originate /ə'rɪdʒə,neit/ *vt* (produce) ocasionar, producir, suscitar, iniciar, engendrar; (create) inventar, crear. *—vi* originarse, surgir, nacer. **to o. in,** tener su origen en, surgir de, emanar de, venir de
origination /ə,rɪdʒə'neiʃən/ *n* origen, principio, génesis, *m*
originator /ə'rɪdʒə,neitər/ *n* iniciador (-ra), fundador (-ra); autor (-ra), creador (-ra)
oriole /'ɔri,oul/ *n Ornith.* oropéndola, *f*
Orion /ə'raiən/ *n Astron.* Orión, *m*
Orkneys, the /'ɔrkniz/ las Orcades, *f pl*
ornament /*n.* 'ɔrnəmənt; *v.* -,mɛnt/ *n* adorno, *m;* decoración, *f; Fig.* ornamento, *m;* (trinket) chuchería, *f, n pl.* **ornaments,** *Eccl.* ornamentos, *m pl. —vt* ornar, adornar, decorar, embellecer
ornamental /,ɔrnə'mɛntl̩/ *a* ornamental, decorativo
ornamentation /,ɔrnəmɛn'teiʃən/ *n* ornamentación, decoración, *f*
ornate /ɔr'neit/ *a* vistoso, ornado en demasía, barroco
ornateness /ɔr'neitnɪs/ *n* elegancia, vistosidad, magnificencia, *f*
ornithological /,ɔrnəθə'lɒdʒɪkəl/ *a* ornitológico
ornithologist /,ɔrnə'θɒlədʒɪst/ *n* ornitólogo, *m*
ornithology /,ɔrnə'θɒlədʒi/ *n* ornitología, *f*
orphan /'ɔrfən/ *a* and *n* huérfano (-na)
orphanage /'ɔrfənɪdʒ/ *n* orfanato, hospicio, *m*
orphanhood /'ɔrfən,hʊd/ *n* orfandad, *f*
Orphean /ɔr'fiən/ *a* órfico
orthodox /'ɔrθə,dɒks/ *a* ortodoxo
orthodoxy /'ɔrθə,dɒksi/ *n* ortodoxia, *f*
orthographic /,ɔrθə'græfɪk/ *a* ortográfico
orthography /ɔr'θɒgrəfi/ *n* ortografía, *f*
orthopedic /,ɔrθə'pidɪk/ *a* ortopédico
orthopedics /,ɔrθə'pidɪks/ *n* ortopedia, *f*
orthopedist /,ɔrθə'pidɪst/ *n* ortopedista, *mf* ortopédico (-ca)
oscillate /'ɒsə,leit/ *vi* oscilar, fluctuar; (hesitate) dudar, vacilar. *—vt* hacer oscilar
oscillation /,ɒsə'leiʃən/ *n* oscilación, fluctuación, vibración, *f; Elec.* oscilación, *f*
oscillator /'ɒsə,leitər/ *n* oscilador, *m*
oscillatory /'ɒsələ,tɔri/ *a* oscilante
osculation /,ɒskyə'leiʃən/ *n* ósculo, *m*
osier /'ouʒər/ *n Bot.* mimbre, *m,* or *f.* **o. bed,** mimbrera, *f*
osmic /'ɔzmɪk/ *a Chem.* ósmico
osmosis /ɒz'mousɪs/ *n* (*Phys. Chem.*) ósmosis, *f*
osprey /'ɒspri, -prei/ *n Ornith.* quebrantahuesos, *m*
osseous /'ɒsiəs/ *a* óseo
ossification /,ɒsəfɪ'keiʃən/ *n* osificación, *f*
ossify /'ɒsə,fai/ *vt* osificar; *vi* osificarse
ossuary /'ɒʃu,ɛri/ *n* osario, *m*
osteitis /,ɒsti'aitɪs/ *n Med.* osteítis, *f*
Ostend /ɒs'tɛnd/ Ostende, *m*
ostensible /ɒ'stɛnsəbəl/ *a* ostensible; aparente, engañoso, ilusorio
ostensibly /ɒ'stɛnsəbli/ *adv* en apariencia, ostensiblemente
ostentation /,ɒstɛn'teiʃən/ *n* ostentación, *f;* aparato, fausto, boato, alarde, *m,* soberbia, *f*
ostentatious /,ɒstɛn'teiʃəs/ *a* ostentoso; aparatoso, fastuoso, rumboso
ostentatiously /,ɒstɛn'teiʃəsli/ *adv* con ostentación
osteology /,ɒsti'ɒlədʒi/ *n* osteología, *f*
osteomyelitis /,ɒstiou,maiə'laitɪs/ *n Med.* osteomielitis, *f*
osteopath /'ɒstiə,pæθ/ *n* osteópata, *m*
osteopathy /,ɒsti'ɒpəθi/ *n* osteopatía, *f*
osteoplasty /'ɒstiə,plæsti/ *n Surg.* osteoplastia, *f*
ostler /'ɒslər/ *n* mozo de cuadras, establero, *m*
ostracism /'ɒstrə,sɪzəm/ *n* ostracismo, *m*
ostracize /'ɒstrə,saiz/ *vt* desterrar; excluir del trato, echar de la sociedad
ostrich /'ɔstrɪtʃ/ *n* avestruz, *m.*
otalgia /ou'tældʒiə/ *n Med.* otalgia, *f,* dolor de oídos, *m*
other /'ʌðər/ *a* otro. *—pron* el otro, *m;* la otra, *f;* lo otro, *neut adv* (with than) de otra manera que, de otro modo que; otra cosa que. **this hand, not the o.,** esta mano, no la otra. **every o. day,** un día sí y otro no, cada dos días. **no o.,** ningún otro, *m;* otra ninguna, *f.* **someone or o.,** alguien. **the others,** los (las) demás, *m, f pl;* los otros, *m pl;* las otras, *f pl.* **o. people,** otros, *m pl,* los demás
otherwise /'ʌðər,waiz/ *adv* de otra manera, de otro modo, otramente; (in other respects) por lo demás, por otra parte; (if not) si no
otitis /ou'taitɪs/ *n Med.* otitis, *f*
otologist /ou'tɒlədʒɪst/ *n* otólogo, *m*
otology /ou'tɒlədʒi/ *n* otología, *f*
otter /'ɒtər/ *n Zool.* nutria, *f.* **o. hound,** perro para cazar la nutria
ottoman /'ɒtəmən/ *a* otomano, turco. *—n* otomana, *f*
ouch! /autʃ/ *interj* ¡ax!, ¡huy!
ought /ɔt/ *v aux* deber, tener la obligación (de); ser conveniente, convenir; ser necesario (que), tener que. **I o. to have done it yesterday,** Debía haberlo hecho ayer. **She o. not to come,** No debe (debiera, debería) venir. **He o. to see them tomorrow,** (should) Conviene que les vea mañana; Tiene la obligación de verles mañana; (must) Es necesario que les vea mañana, Tiene que verles mañana.
ounce /auns/ *n* (animal and weight) onza, *f.* **He hasn't an o. of common sense,** No tiene pizca de sentido común
our /au^{ə}r *unstressed* ɑr/ *a* nuestro
ours /au^{ə}rz/ *pron* nuestro, *m;* nuestra, *f;* nuestros, *m pl;* nuestras, *f pl;* de nosotros, *m pl;* de nosotras, *f pl;* el nuestro, *m;* la nuestra, *f;* lo nuestro, *neut;* los nuestros, *m pl;* las nuestras, *f pl.* **This book is ours,** Este libro es nuestro (or el nuestro)
ourselves /ɑr'sɛlvz/ *pron pl* nosotros mismos, *m pl;* nosotras mismas, *f pl*
oust /aust/ *vt* despedir, desahuciar, expulsar, echar
out /aut/ *adv* afuera; hacia fuera; (gone out) fuera, salido, ausente; (invested) puesto; (published) publicado, salido; (discovered) conocido, descubierto; (on strike) en huelga; (mistaken) en error, equivocado; (of journeys) de ida, (on ships) de navegación (e.g. *on the second day out,* al segundo día de navegación); (of fire, etc.) extinguido; (at sea) en el mar; (of girls in society) puesta de largo, que ha entrado en sociedad; (of fashion) fuera de moda; (of office) fuera del poder; (in holes) roto, agujereado, andrajoso; (exhausted) agotado; (expired) vencido; (of a watch) llevar... minutos (horas) de atraso or de adelanto; (unfriendly) reñido; (way out) salida, *f;* (sport) fuera de juego; (of flowers) abierto; (of chickens) empollado. **a scene out of one of Shakespeare's plays,** una escena de una de las comedias de Shakespeare. **I am**

out $6, He perdido seis dólares. **I am out of tea,** Se me ha acabado el té. **to drink out of a glass,** beber de un vaso. **to read out of a book,** leer en un libro. **to speak out,** hablar claro. **Murder will out,** El asesinato se descubrirá. **out-and-out,** completo; (with rogue, etc.) redomado. **out of,** fuera de; (beyond) más allá de; (through, by) por; (with) con; (without) sin; (from among) entre; (in) en; (with a negative sense) no. **out of breath,** jadeante, sin aliento. **out of character,** impropio. **out of commission,** fuera de servicio. **out of danger,** fuera de peligro. **out of date,** anticuado. **out of hand,** en seguida; indisciplinado. **out of money,** sin dinero. **out of necessity,** por necesidad. **out of one's mind,** loco, demente. **out of order.** See **order. out of print,** agotado. **out of reach,** fuera de alcance, inasequible. **out of season,** fuera de temporada. **out of sight,** fuera del alcance de la vista; invisible. **Out of sight, out of mind,** Ojos que no ven, corazón que no siente. **out of sorts,** indispuesto. **out of temper,** de mal genio. **out of the question,** imposible. **out of the way,** *adv* (of work) terminado, hecho; (remote) fuera del camino; (put aside) arrinconado; donde no estorbe. **out-of-the-way,** *a* remoto, aislado; (unusual) extraordinario, singular. **out of this world,** lo máximo, lo último. **out of touch with,** alejado de; sin relaciones con; sin simpatía con. **out of work,** sin empleo, sin trabajo, en paro forzoso. **out-patient,** enfermo (-ma) de un dispensario. **Out!** *interj* ¡Fuera! ¡Fuera de aquí! ¡Márchate! **Out with it!** ¡Hable Vd.! sin rodeos! ¡Hablen claro!

outbalance /ˌaut'bæləns/ *vt* exceder, sobrepujar

outbid /ˌaut'bɪd/ *vt* pujar, mejorar

outbidding /ˌaut'bɪdɪŋ/ *n* puja, mejora, *f*

outbreak /'autˌbreik/ *n* (of war) declaración, *f;* comienzo, *m;* (of disease) epidemia, *f;* (of crimes, etc.) serie, *f*

outbuilding /'autˌbɪldɪŋ/ *n* dependencia, *f,* edificio accesorio, anexo, *m*

outburst /'autˌbɜrst/ *n* acceso, arranque, *m,* explosión, *f*

outcast /'autˌkæst/ *n* paria, *mf;* desterrado (-da), proscripto (-ta)

outclass /ˌaut'klæs/ *vt* aventajar, ser superior (a), exceder

outcome /'autˌkʌm/ *n* consecuencia, *f,* resultado, *m*

outcry /'autˌkrai/ *n* clamor, grito, *m;* protesta, *f*

outdistance /ˌaut'dɪstəns/ *vt* dejar atrás

outdo /ˌaut'du/ *vt* eclipsar, aventajar, sobrepujar

outdoor /'autˌdɔr/ *a* externo; (of activities) al aire libre; fuera de casa

outdoors /ˌaut'dɔrz/ *adv* fuera de casa; al aire libre

outer /'autər/ *a* externo, exterior

outermost /'autərˌmoust/ *a superl* (el, etc.) más externo, más exterior; extremo, de más allá

outer space espacio extraatmosférico, espacio exterrestre, espacio exterior, espacio sideral, espacio sidéreo, espacio ultraterrestre, *m*

outfit /'autˌfɪt/ *n* equipo, *m;* (of clothes) traje, *m;* (of furniture or trousseau) ajuar, *m;* (gear) pertrechos, avíos, *m pl.* —*vt* aviar equipar

outfitter /'autˌfɪtər/ *n* proveedor (-ra), abastecedor (-ra)

outflank /ˌaut'flæŋk/ *vt Mil.* flanquear; ser más listo (que)

outgoing /'autˌgouɪŋ/ *a* saliente, que sale; cesante. **outgoings,** *n pl* gastos, *m pl*

outgrow /ˌaut'grou/ *vt* hacerse demasiado grande para; crecer más que; (ideas) perder; (illness) curarse de, curarse con la edad; pasar de la edad de, ser ya viejo para. **to o. one's clothes,** quedársele a uno chica la ropa.

outgrowth /'autˌgrouθ/ *n* excrecencia, *f;* resultado, fruto, *m,* consecuencia, *f*

outhouse /'autˌhaus/ *n* edificio accesorio, *m*

outing /'autɪŋ/ *n* excursión, vuelta, *f,* paseo, *m*

outlandish /aut'lændɪʃ/ *a* extraño, singular, raro; absurdo, ridículo

outlast /ˌaut'læst/ *vt* durar más que; (outlive) sobrevivir a

outlaw /'autˌlɔ/ *n* bandido, proscrito, *m, vt* proscribir

outlay /'autˌlei/ *n* gasto, desembolso, *m*

outlet /'autlɛt/ *n* salida, *f;* orificio de salida, *m;* (of drains, etc.) desagüe, *m;* (of streets, rivers) desembocadura, *f; Fig.* escape, *m,* válvula de seguridad, *f*

outline /'autˌlain/ *n* perfil, contorno, *m;* (drawing) esbozo, bosquejo, *m;* idea general, *f;* plan general, *m, vt* esbozar, bosquejar. **in o.,** en esbozo; en perfil. **to be outlined** (against), dibujarse (contra), destacarse (contra)

outlive /ˌaut'lɪv/ *vt* sobrevivir (a); (live down) hacer olvidar

outlook /'autˌlʊk/ *n* (view) perspectiva, vista, *f;* (opinion) actitud, *f,* punto de vista, *m;* aspecto, *m,* apariencia, *f;* (for trade, etc.) perspectiva, *f,* posibilidades, *f pl.* **o. tower,** atalaya, *f*

outlying /'autˌlaiɪŋ/ *a* remoto, lejano, distante

outmaneuver /ˌautmə'nuvər/ *vt* superar en estrategia

outmatch /ˌaut'mætʃ/ *vt* aventajar, superar

outmoded /ˌaut'moudɪd/ *a* anticuado, pasado de moda

outnumber /ˌaut'nʌmbər/ *vt* ser más numerosos que, exceder en número

out-of-court settlement /'aut əv ˌkɔrt/ *n* arreglo pacífico, *m*

out-of-town *a* de las provincias

outpost /'autˌpoust/ *n Mil.* avanzada, *f,* puesto avanzado, *m*

outpouring /'autˌpɔrɪŋ/ *n* derramamiento, *m;* efusión, *f*

output /'autˌpʊt/ *n* producción, *f.* **o. capacity,** capacidad de producción, *f*

outrage /'autreidʒ/ *n* barbaridad infamia, atrocidad, *f;* rapto, *m,* violación, *f.* —*vt* ultrajar; violar;

outrageous /aut'reidʒəs/ *a* atroz, terrible; desaforado, monstruoso; injurioso; ridículo

outrageousness /aut'reidʒəsnɪs/ *n* lo atroz; violencia, furia, *f;* escándalo, *m;* enormidad, *f;* lo excesivo; lo horrible

outré /u'trei/ *a* cursi, extravagante

outride /ˌaut'raid/ *vt* cabalgar más a prisa que

outright /*adv.* 'aut'rait; *a.* 'autˌrait/ *adv* (frankly) de plano (e.g. *to reject outright,* rechazar de plano), francamente, sin reserva; (immediately) en seguida, immediatamente. —*a* categórico; completo; franco

outrival /'autˌraivəl/ *vt* vencer, superar

outrun /ˌaut'rʌn/ *vt* correr más que

outset /'autˌsɛt/ *n* principio, comienzo, *m*

outshine /ˌaut'ʃain/ *vt* brillar más que, eclipsar en brillantez; superar, eclipsar

outside /*adv., prep., a.* ˌaut'said; *n.* 'aut'said/ *adv* afuera, fuera. —*prep* fuera de, al otro lado de, al exterior de; (besides) aparte de, fuera de. —*a* externo, exterior; (of labor, etc.) desde fuera; máximo; ajeno. —*n* exterior, *m;* superficie, *f;* aspecto, *m,* apariencia, *f.* **at the o.,** a lo sumo, cuando más. **from the o.,** de (or desde) fuera. **on the o.,** (externally) por fuera. **o. the door,** a la puerta

outsider /ˌaut'saidər/ *n* forastero (-ra); desconocido (-da); caballo desconocido, *m;* persona poco deseable, *f*

outsize /'autˌsaiz/ *n* artículo de talla mayor que las corrientes, *m*

outskirts /'aut'skɜrts/ *n pl* alrededores, *m pl,* afueras, immediaciones, cercanías, *f pl*

outspoken /'aut'spoukən/ *a* franco. **to be o.,** decir lo que se piensa, no tener pelos en la lengua

outspokenness /'aut'spoukənnɪs/ *n* franqueza, *f,*

outspread /'autˌsprɛd/ *a* extendido; (of wings) desplegadas

outstanding /ˌaut'stændɪŋ/ *a* excelente; sobresaliente, conspicuo; *Com.* pendiente, sin pagar. **to be o.,** *Com.* estar pendiente; *Fig.* sobresalir. **o. account,** *Com.* cuenta pendiente, *f*

outstay /ˌaut'stei/ *vt* quedarse más tiempo que. **to o. one's welcome,** pegársele la silla

outstretched /ˌaut'strɛtʃt/ *a* extendido

outstrip /ˌaut'strɪp/ *vt* dejar atrás, pasar; aventajar, superar

outvote /ˌaut'vout/ *vt* emitir más votos que; rechazar por votación

outward /'autwərd/ *a* exterior, externo; aparente, visible. —*adv* exteriormente; hacia fuera; superficial-

mente. **o. bound,** con rumbo a... **o. voyage,** el viaje de ida
outwardly /'autwərdli/ *adv* exteriormente; hacia fuera; en apariencia
outwear /ˌaut'wɛər/ *vt* durar más que; gastar
outweigh /ˌaut'wei/ *vt* exceder, valer más que
outwit /ˌaut'wɪt/ *vt* ser más listo que; vencer
outworn /'aut'wɔrn/ *a* anticuado, ya viejo
oval /'ouvəl/ *n* óvalo, *m, a* oval, ovalado, aovado
ovarian /ou'vɛəriən/ *a* (*Bot. Zool.*) ovárico
ovary /'ouvəri/ *n* ovario, *m*
ovation /ou'veiʃən/ *n* ovación, recepción entusiasta, *f*
oven /'ʌvən/ *n* horno, *m*. **o. peel,** pala de horno, *f*. **o. rake,** hurgón, *m*
over /'ouvər/ *prep* (above, upon, over) sobre, encima de; (on the other side) al otro lado de; (across) allende, a través de; (more than) más de; (beyond) más allá de; (of rank) superior a; (during) durante; (in addition) además de; (through) por. —*n* en; por encima; al otro lado; de un lado a otro; enfrente; al lado contrario; de un extremo a otro; (finished) terminado; (ruined) arruinado, perdido; (more) más; (excessively) demasiado, excesivamente; (covered) cubierto (de); (extra) en exceso; (completely) enteramente; (from head to foot) de pies a cabeza, de hito en hito; (of time) pasado. **over** is also used as a prefix. Indicating excess, it is generally translated by demasiado or excesivamente. In other meanings, it is either not translated or its meaning forms part of the verb, being translated as re-, super-, trans-, ultra. Very often a less literal translation is more successful than the employment of the above prefixes. **all o.,** (everywhere) en todas partes; (finished) todo acabado; (covered) cubierto (de); (up and down) de pies a cabeza. **all the world o.,** en todo el mundo. **He is o. in Germany,** Está en Alemania. **He trembled all o.,** Estaba todo tembloroso. **that which is o.,** el exceso, lo que queda. **to read o.,** leer, repasar. **o. again,** de nuevo. **o. and above,** por encima de, fuera de, en exceso de. **o. and o.,** repetidamente, muchas veces. **o. my signature,** bajo mi firma. **o. six months since...,** más de seis meses desde que...
overabundance /ˌouvərə'bʌndəns/ *n* sobreabundancia, *f*
overabundant /ˌouvərə'bʌndənt/ *a* sobreabundante
overact /ˌouvər'ækt/ *vt* exagerar (un papel)
overall /'ouvərˌɔl/ *n* bata, *f;* guardapolvo, *m; a* de conjunto (e.g., *overall assessment,* evaluación de conjunto) *pl* **overalls,** mono, *m*
overanxious /ˌouvər'æŋkʃəs/ *a* demasiado ansioso; demasiado inquieto. **to be o.-a.,** preocuparse demasiado
overarch /ˌouvər'ɑrtʃ/ *vt* abovedar
overawe /ˌouvər'ɔ/ *vt* intimidar, acobardar
overbalance /ˌouvər'bæləns/ *vt* hacer perder el equilibrio. hacer caer; preponderar. —*vi* perder el equilibrio, caer
overbalancing /'ouvərˌbælənsɪŋ/ *n* pérdida del equilibrio, caída, *f;* preponderancia, *f*
overbearing /ˌouvər'bɛərɪŋ/ *a* dominante, autoritario, imperioso
overboard /'ouvərˌbɔrd/ *adv* al agua, al mar.
overburden /ˌouvər'bɜrdn̩/ *vt* sobrecargar, agobiar
overcast /*a.* 'ouvər'kæst; *v.* ˌouvər'kæst/ *a* anublado, cerrado, encapotado. —*vt Sew.* sobrehilar. **to become o.,** anublarse
overcharge /*n.* 'ouvərˌtʃɑrdʒ; *v.* ˌouvər'tʃɑrdʒ/ *n* recargo, *m:* (price) recargo de precio, precio excesivo, *m.* —*vt* recargar, cobrar un precio excesivo; *Elec.* sobrecargar. —*vi* cobrar demasiado
overcloud /ˌouvər'klaud/ *vt* anublar; *Fig.* entristecer
overcoat /'ouvərˌkout/ *n* abrigo, sobretodo, gabán, *m*
overcome /ˌouvər'kʌm/ *vt* vencer, rendir, subyugar; (difficulties) triunfar de, allanar, dominar. —*vi* saber vencer. —*a* (by sleep, etc.) rendido; (at a loss) turbado, confundido; (by kindness) agradecidisimo
overconfidence /ˌouvər'kɒnfɪdəns/ *n* confianza excesiva, *f*
overcooked /'ouvərˌkʊkt/ *a* recocido, demasiado cocido
overcrowd /ˌouvər'kraud/ *vt* atestar, llenar de bote en bote; (over-populate) sobrepoblar
overcrowding /'ouvərˌkraudɪŋ/ *n* sobrepoblación, *f*
overdo /ˌouvər'du/ *vt* exagerar; ir demasiado lejos, hacer demasiado; *Cul.* recocer; (overtire) fatigarse demasiado
overdose /'ouvərˌdous/ *n* dosis excesiva, *f*
overdraft /'ouvərˌdræft/ *n Com.* giro en descubierto, *m*
overdraw /ˌouvər'drɔ/ *vt* and *vi Com.* girar en descubierto
over-dressed /'ouvər 'drɛst/ *a* que viste demasiado; cursi
overdue /ˌouvər'du/ *a* atrasado; *Com.* vencido y no pagado
overeat /ˌouvər'it/ *vi* comer demasiado, atracarse
overestimate /ˌouvər'ɛstəˌmeit/ *vt* estimar en valor excesivo; exagerar, sobreestimar, *n* presupuesto excesivo, *m;* estimación excesiva, *f*
overexcite /ˌouvərɪk'sait/ *vt* sobreexcitar
overexposure /ˌouvərɪk'spouʒər/ *n Photo.* exceso de exposición, *m*
overfatigue /ˌouvərfə'tig/ *vt* fatigar demasiado. —*n* cansancio excesivo, *m*
overfeeding /'ouvərˌfidɪŋ/ *n* sobrealimentación, *f*
overflow /*v.* ˌouvər'flou; *n.* 'ouvərˌflou/ *vt* inundar, derramarse por; *Fig.* cubrir, llenar; desbordarse. —*vi* (with) rebosar de. —*n* inundación, *f*, desbordamiento, derrame, *m; Fig.* residuo, resto, exceso, *m;* (plumbing) sumidero, vertedero, *m*, descarga, *f*. **The river overflowed its banks,** El río se desbordó, El río salió de cauce
overflowing /ˌouvər'flouɪŋ/ *a* rebosante; superabundante. **filled to o.,** lleno hasta los bordes.
overgrown /ˌouvər'groun/ *a* (gawky) talludo; (plants) exuberante, vicioso; frondoso, cubierto de verdura
overhang /ˌouvər'hæŋ/ *vt* caer a, mirar a; colgar; *Fig.* amenazar. —*vi* colgar, sobresalir; *Fig.* amenazar
overhanging /'ouvərˌhæŋɪŋ/ *a* saledizo, sobresaliente; colgante, pendiente
overhaul /*v.* ˌouvər'hɔl; *n.* 'ouvərˌhɔl/ *vt* examinar, investigar; componer, hacer una inspección general de; (of boats overtaking) alcanzar. —*n* examen, *m*, investigación, *f; Med.* exploración general, *f*
overhead /'ouvər'hɛd/ *adv* arriba, en lo alto, encima de la cabeza. —*a* aéreo, elevado; general, fijo. **o. cable,** cable eléctrico, *m*. **o. expenses,** gastos generales, *m pl.* **o. railway,** ferrocarril aéreo (or elevado), *m*
overhear /ˌouvər'hɪər/ *vt* (accidentally) oír por casualidad, oír sin querer; (on purpose) alcanzar a oír, lograr oír
overheat /ˌouvər'hit/ *vt* acalorar, hacer demasiado caliente, recalentar. —*vi* (in argument) acalorarse; hacerse demasiado caliente
overheating /ˌouvər'hitɪŋ/ *n* recalentramiento, *m*
overindulge /ˌouvərɪn'dʌldʒ/ *vt* mimar demasiado; dedicarse a algo con exceso; tomar algo con exceso. —*vi* darse demasiada buena vida
overjoyed /'ouvərˌdʒɔid/ *a* contentísimo, lleno de alegría, encantado
overland /'ouvərˌlænd/ *adv* por tierra. —*a* terrestre, trascontinental
overlap /*v.* ˌouvər'læp; *n.* 'ouvərˌlæp/ *vi* traslaparse; coincidir. —*n* traslapo, *m*
overlay /ˌouvər'lei/ *vt* cubrir, dar una capa; (with silver) platear; (with gold) dorar. —*n* capa, *f;* cubierta, *f*
overleaf /'ouvərˌlif/ *adv* a la vuelta
overload /*v.* ˌouvər'loud; *n.* 'ouvərˌloud/ *vt* sobrecargar, recargar. —*n* sobrecarga, *f*
overlook /ˌouvər'lʊk/ *vt* (face) dar a, mirar a, dominar; (supervise) vigilar, examinar, inspeccionar; (not notice) no notar, pasar por alto, no hacer, caso de, no fijarse en; (neglect) desdeñar; (ignore) no darse cuenta de, ignorar; (excuse) perdonar, tolerar, hacer la vista gorda
overlord /'ouvərˌlɔrd/ *n* señor de horca y cuchillo, señor, jefe, *m*
overmuch /'ouvər'mʌtʃ/ *adv* demasiado, en exceso
overnight /*adv.* 'ouvər'nait; *a.* 'ouvərˌnait/ *adv* la noche pasada, durante la noche; toda la noche. —*a* de la víspera, nocturno. **to stay o. with,** pasar la noche con

overpass /'ouvər,pæs/ *n* pasaje elevado, viaducto, *m*

overpay /,ouvər'pei/ *vt* pagar demasiado

overpayment /'ouvər,peimənt/ *n* pago excesivo, *m*

overpopulate /,ouvər'pɒpyə,leit/ *vt* sobrepoblar, become overpopulated recargarse de habitantes (with people), recargarse de animales (with animals)

overpower /,ouvər'pauər/ *vt* vencer, subyugar; (of scents, etc.) trastornar; rendir, dominar

overpowering /,ouvər'pauərıŋ/ *a* irresistible

overpraise /,ouvər'preiz/ *vt* encarecer, alabar mucho

overproduce /,ouvərprə'dus/ *vt* and *vi* sobreproducir

overproduction /,ouvərprə'dʌkʃən/ *n* sobreproducción, *f*

overrate /,ouvər'reit/ *vt* exagerar el valor de; (of property) sobrevalorar

overreach /,ouvər'ritʃ/ *vt* sobrealcanzar. **to o. oneself,** sobrepasarse, ir demasiado lejos

override /,ouvər'raid/ *vt* (trample) pasar por encima (de); *Fig.* rechazar, poner a un lado; (bully) dominar; (a horse) fatigar, reventar

overripe /'ouvər'raip/ *a* demasiado maduro

overrule /,ouvər'rul/ *vt Law.* denegar, no admitir; vencer

overrun /,ouvər'rʌn/ *vt* (flood) inundar; (ravage) invadir; (infest) plagar, infestar, desbordarse, derramarse

overseas /*a.* 'ouvər'siz; *adv.* ,ouvər'siz/ *a* ultramarino, de ultramar. —*adv* en ultramar, allende los mares

oversee /,ouvər'si/ *vt* vigilar, inspeccionar

overseer /'ouvər,siər/ *n* capataz, mayoral, sobrestante, contramaestre, *m;* inspector (-ra), veedor (-ra)

oversell /,ouvər'sɛl/ *vt* and *vi* vender en exceso

oversensitive /,ouvər'sɛnsıtıv/ *a* demasiado sensitivo; vidrioso; susceptible

oversew /'ouvər,sou/ *vt* sobrecoser

overshadow /,ouvər'ʃædou/ *vt* sombrear; *Fig.* eclipsar, obscurecer; (sadden) entristecer

overshoe /'ouvər,ʃu/ *n* chanclo, *m;* (for snow) galocha, *f*

overshoot /,ouvər'ʃut/ *vt* tirar más allá del blanco; *Fig.* exceder, rebasar el límite conveniente, **overshoot the target** (fig.) ir más allá del blanco, ir más allá de lo razonable. **to o. oneself,** exagerar; propasarse, descomedirse

oversight /'ouvər,sait/ *n* inadvertencia, omisión, equivocación, *f;* descuido, *m*

oversimplify /,ouvər'sımplə,fai/ *vt* simplificar en exceso

oversleep /,ouvər'slip/ *vi* dormir demasiado; *Inf.* pegársele a uno las sábanas, levantarse demasiado tarde

overspend /,ouvər'spɛnd/ *vt* and *vi* gastar demasiado

overspread /,ouvər'sprɛd/ *vt* desparramar, salpicar, esparcir, sembrar; cubrir

overstate /,ouvər'steit/ *vt* exagerar, encarecer, ponderar

overstatement /,ouvər'steitmənt/ *n* exageración, ponderación, *f*

overstep /,ouvər'stɛp/ *vt* exceder, pasar, violar; rebasar, pasar más allá (de)

overstrain /,ouvər'strein/ *vt* fatigar demasiado, agotar. —*n* fatiga, *f.* **to o. oneself,** esforzarse demasiado, cansarse demasiado

overstrung /,ouvər'strʌŋ/ *a* nervioso, excitable; (piano) de cuerdas cruzadas

oversubscribe /,ouvərsəb'skraib/ *vt* subscribir en exceso

overt /ou'vɜrt/ *a* abierto, público; manifiesto, evidente

overtake /,ouvər'teik/ *vt* alcanzar, pasar, dejar atrás; adelantarse (a); (surprise) coger, sorprender; (overwhelm) vencer, dominar

overtax /,ouvər'tæks/ *vt* oprimir de tributos; agobiar, cansar demasiado

overthrow /*v.* ,ouvər'θrou; *n.* 'ouvər,θrou/ *vt* volcar, echar por tierra, derribar; *Fig.* vencer, destruir, destronar. —*n* vuelco, derribo, *m; Fig.* destrucción, ruina, *f*

overtime /'ouvər,taim/ *adv* fuera de las horas estipuladas. —*n* horas extraordinarias de trabajo, *f pl.* **to work o.,** trabajar horas extraordinarias

overtone /'ouvər,toun/ *n Mus.* armónico, *m*

overtop /,ouvər'tɒp/ *vt* dominar, sobresalir, elevarse encima de

overture /'ouvərtʃər/ *n Mus.* obertura, *f*

overturn /,ouvər'tɜrn/ *vt* volcar, derribar, echar a rodar, echar abajo; (upset) revolver, desordenar. —*vi* volcar, venirse abajo, allanarse; estar revuelto

overturning /,ouvər'tɜrnıŋ/ *n* vuelco, salto de campana, *m*

overweening /'ouvər'winıŋ/ *a* arrogante, insolente, altivo

overweight /'ouvər,weit/ *n* sobrepeso, exceso en el peso, *m.* **to be o.,** pesar más de lo debido

overwhelm /,ouvər'wɛlm/ *vt* (conquer) vencer, aplastar, derrotar; (of waves, etc.) sumergir, hundir, inundar, engolfar; (in argument) confundir, dejar confuso, avergonzar; (of grief, etc.) vencer, postrar, dominar; (of work) inundar

overwhelming /,ouvər'wɛlmıŋ/ *a* irresistible, invencible, abrumador, apabullante

overwind /,ouvər'waind/ *vt* (a watch) dar demasiada cuerda a; romper la cuerda de

overwork /*v.* ,ouvər'wɜrk; *n.* 'ouvər,wɜrk/ *vt* hacer trabajar demasiado (or con exceso); esclavizar. —*vi* trabajar demasiado. —*n* exceso de trabajo, demasiado trabajo, *m*

overwrought /'ouvər'rɔt/ *a* (overworked) agotado por el trabajo, rendido, muy cansado; nerviosísimo, sobreexcitado, exaltado, muy agitado

ovine /'ouvain/ *a* ovejuno

ovoid /'ouvɔid/ *a* ovoide

ovulation /,ɒvyə'leiʃən/ *n Med.* ovulación, *f*

owe /ou/ *vt* deber, tener deudas (de); deber, estar agradecido (por), estar obligado (a). —*vi* estar en deuda, estar endeudado, tener deudas. **He owes his tailor $30,** Le debe treinta dólares a su sastre. **I owe him thanks for his help,** Le estoy agradecido por su ayuda (*or* Le debo las gracias por...). **He owes his success to good fortune,** Su éxito se debe a la suerte

owing /'ouıŋ/ *a* sin pagar. **o. to,** debido a, a causa de, por. **We had to stay in o. to the rain,** Tuvimos que quedarnos en casa a causa de la lluvia. **What is o. to you now?** ¿Cuánto se le debe ahora?

owl /aul/ *n* búho, mochuelo, *m.* **barn** or **screech owl,** lechuza, *f.* **brown owl,** autillo, *m*

owlish /'aulıʃ/ *a* parecido a un búho, de búho

own /oun/ *a* propio. —*n* (dearest) bien, *m.* —*vt* poseer, tener, ser dueño de; (recognize) reconocer; (admit) confesar. —*vi* confesar. **my (thy, his, our, your) own,** mi (tu, su, nuestro, vuestro) propio, *m,* (*f,* propia); mis (tus, sus, nuestros, vuestros) propios, *m pl,* (*f pl,* propias); (when not placed before a noun) el mío (tuyo, suyo, nuestro, vuestro), la mía (tuya, etc.), los míos (tuyos, etc.), las mías (tuyas, etc.); (relations) los suyos. **in his own house,** en su propia casa. **my (thy, his, etc.) own self,** yo (tú, él) mismo, *m,* (*f,* misma, *m pl,* mismos, *f pl,* mismas). **a room of one's own,** un cuarto para sí (or para uno mismo). **to be on one's own,** ser independiente; estar a solas. **to hold one's own,** mantenerse en sus trece. **to own up,** confesar

owner /'ounər/ *n* dueño (-ña), propietario (-ia), poseedor (-ra)

ownerless /'ounərlıs/ *a* sin dueño, sin amo

ownership /'ounər,ʃıp/ *n* posesión, *f,* dominio, *m;* propiedad, *f*

ox /ɒks/ *n* buey (*pl* bueyes), *m.* **oxeye daisy,** margarita, *f.* **oxstall,** boyera, *f*

oxidation /,ɒksı'deiʃən/ *n Chem.* oxidación, *f*

oxide /'ɒksaid/ *n Chem.* óxido, *m*

oxidization /,ɒksədı'zeiʃən, -,dai-/ *n* oxidación, *f*

oxidize /'ɒksı,daiz/ *vt Chem.* oxidar; *vi* oxidarse

oxygen /'ɒksıdʒən/ *n* oxígeno, *m.* **o. mask,** máscara de oxígeno, *f.* **o. tent,** tienda de oxígeno, *f*

oxygenate /'ɒksıdʒə,neit/ *vt Chem.* oxigenar

oxygenation /,ɒksıdʒə'neiʃən/ *n Chem.* oxigenación, *f*

oyez, oyez! /'ouyei, 'ouyɛs, 'ouɛz/ *interj* ¡oíd!

oyster /'ɔistər/ *n* ostra, *f.* **o. bed,** pescadero (or criadero) de ostras, *m.* **o. culture,** ostricultura, *f*

ozone /'ouzoun/ *n* ozono, *m*

P

p /pi/ *n* (letter) pe, *f.* **to mind one's p's and q's,** poner los puntos sobre las íes; ir con pies de plomo
pabulum /ˈpæbyələm/ *n* pábulo, *m;* sustento, *m*
pace /peis/ *n* paso, *m;* (gait) andar, *m,* marcha, *f;* (of a horse) andadura, *f;* (speed) velocidad, *f.* —*vi* pasear(se), andar; (of a horse) amblar. —*vt* recorrer, andar por; marcar el paso para; (with out) medir a pasos. **at a good p.,** a un buen paso. **to keep p. with,** ajustarse al paso de, ir al mismo paso que; andar al paso de; (events) mantenerse al corriente de. **to p. up and down,** pasearse, dar vueltas. **p.-maker,** el que marca el paso
paced /peist/ *a* de andar...; (of a horse) de andadura...; de paso...
pachyderm /ˈpækɪˌdɜrm/ *n* paquidermo, *m*
pacific /pəˈsɪfɪk/ *a Geog.* pacífico; sosegado, tranquilo, pacífico. **He is of a p. disposition,** Es amigo de la paz
pacification /ˌpæsəfɪˈkeiʃən/ *n* pacificación, *f*
pacificatory /pəˈsɪfɪkəˌtɔri/ *a* pacificador
Pacific, the el (Océano) Pacífico, *m*
pacifier /ˈpæsəˌfaiər/ *n* pacificador (-ra)
pacifism /ˈpæsəˌfɪzəm/ *n* pacifismo, *m*
pacifist /ˈpæsəfɪst/ *a* pacifista. —*n* pacifista, *mf*
pacify /ˈpæsəˌfai/ *vt* pacificar; calmar, tranquilizar; aplacar, conciliar
pack /pæk/ *n* (bundle) fardo, lío, *m;* paquete, *m;* (load) carga, *f;* (of hounds) jauría, *f;* (herd) hato, *m;* (of seals) manada, *f;* (of cards) baraja (de naipes), *f;* (of rogues) cuadrilla, *f;* (of lies, etc.) colección, *f;* masa, *f;* (of ice) témpanos flotantes, *m pl;* (Rugby football) delanteros, *m pl;* (for the face) compresa, *f.* **p.-horse,** caballo de carga, *m.* **p.-needle,** aguja espartera, *f.* **p.-saddle,** albarda, *f.* **p.-thread,** bramante, *m*
pack /pæk/ *vt* embalar; empaquetar; envasar; encajonar; (a suit-case, etc.) hacer; (cram) apretar; (crowd) atestar, llenar; (a pipe joint, etc.) empaquetar; (an animal) cargar. —*vi* llenar; (one's luggage) hacer el equipaje, hacer el baúl, arreglar el equipaje. **packed like sardines,** como sardinas en banasta. **The train was packed,** El tren estababa lleno de bote en bote. **to p. off,** (a person) despachar; poner de partitas en la calle. **to p. up,** hacer el equipaje; empaquetar; embalar; *Inf.* liar el hato
package /ˈpækɪdʒ/ *n* paquete, *m;* bulto, *m;* (bundle) fardo, *m*
packer /ˈpækər/ *n* embalador, *m;* envasador (-ra)
packet /ˈpækɪt/ *n* paquete, *m;* (of cigarettes, etc.) cajetilla, *f;* (boat) paquebote, *m.* **to make one's p.,** *Inf.* hacer su pacotilla
packing /ˈpækɪŋ/ *n* embalaje, *m;* envoltura, *f;* envase, *m;* (on a pipe, etc.) guarnición, *f.* **I must do my p.,** Tengo que hacer las maletas. **p.-case,** caja de embalaje, *f.* **p.-needle,** aguja espartera, *f*
pact /pækt/ *n* pacto, convenio, *m.* **to make a p.,** pactar
pad /pæd/ *n* almohadilla, *f,* cojinete, *m;* (on a bed, chair) colchoneta, *f;* (on a wound) cabezal, *m;* (for polishing) muñeca, *f;* (hockey) defensa, *f;* (cricket) espinillera, *f;* (writing) bloque, *m;* (of a calendar) taco, *m;* (blotting) secafirmas, *m;* (of a quadruped's foot) pulpejo, *m;* (of fox, hare) pata, *f;* (leaf) hoja grande, *f, vt* almohadillar; acolchar; rellenar, forrar; (out, a book, etc.) meter paja en. **inking-pad,** almohadilla de entintar, *f.* **padded cell,** celda acolchonada, *f.* **shoulder-pad,** (in a garment) hombrera, *f*
padding /ˈpædɪŋ/ *n* relleno, *m,* almohadilla, *f;* (material) borra, *f,* algodón, *m; Fig.* paja, *f,* ripio, *m,*
paddle /ˈpædl̩/ *n* (oar) canalete, zagual, *m;* paleta, *f;* (flipper) aleta, *f, vt* and *vi* remar con canalete; (dabble) chapotear. **double p.,** remo doble, *m.* **p.-steamer,** vapor de ruedas, vapor de paleta, *m.* **p.-wheel,** rueda de paletas, *f*
paddler /ˈpædlər/ *n* remero (-ra); el, *m,* (*f,* la) que chapotea
paddling *n* chapoteo, chapaleo, *m*
paddock /ˈpædək/ *n* prado, *m,* dehesa, *f;* parque, *m;* (near a racecourse) en silla dero, picadero, *m;* (toad) sapo, *m*
padlock /ˈpædˌlɒk/ *n* candado, *m, vt* cerrar con candado, acerrojar
Paduan /ˈpædʒuən/ *a* and *n* paduano (-na)
paean /ˈpiən/ *n* himno de alegría, *m*
pagan /ˈpeigən/ *a* and *n* pagano (-na)
paganism /ˈpeigənɪzəm/ *n* paganismo, *m*
page /peidʒ/ *n* (boy) paje, *m;* (squire) escudero, *m;* (of a book, etc.) página, *f; Fig.* hoja, *f.* —*vt* compaginar; (a person) vocear. **on p. nine,** en la página nueve. **to turn the p.,** *Fig.* volver la hoja
pageant /ˈpædʒənt/ *n* espectáculo, *m;* (procession) desfile, *m;* representación teatral, *f;* fiesta, *f; Fig.* pompa, *f,* aparato, *m*
pageantry /ˈpædʒəntri/ *n* pompa, *f,* aparato, *m,* magnificencia, *f*
pager /ˈpeidʒər/ *n* buscapersonas, *m,* bip, *m* (Mexico)
paginate /ˈpædʒəˌneit/ *vt* paginar
pagination /ˌpædʒəˈneiʃən/ *n* paginación, *f*
pagoda /pəˈgoudə/ *n* pagoda, *f*
paid /peid/ *a* pagado; (on a parcel) porte pagado. **p. mourner,** plañidera, *f.* **p.-up share,** acción liberada, *f*
pail /peil/ *n* cubo, pozal, *m,* cubeta, *f*
pailful /ˈpeilˌfʊl/ *n* cubo (de agua, etc.), *m*
pain /pein/ *n* dolor, *m;* sufrimiento, *m;* (mental) tormento, *m,* angustia, *f; Law.* pena, *f; pl* **pains,** (effort) trabajo, esfuerzo, *m.* —*vt* doler; atormentar, afligir. **dull p.,** dolor sordo, *m.* **I have a p. in my head,** Me duele la cabeza. **on p. of death,** so pena de muerte. **to be in great p.,** sufrir mucho. **to take pains,** tomarse trabajo, esforzarse, esmerarse
pained /peind/ *a* dolorido; afligido; de angustia
painful /ˈpeinfəl/ *a* doloroso; angustioso; fatigoso; (troublesome) molesto; (embarrassing) embarazoso; difícil; (laborious) arduo
painfully /ˈpeinfəli/ *adv* dolorosamente; penosamente; fatigosamente; con angustia; laboriosamente
painfulness /ˈpeinfəlnɪs/ *n* dolor, *m;* angustia, aflicción, *f;* tormento, *m;* dificultad, *f*
painless /ˈpeinlɪs/ *a* sin dolor, indoloro
painlessly /ˈpeinlɪsli/ *adv* sin dolor; sin sufrir
painlessness /ˈpeinlɪsnɪs/ *n* falta de dolor, *f*
painstaking /ˈpeinzˌteikɪŋ, ˈpeinˌstei-/ *a* concienzudo; diligente, industrioso; cuidadoso. —*n* trabajo, *m;* diligencia, industria, *f;* cuidado, *m*
paint /peint/ *n* pintura, *f;* (for preserving metal) pavón, *m;* (rouge) colorete, *m.* —*vt* pintar. —*vi* pintar; pintarse. **The door is painted blue,** La puerta está pintada de azul. **p.-box,** caja de pinturas, *f.* **p.-brush,** pincel, *m;* (for house painting) brocha, *f*
painter /ˈpeintər/ *n* pintor (-ra); (house) pintor de brocha gorda, pintor de casas, *m;* (of a boat) boza, *f.* **sign-p.,** pintor de muestras, *m*
painting /ˈpeintɪŋ/ *n* pintura, *f;* (picture) cuadro, *m,* pintura, *f*
pair /pɛər/ *n* par, *m;* (of people) pareja, *f;* (of oxen) yunta, *f.* —*vt* parear, emparejar; (persons) unir, casar; (animals) aparear. —*vi* parearse; casarse; aparearse. **a carriage and p.,** un landó con dos caballos. **a p. of steps,** una escalera de mano. **a p. of pants a p. of trousers,** unos pantalones. **in pairs,** de dos en dos; por parejas. **to p. off,** *vi* formar pareja; *Inf.* casarse
pal /pæl/ *n* camarada, compinche, *mf;* amigote, *m*
palace /ˈpælɪs/ *n* palacio, *m*
paladin /ˈpælədɪn/ *n* paladín, *m*
palatable /ˈpælətəbəl/ *a* sabroso, apetitoso; *Fig.* agradable, aceptable
palatableness /ˈpælɪtəbəlnɪs/ *n* buen sabor, gusto agradable, *m; Fig.* lo agradable
palatably /ˈpælɪtəbli/ *adv* agradablemente
palatal /ˈpælətl̩/ *a* paladial. —*n* letra paladial, *f*
palatalize /ˈpælətl̩ˌaiz/ *vt* palatizar

palate /ˈpælɪt/ *n* paladar, *m.* **hard p.,** paladar, *m.* **soft p.,** velo del paladar, *m*

palatial /pəˈleiʃəl/ *a* (of a palace) palaciego; (sumptuous) magnífico, suntuoso

pale /peil/ *n* (stake) estaca, *f;* límite, *m; Herald.* palo, *m, a* pálido; (wan) descolorido; (of colours) claro, desmayado; (of light) tenue, mortecino; (lustreless) sin brillo, muerto. —*vi* palidecer, perder el color; *Fig.* eclipsarse

palely /ˈpeilli/ *adv* pálidamente; vagamente, indistintamente

paleness /ˈpeilnɪs/ *n* palidez, *f;* (wanness) descoloramiento, *m,* amarillez, *f;* (of light) tenuidad, *f*

paleographer /ˌpeiliˈɒgrəfər/ *n* paleógrafo, *m*

paleography /ˌpeiliˈɒgrəfi; *esp. Brit.* ˌpæli-/ *n* paleografía, *f*

paleolithic /ˌpeiliəˈlɪθɪk/ *a* paleolítico

paleology /ˌpeiliˈɒlədʒi/ *n* paleología, *f*

paleontology /ˌpeiliənˈtɒlədʒi; *esp. Brit.* ˌpæli-/ *n* paleontología, *f*

Palestine /ˈpæləˌstain/ Palestina, *f*

palette /ˈpælɪt/ *n* paleta, *f.* **p.-knife,** espátula, *f*

palimpsest /ˈpælɪmpˌsɛst/ *n* palimpsesto, *m*

palindrome /ˈpælɪnˌdroum/ *n* capicúa *f,* (of numbers), palíndromo *m*

paling /ˈpeilɪŋ/ *n* palizada, estacada, valla, *f*

palisade /ˌpæləˈseid/ *n* palenque, *m,* tranquera, palizada, *f; Mil.* estacada, *f*

palish /ˈpeilɪʃ/ *a* algo pálido; paliducho

pall /pɔl/ *n* (on a coffin) paño mortuorio, *m;* (*Fig.* covering) manto, *m,* capa, *f; Eccl.* palio, *m;* (over a chalice) palia, *f.* —*vi* perder el sabor, hacerse insípido; saciarse (de); aburrirse (de), cansarse (de). **The music of Bach never palls on me,** No me canso nunca de la música de Bach

palladium /pəˈleidiəm/ *n Mineral.* paladio, *m;* (safeguard) paladión, *m*

pallet /ˈpælɪt/ *n* jergón, *m;* camilla, *f; Mech.* fiador de rueda, *m;* torno de alfarero, *m*

palliate /ˈpæliˌeit/ *vt* (pain) paliar, aliviar; mitigar; (excuse) disculpar, excusar

palliation /ˌpæliˈeiʃən/ *n* paliación, *f;* mitigación, *f;* disculpa, *f*

palliative /ˈpæliˌeitɪv, -iətɪv/ *a* paliativo; (extenuating) atenuante. —*n* paliativo, *m*

pallid /ˈpælɪd/ *a* pálido

pallidness /ˈpælɪdnɪs/ *n* palidez, *f*

pallor /ˈpælər/ *n* palidez, *f*

palm /pɑm/ *n* (of the hand, and *Fig.*, victory) palma, *f;* (measurement) ancho de la mano, *m;* (tree) palmera, *f.* —*vt* (a card, etc.) empalmar; (with off) defraudar (con); dar gato por liebre (a). **to bear away the p.,** llevar la palma. **p. branch,** palma, *f.* **p. grove,** palmar, *m.* **p.-oil,** aceite de palma, *m;* (bribe) soborno, *m.* **P. Sunday,** Domingo de Ramos, *m.* **p. tree,** palmera, *f*

palmate /ˈpælmeit, -mɪt, ˈpɑl-, ˈpɑmeit/ *a* palmeado

palmer /ˈpɑmər, ˈpɑl-/ *n* peregrino, *m;* (caterpillar) oruga velluda, *f*

palming /ˈpɑmɪŋ/ *n* (in conjuring, etc.) empalme, *m*

palmist /ˈpɑmɪst/ *n* quiromántico (-ca)

palmistry /ˈpɑməstri/ *n* quiromancía, *f*

palmy /ˈpɑmi/ *a* palmar; (flourishing) floreciente; (happy) dichoso, feliz; (prosperous) próspero; triunfante

Palmyra /pælˈmairə/ Palmira, *f*

palp /pælp/ *n* palpo, *m*

palpability /ˌpælpəˈbɪlɪti/ *n* palpabilidad, *f*

palpable /ˈpælpəbəl/ *a* palpable

palpate /ˈpælpeit/ *vt* palpar

palpation /pælˈpeiʃən/ *n* palpación, *f*

palpitate /ˈpælpɪˌteit/ *vi* palpitar

palpitating /ˈpælpɪˌteitɪŋ/ *a* palpitante

palpitation /ˌpælpɪˈteiʃən/ *n* palpitación, *f*

palsied /ˈpɔlzid/ *a* paralítico

palsy /ˈpɔlzi/ *n* parálisis, *f, vt* paralizar

paltriness /ˈpɔltrinɪs/ *n* mezquindad, pequeñez, *f*

paltry /ˈpɔltri/ *a* mezquino, insignificante, pobre

paludism /ˈpælyəˌdizəm/ *n Med.* paludismo, *m*

pampas /ˈpæmpəz; *attributively* ˈpæmpəs/ *n* pampa, *f*

pamper /ˈpæmpər/ *vt* mimar, consentir demasiado; criar con mimos, regalar; alimentar demasiado bien

pampered /ˈpæmpərd/ *a* mimado, consentido; demasiado bien alimentado

pamphlet /ˈpæmflɪt/ *n* folleto, *m*

pamphleteer /ˌpæmflɪˈtɪər/ *n* folletinista, *mf*

pan /pæn/ *n* (vessel) cazuela, *f;* cacerola, *f;* (brain) cráneo, *m;* (of a balance) platillo, *m;* (of a firelock) cazoleta, *f, Cinema.* toma panorámica *f, prefix* pan-. **to pan off,** separar el oro en una gamella. **to pan out,** dar oro; *Fig.* suceder. **Pan-Americanism,** panamericanismo, *m*

Pan /pæn/ *n* Pan, *m.* **pipes of Pan,** flauta de Pan, *f*

panacea /ˌpænəˈsiə/ *n* panacea, *f*

panache /pəˈnæʃ/ *n* penacho, *m*

panada /pənaˈda/ *n Cul.* panetela, *f*

Panama /ˈpænəˌmɑ/ el Panamá, *m*

Panama /ˈpænəˌmɑ/ *a* panameño. (-ña). **P. hat,** sombrero de jipijapa, panamá *m*

pancake /ˈpænˌkeik/ *n* fruta de sartén, hojuela, *f.* **p. landing,** *Aer.* aterrizaje brusco, *m.* **P. Tuesday,** martes de Carnaval, *m*

panchromatic /ˌpænkrouˈmætɪk, -krə-/ *a* pancromático

pancreas /ˈpænkriəs, ˈpæŋ-/ *n* páncreas, *m*

pancreatic /ˌpænkriˈætɪk/ *a* pancreático

panda /ˈpændə/ *n Zool.* panda, *mf*

pandemic /pænˈdɛmɪk/ *a* pandémico

pandemonium /ˌpændəˈmouniəm/ *n* pandemonio

pander /ˈpændər/ *n* alcahuete, *m, vi* alcahuetear. **to p. to,** prestarse a; favorecer, ayudar

pandore /pænˈdɔr/ *n Mus.* bandola, *f*

pane /pein/ *n* hoja de vidrio, hoja de cristal, *f;* cuadro, *m*

panegyric /ˌpænɪˈdʒɪrɪk/ *a* panegírico. —*n* panegírico, *m*

panegyrist /ˌpænɪˈdʒɪrɪst/ *n* panegirista, *mf*

panel /ˈpænl̩/ *n* panel, entrepaño, *m; Art.* tabla, *f;* (in a dress) paño, *m;* (list) lista, *f,* registro, *m;* (jury) jurado, *m;* lista de jurados, *f, vt* labrar a entrepaños; artesonar. **p. doctor,** médico (-ca) de seguros

paneled /ˈpænl̩d/ *a* entrepañado; (of ceilings) artesonado. **p. ceiling,** artesonado, *m*

paneling /ˈpænl̩ɪŋ/ *n* entrepaños, *m pl*; artesonado, *m*

panful /ˈpænˌfʊl/ *n* cazolada, *f*

pang /pæŋ/ *n* punzada (de dolor), *f,* dolor agudo, *m;* dolor, *m;* (anguish of mind) angustia, *f,* tormento, *m;* (of conscience) remordimiento, *m*

panic /ˈpænɪk/ *n* pánico, *m;* pavor, espanto, *m;* terror súbito, *m, a* pánico. —*vi* espantarse. **p.-monger,** alarmista, *mf* **p.-stricken,** aterrorizado, despavorido

panicky /ˈpænɪki/ *a Inf.* lleno de pánico; nervioso

panicle /ˈpænɪkəl/ *n Bot.* panoja, *f*

pannier /ˈpænyər/ *n* (basket) alforja, *f;* cesto, *m;* (bustle) caderillas, *f pl*

panoply /ˈpænəpli/ *n* panoplia, *f*

panorama /ˌpænəˈræmə, -ˈrɑmə/ *n* panorama, *m*

panoramic /ˌpænəˈræmɪk/ *a* panorámico

pansy /ˈpænzi/ *n* pensamiento, *m,* trinitaria, *f*

pant /pænt/ *vi* jadear; (of dogs) hipar; resollar; (of the heart) palpitar. —*n* jadeo, *m;* palpitación, *f.* **to p. after,** suspirar por

pantaloon /ˌpæntl̩ˈun/ *n* (trouser) pantalón, *m;* (Pantaloon) Pantalón, *m*

pantechnicon /pænˈtɛknɪˌkɒn/ *n* almacén de muebles, *m;* (van) carro de mudanzas, *m*

pantheism /ˈpænθiˌɪzəm/ *n* panteísmo, *m*

pantheist /ˈpænθiɪst/ *n* panteísta, *mf*

pantheistic /ˌpænθiˈɪstɪk/ *a* panteísta

pantheon /ˈpænθiˌɒn, -ən *or, esp. Brit.*, pænˈθiən/ *n* panteón, *m*

panther /ˈpænθər/ *n* pantera, *f*

panties /ˈpæntiz/ *n pl* pantalones, *m pl*

panting /ˈpæntɪŋ/ *a* jadeante, sin aliento. —*n* jadeo, *m;* resuello, *m,* respiración difícil, *f;* palpitación, *f*

pantograph /ˈpæntəˌgræf/ *n* pantógrafo, *m*

pantomime /ˈpæntəˌmaim/ *n* pantomima, *f;* revista, *f.* **in p.,** en pantomima; por gestos

pantry /ˈpæntri/ *n* despensa, *f*

pants /pænts/ *n pl* calzoncillos, *m pl*; (trousers) pantalones, *m pl*
panzer division /'pænzər/ *n* división motorizada, *f*
pap /pæp/ *n* (nipple) pezón, *m;* (soft food) papilla, *f*
papa /'pɑpə, pə'pɑ/ *n* papá, *m*
papacy /'peipəsi/ *n* papado, pontificado, *m*
papal /'peipəl/ *a* papal, pontificio. **p. bull,** bula pontificia, *f.* **p. nuncio,** nuncio del Papa, nuncio apostólico, *m.* **p. see,** sede apostólica, *f*
paper /'peipər/ *n* papel, *m;* hoja de papel, *f;* documento, *m;* (lecture) comunicación, *f;* (newspaper) periódico, *m;* (journal) revista, *f;* (exam.) examen escrito, trabajo, *m;* ejercicio, *m; pl* **papers,** (credentials) documentación, *f,* credenciales, *f pl; Com.* valores negociables, *m pl;* (packet) paquete, *m, a* de papel; para papeles; parecido al papel. —*vt* (a room) empapelar; (a parcel) envolver. **daily p.,** diario, *m.* **in p. covers,** (of books) en rústica. **slip of p.,** papeleta, *f.* **to send in one's papers,** entregar su dimisión. **p. bag,** saco de papel, *m.* **p.-chase,** rally-paper, *m.* **p. clip,** prendedero de oficina, "sujeta papels," *m.* **p.-cutting machine,** guillotina, *f.* **p. folder,** plegadera, *f.* **p.-hanger,** empapelador, *m.* **p.-hanging,** empapelado, *m.* **p.-knife,** cortapapel, *m.* **p.-maker,** fabricante de papel, *m.* **p.-making,** manufactura de papel, *f.* **p.-mill,** fábrica de papel, *f.* **p.-money,** papel moneda, *m.* **p.-pulp,** pasta, *f.* **p.-streamer,** serpentina, *f.* **p.-weight,** pisapapeles, *m*
papering /'peipərɪŋ/ *n* (of a room) empapelado, *m*
papery /'peipəri/ *a* semejante al papel
papier-mâché /ˌpeipərmə'ʃei, pɑˌpyei-/ *n* cartón piedra, *m*
papillary /'pæpəˌlɛri/ *a* papilar
papist /'peipɪst/ *n* papista, *mf;* católico (-ca)
papoose /pæ'pus;/ *n* niño indio, *m*
paprika /pæ'prikə, pə-, pɑ-, 'pæprɪkə/ *n* pimienta húngara, *f*
papyrus /pə'pairəs/ *n* papiro, *m*
par /pɑr/ *n* par, *f.* **at par,** *Com.* a la par. **above (below) par,** *Com.* por encima (*or* debajo) de la par. **He is a little below par,** No está muy bien de salud. **to be on par with,** ser el equivalente de; ser igual a. **par excellence,** por excelencia
parable /'pærəbəl/ *n* parábola, *f*
parabola /pə'ræbələ/ *n Geom.* parábola, *f*
parachute /'pærəˌʃut/ *n* paracaídas, *m; Bot.* vilano, *m* **to p. down,** lanzarse en paracaídas. **p. troops,** cuerpo de paracaidistas, *m*
parachutist /'pærəˌʃutɪst/ *n* paracaidista, *mf*
parade /pə'reid/ *n* alarde, *m; Mil.* parada, revista, *f;* (procession) desfile, *m,* procesión, *f;* (promenade) paseo, *m.* —*vt* (display) hacer alarde de, hacer gala de, ostentar; (troops) formar en parada; pasar revista (a); (patrol) recorrer. —*vi Mil.* tomar parte en una parada; desfilar. **to p. up and down,** pasearse. **p.-ground,** campo de instrucción, *m;* plaza de armas, *f*
paradigm /'pærəˌdaim/ *n* paradigma, *m*
paradise /'pærəˌdais/ *n* paraíso, edén, *m; Fig.* jauja, *f.* **bird of p.,** ave del paraíso, *f*
paradisiac /ˌpærə'diziˌæk/ *a* paradisíaco
paradox /'pærəˌdɒks/ *n* paradoja, *f*
paradoxical /ˌpærə'dɒksɪkəl/ *a* paradójico
paradoxicality /ˌpærəˌdɒksɪ'kælɪti/ *n* lo paradójico
paraffin /'pærəfɪn/ *n* parafina, *f.* —*vt* parafinar. **p.-oil,** parafina líquida, *f*
paragon /'pærəˌgɒn/ *n* modelo perfecto, dechado, *m*
paragraph /'pærəˌgræf/ *n* párrafo, *m;* (in a newspaper) suelto, *m, vt* dividir en párrafos; escribir un suelto sobre. **new p.,** párrafo aparte, *m*
Paraguay /'pærəˌgwai, -ˌgwei/ el Paraguay, *m*
Paraguayan /ˌpærə'gwaɪən/ *a* and *n* paraguayo (-ya)
parakeet /'pærəˌkit/ *n Ornith.* perico, *m*
parallel /'pærəˌlɛl/ *a* paralelo; igual; semejante, análogo. —*n* línea paralela, *f;* paralelo, *m; Mil.* paralela, *f; Geog.* paralelo, *m; Print.* pleca, *f.* —*vt* poner en paralelo; cotejar, comparar; igualar. **to run p. to,** ser paralelo a; ser conforme a. **p. bars,** paralelas, *f pl*
parallelism /'pærəlɛˌlɪzəm/ *n* paralelismo, *m*
parallelogram /ˌpærə'lɛləˌgræm/ *n* paralelogramo, *m*
paralysis /pə'ræləsɪs/ *n* parálisis, *f*
paralytic /ˌpærə'lɪtɪk/ *a* and *n* paralítico (-ca)
paralyzation *n* paralización, *f*
paralyze *vt* paralizar
paramount /'pærəˌmaunt/ *a* supremo, sumo
paramour /'pærəˌmʊr/ *n* amante, querido, *m;* querida, amiga, *f*
paranoia /ˌpærə'nɔiə/ *n* paranoia, *f*
paranoiac /ˌpærə'nɔiæk/ *n* paranoico, *m*
parapet /'pærəpɪt, -ˌpɛt/ *n* (*Archit.* and *Mil.*) parapeto, *m*
paraphernalia /ˌpærəfər'neilyə, -fə'neil-/ *n Law.* bienes parafernales, *m, pl;* (finery) atavíos, adornos, *m pl;* equipo, *m;* arreos, *m pl;* insignias, *f pl*
paraphrase /'pærəˌfreiz/ *n* paráfrasis, *f, vt* parafrasear
parasite /'pærəˌsait/ *n* parásito, *m; Inf.* zángano, *m,* gorrista, *mf*
parasitic /ˌpærə'sɪtɪk/ *a* parásito, parasitario; *Med.* parasítico
parasitology /ˌpærəsai'tɒlədʒi, -sɪ-/ *n* parasitología, *f*
parasol /'pærəˌsɔl, -ˌsɒl/ *n* parasol, quitasol, *m*
parathyroid /ˌpærə'θairɔid/ *a* paratiroides. —*n* paratiroides, *f pl*
paratroops /'pærəˌtrups/ *n pl* paracaidistas, *m pl*
paratyphoid /ˌpærə'taifɔid/ *n* paratifoidea, *f*
parboil /'pɑrˌbɔil/ *vt* sancochar
parcel /'pɑrsəl/ *n* paquete, *m;* fardo, *m;* (of land) parcela, *f.* **to p. out,** repartir, distribuir; dividir. **to p. up,** envolver, empaquetar. **p. post,** servicio de paquetes, *m*
parceling /'pɑrsəlɪŋ/ *n* empaque, *m;* (out) reparto, *m,* distribución, *f;* división, *f*
parch /pɑrtʃ/ *vt* secar; abrasar, quemar; (roast) tostar. —*vi* secarse; quemarse, abrasarse
parched /pɑrtʃt/ *a* seco, sediento. **p. with thirst,** muerto de sed
parchedness /'pɑrtʃɪdnɪs/ *n* sequedad, aridez, *f*
parchment /'pɑrtʃmənt/ *n* pergamino, *m;* (of a drum) parche, *m.* **p.-like,** apergaminado
pardon /'pɑrdn̩/ *n* perdón, *m; Eccl.* indulgencia, *f.* —*vt* perdonar; indultar, amnistiar. **a general p.,** una amnistía. **I beg your p.!** ¡Vd. dispense!; ¡Perdone Vd.! **to beg p.,** pedir perdón; disculparse. **P.?** ¿Cómo?
pardonable /'pɑrdn̩əbəl/ *a* perdonable, disculpable, excusable
pardonableness /'pɑrdn̩əbəlnɪs/ *n* disculpabilidad, *f*
pardonably /'pɑrdn̩əbli/ *adv* disculpablemente, excusablemente
pardoner /'pɑrdn̩ər/ *n* vendedor de indulgencias, *m;* perdonador (-ra)
pardoning /'pɑrdn̩ɪŋ/ *n* perdón, *m;* remisión, *f*
pare /pɛər/ *vt* (one's nails) cortar; (fruit) mondar; (potatoes, etc.) pelar; (remove) quitar; (reduce) reducir
parent /'pɛərənt, 'pær-/ *n* padre, *m;* madre, *f;* (ancestor) antepasado, *m;* (origin) origen, *m,* fuente, *f;* (cause) causa, *f;* (author) autor, *m;* autora, *f; pl* **parents,** padres, *m pl.* —*a* madre, materno; principal
parentage /'pɛərəntɪdʒ, 'pær-/ *n* parentela, *f;* linaje, *m,* familia, alcurnia, *f;* procedencia, *f,* nacimiento, origen, *m*
parental /pə'rɛntl̩/ *a* paternal; maternal, de madre
parentally /pə'rɛntl̩i/ *adv* como un padre; como una madre
parenthesis /pə'rɛnθəsɪs/ *n* paréntesis, *m*
parenthetical /ˌpɛərən'θətɪkəl/ *a* entre paréntesis; de paréntesis
parenthood /'pɛərəntˌhʊd, 'pær-/ *n* paternidad, *f;* maternidad, *f*
pariah /pə'raiə/ *n* paria, *mf*
parietal /pə'raiɪtl̩/ *a* parietal
paring /'pɛərɪŋ/ *n* (act) raedura, *f;* peladura, mondadura, *f;* (shred) brizna, *f;* (refuse) desecho, desperdicio, *m.* **p.-knife,** trinchete, *m*
Paris /'pærɪs/ París, *m*
parish /'pærɪʃ/ *n* parroquia, *f;* feligresía, *f, a* parroquial. **p. church,** parroquia, *f.* **p. clerk,** sacristán de parroquia, *m.* **p. priest,** párroco, *m.* **p. register,** registro de la parroquia, *m*
parishioner /pə'rɪʃənər/ *n* parroquiano (-na); feligrés (-esa)
Parisian /pə'rɪʒən, -'riʒən, -'rɪziən/ *a* parisiense. —*n* parisiense, *mf*
parity /'pærɪti/ *n* paridad, *f*

park /pɑrk/ *n* parque, *m;* jardín, *m.* —*vt* (vehicles) estacionar; (dump) depositar. **car p.,** parque de automóviles, *m.* **p.-keeper,** guardián del parque, *m*
parking /ˈpɑrkɪŋ/ *n* (of vehicles) estacionamiento, *m;* (dumping) depósito, *m.* **p. lights,** *Auto.* luces de estacionamiento, *f pl.* **p. place,** parque de estacionamiento, *m*
parking meter *n* parquímetro, *m* (Argentina)
parlance /ˈpɑrləns/ *n* lenguaje, *m.* **in common p.,** en lenguaje vulgar
parley /ˈpɑrli/ *n* plática, conversación, *f;* discusión, *f; Mil.* parlamento, *m.* —*vi Mil.* parlamentar; discutir; conversar. —*vt* hablar
parliament /ˈpɑrləmənt/ *n* parlamento, *m;* cortes, *f pl;* cuerpo legislativo, *m*
parliamentarian /ˌpɑrləmɛnˈtɛəriən/ *a* and *n* parlamentario; (of an academy) censor, *m*
parliamentarianism /ˌpɑrləmɛnˈtɛəriənɪzəm/ *n* parlamentarismo, *m,*
parliamentary /ˌpɑrləˈmɛntəri, -tri; *sometimes* ˌpɑrlyə-/ *a* parlamentario. **p. immunity,** inviolabilidad parlamentaria, *f*
parlor /ˈpɑrlər/ *n* salón, gabinete, *m;* sala de recibo, *f;* (in a convent) locutorio, *m.* **p. games,** diversión de salón, *f,* juego de sociedad, *m.* **p.-maid,** camarera, *f*
parlous /ˈpɑrləs/ *a* crítico, malo. —*adv* sumamente, muy
Parmesan /ˈpɑrməˌzɑn, ˌpɑrməˈzɑn/ *a* parmesano, de Parma. —*n* parmesano (-na). **P. cheese,** queso de Parma, *m*
Parnassian /pɑrˈnæsiən/ *a* del parnaso; parnasiano. —*n* parnasiano, *m*
Parnassus /pɑrˈnæsəs/ *n* Parnaso, *m*
parochial /pəˈroukiəl/ *a* parroquial, parroquiano; *Fig.* provincial
parochialism /pəˈroukiəˌlɪzəm/ *n* provincialismo, *m*
parochially /pəˈroukiəli/ *adv* por parroquias
parodist /ˈpærədɪst/ *n* parodista, *mf*
parody /ˈpærədi/ *n* parodia, *f, vt* parodiar
parole /pəˈroul/ *n* (of convict) libertad vigilada, *f*
paroxysm /ˈpærəkˌsɪzəm/ *n* paroxismo, *m;* ataque, acceso, *m*
parquet /pɑrˈkei/ (floor) entarimado *m;* (of theater) platea, *f*
parricide /ˈpærəˌsaid/ *n* (act) parricidio, *m;* (person) parricida, *mf*
parrot /ˈpærət/ *n* papagayo, loro, *m*
parry /ˈpæri/ *vt* (a blow, and in fencing) parar; rechazar; evitar. —*n* parada, *f;* (in fencing) quite, *m,* parada, *f*
parse /pɑrs, pɑrz/ *vt* analizar
Parsee /ˈpɑrsi, pɑrˈsi/ *n* parsi, *m*
parsimonious /ˌpɑrsəˈmouniəs/ *a* parsimonioso
parsimoniously /ˌpɑrsəˈmouniəsli/ *adv* con parsimonia
parsimony /ˈpɑrsəˌmouni/ *n* parsimonia, *f*
parsley /ˈpɑrsli/ *n* perejil, *m*
parsnip /ˈpɑrsnɪp/ *n* chirivía, *f*
parson /ˈpɑrsən/ *n* párroco, cura, *m;* (clergyman) clérigo, *m*
parsonage /ˈpɑrsənɪdʒ/ *n* rectoría, *f*
part /pɑrt/ *n* parte, *f;* porción, *f;* trozo, *m; Mech.* pieza, *f;* (*Gram.* and of a literary work) parte, *f;* (of a living organism) miembro, *m;* (duty) deber, *m,* obligación, *f; Theat.* papel, *m; Mus.* voz, *f; pl* **parts,** (region) partes, *f pl,* lugar, *m;* (talents) partes, dotes, *f pl.* **foreign parts,** países extranjeros, *m pl,* el extranjero. **For my p....,** Por lo que a mí toca, Por mi parte. **for the most p.,** en su mayoría. **from all parts,** de todas partes. **in p.,** en parte; parcialmente. **spare p.,** pieza de recambio, *f.* **The funny p. of it is...,** Lo cómico del asunto es... **the latter p. of the month,** los últimos días del mes, la segunda quincena del mes. **to form p. of,** formar parte de. **to play a p.,** hacer un papel. **to take a person's p.,** apoyar a alguien, ser partidario de alguien. **to take in good p.,** tomar bien. **to take p. in,** tomar parte en, participar en. **p. of speech,** parte de la oración, *f.* **p.-owner,** copropietario (-ia). **p.-time job,** trabajo de unas cuantas horas, *m*
part /pɑrt/ *vt* distribuir, repartir; dividir; separar (de); (open) abrir. —*vi* partir, marcharse; despedirse; (of roads, etc.) bifurcarse; dividirse; (open) abrirse. **to p. one's hair,** hacerse la raya. **to p. from,** (things) separarse de; (people) despedirse de. **to p. with,** separarse de; deshacerse de; perder; (dismiss) despedir (a)
partake /pɑrˈteik/ *vt* participar de, compartir; tomar parte en. —*vi* tomar algo (de comer, de beber). **to p. of,** comer (beber) de; tener rasgos de
partaker /pɑrˈteikər/ *n* partícipe, *mf*
Parthian /ˈpɑrθiən/ *a* parto. —*n* parto (-ta). **P. shot,** la flecha del parto
partial /ˈpɑrʃəl/ *a* parcial; (fond of) aficionado (a). **p. eclipse,** eclipse parcial, *m*
partiality /ˌpɑrʃiˈælɪti, pɑrˈʃæl-/ *n* parcialidad, *f;* preferencia, predilección, *f*
partially /ˈpɑrʃəli/ *adv* en parte, parcialmente; (with bias) con parcialidad
participant /pɑrˈtɪsəpənt/ *a* participante. —*n* partícipe, *mf*
participate /pɑrˈtɪsəˌpeit/ *vi* participar (de), compartir; tomar parte (en)
participation /pɑrˌtɪsəˈpeiʃən/ *n* participación, *f*
participial /ˌpɑrtəˈsɪpiəl/ *a Gram.* participial
participle /ˈpɑrtəˌsɪpəl, -səpəl/ *n Gram.* participio, *m.* **past p.,** participio pasado (or pretérito or pasivo), *m.* **present p.,** participio activo (or presente), *m*
particle /ˈpɑrtɪkəl/ *n* partícula, *f; Fig.* átomo, grano, *m,* pizca, *f; Gram.* partícula, *f*
parti-colored /ˈpɑrtiˌkʌlərd/ *a* bicolor
particular /pərˈtɪkyələr/ *a* particular; especial; individual; singular; cierto; exacto; escrupuloso; difícil, exigente. —*n* detalle, pormenor, *m;* circunstancia, *f;* caso particular, *m; pl* **particulars,** informes, detalles, *m pl.* **further particulars,** más detalles. **in p.,** en particular; sobre todo. **He is very p. about...,** Es muy exigente en cuanto a...; Le es muy importante..., Le importa mucho...
particularize /pərˈtɪkyələˌraiz/ *vt* particularizar, detallar; especificar
particularly /pərˈtɪkyələrli/ *adv* en particular; particularmente; sobre todo
parting /ˈpɑrtɪŋ/ *n* despedida, *f;* partida, *f;* separación, *f;* (of the hair) raya, crencha, *f;* (cross roads) bifurcación, *f.* —*a* de despedida. **at p.,** al despedirse. **to reach the p. of the ways,** *Fig.* llegar al punto decisivo
partisan /ˈpɑrtəzən, -sən/ *n* partidario (-ia); (fighter) guerrillero, *m, a* partidario; de guerrilleros
partisanship /ˈpɑrtəˌzənʃɪp/ *n* partidarismo, *m*
partition /pɑrˈtɪʃən, pər-/ *n* partición, *f;* división, *f;* (wall) pared, *f,* tabique, *m.* **the p. of Ireland,** la división de Irlanda
partly /ˈpɑrtli/ *adv* en parte
partner /ˈpɑrtnər/ *n* asociado (-da); *Com.* socio (-ia); (dancing) pareja, *f;* (in games, and companion) compañero (-ra); (spouse) consorte, *mf;* (in crime) codelincuente, *mf* **sleeping p.,** socio comanditario, *m.* **working p.,** socio industrial, *m*
partnership /ˈpɑrtnərˌʃɪp/ *n* asociación, *f; Com.* sociedad, compañía, *f.* **deed of p.,** artículos de sociedad, *m pl.* **to take into p.,** tomar como socio (a). **to form a p.,** asociarse
partridge /ˈpɑrtrɪdʒ/ *n Ornith.* perdiz, *f.* **young p.,** perdigón, *m*
parturient /pɑrˈtʊriənt/ *a f,* parturienta. —*n* parturienta, *f*
parturition /ˌpɑrtʊˈrɪʃən, -tʃʊ-/ *n* parto, *m*
party /ˈpɑrti/ *n* partido, *m;* grupo, *m;* (of pleasure, etc.) partida, *f;* reunión, fiesta, *f; Mil.* pelotón, destacamento, *m; Law.* parte, *f;* (person) interesado (-da); (accessory) cómplice, *mf.* **rescue p.,** pelotón de salvamento, *m.* **to be a p. to,** prestarse a; ser cómplice en. **to give a p.,** dar una fiesta, dar una reunión. **p.-spirit,** espíritu del partido, *m.* **p.-wall,** pared medianera, *f*
parvenu /ˈpɑrvəˌnu/ *n* advenedizo (-za)
parvis /ˈpɑrvɪs/ *n Archit.* atrio, *m*
Paschal /pæˈskæl/ *a* pascual
pass /pæs/ *n* (in an exam.) aprobación, *f;* (crisis) crisis, situación crítica, *f;* estado, *m;* (with the hands) pase, *m;* (permit) permiso, *m; Mil.* licencia, *f;* (safe-conduct) salvoconducto, *m;* (in football, etc.) pase,

m; (membership card) carnet, *m;* (defile) desfiladero, paso, puerto, *m; Naut.* rebasadero, *m;* (fencing) estocada, *f.* **free p.,** billete de favor, *m.* **p.-book,** libreta de banco, *f.* **p. certificate,** (in exams.) aprobado, *m.* **p.-key,** llave maestra, *f*

pass /pæs/ *vi* pasar; (of time) correr, pasar, transcurrir; (happen) occurrir, tomar lugar; (end) cesar, desaparecer; (die) morir. —*vt* pasar; hacer pasar; (the butter, etc.) dar, alargar; (in football, hockey) pasar; (excel) aventajar, exceder; (a bill, an examination) aprobar; (sentence) fallar, pronunciar; (a remark) hacer; (transfer) traspasar; (tolerate) sufrir, tolerar; evacuar. **He passed in psychology,** Aprobó sicología. **to allow to p.,** ceder el paso (a). **to bring to p.,** ocasionar. **to come to p.,** suceder. **to let p.,** (put up with) dejar pasar; no hacer caso de; (forgive) perdonar. **to p. a vote of confidence,** votar una proposición de confianza. **to p. the buck,** *Inf.* echarle a uno el muerto. **pass the hat, pass the plate,** pasar la gorra. **to p. along,** pasar por; pasar. **to p. away,** pasar; desaparecer; (die) morir, fallecer; (of time) transcurrir. **to p. by,** pasar por, pasar delante de, pasar al lado de; (omit) pasar por alto de, omitir; (ignore) pasar sin hacer caso de. **to p. for,** pasar por. **to p. in,** entrar. **to p. in and out,** entrar y salir. **to p. off,** *vi* pasar; cesar, acabarse; desaparecer; evaporarse, disiparse; (of events) tener lugar. —*vt* (oneself) darse por; dar por, hacer pasar por. **to p. a cat off as hare,** dar gato por liebre. **to p. on,** *vi* pasar; seguir su camino, continuar su marcha. —*vt* pasar algo de uno a otro. **to p. out,** salir. **to p. over,** pasar por encima de; pasar; cruzar, atravesar; (transfer) traspasar; (disregard) pasar por alto de, dejar a un lado; omitir. **to p. over in silence,** pasar en silencio (por). **to p. round,** circular. **to p. through,** cruzar, atravesar, pasar por; (pierce) traspasar; *Fig.* experimentar

passable /ˈpæsəbəl/ *a* transitable, pasadero; (fairly good) regular, mediano; tolerable

passably /ˈpæsəbli/ *adv* medianamente, pasaderamente, tolerablemente

passage /ˈpæsɪdʒ/ *n* pasaje, *m;* paso, tránsito, *m;* (voyage) viaje, *m,* travesía, *f;* (corridor) pasillo, *m;* (entrance) entrada, *f;* (way) camino, *m;* (alley) callejón, *m;* (in a mine) galería, *f;* (of time) transcurso, *m;* (of birds) pasa, *f;* (in a book, and *Mus.*) pasaje, *m;* (occurrence) episodio, incidente, *m;* (of a bill) aprobación, *f.* **p. money,** pasaje, *m.* **p. of arms,** lucha, *f,* combate, *m;* disputa, *f*

passementerie /pæsˈmɛntri/ *n* pasamanería, *f*

passenger /ˈpæsəndʒər/ *n* viajero (-ra); (on foot) peatón, *m.* **by p. train,** en gran velocidad

passerby /ˈpæsərˈbai/ *n* transeúnte, paseante, *mf*

passing /ˈpæsɪŋ/ *a* pasajero; fugitivo; momentáneo. —*adv* sumamente, extremadamente. —*n* pasada, *f;* paso, *m;* (death) muerte, *f;* (disappearance) desaparición, *f;* (of a law) aprobación, *f.* **in p.,** de paso. **p.-bell,** toque de difuntos, *m*

passing grade *n* mínima calificación aprobatoria, *f*

passion /ˈpæʃən/ *n* pasión, *f;* (Christ's) Pasión, *f;* (anger) cólera, *f.* **to fly into a p.,** montar en cólera. **p.-flower,** pasionaria, granadilla, *f.* **P. play,** drama de la Pasión, *m.* **P. Sunday,** Domingo de Pasión, *m.* **P. Week,** Semana Santa, *f*

passionate /ˈpæʃənɪt/ *a* apasionado; (quick-tempered) irascible, colérico; (fervid) vehemente, intenso, ardiente

passionately /ˈpæʃənɪtli/ *adv* con pasión, apasionadamente; (irascibly) coléricamente; (fervidly) con vehemencia, ardientemente

passionless /ˈpæʃənlɪs/ *a* sin pasión, frío; impasible; imparcial

passive /ˈpæsɪv/ *a* pasivo. —*n Gram.* pasiva, *f.* **p. resistance,** resistencia pasiva, *f*

passivity /pæˈsɪvɪti/ *n* pasividad, *f*

Passover /ˈpæs,ouvər/ *n* Pascua de los judíos, *f*

passport /ˈpæspɔrt/ *n* pasaporte, *m*

password /ˈpæs,wɜrd/ *n* contraseña, *f*

past /pæst/ *a* pasado; último; (expert) consumado; (former) antiguo, ex-. —*n* pasado, *m;* historia, *f,* antecedentes, *m pl, prep* después de; (in front of) delante de; (next to) al lado de; (beyond) más allá de; (without) sin; fuera de; (of age) más de; (no longer able to) incapaz de. —*adv* más allá. (The translation of **past** as an adverb is often either omitted, or included in the verb, e.g. *The years flew p.,* Los años transcurrieron. *for centuries p.,* durante siglos.) **I am p. caring,** Nada me importa ya. **It is a quarter p. ten,** Son las diez y cuarto. **It is p. four o'clock,** Son las siete pasadas, Son después de las cuatro. **what's p. is p.,** lo pasado, pasado. **p. doubt,** fuera de duda. **p. endurance,** insoportable. **p. help,** sin remedio, irremediable. **p. hope,** sin esperanza. **p.-master,** maestro, consumado, experto, *m.* **p. participle,** participio pasado, *m.* **p. president,** ex-presidente, *m.* **p. tense,** (tiempo) pasado, *m*

paste /peist/ *n* pasta, *f;* (gloy) engrudo, *m.* —*vt* (affix) pegar; (glue) engomar, engrudar

pasteboard /ˈpeist,bɔrd/ *n* cartón, *m,* cartulina, *f, a* de cartón, de cartulina

pastel /pæˈstɛl/ *n Art.* pastel, *m.* **p. drawing,** pintura al pastel, *f*

pastelist /pæˈstɛlɪst/ *n* pastelista, *mf*

pasteurization /,pæstʃərəˈzeiʃən/ *n* pasteurización, *f*

pasteurize /ˈpæstʃə,raiz/ *vt* pasteurizar

pastille /pæˈstil/ *n* pastilla, *f*

pastime /ˈpæs,taim/ *n* pasatiempo, entretenimiento, *m,* diversión, recreación, *f*

pastor /ˈpæstər/ *n* pastor, *m*

pastoral /ˈpæstərəl/ *a* pastoril; *Eccl.* pastoral. —*n Eccl.* pastoral, *f;* (*Poet. Mus.*) pastorela, *f*

pastorate /ˈpæstərɪt/ *n* pastoría, *f*

pastry /ˈpeistri/ *n* (dough) pasta, *f;* pastel, *m,* torta, *f;* pastelería, *f.* **p.-cook,** repostero, *m,* pastelero (-ra)

pasturage /ˈpæstʃərɪdʒ/ *n* (grass, etc.) pasto, *m;* pasturaje, *m;* pastoreo, *m*

pasture /ˈpæstʃər/ *n* (grass, etc.) pasto, herbaje, *m;* pasturaje, *m;* (field) prado, *m,* pradera, dehesa, *f.* —*vi* pacer; pastar. —*vt* apacentar, pastar

pasty /ˈpæsti/ *a* pastoso; (pale) pálido. —*n* empanada, *f*

pat /pæt/ *n* toque, *m;* caricia, *f;* (for butter) molde (de mantequilla), *m.* —*vt* tocar; acariciar, pasar la mano (sobre). —*adv* a propósito; oportunamente; fácilmente. **pat of butter,** pedacito de mantequilla, *m.* **pat on the back,** golpe en la espalda, *m; Fig.* elogio, *m*

Patagonian /,pætəˈgouniən/ *a* and *n* patagón (-ona)

patch /pætʃ/ *n* (mend) remiendo, *m;* (piece) pedazo, *m;* (plaster and *Auto.,* etc.) parche, *m;* (beauty spot) lunar postizo, *m;* (of ground) parcela, *f;* (of flowers, etc.) masa, *f;* (stain, and *Fig.*) mancha, *f.* —*vt* (mend) remendar; poner remiendo (a); pegar; (roughly) chafallar; (the face) ponerse lunares postizos. **p. of blue sky,** pedazo de cielo azul. **patch of green grass,** mancha de hierba verde. **to be not a p. on,** no ser de la misma clase que; (of persons) no llegarle a los zancajos de. **to p. up a quarrel,** hacer las paces

patchwork /ˈpætʃ,wɜrk/ *n* labor de retazos, obra de retacitos, *f; Fig.* mezcla, mezcolanza, *f.* **p. quilt,** centón, *m*

patchy /ˈpætʃi/ *a* desigual; manchado

patella /pəˈtɛlə/ *n Anat.* rótula, *f*

patency /ˈpeitn̩si/ *n* evidencia, claridad, *f*

patent /ˈpætn̩t/ *a* evidente, patente; patentado. —*n* patente, *f.* —*vt* patentar. **p. of nobility,** carta de hidalguía, ejecutoria, *f.* **"P. Applied For,"** «Patente Solicitada.» **Patent Pending** marca en trámite. **p. leather,** *n* charol, *m.* —*a* de charol. **p. medicine,** específico farmacéutico, *m*

patentee /,pætn̩ˈti/ *n* el, *m,* (*f,* la) que obtiene una patente; inventor (-ra)

patently /ˈpætn̩tli/ *adv* evidentemente, claramente

paterfamilias /,peitərfəˈmɪliəs, ,pɑ-, ,pætər-/ *n* padre de familia, *m*

paternal /pəˈtɜrnl̩/ *a* paterno, paternal

paternally /pəˈtɜrnl̩i/ *adv* paternalmente

paternity /pəˈtɜrnɪti/ *n* paternidad, *f*

path /pæθ/ *n* senda, vereda, *f,* sendero, *m;* camino, *m;* (track) pista, *f;* (traject) trayectoria, *f.* **the beaten p.,** el camino trillado

pathetic /pəˈθɛtɪk/ *a* patético

pathless /ˈpæθlɪs/ *a* sin senda

pathogenic /,pæθəˈdʒɛnɪk/ *a Med.* patógeno

pathological /,pæθəˈlɒdʒɪkəl/ *a* patológico

pathologist /pə'θɒlədʒɪst/ *n* patólogo, *m*
pathology /pə'θɒlədʒi/ *n* patología, *f*
pathos /'peiθɒs/ *n* lo patético
patience /'peiʃəns/ *n* paciencia, *f.* **He tries my p. very much,** Me cuesta mucho no impacientarme con él. **to lose p.,** perder la paciencia; (grow angry) perder los estribos. **to play p.,** hacer solitarios
patient /'peiʃənt/ *a* paciente. —*n* paciente, *mf;* (ill person) enfermo (-ma); (of a physician) cliente, *mf*
patiently /'peiʃəntli/ *adv* con paciencia, pacientemente
patina /'pætn̩ə, pə'tinə/ *n* pátina, *f*
patriarch /'peitri,ɑrk/ *n* patriarca, *m*
patriarchal /,peitri'arkəl/ *a* patriarcal
patriarchy /'peitri,ɑrki/ *n* patriarcado, *m*
patrician /pə'trɪʃən/ *a* and *n* patricio (-ia)
patrimonial /,pætrə'mouniəl/ *a* patrimonial
patrimony /'pætrə,mouni/ *n* patrimonio, *m*
patriot /'peitriət/ *n* patriota, *mf*
patriotic /,peitri'ɒtɪk/ *a* patriótico
patriotism /'peitriə,tɪzəm/ *n* patriotismo, *m*
patrol /pə'troul/ *n* patrulla, *f;* ronda, *f, vi* and *vt* patrullar; rondar; recorrer. **p. boat,** lancha escampavía, *f.* **p. flight,** vuelo de patrulla, *m*
patron /'peitrən/ *n* (of a freed slave) patrono, *m;* (of the arts, etc.) mecenas, protector, *m;* (customer) parroquiano (-na), cliente, *mf.* **p. saint,** santo (-ta) patrón (-ona)
patronage /'peitrənɪdʒ/ *n* (protection) patrocinio, *m;* protección, *f; Eccl.* patronato, *m;* (regular custom) clientela, *f;* (of manner) superioridad, *f*
patroness /'peitrənɪs/ *n* patrona, *f;* protectora, *f;* (of a charity, etc.) patrocinadora, *f;* (of a regiment, etc.) madrina, *f*
patronize /'peitrə,naiz/ *vt* patrocinar; proteger, favorecer; (a shop) ser parroquiano de; (treat arrogantly) tratar con superioridad
patronizing /'peitrə,naizɪŋ/ *a* (with air, behavior, etc.) de superioridad, de altivez
patten /'pætn̩/ *n* zueco, chanclo, *m*
patter /'pætər/ *n* (jargon) jerga, *f;* charla, *f;* (of rain) azotes, *m pl;* (of feet) son, *m;* golpecitos, *m pl.* —*vt* (repeat) decir mecánicamente. —*vi* (chatter) charlar; (of rain) azotar, bailar; correr ligeramente
pattern /'pætərn/ *n* modelo, *m;* (*Sew.* and dressmaking) patrón, *m;* (in founding) molde, *m;* (template) escantillón, *m;* (of cloth, etc.) muestra, *f;* (design) dibujo, diseño, *m;* (example) ejemplar, *m.* —*vt* diseñar; estampar. **p. book,** libro de muestras, *m*
patty /'pæti/ *n* empanada, *f,* pastelillo, *m*
paucity /'pɔsɪti/ *n* poquedad, *f;* corto número, *m;* insuficiencia, escasez, *f*
paunch /pɔntʃ/ *n* panza, barriga, *f*
pauper /'pɔpər/ *n* pobre, *mf*
pauperism /'pɔpə,rɪzəm/ *n* pauperismo, *m*
pauperization /,pɔpərə'zeiʃən/ *n* empobrecimiento, *m*
pauperize /'pɔpə,raiz/ *vt* empobrecer, reducir a la miseria
pause /pɔz/ *n* pausa, *f;* intervalo, *m;* silencio, *m;* interrupción, *f; Mus.* pausa, *f.* —*vi* pausar, hacer una pausa; detenerse, interrumpirse; vacilar. **to give p. to,** hacer vacilar (a)
pavan /'pævən/ *n* (dance) pavana, *f*
pave /peiv/ *vt* empedrar, enlosar. **to p. the way for,** facilitar el paso de, preparar el terreno para, abrir el camino de
pavement /'peivmənt/ *n* pavimento, *m;* (sidewalk) acera, *f.* **p.-artist,** pintor callejero, *m*
pavilion /pə'vɪlyən/ *n* pabellón, *m;* (for a band, etc.) quiosco, *m;* (tent) tienda de campaña, *f*
paving /'peivɪŋ/ *n* pavimentación, *f;* empedrado, *m;* see **pavement. p.-stone,** losa, *f*
paw /pɔ/ *n* pata, *f;* (with claws) garra, *f; Inf.* manaza, *f.* —*vt* tocar con la pata; (scratch) arañar; (handle) manosear. —*vi* (of a horse) piafar
pawing /'pɔɪŋ/ *n* (of a horse) el piafar; (handling) manoseo, *m*
pawn /pɔn/ *n* (chess) peón (de ajedrez), *m;* empeño, *m; Fig.* prenda, *f.* —*vt* empeñar, pignorar; dar en prenda. **p.-ticket,** papeleta de empeño, *f*
pawnbroker /'pɔn,broukər/ *n* prestamista, *mf*
pawning /'pɔnɪŋ/ *n* empeño, *m,* pignoración, *f*
pawnshop /'pɔn,ʃɒp/ *n* casa de préstamos, casa de empeño, *f,* monte de piedad, *m*
pay /pei/ *n* paga, *f;* (*Mil. Nav.*) soldada, *f;* salario, *m;* (of a workman) jornal, *m;* (reward) recompensa, compensación, *f;* (profit) beneficio, provecho, *m.* **pay-day,** día de paga, *m.* **pay-office,** pagaduría, *f.* **pay-sheet,** nómina, *f*
pay /pei/ *vt* pagar; (a debt) satisfacer; (spend) gastar; (recompense) remunerar, recompensar; (hand over) entregar; (yield) producir; (a visit) hacer; (attention) prestar; (homage) rendir; (one's respects) presentar. —*vi* pagar; producir ganancia; sacar provecho; ser una ventaja, ser provechoso. **It would not pay him to do it,** No le saldría a cuenta hacerlo. **This job doesn't pay,** Este trabajo no da dinero. **to pay a compliment (to),** cumplimentar, decir alabanzas (a), echar una flor (a). **to pay attention,** prestar atención; hacer caso. **to pay cash,** pagar al contado. **to pay in advance,** pagar adelantado. **to pay in full,** saldar. **to pay off old scores,** ajustar cuentas viejas. **to pay one's addresses to,** hacer la corte (a), pretender en matrimonio (a). **to pay the penalty,** sufrir el castigo, hacer penitencia. **to pay with interest,** *Fig.* pagar con creces. **to pay again,** volver a pagar, pagar de nuevo. **to pay back,** devolver, restituir; (money only) reembolsar; *Fig.* pagar en la misma moneda, vengarse (de). **to pay down,** pagar al contado. **to pay for,** pagar, costear; satisfacer. **to pay in,** ingresar. **to pay off,** (persons) despedir; (a debt) saldar; (a mortgage) cancelar, redimir. **to pay out,** (persons) vengarse de; (money) pagar; (ropes, etc.) arriar. **to pay up,** pagar; pagar por completo; (shares, etc.) redimir
payable /'peiəbəl/ *a* pagadero; a pagar; que puede ser pagado
payee /pei'i/ *n* tenedor, *m*
payer /'peiər/ *n* pagador (-ra)
paying /'peiɪŋ/ *n.* See **payment**
paymaster /'pei,mæstər/ *n* pagador, *m;* tesorero, *m.* **P.-General,** ordenador general de pagos, *m*
payment /'peimənt/ *n* pago, *m,* paga, *f;* remuneración, *f; Fig.* recompensa, satisfacción, *f; Fig.* premio, *m.* **in p. of,** en pago de. **on p. of,** mediante el pago de. **p. in advance,** pago adelantado, anticipo, *m*
pea /pi/ *n* guisante, *m.* **dry or split pea,** guisante seco, *m.* **sweet pea,** guisante de olor, *m.* **pea-flour,** harina de guisantes, *f.* **pea-green,** verde claro, *m.* **pea-jacket,** chaquetón de piloto, *m.* **pea-shooter,** cerbatana, *f*
peace /pis/ *n* paz, *f;* tranquilidad, quietud, *f,* sosiego, *m; Law.* orden público, *m.* **P.!** ¡Silencio! **to hold one's p.,** callarse, guardar silencio. **to make p.,** hacer las paces. **P. be upon this house!** ¡Paz sea en esta casa! **p.-footing,** pie de paz, *m.* **p.-loving,** pacífico. **p.-offering,** sacrificio propiciatorio, *m;* satisfacción, oferta de paz, *f*
peaceable /'pisəbəl/ *a* pacífico; apacible; tranquilo, sosegado
peaceableness /'pisəbəlnɪs/ *n* paz, *f;* apacibilidad, *f;* tranquilidad, quietud, *f,* sosiego, *m*
peaceably /'pisəbli/ *adv* pacíficamente; tranquilamente
peaceful /'pisfəl/ *a* pacífico; tranquilo; silencioso. **to come with p. intentions,** venir de paz
peacefully /'pisfəli/ *adv* en paz; pacíficamente; tranquilamente
peacefulness /'pisfəlnɪs/ *n* paz, *f;* tranquilidad, calma, quietud, *f;* silencio, *m;* carácter pacífico, *m*
peacemaker /'pis,meikər/ *n* pacificador (-ra); conciliador (-ra)
peach /pitʃ/ *n* (fruit) melocotón, *m;* (tree) melocotonero, melocotón, *m;* (girl) breva, *f.* **p.-colour,** color de melocotón, *m*
peacock /'pi,kɒk/ *n* pavo real, pavón, *m.* —*vi* pavonearse; darse humos. **The p. spread its tail,** El pavo real hizo la rueda
peahen /'pi,hɛn/ *n* pava real, *f*
peak /pik/ *n* punta, *f;* (of a cap) visera, *f;* (of a mountain) peñasco, *m,* cumbre, cima, *f;* (mountain itself) pico, *m;* (*Naut.* of a hull) pico, *m; Fig.* auge,

apogeo, *m;* punto más alto, *m.* —*vi* consumirse, enflaquecer. **p. hours,** horas de mayor tráfico, *f pl*

peaked /'pikɪd/ *a* en punta; puntiagudo; picudo; (of a cap) con visera; (wan) ojeroso; (thin) delgaducho, macilento, consumido

peal /pil/ *n* toque (or repique) de campanas, *m;* campanillazo, *m;* carillón, *m;* (noise) estruendo, ruido, *m;* (of thunder) trueno, *m;* (of an organ) sonido, *m.* —*vi* repicar; sonar. —*vt* tañer, echar a vuelo (las campanas); (of a bell that one presses) hacer sonar, tocar. **a p. of laughter,** una carcajada

peanut /'pi,nʌt/ *n* cacahuete, *m.* **p. butter,** mantequilla de cacahuete, *f*

pear /pɛər/ *n* pera, *f.* **p.-shaped,** piriforme, de figura de pera. **p. tree,** peral, *m*

pearl /pɜrl/ *n* perla, *f;* (mother-of-pearl) nácar, *m, a* de perla; perlero. —*vt* (dew) rociar, aljofarar. —*vi* pescar perlas; formar perlas. **seed p.,** aljófar, *m.* **p.-ash,** carbonato potásico, *m.* **p.-barley,** cebada perlada, *f.* **p.-button,** botón de nácar, *m.* **p.-fisher,** pescador de perlas, *m.* **p.-fishery,** pescaduría de perlas, *f.* **p.-grey,** gris de perla, *m*

pearly /'pɜrli/ *a* perlino; de perla; nacarado; (dewy) aljofarado

peasant /'pɛzənt/ *n* campesino (-na), labrador (-ra). —*a* campesino

peasantry /'pɛzəntri/ *n* campesinos, *m pl,* gente del campo, *f*

peat /pit/ *n* turba, *f.* **p.-bog,** turbera, *f*

pebble /'pɛbəl/ *n* guijarro, *m,* pedrezuela, guija, *f;* (gravel) guijo, *m;* cristal de roca, *m;* lente de cristal de roca, *m*

pebbled, pebbly /'pɛbəld; 'pɛbli/ *a* guijarroso, enguijarrado

peccadillo /,pɛkə'dɪlou/ *n* pecadillo, *m*

peck /pɛk/ *n* (of a bird) picotazo, *m,* picada, *f;* (kiss) besito, *m;* (large amount) montón, *m;* multitud, *f.* —*vt* (of a bird) picotear; sacar (or coger) con el pico; (kiss) besar rápidamente. —*vi* (with at) picotear; picar

pectoral /'pɛktərəl/ *a* pectoral

peculiar /pɪ'kyulyər/ *a* particular, peculiar, individual; propio, característico; (marked) especial; (unusual) extraño, raro, extraordinario

peculiarity /pɪ,kyuli'ærɪti/ *n* peculiaridad, particularidad, *f;* singularidad, *f;* (eccentricity) excentricidad, rareza, *f*

peculiarly /pɪ'kyulyərli/ *adv* particularmente, peculiarmente; especialmente; extrañamente

pecuniarily /pɪ,kyuni'ɛərəli/ *adv* pecuniariamente

pecuniary /pɪ'kyuni,ɛri/ *a* pecuniario

pedagogic /,pɛdə'gɒdʒɪk/ *a* pedagógico

pedagogue /'pɛdə,gɒg/ *n* pedagogo, *m*

pedagogy /'pɛdə,goudʒi, -,gɒdʒi/ *n* pedagogía, *f*

pedal /'pɛdl̩/ *n* pedal, *m.* —*vi* pedalear

pedant /'pɛdn̩t/ *n* pedante, *mf*

pedantic /pə'dæntɪk/ *a* pedante

pedantically /pə'dæntɪkli/ *adv* con pedantería, pedantescamente

pedantry /'pɛdn̩tri/ *n* pedantería, *f*

peddle /'pɛdl̩/ *vi* ser buhonero. —*vt* revender

peddling /'pɛdlɪŋ/ *n* buhonería, *f.* —*a* trivial, insignificante; mezquino

pedestal /'pɛdəstl̩/ *n* pedestal, *m; Fig.* fundamento, *m,* base, *f.* **to put on a p.,** *Fig.* poner sobre un pedestal

pedestrian /pə'dɛstriən/ *n* peatón, peón, *m, a* pedestre; *Fig.* patoso. **p. traffic,** circulación de los peatones, *f*

pedestrian crosswalk, cruce peatonal (Argentina), cruce de peatones, *m*

pediatrician /,pidiə'trɪʃən/ *n* pediatra, *mf*

pedigree /'pɛdɪ,gri/ *n* genealogía, *f;* raza, *f;* (of words) etimología, *f.* —*a* (of animals) de raza, de casta. **p. dog,** perro de casta, *m*

pediment /'pɛdəmənt/ *n Archit.* frontón, *m*

pedlar /'pɛdlər/ *n* buhonero, *m*

pedometer /pə'dɒmɪtər/ *n* pedómetro, cuentapasos, *m*

peel /pil/ *n* (baker's) pala, *f;* (of fruit, etc.) piel, *f,* hollejo, *m.* —*vt* pelar, mondar; (bark) descortezar. —*vi* descascararse, desconcharse; (of the bark of a tree) descortezarse

peeling /'pilɪŋ/ *n* (of fruit, etc.) peladura, monda, *f;* (of bark) descortezadura, *f;* (of paint, etc.) desconchadura, *f*

peep /pip/ *vi* (of birds) piar; (of mice) chillar; (peer) atisbar, mirar a hurtadillas; (appear) asomar; mostrarse; (of the dawn) despuntar. —*n* (of birds) pío, *m;* (of mice) chillido, *m;* (glimpse) vista, *f;* (glance) ojeada, mirada furtiva, *f;* **at the p. of day,** al despuntar el día. **p.-hole,** mirilla, *f,* atisbadero, *m;* escucha, *f.* **p.-show,** óptica, *f*

peeper /'pipər/ (eye) avizón *m*

peer /pɪər/ *n* par, *m;* igual, *mf.* —*vi* atisbar; escudriñar; *Fig.* asomar, aparecer

peerage /'pɪərɪdʒ/ *n* nobleza, aristocracia, *f;* dignidad de par, *f*

peeress /'pɪərɪs/ *n* paresa, *f*

peerless /'pɪərlɪs/ *a* sin par, incomparable, sin igual

peevish /'pivɪʃ/ *a* displicente, malhumorado; picajoso, vidrioso, enojadizo

peevishness /'pivɪʃnɪs/ *n* displicencia, *f,* mal humor, *m;* impaciencia, *f*

peg /pɛg/ *n* clavija, *f;* (of a tent) estaca, *f;* (of a barrel) estaquilla, *f;* (of a violin, etc.) clavija, *f;* (for coats, etc.) colgadero, *m;* (of whisky, etc.) trago, *m; Fig.* pretexto, *m.* —*vt* clavar, enclavijar, empernar. **to take down a peg,** bajar los humos (a). **to peg away,** batirse el cobre. **to peg down,** fijar con clavijas; (a tent) sujetar con estacas; (prices) fijar

Pegasus /'pɛgəsəs/ *n* Pegaso, *m*

peignoir /pein'wɑr/ *n* peinador, salto de cama, *m,* bata, *f*

pekinese /,pikə'niz/ *n* perro (-rra) pequinés (-esa)

pelican /'pɛlɪkən/ *n* pelícano, *m*

pellagra /pə'lægrə/ *n Med.* pelagra, *f*

pellet /'pɛlɪt/ *n* bolita, *f;* (pill) píldora, *f;* (shot) perdigón, *m*

pellmell /'pɛl'mɛl/ *adv* a trochemoche; atropelladamente

pellucid /pə'lusɪd/ *a* diáfano

Peloponnesian /,pɛləpə'niʒən/ *a* and *n* peloponense, *mf*

pelota /pə'loutə/ *n* pelota vasca, *f.* **p. player,** pelotari, *m*

pelt /pɛlt/ *n* pellejo, *m;* cuero, *m;* (fur) piel, *f;* (blow) golpe, *m.* —*vt* llover (piedras, etc.) sobre, arrojar... sobre; (questions) disparar; (throw) tirar. —*vi* (of rrain) azotar, diluviar

pelvic /'pɛlvɪk/ *a* pélvico, pelviano

pelvis /'pɛlvɪs/ *n* pelvis, *f*

pen /pɛn/ *n* (for sheep, etc.) aprisco, *m;* corral, *m;* (paddock) parque, *m;* (for hens) pollera, *f;* (for writing and *Fig.*, author, etc.) pluma, *f.* —*vt* (shut up) acorralar; encerrar; (write) escribir (con pluma). **pen-and-ink drawing,** dibujo a la pluma, *m.* **pen-holder,** portaplumas, *m.* **pen-name,** seudónimo, *m.* **pen-wiper,** limpiaplumas, *m*

penal /'pinl̩/ *a* penal. **p. code,** código penal, *m.* **p. colony,** colonia penal, *f.* **p. servitude,** trabajos forzados (or forzosos), *m pl.* **p. servitude for life,** cadena perpetua, *f*

penalization /,pinl̩ə'zeiʃən/ *n* castigo, *m*

penalize /'pinl̩,aiz/ *vt* penar, imponer pena (a); castigar

penalty /'pɛnl̩ti/ *n Law.* penalidad, *f;* castigo, *m;* (fine) multa, *f;* (risk) riesgo, *m; Sports.* sancíon, *m.* **the p. of,** la desventaja de. **under p. of,** so pena de. **p. kick,** (football) penalty, *m*

penance /'pɛnəns/ *n* penitencia, *f.* **to do p.,** hacer penitencia

penchant /'pɛntʃənt;/ *n* tendencia, *f;* inclinación, *f*

pencil /'pɛnsəl/ *n* lápiz, *m;* (automatic) lapicero, *m.* —*vt* escribir (or dibujar or marcar) con lápiz. **p.-case,** estuche para lápices, *m.* **p.-holder,** lapicero, *m.* **p.-sharpener,** cortalápices, afilalápices, *m*

pendant /'pɛndənt/ *n* (jewel) pendiente, *m; Archit.* culo de lámpara, *m;* (*Naut.* rope) amantillo, *m;* (flag) gallardete, *m*

pending /'pɛndɪŋ/ *a* pendiente. —*prep* durante. **to be p.,** pender; amenazar

pendulous /'pɛndʒələs/ *a* péndulo; colgante; oscilante
pendulum /'pɛndʒələm/ *n* péndola, *f*, péndulo, *m*
penetrability /ˌpɛnɪtrə'bɪlɪti/ *n* penetrabilidad, *f*
penetrable /'pɛnɪtrəbəl/ *a* penetrable
penetrate /'pɛnɪˌtreit/ *vt* and *vi* penetrar
penetrating /'pɛnɪˌtreitɪŋ/ *a* penetrante
penetration /ˌpɛnɪ'treiʃən/ *n* penetración, *f*
penguin /'pɛŋgwɪn/ *n* pingüino, pájaro bobo, *m*
penicillin /ˌpɛnə'sɪlɪn/ *n* penicilina, *f*
peninsula /pə'nɪnsələ, -'nɪnsyələ/ *n* península, *f*
peninsular /pə'nɪnsələr, -'nɪnsyələr/ *a* peninsular. **P. War,** Guerra de la Independencia, *f*
penis /'pinɪs/ *n* pene, *m*
penitence /'pɛnɪtəns/ *n* penitencia, *f*
penitent /'pɛnɪtənt/ *a* penitente. —*n* penitente, *mf*
penitential /ˌpɛnɪ'tɛnʃəl/ *a* penitencial
penitentiary /ˌpɛnɪ'tɛnʃəri/ *n Eccl.* penitenciaria, *f;* casa de corrección, *f;* penitenciaria, *f*, presidio, *m;* cárcel modelo, *f*, *a* penitenciario
penknife /'pɛnˌnaif/ *n* cortaplumas, *m*
penmanship /'pɛnmənˌʃɪp/ *n* caligrafía, *f*
pennant /'pɛnənt/ *n Naut.* gallardete, *m;* banderola, *f*, (ensign) insignia, bandera, *f*
penniless /'pɛnɪlɪs/ *a* sin un penique, sin blanca; indigente, pobre de solemnidad. **to leave p.,** dejar en la miseria; *Inf.* dejar sin camisa
pennilessness /'pɛnɪlɪsnɪs/ *n* falta de dinero, extrema pobreza, *f*
penning /'pɛnɪŋ/ *n* escritura, *f;* (drawing up) redacción, *f;* (of bulls, etc.) acorralamiento, *m*
pennon /'pɛnən/ *n* pendón, *m*, banderola, *f;* (ensign) bandera, insignia, *f*
Pennsylvanian /ˌpɛnsəl'veinyən/ *a* and *n* pensilvano (-na)
penny /'pɛni/ *n* de un centavo, penique, *m;* perra gorda, *f.* —*a* de un penique. **p.-a-liner,** gacetillero, *m.* **p. dreadful,** folletín, *m*, novela por entregas, *f.* **p.-in-the-slot machine,** tragaperras, *m*
pennyworth /'pɛniˌwɜrθ/ *n* penique, valor de un penique, *m*
pension /'pɛnʃən/ *n* pensión, *f; Mil.* retiro, *m;* (grant) beca, *f;* (boardinghouse) pensión de familia, *f.* —*vt* pensionar, dar una pensión (a); (with off) jubilar. **old age p.,** pensión para la vejez, *f.* **retirement p.,** pensión vitalicia, *f*
pensioner /'pɛnʃənər/ *n* pensionista, *mf;* (*Mil.* and *Nav.*) inválido, *m*
pensive /'pɛnsɪv/ *a* pensativo, meditabundo; cabizbajo, triste
pensively /'pɛnsɪvli/ *adv* pensativamente; tristemente
pensiveness /'pɛnsɪvnɪs/ *n* reflexión, meditación profunda, *f;* tristeza, melancolía, *f*
pentagon /'pɛntəˌgɒn/ *n* pentágono, *m*
Pentateuch /'pɛntəˌtuk/ *n* pentateuco, *m*
Pentecost /'pɛntɪˌkɔst/ *n* Pentecostés, *m*, Pascua, *f*
pentecostal /ˌpɛntɪ'kɔstl̩/ *a* de Pentecostés, pascual
penthouse /'pɛntˌhaus/ *n* cobertizo, tinglado, *m*, tejavana, *f*
pent-up /pɛnt 'ʌp/ *a* encerrado; enjaulado; (of emotion) reprimido
penultimate /pɪ'nʌltəmɪt/ *a* penúltimo. —*n* penúltimo, *m*
penurious /pə'nʊriəs/ *a* pobre; escaso; (stingy) tacaño, avaro
penury /'pɛnyəri/ *n* penuria, *f*
peony /'piəni/ *n* peonía, *f*, saltaojos, *m*, rosa albardera, rosa montés, *f*
people /'pipəl/ *n* pueblo, *m;* nación, *f;* gente, *f;* personas, *f pl*; (used disparagingly, mob) populacho, vulgo, *m;* (inhabitants) habitantes, *m pl*; (subjects) súbditos, *m pl*; (relations) parientes, *m pl*; familia, *f.* —*vt* poblar. **little p.,** (children) gente menuda, *f.* **respectable p.,** gente de bien, *f.* **the p. of Burgos,** los habitantes de Burgos. **P. say,** Se dice, La gente dice. **Very few p. think as you do,** Hay muy pocas personas que opinan como Vd. **How are your p.** (family)? ¿Cómo están los de tu casa? ¿Cómo está tu familia? **"People Working"** «Trabajadores»
peopling /'piplɪŋ/ *n* población, *f;* colonización, *f*
pep /pɛp/ *n Inf.* energía, *f*, ánimo, *m.* **p. talk,** discurso estimulante, *m.* **p. up,** animar
Pepin the Short /'pɛpɪn/ Pipino el Breve
peplum /'pɛpləm/ *n* peplo, *m*
pepper /'pɛpər/ *n* pimienta, *f;* (plant) pimentero, pimiento, *m*, *vt* sazonar con pimienta; (pelt) acribillar; (with questions) disparar; (a literary work with quotations, etc.) salpimentar. **black p.,** pimienta negra, *f.* **red p.,** pimiento, *m;* (cayenne) pimentón, *m.* **p.-castor,** pimentero, *m*
peppercorn /'pɛpərˌkɔrn/ *n* grano de pimienta, *m*
peppermint /'pɛpərˌmɪnt/ *n* menta, *f.* **p. drop,** pastilla de menta, *f*
peppery /'pɛpəri/ *a* picante; (irascible) colérico, irascible
pepsin /'pɛpsɪn/ *n Chem.* pepsina, *f*
peptic /'pɛptɪk/ *a* péptico
per /pɜr; *unstressed* pər/ *prep* por. **ninety miles per hour,** noventa millas por hora. **ten pesetas per dozen,** diez pesetas la docena. **$60 per annum,** sesenta dólares al año. **per cent.,** por ciento
perambulate /pər'æmbyəˌleit/ *vt* recorrer
perambulator /pər'æmbyəˌleitər/ *n* cochecito para niños, *m*
percale /pər'keil/ *n* percal, *m*
percaline /ˌpɜrkə'lin/ *n* percalina, *f*
perceive /pər'siv/ *vt* percibir, comprender, darse cuenta de; percibir, discernir
percentage /pər'sɛntɪdʒ/ *n* tanto por ciento, *m;* porcentaje, *m*
perceptible /pər'sɛptəbəl/ *a* perceptible, visible; sensible
perceptibly /pər'sɛptəbli/ *adv* visiblemente; sensiblemente
perception /pər'sɛpʃən/ *n* percepción, *f;* sensibilidad, *f*
perceptive /pər'sɛptɪv/ *a* perceptivo
perch /pɜrtʃ/ *n Ichth.* perca, *f;* (for birds) percha, *f;* (measure) pértiga, *f.* —*vi* posarse (en or sobre). —*vt* posar (en or sobre)
percolate /'pɜrkəˌleit/ *vi* filtrar; *Fig.* penetrar. —*vt* filtrar, colar
percolation /ˌpɛrkə'leiʃən/ *n* filtración, *f*
percolator /'pɜrkəˌleitər/ *n* filtro, *m.* **coffee p.,** colador de café, *m*
percussion /pər'kʌʃən/ *n* percusión, *f;* choque, *m.* **p. cap,** fulminante, *m.* **p. instrument,** instrumento de percusión, *m*
perdition /pər'dɪʃən/ *n* perdición, *f;* ruina, *f*
peregrination /ˌpɛrɪgrə'neiʃən/ *n* peregrinación, *f*
peremptorily /pə'rɛmptərəli/ *adv* perentoriamente
peremptoriness /pə'rɛmptərinɪs/ *n* perentoriedad, *f*
peremptory /pə'rɛmptəri/ *a* perentorio; (of manner, etc.) imperioso, autoritario
perennial /pə'rɛniəl/ *a Bot.* vivaz; perenne; eterno, perpetuo. —*n* planta vivaz, *f*
perennially /pə'rɛniəli/ *adv* perennemente
perfect /*a.*, *n.* 'pɜrfɪkt; *v.* pər'fɛkt/ *a* perfecto; (of a work) acabado; completo. —*n Gram.* (tiempo) perfecto, *m.* —*vt* perfeccionar; (oneself) perfeccionarse. **to have a p. knowledge of...,** conocer a fondo... **They are p. strangers to me,** Me son completamente desconocidos
perfectible /pər'fɛktəbəl/ *a* perfectible
perfecting /pər'fɛktɪŋ/ *n* perfeccionamiento, *m;* terminación, *f*
perfection /pər'fɛkʃən/ *n* perfección, *f;* excelencia, *f.* **to p.,** a la perfección, a las mil maravillas
perfectionist /pər'fɛkʃənɪst/ *n* perfeccionista, *mf*
perfidious /pər'fɪdiəs/ *a* pérfido
perfidy /'pɜrfɪdi/ *n* perfidia, *f*
perforate /'pɜrfəˌreit/ *vt* perforar, agujerear
perforating /'pɜrfəˌreitɪŋ/ *a* perforador
perforation /ˌpɜrfə'reiʃən/ *n* perforación, *f;* agujero, *m*
perforce /pər'fɔrs/ *adv* a la fuerza, forzosamente
perform /pər'fɔrm/ *vt* hacer; poner por obra, llevar a cabo; desempeñar, cumplir; ejercer; (a piece of music, etc.) ejecutar; realizar; (a play) representar, dar; (a part in a play) desempeñar (el papel de...); (Divine Service) oficiar. —*vi Theat.* trabajar, representar un

papel; (a musical instrument) tocar; (sing) cantar; (of animals) hacer trucos
performable /pər'fɔrməbəl/ *a* hacedero, practicable, ejecutable; *Theat.* que puede representarse; *Mus.* tocable
performance /pər'fɔrməns/ *n* ejecución, realización, *f;* desempeño, ejercicio, *m;* cumplimiento, *m;* acción, *f;* hazaña, *f;* (work) obra, *f; Theat.* función, representación, *f;* (*Theat.* acting of a part) interpretación, *f; Mus.* ejecución, *f; Mech.* potencia, *f.* **first p.,** *Theat.* estreno, *m*
performer /pər'fɔrmər/ *n Mus.* ejecutante, *mf,* músico, *m; Theat.* actor (-triz), representante, *mf;* artista, *mf*
performing /pər'fɔrmɪŋ/ *a* (of animals) sabio. **p. dog,** perro sabio, *m*
perfume /*n.* 'pɜrfyum; *v.* pər'fyum/ *n* perfume, *m;* fragancia, *f;* aroma, *m.* —*vt* perfumar; embalsamar, aromatizar, llenar con fragancia. **p. burner,** perfumador, *m*
perfumer /pər'fyumər/ *n* perfumista, *mf*
perfumery /pər'fyuməri/ *n* perfumería, *f*
perfuming /'pɜrfyumɪŋ/ *n* acción de perfumar, *f, a* que perfuma
perfunctorily /pər'fʌŋktərəli/ *adv* perfunctoriamente, sin cuidado; superficialmente
perfunctoriness /pər'fʌŋktərinɪs/ *n* descuido, *m,* negligencia, *f;* superficialidad, *f*
perfunctory /pər'fʌŋktəri/ *a* perfunctorio, negligente; superficial; ligero, de cumplido
pergola /'pɜrgələ/ *n* emparrado, cenador, *m*
perhaps /pər'hæps/ *adv* quizá, quizás(s), tal vez
peril /'pɛrəl/ *n* peligro, *m;* riesgo, *m.* —*vt* poner en peligro; arriesgar. **at one's p.,** a su riesgo. **in p.,** en peligro
perilous /'pɛrələs/ *a* peligroso, arriesgado
perimeter /pə'rɪmɪtər/ *n* perímetro, *m*
perineum /ˌpɛrə'niəm/ *n Anat.* perineo, *m*
period /'pɪəriəd/ *n* período, *m;* época, *f;* edad, *f,* tiempo, *m;* duración, *f;* término, plazo, *m; Gram.* período, *m;* (full stop) punto final, *m; Med.* menstruación, regla, *f.* **p. furniture,** muebles de época, *m pl*
periodic /ˌpɪəri'ɒdɪk/ *a* periódico
periodical /ˌpɪəri'ɒdɪkəl/ *a* periódico. —*n* publicación periódica, revista, *f*
periodicity /ˌpɪəriə'dɪsɪti/ *n* periodicidad, *f*
peripatetic /ˌpɛrəpə'tɛtɪk/ *a* peripatético
peripheral /pə'rɪfərəl/ *a* periférico
periphery /pə'rɪfəri/ *n* periferia, *f*
periphrastic /ˌpɛrə'fræstɪk/ *a* perifrástico
periscope /'pɛrəˌskoup/ *n* periscopio, *m*
perish /'pɛrɪʃ/ *vi* perecer; marchitarse; desaparecer, acabar. **to be perished with cold,** estar muerto de frío
perishable /'pɛrɪʃəbəl/ *a* perecedero, frágil
peritoneum /ˌpɛrɪtn̩'iəm/ *n* peritoneo, *m*
peritonitis /ˌpɛrɪtn̩'aitɪs/ *n* peritonitis, *f*
periwig /'pɛrɪˌwɪg/ *n* peluca, *f*
periwinkle /'pɛrɪˌwɪŋkəl/ *n Zool.* caracol marino, *m; Bot.* vincapervinca, *f*
perjure /'pɜrdʒər/ *vt* perjurar. **to p. oneself,** perjurarse
perjurer /'pɜrdʒərər/ *n* perjuro (-ra); perjurador (-ra)
perjury /'pɜrdʒəri/ *n* perjurio, *m.* **to commit p.,** jurar en falso, perjurar
perkiness /'pɜrkinɪs/ *n* desenvoltura, gallardía, *f,* despejo, *m*
perk (up) /pɜrk/ *vi* levantar la cabeza; recobrar sus bríos, alzar la cabeza; sacar la cabeza
perky /'pɜrki/ *a* desenvuelto, gallardo; coquetón; atrevido; (gay) alegre
permanence /'pɜrmənəns/ *n* permanencia, *f;* estabilidad, *f*
permanent /'pɜrmənənt/ *a* permanente; estable; (of posts, etc.) fijo. **p. wave,** ondulación permanente, *f.* **p. way,** *Rail.* vía, *f*
permanganate /pər'mæŋgəˌneit/ *n* permanganato, *m*
permeability /ˌpɜrmiə'bɪlɪti/ *n* permeabilidad, *f*
permeable /'pɜrmiəbəl/ *a* permeable
permeate /'pɜrmiˌeit/ *vt* penetrar; impregnar; *Fig.* infiltrar (en)
permeation /ˌpɜrmi'eiʃən/ *n* penetración, *f;* impregnación, *f; Fig.* infiltración, *f*
permissible /pər'mɪsəbəl/ *a* permisible, admisible; lícito
permission /pər'mɪʃən/ *n* permiso, *m,* licencia, *f*
permissive /pər'mɪsɪv/ *a* permisivo, tolerado; (optional) facultativo
permit / *v* pər'mɪt; *n* 'pɜrmɪt/ *vt* permitir; dar permiso (a), dejar; tolerar, sufrir; admitir. —*n* permiso, *m;* licencia, *f;* pase, *m.* **Will you p. me to smoke?** ¿Me permites fumar?
permutation /ˌpɜrmyʊ'teiʃən/ *n* permutación, *f*
permute /pər'myut/ *vt* permutar
pernicious /pər'nɪʃəs/ *a* pernicioso. **p. anemia,** anemia perniciosa, *f*
perniciousness /pər'nɪʃəsnɪs/ *n* perniciosidad, *f*
pernickety /pər'nɪkɪti/ *a* tiquismiquis
peroration /ˌpɛrə'reiʃən/ *n* peroración, *f*
peroxide /pə'rɒksaid/ *n* peróxido, *m*
perpendicular /ˌpɜrpən'dɪkyələr/ *a* perpendicular. —*n* perpendicular, *f*
perpendicularity /ˌpɜrpənˌdɪkyə'lærɪti/ *n* perpendicularidad, *f*
perpendicularly /ˌpɜrpən'dɪkyələrli/ *adv* perpendicularmente
perpetrate /'pɜrpɪˌtreit/ *vt Law.* perpetrar; cometer
perpetration /ˌpɜrpɪ'treiʃən/ *n Law.* perpetración, *f;* comisión, *f*
perpetrator /'pɜrpɪˌtreitər/ *n* el, *m,* (*f,* la) que comete; *Law.* autor (-ra); perpetrador (-ra)
perpetual /pər'pɛtʃuəl/ *a* perpetuo, perdurable, eterno; incesante, constante; (life-long) perpetuo
perpetually /pər'pɛtʃuəli/ *adv* perpetuamente; sin cesar; continuamente; constantemente
perpetuate /pər'pɛtʃuˌeit/ *vt* perpetuar, eternizar; inmortalizar
perpetuation /pərˌpɛtʃu'eiʃən/ *n* perpetuación, *f*
perpetuity /ˌpɜrpɪ'tuɪti/ *n* perpetuidad, *f.* **in p.,** para siempre
perplex /pər'plɛks/ *vt* dejar perplejo, aturdir, confundir; embrollar
perplexed /pər'plɛkst/ *a* perplejo, irresoluto; confuso; (of questions, etc.) complicado, intrincado
perplexedly /pər'plɛksɪdli/ *adv* perplejamente
perplexing /pər'plɛksɪŋ/ *a* difícil; complicado; confuso
perplexity /pər'plɛksɪti/ *n* perplejidad, *f;* confusión, *f*
perquisites /'pɜrkwəzɪts/ *n pl* emolumentos, *m pl;* gajes, percances, *m pl;* (tips) propinas, *f pl*
persecute /'pɜrsɪˌkyut/ *vt* perseguir; importunar, molestar
persecution /ˌpɜrsɪ'kyuʃən/ *n* persecución, *f*
persecutor /'pɜrsɪˌkyutər/ *n* perseguidor (-ra)
perseverance /ˌpɜrsə'vɪərəns/ *n* perseverancia, *f*
persevere /ˌpɜrsə'vɪər/ *vi* perseverar
persevering /ˌpɜrsə'vɪərɪŋ/ *a* perseverante
perseveringly /ˌpɜrsə'vɪərɪŋli/ *adv* con perseverancia, perseverantemente
Persia /'pɜrʒə/ (la) Persia, *f*
Persian /'pɜrʒən/ *a* persa; de Persia; pérsico. —*n* persa, *mf;* (language) persa, *m.* **P. blinds,** persianas, *f pl.* **P. cat,** gato (-ta) de Angora
persiennes /ˌpɜrzi'ɛnz/ *n pl* persianas, *f pl*
persist /pər'sɪst/ *vi* persistir; persistir (en), empeñarse (en), obstinarse (en)
persistence /pər'sɪstəns/ *n* persistencia, *f*
persistent /pər'sɪstənt/ *a* persistente
persistently /pər'sɪstəntli/ *adv* con persistencia, persistentemente
person /'pɜrsən/ *n* persona, *f.* **first p.,** *Gram.* primera persona, *f.* **in p.,** en persona. **no p.,** nadie
personable /'pɜrsənəbəl/ *a* bien parecido
personage /'pɜrsənɪdʒ/ *n* personaje, *m*
personal /'pɜrsənl̩/ *a* personal; íntimo; particular; en persona; (movable) mueble. **He is to make a p. appearance,** Va a estar presente en persona. **p. column,** (in a newspaper) columna de los suspiros, *f.* **p. equation,** ecuación personal, *f.* **p. estate,** (goods) bienes muebles, *m pl*

personality /ˌpɜrsəˈnælɪti/ *n* personalidad, *f;* (insult) personalismo, *m.* **dual p.,** conciencia doble, *f*
personate /ˈpɜrsəˌneit/ *vt* (in a play) hacer el papel de; (impersonate) hacerse pasar por
personification /pərˌsɒnəfɪˈkeiʃən/ *n* personificación, *f*
personify /pərˈsɒnəˌfai/ *vt* personificar
personnel /ˌpɜrsəˈnɛl/ *n* personal, *m*
perspective /pərˈspɛktɪv/ *n* perspectiva, *f, a* en perspectiva
perspicacious /ˌpɜrspɪˈkeiʃəs/ *a* perspicaz, clarividente, sagaz
perspicacity /ˌpɜrspɪˈkæsɪti/ *n* perspicacia, clarividencia, sagacidad, *f*
perspicuity /ˌpɜrspɪˈkyuɪti/ *n* perspicuidad, claridad, lucidez, *f*
perspicuous /pərˈspɪkyuəs/ *a* perspicuo, claro
perspiration /ˈpɜrspəˈreiʃən/ *n* sudor, *m*
perspire /pərˈspaiər/ *vi* sudar, transpirar
persuadable /pərˈsweidəbəl/ *a* persuasible
persuade /pərˈsweid/ *vt* persuadir; inducir (a), instar (a), mover (a), inclinar (a)
persuasion /pərˈsweiʒən/ *n* persuasión, *f;* persuasiva, *f;* opinión, *f;* creencia, *f;* religión, *f;* secta, *f*
persuasive /pərˈsweisɪv/ *a* persuasivo. —*n* persuasión, *f;* aliciente, atractivo, *m*
persuasively /pərˈsweisɪvli/ *adv* de un modo persuasivo, persuasivamente
persuasiveness /pərˈsweisɪvnɪs/ *n* persuasiva, *f*
pert /pɜrt/ *a* petulante; respondón, desparpajado
pertain /pərˈtein/ *vi* pertenecer (a); tocar (a), incumbir (a), convenir (a); estar relacionado (con)
pertinacious /ˌpɜrtn̩ˈeiʃəs/ *a* pertinaz
pertinaciously /ˌpɜrtn̩ˈeiʃəsli/ *adv* con pertinacia
pertinacity /ˌpɜrtn̩ˈæsɪti/ *n* pertinacia, *f*
pertinence /ˈpɜrtn̩əns/ *n* pertinencia, *f*
pertinent /ˈpɜrtn̩ənt/ *a* pertinente, atinado
pertinently /ˈpɜrtn̩əntli/ *adv* atinadamente
pertly /ˈpɜrtli/ *adv* con petulancia; con descaro
pertness /ˈpɜrtnɪs/ *n* petulancia, *f;* desparpajo, descaro, *m*
perturb /pərˈtɜrb/ *vt* perturbar, agitar, turbar, inquietar
perturbation /ˌpɜrtərˈbeiʃən/ *n* perturbación, agitación, inquietud, *f;* confusión, *f;* desorden, *m*
perturbed /pərˈtɜrbd/ *a* perturbado, agitado, ansioso, intranquilo
perturbing /pərˈtɜrbɪŋ/ *a* perturbador, inquietador
Peru /pəˈru/ el Perú
peruke /pəˈruk/ *n* peluca, *f*
perusal /pəˈruzəl/ *n* lectura, *f;* examen, *m*
peruse /pəˈruz/ *vt* leer con cuidado, estudiar, examinar
Peruvian /pə ˈruvi ən/ *a* and *n* peruano (-na)
pervade /pərˈveid/ *vt* penetrar; llenar, saturar; difundirse por; reinar en
pervasion /pərˈveiʒən/ *n* penetración, *f*
pervasive /pərˈveisɪv/ *a* penetrante
perverse /pərˈvɜrs/ *a* (wicked) perverso, depravado; obstinado; travieso; intratable
perversion /pərˈvɜrʒən/ *n* perversión, *f*
perversity /pərˈvɜrsɪti/ *n* (wickedness) perversidad, *f;* obstinacia, *f;* travesura, *f*
perversive /pərˈvɜrsɪv/ *a* perversivo
pervert /pərˈvɜrt/ *vt* pervertir; (words, etc.) torcer, tergiversar
pervious /ˈpɜrviəs/ *a* penetrable; permeable
pessary /ˈpɛsəri/ *n Surg.* pesario, *m*
pessimism /ˈpɛsəˌmɪzəm/ *n* pesimismo, *m*
pessimist /ˈpɛsəmɪst/ *n* pesimista, *mf*
pessimistic /ˌpɛsəˈmɪstɪk/ *a* pesimista
pessimistically /ˌpɛsəˈmɪstɪkli/ *adv* con pesimismo
pest /pɛst/ *n* insecto nocivo, *m;* animal dañino, *m;* parásito, *m;* (pestilence) peste, *f; Fig.* plaga, *f;* (person) mosca, *f*
pester /ˈpɛstər/ *vt* importunar, molestar, incomodar. **to p. constantly,** *Inf.* no dejar a sol ni a sombra
pestering /ˈpɛstərɪŋ/ *n* importunaciones, *f pl*
pestilence /ˈpɛstl̩əns/ *n* pestilencia, peste, *f;* plaga, *f*
pestilential /ˌpɛstl̩ˈɛnʃəl/ *a* pestilente, pestífero; pernicioso
pestle /ˈpɛsəl/ *n* mano de mortero, *f, vt* pistar, machacar, majar
pet /pɛt/ *n* animal doméstico, *m;* niño (-ña) mimado (-da); favorito (-ta); (dear) querido (-da); (peevishness) despecho, malhumor, *m.* —*vt* acariciar; (spoil) mimar. **to be a great pet,** ser un gran favorito
petal /ˈpɛtl̩/ *n* pétalo, *m,* hoja, *f*
Peter /ˈpitər/ *n* Pedro, *m.* **blue P.,** bandera de salida, *f.* **Peter's pence,** los diezmos de San Pedro
peter (out) *vi* desaparecer; agotarse
petition /pəˈtɪʃən/ *n* petición, *f;* súplica, *f;* instancia, solicitud, *f;* memorial, *m.* —*vt* suplicar; pedir, demandar; dirigir un memorial (a). **to file a p.,** elevar una instancia
petitioner /pəˈtɪʃənər/ *n* peticionario (-ia)
Petrarchan /pɪˈtrɑrkən/ *a* petrarquista
petrel /ˈpɛtrəl/ *n* petrel, *m*
petrifaction /ˌpɛtrəˈfækʃən/ *n* petrificación, *f*
petrify /ˈpɛtrəˌfai/ *vt* petrificar; *Inf.* dejar seco. **to become petrified,** petrificarse
petrol /ˈpɛtrəl/ *n* bencina, gasolina, *f.* —*a* de gasolina, de bencina. **to run out of p.,** tener una pana de bencina. **p. gauge,** indicador del nivel de gasolina, *m.* **p. pump,** surtidor de gasolina, *m.* **p. station,** puesto de bencina, *m,* estación de servicio, *f.* **p. tank,** depósito de bencina, *m*
petroleum /pəˈtrouliəm/ *n* petróleo, *m.* —*a* petrolero; de petróleo. **p. works,** refinería de petróleo, *f*
petrology /pɪˈtrɒlədʒi/ *n* petrografía, *f*
petrous /ˈpɛtrəs/ *a* pétreo
petticoat /ˈpɛtiˌkout/ *n* enagua, *f; pl* **petticoats,** (slang) faldas, *f pl.* —*a* de faldas, de mujeres; de mujer
pettifogger /ˈpɛtɪˌfɒgər/ *n* (lawyer) picapleitos, *m,* rábula, *mf;* (quibbler) sofista, *mf*
pettifogging /ˈpɛtɪˌfɒgɪŋ/ *a* charlatán, mezquino, trivial
pettiness /ˈpɛtinɪs/ *n* trivialidad, insignificancia, *f;* pequeñez, *f;* mezquindad, *f;* ruindad, bajeza, *f*
petty /ˈpɛti/ *a* trivial, sin importancia, insignificante; inferior; pequeño; mezquino; ruin; bajo. **p. cash,** gastos menores de caja, *m pl.* **p. expense,** gasto menudo, *m.* **p. officer,** suboficial, *m.* **p. thief,** ratero (-ra)
petulance /ˈpɛtʃələns/ *n* mal humor, *m,* displicencia, irritabilidad, *f*
petulant /ˈpɛtʃələnt/ *a* malhumorado, displicente, enojadizo, irritable
petulantly /ˈpɛtʃələntli/ *adv* displicentemente, con mal humor
petunia /pɪˈtunyə/ *n* petunia, *f*
pew /pyu/ *n* banco (de iglesia), *m.* **p.-opener,** sacristán, *m*
pewter /ˈpyutər/ *n* peltre, *m, a* de peltre
phalange /ˈfælәndʒ/ *n* falange, *f*
phalanx /ˈfeilæŋks/ *n* falange, *f*
phallic /ˈfælɪk/ *a* fálico
phallus /ˈfæləs/ *n* falo, *m*
phantasmagoria /fænˌtæzməˈgɔriə/ *n* fantasmagoría, *f*
phantasmagoric /fænˌtæzməˈgɔrɪk/ *a* fantasmagórico
phantom /ˈfæntəm/ *n* fantasma, espectro, *m;* sombra, ficción, *f;* visión, *f*
Pharisaical /ˌfærəˈseiɪkəl/ *a* farisaico
Pharisee /ˈfærəˌsi/ *n* fariseo, *m*
pharmaceutical /ˌfɑrməˈsutɪkəl/ *a* farmacéutico; *n* producto farmacéutico, *m*
pharmacist /ˈfɑrməsɪst/ *n* farmacéutico, *m*
pharmacological /ˌfɑrməkəˈlɒdʒɪkəl/ *a* farmacológico
pharmacologist /ˌfɑrməˈkɒlədʒɪst/ *n* farmacólogo, *m*
pharmacology /ˌfɑrməˈkɒlədʒi/ *n* farmacología, *f*
pharmacopeia /ˌfɑrməˈkoupiə/ *n* farmacopea, *f*
pharmacy /ˈfɑrməsi/ *n* farmacia, *f*
pharyngeal /fəˈrɪndʒiəl/ *a* faríngeo
pharyngitis /ˌfærɪnˈdʒaitɪs/ *n* faringitis, *f*
pharynx /ˈfærɪŋks/ *n* faringe, *f*
phase /feiz/ *n* fase, *f;* aspecto, *m; Astron.* fase, *f*
pheasant /ˈfɛzənt/ *n* faisán, *m.* **hen p.,** faisana, *f.* **p. shooting,** caza de faisanes, *f*
phenic /ˈfinɪk/ *a* fénico

phenol /'finɔl/ *n* fenol, *m*

phenomenal /fɪ'nɒmənḷ/ *a* fenomenal

phenomenon /fɪ'nɒmə,nɒn/ *n* fenómeno, *m*

phial /'faiəl/ *n* redoma, *f*

philander /fɪ'lændər/ *vi* galantear

philanderer /fɪ'lændərər/ *n* Tenorio, galanteador, *m*

philandering /fɪ'lændərɪŋ/ *n* galanteo, *m*

philanthropic /,fɪlən'θrɒpɪk/ *a* filantrópico

philanthropist /fɪ'lænθrəpɪst/ *n* filántropo, *m*

philanthropy /fɪ'lænθrəpi/ *n* filantropía, *f*

philatelic /,fɪlə'tɛlɪk/ *a* filatélico

philatelist /fɪ'lætḷɪst/ *n* filatelista, *mf*

philately /fɪ'lætḷi/ *n* filatelia, *f*

philharmonic /,fɪlhɑr'mɒnɪk/ *a* filarmónico

philippic /fɪ'lɪpɪk/ *n* filípica, *f*

Philippine /'fɪlə,pin/ *a* and *n* filipino (-na)

Philippines, the /'fɪlə,pinz/ las (Islas) Filipinas, *f pl*

Philistine /'fɪlə,stin/ *a* and *n* filisteo (-ea)

philological /,fɪlə'lɒdʒɪkəl/ *a* filológico

philologist /fɪ'lɒlədʒɪst/ *n* filólogo, *m*

philology /fɪ'lɒlədʒi/ *n* filología, *f*

philosopher /fɪ'lɒsəfər/ *n* filósofo, *m*. **philosopher's stone,** piedra filosofal, *f*

philosophical /,fɪlə'sɒfɪkəl/ *a* filosófico

philosophize /fɪ'lɒsə,faiz/ *vi* filosofar

philosophy /fɪ'lɒsəfi/ *n* filosofía, *f*. **moral p.,** filosofía moral, *f*. **natural p.,** filosofía natural, *f*

philter /'fɪltər/ *n* filtro, *m*

phlebitis /flə'baitɪs/ *n* flebitis, *f*

phlebotomist /flə'bɒtəmɪst/ *n* sangrador, flebotomiano, *m*

phlebotomy /flə'bɒtəmi/ *n* flebotomía, *f*

phlegm /flɛm/ *n* flema, *f*

phlegmatic /flɛg'mætɪk/ *a* flemático

phlox /flɒks/ *n* flox, *m*

Phoenician /fɪ'nɪʃən/ *a* and *n* fenicio (-ia)

phoenix /'finɪks/ *n* fénix, *f*

phonetic /fə'nɛtɪk/ *a* fonético

phoneticist /fe'nɛtəsɪst/ *n* fonetista, *mf*

phonetics /fə'nɛtɪks, fou-/ *n* fonética, *f*

phonograph /'founə,græf/ *n* fonógrafo, *m*

phonological /,fōnḷɒdʒɪkəl/ *a* fonológico

phonology /fə'nɒlədʒi/ *n* fonología, *f*

phony /'founi/ *a* falso; espurio. **p. war,** guerra tonta, guerra falsa, *f*

phosphate /'fɒsfeit/ *n* fosfato, *m*

phosphoresce /,fɒsfə'rɛs/ *vi* fosforecer, ser fosforescente

phosphorescence /,fɒsfə'rɛsəns/ *n* fosforescencia, *f*

phosphorescent /,fɒsfə'rɛsənt/ *a* fosforescente

phosphoric /fɒs'fɔrɪk/ *a* fosfórico

phosphorus /'fɒsfərəs/ *n* fósforo, *m*

photo /'foutou/ *n* foto, *f*

photochemistry /,foutou'kɛməstri/ *n* fotoquímica, *f*

photogenic /,foutə'dʒɛnɪk/ *a* fotogénico

photograph /'foutə,græf/ *n* fotografía, *f*. —*vt* fotografiar, retratar. **to have one's p. taken,** hacerse retratar

photographer /fə'tɒgrəfər/ *n* fotógrafo, *m*

photographic /,foutə'græfɪk/ *a* fotográfico

photography /fə'tɒgrəfi/ *n* fotografía, *f*

photogravure /,foutəgrə'vyʊr/ *n* fotograbado, *m*

photostat /'foutə,stæt/ *n* fotostato, *m*

photosynthesis /,foutə'sɪnθəsɪs/ *n* fotosíntesis, *f*

phrase /freiz/ *n* frase, *f*; *Mus.* frase musical, *f*. —*vt* expresar, frasear; redactar. **p.-book,** libro de frases, *m*

phraseology /,freizi'ɒlədʒi/ *n* fraseología, *f*

phrasing /'freizɪŋ/ *n* (drawing up) redacción, *f*; (style) estilo, *m*; *Mus.* frases, *f pl*

phrenetic /frɪ'nɛtɪk/ *a* frenético

Phrygian /'frɪdʒiən/ *a* and *n* frigio (-ia)

Phrygian cap *n* gorro frigio, *m*

phthisis /'θaisɪs/ *n* tisis, *f*

phylactery /fɪ'læktəri/ *n* filactria, *f*

phylloxera /fɪ'lɒksərə/ *n* filoxera, *f*

physical /'fɪzɪkəl/ *a* físico. **p. fitness,** buen estado físico, *m*. **p. geography,** geografía física, *f*. **p. jerks,** ejercicios físicos, *m pl*. **p. sciences,** ciencias físicas, *f pl*. **p. training,** educación física, *f*

physician /fɪ'zɪʃən/ *n* médico (-ca)

physicist /'fɪzəsɪst/ *n* físico, *m*

physics /'fɪzɪks/ *n* física, *f*

physiognomist /,fɪzi'ɒgnəmɪst/ *n* fisonomista, *mf*

physiognomy /,fɪzi'ɒgnəmi/ *n* fisonomía, *f*

physiological /,fɪziə'lɒdʒɪkəl/ *a* fisiológico

physiologist /,fɪzi'ɒlədʒɪst/ *n* fisiólogo, *m*

physiology /,fɪzi'ɒlədʒi/ *n* fisiología, *f*

physiotherapy /,fɪziou'θɛrəpi/ *n* fisioterapia, *f*

physique /fɪ'zik/ *n* físico, *m*

pianist /pi'ænɪst, 'piənɪst/ *n* pianista, *mf*

pianola /,piə'noulə/ *n* piano mecánico, *m*

piano, pianoforte /pi'ænou; pi'ænə,fɔrt/ *n* piano, *m*. **baby grand p.,** piano de media cola, *m*. **grand p.,** piano de cola, *m*. **upright p.,** piano vertical, *m*. **p. maker,** fabricante de pianos, *m*. **p. stool,** taburete de piano, *m*. **p. tuner,** afinador de pianos, *m*

picaresque /,pɪkə'rɛsk/ *a* picaresco

piccolo /'pɪkə,lou/ *n* flautín, *m*

pick /pɪk/ *n* (tool) pico, zapapico, *m*, (mattock) piqueta, *f*; (choice) selección, *f*; derecho de elección, *m*; (best) lo mejor, lo más escogido; (*Fig.* cream) flor, nata, *f*. **tooth-p.,** mondadientes, *m*. **p.-a-back,** sobre los hombros, a cuestas. **p.-ax,** zapapico, *m*, alcotana, *f*. **p.-me-up,** tónico, *m*; trago, *m*

pick /pɪk/ *vt* (with a pick-ax, make a hole) picar; (pluck, pick up) coger; (remove) sacar; (clean) limpiar; (one's teeth) mondarse (los dientes); (one's nose) hurgarse (las narices); (a bone) roer; (a lock) abrir con ganzúa; (a pocket) bolsear, robar del bolsillo; (peck) picotear; (choose) escoger; (a quarrel) buscar. —*vi* (steal) hurtar, robar; (nibble) picar. **I have a bone to p. with you,** Tengo que ajustar unas cuentas contigo. **Take your p.!** ¡Escoja! **to p. and choose,** mostrarse difícil. **to p. to pieces,** *Fig.* criticar severamente. **to p. one's way through,** abrirse camino entre; andar con precaución por; andar a tientas por. **to p. off,** coger; arrancar; quitar; (shoot) disparar; fusilar. **to p. out,** entresacar; escoger; (recognize) reconocer; (understand) llegar a comprender; (a tune) tocar de oídas; (a song) cantar de oídas; (of colours) contrastar, resaltar. **to p. up,** *vt* (ground, etc.) romper con pico; coger; tomar; recoger; (raise) levantar, alzar; (information, etc.) cobrar, adquirir; (a living) ganar; (make friends with) trabar amistad con; (recover) recobrar; (find) encontrar, hallar; (buy) comprar; (learn) aprender; (a wireless message) interceptar; (a radio station) oír, tener. —*vi* recobrar la salud; reponerse; mejorar. —*n Mech.* recobro, *m*

picket /'pɪkɪt/ *n* estaca, *f*; (*Mil.* and during strikes) piquete, *m*. —*vt* cercar con estacas; poner piquetes ante (or alrededor de); poner de guardia; estacionar

picking /'pɪkɪŋ/ *n* (gathering) recolección, *f*; (choosing) selección, *f*; (pilfering) robo, *m*; *pl* **pickings,** desperdicios, *m pl*; (perquisites) gajes, *m pl*; ganancias, *f pl*

pickle /'pɪkəl/ *n* (solution) escabeche, *m*; (vegetable, etc.) encurtido, *m*; (plight) apuro, *m*; (child) diablillo, *m*. —*vt* encurtir, escabechar

picklock /'pɪk,lɒk/ *n* (thief and instrument) ganzúa, *f*

pickpocket /'pɪk,pɒkɪt/ *n* carterista, *mf* ratero (-ra)

picnic /'pɪknɪk/ *n* partida de campo, jira, *f*, picnic, *m*. —*vi* llevar la merienda al campo, hacer un picnic

picnicker /'pɪknɪkər/ *n* excursionista, *mf*

pictorial /pɪk'tɔriəl/ *a* pictórico; ilustrado. —*n* revista ilustrada, *f*

pictorially /pɪk'tɔriəli/ *adv* pictóricamente; en grabados; por imágenes

picture /'pɪktʃər/ *n* cuadro, *m*; (of a person) retrato, *m*; imagen, *f*; (illustration) grabado, *m*, lámina, *f*; fotografía, *f*; (outlook) perspectiva, *f*; idea, *f*. —*vt* pintar; describir; imaginar. **to go to the pictures,** ir al cine. **motion p.,** película, *f*. **talking p.,** película sonora, *f*. **p. book,** libro con láminas, *m*. **p. frame,** marco, *m*. **p. gallery,** museo de pinturas, *m*; galería de pinturas, *f*. **p. hat,** pamela, *f*. **p. palace,** cine, *m*. **p. postcard,** tarjeta postal, *f*. **p. restorer,** restaurador de cuadros, *m*. **p. writing,** pictografía, *f*

picturesque /,pɪktʃə'rɛsk/ *a* pintoresco

picturesqueness /,pɪktʃə'rɛsknɪs/ *n* carácter pintoresco, *m*, lo pintoresco; pintoresquismo, *m*

pie /pai/ *n* (savoury) empanada, *f*; (sweet) pastel, *m*, torta, *f*; (of meat) pastelón, *m*; *Print.* pastel, *m*. **apple**

pie, torta de manzanas, *f.* **to eat humble pie,** bajar las orejas. **to have a finger in the pie,** meter baza

piebald /'pai,bɔld/ *a* pío; tordo

piece /pis/ *n* pedazo, *m;* trozo, *m;* parte, porción, *f;* (literary, artistic work, coin, of fabric, at chess, etc. and slang) pieza, *f;* (of luggage) bulto, *m;* (of paper) hoja, *f;* (of ground) parcela, *f;* (of money) moneda, *f, vt* remendar; unir, juntar. **a p. of advice,** un consejo. **a p. of bread,** un pedazo de pan; una rebanada de pan. **a p. of folly,** un acto de locura. **a p. of furniture,** un mueble. **a p. of insolence,** una insolencia. **a p. of news,** una noticia. **a p. of paper,** un papel, una hoja de papel, una cuartilla. **a p. of poetry,** una poesía. **Peter has a five-shilling p.,** Pedro tiene una moneda de cinco chelines. **to break in pieces,** *vt* hacer pedazos, romper. —*vi* hacerse pedazos, romperse. **to come or fall to pieces,** deshacerse; (of machines) desarmarse. **to cut in pieces,** cortar en pedazos; (an army) destrozar. **to give a p. of one's mind (to),** decir cuatro verdades (a), decir cuántas son cinco (a). **to go to pieces,** (of persons) hacerse pedazos. **to take to pieces,** (a machine) desmontar; deshacer. **to tear or pull to pieces,** hacer pedazos, despedazar; desgarrar. **p. goods,** géneros en piezas, *m pl.* **p.-work,** trabajo a destajo, *m.* **to do p.-work,** trabajar a destajo. **p.-worker,** destajista, *mf*

piecemeal /'pis,mil/ *adv* en pedazos; a remiendos; en detalle; poco a poco

piecrust /'pai,krʌst/ *n* pasta, *f*

pied /paid/ *a* bicolor; abigarrado, de varios colores

pier /pɪər/ *n* (jetty) dique, *m;* embarcadero, *m;* malecón, *m;* (of a bridge) pila, *f;* (pillar) columna, *f;* (between windows, etc.) entrepaño, *m.* **p.-glass,** espejo de cuerpo entero, *m.* **p. head,** punta del dique, *f.* **p. table,** consola, *f*

pierce /pɪərs/ *vt* penetrar; (of sorrow, etc.) traspasar, herir; (bore) agujerear, taladrar. —*vi* penetrar

pierced ear /pɪərst/ *n* oreja perforada, *f*

piercing /'pɪərsɪŋ/ *a* penetrante; (of the wind, etc.) cortante; (of the voice, etc.) agudo. —*n* penetración, *f*

piercingly /'pɪərsɪŋli/ *adv* de un modo penetrante, agudamente

pietism /'paiɪ,tɪzəm/ *n* pietismo, *m*

pietist /'paiɪtɪst/ *n* pietista, *mf*

pietistic /,paiɪ'tɪstɪk/ *a* pietista

piety /'paiɪti/ *n* piedad, devoción, *f*

piezometer /,paiə'zɒmɪtər/ *n Phys.* piezómetro, *m*

piffle /'pɪfəl/ *n* patrañas, tonterías, *f pl*

pig /pɪg/ *n* puerco, cerdo, *m; Inf.* cochino, *m;* (metal) lingote, *m.* **to buy a p. in a poke,** cerrar un trato a ciegas. **p.-eyed,** de ojos de cerdo. **p.-iron,** arrabio; hierro colado en barras, lingote de fundición, *m*

pigeon /'pɪdʒən/ *n* paloma, *f,* palomo, *m; Inf.* primo, *m.* —*vt* embaucar, engañar. **carrier p.,** paloma mensajera, *f.* **clay p.,** pichón de barro, platillo de arcilla, *m.* **male p.,** pichón, *m.* **pouter p.,** paloma buchona, *f.* **young p.,** palomino, *m.* **p. fancier,** palomero, *m.* **p.-hole,** casilla, *f.* —*vt* encasillar. **set of p.-holes,** encasillado, *m.* **p.-shooting,** tiro de pichón, *m.* **p.-toed,** patituerto

piggy bank /'pɪgi/ *n* alcancía, *f*

pigheaded /'pɪg,hɛdɪd/ *a* terco, testarudo

pigheadedness /'pɪg,hɛdɪdnɪs/ *n* terquedad, testarudez, *f*

piglet /'pɪglɪt/ *n* cerdito, *m*

pigment /'pɪgmənt/ *n* pigmento, *m*

pigmentary /'pɪgmən,tɛri/ *a* pigmentario

pigmentation /,pɪgmən'teiʃən/ *n* pigmentación, *f*

pigskin /'pɪg,skɪn/ *n* piel de cerdo, *f*

pigsty /'pɪg,stai/ *n* pocilga, *f*

pigtail /'pɪg,teil/ *n* coleta, *f*

pike /paik/ *n Mil.* pica, *f,* chuzo, *m;* (peak) pico, *m*

pilaster /pɪ'læstər/ *n* pilastra, *f*

pile /pail/ *n* estaca, *f;* poste, *m;* (engineering) pilote, *m;* (heap) pila, *f,* montón, *m;* (pyre) pira, *f;* (building) edificio grande, *m; Elec.* pila, *f;* (hair) pelo, *m;* (nap) pelusa, *f; pl* **piles,** *Med.* almorranas, *f pl.* —*vt* clavar pilotes en; apoyar con pilotes; (heap) amontonar; (load) cargar. **to make one's p.,** *Inf.* hacer su pacotilla. **to p. arms,** poner los fusiles en pabellón. **to p. on,** (coal, etc.) echar; (increase) aumentar. **to p. it on,** exagerar, intensificar; (a table) cargar. **to p. up,** amontonarse; acumularse; (of a ship) encallar. **p. -driver,** machina, *f;* martinete, *m.* **p. dwelling,** vivienda palustre, sostenida por pilares, *f*

pilfer /'pɪlfər/ *vt* sisar, sonsacar, hurtar, ratear

pilferer /'pɪlfərər/ *n* sisador (-ra), ratero (-ra)

pilfering /'pɪlfərɪŋ/ *n* sisa, ratería, *f*

pilgrim /'pɪlgrɪm/ *n* peregrino (-na). **pilgrim's staff,** bordón, *m*

pilgrimage /'pɪlgrəmɪdʒ/ *n* peregrinación, *f;* romería, *f.* **to make a p.,** hacer una peregrinación, peregrinar; ir en romería

piling /'pailɪŋ/ *n* amontonamiento, *m;* (of buildings) pilotaje, *m*

pill /pɪl/ *n* píldora, *f.* **to gild the p.,** *Fig.* dorar la píldora. **p.-box,** caja de píldoras, *f;* casamata, *f, Mil.* nido de ametralladoras, *m*

pillage /'pɪlɪdʒ/ *vt* pillar, saquear. —*n* saqueo, *m*

pillager /'pɪlɪdʒər/ *n* saqueador (-ra)

pillaging /'pɪlɪdʒɪŋ/ *n* pillaje, *m, a* pillador, saqueador

pillar /'pɪlər/ *n* pilar, *m,* columna, *f;* (person) sostén, soporte, *m.* **from p. to post,** de Ceca en Meca. **p. of salt,** estatua de sal, *f.* **the Pillars of Hercules,** las Columnas de Hércules. **to be a p. of strength,** *Inf.* ser una roca. **p.-box,** buzón, *m*

pillared /'pɪlərd/ *a* con columnas, sostenido por columnas; en columnas

pillion /'pɪlyən/ *n* (on a horse, etc.) grupera, *f;* (on a motor-cycle) grupa, *f.* **to ride p.,** ir a la grupa

pillory /'pɪləri/ *n* picota, argolla, *f.* —*vt* empicotar; *Fig.* poner en ridículo; censurar duramente

pillow /'pɪlou/ *n* almohada, *f;* (for lace-making) cojín, *m;* (of a machine) cojinete, *m.* —*vt* apoyar; reposar; servir como almohada. **to take counsel of one's p.,** consultar con la almohada. **p.-case,** funda de almohada, *f*

pilot /'pailət/ *n* piloto, *m; Naut.* práctico, piloto (de puerto), *m.* —*vt* guiar, conducir; (*Naut. Aer.*) pilotar, pilotear. **p. boat,** vaporcito del práctico, *m.* **p. jacket,** chaquetón de piloto, *m.* **p. officer,** oficial de aviación, *m*

pilotage /'pailətɪdʒ/ *n* pilotaje, *m; Naut.* practicaje, *m*

pilotless /'pailətlɪs/ *a* sin piloto

pimento /pɪ'mɛntou/ *n* pimiento, *m*

pimp /pɪmp/ *n* rufián, alcahuete, *m, vi* alcahuetear

pimple /'pɪmpəl/ *n* grano, *m*

pimply /'pɪmpli/ *a* con granos

pin /pɪn/ *n* alfiler, *m;* prendedor, *m;* clavija, *f;* clavo, *m,* chaveta, *f;* (bolt) perno, *m.* —*vt* prender con alfileres; (with a peg) enclavijar; fijar; sujetar. **to pin up,** sujetar con alfileres; (the hair) sujetar con horquillas. **I don't care a pin,** No me importa un bledo. **to be on pins,** estar en ascuas. **to suffer from pins and needles,** tener aguijones. **pin-head,** cabeza de alfiler, *f.* **pin-money,** alfileres, *m pl.* **pin-oak,** *Bot.* pincarrasco, *m,* carrasca, *f.* **pin point,** punta de alfiler, *f.* **pin-prick,** alfilerazo, *m*

pinafore /'pɪnə,fɔr/ *n* delantal de niño, *m*

pince-nez /'pæns,nei/ *n* quevedos, *m pl*

pincers /'pɪnsərz/ *n pl* pinzas, tenazas, *f pl,* alicates, *m pl;* (of crustaceans) pinzas, *f pl.* **p. movement,** movimiento de pinzas, *m*

pinch /pɪntʃ/ *vt* pellizcar; (crush) estrujar; aplastar; apretar; (of the cold) helar; (steal) hurtar, birlar; (arrest) coger, prender. —*n* pellizco, torniscón, *m;* pulgarada, *f;* (of snuff) polvo, *m;* (distress) miseria, *f;* (pain) dolor, *m,* angustia, *f.* **at a p.,** en caso de apuro. **to know where the shoe pinches,** saber dónde le aprieta el zapato

pinched /pɪntʃt/ *a* (by the cold) helado; (wan) marchito, descolorido

pincushion /'pɪn,kʊʃən/ *n* acerico, *m*

Pindaric /pɪn'dærɪk/ *a* pindárico

pine /pain/ *n Bot.* pino, *m.* —*vi* languidecer, marchitarse, consumirse. **to p. for,** anhelar, suspirar por, perecer por. **pitch-p.,** pino de tea, *m.* **p.-apple,** piña de las Indias, *f,* ananás, *m.* **p. cone,** piña, *f.* **p. kernel,** piñón, *m.* **p. needle,** pinocha, *f.* **p. wood,** pinar, *m,* pineda, *f*

pineal /'pɪniəl/ *a* en figura de piña; *Anat.* pineal

ping /pɪŋ/ *n* silbido de una bala, *m;* zumbido, *m.* **p. pong,** tenis de mesa, pingpong, *m*
pinion /'pɪnyən/ *n* (wing) ala, *f;* (small feather) piñón, *m;* (in carving) alón, *m;* (wheel) piñón, *m.* —*vt* atar las alas de; cortar un piñón de; (a person) atar; (the arms of) trincar, asegurar
pink /pɪŋk/ *n Bot.* clavel, *m;* color de rosa, *m;* (perfection) modelo, *m;* colmo, *m;* (hunting) color rojo, *m;* levitín rojo de caza, *m.* —*a* de color de rosa, rosado. —*vt Sew.* picar; (pierce) penecrar, atravesar. —*vi* (of an engine) picar
pinking /'pɪŋkɪŋ/ *n Sew.* picadura, *f*
pinkish /'pɪŋkɪʃ/ *a* rosáceo
pinnacle /'pɪnəkəl/ *n Naut.* pinaza, *f*
pinnacle /'pɪnəkəl/ *n* pináculo, *m*
pinpoint /'pɪn,pɔint/ *vt* precisar
pint /paint/ *n* (measure) pinta, *f*
pintle /'pɪntl̩/ *n* (pin) perno, *m*
piolet /,piə'lei/ *n* piolet, *m*
pioneer /,paiə'nɪər/ *n* pionero, explorador, *m;* introductor, *m.* **to be a p. in...,** ser el primero en (or a)... **pioneering role,** papel de iniciador (e.g. *She played a pioneering role,* jugó un papel de iniciadora)
pious /'paiəs/ *a* pío, devoto, piadoso
piously /'paiəsli/ *adv* piadosamente, devotamente
pip /pɪp/ *n* (of fruit) pepita, *f;* (on cards, dice) punto, *m;* (disease) moquillo, *m;* (of an army, etc., officer) insignia, *f*
pipe /paip/ *n* (for tobacco) pipa de fumar, *f; Mus.* caramillo, *m;* (boatswain's) pito, *m;* (of a bird) trino, *m;* (voice) voz aguda, *f;* tubo, *m;* (for water, etc.) cañería, *f;* (of a hose) manga, *f;* (of an organ) cañón, *m;* (of wine) pipa, *f; pl* **pipes,** *Mus.* gaita, *f.* —*vi* tocar el caramillo (or la gaita); empezar a cantar; silbar; (of birds) trinar. —*vt* (a tune) tocar; (sing) cantar; (whistle) llamar con pito; conducir con cañerías; instalar cañerías en. **He smokes a p.,** Fuma una pipa. **I smoked a p.** (of tobacco) **before I went to bed,** Fumé una pipa antes de acostarme. **Put that in your p. and smoke it!** ¡Chúpate eso! **p. clay,** blanquizal, *m.* **p. cleaner,** limpiapipas, *m.* **p. layer,** cañero, fontanero, *m.* **p. laying,** instalación de cañerías, *f.* **p.-line,** cañería, *f;* (oil) oleoducto, *m.* **p. tobacco,** tabaco de pipa, *m*
pipeful /'paipfʊl/ *n* pipa, *f*
piper /'paipər/ *n* (bagpiper) gaitero, *m;* flautista, *mf*
pipette /pai'pɛt/ *n Chem.* pipeta, *f*
piping /'paipɪŋ/ *n* sonido del caramillo, *m;* música de la flauta, etc., *f;* (of birds) trinos, *m pl;* voz aguda, *f;* (for water, etc.) cañería, tubería, *f; Sew.* cordoncillo, *m.* **p.-hot,** hirviente
pipkin /'pɪpkɪn/ *n* ollita de barro, *f*
pippin /'pɪpɪn/ *n* (apple) camuesa, *f*
piquancy /'pikənsi/ *n* picante, *m*
piquant /'pikənt/ *a* picante
pique /pik/ *n* (resentment, and score in game) pique, *m.* **to p. oneself upon,** preciarse de, jactarse de. **to be piqued,** estar enojado; *Inf.* amoscarse
piquet /pɪ'kei/ *n* juego de los cientos, *m*
piracy /'pairəsi/ *n* piratería, *f*
pirate /'pairət/ *n* pirata, *mf.* —*vi* piratear. —*vt* publicar una edición furtiva de. **p. edition,** edición furtiva, *f*
piratical /pɪ'rætɪkəl/ *a* pirata, pirático; de pirata, de piratas
pirouette /,pɪru'ɛt/ *n* pirueta, *f*
Pisces /'paisiz/ *n pl* peces, *m pl*
pisciculture /'pɪsɪ,kʌltʃər/ *n* piscicultura, *f*
Pisgah /'pɪzgə/ Fasga, *f*
pistachio /pɪ'stæʃi,ou/ *n* pistacho, *m*
pistil /'pɪstl̩/ *n Bot.* pistilo, *m*
pistol /'pɪstl̩/ *n* pistola, *f.* **p. belt,** charpa, *f,* cinto de pistolas, *m.* **p. case,** pistolera, *f.* **p. shot,** pistoletazo, *m*
piston /'pɪstən/ *n Mech.* émbolo, pistón, *m; Mus.* pistón, *m,* llave, *f.* **p. ring,** anillo de émbolo, segmento de émbolo, *m.* **p. rod,** biela, *f.* **p. stroke,** carrera del émbolo, *f*
pit /pɪt/ *n* hoyo, *m;* foso, *m;* (in a garage) foso de reparación, *m; Theat.* platea, *f;* (trap) trampa, *f;* (scar) hoyo, *m;* precipicio, *m;* (hell) infierno, *m.* —*vt* (with smallpox) marcar con viruelas; (against) competir con. **pithead,** boca de mina, *f.* **pit of the stomach,** boca del estómago, *f.* **pit stall,** butaca de platea, *f*
pitch /pɪtʃ/ *n Chem.* pez, brea, *f,* alquitrán, *m;* (place) puesto, *m;* (throwing) lanzamiento, *m;* (distance thrown) alcance, *m;* (for cricket) cancha, *f;* (bowling) saque, *m;* (slope) pendiente, inclinación, *f;* (height) elevación, *f; Mus.* tono, *m;* (*Fig.* degree) grado, extremo, *m;* (*Naut. Aer.*) cabeceo, *m;* (of threads of a screw, etc.) paso, *m.* —*vt* (camp) asentar; (a tent, etc.) colocar, poner; (throw) lanzar, arrojar, tirar; (cricket, etc.) lanzar; (fix in) clavar; *Mus.* graduar el tono de; (tell) narrar. —*vi* (fall) caer; *Naut.* cabecear, zozobrar; *Aer.* cabecear. **to paint with p.,** embrear. **to p. into,** (attack) acometer, atacar; (scold) desatarse contra; (food) engullir. **p.-black,** negro como la pez; oscuro como boca de lobo. **p.-pine,** pino de tea, *m.* **p.-pipe,** diapasón vocal, *m*
pitched battle /pɪtʃt/ *n* batalla campal, *f*
pitcher /'pɪtʃər/ *n* jarro, cántaro, *m;* (in baseball) lanzador de pelota, *m*
pitcherful /'pɪtʃər,fʌl/ *n* jarro (de), *m*
pitchfork /'pɪtʃ,fɔrk/ *n* horquilla, *f,* aventador, *m.* —*vt* levantar con horquilla; *Fig.* lanzar
pitching /'pɪtʃɪŋ/ *n* (pavement) adoquinado, *m;* (of a ship) socollada, *f;* cabeceo, *m*
piteous /'pɪtiəs/ *a* lastimero; triste; plañidero; compasivo, tierno
piteousness /'pɪtiəsnɪs/ *n* estado lastimero, *m;* tristeza, *f;* compasión, ternura, *f*
pitfall /'pɪt,fɔl/ *n* trampa, *f; Fig.* añagaza, *f,* lazo, peligro, *m*
pith /pɪθ/ *n Bot.* médula, *f;* médula espinal, *f; Fig.* meollo, *m;* fuerza, *f,* vigor, *m;* substancia, *f;* quinta esencia, *f;* importancia, *f*
pithiness /'pɪθinɪs/ *n* jugosidad, *f;* fuerza, *f,* vigor, *m*
pithy /'pɪθi/ *a* meduloso; *Fig.* jugoso; enérgico, vigoroso
pitiable /'pɪtiəbəl/ *a* lastimoso, digno de compasión; (paltry) despreciable
pitiful /'pɪtɪfəl/ *a* piadoso, compasivo; conmovedor, doloroso, lastimero; (contemptible) miserable
pitifully /'pɪtɪfəli/ *adv* lastimosamente
pitiless /'pɪtɪlɪs/ *a* sin piedad, despiadado
pitilessness /'pɪtɪlɪsnɪs/ *n* crueldad, inhumanidad, *f*
pitman /'pɪtmən/ *n* minero, *m;* aserrador de foso, *m*
pittance /'pɪtn̩s/ *n* pitanza, *f;* pequeña porción, *f;* ración de hambre, *f*
pitted /'pɪtɪd/ *a* picoso
pituitary /pɪ'tuɪ,tɛri/ *a* pituitario
pity /'pɪti/ *n* piedad, compasión, *f;* lástima, *f.* —*vt* compadecerse de, tener lástima (a); compadecer. **It is a p. that...,** Es lástima que... **Have p.!** ¡Ten piedad! **to take p. on,** tener lástima (de). **to move to p.,** dar lástima (a), enternecer
pityingly /'pɪtiɪŋli/ *adv* con lástima
pivot /'pɪvət/ *n* pivote, *m;* eje, *m; Fig.* punto de partida, *m, vi* girar sobre un pivote o eje
pivotal /'pɪvətl̩/ *a Fig.* cardinal, principal, fundamental
pixy /'pɪksi/ *n* duende, *m.* **p. hood,** caperuza, *f*
pizzicato /,pɪtsɪ'kɑtou/ *a* pichigato
placability /,plækə'bɪlɪti/ *n* placabilidad, *f*
placable /'plækəbəl/ *a* aplacable, placable
placard /'plækɑrd/ *n* cartel, *m.* —*vt* fijar carteles (en); publicar por carteles
placate /'pleikeit/ *vt* aplacar, ablandar, apaciguar
placatory /'pleikə,tɔri/ *a* placativo
place /pleis/ *n* lugar, *m;* sitio, *m;* (position) puesto, *m;* (seat) asiento, *m;* (laid at table) cubierto, *m;* (square) plaza, *f;* (house) residencia, *f;* (in the country) casa de campo, finca, *f;* (in a book) pasaje, *m;* (in an examination) calificación, *f;* (rank) posición, *f,* rango, *m;* situación, *f;* (employment) empleo, *m,* colocación, *f.* —*vt* poner; colocar; (in employment) dar empleo (a); (appoint) nombrar; (an order) dar; (money) invertir; (remember) recordar, traer a la memoria; (size up) fijar; (confidence) poner. **in p.,** en su lugar; apropiado. **in p. of,** en vez de, en lugar de. **in the first p.,** en primer lugar, primero. **in the next p.,** luego, después. **out of p.,** fuera de lugar; inoportuno. **It is not my p. to...,** No me toca a mí de... **to give p. to,** ceder el paso (a); ceder (a). **to**

take p., verificarse, tener lugar, ocurrir. **p. of business,** establecimiento, local de negocios, *m*. **p. of worship,** edificio de culto, *m*
placenta /plə'sɛntə/ *n* placenta, *f*
placid /'plæsɪd/ *a* plácido, apacible; calmoso; sereno, sosegado; dulce
placidity /plə'sɪdɪti/ *n* placidez, *f;* serenidad, tranquilidad, *f,* sosiego, *m*
placidly /'plæsɪdli/ *adv* plácidamente
placing /'pleisɪŋ/ *n* colocación, *f;* posición, *f;* localización, *f*
placket /'plækɪt/ *n* abertura (en una falda), *f*
plagiarism /'pleidʒəˌrɪzəm/ *n* plagio, *m*
plagiarist /'pleidʒərɪst/ *n* plagiario (-ia)
plagiarize /'pleidʒəˌraiz/ *vt* plagiar, hurtar
plague /pleig/ *n* plaga, *f;* peste, pestilencia, *f.* —*vt* importunar, atormentar; plagar
plaice /pleis/ *n* (nearest equivalent) platija, *f*
plaid /plæd/ *n* manta escocesa, *f;* género de cuadros, *m, a* a cuadros
plain /plein/ *a* claro; evidente; (simple) sencillo; llano; sin adorno; (flat) liso, igual; (candid) franco; (with truth, etc.) desnudo; mero; puro, sin mezcla; (of words) redondo; (ugly) feo. —*adv* claramente; llanamente; sencillamente; francamente. —*n* llanura, *f,* llano, *m*. **the p. truth,** la pura verdad. **p. clothes,** traje de paisano, *m*. **p. clothes man,** detective, *m*. **p. cooking,** cocina sencilla, cocina casera, *f.* **p. dealing,** buena fe, sinceridad, *f.* **p. dweller,** llanero (-ra). **p. living,** vida sencilla, *f.* **p. people,** gente sencilla, *f.* **p. sailing,** *Fig.* camino fácil, *m*. **p. sewing,** costura, *f.* **p. -song,** canto llano, *m*. **p. speaking,** franqueza, *f.* **p.-spoken,** franco. **in p. English,** sin rodeos, en cristiano (e.g. *Speak in p. English!* Habla sin rodeos! Habla en cristiano!)
plainly /'pleinli/ *adv* claramente; sencillamente; llanamente; francamente; rotundamente
plainness /'pleinnɪs/ *n* claridad, *f;* sencillez, *f;* llaneza, *f;* franqueza, *f;* (ugliness) fealdad, *f*
plainsman /'pleinzmən/ *n* hombre de las llanuras, *m*
plaint /pleint/ *n* queja, *f,* lamento, *m; Law.* demanda, querella, *f*
plaintiff /'pleintɪf/ *n* demandante, *mf,* actor, *m,* parte actora, actora, *f*
plaintive /'pleintɪv/ *a* quejumbroso, dolorido; patético
plaintively /'pleintɪvli/ *adv* quejumbrosamente
plaintiveness /'pleintɪvnɪs/ *n* melancolía, tristeza, *f;* voz quejumbrosa, *f*
plait /pleit/ *n* trenza, *f.* —*vt* trenzar; tejer. **in plaits,** (of hair) en trenzas
plan /plæn/ *n* plan, *m;* (map) plano, *m;* proyecto, *m*. —*vt* planear; proyectar; proponerse. **the Marshall P.,** el Plan Marshall. **to make a p. of,** trazar un plano de. **to make plans,** hacer planes
planchette /plæn'ʃɛt/ *n* mesa giratoria, *f*
plane /plein/ *n* (tree) plátano, *m;* (tool) cepillo, *m; Geom.* plano, *m;* (level) nivel, *m; Aer.* avión, *m,* plano. —*vt* acepillar, alisar. —*vi Aer.* planear
planet /'plænɪt/ *n* planeta, *m*
planetarium /ˌplænɪ'tɛəriəm/ *n* planetario, *m*
planetary /'plænɪˌtɛri/ *a* planetario
planing /'pleinɪŋ/ *n* acepilladura, alisadura, *f,*
plank /plæŋk/ *n* tabla, *f; Fig.* fundamento, principio, *m; pl* **planks,** tablazón, *f.* —*vt* entablar, enmaderar
planking /'plæŋkɪŋ/ *n* entablado, *m,* tablazón, *f*
plankton /'plæŋktən/ *n* plancton, *m*
planned /plænd/ *a* proyectado, planeado; dirigido **p. economy,** economía dirigida, *f*
planner /'plænər/ *n* proyectista, *mf;* autor (-ra) de un plan
planning /'plænɪŋ/ *n* proyecto, *m;* concepción, *f*
plant /plænt/ *n Bot.* planta, *f;* instalación, *f,* material, *m*. —*vt* plantar; (place) colocar; fijar; (a blow) asestar; (people) establecer; (instil) inculcar, imbuir (con); (conceal) esconder. **p. pot,** florero, *m*. **p. stand,** jardinera, *f*
plantain /'plæntɪn/ *n Bot.* llantén, *m*
plantation /plæn'teiʃən/ *n* plantación, *f;* plantío, *m; Fig.* colonia, *f;* introducción, *f,* establecimiento, *m*
planter /'plæntər/ *n* plantador, cultivador, *m*
planting /'plæntɪŋ/ *n* plantación, *f; Fig.* colonia, *f;* introducción, *f.* **p. out,** trasplante, *m*
plantlike /'plæntˌlaik/ *a* como una planta; de planta
plaque /plæk/ *n* placa, *f;* medalla, *f*
plash /plæʃ/ *n* (puddle) charco, *m;* (sound) chapaleteo, *m*. —*vt* and *vi* chapotear, chapalear
plasma /'plæzmə/ *n* plasma, *m*
plaster /'plæstər/ *n* (for walls, etc.) argamasa, *f;* yeso, *m; Med.* parche, emplasto, *m*. —*vt* (walls, etc.) enlucir, enyesar; poner emplastos (a or en); (daub) embadurnar manchar; (cover) cubrir. **p. cast,** vaciado, yeso, *m*. **p. of Paris,** escayola, *f*
plasterer /'plæstərər/ *n* yesero, *m*
plastering /'plæstərɪŋ/ *n* revoque, enyesado, guarnecido, *m*. **p. trowel,** fratás, *m*
plastic /'plæstɪk/ *a* plástico. —*n* plástica, *f; pl* **plastics,** materias plásticas, *f pl.* **p. surgery,** cirugía plástica, cirugía estética, *f*
plasticine /'plæstəˌsin/ *n* plasticina, *f*
plasticity /plæ'stɪsɪti/ *n* plasticidad, *f*
plate /pleit/ *n* plancha, chapa, *f;* (engraving and *Photo.*, of a doctor, etc.) placa, *f;* (illustration) lámina, *f;* (cutlery, etc.) vajilla, *f;* (for eating) plato, *m;* (for money) platillo, *m;* electrotipo, *m;* (dental) dentadura postiza, *f.* —*vt* (with armor) blindar; (with metal) planchear; (silver) platear; (electro-plate) niquelar. **silver p.,** vajilla de plata, plata, *f.* **p.-armor,** armadura, *f;* (of a ship) blindaje, *m*. **p.-draining rack,** escurreplatos, *m*. **p.-glass,** vidrio plano, *m*. **p.-rack,** escurridero para platos, *m*. **p. warmer,** calientaplatos, *m*
plateau /plæ'tou/ *n* meseta, altiplanicie, *f*
plateful /'pleitˌfʌl/ *n* plato (de), *m*
plater /'pleitər/ *n* plateador, *m;* platero, *m*
plateresque /ˌplætə'rɛsk/ *a Archit.* plateresco
platform /'plætfɔrm/ *n* plataforma, *f;* (railway) andén, *m*. **p. ticket,** billete de andén, *m*
plating /'pleitɪŋ/ *n* niquelado, *m;* electrogalvanización, *f;* (with armor) blindaje, *m*
platinum /'plætn̩əm/ *n* platino, *m*. **p. blonde,** rubia platino, *f*
platitude /'plætɪˌtud/ *n* perogrullada, *f,* lugar común, *m;* trivialidad, vulgaridad, *f*
platitudinous /ˌplætɪ'tudn̩əs/ *a* lleno de perogrulladas; trivial
platonic /plə'tɒnɪk/ *a* platónico
Platonism /'pleitn̩ˌɪzəm/ *n* platonismo, *m*
Platonist /'pleitn̩ɪst/ *n* platonista, *mf*
platoon /plə'tun/ *n Mil.* pelotón, *m*
platter /'plætər/ *n* fuente, *f,* trinchero, *m;* plato, *m*
plaudit /'plɔdɪt/ *n* aplauso, *m,* aclamación, *f;* (praise) elogio, *m,* alabanza, *f*
plausibility /ˌplɔzə'bɪlɪti/ *n* plausibilidad, *f*
plausible /'plɔzəbəl/ *a* plausible
plausibly /'plɔzəbli/ *adv* plausiblemente
play /plei/ *vi* jugar; (frolic) juguetear, retozar; recrearse, divertirse; *Mech.* moverse; (on a musical instrument) tocar; (wave) ondear, flotar; *Theat.* representar; (behave) conducirse. —*vt* jugar; (of a searchlight, etc.) enfocar; (direct) dirigir; (a fish) agotar; (a joke, etc.) hacer; (a piece in a game) mover; (a musical instrument or music) tocar; (a string instrument) tañer; (a character in a play) hacer el papel de; (a drama, etc.) representar, poner en escena. **to p. a joke,** gastar una broma, hacer una burla. **to p. fair,** jugar limpio. **to p. false,** jugar sucio, engañar. **to p. the fool,** hacerse el tonto, hacerse el payaso. **to p. at,** jugar a; (pretend) fingir; hacer sin entusiasmo. **to p. off,** confrontar, contraponer. **to p. on.** See **to p. upon. to p. on the...,** (of musical instruments) tocar. **to p. to,** (a person) tocar para. **to p. upon,** tocar; (a person's fears, etc.) explotar. **to p. up to,** (a person) adular, hacer la rueda (a). **to p. with,** jugar con; burlarse de; (an idea) acariciar play, *n* juego, *m;* diversión, *f,* recreo, *m;* (reflection) reflejo, *m;* movimiento libre, *m;* (to the imagination, etc.) rienda suelta, *f; Mech.* holgura, *f; Lit.* pieza dramática, comedia, *f;* (performance) función, representación, *f;* (*Theater.*) teatro, *m*. **fair p.,** juego limpio, *m*. **foul p.,** juego sucio, *m;* traición, perfidia, *f.* **to bring into p.,** poner en juego. **to come into p.,** entrar en juego. **to give**

p. to, dar rienda a. **p. on words,** juego de palabras, *m.* **p.-pen,** cuadro enrejado, *m*

playact /'plei,ækt/ *vi* hacer la comedia

playbill /'plei,bɪl/ *n* cartel, *m;* programa, *m*

played-out /,pleid 'aut/ *a* agotado; viejo

player /'pleiər/ *n* jugador (-ra); *Theat.* actor (-triz), representante, *mf; Mus.* músico (-ca), tocador (-ra)

playfellow /'plei,fɛlou/ *n* camarada, *mf;* compañero (-ra) de juego, compañero de juegos

playful /'pleifəl/ *a* juguetón; travieso; alegre

playfully /'pleifəli/ *adv* en juego, de broma; alegremente

playfulness /'pleifəlnɪs/ *n* carácter juguetón, *m;* travesuras, *f pl;* alegría, *f*

playgoer /'plei,gouər/ *n* persona que frecuenta los teatros, *f;* espectador de comedias, *m*

playground /'plei,graund/ *n* patio de recreo, *m*

playing /'pleiɪŋ/ *n* juego, *m.* **p.-cards,** naipes, *m pl,* cartas, *f pl.* **p.-field,** campo de deportes, *m*

playlet /'pleilɪt/ *n* comedia corta, *f*

playmate /'plei,meit/. See **playfellow**

plaything /'plei,θɪŋ/ *n* juguete, *m*

playtime /'plei,taim/ *n* recreación, *f;* (in schools) hora de recreo, *f,* recreo, *m*

playwright /'plei,rait/ *n* dramaturgo, *m,* autor (-ra) de comedias

plea /pli/ *n Law.* informe, *m;* declaración, *f; Law.* acción, *f,* proceso, *m;* (excuse) pretexto, *m,* excusa, *f;* (entreaty) súplica, *f.* **under p. of,** bajo pretexto de, con excusa de

plead /plid/ *vi Law.* pleitear; *Law.* declarar; suplicar; (of counsel, etc.) abogar (por); interceder (por). *—vt* defender en juicio; aducir, alegar; pretender. **to p. guilty,** confesarse culpable. **to p. not guilty,** negar la acusación. **to p. ignorance,** pretender ignorancia

pleading /'plidɪŋ/ *n* súplicas, *f pl; Law.* defensa, *f; pl* **pleadings,** alegatos, *m pl, a* implorante

pleasant /'plɛzənt/ *a* agradable; placentero; ameno; encantador; dulce; alegre; (of persons) simpático, amable; bueno; divertido

pleasantly /'plɛzəntli/ *adv* agradablemente; de un modo muy amable; alegremente

pleasantness /'plɛzəntnɪs/ *n* agrado, *m;* placer, *m;* amabilidad, *f;* alegría, *f*

pleasantry /'plɛzəntri/ *n* jocosidad, *f;* broma, chanza, *f*

please /pliz/ *vi* dar placer, gustar, dar gusto, agradar; parecer bien, querer, servirse; tener a bien, placer. *—vt* deleitar, agradar, gustar; halagar; contentar, satisfacer. **I will do what I p.,** Haré lo que me parezca bien. **If you p.,** Si te parece bien; Con tu permiso. **She is very easy to p.,** Es muy fácil de darle placer. **When you p.,** Cuando Vd. quiera, Cuando a Vd. le venga bien Cuando Vd. guste. **"Please Do Not Disturb,"** «No Molesten.» **P. sit down!** ¡Haga el favor de sentarse! ¡Sírvase de sentarse! **P. God!** ¡Plegue a Dios!

pleased /plizd/ *a* contento (de or con); encantado (de); alegre (de); satisfecho (de or con). **I am p. with my new house,** Estoy contento con mi nueva casa. **I'm p. to meet you,** Mucho gusto (en conocerle), Mucho gusto (en conocerla). **to be p.,** estar contento; complacerse en

pleasing /'plizɪŋ/ *a* agradable, grato; placentero; halagüeño

pleasurable /'plɛʒərəbəl/ *a* agradable; divertido, entretenido

pleasure /'plɛʒər/ *n* placer, *m;* gusto, *m;* satisfacción, *f;* (will) voluntad, *f;* recreo, *m;* diversión, distracción, *f.* **to give p. (to),** dar placer (a); deleitar, agradar; complacer. **to take p. in,** gustar de, disfrutar de; complacerse en. **I shall do it with great p.,** Lo haré con mucho gusto, Lo haré con mucho placer. **p.-boat,** barco de recreo, *m.* **p.-ground,** parque de atracciones, *m.* **p.-seeking,** amigo de placeres, frívolo. **p. trip,** viaje de recreo, *m;* excursión, *f*

pleasure craft *n* barco de recreo, *m,* (one vessel); barcas de recreo (collectively), *m pl*

pleat /plit/ *n* pliegue, *m, vt* plegar, hacer pliegues en

pleating /'plitɪŋ/ *n* plegado, *m*

plebeian /plɪ'biən/ *a* plebeyo. *—n* plebeyo (-ya)

plebiscite /'plɛbə,sait/ *n* plebiscito, *m.* **to take a p.,** hacer un plebiscito

plectrum /'plɛktrəm/ *n* plectro, *m*

pledge /plɛdʒ/ *n* prenda, *f;* empeño, *m;* garantía, *f;* (hostage) rehén, *m;* (toast) brindis, *m.* *—vt* empeñar, dar en prenda; garantizar; brindar por; prometer. **to p. oneself,** comprometerse. **to p. support for,** prometer apoyo para

Pleiades /'pliə,diz/ *n pl* pléyades, *f pl*

plenary /'plinəri/ *a* pleno; plenario. **p. indulgence,** indulgencia plenaria, *f.* **p. session,** sesión plenaria, *f*

plenipotentiary /,plɛnəpə'tɛnʃi,ɛri/ *a* plenipotenciario. *—n* plenipotenciario, *m*

plenitude /'plɛnɪ,tud/ *n* plenitud, *f*

plentiful /'plɛntəfəli/ *a* copioso, abundante. **to be p.,** abundar

plentifully /'plɛntəfəli/ *adv* en abundancia

plenty /'plɛnti/ *n* abundancia, *f;* en abundancia; de sobra; mucho. *—adv Inf.* bastante. **There is p. of food,** Hay comida en abundancia. **We have p. of time,** Tenemos tiempo de sobra

pleonasm /'pliə,næzəm/ *n* pleonasmo, *m*

plethora /'plɛθərə/ *n* plétora, *f*

pleurisy /'plʊrəsi/ *n* pleuresía, *f*

plexus /'plɛksəs/ *n* plexo, *m*

pliability /,plaiə'bɪlɪti/ *n* flexibilidad, *f;* docilidad, *f*

pliable, pliant /'plaiəbəl; 'plaiənt/ *a* flexible; dócil

pliers /'plaiərz/ *n pl* pinzas, *f pl,* alicates, *m pl,* tenazas, *f pl*

plight /plait/ *vt* (one's word) empeñar, dar; prometer en matrimonio. *—n* (fix) aprieto, apuro, *m.* **to p. one's troth,** dar palabra de matrimonio

plinth /plɪnθ/ *n Archit.* plinto, *m*

Pliny the Elder /'plɪni/ Plinio el Antiguo, Plinio el Mayor

Pliny the Younger Plinio el Menor

plod /plɒd/ *vi* andar despacio, caminar con trabajo; *Fig.* trabajar con ahínco

plodder /'plɒdər/ *n* trabajador lento y concienzudo, *m;* (student) empollón (-ona)

plot /plɒt/ *n* (of land) parcela, *f;* terreno, solar, *m;* (plan) proyecto, *m;* estratagema, *m;* (literary) intriga, trama, *f;* (story) argumento, *m;* (conspiracy) conjuración, *f,* complot, *m.* *—vt* trazar (un plano, etc.); urdir, tramar. *—vi* conspirar, intrigar

plotter /'plɒtər/ *n* conspirador (-ra conjurado (-da)

plotting /'plɒtɪŋ/ *n* trazado (de un plano, una gráfica), *m;* (conspiracy) conspiración, *f;* maquinaciones, *f pl;* (hatching) trama, *f*

plover /'plʌvər, 'plouvər/ *n* ave fría, *f,* chorlito, *m*

plow /plau/ *n* arado, *m; Astron.* el Carro, la Osa Mayor; (in an examination) escabechina, *f.* *—vt* and *vi* arar; *Fig.* surcar; (in examinations) escabechar, dar calabazas (a), suspender. **plow the sands,** arar en el mar. **p. handle,** esteva, *f.* **to p. up,** roturar

plowman /'plaumən/ *n* arador, surcador, *m;* (peasant) labrador, *m*

plowshare /'plau,ʃɛər/ *n* reja de arado, *f*

pluck /plʌk/ *vt* (pick) coger; (a bird) desplumar; *Mus.* puntear; (in an examination) calabacear escabechar. *—vi* tirar (de). *—n* (tug) tirón, *m;* (of an animal) asadura, *f;* (courage) coraje, *m.* **to p. up courage,** tomar coraje, sacar ánimos. **to p. off,** quitar. **to p. out,** arrancar; quitar

pluckily /'plʌkɪli/ *adv* valientemente

pluckiness /'plʌkinɪs/ *n* coraje, valor, *m*

plucky /'plʌki/ *a* valiente, esforzado, resuelto, animoso

plug /plʌg/ *n* tapón, tarugo, *m;* (in building) nudillo, *m;* (of a switchboard) clave, *f; Elec.* enchufe, *m;* (of a w.c.) tirador, *m;* (of a bath, etc.) tapón, *m;* (of tobacco) rollo, *m.* *—vt* atarugar, taponar, obturar; (in building) rellenar. *—vi* (with away) batirse el cobre, sudar la gota gorda. **to p. in,** enchufar

plum /plʌm/ *n* (tree) ciruelo, *m;* (fruit) ciruela, *f;* (raisin) pasa, *f;* (*Inf.* prize) breva, golosina, *f.* **p. cake,** pastel de fruta, *m*

plumage /'plumɪdʒ/ *n* plumaje, *m*

plumb /plʌm/ *n* plomada, *f;* (sounding-lead) escandallo, *m.* *—a* perpendiculo; recto; completo. *—adv* a plomo, verticalmente; exactamente. *—vt* aplomar; *Naut.* sondar; (*Fig.* pierce) penetrar; (understand)

comprender. —*vi* trabajar como plomero. **p.-line,** plomada, *f*
plumbago /plʌm'beigou/ *n* plombagina, *f*
plumber /'plʌmər/ *n* plomero, fontanero, *m;* instalador de cañerías, *m*
plumbic /'plʌmbɪk/ *a Chem.* plúmbico
plumbing /'plʌmɪŋ/ *n* plomería, fontanería, *f;* instalación de cañerías, *f*
plumbless /'plʌmlɪs/ *a Poet.* insondable
plume /plum/ *n* pluma, *f;* penacho, *m.* —*vt* adornar con plumas; desplumar; **to p. itself,** (of a bird) limpiarse las plumas. **to p. oneself on,** echárselas de, hacer alarde de; jactarse de
plumed /plumd/ *a* plumado; con plumas; empenachado
plumelet /'plumlɪt/ *n* agujas, *f pl*
plummet /'plʌmɪt/ *n* plomada, *f;* (weight) plomo, *m;* (sounding-lead) sonda, *f*
plump /plʌmp/ *a* gordito, llenito; rollizo; hinchado. —*adv* de golpe; claramente. —*vt* (swell) hinchar, rellenar; (make fall) hacer (or dejar) caer. —*vi* (swell) hincharse; engordar; (fall) caer a plomo; dejarse caer. **to p. for,** escoger, dar apoyo (a); votar por. **p.-cheeked,** mofletudo
plumpness /'plʌmpnɪs/ *n* gordura, *f;* lo rollizo
plumy /'plumi/ *a* como una pluma; plumado
plunder /'plʌndər/ *vt* saquear; pillar; despojar. —*n* saqueo, pillaje, *m;* (booty) botín, despojo, *m*
plunderer /'plʌndərər/ *n* saqueador (-ra); ladrón (-ona)
plundering /'plʌndərɪŋ/ *n* saqueo, *m;* despojo, *m.* —*a* saqueador
plunge /plʌndʒ/ *vt* chapuzar; sumergir; hundir; meter. —*vi* sumergirse; (into water) zambullirse; (rush) precipitarse, lanzarse; *Naut.* zozobrar; (of a horse) encabritarse; (gamble) jugarse el todo. —*n* sumersión, *f;* zambullida, *f;* chapuz, *m;* (rush) salto, *m;* (*Fig.* step) paso, *m*
plunger /'plʌndʒər/ *n Mech.* émbolo, *m*
plunging /'plʌndʒɪŋ/ *n* (of a ship) zozobra, *f;* (of a horse) cabriolas, *f pl;* saltos, *m pl,* For other meanings, see **plunge**
plural /'plʊrəl/ *a* plural. —*n* plural, *m.* **in the p.,** en el plural. **to make p.,** poner en plural
plurality /plʊ'rælɪti/ *n* pluralidad, *f*
pluralize /'plʊrə,laiz/ *vt* pluralizar
plus /plʌs/ *prep* and *a* más; (*Math. Elec.*) positivo. —*n* signo más, *m; Math.* cantidad positiva, *f.* **p. fours,** pantalones de golf, *m pl*
plush /plʌʃ/ *n* felpa, *f;* velludo, *m*
plushy /'plʌʃi/ *a* felpudo; de felpa
Pluto /'plutou/ *n* Plutón, *m;* (pipe-line) oleoducto, *m*
plutocracy /plu'tɒkrəsi/ *n* plutocracia, *f*
plutocrat /'plutə,kræt/ *n* plutócrata, *mf*
plutocratic /,plutə'krætɪk/ *a* plutocrático
pluviometer /,pluvi'ɒmɪtər/ *n* pluviómetro, *m*
ply /plai/ *n* cabo, *m.* —*vt* emplear, usar; manejar; ejercer; ofrecer, servir (con); importunar (con). —*vi* hacer el trayecto; hacer el servicio; ir y venir; hacer viajes. **to ply for hire,** tomar viajeros; ofrecerse para ser alquilado
plywood /'plai,wʊd/ *n* madera contrachapada, *f*
pneumatic /nʊ'mætɪk/ *a* neumático. —*n* (tire) neumático, *m.* **p. drill,** barreno neumático, *m*
pneumococcus /,numə'kɒkəs/ *n* neumococo, *m*
pneumonia /nʊ'mounyə/ *n* pulmonía, *f.* **double p.,** pulmonía doble, *f*
poach /poutʃ/ *vi* cazar (or pescar) en vedado. —*vt* robar caza de un vedado; *Fig.* invadir; (*Fig.* steal) hurtar; (eggs) escalfar. **to p. upon another's preserves,** meterse en los asuntos de otro
poacher /'poutʃər/ *n* cazador furtivo, *m*
poaching /'poutʃɪŋ/ *n* caza (or pesca) furtiva, *f*
pock /pɒk/ *n* pústula, *f.* **p.-mark,** hoyo, *m.* **p.-marked,** picado de viruelas
pocket /'pɒkɪt/ *n* bolsillo, *m;* bolsillo del reloj, *m;* faltriquera, *f; Mineral.* bolsa, *f,* depósito, *m; Fig.* bolsa, *f;* (in billiards) tronera, *f.* —*vt* meter (or poner) en el bolsillo; (an insult) tragarse; (in billiards) entronerar; (a profit) ganar; apropiarse. **air-p.,** bolsa de aire, *f.* **to be out of p.,** haber perdido, tener una pérdida. **to have a person in one's p.,** calzarse a una persona. **to p. one's pride,** olvidarse de su orgullo. **p. battleship,** acorazado de bolsillo, *m.* **p.-book,** cartera, *f.* **p. dictionary,** diccionario de bolsillo, *m.* **p.-flap,** portezuela, *f.* **p.-handkerchief,** pañuelo (de bolsillo), *m.* **p.-knife,** cortaplumas, *m.* **p.-lighter,** encendedor de bolsillo, *m.* **p.-money,** alfileres, *m pl,* dinero del bosillo, *m.* **p. picking,** ratería de carterista, *f*
pocketful /'pɒkɪt,fʊl/ *n* bolsillo lleno (de), *m;* lo que cabe en un bolsillo
pocket of resistance *n* foco de resistencia, *m*
pod /pɒd/ *n Bot.* vaina, *f;* (of a silkworm) capullo, *m.* —*vt* desvainar; mondar. —*vi* hincharse, llenarse
podgy /'pɒdʒi/ *a* gordo, grueso
poem /'pouəm/ *n* poema, *m; pl* **poems,** poesías, *f pl,* versos, *m pl*
poet /'pouɪt/ *n* poeta, *m.* **p. laureate,** poeta laureado, *m*
poetaster /'pouɪt,æstər/ *n* poetastro, *m*
poetess /'pouɪtɪs/ *n* poetisa, *f*
poetic /pou'ɛtɪk/ *a* poético. **p. licence,** licencia poética, *f*
poeticize /pou'ɛtə,saiz/ *vt* poetizar; hacer un poema (de)
poetics /pou'ɛtɪks/ *n* poética, *f*
poetry /'pouɪtri/ *n* poesía, *f;* versos, poemas, *m pl*
pogrom /pə'grʌm/ *n* pogrom, *m*
poignancy /'pɔinyənsi/ *n* (of emotions) profundidad, violencia, *f,* lo patético; (of a retort, etc.) mordacidad, acerbidad, *f*
poignant /'pɔinyənt/ *a* (moving) conmovedor, hondo, agudo; patético; (mordant) mordaz, agudo
poignantly /'pɔinyəntli/ *adv* de un modo conmovedor, patéticamente; mordazmente
poinsettia /pɔin'sɛtiə/ *n* flor de nochebuena, *f*
point /pɔint/ *n* (usual meanings and *Astrol.*, *Math.*, in cards, in a speech, etc.) punto, *m;* característica, *f;* cualidad, *f;* (purpose) motivo, fin, *m;* (question) cuestión, *f;* asunto, *m;* (wit) agudeza, *f;* (significance) significación, *f;* (detail) detalle, *m;* (in rationing) cupón, *m;* (sharp end) punta, *f;* (of a shawl, etc.) pico, *m;* (of land) promontorio, cabo, *m;* (engraving) buril, *m;* (railway) aguja, *f;* (of horses) cabo, *m.* **Mary has many good points,** María tiene muchas cualidades buenas. **There is no p. in being angry,** No hay para que enfadarse. **in p.,** en cuestión; a propósito. **in p. of fact,** en efecto, en verdad. **on the p. of,** a punto de. **to be to the p.,** venir al caso; ser apropiado. **to carry one's p.,** salir con la suya. **to come to the p.,** ir al grano, ir al caso, ir al mollo del asunto. **to make a p. of,** insistir en; tener por principio. **to win on points,** (boxing) ganar por puntos. **p. at issue,** cuestión bajo consideración, *f,* punto en cuestión, *m.* **p.-blank,** a boca de jarro. **p.-duty,** regulación de tráfico, *f.* **p. lace,** encaje de aguja, *m.* **p. of honor,** punto de honor, *m;* cuestión de honor, *f.* **p. or order,** cuestión de orden, *f.* **p. of view,** punto de vista, *m.* **What's your p.?** ¿A dónde quieres llegar con esto?
point /pɔint/ *vt* sacar punta (a), afilar; (a moral, etc.) inculcar; (in building) rejuntar; *Gram.* puntuar; (of dogs) mostrar la caza. **He pointed his gun at them,** Les apuntó con su fusil. **The hands of the clock pointed to seven o'clock,** Las agujas del reloj marcaban las siete. **to p. with the finger,** señalar con el dedo. **to p. at,** señalar, indicar; (with a gun) apuntar; dirigir. **to p. out,** señalar, indicar; enseñar, mostrar; advertir
pointed /'pɔintɪd/ *a* (sharpened) afilado; (in shape) puntiagudo; picudo; *Archit.* ojival; *Fig.* mordaz; satírico; (of a remark, etc.) directo; personal; aparente, evidente
pointedly /'pɔintɪdli/ *adv* explícitamente, categóricamente; mordazmente; directamente; satíricamente
pointedness /'pɔintɪdnɪs/ *n* forma puntiaguda, *f;* (incisiveness) mordacidad, aspereza, *f;* claridad, *f*
pointer /'pɔintər/ *n* (of a clock, weighing-machine, etc.) aguja, *f;* (of a balance) fiel, *m;* (wand) puntero, *m; Fig.* índice, *m;* (dog) perro de muestra, *m*
pointillism *n Art.* puntillismo, *m*
pointillisme /'pwantḷ,ɪzem/ *n Art.* puntillismo, *m*

pointing /ˈpɔintɪŋ/ *n* (in building) rejuntado, *m;* (of a gun) puntería, *f*
pointless /ˈpɔintlɪs/ *a* sin motivo, innecesario; fútil; sin importancia
pointlessly /ˈpɔintlɪsli/ *adv* sin motivo, sin necesidad; fútilmente
pointsman /ˈpɔintsmən/ *n* (railway) guardagujas, *m;* (policeman) guardia del tráfico, *m*
poise /pɔiz/ *vt* balancear; pesar. —*vi* balancearse; posar, estar suspendido. —*n* equilibrio, *m;* (of mind) serenidad de ánimo, sangre fría, *f;* aplomo, *m;* (bearing) porte, aire, *m*
poison /ˈpɔizən/ *n* veneno, *m; Fig.* ponzoña, *f,* veneno, *m.* —*vt* envenenar; intoxicar; *Fig.* emponzoñar. **p. gas,** gas asfixiante, *m*
poisoner /ˈpɔizənər/ *n* envenenador (-ra); *Fig.* corruptor (-ra)
poisoning /pɔizənɪŋ/ *n* envenenamiento, *m;* intoxicación, *f*
poisonous /ˈpɔizənəs/ *a* venenoso; tóxico; *Fig.* ponzoñoso, pernicioso. **p. snake,** serpiente venenosa
poisonousness /ˈpɔizənəsnɪs/ *n* venenosidad, *f;* toxicidad, *f; Fig.* veneno, *m,* ponzoña, *f*
poke /pouk/ *vt* (thrust) clavar; (make) hacer; (the fire) atizar; hurgar; (push) empujar; (put away) arrinconar. —*vi* andar a tientas; meterse. **Don't p. your nose into other people's business!** ¡No te metas donde no te llaman! **They poked his eyes out,** Le saltaron los ojos. **to p. fun at,** burlarse de, mofarse de. **to p. the fire,** atizar la lumbre (or el fuego). **to p. about for,** buscar a tientas. **p.-bonnet,** capelina, *f*
poker /ˈpoukər/ *n* (game) póker, *m;* (for the fire) hurgón, atizador, *m.* **p. work,** pirograbado, *m*
poky /ˈpouki/ *a* estrecho, ahogado, pequeño; miserable
Poland /ˈpoulənd/ Polonia, *f*
polar /ˈpoulər/ *a* polar. **p. bear,** oso (-sa) blanco (-ca). **p. lights,** aurora boreal, *f*
polarimeter /ˌpouləˈrɪmɪtər/ *n* polarímetro, *m*
polarity /pouˈlærɪti/ *n* polaridad, *f*
polarization /ˌpoulərəˈzeiʃən/ *n* polarización, *f*
polarize /ˈpouləˌraiz/ *vt* polarizar
pole /poul/ *n* palo largo, *m;* poste, *m;* (of a tent) mástil, *m;* (of a cart) pértiga, *f; Sports.* pértiga, garrocha, *f;* (measurement) percha, *f;* (*Astron. Geog. Biol. Math. Elec.*) polo, *m.* —*vt* (a punt) impeler con pértiga. **from p. to p.,** de polo a polo. **greasy p.,** cucaña, *f.* **under bare poles,** *Naut.* a palo seco. **p.-ax,** hachuela de mano, *f;* hacha de marinero, *f;* (butcher's) mazo, *m.* **p. jumping,** salto de pértiga, salto a la garrocha, *m.* **p.-star,** estrella polar, *f*
Pole /poul/ *n* polaco (-ca)
polemic /pəˈlɛmɪk/ *n* polémica, *f*
polemical /pəˈlɛmɪkəl/ *a* polémico
police /pəˈlis/ *n* policía, *f.* —*vt* mantener servicio de policía en; mantener el orden público en; administrar, regular. **mounted p.,** policía montada, *f.* **p. constable,** (agente de) policía, guardia urbano, *m.* **p. court,** tribunal de la policía, *m.* **p. dog,** perro de policía, *m.* **p. force,** cuerpo de policía, *m,* policía, *f.* **p. magistrate,** juez municipal, *m.* **p. station,** comisaría de policía, *f.* **p. trap,** puesto oculto de la policía del tráfico, *m.* **p. woman,** policía, *f*
policeman /pəˈlismən/ *n* policía, guardia, *m*
policy /ˈpɒləsi/ *n* política, *f;* táctica, *f;* sistema, *m;* norma de conducta, *f;* ideas, *f pl,* principios, *m pl;* prudencia, *f;* (insurance) póliza, *f.* **fixed premium p.,** póliza a prima fija, *f.* **p.-holder,** asegurado (-da), tenedor (de una póliza), *m*
poliomyelitis /ˌpouliouˌmaiəˈlaitɪs/ *n* poliomielitis, *f*
polish /ˈpɒlɪʃ/ *vt* (metals and wood) pulir; (furniture and shoes) dar brillo (a); (*Lit.* works) pulir, limar; (persons) descortezar, civilizar. —*n* (shine) brillo, *m;* (furniture) cera para los muebles, *f;* (metal, silver) líquido para limpiar metales, *m;* (for shoes) betún para zapatos, *m;* (varnish) barniz, *m;* (of *Lit.* works) pulidez, elegancia, *f;* (of persons) urbanidad, cultura, *f.* **to p. off,** terminar a prisa; (a person) acabar con; (food) engullir
Polish /ˈpoulɪʃ/ *a* polaco, polonés. —*n* (language) polaco, *m*
polished /ˈpɒlɪʃt/ *a* (of verses, etc.) pulido, elegante; (of person) culto, distinguido; (of manners) fino, cortés
polisher /ˈpɒlɪʃər/ *n* (machine) pulidor, *m;* lustrador, *m.* **floor-p.,** lustrador de piso, *m.* **French p.,** barnizador, *m*
polite /pəˈlait/ *a* cortés, bien educado; atento; elegante
politely /pəˈlaitli/ *adv* cortésmente; atentamente
politeness /pəˈlaitnɪs/ *n* cortesía, *f.* **for p. sake,** por cortesía
politic /ˈpɒlɪtɪk/ *a* político
political /pəˈlɪtɪkəl/ *a* político. **p. agent,** agente político, *m.* **p. economist,** hacendista, *mf* **p. economy,** economía política, *f*
politically /pəˈlɪtɪkli/ *adv* políticamente
politician /ˌpɒlɪˈtɪʃən/ *n* político (-ca)
politics /ˈpɒlɪtɪks/ *n* política, *f.* **to dabble in p.,** meterse en política
polity /ˈpɒlɪti/ *n* forma de gobierno, constitución política, *f*
polka /ˈpoulkə/ *n* polca, *f*
polka-dot /ˈpoukəˌdɒt/ *a* con puntos
poll /poul/ *n* (head of person) cabeza, *f;* (voters' register) lista electoral, *f;* (voting) votación, *f;* (polling booth) colegio electoral, *m;* (counting of votes) escrutinio, *m.* —*vt* (trees) desmochar; (vote) votar, dar su voto (a); (obtain votes) obtenir, recibir; (count votes) escrutar. **p.-tax,** capitación, *f*
pollard /ˈpɒlərd/ *vt* desmochar. —*n* (tree) árbol desmochado, *m*
pollen /ˈpɒlən/ *n* polen, *m*
pollinate /ˈpɒləˌneit/ *vt* fecundar con polen
pollination /ˌpɒləˈneiʃən/ *n* polinización, *f*
polling /ˈpoulɪŋ/ *n* votación, *f.* **p. booth,** colegio electoral, *m*
pollute /pəˈlut/ *vt* contaminar; ensuciar; profanar; (corrupt morally) corromper
polluter /pəˈlutər/ *n* profanador (-ra), corruptor (-ra)
pollution /pəˈluʃən/ *n* contaminación, *f;* profanación, *f;* corrupción, *f*
polo /ˈpoulou/ *n* polo, *m.* **p. mallet,** maza de polo, *f.* **p. player,** jugador de polo, *m,* polista, *mf*
polonaise /ˌpɒləˈneiz/ *n* polonesa, *f*
poltroon /pɒlˈtrun/ *n* cobarde, *m*
polychrome /ˈpɒliˌkroum/ *a* policromo
polygamist /pəˈlɪgəmɪst/ *n* polígamo (-ma)
polygamous /pəˈlɪgəməs/ *a* polígamo
polygamy /pəˈlɪgəmi/ *n* poligamia, *f*
polygenesis /ˌpɒliˈdʒɛnəsɪs/ *n* poligenismo, *m*
polyglot /ˈpɒliˌglɒt/ *n* poligloto (-ta). **p. Bible,** poliglota, *f*
polygon /ˈpɒliˌgɒn/ *n* polígono, *m*
Polynesia /ˌpɒləˈniʒə/ Polinesia, *f*
Polynesian /ˌpɒləˈniʒən/ *n* polinesio (-ia)
polyp /ˈpɒlɪp/ *n* pólipo, *m*
polyphonic /ˌpɒliˈfɒnɪk/ *a* polifónico
polyphony /pəˈlɪfəni/ *n* polifonía, *f*
polytechnic /ˌpɒliˈtɛknɪk/ *a* politécnico
polytheism /ˈpɒliθiˌɪzəm/ *n* politeísmo, *m*
polytheistic /ˌpɒliθiˈɪstɪk/ *a* politeísta
pomade /pɒˈmeid/ *n* pomada, *f*
pomegranate /ˈpɒmˌgrænɪt/ *n* granada, *f*
Pomeranian /ˌpɒməˈreiniən/ *a* pomerano. **P. dog,** perro pomerano, *m*
pommel /ˈpʌməl/ *n* pomo, *m, vt* aporrear
pomp /pɒmp/ *n* pompa, magnificencia, *f,* fausto, aparato, *m;* ostentación, *f*
Pompeian /pɒmˈpeiən/ *a* pompeyano
Pompeii /pɒmˈpei/ Pompeya, *f*
pompom /ˈpɒmˌpɒm/ *n* pompón, *m*
pomposity /pɒmˈpɒsɪti/ *n* pomposidad, presunción, *f;* (of language) ampulosidad, *f*
pompous /ˈpɒmpəs/ *a* pomposo, ostentoso; (of style) ampuloso, hinchado; importante. **to be p.,** (of persons) darse tono
pompously /ˈpɒmpəsli/ *adv* pomposamente
pond /pɒnd/ *n* charca, *f,* estanque, *m*
ponder /ˈpɒndər/ *vt* ponderar, estudiar, considerar. —*vi* meditar (sobre), reflexionar (sobre)
ponderable /ˈpɒndərəbəl/ *a* ponderable

ponderous /'pɒndərəs/ *a* pesado; macizo, abultado; grave; (dull) pesado, aburrido
ponderously /'pɒndərəsli/ *adv* pesadamente; gravemente
ponderousness /'pɒndərəsnɪs/ *n* pesadez, *f;* gravedad, importancia, *f*
poniard /'pɒnyərd/ *n* puñal, *m, vt* apuñalar
pontiff /'pɒntɪf/ *n* pontífice, *m*
pontifical /pɒn'tɪfɪkəl/ *a* pontificio
pontificate /pɒn'tɪfɪˌkɪt/ *n* pontificado, *m*
pontonier /ˌpɒntn̩ɪər/ *n* pontonero, *m*
pontoon /pɒn'tun/ *n* pontón, *m.* **p. bridge,** puente de pontones, *m*
pony /'pouni/ *n* jaca, *f*
poodle /'pudl̩/ *n* perro (-rra) de aguas, perro de lanas, perro lanudo
pooh-pooh /'pu'pu/ *vt* despreciar, desdeñar. **Pooh!** ¡Bah!
pool /pul/ *n* (in a river) rebalsa, *f;* charca, *f,* estanque, *m;* (of blood, etc.) charco, *m;* (in cards) baceta, *f; Com.* asociación, *f; Fig.* fuente, *f; pl* **pools,** (football) apuestas benéficas de fútbol, *f pl.* —*vt* (resources, etc.) combinar; juntar
poop /pup/ *n* popa, *f.* **p. lantern,** fanal, *m*
poor /pʊr/ *a* pobre; malo; (insignificant or unfortunate) infeliz, desgraciado. **the p.,** los pobres. **to be in p. health,** estar mal de salud. **to be p. stuff,** ser de pacotilla. **to be poorer than a church mouse,** ser más pobre que las ratas. **to have a p. opinion of,** tener en poco (a). **P. me!** ¡Ay de mí! ¡Pecador de mí! **p.-box,** cepillo, *m.* **p.-law,** ley de asistencia pública, *f.* **p.-spirited,** apocado
poorhouse /'pʊrˌhaus/ *n* asilo, *m*
poorly /'pʊrli/ *adv* pobremente; mal. —*a* indispuesto, malo
poorness /'pʊrnɪs/ *n* pobreza, *f;* mala calidad, *f;* (lack) carestía, *f;* (of soil) infertilidad, *f;* (of character) mezquindad, *f*
pop /pɒp/ *n* (of a cork) taponazo, *m;* (of a gun) detonación, *f;* (drink) gaseosa, *f, adv* ¡pum! —*vi* (of a cork) saltar; (of guns) detonar. —*vt* (corks) hacer saltar; (a gun, a question, etc.) disparar. **popgun,** escopeta de aire comprimido, *f.* **to pop down,** bajar a presuradamente. **to pop in,** (visit) dejarse caer; entrar rápidamente. **to pop off,** marcharse a prisa; (die) estirar la pata. **to pop up,** subir corriendo; aparecer de pronto
pope /poup/ *n* Papa, *m*
popinjay /'pɒpɪnˌdʒei/ *n* (fop) pisaverde, *m*
popish /'poupɪʃ/ *a* papista
poplar /'pɒplər/ *n* (black) chopo, álamo, *m;* (white) álamo blanco, *m.* **p. grove,** alameda, *f*
poplin /'pɒplɪn/ *n* popelina, *f*
poppy /'pɒpi/ *n* amapola, adormidera, *f*
populace /'pɒpyələs/ *n* pueblo, *m;* (scornful) populacho, *m*
popular /'pɒpyələr/ *a* popular; en boga, de moda; cómun. **He is a p. hero,** Es un héroe popular
popularity /ˌpɒpyə'lærɪti/ *n* popularidad, *f*
popularization /ˌpɒpyələrə'zeiʃən/ *n* vulgarización, *f*
popularize /'pɒpyələˌraiz/ *vt* popularizar, vulgarizar
popularly /'pɒpyələrli/ *adv* popularmente
populate /'pɒpyəˌleit/ *vt* poblar
population /ˌpɒpyə'leiʃən/ *n* población, *f*
populous /'pɒpyələs/ *a* populoso; muy poblado
porcelain /'pɔrsəlɪn/ *n* porcelana, *f*
porch /pɔrtʃ/ *n* pórtico, *m;* (of a house) portal, *m*
porcine /'pɔrsain/ *a* porcino, porcuno
porcupine /'pɔrkyəˌpain/ *n* puerco espín, *m*
pore /pɔr/ *n* poro, *m.* **to p. over,** estar absorto en; examinar cuidadosamente
pork /pɔrk/ *n* carne de cerdo, *f.* **salt p.,** tocino, *m.* **p. butcher,** tocinero, *m.* **p. pie,** pastel de carne de cerdo, *m*
pornographic /ˌpɔrnə'græfɪk/ *a* pornográfico
pornography /pɔr'nɒgrəfi/ *n* pornografía, *f*
porosity /pɔ'rɒsɪti/ *n* porosidad, *f*
porous /'pɔrəs/ *a* poroso
porphyry /'pɔrfəri/ *n* pórfido, *m*
porpoise /'pɔrpəs/ *n* marsopa, *f,* puerco marino, *m*
porridge /'pɔrɪdʒ/ *n* gachas, *f pl, m*
port /pɔrt/ *n* puerto, *m;* (in a ship) porta, *f;* (larboard) babor, *m;* (wine) vino de Oporto, *m;* (mien) porte, *m,* presencia, *f.* —*vt* (the helm) poner a babor; *Mil.* llevar un fusil terciado. **to put into p.,** tomar puerto. **to stop at a p.,** hacer escala en un puerto. **p. dues,** derechos de puerto, *m pl*
portable /'pɔrtəbəl/ *a* portátil; móvil. **p. typewriter,** máquina de escribir portátil (or de viaje), *f.* **p. wireless,** radio portátil, *f*
portal /'pɔrtl̩/ *n* portal, *m*
portcullis /pɔrt'kʌlɪs/ *n* rastrillo, *m*
portend /pɔr'tɛnd/ *vt* presagiar, anunciar
portent /'pɔrtɛnt/ *n* augurio, presagio, *m;* portento, *m*
portentous /pɔr'tɛntəs/ *a* ominoso; portentoso; importante
porter /'pɔrtər/ *n* (messenger) mozo de cordel, *m;* (of a university, hotel) portero, *m;* (of a block of flats) conserje, *m;* (railway) mozo de estación, *m;* (drink) cerveza negra, *f.* **porter's lodge,** portería, *f;* conserjería, *f*
porterage /'pɔrtərɪdʒ/ *n* porte, *m*
portfolio /pɔrt'fouliˌou/ *n* carpeta, *f;* (*Polit.* of a minister) cartera, *f;* (*Polit.* ministry) ministerio, *m*
porthole /'pɔrtˌhoul/ *n* tronera, *f*
portico /'pɔrtɪˌkou/ *n* pórtico, *m*
portiere /pɔr'tyɛər/ *n* antepuerta, *f*
portion /'pɔrʃən/ *n* porción, *f;* parte, *f;* (marriage) dote, *mf;* (piece) pedazo, *m;* (in a restaurant) ración, *f;* (in life) fortuna, *f.* —*vt* dividir; repartir; (dower) dotar
portliness /'pɔrtlinɪs/ *n* corpulencia, *f*
portly /'pɔrtli/ *a* corpulento, grueso
portmanteau /pɔrt'mæntou/ *n* maleta, *f*
portmanteau word *n* palabra de acarreo, *f*
portrait /'pɔrtrɪt/ *n* retrato, *m.* **p. painter,** pintor (-ra) de retratos
portraiture /'pɔrtrɪtʃər/ *n* retratos, *m pl*; descripción, pintura, *f*
portray /pɔr'trei/ *vt* retratar; pintar, representar; (in words) describir, pintar
portrayal /pɔr'treiəl/ *n* pintura, *f;* retrato, *m;* (in words) descripción, *f*
portrayer /pɔr'treiər/ *n* retratista, *mf,* pintor (-ra)
portress /'pɔrtrɪs/ *n* portera, *f;* (in a convent) tornera, *f*
Portuguese /ˌpɔrtʃə'giz/ *a* portugués. —*n* portugués (-esa); (language) portugués, *m*
pose /pouz/ *vt* colocar; (a problem, etc.) plantear; (a question) hacer; *vi* colocarse; (with as) echárselas de, dárselas de, fingir ser; hacerse pasar por. —*n* actitud, postura, *f;* (affected) pose, *f;* (deception) engaño, *m*
poser /'pouzər/ *n* problema difícil, *m;* (in an examination) pega, *f;* pregunta embarazosa, *f*
position /pə'zɪʃən/ *n* posición, *f;* situación, *f;* actitud, postura, *f;* condición, *f,* estado, *m;* (post) puesto, empleo, *m.* **He is not in a p. to...,** No está en condiciones de..., No está para... **to place in p.,** poner en posición, colocar
positive /'pɒzɪtɪv/ *a* positivo; absoluto; (convinced) convencido, seguro; (downright) categórico; *Inf.* completo. —*n* realidad, *f; Photo.* (prueba) positiva, *f*
positively /'pɒzɪtɪvli/ *adv* positivamente; categóricamente
positiveness /'pɒzɪtɪvnɪs/ *n* certitud, seguridad, *f;* terquedad, obstinacia, *f*
positivism /'pɒzɪtəˌvɪzəm/ *n* positivismo, *m*
positivist /'pɒzɪtɪvɪst/ *n* positivista, *mf*
positivistic /ˌpɒzɪtɪ'vɪstɪk/ *a* positivista
posse /'pɒsi/ *n* pelotón, *m;* multitud, muchedumbre, *f*
possess /pə'zɛs/ *vt* poseer; gozar (de); (of ideas, etc.) dominar. **to p. oneself of,** apoderarse de, apropiarse. **What possessed you to do it?** ¿Qué te hizo hacerlo?
possession /pə'zɛʃən/ *n* posesión, *f.* **to take p. of,** tomar posesión de; hacerse dueño de, apoderarse de; (a house, etc.) entrar en, ocupar
possessive /pə'zɛsɪv/ *a* posesivo. —*n* posesivo, *m*
possessor /pə'zɛsər/ *n* poseedor (-ra); dueño (-ña); propietario (-ia)
possibility /ˌpɒsə'bɪlɪti/ *n* posibilidad, *f*
possible /'pɒsəbəl/ *a* posible. **as soon as p.,** cuanto

antes, lo más pronto posible. **to make p.,** hacer posible, posibilitar
possibly /'pɒsəbli/ *adv* posiblemente; (perhaps) quizás. **I shall come as soon as I p. can,** Vendré lo más pronto posible
post /poust/ *n* (pole) poste, *m;* (of a sentry, etc.) puesto, *m;* (employment) empleo, *m;* (mail) correo, *m; Mil.* toque, *m.* —*vt* (a notice) fijar; anunciar; (to an appointment) destinar; (letters, etc.) echar al correo; *Com.* pasar al libro mayor; (inform) tener al corriente. —*vi* viajar en posta. **"P. no bills!"** «Se prohibe fijar carteles.» **registered p.,** correo certificado, *m.* **p. card,** postal, *f.* **p.-chaise,** silla de posta, *f.* **p.-date,** posfecha, *f.* **p.-free,** franco de porte. **p.-haste,** con gran celeridad. **p.-horse,** caballo de posta, *m.* **p.-impressionism,** post-impresionismo, *m.* **p.-mortem,** *n* autopsia, *f.* **p.-natal,** post-natal. **p.-nuptial,** postnupcial. **p. office,** correo, *m,* correos, *m pl*; (on a train) ambulancia de correos, *f.* **p. office box,** apartado de correos, *m.* **p. office savings bank,** caja postal de ahorros, *f.* **p.-paid,** porte pagado; franco. **p.-war,** *n* postguerra, *f.* —*a* de la postguerra
postage /'poustɪdʒ/ *n* porte de correos, franqueo, *m.* **p. stamp,** sello postal, *m*
postage meter *n* franqueadora, *f*
postal /'poustl̩/ *a* postal. **p. order,** orden postal de pago, *f.* **p. packet,** paquete postal, *m*
poster /'poustər/ *n* cartel, *m.* —*vt* fijar carteles (a or en); anunciar por carteles. **bill-p.,** fijador de carteles, *m*
poste restante /ˌpoust rɛ'stɑnt/ *n* lista de correos, *f*
posterior /pɒ'stɪəriər/ *a* posterior. —*n* trasero, *m,* asentaderas, *f pl*
posteriority /pɒˌstɪəri'ɔrɪti/ *n* posterioridad, *f*
posterity /pɒ'stɛrɪti/ *n* posteridad, *f*
postern /'poustərn/ *n* postigo, *m; Mil.* poterna, *f*
postgraduate /poust'grædʒuɪt/ *n* estudiante graduado que hace estudios avanzados, *m.* —*a* avanzado; para estudiantes graduados
posthumous /'pɒstʃəməs/ *a* póstumo
posthumously /'pɒstʃəməsli/ *adv* después de la muerte
postman /'poustmən/ *n* cartero, *m*
postmark /'poustˌmɑrk/ *n* matasellos, *m, vt* poner matasellos (a)
postmaster /'poustˌmæstər/ *n* administrador de correos, *m*
postmeridian /ˌpoustmə'rɪdiən/ *a* postmeridiano
postmistress /'poustˌmɪstrɪs/ *n* administradora de correos, *f*
postpone /poust'poun/ *vt* aplazar, diferir; retrasar; (subordinate) postergar
postponement /poust'pounmənt/ *n* aplazamiento, *m;* tardanza, *f*
postscript /'poustˌskrɪpt/ *n* posdata, *f*
postulate /*n.* 'pɒstʃəlɪt; *v.* -ˌleit/ *n* postulado, *m, vt* postular
posture /'pɒstʃər/ *n* postura, actitud, *f;* (of affairs) estado, *m,* situación, *f.* —*vi* tomar una postura
posy /'pouzi/ *n* (nosegay) ramillete de flores, *m;* flor, *f;* (motto) mote, *m*
pot /pɒt/ *n* pote, *m;* tarro, *m;* (flower-) tiesto, *m;* (for cooking) olla marmita, *f;* jarro, *m.* —*vt* plantar en tiestos; conservar en potes. **pot-bellied,** panzudo. **pot-boiler,** obra literaria escrita con el sólo propósito de ganar dinero, *f.* **pot-herb,** hierba que se emplea para sazonar, hortaliza, *f.* **pot-hole,** bache, **pot-luck,** comida ordinaria, *f.* **pot-shot,** tiro fácil, *m;* tiro al azar, *m*
potable /'poutəbəl/ *a* potable
potage /pou'tɑʒ/ *n* potaje, *m*
potash /'pɒtˌæʃ/ *n* potasa, *f.* **caustic p.,** potasa cáustica, *f*
potassium /pə'tæsiəm/ *n* potasio, *m*
potato /pə'teitou/ *n* patata, *f.* **sweet p.,** batata, *f.* **p. beetle,** coleóptero de la patata, *m.* **p. omelet,** tortilla a la española, *f.* **p. patch,** patatal, *m.* **p. peeler,** pelapatatas, *m*
potency /'poutn̩si/ *n* potencia, *f;* fuerza, eficacia, *f*
potent /'poutn̩t/ *a* potente, fuerte; eficaz
potentate /'poutn̩ˌteit/ *n* potentado, *m*
potential /pə'tɛnʃəl/ *a* potencial; virtual; (*Phys. Gram.*) potencial, *n* poder, *m; Gram.* modo potencial, *m; Phys.* energía potencial, *f; Elec.* tensión potencial, *f*
potentiality /pəˌtɛnʃi'ælɪti/ *n* potencialidad, *f*
pothook /'pɒtˌhʊk/ *n* garabato de cocina, *m;* palote, *m;* (scrawl) garabato, *m*
potion /'pouʃən/ *n* poción, *f,*
potpourri /ˌpoupʊ'ri/ *n* popurrí, *m*
potter /'pɒtər/ *n* alfarero, *m.* —*vi* gandulear. —*vt* perder. **potter's clay,** barro de alfarero, *m.* **potter's wheel,** tabanque, *m.* **potter's workshop,** alfar, *m*
pottery /'pɒtəri/ *n* alfarería, *f;* (china) loza, porcelana, *f*
pouch /pautʃ/ *n* bolsa, *f; Zool.* bolsa marsupial, *f;* (for tobacco) tabaquera, *f;* (for cartridges) cartuchera, *f.* —*vt* embolsar. —*vi* bolsear
poulterer /'poultərər/ *n* pollero (-ra)
poultice /'poultɪs/ *n* apósito, emplasto, *m, vt* poner emplastos (a or en)
poultry /'poultri/ *n* volatería, *f.* **p. dealer,** gallinero (-ra) vendedor (-ra) de volatería. **p. yard,** gallinero, *m*
poultry farming *n* avicultura, *f*
pounce /pauns/ *n* (swoop) calada, *f.* —*vi* (swoop) calarse; saltar (sobre); agarrar, hacer presa (en); *Fig.* atacar; descubrir, hacer patente
pound /paund/ *n* (weight and currency) libra, *f;* (for cattle) corral de concejo, *m;* (thump) golpe, *m.* —*vt* (break up) machacar, pistar; (beat) batir; (thump) golpear, aporrear. **p. sterling,** libra esterlina, *f.* **p. troy,** libra medicinal, *f*
pounding /'paundɪŋ/ *n* machucamiento, *m;* batimiento, *m*
pour /pɔr/ *vt* vaciar, verter; derramar. —*vi* correr; (of rain) diluviar, llover a cántaros; (fill) llenar; (of crowds, words, etc.) derramarse. **to p. out the tea,** servir el té. **The crowd poured in,** La multitud entró en tropel
pouring /'pɔrɪŋ/ *a* (of rain) torrencial
pout /paut/ *vi* torcer el gesto; hacer pucheritos
poverty /'pɒvərti/ *n* pobreza, *f.* **p.-stricken,** menesteroso, indigente, necesitado
powder /'paudər/ *n* polvo, *m;* (face) polvos de arroz, *m pl*; (gun) pólvora, *f.* —*vt* polvorear; (crush) reducir a polvo, pulverizar. —*vi* ponerse polvos. **p.-flash,** fogonazo, *m.* **p.-flask,** polvorín, *m.* **p.-magazine,** santabárbara, *f.* **p.-mill,** fábrica de pólvora, *f.* **p.-puff,** polvera, borla de empolvarse, *f*
powdered /'paudərd/ *a* en polvo
powdery /'paudəri/ *a* polvoriento; friable
power /'pauər/ *n* poder, *m;* facultad, capacidad, *f;* vigor, *m,* fuerza, *f;* (*Polit.* and *Math.*) potencia, *f; Mech.* fuerza, *f;* influencia, *f.* **as far as lies within my p.,** en cuanto me sea posible. **It does not lie within my p.,** No está dentro de mis posibilidades, No está en mi poder. **the Great Powers,** las grandes potencias. **the powers that be,** los que mandan. **to be in p.,** estar en el poder. **p.-house, p.-station,** central eléctrica, *f.* **p. of attorney,** poderes, *m pl,* procuración, *f.* **to grant p. of attorney (to),** dar poderes (a)
powerful /'pauərfəl/ *a* poderoso; fuerte; eficaz; potente; (of arguments, etc.) convincente
powerfully /'pauərfəli/ *adv* poderosamente; fuertemente
powerless /'pauərlɪs/ *a* impotente
power steering *n* dirección asistida *f* (Spain), servo dirección *f*
powwow /'pauˌwau/ *n* conferencia, *f;* conversación, *f*
pox /pɒks/ *n* sífilis, *f;* (smallpox) viruelas, *f pl;* (chicken-pox) viruelas falsas, *f pl*
practicability /ˌpræktɪkə'bɪlɪti/ *n* factibilidad, *f*
practicable /'præktɪkəbəl/ *a* practicable, factible, posible; viable, transitable
practical /'præktɪkəl/ *a* (doable) factible; práctico; virtual. **p. joke,** burla de consecuencias
practically /'præktɪkli/ *adv* prácticamente; en práctica; virtualmente; (in fact) en efecto. **p. nothing,** casi nada
practicalness /'præktɪkəlnɪs/ *n* carácter práctico, *m*
practice /'præktɪs/ *n* (custom) costumbre, *f;* práctica, *f;* ejercicio, *m;* (of a doctor, etc.) clientela, *f;* profe-

sión, *f*; (religious) rito, *m*, ceremonias, *f pl*; (experience) experiencia, *f*. **It is not his p. to...,** No es su costumbre de... **to be out of p.,** estar desentrenado. **to put into p.,** poner en práctica. **P. makes perfect,** El ejercicio hace maestro. —*vt* tener la costumbre de; practicar; (a profession) ejercer; (a game) entrenarse en; (work at) estudiar; (a musical instrument) tocar; (accustom) acostumbrar. **to p. what one preaches,** predicar con el ejemplo

practiced /'præktɪst/ *a* experimentado; experto

practitioner /præk'tɪʃənər/ *n* médico (-ca). **general p.,** médico (-ca) general

pragmatic /præg'mætɪk/ *a* pragmatista; (historical) pragmático; práctico

pragmatism /'prægmə,tɪzəm/ *n* pragmatismo, *m*

pragmatist /'prægmətɪst/ *n* pragmatista, *mf*

Prague /prɑg/ Praga, *f*

prairie /'prɛəri/ *n* pradera, sabana, pampa, *f*, *a* de la pradera, etc.

praise /preiz/ *vt* alabar; ensalzar, glorificar; elogiar. —*n* alabanza, *f*; elogio, *m*; glorificación, *f*, ensalzamiento, *m*. **to p. to the skies,** poner en los cuernos de la luna poner por las nubes, poner sobre las estrellas hacerse lenguas de

praiseworthiness /'preiz,wɜrðinɪs/ *n* mérito, *m*

praiseworthy /'preiz,wɜrði/ *a* digno de alabanza, laudable

prance /præns/ *vi* (of a horse) caracolear, encabritarse, cabriolar; saltar; andar airosamente. —*n* corveta, cabriola, *f*; salto, *m*

prank /præŋk/ *n* travesura, diablura, *f*. **to play pranks,** hacer diabluras

prate, prattle /preit; 'prætḷ/ *vi* charlar, chacharear; (lisp) balbucir; (of brooks, etc.) murmurar, susurrar. —*vt* divulgar. —*n* charla, cháchara, *f*; balbuceo, *m*

prattler /'prætlər/ *n* parlanchín (-ina); (gossip) chismoso (-sa); (child) niño (-ña)

prattling /'prætlɪŋ/ *n* charla, *f*; (lisping) balbuceo, *m*; (of brooks, etc.) murmullo, susurro, ruido armonioso, *m*. —*a* charlatán, gárrulo; balbuciente; (of brooks, etc.) parlero

prawn /prɔn/ *n* camarón, *m*

pray /prei/ *vt* and *vi* suplicar; implorar; rezar, orar. **P. be seated,** Haga el favor de sentarse

prayer /'preiər/ *n* rezo, *m*, plegaria, oración, *f*; súplica, *f*; *Law*. petición, *f*. **p. book,** libro de devociones, devocionario, *m*. **p.-meeting,** reunión para rezar, *f*. **p.-rug,** alfombra de rezo, *f*

praying /'preiɪŋ/ *n* rezo, *m*; suplicación, *f*

pre- *prefix* de antes de (e.g. *pre-World-War-1 publications,* publicaciones de antes de la Primera Guerra Mundial)

preach /pritʃ/ *vt* and *vi* predicar

preacher /'pritʃər/ *n* predicador (-ra). **to turn p.,** meterse a predicar

preaching /'pritʃɪŋ/ *n* predicación, *f*, *a* predicador

preamble /'pri,æmbəl/ *n* preámbulo, *m*

prearrange /,priə'reindʒ/ *vt* preparar de antemano, predisponer

precarious /prɪ'kɛəriəs/ *a* precario; inseguro; incierto, arriesgado

precariousness /prɪ'kɛəriəsnɪs/ *n* condición precaria, *f*; inseguridad, *f*; incertidumbre, *f*

precaution /prɪ'kɔʃən/ *n* precaución, *f*. **to take precautions,** tomar precauciones

precautionary /prɪ'kɔʃə,nɛri/ *a* de precaución; preventivo

precede /prɪ'sid/ *vt* preceder (a), anteceder (a); tomar precedencia (a), exceder en importancia (a). —*vi* ir delante; tener la precedencia

precedence /'prɛsɪdəns/ *n* precedencia, *f*; prioridad, *f*; superioridad, *f*. **to take p. over,** tomar precedencia (a), preceder (a)

precedent /*n*. 'prɛsɪdənt; *a*. prɪ'sidnt/ *n* precedente, *m*, *a* precedente. **without p.,** sin precedente

preceding /prɪ'sidɪŋ/ *a* anterior, precedente

precept /'prisɛpt/ *n* precepto, *m*

preceptor /prɪ'sɛptər/ *n* preceptor, *m*

precinct /'prisɪŋkt/ *n* (police station) comisaría de sección (Argentina), delegación (Mexico), *f*

precincts /'prisɪŋkts/ *n pl* recinto, *m*; ámbito, *m*; distrito, barrio, *m*

preciosity /,prɛʃi'ɒsɪti/ *n* afectación, *f*

precious /'prɛʃəs/ *a* precioso; de gran valor; hermoso; amado; muy querido; (with rogue, etc.) redomado; completo. **p. little,** muy poco. **p. nearly,** casi, por poco... **p. stone,** piedra preciosa, *f*

preciousness /'prɛʃəsnɪs/ *n* preciosidad, *f*; gran valor, *m*

precipice /'prɛsəpɪs/ *n* precipicio, *m*

precipitancy /prɪ'sɪpɪtənsi/ *n* precipitación, *f*

precipitant /prɪ'sɪpɪtənt/ *a* precipitado

precipitate /*v*. prɪ'sɪpɪ,teit; *n*., *a*. -tɪt/ *vt* precipitar, despeñar, arrojar; acelerar; *Chem*. precipitar. —*vi* precipitarse. —*n* precipitado, *m*. —*a* precipitado, súbito. **to p. oneself,** tirarse, lanzarse

precipitately /prɪ'sɪpɪtɪtli/ *adv* precipitadamente

precipitation /prɪ,sɪpɪ'teiʃən/ *n* *Chem*. precipitación, *f*; *Chem*. precipitado, *m*; (rain, etc.) precipitación pluvial, *f*

precipitous /prɪ'sɪpɪtəs/ *a* precipitoso, escarpado, acantilado

precipitously /prɪ'sɪpɪtəsli/ *adv* en precipicio

precise /prɪ'sais/ *a* preciso; exacto; justo; puntual; escrupuloso; formal; claro; pedante, afectado; ceremonioso

precisely /prɪ'saisli/ *adv* precisamente; exactamente; puntualmente; escrupulosamente; claramente; con afectación; ceremoniosamente. **at six o'clock p.,** a las seis en punto

precision /prɪ'sɪʒən/ *n* precisión, *f*; exactitud, *f*; puntualidad, *f*; escrupulosidad, *f*; claridad, *f*; afectación, *f*; ceremonia, *f*

preclude /prɪ'klud/ *vt* excluir; impedir, hacer imposible

preclusion /prɪ'kluʒən/ *n* exclusión, *f*; imposibilidad, *f*

precocious /prɪ'kouʃəs/ *a* precoz

precocity /prɪ'kɒsɪti/ *n* precocidad, *f*

preconceived /,prikən'sivd/ *a* preconcebido

preconception /,prikən'sɛpʃən/ *n* idea preconcebida, *f*; (prejudice) prejuicio, *m*

preconcerted /,prikən'sɛrtɪd/ *a* concertado de antemano

precursor /prɪ'kɜrsər/ *n* precursor (-ra)

precursory /prɪ'kɜrsəri/ *a* precursor

predatory /'prɛdə,tɔri/ *a* rapaz; de rapiña; voraz

predecease /,pridɪ'sis/ *vt* morir antes (de or que); *Law*. premorir. —*n* *Law*. premuerto, *m*

predecessor /'prɛdə,sɛsər/ *n* predecesor (-ra); (ancestor) antepasado, *m*

predestination /prɪ,dɛstə'neiʃən/ *n* predestinación, *f*

predestine /prɪ'dɛstɪn/ *vt* predestinar

predetermination /,pridɪ,tɜrmɪ'neiʃən/ *n* predeterminación, *f*

predetermine /,pridɪ'tɜrmɪn/ *vt* predeterminar

predicament /prɪ'dɪkəmənt/ *n* /'prɛdɪkəmənt/ (logic) predicamento, *m*; situación, *f*; (fix) apuro, *m*; *pl* **predicaments,** categorías, *f pl*

predicate /*v*. 'prɛdɪ,keit; *n*. -kɪt/ *vt* afirmar. —*n* (logic, *Gram*.) predicado, *m*

predict /prɪ'dɪkt/ *vt* predecir, pronosticar, profetizar

prediction /prɪ'dɪkʃən/ *n* predicción, *f*; pronóstico, vaticinio, *m*, profecía, *f*

predilection /,prɛdḷ'ɛkʃən/ *n* predilección, *f*

predispose /,pridɪ'spouz/ *vt* predisponer

predisposition /,pridɪspə'zɪʃən/ *n* predisposición, *f*

predominance /prɪ'dɒmənəns/ *n* predominio, *m*

predominant /prɪ'dɒmənənt/ *a* predominante

predominate /prɪ'dɒmə,neit/ *vi* predominar

preeminence /pri'ɛmənəns/ *n* preeminencia, *f*; primacía, superioridad, *f*

preeminent /pri'ɛmənənt/ *a* preeminente; superior; extraordinario

preeminently /pri'ɛmənəntli/ *adv* preeminentemente; extraordinariamente; por excelencia; entre todos

preen /prin/ *vt* (of birds) limpiarse; (of people) darse humos, jactarse

preexist /,priɪg'zɪst/ *vi* preexistir

preexistence /,priɪg'zɪstəns/ *n* preexistencia, *f*

prefabricated /pri'fæbrɪ,keitɪd/ *a* prefabricado

preface /'prɛfɪs/ *n* prólogo, *m*; *Eccl*. prefacio, *m*; introducción, *f*. —*vt* dar principio (a), empezar. **He**

prefaced his remarks by..., Dijo a modo de introducción
prefatory /ˈprɛfəˌtɔri/ *a* preliminar, introductorio; a manera de prólogo
prefect /ˈprifɛkt/ *n* prefecto, *m*
prefecture /ˈprifɛktʃər/ *n* prefectura, *f*
prefer /prɪˈfɜr/ *vt* preferir, gustar más (a); (promote) ascender, elevar; (a charge, etc.) presentar. **to p. a charge against,** pedir en juicio (a). **I p. oranges to apples,** Me gustan más las naranjas que las manzanas, Prefiero las naranjas a las manzanas
preferability /ˌprɛfərəˈbɪlɪti/ *n* preferencia, ventaja, *f*
preferable /ˈprɛfərəbəl/ *a* preferible
preferably /ˈprɛfərəbli/ *adv* preferiblemente, con preferencia
preference /ˈprɛfərəns/ *n* preferencia, *f;* privilegio, *m.* **p. share,** acción privilegiada, acción preferente, *f*
preferential /ˌprɛfəˈrɛnʃəl/ *a* preferente
preferment /prɪˈfɜrmənt/ *n* promoción, *f,* ascenso, *m;* puesto eminente, *m*
preferred /prɪˈfɜrd/ *a* preferente; favorito, predilecto. **p. share,** acción preferente, *f*
prefix /ˈprifɪks/ *vt* anteponer, prefijar; (to a word) poner prefijo (a). —*n* prefijo, *m*
pregnancy /ˈprɛgnənsi/ *n* embarazo, *m,* preñez, *f*
pregnant /ˈprɛgnənt/ *a* embarazada, encinta, preñada, *f; Fig.* fértil; *Fig.* preñado
prehensile /prɪˈhɛnsɪl/ *a* prensil
prehistoric /ˌprihɪˈstɔrɪk/ *a* prehistórico
prehistory /priˈhɪstəri/ *n* prehistoria, *f*
prejudge /priˈdʒʌdʒ/ *vt* prejuzgar
prejudice /ˈprɛdʒədɪs/ *n* prejuicio, *m; Law.* perjuicio, *m.* —*vt* influir, predisponer; (damage) perjudicar. **without p.,** sin perjuicio
prejudiced /ˈprɛdʒədɪst/ *a* parcial; con prejuicios
prejudicial /ˌprɛdʒəˈdɪʃəl/ *a* perjudicial
prelacy /ˈprɛləsi/ *n* prelacía, *f;* episcopado, *m*
prelate /ˈprɛlɪt/ *n* prelado, *m*
preliminarily /prɪˌlɪməˈnɛərəli/ *adv* preliminarmente
preliminary /prɪˈlɪməˌnɛri/ *a* preliminar. —*n* preliminar, *m*
prelude (to) /ˈprɛlyud/ *n* preludio (de) *m;* presagio (de) *m, vt* and *vi* preludiar
premature /ˌpriməˈtʃʊr/ *a* prematuro
prematurely /ˌpriməˈtʃʊrli/ *adv* prematuramente
prematureness /ˌpriməˈtʃʊrnɪs/ *n* lo prematuro
premeditate /prɪˈmɛdɪˌteit/ *vt* premeditar
premeditatedly /prɪˈmɛdɪˌteitɪdli/ *adv* premeditadamente, con premeditación
premeditation /prɪˌmɛdɪˈteiʃən/ *n* premeditación, *f*
premier /prɪˈmɪər/ *a* primero, principal. —*n* primer ministro, *m;* (in Spain) presidente del Consejo de Ministros, *m*
premiere /prɪˈmɪər/ *n* estreno, *m*
premiership /prɪˈmɪərʃɪp/ *n* puesto de primer ministro, *m;* (in Spain) presidencia del Consejo de Ministros, *f*
premise /ˈprɛmɪs/ *n* (logic) premisa, *f; pl* **premises,** local, *m;* recinto, *m;* establecimiento, *m;* propiedad, *f;* tierras, *f pl.* **on the premises,** en el local; en el establecimiento
premium /ˈprimiəm/ *n* (prize) premio, *m,* recompensa, *f; Com.* prima, *f;* precio, *m.* **at a p.,** a premio; a una prima; (of shares) sobre la par; *Fig.* en boga, muy solicitado, en gran demanda
premonition /ˌpriməˈnɪʃən/ *n* presentimiento, presagio, *m*
premonitory /prɪˈmɒnɪˌtɔri/ *a* premonitorio
prenatal /priˈneitl̩/ *a* prenatal, antenatal
preoccupation /priˌɒkyəˈpeiʃən/ *n* preocupación, *f*
preoccupied /priˈɒkyəˌpaid/ *a* preocupado; abstraído, absorto
preoccupy /priˈɒkyəˌpai/ *vt* preocupar
prepaid /priˈpeid/ *a* porte pagado, franco de porte
preparation /ˌprɛpəˈreiʃən/ *n* preparación, *f;* preparativo, *m,* disposición, *f;* (patent food) preparado, *m.* **I have made all my preparations,** He hecho todos mis preparativos. **The book is in p.,** El libro está en preparación
preparative /prɪˈpærətɪv/ *a* preparativo. —*n* preparativo, *m*
preparatory /prɪˈpærəˌtɔri/ *a* preparatorio, preparativo; preliminar. **p. school,** escuela preparatoria, *f, m.* **p. to,** como preparación para; antes de
prepare /prɪˈpɛər/ *vt* preparar; aparejar, aviar; equipar; (cloth) aprestar. —*vi* prepararse; hacer preparativos
preparedness /prɪˈpɛərɪdnɪs/ *n* estado de preparación, *m;* preparación, *f,* apercibimiento, *m*
prepay /priˈpei/ *vt* pagar adelantado; (a letter, etc.) franquear
prepayment /priˈpeimənt/ *n* pago adelantado, *m;* (of a letter, etc.) franqueo, *m*
preponderance /prɪˈpɒndərəns/ *n* preponderancia, *f*
preponderant /prɪˈpɒndərənt/ *a* preponderante, predominante
preponderantly /prɪˈpɒndərəntli/ *adv* predominantemente; en su mayoría
preponderate /prɪˈpɒndəˌreit/ *vi* preponderar; prevalecer (sobre), predominar (sobre)
preposition /ˌprepəˈzɪʃən/ *n* preposición, *f*
prepossess /ˌpripəˈzɛs/ *vt* predisponer; causar buena impresión (a)
prepossessing /ˌpripəˈzɛsɪŋ/ *a* atractivo
preposterous /prɪˈpɒstərəs/ *a* ridículo, absurdo
preposterously /prɪˈpɒstərəsli/ *adv* absurdamente
preposterousness /prɪˈpɒstərəsnɪs/ *n* ridiculez, *f*
Prep School /prɛp/ *n* preparatoria, *f*
prepuce /ˈpripyus/ *n* prepucio, *m*
Pre-Raphaelite /priˈræfiəˌlait/ *a* and *n* prerrafaelista, *mf*
prerequisite /prɪˈrɛkwəzɪt/ *n* requisito necesario, esencial, *m, a* previamente necesario, esencial
prerogative /prɪˈrɒgətɪv/ *n* prerrogativa, *f*
presage /ˈprɛsɪdʒ/ *n* presagio, *m;* anuncio, *m.* —*vt* presagiar; anunciar
Presbyterian /ˌprɛzbɪˈtɪəriən/ *a* and *n* presbiteriano (-na)
prescience /ˈprɛʃəns/ *n* presciencia, previsión, *f*
prescient /ˈprɛʃənt/ *a* presciente
prescind /prɪˈsɪnd/ *vt* prescindir (de); separar (de). —*vi* separarse
prescribe /prɪˈskraib/ *vt* and *vi* prescribir; *Med.* recetar; dar leyes; *Law.* prescribir
prescription /prɪˈskrɪpʃən/ *n* prescripción, *f; Med.* receta, *f*
presence /ˈprɛzəns/ *n* presencia, *f;* (ghost) aparición, *f.* **in the p. of,** en presencia de, delante; a vista de. **p. of mind,** presencia de ánimo, serenidad de ánimo, *f*
present /ˈprɛzənt/ *a* presente; actual; (with month) corriente; *Gram.* presente. **at p.,** al presente, actualmente. **at the p. day,** a la fecha, en la actualidad, hoy día. **P. company excepted!** ¡Mejorando lo presente! **the present writer,** el que suscribe, el que esto escribe, el que estas líneas traza. **to be p. at,** presenciar, ser testigo de; asistir a, acudir a; hallarse en. **p.-day,** de hoy, actual. **p. tense,** *Gram.* tiempo presente, *m*
present /ˈprɛzənt/ *n* (time) presente, *m;* actualidad, *f; Gram.* tiempo presente, *m;* (gift) regalo, *m,* dádiva, *f.* **By these presents...,** *Law.* Por estas presentes... **to make a p. of,** regalar. **Jane made me a p. of a watch,** Juana me regaló un reloj
present /prɪˈzɛnt/ *vt* presentar; ofrecer; manifestar; (a gift) regalar, dar; (*Eccl. Mil.*) presentar. **New problems presented themselves,** Nuevos problemas surgieron. **to p. arms,** presentar las armas. **He presented himself in the office,** Se presentó en la oficina. **He presented his friend Mr. Moreno to me,** Me presentó a su amigo el Sr. Moreno
presentable /prɪˈzɛntəbəl/ *a* presentable
presentation /ˌprɛzənˈteiʃən/ *n* presentación, *f;* homenaje, *m;* (exhibition) exposición, *f.* **on p.,** *Com.* a presentación
presentiment /prɪˈzɛntəmənt/ *n* presentimiento, *m,* corazonada, *f.* **I had a p. that...,** Tuve el presentimiento de que..., Tuve una corazonada que... **to have a p. about,** presentir
presently /ˈprɛzəntli/ *adv* pronto; en seguida; dentro de poco
preservation /ˌprɛzərˈveiʃən/ *n* conservación, *f;* (from harm) preservación, *f*

preservative /prɪ'zɜrvətɪv/ *a* preservativo. *—n* preservativo, *m*
preserve /prɪ'zɜrv/ *vt* preservar (de); guardar; proteger; conservar; *Cul.* hacer conservas de; (in syrup) almibarar. *—n Cul.* conserva, *f;* (of fruit) compota, confitura, *f;* (covert) coto, *m.* **preserved fruit,** dulce de almibar, *m.* **p. dish,** compotera, *f*
preserver /prɪ'zɜrvər/ *n* conservador (-ra); (saviour) salvador (-ra); (benefactor) bienhechor (-ra)
preserving /prɪ'zɜrvɪŋ/ *n* (from harm) preservación, *f;* conservación, *f.* **p. pan,** cazuela para conservas, *f*
preside /prɪ'zaid/ *vi* (over) presidir; dirigir, gobernar. **He presided at the meeting,** Presidio la reunión
presidency /'prɛzɪdənsi/ *n* presidencia, *f*
president /'prɛzɪdənt/ *n* presidente, *m;* (of a college) rector, *m.* **lady p.,** presidenta, *f*
presidential /ˌprɛzɪ'dɛnʃəl/ *a* presidencial
presidentship /'prɛzɪdəntˌʃɪp/ *n* presidencia, *f*
press /prɛs/ *vt* prensar; (juice out of) exprimir; (clothes) planchar; (a bell, a hand, and of a shoe, etc.) apretar; (embrace) dar un abrazo (a); (a stamp, a kiss, etc.) imprimir; (an enemy) hostigar, acosar; (in a game) apretar; (crowd upon) oprimir; (emphasize) insistir en; (urge) instar, instigar; (compel) obligar; apremiar; (oppress) abrumar, agobiar; (paper) satinar; (an advantage) aprovecharse de. **Lola pressed his hand,** Lola le apretó la mano. **Time presses,** El tiempo es breve. **I did not p. the point,** No insistí. **to p. against,** pegar(se) contra. **to p. down,** comprimir; *Fig.* agobiar. **to p. for,** exigir, reclamar. **to p. forward, on,** avanzar; seguir el camino, continuar la marcha; (hurry) apretar el paso
press /prɛs/ *n* (pressure) apretón, *m;* (push) golpe, *m;* (throng) muchedumbre, *f;* (of business, etc.) urgencia, *f;* (apparatus) prensa, *f;* (printing press and publishing firm) imprenta, *f;* (cupboard) armario, *m.* **Associated P.,** Prensa Asociada, *f.* **freedom of the p.,** libertad de la prensa, *f.* **in p., in the p.,** en prensa. **in the p. of battle,** en lo más reñido de la batalla. **to go to p.,** entrar en prensa. **p.-agent,** agente de publicidad, *m.* **p.-box,** tribuna de la prensa, *f.* **p. clipping, p.-cutting,** recorte de prensa, *m.* **p.-gallery,** tribuna de la prensa, *f.* **p.-gang,** ronda de enganche, *f.* **p.-mark,** número de catálogo, *m.* **p. proof,** prueba de imprenta, *f.* **p.-room,** taller de imprenta, *m.* **p.-stud,** botón automático, *m.* **p. conference,** rueda de prensa, entrevista de prensa, conferencia de pensa, *f*
pressing /'prɛsɪŋ/ *a* urgente, apremiante; importuno. *—n* prensado, *m,* prensadura, *f;* expresión, *f;* (of a garment) planchado, *m*
pressingly /'prɛsɪŋli/ *adv* urgentemente, con urgencia; importunamente
pressman /'prɛsmən/ *n* tirador, *m;* (journalist) periodista, *m*
pressure /'prɛʃər/ *n* presión, *f;* (of the hand) apretón, *m;* apremio, *m;* opresión, *f;* (weight) peso, *m;* (force) fuerza, *f;* urgencia, *f.* **p.-cooker,** cazuela de presión, olla de presión, *f,* presto, *m.* **p.-gauge,** manómetro, *m*
prestidigitation /ˌprɛstɪˌdɪdʒɪ'teiʃən/ *n* prestidigitación, *f,* juegos de manos, *m pl*
prestige /prɛ'stiʒ/ *n* prestigio, *m*
prestigious /prɛ'stɪdʒəs/ *a* prestigiado
presumable /prɪ'zuməbəl/ *a* presumible
presume /prɪ'zum/ *vt* presumir; suponer, sospechar; (attempt) pretender. *—vi* presumir; tomarse libertades; abusar (de)
presumption /prɪ'zʌmpʃən/ *n* presunción, *f;* suposición, *f;* (effrontery) atrevimiento, *m;* insolencia, *f*
presumptive /prɪ'zʌmptɪv/ *a* presuntivo; (with heir, etc.) presunto
presumptuous /prɪ'zʌmptʃuəs/ *a* presumido, insolente, presuntuoso; atrevido
presumptuously /prɪ'zʌmptʃuəsli/ *adv* presuntuosamente
presumptuousness /prɪ'zʌmptʃuəsnɪs/ *n* presunción, presuntuosidad, *f;* atrevimiento, *m*
presuppose /ˌprisə'pouz/ *vt* presuponer
presupposition /ˌprisʌpə'zɪʃən/ *n* presuposición, *f*
pretence /prɪ'tɛns/ *n* (claim) pretensión, *f;* afectación, *f;* (simulation) fingimiento, *m;* pretexto, *m.* **false pretences,** apariencias fingidas, *f pl;* engaño, *m,* estafa, *f.* **to make a p. of,** fingir. **under p. of,** bajo pretexto de
pretend /prɪ'tɛnd/ *vt* dar como pretexto de; aparentar, fingir, simular, hacer el papel (de). *—vi* pretender (a); tener pretensiones (de); ser pretendiente (a); fingir
pretended /prɪ'tɛndɪd/ *a* supuesto, fingido; falso
pretender /prɪ'tɛndər/ *n* pretendiente, *m;* hipócrita, *mf*
pretension /prɪ'tɛnʃən/ *n* pretensión, *f;* afectación, simulación, *f*
pretentious /prɪ'tɛnʃəs/ *a* pretencioso; (of persons) presumido
pretentiousness /prɪ'tɛnʃəsnɪs/ *n* pretensiones, *f pl,* lo pretencioso
preterite /'prɛtərɪt/ *n* (tiempo) pretérito, *m, a* pretérito, pasado
pretext /'pritɛkst/ *n* pretexto, *m.* *—vt* pretextar. **under p. of,** bajo pretexto de, so color de
prettily /'prɪtḷi/ *adv* lindamente; con gracia; agradablemente
prettiness /'prɪtinɪs/ *n* lo bonito; elegancia, *f;* gracia, *f*
pretty /'prɪti/ *a* bonito; (of women, children) guapo, mono; (of men) lindo; elegante; excelente; *Ironic.* bueno. *—adv* bastante; medianamente; (very) muy; (almost) casi. **p. good,** bastante bueno. **p.-p.,** de muñeca; mono. *—n* chuchería, *f,* guapos, *m pl.* **p. ways,** monerías, *f pl*
prevail /prɪ'veil/ *vi* prevalecer, predominar; ser la costumbre. **to p. against or over,** triunfar de, vencer (a). **to p. on, upon,** inducir, convencer, persuadir. **to be prevailed upon to,** dejarse persuadir a
prevailing /prɪ'veilɪŋ/ *a* prevaleciente; dominante; predominante, reinante; general; común; (fashionable) en boga
prevalence /'prɛvələns/ *n* predominio, *m;* existencia, *f;* (habit) costumbre, *f;* (fashion) boga, *f*
prevalent /'prɛvələnt/ *a* prevaleciente; predominante; general; común; corriente; (fashionable) en boga
prevaricate /prɪ'værɪˌkeit/ *vi* tergiversar; *Law.* prevaricar
prevarication /prɪˌværɪ'keiʃən/ *n* tergiversación, *f,* equívoco, *m*
prevaricator /prɪ'værɪˌkeitər/ *n* tergiversador (-ra)
prevent /prɪ'vɛnt/ *vt* evitar; (hinder) impedir (a)
preventable /prɪ'vɛntəbəl/ *a* evitable
prevention /prɪ'vɛnʃən/ *n* prevención, *f;* (preventive) estorbo, obstáculo, *m*
preventive /prɪ'vɛntɪv/ *a* preventivo. *—n* preservativo, *m*
preview /'priˌvyu/ *n* vista de antemano, *f;* (of a film) avances, *m pl* (Cuba, Mexico), colas, *f pl* (Argentina), cortos *m pl* (Venezuela), sinopsis, *f* (Uruguay), tráiler, *m* (Spain)
previous /'priviəs/ *a* previo, anterior. **p. to,** antes de
previously /'priviəsli/ *adv* anteriormente, antes, previamente
previousness /'priviəsnɪs/ *n* anterioridad, *f;* inoportunidad, *f*
prevision /prɪ'vɪʒən/ *n* previsión, *f*
prewar /'pri'wɔr/ *a* de antes de la guerra
prey /prei/ *n* presa, *f; Fig.* víctima, *f;* (booty) botín, *m.* *—vi* (of animals) devorar; (plunder) robar, pillar; (of sorrow, etc.) hacer presa (de); agobiar, consumir; (sponge on) vivir a costa de. **to fall a p. to,** ser víctima de
price /prais/ *n* precio, *m;* valor, *m;* costa, *f.* *—vt* evaluar, tasar; poner precio a; preguntar el precio de; fijar el precio de. **at any p.,** a cualquier precio; (whatever the cost) cueste lo que cueste. **at a reduced p.,** a precio reducido. **fixed p.,** precio fijo, *m.* **p. ceiling,** precio máximo, precio tope, *m.* **p. control,** control de precios, *m.* **price list,** lista de precios, *f;* tarifa, *f;* (of shares, etc.) boletín de cotización, *m.* **Prices are subject to change without notice,** Los precios están sujetos a variación sin previo aviso.
priceless /'praislɪs/ *a* sin precio; (amusing) divertidisimo. **These jewels are p.,** Estas joyas no tienen precio
prick /prɪk/ *n* pinchazo, *m;* picadura, *f;* punzada, *f;* (prickle) espina, *f;* (with a goad) aguijonazo, *m;*

(with a pin) alfilerazo, *m;* (with a spur) espolada, *f;* (of conscience) remordimiento, escrúpulo, *m.* —*vt* pinchar, punzar; picar; (with remorse) atormentar, causar remordimiento (a); (urge on) incitar. **to p. the ears,** aguzar las orejas

pricking /ˈprɪkɪŋ/ *n* picadura, *f;* punzada, *f.* **prickings of conscience,** remordimientos, *m pl*

prickle /ˈprɪkəl/ *n* espina, *f;* (irritation) escozor, *m*

prickly /ˈprɪkli/ *a* espinoso; erizado. **p. heat,** salpullido causado por exceso de calor, *m.* **p. pear,** higo chumbo, *m,* chumbera, *f*

pride /praid/ *n* orgullo, *m;* arrogancia, *f;* (splendour) pompa, *f,* fausto, aparato, *m;* belleza, *f;* vigor, *m;* (of lions) manada, *f.* **to take p. in,** estar orgulloso de. **to p. oneself,** sentirse orgulloso, ufanarse. **to p. oneself upon,** jactarse de, preciarse de

prie-dieu /priˈdyʊ/ *n* reclinatorio, *m*

prier /ˈpraiər/ *n* espía, *mf;* curioso (-sa)

priest /prist/ *n* sacerdote, *m;* cura, *m.* **high-p.,** sumo sacerdote, *m.* **p.-ridden,** dominado por el clero

priestess /ˈpristɪs/ *n* sacerdotisa, *f*

priesthood /ˈpristhʊd/ *n* sacerdocio, *m*

priestly /ˈpristli/ *a* sacerdotal

prig /prɪg/ *n* fatuo (-ua), mojigato (-ta)

priggish /ˈprɪgɪʃ/ *a* fatuo, gazmoño

priggishness /ˈprɪgɪʃnɪs/ *n* gazmoñería, fatuidad, *f*

prim /prɪm/ *a* almidonado, etiquetero; peripuesto; afectado

primacy /ˈpraiməsi/ *n* primacía, *f*

prima donna /ˌprimə ˈdɒnə/ *n* cantatriz, *f*

primarily /praiˈmɛərəli/ *adv* en primer lugar principalmente

primary /ˈpraimɛri/ *a* primario; primitivo; principal. **p. education,** enseñanza primaria, *f.* **p. color,** color primario, *m.* **p. school,** escuela primaria, *f.* **p. election,** elección interna (dentro de un partido), *f*

primate /ˈpraimeit/ *n* primado, *m*

prime /praim/ *a* primero; principal; excelente; de primera calidad; de primera clase. —*n* (spring) primavera, *f;* (of life, etc.) flor, *f,* vigor, *m;* (best) nata, crema, *f; Eccl.* prima, *f;* (number) número primo, *m.* —*vt* preparar, aprestar; (fire-arms) cebar. **p. the pump**, cebar la bomba; (with paint, etc.) imprimar; (instruct) dar instrucciones (a), informar. **in his p.,** en la flor de su edad. **of p. quality,** de primera calidad. **P. Minister,** Primer Ministro, *m.* **p. necessity,** artículo de primera necesidad, *m*

primer /ˈpraimər/ *n* cartilla, *f,* abecedario, *m;* libro de lectura, *m;* (prayer book) devocionario, *m*

primeval /praiˈmivəl/ *a* primevo, primitivo

priming /ˈpraimɪŋ/ *n* preparación, *f;* (of fire-arms) cebo, *m;* (of paint, etc.) imprimación, *f;* instrución, *f*

primitive /ˈprɪmɪtɪv/ *a* primitivo; anticuado. —*n* primitivo, *m*

primitiveness /ˈprɪmɪtɪvnɪs/ *n* lo primitivo; carácter primitivo, *m*

primly /ˈprɪmli/ *adv* afectadamente, con afectación; gravemente

primness /ˈprɪmnɪs/ *n* afectación, *f;* gravedad, *f*

primogeniture /ˌpraiməˈdʒɛnɪtʃər/ *n* primogenitura, *f*

primordial /praiˈmɔrdiəl/ *a* primordial

primrose /ˈprɪmˌrouz/ *n* primavera, *f;* color amarillo pálido, *m*

prince /prɪns/ *n* príncipe, *m.* **P. Consort,** príncipe consorte, *m.* **P. of Wales,** (Britain) príncipe heredero, *m;* (Spanish equivalent) Príncipe de Asturias, *m.* **p. regent,** príncipe regente, *m.* **P. Charming,** el Príncipe Azul, *m*

princeliness /ˈprɪnslinɪs/ *n* magnificencia, *f;* nobleza, *f*

princely /ˈprɪnsli/ *a* principesco; magnífico; noble

princess /ˈprɪnsɪs/ *n* princesa, *f*

principal /ˈprɪnsəpəl/ *a* principal; fundamental; mayor. —*n* principal, jefe, *m;* (of a university) rector, *m;* (of a school) director (-ra); *Law.* causante, *m; Com.* capital, *m*

principality /ˌprɪnsəˈpælɪti/ *n* principado, *m*

principally /ˈprɪnsəpli/ *adv* principalmente

principle /ˈprɪnsəpəl/ *n* principio, *m.* **in p.,** en principio

principled /ˈprɪnsəpəld/ *a* de principios...

print /prɪnt/ *n* (mark) impresión, marca, *f;* (type) letra de molde, *f,* tipo, *m;* (of books) imprenta, *f;* (fabric) estampado, *m;* (picture) grabado, *m;* (photograph) positiva impresa, *f;* (mold) molde, *m.* —*vt* marcar; imprimir; (on the mind) grabar; *Print.* tirar, hacer una tirada (de); (in photography) tirar una prueba (de); (publish) sacar a luz, publicar; (fabrics) estampar. **in p.,** impreso; publicado; **He likes to see his name in print,** Le gusta ver su nombre en letras de molde; (available) existente. **to be out of p.,** estar agotado. **p. dress,** vestido estampado, *m*

printed /ˈprɪntɪd/ *a* impreso. **p. fabric,** estampado, *m.* **p. matter,** impresos, *m pl*

printer /ˈprɪntər/ *n* impresor, *m;* tipógrafo, *m.* **printer's devil,** aprendiz de impresor, *m.* **printer's ink,** tinta de imprenta, tinta tipográfica, *f.* **printer's mark,** pie de imprenta, *m*

printing /ˈprɪntɪŋ/ *n* imprenta, *f;* impresión, *f;* (of fabrics) estampación, *f;* (art of) tipografía, *f.* **p. house,** imprenta, *f.* **p. machine,** máquina de imprimir, *f.* **p. press,** prensa tipográfica, *f.* **p. types,** caracteres de imprenta, *m pl*

prior /ˈpraiər/ *n* prior, *m, a* anterior, previo. **p. to,** anterior a, antes de

prioress /ˈpraiərɪs/ *n* priora, *f*

priority /praiˈɔrɪti/ *n* prioridad, *f*

prism /ˈprɪzəm/ *n* prisma, *m;* espectro solar, *m*

prismatic /prɪzˈmætɪk/ *a* prismático

prison /ˈprɪzən/ *n* prisión, cárcel, *f.* **p.-breaking,** huida de la prisión, *f.* **p. camp,** campo de prisioneros, *m.* **p. van,** coche celular, *m.* **p. yard,** patio de la prisión, *m*

prisoner /ˈprɪzənər/ *n* prisionero (-ra), preso (-sa). **to take p.,** prender, hacer prisionero (a)

pristine /ˈprɪstin/ *a* pristino, original

privacy /ˈpraivəsi/ *n* soledad, *f,* aislamiento, retiro, *m;* intimidad, *f;* secreto, *m*

private /ˈpraivɪt/ *a* particular; privado; secreto; confidencial; reservado; íntimo; personal; doméstico; (of hearings, etc.) a puertas cerradas, secreto; (own) propio. —*n* (soldier) soldado raso, *m.* **in p.,** en secreto; confidencialmente, de persona a persona. **They wish to be p.,** Quieren estar a solas. **p. company,** sociedad en comandita, *f.* **p. hotel,** pensión, *f.* **p. house,** casa particular, *f.* **p. individual,** particular, *mf.* **p. interview,** entrevista privada, *f.* **p. life,** vida privada, *f.* **p. office,** despacho particular, *m.* **p. secretary,** secretario (-ia) particular. **p. viewing, (of a film)** función privada, *f;* **(of an exhibition)** día de inauguración, *m*

privateer /ˌpraivəˈtɪər/ *n* corsario, *m*

privately /ˈpraivɪtli/ *adv* privadamente; en secreto; personalmente; confidencialmente; (of hearings) a puertas cerradas

privation /praiˈveiʃən/ *n* privación, *f;* carencia, escasez, *f*

privet /ˈprɪvɪt/ *n* alheña, *f*

privilege /ˈprɪvəlɪdʒ/ *n* privilegio, *m;* derecho, *m;* inmunidad, *f.* —*vt* privilegiar

privileged /ˈprɪvəlɪdʒd/ *a* privilegiado; confidencial

privy /ˈprɪvi/ *a* privado; cómplice; enterado; personal, particular. —*n* (latrine) retrete, *m.* **p. council,** consejo privado, *m*

prize /praiz/ *n* premio, *m;* recompensa, *f,* galardón, *m;* (capture) presa, *f.* —*a* que ha ganado un premio; premiado; (huge) enorme; (complete) de primer orden. —*vt* estimar, apreciar. **to p. open,** abrir con una palanca. **to carry off the p.,** ganar el premio. **cash p.,** premio en metálico, *m.* **first p.,** primer premio, *m;* (in a lottery) premio gordo, *m.* **p. court,** tribunal de presas, *m.* **p. fight,** partido de boxeo, *m.* **p. fighter,** boxeador, *m.* **p. giving,** distribución de premios, *f.* **p. money,** premio en metálico, *m;* (boxing) bolsa, *f*

pro /prou/ *prep* pro. **pro forma invoice,** factura simulada, *f*

probability /ˌprɒbəˈbɪlɪti/ *n* probabilidad, *f*

probable /ˈprɒbəbəl/ *a* probable

probably /ˈprɒbəbli/ *adv* probablemente

probate /ˈproubeit/ *n* verificación de un testamento, *f*

probation /prouˈbeiʃən/ *n* probación, *f; Law.* libertad vigilada, *f*

probationary /prouˈbeiʃəˌnɛri/ *a* de probación; de prueba

probationer /prou'beiʃənər/ *n* novicio, *m;* estudiante de enfermera, *f;* candidato, *m;* aspirante, *m*

probe /proub/ *n Surg.* sonda, cala, tienta, *f.* —*vt Surg.* tentar; escudriñar

probing /'proubɪŋ/ *n* sondeo, *m*

probity /'proubɪti/ *n* probidad, integridad, *f*

problem /'prɒbləm/ *n* problema, *m;* cuestión, *f.* **p. play,** drama de tesis, *m*

problematic /ˌprɒblə'mætɪk/ *a* problemático

problem child *n* niño problemático, *m* (male), niña problemática, *f* (female)

proboscis /prou'bɒsɪs/ *n* (of an elephant) trompa, *f;* (of an insect) trompetilla, *f*

Probus /'proubəs/ Probo, *m*

procedure /prə'sidʒər/ *n* procedimiento, *m*

proceed /prə'sid/ *vi* seguir el camino, continuar la marcha; avanzar, seguir adelante; ir; proceder; ponerse (a); empezar (a); (say) proseguir; (come to) llegar a, ir a; (of a play, etc.) desarrollarse. **Before we p. any further...** Antes de ir más lejos... **to p. to blows,** llegar a las manos. **to p. against,** proceder contra, procesar. **to p. from,** venir de. **to p. with,** proseguir; poner por obra; usar

proceeding /prə'sidɪŋ/ *n* modo de obrar, *m;* conducta, *f;* procedimiento, *m;* transacción, *f; pl* **proceedings,** (measures) medidas, *f pl,* actos, *m pl;* (of a learned society or a conference) actas, *f pl.* **to take proceedings against,** *Law.* procesar

proceeds /'prousidz/ *n pl* producto, *m;* ganancias, *f pl;* beneficios, *m pl.* **net p.,** producto neto, *m*

process /'prɒsɛs/ *n* proceso, *m;* (method) procedimiento, *m;* (course) curso, *m;* marcha, *f;* (*Law. Zool.*) proceso, *m.* —*vt* beneficiar (ore), trasformar, elaborar. **in p. of,** en curso de. **in the p. of time,** con el tiempo marchando el tiempo

processing industry /'prɒsɛsɪŋ/ *n* industria de trasformación, industria de elaboración, *f*

procession /prə'sɛʃən/ *n* desfile, *m;* cortejo, *m;* (religious) procesión, *f.* **funeral p.,** cortejo fúnebre, *m.* **to walk in p.,** desfilar

processional /prə'sɛʃənl̩/ *a* procesional

proclaim /prou'kleim/ *vt* proclamar; publicar, pregonar; anunciar; (reveal) revelar; (outlaw) denunciar

proclamation /ˌprɒklə'meiʃən/ *n* proclamación, *f;* proclama, *f,* anuncio, *m;* declaración, *f*

proclivity /prou'klɪvɪti/ *n* proclividad, propensión, *f*

procrastinate /prou'kræstəˌneit/ *vi* tardar (en decidirse), aplazar su decisión; vacilar; perder el tiempo

procrastination /prouˌkræstə'neiʃən/ *n* dilación, tardanza, *f;* vacilación, *f;* pereza, *f*

procrastinator /prou'kræstəˌneitər/ *n* perezoso (-sa)

procreate /'proukriˌeit/ *vt* procrear

procreation /ˌproukri'eiʃən/ *n* procreación, *f*

procreator /'proukriˌeitər/ *n* procreador (-ra)

proctor /'prɒktər/ *n* procurador, *m; Educ.* censor, *m*

procurable /prou'kyʊrəbəl/ *a* procurable; asequible

procure /prou'kyʊr/ *vt* obtener, conseguir, lograr

procurement /prou'kyʊrmənt/ *n* obtención, *f,* logro, *m*

procurer /prou'kyʊrər/ *n* alcahuete, *m*

procuress /prou'kyʊrɪs/ *n* alcahueta, celestina, trotaconventos, *f*

prod /prɒd/ *n* (with a bayonet, etc.) punzada, *f; Fig.* pinchazo, *m.* —*vt* punzar; (in the ribs, etc.) clavar; *Fig.* pinchar

prodigal /'prɒdɪgəl/ *a* and *n* pródigo (-ga)

prodigality /ˌprɒdɪ'gælɪti/ *n* prodigalidad, *f*

prodigally /'prɒdɪgəli/ *adv* pródigamente

prodigious /prə'dɪdʒəs/ *a* prodigioso

prodigiousness /prə'dɪdʒəsnɪs/ *n* prodigiosidad, *f;* enormidad, *f*

prodigy /'prɒdɪdʒi/ *n* prodigio, *m;* portento, *m.* **child p.,** niño prodigio

produce /*v.* prə'dus; *n.* 'prɒdus, 'proudus/ *vt* producir; dar frutos; (show) mostrar, presentar; (take out) sacar; (occasion) causar, traer consigo, ocasionar; (goods) fabricar, manufacturar; (of shares, etc.) rendir; *Geom.* prolongar; (a play) poner en escena. —*n* producto, *m;* víveres, comestibles, *m pl*

producer /prə'dusər/ *n* productor (-ra); *Theat.* director de escena, *m*

product /'prɒdəkt/ *n* producto, *m;* (result) fruto, resultado, *m,* consecuencia, *f; Math.* producto, *m*

production /prə'dʌkʃən/ *n* producción, *f;* producto, *m; Geom.* prolongación, *f;* (of a play) dirección escénica, *f;* (performance) producción, *f.* **p. cost,** coste de producción, *m*

productive /prə'dʌktɪv/ *a* productivo

productivity /ˌproudʌk'tɪvɪti/ *n* productividad, *f*

profanation /ˌprɒfə'neiʃən/ *n* profanación, *f*

profane /prə'fein/ *a* profano; sacrílego, blasfemo. —*vt* profanar

profaner /prə'feinər/ *n* profanador (-ra)

profanity /prə'fænɪti/ *n* profanidad, *f;* blasfemia, *f*

profess /prə'fɛs/ *vt* (assert) afirmar, manifestar; declarar; (a faith, a profession, teach) profesar; (feign) fingir; (pretend) tener pretensiones de. —*vi* (as a monk or nun) tomar estado, entrar en religión. **He professed himself surprised,** Se declaró sorprendido

professed /prə'fɛst/ *a* declarado; *Eccl.* profeso; ostensible, fingido

profession /prə'fɛʃən/ *n* profesión, *f;* carrera, *f;* declaración, *f.* **p. of faith,** profesión de fe, *f.* **the learned professions,** las carreras liberales

professional /prə'fɛʃənl̩/ *a* profesional; de la profesión; de profesión; de carrera. **p. diplomat,** diplomático (-ca) de carrera. **p. etiquette,** etiqueta profesional, *f.* **p. man,** hombre profesional, *m;* hombre de carrera liberal, *m*

professor /prə'fɛsər/ *n* catedrático (-ca), profesor (-ra)

professorate /prə'fɛsərɪt/ *n* profesorado, *m*

professorial /ˌproufə'sɔriəl/ *a* de catedrático; de profesor

professorship /prə'fɛsərˌʃɪp/ *n* cátedra, *f*

proffer /'prɒfər/ *vt* proponer; ofrecer. —*n* oferta, *f*

proficiency /prə'fɪʃənsi/ *n* pericia, habilidad, *f*

proficient /prə'fɪʃənt/ *a* proficiente, experto, adepto, perito

profile /'proufail/ *n* perfil, *m.* —*vt* perfilar. **in p.,** de perfil

profit /'prɒfɪt/ *n* provecho, *m;* utilidad, *f;* ventaja, *f; Com.* ganancia, *f, vt* aprovechar. —*vi* ganar; *Com.* sacar ganancia. **to p. by,** aprovechar. **gross p.,** ganancia total, *f.* **p. and loss,** ganancias y pérdidas, *f pl.* **p. sharing,** participación en las ganancias, participación de utilidades, *f*

profitable /'prɒfɪtəbəl/ *a* provechoso, útil, ventajoso; lucrativo. **p. use,** aprovechamiento, *m*

profitably /'prɒfɪtəbli/ *adv* con provecho, provechosamente; lucrativamente

profiteer /ˌprɒfɪ'tɪər/ *n* estraperlista, *mf*

profit incentive *n* acicate del lucro, *m*

profitless /'prɒfɪtlɪs/ *a* sin provecho, infructuoso, inútil

profligacy /'prɒflɪgəsi/ *n* libertinaje, *m*

profligate /'prɒflɪgɪt/ *a* licencioso, disoluto. —*n* libertino, *m*

profound /prə'faund/ *a* profundo

profundity /prə'fʌndɪti/ *n* profundidad, *f*

profuse /prə'fyus/ *a* profuso; pródigo; lujoso

profusely /prə'fyusli/ *adv* profusamente; pródigamente; lujosamente

profusion /prə'fyuʒən/ *n* profusión, abundancia, *f;* prodigalidad, *f;* exceso, *m*

progenitor /prou'dʒɛnɪtər/ *n* progenitor, *m;* (ancestor) antepasado, *m*

progeny /'prɒdʒəni/ *n* prole, *f*

prognosis /prɒg'nousɪs/ *n* prognosis, *f;* presagio, *m; Med.* pronóstico, *m*

prognosticate /prɒg'nɒstɪˌkeit/ *vt* pronosticar, presagiar

prognostication /prɒgˌnɒstɪ'keiʃən/ *n* pronosticación, *f;* pronóstico, presagio, augurio, *m*

program /'prougræm/ *n* programa, *m*

progress /*n.* 'prɒgrɛs; *v.* prə'grɛs/ *n* progreso, *m;* avance, *m;* (betterment) mejora, *f;* (of events) marcha, *f.* —*vi* avanzar, marchar; (improve) progresar, adelantar; mejorar. **to make p.,** adelantarse; hacer progresos

progression /prə'grɛʃən/ *n* progresión, *f*

progressive /prə'grɛsɪv/ *a* progresivo; avanzado; *Polit.* progresista. —*n Polit.* progresista, *mf*

progressiveness /prə'gresɪvnɪs/ *n* carácter progresivo, *m*
prohibit /prou'hɪbɪt/ *vt* prohibir; defender; (prevent) impedir, privar. **His health prohibited him from doing it,** Su salud le impidió hacerlo
prohibition /ˌprouə'bɪʃən/ *n* prohibición, *f;* interdicción, *f;* (of alcohol) prohibicionismo, *m*
prohibitionist /ˌprouə'bɪʃənɪst/ *n* prohibicionista, *mf*
prohibitive /prou'hɪbɪtɪv/ *a* prohibitivo, prohibitorio
project /*v.* prə'dʒɛkt; *n.* 'prɒdʒɛkt/ *vt* (all meanings) proyectar. —*vi* sobresalir; destacarse. —*n* proyectil, plan, *m*
projectile /prə'dʒɛktɪl/ *n* proyectil, *m, a* arrojadizo
projecting /prə'dʒɛktɪŋ/ *a* saliente; (of teeth) saltón
projection /prə'dʒɛkʃən/ *n* (hurling) lanzamiento, *m;* prominencia, protuberancia, *f;* (other meanings) proyección, *f*
projector /prə'dʒɛktər/ *n* proyectista, *mf;* proyector, *m*
proletarian /ˌproulɪ'tɛəriən/ *a* proletario
proletariate /ˌproulɪ'tɛəriɪt/ *n* proletariado, *m*
prolific /prə'lɪfɪk/ *a* prolífico; fecundo, fértil
prolix /prou'lɪks/ *a* prolijo
prolixity /prou'lɪksɪti/ *n* prolijidad, *f*
prolog /'prouˌlɔg/ *n* prólogo, *m, vt* prologar
prolong /prə'lɔŋ/ *vt* prolongar
prolongation /ˌproulɔŋ'geiʃən/ *n* prolongación, *f*
promenade /ˌprɒmə'neid, -'nɑd/ *n* paseo, *m;* bulevar, *m;* avenida, *f.* —*vi* pasearse. —*vt* recorrer, andar por, pasearse por. **p. deck,** cubierta de paseo, *f*
Promethean /prə'miθiən/ *a* de Prometeo
prominence /'prɒmənəns/ *n* prominencia, *f;* protuberancia, *f;* eminencia, *f;* importancia, *f*
prominent /'prɒmənənt/ *a* prominente, saliente; (of eyes, teeth) saltón; (distinguished) eminente, distinguido. **They placed the vase in a p. position,** Pusieron el florero muy a la vista. **to play a p. part,** desempeñar un papel importante. **p. eyes, ojos** saltones, *m pl*
promiscuous /prə'mɪskyuəs/ *a* promiscuo
promiscuousness /prə'mɪskyuəsnɪs/ *n* promiscuidad, *f*
promise /'prɒmɪs/ *n* promesa, *f;* (hope) esperanza, *f;* (word) palabra, *f;* (future) porvenir, *m.* —*vt* and *vi* prometer. **a young man of p.,** un joven de porvenir. **to break one's p.,** faltar a su palabra; no cumplir una promesa. **to keep one's p.,** guardar su palabra; cumplir su promesa. **to p. and do nothing,** apuntar y no dar. **under p. of,** bajo palabra de. **p. of marriage,** palabra de matrimonio, *f*
promised /'prɒmɪst/ *a* prometido. **P. Land,** Tierra de promisión, *f*
promising /'prɒməsɪŋ/ *a* que promete bien, que promete mucho; prometedor; (of the future, etc.) halagüeño; (of persons) que llegará
promissory /'prɒməˌsɔri/ *a* promisorio. **p. note,** pagaré, abonaré, *m*
promontory /'prɒmənˌtɔri/ *n* promontorio, *m*
promote /prə'mout/ *vt* fomentar, promover; provocar; (aid) favorecer, proteger; avanzar; estimular; (to a post) ascender; (an act bill) promover; *Com.* negociar
promoter /prə'moutər/ *n* promotor (-ra); instigador (-ra); (*Theat.* etc.) empresario, *m*
promotion /prə'mouʃən/ *n* (encouragement) fomento, *m;* (furtherance) adelanto, *m;* protección, *f,* favorecimiento, *m;* (in employment, etc.) promoción, *f,* ascenso, *m;* (of a company, etc.) creación, *f*
prompt /prɒmpt/ *a* pronto; diligente; presuroso; puntual; rápido; *Com.* inmediato. —*vt* impulsar, incitar, mover; dictar; insinuar; *Theat.* apuntar; (remind) recordar. **He came at five o'clock p.,** Vino a las cinco en punto. **p. book,** libro del traspunte, *m.* **p. box,** concha (del apuntador), *f*
prompter /'prɒmptər/ *n* *Theat.* apuntador, (in the wings) traspunte, *m*
prompting /'prɒmptɪŋ/ *n* sugestión, *f;* instigación, *f; pl* **promptings,** impulso, *m;* (of the heart, etc.) dictados, *m pl*
promptitude /'prɒmptɪˌtud/ *n* prontitud, presteza, *f;* prisa, expedición, *f;* puntualidad, *f*
promptly /'prɒmptli/ *adv* inmediatamente, en seguida; con prontitud, con celeridad; puntualmente
promptness /'prɒmptnɪs/ *n* See **promptitude**
promulgate /'prɒməlˌgeit/ *vt* promulgar; divulgar, diseminar
promulgation /'prɒməl'geiʃən/ *n* promulgación, *f;* divulgación, diseminación, *f*
prone /proun/ *a* postrado; inclinado, propenso
proneness /'prounɪs/ *n* postración, *f;* inclinación, tendencia, propensión, *f*
prong /prɔŋ/ *n* (pitchfork) horquilla, *f;* (of a fork) diente, *m,* púa, *f*
pronged /prɔŋd/ *a* dentado, con púas
pronoun /'prouˌnaun/ *n* pronombre, *m*
pronounce /prə'nauns/ *vt* pronunciar; declarar; articular
pronounced /prə'naunst/ *a* marcado; perceptible; bien definido
pronouncement /prə'naunsmənt/ *n* pronunciamiento, *m*
pronunciation /prəˌnʌnsi'eiʃən/ *n* pronunciación, *f;* articulación, *f*
proof /pruf/ *n* prueba, *f;* demostración, *f;* ensayo, *m; Law.* testimonio, *m;* (*Photo. Print.*) prueba, *f; Math.* comprobación, *f, a* hecho a prueba (de); impenetrable (a); *Fig.* insensible (a). —*vt* (raincoats, etc.) impermeabilizar. **in p. whereof,** en fe de lo cual. **p. against bombs,** a prueba de bombas. **p. reading,** corrección de pruebas, *f*
prop /prɒp/ *n* apoyo, puntal, estribadero, *m;* (for a tree) horca, *f,* rodrigón, *m; Naut.* escora, *f; Fig.* báculo, *m,* columna, *f,* apoyo, *m.* —*vt* apoyar; apuntalar; (a tree) ahorquillar; (a building) acodalar; *Naut.* escorar; *Fig.* sostener. **He propped himself against the wall,** Se apoyó en el muro, Se arrimó al muro
propaganda /ˌprɒpə'gændə/ *n* propaganda, *f*
propagandist /ˌprɒpə'gændɪst/ *n* propagandista, *mf*
propagate /'prɒpəˌgeit/ *vt* propagar. —*vi* propagarse
propagation /ˌprɒpə'geiʃən/ *n* propagación, *f*
propagator /'prɒpəˌgeitər/ *n* propagador (-ra)
propel /prə'pɛl/ *vt* propulsar, empujar, mover
propeller /prə'pɛlər/ *n* propulsor, *m; Mech.* hélice, *f*
propelling /prə'pɛlɪŋ/ *n* propulsión, *f.* **p. pencil,** lapicero, *m*
propensity /prə'pɛnsɪti/ *n* propensión, tendencia, inclinación, *f*
proper /'prɒpər/ *a* propio; apropiado; correcto; decente; (prim) afectado; serio, formal; (exact) justo, exacto; (suitable (for)) bueno (para), apto (para); (true) verdadero; (characteristic) peculiar; *Herald.* natural; (with rascal, etc.) redomado; (handsome) guapo. **If you think it p.,** Si te parece bien. **p. noun,** nombre propio, *m*
properly /'prɒpərli/ *adv* decentemente; correctamente; propiamente; bien. **to do (a thing) p.,** hacer algo bien. **p. speaking,** propiamente dicho, hablando con propiedad
propertied /'prɒpərtid/ *a* propietario, hacendado; (rich) pudiente, adinerado
property /'prɒpərti/ *n* propiedad, *f;* (belongings) bienes, *m pl;* posesiones, *f pl;* (estate) hacienda, *f;* (quality) cualidad, *f; pl* **properties,** *Theat.* accesorios, *m pl.* **personal p.,** bienes muebles, *m pl;* cosas personales, *f pl.* **real p.,** bienes raíces, *m pl.* **p. man,** *Theat.* encargado de los accesorios, *m.* **p. owner,** propietario (-ia). **p. tax,** contribución sobre la propiedad, *f*
prophecy /'prɒfəsi/ *n* profecía, *f;* predicción, *f*
prophesier /'prɒfəˌsiər/ *n* See **prophet**
prophesy /'prɒfəˌsai/ *vt* profetizar; presagiar, predecir. —*vi* hacer profecías
prophet /'prɒfɪt/ *n* profeta, *m*
prophetess /'prɒfɪtɪs/ *n* profetisa, *f*
prophetic /prə'fɛtɪk/ *a* profético
prophylactic /ˌproufə'læktɪk/ *a* and *n* profiláctico, *m*
propinquity /prou'pɪŋkwɪti/ *n* propincuidad, proximidad, *f;* (relationship) parentesco, *m*
propitiate /prə'pɪʃiˌeit/ *vt* propiciar; apaciguar, conciliar
propitiation /prəˌpɪʃi'eiʃən/ *n* propiciación, *f*
propitiator /prə'pɪʃiˌeitər/ *n* propiciador (-ra)

propitiatory /prə'pɪʃiə,tɔri/ *a* propiciador
propitious /prə'pɪʃəs/ *a* propicio, favorable
propitiousness /prə'pɪʃəsnɪs/ *n* lo propicio
proportion /prə'pɔrʃən/ *n* proporción, *f;* parte, *f;* porción, *f; pl* **proportions,** proporciones, *f pl;* dimensiones, *f pl.* —*vt* proporcionar; repartir, distribuir. **in p.,** en proporción; conforme (a), según; *Com.* a prorrata. **in p. as,** a medida que. **out of p.,** desproporcionado. **He has lost all sense of p.,** Ha perdido su equilibrio (mental)
proportional /prə'pɔrʃənḷ/ *a* proporcional; en proporción (a); proporcionado (a). **p. representation,** representación proporcional, *f*
proportionally /prə'pɔrʃənḷi/ *adv* proporcionalmente, en proporción
proportionate /*a.* prə'pɔrʃənɪt; *v.* -,neit/ *a* proporcionado; proporcional. —*vt* proporcionar
proportionately /prə'pɔrʃənɪtli/ *adv* See **proportionally**
proposal /prə'pouzəl/ *n* proposición, *f;* oferta, *f;* (plan) propósito, proyecto, *m.* **p. of marriage,** oferta de matrimonio, *f*
propose /prə'pouz/ *vt* proponer; ofrecer; (a toast) dar, brindar. —*vi* pretender, intentar, tener la intención de; pensar; (marriage) declararse
proposer /prə'pouzər/ *n* proponente, *m;* (of a motion) autor (-ra) de una proposición
proposition /,prɒpə'zɪʃən/ *n* proposición, *f;* (plan) proyecto, propósito, *m*
propound /prə'paund/ *vt* proponer; plantear, presentar
proprietary /prə'praiɪ,tɛri/ *a* propietario; de propiedad
proprietor /prə'praiɪtər/ *n* propietario, *m;* dueño, *m*
proprietorship /prə'praitər,ʃɪp/ *n* propiedad, pertenencia, *f*
proprietress /prə'praiɪtrɪs/ *n* propietaria, *f;* dueña, *f*
propriety /prə'praiɪti/ *n* decoro, *m;* conveniencia, *f;* corrección, *f*
propulsion /prə'pʌlʃən/ *n* propulsión, *f*
propulsive /prə'pʌlsɪv/ *a* propulsor
prorogation /,prourou'geiʃən/ *n* prorrogación, *f*
prorogue /prou'roug/ *vt* prorrogar, suspender (la sesión de una asamblea legislativa)
prosaic /prou'zeiɪk/ *a* prosaico
pros and cons /'prouz ən 'kɒnz/ el pro y el contra
proscenium /prou'siniəm/ *n* proscenio, *m*
proscribe /prou'skraib/ *vt* proscribir
proscription /prou'skrɪpʃən/ *n* proscripción, *f*
prose /prouz/ *n* prosa, *f.* **p. writer,** prosista, *mf*
prosecute /'prɒsɪ,kyut/ *vt* proseguir, llevar adelante; (*Law.* a person) procesar; (*Law.* a claim) pedir en juicio
prosecution /,prɒsɪ'kyuʃən/ *n* prosecución, *f;* cumplimiento, *m; Law.* acusación, *f;* (*Law.* party) parte actora, *f.* **in the p. of his duty,** en el cumplimiento de su deber
prosecutor /'prɒsɪ,kyutər/ *n* demandante, actor, *m.* **public p.,** fiscal, *m*
proselyte /'prɒsə,lait/ *n* prosélito, *m*
proselytism /'prɒsəlɪ,tɪzəm/ *n* proselitismo, *m*
prose writer *n* prosador, *m*
prosody /'prɒsədi/ *n* prosodia, *f*
prospect /'prɒspɛkt/ *n* perspectiva, *f;* esperanza, *f;* probabilidad, *f;* (in mining) indicio de filón, *m;* criadero (de oro, etc.), *m.* —*vi* explorar; (of a mine) prometer (bien), dar buenas esperanzas. —*vt* explorar, inspeccionar; examinar. **He is a man with good prospects,** Es un hombre de porvenir
prospecting /'prɒspɛktɪŋ/ *n* la prospección, *f*
prospective /prə'spɛktɪv/ *a* en expectativa, futuro; previsor
prospector /'prɒspɛktər/ *n* explorador, operador, *m*
prospectus /prə'spɛktəs/ *n* prospecto, programa, *m*
prosper /'prɒspər/ *vi* prosperar. —*vt* favorecer, prosperar
prosperity /prɒ'spɛrɪti/ *n* prosperidad, *f*
prosperous /'prɒspərəs/ *a* próspero; favorable
prostate /'prɒsteit/ *n* próstata, *f*
prostitute /'prɒstɪ,tut/ *n* prostituta, *f, vt* prostituir
prostitution /,prɒstɪ'tuʃən/ *n* prostitución, *f*
prostrate /'prɒstreit/ *a* tendido; postrado; abatido. —*vt* derribar; arruinar; (by grief, etc.) postrar; (oneself) postrarse
prostration /prɒ'streiʃən/ *n* postración, *f;* abatimiento, *m.* **nervous p.,** neurastenia, *f*
prosy /'prouzi/ *a* aburrido, árido; pedestre, prosaico; verboso, prolijo
protagonist /prou'tægənɪst/ *n* protagonista, *mf*
protean /'proutiən/ *a* proteico
protect /prə'tɛkt/ *vt* proteger
protection /prə'tɛkʃən/ *n* protección, *f;* defensa, *f;* garantía, *f;* abrigo, *m;* refugio, *m;* (passport) salvoconducto, *m; Polit.* proteccionismo, *m*
protectionism /prə'tɛkʃə,nɪzəm/ *n* proteccionismo, *m*
protectionist /prə'tɛkʃənɪst/ *n* proteccionista, *mf*
protective /prə'tɛktɪv/ *a* protector; *Polit.* proteccionista
protector /prə'tɛktər/ *n* protector, *m*
protectorate /prə'tɛktərɪt/ *n* protectorado, *m*
protectress /prou 'tɛktrɪs/ *n* protectriz, *f*
protein /'proutin, -tiɪn/ *n* proteína, *f*
protest /*v.* prə'tɛst, 'proutɛst; *n.* 'proutɛst/ *vt* protestar; *Law.* hacer el protesto de una letra de cambio. —*vi* declarar; insistir (en); hacer una protesta. —*n* protesta, *f; Law.* protesto, *m.* **under p.,** bajo protesta. **to p. against,** protestar contra
Protestant /'prɒtəstənt/ *a* and *n* protestante, *mf*
Protestantism /'prɒtəstən,tɪzəm/ *n* protestantismo, *m*
protestation /,prɒtə'steiʃən/ *n* protestación, *f*
protester /'proutɛstər/ *n* el, *m,* (*f,* la) que protesta
protest literature *n* literatura de denuncia, *f*
protocol /'proutə,kɔl/ *n* protocolo, *m, vt* protocolizar
protoplasm /'proutə,plæzəm/ *n* protoplasma, *m*
prototype /'proutə,taip/ *n* prototipo, *m*
protract /prou'trækt/ *vt* prolongar; dilatar
protracted /prou'træktɪd/ *a* prolongado; largo
protraction /prou'trækʃən/ *n* prolongación, *f*
protractor /prou'træktər/ *n* (*Geom.* and *Surv.*) transportador, *m.* **p. muscle,** músculo extensor, *m*
protrude /prou'trud/ *vt* sacar fuera. —*vi* salir fuera; sobresalir
protuberance /prou'tubərəns/ *n* protuberancia, *f*
protuberant /prou'tubərənt/ *a* protuberante, prominente
proud /praud/ *a* orgulloso; arrogante; noble; glorioso; magnífico; soberbio. **to be p.,** enorgullecerse. **to make p.,** enorgullecer; hacer orgulloso. **to be p. of,** ser orgulloso de, pagarse de, gloriarse en. **p. flesh,** carnosidad, *f,* bezo, *m*
proudly /'praudli/ *adv* con orgullo, orgullosamente
provable /'pruvəbəl/ *a* demostrable
prove /pruv/ *vt* probar; demostrar; (experience) experimentar, sufrir; poner a prueba; (a will) verificar; (show) mostrar; confirmar. —*vi* resultar, salir (bien or mal)
provenance /'prɒvənəns/ *n* origen, *m*
Provençal /,prouvən'sɑl, ,prɔvɑ̃-/ *a* provenzal. —*n* provenzal, *mf;* (language) provenzal, *m*
Provence /prə'vɑns/ Provenza, *f*
provender /'prɒvəndər/ *n* forraje, *m; Inf.* provisiones, *f pl*
proverb /'prɒvərb/ *n* refrán, *m;* proverbio, *m.* **collection of proverbs,** refranero, *m.* **Book of Proverbs,** Proverbios, *m pl*
proverbial /prə'vɜrbiəl/ *a* proverbial
proverbially /prə'vɜrbiəli/ *adv* proverbialmente
provide /prə'vaid/ *vt* proporcionar, dar; proveer, surtir, suplir; (stipulate) estipular; preparar (por); tomar precauciones (contra); sufragar los gastos (de); proporcionar medios de vida (a); señalar una pensión (a). **to p. oneself with,** proveerse de
provided (that) /prə'vaidɪd/ *conjunc* si; a condición de que, siempre que, con tal que
providence /'prɒvɪdəns/ *n* providencia, *f*
provident /'prɒvɪdənt/ *a* próvido, previsor, prudente; económico
providential /,prɒvɪ'dɛnʃəl/ *a* providencial
providentially /,prɒvɪ'dɛnʃəli/ *adv* providencialmente
providently /'prɒvɪdəntli/ *adv* próvidamente, prudentemente
provider /prə'vaidər/ *n* proveedor (-ra)

province /'prɒvɪns/ *n* provincia, *f;* esfera, *f;* función, incumbencia, *f*
provincial /prə'vɪnʃəl/ *a* provincial, de provincia; provinciano. —*n* provinciano (-na); *Eccl.* provincial, *m*
provincialism /prə'vɪnʃə,lɪzəm/ *n* provincialismo, *m*
provision /prə'vɪʒən/ *n* provisión, *f;* (stipulation) estipulación, *f; pl* **provisions,** provisiones, *f pl;* víveres, comestibles, *m pl.* —*vt* abastecer, aprovisionar. **to make p. for,** hacer provisión para, proveer de. **to make p. for one's family,** asegurar el porvenir de su familia. **p. merchant,** vendedor (-ra) de comestibles
provisional /prə'vɪʒənl̩/ *a* provisional, interino
provisioning /prə'vɪʒənɪŋ/ *n* aprovisionamiento, abastecimiento, *m*
proviso /prə'vaizou/ *n* condición, estipulación, disposición, *f*
provisory /prə'vaizəri/ *a* provisional; condicional
provocation /,prɒvə'keiʃən/ *n* provocación, *f*
provocative /prə'vɒkətɪv/ *a* provocativo, provocador
provocatively /prə'vɒkətɪvli/ *adv* de un modo provocativo
provoke /prə'vouk/ *vt* provocar; suscitar; incitar, excitar; (irritate) sacar de madre (a), indignar
provoker /prə'voukər/ *n* provocador (-ra); instigador (-ra)
provoking /prə'voukɪŋ/ *a* provocativo; (irritating) enojoso, irritante
provost /'prouvoust *or, esp. in military usage,* 'prouvou/ *n* preboste, *m;* (of a college) director, *m;* (in Scotland) alcalde, *m.* **p.-marshal,** capitán preboste, *m*
prow /prau/ *n* proa, *f*
prowess /'prauɪs/ *n* valor, *m,* destreza, *f;* proeza, *f*
prowl /praul/ *vi* and *vt* rondar; cazar al acecho
prowler /'praulər/ *n* rondador (-ra); ladrón (-ona)
proximity /prɒk'sɪmɪti/ *n* proximidad, *f*
proximo /'prɒksə,mou/ *adv* en (or del) mes próximo
proxy /'prɒksi/ *n* poder, *m;* delegación, *f;* apoderado, *m;* delegado (-da); substituto (-ta). **to be married by p.,** casarse por poderes
prude /prud/ *n* mojigata, beata, *f*
prudence /'prudn̩s/ *n* prudencia, *f*
prudent /'prudn̩t/ *a* prudente
prudently /'prudn̩tli/ *adv* con prudencia
prudery /'prudəri/ *n* mojigatería, beatería, damería, gazmoñería, *f*
prudish /'prudɪʃ/ *a* mojigato, gazmoño, remilgado
prune /prun/ *n* ciruela pasa, *f;* color de ciruela, *m, vt* podar; (cut) cortar; reducir
pruning /'prunɪŋ/ *n* poda, *f;* reducción, *f.* **p. knife,** podadera, *f*
prurient /'prʊriənt/ *a* lascivo, lujurioso, salaz
Prussia /'prʌʃə/ Prusia, *f*
Prussian /'prʌʃən/ *a* and *n* prusiano (-na). **P. blue,** azul de Prusia, *m*
prussic acid /'prʌsɪk/ *n* acido prúsico, *m*
pry /prai/ *vi* escudriñar; acechar, espiar, fisgonear; (meddle) entremeterse, meterse donde no le llaman. —*vt* See **prize**
prying /'praiɪŋ/ *n* fisgoneo, *m;* curiosidad, *f, a* fisgón, curioso
psalm /sɑm/ *n* salmo, *m.* **to sing psalms,** salmodiar
psalmist /'sɑmɪst/ *n* salmista, *m*
psaltery /'sɔltəri/ *n* salterio, *m*
pseudo- *a* seudo. **p.-learned,** erudito a la violeta
pseudonym /'sudn̩ɪm/ *n* seudónimo, *m*
psychiatrist /sɪ'kaiətrɪst, sai-/ *n* siquiatra, *m*
psychiatry /sɪ'kaiətri, sai-/ *n* siquiatría, *f*
psychic /'saikɪk/ *a* síquico
psychoanalysis /,saikouə'næləsɪs/ *n* sicoanálisis, *mf*
psychoanalyst /,saikou'ænl̩ɪst/ *n* sicoanalista, *mf*
psychoanalyze /,saikou'ænl̩,aiz/ *vt* sicoanalizar
psychological /,saikə'lɒdʒɪkəl/ *a* sicológico
psychologist /sai'kɒlədʒɪst/ *n* sicólogo (-ga)
psychology /sai'kɒlədʒi/ *n* sicología, *f*
psychopathic /,saikə'pæθɪk/ *a* sicopático
psychosis /sai'kousɪs/ *n* sicosis, *f*
psychotherapy /,saikou'θɛrəpi/ *n* sicoterapia, *f*
ptomaine poisoning /'toumein/ *n* intoxicación por tomaínas, *f*
puberty /'pyubərti/ *n* pubertad, *f*
pubescent /pyu'bɛsənt/ *a* púber
pubic /'pyubɪk/ *a* púbico
pubis /'pyubɪs/ *n* pubis, *m*
public /'pʌblɪk/ *a* and *n* público *m.* **in p.,** en público. **p. assistance,** asistencia pública, *f.* **p. funds,** hacienda pública, *f.* **p. health,** higiene pública, *f.* **p.-house,** taberna, *f.* **p. opinion,** opinión pública, *f. Inf.* el qué dirán. **p.-spirited,** patriótico. **p. thoroughfare,** vía pública, *f.* **p. works,** obras públicas, *f pl*
publican /'pʌblɪkən/ *n* tabernero, *m*
publication /,pʌblɪ'keiʃən/ *n* publicación, *f*
publicist /'pʌbləsɪst/ *n* publicista, *mf*
publicity /pʌ'blɪsɪti/ *n* publicidad, *f*
publicity agent *n* publicista, *mf*
publish /'pʌblɪʃ/ *vt* publicar, divulgar, difundir; (a book, etc.) dar a luz, dar a la prensa, publicar; (of a publisher) editar. **to p. abroad,** pregonar a los cuatro vientos. **to p. banns of marriage,** correr las amonestaciones
publisher /'pʌblɪʃər/ *n* publicador (-ra); (of books) editor (-ra)
publishing /'pʌblɪʃɪŋ/ *n* publicación, *f.* **p. house,** casa editorial, *f.* **the p. world,** el mundo de la edición, *m*
puck /pʌk/ *n* trasgo, *m;* diablillo, picaruelo, *m*
pucker /'pʌkər/ *vt* (one's brow, etc.) fruncir; (crease) arrugar. —*vi* arrugarse. —*n* frunce, *m;* arruga, *f;* (fold) bolsa, *f*
puckering /'pʌkərɪŋ/ *n* fruncido, *m;* arrugas, *f pl*
puckish /'pʌkɪʃ/ *a* travieso
pudding /'pʊdɪŋ/ *n* pudín, budín, *m.* **black p.,** morcilla, *f*
puddle /'pʌdl̩/ *n* charco, *m*
puerile /'pyuərɪl/ *a* pueril
puerility /pyuə'rɪlɪti/ *n* puerilidad, *f*
puerperal /pyu'ɜrpərəl/ *a* puerperal. **p. fever,** fiebre puerperal, *f*
Puerto Rican /'pwɛrtə 'rikən, 'pɔr-/ *a* and *n* puertorriqueño (-ña)
puff /pʌf/ *vt* and *vi* (blow) soplar; (at a pipe, etc.) chupar; (smoke) lanzar bocanadas de humo; (make pant) hacer jadear; (advertise) dar bombo (a); (distend) hinchar; (make conceited) envanecerse; (of a train, etc.) bufar; resoplar. —*n* soplo, *m;* (of smoke, etc.) bocanada, *f;* (of an engine, etc.) resoplido, bufido, *m;* (for powder) borla (para polvos), *f;* (pastry) bollo, *m;* (advertisement) bombo, *m.* **to be puffed up,** *Fig.* hincharse, inflarse. **p. of wind,** ráfaga de aire, *f.* **p.-ball,** bejín, *m.* **p.-pastry,** hojaldre, *m,* or *f.* **p.-sleeve,** manga de bullón, *f*
puffiness /'pʌfinɪs/ *n* hinchazón, *f*
puffy /'pʌfi/ *a* (of the wind) a ráfagas; (panting) jadeante; (swollen) hinchado
pug /pʌg/ *n* (dog) doguino, *m.* **p.-nosed,** de nariz respingona
pugilism /'pyudʒə,lɪzəm/ *n* boxeo, pugilato, *m*
pugilist /'pyudʒəlɪst/ *n* pugilista, *mf,* boxeador, *m*
pugnacious /pʌg'neiʃəs/ *a* pugnaz, belicoso
pugnacity /pʌg'næsɪti/ *n* pugnacidad, belicosidad, *f*
pull /pʊl/ *n* tirón, *m;* sacudida, *f;* golpe, *m;* (row) paseo en barco, *m;* (with the oars) golpe (de remos), *m;* (at a bell) tirón, *m;* (bell-rope) tirador, *m;* (at a bottle) trago, *m;* (strain) fuerza, *f;* atracción, *f;* (struggle) lucha, *f;* (advantage) ventaja, *f;* (influence) influencia, *f.* **to give a p.,** tirar (de), dar un tirón (a). **to have plenty of p.,** *Inf.* tener buenas aldabas
pull /pʊl/ *vt* tirar (de); (drag) arrastrar; (extract) sacar; (a boat) remar; (gather) coger; *Print.* imprimir. **He pulled the trigger (of his gun),** Apretó el gatillo. **He was sitting by the fire pulling at his pipe,** Estaba sentado cerca del fuego fumando su pipa. **to p. a hat well down on the head,** calarse el sombrero. **to p. a person's leg,** tomar el pelo (a). **to p. oneself together,** componer el semblante, serenarse; recobrar el aplomo; (tidy oneself) arreglarse. **to p. apart,** *vt* separar; romper en dos. —*vi* separarse; romperse en dos. **to p. away,** *vt* arrancar; quitar. —*vi* tirar con esfuerzo. **to p. back,** tirar hacia atrás; hacer retroceder (a); retener. **to p. down,** hacer bajar, obligar a bajar; (objects) bajar; (buildings) derribar, demoler; (humble) humillar; degradar; (weaken) debilitar. **to p. in,** tirar hacia dentro; hacer entrar; (a horse) enfrenar;

(expenditure) reducir. **to p. off,** arrancar; (clothes) quitarse; (a deal) cerrar (un trato), concluir con éxito; (win) ganar. **to p. on,** *vt* (gloves, etc.) meterse, ponerse. —*vi* seguir remando. **to p. open,** abrir; abrir rápidamente. **to p. out,** hacer salir; obligar a salir; (teeth, daggers, etc.) sacar; (hair) arrancar. **to p. round, through,** *vt* ayudar a reponerse (a); sacar de un aprieto. —*vi* restablecerse; reponerse, cobrar la salud, sanar. **to p. together,** obrar de acuerdo; (get on) llevarse (bien or mal). **He pulled himself together very quickly,** Se repuso muy pronto. **to p. up,** *vt* montar, subir; (a horse) sofrenar; (stop) parar; (by the root) desarraigar, extirpar; (interrupt) interrumpir; (scold) reñir. —*vi* parar(se); (restrain oneself) reprimirse, contenerse

pullet /'pʊlɪt/ *n* polla, *f*

pulley /'pʊli/ *n* polea, *f; Naut.* garrucha, *f.* **p. wheel,** roldana, *f*

pulling /'pʊlɪŋ/ *n* tracción, *f;* tirada, *f;* arranque, *m*

pullover /'pʊl,ouvər/ *n* jersey, *m*

pullulate /'pʌlyə,leit/ *vi* pulular

pulmonary /'pʌlmə,nɛri/ *a* pulmonar

pulp /pʌlp/ *n* pulpa, *f;* (of fruit) carne, *f;* (paper) pasta, *f;* (of teeth) bulbo dentario, *m.* —*vt* reducir a pulpa; deshacer (el papel). **to beat to a p.,** *Inf.* poner como un pulpo

pulpit /'pʊlpɪt, 'pʌl-/ *n* púlpito, *m*

pulpy /'pʌlpi/ *a* pulposo; *Bot.* carnoso

pulsate /'pʌlseit/ *vi* pulsar, latir

pulsation /pʌl'seiʃən/ *n* pulsación, *f,* latido, *m*

pulsatory /'pʊlsə,tɔri/ *a* pulsante, pulsativo, latiente

pulse /pʌls/ *n* pulso, *m;* pulsación, *f,* latido, *m;* vibración, *f;* (vegetable) legumbre, *f, vi* pulsar, latir; vibrar. **to take a person's p.,** tomar el pulso (a)

pulverization /,pʊlvərə'zeiʃən/ *n* pulverización, *f*

pulverize /'pʌlvə,raiz/ *vt* pulverizar

puma /'pyumə, 'pu-/ *n* puma, *f*

pumice /'pʌmɪs/ *n* piedra pómez, *f*

pummel /'pʌməl/ *vt* aporrear

pump /pʌmp/ *n Mech.* bomba, *f;* (for water, etc.) aguatocha, *f; Naut.* pompa, *f;* (slipper) escarpín, *m, vt* bombear, extraer por medio de una bomba; (inflate) inflar; (for information) sondear, sonsacar. **hand-p.,** bomba de mano, *f.* **to work a p.,** darle a la bomba

pumpkin /'pʌmpkɪn/ *n* calabaza, *f,* (Chile) zapallo *m;* (plant) calabacera, *f*

pun /pʌn/ *n* retruécano, *m*

punch /pʌntʃ/ *n* (drink) ponche, *m;* (blow) puñetazo, golpe, *m; Mech.* punzón, *m;* (for tickets, etc.) taladro, *m; Inf.* fuerza, *f.* —*vt* (perforate) taladrar, punzar; estampar; (hit) dar un puñetazo (a). **p.-ball,** pelota de boxeo, *f.* **p.-bowl,** ponchera, *f*

Punchinello /,pʌntʃə'nɛlou/ *n* Polichinela, *m.* **Punch and Judy show,** títeres, *m pl*

punctilious /pʌŋk'tɪliəs/ *a* formal, puntual, puntilloso

punctiliousness /pʌŋk'tɪliəsnɪs/ *n* formalidad, punctualidad, *f*

punctual /'pʌŋktʃuəl/ *a* puntual

punctually /'pʌŋktʃuəli/ *adv* puntualmente

punctuate /'pʌŋktʃu,eit/ *vt* puntuar

punctuation /,pʌŋktʃu'eiʃən/ *n* puntuación, *f*

puncture /'pʌŋktʃər/ *n* pinchazo, *m;* perforación, *f; Surg.* punción, *f.* —*vt* pinchar; perforar; punzar. **We have a p. in the right tire,** Tenemos un pinchazo en el neumático derecho

pungency /'pʌndʒənsi/ *n* picante, *m;* acerbidad, mordacidad, *f*

pungent /'pʌndʒənt/ *a* picante; acerbo, mordaz

Punic /'pyunɪk/ *a* púnico, cartaginés

punish /'pʌnɪʃ/ *vt* castigar; maltratar

punishable /'pʌnɪʃəbəl/ *a* punible

punishment /'pʌnɪʃmənt/ *n* castigo, *m;* pena, *f;* maltrato, *m*

punitive /'pyunɪtɪv/ *a* punitivo

punt /pʊnt/ *n* batea, *f.* —*vt* impeler una batea con una pértiga; ir en batea; (a ball) golpear, dar un puntapié (a)

puny /'pyuni/ *a* débil, encanijado; insignificante; pequeño

pup /pʌp/ *n* cachorro (-rra). —*vi* parir la perra

pupa /'pyupə/ *n* crisálida, *f*

pupil /'pyupəl/ *n* alumno (-na), discípulo (-la); (of the eye) pupila, niña (del ojo), *f; Law.* pupilo (-la). —*a* escolar. **day p.,** alumno (-na) externo (-na). **p. teacher,** maestro (-tra) alumno (-na)

puppet /'pʌpɪt/ *n* títere, *m,* marioneta, *f;* muñeca, *f;* (person) maniquí, *m.* **p. show,** función de títeres, *f.* **p. showman,** titiritero, titerero, *m*

puppy /'pʌpi/ *n* perrito (-ta), cachorro (-rra)

purblind /'pɜr,blaind/ *a* ciego; (short-sighted and *Fig.*) miope

purchasable /'pɜrtʃəsəbəl/ *a* comprable, que puede comprarse; *Fig.* sobornable

purchase /'pɜrtʃəs/ *vt* comprar; adquirir; *Fig.* lograr, conseguir. —*n* compra, *f;* adquisición, *f; Mech.* apalancamiento, *m;* fuerza, *f;* (lever) palanca, *f,* aparejo, *m; Fig.* influencia, *f.* **p. tax,** impuesto de lujo, *m*

purchaser /'pɜrtʃəsər/ *n* comprador (-ra)

purchasing /'pɜrtʃəsɪŋ/ *n* See **purchase. p. power,** poder de adquisición, *m*

pure /pyʊr/ *a* puro. **p.-bred,** de raza

pureness /pyʊrnɪs/ *n* pureza, *f*

purgation /pɜr'geiʃən/ *n* purgación, *f*

purgative /'pɜrgətɪv/ *a* purgativo. —*n* purga, *f*

purgatorial /,pɜrgə'tɔriəl/ *a* del purgatorio; (expiatory) purgatorio

purgatory /'pɜrgə,tɔri/ *n* purgatorio, *m*

purge /pɜrdʒ/ *n* purgación, *f;* (laxative) purga, *f; Polit.* depuración, *f;* purificación, *f.* —*vt* purgar; *Polit.* depurar; purificar; expurgar

purging /'pɜrdʒɪŋ/ *n* purgación, *f; Polit.* depuración, *f; Fig.* purificación, *f*

purification /,pyʊrəfɪ'keiʃən/ *n* purificación, *f*

purificatory /pyʊ'rɪfɪkə,tɔri/ *a* purificador, purificatorio, que purifica

purifier /'pyʊrə,faiər/ *n* purificador (-ra)

purify /'pyʊrə,fai/ *vt* purificar; (metals) acrisolar; refinar; depurar; (purge) purgar

purist /'pyʊrɪst/ *n* purista, *mf*

puritan /'pyʊrɪtn̩/ *a* and *n* puritano (-na)

Puritanism /'pyʊrɪtn̩,ɪzəm/ *n* puritanismo, *m*

purity /'pyʊrɪti/ *n* pureza, *f*

purl /pɜrl/ *vi* (of a stream, etc.) murmurar, susurrar. —*n* (of a stream, etc.) susurro, murmullo, *m*

purlieu /'pɜrlu/ *n* límite, *m; pl* **purlieus,** alrededores, *m pl,* inmediaciones, *f pl;* (slums) barrios bajos, *m pl*

purling /'pɜrlɪŋ/ *a* murmurante, que susurra, parlero. —*n* murmullo, susurro, *m*

purloin /pər'lɔin/ *vt* hurtar, robar

purple /'pɜrpəl/ *n* púrpura, *f, a* purpúreo. —*vt* purpurar, teñir de púrpura. —*vi* purpurear

purplish /'pɜrplɪʃ/ *a* purpurino, algo purpúreo

purport /*v.* pər'pɔrt; *n.* 'pɜrpɔrt/ *vt* dar a entender, querer decir; significar; indicar; parecer; tener el objeto de; pretender. —*n* importe, *m;* sentido, significado, *m;* objeto, *m*

purpose /'pɜrpəs/ *n* objeto, *m;* propósito, fin, *m;* intención, *f;* proyecto, *m;* designio, *m;* determinación, voluntad, *f;* efecto, *m;* ventaja, utilidad, *f, vi* and *vt* proponerse; pensar, tener el propósito (de), intentar. **It will serve my p.,** Servirá para lo que yo quiero. **for the p. of...,** con el propósito de..., con el fin de... for purposes of... para efectos de... **on p.,** de propósito, expresamente. **to no p.,** inútilmente; en vano

purposeful /'pɜrpəsfəl/ *a* resuelto; de substancia

purposeless /'pɜrpəslɪs/ *a* irresoluto, vacilante, vago; sin objeto; inútil

purposely /'pɜrpəsli/ *adv* expresamente, de intento

purr /pɜr/ *vi* ronronear. —*n* ronroneo, *m*

purse /pɜrs/ *n* bolsa, *f;* monedero, portamonedas, *m.* **to p. one's lips,** apretar los labios

purser /'pɜrsər/ *n Naut.* contador, sobrecargo, *m.* **purser's office,** contaduría, *f*

pursuance /pər'suəns/ *n* cumplimiento, desempeño, *m,* prosecución, *f.* **in p. of,** en cumplimiento de; en consecuencia de

pursuant /pər'suənt/ *a* and *adv* según; conforme (a), de acuerdo (con); en consecuencia (de)

pursue /pər'su/ *vt* perseguir; seguir; (search) buscar; (hunt) cazar; (a submarine, etc.) dar caza (a); (continue) proseguir, continuar; (an occupation) dedicarse (a), ejercer

pursuer /pər'suər/ *n* perseguidor (-ra)

pursuit /pər'sut/ *n* perseguimiento, *m;* (search) busca, *f;* (hunt) caza, *f;* (performance) prosecución, *f,* desempeño, *m;* (employment) ocupación, *f.* **in p. of,** en busca de. **p. plane,** avión de caza, *m*
purulence /'pyʊrələns/ *n* purulencia, *f*
purulent /'pyʊrələnt/ *a* purulento
purvey /pər'vei/ *vt* proveer, surtir, suministrar; abastecer; procurar
purveyance /pər'veiəns/ *n* suministro, abastecimiento, *m;* provisión, *f*
purveyor /pər'veiər/ *n* suministrador (-ra), proveedor (-ra), bastecedor (-ra)
pus /pʌs/ *n* pus, *m*
push /pʊʃ/ *n* empujón, *m;* empellón, *m;* impulso, *m;* (of a person) empuje, *m,* energía, *f;* (attack) ataque, *m;* ofensiva, *f;* (effort) esfuerzo, *m;* crisis, *f,* momento crítico, *m.* **at a push,** *Inf.* en caso de necesidad; en un aprieto, si llegara el caso. **to give the p. to,** *Inf.* despedir (a). **p.-bicycle,** bicicleta, *f.* **p.-button,** botón, *m;* botón de llamada, *m.* **p.-cart,** carretilla de mano, *f;* (child's) cochecito de niño, *m*
push /pʊʃ/ *vt* empujar; (jostle) empellar, dar empellones (a); (a finger in one's eye, etc.) clavar; (a button) apretar; (*Fig.* a person) proteger, ayudar; dar publicidad (a); (a claim, etc.) insistir en; (compel) obligar. —*vi* empujar; dar empujones, empellar. **I am pushed for time,** Me falta tiempo. **He is pushed for money,** Está apurado por dinero. **I have pushed my finger in my eye,** Me he clavado el dedo en el ojo. **to p. against,** empujar contra; lanzarse contra; empellar, dar empellones (a). **to p. aside, away,** apartar con la mano; rechazar, alejar. **to p. back,** (hair, etc.) echar hacia atrás; (people) hacer retroceder; rechazar. **to p. by,** pasar. **to p. down,** hacer bajar; hacer caer; (demolish) derribar. **to p. forward,** *vt* empujar hacia delante, hacer avanzar; (a plan, etc.) llevar adelante. —*vi* adelantarse a empujones; avanzar; seguir el camino. **to p. oneself forward,** *Fig.* abrirse camino; entremeterse; darse importancia. **to p. in,** *vt* empujar; hacer entrar; clavar, hincar. —*vi* entrar a la fuerza; entremeterse. **to p. off,** *vt* apartar con la mano (a); *Inf.* quitar de encima (a). —*vi Naut.* desatracar; *Inf.* ponerse en camino. **to p. open,** empujar, abrir. **to p. out,** *vt* empujar hacia fuera; hacer salir; echar. —*vi Naut.* zarpar. **to p. through,** *vt* (business, etc.) despachar rápidamente; (a crowd) abrirse camino por. —*vi* aparecer, mostrarse. **to p. to,** cerrar. **to p. up,** empujar; hacer subir; (windows, etc.) levantar. **be pushing up the daises,** mirar los árboles de raíz
pushing /'pʊʃɪŋ/ *a* enérgico, emprendedor; ambicioso; agresivo. **by p. and shoving,** a empellones, a empujones
pusillanimity /ˌpyusələ'nɪmɪti/ *n* pusilanimidad, *f*
pusillanimous /ˌpyusə'lænəməs/ *a* pusilánime
puss /pʊs/ *n* micho (-cha). **P.! P.!** ¡Miz, Miz!
pustule /'pʌstʃʊl/ *n* pústula, *f*
put /pʊt/ *vt* poner; colocar; (pour out) echar; aplicar; emplear; (estimate) calcular; presentar; (ask) preguntar; (say) decir; (express) expresar; (a question) hacer; (a problem) plantear; (the weight) lanzar; (rank) estimar. **As the Spanish put it,** Como dicen los españoles. **If I may put it so,** Si puedo expresarlo así, Por así decirlo. **hard put to it,** en dificultades, apurado. **How will you put it to her?** ¿Cómo se lo vas a explicar a ella? **to put ashore,** echar en tierra (a). **to put a child to bed,** acostar a un niño. **to put in order,** arreglar; ordenar. **to put out of joint,** dislocar. **to put out of order,** estropear. **to put to death,** matar; (judicially) ajusticiar. **to put about,** *vt* (a rumor) diseminar, divulgar; (worry) preocupar. —*vi Naut.* virar, cambiar de rumbo. **to put aside,** poner a un lado; descartar; (omit) omitir, pasar por alto de; (fears, etc.) desechar. **to put away,** quitar; guardar; poner en salvo; arrinconar; (thoughts) desechar, ahuyentar; (save) ahorrar; (banish) despedir, alejar; (a wife) repudiar, divorciar; (food) tragar. **to put back,** *vt* echar hacia atrás; hacer retroceder; (replace) devolver, restituir; (the clock) retrasar; (retard) retardar, atrasar. —*vi* volver; *Naut.* volver a puerto. **to put down,** depositar; poner en el suelo; (the blinds) bajar; (an umbrella) cerrar; (a rebellion) sofocar; (gambling, etc.) suprimir; (humble) abatir, humillar; degradar; (silence) hacer callar; (reduce) reducir, disminuir; (write) apuntar, anotar; (a name) inscribir; (to an account) poner a la cuenta de; (estimate) juzgar, creer; (impute) atribuir. **The book is so interesting that it's hard to put down,** El libro es tan interesante que es difícil dejarlo. **to put forth,** (leaves, flowers, sun's rays) echar; (a book) publicar, dar a luz; (a hand) alargar; (an arm) extender; (show) manifestar, mostrar; (strength, etc.) desplegar; (use) emplear. **to put forward,** avanzar; (a clock) adelantar; (a suggestion, etc.) hacer; (propose) proponer; (a case) presentar. **to put oneself forward,** ponerse en evidencia. **to put in,** poner dentro; (a hand, etc.) introducir; (liquids) echar en; (a government) poner en el poder; (an employment) nombrar, colocar; (insert) insertar; (a claim) presentar; (say) decir. **I shall put in two hours' work before bedtime,** Trabajaré por dos horas antes de acostarme. **He put in a good word for you,** Habló en tu favor. **to put in writing,** poner por escrito. **to put in for,** (an employment) solicitar (un empleo); (as a candidate) presentarse como candidato para. **to put into,** meter dentro (de); (words) expresar; (port) arribar, hacer escala en (un puerto). **to put off,** desechar; (garments) quitarse, despojarse (de); (postpone) diferir, aplazar; (evade) evadir, entretener; quitarse de encima (a), desembarazarse (de); (confuse) desconcertar; (discourage) desanimar; quitar el apetito (a). **to put on,** poner sobre; (clothes) ponerse; (pretend) fingir, afectar; poner; (a play) poner en escena; (the hands of a clock) adelantar; (weight) engordar, poner carnes; (add) añadir; (*Sports.* score) hacer; (bet) apostar; (the light) encender; (assume) tomar; (the brake) frenar; (abuse) abusar (de). engañar. **He put the kettle on the fire,** Puso la tetera en el fuego. **to put on airs and graces,** darse humos. **to put on probation,** dar el azul a, poner a prueba a. **to put on more trains,** poner más trenes. **put one's foot down,** ponerle a fulano el alto. **to put out,** *vt* (eject) echar, expulsar; hacer salir; poner en la calle; (a tenant) desahuciar; (one's hand) alargar; (one's arm) extender; (one's tongue) sacar; (eyes) saltar; (fire, light) apagar, extinguir; (leaves, etc.) echar; (horns) sacar; (head) asomar, sacar; (use) emplear; (give) entregar, dar; (at interest) dar a interés; (finish) terminar; (dislocate) dislocar; (worry) desconcertar; turbar; poner los nervios en punta (a); (anger) enojar; (inconvenience) incomodar; (a book) publicar; (a boat) echar al mar. —*vi* (of a ship) hacerse a la vela, zarpar. **to put out to grass,** mandar a pacer. **We put out to sea,** Nos hicimos a la mar. **to put the cart before the horse,** poner la carreta por delante de los bueyes. **to put through,** (perform) desempeñar; concluir, terminar; (thrust) meter; (subject to) someter a; (exercise) ejercitar; (on the telephone) poner en comunicación (con). **to put together,** juntar; (a machine, etc.) montar, armar. **to put two and two together,** atar cabos. **to put up,** *vt* (sails, a flag) izar; (raise a window) levantar, cerrar; (open a window, or an umbrella) abrir; (one's hands, etc.) poner en alto; (one's fists) alzar; (a prayer) ofrecer, hacer; (as a candidate) nombrar; (for sale) poner (a la venta); (the price) aumentar; (a prescription) preparar; (food) conservar; (pack) empaquetar; (a sword) envainar; (lodge) alojar; (a petition) presentar; (build) construir; *Mech.* montar; (*Inf.* plan) arreglar. —*vi* alojarse. **to put upon,** abusar (de); oprimir; (accuse) imputar, acusar (de). **to put up to,** incitar (a), instigar (a); dar informaciones sobre; poner al corriente (de). **to put up with,** tolerar, soportar, aguantar; resignarse a; contentarse con, conformarse con
putative /'pyutətɪv/ *a* supuesto; (of relationship) putativo
putrefaction /ˌpyutrə'fækʃən/ *n* putrefacción, *f*
putrefy /'pyutrəˌfai/ *vt* pudrir. —*vt* pudrirse, descomponerse
putrid /'pyutrɪd/ *a* pútrido; *Inf.* apestoso
putt /pʌt/ *vt* and *vi* patear.
putting /'pʊtɪŋ/ *n* acción de poner, *f;* colocación, *f.* **p. forward of the clock,** adelanto de la hora, *m.* **p. off,** tardanza, dilación, *f.* **p. the weight,** lanzamiento del peso, *m.* **p. up,** (for office) candidatura, *f.* /'pʌtɪŋ/ **p. green,** pista de golf en miniatura, *f*

putty /ˈpʌti/ *n* masilla, *f*, *vt* enmasillar, rellenar con masilla
puzzle /ˈpʌzəl/ *vt* dejar perplejo; desconcertar; confundir; embrollar. —*n* problema, *m;* dificultad, *f;* enigma, *m;* (perplexity) perplejidad, *f;* (game) rompecabezas, *m.* **to p. out,** procurar resolver; encontrar la solución de. **to p. over,** pensar en, meditar sobre. **I am puzzled by...,** Me trae (or tiene) perplejo...
pygmy /ˈpɪgmi/ *a* and *n* pigmeo (-ea)
pyjamas /pəˈdʒɑməz, -ˈdʒæməz/ *n* pijama, *m*
pylon /ˈpailɒn/ *n* pilón, *m;* poste, *m;* (at an airport) poste de señales, *m*
pylorus /paiˈlɔrəs/ *n* píloro, *m*
pyorrhea /ˌpaiəˈriə/ *n* piorrea, *f*
pyramid /ˈpɪrəmɪd/ *n* pirámide, *f*
pyramidal /pɪˈræmɪdl̩/ *a* piramidal
pyre /paiᵊr/ *n* pira, *f*
Pyrenean /ˌpɪərəˈniən/ *a* pirineo, pirenaico
Pyrenees, the /ˈpɪərəˌniz/ los Pirineos, *m pl*
pyrites /paiˈraitiz/ *n* pirita, *f*
pyromancy /ˈpairəˌmænsi/ *n* piromancia, *f*
pyrotechnic /ˌpairəˈtɛknɪk/ *a* pirotécnico
pyrotechnics /ˌpairəˈtɛknɪks/ *n* pirotecnia, *f*
pyrotechnist /ˌpairəˈtɛknɪst/ *n* pirotécnico, *m*
Pyrrhic /ˈpɪrɪk/ *a* pírrico
Pythagorean /pɪˌθægəˈriən/ *a* and *n* pitagórico (-ca)
Pythian /ˈpɪθiən/ *a* pitio
python /ˈpaiθɒn/ *n* pitón, *m*
pythoness /ˈpaiθənɪs/ *n* pitonisa, *f*

Q

q /kyu/ *n* (letter) cu, *f*
quack /kwæk/ *vi* (of a duck) graznar. —*n* (of a duck) graznido, *m;* (charlatan) charlatán, farsante, *m;* curandero, *m.* **q. doctor,** matasanos, medicastro, curandero, *m.* **q. medicine,** curanderismo, *m*
quackery /'kwækəri/ *n* charlatanería, *f,* charlatanismo, *m*
quadrangle /'kwɒd,ræŋgəl/ *n* cuadrángulo, *m;* (courtyard) patio, *m*
quadrangular /kwɒd'ræŋgyələr/ *a* cuadrangular
quadrant /'kwɒdrənt/ *n* (*Geom. Astron.* etc.) cuadrante, *m*
quadratic /kwɒ'drætɪk/ *a* cuadrático. **q. equation,** cuadrática, ecuación de segundo grado, *f*
quadrature /'kwɒdrətʃər/ *n* (*Math. Astron.*) cuadratura, *f*
quadrennial /kwɒ'drɛniəl/ *a* cuadrienal
quadrilateral /ˌkwɒdrə'lætərəl/ *a* and *n* cuadrilátero *m*
quadrille /kwɒ'drɪl/ *n* cuadrilla, *f;* (card game) cuatrillo, *m*
quadruped /'kwɒdrʊˌpɛd/ *a* and *n* cuadrúpedo *m*
quadruple /kwɒ'drupəl/ *a* cuádruple. —*vt* cuadruplicar. —*n* cuádruplo, *m*
quadruplet /kwɒ'drʌplɪt/ *n* serie de cuatro cosas, *f;* bicicleta de cuatro asientos, *f;* uno (una) de cuatro niños (-as) gemelos (-as)
quadruplication /kwɒˌdruplɪ'keiʃən/ *n* cuadruplicación, *f*
quaff /kwɒf/ *vt* beber a grandes tragos, vaciar de un trago
quagmire /'kwægˌmaiᵊr/ *n* tremedal, pantano, *m; Fig.* cenagal, *m*
quail /kweil/ *n* codorniz, *f;* (U.S.A.) parpayuela, *f.* —*vi* cejar, retroceder; temblar, acobardarse
quaint /kweint/ *a* pintoresco; curioso, raro; (eccentric) excéntrico, extravagante
quaintly /'kweintli/ *adv* de un modo pintoresco; curiosamente; con extravagancia
quaintness /'kweintnɪs/ *n* lo pintoresco; rareza, singularidad, *f;* (eccentricity) extravagancia, *f*
quake /kweik/ *vi* estremecerse, vibrar; temblar. —*n* estremecimiento, *m;* (of the earth) terremoto, *m.* **to q. with fear,** temblar de miedo
Quaker /'kweikər/ *n* cuáquero (-ra)
Quakerism /'kweikəˌrɪzəm/ *n* cuaquerismo, *m*
quaking /'kweikɪŋ/ *a* temblón; tembloroso. —*n* temblor, *m;* estremecimiento, *m.* **q. ash,** álamo temblón, *m*
quakingly /'kweikɪŋli/ *adv* trémulamente
qualifiable /'kwɒləˌfaiəbəl/ *a* calificable
qualification /ˌkwɒləfɪ'keiʃən/ *n* calificación, *f;* requisito, *m;* capacidad, aptitud, *f;* (reservation) reservación, salvedad, *f*
qualified /'kwɒləˌfaid/ *a* apto, competente; (of professions) con título universitario; habilitado; limitado
qualify /'kwɒləˌfai/ *vt* habilitar; calificar; modificar; suavizar; *vi* habilitarse; prepararse; llenar los requisitos
qualifying /'kwɒləˌfaiɪŋ/ *a Gram.* calificativo
qualitative /'kwɒlɪˌteitɪv/ *a* cualitativo
quality /'kwɒlɪti/ *n* cualidad, *f;* calidad, *f;* propiedad, *f.* **This cloth is of good q.,** Esta tela es de buena calidad. **the q.,** la alta sociedad, la aristocracia
qualm /kwɑm/ *n* náusea, *f;* mareo, desmayo, *m;* (of conscience) escrúpulo, remordimiento, *m*
quandary /'kwɒndəri/ *n* incertidumbre, perplejidad, *f;* dilema, apuro, *m.* **to be in a q.,** estar perplejo
quantitative /'kwɒntɪˌteitɪv/ *a* cuantitativo
quantity /'kwɒntɪti/ *n* cantidad, *f;* gran cantidad, *f.* **unknown q.,** incógnita, *f*
quantum /'kwɒntəm/ *n* cantidad, *f;* tanto, *m.* **q. theory,** teoría de la quanta, *f*
quarantine /'kwɔrənˌtin/ *n* cuarentena, *f, vt* someter a cuarentena
quarrel /'kwɔrəl/ *vi* pelear, disputar; (scold) reñir; (find fault) criticar. —*n* pelea, disputa, *f;* (glazier's) diamante de vidriero, *m.* **to pick a q. with,** armar pleito con, reñir con. **to q. with,** reñir con, romper con; quejarse de
quarreller /'kwɔrələr/ *n* reñidor (-ra)
quarrelling /'kwɔrəlɪŋ/ *n* disputas, altercaciones, *f pl*
quarrelsome /'kwɔrəlsəm/ *a* pendenciero, peleador, belicoso
quarrelsomeness /'kwɔrəlsəmnɪs/ *n* belicosidad, pugnacidad, *f*
quarry /'kwɔri/ *n* cantera, *f; Fig.* mina, *f;* (prey) presa, *f;* víctima, *f.* —*vt* explotar una cantera; examinar
quarrying /'kwɔriɪŋ/ *n* explotación de canteras, *f;* cantería, *f*
quarryman /'kwɔrimən/ *n* cantero, *m*
quart /kwɔrt/ *n* cuarto de galón, *m*
quartan /'kwɔrtn̩/ *a* cuartanal. —*n* (fever) cuartana, *f*
quarter /'kwɔrtər/ *n* (fourth part) cuarta parte, *f,* cuarto, *m;* (of a year) trimestre, *m;* (of an hour, the moon, a ton, an animal, etc.) cuarto, *m;* (of the compass) cuarta, *f; Naut.* cuartelada, *f;* (of a town) barrio, *m;* (mercy) cuartel, *m; Herald.* cuartel, *m;* dirección, *f;* origen, *m,* fuente, *f; pl* **quarters,** vivienda, *f;* alojamiento, *m;* (barracks) cuartel, *m.* —*vt* cuartear; (a body) descuartizar, hacer cuartos (a); (troops) alojar; (in barracks) acuartelar; *Herald.* cuartelar. **a q. of an hour,** un cuarto de hora. **at close quarters,** de cerca. **hind quarters,** cuartos traseros, *m pl.* **It is a q. to four,** Son las cuatro menos cuarto. **It is a q. past four,** Son las cuatro y cuarto. **q.-day,** primer día de un trimestre, *m.* **q.-deck,** alcázar, *m;* cuerpo de oficiales de un buque, *m.* **q.-mile,** cuarto de milla, *m.* **q.-plate,** cuarto de placa, *m.* **q.-sessions,** sesión trimestral de los juzgados municipales, *f.* **q.-staff,** barra, *f.* **q.-tone,** cuarto de tono, *m*
quartering /'kwɔrtərɪŋ/ *n* (punishment) descuartizamiento, *m; Herald.* cantón, *m*
quarterly /'kwɔrtərli/ *a* trimestral, trimestre. —*n* publicación trimestral, *f, adv* trimestralmente
quartermaster /'kwɔrtərˌmæstər/ *n Mil.* cabo furriel, *m; Nav.* maestre de víveres, cabo de mar, *m.* **q.-general,** intendente de ejército, *m*
quartet /kwɔr'tɛt/ *n* cuarteto, *m*
quarto /'kwɔrtou/ *n* papel en cuarto, *m;* libro en cuarto, *m.* **in q.,** en cuarto
quartz /kwɔrts/ *n* cuarzo, *m*
quash /kwɒʃ/ *vt Law.* anular, derogar; *Inf.* sofocar, reprimir
quasi /'kweizai, 'kwɑsi/ *a* and *adv* cuasi
quasimodo /ˌkwɑsə'moudou/ *n* cuasimodo, *m*
quatrain /'kwɒtrein/ *n* cuarteta, *f*
quaver /'kweivər/ *vi* vibrar; temblar; (trill) trinar, hacer quiebros. —*vt* decir con voz temblorosa. —*n* vibración, *f;* trémolo, *m;* (trill) trino, *m;* (musical note) corchea, *f*
quaveringly /'kweivərɪŋli/ *adv* con voz temblorosa
quavery /'kweivəri/ *a* trémulo, tembloroso
quay /ki, kei/ *n* muelle, *m*
queasiness /'kwizinɪs/ *n* náusea, *f;* escrupulosidad, *f*
queasy /'kwizi/ *a* propenso a la náusea; nauseabundo; delicado, escrupuloso
queen /kwin/ *n* reina, *f;* (in a Spanish pack of cards) caballo, *m;* (in a French or English pack and in chess) reina, *f.* **to q. it,** conducirse como una reina; mandar. **q. bee,** maestra, abeja reina, *f.* **q. cell,** maestril, *m.* **q. mother,** reina madre, *f.* **q. regent,** reina regente, *f*
queenliness /'kwinlinɪs/ *n* majestad de reina, *f*
queenly /'kwinli/ *a* de reina; regio
queer /kwɪər/ *a* raro; extraño, singular; ridículo; (shady) sospechoso; (ill) malucho, algo enfermo; (mad) chiflado
queerly /'kwɪərli/ *adv* extrañamente; ridiculamente
queerness /'kwɪərnɪs/ *n* rareza, extrañeza, singularidad, *f;* ridiculez, *f*

quell /kwɛl/ *vt* subyugar; reprimir; apaciguar, calmar
quench /kwɛntʃ/ *vt* apagar; calmar; satisfacer. **to q. one's thirst,** apagar la sed
quenching /'kwɛntʃɪŋ/ *n* apagamiento, *m;* satisfacción, *f*
querulous /'kwɛrələs/ *a* quejumbroso
querulousness /'kwɛrələsnɪs/ *n* hábito de quejarse, *m;* quejumbre, *f*
query /'kwɪəri/ *n* pregunta, *f;* duda, *f;* punto de interrogación, *m.* —*vt* preguntar; dudar (de); poner en duda. —*vi* hacer una pregunta; expresar una duda
quest /kwɛst/ *n* busca, *f;* (adventure) demanda, *f.* **in q. of,** en busca de
question /'kwɛstʃən/ *n* pregunta, *f;* problema, *m;* asunto, *m;* cuestión, *f;* (discussion) debate, *m,* discusión, *f.* —*vt* and *vi* interrogar; examinar; poner en duda, dudar de; preguntarse; hacer preguntas. **beyond q.,** fuera de duda. **to ask a q.,** hacer una pregunta. **without q.,** sin duda. **It is out of the q.,** Es completamente imposible. **It is a q. of whether...,** Se trata de si... **q.-mark,** punto interrogante, *m*
questionable /'kwɛstʃənəbəl/ *a* cuestionable, discutible, dudoso; equívoco, sospechoso
questionableness /'kwɛstʃənəbəlnɪs/ *n* lo discutible; carácter dudoso, *m;* carácter sospechoso, *m*
questioner /'kwɛstʃənər/ *n* preguntador (-ra); interrogador (-ra)
questioning /kwəstʃənɪŋ/ *n* preguntas, *f pl;* interrogatorio, *m*
questioningly /kwɛstʃənɪŋli/ *adv* interrogativamente
questionnaire /ˌkwɛstʃə'nɛər/ *n* cuestionario, *m*
quetzal /kɛt'sɑl/ *n* (money and *Ornith.*) quetzal, *m*
queue /kyu/ *n* coleta, *f;* cola, *f, vi* formar cola; hacer cola
quibble /'kwɪbəl/ *n* equívoco, subterfugio, *m;* sutileza, *f;* (pun) retruécano, *m.* —*vi* hacer uso de subterfugios; sutilizar
quibbler /'kwɪblər/ *n* sofista, *mf*
quibbling /'kwɪblɪŋ/ *n* sofistería, *f,* sofismas, *m pl,* sutilezas, *f pl*
quick /kwɪk/ *a* vivo; agudo; penetrante; sagaz; rápido, veloz; (ready) pronto; ágil, activo; (light) ligero. —*adv* rápidamente; (soon) pronto. —*n* carne viva, *f; Fig.* lo vivo. **Be q.!** ¡Date prisa! **He was very q.,** Lo hizo muy aprisa; Volvió (or Fue, according to sense) rápidamente. **the q. and the dead,** los vivos y los muertos. **to cut to the q.,** herir en lo más vivo. **q. march,** paso doble, *m.* **q.-sighted,** de vista aguda; perspicaz. **q. step,** paso rápido, *m.* **q.-tempered,** de genio vivo, colérico. **q. time,** compás rápido, *m; Mil.* paso doble, *m.* **q.-witted,** de ingenio agudo
quicken /'kwɪkən/ *vt* vivificar; animar; acelerar; excitar, avivar. —*vi* vivificarse; despertarse; renovarse; acelerarse; (stir) moverse. **to q. one's step,** acelerar el paso
quicklime /'kwɪkˌlaim/ *n* cal viva, *f*
quickly /'kwɪkli/ *adv* rápidamente; (soon) pronto; (immediately) en seguida; (promptly) con presteza; vivamente
quickness /'kwɪknɪs/ *n* viveza, *f;* (of wit, etc.) agudeza, *f;* rapidez, velocidad, *f;* (promptness) prontitud, *f;* agilidad, *f;* (lightness) ligereza, *f;* (understanding) penetración, sagacidad, *f*
quicksand /'kwɪkˌsænd/ *n* arena movediza, *f; Fig.* cenagal, *m*
quicksilver /'kwɪkˌsɪlvər/ *n* azogue, mercurio, *m, vt* azogar
quiescence /kwi'ɛsəns/ *n* reposo, *m;* quietud, tranquilidad, *f;* inactividad, *f;* pasividad, *f*
quiescent /kwi'ɛsənt/ *a* quieto; inactivo; pasivo
quiet /'kwaiɪt/ *a* tranquilo; quieto; silencioso; quedo; monótono; inactivo; (informal) sin ceremonia; (simple) sencillo; (of the mind) sereno; (of colours, etc.) suave. —*n* tranquilidad, quietud, *f;* silencio, *m;* paz, *f;* (of mind) serenidad, *f.* —*vt* tranquilizar, sosegar; calmar. **to be q.,** callarse; no hacer ruido. **Be q.!** ¡Estate quieto! ¡A callar!
quietism /'kwaiɪˌtɪzəm/ *n* quietismo, *m*
quietist /'kwaiɪtɪst/ *n* quietista, *mf*
quietistic /ˌkwaiɪ'tɪstɪk/ *a* quietista
quietly /'kwaiɪtli/ *adv* tranquilamente; en silencio; sin ruido; en calma; (simply) sencillamente; dulcemente
quietness /'kwaiɪtnɪs/ *n* tranquilidad, quietud, *f;* calma, *f;* paz, *f;* silencio, *m*
quietus /kwai'itəs/ *n* (quittance) quitanza, *f,* finiquito, *m;* golpe de gracia, *m;* muerte, *f*
quill /kwɪl/ *n* pluma de ave, *f;* (of a feather) cañón, *m;* (pen) pluma, *f;* (of a porcupine) púa, *f.* **q.-driver,** cagatintas, *mf*
quilt /kwɪlt/ *n* colcha, *f,* edredón, *m.* —*vt* acolchar. **q. maker,** colchero, *m*
quilting /'kwɪltɪŋ/ *n* acolchamiento, *m;* colchadura, *f*
quince /kwɪns/ *n* (tree and fruit) membrillo, *m.* **q. cheese,** carne de membrillo, *f.* **q. jelly,** jalea de membrillo, *f*
quincentenary /ˌkwɪnsɛn'tɛnəri/ *n* quinto centenario, *m*
quinine /'kwainain/ *n* quinina, *f*
quinsy /'kwɪnzi/ *n* angina, *f*
quintessence /kwɪn'tɛsəns/ *n* quinta esencia, *f*
quintessential /ˌkwɪntə'sɛnʃəl/ *a* quintaesenciado
quintet /kwɪn'tɛt/ *n* quinteto, *m*
quintuple /kwɪn'tupəl/ *a* quíntuplo
quintuplet /kwɪn'tʌplɪt/ *n* quintupleto, *m;* uno (una) de cinco niños (-as) gemelos (-as)
quip /kwɪp/ *n* agudeza, salida, *f;* (hint) indirecta, *f;* donaire, *m,* chanza, burla, *f*
quire /kwaiᵊr/ *n* (of paper) mano (de papel), *f*
quirk /kwɜrk/ *n* (quip) agudeza, salida, *f;* (quibble) sutileza, evasiva, *f,* (gesture) gesto, *m*
quit /kwɪt/ *vt* abandonar; dejar; renunciar (a). —*vi* marcharse, *Inf.* tomar las de Villadiego, poner pies en polvorosa; (slang) dejar de, cesar de. **notice to q.,** aviso de desahúcio, *m*
quite /kwait/ *adv* completamente, enteramente; totalmente; del todo; (very) muy; (fairly) bastante. **It is not q. the thing to do,** Esto es algo que no se hace. **Q. so!** ¡Claro!; ¡Eso es! Se comprende. **It is not q. so good as we hoped,** No es tan bueno como esperábamos. **Peter is q. grown-up,** Pedro está hecho un hombre (*or* es todo un hombre)
quits /kwɪts/ *adv* quito, descargado. **be q.,** estar en paz
quittance /'kwɪtns/ *n* quitanza, *f;* recibo, *m;* recompensa, *f*
quitter /'kwɪtər/ *n* desertor (-ra); cobarde, *mf*
quiver /'kwɪvər/ *vi* temblar; vibrar; estremecerse; palpitar; (of light) titilar. —*n* (for arrows) aljaba, *f,* carcaj, *m.* See also **quivering**
quivering /'kwɪvərɪŋ/ *a* tremulante; vibrante; palpitante. —*n* temblor, *m;* estremecimiento, *m*
quixotic /kwɪk'sɒtɪk/ *a* quijotesco
quixotism /'kwɪksəˌtɪzəm/ *n* quijotismo, *m*
quiz /kwɪz/ *n* examen parcial, *m.* —*vt* tomar el pelo (a); burlarse (de); (stare) mirar de hito en hito (a)
quizzical /'kwɪzɪkəl/ *a* burlón; cómico; estrafalario
quizzically /'kwɪzɪkli/ *adv* burlonamente; cómicamente
quoin /kɔin, kwɔin/ *n* piedra angular, *f;* ángulo, *m;* (wedge) cuña, *f.* —*vt* meter cuñas (a)
quoit /kwɔit/ *n* tejo, *m; pl* **quoits,** juego de tejos, *m*
quondam /'kwɒndəm/ *a* antiguo
quorum /'kwɔrəm/ *n* quórum, *m.* **to form a q.,** hacer un quórum
quota /'kwoutə/ *n* cuota, *f*
quotable /'kwoutəbəl/ *a* citable; (Stock Exchange) cotizable
quota system *n* tablas diferenciales, *f pl*
quotation /kwou'teiʃən/ *n* citación, *f;* cita, *f; Com.* cotización, *f.* **q. mark,** comilla, *f*
quote /kwout/ *vt* citar; *Com.* cotizar. —*n Inf.* comilla, *f*
quoth /kwouθ/ *vt* **q. I,** dije yo. **q. he,** dijo él
quotient /'kwouʃənt/ *n* cociente, *m.* **intelligence q.,** cociente intelectual, *m*

r /ar/ *n* (letter) erre, *f*

rabbet /'ræbɪt/ *n* ranura, *f,* rebajo, *m.* —*vt* ensamblar a rebajo. **r.-joint,** junta a rebajo, *f*

rabbi /'ræbai/ *n* rabí, rabino, *m.* **grand r.,** gran rabino, *m*

rabbinical /rə'bɪnɪkəl/ *a* rabínico

rabbinism /'ræbə,nɪzəm/ *n* rabinismo, *m*

rabbit /'ræbɪt/ *n* conejo (-ja). —*a* conejuno, de conejo. —*vi* cazar conejos. **young r.,** gazapo, *m.* **r.-hutch,** jaula para conejos, *f.* **r.-warren,** conejera, *f*

rabble /'ræbəl/ *n* populacho, vulgo, *m,* plebe, *f*

Rabelaisian /,ræbə'leiziən/ *a* rabelasiano

rabid /'ræbɪd/ *a* rabioso; fanático; furioso, violento

rabies /'reibiz/ *n* rabia, hidrofobia, *f*

raccoon /ræ'kun/ *n* mapache, *m*

race /reis/ *n* carrera, *f;* (current) corriente, *f;* (prize) premio, *m;* (breed) raza, *f;* casta, estirpe, *f;* (family) linaje, *m,* familia, *f;* (scornful) ralea, *f;* (struggle) lucha, *f.* —*vi* tomar parte en una carrera; correr de prisa; asistir a concursos de carreras de caballos; (of a machine) dispararse. —*vt* (hacer) correr; competir en una carrera (con); desafiar a una carrera. **flat r.,** carrera llana, *f.* **mill-r.,** caz, *m.* **to run a r.,** tomar parte en una carrera; *Fig.* hacer una carrera. **r.-card,** programa de carreras de caballos, *m.* **r. hatred,** odio de razas, *m.* **r.-meeting,** concurso de carreras de caballos, *m.* **r. suicide,** suicidio de la raza, *m.* **r.-track,** pista, *f*

racecourse /'reis,kɔrs/ hipódromo, *m;* estadio, *m*

racehorse /'reis,hɔrs/ *n* caballo de carrera, *m*

racer /'reisər/ *n* (horse) caballo de carreras, *m;* (person) carrerista, *mf;* (car) coche de carreras, *m;* (boat) yate de carreras, *m;* (bicycle) bicicleta de carreras, *f*

rachitic /rə'kɪtɪk/ *a* raquítico

racial /'reiʃəl/ *a* racial, de raza

racialism /'reiʃə,lɪzəm/ *n* rivalidad de razas, *f*

raciness /'reisinɪs/ *n* sabor, *m;* savia, *f,* picante, *m*

racing /'reisɪŋ/ *n* carreras, *f pl; Mech.* disparo, *m, a* de carreras; hípico. **r. calendar,** calendario de concursos de carreras de caballos, *m.* **r. car,** coche de carreras, *m.* **r. cycle,** bicicleta de carreras, *f*

rack /ræk/ *n* (for hay) percha (del pesebre), *f;* (in a railway compartment) rejilla, *f;* (for billiard cues) taquera, *f;* (for clothes) percha, *f;* (for torture) potro, *m; Mech.* cremallera, *f.* —*vt* poner en el potro, torturar; atormentar. **to be on the r.,** estar en el potro **to r. one's brains,** devanarse los sesos, quebrarse la cabeza. **r. and ruin,** ruina total, *f.* **r. railway,** ferrocarril de cremallera, *m,*

racket /'rækɪt/ *n Sports.* raqueta, *f;* (din) barahúnda, *f;* ruido, estrépito, *m;* confusión, *f;* (bustle) bullicio, *m,* agitación, *f;* (swindle) estafa, *f;* (binge) parranda, *f.* **to play rackets,** jugar a la raqueta

racking /'rækɪŋ/ *n* tortura, *f;* (of wine) trasiego, *m, a* torturante; (of a pain or cough) persistente

racoon /ræ'kun/ *n* mapache, *m*

racquet /'rækɪt/ *n* See **racket**

racy /'reisi/ *a* picante; sabroso

radar /'reidɑr/ *n* radar, *m*

raddled /'rædḷd/ *a* pintado de almagre; mal pintado

radial /'reidiəl/ *a* radial

radiance /'reidiəns/ *n* resplandor, brillo, *m,* luminosidad, *f*

radiant /'reidiənt/ *a* radiante; brillante, luminoso. —*n Geom.* línea radial, *f.* **r. heat,** calor radiante, *m*

radiantly /'reidiəntli/ *adv* con resplandor; brillantemente; con alegría

radiate /'reidi,eit/ *vi* radiar. —*vt* irradiar

radiation /,reidi'eiʃən/ *n* irradiación, *f; Geom.* radiación, *f*

radiator /'reidi,eitər/ *n* (for central heating and of a car) radiador, *m;* (stove) calorífero, *m*

radical /'rædɪkəl/ *a* radical. —*n* (*Math. Chem.*) radical, *m; Polit.* radical, *mf*

radicalism /'rædɪkə,lɪzəm/ *n* radicalismo, *m*

radio /'reidi,ou/ *n* radio, *f;* radiocomunicación, *f.* **r. amateur, r. enthusiast,** radioaficionado (-da). **r. announcer,** locutor (-ra). **r. broadcast,** radioemisión, radiodifusión, *f.* **r. listener,** radiooyente, *mf* **r. receiver,** (technical) radiorreceptor, *m;* (usual word) aparato de radio, *m.* **r. transmitter,** radiotransmisor, *m*

radioactive /,reidiou'æktɪv/ *a* radiactivo

radioactive fallout *n* caída radiactiva, llovizna radiactiva, precipitación radiactiva, *f*

radioactivity /,reidiouæk'tɪvɪti/ *n* radiactividad, *f*

radiofrequency /,reidiou'frikwənsi/ *n* radiofrecuencia, *f*

radiolocation /,reidioulou'keiʃən/ radiolocación, *f*

radiologist /,reidi'ɒləgɪst/ *n* radiólogo, *m*

radiology /reidi'ɒlədʒi/ *n* radiología, *f*

radiometer /,reidi'ɒmɪtər/ *n* radiómetro, *m*

radiometry /,reidi'ɒmɪtri/ *n* radiometría, *f*

radioscopy /,reidi'ɒskəpi/ *n* radioscopia, *f*

radiotherapeutics, radiotherapy /,reidiou,θɛrə'pyutɪks; ,reidiou'θɛrəpi/ *n* radioterapia, *f*

radish /'rædɪʃ/ *n* rábano, *m.* **horse-r.,** rábano picante, *m*

radium /'reidiəm/ *n* radio, *m*

radius /'reidiəs/ *n* (*Geom. Anat.*) radio, *m;* (of a wheel) rayo, *m;* (scope) alcance, *m*

raffia /'ræfiə/ *n* rafia, *f*

raffish /'ræfɪʃ/ *a* disoluto, libertino

raffle /'ræfəl/ *n* rifa, *f,* sorteo, *m;* lotería, *f.* —*vt* rifar, sortear

raffling /'ræflɪŋ/ *n* sorteo, *m,* rifa, *f*

raft /ræft/ *n* balsa, *f;* (timber) armadía, *f.* —*vt* transportar en balsa; cruzar en balsa

rafter /'ræftər/ *n* (of a roof) viga, traviesa, *f;* (raftsman) balsero, *m*

raftered /'ræftərd/ *a* con vigas

rag /ræg/ *n* jirón, guiñapo, *m;* (for cleaning) paño, trapo, *m;* (for papermaking) estraza, *f;* (of smoke, etc.) penacho, *m;* (newspaper) papelucho, *m; pl* **rags,** harapos, *m pl; Inf.* viejos hábitos, *m pl.* —*vt* (tease) tomar el pelo (a); burlarse de; hacer una broma pesada (a). **r.-and-bone-man, ragpicker,** andrajero, trapero (Mexico), pepinador, *m.* **r. doll,** muñeca de trapo, *f*

ragamuffin /'rægə,mʌfɪn/ *n* galopín, *m*

rage /reidʒ/ *n* (anger) cólera, rabia, ira, *f;* (of the elements) furia, violencia, *f;* (ardour) entusiasmo, ardor, *m;* (fashion) boga, moda, *f;* (craze) manía, *f;* (of the poet) furor, *m.* —*vi* (be angry) rabiar, estar furioso; (of the sea) encresparse, alborotarse, enfurecerse; (of wind, fire, animals) bramar, rugir; (of pain) rabiar; (be prevalent) prevalecer, desencadenarse. **to r. against,** protestar furiosamente contra; culpar amargamente (de). **to be all the r.,** *Inf.* ser la ultima moda. **to fly into a r.,** montar en cólera. **to put into a r.,** hacer rabiar

ragged /'rægɪd/ *a* harapiento, andrajoso; roto; (uneven) desigual; (rugged) peñascoso, áspero, escabroso; (serrated) serrado; dentellado; (of a coastline) accidentado; (unfinished) inacabado, sin terminar; (of style) descuidado, sin pulir

raggedness /'rægɪdnɪs/ *n* harapos, *m pl;* estado andrajoso, *m;* aspereza, escabrosidad, *f;* lo serrado; lo accidentado; (of style) falta de elegancia, tosquedad, *f*

raging /'reidʒɪŋ/ *a* furioso, rabioso; violento; (roaring) bramante; (of the sea) bravío; intenso. —*n* furia, *f;* violencia, *f;* intensidad, *f*

raglan /'ræglən/ *n* raglán, *m.* **r. sleeve,** manga raglán, *f*

ragout /ræ'gu/ *n* estofado, *m*

ragpicker /'ræg,pɪkər/ *n* trapero (-ra)

ragtime /'ræg,taim/ *n* música sincopada, *f*

raid /reid/ *n* incursión, correría, *f;* asalto, ataque, *m;* (by the police) razzia, *f;* (by aircraft) bombardeo, *m, vt* invadir; atacar, asaltar; apoderarse de; hacer una razzia en; (by aircraft) bombear, bombardear; (pil-

lage) pillar, saquear. **obliteration r.,** hombardeo de saturación, *m*
raider /'reidər/ *n* corsario, *m;* atacador, asaltador, *m;* (aircraft) avión enemigo, *m*
rail /reil/ *n* barra, *f;* antepecho, *m;* (of a staircase) barandilla, *f,* pasamano, *m;* (track) riel, *m;* (railway) ferrocarril, *m;* (of a ship) barandilla, *f;* (of a chair) travesaño, *m pl.* **rails,** (fence) cerca, barrera, palizada, *f.* —*vt* cercar con una palizada, poner cerca a; mandar por ferrocarril. **by r.,** por ferrocarril. **to run off the rails,** descarrilar. **to r. at,** protestar contra; prorrumpir en invectivas contra, injuriar de palabra (a)
railing /'reilɪŋ/ *n* barandilla, *f;* antepecho, *m,* enrejado, *m;* (grille) reja, *f;* (jeers) burlas, *f pl;* insultos, *m pl,* injurias, *f pl;* quejas, *f pl*
raillery /'reiləri/ *n* jocosidad, tomadura de pelo, *f;* sátiras, *f pl*
railway /'reil,wei/ *n* ferrocarril, *m;* vía férrea, *f,* camino de hierro, *m, a* de ferrocarril, ferroviario. **elevated r.,** ferrocarril aéreo, *m.* **narrow gauge r.,** ferrocarril de vía estrecha, *m.* **r. buffet,** fonda, *f,* (or restaurante, *m*) de estación. **r. carriage,** departamento de tren, *m.* **r. company,** compañía de ferrocarriles, *f.* **r. crossing,** paso a nivel, *m.* **r. engine,** locomotora, *f.* **r. guard,** jefe del tren, *m.* **r. guide,** guía de ferrocarriles, *f.* **r. line,** vía férrea, *f.* **r. marshalling yard,** apartadero ferroviario, *m.* **r. passenger,** viajero (-ra) en un tren. **r. platform,** andén, *m.* **r. porter,** mozo de estación, *m.* **r. siding,** vía muerta, *f.* **r. signal,** disco de señales, *m.* **r. station,** estación (de ferrocarril), *f.* **r. system,** sistema ferroviario, *m.* **r. ticket,** billete de tren, *m*
railwayman /'reil,weimən/ *n* ferroviario, empleado de los ferrocarriles, *m*
raiment /'reimənt/ *n* ropa, *f; Poet.* hábitos, *m pl*
rain /rein/ *n* lluvia, *f.* —*vi* and *vt* llover. **a r. of arrows,** una lluvia de flechas. **fine r.,** llovizna, *f.* **to r. cats and dogs,** llover a cántaros. **to r. hard,** diluviar. **r. cloud,** nubarrón, *m.* **r.-gauge,** pluviómetro, *m*
rainbow /'rein,bou/ *n* arco iris, arco de San Martín, *m*
raincoat /'rein,kout/ *n* abrigo impermeable, *m*
raindrop /'rein,drɒp/ *n* gota de lluvia, *f*
rainfall /'rein,fɔl/ *n* cantidad llovida, *f;* (shower) aguacero, *m*
rainless /'reinlɪs/ *a* sin lluvia, seco
rainstorm /'rein,stɔrm/ *n* chaparrón, *m,* tempestad de lluvia, *f*
rainwater /'rein,wɔtər/ *n* lluvia, *f;* agua lluvia, *f*
rainy /'reini/ *a* lluvioso. **r. day,** día de lluvia, *m; Fig.* tiempo de escasez, *m*
raise /reiz/ *vt* levantar; alzar; (the hat) quitar; solevantar; (dough) fermentar; (erect) erigir, edificar; (dust) levantar; elevar; (promote) ascender; (increase) aumentar; hacer subir; (spirits, memories) evocar; (the dead) resucitar; (cause) causar; dar lugar (a); hacer concebir; (a question, a point) hacer; plantear; (breed or educate) criar; (a crop) cultivar; (an army) alistar; (gather together) juntar; (a subscription) hacer; (money, etc.) obtener, hallar; (a siege, etc.) levantar, alzar; (a laugh, a protest, etc.) suscitar, provocar; (utter) poner, dar; (a fund) abrir. **to r. oneself,** incorporarse. **He succeeded in raising himself,** Logró alzarse; Logró mejorar su posición. **He raised their hopes unduly,** Les hizo concebir esperanzas desmesuradas. **to r. an objection (to),** poner objeción (a). **to r. an outcry,** armar un alboroto. **to r. a point,** hacer una observación; plantear una cuestión. **to r. a siege,** levantar un sitio. **to r. Cain,** armar lo de Dios es Cristo. **to r. one's voice,** alzar la voz
raised /reizd/ *a* (in relief) en relieve; (embossed) de realce
raiser /'reizər/ *n* (breeder) criador (-ra); (cultivator) cultivador (-ra); (educator) educador (-ra); autor (-ra); fundador (-ra); (of objections, etc.) suscitador (-ra)
raisin /'reizɪn/ *n* pasa, *f*
raising /'reizɪŋ/ *n* levantamiento, *m;* alzamiento, *m;* (of a building, monument) erección, *f;* elevación, *f;* (increase) aumento, *m;* provocación, *f;* fundación, *f;* (breeding or education) crianza, *f;* (of spirits) evocación, *f;* (of the dead) resucitación, *f;* producción, *f;* (of crops) cultivo, *m*
rake /reik/ *n Agr.* rastrillo, *m,* rastra, *f;* (for the fire) hurgón, *m;* (croupier's) raqueta, *f;* (of a mast, funnel) inclinación, *f;* (person) tenorio, calavera, *m.* —*vt Agr.* rastrillar; (a fire, etc.) hurgar; (sweep) barrer; recoger; (ransack) buscar (en); (with fire) enfilar, tirar a lo largo de; (scan) escudriñar. —*vi* trabajar con el rastrillo; (slope) inclinarse. **r. off,** tajada, *f.* **to r. together,** juntar con el rastrillo; amontonar; ahorrar. **to r. up,** (revive) resucitar, desenterrar
raking /'reikɪŋ/ *n* rastrillaje, *m;* (the fire, etc.) hurgonada, *f*
rakish /'reikɪʃ/ *a* (of a ship) de palos muy inclinados, (dissolute) disoluto, libertino; (dashing) elegante
rakishly /'reikɪʃli/ *adv* disolutamente; elegantemente
rakishness /'reikɪʃnɪs/ *n* (licentiousness) libertinaje, *m,* disipación, disolución, *f;* (elegance) elegancia, *f*
rally /'ræli/ *vt* reunir; *Mil.* rehacer; (faculties) concentrar; (tease) tomar el pelo (a). —*vi* reunirse; *Mil.* rehacerse; (revive) mejorar, recobrar las fuerzas; (of markets, etc.) mejorar *n* reunión, *f*
rallying /'ræliɪŋ/ *n* reunión, *f;* (of faculties, etc.) concentración, *f;* (recovery) mejora, *f.* **r. point,** punto de reunión, *m*
ram /ræm/ *n Zool.* carnero, morueco, *m; Astron.* Aries, Carnero, *m;* (*Mil.* etc.) ariete, *m;* (tool) pisón, *m; Nav.* espolón, *m, vt* golpear con ariete o espolón; (of a gun) atacar; apisonar; meter a la fuerza; hacer tragar a la fuerza; (squeeze) apretar; (crowd) atestar
Ramadan /,ræmə'dɑn/ *n* ramadán, *m*
ramble /'ræmbəl/ *vi* vagar, vagabundear; hacer una excursión. —*vt* errar por
rambler /'ræmblər/ *n* excursionista, *mf;* paseante, *mf; Bot.* rosa trepante, *f*
rambling /'ræmblɪŋ/ *a* (of houses) encantado; laberíntico; (straggly) disperso; (of thought, etc.) incoherente, inconexo. —*n* vagabundeo, *m;* excursiones, *f pl;* paseo, *m;* (digression) digresiones, *f pl;* (delirium) desvaríos, *m pl*
ramification /,ræməfɪ'keiʃən/ *n* ramificación, *f*
ramify /'ræmə,fai/ *vi* ramificarse, tener ramificaciones. —*vt* ramificar; dividir en ramales
rammer /'ræmər/ *n* pisón de empedrador, *m;* baqueta (de fusil), *f;* (of a ship) espolón, *m*
ramp /ræmp/ *n* rampa, *f;* (swindle) estafa, *f;* (storm, commotion) tormenta, *f*
rampage /'ræmpeidʒ/ *vi* alborotarse; bramar
rampant /'ræmpənt/ *a* salvaje; *Herald.* rampante; (of persons) impaciente, furioso; (of plants, growth) lozano, exuberante; desenfrenado; (rife) prevaleciente, predominante
rampart /'ræmpɑrt/ *n* muralla, *f;* terraplén, *m; Fig.* baluarte, *m.* —*vt* abaluartar, abastionar
ramrod /'ræm,rɒd/ *n* baqueta, *f*
ramshackle /'ræm,ʃækəl/ *a* destartalado, ruinoso; desvencijado; (badly made) mal hecho
ranch /ræntʃ/ *n* rancho, *m,* hacienda (de ganado), *f*
rancher /'ræntʃər/ *n* ranchero, *m*
rancid /'rænsɪd/ *a* rancio
rancidness /'rænsɪdnɪs/ *n* rancidez, *f*
rancor /'ræŋkər/ *n* rencor, encono, *m*
rancorous /'ræŋkərəs/ *a* rencoroso
random /'rændəm/ *n* azar, *m, a* fortuito, al azar; sin orden ni concierto. **at r.,** a la ventura, al azar; sin pensar; (of shooting) sin apuntar. **to talk at r.,** hablar a trochemoche
range /reindʒ/ *n* línea, hilera, *f;* (of mountains) cadena, *f;* serie, *f;* clase, *f;* variedad, *f;* (of goods) surtido, *m;* (of a gun, voice, vision, etc.) alcance, *m;* (area) extensión, área, *f;* esfera de actividad, *f;* (scope) alcance, *m;* (of voice, musical instrument) compás, *m;* (of colors) gama, *f;* (for shooting) campo de tiro, *m;* (for cooking) cocina económica, *f.* **at close r.,** de cerca. **out of r.,** fuera de alcance. **within r.,** al alcance. **r.-finder,** (of guns, cameras) telémetro, *m.* **r. of mountains,** cadena de montañas, *f;* sierra, *f*
range /reindʒ/ *vt Poet.* arreglar; alinear; ordenar; clasificar; (a gun, etc.) apuntar; (place oneself) ponerse; sumarse (a); (roam) recorrer; (scan) escudriñar. —*vi* extenderse; (roam) vagar; (of plants) crecer (en);

variar, fluctuar; oscilar, vacilar; (of guns, etc.) alcanzar; (of the mind) pasar (por); (include) incluir
ranger /'reindʒər/ *n* (wanderer) vagabundo, *m;* (keeper) guardabosque, *m; Mil.* batidor, *m*
ranging /'reindʒɪŋ/ *n* arreglo, *m;* alineación, *f;* ordenación, *f;* clasificación, *f;* (roving) vida errante, *f*
rank /ræŋk/ *n* línea, *f;* fila, *f;* grado, *m;* clase, *f;* rango, *m;* categoría, *f;* posición, *f;* calidad, *f;* distinción, *f.* —*vt* ordenar; clasificar; (estimate) estimar; poner (entre). —*vi* ocupar un puesto; tener un grado, rango, etc.; estar al nivel (de); ser igual (a); contarse (entre). —*a* (luxuriant) lozano, exuberante; fértil; (thick) espeso; (rancid) rancio; (complete) consumado; completo; (foul-smelling) fétido; *Fig.* repugnante, aborrecible; (very) muy. **of the first r.,** de primera calidad; de primera clase; de distinción. **the r. and file,** los soldados, la tropa; las masas, hombres de filas, *m pl,* mujeres de fila, *f pl,* la mayoría; los socios ordinarios (de un club, etc.). **to break ranks,** *Mil.* romper filas. **to rise from the ranks,** ascender de las filas. **to r. high,** ocupar alta posición; ser de los mejores (de). **to r. with,** estar al nivel de; (be numbered among) contarse entre, figurar entre
rankle /'ræŋkəl/ *vi Fig.* irritar, molestar; envenenarse la vida, hacerse odioso
rankly /'ræŋkli/ *adv* ranciamente; lozanamente; con exuberancia; abundantemente; groseramente
rankness /'ræŋknɪs/ *n* rancidez, *f;* olor rancio, *m;* fertilidad, lozanía, *f;* exuberancia, *f,* vigor, *m;* enormidad, *f*
ransack /'rænsæk/ *vt* (search) registrar; (pillage) saquear; *Fig.* buscar en
ransacking /'rænsækɪŋ/ *n* (searching) registro, *m;* (sacking) saqueo, *m*
ransom /'rænsəm/ *n* rescate, *m,* redención, *f;* liberación, *f.* —*vt* rescatar, redimir
ransomer /'rænsəmər/ *n* rescatador (-ra)
ransoming /'rænsəmɪŋ/ *n* redención, *f;* liberación, *f*
rant /rænt/ *vi* declamar a gritos, vociferar; despotricar (contra); desvariar; hablar por hablar, hablar sin ton ni son. —*n* declamación, vociferación, *f;* desvarío, *m*
ranter /'ræntər/ *n* declamador (-ra); agitador populachero, *m;* predicador chillón, *m*
rap /ræp/ *n* golpecito, *m;* toque, *m;* (with the knocker) aldabada, *f;* (worthless trifle) ardite, maravedí, *m.* —*vt* and *vi* golpear; tocar. **He doesn't care a rap,** No le importa un ardite. **to rap at the door,** tocar a la puerta. **to rap with the knuckles,** golpear con los nudillos. **to rap out an oath,** proferir una blasfemia
rapacious /rə'peiʃəs/ *a* rapaz
rapaciously /rə'peiʃəsli/ *adv* con rapacidad
rapacity /rə'pæsɪti/ *n* rapacidad, *f*
rape /reip/ *n* (carrying off) rapto, *m.* **the Rape of the Sabine Women,** el Rapto de las Sabinas, *m; Law.* estupro, *m;* violación, *f; Bot.* nabo silvestre, *m.* —*vt* (carry off) raptar, robar; violar, forzar
rapid /'ræpɪd/ *a* rápido. —*n* rápido, *m.* **r. combustion,** combustión activa, *f*
rapidity /rə'pɪdɪti/ *n* rapidez, *f*
rapidly /'ræpɪdli/ *adv* rápidamente, con rapidez
rapier /'reipiər/ *n* estoque, *m;* espadin, *m*
rapine /'ræpɪn/ *n* rapiña, *f*
rapping /'ræpɪŋ/ *n* golpecitos, *m pl;* golpeo, *m;* toques, *m pl;* (of the knocker) aldabeo, *m*
rapscallion /ræp'skælyən/ *n* bribón, *m*
rapt /ræpt/ *past part* and *a* arrebatado; absorto; extático, extasiado
rapture /'ræptʃər/ *n* arrebato, *m;* éxtasis, *m;* transporte, *m;* embriaguez, *f;* entusiasmo, *m*
rapturous /'ræptʃərəs/ *a* embelesado; extático; entusiasta
rapturously /'ræptʃərəsli/ *adv* extáticamente; con entusiasmo
rare /rɛər/ *a* raro; extraordinario; exótico; infrecuente
raree show /'rɛəri/ *n* barracón de los fenómenos, barracón de las atracciones, *m*
rarefaction /ˌrɛərə'fækʃən/ *n* rarefacción, *f*
rarefy /'rɛərəˌfai/ *vt* rarefacer. —*vi* rarefacerse
rareness /'rɛərnɪs/ *n* rareza, *f;* singularidad, *f;* infrecuencia, *f*
rarity /'rɛərɪti/ *n* raridad, *f;* (uncommonness and rare object) rareza, *f*
rascal /'ræskəl/ *n* sinvergüenza, *m;* truhán, bribón, pícaro, *m;* (affectionately) picaruelo, *m*
rascality /ræ'skælɪti/ *n* bellaquería, truhanería, *f*
rascally /'ræskəli/ *a* redomado; vil, ruin, canallesco
rash /ræʃ/ *a* temerario, precipitado; imprudente. —*n* erupción, *f,* salpullido, *m*
rasher /'ræʃər/ *n* magra, *f;* (of bacon) torrezno, *m*
rashly /'ræʃli/ *adv* temerariamente, precipitadamente; imprudentemente, con imprudencia
rashness /'ræʃnɪs/ *n* temeridad, precipitación, *f;* imprudencia, *f*
rasp /ræsp/ *n* escofina, *f,* rallo, *m,* sonido áspero, *m.* —*vt* raspar, escofinar; (get on one's nerves) poner los nervios en punta (a)
raspberry /'ræzˌbɛri/ *n* frambuesa, *f.* **r.-cane,** frambueso, *m.* **r. jam,** mermelada de frambuesa, *f*
rasping /'ræspɪŋ/ *a* (of the voice) áspero, estridente
rat /ræt/ *n* rata, *f;* desertor, *m;* (black leg) esquirol, *m.* —*vi* cazar ratas; ser desertor; ser esquirol. **rat-catcher,** cazador de ratas, *m.* **rat poison,** matarratas, *m,* raticida, *f.* **rat-trap,** ratonera, *f*
ratable /'reitəbəl/ *a* sujeto a contribución; imponible; valuable
ratafia /ˌrætə'fiə/ *n* ratafía, *f*
rataplan /ˌrætə'plæn/ *n* rataplán, *m*
ratchet /'rætʃɪt/ *n Mech.* trinquete, *m;* (of a watch) disparador, *m.* **r.-drill,** carraca, *f.* **r.-wheel,** rueda dentada con trinquete, *f*
rate /reit/ *n* velocidad, *f;* razón, proporción, *f;* (of exchange) tipo, *m;* tanto, *m;* precio, *m;* clase, *f;* modo, *m,* manera, *f; Naut.* clasificación, *f;* (tax) contribución, *f,* impuesto, *m; pl* **rates,** (of a house) inquilinato, *m.* —*vt* tasar; estimar; fijar el precio (a); *Naut.* clasificar; imponer una contribución (de); (scold) reñir. **at a great r.,** rápidamente, velozmente. **at a r. of,** a razón de; a una velocidad de. **at any r.,** de todos modos; por lo menos; sea como fuere. **at this r.,** de este modo; a este paso; a esa cuenta; en esta proporción; (with seguir) así. **first-r.,** de primera clase. **rates and taxes,** contribuciones e impuestos, *f pl.* **r. of climb,** *Aer.* velocidad ascensional, *f.* **r. of exchange,** tipo de cambio, *m.* **r.-payer,** contribuyente, *mf*
rather /'ræðər/ *adv* más bien; antes; (more willingly) de mejor gana; (somewhat) algo, un poco; (perhaps) quizás; mejor dicho; (fairly) bastante; (very) muy; mucho; al contrario. **R.!** ¡Ya lo creo! **or r.,** o más bien. **anything r. than...,** todo menos... **He had r.,** Preferiría. **r. than,** antes que, en vez de
ratification /ˌrætəfɪ'keiʃən/ *n* ratificación, *f;* (of a bill) aprobación, *f*
ratifier /'rætəˌfaiər/ *n* ratificador (-ra)
ratify /'rætəˌfai/ *vt* ratificar
ratifying /'rætəˌfaiɪŋ/ *n* ratificación, *f, a* ratificatorio
rating /'reitɪŋ/ *n* tasación, *f;* valuación, *f;* clasificación, *f;* impuesto, *m,* contribución, *f;* repartición de impuestos, *f;* (of a ship's company) graduación, *f;* (scolding) reprensión, *f*
ratio /'reiʃou/ *n* razón, *f;* proporción, *f.* **in direct r.,** en razón directa
ratiocinate /ˌræʃi'ɒsəˌneit/ *vi* raciocinar
ratiocination /ˌræʃiˌɒsə'neiʃən/ *n* raciocinación, *f*
ration /'ræʃən, 'reiʃən/ *n* ración, *f.* —*vt* racionar. **r.-book,** cartilla de racionamiento, *f*
rational /'ræʃənl̩/ *a* racional; razonable, juicioso. —*n* ser racional, *m*
rationalism /'ræʃənl̩ˌɪzəm/ *n* racionalismo, *m*
rationalist /'ræʃənl̩ɪst/ *n* racionalista, *mf*
rationalistic /ˌræʃənl̩'ɪstɪk/ *a* racionalista
rationality /ˌræʃə'nælɪti/ *n* racionalidad, *f;* justicia, *f*
rationalization /ˌræʃənl̩ə'zeiʃən/ *n* racionalización, *f;* justificación, *f*
rationalize /'ræʃənl̩ˌaiz/ *vt* hacer racional; concebir racionalmente; *Math.* quitar los radicales (a); justificar
rationing /'ræʃənɪŋ, 'rei-/ *n* racionamiento, *m*
rattan /ræ'tæn/ *n* rota, *f,* bejuco, *m;* junquillo, *m*
ratteen /ræ'tin/ *n* ratina, *f*
ratter /'rætər/ *n* perro ratonero, *m;* gato que caza ratas, *m*

ratting /'rætɪŋ/ *n* caza de ratas, *f;* deserción, *f*

rattle /'rætl̩/ *vi* hacer ruido; rechinar, crujir; (of loose windows, etc.) zangolotearse; (knock) golpear; tocar; (patter) bailar; sonar; (of the dying) dar un estertor. —*vt* (shake) sacudir; hacer vibrar; (jolt) traquetear; (do rapidly) acabar rápidamente; (confuse) aturdir, hacer perder la cabeza (a); desconcertar. **to r. along,** deslizarse (or correr) rápidamente. **to r. off,** (repeat) decir rápidamente; terminar apresuradamente. **to r. on about,** charlar mucho de, hablar sin cesar sobre

rattle /'rætl̩/ *n* rechinamiento, crujido, *m;* zangoloteo, *m;* ruido, *m;* son (de la lluvia, etc.), *m;* (in the throat) estertor, *m;* (of a rattlesnake) cascabel, *m;* (child's) sonajero, *m;* matraca, *f;* carraca, *f;* (chatter) charla, *f.* **r.-headed,** de cabeza de chorlito, casquivano

rattlesnake /'rætl̩ˌsneik/ *n* serpiente de cascabel, *f,* crótalo, *m*

rattling /'rætlɪŋ/ *n* See **rattle**

raucous /'rɔkəs/ *a* ronco, estridente

raucousness /'rɔkəsnɪs/ *n* ronquedad, *f,* estridor, *m*

ravage /'rævɪdʒ/ *vt* devastar; (pillage) saquear; destruir; (spoil) estropear. —*n* devastación, *f;* destrucción, *f;* estrago, *m*

ravager /'rævɪdʒər/ *n* devastador (-ra), saqueador (-ra)

rave /reiv/ *vi* desvariar, delirar; (of the elements) bramar, rugir. **to r. about,** hablar con entusiasmo de; delirar por. **to r. against,** vociferar contra, despotricarse contra

ravel /'rævəl/ *vt* deshilar, destejer; *Fig.* enredar. **to r. out,** deshilarse; *Fig.* desenredarse, desenmarañarse

raven /'reivən/ *n* cuervo, *m, a* negro como el azabache

ravening /'rævənɪŋ/ *a* rapaz, salvaje

Ravenna /rə'vɛnə/ Rávena, *f*

ravenous /'rævənəs/ *a* voraz

ravenously /'rævənəsli/ *adv* vorazmente

ravenousness /'rævənəsnɪs/ *n* voracidad, *f*

ravine /rə'vin/ *n* cañada, *f,* barranco, cañón, *m*

raving /'reivɪŋ/ *n* delirio, *m,* desvaríos, *m pl.* —*a* delirante; violento; bravío

ravioli /ˌrævi'ouli/ *n pl* ravioles, *m pl*

ravish /'rævɪʃ/ *vt* (carry off) arrebatar, raptar; extasiar, encantar; (rape) violar, forzar

ravisher /'rævɪʃər/ *n* raptador, *m;* violador, *m*

ravishing /'rævɪʃɪŋ/ *n* violación, *f, a* encantador

ravishment /'rævɪʃmənt/ *n* violación, *f;* arrobamiento, *m;* transporte, éxstasis, *m*

raw /rɔ/ *a* (of meat, etc., silk, leather, weather) crudo; bruto; (inexpert) bisoño; (of flesh) vivo; *Com.* en bruto. **raw-boned,** huesudo. **raw hand,** novato (-ta). **raw material,** primera materia, *f.* **raw materials,** materias primas, *f pl.* **raw score,** puntuación bruta, *f.* **raw silk,** seda cruda, seda en rama, *f.* **raw sugar,** azúcar bruto, *m*

rawhide /'rɔˌhaid/ *a* de cuero crudo

rawness /'rɔnɪs/ *n* crudeza, *f;* inexperiencia, *f;* (of weather) humedad, *f*

ray /rei/ *n* rayo, *m;* (line) raya, *f;* (radius) radio, *m;* (fish) raya, *f.* **cathode rays,** rayos catódicos, *m pl*

rayon /'reiɒn/ *n* rayón, *m*

raze /reiz/ *vt* arrasar, asolar; demoler; (erase) borrar, tachar

razor /'reizər/ *n* navaja, *f.* **electric r.,** máquina de afeitar eléctrica, *f.* **safety r.,** máquina de afeitar, *f.* **slash with a r.,** navajada, *f.* **r. blade,** hoja de afeitar, *f.* **r. case,** navajero, *m.* **r. strop,** suavizador, *m*

re /ri, rei/ *n Mus.* re, *m; prep Law.* causa, *f; Com.* concerniente a

re /ri/ *prefix* (attached to verb) re-; (after the verb) de nuevo; (followed by infin.) volver a... **to re-count,** volver a contar, contar de nuevo, recontar

reabsorb /ˌriəb'sɔrb, -'zɔrb/ *vt* resorber

reabsorption /ˌriəb'sɔrpʃən, -'zɔrp-/ *n* reabsorción, resorción, *f*

reach /ritʃ/ *vt* (stretch out) alargar; extender; alcanzar; llegar hasta; (arrive at) llegar a; (achieve) lograr, obtener. —*vi* extenderse; alcanzar; penetrar. —*n* alcance, *m;* extensión, *f;* poder, *m;* capacidad, *f;* (of a river) tabla, *f.* **as far as the eye could r.,** hasta donde alcanzaba la vista. **He reached home very soon,** Llegó muy pronto a casa. **out of r.,** fuera de alcance. **to r. a deadlock,** llegar a un punto muerto. **within r.,** al alcance. **within easy r.,** de fácil acceso; a corta distancia. **to r. after,** procurar alcanzar; hacer esfuerzos para obtener. **to r. back,** (of time) remontarse. **to r. down,** bajar. **r.-me-downs,** ropa hecha, *f*

react /ri'ækt/ *vi* reaccionar. —*vt* hacer de nuevo; *Theat.* volver a representar

reaction /ri'ækʃən/ *n* reacción, *f*

reactionary /ri'ækʃəˌnɛri/ *a* and *n* reaccionario (-ia)

reactive /ri'æktɪv/ *a* reactivo

read /rid/ *vt* leer; (a riddle, etc.) adivinar; descifrar; interpretar; (study) estudiar; (the Burial Service, etc.) decir; (correct) corregir; (of thermometers, etc.) marcar. —*vi* leer; estudiar; (be written) estar escrito, decir. **The play acts better than it reads,** La comedia es mejor representada que leída. **to r. aloud,** leer en voz alta. **to r. between the lines,** leer entre líneas. **to r. proofs,** corregir pruebas. **to r. to oneself,** leer para sí. **to r. about,** leer; (learn) enterarse de. **to r. again,** volver a leer, leer otra vez. **to r. on,** continuar leyendo. **to r. out,** leer en alta voz. **to r. over,** leer; leerlo todo. **to r. over and over again,** leer muchas veces, leer y releer.

read /rɛd/ *past part* leído, etc. **well-r.,** leído; instruido, culto

readability /ˌridə'bɪlɪti/ *n* legibilidad, *f;* interés, *m,* amenidad, *f*

readable /'ridəbəl/ *a* legible; interesante

readdress /ˌriə'drɛs/ *vt* dirigir de nuevo (una carta, etc.); poner la nueva dirección en (una carta, etc.)

reader /'ridər/ *n* lector (-ra); *Eccl.* lector, *m;* (proof) corrector de pruebas, *m;* (citation collector for a dictionary) cedulista, *mf;* (university) profesor (-ra) auxiliar a cátedra; (book) libro de lectura, *m.* **to be a great r.,** leer mucho. **the Spanish r.** (reader of Spanish books) el lector de español

readily /'rɛdl̩i/ *adv* fácilmente; en seguida, inmediatamente; de buena gana, con placer

readiness /'rɛdinɪs/ *n* prontitud, expedición, *f;* buena voluntad, *f;* (of speech, etc.) facilidad, *f.* **in r.,** preparado. **r. of wit,** viveza de ingenio, *f*

reading /'ridɪŋ/ *n* lectura, *f;* (erudition) conocimientos, *m pl;* (recital) declamación, *f;* (lecture) conferencia, *f;* (study) estudio, *m;* interpretación, *f;* (of a thermometer, etc.) registro, *m;* (of a will) apertura, *f.* **r.-book,** libro de lectura, *m.* **r.-desk,** atril, *m.* **r.-glass,** lente para leer, *m,* carlita, *f.* **r.-lamp,** lámpara de sobremesa, *f.* **r.-matter,** material de lectura, *m.* **r.-room,** gabinete de lectura, *m,* sala de lectura, *f*

readjourn /ˌriə'dʒɜrn/ *vt* (a meeting) suspender (la sesión) de nuevo

readjust /ˌriə'dʒʌst/ *vt* reajustar, reacomdar; *vi* reacomodarse

readjustment /ˌriə'dʒ½stmənt/ *n* reajuste, *m,* reacomodación, *f*

readmission /ˌriəd'mɪʃən/ *n* readmisión, *f*

readmit /ˌriəd'mɪt/ *vt* readmitir

ready /'rɛdi/ *a* listo, preparado; dispuesto; pronto; (on the point of) a punto de; (easy) fácil; (near at hand) a la mano; (with money) contante; (with wit, etc.) vivo; (available) disponible; (nimble) ágil, ligero. **I am r. to do it,** Estoy dispuesto a hacerlo. **in r. cash,** en dinero contante. **to get r.,** prepararse; (dress) vestirse. **to make r.,** *vt* preparar; aprestar; *Print.* imponer. —*vi* prepararse, disponerse. **r.-made,** hecho; confeccionado. **r.-made clothing,** ropa hecha, *f.* **r. money,** dinero contante, *m.* **r.-witted,** de ingenio vivo

reaffirm /ˌriə'fɜrm/ *vt* afirmar de nuevo; reiterar, volver a repetir

reaffirmation /ˌriæfər'meiʃən/ *n* reiteración, *f*

reagent /ri'eidʒənt/ *n* reactivo, *m*

real /rei'ɑl/ *a* real; verdadero; efectivo; (with silk, etc.) puro; sincero. **r. estate, r. property,** bienes raíces, *m pl*

realism /'riəˌlɪzəm/ *n* realismo, *m*

realist /'riəlɪst/ *n* realista, *mf*

realistic /ˌriə'lɪstɪk/ *a* realista

reality /ri'ælɪti/ *n* realidad, *f;* verdad, *f*

realizable /ˌriə'laizəbəl/ *a* realizable; factible

realization /ˌriələ'zeiʃən/ *n* realización, *f;* comprensión, *f*
realize /'riəˌlaiz/ *vt* (understand) darse cuenta de, hacerse cargo de; realizar; (make real) dar vida (a); (accomplish) llevar a cabo; *Com.* realizar; (gain) adquirir
really /'riəli/ *adv* realmente; en verdad; en realidad; en efecto; (frankly) francamente. **R.?** ¿De veras?
realm /rɛlm/ *n* reino, *m,* dominios, *m pl; Fig.* esfera, *f*
realty /'riəlti/ *n* bienes raíces, *m pl*
ream /rim/ *n* resma, *f*
reanimate /ˌri'ænəˌmeit/ *vt* reanimar
reap /rip/ *vt* segar; *Fig.* cosechar, recoger
reaper /'ripər/ *n* segador (-ra); (machine) segadora mecánica, *f*
reaping /'ripɪŋ/ *n* siega, *f; Fig.* cosecha, *f.* **r.-machine,** segadora mecánica, *f*
reappear /ˌriə'pɪər/ *vi* reaparecer
reappearance /ˌriə'pɪərəns/ *n* reaparición, *f*
reapplication /ˌriæplɪ'keiʃən/ *n* nueva aplicación, *f;* (of paint, etc.) otra capa, *f;* (for a post, etc.) neuva solicitud, *f*
reapply /ˌriə'plai/ *vt* aplicar de nuevo; (paint, etc.) dar otra capa (de); (for a post, etc.) mandar una nueva solicitud
reappoint /ˌriə'pɔint/ *vt* designar de nuevo
rear /rɪər/ *vt* (lift) alzar, levantar; (breed, educate) criar; (build) erigir, construir. *—vi* (of horses) encabritarse, corcovear
rear /rɪər/ *n* cola, *f;* parte de atrás, *f;* parte posterior, *f;* última fila, *f;* (background) fondo, *m; Inf.* trasera, *f; Mil.* retaguardia, *f.* *—a* de atrás; trasero; último; posterior; de última fila; *Mil.* de retaguardia. **in the r.,** por detrás; a la cola; a retaguardia. **to bring up the r.,** cerrar la marcha. **r.-admiral,** contra almirante, *m.* **r.-axle,** eje trasero, *m.* **r.-guard,** retaguardia, *f.* **r. lamp,** faro trasero, *m.* **r. rank,** última fila, *f.* **r. view,** vista por detrás, *f;* vista posterior, *f*
rearing /'rɪərɪŋ/ *n* (breeding) cría, *f;* (education) crianza, *f*
rearm /ri'ɑrm/ *vt* rearmar. *—vi* rearmarse
rearmament /ri'arməmənt/ *n* rearmamento, *m*
rearrange /ˌriə'reindʒ/ *vt* volver a arreglar; arreglar de otra manera; (a literary work) refundir, adaptar
rearrangement /ˌriə'reindʒmənt/ *n* nuevo arroglo, *m;* (of a literary work) refundición, adaptación, *f*
reascend /ˌriə'sɛnd/ *vi* and *vt* subir de nuevo, subir otra vez; montar de nuevo (sobre)
reason /'rizən/ *n* razón, *f.* **I have plenty of r. to...** No me faltarían motivos para... *—vi* and *vt* razonar. **to r. out of,** disuadir de. **by r. of,** a causa de, con motivo de; en virtud de. **for this r.,** por esto, por esta razón. **out of all r.,** fuera de razón. **to stand to r.,** ser lógico, estar puesto en razón. **with r.,** con razón. **r. of state,** razón de estado, *f*
reasonable /'rizənəbəl/ *a* razonable; racional
reasonableness /'rizənəbəlnɪs/ *n* lo razonable; moderación, *f;* justicia, *f;* racionalidad, *f*
reasonably /'rizənəbli/ *adv* razonablemente; con razón; bastante
reasoning /'rizənɪŋ/ *n* razonamiento, *m*
reassemble /ˌriə'sɛmbəl/ *vt* reunir otra vez. *—vi* juntarse de nuevo
reassert /ˌriə'sɜrt/ *vt* afirmar de nuevo, reiterar
reassertion /ˌriə'sɜrʃən/ *n* reiteración, *f*
reassess /ˌriə'sɛs/ *vt* tasar de nuevo; repartir de nuevo; (a work of art) hacer una nueva apreciación (de)
reassessment /ˌriə'sɛsmənt/ *n* nueva tasación, *f;* nuevo repartimiento, *m;* (of a work of art) nueva estimación, *f*
reassume /ˌriə'sum/ *vt* reasumir
reassumption /ˌriə'sʌmpʃən/ *n* reasunción, *f*
reassurance /ˌriə'sʊrəns/ *n* afirmación repetida, *f;* confianza restablecida, *f*
reassure /ˌriə'ʃʊr/ *vt* asegurar de nuevo; tranquilizar, confortar
reassuring /ˌriə'ʃʊrɪŋ/ *a* tranquilizador, consolador
rebate /'ribeit/ *n* rebaja, *f,* descuento, *m;* reducción, *f.* *—vt* rebajar, descontar; reducir. **to r. pro rata,** ratear
rebec /'ribɛk/ *n Mus.* rabel, *m*
rebel / *n.* 'rɛbəl; *v.* rɪ'bɛl/ *n* rebelde, *mf,* insurrecto (-ta). *—vi* rebelarse, sublevarse. **r. leader,** cabecilla, *m*
rebellion /rɪ'bɛlyən/ *n* rebelión, *f*
rebellious /rɪ'bɛlyəs/ *a* rebelde; revoltoso; refractario
rebelliousness /rɪ'bɛlyəsnɪs/ *n* rebeldía, *f*
rebind /ri'baind/ *vt* atar de nuevo; (a book) reencuadernar
rebirth /ri'bɜrθ/ *n* renacimiento, *m*
rebore /ri'bɔr/ *vt* (an engine) descarbonizar
reboring /ri'bɔrɪŋ/ *n* (of an engine) descarburación, *f*
reborn, to be /ri'bɔrn/ *vi* renacer; ser reincarnado
rebound /*v.* rɪ'baund; *n.* 'riˌbaund/ *a* (of books) reencuadernado. *—vi* rebotar; repercutir; (revive) reavivarse. *—n* rebote, resalto, *m;* reacción, *f,* rechazo, *m*
rebuff /rɪ'bʌf/ *n* repulsa, *f,* desaire, *m;* contrariedad, *f.* *—vt* rechazar; contrariar
rebuild /ri'bɪld/ *vt* reedificar
rebuilding /ri'bɪldɪŋ/ *n* reedificación, *f*
rebuke /rɪ'byuk/ *n* reconvención, reprensión, censura, *f,* reproche, *m, vt* reprender, censurar, reprochar
rebukingly /rɪ'byukɪŋli/ *adv* en tono de censura; con reprensión, con reprobación
rebut /rɪ'bʌt/ *vt* refutar
rebuttal /rɪ'bʌtl̩/ *n* refutación, *f*
recalcitrance /rɪ'kælsɪtrəns/ *n* terquedad, obstinacia, *f;* rebeldía, *f*
recalcitrant /rɪ'kælsɪtrənt/ *a* reacio, recalcitrante
recall / *v.* rɪ'kɔl; *n. also* 'rikɔl/ *vt* llamar; hacer volver; (dismiss) destituir; (ambassador, etc.) retirar; (remind or remember) recordar; (revoke) revocar. *—n* llamada, *f; Mil.* toque de llamada, *m;* (of ambassadors, etc.) retirada, *f;* (dismissal) destitución, *f.* **beyond r.,** irrevocable; (forgotten) olvidado
recant /rɪ'kænt/ *vt* retractar, retirar. *—vi* desdecirse (de), retractarse
recantation /ˌrikæn'teiʃən/ *n* recantación, *f*
recapitulate /ˌrikə'pɪtʃəˌleit/ *vt* recapitular, resumir
recapitulation /ˌrikəˌpɪtʃə'leiʃən/ *n* recapitulación, *f*
recapture /ri'kæptʃər/ *vt* volver a prender, hacer prisionero nuevamente; (a place) volver a tomar; (a ship) represar
recast /ri'kæst/ *vt* (metals, a literary work) refundir; (alter) cambiar; (reckon) volver a calcular
recasting /ri'kæstɪŋ/ *n* (metals, a literary work) refundición, *f*
recede /ri'sid/ *vi* retroceder; alejarse (de), separarse (de); desviarse (de); retirarse; desaparecer; (diminish) disminuir; (of prices) bajar
receding /ri'sidɪŋ/ *a* que retrocede, etc.
receipt /rɪ'sit/ *n* recibo, *m;* (for money) recibí, *m;* (recipe) receta, *f; pl* **receipts,** ingresos, *m pl.* *—vt* firmar (or extender) recibo. **on r. of,** al recibir. **to acknowledge the r. of,** acusar recibo de. **r. book,** libro talonario, *m*
receive /rɪ'siv/ *vt* and *vi* recibir; admitir, aceptar; acoger; (money) percibir, cobrar; (lodge) hospedar, alojar; (contain) contener. **to be well received,** tener buena acogida
receiver /rɪ'sivər/ *n* recibidor (-ra); (of stolen goods) receptador (-ra); (in bankruptcies) síndico, *m;* (for other legal business) receptor, *m;* (of a telephone) auricular, *m; Elec.* receptor, *m; Radio.* radiorreceptor, *m.* **to hang up (the r.),** colgar (el auricular)
receivership /rɪ'sivərˌʃɪp/ *n* sindicatura, *f;* receptoría, *f*
receiving /rɪ'sivɪŋ/ *n* recibimiento, *m;* (of money, etc.) cobranza, *f,* percibo, *m;* (of stolen goods) encubrimiento, *m.* *—a* que recibe; recipiente; de recepción. **r. set,** aparato de radio, *m*
recency /'risənsi/ *n* lo reciente; novedad, *f*
recent /'risənt/ *a* reciente; nuevo. **in r. years,** en estos últimos años
recently /'risəntli/ *adv* recientemente; (before past participles) recién. **until r.,** hasta hace poco. **r. painted,** recién pintado
receptacle /rɪ'sɛptəkəl/ *n* receptáculo, recipiente, *m; Bot.* receptáculo, *m*
reception /rɪ'sɛpʃən/ *n* recepción, *f;* recibo, *m;* (welcome) acogida, *f;* (of evidence) recepción, *f.* **r. room,** pieza de recibo, *f,* gabinete, *m*
receptive /rɪ'sɛptɪv/ *a* receptivo; susceptible

receptiveness /rɪ'sɛptɪvnɛs/ *n* sensibilidad, susceptibilidad, *f*

recess /rɪ'sɛs, 'risɛs/ *n* (holiday) vacaciones, *f pl*; (during school hours) hora de recreo, *f;* (*Fig.* heart) seno, *m*, entrañas, *f pl;* (of the soul, heart) hondón, *m;* (in a coastline, etc.) depresión, *f;* (in a wall) nicho, *m;* (alcove) alcoba, *f.* **parliamentary r.,** interregno parlamentario, *m*

recessional /rɪ'sɛʃənḷ/ *n* himno que se canta mientras se retiran los eclesiásticos y el coro, *m*

recharge /ri'tʃɑrdʒ/ *vt* (a gun, etc.) recargar; acusar de nuevo

recipe /'rɛsəpi/ *n* receta, *f*

recipient /rɪ'sɪpiənt/ *n* recibidor (-ra); el, *m*, (*f*, la) que recibe. —*a* recipiente; receptivo

reciprocal /rɪ'sɪprəkəl/ *a* recíproco

reciprocate /rɪ'sɪprəˌkeit/ *vt* reciprocar; *Mech.* producir movimiento de vaivén. —*vi Mech.* oscilar, tener movimiento alternativo; corresponder; ser recíproco

reciprocation /rɪˌsɪprə'keiʃən/ *n* reciprocación, *f;* reciprocidad, correspondencia, *f*

reciprocity /ˌrɛsə'prɒsɪti/ *n* reciprocidad, *f*

recital /rɪ'saitḷ/ *n* narración, relación, *f;* enumeración, *f;* recitación, *f; Mus.* recital, *m*

recitation /ˌrɛsɪ'teiʃən/ *n* recitación, *f*

recitative /ˌrɛsɪtə'tiv/ *n* recitado, *m*

recite /rɪ'sait/ *vt* recitar, repetir; narrar; declamar. —*vi* decir una recitación

reciter /rɪˌsaitər/ *n* recitador (-ra); declamador (-ra)

reckless /'rɛklɪs/ *a* temerario, audaz; precipitado; descuidado (de); indiferente (a); excesivo; imprudente

recklessly /'rɛklɪsli/ *adv* temerariamente; descuidadamente; imprudentemente

recklessness /'rɛklɪsnɪs/ *n* temeridad, audacia, *f;* descuido, *m;* imprudencia, *f;* indiferencia, *f*

reckon /'rɛkən/ *vt* calcular, computar; contar; enumerar; (believe) considerar, juzgar; (attribute) atribuir; (think) creer (que). **to r. up,** echar cuentas, calcular. **to r. with,** contar con; tomar en serio

reckoner /'rɛkənər/ *n* calculador (-ra). **ready r.,** tablas matemáticas, *f pl*

reckoning /'rɛkənɪŋ/ *n* cálculo, *m*, calculación, *f;* cuenta, *f; Fig.* retribución, *f*, castigo, *m; Naut.* estima, *f.* **the day of r.,** el día de ajuste de cuentas; el día del juicio final. **to be out in one's r.,** equivocarse en el cálculo; engañarse en el juicio

reclaim /rɪ'kleim/ *vt* (land) entarquinar; (reform) reformar; (tame) domesticar; (claim) reclamar; (restore) restaurar

reclamation /ˌrɛklə'meiʃən/ *n* (of land) entarquinamiento, *m;* cultivo, *m;* (reform) reformación, *f;* (restoration) restauración, *f;* (claiming) reclamación, *f*

recline /rɪ'klain/ *vt* apoyar; recostar; reclinar; descansar, reposar. —*vi* recostarse, reclinarse; estar tumbado; apoyarse; descansar

reclining /rɪ'klainɪŋ/ *n* reclinación, *f.* —*a* inclinado; acostado; (of statues) yacente

recluse /'rɛklus, rɪ'klus/ *a* solitario, *n* recluso (-sa); solitario (-ia); ermitaño, *m*, anacoreta, *mf*

recognition /ˌrɛkəg'nɪʃən/ *n* reconocimiento, *m*

recognizable /ˌrɛkəg'naizəbəl/ *a* que puede reconocerse; identificable

recognizance /rɪ'kɒgnəzəns, -'kɒnə-/ *n* reconocimiento, *m; Law.* obligación, *f*

recognize /'rɛkəgˌnaiz/ *vt* reconocer; confesar

recoil /*n.* 'riˌkɔil; *v.* rɪ'kɔil/ *n* reculada, *f;* (of a gun) culatazo, *m;* (refusal) rechazo, *m;* (result) repercusión, *f;* (repugnance) aversión, repugnancia, *f.* —*vi* recular; retroceder; repercutir; sentir repugnancia

recoin /ri'kɔin/ *vt* acuñar de nuevo

recollect /ˌrɛkə'lɛkt/ *vt* acordarse de, recordar. **to r. oneself,** reponerse, recobrarse

recollection /ˌrɛkə'lɛkʃən/ *n* recuerdo, *m*, memoria, *f*

recommence /ˌrikə'mɛns/ *vt* and *vi* empezar de nuevo

recommend /ˌrɛkə'mɛnd/ *vt* recomendar; aconsejar; encargar

recommendable /ˌrɛkə'mɛndəbəl/ *a* recomendable

recommendation /ˌrɛkəmɛn'deiʃən/ *n* recomendación, *f*

recommendatory /ˌrɛkə'mɛndəˌtɔri/ *a* recomendatario

recommender /ˌrɛkə'mɛndər/ *n* el, *m*, (*f*, la) que recomienda

recompense /'rɛkəmˌpɛns/ *n* recompensa, *f*, *vt* recompensar

recomposition /ˌrikɒmpə'zɪʃən/ *n* recomposición, *f*

reconcilability /ˌrɛkənˌsailə'bɪlɪti/ *n* posibilidad de reconciliación, *f;* compatibilidad, *f*

reconcilable /ˌrɛkən'sailəbəl/ *a* reconciliable; compatible; conciliable

reconcile /'rɛkənˌsail/ *vt* reconciliar; (quarrels) componer, ajustar; (opposing theories, etc.) conciliar. **to r. oneself** (**to**)**,** aceptar; acostumbrarse (a); resignarse (a)

reconciler /'rɛkənˌsailər/ *n* reconciliador (-ra)

reconciliation /ˌrɛkənˌsɪli'eiʃən/ *n* reconciliación, *f;* (of theories, etc.) conciliación, *f*

reconciliatory /ˌrɛkən'sɪliəˌtɔri/ *a* reconciliador

recondite /'rɛkənˌdait/ *a* recóndito

recondition /ˌrikən'dɪʃən/ *vt* recondicionar

reconnaissance /rɪ'kɒnəsəns, -zəns/ *n* reconocimiento, *m;* exploración, *f.* **r. flight,** vuelo de reconocimiento, *m.* **r. plane,** avión de reconocimiento, *m*

reconnoiter /ˌrikə'nɔitər/ *vt Mil.* reconocer; explorar. —*vi Mil.* practicar un reconocimiento; correr la campaña

reconnoitering /ˌrikə'nɔitərɪŋ/ *n* reconocimiento, *m*, *a* de reconocimiento

reconquer /ri'kɒŋkər/ *vt* reconquistar

reconquest /ri'kɒŋkwɛst/ *n* reconquista, *f*

reconsecrate /ri'kɒnsɪˌkreit/ *vt* consagrar de nuevo

reconsider /ˌrikən'sɪdər/ *vt* considerar de nuevo, volver a considerar; volver a discutir

reconsideration /ˌrikənˌsɪdə'reiʃən/ *n* nueva consideración, *f;* nueva discusión, *f*

reconstitute /ri'kɒnstɪˌtut/ *vt* reconstituir

reconstitution /riˌkɒnstɪ'tuʃən/ *n* reconstitución, *f*

reconstruct /ˌrikən'strʌkt/ *vt* reconstruir

reconstruction /ˌrikən'strʌkʃən/ *n* reconstrucción, *f*

reconversion /ˌrikən'vɜrʒən/ *n* reconversión, *f*

recopy /ri'kɒpi/ *vt* copiar de nuevo

record /*v.* rɪ'kɔrd; *n.* 'rɛkərd/ *vt* apuntar; inscribir; (recount) contar, escribir; recordar; registrar; (of thermometers, etc.) marcar, registrar; hacer un disco de gramófono de; (radio, cinema) impresionar. —*n* relación, *f;* crónica, *f;* historia, *f;* (soldier's) hoja de servicios, *f;* (past) antecedentes, *m pl;* documento, *m;* inscripción, *f;* (entry) partida, *f;* testimonio, *m;* (memory) recuerdo, *m;* registro, *m;* (gramophone) disco de gramófono, *m; Sports.* record, *m*, plusmarca, *f; pl* **records,** *m pl;* (notes) notas, *f pl;* (facts) datos, *m pl;* anales, *m pl.* **keeper of the records,** archivero, *m.* **off the r.,** confidencialmente. **on r.,** escrito; registrado; inscrito en los anales de la historia. **to break a r.,** supremar precedentes. **r.-holder,** plusmarquista, *mf*

recorder /rɪ'kɔrdər/ *n* registrador, *m;* archivero, *m; Law.* juez, *m;* (historian) historiador, *m; Mus.* caramillo, *m; Mech.* contador, indicador, *m;* (scientific) aparato registrador, *m*

recording /rɪ'kɔrdɪŋ/ *a* registrador. **r. apparatus,** (cinema, radio, gramophone) máquina de impresionar, *f;* (scientific) aparato registrador, *m.* **r. van,** carro de sonido, *m*

recount /rɪ'kaunt/ *vt* contar de nuevo; (tell) referir, narrar, contar

recoup /rɪ'kup/ *vt* compensar, indemnizar; recobrar, desquitarse de

recourse /'rikɔrs/ *n* recurso, *m.* **to have r. to,** recurrir, *a*

recover /rɪ'kʌvər/ *vt* (regain) recobrar; *Fig.* reconquistar; (retrieve) rescatar; *Law.* reivindicar. —*vi* reponerse; (in health) recobrar la salud, sanar, curarse; *Law.* ganar un pleito. **to r. consciousness,** volver en sí

recoverable /rɪ'kʌvərəbəl/ *a* recuperable

recovery /rɪ'kʌvəri/ *n* (regaining) recobro, *m*, recuperación, *f;* (of money) cobranza, *f;* (retrieval) rescate, *m; Fig.* reconquista, *f;* (from illness) mejoría, convalecencia, *f;* restablecimiento, *m; Law.* reivindicación, *f*

recreant /'rɛkriənt/ *a* traidor, falso, desleal. —*n* apóstata, *mf* traidor (-ra)

recreate /'rɛkriˌeit/ *vt* recrear

recreation /ˌrɛkri'eiʃən/ *n* recreación, *f;* (break in schools) recreo, *m.* **r. hall,** sala de recreo, *f*
recreative /'rɛkriˌeitɪv/ *a* recreativo
recriminate /rɪ'krɪməˌneit/ *vi* recriminar
recrimination /rɪˌkrɪmə'neiʃən/ *n* recriminación, reconvención, *f*
recriminator /rɪ'krɪməˌneitər/ *n* recriminador (-ra)
recriminatory /rɪ'krɪmənəˌtɔri/ *a* recriminador
recross /ri'krɔs/ *vt* volver a cruzar, cruzar de nuevo
recrudesce /ˌrikru'dɛs/ *vi* recrudecer
recrudescence /ˌrikru'dɛsəns/ *n* recrudescencia, *f*
recrudescent /ˌrikru'dɛsənt/ *a* recrudescente
recruit /rɪ'krut/ *n* recluta, *m.* —*vt* reclutar; (restore) reponer
recruiting /rɪ'krutɪŋ/ *n* reclutamiento, *m.* **r. office,** caja de reclutamiento, *f*
recruiting flag *n* bandera de enganche, *f*
rectal /'rɛktl̩/ *a* rectal
rectangle /'rɛkˌtæŋgəl/ *n* rectángulo, *m*
rectangular /rɛk'tæŋgyələr/ *a* rectangular
rectifiable /'rɛktəˌfaiəbəl/ *a* rectificable
rectification /ˌrɛktəfɪ'keiʃən/ *n* rectificación, *f*
rectifier /'rɛktəˌfaiər/ *n* rectificador, *m*
rectify /'rɛktəˌfai/ *vt* rectificar
rectilinear /ˌrɛktl̩'ɪniər/ *a* rectilíneo
rectitude /'rɛktɪˌtud/ *n* rectitud, *f*
rector /'rɛktər/ *n* (of a university or school) rector, *m;* (priest) párroco, *m*
rectorship /'rɛktərˌʃɪp/ *n* rectorado, *m*
rectory /'rɛktəri/ *n* rectoral, rectoría, *f*
rectum /'rɛktəm/ *n* recto, *m*
recumbent /rɪ'kʌmbənt/ *a* recostado, reclinado; (of a statue) yacente
recuperable /rɪ'kupərəbəl/ *a* recuperable
recuperate /rɪ'kupəˌreit/ *vt* recuperar, recobrar. —*vi* restablecerse, reponerse; recuperarse
recuperation /rɪkupə'reiʃən/ *n* recuperación, *f*
recuperative /rɪ'kupərətɪv/ *a* recuperativo
recur /rɪ'kɜr/ *vi* presentarse a la imaginación; volver (sobre); presentarse de nuevo, aparecer otra vez; repetirse; reproducirse
recurrence /rɪ'kɜrəns/ *n* reaparición, *f;* repetición, *f*
recurrent /rɪ'kɜrənt/ *a* periódico; *Med.* recurrente
red /rɛd/ *a* rojo; (of wine) tinto. —*n* color rojo, *m;* (in billiards) mingo, *m,* bola roja, *f; Polit.* rojo, *m.* **to catch red-handed,** coger con el hurto en las manos; coger con las manos en la masa, coger en el acto. **to grow red,** enrojecerse, ponerse rojo; volverse rojo. **red-berried,** con bayas rojas. **red cabbage,** lombarda, *f.* **red cedar,** cedro dulce, *m.* **red corpuscle,** glóbulo rojo, *m.* **Red Cross,** Cruz Roja, *f.* **red currant,** grosella, *f.* **red currant bush,** grosellero, *m.* **red-eyed,** con los ojos inyectados. **red fir,** pino silvestre, *m.* **red flush,** (in the sky) arrebol, *m.* **red-gold,** bermejo; (of hair, etc.) rojo. **red-haired,** pelirrojo, de pelo rojo. **red-handed,** con las manos ensangrentadas; *Fig.* en el acto. **red-head** (person) pelirrojo (-ja). **red-heat,** incandescencia, *f.* **red-hot,** candente. *m.* **red-lead,** minio, *m.* **red-letter,** de fiesta; extraordinario. **red-letter day,** día de fiesta, *m;* día extraordinario, *m.* **red mullet,** salmonete, *m,* trilla, *f.* **red ocher,** almagre, *m.* **red pepper,** pimiento, *m;* (cayenne) pimentón, *m,* **Red Sea,** mar Rojo, mar Bermejo, *m.* **red tape,** balduque, *m;* formulismo, *m;* burocracia, *f.* **red wine,** vino tinto, *m*
redbreast /'rɛdˌbrɛst/ *n* petirrojo, *m*
redden /'rɛdn̩/ *vt* rojear, enrojecer; pintar de rojo. —*vi* enrojecerse, ponerse rojo; volverse rojo
reddish /'rɛdɪʃ/ *a* rojizo
redeem /rɪ'dim/ *vt* (a mortgage, bonds, etc.) amortizar; (from pawn) desempeñar; (a promise, etc.) cumplir; libertar; redimir; compensar; (a fault) expiar; (reform) reformar; (rescue) rescatar
redeemable /rɪ'diməbəl/ *a* redimible; amortizable
redeemer /rɪ'dimər/ *n* rescatador (-ra); salvador (-ra); *Theol.* Redentor, *m*
redeeming /rɪ'dimɪŋ/ *a* redentor; compensatorio. **r. feature,** compensación, *f;* rasgo bueno, *m.* **There is no r. feature in his work,** No hay nada bueno en su obra
redemption /rɪ'dɛmpʃən/ *n* (of a mortgage, etc.) amortización, *f;* (from pawn) desempeño, *m;* (of a promise, etc.) cumplimiento, *m;* (ransom, etc.) rescate, *m; Theol.* redención, *f;* compensación, *f;* (of a fault) expiación, *f;* reformación, *f*
redemptive /rɪ'dɛmptɪv/ *a* redentor
redescend /ˌridɪ'sɛnd/ *vi* bajar de nuevo
rediscovery /ˌridə'skʌvəri/ *n* nuevo descubrimiento, *m*
redistribute /ˌridɪ'strɪbyut/ *vt* distribuir de nuevo, volver a distribuir
redistribution /ˌridɪstrə'byuʃən/ *n* nueva distribución, *f*
redness /'rɛdnɪs/ *n* rojez, *f,* color rojo, *m*
redolent /'rɛdl̩ənt/ *a* fragante, oloroso; *Fig.* evocador (de)
redouble /ri'dʌbəl/ *vt* redoblar. —*vi* redoblarse
redoubling /ri'dʌblɪŋ/ *n* redoblamiento, *m*
redoubt /rɪ'daut/ *n* reducto, *m*
redoubtable /rɪ'dautəbəl/ *a* formidable, terrible; valiente
redound /rɪ'daund/ *vi* redundar (en)
redress /rɪ'drɛs/ *vt* rectificar; reparar; remediar; hacer justicia (a); corregir
reduce /rɪ'dus/ *vt* reducir; disminuir; (in price) rebajar; abreviar; (exhaust, weaken) agotar; (impoverish) empobrecer; (degrade) degradar. **to r. to the ranks,** *Mil.* volver a las filas; degradar. **to be in reduced circumstances,** estar en la indigencia
reducible /rɪ'dusəbəl/ *a* reducible
reduction /rɪ'dʌkʃən/ *n* reducción, *f;* (in price) rebaja, *f*
redundance /rɪ'dʌndəns/ *n* redundancia, *f*
redundant /rɪ'dʌndənt/ *a* redundante; superfluo, excesivo
reduplicate /rɪ'duplɪˌkeit/ *vt* reduplicar
reduplication /rɪˌduplɪ'keiʃən/ *n* reduplicación, *f*
reecho /ri'ɛkou/ *vt* repetir; devolver el son de, hacer reverberar. —*vi* repercutirse, reverberar
reed /rid/ *n Bot.* caña, *f;* (arrow) saeta, *f;* (pipe) caramillo, *m;* (in wind-instruments) lengüeta, *f; Archit.* junquillo, *m;* (in a loom) peine, *m;* (pastoral poetry) poesía bucólica, *f.* —*vt* (thatch) bardar con cañas
reedit /ri'ɛdɪt/ *vt* reeditar, volver a editar
reedy /'ridi/ *a* juncoso, lleno de cañas; (of the voice) silbante
reef /rif/ *n* arrecife, escollo, encalladero, *m; Mineral.* filón, *m; Naut.* rizo, *m.* —*vt Naut.* arrizar. **to take in reefs,** *Naut.* hacer el rizo. **r.-knot,** nudo de marino, *m*
reek /rik/ *n* humo, *m;* olor, *m.* —*vi* humear; oler (de); *Fig.* recordar, hacer pensar (en)
reeky /'riki/ *a* humoso
reel /ril/ *n* carrete, *m;* devanadera, *f;* (of a fishing rod) carrete, carretel, *m;* (cinema) cinta, *f;* (dance) baile escocés, *m.* —*vt* devanar. —*vi* tambalear, titubear; (of ships, etc.) cabecear; temblar; oscilar. **to r. about drunkenly,** (of persons) andar haciendo eses, arrimarse a las paredes. **to r. off,** recitar; enumerar; decir rápidamente
reelect /ˌriɪ'lɛkt/ *vt* reelegir
reelection /ˌriɪ'lɛkʃən/ *n* reelección, *f*
reeligible /ri'ɛlɪdʒəbəl/ *a* reelegible
reeling /'rilɪŋ/ *n* tambaleo, *m;* andar vacilante, *m;* (of a ship, etc.) cabeceo, *m;* oscilación, *f*
reembarcation /ˌriɛmbar'keiʃən/ *n* reembarque, *m*
reembark /ˌriɛm'bark/ *vt* reembarcar. —*vi* reembarcarse
reemerge /ˌriɪ'mɜrdʒ/ *vi* reaparecer
reemergence /ˌriɪ'mɜrdʒəns/ *n* reaparición, *f*
reenact /ˌriɪ'nækt/ *vt* revalidar (una ley); decretar de nuevo
reenactment /ˌriɪ'næktmənt/ *n* revalidación (de una ley), *f;* nuevo decreto, *m*
reengage /ˌriɪn'geidʒ/ *vt* contratar de nuevo
reengagement /ˌriɪn'geidʒmənt/ *n* nuevo contrato, *m*
reenlist /ˌriɪn'lɪst/ *vt* and *vi* alistar(se) de nuevo
reenlistment /ˌriɪn'lɪstmənt/ *n* reenganche, *m*
reenter /ri'ɛntər/ *vt* volver a entrar (en); reingresar (en)
reentry /ri'ɛntri/ *n* segunda entrada, *f,* reingreso, *m*

reequip /ˌriɪ'kwɪp/ *vt* equipar de nuevo

reestablish /ˌriɪ'stæblɪʃ/ *vt* restablecer; restaurar

reestablishment /ˌriɪ'stæblɪʃmənt/ *n* restablecimiento, *m;* restauración, *f*

reeve /riv/ *vt Naut.* laborear, guarnir

reexamination /ˌriɪgˌzæmɪ'neiʃən/ *n* reexaminación, *f;* nuevo examen, *m; Law.* nuevo interrogatorio, *m*

reexamine /ˌriɪg'zæmɪn/ *vt* reexaminar; *Law.* interrogar de nuevo

reexport /ˌriɛk'spɔrt/ *vt* reexportar

reexportation /ˌriɛkspɔr'teiʃən/ *n* reexportación, *f*

refashion /ri'fæʃən/ *vt* volver a hacer; formar de nuevo

refection /rɪ'fɛkʃən/ *n* refección, *f*

refectory /rɪ'fɛktəri/ *n* refectorio, *m*

refer /rɪ'fɜr/ *vt* atribuir (a); (send) enviar, remitir; (assign) referir (a), relacionar (con). *—vi* referirse (a); aludir (a); hablar (de)

referee /ˌrɛfə'ri/ *n* árbitro, *m; Law.* juez arbitrador, *m;* (reference) garante, *mf* fiador (-ra). *—vi* servir de árbitro

reference /'rɛfərəns/ *n* referencia, *f;* consulta, *f;* mención, *f;* alusión, *f;* (relation) relación, *f; pl* **references,** *Com.* referencias, *f pl.* **for r.,** para consulta. **in r. to,** con referencia a, respecto a, en cuanto a. **terms of r.,** puntos de consulta, *m pl.* **work of r.,** libro de consulta, *m*

reference book *n* libro de consulta, *m*

referendum /ˌrɛfə'rɛndəm/ *n* referéndum, *m*

refill /*v.* ri'fɪl; *n.* 'riˌfɪl/ *vt* rellenar; rehenchir; (pen) llenar de nuevo con tinta. *—n* (for a pencil) mina de recambio, *f*

refine /rɪ'fain/ *vt* refinar; (metals) acrisolar; (fats) clarificar; *Fig.* perfeccionar, pulir, refinar

refined /rɪ'faind/ *a* refinado; fino; culto; cortés; elegante; delicado; (subtle) sutil; (affected) afectado

refinement /rɪ'fainmənt/ *n* refinamiento, *m;* finura, *f;* cultura, *f;* cortesía, *f;* elegancia, *f;* delicadeza, *f;* (subtlety) sutileza, *f;* (affectation) afectación, *f*

refiner /rɪ'fainər/ *n* refinador, *m*

refinery /rɪ'fainəri/ *n* refinería, *f*

refining /rɪ'fainɪŋ/ *n* refinación, *f; Fig.* refinamiento, *m*

refit /ri'fɪt/ *vt* reparar; *Naut.* embonar

refitting /ri'fɪtɪŋ/ *n* reparación, *f; Naut.* embonada, *f*

reflect /rɪ'flɛkt/ *vt* reflejar; reflexionar. *—vi* reflejar; reflexionar (sobre), pensar (en), meditar (sobre). **This offer reflects credit on him,** Esta oferta le hace honor. **to r. on, upon,** reflexionar sobre; (disparage) desacreditar; (affect unfavorably) perjudicar

reflecting /rɪ'flɛktɪŋ/ *a* reflector

reflection /rɪ'flɛkʃən/ *n Phys.* reflexión, *f;* reflejo, *m;* consideración, *f,* pensamiento, *m;* (aspersion) censura, *f,* reproche, *m.* **upon mature r.,** después de pensarlo bien

reflective /rɪ'flɛktɪv/ *a Phys.* reflector; reflexivo, pensativo, meditabundo

reflectively /rɪ'flɛktɪvli/ *adv* reflexivamente

reflector /rɪ'flɛktər/ *n* reflector, *m;* (shade) pantalla, *f*

reflex /'riflɛks/ *a* reflejo. *—n* reflejo, *m;* acción refleja, *f.* **r. action,** acción refleja, *f*

refloat /ri'flout/ *vt* (a ship) poner otra vex a flote, desvarar

reflux /'riˌflʌks/ *n* reflujo, *m*

reforestation *n* nuevas plantaciones, *f pl*

reform /rɪ'fɔrm/ *n* reforma, *f.* *—a* de reforma; reformista. *—vt* reformar; formar de nuevo. *—vi* reformarse

reformation /ˌrɛfər'meiʃən/ *n* reformación, *f;* **Reformation,** Reforma, *f*

reformatory /rɪ'fɔrməˌtɔri/ *a* reformatorio, reformador. *—n* reformatorio, *m,* casa de corrección, *f*

reformer /rɪ'fɔrmər/ *n* reformador (-ra), reformista, *mf*

refract /rɪ'frækt/ *vt* refractar

refraction /rɪ'frækʃən/ *n* refracción, *f*

refractive /rɪ'fræktɪv/ *a* refringente

refractoriness /rɪ'fræktərinɪs/ *n* terquedad, obstinacia, *f;* rebeldía, indocilidad, *f*

refractory /rɪ'fræktəri/ *a* (of substances) refractario; recalcitrante, intratable, rebelde

refrain /rɪ'frein/ *n* estribillo, estrambote, *m*

refrain /rɪ'frein/ *vi* abstenerse (de), evitar

refresh /rɪ'frɛʃ/ *vt* refrescar

refreshing /rɪ'frɛʃɪŋ/ *a* refrescante; atractivo; estimulante; interesante

refreshment /rɪ'frɛʃmənt/ *n* (solace) solaz, reposo, *m;* recreación, *f,* deleite, *m;* (food and (or) drink) refresco, *m.* **r.-room,** (at a station) fonda, *f*

refrigerate /rɪ'frɪdʒəˌreit/ *vt* refrigerar; enfriar; refrescar

refrigeration /rɪˌfrɪdʒə'reiʃən/ *n* refrigeración, *f;* enfriamiento, *m.* **r. chamber,** cámara frigorífica, *f*

refrigerative /rɪ'frɪdʒərətɪv/ *a* refrigerante, frigorífico

refrigerator /rɪ'frɪdʒəˌreitər/ *n* refrigerador, *m,* nevera, *f*

refringent /rɪ'frɪndʒənt/ *a* refringente

refuel /ri'fyuəl/ *vt* (a furnace) cargar con carbón, etc.; (of a ship) tomar carbón; (of an airplane, motor vehicle) tomar bencina

refuge /'rɛfyudʒ/ *n* refugio, *m;* asilo, *m;* (resort) recurso, *m;* subterfugio, *m;* (traffic island) refugio para peatones, *m.* **to take r.,** refugiarse; resguardarse (de)

refugee /ˌrɛfyʊ'dʒi/ *a* refugiado. *—n* refugiado (-da)

refulgence /rɪ'fʌldʒəns/ *n* refulgencia, *f*

refulgent /rɪ'fʌldʒənt/ *a* refulgente

refund /ri'fʌnd/ *vt* reembolsar; devolver

refunding /ri'fʌndɪŋ/ *n* reembolso, *m;* devolución, *f*

refurbish /ri'fɜrbɪʃ/ *vt* restaurar; renovar; (a literary work) refundir

refurnish /ri'fɛrnɪʃ/ *vt* amueblar de nuevo

refusal /rɪ'fyuzəl/ *n* negativa, *f;* (rejection) rechazo, *m;* (option) opción, *f;* preferencia, *f*

refuse /rɪ'fyuz/ *vt* negar; (reject) rechazar. *—vi* negarse (a), rehusar; (of a horse) resistirse a saltar

refuse /'rɛfyus/ *n* desecho, *m;* desperdicios, *m pl;* residuo, *m;* basura, *f.* *—a* de desecho. **r. dump,** muladar, *m*

refutable /rɪ'fyutəbəl/ *a* refutable

refutation /ˌrɛfyʊ'teiʃən/ *n* refutación, *f*

refute /rɪ'fyut/ *vt* refutar

regain /ri'gein/ *vt* recobrar, recuperar; cobrar; ganar de nuevo; *Fig.* reconquistar. **to r. one's breath,** cobrar aliento. **to r. consciousness,** volver en sí

regal /'rigəl/ *a* regio, real

regale /rɪ'geil/ *vt* regalar, agasajar; recrear, deleitar

regalia /rɪ'geiliə/ *n* regalía, *f;* insignias reales, *f pl;* distintivos, *m pl,* insignias, *f pl*

regally /'rigəli/ *adv* regiamente

regard /rɪ'gɑrd/ *vt* mirar; observar; considerar; (respect) respetar; (concern) importar, concernir; relacionarse con. *—n* mirada, *f;* atención, *f;* (esteem) aprecio, *m,* estimación, *f;* respeto, *m;* veneración, *f;* (relation) referencia, *f; pl* **regards,** recuerdos, saludos, *m pl.* **He has little r. for their feelings,** Le importan poco sus susceptibilidades. **With kindest regards,** Con mis saludos más afectuosos. **as regards, with r. to,** con referencia a, respecto a, en cuanto a

regardful /rɪ'gɑrdfəl/ *a* atento (a), cuidadoso (de); que se preocupa (de)

regarding /rɪ'gɑrdɪŋ/ *prep* tocante a, en cuanto a, respecto de

regardless /rɪ'gɑrdlɪs/ *a* negligente (de); indiferente (a), insensible (a); que no se interesa (en); que no se inqueta (por); sin preocuparse (de)

regatta /rɪ'gætə, -'gɑtə/ *n* regata, *f*

regency /'ridʒənsi/ *n* regencia, *f*

regeneracy /rɪ'dʒɛnərəsi/ *n* regeneración, *f*

regenerate /rɪ'dʒɛnəˌreit/ *vt* regenerar. *—a* regenerado

regeneration /rɪˌdʒɛnə'reiʃən/ *n* regeneración, *f*

regenerative /rɪ'dʒɛnərətɪv/ *a* regenerador

regenerator /rɪ'dʒɛnəˌreitər/ *n* regenerador (-ra)

regent /'ridʒənt/ *n* regente, *mf*

régime /rei'ʒim/ *n* régimen, *m*

regimen /'rɛdʒəmən/ *n* (*Gram. Med.*) régimen, *m,*

regiment /*n.* 'rɛdʒəmənt; *v.* -ˌmɛnt/ *n* regimiento, *m.* *—vt* regimentar. **r. of the line,** tropa de línea, *f*

regimental /ˌrɛdʒə'mɛntl̩/ *a* de (un) regimiento, perteneciente a un regimiento

regimentation /ˌrɛdʒəmən'teiʃən/ *n* regimentación, *f*

region /'ridʒən/ *n* región, *f*
regional /'ridʒənl̩/ *a* regional
regionalism /'ridʒənl̩ˌɪzəm/ *n* regionalismo, *m*
regionalist /'ridʒənl̩ɪst/ *n* regionalista, *mf*
regionalistic /'ridʒənl̩ɪstɪk/ *a* regionalista
register /'rɛdʒəstər/ *n* (record and *Mech. Mus. Print.*) registro, *m;* (of ships, etc.) matrícula, *f;* lista, *f.* —*vt* registrar; matricular; (a ship) abanderar; inscribir; (one's child in a school) anotar (Argentina), inscribir; (of thermometers, etc.) marcar; (letters) certificar; (luggage) facturar; (in one's mind) grabar; (emotion) mostrar, manifestar. —*vi* (at a hotel, etc.) registrarse; *Print.* estar en registro. **cash r.,** caja registradora, *f.* **r. of births, marriages and deaths,** registro civil, *m*
registered letter /'rɛdʒəstərd/ *n* carta certificada, *f*
registrar /'rɛdʒəˌstrɑr/ *n* registrador, *m;* archivero, *m;* secretario, *m;* (of a school) jefe de inscripciones, secretario general (the latter has many more duties). **r. of births, marriages and deaths,** secretario del registro civil, *m.* **registrar's office,** oficina del registro civil, *f*
registration /ˌrɛdʒə'streiʃən/ *n* registro, *m;* inscripción, *f;* (of a vehicle, etc.) matrícula, *f; Naut.* abanderamiento, *m;* (of a letter, etc.) certificación, *f.* **r. number,** número de matrícula, *m*
registry /'rɛdʒəstri/ *n* registro, *m;* inscripción, *f;* matrícula, *f.* **r. office,** oficina del registro civil, *f;* (for servants) agencia doméstica, *f*
regression /rɪ'grɛʃən/ *n* regresión, *f,* retroceso, *m*
regret /rɪ'grɛt/ *vt* sentir; lamentar, pesar; arrepentirse (de); (miss) echar de menos (a). —*n* sentimiento, pesar, *m;* (remorse) remordimiento, *m.* **I r. very much that...,** Me pesa mucho que..., Siento mucho que... **to send one's regrets,** mandar sus excusas
regretful /rɪ'grɛtfəl/ *a* lleno de pesar; arrepentido; lamentable, deplorable. **He was most r. that...,** Lamentaba mucho que...
regretfully /rɪ'grɛtfəli/ *adv* con pesar
regrettable /rɪ'grɛtəbəl/ *a* lamentable, deplorable; doloroso; (with loss, etc.) sensible
regrettably /rɪ'grɛtəbli/ *adv* lamentablemente; sensiblemente
regroup /ri'grup/ *vt* arreglar de nuevo; formar de nuevo; reorganizar
regular /'rɛgyələr/ *a* regular; normal; (ordinary) corriente, común; (in order) en regla; (*Gram. Bot. Eccl. Mil. Geom.*) regular. —*n Eccl.* regular, *m;* (soldier) soldado de línea, *m;* (officer) militar de carrera, *m;* (client) parroquiano habitual, *m*
regularity /ˌrɛgyə'lærɪti/ *n* regularidad,
regularization /ˌrɛgyələrə'zeiʃən/ *n* regularización, *f*
regularize /'rɛgyələˌraiz/ *vt* regularizar
regularly /'rɛgyələrli/ *adv* regularmente
regulate /'rɛgyəˌleit/ *vt* regular; ajustar, arreglar; (direct) dirigir; reglamentar
regulation /ˌrɛgyə'leiʃən/ *n* regulación, *f;* arreglo, *m;* (rule) reglamento, *m, a* de reglamento; normal
regulative /'rɛgyəˌleitɪv/ *a* regulador
regulator /'rɛgyəˌleitər/ *n Mech.* regulador, *m*
regurgitate /rɪ'gɜrdʒɪˌteit/ *vt* and *vi* regurgitar
regurgitation /rɪˌgɜrdʒɪ'teiʃən/ *n* regurgitación, *f*
rehabilitate /ˌrihə'bɪlɪˌteit/ *vt* rehabilitar
rehabilitation /ˌrihəˌbɪlɪ'teiʃən/ *n* rehabilitación, *f*
rehash /ri'hæʃ/ *vt* (a literary work, etc.) refundir
rehearing /ri'hɪərɪŋ/ *n* nueva audición, *f,* (of a case) revisión, *f*
rehearsal /rɪ'hɜrsəl/ *n Theat.* ensayo, *m;* recitación, *f;* relación, narración, *f.* **dress r.,** ensayo general, *m*
rehearse /rɪ'hɜrs/ *vt Theat.* ensayar; recitar; (narrate) narrar; enumerar
reheat /ri'hit/ *vt* recalentar
reign /rein/ *n* reinado, *m.* —*vi* reinar; predominar
reigning /'reinɪŋ/ *a* reinante; predominante
reimburse /ˌriɪm'bɜrs/ *vt* reembolsar
reimbursement /ˌrilm'bDrsmənt/ *n* reembolso, *m*
reimport /ri'ɪmpɔrt/ *vt* importar de nuevo, reimportar, *n* reimporte, *m*
reimportation /ˌriɪmpɔr'teiʃən/ *n* reimportación, *f*
reimpose /ˌriɪm'pouz/ *vt* reimponer
reimposition /ˌriɪmpə'zɪʃən/ *n* reimposición, *f*
reimprison /ˌriɪm'prɪzən/ *vt* encarcelar de nuevo, reencarcelar
reimprisonment /ˌriɪm'prɪzənmənt/ *n* reencarcelamiento, *m*
rein /rein/ *n* rienda, *f.* —*vt* llevar las riendas (de); (hold back) refrenar. **to give r. to,** *Fig.* dar rienda suelta (a)
reincarnation /ˌriɪnkɑr'neiʃən/ *n* reencarnación, *f*
reincorporate /ˌriɪn'kɔrpəˌreit/ *vt* reincorporar
reincorporation /ˌrilnˌkɔrpə'reiSən/ *n* reincorporación, *f*
reindeer /'reinˌdɪər/ *n* reno, *m*
reinforce /ˌriɪn'fɔrs/ *vt* reforzar; (concrete) armar; fortalecer. **reinforced concrete,** *n* hormigón armado, *m*
reinforcement /ˌriɪn'fɔrsmənt/ *n* reforzamiento, *m;* (*Mil. Nav. Fig.*) refuerzo, *m*
reins. *n* See **rein**
reinsert /ˌriɪn'sɛrt/ *vt* volver a insertar
reinstall /ˌriɪn'stɔl/ *vt* reinstalar; rehabilitar
reinstallment /ˌriɪn'stɔlmənt/ *n* reinstalación, *f;* rehabilitación, *f;* restablecimiento, *m*
reinstate /ˌriɪn'steit/ *vt* reponer, restablecer; reinstalar; rehabilitar
reinstatement /ˌriɪn'steitmənt/ *n* restablecimiento, *m;* rehabilitación, *f*
reinsurance /ˌriɪnʃʊrəns/ *n* reaseguro, *m*
reinsure /ˌriɪn'ʃʊr, -'ʃɜr/ *vt* reasegurar
reintegrate /ri'ɪntəˌgreit/ *vt* reintegrar
reintegration /ˌriɪntə'greiʃən/ *n* reintegración, *f*
reinter /ˌriɪn'tɛr/ *vt* enterrar de nuevo
reinvest /ˌriɪn'vɛst/ *vt* reinvertir
reinvestment /ˌriɪn'vɛstmənt/ *n* reinversión, *f*
reinvigorate /ˌriɪn'vɪgəˌreit/ *vt* reanimar, dar nuevo vigor (a)
reinvite /ˌriɪn'vait/ *vt* invitar de nuevo (a)
reissue /ri'ɪʃu/ *n* nueva emisión, *f;* (of a book, etc.) nueva edición, reimpresión, *f.* —*vt* hacer una nueva emisión (de); reeditar, publicar de nuevo
reiterate /ri'ɪtəˌreit/ *vt* reiterar, repetir
reiteration /riˌɪtə'reiʃən/ *n* reiteración, *f*
reiterative /ri'ɪtəˌreitiv/ *a* reiterativo
reject /*v.* rɪ'dʒɛkt/ *vt* rechazar, rehusar; repudiar; repulsar; desechar
rejection /rɪ'dʒɛkʃən/ *n* rechazamiento, *m;* repudiación, refutación, *f;* repulsa, *f*
rejoice /rɪ'dʒɔis/ *vt* alegrar, regocijar. —*vi* alegrarse (de), regocijarse (de), gloriarse (en)
rejoicing /rɪ'dʒɔisɪŋ/ *n* regocijo, júbilo, *m,* alegría, *f;* algazara, *f,* fiestas, *f pl*
rejoin /rɪ'dʒɔin/ *vt* and *vi* juntar de nuevo; volver a; reunirse con; (reply) contestar, replicar
rejoinder /rɪ'dʒɔindər/ *n* contestación, respuesta, *f*
rejuvenate /rɪ'dʒuvəˌneit/ *vt* rejuvenecer
rejuvenation /rɪˌdʒuvə'neiʃən/ *n* rejuvenecimiento, *m*
rekindle /ri'kɪndl̩/ *vt* encender de nuevo; despertar, reavivar. —*vi* encenderse de nuevo; reavivarse
relapse /*rI'l{ps; n. also* 'rilæps/ *n* reincidencia, recaída, *f; Med.* recidiva, *f.* —*vi* reincidir (en); *Med.* recaer
relapsed /rɪ'læpst/ *a* relapso
relate /rɪ'leit/ *vt* (recount) relatar, narrar; relacionar; unir; (of kinship) emparentar. —*vi* ajustarse (a); referirse (a). **The first fact is not related to the second,** El primer hecho no tiene nada que ver con el segundo
related /rɪ'leitɪd/ *a* relacionado; (by kinship) emparentado. **John is well-r.,** Juan es de buena familia; Juan es de familia influyente; Juan tiene buenas relaciones
relater /rɪˌleitər/ *n* narrador (-ra)
relation /rɪ'leiʃən/ *n* (narrative) relación, narración, *f;* conexión, *f;* relación, *f;* (kinship) parentesco, *m;* (person) pariente (-ta). **in r. to,** con relación a, en cuanto a
relationship /rɪ'leiʃənˌʃɪp/ *n* parentesco, *m;* conexión, relación, *f*
relative /'rɛlətɪv/ *a* relativo. —*n* pariente (-ta); *pl* **relatives,** parientes, *m pl,* parentela, *f*
relativism /'rɛlətəˌvɪzəm/ *n* relativismo, *m*
relativity /ˌrɛlə'tɪvɪti/ *n* relatividad, *f*

relator /rɪ'leitər/ *n Law.* relator, *m*

relax /rɪ'læks/ *vt* relajar; aflojar; soltar; (make less severe) ablandar; (decrease) mitigar. —*vi* relajarse; aflojar; (rest) descansar

relaxation /ˌrilæk'seiʃən/ *n* relajación, *f;* aflojamiento, *m;* ablandamiento, *m;* mitigación, *f;* (rest) descanso, reposo, *m;* (pastime) pasatiempo, *m;* (amusement) diversión, *f*

relaxing /rɪ'læksɪŋ/ *a* relajante; (of climate) enervante

relay /'rilei; v. rɪ'lei/ *n* (of horses) parada, *f;* (shift) tanda, *f;* relevo, *m; Elec.* relais, *m; Radio.* redifusión, *f.* —*vt* enviar por posta; *Elec.* reemitir; *Radio.* retransmitir; (lay again) colocar de nuevo. **r. race,** carrera de equipo, carrera de relevos, *f*

release /rɪ'lis/ *vt* soltar; (hurl) lanzar; (set free) poner en libertad (a); librar (de); absolver; (surrender) renunciar (a); dar al público, poner en circulación; (lease again) realquilar. —*n* soltura, *f;* lanzamiento, *m;* liberación, *f;* (from pain) alivio, *m;* remisión, *f;* exoneración, *f;* publicación, *f;* (of films) representación, *f; Law.* soltura, *f*

relegate /'rɛlɪˌgeit/ *vt* relegar

relegation /ˌrɛlɪ'geiʃən/ *n* relegación, *f*

relent /rɪ'lɛnt/ *vi* ablandarse, enternecerse; ceder

relenting /rɪ'lɛntɪŋ/ *n* enternecimiento, desenojo, *m*

relentless /rɪ'lɛntlɪs/ *a* implacable, inexorable; despiadado

relentlessly /rɪ'lɛntlɪsli/ *adv* inexorablemente; sin piedad

relentlessness /rɪ'lɛntlɪsnɪs/ *n* inexorabilidad, *f;* falta de piedad, *f*

relet /ri'lɛt/ *vt* realquilar

relevance /'rɛləvəns/ *n* conexión, *f;* pertinencia, *f;* aplicabilidad, *f*

relevant /'rɛləvənt/ *a* relativo; pertinente, a propósito, oportuno; aplicable

reliability /rɪˌlaiə'bɪlɪti/ *n* seguridad, *f;* formalidad, *f;* confianza, *f;* exactitud, *f;* veracidad, *f*

reliable /rɪ'laiəbəl/ *a* seguro; formal; digno de crédito, de confianza, solvente digno de confianza; exacto; veraz

reliably /rɪ'laiəbli/ *adv* seguramente; de una manera digna de confianza; exactamente

reliance /rɪ'laiəns/ *n* confianza, *f.* **to place r. on,** tener confianza en

reliant /rɪ'laiənt/ *a* confiado

relic /'rɛlɪk/ *n* vestigio, rastro, *m; Eccl.* reliquia, *f*

relict /'rɛlɪkt/ *n* viuda, *f*

relief /rɪ'lif/ *n* (alleviation) alivio, *m;* desahogo, *m;* (help) socorro, *m,* ayuda, *f;* beneficencia, *f; Mil.* relevo, *m;* (pleasure) placer, *m,* satisfacción, *f;* (consolation) consuelo, *m; Law.* remisión, *f; Art.* relieve, *m.* **high r.,** alto relieve, *m.* **low r.,** bajo relieve, *m.* **r. map,** mapa en relieve, *m.* **r. train,** tren de socorro, *m*

relieve /rɪ'liv/ *vt* aliviar; aligerar, suavizar; mitigar; (one's feelings, etc.) desahogar; (*Mil.* and to take the place of) relevar; (free) librar; (dismiss) destituir; (remove) quitar; (rob) robar; (help) socorrer, remediar; (redeem) redimir; (ornament) adornar; (from a wrong) hacer justicia (a)

relieving /rɪ'livɪŋ/ *n* alivio, *m;* aligeramiento, *m;* mitigación, *f;* (of the feelings) desahogo, *m; Mil.* relevo, *m;* (help) socorro, *m.* **r. arch,** sobrearco, *m*

relight /ri'lait/ *vt* volver a encender. —*vi* encenderse de nuevo

religion /rɪ'lɪdʒən/ *n* religión, *f*

religiosity /rɪˌlɪdʒi'ɒsɪti/ *n* religiosidad, *f*

religious /rɪ'lɪdʒəs/ *a* religioso; en religión; piadoso, creyente; devoto. —*n* religioso (-sa). **r. orders,** órdenes religiosas, *f pl.* **r. toleration,** libertad de cultos, *f*

religiousness /rɪ'lɪdʒəsnɪs/ *n* religiosidad, *f*

relinquish /rɪ'lɪŋkwɪʃ/ *vt* abandonar; (one's grip) soltar; renunciar; desistir (de), dejar (de); (a post) dimitir (de)

relinquishment /rɪ'lɪŋkwɪʃmənt/ *n* abandono, *m;* renuncia, *f;* dejamiento, *m;* (of a post) dimisión, *f*

reliquary /'rɛlɪˌkwɛri/ *n* relicario, *m*

relish /'rɛlɪʃ/ *n* gusto, *m;* sabor, *m;* (touch, smack) dejo, *m;* condimento, *m;* apetito, *m,* gana, *f.* —*vt* gustar de; comer con apetito; saborear, paladear; *Fig.* seducir, atraer, gustar. —*vi* tener gusto (de). **I do not much r. the idea,** No me seduce la idea

relishing /'rɛlɪʃɪŋ/ *n* saboreo, *m;* (enjoyment) goce, *m,* fruición, *f;* consideración, *f*

relive /ri'lɪv/ *vt* vivir de nuevo, volver a vivir

reload / ri'loud/ *vt* recargar

reluctance /rɪ'lʌktəns/ *n* repugnancia, desgana, *f.* **with r.,** a regañadientes, de mala gana

reluctant /rɪ'lʌktənt/ *a* poco dispuesto (a), que tiene repugnancia a (hacer algo), sin gana; (forced) forzado; artificial; (hesitating) vacilante

reluctantly /rɪ'lʌ́ktəntli/ *adv* de mala gana, con repugnancia, a disgusto

rely on /rɪ'lai/ *vi* contar con, confiar en, depender de

remain /rɪ'mein/ *vi* quedar; permanecer; (be left over) sobrar; continuar. **I r. yours faithfully...,** (in a letter) Queda de Vd. su att. s.s.... **It remains to be written,** Queda por escribir

remainder /rɪ'meindər/ *n* resto, *m;* restos, *m pl,* sobras, *f pl;* residuo, *m.* **The r. of the people went away,** Los demás se marcharon

remaining /rɪ'meinɪŋ/ *pres part* and *a* que queda; sobrante

remains /rɪ'meinz/ *n pl* restos, *m pl;* sobras, *f pl,* desperdicios, *m pl;* ruinas, *f pl*

remake /*v.* ri'meik/ *vt* rehacer; reformar

remand /rɪ'mænd/ *vt Law.* reencarcelar. —*n Law.* reencarcelamiento, *m*

remark /rɪ'mɑrk/ *n* observación, *f;* nota, *f;* comentario, *m.* —*vt* and *vi* observar; notar. **to r. on,** comentar, hacer una observación sobre

remarkable /rɪ'mɑrkəbəl/ *a* notable, singular, extraordinario

remarkableness /rɪ'markəbəlnɪs/ *n* singularidad, *f,* lo extraordinario

remarkably /rɪ'markəbli/ *adv* singularmente

remarriage /'riˌmærɪdʒ/ *n* segundas nupcias, *f pl,* segundo casamiento, *m*

remarry /ri'mæri/ *vt* volver a casar (a). —*vi* casarse en segundas nupcias; volver a casarse

remediable /rɪ'midiəbəl/ *a* remediable

remedial /rɪ'midiəl/ *a* remediador; curativo, terapéutico

remedy /'rɛmɪdi/ *n* remedio, *m;* recurso, *m, vt* remediar; curar

remember /rɪ'mɛmbər/ *vt* recordar; tener presente; acordarse de. —*vi* acordarse; no olvidarse. **R. me to your mother,** Dale recuerdos míos a tu madre. **If I r. rightly...,** Si bien me acuerdo... **And r. that I shall do no more!** ¡Y no olvides que no haré más!

remembrance /rɪ'mɛmbrəns/ *n* recuerdo, *m;* memoria, *f; pl* **remembrances,** recuerdos, *m pl*

remind /rɪ'maind/ *vt* recordar

reminder /rɪ'maindər/ *n* recuerdo, *m;* (warning) advertencia, *f.* **a gentle r.,** una indirecta, una insinuación

reminisce /ˌrɛmə'nɪs/ *vi Inf.* recordar viejas historias

reminiscence /ˌrɛmə'nɪsəns/ *n* reminiscencia, *f,* recuerdo, *m*

reminiscent /ˌrɛmə'nɪsənt/ *a* evocador, que recuerda; de reminiscencia; que piensa en el pasado. **to be r. of,** recordar; *Inf.* oler a

reminiscently /ˌrɛmə'nɪsəntli/ *adv* evocadoramente, como si recordara

remiss /rɪ'mɪs/ *a* negligente, descuidado

remission /rɪ'mɪʃən/ *n* remisión, *f*

remissly /rɪ'mɪsli/ *adv* negligentemente

remissness *n* negligencia, *f,* descuido, *m*

remit /rɪ'mɪt/ *vt* remitir; *Com.* remesar, enviar. —*vi* (pay) pagar

remittance /rɪ'mɪtns/ *n* remesa, *f,* envío, *m*

remitter /rɪ'mɪtər/ *n* remitente, *mf*

remnant /'rɛmnənt/ *n* resto, *m;* (of fabric) retal, retazo, *m;* (relic) vestigio, *m,* reliquia, *f.* **r. sale,** saldo, *m*

remodel /ri'mɒdḷ/ *vt* rehacer; reformar; modelar de nuevo; (a play, etc.) refundir

remodeling /ri'mɒdḷɪŋ/ *n* reformación, *f;* (of a play, etc.) refundición, *f*

remonstrance /rɪ'mɒnstrəns/ *n* protesta, *f;* reconvención, *f*

remonstrate /rɪ'mɒnstreit/ *vi* protestar, objetar. **to r. with,** reprochar, reconvenir
remorse /rɪ'mɔrs/ *n* remordimiento, *m*
remorseful /rɪ'mɔrsfəl/ *a* lleno de remordimientos; penitente, arrepentido
remorsefully /rɪ'mɔrsfəli/ *adv* con remordimiento
remorseless /rɪ'mɔrslɪs/ *a* sin conciencia, sin remordimientos; despiadado, inflexible
remorselessness /rɪ'mɔrslɪsnɪs/ *n* inexorabilidad, crueldad, dureza, *f*
remote /rɪ'mout/ *a* distante, lejano; remoto; aislado; ajeno; (slight) leve, vago. **r. control,** mando a distancia, *m*
remotely /rɪ'moutli/ *adv* remotamente
remoteness /rɪ'moutnɪs *n* distancia, *f;* aislamiento, *m;* alejamiento, *m;* (vagueness) vaguedad, *f*
remount /*v.* ri'maunt; *n.* 'ri,maunt/ *vt* subir de nuevo, montar de nuevo; *Mil.* remontar. —*vi* (go back to) remontar (a), derivarse (de). —*n Mil.* remonta, *f*
removable /rɪ'muvəbəl/ *a* que puede quitarse; (of collars, etc.) de quita y pon; transportable; (of officials, etc.) amovible
removal /rɪ'muvəl/ *n* acción de quitar o levantar, *f;* sacamiento, *m;* separación, *f;* eliminación, *f;* alejamiento, *m;* traslado, *m;* (from office, etc.) deposición, *f;* supresión, *f;* asesinato, *m.* **r. van,** carro de mudanzas, *m*
remove /rɪ'muv/ *vt* quitar; retirar; levantar; sacar; apartar; separar; eliminar; trasladar; (from office) destituir; suprimir; asesinar. —*vi* trasladarse. —*n* grado, *m;* distancia, *f;* (departure) partida, *f.* **to r. oneself,** quitarse de en medio. **to r. one's hat,** descubrirse. **first cousin once removed,** hijo de primo carnal, primo hermano del padre, primo hermano de la madre, *m*
remunerate /rɪ'myunə,reit/ *vt* remunerar
remuneration /rɪ,myunə'reiʃən/ *n* remuneración, *f*
remunerative /rɪ'myunərətɪv/ *a* remunerador
renaissance /'rɛnə,sans/ *n* renacimiento, *m, a* renacentista
Renaissance man /'rɛnə,sans/ *n* hombre del Renacimiento, *m*
Renaissance woman *n* mujer del Renacimiento, *f*
renal /'rinl̩/ *a* renal
rename /ri'neim/ *vt* poner otro nombre (a)
renascent /rɪ'næsənt, -'neisənt/ *a* renaciente, que renace
rend /rɛnd/ *vt* desgarrar, rasgar; *Fig.* lacerar; (split) hender; *Fig.* dividir. **to r. from,** arrancar (a). **to r. the air,** (with cries, etc.) llenar el aire
render /'rɛndər/ *vt* (return) devolver; dar; rendir; (make) hacer; (help, service) prestar; interpretar; (translate) traducir; (fat) derretir y clarificar
rendering /'rɛndərɪŋ/ *n* versión, *f;* interpretación, *f*
rendezvous /'rɑndə,vu, -dei-/ *n* cita, *f;* lugar de cita, *m;* reunión, *f.* —*vi* reunirse
rending /'rɛndɪŋ/ *n* desgarro, *m;* hendimiento, *m*
renegade /'rɛnɪ,geid/ *a* renegado. —*n* renegado (-da)
renew /rɪ'nu/ *vt* renovar; (resume) reanudar; (a lease, etc.) prorrogar
renewable /rɪ'nuəbəl/ *a* renovable
renewal /rɪ'nuəl/ *n* renovación, *f;* (resumption) reanudación, *f;* (of a lease, etc.) prorrogación, *f*
renewed /rɪ'nud/ *a* renovado; nuevo
rennet /'rɛnɪt/ *n* cuajo, *m*
renounce /rɪ'nauns/ *vt* renunciar; (a throne) abdicar; renegar (de), repudiar; abandonar. —*vi Law.* desistir; (cards) renunciar
renouncement /rɪ'naunsmənt/ *n* renuncia, *f;* (of a throne) abdicación, *f;* repudiación, *f*
renovate /'rɛnə,veit/ *vt* renovar; limpiar; restaurar
renovation /,rɛnə'veiʃən/ *n* renovación, *f;* limpiadura, *f;* restauración, *f*
renovator /'rɛnə,veitər/ *n* renovador (-ra)
renown /rɪ'naun/ *n* renombre, *m,* fama, *f*
renowned /rɪ'naund/ *a* renombrado, famoso
rent /rɛnt/ *n* (tear) rasgadura, *f;* desgarro, *m;* abertura, *f;* raja hendedura, *f;* (discord) división, *f;* (hire) alquiler, *m;* arrendamiento, *m.* —*vt* arrendar, alquilar. **r.-free,** sin pagar alquiler
rentable /'rɛntəbəl/ *a* alquilable, arrendable
rental /'rɛntl̩/ See **rent**
renter /'rɛntər/ *n* arrendador (-ra)
rentier *n* rentista, *mf*
renting /'rɛntɪŋ/ *n* alquiler, arrendamiento, *m*
renumber /ri'nʌmbər/ *vt* numerar de nuevo
renunciation /rɪ,nʌnsi'eiʃən/ *n* renunciación, renuncia, *f*
reoccupy /ri'ɒkyʊ,pai/ *vt* volver a ocupar, ocupar otra vez
reopen /ri'oupən/ *vt* abrir de nuevo, volver a abrir. —*vi* abrirse nuevamente, abrirse otra vez
reopening /ri'oupənɪŋ/ *n* reapertura, *f*
reorder /ri'ɔrdər/ *vt* ordenar de nuevo, *Com.* volver a pedir. —*n Com.* nuevo pedido, *m*
reorganization /,riɔrgənə'zeiʃən/ *n* reorganización, *f*
reorganize /ri'ɔrgə,naiz/ *vt* reorganizar
reorganizing /ri'ɔrgə,naizɪŋ/ *a* reorganizador
repack /ri'pæk/ *vt* reembalar; reenvasar; volver a hacer (una maleta)
repaint /ri'peint/ *vt* pintar de nuevo
repainting /ri'peintɪŋ/ *n* nueva pintura, *f*
repair /rɪ'pɛər/ *vt* arreglar (e.g. a machine) componer, remendar; reparar; restaurar; rehacer. —*vi* (with to) dirigirse a, ir a; acudir a. —*n* arreglo *m,* reparación, *f;* compostura, *f;* restauración, *f.* **to keep in r.,** conservar en buen estado
repairable /rɪ'pɛərəbəl/ *a* que se puede componer
repairer /rɪ'pɛərər/ *n* componedor (-ra); restaurador (-ra)
repairing /rɪ'pɛərɪŋ/ *a* reparador
reparable /'rɛpərəbəl/ *a* reparable; remediable
reparation /,rɛpə'reiʃən/ *n* reparación, *f*
repartee /,rɛpər'ti, -'tei, -ɑr-/ *n* respuestas, agudezas, *f pl; Inf.* dimes y diretes, *m pl*
repast /rɪ'pæst/ *n* comida, *f;* (light) colación, *f*
repatriate /*v.* ri'peitri,eit/ *vt* repatriar
repatriation /ri,peitri'eiʃən/ *n* repatriación, *f*
repay /rɪ'pei/ *vt* reembolsar; recompensar, pagar; pagar en la misma moneda. —*vi* pagar. **It well repays a visit,** Vale la pena de visitarse
repayable /rɪ'peiəbəl/ *a* reembolsable
repayment /rɪ'peimeənt/ *n* reembolso, *m;* pago, retorno, *m*
repeal /rɪ'pil/ *n* abrogación, revocación, *f, vt* abrogar, rescindir, revocar
repeat /rɪ'pit/ *vt* repetir; reiterar; (renew) renovar; duplicar. —*n* repetición, *f*
repeated /rɪ'pitɪd/ *a* reiterado; redoblado
repeatedly /rɪ'pitɪdli/ *adv* reiteradamente, repetidamente
repeater /rɪ'pitər/ *n* repetidor (-ra); reloj de repetición, *m;* arma de repetición, *f*
repel /rɪ'pɛl/ *vt* repeler; ahuyentar; (spurn) rechazar; *Phys.* resistir; repugnar
repellent /rɪ'pɛlənt/ *a* repulsivo
repent /rɪ'pɛnt/ *vt* arrepentirse de. —*vi* arrepentirse
repentance /rɪ'pɛntn̩s/ *n* arrepentimiento, *m,* penitencia, *f*
repentant /rɪ'pɛntn̩t/ *a* arrepentido, penitente, contrito
repentantly /rɪ'pɛntn̩tli/ *adv* arrepentidamente, con contrición
repeople /ri'pipəl̩/ *vt* repoblar
repeopling /ri'pipəlɪŋ/ *n* repoblación, *f*
repercuss /,ripər'kʌs/ *vt* repercutir (en)
repercussion /,ripər'kʌʃən/ *n* repercusión, *f*
repercussive /,ripər'kʌsɪv/ *a* repercusivo
repertory /'rɛpər,tɔri/ *n* repertorio, *m*
repetition /,rɛpɪ'tɪʃən/ *n* repetición, *f;* recitación, *f*
repetitive /rɪ'pɛtɪtɪv/ *a* iterativo
repine /rɪ'pain/ *vi* afligirse (de); quejarse (de); padecer nostalgia
repining /rɪ'painɪŋ/ *n* pesares, *m pl;* quejas, *f pl,* descontento, *m;* nostalgia, *f*
replace /rɪ'pleis/ *vt* (put back) reponer, colocar de nuevo; restituir, devolver; (renew) renovar; (in a post, etc.) reemplazar, substituir
replaceable /rɪ'pleisəbəl/ *a* restituible; renovable; reemplazable
replacement /rɪ'pleismənt/ *n* reposición, *f;* restitución, devolución, *f;* renovación, *f;* reemplazo, *m*

replant /ri'plænt/ *vt* replantar
replanting /ri'plæntɪŋ/ *n* replantación, *f*
replenish /rɪ'plɛnɪʃ/ *vt* rellenar
replenishment /ri'plɛnɪʃmənt/ *n* relleno, *m*
replete /rɪ'plit/ *a* repleto
repletion /rɪ'pliʃən/ *n* repleción, *f*
replica /'rɛplɪkə/ *n* réplica, *f*
reply /rɪ'plai/ *n* respuesta, contestación, *f*, *vi* responder, contestar. **Awaiting your r.,** En espera de sus noticias. **in his r.,** en su respuesta
repolish /ri'pɒlɪʃ/ *vt* repulir
repopulate /ri'pɒpyə,leit/ *vt* repoblar
repopulation /ri,pɒpyə'leiʃən/ *n* repoblación, *f*
report /rɪ'pɔrt/ *n* (rumor) voz, *f*, rumor, *m;* (reputation) fama, *f;* (news) noticia, *f;* (journalistic) reportaje, *m;* (*Mil. Nav.* and from school) parte, *f;* (weather) boletín, *m;* (proceedings) actas, *f pl*; (statement) informe, *m;* relación, *f;* (of a gun, etc.) detonación, *f;* explosión, *f.* —*vt* dar cuenta de, relatar; informar; (measure) registrar; (*Mil. Nav.*) dar parte de; comunicar; (journalistic) hacer un reportaje de; (transcribe) transcribir; (accuse) denunciar; quejarse de. —*vi* presentar informe; ser reportero; (present oneself) presentarse, comparecer. **It is reported that...,** Se informa que...
report card *n* boletín de calificaciones, *m*
reporter /rɪ'pɔrtər/ *n* reportero (-ra); *Law.* relator, *m*
reporting /rɪ'pɔrtɪŋ/ *n* reporterismo, *m*
repose /rɪ'pouz/ *n* reposo, *m;* quietud, *f;* tranquilidad, serenidad, *f.* —*vt* reposar, descansar; reclinar; (place) poner. —*vi* reposar; tener confianza (en); basarse (en)
repository /rɪ'pɒzɪ,tɔri/ *n* repositorio, depósito, *m;* almacén, *m;* (furniture) guardamuebles, *m;* (person) depositario (-ia)
repoussé /,rəpu'sei/ *n* repujado, *m.* **to work in r.,** repujar
reprehend /,rɛprɪ'hɛnd/ *vt* reprender, reprobar
reprehensible /,rɛprɪ'hɛnsəbəl/ *a* reprensible
reprehension /,rɛprɪ'hɛnʃən/ *n* reprensión, *f*
represent /,rɛprɪ'zɛnt/ *vt* representar; significar
representation /,rɛprɪzɛn'teiʃən/ *n* representación, *f*
representational /,rɛprɪzɛn'teiʃənl̩/ *a Art.* realista
representative /,rɛprɪ'zɛntətɪv/ *a* que representa; representativo. —*n* representante, *mf*
repress /rɪ'prɛs/ *vt* reprimir
repression /rɪ'prɛʃən/ *n* represión, *f*
repressive /rɪ'prɛsɪv/ *a* represivo
reprieve /rɪ'priv/ *vt Law.* aplazar la ejecución (de); *Fig.* dar una tregua (a)
reprimand /'rɛprə,mænd/ *n* reprimenda, *f*, *vt* reprender
reprint /*n.* 'ri,prɪnt; v. ri'prɪnt; / *n* reimpresión, tirada aparte, separata, *f*, *vt* reimprimir
reprinting /'ri,prɪntɪŋ/ *n* reimpresión, *f*
reprisal /rɪ'praizəl/ *n* represalia, *f.* **to take reprisals,** tomar represalias
reproach /rɪ'proutʃ/ *n* reproche, *m;* censura, *f;* (shame) vergüenza, *f.* —*vt* reprochar; censurar, echar en cara, afear
reproachful /rɪ'proutʃfəl/ *a* severo; lleno de reproches; de censura; (shameful) vergonzoso
reproachfully /rɪ'proutʃfəli/ *adv* con reprobación, con reprensión, severamente
reproachfulness /rɪ'proutʃfəlnɪs/ *n* severidad, *f.* **the r. of my gaze,** mi mirada llena de reproches
reprobate /'rɛprə,beit/ *n* réprobo (-ba)
reproduce /,riprə'dus/ *vt* reproducir. —*vi* reproducirse
reproducible /,riprə'dusəbəl/ *a* reproductible
reproduction /,riprə'dʌkʃən/ *n* reproducción, *f*
reproductive /,riprə'dʌktɪv/ *a* reproductor; de reproducción
reproof /rɪ'pruf/ *n* reconvención, *f*
reprove /rɪ'pruv/ *vt* censurar, culpar; reprender
reprovingly /rɪ'pruvɪŋli/. See **rebukingly**
reptile /'rɛptɪl, -tail/ *a* and *n* reptil, *m*
republic /rɪ'pʌblɪk/ *n* república, *f.* **the r. of letters,** la república de las letras
republican /rɪ'pʌblɪkən/ *a* and *n* republicano (-na)
republicanism /rɪ'pʌblɪkə,nɪzəm/ *n* republicanismo, *m*
republish /ri'pʌblɪʃ/ *vt* publicar de nuevo; volver a editar
repudiate /rɪ'pyudi,eit/ *vt* repudiar; negar, rechazar
repudiation /rɪ,pyudi'eiʃən/ *n* repudiación, *f*
repugnance /rɪ'pʌgnəns/ *n* repugnacia, *f*
repugnant /rɪ'pʌgnənt/ *a* repugnante; contrario; opuesto. **to be r. to,** repugnar (a)
repulse /rɪ'pʌls/ *vt* repulsar, repeler; rebatir, refutar; (refuse) rechazar, *n* repulsa, *f;* refutación, *f;* rechazo, *m*
repulsion /rɪ'pʌlʃən/ *n Phys.* repulsión, *f;* repugnancia, aversión, *f*
repulsive /rɪ'pʌlsɪv/ *a* repulsivo, repugnante, repelente
repulsiveness /rɪ'pʌlsɪvnɪs/ *n* carácter repulsivo, *m;* aspecto repugnante, *m*
reputable /'rɛpyətəbəl/ *a* honrado, respetable, formal
reputation /,rɛpyə'teiʃən/ *n* reputación, *f;* fama, *f*, renombre, *m.* **to have the r. of,** ser reputado como, pasar por
reputed /rɪ'pyutɪd/ *a* supuesto; putativo
reputedly /rɪ'pyutɪdli/ *adv* según la opinión común, según dice la gente
request /rɪ'kwɛst/ *n* ruego, *m*, petición, *f;* instancia, *f;* solicitud, *f; Com.* demanda, *f.* —*vt* pedir, rogar; suplicar; solicitar. **in r.,** en boga; solicitado; en demanda, **on r.,** a solicitud. **r. stop,** (for buses) parada discrecional, *f*
requiem /'rɛkwiəm/ *n* réquiem, *m.* **r. mass,** misa de difuntos, *f*
require /rɪ'kwaiᵊr/ *vt* exigir, requerir; necesitar; (wish) desear; invitar. —*vi* ser necesario
required /rɪ'kwaiərd/ *a* necesario; obligatorio
requirement /rɪ'kwaiᵊrmənt/ *n* deseo, *m;* requisito, *m;* formalidad, *f;* estipulación, *f;* necesidad, *f*
requisite /'rɛkwəzɪt/ *n* requisito, *m.* —*a* necesario, requisito, preciso. **to be r.,** ser necesario, ser menester hacer falta
requisition /,rɛkwə'zɪʃən/ *vt Mil.* requisar
requisitioning /,rɛkwə'zɪʃənɪŋ/ *n* requisa, *f*
requital /rɪ'kwaitl̩/ *n* recompensa, *f;* compensación, satisfacción, *f*
requite /rɪ'kwait/ *vt* pagar, recompensar; (affection) corresponder a
reread /ri'rid/ *vt* releer
reredos /'rɪərdɒs/ *n* retablo, *m*
resale /'ri,seil/ *n* reventa, *f*
rescind /rɪ'sɪnd/ *vt* rescindir
rescission /rɪ'sɪʒən/ *n* rescisión, *f*
rescue /'rɛskyu/ *vt* salvar; librar; *Mil.* rescatar. —*n* socorro, *m;* salvamento, *m; Mil.* rescate, *m.* **to go to the r. of,** ir al socorro de. **r. party,** expedición de salvamento, *f; Mil.* expedición de rescate, *f*
rescuer /'rɛskyuər/ *n* salvador (-ra)
reseal /ri'sil/ *vt* resellar
research /rɪ'sɜrtʃ, 'risɜrtʃ/ *n* investigación, *f*, *vt* investigar
researcher /rɪsɜrtʃər, 'risɜrtʃər/ *n* investigador (-ra)
reseda /rɪ'sidə/ *n Bot.* reseda, *f*
resell /ri'sɛl/ *vt* revender
resemblance /rɪ'zɛmbləns/ *n* parecido, *m*, semejanza, *f.* **The two sisters bear a strong r. to each other,** Las dos hermanas se parecen mucho
resemble /rɪ'zɛmbəl/ *vt* parecerse (a). **Mary doesn't r. her mother,** María no se parece a su madre
resent /rɪ'zɛnt/ *vt* resentirse de; ofenderse por, indignarse por; tomar a mal
resentful /rɪ'zɛntfəl/ *a* resentido; ofendido, indignado, agraviado; vengativo
resentfully /rɪ'zɛntfəli/ *adv* con resentimiento; con indignación
resentment /rɪ'zɛntmənt/ *n* resentimiento, *m*
reservation /,rɛzər'veiʃən/ *n* reservación, *f;* reserva, *f;* territorio reservado, *m;* santuario, *m.* **mental r.,** reserva mental, *f*
reserve /rɪ'zɜrv/ *n* reserva, *f.* —*vt* reservar. —*a* de reserva. **without r.,** sin reserva
reserved /rɪ'zɜrvd/ *a* reservado; callado, taciturno. **r.**

compartment, reservado, *m.* **r. list,** (*Mil. Nav.*) sección de reserva, *f*
reservedly /rɪ'zɜrvɪdli/ *adv* con reserva
reservist /rɪ'zɜrvɪst/ *n* reservista, *mf*
reservoir /'rɛzər,vwɑr/ *n* depósito, *m;* cisterna, *f,* aljibe, tanque, *m*
reset /*v.* ri'sɛt/ *vt* montar de nuevo
resettle /ri'sɛtl̩/ *vt* repoblar; rehabilitar; (a dispute) llegar a un nuevo acuerdo sobre
resettlement /ri'sɛtl̩mənt/ *n* repoblación, *f;* rehabilitación, *f;* (of a dispute) nuevo acuerdo, *m*
reshape /ri'ʃeip/ *vt* reformar
reship /ri'ʃɪp/ *vt* reembarcar
reshipment /ri'ʃɪpmənt/ *n* reembarque, *m*
reshuffle /ri'ʃʌfəl/ *vt* volver a barajar; *Fig.* cambiar
reside /rɪ'zaid/ *vi* residir, habitar; vivir
residence /'rɛzɪdəns/ *n* residencia, *f;* permanencia, estada, *f;* domicilio, *m*
resident /'rɛzɪdənt/ *a* residente; (of a servant) que duerme en casa; interno. —*n* residente, *mf;* (diplomacy) residente, *m*
residential /ˌrɛzɪ'dɛnʃəl/ *a* residencial
residue /'rɛzɪˌdu/ *n* resto, *m;* (*Law., Chem.*) residuo, *m*
residuum /rɪ'zɪdʒuəm/ *n* residuo, *m*
resign /rɪ'zain/ *vt* renunciar (a); ceder; resignar. —*vi* dimitir. **to r. oneself,** resignarse
resignation /ˌrɛzɪg'neiʃən/ *n* resignación, *f;* (from a post) dimisión, *f.* **to send in one's r.,** dimitir
resigned /rɪ'zaind/ *a* resignado
resignedly /rɪ'zainɪdli/ *adv* con resignación
resilience /rɪ'zɪlyəns/ *n* elasticidad, *f*
resilient /rɪ'zɪlyənt/ *a* elástico
resin /'rɛzɪn/ *n* resina, *f;* (solid, for violin bows, etc.) colofonia, *f*
resinous /'rɛzənəs/ *a* resinoso
resist /rɪ'zɪst/ *vt* and *vi* (bear) aguantar; (impede) impedir; (repel, ward off) resistir; rechazar; hacer frente (a); oponerse (a); negarse (a)
resistance /rɪ'zɪstəns/ *n* resistencia, *f;* aguante, *m,* tenacidad, *f;* oposición, *f;* repugnancia, *f.* **passive r.,** resistencia pasiva, *f.* **r. coil,** *Elec.* resistencia, *f.* **r. movement,** movimiento de resistencia, *m*
resistant /rɪ'zɪstənt/ *a* resistente
resister /rɪ'zɪstər/ *n* el, *m,* (*f,* la) que resiste
resole /ri'soul/ *vt* remontar
resoling /ri'soulɪŋ/ *n* remonta, *f*
resolute /'rɛzəˌlut/ *a* resuelto, decidido
resolutely /ˌrɛzə'lutli/ *adv* resueltamente
resolution /ˌrɛzə'luʃən/ *n* resolución, *f;* (proposal placed before a legislative body, etc.) proposición, *f;* propósito, *m*
resolve /rɪ'zɒlv/ *vt* resolver; desarrollar, deshacer (an abbreviation, acronym, or initialism). —*vi* resolverse. —*n* propósito, *m;* (of character) resolución, firmeza, *f*
resonance /'rɛzənəns/ *n* resonancia, *f;* sonoridad, *f*
resonant /'rɛzənənt/ *a* resonante; reverberante, sonoro
resort /rɪ'zɔrt/ *n* recurso, *m;* punto de reunión. *m;* (frequentation) frecuentación, *f;* (gathering) concurrencia, *f;* reunión, *f.* —*vi* acudir (a), acogerse (a); hacer uso (de); pasar (a); (frequent) frecuentar, concurrir. **health r.,** balneario, *m.* **holiday r.,** playa de verano, *f;* pueblo de veraneo, *m.* **in the last r.,** en último recurso
resound /rɪ'zaund/ *vi* resonar, retumbar, retronar; *Fig.* tener fama, ser celebrado. —*vt* hacer reverberar; *Fig.* celebrar
resounding /rɪ'zaundɪŋ/ *a* retumbante, resonante
resource /'risɔrs/ *n* recurso, *m;* (of character) inventiva, *f; pl* **resources**; recursos, fondos, *m pl*
resourceful /rɪ'sɔrsfəl/ *a* ingenioso
resourcefully /rɪ'sɔrsfəli/ *adv* ingeniosamente
resourcefulness /rɪ'sɔrsfəlnɪs/ *n* ingeniosidad, *f*
respect /rɪ'spɛkt/ *n* respeto, *m;* consideración, *f;* (reference, regard) respecto, *m; pl* **respects,** (greetings) saludos, *m pl*; homenaje, *m.* —*vt* respetar; honrar; (concern, regard) concernir, tocar (a). **in other respects,** por lo demás. **in r. of,** tocante a, respecto a. **in some respects,** desde algunos puntos de vista. **out of r. for,** por consideración a
respectability /rɪˌspɛktə'bɪlɪti/ *n* respetabilidad, *f*
respectable /rɪ'spɛktəbəl/ *a* respetable; pasable; considerable
respectably /rɪ'spɛktəbli/ *adv* respetablemente
respected /rɪ'spɛktɪd/ *a* and *part* respetado; apreciado, estimado; digno de respeto, honrado
respectful /rɪ'spɛktfəl/ *a* respetuoso
respectfully /rɪ'spɛktfəli/ *adv* respetuosamente
respectfulness /rɪ'spɛktfəlnɪs/ *n* aire respetuoso, *m;* conducta respetuosa, *f*
respecting /rɪ'spɛktɪŋ/ *prep* con respecto a, en cuanto a, tocante a; a propósito de
respective /rɪ'spɛktɪv/ *a* respectivo; relativo
respectively /rɪ'spɛktɪvli/ *adv* respectivamente
respiration /ˌrɛspə'reiʃən/ *n* respiración, *f*
respirator /'rɛspəˌreitər/ *n* respirador, *m*
respiratory /'rɛspərəˌtɔri/ *a* respiratorio
respire /rɪ'spaiər/ *vt* and *vi* respirar; exhalar; descansar
respite /'rɛspɪt/ *n* tregua, pausa, *f;* respiro, *m; Law.* espera, *f.* —*vt* dar tregua (a); (postpone) aplazar; (relieve) aliviar
resplendence /rɪ'splɛndəns/ *n* resplandor, *m,* refulgencia, *f,* esplendor, fulgor, *m*
resplendent /rɪ'splɛndənt/ *a* resplandeciente, refulgente, relumbrante. **He was r. in a new uniform,** Lucía (or Ostentaba) un nuevo uniforme. **to be r.,** ser resplandeciente; relumbrar, refulgir
resplendently /rɪ'splɛndəntli/ *adv* esplendorosamente
respond /rɪ'spɒnd/ *vi* responder; contestar; (obey) obedecer; reaccionar
respondent /rɪ'spɒndənt/ *n* (in a suit) demandado (-da)
response /rɪ'spɒns/ *n* respuesta, *f; Eccl.* responso, *m*
responsibility /rɪˌspɒnsə'bɪlɪti/ *n* responsabilidad, *f*
responsible /rɪ'spɒnsəbəl/ *a* responsable
responsive /rɪ'spɒnsɪv/ *a* simpático; sensible, sensitivo
responsiveness /rɪ'spɒnsɪvnɪs/ *n* simpatía, *f;* sensibilidad, *f*
rest /rɛst/ *n* descanso, *m;* reposo, *m;* (the grave) última morada, *f;* tranquilidad, paz, *f;* inacción, *f;* (prop) soporte, apoyo, *m;* base, *f;* (for a lance) ristre, *m;* (for a rifle) apoyo, *m; Mus.* silencio, *m,* pausa, *f;* (in verse) cesura, *f.* **in r.,** en ristre. **the r.,** el resto; los demás, los otros. **to set at r.,** calmar, tranquilizar; (remove) quitar. **r.-cure,** cura de reposo, *f.* **r.-house,** hospedería, *f;* refugio, *m.* **r.-room, lounge,** sala de descanso, *f;* (toilet) excusado, retrete, *m;* (in theaters) saloncillo, *m*
rest /rɛst/ *vi* reposar, descansar; (lie down) acostarse, echarse; (stop) cesar, parar; estar en paz; apoyarse (en); descansar (sobre); posar; depender (de); (remain) quedar. —*vt* descansar; dar un descanso (a); (lean) apoyar; basar (en). **It rests with them,** Depende de ellos. **These valuable documents now rest in the Library of Congress,** Estos valiosos documentos han parado en la Biblioteca del Congresso. **May he r. in peace!** ¡Que en paz descanse! **to r. assured,** estar seguro. **to r. on one's oars,** cesar de remar; descansar
restate /ri'steit/ *vt* repetir, afirmar de nuevo
restatement /ri'steitmənt/ *n* repetición, *f*
restaurant /'rɛstərənt/ *n* restaurante, restorán, *m.* **r.-car,** coche-comedor, *m*
restful /'rɛstfəl/ *a* descansado; tranquilo, sosegado
resting /'rɛstɪŋ/ *n* reposo, *m.* **last r.-place,** última morada, *f.* **r.-place,** descansadero, *m;* refugio, *m*
restitution /ˌrɛstɪ'tuʃən/ *n* restitución, *f*
restive /'rɛstɪv/ *a* (of a horse) repropio, ingobernable; inquieto, agitado; impaciente
restiveness /'rɛstɪvnɪs/ *n* inquietud, agitación, *f;* impaciencia, *f*
restless /'rɛstlɪs/ *a* agitado; inquieto, intranquilo; turbulento; sin reposo; (wakeful) desvelado; (ceaseless) incesante. **r. night,** noche desvelada, noche intranquila, *Inf.* noche toledana, *f*
restlessly /'rɛstlɪsli/ *adv* agitadamente; con inquietud; turbulentamente; incesantemente
restlessness /'rɛstlɪsnɪs/ *n* agitación, *f;* inquietud, intranquilidad, *f;* turbulencia, *f;* falta de reposo, *f;* (wakefulness) desvelo, *m;* movimiento incesante, *m*

restock /ri'stɔk/ *vt* (with goods) surtir de nuevo; proveer de nuevo; restablecer; repoblar
restoration /ˌrɛstə'reiʃən/ *n* restauración, *f;* renovación, *f;* restablecimiento, *m;* (returning) restitución, *f*
restorative /rɪ'stɔrətɪv/ *a* and *n* restaurativo *m*
restore /rɪ'stɔr/ *vt* restaurar; restituir; devolver; restablecer; reponer; (repair) reformar, reparar; reconstruir; (to former rank, etc.) rehabilitar. **He restored the book to its place,** Devolvió el libro a su sitio
restorer /ri'stɔrər/ *n* restaurador (-ra)
restrain /rɪ'strein/ *vt* refrenar; reprimir; (restrict) limitar, restringir; (prevent) impedir; desviar; (detain) recluir. **to r. oneself,** contenerse
restrained /rɪ'streind *a* moderado, mesurado; sobrio; (of emotion) contenido
restraining /rɪ'streinɪŋ/ *a* restrictivo; moderador, calmante
restraint /rɪ'streint/ *n* freno, *m;* restricción, *f;* limitación, *f;* prohibición, *f;* compulsión, *f;* (reserve) reserva, *f;* moderación, *f*
restrict /rɪ'strɪkt/ *vt* restringir; limitar
restriction /rɪ'strɪkʃən/ *n* restricción, *f;* limitación, *f*
restrictive /rɪ'strɪktɪv/ *a* restrictivo
result /rɪ'zʌlt/ *n* resultado, *m;* consecuencia, resulta, *f,* solución, *f.* —*vi* resultar. **as the r. of,** de resultas de
resultant /rɪ'zʌltnt/ *a* resultante; consecuente. —*n* resultado, *m; Mech.* resultante, *f*
resume /rɪ'zum/ *vt* reasumir; (continue) reanudar, continuar; (summarize) resumir
résumé *n* resumen, *m*
resummon /ri'sʌ́mən/ *vt* convocar de nuevo (a); citar de nuevo (a)
resumption /rɪ'zʌmpʃən/ *n* (renewal) reanudación, *f;* reasunción, *f*
resurgence /rɪ'sɜrdʒəns/ *n* resurgimiento, *m*
resurrect /ˌrɛzə'rɛkt/ *vt Inf.* desenterrar; resucitar
resurrection /ˌrɛzə'rɛkʃən/ *n* resurrección, *f*
resuscitate /rɪ'sʌsɪˌteit/ *vt* and *vi* resucitar
resuscitation /rɪˌsʌ́sɪ'teiʃən/ *n* resurrección, *f;* renovación, *f;* renacimiento, *m*
retail /'riteil/ *n* venta al por menor, reventa, *f.* —*adv* al por menor. —*vt* (goods) vender al por menor, revender; (tell) contar; repetir. **r. trade,** comercio al por menor, *m*
retailer /'riteilər/ *n* vendedor (-ra) al por menor; (of a story) narrador (-ra); el, *m,* (*f,* la) que cuenta algo
retain /rɪ'tein/ *vt* retener; guardar; conservar; (a barrister) ajustar; (hire) contratar
retainer /rɪ'teinər/ *n* (dependent) criado, dependiente, *m;* partidario, adherente, *m;* (fee) honorario, *m; pl* **retainers,** séquito, *m,* adherentes, *m pl,* gente, *f*
retaining wall /rɪ'teinɪŋ/ *n* muro de contención, *m*
retake /*ri'teik/ vt* volver a tomar; reconquistar
retaking /'riˌteikɪŋ/ *n* reconquista, *f*
retaliate /rɪ'tæliˌeit/ *vt* vengarse de, desquitarse de. —*vi* vengarse, tomar represalias
retaliation /rɪˌtæli'eiʃən/ *n* represalias, *f pl*; desquite, *m,* satisfacción, *f.* **law of r.,** talión, *m,*
retaliatory /rɪ'tæliəˌ tɔri/ *a* de represalias; de desquite
retard /rɪ'tɑrd/ *vt* retardar
retch /rɛtʃ/ *vi* tener náuseas, procurar vomitar
retching *n* náusea, basca, *f*
retell /ri'tɛl/ *vt* repetir, volver a contar
retention /rɪ'tɛnʃən/ *n* retención, *f;* conservación, *f*
retentive /rɪ'tɛntɪv/ *a* retentivo
retentiveness /rɪ' tDntIvnIs/ *n* poder de retención, *m;* (memory) retentiva, *f*
reticence /'rɛtəsəns/ *n* reticencia, reserva, *f*
reticent /'rɛtəsənt/ *a* reservado, inexpresivo, taciturno
retina /'rɛtn̩ə, 'rɛtnə/ *n* retina, *f*
retinue /'rɛtn̩ˌu, -ˌyu/ *n* séquito, acompañamiento, *m,* comitiva, *f*
retire /rɪ'taiᵊr/ *vi* retirarse; (to bed) recogerse, acostarse; (from a post) jubilarse. —*vt* retirar; jubilar. **to r. from a post,** *Mil.* rendir el puesto
retired /rɪ'taiᵊrd/ *a* retirado; (remote) apartado, aislado; (hidden) escondido; (former) antiguo; (from employment, etc.) jubilado; (of an officer) retirado. **to place on the r. list,** jubilar; (*Mil. Nav.*) dar el retiro (a)
retirement /rɪ'taiᵊrmənt/ *n* retirada, *f;* (solitude) apartamiento, aislamiento, *m;* retiro, *m;* (superannuation) jubilación, *f*
retiring /rɪ'taiᵊrɪŋ/ *a* que se retira; (from a post) dimitente; (with pension, etc.) de jubilación; (reserved) reservado; modesto
retort /rɪ'tɔrt/ *vi* replicar. —*vt* retorcer; devolver (una acusación, etc.). —*n* réplica, *f;* contestación, *f; Chem.* retorta, *f*
retouch /*v.* ri'tʌtʃ/ *vt* retocar
retrace /rɪ'treis/ *vt* volver a trazar; volver a andar (un camino); (one's steps) volver sobre sus pasos, volver atrás; (in memory) rememorar, recordar; buscar el origen (de); (recount) narrar, contar
retract /rɪ'trækt/ *vt* retractar, retirar; (draw back) retraer. —*vi* retractarse
retraction /rɪ'trækʃən/ *n* retracción, *f*
retranslate /ri'trænsleit/ *vt* hacer una nueva traducción (de)
retransmission /ˌritrænsm'mɪʃən/ *n* retransmisión, *f*
retread /*v.* ri'trɛd/ *vt* pisar de nuevo; (tires) recauchetear
retreat /rɪ'trit/ *n* retirada, *f;* (*Mil.* signal) retreta, *f;* (refuge and *Eccl.*) retiro, *m.* —*vi* retirarse; retroceder; refugiarse
retreat house *n* casa de ejercicios, *f*
retreating /rɪ'tritɪŋ/ *a* que se retira; que retrocede; *Mil.* que se bate en retirada
retrench /rɪ'trɛntʃ/ *vt* reducir; disminuir; *vi* economizar, hacer economías
retrenchment /rɪ'trɛntʃmənt/ *n* disminución, reducción, *f;* economías, *f pl*
retrial /'rɪtrail/ *n* (of a person) nuevo proceso, *m;* (of a case) revisión, *f*
retribution /ˌrɛtrə'byuʃən/ *n* retribución, *f;* justo castigo, *m,* pena merecida, *f*
retrievable /rɪ'trivəbəl/ *a* recuperable, que puede recobrarse; reparable
retrieval /rɪ'trivəl/ *n* recuperación, *f;* reparación, *f;* (of game) cobra, *f;* (of one's character) rehabilitación, *f*
retrieve /rɪ'triv/ *vt* (game, of dogs) cobrar; (regain) recobrar, recuperar; restaurar; reparar; restablecer; (one's character) rehabilitar. —*vi* cobrar la caza
retriever /rɪ'trivər/ *n* (dog) perdiguero (-ra)
retroactive /ˌrɛtrou'æktɪv/ *a* retroactivo
retrocede /ˌrɛtrə'sid/ *vi* retroceder
retrograde /'rɛtrəˌgreid/ *a* retrógrado
retrogression /ˌrɛtrə'grɛʃən/ *n* retrogradación, regresión, *f; Med.* retroceso, *m*
retrogressive /ˌrɛtrə'grɛsɪv/ *a* retrógrado
retrospect /'rɛtrəˌspɛkt/ *n* mirada retrospectiva, *f,* examen del pasado, *m.* **in r.,** retrospectivamente
retrospection /ˌrɛtrə'spɛkʃən/ *n* retrospección, *f*
retrospective /ˌrɛtrə'spɛktɪv/ *a* retrospectivo
retrospectively /ˌrɛtrə'spɛktɪvli/ *adv* retrospectivamente
retry /ri'trai/ *vt* (a case) rever; (a person) procesar de nuevo
return /rɪ'tɜrn/ *vi* regresar; volver; reaparecer; presentarse de nuevo; *Law.* revertir; (answer) contestar, responder. —*vt* (give back or put back) devolver; (a ball) restar; (a kindness, visit) pagar; restituir; (reciprocate) corresponder (a); recompensar; contestar (a); dar; rendir; (yield) producir; (a verdict) fallar, pronunciar; (report) dar parte de; anunciar; (exchange) cambiar; (elect) elegir. —*n* regreso, *m;* vuelta, *f;* (giving or putting back) devolución, *f;* pago, *m;* restitución, *f;* correspondencia, *f;* recompensa, *f;* (reply) respuesta, *f;* (reappearance) reaparición, *f;* reinstalación, *f;* repetición, *f;* (gain) ganancia, *f,* pro vecho, *m;* rendimiento, *m;* (exchange) cambio, *m;* (report) parte oficial, *f;* informe, *m;* lista, *f;* (election) elección, *f; pl* **returns,** tablas estadísticas, *f pl*; (of an election) resultados, *m pl.* **Many happy returns!** ¡Feliz cumpleaños! **by return mail,** a vuelta de correo. **on my (his, etc.) r.,** a la vuelta, cuando vuelva. **to r. like for like,** pagar en la misma moneda. **r. journey, r. trip,** viaje de vuelta, *m.* **r. match,** partido de vuelta, *m.* **r. ticket,** billete de ida y vuelta, *m;* billete de vuelta, *m*
returnable /rɪ'tɜrnəbəl/ *a* restituible; susceptible a

ser devuelto; (on approval) a prueba; *Law.* devolutivo
returning /rɪ'tɜrnɪŋ/ *a* que vuelve. —*n* See **return**
"Return to Sender" «Al remitente»
reunion /ri'yunyən/ *n* reunión, *f*
reunite /ˌriyu'nait/ *vt* reunir. —*vi* reunirse
revaccinate /ri'væksəˌneit/ *vt* revacunar
revaccination /riˌvæksə'neiʃən/ *n* revacunación, *f*
reveal /rɪ'vil/ *vt* revelar; descubrir
revealer /rɪ'vilər/ *n* revelador (-ra)
revealing /rɪ'vilɪŋ/ *a* revelador. —*n* revelación, *f;* descubrimiento, *m*
reveille /'rɛvəli; *Brit.* rɪ'væli/ *n Mil.* diana, *f*
revel /'rɛvəl/ *vi* divertirse; regocijarse (en), gozarse (en); entregarse (a); (carouse) ir de parranda; emborracharse. —*n* algazara, jarana, *f; pl* **revels,** fiestas, festividades, *f pl*
revelation /ˌrɛvə'leiʃən/ *n* revelación, *f;* descubrimiento, *m;* (in the Bible) Apocalipsis, *m*
reveler /'rɛvələr/ *n* convidado alegre, *m;* (at night) trasnochador (-ra); (drunk) borracho (-cha); (masked) máscara, *mf*
revelry /'rɛvəlri/ *n* festividades, *f pl,* regocijo, *m;* orgías, *f pl*
revenge /rɪ'vɛndʒ/ *n* venganza, *f.* —*vt* vengarse de; desquitarse de
revengeful /rɪ'vɛndʒfəl/ *a* vengativo
revengefully /rɪ'vɛndʒfəli/ *adv* vengativamente
revengefulness /rɪ'vɛndʒfəlnɪs/ *n* deseo de venganza, *m;* carácter vengativo, *m*
revenger /rɪ'vɛndʒər/ *n* vengador (-ra)
revenue /'rɛvənˌyu, -əˌnu/ *n* rentas públicas, *f pl;* (treasury) fisco, *m; Com.* rédito, *m,* ingresos, *m pl;* beneficio, *m.* **Inland R.,** delegación de contribuciones, *f.* **r. officer,** agente fiscal, *m*
reverberate /rɪ'v˘rb@ˌreit/ *vt* and *vi* (of sound) retumbar, resonar; (of light, etc.) reverberar
reverberation /rɪˌvɜrbə'reiʃən/ *n* (reflection) reverberación, *f;* (of sound) retumbo, eco, *m*
revere /rɪ'vɪər/ *vt* reverenciar, venerar, honrar
reverence /'rɛvərəns/ *n* reverencia, *f, vt* reverenciar
reverend /'rɛvərənd/ *a* reverendo
reverent /'rɛvərənt/ *a* reverente
reverently /'rɛvərəntli/ *adv* reverentemente, con reverencia
reverie /'rɛvəri/ *n* ensueño, *m*
reversal /rɪ'vɜrsəl/ *n* inversión, *f;* (of a verdict) revocación, *f*
reverse /rɪ'vɜrs/ *vt* invertir; (a steam engine) dar contra vapor (a); (a vehicle) poner en marcha atrás; (arms) llevar a la funerala; (a judgment, etc.) revocar, derogar. —*vi* (dancing) dar vueltas al revés. —*n* lo contrario, lo opuesto; (back) dorso, revés, *m;* (change) cambio, *m;* (check) revés, *m,* vicisitud, *f;* (loss) pérdida, *f;* (defeat) derrota, *f; Mech.* marcha atrás, *f, a* inverso; contrario, opuesto. **quite the r.,** todo el contrario. **r. turn,** (of an engine) cambio de dirección, *m;* (in dancing) vuelta al revés, *f*
reversible /rɪ'vɜrsəbəl/ *a* reversible
reversion /rɪ'vɜrʒən, -ʃən/ *n* reversión, *f; Biol.* atavismo, *m;* (of offices) futura, *f;* (of property) reversión, *f*
revert /rɪ'vɜrt/ *vi Law.* revertir; volver (a)
review /rɪ'vyu/ *n* examen, análisis, *m;* juicio crítico, *m;* (journal and *Mil.*) revista, *f;* (criticism) revista, reseña, *f; Law.* revisión, *f.* —*vt* examinar, analizar; (*Mil.* etc.) pasar revista (a); revisar; repasar; (a book, etc.) reseñar; *Law.* revisar. —*vi* escribir revistas
review article *n* artículo de reseña, *m*
reviewer /rɪ'vyuər/ *n* revistero (-ra), crítico, *m*
revile /rɪ'vail/ *vt* injuriar, maldecir, difamar
reviler /rɪ'vailər/ *n* maldiciente, *m,* insultador (-ra)
reviling /rɪ'vailɪŋ/ *n* insultos, *m pl,* injurias, *f pl*
revisal /rɪ'vaizəl/ *n* revisión, *f*
revise /rɪ'vaiz/ *vt* revisar; repasar; corregir; (change) cambiar
reviser /rɪ'vaizər/ *n* revisor, *m;* corrector de pruebas, *m*
revision /rɪ'vɪʒən/ *n* revisión, *f;* repaso, *m;* corrección de pruebas, *f*
revisit /rɪ'vɪzɪt/ *vt* volver a visitar, visitar de nuevo
revival /rɪ'vaivəl/ *n* resurgimiento, *m;* renovación, *f;* (awakening) despertamiento, *m;* restablecimiento, *m;* resurrección, *f;* (of learning) renacimiento, *m; Theat.* reposición, *f;* (religious) despertar religioso, *m*
revive /rɪ'vaiv/ *vi* reponerse; restablecerse; resucitar; renovarse; renacer; cobrar fuerzas; (recover consciousness) volver en sí. —*vt* hacer revivir; resucitar; restablecer; renovar; restaurar; despertar; (fire, colors) avivar
reviver /rɪ'vaivər/ *n* resucitador (-ra)
revivification /rɪˌvɪvəfɪ'keiʃən/ *n* revivificación, *f*
revivify /rɪ'vɪvəˌfai/ *vt* revivificar
revocable /'rɛvəkəbəl, rɪ'vou-/ *a* revocable
revocation /ˌrɛvə'keiʃən/ *n* revocación, *f*
revoke /rɪ'vouk/ *vt* revocar, anular, derogar; (wills) quebrantar. —*vi* revocar, anular; (at cards) renunciar. —*n* (cards) renuncio, *m*
revolt /rɪ'voult/ *n* rebelión, *f, vi* rebelarse, sublevarse. —*vt* repugnar, indignar, dar asco (a)
revolting /rɪ'voultɪŋ/ *a* repugnante, asqueroso; (rebellious) rebelde
revolution /ˌrɛvə'luʃən/ *n* revolución, *f;* (turn) vuelta, *f,* giro, *m*
revolutionary /ˌrɛvə'luʃəˌnɛri/ *a* and *n* revolucionario (-ia)
revolutionize /ˌrɛvə'luʃəˌnaiz/ *vt* revolucionar
revolve /rɪ'vɒlv/ *vi* dar vueltas, girar; suceder periódicamente. —*vt* hacer girar; (ponder) revolver, discurrir
revolver /rɪ'vɒlvər/ *n* revólver, *m*
revolving /rɪ'vɒlvɪŋ/ *a* giratorio; que vuelve; periódico. **r. chair,** silla giratoria, *f.* **r. door,** puerta giratoria, *f.* **r. stage,** escenario giratorio, *m*
revue /rɪ'vyu/ *n Theat.* revista, *f*
revulsion /rɪ'vʌlʃən/ *n* revulsión, *f*
revulsive /rɪ'vʌlsɪv/ *a Med.* revulsivo
rev up /rɛv/ *vt* (an engine) calentar
reward /rɪ'wɔrd/ *n* recompensa, *f;* retribución, *f.* —*vt* recompensar; satisfacer, premiar
rewarding /rɪ'wɔrdɪŋ/ *a* premiador; que recompensa. —*n* recompensación, *f.* **a rewarding experience,** una experiencia compensadora, *f*
rewrite /*v.* ri'rait/ *vt* escribir de nuevo; volver a escribir; redactar otra vez
rhapsody /'ræpsədi/ *n* rapsodia, *f*
rheostat /'riəˌstæt/ *n* reóstato, *m*
rhetoric /'rɛtərɪk/ *n* retórica, *f*
rhetorical /rɪ'tɔrɪkəl/ *a* retórico; declamatorio
rhetorician /ˌrɛtə'rɪʃən/ *n* retórico (-ca)
rheumatic /rʊ'mætɪk/ *a* reumático. **r. fever,** reumatismo poliarticular agudo, *m*
rheumatism /'ruməˌtɪzəm/ *n* reumatismo, reuma, *m*
rheumy /'rumi/ *a* catarroso; (of the eyes) legañoso
rhinestone /'rainˌstoun/ circón, *m*
Rhine, the /rain/ el Rin, *m*
rhinoceros /rai'nɒsərəs/ *n* rinoceronte, *m*
Rhodes /roudz/ Rodas, *f*
rhododendron /ˌroudə'dɛndrən/ *n* rododendro, *m*
rhubarb /'rubɑrb/ *n* ruibarbo, *m*
rhyme /raim/ *n* rima, *f;* verso, *m.* —*vi* and *vt* rimar. **without r. or reason,** sin ton ni son; a tontas y a locas
rhymer /'raimər/ *n* rimador (-ra)
rhyming /'raimɪŋ/ *a* rimador
rhythm /'rɪðəm/ *n* ritmo, *m*
rhythmic /'rɪðmɪk/ *a* rítmico
rib /rɪb/ *n* (*Anat. Bot. Aer. Naut. Archit.*) costilla, *f;* (of an umbrella or fan) varilla, *f;* (in cloth) cordoncillo, *m,* lista, *f*
ribald /'rɪbəld/ *a* escabroso, ribaldo, indecente
ribaldry /'rɪbəldri/ *n* ribaldería, escabrosidad, indecencia, *f*
ribbed /rɪbd/ *a* con costillas; (of cloth) listado, con listas
ribbon /'rɪbən/ *n* cinta, *f;* tira, *f;* (tatter) jirón, *m.* **to tear to ribbons,** hacer jirones
rice /rais/ *n* arroz, *m.* —*a* de arroz; con arroz. **r. field,** arrozal, *m.* **r.-paper,** papel de paja de arroz, *m.* **r.-pudding,** arroz con leche, *m*
rich /rɪtʃ/ *a* rico; opulento; (happy) dichoso; (of land, etc.) fértil; abundante; (of objects) magnífico, suntuoso, hermoso; precioso; (of food) exquisito;

suculento; (highly seasoned) muy sazonado; (creamy) con mucha nata; (of colours) brillante, vivo. **new r.,** ricacho (-cha). **newly-r.,** advenedizo. **to grow r.,** enriquecerse

riches /ˈrɪtʃɪz/ *n* riqueza, *f*

richly /ˈrɪtʃli/ *adv* ricamente; abundantemente; magníficamente; bien

richness /ˈrɪtʃnɪs/ *n* riqueza, *f;* opulencia, *f;* (of land, etc.) fertilidad, *f;* abundancia, *f;* (of objects) magnificencia, suntuosidad, hermosura, *f;* preciosidad, *f;* (of food) gusto exquisito, *m;* suculencia, *f;* (piquancy) gusto picante, *m;* (of colours) viveza, *f*

rickets /ˈrɪkɪts/ *n* raquitismo, *m*

rickety /ˈrɪkɪti/ *a Med.* raquítico; destartalado, desvencijado; (unsteady) tambaleante; cojo

rickshaw /ˈrɪkʃɔ/ *n* riksha, *m*

ricochet /ˌrɪkəˈʃei/ *n* rebote, *m, vi* rebotar

rid /rɪd/ *vt* librar (de). **to get rid of,** librarse de; quitarse de encima (a); perder, quitarse; (dismiss) despedir. **to rid oneself of,** librarse de, deshacerse de

riddance /ˈrɪdns/ *n* libramiento, *m*

riddle /ˈrɪdl̩/ *n* acertijo, *m;* enigma, problema, *m;* misterio, *m;* (sieve) tamiz de alambre, *m; vt* (guess) adivinar; (sift) cribar; (with holes) acribillar

ride /raid/ *vi* (a horse) montar a caballo, cabalgar; pasear a caballo; (a mule, a bicycle) montar en, pasear en; (a vehicle, train) ir en; (a carriage, car) andar en, pasear en; (float) flotar; (on the wind) dejarse llevar por el viento; ser llevado por el viento; (go) ir; (come) venir; (a distance) hacer... a caballo, en coche, etc.; *Naut.* estar al ancla; *Mech.* tener juego. —*vt* (a horse, mule, bicycle) montar; ir montado sobre; manejar; (a race) hacer; (float) flotar en; (cleave, the sea, etc.) surcar. —*n* paseo (a caballo, en bicicleta, en coche, etc.), *m;* viaje (en un autobús, de tren, etc.), *m;* (bridle path) camino de herradura, *m;* cabalgata, *f,* desfile a caballo, *m.* **a r. on horseback,** un paseo a caballo. **They gave me a r. in their car,** (e.g. to see the sights) Me llevaron a paseo en su auto, (a lift to a certain place) Me dieron un aventón. **ride at anchor,** estar fondeado. **to r. a bicycle,** montar en bicicleta. **to r. rough-shod over,** mandar a la baqueta (a), mandar a puntapiés (a). **to r. sidesaddle,** cabalgar a mujeriegas. **to r. at,** embestir con. **to r. away,** marcharse, alejarse; marcharse a caballo, etc. **to r. back,** volver; volver a caballo, en bicicleta, etc. **to r. behind,** seguir a caballo; ir inmediatamente detrás (de); (on the back seat) ocupar el asiento de atrás; (on the same animal) cabalgar en la grupa. **to r. down,** atropellar; (trample) pisotear, pasar por encima de. **to r. on,** seguir su camino. **to r. out,** salir a paseo en caballo, etc.; irse a paseo en coche, etc.; (a storm) hacer frente a, luchar con. **to r. over,** pasar por encima de; recorrer. **to r. up,** *vi* llegar, acercarse; (of a tie, etc.) subir. —*vt* montar

rider /ˈraidər/ *n* cabalgador (-ra); jinete, *m;* persona que va en coche, etc., *f;* (on a bicycle) ciclista, *mf;* (on a motorcycle) motociclista, *mf;* (horsebreaker) domador de caballos, *m;* (clause) añadidura, *f;* corolario, *m*

ridge /rɪdʒ/ *n* cumbre, cima, *f;* (of mountains) cordillera, sierra, *f;* (of a roof, of a nose) caballete, *m; Agr.* lomo, caballón, *m;* (wrinkle) arruga, *f;* (on coins) cordoncillo, *m.* —*vt* surcar; formar lomos (en); (wrinkle) arrugar

ridicule /ˈrɪdɪˌkyul/ *n* ridículo, *m, vt* poner en ridículo, ridiculizar, burlarse (de), mofarse (de)

ridiculous /rɪˈdɪkyələs/ *a* ridículo, absurdo

ridiculously /rɪˈdɪkyələsli/ *adv* absurdamente

ridiculousness /rɪˈdɪkyələsnɪs/ *n* ridiculez, *f*

riding /ˈraidɪŋ/ *a* cabalgante; que va a caballo; montado (a, en, sobre); *Naut.* al ancla; (in compounds) de equitación; de montar. —*n* equitación, *f;* paseo a caballo; en bicicleta, etc., *m;* acción de ir a caballo, etc., *f;* (district) comarca, *f.* **r.-boots,** botas de montar, *f pl.* **r.-habit,** traje de montar, *m;* (woman's) amazona, *f.* **r.-master,** profesor de equitación, *m.* **r.-saddle,** silla de montar, *f.* **r.-school,** escuela de equitación, *f*

rife /raif/ *a* común; corriente; frecuente; prevalente; abundante; general. **r. with,** abundante en; lleno de

riffraff /ˈrɪfˌræf/ *n* desperdicios, *m pl;* (rabble) gentuza, canalla, *f*

rifle /ˈraifəl/ *n* rifle, fusil rayado, *m.* —*vt* robar; (a suitcase, etc.) desvalijar; (a gun) rayar. **r.-range,** campo de tiro, *m.* **r.-sling,** portafusil, *m.* **r.-shot,** fusilazo, *m*

rifleman /ˈraifəlmən/ *n* fusilero, *m*

rifler /ˈraiflər/ *n* saqueador (-ra)

rifling /ˈraiflɪŋ/ *n* (robbing) saqueo, robo, *m;* (of a suitcase, etc.) desvalijamiento, *m*

rift /rɪft/ *n* hendedura, abertura, *f;* grieta, *f*

rig /rɪg/ *n Naut.* aparejo, *m; Inf.* atavío, *m.* —*vt* (a ship) aparejar; equipar; (elections) falsificar. **to rig out,** proveer de; equipar con; ataviar. **to rig up,** arreglar; armar, construir

rigging /ˈrɪgɪŋ/ *n* (of a ship) aparejo, *m*

right /rait/ *a* recto; correcto; conveniente, debido; apropiado; exacto; (opposite of left hand) derecho; (straight) directo; en línea recta; razonable; (true) verdadero, genuino, legítimo; (just) justo; (prudent) prudente; (in health) sano. **All r.!** ¡Está bien! **I feel all r.,** Me siento perfectamente bien, Estoy bien. **He is the r. man for the job,** Él es el hombre que hace falta para el puesto. **It is the r. word,** Es la palabra apropiada. **on the r.,** a la derecha. **to be r.,** (of persons) tener razón. **to make r.,** poner en orden; arreglar. **r.-angle,** ángulo recto, *m.* **r.-angled,** rectangular. **r.-angled triangle,** triángulo rectángulo, *m.* **the R. Bank (of Paris)**, la Orilla derecha, la Ribera derecha, *f.* **r. hand,** *n* (mano) derecha, diestra, *f;* derecha, *f;* (person) brazo derecho, *m.* —*a* de la mano derecha; de la derecha; a la derecha. **r.-handed,** derecho; diestro, hábil. **r. mind,** entero juicio, *m.* **r.-minded,** juicioso, prudente; honrado. **r.-of-way,** derecho a la vía, *m*

right /rait/ *adv* directamente; inmediatamente; derechamente; correctamente; debidamente; exactamente; bien; (quite, thoroughly) completamente; honradamente; (very) muy. **r. on,** adelante; en frente. **R. about face!** ¡Media vuelta a la derecha! **r. at the bottom,** al fondo; al final; el último (de la clase, etc.). **r. at the end of his speech,** al fin de su discurso. **r. away,** en seguida, inmediatamente

right /rait/ *n* razón, *f;* verdad, *f;* justicia, *f;* (good) bien, *m;* derecho, *m;* (not left side) derecha, *f;* (of political parties) derechas, *f pl.* **r. and wrong,** el bien y el mal. **"All rights reserved,"** «Derechos reservados.» **by rights,** por derecho. **It is on the r.,** Está a la derecha. **to exercise one's r.,** usar de su derecho. **r. of association,** derecho de asociación, *m.* **r. of way,** derecho de paso, *m.* **to be in the r.,** tener razón; estar en su derecho

right /rait/ *vt* enderezar; rectificar; corregir; poner en orden; *Naut.* enderezar; hacer justicia (a). **to r. wrongs,** deshacer agravios

righteous /ˈraitʃəs/ *a* recto, virtuoso, justo; justificado

righteously /ˈraitʃəsli/ *adv* virtuosamente; justamente

righteousness /ˈraitʃəsnɪs/ *n* rectitud, integridad, virtud, *f;* justicia, *f*

rightful /ˈraitfəl/ *a* justo; legítimo; verdadero

rightfully /ˈraitfəli/ *adv* justamente; legitimamente; verdaderamente

rightfulness /ˈraitfəlnɪs/ *n* justicia, *f;* legitimidad, *f;* verdad, *f*

rightly /ˈraitli/ *adv* justamente; debidamente; correctamente; bien. **r. or wrongly,** mal que bien

rightness /ˈraitnɪs/ *n* rectitud, *f;* derechura, *f;* justicia, *f;* exactitud, *f*

rigid /ˈrɪdʒɪd/ *a* rígido; inflexible; severo, riguroso

rigidity /rɪˈdʒɪdɪti/ *n* rigidez, *f;* inflexibilidad, *f;* severidad, *f*

rigmarole /ˈrɪgməˌroul/ *n* monserga, *f,* galimatías, *m,* jerigonza, *f*

rigor /ˈrɪgər/ *n* rigor, *m*

rigorous /ˈrɪgərəs/ *a* riguroso

rigorously /ˈrɪgərəsli/ *adv* rigurosamente

rile /rail/ *vt Inf.* irritar, sacar de tino (a)

rim /rɪm/ *n* borde, *m;* orilla, *f;* (of a wheel) llanta, *f,* aro, *m*

rime /raim/ *n* escarcha, *f, vt* cubrir con escarcha. See also **rhyme**

rind /raind/ *n* (of fruit) cáscara, corteza, *f;* (of cheese) costra, *f;* (of bacon) piel, *f*
ring /rɪŋ/ *n* círculo, *m;* (round the eyes) ojera, *f;* (for curtains, etc.) anilla, *f;* (for the finger) anillo, *m,* sortija, *f;* (for children's games, etc.) corro, *m;* (for the ears) arete, *m;* (of smoke and for the nose) anillo, *m;* (for hitching, etc.) argolla, *f;* (for boxing) cuadrilátero, *m;* (on a racecourse) picadero, *m;* (at a circus, bull-fight) ruedo, redondel, *m; Fig.* arena, *f;* (group) camarilla, *f,* grupo, *m;* (metallic sound) sonido metálico, *m;* resonancia, *f;* (tinkle) tintín, *m;* (of a bell) repique, tañido, son (de la campana), *m;* (of bells) juego de campanas, *m;* (of laughter, etc.) ruido, *m;* (of truth, etc.) apariencia, *f.* **r.-bolt,** *Naut.* cáncamo, *m.* **r. finger,** dedo anular, *m.* **r.-master,** director de circo, *m*
ring /rɪŋ/ *vt* (surround) cercar, rodear; (a bull, etc.) poner un anillo (a); (sound) hacer sonar; sonar; (a door bell, etc.) tocar, apretar; (bells) echar a vuelo; (announce by pealing the bells) anunciar, proclamar; sonar, tañer. *—vi* (of bells) sonar; (re-echo) resonar; (of the ears) zumbar; (tinkle) tintinar. **to r. the bell,** tocar la campana; tocar el timbre. **to r. off,** colgar el teléfono. **to r. up,** llamar por teléfono, telefonear
ringing /'rɪŋɪŋ/ *n* acción de tocar las campanas o el timbre, *f;* toque, *m;* repique, *m;* campanilleo, *m;* (in the ears) zumbido, *m. —a* resonante, sonoro. **r. signal,** señal de llamada, *f.* **the r. of the bells,** el son de las campanas
ringleader /'rɪŋˌlidər/ *n* cabecilla, *m*
ringlet /'rɪŋlɪt/ *n* rizo, bucle, *m*
ringworm /'rɪŋˌwɜrm/ *n* tiña, *f*
rink /rɪŋk/ *n* pista, *f.* **skating-r.,** sala de patinar, *f;* pista de patinar, *f*
rinse /rɪns/ *n* enjuague, *m;* enjuagadura, *f;* (of clothes) aclarado, *m. —vt* enjuagar; (clothes) aclarar; lavar
rinsing /'rɪnsɪŋ/ *n* See **rinse;** *—pl* **rinsings,** lavazas, *f pl, a* de aclarar
riot /'raiət/ *n* motín, *m;* tumulto, *m;* desorden, *m;* exceso, *m;* orgía, *f;* disipación, *f. —vi* amotinarse; alborotarse; entregarse a la disipación (or al placer); (enjoy) gozar, disfrutar. **to run r.,** hacer excesos; perder el freno; desmandarse; *Fig.* extenderse por todas partes; crecer en abundancia, cubrir todo
rioter /'raiətər/ *n* amotinador (-ra); alborotador (-ra)
riotous /'raiətəs/ *a* sedicioso; bullicioso; disoluto; desordenado; desenfrenado
riotously /'raiətəs/ *adv* sediciosamente; bulliciosamente; disolutamente; con exceso
riotousness /'raiətəsnɪs/ *n* sedición, *f;* disolución, *f;* excesos, *m pl,* desenfreno, *m;* desorden, *m*
rip /rɪp/ *vt* rasgar; (unsew) descoser; (wood, etc.) partir; (make) hacer. *—vi* rasgarse. *—n* rasgón, *m;* rasgadura, *f;* desgarro, *m;* (libertine) calavera, *m.* **to rip off,** arrancar; quitar. **to rip open,** abrir; (an animal) abrir en canal
riparian /rɪ'pɛəriən/ *a* and *n* ribereño (-ña)
ripe /raip/ *a* maduro; preparado; perfecto, acabado
ripen /'raipən/ *vt* and *vi* madurar
ripeness /'raipənɪs/ *n* madurez, *f*
ripening /'raipənɪŋ/ *n* maduración, *f*
ripping /'rɪpɪŋ/ *n* rasgadura, *f;* (unstitching) deshiladura, *f. —a Inf.* estupendo
ripple /'rɪpəl/ *n* rizo, *m;* onda, *f;* (of sound) murmullo, *m. —vt* rizar. *—vi* rizarse; murmurar
rippling /'rɪplɪŋ/ *n* rizado, *m;* murmullo, *m*
rise /raiz/ *vi* ascender; subir; levantarse; ponerse de pie; (of a meeting) suspenderse; (from the dead) resucitar; (grow) crecer; (swell) hincharse; (of sun, moon) salir; (of sound, gradient, price, stock exchange quotations) subir; (of river source) nacer; (in revolt) sublevarse, rebelarse; (to the mind) presentarse, surgir; (appear) aparecer; (of buildings, etc.) elevarse, alzarse; (in the world) mejorar de posición; (originate) originarse (en), proceder (de); (of mercury) alzarse; (of fish) picar. **He has risen in my estimation,** Ha ganado en mi estimación. **She rose early,** Se levantó temprano. **The color rose in her cheeks,** Se le subieron los colores a la cara. **to r. to the occasion,** estar al nivel de las circunstancias. **to r. to one's feet,** ponerse de pie. **to r. to the bait,** morder el anzuelo. **to r. again,** levantarse de nuevo; resucitar; renovarse, suscitarse otra vez. **to r. above,** alzarse por encima de; mostrarse superior a
rise /raiz/ *n* ascensión, *f;* subida, *f;* levantamiento, *m;* (in price, temperature) alza, *f;* (increase) aumento, *m;* (of the sun, moon) salida, *f;* (of a river) nacimiento, *m;* (origin) origen, *m;* (growth, development) desarrollo, crecimiento, *m;* (promotion) ascenso, *m;* (slope) cuesta, *f;* pendiente, *f;* (high ground) eminencia, altura, *f.* **to give r. to,** dar lugar a, causar. **r. and fall,** subida y baja, *f;* (of the voice) ritmo, *m;* (of music) cadencia, *f;* (of institutions) grandeza y decadencia, *f.* **r. to power,** subida al poder, *f*
riser /'raizər/ *n* el, *m,* (*f,* la) que se levanta; (of a step) contrahuella, *f.* **early r.,** madrugador (-ra). **late r.,** el, *m,* (*f,* la) que se levanta tarde
risibility /ˌrɪzə'bɪlɪti/ *n* risibilidad, *f*
risible /'rɪzəbəl/ *a* risible
rising /'raizɪŋ/ *n* subida, *f;* (of the source of rivers) nacimiento, *m;* (overflowing of rivers) crecimiento, *m;* (of sun, moon) salida, *f;* (from the dead) resurrección, *f;* (rebellion) sublevación, insurrección, *f;* (of the tide) crecida, *f;* (of bread) levadura, *f;* (of an assembly) suspensión, *f;* (of a theater curtain) subida, *f;* (literary) renacimiento, *m, a* creciente; naciente; saliente; (promising) de porvenir; (young) joven. **the r. generation,** los jóvenes, la generación joven. **He is r. forty,** Raya en los cuarenta. **He likes early r.,** Le gusta madrugar. **On the r. of the curtain...,** Al levantarse el telón... **the r. of the moon,** la salida de la luna, *f.* **the r. tide,** la marea creciente
risk /rɪsk/ *n* riesgo, *m;* peligro, *m. —vt* arriesgar; atreverse (a), osar. **at the r. of,** al riesgo de. **to take a r.,** tomar un riesgo; correr peligro. **to r. everything on the outcome,** jugar el todo por el todo
risk capital *n* capital-riesgo, *m*
riskiness /'rɪskinɪs/ *n* peligro, *m*
risky /'rɪski/ *a* arriesgado, peligroso
rissole /rɪ'soul/ *n* risol, *m,* (*pl* risoles)
rite /rait/ *n* rito, *m*
rite of passage *n* rito de tránsito, *m*
ritual /'rɪtʃuəl/ *a* ritual. *—n* rito, *m,* ceremonia, *f*
ritualist /'rɪtʃuəlɪst/ *n* ritualista, *mf*
ritualistic /ˌrɪtʃuə'lɪstɪk/ *a* ritualista
rival /'raivəl/ *n* rival, *mf a* competidor; rival. *—vt* rivalizar con, competir con
rivalry /'raivəlri/ *n* rivalidad, *f*
river /'rɪvər/ *n* río, *m. —a* del río; fluvial. **r.-basin,** cuenca de un río, *f.* **r.-bed,** lecho, cauce (de un río), *m.* **r. civilization,** civilización fluvial, *f.* **r.-god,** dios de los ríos, *m.* **r.-mouth,** ría, *f.* **r. port,** puerto fluvial, *m*
riverside /'rɪvərˌsaid/ *n* ribera, orilla de un río, *f. —a* de la(s) orilla(s) de un río; situado a la orilla de un río; ribereño
rivet /'rɪvɪt/ *n* remache, roblón, *m. —vt* remachar; clavar; *Fig.* fijar, concentrar; *Fig.* cautivar, absorber
riveter /'rɪvɪtər/ *n* remachador, *m*
riveting /'rɪvɪtɪŋ/ *n* remachado, remache, *m; Fig.* fijación, concentración, *f; Fig.* absorción, *f.* **r. machine,** remachadora, *f*
Riviera, the /ˌrɪvi'ɛrə/ la Riviera, *f*
rivulet /'rɪvyəlɪt/ *n* riachuelo, arroyo, *m*
road /roud/ *n* camino, *m;* carretera, *f;* ruta, *f; pl* **roads,** *Naut.* rada, *f.* **high r.,** camino real, *m.* **main r.,** carretera, *f.* **secondary r.,** carretera de segunda clase, *f.* **on the r. to...,** en el camino de... **to get out of the r.,** *Inf.* quitarse de en medio. **to go by r.,** ir por carretera. **"R. up!"** «Carretera en reparaciones.» **r.-book,** guía de carreteras, *f.* **r. house,** albergue de carretera, *m.* **r. maker,** constructor de caminos, *m;* (navvy) peón caminero, *m.* **r. making,** construcción de caminos, *f.* **r. map,** mapa de carreteras, *m.* **r. sign,** señal de carretera, señal de tránsito, señal vial, *f,* poste indicador, *m.* **The r. to hell is paved with good intentions,** El camino del infierno está empedrado de buenas intenciones. **"R. Repairs,"** «Camino en Reparación»
roadmender /'roudˌmɛndər/ *n* peón caminero, *m*
roadside /'roudˌsaid/ *n* borde del camino, *m, a* al lado del camino
roadstead /'roudˌstɛd/ *n* rada, *f*

roadster /'roudstər/ *n* automóvil de turismo, *m;* bicicleta de carreras, *f;* caballo de aguante, *m;* buque fondeado en rada, *m*
roadway /'roud,wei/ *n* calzada, carretera, *f*
roam /roum/ *vi* vagar, vagabundear, andar errante. —*vt* errar por
roamer /'roumər/ *n* vagabundo (-da), hombre errante, *m*
roaming /'roumɪŋ/ *n* vagabundeo, *m;* excursiones, *f pl,* paseos, *m pl;* *a* errante, vagabundo; nómada
roan /roun/ *a* roano, sabino. —*n* caballo roano, *m*
roar /rɔr/ *vi* rugir; (of a bull, of the wind, of a person in anger) bramar; dar voces; (of the fire) crepitar; (of cannon) retumbar; (of thunder) estallar. —*vt* gritar. —*n* rugido, bramido, *m;* (shout) grito, *m;* (of the fire) crepitación, *f;* (of cannon, thunder) estallido, *m;* (noise) ruido, *m.* **to r. with laughter,** reírse a carcajadas
roaring /'rɔrɪŋ/ *n* (of horses) asma de los caballos, *f,* For other meanings, see under **roar.** *a* rugiente, bramante; *Inf.* magnífico. **to do a r. trade,** hacer un buen negocio
roast /roust/ *n* asado, *m,* carne asada, *f.* —*a* asado; tostado. —*vt* asar; (coffee and to warm one's feet, etc.) tostar, (metals) calcinar, (scold) desollar vivo (a). —*vi* asarse; tostarse. **r. beef,** rosbif, *m*
roaster /'roustər/ *n* asador, *m;* (for coffee or peanuts) tostador, *m;* (for chestnuts, etc.) tambor, *m*
roasting /'roustɪŋ/ *n* asación, *f;* (of coffee) tostado, *m;* (of metals) calcinación, *f.* **r. spit,** asador, *m*
rob /rɒb/ *vt* robar; quitar, privar (de). **They have robbed her of her pocketbook,** Le han robado la cartera
robber /'rɒbər/ *n* ladrón (-ona); (footpad) salteador de caminos, *m;* (brigand) bandido, *m*
robbery /'rɒbəri/ *n* robo, *m.* **It's daylight r.!** ¡Es un desuello! **to commit a r.,** cometer un robo. **r. with violence,** robo armado, *m*
robe /roub/ *n* traje talar, *m,* toga, *f;* (of a monk, nun) hábito, *m;* (of a priest, etc.) sotana, *f; Poet.* manto, *m;* (infant's) mantillas, *f pl; pl* **robes,** traje de ceremonia, *m.* —*vt* vestir; cubrir, revestir (de). —*vi* vestirse. **bath r.,** albornoz, *m*
robin /'rɒbɪn/ *n* petirrojo, *m*
robot /'roubət, -bɒt/ *n* hombre mecánico, *m; Aer.* piloto mecánico, *m.* **traffic r.,** torre del tráfico, *f,* aparato automático, *m.* **r. plane,** avión sin piloto, *m*
robust /rou'bʌst/ *a* robusto; fuerte, vigoroso. **to make r.,** robustecer
robustness /rou'bʌstnɪs/ *n* robustez, *f;* vigor, *m,* fuerza, *f*
rock /rɒk/ *n* roca, *f;* (in the sea) abrojo, escollo, *m;* peña, *f,* peñasco, *m.* **as firm as a r.,** como una roca. **to be on the rocks,** *Inf.* estar a la cuarta pregunta. **r. bottom,** *n* fondo, *m.* —*a* mínimo, más bajo. **r. crystal,** cuarzo, *m.* **r.-garden,** jardincito rocoso, jardin alpestre, *m.* **r.-plant,** planta alpestre, *f.* **r.-rose,** heliantemo, *m.* **r.-salt,** sal gema, *f*
rock /rɒk/ *vt* mecer; (shake) hacer temblar, sacudir; (to sleep) arrullar. —*vi* mecerse, balancearse; tambalearse; agitarse; temblar
rocker /'rɒkər/ *n* (of a chair, cradle) balancín, *m;* (chair) mecedora, *f*
rockery /'rɒkəri/ *n* jardincito rocoso, *m*
rocket /'rɒkɪt/ *n* cohete, volador, *m.* —*vi* lanzarse. **r.-launching aircraft,** caza lanzacohetes, *f*
rockiness /'rɒkinɪs/ *n* abundancia de rocas, *f;* fragosidad, escabrosidad, *f*
rocking /'rɒkɪŋ/ *n* balanceo, *m,* (staggering) tambaleo, *m;* oscilación, *f;* (of an infant) arrullo, *m.* **r.-chair,** mecedora, *f.* **r.-horse,** caballo balancín, caballo mecedor, *m*
rocky /'rɒki/ *a* rocoso; de roca; roqueño; (rough) fragoso, escabroso; (rugged) peñascoso, escarpado. **the R. Mountains,** las Montañas Rocosas, *f pl*
rococo /rə'koukou/ *n* rococó, *m*
rod /rɒd/ *n* vara, *f;* bastón de mando, *m;* (for fishing) caña, *f;* (measure) pértiga, *f;* (surveying) jalón, *m;* palo, *m;* (for punishment) vergajo, *m; Mech.* vástago, *m.* **connecting rod,** biela, *f.* **to fish with rod and line,** pescar con caña
rodent /'roudn̩t/ *a* and *n* roedor, *m*
roe /rou/ *n* (deer) corzo (-za); (of fish) hueva, *f.* **soft roes,** lechas, *f pl*
rogue /roug/ *n* bribón, pícaro, pillo, *m; Law.* vago, *m;* (affectionate) picaruelo (-la)
roguery /'rougəri/ *n* truhanería, picardía, *f;* (knaves) pícaros, *m pl;* (mischief) travesuras, *f pl.* **novel of r.,** novela picaresca, *f*
roguish /'rougɪʃ/ *a* picaresco, bellaco; (mischievous) travieso, juguetón; malicioso
roguishly /'rougɪʃli/ *adv* como un pícaro; con malicia
roguishness /'rougɪʃnɪs/ *n* picardía, bribonería, bellaquería, *f;* (mischievousness) travesuras, *f pl;* malicia, *f*
role /roul/ *n* papel, *m*
roll /roul/ *n* rollo, *m;* (list) rol, *m,* lista, *f;* (of bread) panecillo, *m;* (of a drum) redoble, *m;* (of thunder) tronido, *m;* (of cloth) pieza, *f;* (of tobacco) rollo, *m;* (of meat, etc.) pastel, *m;* (of a ship) balanceo, *m; pl* **rolls,** (records) archivos, *m pl.* **He has a nautical r.,** Tiene un andar de marinero. **to call the r.,** pasar lista. **r. film,** película fotográfica, *f.* **r. of honour,** lista de honor, *f.* **r.-on corset,** faja elástica, *f,* corsé de goma, *m.* **r.-top desk,** buró de cierre enrollable, *m*
roll /roul/ *vi* rodar; dar vueltas; (wallow) revolcarse; (of a ship) balancearse, bambolearse, (in money, etc.) nadar; (flow) correr, fluir; (*Fig.* of time) pasar tranquilamente; (of vehicle) rodar; pasar rodando; (of country) ondular; (of the sea) ondear; (of drums) redoblar; (of thunder) retumbar. —*vt* hacer rodar; arrollar; (a cigarette) liar; (metals) laminar; (move) mover; (the eyes) guiñar (los ojos); (the ground) apisonar; (pastry) aplanar; (of an organ) sonar; (a drum) redoblar. **Mary rolled her eyes heavenwards,** María puso los ojos en blanco. **to r. away,** alejarse; desaparecer; (of time) pasar. **to r. back,** volver, retirarse; desaparecer. **to r. by,** pasar rodando; desaparecer. **to r. down,** bajar rodando, rodar por. **to r. in,** llegar en gran cantidad (or en gran número). **to r. off,** caer de. **to r. on,** seguir su marcha; fluir sin cesar; seguir su curso; (of time) avanzar. **to r. out,** (metal) laminar; (pastry) aplanar; (bring out) sacar; desenrollar. **to r. over,** *vt* volcar; tumbar; dar la vuelta (a). —*vi* dar la vuelta; volverse al otro lado. **to r. up,** arrollar; envolver; (of hedgehogs, etc.) enroscarse, hacerse un ovillo
roll-call vote /'roul,kɔl/ *n* votación nominal, *f*
roller /'roulər/ *n* rodillo, *m;* cilindro, *m;* (wheel, castor) rueda, *f;* (for flattening the ground) apisonadora, *f; Print.* rodillo, *m;* (wave) ola grande, *f.* **r.-bandage,** venda, *f.* **r. canary,** canario de raza flauta, *m.* **r.-skate,** patín de ruedas, *m.* **r.-skating,** patinaje de ruedas, *m.* **r.-towel,** toalla continua, *f*
rollicking /'r`lIkIŋ/ *a* alegre, jovial; juguetón
rolling /'roulɪŋ/ *a* rodante; (of landscape) ondulante, quebrado. —*n* rodadura, *f;* (wallowing) revuelco, *m;* (of metals) laminación, *f;* (of a ship) balanceo, *m;* (rolling up) enrollamiento, *m.* **r.-pin,** rollo, rodillo de pastelero, *m.* **r.-stock,** material móvil ferroviario, *m*
Roman /'roumən/ *a* romano, de los romanos; (of noses and *Print.*) romano. —*n* romano (-na). **in R. fashion,** a la romana. **R. Catholic,** *a* católico; católico apostólico romano. —*n* el católico (-ca). **R. Catholicism,** catolicismo, *m.* **R. figures,** números romanos, *m pl.* **R. nose,** nariz romana, *f.* **R. road,** vía romana, *f.* **R. type,** *Print.* tipo romano, *m*
Romance /'roumæns/ *a* (of languages) romance. —*n* (language) romance, *m*
romance /rou'mæns/ *n* novela de caballería, *f;* romance, *m;* aventura, *f;* cuento, *m,* novela, *f;* romanticismo, *m; Mus.* romanza, *f.* —*vi* inventar ficciones; exagerar
romancer /rou'mænsər/ *n* romancerista, *mf;* mentiroso (-sa), embustero (-ra)
Romanesque /,roumə'nɛsk/ *a* románico; romanesco
Romanian /rʊ'meiniən, -'meinyən/ *a* rumano. —*n* rumano (-na); (language) rumano, *m*
romantic /rou'mæntɪk/ *a* and *n* romántico (-ca)
romantically /rou'mæntɪkli/ *adv* románticamente; de un modo romántico
romanticism /rou'mæntə,sɪzəm/ *n* romanticismo, *m*
romanticist /rou'mæntəsɪst/ *n* romántico (-ca)
Rome /roum/ Roma, *f*

romp /rɒmp/ *vi* juguetear, brincar, retozar, loquear; correr rápidamente. —*n* locuelo (-la), saltaparedes, *mf;* (game) retozo, *m.* **The horse romped home easily,** El caballo ganó la carrera fácilmente
rompers /ˈrɒmpərz/ *n* mono, *m*
romping /ˈrɒmpɪŋ/ *n* juegos, *m pl,* travesuras, *f pl*
rondo /ˈrɒndou/ *n* rondó, *m*
rood /rud/ *n* cruz, *f;* crucifijo, *m;* cuarto de acre, *m.* **By the r.!** ¡Por mi santiguada!
roof /ruf/ *n* tejado, techado, *m;* (of a motor-car, bus) tejadillo, *m;* (of coaches, etc.) imperial, *f;* cubierta, *f;* (of the mouth) paladar, *m;* (bower) enramada, *f;* (of heaven) bóveda (del cielo), *f.* —*vt* techar, tejar; (shelter) abrigar. **r.-garden,** azotea, *f.* **r.-gutter,** canalera, *f*
roofer /ˈrufər/ *n* techador, *m;* constructor de tejados, *m*
rook /rʊk/ *n* chova, *f,* grajo, *m;* (chess) torre, *f.* —*vt* engañar, estafar; (overcharge) desollar vivo (a)
rookery /ˈrʊkəri/ *n* manada de grajos, *f;* colonia de grajos, aves marinas or focas, *f*
room /rum/ *n* (in a house) habitación, *f,* cuarto, *m;* sala, *f;* cámara, *f;* (behind a shop) trastienda, *f;* (space) sitio, espacio, *m;* lugar, *m;* (opportunity) oportunidad, *f;* (cause) motivo, *m,* causa, *f.* —*vi* alojarse. **bath-r.,** cuarto de baño, *m.* **dining-r.,** comedor, *m.* **drawing-r.,** salón, *m.* **There is no r. for us in this car,** No cabemos en este coche. **There is still r. for improvement,** Se puede mejorar todavía. **There isn't r. for anything else,** No cabe más. **to be r.,** caber, haber sitio. **to make r.,** hacer sitio
roomed /rumd/ *a* (in compounds) de... habitaciones; de... salas
roominess /ˈruminɪs/ *n* espaciosidad, amplitud, amplitud de habitación, *f;* (of garments) holgura, *f*
rooming house /ˈrutɪd/ *n* casa de huéspedes, *f*
roommate /ˈrum,meit, ˈrʊm-/ *n* compañero de cuarto, compañero de pieza, *m*
roomy /ˈrumi, ˈrʊmi/ *a* espacioso, amplio; (of garments) holgado
roost /rust/ *n* percha de gallinero, *f.* —*vi* dormir en una percha; recogerse. **to rule the r.,** ser el amo del cotarro
rooster /ˈrustər/ *n* gallo, *m,*
root /rut *or, sometimes,* rʊt/ *n* raíz, *f; Gram.* radical, *m; Mus.* base, *f;* origen, *m;* explicación, *f.* —*vt* arraigar; *Fig.* fijar, clavar. —*vi* echar raíces; *Fig.* arraigarse; (of pigs, etc.) hozar, escarbar; revolver. **to r. out,** arrancar de raíz; *Fig.* desarraigar; (destroy) extirpar. **cubed r.,** raíz cúbica, *f.* **from the r.,** (entirely) de raíz. **square r.,** raíz cuadrada, *f.* **to cut close to the r.,** cortar a raíz
rooted *a* (in compounds) de raíces...; arraigado
rope /roup/ *n* soga, cuerda, *f;* (hawser) maroma, *f; Naut.* cabo, *m;* (tight-rope) cable, *m,* cuerda de volatinero, *f;* (string) ristra, sarta, *f;* hilo, *m; pl* **ropes,** (boxing) cuerdas del cuadrilátero, *f pl.* —*vt* encordelar, atar con cuerdas. **to r. in,** encerrar; (a person) enganchar, coger. **a r. of pearls,** una sarta de perlas. **to give a person plenty of r.,** dar mucha latitud (a). **to know the ropes,** conocer todos los trucos. **r.-ladder,** escala de cuerda, *f.* **r.-maker,** cordelero (-ra), soguero, *m.* **r.-making,** cordelería, soguería, *f.* **r.-trick,** truco de la cuerda, *m.* **r.-walk,** cordelería, *f.* **r.-yarn,** *Naut.* filástica, *f*
rosary /ˈrouzəri/ *n* rosario, *m.* **to say the r.,** rezar el rosario
rose /rouz/ *n* rosa, *f;* color de rosa, *m;* (rosette) roseta, *f; Archit.* rosetón, *m;* (of watering-can) pomo, *m,* roseta, *f.* —*a* de rosa, rosado. **to see the world through r.-colored spectacles,** ver las cosas en color de rosa. **to turn to r.,** volverse color de rosa, rosear. **r.-bay,** *Bot.* rododafne, adelfa, *f.* **r.-bush,** rosal, *m.* **r.-color,** color de rosa, rosa, *m.* **r.-colored,** de color de rosa, rosado. **r.-garden,** rosalera, rosaleda, *f.* **r. grower,** cultivador (-ra) de rosas. **r. hip,** escaramujo, *m.* **r. leaf,** hoja de rosa, *f;* pétalo de rosa, *m.* **r.-like,** como una rosa, de rosa. **r.-red,** de color de rosa; como una rosa. **climbing r.-tree,** rosal trepador, *m.* **dwarf r.-tree,** rosal bajo, *m.* **standard r.-tree,** rosal de tallo, *m.* **r.-water,** agua de rosas, *f.* **r.-window,** rosetón, *m,* rosa, *f.* **r.-wood,** palo de rosa, *m*
rosé *a* (of wines) rosado
rosebud /ˈrouz,bʌd/ *n* capullo de rosa, *m*
rosemary /ˈrouz,mɛəri/ *n* romero, *m*
rosin /ˈrɒzɪn/ *n* (solid, for violin-bows, etc.) colofonia, *f;* resina, *f.* —*vt* dar con colofonia; dar con resina
rosiness /ˈrouzinɪs/ *n* color de rosa, *m*
roster /ˈrɒstər/ *n* lista, *f;* registro, *m,* matrícula, *f*
rostrum /ˈrɒstrəm/ *n* tribuna, *f; Zool.* pico, *m;* (of a ship) espolón, *m*
rosy /ˈrouzi/ *a* róseo, rosado; sonrosado; *Fig.* de color de rosa, halagüeño; optimista. **r.-cheeked,** con (de) mejillas sonrosadas
rot /rɒt/ *n* putrefacción, podredumbre, *f;* (in trees) caries, *f;* (in sheep) comalía, *f;* (slang) patrañas, *f pl,* disparates, *m pl, vi* pudrirse; descomponerse; *Fig.* echarse a perder; (slang) decir disparates. —*vt* pudrir; *Fig.* corromper; (slang) tomar el pelo (a)
rota /ˈroutə/ *n* lista, *f;* orden del día, *m*
rotary /ˈroutəri/ *a* rotativo. **r. printing press,** rotativa, *f*
rotary telephone *n* teléfono de discado, *m*
rotate /ˈrouteit/ *vi* girar, dar vueltas; alternarse. —*vt* hacer girar
rotating /ˈrouteitɪŋ/ *a* rotativo; giratorio
rotation /rouˈteiʃən/ *n* rotación, *f;* turno, *m.* **in r.,** por turnos. **r. of crops,** rotación de cultivos, *f*
rotatory /ˈroutə,tɔri/ *a* rotatorio
rote, to learn by /rout/ *vt* aprender de memoria, aprender por repetición, aprender de cotorra
rotogravure /,routəgrəˈvyʊr/ *n* rotograbado, *m*
rotten /ˈrɒtn̩/ *a* putrefacto; podrido; (of bones, teeth) cariado; dañado, echado a perder; *Fig.* corrompido; (slang) pésimo. **to smell r.,** oler a podredumbre; apestar
rottenness /ˈrɒtn̩nɪs/ *n* putrefacción, podredumbre, *f; Fig.* corrupción, *f*
rotter /ˈrɒtər/ *n* (slang) perdido, *m*
rotting /ˈrɒtɪŋ/ *n* pudrición, *f, a* que se pudre
rotund /rouˈtʌnd/ *a* rotundo
rotunda /rouˈtʌndə/ *n* rotonda, *f*
rotundity /rouˈtʌ́ndɪti/ *n* redondez, *f;* rotundidad, *f*
roué /ruˈei, ˈruei/ *n* calavera, libertino, *m*
rouge /ruʒ / *n* colorete, *m, vt* and *vi* pintar de rojo, poner(se) colorete
rough /rʌf/ *a* áspero; duro; (of country) fragoso, escabroso; (uneven) desigual; (stormy) borrascoso, tempestuoso; (of the sea) encrespado, bravo; (of movement) violento; (bristling) erizado; (of the hair) despeinado; (unpolished) tosco; basto; (unskilled, clumsy) torpe; (of sounds, tastes) áspero; (of persons) rudo, inculto; (severe) severo; (of behavior) brutal; (of manners) brusco; (rude) grosero; (approximate) aproximado. —*adv* duramente, mal. —*n* estado tosco, *m;* (person) matón, *m.* **in the r.,** en bruto; (roughed out) bosquejado. **to grow r.,** (of the sea) encresparse, embravecerse. **to take the r. with the smooth,** *Fig.* aceptar la realidad; tomar lo bueno con lo malo. **to r. it,** luchar contra las dificultades, pasar apuros; llevar una vida sencilla; vivir mal. **to r. out,** bosquejar. **r. and ready,** improvisado; provisional. **r. and tumble,** *n* camorra, pendencia, *f.* **r.-cast,** *vt* dar una primera capa de mezcla gruesa (a); bosquejar. **r. diamond,** diamante bruto (or en bruto), *m.* **r.-draft,** borrador, *m;* bosquejo, *m.* **r.-haired,** (of a dog) de pelo crespo. **r.-hewn,** modelado toscamente; desbastado; *Fig.* cerril, tosco. **r.-house,** jarana, *f.* **r.-rider,** domador (de caballos), *m.* **r. sketch,** bosquejo, esbozo, *m.* **r.-spoken,** malhablado
roughen /ˈrʌfən/ *vt* poner áspero. —*vi* ponerse áspero
roughly /ˈrʌ́fli/ *adv* rudamente, toscamente; duramente; brutalmente; bruscamente; (of tastes, sounds) ásperamente; (approximately) aproximadamente, más o menos
roughness /ˈrʌ́fnɪs/ *n* aspereza, *f;* dureza, *f;* tosquedad, *f;* rudeza, *f;* (of the sea, wind) braveza, *f;* violencia, *f;* (of manner) brusquedad, *f;* brutalidad, *f;* (vulgarity) grosería, *f.* **the r. of the way,** la aspereza del camino
roulette /ruˈlɛt/ *n* ruleta, *f*
round /raund/ *a* redondo; (plump) rollizo; rotundo, categórico; sonoro. **a r. sum,** una cantidad redonda;

un número redondo. **to walk at a r. pace,** andar a un buen paso. **r. dance,** baile en ruedo, *m.* **r.-faced,** carilleno, de cara redonda. **r.-house,** cuerpo de guardia, *m; Naut.* tumbadillo, *m.* **r.-shouldered,** cargado de espaldas. **r. table,** mesa redonda, *f;* (of King Arthur) Tabla Redonda, *f.* **r. trip,** viaje redondo, viaje de ida y vuelta, *m.* **r.-up,** rodeo de ganado, *m;* arresto, *m*

round /raund/ *n* círculo, *m;* esfera, *f;* redondez, *f;* (slice) rodaja, *f;* (of a ladder) peldaño, *m;* (patrol and *Mil.*) ronda, *f;* circuito, *m;* vuelta, *f,* giro, *m;* serie, *f;* rutina, *f;* (of ammunition) andanada, descarga, *f;* (of cartridge) cartucho con bala, *m;* (of applause, etc.) salva, *f;* (of golf) partido, *m;* (in a fight) asalto, *m; Sports.* vuelta, *f;* (of drinks) ronda, *f;* (doctor's) visitas, *f pl*

round /raund/ *vt* redondear; (*Fig.* complete) acabar, perfeccionar; (go round, e.g. a corner) dar vuleta (a), doblar, trasponer; rodear, cercar; (of a ship) doblar. —*vi* redondearse. **to r. off,** redondear; terminar; coronar. **to r. up,** (cattle) rodear. **to r. upon,** volverse contra

round /raund/ *adv* alrededor, en derredor; por todos lados; a la redonda, en torno; en circunferencia; en conjunto (r. is not translated in Spanish, e.g. *I shall come r. to your house,* Vendré a tu casa). —*prep* alrededor de. **all the year r.,** todo el año, el año entero. **r. about,** a la redonda de, al derredor de; (nearly) cerca de; (of time by the clock) a eso de. **The road is closed and we shall have to go r.,** El camino está cerrado y tendremos que dar una vuelta. **to come r.,** volver; dejarse persuadir; recobrar su buen humor. **to go r.,** (spin) dar vueltas; (of the wind) cambiar. **There is enough to go r.,** Hay bastante para todos

roundabout /*a.* ˌraundə'baut, *n.* 'raundəˌbaut/ *a* indirecto; desviado; vago. —*n* tiovivo, *m;* (traffic) redondel, *m.* **He spoke in a r. way,** Hablaba con circunloquios. **We went there by a r. way,** Fuimos dando un rodeo

roundly /'raundli/ *adv* en redondo; rotundamente, claramente

roundness /'raundnɪs/ *n* redondez, *f;* rotundidad, *f*

rouse /rauz/ *vt* despertar; animar; excitar; suscitar, provocar. **to r. oneself,** despertarse; animarse (a hacer algo)

rousing /'rauzɪŋ/ *a* que despierta; (moving) emocionante; (enthusiastic) entusiasta; grande, bueno

rout /raut/ *n* (rabble) chusma, *f;* (party) sarao, *m;* (defeat) derrota, *f;* (meeting) reunión, *f.* —*vt* derrotar, poner en fuga; vencer

route /rut, raut/ *n* ruta, *f;* camino, *m;* itinerario, *m.* **r. march,** marcha de maniobras, *f*

routine /ru'tin/ *n* rutina, *f, a* rutinario, de rutina

rove /rouv/ *vi* vagar, errar

rover /'rouvər/ *n* vagabundo (-da); pirata, *m*

roving /'rouvɪŋ/ *a* vagabundo, errante; ambulante

row /rou/ *n* (line) hilera, fila, hila, *f;* (in a theater, etc.) fila, *f;* (string) ristra, *f;* (in a boat) paseo en bote, *m;* (commotion) alboroto, *m;* (noise) ruido, *m;* (shindy) gresca, camorra, *f;* (scolding) regaño, *m, vi* (a boat) remar, bogar. —*vt* conducir remando; (scold) regañar. **to be a row,** (shindy) haber la de San Quintín. **to start a row,** (shindy) armar camorra.

rowboat /'rouˌbout/ *n* bote de remos, *m*

rowdiness /'raudinɪs/ *n* alboroto, *m*

rowdy /'raudi/ *a* alborotador. —*n* trafalmejas, *mf* rufián, *m*

rower /'rouər/ *n* remero (-ra), bogador (-ra)

rowing /'rouɪŋ/ *a* que rema; de remos. —*n* deporte del remo, *m;* paseo en bote, *m.* **r.-boat,** bote de remos, *m.* **r.-club,** club náutico, *m.* **r.-seat,** bancada, *f.* **r.-stroke,** bogada, *f*

royal /'rɔiəl/ *a* real; regio. —*n Naut.* sobrejuanete, *m.* **r. academy,** real academia, *f.* **r. eagle,** águila real, *f.* **R. Highness,** Alteza Real, *f.* **r. letters patent,** cédula real, *f.* **R. Mail,** mala real, *f.* **R. Standard,** estandarte real, *m*

royalism /'rɔiəˌlɪzəm *n* realismo, *m*

royalist /'rɔiəlɪst/ *a* and *n* realista, *mf*

royally /'rɔiəli/ *adv* realmente; regiamente

royalty /'rɔiəlti/ *n* realeza, *f;* miembro de la familia real, *m;* tanto por ciento de los ingresos, *m;* derechos de autor, *m pl*

R.R. (abbrev. of *Railroad*) F.R. (abbrev. of *ferrocarril*)

rub /rʌb/ *vt* frotar, estregar; fregar; rozar; friccionar; (make sore) raspar. **to rub one's hands together,** frotarse las manos. **to rub the wrong way,** frotar a contrapelo. **to rub against,** rozar. **to rub along,** *Inf.* ir tirando. **to rub down,** (a horse) bruzar; limpiar; (dry) secar; (wear down) desgastar. **to rub in,** dar fricciones con; frotar con; (an idea, etc.) machacar. **to rub off,** *vt* quitar (frotando); borrar. —*vi* borrarse; separarse (de). **to rub out,** *vt* borrar. —*vi* borrarse. **to rub up,** (polish) limpiar; *Fig.* refrescar

rub /rʌb/ *n* frotación, *f;* roce, *m;* fricción, *f; Fig.* obstáculo, *m;* dificultad, *f.* **to give a rub,** frotar, etc. **rub-a-dub,** rataplán, *m*

rubber /'rʌbər/ *a* de caucho, de goma. —*n* caucho, *m,* goma, *f;* (for erasing) goma de borrar, *f;* (masseur) masajista, *mf;* (at whist, etc.) partida, *f; pl* **rubbers,** zapatos de goma, chanclos, *m pl.* **synthetic r.,** caucho artificial, *m.* **r. band,** goma, banda de goma, *f.* **r. belt,** *Mech.* correa de transmisión de caucho, *f.* **r. -plant, tree,** cauchera, *f.* **r. plantation,** cauchal, *m.* **r. planter,** cauchero, *m.* **r. stamp,** estampilla, *f*

rubbing /'rʌbɪŋ/ *n* frotación, *f;* fricción, *f;* roce, *m;* (of floors, dishes, etc.) fregado, *m*

rubbish /'rʌbɪʃ/ *n* basura, *f;* desperdicios, *m pl,* desecho, *m;* (of goods) pacotilla, *f;* (nonsense) pamplinas, patrañas, *f pl,* disparates, *m pl.* **r. cart,** carro del basurero, *m*

rubbishy /'rʌ́bɪʃi/ *a* sin valor, malo; (of goods) de pacotilla, de calidad inferior

rubble /'rʌbəl/ *n* escombros, *m pl;* cascote, *m;* piedra bruta, *f*

rubicund /'rubɪˌkʌnd/ *a* rubicundo

ruble /'roublei/ *n* rublo, *m*

rubric /'rubrɪk/ *n* rúbrica, *f*

ruby /'rubi/ *n* rubí, *m.* —*a* de rubíes; de rubí. **r. lips,** labios de rubí, *m pl*

rucksack /'rʌkˌsæk, 'rʊk-/ *n* mochila, *f*

rudder /'rʌdər/ *n* timón, gobernalle, *m*

ruddiness /'rʌ́dinɪs/ *n* rubicundez, *f;* rojez, *f;* frescura, *f*

ruddy /'rʌdi/ *a* rubicundo; rojo; frescote; (of animals) barcino

rude /rud/ *a* rudo; tosco; vigoroso; grosero, descortés

rudely /'rudli/ *adv* toscamente; groseramente

rudeness /'rudnɪs/ *n* rudeza, *f;* tosquedad, *f;* grosería, incivilidad, descortesía, *f*

rudiment /'rudəmənt/ *n* rudimento, *m*

rudimentary /ˌrudə'mɛntəri/ *a* rudimentario

rue /ru/ *vt* lamentar, llorar. —*n Bot.* ruda, *f*

rueful /'rufəl/ *a* triste, melancólico; lamentable

ruefully /'rufəli/ *adv* tristemente

ruefulness /'rufəlnɪs/ *n* tristeza, *f*

ruff /rʌf/ *n* golilla, lechuguilla, *f;* (of a bird) collarín de plumas, *m;* (of an animal) collarín de pelo, *m*

ruffian /'rʌfiən/ *n* rufián, *m*

ruffle /'rʌfəl/ *n Sew.* volante fruncido, *m;* (of a bird) collarin de plumas, *m;* (of an animal) collarín de pelo, *m;* (ripple) rizo, *m;* (annoyance) irritación, *f.* —*vt* (ripple) rizar; (pleat) fruncir; (feathers) erizar; (hair) despeinar; agitar; (annoy) irritar, incomodar

ruffling /'rʌ́flɪŋ/ *n* (rippling) rizado, *m;* (pleating) fruncido, *m;* (of the temper) irritación, *f*

rug /rʌg/ *n* (floor) alfombra, *f;* manta de viaje, *f.* **rug strap,** portamantas, *m*

rugged /'rʌgɪd/ *a* áspero, escabroso; escarpado, abrupto, (wrinkled) arrugado, tosco; (harsh) duro, severo; inculto; rudo; mal acabado; vigoroso

ruggedness /'rʌ́gɪdnɪs/ *n* aspereza, escabrosidad, *f;* lo escarpado; dureza, severidad, *f;* rudeza, *f;* vigor, *m*

ruin /'ruɪn/ *n* ruina, *f.* —*vt* arruinar; echar a perder, estropear por completo; (a woman) perder

ruination /ˌruə'neiʃən/ *n* ruina, perdición, *f*

ruined /'ruɪnd/ *a* arruinado; en ruinas

ruinous /'ruənəs/ *a* ruinoso; en ruinas

ruinously /'ruənəsli/ *adv* ruinosamente

rule /rul/ *n* regla, *f;* gobierno, *m;* autoridad, *f,* mando, *m;* administración, *f;* (reign) reinado, *m;* (of a court, etc.) orden, *f;* (for measuring) regla, *f; Print.*

regleta, *f; pl* **rules,** reglas, *f pl;* reglamento, *m.* —*vt* gobernar; regentar, regir; (control) dominar; (of a chairman, etc.) disponer, decidir; (guide) guiar; (lines) reglar. —*vi* gobernar; (of a monarch) reinar; (of prices) mantenerse; estar en boga, prevalecer. **as a r.,** por regla general, en general. **slide-r.,** regla de cálculo, *f.* **to make it a r.,** tener por regla; tener por costumbre; tener por máxima. **to r. out,** excluir; *Law.* no admitir. **to r. over,** (of a king, etc.) reinar sobre. **r. of the road,** reglamento del tráfico, *m.* **r. of thumb,** regla empírica, *f;* rutina, *f*

ruler /'rulər/ *n* gobernador (-ra); soberano (-na); (master) amo (ama); (for ruling lines) regla, *f*

ruling /'rulɪŋ/ *a* regente; dominante; (current) vigente. —*n* gobierno, *m; Law.* decisión, *f,* fallo, *m;* (with lines) rayado, *m.* **r. pen,** tiralíneas, *m*

rum /rʌm/ *n* ron, *m*

rumble /'rʌmbəl/ *vi* retumbar, tronar; (of vehicles) rugir; crujir. —*n* retumbo, trueno, *m;* rugido, *m;* ruido sordo, *m;* rumor, *m;* crujido, *m*

rumbling /'rʌmblɪŋ/ *a* que retumba, etc. —*n* ruido sordo, *m;* retumbo, *m;* crujido, *m;* (in the bowels) rugido, *m*

ruminant /'rumənənt/ *a* and *n* rumiante, *mf*

ruminate /'ruməˌneit/ *vi* and *vt* rumiar

rumination /ˌruməˈneiʃən/ *n* rumia, *f;* meditación, reflexión, *f*

rummage /'rʌmɪdʒ/ *vt* revolver, desordenar, trastornar; explorar. **to r. out,** desenterrar

rumor /'rumər/ *n* rumor, *m,* fama, *f.* **It is rumored that...,** Hay rumores de que..., La voz corre que..., Se dice que...

rump /rʌmp/ *n* (of an animal) nalgas, ancas, *f pl;* cuarto trasero, *m;* (of a bird) rabadilla, *f;* (scornful) culo, *m,* posaderas, *f pl.* **r.-steak,** solomillo, *m*

rumple /'rʌmpəl/ *vt* arrugar; desordenar

run /rʌn/ *vi* correr; acudir; (flee) huir; (rush) precipitarse, lanzarse; (in a race) tomar parte en una carrera; competir; (pass over) deslizarse (por); (of machines) andar, marchar; (of traffic) circular; (leave, of trains, ships, etc.) salir; (ply between) hacer el trayecto entre... y...; (flow) fluir, correr; (into the sea, of rivers) desembocar (en); (spurt) chorrear, manar; (drip) gotear; (leak) dejar fugar (el agua, etc.); (of colors) correrse; caer; (of tears) correr; derramarse; (of eyes) llorar; (melt) derretirse; (of a sore) supurar; (travel or go) ir; moverse; (work) trabajar; funcionar; (of editions of a book) agotarse; (of a play) representarse; (cross) cruzar; (elapse) correr; transcurrir, pasar; (become) hacerse; (of wording) decir; (be current) correr; (for parliament, etc.) hacerse candidato; (navigate) navegar; (spread) extenderse; (be) estar; ser; (of thoughts) pasar; (last) durar; (tend) tender (a). —*vt* (a race, a horse) correr; (drive) conducir; (a business, etc.) administrar; dirigir; (govern) gobernar, regir; (hunt) cazar; perseguir; (water, etc.) hacer correr; (pierce) clavar; introducir; (push) empujar; (one's hand, eye, etc.) pasar; (risks, etc.) correr; (possess) tener; establecer un servicio de (autobuses, etc.); (smuggle) hacer contrabando de. **The ship ran aground,** El barco encalló. **to run dry,** secarse; agotarse. **to run in the family,** estar en la familia. **to run into debt,** endeudarse, contraer deudas. **to run to seed,** granar; agotarse. **Steamers run daily between Barcelona and Mallorca,** Hay servicio diario de vapores entre Barcelona y Mallorca. **A stab of pain ran up his leg,** Sintió un dolor agudo en la pierna. **Feeling was running high,** Los ánimos estaban excitados. **My arrangements ran smoothly,** Mis planes marchaban bien. **Funds are running low,** El dinero escasea. **The tune runs in my head,** Tengo la canción metida en la cabeza. **The message runs like this,** El mensaje reza así, El mensaje dice así. **He ran his fingers through his hair,** Se mesaba los cabellos. **to run about,** andar de un lado a otro, correr por todas partes; (gad) corretear. **to run across,** cruzar corriendo; (meet) topar con, tropezar con. **to run after,** correr detrás (de); perseguir; buscar. **to run against,** (collide with) dar contra; (meet) tropezar con. **to run at,** abalanzarse hacia, precipitarse sobre; atacar. **to run away,** huir, escaparse; (slip away) escurrirse; (of a horse) dispararse, desbocarse. **to run away with,** huir con, fugarse con; (carry off) arrebatar; (steal) llevarse; (imagine) imaginarse, figurarse; (of temper, etc.) dominar, poseer. **to run back,** volver corriendo; llegar corriendo; retroceder rápidamente, correr hacia atrás. **to run backwards,** correr hacia atrás; **to run backwards and forwards,** ir y venir. **to run behind,** correr detrás (de); quedarse atrás; (be late) estar atrasado. **to run down,** *vi* bajar corriendo; descender, bajar; (of a clock) parar; (of a battery) gastarse; (of liquids) correr; fluir; (drop by drop) destilar. —*vt* (capture) coger; alcanzar; (a person by a vehicle) atropellar; (a ship) echar a pique; (disparage) hablar mal de. **run-down,** (in health) agotado; (of a clock) parado. **to run for,** buscar corriendo; correr para coger (el autobús, etc.); (president, etc.) ser candidato para. **to run in,** *vi* entrar corriendo. —*vt* arrestar; hacer prisionero; *Print.* encerrar. **to run into,** tropezar con; chocar con; (plunge into) meterse de cabeza en; (of sums of money, etc.) ascender a; (of streets, rivers, etc.) desembocar en. **to run off,** *vi* escaparse corriendo; marcharse corriendo. —*vt* deslizarse por; (drain) vaciar; *Print.* imprimir; (compose) componer. **to run off with,** huir con. **to run on,** correr delante; continuar; (of the mind) pensar en, entregarse a; hablar sin cesar; *Print.* recorrer. **to run out,** *vi* salir corriendo; (of liquids) derramarse; salir; (end) acabarse; agotarse; (project) sobresalir. —*vt* (cricket) coger al lanzador fuera de la línea de saque. **to run out of,** no tener más de, haber terminado. **to run over,** *vi* rebosar; derramarse. —*vt* (of a vehicle) atropellar, pasar por encima de; (peruse) repasar; revisar. **run pell-mell,** salir pitando, salir volando, salvarse por pies. **to run through,** correr por; pasar por; recorrer; (go directly) ir directamente (a); (pierce) traspasar, pasar de parte a parte; (squander) derrochar, malbaratar; (read) hojear, leer por encima. **to run up,** *vt* (hoist) izar; hacer de prisa; construir rápidamente; (incur) incurrir. —*vi* subir corriendo; (of plants) trepar (por); (shrink) encogerse; (of expenses) aumentar. **to run up to time,** llegar a su hora. **to run up against,** tropezar con; (opposition, etc.) encontrar.

run /rʌn/ *n* carrera, corrida, *f;* (excursion) visita, excursión, *f;* (cricket) carrera, *f;* (walk) paseo, *m;* (by train or sea) viaje, *m;* (by bus, tram) trayecto, *m;* (sea crossing) travesía, *f;* (distance run) recorrido, *m;* (of events, etc.) curso, *m;* marcha, *f;* (of markets, etc.) tendencia, *f;* (rhythm) ritmo, *m;* dirección, *f;* distancia, *f; Mus.* serie de notas, *f;* serie, *f;* duración, *f; Theat.* serie de representaciones, *f;* (freedom to use) libre uso, *m;* (majority) mayoría, *f;* (on a bank) asedio, *m;* (on a book, etc.) d > f; (for sheep, etc.) terreno de pasto, *m;* (for fowls) gallinero, *m.* **a run of bad luck,** una temporada de mala suerte. **at a run,** corriendo. **in the long run,** a la larga, al fin y al cabo. **on the run,** en fuga; ocupado. **Prices came down with a run,** Los precios bajaron de golpe. **take-off run,** *Aer.* recorrido de despegue, *m*

runaway /'rʌnəˌwei/ *a* fugitivo; (of a horse) desbocado

rune /run/ *n* runa, *f*

rung /rʌŋ/ *n* (of a ladder) peldaño, *m;* (of a chair) travesaño, *m;* (lath) listón, *m*

runic /'runɪk/ *a* rúnico

runner /'rʌnər/ *n* corredor (-ra); (carrier of sedan chair, etc.) silletero, *mf;* (smuggler) contrabandista, *m;* (courier) estafeta, *f;* (messenger) mensajero, *m;* (ring) anillo movible, pasador corredizo, *m;* rueda móvil, *f;* (of a sledge) patín, *m; Bot.* tallo rastrero, *m.* **r.-up,** el segundo

running /'rʌnɪŋ/ *a* corredor; (of water, bank accounts) corriente; (of a knot) corredizo; (of a sore) supurante; (continuous) continuo; (consecutive) consecutivo. —*n* carrera, *f;* marcha, *f;* funcionamiento, *m;* administración, *f;* gobierno, *m;* dirección, *f;* (flowing) derrame, *m;* (of trains, buses, etc.) servicio, *m;* (smuggling) contrabando, *m;* (of a sore) supuración, *f.* **six times r.,** seis veces consecutivas. **The car is in r. order,** El auto está en buen estado. **r. away,** fuga, *f.* **r.-board,** (of a car, etc.) estribo, *m;* (of a locomotive) plataforma, *f.* **r. costs,** gastos de mantenimiento, *m pl;* (railway) gastos de tracción, *m pl.* **r.**

fight, acción de retirada, *f.* **r.-knot,** lazo corredizo, *m.* **r. title,** *Print.* título de la columna, *m*

run-off match /'rʌ́nɔf/ *n* desempate, *m*

runway /'rʌn,wei/ *n* (for launching a ship) grada, *f;* (of an airfield) pista de aterrizaje, *f*

rupee /ru'pi, 'rupi/ *n* rupia, *f*

rupestrian /ru'pɛstriən/ *a* rupestre

rupture /'rʌptʃər/ *n* rompimiento, *m,* rotura, *f;* ruptura, *f; med* hernia, *f*

ruptured /'rʌ́ptʃərd/ *a med* herniado, quebrado

rupturing /'rʌ́ptʃərɪŋ/ *n* ruptura, *f*

rural /'rʊrəl/ *a* rural, campestre, del campo; agrario

ruse /ruz/ *n* artimaña, treta, ardid, *f*

rush /rʌʃ/ *n Bot.* junco, *m;* acometida, *f;* ataque, *m;* (of water) torrente, *m;* (bustle) bullicio, *m;* (speed) prisa, *f;* precipitación, *f;* acceso, *m;* (crowd) tropel, *m,* masa, *f;* (struggle) lucha, *f;* furia, *f.* —*vi* precipitarse, lanzarse; agolparse. —*vt* llevar rápidamente (a); despachar rápidamente; precipitar; (attack) asaltar, atacar; (capture) tomar, capturar; hacer de prisa; (a bill) hacer aprobar de prisa. **to r. upon,** abalanzarse hacia; embestir. **in a r.,** en tropel, en masa; de prisa. **to r. to a conclusion,** precipitarse a una conclusión. **r.-bottomed,** con asiento de enea. **r. hour,** hora de mayor circulación, *f,* hora de aglomeración, hora-pico (Argentina), hora brava (Argentina, informal). **r. order,** pedido urgente, *m*

rushy /'rʌ́ʃi/ *a* juncoso

russet /'rʌsɪt/ *a* rojizo; rojo. **r. apple,** manzana asperiega, *f*

Russia /'rʌʃə/ Rusia, *f*

Russian /'rʌʃən/ *a* ruso. —*n* ruso (-sa); (language) ruso, *m.* **R. leather,** piel de Rusia, *f*

rust /rʌst/ *n* herrumbre, *f,* orín, *m;* moho, *m;* (disease) añublo, tizón, *m.* —*vt* aherrumbrar; enmohecer. —*vi* aherrumbrarse; enmohecerse

rustic /'rʌstɪk/ *a* rústico; campesino, aldeano; (scornful) palurdo, grosero. —*n* aldeano, *m;* (scornful) patán, *m*

rusticate /'rʌstɪ,keit/ *vi* rusticar, vivir en el campo. —*vt* enviar al campo

rustication /,rʌ́stɪ'keiʃən/ *n* rusticación, *f*

rusticity /rʌ́'stɪsɪti/ *n* rusticidad, *f*

rustiness /'rʌ́stinɪs/ *n* herrumbre, *f;* enmohecimiento, *m;* color rojizo, *m; Fig.* falta de práctica, *f*

rustle /'rʌsəl/ *n* susurro, *m;* murmurio, *m;* (of silk, a dress, etc.) frufru, *m;* (of paper, etc.) crujido, *m.* —*vi* susurrar; murmurar; crujir. —*vt* (a paper) hacer crujir

rustless /'rʌ́stlɪs/ *a* inoxidable

rustling /'rʌ́slɪŋ/ *n* see **rustle**

rusty /'rʌsti/ *a* herrumbroso; enmohecido, mohoso; (red) rojizo, (worn out) usado, viejo; (out of practice) desacostumbrado; (forgotten) empolvorado, oxidado (e.g. *My Portuguese is rusty,* Mi portugués está empolvorado)

rut /rʌt/ *n* rodera, *f,* bache, surco, *m; fig* sendero trillado, *m; fig* rutina, *f;* (sexual appetite) celo, *m, vi* estar en celo

ruthless /'ruθlɪs/ *a* inhumano, insensible, despiadado; inexorable, inflexible

ruthlessly /'ruθlɪsnɪs/ *adv* inhumanamente; inflexiblemente, inexorablemente

ruthlessness *n* inhumanidad, *f;* inflexibilidad, inexorabilidad, *f*

Rwanda /ru'ɑndə/ Ruanda, *f*

rye /rai/ *n* centeno, *m.* **rye field,** centenar, *m*

S

s /ɛs/ *n* (letter) ese, *f*
sabbatarian /ˌsæbəˈtɛəriən/ *a* sabatario
Sabbath /ˈsæbəθ/ *n* (Jewish) sábado, *m;* (Christian) domingo, *m*
sabbatical /səˈbætɪkəl/ *a* sabático
saber /ˈseibər/ *n* sable, *m;* (soldier) jinete, *m.* *—vt* dar sablazos (a), acuchillar. **s. cut, thrust,** sablazo, *m*
sable /ˈseibəl/ *n* (animal and fur) marta, *f; herald* sable, *m.* *—a herald* sable; *poet* negro
sabotage /ˈsæbəˌtɑʒ/ *n* sabotaje, *m, vt* cometer un acto de sabotaje en
saboteur /ˌsæbəˈtɜr/ *n* saboteador, *m*
sac /sæk/ *n biol* saco, *m*
saccharin /ˈsækərɪn/ *n* sacarina, *f*
sachet /sæˈʃei/ *n* sachet, *m;* bolsa, *f.* **handkerchief s.,** bolsa para pañuelos, *f*
sack /sæk/ *n* (bag) saco, *m; mil* saqueo, saqueamiento, saco, *m.* *—vt* meter en sacos; (dismiss) dar pasaporte (a), despedir; *mil* saquear. **to get the s.,** recibir el pasaporte. **to give the s.,** dar el pasaporte (a), poner de patitas en la calle (a). **s. coat,** saco, *m*
sackcloth /ˈsækˌklɔθ/ *n* harpillera, *f.* **to repent in s. and ashes,** ponerse cenizas en la cabeza
sacking /ˈsækɪŋ/ *n* harpillera, *f; mil* saqueo, *m*
sacrament /ˈsækrəmənt/ *n* sacramento, *m;* Eucaristía, *f.* **the Blessed S.,** el Santísimo Sacramento. **to receive the Holy S.,** comulgar. **to receive the last sacraments,** recibir los sacramentos, recibir la Extremaunción
sacramental /ˌsækrəˈmɛntl̩/ *a* sacramental
sacramentalist /ˌsækrəˈmɛntl̩ɪst/ *n* sacramentario (-ia)
sacred /ˈseikrɪd/ *a* sagrado; sacro, santo; consagrado. **Nothing is s. to them,** No hay nada sagrado para ellos, No respetan nada. **the S. Heart of Jesus,** el Sagrado Corazón (de Jesús). **S. to the memory of...** Consagrado a la memoria de... **s. music,** música sagrada, *f*
sacredness /ˈseikrɪdnɪs/ *n* carácter sagrado, *m;* santidad, *f;* inviolabilidad, *f*
sacrifice /ˈsækrəˌfais/ *n* sacrificio, *m.* *—vt and vi* sacrificar. **s. of the mass,** sacrificio del altar, *m*
sacrificial /ˌsækrəˈfɪʃəl/ *a* sacrificador; del sacrificio
sacrilege /ˈsækrəlɪdʒ/ *n* sacrilegio, *m*
sacrilegious /ˌsækrəˈlɪdʒəs/ *a* sacrílego
sacristan /ˈsækrɪstən/ *n* sacristán, *m*
sacristy /ˈsækrɪsti/ *n* sacristía, *f*
sacrosanct /ˈsækrouˌsæŋkt/ *a* sacrosanto
sacrum /ˈsækrəm, ˈseikrəm/ *n anat* sacro, *m*
sad /sæd/ *a* triste; melancólico; (of a mistake) deplorable, funesto; *Inf.* redomado; (pensive) pensativo. **How s.!** ¡Qué lástima! ¡Qué triste! **It made me s.,** Me entristeció
sadden /ˈsædn̩/ *vt* entristecer, acongojar, afligir
saddle /ˈsædl̩/ *n* (riding) silla de montar, *f;* (of a bicycle, etc.) sillín, *m; mech* silla, *f; Anat.* espalda, *f.* *—vt* ensillar. **to s. with the responsibility of,** echar la responsabilidad de (a). **s. of mutton,** lomo de carnero, *m.* **s.-bag,** alforja, *f.* **s.-cloth,** mantilla de silla, *f.* **s.-tree,** arzón, *m*
saddler /ˈsædlər/ *n* sillero, guarnicionero, *m*
Sadducee /ˈsædʒəˌsi/ *n* saduceo (-ea)
sadism /ˈseidɪzəm/ *n* sadismo, *m*
sadist /ˈseidɪst/ *n* sadista, *mf*
sadistic /səˈdɪstɪk/ *a* sadístico
sadly /ˈsædli/ *adv* tristemente; (very) muy
sadness /ˈsædnɪs/ *n* tristeza, melancolía, *f*
safe /seif/ *a* al abrigo (de); seguro; salvo; (certain) cierto; prudente; digno de confianza. *—n* caja de caudales, *f;* (for food) alacena, *f.* **I stood beneath a tree s. from the rain,** Estaba de pie bajo un árbol, al abrigo de la lluvia. **to put something in a s. place,** poner algo en salvo; poner algo en un lugar seguro. **s. and sound,** sano y salvo. **s.-conduct,** salvoconducto, *m.* **s.-keeping,** lugar seguro, *m;* (of a person) buenas manos, *f pl*
safeguard /ˈseifˌgɑrd/ *n* protección, garantía, *f;* precaución, *f.* *—vt* proteger, guardar; tomar precauciones (contra)
safely /ˈseifli/ *adv* seguramente; sin accidente, sin novedad, sano y salvo; sin peligro. **You may s. tell him,** Puedes decírselo con toda seguridad. **to put** (something) **away s.,** poner (algo) en un lugar seguro
safety /ˈseifti/ *n* seguridad, *f.* *—a* de seguridad; (of locks) de golpe. **a place of s.,** un lugar seguro. **in s.,** en salvo, en seguro; con seguridad. **to believe in s. first,** poner la seguridad en primer lugar. **to play for s.,** jugar seguro. **with complete s.,** con toda seguridad. **s.-belt,** (cinto) salvavidas, *m.* **s.-catch,** fiador, *m.* **s.-curtain,** telón de seguridad, telón contra incendios, *m.* **s.-fuse,** espoleta de seguridad, *f.* **s.-glass,** vidrio inastillable, *m.* **s.-island,** refugio para peatones, *m.* **s.-lamp,** lámpara de seguridad, *f.* **s.-latch,** pestillo de golpe, *m.* **s.-lock,** (of fire-arms) seguro, *m;* (of doors, etc.) cerradura de seguridad, *f.* **s.-pin,** imperdible, *m.* **s.-razor,** máquina de afeitar, *f.* **s.-valve,** válvula de seguridad, *f*
saffron /ˈsæfrən/ *n* azafrán, *m, a* azafranado, de color de azafrán.
sag /sæg/ *vi* doblegarse, ceder; inclinarse; *naut* caer a sotavento; (of prices) bajar; (of spirits, etc.) flaquear
saga /ˈsɑgə/ *n* saga, *f;* epopeya, *f*
sagacious /səˈgeiʃəs/ *a* sagaz, perspicaz; (of animals) sabio
sagacity /səˈgæsɪti/ *n* sagacidad, perspicacia, *f;* (of animals) sagacidad, *f*
sage /seidʒ/ *n* sabio, *m; bot* salvia, *f.* *—a* sabio; sagaz; cuerdo
Sagittarius /ˌsædʒɪˈtɛəriəs/ *n* Sagitario, *m*
Sahara, the /səˈhærə/ el Sáhara, *m*
said /sɛd/ *a* antedicho; tal dicho. **No sooner s. than done,** Dicho y hecho. **the s. Mr. Martínez,** el tal Sr. Martínez
sail /seil/ *n* (of a ship) vela, *f;* (sailing-ship) velero, *m;* (of a windmill) aspa, *f; mech* ala, *f;* (trip) paseo en barco, *m.* *—vi* navegar; ir en barco; dar un paseo en barco; (leave) salir en barco; zarpar; (of swans, etc.) deslizarse; (of clouds, etc.) flotar. *—vt* (a ship) gobernar; (the sea) navegar por. **She sailed into the room,** Entró majestuosamente en la sala. **The ship sailed at eight knots,** El buque navegaba a ocho nudos. **to go for a s.,** dar un paseo en barco. **to s. round the world,** dar la vuelta al mundo. **to s. the seas,** navegar por los mares. **to set s.,** darse a la vela, zarpar. **to take in the sails,** amainar. **s.-maker,** velero, *m.* **to s. into,** entrar en. **to s. round,** (the Cape, etc.) doblar. **to s. up,** subir en barco; (of a boat) ir río arriba
sailcloth /ˈseilˌklɔθ/ *n* lona, *f*
sailing /ˈseilɪŋ/ *n* navegación, *f;* (departure) salida, *f.* **It's all plain s.,** Todo va viento en popa. **s.-boat,** bote de vela, *m.* **s.-ship,** buque de vela, velero, *m*
sailor /ˈseilər/ *n* marinero, *m.* **John is a bad s.,** Juan se marea fácilmente. **to be a good s.,** no marearse. **s. -blouse,** marinera, *f.* **s.-suit,** traje de marinero, *m*
saint /seint/ *n* santo (-ta); (before masculine names of Sts., excluding Sts. Dominic and Thomas) San; *Inf.* ángel, *m.* **All Saints' Day,** el día de Todos los Santos. **saint's day,** fiesta de un santo (or de una santa), *f;* (of a person) santo, *m.* **St. Bernard dog,** perro de San Bernardo, *m.* **St. John the Baptist,** San Juan Bautista. **St. Martin's summer,** el veranillo de San Martín. **St. Vitus's dance,** el baile de San Vito
sainthood /ˈseinthʊd/ *n* santidad, *f*
saintliness /ˈseintlinɪs/ *n* santidad, *f*
saintly /ˈseintli/ *a* de santo; de santa; santo; inf angelical
Saint Petersburg /seint ˈpitərzˌbɜrg/ San Petersburgo, *m*
sake /seik/ *n* amor, *m;* causa, *f.* **for God's s.,** por el amor de Dios. **for the s. of,** para; por amor de. **to talk for talking's s.,** hablar por hablar

salable /'seiləbəl/ *a* vendible
salaciousness /sə'leiʃəsnɪs/ *n* salacidad, *f*
salad /'sæləd/ *n* ensalada, *f;* (lettuce) lechuga, *f.* **fruit s.,** macedonia de frutas, *f.* **s.-bowl,** ensaladera, *f.* **s.-dressing,** aderezo, aliño, *m,* salsa para ensalada, *f.* **s.-oil,** aceite para ensaladas, *m*
salamander /'sælə,mændər/ *n* salamandra, *f*
salaried /'sælərid/ *a* a sueldo; (of posts) retribuido
salary /'sæləri/ *n* sueldo, salario, *m*
sale /seil/ *n* venta, *f;* (auction) almoneda, subasta pública, *f.* **clearance s.,** liquidación, *f,* saldo, *m.* **to be on s.,** estar de venta. **"Piano for s.,"** «Se vende un piano.» **s. price,** precio de venta, *m;* precio de saldo, *m*
sales contract *n* contrato de compraventa, *m*
salesman /'seilzmən/ *n* dependiente de tienda, *m;* (traveller) viajante, *m*
salesmanship /'seilzmən,ʃɪp/ *n* arte de vender, *mf*
salesroom /'seilz,rum/ *n* salón de ventas, *m*
saleswoman /'seilz,wʊmən/ *n* dependiente de tienda, vendedera, *f*
salient /'seiliənt/ *a* saliente; *Fig.* prominente, conspicuo, notable, *n* saliente, *m.* **s. angle,** ángulo saliente, *m*
saline /'seilin/ *a* salino. —*n* (marsh) saladar, *m; med* salino, *m*
saliva /sə'laivə/ *n* saliva, *f*
salivary /'sælə,vɛri/ *a* salival
salivate /'sælə,veit/ *vi* salivar
salivation /,sælə'veiʃən/ *n* salivación, *f*
sallow /'sælou/ *a* cetrino, oliváceo, lívido
sallowness /'sælounɪs/ *n* amarillez, lividez, *f;* palidez, *f*
sally /'sæli/ *n* (*mil.* etc) salida, *f;* (quip) ocurrencia, salida, *f.* —*vi* hacer una salida, salir. **to s. forth,** ponerse en camino
salmon /'sæmən/ *n* salmón, *m;* color de salmón, *m.* **s.-net,** salmonera, *f.* **s. trout,** trucha asalmonada, *f*
salon /sə'lɒn/ *n* salón, *m*
Salonika /sə'lɒnɪkə/ Salónica, *f*
saloon /sə'lun/ *n* sala, *f;* (of a steamer) cámara, *f,* salón, *m;* (on train, for sleeping) departamento de coche cama, *m;* (on train, for dining) coche comedor, *m; auto* coche cerrado, *m.* **billiard s.,** salón de billares, *m.* **dancing s.,** salón de baile, *m.* **hair-dresser's s.,** salón de peluquero, *m.* **s. bar,** bar, *m*
salsify /'sælsəfi/ *n bot* salsifí, *m*
salt /sɔlt/ *n* sal, *f;* (spice) sabor, *m;* (wit) sal, agudeza, *f.* —*a* salobre, salino; salado; (of land) salitroso. —*vt* (season) poner sal en; (cure) salar. **kitchen s.,** sal de cocina, *f.* **old s.,** *inf* lobo de mar, *m.* **rock s.,** sal gema, *f.* **sea s.,** sal marina, *f.* **to be not worth one's s.,** no merecer el pan que se come. **to take with a pinch of s.,** tomar con su grano de sal. **s.-cellar,** salero, *m.* **s. lagoon,** albufera, *f.* **s. lake,** lago salado, *m.* **s. marsh,** saladar, *m.* **s. meat,** carne salada, cecina, *f.* **s. merchant,** salinero, *m.* **s.-mine,** mina de sal, *f.* **s.-spoon,** cucharita de sal, *f.* **s. water,** agua salada, *f;* agua de mar, *f.* **s.-water fish,** pez de mar, *m.* **s.-works,** salinas, *f pl*
saltiness /'sɔltinɪs/ *n* sabor de sal, *m;* salobridad, *f*
salting /'sɔltɪŋ/ *n* saladura, *f;* (salt marsh) saladar, *m*
saltless /'sɔltlɪs/ *a* sin sal, soso, insípido; *Fig.* soso
saltpeter /,sɔlt'pitər/ *n* salitre, *m.* **s. bed,** salitral, *m.* **s. works,** salitrería, *f*
salty /'sɔlti/ *a* salado; salobre
salubrious /sə'lubriəs/ *a* salubre, saludable, sano
salubriousness /sə'lubriəsnɪs/ *n* salubridad, *f*
salutary /'sælyə,tɛri/ *a* saludable, beneficioso
salutation /,sælyə'teiʃən/ *n* salutación, *f,* saludo, *m*
salute /sə'lut/ *vt* and *vi* saludar. —*n* saludo, *m;* (of guns) salva, *f.* **to fire a s.,** hacer salvas, saludar con... salvas. **The soldier saluted them,** El soldado les saludó. **to take the s.,** tomar el saludo. **saluting base,** puesto de mando, *m*
Salvadoran, Salvadorian /,sælvə'dɔrən; -'dɔriən/ *a* and *n* salvadoreño (-ña)
salvage /'sælvɪdʒ/ *n* salvamento, *m, vt* salvar
salvation /sæl'veiʃən/ *n* salvación, *f.* **to work out one's own s.,** salvar el alma. **the S. Army,** el Ejército de la Salvación, *m*
salve /sælv/ *n* pomada, *f; fig* bálsamo, *m.* —*vt* curar; (overcome) vencer; (soothe) tranquilizar; *naut* salvar. **to s. one's conscience,** tranquilizar la conciencia
salver /'sælvər/ *n* salva, bandeja, *f*
salvo /'sælvou/ *n* (of guns or applause) salva, *f;* (reservation) salvedad, reservación, *f.* **s. of applause,** salva de aplausos, *f*
Samaritan /sə'mærɪtn̩/ *a* and *n* samaritano (-na)
same /seim/ *a* mismo; igual; parecido; idéntico. —*adv* lo mismo; del mismo modo. **all the s.,** sin embargo; con todo, a pesar de eso. **at the s. time,** al mismo tiempo; a la vez. **just the s.,** igual; (nevertheless) sin embargo. **He bowed deeply and I did the s.,** Él hizo una profunda reverencia y yo hice lo mismo. **They do not look at things the s. as we do,** No ven las cosas del mismo modo que nosotros. **If it is the s. to her,** Si le da igual. **It's all the s.,** Es igual, Lo mismo da, Es todo uno. **Ávila, capital of the province of the s. name,** Ávila, capital de la provincia de su nombre
"Same-Day Service" /'seimdei/ «En el día» (Argentina)
sameness /'seimnɪs/ *n* identidad, *f;* semejanza, *f,* parecido, *m;* monotonía, *f*
samovar /'sæmə,vɑr/ *n* samovar, *m*
sampan /'sæmpæn/ *n* (boat) champán, *m*
sample /'sæmpəl/ *n* muestra, *f;* prueba, *f;* ejemplo, *m.* —*vt* sacar una muestra de; (try) probar. **s. book,** muestrario, *m*
sampler /'sæmplər/ *n* probador, *m;* (of wines) catador, *m; sew* dechado, *m*
sanatorium /,sænə'tɔriəm/ *n* sanatorio, *m*
sanctification /,sæŋktəfɪ'keiʃən/ *n* santificación, *f;* consagración, *f*
sanctify /'sæŋktə,fai/ *vt* santificar; consagrar
sanctimonious /,sæŋktə'mouniəs/ *a* santurrón, mojigato, beato
sanctimoniousness /,sæŋktə'mouniəsnɪs/ *n* beatería, mojigatería, santurronería, *f*
sanction /'sæŋkʃən/ *n* sanción, *f.* —*vt* sancionar; autorizar. **to apply sanctions,** *polit* aplicar sanciones
sanctity /'sæŋktɪti/ *n* santidad, *f;* lo sagrado; inviolabilidad, *f.* **odor of s.,** olor de santidad, *f*
sanctuary /'sæŋktʃu,ɛri/ *n* santuario, *m;* (historical) sagrado, sagrado asilo, *m;* refugio, asilo, *m.* **to take s.,** acogerse a sagrado; refugiarse
sand /sænd/ *n* arena, *f;* (for drying writing) arenilla, *f;* granos de arena, *m pl*; *pl* **sands,** playa, *f;* (of life) horas de la vida, *f pl.* —*vt* arenar. **to plough the s.,** arar en el mar. **s.-bag,** *n* saco de arena, *m.* —*vt* (a building) proteger con sacos de arena; (a person) golpear con un saco de arena. **s.-bank,** banco de arena, *m,* barra, *f.* **to run on a s.-bank,** encallar. **s.-colored,** de color de arena. **s.-dune,** médano, *m.* **s.-paper,** *n* papel de lija, *m.* —*vt* pulir con papel de lija, lijar. **s.-pit,** arenal, *m.* **s. shoes,** alpargatas, *f pl*
sandal /'sændl̩/ *n* sandalia, *f;* (rope-soled) alpargata, *f.* **s.-wood,** sándalo, *m*
sandiness /'sændinɪs/ *n* naturaleza arenosa, *f;* (of hair) color bermejo, *m*
sandstone /'sænd,stoun/ *n* arenisca, *f*
sandstorm /'sænd,stɔrm/ *n* tempestad de arena, *f;* simún, *m*
sandwich /'sændwɪtʃ, 'sæn-/ *n* emparedado, bocadillo, *m.* —*vt* insertar. **I found myself sandwiched between two fat men,** Me encontré aplastado entre dos hombres gordos. **s.-man,** hombre sándwich, *m*
sandy /'sændi/ *a* arenoso; sabuloso; (of hair) rojo, rufo, bermejo. **a s. beach,** una playa arenosa
sane /sein/ *a* de juicio sano; razonable, prudente; sesudo. **He is a very s. person,** Es un hombre con mucho sentido común. **to be s.,** estar en su juicio; (of a policy, etc.) ser prudente, ser razonable
sangfroid /san'frwa/ *n* sangre fría, *f;* aplomo, *m*
sanguinary /'sæŋgwə,nɛri/ *a* sanguinario
sanguine /'sæŋgwɪn/ *a* (of complexion) rubicundo; sanguíneo; optimista, confiado. —*n* (drawing) sanguina, *f.* **to be s. about the future,** ser optimista acerca del porvenir, tener confianza en el porvenir
sanhedrin /sæn'hɛdrɪn/ *n* sanedrín, *m*
sanitary /'sænɪ,tɛri/ *a* sanitario; higiénico, **s. inspector,** inspector de sanidad, *m.* **s. napkin, s. towel,** ser-

villeta higiénica, toalla sanitaria, *mf,* paño higiénico, *m*
sanitation /ˌsænɪ'teiʃən/ *n* higiene, *f;* sanidad pública, *f;* (apparatus) instalación sanitaria, *f*
sanity /'sænɪti/ *n* juicio sano, *m;* prudencia, *f;* (common sense) sentido común, *m,* sensatez, *f*
Sanskrit /'sænskrɪt/ *a* and *n* sánscrito, *m*
Santa Claus /'sæntə klɔz/ *n* (Spanish equivalent) los Reyes Magos, *m pl*
São Paulo /'sau 'paulou, -lʊ/ San Pablo, *m*
sap /sæp/ *n* (*bot* and *fig*) savia, *f; mil* zapa, *f.* —*vt* (undermine) debilitar, agotar; *mil* zapar
sapidity /sæ'pɪdɪti/ *n* sapidez, *f*
sapling /'sæplɪŋ/ *n* arbolillo, *m*
sapper /'sæpər/ *n mil* zapador, *m*
Sapphic /'sæfɪk/ *a* sáfico. **S. verse,** verso sáfico, *m*
sapphire /'sæfaiᵊr/ *n* zafiro, *m.* —*a* de zafiros; cerúleo, de zafiro
Saracen /'særəsən/ *a* and *n* sarraceno (-na)
Saragossa /ˌsærə'gɒsə/ Zaragoza, *f*
sarcasm /'sɑrkæzəm/ *n* sarcasmo, *m*
sarcastic /sɑr'kæstɪk/ *a* sarcástico
sarcastically /sar'kæstɪkli/ *adv* con sarcasmo, sarcásticamente
sarcophagus /sɑr'kɒfəgəs/ *n* sarcófago, *m*
sardine /sɑr'din/ *n* sardina, *f.* **packed like sardines,** como sardinas en banasta. **s.-net,** sardinal, *m*
Sardinia /sɑr'dɪniə/ Cerdeña, *f*
Sardinian /sɑr'dɪniən/ *a* and *n* sardo (-da)
sardonic /sɑr'dɒnɪk/ *a* sardónico
sarsaparilla /ˌsæspə'rɪ, ˌsɑrspə-/ *n* zarzaparrilla, *f*
sash /sæʃ/ *n* (with uniform) faja, *f;* (belt) cinto, cinturón, *m;* (of a window) cerco, *m.* **s. window,** ventana de guillotina, *f*
Satan /'seitn̩/ *n* Satanás, *m*
satanic /sə'tænɪk, sei-/ *a* satánico
satchel /'sætʃəl/ *n* saquito de mano, *m,* bolsa, *f;* (school) vademécum, *m;* cartapacio, *m,* cartera, *f*
sate /seit/ *vt* saciar, hartar; satisfacer
sateen /sæ'tin/ *n* satén, *m*
satellite /'sætl̩ˌait/ *n* satélite, *m*
satiable /'seiʃəbəl/ *a* saciable
satiate /*v.* 'seiʃiˌeit; -ɪt, -ˌeit/ *vt* saciar, hartar; satisfacer. —*a* harto; repleto
satiety /sə'taiɪti/ *n* saciedad, *f*
satin /'sætn̩/ *n* raso, *m.* —*a* de raso; (glossy) lustroso, terso. —*vt* (paper) satinar
satiny /'sætn̩i/ *a* arrasado; lustroso, brillante
satire /'sætaiᵊr/ *n* sátira, *f*
satiric /sə'tɪərɪk/ *a* satírico
satirist /'sætərɪst/ *n* escritor (-ra) satírico (-ca)
satirize /'sætəˌraiz/ *vt* satirizar
satisfaction /ˌsætɪs'fækʃən/ *n* satisfacción, *f;* (contentment) contento, *m,* satisfacción, *f;* (for sin) expiación, *f;* (of a debt) pago, *m;* desquite, *m;* recompensa, *f.* **to demand s.,** pedir satisfacción. **to give** (someone) **s.,** dar contento (a), alegrar
satisfactorily /ˌsætɪs'fæktərəli/ *adv* satisfactoriamente
satisfactoriness /ˌsætɪs'fæktərinɪs/ *n* carácter satisfactorio, *m,* lo satisfactorio
satisfactory /ˌsætɪs'fæktəri/ *a* satisfactorio; (for sin) expiatorio
satisfy /'sætɪsˌfai/ *vt* satisfacer; (convince) convencer; (allay) tranquilizar, apaciguar. **I am satisfied with him,** Estoy satisfecho (Estoy contento) con él. **The explanation did not s. me,** La explicación no me convenció. **to s. oneself that...,** asegurarse de que... **to s. one's thirst,** apagar la sed
satisfying /'sætɪsˌfaiɪŋ/ *a* que satisface; satisfactorio; (of food) nutritivo
satrap /'seitræp, 'sæ-/ *n* sátrapa, *m*
saturate /'sætʃəˌreit/ *vt* saturar (de), empapar (de); *chem* saturar; *fig* imbuir; *fig* empapar. **to s. oneself in,** (a subject) empaparse en
saturation /ˌsætʃə'reiʃən/ *n* saturación, *f.* **s. point,** (*chem* etc.) punto de saturación, *m*
Saturday /'sætərˌdei/ *n* sábado, *m*
Saturn /'sætərn/ *n* Saturno, *m*
saturnine /'sætərˌnain/ *a* saturnino, taciturno
satyr /'seitər, 'sætər/ *n* sátiro, *m*
sauce /sɔs/ *n* salsa, *f;* (thick fruit) compota, *f; inf* insolencia, *f.* **s.-boat,** salsera, *f*
saucepan /'sɔsˌpæn/ *n* cazuela, cacerola, *f.* **double s.,** baño de María, *m*
saucer /'sɔsər/ *n* platillo, *m.* **flying s.,** platillo volante, *m.* **s.-eyed,** con ojos redondos
sauciness /'sɔsinɪs/ *n* impertinencia, insolencia, *f*
saucy /'sɔsi/ *a* respondón, descarado; (cheerful) alegre; (of hats, etc.) coquetón, majo
sauerkraut /'sauᵊrˌkraut/ *n* chucruta, *f*
saunter /'sɔntər/ *vi* pasearse, vagar, *n* paseo, *m,* vuelta, *f*
sausage /'sɔsɪdʒ/ *n* chorizo, *m;* salchicha, *f.* **s.-balloon,** globo cautivo, *m.* **s.-curl,** bucle, *m.* **s.-machine,** choricera, *f.* **s.-maker,** choricero (-ra)
savage /'sævɪdʒ/ *a* salvaje; feroz; (cruel) inhumano, cruel; (furious) furioso. —*n* salvaje, *mf*
savagely /'sævɪdʒli/ *adv* bárbaramente; ferozmente; furiosamente
savagery /'sævɪdʒri/ *n* salvajismo, *m;* ferocidad, *f;* brutalidad, crueldad, *f*
savannah /sə'vænə/ *n* sabana, *f.* **s. dweller,** sabanero (-ra)
save /seiv/ *vt* salvar; (keep) guardar; conservar; reservar; (money, one's clothes, etc.) ahorrar; (time) ganar; (avoid) evitar. —*vi* salvar; hacer economías; ahorrar. **He saved my life,** Me salvó la vida. **They have saved a room for me,** Me han reservado una habitación. **to s. appearances,** guardar las apariencias. **to s. oneself trouble,** ahorrarse molestias. **to s. the situation,** estar al nivel de las circunstancias
save /seiv/ *prep* salvo, excepto, menos. —*conjunc* sino, a menos que; con la excepción de. **all s. one,** todos menos uno. **all the conspirators s. he,** todos los conspiradores con la excepción de él
saving /'seivɪŋ/ *a* frugal, económico; (stingy) tacaño, avaricioso; (clause) condicional. —*n* salvación, *f;* (of money, time, etc.) ahorro, *m,* economía, *f; pl* **savings,** ahorros, *m pl.* —*prep* salvo, excepto, fuera de. —*conjunc* con excepción de que, fuera de que. **s. grace,** único mérito, *m.* **savings bank,** caja de ahorros, *f.* **savings fund,** montepío, *m*
savior /'seivyər/ *n* salvador (-ra). **the S.,** el Salvador, el Redentor
savor /'seivər/ *n* sabor, gusto, *m;* (aftertaste) dejo, *m;* (zest) salsa, *f.* —*vi* saber (a), tener sabor (de); *fig* oler (a). —*vt* saborear, paladear; (flavor) sazonar
savoriness /'seivərinɪs/ *n* buen sabor, *m;* (of a district) respetabilidad, *f*
savory /'seivəri/ *a* sabroso, apetitoso; (not sweet) no dulce; (of places) respetable; (of reputation, etc.) bueno. —*n* entremés salado, *m.* **s. omelette,** tortilla, *f*
Savoy /sə'vɔi/ Saboya, *f*
saw /sɔ/ *n* (maxim) sentencia, *f;* (proverb) refrán, decir, *m;* (tool) sierra, *f.* —*vt* aserrar; (the air) cortar. —*vi* usar una sierra. **two-handled saw,** tronzador, *m.* **saw-fish,** pez sierra, *m.* **saw-mill,** molino de aserrar, *m.* **saw-pit,** aserradero, *m*
sawdust /'sɔˌdʌst/ *n* aserrín, *m*
sawhorse /'sɔˌhɔrs/ *n* caballete de aserrar, *m*
sawyer /'sɔyər/ *n* aserrador, *m*
Saxon /'sæksən/ *a* and *n* sajón (-ona)
Saxony /'sæksəni/ Sajonia, *f*
saxophone /'sæksəˌfoun/ *n* saxófono, saxofón *m*
say /sei/ *vt* decir; recitar. —*vi* decir. **Let us say that the house is worth $100,000,** Pongamos por ejemplo que la casa vale cien mil dólares. **He has no say in the matter,** No entra ni sale en el asunto. **I have said my say,** He dicho lo que quería. **They say,** Se dice, Dicen, La gente dice. **You don't say!** ¡Calle! ¿De veras? ¡Imposible! **that is to say...,** es decir...; esto es..., a saber... **to say one's prayers,** rezar, decir sus oraciones. **to say again,** volver a decir; decir otra vez, repetir. **to say over and over again,** repetir muchas veces, decir repetidamente. **What do you say to that?** ¿Qué dices a esto?
saying /'seiɪŋ/ *n* decir, *m;* (proverb) refrán, *m;* (maxim) sentencia, *f.* **As the s. is,** Como suele decirse; Según el refrán. **It goes without s.,** Huelga decir. **It's only a s.,** Es un decir, nada más

scab /skæb/ *n* (of a wound) costra, *f;* (disease) escabro, *m;* (blackleg) esquirol, *m*

scabbard /ˈskæbərd/ *n* vaina (de espada), *f*

scabby /ˈskæbi/ *a* costroso; (diseased) roñoso, sarnoso

scabies /ˈskeibiz/ *n* sarna, *f.* **s. mite,** arador de la sarna, *m*

scaffold /ˈskæfəld/ *n* (in building) andamio, *m;* (for execution) cadalso, patíbulo, *m.* **to go to the s.,** ir al patíbulo; acabar en el patíbulo

scaffolding /ˈskæfəldɪŋ/ *n* andamiada, *f;* (building, scaffold) andamio, *m*

scald /skɔld/ *vt* escaldar; quemar; (instruments) esterilizar. —*n* quemadura, escaldadura, *f.* **to s. oneself,** escaldarse. **scalding hot,** hirviendo

scale /skeil/ *n* (of a balance) platillo, *m; zool* escama, *f; bot* bráctea, *f; bot* hojuela, *f;* (flake) laminita, *f;* (*mus, math*) escala, *f;* (of charges, etc.) tarifa, *f;* (of salaries) escalafón, *m;* (of a thermometer) escala, *f.* —*vt* escalar; (fish) escamar. **major s.,** escala mayor, *f.* **minor s.,** escala menor, *f.* **on a grand s.,** en gran escala. **on a small s.,** en pequeña escala. **pair of scales,** balanza, *f;* (for heavy weights) báscula, *f.* **social s.,** escala social, *f.* **The Scales,** *Astron.* Libra, *f.* **to draw to s.,** dibujar a escala. **to turn the scales,** pesar; *Fig.* inclinar la balanza. **to s. down,** (*Art.* and of charges) reducir

scaling /skeilɪŋ/ *n* (of fish) escamadura, *f;* (of buildings) desconchadura, *f;* (ascent) escalamiento, *m*

scallop /ˈskɒləp, ˈskæl-/ *n* (*ichth* and badge) venera, *f;* concha, *f; sew* onda, *f,* festón, *m.* —*vt Cul.* guisar en conchas; *sew* ondear, festonear

scalp /skælp/ *n anat* pericráneo, *m;* cuero cabelludo, *m; fig* trofeo, *m.* —*vt* escalpar. **s.-hunter,** cazador de cabelleras, *m*

scalpel /ˈskælpəl/ *n* escalpelo, *m*

scaly /ˈskeili/ *a* escamoso, conchado; (of boilers) incrustado

scamp /skæmp/ *n* bribón, granuja, *m, vt* (work) frangollar

scamper /ˈskæmpər/ *vi* retozar, brincar; correr. —*n* carrerita, *f.* **to s. off,** salvarse por los pies, huir; marcharse corriendo

scan /skæn/ *vt* (verse) medir, escandir; (examine) escudriñar, examinar; (glance at) dar un vistazo (a)

scandal /ˈskændl̩/ *n* escándalo, *m;* maledicencia, *f;* (slander) calumnia, *f.* **to talk s.,** murmurar

scandalize /ˈskændl̩ˌaiz/ *vt* escandalizar

scandalous /ˈskændl̩əs/ *a* escandaloso; infame; calumnioso

scandalously /ˈskændl̩əsli/ *adv* escandalosamente

scandalousness /ˈskændl̩əsnɪs/ *n* carácter escandaloso, *m*

Scandinavia /ˌskændəˈneiviə/ Escandinavia, *f*

Scandinavian /ˌskændəˈneiviən/ *a* escandinavo. —*n* escandinavo (-va);

scant /skænt/ *a* escaso; insuficiente

scantily /ˈskæntl̩i/ *adv* insuficientemente

scantiness /ˈskæntinɪs/ *n* escasez, *f;* insuficiencia, *f*

scanty /ˈskænti/ *a* insuficiente; escaso; (of hair) ralo; (of crops, etc.) pobre

scapegoat /ˈskeipˌgout/ *n* víctima propiciatoria, *f;* cabeza de turco, *f.* **to be a s. for,** pagar el pato por

scapegrace /ˈskeipˌgreis/ *n* bribón, *m*

scapula /ˈskæpyələ/ *n anat* escápula, *f*

scapulary /ˈskæpyəˌlɛri// *n eccl* escapulario, *m*

scar /skɑr/ *n* cicatriz, *f; fig* señal, *f.* —*vt* marcar con una cicatriz. **to s. over,** cicatrizarse

scarab /ˈskærəb/ *n* escarabajo, *m;* escarabajo sagrado, *m*

scarce /skɛərs/ *a* escaso; insuficiente; raro. —*adv poet* apenas. **to make oneself s.,** largarse, pirarse, escabullirse; ausentarse, esconderse

scarcely /ˈskɛərsli/ *adv* apenas; no bien; casi; (with difficulty) a duras penas, con dificultad. **It is s. likely he said that,** No es muy probable que lo hubiese dicho. **There were s. twenty people in the building,** Había apenas veinte personas en el edificio. **S. anyone likes his pictures,** Sus cuadros no le gustan a casi nadie

scarcity /ˈskɛərsɪti/ *n* escasez, insuficiencia, *f;* (famine) carestía, *f;* (rarity) rareza, *f*

scare /skɛər/ *vt* asustar, espantar, llenar de miedo (a); intimidar. —*n* susto, pánico, *m;* alarma, *f.* **What a s. I got!** ¡Qué susto me he llevado! **to s. away,** ahuyentar

scarecrow /ˈskɛərˌkrou/ *n* espantapájaros, *m; Inf.* estantigua, *f,* mamarracho, espantajo, *m*

scaremonger /ˈskɛərˌmʌŋgər/ *n* alarmista, *mf*

scarf /skɑrf/ *n* bufanda, *f;* (tie) corbata, *f; mil* faja, *f*

scarlatina /ˌskɑrləˈtinə/ *n med* escarlatina, *f*

scarlet /ˈskɑrlɪt/ *n* escarlata, *f.* —*a* de color escarlata. **to turn s.,** (of persons) enrojecerse. **s. fever,** escarlatina, *f.* **s. hat,** *eccl* capelo (cardenalicio), *m.* **s. runner,** *bot* judía verde, *f*

scatheless ˈskeiðlɪs/ *a* ileso, sano y salvo

scathing /ˈskeiðɪŋ/ *a* mordaz, cáustico

scathingly /ˈskeiðɪŋli/ *adv* mordazmente, cáusticamente

scatter /ˈskætər/ *vt* esparcir, sembrar con; (benefits, etc.) derramar; (put to flight) derrotar; dispersar; disipar; *fig* frustrar; (squander) derrochar, desparramar. —*vi* dispersarse. **The crowd scattered,** La muchedumbre se dispersó. **s.-brained,** de cabeza de chorlito, atolondrado

scattered /ˈskætərd/ *a* disperso; esparcido

scattered showers *n* lluvias aisladas, *f pl*

scattering /ˈskætərɪŋ/ *n* dispersión, *f;* (defeat) derrota, *f;* esparcimiento, *m;* (small number) número pequeño, *m*

scavenge /ˈskævɪndʒ/ *vt* (streets) recoger la basura de, barrer

scavenger /ˈskævɪndʒər/ *n* (of the streets) barrendero, *m;* (dustman) basurero, *m; zool* animal que se alimenta de carne muerta, *m;* insecto que se alimenta de estiércol, *m.* —*vt* See **scavenge**

scenario /sɪˈnɛəriˌou, -ˈnɑr-/ *n* escenario, *m*

scene /sin/ *n* escena, *f;* teatro, lugar, *m;* espectáculo, *m;* (*theat* décor) decoración, *f;* (of a play) escena, *f;* (view) vista, perspectiva, *f.* **behind the scenes,** entre bastidores. **The s. is laid...,** La acción pasa... **to come on the s.,** entrar en escena. **to make a s.,** hacer una escena. **s.-painter,** *n* escenógrafo (-fa). **s.-shifter,** tramoyista, *mf*

scenery /ˈsinəri/ *n theat* decorado, *m;* (landscape) paisaje, *m*

scenic /ˈsinɪk/ *a* dramático; escénico; pintoresco. **s. railway,** montaña rusa, *f*

scenography /siˈnɒgrəfi/ *n* escenografía, *f*

scent /sɛnt/ *vt* perfumar; (smell) oler; (out) husmear, olfatear; (suspect) sospechar. —*n* perfume, *m;* fragancia, *f,* aroma, *m;* (smell) olor, *m;* (of hounds) viento, *m;* (of game, etc.) rastro, viento, *m;* (*fig* of person) nariz, *f;* (trail) pista, *f.* **to lose the s.,** perder la pista. **to s. danger,** oler el peligro. **to throw off the s.,** despistar. **s.-bottle,** frasco de perfume, *m.* **s.-spray,** pulverizador, *m*

scented /ˈsɛntɪd/ *a* perfumado; (of roses, etc.) de olor, oloroso; (in compounds) de... olfato. **s. sweet pea,** guisante de olor, *m*

scentless /ˈsɛntlɪs/ *a* sin olor; inodoro

scepter /ˈsɛptər/ *n* cetro, *m*

sceptic /ˈskɛptɪk/ *n* escéptico (-ca)

sceptical /ˈskɛptɪkəl/ *a* escéptico

scepticism /ˈskɛptəˌsɪzəm/ *n* escepticismo, *m*

schedule /ˈskɛdʒul/ *n* lista, *m;* programa, *m;* (of taxes) clase, *f;* (of trains, etc.) horario, *m.* —*vt* poner en una lista; inventariar

scheme /skim/ *n* plan, *m;* proyecto, *m;* diagrama, esquema, *m;* (summary) resumen, *m;* (of colors, etc.) combinación, *f;* (plot) intriga, maquinación, *f.* —*vt* proyectar. —*vi* planear, formar planes; (intrigue) intrigar, conspirar. **color s.,** combinación de colores, *f*

schemer /ˈskimər/ *n* (plotter) intrigante, *mf*

scheming /ˈskimɪŋ/ *a* intrigante; astuto. —*n* planes, proyectos, *m pl;* intrigas, maquinaciones, *f pl*

schism /ˈsɪzəm, ˈskɪz-/ *n* cisma, *mf*

schismatic /sɪzˈmætɪk, skɪz-/ *a* cismático. —*n* cismático (-ca)

scholar /ˈskɒlər/ *n* (at school) colegial (-la); (disciple) alumno (-na); (student) estudiante, *mf;* (learned person) erudito (-ta), hombre de letras, *m;* (scholarship holder) becario, *m.*

scholarly /'skɒlərli/ *a* de sabio, de hombre de letras; erudito

scholarship /'skɒlər,ʃɪp/ *n* erudición, *f;* saber, *m;* (exhibition) beca, *f.* **s. holder,** becario, *m*

scholastic /skə'læstɪk/ *a* escolar, escolástico; pedante; (medieval) escolástico. —*n* escolástico, *m.* **the s. profession,** el magisterio

school /skul/ *n* escuela, *f;* colegio, *m;* academia, *f;* *educ* departamento, *m;* (faculty) facultad, *f;* (of fish) banco, *m.* —*vt* enseñar, instruir; formar; disciplinar. **in s.,** en clase. **day s.,** escuela, *f,* colegio, *m.* **the Florentine s.,** (of painting) la escuela florentina. **the lower s.,** los alumnos del preparatorio. **private s.,** colegio particular, *m.* **s.-bag,** vademécum, *m.* **s.-book,** libro escolar, *m.* **s.-days,** los días de escuela; los años de colegio. **in his s.-days,** cuando él iba a la escuela. **s.-fees,** gastos de la enseñanza, *m pl,* cuota escolar, *f,*

schoolboy /'skul,bɔi/ *n* muchacho de escuela, colegial, *m*

school district *n* sector escolar, *m*

schoolfellow /'skul,fɛlou/ *n* compañero de colegio, condiscípulo, *m*

schoolgirl /'skul,gɜrl/ *n* colegiala, *f*

schooling /'skulɪŋ/ *n* educación, enseñanza, *f*

schoolmaster /'skul,mæstər/ *n* maestro de escuela, professor, *m*

schoolmistress /'skul,mɪstrɪs/ *n* maestra de escuela, profesora, *f*

school of hard knocks *n* universidad sin tejados, *f*

schoolroom /'skul,rum/ *n* aula, sala de clase, salón de clase, *m*

schooner /'skunər/ *n* *naut* escuna, goleta, *f*

sciatic /sai'ætɪk/ *a* ciático

sciatica /sai'ætɪkə/ *n* ciática, *f*

science /'saiəns/ *n* ciencia, *f*

scientific /,saiən'tɪfɪk/ *a* científico; exacto, sistemático

scientifically /,saiən'tɪfɪkli/ *adv* científicamente

scientist /'saiəntɪst/ *n* hombre de ciencia, *m,* científico (-ca)

scimitar /'sɪmɪtər, -,tɑr/ *n* cimitarra, *f*

scintilla /sɪn'tɪlə/ *n* *fig* átomo, vestigio, *m*

scintillate /'sɪntḷ,eit/ *vi* centellear, lucir, chispear; (of persons) brillar

scion /'saiən/ *n* (sucker) acodo, *m;* (shoot) vástago, renuevo, *m;* (human) descendiente, *mf.* **s. of a noble race,** vástago de una raza noble, *m*

scissors /'sɪzərz/ *n pl* tijeras, *f pl.* **s.-sharpener,** amolador, *m*

sclerosis /sklɪ'rousɪs/ *n* *med* esclerosis, *f*

sclerotic /sklɪ'rɒtɪk/ *n* *anat* esclerótica, *f*

scoff /skɔf, skɒf/ *n* burla, mofa, *f.* —*vi* burlarse. **to s. at,** burlarse de, mofarse de

scoffer /'skɔfər, 'skɒf-/ *n* mofador (-ra); (at religion, etc.) incrédulo (-la)

scoffing /'skɔfɪŋ, 'skɒf-/ *a* burlón. —*n* mofas, burlas, *f pl*

scold /skould/ *n* virago, *f, vt* reñir, reprender

scolding /'skouldɪŋ/ *n* reprensión, increpación, *f*

sconce /skɒns/ *n* cubo de candelero, *m;* candelabro de pared, *m;* cornucopia, *f*

scone /skoun, skɒn/ *n* bollo, *m*

scoop /skup/ *n* pala de mano, *f;* cuchara de draga, *f;* (boat) achicador, *m;* (financial) golpe, *m;* (journalistic) éxito periodistico, *m.* —*vt* sacar con pala (de); sacar con cuchara (de); (shares, etc.) comprar, obtener. **to s. out,** vaciar; excavar; (bail) achicar

scooter /'skutər/ *n* (child's) patinete, patín del diablo, *m;* monopatín, *m*

scope /skoup/ *n* alcance, *m;* esfera de acción, *f;* lugar, *m.* **to give full s. to,** dar rienda suelta a. **to have full s.,** tener plena oportunidad; tener todas las facilidades. **within the s. of,** dentro del alcance de

scorbutic /skɔr'byutɪk/ *a* *med* escorbútico

scorch /skɔrtʃ/ *vt* chamuscar; (the skin) tostar; (of the sun) abrasar, quemar; (wither) agostar. **to s. along,** ir como un relámpago. **scorching,** *a* abrasador, ardiente; *fig* mordaz

score /skɔr/ *n* (scratch) rasguño, *m;* señal, *f;* (crossing out) raya, *f;* (reckoning) cuenta, *f,* escote, *m;* (notch) muesca, *f;* *sports* tanteo, *m,* puntuación, *f;* (point) punto, tanto, *m;* (twenty) veintena, *f;* (reason) motivo, *m,* causa, *f;* respecto, *m;* *mus* partitura, *f.* —*vt* marcar; rayar; (erase) tachar, borrar; (cricket runs, etc.) hacer; (goals) marcar; (points) ganar; (reckon) apuntar. **s. a triumph,** apuntarse un triunfo; *mus* instrumentar; (for orchestra) orquestar. —*vi* (be fortunate) llevar la ventaja. **to pay off old scores,** ajustar cuentas viejas. **to s. off someone,** ganar un punto (a), triunfar de. **upon that s.,** a ese respecto; por esa causa. **Upon what s.?** ¿Con qué motivo? **s.-board,** marcador, *m*

scorer /'skɔrər/ *n* (of a goal, etc.) tanteador, *m;* (keeper of score) marcador, *m*

scoria /'skɔriə/ *n* escoria, *f*

scorn /skɔrn/ *n* desprecio, desdén, *m.* —*vt* despreciar, desdeñar; reírse de. **to s. to do,** no dignarse hacer

scornful /'skɔrnfəl/ *a* desdeñoso, despreciativo

scornfully /'skɔrnfəli/ *adv* desdeñosamente, con desprecio

Scorpion /'skɔrpiən/ *n* Escorpión, *m*

scorpion /'skɔrpiən/ *n* escorpión, alacrán, *m;* *astron* Escorpión, *m*

Scot /skɒt/ *n* escocés, *m*

scotch /skɒtʃ/ *vt* (kill) matar; (thwart) frustrar; (a wheel) calzar

Scotland /'skɒtlənd/ Escocia, *f*

Scotswoman /'skɒts,wʊmən/ *n* escocesa, *f*

Scottish /'skɒtɪʃ/ *a* escocés

scoundrel /'skaundrəl/ *n* canalla, sinvergüenza, *mf*

scour /skauər/ *vt* (traverse) recorrer, batir; (pans, etc.) fregar, estregar; (free from) limpiar (de); (of water) arrastrar

scourge /skɜrdʒ/ *vt* azotar, flagelar; castigar, mortificar. —*n* disciplinas, *f pl;* *fig* verdugo, *m,* plaga, *f*

scout /skaut/ *n* *mil* batidor, explorador, *m.* —*vi* *mil* explorar, reconocer. —*vt* (flout) rechazar a mano airada, rechazar con desdén. **boy s.,** muchacho explorador, *m*

scowl /skaul/ *vi* fruncir el ceño. —*n* ceño, *m.* **to s. at,** mirar con ceño

scowling /'skaulɪŋ/ *a* amenazador

scragginess /'skrægin ɪs/ *n* magrez, flaqueza, *f*

scraggy /'skrægi/ *a* flaco, magro, descarnado

scramble /'skræmbəl/ *vi* trepar. —*vt* (throw) arrojar; (eggs) revolver. **scrambled eggs,** huevos revueltos, *m pl.* **to s. for,** andar a la rebatiña por; (for coins, etc.) luchar para. **to s. up,** escalar; subir a gatas

scrap /skræp/ *n* pedazo, *m;* fragmento, *m;* pizca, brizna, *f;* (shindy) suiza, camorra, *f;* (boxing) combate de boxeo, *m;* *pl* **scraps,** desperdicios, *m pl;* (food) restos de la comida, *m pl.* —*vt* desechar; (expunge) borrar; *vi* (fight) armar camorra. **a few scraps of news,** algunas noticias. **Do you mind not coming? Not a s.,** ¿Te importa no venir? Ni pizca. **s.-book,** álbum de recortes, *m;* **s.-heap,** depósito de basura, *m;* *fig* olvido, *m.* **s. iron,** chatarra, *f,* hierro viejo, *m*

scrape /skreip/ *vt* raspar, rascar, raer; (one's shoes) restregar; (a musical instrument) rascar. —*n* rasguño, *m;* ruido de raspar, *m;* (predicament) lío, apuro, *m;* dificultad, *f.* **to s. acquaintance with,** trabar amistad con. **to s. along,** *inf* ir tirando. **to s. away,** rascar; quitar. **to s. through,** (an examination) aprobar justo. **to s. together,** amontonar poco a poco

scrappy /'skræpi/ *a* escaso; fragmentario; (incoherent) descosido. **a s. meal,** una comida escasa

scratch /skrætʃ/ *vt* arañar; (the earth) escarbar; (rub) rascar; (a hole) hacer; (sketch) dibujar, trazar; (a horse) retirar de una carrera. —*vi* arañar; rascar; escarbar; (of a pen) rasguear; (back out) retirarse. —*n* arañazo, *m;* (of a pen) rasgueo, *m;* (in a race) línea de salida, *f;* (in games) cero, *m.* —*a* improvisado. **The dog scratched at the door,** El perro arañó la puerta. **to come up to s.,** estar al nivel de las circunstancias. **to s. one's head,** rascarse la cabeza. **to s. a person's eyes out,** sacar los ojos con las uñas (a). **to s. the surface of,** (a subject) tratar superficialmente. **to s. out,** tachar

scrawl /skrɔl/ *vi* hacer garabatos. —*vt* garabatear, garrapatear. —*n* garabato, *m*

scream /skrim/ *vt* and *vi* chillar. —*n* chillido, *m.* **It was a perfect s.** Era para morirse de risa. **to s. with laughter,** reírse a carcajadas, morirse de risa

screaming /'skrimɪŋ/ *n* chillidos, *m pl.* —*a* chillador; (piercing) penetrante, agudo; (funny) divertidisimo
screech /skritʃ/ *vi* chillar; (of owls, etc.) ulular; graznar. —*n* chillido, *m,* ululación, *f;* graznido, *m.* **s.-owl,** úlula, *f*
screed /skrid/ *n* arenga, *f;* cita larga, *f*
screen /skrin/ *n* biombo, *m;* (wire) tela metálica, *f;* (nonfolding) mampara, *f;* (*ecol*) cancel, *m;* (cinema, television) pantalla, *f;* (of trees, etc., and *mil*) cortina, *f;* (*fig* protection) abrigo, *m.* —*vt* proteger; (shelter) abrigar; (hide) esconder, ocultar; (a light) proteger con pantalla; (a film) proyectar; (sieve) cribar, cerner; (examine) investigar. **to s. from view,** ocultar la vista (de), esconder. **s. star,** estrella de la pantalla, *f*
screw /skru/ *n* tornillo, *m;* (propeller) hélice, *f;* vuelta de tornillo, *f;* presión, *f;* (miser) tacaño, *m;* (salary) salario, *m.* —*vt* atornillar; torcer; apretar, oprimir. **He has a s. loose,** Le falta un tornillo. **to s. down,** sujetar con tornillos. **to s. up,** cerrar con tornillos. **to s. up one's courage,** tomar coraje. **to s. up one's eyes,** desojarse, entornar los ojos. **s.-driver,** destornillador, *m*
scribble /'skrɪbəl/ *vt* escribir de prisa, *vi* garabatear, garrapatear; escribir, ser autor. —*n* garabato, garrapato, *m;* mala letra, letra ilegible, *f;* (note) billete, *m*
scribbler /'skrɪblər/ *n* el, *m,* (*f,* la) que tiene mala letra; (author) autor (-ra) malo (-la)
scribbling /'skrɪblɪŋ/ *n* garabateo, *m.* **s.-block,** bloque de papel, *m*
scribe /skraib/ *n* escribiente, copista, *mf;* (Jewish history) escriba, *m*
scrimmage /'skrɪmɪdʒ/ *n* reyerta, pelea, camorra, *f;* (Rugby) mêlée, *f*
script /skrɪpt/ *n* letra cursiva, *f; print* plumilla, *f;* manuscrito, *m; law* escritura, *f;* examen escrito, *m;* (film) escenario, *m*
scriptural /'skrɪptʃərəl/ *a* bíblico
Scripture /'skrɪptʃər/ *n* Sagrada Escritura, *f.* **Scriptures,** Escrituras, *f pl;* (of non-Christian religions) los libros sagrados
scrivener /'skrɪvnər/ *n* chupatintas, *mf*
scrofula /'skrɒfyələ/ *n* escrófula, *f*
scrofulous /'skrɒfyələs/ *a* escrofuloso
scroll /skroul/ *n* (of paper, etc.) rollo, *m;* pergamino, *m;* (flourish) rúbrica, *f;* (of an Ionic capital) voluta, *f.* **s. of fame,** lista de la fama, *f*
scrotum /'skroutəm/ *n anat* escroto, *m*
scrounge /skraundʒ/ *vi* sablear. —*vt* dar un sablazo (a); hurtar
scrounger /'skraundʒər/ *n* sablista, *mf*
scrub /skrʌb/ *vt* fregar; limpiar; restregar. —*n* fregado, *m;* limpieza, *f;* fricción, *f;* (brushwood) matorral, breñal, *m,* maleza, *f*
scrubbing /'skrʌbɪŋ/ *n* fregado, *m.* **s.-brush,** cepillo para el suelo, *m*
scrubby /'skrʌbi/ *a* (of plants) anémico; (of persons) insignificante, pobre; (of land) cubierto de maleza
scruff /skrʌf/ *n* nuca, *f,* pescuezo, *m*
scruple /'skrupəl/ *n* escrúpulo, *m.* —*vi* tener escrúpulos. **to have no scruples,** no tener escrúpulos
scrupulous /'skrupyələs/ *a* escrupuloso; exacto, meticuloso
scrupulously /'skrupyələsli/ *adv* escrupulosamente; meticulosamente
scrupulousness /'skrupyələsnɪs/ *n* escrupulosidad, *f;* meticulosidad, *f*
scrutinize /'skrutn̩ˌaiz/ *vt* escudriñar, examinar; (votes) escrutar
scrutinizer /'skrutn̩ˌaizər/ *n* escudriñador (-ra); (of votes) escrutador (-ra)
scrutinizing /'skrutn̩ˌaizɪŋ/ escrutador
scrutiny /'skrutn̩i/ *n* escrutinio, *m*
scud /skʌd/ *vi* correr; deslizarse; flotar. **to s. before the wind,** ir viento en popa
scuffle /'skʌfəl/ *vi* pelear, forcejear, andar a la rebatiña. —*n* refriega, pelea, sarracina, arrebatiña, *f*
scull /skʌl/ *n* remo, *m, vi* remar
scullery /'skʌləri/ *n* fregadero, *m.* **s. maid,** fregona, *f*
sculptor /'skʌlptər/ *n* escultor, *m,* escultora, *f*
sculptural /'skʌlptʃərəl/ *a* escultural, escultórico
sculpture /'skʌlptʃər/ *n* escultura, *f, vt* esculpir
scum /skʌm/ *n* espuma, *f;* (dregs) heces, *f pl.* —*vt* espumar. **s. of the earth,** las heces de la sociedad
scupper /'skʌpər/ *n Naut.* clava, *f.* —*vt* abrir las clavas (de); (frustrate) frustrar, destruir
scurrility /skə'rɪlɪti/ *n* grosería, indecencia, *f*
scurrilous /'skɜrələs/ *a* grosero, indecente
scurry /'skɜri/ *vi* echar a correr. —*n* fuga precipitada, *f;* (of rain) chaparrón, *m;* (of snow) remolino, *m.* **to s. off,** escabullirse. **to s. through,** hacer de prisa, terminar rápidamente
S-curve /'ɛsˌkɜrv/ *n* curva doble, *f*
scurvy /'skɜrvi/ *a* tiñoso, vil, ruin. —*n* escorbuto, *m.* **a s. trick,** una mala pasada
scuttle /'skʌtl̩/ *n* (trap-door) escotillón, *m; naut* escotilla, *f;* (for coal) carbonera, *f;* (flight) huida precipitada, *f.* —*vt* (a boat) echar a pique, *vi* (run away) escabullirse, apretar a correr
scythe /saið/ *n* dalle, *m,* guadaña, *f, vt* dallar, segar
sea /si/ *n* mar, *m,* or *f;* ola, *f;* multitud, *f.* **Black Sea,** Mar Negro. **Mediteranean Sea,** (Mar) Mediterráneo, *m.* **at sea,** en el mar; perplejo. **beyond the seas,** allende los mares. **by sea,** por mar. **by the sea,** a la orilla del mar. **high seas,** alta mar, *f.* **the seven seas,** todos los mares del mundo. **to go to sea,** hacerse marinero. **to put to sea,** hacerse a la mar, hacerse a la vela. **sea-anemone,** anémone de mar. *f.* **sea-bathing,** baños de mar, *m pl.* **sea-breeze,** brisa de mar, *f.* **sea captain,** capitán de mar, *m.* **sea chart,** carta de marear, *f.* **sea-coast,** litoral, *m,* costa marítima, *f.* **sea-cow,** manatí, *m.* **sea dog,** lobo de mar, *m.* **sea-fight,** combate naval, *m.* **sea-foam,** espuma de mar, *f.* **sea-girt,** rodeado por el mar. **sea-going,** de altura; navegante. **sea-going craft,** embarcación de alta mar, *f.* **sea-green,** verdemar, *m.* **sea-gull,** gaviota, *f.* **sea-horse,** caballo marino, *m.* **sea-legs,** piernas de marino, *f pl.* **sea-level,** nivel del mar, *m.* **sea-lion,** león marino, *m.* **sea-mist,** bruma, *f.* **sea-nymph,** nereida, *f.* **sea-power,** potencia naval, *f.* **sea-serpent,** serpiente de mar, *f.* **sea-sick,** mareado. **to be sea-sick,** marearse. **sea-sickness,** mal de mar, *m.* **sea-trip,** viaje por mar, *m.* **sea-urchin,** erizo de mar, *m.* **sea-wall,** dique de mar, *m*
seafarer /'siˌfɛərər/ *n* (traveller) viajero (-ra) por mar; (sailor) marinero, *m*
seafaring /'siˌfɛərɪŋ/ *a* marinero, marino. —*n* viajes por mar, *m pl;* vida del marinero, *f*
seal /sil/ *n zool* foca, *f,* lobo marino, *m;* piel de foca, *f;* sello, *m;* (stamp) estampillo, timbre, *m; vt* sellar; (stamp) estampar; (letters, etc.) cerrar; *vi* cazar focas. **His fate is sealed,** Su suerte está determinada. **His lips were sealed,** Sus labios estaban cerrados. **under my hand and s.,** firmado y sellado por mí. **s.-ring,** sortija de sello, *f*
sealing wax /'silɪŋ/ *n* lacre, *m*
sealskin /'silˌskɪn/ *n* piel de foca, *f*
seam /sim/ *n sew* costura, *f; naut* costura de los tablones, *f; anat* sutura, *f; surg* cicatriz, *f;* (wrinkle) arruga, *f,* surco, *m; geol* capa, *f,* yacimiento, *m; mineral* vena, *f,* filón, *m.* —*vt* coser; juntar; (a face) surcar, arrugar
seaman /'simən/ *n* marinero, *m;* hombre de mar, *m;* navegante, *m.* **able-bodied s.,** marinero práctico, *m*
seamanlike /'simənˌlaik/ *a* de marinero, marino; de buen marinero
seamanship /'simənˌʃɪp/ *n* marinería, *f;* náutica, *f*
seamstress /'simstrɪs/ *n* costurera, *f*
seamy /'simi/ *a* con costuras. **the s. side of life,** el lado peor de la vida
seance /'seians/ *n* sesión, junta, *f;* sesión de espiritistas, *f*
seaplane /'siˌplein/ *n* hidroavión, hidroplano, *m*
seaport /'siˌpɔrt/ *n* puerto de mar, *m*
sear /sɪər/ *a* marchito. —*vt* agostar, secar; (a wound) cauterizar; marchitar, ajar; (a conscience) endurecer
search /sɜrtʃ/ *vt* registrar; (a wound) explorar; examinar; escudriñar; investigar. —*vi* buscar. —*n* busca, *f;* (of luggage, etc.) reconocimiento, *m.* **in s. of,** en busca de. **to s. after, for,** buscar; ir al encuentro de. **to s. out,** ir en busca de; preguntar por. **right of s.,** (international law) derecho de visita, *m.* **s.-party,** pelotón de salvamento, *m.* **s.-warrant,** auto de recono-

cimiento, auto de registro domiciliario, orden de allanamiento, orden de cateo, *m*

searching /ˈsɜrtʃɪŋ/ *a* escrutador; penetrante; minucioso. **a s. look,** una mirada penetrante. **a s. wind,** un viento penetrante. **a s. question,** una pregunta perspicaz

searchlight /ˈsɜrtʃˌlait/ *n* reflector, proyector, *m*

seashore /ˈsiˌʃɔr/ *n* playa, *f;* orilla del mar, *f*

seaside /ˈsiˌsaid/ *n* orilla del mar, *f;* playa, *f.* **to go to the s.,** ir al mar, ir a la playa

season /ˈsizən/ *n* estación, *f;* sazón, *f;* temporada, *f;* tiempo, *m.* —*vt* (food) sazonar; (wood, wine) madurar; (accustom) acostumbrar, aclimatar; (with wit, etc.) salpimentar; (temper) templar, moderar. —*vi* madurarse. **at that s.,** a la sazón. **close s.,** veda, *f.* **in s.,** en sazón; a su tiempo. **out of s.,** fuera de sazón; fuera de tiempo, inoportuno. **the dead s.,** la estación muerta. **the autumn s.,** el otoño; (for social functions, etc.) la temporada de otoño. **s. ticket,** billete de abono, *m*

seasonable /ˈsizənəbəl/ *a* de estación; tempestivo, oportuno

seasonably /ˈsizənəbli/ *adv* en sazón; oportunamente

seasonal /ˈsizənl̩/ *a* estacional; de temporada

seasonal worker *n* trabajador por temporada, *m*

seasoned /ˈsizənd/ *a* (of food) sazonado; (of wood, etc.) maduro. **highly-s.,** (of a dish) picante, con muchas especies

seasoning /ˈsizənɪŋ/ *n cul* condimento, *m;* madurez, *f;* aclimatación, *f; fig* salsa, sal, *f*

seat /sit/ *n* asiento, *m;* (bench) banco, *m;* (chair) silla, *f;* (in a cinema, etc.) localidad, *f;* (*theat* etc., ticket) entrada, *f;* (of a person) trasero, *m,* asentaderas, *f pl;* (of trousers) fondillos, *m pl;* (of government, etc.) sede, capital, *f;* (of war, etc.) teatro, *m;* (place) sitio, lugar, *m;* (house) casa solar, *f.* —*vt* sentar; poner en una silla (a); encontrar sitio; (of buildings) tener... asientos; (a chair) poner asiento (a). **The hall seats a thousand,** La sala tiene mil asientos, Hay mil asientos en la sala. **Please be seated!** ¡Haga el favor de sentarse! **to be seated,** estar sentado; sentarse. **to have a good s.,** (on a horse) caer bien a caballo. **to hold a s. in parliament,** ser diputado a Cortes. **to keep one's s.,** permanecer sentado. **to take a s.,** tomar asiento, sentarse. **s.-back,** respaldo, *m.* **s. belt,** cinturón de seguridad, *m*

seater /ˈsitər/ *n* de... asientos. **four-s.,** automóvil de cuatro asientos, *m*

seaweed /ˈsiˌwid/ *n* alga marina, *f*

seaworthy /ˈsiˌwɜrði/ *a* (of a ship) en buen estado; marinero

sebaceous /sɪˈbeiʃəs/ *a* sebáceo

secede /sɪˈsid/ *vi* retirarse (de); separarse (de)

secession /sɪˈsɛʃən/ *n* secesión, *f*

secessionist /sɪˈsɛʃənɪst/ *n* secesionista, *mf; polit* separatista, *mf.* —*a* secesionista; *polit* separatista

secluded /sɪˈkludɪd/ *a* apartado, retirado; solitario

seclusion /sɪˈkluʒən/ *n* reclusión, *f;* apartamiento, retiro, *m;* soledad, *f*

second /sɪˈkɒnd/ *a* segundo; otro; igual. —*adv* en segundo lugar; después. —*n* segundo, *m;* (in a duel) padrino, *m;* (helper) ayudante, *m;* (boxing) segundo, *m;* (railway compartment) departamento de segunda (clase), *m; mus* segunda, *f;* (of time) segundo, *m;* (moment) instante, momento, *m.* —*vt* secundar; (a motion) apoyar; *mil* ayudar. **the s. of May,** el dos de mayo. **James the S.,** Jaime el segundo. **on s. thoughts,** después de pensarlo bien. **every s. day,** cada dos días. **They live on the s. floor,** Viven en el primer piso (since the ground floor is not counted separately in Spanish speaking areas, the American second floor = the Spanish **primer piso**). **the s. largest,** el más grande menos uno. **to be s. to none,** no ser inferior a ninguno; (of persons) no ser inferior a nadie; no ceder a nadie. **to come off s.,** llegar el segundo; ser vencido. **seconds hand,** (of watch) segundero, *m.* **s.-in-command,** segundo, *m;* subjefe, *m.* **s.-best,** segundo. **My s.-best hat,** Mi sombrero número dos. **to come off s.-best,** salir mal parado, ser vencido. **s. class,** segunda clase, *f.* **s.-class,** de segunda clase; de calidad inferior; mediocre. **s. cousin,** primo (-ma) segundo (-a). **s. gear,** segunda velocidad, *f.* **s.-hand,** *a* usado; de ocasión; no nuevo. —*adv* de segunda mano. **s.-hand car,** un coche de segunda mano. **s.-hand clothing,** ropa usada, *f.* **s. lieutenant,** *mil* subteniente, segundo teniente, *m; nav* alférez de fragata, *m.* **s.-rate,** *a* inferior, mediocre. **s. sight,** doble vista, *f*

secondary /ˈsɛkənˌdɛri/ *a* secundario; subordinado; accesorio; poco importante. **s. education,** enseñanza secundaria, *f*

seconder /ˈsɛkəndər/ *n* ayudante, *m;* el, *m,* (*f,* la) que apoya una proposición

secondly /ˈsɛkəndli/ *adv* en segundo lugar

secrecy /ˈsikrəsi/ *n* secreto, *m;* reserva, *f,* silencio, *m.* **in the s. of one's own heart,** en lo más íntimo de su corazón

secret /ˈsikrɪt/ *a* secreto; clandestino; (of persons) reservado, taciturno; (secluded) remoto, apartado; oculto; misterioso. —*n* secreto, *m;* (key) clave, *f.* **a s. code,** un código secreto. **in s.,** en secreto, secretamente. **open s.,** secreto a voces. **to keep a s.,** guardar un secreto. **to keep s.,** tener secreto, ocultar. **s. drawer,** secreto, *m.*

secretaire /ˌsɛkrɪˈtɛər/ *n* secreter, escritorio, *m*

secretarial /ˌsɛkrɪˈtɛəriəl/ *a* de secretario. **s. college,** academia comercial, *f*

secretariat /ˌsɛkrɪˈtɛəriət/ *n* secretaría, *f*

secretary /ˈsɛkrɪˌtɛri/ *n* secretario (-ia). **private s.,** secretario (-ia) particular. **S. of State,** ministro, *m;* Ministro de Estado, *m*

secrete /sɪˈkrit/ *vt* esconder, ocultar; *med* secretar

secretion /sɪˈkriʃən/ *n* escondimiento, *m; med* secreción, *f*

secretive /ˈsikrɪtɪv/ *a* reservado, callado

secretly /ˈsikrɪtli/ *adv* en secreto, secretamente; ocultamente, a escondidas

sect /sɛkt/ *n* secta, *f*

sectarian /sɛkˈtɛəriən/ *a* and *n* sectario (-ia)

sectarianism /sɛkˈtɛəriəˌnɪzəm/ *n* sectarismo, *m*

section /ˈsɛkʃən/ *n* sección, *f;* porción, *f;* subdivisión, *f;* (of a law) artículo, *m.* —*vt* seccionar. **conic s.,** sección cónica, *f*

sectional /ˈsɛkʃənl̩/ *a* en secciones. **s. bookcase,** biblioteca desmontable, *f*

sector /ˈsɛktər/ *n* sector, *m*

secular /ˈsɛkyələr/ *a* (very old) secular; (lay) seglar; laico; profano. **s. music,** música profana, *f.* **s. school,** escuela laica, *f*

secularization /ˌsɛkyələrəˈzeiʃən/ *n* secularización, *f*

secularize /ˈsɛkyəlaˌraiz/ *vt* secularizar

secure /sɪˈkyʊr/ *a* seguro; (certain) asegurado; (safe) en seguridad; sano y salvo; (firm) firme; fijo; (confident (in)) confiado (en). —*vt* asegurar; (insure) garantizar; (lock) cerrar; (confine) prender; (acquire) adquirir, obtener; lograr, conseguir

securely /sɪˈkyʊrli/ *adv* seguramente; en seguridad, sin peligro; con confianza; (firmly) firmemente

security /sɪˈkyʊrɪti/ *n* seguridad, *f;* protección, defensa, *f;* garantía, *f;* (faith) confianza, *f; com* fianza, *f;* (person) fiador, *m; pl* **securities,** valores, títulos, *m pl.* **government securities,** papel del Estado, *m.* **to give s.,** *com* dar fianza. **to stand s. for,** *com* salir fiador de

sedan-chair /sɪˈdænˌtʃɛər/ *n* silla de manos, *f*

sedate /sɪˈdeit/ *a* tranquilo, sosegado; formal, serio, grave

sedately /sɪˈdeitli/ *adv* sosegadamente; seriamente

sedateness /sɪˈdeitnɪs/ *n* sosiego, *m,* tranquilidad, *f;* formalidad, compostura, *f*

sedative /ˈsɛdətɪv/ *a* and *n* sedativo, calmante *m*

sedentary /ˈsɛdn̩ˌtɛri/ *a* sedentario

sediment /ˈsɛdəmənt/ *n* sedimento, *m*

sedimentation /ˌsɛdəmənˈteiʃən/ *n* sedimentación, *f*

sedition /sɪˈdɪʃən/ *n* sedición, *f*

seditious /sɪˈdɪʃəs/ *a* sedicioso

seduce /sɪˈdus/ *vt* seducir

seducer /sɪˈdusər/ *n* seductor, *m*

seduction /sɪˈdʌkʃən/ *n* seducción, *f*

seductive /sɪˈdʌktɪv/ *a* seductivo, atractivo; persuasivo

sedulous /ˈsɛdʒələs/ *a* asiduo, diligente

see /si/ *n* sede, *f.* **The Holy S.,** la Santa Sede, *f*

see /si/ *vt* and *vi* ver; mirar; (understand) comprender; (visit) visitar; (attend to) atender a; ocuparse de. **He sees the matter quite differently,** Él mira el asunto de un modo completamente distinto, Su punto de vista sobre el asunto es completamente distinto. **You are not fit to be seen,** No eres nada presentable. **See you next Tuesday!** ¡Hasta el miércoles que viene! **I see!** ¡Ya! ¡Ahora comprendo! **Let's see!** ¡Vamos a ver! **Shall I see you home?** ¿Quieres que te acompañe a casa? **to go and see,** ir a ver. **to see red,** echar chispas. **to see the sights,** visitar los monumentos. **to see life,** ver mundo. **to see service,** servir (en el ejército, etc.). **to see about,** atender a; pensar en; ocuparse de. **to see after,** cuidar de; atender (a); ocuparse de. **to see again,** volver a ver. **to see into,** investigar, examinar. **to see off,** (at the station, etc.) ir a despedir; acompañar. **to see out,** (a person) acompañar a la puerta; (a play, etc.) quedarse hasta el fin (de); no dejar el puesto. **to see over,** inspeccionar. **to see through,** (a house, etc.) inspeccionar; (a person) calarle las intenciones; (a mystery) penetrar; (a person through trouble) ayudar. **to see it through,** llevarlo al cabo; quedarse hasta el fin. **to see to,** atender a; ocuparse de; encargarse de. **to see to everything,** encargarse de todo

seed /sid/ *n* semilla, *f;* simiente, *f;* (of fruit) pepita, *f,* grano, *m; fig* germen, *m;* (offspring) prole, descendencia, *f.* —*vi* granar. —*vt* sembrar. **s.-bed,** almáciga, *f,* semillero, *m.* **s.-pearl,** aljófar, *m.* **s.-plot,** sementera, *f; fig* semillero, *m.* **s.-time,** tiempo de sembrar, *m*

seedling /'sidlɪŋ/ *n* planta de semilla, *f*

seedsman /'sidzmən/ *n* tratante en semillas, *m*

seedy /'sidi/ *a* granado; (of clothes) raído, roto; (of persons) andrajoso, desharrapado; infeliz, desgraciado; (ill) indispuesto, malucho

seeing /'siɪŋ/ *n* vista, *f;* visión, *f.* **It is worth s.,** Vale la pena de verse. **s. that...,** visto que, dado que, como que. **S. is believing,** Ver es creer

seek /sik/ *vt* buscar; solicitar, pretender; (demand) pedir; (investigate) investigar; (to do something) procurar, tratar de. **They are much sought after,** Son muy populares, Están en demanda. **to s. after,** buscar; perseguir. **to s. for,** buscar

seeker /'siker/ *n* el, *m,* (*f,* la) que busca; investigador (-ra)

seem /sim/ *vi* parecer. **He seemed honest,** Parecía honrado. **It seemed to me,** Me pareció a mí. **It seems that they were both at home last night,** Parece ser que ambos estaban en casa anoche

seeming /'simɪŋ/ *a* aparente; supuesto

seemingly /'simɪŋli/ *adv* aparentemente; en apariencia

seemliness /'simlinɪs/ *n* decoro, *m*

seemly /'simli/ *a* decoroso, decente

seep /sip/ *vi* filtrar; rezumarse

seer /sɪər/ *n* profeta, *m*

seesaw /'siˌsɔ/ *n* columpio, *m;* vaivén, *m.* —*vi* columpiarse; balancearse, oscilar. —*a* de vaivén, oscilante

seethe /sið/ *vi* hervir; *fig* bullir

segment /'sɛgmənt/ *n* segmento, *m*

segregate /*v.* 'sɛgrɪˌgeit; *a.* -gɪt/ *vt* segregar. —*vi* segregarse. —*a* segregado

segregation /ˌsɛgrɪ'geiʃən/ *n* segregación, *f*

Seine, the /sɛn/ el Sena, *m*

seismic /'saizmɪk/ *a* sísmico

seismograph /'saizməˌgræf/ *n* sismógrafo, *m*

seismological /ˌsaizmə'lɒdʒɪkəl/ *a* sismológico

seismology /saiz'mɒlədʒi/ *n* sismología, *f*

seize /siz/ *vt law* embargar; apoderarse de; asir; (a person) prender; coger; (a meaning) comprender; (an occasion, etc.) aprovecharse de; (of emotions) dominar; (of illnesses) atacar. —*vi mech* atascarse. **He was seized by fear,** Le dominó el miedo. **to s. the opportunity,** aprovecharse de la oportunidad. **to s. upon a pretext,** valerse de un pretexto

seizure /'siʒər/ *n* asimiento, *m;* (of property) embargo, secuestro, *m;* (of a person) captura, *f;* arresto, *m; med* ataque, *m*

seldom /'sɛldəm/ *adv* rara vez, raramente; pocas veces

select /sɪ'lɛkt/ *a* escogido, selecto; exclusivista. —*vt* escoger

selection /sɪ'lɛkʃən/ *n* selección, *f.* **selections from Cervantes,** trozos escogidos de Cervantes, *m pl.* **to make a s. from,** escoger entre. **s. committee,** comité de selección, *m*

selective /sɪ'lɛktɪv/ *a* selectivo

self /sɛlf/ *n* mismo (-a), propio (-a); sí mismo (-a), se; personalidad, *f;* ser, *m.* **all by one's s.,** sin ayuda de nadie; solo; *inf* solito. **my other s.,** mi otro yo. **my better s.,** mi mejor parte. **the s.,** el yo. **s.-abasement,** humillación de sí mismo, *f.* **s.-acting,** automático. **s.-apparent,** evidente, patente. **s.-appointed,** nombrado por uno mismo. **s.-assertion,** presunción, *f.* **s.-assertive,** presumido. **s.-assurance,** confianza en sí mismo, *f;* aplomo, *m;* (impertinence) cara dura, frescura, *f.* **s.-centered,** egocéntrico. **s.-colored,** del mismo color; de su color natural. **s.-command,** dominio de sí mismo, *m;* sangre fría, ecuanimidad, *f.* **s.-complacent,** satisfecho de sí mismo. **s.-conceit,** vanidad, arrogancia, petulancia, *f.* **s.-confidence,** confianza en sí mismo, *f;* aplomo, *m.* **s.-confident,** seguro de sí mismo, lleno de confianza en sí mismo. **s.-conscious,** turbado, confuso, apocado. **s.-consciousness,** turbación, confusión, *f,* apocamiento, azoramiento, *m.* **s.-contained,** (of a person) reservado, poco comunicativo; dueño de sí mismo; (of things) completo; (of flats, etc.) independiente; con entrada independiente. **s.-contradictory,** contradictorio. **s.-control,** dominio de sí mismo, *m;* ecuanimidad, serenidad, sangre fría, *f.* **s.-controlled,** dueño de sí mismo; ecuánime, sereno. **s.-deception,** engaño de sí mismo, *m;* ilusiones, *f pl.* **s.-defense,** defensa propia, *f.* **s.-denial,** abnegación, *f;* renunciación, *f;* frugalidad, *f.* **s.-destruction,** suicidio, *m.* **s.-determination,** libre albedrío, *m;* (of peoples) autonomía, *f;* independencia, *f.* **s.-educating,** autodidacto. **s.-esteem,** respeto para uno mismo, *m;* amor propio, *m.* **s.-evident,** aparente, que salta a la vista. **s.-explanatory,** que se explica a sí mismo; evidente. **s.-generating,** autógeno. **s.-government,** (of a person) dominio de sí mismo, *m;* (of a state) autonomía, *f.* **s.-importance,** presunción, petulancia, *f.* **s.-important,** pagado de sí mismo. **to be s.-important,** darse importancia, darse tono. **s.-indulgence,** indulgencia con sí mismo, *f;* (of food, drink, etc.) excesos, *m pl,* falta de moderación, *f.* **s.-indulgent,** indulgente con sí mismo; dado a los placeres, sibarita. **s.-interest,** propio interés, *m.* **s.-knowledge,** conocimiento de sí mismo, *m.* **s.-love,** egolatría, *f.* **s.-made man,** hombre que ha llegado a su posición actual por sus propios esfuerzos, *m.* **self-medication,** automedicación, *f.* **s.-opinionated,** terco, obstinaz. **s.-portrait,** autorretrato, *m.* **s.-possessed,** dueño de sí mismo; reservado; de sangre fría. **s.-possession,** aplomo, *m,* sangre fría, serenidad, *f.* **s.-preservation,** protección de sí mismo, *f.* **s.-reliance,** independencia, *f;* confianza en sí mismo, *f.* **s.-reliant,** independiente; confiado en sí mismo. **s.-reproach,** remordimiento, *m.* **s.-respect,** respeto de sí mismo, *m;* amor propio, *m,* dignidad, *f.* **s.-respecting,** que se respeta; que tiene amor propio. **s.-restraint,** dominio de sí mismo, *m;* moderación, *f.* **s.-righteous,** farisaico. **s.-sacrifice,** abnegación, *f.* **s.-sacrificing,** abnegado. **s.-same,** mismo, idéntico. **s.-satisfaction,** satisfacción de sí mismo, *f;* vanidad, *f;* (of desires, etc.) satisfacción, indulgencia, *f.* **s.-satisfied,** satisfecho de sí mismo, pagado de sí mismo. **s.-seeking,** *a* egoísta, interesado. —*n* egoísmo, *m.* **s.-starter,** *Mech.* arranque automático, *m.* **s.-styled,** autodenominado, autotitulado, llamado por sí mismo. **s.-sufficiency,** suficiencia, *f;* presunción, *f.* **s.-sufficient,** que basta a sí mismo; contento de sí mismo. **s.-supporting,** que vive de su propio trabajo; (of an institution, business) independiente. **s. -taught,** autodidacto. **s.-willed,** voluntarioso

selfish /'sɛlfɪʃ/ *a* egoísta, interesado

selfishly /'sɛlfɪʃli/ *adv* interesadamente; por egoísmo

selfishness /'sɛlfɪʃnɪs/ *n* egoísmo, *m*

sell /sɛl/ *vt* vender. —*vi* vender; venderse. **They sold him to his enemies,** Le vendieron a sus enemigos. **House to s.,** «Se vende una casa.» **to s. at a loss,** malvender, vender con pérdida. **to s. for cash,** vender al contado. **to s. retail,** vender al por menor.

to s. wholesale, vender al por mayor. **to s. one's life dearly,** vender cara la vida. **They sold the chair for $10,** Vendieron la silla por diez dólares. **to s. off,** (goods) liquidar, saldar. **to s. out,** vender; agotar. **The best edition is sold out,** La mejor edición está agotada. **All the nylons have been sold out,** Se han vendido todas las medias de nilón (de cristal). **to s. up,** vender

seller /ˈsɛlər/ *n* vendedor (-ra); comerciante (en), *m*

selling /ˈsɛlɪŋ/ *n* venta, *f.* **s. off,** liquidación, *f.* **s. price,** precio de venta, *m*

selvage /ˈsɛlvɪdʒ/ *n* (in cloth) orillo, *m*

semantics /sɪˈmæntɪks/ *n* semántica, *f*

semaphore /ˈsɛməˌfɔr/ *n* semáforo, *m, vt* and *vi* hacer señales semafóricas (a)

semaphoric /ˌsɛməˈfɔrɪk/ *a* semafórico

semblance /ˈsɛmbləns/ *n* apariencia, *f.* **to put on a s. of woe,** aparentar ser triste

semen /ˈsimən/ *n* semen, *m,* esperma, *f*

semester /sɪˈmɛstər/ *n* semestre, *m*

semi- *prefix* semi; medio. **s.-conscious,** medio consciente. **s.-detached house,** casa doble, *f*

semicircle /ˈsɛmɪˌsɜrkəl/ *n* semicírculo, *m*

semicircular /ˌsɛmɪˈsɜrkyələr/ *a* semicircular

semicolon /ˈsɛmɪˌkoulən/ *n* punto y coma, *m*

semidetached /ˌsɛmidɪˈtætʃt, ˌsɛmai-/ *a* (house) apartado

semiformal /ˌsɛmiˈfɔrməl, ˌsɛmai-/ *a* de media ceremonia

seminarist /ˈsɛmɪnərɪst/ *n* seminarista, *mf*

seminary /ˈsɛməˌnɛri/ *n* seminario, *m;* (for girls) colegio interno, *m*

Semite /ˈsɛmait/ *n* semita, *mf*

Semitic /səˈmɪtɪk/ *a* semítico, semita

Semitism /ˈsɛmɪˌtɪzəm/ *n* semitismo, *m*

semolina /ˌsɛməˈlinə/ *n* sémola, *f*

senate /ˈsɛnɪt/ *n* senado, *m*

senator /ˈsɛnətər/ *n* senador, *m*

senatorial /ˌsɛnəˈtɔriəl/ *a* senatorio

send /sɛnd/ *vt* enviar, mandar; *com* remitir; (a ball) lanzar; (grant) conceder; permitir; (inflict) afligir (con). **I sent Jane for it,** Envié a Juana a buscarlo. **He sent us word that he could not come,** Nos mandó un recado diciéndonos que no podía venir. **to s. mad,** hacer enloquecer. **to s. packing,** mandar a paseo. **to s. again,** volver a mandar. **to s. away,** *vt* enviar; (dismiss) destituir; despedir; (scare off) ahuyentar, *vi* enviar a otra parte. **to s. back,** (goods) devolver; (persons) volver. **to s. down,** hacer bajar; (rain, etc.) mandar, derramar; (a student) suspender, expulsar. **to s. in,** mandar; (persons) hacer entrar, introducir; (food) servir; (a bill) presentar; (one's name) dar. **Please s. him in!** ¡Sírvase de invitarle a entrar! **to s. in one's resignation,** mandar su dimisión. **to s. off,** enviar, mandar; (goods) despachar; (persons) destituir; (scare) ahuyentar. **s.-off,** *n* despedida, *f.* **a good s.-off,** una despedida afectuosa. **to s. on,** (a letter) hacer seguir; (instructions) trasmitir. **to s. out,** hacer salir; mandar; (emit) despedir, dar; (new shoots, etc.) echar. **to s. round,** (the hat, etc.) hacer circular. **to s. up,** enviar arriba; mandar subir, hacer subir; mandar, enviar; (a ball) lanzar

sender /ˈsɛndər/ *n* remitente, *mf; elec* transmisor, *m*

sending /ˈsɛndɪŋ/ *n* envío, *m*

Senegal /ˌsɛnɪˈgɔl, -ˈgɑl/ Senegal, *m*

Senegalese /ˌsɛnəgəˈliz/ *a* and *n* senegalés (-esa)

senile /ˈsinail/ *a* senil

senility /sɪˈnɪlɪti/ *n* senilidad, *f*

senior /ˈsinyər/ *a* mayor, de mayor edad; más antiguo. **Martinez s.,** Martínez padre. **Charles is Mary's s. by five years,** Carlos es cinco años mayor que María. **s. member,** decano, *m*

seniority /sinˈyɔrɪti/ *n* ancianidad, *f;* antigüedad, *f*

senna /ˈsɛnə/ *n bot* sena, *f*

sensation /sɛnˈseiʃən/ *n* sensación, *f;* sentimiento, *m;* impresión, *f.* **to create a s.,** causar una sensación

sensational /sɛnˈseiʃənl̩/ *a* sensacional

sensationalism /sɛnˈseiʃənl̩ˌɪzəm/ *n philos* sensualismo, *m;* efectismo, *m*

sensationalist /sɛnˈseiʃənl̩ɪst/ *n philos* sensualista, *mf;* efectista, *mf*

sense /sɛns/ *n* sentido, *m.* —*vt* sentir. **in a s.,** hasta cierto punto; desde un punto de vista. **in the full s. of the word,** en toda la extensión de la palabra. **common s.,** sentido común, *m.* **He has no s. of smell,** No tiene olfato. **the five senses,** los cinco sentidos. **to be out of one's senses,** estar fuera de sí, estar trastornado. **You must be out of your senses!** ¡Debes de haber perdido el juicio! ¡Estás loco! **to come to one's senses,** (after unconsciousness) volver en sí; (after folly) recobrar el sentido común. **to talk s.,** hablar con sentido común, hablar razonablemente. **s. organ,** órgano de los sentidos, *m.* **have a good s. of direction,** saber orientarse, tener buena orientación. **have no s. of smell,** ser incapaz de percibir olores. **have no s. of taste,** ser incapaz de distinguir gustos

senseless /ˈsɛnslɪs/ *a* (unconscious) sin sentido, insensible; desmayado; (silly) necio, estúpido. **to knock s.,** derribar, tumbar

senselessness /ˈsɛnslɪsnɪs/ *n* falta de sentido común, *f;* locura, absurdidad, *f*

sensibility /ˌsɛnsəˈbɪlɪti/ *n* sensibilidad, *f*

sensible /ˈsɛnsəbəl/ *a* sensible; (conscious) consciente (de); sesudo. **to be s. of,** estar consciente de; estar persuadido de

sensibly /ˈsɛnsəbli/ *adv* sensiblemente; sesudamente, cuerdamente

sensitive /ˈsɛnsɪtɪv/ *a* sensitivo; susceptible (a); impresionable. **s. plant,** sensitiva, *f*

sensitivity /ˌsɛnsɪˈtɪvɪti/ *n* sensibilidad, *f;* susceptibilidad, *f;* delicadeza, *f*

sensitize /ˈsɛnsɪˌtaiz/ *vt photo* sensibilizar

sensory /ˈsɛnsəri/ *a* sensorio

sensual /ˈsɛnʃuəl/ *a* sensual; voluptuoso

sensualism /ˈsɛnʃuəˌlɪzəm/ *n* sensualismo, *m*

sensualist /ˈsɛnʃuəlɪst/ *n* sensualista, *mf*

sensuality /ˌsɛnʃuˈælɪti/ *n* sensualidad, *f*

sensually /ˈsɛnʃuəli/ *adv* sensualmente

sensuous /ˈsɛnʃuəs/ *a* sensorio

sensuousness /ˈsɛnʃuəsnɪs/ *n* sensualidad, *f*

sentence /ˈsɛntn̩s/ *n law* sentencia, *f;* (penalty) pena, *f; gram* frase, *f;* (maxim) máxima, sentencia, *f.* —*vt* sentenciar, condenar. **to pass s.,** pronunciar sentencia, fallar. **under s. of,** bajo pena de

sententious /sɛnˈtɛnʃəs/ *a* sentencioso

sentient /ˈsɛnʃənt/ *a* sensible

sentiment /ˈsɛntəmənt/ *n* sentimiento, *m;* (sentimentality) sentimentalismo, *m;* opinión, *f*

sentimental /ˌsɛntəˈmɛntl̩/ *a* sentimental; (mawkish) sensiblero

sentimentalist /ˌsɛntəˈmɛntl̩ɪst/ *n* romántico (-ca), persona sentimental, *f*

sentimentality /ˌsɛntəmɛnˈtælɪti/ *n* sentimentalismo, *m,* sensiblería, *f*

sentimentalize /ˌsɛntəˈmɛntl̩ˌaiz/ *vt* idealizar

sentimentally /ˌsɛntəˈmɛntl̩i/ *adv* sentimentalmente

sentinel /ˈsɛntn̩l/ *n* centinela, *mf*

sentry /ˈsɛntri/ *n* centinela, *m.* **to be on s. duty,** estar de guardia. **s.-box,** garita de centinela, *f*

separable /ˈsɛpərəbəl/ *a* separable

separate /*a.* ˈsɛpərɪt; *v.* ɹreit/ *a* separado; distinto; independiente. —*vt* separar; dividir. —*vi* separarse; (of husband and wife) separarse de bienes y de cuerpos

separately /ˈsɛpərɪtli/ *adv* separadamente; aparte

separation /ˌsɛpəˈreiʃən/ *n* separación, *f; law* separación de bienes y de cuerpos, *f*

separatism /ˈsɛpərəˌtɪzəm/ *n* separatismo, *m*

separatist /ˈsɛpərətɪst/ *a* and *n* separatista *mf*

Sephardic /səˈfardɪk/ *a* Sefaradí

sepia /ˈsipiə/ *n* (color and fish) sepia, *f*

September /sɛpˈtɛmbər/ *n* setiembre, septiembre, *m*

septic /ˈsɛptɪk/ *a* séptico

septicemia /ˌsɛptəˈsimiə/ *n* septicemia, *f*

septuagenarian /ˌsɛptʃuədʒəˈnɛəriən/ *n* setentón (-ona); septuagenario (-ia)

septum /ˈsɛptəm/ septo, tabique, *m*

sepulcher /ˈsɛpəlkər/ *n* sepulcro, *m*

sepulchral /səˈpʌlkrəl/ *a* sepulcral

sequel /ˈsikwəl/ *n* (of a story, etc.) continuación, *f;* consecuencia, *f;* resultado, *m*

sequence /ˈsikwəns/ *n* sucesión, *f;* serie, *f;* orden, *mf;* (at cards) serie, *f; gram* correspondencia, *f;* (*eccl* and cinema) secuencia, *f.* **s. of tenses,** correspondencia de los tiempos, *f*

sequestered /sɪ'kwɛstərd/ *a* aislado, remoto

sequestrate /sɪ'kwɛstreit/ *vt* secuestrar

sequestration /ˌsikwɛs'treiʃən/ *n* secuestro, *m,*

sequin /'sikwɪn/ *n* lentejuela, *f*

seraglio /sɪ'rælyou/ *n* serrallo, *m*

seraph /'sɛrəf/ *n* serafín, *m*

seraphic /sɪ'ræfɪk/ *a* seráfico

seraphim /'sɛrəfɪm/ *n* serafín, *m*

Serbia /'sɜrbiə/ Servia, *f*

Serbian /'sɜrbiən/ *a* servio. —*n* servio (-ia); (language) servio, *m*

serenade /ˌsɛrə'neid/ *n* serenata, *f, vt* dar una serenata (a)

serene /sə'rin/ *a* sereno. **His S. Highness,** Su Alteza Serenísima

serenity /sə'rɛnɪti/ *n* serenidad, *f;* tranquilidad, *f*

serf /sɜrf/ *n* siervo (-va)

serfdom /'sɜrfdəm/ *n* servidumbre, *f*

serge /sɜrdʒ/ *n* estameña, *f;* (silk) sarga, *f*

sergeant /'sɑrdʒənt/ *n mil* sargento, *m;* (police) sargento de policía, *m.* **s.-at-arms,** macero, *m.* **s.-major,** sargento instructor, *m*

serial /'sɪəriəl/ *a* en serie; (of a story) por entregas. —*n* novela por entregas, *f.* **s. number,** número de serie, *m*

sericulture /'sɜrɪˌkʌltʃər/ *n* sericultura, *f*

series /'sɪəriz/ *n* serie, *f;* cadena, *f; math* serie, progresión, *f.* **in s.,** en serie

serious /'sɪəriəs/ *a* serio; sincero; verdadero; (of illness, etc.) grave; importante. **He was s.** (not laughing) **when he said it,** Lo dijo en serio. **He is very s. about it,** Lo toma muy en serio. **to grow s.,** (of persons) ponerse serio; (of events) hacerse grave

seriously /'sɪəriəsli/ *adv* seriamente; en serio; gravemente. **to take** (something) **s.,** tomar (algo) en serio. **to take oneself s.,** tomarse muy en serio

seriousness /'sɪəriəsnɪs/ *n* seriedad, *f;* gravedad, *f.* **in all s.,** en serio, seriamente

sermon /'sɜrmən/ *n* sermón, *m*

sermonize /'sɜrməˌnaiz/ *vt* and *vi* sermonear

serpent /'sɜrpənt/ *n* serpiente, *f; mus* serpentón, *m*

serpentine /'sɜrpənˌtin, -ˌtain/ *a* serpentino; (of character) tortuoso. —*n mineral* serpentina, *f*

serrated /'sɛreitɪd/ *a* serrado; dentellado

serried /'sɛrid/ *a* apretado, apiñado

serum /'sɪərəm/ *n* suero, *m*

servant /'sɜrvənt/ *n* servidor (-ra); (domestic) criado (-da); (employee) empleado (-da); (slave and *fig*) siervo (-va); *pl* **servants,** (domestic) servidumbre, *f,* servicio, *m.* **I remain your obedient s.,** Quedo de Vd. atento y seguro servidor (att. y s.s.). **civil s.,** empleado del estado, *m.* **general s.,** criada para todo, *f.* **man s.,** criado, *m.* **the s. problem,** el problema del servicio. **Your s., sir,** Servidor de Vd., señor. **s.-girl,** criada, *f*

serve /sɜrv/ *vt* servir (a); ser útil (a); satisfacer; (in a shop) despachar; (an apprenticeship, etc.) hacer; (a prison sentence) cumplir; (treat) tratar; (of stallion) cubrir; (a warrant, etc.) ejecutar; (a notice) entregar; (a ball) servir; (on a jury, etc.) formar parte de; *naut* aforrar. —*vi* servir; (*mil, nav*) hacer el servicio. —*n sports* saque, *m.* **It serves you right!** ¡Lo tienes merecido! **to s. at table,** servir a la mesa. **to s. as,** servir de. **to s. out,** distribuir; servir. **Serves 8,** (recipe) Da 8 porciones

server /'sɜrvər/ *n eccl* acólito, *m; sports* saque, *m;* (tray) bandeja, *f;* (for fish, etc.) pala, *f*

service /'sɜrvɪs/ *n* servicio, *m; eccl* oficio, *m;* servicio de mesa, *m;* (of a writ) entrega, *f; sports* saque, *m.* **coffee s.,** juego de café, *m.* **diplomatic s.,** cuerpo diplomático, *m.* **At your s.,** Para servir a Vd., A su disposición. **on active s.,** en acto de servicio; en el campo de batalla. **to go into s.,** (of servants) ir a servir. **to render s.,** prestar servicios. **s. tree,** serbal, *m*

serviceable /'sɜrvəsəbəl/ *a* (of persons) servicial; (of things) servible, utilizable; útil; práctico; (lasting) duradero

service road *n* vía de servicio, *f*

serviette /ˌsɜrvi'ɛt/ *n* servilleta, *f.* **s. ring,** servilletero, *m*

servile /'sɜrvɪl/ *a* servil

servility /sər'vɪlɪti/ *n* servilismo, *m*

serving /'sɜrvɪŋ/ *a* sirviente; al servicio (de). **s. maid,** criada, *f.* **s. table,** trinchero, *m*

servitude /'sɜrvɪˌtud/ *n* servidumbre, esclavitud, *f.* **penal s.,** cadena perpetua, *f*

session /'sɛʃən/ *n* sesión, *f;* junta, *f.* **petty sessions,** tribunal de primera instancia, *m*

set /sɛt/ *vt* poner; colocar; fijar; (seeds, etc.) plantar; (bones) reducir, componer; (gems) engastar, montar; (a clock) regular; (sails) desplegar; (the teeth of a saw) trabar, triscar; (congeal) hacer coagular; (a trap) armar; (a snare) tender; (a razor) afilar; (make ready) preparar; (type) componer; (cause) hacer; *mus* poner en música; *mus* adaptar; (order) mandar; (prescribe) dar, asignar; (estimate) estimar, evaluar; (an example, etc.) dar; (establish) establecer, crear. —*vi* (of the sun, etc.) ponerse; (solidify) coagularse; solidificarse; (of tides) fluir; (of the wind) soplar; (of dogs) hacer punta. **The joke set him laughing,** El chiste le hizo reír. **set an example,** dar ejemplo, dar el ejemplo. **set a precedent,** sentar precedente. **to set a person's mind at rest,** tranquilizar, sosegar. **to set a trap,** armar lazo. **to set at ease,** poner a sus anchas (a), hacer cómodo (a). **to set at naught,** despreciar. **to set eyes on,** poner los ojos en. **to set fire to,** pegar fuego a, incendiar. **to set free,** poner en libertad, librar (de). **to set in motion,** poner en marcha. **to set one's teeth,** apretar los dientes. **to set people talking,** dar que hablar a la gente. **to set the fashion,** fijar la moda; poner de moda. **to set the alarm at seven o'clock,** poner el despertador a las siete. **to set the table,** poner la mesa. **to set to work,** ponerse a trabajar. **to set about,** *vi* (begin) ponerse (a); empezar; (undertake) emprender. —*vt* (a rumor, etc.) divulgar. **They set about each other,** Empezaron a golpearse, Vinieron a las manos. **to set against,** indisponer (con), enemistar (con); hacer el enemigo (de), ser hostil (a); (balance) oponer, balancear. **to set oneself against,** oponerse a; atacar, luchar contra. **to set aside,** poner a un lado; apartar; (discard) desechar; (omit) omitir, pasar por alto de; dejar aparte, excluir; (keep) reservar; (money, etc.) ahorrar; (reject) rechazar; (quash) anular. **to set back,** retrasar; hacer retroceder. **set-back,** *n* revés, *m;* contrariedad, *f.* **to set before,** poner ante; (facts) exponer; (introduce) presentar. **to set down,** poner en tierra; depositar; (of a bus, etc.) dejar; (in writing) poner por escrito; anotar, apuntar; narrar, contar; (attribute) atribuir; (fix) fijar, formular; (believe to be) creer. **Passengers are set down at...,** Los viajeros pueden apearse en... **to set forth,** *vt* (one's opinions, etc.) exponer; publicar; (display) exhibir, mostrar; (make) hacer. —*vi* ponerse en camino. **to set going,** poner en marcha; echar a andar. **to set in,** empezar; (of the tide) fluir. **A reaction has set in,** Se ha hecho sentir una reacción. **to set off,** *vt* (explode) hacer estallar; (cause) hacer; (heighten) realzar; hacer resaltar; (counterbalance) contraponer. —*vi* partir; ponerse en camino. **set-off,** *n* contraste, *m,* contraposición, *f.* **to set off against,** contraponer. **to set on,** *vt* (a dog) azuzar; (incite) instigar, incitar. —*vi* atacar. **to set out,** *vt* (state) exponer, manifestar; (embellish) realzar; (display) arreglar, disponer. —*vi* ponerse en camino, partir. **to set over,** (rule) tener autoridad sobre, gobernar. **to set to,** (begin to) ponerse a, empezar a; (work) ponerse a trabajar. **set-to,** *n* lucha, *f;* (boxing) asalto, *m;* (quarrel) pelea, riña, *f.* **to set up,** *vt* (a monument, etc.) erigir, levantar; (fix) fijar; (apparatus, machinery) montar; (exalt) exaltar; (found) establecer; crear; (propound) exponer; (a howl, etc.) dar; (equip with) proveer de; instalar; (make strong) robustecer; fortificar; (type) componer; (raise) alzar. —*vi* establecerse; dárselas de. **He sets himself up as a painter,** Se las da de pintor. **to set** (a person) **up as a model,** poner como modelo (a). **to set up house,** poner casa. **to set up a business,** establecer un comercio. **set-up,** *n* establecimiento, *m;* arreglo, *m.* **to set upon,** atacar

set /sɛt/ *n* (of sun, etc.) puesta, *f,* ocaso, *m;* (of the head, etc.) porte, *m;* (of a garment) corte, *m;* (of the tide, etc.) dirección, *f;* (slant) inclinación, *f;* (*fig* drift) tendencia, *f,* movimiento, *m;* (of the teeth of a saw) triscamiento, *m;* (of men, houses, etc.) grupo, *m;* (of tools, golf clubs, china, etc.) juego, *m;* (gang) pandilla, camarilla, *f;* clase, *f;* (*dance*) tanda, *f;* (tennis) partido, *f; theat* decoración, *f; radio* aparato de radio, *m,* radio, *f.* **coffee set,** juego de café, *m.* **all-mains set,** radio de corriente eléctrica, *f.* **battery set,** radio de batería, *f.* **portable set,** radio portátil, *f.* **the smart set,** el mundo elegante. **to have a shampoo and set,** hacerse lavar y marcar (el pelo). **to make a set,** hacer juego. **to make a dead set at,** hacer un ataque vigoroso (a), atacar resueltamente; procurar insinuarse en el favor de. **set of teeth,** dentadura, *f*

set /sɛt/ *a* fijo; inmóvil; (of a smile) forzado; (of a task) asignado; (of times) señalado, fijo; (prescribed) prescrito, establecido; (firm) firme; (resolved) resuelto; (well-known) consabido; (obstinate) terco, nada adaptable. **well set-up,** apuesto, bien plantado. **He is set on doing it,** Se empeña en **to be dead set against,** estar completamente opuesto a. **set phrase,** frase hecha, *f.* **set-square,** cartabón, *m*

settee /sɛ'ti/ *n* canapé, *m.* **s.-bed,** cama turca, *f*

setter /'sɛtər/ *n* (perro) séter, perdiguero, *m.* **s.-on,** instigador (-ra)

setting /'sɛtɪŋ/ *n* (of the sun, etc.) puesta, *f;* (of mortar, etc.) fraguado, *m;* (of a jelly) solidificación, *f;* (of jewels) engaste, *m,* montadura, *f;* (of bones) aliño, *m;* (of teeth of saw) traba, *f;* (of razor) afiladura, *f;* (of a trap) armadura, *f;* (of a machine, etc.) ajuste, *m;* (frame) marco, *m; mus* arreglo, *m; theat* decorado, *m;* (emplacement) lecho, *m.* **the s. sun,** el sol poniente. **s. free,** liberación, *f.* **s. off,** partida, salida, *f.* **s. out,** ida, marcha, *f;* principio, *m.* **s.-up,** creación, institución, *f,* establecimiento, *m;* (of a machine) montaje, *m; print* composición, *f*

settle /'sɛtl̩/ *vt* colocar; asegurar, afirmar; (a country) colonizar; (live in) establecer (en); (populate) poblar; (in a profession, etc.) dar; (install) instalar; (the imagination, etc.) sosegar, calmar; (resolve) resolver; (arrange) disponer, arreglar; (differences) componer, concertar; (an opponent, etc.) confundir; (a bill) saldar, pagar; (a claim) satisfacer; (clarify) depositar, clarificar; (end) poner fin (a). —*vi* establecerse; (of weather) serenarse; (to work, etc.) empezar a, ponerse a; aplicarse a; (decide) decidirse; (alight) posarse; (of foundations, etc.) asentarse; (of a ship) zozobrar; (of sediment) depositarse; (of liquid) clarificarse. **to s. accounts with,** *fig* ajustar cuentas con. **to s. down,** establecerse, arraigarse; adaptarse (a); (become calm) sosegarse, calmarse; sentar el juicio; (of foundations) asentarse; (of a ship) zozobrar; (of sediment) depositarse. **to s. in,** *vt* instalar. —*vi* instalarse. **to s. on,** (choose) escoger; (decide on) decidirse (a). **to s. a pension on,** señalar pensión (a). **to s. up,** *vt* (one's affairs) poner en orden; (bill) pagar, saldar. —*vi* llegar a un acuerdo; pagar cuentas

settled /'sɛtl̩d/ *a* fijo; permanente; invariable; (of countries) colonizado; (of weather) sereno

settlement /'sɛtl̩mənt/ *n* (of a country) colonización, *f;* (of a dispute) arreglo, ajuste, *m;* (of a question) solución, *f;* decisión, *f;* (of a bill) saldo, pago, *m,* liquidación, *f;* (of an obligation) satisfacción, *f;* (colony) colonia, *f;* (creation) creación, institución, *f;* establecimiento, arraigo, *m.* **deed of s.,** escritura de donación, *f.* **marriage s.,** contrato matrimonial, *m;* **s. out of court,** arreglo pacífico, *m*

settler /'sɛtlər/ *n* colono, *m;* colonizador (-ra)

seven /'sɛvən/ *a* and *n* siete *m.* **It is s. o'clock,** Son las siete. **the s. deadly sins,** los siete pecados capitales

seventeen /'sɛvən'tin/ *a* diecisiete, diez y siete. —*n* diecisiete, *m.* **She is just s.,** Acaba de cumplir los diez y siete años

seventeenth /'sɛvən'tinθ/ *a* décimoséptimo; (of monarchs and of the month) diez y siete. —*n* décimoséptimo, *m.* **Louis the S.,** Luis diez y siete. **the s. of June,** el diez y siete de junio

seventh /'sɛvənθ/ *a* séptimo; (of the month) siete. —*n* séptimo, *m;* séptima parte, *f; mus* séptima, *f.* **Edward the S.,** Eduardo séptimo. **the s. of August,** el siete de agosto

seventieth /'sɛvəntiɪθ/ *a* septuagésimo, setentavo. —*n* setentavo, *m*

seventy /'sɛvənti/ *a* and *n* setenta, *m*

sever /'sɛvər/ *vt* separar; romper; dividir

several /'sɛvərəl/ *a* distinto, diferente; respectivo; varios, *m pl,* (*f pl,* varias); algunos, *m pl,* (*f pl,* algunas)

severally /'sɛvərəli/ *adv* separadamente; individualmente; independientemente

severance /'sɛvərəns/ *n* separación, *f;* (of friendship, etc.) ruptura, *f*

severe /sə'vɪər/ *a* severo; riguroso; fuerte; duro; (of style) austero; (of pain) agudo; (of illness) grave

severely /sə'vɪərli/ *adv* severamente; intensamente; gravemente

severity /sə'vɛrɪti/ *n* severidad, *f;* intensidad, *f;* (of weather) inclemencia, *f;* (of illness) gravedad, *f*

sew /sou/ *vt* and *vi* coser. **to sew on,** coser, pegar

sewage /'suɪdʒ/ *n* aguas residuales, *f pl.* **s. system,** alcantarillado, *m*

sewer /'suər/ *n* alcantarilla, cloaca, *f,* albañal, *m*

sewing /'souɪŋ/ *n* costura, *f.* **s. bag,** costurero, *m.* **s. cotton,** hilo de coser, *m.* **s.-machine,** máquina de coser, *f.* **s. silk,** torzal, *m*

sex /sɛks/ *n* sexo, *m.* **the fair sex,** el bello sexo. **the weaker sex,** el sexo débil. **sex appeal,** atractivo, *m*

sexagenarian /ˌsɛksədʒə'nɛəriən/ *n* sexagenario (-ia)

sexless /'sɛkslɪs/ *a* neutro; frígido

sexologist /sɛk'sɒlədʒɪst/ *n* sexólogo (-ga)

sexology /sɛk'sɒlədʒi/ *n* sexología, *f*

sextant /'sɛkstənt/ *n* sextante, *m*

sexton /'sɛkstən/ *n* sacristán, *m;* sepulturero, *m;* (bell-ringer) campanero, *m*

sexual /'sɛkʃuəl/ *a* sexual

sexuality /ˌsɛkʃu'ælɪti/ *n* sexualidad, *f*

Sforza /'sfɔrtsa/ Esforcia, *f*

sh! /ʃ/ *interj* ¡Chitón! ¡Chis!

shabbily /'ʃæbəli/ *adv* (of dressing) pobremente; (of treatment) mezquinamente

shabbiness /'ʃæbinɪs/ *n* pobreza, *f;* estado andrajoso, *m;* (of behavior) mezquindad, ruindad, *f*

shabby /'ʃæbi/ *a* (of persons) desharrapado, andrajoso; (of garments) raído, roto; (of a neighborhood, etc.) pobre; (mean) ruin, mezquino

shack /ʃæk/ *n* choza, *f*

shackle /'ʃækəl/ *n* traba, *f; pl* **shackles,** grillos, *m pl,* esposas, *f pl; fig* cadenas, *f pl.* —*vt* poner esposas (a), encadenar; (a horse) apear; *fig* atar; (impede) estorbar

shad /ʃæd/ *n* sábalo, *m*

shade /ʃeid/ *n* sombra, *f;* (in a picture) toque de obscuro, *m;* (for the eyes) visera, *f;* (of a lamp) pantalla, *f;* (ghost) espectro, fantasma, *m;* (of color) matiz, *m;* (tinge) dejo, *m.* —*vt* sombrear, dar sombra (a); (the face, etc.) proteger, resguardar; (a drawing) esfumar. **in the s.,** a la sombra. **80° in the s.,** ochenta grados a la sombra. **to put** (a person) **in the s.,** eclipsar

shadiness /ʃeidinɪs/ *n* sombra, *f*

shading /'ʃeidɪŋ/ *n* sombra, *f; art* degradación, *f*

shadow /'ʃædou/ *n* sombra, *f;* obscuridad, *f;* (in a picture) toque de obscuro, *m.* —*vt* sombrear; obscurecer; (a person) seguir **to cast a s.,** proyectar una sombra. **to s. forth,** indicar; simbolizar. **s. show,** sombras chinescas, *f pl*

shadowy /'ʃædoui/ *a* umbroso; vago, indistinto, indefinido

shady /'ʃeidi/ *a* sombreado, umbrío; sombrío; (of persons, etc.) sospechoso. **It was s. in the wood,** Hacía sombra en el bosque

shaft /ʃæft/ *n* fuste, *m;* (arrow) flecha, saeta, *f,* dardo, *m;* (of a golf club, etc.) mango, *m;* (of a cart) vara, *f; mech* árbol, eje, *m;* (of a column and a feather) cañón, *m;* (of light) rayo, *m;* (of a mine) pozo, tiro, *m;* (air-shaft) conducto de aire, ventilador, *m.* **cam-s.,** árbol de levas, *m.* **driving s.,** árbol motor, *m*

shaggy /'ʃægi/ *a* peludo; lanudo

shagreen /ʃə'grin/ *n* chagrén, *m*

shah /ʃɑ, ʃɔ/ *n* cha, *m*

shake /ʃeik/ *vt* sacudir; agitar; hacer temblar; (weaken) debilitar, hacer flaquear. —*vi* estremecerse; temblar; (trill) trinar. **He managed to s. himself**

free, Consiguió librarse por una sacudida. **to s. hands,** darse la mano, estrecharse la mano. **to s. one's finger at,** señalar con el dedo (a). **to s. one's fist at,** amenazar con el puño (a). **to s. one's head,** mover la cabeza; negar con la cabeza. **to s. one's sides,** (with laughter) reírse a carcajadas. **to s. with fear,** temblar de miedo. **to s. down,** sacudir, hacer caer. **s.-down,** *n* cama improvisada, *f.* **to s. off,** sacudirse; librarse (de), perder; quitar de encima (a). **to s. out,** (unfurl) desplegar; sacudir. **to s. up,** agitar; sacudir, remover

shake /ʃeik/ *n* sacudida, *f;* (of the head) movimiento (de la cabeza), *m;* (of the hand) apretón (de manos), *m;* temblor, *m; mus* trino, gorjeo, *m.* **in two shakes,** *Inf.* en un periquete. **to give a person a good s.,** sacudir violentamente (a)

Shakespearean /ʃeik'spɪəriən/ *a* shakespeariano

shakiness /'ʃeikinɪs/ *n* inestabilidad, *f;* poca firmeza, *f;* temblor, *m;* lo dudoso. **the s. of his voice,** su voz trémula

shaking /'ʃeikɪŋ/ *n* sacudimiento, *m;* temblor, *m;* (of windows, etc.) zangoloteo, *m*

shaky /'ʃeiki/ *a* inestable; poco firme; (of hands, etc.) tembloroso; (of the voice) trémulo; (of gait) vacilante, dudoso

shale /ʃeil/ *n* esquisto, *m*

shall /ʃæl; *unstressed* ʃəl/ *v aux* (expressing simple future) **I s. arrive tomorrow,** Llegaré mañana. **S. we go to the sea next week?** ¿Iremos al mar la semana próxima?; (expressing obligation, compulsion) **You s. not go out,** No has de salir, No quiero que salgas. **He s. see her immediately,** Tiene que verla en seguida; (as a polite formula) **S. I go?** ¿Quiere Vd. que vaya? **S. we buy the soap?** ¿Quiere Vd. que compremos el jabón? ¿Compraremos el jabón?

shallot /'ʃælət, ʃə'lɒt/ *n bot* chalote, *m,* ascalonia, *f*

shallow /'ʃælou/ *a* poco profundo; (of a receptacle) llano; (of persons) superficial, frívolo; (of knowledge, etc.) superficial, ligero, somero. *—n* bajío, *m*

shallowness /'ʃælounɪs/ *n* poca profundidad, *f;* superficialidad, *f*

sham /ʃæm/ *vt* fingir, simular. *—n* farsa, *f;* imitación, *f;* engaño, *m;* (person) farsante, *m.* *—a* fingido; falso; espurio. **to s. illness,** fingirse enfermo. **to s. dead,** hacer la mortecina. **You're just a s.,** Eres un farsante

sham battle *n mil* simulacro de combate, simulacro guerrero, *m*

shamble /'ʃæmbəl/ *vi* andar arrastrándose. *—n* andar pesado, *m; pl* **shambles,** matadero, *m; fig* carnicería, *f*

shambling /'ʃæmblɪŋ/ *a* pesado, lento

shame /ʃeim/ *n* vergüenza, *f;* ignominia, *f;* deshonra, *f.* *—vt* avergonzar; deshonrar. **For s.!** ¡Qué vergüenza! **What a s.!** ¡Qué lástima! **to put to s.,** avergonzar

shamefaced /'ʃeim,feist/ *a* (bashful) vergonzoso, tímido; (ashamed) avergonzado

shamefacedly /,ʃeim'feisɪdli/ *adv* vergonzosamente, tímidamente; con vergüenza

shameful /'ʃeimfəl/ *a* vergonzoso, escandaloso; indecente

shamefully /'ʃeimfəli/ *adv* escandalosamente

shamefulness /'ʃeimfəlnɪs/ *n* vergüenza, infamia, *f;* indecencia, *f*

shameless /'ʃeimlɪs/ *a* desvergonzado; impúdico, indecente

shamelessly /'ʃeimlɪsli/ *adv* desvergonzadamente

shamelessness /'ʃeimlɪsnɪs/ *n* desvergüenza, poca vergüenza, *f;* impudicia, deshonestidad, *f*

shampoo /ʃæm'pu/ *n* champú, *m.* *—vt* dar un champú (a); dar un masaje (a). **dry s.,** champú seco, *m*

shamrock /'ʃæmrɒk/ *n* trébol blanco, *m*

shank /ʃæŋk/ *n* zanca, *f; mech* pierna, *f;* (handle) mango, *m;* (of a button) rabo, *m,* cola, *f.* **go on Shank's mare, ride on Shank's mare,** caminar en coche de San Francisco, ir en la boridad de Villadiego

shanty /'ʃænti/ *n* choza, *f*

shanty town *n* barriada (Peru), callampa, población, población callampa (Chile), *f.* Rancho (Venezuela), *m,* villa-miseria (Argentina), *f*

shape /ʃeip/ *n* forma, *f;* bulto, *m;* fantasma, *m;* (of a garment) corte, *m;* (of a person) talle, *m; cul* molde, *m;* (of a hat) forma, *f.* *—vt* formar; (a garment) cortar; (ideas) dar forma (a); adaptar; (stone, etc.) labrar; (one's life) dominar. *—vi* (of events) desarrollarse. **to go out of s.,** perder la forma. **to take s.,** tomar forma. **to s. one's course,** dirigirse (hacia, a); *naut* dar el rumbo. **to s. well,** prometer bien

shaped /ʃeipt/ *a* de forma de..., que tiene figura de... **pear-s.,** piriforme

shapeless /'ʃeiplɪs/ *a* informe; disforme

shapelessness /'ʃeiplɪsnɪs/ *n* informidad, *f;* deformidad, *f*

shapeliness /'ʃeiplinɪs/ *n* belleza de forma, *f;* simetría, *f*

shapely /'ʃeipli/ *a* bien formado; simétrico

share /ʃɛər/ *n* porción, *f;* parte, *f;* cuota, *f;* contribución, *f;* (part ownership) interés, *m;* (in a company) acción, *f.* *—vt* distribuir; compartir; dividir; tomar parte en. *—vi* participar (de); tomar parte (en). **to fall to one's s.,** tocar, corresponder. **to go shares with,** dividir con, compartir con. **to take a s. in the conversation,** tomar parte en la conversación. **paid-up s.,** *com* acción liberada, *f.* **to s. out,** repartir, distribuir

shareholder /'ʃɛər,houldər/ *n* accionista, *mf*

sharer /'ʃɛərər/ *n* partícipe, *mf*

shark /ʃɑrk/ *n ichth* tiburón, *m; inf* caimán, *m*

sharp /ʃɑrp/ *a* (of edges) afilado, cortante; (of points) punzante, puntiagudo; (of features, etc.) anguloso; (of bends, etc.) brusco; (of outlines, etc.) definido, distinto; (of pain, sound) agudo; (marked) marcado; (intense) intenso; (of winds, glance, etc.) penetrante; (of hearing) fino; (of appetite) bueno; (of showers) fuerte; (quick) rápido; (clever, etc.) vivo, listo; perspicaz; (of children) despierto, precoz; (unscrupulous) astuto, sin escrúpulos; (of criticism, remarks) mordaz; (of rebukes, sentences, etc.) severo; (of winters, etc.) riguroso; (of fighting) encarnizado; (of taste) picante; (sour) ácido; *mus* sostenido. *—adv* en punto; puntualmente. *—n mus* sostenido, *m.* **at five o'clock s.,** a las cinco en punto. **Look s.!** ¡Date prisa! **s.-edged,** afilado. **s.-eyed,** con ojos de lince; de mirada penetrante. **s.-featured,** de facciones angulosas. **s.-nosed,** de nariz puntiaguda. **s.-pointed,** puntiagudo. **s. practice,** procedimientos poco honrados, *m pl.* **s.-tongued,** de lengua áspera. **s. turn,** curva brusca, curva cerrada, *f.* **s.-witted,** de inteligencia viva, listo

sharpen /'ʃɑrpən/ *vt* (knives) afilar, amolar; (pencils, etc.) sacar punta (a); (wits, etc.) despabilar; (appetite) abrir. **This walk has sharpened my appetite,** Este paseo me ha abierto el apetito. **to s. one's claws,** afilarse las uñas

sharper /'ʃɑrpər/ *n inf* caballero de industria, timador, *m;* (at cards) fullero, *m*

sharply /'ʃɑrpli/ *adv* claramente; bruscamente; severamente; ásperamente

sharpness /'ʃɑrpnɪs/ *n* (of cold, etc.) intensidad, *f;* severidad, *f;* (cleverness) agudeza, perspicacia, *f;* (of a child) precocidad, *f;* (sarcasm, etc.) mordacidad, *f;* aspereza, *f;* brusquedad, *f*

sharpshooter /'ʃɑrp,ʃutər/ *n* franco tirador, *m*

sharpsighted /'ʃɑrp,saitɪd/ *a* de vista penetrante, listo, perspicaz

shatter /'ʃætər/ *vt* romper, quebrantar; hacer añicos; *fig* destrozar. **You have shattered my illusions,** Has destrozado todas mis ilusiones

shave /ʃeiv/ *vt* afeitar, rasurar; (wood, etc.) acepillar. *—vi* afeitarse; (of razors) afeitar. *—n* afeitada, *f.* **to have a s.,** hacerse afeitar. **to have a close s.,** *inf* escapar por un pelo

shaving /'ʃeivɪŋ/ *n* afeitada, *f;* (of wood, etc.) viruta, acepilladura, *f.* **s.-bowl,** bacía, *f.* **s.-brush,** brocha de afeitar, *f.* **s.-glass,** espejo de afeitar, *m.* **s.-soap,** jabón de afeitar, *m.* **s.-stick,** barra de jabón de afeitar, *f*

shawl /ʃɔl/ *n* chal, mantón, rebozo, *m*

she /ʃi/ *pers pron* ella; la; (female) hembra, *f;* (translated by fem. ending in the case of animals, etc., e.g. *she bear,* osa, *she cat,* gata). **It is her,** Es ella. **she who is dancing,** la que baila

sheaf /ʃif/ *n* (of corn, etc.) gavilla, garba, *f;* (of ar-

rows) haz, *m;* (of papers, etc.) paquete, atado, *m.* **to bind in sheaves,** agavillar
shear /ʃıər/ *vt* (sheep) esquilar, trasquilar; tonsurar; cortar; (cloth) tundir
shearer /'ʃıərər/ *n* (of sheep) esquilador, *m*
shearing /'ʃıərıŋ/ *n* (of sheep) esquileo, *m,* tonsura, *f;* (of cloth) tunda, *f.* **s. machine,** esquiladora, *f.* **s. season,** esquileo, *m*
shears /ʃıərz/ *n pl* tijeras grandes, *f pl,* cizalla, *f*
sheath /ʃiθ/ *n* vaina, *f.* **s.-knife,** cuchillo de monte, *m*
sheathe /ʃið/ *vt* envainar; *naut* aforrar
shed /ʃɛd/ *vt* derramar; (skin, etc.) mudar; perder; (remove) quitarse, desprenderse de; (get rid of) deshacerse de. —*n* cobertizo, sotechado, *m;* cabaña, *f.* **to s. light on,** echar luz sobre, iluminar
sheen /ʃin/ *n* lustre, *m;* brillo, *m*
sheep /ʃip/ *n* oveja, *f;* carnero, *m;* ganado lanar, *m.* **He is the black s. of the family,** Es el garbanzo negro de la familia. **to cast sheep's eyes at,** lanzar miradas de carnero degollado. **s. breeder,** ganadero, *m.* **s.-dip,** desinfectante para ganado, *m.* **s.-dog,** perro de pastor, *m.* **s.-like,** ovejuno, de oveja. **s.-shearing,** esquileo, *m*
sheepfold /'ʃip,fould/ *n* aprisco, redil, *m*
sheepish /'ʃipıʃ/ *a* tímido, vergonzoso; estúpido
sheepishly /'ʃipıʃli/ *adv* tímidamente
sheepishness /'ʃipıʃnıs/ *n* timidez, cortedad, *f;* estupidez, *f*
sheepskin /'ʃip,skın/ *n* piel de carnero, *f.* **s. jacket,** zamarra, *f*
sheer /ʃıər/ *a* puro; completo, absoluto; (steep) escarpado, acantilado; a pico; (of fabrics) transparente; ligero, fino. —*adv* completamente; de un golpe; (perpendicularly) a pico. **to s. off,** desviarse; largarse, marcharse
sheet /ʃit/ *n* (bed) sábana, *f;* (shroud) mortaja, *f;* (of paper) hoja, *f;* cuartilla, *f;* (pamphlet) folleto, *m;* (news) periódico, *m,* hoja, *f;* (of metal, etc.) lámina, plancha, *f;* (of water, etc.) extensión, *f; naut* escota, *f.* —*vt* poner sábanas en; envolver en sábanas; (a corpse) amortajar. **to be as white as a s.,** estar pálido como un muerto. **s. bend,** (knot) nudo de tejedor, *m.* **s. glass,** vidrio en lámina, *m.* **s. iron,** hierro en planchas, *m*
sheik /ʃik/ *n* jeque, *m*
shekel /'ʃɛkəl/ *n* (coin) siclo, *m; pl* **shekels,** dinero, *m*
shelf /ʃɛlf/ *n* estante, anaquel, *m;* (reef) banco de arena, bajío, *m;* (of rock) escalón, *m.* **to be on the s.,** *inf* quedarse para tía, quedarse para vestir imágenes
shell /ʃɛl/ *n* (of small shellfish) concha, *f;* (of tortoise) coraza, *f;* (of insects, lobsters, etc.) caparazón, *m;* (of a nut) cáscara, *f;* (of an egg) cascarón, *m;* (of peas, beans) vaina, *f;* (*com* and *mus*) concha, *f;* (of a building) casco, *m;* (outside) exterior, *m;* (empty form) apariencia, *f; mil* granada, *f.* —*vt* pelar; (nuts) descascarar; (beans, etc.) desvainar; *mil* bombardear. **to be under s.-fire,** sufrir un bombardeo. **s. shock,** neurosis de guerra, *f*
shellfish /'ʃɛl,fıʃ/ *n* crustáceo, *m;* (as food) marisco, *m*
shelling /'ʃɛlıŋ/ *n mil* bombardeo, *m*
shelter /'ʃɛltər/ *n* abrigo, amparo, *m;* refugio, *m;* asilo, *m.* —*vt* dar asilo (a); abrigar; (defend) amparar, proteger; (hide) esconder. —*vi* refugiarse; resguardarse; esconderse
sheltered /'ʃɛltərd/ *a* abrigado
sheltering /'ʃɛltərıŋ/ *a* protector
shelve /ʃɛlv/ *vt* (books) poner en un estante; (persons) destituir; (questions, etc.) aplazar, arrinconar; proveer de estantes, *vi* (slope) inclinarse, formar declive; (of sea bed) formar escalones
shelving /'ʃɛlvıŋ/ *a* inclinado; (of ocean bed) acantilado
shepherd /'ʃɛpərd/ *n* pastor, *m.* —*vt* guardar; guiar, conducir. **s. boy,** zagal, *m.* **shepherd's pouch,** zurrón, *m*
shepherdess /'ʃɛpərdıs/ *n* pastora, *f*
sherbet /'ʃɜrbıt/ *n* sorbete, *m*
sheriff /'ʃɛrıf/ *n* (in U.K.) sheriff, *m;* (U.S.A.) jefe de la policía, *m*
sherry /'ʃɛri/ *n* (vino de) jerez, *m.* **dry s.,** jerez seco, *m*
Shetlands, the /'ʃɛtləndz/ las Islas de Shetland, *f pl*
shield /ʃild/ *n* escudo, *m;* (round) rodela, *f; herald* escudo de armas, *m; fig* defensa, *f,* amparo, *m.* —*vt* proteger, amparar. **to s. a person,** proteger a una persona. **to s. one's eyes from the sun,** proteger los ojos del sol. **s.-bearer,** escudero, *m*
shift /ʃıft/ *vt* mover; trasladar; quitar, librarse de; cambiar. —*vi* moverse; (of the wind) girar; cambiar. —*n* cambio, *m;* (expedient) recurso, expediente, *m;* (dodge) artificio, *m,* trampa, *f;* (of workmen) tanda, *f,* turno, *m.* **to make s.,** arreglárselas (para hacer algo); procurar (hacer algo); (manage) ir tirando. **to s. for oneself,** componérselas, arreglárselas. **to s. the scenes,** *theat* cambiar de decoración. **to s. the helm,** *naut* cambiar el timón. **to work in shifts,** trabajar por turnos
shiftiness /'ʃıftinıs/ *n* falta de honradez, informalidad, *f;* astucia, *f*
shifting /'ʃıftıŋ/ *a* (of light, etc.) cambiante; (of sand, etc.) movedizo; (of wind) mudable; (of moods) voluble. **s. sand,** arena movediza, *f*
shiftless /'ʃıftlıs/ *a* perezoso; sin energía, ineficaz
shiftlessness /'ʃıftlısnıs/ *n* pereza, *f;* falta de energía, *f*
shifty /'ʃıfti/ *a* (tricky) tramposo, astuto; (dishonest) informal, falso; (of gaze) furtivo. **s.-eyed,** *a* de mirada furtiva
Shiite /'ʃiait/ *a* and *n* chiita
shilling /'ʃılıŋ/ *n* chelín, *m.* **nine shillings in the £,** nueve chelines por libra. **to cut off with a s.,** desheredar
shilly shally /'ʃıli ,ʃæli/ *n* irresolución, vacilación, *f, vi* estar irresoluto, titubear, no saber qué hacer
shimmer /'ʃımər/ *vi* rielar; relucir. —*n* luz trémula, *f;* resplandor, *m;* viso, *m*
shin /ʃın/ *n* espinilla, *f;* (of beef) corvejón, *m.* **to s. up,** trepar
shindy /'ʃındi/ *n* suiza, reyerta, tasquera, *f.* **to kick up a s.,** armar camorra
shine /ʃain/ *vi* brillar; resplandecer, relucir, relumbrar. —*vt* (shoes) dar lustre (a). —*n* brillo, *m;* lustre, *m.* **in rain or s.,** en buen o mal tiempo. **to s. with happiness,** radiar felicidad. **to take the s. out of,** eclipsar
shingle /'ʃıŋgəl/ *n* (pebbles) guijarros, *m pl*; cascajo, *m;* barda, *f;* (hair) pelo a la garçonne, *m; pl* **shingles,** *med* zona, *f,* herpe zóster, *m.* —*vt* (the hair) cortar a la garçonne
shining /'ʃainıŋ/ *a* resplandeciente, brillante, reluciente; radiante. **s. with happiness,** radiante de felicidad. **s. example,** ejemplo notable, *m*
shintoism /'ʃıntou,ızəm/ *n* sintoísmo, *m*
shiny /'ʃaini/ *a* brillante; lustroso, terso; (of trousers, etc.) reluciente; (of paper) glaseado
ship /ʃıp/ *n* buque, barco, *m;* (sailing) velero, *m.* —*vt* embarcar; (oars) armar. —*vi* embarcar; (as a member of crew) embarcarse. **on board s.,** a bordo. **to s. a sea,** embarcar agua. **to take s.,** embarcar. **to s. off,** mandar. **ship's boat,** lancha, *f.* **ship's boy,** grumete, *m.* **ship's carpenter,** carpintero de ribera, *m.* **ship's company,** tripulación, *f.* **s.-breaker,** desguazador, *m.* **s.-canal,** canal de navegación, *m.* **s.-load,** cargamento, *m*
shipbuilder /'ʃıp,bıldər/ *n* constructor de buques, arquitecto naval, *m*
shipbuilding /'ʃıp,bıldıŋ/ *n* construcción naval, *f*
shipment /'ʃıpmənt/ *n* embarque, *m;* despacho por mar, *m;* (consignment) remesa, *f*
shipowner /'ʃıp,ounər/ *n* naviero, *m*
shipper /'ʃıpər/ *n* naviero, *m;* importador, *m;* exportador, *m*
shipping /'ʃıpıŋ/ *n* embarque, *m;* buques, barcos, *m pl*; (of a country) marina, *f.* **s. agent,** consignatario de buques, *m.* **s. company,** compañía de navegación, *f.* **s. offices,** oficinas de una compañía de navegación, *f pl*
shipshape /'ʃıp,ʃeip/ *a* en buen orden; bien arreglado
shipwreck /'ʃıp,rɛk/ *n* naufragio, *m, vt* hacer naufragar, echar a pique

shipwrecked person /'ʃɪp,rɛkt/ *n* náufrago (-ga). **to be shipwrecked,** naufragar
shipyard /'ʃɪp,yɑrd/ *n* astillero, varadero, *m*
shire /ʃaiᵊr/ *n* condado, *m*
shirk /ʃɜrk/ *vt* eludir, esquivar; desentenderse de. —*vi* faltar al deber
shirker /'ʃɜrkər/ *n* gandul (-la); persona que no cumple con su deber, *f*
shirr /ʃɜr/ *vt* fruncir
shirt /ʃɜrt/ *n* camisa, *f.* **dress s.,** camisa de pechera dura, *f.* **hair-s.,** cilicio, *m.* **in one's s.-sleeves,** en mangas de camisa. **s.-blouse,** blusa sencilla, *f.* **s.-collar,** cuello de camisa, *m.* **s. factory** or **shop,** camisería, *f.* **shirt-front,** pechera, *f.* **s.-maker,** camisero (-ra)
shirting /'ʃɜrtɪŋ/ *n* tela para camisas, *f*
shiver /'ʃɪvər/ *vi* temblar, tiritar; dar diente con diente; (of a boat) zozobrar. —*vt* (break) hacer añicos, romper; (sails) sacudir. —*n* temblor, estremecimiento, *m;* escalofrío, *m;* (of glass, etc.) fragmento, *m,* astilla, *f.* **You give me the shivers,** Me das escalofríos
shivery /'ʃɪvəri/ *a* tembloroso; friolero. **I feel s.,** Tengo escalofríos
shoal /ʃoul/ *n* (of fish) banco, *m;* gran cantidad, *f;* (of people) multitud, muchedumbre, *f;* (water) bajo fondo, *m;* (sand-bank) banco, bajío, *m, a* poco profundo. **I know shoals of people in Valencia,** Conozco a muchísima gente de Valencia
shock /ʃɒk/ *n* choque, *m; elec* conmoción, *f; med* shock, *m;* (*med* stroke) conmoción cerebral, *f;* (fright) sobresalto, susto, *m.* —*vt* sacudir, dar una sacudida (a); chocar; escandalizar, horrorizar. —*vi* chocar. **electric s.,** conmoción eléctrica, *f.* **She is easily shocked,** Ella se escandaliza fácilmente. **s. of hair,** mata de pelo, *f.* **s. absorber,** *ech* amortiguador, *m; auto* amortiguador (de los muelles), *m.* **s. troops,** tropas de asalto, *f pl,* elementos de choque, *m pl*
shocking /'ʃɒkɪŋ/ *a* escandaloso; repugnante, horrible; espantoso. **How s.!** ¡Qué horror! **s. bad,** malísimo
shockingly /'ʃɒkɪŋli/ *adv* horriblemente
shod /ʃɒd/ *a* calzado; (of horses) herrado
shoddy /'ʃɒdi/ *n* pacotilla, *f.* —*a* de pacotilla; espurio, falso
shoe /ʃu/ *n* zapato, *m;* (horse) herradura, *f;* (*naut mech*) zapata, *f.* —*vt* (horses) herrar. **I should not like to be in his shoes,** No me gustaría estar en su pellejo. **That is quite another pair of shoes,** Eso es harina de otro costal. **to cast a s.,** (of horses) desherrarse, perder una herradura. **to put on one's shoes,** ponerse los zapatos, calzarse. **to remove one's shoes,** quitarse los zapatos, descalzarse. **wooden shoes,** zuecos, *m pl.* **s.-buckle,** hebilla de zapato, *f.* **s.-lace,** cordón de zapato, *m.* **s.-leather,** cuero para zapatos, *m;* calzado, *m.* **s.-scraper,** limpiabarros, *m,* estregadera, *f.* **s.-shop,** zapatería, *f*
shoeblack /'ʃu,blæk/ *n* betún, *m;* (person) limpiabotas, *m*
shoehorn /'ʃu,hɔrn/ *n* calzador, *m*
shoemaker /'ʃu,meikər/ *n* zapatero (-ra)
shoemaking /'ʃu,meikɪŋ/ *n* fabricación de calzado, zapatería, *f*
shoo! /ʃu/ *interj* ¡fuera!; ¡zape! —*vt* ahuyentar
shoot /ʃut/ *vt* (throw) lanzar; precipitar; (empty) vaciar; (a rapid) salvar; (rays, etc.) echar; (an arrow, a gun, etc.) disparar; (a person, etc.) pegar un tiro (a); *sports* tirar; *mil* fusilar, pasar por las armas; (a film) hacer, impresionar. —*vi* lanzarse, precipitarse; (of pain) latir; (sprout) brotar; disparar; tirar; (at football) tirar a gol, chutar. **to s. a glance at,** lanzar una mirada (a). **I was shot in the foot,** Una bala me hirió en el pie. **to s. the sun,** *naut* tomar el sol. **to s. ahead,** tomar la delantera. **to s. at,** tirar a. **to s by,** pasar como una bala. **to s. down,** *aer* derribar; matar de un tiro. **to s. up,** (of children) espigarse; (of prices) subir mucho; (of cliffs, etc.) elevarse
shoot /ʃut/ *n* partida de caza, *f;* tiro, *m; bot* renuevo, retoño, *m*
shooting /'ʃutɪŋ/ *n* tiro, *m;* caza con escopeta, *f;* (of guns) tiroteo, *m;* (of an arrow) disparo, *m;* (of a film) rodaje, *m.* **to go s.,** ir a cazar con escopeta. **s.-box,** pabellón de caza, *m.* **s. butts,** tiradero, *m.* **s. dog,** perro de caza, *m.* **s.-gallery,** tiro al blanco, *m.* **s. match,** concurso de tiro, *m.* **s. pain,** punzada de dolor, *f.* **s. party,** partida de caza, *f.* **s. practice,** ejercicios de tiro, *m pl.* **s.-range,** campo de tiro, *m.* **s. star,** estrella fugaz, *f*
shop /ʃɒp/ *n* tienda, *f;* (workshop) taller, *m.* —*vi* ir de compras, ir de tiendas; comprar. **to talk s.,** hablar de negocios. **s.-assistant,** dependiente (-ta). **s.-soiled,** deslucido. **s.-steward,** representante de los obreros de una fábrica o taller, *m.* **s. window,** escaparate, *m*
shopkeeper /'ʃɒp,kipər/ *n* tendero (-ra)
shoplifter /'ʃɒp,lɪftər/ *n* ladrón (-ona) de tiendas, ratero (-ra) de las tiendas
shoplifting /'ʃɒp,lɪftiŋ/ *n* ratería en las tiendas, *f*
shopper /'ʃɒpər/ *n* comprador (-ra)
shopping /'ʃɒpɪŋ/ *n* compra, *f;* compras, *f pl.* **to go s.,** ir de compras. **s. basket,** cesta para compras, *f.* **s. center,** centro comercial, *m*
shopwalker /'ʃɒp,wɔkər/ *n* jefe de recepción, *m*
shore /ʃɔr/ *n* orilla, ríbera, *f;* costa, *f;* (sands) playa, *f.* **off s.,** en alta mar. **on s.,** en tierra. **to come on s.,** desembarcar. **to s. up,** apuntalar, acodalar; *fig* apoyar
short /ʃɔrt/ *a* corto; (of persons) bajo; breve; (of temper) vivo; insuficiente; distante (de); (brusque) seco; (of money) alcanzado. —*adv* súbitamente; brevemente. —*n* (vowel) vocal breve, *m; pl* **shorts,** calzones cortos, *m pl.* **for s.,** para mayor brevedad. **for a s. time,** por poco tiempo. **in a s. time,** dentro de poco. **in s.,** en breve, en resumen, en pocas palabras. **on s. notice,** con poco tiempo de aviso. **s. of,** con la excepción de, menos. **to be s.,** faltar, ser escaso. **to be s. with someone,** tratar con sequedad (a). **to fall s. of expectations,** no cumplir las esperanzas. **to go s. of,** pasarse sin. **to grow s.,** escasear. **s.-circuit,** corto circuito, *m.* **s. cut,** atajo, *m.* **s.-haired,** pelicorto. **s.-handed,** falto de mano de obra. **s.-lived,** de vida corta; efímero, fugaz. **to be short-lived,** tener vida corta. **s.-sighted,** corto de vista. **s.-sightedness,** miopía, cortedad de vista, *f.* **s. story,** cuento, *m.* **s.-tempered,** iracible, irritable, de genio vivo. **s.-waisted,** corto de talle. **s.-winded,** corto de resuello; asmático
shortage /'ʃɔrtɪdʒ/ *n* falta, escasez, *f;* carestía, *f.* **water s.,** carestía de agua, *f*
shortcoming /'ʃɔrt,kʌmɪŋ/ *n* defecto, *m;* imperfección, *f*
shorten /'ʃɔrtn̩/ *vt* acortar; reducir, disminuir; abreviar. —*vi* acortarse
shorthand /'ʃɔrt,hænd/ *n* taquigrafía, estenografía, *f.* —*a* taquigráfico, estenográfico. **to take down in s.,** taquigrafiar. **s. writer,** estenógrafo (-fa); taquígrafo (-fa)
shortly /'ʃɔrtli/ *adv* dentro de poco, pronto; brevemente, en resumen, en pocas palabras; (curtly) bruscamente, secamente
shortness /'ʃɔrtnɪs/ *n* cortedad, *f;* brevedad, *f;* (of a person) pequeñez, *f;* (lack) falta, *f;* (of memory, sight) cortedad, *f;* brusqueness) sequedad, brusquedad, *f.* **s. of breath,** falta de aliento, respiración difícil, *f*
shot /ʃɒt/ *n* perdigón, *m; inf* perdigones, *m pl*; bala, *f;* (firing) tiro, *m;* (person) tirador (-ra); (stroke, etc.) golpe, *m,* tirada, *f;* (cinema) fotograma, *m.* —*a* (of silk) tornasolado. **at one s.,** de un tiro. **like a s.,** *fig* como una bala. **to exchange shots,** tirotearse. **to fire a s.,** disparar un tiro. **to have a s. at,** probar suerte. **s.-gun,** escopeta, *f.* **s. silk,** seda tornasolada, *f*
should /ʃʊd/ *v aux* (expressing future) **I s. like to go to the sea,** Me gustaría ir al mar; (expressing conditional) **I s. like to see them if I could,** Me gustaría verlos si pudiera; (expressing obligation) **You s. go at once,** Debes ir en seguida; (expressing probability) **They s. arrive tomorrow,** Seguramente llegarán mañana; (expressing doubt) **If the moment s. be opportune,** Si el momento fuera oportuno. **I s. just think so!** ¡Ya lo creo! ¡No lo dudo!
shoulder /'ʃouldər/ *n* hombro, *m;* (of mutton) espalda, *f;* (of a hill) falda, *f.* —*vt* echar al hombro, echar sobre sí; (a responsibility) cargar con, hacerse responsable para; (jostle) dar codazos (a). **s. to s.,** hombro a hombro. **S. arms!** ¡Armas al hombro! **s.-**

blade, omoplato, *m.* **s.-knot,** charretera, *f.* **s.-pad,** hombrera, *f.* **s.-strap,** *mil* dragona, *f;* (of a dress, etc.) tirante, *m;* (of a water carrier, etc.) correón, *m*
shouldered /ˈʃouldərd/ *a* de hombros..., de espaldas... **round-s.,** cargado de espaldas
shout /ʃaut/ *vi* gritar, hablar a gritos. —*vt* gritar. —*n* grito, *m.* **shouts of applause,** aclamaciones, *f pl,* aplausos, *m pl.* **to s. from the housetops,** pregonar a los cuatro vientos. **to s. with laughter,** reírse a carcajadas. **to s. down,** silbar. **to s. out,** gritar
shouting /ˈʃautɪŋ/ *n* gritos, *m pl,* vocerío, clamor, *m;* (applause) aclamaciones, *f pl*
shove /ʃʌv/ *vt* empujar; poner. —*n* empujón, *m.* **to s. along,** empujar. **to s. aside,** empujar a un lado; apartar a codazos. **to s. away,** rechazar. **to s. back,** hacer retroceder. **to s. forward,** hacer avanzar, empujar hacia adelante. **to s. off,** (a boat) echar afuera. **to s. out,** empujar hacia fuera
shovel /ˈʃʌvəl/ *n* pala, *f.* —*vt* traspalar. **s. hat,** sombrero de teja, *m*
show /ʃou/ *vt* mostrar; hacer ver; (disclose) descubrir; revelar; (exhibit) exhibir; (indicate) indicar; (prove) demostrar, probar; (conduct) conducir, llevar, guiar; (explain) explicar; (oneself) presentarse. —*vi* mostrarse; verse; parecer. **to s. cause,** mostrar causa. **to s. fight,** ofrecer resistencia. **s. signs of,** dar señales de. **to s. itself,** declararse, asomarse, surgir. **to s. to the door,** acompañar a la puerta. **to s. in,** (a person) hacer entrar, introducir (en). **to s. off,** *vt* exhibir; realzar; (new clothes, etc.) lucir. —*vi* darse importancia; pavonearse. **to s. out,** (a person) acompañar a la puerta; (in anger) poner de patitas en la calle. **to s. through,** *vi* trasparentarse. —*vt* conducir por. **to s. up,** *vt* invitar a subir; (a fraud, etc.) descubrir; (a swindler) desenmascarar; (defects) revelar. —*vi* (stand out) destacarse; (be present) asomarse, asistir
show /ʃou/ *n* (exhibition) exposición, *f;* espectáculo, *m;* (sign) indicio, *m,* señal, *f;* (ostentation) pompa, *f,* aparato, *m,* ostentación, *f;* (appearance) apariencia, *f;* (affair) negocio, *m.* **to give the s. away,** echar los títeres a rodar. **to make a s. of,** hacer gala de. **s.-case,** escaparate, *m,* vitrina, *f.* **s. of hands,** votación por manos levantadas, *f.* **s.-room,** salón de muestras, *m*
showdown /ˈʃouˌdaun/ *n* cartas boca arriba, *m*
shower /ˈʃauər/ *n* chaparrón, chubasco, *m;* (of spray, etc.) chorro, *m;* (of stones, arrows, etc.) lluvia, *f;* (of honors) cosecha, *f,* (bridal) despedida de soltera, despedida de soltería, *f.* —*vt* derramar; rociar; mojar; llover. —*vi* chaparrear, llover. **s.-bath,** ducha, *f*
shower cap *n* gorro de ducha, *m*
showery /ˈʃauəri/ *a* lluvioso
showily /ˈʃouəli/ *adv* aparatosamente, con ostentación
showiness /ˈʃouinɪs/ *n* ostentación, *f;* esplendor, *m,* magnificencia, *f*
showman /ˈʃoumən/ *n* director de un espectáculo de feria, *m;* titiritero, *m;* pregonero, *m*
showy /ˈʃoui/ *a* vistoso; ostentoso
shrapnel /ˈʃræpnl̩/ *n* granada, *m,* granada de metralla, *f*
shred /ʃrɛd/ *n* fragmento, *m;* (of cloth) jirón, *m;* brizna, *f;* *fig* pizca, *f.* —*vt* desmenuzar. **to tear in shreds,** hacer pedazos
shrew /ʃru/ *n zool* musaraña, *f;* (woman) fiera, *f*
shrewd /ʃrud/ *a* sagaz, perspicaz; prudente; (of the wind) penetrante; (pain) punzante. **to have a s. idea of,** tener una buena idea de. **a s. diplomat,** un fino diplomático
shrewdly /ˈʃrudli/ *adv* sagazmente, con perspicacia; prudentemente
shrewdness /ˈʃrudnɪs/ *n* sagacidad, perspicacia, *f;* prudencia, *f*
shrewish /ˈʃruɪʃ/ *a* regañón
shrewishness /ˈʃruɪshnɪs/ *n* mal genio, *m*
shriek /ʃrik/ *vi* chillar, gritar. —*vt* decir a voces, gritar. —*n* chillido, *m;* grito agudo, *m.* **shrieks of laughter,** carcajadas, *f pl*
shrieking /ˈʃrikɪŋ/ *n* gritos, chillidos, *m pl*
shrift /ʃrɪft/ **to give short,** enviar normala (a), enviar a paseo (a)
shrill /ʃrɪl/ *a* estridente, agudo
shrillness /ˈʃrɪlnɪs/ *n* estridencia, *f*
shrimp /ʃrɪmp/ *n* camarón, *m,* gamba, *f, vi* pescar camarones
shrine /ʃrain/ *n* relicario, *m;* sepulcro de santo, *m;* templete, *m,* capilla, *f;* santuario, *m*
shrink /ʃrɪŋk/ *vi* encogerse; contraerse; disminuir, reducirse. —*vt* encoger; reducir, disminuir; desaparecer; disiparse. **I shrank from doing it,** Me repugnaba hacerlo. **to s. away from,** retroceder ante; recular ante; huir de. **to s. back,** recular (ante)
shrinkage /ˈʃrɪŋkɪdʒ/ *n* encogimiento, *m;* contracción, *f;* reducción, disminución, *f*
shrinking /ˈʃrɪŋkɪŋ/ *a* tímido
shrive /ʃraiv/ *vt* confesar
shrivel /ˈʃrɪvəl/ *vi* avellanarse; (of persons, through old age) acartonarse, apergaminarse; (wither) marchitarse; arrugarse. —*vt* arrugar; secar, marchitar
shroud /ʃraud/ *n* sudario, *m,* mortaja, *f;* *Naut.* obenque, *m.* **to wrap in a s.,** amortajar
Shrove Tuesday /ʃrouv/ *n* martes de carnaval, *m*
shrub /ʃrʌb/ *n* arbusto, *m;* matajo, *m*
shrubbery /ˈʃrʌbəri/ *n* arbustos, *m pl,* maleza, *f;* bosquecillo, *m*
shrug /ʃrʌg/ *vi* encogerse de hombros. —*n* encogimiento de hombros, *m*
shrunken /ˈʃrʌŋkən/ *a* contraído; acartonado, apergaminado; seco, marchito. **shrunken head,** cabeza reducida, *f*
shudder /ˈʃʌdər/ *vi* estremecerse; vibrar. —*n* estremecimiento, *m;* escalofrío, *m;* (of an engine, etc.) vibración, *f*
shuffle /ˈʃʌfəl/ *vt* (the feet) arrastrar; (scrape) restregar; (cards) barajar; (papers) mezclar. —*vi* arrastrar los pies, arrastrarse; (cards) barajar; *fig* tergiversar. —*n* (of the cards) barajadura, *f;* *fig* evasiva, *f;* embuste, *m.* **to s. along,** andar arrastrando los pies
shuffling /ˈʃʌflɪŋ/ *n* el arrastrar, *m,* (e.g. *the shuffling of chairs,* el arrastrar de sillas)
shun /ʃʌn/ *vt* evitar, rehuir, esquivar
shunt /ʃʌnt/ *vt rail* apartar; *elec* shuntar. —*vi rail* hacer maniobras
shunting /ˈʃʌntɪŋ/ *n* (of trains) maniobras, *f pl*
shut /ʃʌt/ *vt* and *vi* cerrar. **to s. again,** volver a cerrar. **to s. down,** *vt* cerrar; (a machine) parar. —*vi* (of factories, etc.) cerrar. **to s. in,** encerrar; (surround) cercar, rodear. **to s. off,** (water, etc.) cortar; (isolate) aislar (de). **to s. out,** excluir; obstruir, impedir; negar la entrada (a). **to s. up,** *vt* cerrar; encerrar; *inf* hacer callar (a); *vi inf* callarse, cerrar la boca. **to s. oneself up,** encerrarse
shutter /ˈʃʌtər/ *n* (window) contraventana, *f,* postigo, *m;* (of a camera) obturador, *m;* (of a fireplace) campana (de hogar), *f.* —*vt* poner contraventanas (a); cerrar los postigos de
shuttle /ˈʃʌtl̩/ *n* (weaver's, and sewing-machine) lanzadera, *f,* (airplane service) puente aéreo, *m.* **s.-cock,** volante, gallito, *m*
shy /ʃai/ *a* (of animals) tímido, salvaje; (of persons) huraño, tímido; vergonzoso. —*vi* (of a horse) respingar; (of persons) asustarse (de). —*vt* (a ball, etc.) lanzar. —*n* (of a horse) respingo, *m;* (of a ball) lanzamiento, *m;* (try) prueba, tentativa, *f.* **to fight shy of,** procurar evitar. **to have a shy at,** probar
shyly /ˈʃaili/ *adv* tímidamente; con vergüenza, vergonzosamente
shyness /ˈʃainɪs/ *n* timidez, *f;* hurañía, *f;* vergüenza, *f*
Siamese /ˌsaiəˈmiz/ *a* siamés. —*n* siamés (-esa); (language) siamés, *m.* **S. cat,** gato siamés, *m*
Siberia /saiˈbɪəriə/ Siberia, *f*
Siberian /saiˈbɪəriən/ *a* and *n* siberiano (-na)
sic /sɪk/ *vt* atacar; abijar, azuzar (a dog); *adv* así (in academic prose)
Sicilian /sɪˈsɪlyən/ *a* and *n* siciliano (-na)
Sicily /ˈsɪsəli/ Sicilia, *f*
sick /sɪk/ *a* enfermo; mareado. **the s.,** los enfermos. **to be s.,** vomitar; estar enfermo. **to be s. of,** estar harto de. **to feel s.,** sentirse mareado. **to be on the s.-list,** estar enfermo. **s.-bed,** lecho de dolor, *m.* **s.-headache,** jaqueca, con náuseas, *f.* **s.-leave,** *mil* permiso por enfermedad, *m.* **s.-nurse,** enfermera, *f*
sicken /ˈsɪkən/ *vi* caer enfermo, enfermar; (feel sick) marearse; (recoil from) repugnar; (weary of) cansarse (de), aburrirse (de). —*vt* marear; dar asco (a), repug-

nar; cansar, aburrir. **It sickens me,** Me da asco. **He is sickening for measles,** Muestra síntomas de sarampión

sickening /ˈsɪkənɪŋ/ *a* nauseabundo; repugnante; (tedious) fastidioso

sickle /ˈsɪkəl/ *n* hoz, segadera, *f*

sickliness /ˈsɪklinɪs/ *n* falta de salud, *f;* náusea, *f;* (paleness) palidez, *f*

sickly /ˈsɪkli/ *a* enfermizo, achacoso, malucho; (of places, etc.) malsano; (pale) pálido; débil; (of a smell) nauseabundo; (mawkish) empalagoso

sickness /ˈsɪknɪs/ *n* enfermedad, *f;* mal, *m;* náusea, *f,* mareo, *m*

side /said/ *n* lado, *m;* (hand) mano, *f;* (of a river, etc.) orilla, *f,* margen, *m;* (of a person) costado, *m;* (of an animal) ijada, *f;* (of a hill) falda, pendiente, ladera, *f;* (of a ship) banda, *f,* costado, *m;* (aspect) aspecto, *m;* punto de vista, *m;* (party) partido, grupo, *m;* (team) equipo, *m;* (of descent) lado, *m.* —*a* lateral, de lado; oblicuo. **on all sides,** por todas partes. **on both sides,** por ambos lados. **s. by s.,** lado a lado. **the other s. of the picture,** el revés de la medalla. **to change sides,** cambiar de partido. **to pick sides,** escoger el equipo. **to put on s.,** darse tono, alzar el gallo. **to split one's sides,** desternillarse de risa, reírse a carcajadas. **to s. with,** declararse por, ponerse al lado de, tomar el partido de. **wrong s. out,** al revés. **s.-car,** sidecar, asiento lateral, *m.* **s.-chain,** *chem* cadena lateral, *f.* **s.-dish,** entremés, *m.* **s. door,** puerta lateral, *f.* **s.-face,** *a* de perfil. —*n* perfil, *m.* **s.-glance,** mirada de soslayo, *f.* **s.-issue,** cuestión secundaria, *f.* **s.-line,** negocio accesorio, *m;* ocupación secundaria, *f;* *rail* vía secundaria, *f.* **s.-saddle,** silla de señora, silla de montar de lado, *f.* **s.-show,** (at a fair) barraca, *f,* puesto de feria, *m;* exhibición secundaria, *f;* función secundaria, *f.* **s.-table,** trinchero, *m.* **s.-track,** *n* *rail* apartadero, *m.* —*vt* desviar (de), apartar (de). **s.-view,** perfil, *m.* **s.-walk,** acera, *f.* **s.-whiskers,** patillas, *f pl*

sidelight /ˈsaidˌlait/ *n* luz lateral, *f;* (on a ship) ojo de buey, *m;* *fig* información incidental, *f*

sidelong /ˈsaidˌlɔŋ/ *adv* de lado, lateralmente; (of glances) de soslayo. —*a* oblicuo

side road *n* camino lateral, *m*

sideways /ˈsaidˌweiz/ *adv* oblicuamente, de lado; (edgewise) de soslayo. —*a* de soslayo

siding /ˈsaidɪŋ/ *n* *rail* apartadero, *m*

sidle /ˈsaidl̩/ *vi* andar (or ir) de lado. **to s. up to,** acercarse servilmente a; arrimarse (a)

siege /sidʒ/ *n* asedio, sitio, cerco, *m.* **to lay s. to,** poner cerco (a), sitiar, asediar cercar. **to raise a s.,** levantar un sitio

sienna /siˈɛnə/ *n* tierra de siena natural, *f.* **burnt s.,** tierra de siena tostada, *f*

sieve /sɪv/ *n* cedazo, tamiz, *m,* criba, *f, vt* tamizar, cerner, cribar

sift /sɪft/ *vt* (sieve) cerner, cribar; (sugar, etc.) salpicar (con); (a question) escudriñar, examinar minuciosamente

sifting /ʃɪftɪŋ/ *n* cribado, *m;* (of a question) investigación minuciosa, *f;* *pl* **siftings,** cerniduras, *f pl*

sigh /sai/ *vi* suspirar; (of the wind) susurrar. —*n* suspiro, *m;* (of the wind) susurro, *m.* **to s. for,** suspirar por; lamentar

sighing /ˈsaiɪŋ/ *n* suspiros, *m pl*; (of the wind) susurro, *m*

sight /sait/ *n* vista, *f;* visión, *f;* espectáculo, *m;* (fright) estantigua, *f.* —*vt* ver, divisar; (aim) apuntar. **front s.,** (of guns) alza, *f.* **short s.,** (of eyes) vista corta, *f.* **at first s.,** a primera vista. **in s.,** a la vista. **in s. of,** a vista de. **out of s.,** que no está a la vista; perdido de vista. **Out of s., out of mind,** Ojos que no ven, corazón que no siente. **to be lost to s.,** perderse de vista. **to lose s. of,** perder de vista (a). **to catch a s. of,** vislumbrar. **to come in s.,** aparecer, asomarse. **to know by s.,** conocer de vista (a). **s.-reading,** lectura a primera vista, *f*

sightly /ˈsaitli/ *a* hermoso; deleitable

sightseeing /ˈsaitˌsiɪŋ/ *n* turismo, *m.* **to go s.**, visitar los monumentos, ver los puntos de interés

sightseer /ˈsaitˌsiər/ *n* curioso (-sa); turista, *mf*

sign /sain/ *n* señal, *f;* seña, *f;* indicio, *m;* (of the zodiac and *mus*) signo, *m;* marca, *f;* *eccl* símbolo, *m;* (of a shop, etc.) muestra, *f,* rótulo, *m;* (symptom) síntoma, *m.* —*vt* firmar; indicar; *eccl* persignar. **as a s. of,** en señal de. **to converse by signs,** hablar por señas. **to make the s. of the cross over,** santiguar. **to show signs (of),** dar señas (de); indicar. **s.-painter,** pintor de muestras, *m*

signal /ˈsɪgnl̩/ *n* señal, *f.* —*vt* señalar; hacer señas (a). —*vi* hacer señales. —*a* insigne, notable. **fog-s.,** señal de niebla, *f.* **landing s.,** *aer* señal de aterrizaje, *f.* **to give the s. for,** dar la señal para. **s.-box,** garita de señales, *f.* **s. code,** *naut* código de señales, *m*

signaler /ˈsɪgnl̩ər/ *n* señalador, *m*

signalize /ˈsɪgnl̩ˌaiz/ *vt* señalar, distinguir

signalman /ˈsɪgnl̩mən/ *n* *rail* guardavía, *m*

signatory /ˈsɪgnəˌtɔri/ *a* and *n* signatario (-ia)

signature /ˈsɪgnətʃər/ *n* firma, *f;* (*mus* and *print*) signatura, *f*

signboard /ˈsainˌbɔrd/ *n* letrero, *m,* muestra, *f*

signet /ˈsɪgnɪt/ *n* sello, *m.* **s.-ring,** anillo de sello, *m*

significance /sɪgˈnɪfɪkəns/ *n* significación, *f,* significado, *m;* importancia, *f*

significant /sɪgˈnɪfɪkənt/ *a* significativo, significante; expresivo; importante

significantly /sɪgˈnɪfɪkəntli/ *adv* significativamente; expresivamente

signify /ˈsɪgnəˌfai/ *vt* significar; querer decir; importar. —*vi* significar, tener importancia; importar

signpost /ˈsainˌpoust/ *n* indicador de dirección, *m*

Sikh /sik/ *n* sik, *mf* (*pl* siks)

silage /ˈsailɪdʒ/ *n* forraje conservado en silo, *m*

silence /ˈsailəns/ *n* silencio, *m, interj* ¡silencio! —*vt* hacer callar, imponer silencio (a); silenciar. **to keep s.,** guardar silencio, callarse. **to pass over in s.,** pasar en silencio (por), pasar por alto de. **S. gives consent,** Quien calla otorga

silencer /ˈsailənsər/ *n* (of fire-arms) silencioso, *m;* *auto* silenciador, silencioso, *m*

silent /ˈsailənt/ *a* silencioso. **to become s.,** enmudecer; callar. **to remain s.,** callarse, guardar silencio; permanecer silencioso. **s. partner,** *n* socio (-ia) comanditario (-ia)

silent film *n* película muda, *f*

silently /ˈsailəntli/ *adv* silenciosamente, en silencio

silhouette /ˌsɪluˈɛt/ *n* silueta, *f.* —*vt* representar en silueta; destacar. **in s.,** en silueta. **to be silhouetted against the sky,** destacarse contra el sielo

silica /ˈsɪlɪkə/ *n* sílice, *f*

silk /sɪlk/ *n* seda, *f, a* de seda. **artificial s.,** seda artificial, *f.* **floss s.,** seda ocal, *f.* **sewing s.,** seda de coser, *f.* **twist s.,** seda cordelada, *f.* **as smooth as s.,** como una seda. **s. growing,** sericultura, *f.* **s. hat,** sombrero de copa, *m.* **s. merchandise,** sedería, *f.* **s. stocking,** media de seda, *f*

silken /ˈsɪlkən/ *a* de seda; sedoso

silkiness /ˈsɪlkinɪs/ *n* carácter sedoso, *m;* suavidad, *f*

silk-screen process /ˈsɪlkˌskrin/ *n* imprenta por tamiz, imprenta serigráfica, imprenta tamigráfica, impresión con estarcido de seda, *f,* proceso tamigráfico, *m,* serigrafía, tamigrafía, *f*

silkworm /ˈsɪlkˌwɜrm/ *n* gusano de seda, *m*

silky /ˈsɪlki/ *a* sedoso; (of wine) suave

sill /sɪl/ *n* (of a window) alféizar, antepecho, *m;* (of a door) umbral, *m*

silliness /ˈsɪlinɪs/ *n* tontería, estupidez, *f*

silly /ˈsɪli/ *a* tonto, estúpido; imbécil. —*n* tonto (-ta). **You are a s. ass,** Eres un imbécil

silo /ˈsailou/ *n* silo, *m*

silt /sɪlt/ *n* aluvión, *m,* sedimentación, *f.* **to s. up,** *vt* cegar (or obstruir) con aluvión. —*vi* cegarse con aluvión

silver /ˈsɪlvər/ *n* plata, *f.* —*a* de plata; argénteo; (of the voice, etc.) argentino. —*vt* platear; (mirrors) azogar; (hair) blanquear. **s. birch,** abedul, *m.* **s. fox,** zorro plateado, *m.* **s.-gry,** gris perla, *m.* **s.-haired,** de pelo entrecano. **s.-paper,** papel de estaño, *m.* **s.-plate,** *n* vajilla de plata, *f.* —*vt* platear. **s.-tongued,** de pico de oro; de voz argentina. **s. wedding,** bodas de plata, *f pl*

silversmith /ˈsɪlvərˌsmɪθ/ *n* platero, *m.* **silversmith's shop,** platería, *f*

silvery /'sılvəri/ *a* plateado, argentado; (of sounds) argentino

simian /'sımiən/ *a* símico

similar /'sımələr/ *a* parecido (a), semejante (a); similar; *geom* semejante. **to be s. to,** asemejarse (a), parecerse (a)

similarity /ˌsımə'lærıti/ *n* parecido, *m,* semejanza, similitud, *f*

similarly /'sımələrli/ *adv* de un modo parecido, asimismo

simile /'sıməli/ *n* símil, *m*

simmer /'sımər/ *vi* hervir a fuego lento; *fig* estar a punto de estallar. **to s. down,** *fig* moderarse poco a poco. **to s. over,** *fig* estallar

simper /'sımpər/ *vi* sonreírse bobamente

simpering /'sımpərıŋ/ *n* sonrisilla tonta, *f*

simperingly /'sımpərıŋli/ *adv* con sonrisa necia

simple /'sımpəl/ *a* sencillo; simple; ingenuo, inocente; crédulo; (humble) humilde; (mere) mero. **s.-hearted,** inocente, cándido, sin malicia. **s.-minded,** ingenuo; crédulo. **s.-mindedness,** ingenuidad, *f;* credulidad, *f*

simpleton /'sımpəltən/ *n* primo (-ma); papanatas, *m,* tonto (-ta)

simplicity /sım'plısıti/ *n* sencillez, *f;* simplicidad, candidez, *f*

simplifiable /ˌsımplə'faiəbəl/ *a* simplificable

simplification /ˌsımpləfı'keiʃən/ simplificación, *f*

simplify /'sımpləˌfai/ *vt* simplificar

simply /'sımpli/ *adv* sencillamente; simplemente, meramente; absolutamente

simulacrum /ˌsımyə'leikrəm/ *n* simulacro, *m*

simulate /'sımyəˌleit/ *vt* fingir, aparentar, simular

simulation /ˌsımyə'leiʃən/ *n* simulación, *f,* fingimiento, *m*

simultaneous /ˌsaiməl'teiniəs/ *a* simultáneo

simultaneously /ˌsaiməl'teiniəsli/ *adv* simultáneamente; al mismo tiempo (que)

simultaneousness /ˌsaiməl'teiniəsnıs/ *n* simultaneidad, *f*

sin /sın/ *n* pecado, *m, vi* pecar; faltar (a)

since /sıns/ *adv* desde entonces, desde (que). *—prep* desde. *—conjunc* desde que; ya que, puesto que. **a long time s.,** hace mucho. **not long s.,** hace poco. **How long is it s...?** ¿Cuánto tiempo hace que...? **s. then,** desde entonces

sincere /sın'sıər/ *a* sincero

sincerely /sın'sıərli/ *adv* sinceramente. **Yours s.,** Su afectísimo...

sincerity /sın'sɛrıti/ *n* sinceridad, *f*

sine /sain/ *n math* seno, *m*

sinecure /'sainıˌkyʊr/ *n* canonjía, sinecura, *f,* empleo de aviador (Mexican slang), *m*

sinew /'sınyu/ *n* tendón, *m; pl* **sinews,** nervio, *m,* fuerza, *f*

sinewy /'sınyui/ *a* (stringy) fibroso; musculoso, nervudo

sinful /'sınfəl/ *a* (of persons) pecador; (of thoughts, acts) pecaminoso

sinfulness /'sınfəlnıs/ *n* pecado, *m;* culpabilidad, perversidad, maldad, *f*

sing /sıŋ/ *vi* cantar; (of the ears) zumbar; (of wind, water) murmurar, susurrar; (of a cat) ronronear. *—vt* cantar. **to s. a child to sleep,** dormir a un niño cantando. **to s. another song,** *inf* bajar el tono. **to s. small,** hacerse el chiquito. **to s. the praises of,** hacer las alabanzas de. **to s. out,** vocear, gritar. **s.-song,** *n* canturía, *f;* concierto improvisado, *m.* *—a* monótono

Singapore /'sıŋgəˌpɔr/ Singapur, *m*

singe /sındʒ/ *vt* chamuscar; (a fowl) aperdigar; (hair) quemar las puntas de los cabellos

singer /'sıŋər/ *n* cantor (-ra); (professional) cantante, *mf;* (bird) ave cantora, *f*

singing /sıŋıŋ/ *n* canto, *m;* (of the ears) zumbido, *m.* *—a* cantante. **s.-bird,** ave cantora, *f.* **s.-master,** maestro de cantar, *m*

single /'sıŋgəl/ *a* único; sencillo; solo; simple; (individual) particular; individual; (unmarried) soltero. *—n* (tennis) juego sencillo, individual, *m.* **in s. file,** de reata. **to s. out,** escoger; singularizar. **s. bed,** cama de monja, *f.* **s. bedroom,** habitación individual, habitación con una sola cama, *f.* **s.-breasted,** (of coats) recto. **s. combat,** combate singular, *m.* **s. entry,** *Com.* partida simple, *f.* **s.-handed,** de una mano; para una sola persona; sin ayuda, solo, en solitario. **s. -minded,** sin doblez, sincero de una sola idea. **s. ticket,** billete sencillo, *m*

singleness /'sıŋgəlnıs/ *n* celibato, *m,* soltería, *f.* **with s. of purpose,** con un solo objeto

singlet /'sıŋglıt/ *n* camiseta, *f*

singly /'sıŋgli/ *adv* separadamente, uno a uno; a solas, solo; sin ayuda

singular /'sıŋgyələr/ *a* and *n* singular, *m*

singularity /ˌsıŋgyə'lærıti/ *n* singularidad, *f*

singularly /'sıŋgyələrli/ *adv* singularmente

sinister /'sınəstər/ *a* siniestro

sink /sıŋk/ *vi* ir al fondo; bajar; hundirse; (of ships) irse a pique, naufragar; sumergirse; disminuir; caer (en); penetrar; (of persons, fires) morir; (of the sun, etc.) ponerse. *—vt* (a ship) echar a pique; sumergir; hundir; dejar caer; bajar; (wells) cavar; reducir, disminuir; (invest) invertir; (one's identity, etc.) tener secreto; (differences) olvidar; (engrave) grabar. **My heart sank,** Se me cayeron las alas del corazón. **He sank to his knees,** Cayó de rodillas. **He is sinking fast,** Está en las últimas. **Their words began to s. in,** Sus palabras empezaban a tener efecto (or hacer mella). **I found her sunk in thought,** La encontré ensimismada. **to s. one's voice,** bajar la voz. **to s. down on a chair,** dejarse caer en una silla. **to s. into misery,** caer en la miseria. **to s. under,** (a responsibility, etc.) estar agobiado bajo

sink /sıŋk/ *n* (kitchen) fregadero, *m;* sumidero, *m,* sentina, *f.* **s. of iniquity,** sentina, *f*

sinker /'sıŋkər/ *n* (engraver) grabador (-ra); (of a fishing line) plomada, *f*

sinking /'sıŋkıŋ/ *n* hundimiento, *m;* (of the sun) puesta, *f;* (of wells) cavadura, *f;* sumergimiento, *m.* **the s. of a boat,** el hundimiento de un buque. **with s. heart,** con la muerte en el alma. **s. fund,** fondo de amortización, *m*

sinless /'sınlıs/ *a* sin pecado, inocente, puro

sinner /'sınər/ *n* pecador (-ra)

sinuosity /ˌsınyu'ɒsıti/ *n* sinuosidad, *f;* flexibilidad, agilidad, *f*

sinuous /'sınyuəs/ *a* sinuoso, tortuoso; flexible, ágil

sinus /'sainəs/ *n* (*anat* etc.) seno, *m*

sip /sıp/ *vt* sorber; (wine) saborear, paladear. *—n* sorbo, *m*

siphon /'saifən/ *n* sifón, *m, vt* sacar con sifón

sir /sɜr/ *n* señor, *m;* (British title) sir. **Dear s.,** Muy Señor mío

sire /saiᵊr/ *n* (to a monarch) Señor, *m;* (father) padre, *m;* (stallion) semental, *m.* *—vt* procrear, engendrar

siren /'sairən/ *n* sirena, *f.* **s. suit,** mono, *m*

sirloin /'sɜrlɔin/ *n* solomillo, *m*

sirocco /sə'rɒkou/ *n* siroco, *m*

sister /'sıstər/ *n* hermana, *f;* (before nun's christian name) Sor; (hospital) hermana del hospital, *f;* enfermera, *f.* **s. language,** lengua hermana, *f.* **s. ship,** buque gemelo, *m.* **s.-in-law,** cuñada, hermana política, *f.* **S. of Mercy,** Hermana de la Caridad, *f*

sisterhood /'sıstərˌhʊd/ *n* hermandad, *f;* comunidad de monjas, *f*

sisterly /'sıstərli/ *a* de hermana

sit /sıt/ *vi* sentarse; estar sentado; (of birds) posarse; (of hens) empollar; (in Parliament, etc.) ser diputado; (of a committee, etc.) celebrar sesión; (on a committee, etc.) formar parte de; (function) funcionar; (of garments, food, and *fig*) sentar. **to sit a horse,** mantenerse a caballo; montar a caballo. **to sit oneself,** sentarse, tomar asiento. **to sit by,** (a person) sentarse (or estar sentado) al lado de. **to sit for** (a portrait) servir de modelo para; hacerse retratar. **to sit tight,** no moverse. **to sit down,** sentarse; (besiege) sitiar. **to sit on,** sentarse (en or sobre); (eggs) empollar; (a committee, etc.) formar parte de; (investigate) investigar; (snub) dejar aplastado (a). **to sit out,** quedarse hasta el fin (de). **to sit out a dance,** conversar un baile. **to sit up,** incorporarse en la cama; tenerse derecho; (at night) velar; (of dogs, etc.) pedir. **to sit up and take notice,** abrir los ojos. **to sit up in bed,** incorporarse en la cama. **to sit up late,** estar de pie hasta muy tarde

sit-down strike /ˈsɪtˌdaun/ *n* huelga de brazos caídos, huelga de sentados, *f*
site /sait/ *n* sitio, local, *m;* (for building) solar, *m*
sitting /ˈsɪtɪŋ/ *n* asentada, *f;* (of Parliament, etc.) sesión, *f;* (for a portrait) estadia, *f;* (of eggs) nidada, *f.* **at a s.,** de una asentada. **s.-room,** sala de estar, *f*
situated /ˈsɪtʃuˌeitɪd/ *a* situado. **How is he s.?** ¿Cómo está situado? ¿Cuál es su situación?
situation /ˌsɪtʃuˈeiʃən/ *n* situación, *f;* (job) empleo, *m*
six /sɪks/ *a* and *n* seis, *m.* **It is six o'clock,** Son las seis. **Everything is at sixes and sevens,** Todo está en desorden. **six-foot,** de seis pies. **six hundred,** seiscientos (-as)
sixfold /ˈsɪksˌfould/ *a* séxtuplo
sixteen /ˈsɪksˈtin/ *a* and *n* diez y seis, dieciséis, *m.* **John is s.,** Juan tiene dieciséis años
sixteenth /ˈsɪksˈtinθ/ *a* décimosexto; (of the month) (el) diez y seis; (of monarch) diez y seis. —*n* dieciseisavo, *m*
sixth /sɪksθ/ *a* sexto; (of the month) (el) seis; (of monarchs) sexto. —*n* seisavo, *m;* sexta parte, *f; mus* sexta, *f.* **Henry the S.,** Enrique sexto. **May the s.,** el seis de mayo
sixtieth /ˈsɪkstiɪθ/ *a* sexagésimo. —*n* sesentavo, *m;* sexagésima parte, *f*
sixty /ˈsɪksti/ *a* and *n* sesenta *m.* **John has turned s.,** Juan ha pasado los sesenta
sizable /ˈsaizəbəl/ *a* bastante grande
size /saiz/ *n* tamaño, *m;* dimensión, *f;* (height) altura, *f;* (measurement) medida, *f;* talle, *m;* (in gloves, etc.) número, *m;* (glue) cola, *f.* —*vt* clasificar por tamaños; (glaze, etc.) encolar. **to s. up,** tomar las medidas (a).
sizzle /ˈsɪzəl/ *vi* chisporrotear, chirriar. —*n* chisporroteo, chirrido, *m*
skate /skeit/ *n* patín, *m; ichth* raya, *f, vi* patinar
skater /ˈskeitər/ *n* patinador (-ra)
skating /ˈskeitɪŋ/ *n* patinaje, *m.* **s. rink,** sala de patinar, *f;* pista de hielo, pista de patinar, *f,* patinadero, *m*
skein /skein/ *n* madeja, *f*
skeleton /ˈskɛlɪtn̩/ *n* esqueleto, *m;* (of a building) armadura, *f;* (of a literary work) esquema, *m.* **s. key,** ganzúa, *f*
sketch /skɛtʃ/ *n* croquis, apunte, *m;* (for a literary work) esbozo, esquema, *m;* (article) cuadro, artículo, *m;* descripción, *f; theat* entremés, sainete, *m.* —*vt* dibujar; esbozar, bosquejar; trazar; describir. **s.-book,** álbum de croquis, *m*
sketchily /ˈskɛtʃəli/ *adv* incompletamente
sketching /ˈskɛtʃɪŋ/ *n* arte de dibujar, *mf.* **He likes s.,** Le gusta dibujar
sketchy /ˈskɛtʃi/ *a* bosquejado; incompleto; escaso
skewer /ˈskyuər/ *n* broqueta, *f, vt* espetar
ski /ski/ *n* esquí, *m, vi* esquiar
skid /skɪd/ *n* (of a vehicle) patinazo, *m, vi* patinar
skidding /ˈskɪdɪŋ/ *n* patinaje, *m*
skier /ˈskiər/ *n* esquiador, *m*
skiff /skɪf/ *n* esquife, *m*
skiing /ˈskiɪŋ/ *n* patinaje sobre la nieve, *m,* el esquiar. **to go s.,** ir a esquiar
skill /skɪl/ *n* habilidad, *f*
skilled /skɪld/ *a* hábil; experto
skilled worker *n* obrero calificado, *m*
skillful /ˈskɪlfəl/ *a* hábil
skim /skɪm/ *vt* espumar; (milk) desnatar; (touch lightly) deslizarse sobre, rozar; (a book) hojear
skimp /skɪmp/ *vt* escatimar; escasear; (work) frangollar. —*vi* ser parsimonioso
skimpy /ˈskɪmpi/ *a* escaso
skin /skɪn/ *n* tez, *f,* cutis, *m;* piel, *f;* (of fruit) pellejo, *m,* piel, *f;* (for wine) odre, pellejo, *m;* (on milk) espuma, *f.* —*vt* despellejar; pelar, mondar; (graze) hacerse daño (a); *inf* desollar. **next to one's s.,** sobre la piel. **to s. over,** cicatrizarse. **to have a thin s.,** *fig* ser muy susceptible. **to save one's s.,** salvar el pellejo. **s.-deep,** superficial. **s.-tight,** escurrido, muy ajustado
skinflint /ˈskɪnˌflɪnt/ *n* avaro (-ra)
skinned /skɪnd/ *a* de... piel
skinny /ˈskɪni/ *a* flaco, descarnado, magro
skip /skɪp/ *vi* retozar, brincar, saltar; saltar a la comba; (bolt) largarse, escaparse. —*vt* saltar; (a book) hojear; (omit) omitir; pasar por alto de. —*n* brinco, pequeño salto, *m*
skipper /ˈskɪpər/ *n naut* patrón, *m;* (*inf* and *sports*) capitán, *m*
skirmish /ˈskɜrmɪʃ/ *vi* escaramuzar. —*n* escaramuza, *f*
skirt /skɜrt/ *n* falda, *f;* (edge) margen, borde, *m,* orilla, *f;* (of a jacket, etc.) faldón, *m* —*vt* ladear; (hug) rodear, ceñir
skit /skɪt/ *n* sátira, *f;* parodia, *f*
skittish /ˈskɪtɪʃ/ *a* (of a horse) retozón; (of persons) frívolo; caprichoso
skittle /ˈskɪtl̩/ *n* bolo, *m; pl* **skittles,** juego de bolos, *m.* **s. alley,** pista de bolos, bolera, *f*
skulk /skʌlk/ *vi* estar en acecho; esconderse; rondar
skull /skʌl/ *n* cráneo, *m;* calavera, *f.* **s.-cap,** gorro, casquete, *m;* (for ecclesiastics) solideo, *m*
skunk /skʌŋk/ *n zool* mofeta, *f,* chingue, mapurite, yaguré, zorrillo, zorrino, zorro hediondo, *m*
sky /skai/ *n* cielo, *m.* **to praise to the skies,** poner en los cuernos de la luna. **s.-blue,** *n* azul celeste, *m.* —*a* de color azul celeste, cerúleo. **s.-high,** hasta las nubes, hasta el cielo. **s.-line,** horizonte, *m.* **s.-scraper,** rascacielos, *m.* **s.-sign,** anuncio luminoso, *m*
skylight /ˈskaiˌlait/ *n* claraboya, *f,* tragaluz, *m*
slab /slæb/ *n* bloque, *m;* losa, *f;* plancha, *f*
slack /slæk/ *a* lento; flojo; (lazy) perezoso; negligente, descuidado; *com* encalmado; débil. —*vi* ser perezoso. **the s. season,** la estación muerta. **to be s. in one's work,** ser negligente en el trabajo. **to s. off,** disminuir sus esfuerzos; dejar de trabajar
slacken /ˈslækən/ *vt* and *vi* aflojar; disminuir, reducir. **The wind slackened,** El viento amainaba, El viento aflojaba. **to s. one's efforts,** disminuir sus esfuerzos. **to s. speed,** disminuir la velocidad
slackening /ˈslækənɪŋ/ *n* aflojamiento, *m;* disminución, *f*
slacker /ˈslækər/ *n* gandul (-la)
slackness /ˈslæknɪs/ *n* flojedad, *f;* pereza, falta de energía, *f;* negligencia, *f; com* desanimación, *f*
slacks /slæks/ *n pl* pantalones, *m pl*
slag /slæg/ *n* escoria, *f.* **s. heap,** escorial, *m*
slake /sleik/ *vt* (one's thirst and lime) apagar; satisfacer
slam /slæm/ *vt* cerrar de golpe; golpear. —*n* (of a door) portazo, *m;* golpe, *m;* (cards) capote, *m.* **He went out and slammed the door,** Salió dando un portazo
slander /ˈslændər/ *n* calumnia, *f, vt* calumniar
slanderer /ˈslændərər/ *n* calumniador (-ra)
slanderous /ˈslændərəs/ *a* calumnioso
slang /slæŋ/ *n* argot, *m,* jerga, *f, vt* poner como un trapo (a), llenar de insultos
slant /slænt/ *vi* estar al sesgo; inclinarse; ser oblicuo. —*vt* inclinar. —*n* inclinación, *f;* oblicuidad, *f.* **on the s.,** inclinado; oblicuo
slanting /ˈslæntɪŋ/ *a* al sesgo, inclinado; oblicuo
slap /slæp/ *vt* pegar con la mano. —*n* bofetada, *f;* palmada, *f.* **to s. on the back,** golpear en la espalda. **s.-dash,** (of persons) irresponsable, descuidado; (of work) chapucero, sin cuidado.
slash /slæʃ/ *vt* (gash, also sleeves, etc.) acuchillar; cortar; (with a whip) dar latigazos (a). —*n* cuchillada, *f;* corte, *m;* latigazo, *m*
slashing /ˈslæʃɪŋ/ *a* mordaz, severo
slat /slæt/ *n* tablilla, *f, vi* (of sails) dar zapatazos, zapatear
slate /sleit/ *n* pizarra, *f,* esquisto, *m;* (for roofs and for writing) pizarra, *f, vt* (a roof) empizarrar; (censure) criticar severamente, censurar. **s.-colored,** apizarrado. **s. pencil,** pizarrín, *m.* **s. quarry,** pizarrería, *f,* pizarral, *m*
slater /ˈsleitər/ *n* pizarrero, *m*
slating /ˈsleitɪŋ/ *n* empizarrado, *m;* (criticism) crítica severa, censura, *f;* (scolding) peluca, *f*
slattern /ˈslætərn/ *n* pazpuerca, *f*
slatternly /ˈslætərnli/ *a* desgarbado, desaliñado
slaughter /ˈslɔtər/ *n* matanza, *f;* carnicería, *f;* —*vt* (animals) sacrificar, matar; matar, hacer una carnicería de. **s.-house,** matadero, *m*
slaughterer /ˈslɔtərər/ *n* jifero, carnicero, *m*
Slav /slɑv, slæv/ *a* and *n* eslavo (-va)

slave /sleiv/ *n* esclavo (-va). —*vi* trabajar mucho. **white s. traffic,** trata de blancas, *f.* **s.-bangle,** esclava, *f.* **s.-driver,** capataz de esclavos, negrero, *m; fig* negrero, sayón de esclavos, *m.* **s.-trade,** trata de esclavos, *f*
slaver /'sleivər/ *n* negrero, *m*
slaver /'slævər/ *vi* babear. —*n* baba, *f*
slavering /'slævərɪŋ/ *a* baboso
slavery /'sleivəri/ *n* esclavitud, *f;* trabajo muy arduo, *m*
slavish /'sleivɪʃ/ *a* de esclavo; servil
slavishly /'sleivɪʃli/ *adv* como esclava; servilmente
Slavonic /slə'vɒnɪk/ *a* eslavo. —*n* (language) eslavo, *m,* lengua eslava, *f*
slay /slei/ *vt* matar; asesinar
slayer /'sleiər/ *n* matador (-ra); asesino, *mf*
slaying /'sleiɪŋ/ *n* matanza, *f;* asesinato, *m*
sled /slɛd/ *n* trineo, *m,* rastra, *f*
sledge /slɛdʒ/ *n* trineo, *m.* —*vi* ir en trineo. —*vt* transportar por trineo. **s.-hammer,** acotillo, *m*
sleek /slik/ *a* liso, lustroso; (of general appearance) pulcro, bien aseado, elegante; (of manner) obsequioso
sleekness /'sliknɪs/ *n* lustre, *m,* lisura, *f;* (of an animal) gordura, *f;* elegancia, *f*
sleep /slip/ *n* sueño, *m.* —*vi* dormir; reposar, descansar. —*vt* dormir. **a deep s.,** un sueño pesado. **He walks in his s.,** Es un sonámbulo. **to court s.,** conciliar el sueño. **to go to s.,** dormirse; entumecerse. **My foot has gone to s.,** Se me ha dormido (*or* Se me ha entumecido) el pie. **to send a person to s.,** adormecer. **to s. like a top,** dormir como un lirón. **to s. oneself sober,** dormir la mona. **to s. in,** dormir tarde; dormir en casa. **to s. off,** (a cold, etc.) curarse... durmiendo; (drunkenness) dormirla. **to s. on,** *vt* (consider) dormir sobre, consultar con la almohada. —*vi* seguir durmiendo. **to s. out,** dormir fuera de casa; dormir al aire libre
sleeper /'slipər/ *n* durmiente, *mf; rail* traviesa, *f;* (on a train) coche cama, *m.* **to be a bad s.,** dormir mal. **to be a good s.,** dormir bien.
sleepily /'slipəli/ *adv* soñolientamente
sleepiness /'slipinɪs/ *n* somnolencia, *f;* letargo, *m*
sleeping /'slipɪŋ/ *a* durmiente. —*n* el dormir. **between s. and waking,** entre duerme y vela. **s.-bag,** saco-cama, *m.* **s.-car,** coche camas, *m.* **s.-draught,** narcótico, *m.* **s. partner,** *n* socio (-ia) comanditario (-ia). **s. sickness,** enfermedad del sueño, *f*
sleepless /'sliplɪs/ *a* (of persons) insomne, desvelado; (unremitting) incansable; (of the sea, etc.) en perpetuo movimiento. **to spend a s. night,** pasar una noche en vela, pasar una noche toledana, pasar una noche sin dormir
sleeplessness /'sliplɪsnɪs/ *n* insomnio, *m*
sleepwalker /'slip,wɔkər/ *n* sonámbulo (-la)
sleepwalking /'slip,wɔkɪŋ/ *n* sonambulismo, *m*
sleepy /'slipi/ *a* soñoliento; letárgico. **to be s.,** tener sueño. **s.-head,** lirón, *m,* marmota, *f*
sleet /slit/ *n* aguanieve, cellisca, nevisca, *f, vi* caer aguanieve, cellisquear, neviscar
sleeve /sliv/ *n* manga, *f;* (of a hose pipe, etc.) manguera, *f; mech* manguito, *m.* **to have something up one's s.,** traer algo en la manga
sleeved /slivd/ *a* con mangas...; de... manga(s)
sleeveless /'slivlɪs/ *a* sin manga
sleigh /slei/ *n* trineo, *m, vi* ir en trineo
sleight of hand /sleit/ *n* prestidigitación, *f;* juego de manos, *m*
slender /'slɛndər/ *a* delgado; esbelto; tenue; escaso; pequeño; ligero. **Their means are very s.,** Sus recursos son muy escasos. **It is a very s. hope,** Es una esperanza muy remota
slenderness /'slɛndərnɪs/ *n* delgadez, *f;* esbeltez, *f;* tenuidad, *f;* escasez, *f*
sleuth /sluθ/ *n* (dog) sabueso, *m; inf* detective, *m*
slice /slais/ *n* lonja, tajada, *f;* (of fruit) raja, *f;* (of bread, etc.) rebanada, *f;* (share) parte, porción, *f;* (for fish, etc.) pala, *f.* —*vt* cortar en tajadas, etc.; rajar; cortar
slick /slɪk/ *a* hábil, diestro
slide /slaid/ *vi* deslizarse, resbalar; (over a question) pasar por alto de; (into a habit, etc.) caer (en). —*n* resbalón, *m;* pista de hielo, *f;* (chute) tobogán, *m;* (of a microscope) portaobjetos, *m;* (lantern) diapositiva, *f;* (for the hair) pasador, *m;* (of rock, etc.) desprendimiento, *m; mech* guía, *f.* **to let things s.,** dejar rodar la bola. **s.-rule,** regla de cálculo, *f*
sliding /'slaidɪŋ/ *a* resbaladizo; corredizo; movible. **s.-door,** puerta corrediza, puerta de corradera, *f.* **s.-roof,** techo corredizo, *m.* **s.-scale,** escala graduada, *f.* **s.-seat,** asiento movible, *m;* (in a rowing-boat) bancada corrediza, *f*
slight /slait/ *a* delgado; débil, frágil; ligero; (small) pequeño; escaso; (trivial) insignificante, poco importante. —*vt* desairar, despreciar. —*n* desaire, desprecio, *m;* falta de respeto, *f*
slighting /'slaitɪŋ/ *a* despreciativo, de desprecio
slightingly /'slaitɪŋli/ *adv* con desprecio
slightly /'slaitli/ *adv* ligeramente; poco. **I only know her s.,** La conozco muy poco. **s. built,** de talle delgado
slightness /'slaitnɪs/ *n* (slimness) delgadez, *f;* ligereza, *f;* (triviality) poca importancia, insignificancia, *f*
slim /slɪm/ *a* delgado; escaso. —*vi* adelgazarse. **He has very s. chances of success,** Tiene muy pocas posibilidades de conseguir el éxito
slime /slaim/ *n* légamo, limo, lodo, cieno, *m;* (of a snail) limazo, *m; fig* cieno, *m*
sliminess /'slaiminɪs/ *n* limosidad, *f;* viscosidad, *f*
slimness /'slɪmnɪs/ *n* delgadez, *f;* escasez, *f*
slimy /'slaimi/ *a* limoso, legamoso; pecinoso, viscoso; (of persons) rastrero, servil
sling /slɪŋ/ *vt* arrojar, lanzar; tirar con honda; (a sword, etc.) suspender; (lift) embragar; (a limb) poner en cabestrillo. —*n* (for missiles) honda, *f; Naut* balso, *m;* (for a limb) cabestrillo, *m,* charpa, *f*
slink /slɪŋk/ *vi* (away, off) escurrirse, escabullirse
slip /slɪp/ *vi* resbalar, deslizar; (stumble) resbalar, tropezar; (fall) caer; (out of place) salirse; (become untied) desatarse; (steal away) escabullirse; (glide) deslizarse; (of years) correr, pasar; (skid) patinar. —*vt* deslizar; (garments, shoes) ponerse; (dogs, cables) soltar; (an arm round, etc.) pasar; *Rail* desacoplar; (escape) escaparse de; (free oneself of) librarse de. —*n* resbalón, *m;* (skid) patinazo, *m;* (stumble) tropezón, traspié, *m;* (oversight) inadvertencia, *f;* (mistake) falta, equivocación, *f;* (moral lapse) desliz, *m;* (petticoat) combinación, *f;* (cover) funda, *f; Bot* vástago, *m; Print* galerada, *f;* (of paper) papeleta, *f; pl* **slips,** *Naut* anguilas, *f pl.* **It slipped my memory,** Se me fue de la memoria. **There's many a s. 'twixt the cup and the lip,** Del dicho al hecho hay muy gran trecho, De la mano a la boca desaparece la sopa. **to give** (someone) **the slip,** escaparse de. **You ought not to let the opportunity s.,** No debes perder la oportunidad. **to let s. a secret,** revelar un secreto. **to let s. an exclamation,** soltar (dar) una exclamación. **to s. into,** colarse en, deslizarse en. **to s. into,** colarse en, deslizarse en. **to s. into one's clothes,** vestirse rápidamente. **to s. on,** (a garment) ponerse. **to s. out,** salir a hurtadillas; escaparse; (of information) divulgarse. **s. of a boy,** mozalbete, joven imberbe, *m.* **s. of the tongue,** error de lengua, *m.* **s.-knot,** nudo corredizo, *m*
slipcover /'slɪp,kʌvər/ *n* cubierta, cubierta para muebles, funda, funda para muebles, *f*
slipper /'slɪpər/ *n* babucha, chinela, *f,* pantuflo, *m;* (heelless) chancleta, *f;* (dancing) zapatilla de baile, *f.* **s.-shaped,** achinelado
slippered /'slɪpərd/ *a* en zapatillas
slipperiness /'slɪpərinɪs/ *n* lo resbaladizo; (of persons) informalidad, *f*
slippery /'slɪpəri/ *a* resbaladizo; poco firme, inestable; (of persons) informal, sin escrúpulos
slipshod /'slɪp,ʃɒd/ *a* descuidado, negligente; poco correcto
slipway /'slɪp,wei/ *n* surtida, *f,* anguilas, *f pl*
slit /slɪt/ *vt* cortar; hender, rajar; (the throat) degollar. —*n* cortadura, *f;* resquicio, *m.* **to s. open,** abrir de un tajo
slither /'slɪðər/ *vi* resbalar; deslizarse
sliver /'slɪvər/ *n* raja, *f;* (of wood) astilla, *f;* (of cloth) tira, *f*

slobber /ˈslɒbər/ *vi* babear; (blubber) gimotear, *n* baba, *f*

sloe /slou/ *n* (fruit) endrina, *f;* (tree) endrino, *m.* **s.-colored,** endrino. **s.-eyed,** con ojos de mora

slog /slɒg/ *vt* golpear duramente. **to s. away,** batirse el cobre, trabajar como un negro

slogan /ˈslougən/ *n* grito de batalla, *m;* reclamo, *m;* frase hecha, *f;* mote, *m*

slop /slɒp/ *n* charco, *m; pl* **slops,** agua sucia, *f;* alimentos líquidos, *m pl.* —*vi* derramarse, verterse. —*vt* verter, derramar

slope /sloup/ *n* inclinación, *f;* pendiente, *f;* (of a mountain, etc.) falda, ladera, cuesta, *f;* vertiente, *mf.* —*vi* inclinarse; estar en declive; bajar (hacia). **to s. down,** declinar

sloping /ˈsloupɪŋ/ *a* inclinado; en declive; (of shoulders) caídos, *m pl*

sloppy /ˈslɒpi/ *a* casi líquido; (muddy) lodoso, lleno de barro; (of work) chapucero; (of persons) baboso, sobón. **s. sentiment,** sensiblería, *f*

slot /slɒt/ *n* ranura, muesca, *f.* **s.-machine,** máquina expendedora, *f,* expendedor, *m;* (in amusement arcades, etc.) tragaperras, *m*

sloth /slɔθ *or, esp. for 2,* slouθ/ *n* pereza, indolencia, *f, zool* perezoso, *m*

slothful /ˈslɔθfəl, ˈslouθ-/ *a* perezoso, indolente

slouch /slautʃ/ *n* inclinación del cuerpo, *f.* —*vi* andar cabizbajo, andar arrastrando los pies. **to s. about,** vagar, golfear. **s.-hat,** sombrero gacho, *m*

slough /slʌf/ *n* (bog) cenagal, pantano, *m,* marisma, *f;* (of a snake) camisa, *f.* —*vt* (a skin) mudar; (prejudices, etc.) desechar

Slovak /ˈslouvɑk/ *n* eslovaco (-ca)

Slovakian /slouˈvakiən/ *a* eslovaco

sloven /ˈslʌvən/ *n* puerco, *m;* (at work) chapucero, *m*

Slovene /slouˈvin/ *a* and *n* esloveno (-na)

slovenliness /ˈslʌvənlinɪs/ *n* desaseo, desaliño, *m;* (carelessness) descuido, *m,* negligencia, *f;* (of work) chapucería, *f*

slovenly /ˈslʌvənli/ *a* desgarbado, desaseado; (careless) descuidado, negligente; (of work) chapucero

slow /slou/ *a* despacio; lento; (stupid) torpe; tardo; (of clocks) atrasado; (boring) aburrido; (inactive) flojo. —*adv* despacio, lentamente. **I was not s. to...,** No tardé en... **The clock is ten minutes s.,** El reloj lleva diez minutos de atraso. **to s. down,** aflojar el paso; ir más despacio. **s.-motion,** velocidad reducida, *f.* **s. train,** tren ómnibus, *m.* **s.-witted,** lerdo tardo

slowcoach /ˈslouˌkoutʃ/ *n* perezoso (-sa)

"Slow Down" «Moderar Su Velocidad»

slow learner *n* alumno de lento aprendizaje, *m*

slowly /ˈslouli/ *adv* despacio, lentamente; poco a poco

slowness /ˈslounɪs/ *n* lentitud, *f;* (delay) tardanza, *f;* (stupidity) torpeza, estupidez, *f*

slug /slʌg/ *n* babosa, *f*

sluggard /ˈslʌgərd/ *n* gandul (-la), perezoso (-a)

sluggish /ˈslʌgɪʃ/ *a* perezoso; (of the market) flojo; (of temperament, etc.) calmoso, flemático; (slow) lento

sluggishness /ˈslʌgɪʃnɪs/ *n* pereza, *f;* (of the market) flojedad, *f;* (slowness) lentitud, *f*

sluice /slus/ *n* esclusa, *f;* canal, *m,* acequia, *f* **to s. down,** lavar; echar agua sobre; (a person) dar una ducha (a), dar un baño (a). **s.-gate,** compuerta de esclusa, *f;* tajaderas, *f pl,* tablacho, *m*

slum /slʌm/ *n* barrio pobre, *m,* banda de miseria (Argentina), barriada (Peru), población (Chile), villa-miseria (Argentina), *f,* tugurio (Colombia), *m; pl* **slums,** barrios bajos, *m pl*

slumber /ˈslʌmbər/ *vi* dormir; (go to sleep) dormirse, caer dormido; (be latent) estar latente. —*n* sueño, *m*

slump /slʌmp/ *n com* baja repentina, *f; fig* baja, racha mala, *f.* —*vi com* bajar repentinamente. **the s.,** la crisis económica. **to s. into an armchair,** dejarse caer en un sillón

slur /slɜr/ *vt* (words) comerse sílabas o letras (de); (in writing) unir (las palabras); (*mus* of notes) ligar. **to cast a s. on,** difamar, manchar. **to s. over,** pasar por alto de, omitir, suprimir

slush /slʌʃ/ *n* lodo, *m;* agua nieve, *f;* (sentimentality) ñoñería, *f*

slushy /ˈslʌʃi/ *a* lodoso, fangoso

slut /slʌt/ *n* pazpuerca, marrana, *f*

sly /slai/ *a* astuto, taimado, socarrón; disimulado; (arch) malicioso. **on the sly,** a hurtadillas

slyly /ˈslaili/ *adv* astutamente; disimuladamente; (archly) maliciosamente

slyness /ˈslainɪs/ *n* astucia, socarronería, *f;* disimulo, *m;* malicia, *f*

smack /smæk/ *n* (taste) sabor, gusto, *m;* (tinge) dejo, *m;* (blow) golpe, *m;* (with the hand) bofetada, palmada, *f;* (with a whip) latigazo, *m;* (crack of whip) restallido, chasquido, *m;* (kiss) beso sonado, *m;* (boat) lancha de pescar, *f.* —*vi* (taste of) tener gusto de, saber a; (be tinged with) oler a. —*vt* (a whip) hacer restallar; (slap) pegar con la mano. **to s. one's lips over,** chuparse los dedos

small /smɔl/ *a* pequeño; menudo; menor; poco; (petty) mezquino, vulgar. —*n* parte estrecha, *f.* **a s. number,** un pequeño número. **to make a person look s.,** humillar. **to make oneself s.,** hacerse chiquito. **s.-arms,** armas portátiles, *f pl.* **s. change,** suelto, *m.* **s. craft,** embarcaciones menores, *f pl.* **s. fry,** pececillos, *m pl;* (children) gente menuda, *f;* gente sin importancia, *f.* **s. hours,** altas horas de la noche, *f pl.* **s.-minded,** adocenado, de cortos alcances. **s.-talk,** trivialidades, *f pl,* charla frívola, *f*

smallish /ˈsmɔlɪʃ/ *a* bastante pequeño; más bien pequeño que grande

smallness /ˈsmɔlnɪs/ *n* pequeñez, *f;* escasez, exigüidad, *f*

smallpox /ˈsmɔlˌpɒks/ *n* viruelas, *f pl*

smart /smɑrt/ *vi* picar; dolerse (de). —*n* escozor, *m;* dolor, *m.* —*a* severo; vivo; rápido; pronto; (competent) hábil; (clever) listo; (unscrupulous) cuco, astuto; (of personal appearance) majo; elegante, distinguido; (neat) aseado; (fashionable, etc.) de moda; de buen tono. **to s. for,** ser castigado por. **to s. under,** sufrir

smarten /ˈsmɑrtn̩/ *vt* embellecer. —*vi* (up) ponerse elegante; mejorar. **I must go and s. myself up a little,** Tengo que arreglarme un poco

smartly /ˈsmartli/ *adv* severamente; vivamente; rápidamente; hábilmente; elegantemente

smartness /ˈsmartnɪs/ *n* viveza, *f;* prontitud, rapidez, *f;* (cleverness) despejo, *m,* habilidad, *f;* (wittiness) agudeza, *f;* (astuteness) cuquería, astucia, *f;* (of dress, etc.) elegancia, *f;* buen tono, *m*

smash /smæʃ/ *vt* romper, quebrar; (a ball, etc.) golpear; (annihilate) destruir; (an opponent) aplastar. —*vi* romperse, quebrarse; hacerse pedazos; (collide) chocar (con, contra); estallarse (contra); (financially) hacer bancarrota. —*n* rotura, *f;* quebrantamiento, *m;* estruendo, *m;* (financial) quiebra, ruina, *f;* (car, etc.) accidente, *m;* desastre, *m,* catástrofe, *f.* **to s. to atoms,** hacer trizas. **to s. up,** hacer pedazos. **s. and grab raid,** atraco a mano armada, *m*

smash hit *n* éxito arrollador, éxito rotundo, *m*

smattering /ˈsmætərɪŋ/ *n* conocimiento superficial, *m,* tintura, *f,* barniz, *m*

smear /smɪər/ *n* mancha, *f; biol* frotis, *m.* —*vt* embadurnar (de); manchar (con), ensuciar (con); (oneself) untarse; (blur) borrar

smell /smɛl/ *n* (sense of) olfato, *m;* (odor) olor, *m.* —*vt* oler. —*vi* oler; tener olor; (disagreeably) oler mal, tener mal olor; (stink) apestar. **How good it smells!** ¡Qué bien huele! **to s. of,** oler a. **to s. out,** husmear

smelling /ˈsmɛlɪŋ/ *n* olfateo, *m.* **s.-bottle,** frasco de sales, *m.* **s.-salts,** sales (inglesas), *f pl*

smelt /smɛlt/ *vt* fundir. —*n ichth* eperlano, *m*

smelter /ˈsmɛltər/ *n* fundidor, *m*

smelting /ˈsmɛltɪŋ/ *n* fundición, *f.* **s. furnace,** horno de fundición, *m*

smile /smail/ *vi* sonreír; reírse. —*vt* expresar con una sonrisa. —*n* sonrisa, *f.* **Mary smiled her thanks,** María dio las gracias con una sonrisa. **smile at adversity,** ponerse buena cara a mal tiempo. **to s. at threats,** reírse de las amenazas

smiling /ˈsmailɪŋ/ *a* sonriente, risueño

smilingly /'smailɪŋli/ *adv* sonriendo, con una sonrisa, con cara risueña
smirch /smɜrtʃ/ *vt* manchar. —*n* mancha, *f*
smirk /smɜrk/ *vi* sonreír con afectación; hacer visajes. —*n* sonrisa afectada, *f*
smirking /'smɜrkɪŋ/ *a* afectado; sonriente
smite /smait/ *vt* golpear; (kill) matar; (punish) castigar; (pain) doler; (of bright light, sounds, etc.) herir; (cause remorse) remorder. **My conscience smites me,** Tengo remordimientos de conciencia. **to be smitten by,** *inf* estar prendado de. **I was smitten by a desire to smoke,** Me entraron deseos de fumar
smith /smɪθ/ *n* herrero, *m*. **smith's hammer,** destajador, *m*
smithereens /ˌsmɪðə'rinz/ *n pl* añicos, *m pl*
smithy /'smɪθi, 'smɪði/ *n* herrería, *f*
smock /smɒk/ *n* blusa, *f;* (child's) delantal, *m*
smoke /smouk/ *n* humo, *m*. —*vi* humear, echar humo; (tobacco) fumar. —*vt* ahumar; ennegrecer; (tobacco) fumar. **smoked glasses,** gafas ahumadas, *f pl*. **s. helmet,** casco respiratorio, *m*. **s.-screen,** cortina de humo, *f*. **s. signal,** ahumada, *f*. **s.-stack,** chimenea, *f*
smokeless /'smouklɪs/ *a* sin humo
smoker /'smoukər/ *n* fumador (-ra)
smoking /'smoukɪŋ/ *a* humeante. —*n* el fumar. **"S. Prohibited,"** «Se prohibe fumar.» **non-s. compartment,** *rail* departamento de no fumadores, *m*. **s.-carriage,** *rail* departamento para fumadores, *m*. **s.-room,** fumadero, *m*
smoky /'smouki/ *a* humeante; lleno de humo; (black) ahumado
smooth /smuð/ *a* liso; igual; (of the skin, etc.) suave; (of water) calmo, tranquilo; (flattering, etc.) lisonjero; obsequioso; afable. —*vt* allanar; (hair, etc.) alisar; (paths, etc.) igualar. **to s. down,** (a person) tranquilizar, calmar. **to s. over,** (faults) exculpar. **to s. the way for,** allanar el camino para. **s.-faced,** barbilampiño, lampiño, bien afeitado, todo afeitado; *fig* obsequioso, untuoso. **s.-haired,** de pelo liso. **s.-spoken,** de palabras lisonjeras; obsequioso
smoothly /'smuðli/ *adv* lisamente; (of speech) afablemente; con lisonjeras. **Everything was going s.,** Todo iba viento en popa
smoothness /'smuðnɪs/ *n* igualdad, *f;* lisura, *f;* (of skin, etc.) suavidad, *f;* (of water) calma, tranquilidad, *f;* (of manner, etc.) afabilidad, *f*
smother /'smʌðər/ *vt* ahogar, sofocar; (a fire) apagar; (cover) envolver, cubrir
smoulder /'smouldər/ *vi* arder sin llama, arder lentamente; (of passions, etc.) arder; estar latente
smouldering /'smouldərɪŋ/ *a* que arde lentamente; *fig* latente
smudge /smʌdʒ/ *vt* manchar, ensuciar; (blur) borrar. —*n* mancha, *f*
smug /smʌg/ *a* satisfecho de sí mismo, pagado de sí mismo; farisaico
smuggle /'smʌgəl/ *vt* pasar de contrabando. —*vi* hacer contrabando
smuggler /'smʌglər/ *n* contrabandista, *mf*
smuggling /'smʌglɪŋ/ *n* contrabando, *m*
smugly /'smʌgli/ *adv* con presunción, de un aire satisfecho
smugness /'smʌgnɪs/ *n* satisfacción de sí mismo, *f;* fariseísmo, *m*
smut /smʌt/ *n* copo de hollín, *m;* mancha, *f;* (disease) tizón, *m*
smutty /'smʌti/ *a* tiznado; ahumado; *inf* verde
snack /snæk/ *n* tentempié, piscolabis, bocado, *m*. **to take a s.,** tomar un piscolabis
snack bar *n* merendero, *m*
snaffle /'snæfəl/ *n* filete, *m*. —*vt* (a horse) refrenar. **s.-bridle,** bridón, *m*
snag /snæg/ *n* (of a tree) tocón, *m;* (of a tooth) raigón, *m;* (problem) busilis, *m;* obstáculo inesperado, *m*
snail /sneil/ *n* caracol, *m*. **at a snail's pace,** a paso de tortuga
snake /sneik/ *n* serpiente, *f*. **s.-charmer,** encantador de serpientes, *m*
snakelike /'sneikˌlaik/ *a* de serpiente; serpentino
snap /snæp/ *vt* morder; (break) romper; (one's fingers) castañetear; (a whip) chasquear; (down a lid, etc.) cerrar de golpe; (beaks, etc.) cerrar ruidosamente; *photo* sacar una instantánea de. —*vi* partirse; quebrarse; hablar bruscamente. —*n* (bite) mordedura, *f;* golpe seco, *m;* chasquido, *m;* rotura, *f;* (clasp) cierre, *m;* (of weather) temporada, *f;* (spirit) vigor, brío, *m; photo* instantánea, *f*. **to s. at,** procurar morder; (an invitation, etc.) aceptar gustoso. **to s. one's fingers at,** *fig* burlarse de. **to s. up,** coger, agarrar; (a person) cortar la palabra (a), interrumpir. **s.-fastener,** botón de presión, *m*
snapdragon /'snæpˌdrægən/ *n* dragón, *m*, becerra, boca de dragón, *f*
snappily /'snæpəli/ *adv* irritablemente
snappishness /'snæpɪʃnɪs/ *n* irritabilidad, *f*
snappy /'snæpi/ *a* irritable; vigoroso
snapshot /'snæpˌʃɒt/ *n* instantánea, foto, *f*
snare /snɛər/ *n* cepo, lazo, *m*, trampa, *f; fig* red, *f*. —*vt* coger en el lazo; *fig* enredar
snarl /snɑrl/ *vi* (of dogs) regañar; (cats, etc.) gruñir. —*n* regañamiento, *m;* gruñido, *m*
snarling /'snɑrlɪŋ/ *n* regañamiento, *m;* gruñidos, *m pl*, *a* gruñidor
snatch /snætʃ/ *vt* asir; agarrar; (enjoy) disfrutar; (an opportunity) tomar, aprovecharse de. —*n* asimiento, agarro, *m;* (of time) rato, *m;* instante, *m;* (of song) fragmento, *m*. **to make a s. at,** procurar agarrar; alargar la mano hacia. **to s. a hurried meal,** comer aprisa. **to s. away,** arrebatar, quitar; (carry off) robar. **to s. up,** coger rápidamente; coger en brazos
sneak /snik/ *vi* deslizarse (en), colarse (en); (lurk) rondar; (inform) acusar. —*n* mandilón, *m;* (accuser) acusón (-ona). **to s. off,** escabullirse, irse a hurtadillas. **s.-thief,** *n* garduño (-ña)
sneaker /'snikər/ *n* (shoe) zapatilla de tenis, *f*
sneaking /'snikɪŋ/ *a* furtivo, ruin, mezquino; secreto
sneer /snɪər/ *vi* sonreír irónicamente; burlarse, mofarse. —*n* sonrisa sardónica, sonrisa de desprecio, *f;* burla, mofa, *f*. **to s. at,** mofarse de, burlarse de; hablar con desprecio de
sneering /'snɪərɪŋ/ *a* mofador, burlón
sneeringly /'snɪərɪŋli/ *adv* con una sonrisa sardónica; burlonamente
sneeze /sniz/ *vi* estornudar. —*n* estornudo, *m*. **It's not to be sneezed at,** No es moco de pavo
sniff /snɪf/ *vi* respirar fuertemente; resollar. —*vt* oler, olfatear; aspirar. **to s. at,** oler. **to s. out,** *Inf.* husmear
snigger /'snɪgər/ *vi* reírse por lo bajo, reírse disimuladamente. —*n* risa disimulada, *f*
snip /snɪp/ *vt* cortar con tijeras; cortar, quitar. —*n* tijeretada, *f;* (of cloth, etc.) recorte, pedacito, *m*
snipe /snaip/ *n ornith* agachadiza, *f*. **to s. at,** *Mil.* pacar
sniper /'snaipər/ *n Mil.* paco, *m*
snippet /'snɪpɪt/ *n* pedacito, fragmento, *m;* (of prose, etc.) trocito, *m;* (of news) noticia, *f*
snivel /'snɪvəl/ *vi* lloriquear, gimotear
sniveling /'snɪvəlɪŋ/ *n* lloriqueo, gimoteo, *m*. —*a* llorón; mocoso
snob /snɒb/ *n* esnob, *mf*
snobbery /'snɒbəri/ *n* snobismo, *m*
snobbish /'snɒbɪʃ/ *a* esnob
snood /snud/ *n* (for the hair) redecilla, *f;* (turkey's) moco (de pavo), *m;* (fishing) cendal, *m*
snoop /snup/ *vi* espiar; entremeterse
snooze /snuz/ *vi* dormitar, echar un sueño. —*n* sueñecito, *m;* (afternoon) siesta, *f*
snore /snɔr/ *vi* roncar. —*n* ronquido, *m*
snoring /'snɔrɪŋ/ *n* ronquidos, *m pl*
snort /snɔrt/ *vi* bufar; resoplar. —*n* bufido, *m;* resoplido, *m*
snout /snaut/ *n* hocico, *m;* (of a pig) jeta, *f*
snow /snou/ *n* nieve, *f*. —*vi* nevar. —*vt* nevar; *fig* inundar. **to s. under** (with), inundar con. **to be snowed up,** estar aprisionado por la nieve. **s.-blindness,** deslumbramiento causado por la nieve, *m*. **s.-boot,** bota para la nieve, *f*. **s.-bound,** aprisionado por la nieve; bloqueado por la nieve. **s.-capped,** coronado de nieve. **s.-clad,** cubierto de nieve. **s.-drift,** acumulación de nieve, *f*. **s.-field,** ventisquero, *m*. **s.-goggles,** gafas ahumadas, *f pl*. **s.-line,** límite de las

nieves perpetuas, *m.* **s.-man,** figura de nieve, *f.* **s.-plough,** quitanieve, *m.* **s.-shoe,** raqueta de nieve, *f.* **s.-white,** blanco como la nieve
snowball /'snouˌbɔl/ *n* bola de nieves, *f; bot* bola de nieve, *f*
snowdrop /'snouˌdrɒp/ *n* campanilla de invierno, violeta de febrero, *f*
snowfall /'snouˌfɔl/ *n* nevada, *f*
snowflake /'snouˌfleik/ *n* copo de nieve, *m*
snowstorm /'snouˌstɔrm/ *n* ventisca, *f*
snowy /'snoui/ *a* nevoso; de nieve
snub /snʌb/ *vt* repulsar; desairar, tratar con desdén. —*n* repulsa, *f,* desaire, *m;* (nose) nariz respingona, *f.* **s.-nosed,** de nariz respingona
snuff /snʌf/ *vt* (breathe) oler, olfatear; inhalar; (a candle) atizar, despabilar. —*n* (of a candle) moco, *m,* despabiladura, *f;* (tobacco) rapé, *m.* **to take s.,** tomar rapé. **to s. out,** extinguir. **s.-box,** caja de rapé, tabaquera, *f*
snuffers /'snʌfərz/ *n pl* tenacillas, despabiladeras, *f pl*
snuffle /'snʌfəl/ *vi* hacer ruido con la nariz; respirar fuerte; (in speaking) ganguear
snuffling /'snʌflɪŋ/ *a* mocoso; (of the voice) gangoso
snug /snʌg/ *a* caliente; cómodo; (hidden) escondido, **to have a s. income,** tener el riñón bien cubierto, ser acomodado
snuggle /'snʌgəl/ *vi* hacerse un ovillo; acomodarse; ponerse cómodo. **to s. up to,** arrimarse a, apretarse contra
snugly /'snʌgli/ *adv* cómodamente
snugness /'snʌgnɪs/ *n* comodidad, *f*
so /sou/ *adv* así; de este modo, de esta manera; por lo tanto; tanto; (before adjs. and advs. but not before **más, mejor, menos, peor,** where **tanto** is used) tan; (in the same way) del mismo modo, de igual modo; (therefore) de modo que, de manera que; (also) también; (approximately) más o menos, aproximadamente. **Is that so?** ¿De veras? **if so...,** si así es... **He has not yet done so,** no lo ha hecho todavía. **I told you so!** ¡Ya te lo dije yo! **So be it!** ¡Así sea! **so far,** hasta aquí; hasta ahora. **so forth,** etcétera. **So long!** ¡Nos vemos! **so much,** tanto. **So much the worse for them,** Tanto peor para ellos. **so to speak,** por decirlo así. **so as to,** a fin de, para. **so long as,** con tal que, a condición de que. **so on,** etcétera. **so soon as,** tan pronto como. **so that,** de suerte que, de modo que, para que; con que. **so-and-so,** *n* fulano (-na); mengano (-na). **so-called.** así llamado, supuesto. **so-so,** así-así, regular
soak /souk/ *vt* remojar; empapar; (skins) abrevar. —*vi* estar en remojo. —*n* remojo, *m;* (rain) diluvio, *m;* (booze) borrachera, *f.* **to s. into,** filtrar en; penetrar. **to s. through,** penetrar; filtrar **so-called,** así llamado, supuesto. **so-so,** así, regular
soaked /soukt/ *a* remojado. **He is s. to the skin,** Está calado hasta los huesos
soaking /'soukɪŋ/ *n* remojo, *m;* empapamiento, *m,*
soap /soup/ *n* jabón, *m.* —*vt* jabonar; (flatter) enjabonar. **a tablet of s.,** una pastilla de jabón. **soft s.,** jabón blando, *m.* **toilet s.,** jabón de tocador, jaboncillo, *m.* **s.-bubble,** burbuja de jabón, *f.* **s. dish,** jabonera, *f.* **s. factory,** jabonería, *f.* **s.-flakes,** copos de jabón, *m pl*
soapbark tree /'soupˌbark/ *n* quillay, palo de jabón, *m*
soap box *n lit* caja de jabón, *f; fig* tribuna callejera, *f*
soap opera /'ɒpərə/ *n* radionovela (on radio), telenovela (on television), *f,* serial lacrimógeno (derogatory), *m*
soapsuds /'soupˌsʌdz/ *n pl* jabonaduras, *f pl*
soapy /'soupi/ *a* cubierto de jabón; jabonoso
soar /sɔr/ *vi* remontarse; *fig* elevarse; (of prices, etc.) subir de golpe
soaring /'sɔrɪŋ/ *n* remonte, vuelo, *m; fig* aspiración, *f;* (of prices, etc.) subida repentina, *f*
sob /sɒb/ *vi* sollozar. —*n* sollozo, *m.* **to sob one's heart out,** llorar a lágrima viva. **to sob out,** decir sollozando, decir entre sollozos
sobbing /'sɒbɪŋ/ *n* sollozos, *m pl, a* sollozante
sober /'soubər/ *a* sobrio; moderado; (of colors) obscuro. **s.-minded,** serio; reflexivo
sobriety /sə'braiɪti/ *n* sobriedad, *f;* moderación, *f;* seriedad, *f;* calma, tranquilidad, *f*
sobriquet /'soubrɪˌkei, -ˌkɛt/ *n* apodo, *m*
soccer /'sɒkər/ *n* fútbol (Asociación), *m*
sociability /ˌsɒʃə'bɪlɪti/ *n* sociabilidad, *f*
sociable /'souʃəbəl/ *a* sociable; amistoso
sociably /'souʃəbli/ *adv* sociablemente; amistosamente
social /'souʃəl/ *a* social; sociable. —*n* reunión, velada, *f.* **s.-democrat,** *a* and *n* socialdemócrata, *mf.* **s. event,** acontecimiento social, *m.* **s. insurance,** previsión social, *f.* **s. services,** servicios sociales, *m pl.* **s. work,** asistencia social, *f*
socialism /'souʃəˌlɪzəm/ *n* socialismo, *m*
socialist /'souʃəlɪst/ *a* socialista, laborista. —*n* socialista, *mf*
socialization /ˌsouʃələ'zeiʃən/ *n* socialización, *f*
socialize /'souʃəˌlaiz/ *vt* socializar
socially /'souʃəli/ *adv* socialmente
society /sə'saiɪti/ *n* sociedad, *f;* (fashionable) mundo elegante, *m,* alta sociedad, *f;* compañía, *f.* **to go into s.,** (of girls) ponerse de largo; entrar en el mundo elegante. **s. hostess,** dama de sociedad, *f.* **Society for the Prevention of Cruelty to Animals,** sociedad protectora de animales, *f.* **s. news,** noticias de sociedad, *f pl*
sociological /ˌsousiə'lɒdʒɪkəl/ *a* sociológico
sociologist /ˌsousiˌɒlədʒɪst/ *n* sociólogo (-ga)
sociology /ˌsousi'ɒlədʒi/ *n* sociología, *f*
sock /sɒk/ *n* calcetín, *m;* (for a shoe) plantilla, *f*
socket /'sɒkɪt/ *n mech* encaje, cubo, ojo, *m;* (of a lamp, and *elec*) enchufe, *m;* (of the eye) órbita, cuenca, *f;* (of a tooth) alvéolo, *m;* (of a joint) fosa, *f.* **His eyes started out of their sockets,** Sus ojos estaban fuera de su órbita
Socratic /sə'krætɪk/ *a* socrático
sod /sɒd/ *n* césped, *m;* (cut) tepe, *m*
soda /'soudə/ *n* sosa, *f.* **caustic s.,** sosa cáustica, *f.* **s.-ash,** carbonato sódico, *m.* **s.-fountain,** aparato de aguas gaseosas, *m.* **s.-water,** sifón, *m*
sodden /'sɒdn̩/ *a* saturado, empapado
sodium /'soudiəm/ *n* sodio, *m*
Sodomite /'sɒdəˌmait/ *n* sodomita, *mf*
sodomy /'sɒdəmi/ *n* sodomía, *f*
sofa /'soufə/ *n* sofá, *m*
soft /sɔft/ *a* blando; suave; muelle; (flabby) flojo; (of disposition, etc.) dulce; (effeminate) muelle, afeminado; (lenient) indulgente; (easy) fácil; (silly) tonto. **to have a s. spot for,** (a person) tener una debilidad para. **s. coal,** carbón bituminoso, *m.* **s. drink,** bebida no alcohólica, *f.* **s. felt hat,** sombrero flexible, *m.* **s. fruit,** fruta blanda, *f.* **s.-boiled,** (of eggs) pasado por agua; (of persons) inocente, ingenuo. **s.-hearted,** de buen corazón; compasivo, bondadoso. **s.-heartedness,** buen corazón, *m,* bondad, *f.* **s.-spoken,** de voz suave; que habla con dulzura, meloso. **s. water,** agua blanda, *f*
soften /'sɔfən/ *vt* ablandar, reblandecer) (weaken) debilitar; (mitigate; mitigar, suavizar; (the heart, etc.) enternecer. —*vi* reblandecerse; enternecerse
softening /'sɔfənɪŋ/ *n* reblandecimiento, *m;* (relenting) enternecimiento, *m*
softly /'sɔftli/ *adv* suavemente; dulcemente, tiernamente; sin ruido, silenciosamente
softness /'sɔftnɪs/ *n* blandura, *f;* suavidad, *f;* (sweetness, etc.) dulzura, *f;* (of character) debilidad de carácter, *f;* (silliness) necedad, estupidez, *f*
soggy /'sɒgi/ *a* empapado de agua; saturado
soil /sɔil/ *n* tierra, *f;* (country) país, *m,* tierra, *f.* —*vt* ensuciar; *Fig.* manchar. **my native s.,** mi tierra, mi patria
soiled /sɔild/ *a* sucio. **s. linen,** ropa sucia, *f*
soiree /swɑ'rei/ *n* velada, *f*
sojourn /'soudʒɜrn/ *vi* morar, residir, permanecer. —*n* residencia, permanencia, *f*
sojourner /'soudʒɜrnər/ *n* morador (-ra), residente, *mf*
sol /sɔl/ *n mus* sol, *m.* **sol-fa,** *n* solfa, *f,* solfeo, *m.* —*vt* solfear
solace /'sɒlɪs/ *n* consuelo, solaz, *m.* —*vt* consolar; solazar

solar /ˈsoulər/ *a* solar. **s. plexus,** *anat* plexo solar, *m.* **s. system,** sistema solar, *m*
solder /ˈsɒdər/ *n* soldadura, *f, vt* soldar
soldering /ˈsɒdərɪŋ/ *n* soldadura, *f*
soldier /ˈsouldʒər/ *n* soldado, *m;* militar, *m.* **He wants to be a s.,** Quiere ser militar
soldierly /ˈsouldʒərli/ *a* militar; marcial
soldiery /ˈsouldʒəri/ *n* soldadesca, *f*
sole /soul/ *n* (of a foot) planta, *f;* (of a shoe) suela, *f;* (of a plough) cepa, *f; ichth* lenguado, *m,* suela, *f.* —*vt* (shoes) solar, poner suela (a). —*a* solo, único; exclusivo. **s. right,** exclusiva, *f,* derecho exclusivo, *m*
solecism /ˈsɒləˌsɪzəm/ *n* solecismo, *m*
solely /ˈsoulli/ *adv* sólo; únicamente, puramente; meramente
solemn /ˈsɒləm/ *a* solemne; grave; serio; (sacred) sagrado. **Why do you look so s.?** ¿Por qué estás tan serio?
solemnity /səˈlɛmnɪti/ *n* solemnidad, *f*
solemnization /ˌsɒləmnəˈzeiʃən/ *n* solemnización, celebración, *f*
solemnize /ˈsɒləmˌnaiz/ *vt* solemnizar
solemnly /ˈsɒləmli/ *adv* solemnemente; gravemente
solicit /səˈlɪsɪt/ *vt* solicitar; implorar, rogar encarecidamente
solicitation /səˌlɪsɪˈteiʃən/ *n* solicitación, *f*
solicitor /səˈlɪsɪtər/ *n* abogado (-da)
solicitous /səˈlɪsɪtəs/ *a* ansioso (de), deseoso (de); solícito, atento; (worried) preocupado
solicitude /səˈlɪsɪˌtud/ *n* solicitud, *f,* cuidado, *m;* (anxiety) preocupación, *f*
solid /ˈsɒlɪd/ *a* sólido; macizo; (of persons) serio, formal; (unanimous) unánime. —*n* sólido, *m.* **a s. meal,** una comida fuerte. **He slept for ten s. hours,** Durmió por diez horas seguidas. **solid-colored material,** tela lisa, *f.* **s. food,** alimentos sólidos, *m pl.* **s. geometry,** geometría del espacio, *f.* **solid gold,** oro de ley, *m.* **s. tire,** llanta de goma maciza, *f*
solidarity /ˌsɒlɪˈdærɪti/ *n* solidaridad, *f*
solidification /səˌlɪdəfɪˈkeiʃən/ *n* solidificación, *f*
solidify /səˈlɪdəˌfai/ *vt* solidificar. —*vi* solidificarse; congelarse
solidity /səˈlɪdɪti/ *n* solidez, *f;* unanimidad, *f*
solidly /ˈsɒlɪdli/ *adv* sólidamente
soliloquize /səˈlɪləˌkwaiz/ *vi* soliloquiar, hablar a solas
soliloquy /səˈlɪləkwi/ *n* soliloquio, *m*
solitaire /ˈsɒlɪˌtɛər/ *n* (diamond and game) solitario, *m*
solitary /ˈsɒlɪˌtɛri/ *a* solitario; solo, aislado, único. **He was in s. confinement for three months,** Estuvo incomunicado durante tres meses. **There is not a s. one,** No hay ni uno
solitude /ˈsɒlɪˌtud/ *n* soledad, *f*
solo /ˈsoulou/ *n* (performance and cards) solo, *m.* **to sing a s.,** cantar un solo. **It was his first s. flight,** Era su primer vuelo a solas
soloist /ˈsoulouɪst/ *n* solista, *mf*
solstice /ˈsɒlstɪs, ˈsoul-/ *n* solsticio, *m.* **summer s.,** solsticio vernal, *m.* **winter s.,** solsticio hiemal, *m*
solubility /ˌsɒlyəˈbɪlɪti/ *n* solubilidad, *f*
soluble /ˈsɒlyəbəl/ *a* soluble
solution /səˈluʃən/ *n* solución, *f*
solvable /ˈsɒlvəbəl/ *a* que se puede resolver, soluble
solve /sɒlv/ *vt* resolver, hallar la solución de
solvency /ˈsɒlvənsi/ *n* solvencia, *f*
solvent /ˈsɒlvənt/ *a com* solvente; (*chem* and *fig*) disolvente. —*n* disolvente, *m*
somatic /souˈmætɪk/ *a* somático
somber /ˈsɒmbər/ *a* sombrío
somberly /ˈsɒmbərli/ *adv* sombríamente
somberness /ˈsɒmbərnɪs/ *n* lo sombrío; sobriedad, *f;* melancolía, *f*
some /sʌm; *unstressed* səm/ *a* alguno (-a), algunos (-as); (before a masculine sing. noun) algún; unos (-as); un poco de, algo de; (as a partitive, often not translated, e.g. *Give me s. wine,* Dame vino); (approximately) aproximadamente, unos (-as). —*pron* algunos (-as), unos (-as); algo, un poco. **I should like s. strawberries,** Me gustaría comer unas fresas. **s. day,** algún día. **S. say yes, others no,** Algunos dicen que sí, otros que no. **There are s. sixty people in the garden,** Hay unas sesenta personas en el jardín
somebody, someone /ˈsʌmbɒdi; ˈsʌmˌwʌn/ *n* alguien, *mf.* **s. else,** otro (-a), otra persona, *f.* **S. or other said that the book is worth reading,** No sé quién dijo que el libro vale la pena de leerse. **to be s.,** *inf* ser un personaje
somehow /ˈsʌmˌhau/ *adv* de un modo u otro, de alguna manera. **S. I don't like them,** No sé por qué, pero no me gustan
somersault /ˈsʌmərˌsɔlt/ *n* salto mortal, *m, vi* dar un salto mortal
something /ˈsʌmˌθɪŋ/ *n* algo, *m,* alguna cosa, *f.* —*adv* algún tanto. **Would you like s. else?** ¿Quiere Vd. otra cosa? **He left s. like fifty thousand dollars,** Dejó algo así como cincuenta mil dolares. **He has s. to live for,** Tiene para que vivir
sometime /ˈsʌmˌtaim/ *adv* algún día, alguna vez; en algún tiempo. —*a* ex-. **Come and see me s. soon,** Ven a verme algún día de estos. **He will have to go abroad s. or another,** Tarde o temprano, tiene que ir al extranjero. **s. last month,** durante el mes pasado
sometimes /ˈsʌmˌtaimz/ *adv* algunas veces, a veces. **s. happy, s. sad,** algunas veces feliz y otras triste, ora feliz ora triste
somewhat /ˈsʌmˌwʌt/ *adv* algo; algún tanto, un tanto; un poco. **I am s. busy,** Estoy algo ocupado. **He is s. of a lady-killer,** Tiene sus puntos de castigador, Tiene algo de castigador
somewhere /ˈsʌmˌwɛər/ *adv* en alguna parte. **s. about,** por ahí. **s. else,** en otra parte
somnambulism /sɒmˈnæmbyəˌlɪzəm/ *n* somnambulismo, *m*
somnambulist /sɒmˈnæmbyəlɪst/ *n* somnámbulo (-la)
somnolence /ˈsɒmnələns/ *n* somnolencia, *f*
somnolent /ˈsɒmnələnt/ *a* soñoliento; soporifero
son /sʌn/ *n* hijo, *m.* **son-in-law,** yerno, hijo político, *m*
sonata /səˈnɑtə/ *n* sonata, *f*
song /sɔŋ/ *n* canto, *m;* canción, *f;* (poem) poema, verso, *m.* **It's nothing to make a s. about,** No es para tanto. **to break into s.,** ponerse a cantar. **the S. of Songs,** Cantar de los Cantares, *m.* **s.-bird,** ave canora, *f.* **s.-book,** libro de canciones, *m.* **s.-writer,** compositor (-ra) de canciones
sonic /ˈsɒnɪk/ *a* sónico. **sonic boom,** estampido sónico, *m*
sonnet /ˈsɒnɪt/ *n* soneto, *m*
sonorous /səˈnɔrəs/ *a* sonoro
sonorousness /səˈnɔrəsnɪs/ *n* sonoridad, *f*
soon /sun/ *adv* pronto; dentro de poco, luego. **as s. as,** así que, en cuanto, luego que, no bien... **as s. as possible,** lo antes posible, lo más pronto posible, con la mayor antelación posible, cuanto antes. **s. after,** poco después (de). **See you s.!** ¡Hasta pronto! **sooner or later,** tarde o temprano. **the sooner the better,** cuanto antes mejor. **No sooner had he left the house, when...** Apenas hubo dejado la casa, cuando... **Emily would sooner go to London,** Emilia preferiría ir a Londres (A Emilia le gustaría más ir a Londres)
soot /sʊt/ *n* hollín, *m, vt* cubrir de hollín
soothe /suð/ *vt* tranquilizar, calmar, (pain) aliviar, mitigar
soothing /ˈsuðɪŋ/ *a* calmante, tranquilizador, sosegador; (of powders, etc.) calmante
soothingly /ˈsuðɪŋli/ *adv* con dulzura; suavemente; como un consuelo
soothsayer /ˈsuθˌseiər/ *n* adivino (-na), adivinador (-ra)
soothsaying /ˈsuθˌseiɪŋ/ *n* adivinanza, *f*
sooty /ˈsʊti/ *a* cubierto de hollín; negro como el hollín
sop /sɒp/ *n* sopa, *f;* (bribe) soborno, *m*
sophism /ˈsɒfɪzəm/ *n* sofisma, *m*
sophist /ˈsɒfɪst/ *n hist* sofista, *m;* (quibbler) sofista, *mf*
sophistic /səˈfɪstɪk/ *a philos* sofista; (of persons, arguments) sofístico
sophisticated /səˈfɪstɪˌkeitɪd/ *a* nada ingenuo; mundano; (cultured) culto

sophistication /sə,fɪstɪ'keiʃən/ *n* falta de simplicidad, *f;* mundanería, *f;* cultura, *f*
sophistry /'sɒfəstri/ *n* sofistería, *f*
Sophoclean /,sɒfə'kliən/ *a* sofocleo
soporific /,sɒpə'rɪfɪk/ *a* soporífico
sopping /'sɒpɪŋ/ *a* muy mojado. **s. wet,** hecho una sopa
soprano /sə'prænou/ *n* (voice and part) soprano, *m;* (singer) soprano, tiple, *mf*
sorcerer /'sɔrsərər/ *n* encantador, mago, brujo, *m*
sorceress /'sɔrsərɪs/ *n* hechicera, bruja, *f*
sorcery /'sɔrsəri/ *n* sortilegio, *m,* hechicería, brujería, *f;* encanto, *m*
sordid /'sɔrdɪd/ *a* sórdido; (of motives, etc.) ruin, vil
sordidness /'sɔrdɪdnɪs/ *n* sordidez, *f;* (of motives, etc.) vileza, bajeza, *f*
sordine /sɔrdɛn/ *n Mus.* sordina, *f*
sore /sɔr/ *a* doloroso, malo; (sad) triste; (annoyed) enojado; (with need, etc.) extremo. *—n* llaga, *f;* (on horses, etc., caused by girths) matadura, *f; Fig.* herida, *f;* recuerdo doloroso, *m.* **to open an old s.,** *Fig.* renovar la herida. **running s.,** úlcera, *f.* **s. throat,** dolor de garganta, *m*
sorely /'sɔrli/ *adv* grandemente; muy; urgentemente. **He was s. tempted,** Tuvo grandes tentaciones
soreness /'sɔrnɪs/ *n* dolor, *m;* (resentment) amargura, *f,* resentimiento, *m;* (ill-feeling) rencor, *m*
sorrel /'sɔrəl, 'sɒr-/ *a* alazán. *—n* (horse) alazán, *m; Bot.* acedera, *f*
sorrow /'sɒrou/ *n* pesar, *m,* aflicción, pesadumbre, *f;* tristeza, *f.* *—vi* afligirse; entristecerse. **To my great s.,** Con gran pesar mío. **s.-stricken,** afligido, agobiado de pena
sorrowful /'sɒrəfəl/ *a* afligido, angustiado; triste
sorrowfully /'sɒrəfəli/ *adv* con pena, tristemente
sorrowing /'sɒrouɪŋ/ *a* afligido. *—n* aflicción, *f;* lamentación, *f*
sort /sɔrt/ *n* especie, *f;* clase, *f;* tipo, *m.* *—vt* separar (de); clasificar. **a s. of hat,** una especie de sombrero. **all sorts of,** toda clase de. **He is a good s.,** Es buen chico. **He is a queer s.,** Es un tipo raro. **in some s.,** hasta cierto punto. **I am out of sorts,** Estoy destemplado. **Nothing of the s.!** ¡Nada de eso!
sorter /'sɔrtər/ *n* oficial de correos, *m;* clasificador (-ra)
sorting /'sɔrtɪŋ/ *n* clasificación, *f*
sot /sɒt/ *n* zaque, pellejo, *m*
sotto voce /'sɒt'ou voutʃi/ *adv* a sovoz, en voz baja
soul /soul/ *n* alma, *f;* espíritu, *m;* (departed) ánima, *f;* (being) ser, *m;* (life) vida, *f;* (heart) corazón, *m.* **All Souls' Day,** Día de los Difuntos, *m.* **He is a good s.!** ¡Es un bendito! **She is a simple s.,** Ella es una alma de Dios. **without seeing a living s.,** sin ver un bicho viviente. **Upon my s.!** ¡Por mi vida! **s. in purgatory,** alma en pena, *f.* **s.-stirring,** emocionante
soulful /'soulfəl/ *a* sentimental, emocional; espiritual; romántico
soulless /'soullɪs/ *a* sin alma; mecánico
sound /saund/ *n* sonido, *m;* son, *m;* ruido, *m;* (strait) estrecho, *m.* *—vi* sonar; hacer ruido; resonar; (seem) parecer. *—vt* sonar; (the horn, the alarm, musical instrument) tocar; (express) expresar; proclamar; (praise) celebrar; *Naut.* hondear; *Med.* tentar; (the chest) auscultar; (try to discover) tentar, sondar; (experience) experimentar. **to the s. of,** al son de. **s.-box,** (of a gramophone) diafragma, *m.* **s.-detector,** fonolocalización de aviones, *f.* **s.-film,** película sonora, *f.* **s.-proof,** (of radio studios, etc.) aislado de todo sonido. **s.-track,** guía sonora, banda sonora, *f.* **s.-wave,** onda sonora, *f*
sound /saund/ *a* sano; (of a person) perspicaz; (reasonable) lógico, razonable; (of a policy, etc.) prudente; (of an argument, etc.) válido; (of an investment) seguro; (solvent) solvente; (good) bueno; (deep) profundo. *—adv* profundamente, bien
sounding /'saundɪŋ/ *n Naut.* sondeo, *m; pl* **soundings,** sondas, *f pl.* *—a* sonoro. **to take soundings,** sondar, echar la plomada. **s.-board,** tabla de armonía, *f*
soundless /'saundlɪs/ *a* sin ruido, silencioso
soundly /'saundli/ *adv* sanamente; juiciosamente, prudentemente; bien; (deeply) profundamente
soundness /'saundnɪs/ *n* (of a person) perspicacia, *f;* (of a policy, etc.) prudencia, *f;* (of an argument, etc.) validez, fuerza, *f;* (financial) solvencia, *f*
soup /sup/ *n* sopa, *f.* **clear s.,** consommé, *m.* **thick s.,** puré, *m.* **to be in the s.,** *Inf.* estar aviado. **s.-ladle,** cucharón, *m.* **s.-plate,** plato sopero, *m.* **s.-tureen,** sopera, *f*
sour /sauᵊr/ *a* ácido, agrio; (of milk) agrio; (of persons, etc.) agrio, desabrido. *—vt* agriar. **to go s.,** volverse agrio. **S. grapes!** ¡Están verdes!
source /sɔrs/ *n* (of a river, etc.) nacimiento, *m;* fuente, *f;* (of infection) foco, *m.* **to know from a good s.,** saber de buena tinta
sourly /'sauᵊrli/ *adv* agriamente
sourness /'sauᵊrnɪs/ *n* acidez, agrura, *f;* acrimonia, *f*
south /sauθ/ *n* sur, *m;* mediodía, *m.* *—a* del sur. *—adv* hacia el sur. **S. African,** *a* and *n* sudafricano (-na). **S. American,** *a* and *n* sudamericano (-na). **s.-east,** *n* sudeste, *m.* *—a* del sudeste. *—adv* hacia el sudeste. **s.-easter,** viento del sudeste, *m.* **s.-easterly,** *a* del sudeste; al sudeste. *—adv* hacia el sudeste. **s.-eastern,** del sudeste. **s.-s.-east,** *n* sudsudeste, *m.* **s.-s.-west,** sudsudoeste, *m.* **s.-west,** *n* sudoeste, *m.* *—a* del sudoeste. *—adv* hacia el sudoeste. **s.-west wind,** viento sudoeste, ábrego, *m.* **s.-westerly,** *a* del sudoeste. *—adv* hacia el sudoeste. **s.-western,** *a* del sudoeste
South Africa República Sudafricana, *f*
South America América del Sur, Sudamérica, *f*
southerly /'sʌðərli/ *a* del sur; hacia el sur. **The house has a s. aspect,** La casa está orientada al sur
southern /'sʌðərn/ *a* del sur; del mediodía; meridional. **S. Cross,** Cruz, *f,* Crucero, *m.* **s. express,** sudexpreso, *m*
southerner /'sʌðərnər/ *n* habitante del sur, *m*
South Sea Mar del Sur, Mar del Pacífico, *m*
southward /'sauθwərd; *Naut.* 'sʌðərd/ *a* del sur; al sur. *—adv* hacia el sur
souvenir /,suvə'nɪər/ *n* recuerdo, *m*
sovereign /'sɒvrɪn/ *a* soberano. *—n* soberano (-na); (coin) soberano, *m*
sovereignty /'sɒvrɪnti/ *n* soberanía, *f*
soviet /'souvi,ɛt/ *n* soviet, *m, a* soviético
Soviet Union, the la Unión Soviética, *f*
sow /sau/ *n* cerda, puerca, marrana, *f;* (of a wild boar) jabalina, *f;* (of iron) galápago, *m*
sow /sou/ *vt* sembrar; esparcir; diseminar
sower /'souər/ *n* sembrador (-ra)
sowing /'souɪŋ/ *n* sembradura, siembra, *f.* **s. machine,** sembradera, *f.*
soya bean /'sɔiə/ *n* soja, *f*
spa /spɑ/ *n* balneario, *m;* (spring) manantial mineral, *m,* caldas, *f pl*
space /speis/ *n* espacio, *m;* (of time) temporada, *f;* intervalo, *m;* (*Print., Mus.*) espacio, *m.* *—vt* espaciar. **blank s.,** blanco, *m.* **s.-bar,** tecla de espacios, *f,* espaciador, *m*
spacious /'speiʃəs/ *a* espacioso; amplio
spaciousness /'speiʃəsnɪs/ *n* espaciosidad, *f;* amplitud, *f*
spade /speid/ *n* pala, azada, *f;* (cards) espada, *f.* **to call a s. a s.,** llamar al pan pan y al vino vino, llamar a las cosas por su nombre. **s.-work,** trabajo preparatorio, *m,* labor de pala, *f*
spaghetti /spə'gɛti/ *n* fideos, macarrones, *m pl*
Spain /spein/ España, *f*
span /spæn/ *vt* medir a palmos; rodear; medir; (cross) atravesar, cruzar. *—n* palmo, *m;* espacio, *m,* duración, *f;* (of a bridge) vano, *m;* (of wing, *Aer., Zool.*) envergadura, *f;* (distance) distancia, *f.* **single-s. bridge,** puente de vano único. **the brief s. of human life,** la corta duración de la vida humana
spangle /'spæŋgəl/ *n* lentejuela, *f;* (tinsel) oropel, *m.* *—vt* adornar con lentejuelas; sembrar (de), esparcir (de). **spangled with stars,** sembrado de estrellas
Spaniard /'spænyərd/ *n* español (-la). **a young S.,** un joven español
spaniel /'spænyəl/ *n* perro de aguas, perro sabueso español *m;* (cocker) sabueso, *m*
Spanish /'spænɪʃ/ *a* español. *—n* (language) español, castellano, *m.* **a S. girl,** una muchacha española. **in S. fashion,** a la española. **S. American,** *a* and *n* his-

panoamericano (-na). **S. broom,** retama de olor, *f.* **S. fly,** cantárida, *f*
Spanish America Hispanoamérica, *f*
spank /spæŋk/ *vt* pegar con la mano, azotar. —*n* azotazo, *m.* **to s. along,** correr rápidamente; (of a horse) galopar
spanking /'spæŋkɪŋ/ *n* azotamiento, vapuleo, *m*
spanner /'spænər/ *n* llave inglesa, llave de tuercas, *f*
spar /spɑr/ *n Naut.* mastel, *m; Mineral.* espato, *m;* (boxing) boxeo, *m;* (quarrel) disputa, *f.* —*vi* boxear; (argue) disputar
spare /spɛər/ *a* (meager) frugal, escaso; (of persons) enjuto, flaco; (available) disponible; (extra) de repuesto. —*n* recambio, *m.* **s. part,** pieza de recambio, pieza de repuesto, *f.* **s. room,** cuarto de amigos, *m.* **s. time,** ratos de ocio, *m pl,* tiempo disponible, *m.* **s. wheel,** rueda de repuesto, *f*
spare /spɛər/ *vt* (expense, etc.) escatimar; ahorrar; (do without) pasarse sin; (give) dar; (a life, etc.) perdonar; (avoid) evitar; dispensar de; (grant) hacer gracia de; (time) dedicar. **I cannot s. her,** No puedo estar sin ella. **They have no money to s.,** No tienen dinero de sobra. **to be sparing of,** ser avaro de
sparingly /'spɛərɪŋli/ *adv* frugalmente; escasamente. **to eat s.,** comer con frugalidad
spark /spɑrk/ *n* chispa, *f;* (gallant) pisaverde, *m.* —*vi* chispear, echar chispas
sparking /'spɒrkɪŋ/ *a* chispeante. —*n* emisión de chispas, *f.* **s.-plug,** bujía de encendido, *f*
sparkle /'spɑrkəl/ *vi* centellear, rutilar, destellar; *Fig.* brillar; (of wines) ser espumoso. —*n* centelleo, destello, *m; Fig.* brillo, *m*
sparkling /'spɒrklɪŋ/ *a* rutilante, centelleante, reluciente; *Fig.* brillante, chispeante; (of wines) espumante
sparring match /'spɒrɪŋ/ *n* combate de boxeo amistoso, *m*
sparrow /'spærou/ *n* gorrión, *m.* **s.-hawk,** gavilán, esparaván, *m*
sparse /spars/ *a* claro, ralo; esparcido
sparsely /'sparsli/ *adv* escasamente
Sparta /'spɑrtə/ Esparta, *f*
Spartan /'spɑrtn̩/ *a* and *n* espartano (-na)
spasm /'spæzəm/ *n* espasmo, *m;* ataque, *m;* acceso, *m*
spasmodic /spæz'mɒdɪk/ *a* espasmódico; intermitente
spasmodically /spæz'mɒdɪkli/ *adv* espasmódicamente
spat /spæt/ *n* (gaiter) polaina de tela, *f*
spate /speit/ *n* crecida, *f; Fig.* torrente, *m.* **in s.,** crecido
spatter /'spætər/ *vt* salpicar; (*Fig.* smirch) manchar. —*vi* rociar. —*n* salpicadura, *f;* rociada, *f*
spatula /'spætʃələ/ *n* espátula, *f*
spawn /spɔn/ *vt* and *vi* desovar; engendrar. —*n* huevas, *f pl,* freza, *f;* (offspring) producto, *m*
spawning /'spɔnɪŋ/ *n* desove, *m*
speak /spik/ *vi* hablar; pronunciar un discurso; (sound) sonar. —*vt* decir; (French, etc.) hablar. **She never spoke to him again,** Nunca volvió a dirigirle la palabra. **roughly speaking,** aproximadamente, más o menos. **Speaking for myself,** En cuanto a mí, Por mi parte. **without speaking,** sin decir nada, sin hablar. **to s. for,** (a person) hablar por. **to s. for itself,** hablar por sí mismo, ser evidente. **to s. one's mind,** decir lo que se piensa. **to s. of,** hablar de. **to s. out,** hablar claro; hablar alto. **to s. up for,** (a person) hablar en favor de (alguien)
speaker /'spikər/ *n* el, *m,* (*f,* la) que habla; (public) orador (-ra). **the S.,** el Presidente de la Cámara de los Comunes
speaking /'spikɪŋ/ *a* hablante; para hablar; elocuente, expresivo. —*n* habla, *f,* discurso, *m.* **They are not on s. terms,** No se hablan. **within s. distance,** al habla. **s.-trumpet,** portavoz, *m.* **s.-tube,** tubo acústico, *m*
spear /spɪər/ *n* lanza, *f;* (javelin) venablo, *m;* (harpoon) arpón, *m.* —*vt* herir con lanza, alancear; (fish) arponear. **s.-head,** punta de la lanza, *f.* **s.-thrust,** lanzada, *f*
special /'spɛʃəl/ *a* especial; particular; extraordinario. —*n* (train) tren extraordinario, *m.* **s. correspondent,** corresponsal extraordinario, *m.* **s. friend,** amigo (-ga) del alma, amigo intimo
specialist /'spɛʃəlɪst/ *n* especialista, *mf*
specialization /ˌspɛʃələ'zeiʃən/ *n* especialización, *f*
specialize /'spɛʃəˌlaiz/ *vt* especializar. —*vi* especializarse
specially /'spɛʃəli/ *adv* especialmente; particularmente; sobre todo
specialty /ˌspɛʃi'ælɪti/ *n* particularidad, *f;* especialidad, *f*
species /'spiʃiz, -siz/ *n* especie, *f;* raza, *f*
specific /spɪ'sɪfɪk/ *a* específico; explícito. —*n* específico, *m.* **s. gravity,** peso específico, *m,* densidad, *f*
specifically /spɪ'sɪfɪkli/ *adv* específicamente; explícitamente
specification /ˌspɛsəfɪ'keiʃən/ *n* especificación, *f*
specify /'spɛsəˌfai/ *vt* especificar
specimen /'spɛsəmən/ *n* espécimen, *m;* ejemplo, *m; Inf.* tipo, *m*
specious /'spiʃəs/ *a* especioso
speciousness /'spiʃəsnɪs/ *n* plausibilidad, *f;* apariencia engañosa, *f*
speck /spɛk/ *n* pequeña mancha, *f;* punto, *m;* átomo, *m;* (on fruit) maca, *f*
speckle /'spɛkəl/ *vt* motear, manchar
speckled /'spɛkəld/ *a* abigarrado; con manchas
spectacle /'spɛktəkəl/ *n* espectáculo, *m;* escena, *f; pl* **spectacles,** gafas, *f pl,* anteojos, *m pl.* **s.-case,** cajita para las gafas, *f*
spectacled /'spɛktəkəld/ *a* con gafas, que lleva gafas
spectacular /spɛk'tækyələr/ *a* espectacular
spectator /'spɛkteitər/ *n* espectador (-ra)
specter /'spɛktər/ *n* espectro, fantasma, *m*
spectral /'spɛktrəl/ *a* espectral
spectroscope /'spɛktrəˌskoup/ *n* espectroscopio, *m*
spectrum /'spɛktrəm/ *n Phys.* espectro, *m*
speculate /'spɛkyəˌleit/ *vi* especular (sobre, acerca de); *Com.* especular (en)
speculation /ˌspɛkyə'leiʃən/ *n* especulación, *f*
speculative /'spɛkyəˌlətɪv/ *a* especulativo
speculator /'spɛkyəˌleitər/ *n* especulador (-ra)
speech /spitʃ/ *n* habla, *f;* palabra, *f;* (idiom) lenguaje, *m;* (language) idioma, *m; Gram.* oración, *f;* (address) discurso, *m;* disertación, *f.* **part of s.,** parte de la oración, *f.* **to make a s.,** pronunciar un discurso. **s. maker,** orador (-ra)
speechless /'spitʃlɪs/ *a* mudo; sin habla; desconcertado, turbado
speed /spid/ *n* prisa, rapidez, *f;* velocidad, *f.* —*vt* dar la bienvenida (a); conceder éxito (a); (accelerate) acelerar. —*vi* darse prisa; correr a toda prisa; (of arrows) volar. **at full s.,** a toda prisa; a toda velocidad; a todo correr. **maximum s.,** velocidad máxima, *f.* **with all s.,** a toda prisa. **s. of impact,** velocidad del choque, *f.* **s.-boat,** lancha de carrera, *f.* **s.-limit,** velocidad máxima, *f,* límite de velocidad, *m*
speedily /'spidl̩i/ *adv* aprisa, rápidamente; prontamente
speediness /'spidinɪs/ *n* rapidez, prisa, celeridad, *f;* prontitud, *f*
speeding /'spidɪŋ/ *n* exceso de velocidad, *m.* **s. up,** aceleración, *f*
speedometer /spi'dɒmɪtər/ *n* cuentakilómetros, *m*
speedway /'spidˌwei/ *n* autódromo, *m,* pista de ceniza, *f*
speedy /'spidi/ *a* rápido, pronto
spell /spɛl/ *n* ensalmo, hechizo, *m;* encanto, *m;* (bout) turno, *m;* (interval) rato, *m;* temporada, *f.* —*vt* (a word) deletrear; (a word in writing) escribir; (mean) significar; (be) ser. **a s. of good weather,** una temporada de buen tiempo. **by spells,** a ratos. **to learn to s.,** aprender la ortografía. **s.-bound,** encantado, fascinado; asombrado
spelling /'spɛlɪŋ/ *n* deletreo, *m;* ortografía, *f.* **s.-book,** silabario, *m;* **s. mistake,** falta de ortografía, *f*
spelling bee *n* certamen de deletreo, *m*
spend /spɛnd/ *vt* gastar; (time, etc.) pasar; perder; consumir, agotar. —*vi* gastar, hacer gastos. **to s. oneself,** agotarse

spendthrift /'spɛnd,θrɪft/ *n* derrochador (-ra), manirroto (-ta). —*a* despilfarrado, pródigo

spent /spɛnt/ *a* agotado, rendido. **The night is far s.,** La noche está avanzada. **s. bullet,** bala fría, *f*

sperm /spɜrm/ *n Biol.* esperma, *f;* (whale) cachalote, *m*

spermaceti /,spɜrmə'sɛti/ *n* esperma de ballena, *f*

sphere /sfɪər/ *n* esfera, *f.* **s. of influence,** zona de influencia, *f*

spherical /'sfɛrɪkəl, 'sfɪər-/ *a* esférico

sphinx /sfɪŋks/ *n* esfinge, *f.* **s.-like,** de esfinge

spice /spais/ *n* especia, *f; Fig.* sabor, *m;* (trace) dejo, *m.* —*vt* especiar. **s. cupboard,** especiero, *m*

spick and span /'spɪk ən 'spæn/ *a* limpio como una patena; (brand-new) flamante; (of persons) muy compuesto

spicy /'spaisi/ *a* especiado; aromático; *Fig.* picante

spider /'spaidər/ *n* araña, *f.* **spider's web,** telaraña, *f*

spidery /'spaidəri/ *a* de araña; lleno de arañas. **s. writing,** letra de patas de araña, *f*

spigot /'spɪgət/ *n* espiche, *m*

spike /spaik/ *n* punta (de hierro, etc.), *f;* escarpia, *f;* (for boots) clavo, *m; Bot.* espiga, *f.* —*vt* clavetear; (a cannon) clavar

spill /spɪl/ *vt* derramar. —*n* (fall) caída, *f*

spilling /'spɪlɪŋ/ *n* derramamiento, derrame, *m*

spin /spɪn/ *vt* hilar; (a cocoon) tejer; (a top) bailar; (a ball) tornear; (a coin) lanzar. —*vi* hilar; girar, bailar. —*n* vuelta, *f;* paseo, *m.* **to send spinning downstairs,** hacer rodar por la escalera (a). **to s. a yarn,** contar un cuento. **to s. out,** prolongar

spinach /'spɪnɪtʃ/ *n* espinaca, *f*

spinal /'spainl̩/ *a* espinal. **s. anaesthesia,** raquianestesia, *f.* **s. column,** columna vertebral, *f*

spindle /'spɪndl̩/ *n* huso, *m; Mech.* eje, *m.* **s.-shaped,** ahusado

spine /spain/ *n Anat.* espinazo, *m,* columna vertebral, *f; Bot.* espina, *f;* (of a porcupine, etc.) púa, *f*

spineless /'spainlɪs/ *a Zool.* invertebrado; *Fig.* débil

spinet /'spɪnɪt/ *n* espineta, *f*

spinner /'spɪnər/ *n* hilandero (-ra); máquina de hilar, *f*

spinney /'spɪni/ *n* arboleda, *f;* bosquecillo, *m*

spinning /'spɪnɪŋ/ *n* hilado, *m;* hilandería, *f.* **s.-machine,** máquina de hilar, *f.* **s.-top,** trompo, *m,* peonza, *f.* **s.-wheel,** rueca, *f*

spinster /'spɪnstər/ *n* soltera, *f.* **confirmed s.,** solterona, *f*

spiny /'spaini/ *a* con púas; espinoso

spiral /'spairəl/ *a* espiral; en espiral. —*n* espiral, *f*

spirally /'spairəli/ *adv* en espiral

spire /spaiər/ *n* (of a church) aguja, *f;* espira, *f*

spirit /'spɪrɪt/ *n* espíritu, *m;* alma, *f;* (ghost) aparecido, fantasma, *m;* (outstanding person) ingenio, *m,* inteligencia, *f;* (disposition) ánimo, *m;* (courage) valor, espíritu, *m;* (for a lamp, etc.) alcohol, *m.* **the Holy S.,** El Espíritu Santo. **to be in high spirits,** no caber de contento, saltar de alegría. **to be in low spirits,** estar desalentado, estar deprimido. **to be full of spirits,** ser bullicioso, tener mucha energía. **to keep up one's spirits,** sostener el valor. **to s. away,** quitar secretamente, hacer desaparecer; (kidnap) secuestrar. **s.-level,** nivel de burbuja, *m.* **s.-stove,** cocinilla, *f*

spirited /'spɪrɪtɪd/ *a* animado, vigoroso; fogoso, animoso, brioso

spiritless /'spɪrɪtlɪs/ *a* sin espíritu, apático; flojo, débil; (depressed) abatido, desalentado; (cowardly) sin valor, cobarde

spiritual /'spɪrɪtʃuəl/ *a* espiritual

spiritualism /'spɪrɪtʃuə,lɪzəm/ *n* espiritismo, *m; Philos.* espiritualismo, *m*

spiritualist /'spɪrɪtʃuəlɪst/ *n* espiritista, *mf; Philos.* espiritualista, *mf*

spiritualistic /,spɪrɪtʃuə'lɪstɪk/ *a* espiritista; *Philos.* espiritualista. **s. séance,** sesión espiritista, *f*

spirituality /,spɪrɪtʃu'ælɪti/ ' *n* espiritualidad, *f*

spiritually /'spɪrɪtʃuəli/ *adv* espiritualmente

spirituous /'spɪrɪtʃuəs/ *a* espiritoso

spirt /spɜrt/ *vi, vt, n.* See **spurt**

spit /spɪt/ *n* (for roasting) espetón, asador, *m;* (sandbank) banco de arena, *m;* (of land) lengua de tierra, *f;* (spittle) saliva, *f.* **the spit of, the spit and image of, the spitting image of,** la imagen viva de, la segunda edición de, *f.* —*vt* (skewer) espetar; (saliva, etc.) escupir; (curses, etc.) vomitar. —*vi* escupir, expectorar; (of a cat) fufear, decir fu; (sputter) chisporrotear; (rain) lloviznar

spite /spait/ *n* malevolencia, mala voluntad, hostilidad, *f;* rencor, *m,* ojeriza, *f.* —*vt* contrariar, hacer daño (a). **He has a s. against them,** Les tiene rencor. **in s. of,** a pesar de; a despecho de

spiteful /'spaitfəl/ *a* rencoroso, malévolo

spitefully /'spaitfəli/ *adv* malévolamente; con rencor; por maldad; por despecho

spitefulness /'spaitfəlnɪs/ *n* malevolencia, *f;* rencor, *m*

spitfire /'spɪt,faiər/ *n* cascarrabias, *mf,* furia, *f*

spittle /'spɪtl̩/ *n* saliva, *f*

splash /splæʃ/ *vt* salpicar (de); manchar (con). —*vi* derramarse, esparcirse; chapotear, chapalear. —*n* chapoteo, *m;* (of rain, etc.) chapaleteo, *m;* (stain or patch) mancha, *f.* **John was splashing about in the sea,** Juan chapoteaba en el mar. **to make a s.,** *Fig.* causar una sensación. **s.-board,** alero, *m*

spleen /splin/ *n Anat.* bazo, *m;* esplín, *m*

splendid /'splɛndɪd/ *a* espléndido; magnífico; glorioso; excelente

splendidly /'splɛndɪdli/ *adv* espléndidamente; magníficamente; excelentemente

splendor /'splɛndər/ *n* resplandor, *m;* magnificencia, *f;* (of exploits, etc.) esplendor, brillo, *m*

splice /splais/ *vt* (ropes, timbers) empalmar; (marry) unir, casar. —*n* empalme, *m*

splint /splɪnt/ *n Surg.* férula, *f.* **to put in a s.,** entablar

splinter /'splɪntər/ *vt* astillar, hacer astillas. —*vi* hacerse astillas

splintery /'splɪntəri/ *a* astilloso

split /splɪt/ *vi* henderse; resquebrajarse; (of seams) nacerse; abrirse; dividirse. —*vt* hender; partir; dividir; abrir; (the atom) escindir. —*n* hendedura, *f;* grieta, *f;* división, *f;* (in fabric) rasgón, *m;* (quarrel) ruptura, *f.* **to s. hairs,** andar en quisquillas, pararse en pelillos, sutilizar. **I have a splitting headache,** Tengo un dolor de cabeza que me trae loco. **to s. one's sides,** reírse a carcajadas, desternillarse de risa. **to s. on a rock,** estrellarse contra una roca. **to s. the difference,** partir la diferencia. **The blow s. his head open,** El golpe le abrió la cabeza. **to s. on,** *Inf.* delatar, denunciar

splotch /splatʃ/ *n* mancha, *f,* borrón, *m*

splutter /'splʌtər/ *vi* chisporrotear; (of a person) balbucir. —*n* chisporroteo, *m.* **to s. out,** decir tartamudeando

spoil /spɔil/ *n* botín, despojo, *m;* (of war) trofeo, *m.* —*vt* estropear; echar a perder; (diminish) mitigar; (a child) mimar; (injure) dañar; (destroy) arruinar, destruir. —*vi* estropearse; echarse a perder. **to be spoiling for a fight,** tener ganas de pelearse. **You have spoilt my fun,** Me has aguado la fiesta. **s.-sport,** aguafiestas, *mf*

spoiled /spɔild/ *a* (of a child, etc.) mimado, consentido, malacostumbrado

spoke /spouk/ *n* (of a wheel) rayo, *m;* (of a ladder) travesaño, peldaño, *m; Naut.* cabilla (de la rueda del timón), *f*

spoken /'spoukən/ *a* hablado. **well-s.,** bien hablado; cortés

spokesman /'spouksmən/ *n* portavoz, *m.* **to be s.,** llevar la palabra

spoliation /,spouli'eiʃən/ *n* expoliación, *f;* despojo, *m*

sponge /spʌndʒ/ *n* esponja, *f;* (cadger) gorrón (-ona); (cake) bizcocho, *m.* —*vt* limpiar con esponja. **to s.,** *Inf.* vivir de gorra. **s.-holder,** esponjera, *f*

sponger /'spʌndʒər/ *n* gorrón (-ona), vividor, *m,* sablista, *mf*

sponginess /'spʌndʒinɪs/ *n* esponjosidad, *f*

sponging *n* esponjadura, *f; Inf.* sablazo, *m*

spongy /'spʌndʒi/ *a* esponjoso

sponsor /'spɒnsər/ *n* garante, *mf;* valedor (-ra), patron (-na); (godfather) padrino, *m;* (godmother) madrina, *f,* (radio and TV) auspiciador, patrocinador, *m*

spontaneity /ˌspɒntəˈniːti, -ˈnei-/ *n* espontaneidad, *f*
spontaneous /spɒnˈteiniəs/ *a* espontáneo. **s. combustion,** combustión espontánea, *f*
spontaneously /spɒnˈteiniəsli/ *adv* espontáneamente
spook /spuk/ *n* fantasma, espectro, *m*
spool /spul/ *n* (for thread) bobina, *f*, carrete, *m;* (in a sewing machine) canilla, *f;* (of a fishing rod) carrete, *m*
spoon /spun/ *n* cuchara, *f.* —*vt* sacar con cuchara. —*vi* (slang) besuquearse. **to s.-feed,** dar de comer con cuchara (a); tratar como un niño (a)
spoonful /ˈspunfʊl/ *n* cucharada, *f*
spoor /spʊr, spɔr/ *n* pista, huella de animal, *f;* rastro, *m*
sporadic /spəˈrædɪk/ *a* esporádico
spore /spɔr/ *n Bot.* espora, *f; Zool.* germen, *m*
sport /spɔrt/ *n* deporte, sport, *m;* deportismo, *m;* (jest) broma, *f;* (game) juego, *m;* (plaything) juguete, *m;* (pastime) pasatiempo, *m.* —*vi* jugar; recrearse, divertirse. —*vt* llevar; ostentar, lucir. **He is a s.,** Es un buen chico. **to make s. of,** burlarse de. **sports car,** coche de deporte, *m.* **sports ground,** campo de recreo, *m.* **sports jacket,** chaqueta de deporte, americana, *f.* **sports shirt,** camisa corta, *f*
sporting /ˈspɔrtɪŋ/ *a* deportista; caballeroso. **I think there is a s. chance,** Me parece que hay una posibilidad de éxito
sporting goods *n* artículos de deporte, efectos de deportes, *m pl*
sportive /ˈspɔrtɪv/ *a* juguetón; bromista
sportsman /ˈspɔrtsmən/ *n* deportista, *m;* aficionado al sport, *m; Fig.* caballero, señor, *m;* buen chico, *m*
sportsmanlike /ˈspɔrtsmənˌlaik/ *a* de deportista; caballeroso
sportsmanship /ˈspɔrtsmənˌʃɪp/ *n* deportividad, *f*
spot /spɒt/ *n* mancha, *f;* pinta, *f;* (on the face, etc.) peca, *f;* grano, *m;* (place) sitio, *m;* lugar, *m;* (of liquor) trago, *m;* (of food) bocado, *m;* (of rain) gota, *f.* —*vt* manchar; motear; (recognize) reconocer; (understand) darse cuenta de, comprender. **a tender s.,** *Fig.* debilidad, *f.* **on the s.,** en el acto. **s. ball,** (billiards) pinta, *f.* **s. cash,** dinero contante, *m*
spotless /ˈspɒtlɪs/ *a* saltando de limpio; sin mancha; inmaculado; puro; virgen
spotlight /ˈspɒtˌlait/ *n* luz del proyector, *f;* proyector, *m*
spotted /ˈspɒtɪd/ *a* (stained) manchado; (of animals, etc.) con manchas; (of garments, etc.) con pintas
spotty /ˈspɒti/ *a* lleno de manchas; moteado; (pimply) con granos
spouse /spaus/ *n* esposo, *m;* esposa, *f*
spout /spaut/ *vi* chorrear; *Inf.* hablar incesantemente. —*vt* arrojar; vomitar; *Inf.* declamar, recitar. —*n* (of a jug, etc.) pico, *m;* (for water, etc.) tubo, *m*, cañería, *f;* canalón, *m;* (gust) ráfaga, nube, *f.* **down s.,** tubo de bajada, *m*
spouting /ˈspautɪŋ/ *n* chorreo, *m; Inf.* declamación, *f*
Sprachgefühl /ˈʃpraxgəˌfil/ *n* sentido del idioma, *m*
sprain /sprein/ *vt* dislocar, torcer. —*n* dislocación, *f*, esguince, *m.* **Victoria has sprained her foot,** Victoria se ha torcido el pie
sprat /spræt/ *n* sardineta, *f*
sprawl /sprɔl/ *vi* recostarse (en); extenderse; (of plants) trepar. **He went sprawling,** Cayó cuan largo era
spray /sprei/ *n* (branch) ramo, *m;* (of water, etc.) rocío, *m;* (of the sea) espuma, *f;* (mechanical device) pulverizador, *m.* —*vt* pulverizar; rociar; regar; (the throat) jeringar
spread /sprɛd/ *vt* tender; cubrir (de); poner; (stretch out) extender; (open out) desplegar; (of disease, etc.) propagar; diseminar; divulgar, difundir. —*vi* extenderse; propagarse; difundirse; divulgarse; (become general) generalizarse. —*n* extensión, *f;* expansión, *f;* propagación, *f;* divulgación, *f;* (*Aer.* and of birds) envergadura, *f.* **Carmen s. her hands to the fire,** Carmen extendió las manos al fuego. **The peacock s. its tail,** El pavo real hizo la rueda. **The dove s. its wings,** La paloma desplegó sus alas. **to s. out,** *vt* extender; desplegar; (scatter) esparcir, *vi* extenderse. **spread like wildfire,** correr como pólvora en reguero, propagarse como un reguero de pólvora, ser un reguero de pólvora
spreading /ˈsprɛdɪŋ/ *n* (of a disease) propagación, *f;* (of knowledge, etc.) divulgación, *f;* expansión, *f;* extensión, *f*
spreadsheet /ˈsprɛdˌʃit/ *n* hoja de cálculo, *f*
spree /spri/ *n* juerga, parranda, *f;* excursión, *f.* **to go on the s.,** ir de juerga, ir de picos pardos
sprig /sprɪg/ *n* ramita, *f;* (of heather, etc.) espiga, *f;* (scion) vástago, *m*
sprightliness /ˈspraitlinɪs/ *n* vivacidad, *f*, despejo, *m;* energía, *f*
sprightly /ˈspraitli/ *a* vivaracho, despierto; enérgico
spring /sprɪŋ/ *vi* saltar, brincar; (become) hacerse; (seek) buscar; (of plants, water) brotar; (of tears) arrasar, llenar; (from) originarse (en), ser causado (por); inspirarse (en). —*vt* (a mine) volar; (a trap) soltar. **to s. a surprise,** dar una sorpresa. **to s. a surprise on a person,** coger a la imprevista (a). **to s. at a person,** precipitarse sobre. **to s. to one's feet,** ponerse de pie de un salto. **to s. back,** saltar hacia atrás; recular; volver a su sitio. **to s. open,** abrirse súbitamente. **to s. up,** (of plants) brotar, crecer; (of difficulties, etc.) surgir, asomarse
spring /sprɪŋ/ *n* (jump) salto, brinco, *m;* (of water) fuente, *f*, manantial, *m;* (season) primavera, *f;* (of a watch, etc.) resorte, *m;* (of a mattress, etc.) muelle, *m.* —*a* primaveral. —*vi* saltar, brincar. **at one s.,** en un salto. **to give a s.,** dar un salto. **s.-board,** trampolín, *m.* **s.-mattress,** colchón de muelles, *m.* **s.-tide,** marea viva, *f*
springiness /ˈsprɪŋinɪs/ *n* elasticidad, *f*
springlike /ˈsprɪŋˌlaik/ *a* primaveral
springtime /ˈsprɪŋˌtaim/ *n* primavera, *f*
sprinkle /ˈsprɪŋkəl/ *vt* esparcir; salpicar; rociar
sprinkling /ˈsprɪŋklɪŋ/ *n* salpicadura, *f;* rociadura, *f;* pequeño número, *m.* **a s. of snow,** una nevada ligera
sprint /sprɪnt/ *vi* sprintar. —*n* sprint, *m*
sprite /sprait/ *n* trasgo, *m;* hada, *f*
sprout /spraut/ *vi* brotar, despuntar, retoñar, tallecer; germinar. —*vt* salir. —*n* brote, retoño, pimpollo, *m;* germen, *m.* **Brussels sprouts,** coles de Bruselas, *f pl*
spruce /sprus/ *a* peripuesto, muy aseado, pulido; elegante, *n Bot.* pícea, *f.* **to s. oneself up,** arreglarse, ponerse elegante
spruceness /ˈsprusnɪs/ *n* aseo, buen parecer, *m*, elegancia, *f*
spry /sprai/ *a* activo, ágil
spur /spɜr/ *n* espuela, *f;* aguijada, *f;* (of a bird) espólon, *m; Bot.* espuela, *f;* (of a mountain range) espolón, estribo, *m; Fig.* estímulo, *m.* —*vt* espolear, picar con la espuela; calzarse las espuelas; *Fig.* estimular, incitar. **on the s. of the moment,** bajo el impulso del momento
spurious /ˈspyʊriəs/ *a* espurio; falso
spurn /spɜrn/ *vt* rechazar; tratar con desprecio; menospreciar
spurt /spɜrt/ *vi* (gush) chorrear, borbotar; brotar, surgir; (in racing, etc.) hacer un esfuerzo supremo. —*vt* hacer chorrear; lanzar. —*n* (jet) chorro, *m;* esfuerzo supremo, *m*
sputter /ˈspʌtər/ *vi* chisporrotear; crepitar; (of a pen) escupir; (of a person) balbucir
sputtering /ˈspʌtərɪŋ/ *n* chisporroteo, *m;* crepitación, *f;* (of a person) balbuceo, *m*
sputum /ˈspyutəm/ *n* esputo, *m*
spy /spai/ *vt* observar, discernir. —*vi* espiar, ser espía. —*n* espía, *mf.* **to spy out the land,** explorar el terreno. **to spy upon,** espiar; seguir los pasos (a). **spy-glass,** catalejo, *m*
spying /ˈspaiɪŋ/ *n* espionaje, *m*
squabble /ˈskwɒbəl/ *n* disputa, *f;* riña, *f.* —*vi* pelearse; disputar
squabbling /ˈsqwɒblɪŋ/ *n* riñas, querellas, *f pl*; disputas, *f pl*
squad /skwɒd/ *n* escuadra, *f;* pelotón, *m*
squadron /ˈskwɒdrən/ *n Mil.* escuadrón, *m; Nav.* escuadra, *f; Aer.* escuadrilla, *f;* (of persons) pelotón, *m.* **s.-leader,** comandante, *m*
squalid /ˈskwɒlɪd/ *a* escuálido; (of quarrels, etc.) sórdido, mezquino
squall /skwɔl/ *vi* berrear; chillar. —*n* berrido, *m;*

chillido, *m;* (storm) chubasco, turbión, *m;* (storm) chubasco, turbión, *m; Fig.* tormenta, tempestad, *f*

squalor /ˈskwɒlər/ *n* escualidez, *f;* sordidez, mezquindad, *f*

squander /ˈskwɒndər/ *vt* derrochar, tirar, desperdiciar; (time, etc.) malgastar

squanderer /ˈskwɒndərər/ *n* derrochador (-ra)

squandering /ˈskwɒndərɪŋ/ *n* derroche, desperdicio, dispendio, *m;* (of time, etc.) pérdida, *f,* desperdicio, *m*

square /skwɛər/ *n Math.* cuadrado, *m;* rectángulo, *m;* (of a chessboard) escaque, *m;* (of a draughtboard and of graph paper) casilla, *f;* (in a town) plaza, *f;* (of troops) cuadro, *m, a* cuadrado; justo; igual; (honest) honrado, formal; (unambiguous) redondo, categórico; *Math.* cuadrado. **She wore a silk s. on her head,** Llevaba un pañuelo de seda en la cabeza. **five s. feet,** cinco pies cuadrados. **nine feet s.,** nueve pies en cuadro. **on the s.,** honradamente. **a s. dance,** contradanza, *f.* **a s. meal,** una buena comida. **s. dealing,** trato limpio, *m.* **The account is s.,** La cuenta está justa. **to get s. with,** desquitarse (de), vengarse de. **s. measure,** medida de superficie, *f.* **s. root,** raíz cuadrada, *f.* **s.-shouldered,** de hombros cuadrados

square /skwɛər/ *vt* cuadrar, escuadrar, (arrange) arreglar; (bribe) sobornar; (reconcile) acomodar; *Math.* cuadrar. —*vi* conformarse (con), cuadrar (con). **to s. the circle,** cuadrar el círculo. **to s. one's shoulders,** enderezarse. **to s. accounts with,** saldar cuentas con. **to s. up to,** (a person) avanzar belicosamente hacia

squarely /ˈskwɛərli/ *adv* en cuadro; directamente; sin ambigüedades, rotundamente; (honestly) de buena fe, honradamente

squareness /ˈskwɛərnɪs/ *n* cuadratura, *f;* (honesty) honradez, buena fe, *f*

squash /skwɒʃ/ *vt* aplastar. —*vi* aplastarse; apretarse. —*n* aplastamiento, *m;* (of fruit, etc.) pulpa, *f;* (of people) agolpamiento, *m;* muchedumbre, *f;* (drink) refresco (de limón, etc.), *m,* (sport) frontón con raqueta, *m*

squashy /ˈskwɒʃi/ *a* blando y húmedo

squat /skwɒt/ *vi* acuclillarse, agacharse, agazaparse ponerse en cuclillas; estar en cuclillas; (on land, etc.) apropiarse sin derecho. —*a* rechoncho

squatter /ˈskwɒtər/ *n* intruso (-sa); colono usurpador, *m*

squatter town *n.* See **shanty town**

squawk /skwɔk/ *vi* graznar; lanzar gritos agudos. —*n* graznido, *m;* grito agudo, *m*

squeak /skwik/ *vi* (of carts, etc.) chirriar, rechinar; (of shoes) crujir; (of persons, mice, etc.) chillar; (slang) cantar. —*n* chirrido, crujido, *m;* chillido, *m.* **to have a narrow s.,** escapar por un pelo

squeaking /ˈskwikɪŋ/ *n* chirrido, rechinamiento, *m;* crujido, *m;* (of humans, mice, etc.) chillidos, *m pl*

squeal /skwil/ *vi* lanzar gritos agudos, chillar; (complain) quejarse; (slang) cantar. —*n* grito agudo, chillido, *m*

squealing /ˈskwilɪŋ/ *n* gritos agudos, chillidos, *m pl*

squeamish /ˈskwimɪʃ/ *a* que se marea fácilmente; mareado; (nauseated) asqueado; delicado; remilgado

squeamishness /ˈskwimɪʃnɪs/ *n* tendencia a marearse, *f;* delicadeza, *f;* remilgos, *m pl*

squeeze /skwiz/ *vt* apretar; estrujar; (fruit) exprimir; (extort) arrancar; (money from) sangrar. —*n* (of the hand, etc.) apretón, *m;* estrujón, *m;* (of fruit juice) algunas gotas (de). **It was a tight s. in the car,** Íbamos muy apretados en el coche. **He was in a tight s.,** Se encontraba en un aprieto. **to s. one's way through the crowd,** abrirse camino a codazos por la muchedumbre. **to s. in,** *vt* hacer sitio para. —*vi* introducirse con dificultad (en)

squelch /skwɛltʃ/ *vi* gorgotear, chapotear. —*vt* aplastar

squib /skwɪb/ *n* (firework) rapapiés, buscapiés, *m;* (lampoon) pasquinada, *f*

squid /skwɪd/ *n* calamar, *m*

squint /skwɪnt/ *n* estrabismo, *m;* mirada furtiva, *f; Inf.* vistazo, *m,* mirada, *f.* —*vi* ser bizco; bizcar. **to s. at,** mirar de soslayo. **s.-eyed,** bizco. **to be s.-eyed,** mirar contra el gobierno

squire /skwaiər/ *n* escudero, *m;* hacendado, *m.* —*vt* escoltar, acompañar

squirm /skwɜrm/ *vi* retorcerse; (with embarrassment) no saber dónde meterse. —*n* retorcimiento, *m.* **to s. along the ground,** arrastrarse por el suelo

squirrel /ˈskwɜrəl// *n* ardilla, *f*

squirt /skwɜrt/ *vt* (liquids) lanzar. —*vi* chorrear, salir a chorros. —*n* chorro, *m;* (syringe) jeringa, *f*

stab /stæb/ *vt* apuñalar, dar de puñaladas (a); herir. —*n* puñalada, *f;* herida, *f;* (of pain, and *Fig.*) pinchzo, *m.* **a s. in the back,** una puñalada por la espalda

stability /stəˈbɪlɪti/ *n* estabilidad, *f;* solidez, firmeza, *f*

stabilize /ˈsteibəˌlaiz/ *vt* estabilizar

stable /ˈsteibəl/ *a* estable; fijo, firme. —*n* cuadra, caballeriza, *f;* (for cows, etc.) establo, *m.* —*vt* poner en la cuadra; alojar. **s.-boy,** mozo de cuadra, *m*

stack /stæk/ *n* (of hay) niara, *f,* almiar, *m;* (heap) montón, *m;* (of rifles) pabellón, *m;* (of a chimney) cañón, *m.* —*vt Agr.* hacinar; amontonar; *Mil.* poner (las armas) en pabellón

stacked /stækt/ *a* (woman) abultada de pechera

stadium /ˈsteidiəm/ *n* estadio, *m*

staff /stæf/ *n* vara, *f;* (bishop's, and *Fig.*) báculo, *m;* (pilgrim's) bordón, *m;* (pole) palo, *m;* (flagstaff) asta, *f;* (of an office, etc.) personal, *m;* (editorial) redacción, *f;* (corps) cuerpo, *m; Mil.* plana mayor, *f,* estado mayor, *m; Mus.* pentagrama, *m.* —*vt* proveer de personal. **general s.,** estado mayor general, *m.* **s. officer,** *Mil.* oficial de estado mayor, *m*

stag /stæg/ *n* ciervo, *m.* **s.-beetle,** ciervo volante, *m.* **s.-hunting,** caza del ciervo, *f*

stage /steidʒ/ *n* (for workmen) andamio, *m;* (of a microscope) portaobjetos, *m; Theat.* escena, *f,* tablas, *f pl;* teatro, *m;* (of development, etc.) etapa, *f;* fase, *f.* —*vt Theat.* escenificar, poner en escena; *Theat.* representar; (a demonstration, etc.) arreglar. **by easy stages,** poco a poco; (of a journey) a pequeñas etapas. **to come on the s.,** salir a la escena. **to go on the s.,** hacerse actor (actriz), dedicarse al teatro. **s. carpenter,** tramoyista, *m.* **s.-coach,** diligencia, *f.* **s.-craft,** arte de escribir para el teatro, *f;* arte escénica, *f.* **s.-direction,** acotación, *f.* **s.-door,** entrada de los artistas, *f.* **s.-effect,** efecto escénico, *m.* **s.-fright,** miedo al público, *m.* **s.-hand,** tramoyista, sacasillas, metesillas y sacamuertos, *m.* **s. manager,** director de escena, *m.* **s.-whisper,** aparte, *m*

stagger /ˈstægər/ *vi* tambalear; andar haciendo eses; (hesitate) titubear, vacilar. —*vt* desconcertar. —*n* titubeo, tambaleo, *m; Aer.* decalaje, *m.* **staggered working hours,** horas de trabajo escalonadas, *f pl*

staggering /ˈstægərɪŋ/ *a* tambaleante; (surprising) asombroso, sorprendente; (dreadful) espantoso. **a s. blow,** un golpe que derriba

staging /ˈsteidʒɪŋ/ *n* (scaffolding) andamio, *m; Theat.* producción, *f;* representación, *f;* decorado, *m*

stagnancy /ˈstægnənsi/ *n* (of water) estancación, *f;* (inactivity) estagnación, *f;* paralización, *f*

stagnant /ˈstægnənt/ *a* estancado; paralizado. **to be s.,** estar estancado. **s. water,** agua estancada, *f*

stagnate /ˈstægneit/ *vi* estancarse; estar estancado; (of persons) vegetar

stagnation /stægˈneiʃən/ *n* (of water) estancación, *f;* estagnación, *f;* parálisis, *f*

staid /steid/ *a* serio, formal, juicioso

staidness /ˈsteidnɪs/ *n* seriedad, formalidad, *f*

stain /stein/ *vt* manchar; (dye) teñir. —*n* mancha, *f;* colorante, *m.* **without a s.,** *Fig.* sin mancha. **stained glass,** vidrio de color, *m.* **s.-remover,** quitamanchas, *m*

stainless /ˈsteinlɪs/ *a* sin mancha; inmaculado, puro

stair /stɛər/ *n* escalón, peldaño, *m;* escalera, *f; pl* **stairs,** escalera, *f.* **a flight of stairs,** una escalera; un tramo de escaleras. **below stairs,** escalera abajo. **s.-carpet,** alfombra de escalera, *f.* **s.-rod,** varilla para alfombra de escalera, *f*

staircase /ˈstɛərˌkeis/ *n* escalera, *f.* **spiral s.,** escalera de caracol, *f*

stake /steik/ *n* estaca, *f;* (for plants) rodrigón, *m;* (gaming) envite, *m,* apuesta, *f;* (in an undertaking) interés, *m; pl* **stakes,** (prize) premio, *m;* (race) carrera, *f.* —*vt* estacar; (plants) rodrigar; (bet) jugar. **at s.,**

en juego; en peligro. **to be burnt at the s.,** morir en la hoguera. **to s. one's all,** jugarse el todo por el todo. **to s. a claim,** hacer una reclamación. **to s. out,** jalonar

stalactite /stə'læktait/ *n* estalactita, *f*

stalagmite /stə'lægmait/ *n* estalagmita, *f*

stale /steil/ *a* no fresco; (of bread, etc.) duro, seco; (of air) viciado; viejo; pasado de moda; (tired) cansado

stalemate /'steil,meit/ *n* (chess, checkers) tablas, *f pl; Fig.* punto muerto, *m.* **to reach a s.,** llegar a un punto muerto

staleness /steilnɪs/ *n* rancidez, *f;* (of bread, etc.) dureza, *f;* (of news, etc.) falta de novedad, *f*

stalk /stɔk/ *n Bot.* tallo, *m; Bot.* pedúnculo, *m;* (of a glass) pie, *m.* —*vi* andar majestuosamente; *Fig.* rondar. —*vt* (game) cazar al acecho; (a person) seguir los pasos (a)

stalking horse /'stɔkɪŋ/ *n* boezuelo, *m; Fig.* pretexto, disfraz, *m*

stall /stɔl/ *n* (in a stable) puesto (individual), *m;* (stable) establo, *m;* (choir) silla de coro, *f;* (in a fair, etc.) barraca, *f,* puesto, *m; Theat.* butaca, *f;* (fingerstall) dedal, *m.* —*vt* (an engine) cortar accidentalmente. —*vi Auto.* pararse de pronto; *Aer.* perder velocidad; (of a cart, etc.) atascarse. **pit s.,** *Theat.* butaca de platea, *f*

stalling /stɔlɪŋ/ *n Auto.* parada accidental, *f; Aer.* pérdida de velocidad, *f.* **Stop s.!** ¡Déjate de rodeos!

stallion /'stælyən/ *n* semental, *m*

stalwart /'stɔlwərt/ *a* robusto, fornido; leal; valiente

stalwartness /'stɔlwərtnɪs/ *n* robustez, *f;* lealtad, *f;* valor, *m*

stamen /'steimən/ *n Bot.* estambre, *m*

stamina /'stæmənə/ *n* resistencia, *f*

stammer /'stæmər/ *vi* tartamudear; (hesitate in speaking) titubear, balbucir. —*n* tartamudez, *f;* titubeo, balbuceo, *m*

stammerer /'stæmərər/ *n* tartamudo (-da)

stammering /'stæmərɪŋ/ *a* tartamudo; balbuciente. —*n* tartamudeo, *m;* balbuceo, *m*

stamp /stæmp/ *vt* estampar; imprimir; (documents) timbrar; pegar el sello de correo (a); (characterize) sellar; (*Fig.* engrave) grabar; (coins) acuñar; (press) apisonar; (with the foot) golpear con los pies, patear; (in dancing) zapatear. —*n* (with the foot) patada, *f,* golpe con los pies, *m;* (mark, etc.) marca, *f;* (rubber, etc.) estampilla, *f;* matasellos, *m;* cuño, *m;* (for documents) póliza, *f;* timbre, *m;* (for letters) sello, *m;* (machine) punzón, *m;* mano de mortero, *f;* (*Fig.* sign) sello, *m;* (kind) temple, *m,* clase, *f.* **The events of that day are stamped on my memory,** Los acontecimientos de aquel día están grabados en mi memoria. **to s. out,** (a fire, etc.) extinguir, apagar; (resistance, etc.) vencer; destruir. **postage-s.,** sello de correos, *m.* **s.-album,** álbum de sellos, *m.* **s.-duty,** impuesto del timbre, *m.* **s.-machine,** expendedor automático de sellos de correo, *m*

stampede /stæm'pid/ *n* fuga precipitada, *f;* pánico, *m.* —*vi* huir precipitadamente; (of animals) salir de estampía; huir en desorden. —*vt* hacer perder la cabeza (a), sembrar el pánico entre

stamping /'stæmpɪŋ/ *n* selladura, *f;* (of documents) timbrado, *m;* (of fabrics, etc.) estampado, *m;* (with the feet) pataleo, *m;* (in dancing) zapateo, *m*

stance /stæns/ *n* posición de los pies, *f;* postura, *f*

stanch /stɔntʃ/ *vt* restañar

stand /stænd/ *vi* estar de pie; ponerse de pie, incorporarse; estar; hallarse; sostenerse; ser; ponerse; (halt) parar; (remain) permanecer, quedar. —*vt* poner; (endure) resistir; tolerar; sufrir; (entertain) convidar. **S.!** ¡Alto! **as things s.,** tal como están las cosas. **I cannot s. any more,** No puedo más. **I cannot s. him,** No le puedo ver. **Nothing stands between them and ruin,** No hay nada entre ellos y la ruina. **I stood him a drink,** Le convidé a un trago. **How do we s.?** ¿Cómo estamos? **It stands to reason that...,** Es lógico que... **Edward stands six feet,** Eduardo tiene seis pies de altura. **to s. accused of,** ser acusado de. **to s. godfather** (or **godmother**) **to,** sacar de pila (a). **to s. in need (of),** necesitar, tener necesidad (de). **to s. on end,** (of hair) ponerse de punta, despeluzarse, **to s. one in good stead,** ser útil, ser ventajoso. **to s. one's ground,** no ceder, tenerse fuerte. **to s. to attention,** cuadrarse, permanecer en posición de firmes. **to s. well with,** tener buenas relaciones con, ser estimado de. **to s. aside,** tenerse a un lado; apartarse; (in favor of someone) retirarse. **to s. back,** quedarse atrás; recular, retroceder. **to s. by,** estar de pie cerca de; estar al lado de; estar presente (sin intervenir); ser espectador; estar preparado; (one's friends) ayudar, proteger; (a promise, etc.) atenerse (a); ser fiel (a); (of a ship) mantenerse listo. **s.-by,** *n* recurso, *m.* **to s. for,** representar; simbolizar; (mean) significar; (Parliament, etc.) presentarse como candidato; (put up with) tolerar, sufrir. **to s. in,** colaborar. **to s. in with,** estar de acuerdo con, ser partidario de; compartir. **to s. off,** mantenerse a distancia. **to s. out,** (in relief, and *Fig.* of persons) destacarse; (be firm) resistir, mantenerse firme; *Naut.* gobernar más afuera. **S. out of the way!** ¡Quítate del medio! **to s. over,** (be postponed) quedar aplazado. **to s. up,** estar de pie; ponerse de pie, incorporarse; tenerse derecho. **to s. up against,** resistir; oponerse a. **to s. up for,** defender; volverpor. **to s. up to,** hacer cara a

stand /stænd/ *n* puesto, *m;* posición, actitud, *f;* (for taxis, etc.) punto, *m;* (in a market, etc.) puesto, *m; Sports.* tribuna, *f;* (for a band) quiosco, *m;* (of a dish, etc.) pie, *m; Mech.* sostén, *m;* (opposition) resistencia, oposición, *f.* **to make a s. against,** oponerse resueltamente (a); ofrecer resistencia (a). **to take one's s.,** fundarse (en), apoyarse (en). **to take up one's s. by the fire,** ponerse cerca del fuego

standard /'stændərd/ *n* (flag) estandarte, *m,* bandera, *f;* (for gold, weights, etc.) marco, *m;* norma, *f;* convención, regla, *f;* (of a lamp) pie, *m;* (pole) poste, *m;* columna, *f;* (level) nivel, *m.* —*a* corriente; normal; típico; clásico. **It is a s. type,** Es un tipo corriente. **gold s.,** patrón de oro, *m.* **s. author,** autor clásico, *m.* **s. formula,** fórmula clásica, *f.* **s. of living,** nivel de vida, *m.* **s.-bearer,** abanderado, *m.* **s.-lamp,** lámpara vertical, *f*

standardization /ˌstændərdə'zeiʃən/ *n* (of armaments, etc.) unificación de tipos, *f;* (of dyestuffs, medicinals, etc.) control, *m,* estandardización, *f*

standardize /'stændərˌdaiz/ *vt* hacer uniforme; controlar

standing /'stændɪŋ/ *a* de pie, derecho; permanente, fijo; constante. —*n* posición, *f;* reputación, *f;* importancia, *f;* antigüedad, *f.* **It is a quarrel of long s.,** Es una riña antigua. **s. committee,** comisión permanente, *f.* **s. room,** sitio para estar de pie, *m.* **s. water,** agua estancada, *f.* **standoffish,** frío, etiquetero; altanero. **stand-offishness,** frialdad, *f;* altanería, *f.* **standpoint,** punto de vista, *m*

standstill /'stændˌstɪl/ *n* parada, *f;* pausa, *f.* **at a s.,** parado; (of industry) paralizado

stanza /'stænzə/ *n* estrofa, estancia, *f*

staple /'steipəl/ *n* (fastener) grapa, *f;* (of wool, etc.) hebra, fibra, *f;* producto principal (de un pais), *m;* (raw material) materia prima, *f; a* principal; más importante; corriente

stapler /'steiplər/, (device) cosepapeles, engrapador, *m,* atrochadora (Argentina), *f*

star /stɑr/ *n* (all meanings) estrella, *f;* (asterisk) asterisco, *m.* —*vt* estrellar, sembrar de estrellas; marcar con asterisco. —*vi* (*Theat.* cinema) presentarse como estrella, ser estrella. **stars and stripes,** las barras y las estrellas. **to be born under a lucky s.,** tener estrella. **to see stars,** ver estrellas. **s.-gazing,** observación de las estrellas, *f;* ensimismamiento, *m.* **s.-spangled,** estrellado, tachonado de estrellas, sembrado de estrellas. **s.-turn,** gran atracción, *f*

starboard /'stɑrbərd/ *n Naut.* estribor, *m*

starch /stɑrtʃ/ *n* almidón, *m,* las harinas, *f pl, vt* almidonar

starchy /'stɑrtʃi/ *a* almidonado; (of food) feculento; *Fig.* tieso, entonado, etiquetero

stare /stɛər/ *vi* mirar fijamente; abrir mucho los ojos. —*n* mirada fija, *f.* **stony s.,** mirada dura, *f.* **to s. at,** (a person) clavar la mirada en; mirar de hito en hito (a). **The explanation stares one in the face,** La explicación salta a la vista (or está evidente). **to s. into**

space, mirar las telarañas. **to s. out of countenance,** avergonzar con la mirada

starfish /'stɑrˌfɪʃ/ *n* estrella de mar, *f*

staring /'stɛərɪŋ/ *a* (of colors) chillón, llamativo, encendido. **s. eyes,** ojos saltones, *m pl*; ojos espantados, *m pl*

stark /stɑrk/ *a* rígido; *Poet.* poderoso; absoluto. **s. staring mad,** loco de atar. **s.-naked,** en cueros vivos, en pelota

starless /'starlɪs/ *a* sin estrellas

starlight /'stɑrˌlait/ *n* luz de las estrellas, *f*, *a* estrellado

starry /'stɑri/ *a* estrellado, sembrado de estrellas

start /stɑrt/ *vi* estremecerse, asustarse; saltar; (set out) salir; ponerse en camino; (of a train, a race) arrancar; ponerse en marcha; *Aer.* despegar; (begin) empezar; (of timbers) combarse. —*vt* empezar; (a car, etc.) poner en marcha; (a race) dar la señal de partida; (a hare, etc.) levantar; (cause) provocar, causar; (a discussion, etc.) abrir; iniciar. —*n* (fright) susto, *m;* (setting out) partida, salida, *f;* (beginning) principio, comienzo, *m;* (starting-point of a race) arrancadero, *m; Aer.* despegue, *m;* (advantage) ventaja, *f.* **at the s.,** al principio. **for a s.,** para empezar. **from s. to finish,** desde el principio hasta el fin. **She started to cry,** Se puso a llorar. **He has started his journey to Canada,** Ha empezado su viaje al Canadá. **I started up the engine,** Puse el motor en marcha. **to get a s.,** asustarse; tomar la delantera. **to give** (a person) **a s.,** asustar, dar un susto (a); dar la ventaja (a). **to give** (a person) **a s. in life,** ayudar a alguien a situarse en la vida. **to make a fresh s. (in life),** hacer vida nueva, empezar la vida de nuevo. **to s. after,** lanzarse en busca de; salir tras. **to s. back,** retroceder; emprender el viaje de regreso; marcharse. **to s. off,** salir, partir; ponerse en camino. **to s. up,** *vi* incorporarse bruscamente, ponerse de pie de un salto; (appear) surgir, aparecer. —*vt* (an engine) poner en marcha

starter /'stɑrtər/ *n* iniciador (-ra); (for a race) starter, juez de salida, *m;* (competitor in a race) corredor, *m;* (of a car, etc.) arranque, *m*

starting /'startɪŋ/ *n* (setting out) salida, partida, *f;* (beginning) principio, *m;* (fear) estremecimiento, *m;* susto, *m.* **s.-gear,** palanca de arranque, *f.* **s.-handle,** manivela de arranque, *f.* **s.-point,** punto de partida, *m; Fig.* arrancadero, punto de arranque, *m.* **s.-post,** puesto de salida, *m*

startle /'stɑrtl̩/ *vt* asustar, sobresaltar, alarmar. **The news startled him out of his indifference,** Las noticias le hicieron salir de su indiferencia

startling /'stɑrtlɪŋ/ *a* alarmante; (of dress, etc.) exagerado; (of colors) chillón

starvation /stɑr'veiʃən/ *n* hambre, *f; Med.* inanición, *f.* **s. diet,** régimen de hambre, *m.* **s. wage,** ración de hambre, *f*

starve /stɑrv/ *vi* morir de hambre; pasar hambre, no tener bastante que comer; no comer. —*vt* matar de hambre; privar de alimentos (a). **I am simply starving,** Tengo una hambre canina, Me muero de hambre. **to s. with cold,** *vi* morir de frío. —*vt* matar de frío

starved /starvd/ *a* muerto de hambre, hambriento. **s. of affection,** hambriento de cariño

starving /'starvɪŋ/ *a* que muere de hambre, hambriento

state /steit/ *n* estado, *m;* condición, *f;* (anxiety) agitación, ansiedad, *f;* (social) rango, *m;* (pomp) magnificencia, pompa, *f;* (government, etc.) Estado, *m;* nación, *f.* —*a* de Estado; de gala, de ceremonia. **the married s.,** el estado matrimonial. **s. of war,** estado de guerra. **in s.,** con gran pompa. **to lie in s.,** (of a body) estar expuesto. **s. apartments,** habitaciones de gala, *f pl.* **s. banquet,** comida de gala, *f.* **s. coach,** coche de gala, *m.* **s. control,** control por el Estado, *m.* **S. Department,** Ministerio de Estado, *m.* **s. education,** instrucción pública, *f.* **State of the Union message,** Mensaje al Congreso, *m.* **s. papers,** documentos de Estado, *m pl*

state /steit/ *vt* decir (que), afirmar (que); (one's case, etc.) exponer; explicar; *Math.* proponer

statecraft /'steitˌkræft/ *n* arte de gobernar, *m*

stated /'steitɪd/ *a* arreglado, indicado; fijo. **the s. date,** la fecha indicada. **at s. intervals,** a intervalos fijos

statehood /'steithʊd/ *n* estadidad, *f*

stateliness /'steitlinɪs/ *n* dignidad, *f;* majestad, *f*

stately /'steitli/ *a* majestuoso; imponente; noble; digno

statement /'steitmənt/ *n* afirmación, declaración, *f;* resumen, *m;* exposición, *f; Law.* deposición, *f; Com.* estado de cuenta, *m.* **to make a s.,** hacer una declaración

stateroom /'steitˌrum/ *n* sala de recepción, *f;* (on a ship) camarote, *m*

statesman /'steitsmən/ *n* hombre de estado, *m*

statesmanlike /'steitsmənˌlaik/ *a* de hombre de estado

statesmanship /'steitsmənˌʃɪp/ *n* arte de gobernar, *m*

static /'stætɪk/ *a* estático

statics /'stætɪks/ *n* estática, *f*

station /'steiʃən/ *n* (place) puesto, sitio, *m;* (*Rail.* and *Eccl.*) estación, *f;* (social) posición social, *f; Naut.* apostadero, *m; Surv.* punto de marca, *m.* —*vt* estacionar, colocar, poner. **to s. oneself,** colocarse. **Stations of the Cross,** Estaciones, *f pl.* **s.-master,** jefe de la estación, *m*

stationary /'steiʃəˌnɛri/ *a* estacionario; inmóvil; *Astron.* estacional

stationer /'steiʃənər/ *n* papelero (-ra). **stationer's shop,** papelería, *f*

stationery /'steiʃəˌnɛri/ *n* papelería, *f*, efectos de escritorio, *m pl*; papel de escribir, *m*

station wagon *n* pisicorre, coche camioneta, coche rural, *m*

statistical /stə'tɪstɪkəl/ *a* estadístico

statistician /ˌstætɪ'stɪʃən/ *n* estadista, *m*

statistics /stə'tɪstɪks/ *n* estadística, *f*

statuary /'stætʃuˌɛri/ *a* estatuario. —*n* estatuaria, *f;* estatuas, *f pl;* (sculptor) estatuario, *m*

statue /'stætʃu/ *n* estatua, *f;* imagen, *f*

statuesque /ˌstætʃu'ɛsk/ *a* escultural

statuette /ˌstætʃu'ɛt/ *n* figurilla, *f*

stature /'stætʃər/ *n* estatura, *f;* (moral, etc.) valor, *m*

status /'steitəs, 'stætəs/ *n* (*Law.* etc.) estado, *m;* posición, *f;* rango, *m.* **What is his s. as a physicist?** ¿Cómo se le considera entre los físicos? **social s.,** posición social, *f;* rango social, *m*

statute /'stætʃut/ *n* ley, *f;* acto legislativo, *m;* estatuto, *m;* regla, *f.* **s. book,** código legal, *m*

statutory /'stætʃʊˌtɔri/ *a* establecido; reglamentario; estatutario

staunch /stɔntʃ/ *a* leal, fiel; firme, constante. —*vt* restañar

staunchness /'stɔntʃnɪs/ *n* lealtad, fidelidad, *f;* firmeza, *f*

stave /steiv/ *n* (of a barrel, etc.) duela, *f;* (of a ladder) peldaño, *m;* (stanza) estrofa, *f; Mus.* pentagrama, *m.* **to s. in,** abrir boquete en; romper a golpes; quebrar. **to s. off,** apartar, alejar; (delay) aplazar, diferir; (avoid) evitar; (thirst, etc.) dominar

stay /stei/ *vt* detener; (a judgment, etc.) suspender. —*vi* permanecer; quedarse; detenerse; (of weather, etc.) durar; (lodge) hospedarse, vivir. **to come to s.,** venir a ser permanente. **to s. a person's hand,** detenerle a fulano el brazo. **to s. at home,** quedarse en casa. **s.-at-home,** *a* casero. —*n* persona casera, *f.* **to s. the course,** terminar la carrera. **S.! Say no more!** ¡Calle! ¡No diga más! **to s. away,** ausontarse. **to s. up,** no acostarse; velar. **to s. with,** quedarse con; alojarse con; quedarse en casa de, vivir con

stay /stei/ *n* estancia, permanencia, *f;* residencia, *f;* (restraint) freno, *m; Law.* suspensión, *f;* (endurance) aguante, *m,* resistencia, *f; Naut.* estay, *m;* (prop) puntal, *m; Fig.* apoyo, soporte, *m; pl* **stays,** corsé, *m*

stead /stɛd/ *n* lugar, *m.* **in the s. of,** en el lugar de, como substituto de. **It has stood me in good s.,** Me ha sido muy útil

steadfast /'stɛdˌfæst/ *a* fijo; constante; firme; tenaz. **s. gaze,** mirada fija, *f*

steadfastly /'stɛdˌfæstli/ *adv* fijamente; con constancia; firmemente; tenazmente

steadfastness /'stɛdˌfæstnɪs/ *n* fijeza, *f;* constancia, *f;* firmeza, *f;* tenacidad, *f*

steadily /'stɛdl̩i/ *adv* firmemente; (without stopping) sin parar; continuamente; (assiduously) diligentemente; (uniformly) uniformemente. **Prices have gone up s.,** Los precios no han dejado de subir. **He looked at it s.,** Lo miraba sin pestañear (or fijamente)

steadiness /'stɛdinɪs/ *n* estabilidad, *f;* firmeza, *f;* constancia, *f;* (of persons) seriedad, formalidad, *f;* (of workers) diligencia, asiduidad, *f*

steady /'stɛdi/ *a* firme; seguro; fijo; constante; uniforme; continuo; estacionario; (of persons) serio, formal, juicioso; (of workers) diligente, asiduo. *—vt* afirmar; (persons) hacer más serio (a); (nerves, etc.) calmar, fortificar. **a s. job,** un empleo seguro. **S.!** ¡Calma!; *Naut.* ¡Seguro! **He steadied himself against the table,** Se apoyó en la mesa

steak /steik/ *n* tajada, *f;* biftec, *m*

steal /stil/ *vt* robar, hurtar; tomar. *—vi* robar, ser ladrón; (glide) deslizarse; (overwhelm) dominar, ganar insensiblemente (a). **to s. a kiss,** robar un beso. **to s. a look at,** mirar de soslayo (or de lado). **to s. away,** escurrirse, escabullirse; marcharse a hurtadillas. **to s. in,** deslizarse en, colarse en

stealthily /'stɛlθəli/ *adv* a hurtadillas; a escondidas, furtivamente

stealthiness /'stɛlθinɪs/ *n* carácter furtivo, *m*

stealthy /'stɛlθi/ *a* furtivo; cauteloso

steam /stim/ *n* vapor, *m.* *—a* de vapor. *—vi* echar vapor. *—vt Cul.* cocer al vapor; (clothes) mojar; (windows, etc.) empañar. **to have the s. up,** estar bajo presión. **The windows are steamed,** Los cristales están empañados. **s.-boiler,** caldera de vapor, *f.* **s.-engine,** máquina de vapor, *f.* **s.-hammer,** maza de fragua, *f.* **s.-heat,** calefacción por vapor, *f.* **s.-roller,** *Lit.* apisonadora, *Fig.* fuerza arrolladora, *f*

steamboat /'stim,bout/ *n* vapor, *m*

steamer /'stimər/ *n Cul.* marmita al vacío, *f; Naut.* buque de vapor, *m*

steamship /'stim,ʃɪp/ *n* buque de vapor, piróscafo, *m*

steamy /'stimi/ *a* lleno de vapor

steed /stid/ *n* corcel, *m*

steel /stil/ *n* (metal, and *Poet.* sword) acero, *m,* (for sharpening) afilón, *m.* *—a* de acero; acerado. *—vt* acerar; *Fig.* endurecer. **to be made of s.,** *Fig.* ser de bronce. **He cannot s. himself to do it,** No puede persuadirse a hacerlo. **to s. one's heart,** hacerse duro de corazón. **cold s.,** arma blanca, *f.* **stainless s.,** acero inoxidable, *m.* **s.-engraving,** grabado en acero, *m*

steel mill *n* fábrica de acero, *f*

steep /stip/ *a* acantilado, escarpado; precipitoso; (of stairs, etc.) empinado; (of price) exorbitante. *—vt* (soak) remojar, empapar; *Fig.* absorber; (in a subject) empaparse (en). *—n* remojo, *m.* **It's a bit s.!** *Inf.* ¡Es un poco demasiado!

steeping /'stipɪŋ/ *n* remojo, *m,* maceración, *f*

steeple /'stipəl/ *n* campanario, *m,* torre, *f;* aguja, *f*

steeplechase /'stipəl,tʃeis/ *n* steeplechase, *m,* carrera de obstáculos, *f*

steepness /'stipnɪs/ *n* carácter escarpado, *m,* lo precipitoso

steer /stɪər/ *vt Naut.* gobernar; (a car, etc.) conducir; *Fig.* guiar, conducir. *—vi Naut.* timonear; *Naut.* navegar; *Auto.* conducir. *—n Zool.* novillo, *m.* **to s. clear of,** evitar. **to s. one's way through the crowd,** abrirse paso entre la muchedumbre

steerage /'stɪərɪdʒ/ *n* gobierno, *m;* (stern) popa, *f;* (quarters) entrepuente, *m.* **to go s.,** viajar en tercera clase

steering /'stirɪŋ/ *n Naut.* gobierno, *m;* (tiller, etc.) gobernalle, timón, *m;* (of a vehicle) conducción, *f.* **s.-column,** barra de dirección, *f.* **s.-wheel,** *Auto.* volante de dirección, *m; Naut.* rueda del timón, *f*

stellar /'stɛlər/ *a* estelar

stem /stɛm/ *n* (of a tree) tronco, *m;* (of a plant) tallo, *m;* (of a glass, etc.) pie, *m;* (*Mus.* of a note) rabo, *m;* (of a pipe) tubo, *m;* (of a word) radical, *m.* *—vt* (check) contener; (the tide) ir contra; (the current) vencer; (dam) estancar. **from s. to stern,** de proa a popa

stench /stɛntʃ/ *n* tufo, hedor, *m,* hediondez, *f*

stencil /'stɛnsəl/ *n* patrón para estarcir, *m;* estarcido, *m.* *—vt* estarcir

stenographer /stə'nɒgrəfər/ *n* estenógrafo (-fa), taquígrafo (-fa)

stenography /stə'nɒgrəfi/ *n* estenografía, taquigrafía, *f*

stentorian /stɛn'tɔriən/ *a* estentóreo

step /stɛp/ *n* paso, *m;* (footprint) huella, *f;* (measure) medida, *f;* (of a stair, etc.) escalón, peldaño, *m,* grada, *f;* (of a ladder) peldaño, *m;* (of vehicles) estribo, *m;* (grade) escalón, *m; Mus.* intervalo, *m.* **at every s.,** a cada paso. **flight of steps,** escalera, *f;* (before a building, etc.) escalinata, *f.* **in steps,** en escalones. **to bend one's steps towards,** dirigirse hacia. **to keep in s.,** llevar el paso. **to take a s.,** dar un paso. **to take steps,** tomar medidas. **s. by s.,** paso a paso; poco a poco. **s.-dance,** baile típico, *m.* **s.-ladder,** escalera de tijera, *f*

step /stɛp/ *vi* dar un paso; pisar; andar. **Please s. in!** Sírvase de entrar. **Will you s. this way, please?** ¡Haga el favor de venir por aquí! **to s. aside,** ponerse a un lado; desviarse; *Fig.* retirarse (en favor de). **to s. in,** entrar; intervenir (en); (meddle) entrometerse. **He stepped into the train,** Subió al tren. **to s. on,** pisar. **to s. on board,** *Naut.* ir a bordo. **to s. out,** salir; (from a vehicle) bajar; (a dance) bailar. **He stepped out a moment ago,** Salió hace un instante

stepbrother /'stɛp,brʌðər/ *n* hermanastro, medio hermano, *m*

stepchild /'stɛp,tʃaild/ *n* hijastro (-ra)

stepdaughter /'stɛp,dɔtər/ *n* hijastra, *f*

stepfather /'stɛp,fɑðər/ *n* padrastro, *m*

stepmother /'stɛp,mʌðər/ *n* madrastra, *f*

steppe /stɛp/ *n* estepa, *f*

steppingstone /'stɛpɪŋ,stoun/ *n* pasadera, *f; Fig.* escabel, escalón, *m*

stepsister /'stɛp,sɪstər/ *n* hermanastra, media hermana, *f*

stepson /'stɛp,sʌn/ *n* hijastro, *m*

stereotype /'stɛriə,taip/ *n* estereotipia, *f,* clisé, *m, vt* (*Print.* and *Fig.*) estereotipar

sterile /'stɛrɪl/ *a* estéril; árido

sterility /stə'rɪlɪti/ *n* esterilidad, *f;* aridez, *f*

sterilization /,stɛrələ'zeiʃən/ *n* esterilización, *f*

sterilize /'stɛrə,laiz/ *vt* esterilizar

sterilizer /'stɛrə,laizər/ *n* esterilizador, *m*

sterling /'stɜrlɪŋ/ *a* esterlina *f; Fig.* genuino. **pound s.,** libra esterlina, *f*

stern /stɜrn/ *a* severo, austero; duro. *—n Naut.* popa, *f*

sternly /'stɜrnli/ *adv* con severidad, severamente, duramente

sternness /'stɜrnnɪs/ *n* severidad, *f;* dureza, *f*

sternum /'stɜrnəm/ *n Anat.* esternón, *m*

stethoscope /'stɛθə,skoup/ *n* estetoscopio, *m*

stevedore /'stivɪ,dɔr/ *n* estibador, *m*

stew /stu/ *vt* guisar a la cazuela, estofar; (mutton, etc.) hervir; (fruit) cocer. *—n* estofado, *m; Inf.* agitación, *f.* **to be in a s.,** *Inf.* sudar la gota gorda. **stewed fruit,** compota de frutas, *f.* **s.-pot,** cazuela, olla, *f,* puchero, *m*

steward /'stuərd/ *n* administrador, *m;* mayordomo, *m;* (provision) despensero, *m; Naut.* camarero, *m*

stewardess /'stuərdɪs/ *n Naut.* camarera, *f*

stick /stɪk/ *vt* clavar (en), hundir (en); (put) poner; sacar; (stamps, etc.) pegar; fijar; (endure) resistir; tolerar. *—vi* clavarse, hundirse; estar clavado; pegarse; (remain) quedar; (in the mud, etc.) atascarse, embarrancarse, (on a reef) encallarse; (in the throat, etc.) atravesarse; (stop) detenerse. **It sticks in my throat,** *Inf.* No lo puedo tragar. **Friends always s. together,** Los amigos no se abandonan. **The nickname stuck to him,** El apodo se le quedó. **to s. at,** persistir en; desistir (ante); pararse (ante); tener escrúpulos sobre. **to s. at nothing,** no tener escrúpulos. **He stuck at his work,** Siguió trabajando. **to s. down,** pegar. **to s. out,** *vi* proyectar; sobresalir. *—vt* (one's chest) inflar; (one's tongue) sacar. **His ears s. out,** Tiene las orejas salientes. **to s. to,** (one's job) no dejar; (one's plans) adherirse (a); (one's principles) ser fiel (a); (one's friends) no abandonar; (one's word, etc.) cumplir; atenerse a. **to s. up,** *vi* (of hair) erizarse, ponerse de punta; salirse. *—vt* clavar; (a notice) fijar. **to s. up for,** (a person) defender

stick /stɪk/ *n* estaca, *f;* (for the fire) leña, *f;* (walking-s.) bastón, *m;* (of office) vara, *f;* (of sealing-wax, etc.) barra, *f;* palo, *m;* (baton) batuta, *f;* (of celery) tallo, *m.* **in a cleft s.,** entre la espada y la pared. **to give** (a person) **the s.,** dar palo (a)

stickiness /'stɪkinɪs/ *n* viscosidad, *f*

sticking plaster *n* esparadrapo, *m*

stick-in-the-mud /'stɪkɪnðəˌmʌd/ *n* chapado a la antigua, *m*

stickler /'stɪklər/ *n* rigorista, *mf.* **to be a s. for etiquette,** ser etiquetero

sticky /'stɪki/ *a* pegajoso, viscoso; *Fig.* difícil

stiff /stɪf/ *a* rígido; inflexible; tieso; (of paste, etc.) espeso; (of manner) distante; (of a bow, etc.) frío; (of a person) almidonado, etiquetero; severo; (of examinations, etc.) difícil; (strong) fuerte; (of price, etc.) alto, exorbitante; (of a shirt front, etc.) duro. **s. with cold,** aterido de frío. **s. neck,** torticolis, *m.* **s.-necked,** terco, obstinaz

stiffen /'stɪfən/ *vt* reforzar; atiesar; (paste, etc.) hacer más espeso; (*Fig.* strengthen) robustecer; (make more obstinate) hacer más tenaz. *—vi* atiesarse; endurecerse; (straighten oneself) enderezarse; (of manner) volverse menos cordial; (become firmer) robustecerse; (become more obstinate) hacerse más tenaz. **The breeze stiffened,** Refrescó el viento

stiffly /'stɪfli/ *adv* tiesamente, rígidamente, obstinadamente

stiffness /'stɪfnɪs/ *n* rigidez, *f;* tiesura, *f;* dureza, *f;* (of manner) frialdad, *f;* (obstinacy) terquedad, obstinación, *f;* (of an examination, etc.) dificultad, *f*

stifle /'staifəl/ *vt* ahogar, sofocar; apagar; suprimir

stifling /'staiflɪŋ/ *a* sofocante, bochornoso

stigma /'stɪgmə/ *n* estigma, *m*

stigmatize /'stɪgməˌtaiz/ *vt* estigmatizar

stile /stail/ *n* (nearest equivalent) portilla con escalones, *f*

stiletto /stɪ'lɛtou/ *n* estilete, *m*

still /stɪl/ *a* tranquilo; inmóvil; quedo; silencioso; (of wine) no espumoso. *—n* silencio, *m.* **in the s. of the night,** en el silencio de la noche. **Keep s.!** ¡Estate quieto! **to keep s.,** quedarse inmóvil, no moverse. **s.-birth,** nacimiento de un niño muerto, *m.* **s.-born,** nacido muerto. **s. life,** *Art.* bodegón, *m,* naturaleza muerta, *f*

still /stɪl/ *vt* hacer callar, acallar; calmar, tranquilizar; apaciguar; (pain) aliviar

still /stɪl/ *adv* todavía, aún; (nevertheless) sin embargo, no obstante; (always) siempre. **I think she s. visits them every week,** Me parece que sigue visitándoles cada semana. **s. and all,** con todo y eso. **s. more,** aún más

still /stɪl/ *n* alambique, *m.* **salt water s.,** adrazo, *m*

stillness /'stɪlnɪs/ *n* quietud, tranquilidad, *f;* silencio, *m.* **in the s. of the night,** en el silencio de la noche

stilt /stɪlt/ *n* zanco, *m*

stilted /'stɪltɪd/ *a* ampuloso, campanudo, hinchado

stimulant /'stɪmyələnt/ *a* and *n* estimulante, *m*

stimulate /'stɪmyəˌleit/ *vt* estimular; incitar (a), excitar (a)

stimulating /'stɪmyəˌleitɪŋ/ *a* estimulante; (encouraging) alentador; (inspiring) sugestivo, inspirador

stimulation /ˌstɪmyə'leiʃən/ *n* excitación, *f;* (stimulus) estímulo, *m*

stimulus /'stɪmyələs/ *n* estímulo, *m; Med.* estimulante, *m;* (incentive) impulso, incentivo, *m;* acicate, aguijón, *m*

sting /stɪŋ/ *vt* picar, pinchar; (of snakes, etc.) morder; (of hot dishes) resquemar; (of hail, etc.) azotar; (pain) atormentar; (provoke) provocar (a), incitar (a). *—n* (*Zool.* organ) aguijón, *m; Bot.* púa, *f;* (of a scorpion) uña, *f;* (of a serpent) colmillo, *m;* (pain and wound) pinchazo, *m;* (serpent's) mordedura, *f;* (stimulus) acicate, estímulo, *m;* (torment) tormento, dolor, *m*

stingily /'stɪndʒəli/ *adv* avaramente, tacañamente

stinginess /'stɪndʒinɪs/ *n* tacañería, avaricia, *f*

stinging /'stɪŋɪŋ/ *a* picante; *Fig.* mordaz; (of blows) que duele

stingy /'stɪndʒi/ *a* tacaño, avaro, mezquino

stink /stɪŋk/ *vi* apestar, heder, oler mal. *—n* tufo, *m,* hediondez, *f*

stinking /'stɪŋkɪŋ/ *a* apestoso, hediondo, fétido, mal oliente

stint /stɪnt/ *vt* escatimar; limitar. *—n* límite, *m,* restricción, *f.* **without s.,** sin límite; sin restricción.

stipend /'staipɛnd/ *n* estipendio, salario, *m*

stipple /'stɪpəl/ *vt Art.* puntear. *—n* punteado, *m*

stipulate /'stɪpyəˌleit/ *vi* estipular, poner como condición. *—vt* estipular, especificar. **They stipulated for a five-day week,** Pusieron como condición (*or* Estipularon) que trabajasen cinco días por semana

stipulation /ˌstɪpyə'leiʃən/ *n* estipulación, *f;* condición, *f*

stir /stɜr/ *vt* agitar; revolver; (the fire) atizar; (move) mover; (emotionally) conmover, impresionar; (the imagination) estimular. *—vi* moverse. *—n* movimiento, *m;* conmoción, *f;* (bustle) bullicio, *m;* sensación, *f.* **to make a s.,** causar una sensación. **to s. one's coffee,** revolver el café. **to s. up discontent,** fomentar el descontento

stirring /'stɜrɪŋ/ *a* conmovedor, emocionante, impresionante; (of times, etc.) turbulento, agitado

stirrup /'stɜrəp, 'stɪr-/ *n* estribo, *m.* **s.-cup,** última copa, *f.* **s.-pump,** bomba de mano (para líquidos), *f*

stitch /stɪtʃ/ *n* (action) puntada, *f;* (result) punto, *m; Surg.* punto de sutura, *m;* (pain) punzada, *f,* pinchazo, *m.* *—vt* coser; *Surg.* suturar

stoat /stout/ *n* armiño, *m;* (weasel) comadreja, *f*

stock /stɒk/ *n* (of a tree) tronco, *m;* (of a rifle) culata, *f;* (handle) mango, *m;* (of a horse's tail) nabo, *m;* (stem for grafting etc.) injerto, *m;* (race) raza, *f;* (lineage) linaje, *m,* estirpe, *f;* (supply) provisión, *f;* reserva, *f;* (of merchandise) surtido, *m; Cul.* caldo, *m;* (collar) alzacuello, *m; Bot.* alhelí, *m;* (government) papel del estado, *m,* valores públicos, *m pl;* (financial) valores, *m pl,* (of a company) capital, *m; pl* **stocks,** *Hist.* cepo, *m;* (of goods) existencias, *f pl,* stock, *m, a* corriente; del repertorio. **in s.** en existencia. **lives.,** ganado *m.* **rolling-s.,** *Rail.* materia móvil ferroviario, *m.* **s. phrase** frase hecha, *f.* **s. size,** talla corriente, *f.* **to lay in a s. of,** hacer provisión de, almacenar, **to stand s.-still,** quedarse completamente inmóvil. **to take s.,** *Com.* hacer inventario. **to take s. of,** inventariar; examinar, considerar. **s.-breeder,** ganadero, *m.* **s.-broker,** corredor de bolsa, bolsista, *m.* **s. exchange,** bolsa, *f.* **s.-in-hand,** *Com.* existencias, *f pl.* **s.-in-trade** (*Com.* etc.) capital, *m.* **s.-raising,** cría de ganados, ganadería, *f.* **s.-taking,** *Com.* inventario, *m*

stock /stɒk/ *vt* proveer (de), abastecer (de); (of shops) tener existencia de

stockade /stɒ'keid/ *n* estacada, empalizada, *f, vt* empalizar

stocking /'stɒkɪŋ/ *n* media, *f.* **nylon stockings,** medias de cristal (or de nilón), *f pl*

stocky /'stɒki/ *a* rechoncho, doblado, achaparrado

stodgy /'stɒdʒi/ *a* (of food) indigesto; (of style, etc.) pesado, amazacotado

stoic /'stouɪk/ *a* and *n* estoico (-ca)

stoical /'stouɪkəl/ *a* estoico

stoicism /'stouəˌsɪzəm/ *n* estoicismo, *m*

stoke /stouk/ *vt* (a furnace, etc.) cargar, alimentar; (a fire) echar carbón, etc., en. **s.-hole,** cuarto de fogoneros, *m; Naut.* cámara de calderas, *f*

stoker /'stoukər/ *n* fogonero, *m;* (mechanical) cargador, *m*

stole /stoul/ *n* (*Eccl.* and of fur, etc.) estola, *f*

stolid /'stɒlɪd/ *a* impasible, imperturbable

stolidity /stə'lɪdɪti/ *n* imperturbabilidad, impasibilidad, *f*

stolidly /'stɒlɪdli/ *adv* imperturbablemente

stomach /'stʌmək/ *n* estómago, vientre, *m;* apetito, estómago, *m;* (courage) corazón, valor, *m.* *—vt* digerir; (tolerate) tragar, sufrir. **s.ache,** dolor de estómago, *m*

stone /stoun/ *n* piedra, *f;* (gem) piedra preciosa, *f;* (of cherries, etc.) hueso, *m;* (of grapes, etc.) pepita, *f; Med.* cálculo, *m.* *—a* de piedra. *—vt* apedrear; (a wall, etc.) revestir de piedra; (fruit) deshuesar. **to pave with stones,** empedrar. **to leave no s. unturned,** no dejar piedra sin remover. **within a stone's throw,** a corta distancia, a un paso. **S. Age,** edad de piedra, *f.* **s.-breaker,** cantero, picapedrero, *m.* **s.-cold,** muy frío, completamente frío **s.-deaf,** *a* completamente sordo. **s.-fruit,** fruta de hueso, *f.* **s.-

mason, mazonero, albañil, *m;* picapedrero, *m.* **s.-quarry,** pedrera, cantera, *f*
stonily /'stounḷi/ *adv* fríamente; fijamente, sin pestañear
stoniness /'stouninıs/ *n* lo pedregoso; (of hearts, etc.) dureza, *f;* (of stares, etc.) fijeza, inmovilidad, *f*
stoning /'stounıŋ/ *n* apedreamiento, *m,* lapidación, *f*
stony /'stouni/ *a* pedregoso; (of hearts, etc.) duro, insensible, empedernido; (of a stare, etc.) fijo, duro
stool /stul/ *n* banquillo, taburete, *m;* (feces) excremento, *m*
stoop /stup/ *vi* inclinarse, doblarse; encorvarse; ser cargado de espaldas; andar encorvado; (demean oneself) rebajarse (a). —*vt* inclinar, doblar. —*n* inclinación, *f;* cargazón de espaldas, *f*
stooping /'stupıŋ/ *a* inclinado, doblado; (of shoulders) cargado
stop /stɒp/ *vt* (a hole) obstruir, atascar; (a leak) cegar, tapar; (a tooth) empastar; (stanch) restañar; (the traffic, etc.) parar; detener; (prevent) evitar; (discontinue) cesar (de), dejarse de; (cut off) cortar; (end) poner fin (a), acabar con; (payment) suspender. —*vi* parar; detenerse; cesar; terminar; (stay) quedarse, permanecer. **I stopped myself from saying what I thought,** Me abstuve de decir lo que pensaba, Me mordí la lengua. **They stopped the food-supply,** Cortaron las provisiones. **to s. beating about the bush,** dejarse de historias. **to s. one's ears,** *Fig.* taparse los oídos. **to s. payments,** suspender pagos
stop /stɒp/ *n* parada, *f;* pausa, *f;* interrupción, *f;* cesación, *f;* (of an organ) registro, *m.* **"Stop,"** (road sign) «Alto.» **full s.,** *Gram.* punto, *m.* **tram s.,** parada de tranvía, *f.* **to come to a full s.,** pararse de golpe; cesar súbitamente. **to put a s. to,** poner fin a, poner coto a, acabar con. *f pl.* **s.-watch,** cronógrafo, *m*
stopgap /'stɒp,gæp/ *n* (person) tapagujeros, *m;* substituto, *m*
stoppage /'stɒpıdʒ/ *n* parada, *f;* cesación, *f;* suspensión, *f;* interrupción, *f;* pausa, *f;* (obstruction) impedimento, *m;* obstrucción, *f.* **s. of work,** suspensión de trabajo, *f*
stopper /'stɒpər/ *n* tapón, *m;* obturador, *m, vt* cerrar con tapón, taponar
stopping /'stɒpıŋ/ *n* parada, *f;* cesación, *f;* suspensión, *f;* (of a tooth) empaste, *m.* **without s.,** sin parar. **without s. to draw breath,** de un aliento. **s.-place,** paradero, *m;* (of buses, etc.) parada, *f.* **s. train,** tren ómnibus, *m.* **s. up,** obturación, *f*
storage /'stɔrıdʒ/ *n* almacenamiento, *m;* (charge) almacenaje, *m;* (place) depósito, *m.* **cold s.,** cámara frigorífica, *f.* **s. battery,** acumulador, *m*
store /stɔr/ *n* provisión, *f;* abundancia, *f;* reserva, *f;* (of knowledge, etc.) tesoro, *m;* (for furniture, etc.) depósito, almacén, *m; pl* **stores,** (shop) almacenes, *m pl;* (food) provisiones, *f pl;* (*Mil.* etc.) pertrechos, *m pl.* —*vt* proveer; guardar, acumular; tener en reserva; (furniture, etc.) almacenar; (hold) caber en, tomar. **in s.,** en reserva; en depósito, en almacén. **to set s. by,** estimar en mucho; dar importancia a. **to set little s. by,** estimar en poco; conceder poca importancia a. **s.-room,** despensa, *f*
storehouse /'stɔr,haus/ *n* almacén, *m; Fig.* mina, *f,* tesoro, *m*
storied /'stɔrid/ *a* de...pisos. **two-s.,** de dos pisos
stork /stɔrk/ *n* cigüeña, *f*
storm /stɔrm/ *n* tempestad, tormenta, *f,* temporal, *m; Fig.* tempestad, *f; Mil.* asalto, *m.* —*vt Mil.* tomar por asalto, asaltar. —*vi* (of persons) bramar de cólera. **to take by s.,** tomar por asalto; *Fig.* cautivar, conquistar. **s. cloud,** nubarrón, *m.* **s.-signal,** señal de temporal, *f.* **s.-tossed,** *a* sacudido por la tempestad. **s. troops,** tropas de asalto, *f pl.* **s. window,** contravidriera, *f*
stormily /'stɔrməli/ *adv* tempestuosamente; con tormenta
storming /'stɔrmıŋ/ *n* (*Mil.* etc.) asalto, *m;* violencia, *f.* **s.-party,** pelotón de asalto, *m*
stormy /'stɔrmi/ *a* tempestuoso; de tormenta; (of life, etc.) borrascoso; (of meetings, etc.) tempestuoso
story /'stɔri/ *n* historia, *f;* cuento, *m;* anécdota, *f;* (funny) chiste, *m;* (plot) argumento, enredo, *m;* (fib) mentira, *f;* (floor) piso *m.* **It's always the same old s.,** Es siempre la misma canción (or historia). **That is quite another s.,** Eso es harina de otro costal. **short s.,** cuento, *m.* **s. book,** libro de cuentos, *m.* **s. teller,** cuentista, *mf;* (fibber) mentiroso (-sa)
stoup /stup/ *n* copa, *f;* pila de agua bendita, *f*
stout /staut/ *a* fuerte; (brave) intrépido, indómito; (fat) gordo, grueso; (firm) sólido, firme; (decided) resuelto; vigoroso. —*n* (drink) cerveza negra, *f.* **s.-hearted,** valiente, intrépido
stove /stouv/ *n* estufa, *f;* (open, for cooking) cocina económica, *f;* (gas, etc., for cooking) cocina, *f,* fogón, *m.* **s. pipe,** tubo de la chimenea, *m*
stow /stou/ *vt* meter, poner; colocar; (hide) esconder; (cargo) estibar, arrimar
stowaway /'stouə,wei/ *n* polizón, llovido, *m, vi* embarcarse secretamente
straddle /'strædḷ/ *vi* (*Nav.* etc.) graduar el tiro. —*vt* montar a horcajadas en. **s.-legged,** patiabierto
strafe /streif/ *vt* bombardear concentradamente; castigar; reñir
straggle /'strægəl/ *vi* rezagarse; vagar en desorden; dispersarse; estar esparcido; extenderse.
straggler /'stræglər/ *n* rezagado (-da)
straggling /'stræglıŋ/ *a* disperso; esparcido
straight /streit/ *a* derecho; recto; (of hair) lacio; directo; (tidy) en orden; (frank) franco; (honest) honrado. —*adv* derecho; en línea recta; directamente. **Keep s. on!** ¡Siga Vd. derecho! **to go s. to the point,** dejarse de rodeos, ir al grano. **to look s. in the eyes,** mirar derecho en los ojos. **s. away,** inmediatamente, en seguida. **s. out,** sin rodeos
straighten /'streitn̩/ *vt* enderezar; poner derecho; poner en orden; arreglar. —*vi* ponerse derecho; enderezarse. **to s. one's face,** componer el semblante. **to s. the line,** *Mil.* rectificar el frente. **to s. out,** poner en orden; *Fig.* desenredar. **to s. oneself up,** erguirse
straightforward /,streit'fɔrwərd/ *a* honrado, sincero; franco; (simple) sencillo. **s. answer,** respuesta directa, *f*
straightforwardly /,streit,fɔrwərdli/ *adv* honradamente; francamente
straightforwardness /,streit'fɔrwərdnıs/ *n* honradez, integridad, *f;* franqueza, *f;* (simplicity) sencillez, *f*
straightness /'streitnıs/ *n* derechura, rectitud, *f;* (of persons) honradez, probidad, *f*
straightway /'streit'wei, -,wei/ *adv* al instante, inmediatamente
strain /strein/ *vt* estirar; forzar; esforzar; (one's eyes) quebrarse; (one's ears) aguzar (el oído); (a muscle, etc.) torcer; (a friendship) pedir demasiado (a), exigir demasiado (de); (a person's patience, etc.) abusar (de); (words) tergiversar; (embrace) abrazar estrechamente (a); (filter) filtrar; *Cul.* colar. —*vi* hacer un gran esfuerzo, esforzarse (para). —*n* tirantez, *f;* tensión, *f;* (effort) esfuerzo, *m;* (sprain) torcedura, *f;* (nervous) tensión nerviosa, *f; Mech.* esfuerzo, *m;* (breed) raza, *f; Biol.* cepa, *f;* (tendency) tendencia, *f;* (heredity) herencia, *f;* rasgo, *m,* vena, *f;* (style) estilo, *m; Mus.* melodia, *f;* (of mirth, etc.) son, ruido, *m;* (poetry) poesía, *f.* **to s. a point,** hacer una excepción. **to s. after effect,** buscar demasiado el efecto
strained /streind/ *a* tenso; (of muscles, etc.) torcido; (of smiles, etc.) forzado. **s. relations,** *Polit.* estado de tirantez, *m*
strainer /'streinər/ *n* filtro, *m;* coladero, *m*
strait /streit/ *n Geog.* estrecho, *m.* **to be in great straits,** estar en un apuro. **s. laced,** *Fig.* de manga estrecha
straiten /'streitn̩/ *vt* estrechar; limitar, **in straitened circumstances,** en la necesidad
Strait of Magellan /mə'dʒɛlən/ Estrecho de Magallanes, *m*
Straits Settlements Establecimientos del Estrecho, *m pl*
strand /strænd/ *n* (shore) playa, *f;* (of a river) ribera, orilla, *f;* (of rope) cabo, ramal, *m;* (of thread, etc.) hebra, *f;* (of hair) trenza, *f.* —*vt* and *vi* (a ship) encallar, varar. **to be stranded,** hallarse abandonado; (by missing a train, etc.) quedarse colgado. **to leave stranded,** abandonar, dejar plantado (a)
strange /streindʒ/ *a* (unknown) desconocido; nuevo; (exotic, etc.) extraño, singular; extraordinario; raro;

exótico. **I felt very s. in a s. country,** Me sentía muy solo en un país desconocido. **He is a very s. person,** Es una persona muy rara
strangely /'streindʒli/ *adv* extrañamente, singularmente; de un modo raro
strangeness /'streindʒnɪs/ *n* novedad, *f;* singularidad, *f;* rareza, *f*
stranger /'streindʒər/ *n* desconocido (-da); (from a foreign country) extranjero (-ra); (from another region, etc.) forastero (-ra).
strangle /'stræŋgəl/ *vt* estrangular; (a sob, etc.) ahogar
stranglehold /'stræŋgəl,hould/ *n* collar de fuerza, *m.* **to have a s. (on),** tener asido por la garganta; paralizar
strap /stræp/ *n* correa, *f;* tirante de botas, *m, vt* atar con correas
strapping /'stræpɪŋ/ *a* rozagante, robusto
stratagem /'strætədʒəm/ *n* estratagema, *f,* ardid, *m*
strategic /strə'tidʒɪk/ *a* estratégico
strategist /'strætɪdʒɪst/ *n* estratego, *m*
strategy /'strætɪdʒi/ *n* estrategia, *f*
stratification /,strætəfɪ'keiʃən/ *n* estratificación, *f*
stratosphere /'strætə,sfɪər/ *n* estratosfera, *f*
stratum /'streɪtəm, 'strætəm/ *n Geol.* estrato, *m,* capa, *f;* (social, etc.) estrato, *m*
straw /strɔ/ *n* paja, *f.* **I don't care a s.,** No se me da un bledo. **to be not worth a s.,** no valer un ardite. **to be the last s.,** ser el colmo. **to drink through a s.,** sorber con una paja. **s. hat,** sombrero de paja, *m.* **s.-colored,** pajizo
strawberry /'strɔ,bɛri/ *n* (plant and fruit, especially small or wild) fresa, *f;* (large cultivated) fresón, *m.* **s. bed,** fresal, *m.* **s. ice,** helado de fresa, *m*
stray /strei/ *vi* errar, vagar; perderse; (from a path, etc., also *Fig.*) descarriarse. —*n* animal perdido, *m;* niño (-ña) sin hogar. —*a* descarriado, perdido; errante; (sporadic) esporádico
stray bullet *n* bala perdida, *f*
streak /strik/ *n* raya, *f;* (in wood and stone) vena, *f;* (of light) rayo, *m;* (of humor, etc.) rasgo, *m.* —*vt* rayar. **like a s. of lightning,** como un relámpago
streaky /'striki/ *a* rayado; (of bacon) entreverado
stream /strim/ *n* arroyo, riachuelo, *m;* río, *m;* (current) corriente, *f;* (of words, etc.) torrente, *m.* —*vi* correr, fluir; manar, brotar; (float) flotar, ondear. —*vt* (blood, etc.) manar, echar. **The tears streamed down Jean's cheeks,** Las lágrimas corrían por las mejillas de Juana. **s.-lined,** fuselado
streamer /'strimər/ *n* gallardete, *m,* serpentina, *f;* (on a hat, etc.) cinta colgante, *f,* siguemepollo, *m*
stream-of-consciousness *n* escritura automática, *f,* fluir de la conciencia, *m,* flujo de la subconciencia, monólogo interior, *m*
street /strit/ *n* calle, *f.* **the man in the s.,** el hombre medio. **at s. level,** a ras de suelo. **s. arab,** golfo, *m.* **s. cries,** gritos de vendedores ambulantes, *m pl.* **s. entertainer,** saltabanco, *m.* **s. brawl, s. fight,** algarada callejera, *f.* **s. fighting,** luchas en las calles, *f pl.* **s. musician,** músico ambulante, *m.* **s.-sweeper,** barrendero, *m.* **s.-walker,** buscona, prostituta, *f*
strength /strɛŋkθ, strɛnθ/ *n* fuerza, *f;* (of colors, etc.) intensidad, *f;* (of character) firmeza (de carácter), *f;* (of will) resolución, decisión, *f; Mil.* complemento, *m.* **by sheer s.,** a viva fuerza. **on the s. of,** confiando en, en razón de
strengthen /'strɛŋkθən, 'strɛn-/ *vt* fortificar; consolidar; reforzar. —*vi* fortificarse; consolidarse; reforzarse
strengthening /'strɛŋkθənɪŋ, 'strɛn-/ *a* fortificante; tonificante. —*n* refuerzo, *m;* fortificación, *f;* consolidación, *f*
strenuous /'strɛnyuəs/ *a* activo, enérgico; vigoroso; (arduous) arduo
strenuously /'strɛnyuəsli/ *adv* enérgicamente, vigorosamente
strenuousness /'strɛnyuəsnɪs/ *n* energía, *f;* vigor, *m;* (arduousness) arduidad, *f*
streptococcus /,strɛptə'kɒkəs/ *n Med.* estreptococo, *m*
streptomycin /,strɛptə,maisɪn/ *n Med.* estreptomicina, *f*
stress /strɛs/ *n* tensión, *f;* impulso, *m;* importancia, *f,* énfasis, *m; Gram.* acento (tónico), *m;* acentuación, *f; Mech.* esfuerzo, *m.* —*vt* acentuar; poner énfasis en, insistir en. **under s. of circumstance,** impulsado por las circunstancias. **times of s.,** tiempos turbulentos, *m pl.* **to lay great s. on,** insistir mucho en; dar gran importancia a
stretch /strɛtʃ/ *vt* (make bigger) ensanchar; (pull) estirar; (one's hand, etc.) alargar, extender; (knock down) tumbar. —*vi* ensancharse; dar de sí; ceder; extenderse. **to s. oneself,** estirarse, desperezarse. **to s. as far as,** llegar hasta, extenderse hasta. **to s. a point,** hacer una concesión. **to s. one's legs,** estirar las piernas
stretch /strɛtʃ/ *n* estirón, *m;* tensión, *f;* (of country, etc.) extensión, *f;* (scope) alcance, *m.* **by a s. of the imagination,** con un esfuerzo de imaginación. **He can sleep for hours at a s.,** Puede dormir durante horas enteras
stretcher /'strɛtʃər/ *n* (for gloves) ensanchador, *m;* dilatador, *m;* (for canvas) bastidor, *m;* (for wounded, etc.) camilla, *f.* **s.-bearer,** camillero, *m*
strew /stru/ *vt* esparcir; derramar
stricken /'strɪkən/ *a* (wounded) herido; (ill) enfermo; (with grief) afligido, agobiado de dolor. **s. in years,** entrado en años
strict /strɪkt/ *a* exacto; estricto; escrupuloso; severo
strictly /'strɪktli/ *adv* exactamente; estrictamente; severamente, con severidad. **s. speaking,** en rigor, en realidad
strictness /'strɪktnɪs/ *n* exactitud, *f;* escrupulosidad, *f;* rigor, *m;* severidad, *f*
stricture /'strɪktʃər/ *n Fig.* crítica severa, censura, *f.* **to pass strictures on,** criticar severamente
stride /straid/ *vi* andar a pasos largos, dar zancadas; cruzar a grandes trancos. —*vt* cruzar de un tranco; poner una pierna en cada lado de. —*n* zancada, *f,* paso largo, tranco, *m.* **to s. up and down,** dar zancadas
strident /'straidnt/ *a* estridente; (of colors) chillón
strife /straif/ *n* lucha, *f,* conflicto, *m*
strike /straik/ *vt* golpear; pegar, dar una bofetada (a); (wound) herir; (a coin) acuñar; (a light) encender; (of a snake) morder; (a blow) asestar, dar; (of ships, a rock, etc.) chocar contra; estrellarse contra; (flags) bajar, arriar; (a tent) desmontar; (camp) levantar; (come upon) llegar a; (discover) encontrar por casualidad, tropezar con; hallar, descubrir; (seem) parecer; (impress) impresionar; (of ideas) ocurrirse; (an attitude) tomar, adoptar; (of a clock) dar; (a balance) hacer; (a bargain) cerrar, llegar a; (level) nivelar; (cuttings) enraciar. —*vi* golpear; (of a clock) dar la hora; (of a ship) encallar; (go) ir; (penetrate) penetrar; (of a cutting) arraigar; (sound) sonar. **He struck the table with his fist,** Golpeó la mesa con el puño. **I was very much struck by the city's beauty,** La belleza de la ciudad me impresionó mucho. **The news struck fear into their hearts,** La noticia les llenó el corazón de miedo. **The clock struck three,** El reloj dio las tres. **The hour has struck,** *Fig.* Ha llegado la hora. **How did the house s. you?** ¿Qué te pareció la casa? **to s. a bargain,** cerrar un trato. **to s. a blow,** asestar un golpe. **to s. across country,** ir a campo traviesa. **to s. an attitude,** tomar una actitud. **to s. home,** dar en el blanco; herir; herir en lo más vivo; hacerse sentir. **to s. at,** asestar un golpe (a); acometer, embestir; atacar. **to s. down,** derribar; (of illness) acometer. **to s. off,** (a head, etc.) cortar; (a name) borrar, tachar; (print) imprimir. **to s. out,** *vi* asestar un golpe (a); (of a swimmer) nadar; echarse, lanzarse. —*vt* (a word, etc.) borrar, rayar; (begin) iniciar. **to s. through,** (cross out) rayar, tachar; (of the sun's rays, etc.) penetrar. **to s. up,** *vt* tocar; empezar a cantar; (a friendship) trabar. —*vi* empezar a tocar. **to s. up a march,** *Mil.* batir la marcha
strike /straik/ *n* huelga, *f.* —*vi* declararse en huelga. **go-slow s.,** tortuguismo, *m.* **lock-out s.,** huelga patronal, *f.* **sit-down s.,** huelga de brazos caídos, *f.* **to go on s.,** declararse en huelga. **s.-breaker,** esquirol, *m.* **s.-pay,** subsidio de huelga, *m*
striker /'straikər/ *n* huelguista, *mf*

striking /ˈstraikɪŋ/ *a* notable, sorprendente; (impressive) impresionante; que llama la atención; llamativo
string /strɪŋ/ *n* bramante, *m;* cuerda, *f;* (ribbon) cinta, *f;* (of beads, etc.) sarta, *f;* (of onions) ristra, *f;* (of horses, etc.) reata, *f;* hilera, *f;* (of a bridge) cable, *m;* (of oaths, lies) sarta, serie, *f;* (of beans) fibra, *f.* —*vt* encordar; (beads, etc.) ensartar; (beans) quitar las fibras (de). **He is all strung up,** Se le crispan los nervios. **the strings,** los instrumentos de cuerda. **a s. of pearls,** un collar de perlas. **for strings,** *Mus.* para arco. **to pull strings,** *Fig.* manejar los hilos. **to s. up,** (an instrument) templar; (a person) pender, ahorcar. **s. bean,** judía verde, *f*
stringed /strɪŋd/ *a* (of musical instruments) de cuerda. **s. instrument,** instrumento de cuerda, *m*
stringency /ˈstrɪndʒənsi/ *n* severidad, *f;* estrechez, *f*
stringent /ˈstrɪndʒənt/ *a* estricto, severo
stringy /ˈstrɪŋi/ *a* fibroso; filamentoso; correoso; arrugado
strip /strɪp/ *vt* desnudar; despojar (de), quitar; robar; (a cow) ordeñar hasta agotar la leche. —*vi* desnudarse. —*n* (tatter) jirón, *m;* tira, lista, *f;* (of wood) listón, *m;* (of earth) pedazo, *m;* (*Geog.* of land) zona, *f.* **to s. off,** *vt* quitar; (bark from a tree) descortezar; (one's clothes) despojarse de. —*vi* desprenderse, separarse
stripe /straip/ *n* raya, lista, *f;* (*Mil.* etc.) galón, *m;* (lash) azote, *m.* —*vt* rayar. **the stripes of the tiger,** las rayas del tigre
striped /straipt, ˈstraipɪd/ *a* listado, a rayas; con rayas. **s. trousers,** pantalón de corte, *m*
stripling /ˈstrɪplɪŋ/ *n* joven imberbe, pollo, mancebo, *m*
strive /straiv/ *vi* esforzarse (a); pugnar (por, para); trabajar (por); (fight against) luchar contra; pelear con. **He was striving to understand,** Pugnaba por (or Se esforzaba a) comprender
stroke /strouk/ *n* (blow) golpe, *m;* (of the oars) golpe del remo, *m,* remada, *f;* (at billards) tacada, *f;* (in golf) tirada, *f;* (in swimming) braza, *f;* (of a clock) campanada, *f;* (of a pen) rasgo de la pluma, *m;* (of a brush) pincelada, *f; Mech.* golpe de émbolo, *m;* (caress) caricia con la mano, *f.* —*vt* acariciar con la mano. **on the s. of six,** al acabar de dar las seis. **to have a s.,** tener un ataque de apoplejía. **s. of genius,** rasgo de ingenio, *m.* **s. of good luck,** racha de buena suerte, *f*
stroll /stroul/ *vi* pasearse, vagar. —*n* vuelta, *f,* paseo, *m.* **to go for a s.,** dar una vuelta
stroller /ˈstroulər/ *n* paseante, *mf*
strolling /ˈstroulɪŋ/ *a* errante; ambulante. **s. player,** *n* cómico (-ca) ambulante
strong /strɔŋ/ *a* fuerte; vigoroso; robusto; enérgico; firme; poderoso; (of colours) intenso, vivo; (of tea, coffee) cargado; *Gram.* fuerte. **The government took s. measures,** El gobierno tomó medidas enérgicas. **They gave very s. reasons,** Alegaron unas razones muy poderosas. **Grammar is not his s. point,** La gramática no es su punto fuerte. **The enemy is s. in numbers,** El enemigo es numéricamente fuerte. **The society is four thousand s.,** La sociedad tiene cuatro mil miembros. **s. box,** caja de caudales, *f.* **s. man,** hombre fuerte, *m;* (in a circus) hércules, *m.* **s.-minded,** de espíritu fuerte; independiente. **s. room,** cámara acorazada, *f*
stronghold /ˈstrɔŋˌhould/ *n* fortaleza, *f;* refugio, *m*
strongly /ˈstrɔŋli/ *adv* vigorosamente; fuertemente; firmemente
strop /strɒp/ *n* (razor) suavizador, *m, vt* suavizar
strophe /ˈstroufi/ *n* estrofa, *f*
structural /ˈstrʌktʃərəl/ *a* estructural
structurally /ˈstrʌktʃərəli/ *adv* estructuralmente, desde el punto de vista de la estructura
structure /ˈstrʌktʃər/ *n* estructura, *f;* edificio, *m;* construcción, *f*
struggle /ˈstrʌgəl/ *vi* luchar; pelear; disputarse. —*n* lucha, *f;* combate, *m;* conflicto, *m.* **to s. to one's feet,** luchar por levantarse. **without a s.,** sin luchar
struggling /ˈstrʌglɪŋ/ *a* pobre, indigente, que lucha para vivir
strum /strʌm/ *vt* (a stringed instrument) rascar; tocar mal
strumpet /ˈstrʌmpɪt/ *n* ramera, *f*
strut /strʌt/ *vi* pavonearse. —*vt* (prop) apuntalar. —*n* pavonada, *f;* (prop) puntal, *m.* **to s. out,** salir de un paso majestuoso
strychnine /ˈstrɪknin/ *n* estricnina, *f*
stub /stʌb/ *n* (of a tree) tocón, *m;* (of a pencil, candle, etc.) cabo, *m;* pedazo, fragmento, *m;* (of a cigarette or cigar) colilla, *f.* **s.-book,** talonario, *m*
stubble /ˈstʌbəl/ *n* rastrojo, *m;* (beard) barba de tres días, *f*
stubborn /ˈstʌbərn/ *a* inquebrantable, tenaz; persistente; (pig-headed) terco, testarudo
stubbornness /ˈstʌbərnɪs/ *n* tenacidad, *f;* terquedad, testarudez, *f*
stucco /ˈstʌkou/ *n* estuco, *m, vt* estucar
stud /stʌd/ *n* (of horses) caballeriza, *f;* (nail) tachón, *m;* (for collars) pasador para camisas, *m.* —*vt* tachonar; sembrar. **dress s.,** botón de la pechera, *m.* **s.-farm,** potrero, *m*
student /ˈstudnt/ *n* estudiante, *mf.* —*a* estudiantil
studied /ˈstʌdid/ *a* estudiado; calculado; (of style) cerebral, reflexivo; (intentional) deliberado
studio /ˈstudiˌou/ *n* estudio, *m.* **broadcasting s.,** estudio de emisión, *m*
studious /ˈstudiəs/ *a* estudioso, aplicado; (deliberate) intencional, deliberate; (eager) solícito, ansioso
studiously /ˈstudiəsli/ *adv* estudiosamente; con intención, deliberadamente; solícitamente
study /ˈstʌdi/ *n* estudio, *m;* solicitud, *f,* cuidado, *m;* investigación, *f;* (room) gabinete, cuarto de trabajo, *m.* —*vt* ocuparse de, cuidar de, atender a; considerar; estudiar; examinar; (the stars) observar; (try) procurar. —*vi* estudiar. **in a brown s.,** en Babia. **to make a s. of,** hacer un estudio de, estudiar. **to s. for an examination,** prepararse para un examen
stuff /stʌf/ *n* substancia, materia, *f;* (fabric) tela, *f,* paño, *m;* (rubbish) cachivaches, *m pl,* cosas, *f pl.* —*a* de estofa. —*vt* henchir; llenar; *Cul.* rellenar; (with food) ahitar (de); (cram) atestar, apretar; (furniture) rehenchir; (an animal, bird) disecar; (put) meter, poner. **S. and nonsense!** ¡Patrañas! **to be poor s.,** ser de pacotilla; no valer para nada
stuffed animal /stʌft/ *n* animal disecado, *m*
stuffiness /ˈstʌfinɪs/ *n* mala ventilación, *f;* falta de aire, *f;* calor, *m*
stuffing /ˈstʌfɪŋ/ *n* (of furniture) rehenchimiento, *m; Cul.* relleno, *m*
stuffy /ˈstʌfi/ *a* mal ventilado, poco aireado, ahogado
stultify /ˈstʌltəˌfai/ *vt* hacer inútil; invalidar; hacer ridiculo
stumble /ˈstʌmbəl/ *vi* tropezar; dar un traspié; (in speaking) tartamudear. —*n* tropezón, *m;* traspié, *m.* **to s. through a speech,** pronunciar un discurso a tropezones. **to s. against,** tropezar contra. **to s. upon, across,** tropezar con; encontrar por casualidad
stumbling block *n* tropiezo, impedimento, *m*
stump /stʌmp/ *n* (of a tree) tocón, *m;* (of an arm, leg) muñón, *m;* (of a pencil, candle) cabo, *m;* (of a tooth) raigón, *m;* (of a cigar) colilla, *f;* (cricket) poste, montante, *m; Art.* esfumino, *m;* (leg) pata, *f.* —*vt* (disconcert) desconcertar; *Art.* esfumar; recorrer. **to s. up,** *Inf.* pagar
stun /stʌn/ *vt* dejar sin sentido (a); aturdir de un golpe (a); (astound) pasmar
stunning /ˈstʌnɪŋ/ *a* aturdidor; que pasma; *Inf.* estupendo
stunt /stʌnt/ *vt* impedir el crecimiento de; encanijar. —*n* (advertising) anuncio de reclamo, *m;* recurso (para conseguir algo), *m;* proeza, *f*
stunted /ˈstʌntɪd/ *a* (of trees, etc.) enano; (of children) encanijado; (of intelligence) inmaduro
stupefaction /ˌstupəˈfækʃən/ *n* estupefacción, *f;* estupor, *m*
stupefy /ˈstupəˌfai/ *vt* atontar, embrutecer; causar estupor (a), asombrar
stupendous /stuˈpɛndəs/ *a* asombroso; enorme
stupid /ˈstupɪd/ *a* (with sleep, etc.) atontado; (silly) estúpido, tonto. —*n* tonto (-ta)
stupidity /stuˈpɪdɪti/ *n* estupidez, *f;* tontería, *f*
stupor /ˈstupər/ *n* estupor, *m*
sturdiness /ˈstɜrdinɪs/ *n* robustez, *f,* vigor, *m;* firmeza, tenacidad, *f*

sturdy /'stɜrdi/ *a* robusto, vigoroso, fuerte; firme, tenaz

sturgeon /'stɜrdʒən/ *n Ichth.* esturión, *m*

stutter /'stʌtər/ *vi* tartamudear. —*vt* balbucir. —*n* tartamudeo, *m*

stutterer /'stʌtərər/ *n* tartamudo (-da)

stuttering /'stʌtərɪŋ/ *a* tartamudo; balbuciente. —*n* tartamudeo, *m*

sty /stai/ *n* (pig) pocilga, *f; Med.* orzuelo, *m*

Stygian /'stɪdʒiən/ *a* estigio

style /stail/ *n* (for etching) buril, *m;* (*Lit., Art., Archit.,* etc.) estilo, *m;* (fashion) moda, *f;* (model) modelo, *m;* (behavior, etc.) tono, *m;* elegancia, *f;* (kind) especie, clase, *f;* (designation) tratamiento, *m; vt* llamar, nombrar. **the latest styles from Madrid,** los últimos modelos de Madrid. **He has a very individual s.,** Su estilo es muy personal. **They live in great s.,** Viven en gran lujo

stylet /'stailɪt/ *n* estilete, *m*

stylish /'stailɪʃ/ *a* elegante

stylishness /'stailɪʃnɪs/ *n* elegancia, *f*

stylist /'stailɪst/ *n* estilista, *mf*

stylize /'stailaiz/ *vt* estilizar

suasion /'sweiʒən/ *n* persuasión, *f*

suasive /'sweisɪv/ *a* suasorio, persuasivo

suave /swɑv/ *a* afable, cortés, urbano; (of wine) suave

suavity /'swɒvɪti/ *n* afabilidad, urbanidad, *f*

subaltern /sʌb'ɔltərn/ *n Mil.* subalterno, *m, a* subalterno, subordinado

subcommittee /'sʌbkəˌmɪti/ *n* subcomisión, *f*

subconscious /sʌb'kɒnʃəs/ *a* subconsciente. **the s.,** la subconsciencia

subconsciously /sʌb'kɒnʃəsli/ *adv* subconscientemente

subcutaneous /ˌsʌbkyu'teiniəs/ *a* subcutáneo

subdivide /ˌsʌbdɪ'vaid/ *vt* subdividir. —*vi* subdividirse

subdivision /'sʌbdɪˌvɪʒən/ *n* subdivisión, *f*

subdominant /sʌb'dɒmənənt/ *n Mus.* subdominante, *f*

subdue /səb'du/ *vt* subyugar, sojuzgar, vencer; (one's passions) dominar; (colors, voices) suavizar; (lessen) mitigar; apagar

subdued /səb'dud/ *a* (of colors) apagado; (of persons) sumiso; (depressed) deprimido, melancólico. **in a s. voice,** en voz baja

subheading /'sʌbˌhɛdɪŋ/ *n* subtítulo, *m*

subhuman /sʌb'hyumən/ *a* subhumano

subject /*n.* 'sʌbdʒɪkt; *v.* səb'dʒɛkt/ *a* sujeto; sometido (a); expuesto (a). —*n* (of a country) súbdito (-ta); sujeto, *m;* (of study) asignatura, materia, *f;* (theme) tema, *m;* (*Gram., Philos.*) sujeto, *m.* —*vt* subyugar; someter. **It can only be done s. to his consent,** Podrá hacerse únicamente si él lo consiente. **to change the s.,** cambiar de conversación. **to s. to criticism,** criticar (a). **s.-matter,** materia, *f;* (of a letter) contenido, *m*

subjection /səb'dʒɛkʃən/ *n* sujeción, *f;* sometimiento, *m.* **He was in a state of complete s.,** Estaba completamente sumiso. **to bring into s.,** subyugar

subjective /səb'dʒɛktɪv/ *a* subjetivo

subjectiveness /səb'dʒɛktɪvnɪs/ *n* subjetividad, *f*

subjectivism /səb'dʒɛktəˌvɪzəm/ *n* subjetivismo, *m*

subjoin /səb'dʒɔin/ *vt* añadir, adjuntar

subjugate /'sʌbdʒəˌgeit/ *vt* subyugar, someter

subjugation /ˌsʌbdʒə'geiʃən/ *n* subyugación, *f*

subjunctive /səb'dʒʌŋktɪv/ *a* and *n* subjuntivo *m*

sublet /*v.* sʌb'lɛt; *n.* 'sʌbˌlɛt/ *vt* subarrendar. —*n* subarriendo, *m*

sublimate /*v.* 'sʌbləˌmeit; *n.* -mɪt/ *vt* sublimar. —*n* sublimado, *m*

sublimation /ˌsʌblɪ'meiʃən/ *n* sublimación, *f*

sublime /sə'blaim/ *a* sublime; absoluto, completo; extremo. **the s.,** lo sublime

sublimely /sə'blaimli/ *adv* sublimemente; completamente

submachine gun /ˌsʌbmə'ʃin/ *n* pistola ametralladora, metralleta, *f,* subfusil ametrallador, *m*

submarine /ˌsʌbmə'rin/ *a* submarino. —*n* submarino, *m.* **midget s.,** submarino enano, submarino de bolsillo, *m.* **s. chaser,** cazasubmarino, *m*

submerge /səb'mɜrdʒ/ *vt* sumergir; inundar. —*vi* sumergirse. **The submarine submerged,** El submarino se sumergió

submergence /səb'mɜrdʒəns/ *n* sumergimiento, *m,* sumersión, *f;* hundimiento, *m*

submersible /səb'mɜrsəbəl/ *a* sumergible

submersion /səb'mɜrʒən/ *n* sumersión, *f;* hundimiento, *m*

submission /səb'mɪʃən/ *n* sometimiento, *m;* sumisión, resignación, *f;* docilidad, *f*

submissive /səb'mɪsɪv/ *a* sumiso, dócil, manso

submissively /səb'mɪsɪvli/ *adv* sumisamente, con docilidad

submissiveness /səb'mɪsɪvnɪs/ *n* sumisión, docilidad, *f*

submit /səb'mɪt/ *vt* someterse (a); doblarse ante; (a scheme, etc.) someter; presentar; (urge) proponer. —*vi* someterse; resignarse; (surrender) rendirse, entregarse. **to s. to arbitration,** someter a arbitraje

subnormal /sʌb'nɔrməl/ *a* anormal

subordinate /*adj., n.* sə'bɔrdn̩ɪt; *v.* -dn̩ˌeit/ *a* subordinado; subalterno, inferior; secundario. —*n* subordinado (-da). —*vt* subordinar

subordination /səˌbɔrdn̩'eiʃən/ *n* subordinación, *f*

suborn /sə'bɔrn/ *vt* sobornar, cohechar

subplot /'sʌbˌplɒt/ *n* intriga secundaria, trama secundaria, *f*

subpoena /sə'pinə/ *n* citación, *f, vt* citar

subscribe /səb'skraib/ *vt* and *vi* subscribir; (to a periodical, etc.) abonarse (a)

subscriber /səb'skraibər/ *n* subscriptor (-ra); abonado (-da)

subscription /səb'skrɪpʃən/ *n* subscripción, *f;* (to a periodical, series of concerts, etc.) abono, *m;* (to a club) cuota, *f*

subsection /'sʌbˌsɛkʃən/ *n* subsección, *f*

subsequent /'sʌbsɪkwənt/ *a* subsiguiente, subsecuente; posterior. **s. to,** después de, posterior a. **s. upon,** de resultas de

subsequently /'sʌbsikwəntli/ *adv* más tarde; subsiguientemente; posteriormente

subservience /səb'sɜrviens/ *n* servilidad, *f;* utilidad, *f*

subservient /səb'sɜrviənt/ *a* servil; subordinado; útil

subside /səb'said/ *vi* (of water) bajar; (of ground) hundirse; (of foundations) asentarse; disminuir; calmarse; (be quiet) callarse. **to s. into a chair,** dejarse caer en un sillón

subsidence /səb'saidn̩s/ *n* hundimiento, *m;* desplome, derrumbamiento, *m;* (of floods) bajada, *f;* (of anger, etc.) apaciguamiento, *m*

subsidiary /səb'sɪdiˌɛri/ *a* subsidiario

subsidize /'sʌbsɪˌdaiz/ *vt* subvencionar

subsidy /'sʌbsɪdi/ *n* subvención, *f,* subsidio, *m;* prima, *f*

subsist /səb'sɪst/ *vi* subsistir

subsistence /səb'sɪstəns/ *n* subsistencia, *f*

subsoil /'sʌbˌsɔil/ *n* subsuelo, *m*

substance /'sʌbstəns/ *n* substancia, *f*

substantial /səb'stænʃəl/ *a* substancial; sólido; importante

substantially /səbˌstænʃəli/ *adv* substancialmente; sólidamente

substantiate /səb'stænʃiˌeit/ *vt* establecer, verificar; justificar

substantiation /səbˌstænʃi'eiʃən/ *n* comprobación, verificación, *f;* justificación, *f*

substantive /'sʌbstəntɪv/ *a* real, independiente; *Gram.* substantivo. —*n Gram.* substantivo, *m*

substitute /'sʌbstɪˌtut/ *n* substituto (-ta); (material) substituto, *m.* —*vt* substituir, reemplazar. **to be a s. for,** hacer las veces de

substitution /ˌsʌbstɪ'tuʃən/ *n* substitución, *f,* reemplazo, *m*

substratum /'sʌbˌstreitəm, -ˌstrætəm/ *n* substrato, *m*

subterfuge /'sʌbtərˌfyudʒ/ *n* subterfugio, *m;* evasiva, *f*

subterranean /ˌsʌbtə'reiniən/ *a* subterráneo

subtitle /'sʌbˌtaitl̩/ *n* subtítulo, *m;* (on films) guión, *m*

subtle /ˈsʌtl̩/ *a* sutil; delicado; penetrante; (crafty) astuto
subtlety /ˈsʌtl̩ti/ *n* sutileza, *f;* delicadeza, *f;* (craftiness) astucia, *f*
subtly /ˈsʌtli/ *adv* sutilmente; con delicadeza
subtract /səbˈtrækt/ *vt* restar, substraer
subtraction /səbˈtrækʃən/ *n* resta, substracción, *f*
suburb /ˈsʌbɜrb/ *n* suburbio, *m; pl* **suburbs,** las afueras, *f pl* los arrabales, *m pl*
suburban /səˈbɜrbən/ *a* suburbano
subvention /səbˈvɛnʃən/ *n* subvención, *f*
subversion /səbˈvɜrʒən/ *n* subversión, *f*
subversive /səbˈvɜrsɪv/ *a* subversivo
subvert /səbˈvɜrt/ *vt* subvertir
subway /ˈsʌbˌwei/ *n* (passageway) pasaje subterráneo, *m;* (underground railway) metro (Spain, Puerto Rico), subte (Argentina), *m*
succeed /səkˈsid/ *vt* seguir (a); suceder (a); heredar. —*vi* seguir (a); suceder (a); (be successful) tener éxito. **I did not s. in doing it,** No logré hacerlo. **to s. to the throne,** subir al trono
succeeding /səkˈsidɪŋ/ *a* subsiguiente; futuro; consecutivo; sucesivo
success /səkˈsɛs/ *n* éxito, *m;* triunfo, *m.* **to be a s.,** tener éxito. **The film was a great s.,** La película tuvo mucho éxito
successful /səkˈsɛsfəl/ *a* que tiene éxito; afortunado, venturoso; próspero.
successfully /səkˈsɛsfəli/ *adv* con éxito; prósperamente
succession /səkˈsɛʃən/ *n* sucesión, *f;* (series) serie, *f;* (inheritance) herencia, *f;* (descendants) descendencia, *f.* **in s.,** sucesivamente
successive /səkˈsɛsɪv/ *a* sucesivo
successor /səkˈsɛsər/ *n* sucesor (-ra)
succinct /səkˈsɪŋkt/ *a* sucinto, conciso
succinctly /səkˈsiŋktli/ *adv* sucintamente, brevemente, en pocas palabras
succor /ˈsʌkər/ *vt* socorrer, auxiliar. —*n* socorro, *m,* ayuda, *f*
succulence /ˈsʌkyələns/ *n* suculencia, *f*
succulent /ˈsʌkyələnt/ *a* suculento
succumb /səˈkʌm/ *vi* sucumbir; someterse, ceder
such /sʌtʃ/ *a* tal; parecido, semejante; así; tanto; (before an adjective, adverb) tan. —*n* el, *m,* (*f,* la) que, los, *m pl,* (*f pl,* las) que; tal. **s. men,** tales hombres. **I have never seen s. magnificence,** Nunca no he visto tanta magnificencia. **s. an important man,** un hombre tan importante. **s. pictures as these,** cuadros como estos. **S. is life!** ¡Así es la vida! **science as s.,** la ciencia como tal. **s.-and-s.,** tal y tal
suchlike /ˈsʌtʃˌlaik/ *a* parecido, semejante; de esta clase
suck /sʌk/ *vt* chupar; (the breast) mamar; sorber; (of a vacuum cleaner, etc.) aspirar. —*n* chupada, *f;* succión, *f.* **to s. down,** tragar. **to s. up,** aspirar; absorber
sucker /ˈsʌkər/ *n Zool.* ventosa, *f; Bot.* acodo, mugrón, *m;* (greenhorn) primo, *m;* (pig) lechón, *m*
suckle /ˈsʌkəl/ *vt* amamantar, dar el pecho (a)
suckling pig /ˈsʌklɪŋ/ *n* lechón, cochinillo, *m*
suction /ˈsʌkʃən/ *n* succión, *f;* aspiración, *f.* **s.-pump,** bomba aspirante, *f*
Sudanese /ˌsudn̩ˈiz/ *a* and *n* sudanés (-esa)
Sudan, the /suˈdæn/ el Sudán, *m*
sudden /ˈsʌdn̩/ *a* súbito; (unexpected) inesperado, impensado; (of bends) brusco. **all of a s.,** de repente; súbitamente
suddenly /ˈsʌdn̩li/ *adv* súbitamente; de pronto, de repente
suddenness /ˈsʌdn̩nɪs/ *n* carácter repentino, *m;* (of a bend, etc.) brusquedad, *f*
suds /sʌdz/ *n pl* jabonaduras, *f pl;* espuma, *f*
sue /su/ *vt Law.* proceder contra, pedir en juicio; *Law.* demandar; (beg) suplicar. **to sue for peace,** pedir la paz
suede /sweid/ *n* ante, *m.* **s. glove,** guante de ante, *m*
suet /ˈsuɪt/ *n* sebo, *m*
Suez Canal, the /suˈɛz/ el Istmo de Suez, *m*
suffer /ˈsʌfər/ *vt* sufrir, padecer; pasar, experimentar; (tolerate) tolerar, sufrir; (allow) permitir. —*vi* sufrir. **She suffers from her environment,** es la víctima de su medio ambiente
sufferance /ˈsʌfərəns/ *n* tolerancia, *f.* **on s.,** por tolerancia
sufferer /ˈsʌfərər/ *n* enfermo (-ma); víctima, *f*
suffering /ˈsʌfərɪŋ/ *n* sufrimiento, padecimiento, *m;* dolor, *m.* —*a* sufriente
suffice /səˈfais/ *vi* ser suficiente, bastar. —*vt* satisfacer
sufficiency /səˈfɪʃənsi/ *n* suficiencia, *f;* (of money) subsistencia, *f*
sufficient /səˈfɪʃənt/ *a* suficiente, bastante. **to be s.,** bastar, ser suficiente
sufficiently /səˈfɪʃəntli/ *adv* suficientemente, bastante
suffix /ˈsʌfɪks/ *n Gram.* sufijo, *m*
suffocate /ˈsʌfəˌkeit/ *vt* ahogar, sofocar, asfixiar. —*vi* sofocarse, asfixiarse
suffocating /ˈsʌfəˌkeitɪŋ/ *a* sofocante, asfixiante
suffocation /ˌsʌfəˈkeiʃən/ *n* sofocación, asfixia, *f;* ahogo, *m*
suffrage /ˈsʌfrɪdʒ/ *n* sufragio, *m;* voto, *m.* **universal s.,** sufragio universal, *m*
suffragette /ˌsʌfrəˈdʒɛt/ *n* sufragista, *f*
suffuse /səˈfyuz/ *vt* bañar, inundar, cubrir
sugar /ˈʃʊgər/ *n* azúcar, *m.* —*vt* azucarar. **brown s.,** azúcar moreno, *m.* **loaf s.,** azúcar de pilón, *m.* **white s.,** azúcar blanco, *m.* **to s. the pill,** dorar la píldora. **s.-almond,** peladilla, *f.* **s.-basin,** azucarera, *f.* **s.-beet,** remolacha, *f.* **s.-candy,** azúcar candi, *m.* **s.-cane,** caña de azúcar, *f.* **s.-cane syrup,** miel de caña, *f.* **s.-paste,** alfeñique, *m,* alcorza, *f.* **s.-refinery,** fábrica de azúcar, *f.* **s.-tongs,** tenacillas para azúcar, *f pl*
sugary /ˈʃʊgəri/ *a* azucarado; *Fig.* meloso, almibarado
suggest /səgˈdʒɛst/ *vt* implicar; indicar, dar a entender; sugerir; (advise) aconsejar; (hint) insinuar; (evoke) evocar. **I suggested they should go to London,** Les aconsejé que fueran a Londres. **An idea suggested itself to him,** Se le ocurrió una idea
suggestion /səgˈdʒɛstʃən/ *n* sugestión, *f;* insinuación, *f*
suggestive /səgˈdʒɛstɪv/ *a* sugestivo; estimulante
suicidal /ˌsuəˈsaidl̩/ *a* suicida. **s. tendency,** tendencia suicida, tendencia al suicidio, *f*
suicide /ˈsuəˌsaid/ *n* (act) suicidio, *m;* (person) suicida, *mf.* **to commit s.,** darse la muerte, quitarse la vida suicidarse
suit /sut/ *n* (request) petición, súplica, *f;* oferta de matrimonio, *f; Law.* pleito, *m;* (of clothes) traje, *m;* (cards) palo, *m;* (of cards held) serie, *f, vt* convenir; sentar; ir bien (a); venir bien (a); (adapt) adaptar. **S. yourself!** ¡Haz lo que quieras! **The arrangement suits me very well,** El arreglo me viene muy bien. **The climate doesn't s. me,** El clima no me sienta bien. **The color does not s. you,** El color no te va bien. **to follow s.,** seguir el ejemplo (de); (cards) jugar el mismo palo. **s.-case,** maleta, *f*
suitability /ˌsutəˈbɪlɪti/ *n* conveniencia, *f;* aptitud, *f*
suitable /ˈsutəbəl/ *a* conveniente; apropiado; apto; a propósito. **Not s. for children,** No apto para menores. **to make s. for,** adaptar a las necesidades de
suitably /ˈsutəbli/ *adv* convenientemente; apropiadamente
suite /swit/ *n* (of retainers, etc.) séquito, acompañamiento, *m;* (of furniture, etc.) juego, *m; Mus.* suite, *f.* **private s.,** habitaciones particulares, *f pl.* **s. of rooms,** apartamiento, *m*
suitor /ˈsutər/ *n Law.* demandante, *m;* pretendiente, *m*
sulk /sʌlk/ *vi* ponerse malhumorado, ser mohíno
sulkiness /ˈsʌlkinɪs/ *n* mohína, *f,* mal humor, *m*
sulky /ˈsʌlki/ *a* mohíno, malhumorado
sullen /ˈsʌlən/ *a* taciturno, hosco; malhumorado, sombrío; (of a landscape, etc.) triste, sombrío
sullenly /ˈsʌlənli/ *adv* taciturnamente, hoscamente
sullenness /ˈsʌlənnɪs/ *n* taciturnidad, hosquedad, *f,* mal humor, *m*
sully /ˈsʌli/ *vt* desdorar, empañar; manchar
sulphur /ˈsʌlfər/ *n* azufre, *m*
sulphuric /sʌlˈfyʊrɪk/ *a* sulfúrico
sulphurous /ˈsʌlfərəs/ *a* sulfuroso
sultan /ˈsʌltn̩/ *n* sultán, *m*
sultriness /ˈsʌltrinɪs/ *n* bochorno, calor sofocante, *m*

sultry /'sʌltri/ *a* bochornoso, sofocante
sum /sʌm/ *n* suma, *f;* total, *m;* cantidad, *f;* (in arithmetic) problema (de aritmética), *m.* —*vt* sumar, calcular. **in sum,** en suma; en resumen. **to sum up,** recapitular; resumir; (a person) tomar las medidas (a)
summarily /sə'mɛərəli/ *adv* someramente; *Law.* sumariamente
summarize /'sʌmə,raiz/ *vt* resumir brevemente; compendiar
summary /'sʌməri/ *a* somero; *Law.* sumario. —*n* resumen, sumario, compendio, *m.* **summary records,** actas resumidas, *f pl*
summer /'sʌmər/ *n* verano, estío, *m.* **to spend the s.,** veranear. **s.-house,** cenador, *m.* **s.-time,** verano, *m;* hora de verano, *f.* **s. wheat,** trigo tremesino, *m*
summing-up /'sʌmɪŋ,ʌp/ *n* recapitulación, *f*
summit /'sʌmɪt/ *n* cima, cumbre, *f; Fig.* apogeo, *m*
summitry /'sʌmɪtri/ *n* diplomacia en la cumbre, *f*
summon /'sʌmən/ *vt* llamar, hacer venir; mandar, requerir; *Law.* citar. **to s. up one's courage,** cobrar ánimos
summons /'sʌmənz/ *n* llamamiento, *m; Mil.* intimación, *f; Law.* citación, *f.* —*vt Law.* citar
sump /sʌmp/ *n* (of a motor-car) pozo colector, *m; Mineral.* sumidero, *m*
sumptuous /'sʌmptʃuəs/ *a* suntuoso, lujoso, magnífico
sumptuousness /'sʌmptʃuəsnɪs/ *n* suntuosidad, magnificencia, *f*
sun /sʌn/ *n* sol, *m.* **The sun was shining,** Hacía sol, El sol brillaba. **to bask in the sun,** tomar el sol. **sun-bathing,** baños de sol, *m pl.* **sun-blind,** toldo para el sol, *m.* **sun-bonnet,** capelina, *f.* **sun-glasses,** gafas ahumadas, *f pl.* **sun-helmet,** casco colonial, *m.* **sun-spot,** *Astron.* mancha del sol, *f;* (freckle) peca, *f.* **sun-worship,** adoración del sol, *f*
sunbeam /'sʌn,bim/ *n* rayo de sol, *m*
sunburn /'sʌn,bɜrn/ *n* quemadura del sol, *f;* bronceado, *m*
sunburnt /'sʌn,bɜrnt/ *a* quemado por el sol; bronceado, tostado por el sol
sundae /'sʌndei/ *n* helado de frutas, *m*
Sunday /'sʌndei/ *n* domingo, *m.* **in his S. best,** en su traje dominguero, endomingado. **S. school,** escuela dominical, *f*
Sunday's child *n* niño nacido de pies, niño nacido un domingo, niño mimado de la fortuna
sunder /'sʌndər/ *vt* dividir en dos, hender; separar
sundial /'sʌn,daiəl/ *n* reloj de sol, reloj solar, *m*
sundown /'sʌn,daun/ *n* puesta del sol, *f*
sundry /'sʌndri/ *a* varios (-as). —*n pl* **sundries,** artículos diversos, *m pl; Com.* varios, *m pl.* **all and s.,** todo el mundo, todos y cada uno
sunflower /'sʌn,flauər/ *n* girasol, tornasol, *m,* trompeta de amor, *f*
sunken /'sʌŋkən/ *a* (of eyes, etc.) hundido
sunless /'sʌnlɪs/ *a* sin sol
sun letter *n* letra solar, *f*
sunlight /'sʌn,lait/ *n* luz del sol, *f,* rayos del sol, *m pl.* **artificial s.,** sol artificial, *m.* **in the s.,** al sol
sunny /'sʌni/ *a* de sol; bañado de sol; asoleado; expuesto al sol; (face) risueño; (of disposition, etc.) alegre. **to be s.,** hacer sol
sunrise /'sʌn,raiz/ *n* salida del sol, *f.* **from s. to sunset,** de sol a sol
sunset /'sʌn,sɛt/ *n* puesta del sol, *f.* **at s.,** a la caída (or puesta) del sol
sunshade /'sʌn,ʃeid/ *n* parasol, quitasol, *m,* sombrilla, *f*
sunshine /'sʌn,ʃain/ *n* luz del sol, *f.* **in the s.,** al sol
sunstroke /'sʌn,strouk/ *n* insolación, *f*
sup /sʌp/ *vt* sorber. —*vi* cenar. —*n* sorbo, *m*
super /'supər/ *n* (actor) comparsa, *mf;* (film) superproducción, *f;* (of a beehive) alza, *f*
superabundance /,supərə'bʌndəns/ *n* superabundancia, sobreabundancia, *f*
superabundant /,supərə'bʌndənt/ *a* superabundante, sobreabundante. **to be s.,** sobreabundar
superannuate /,supər'ænyu,eit/ *vt* (retire) jubilar
superannuated /,supər'ænyu,eitɪd/ *a* (retired) jubilado; (out-of-date) anticuado
superannuation /,supər,ænyu'eiʃən/ *n* (retirement and pension) jubilación, *f*
superb /sʊ'pɜrb/ *a* magnífico, espléndido
superbly /sʊ'pɜrbli/ *adv* magníficamente
supercargo /,supər'kɑrgou/ *n Naut.* sobrecargo, *m*
supercharger /'supər,tʃɑrdʒər/ *n* (*Auto., Aer.*) compresor, *m*
supercilious /,supər'sɪliəs/ *a* altanero, altivo, orgulloso; desdeñoso
superciliousness /,supər'sɪliəsnɪs/ *n* altanería, altivez, *f,* orgullo, *m;* desdén, *m*
superficial /,supər'fɪʃəl/ *a* superficial
superficiality /,supər,fɪʃi'ælɪti/ *n* superficialidad, *f*
superficially /,supər'fɪʃəli/ *adv* superficialmente
superfine /,supər'fain/ *a* superfino
superfluity /,supər'fluɪti/ *n* superfluidad, *f*
superfluous /sʊ'pɜrfluəs/ *a* superfluo. **to be s.,** sobrar
superfortress /'supər,fɔrtrɪs/ *n Aer.* superfortaleza volante, *f*
superhuman /,supər'hyumən/ *a* sobrehumano
superimpose /,supərɪm'pouz/ *vt* sobreponer
superintend /,supərɪn'tɛnd/ *vt* superentender, dirigir
superintendent /,supərɪn'tɛndənt/ *n* superintendente, *mf;* director (-ra); (school) inspector; (police) subjefe de la policía, *m*
superior /sə'pɪəriər/ *a* superior; (in number) mayor; (smug) desdeñoso. —*n* superior (-ra). **Mother S.,** (madre) superiora, *f.* **s. to,** superior a; encima de
superiority /sə,pɪəri'ɔrɪti/ *n* superioridad, *f*
superlative /sə'pɜrlətɪv/ *a* extremo, supremo; *Gram.* superlativo. —*n Gram.* superlativo, *m*
superlatively /sə'pɜrlətɪvli/ *adv* en sumo grado, superlativamente
superman /'supər,mæn/ *n* superhombre, *m*
supermarket /'supər,mɑrkɪt/ *n* supermercado, *m*
supernatural /,supər'nætʃərəl/ *a* sobrenatural
supernumerary /,supər'numə,rɛri/ *a* and *n* supernumerario (-ia)
superposition /,supərpə'zɪʃən/ *n* superposición, *f*
superscribe /'supər,skraib/ *vt* sobrescribir; poner el sobrescrito (a)
superscription /,supər'skrɪpʃən/ *n* (on letters, documents) sobrescrito, *m;* leyenda, *f*
supersede /,supər'sid/ *vt* reemplazar; suplantar
supersensible /,supər'sɛnsəbəl/ *a* suprasensible
superstition /,supər'stɪʃən/ *n* superstición, *f*
superstitious /,supər'stɪʃəs/ *a* supersticioso
supertax /'supər,tæks/ *n* impuesto suplementario, *m*
supervene /,supər'vin/ *vi* sobrevenir
supervise /'supər,vaiz/ *vt* superentender, vigilar; dirigir
supervision /,supər'vɪʒən/ *n* superintendencia, *f;* dirección, *f*
supervisor /'supər,vaizər/ *n* superintendente, *mf;* inspector (-ra); director (-ra)
supine /*a.* su'pain; *n.* 'supain/ *a* supino; indolente, negligente. —*n Gram.* supino, *m*
supper /'sʌpər/ *n* cena, *f.* **the Last S.,** la Última Cena. **to have s.,** cenar. **s.-time,** hora de cenar, *f*
supplant /sə'plænt/ *vt* suplantar; usurpar; reemplazar
supplanter /sə'plæntər/ *n* suplantador (-ra)
supple /'sʌpəl/ *a* flexible; dócil, manso; (fawning) adulador, servil, lisonjero
supplement /'sʌpləmənt/ *n* suplemento, *m;* (of a book) apéndice, *m*
supplementary /,sʌplə'mɛntəri/ *a* suplementario; adicional
suppleness /'sʌpəlnɪs/ *n* flexibilidad, *f;* docilidad, *f;* servilidad, *f*
suppliant /'sʌpliənt/ *a* and *n* suplicante, *mf*
supplicate /'sʌplɪ,keit/ *vt* and *vi* suplicar
supplication /, s½plI'keiSən/ *n* suplicación, *f;* súplica, *f*
supply /sə'plai/ *vt* proveer (de); suministrar; proporcionar, dar; (a deficiency) suplir; (a post) llenar; (a post temporarily) reemplazar. —*n* suministro, surtimiento, *m;* provisión, *f;* (of electricity, etc.) suministro, *m; Com.* oferta, *f;* (person) substituto (-ta); *pl* **supplies,** *Com.* existencias, *f pl; Mil.* pertrechos, *m pl;*

víveres, *m pl,* provisiones, *f pl.* **s. and demand,** oferta y demanda, *f*

support /sə'pɔrt/ *vt* apoyar, sostener; mantener; (endure) soportar; (a cause) apoyar, defender; (corroborate) confirmar, vindicar. *—n* apoyo, *m;* sostén, *m;* soporte, *m.* **to speak in s. of,** defender, abogar por. **to s. oneself,** ganarse la vida, mantenerse

supporter /sə'pɔrtər/ *n* apoyo, *m;* defensor (-ra); partidario (-ia)

suppose /sə'pouz/ *vt* suponer; imaginar(se); creer. **always supposing,** dado que, en el caso de que. **Supposing he had gone out?** ¿Y si hubiera salido? **I don't s. they will go to Spain,** No creo que vayan a España. **He is supposed to be clever,** Tiene fama de listo

supposed /sə'pouzd, -'pouzɪd/ *a* supuesto; que se llama a sí mismo

supposition /ˌsʌpə'zɪʃən/ *n* suposición, hipótesis, *f*

suppress /sə'prɛs/ *vt* reprimir; (yawns, etc.) ahogar; contener; (heresies, rebellions, books, etc.) suprimir; (dissemble) disimular, esconder; (a heckler, etc.) hacer callar

suppressed /sə'prɛst/ *a* reprimido; contenido; disimulado

suppression /sə'prɛʃən/ *n* represión, *f;* supresión, *f;* disimulación, *f*

suppurate /'sʌpyəˌreit/ *vi* supurar

suppuration /ˌsʌpyə'reiʃən/ *n* supuración, *f*

supremacy /sə'prɛməsi/ *n* supremacía, *f*

supreme /sə'prim/ *a* supremo; sumo. **with s. indifference,** con suma indiferencia. **s. court,** tribunal supremo, *m*

surcharge /'sɜrˌtʃɑrdʒ/ *n* sobrecarga, *f*

sure /ʃʊr/ *a* seguro; cierto. *—adv* seguramente. **Be s. to...!** ¡Ten cuidado de...! ¡No dejes de...! **to be s.,** seguramente, sin duda; ¡claro!; (fancy!) ¡no me digas!; ¡qué sorpresa! **I am not so s. of that,** No diría yo tanto. **Come on Thursday for s.,** Venga el jueves sin falta. **It is s. to rain tomorrow,** Seguramente va a llover mañana. **to make s. of,** asegurarse de. **to be (or feel) s.,** estar seguro. **s.-footed,** de pie firme, seguro

surely /'ʃʊrli/ *adv* seguramente; sin duda, ciertamente; por supuesto

sureness /'ʃʊrnɛs/ *n* seguridad, *f;* certeza, *f*

surety /'ʃʊrɪti/ *n* garantía, fianza, *f;* (person) garante, *mf.* **to go s. for,** ser fiador (de), salir garante (por)

surf /sɜrf/ *n* resaca, *f;* rompiente, *m;* oleaje, *m.* **s.-board,** aquaplano, *m.* **s.-riding,** patinaje sobre las olas, *m*

surface /'sɜrfɪs/ *n* superficie, *f;* exterior, *m. —a* superficial. *—vi* (of a submarine) salir a la superficie. **on the s.,** en apariencia

surface mail *n* correo por vía ordinaria, servicio ordinario, servicio per vía de superficie, *m*

surfeit /'sɜrfɪt/ *n* exceso, *m,* superabundancia, *f;* saciedad, *f. —vt* hartar; saciar

surge /sɜrdʒ/ *vi* (of waves) embravecerse, hincharse; (of crowds) agitarse, bullir; (of emotions) despertarse. *—n* (of sea, crowd, blood) oleada, *f;* (of anger) ola, *f.* **The blood surged into his face,** La sangre se le subió a las mejillas

surgeon /'sɜrdʒən/ *n* cirujano, *m;* (*Nav., Mil.*) médico, *m*

surgery /'sɜrdʒəri/ *n* cirugía, *f;* (doctor's) consultorio, *m;* (dispensary) dispensario, *m*

surgical /'sɜrdʒɪkəl/ *a* quirúrgico

surliness /'sɜrlinɪs/ *n* mal genio, *m,* taciturnidad, *f;* brusquedad, *f*

surly /'sɜrli/ *a* taciturno, huraño, malhumorado; brusco

surmise /sər'maiz/ *n* conjetura, suposición, *f. —vt* conjeturar, adivinar; imaginar, suponer. *—vi* hacer conjeturas

surmount /sər'maunt/ *vt* superar, vencer; coronar

surname /'sɜrˌneim/ *n* apellido, *m, vt* denominar, nombrar

surpass /sər'pæs/ *vt* superar, exceder; aventajarse (a); eclipsar

surpassing /sər'pæsɪŋ/ *a* sin par, incomparable

surplus /'sɜrplʌs/ *n* exceso, sobrante, *m;* (*Com.* of accounts) superávit, *m.* **sale of s. stock,** liquidación de saldos, *f*

surprise /sər'praiz, sə-/ *n* sorpresa, *f;* asombro, *m. —vt* sorprender; asombrar. **to s.** (someone) **in the act,** coger en el acto. **to take** (a person) **by s.,** sorprender (a). **He was surprised into admitting it,** Cogido a la imprevista, lo confesó

surprising /sər'praizɪŋ, sə-/ *a* sorprendente

surrealism /sə'riəˌlɪzəm/ *n* surrealismo, *m*

surrealist /sə'riəlɪst/ *a* and *n* surrealista, *mf*

surrender /sə'rɛndər/ *vt* rendir, entregar; (goods) ceder, renunciar (a). *—vi* rendirse, entregarse; abandonarse. *—n* rendición, capitulación, *f;* entrega, *f;* (of goods) cesión, *f;* (of an insurance policy) rescate, *m.* **to s. oneself to remorse,** abandonarse (or entregarse) al remordimiento. **to s. unconditionally,** entregarse a discreción

surreptitious /ˌsɜrəp'tɪʃəs/ *a* subrepticio

surreptitiously /ˌsɜrəp'tɪʃəsli/ *adv* subrepticiamente, a hurtadillas

surround /sə'raund/ *vt* rodear; cercar; *Mil.* asediar, sitiar. *—n* borde, *m.* **Peter was surrounded by his friends,** Pedro estaba rodeado por sus amigos

surrounding /sə'raundɪŋ/ *a* (que está) alrededor de; vecino. **the s. country,** los alrededores

surroundings /sə'raudɪŋz/ *n pl* cercanías, *f pl,* alrededores, *m pl;* (environment) medio, *m;* (medio) ambiente, *m*

surtax /'sɜrˌtæks/ *n* impuesto suplementario, *m*

surveillance /sər'veiləns/ *n* vigilancia, *f*

survey /*v.* sər'vei; *n.* 'sɜrvei/ *vt* contemplar, mirar; (events, etc.) pasar en revista; estudiar; (land, etc.) apear; (a house, etc.) inspeccionar. *—n* vista general, *f;* inspección, *f;* (of facts, etc.) examen, *m;* estudio, *m;* (of land, etc.) apeo, *m;* (of literature, etc.) bosquejo, breve panorama, *m*

surveying /sər'veiɪŋ/ *n* agrimensura, *f*

surveyor /sər'veiər/ *n* agrimensor, *m;* (superintendent) inspector, *m;* superintendente, *m*

survival /sər'vaivəl/ *n* supervivencia, *f.* **s. of the fittest,** supervivencia de los más aptos, *f*

survive /sər'vaiv/ *vt* sobrevivir a. *—vi* sobrevivir; (of customs) subsistir, durar

survivor /sər'vaivər/ *n* sobreviviente, *mf*

susceptibility /səˌsɛptə'bɪlɪti/ *n* susceptibilidad, *f;* tendencia, *f; pl* **susceptibilities,** sensibilidad, *f*

susceptible /sə'sɛptəbəl/ *a* susceptible; impresionable; sensible; (to love) enamoradizo. **He is s. to bronchitis,** Es susceptible a la bronquitis

suspect /*a., n.* 'sʌspɛkt; *v.* sə'spɛkt/ *a* and *n* sospechoso (-sa). *—vt* sospechar; dudar; imaginar, suponer. *—vi* tener sospechas

suspend /sə'spɛnd/ *vt* suspender. **suspended animation,** muerte aparente, *f*

suspender /sə'spɛndər/ *n* liga, *f; pl* **suspenders,** (braces) tirantes del pantalón, *m pl.* **s.-belt,** faja, *f*

suspense /sə'spɛns/ *n* incertidumbre, *f.* **to keep** (a person) **in s.,** dejar en la incertidumbre (a)

suspension /sə'spɛnʃən/ *n* suspensión, *f.* **s.-bridge,** puente colgante, *m.* **s. of payments,** suspensión de pagos, *f,*

suspicion /sə'spɪʃən/ *n* sospecha, *f;* (touch) dejo, *m;* cantidad muy pequeña, *f.* **to be above s.,** estar por encima de toda sospecha. **to be under s.,** estar bajo sospecha. **I had no suspicions...,** No sospechaba...

suspicious /sə'spɪʃəs/ *a* (by nature) suspicaz; sospechoso. **to make s.,** hacer sospechar

suspiciously /sə'spɪʃəsli/ *adv* suspicazmente, desconfiadamente; de un modo sospechoso. **It seems s. like...,** Tiene toda la apariencia de...

suspiciousness /sə'spɪʃəsnɪs/ *n* carácter sospechoso, *m,* lo sospechoso; suspicacia, *f*

sustain /sə'stein/ *vt* sostener; mantener; sustentar; apoyar; corroborar, confirmar; (a note) prolongar. **to s. injuries,** recibir heridas

sustenance /'sʌstənəns/ *n* mantenimiento, *m;* sustento, *m,* alimentos, *m pl*

suture /'sutʃər/ *n* sutura, *f*

svarabhakti /ˌsfarə'bakti/ *a* esvarabático

svelte /svɛlt/ *a* esbelto, gentil

swab /swɒb/ *vt Naut.* lampacear; limpiar con lam-

pazo; *Surg.* tamponar. —*n* lampazo, *m; Surg.* torunda, *f,* tampón, *m*
swaddle /'swɒdl̩/ *vt* envolver; (infants) fajar
swaddling clothes /'swɒdlɪŋ/ *n pl* pañales, *m pl.* **to be still in s. clothes,** *Fig.* estar en mantillas, estar en pañales
swag /swæg/ *n* botín, *m*
swagger /'swægər/ *vi* fanfarronear, pavonearse; darse importancia. —*n* pavoneo, *m;* aire importante, *m;* (coat) tonto, *m.* —*a* majo; de última moda
swaggering /'swægərɪŋ/ *a* fanfarrón, jactancioso; importante
Swahili /swɑ'hili/ suaili; *n* suaili, *m*
swain /swein/ *n* zagal, *m;* enamorado, *m;* pretendiente, amante, *m*
swallow /'swɒlou/ *vt* tragar, engullir. —*n* trago, *m;* sorbo, *m; Ornith.* golondrina, *f.* **to s. an insult (a story),** tragar un insulto (una historia). **to s. one's words,** retractarse. **to s. one's pride,** bajar la cerviz, humillarse. **to s. up,** tragar; absorber.
swamp /swɒmp/ *n* pantano, *m,* marisma, *f.* —*vt* sumergir; (a boat) echar a pique, hundir; (inundate) inundar
swampy /'swɒmpi/ *a* pantanoso
swan /swɒn/ *n* cisne, *m.* **swan's down,** plumón de cisne, *m.* **s.-song,** canto del cisne, *m*
swank /swæŋk/ *n* pretensiones, *f pl, vi* darse humos
sward /swɔrd/ *n* césped, *m,* hierba, *f*
swarm /swɔrm/ *n* enjambre, *m;* (of people) muchedumbre, multitud, *f;* tropel, *m.* —*vi* (of bees) enjambrar; (of other insects) pulular; (of people) hormiguear, bullir, pulular. —*vt* (climb) trepar. **to s. with,** estar infestado de
swarthiness /'swɔrðinɪs/ *n* tez morena, *f;* color moreno, *m*
swarthy /'swɔrði/ *a* moreno
swashbuckler /'swɒʃˌbʌklər, 'swɔʃ-/ *n* perdonavidas, matasiete, *m*
swashbuckling /'swɒʃˌbʌklɪŋ/ *a* matamoros, valentón, fanfarrón
swastika /'swɒstɪkə/ *n* esvástica, cruz gamada, *f*
swathe /swɒð/ *vt* envolver; fajar; (with bandages) vendar
swathing /'swɒðɪŋ/ *n* envoltura, *f;* (bandages) vendas, *f pl*
sway /swei/ *vi* balancearse; oscilar; (stagger, of persons) bambolearse; (totter, of things) tambalearse; (of carriages) cabecear; (gracefully, in walking) cimbrarse. —*vt* balancear, mecer; oscilar; hacer tambalear; (influence) influir, inclinar; (govern) regir, gobernar. —*n* balanceo, *m;* oscilación, *f;* vaivén, *m;* tambaleo, *m;* (influence) ascendiente, dominio, *m,* influencia, *f;* (rule) imperio, poder, *m.* **to hold s. over,** gobernar, regir
swear /swɛər/ *vt* jurar; (*Law.* etc.) declarar bajo juramento. —*vi* jurar; (curse) echar pestes, blasfemar. **to s. at,** maldecir. **to s. by,** jurar por; poner fe implícita en. **to be sworn in,** prestar juramento. **to s. in,** tomar juramento (a). **to s. to,** atestiguar
sweat /swɛt/ *n* sudor, *m; Inf.* trabajo arduo, *m.* —*vi* sudar. —*vt* sudar; hacer sudar; (workers) explotar. **by the s. of one's brow,** con el sudor de la frente, con el sudor del rostro. **s.-gland,** glándula sudorípara, *f*
sweated /'swɛtɪd/ *a* (of persons) explotado; (of labor) mal retribuido
sweater /'swɛtər/ *n* suéter, jersey, *m*
sweating /'swɛtɪŋ/ *n* transpiración, *f;* (of workers) explotación, *f*
sweaty /'swɛti/ *a* sudoroso
Swede /swid/ *n* sueco (-ca); (vegetable) naba, *f*
Sweden /'swidn̩/ Suecia, *f*
Swedish /'swidɪʃ/ *a* sueco. —*n* (language) sueco, *m*
sweep /swip/ *vi* extenderse (por); (cleave) surcar; pasar rápidamente (por); invadir; dominar; andar majestuosamente; (with a brush) barrer. —*vt* barrer; pasar (por); (the strings of a musical instrument) rasguear; (the sea) navegar por; (mines) barrer; (the horizon, etc.) examinar; (a chimney) deshollinar; (with a brush) barrer; (remove) arrebatar; quitar; llevarse; (abolish) suprimir. **to s. along,** *vt* (of the current, crowds, etc.) arrastrar. —*vi* pasar majestuosamente; correr rápidamente (por). **to s. aside,** apartar con la mano; abandonar; (a protest) desoír, no hacer caso de. **to s. away,** barrer; (remove) llevarse; destruir; suprimir. **to s. down,** *vt* barrer; (carry) arrastrar. —*vi* (of cliffs, etc.) bajar; (of an enemy) abalanzarse (sobre); lanzarse (por). **to s. off,** barrer; (a person) llevarse sin perder tiempo; arrebatar con violencia (a). **to be swept off one's feet,** ser arrastrado (por); perder el balance; (of emotion) ser dominado por. **to s. up,** recoger, barrer
sweep /swip/ *n* barredura, *f;* (of a chimney) deshollinador, *m;* (of the tide) curso, *m;* (of a scythe, etc.) golpe, *m;* (range) alcance, *m;* (fold) pliegue, *m;* (curve) curva, *f;* (of water, etc.) extensión, *f;* (of wings) envergadura, *f.* **with a s. of the arm,** con un gesto del brazo. **to make a clean s. of,** hacer tabla rasa de
sweeping /'swipɪŋ/ *a* completo; comprensivo; demasiado general; radical. **a s. judgment,** un juicio demasiado general. **s. change,** cambio radicale, *m pl.* **s. brush,** escoba, *f*
sweepings /'swipɪŋz/ *n pl* barreduras, *f pl;* residuos, *m pl;* (of society) heces, *f pl*
sweepstake /'swipˌsteik/ *n* lotería, *f*
sweet /swit/ *a* dulce; (of scents) oloroso, fragante; (of sounds) melodioso, dulce; (charming) encantador; amable; (pretty) bonito. —*n* bombón, *m;* golosina, *f;* (at a meal) (plato) dulce, *m;* dulzura, *f;* (beloved) amor, *m,* querido (-da). **How s. it smells!** ¡Qué buen olor tiene! **the sweets of life,** las dulzuras de la vida. **s.-pea,** guisante de olor, *m,* haba de las Indias, *f.* **s.-potato,** batata, *f.* **s.-scented,** perfumado, fragante. **s.-tempered,** amable, de carácter dulce. **s.-toothed,** goloso. **s.-william,** *Bot.* clavel de la China, clavel de ramillete, clavel de San Isidro, ramillete de Constantinopla, *m,* minutisa, *f*
sweetbread /'switˌbrɛd/ *n* lechecillas, *f pl*
sweeten /'switn̩/ *vt* azucarar; endulzar. **Cervantes sweetens one's bitter moments,** Cervantes endulza los momentos ásperos
sweetheart /'switˌhɑrt/ *n* amante, *mf,* amado (-da); (as address) querido (-da)
sweetish /'switɪʃ/ *a* algo dulce
sweetly /'switli/ *adv* dulcemente; (of scents) olorosamente; (of sounds) melodiosamente; (of behavior, etc.) amablemente
sweetmeat /'switˌmit/ *n* bombón, dulce, *m*
sweetness /'switnɪs/ *n* dulzura, *f;* (of scents) buen olor, *m,* fragancia, *f;* (of sounds) melodía, dulzura, *f;* (of character) bondad, amabilidad, *f*
sweet potato *n* batata, *f,* boniato, buniato, camote, *m*
sweet sixteen *n* (age) los dieciséis abriles, *m pl;* (party) quinceañera (at age fifteen) *f*
swell /swɛl/ *vi* hincharse; (of the sea) entumecerse; crecer; aumentarse. —*vt* hinchar; aumentar. —*n* (of the sea) oleada, *f,* oleaje, *m;* (of the ground) ondulación, *f;* (of sound) crescendo, *m;* (increase) aumento, *m;* (dandy) pisaverde, elegante, *m;* (important person) pájaro gordo, *m;* (at games, etc.) espada, *m.* —*a* estupendo; elegantísimo; de primera, excelente. **to suffer from swelled head,** tener humos, darse importancia. **This foot is swollen,** Este pie está hinchado (or tumefacto). **The refugees have swelled the population,** Los refugiados han aumentado la población. **eyes swollen with tears,** ojos arrasados de lágrimas. **to s. with pride,** hincharse de orgullo
swelling /'swɛlɪŋ/ *n* hinchazón, *f; Med.* tumefacción, *f;* (bruise, etc.) chichón, *m*
swelter /'swɛltər/ *vi* abrasarse, arder. —*n* bochorno, calor sofocante, *m*
swerve /swɜrv/ *vi* desviarse; apartarse (de); torcerse. —*n* desvío, *m*
swift /swɪft/ *a* rápido, veloz; pronto. —*adv* velozmente, rápidamente. —*n Ornith.* vencejo, *m.* **s.-flowing,** (of rivers, etc.) de corriente rápida. **s.-footed,** de pies ligeros
swiftly /'swɪftli/ *adv* rápidamente, velozmente
swiftness /'swɪftnɪs/ *n* rapidez, velocidad, *f;* prontitud, *f*
swim /swɪm/ *vi* nadar; flotar; (glide) deslizarse; (fill) inundarse. —*vt* (a horse) hacer nadar; pasar a nado; nadar. —*n* natación, *f.* **eyes swimming with tears,**

ojos inundados de lágrimas. **He enjoys a s.,** Le gusta nadar. **My head swims,** Se me va la cabeza. **Everything swam before my eyes,** Todo parecía bailar ante mis ojos. **to be in the s.,** formar parte (de), ser (de); (be up to date) estar al corriente. **to s. with the tide,** ir con la corriente

swimmer /'swɪmər/ *n* nadador (-ra). **He is a bad s.,** Él nada mal

swimming /'swɪmɪŋ/ *n* natación, *f;* (of the head) vértigo, *m.* **s.-bath,** piscina, *f.* **s.-costume,** traje de baño, *m.* **s.-pool,** piscina al aire libre, *f*

swindle /'swɪndl̩/ *vt* engañar, estafar; defraudar (de). —*n* estafa, *f,* timo, *m;* engaño, *m;* impostura, *f*

swindler /'swɪndlər/ *n* estafador (-ra), trampeador (-ra); engañador (-ra)

swine /swain/ *n* cerdo, puerco, *m;* (person) cochino (-na). **a herd of s.,** una manada de cerdos

swineherd /'swain,hɜrd/ *n* porquero, *m*

swing /swɪŋ/ *vi* balancearse; oscilar; (hang) colgar, pender; columpiarse; girar; dar la vuelta; (of a boat) bornear. —*vt* balancear; (hang) colgar; (rock) mecer; (in a swing, etc.) columpiar; hacer oscilar; (raise) subir. —*n* oscilación, *f;* vaivén, *m;* balanceo, *m;* (rhythm) ritmo, *m;* (seat, etc.) columpio, *m;* (reach) alcance, *m.* **The door swung open,** La puerta se abrió silenciosamente. **He swung the car round,** Dio la vuelta al auto. **He swung himself into the saddle,** Montó de un salto. **to be in full s.,** estar a toda marcha. **to go with a s.,** tener mucho éxito. **s.-bridge,** puente giratorio, *m.* **s.-door,** puerta giratoria, *f*

swinging /'swɪŋɪŋ/ *a* oscilante; pendiente; rítmico. —*n* balanceo, *m;* oscilación, *f;* vaivén, *m;* ritmo, *m.* **s. stride,** andar rítmico, *m*

swinish /'swainɪʃ/ *a* porcuno, de cerdo; cochino, sucio

swipe /swaip/ *vt* golpear duro; aplastar. —*n* golpe fuerte, *m*

swirl /swɜrl/ *vi* arremolinarse. —*n* remolino, *m*

swish /swɪʃ/ *vt* (of an animal's tail) agitar, mover, menear; (of a cane) blandir; (thrash) azotar. —*vi* silbar; (of water) susurrar; (of a dress, etc.) crujir. —*n* silbo, *m;* (of water) susurro, murmullo, *m;* (of a dress, etc.) crujido, *m*

Swiss /swɪs/ *a* and *n* suizo (-za)

switch /swɪtʃ/ *n* vara, *f;* (riding) látigo, *m;* (of hair) trenza, *f; Elec.* interruptor, *m; Rail.* aguja, *f;* (*Rail.* siding) desviadero, *m.* —*vt* azotar; (a train) desviar; *Elec.* interrumpir; (transfer) trasladar; (of an animal, its tail) remover, mover rápidamente. **to s. off,** (*Elec.* and telephone) cortar; (*Radio.* and *Auto.*) desconectar. **to s. on,** conectar; (a light) poner (la luz); (a radio) encender

switchback /'swɪtʃ,bæk/ *n* subida en zigzag, *f;* (amusement) montañas rusas, *f pl*

switchboard /'swɪtʃ,bɔrd/ *n* cuadro de distribución, *m*

Switzerland /'swɪtsərlənd/ Suiza, *f*

swivel /'swɪvəl/ *n* torniquete, *m;* anillo móvil, *m;* pivote, *m.* —*vi* girar sobre un eje; dar una vuelta. **s.-chair,** silla giratoria, *f.* **s.-door,** puerta giratoria, *f*

swoon /swun/ *vi* desvanecerse, desmayarse. —*n* desmayo, desvanecimiento, *m*

swoop /swup/ *vi* calarse, abatirse; (of robbers, etc.) abalanzarse (sobre). —*n* calada, *f.* **at one fell s.,** de un solo golpe

sword /sɔrd/ *n* espada, *f;* sable, *m.* **to measure swords with,** cruzar espadas con. **to put to the s.,** pasar a cuchillo (a). **s.-arm,** brazo derecho, *m.* **s.-cut,** sablazo, *m.* **s.-dance,** danza de espadas, *f.* **s.-fish,** pez espada, pez sierra, espadarte, *m,* jifia, *f.* **s.-play,** esgrima, *f;* manejo de la espada, *m.* **s.-thrust,** golpe de espada, *m;* estocada, *f*

swordsman /'sɔrdzmən/ *n* espadachín, *m;* esgrimidor, *m*

swordsmanship /'sɔrdzmən,ʃɪp/ *n* manejo de la espada, *m;* esgrima, *f*

sybarite /'sɪbə,rait/ *a* and *n* sibarita, *mf*

sybaritic /,sɪbə'rɪtɪk/ *a* sibarítico, sibarita

sycamore /'sɪkə,mɔr/ *n* sicomoro, *m;* falso plátano, *m*

sycophancy /'sɪkəfənsi/ *n* servilismo, *m*

sycophant /'sɪkəfənt/ *n* sicofanta, *m*

syllabic /sɪ'læbɪk/ *a* silábico

syllable /'sɪləbəl/ *n* sílaba, *f*

syllabus /'sɪləbəs/ *n* programa, *m;* compendio, *m*

syllogism /'sɪlə,dʒɪzəm/ *n* silogismo, *m*

sylph /sɪlf/ *n* sílfide, *f,* silfo, *m;* (woman) sílfide, *f;* (hummingbird) colibrí, *m.* **s.-like,** de sílfide; como una sílfide

sylvan /'sɪlvən/ *a* selvático, silvestre; rústico

symbiosis /,sɪmbi'ousɪs/ *n* simbiosis, *f*

symbol /'sɪmbəl/ *n* símbolo, emblema, *m; Math.* símbolo, *m;* (of rank, etc.) insignia, *f*

symbolical /sɪm'bɒlɪkəl/ *a* simbólico

symbolism /'sɪmbə,lɪzəm/ *n* simbolismo, *m*

symbolist /'sɪmbəlɪst/ *n* simbolista, *mf*

symbolize /'sɪmbə,laiz/ *vt* simbolizar

symmetrical /sɪ'mɛtrɪkəl/ *a* simétrico

symmetry /'sɪmɪtri/ *n* simetría, *f*

sympathetic /,sɪmpə'θɛtɪk/ *a* simpático; compasivo; (of the public, etc.) bien dispuesto. —*n Anat.* gran simpático, *m.* **s. words,** palabras de simpatía, *f pl.* **s. ink,** tinta simpática, *f*

sympathetically /,sɪmpə'θɛtɪkli/ *adv* simpáticamente; con compasión

sympathize /'sɪmpə,θaiz/ *vi* simpatizar (con); (understand) comprender; (condole) compadecerse (de), condolerse (de); dar el pésame

sympathizer /'sɪmpə,θaizər/ *n* partidario (-ia)

sympathy /'sɪmpəθi/ *n* simpatía, *f;* compasión, *f.* **Paul is in s. with their aims,** Pablo está de acuerdo con sus objetos. **Please accept my s.,** (on a bereavement) Le acompaño a Vd. en su sentimiento

symphonic /sɪm'fɒnɪk/ *a* sinfónico

symphony /'sɪmfəni/ *n* sinfonía, *f*

symposium /sɪm'pouziəm/ *n* colección de artículos, *f*

symptom /'sɪmptəm/ *n* síntoma, *m;* señal, *f,* indicio, *m.* **to show symptoms of,** dar indicios de

symptomatic /,sɪmptə'mætɪk/ *a* sintomático

synagogue /'sɪnə,gɒg/ *n* sinagoga, *f*

synchronization /,sɪŋkrənə'zeiʃən/ *n* sincronización, *f*

synchronize /'sɪŋkrə,naiz/ *vi* coincidir, tener lugar simultáneamente; sincronizarse. —*vt* sincronizar

synchronous /'sɪŋkrənəs/ *a* sincrónico

syncopate /'sɪŋkə,peit/ *vt* (*Gram. Mus.*) sincopar

syncopation /,sɪŋkə'peiʃən/ *n Mus.* síncopa, *f*

syndical /'sɪndɪkəl/ *a* sindical

syndicalism /'sɪndɪkə,lɪzəm/ *n* sindicalismo, *m*

syndicalist /'sɪndɪkəlɪst/ *n* sindicalista, *mf*

syndicate /*n.* 'sɪndɪkɪt; *v.* -,keit/ *n* sindicato, *m, vt* sindicar

syndication /,sɪndɪ'keiʃən/ *n* sindicación, *f*

synod /'sɪnəd/ *n Eccl.* sínodo, *m*

synonym /'sɪnənɪm/ *n* sinónimo, *m*

synonymous /sɪ'nɒnəməs/ *a* sinónimo

synopsis /sɪ'nɒpsɪs/ *n* sinopsis, *f*

synoptic /sɪ'nɒptɪk/ *a* sinóptico

syntax /'sɪntæks/ *n* sintaxis, *f*

synthesis /'sɪnθəsɪs/ *n* síntesis, *f*

synthetic /sɪn'θɛtɪk/ *a* sintético

synthetize /'sɪnθə,taiz/ *vt* sintetizar

syphilis /'sɪfəlɪs/ *n* sífilis, *f*

syphilitic /,sɪfə'lɪtɪk/ *a* and *n* sifilítico (-ca)

Syracuse /'sɪrə,kyus, -,kyuz/ Siracusa, *f*

syren /'sairən/ *n.* See **siren**

Syria /'sɪəriə/ Siria, *f*

Syrian /'sɪəriə/ *a* and *n* siríaco (-ca), sirio (-ia)

syringe /sə'rɪndʒ/ *n* jeringa, *f, vt* jeringar

syrup /'sɪrəp, 'sɜr-/ *n* jarabe, *m;* (for bottling fruit, etc.) almíbar, *m*

syrupy /'sɪrəpi, 'sɜr-/ *a* siroposo

system /'sɪstəm/ *n* sistema, *m;* régimen, *m;* método, *m;* (body) organismo, *m.* **He has no s. in his work,** No tiene método en su trabajo. **the nervous s.,** el sistema nervioso. **the feudal s.,** el feudalismo, el sistema feudal

systematic /,sɪstə'mætɪk/ *a* sistemático, metódico

systematically /,sɪstə'mætɪkli/ *adv* sistemáticamente, metódicamente

systematization /,sɪstəmətə'zeiʃən/ *n* sistematización, *f*

systematize /'sɪstəmə,taiz/ *vt* sistematizar

systole /'sɪstə,li/ *n Med.* sístole, *f*

T

t /ti/ *n* (letter) te, *f.* —*a* en T, en forma de T. **T bandage,** vendaje en T, *m.* **T square,** regla T, *f*

tab /tæb/ *n* oreja, *f*

tabby /ˈtæbi/ *n* gato romano, *m;* (female) gata, *f; Inf.* vieja chismosa, *f*

tabernacle /ˈtæbərˌnækəl/ *n* tabernáculo, *m;* templo, *m; Archit.* templete, *m; Eccl.* custodia, *f*

tabes /ˈteibiz/ *n Med.* tabes, *f*

table /ˈteibəl/ *n* mesa, *f;* (food) comida, mesa, *f;* (of the law, weights, measures, contents, etc.) tabla, *f;* (of land) meseta, *f;* (of prices) lista, tarifa, *f.* —*vt* (parliament) poner sobre la mesa; enumerar, apuntar, hacer una lista de. **to clear the t.,** alzar (or levantar) la mesa. **to lay the t.,** cubrir (or poner) la mesa. **to have a table d'hôte meal,** tomar el menú. **to rise from the t.,** levantarse de la mesa. **to sit down at the t.,** ponerse a la mesa. **The tables are turned,** Se volvió la tortilla. **side t.,** aparador, trinchero, *m.* **small t.,** mesilla, *f.* **t. of contents,** tabla de materias, *f,* índice, índice de materias, índice general, *m.* **t.-centrepiece,** centro de mesa, *m.* **t.-cloth,** mantel, *m.* **t.-companion,** comensal, *mf* **t.-knife,** cuchillo de mesa, *m.* **t.-lamp,** quinqué, *m;* lampara de mesa, *f.* **t.-land,** meseta, *f.* **t.-leg,** pata de una mesa, *f.* **t.-linen,** mantelería, *f.* **t.-napkin,** servilleta, *f.* **t.-runner,** camino de mesa, *m.* **t.-spoon,** cuchara para los legumbres, *f.* **t.-talk,** conversación de sobremesa, *f.* **t.-turning,** mesas que dan vueltas, *f pl.* **t.-ware,** artículos para la mesa, *m pl*

tableau /tæˈblou/ *n* cuadro, *m.* **tableaux vivants,** cuadros vivos, *m pl*

tablespoonful /ˈteibəlspunˌfʊl/ *n* cucharada, *f*

tablet /ˈtæblɪt/ *n* tabla, *f;* (with inscription) tarjeta, losa, lápida, *f; Med.* comprimido, *m,* tableta, *f;* (of soap, chocolate) pastilla, *f.* **writing t.,** taco de papel, *m*

tabloid /ˈtæblɔid/ *n* comprimido, *m,* pastilla, *f*

taboo /təˈbu, tæ-/ *n* tabú, *m.* —*a* prohibido, tabú. —*vt* declarar tabú, prohibir

tabor /ˈteibər/ *n Mus.* tamboril, tamborín, *m.* **t. player,** tamborilero, *m*

tabouret /ˌtæbəˈrɛt/ *n* (stool) taburete, *m;* (for embroidery) tambor de bordar, *m; Mus.* tamborilete, *m*

tabulate /ˈtæbyəˌleit/ *vt* resumir en tablas; hacer una lista de, catalogar

tabulation /ˌtæbyəˈleiʃən/ *n* distribución en tablas, *f*

tacit /ˈtæsɪt/ *a* tácito

taciturn /ˈtæsɪˌtɜrn/ *a* taciturno, sombrío, reservado, de pocas palabras

taciturnity /ˌtæsɪˈtɜrnɪti/ *n* taciturnidad, *f;* reserva, *f*

tack /tæk/ *n* (nail) tachuela, puntilla, *f; Sew.* hilván, embaste, *m; Naut.* amura, *f; Naut.* puño de amura, *m; Naut.* bordada, *f; Fig.* cambio de política, *m.* —*vt* clavar con tachuelas; *Sew.* hilvanar, embastar; *Fig.* añadir. —*vi Naut.* virar; *Fig.* cambiar de política, adoptar un nuevo plan de acción. **t. puller,** sacabrocas, *m*

tackle /ˈtækəl/ *n* aparejo, *m;* maniobra, *f; Naut.* cuadernal, *m,* jarcia, *f;* (gear) aparejos, avíos, *m pl;* (football) carga, *f.* —*vt* agarrar, asir; *Fig.* atacar, abordar; (football) cargar; (undertake) emprender; (a problem) luchar con. **t.-block,** polea, *f*

tackling /ˈtæklɪŋ/ *n* aparejo, *m,* maniobra, *f; Naut.* cordaje, *m*

tacky /ˈtæki/ *a* pegajoso, viscoso

tact /tækt/ *n* tacto, *m,* discreción, diplomacia, delicadeza, *f*

tactful /ˈtæktfəl/ *a* lleno de tacto, diplomático, discreto

tactfully /ˈtæktfəli/ *adv* discretamente, diplomáticamente

tactical /ˈtæktɪkəl/ *a* táctico

tactically /ˈtæktɪkli/ *adv* según la táctica; del punto de vista táctico

tactician /tækˈtɪʃən/ *n* táctico, *m*

tactics /ˈtæktɪks/ *n pl* táctica, *f*

tactile /ˈtæktɪl/ *a* táctil; tangible

tactless /ˈtæktlɪs/ *a* que no tiene tacto, sin tacto alguno, indiscreto

tactlessly /ˈtæktlɪsli/ *adv* impolíticamente, indiscretamente

tactlessness *n* falta de tacto, *f*

tadpole /ˈtædpoul/ *n* renacuajo, *m*

taffeta /ˈtæfɪtə/ *n* tafetán, *m*

tag /tæg/ *n* herrete, *m;* (label) marbete, *m,* etiqueta, *f;* (of tail) punta del rabo, *f;* (of boot) tirador de bota, *m;* (game) marro, *m;* (rag) arrapiezo, *m;* (quotation) cita bien conocida, *f;* (of song, poem) refrán, *m.* **to play t.,** jugar al marro

Tagus /ˈteigəs/ el Tajo, *m*

Tahiti /təˈhiti/ Taiti, Tahiti, *m*

tail /teil/ *n* cola, *f,* rabo, *m;* (plait) trenza, *f;* (wisp of hair) mechón, *m;* (of a comet) cola, cabellera, *f;* (of a note in music) rabito, *m;* (of a coat) faldon, *m;* (of a kite) cola, *f;* (of the eye) rabo, *m;* (retinue) séquito, *m,* banda, *f;* (of an aeroplane) cola, *f;* (end) fin, *m;* (of coin) cruz, *f;* (line) fila, cola, *f.* —*vt* seguir de cerca, pisarle (a uno) los talones. **to t. after,** seguir de cerca. **to t. away,** disminuir; desaparecer, perderse de vista. **to t. on,** unir, juntar. **to turn t.,** volver la espalda, poner los pies en polvorosa. **with the t. between the legs,** con el rabo entre piernas. **t.-board,** (of a cart) escalera, *f.* **t.-coat,** frac, *m.* **t.-end,** extremo, *m;* fin, *m;* lo último. **t.-feather,** pena, *f.* **t.-fin,** aleta caudal, *f; Aer.* timón de dirección, *m.* **t.-light,** farol trasero, *m.* **t.-piece,** (of a violin, etc.) cola, *f; Print.* marmosete, culo de lámpara, *m.* **t. spin** *Aer.* barrena de cola, *f.* **t. wind,** viento de cola, *m*

tailed /teild/ *a* de rabo. **big-t.,** rabudo, de cola grande. **long-t.,** rabilargo. **short-t.,** rabicorto

tailless /ˈteillɪs/ *a* rabón, sin rabo

tailor /ˈteilər/ *n* sastre (-ra). **t.-made,** *n* traje sastre, *m, a* de hechura de sastre. **tailor's shop,** sastrería, *f*

tailoring /ˈteilərɪŋ/ *n* sastrería, *f;* (work) corte, *m*

taint /teint/ *n* corrupción, *f;* infección, *f;* (blemish) mancha, *f;* (tinge) dejo, *m.* —*vt* corromper, pervertir; inficionar; (meat) corromper. —*vi* corromperse, inficionarse; (meat) corromperse

take /teik/ *vt* tomar; (receive) aceptar; (remove) quitar; (pick up) coger; (grab) asir, agarrar; *Math.* restar; (carry) llevar; (a person) traer, llevar; (guide) conducir, guiar; (win) ganar; (earn) cobrar, percibir; obtener; (make prisoner) hacer prisionero, prender; (a town, etc.) tomar, rendir, conquistar; (appropriate) apoderarse de, apropiarse; (steal) robar, hurtar; (ensnare) coger, cazar con trampas; (fish) pescar, coger; (a trick, in cards) hacer (una baza); (an illness) contraer, coger; (by surprise) sorprender, coger desprevenido (a); (attract) atraer; (drink) beber; (a meal) tomar; (select) escoger; (hire) alquilar; (suppose) suponer; (use) emplear, usar; (impers., require) necesitarse, hacer falta; (purchase) comprar; (assume) adoptar, asumir; (a leap) dar (un salto); (a walk) dar (un paseo); (a look) echar (un vistazo); (measures) tomar (medidas); (the chair) presidir; (understand) comprender; (a photograph) sacar (una fotografía); (believe) creer; (consider) considerar; (a note) apuntar; (jump over) saltar; (time) tomar, emplear. **I t. size three in shoes,** Calzo el número tres. **to t. to be,** (believe) suponer; (mistake) creer quivocadamente. **to t. (a thing) badly,** tomarlo (or llevarlo) a mal. **The book took me two hours to read,** Necesité dos horas para leer el libro, Leí el libro en dos horas. **And this, I t. it, is Mary?** ¿Y supongo que ésta será María? **to be taken with,** ser entusiasta de; (of persons) estar prendado de. **to t. aback,** desconcertar, coger desprevenido (a). **to t. again,** volver a tomar; llevar otra vez; (a photograph) retratar otra vez. **to t. along,** llevar; traer. **to t. away,** quitar; llevarse. **to t. back,** devolver; (retract) retractar; (receive) recibir (algo) devuelto. **to t. down,** bajar; (a building) derribar; (machinery) desmontar; (hair) deshacerse (el cabello); (swallow) tragar; (in writing) apuntar;

(humble) quitar los humos (a), humillar. **to t. for,** creer, imaginar; (a walk, etc.) llevar a; (mistake) creer erróneamente; tomar por. **Whom do you t. me for?** ¿Por quién me tomas? **to. t. for granted (assume),** dar por descontado, dar por lecho, dar por sentado, dar por supuesto; (underestimate) no hacer caso de, tratar con indiferencia. **t. the lion's share (of),** llevarse la parte del león (de), llevarse la tajada del león (de). **t. shape,** cobrar perfiles más nítidos, estructurarse con más nitidez, ir adquiriendo consistencia, tomar forma. **t. the law into one's own hands,** tomar la justicia por la mano. **to t. from,** privar, quitar de; (subtract) restar; substraer de. **to t. in,** (believe) tragar, creer; (sail) acortar las velas; (deceive) engañar; (lead in) hacer entrar; (accept) recibir, aceptar. **to t. off,** quitar; (surgically) amputar; (one's hat, etc.) quitarse (el sombrero); (eyes) sacar; (take away) llevarse; (mimic) imitar; (ridicule) ridiculizar; (unstick) despegar; (discount) descontar. **to t. on,** emprender; aceptar; (at sports) jugar. **to t. on oneself,** encargarse de, tomar por su cuenta, asumir. **to t. out,** sacar; extraer; (remove) quitar; (outside) llevar fuera; (for a walk) llevar a paseo; (obtain) obtener, sacar; (tire) agotar, rendir. **to t. over,** tomar posesión de; asumir; (show) mostrar, conducir por. **t. the bull by the horns,** ir al toro por los cuernos. **take seriously,** tomar en serio. **to t. up,** subir; (pick up) recoger; tomar; (a challenge, etc.) aceptar; (a dress, etc.) acortar; (absorb) absorber; (of space) ocupar; (of time) ocupar, hacer perder; (buy) comprar; (adopt) dedicarse a; (arrest) arrestar, prender; (criticize) censurar, criticar; (begin) empezar; (resume) continuar

take /teik/ *vi* tomar; (be successful) tener éxito; (of vaccination, etc.) prender; (a good (bad) photograph) salir bien (mal). **to t. after,** salir a, parecerse a; (of conduct) seguir el ejemplo de; **to t. off,** salir; *Aer.* despegar. **to t. on,** *Inf.* lamentarse. **to t. to,** dedicarse a; darse a; (of persons) tomar cariño a; (grow accustomed) acostumbrarse a. **to t. up with,** hacerse amigo de

take /teik/ *n* toma, *f;* cogida, *f; Print.* tomada, *f; Theat.* taquilla, *f.* **t.-in,** engaño, *m.* **t.-off,** *Aer.* (recorrido de) despegue, *m;* caricatura, *f;* sátira, *f*

taker /'teikər/ *n* tomador (-ra)

taking /'teikıŋ/ *n* toma, *f;* secuestro, *m, n pl* **takings,** ingresos, *m pl; Theat.* taquilla, entrada, *f.* —*a* atractivo, encantador; simpático; (of disease) contagioso

talc /tælk/ *n Mineral.* talco, *m*

talcum powder /'tælkəm/ *n* talco, polvo de talco, *m*

tale /teil/ *n* (recital) narración, historia, *f;* relato, *m;* cuento, *m;* leyenda, historia, fábula, *f;* (number) cuenta, *f,* número, *m;* (gossip) chisme, *m.* **old wives' t.,** cuento de viejas, *m.* **to tell a t.,** contar una historia. **to tell tales,** contar cuentos; revelar secretos, chismear

talebearer /'teil,bɛərər/ *n* correveidile, *mf;* chismoso (-sa), soplón (-ona)

talebearing /'teil,bɛarıŋ/ *n* el chismear, *m*

talent /'tælənt/ *n* (coin) talento, *m;* (ability) ingenio, *m;* habilidad, *f.* **the best t. in Spain,** la flor de la cultura española

talented /'tæləntıd/ *a* talentoso, ingenioso

talisman /'tælısmən/ *n* talismán, *m*

talit /'talıs, talit/ taled, *m*

talk /tɔk/ *vi* and *vt* hablar, decir. **to t. business,** hablar de negocios. **to t. for talking's sake,** hablar por hablar. **to t. French,** hablar francés. **to t. nonsense,** decir disparates. **to t. too much,** hablar demasiado; *Inf.* hablar por los codos, irse (a uno) la lengua. **to t. about,** hablar de; conversar sobre. **to t. at,** decir algo a alguien para que lo entienda otro. **Are you talking at me?** ¿Lo dices por mí? **to t. away,** seguir hablando; disipar. **to t. into,** persuadir, inducir (a). **to t. of,** hablar de; charlar sobre. **to t. on,** hablar acerca de (or sobre); (continue) seguir hablando. **to t. out of,** disuadir de. **to t. out of turn,** meterse donde no le llaman, meter la pata. **to t. over,** hablar de; discutir, considerar. **to t. round,** persuadir. **to t. to,** (address) hablar a; (consult) hablar con; (scold) reprender. **to t. to each other,** hablarse. **to t. up,** hablar claro

talk /tɔk/ *n* conversación, *f;* (informal lecture) charla, *f;* (empty words) palabras, *f pl;* (notoriety) escándalo, *m;* rumor, *m.* **There is t. of...,** Se dice que...; Se habla de que. **to give a t.,** dar una charla. **to indulge in small t.,** hablar de cosas sin importancia, hablar de naderías

talkative /'tɔkətıv/ *a* locuaz, gárrulo, hablador, decidor. **to be very t.,** ser muy locuaz; *Inf.* tener mucha lengua

talkativeness /'tɔkətıvnıs/ *n* locuacidad, garrulidad, *f*

talker /'tɔkər/ *n* hablador (-ra), conversador (-ra); (lecturer) orador (-ra); (in a derogatory sense) fanfarrón (-ona), charlatán (-ana). **to be a good t.,** hablar bien, ser buen conversacionista

talking /'tɔkıŋ/ *a* que habla, hablante; (of birds, dolls, etc.) parlero. **to give a good t. to,** dar una peluca (a). **t.-film,** película sonora, *f.* **t.-machine,** fonógrafo, *m*

tall /tɔl/ *a* alto; (of stories) exagerado. **five feet tall,** de cinco pies de altura

tallboy /'tɔl,bɔi/ *n* cómoda alta, *f*

tallness /'tɔlnıs/ *n* altura, *f;* estatura, talla, *f;* (of stories) lo exagerado

tallow /'tælou/ *n* sebo, *m.* **t. candle,** vela de sebo, *f.* **t. chandler,** velero (-ra). **t.-faced,** con cara de color de cera

tallowy /'tæloui/ *a* seboso

tally /'tæli/ *n* tarja, tara, *f;* cuenta, *f.* —*vt* llevar la cuenta (de). —*vi* estar conforme, cuadrar

Talmud /'talmʊd/ *n* Talmud, *m*

Talmudic /tal'mʊdık/ *a* talmúdico

tamable /'teiməbəl/ *a* domable, domesticable

tambour /'tæmbʊr, tæm'bʊr/ *n Mus.* tambor, *m;* (for embroidery) tambor (or bastidor) para bordar, *m*

tambourine /,tæmbə'rin/ *n* pandereta, *f*

tame /teim/ *a* domesticado, manso; (spiritless) sumiso; (dull) aburrido, soso. —*vt* domar, domesticar; (curb) reprimir, gobernar, domar, suavizar. **to grow t.,** domesticarse

tameness /'teimnıs/ *n* mansedumbre, *f;* sumisión, timidez, *f*

tamer /'teimər/ *n* domador (-ra)

taming /'teimıŋ/ *n* domadura, *f.* **The T. of the Shrew,** La Fierecilla Domada

tamp /tæmp/ *vt* apisonar; (in blasting) atacar (un barreno)

tamper /'tæmpər/ *vi* (with) descomponer, estropear; (meddle with) meterse con; (witnesses) sobornar; (documents) falsificar

tampon /'tæmpɒn/ *n Surg.* tampón, tapón, *m, vt* taponar

tan /tæn/ *vt* curtir, adobar; (of sun) tostar, quemar; (slang) zurrar. —*vi* tostarse por el sol. —*n* color café claro, *m;* bronceado, cutis tostado, *m.* —*a* de color café claro

tandem /'tændəm/ *n* tándem, *m*

tang /tæŋ/ *n* (of sword, etc.) espiga, *f;* (flavor) fuerte sabor, *m;* (sound) retintín, *m*

tangent /'tændʒənt/ *a* and *n* tangente *f.* **to go off on a t.,** *Fig.* salir por la tangente

tangerine /,tændʒə'rin/ *a* and *n* tangerino (-na). **t. orange,** naranja mandarina, *f*

tangible /'tændʒəbəl/ *a* tangible; *Fig.* real

Tangier /tæn'dʒıər/ Tánger, *m*

tangle /'tæŋgəl/ *n* embrollo, enredo, nudo, *m;* (of streets) laberinto, *m; Fig.* confusión, *f.* —*vt* embrollar, enmarañar; (entangle) enredar; *Fig.* poner en confusión, complicar. —*vi* enmarañarse

tank /tæŋk/ *n* tanque, depósito (de agua, etc.), *m;* cisterna, *f;* (as a reservoir) aljibe, estanque, *m; Mil.* tanque, carro de asalto, *m*

tankard /'tæŋkərd/ *n* pichel, bock, *m*

tanker /'tæŋkər/ *n* petrolero, *m*

tanned /tænd/ *a* bronceado, quemado por el sol, dorado por el sol

tanner /'tænər/ *n* curtidor, *m;* (slang) medio chelín, *m.* **tanner's scraper,** descarnador, *m.* **tanner's vat,** noque, *m*

tannery /'tænəri/ *n* curtiduría, *f*

tannic /ˈtænɪk/ *a Chem.* tánico. **t. acid,** ácido tánico, *m*

tannin /ˈtænɪn/ *n Chem.* tanino, *m*

tanning /ˈtænɪŋ/ *n* curtido, adobamiento, *m*

tantalize /ˈtæntḷˌaiz/ *vt* tentar, atormentar, provocar

tantalizing /ˈtæntḷˌaizɪŋ/ *a* tentador, atormentador; provocativo

tantamount /ˈtæntəˌmaunt/ *a* equivalente, igual. **to be t. to,** ser equivalente a

tantrum /ˈtæntrəm/ *n* pataleta, rabieta, *f*, berrinche, *m*

taoism /ˈdauɪzəm/ *n* taoísmo, *m*

taoist /ˈdauɪst/ *n* taoísta, *mf*

tap /tæp/ *n* (blow) pequeño golpe, toque ligero, *m;* palmadita, *f;* (for drawing water, etc.) grifo, *m*, llave, *f;* (of a barrel) canilla, *f;* (brew of liquor) clase de vino, *f;* (tap-room) bar con mostrador, *m;* (tool) macho de terraja, *m;* (piece of leather on shoe) tapa, *f; pl* **taps,** *Mil.* toque de apagar las luces, *m.* —*vt* (strike) golpear ligeramente, dar una palmadita a; (pierce) horadar; (a barrel) decentar; *Surg.* hacer una puntura en; (trees) sangrar; *Elec.* derivar (una corriente); (of water, current) tomar; (information) descubrir; (telephone) escuchar las conversaciones telefónicas. —*vi* golpear ligeramente. **to tap at the door,** llamar suavemente a la puerta. **on tap,** en tonel. **screw-tap,** terraja, *f.* **tap-dance,** claqué, *m.* **tap-root,** raíz pivotante, *f*

tape /teip/ *n* (linen) cinta de hilo, *f;* (cotton) cinta de algodón, *f;* (telegraph machine) cinta de papel, *f;* (surveying) cinta para medir, *f.* **adhesive t.,** cinta adhesiva, *f.* **red t.,** balduque, *m; Fig.* burocracia, *f;* formulismo, *m.* **t.-machine,** telégrafo de cotizaciones, bancarias, *m.* **t.-measure,** cinta métrica, *f*

taper /ˈteipər/ *n* bujía, cerilla, *f; Eccl.* cirio, *m.* —*vi* ahusarse, rematar en punta. —*vt* afilar

tapering /ˈteipərɪŋ/ *a* cónico, piramidal; (of fingers) afilado

tapestried /ˈtæpəstrid/ *a* cubierto de tapices, tapizado

tapestry /ˈtæpəstri/ *n* tapiz, *m.* **t. weaver,** tapicero, *m*

tapeworm /ˈteipˌwɜrm/ *n* tenia, lombriz solitaria, *f*

tapioca /ˌtæpiˈoukə/ *n* tapioca, *f*

tapir /ˈteipər/ *n Zool.* danta, *f*

tar /tɑr/ *n* alquitrán, *m*, brea, *f.* —*vt* embrear, alquitranar. **to tar and feather,** emplumar. **coal t.,** alquitrán mineral, *m*

tarantella /ˌtærənˈtɛlə/ *n* tarantela, *f*

tarantula /təˈræntʃələ/ *n* tarántula, *f*

tardily /ˈtardḷi/ *adv* tardíamente; lentamente

tardiness /ˈtardinɪs/ *n* tardanza, lentitud, *f*

tardy /ˈtɑrdi/ *a* (late) tardío; (slow) lento; (reluctant) desinclinado

tare /tɛər/ *n Bot.* yero, *m;* (in the Bible) cizaña, *f; Com.* tara, *f;* (of a vehicle) peso en vacío, *m*

target /ˈtɑrgɪt/ *n* blanco (de tiro), *m;* (shield) rodela, tarja, *f.* **t. practice,** tiro al blanco, *m*

tariff /ˈtærɪf/ *n* tarifa, *f.* **to put a t. on,** tarifar

tarlatan /ˈtɑrlətṇ/ *n* tarlatana, *f*

tarmac /ˈtarmæk/ *n* alquitranado, *m*

tarn /tɑrn/ *n* lago de montaña, *m*

tarnish /ˈtɑrnɪʃ/ *n* deslustre, *m.* —*vt* deslustrar, empañar; *Fig.* obscurecer, manchar. —*vi* deslustrarse

tarpaulin /tɑrˈpɔlɪn, ˈtɑrpəlɪn/ *n* alquitranado, encerado, *m*

tarred /tard/ *a* alquitranado, embreado

tarring /ˈtɑrɪŋ/ *n* embreadura, *f*

tarry /ˈtɑri/ *vi* tardar, detenerse

tart /tɑrt/ *a* ácido, acerbo, agridulce; *Fig.* áspero. —*n* tarta, *f;* pastelillo de fruta, *m*

tartan /ˈtɑrtṇ/ *n Naut.* tartana, *f;* (plaid) tartán, *m*

tartar /ˈtɑrtər/ *n Chem.* tártaro, *m;* (in teeth) sarro, tártaro, *m;* **cream of t.,** (cremor) tártaro, *m.* **t. emetic,** tártaro emético, *m.* **Tartar,** *a* and *n* tártaro (-ra)

Tartary /ˈtɑrtəri/ Tartaria, *f*

tartly /ˈtartli/ *adv* ásperamente, agriamente

tartness /tartnɪs/ *n* acidez, *f; Fig.* aspereza, *f*

task /tæsk/ *n* tarea, labor, *f;* empresa, *f;* misión, *f.* **to take to t.,** regañar, censurar. **t.-force,** (naval or military) contingente, *m*

taskmaster /ˈtæskˌmæstər/ *n* el que señala una tarea; amo, *m*

tassel /ˈtæsəl/ *n* borla, *f;* (of corn) panoja, espiga, *f*

taste /teist/ *n* gusto, *m;* (flavor) sabor, *m;* (specimen) ejemplo, *m*, idea, *f;* (small quantity) un poco, muy poco; (liking) afición, inclinación, *f;* (of drink) sorbo, trago, *m;* (tinge) dejo, *m.* —*vt* (appraise) probar; gustar, percibir el gusto de; (experience) experimentar, conocer. —*vi* tener gusto, tener sabor. **a matter of t.,** cuestión de gusto. **Each to his own t.,** Entre gustos no hay disputa. **He had not tasted a bite,** No había probado bocado. **in bad (good) t.,** de mal (buen) gusto; de mal (buen) tono. **to have a t. for,** ser aficionado a, gustar de. **to t.,** *Cul.* a gusto, a sabor. **to t. of,** tener gusto de, saber a

tasted /ˈteistɪd/ *a* (in compounds) de sabor...

tasteful /ˈteistfəl/ *a* de buen gusto

tastefully /ˈteistfəli/ *adv* con buen gusto

tastefulness /ˈteistfəlnɪs/ *n* buen gusto, *m*

tasteless /ˈteistlɪs/ *a* insípido, soso, insulso; de mal gusto

tastelessness /ˈteistlɪsnɪs/ *n* insipidez, insulsez, *f;* mal gusto, *m*

taster /ˈteistər/ *n* catador, *m;* (vessel) catavino, *m*

tasting /ˈteistɪŋ/ *n* saboreo, *m*, gustación, *f*, *a* (in compounds) de sabor...

tasty /ˈteisti/ *a* apetitoso, sabroso

tatter /ˈtætər/ *n* andrajo, harapo, *m;* jirón, *m.* **to tear in tatters,** hacer jirones

tattered /ˈtætərd/ *a* andrajoso, haraposo

tatting /ˈtætɪŋ/ *n* frivolité, *m*

tattoo /tæˈtu/ *n* tatuaje, *m; Mil.* retreta, *f;* (display) parada militar, *f.* —*vt* tatuar

tattooing /tæˈtuɪŋ/ *n* tatuaje, *m;* tamboreo, *m*

taunt /tɔnt/ *n* mofa, *f*, insulto, escarnio, *m.* —*vt* insultar, atormentar. **to t. with,** echar en cara

taunting /ˈtɔntɪŋ/ *a* insultante, burlón, insolente

tauntingly /ˈtɔntɪŋli/ *adv* burlonamente, insolentemente

Taurus /ˈtɔrəs/ *n* tauro, toro, *m*

taut /tɔt/ *a* tieso, tirante, tenso; en regla; *Naut.* **to make t.,** tesar

tauten /ˈtɔtṇ/ *vt* tesar; poner tieso

tautness /ˈtɔtnɪs/ *n* tensión, *f*

tautological /ˌtɔtḷˈɒdʒɪkəl/ *a* tautológico

tautology /tɔˈtɒlədʒi/ *n* tautología, *f*

tavern /ˈtævərn/ *n* taberna, *f;* (inn) mesón, *m*, posada, *f.* **t.-keeper,** tabernero, *m*

tawdrily /ˈtɔdrɪli/ *adv* llamativamente, de un modo cursi

tawdriness /ˈtɔdrinɪs/ *n* charrería, *f*

tawdry /ˈtɔdri/ *a* chillón, charro, cursi

tawny /ˈtɔni/ *a* leonado

tax /tæks/ *n* contribución, gabela, imposición, *f; Fig.* carga, *f; vt* imponer contribuciones (a); *Law.* tasar; *Fig.* cargar, abrumar. **to tax with,** tachar (de), acusar (de). **direct (indirect) tax,** contribución directa (indirecta), *f.* **tax-collector,** recaudador de contribuciones, *m.* **tax-free,** libre de impuestos. **tax-rate,** tarifa de impuestos, *f*, cupo, *m.* **tax-register,** lista de contribuyentes, *f*

taxable /ˈtæksəbəl/ *a* imponible, sujeto a impuestos

taxation /tækˈseiʃən/ *n* imposición de contribuciones (or impuestos), *f*

tax evasion *n* evasión tributaria, *f*

taxi /ˈtæksi/ *n* taxi, *m.* —*vi* ir en un taxi; *Aer.* correr por tierra. **t. driver,** chófer de un taxi, taxista, *m.* **t. rank, taxi stand,** parada de taxis, *f*

taxidermist /ˈtæksɪˌdɜrmɪst/ *n* taxidermista, *mf*

taxidermy /ˈtæksɪˌdɜrmi/ *n* taxidermia, *f*

taximeter /ˈtæksiˌmitər/ *n* taxímetro, *m*

taxpayer /ˈtæksˌpeiər/ *n* contribuyente, *mf*

taxpaying /ˈtæksˌpeiɪŋ/ *a* tributario, que paga contribuciones

tax reform *n* reforma impositiva, reforma tributaria, *f*

tea /ti/ *n* (liquid) té, *m;* (meal) merienda, *f.* **to have tea,** tomar el té, merendar. **tea-caddy,** bote para té, *m.* **tea-chest,** caja para té, *f.* **tea-cosy,** cubretetera, *m.* **tea-cup,** taza para té, *f.* **tea-dance,** té baile, *m.* **tea-kettle** or **tea-pot,** tetera, *f.* **tea-leaf,** hoja de té, *f.* **tea-party,** reunión para tomar el té, *f.* **tea-room,** salón de té, *m.* **tea-rose,** rosa de té, *f.* **tea-set,** juego de té, *m.* **tea-strainer,** colador de té, *m.* **tea-time,** hora de té, *f.* **tea-urn,** samowar, *m,* tetera para hacer té, *f.* **tea-waggon,** carrito para el té, *m*

teach /titʃ/ *vt* (a person) enseñar, instruir; (a subject) enseñar; (to lecture on) ser profesor de; (a lesson) dar una lección (de). —*vi* (be a teacher) dedicarse a la enseñanza. **to teach at...,** desempeñor una cátedra en... **to t. a person Spanish,** enseñar el castellano a alguien. **to t. how to,** enseñar a (followed by infin.)

teachability /ˌtitʃə'bɪlɪti/ *n* docilidad, *f*

teachable /'titʃəbəl/ *a* educable; dócil

teacher /'titʃər/ *n* preceptor, *m;* profesor, maestro, *m.* **woman t.,** profesora, maestra, *f*

teaching /'titʃɪŋ/ *n* enseñanza, *f;* (belief) doctrina, *f, a* docente. **t. profession,** magisterio, *m*

teaching method *n* método didáctico, *f*

teak /tik/ *n Bot.* teca, *f;* (wood) madera de teca, *f*

team /tim/ *n* (of horses) tiro, *m;* (of oxen, mules) par, *m,* pareja, yunta, *f; Sports.* partido, equipo, *m;* compañía, *f,* grupo, *m.* —*vt* enganchar, uncir. **t.-work,** cooperación, *f*

teamster /'timstər/ *n* gañán, *m*

tear /tɪər/ *vt* rasgar; romper; lacerar; (in pieces) hacer pedazos, despedazar; (scratch) arañar; *Fig.* atormentar. **to t. asunder,** romper; desmembrar. **to t. away,** arrancar, quitar violentamente. **to t. down,** derribar, echar abajo. **to t. off,** arrancar; desgajar. **to t. oneself away,** arrancarse, desgarrarse. **to t. one's hair,** arrancarse los pelos, mesarse. **to t. open,** abrir apresuradamente. **to t. up,** hacer pedazos; (uproot) arrancar, desarraigar.

tear /tɛər/ *vi* rasgarse; romper; correr precipitadamente. **to t. along,** correr rápidamente (por). **to t. away,** marcharse corriendo. **to t. down,** bajar corriendo. **to t. into,** entrar corriendo en. **to t. off,** irse precipitadamente, marcharse corriendo. **to t. up,** subir corriendo; llegar corriendo; atravesar rápidamente

tear /tɛər/ *n* lágrima, *f;* (drop) gota, *f.* **with tears in one's eyes,** con lágrimas en los ojos. **to shed tears,** llorar, lagrimear. **to wipe away one's tears,** secarse las lágrimas. **t.-drop,** lágrima, *f.* **t.-duct,** conductor lacrimal, *m.* **t.-gas,** gas lacrimante, *m.* **t.-stained,** mojado de lágrimas

tear /tɛər/ *n* (rent) rasgón, *m*

tearful /'tɪərfəl/ *a* lloroso, lacrimoso

tearfully /'tɪərfəli/ *adv* con lágrimas en los ojos

tearing *n* rasgadura, *f,* desgarro, *m*

tearjerker /'tɪərˌdʒ3rkər/ *n* drama lacrimón, *m*

tease /tiz/ *vt* (card) cardar; (annoy) fastidiar, irritar, molestar; (chaff) tomar el pelo (a), embromar; (pester) importunar. —*n* bromista, *mf*

teasel /'tizəl/ *n Bot.* cardencha, *f, vt* cardar

teaser /'tizər/ *n* (problem) rompecabezas, *m;* (person) bromista, *mf*

teaspoon /'tiˌspun/ *n* cucharita, *f*

teaspoonful /'tispunˌfʊl/ *n* cucharadita, *f*

teat /tit, tɪt/ *n* pezón, *m;* (of animals) teta, *f*

technical /'tɛknɪkəl/ *a* técnico. **t. offence,** *Law.* cuasidelito, *m.* **t. school,** escuela industrial, *f*

technicality /ˌtɛknɪ'kælɪti/ *n* carácter técnico, *m;* tecnicismo, *m;* detalle técnico, *m*

technician /tɛk'nɪʃən/ *n* técnico, *m*

technicolor /'tɛknɪˌkʌlər/ *n* tecnicolor, *m*

technique /tɛk'nik/ *n* técnica, *f;* ejecución, *f;* mecanismo, *m*

technological /ˌtɛknə'lɒdʒɪkəl/ *a* tecnológico

technologist /tɛk'nɒlədʒɪst/ *n* tecnólogo, *m*

technology /tɛk'nɒlədʒi/ *n* tecnología, *f*

teddy bear /'tɛdi/ *n* osito de trapo, *m*

tedious /'tidiəs/ *a* aburrido, tedioso, pesado

tediously /'tidiəsli/ *adv* aburridamente

tediousness /'tidiəsnɪs/ *n* aburrimiento, *m,* pesadez, *f*

tedium /'tidiəm/ *n* tedio, *m,* monotonía, *f*

tee /ti/ *n Sports.* meta, *f;* (golf) tee, *m;* (letter) te, *f;* cosa en forma de te, *f.* —*vt* (golf) colocar la pelota en el tee

teem /tim/ *vi* rebosar (de), abundar (en); pulular, hormiguear, estar lleno (de); (with rain) diluviar

teeming /'timɪŋ/ *a* prolífico, fecundo. **t. with,** abundante en, lleno de

teens /tinz/ *n pl* números y años desde trece hasta diez y nueve; edad de trece a diez y nueve años de edad. **to be still in one's t.,** no haber cumplido aún los veinte

teeter /'titər/ *vi* balancearse, columpiarse

teethe /tið/ *vi* endentecer, echar los dientes

teething /'tiðɪŋ/ *n* dentición, *f.* **t.-ring,** chupador, *m*

teetotal /ti'toutl̩/ *a* abstemio

teetotalism /ti'toutl̩ˌɪzəm/ *n* abstinencia completa de bebidas alcohólicas, *f*

teetotaller /'tiˌtoutlər/ *n* abstemio (-ia)

teetotum /ti'toutəm/ *n* perinola, *f*

telecast /'tɛlɪˌkæst/ *vt* telefundir

telecommunication /ˌtɛlɪkəˌmyunɪ'keɪʃən/ *n* telecomunicación, *f*

telegram /'tɛlɪˌgræm/ *n* telegrama, *m*

telegraph /'tɛlɪˌgræf/ *n* telégrafo, *m.* —*vi* telegrafiar; *Fig.* hacer señas. —*vt* telegrafiar, enviar por telégrafo. **t. line,** línea telegráfica, *f.* **t. office,** central de telégrafos, *f.* **t. pole,** poste telegráfico, *m.* **t. wire,** hilo telegráfico, *m*

telegraphic /ˌtɛlɪ'græfɪk/ *a* telegráfico

telegraphist /tə'lɛgrəfɪst/ *n* telegrafista, *mf*

telegraphy /tə'lɛgrəfi/ *n* telegrafía, *f.* **wireless t.,** telegrafía sin hilos, *f*

telemetry /tə'lɛmɪtri/ *n* telemetría, *f*

teleology /ˌtɛli'ɒlədʒi/ *n* teleología, *f*

telepathic /ˌtɛlə'pæθɪk/ *a* telepático

telepathy /tə'lɛpəθi/ *n* telepatía, *f*

telephone /'tɛləˌfoun/ *n* teléfono, *m.* —*vi* telefonear. —*vt* telefonear, llamar por teléfono. **to be on the t.,** (speaking) estar communicando; (of subscribers) tener teléfono. **dial t.,** teléfono automático, *m.* **t. call,** comunicación telefónica, *f;* conversación telefónica, *f.* **t. call box,** teléfono público, *m.* **t. directory,** guía de teléfonos, *f.* **t. exchange,** central telefónica, *f.* **t. number,** número de teléfono, *m.* **t. operator,** telefonista, *mf* **t. receiver,** receptor telefónico, *m.* **t. wire,** hilo telefónico, *m*

telephonic /ˌtɛlə'fɒnɪk/ *a* telefónico

telephonist /tə'lɛfənɪst/ *n* telefonista, *mf*

telephony /tə'lɛfəni/ *n* telefonía, *f.* **wireless t.,** telefonía sin hilos, *f*

teleprinter /'tɛləˌprɪntər/ *n* teletipo, *m*

telescope /'tɛləˌskoup/ *n* telescopio, catalejo, *m.* —*vt* enchufar. —*vi* enchufarse, meterse una cosa dentro de otra

telescopic /ˌtɛlə'skɒpɪk/ *a* telescópico; de enchufe

televise /'tɛləˌvaiz/ *vt* trasmitir por televisión

television /'tɛləˌvɪʒən/ *n* televisión, *f.* **on television,** por televisión. **I saw her on television,** La vi por televisión

television series *n* serie televisiva, *f*

tell /tɛl/ *vt* contar, narrar; decir; revelar; expresar; (the time, of clocks) marcar; (inform) comunicar, informar; (show) indicar, manifestar; (explain) explicar; distinguir; (order) mandar; (compute) contar. —*vi* decir; (have effect) producir efecto. **We cannot t.,** No sabemos. **Who can t.?** ¿Quién sabe? **T. that to the marines!;** Cuéntaselo a tu tía! **to t. its own tale,** hacer ver por sí mismo lo que hay. **to t. again,** volver a decir; contar otra vez. **to t. off,** regañar, reñir; (on a mission) despachar, mandar. **to t. on,** delatar. **to t. upon,** afectar

teller /'tɛlər/ *n* narrador (-ra); (of votes) escrutador (-ra) de votos; (payer) pagador; (bank) cajero (-ra), *m*

telling /'tɛlɪŋ/ *a* notable, significante. —*n* narración, *f*

telltale /'tɛlˌteil/ *n* chismoso (-sa), soplón (-ona); (informer) acusón (-ona); *Fig.* indicio, *m,* señal, *f, a* revelador

temerity /tə'mɛrɪti/ *n* temeridad, *f*

temper /'tɛmpər/ *n* (of metals) temple, *m;* (nature) naturaleza, *f,* carácter, *m;* espíritu, *m;* (mood) humor, *m;* (anger) mal genio, *m.* —*vt* (of metals) templar; moderar, mitigar; mezclar. —*vi* templarse. **bad (good) t.,** mal (buen) humor. **to keep one's t.,** no enojarse, no impacientarse. **to lose one's t.,** enojarse, perder la paciencia

tempera /'tɛmpərə/ *n Art.* templa, *f.* **in t.,** al temple, *m*

temperament /'tɛmpərəmənt, -prəmənt/ *n* tempera-

mento, *m;* modo de ser, natural, *m,* naturaleza, índole, *f; Mus.* temple, *m*
temperamental /ˌtɛmpərəˈmɛntl̩, -prəˈmɛn-/ *a* natural, innato; caprichoso
temperamentally /ˌtɛmpərəˈmɛntl̩i, -prəˈmɛn- *adv* por naturaleza
temperance /ˈtɛmpərəns/ *n* moderación, templanza, *f;* sobriedad, abstinencia, *f*
temperate /ˈtɛmpərɪt/ *a* moderado; sobrio; (of regions) templado. **t. zone,** zona templada, *f*
temperately /ˈtɛmpərɪtli/ *adv* sobriamente
temperateness /ˈtɛmpərɪtnɪs/ *n* moderación, sobriedad, mesura, *f;* (of regions) templanza, *f*
temperature /ˈtɛmpərətʃər/ *n* temperatura, *f.* **to have a t.,** tener fiebre
tempered /ˈtɛmpərd/ *a* de humor..., de genio... **to be good (bad) t.,** ser de buen (mal) humor
tempering /ˈtɛmpərɪŋ/ *n* temperación, *f*
tempest /ˈtɛmpɪst/ *n* tempestad, borrasca, *f,* temporal, *m; Fig.* tormenta, *f*
tempest in a teapot borrasca en un vaso de agua, *m*
tempestuous /tɛmˈpɛstʃuəs/ *a* tempestuoso, borrascoso; *Fig.* impetuoso, violento
tempestuousness /tɛmˈpɛstʃuəsnɪs/ *n* lo tempestuoso; *Fig.* impetuosidad, violencia, *f*
temple /ˈtɛmpəl/ *n* templo, *m; Anat.* sien, *f*
tempo /ˈtɛmpou/ *n Mus.* tiempo, *m*
temporal /ˈtɛmpərəl/ *a* temporal; (transient) transitorio, fugaz; *Anat.* temporal. *—n Anat.* hueso temporal, *m*
temporality /ˌtɛmpəˈrælɪti/ *n* temporalidad, *f*
temporarily /ˌtɛmpəˈrɛərəli/ *adv* provisionalmente
temporariness /ˈtɛmpəˌrɛrinɪs/ *n* interinidad, *f*
temporary /ˈtɛmpəˌrɛri/ *a* provisional, interino
temporize /ˈtɛmpəˌraiz/ *vi* ganar tiempo; contemporizar
temporizing /ˈtɛmpəˌraizɪŋ/ *n* contemporización, *f, a* contemporizador
tempt /tɛmpt/ *vt* tentar; atraer, seducir
temptation /tɛmpˈteiʃən/ *n* tentación, *f;* aliciente, atractivo, *m*
tempter /ˈtɛmptər/ *n* tentador (-ra)
tempting /ˈtɛmptɪŋ/ *a* tentador, atrayente; seductor
ten /tɛn/ *a* diez; (of the clock) las diez, *f pl;* (of age) diez años, *m pl, n* diez, *m;* (a round number) decena, *f;* **ten-millionth,** *a* and *n* diezmillonésimo *m.* **ten months old,** diezmesino. **ten syllable,** decasílabo. **ten thousand,** *a* and *n* diez mil *m.* **There are ten thousand soldiers,** Hay diez mil soldados. **ten-thousandth,** *a* and *n* diezmilésimo *m*
tenable /ˈtɛnəbəl/ *a* sostenible, defendible
tenacious /təˈneiʃəs/ *a* tenaz; (stubborn) porfiado, obstinaz, terco; (sticky) adhesivo. **to be t. of life,** estar muy apegado a la vida
tenaciously /təˈneiʃəsli/ *adv* tenazmente; porfiadamente
tenacity /təˈnæsɪti/ *n* tenacidad, *f;* porfía, *f;* tesón, *m*
tenancy /ˈtɛnənsi/ *n* inquilinato, *m;* tenencia, *f*
tenant /ˈtɛnənt/ *n* arrendatario (-ia), inquilino (-na); habitante, *m;* morador (-ra)
tench /tɛntʃ/ *n Ichth.* tenca, *f*
tend /tɛnd/ *vt* cuidar, atender; guardar; vigilar. *—vi* tender; inclinarse (a), propender (a)
tendency /ˈtɛndənsi/ *n* tendencia, inclinación, propensión, *f;* proclividad, *f*
tendentious /tɛnˈdɛnʃəs/ *a* tendencioso
tender /ˈtɛndər/ *n* guardián, *m; Com.* oferta, propuesta, *f; Naut.* falúa, *f;* (of a railway engine) ténder, *m.* **legal t.,** moneda corriente, *f*
tender /ˈtɛndər/ *a* tierno; delicado; (of conscience) escrupuloso; (of a subject) espinoso; compasivo, afectuoso, sensible; muelle, blando. **t.-hearted,** compasivo, tierno de corazón
tender /ˈtɛndər/ *vt* ofrecer; dar; presentar. *—vi* hacer una oferta. **to t. condolences,** dar el pésame. **to t. one's resignation,** presentar la dimisión. **to t. thanks,** dar las gracias
tenderly /ˈtɛndərli/ *adv* tiernamente
tenderness /ˈtɛndərnɪs/ *n* ternura, *f;* sensibilidad, *f;* delicadeza, *f;* dulzura, *f;* indulgencia, *f;* compasividad, benevolencia, *f;* escrupulosidad, *f;* mimo, cariño, *m*
tendon /ˈtɛndən/ *n Anat.* tendón, *m.* **t. of Achilles,** tendón de Aquiles, *m*
tenement /ˈtɛnəmənt/ *n* casa de vecindad, *f;* vivienda, *f; Poet.* morada, *f*
Teneriffe /ˌtɛnəˈrif/ Tenerife, *f*
tenet /ˈtɛnɪt/ *n* principio, dogma, *m,* doctrina, *f*
tenfold /*a.*ˈtɛnˌfould; *adv.* -ˈfould/ *a* décuplo. *—adv* diez veces
tennis /ˈtɛnɪs/ *n* tenis, *m.* **to play t.,** jugar al tenis. **t. ball,** pelota de tenis, *f.* **t. court,** campo de tenis, *m,* cancha de tenis, pista de tenis, *f.* **tennis club,** club de tenis, *m.* **t. racket,** raqueta de tenis, *f;* **tennis shoe,** zapatilla de tenis, *f*
tenon /ˈtɛnən/ *n* espiga, *f, vt* espigar
tenor /ˈtɛnər/ *n* curso, *m;* tenor, contenido, *m; Mus.* tenor, *m; Mus.* alto, *m;* (mus. instrument) viola, *f.* *—a Mus.* de tenor
tense /tɛns/ *n Gram.* tiempo, *m.* *—a* tirante, estirado, tieso; tenso
tenseness /ˈtɛnsnɪs/ *n* tirantez, *f;* tensión, *f*
tensile /ˈtɛnsəl/ *a* tensor; extensible
tension /ˈtɛnʃən/ *n* tensión, *f; Elec.* voltaje, *m,* tensión, *f;* (of sewing-machine) tensahílo, *m.* **state of t.,** (diplomatic) estado de tirantez, *m*
tent /tɛnt/ *n* tienda (de campaña), *f;* (bell) pabellón, *m; Surg.* tienda, *f.* **oxygen t.,** tienda oxígena, *f.* **to pitch tents,** armar las tiendas de campaña; acamparse. **to strike tents,** plegar tiendas. **t. fly,** toldo de tienda, *m.* **t. maker,** tendero, *m.* **t. peg,** clave que sujeta las cuerdas de una tienda, *f.* **t. pole,** mástil (or montante) de tienda, *m*
tentacle /ˈtɛntəkəl/ *n* tentáculo, *m*
tentative /ˈtɛntətɪv/ *a* tentativo, interino, provisional, de prueba, *n* tentativa, *f,* ensayo, *m*
tentatively /ˈtɛntətɪvli/ *adv* por vía de ensayo, experimentalmente
tenth /tɛnθ/ *a* décimo; (of monarchs) diez; (of the month) (el) diez. *—n* décimo, *m;* (part) décima parte, *f; Mus.* decena, *f*
tenthly /ˈtɛnθli/ *adv* en décimo lugar
tenuity /təˈnuɪti/ *n* tenuidad, *f;* sutilidad, *f;* delgadez, *f*
tenuous /ˈtɛnyuəs/ *a* tenue; sutil; delgado; fino
tenure /ˈtɛnyər/ *n* tenencia, posesión, *f;* (duration) duración, *f;* (of office) administración, *f*
tepid /ˈtɛpɪd/ *a* tibio
tepidity /tɛˈpɪdɪti/ *n* tibieza, *f*
tercentenary /ˌtɜrsɛnˈtɛnəri/ *n* tercer centenario, *m*
tercet /ˈtɜrsɪt/ *n* terceto, *m*
term /tɜrm/ *n* (limit) límite, fin, *m;* (period) plazo, tiempo, período, *m;* (schools, universities) trimestre, *m;* (*Math. Law. Logic.*) término, *m;* (word) expresión, palabra, *f pl.* **terms,** (conditions) condiciones, *f pl;* (charges) precios, *m pl,* tarifa, *f;* (words) términos, *m pl,* palabras, *f pl.* *—vt* llamar, calificar. **for a t. of years,** por un plazo de años. **in plain terms,** en palabras claras. **on equal terms,** en condiciones iguales. **to be on bad (good) terms with,** estar en (or tener) malas (buenas) relaciones con. **to come to terms,** llegar a un acuerdo; hacer las paces. **What are your terms?** ¿Cuáles son sus condiciones? (price) ¿Cuáles son sus precios? **terms of sale,** condiciones de venta, *f pl*
termagant /ˈtɜrməgənt/ *n* arpía, fiera, *f*
terminable /ˈtɜrmənəbəl/ *a* terminable
terminal /ˈtɜrmənl̩/ *a* terminal, final; (of schools, universities) trimestre. *—n* término, *m; Elec.* borne, *m;* (schools, universities) examen de fin de trimestre, *m;* (railway) estación terminal, *f;* (*Archit.* and figure) término, *m; Archit.* remate, *m*
terminate /ˈtɜrməˌneit/ *vt* limitar; terminar, concluir, poner fin (a). *—vi* terminarse, concluirse (por); cesar
termination /ˌtɜrməˈneiʃən/ *n* terminación, conclusión, *f;* fin, *m; Gram.* terminación, *f;* cabo, remate, *m*
terminology /ˌtɜrməˈnɒlədʒi/ *n* nomenclatura, terminología, *f*
terminus /ˈtɜrmənəs/ *n* (railway) estación terminal, *f;* (*Archit.* and figure) término, *m; Archit.* remate, *m; Myth.* Término
termite /ˈtɜrmait/ *n Ent.* termita, *m*

term paper *n* trabajo de examen, *m*
terms of trade *n* relación de los precios de intercambio, *f*
terrace /ˈtɛrəs/ *n* terraza, *f, vt* terraplenar
terraced /ˈtɛrəst/ *a* en terrazas; con terrazas
terracotta /ˌtɛrəˈkɒtə/ *n* terracota, *f*
terrain /təˈrein/ *n* terreno, campo, *m*, región, *f*
terrapin /ˈtɛrəpɪn/ *n* tortuga de agua dulce, *f*
terrestrial /təˈrɛstriəl/ *a* terrestre, terrenal
terrible /ˈtɛrəbəl/ *a* terrible, pavoroso, espantoso; *Inf.* tremendo
terribleness /ˈtɛrəbəlnɪs/ *n* terribilidad, *f*, lo horrible
terrier /ˈtɛriər/ *n* terrier, *m; Inf.* soldado del ejército territorial, *m*
terrific /təˈrɪfɪk/ *a* espantoso, terrible; *Inf.* atroz, tremendo
terrify /ˈtɛrəˌfai/ *vt* aterrorizar, espantar, horrorizar
terrifying /ˈtɛrəˌfaiɪŋ/ *a* aterrador, espantoso
territorial /ˌtɛrɪˈtɔriəl/ *a* territorial. —*n* soldado del ejército territorial, *m*
territoriality /ˌtɛrɪˌtɔriˈælɪti/ *n* territorialidad, *f*
territory /ˈtɛrɪˌtɔri/ *n* región, comarca, *f;* (state) territorio, *m;* jurisdicción, *f.* **mandated territory,** territorio bajo mandato, *m pl*
terror /ˈtɛrər/ *n* terror, pavor, espanto, *m.* **the Reign of T.,** el Reinado del Terror, *m.* **t.-stricken,** espantado, muerto de miedo
terrorism /ˈtɛrəˌrɪzəm/ *n* terrorismo, *m*
terrorist /ˈtɛrərɪst/ *n* terrorista, *m*
terrorization /ˌtɛrərəˈzeiʃən/ *n* aterramiento, *m*
terrorize /ˈtɛrəˌraiz/ *vt* aterrorizar
terse /tɜrs/ *a* conciso, sucinto; seco, brusco
tersely /ˈtɜrsli/ *adv* concisamente; secamente
terseness /ˈtɜrsnɪs/ *n* concisión, *f;* brusquedad, *f*
tertiary /ˈtɜrʃiˌɛri, -ʃəri/ *a* tercero; *Geol.* terciario. —*n Eccl.* terciario, *m*
tessera /ˈtɛsərə/ *n* tesela, *f*
test /tɛst/ *n* (proof) prueba, *f;* examen, *m;* investigación, *f;* (standard) criterio, *m,* piedra de toque, *f; Chem.* análisis, *m;* (trial) ensayo, *m; Zool.* concha, *f.* —*vt Chem.* ensayar; probar, poner a prueba; examinar; (eyes) graduar (la vista). **to put to the t.,** poner a prueba. **to stand the t.,** soportar la prueba. **t. match,** partido internacional de cricket, *m.* **t. meal,** *Med.* comida de prueba, *f.* **t. pilot,** *Aer.* piloto de pruebas, *m.* **t. tube,** tubo de ensayo, *m*
testament /ˈtɛstəmənt/ *n* testamento, *m.* **the New T.,** el Nuevo Testamento, *m.* **the Old T.,** el Antiguo Testamento, *m*
testamentary /ˌtɛstəˈmɛntəri/ *a* testamentario
testate /ˈtɛsteit/ *a* testado
testator /ˈtɛsteitər/ *n* testador, *m,* (**testatrix,** testadora, *f*)
testicle /ˈtɛstɪkəl/ *n* testículo, *m*
testification /ˌtɛstəfɪˈkeiʃən/ *n* testificación, *f*
testify /ˈtɛstəˌfai/ *vt* and *vi* declarar, atestar; *Law.* atestiguar, testificar, dar fe
testily /ˈtɛstəli/ *adv* malhumoradamente
testimonial /ˌtɛstəˈmouniəl/ *n* recomendación, *f;* certificado, *m;* (tribute) homenaje, *m*
testimony /ˈtɛstəˌmouni/ *n* testimonio, *m,* declaración, *f;* (proof) prueba, *f.* **in t. whereof,** en fe de lo cual. **to bear t.,** atestar
testiness /ˈtɛstinɪs/ *n* mal humor, *m,* irritación, *f*
testing grounds /ˈtɛstɪŋ/ *n* campo de experimentación, campo de pruebas, *m*
testy /ˈtɛsti/ *a* enojadizo, irritable, irascible, quisquilloso
tetanus /ˈtɛtn̩əs/ *n* tétano, *m*
tether /ˈtɛðər/ *n* traba, atadura, maniota, *f.* —*vt* atar con una correa. **to be at the end of one's t.,** acabarse la resistencia; acabarse la paciencia
Teuton /ˈtutn̩/ *n* teutón (-ona)
Teutonic /tuˈtɒnɪk/ *a* teutónico
text /tɛkst/ *n* texto, *m;* (subject) tema, *m;* (motto) lema, *m;* (of a musical composition) letra, *f.* **t.-book,** libro de texto, *m*
textile /ˈtɛkstail/ *a* textil, de tejer. —*n* textil, *m,* materia textil, *f;* tejido, *m*
textual /ˈtɛkstʃuəl/ *a* textual
texture /ˈtɛkstʃər/ *n* (material and *Biol.*) tejido, *m;* textura, *f*
Thailand /ˈtaiˌlænd/ Tailandia, *f*
thalamus /ˈθæləməs/ *n* (*Anat., Bot.*) tálamo, *m*
Thames, the /tɛmz/ *n* el Támesis, *m.* **to set the T. on fire,** descubrir la pólvora
than /ðæn, ðɛn; *unstressed* ðən, ən/ *conjunc* que; (between **more, less,** or **fewer** and a number) de; (in comparisons of inequality) que, but que becomes(*a*) del (de la, de los, de las) que if the point of comparison is a noun in the principal clause, which has to be supplied mentally to fill up the ellipsis; (*b*) de lo que if there is no noun to act as a point of comparison, e.g. **He was older than I thought,** Era más viejo de lo que yo pensaba. **They have less than they deserve,** Tienen menos de lo que merecen. **They lose more money than (the money) they earn,** Pierden más dinero del que ganan. **He will meet with more opposition than he thought,** Va a encontrar más oposición de la que pensaba. **I have more books than you,** Tengo más libros que tú. **She has fewer than nine and more than five,** Ella tiene menos de nueve y más de cinco
thank /θæŋk/ *vt* agradecer, dar las gracias (a). **to t. for,** agradecer. **I will t. you to be more polite,** Le agradecería que fuese más cortés. **He has himself to t. for it,** Él mismo tiene la culpa de ello. **No, t. you,** No, muchas gracias. **T. goodness!** ¡Gracias a Dios!
thank /θæŋks/ *n* (now in pl. only, **thanks**) gracias, *f pl.* **a vote of thanks,** un voto de gracias. **Many thanks!** ¡Muchas gracias! **to return thanks,** dar las gracias. **thanks to,** merced a, debido a. **thanks to you,** gracias a tí. **t.-offering,** ofrecimiento en acción de gracias, *m*
thankful /ˈθæŋkfəl/ *a* agradecido. **I am t. to see,** Me alegro de ver, Me es grato ver
thankfully /ˈθæŋkfəli/ *adv* con gratitud, agradecido
thankfulness /ˈθæŋkfəlnɪs/ *n* agradecimiento, *m;* gratitud, *f*
thankless /ˈθæŋklɪs/ *a* ingrato; desagradecido; desagradable
thanksgiving /ˌθæŋksˈgɪvɪŋ/ *n* acción de gracias, *f.* **t. service,** servicio de acción de gracias, *m.* **Thanksgiving (Day),** *n* día de acción de dar gracias, día de gracias, *m*
that /ðæt; *unstressed* ðət/ *dem a* ese, *m;* esa, *f;* aquel, *m;* aquella, *f, dem. pron* ése, *m;* ésa, *f;* eso, *neut;* aquél, *m;* aquélla, *f;* aquello, *neut;* (standing for a noun) el, *m;* la, *f;* lo, *neut* **All t. there is,** Todo lo que hay. **His temperament is t. of his mother,** Su temperamento es el de su madre. **We have not come to t. yet,** Todavía no hemos llegado a ese punto. **T. is what I want to know,** Eso es lo que quiero saber. **with t.,** con eso; (thereupon) en eso. **Go t. way,** Vaya Vd. por allí; Tome Vd. aquel camino. **T. is to say...,** Es decir.... **What do you mean by t.?** ¿Qué quieres decir con eso? **The novel is not as bad as all t.,** La novela no es tan mala como tú piensas (*or* como dicen, etc.)
that /ðæt; *unstressed* ðət/ *pron rel* que; el cual, *m;* la cual, *f;* lo cual, *neut;* (of persons) a quien, *mf;* a quienes, *mf pl*; (with from) de quien, *mf;* de quienes, *mf pl*; (of place) donde. **The letter t. I sent you,** la carta que te mandé. **The box t. John put them in,** la caja en la cual los puso Juan. **The last time t. I saw her,** La última vez que la vi
that /ðæt; *unstressed* ðət/ *conjunc* que; (of purpose) para que, afin de que, (before infin.) para, (because) porque. **O t. he would come!** ¡Ojalá que viniese! **so t.,** para que; (before infin.) para; (as a result) de manera que; de modo que. **It is better t. he should not come,** Es mejor que no venga. **now t.,** ahora que
thatch /θætʃ/ *n* barda, *f, vt* bardar
thaw /θɔ/ *n* deshielo, *m.* —*vt* deshelar; derretir. —*vi* deshelarse; derretirse
the /*stressed* ði; *unstressed before a consonant* ðə, *unstressed before a vowel* ði/ *def art* el, *m;* la, *f;* lo, *neut;* los, *m pl*; las, *f pl*; (before feminine sing. noun beginning with stressed a or ha) el; (untranslated between the name and number of a monarch, pope, ruler, e.g. *Charles the Tenth,* Carlos diez). —*adv* (before a comparative) cuanto, tanto más. **at the** or

to the, al, *m,* (also before feminine sing. noun beginning with a or ha); a la, *f;* a lo, *neut;* a los, *m pl;* a las, *f pl.* **from the** or **of the,** del, *m,* (also before feminine sing. noun beginning with stressed a or ha); de la, *f;* de lo, *neut;* de los, *m pl;* de las, *f pl.* **the one,** see **one. The sooner the better,** Cuanto antes mejor. **The room will be all the warmer,** El cuarto estará tanto más caliente

theater /'θiətər/ *n* teatro, *m;* (lecture) anfiteatro, *m;* (drama) teatro, *m,* obra dramática, *f;* (scene) teatro, *m,* escena, *f.* **t. attendant,** acomodador (-ra)

theater-in-the-round /'θiətərınðə'raund/ *n* teatro circular, teatro en círculo, *m*

Theatine /θi'ətin, ˌɹtın/ *a* and *n Eccl.* teatino *m*

theatrical /θi'ætrıkəl/ *a* teatral. —*n pl* **theatricals,** funciones teatrales, *f pl.* **amateur theatricals,** función de aficionados, *f.* **t. company,** compañía de teatro, *f.* **t. costumier,** mascarero (-ra), alquilador (-ra) de disfraces. **t. manager,** empresario de teatro, *m*

theatricality /θiˌætrı'kælıti/ *n* teatralidad, *f*

Theban *a* and *n* tebeo (-ea), tebano (-na)

Thebes /θibz/ Tebas, *f*

thee /ði/ *pers pron* te; (after prep.) tí. **with t.,** contigo

theft /θɛft/ *n* robo, hurto, *m*

their /ðɛər; *unstressed* ðər/ *poss a* su, *mf sing;* sus, *pl;* de ellos, *m pl;* de ellas, *f pl.* **They have t. books,** Tienen sus libros. **I have t. books,** Tengo los libros de ellos

theirs /ðɛərz/ *poss pron* (el) suyo, *m;* (la) suya, *f;* (los) suyos, *m pl;* (las) suyas, *f pl;* de ellos, *m pl;* de ellas, *f pl.* **These hats are t.,** Estos sombreros son los suyos

them /ðɛm; *unstressed* ðəm, əm/ *pers pron* ellos, *m pl;* ellas, *f pl;* (as object of a verb) los, *m pl;* las, *f pl;* (to them) les

thematic /θi'mætık/ *a* temático

theme /θim/ *n* tema, asunto, *m;* tesis, *f; Mus.* tema, motivo, *m*

themselves /ðəm'sɛlvz, ˌðɛm-/ *pers pron pl* ellos mismos, *m pl;* ellas mismas, *f pl, reflexive pron* sí; sí mismos; (with a reflexive verb) se. **They t. told me about it,** Ellos mismos me lo dijeron. **They left it for t.,** Lo dejaron para sí (mismos)

then /ðɛn/ *adv* (of future time) entonces; (of past time) a la sazón, en aquella época, entonces; (next, afterwards) luego, después, en seguida; (in that case) en este caso, entonces; (therefore) por consiguiente. —*a* de entonces. —*n* entonces, *m.* —*conjunc* (moreover) además; pues. **And what t.?** ¿Y qué pasó después?; ¿Y qué pasará ahora?; ¿Y qué más? **by t.,** por entonces. **now and t.,** de vez en cuando. **now... t.,** ya... ya, ora... ora. **since t.,** desde aquel tiempo; desde entonces; desde aquella ocasión. **until t.,** hasta entonces; hasta aquella época. **well t.,** bien, pues. **t. and there,** en el acto, en seguida; allí mismo

thence /ðɛns/ *adv* desde allí, de allí; (therefore) por eso, por esa razón, por consiguiente

thenceforth /ˌðɛns'fɔrθ/ *adv* de allí en adelante, desde entonces

theocracy /θi'ɒkrəsi/ *n* teocracia, *f*

theocratic /ˌθiə'krætık/ *a* teocrático

theologian /ˌθiə'loudʒən/ *n* teólogo, *m*

theological /ˌθiə'lɒdʒıkəl/ *a* teológico, teologal

theologize /θi'ɒləˌdʒaiz/ *vi* teologizar

theology /θi'ɒlədʒi/ *n* teología, *f*

theorem /'θiərəm/ *n* teorema, *m*

theoretical /ˌθiə'rɛtıkəl/ *a* teórico

theoretically /ˌθiə'rɛtıkli/ *adv* teóricamente, en teoría

theorist /'θiərıst/ *n* teórico, *m*

theorize /'θiəˌraiz/ *vi* teorizar

theory /'θiəri/ *n* teoría, *f*

theosophical /ˌθiə'sɒfıkəl/ *a* teosófico

theosophist /θi'ɒsəfıst/ *n* teósofo, *m*

theosophy /θi'ɒsəfi/ *n* teosofía, *f*

therapeutic /ˌθɛrə'pyutık/ *a* terapéutico. —*n* **therapeutics,** terapéutica, *f*

therapeutist /ˌθɛrə'pyutıst/ *n* terapeuta, *mf*

therapy /'θɛrəpi/ *suffix* terapia, *f*

there /ðɛər; *unstressed* ðər/ *adv* allí; ahí, allá; (at that point) en eso; (used pronominally as subject of verb) haber, e.g. *T. was once a king,* Hubo una vez un rey; *What is t. to do here?* ¿Qué hay que hacer aquí? —*interj* ¡vaya!; (I told you so!) ¡ya ves! ¡ya te lo dije yo!; (in surprise) ¡toma! **about t.,** cerca de allí. **down t.,** allí abajo. **in t.,** allí dentro. **out t.,** allí fuera. **over t.,** ahí; allá a lo lejos. **up t.,** allí arriba. **T. came a time when...,** Llegó la hora cuando... **T. it is!** ¡Allí está! **t. is** or **t. are,** hay. **t. was** or **t. were,** había, hubo. **t. may be,** puede haber, quizás habrá. **t. must be,** tiene que haber. **t. will be,** habrá. **T., t.!** (to a child, etc.) ¡Vamos!

thereabouts /'ðɛərəˌbauts/ *adv* (near to a place) cerca de allí, por ahí, allí cerca; (approximately) approximadamente, cerca de

thereafter /ˌðɛər'æftər/ *adv* después, después de eso

thereby /ˌðɛər'bai/ *adv* (near to that place) por allí cerca; (by that means) con lo cual, de este modo

therefore /'ðɛərˌfɔr/ *adv* por lo tanto, por eso, así, por consiguiente; por esta razón

therein /ˌðɛər'ın/ *adv* (inside) allí dentro; (in this, that particular) en estre, en eso, en ese particular

thereinafter /ˌðɛərın'æftər/ *adv* posteriormente, más adelante

thereupon /'ðɛərəˌpɒn/ *adv* (in consequence) por consiguiente, por lo tanto; (at that point) luego, en eso; (immediately afterwards) inmediatamente después, en seguida

thermal /'θɜrməl/ *a* termal. **t. springs,** aguas termales, termas, *f pl*

thermodynamics /ˌθɜrmoudai'næmıks/ *n* termodinámica, *f*

thermoelectric /ˌθɜrmouı'lɛktrık/ *a* termoeléctrico

thermometer /θər'mɒmıtər/ *n* termómetro, *m*

Thermopylae /θər'mɒpəˌli/ Termópilas, *f*

thermos flask /'θɜrməs/ *n* termos, *m*

thermostat /'θɜrməˌstæt/ *n* termostato, *m*

thermostatic /ˌθɜrmə'stætık/ *a* termostático

thesaurus /θı'sɔrəs/ *n* tesoro, tesauro, *m*

these /ðiz/ *dem pron pl* of **this,** éstos, *m pl;* éstas, *f pl, dem a* estos, *m pl;* estas, *f pl.* **Aren't t. your flowers?** ¿No son éstas tus flores? **T. pictures have been sold,** Estos cuadros han se han vendito

thesis /'θisıs/ *n* tesis, *f*

Thespian /'θɛspiən/ *a* dramático

Thessaly /'θɛsəli/ Tesalia, *f*

they /ðei/ *pers pron pl* ellos, *m pl;* ellas, *f pl;* (people) se (followed by sing. verb). **T. say,** Dicen, Se dice

thick /θık/ *a* espeso; (big) grueso, (wall) grueso, (string, cord) gordo; (vapors) denso; (muddy) turbio; (dense, close) tupido apretado; (numerous) numeroso, repetido, continuo; (full of) lleno (de); (of voice) velado, indistinto; (obtuse) estúpido, lerdo; (friendly) íntimo. —*adv* densamente; continuamente, sin cesar. **three feet t.,** de tres pies de espesor. **That's a bit t.!** ¡Eso es un poco demasiado! **to be as t. as thieves,** estar unidos como los dedos de la mano. **t.-lipped,** con labios gruesos, bezudo. **t.-headed,** estúpido, lerdo. **t.-skinned,** de piel gruesa; *Zool.* paquidermo; *Fig.* sin vergüenza, insensible. **t. stroke,** (of letters) grueso, *m*

thick /θık/ *n* espesor, *m;* parte gruesa, *f;* lo más denso; (of a fight) lo más reñido; centro, *m.* **in the t. of,** en el centro (de), en medio de

thicken /'θıkən/ *vt* espesar; (increase) aumentar, multiplicar; *Cul.* espesar. —*vi* espesarse; condensar; aumentar, multiplicarse; (of a mystery, etc.) complicarse; hacerse más denso; *Cul.* espesarse

thickening /'θıkənıŋ/ *n* hinchamiento, *m;* gordura, *f;* (*Cul.* and of paints) espesante, *m*

thicket /'θıkıt/ *n* matorral, soto, *m,* maleza, *f;* (grove) boscaje, *m*

thickly /'θıkli/ *adv* densamente; espesamente; continuamente, sin cesar; (of speech) indistintamente

thickness /'θıknıs/ *n* espesor, *m;* grueso, *m;* densidad, *f;* (of liquids) consistencia, *f;* (layer) capa, *f;* (of speech) dificultad (en el hablar), *f*

thickset /'*TIk'sEt*/ *a* doblado

thief /θif/ *n* ladrón (-ona); (in a candle) moco de vela, *m.* **Stop t.!** ¡Ladrones! **thieves' den,** *Fig.* cueva de ladrones, *f*

thieve /θiv/ *vi* hurtar, robar. —*vt* robar

thievish /'θivıʃ/ *a* ladrón

thigh /θai/ *n* muslo, *m.* **t.-bone,** fémur, *m*
thimble /ˈθɪmbəl/ *n* dedal, *m*
thimbleful /ˈθɪmbəlˌfʊl/ *n* lo que cabe en un dedal; *Fig.* dedada, *f*
thin /θɪn/ *a* delgado; (lean) flaco; (small) pequeño; delicado; fino; (of air, light) tenue, sutil; (clothes) ligero; (sparse) escaso; transparente; (watery) aguado; (of wine) bautizado; (not close) claro; (of arguments) flojo. —*vt* adelgazar; aclarar; *Agr.* limpiar; reducir. —*vi* adelgazarse; afilarse; reducirse. **somewhat t.,** (of persons) delgaducho, algo flaco. **to grow t.,** enflaquecer; afilarse. **to make t.,** hacer adelgazar volver flaco. **t.-clad,** ligero de ropa; mal vestido. **t.-faced,** de cara delgada. **t.-lipped,** de labios apretados. **t.-skinned,** de piel fina; *Fig.* sensitivo, sensible
thine /ðain/ See **theirs.** *poss pron* (el) tuyo, *m;* (la) tuya, *f;* (los) tuyos, *m pl;* (las) tuyas, *f pl;* tu, *mf;* tus, *mf pl;* de tí. **The fault is t.,** La culpa es tuya, La culpa es de tí
thing /θɪŋ/ *n* cosa, *f;* objeto, artículo, *m;* (affair) asunto, *m;* (contemptuous) sujeto, tipo, *m;* (creature) ser, *m,* criatura, *f; pl* **things,** (belongings) efectos, trastos, *m pl;* (luggage) equipaje, *m;* (clothes) trapitos, *m pl;* (circumstances) circunstancias, condiciones, *f pl.* **above all things,** ante todo, sobre todo. **a very pretty little t.,** (child) una pequeña muy mona. **as things are,** tal como están las cosas. **for one t.,** en primer lugar. **Her behavior is not quite the t.,** La conducta de ella no está bien vista. **The bad t. is that...,** Lo malo es que... **The good t. is that...,** Menos mal que...; Lo bueno es que... **No such t.!** ¡No hay tal!; ¡Nada de eso! **Poor t.!** ¡Pobrecito!; (woman) ¡Pobre mujer!; (man) ¡Pobre hombre! **to be just the t.,** venir al pelo. **with one t. and another,** entre unas cosas y otras. **I like things Spanish,** Me gusta lo español
think /θɪŋk/ *vt* and *vi* pensar; (believe) creer; (deem) considerar, juzgar; imaginar; (suspect) sospechar; (opine) ser de opinión (que). **And to t. that...!** ¡Y pensar que...! **As you t. fit,** Como usted quiera, Como a usted le parezca bien. **He thought as much,** Se lo figuraba. **He little thought that...!** ¡Cuán lejos estaba de pensar que...! **He thinks nothing of...,** No le importa...; Desprecia..., Tiene una opinión bastante mala de.... **I don't t. so,** No lo creo. **I should t. not!** ¡Claro que no! ¡Eso sí que no! **I should t. so!** ¡Claro! ¡Ya lo creo! **It makes me t. of...,** Me hace pensar en... **One might t.,** Podría creerse... **to t. better of something,** cambiar de opinión, considerar mejor. **to t. highly (badly) of,** tener buen (mal) concepto sobre. **to t. over carefully,** pensarlo bien, considerar detenidamente; *Inf.* consultar con la almohada. **to t. proper,** creer conveniente. **to t. to oneself,** pensar para sí (or entre sí). **to t. too much of oneself,** pensar demasiado en sí; tener demasiada buena opinión de sí mismo; tener humos. **What do you t. about it?** ¿Qué te parece? **to t. about,** (of persons) pensar en; (of things) pensar de (or sobre); meditar, considerar, reflexionar sobre. **to t. for,** pensar por. **to t. of,** pensar en; pensar de (or sobre). **What do you t. of this?** ¿Qué te parece esto? **to t. out,** idear, proyectar, hacer planes para; (a problem) resolver. **to t. over,** pensar; reflexionar sobre, meditar sobre. **I shall t. it over,** Lo pensaré.
thinker /ˈθɪŋkər/ *n* pensador, *m*
thinking /ˈθɪŋkɪŋ/ *n* pensamiento, *m,* reflexión, meditación, *f;* juicio, *m;* opinión, *f,* parecer, *m.* —*a* pensador; inteligente; racional; serio. **To my way of t.,** Según pienso yo, A mi parecer. **way of t.,** modo de pensar, *m*
thinly /ˈθɪnli/ *adv* delgadamente; esparcidamente; (lightly) ligeramente; poco numeroso
thinness /ˈθɪnnɪs/ *n* delgadez, *f;* (leanness) flaqueza, *f;* sutileza, tenuidad, *f;* (lack) escasez, *f;* pequeño número, *m;* poca consistencia, *f*
third /θɜrd/ *a* tercero (tercer before *m, sing* noun); (of monarchs) tercero; (of the month) (el) tres. —*n* tercio, *m,* tercera parte, *f; Mus.* tercera, *f.* **T. time lucky!** ¡A la tercera va la vencida! **t. class,** *n* tercera clase, *f.* —*a* de tercera clase. **t. party,** tercera persona, *f.* **t.-party insurance,** seguro contra tercera persona, *m.* **t. person,** tercero (-ra); *Gram.* tercera persona, *f.* **t.-rate,** de tercera clase
thirdly /ˈθɜrdli/ *adv* en tercer lugar
thirst /θɜrst/ *n* sed, *f; Fig.* deseo, *m,* ansia, *f;* entusiasmo, *m.* **to satisfy one's t.,** apagar (or matar) la sed
thirsty /ˈθɜrsti/ *a* sediento. **to be t.,** tener sed. **to make t.,** dar sed.
thirteen /ˈθɜrˈtin/ *a* and *n* trece *m.* **t. hundred,** *a* and *n* mil trescientos *m*
thirteenth /θɜrˈtinθ/ *a* décimotercio; (of monarchs) trece; (of month) (el) trece, *m, n* décimotercio, trezavo, *m*
thirtieth /ˈθɜrtiəθ/ *a* trigésimo; (of month) (el) treinta, *m.* —*n* treintavo, *m*
thirty /ˈθɜrti/ *a* and *n* treinta, *m.* **t.-first,** treinta y uno
this /ðɪs/ *dem a* este, *m;* esta, *f, dem pron* éste, *m;* ésta, *f;* esto, *neut* **by t. time,** a esta hora, ya. **like t.,** de este modo, así. **T. is Wednesday,** Hoy es miércoles. **What is all t.?** ¿Qué es todo esto?
thistle /ˈθɪsəl/ *n* cardo, *m.* **t.-down,** papo de cardo, vilano de cardo, *m*
thither /ˈθɪðər, ˈðɪð-/ *adv* allá, hacia allá; a ese fin. —*a* más remoto
thong /θɔŋ/ *n* correa, tira, *f*
thoracic /θɔˈræsɪk/ *a* torácico
thorax /ˈθɔræks/ *n* tórax, *m*
thorn /θɔrn/ *n* espina, *f;* (tree) espino, *m; Fig.* abrojo, *m,* espina, *f.* **to be a t. in the flesh of,** ser una espina en el costado de. **t. brake,** espinar, *m*
thornless /ˈθɔrnlɪs/ *a* sin espinas
thorny /ˈθɔrni/ *a* espinoso; *Fig.* difícil, arduo
thorough /ˈθɜrou/ *a* completo; perfecto; (conscientious) concienzudo; (careful) cuidadoso. **t.-bred,** (of animals) de pura raza, de casta; (of persons) bien nacido. **t.-paced,** cabal, consumado
thoroughfare /ˈθɜrəˌfɛər/ *n* vía pública, *f.* **"No t.,"** «Prohibido el paso», «Calle cerrada»
thoroughly /ˈθɜrəli/ *adv* completamente; (of knowing a subject) a fondo; concienzudamente
thoroughness /ˈθɜrənɪs/ *n* perfección, *f;* minuciosidad, *f*
those /ðouz/ *dem a pl* of **that,** esos, *m pl;* esas, *f pl;* aquellos, *m pl;* aquellas, *f pl, dem pron* ésos, *m pl;* ésas, *f pl;* aquéllos, *m pl;* aquéllas, *f pl;* (standing for a noun) los, *m pl;* las, *f pl.* **t. who,** quienes, *mf pl;* los que, *m pl;* las que, *f pl.* **t. that** or **which,** los que, *m pl;* las que, *f pl.* **Your eyes are t. of your mother,** Tus ojos son los de tu madre
thou /θau/ *pers pron* tú
though /ðou/ *conjunc* (followed by subjunc. when doubt is implied or uncertain future time) aunque, bien que; (nevertheless) sin embargo, no obstante; (in spite of) a pesar de que; (but) pero. **as t.,** como si (followed by subjunc.). **even t.,** aunque (followed by subjunc.)
thought /θɔt/ *n* pensamiento, *m;* meditación, reflexión, *f.* **some thoughts on...** algunas reflexiones sobre...; opinión, *f;* consideración, *f;* idea, *f,* propósito, *m;* (care) cuidado, *m,* solicitud, *f; Inf.* pizca, *f.* **on second thought,** después de pensarlo bien. **The t. struck him,** Se le ocurrió la idea. **to collect one's thoughts,** orientarse; informarse (de). **t.-reading,** adivinación del pensamiento, *f.* **t.-transference,** telepatía, transmisión del pensamiento, *f*
thoughtful /ˈθɔtfəl/ *a* pensativo, meditabundo; serio; especulativo; (provident) previsor; (kind) atento, solícito; cuidadoso; (anxious) inquieto, intranquilo
thoughtfully /ˈθɔtfəli/ *adv* pensativamente; seriamente; (providently) con previsión; (kindly) atentamente, solícitamente
thoughtfulness /ˈθɔtfəlnɪs/ *n* natural reflexivo, *m,* seriedad, *f;* (kindness) solicitud, atención, *f;* (forethought) previsión, *f*
thoughtless /ˈθɔtlɪs/ *a* irreflexivo; (careless) descuidado, negligente; (unkind) inconsiderado; (silly) necio, estúpido
thoughtlessly /ˈθɔtlɪsli/ *adv* sin pensar, irreflexivamente; negligentemente
thoughtlessness /ˈθɔtlɪsnɪs/ *n* irreflexión, *f;* descui-

do, *m,* negligencia, *f;* (unkindness) inconsideración, *f;* (silliness) neciedad, *f*

thousand /'θauzənd/ *a* mil. *—n* mil, *m;* millar, *m.* **one t.,** mil, *m.* **one t. three hundred,** *a* mil trescientos, *m pl;* mil trescientas, *f pl.* *—n* mil trescientos, *m pl.* **two** (**three**) **t.,** dos (tres) mil. **by thousands,** por millares; por miles. **t.-fold,** mil veces más

thousandth /'θauzəndθ/ *a* and *n* milésimo *m*

Thrace /θreis/ Tracia, *f*

thrall /θrɔl/ *n* esclavo (-va); esclavitud, *f*

thrash /θræʃ/ *vt* azotar, apalear; *Agr.* trillar, desgranar; *Inf.* triunfar sobre, derrotar. *—vi Agr.* trillar el grano; arrojarse, agitarse. *Fig.* **to t. out,** ventilar

thrashing /'θræʃɪŋ/ *n* apaleamiento, *m,* paliza, *f; Agr.* See **threshing**

thread /θrɛd/ *n* hilo, *m;* (fibre) hebra, fibra, *f,* filamento, *m;* (of a screw) filete, *m; Fig.* hilo, *m, a* de hilo. *—vt* (a needle) enhebrar; (beads) ensartar; (make one's way) colarse a través de, atravesar; pasar por. **to hang by a t.,** pender de un hilo. **to lose the t. of,** *Fig.* perder el hilo de

threadbare /'θrɛd,bɛər/ *a* raído; muy usado; *Fig.* trivial, viejo

threadlike /'θrɛd,laik/ *a* como un hilo, filiforme

threadworm /'θrɛd,wɜrm/ *n m,* lombriz intestinal, *f*

threat /θrɛt/ *n* amenaza, *f*

threaten /'θrɛtn̩/ *vt* and *vi* amenazar. **to t. with,** amenazar con

threatening /'θrɛtn̩ɪŋ/ *a* amenazador. *—n* amenazas, *f pl*

threateningly /'θrɛtn̩ɪŋli/ *adv* con amenazas

three /θri/ *a* and *n* tres *m;* (of the clock) las tres, *f pl;* (of one's age) tres años, *m pl.* **t.-color process,** tricromía, *f.* **t.-colored,** tricolor. **t.-cornered,** triangular; (of hats) de tres picos, tricornio. **t.-cornered hat,** sombrero de tres picos, tricornio, *m.* **t. decker,** *Naut.* navío de tres puentes, *m;* novela larga, *f.* **t. deep,** en tres hileras. **t. hundred,** *a* and *n* trescientos *m.* **t.-hundredth,** *a* and *n* tricentésimo *m.* **t.-legged,** de tres patas. **t.-legged stool,** banqueta, *f.* **t.-per-cents,** accion al tres por ciento (3%), *f.* **t.-phase,** *Elec.* trifásico. **t.-ply,** (of yarn) triple; (of wood) de tres capas. **t.-quarter,** de tres cuartos. **t. quarters of an hour,** tres cuartos de hora, *m pl.* **t.-sided,** trilátero. **t. speed gear box,** cambio de marcha de tres velocidades, *m.* **t.-stringed,** *Mus.* de tres cuerdos. **t. thousand,** *a* tres mil, *mf pl; n* tres mil, *m*

threefold /'θri,fould/ *a* triple

Three Musketeers, the los Tres Mosqueteros

threescore /'θri'skɔr/ *a* and *n* sesenta, *m pl*

threesome /'θrisəm/ *n* partido de tres, *m*

threnody /'θrɛnədi/ *n* treno, *m*

thresh /θrɛʃ/ *vt* trillar, desgranar. *—vi* trillar el grano. **to t. out,** ventilar

threshing /'θrɛʃɪŋ/ *n* trilla, *f.* **t. floor,** era, *f.* **t. machine,** trilladora, *f*

threshold /'θrɛʃould/ *n* umbral, *m; Psychol.* limen, *m; Fig.* comienzo, principio, *m;* (entrance) entrada, *f.* **to cross the t.,** atravesar (or pisar) los umbrales

thrice /θrais/ *adv* tres veces

thrift /θrɪft/ *n* frugalidad, parsimonia, *f*

thriftless /'θrɪftlɪs/ *a* malgastador, manirroto

thrifty /'θrɪfti/ *a* frugal, económico

thrill /θrɪl/ *n* estremecimiento, *m;* emoción, *f.* *—vt* conmover, emocionar; penetrar. *—vi* estremecerse, emocionarse

thriller /'θrɪlər/ *n* libro, *m,* (or comedia, *f*) sensacional; (detective novel) novela policíaca, *f*

thrilling /'θrɪlɪŋ/ *a* sensacional, espeluznante; (moving) emocionante, conmovedor

thrive /θraiv/ *vi* prosperar, medrar; enriquecerse, tener éxito; (grow) desarrollarse, robustecerse; florecer; (of plants) acertar

thriving /'θraivɪŋ/ *a* próspero; floreciente; robusto, vigoroso

throat /θrout/ *n* garganta, *f;* orificio, *m;* (narrow entry) paso, *m.* **sore t.,** dolor de garganta, *m.* **to cut one's t.,** cortarse la garganta. **to take by the t.,** asir (or agarrar) por la garganta

throat cancer *n* cáncer de la garganta, *m*

throaty /'θrouti/ *a* indistinto, ronco

throb /θrɒb/ *n* latido, *m;* pulsación, *f;* vibración, *f; Fig.* estremecimiento, *m.* *—vi* palpitar, latir; vibrar

throbbing /'θrɒbɪŋ/ *n* pulsación, *f;* vibración, *f.* *—a* palpitante; vibrante. **t. pain,** dolor pungente, *m*

throe /θrou/ *n* dolor, *m,* agonía, angustia, *f.* **in the throes of,** en medio de; luchando con; en las garras de. **throes of childbirth,** dolores de parto, *m pl.* **throes of death,** agonía de la muerte, *f*

thrombosis /θrɒm'bousɪs/ *n Med.* trombosis, *f*

throne /θroun/ *n* trono, *m;* (royal power) corona, *f,* poder real, *m.* *—vt* elevar al trono. **speech from the t.,** el discurso de la corona, *m*

throng /θrɔŋ/ *n* muchedumbre, multitud, *f.* *—vi* apiñarse remolinarse, acudir. *—vt* atestar, llenar de bote en bote

throstle /'θrɒsəl/ *n Ornith.* tordo, malvís, *m*

throttle /'θrɒtl̩/ *n Mech.* regulador, *m; Auto.* estrangulador, *m; Inf.* garganta, *f.* *—vt* estrangular; *Fig.* ahogar, suprimir. **to open** (**close**) **the t.,** abrir (cerrar) el estrangulador

throttling /'θrɒtlɪŋ/ *n* estrangulación, *f*

through /θru/ *prep* por; al través de; de un lado a otro de; por medio de; (between) entre; por causa de; gracias a. *—adv* al través; de un lado a otro; (whole) entero, todo; (from beginning to end) desde el principio hasta el fin; (to the end) hasta el fin. *—a* (of passages, etc.) que va desde... hasta...; (of trains) directo. **to look t. the window,** mirar por la ventana, asomarse a la ventana. **to be wet t.,** estar calado hasta los huesos; estar muy mojado. **to carry t.,** llevar a cabo. **to fall t.,** caer por; (fail) fracasar. **to sleep the whole night t.,** dormir durante toda la noche, dormir la noche entera. **t. and t.,** completamente. **through the length and breadth of,** a lo largo y a lo ancho de, hasta los últimos rincones de. **t. traffic,** tráfico directo, *m.* **t. train,** tren directo, *m*

throughout /θru'aut/ *prep* por todo; durante todo. *—adv* completamente; (from beginning to end) desde el principio hasta el fin; (everywhere) en todas partes

throw /θrou/ *vt* arrojar, lanzar, echar; (fire) disparar; (pottery) plasmar; (knock down) derribar; (slough) mudar (la piel); (cast off) despojarse de; (a rider) desmontar; (a glance) echar, dirigir (una mirada, etc.); (silk) torcer; (dice) echar; (light) dirigir, enfocar. **to t. oneself at the head of,** echarse a la cabeza de. **to t. open,** abrir de par en par; abrir. **to t. overboard,** *Naut.* echar al mar; desechar; (desert) abandonar. **to t. about,** esparcir, desparramar; derrochar. **to t. aside,** echar a un lado, desechar; abandonar, dejar. **to t. away,** tirar; desechar; (spend) malgastar, derrochar; (waste) sacrificar; (of opportunities) malograr, perder. **to t. back,** devolver; echar hacia atrás. **to t. down,** derribar, dar en el suelo con; echar abajo; (arms) rendir. **to t. down the glove,** arrojar el guante. **to t. oneself down,** tumbarse, echarse; (descend) echarse abajo. **to t. oneself down from,** arrojarse de. **to t. in,** echar dentro; (give extra) añadir; (the clutch) embragar; insertar; (a remark) hacer (una observación). **to t. off,** despojarse de; quitarse; (refuse) rechazar; sacudirse; (get rid of) despedir; (renounce) renunciar; (exhale) emitir, despedir; (verses) improvisar. **to t. on,** echar sobre; (garments) ponerse. **to t. oneself upon,** lanzarse sobre. **to t. out,** expeler; hacer salir; plantar en la calle; (utter) proferir, soltar; (one's chest) inflar. **to t. over,** (desert) abandonar, dejar. **to t. up,** (build) levantar; lanzar en el aire; (a post, etc.) renunciar (a), abandonar; vomitar

throw /θrou/ *n* echada, *f;* tiro, *m;* (at dice) lance, *m;* jugada, *f;* (wrestling) derribo, *m.* **within a stone's t.,** a tiro de piedra. **t.-back,** retroceso, *m; Biol.* atavismo, *m*

thrower /'θrouər/ *n* tirador (-ra), lanzador (-ra)

throwing /'θrouɪŋ/ *n* lanzamiento, *m,* lanzada, *f.* **t. the hammer,** lanzamiento del martillo, *m*

thrum /θrʌm/ *vt* and *vi* tocar mal; (of keyed instruments) teclear; (of stringed instruments) rascar las cuerdas (de)

thrush /θrʌʃ/ *n Ornith.* tordo, *m*

thrust /θrʌst/ *n* empujón, *m;* (with a sword) estocada, *f;* (fencing) golpe, *m;* (with a lance) bote, *m;* ataque, *m;* asalto, *m.* *—vt* empujar; (put) meter; (insert) introducir; (pierce) atravesar; (out, through, of the head, etc.) asomar. —*vi* acometer, atacar, embestir; meterse, introducirse; (intrude) entrometerse; (fencing) dar un golpe. **to t. aside,** empujar a un lado; (proposals) rechazar. **to t. back,** hacer retroceder, empujar hacia atrás; (words) tragarse; (thoughts) apartar, rechazar. **to t. down,** empujar hacia abajo; hacer bajar; *Fig.* reprimir. **to t. forward,** empujar hacia delante; hacer seguir. **to t. oneself forward,** adelantarse; *Fig.* ponerse delante de los otros, darse importancia. **to t. in,** introducir; (stick) hincar; (insert) intercalar. **to t. on,** hacer seguir; empujar sobre; (garments) ponerse rápidamente. **to t. oneself in,** introducirse; entrometerse. **to t. out,** echar fuera; hacer salir, echar; expulsar; (the tongue) sacar (la lengua); (the head, etc.) asomar. **to t. through,** atravesar; (pierce) traspasar. **to t. one's way through,** abrirse paso por. **to t. upon,** imponer, hacer aceptar

thud /θʌd/ *n* sonido sordo, *m;* golpe sordo, *m*

thug /θʌg/ *n* asesino, criminal, *m*

thumb /θʌm/ *n* pulgar, *m.* —*vt* hojear; ensuciar con los dedos. **under the t. of,** *Fig.* en el poder de. **t. index,** índice pulgar, *m.* **t.-mark,** huella del dedo, *f.* **t.-screw,** tornillo de orejas, *m,* **t.-stall,** dedil, *m.* **t.-tack,** chinche, *m*

thump /θʌmp/ *n* golpe, porrazo, *m.* —*vt* and *vi* golpear, aporrear; (the ground, of rabbits) zapatear

thunder /ˈθʌndər/ *n* trueno, *m;* (of hooves, etc.) estampido, *m;* estruendo, *m.* —*vi* tronar; retumbar; *Fig.* fulminar. —*vt* gritar en una voz de trueno, rugir. **to t. along,** avanzar como el trueno; galopar ruidosamente. **t.-clap,** trueno, *m.* **t.-cloud,** nube de tormenta, *f,* nubarrón, *m.* **t.-storm,** tronada, *f.* **t. struck,** muerto, estupefacto. **to be thunderstruck,** quedarse frío

thunderbolt /ˈθʌndərˌboult/ *n* rayo, *m*

thunderer /ˈθʌndərər/ *n* fulminador, *m.* **the Thunderer,** Júpiter tonante, Júpiter tronante, *m;* el «Times» londinense, *m*

Thuringia /θʊˈrɪndʒiə/ Turingia, *f*

Thursday /ˈθɜrzdei/ *n* jueves, *m.* **Holy T.,** Jueves Santo, *m*

thus /ðʌs/ *adv* así; de este modo; en estos términos; hasta este punto. **t. far,** hasta ahora; hasta este punto; hasta aquí. **Thus it is that...,** Así es que...

thwack /θwæk/ *n* golpe, *m; vt* golpear

thwart /θwɔrt/ *vt* frustrar, impedir

thy /ðai/ *poss a* tu, *mf;* tus, *m pl,* and *f pl*

thyme /taim/ *n Bot.* tomillo, *m*

thymus /ˈθaiməs/ *n Anat.* timo, *m*

thyroid /ˈθairɔid/ *a* tiroideo. **t. gland,** tiroides, *f*

thyself /ðaiˈsɛlf/ *poss pron* tu mismo, *m;* tu misma, *f;* (with prep.) tí mismo, *m;* tí misma, *f;* (in a reflexive verb) te

tiara /tiˈærə, -ˈɑrə/ *n* tiara, *f*

Tiberias /taiˈbɪəriəs/ Tiberíades, *f*

Tibetan /tɪˈbɛtn̩/ *a* and *n* tibetano (-na); (language) tibetano, *m*

tibia /ˈtɪbiə/ *n Anat.* tibia, *f*

tic /tɪk/ *n* (twitch) tic nervioso, *m*

tick /tɪk/ *n Ent.* ácaro, *m;* (sound) tictac, *m;* (cover) funda de colchón, *f; Inf.* fiado, crédito, *m;* (mark) marca, *f vi* hacer tictac. —*vt* poner una marca contra. **on t.,** *Inf.* al fiado. **to t. off,** poner una marca contra; *Inf.* reñir. **to t. over,** *Auto.* andar, marchar

ticket /ˈtɪkɪt/ *n* billete, *m;* (for an entertainment) entrada, localidad, *f,* (label) etiqueta, *f,* (pawn) papeleta de empeño, *f;* (for luggage) talón, *m;* (*Polit.* U.S.A.) candidatura, *f, vt* marcar. **to take one's t.,** sacar el billete (or for entertainment) la entrada, *f*). **excursion t.,** billete de excursión, *m.* **return t.,** billete de ida y vuelta, *m.* **season t.,** billete de abono, *m.* **single t.,** billete sencillo, *m.* **t. agency,** (for travel) agencia de viajes, *f;* (for entertainments) agencia de teatros, *f.* **t. collector or inspector,** revisor, *m.* **t. holder,** tenedor de billete, *m;* abonado (-da). **t. office,** (railway) despacho de billetes, *m;* taquilla, *f.* **t.-of-leave,** libertad condicional, *f.* **t. punch,** sacabocados, *m;* (on tramcars) clasificador de billetes, *m*

ticking /ˈtɪkɪŋ/ *n* (sound) tictac, *m;* (cloth) cotí, *m*

tickle /ˈtɪkəl/ *vt* hacer cosquillas (a), cosquillear; irritar; (gratify) halagar; (amuse) divertir. —*vi* tener cosquillas; hacer cosquillas; ser irritante

ticklish /ˈtɪklɪʃ/ *a* cosquilloso; (of persons) difícil, vidrioso; (of affairs) espinoso, delicado

tidal /ˈtaidl̩/ *a* de marea. **t. wave,** marejada, *f; Fig.* ola popular, *f*

tidbit /ˈtɪdˌbɪt/ *n* See **titbit**

tiddlywinks /ˈtɪdliˌwɪŋks/ *n* juego de la pulga, *m*

tide /taid/ *n* marea, *f;* (season) tiempo, *m,* estación, *f;* (trend) corriente, *f;* (progress) curso, *m;* marcha, *f.* —*vi* (with over) vencer, superar; aguardar la ocasión. **to go against the t.,** ir contra la corriente. **to go with the t.,** seguir la corriente. **high t.,** marea alta, *f.* **low t.,** marea baja, *f,* bajamar, *m.* **neap t.,** marea muerta, *f.* **t. mark,** lengua del agua, *f*

tideless /ˈtaidlɪs/ *a* sin mareas

tidily /ˈtaidl̩i/ *adv* aseadamente; en orden, metódicamente

tidiness /ˈtaidnɪs/ *n* aseo, *m;* buen orden, *m*

tidings /ˈtaidɪŋz/ *n pl* noticias, nuevas, *f pl*

tidy /ˈtaidi/ *a* aseado; metódico, en orden; pulcro; *Inf.* considerable. —*vt* poner en orden, asear; limpiar; (oneself) arreglarse

tie /tai/ *n* lazo, *m,* atadura, *f;* (knot) nudo, *m;* (for the neck) corbata, *f; Sports.* empate, *m; Mus.* ligado, *m; Archit.* tirante, *m;* (spiritual bond) lazo, *m;* (burden) carga, responsabilidad, **tie clasp,** pisa corbata, *mf.* **tie-pin,** alfiler de corbata, *m.* **tie seller,** corbatero (-ra)

tie /tai/ *vt* atar; (bind) ligar; (lace) lacear; (a knot) hacer; (with a knot) anudar; (unite) unir; (*Fig.* bind) constreñir, obligar; (limit) limitar, restringir; (occupy) ocupar, entretener; (hamper) estorbar, impedir. —*vi* atarse; *Sports.* empatar. **to tie one's tie,** hacer la corbata. **to tie down,** atar a; limitar; obligar. **They tied him down to a chair,** Le ataron a una silla. **to tie together,** enlazar, ligar; unir. **to tie up,** liar, atar; (wrap) envolver; recoger; *Naut.* amarrar, atracar; (restrict) limitar, restringir; (invest) invertir

tie-breaker /ˈtaiˌbreikər/ *n* desempate, *m*

tier /ˈtɪər/ *n* fila, hilera, *f.* **in tiers,** en gradas; (of a dress) en volantes

tiff /tɪf/ *n* disgusto, *m*

tiger /ˈtaigər/ *n* tigre, *m.* **t.-cat,** gato (-ta) atigrado (-da). **t.-lily,** tigridia, *f*

tigerish /ˈtaigərɪʃ/ *a* atigrado, de tigre; salvaje, feroz

tight /tait/ *a* apretado; (not leaky) hermético, impermeable; (taut) tieso, tirante; (narrow) estrecho; (trim) compacto; (of clothes) muy ajustado; (shut) bien cerrado; *Naut.* estanco; (risky) peligroso, difícil; (miserly) tacaño; (of money, goods) escaso; **to be t.-fisted,** ser como un puño. **to hold t.,** agarrar fuerte. **t. corner,** *Fig.* aprieto, lance apretado, *m.* **t.-rope,** cuerda de volatinero, *f.* **t.-rope walker,** alambrista, equilibrista, *mf;* volatinero (-ra), bailarín de la cuerda floja, *m.* **t.-rope walker's pole,** balancín, *m*

tighten /ˈtaitn̩/ *vt* estrechar, apretar; (stretch) estirar; (of saddle girths) cinchar. —*vi* estrecharse; estirarse

tightly /ˈtaitli/ *adv* estrechamente

tightness /ˈtaitnɪs/ *n* estrechez, *f;* tirantez, tensión, *f;* (feeling of constriction) opresión, *f;*

tights /taits/ *n pl* mallas, *f pl*

tigress /ˈtaigrɪs/ *n* tigresa, *f*

tile /tail/ *n* teja, *f;* (for flooring) baldosa, losa, *f;* (ornamental) azulejo, *m;* (hat) chistera, *f.* —*vt* tejar; embaldosar. **t. floor,** enlosado, embaldosado, *m.* **t. manufacturer,** tejero, *m.* **t. works** or **yard,** tejar, *m.* (Colombia) galpón *m*

tiler /ˈtailər/ *n* solador, *m;* tejero, *m*

till /tɪl/ *n* (for money) cajón, *m.* —*vt Agr.* cultivar, labrar. —*prep* hasta. —*conjunc* hasta que

tillable /ˈtɪləbəl/ *a* laborable

tillage /ˈtɪlɪdʒ/ *n* labranza, *f,* cultivo, *m;* tierra de labrantío, *f*

tiller /ˈtɪlər/ *n Agr.* labrador, *m; Bot.* mugrón, renuevo, vástago, *m; Naut.* caña del timón, *f*

tilling /ˈtɪlɪŋ/ *n Agr.* cultivo, laboreo, *m*

tilt /tɪlt/ *n* inclinación, *f;* ladeo, *m;* (fight) torneo, *m,* justa, *f.* —*vt* inclinar; ladear; (a drinking vessel) empinar. —*vi* inclinarse; ladearse; (fight) justar. **to t. against,** *Fig.* arremeter contra, atacar. **at full t.,** a todo correr. **t. hammer,** martinete de báscula, *m.* **t.-yard,** palestra, *f*

tilting /'tɪltɪŋ/ *n* incinación, *f;* (fighting) justas, *f pl.* —*a* inclinado

timber /'tɪmbər/ *n* madera de construcción, *f;* (trees) árboles de monte, *m pl;* bosque, *m;* (beam) viga, *f; Naut.* cuaderna, *f.* —*vt* enmaderar. **t. line,** límite del bosque maderable, *m.* **t. merchant,** maderero, *m.* **t. wolf,** lobo gris, *m.* **t. work,** maderaje, *m.* **t. yard,** madererría, *f,* corral de madera, *m*

timbered /'tɪmbərd/ *a* enmaderado; (with trees) arbolado

timbre /'tæmbər, 'tɪm-/ *n Mus.* timbre, *m*

timbrel /'tɪmbrəl/ *n Mus.* tamborete, tamboril, *m*

time /taim/ *n* (in general) tiempo, *m;* (epoch) época, edad, *f;* tiempos, *m pl;* (of the year) estación, *f;* (by the clock) hora, *f,* (lifetime) vida, *f,* (particular moment of time) momento, *m;* (occasion) sazón, ocasión, *f;* (day) día, *m;* (time allowed) plazo, *m;* (in repetition) vez, *f; Mus.* compás, *m; Mil.* paso, *m.* —*vt* ajustar al tiempo; hacer con oportunidad; (regulate) regular; calcular el tiempo que se emplea en hacer una cosa; (a blow) calcular. **all the t.,** todo el tiempo; continuamente, sin cesar. **a long t.,** mucho tiempo. **a long t. ago,** mucho tiempo ha, hace mucho tiempo. **at a t.,** a la vez, al mismo tiempo; (of period) en una época. **at any t.,** a cualquier hora; en cualquier momento; (when you like) cuando gustes. **at no t.,** jamás, nunca. **at some t.,** alguna vez; en alguna época. **at some t. or another,** un día u otro; en una u otra ocasión; en alguna época. **at that t.,** en aquella época; en la sazón; en aquel instante. **at the one t.,** de una vez. **at the present t.,** en la actualidad, al presente. **at the proper t.,** a su debido tiempo; a la hora señalada; a la hora conveniente. **at the same t.,** al mismo tiempo. **at the same t. as,** mientras, a medida que; al mismo instante que, **at times,** a veces, en ocasiones. **behind the times,** *Fig.* atrasado de noticias; pasado de moda. **behind t.,** atrasado. **by that t.,** para entonces. **every t.,** cada vez; siempre. **for some t.,** durante algún tiempo. **for some t. past,** de algún tiempo a esta parte. **for the t. being,** de momento, por ahora, por lo pronto. **from this t.,** desde hoy; desde esta fecha. **from this t. forward,** de hoy en adelante. **from t. to t.,** de vez en cuando, de cuando en cuando, de tarde en tarde. **in a month's t.,** en un mes. **in a short t.,** en breve, dentro de poco. **in good t.,** puntualmente; temprano. **in my t.,** en mis días, en mis tiempos. **in olden times,** antiguamente, en otros tiempos. **in the course of t.,** andando el tiempo, en el transcurso de los años. **in the t. of,** en la época de. **in t.,** (promptly) a tiempo; con el tiempo. **in t. to come,** en el porvenir. **It is t. to...,** Es hora de.... **many times,** frecuentemente, muchas veces. **Once upon a t.,** Érase una vez, Una vez había, Érase que érase, Érase que se era. **Since t. out of mind,** Desde tiempo inmemorial. **the last (next) t.,** la última (próxima) vez. **this t. of year,** esta estación del año. **T. hangs heavy on his hands,** El tiempo se le hace interminable. **T. flies,** El tiempo vuela. **T. will tell!** ¡El tiempo lo dirá! ¡Veremos lo que veremos! **What t. is it?** ¿Qué hora es? **The t. is...,** La hora es... **within a given t.,** dentro de un plazo dado. **to be out of t.,** estar fuera de compás. **to gain t.,** ganar tiempo. **to have a good t.,** pasarlo bien, divertirse. **to have a bad t.,** pasarlo mal; *Inf.* tener un mal cuarto de hora. **to have no t. to,** no tener tiempo para + noun or pronoun, no tener tiempo de + infinitive. **to keep t.,** guardar el compás. **to kill t.,** engañar (or entretener) el tiempo. **to mark t.,** marcar el paso; *Fig.* hacer tiempo. **to pass the t.,** pasar el rato; pasar el tiempo. **to pass the t. of day,** saludar. **to serve one's t.,** (to a trade) servir el aprendizaje; (in prison) cumplir su condena; *Mil.* hacer el servicio militar. **to take t. to,** tomar tiempo para. **to take t. by the forelock,** asir la ocasión por la melena. **to waste t.,** perder el tiempo. **t. exposure,** pose, *f.* **t. fuse,** espoleta de tiempo, espoleta graduada, *f.* **t.-honored,** tradicional, consagrado por el tiempo. **t.-keeper,** capataz, *m;* reloj, *m.* **t.-saving,** que ahorra el tiempo. **t.-server,** lameculos, *mf.* **t.-signal,** señales horarias, *f pl.* **t.-table,** horario, *m;* itinerario, programa, *m* (railway) guía de ferrocarriles, *f.* **t. to come,** porvenir, *m,* lo venidero

timed /taimd/ *a* calculado; (**ill-**) intempestivo; (**well-**) oportuno

timeless /'taimlɪs/' *a* eterno

timeliness /'taimlinɪs/ *n* tempestividad, oportunidad, *f*

timely /'taimli/ *a* oportuno

timepiece /'taim,pis/ *n* reloj, *m*

time zone *n* huso esférico, huso horario, *m*

timid /'tɪmɪd/ *a* tímido, asustadizo, medroso; (shy) vergonzoso

timidity /tɪ'mɪdɪti/ *n* timidez, *f;* vergüenza, *f*

timing /'taimɪŋ/ *n* medida del tiempo, *f; Mech.* regulación, *f;* (timetable) horario, *m*

timorous /'tɪmərəs/ *a* timorato, apocado, asustadizo

timorousness /'tɪmərəsnɪs/ *n* encogimiento, *m,* timidez, *f*

tin /tɪn/ *n* (metal) estaño, *m;* (container) lata, *f;* (sheet) hojalata, *f;* (money) plata, *f.* —*vt* estañar; (place in tins) envasar en lata; cubrir con hojalata, hoja de aluminio, *f.* **tin-foil,** papel de estaño, *m.* **tin hat,** casco de acero, *m.* **tin opener,** abrelatas, abridor de latas, *m.* **tin-plate,** hojalata, *f.* **tin soldier,** soldado de plomo, *m.* **tin ware,** hojalatería, *f*

tincture /'tɪŋktʃər/ *n* tintura, *f,* tinte, *m; Med.* tintura, *f;* (trace) dejo, *m;* (veneer) capa, *f.* —*vt* teñir, tinturar

tinder /'tɪndər/ *n* yesca, *f.* **t. box,** yescas, lumbres, *f pl*

tinge /tɪndʒ/ *n* tinte, matiz, *m; Fig.* dejo, toque, *m.* —*vt* matizar, tinturar; *Fig.* tocar

tingle /'tɪŋgəl/ *n* picazón, comezón, *f;* (thrill) estremecimiento, *m.* —*vi* picar; (of ears) zumbar; (thrill) estremecerse (de); vibrar

tingling /'tɪŋglɪŋ/ *n* picazón, *f;* (of the ears) zumbido, *m;* (thrill) estremecimiento, *m*

tinker /'tɪŋkər/ *n* calderero remendón, *m.* —*vt* remendar. —*vi* chafallar. **to t. with,** jugar con

tinkle /'tɪŋkəl/ *n* tilín, retintín, *m;* campanilleo, *m;* cencerreo, *m.* —*vi* tintinar. —*vt* hacer tintinar

tinkling /'tɪŋklɪŋ/ *n* retintín, tintineo, *m;* campanilleo, *m*

tinned /tɪnd/ *a* (of food) en lata, en conserva

tinsel /'tɪnsəl/ *n* oropel, *m;* (cloth) lama de oro o plata, *f,* brocadillo, *m; Fig.* oropel, *m.* —*a* de oropel; de brocadillo; *Fig.* charro. —*vt* adornar con oropel

tinsmith /'tɪn,smɪθ/ *n* hojalatero, estañador, *m*

tint /tɪnt/ *n* tinta, *f,* color, *m;* matiz, *m;* tinte, *m.* —*vt* colorar, teñir; matizar

tinting /'tɪntɪŋ/ *n* tintura, *f,* teñido, *m*

tiny /'taini/ *a* diminuto, minúsculo, menudo, chiquito

tip /tɪp/ *n* punta, *f;* cabo, *m,* extremidad, *f;* (of an umbrella, etc.) regatón, *m;* (of a lance) borne, *m;* (of a cigarette) boquilla, *f;* (of a shoe) puntera, *f;* (of a finger) yema, *f;* (for rubbish) depósito de basura, *m;* (gratuity) propina, *f;* (information) informe oportuno, *m;* (tap) golpecito, *m.* **to have on the tip of one's tongue,** tener en la punta de la lengua. **tip-cart,** volquete, *m.* **tip-up seat,** asiento plegable, *m*

tip /tɪp/ *vt* inclinar; volcar, voltear; (drinking vessel) empinar; poner regatón, etc. (a); *Poet.* tocar, golpear ligeramente; (reward) dar propina (a). —*vi* inclinarse; (topple) tambalearse; (reward) dar propina. **to tip the wink,** guiñar el ojo (a). **to tip off,** (liquids) echar; hacer caer; (inform) decir en secreto; informar oportunamente. **to tip over,** *vt* volcar; hacer caer. —*vi* volcarse; caer; (of a boat) zozobrar. **to tip up,** *vt* (a seat) levantar; (money) proporcionar (el dinero); (upset) volcar; hacer perder el equilibrio. —*vi* volcarse; (of a seat) levantarse; (lose the balance) perder el equilibrio

tipple /'tɪpəl/ *n* bebida, *f.* —*vt* beber, sorber. —*vi* empinar el codo

tippler /'tɪplər/ *n* borracho (-cha)

tipsily /'tɪpsəli/ *adv* como borracho

tipsiness /'tɪpsinɪs/ *n* borrachera, *f*

tipsy /'tɪpsi/ *a* achispado, algo borracho. **to be t.,** estar entre dos luces, estar entre dos velas

tiptoe /'tɪp,tou/ (**on**) *adv* de puntillas; *Fig.* excitado, ansioso. **to stand on t.,** ponerse de puntillas, empinarse

tirade /'taireid/ *n* diatriba, *f*

tire /taiᵊr/ *n* (of a cart, etc.) llanta, *f; Auto.* neumático, *m;* (of a perambulator, etc.) rueda de goma, *f.* **balloon t.,** neumático balón, *m.* **pneumatic t.,** neumático, *m.* **slack t.,** neumático desinflado, *m.* **solid t.,** neumático macizo, *m.* **spare t.,** neumático de recambio (or de repuesto), *m.* **t. burst,** estallido de un neumático, *m.* **t. valve,** válvula de cámara (del neumático), *f*

tire /taiᵊr/ *vt* cansar, fatigar; (bore) aburrir. *—vi* cansarse, fatigarse; aburrirse. **to be tired of,** estar cansado de. **to grow tired,** empezar a cansarse. **to t. out,** rendir de cansancio

tired /taiᵊrd/ *a* cansado, fatigado. **to be sick and t. of,** estar hasta la coronilla (de), (of persons) con. **t. of,** cansado de; disgustado de

tiredness /ˈtaɪᵊrdnɪs/ *n* cansancio, *m,* fatiga, *f;* aburrimiento, *m*

tireless /ˈtaiᵊrlɪs/ *a* infatigable, incansable

tirelessly /ˈtaiᵊrlɪsli/ *adv* sin tregua, sin cesar

tiresome /ˈtaiᵊrsəm/ *a* fastidioso, molesto, pesado; (dull) aburrido

tiresomeness /ˈtaiᵊrsəmnɪs/ *n* pesadez, *f,* fastidio, *m;* tedio, aburrimiento, *m*

tiring /ˈtaiᵊrɪŋ/ *a* fatigoso

tissue /ˈtɪʃu/ *n* (cloth) tisú, *m,* lama, *f;* (paper) pañuelito *m; Biol.* tejido, *m;* (series) serie, sarta, *f.* **t. paper,** papel de seda, *m*

tit /tɪt/ *n Ornith.* paro, *m.* **tit for tat,** tal para cual

Titan /ˈtaitn̩/ *n* titán, *m*

titanic /taiˈtænɪk/ *a* titánico

titbit /ˈtɪtˌbɪt/ *n* golosina, *f*

tithe /taið/ *n* décima, *f;* fracción, pequeña parte, *f, vt* diezmar. **t. gatherer,** diezmero (-ra)

titillate /ˈtɪtl̩ˌeit/ *vt* titilar, estimular

titivate /ˈtɪtəˌveit/ *vi* arreglarse

title /ˈtaitl̩/ *n* título, *m;* (right) derecho, *m;* documento, *m.* **to give a t. to,** intitular; ennoblecer. **t. deed,** títulos de propiedad, *m.* **t. page,** portada, *f.* **t. role,** papel principal, *m*

titter /ˈtɪtər/ *vi* reírse disimuladamente. *—n* risa disimulada, *f*

tittle /ˈtɪtl̩/ *n* adarme, tilde, ápice, *m*

titular /ˈtɪtʃələr/ *a* titular; nominal

to /tu; *unstressed* tʊ, tə/ *prep* a; (as far as) hasta; (in the direction of) en dirección a, hacia; (with indirect object) a; (until) hasta; (compared with) en comparación con, comparado con; (against) contra; (according to) según; (as) como; (in) en; (so that, in order to, for the purpose of) para; (indicating possession) a, de; (of time by the clock) menos; (by) por; (before verbs of motion or which imply motion) a (sometimes para); (before some other verbs) de; en; (before verbs of beginning, inviting, exhorting, obliging) a; (indicating indirect object) a; (before a subjunctive or infinitive indicating future action or obligation) que. **To** is often not translated. With most Spanish infinitives no separate translation is necessary, e.g. leer, decir, to read, to speak. Some verbs are always followed by a preposition (e.g. *to begin to speak,* empezar a hablar, etc.). *—adv* (shut) cerrado. **to come to,** volver en sí. **to lie to,** *Naut.* ponerse a la capa. **to and from,** de un lado a otro. **face to face,** cara a cara. **He has been a good friend to them,** Ha sido un buen amigo para ellos. **That is new to me,** Eso es nuevo para mí. **He went to London,** Se fue a Londres. **to go to France (Canada),** ir a Francia (al Canadá). **the road to Madrid,** la carretera de Madrid. **She kept the secret to herself,** Guardó el secreto para sí. **to go to the dentist,** ir al dentista. **We give it to them,** Se lo damos a ellos. **It belongs to me,** Pertenece a mí. **What does it matter to you?** ¿Qué te importa a tí? **I wish to see him,** Quiero verle. **They did it to help us,** Lo hicieron para ayudarnos. **I have to go to see her,** Tengo que ir a verla. **to this day,** hasta hoy, hasta el presente. **It is a quarter to six,** Son las seis menos cuarto. **to the last shilling,** hasta el último chelín. **the next to me,** el que me sigue. **closed to the public,** cerrado para el público

toad /toud/ *n* sapo, *m*

toadstool /ˈtoudˌstul/ *n* hongo, *m.* **poisonous t.,** seta venenosa, *f*

toady /ˈtoudi/ *n* lameculos, *mf* adulador (-ra). *—vt* lamer el culo (a), adular

toast /toust/ *n Cul.* tostada, *f;* (drink) brindis, *m.* *—vt* tostar; brindar, beber a la salud de. *—vi* brindar. **buttered t.,** mantecada, *f.* **t.-rack,** portatostadas, *m*

toaster /ˈtoustər/ *n* (device) tostador, *m;* (person) brindador, *m*

toasting /ˈtoustɪŋ/ *n* tostadura, *f,* tueste, *m, a* de tostar. **t.-fork,** tostadera, *f*

tobacco /təˈbækou/ *n* tabaco, *m.* *—a* tabacalero. **black** or **cut t.,** picadura, *f.* **leaf t.,** tabaco de hoja, *m.* **mild t.,** tobaco flojo, *m.* **pipe t.,** tabaco de pipa, *m.* **plug t.,** tabaco para mascar, *m.* **strong t.,** tabaco fuerte, *m.* **Turkish t.,** tabaco turco, *m.* **Virginian t.,** tabaco rubio, *m.* **t.-pipe,** pipa (de tabaco), *f.* **t.-pipe cleaner,** escobillón para limpiar pipas, *m.* **t. plantation,** tabacal, *m.* **t. planter,** tabacalero (-ra). **t. poisoning,** tabaquismo, *m.* **t.-pouch** or **jar,** tabaquera, *f*

tobacconist /təˈbækənɪst/ *n* tabaquero (-ra). **tobacconist's shop,** tabaquería, *f*

toboggan /təˈbɒgən/ *n* tobogán, *m.* *—vi* ir en tobogán. **t. run,** pista de tobogán, *f*

tocsin /ˈtɒksɪn/ *n* rebato, *m*

today /təˈdei/ *adv* hoy; ahora, actualmente, al presente, hoy día. *—n* el día de hoy. **from t.,** desde hoy. **from t. forward,** de hoy en adelante

toddle /ˈtɒdl̩/ *vi* hacer pinos, empezar a andar; (stroll) dar una vuelta; (leave) marcharse

toddy /ˈtɒdi/ *n* ponche, *m*

toe /tou/ *n* dedo del pie, *m;* (cloven) pezuña, *f;* uña, *f;* (of furniture) base, *f,* pie, *m;* (of stockings, shoes) punta, *f.* **He stepped on my toe,** Me pisó el dedo del pie. **big toe,** dedo pulgar del pie, dedo gordo del pie, *m.* **little toe,** dedo pequeño del pie, *m.* **to toe the line,** ponerse en la raya; *Fig.* cumplir con su deber. **toe-cap,** puntera, *f.* **toe-dancing,** baile de puntillas, *m.* **toe-nail,** uña del dedo del pie, *f*

toffee /ˈtɔfi/ *n* caramelo, *m*

toga /ˈtougə/ *n* toga, *f*

together /təˈgɛðər/ *adv* junto; (uninterruptedly) sin interrupción; (in concert) simultáneamente, a la vez, al mismo tiempo; (consecutively) seguido. **t. with,** con; junto con; en compañía de; (simultaneously) a la vez que

toil /tɔil/ *n* labor, *f,* trabajo, *m* *—pl.* **toils,** lazos, *m pl; Fig.* redes, *f pl.* *—vi* trabajar, afanarse. **to t. along,** caminar penosamente (por); adelantar con dificultad. **to t. up,** subir penosamente

toiler /ˈtɔilər/ *n* trabajador (-ra)

toilet /ˈtɔilɪt/ *n* tocado, *m;* atavío, *m;* vestido, *m;* (w.c.) retrete, excusado, *m;* (for ladies) tocador, *m.* **to make one's t.,** arreglarse. **t. case,** neceser, *m.* **t.-paper,** papel higiénico, *m.* **t.-powder,** polvos de arroz, *m pl.* **t. roll,** rollo de papel higiénico, *m.* **t.-set,** juego de tocador, *m.* **t. soap,** jabón de olor, jabón de tocador, *m*

toiling /ˈtɔilɪŋ/ *n* trabajo duro, *m, a* laborioso, trabajador

token /ˈtoukən/ *n* señal, muestra, *f;* prueba, *f;* (presage) síntoma, indicio, *m;* (remembrance) recuerdo, *m.* **as a t. of,** en señal de; como recuerdo de

Tokyo /ˈtoukiˌou/ Tokio, *m*

tolerable /ˈtɒlərəbəl/ *a* tolerable, soportable, llevadero; (fairly good) mediano, mediocre, regular

tolerably /ˈtɒlərəbli/ *adv* bastante

tolerance /ˈtɒlərəns/ *n* tolerancia, *f;* paciencia, indulgencia, *f*

tolerant /ˈtɒlərənt/ *a* tolerante; indulgente

tolerate /ˈtɒləˌreit/ *vt* tolerar, sufrir, soportar; permitir

toleration /ˌtɒləˈreiʃən/ *n* tolerancia, *f;* indulgencia, paciencia, *f.* **religious t.,** libertad de cultos, *f*

toll /toul/ *n* (of a bell) tañido, doble, *m;* (for passage) peaje, portazgo, *m;* (for grinding) derecho de molienda, *m.* *—vt* and *vi* doblar, tañer. **to t. the hour,** dar la hora. **t. call,** conferencia telefónica interurbana, llamada a larga distancia, *f.* **t. gate,** barrera de peaje, *f.* **t. house,** oficina de portazgos, *f*

toll booth *n* caseta de pago, *f*

tolling /ˈtoulɪŋ/ *n* tañido, clamor (de las campanas), *m*

Tom /tɒm/ *n* Tomás, *m;* (cat) gato, *m.* **Tom, Dick and Harry,** Fulano, Zutano y Mengano

tomahawk /'tɒmə,hɔk/ *n* hacha de guerra de los indios, *f*

tomato /tə'meitou/ *n* tomate, jitomate, (Mexico) *m.* **t. plant,** tomatera, *f.* **t. sauce,** salsa de tomate, *f*

tomb /tum/ *n* tumba, *f,* sepulcro, *m*

tombac /'tɒmbæk/ *n* tombac, *m,* tumbaga, *f*

tomboy /'tɒm,bɔi/ *n* muchachote, torbellino, *m*

tombstone /'tum,stoun/ *n* piedra mortuoria, *f,* monumento funerario, *m*

tome /toum/ *n* tomo, volumen, *m*

tomfoolery /,tɒm'fuləri/ *n* necedad, tontería, *f;* payasada, *f*

tommy gun /'tɒmi/ *n* pistola automática

tomorrow /tə'mɔrou/ *adv* and *n* mañana, *f.* **a fortnight t.,** mañana en quince. **the day after t.,** pasado mañana. **t. afternoon (morning),** mañana por la tarde (mañana). **T. is Friday,** Mañana es viernes

ton /tʌn/ *n* tonelada, *f*

tonality /tou'nælıti/ *n* tonalidad, *f*

tone /toun/ *n* tono, *m;* (*Mus. Med. Art.*) tono, *m;* (of the voice) acento, *m,* entonación, *f;* (of musical instruments) sonido, *m;* (shade) matiz, *m.* —*vt* entonar; *Photo* virar. **to t. down,** *vt* (*Art. Mus.*) amortiguar; *Fig.* suavizar, modificar. —*vi* (*Art. Mus.*) amortiguarse; *Fig.* suavizarse, modificarse. **to t. in with,** (of colors) *vt* armonizar con. —*vi* armonizarse, corresponder en tono o matiz. **to t. up,** *vt* subir de color, intensificar el color de; *Med.* entonar, robustecer. **t. poem,** poema sinfónico, *m*

tonelessly /'tounlısli/ *adv* sin tono; apáticamente

tongs /tɔŋz/ *n pl* tenazas, *f pl;* tenacillas, *f pl.* **curling t.,** tenacillas para el pelo, *f pl.* **sugar t.,** tenacillas para azúcar, *f pl*

tongue /tʌŋ/ *n Anat.* lengua, *f;* (language) idioma, *m,* lengua, *f;* (speech) modo de hablar, *m,* habla, *f;* *Mus.* lengüeta, *f;* (of buckle) diente, *m;* (of shoe) oreja, *f;* (of land) lengua, *f;* (of a bell) badajo, *m;* (flame) lengua, *f.* **My t. ran away with me,** *Inf.* Se me fue la mula. **to give t.,** ladrar. **to hold one's t.,** cerrar el pico, tener la boca. **t. of fire,** lengua de fuego, *f.* **t. tied,** con impedimento en el habla; turbado, confuso; mudo. **t.-twister,** trabalenguas, *m*

-tongued *a* de voz...

tonic /'tɒnık/ *a* tónico. —*n Med.* tónico, reconstituyente, *m;* *Mus.* tónica, *f*

tonight /tə'nait/ *adv* and *n* esta noche

tonnage /'tʌnıdʒ/ *n* tonelaje, porte, *m;* (duty) derecho de tonelaje, *m*

tonner /'tʌnər/ *n Naut.* de... toneladas

tonsil /'tɒnsəl/ *n* amígdala, *f*

tonsillitis /,tɒnsə'laitıs/ *n* amigdalitis, *f*

tonsure /'tɒnʃər/ *n Eccl.* tonsura, *f, vt* tonsurar

tonsured /'tɒnʃərd/ *a* tonsurado

too /tu/ *adv* demasiado; (very) muy; también; además. **too hard,** demasiado difícil, demasiado rígido; (of persons) demasiado duro. **too much,** demasiado. **too often,** con demasiada frecuencia

tool /tul/ *n* herramienta, *f;* utensilio, *m;* instrumento, *m;* (person) criatura, *f.* —*vt* labrar con herramienta; (a book) estampar en seco. **t.-bag,** capacho, *m.* **t. box,** caja de herramientas, *f*

tooling /'tulıŋ/ *n* (of books) estampación en seco, *f*

toot /tut/ *n* sonido de bocina, *m, vi* sonar una bocina

tooth /tuθ/ *n* diente, *m;* muela, *f;* (of comb) púa, *f;* (taste) gusto, paladar, *m;* (cog) diente de rueda, *m;* (of saw) diente, *m.* —*vt* dentar; mellar. —*vi Mech.* engranar. **armed to the teeth,** armado hasta los dientes. **double t.,** muela, *f.* **false teeth,** dentadura postiza, *f.* **set of teeth,** dentadura, *f.* **to cut one's teeth,** echar los dientes. **to have a sweet t.,** ser muy goloso. **to show one's teeth,** enseñar los dientes. **t.-brush,** cepillo para los dientes, *m.* **t. drawing,** extracción de un diente, *f.* **t.-paste,** pasta dentífrica, *f*

toothache /'tuθ,eik/ *n* dolor de muelas, *m*

toothed /tuθt/ *a* con dientes; dentado

toothless /'tuθlıs/ *a* desdentado, sin dientes; (of combs) sin púas

toothpick /'tuθ,pık/ *n* mondadientes, *m*

top /tɒp/ *n* (summit) cima, cumbre, *f;* (of a tree) copa, *f;* (of the head) coronilla, *f;* (of a page) cabeza, *f;* (crest) copete, *m,* cresta, *f;* (surface) superficie, *f;* (of a wall) coronamiento, *m;* (tip) punta, *f;* (point) ápice, *m;* (of a tram, bus) imperial, baca, *f;* (of a wave) cresta, *f;* (acme) auge, *m;* (of a class) primero (de la clase), *m;* (highest rank) último grado, *m;* (of a plant) hojas, *f pl;* (of a piano) cima, *f; Naut.* cofa, *f;* (head of a bed, etc.) cabeza, *f;* (lid) tapadera, *f;* (toy) trompo, peón, *m;* (humming) trompa, *f, a* más alto; máximo; (chief) principal, primero. —*vt* (cover) cubrir de; (cut off) desmochar; (come level with) llegar a la cima de; (rise above) elevarse por encima (de), coronar, dominar; (be superior to) exceder, aventajar; (golf) topear. **at the top,** a la cabeza; a la cumbre. **from top to bottom,** de arriba abajo. **on top of,** encima de; (besides) en adición a, además de. **to be top-dog,** ser un gallito. **to sleep like a top,** dormir como un lirón. **top boots,** botas de campaña, *f pl.* **top-dog,** vencedor, *m;* poderoso, *m.* **top-hat,** sombrero de copa, *m.* **top-heavy,** más pesado por arriba que por abajo

topaz /'toupæz/ *n* topacio, jacinto occidental, *m*

topcoat /'tɒp,kout/ *n* sobretodo, gabán, *m*

top floor *n* piso alto, *m*

topic /'tɒpık/ *n* asunto, tema, *m*

topical /'tɒpıkəl/ *a* tópico; actual

topknot /'tɒp,nɒt/ *n* cresta, *f,* penacho, *m;* (of birds) moño, *m;* copete, *m*

topmast /'tɒp,mæst, *Naut.* -məst/ *n* mastelero, *m*

topmost /'tɒp,moust/ *a* más alto; más importante

topographer /tə'pɒgrəfər/ *n* topógrafo, *m*

topographical /,tɒpə'græfıkəl/ *a* topográfico

topography /tə'pɒgrəfi/ *n* topografía, *f*

topple /'tɒpəl/ *vi* tambalearse, estar al punto de caer. **to t. down,** volcarse; derribarse; caer. **to t. over,** *vi* venirse abajo; perder el equilibrio. —*vt* derribar, hacer caer

topsail /'tɒp,seil; *Naut.* -səl/ *n* gavia, *f*

topsy-turvy /'tɒpsi'tɜrvi/ *a* desordenado. —*adv* en desorden, patas arriba, de arriba abajo

toque /touk/ *n* toca, *f*

torch /tɔrtʃ/ *n* antorcha, hacha, tea, *f.* **electric t.,** lamparilla eléctrica, *f.* **t.-bearer,** hachero, *m*

torchlight /'tɔrtʃ,lait/ *n* luz de antorcha, *f.* **by t.,** a la luz de las antorchas

torment /*v.* tɔr'mɛnt, *n.* 'tɔrmɛnt/ *n* tormento, *m,* angustia, *f;* (torture) tortura, *f;* suplicio, *m;* mortificación, *f;* disgusto, *m.* —*vt* atormentar, martirizar; (torture) torturar; molestar

tormentor /tɔr'mɛntər/ *n* atormentador (-ra)

tornado /tɔr'neidou/ *n* tornado, *m*

torpedo /tɔr'pidou/ *n* torpedo, *m; Ichth.* pez torpedo, *m.* —*vt* torpedear. **self-propelling t.,** torpedo automóvil, *m.* **t.-boat,** torpedero, *m.* **t.-boat destroyer,** cazatorpedero, contratorpedero, *m.* **t. netting,** red contra torpedos, *f.* **t. station,** base de torpederos, *f.* **t. tube,** tubo lanzatorpedos, *m*

torpedoing /tɔr'pidouıŋ/ *n* torpedeamiento, torpedeo, *m*

torpid /'tɔrpıd/ *a* aletargado, entorpecido; (of the mind) torpe, tardo, apático

torpidity, torpor /tɔr'pıdıti, 'tɔrpər/ *n* letargo, *m;* apatía, *f*

torrent /'tɔrənt/ *n* torrente, *m*

torrential /tɔ'rɛnʃəl/ *a* torrencial

torrid /'tɔrıd/ *a* tórrido. **t. zone,** zona tórrida, *f*

torsion /'tɔrʃən/ *n* torsión, *f*

torso /'tɔrsou/ *n* torso, *m*

tort /tɔrt/ *n Law.* tuerto, *m*

tortoise /'tɔrtəs/ *n* tortuga, *f.* **t.-shell,** carey, *m.* —*a* de carey

tortuous /'tɔrtʃuəs/ *a* tortuoso

tortuousness /'tɔrtʃuəsnıs/ *n* tortuosidad, *f*

torture /'tɔrtʃər/ *n* tortura, *f,* tormento, *m;* angustia, *f.* —*vt* torturar, dar tormento (a); martirizar

torturer /'tɔrtʃərər/ *n* atormentador (-ra)

torturing /'tɔrtʃərıŋ/ *a* torturador, atormentador; angustioso

toss /tɔs/ *n* sacudimiento, *m,* sacudidad, *f;* (of the head) movimiento (de cabeza), *m;* (bull fighting) cogida, *f;* (from a horse) caída de caballo, *f.* —*vt* echar, lanzar; agitar, sacudir; (of bulls) acornear. —*vi* agitarse; (of plumes, etc.) ondear; (in a boat) balancearse a la merced de las olas; jugar a cara o cruz. **to t. in a blanket,** mantear, dar una manta (a). **to t. aside,** echar a un lado; abandonar. **to t. off,** beber de un trago. **to t. up,** jugar a cara o cruz

tot /tɒt/ *n* (child) nene (-na), crío (-ía); (of drink) vaso pequeño, *m.* **to tot up,** sumar

total /ˈtoutḷ/ *a* total; absoluto, completo, entero. —*n* total, *m,* suma, *f.* —*vt* sumar. —*vi* ascender (a). **t. employment,** ocupación total, *f.* **t. war,** guerra total, *f*

totalitarian /touˌtælɪˈtɛəriən/ *a* totalitario

totality /touˈtælɪti/ *n* totalidad, *f*

totally /ˈtoutḷi/ *adv* totalmente, completamente

totem /ˈtoutəm/ *n* tótem, *m*

totemism /ˈtoutəˌmɪzəm/ *n* totemismo, *m*

totter /ˈtɒtər/ *vi* (of persons) bambolearse; tambalear, estar al punto de caer; *Fig.* aproximarse a su fin

tottering /ˈtɒtərɪŋ/ *a* vacilante; tambaleante. —*n* bamboleo, *m;* tambaleo, *m*

toucan /ˈtukæn/ *n* *Ornith.* tucán, *m*

touch /tʌtʃ/ *vt* tocar; (brush against) rozar; (reach) alcanzar; (musical instruments) tocar; (move) emocionar, enternecer; (spur on) aguijar; (food) tomar; (affect) influir, afectar; (arouse) despertar, estimular; (equal) compararse con, igualar; (consider) tratar ligeramente (de); (money) dar un sablazo (a). —*vi* tocarse; imponer las manos para curar. **I have not touched a bite,** No he probado un bocado. **This touches me dearly,** Esto me toca de cerca. **to t. at,** hacer escala en, tocar en (un puerto). **to t. off,** descargar. **to t. up,** retocar; corregir. **to t. upon,** (a subject) tratar superficialmente de, tratar ligeramente de; hablar de; considerar

touch /tʌtʃ/ *n* (sense of) tacto, *m;* (contact) toque, contacto, *m;* (brushing) roce, *m;* (tap) golpe ligero, *m;* palmadita, *f;* (of an illness) ataque ligero, *m;* *Mus.* dedeo, *m;* (little) dejo, *m;* (test) prueba, *f,* toque, *m;* *Art.* toque, *m,* pincelada, *f.* **by the t.,** a tiento. **in t. with,** en relaciones con; en comunicación con; al corriente de. **to give the finishing t.,** dar la última pincelada; dar el último toque. **t.-line,** (football) línea de toque, línea lateral, *f.* **t.-me-not,** *Inf.* erizo, *m.* **t.-stone,** piedra de toque, *f*

touched /tʌtʃt/ *a* emocionado, conmovido

touchiness /ˈtʌtʃinɪs/ *n* susceptibilidad, *f*

touching /ˈtʌtʃɪŋ/ *a* patético, conmovedor. —*prep* tocante a, acerca de. —*n* tocamiento, *m*

touchy /ˈtʌtʃi/ *a* susceptible, quisquilloso, vidrioso

tough /tʌf/ *a* (hard) duro; vigoroso, fuerte, robusto; resistente; (of character) tenaz, firme; (of a job) difícil; espinoso. —*n* chulo, *m*

toughen /ˈtʌfən/ *vt* endurecer. —*vi* endurecerse

toughness /ˈtʌfnɪs/ *n* dureza, *f;* vigor, *m,* fuerza, *f;* resistencia, *f;* tenacidad, firmeza, *f;* dificultad, *f*

Toulouse /tʊˈluz/ Tolosa, *f*

toupee /tuˈpei/ *n* tupé, *m*

tour /tʊr/ *n* viaje, *m,* excursión, *f.* —*vi* viajar. —*vt* viajar por. **circular t.,** viaje redondo, *m.* **on t.,** *Theat.* en tour, de gira

touring /ˈtʊrɪŋ/ *a* de turismo. —*n* turismo, *m;* viaje, *m.* **t. car,** coche de turismo, *m*

tourist /ˈtʊrɪst/ *n* turista, *mf;* viajero (-ra). **t. agency,** agencia de turismo, *f,* patronato de turismo, *m.* **t. ticket,** billete kilométrico, *m*

tournament /ˈtʊrnəmənt/ *n* torneo, *m,* justa, *f;* (of games) concurso, *m*

tourniquet /ˈtɜrnɪkɪt, ˈtʊr-/ *n* torniquete, *m*

tousle /ˈtauzəl, -səl/ *vt* despeinar; desordenar el pelo

tout /taut/ *n* buhonero, *m.* **to t. for,** pescar, solicitar

tow /tou/ *n* remolque, *m;* (rope) estopa, *f.* —*vt* (*Naut. Auto.*) remolcar. **on tow,** a remolque. **tow-path,** camino de sirga, *m.* **tow rope,** cable de remolque, *m*

towage /ˈtouɪdʒ/ *n* remolque, *m;* (fee) derechos de remolque, *m pl*

towards /tɔrdʒ/ *prep* hacia, en dirección a; (of time) sobre, cerca de; (concerning) tocante a; (with persons) para, con

towel /ˈtauəl/ *n* toalla, *f.* **roller t.,** toalla continua, *f.* **t. rail,** toallero, *m*

toweling /ˈtauəlɪŋ/ *n* tela para toallas, *f*

tower /ˈtauər/ *n* torre, *f;* (fortress) fortaleza, *f;* (belfry) campanario, *m;* (large) torreón, *m.* —*vi* elevarse. **to t. above,** destacarse sobre, sobresalir; *Fig.* sobrepujar, superar

towered /ˈtauərd/ *a* torreado; de las... torres. **high t.,** de las altas torres

towering /ˈtauərɪŋ/ *a* elevado; dominante; orgulloso; *Fig.* violento, terrible

town /taun/ *n* población, *f,* pueblo, *m;* ciudad, *f.* **t. clerk,** secretario de ayuntamiento, *m.* **t. council,** concejo municipal, *m.* **t. councilor,** concejero municipal, *m.* **t. crier,** pregonero, *m.* **t. hall,** (casa de) ayuntamiento, casa consistorial, *f.* **t. house,** casa de ciudad, *f* **t. planning,** urbanismo, *m;* reforma urbana, *f.* **t. wall,** muralla, *f*

"Town Ahead" «Poblado Próximo»

townsman /ˈtaunzmən/ *n* ciudadano, *m*

town worthy *n* persona principal de la ciudad, *f*

toxic /ˈtɒksɪk/ *a* tóxico

toxicological /ˌtɒksɪkəˈlɒdʒɪkəl/ *a* toxicológico

toxicologist /ˌtɒksɪˈkɒlədʒɪst/ *n* toxicólogo, *m*

toxicology /ˌtɒksɪˈkɒlədʒi/ *n* toxicología, *f*

toxin /ˈtɒksɪn/ *n* toxina, *f*

toy /tɔi/ *n* juguete, *m.* —*vi* (with) jugar con; acariciar. **toy maker,** fabricante de juguetes, *m*

toyshop /ˈtɔiˌʃɒp/ *n* juguetería, tienda de juguetes, *f*

trace /treis/ huella, pista, *f,* rastro, *m;* vestigio, *m;* indicio, *m,* evidencia, *f;* (of a harness) tirante, *m;* (touch) dejo, *m;* (of fear, etc.) sombra, *f.* —*vt* trazar; (through transparent paper) calcar; seguir la pista (de); (write) escribir; (discern) distinguir; investigar; descubrir; determinar; (walk) atravesar, recorrer. **to t. back,** (of ancestry, etc.) hacer remontar (a)

traceable /ˈtreisəbəl/ *a* que se puede trazar; atribuible

tracer /ˈtreisər/ *n* trazador (-ra). **t. bullet,** bala luminosa, *f*

tracery /ˈtreisəri/ *n* tracería, *f*

trachea /ˈtreikiə/ *n* *Anat.* tráquea, *f*

trachoma /trəˈkoumə/ *n* *Med.* tracoma, *f*

tracing /ˈtreisɪŋ/ *n* calco, *m;* trazo, *m;* seguimiento, *m.* **t.-paper,** papel de calcar, *m*

track /træk/ *n* huella, *f,* rastro, *m;* (for racing, etc.) pista, *f;* (of wheels) rodada, *f;* (railway) vía, *f;* (of a boat) estela, *f;* (path) senda, vereda, *f;* (sign) señal, evidencia, *f;* (course) ruta, *f.* —*vt* rastrear, seguir la pista (de); *Naut.* sirgar. **to t. down,** seguir y capturar. **double t.,** vía doble, *f.* **off the t.,** extraviado; (of a train) descarrilado; *Fig.* por los cerros de Úbeda. **side t.,** desviadero, *m.* **to keep t. of,** *Inf.* no perder de vista (a); seguir las fortunas de

trackless /ˈtræklɪs/ *a* sin camino; sin huella; (of trams, etc.) sin rieles; (untrodden) no pisado

tract /trækt/ *n* tracto, *m;* región, *f;* *Anat.* vía, *f;* (written) tratado, *m*

tractability /ˌtræktəbɪlɪti/ *n* docilidad, *f*

tractable /ˈtræktəbəl/ *a* dócil

traction /ˈtrækʃən/ *n* tracción, *f.* **t.-engine,** máquina de arrastre (or de tracción), *f*

tractor /ˈtræktər/ *n* máquina de arrastre, *f;* tractor, *m*

trade /treid/ *n* comercio, *m;* tráfico, *m;* negocio, *m;* industria, *f;* (calling) oficio, *m,* profesión, *f;* (dealers) comerciantes, *mf pl.* —*vi* comerciar, traficar. —*vt* cambiar. **to t. on,** explotar, aprovecharse de. **by t.,** de oficio, por profesión. **t.-mark,** marca de fábrica, *f.* **t.-name,** razón social, *f.* **t. price,** precio para el comerciante, *m.* **t. union,** sindicato, *m.* **T. Union Congress,** Congreso de Sindicatos, *m.* **t. unionism,** sistema de sindicatos obreros, *m.* **t.-winds,** vientos alisios, *m pl*

trader /ˈtreidər/ *n* comerciante, traficante, *mf;* mercader, *m;* (boat) buque mercante, *m*

tradesman /ˈtreidzmən/ *n* tendero, *m.* **tradesmen's entrance,** puerta de servicio, *f*

trading /ˈtreidɪŋ/ *n* comercio, tráfico, *m.* —*a* mercantil, comerciante, mercante. **t. ship,** buque mercante, *m.* **t. station,** factoría, *f*

tradition /trəˈdɪʃən/ *n* tradición, *f*

traditional /trəˈdɪʃənḷ/ *a* tradicional; del lugar

traditionalism /trəˈdɪʃənḷˌɪzəm/ *n* tradicionalismo, *m*

traditionalist /trəˈdɪʃənḷɪst/ *n* tradicionalista, *mf*

traditionally /trəˈdɪʃənḷi/ *adv* según la tradición, tradicionalmente

traduce /trə'dus/ *vt* calumniar, denigrar, vituperar

traducer /trə'dusər/ *n* calumniador (-ra)

traffic /'træfık/ *n* comercio, negocio, tráfico, *m;* (in transit) transporte, *m;* (in movement) circulación, *f.* —*vi* comerciar, traficar, negociar. **to cause a block in the t.,** interrumpir la circulación. **t. block,** obstrución del tráfico, *f,* atasco en la circulación, *m.* **t. indicator,** (on a car) indicador de dirección, *m.* **t. island,** refugio para peatones, salvavidas, *m.* **t. light,** disco, *m,* luz (de tráfico), *f,* semáforo, *m.* **t. roundabout,** redondel, *m*

trafficker /'træfıkər/ *n* traficante, *mf*

tragedian /trə'dʒidiən/ *n* trágico, *m*

tragedy /'trædʒıdi/ *n* tragedia, *f*

tragic /'trædʒık/ *a* trágico

tragicomedy /ˌtrædʒı'kɒmıdi/ *n* tragicomedia, *f*

tragicomic /ˌtrædʒı'kɒmık/ *a* tragicómico

trail /treil/ *n* rastro, *m,* pista, huella, *f;* (path) sendero, *m;* (of a comet) cola, cabellera, *f.* —*vt* rastrear, seguir el rastro de; (drag) arrastrar; (the anchor) garrar. —*vi* arrastrar; (of plants) trepar. **on the t. of,** en busca de; siguiendo el rastro de; **put somebody on the t. of...** darle a fulano la pista de...

trailer /'treilər/ *n* cazador (-ra); perseguidor (-ra); *Auto.* remolque, *m;* (cinema) anuncio de próximas atracciones, *m; Bot.* talle rastrero, *m*

train /trein/ *n* (railway) tren, *m;* (of a dress) cola, *f;* (retinue) séquito, *m;* (procession) desfile, *m,* comitiva, *f;* (series) serie, sucesión, *f;* (of gunpowder) reguero de pólvora, *m.* **down t.,** tren descendente, *m.* **excursion t.,** tren de excursionistas, *m.* **express t.,** exprés, tren expreso, *m.* **fast t.,** rápido, *m.* **goods t.,** tren de mercancías, *m.* **mail t.,** tren correo, *m.* **next t.,** próximo tren, *m.* **passenger t.,** tren de pasajeros, *m.* **stopping t.,** tren ómnibus, *m.* **through t.,** tren directo, *m.* **up t.,** tren ascendente, *m.* **t.-bearer,** paje que lleva la cola, *m;* dama de honor, *f;* (of a cardinal, etc.) caudatario, *m.* **t.-ferry,** buque transbordador, *m.* **t.-oil,** aceite de ballena, *m.* **t. service,** servicio de trenes, *m*

train /trein/ *vt* educar; adiestrar; enseñar; *Sports.* entrenar; (firearms) apuntar; (plants) guiar; (accustom) habituar, acostumbrar; (a horse for racing) entrenar; (circus) amaestrar. —*vi* educarse; adiestrarse; *Sports.* entrenarse

trainer /'treinər/ *n* (of men and racehorses) entrenador, *m;* (of performing animals) domador, *m*

training /'treinıŋ/ *n* educación, *f;* enseñanza, instrucción, *f; Sports.* entrenamiento, *m.* **t.-college,** escuela normal, *f.* **t.-ship,** buque escuela, *m*

trait /treit/ *n* rasgo, *m,* característica, *f*

traitor /'treitər/ *n* traidor, *m*

traitress /'treitrıs/ *n* traidora, *f*

trajectory /trə'dʒɛktəri/ *n* trayectoria, *f*

tram /træm/ *n* tranvía, *m.* —*a* tranviario. **t. conductor,** cobrador de tranvía, *m.* **t. depot,** cochera de tranvías, *f.* **t. stop,** parada de tranvía, *f*

trammel /'træməl/ *n* (of a horse) traba, *f; Fig.* obstáculo, estorbo, *m.* —*vt* travar; *Fig.* estorbar, impedir

tramp /træmp/ *n* (person) vagabundo (-da); vago (-ga); (walk) caminata, *f,* paseo largo, *m;* ruido de pasos, *m; Naut.* vapor volandero, *m.* —*vi* ir a pie; patear; vagabundear. —*vt* vagar por

trample /'træmpəl/ *n* pisoteo, *m;* (of feet) ruido de pasos, *m.* —*vt* pisotear, pisar, hollar. —*vi* pisar fuerte. **to t. on,** *Fig.* atropellar humillar

trance /træns/ *n* rapto, arrobamiento, *m; Med.* catalepsia, *f*

tranquil /'træŋkwıl/ *a* tranquilo, apacible; sereno, sosegado

tranquility /træŋ'kwılıti/ *n* tranquilidad, paz, quietud, *f;* serenidad, *f,* sosiego, *m;* calma, *f*

tranquilize /'træŋkwəˌlaiz/ *vt* tranquilizar, sosegar, calmar

tranquilizer /'træŋkwəˌlaizər/ *n* calmante, *m*

tranquilizing /'træŋkwəˌlaizıŋ/ *a* sosegador, tranquilizador

trans- *prefix* trans-. **t.-Pyrenean,** *a* traspirenaico. **to t. -ship,** trasbordar. **t.-shipment,** trasbordo, *m.* **t.-Siberian,** trasiberiano

trans- *prefix* trans-. **t.-Pyrenean,** *a* traspirenaico. **to t. -ship,** trasbordar. **t.-shipment,** trasbordo, *m.* **t.-Siberian,** trasiberiano

transact /træn'sækt/ *vt* despachar, hacer. —*vi* despachar un negocio

transaction /træn'sækʃən/ *n* desempeño, *m;* negocio, *m;* transacción, operación, *f; pl* **transactions** (of a society) actas, *f pl*

transatlantic /ˌtrænsət'læntık/ *a* transatlántico. **t. liner,** transatlántico, *m*

transcend /træn'sɛnd/ *vt* exceder, superar, rebasar. —*vi* trascender

transcendence /træn'sɛndəns/ *n* superioridad, *f;* trascendencia, *f*

transcendental /ˌtrænsɛn'dɛntl̩/ *a* trascendental

transcontinental /ˌtrænskɒntn̩'ɛntl̩/ *a* transcontinental

transcribe /træn'skraib/ *vt* trascribir, copiar; *Mus.* trascribir, adaptar

transcriber /træn'skraibər/ *n* copiador (-ra); *Mus.* adaptador (-ra)

transcript /'trænskrıpt/ *n* traslado, trasunto, *m;* (student's) certificado de estudios, certificado de materias aprobadas, *m,* constancia de estudios, copia del expediente académico, hoja de estudios, *f*

transcription /træn'skrıpʃən/ *n* trascripción, copia, *f,* trasunto, *m; Mus.* trascripción, adaptación, *f,* arreglo, *m*

transept /'trænsɛpt/ *n Archit.* transepto, crucero, *m*

transfer /*v.* træns'fɜr, *n.* 'trænsfər/ *n* traslado, *m;* trasferencia, *f,* traspaso, *m; Law.* cesión, enajenación, *f;* (picture) calcomanía, *f.* —*vt* trasladar; trasferir; pasar; *Law.* enajenar, ceder; estampar; calcografiar. —*vi* trasbordarse. **deed of t.,** escritura de cesión, *f.* **t. -paper,** papel de calcar, *m*

transferable /træns'fɜrəbəl/ *a* trasferible

transferee /ˌtrænsfə'ri/ *n* cesionario (-ia)

transference /træns'fɜrəns/ *n* traslado, *m;* transferencia, *f; Law.* cesión, enajenación, *f*

transferor /træns'fɜrər/ *n* cesionista, *mf*

transfiguration /ˌtrænsfıgyə'reiʃən/ *n* trasfiguración, *f*

transfigure /træns'fıgyər/ *vt* trasfigurar, trasformar

transfix /træns'fıks/ *vt* traspasar; *Fig.* paralizar

transfixion /træns'fıkʃən/ *n* trasfixión, *f*

transform /træns'fɔrm/ *vt* trasformar; convertir, cambiar. **It is completely transformed,** Está completamente trasformado

transformation /ˌtrænsfər'meiʃən/ *n* trasformación, *f;* conversión, *f,* cambio, *m*

transformative /træns'fɔrmətıv/ *a* trasformador

transformer /træns'fɔrmər/ *n Elec.* trasformador, *m*

transfuse /træns'fyuz/ *vt* trasfundir

transfusion /træns'fyuʒən/ *n* trasfusión, *f.* **blood t.,** trasfusión de sangre, *f*

transgress /træns'grɛs/ *vt* exceder, sobrepasar; (violate) contravenir, violar, pecar contra. —*vi* pecar

transgression /træns'grɛʃən/ *n* contravención, trasgresión, *f;* pecado, *m*

transgressor /træns'grɛsər/ *n* trasgresor (-ra), pecador (-ra)

transient /'trænʃənt, -ʒənt/ *a* transitorio, fugaz, pasajero; perecedero

transiently /'trænʃəntli, -ʒənt-/ *adv* pasajeramente

transit /'trænsıt/ *n* tránsito, paso, *m;* trasporte, *m; Astron.* tránsito, *m.* **in t.,** de tránsito

transition /træn'zıʃən/ *n* transición, *f;* cambio, *m;* tránsito, paso, *m*

transitional /træn'zıʃənl̩/ *a* de transición, transitorio

transitive /'trænsıtıv/ *a Gram.* transitivo, activo. **t. verb,** verbo transitivo, verbo activo, *m*

transitively /'trænsıtıvli/ *adv* transitivamente

transitorily /ˌtrænsı'tɔrəli/ *adv* transitoriamente; provisionalmente

transitoriness /'trænsıˌtɔrinıs/ *n* brevedad, *f,* lo fugaz

transitory /'trænsıˌtɔri/ *a* transitorio, fugaz, pasajero, breve

translatable /træns'leitəbəl/ *a* traducible

translate /træns'leit/ *vt* traducir; interpretar; (transfer) trasladar

translation /træns'leiʃən/ *n* traducción, *f;* versión, *f;* traslado, *m*

translator /træns'leitər/ *n* traductor (-ra)
translucence /træns'lusəns/ *n* traslucidez, *f*
translucent /træns'lusənt/ *a* traslúcido, trasparente
transmigrate /træns'maigreit/ *vi* trasmigrar
transmigration /ˌtrænsmai'greiʃən/ *n* trasmigración, *f*
transmissibility /trænsˌmɪsə'bɪlɪti/ *n* trasmisibilidad, *f*
transmissible /træns'mɪsəbəl/ *a* trasmisible
transmission /træns'mɪʃən/ *n* trasmisión, *f*
transmit /træns'mɪt/ *vt* trasmitir; remitir, dar
transmitter /træns'mɪtər/ *n* trasmisor (-ra); *Radio.* radiotrasmisor, *m; Elec.* trasmisor, *m*
transmutable /træns'myutəbəl/ *a* trasmutable
transmutation /ˌtrænsmyu'teiʃən/ *n* trasmutación, *f*
transmute /træns'myut/ *vt* trasmutar
transoceanic /ˌtrænsouʃi'ænɪk/ *a* transoceánico
transom /'trænsəm/ *n* travesaño, *m; Naut.* yugo de popa, *m*
transpacific /ˌtrænspə'sɪfɪk/ *a* traspacífico
transparency /træns'pɛərənsi/ *n* trasparencia; diafanidad, *f;* (picture) trasparente, *m*
transparent /træns'pɛərənt/ *a* trasparente; diáfano; (of style) claro, limpio
transpiration /ˌtrænspə'reiʃən/ *n* traspiración, *f*
transpire /træn'spaiᵊr/ *vi* traspirar; rezumarse; hacerse público; *Inf.* acontecer. —*vt* exhalar
transplant /træns'plænt/ *vt* trasplantar
transplantation /ˌtrænsplæn'teiʃən/ *n* trasplante, *m,* trasplantación, *f,*
transport /*v.* træns'pɔrt, *n.* 'trænspɔrt/ *n* trasporte, *m; Naut.* navío de trasporte, *m; Aer.* avión de trasporte, *m;* (fit) acceso, paroxismo, *m.* —*vt* trasportar; (convicts) deportar; *Fig.* (joy) colmar; (rage) llenar
transportable /træns'pɔrtəbəl/ *a* trasportable
transportation /ˌtrænspər'teiʃən/ *n* trasporte, *m;* (convicts) deportación, *f*
transporter /trænsˌpɔrtər/ *n* trasportador (-ra)
transpose /træns'pouz/ *vt* trasponer; *Mus.* trasportar
transposition /ˌtrænspə'zɪʃən/ *n* trasposición, *f*
transversal /træns'vɜrsəl/ *a* and *n* trasversal, *m*
transverse /træns'vɜrs/ *a* trasverso, trasversal
transversely /træns'vɜrsli/ *adv* trasversalmente
trap /træp/ *n* trampa, *f;* cepo, *m;* (net) lazo, *m,* red, *f;* (for mice, rats) ratonera, *f; Mech.* sifón de depósito, *m;* pequeño carruaje de dos ruedas, *m;* (door) puerta caediza, *f; Theat.* escotillón, *m; pl* **traps,** trastos, *m pl;* equipaje, *m.* —*vt* coger con trampa; hacer caer en el lazo; *Fig.* tender el lazo. —*vi* armar una trampa; armar lazo. **to fall into a t.,** *Fig.* caer en la trampa. **to pack one's traps,** liar el hato
trapeze /træ'piz/ *n* trapecio (de gimnasia), *m*
trapper /'træpər/ *n* cazador de animales de piel, *m*
trappings /'træpɪŋz/ *n pl* arneses, jaeces, *m pl;* arreos, aderezos, *m pl,* galas, *f pl*
trash /træʃ/ *n* paja, hojarasca, *f;* (of sugar, etc.) bagazo, *m;* trastos viejos, *m pl;* cachivaches, *m pl;* (literary) paja, *f*
trashy /'træʃi/ *a* de ningún valor, inútil, despreciable
traumatic /trə'mætɪk/ *a Med.* traumático
traumatism /'traumәˌtɪzəm/ *n Med.* traumatismo, *m*
travail /trə'veil/ *n* dolores de parto, *m pl.* —*vi* estar de parto; trabajar
travel /'trævəl/ *n* el viajar, viajes, *m pl.* —*vi* viajar; ver mundo; (of traffic) circular, pasar, ir. —*vt* viajar por; recorrer; (with number of miles) hacer. **to t. over,** viajar por; recorrer. **t. worn,** fatigado por el viaje
travel agent *n* agente de viajes, *mf*
traveled /'trævəld/ *a* que ha viajado, que ha visto muchas partes
traveler /'trævələr/ *n* viajero (-ra); pasajero (-ra). **commercial t.,** viajante, *mf* **traveler's check,** cheque de viajeros, *m.* **traveler's joy,** *Bot.* clemátide, *f*
traveling /'trævəlɪŋ/ *n* viajes, *m pl.* —*a* viajero; para (or de) viajar; (itinerant) ambulante. **t. crane,** grúa móvil, *f.* **t. expenses,** gastos de viaje, *m pl.* **t. requisites,** objetos de viaje, *m pl.* **t. rug,** manta, *f.* **t. show,** circo ambulante, *m*
traversable /trə'vɜrsəbəl/ *a* atravesable, transitable, practicable
traverse /*n., a.* 'trævərs; *v.* trə'vɜrs/ *n* travesaño, *m; Law.* negación, *f;* (*Mil. Archit.*) través, *m;* (crossing) travesía, *f, a* transversal. —*vt* atravesar, cruzar; *Law.* negar
travesty /'trævəsti/ *n* parodia, *f, vt* parodiar
trawl /trɔl/ *vt* rastrear. —*vi* pescar a la rastra. **t.-net,** red de arrastre, *f*
trawler /'trɔlər/ *n* barco barredero, *m;* pescador a la rastra, *m*
trawling /'trɔlɪŋ/ *n* pesca a la rastra, *f*
tray /trei/ *n* bandeja, *f;* (of a balance) platillo, *m;* (in a wardrobe, etc.) cajón, *m;* (trough) artesa, *f*
treacherous /'trɛtʃərəs/ *a* traidor, falso, pérfido, fementido; (of memory) infiel; engañoso; (of ice, etc.) peligroso
treacherously /'trɛtʃərəsli/ *adv* traidoramente, a traición
treachery /'trɛtʃəri/ *n* perfidia, traición, falsedad, *f*
treacle /'trikəl/ *n* melado, *m*
tread /trɛd/ *n* pisada, *f;* paso, *m;* (of a stair) peldaño, *m;* (of tire) pastilla, *f;* (walk) andar, porte, *m, vi* pisar; (trample) pisotear; hollar; (oppress) oprimir. —*vt* hollar; (a path) abrir; recorrer; caminar por; bailar. **to t. the grapes,** pisar las uvas. **to t. the stage,** pisar las tablas. **to t. under foot,** hollar; pisotear. **to t. on,** pisar. **to t. on one's heels,** pisarle los talones a uno; seguir de cerca. **to t. out,** (a measure) bailar
treading /'trɛdɪŋ/ *n* pisoteo, *m*
treadle /'trɛdl̩/ *n* pedal, *m;* (of a loom) cárcola, *f*
treadmill /'trɛdˌmɪl/ *n* molino de rueda de escalones, *m; Fig.* rueda, *f*
treason /'trizən/ *n* traición, *f.* **high t.,** alta traición, lesa majestad, *f*
treasonable /'trizənəbəl/ *a* desleal, traidor
treasonably /'trizənəbli/ *adv* traidoramente
treasure /'trɛʒər/ *n* tesoro, *m;* riqueza, *f,* caudal, *m; Fig.* perla, *f.* —*vt* atesorar; acumular (or guardar) riquezas; (a memory) guardar. **t. trove,** tesoro hallado, *m*
treasurer /'trɛʒərər/ *n* tesorero (-ra)
treasury /'trɛʒəri/ *n* tesorería, *f;* (government department) Ministerio de Hacienda, *m;* (anthology) tesoro, *m.* **t. bench,** banco del Gobierno, *m*
treat /trit/ *n* (pleasure) gusto, placer, *m;* (present) obsequio, *m;* (entertainment) fiesta, *f.* —*vt* tratar; *Med.* tratar, curar; (regale) obsequiar. —*vi* (stand host) convidar; (of) tratar de, versar sobre; (with) negociar con
treatise /'tritɪs/ *n* tesis, monografía, disertación, *f,* tratado, *m*
treatment /'tritmənt/ *n* tratamiento, *m;* (of persons) conducta hacia, *f,* modo de obrar con, *m; Med.* tratamiento, *m;* (*Lit., Art.*) procedimiento, *m,* técnica, *f*
treaty /'triti/ *n* tratado, pacto, *m;* (bargain) contrato, *m*
treble /'trɛbəl/ *n Mus.* tiple, *m;* voz de tiple, *f.* —*a* triple; *Mus.* sobreagudo. —*vt* triplicar; *vi* triplicarse. **t. clef,** clave de sol, *f*
trebling /'trɛblɪŋ/ *n* triplicación, *f*
tree /tri/ *n* árbol, *m;* (for shoes) horma, *f;* (of a saddle) arzón, *m.* **breadfruit t.,** árbol del pan, *m.* **Judas t.,** árbol de amor, *m.* **t. of knowledge,** árbol de la ciencia, *m.* **t.-covered,** arbolado. **t.-frog,** rana de San Antonio, *f*
treeless /'trilɪs/ *a* sin árboles
trefoil /'trifɔil/ *n* trébol, trifolio, *m*
trek /trɛk/ *vi* caminar, andar
trellis /'trɛlɪs/ *n* enrejado, *m;* (for plants) espaldera, *f.* —*vt* cercar con un enrejado; construir espalderas
tremble /'trɛmbəl/ *vi* temblar; estremecerse; trepidar; vibrar; (sway) oscilar; (of flags) ondear; agitarse; ser tembloroso. **His fate trembled in the balance,** Su suerte estaba en la balanza. **to t. all over,** temblar de pies a cabeza
trembling /'trɛmblɪŋ/ *n* temblor, *m;* estremecimiento, *m;* trepidación, *f;* vibración, *f;* (fear) agitación, ansiedad, *f;* temor, *m.* —*a* tembloroso; trémulo
tremendous /trɪ'mɛndəs/ *a* terrible, espantoso; formidable; grande; importante; *Inf.* tremendo; enorme
tremendously /trɪ'mɛndəsli/ *adv* terriblemente; *Inf.* enormemente
tremor /'trɛmər/ *n* temblor, movimento sísmico, *m;* (thrill) estremecimiento, *m;* vibración, *f*

tremulous /ˈtrɛmyələs/ *a* trémulo, tembloroso; vacilante; tímido
tremulously /ˈtrɛmyələsli/ *adv* trémulamente; tímidamente
tremulousness /ˈtrɛmyələsnɪs/ *n* lo tembloroso; vacilación, *f;* timidez, *f*
trench /trɛntʃ/ *n* zanja, *f,* foso, *m;* (for irrigation) acequia, *f; Mil.* trinchera, *f.* —*vt* hacer zanjas (en); acequiar; *Mil.* atrincherar. **t.-fever,** tifus exantemático, *m.* **t.-foot,** pie de trinchera, *m.* **t.-mortar,** mortero de trinchera, *m*
trenchant /ˈtrɛntʃənt/ *a* mordaz
trencher /ˈtrɛntʃər/ *n* trinchero, *m*
trend /trɛnd/ *n* curso, rumbo, *m; Fig.* tendencia, *f;* dirección, *f.* —*vi Fig.* tender
trepan /trɪˈpæn/ *vt Surg.* trepanar
trepanning /trɪˈpænɪŋ/ *n Surg.* trepanación, *f*
trepidation /ˌtrɛpɪˈdeiʃən/ *n* trepidación, *f*
trespass /ˈtrɛspəs, -pæs/ *n* violación de propiedad, *f;* ofensa, *f;* pecado, *m;* (in the Lord's Prayer) deuda, *f.* —*vi* (on land) entrar sin derecho, violar la propiedad; (upon) entrar sin permiso en; (with patience, etc.) abusar de; (against) pecar contra, infringir
trespasser /ˈtrɛspəsər, -pæs-/ *n* violador (-ra) de la ley de propiedad. **"Trespassers will be prosecuted,"** «Entrada prohibida,» «Prohibido el paso»
tress /trɛs/ *n* (plait) trenza, *f;* rizo, bucle, *m; pl* **tresses,** cabellera, *f*
trestle /ˈtrɛsəl/ *n* caballete, *m;* armazón, *m.* **trestle-table,** mesa de caballete, *f*
triad /ˈtraiæd/ *n* terna, *f; Mus.* acorde, *m*
trial /ˈtraiəl/ *n* prueba, *f,* ensayo, *m;* examen, *m;* (experiment) tentativa, *f,* experimento, *m;* (misfortune) desgracia, pena, *f;* (nuisance) molestia, *f; Law.* vista de una causa, *f.* **on t.,** a prueba; *Law.* en proceso. **to bring to t.,** procesar. **to stand one's t.,** ser procesado. **t. run,** marcha de ensayo, *f.* **t. trip,** *Naut.* viaje de ensayo, *m*
trial and error *n* tanteos, *m.* **by trial and error,** por tanteos.
triangle /ˈtraiˌæŋgəl/ *n* triángulo, *m.* **acute-angled t.,** triángulo acutángulo, *m.* **obtuse-angled t.,** triángulo obtusángulo, *m.* **right-angled t.,** triángulo rectángulo, *m.* **the eternal t.,** el eterno triángulo
triangular /traiˈæŋgyələr/ *a* triangular, triángulo
triangulation /traiˌæŋgyəˈleiʃən/ *n* (in surveying) triangulación, *f*
tribal /ˈtraibəl/ *a* tribal
tribe /traib/ *n* tribu, *f*
tribesman /ˈtraibzmən/ *n* miembro de una tribu, *m*
tribulation /ˌtrɪbyəˈleiʃən/ *n* tribulación, *f;* pena, aflicción, desgracia, *f*
tribunal /traiˈbyunl̩/ *n* (seat) tribunal, *m;* (court) juzgado, *m;* (confessional) confesionario, *m*
tribunate /ˈtrɪbyənɪt/ *n* tribunado, *m*
tribune /ˈtrɪbyun/ *n* (person) tribuno, *m;* tribuna, *f*
tribunicial *a* tribúnico
tributary /ˈtrɪbyəˌtɛri/ *a* and *n* tributario *m*
tribute /ˈtrɪbyut/ *n* tributo, *m;* contribución, imposición, *f*
trice /trais/ *n* tris, soplo, *m.* **in a t.,** en un periquete, en un avemaría, en dos trancos
tricentennial /ˌtraisɛnˈtɛniəl/ *a* de trescientos años; *n* tercer centenario, tricentenario, *m*
trick /trɪk/ *n* (swindle) estafa, *f,* engaño, *m;* (ruse) truco, *m,* estratagema, ardid, *f;* (mischief) travesura, *f;* burla, *f;* (illusion) ilusión, *f;* (habit) costumbre, *f;* (affectation) afectación, *f;* (jugglery) juego de manos, *m;* (knack) talento, *m;* (at cards) baza, *f.* —*vt* engañar, estafar; (with out) adornar, ataviar; (with into) inducir fraudulentamente. —*vi* trampear. **dirty t.,** *Inf.* mala pasada, perrada, *f.* **His memory plays him tricks,** La memoria le engaña. **to play a t. on,** gastar una broma (a). **to play tricks,** hacer travesuras. **t. riding,** acrobacia ecuestre, *f*
trickery /ˈtrɪkəri/ *n* maullería, superchería, *f;* fraude, engaño, *m*
trickle /ˈtrɪkəl/ *n* chorrito, hilo (de agua, etc.) *m.* —*vi* gotear. **to t. down,** deslizar por, correr por, escurrir por
trickling /ˈtrɪklɪŋ/ *n* goteo, *m;* (sound) murmullo, *m*
trickster /ˈtrɪkstər/ *n* embustero (-ra), trampeador (-ra). **to be a t.,** ser buena maula
tricky /ˈtrɪki/ *a* informal, maullero; (of things) difícil; complicado; (clever) ingenioso
tricolor /ˈtraiˌkʌlər/ *a* tricolor
tricycle /ˈtraisɪkəl/ *n* triciclo, *m*
tried /traid/ *a* probado
triennial /traiˈɛniəl/ *a* trienal
trifle /ˈtraifəl/ *n* (object) baratija, fruslería, *f;* pequeñez, tontería, bagatela, *f; Culin, f;* (small amount) pequeña cantidad, *f,* muy poco (de); (adverbially) algo. —*vi* entretenerse, jugar. —*vt* (away) malgastar. **to t. with,** jugar con
trifler /ˈtraiflər/ *n* persona frívola, *f;* (with affections) seductor (-ra)
trifling /ˈtraiflɪŋ/ *a* insignificante, sin importancia, trivial
trigger /ˈtrɪgər/ *n* (of a fire-arm) gatillo, *m; Mech.* tirador, *m*
trigonometric /ˌtrɪgənəˈmɛtrɪk/ *a* trigonométrico
trigonometry /ˌtrɪgəˈnɒmɪtri/ *n* trigonometría, *f*
trilingual /traiˈlɪŋgwəl/ *a* trilingüe
trill /trɪl/ *n* trino, *m, vi* trinar
trillion /ˈtrɪlyən/ *n* trillón, *m*
trilogy /ˈtrɪlədʒi/ *n* trilogía, *f*
trim /trɪm/ *a* aseado; bien arreglado; bien ajustado; elegante; bonito; (of sail) orientado. **She has a t. waist,** *Inf.* Tiene un talle juncal. —*n* orden, *m;* buen estado, *m;* buena condición, *f;* (toilet) atavío, *m.* —*vt* arreglar; (tidy) asear; pulir; (ornament) ornar, adornar; (adapt) ajustar, adaptar; *Sew.* guarnecer; (lamps) despabilar; (a fire) atizar; (hair, moustache) atusar, recortar; (trees) mondar, atusar; alisar; (sails) templar, orientar; (distribute weight in a boat) equilibrar; (of quill pens) tajar. —*vi* (waver) nadar entre dos aguas. **to t. oneself up,** arreglarse
trimly /ˈtrɪmli/ *adv* aseadamente; lindamente
trimmer /ˈtrɪmər/ *n* guarnecedor (-ra); contemporizador (-ra)
trimming /ˈtrɪmɪŋ/ *n* arreglo, *m;* guarnición, *f;* (on a dress) pasamanería, *f;* adorno, *m; Agr.* poda, *f;* adaptación, *f,* ajuste, *m; pl* **trimmings,** accesorios, *m pl*
trimness /ˈtrɪmnɪs/ *n* aseo, buen orden, *m;* buen estado, *m;* elegancia, lindeza, *f;* (slimness) esbeltez, *f*
Trinidad and Tobago /ˈtrɪnɪdæd; təˈbeigou/ Trinidad, *f,* y Tobago, *m*
Trinidadian /ˌtrɪnɪˈdeidiən/ *n* and *a* trinitario
Trinity /ˈtrɪnɪti/ *n* Trinidad, *f*
trinket /ˈtrɪŋkɪt/ *n* joya, alhaja, *f;* dije, *m,* chuchería, baratija, *f*
trinomial /traiˈnoumiəl/ *a Math.* de tres términos. —*n Math.* trinomio, *m*
trio /ˈtriou/ *n* trío, *m*
trip /trɪp/ *n* excursión, *f;* viaje, *m;* (slip) traspié, tropiezo, *m;* (in wrestling) zancadilla, *f;* (mistake) desliz, *m.* —*vi* (stumble) tropezar, caer; (move nimbly) andar airosamente, ir (or correr) ligeramente; (frolic) bailar, saltar; (wrestling, games) echar la zancadilla; (err) equivocarse; cometer un desliz. —*vt* (up) hacer caer; echar la zancadilla (a); coger en una falta; hacer desdecirse; coger en un desliz; *Naut.* levantar (el ancla)
tripartite /traiˈpɑrtait/ *a* tripartito
tripartition /ˌtraiparˈtɪʃən/ *n* tripartición, *f*
tripe /traip/ *n* callos, *m pl*
triple /ˈtrɪpəl/ *a* triple. —*vt* triplicar. —*vi* triplicarse
triplet /ˈtrɪplɪt/ *n Poet.* terceto, *m; Mus.* tresillo, *m;* cada uno (una) de tres hermanos (hermanas) gemelos (-as)
triplicate /*a.* ˈtrɪplɪkɪt, *v.* -ˌkeit/ *a* triplicado. —*vt* triplicar
triplication /ˌtrɪplɪˈkeiʃən/ *n* triplicación, *f*
tripod /ˈtraipɒd/ *n* trípode, *m*
Tripoli /ˈtrɪpəli/ Trípoli, *m*
tripper /ˈtrɪpər/ *n* turista, excursionista, *mf*
tripping /ˈtrɪpɪŋ/ *a* ligero, ágil
trippingly /ˈtrɪpɪŋli/ *adv* ligeramente
triptych /ˈtrɪptɪk/ *n* tríptico, *m*
trite /trait/ *a* vulgar, trivial
triteness /ˈtraitnɪs/ *n* trivialidad, vulgaridad, *f*

triumph /'traiəmf/ *n* triunfo, *m.* —*vi* triunfar; (over) triunfar de, vencer
triumphal /trai'ʌmfəl/ *a* triunfal. **t. arch,** arco de triunfo, *m*
triumphant /trai'ʌmfənt/ *a* triunfante, victorioso
triumvirate /trai'ʌmvərɪt/ *n* triunvirato, *m*
trivet /'trɪvɪt/ *n* trébedes, *f pl,* trípode, *m*
trivial /'trɪviəl/ *a* trivial, frívolo; insignificante, sin importancia
triviality /ˌtrɪvi'ælɪti/ *n* trivialidad, frivolidad, *f;* insignificancia, *f*
trochlea /'trɒkliə/ *n Anat.* tróclea, *f*
trodden /'trɒdn̩/ *a* trillado, batido
troglodyte /'trɒgləˌdait/ *a* and *n* troglodita, *mf*
Trojan /'troudʒən/ *a* and *n* troyano (-na). **the T. War,** la guerra de Troya, *f*
trolley /'trɒli/ *n Elec.* trole, *m;* (for children) carretón, *m.* **t.-bus,** trolebús, *m.* —*n* **trolley car** tranvía, *m.* **t.-pole,** trole, *m*
trollop /'trɒləp/ *n* tarasca, ramera, *f*
trombone /trɒm'boun/ *n* trombón, *m.* **t. player,** trombón, *m*
troop /trup/ *n* banda, muchedumbre, *f; Theat.* compañía, *f;* (of cavalry) escuadrón, *m; pl* **troops,** *Mil.* tropas, *f pl;* ejército, *m.* —*vi* ir en tropel, congregarse; (with away) marcharse en tropel, retirarse; (with out) salir en masa. **fresh troops,** tropas frescas, *f pl.* **storm troops,** tropas de asalto, *f pl.* **t.-ship,** transporte de guerra, *m*
trooper /'trupər/ *n* soldado de caballería, *m*
trope /troup/ *n* tropo, *m*
trophy /'troufi/ *n* trofeo, *m*
tropic /'trɒpɪk/ *a* and *n* trópico, *m*
tropical /'trɒpɪkəl/ *a* tropical
tropism /'troupɪzəm/ *n* tropismo, *m*
trot /trɒt/ *n* trote, *m.* —*vi* trotar. —*vt* hacer trotar. **to t. out,** *Inf.* sacar a relucir
troth /trɔθ/ *n* fe, *f;* palabra, *f.* **to plight one's t.,** dar palabra de matrimonio, desposarse
trotting /'trɒtɪŋ/ *a* trotón. —*n* trote, *m*
troubadour /'trubəˌdɔr/ *n* trovador, *m, a* trovadoresco
trouble /'trʌbəl/ *n* (grief) aflicción, angustia, *f;* (difficulty) dificultad, *f;* (effort) esfuerzo, *m;* pena, desgracia, *f;* (annoyance) disgusto, sinsabor, *m;* (unrest) confusión, *f,* disturbio, *m;* (illness) enfermedad, *f;* mal, *m;* (disagreement) desavenencia, *f.* **The t. is....,** Lo malo es; La dificultad está en que... **to be in t.,** estar afligido; estar en un apuro, estar entre la espada y la pared. **to be not worth the t.,** no valer la pena. **to stir up t.,** revolver el ajo; armar un lío. **to take the t. to,** tomarse la molestia de
trouble /'trʌbəl/ *vt* turbar; agitar; afligir, inquietar; (badger) importunar; (annoy) molestar; (cost an effort) costar trabajo (e.g., *Learning Spanish did not t. him much,* No le costó mucho trabajo aprender el castellano). —*vi* preocuparse; darse la molestia; inquietarse
troubled /'trʌbəld/ *a* agitado; inquieto; preocupado; (of life) accidentado, borrascoso. **to fish in t. waters,** pescar en agua turbia, pescar en río revuelto
troublesome /'trʌbəlsəm/ *a* dificultoso; molesto; inconveniente; importuno; fastidioso
trough /trɔf/ *n* gamella, *f;* (for kneading bread) artesa, *f;* (of the waves) seno, *m;* (meteorological) mínimo, *m.* **drinking t.,** abrevadero, *m.* **stone t.,** pila, *f*
trounce /trauns/ *vt* zurrar, apalear; *Fig.* fustigar
troupe /trup/ *n* compañía, *f*
trousers /'trauzərz/ *n pl* pantalones, *m pl.* **plus four t.,** pantalones de golf, *m pl.* **striped t.,** pantalón de corte, *m.* **t. pocket,** bolsillo del pantalón, *m.* **t. press,** prensa para pantalones, *f*
trousseau /'trusou/ *n* ajuar de novia, *m*
trout /traut/ *n* trucha, *f*
trowel /'trauəl/ *n Agr.* almocafre, *m;* (mason's) paleta, *f,* palustre, *m*
Troy /trɔi/ Troya, *f*
troy weight /trɔi/ *n* peso de joyería, *m*
troy weight *n* peso de joyería, *m*
truant /'truənt/ *n* novillero, *m;* haragán (-ana). —*a* haragán, perezoso. **to play t.,** (from school) hacer novillos; ausentarse
truce /trus/ *n* tregua, *f;* suspensión, cesación, *f*
truck /trʌk/ *n* (lorry) camión, *m;* carretilla de mano, *f;* (railway) vagón de carga, *m;* (intercourse) relaciones, *f pl;* (trash) cachivaches, *m pl,* cosas sin valor, *f pl*
truckage /'trʌkɪdʒ/ *n* camionaje, *m;* acarreo, *m*
truckle /'trʌkəl/ *vi* humillarse, no levantar los ojos. **t. bed,** carriola, *f*
truculence /'trʌkyələns/ *n* truculencia, agresividad, *f*
truculent /'trʌkyələnt/ *a* truculento, agresivo
trudge /trʌdʒ/ *vi* caminar a pie; andar con dificultad, caminar lentamente, andar trabajosamente, *n* caminata, *f*
true /tru/ *a* verdadero; real; leal, sincero; fiel; exacto; honesto; genuino; auténtico; alineado, a plomo. **That is t. of...** Es propio de.... —*adv* realmente; exactamente. **t.-bred,** de casta legítima. **t.-hearted,** leal, fiel, sincero
truffle /'trʌfəl/ *n* trufa, *f.* **to stuff with truffles,** trufar
truism /'truɪzəm/ *n* perogrullada, *f*
truly /'truli/ *adv* lealmente; realmente, verdaderamente; en efecto, por cierto; sinceramente, de buena fe. **Yours t.,** su seguro servidor (su s.s.)
trump /trʌmp/ *n* (cards) triunfo, *m;* son de la trompeta, *m; Inf.* gran persona, joya, *f.* —*vt* ganar con el triunfo. **to t. up,** inventar. **t.-card,** naipe de triunfo, *m*
trumpery /'trʌmpəri/ *a* de pacotilla; ineficaz. —*n* oropel, *m*
trumpet /'trʌmpɪt/ *n* trompeta, *f.* —*vt* trompetear; *Fig.* pregonar. —*vi* (of elephant) barritar. **ear.-t.,** trompetilla (acústica), *f.* **speaking t.,** portavoz, *m.* **t. blast,** trompetazo, *m.* **t. shaped,** en trompeta
trumpeter /'trʌmpɪtər/ *n* trompetero, trompeta, *m*
trumpeting /'trʌmpɪtɪŋ/ *n* trompeteo, *m;* (of elephant) barrito, *m*
truncate /'trʌŋkeit/ *a* truncado. —*vt* truncar
truncheon /'trʌntʃən/ *n* porra (de goma), *f;* bastón de mando, *m.* **blow with a t.,** porrazo, *m*
trundle /'trʌndl̩/ *vt* and *vi* rodar
trunk /trʌŋk/ *n* (*Anat. Bot.*) tronco, *m;* (elephant's) trompa, *f;* (railway) línea principal, *f;* baúl, *m;* coíre, *m; pl* **trunks,** (Elizabethan, etc.) trusas, *f pl;* calzoncillos cortos, *m pl.* **wardrobe t.,** baúl mundo, *m.* **t.-call,** conferencia telefónica, *f.* **t.-line,** tronco, *m.* **t.-road,** carretera de primera clase, carretera mayor, *f*
truss /trʌs/ *n Med.* braguero, *m;* (of straw, etc.) haz, *m;* (of blossom) racimo, *m;* (framework) armazón, *f.* —*vt* atar; *Cul.* espetar; (a building) apuntalar
trust /trʌst/ *n* fe, confianza, *f;* deber, *m; Law.* fideicomiso, *m;* (credit) crédito, *m;* esperanza, expectación, *f; Com.* trust, *m.* —*vt* tener confianza en; confiar en; esperar; creer; *Com.* dar crédito (a). —*vi* confiar; *Com.* dar crédito. **in t.,** en confianza; en administración, en depósito. **on t.,** al fiado
trustee /trʌ'sti/ *n* guardián, *m; Law.* fideicomisario, depositario, consignatario, *m*
trustful /'trʌstfəl/ *a* confiado
trustingly /'trʌstɪŋli/ *adv* confiadamente
trust release *n* extinción de fideicomiso, *f*
trustworthiness /'trʌstˌwɜrðinɪs/ *n* honradez, probidad, integridad, *f;* (of statements) exactitud, *f*
trustworthy /'trʌstˌwɜrði/ *a* digno de confianza, honrado; fidedigno, seguro; exacto
trusty /'trʌsti/ *a* leal, fiel; firme, seguro
truth /truθ/ *n* verdad, *f;* realidad, *f;* exactitud, *f.* **the plain t.,** la pura verdad. **to tell the t.,** decir la verdad
truthful /'truθfəl/ *a* veraz; exacto, verdadero
truthfulness /'truθfəlnɪs/ *n* veracidad, *f;* exactitud, *f*
try /trai/ *vt* and *vi* procurar, tratar de; (test) probar, ensayar; (a case, *Law.*) ver (el pleito); (strain) poner a prueba; (tire) cansar, fatigar; (annoy) molestar, exasperar; (afflict) hacer sufrir, afligir; (attempt) intentar; (judge) juzgar; (the weight of) tomar a pulso; (assay) refinar. —*n* tentativa, *f;* (football) tiro, *m.* **Try as he would....,** Por más que hizo... **to try hard to,** hacer un gran esfuerzo para. **to try one's luck,** probar fortuna. **to try on clothes,** probarse (un vestido,

etc.). **to try out,** poner a prueba, probar. **to try to,** tratar de, procurar
trying /'traiıŋ/ *a* molesto; fatigoso; irritante; (painful) angustioso, penoso
tryst /trıst/ *n* cita, *f;* lugar de cita, *m.* —*vt* citar. —*vi* citarse
tsar /zɑr, tsɑr/ *n* zar, *m*
tsarina /za'rinə, tsa-/ *n* zarina, *f*
tsetse fly /tset'se, 'titsi/ *n* mosca tsetsé, *f*
tub /tʌb/ *n* cuba, *f,* artesón, *m;* cubeta, *f.* —*vi* bañarse. **tub thumper,** *Inf.* gerundio, *m*
tuba /'tubə/ *n Mus.* tuba, *f*
tube /tub/ *n* tubo, *m;* (railway) metro, ferrocarril subterráneo, *m;* tubo, *m; Anat.* trompa, *f.* **Eustachian t.,** *Anat.* trompa de Eustaquio, *f.* **Fallopian t.,** trompa de Falopio, *f.* **inner t.,** *Auto.* cámara de aire, *f.* **speaking t.,** tubo acústico, *m.* **test t.,** tubo de ensayo, *m*
tuber /'tubər/ *n* tubérculo, *m*
tubercular /tʊ'bɜrkyələr/ *a* tuberculoso
tuberculosis /tʊˌbɜrkyə'lousıs/ *n* tuberculosis, *f*
tuberose /'tubˌrouz/ *n* nardo, *m,* tuberosa, *f*
tubing /'tubıŋ/ *n* tubería, *f*
tubular /'tubyələr/ *a* tubular
tuck /tʌk/ *n Sew.* alforzar, *f;* pliegue, *m.* —*vt* recoger; *Sew.* alforzar. —*vi* hacer alforzas. **to t. in,** (in bed) arropar; *Inf.* tragar. **to t. under,** poner debajo; doblar. **to t. up,** (in bed) arropar; (skirt) sofaldar; (sleeves) arremangar
tucker /'tʌkər/ *n* camisolín, *m*
Tuesday /'tuzdei/ *n* martes, *m.* **Shrove T.,** martes de carnaval, *m*
tuft /tʌft/ *n* (bunch) manojo, *m;* (on the head) copete, moño, *m,* cresta, *f;* (tassel) borla, *f;* mechón, *m*
tug /tʌg/ *n* tirón, *m;* sacudida, *f;* (boat) remolcador, *m.* —*vt* tirar de; halar; sacudir. —*vi* tirar con fuerza. **to give a tug,** dar una sacudida. **tug of war,** *Lit.* lucha de la cuerda, *f; Fig.* estira y afloja, *m sing*
tuition /tu'ıʃən/ *n* (teaching) instrucción, enseñanza, *f;* lecciones, *f pl;* (fee) cuota, *f*
tulip /'tulıp/ *n* tulipán, *m.* **t. wood,** palo de rosa, *m*
tulle /tul/ *n* tul, *m*
tumble /'tʌmbəl/ *n* caída, *f;* (somersault) tumbo, *m;* voltereta, *f.* —*vi* caer; (acrobats) voltear, dar saltos. —*vt* hacer caer; desarreglar. **to t. down,** venirse abajo; caer por. **t. down,** ruinoso, destartalado. **to t. off,** caer de. **to t. out,** *vt* hacer salir; arrojar. —*vi* salir apresuradamente. **to t. over,** *vt* tropezar con. —*vi* volcarse. **to t. to,** *Inf.* caer en la cuenta
tumbler /'tʌmblər/ *n* (acrobat) volteador (-ra); vaso para beber, *m*
tumbrel /'tʌmbrəl/ *n* carreta, *f*
tumefaction /ˌtumə'fækʃən/ *n* tumefacción, *f*
tumid /'tumıd/ *a* túmido, hinchado
tumor /'tumər/ *n* tumor, *m*
tumult /'tumʌlt/ *n* alboroto, tumulto, *m;* conmoción, agitación, *f;* confusión, *f*
tumultuous /tu'mʌltʃuəs/ *a* tumultuoso, alborotado; ruidoso; confuso; turbulento, violento
tumulus /'tumyələs/ *n* túmulo, *m*
tun /tʌn/ *n* tonel, *m,* cuba, *f, vt* entonelar, embarrilar
tuna /'tʌni/ *n* atún, *m.*
tune /tun/ *n* melodía, *f;* son, *m;* armonía, *f; Fig.* tono, *m; Inf.* suma, *f.* —*vt Mus.* afinar, templar; *Radio.* sintonizar; (up, an engine) ajustar (un motor). —*vi* (in) sintonizar el receptor; (up, *Mus.*) templar (afinar) los instrumentos. **in t.,** *Mus.* afinado, templado; *Fig.* armonioso; (agreement) de acuerdo, conforme. **out of t.,** *Mus.* desafinado, destemplado. **to be out of t.,** desentonar, discordar; *Fig.* no armonizar, no estar en armonía. **to go out of t.,** desafinar. **to put out of t.,** destemplar. **to change one's t.,** *Inf.* bajar el tono
tuneful /'tunfəl/ *a* melodioso
tunefully /'tunfəli/ *adv* melodiosamente, armoniosamente
tunefulness /'tunfəlnıs/ *n* melodía, *f*
tuneless /'tunlıs/ *a* disonante, discordante
tuner /'tunər/ *n* afinador, templador, *m; Radio.* sintonizador, *m*
tungsten /'tʌŋstən/ *n* tungsteno, *m*
tunic /'tunık/ *n* túnica, *f*
tuning /'tunıŋ/ *n* afinación, *f; Radio.* sintonización, *f.* **t. fork,** diapasón normal, *m.* **t. key,** templador, *m*
Tunis /'tunıs/ Túnez, *m*
Tunisian /tu'niʒən/ *a* and *n* tunecino (-na)
tunnel /'tʌnl̩/ *n* túnel, *m.* —*vt* hacer (or construir) un túnel por. —*vi* hacer un túnel
tunneling /'tʌnl̩ıŋ/ *n* construcción de túneles, *f;* horadación, *f*
turban /'tɜrbən/ *n* turbante, *m*
turbid /'tɜrbıd/ *a* turbio; *Fig.* confuso, **to make t.,** enturbiar
turbine /'tɜrbın, -bain/ *n* turbina, *f*
turbulence /'tɜrbyələns/ *n* turbulencia, *f;* desorden, *m;* agitación, *f*
turbulent /'tɜrbyələnt/ *a* turbulento; alborotado; (stormy) borrascoso; agitado
tureen /tʊ'rin/ *n* sopera, *f*
turf /tɜrf/ *n* césped, *m;* (fuel) turba, *f;* (racing) carreras de caballos, *f pl*
turgid /'tɜrdʒıd/ *a* turgente, hinchado; (of style) pomposo
turgidity /tər'dʒıdıti/ *n* turgencia, *f;* pomposidad, *f*
Turk /tɜrk/ *n* turco (-ca). **Turk's head,** (duster) deshollinador, *m; Naut.* cabeza de turco, *f*
Turkey /'tɜrki/ Turquía, *f*
turkey /'tɜrki/ *n* (cock) pavo, *m;* (hen) pava, *f;* **t. red,** rojo turco, *m*
Turkish /'tɜrkıʃ/ *a* turco. —*n* (language) turco, idioma turco, *m.* **T. bath,** baño turco, *m.* **T. slipper,** babucha, *f.* **T. towel,** toalla rusa, *f*
turmeric /'tɜrmərık/ *n* cúrcuma, *f.* **t. paper,** papel de cúrcuma, *m*
turmoil /'tɜrmɔil/ *n* alboroto, tumulto, desorden, *m*
turn /tɜrn/ *n* turno, *m;* (twist) torcimiento, *m;* (bend) recodo, *m,* vuelta, *f;* (in a river) meandro, *m;* (in a road) viraje, *m;* (revolution) vuelta, revolución, *f;* (direction) dirección, *f;* (in spiral stair) espira, *f; Theat.* número, *m;* (change) cambio, *m;* vicisitud, *f;* (appearance) aspecto, *m;* (service) servicio, *m;* (nature) índole, naturaleza, *f;* (of phrase) giro, *m,* expresión, *f;* (walk) vuelta, *f,* paseo, *m;* (talent) talento, *m.* **a sharp t.,** (in a road) un viraje rápido. **at every t.,** a cada instante; en todas partes. **bad t.,** flaco servicio, *m.* **by turns,** por turnos. **good t.,** servicio, favor, *m.* **in its t.,** a su vez. **in t.,** sucesivamente. **Now it's my t.,** Ahora me toca a mí. **The affair has taken a new t.,** El asunto ha cambiado de aspecto. **turn of the century,** vuelta del siglo, *f.* **turn of the millenium,** vuelta del milenio, *f.* **to a t.,** *Cul.* a la perfección. **to have a t. for,** tener talento para. **to take turns at,** alternar en. **t.-table,** (railway) plataforma, *f;* (of a gramophone) disco giratorio, *m.* **t. up,** barahúnda, conmoción, *f;* (of trousers) dobladillo (del pantalón), *m*
turn /tɜrn/ *vt* (on a lathe) tornear; (revolve) dar vueltas a, girar; (a key, door handle, etc.) torcer; (the leaves of a book) hojear; (the brain) trastornar; (a screw) enroscar; (the stomach) revolver (el estómago), marear; (go round) doblar, dar la vuelta a; (change) cambiar, mudar; (translate) traducir, verter; (dissuade) disuadir; (deflect) desviar; (apply) adaptar; (direct, move) volver; (concentrate) dirigir; concentrar; (turn over) volver del revés al derecho; (upside-down) volver lo de arriba abajo; (make) hacer, volver; (make sour) volver agrio; (transform) transformar convertir; *Mil.* envolver. **He has turned thirty,** Ha cumplido los treinta. **He said it without turning a hair,** Lo dijo sin pestañear. **He turned his head,** Volvió la cabeza. **They have turned the corner,** Han doblado la esquina; *Fig.* Han pasado la crisis. **"Please t. over,"** «A la vuelta (de la página).» **to t. a deaf ear to,** no dar oídos a, no hacer caso de. **to t. one's hand to,** aplicarse a. **to t. to account,** sacar ventaja (de). **to t. adrift,** dejar a la merced de las olas; echar de casa, poner en la calle; abandonar. **to t. against,** causar aversión, hacer hostil. **to t. aside,** desviar. **to t. away,** despedir; rechazar; (the head, etc.) volver; desviar. **to t. back,** hacer volver; enviar de nuevo; (raise) alzar; (fold) doblar; (the clock) retrasar. **to t. down,** doblar; (gas) bajar; (a glass, etc.) poner boca abajo; (reject) rechazar; (a suitor) dar calabazas (a). **to t. from,** alejar de, desviar de. **to t. in,**

doblar hacia dentro; entregar. **to t. in one's toes,** ser patizambo. **to t. inside out,** volver al revés. **to t. into,** (enter) entrar en; (change) cambiar en, transformar en; convertir en; (translate) traducir a. **to t. off,** (dismiss) despedir; (from) desviarse de, dejar; (light) apagar; (water) cortar; *Mech.* cerrar; (disconnect) desconectar; (avoid) evitar; (refuse) rechazar. **to t. off the tap,** (water, gas) cerrar la llave (del agua, del gas). **to t. on,** (light) encender; (water, gas, etc.) abrir la llave (del agua, del gas); (steam) dar (vapor); (electric current) establecer (la corriente eléctrica); (eyes) fijar. **to t. out,** (expel) expeler, echar; (dismiss) despedir; (animals) echar al campo; (produce) producir; (dress) vestir; (equip) equipar, guarnecer; (a light) apagar. **to t. over,** (the page) volver (la hoja); (transfer) ceder, traspasar; revolver; (upset) volcar; considerar, pensar. **to t. round,** dar vuelta (a); girar; (empty) descargar. **to t. up,** levantar; apuntar; hacia arriba; (the earth) labrar, cavar; (a glass) poner boca arriba; (one's sleeves, skirt) arremangar; (fold) doblar. **to t. up one's nose at,** mirar con desprecio. **to t. upon,** atacar, volverse contra, acometer; depender de, estribar en. **to t. upside down,** volver lo de arriba abajo; revolver; revolcar

turn /tɜrn/ *vi* (in a lathe) tornear; (revolve) girar, dar vueltas; (depend) depender (de); torcer; volverse; dar la vuelta; girar sobre los talones; dirigirse (a, hacia); (move) mudar de posición; (deviate) desviarse (de); (be changed) convertirse (en); (become) hacerse, venir a ser; (begin) meterse (a); (take to) dedicarse a; (seek help) acudir; (change behavior) enmendarse, corregirse; (the stomach) revolver (el estómago); (go sour) agriarse, avinagrarse; (rebel) sublevarse. **He turned to the left,** Dio la vuelta a la izquierda; Torció hacia la izquierda. **My head turns,** (with giddiness) Se me va la cabeza. **to t. about,** voltearse, dar la vuelta. **to t. against,** coger aversión (a), disgustarse con; volverse hostil (a). **to t. aside,** desviarse; dejar el camino. **to t. away,** volver la cabeza; apartarse; alejarse. **to t. back,** volver atrás; volver de nuevo; retroceder; volver sobre sus pasos. **to t. down,** doblarse; reducirse. **to t. from,** alejarse de; apartarse de, huir de. **to t. in,** doblarse hacia dentro; (retire) acostarse. **to t. into,** transformarse en; convertirse en. **to t. off,** (depart from) desviarse (de); (fork) torcer, bifurcarse. **to t. out,** estar vuelto hacia fuera; (leave ome) salir de casa; (rise) levantarse (de la cama); (arrive) llegar, presentarse; (attend) asistir, acudir; (result) resultar. **to t. over,** mudar (or cambiar) de posición, revolverse; (upset) voltearse, volcarse. **to t. round,** girar; volverse; cambiar de frente; cambiar de dirección, dar la vuelta; (*Auto., Aer.*) virar; (change views) cambiar de opinión; (change sides) cambiar de partido. **to t. round and round,** dar vueltas, girar. **to t. to,** (apply to) acudir a; (begin) ponerse a; (become) convertirse en; (face) dirigirse hacia; (address) dirigirse a. **to t. up,** (crop up), surgir, aparecer; (arrive) llegar; (happen) acontecer; (be found again) volver a hallarse, reaparecer; (cards) venir; (of hats) levantar el ala; (of hair, etc.) doblarse. **His nose turns up,** Tiene la nariz respingona

turncoat /ˈtɜrnˌkout/ *n* desertor (-ra), renegado (-da). **to become a t.,** volver la casaca

turned-up /ˈtɜrndˈʌp/ *a* (of hats) con el ala levantada; (of noses) respingona

turner /ˈtɜrnər/ *n* (craftsman) tornero, torneador, *m*

turnery /ˈtɜrnəri/ *n* tornería, *f*

turning /ˈtɜrnɪŋ/ *n* (bend) vuelta, *f;* (turnery) tornería, *f;* (of milk, etc.) agrura, *f; pl* **turnings,** *Sew.* ensanche, *m.* **t.-point,** punto decisivo, *m,* crisis, *f*

turnip /ˈtɜrnɪp/ *n* nabo, *m.* **t. field,** nabar, *m*

turnover /ˈtɜrnˌouvər/ *n Com.* ventas, *f pl*; *Cul.* pastelillo, *m*

turnpike /ˈtɜrnˌpaik/ *n* barrera de portazgo, *f*

turnstile /ˈtɜrnˌstail/ *n* torniquete, *m*

turpentine /ˈtɜrpənˌtain/ *n* aguarrás, *m,* trementina, *f*

turpitude /ˈtɜrpɪˌtud/ *n* infamia, maldad, *f*

turquoise /ˈtɜrkɔiz, -kwɔiz/ *n* turquesa, *f*

turret /ˈtɜrɪt/ *n* torrecilla, almenilla, *f; Naut.* torre blindada, *f*

turreted /ˈtɜrɪtɪd/ *a* con torres, guarnecido de torres; en forma de torre

turtle /ˈtɜrtl̩/ *n* tortuga (dove) tórtolo (-la); (sea) tortuga de mar, *f.* **to turn t.,** voltearse patas arriba; *Naut.* zozobrar. **t. soup,** sopa de tortuga, *f*

Tuscan /ˈtʌskən/ *a* and *n* toscano (-na)

Tuscany /ˈtʌskəni/ Toscana, *f*

tusk /tʌsk/ *n* colmillo, *m*

tussle /ˈtʌsəl/ *n* lucha, *f;* agarrada, *f.* —*vi* luchar, pelear; tener una agarrada

tutelage /ˈtutl̩ɪdʒ/ *n* tutela, *f*

tutelar /ˈtutl̩ər/ *a* tutelar

tutor /ˈtutər/ *n* (private) ayo, *m;* profesor (-ra); (Roman law) tutor, *m;* (supervisor of studies) preceptor. —*vt* enseñar, instruir. —*vi* ser profesor, dar clases

tutorial /tuˈtɔriəl/ *n* (university) seminario, *m;* (private) clase particular, *f*

tutoring /ˈtutərɪŋ/ *n* enseñanza, instrucción, *f*

twaddle /ˈtwɒdl̩/ *n* disparates, *m pl,* tonterías, patrañas, *f pl*

twain /twein/ *a* and *n* dos, *m*

twang /twæŋ/ *n* punteado de una cuerda, *m;* (of a guitar) zumbido, *m;* (in speech) gangueo, *m.* —*vt* puntear; (las cuerdas de un instrumento) rasguear. —*vi* zumbar. **to speak with a t.,** hablar con una voz gangosa

tweak /twik/ *n* pellizco, *m;* sacudida, *f,* tirón, *m.* —*vt* pellizcar; sacudir, tirar

tweed /twid/ *n* mezcla, *f,* cheviot, *m*

tweezers /ˈtwizərz/ *n pl* pinzas, tenacillas, *f pl*

twelfth /twɛlfθ/ *a* duodécimo; (of the month) (el) doce; (of monarchs) doce. —*n* duodécimo, *m;* (part) dozavo, *m,* duodécima parte, *f.* **T.-night,** Día de Reyes, *m,* Epifanía, *f*

twelve /twɛlv/ *a* and *n* doce *m;* (of age) doce años, *m pl.* **t. o'clock,** las doce; (mid-day) mediodía, *m;* (midnight) media noche, *f,* las doce de la noche. **t.-syllabled,** dodecasílabo

twentieth /ˈtwɛntiɪθ/ *a* vigésimo; (of the month) (el) veinte; (of monarchs) veinte, *n* vigésimo, *m;* (part) vientavo, *m,* vigésima parte, *f*

twenty /ˈtwɛnti/ *a* veinte; (of age) veinte años, *m pl, n* veinte, *m;* (score) veintena, *f.* **t.-first,** vigésimo primero; (of date) (el) veintiuno, *m,* (In modern Spanish the ordinals above *décimo* "tenth" are generally replaced by the cardinals, e.g. *the twenty-ninth chapter,* el capítulo veintinueve.)

twice /twais/ *adv* dos veces. **t. as many** or **as much,** el doble

twiddle /ˈtwɪdl̩/ *vt* jugar con; hacer girar. —*vi* girar; vibrar. —*n* vuelta, *f.* **to t. one's thumbs,** dar vuelta a los pulgares, estar mano sobre mano

twig /twɪg/ *n* ramita, pequeña rama, *f*

twilight /ˈtwaiˌlait/ *n* crepúsculo, *m;* media luz, *f.* —*a* crepuscular. **in the t.,** en el crepúsculo; en la media luz. **t. sleep,** parto sin dolor, *m*

twin /twɪn/ *a* gemelo, mellizo; doble. —*n* gemelo (-la), mellizo (-za); (of objects) pareja, *f,* par, *m.* **t.-engined,** bimotor. **t. screw,** (*Naut. Aer.*) de dos hélices

twine /twain/ *n* bramante, cordel, *m;* guita, *f.* —*vt* enroscar; (weave) tejer; (encircle) ceñir; (round, about) abrazar. —*vi* (of plants) trepar; entrelazarse; (wind) serpentear

twinge /twɪndʒ/ *n* punzada, *f,* dolor agudo, *m; Fig.* remordimiento, tormento, *m.* —*vi* causar un dolor agudo

twining /ˈtwainɪŋ/ *a Bot.* trepante, voluble. **t. plant,** planta enredadera (or trepante), *f*

twinkle /ˈtwɪŋkəl/ *vi* centellear, chispear, titilar; (of eyes) brillar; (of feet) moverse rápidamente, bailar. —*n* (in the eye) chispa, *f*

twinkling /ˈtwɪŋklɪŋ/ *n* centelleo, *m;* titilación, *f;* (of the eye) brillo, *m;* (glimpse) vislumbre, *m; Fig.* instante, momento, *m.* —*a* titilante, centelleador. **in a t.,** en un dos por tres. **in the t. of an eye,** en un abrir y cerrar de ojos

twin-tailed comet /ˈtwɪnˌteild/ *n* ceratias, *m*

twirl /twɜrl/ *n* rotación, vuelta, *f;* pirueta, *f.* —*vi* hacer girar; voltear; torcer; (a stick, etc.) dar vueltas (a). —*vi* girar, dar vueltas; dar piruetas

twirp /twɜrp/ *n Inf.* renacuajo, *m*

twist /twɪst/ *n* (skein) mecha, *f;* trenza, *f;* (yarn) torzal, *m;* (of tobacco) rollo, *m;* (of bread) rosca de pan, *f;* (act of twisting) torcimiento, *m,* torsión, *f;* (in a road, etc.) recodo, *m,* curva, vuelta, *f;* (pull) sacudida, *f;* (contortion) regate, esguince, *m;* (in a winding stair) espira, *f;* (in ball games) efecto, *m;* (in a person's nature) peculiaridad, *f;* falta de franqueza, *f;* (to words) interpretación, *f.* —*vt* torcer; enroscar; (plait) trenzar; (wring) estrujar; (weave) tejer; (encircle) ceñir; (a stick, etc.) dar vueltas a; (of hands) crispar; (distort) interpretar mal, torcer. —*vi* torcerse; enroscarse; (wind) serpentear; dar vueltas; (coil) ensortijarse; (writhe) undular, retorcerse; (of a stair) dar vueltas

twisted /'twɪstɪd/ *a* torcido; (of persons) contrahecho

twisting /'twɪstɪŋ/ *n* torcimiento, *m;* torcedura, *f;* serpenteo, *m;* (interlacing) entrelazamiento, *m.* —*a* sinuoso, serpenteado

twit /twɪt/ **(with)** *vt* echar en cara

twitch /twɪtʃ/ *n* sacudida, *f,* tirón, *m;* (nervous) contracción nerviosa, *f.* —*vt* tirar bruscamente, quitar rápidamente; agarrar; (ears, etc.) mover; (hands) &crispar, retorcer. —*vi* crisparse; (of ears, nose) moverse

twitching /'twɪtʃɪŋ/ *n* sacudida, *f;* (contraction) crispamiento, *m,* contracción nerviosa, *f;* (pain) punzada, *f;* (of conscience) remordimiento, *m*

twitter /'twɪtər/ *n* piada, *f,* gorjeo, *m.* —*vi* piar, gorjear

two /tu/ *a* and *n* dos, *m;* (of the clock) (las) dos, *f pl;* (of age) dos años, *m pl.* —*a* de dos. **in two,** en dos partes. **in two's,** de dos en dos. **one or two,** uno o dos; algunos, *m pl;* algunas, *f pl.* **two against two,** dos a dos. **two by two,** de dos en dos, a pares. **Two can live as cheaply as one,** Donde come uno comen dos. **to put two and two together,** atar cabos. **two-edged,** de dos filos. **two-faced,** de dos caras; *Fig.* de dos haces. **to be two-faced,** hacer a dos caras. **two-headed,** de dos cabezas; bicéfalo. **two hundred,** *a* and *n* doscientos, *m.* **two hundredth,** *a* ducentésimo. —*n* ducentésima parte, *f;* doscientos, *m.* **two-legged,** bípedo. **two-ply,** de dos hilos. **two-seater,** *a* de dos asientos. **two-speed gear box,** cambio de marcha de dos velocidades, *m.* **two-step,** paso doble, *m.* **two of a kind,** (well-matched) tal para cual. **two-way switch,** *Elec.* interruptor de dos direcciones, *m*

twofold /*a.* 'tuˌfould; *adv.* -'fould/ *a* doble. —*adv* doblemente, dos veces

twosome /'tusəm/ *n* partido de dos, *m*

two's words theory *n* teoría de los dos gladios, *f*

tying /'taiɪŋ/ *n* ligadura, *f;* atadura, *f*

tympanum /'tɪmpənəm/ *n* (*Anat., Archit.*) tímpano, *m*

type /taip/ *n* tipo, *m; Print.* carácter, *m,* letra de imprenta, *f,* tipo, *m.* —*vt* and *vi* escribir a máquina. **t. case,** caja de imprenta, *f.* **t. founder,** fundidor de letras de imprenta, *m.* **t. foundry,** fundición de tipos, *f.* **t.-setter,** cajista, *mf* **t.-setting,** composición tipográfica, *f*

typewrite /'taipˌrait/ *vt* and *vi* escribir a máquina

typewriter /'taipˌraitər/ *n* máquina de escribir, *f*

typewriting /'taipˌraitɪŋ/ *n* mecanografía, *f, a* mecanográfico

typewritten /'taipˌrɪtn/ *a* escrito a máquina

typhoid /'taifɔid/ *n* tifoidea, fiebre tifoidea, *f*

typhoon /tai'fun/ *n* tifón, *m*

typhus /'taifəs/ *n* tifus, tabardillo pintado, *m*

typical /'tɪpɪkəl/ *a* típico, característico; simbólico

typify /'tɪpəˌfai/ *vt* simbolizar, representar; ser ejemplo de

typist /'taipɪst/ *n* mecanografista, *mf;* mecanógrafo (-fa)

typographer /tai'pɒgrəfər/ *n* tipógrafo, *m*

typographic /ˌtaipə'græfɪk/ *a* tipográfico

typography /tai'pɒgrəfi/ *n* tipografía, *f*

tyrannical /tɪ'rænɪkəl/ *a* tiránico, despótico

tyrannization /ˌtɪrənə'zeiʃən/ *n* tiranización, *f*

tyrannize /'tɪrəˌnaiz/ *vi* tiranizar

tyranny /'tɪrəni/ *n* tiranía, *f,* despotismo, *m*

tyrant /'tairənt/ *n* déspota, *m,* tirano (-na)

Tyre /taiᵊr/ Tiro, *m*

Tyrolese /ˌtairə'liz/ *a* and *n* tirolés (-esa)

Tyrol, the /tɪ'roul/ el Tirol

Tyrrhenian /tɪ'riniən/ *a* tirreno

Tyrrhenian Sea, the el Mar Tirreno, *m*

U

u /yu/ *n* (letter) u, *f.* **U-boat,** submarino, *m.* **u-shaped,** en forma de U
ubiquitous /yu'bɪkwɪtəs/ *a* ubicuo, omnipresente
ubiquity /yu'bɪkwɪti/ *n* ubicuidad, omnipresencia, *f*
udder /'ʌdər/ *n* ubre, teta, mama, *f*
ugh /ʊx, ʌg/ *interj* ¡uf!
ugliness /'ʌglinɪs/ *n* fealdad, *f;* (moral) perversidad, *f;* (of a situation) peligro, *m,* lo difícil
ugly /'ʌgli/ *a* feo; (morally) repugnante, asqueroso, perverso; (of a situation) peligroso, difícil; (of a wound) grave, profundo; (of a look) amenazador; *Inf.* desagradable; (of weather) borrascoso. **to make u.,** afear, hacer feo
Ukraine /yu'krein/ Ucrania, *f*
Ukrainian /yu'kreiniən/ *a* and *n* ucranio (-ia)
ukulele /ˌyukə'leili/ *n Mus.* ucelele, *m*
ulcer /'ʌlsər/ *n* úlcera, *f*
ulcerate /'ʌlsəˌreit/ *vt* ulcerar. —*vi* ulcerarse
ulceration /ˌʌlsə'reiʃən/ *n* ulceración, *f*
ulcerous /'ʌlsərəs/ *a* ulceroso
ulterior /ʌl'tɪəriər/ *a* (of place) ulterior; (of time) posterior, ulterior; (of motives) interesado, oculto; **ulterior motive,** segunda intención, *f*
ultimate /'ʌltəmɪt/ *a* último; fundamental, esencial
ultimately /'ʌltəmɪtli/ *adv* por fin, al final; esencialmente
ultimatum /ˌʌltə'meitəm/ *n* ultimátum, *m*
ultimo /'ʌltəˌmou/ *adv* del mes anterior
ultra /'ʌltrə/ *a* exagerado, extremo. —*prefix* ultra-. **u-red,** ultrarrojo. **u.-violet,** ultravioleta
ultramarine /ˌʌltrəmə'rin/ *a* ultramarino. —*n* azul de ultramar, *m*
ultramontane /ˌʌltrəmɒn'tein/ *a* ultramontano
ululation /ˌʌlyə'leiʃən/ *n* ululación, *f,* ululato, *m*
umbilical /ʌm'bɪlɪkəl/ *a* umbilical
umbilicus /ʌm'bɪlɪkəs/ *n* ombligo, *m*
umbra /'ʌmbrə/ *n Astron.* cono de sombra, *m*
umbrage /'ʌmbrɪdʒ/ *n Poet.* sombra, *f;* resentimiento, enfado, *m.* **to take u.,** ofenderse, resentirse
umbrella /ʌm'brɛlə/ *n* paraguas, *m.* **u. maker,** paragüero (-ra). **u. shop,** paragüería, *f.* **u. stand,** paragüero, *m*
umpire /'ʌmpaiər/ *n Sports.* árbitro, *m; Law.* juez arbitrador, tercero en discordia, *m.* —*vt* arbitrar
un- *prefix* Used before adjectives, adverbs, abstract nouns, verbs and translated in Spanish by **in-, des-, nada, no, poco, sin,** as well as in other ways
unabashed /ˌʌnə'bæʃt/ *a* desvergonzado, descarado, insolente; (calm) sereno, sosegado
unabashedly /ˌʌnə'bæʃɪdli/ *adv* sin rubor
unabated /ˌʌnə'beitɪd/ *a* no disminuido; cabal, entero
unabbreviated /ˌʌnə'briviˌeitɪd/ *a* íntegro, sin abreviar
unable /ʌn'eibəl/ *a* incapaz, impotente; (physical defect) imposibilitado. **to be u. to,** no poder, serle a uno imposible. **to be u. to control,** no poder controlar
unabridged /ˌʌnə'brɪdʒd/ *a.* See **unabbreviated**
unaccented /ʌn'æksɛntɪd/ *a* sin acento
unacceptability /ˌʌnækˌsɛptə'bɪlɪti/ *n* lo inaceptable
unacceptable /ˌʌnækˌsɛptəbəl/ *a* inaceptable
unaccepted /ˌʌnækˌsɛptɪd/ *a* rechazado, no aceptado
unaccommodating *a* poco complaciente, nada servicial
unaccompanied /ˌʌnə'kʌmpənid/ *a* solo, sin compañía; *Mus.* sin acompañamiento
unaccomplished /ˌʌnə'kɒmplɪʃt/ *a* incompleto, sin terminar, inacabado; (not clever) sin talento
unaccountability /ˌʌnəˌkauntə'bɪlɪti/ *n* lo inexplicable; falta de responsabilidad, irresponsabilidad, *f*
unaccountable /ˌʌnə'kauntəbəl/ *a* inexplicable; irresponsable
unaccountably /ˌʌnə'kauntəbli/ *adv* inexplicablemente, extrañamente
unaccredited /ˌʌnæ'krɛdɪtɪd/ *a* no acreditado, extraoficial
unaccustomed /ˌʌnə'kʌstəmd/ *a* no habituado; (unusual) desacostumbrado, insólito, inusitado
unacknowledged /ˌʌnæk'nɒlɪdʒd/ *a* no reconocido; (of letter) sin contestación, por contestar; no correspondido, sin devolver; (of crimes, etc.) inconfeso, no declarado
unacquainted /ˌʌnə'kweintɪd/ *a* que no conoce; que desconoce, que ignora; no habituado. **to be u. with,** no conocer; ignorar; no estar acostumbrado a
unadaptable /ˌʌnə'dæptəbəl/ *a* inadaptable (also of persons)
unadorned /ˌʌnə'dɔrnd/ *a* sin adorno sencillo, que no tiene adornos
unadulterated /ˌʌnə'dʌltəˌreitɪd/ *a* sin mezcla, no adulterado, natural; genuino, verdadero; puro
unadventurous /'ʌnæd'vɛntʃərəs/ *a* nada aventurero, que no busca aventuras, tímido; tranquilo, sin incidente
unadvisability /ˌʌnædˌvaizə'bɪlɪti/ *n* imprudencia, *f;* inoportunidad, *f*
unadvisable /ˌʌnædˌvaizə'bəl/ *a* imprudente; inoportuno, no conveniente
unadvisedly /ˌʌnædˌvaizɪdli/ *adv* imprudentemente
unaffected /ˌʌnə'fɛktɪd/ *a* natural, llano, sin melindres; impasible; genuino, sincero. **u. by,** no afectado por
unaffectedly /ˌʌnə'fɛktɪdli/ *adv* sin afectación
unaffectedness /ˌʌnə'fɛktɪdnɪs/ *n* naturalidad, sencillez, *f;* sinceridad, franqueza, *f*
unaffiliated /ˌʌnə'fɪliˌeitɪd/ *a* no afiliado
unafraid /ˌʌnə'freid/ *a* sin temor
unaided *a* sin ayuda, solo a solas
unaired /ʌn'ɛərd/ *a* sin ventilar, no ventilado; húmedo, sin airear
unalloyed /ˌʌnə'lɔid/ *a* sin mezcla, puro
unalterability /ʌnˌɔltərə'bɪlɪti/ *n* lo inalterable; constancia, *f*
unalterable /ʌn'ɔltərəbəl/ *a* inalterable; invariable, constante
unambiguous /ˌʌnæm'bɪgyuəs/ *a* no ambiguo, nada dudoso, claro
unambitious /ˌʌnæm'bɪʃəs/ *a* sin ambición; modesto
unamusing /ˌʌnə'myuzɪŋ/ *a* nada divertido
unanimity /ˌyunə'nɪmɪti/ *n* unanimidad, *f*
unanimous /yu'nænəməs/ *a* unánime
unanimously /yu'nænəməsli/ *adv* unánimemente, por unanimidad. **carried u.,** adoptado por unanimidad
unanswerability /ʌnˌænsərə'bɪlɪti/ *n* imposibilidad de negar, *f;* lo irrefutable
unanswerable /ʌn'ænsərəbəl/ *a* incontestable, incontrovertible, incontrastable, irrefutable
unanswered /ʌn'ænsərd/ *a* no contestado, sin contestar; (unrequited) no correspondido
unapparent /ˌʌnə'pærənt/ *a* no aparente
unappealable /ˌʌnə'piləbəl/ *a* inapelable
unappeasable /ˌʌnə'pizəbəl/ *a* implacable
unappeased /ˌʌnə'pizd/ *a* no satisfecho; implacable
unappetizing /ʌn'æpɪˌtaizɪŋ/ *a* no apetitoso; (unattractive) repugnante, feo
unappreciated /ˌʌnə'priʃiˌeitɪd/ *a* desestimado, no apreciado, tenido en poco; (misunderstood) mal comprendido
unapproachable /ˌʌnə'proutʃəbəl/ *a* inaccesible
unapproachableness /ˌʌnə'proutʃəbəlnɪs/ *n* inaccesibilidad, *f*
unappropriated /ˌʌnə'proupriˌeitɪd/ *a* no concedido; libre
unapproved /ˌʌnə'pruvd/ *a* sin aprobar, no aprobado
unarm /ʌn'ɑrm/ *vt* desarmar. —*vi* desarmarse, quitarse las armas
unarmed /ʌn'ɑrmd/ *a* desarmado; indefenso; (*Zool., Bot.*) inerme

unarranged /ˌʌnəˈreindʒd/ *a* no arreglado, sin clasificar; (accidental) fortuito, casual
unartistic /ˌʌnarˈtɪstɪk/ *a* no artístico
unascertainable /ˌʌnæsərˈteinəbəl/ *a* no verificable
unashamed /ˌʌnəˈʃeimd/ *a* sin vergüenza; tranquilo, sereno; insolente, descarado
unasked /ʌnˈæskt/ *a* sin pedir; no solicitado; espontáneo; (uninvited) no convidado
unassailable /ˌʌnəˈseiləbəl/ *a* inexpugnable; irrefutable; incontestable
unassisted /ˌʌnəˈsɪstɪd/ *a*. See **unaided**
unassuming /ˌʌnəˈsumɪŋ/ *a* modesto, sin pretensiones
unattached /ˌʌnəˈtætʃt/ *a* suelto; *Law.* no embargado; *Mil.* de reemplazo; independiente
unattainable /ˌʌnəˈteinəbəl/ *a* inasequible, irrealizable
unattainableness /ˌʌnəˈteinəbəlnɪs/ *n* imposibilidad de alcanzar (or realizar), *f;* inaccesibilidad
unattended /ˌʌnəˈtɛndɪd/ *a* solo, sin acompañamiento; (of ill person) sin tratamiento; (of entertainment, etc.) no concurrido
unattested /ˌʌnəˈtɛstɪd/ *a* sin atestación
unattractive /ˌʌnəˈtræktɪv/ *a* poco atrayente, desagradable, antipático, feo
unattractiveness /ˌʌnəˈtræktɪvnɪs/ *n* fealdad, falta de hermosura, *f;* lo desagradable
unauthentic /ˌʌnɔˈθɛntɪk/ *a* no auténtico, sin autenticidad; apócrifo
unauthorized /ʌnˈɔθəˌraizd/ *a* no autorizado
unavailable ˌ½nəˈveiləbəl/ *a* inaprovechable
unavailing /ˌʌnəˈveilɪŋ/ *a* inútil, vano
unavenged /ˌʌnəˈvɛndʒd/ *a* no vengado, sin castigo
unavoidable /ˌʌnəˈvɔidəbəl/ *a* inevitable, preciso, necesario. **to be u.,** no poder evitarse, no tener remedio
unavoidableness /ˌʌnəˈvɔidəbəlnɪs/ *n* inevitabilidad, necesidad, *f*
unavoidably /ˌʌnəˈvɔidəbli/ *adv* irremediablemente
unaware /ˌʌnəˈwɛər/ *a* ignorante; inconsciente. **to be u. of,** ignorar, desconocer; no darse cuenta de
unawareness /ˌʌnəˈwɛərnɪs/ *n* ignorancia, *f,* desconocimiento, *m;* inconsciencia, *f*
unawares /ˌʌnəˈwɛərz/ *adv* (by mistake) sin querer, inadvertidamente; (unprepared) de sobresalto, de improviso, inopinadamente. **He caught me u.,** Me cogió desprevenido
unbalance /ʌnˈbæləns/ *vt* desequilibrar, hacer perder el equilibrio; *Fig.* trastornar
unbalanced /ʌnˈbælənst/ *a* desequilibrado; *Fig.* trastornado; *Com.* no balanceado
unbaptized /ʌnˈbæptaizd/ *a* no bautizado, sin bautizar
unbar /ʌnˈbɑr/ *vt* desatrancar; *Fig.* abrir
unbearable /ʌnˈbɛərəbəl/ *a* intolerable, insufrible, inaguantable, inllevable, insoportable
unbearably /ʌnˈbɛərəbli/ *adv* insoportablemente
unbeatable /ʌnˈbitəbəl/ *a* inmejorable
unbeaten /ʌnˈbitn̩/ *a* (of paths) no frecuentado, no pisado; (of armies) no derrotado, no batido; invicto
unbecoming /ˌʌnbɪˈkʌmɪŋ/ *a* impropio, inapropiado, inconveniente; indecoroso, indigno; indecente; (of clothes) que no va bien, que sienta mal
unbelief /ˌʌnbɪˈlif/ *n* incredulidad, *f*
unbelievable /ˌʌnbɪˈlivəbəl/ *a* increíble
unbelievably /ˌʌnbɪˈlivəbli/ *adv* increíblemente
unbeliever /ˌʌnbɪˈlivər/ *n* incrédulo (-la), descreído (-da)
unbeloved /ˌʌnbɪˈlʌvd/ *a* no amado
unbend /ʌnˈbɛnd/ *vt* desencorvar, enderezar; entretenerse, descansar; (*Naut.* of sails) desenvergar; (*Naut.* of cables) desamarrar. —*vi* enderezarse; mostrarse afable
unbending /ʌnˈbɛndɪŋ/ *a* inflexible, rígido, tieso; *Fig.* inexorable, inflexible, duro, terco; (amiable) afable, jovial
unbiased /ʌnˈbaiəst/ *a* imparcial, ecuánime
unbidden /ʌnˈbɪdn̩/ *a* espontáneo; (uninvited) no convidado, no invitado
unbind /ʌnˈbaind/ *vt* desligar, desatar; (bandages) desvendar; (books) desencuadernar
unbleached /ʌnˈblitʃt/ *a* crudo, sin blanquear
unblemished /ʌnˈblɛmɪʃt/ *a* no manchado; (pure) sin mancha, inmaculado, puro
unblessed /ʌnˈblɛst/ *a* no bendecido, no consagrado; (accursed) maldito; (unhappy) desdichado
unblushing /ʌnˈblʌʃɪŋ/ *a* desvergonzado, insolente
unbolt /ʌnˈboult/ *vt* descerrojar, desempernar
unborn /ʌnˈbɔrn/ *a* sin nacer, no nacido todavía; venidero
unbosom /ʌnˈbʊzəm/ *vt* confesar, declarar. **to u. oneself,** abrir su pecho (a) or (con)
unbought /ʌnˈbɔt/ *a* no comprado; gratuito, libre; (not bribed) no sobornado
unbound /ʌnˈbaund/ *a* suelto, libre; (of books) en rama, no encuadernado
unbounded /ʌnˈbaundɪd/ *a* ilimitado, infinito; inmenso
unbowed /ʌnˈbaud/ *a* erguido; no encorvado; (undefeated) invicto
unbreakable /ʌnˈbreikəbəl/ *a* irrompible, inquebrantable
unbridled /ʌnˈbraidld/ *a* desenfrenado, violento; licencioso
unbroken /ʌnˈbroukən/ *a* no quebrantado, intacto, entero; continuo, incesante; no interrumpido; (of soil) virgen; (of a horse) indomado; inviolado; (of the spirit) indómito; (of a record) no batido
unbrotherly /ʌnˈbrʌðərli/ *a* poco fraternal, indigno de hermanos
unbuckle /ʌnˈbʌkəl/ *vt* deshebillar
unburden /ʌnˈbɜrdn̩/ *vt* descargar; aliviar. **to u. oneself,** (express one's feelings) desahogarse
unburied /ʌnˈbɛrid/ *a* insepulto
unburnt /ʌnˈbɜrnt/ *a* no quemado; incombusto
unbusinesslike /ʌnˈbɪznɪsˌlaik/ *a* informal; poco comercial, descuidado
unbutton /ʌnˈbʌtn̩/ *vt* desabrochar, desabotonar
uncalled /ʌnˈkɔld/ *a* no llamado, no invitado. **u.-for,** impertinente; innecesario
uncannily /ʌnˈkænl̩i/ *adv* misteriosamente
uncanniness /ʌnˈkænɪnɪs/ *n* lo misterioso
uncanny /ʌnˈkæni/ *a* misterioso, horroroso, pavoroso
uncared-for /ʌnˈkɛərdˌfɔr/ *a* abandonado, desatendido, desamparado
uncarpeted /ʌnˈkarpɪtɪd/ *a* sin alfombra
uncaught /ʌnˈkɔt/ *a* no prendido, libre
unceasing /ʌnˈsisɪŋ/ *a* continuo, incesante, sin cesar, constante
unceasingly /ʌnˈsisɪŋli/ *adv* incesantemente, sin cesar
uncensored /ʌnˈsɛnsərd/ *a* no censurado
unceremonious /ˌʌnsɛrəˈmouniəs/ *a* sin ceremonia, familiar; descortés, brusco
unceremoniousness /ˌʌnsɛrɛˈmouniəsnɪs/ *n* falta de ceremonia, familiaridad, *f;* incivilidad, descortesía, *f*
uncertain /ʌnˈsɜrtn̩/ *a* incierto, dudoso; inseguro; precario; (hesitant) indeciso, vacilante, irresoluto
uncertainly /ʌnˈsɜrtn̩li/ *adv* inciertamente
uncertainty /ʌnˈsɜrtn̩ti/ *n* incertidumbre, duda, *f;* inseguridad, *f;* irresolución, *f*
uncertificated /ˌʌnsərˈtɪfɪˌkeitɪd/ *a* sin certificado (of teachers, etc.) sin título
uncertified /ʌnˈsɜrtəˌfaid/ *a* sin garantía; no garantizado; (of lunatics) sin certificar
unchain /ʌnˈtʃein/ *vt* desencadenar
unchallenged /ʌnˈtʃæləndʒd/ *a* incontestable
unchangeable /ʌnˈtʃeindʒəbəl/ *a* invariable, inalterable, inmutable
unchangeableness /ʌnˈtʃeindʒəbəlnɪs/ *n* invariabilidad, inalterabilidad, *f*
unchanging /ʌnˈtʃeindʒɪŋ/ *a* inmutable, invariable
uncharitable /ʌnˈtʃærɪtəbəl/ *a* nada caritativo, duro; intolerante, intransigente
uncharitableness /ʌnˈtʃærɪtəbəlnɪs/ *n* falta de caridad, *f;* intolerancia, intransigencia
uncharitably /ʌnˈtʃærɪtəbli/ *adv* sin caridad; con intolerancia
unchaste /ʌnˈtʃeist/ *a* incasto, incontinente; deshonesto, impuro, lascivo
unchecked /ʌnˈtʃɛkt/ *a* desenfrenado; (unproved) no comprobado; *Com.* no confrontado

unchivalrous /ʌn'ʃɪvəlrəs/ *a* nada galante, nada caballeroso
unchristened /ʌn'krɪsənd/ *a* no bautizado, sin bautizar
unchristian /ʌn'krɪstʃən/ *a* (heathen) pagano; poco cristiano, indigno de un cristiano, nada caritativo
uncircumcised /ʌn'sɜrkəm,saizd/ *a* incircunciso
uncircumscribed /ʌn'sɜrkəm,skraibd/ *a* incircunscripto
uncivil /ʌn'sɪvəl/ *a* descortés, incivil
uncivilizable /ʌn'sɪvə,laizəbəl/ *a* reacio a la civilización
uncivilized /ʌn'sɪvə,laizd/ *a* no civilizado, bárbaro, salvaje, inculto
uncivilly /ʌn'sɪvəli/ *adv* descortésmente
unclad /ʌn'klæd/ *a* sin vestir; desnudo
unclasp /ʌn'klæsp/ *vt* (jewelery) desengarzar; desabrochar; (of hands) soltar, separar
unclassifiable /ʌn'klæsə,faiəbəl/ *a* inclasificable
unclassified /ʌn'klæsə,faid/ *a* sin clasificar
uncle /'ʌŋkəl/ *n* tío, *m;* (pawnbroker) prestamista, *m*
unclean /ʌn'klin/ *a* sucio, puerco, inmundo; desaseado; impuro, obsceno; (ritually) poluto
uncleanliness /ʌn'klɛnlinɪs/ *n* suciedad, porquería, *f;* desaseo, *m;* falta de limpieza, *f*
uncleanly /ʌn'klɛnli/ *a* sucio, puerco; desaseado
uncleanness /ʌn'klinnɪs/ *n* suciedad, *f;* impureza, obscenidad, inmoralidad, *f*
unclench /ʌn'klɛntʃ/ *vt* (of hands) abrir
Uncle Tom's Cabin La Cabaña del Tío Tom
unclouded /ʌn'klaudɪd/ *a* sin nubes, despejado, claro
uncoil /ʌn'kɔil/ *vt* desarrollar. —*vi* desovillarse; (of snakes) desanillarse
uncollected /,ʌnkə'lɛktɪd/ *a* disperso; no cobrado; (in confusion) confuso, desordenado
uncolored /ʌn'kʌlərd/ *a* incoloro; *Fig.* imparcial, objetivo, sencillo
uncombed /ʌn'koumd/ *a* despeinado, sin peinar
uncomfortable /ʌn'kʌmftəbəl/ *a* incómodo; (anxious) intranquilo, inquieto, desasosegado, preocupado; (awkward) molesto, difícil, desagradable. **to be u.,** (people) estar incómodo; (anxious) estar preocupado; (of things) ser incómodo
uncomfortableness /ʌn'kʌmfərtəbəlnɪs/ *n* incomodidad, *f;* malestar, *m;* intranquilidad, preocupación, *f;* dificultad, *f;* lo desagradable
uncomfortably /ʌn'kʌmfərtəbli/ *adv* incómodamente; intranquilamente; desagradablemente
uncomforted /ʌn'kʌmfərtɪd/ *a* desconsolado, sin consuelo
uncommercial /,ʌnkə'mɜrʃəl/ *a* no comercial
uncommon /ʌn'kɒmən/ *a* poco común, extraordinario, singular, raro, extraño; infrecuente; insólito
uncommonly /ʌn'kɒmənli/ *adv* extraordinariamente, muy; infrecuentemente, raramente
uncommonness /ʌn'kɒmənnɪs/ *n* infrecuencia, rareza, *f;* singularidad, *f*
uncommunicative /,ʌnkə'myunɪkətɪv/ *a* reservado, poco expresivo
uncommunicativeness /,ʌnkə'myunɪkətɪvnɪs/ *n* reserva, *f*
uncomplaining /,ʌnkəm'pleinɪŋ/ *a* resignado, que no se queja
uncomplainingly /,ʌnkəm'pleinɪŋli/ *adv* con resignación
uncompliant /,ʌnkəm'plaiənt/ *a* sordo, inflexible
uncomplicated /ʌn'kɒmplɪ,keitɪd/ *a* sencillo, sin complicaciones
uncomplimentary /,ʌnkɒmplə'mɛntəri/ *a* descortés, poco halagüeño, ofensivo
uncompromising /ʌn'kɒmprə,maizɪŋ/ *a* inflexible, estricto, intolerante; irreconciliable
unconcealed /,ʌnkən'sild/ *a* no oculto; abierto
unconcern /,ʌnkən'sɜrn/ *n* indiferencia, frialdad, *f,* desapego, *m;* (lack of interest) apatía, despreocupación, *f;* (nonchalance) desenfado, *m,* frescura, *f*
unconcerned /,ʌnkən'sɜrnd/ *a* indiferente, frío, despegado; apático, despreocupado; desenfadado, fresco
unconcernedly / ,ʌnkən'sɜrnɪdli/ *adv* con indiferencia; sin preocuparse; con desenfado
unconditional /,ʌnkən'dɪʃənḷ/ *a* incondicional, absoluto. **u. surrender,** rendición incondicional, *f*
unconditionally /,ʌnkən'dɪʃənḷi/ *adv* incondicionalmente; *Mil.* a discreción
unconfessed /,ʌnkən'fɛst/ *a* inconfeso
unconfined /,ʌnkən'faind/ *a* suelto, libre; ilimitado; sin estorbo
unconfirmed /,ʌnkən'fɛrmd/ *a* no confirmado; (report) sin confirmar
uncongenial /,ʌnkən'dʒinyəl/ *a* incompatible, antipático; desagradable, repugnante
uncongeniality /,ʌnkən,dʒini'ælɪti/ *n* incompatibilidad, antipatía, *f;* repugnancia, *f;* lo desagradable
unconnected /,ʌnkə'nɛktɪd/ *a* inconexo; *Mech.* desconectado; (relationship) sin parentesco; (confused) incoherente
unconquerable /ʌn'kɒŋkərəbəl/ *a* invencible, indomable, inconquistable
unconquered /ʌn'kɒŋkərd/ *a* no vencido
unconscientious /,ʌnkɒnʃi'ɛnʃəs/ *a* poco concienzudo
unconscionable /ʌn'kɒnʃənəbəl/ *a* excesivo, desmedido; sin conciencia
unconscious /ʌn'kɒnʃəs/ *a* inconsciente; (senseless) insensible, sin sentido; espontáneo; (unaware) ignorante. **to be u. of,** ignorar; perder la consciencia de. **to become u.,** perder el sentido
unconsciously /ʌn'kɒnʃəsli/ *adv* inconscientemente, involuntariamente
unconsciousness /ʌn'kɒnʃəsnɪs/ *n* inconsciencia, *f;* (hypnosis, swoon) insensibilidad, *f;* (unawareness) ignorancia, falta de conocimiento, *f*
unconsecrated /ʌn'kɒnsɪ,kreitɪd/ *a* no consagrado
unconsidered /,ʌnkən'sɪdərd/ *a* indeliberado; sin importancia, trivial
unconstitutional /,ʌnkɒnstɪ'tuʃənḷ/ *a* anticonstitucional, inconstitucional
unconstitutionally /,ʌnkɒnstɪ'tuʃənḷi/ *adv* inconstitucionalmente
unconstrained /,ʌnkən'streind/ *a* libre; voluntario; sin freno
uncontaminated /,ʌnkəntæmɪ'neitɪd/ *a* incontaminado; puro, sin mancha, impoluto
uncontested /,ʌnkən'tɛstɪd/ *a* sin oposición
uncontradicted /,ʌnkɒntrə'dɪktɪd/ *a* sin contradicción; incontestable
uncontrollable /,ʌnkən'trouləbəl/ *a* irrefrenable, incontrolable, inmanejable; (temper) ingobernable; indomable
uncontrolled /,ʌnkən'trould/ *a* libre, no controlado; desenfrenado, desgobernado
unconventional /,ʌnkən'vɛnʃənḷ/ *n* poco convencional; bohemio, excéntrico, extravagante; original
unconventionality /,ʌnkən,vɛnʃə'nælɪti/ *a* excentricidad, extravagancia, independencia de ideas, *f;* (of a design) originalidad, *f*
unconversant /,ʌnkən'vɜrsənt/ *a* poco familiar, poco versado (en)
unconverted /,ʌnkən'vɜrtɪd/ *a* no convertido; sin transformar
unconvinced /,ʌnkən'vɪnst/ *a* no convencido
unconvincing /,ʌnkən'vɪnsɪŋ/ *a* no convincente, poco convincente, que no me (nos, etc.) convence; frívolo
uncooked /ʌn'kʊkt/ *a* crudo, no cocido, sin cocer
uncork /ʌn'kɔrk/ *vt* destapar, descorchar, quitar el corcho
uncorrected /,ʌnkə'rɛktɪd/ *a* sin corregir, no corregido
uncorroborated /,ʌnkə'rɒbə,reitɪd/ *a* no confirmado, sin confirmar
uncorrupted /,ʌnkə'rʌptɪd/ *a* incorrupto; puro, no pervertido; (unbribed) no sobornado, honrado
uncorruptible /,ʌnkə'rʌptəbəl/ *a* incorruptible
uncountable /ʌn'kauntəbəl/ *a* innumerable
uncounted /ʌn'kauntɪd/ *a* no contado, sin cuenta
uncouple /ʌn'kʌpəl/ *vt* soltar; desenganchar, desconectar
uncouth /ʌn'kuθ/ *a* grosero, chabacano, tosco, patán
uncouthness /ʌn'kuθnɪs/ *n* grosería, tosquedad, patanería, *f*

uncover /ʌn'kʌvər/ *vt* descubrir; (remove lid of) destapar; (remove coverings of) desabrigar, desarropar; (leave unprotected) desamparar; (disclose) revelar, dejar al descubierto. —*vi* descubrirse, quitar el sombrero
uncovered /ʌn'kʌvərd/ *a* descubierto; desnudo; sin cubierta
uncreated /ˌʌnkri'eitɪd/ *a* increado
uncritical /ʌn'krɪtɪkəl/ *a* sin sentido crítico, poco juicioso
uncross /ʌn'krɔs/ *vt* (of legs) descruzar
uncrossed /ʌn'krɔst/ *a* (of check) sin cruzar
uncrowned /ʌn'kraund/ *a* antes de ser coronado; sin corona
unction /'ʌŋkʃən/ *n* unción, *f;* untadura, *f,* untamiento, *m;* (unguent) ungüento, *m;* (zeal) fervor, *m;* (flattery) insinceridad, hipocresía, *f;* (relish) gusto, entusiasmo, *m.* **extreme u.,** extremaunción, *f*
unctuous /'ʌŋktʃuəs/ *a* untuoso, craso; insincero, zalamero
uncultivable /ʌn'kʌltəvəbəl/ *a* incultivable
uncultivated /ʌn'kʌltəˌveitɪd/ *a* inculto, yermo; (barbarous) salvaje, bárbaro; (uncultured) inculto, tosco; no cultivado
uncultured /ʌn'kʌltʃərd/ *a* inculto, iletrado
uncurbed /ʌn'kɜrbd/ *a* sin freno; *Fig.* desenfrenado
uncurl /ʌn'kɜrl/ *vt* desrizar *vi* desrizarse; desovillarse
uncurtained /ʌn'kɜrtn̩d/ *a* sin cortinas; con las cortinas recogidas
uncut /ʌn'kʌt/ *a* sin cortar, no cortado; (of gems) sin labrar
undamaged /ʌn'dæmɪdʒd/ *a* indemne, sin daño
undated /ʌn'deitɪd/ *a* sin fecha
undaunted /ʌn'dɔntɪd/ *a* intrépido, atrevido
undeceive /ˌʌndɪ'siv/ *vt* desengañar, desilusionar
undecided /ˌʌndɪ'saidɪd/ *a* (of question) pendiente, indeciso; dudoso; vacilante, irresoluto
undecipherable /ˌʌndɪ'saifərəbəl/ *a* indescifrable; ilegible
undeclared /ˌʌndɪ'klɛərd/ *a* no declarado
undefended /ˌʌndɪ'fɛndɪd/ *a* indefenso
undeferable /ˌʌndɪ'fɜrəbəl/ *a* inaplazable
undefiled /ˌʌndɪ'fail̩d/ *a* impoluto, incontaminado; puro
undefinable /ˌʌndɪ'fainəbəl/ *a* indefinible; inefable, vago
undefined /ˌʌndɪ'faind/ *a* indefinido; indeterminado
undelivered /ˌʌndɪ'lɪvərd/ *a* no recibido; (speech) no pronunciado; (not sent) no enviado
undemonstrative /ˌʌndə'mɒnstrətɪv/ *a* poco expresivo, reservado
undeniable /ˌʌndɪ'naiəbəl/ *a* incontestable, innegable, indudable; excelente; inequívoco, evidente
undeniably /ˌʌndɪ'naiəbli/ *adv* indudablemente
undenominational /ˌʌndɪˌnɒmə'neiʃənl̩/ *a* sin denominación
undependable /ˌʌndɪ'pɛndəbəl/ *a* indigno de confianza
under /'ʌndər/ *prep* debajo de; bajo; (in) en; (less than) menos de, menos que; (at the orders of) a las órdenes de, al mando de; (in less time than) en menos de; (under the weight of) bajo el peso de; (at the foot of) al abrigo de; (for less than) por menos de; (at the time of) en la época de, en tiempos de; (according to) según, conforme a, en virtud de (e.g. *under the law,* en virtud de la ley); (of monarchs) bajo (or durante) el reinado de; (of rank) inferior a; (in virtue of) en virtud de; (of age) menor de; (with penalty, pretext, etc.) so; en; a (see below for examples); (*Agr.* of fields) plantado de, sembrado de. **u. arms,** bajo las armas. **u. contract,** bajo contrato. **u. cover,** al abrigo, bajo cubierto. **u. cover of,** bajo pretexto de, so color de. **u. fire,** bajo fuego. **u. oath,** bajo juramento. **u. pain of,** so pena de. **u. sail,** a la vela. **u. separate cover,** bajo cubierta separada, en sobre apartado, por separado. **u. steam,** al vapor. **u. way,** en camino; en marcha; en preparación. **to be u. an obligation,** deber favores; (to) tener obligacion de; estar obligado a
under /'ʌndər/ *a* inferior; (of rank) subalterno, subordinado; bajo, bajero. —*adv* debajo; abajo; más abajo; menos; (for less) para menos; (ill) mal; (insufficient) insuficiente. **to bring u.,** someter. **to keep u.,** dominar, subyugar
underact /ˌʌndər'ækt/ *vt* hacer un papel sin fogosidad
underarm /'ʌndərˌɑrm/ *n* sobaco, *m.* —*a* sobacal; (of bowling) de debajo del brazo. **to serve u.,** sacar por debajo
underbid /ˌʌndər'bɪd/ *vt* ofrecer menos que
underbred /ˌʌndər'brɛd/ *a* mal criado, mal educado
undercharge /ˌʌndər'tʃɑrdʒ/ *vt* cobrar menos de lo debido
underclothes /'ʌndərˌklouz, -ˌklouðz/ *n* ropa interior, *f,* paños menores, *m pl*
undercurrent /'ʌndərˌkɜrənt/ *n* corriente submarina, *f; Fig.* tendencia oculta, *f*
undercut /'ʌndərˌkʌt/ *n* (of meat) filete, *m*
underdeveloped /ˌʌndərdɪ'vɛləpt/ *a* de desarrollo atrasado; *Photo.* no revelado lo suficiente
underdog /'ʌndərˌdɔg/ *n* víctima, *f;* débil, paciente, *m.* **underdogs,** los de abajo, *m pl*
underdone /'ʌndər'dʌn/ *a* (of meat) crudo, medio asado
underdress /ˌʌndər'drɛs/ *vt* and *vi* vestir(se) sin bastante elegancia
underestimate /ˌʌndər'ɛstəˌmeit/ *vt* tasar en menos; desestimar, menospreciar
underfeed /ˌʌndər'fid/ *vt* alimentar insuficientemente
underfoot /ˌʌndər'fʊt/ *adv* debajo de los pies, en el suelo
undergo /ˌʌndər'gou/ *vt* sufrir, padecer, pasar por. **undergo surgery,** someterse a la cirugía
undergraduate /ˌʌndər'grædʒuɪt/ *n* estudiante no graduado, *m*
underground /*a., n.* 'ʌndərˌgraund; *adv.* -'graund/ *a* subterráneo; *Fig.* oculto, secreto. —*adv* bajo tierra, debajo de la tierra; *Fig.* en secreto, ocultamente. —*n* sótano, *m;* metro, ferrocarril subterráneo, *m*
undergrown /'ʌndərˌgroun/ *a* enclenque
undergrowth /'ʌndərˌgrouθ/ *n* maleza, *f*
underhand /'ʌndərˌhænd/ *adv Fig.* bajo mano, ocultamente, a escondidas. —*a Fig.* secreto, oculto
underlie /ˌʌndər'lai/ *vt* estar debajo de; servir de base a, caracterizar
underline /'ʌndərˌlain/ *vt* subrayar
underling /'ʌndərlɪŋ/ *n* subordinado (-da)
underlying /'ʌndərˌlaiɪŋ/ *a* fundamental, básico, esencial
undermentioned /ˌʌndər'mɛnʃən/d *a* abajo citado
undermine /ˌʌndər'main/ *vt* socavar, excavar; minar, destruir poco a poco
undermining /'ʌndərˌmainɪŋ/ *n* socava, excavación, *f;* destrucción, *f, a* minador
underneath /ˌʌndər'niθ/ *adv* debajo. —*prep* bajo, debajo de
undernourished /ˌʌndər'nɜrɪʃt/ *a* mal alimentado
undernourishment /ˌʌndər'nɜrɪʃmənt/ *n* desnutrición, *f*
underpaid /ˌʌndər'peid/ *a* insuficientemente retribuido, mal pagado
underpass /'ʌndərˌpæs, -ˌpɑs/ *n* pasaje por debajo, *m*
underpay /ˌʌndər'pei/ *vt* pagar mal, remunerar (or retribuir) deficientemente
underpayment /'ʌndərˌpeimənt/ *n* retribución mezquina, *f,* pago insuficiente, *m*
underpin /ˌʌndər'pɪn/ *vt* apuntalar, socalzar
underpopulated /ˌʌndər'pɒpyəˌleitɪd/ *a* con baja densidad de población
underprivileged /'ʌndər'prɪvəlɪdʒd/ *a* menesteroso, pobre, necesitado
underrate /ˌʌndər'reit/ *vt* tasar en menos; tener en poco, desestimar, menospreciar
underripe /'ʌndərˌraip/ *a* verde
undersecretary /'ʌndərˌsɛkrəˌtɛri/ *n* subsecretario (-ia)
undersell /ˌʌndər'sɛl/ *vt* vender a un precio más bajo que
underside /'ʌndərˌsaid/ *n* revés, envés, *m*
undersigned /'ʌndərˌsaind/ *a* infrascrito, suscrito. **the u.,** el abajo firmado, el infrascrito
undersized /'ʌndər'saizd/ *a* muy pequeño, enclenque, enano
underskirt /'ʌndərˌskɜrt/ *n* enagua, *f;* refajo, *m*

underslung /'ʌndər'slʌŋ/ *a Auto.* con bajo centro de gravedad
understand /ˌʌndər'stænd/ *vt* comprender, entender; (know) saber; (be acquainted with) conocer; (hear) oír, tener entendido; (mean) sobrentender. *—vi* comprender, entender; oír, tener entendido. **to u. each other,** comprenderse. **It being understood that...,** Bien entendido que...
understandable /ˌʌndər'stændəbəl/ *a* comprensible; inteligible. **It is very u. why he does not wish to come,** Se comprende muy bien por qué no quiere venir
understanding /ˌʌndər'stændɪŋ/ *n* (intelligence) entendimiento, *m,* inteligencia, *f;* (agreement) acuerdo, *m;* (knowledge) conocimiento, *m;* (wisdom) comprensión, sabiduría, *f. —a* inteligente; sabio; (sympathetic) comprensivo, simpático. **to come to an u.,** ponerse de acuerdo
understandingly /ˌʌndərstændɪŋ/ *adv* con inteligencia; con conocimiento (de); con simpatía
understate /ˌʌndər'steit/ *vt* decir menos que, rebajar, describir sin énfasis
understatement /'ʌndərsteitmənt/ *n* moderación, *f*
understudy /'ʌndərˌstʌdi/ *n* sobresaliente, *mf. —vt* sustituir
undertake /ˌʌndər'teik/ *vt* comprometerse a, encargarse de; emprender, abarcar, acometer
undertaker /'ʌndərˌteikər/ *n* empresario, director de pompas fúnebres, *m*
undertaking /ˌʌndər'teikɪŋ/ *n* empresa, tarea, *f;* garantía, promesa, *f;* (funerals) funeraria, *f*
undertone /'ʌndərˌtoun/ *n* voz baja, *f; Art.* color tenue (or apagado), *m.* **in an u.,** en voz baja
undervalue /ˌʌndər'vælyu/ *vt* tasar en menos; tener en poco, despreciar
underwater /'ʌndər'wɔtər/ *a* subacuático, submarino. **underwater flipper,** aleta de bucear
underweight /'ʌndər'weit/ *a* de bajo peso, que pesa menos de lo debido, flaco
underworld /'ʌndərˌwɜrld/ *n* (hell) infierno, averno, *m;* (slums) hampa, *f,* fondos bajos de la sociedad, *m pl;* heces de la sociedad, *f pl*
underwrite /ˌʌndər'rait/ *vt Com.* asegurar contra riesgos; reasegurar; obligarse a comprar todas las acciones de una compañía no subscritas por el público, mediante un pago convenido
underwriter /'ʌndərˌraitər/ *n* asegurador, *m;* reasegurador, *m*
underwriting /'ʌndərˌraitɪŋ/ *n* aseguro, *m;* reaseguro, *m*
undeserved /ˌʌndɪ'zɜrvd/ *a* inmerecido, no merecido
undeserving /ˌndɪ'zɜrvɪŋ/ *a* indigno, desmerecedor; que no merece
undesirable /ˌʌndɪ'zaiᵊrəbəl/ *a* no deseable; nocivo, pernicioso; (unsuitable) inconveniente
undesired /ˌʌndɪ'zaiᵊrd/ *a* no deseado; no solicitado, no buscado
undesirous /ˌʌndɪ'zaiᵊrəs/ *a* no deseoso
undestroyed /ˌʌndɪ'strɔid/ *a* sin destruir, no destruido, intacto
undetected /ˌʌndɪ'tɛktɪd/ *a* no descubierto
undeveloped /ˌʌndɪ'vɛləpt/ *a* no desarrollado; rudimentario; inmaturo; (of a country) no explotado, virgen; *Photo.* no revelado; (of land) sin cultivar
undeviating /ʌn'diviˌeitɪŋ/ *a* directo; constante, persistente
undigested /ˌʌndɪ'dʒɛstɪd/ *a* no digerido, indigesto
undignified /ʌn'dɪgnəˌfaid/ *a* sin dignidad; poco serio; indecoroso
undiluted /ˌndɪ'lutɪd/ *a* sin diluir, puro
undiminished /ˌʌndɪ'mɪnɪst/ *a* no disminuido, sin disminuir, cabal, íntegro
undimmed /ʌn'dɪmd/ *a* no obscurecido, brillante
undiplomatic /ˌʌndɪplə'mætɪk/ *a* impolítico, indiscreto
undirected /ˌʌndɪ'rɛktɪd/ *a* sin dirección; (of letters) sin señas
undiscernible /ˌʌndɪ'sɜrnəbəl/ *a* imperceptible, invisible
undiscerning /ˌʌndɪ'sɜrnɪŋ/ *a* sin percepción, obtuso, sin discernimiento
undisciplined /ʌn'dɪsəplɪnd/ *a* indisciplinado
undisclosed /ˌʌndɪ'sklouzd/ *a* no revelado, secreto
undiscouraged /ˌʌndɪ'skɜrɪdʒd/ *a* animoso, sin flaquear, sin desaliento
undiscovered /ˌʌndɪ'skʌvərd/ *a* no descubierto, ignoto
undiscriminating /ˌʌndɪ'skrɪməˌneitɪŋ/ *a* sin distinción; sin sentido crítico
undisguised /ˌʌndɪ'skaizd/ *a* sin disfraz; abierto, claro
undismayed /ˌʌndɪs'meid/ *a* intrépido, impávido; sin desaliento
undisposed /ˌʌndɪ'spouzd/ *a* desinclinado; (of property) no enajenado, no invertido
undisputed /ˌʌndɪ'spyutɪd/ *a* incontestable, indisputable
undistinguishable /ˌʌndɪ'stɪŋgwɪʃəbəl/ *a* indistinguible
undistinguished /ˌʌndɪ'stɪŋgwɪʃt/ *a* (of writers) poco conocido; indistinto; sin distinción
undisturbed /ˌʌndɪ'stɜrbd/ *a* sin tocar; tranquilo, sereno, impasible
undivided /ˌʌndɪ'vaidɪd/ *a* indiviso, íntegro; junto; completo, entero
undo /ʌn'du/ *vt* anular; reparar; desatar, deshacer; desasir; abrir
undoing /ʌn'duɪŋ/ *n* anulación, *f;* (reparation) reparación, *f;* (opening) abrir, *m;* ruina, *f*
undomesticated /ˌʌndə'mɛstɪˌkeitɪd/ *a* salvaje, no domesticado; poco casero
undone /ʌn'dʌn/ *a* and *part* sin hacer; deshecho; arruinado, perdido. **I am undone!** ¡Estoy perdido! **to come u.,** desatarse. **to leave u.,** dejar sin hacer
undoubted /ʌn'dautɪd/ *a* indudable, evidente, incontestable
undoubtedly /ʌn'dautɪdli/ *adv* sin duda
undrained /ʌn'dreind/ *a* sin drenaje
undramatic /ˌʌndrə'mætɪk/ *a* no dramático
undreamed /ʌn'drimd/ *a* no soñado. **u. of,** inopinado, no imaginado
undress /ʌn'drɛs/ *vt* desnudar, desvestir. *—vi* desnudarse. *—n* traje de casa, *m;* paños menores, *m pl; Mil.* traje de cuartel, *m*
undressed /ʌn'drɛst/ *a* desnudo; en paños menores; (of wounds) sin curar; *Com.* en rama, en bruto
undrinkable /ʌn'driŋkəbəl *a* impotable
undue /ʌn'du/ *a* excesivo, indebido; injusto; impropio; (of a bill of exchange) por vencer
undulant /'ʌndʒələnt/ *a* ondulante. **u. fever,** fiebre mediterránea, fiebre de Malta, *f*
undulate /'ʌndʒəˌleit/ *vi* ondular, ondear
undulating /'ʌndʒəˌleitɪŋ/ *a* ondulante
undulation /ˌʌndʒə'leiʃən/ *n* ondulación, undulación, *f,* ondeo, *m;* fluctuación, *f*
undulatory /'ʌndʒələˌtɔri/ *a* ondulatorio, undoso
unduly /ʌn'duli/ *adv* excesivamente, demasiado, indebidamente; injustamente
undutiful /ʌn'dutəfəl/ *a* desobediente, irrespetuoso
undutifulness /ʌn'dutəfəlnɪs/ *n* desobediencia, falta de respeto, *f*
undying /ʌn'daiɪŋ/ *a* inmortal, imperecedero; eterno
unearned /ʌn'ɜrnd/ *a* no ganado; inmerecido
unearth /ʌn'ɜrθ/ *vt* desenterrar; *Fig.* descubrir, sacar a luz
unearthing /ʌn'ɜrθɪŋ/ *n* desenterramiento, *m; Fig.* descubrimiento, *m,* revelación, *f*
unearthly /ʌn'ɜrθli/ *a* sobrenatural; misterioso, aterrador, espantoso
uneasily /ʌn'izəli/ *adv* con dificultad; incómodamente; inquietamente
uneasiness /ʌn'izinɪs/ *n* malestar, *m;* (discomfort) incomodidad, *f;* (anxiety) inquietud, intranquilidad, *f,* desasosiego, *m*
uneasy /ʌn'izi/ *a* incómodo; inseguro; inquieto, intranquilo, desasosegado; aturdido, turbado. **to become u.,** inquietarse
uneatable /ʌn'itəbəl/ *a* incomible
uneaten /ʌn'itn̩/ *a* no comido
uneconomical /ˌʌnɛkə'nɒmɪkəl/ *a* poco económico, costoso, caro
unedifying /ʌn'ɛdəˌfaiɪŋ/ *a* poco edificante
unedited /ʌn'ɛdɪtɪd/ *a* inédito

uneducated /ʌn'ɛdʒəˌkeitɪd/ *a* ignorante; ineducado, inculto, indocto

unembarrassed /ˌʌnɛm'bærəst/ *a* sereno, tranquilo, imperturbable; (financially) sin deudas, acomodado

unemotional /ˌʌnɪ'mouʃənḷ/ *a* frío, impasible

unemployable /ˌʌnɛm'plɔiəbəl/ *a* sin uso, inservible; (of persons) inútil para el trabajo

unemployed /ˌʌnɛm'plɔid/ *a* sin empleo; (out of work) sin trabajo, parado; desocupado, ocioso; inactivo. —*n* paro obrero, *m.* **the u.,** los sin trabajo, los cesantes, los desocupados

unemployment /ˌʌnɛm'plɔimənt/ *n* paro forzoso, *m.* **u. benefit,** subvención contra el paro obrero, *f.* **u. insurance,** seguro contra el paro obrero, *m,*

unencumbered /ˌʌnɛn'kʌmbərd/ *a* libre, independiente; (of estates) libre de gravamen; (untaxable) saneado

unending /ʌn'ɛndɪŋ/ *a* perpetuo, eterno, sin fin; inacabable, constante, continuo, incesante

unendurable /ˌʌnɛn'dʊrəbəl/ *a* insoportable, insufrible, intolerable

unenlightened /ˌʌnɛn'laitṇd/ *a* ignorante

unenterprising /ʌn'ɛntɜrˌpraizɪŋ/ *a* poco emprendedor, tímido

unenthusiastic /ˌʌnɛnˌθuzi'æstɪk/ *a* sin entusiasmo, tibio

unenviable /ʌn'ɛnviəbəl/ *a* no envidiable

unequal /ʌn'ikwəl/ *a* desigual; inferior; (out of proportion) desproporcionado; injusto; insuficiente; incapaz; (of ground) escabroso. **to be u. to the task,** ser incapaz de la tarea; no tener fuerzas para la tarea

unequalled /ʌn'ikwəld/ *a* sin igual, incomparable, sin par, único

unequally /ʌn'ikwəli/ *adv* desigualmente

unequivocal /ˌʌnɪ'kwɪvəkəl/ *a* inequívoco; redondo, claro, franco

unerring /ʌn'ɜrɪŋ, -'ɛr-/ *a* infalible; seguro

unerringly /ʌn'ɜrɪŋli, -'ɛr- *adv* infaliblemente; sin equivocarse

unessential /ˌʌnə'sɛnʃəl/ *a* no esencial

unesthetic /ˌʌnɛs'θɛtɪk/ *a* antiestético

uneven /ʌn'ivən/ *a* desigual; (of roads) escabroso, quebrado; (of numbers) impar; irregular

unevenly /ʌn'ivənli/ *adv* desigualmente

unevenness /ʌn'ivənnɪs/ *n* desigualdad, *f;* desnivel, *m,* irregularidad, *f.* **the unevenness of the terrain,** lo desigual del terreno, lo accidentado del terreno, *m*

uneventful /ˌʌnɪ'vɛntfəl/ *a* sin incidentes, sin acontecimientos notables; tranquilo

unexaggerated /ˌʌnɪg'zædʒəˌreitɪd/ *a* nada exagerado

unexamined /ˌʌnɪg'zæmɪnd// *a* no examinado, sin examinar

unexampled /ˌʌnɪg'zæmpəld/ *a* sin igual, sin par

unexceptionable /ˌʌnɪk'sɛpʃənəbəl/ *a* intachable, irreprensible; correcto; impecable, perfecto

unexhausted /ˌʌnɪg'zɔstɪd/ *a* no agotado; inexhausto

unexpected /ˌʌnɪk'spɛktɪd/ *a* inesperado, imprevisto, inopinado, impensado; repentino, súbito

unexpectedly /ˌʌnɪk'spɛktɪdli/ *adv* inesperadamente; de repente

unexpectedness /ˌʌnɪk'spɛktɪdnɪs/ *n* lo inesperado

unexpired /ˌʌnɪk'spaiᵊrd/ *a* (of bill of exchange) no vencido; (of lease) no caducado

unexplored /ˌʌnɪk'splɔrd/ *a* inexplorado

unexpressed /ˌʌnɪk'sprɛst/ *a* no expresado; tácito, sobrentendido

unexpurgated /ʌn'ɛkspərˌgeitɪd/ *a* sin expurgar, completo

unfading /ʌn'feidɪŋ/ *a* inmarcesible, inmarchitable; eterno, inmortal

unfailing /ʌn'feilɪŋ/ *a* inagotable; inexhausto; seguro; indefectible

unfailingly /ʌn'feilɪŋli/ *adv* siempre, constantemente; sin faltar

unfair /ʌn'fɛər/ *a* injusto; vil, bajo, soez; de mala fe, engañoso; (of play) sucio

unfairly /ʌn'fɛərli/ *adv* injustamente; de mala fe

unfairness /ʌn'fɛərnɪs/ *n* injusticia, *f;* mala fe, *f*

unfaithful /ʌn'feiθfəl/ *a* infiel; desleal; inexacto, incorrecto. **to be u. to,** ser infiel a; faltar a

unfaithfulness /ʌn'feiθfəlnɪs/ *n* infidelidad, *f;* deslealtad, *f;* inexactitud, *f*

unfaltering /ʌn'fɔltərɪŋ/ *a* sin vacilar; resuelto, firme

unfamiliar /ˌʌnfə'mɪlyər/ *a* poco familiar; desconocido. **to be u. with,** ser ignorante de

unfashionable /ʌn'fæʃənəbəl/ *a* pasado de moda, fuera de moda; poco elegante

unfashionableness /ʌn'fæʃənəbəlnɪs/ *n* falta de elegancia, *f*

unfashionably /ʌn'fæʃənəbli/ *adv* contra la tendencia de la moda; sin elegancia

unfasten /ʌn'fæsən/ *vt* desatar; desabrochar, desenganchar; abrir; aflojar; soltar

unfathomable /ʌn'fæðəməbəl/ *a* insondable; impenetrable, inescrutable

unfavorable /ʌn'feivərəbəl/ *a* desfavorable, adverso, contrario

unfavorably /ʌn'feivərəbli/ *adv* desfavorablemente

unfeathered /ʌn'fɛðərd/ *a* implume, sin plumas

unfeeling /ʌn'filɪŋ/ *a* insensible, impasible, frío; duro, cruel

unfeigned /ʌn'feind/ *a* sincero, natural, verdadero

unfenced /ʌn'fɛnst/ *a* descercado, sin tapia; abierto

unfermented /ˌʌnfɜr'mɛntɪd/ *a* no fermentado;

unfetter /ʌn'fɛtər/ *vt* desencadenar, destrabar; poner en libertad, librar

unfilial /ʌn'fɪliəl/ *a* poco filial, desobediente

unfinished /ʌn'fɪnɪʃt/ *a* incompleto, inacabado; sin acabar; imperfecto

unfit /ʌn'fɪt/ *a* incapaz; incompetente, inepto; (unsuitable) impropio; (useless) inservible, inadecuado; (unworthy) indigno; (ill) enfermo, malo. —*vt* inhabilitar, incapacitar. **u. for human consumption,** impropio para el consumo humano

unfitness /ʌn'fɪtnɪs/ *n* incapacidad, *f;* incompetencia, ineptitud, *f;* impropiedad, *f;* falta de mérito, *f;* falta de salud, *f*

unfix /ʌn'fɪks/ *vt* desprender, despegar, descomponer; soltar. **to come unfixed,** desprenderse

unflagging /ʌn'flægɪŋ/ *a* incansable, infatigable; persistente, constante

unflattering /ʌn'flætərɪŋ/ *a* poco halagüeño

unflinching /ʌn'flɪntʃɪŋ/ *a* inconmovible, resuelto, firme

unfold /ʌn'fould/ *vt* desplegar, desdoblar; tender; abrir; (plans) revelar, descubrir; contar, manifestar. —*vi* abrirse

unfolding /ʌn'fouldɪŋ/ *a* que se abre. —*n* despliegue, *m;* revelación, *f;* narración, *f*

unforced /ʌn'fɔrst/ *a* libre; espontáneo; fácil; natural

unforeseen /ˌʌnfɔr'sin/ *a* imprevisto, inesperado

unforgettable /ˌʌnfər'gɛtəbəl/ *a* involvidable

unforgivable /ˌʌnfər'gɪvəbəl/ *a* inexcusable, imperdonable

unforgiving /ˌʌnfər'gɪvɪŋ/ *a* implacable, que no perdona, inexorable

unforgotten /ˌʌnfər'gɒtṇ/ *a* no olvidado

unformed /ʌn'fɔrmd/ *a* informe; rudimentario; inmaturo; (inexperienced) inexperto, sin experiencia

unfortunate /ʌn'fɔrtʃənɪt/ *a* desdichado, infortunado, desgraciado, desventurado. —*n* desdichado (-da); pobre, *mf;* (prostitute) perdida, *f*

unfortunately /ʌn'fɔrtʃənɪtli/ *adv* por desdicha, desgraciadamente

unfounded /ʌn'faundɪd/ *a* infundado, inmotivado, sin fundamento, injustificado

unframed /ʌn'freimd/ *a* sin marco

unfrequented /ʌn'frikwəntɪd/ *a* poco frecuentado, solitario, retirado, aislado

unfriendliness /ʌn'frɛndlinɪs/ *n* hostilidad, falta de amistad, frialdad, *f;* hurañía, insociabilidad, *f*

unfriendly /ʌn'frɛndli/ *a* hostil, enemigo; (of things, events) perjudicial; huraño, insociable

unfrock /ʌn'frɒk/ *vt* degradar, exclaustrar

unfruitful /ʌn'frutfəl/ *a* estéril, infecundo; infructuoso, improductivo, vano

unfulfilled /ˌʌnfəl'fɪld/ *a* incumplido, sin cumplir; malogrado

unfurl /ʌn'fɜrl/ *vt* desplegar; *Naut.* izar (las velas)

unfurnished /ʌn'fɜrnɪʃt/ *a* desamueblado, sin muebles; desprovisto (de), sin

ungainliness /ʌn'gɛinlinɪs/ *n* falta de gracia, torpeza, *f*, desgarbo, *m*
ungainly /ʌn'geinli/ *a* desgarbado
ungallant /ʌn'gælənt/ *a* poco caballeroso, nada galante
ungenerous /ʌn'dʒɛnərəs/ *a* poco generoso; avaro, tacaño, mezquino; injusto
ungentlemanly /ʌn'dʒɛntḷmənli/ *a* poco caballeroso, indigno de un caballero
unglazed /ʌn'gleizd/ *a* sin vidriar; (paper) sin satinar; deslustrado
ungloved /ʌn'glʌvd/ *a* sin guante(s)
unglue /ʌn'glu/ *vt* desencolar, despegar
ungodliness /ʌn'gɒdlinɪs/ *n* impiedad, *f*
ungodly /ʌn'gɒdli/ *a* impío, irreligioso
ungovernable /ʌn'gʌvərnəbəl/ *a* ingobernable, indomable; irrefrenable
ungraceful /ʌn'greisfəl/ *a* desagraciado, desgarbado, sin gracia
ungracious /ʌn'greiʃəs/ *a* desagradable, poco cortés, desdeñoso
ungraciousness /ʌn'greiʃəsnɪs/ *n* descortesía, aspereza, inurbanidad, *f*
ungrammatical /ˌʌngrə'mætɪkəl/ *a* antigramatical, incorrecto
ungrateful /ʌn'greitfəl/ *a* ingrato, desagradecido; desagradable, odioso
ungratefulness /ʌn'greitfəlnɪs/ *n* ingratitud, *f;* lo desagradable
ungrounded /ʌn'graundɪd/ *a* infundado; sin motivo
ungrudging /ʌn'grʌdʒɪŋ/ *a* no avaro, liberal; generoso, magnánimo
ungrudgingly /ʌn'grʌdʒɪŋli *adv* de buena gana
unguarded /ʌn'gɑrdɪd/ *a* indefenso, sin protección; descuidado; indiscreto, imprudente; sin reflexión
unguided /ʌn'gaidɪd/ *a* sin guía
unhallowed /ʌn'hæloud/ *a* impío, profano
unhampered /ʌn'hæmpərd/ *a* desembarazado, libre
unhappily /ʌn'hæpəli/ *adv* desafortunadamente, por desgracia
unhappiness /ʌn'hæpinɪs/ *n* infelicidad, desgracia, desdicha, tristeza, *f*
unhappy /ʌn'hæpi/ *a* infeliz, desgraciado, desdichado, triste; (ill-fated) aciago, funesto, malhadado; (remark) inoportuno, inapropiado
unharmed /ʌn'harmd/ *a* ileso, sano y salvo; (of things) indemne, sin daño
unharness /ʌn'hɑrnɪs/ *vt* desaparejar; desenganchar; desarmar
unhealthiness /ʌn'hɛlθinɪs/ *n* falta de salud, *f;* (of place) insalubridad, *f*
unhealthy /ʌn'hɛlθi/ *a* enfermizo; malsano, insalubre
unheard /ʌn'hɜrd/ *a* no oído; sin ser escuchado; desconocido. **u.-of,** inaudito, no imaginado
unheeding /ʌn'hidɪŋ/ *a* distraído; desatento, sin prestar atención (a); descuidado
unhelpful /ʌn'hɛlpfəl/ *a* poco servicial; inútil
unhesitating /ʌn'hɛzɪˌteitɪŋ/ *a* resuelto, decidido; pronto, inmediato
unhesitatingly /ʌn'hɛzɪˌteitɪŋli/ *adv* sin vacilar
unhinge /ʌn'hɪndʒ/ *vt* desgoznar, desquiciar; (of the mind) trastornar
unhitch /ʌn'hɪtʃ/ *vt* desenganchar; descolgar
unholy /ʌn'houli/ *a* impío, sacrílego
unhonored /ʌn'ɒnərd/ *a* sin que se reconociese sus méritos; despreciado; (check) protestado
unhook /ʌn'hʊk/ *vt* desenganchar; desabrochar; descolgar
unhoped-for /ʌn'houptfɔr/ *a* inesperado
unhurt /ʌn'hɜrt/ *a* ileso, incólume, sano y salvo; (of things) sin daño
unicellular /ˌyunə'sɛlyələr/ *a* unicelular
unicolored /'yunɪˌkʌlərd/ *a* unicolor
unicorn /'yunɪˌkɔrn/ *n* unicornio, *m*
unidentified /ˌʌnai'dɛntəˌfaid/ *a* no reconocido, no identificado
unification /ˌyunəfɪ'keiʃən/ *n* unificación, *f*
uniform /'yunəˌfɔrm/ *a* uniforme; igual, constante, invariable; homogéneo. —*n* uniforme, *m*. **in full u.,** de gran uniforme. **to make u.,** uniformar, igualar, hacer uniforme
uniformity /ˌyunə'fɔrmɪti/ *n* uniformidad, igualdad, *f*
uniformly /'yunəˌfɔrmli/ *adv* uniformemente
unify /'yunəˌfai/ *vt* unificar; unir
unilateral /ˌyunə'lætərəl/ *a* unilateral
unimaginable /ˌʌnɪ'mædʒənəbəl/ *a* inimaginable, no imaginable
unimaginative /ˌʌnɪ'mædʒənətɪv/ *a* sin imaginación
unimpaired /ˌʌnɪm'pɛərd/ *a* no disminuido; sin alteración; intacto, entero; sin menoscabo
unimpeachable /ˌʌnɪm'pitʃəbəl/ *a* irreprochable, intachable
unimportance /ˌʌnɪm'pɔrtṇs/ *n* no importancia, insignificancia, trivialidad, *f*
unimportant /ˌʌnɪm'pɔrtṇt/ *a* sin importancia, nada importante, insignificante, trivial
unimpressive /ˌʌnɪm'prɛsɪv/ *a* poco impresionante; nada conmovedor; (of persons) insignificante
uninflammable /ˌʌnɪn'flæməbəl/ *a* no inflamable, incombustible
uninfluenced /ˌʌnɪn'fluənsd/ *a* no afectado (por), libre (de)
uninformed /ˌʌnɪn'fɔrmd/ *a* ignorante
uninhabitable /ˌʌnɪn'hæbɪtəbəl/ *a* inhabitable
uninhabited /ˌʌnɪn'hæbɪtɪd/ *a* deshabitado, inhabitado, vacío, desierto
uninjured /ʌn'ɪndʒərd/ *a* ileso; sin daño
uninspired /ˌʌnɪn'spaiərd/ *a* sin inspiración; pedestre, mediocre
uninstructive /ˌʌnɪn'strʌktɪv/ *a* nada instructivo
uninsured /ˌʌnɪn'ʃʊrd/ *a* no asegurado
unintelligent /ˌʌnɪn'tɛlɪdʒənt/ *a* nada inteligente, corto de alcances, tonto
unintelligibility /ˌʌnɪn'tɛlɪdʒə'bɪlɪti/ *n* incomprensibilidad, *f*, lo ininteligible
unintelligible /ˌʌnɪn'tɛlɪdʒəbəl/ *a* ininteligible, incomprensible
unintentional /ˌʌnɪn'tɛnʃənḷ/ *a* involuntario, inadvertido
unintentionally /ˌʌnɪn'tɛnʃənḷi/ *adv* sin querer, involuntariamente
uninterested /ʌn'ɪntərəstɪd/ *a* no interesado, despreocupado
uninteresting /ʌn'ɪntərəstɪŋ/ *a* sin interés, poco interesante, soso
uninterrupted /ˌʌnɪntə'rʌptɪd/ *a* ininterrum pido, sin interrupción; continuo, incesante
uninvited /ˌʌnɪn'vaitɪd/ *a* no invitado, no convidado, sin invitación; (unlooked-for) no buscado
uninviting /ˌʌnɪn'vaitɪŋ/ *a* poco atrayente; inhospitalario
union /'yunyən/ *n* unión, *f; Mech.* manguito de unión, *m;* conexión, *f;* (poverty) asociación, *f;* (of trade) gremio de oficios, *m;* sindicato (obrero), *m;* (workhouse) asilo, *m;* (U.S.A.) Estados Unidos de América, *m pl*
unionism /'yunyəˌnɪzəm/ *n* unionismo, *m*
unionist /'yunyənɪst/ *n Polit.* unionista, *mf*
unique /yu'nik/ *a* único, sin igual, sin par
uniqueness /yu'niknɪs/ *n* unicidad, *f;* lo singular
unisexual /ˌyunə'sɛkʃuəl/ *a* unisexual
unison /'yunəsən,/ *n* unisonancia, *f*. **in u.,** al unísono
unit /'yunɪt/ *n* unidad, *f*. **u. bookcase,** librería en secciones, *f*
Unitarian /ˌyunɪ'tɛəriən/ *a* and *n* unitario (-ia)
Unitarianism /ˌyunɪ'tɛəriəˌnɪzəm/ *n* unitarismo, *m*
unite /yu'nait/ *vt* unir, juntar; combinar, incorporar; (of countries) unificar; (of energies, etc.) reunir. —*vi* unirse, juntarse; reunirse, concertarse; convenirse
united /yu'naitɪd/ *a* unido; junto. **the U. Nations,** las Naciones Unidas, *f pl*
unitedly /yu'naitɪdli/ *adv* unidamente; armoniosamente, de acuerdo
United States of America los Estados Unidos, *m pl*
unity /'yunɪti/ *n* unidad, *f; Math.* la unidad; unión, *f;* conformidad, armonía, *f*. **the three unities,** las tres unidades
universal /ˌyunə'vɜrsəl/ *a* universal; general; común. **to make u.,** universalizar, generalizar. **u. joint,** junta universal, *f; Auto.* cardán, *m*
universality /ˌyunəvər'sælɪti/ *n* universalidad, *f*
universalize /ˌyunə'vɜrsəˌlaiz/ *vt* universalizar

universe /'yunə,vɜrs/ *n* universo, *m;* creación, *f,* mundo, *m*
university /,yunə'vɜrsɪti/ *n* universidad, *f.* —*a* universitario. **u. degree,** grado universitario, *m*
unjust /ʌn'dʒʌst/ *a* injusto
unjustifiable /ʌn,dʒʌstə'faiəbəl/ *a* injustificable, indisculpable, inexcusable
unjustifiably /ʌn,dʒʌstə'faiəbli/ *adv* injustificadamente, inexcusablemente
unjustly /ʌn'dʒʌstli/ *adv* injustamente, sin razón
unkempt /ʌn'kɛmpt/ *a* despeinado; desaseado, sucio
unkind /ʌn'kaind/ *a* nada bondadoso, nada amable; poco complaciente; duro, cruel; desfavorable, nada propicio
unkindly /ʌn'kaindli/ *adv* sin bondad; con dureza, cruelmente
unkindness /ʌn'kaindnɪs/ *n* falta de bondad, *f;* severidad, crueldad, dureza, *f,* rigor, *m;* acto de crueldad, *m*
unknowable /ʌn'nouəbəl/ *a* impenetrable, incomprehensible, insondable
unknowingly /ʌn'nouɪŋli/ *adv* sin querer, involuntariamente; sin saberlo; insensiblemente
unknown /ʌn'noun/ *a* ignoto, desconocido; *Math.* incógnito. —*n* lo desconocido, misterio, *m; Math.* incógnita, *f;* (person) desconocido (-da), forastero (-ra). *Math.* **u. quantity,** incógnita, *f*
unlabeled /ʌn'leibəld/ *a* sin etiqueta
unlace /ʌn'leis/ *vt* desenlazar; desatar
unladylike /ʌn'lɛidi,laik/ *a* indigno (or impropio) de una dama; vulgar, ordinario, cursi
unlamented /,ʌnlə'mɛntɪd/ *a* no llorado, no lamentado
unlatch /ʌn'lætʃ/ *vt* alzar el pestillo de, abrir
unlawful /ʌn'lɔfəl/ *a* ilegal, ilícito
unlawfulness /ʌn'lɔfəlnɪs/ *n* ilegalidad, *f*
unlearn /ʌn'lɜrn/ *vt* olvidar, desaprender
unleash /ʌn'liʃ/ *vt* soltar
unleavened /ʌn'lɛvənd/ *a* ázimo, sin levadura
unless /ʌn'lɛs/ *conjunc* a no ser que, a menos que, como no, si no (all followed by subjunc.); salvo, excepto, con excepción de
unlicensed /ʌn'laisənst/ *a* no autorizado, sin licencia
unlike /ʌn'laik/ *a* disímil, desemejante; distinto, diferente. —*prep* a distinción de, a diferencia de, al contrario de. **They are quite u.,** No se parecen nada
unlikeliness /ʌn'laiklinɪs/ *n* improbabilidad, *f*
unlikely /ʌn'laikli/ *a* improbable, inverosímil; arriesgado
unlikeness /ʌn'laiknɪs/ *n* desemejanza, diferencia, *f*
unlimited /ʌn'lɪmɪtɪd/ *a* ilimitado, infinito, inmenso; sin restricción; excesivo, exagerado. **unlimited telephone,** teléfono no medido (Argentina)
unlined /ʌn'laind/ *a* no forrado, sin forro; sin rayas; (of face) sin arrugas
unlit /ʌn'lɪt/ *a* no iluminado, oscuro, sin luz
unload /ʌn'loud/ *vt* descargar; aligerar; *Naut.* hondear; (of shares) deshacerse de. —*vi* descargar
unloading /ʌn'loudɪŋ/ *n* descarga, *f,* descargue, *m*
unlock /ʌn'lɒk/ *vt* desencerrar, abrir; *Fig.* revelar, descubrir
unlooked-for /ʌn'lʊktfɔr/ *a* inopinado, inesperado
unloose /ʌn'lus/ *vt* desatar; soltar; poner en libertad
unlovable /ʌn'lʌvəbəl/ *a* indigno del querer; antipático, poco amable; repugnante
unloveliness /ʌn'lʌvlinɪs/ *n* falta de hermosura, fealdad, *f*
unlovely /ʌn'lʌvli/ *a* nada hermoso, feo; desagradable
unluckily /ʌn'lʌkəli/ *adv* desafortunadamente, por desgracia
unluckiness /ʌn'lʌkinɪs/ *n* mala suerte, *f;* (unsuitability) inoportunidad, *f;* lo nefasto, lo malo
unlucky /ʌn'lʌki/ *a* de mala suerte; desdichado, desgraciado, infeliz; (ill-omened) funesto, nefasto, fatal; inoportuno, inconveniente
unmanageable /ʌn'mænɪdʒəbəl/ *a* indomable, indócil; ingobernable, inmanejable; (unwieldy) difícil de manejar, pesado
unmannerliness /ʌn'mænərlinɪs/ *n* mala crianza, descortesía, *f*
unmannerly /ʌn'mænərli/ *a* mal educado, descortés
unmarketable /ʌn'markɪtəbəl/ *a* invendible
unmarriageable /ʌn'mærɪdʒəbəl/ *a* incasable
unmarried /ʌn'mærid/ *a* soltero, célibe
unmask /ʌn'mæsk/ *vt* desenmascarar; *Fig.* quitar la careta (a). —*vi* quitarse la máscara; *Fig.* quitarse la careta, descubrirse
unmeaning /ʌn'minɪŋ/ *a* sin sentido, vacío, sin significación
unmelodious /,ʌnmə'loudiəs/ *a* sin melodía, discorde
unmendable /ʌn'mɛndəbəl/ *a* incomponible
unmentionable /ʌn'mɛnʃənəbəl/ *a* que no se puede mencionar; indigno de mencionarse
unmerciful /ʌn'mɜrsɪfəl/ *a* sin piedad, sin compasión; cruel, despiadado, duro
unmerited /ʌn'mɛrɪtɪd/ *a* inmerecido, desmerecido
unmethodical /,ʌnmə'θɒdɪkəl/ *a* poco metódico
unmindful /ʌn'maindfəl/ *a* olvidadizo; desatento; negligente. **u. of,** sin pensar en, olvidando
unmistakable /,ʌnmɪ'steikəbəl/ *a* inequívoco; manifiesto, evidente, indudable
unmistakably /,ʌnmɪ'steikəbli/ *adv* indudablemente
unmitigated /ʌn'mɪtɪ,geitɪd/ *a* no mitigado; completo, absoluto; (of rogue) redomado
unmixed /ʌn'mɪkst/ *a* sin mezcla; puro, sencillo, (free) limpio
unmoor /ʌn'mʊr/ *vt* desamarrar
unmoral /ʌn'mɔrəl, -'mɒr-/ *a* amoral, no moral; sin fin didáctico
unmounted /ʌn'mauntɪd/ *a* desmontado
unmoved /ʌn'muvd/ *a* fijo; (unemotional) impasible, frío; (determined) firme, inflexible, inexorable
unmuffle /ʌn'mʌfəl/ *vt* desembozar, descubrir
unmusical /ʌn'myuzɪkəl/ *a* sin afición a la música; sin oído (para la música); inarmónico
unnamable /ʌn'neiməbəl/ *a* que no se puede nombrar, innominable
unnatural /ʌn'nætʃərəl/ *a* desnaturalizado; (of vices, etc.) contra natural; innatural; (of style) rebuscado; artificial; inhumano, cruel
unnaturalness /ʌn'nætʃərəlnɪs/ *n* lo monstruoso; lo innatural; artificialidad, *f;* inhumanidad, *f*
unnavigable /ʌn'nævɪgəbəl/ *a* innavegable, no navegable
unnecessarily /,ʌnnɛsə'sɛrəli/ *adv* inútilmente, innecesariamente, sin necesidad
unnecessariness /ʌn'nɛsə,sɛrinɪs/ *n* inutilidad, *f;* superfluidad, *f;* lo innecesario
unnecessary /ʌn'nɛsə,sɛri/ *a* innecesario, superfluo, inútil
unneighborly /ʌn'neibərli/ *a* de mala vecindad, impropio de vecinos, poco servicial
unnerve /ʌn'nɜrv/ *vt* acobardar quitar el valor, desanimar
unnoticed /ʌn'noutɪst/ *a* inadvertido, no observado
unobliging /ʌnə'blaidʒɪŋ/ *a* nada servicial
unobservable /,ʌnbə'zɛrvəbəl/ *a* inobservable
unobservant /,ʌnəb'zɜrvənt/ *a* inobservante
unobserved /,ʌnəb'zɜrvd/ *a* sin ser notado, desapercibido
unobstructed /,ʌnəb'strʌktɪd/ *a* no obstruido; sin obstáculos; libre
unobtainable /,ʌnəb'teinəbəl/ *a* inalcanzable, inasequible
unobtrusive /,ʌnəb'trusɪv/ *a* discreto, modesto
unobtrusiveness /,ʌnəb'trusɪvnɪs/ *n* discreción, modestia, *f*
unoccupied /ʌn'ɒkyə,paid/ *a* (at leisure) desocupado, ocioso, sin ocupación; vacío, vacante, libre; (untenanted) deshabitado
unofficial /,ʌnə'fɪʃəl/ *a* no oficial
unopened /ʌn'oupənd/ *a* sin abrir, cerrado; (of exhibitions, etc.) no inaugurado
unopposed /,ʌnə'pouzd/ *a* sin oposición
unorganized /ʌn'ɔrgə,naizd/ *a* inorganizado; *Biol.* inorgánico
unoriginal /,ʌnə'rɪdʒənl̩/ *a* poco original
unorthodox /ʌn'ɔrθə,dɒks/ *a* heterodoxo
unostentatious /,ʌnɒstən'teiʃəs/ *a* sencillo, modesto, sin ostentación

unostentatiousness /ˌʌnɒstən'teiʃəsnɪs/ *n* sencillez, modestia, falta de ostentación, *f*
unpack /ʌn'pæk/ *vt* desempaquetar; (trunks) vaciar; (bales) desembalar. —*vi* desempaquetar; deshacer las maletas
unpacking /ʌn'pækɪŋ/ *n* desembalaje, *m*
unpaid /ʌn'peid/ *a* sin pagar, no pagado
unpalatable /ʌn'pælətəbəl/ *a* de mal sabor; desagradable
unparalleled /ʌn'pærəˌlɛld/ *a* sin paralelo, sin par, sin igual
unpardonable /ʌn'pardn̩əbəl/ *a* imperdonable, inexcusable, irremisible
unparliamentary /ˌʌnparlə'mɛntəri/ *a* poco parlamentario
unpatriotic /ˌpeitri'ɒtɪk/ *a* antipatriótico
unpaved /ʌn'peivd/ *a* sin empedrar
unperceived /ˌʌnpər'sivd/ *a* inadvertido, sin ser notado
unperturbed /ˌʌnpər'tɜrbd/ *a* impasible, sin alterarse, sereno
unpleasant /ʌn'plɛzənt/ *a* desagradable, desapacible; ofensivo; (troublesome) enfadoso, molesto
unpleasantly /ʌn'plɛzəntli/ *adv* desagradablemente
unpleasantness /ʌn'plɛzəntnɪs/ *n* lo desagradable; disgusto, sinsabor, *m;* (disagreement) disputa, riña, *f*
unpleasing /ʌn'plizɪŋ/ *a* nada placentero; desagradable, sin atractivos
unplug /ʌn'plʌg/ *vt* desenchufar
unpoetic, unpoetical, /ˌʌnpou'ɛtɪk; ˌʌnpou'ɛtɪkəl/ *a* poco poético
unpolished /ʌn'pɒlɪʃt/ *a* sin pulir, tosco, mate; *Fig.* inculto, cerril. **u. diamond,** diamante en bruto, *m*
unpolluted /ˌʌnpə'lutɪd/ *a* impoluto, incontaminado; puro, sin pervertir
unpopular /ʌn'pɒpyələr/ *a* impopular
unpopularity /ˌʌnpɒpyə'lærɪti/ *n* impopularidad, *f*
unpractical /ʌn'præktɪkəl/ *a* impracticable, imposible; (of persons) sin sentido práctico
unpracticed /ʌn'præktɪst/ *a* no practicado; inexperto, inhábil
unpraiseworthy /ʌn'preizˌwɜrði/ *a* inmeritorio
unprecedented /ʌn'prɛsɪˌdɛntɪd/ *a* sin precedente, inaudito
unprejudiced /ʌn'prɛdʒədɪst/ *a* sin prejuicios, imparcial
unpremeditated /ˌʌnpri'mɛdɪˌteitɪd/ *a* sin premeditación, indeliberado, impremeditado
unprepared /ˌʌnprɪ'pɛərd/ *a* sin preparación, no preparado; desprevenido; desapercibido (unready)
unpreparedness /ˌʌnprɪ'pɛərɪdnɪs *n* falta de preparación, imprevisión, *f,* desapercibimiento, *m*
unprepossessing /ˌʌnpripə'zɛsɪŋ/ *a* poco atrayente, antipático
unpresentable /ˌʌnprɪ'zɛntəbəl/ *a* impresentable
unpretentious /ˌʌnprɪ'tɛnʃəs/ *a* sin pretensiones, modesto
unpriced /ʌn'praist/ *a* sin precio
unprincipled /ʌn'prɪnsəpəld/ *a* sin consciencia, sin escrúpulos
unprinted /ʌn'prɪntɪd/ *a* sin imprimir, no impreso
unprocurable /ˌʌnprou'kyʊrəbəl/ *a* inalcanzable, inasequible
unproductive /ˌʌnprə'dʌktɪv/ *a* improductivo; infructuoso, estéril
unproductiveness /ˌʌnprə'dʌktɪvnɪs/ *n* infructuosidad, *f;* esterilidad, *f*
unprofessional /ˌʌnprə'fɛʃənl̩/ *a* sin profesión; contrario a la ética profesional
unprofitable /ʌn'prɒfɪtəbəl/ *a* improductivo, infructuoso; sin provecho; inútil; nada lucrativo
unprogressive /ˌʌnprə'grɛsɪv/ *a* reaccionario
unpromising /ʌn'prɒməsɪŋ/ *a* poco halagüeño
unpronounceable /ˌʌnprə'naunsəbəl/ *a* impronunciable
unpropitious /ˌʌnprə'pɪʃəs/ *a* desfavorable, nada propicio, nada halagüeño
unprosperous /ʌn'prɒspərəs/ *a* impróspero
unprotected /ˌʌnprə'tɛktɪd/ *a* sin protección; (of persons) indefenso, desválido
unproved /ʌn'pruvd/ *a* no probado, sin demostrar
unprovided /ˌʌnprə'vaidɪd/ *a* desapercibido, desprovisto. **u. for,** sin provisión (para); sin medios de vida, desamparado
unprovoked /ˌʌnprə'voukt/ *a* no provocado, sin provocación; sin motivo
unpublished /ʌn'pʌblɪʃt/ *a* inédito, no publicado, sin publicar
unpunctual /ʌn'pʌŋktʃuəl/ *a* no puntual, retrasado
unpunctuality /ʌnˌpʌŋktʃu'ælɪti/ *n* falta de puntualidad, *f,* retraso, *m*
unpunctually /ʌn'pʌŋktʃuəli/ *adv* sin puntualidad, tarde, con retraso
unpunishable /ʌn'pʌnɪʃə bəl/ *a* no punible
unpunished /ʌn'pʌnɪʃt/ *a* impune, sin castigo
unpurchasable /ʌn'pɛrtʃɪsəbəl/ *a* que no puede comprarse
unqualified /ʌn'kwɒləˌfaid/ *a* incapaz, incompetente; (with professions) sin título; (downright) incondicional, absoluto
unquenchable /ʌn'kwɛntʃəbəl/ *a* inextinguible, inapagable; insaciable
unquestionable /ʌn'kwɛstʃənəbəl/ *a* indiscutible, indudable, indubitable
unquestionably /ʌn'kwɛstʃənəbli/ *adv* indudablemente
unquiet /ʌn'kwaiɪt/ *a* inquieto, intranquilo; agitado
unravel /ʌn'rævəl/ *vt* deshilar; destejer; (a mystery, etc.) desentrañar, desembrollar, descifrar
unraveling /ʌn'rævəlɪŋ/ *n* deshiladura, *f;* aclaración, *f*
unreadable /ʌn'ridəbəl/ *a* ilegible
unreadiness /ʌn'rɛdinɪs/ *n* falta de preparación, *f,* desapercibimiento, *m;* lentitud, *f*
unready /ʌn'rɛdi/ *a* desapercibido, desprevenido; lento
unreal /ʌn'riəl/ *a* irreal; falso, imaginario, ilusorio; ficticio; artificial; insincero, hipócrita; ideal; incorpóreo
unreality /ˌʌnri'ælɪti/ *n* irrealidad, *f;* falsedad, *f;* artificialidad, *f;* lo quimérico
unreasonable /ʌn'rizənəbəl/ *a* irrazonable, irracional; disparatado, extravagante; (with price, etc.) exorbitante, excesivo
unreasonableness /ʌn'rizənəbəlnɪs/ *n* irracionalidad, *f;* exorbitancia, *f*
unreasonably /ʌn'rizənəbli/ *adv* irracionalmente
unreasoning /ʌn'rizənɪŋ/ *a* irracional; sin motivo, sin causa
unreceipted /ˌʌnrɪ'sitɪd/ *a* sin recibo
unrecognizable /ʌn'rɛkəgˌnaizəbəl/ *a* que no puede reconocerse; imposible de reconocer
unrecognized /ʌn'rɛkəgˌnaizd/ *a* no reconocido
unreconciled /ʌn'rɛkənˌsaild/ *a* no resignado, no reconciliado
unrectified /ʌn'rɛktəˌfaid/ *a* no corregido, sin rectificar
unredeemed /ˌʌnrɪ'dimd/ *a* no redimido; no mitigado; (of pledges) sin desempeñar
unrefined /ˌʌnrɪ'faind/ *a* no refinado, impuro; inculto, grosero
unreformed /ˌʌnrɪ'fɔrmd/ *a* no reformado
unrefuted /ˌʌnrɪ'fyutɪd/ *a* no refutado
unregenerate /ˌʌnrɪ'dʒɛnərɪt/ *a* no regenerado
unregretted /ˌʌnrɪ'grɛtɪd/ *a* no llorado, sin lamentar
unrehearsed /ˌʌnrɪ'hɜrst/ *a* sin preparación; *Theat.* sin ensayar; (extempore) improvisado
unrelated /ˌʌnrɪleitɪd/ *a* inconexo; (of persons) sin parentesco
unrelenting /ˌʌnrɪ'lɛntɪŋ/ *a* implacable, inflexible, inexorable
unreliability /ˌʌnrɪˌlaiə'bɪlɪti/ *n* incertidumbre, *f;* el no poder confiar en, informalidad, inestabilidad, *f*
unreliable /ˌʌnrɪˌlaiəbəl/ *a* incierto, dudoso, indigno de confianza; (of persons) informal
unrelieved /ˌnrɪ'livd/ *a* no aliviado; absoluto, completo, total
unremitting /ˌʌnrɪ'mɪtɪŋ/ *a* incansable
unremunerative /ˌʌnrɪ'myunərətɪv/ *a* sin remuneración, no remunerado
unrepealed /ˌʌnrɪ'pild/ *a* vigente
unrepentant /ˌʌnrɪ'pɛntn̩t/ *a* impenitente

unrepresentative /ˌʌnrɛprɪ'zɛntətɪv/ *a* poco representativo
unrepresented /ˌʌnrɛprɪ'zɛntɪd/ *a* sin representación
unrequited /ˌʌnrɪ'kwaitɪd/ *a* no correspondido
unreserved /ˌʌnrɪ'zɜrvd/ *a* no reservado; expresivo, comunicativo, expansivo, franco
unreservedly /ˌʌnrɪ'zɜrvɪdli/ *adv* sin reserva; con toda franqueza
unresisting /ˌʌnrɪ'zɪstɪŋ/ *a* sin oponer resistencia
unresolved /ˌʌnrɪ'zɒlvd/ *a* sin resolverse, vacilante; incierto, dudoso, inseguro; sin solución
unresponsive /ˌʌnrɪ'spɒnsɪv/ *a* flemático; insensible, sordo
unresponsiveness /ˌʌnrɪ'spɒnsɪvnɪs/ *n* flema, *f;* insensibilidad, *f*
unrest /ʌn'rɛst/ *n* desasosiego, *m,* agitación, inquietud, *f*
unrestful /ʌn'rɛstfəl/ *a* agitado, inquieto, intranquilo
unrestrained /ˌʌnrɪ'streind/ *a* desenfrenado; ilimitado, sin límites; sin reserva
unrestricted /ˌʌnrɪ'strɪktɪd/ *a* sin restricción; ilimitado
unrevealed /ˌʌnrɪ'vild/ *a* no revelado, por descubrir, no descubierto
unrewarded /ˌʌnrɪ'wɔrdɪd/ *a* sin premio, no recompensado
unrighteous /ʌn'raitʃəs/ *a* injusto, malo, perverso
unrighteousness /ʌn'raitʃəsnɪs/ *n* injusticia, *f;* maldad, perversidad, *f*
unripe /ʌn'raip/ *a* verde, inmaturo
unripeness /ʌn'raipnɪs/ *n* falta de madurez, *f*
unrivaled /ʌn'raivəld/ *a* sin igual, sin par
unroll /ʌn'roul/ *vt* desarrollar. —*vi* desarrollarse; (unfold) desplegarse (a la vista)
unromantic /ˌʌnrou'mæntɪk/ *a* poco (or nada) romántico
unruffled /ʌn'rʌfəld/ *a* sereno, plácido, ecuánime; no arrugado; (of hair) liso
unruliness /ʌn'rulinɪs/ *n* turbulencia, indisciplina, *f;* insubordinación, rebeldía, *f*
unruly /ʌn'ruli/ *a* ingobernable, revoltoso; refractario, rebelde; (of hair) indomable
unsaddle /ʌn'sædḷ/ *vt* desensillar; derribar (del caballo, etc.)
unsafe /ʌn'seif/ *a* inseguro; peligroso; arriesgado; (to eat) nocivo
unsafeness /ʌn'seifnɪs/ *n* inseguridad, *f;* peligro, riesgo, *m*
unsaid /ʌn'sɛd/ *a* sin decir, no dicho
unsalable / ½n'seiləbəl/ *a* invendible
unsalaried /ʌn'sælərid/ *a* no asalariado
unsalted /ʌn'sɔltɪd/ *a* soso, sin sal
unsanctioned /ʌn'sæŋkʃənd/ *a* no permitido, sin sancionar
unsanitary /ʌn'sænɪˌtɛri/ *a* antihigiénico
unsatisfactoriness /ˌʌnsætɪs'fæktərinɪs/ *n* lo insatisfactorio
unsatisfactory /ˌʌnsætɪs'fæktəri/ *a* poco (or nada) satisfactorio; no aceptable
unsatisfied /ʌn'sætɪsˌfaid/ *a* no satisfecho; descontento; no convencido; (hungry) no harto; *Com.* no saldado
unsatisfying /ʌn'sætɪsˌfaiɪŋ/ *a* que no satisface
unsavoriness /ʌn'seivərinɪs/ *n* insipidez, *f,* mal sabor, *m;* lo desagradable; sordidez, suciedad, *f*
unsavory /ʌn'seivəri/ *a* insípido, de mal sabor; desagradable; sórdido, sucio
unscalable /ʌn'skeiləbəl/ *a* inascendible, virgen
unscathed /ʌn'skeiðd/ *a* sin daño, ileso
unscented /ʌn'sɛntɪd/ *a* sin perfume, sin olor, no fragante
unscholarly /ʌn'skɒlərli/ *a* nada erudito; indigno de un erudito
unscientific /ˌʌnsaiən'tɪfɪk/ *a* no científico
unscrew /ʌn'skru/ *vt* destornillar. —*vi* destornillarse
unscrewing /ʌn'skruɪŋ/ *n* destornillamiento, *m*
unscrupulous /ʌn'skrupyələs/ *a* sin escrúpulos, poco escrupuloso, desaprensivo
unscrupulousness /ʌn'skrupyələsnɪs/ *n* falta de escrúpulos, desaprensión, *f*
unseal /ʌn'sil/ *vt* desellar, romper (*or* quitar) el sello (de)
unseasonable /ʌn'sizənəbəl/ *a* intempestivo, fuera de sazón; inoportuno, inconveniente. **at an u. hour,** a una hora inconveniente, a deshora
unseasonableness /ʌn'sizənəbəlnɪs/ *n* lo intempestivo, inoportunidad, *f*
unseasonably /ʌn'sizənəbli/ /*adv* intempestivamente; a deshora; inoportunamente
unseasoned /ʌn'sizənd/ *a Cul.* sin sazonar, soso; (wood) verde; no maduro, sin madurar
unseat /ʌn'sit/ *vt* (from horse) tirar, echar al suelo; *Polit.* desituir
unseaworthy /'ʌn'siˌwɜrði/ *a* innavegable
unseemliness /ʌn'simlinɪs/ *n* falta de decoro, *f;* indecencia, *f*
unseemly /ʌn'simli/ *a* indecoroso, indigno; indecente; impropio
unseen /ʌn'sin/ *a* no visto, invisible; inadvertido; secreto, oculto. —*n* versión al libro abierto, *f.* **the u.,** lo invisible
unselfish /ʌn'sɛlfɪʃ/ *a* desinteresado, abnegado, nada egoísta; generoso
unselfishness /ʌn'sɛlfɪʃnɪs/ *n* abnegación, *f;* desinterés, *m;* generosidad, *f*
unsentimental /ˌʌnsɛntə'mɛntḷ/ *a* no sentimental
unserviceable /ʌn'sɜrvɪsəbəl/ *a* inservible, inútil, que no sirve para nada, sin utilidad.
unsettle /ʌn'sɛtḷ/ *vt* desarreglar; desorganizar; hacer inseguro; agitar, perturbar
unsettled /ʌn'sɛtld/ *a* inconstante, variable; *Com.* pendiente, sin pagar; incierto; sin resolver; (of estates) sin solucionar
unshackle /ʌn'ʃækəl/ *vt* desencadenar
unshakable /ʌn'ʃeikəbəl/ *a* inconmovible, firme
unshapely /ʌn'ʃeipli/ *a* desproporcionado
unshaven /ʌn'ʃeivən/ *a* sin afeitar
unsheathe /ʌn'ʃið/ *vt* desenvainar, sacar
unsheltered /ʌn'ʃɛltərd/ *a* desabrigado, desamparado; no protegido, sin protección; (of places) sin abrigo, expuesto; (from) sin defensa contra
unship /ʌn'ʃɪp/ *vt* desembarcar; (the oars) desarmar
unshod /ʌn'ʃɒd/ *a* descalzo; (of a horse) sin herraduras
unshorn /ʌn'ʃɔrn/ *a* sin esquilar; intonso
unshrinkable /ʌn'ʃrɪŋkəbəl/ *a* que no se encoge
unshrinking /ʌn'ʃrɪŋkɪŋ/ *a* intrépido; resoluto, sin vacilar
unsightly /ʌn'saitli/ *a* feo, horrible, repugnante, antiestético
unsinkable /ʌn'sɪŋkəbəl/ *a* insumergible
unskilled /ʌn'skɪld/ *a* inexperto, inhábil, imperito, torpe
unsmokable /ʌn'smoukəbəl/ *a* (of tobacco) infumable
unsociability /ˌʌnsouʃə'bɪlɪti/ *n* insociabilidad, huraňía, esquivez, *f*
unsociable /ʌn'souʃəbəl/ *a* insociable, huraño, esquivo, arisco
unsocial /ʌn'souʃəl/ *a* insocial, antisocial
unsold /ʌn'sould/ *a* no vendido, sin vender
unsolder /ʌn'sɒdər/ *vt* desoldar, desestañar
unsoldierly /ʌn'souldʒərli/ *a* indigno de un soldado; poco marcial
unsophisticated /ˌʌnsə'fɪstɪˌkeitɪd/ *a* ingenuo, inocente, cándido
unsought /ʌn'sɔt/ *a* no solicitado; no buscado
unsound /ʌn'saund/ *a* enfermo, defectuoso; (rotten) podrido; (fallacious) erróneo, poco convincente; (of persons) informal, indigno de confianza; (of religious views) heterodoxo. **of u. mind,** insano
unsoundness /ʌn'saundnɪs/ *n* lo defectuoso; mal estado, *m;* falsedad, *f;* informalidad, *f;* heterodoxia, *f*
unsparing /ʌn'spɛərɪŋ/ *a* severo, implacable; generoso, pródigo
unspeakable /ʌn'spikəbəl/ *a* indecible, inefable; que no puede mencionarse, horrible
unspecified /ʌn'spɛsəˌfaid/ *a* no especificado
unspoiled /ʌn'spɔilt/ *a* intacto; ileso, indemne; no corrompido; no estropeado; (of children) no mimado
unspoken /ʌn'spoukən/ *a* no pronunciado

unsportsmanlike /ʌn'spɔrtsmən,laik/ *a* indigno de un cazador; indigno de un deportista; nada caballeroso. **to play in an u. way,** jugar sucio
unstable /ʌn'steibəl/ *a* inestable; variable; inconstante; vacilante, irresoluto
unstained /ʌn'steind /*a* no manchado; no teñido; inmaculado, sin mancha
unstamped /ʌn'stæmpt/ *a* sin sello; no sellado
unstatesmanlike /ʌn'steitsmən,laik/ *a* impropio (*or* indigno) de un hombre de estado
unsteadiness /ʌn'stɛdinɪs/ *n* inestabilidad, falta de firmeza, *f;* inconstancia, *f*
unsteady /ʌn'stɛdi/ *a* inestable, inseguro; inconstante
unstick /ʌn'stɪk/ *vt* desapegar
unstitch /ʌn'stɪtʃ/ *vt* desapuntar
unstressed /ʌn'strɛst/ *a* sin énfasis; (of syllables) sin acento
unstudied /ʌn'stʌdid/ *a* no estudiado; natural, espontáneo
unsubstantial /,ʌnsəb'stænʃəl/ *a* insubstancial; ligero; irreal, imaginario; incorpóreo; aparente
unsuccessful /,ʌnsək'sɛsfəl/ *a* sin éxito; infructuoso. **to be u.,** no tener éxito
unsuccessfully /,ʌnsək'sɛsfəli/ *adv* en vano, sin éxito
unsuitability /,ʌnsutə'bɪlɪti/ *n* impropiedad, *f;* inconveniencia, incongruencia, *f;* incapacidad, *f;* inoportunidad, *f*
unsuitable /ʌn'sutəbəl/ *a* inapropiado; inconveniente; impropio; inservible; incapaz; inoportuno
unsung /ʌn'sʌŋ/ *a* no cantado; no celebrado en verso
unsupported /,ʌnsə'pɔrtɪd/ *a* sin apoyo; sin defensa; no favorecido
unsurmountable /,ʌnsər'mauntəbəl/ *a* insuperable, infranqueable
unsurpassable /,ʌnsər'pæsəbəl/ *a* inmejorable, insuperable
unsurpassed /,ʌnsər'pæst/ *a* sin par
unsuspecting /,ʌnsə'spɛktɪŋ/ *a* no suspicaz, confiado, no receloso
unswerving /ʌn'swɜrvɪŋ/ *a* directo; sin vacilar, constante
unsymmetrical /,ʌnsɪ'mɛtrɪkəl/ *a* asimétrico
unsympathetic /,ʌnsɪmpə'θɛtɪk/ *a* indiferente, incompasivo; antipático
unsystematic /,ʌnsɪstə'mætɪk/ *a* sin sistema, asistemático, no metódico
untalented /ʌn'tæləntɪd/ *a* sin talento
untamed /ʌn'tɛimd/ *a* indomado, cerril, bravío, no domesticado; desenfrenado, violento
unteach /ʌn'titʃ/ *vt* desenseñar
untenable /ʌn'tɛnəbəl/ *a* insostenible
untenanted /ʌn'tɛnəntɪd/ *a* desalquilado, deshabitado; vacío, desierto
unthankful /ʌn'θæŋkfəl/ *a* ingrato, desagradecido
unthinkable /ʌn'θɪŋkəbəl/ *a* inconcebible; imposible
unthinking /ʌn'θɪŋkɪŋ/ *a* sin reflexión; desatento; indiscreto
unthinkingly /ʌn'θɪŋkɪŋli/ *adv* sin pensar
unthread /ʌn'θrɛd/ *vt* deshebrar
untidily /ʌn'taidḷi/ *adv* en desorden, sin aseo
untidiness /ʌn'taidinɪs/ *n* desorden, *m;* desaseo, desaliño, *m;* falta de pulcritud, *f*
untidy /ʌn'taidi/ *a* desarreglado; desaseado; abandonado; en desorden, sin concierto
untie /ʌn'tai/ *vt* desatar, desanudar; (knots) deshacer
until /ʌn'tɪl/ *prep* hasta. *—conjunc* hasta que. (The subjunc. is required in clauses referring to future time, e.g. *No venga usted hasta que le avise yo,* Don't come until I tell you. In clauses referring to past or present time the indicative is generally used, e.g. *No la reconocí hasta que se volvió,* I didn't recognize her until she turned round)
untilled /ʌn'tɪld/ *a* sin cultivar
untimeliness /ʌn'taimlinɪs/ *n* inoportunidad, *f;* lo prematuro
untimely /ʌn'taimli/ *a* inoportuno, intempestivo; prematuro
untiring /ʌn'taiᵊrɪŋ/ *a* incansable, infatigable
unto /'ʌntu; *unstressed* -tə/ *prep* hacia
untold /ʌn'tould/ *a* no revelado; no narrado; sin decir, no dicho; incalculable
untouchable /ʌn'tʌtʃəbəl/ *a* que no puede tocarse, intangible; (of castes) intocable
untouched /ʌn'tʌtʃt/ *a* sin tocar; intacto, incólume
untrained /ʌn'treind/ *a* indisciplinado; inexperto; no adiestrado
untranslatable /,ʌntræns'leitəbəl/ *a* intraducible
untraveled /ʌn'trævəld/ *a* no frecuentado; (of persons) provinciano
untried /ʌn'traid/ *a* no experimentado. **u. knight,** caballero novel, *m*
untrodden /ʌn'trɒdṇ/ *a* no hollado, no frecuentado; inexplorado, virgen
untroubled /ʌn'trʌbəld/ *a* tranquilo, sosegado
untrue /ʌn'tru/ *a* mentiroso, falso, engañoso; ficticio, imaginario; traidor, desleal; infiel
untrustworthiness /ʌn'trʌst,wɜrðinɪs/ *n* incertidumbre, inseguridad, *f;* (of persons) informalidad, *f*
untrustworthy /ʌn'trʌst,wɜrði/ *a* indigno de confianza; incierto, dudoso; desleal
untruth /ʌn'truθ/ *n* mentira, falsedad, *f;* ficción, *f*
untruthful /ʌn'truθfəl/ *a* mentiroso; falso
untruthfulness /ʌn'truθfəlnɪs/ *n* falsedad, *f*
untwist /ʌn'twɪst/ *vt* destorcer
unused /ʌn'yuzd/ *a* no empleado; /ʌn'yust/ desacostumbrado; inusitado; (postage stamp) sin sellar
unusual /ʌn'yuʒuəl/ *a* fuera de lo común, desacostumbrado; extraño, raro, peregrino, extraordinario
unusually /ʌn'yuʒuəli/ *adv* excepcionalmente; infrecuentemente
unusualness /ʌn'yuʒuəlnɪs/ *n* lo insólito; rareza, *f*
unutterable /ʌn'ʌtərəbəl/ *a* indecible, inexpresable
unvarnished /ʌn'vɑrnɪʃt/ *a* sin barnizar; *Fig.* sencillo
unvarying /ʌn'vɛəriɪŋ/ *a* invariable, constante, uniforme
unveil /ʌn'veil/ *vt* quitar el velo; (memorial) descubrir; *Fig.* revelar. *—vi* quitarse el velo; revelarse, quitarse la careta
unventilated /ʌn'vɛntḷeitɪd/ *a* sin ventilación; sin aire, ahogado; (of topics) no discutido
unverifiable /ʌn,vɛrə'faiəbəl/ *a* que no puede verificarse
unverified /ʌn,vɛrə'faid/ *a* sin verificar
unvisited /ʌn 'vIsItId/ no visitado; no frecuentado
unvoiced /ʌn'vɔist/ *a* no expresado
unwanted /ʌn'wɒntɪd/ *a* no deseado; superfluo, de más
unwarlike /ʌn'wɔr,laik/ *a* nada marcial, pacífico
unwarranted /ʌn'wɔrəntɪd/ *a* sin garantía; inexcusable, injustificable
unwary /ʌn'wɛəri/ *a* incauto, imprudente
unwashed /ʌn'wɒʃt/ *a* sin lavar; sucio
unwatched /ʌn'wɒtʃt/ *a* no vigilado
unwavering /ʌn'weivərɪŋ/ *a* resuelto, firme; inexorable; (gaze) fijo
unwaveringly /ʌn'weivərɪŋli/ *adv* sin vacilar; inexorablemente
unwearied /ʌn'wiərid/ *a* incansable; infatigable
unwelcome /ʌn'wɛlkəm/ *a* mal acogido; inoportuno; desagradable
unwell /ʌn'wɛl/ *a* indispuesto
unwholesome /ʌn'houlsəm/ *a* malsano, nocivo, insalubre
unwholesomeness /ʌn'houlsəmnɪs/ *n* insalubridad, *f*
unwieldiness /ʌn'wildinɪs/ *n* pesadez, dificultad de manejarse, *f*
unwieldy /ʌn'wildi/ *a* pesado, abultado, difícil de manejar
unwilling /ʌn'wɪlɪŋ/ *a* desinclinado, reluctante
unwillingly /ʌn'wɪlɪŋli/ *adv* de mala gana
unwillingness /ʌn'wɪlɪŋnɪs/ *n* falta de inclinación, repugnancia, *f*
unwind /ʌn'waind/ *vt* desenvolver; (thread) desdevanar, desovillar. *—vi* desarrollarse; desdevanarse
unwise /ʌn'waiz/ *a* imprudente, indiscreto, incauto; (lacking wisdom) tonto
unwisely /ʌn'waizli/ *adv* imprudentemente, indiscretamente
unwitting /ʌn'wɪtɪŋ/ *a* inconsciente
unwittingly /ʌn'wɪtɪŋli/ *adv* sin darse cuenta
unwomanly /ʌn'wʊmənli/ *a* poco femenino
unwonted /ʌn'wɔntɪd/ *a* insólito, inusitado

unworkable /ʌn'wɜrkəbəl/ *a* impráctico
unworkmanlike /ʌn'wɜrkmənˌlaik/ *a* chapucero, charanguero
unworldly /ʌn'wɜrldli/ *a* poco, mundano, espiritual
unworn /ʌn'wɔrn/ *a* sin llevar, nuevo
unworthiness /ʌn'wɜrðinɪs/ *n* indignidad, *f*
unworthy /ʌn'wɜrði/ *a* indigno
unwounded /ʌn'wundɪd/ *a* no herido, sin herida, ileso
unwrap /ʌn'ræp/ *vt* desenvolver, desempapelar
unwritten /ʌn'rɪtn̩/ *a* no escrito. **u. law,** ley consuetudinaria, *f*
unyielding /ʌn'yildɪŋ/ *a* duro, firme; (of persons) inflexible, terco, resuelto, obstinado
unyoke /ʌn'youk/ *vt* desuncir, quitar el yugo
up /ʌp/ *adv* (high) arriba, en alto; (higher) hacia arriba; (out of bed) levantado; (standing) de pie; (finished) concluido, terminado; (of time) llegado; (excited) agitado; (rebellious) sublevado; (of sun, etc.) salido; (come or gone up) subido; (of universities) en residencia; (for discussion) bajo consideración; (abreast of) al lado, al nivel; (incapable) incapaz, incompetente; (ill) enfermo, indispuesto. **"Up,"** (on elevators) «Para subir.» (For various idiomatic uses of **up** after verbs, see verbs themselves.) *a* (in a few expressions only) ascendente. *—prep* en lo alto de; hacia arriba de; a lo largo de; (with country) en el interior de; (with current) contra. **to be up in arms,** sublevarse, rebelarse. **to be very hard up,** ser muy pobre, estar a la cuarta pregunta. **to drink up,** beberlo todo. **to go or come up,** subir. **to lay up,** acumular. **to speak up,** hablar en voz alta. **He has something up his sleeve,** Tiene algo en la manga. **It is all up,** Todo se acabó, Mi gozo en el pozo. **It is not up to much,** Vale muy poco; No es muy fuerte. **It is up to you,** Tú dirás, Tú harás lo que te parezca. **What is he up to?** ¿Qué está tramando? **What's up?** ¿Qué pasa? ¿Qué hay? **up and down,** *adv* bajando y subiendo, de arriba abajo; de un lado a otro; por todas partes. **up-and-down,** *a* fluctuante; (of roads) undulante; (of life) accidentado, borrascoso. **ups and downs,** vicisitudes, *f pl,* altibajos, *m pl.* **up-grade,** subida, *f.* **up in,** versado en, perito en. **well up in,** fuerte en. **up North,** al norte; en el norte; hacia el norte. **up there,** allí arriba, allí en lo alto. **up to,** hasta; (aware) al corriente de, informado de. **up to date,** *adv* hasta la fecha. **up-to-date,** *a* de última moda; al día. **up to now,** hasta ahora. **up train,** tren ascendente. **Up with...!** ¡Arriba! **Up you go!** (to children) ¡Upa!
upbraid /ʌp'breid/ *vt* reprender, echar en cara
upbringing /'ʌpˌbrɪŋɪŋ/ *n* crianza, educación, *f*
upcountry /*n., a* 'ʌpˌkʌntri; *adv.* ʌp'kʌntri/ *n* tierra adentro, *f;* lo interior (de un país). *—a* de tierra adentro, del interior. *—adv* tierra adentro, hacia el interior
update /'ʌpˌdeit/ *vt* actualizar, poner al día
upheaval /ʌp'hivəl/ *n* solevantamiento, *m;* trastorno, *m*
uphill /*a, adv.* 'ʌp'hɪl; *n.* 'ʌpˌhɪl/ *a* ascendente; penoso, fatigoso, difícil. *—adv* cuesta arriba, pecho arriba
uphold /ʌp'hould/ *vt* sostener, apoyar; (help) ayudar, consolar; (protect) defender; (countenance) aprobar; *Law.* confirmar
upholder /ʌp'houldər/ *n* sostenedor (-ra), defensor (-ra)
upholster /ʌp'houlstər, ə'poul-/ *vt* entapizar, tapizar
upholsterer /ʌp'houlstərər, ə'poul-/ *n* tapicero, *m*
upholstery /ʌp'houlstəri, ə'poul-/ *n* tapicería, *f;* (of car) almohadillado, *m*
upkeep /'ʌpˌkip/ *n* mantenimiento, *m,* conservación, *f*
upland /'ʌplənd/ *n* tierra alta, *f, a* alto, elevado
uplift /*v.* ʌp'lɪft; *n.* 'ʌpˌlɪft/ *vt* elevar. *—n* elevación, *f; Inf.* fervor, *m*
upon /ə'pɒn/ *prep.* See **on**
upper /'ʌpər/ *a compar* superior; alto; de arriba. *—n* (of shoe) pala, *f, Sports.* **u.-cut,** golpe de abajo arriba, upper-cut, *m.* **U. Egypt,** Alto Egipto, *m.* **u. hand,** dominio, *m;* superioridad, ventaja, *f.* **u. house,** cámara alta, *f;* senado, *m.* **u. ten,** los diez primeros
upper classes *a* clases altas, capas altas, *f pl*
uppermost /'ʌpərˌmoust/ *a* más alto, más elevado; predominante, principal; más fuerte. *—adv* en primer lugar; en lo más alto. **to be u.,** predominar
upright /'ʌpˌrait/ *a* recto, derecho; vertical; (honorable) honrado, digno, recto. *—n* (stanchion) mástil, soporte, palo derecho, montante, *m.* *—adv* en pie; derecho
uprightly /'ʌpˌraitli/ *adv* rectamente, honradamente
uprightness /'ʌpˌraitnɪs/ *n* rectitud, honradez, probidad, *f*
uprising /'ʌpˌraizɪŋ/ *n* insurrección, sublevación, *f*
uproar /'ʌpˌrɔr/ *n* alboroto, tumulto, estrépito, *m,* conmoción, *f*
uproarious /ʌp'rɔriəs/ *a* tumultuoso, estrepitoso
uproot /ʌp'rut/ *vt* desarraigar; *Fig.* arrancar; (destroy) extirpar
uprooting /ʌp'rutɪŋ/ *n* desarraigo, *m;* arranque, *m;* extirpación, *f*
upset /*v.* ʌp'sɛt; *n.* 'ʌpˌsɛt/ *vt* volcar; (overthrow) derribar, echar abajo; (frustrate) contrariar; desarreglar; (distress) trastornar, turbar; (of food) hacer mal. *—vi* volcarse. *—n* vuelco, *m;* trastorno, *m.* **u. price,** tipo de subasta, *m*
upsetting /ʌp'sɛtɪŋ/ *a* turbante, inquietante
upshot /'ʌpˌʃɒt/ *n* resultado, *m;* consecuencia, *f*
upside /'ʌpˌsaid/ *n* lado superior, *m;* parte superior, *f;* (of trains) andén ascendente, *m.* **u. down,** al revés, de arriba abajo; en desorden
upstairs /'ʌp'stɛərz/ *adv* arriba, en el piso de arriba; (with go or come) al piso de arriba
upstanding /ʌp'stændɪŋ/ *a* gallardo, guapo. **an u. young man (woman),** un buen mozo (una buena moza)
upstart /'ʌpˌstɑrt/ *n* arribista, *mf;* advenedizo (-za), insolente, *mf;* presuntuoso (-sa)
upstream /'ʌp'strim/ *a* and *adv* contra la corriente, agua arriba, río arriba
upturned /'ʌpˌtɛrnd/ *a* (of noses) respingada
upward /'ʌpwərd/ *a* ascendente, hacia arriba
upwards /'ʌpwərdz/ *adv* hacia arriba; en adelante. **u. of,** más de
Urals, the /'yʊrəlz/ los Urales, *m pl*
uranium /yʊ'reiniəm/ *n Mineral.* uranio, *m*
Uranus /'yʊrənəs, yʊ'rei-/ *n Astron.* Urano, *m*
urban /'ɜrbən/ *a* urbano, ciudadano
urbane /ɜr'bein/ *a* cortés, urbano, fino
urbanity /ɜr'bænɪti/ *n* urbanidad, cortesía, finura, *f*
urbanization /ˌɜrbənə'zeiʃən/ *n* urbanización, *f*
urbanize /'ɜrbəˌnaiz/ *vt* urbanizar
urban renewal *n* renovación urbana, renovación urbanística, *f*
urchin /'ɜrtʃɪn/ *n* galopín, granuja, pilluelo, *m*
ureter /yʊ'ritər/ *n Anat.* uréter, *m*
urethra /yʊ'riθrə/ *n Anat.* uretra, *f*
urge /ɜrdʒ/ *vt* empujar, impeler; incitar, estimular, azuzar, animar; pedir con urgencia, recomendar con ahínco, instar, insistir (en). *—n* instinto, impulso, *m;* deseo, *m;* ambición, *f*
urgency /'ɜrdʒənsi/ *n* urgencia, *f;* importancia, perentoriedad, *f*
urgent /'ɜrdʒənt/ *a* urgente; importante, apremiante, perentorio. **to be u.,** urgir
urgently /'ɜrdʒəntli/ *adv* urgentemente
uric /'yʊrɪk/ *a* úrico
urinal /'yʊrənl̩/ *n* orinal, urinario, *m*
urinalysis /ˌyʊrə'næləsɪs/ *n* análisis de orina, urinálisis, *m*
urinary /'yʊrəˌnɛri/ *a* urinario
urinary tract *n* conducto urinario, *m,* vías urinarias, *f pl*
urinate /'yʊrəˌneit/ *vi* orinar
urine /'yʊrɪn/ *n* orín, *m*
urn /ɜrn/ *n* urna, *f;* (for coffee) cafetera, *f;* (for tea) tetera, *f*
Ursa /'ɜrsə/ *n Astron.* osa, *f.* **U. Major,** osa mayor, *f.* **U. Minor,** osa menor, *f*
urticaria /ˌɜrtɪ'kɛəriə/ *n Med.* urticaria, *f*
Uruguayan /ˌyʊrə'gweiən/ *a* and *n* uruguayo (-ya)
us /ʌs/ *pron* nos; (with prep.) nosotros. **He came toward us,** Vino hacia nosotros

usable /'yuzəbəl/ *a* aprovechable, servible
usage /'yusɪdʒ/ *n* (handling) tratamiento, *m;* uso, *m,* costumbre, *f*
use /yus/ *n* uso, *m;* manejo, empleo, *m;* (custom) costumbre práctica, *f;* (need) necesidad, *f;* (usefulness) aprovechamiento, *m; Law.* usufructo, *m.* **directions for use,** direcciones para el uso, *f pl,* **for the use of...,** para uso de... **in use,** en uso. **out of use,** anticuado; fuera de moda. **to be of no use,** no servir; ser inútil. **to have no use for,** no tener necesidad de; *Inf.* tener en poco. **to make use of,** servirse de, aprovechar; *Law.* ejercer. **to put to use,** poner en uso, poner en servicio
use /yuz/ *vt* usar; (employ) emplear; (utilize) servirse de, utilizar; (handle) manejar; hacer uso de; (consume) gastar, consumir; (treat) tratar; practicar. **to use up,** agotar, acabar con; consumir. —*vi impers* acostumbrar, soler (e.g. *It used to happen that...,* Solía ocurrir que...). (**Used to** and the verb which follows are often translated simply by the imperfect tense of the following verb, e.g. *I used to see her every day,* La veía todos los días. Use of the verbs *acostumbrar* or *soler* to translate used to adds emphasis to the statement)
used /yuzd/ *a* and *past part* /yust/ acostumbrado, habituado; empleado; (clothes) usado; (postage stamp) sellado. **to become u. to,** acostumbrarse a
useful /'yusfəl/ *a* útil; provechoso; servicial
usefully /'yusfəli/ *adv* útilmente; con provecho
usefulness /'yusfəlnɪs/ *n* utilidad, *f;* valor, *m*
useless /'yuslɪs/ *a* inútil; vano, infructuoso. **to render u.,** inutilizar
uselessness /'yuslɪsnɪs/ *n* inutilidad, *f*
user /'yuzər/ *n* el, *m,* (*f,* la) que usa, comprador (-ra)
usher /'ʌʃər/ *n* ujier, *m;* (in a theater) acomodador (-ra). —*vt* introducir, anunciar; acomodar
usual /'yuʒuəl/ *a* usual, acostumbrado, habitual; normal, común. **as u.,** como siempre. **in the u. form,** *Com.* al usado; como de costumbre. **with their usual courtesy,** con la cortesía que les es característica
usually /'yuʒuəli/ *adv* por lo general, ordinariamente. **We u. go out on Sundays,** Acostumbramos salir los domingos
usurer /'yuʒərər/ *n* usurero (-ra)
usurious /yu'ʒʊriəs/ *a* usurario
usurp /yu'sɜrp/ *vt* usurpar; asumir, arrogarse
usurpation /ˌyusər'peiʃən/ *n* usurpación, *f;* arrogación, *f*
usurper /yu'sɜrpər/ *n* usurpador (-ra)
usurping /yu'sɜrpɪŋ/ *a* usurpador
usury /'yuʒəri/ *n* usura, *f.* **to practice u.,** usurear, dar (or tomar) a usura
utensil /yu'tɛnsəl/ *n* utensilio, instrumento, *m;* herramienta, *f.* **kitchen utensils,** batería de cocina, *f*
uterine /'yutərɪn/ *a Med.* uterino
uterus /'yutərəs/ *n* útero, *m*
utilitarian /yuˌtɪlɪ'tɛəriən/ *a* utilitario
utilitarianism /yuˌtɪlɪ'tɛəriəˌnɪzəm/ *n* utilitarismo, *m*
utility /yu'tɪlɪti/ *n* utilidad, *f;* ventaja, *f,* beneficio, provecho, *m.* **u. goods,** artículos fabricados bajo la autorizacion del gobierno, *m pl*
utilizable /ˌyutḷ'aizəbəl/ *a* utilizable, aprovechable
utilization ˌyut*W*ə'zeiSən/ *n* empleo, aprovechamiento, *m*
utilize /'yutḷˌaiz/ *vt* utilizar, servirse de; aprovechar
utmost /'ʌtˌmoust/ *a* (outermost) extremo; (farthest) más remoto, más distante; (greatest) mayor, más grande. —*n* lo más; todo lo posible. **to do one's u.,** hacer todo lo posible, hacer todo lo que uno pueda
utopian /yu'toupiən/ *a* utópico
utter /'ʌtər/ *a* completo, total; terminate, absoluto; sumo, extremo. **He is an u. fool,** Es un tonto de capirote
utter /'ʌtər/ *vt* pronunciar, proferir, decir, hablar; (a sigh, cry, etc.) dar; (express) manifestar, expresar, explicar; (coin) poner en circulación; (a libel) publicar; (disclose) revelar, descubrir
utterance /'ʌtərəns/ *n* expresión, manifestación, *f;* pronunciación, *f;* (style) lenguaje, *m*
utterly /'ʌtərli/ *adv* enteramente, completamente
uttermost /'ʌtərˌmoust/ *a.* See **utmost**
uvula /'yuvyələ/ *n Anat.* úvula, *f*
uxorious /ʌk'sɔriəs/ *a* uxorio

V

v /vi/ *n* (letter) ve, *f;* pieza en forma de V, *f*
vacancy /ˈveikənsi/ *n* vacío, *m;* vacancia, *f;* (mental) vacuidad, *f;* (of offices, posts) vacante, *f;* (leisure) desocupación, ociosidad, *f;* (gap, blank) vacío, *m,* laguna, *f*
vacant /ˈveikənt/ *a* vacío; despoblado, deshabitado; (free) libre; (of offices, etc.) vacante; (leisured) ocioso; (absent-minded) distraído; (vague) vago; (foolish) estúpido, estólido
vacantly /ˈveikəntli/ *adv* distraídamente; estúpidamente
vacate /ˈveikeit/ *vt* dejar vacío; (a post) dejar; (a throne) renunciar a; dejar vacante; *Mil.* evacuar; *Law.* anular, rescindir
vacation /veiˈkeiʃən/ *n* (of offices) vacante, *f;* (holiday) vacaciones, *f pl, f.* **the long v.,** las vacaciones de verano. **to be on a v.,** estar de vacaciones
vaccinate /ˈvæksəˌneit/ *vt* vacunar
vaccination /ˌvæksəˈneiʃən/ *n* vacunación, *f*
vaccine /vækˈsin/ *n* vacuna, *f*
vacillate /ˈvæsəˌleit/ *vi* (sway) oscilar; (hesitate) vacilar, titubear, dudar
vacillating /ˈvæsəˌleitɪŋ/ *a* vacilante
vacillation *n* vacilación, *f*
vacuity /væˈkyuɪti/ *n* vacuidad, *f*
vacuous /ˈvækyuəs/ *a* desocupado, ocioso; estúpido, vacío
vacuum /ˈvækyum/ *n* vacío, *m.* **v. brake,** freno al vacío, *m.* **v. cleaner,** aspirador de polvo, *m.* **v. flask,** termos, *m.* **v. pump,** bomba neumática, *f.* **vacuum-shelf dryer,** secador al vacío, *m*
vade mecum /ˈveiˈdi mikəm, ˈvɑ-/ *n* vademécum, *m*
vagabond /ˈvægəˌbɒnd/ *n* vagabundo (-da); vago, *m;* (beggar) mendigo (-ga). —*a* vagabundo, errante
vagabondage /ˈvægəˌbɒndɪdʒ/ *n* vagabundeo, *m,* vagancia, *f*
vagary /vəˈgɛəri, ˈveigəri/ *n* (whim) capricho, antojo, *m,* extravagancia, *f;* (of the mind) divagación, *f*
vagina /vəˈdʒainə/ *n* vagina, *f*
vaginal /ˈvædʒənl̩/ *a* vaginal
vagrancy /ˈveigrənsi/ *n* vagancia, *f*
vagrant /ˈveigrənt/ *n* vago, *m, a* vagabundo, errante
vague /veig/ *a* vago; indistinto; equívoco, ambiguo; (uncertain) incierto
vaguely /ˈveigli/ *adv* vagamente
vagueness /ˈveignɪs/ *n* vaguedad, *f*
vain /vein/ *a* vano; (fruitless) infructuoso; (useless) inútil; (unsubstantial) fútil, insubstancial; fantástico; (empty) vacío; (worthless) despreciable; (conceited) vanidoso, presumido. **in v.,** en vano, en balde, inútilmente. **v. about,** orgulloso de
vainglorious /veinˈglɔriəs, -ˈglour-/ *a* vanaglorioso
vaingloriousness /veinˈglɔriəsnɪs/ *n* vanagloria, *f*
vainly /ˈveinli/ *adv* vanamente; inútilmente; (conceitedly) vanidosamente, con vanidad
valance /ˈvæləns/ *n* cenefa, *f*
vale /veil/ *n* (valley) valle, *m.* —*interj* ¡adiós! —*n* (good-bye) vale, *m*
valediction /ˌvælɪˈdɪkʃən/ *n* despedida, *f;* vale, *m*
valedictory /ˌvælɪˈdɪktəri/ *a* de despedida
Valencian /vəˈlɛnʃiən/ *a* and *n* valenciano (-na)
valency /ˈveilənsi/ *n Chem.* valencia, *f*
valet /væˈlei, ˈvælɪt/ *n* criado, *m.* **v. de chambre,** ayuda de cámara, *m*
valetudinarian /ˌvælɪˌtudn̩ˈɛəriən/ *a* valetudinario
Valhalla /vælˈhælə, vɑlˈhɑlə/ *n* el Valhala, *m*
valiant /ˈvælyənt/ *a* valiente, esforzado, animoso, bravo
valiantly /ˈvælyəntli/ *adv* valientemente
valid /ˈvælɪd/ *a* válido, valedero; (of laws in force) vigente
validate /ˈvælɪˌdeit/ *vt* validar
validation /ˌvælɪˈdeiʃən/ *n* validación, *f*
validity /vəˈlɪdɪti/ *n* validez, *f*
validly /ˈvælɪdli/ *adv* válidamente
valise /vəˈlis/ *n* valija, *f,* saco de viaje, *m*
Valkyrie /vælˈkɪəri/ *n* Valquiria, *f*
valley /ˈvæli/ *n* valle, *m*
valor /ˈvælər/ *n* valor, *m,* valentía, *f*
valorous /ˈvælərəs/ *a* valoroso, esforzudo, intrépido
valuable /ˈvælyuəbəl/ *a* valioso; costoso; precioso; estimable; excelente. —*n pl* **valuables,** objetos de valor, *m pl*
valuableness /ˈvælyuəbəlnɪs/ *n* valor, *m*
valuation /ˌvælyuˈeiʃən/ *n* valuación, tasación, *f;* estimación, *f*
valuator /ˈvælyuˌeitər/ *n* tasador, *m*
value /ˈvælyu/ *n* valor, *m;* precio, *m;* estimación, *f;* importancia, *f;* (*Gram. Mus.*) valor, *m; pl* **values,** valores morales, principios, *m pl.* —*vt* tasar, valorar; estimar; apreciar; tener en mucho; hacer caso de; considerar. **to be of v.,** ser de valor
valued /ˈvælyud/ *a* apreciado, estimado; precioso
valueless /ˈvælyulɪs/ *a* sin valor; insignificante
valuer /ˈvælyuər/ *n* tasador, *m*
valve /vælv/ *n* (*Elec., Mech., Anat.*) válvula, *f;* (*Bot., Zool.*) valva, *f*
valved /vælvd/ *a* con válvulas; (in compounds) de... válvulas
valvular /ˈvælvyələr/ *a* valvular
vamp /væmp/ *n* (of a shoe) pala (de zapato), *f;* (patch) remiendo, *m; Mus.* acompañamiento improvisado, *m; Inf.* aventurera, *f.* —*vt* (of shoes) poner palas (a); (patch) remendar; *Mus.* improvisar un acompañamiento; (of a woman) fascinar, engatusar
vampire /ˈvæmpaiᵊr/ *n* vampiro, *m*
van /væn/ *n* (*Mil., Nav., Fig.*) vanguardia, *f;* camión, *m;* (for delivery) camión de reparto, *m;* (for furniture) conductora de muebles, *f;* (removal) carro de mudanzas, *m;* (mail) camión postal, *m;* (for bathing) caseta de baño, *f;* (for guard on trains) furgón de equipajes, *m;* (railroad car) vagón, *m*
vandal /ˈvændl̩/ *a* and *n* vándalo (-la); bárbaro (-ra)
vandalism /ˈvændl̩ˌɪzəm/ *n* vandalismo, *m*
Vandyke /vænˈdaik/ *n* cuadro de Vandyke, *m.* **V. beard,** perilla, *f.* **V. collar,** cuello de encaje, *m*
vane /vein/ *n* (weathercock) veleta, *f;* (of a windmill) aspa, *f;* (of a propeller) paleta, *f;* (of a feather) barba, *f;* (of a surveying instrument) pínula, *f*
vanguard /ˈvænˌgɑrd/ *n* vanguardia, *f.* **in the v.,** a vanguardia; *Fig.* en la vanguardia
vanilla /vəˈnɪlə/ *n* vainilla, *f*
vanish /ˈvænɪʃ/ *vi* desaparecer; desvanecerse; disiparse
vanishing /ˈvænɪʃɪŋ/ *n* desaparición, *f;* disipación, *f.* **v. cream,** crema desvanecedora, *f.* **v. point,** punto de la vista, *m*
vanity /ˈvænɪti/ *n* vanidad, *f.* **v. case,** polvera de bolsillo, *f*
vanquish /ˈvæŋkwɪʃ/ *vt* vencer, derrotar
vanquisher /ˈvæŋkwɪʃər/ *n* vencedor (-ra)
vantage /ˈvæntɪdʒ, ˈvɑn-/ *n* ventaja (also in tennis), *f.* **v.-ground,** posición ventajosa, *f,* sitial de privilegio, *m*
vapid /ˈvæpɪd/ *a* insípido, insulso; (of speeches, etc.) soso, aburrido, insípido
vapidity /væˈpɪdɪti/ *n* insipidez, sosería, *f*
vapor /ˈveipər/ *n* vapor, *m; pl* **vapors,** (hysteria) vapores, *m pl.* —*vi* (boast) jactarse, baladronear; decir disparates. **v. bath,** baño de vapor, *m*
vaporizable /ˌveipəˈraizəbəl/ *a* vaporizable
vaporization /ˌveipərəˈzeiʃən/ *n* vaporización, *f*
vaporize /ˈveipəˌraiz/ *vt* vaporizar. —*vi* vaporizarse
vaporizer /ˈveipəˌraizər/ *n* vaporizador, *m*
vaporous /ˈveipərəs/ *a* vaporoso
variability /ˌvɛəriəˈbɪlɪti/ *n* variabilidad, *f*
variable /ˈvɛəriəbəl/ *a* variable. —*n Math.* variable, *f*
variably /ˈvɛəriəbli/ *adv* variablemente
variance /ˈvɛəriəns/ *n* variación, *f,* cambio, *m;* desacuerdo, *m,* disensión, *f;* diferencia, contradicción, *f.* **at v.,** en desacuerdo, reñidos; hostil (a), opuesto (a); (of things) distinto (de), en contradicción (con)

variant /'vɛəriənt/ *n* variante, *f*
variation /ˌvɛəri'eiʃən/ *n* variación, *f;* cambio, *m;* variedad, *f;* diferencia, *f;* (*Mus.* magnetism) variación, *f*
varicose /'værɪˌkous/ *a* varicoso
varied success /'vɛərid/ éxito vario, *m*
variegate /'vɛəriɪˌgeit/ *vt* abigarrar, matizar, salpicar
variegated /'vɛəriɪˌgeitɪd/ *a* abigarrado; variado; mezclado
variegation /ˌvɛəriɪgeiʃən/ *n* abigarramiento, *m;* diversidad de colores, *f*
variety /və'raiɪti/ *n* variedad, *f;* diversidad, *f;* (choice) surtido, *m.* **v. show,** función de variedades, *f*
various /'vɛəriəs/ *a* vario, diverso; diferente
variously /'vɛəriəsli/ *adv* diversamente
varix /'vɛərɪks/ *n* várice, *f*
varnish /'vɑrnɪʃ/ *n* barniz, *m.* —*vt* barnizar; (pottery) vidriar; (conceal) disimular. **copal v.,** barniz copal, *m.* **japan v.,** charol japonés, *m.* **lacquer v.,** laca, *f.* **v. remover,** (for nails) quitaesmalte, *m*
varnishing /'vɑrnɪʃɪŋ/ *n* barnizado, *m;* (of pottery) vidriado, *m*
vary /'vɛəri/ *vt* variar; cambiar; diversificar; modificar. —*vi* variar; cambiar; (be different) ser distinto (de); (deviate) desviarse (de); (disagree) estar en desacuerdo, distar, estar en contradicción. **to v. directly (indirectly),** *Math.* variar en razón directa (inversa)
varying /'vɛəriɪŋ/ *a* variante, cambiante, diverso
vascular /'væskyələr/ *a* vascular
vase /veis, veiz, vɑz/ *n* vaso, jarrón, *m;* urna, *f*
vaseline /'væsəˌlin/ *n* vaselina, *f*
vassal /'væsəl/ *n* vasallo (-lla); esclavo (-va), siervo (-va). —*a* tributario
vast /væst/ *a* vasto, extenso; enorme; grande. —*n* vastedad, inmensidad, *f*
vastly /'væstli/ *adv* enormemente; muy; con mucho
vastness /'væstnɪs/ *n* vastedad, extensión, *f;* inmensidad, *f;* enormidad, *f,* gran tamaño, *m;* grandeza, *f*
vat /væt/ *n* cuba, tina, *f;* alberca, *f,* estanque, *m.* **dyeing vat,** cuba de tintorero, *f.* **tanning vat,** noque, *m.* **wine vat,** lagar, *m*
Vatican /'vætɪkən/ *a* and *n* Vaticano, *m*
vaticinate /və'tɪsəˌneit/ *vt* and *vi* vaticinar, profetizar
vaticination /vəˌtɪsə'neiʃən/ *n* vaticinio, *m,* predicción, *f*
vaudeville /'vɔdvɪl/ *n* vodevil, *m,* zarzuela cómica, *f*
vault /vɔlt/ *n Archit.* bóveda, *f;* caverna, *f;* (for wine) bodega, cueva, *f;* (in a bank) cámara acorazada, *f;* (in a church) cripta, *f;* sepultura, *f;* (of the sky) bóveda celeste, *f;* (leap) salto, *m;* voltereta, *f.* —*vi* (jump) saltar; (with a pole) saltar con pértiga; saltar por encima de; voltear. —*vt Archit.* abovedar; saltar
vaulted /'vɔltɪd/ *a* abovedado
vaulter /'vɔltər/ *n* saltador (-ra)
vaulting /'vɔltɪŋ/ *n* construcción de bóvedas, *f;* bóvedas, *f pl;* edificio abovedado, *m;* (jumping) salto, *m.* **v.-horse,** potro de madera, *m*
vaunt /vɔnt/ *vi* jactarse (de), hacer gala (de); triunfar (sobre). —*vt* ostentar, sacar a relucir; (praise) alabar. —*n* jactancia, *f*
veal /vil/ *n* ternera, *f.* **v.-cutlet,** chuleta de ternera, *f*
vector /'vɛktər/ *n* vector, *m*
Veda /'veidə/ *n* Veda, *m*
veer /vɪər/ *vi* (of the wind) girar; (of a ship) virar; *Fig.* cambiar (de opinión, etc.). —*vt* virar
vegetable /'vɛdʒtəbəl/ *n* vegetal, *m;* legumbre, *f; pl* **vegetables,** (green and generally cooked) verduras, *f pl;* (raw green) hortalizas, *f pl.* **v. dish,** fuente de legumbres, *f.* **v. garden,** huerto de legumbres, *m;* **v. ivory,** marfil vegetal, *m.* **v. kingdom,** reino vegetal, *m.* **v. soup,** sopa de hortelano, *f*
vegetal /'vɛdʒɪtl̩/ *a* vegetal
vegetarian /ˌvɛdʒɪ'tɛəriən/ *a* and *n* vegetariano (-na)
vegetarianism /ˌvɛdʒɪ'tɛəriəˌnɪzəm/ *n* vegetarianismo, *m*
vegetate /'vɛdʒɪˌteit/ *vi* vegetar
vegetation /ˌvɛdʒɪ'teiʃən/ *n* vegetación, *f*
vehemence /'viəməns/ *n* vehemencia, *f;* violencia, *f;* impetuosidad, *f;* pasión, *f,* ardor, *m*
vehement /'viəmənt/ *a* vehemente; violento; impetuoso; apasionado
vehemently /'viəməntli/ *adv* con vehemencia; violentamente; con impetuosidad; apasionadamente
vehicle /'viɪkəl/ *n* vehículo, *m;* (means) medio, *m;* instrumento, *m*
vehicular /vi'hɪkyələr/ *a* vehicular, de los vehículos; de los coches. **v. traffic,** circulación de los coches, *f;* los vehículos
veil /veil/ *n* velo, *m;* (curtain) cortina, *f;* (disguise) disfraz, *m;* (excuse) pretexto, *m;* (appearance) apariencia, *f.* —*vt* velar; cubrir con un velo; (hide) tapar, encubrir; (dissemble) disimular; (disguise) disfrazar. **to take the v.,** tomar el velo, profesar
vein /vein/ *n* (*Anat., Bot.*) vena, *f;* (*Geol., Mineral.*) veta, *f,* filón, *m;* (in wood) fibra, hebra, *f;* (*Fig.* streak) rasgo, *m;* (inspiration) vena, *f;* (mood) humor, *m*
veined, veiny /veind; 'veini/ *a* venoso; de venas; veteado
velar /'vilər/ *a* velar
vellum /'vɛləm/ *n* vitela, *f*
velocity /və'lɒsɪti/ *n* velocidad, *f;* rapidez, *f*
velodrome /'viləˌdroum/ *n* velódromo, *m*
velours /və'lʊr/ *n* terciopelo, *m*
velvet /'vɛlvɪt/ *n* terciopelo, *m, a* hecho de terciopelo; aterciopelado
velveteen /ˌvɛlvɪ'tin/ *n* pana, *f,* velludillo, *m*
velvety /'vɛlvɪti/ *a* aterciopelado
venal /'vinl̩/ *a* venal
venality /vi'nælɪti/ *n* venalidad, *f*
vend /vɛnd/ *vt* vender
vendor /'vɛndər/ *n* vendedor (-ra)
veneer /və'nɪər/ *vt* chapear, taracear; (conceal) disimular, disfrazar. —*n* taraceado, chapeado, *m;* (plate) chapa, hoja para chapear, *f;* (*Fig.* gloss) barniz, *m,* apariencia, *f*
venerability /ˌvɛnərə'bɪlɪti/ *n* venerabilidad, respetabilidad, *f*
venerable /'vɛnərəbəl/ *a* venerable
venerate /'vɛnəˌreit/ *vt* venerar, reverenciar
veneration /ˌvɛnə'reiʃən/ *n* veneración, *f*
venerator /'vɛnəˌreitər/ *n* venerador (-ra)
venereal /və'nɪəriəl/ *a* venéreo. **v. disease,** enfermedad venérea, *f*
Venetian /və'niʃən/ *a* and *n* veneciano (-na). **v. blinds,** persianas, celosías, *f pl*
Venezuelan /ˌvɛnə'zweilən/ *a* and *n* venezolano (-na)
vengeance /'vɛndʒəns/ *n* venganza, *f*
vengeful /'vɛndʒfəl/ *a* vengativo
venial /'viniəl/ *a* venial
veniality /ˌvini'ælɪti/ *n* venialidad, *f*
Venice /'vɛnɪs/ Venecia, *f*
venison /'vɛnəsən/ *n* venado, *m*
venom /'vɛnəm/ *n* veneno, *m*
venomous /'vɛnəməs/ *a* venenoso; maligno, malicioso
venomously /'vɛnəməsli/ *adv* con malignidad, maliciosamente
venomousness /'vɛnəməsnɪs/ *n* venenosidad, *f;* malignidad, *f*
venous /'vinəs/ *a* venoso
vent /vɛnt/ *n* abertura, *f;* salida, *f;* (air-hole) respiradero, *m;* (in pipes) ventosa, *f;* (in fire-arms) oído, *m; Anat.* ano, *m;* (*Fig.* outlet) desahogo, *m;* expresión, *f.* —*vt* dejar escapar; (pierce) agujerear; (discharge) emitir, vomitar; (relieve) desahogar; expresar, dar expresión (a), dar rienda suelta (a)
venter /'vɛntər/ *n Law.* vientre, *m*
ventilate /'vɛntl̩ˌeit/ *vt* ventilar; discutir
ventilation /ˌvɛntl̩'eiʃən/ *n* ventilación, *f*
ventilator /'vɛntl̩ˌeitər/ *n* ventilador, *m*
ventricle /'vɛntrɪkəl/ *n* ventrículo, *m*
ventriloquism /vɛn'trɪləˌkwɪzəm/ *n* ventriloquia, *f*
ventriloquist /vɛn'trɪləkwɪst/ *n* ventrílocuo (-ua)
venture /'vɛntʃər/ *n* ventura, *f;* riesgo, *m;* aventura, *f;* especulación, *f.* —*vt* arriesgar, aventurar; (stake) jugar; (state) expresar. —*vi* aventurarse; (dare) atreverse, osar; permitirse. **at a v.,** a la ventura. **to v. on,** arriesgarse a; probar ventura con; lanzarse a; (a remark) permitirse. **to v. out,** atreverse a salir

venturesome /ˈvɛntʃərsəm/ *a* atrevido, audaz; (dangerous) arriesgado, peligroso
venturesomeness /ˈvɛntʃərsəmnɪs/ *n* atrevimiento, *m*, temeridad, *f;* (risk) riesgo, peligro, *m*
Venus /ˈvinəs/ *n* (planet) Venus, *m;* (woman) venus, *f*
veracious /vəˈreiʃəs/ *a* veraz, verídico; verdadero
veracity /vəˈræsɪti/ *n* veracidad, *f;* verdad, *f*
veranda /vəˈrændə/ *n* veranda, *f*
verb /vɜrb/ *n* verbo, *m.* **auxiliary v.,** verbo auxiliar, *m.* **intransitive v.,** verbo intransitivo (neutro), *m.* **reflexive v.,** verbo reflexivo, *m.* **transitive v.,** verbo transitivo, *m*
verbal /ˈvɜrbəl/ *a* verbal
verbally /ˈvɜrbəli/ *adv* de palabra, verbalmente
verbatim /vərˈbeitɪm/ *a* textual. —*adv* textualmente, palabra por palabra
verbiage /ˈvɜrbiɪdʒ/ *n* verbosidad, palabrería, *f*
verbose /vərˈbous/ *a* verboso, prolijo
verbosity /vərˈbɒsɪti/ *n* verbosidad, *f*
verdancy /ˈvɜrdn̩si/ *n* verdura, *f,* verdor, *m*
verdant /ˈvɜrdnt/ *a* verde
verdict /ˈvɜrdɪkt/ *n Law.* veredicto, fallo, *m,* sentencia, *f;* opinión, *f,* juicio, *m.* **to bring in a v.,** fallar sentencia.
verdigris /ˈvɜrdɪˌgris/ *n* cardenillo, verdin, *m*
verdure /ˈvɜrdʒər/ *n* verdura, *f,* verdor, *m; Fig.* lozanía, *f*
verge /vɜrdʒ/ *n* (wand) vara, *f;* (edge) margen, borde, *m;* (of a lake, etc.) orilla, *f;* (horizon) horizonte, *m; Fig.* víspera, *f,* punto, *m.* **on the v. of,** al margen de, a la orilla de. **to be on the v. of,** *Fig.* estar a punto de; estar en vísperas de
verger /ˈvɜrdʒər/ *n* macero, *m;* (in a church) pertiguero, *m*
verifiable /ˌvɛrəˈfaiəbəl/ *a* verificable
verification /ˌvɛrəfɪˈkeiʃən/ *n* verificación, *f*
verifier /ˈvɛrəˌfaiər/ *n* verificador (-ra)
verify /ˈvɛrəˌfai/ *vt* verificar, confirmar; probar
verily /ˈvɛrəli/ *adv* de veras, en verdad
verisimilitude /ˌvɛrəsɪˈmɪlɪˌtud/ *n* verosimilitud, *f*
veritable /ˈvɛrɪtəbəl/ *a* verdadero
veritably /ˈvɛrɪtəbli/ *adv* verdaderamente
verity /ˈvɛrɪti/ *n* verdad, *f*
vermicelli /ˌvɜrmɪˈtʃɛli/ *n* fideos, *m pl*
vermilion /vərˈmɪlyən/ *n* bermellón, *m*
vermin /ˈvɜrmɪn/ *n* bichos dañinos, *m pl;* (insects) parásitos, *m pl*
vermouth /vərˈmuθ/ *n* vermut, *m*
vernacular /vərˈnækyələr/ *a* vernáculo; nativo; vulgar. —*n* lengua popular, *f;* lenguaje vulgar, *m*
versatile /ˈvɜrsətl̩/ *a Zool.* versátil; inconstante, voluble; (clever) de muchos talentos; de muchos intereses; adaptable; completo, cabal
versatility /ˌvɜrsəˈtɪlɪti/ *n* (cleverness) muchos talentos, *m pl;* adaptabilidad, *f*
verse /vɜrs/ *n* verso, *m;* (stanza) estrofa, *f;* (in the Bible) versículo, *m;* (poetry) poesía, *f,* versos, *m pl.* **to make verses,** escribir versos
versed /vɜrst/ *a* versado, experimentado
versicle /ˈvɜrsɪkəl/ *n* versículo, *m*
versification /ˌvɜrsəfɪˈkeiʃən/ *n* versificación, *f*
versifier /ˈvɜrsəˌfaiər/ *n* versificador (-ra)
versify /ˈvɜrsəˌfai/ *vt* and *vi* versificar
version /ˈvɜrʒən/ *n* versión, *f;* traducción, *f;* interpretación, *f*
versus /ˈvɜrsəs/ *prep* contra
vertebra /ˈvɜrtəbrə/ *n* vértebra, *f*
vertebral /ˈvɜrtəbrəl/ *a* vertebral
vertebrate /ˈvɜrtəbrɪt/ *n* vertebrado, *m*
vertex /ˈvɜrtɛks/ *n* (*Geom., Anat.*) vértice, *m; Astron.* cenit, *m;* cumbre, *f*
vertical /ˈvɜrtɪkəl/ *a* vertical
verticality /ˌvɜrtɪˈkælɪti/ *n* verticalidad, *f*
vertiginous /vərˈtɪdʒənəs/ *a* vertiginoso
vertigo /ˈvɜrtɪˌgou/ *n* vértigo, *m*
verve /vɜrv/ *n* brío, *m,* fogosidad, *f*
very /ˈvɛri/ *a* mismo; (mere) mero; (true) verdadero; (with adjective and comparative) más grande; *Inf.* mismísimo; (complete) perfecto, completo. **The v. thought of it made him laugh,** Sólo con pensarlo se rió (*or* La mera idea le hizo reír). **this v. minute,** este mismísimo instante. **the v. day,** el mismo día
very /ˈvɛri/ *adv* muy; mucho; demasiado; (exactly) exactamente; completamente; absolutamente. **He is v. worried,** Está muy preocupado. **He is not v. well,** (i.e. rather ill) Está bastante bien. **This cloth is the v. best,** Esta tela es la mejor que hay. **I like it v. much,** Me gusta muchísimo. **He is v. much pleased,** Está muy contento. **so v. little,** tan poco; tan pequeño. **v. well,** muy bien
vesicle /ˈvɛsɪkəl/ *n* vesícula, *f*
vesper /ˈvɛspər/ *n* estrella vespertina, *f,* héspero, *m; pl* **vespers,** *Eccl.* vísperas, *f pl*
vessel /ˈvɛsəl/ *n* vasija, *f,* recipiente, *m;* (boat) barco, buque, *m;* (*Anat., Bot.*) vaso, *m*
vest /vɛst/ *n* camiseta, *f;* (waistcoat) chaleco, *m.* —*vt* vestir; (with authority, etc.) revestir de; (property, etc.) hacer entrega de, ceder. —*vi* tener validez; (dress) vestirse. **vested interests,** intereses creados, *m pl.* **v.-pocket,** bolsillo del chaleco, *m.* **v.-pocket camera,** cámara de bolsillo, *f*
vestal /ˈvɛstl̩/ *a* vestal; virgen, casto. —*n* vestal, *f;* virgen, *f*
vestibule /ˈvɛstəˌbyul/ *n* vestíbulo, *m;* (anteroom) antecámara, *f;* (of a theatre box) antepalco, *m; Anat.* vestíbulo, *m*
vestige /ˈvɛstɪdʒ/ *n* vestigio, rastro, *m;* sombra, *f; Biol.* rudimento, *m*
vestment /ˈvɛstmənt/ *n* hábito, *m; Eccl.* vestidura, *f*
vestry /ˈvɛstri/ *n* vestuario, *m,* sacristía, *f*
vesture /ˈvɛstʃər/ *n* traje, hábito, *m,* vestidura, *f*
Vesuvius /vəˈsuviəs/ Vesubio, *m*
veteran /ˈvɛtərən/ *a* veterano; de los veteranos; aguerrido; anciano; experimentado. —*n* veterano (-na)
veterinary /ˈvɛtərəˌnɛri/ *a* veterinario. **v. science,** veterinaria, *f.* **v. surgeon,** veterinario, *m*
veto /ˈvitou/ *n* veto, *m;* prohibición, *f.* —*vt* poner el veto; prohibir
vex /vɛks/ *vt* contrariar, irritar; enojar; (make impatient) impacientar; fastidiar; (afflict) afligir, acongojar; (worry) inquietar
vexation /vɛkˈseiʃən/ *n* contrariedad, irritación, *f;* enojo, enfado, *m;* (impatience) impaciencia, *f;* fastidio, *m;* aflicción, *f;* inquietud, *f;* disgusto, *m*
vexatious /vɛkˈseiʃəs/ *a* irritante; enojoso, enfadoso; fastidioso, molesto
vexatiousness /vɛkˈseiʃəsnɪs/ *n* fastidio, *m,* molestia, *f;* incomodidad, *f;* contrariedad, *f*
vexed /vɛkst/ *a* discutido; contencioso; (thorny) espinoso, difícil
vexing /ˈvɛksɪŋ/ *a* irritante; molesto; enfadoso
via /ˈvaiə, ˈviə/ *n* vía, *f, prep* por, por la vía de
viability /ˌvaiəˈbɪlɪti/ *n* viabilidad, *f*
viable /ˈvaiəbəl/ *a* viable
viaduct /ˈvaiəˌdʌkt/ *n* viaducto, *m*
vial /ˈvaiəl/ *n* frasco, *m,* ampolleta, *f*
vibrant /ˈvaibrənt/ *a* vibrante
vibrate /ˈvaibreit/ *vi* vibrar; (of machines) trepidar; oscilar. —*vt* hacer vibrar, vibrar
vibration /vaiˈbreiʃən/ *n* vibración, *f;* trepidación, *f;* oscilación, *f*
vibrator /ˈvaibreitər/ *n Elec.* vibrador, *m; Radio.* oscilador, *m*
vicar /ˈvɪkər/ *n* vicario, *m;* (of a parish) cura, *m.* **v.-general,** vicario general, *m*
vicarious /vaiˈkɛəriəs/ *a* vicario; sufrido por otro; experimentado por otro
vicariously /vaiˈkɛəriəsli/ *adv* por delegación; por substitución. **I know it only vicariously,** Lo conozco sólo por referencia
vice /vais/ *n* vicio, *m;* defecto, *m;* (in a horse) vicio, resabio, *m;* (tool) tornillo de banco, *m, prefix* vice. **v.-admiral,** vicealmirante, *m.* **v.-chairman,** vicepresidente (-ta). **v.-chancellor,** vicecanciller, *m.* **v.-consul,** vice-cónsul, *m.* **v.-consulate,** vice-consulado, *m.* **v.-president,** vicepresidente (-ta)
viceroy /ˈvaisrɔi/ *n* virrey, *m*
vice versa /ˈvaisəˌvɜrsə, ˈvais- *adv* viceversa
vicinity /vɪˈsɪnɪti/ *n* vecindad, *f;* (nearness) cercanía, proximidad, *f.* **to be in the v. of,** estar en la vecindad de

vicious /'vɪʃəs/ *a* vicioso. **v. circle,** círculo vicioso, *m*

viciousness /'vɪʃəsnɪs/ *n* viciosidad, *f;* (in a horse) resabios, *m pl*

vicissitude /vɪ'sɪsɪˌtud/ *n* vicisitud, *f*

vicissitudinous /vɪˌsɪsɪ'tudn̩əs/ *a* accidentado, vicisitudinario

victim /'vɪktəm/ *n* víctima, *f*

victimization /ˌvɪktəmə'zeiʃən/ *n* sacrificio, *m;* tormento, *m*

victimize /'vɪktəˌmaiz/ *vt* hacer víctima (de); sacrificar; ser víctima (de), sufrir; (cheat) estafar, engañar

victor /'vɪktər/ *n* víctor, vencedor, *m*

victoria /vɪk'tɔriə/ *n* victoria, *f*

Victorian /vɪk'tɔriən/ *a* victoriano

victorious /vɪk'tɔriəs/ *a* victorioso, triunfante. **to be v.,** triunfar, salir victorioso

victoriously /vɪk'tɔriəsli/ *adv* victoriosamente, triunfalmente

victory /'vɪktəri/ *n* victoria, *f*

victual /'vɪtl̩/ *n* vitualla, vianda, *f; pl* **victuals,** víveres, *m pl,* provisiones, *f pl.* —*vt* avituallar; abastecer. —*vi* tomar provisiones

victualler /'vɪtl̩ər/ *n* abastecedor (-ra), proveedor (-ra)

victualling /'vɪtl̩ɪŋ/ *n* abastecimiento, *m*

vide /wɪde, 'vaidi, 'videi/ *Latin imperative* véase, véanse

videlicet /wɪ'deilɪˌkɛt, vi'dɛləsɪt/ *adv* a saber

video /'vɪdiˌou/, *n* vídeo, *m*

videotape /'vɪdiouˌteip/ *n* videograbación, videocinta, *f*

vie /vai/ *vi* (with) competir con; rivalizar con; (with a person for) disputar; luchar con

Vienna /vi'ɛnə/ Viena, *f*

Viennese /ˌviə'niz/ *a* and *n* vienés (-esa)

view /vyu/ *n* vista, *f;* perspectiva, *f,* panorama, *m;* (landscape) paisaje, *m;* escena, *f;* inspección, *f;* (judgment) opinión, *f,* parecer, *m;* consideración, *f;* (appearance) apariencia, *f;* aspecto, *m;* (purpose) propósito, *m,* intención, *f;* (sight) alcance de la vista, *m;* (show) exposición, *f.* —*vt* examinar; inspeccionar; (look at) mirar; (see) ver, contemplar; considerar. **in v. of,** en vista de. **in my v.,** en mi opinión, segun creo yo. **on v.,** a la vista. **to keep in v.,** no perder de vista; *Fig.* no olvidar, tener presente. **to take a different v.,** pensar de un modo distinto. **to v. a house,** inspeccionar una casa. **with a v. to,** con el propósito de. **v.-finder,** enfocador, *m.* **v.-point,** punto de vista, *m*

viewer /'vyuər/ *n* espectador (-ra); examinador (-ra)

viewing /'vyuɪŋ/ *n* inspección, *f,* examen, *m*

vigil /'vɪdʒəl/ *n* vela, vigilia, *f; Eccl.* vigilia, *f*

vigilance /'vɪdʒələns/ *n* vigilancia, *f,* desvelo, *m*

vigilant /'vɪdʒələnt/ *a* vigilante, desvelado

vigilantly /'vɪdʒələntli/ *adv* vigilantemente

vignette /vɪn'yɛt/ *n* viñeta, *f*

vigor /'vɪgər/ *n* vigor, *m,* fuerza, *f*

vigorous /'vɪgərəs/ *a* vigoroso, enérgico, fuerte

vigorously /'vɪgərəsli/ *adv* con vigor

Viking /'vaikɪŋ/ *n* vikingo, *m*

vile /vail/ *a* vil; bajo; despreciable; infame; *Inf.* horrible

vilely /'vailli/ *adv* vilmente; *Inf.* mal, horriblemente

vileness /'vailnɪs/ *n* vileza, *f;* bajeza, *f;* infamia, *f*

vilification /ˌvɪləfɪ'keiʃən/ *n* vilipendio, *m,* difamación, *f*

vilifier /'vɪləˌfaiər/ *n* difamador (-ra)

vilify /'vɪləˌfai/ *vt* vilipendiar, difamar

villa /'vɪlə/ *n* villa, torre, casa de campo, *f;* hotel, *m*

village /'vɪlɪdʒ/ *n* aldea, *f,* pueblo, *m*

villager /'vɪlɪdʒər/ *n* aldeano (-na)

villain /'vɪlən/ *n Hist.* villano, *m;* malvado, *m*

villainous /'vɪlənəs/ *a* malvado; infame; vil

villainously /'vɪlənəsli/ *adv* vilmente

villainy /'vɪləni/ *n* vileza, infamia, maldad, *f*

vindicate /'vɪndɪˌkeit/ *vt* vindicar, justificar; defender

vindication /ˌvɪndɪ'keiʃən/ *n* vindicación, justificación, *f;* defensa, *f*

vindicative /vɪn'dɪkətɪv/ *a* vindicativo, vindicador, justificativo

vindicator /'vɪndɪˌkeitər/ *n* vindicador (-ra)

vindictive /vɪn'dɪktɪv/ *a* vengativo; rencoroso

vindictively /vɪn'dɪktɪvli/ *adv* vengativamente; rencorosamente

vindictiveness /vɪn'dɪktɪvnɪs/ *n* deseo de venganza, *m;* rencor, *m*

vine /vain/ *n* vid, parra, *f;* (twining plant) enredadera, *f.* **v.-arbor,** emparrado, *m.* **v.-branch,** sarmiento, *m.* **v.-clad,** cubierto de parras. **v.-grower,** vinicultor, *m.* **v.-growing,** vinicultura, *f.* **v.-leaf,** hoja de parra, *f.* **v.-pest,** filoxera, *f.* **v.-stock,** cepa, *f*

vinegar /'vɪnɪgər/ *n* vinagre, *m.* **v.-cruet,** vinagrera, *f.* **v.-sauce,** vinagreta, *f*

vinegary /'vɪnɪgəri/ *a* vinagroso

vineyard /'vɪnyərd/ *n* viña, *f,* viñedo, *m.* **v.-keeper,** viñador, *m*

vinification /ˌvɪnəfɪ'keiʃən/ *n* vinificación, *f*

vinosity /vai'nɒsɪti/ *n* vinosidad, *f*

vinous /'vainəs/ *a* vinoso

vintage /'vɪntɪdʒ/ *n* vendimia, *f;* (of wine) cosecha (de vino), *f*

vintner /'vɪntnər/ *n* vinatero, *m*

viola /vi'oulə/ *n* (*Mus., Bot.*) viola, *f.* **v. player,** viola, *mf*

violate /'vaiəˌleit/ *vt* (desecrate) profanar; (infringe) contravenir, infringir; (break) romper; (ravish) violar

violation /ˌvaiə'leiʃən/ *n* profanación, *f;* (infringement) contravención, *f;* (rape) violación, *f*

violator /'vaiəˌleitər/ *n* violador (-ra); (ravisher) violador, *m*

violence /'vaiələns/ *n* violencia, *f*

violent /'vaiələnt/ *a* violento

violently /'vaiələntli/ *adv* con violencia

violet /'vaiəlɪt/ *n* violeta, *f.* —*a* violado, **v. color,** violeta, color violado, *m*

violin /ˌvaiə'lɪn/ *n* violín, *m*

violinist /ˌvaiə'lɪnɪst/ *n* violinista, *mf*

violoncellist /ˌviələn'tʃɛlɪst/ *n* violoncelista, *mf*

violoncello /ˌviələn'tʃɛlou/ *n* violoncelo, *m*

viper /'vaipər/ *n* víbora, *f*

viperish /'vaipərɪʃ/ *a* viperino

virago /vɪ'rɑgou/ *n* virago, *f,*

Virgilian /vər'dʒɪliən/ *a* virgiliano

virgin /'vɜrdʒɪn/ *n* virgen, *f;* (sign of the zodiac) Virgo, *m.* —*a* virginal; (untouched) virgen. **the V.,** la Virgen. **v. soil,** tierra virgen, *f*

virginal /'vɜrdʒənl̩/ *a* virginal

virginity /vər'dʒɪnɪti/ *n* virginidad, *f*

Virgo /'vɜrgou/ *n* Virgo, *m*

virile /'vɪrəl/ *a* viril

virility /və'rɪlɪti/ *n* virilidad, *f*

virtual /'vɜrtʃuəl/ *a* virtual

virtue /'vɜrtʃu/ *n* virtud, *f*

virtuosity /ˌvɜrtʃu'ɒsɪti/ *n* virtuosidad, *f*

virtuoso /ˌvɜrtʃu'ousou/ *n* virtuoso (-sa)

virtuous /'vɜrtʃuəs/ *a* virtuoso

virulence /'vɪryələns/ *n* virulencia, *f*

virulent /'vɪryələnt/ *a* virulento

virulently /'vɪryələntli/ *adv* con virulencia

virus /'vairəs/ *n* virus, *m*

visa /'vizə/ *n* visado, *m*

visage /'vɪzɪdʒ/ *n* cara, *f,* rostro, *m;* semblante, aspecto, *m*

viscera /'vɪsərə/ *n* víscera, *f*

visceral /'vɪsərəl/ *a* visceral

viscid /'vɪsɪd/ *a* viscoso

viscosity /vɪ'skɒsɪti/ *n* viscosidad, *f*

viscount /'vaiˌkaunt/ *n* vizconde, *m*

viscountess /'vaiˌkauntɪs/ *n* vizcondesa, *f*

viscous /'vɪskəs/ *a* viscoso

visé /'vizei/ *n* visado, *m, vt* visar

visibility /ˌvɪzə'bɪlɪti/ *n* visibilidad, *f.* **poor v.,** mala visibilidad, *f*

visible /'vɪzəbəl/ *a* visible; aparente, evidente

visibly /'vɪzəbli/ *adv* visiblemente; a ojos vistas

Visigoth /'vɪzɪˌgɒθ/ *n* visigodo (-da)

Visigothic /ˌvɪzɪ'gɒθɪk/ *a* visigodo, visigótico

vision /'vɪʒən/ *n* visión, *f;* (eyesight) vista, *f.* **field of v.,** campo visual, *m*

visionary /'vɪʒəˌnɛri/ *a* and *n* visionario (-ia)

visit /'vɪzɪt/ *n* visita, *f;* (inspection) inspección, *f;* (doctor's) visita de médico, *f.* —*vt* visitar; hacer una visita (a); ir a ver; inspeccionar; (frequent) frecuen-

tar; (Biblical) visitar. **to be visited by an epidemic,** sufrir una epidemia. **to go visiting,** ir de visita. **to pay a v.,** hacer una visita
visitation /ˌvɪzɪ'teiʃən/ *n* visita, *f; Eccl.* visitación, *f;* (inspection) inspección, *f;* (punishment) castigo, *m*
visiting /'vɪzɪtɪŋ/ *a* de visita. **v. card,** tarjeta de visita, *f.* **v. card case,** tarjetero, *m.* **visiting hours,** horas de visita, *f pl*
visitor /'vɪzɪtər/ *n* visita, *f;* (official) visitador, *m*
visor /'vaizər/ *n* visera, *f*
vista /'vɪstə/ *n* vista, perspectiva, *f*
visual /'vɪʒuəl/ *a* visual. **the v. arts,** las artes visuales
visualize /'vɪʒuəˌlaiz/ *vt* and *vi* imaginarse, ver mentalmente
vital /'vaitl̩/ *a* vital; esencial; trascendental
vitalism /'vaitl̩ˌɪzəm/ *n* vitalismo, *m*
vitality /vai'tælɪti/ *n* vitalidad, *f*
vitalize /'vaitl̩ˌaiz/ *vt* vitalizar, vivificar; reanimar
vitals /'vaitlz/ *n pl* partes vitales, *f pl; Fig.* entrañas, *f pl*
vitamin /'vaitəmɪn/ *n* vitamina, *f*
vitiate /'vɪʃiˌeit/ *vt* viciar; corromper, contaminar
viticultural /ˌvɪtɪ'kʌltʃərl/ *a* vitícola
viticulture /'vɪtɪˌkʌltʃər/ *n* viticultura, *f*
vitreous /'vɪtriəs/ *a* vítreo, vidrioso
vitrification /ˌvɪtrəfɪ'keiʃən/ *n* vitrificación, *f*
vitrify /'vɪtrəˌfai/ *vt* vitrificar. *—vi* vitrificarse
vitriol /'vɪtriəl/ *n* vitriolo, ácido sulfúrico, *m*
vitriolic /ˌvɪtri'ɒlɪk/ *a* vitriólico
Vitruvius /vɪ'truviəs/ Vitrubio, *m*
vituperable /vai'tupərəbəl/ *a* vituperable
vituperate /vai'tupəˌreit/ *vt* vituperar
vituperation /vaiˌtupə'reiʃən/ *n* vituperio, *m*
vituperative /vai'tupərətɪv/ *a* vituperador
vivacious /vɪ'veiʃəs, vai-/ *a* animado, vivaracho
vivaciously /vɪ'veiʃəsli, vai-/ *adv* animadamente
vivacity /vɪ'væsɪti, vai-/ *n* vivacidad, animación, *f*
viva voce /'vai'və vousi, 'vivə/ *a* oral. *—n* examen oral, *m*
vivid /'vɪvɪd/ *a* vivo; brillante; intenso; (of descriptions, etc.) gráfico
vividly /'vɪvɪdli/ *adv* vivamente; brillantemente
vividness /'vɪvɪdnɪs/ *n* vivacidad, *f;* intensidad, *f;* (strength) fuerza, *f*
vivification /ˌvɪvəfɪ'keiʃən/ *n* vivificación, *f*
vivify /'vɪvəˌfai/ *vt* vivificar, avivar
vivifying /'vɪvəˌfaiɪŋ/ *a* vivificante
vivisection /ˌvɪvə'sɛkʃən/ *n* vivisección, *f*
vixen /'vɪksən/ *n* raposa, zorra, *f;* (woman) arpía, *f*
viz. a saber
vizier /vɪ'zɪər, 'vɪzyər/ *n* visir, *m.* **grand v.,** gran visir, *m*
vocabulary /vou'kæbyəˌlɛri/ *n* vocabulario, *m*
vocal /'voukəl/ *a* vocal. **v. cords,** cuerdas vocales, *f pl*
vocalist /'voukəlɪst/ *n* cantante, *mf.* voz, *f*
vocalization /ˌvoukələ'zeiʃən/ *n* vocalización, *f*
vocalize /'voukəˌlaiz/ *vt* vocalizar
vocation /vou'keiʃən/ *n* vocación, *f;* oficio, *m;* empleo, *m;* profesión, *f*
vocational /vou'keiʃənl̩/ *a* profesional; práctico. **vocational guidance,** guía vocacional, orientación profesional, *f.* **v. training,** instrucción práctica, *f;* enseñanza de oficio, *f*
vociferate /vou'sɪfəˌreit/ *vt* gritar. *—vi* vociferar, vocear
vociferation /vouˌsɪfə'reiʃən/ *n* vociferación, *f*
vociferous /vou'sɪfərəs/ *a* (noisy) ruidoso; vocinglero, clamoroso
vociferously /vou'sɪfərəsli/ *adv* ruidosamente; a gritos
vodka /'vɒdkə/ *n* vodca, *m*
vogue /voug/ *n* moda, *f.* **in v.,** en boga, de moda
voice /vɔis/ *n* voz, *f.* *—vt* expresar, interpretar, hacerse eco de; hablar. **in a loud v.,** en voz alta. **in a low v.,** en voz baja
voiced /vɔist/ *a* (in compounds) de voz...; hablado
void /vɔid/ *a* (empty) vacío; (vacant) vacante; deshabitado; (lacking in) privado (de), desprovisto (de); (without) sin; *Law.* inválido, nulo; sin valor. *—n* vacío, *m.* *—vt* evacuar; *Law.* anular; invalidar
voile /vɔil/ *n* espumilla, *f*
volatile /'vɒlətl̩/ *a* volátil; (light) ligero; (changeable) voluble, inconstante
volatility /ˌvɒlə'tɪlɪti/ *n* volatilidad, *f;* ligereza, *f;* volubilidad, *f*
volatilization /ˌvɒlətl̩ə'zeiʃən/ *n* volatilización, *f*
volatilize /'vɒlətl̩ˌaiz/ *vt* volatilizar. *—vi* volatilizarse
volcanic /vɒl'kænɪk/ *a* volcánico
volcano /vɒl'keinou/ *n* volcán, *m.* **extinct v.,** volcán extinto, *m*
volition /vou'lɪʃən/ *n* volición, *f;* voluntad, *f*
volley /'vɒli/ *n* (of stones, etc.) lluvia, *f;* (of firearms) descarga, *f;* (of cannon, naval guns) andanada, *f; Sports.* voleo, *m;* (of words, etc.) torrente, *m;* (of applause and as a salute) salva, *f.* *—vt Sports.* volear; (abuse, etc.) dirigir. *—vi* lanzar una descarga, hacer una descarga
volt /voult/ *n Elec.* voltío, *m;* (of a horse and in fencing) vuelta, *f.* **v.-ampere,** voltamperio, *m*
voltage /'voultɪdʒ/ *n* voltaje, *m.* **v. control,** mando del voltaje, *m*
voltaic /vɒl'teiɪk/ *a* voltaico
Voltairian /voul'tɛəriən/ *a* volteriano
voltmeter /'voultˌmitər/ *n* voltímetro, *m*
volubility /ˌvɒlyə'bɪlɪti/ *n* garrulidad, locuacidad, *f*
voluble /'vɒlyəbəl/ *a* gárrulo, locuaz
volume /'vɒlyum/ *n* (book) tomo, *m;* (amount, size, space) volumen, *m;* (of water) caudal (de río), *m;* (mass) masa, *f;* (of smoke) humareda, *f,* nubes de humo, *f pl*
volumed /'vɒlyumd/ *a* (in compounds) en... volúmenes, de... tomos
volumetric /ˌvɒlyə'mɛtrɪk/ *a* volumétrico
voluminous /və'lumənəs/ *a* voluminoso
voluminousness /və'lumənəsnɪs/ *n* lo voluminoso
voluntarily /ˌvɒlən'tɛrəli/ *adv* voluntariamente
voluntariness /ˌvɒlən'tɛrinɪs/ *n* carácter voluntario, *m*
voluntary /'vɒlənˌtɛri/ *a* voluntario; espontáneo; libre; (charitable) benéfico; (intentional) intencional, deliberado. *—n* solo de órgano, *m*
volunteer /ˌvɒlən'tɪər/ *n Mil.* voluntario (-ia). *—a* de voluntarios. *—vt* ofrecer; contribuir; expresar. *—vi* ofrecerse para hacer algo; *Mil.* alistarse, ofrecerse a servir como voluntario
volunteering /ˌvɒlən'tɪərɪŋ/ *n* voluntariado, *m*
voluptuary /və'lʌptʃuˌɛri/ *n* voluptuoso (-sa); sibarita, *mf*
voluptuous /və'lʌptʃuəs/ *a* voluptuoso
voluptuously /və'lʌptʃuəsli/ *adv* voluptuosamente
voluptuousness /və'lʌptʃuəsnɪs/ *n* voluptuosidad, *f;* sensualidad, *f*
volute /və'lut/ *n Archit.* voluta, *f*
vomit /'vɒmɪt/ *vt* and *vi* vomitar; arrojar, devolver. *—n* vómito, *m*
vomiting /'vɒmɪtɪŋ/ *n* vómito, *m*
voodoo /'vudu/ *n* vudú, *m*
voracious /vɔ'reiʃəs/ *a* voraz
voracity /vɔ'ræsɪti/ *n* voracidad, *f*
vortex /'vɔrtɛks/ *n* torbellino, *m,* vorágine, *f; Fig.* vórtice, *m*
vortical /'vɔrtɪkəl/ *a* vortiginoso
votary /'voutəri/ *n* devoto (-ta), adorante, *mf;* partidario (-ia)
vote /vout/ *n* voto, *m;* (voting) votación, *f;* (suffrage) sufragio, *m;* (election) elección, *f.* *—vt* votar; asignar; nombrar; elegir; (consider) tener por. *—vi* votar, dar el voto. **casting v.,** voto de calidad, *m.* **to put to the v.,** poner a votación. **to v. down,** desechar, rechazar. **v. of confidence,** voto de confianza, *m.* **v. of thanks,** voto de gracias, *m*
voter /'voutər/ *n* votante, *mf,* votador (-ra); elector (-ra)
voting /'voutɪŋ/ *n* votación, *f;* elección, *f.* *—a* de votar; electoral. **v. paper,** papeleta de votación, *f*
votive /'voutɪv/ *a* votivo. **v. offering,** exvoto, *m*
vouch /vautʃ/ *vi* atestiguar, afirmar; garantizar; responder (de)
voucher /'vautʃər/ *n* (guarantor) fiador (-ra); (guarantee) garantía, *f;* (receipt) recibo, *m;* (proof) prueba, *f;* documento justificativo, *m;* vale, bono, *m*

vouchsafe /vautʃ'seif/ *vt* conceder, otorgar
vouchsafement /vautʃ'seifmənt/ *n* concesión, *f,* otorgamiento, *m*
vow /vau/ *n* voto, *m;* promesa solemne, *f.* —*vt* hacer voto (de), hacer promesa solemne (de); jurar. **to take a vow,** hacer un voto
vowel /'vauəl/ *n* vocal, *f*
voyage /'vɔiɪdʒ/ *n* viaje (por mar), *m;* travesía, *f.* —*vi* viajar por mar. **Good v.!** ¡Buen viaje!, Feliz viaje!
voyager /'vɔiɪdʒər/ *n* viajero (-ra)
vulcanite /'vʌlkəˌnait/ *n* ebonita, *f*
vulcanization /ˌvʌlkənə'zeiʃən/ *n* vulcanización, *f*
vulcanize /'vʌlkəˌnaiz/ *vt* vulcanizar
vulgar /'vʌlgər/ *a* vulgar; (ill-bred) ordinario, cursi; (in bad taste) de mal gusto; trivial; adocenado; (coarse) grosero. —*n* vulgo, populacho, *m.* **v. fraction,** fracción común, *f*
vulgarism /'vʌlgəˌrɪzəm/ *n* vulgarismo, *m;* vulgaridad, *f*
vulgarity /vʌl'gærɪti/ *n* vulgaridad, *f;* grosería, *f;* mal tono, *m,* cursilería, *f*
vulgarize /'vʌlgəˌraiz/ *vt* vulgarizar; popularizar
vulgarly /'vʌlgərli/ *adv* vulgarmente; comúnmente; groseramente
Vulgate /'vʌlgeit/ *n* Vulgata, *f*
vulnerability /ˌvʌlnərə'bɪti/ *n* vulnerabilidad, *f*
vulnerable /'vʌlnərəbəl/ *a* vulnerable
vulpine /'vʌlpain/ *a* vulpino; astuto
vulture /'vʌltʃər/ *n* buitre, *m*
vulva /'vʌlvə/ *n* vulva, *f*

W

w /ˈdʌbəlˌyu/ *n* ve doble, *f*
wabble /ˈwɒbəl/ *vi*. See **wobble**
wad /wɒd/ *n* (of straw, etc.) atado, *m;* (of notes, etc.) rollo, *m;* (in a gun) taco, *m.* —*vt Sew.* acolchar; (furniture) emborrar; (guns) atacar; (stuff) rellenar
wadding /ˈwɒdɪŋ/ *n* borra, *f;* (lining) entretela, *f;* (for guns) taco, *m;* (stuffing) relleno, *m*
waddle /ˈwɒdl̩/ *n* anadeo, *m, vi* anadear
waddling /ˈwɒdlɪŋ/ *a* patojo, que anadea
wade /weid/ *vi* and *vt* andar (en el agua, etc.); vadear; (paddle) chapotear. **to w. in,** entrar en (el agua, etc.); *Fig.* meterse en. **to w. through,** (a book) leer con dificultad; estudiar detenidamente; ir por
wader /ˈweidər/ *n* el, *m,* (*f,* la) que vadea; (bird) ave zancuda, *f; pl* **waders,** botas de vadear, *f pl*
wafer /ˈweifər/ *n* (host) hostia, *f;* (for sealing) oblea, *f;* (for ices) barquillo, *m*
waffle /ˈwɒfəl/ *n Cul.* fruta de sartén, *f*
waft /wɑft/ *vt* llevar por el aire o encima del agua, hacer flotar; (stir) mecer; (of the wind) traer. —*n* (fragrance) ráfaga de olor, *f*
wag /wæg/ *n* (of the tail) coleada, *f;* movimiento, *m;* meneo, *m;* (jester) bromista, *mf.* —*vt* mover ligeramente; agitar; (of the tail) menear (la cola), colear. —*vi* menearse; moverse; oscilar; (of the world) ir. **And thus the world wags,** Y así va el mundo
wage /weidʒ/ *vt* emprender; sostener; hacer. **to w. war,** hacer guerra. —*n pl.* **wages,** salario, *m*
wager /ˈweidʒər/ *n* (bet) apuesta, *f;* (test) prueba, *f, vt* (bet) apostar; (pledge) empeñar. **to lay a w.,** hacer una apuesta
waggish /ˈwægɪʃ/ *a* zumbón, jocoso; cómico
waggishness /ˈwægɪʃnɪs/ *n* jocosidad, *f*
waggle /ˈwægəl/ *vt* menear; mover; agitar; oscilar. —*vi* menearse; moverse; agitarse; oscilar. —*n* meneo, movimiento, *m;* oscilación, *f*
Wagnerian /vɑgˈnɪəriən/ *a* wagneriano
wagon /ˈwægən/ *n* carro, *m;* carreta, *f;* (railway) vagón, *m.* **w.-lit,** coche cama, *m.* **w.-load,** carretada, *f;* vagón, *m*
wagoner /ˈwægənər/ *n* carretero, *m*
waif /weif/ *n* niño (-ña) sin hogar; animal perdido o abandonado, *m;* objeto extraviado, *m;* objeto sin dueño, *m.* **waifs and strays,** niños abandonados, *m pl*
wail /weil/ *n* lamento, gemido, *m;* (complaint) queja, *f.* —*vi* lamentarse, gemir; quejarse (de). —*vt* lamentar, deplorar
wailer /ˈweilər/ *n* lamentador (-ra)
wailing /ˈweilɪŋ/ *n* lamentaciones, *f pl,* gemidos, *m pl, a* lamentador, gemidor
wainscot /ˈweinskət, -skɒt/ *n* entablado de madera, *m.* —*vt* enmaderar; poner friso de madera (a)
waist /weist/ *n* cintura, *f;* (blouse) blusa, *f;* (belt) cinturón, *m;* (bodice) corpiño, *m;* (narrowest portion) cuello, *m,* garganta, *f; Naut.* combés, *m.* **w.-band,** pretina, *f.* **w.-deep,** hasta la cintura. **w.-line,** cintura, *f.* **w. measurement,** medida de la cintura, *f.* **w.-coat,** chaleco, *m.* **w. strap,** trincha, *f*
wait /weit/ *vi* and *vt* esperar, aguardar; (serve) servir. **to keep waiting,** hacer esperar. **to w. at table,** servir a la mesa. **to w. on oneself,** servirse a sí mismo; cuidarse a sí mismo; hacer las cosas por sí solo. **to w. one's time,** aguardar la ocasión. **to w. for,** (until) esperar hasta que; (of persons) esperar (a), aguardar (a); (in ambush) acechar. **to w. upon,** (serve) servir (a); (visit) visitar; presentar sus respetos (a); (*Fig.* accompany) acompañar; (follow) seguir a
wait /weit/ *n* espera, *f;* (pause) pausa, *f,* intervalo, *m;* (ambush) asechanza, *f; pl* **waits,** coro de nochebuena, *m.* **to lie in w. for,** estar en acecho para
waiter /ˈweitər/ *n* camarero, mozo, *m;* (tray) bandeja, *f*
waiting /ˈweitɪŋ/ *n* espera, *f.* —*a* que espera; de espera; de servicio. **lady-in-w.,** dama de servicio, *f.* **w.-maid,** camarera, doncella, *f.* **w.-room,** (of a bus station, etc.) sala de espera, *f;* (of an office) antesala, *f*
waitress /ˈweitrɪs/ *n* camarera, *f*
waive /weiv/ *vt* renunciar (a); desistir (de)
wake /weik/ *vi* estar despierto; despertarse; (watch) velar. —*vt* despertar; (a corpse) velar (a). —*n* vela, *f;* vigilia, *f;* (of a corpse) velatorio, *m;* (holiday) fiesta, *f;* (of a ship) estela, *f.* **in the w. of,** *Naut.* en la estela de; después de; seguido por
wakeful /ˈweikfəl/ *a* vigilante; (awake) despierto. **to be w.,** pasar la noche en vela
wakefulness /ˈweikfəlnɪs/ *n* vigilancia, *f;* (sleeplessness) insomnia, *f*
waken /ˈweikən/ *vi* despertarse. —*vt* despertar; (call) llamar
waking /ˈweikɪŋ/ *a* despierto; de vela. —*n* despertar, *m;* (watching) vela, *f*
wale /weil/ *n* (weal) verdugo, *m,* huella de azote, *f, vt* azotar
Wales /weilz/ (País de) Gales, *m*
walk /wɔk/ *n* (pace) paso, *m;* (modo de) andar, *m;* (journey on foot) paseo, *m,* vuelta, *f;* (long) caminata, *f;* (promenade) paseo, *m,* avenida, *f;* (path) senda, *f;* (rank) clase social, *f;* esfera, *f;* profesión, *f;* ocupación, *f.* **quick w.,** paseo rápido, *m;* (pace) andar rápido, *m.* **to go for a w.,** ir de paseo. **to take a w.,** dar un paseo (or una vuelta), pasear. **to take for a w.,** llevar a paseo, sacar a paseo. **w.-out,** (strike) huelga, *f.* **w.-over,** triunfo, *m,* (or victoria, *f*) fácil. **w. past,** desfile, *m*
walk /wɔk/ *vi* andar; caminar; ir a pie; (take a walk) pasear, dar un paseo; (of ghosts) aparecer; (behave) conducirse. —*vt* hacer andar; (take for a walk) sacar a paseo; andar de una parte a otra (de), recorrer; (a specified distance) hacer a pie, andar; (a horse) llevar al paso. **to w. abroad,** dar un paseo; salir. **to w. arm in arm,** ir de bracero. **to w. past,** pasar; (in procession) desfilar. **to w. quickly,** andar de prisa. **to w. slowly,** andar despacio, andar lentamente. **to w. the hospitals,** estudiar en los hospitales. **to w. the streets,** recorrer las calles; vagar por las calles. **to w. about,** pasearse; ir y venir. **to w. after,** seguir (a), ir detrás de. **to w. along,** andar por; recorrer. **to w. away,** marcharse, irse. **to w. away with,** (win) ganar, llevarse; (steal) quitar, tomar, alzarse con. **to w. back,** volver; volver a pie, regresar a pie. **to w. down,** bajar; bajar a pie; andar por. **to w. in,** entrar en; entrar a pie en; (walk about) pasearse en. **to w. on,** seguir andando; (step on) pisar. **to w. out,** salir. **to w. over,** andar por; llevar la victoria (a); triunfar fácilmente sobre. **to w. round,** dar la vuelta a. **to w. round and round,** dar vueltas. **to w. up,** subir andando; subir. **to w. up and down,** dar vueltas, ir y venir
walker /ˈwɔkər/ *n* (pedestrian) peatón, *m;* andador (-ra); (promenader) paseante, *mf*
walking /ˈwɔkɪŋ/ *n* el andar; (excursion on foot) paseo, *m.* —*a* andante; de andar; a pie; ambulante. **at a w. pace,** a un paso de andadura. **w. encyclopedia,** enciclopedia ambulante, *f.* **w. match,** marcha atlética, *f.* **w.-stick,** bastón, *m.* **w. tour,** excursión a pie, *f*
Walkyrie /walˈkɪəri/ *n* valquiria, *f*
wall /wɔl/ *n* muro, *m;* (rampart) muralla, *f;* (*Fig.* and of an organ, cavity, etc.) pared, *f.* **partition w.,** tabique, *m.* **Walls have ears,** Las paredes oyen. **w. lizard,** lagartija, *f.* **w. map,** mapa mural, *m.* **w.-painting,** pintura mural, *f.* **w.-paper,** papel pintado, *m.* **w. socket,** *Elec.* enchufe, *m*
wall /wɔl/ *vt* cercar con un muro; amurallar. **to w. in,** murar. **to w. up,** tapiar, tabicar
wallet /ˈwɒlɪt/ *n* cartera, *f;* bolsa de cuero, *f*
wallflower /ˈwɔlˌflauər/ *n* alhelí, *m*
Walloon /wɒˈlun/ *a* and *n* valón (-ona)
wallop /ˈwɒləp/ *n* golpe, *m, vt* tundir, zurrar
wallow /ˈwɒlou/ *vi* revolcarse; encenagarse; (in riches, etc.) nadar (en). —*n* revuelco, *m*

walnut /ˈwɔlˌnʌt/ *n* (tree and wood) nogal, *m;* (nut) nuez de nogal, *f*

walrus /ˈwɔlrəs/ *n* morsa, *f*

waltz /wɔlts/ *n* vals, *m, vi* valsar

wan /wɑn/ *a* ojeroso, descolorido; (of the sky, etc.) pálido, sin color

wand /wɒnd/ *n* vara, *f;* (conductor's) batuta, *f.* **magic w.,** varita mágica, *f*

wander /ˈwɒndər/ *vi* errar, vagar; (deviate) extraviarse; (from the subject) desviarse del asunto; divagar; (be delirious) delirar. *—vt* vagar por, errar por, recorrer

wanderer /ˈwɒndərər/ *n* vagabundo (-da); hombre, *m,* (*f,* mujer) errante; (traveler) viajero (-ra)

wandering /ˈwɒndərɪŋ/ *a* errante; vagabundo; nómada; (traveling) viajero; (delirious) delirante; (of thoughts, the mind) distraído; (of cells, kidneys, etc.) flotante. *—n* vagancia, *f;* viaje, *m;* (delirium) delirio, *m;* (digression) divagación, *f;* (of a river, etc.) meandro, *m.* **the w. Jew,** el judío errante

wane /wein/ *vi* (of the moon, etc.) menguar; (decrease) disminuir; (*Fig.* decay) decaer. *—n* (of the moon) menguante de la luna, *f;* mengua, *f;* disminución, *f;* decadencia, *f*

waning /ˈweinɪŋ/ *a* menguante

wanly /ˈwanli/ *adv* pálidamente; *Fig.* tristemente

wanness /ˈwannɪs/ *n* palidez, *f; Fig.* tristeza, *f*

want /wɒnt/ *vt* (lack) carecer de, faltar; (need) necesitar, haber menester de; (require or wish) querer, desear; (demand) exigir; (ought) deber; (do without) pasarse sin. *—vi* hacer falta; carecer (de); (be poor) estar necesitado. **I don't w. to,** No quiero, No me da la gana. **to be wanted,** hacer falta; (called) ser llamado. **You are wanted on the telephone,** Te llaman por teléfono

want /wɒnt/ *n* (lack) falta, *f;* escasez, carestía, *f;* (need) necesidad, *f;* (poverty) pobreza, indigencia, *f;* (absence) ausencia, *f;* (wish) deseo, *m;* exigencia, *f.* **in w. of,** por falta de; en la ausencia de. **to be in w.,** estar en la necesidad, ser indigente

wanted /ˈwɒntɪd/ se necesita; (advertisement) demanda, *f.* **Estelle wants me to write a letter,** Estrella quiere que escriba una carta. **What do you w. me to do?** ¿Qué quiere Vd. que haga?; ¿En qué puedo servirle? **What does Paul w.?** ¿Qué quiere Pablo?; (require) ¿Qué necesita Pablo? **He wants (needs) a holiday,** Le hacen falta unas vacaciones, Necesita unas vacaciones

wanting /ˈwɒntɪŋ/ *a* deficiente (en); falto (de); (scarce) escaso; ausente; (in intelligence) menguado. *—prep* (less) menos; (without) sin. **to be w.,** faltar. **to be w. in,** carecer de

wanton /ˈwɒntn̩/ *a* (playful) juguetón; (wilful) travieso; (loose) suelto, libre; (unrestrained) desenfrenado; extravagante; excesivo; caprichoso; (dishevelled) en desorden; (reckless) indiscreto; (of vegetation) lozano; (purposeless) inútil; imperdonable; frívolo; (unchaste) disoluto; lascivo. *—n* mujer disoluta, *f;* ramera, *f;* (child) niño (-ña) juguetón (-ona)

wantonly /ˈwɒntnli/ *adv* innecesariamente; sin motivo; excesivamente; lascivamente

war /wɑr/ *n* guerra, *f.* *—a* de guerra; guerrero. *—vi* guerrear. **at war with,** en guerra con. **cold war,** guerra tonta, *f.* **on a war footing,** en pie de guerra. **We are at war,** Estamos en guerra. **to be on the war-path,** *Fig. Inf.* buscar pendencia, tratar de armarla. **to declare war on,** declarar la guerra (a). **to make war on,** hacer la guerra (a). **war to the death,** guerra a muerte, *f.* **war correspondent,** corresponsal en el teatro de guerra, *m.* **war-cry,** alarido de guerra, grito de combate, grito de guerra *m.* **war-dance,** danza guerrera, *f.* **war horse,** caballo de batalla, *m.* **war loan,** empréstito de guerra, *m.* **war-lord,** adalid, caudillo, jefe militar, *m.* **war material,** pertrechos de guerra, *m pl;* municiones, *f pl.* **war memorial,** monumento a los caídos, *m.* **war minister,** Ministro de la Guerra, *m.* **war neurosis,** neurosis de guerra, *f.* **War Office,** Ministerio de la Guerra, *m.* **war plane,** avión de guerra, *m.* **war-ship,** barco (*or* buque) de guerra, *m.* **war-wearied,** agotado por la guerra

warble /ˈwɔrbəl/ *vt* and *vi* trinar; gorjear; murmurar. *—n* trino, *m;* gorjeo, *m;* murmurio, *m*

ward /wɔrd/ *n* protección, *f;* (of a minor) pupilo (-la); (of locks, keys) guarda, *f;* (of a city) barrio, distrito, *m;* (of a hospital, etc.) sala, *f;* (of a prison) celda, *f;* (fencing) guardia, *f.* **w.-room,** cuarto de los oficiales, *m.* **w. sister,** hermana de una sala de hospital, *f*

ward /wɔrd/ *vt* proteger, defender. **to w. off,** desviar; evitar

warden /ˈwɔrdn̩/ *n* guardián, *m;* director (-ra); (of a prison) alcaide, *m;* (of a church) mayordomo de la iglesia, *m;* (of a port) capitán, *m*

warder /ˈwɔrdər/ *n* (jailer) guardián, *m;* alabardero, guardia, *m*

wardress /ˈwɔrdrɪs/ *n* guardiana, *f*

wardrobe /ˈwɔrdroub/ *n* guardarropa, ropero, *m;* (clothes) ropa, *f; Theat.* vestuario, *m.* **w. trunk,** baúl mundo, *m*

ware /wɛər/ *n* mercadería, *f;* (pottery) loza, *f; pl* **wares,** mercancías, *f pl*

war effort *n* esfuerzo bélico, esfuerzo de guerra, esfuerzo guerrero, *m*

warehouse /*n.* ˈwɛərˌhaus; *v.* -ˌhauz/ *n* almacén, *m, vt* almacenar

warehouseman /ˈwɛərˌhausmən/ *n* almacenero, *m*

warfare /ˈwɔrˌfɛər/ *n* guerra, *f;* lucha, *f;* arte militar, *m,* or *f.* **chemical w.,** guerra química, *f*

war head *n* (of torpedo) cabeza de combate, punto de combate, *f;* (of missile) detonante, *m*

war hero *n* héroe de guerra, *m*

war heroine *n* heroína de guerra, *f*

warily /ˈwɛərəli/ *adv* con cautela, cautelosamente; prudentemente

wariness /ˈwɛərinɪs/ *n* cautela *f;* prudencia, *f*

warlike /ˈwɔrˌlaik/ *a* belicoso, guerrero; militar, de guerra; marcial. **war-spirit,** espíritu belicoso, *m,* marcialidad, *f*

warm /wɔrm/ *a* caliente; (lukewarm) tibio; (hot) caluroso; (affectionate) cordial, cariñoso, afectuoso; (angry) acalorado; (enthusiastic) entusiasta, ardiente; (art) cálido; (of coats, etc.) de abrigo; (fresh) fresco, reciente; *Inf.* adinerado. *—vt* calentar; *Fig.* encender; entusiasmar. *—vi* calentarse; *Fig.* entusiasmarse (con). **to have a w. at the fire,** calentarse al lado del fuego. **to be w.,** (of things) estar caliente; (of coats, etc.) ser de abrigo; (of the weather) hacer calor; (of people) tener calor. **to grow w.,** calentarse; (grow angry) excitarse, agitarse; (of a discussion) hacerse acalorado. **to keep w.,** conservar caliente; calentar. **to keep oneself w.,** estar caliente, no enfriarse. **to w. up,** calentar. **w.-blooded,** de sangre caliente; ardiente. **w.-hearted,** de buen corazón; generoso; afectuoso, cordial. **w.-heartedness,** buen corazón, *m;* generosidad, *f;* cordialidad, *f*

warming /ˈwɔrmɪŋ/ *n* calentamiento, *m;* calefacción, *f.* *—a* calentador; para calentar. **w.-pan,** calentador, *m*

warmly /ˈwɔrmli/ *adv* (affectionately) cordialmente, afectuosamente; con entusiasmo; (angrily) acaloradamente. **to be w. wrapped up,** estar bien abrigado

warmonger /ˈwɔrˌmʌŋgər/ *n* atizador de guerra, belicista, fautor de guerra, fomentador de guerra, propagador (-ra) de guerra

warmth /wɔrmθ/ *n* calor, *m*

warn /wɔrn/ *vt* advertir; prevenir; amonestar; (inform) avisar

warning /ˈwɔrnɪŋ/ *n* advertencia, *f;* aviso, *m;* amonestación, *f;* (lesson) lección, *f,* escarmiento, *m;* alarma, *f.* *—a* amonestador; de alarma. **to give w.,** prevenir, advertir; (dismiss) despedir. **to take w.,** escarmentar

warningly /ˈwɔrnɪŋli/ *adv* indicando el peligro; con alarma; con amenaza

warp /wɔrp/ *vt* torcer; combar; *Naut.* espiar; (the mind) pervertir. *—vi* torcerse; combarse, bornearse; *Naut.* espiarse. *—n* (in a fabric) urdimbre, *f;* (in wood) comba, *f,* torcimiento, *m; Naut.* espía, *f.* **w. and woof,** trama y urdimbre, *f*

warping /ˈwɔrpɪŋ/ *n* (of wood) combadura, *f;* (weaving) urdidura, *f; Naut.* espía, *f;* (of the mind) perversión, *f.* **w. frame,** urdidera, *f*

warrant /ˈwɔrənt, ˈwɒr-/ *n* autoridad, *f;* justificación, *f;* autorización, *f;* garantía, *f;* decreto de prisión, *m;* orden, *f; Com.* orden de pago, *f; Mil.* nombramiento, *m;* motivo, *m,* razón, *f.* —*vt* justificar; autorizar; garantizar, responder por; asegurar. **pay w.,** boletín de pago, *m*

warrantable /ˈwɔrəntəbəl/ *a* justificable

warrantor /ˈwɔrən,tɔr/ *n* garante, *mf*

warranty /ˈwɔrənti/ *n* autorización, *f;* justificación, *f; Law.* garantía, *f*

warren /ˈwɔrən/ *n* (for hunting) vedado, *m;* (rabbit) conejera, *f;* vivar, *m,* madriguera, *f*

warrior /ˈwɔriər/ *n* guerrero, *m;* soldado, *m*

Warsaw /ˈwɔrsɔ/ Varsovia, *f*

wart /wɔrt/ *n* verruga, *f*

wary /ˈwεəri/ *a* cauto, cauteloso; prudente

wash /wɒʃ/ *vt* lavar; (dishes) fregar; (lave) bañar; (clean) limpiar; (furrow) surcar; (wet) regar, humedecer; (with paint) dar una capa de color o de metal. —*vi* lavarse; lavar ropa. **Two of the crew were washed overboard,** El mar arrastró a dos de los tripulantes. **Will this material w.?** ¿Se puede lavar esta tela? ¿Es lavable esta tela? **to w. ashore,** echar a la playa. **w. away,** (remove by washing) quitar lavando; derrubiar; (water or waves) arrastrar, llevarse. **to w. one's hands,** lavarse las manos. **to look washed out,** estar ojeroso. **to w. down,** lavar; limpiar; (remove) llevarse; (accompany with drink) regar. **to w. off,** *vt* quitar lavando; hacer desaparecer; borrar; (of waves, etc.) llevarse; (of color) desteñir. —*vi* borrarse; desteñirse. **to w. up,** lavar los platos, fregar la vajilla; (cast up) desechar. **w. one's dirty laundry in public,** sacar los más sucios trapillos a la colada

wash /wɒʃ/ *n* lavadura, *f,* lavado, *m;* baño, *m;* (clothes) ropa para lavar, ropa sucia, *f;* colada, *f;* (of the waves) chapoteo, *m;* (lotion) loción, *f;* (coating) capa, *f;* (silt) aluvión, *m.* **w.-basin,** palangana, *f;* lavabo, *m.* **w.-board,** tabla de lavar, *f.* **w.-house,** lavadero, *m.* **w.-leather,** gamuza, badana, *f.* **w.-out,** fracaso, *m.* **w.-stand,** aguamanil, lavabo, *m.* **w.-tub,** cuba de lavar, *f*

washable /ˈwɒʃəbəl/ *a* lavable

washer /ˈwɒʃər/ *n* lavador (-ra); (washerwoman) lavandera, *f;* (machine) lavadora, *f; Mech.* arandela, *f*

washerwoman /ˈwɒʃər,wʊmən/ *n* lavandera, *f*

washing /ˈwɒʃɪŋ/ *n* lavamiento, *m;* ropa sucia, ropa para lavar, *f;* ropa limpia, *f;* ropa, *f;* (bleaching) blanqueadura, *f;* (toilet) abluciones, *f pl; Eccl.* lavatorio, *m; pl* **washings,** lavazas, *f pl.* **There is a lot of w. to be done,** Hay mucha ropa que lavar. **w.-board,** tabla de lavar, *f.* **w.-day,** día de colada, *m.* **w.-machine,** lavadora, máquina de lavar, *f.* **w.-soda,** carbonato sódico, *m.* **w.-up,** lavado de los platos, *m.* **w.-up machine,** fregador mecánico de platos, *m*

wasp /wɒsp/ *n* avispa, *f.* **wasp's nest,** avispero, *m.* **w.-waisted,** (of clothes) ceñido, muy ajustado

waspish /ˈwɒspɪʃ/ *a* enojadizo, irascible; malicioso; mordaz

wastage /ˈweistɪdʒ/ *n* desgaste, desperdicio, *m*

waste /weist/ *vt* desperdiciar, derrochar, malgastar; (time) perder; consumir; corroer; (devastate) asolar, devastar; echar a perder; malograr; disipar; agotar. —*vi* gastarse; consumirse; perderse. **to w. time,** perder el tiempo. **to w. away,** (of persons) demacrarse, consumirse

waste /weist/ *n* (wilderness) yermo, desierto, *m;* (vastness) inmensidad, vastedad, *f;* (loss) pérdida, *f;* (squandering) despilfarro, derroche, *m;* disminución, *f;* (refuse) desechos, *m pl;* (of cotton, etc.) borra, *f;* disipación, *f.* —*a* (of land) sin cultivar; yermo; inútil; desechado, de desecho; superfluo. **to lay w.,** devastar. **w. land,** yermo, *m;* tierras sin cultivar, *f pl.* **w. paper,** papel usado, papel de desecho, *m.* **w.-paper basket,** cesto para papeles, *m.* **w.-pipe,** desaguadero, tubo de desagüe, *m*

wasteful /ˈweistfəl/ *a* pródigo, derrochador, manirroto; antieconómico; ruinoso; inútil

wastefully /ˈweistfəli/ *adv* pródigamente; antieconómicamente; inútilmente

wastefulness /ˈweistfəlnɪs/ *n* prodigalidad, *f,* despilfarro, *m;* pérdida, *f;* gasto inútil, *m;* falta de economía, *f*

waster /ˈweistər/ *n* gastador (-ra); disipador (-ra); (loafer) golfo, *m*

watch /wɒtʃ/ *vi* velar; mirar. —*vt* mirar; observar; guardar; (await) esperar; (spy upon) espiar, acechar. **to w. for,** buscar aguardar. **to w. over,** vigilar, guardar; (care for) cuidar; proteger

watch /wɒtʃ/ *n* (at night) vela, *f;* (wakefulness) desvelo, *m;* observación, vigilancia, *f;* (*Mil. Naut.*) guardia, *f;* (sentinel) centinela, *m;* (watchman) sereno, vigilante, *m;* (guard) ronda, *f;* (timepiece) reloj de bolsillo, *m.* **to be on the w.,** estar al acecho, estar al alerta, estar a la mira. **to keep w.,** vigilar. **dog w.,** media guardia, *f.* **pocket w.,** reloj de bolsillo, *m.* **wrist w.,** reloj de pulsera, *m.* **w.-case,** caja de reloj, relojera, *f.* **w.-chain,** cadena de reloj, leontina, *f.* **w.-dog,** perro guardián, *m.* **w.-glass,** cristal de reloj, *m.* **w.-making,** relojería, *f.* **w.-night,** noche vieja, *f.* **w.-spring,** muelle de reloj, *m,* espiral, *f.* **w.-tower,** vigía, atalaya, *f*

watcher /ˈwɒtʃər/ *n* observador (-ra); espectador (-ra); (at a sick bed) el, *m,* (*f,* la) que vela a un enfermo

watchful /ˈwɒtʃfəl/ *a* vigilante, alerto; observador; atento, cuidadoso

watchfully /ˈwɒtʃfəli/ *adv* vigilantemente; atentamente

watchfulness /ˈwɒtʃfəlnɪs/ *n* vigilancia, *f;* cuidado, *m;* desvelo, *m*

watching /ˈwɒtʃɪŋ/ *n* observación, *f;* (vigil) vela, *f*

watchmaker /ˈwɒtʃ,meikər/ *n* relojero (-ra). **watchmaker's shop,** relojería, *f*

watchman /ˈwɒtʃmən/ *n* vigilante, sereno, *m;* guardián, *m*

watchword /ˈwɒtʃ,wɜrd/ *n* (password) consigna, contraseña, *f;* (motto) lema, *m*

water /ˈwɔtər/ *n* agua, *f;* (tide) marea, *f;* (of precious stones) aguas, *f pl;* (urine) orina, *f;* (quality) calidad, clase, *f.* —*a* de agua; por agua; acuático; hidráulico. **fresh w.,** (not salt) agua dulce, *f;* agua fresca, *f.* **hard w.,** agua cruda, *f.* **high w.,** marea alta, *f.* **low w.,** marea baja, *f.* **of the first w.,** de primera clase. **running w.,** agua corriente, *f.* **soft w.,** agua blanda, *f.* **to make w.,** *Naut.* hacer agua; orinar. **to take the waters,** tomar las aguas. **under w.,** *adv* debajo del agua. —*a* acuático. **w.-bird,** ave acuática, *f.* **w. blister,** ampolla, *f.* **w.-boatman,** chinche de agua, *f.* **w.-borne,** flotante. **w.-bottle,** cantimplora, *f.* **w.-brash,** acedia, *f.* **w.-butt,** barril, *m,* pipa, *f.* **w.-carrier,** aguador (-ra). **w.-cart,** carro de regar, *m.* **w.-closet,** retrete, excusado, *m.* **w.-color,** acuarela, *f.* **w.-color painting,** pintura a la acuarela, *f.* **w.-colorist,** acuarelista, *mf* **w.-cooled,** enfriado por agua. **w.-cooler,** cantimplora, *f.* **w.-finder,** zahorí, *m.* **w. front,** (wharf) muelle, *m;* puerto, *m;* litoral, *m.* **w.-gauge,** indicador de nivel de agua, *m,* vara de aforar, *f.* **w.-glass,** vidrio soluble, silicato de sosa, *m.* **w. heater,** calentador de agua, *m.* **w.-ice,** helado, *m.* **w.-level,** nivel de las aguas, *m.* **w.-lily,** nenúfar, *m,* azucena de agua, *f.* **w.-line,** lengua de agua, *f;* (of a ship) línea de flotación, *f.* **w.-logged,** anegado en agua. **w.-main,** cañería maestra de agua, *f.* **w. man,** barquero, *m.* **w.-melon,** sandía, *f.* **w. mill,** aceña, *f.* **w.-nymph,** náyade, *f.* **w.-pipe,** cañería del agua, *f.* **w. pitcher,** jarro, *m.* **w. plant,** planta acuática, *f.* **w.-polo,** polo acuático, *m.* **w.-power,** fuerza hidráulica, *f.* **w.-rate,** cupo del consumo de agua, *m.* **w. snake,** culebra de agua, *f.* **w. softener,** generador de agua dulce, *m;* purificador de agua, *m.* **w. spaniel,** perro (-rra) de aguas. **w. sprite,** ondina, *f.* **w.-supply,** abastecimiento de agua, *m;* traída de aguas, *f.* **w. tank,** depósito para agua, *m.* **w. tower,** arca de agua, *f.* **w. wave,** ondulado al agua, *m.* **w.-way,** canal, río *m,* o vía *f,* navegable. **w.-wheel,** rueda hidráulica, *f,* azud, *m;* (for irrigation) aceña, *f.* **w. wings,** nadaderas, *f pl*

water /ˈwɔtər/ *vt* (irrigate, sprinkle) regar; (moisten) mojar; (cattle, etc.) abrevar; (wine, etc.) aguar; diluir con agua; (bathe) bañar. —*vi* (of animals) beber agua; (of engines, etc.) tomar agua; (of the eyes, mouth) hacerse agua. **My mouth waters,** Se me hace agua la boca

watercourse /ˈwɔtərˌkɔrs/ *n* corriente de agua, *f;* cauce, *m;* lecho de un río, *m*
watercress /ˈwɔtərˌkrɛs/ *n* berro, mastuerzo, *m*
watered /ˈwɔtərd/ *a* regado, abundante en agua; (of silk) tornasolado
watered-down /ˈwɔtərdˈdaun/ *Fig.* pasado por agua
waterfall /ˈwɔtərˌfɔl/ *n* salto de agua, *m,* cascada, catarata, *f*
wateriness /ˈwɔtərinɪs/ *n* humedad, *f;* acuosidad, *f*
watering /ˈwɔtərɪŋ/ *n* riego, *m;* irrigación, *f;* (of eyes) lagrimeo, *m;* (of cattle, etc.) el abrevar (a); *Naut.* aguada, *f.* **w.-can,** regadera, *f.* **w.-cart,** carro de regar, *m.* **w.-place,** (for animals) aguadero, *m;* (for cattle) abrevadero, *m;* (spa) balneario, *m;* (by the sea) playa de veraneo, *f*
watermark /ˈwɔtərˌmɑrk/ *n* (in paper) filigrana, *f;* nivel del agua, *m.* —*vt* filigranar
waterproof /ˈwɔtərˌpruf/ *a* impermeable; a prueba de agua. —*n* impermeable, *m.* —*vt* hacer impermeable, impermeabilizar
water-repellent /ˈwɔtərrɪˌpɛlənt/ *a* repelente al agua
watershed /ˈwɔtərˌʃɛd/ *n* vertiente, *f;* línea divisoria de las aguas, *f;* (river-basin) cuenca, *f*
waterspout /ˈwɔtərˌspaut/ *n* bomba marina, manga, trompa, *f*
watertight /ˈwɔtərˌtait/ *a* impermeable, estanco; a prueba de agua; (of arguments, etc.) irrefutable
watertightness /ˈwɔtərˌtaitnɪs/ *n* impermeabilidad, *f*
waterworks /ˈwɔtərˌwɜrks/ *n* establecimiento para la distribución de las aguas, *m;* obras hidráulicas, *f pl*
watery /ˈwɔtəri/ *a* (wet) húmedo; acuoso; (of the sky) de lluvia; (of eyes) lagrimoso, lloroso; (sodden) mojado; (of soup, etc.) claro; insípido
watt /wɒt/ *n* vatio, *m.* **w. hour,** vatio hora, *m.* **w.-meter,** vatímetro, *m*
wattage /ˈwɒtɪdʒ/ *n* vatiaje, *m*
wattle /ˈwɒtl̩/ *n* zarzo, *m;* (of turkey) barba, *f;* (of fish) barbilla, *f*
wave /weiv/ *vi* ondear; ondular; flotar; hacer señales. —*vt* (brandish) blandir; agitar; (the hair) ondular; ondear; hacer señales (de). **They waved goodby to him,** Le hicieron adiós con la mano; Le hicieron señas de despedida; Se despidieron de él agitando el pañuelo
wave /weiv/ *n* (of the sea) ola, *f; Phys.* onda, *f;* (in hair or a surface) ondulación, *f;* (movement) movimiento, *m;* (of anger, etc.) ráfaga, *f.* **long w.,** onda larga, *f.* **medium w.,** onda media, *f.* **short w.,** onda corta, *f.* **sound w.,** onda sonora, *f.* **to have one's hair waved,** hacerse ondular el pelo. **w. band,** franja undosa, escala de longitudes de onda, *f.* **w. crest,** cresta de la ola, cabrilla, *f.* **w.-length,** longitud de onda, *f*
wavelet /ˈweivlɪt/ *n* pequeña ola, olita, *f;* (ripple) rizo (del agua), *m*
wave of immigration una imigración, *f*
waver /ˈweivər/ *vi* ondear; oscilar; (hesitate) vacilar, titubear; (totter) tambalearse; (weaken) flaquear
waverer /ˈweivərər/ *n* irresoluto (-ta), vacilante, *m*
wavering /ˈweivərɪŋ/ *n* vacilación, irresolución, *f.* —*a* oscilante; vacilante, irresoluto; flotante
waving /ˈweivɪŋ/ *n* ondulación, *f;* oscilación, *f;* agitación, *f;* movimiento, *m.* —*a* ondulante; oscilante; que se balancea
wavy /ˈweivi/ *a* ondulado; flotante
wax /wæks/ *n* cera, *f;* (cobblers') cerote, *m;* (in the ear) cerilla, *f.* —*a* de cera. —*vt* encerar. —*vi* crecer; hacerse; ponerse. **to wax enthusiastic,** entusiasmarse. **waxed paper,** papel encerado, *m.* **wax chandler,** cerero, *m.* **wax doll,** muñeca de cera, *f.* **wax modeling,** modelado en cera, *m,* ceroplástica, *f.* **wax taper,** blandón, *m*
waxen /ˈwæksən/ *a* de cera; como la cera; de color de cera
waxing /ˈwæksɪŋ/ *n* enceramiento, *m;* (of the moon) crecimiento, *m;* aumento, *m*
wax museum *n* museo de cera, *m*
waxwork /ˈwæksˌwɜrk/ *n* figura de cera, *f*
waxy /ˈwæksi/ *a.* See **waxen**
way /wei/ *n* camino, *m;* senda, *f;* paso, *m;* ruta, *f;* (railway, etc.) vía, *f;* dirección, *f;* rumbo, *m;* distancia, *f;* (journey) viaje, *m;* (sea crossing) travesía, *f;* avance, progreso, *m;* (*Naut.* etc.) marcha, *f;* método, *m;* modo, *m;* (means) medio, *m;* manera, *f;* (habit) costumbre, *f;* (behavior) conducta, *f,* modo de obrar, *m;* (line of business, etc.) ramo, *m;* (state) estado, *m,* condición, *f;* (course) curso, *m;* (respect) punto de vista, *m;* (particular kind) género, *m;* (scale) escala, *f.* **a long way off,** a gran distancia, a lo lejos. **a short way off,** a poca distancia, no muy lejos. **by way of,** pasando por; por vía de; como; por medio de; a modo de. **by the way,** de paso; durante el viaje; durante la travesía; a propósito, entre paréntesis. **in a small way,** en pequeña escala. **in a way,** hasta cierto punto; desde cierto punto de vista. **in many ways,** de muchos modos; por muchas cosas. **in no way,** de ningún modo; nada. **in the way,** en el medio. **in the way of,** en cuanto a, tocante a; en materia de. **I went out of my way to,** Dejé el camino para; Me di la molestia de. **Is this the way to...?** ¿Es este el camino a...? **Make way!** ¡Calle! **Milky Way,** vía láctea, *f.* **on the way,** en camino; al paso; durante el viaje. **out of the way,** puesto a un lado; arrinconado; apartado, alejado; (imprisoned) en prisión; fuera del camino; remoto; (unusual) original. **over the way,** en frente; al otro lado (de la calle, etc.). **right of w.,** derecho de paso, *m.* **The ship left on its way to...,** El barco zarpó con rumbo a... **the Way of the Cross,** vía crucis, *f.* **This way!** ¡Por aquí!; De este modo, Así. **this way and that,** en todas direcciones, por todos lados. **"This way to...,"** «Dirección a...» A... **under way,** en camino; en marcha; en preparación. **to bar the way,** cerrar el paso. **to be in the way,** estorbar. **to be out of the way of doing,** haber perdido la costumbre de hacer (algo). **to clear the way,** abrir paso, abrir calle; *Fig.* preparar el terreno. **to force one's way through,** abrirse paso por. **to find a way,** encontrar un camino; *Fig.* encontrar medios. **to find one's way,** hallar el camino; orientarse. **to get into the way of,** contraer la costumbre de. **to get under way,** *Naut.* zarpar, hacerse a la vela; ponerse en marcha. **to give way,** ceder; (break) romper. **to go a long way,** ir lejos; contribuir mucho (a). **to have one's own way,** salir con la suya. **to keep out of the way,** *vt* and *vi* esconder(se); mantener(se) alejado; mantener(se) apartado. **to lose one's way,** perder el camino; desorientarse; *Fig.* extraviarse. **to make one's way,** abrirse paso. **to make one's way down,** bajar. **to make one's way round,** dar la vuelta a. **to make one's way up,** subir. **to make way,** hacer lugar; hacer sitio; dar paso (a). **to pay one's way,** ganarse la vida; pagar lo que se debe. **to prepare the way for,** preparar el terreno para. **to put out of the way,** poner a un lado; apartar; (kill) matar; (imprison) poner en la cárcel; hacer cautivo (a). **to see one's way,** poder ver el camino; poder orientarse; ver el modo de hacer algo; ver cómo se puede hacer algo. **ways and means,** medios y arbitrios, *m pl.* **way back,** camino de regreso, *m;* vuelta, *f.* **way down,** bajada, *f.* **way in,** entrada, *f.* **way out,** salida, *f.* **way round,** camino alrededor, *m;* solución, *f;* modo de evitar..., *m.* **way through,** paso, *m.* **way up,** subida, *f*
wayfarer /ˈweiˌfɛərər/ *n* transeúnte, *mf;* viajero (-ra)
wayfaring /ˈweiˌfɛərɪŋ/ *a* que va de viaje; errante, ambulante
waylay /ˈweiˌlei/ *vt* asechar, salir al paso (de)
wayside /ˈweiˌsaid/ *n* borde del camino, *m.* —*a* (of flowers) silvestre; (by the side of the road) en la carretera
wayward /ˈweiwərd/ *a* caprichoso; desobediente; voluntarioso; travieso; rebelde
waywardness /ˈweiwərdnɪs/ *n* desobediencia, indocilidad, *f;* voluntariedad, *f;* travesura, *f;* rebeldía, *f*
we /wi/ *pron* nosotros, *m pl;* nosotras, *f pl,* (Usually omitted except for emphasis or for clarity.) **We are in the garden,** Estamos en el jardín. **We have come, but they are not here,** Nosotros hemos venido pero ellos no están aquí
weak /wik/ *a* débil; flojo; frágil; delicado; (insecure) inseguro; (of arguments) poco convincente; (of prices, markets, etc.) flojo, en baja. **w.-eyed,** de vista floja. **w.-kneed,** débil de rodillas; *Fig.* sin voluntad.

w.-minded, sin carácter; pusilánime; **w. spot,** debilidad, *f;* flaco, *m;* lado débil, *m;* desventaja, *f*

weaken /ˈwikən/ *vt* debilitar; (diminish) disminuir. —*vi* debilitarse; flaquear, desfallecer; (give way) ceder

weakening /ˈwikənɪŋ/ *n* debilitación, *f.* —*a* debilitante; enervante

weaker /ˈwikər/ *a compar* más débil. **the w. sex,** el sexo débil

weakling /ˈwiklɪŋ/ *n* ser delicado, *m,* persona débil, *f;* cobarde, *m; Inf.* alfeñique, *m*

weakly /ˈwikli/ *a* enfermizo, delicado, enclenque. —*adv* débilmente

weakness /ˈwiknɪs/ *n* debilidad, *f;* imperfección, *f*

weal /wil/ *n* bienestar, *m;* prosperidad, *f;* (blow) verdugo, *m*

wealth /wɛlθ/ *n* riqueza, *f;* abundancia, *f;* bienes, *m pl*

wealthy /ˈwɛlθi/ *a* rico, adinerado, acaudalado; abundante (en)

wean /win/ *vt* destetar, ablactar; separar (de); privar (de); enajenar el afecto de; (of ideas) desaferrar (de)

weaning /ˈwinɪŋ/ *n* ablactación, *f,* destete, *m*

weapon /ˈwɛpən/ *n* arma, *f; pl* **weapons,** (*Zool., Bot.*) medios de defensa, *m pl.* **steel w.,** arma blanca, *f*

wear /wɛər/ *n* uso, *m;* gasto, *m;* deterioro, *m;* (fashion) moda, boga, *f.* **for hard w.,** para todo uso. **for one's own w.,** para su propio uso. **for evening w.,** para llevar de noche. **for summer w.,** para llevar en verano. **w. and tear,** uso y desgaste, *m;* deterioro natural, *m*

wear /wɛər/ *vt* llevar; llevar puesto; traer; usar; (have) tener; (exhibit) mostrar; (be clad in) vestir; (waste) gastar; deteriorar; (make) hacer; (exhaust) agotar, cansar, consumir. —*vi* (last) durar; (of persons) conservar(se); (of time) correr; avanzar. **She wears well,** Está bien conservada. **to w. one's heart on one's sleeve,** tener el corazón en la mano. **to w. the trousers,** *Fig. Inf.* llevar los pantalones. **to w. well,** durar mucho. **to w. away,** *vt* gastar, roer; (rub out) borrar; consumir. —*vi* (of time) pasar lentamente, transcurrir despacio. **to w. down,** gastar; consumir; reducir; agotar las fuerzas de; destruir; (tire) fatigar. **to w. off,** *vt* destruir; borrar. —*vi* quitarse; borrarse; *Fig.* desaparecer, pasar. **to w. on,** (of time) transcurrir, correr, pasar. **to w. out,** *vt* usar; romper con el uso; consumir, acabar con; (exhaust) agotar; (tire) rendir. —*vi* usarse; romperse con el uso; consumirse

wearable /ˈwɛərəbəl/ *a* que se puede llevar

wearer /ˈwɛərər/ *n* el, *m,* (*f,* la) que lleva alguna cosa

weariness /ˈwɪərinɪs/ *n* cansancio, *m,* fatiga, lasitud, *f;* aburrimiento, *m;* aversión, repugnancia, *f*

wearing /ˈwɛərɪŋ/ *n* uso, *m;* desgaste, *m.* —*a* (tiring) agotador; cansado. **w. apparel,** ropa, *f*

wearisome /ˈwɪərisəm/ *a* cansado; laborioso; aburrido, tedioso, pesado

wearisomely /ˈwɪərisəmli/ *adv* tediosamente

wearisomeness /ˈwɪərisəmnɪs/ *n* cansancio, *m;* aburrimiento, tedio, hastío, *m*

weary /ˈwɪəri/ *a* cansado, fatigado; aburrido; hastiado; impaciente; tedioso, enfadoso. —*vt* cansar, fatigar; aburrir; hastiar; molestar. —*vi* cansarse, fatigarse; aburrirse. **to w. for,** anhelar, suspirar por; (miss) echar de menos (a). **to w. of,** aburrirse de; (things) impacientarse de; (people) impacientarse con

weasel /ˈwizəl/ *n* comadreja, *f*

weather /ˈwɛðər/ *n* tiempo, *m;* intemperie, *f;* (storm) tempestad, *f.* —*a Naut.* del lado del viento; de barlovento. —*vt* (of rain, etc.) desgastar; curtir; secar al aire; *Naut.* pasar a barlovento; (bear) aguantar, capear; (survive) sobrevivir a; luchar con. —*vi* curtirse a la intemperie. **Andrew is a little under the w.,** Andrés está algo destemplado; (with drink) Andrés tiene una mona; (depressed) Andrés está melancólico. **to be bad (good) w.,** hacer mal (buen) tiempo. **What is the w. like?** ¿Qué tiempo hace? ¿Cómo está el tiempo? **w.-beaten,** curtido por la intemperie. **w. chart,** carta meteorológica, *f.* **w. conditions,** condiciones meteorológicas, *f pl.* **w. forecast,** pronóstico del tiempo, *m.* **w.-hardened,** endurecido a la intemperie. **w. prophet,** meteorologista, *mf* **w. report,** boletín meteorológico, *m.* **w.-worn,** gastado por la intemperie; curtido por la intemperie

weathercock /ˈwɛðərˌkɒk/ *n* veleta, *f*

weathering /ˈwɛðərɪŋ/ *n* desintegración por la acción atmosférica, *f*

weather-resistant /ˈwɛðərrɪˌzɪstənt/ *a* resistente a la intemperie

weave /wiv/ *vt* tejer; trenzar; entrelazar; *Fig.* tejer. —*vi* tejer. —*n* tejido, *m;* textura, *f*

weaver /ˈwivər/ *n* tejedor (-ra)

weaving /ˈwivɪŋ/ *n* tejido, *m;* tejeduría, *f.* **w. machine,** telar, *m*

web /wɛb/ *n* tejido, *m;* tela, *f;* (network) red, *f;* (spider's) telaraña, *f;* (of a feather) barba, *f;* (of birds, etc.) membrana interdigital, *f;* (of intrigue) red, *f;* (snarl) lazo, *m,* trampa, *f.* **web-foot,** pie palmado, *m.* **web-footed,** palmípedo.

webbed /wɛbd/ *a* (of feet) unido por una membrana

wed /wɛd/ *vt* casarse con; (join in marriage, cause to marry) casar; *Fig.* unir. —*vi* estar casado; casarse

wedded /ˈwɛdɪd/ *a* casado; matrimonial, conyugal; *Fig.* unido (a); aficionado (a), entusiasta (de), devoto (de); aferrado (a). **to be w. to one's own opinion,** estar aferrado a su propia opinión

wedding /ˈwɛdɪŋ/ *n* boda, *f,* casamiento, *m;* (with golden, etc.) bodas, *f pl;* (union) enlace, *m, a* de boda, nupcial, matrimonial, conyugal; de novios, de la novia. **golden w.,** bodas de oro, *f pl.* **silver w.,** bodas de plata, *f pl.* **w. bouquet,** ramo de la novia, *m.* **w.-breakfast,** banquete de bodas, *m.* **w.-cake,** torta de la boda, *f,* pan de la boda, *m.* **w.-day,** día de la boda, *m.* **w.-march,** marcha nupcial, *f.* **w.-present,** regalo de boda, regalo de la boda, *m.* **w.-ring,** anillo de la boda, *m.* **w. trip,** viaje de novios, *m*

wedge /wɛdʒ/ *n* cuña, *f;* (under a wheel) calza, alzaprima, *f; Mil.* cuña, mella, *f;* (of cheese) pedazo, *m.* —*vt* acuñar, meter cuñas; (a wheel) calzar; (fix) sujetar. **to be the thin end of the w.,** ser el principio, ser el primer paso. **to drive a w.,** *Mil.* hacer mella, practicar una cuña. **to w. oneself in,** introducirse con dificultad (en). **w.-shaped,** cuneiforme

wedlock /ˈwɛdˌlɒk/ *n* matrimonio, *m*

Wednesday /ˈwɛnzdei/ *n* miércoles, *m*

wee /wi/ *a* pequeñito, chiquito. **a wee bit,** un poquito

weed /wid/ *n* mala hierba, *f;* tabaco, *m;* (cigar) cigarro, *m;* (person) madeja, *f;* (*Fig.* evil) cizaña, *f.* —*vt* carpir, desherbar, sachar, sallar, escardar; *Fig.* extirpar, arrancar. **w.-grown,** cubierto de malas hierbas. **to w. out,** extirpar; quitar

weeder /ˈwidər/ *n* (person) escardador (-ra); (implement) sacho, *m*

weeding /ˈwidɪŋ/ *n* (also *Fig.*) escarda, *f*

weedy /ˈwidi/ *a* lleno de malas hierbas; *Fig.* raquítico

week /wik/ *n* semana, *f.* **in a w.,** de hoy en ocho (días); en una semana; después de una semana. **once a w.,** una vez por semana. **a w. ago,** hace una semana. **Michael will come a w. from today,** Miguel llegará hoy en ocho. **w. in, w. out,** semana tras semana. **w.-day,** día de trabajo, día laborable, día de la semana que no sea el domingo. **on weekdays,** entre semana, *m.* **w.-end,** fin de semana, *m.* **w.-end case,** saco de noche, *m*

weekly /ˈwikli/ *a* semanal, semanario; de cada semana. —*adv* semanalmente, cada semana. —*n* semanario, *m,* revista semanal, *f*

weep /wip/ *vt* and *vi* llorar. **to w. for,** (a person) llorar (a); (on account of) llorar por; (with happiness, etc.) llorar de. **They wept for joy,** Lloraron de alegría

weeping /ˈwipɪŋ/ *n* lloro, llanto, *m,* lágrimas, *f pl.* —*a* lloroso, que llora; (of trees) llorón. **w.-willow,** sauce llorón, *m*

weevil /ˈwivəl/ *n* gorgojo, *m*

weigh /wei/ *vt* pesar; (consider) considerar, ponderar, tomar en cuenta; comparar; (the anchor) levar. —*vi* pesar; ser de importancia. **to w. anchor,** zarpar, levar el ancla, hacerse a la vela. **to w. down,** pesar sobre; sobrecargar; hacer inclinarse bajo; *Fig.* agobiar. **to be weighed down,** hundirse por su propio peso; *Fig.* estar agobiado. **to w. out,** pesar. **to w. with,** influir (en). **w.-bridge,** báscula, *f*

weighing /'weiıŋ/ *n* pesada, *f;* (weight) peso, *m;* (of the anchor) leva, *f;* (consideration) ponderación, consideración, *f.* **w.-machine,** báscula, *f*
weight /weit/ *n* peso, *m;* (heaviness) pesantez, *f;* cargo, *m;* (of a clock and as part of a system) pesa, *f; Fig.* peso, *m,* importancia, *f.* —*vt* cargar; (a stick) emplomar; aumentar el peso (de); poner un peso (a). **gross w.,** peso bruto, *m.* **heavy w.,** peso pesado, *m.* **light w.,** peso ligero, *m.* **middle w.,** peso medio, *m.* **net w.,** peso neto, *m.* **to lose w.,** adelgazar. **loss of w.,** (of a person) adelgazamiento, *m.* **to put on w.,** cobrar carnes, hacerse más gordo. **to put the w.,** *Sports.* lanzar el peso. **to throw one's w. about,** *Inf.* darse importancia. **to try the w. of,** sopesar. **weights and measures,** pesas y medidas, *f pl.* **weightlifting,** halterofilia, *f*
weighty /'weiti/ *a* pesado; (influential) influyente; importante, de peso; grave
weir /wıər/ *n* presa, esclusa, *f;* (for fish) cañal, *m*
weird /wıərd/ *a* misterioso, sobrenatural; fantástico; mágico; (queer) raro, extraño. **the W. Sisters,** las Parcas
weirdly /'wıərdli/ *adv* misteriosamente; fantásticamente; (queerly) de un modo raro, extrañamente
weirdness /'wıərdnıs/ *n* misterio, *m;* cualidad fantástica, *f;* lo sobrenatural; (queerness) rareza, *f*
welcome /'wɛlkəm/ *a* bienvenido; (pleasant) grato, agradable. —*n* bienvenida, *f;* buena acogida, *f;* (reception) acogida, *f.* —*vt* dar la bienvenida (a); acoger con alegría, acoger con entusiasmo; agasajar, festejar; (receive) acoger, recibir; recibir con gusto. **W.!** ¡Bienvenido! **to bid w.,** dar la bienvenida (a). **You are w.,** Estás bienvenido. **You are w. to it,** Está a su disposición
welcoming /'wɛlkəmıŋ/ *a* acogedor, cordial, amistoso
weld /wɛld/ *vt* soldar; combinar; unificar
welder /'wɛldər/ *n* soldador, *m*
welding /'wɛldıŋ/ *n* soldadura, *f;* unión, fusión, *f*
welfare /'wɛl,fɛər/ *n* bienestar, bien, *m;* (health) salud, *f;* prosperidad, *f;* intereses, *m pl.* **w. state,** estado benefactor, estado de beneficencia, estado socializante, *m.* **w. work,** trabajo social, *m*
well /wɛl/ *a* bien; bien de salud; bueno; conveniente; (advantageous) provechoso; favorable; (happy) feliz; (healed) curado; (recovered) repuesto. **I am very w.,** Estoy muy bien. **to get w.,** ponerse bien. **to make w.,** curar. **w. enough,** bastante bien
well /wɛl/ *adv* bien; (very) muy; favorablemente; convenientemente; (easily) sin dificultad. **as w.,** también. **as w. as,** tan bien como; además de. **That is all very w. but...,** Todo eso está muy bien pero... **to be w. up in,** estar versado en. **to get on w. with,** llevarse bien con. **Very w.!** ¡Está bien!; Muy bien. **w. and good,** bien está. **w. now,** ahora bien. **w. then,** conque; pues bien. **w.-advised,** bien aconsejado; prudente. **w.-aimed,** certero. **w.-appointed,** bien provisto; (furnished) bien amueblado. **w.-attended,** concurrido. **w.-balanced,** bien equilibrado. **w.-behaved,** bien educado; (of animals) manso. **w.-being,** bienestar, *m;* felicidad, *f.* **w.-born,** bien nacido, de buena familia. **w.-bred,** bien criado, bien educado; (of animals) de pura raza. **w.-chosen,** bien escogido. **w.-defined,** bien definido. **w.-deserved,** bien merecido. **w.-disposed,** bien dispuesto; favorable; bien intencionado. **w.-doing,** *n* el obrar bien; obras de caridad, *f pl, a* bondadoso, caritativo. **w.-done,** *a* bien hecho. —*interj* ¡bravo! **w.-educated,** instruido, culto. **w.-favored,** guapo, de buen parecer. **w.-founded,** bien fundado. **w.-groomed,** elegante. **w.-grounded,** bien fundado; bien instruido. **w.-informed,** instruido; culto, ilustrado. **w.-intentioned,** bien intencionado. **w.-known,** bien conocido, notorio. **w.-meaning,** bien intencionado. **w.-modulated,** armonioso. **w.-off,** acomodado, adinerado; feliz. **w.-read,** culto, instruido. **w.-shaped,** bien hecho; bien formado. **w.-shaped nose,** nariz perfilada, *f.* **w.-spent,** bien empleado. **w.-spoken,** bien hablado; bien dicho. **w.-stocked,** bien provisto. **w.-suited,** apropiado. **w.-timed,** oportuno. **w.-to-do,** acomodado, rico. **w.-wisher,** amigo (-ga). **w.-worn,** raído; (of paths) trillado
well /wɛl/ *n* pozo, *m;* (of a stair) caja, *f;* cañón de escalera, *m;* (fountain) fuente, *f,* manantial, *m;* (of a fishing boat) vivar, *m;* (of a ship) sentina, *f.* **w.-sinker,** pocero, *m*
well /wɛl/ *vi* chorrear, manar, brotar, fluir
Welsh /wɛlʃ/ *a* galés, de Gales. —*n* (language) galés, *m.* **the W.,** los galeses
Welshman /'wɛlʃmən/ *n* galés, *m*
Welshwoman /'wɛlʃ,wʊmən/ *n* galesa, *f*
welt /wɛlt/ *n* (of shoe) vira, *f,* cerquillo, *m;* (in knitting) ribete, *m;* (weal) verdugo, *m*
Weltanschauung /'vɛltən,ʃauəŋ/ *n* cosmovisión, postura de vida, *f*
welter /'wɛltər/ *vi* revolcarse; bañarse (en), nadar (en). —*n* confusión, *f,* tumulto, *m;* mezcla, *f.* **w.-weight,** peso welter, *m*
wench /wɛntʃ/ *n* mozuela, muchacha, *f*
wend /wɛnd/ *vt* dirigir, encaminar. —*vi* ir. **to w. one's way,** dirigir sus pasos, seguir su camino
Wesleyan /'wɛsliən/ *a* wesleyano, metodista. —*n* metodista, *mf*
west /wɛst/ *n* oeste, *m;* poniente, *m;* occidente, *m.* —*a* del oeste; occidental. —*adv* hacia el oeste, a poniente; al occidente. **W. Indian,** de las Antillas, de las Indias Occidentales. **w.-north-w.,** oesnorueste, *m.* **w. -south-w.,** oessudueste, *m.* **w. wind,** viento del oeste, poniente, *m*
westerly /'wɛstərli/ *a* del oeste; hacia el oeste; occidental
western /'wɛstərn/ *a* occidental; del oeste. —*n* (novel) novela caballista, *f;* (film) película del oeste, *f*
westernized /'wɛstər,naizd/ *a* influido por el occidente
westernmost /'wɛstərn,moust/ *a* más al oeste
West Indies Indias Occidentales, *f pl*
westward /'wɛstwərd/ *a* que está al oeste. —*adv* hacia el oeste; hacia el occidente
wet /wɛt/ *a* mojado; húmedo; (rainy) lluvioso. —*vt* mojar; humedecer. —*n* (rain) lluvia, *f.* **"Mind the wet paint!"** «¡Cuidado, recién pintado!» **to be wet,** estar mojado; (of the weather) llover. **to get wet,** mojarse. **wet blanket,** *Fig.* aguafiestas, *mf* **wet through,** (of persons) calado, hecho una sopa. **wet-nurse,** nodriza, *f*
wetness /'wɛtnıs/ *n* humedad, *f;* (rain) lluvia, *f*
wetting /'wɛtıŋ/ *n* mojada, *f;* humectación, *f;* (soaking) remojo, *m*
whack /wæk/ *n* golpe, *m;* (try) tentativa, *f;* (portion) porción, parte, *f.* —*vt* golpear, aporrear, pegar
whale /weil/ *n* ballena, *f.* **sperm w.,** cachalote, *m.* **w.-oil,** aceite de ballena, *m*
whalebone /'weil,boun/ *n* barbas de ballena, *f pl,* ballena, *f*
whaler /'weilər/ *n* (man) ballenero, pescador de ballenas, *m;* (boat) buque ballenero, *m*
whaling /'weilıŋ/ *a* ballenero. —*n* pesca de ballenas, *f.* **w.-gun,** cañón arponero, *m*
wharf /wɔrf/ *n* muelle, embarcadero, descargadero, *m, vt* amarrar al muelle
what /wʌt; *unstressed* wət/ *a pron* (interrogative and exclamatory) qué; cómo; (relative) que; el que, *m;* la que, *f;* lo que, *neut;* los que, *m pl;* las que, *f pl;* (which, interrogative) cuál, *mf;* cuáles, *mf pl;* (how many) cuantos, *m pl;* cuantas, *f pl;* (interrogative and exclamatory) cuántos, *m pl;* cuántas, *f pl;* (how much, interrogative and exclamatory) cuánto, *m;* cuánta, *f.* **And w. not,** Y qué sé yo qué más. **Make w. changes you will,** Haz los cambios que quieras. **W. confidence he had...,** La confianza que tenía... **W. is this called?** ¿Cómo se llama esto? **W. did they go there for?** ¿Por qué fueron? **W. do you take me for?** ¿Por quién me tomas? **That was not w. he said,** No fue eso lo que dijo. **to know what's w.,** saber cuántas son cinco. **You have heard the latest news, w.?** Has oído las últimas noticias, ¿verdad? **W. a pity!** ¡Qué lástima! **W., do you really believe it?** ¿Lo crees de veras? **W. else?** ¿Qué más? **W. for?** ¿Para qué? **what's-his-name,** fulano (-na) de tal, *m.* **W. ho!** ¡Hola! **W. if...?** ¿Qué será si...? **W. is the matter?** ¿Qué pasa? ¿Qué hay? **w. though...,** aun cuando...; ¿Qué importa qué? **w. with one thing, w. with another,** entre una cosa y otra. **What's more,...** Es más,...

whatever /wʌt'ɛvər/ *a pron* cuanto; todo lo que; cualquier cosa que; cualquier. **W. sacrifice is necessary,** Cualquier sacrificio que sea necesario. **W. I have is yours,** Todo lo que tenga es vuestro. **W. happens,** Venga lo que venga. **It is of no use w.,** No sirve absolutamente para nada

wheal /wil/ *n.* See **weal**

wheat /wit/ *n* trigo, *m.* —*a* de trigo. **summer w.,** trigo tremesino, *m.* **whole w.,** *a* de trigo entero. **w.-ear,** espiga de trigo, *f.* **w.-field,** trigal, *m.* **w.-sheaf,** gavilla de trigo, *f*

wheaten /'witn̩/ *a* de trigo; del color del trigo

wheedle /'widl̩/ *vt* lagotear, engatusar; (flatter) halagar; (with out) sacar con mimos

wheedling /'widlıŋ/ *a* zalamero, mimoso; marrullero. —*n* lagotería, *f,* mimos, *m pl;* (flattery) halagos, *m pl;* marrullería, *f*

wheel /wil/ *n* rueda, *f;* (bicycle) bicicleta, *f;* (for steering a ship) timón, *m;* rueda del timón, *f;* (for steering a car) volante, *m;* (for spinning) rueca, *f;* (potter's) rueda de alfarero, *f;* (of birds) vuelo, *m;* (turn) vuelta, *f; Mil.* conversión, *f.* **Catherine w.,** (firework) rueda de Santa Catalina, *f.* **back w.,** rueda trasera, *f.* **front w.,** rueda delantera, *f.* **to break on the w.,** enrodar. **to go on wheels,** ir en ruedas; *Fig.* ir viento en popa. **to take the w.,** (in a ship) tomar el timón; tomar el volante. **w. of fortune,** rueda de la fortuna, *f.* **w.-chair,** silla de ruedas, *f.* **w.-house,** timonera, *f.* **w.-mark,** rodada, *f*

wheel /wil/ *vt* hacer rodar; (push) empujar; (drive) conducir; transportar; llevar; pasear; (turn) hacer girar. —*vi* girar; dar vueltas; ir en bicicleta. **to w. about,** cambiar de frente; volverse; cambiar de rumbo

wheelbarrow /'wil,bærou/ *n* carretilla, *f*

wheeled /wild/ *a* de... ruedas; con ruedas. **w. chair,** silla de ruedas, *f*

wheeling /'wilıŋ/ *n* rodaje, *m; Mil.* conversión, *f;* (of birds) vuelos, *m pl,* vueltas, *f pl.* **free-w.,** rueda libre, *f*

wheelwright /'wil,rait/ *n* carpintero de carretas, ruedero, *m*

wheeze /wiz/ *vi* ser asmático, jadear, respirar fatigosamente, resollar

wheezing /'wizıŋ/ *n* resuello, jadeo, *m;* respiración fatigada, *f*

whelp /wɛlp/ *n* cachorro (-rra). —*vi* and *vt* parir

when /wɛn; *unstressed* wən/ *adv* cuando (interrogative, cuándo); (as soon as) tan pronto como, en cuanto; (meaning "and then') y luego, y entonces; (although) aunque. **I will see you w. I return,** Te veré cuando vuelva. **W. he came to see me he was already ill,** Cuando vino a verme estaba enfermo ya. **We returned a week ago, since w. I have not been out,** Volvimos hace ocho días y desde entonces no he salido. **Since w.?** ¿Desde cuándo?

whence /wɛns/ *adv* de donde (*interrogative,* de dónde); a donde (*interrogative* a dónde); por donde, de que; por lo que. **W. does he come?** ¿De dónde viene? **W. comes it that?** ¿Cómo es que...?

whenever /wɛn'ɛvər/ *adv* cuando quiera que, siempre que; cada vez que, todas las veces que; cuando

where /wɛəı/ *adv pron* donde (*interrogative,* dónde); en donde; en que (*interrogative,* en qué); (to where with verbs of motion) a donde (*interrogative,* a dónde); (from where with verbs of motion) de donde (*interrogative,* de dónde). **W. are you going to?** ¿A dónde va Vd.? **This is w. we get out,** (of a bus, etc.) Nos apeamos aquí

whereabouts /'wɛərə,bauts/ *adv* (*interrogative*) dónde; (relative) donde. —*n* paradero, *m*

whereas /wɛər'æz/ *conjunc* (inasmuch as) visto que, ya que; (although) mientras (que)

whereat /wɛər'æt/ *adv* por lo cual; a lo cual

whereby /wɛər'bai/ *adv* cómo; por qué; por el cual, con el cual

wherefore /'wɛər,fɔr/ *adv* (why) por qué; por lo cual. —*n* porqué, *m*

wherein /wɛər'ın/ *adv* en donde (*interrogative,* en dónde); en que (*interrogative,* en qué)

whereinto /wɛər'ıntu/ *adv* en donde; dentro del cual; en lo cual

whereof /wɛər'ʌv/ *adv* de que; (whose) cuyo

whereon /wɛər'ɒn/ *adv* sobre que; en qué

whereto /wɛər'tu/ *adv* adonde; a lo que

whereupon /,wɛərə'pɒn/ *adv* dónde; sobre lo cual, con lo cual; en consecuencia de lo cual

wherever /wɛər'ɛvər/ *adv* dondequiera (que), en cualquier sitio; adondequiera (que). **Sit w. you like,** Siéntate donde te parezca bien

wherewith /wɛər'wıθ, -'wıð/ *adv* con que (*interrogative,* con qué)

wherewithal /'wɛərwıð,ɔl, -wıθ-/ *n* lo necesario; dinero necesario, *m*

whet /wɛt/ *vt* (knives, etc.) afilar, amolar, aguzar; (curiosity, etc.) excitar, estimular

whether /'wɛðər/ *conjunc* si; que; sea que, ya que. **W. he will or no,** Que quiera, que no quiera. **w. or not,** si o no

whetstone /'wɛt,stoun/ *n* afiladera, amoladera, piedra de amolar, *f*

whetting /'wɛtıŋ/ *n* aguzadura, amoladura, *f;* (of curiosity, etc.) estimulación, excitación, *f*

whey /wei/ *n* suero (de la leche), *m*

which /wıtʃ/ *a* and *pron* cuál, *mf;* cuáles, *mf pl;* que (interrogative, qué); el cual, *m;* la cual, *f;* lo cual, *neut;* los cuales, *m pl;* las cuales, *f pl;* el que, *m;* la que, *f;* lo que, *neut;* los que, *m pl;* las que, *f pl;* (who) quien. **all of w.,** todo lo cual, etc. **in w.,** en donde, en el que; donde. **the w.,** el cual, la cual, etc. **W. would you like?** ¿Cuál quieres? **The documents w. I have seen,** Los documentos que he visto. **W. way have we to go?** ¿Por dónde hemos de ir?

whichever /wıtʃ'ɛvər/ *a* and *pron* cualquiera (que), *mf;* cualesquiera, *mf pl;* el que, *m;* la que, *f;* (of persons only) quienquiera (que), *mf;* quienesquiera (que), *mf pl* **Give me w. you like,** Dame el que quieras. **I shall take w. of you would like to come,** Me llevaré a cualquiera de Vds. que guste de venir

whiff /wıf/ *n* (of air) soplo, *m;* vaho, *m;* fragancia, *f*

while /wail/ *n* rato, *m;* momento, *m;* tiempo, *m.* **after a w.,** al cabo de algún tiempo, después de algún tiempo. **a little w. ago,** hace poco. **all this w.,** en todo este tiempo. **at whiles,** a ratos, de vez en cuando. **between whiles,** de cuando en cuando; entre tanto. **It is worth your w. to do it,** Vale la pena de hacerse. **Mary smiled the w.,** María mientras tanto se sonreía. **once in a w.,** de vez en cuando; en ocasiones

while /wail/ *conjunc* mientras (que); al (followed by an infinitive); al mismo tiempo que; a medida que; (although) aunque; si bien. **w. I was walking down the street,** mientras andaba por la calle, al andar yo por la calle. —*vt* **to w. (away),** pasar, entretener. **to w. away the time,** pasar el rato

whim /wım/ *n* capricho, antojo, *m;* manía, *f;* extravagancia, *f;* fantasía, *f*

whimper /'wımpər/ *n* quejido, sollozo, gemido, *m, vi* lloriquear, quejarse, sollozar, gemir

whimpering /'wımpərıŋ/ *n* lloriqueo, llanto, *m, a* que lloriquea

whimsical /'wımzıkəl/ *a* antojadizo, caprichoso; fantástico

whimsicality /,wımzı'kælıti/ *n* capricho, *m,* extravagancia, *f;* fantasía, *f*

whimsically /'wımzıkli/ *adv* caprichosamente; fantásticamente

whine /wain/ *vi* gimotear, lloriquear; quejarse

whining /'wainıŋ/ *n* gimoteo, lloriqueo, *m;* quejumbres, *f pl.* —*a* que lloriquea; quejumbroso

whinny /'wıni/ *n* relincho, hin, *m, vi* relinchar

whip /wıp/ *vt* azotar; pegar; *Cul.* batir; *Sew.* sobrecoser; (ropes, etc.) ligar; (defeat) vencer. —*vi* moverse rápidamente. **to w. down,** *vi* bajar volando, bajar corriendo. —*vt* arrebatar (de). **to w. in,** entrar precipitadamente (en), penetrar apresuradamente (en). **to w. off,** cazar a latigazos, despachar a golpes; (remove) quitar rápidamente; (persons) llevar corriendo, llevar aprisa. **to w. open,** abrir rápidamente. **to w. out,** *vt* (draw) sacar rápidamente; (utter) saltar diciendo (que); proferir. —*vi* escabullirse, escaparse, salir apresuradamente. **to w. round,** volverse de repente. **to w. up,** *vt* (horses, etc.) avivar con el látigo;

(snatch) coger de repente agarrar; (gather) reunir. —*vi* (mount) subir corriendo

whip /wɪp/ *n* azote, zurriago, *m;* (riding) látigo, *m.* **blow with a w.,** latigazo, *m.* **to have the w.-hand,** mandar, tener la sartén por el mango; tener la ventaja. **w.-cord,** tralla del látigo, *f*

whippet /ˈwɪpɪt/ *n* especie de perro (-rra) lebrero (-ra)

whipping /ˈwɪpɪŋ/ *n* paliza, *f,* vapuleo, azotamiento, *m.* **w. post,** picota, *f.* **w. top,** trompo, *m,* peonza, *f*

whirl /wɜrl/ *n* vuelta, *f,* giro, *m;* rotación, *f; Fig.* torbellino, *m.* —*vi* girar; dar vueltas; (dance) bailar, danzar. —*vt* hacer girar; dar vueltas (a); (carry) llevar rápidamente. **to w. along,** volar (por), pasar aprisa (por); dejar atrás los vientos, correr velozmente. **to w. past,** pasar volando (por); pasar como una exhalación. **to w. through,** atravesar rápidamente, cruzar volando

whirligig /ˈwɜrlɪˌgɪg/ *n* perinola, *f;* (merry-go-round) tiovivo, *m*

whirlpool /ˈwɜrlˌpul/ *n* vórtice, remolino, *m; Fig.* vorágine, *f*

whirlwind /ˈwɜrlˌwɪnd/ *n* torbellino, *m,* manga de viento, *f*

whirr /wɜr/ *n* zumbido, *m;* (of wings) ruido (de las alas), *m.* —*vi* girar; zumbar

whirring /ˈwɜrɪŋ/ *n* zumbido, *m;* ruido, *m.* —*a* que gira; que zumba

whisk /wɪsk/ *n* cepillo, *m; Cul.* batidor, *m;* (movement) movimiento rápido, *m.* —*vt Cul.* batir; (wag) menear, mover rápidamente; (with off, away) quitar rápidamente; sacudirse; arrebatar; (take away a person) llevarse (a). —*vi* moverse rápidamente; andar rápidamente

whiskered /ˈwɪskərd/ *a* bigotudo

whiskers /ˈwɪskərz/ *n pl* mostacho, *m,* patillas, barbas, *f pl;* (of a feline) bigotes, *m pl*

whisky /ˈwɪs-/ *n* güísqui, *m*

whisper /ˈwɪspər/ *n* cuchicheo, *m;* (rumour) voz, *f;* (of leaves, etc.) susurro, murmullo, *m.* —*vi* and *vt* cuchichear, hablar al oído; (of leaves, etc.) susurrar; (of rumors) murmurar. **in a w.,** al oído, en un susurro

whisperer /ˈwɪspərərsol; *n* cuchicheador (-ra); (gossip) murmurador (-ra)

whispering /ˈwɪspərɪŋ/ *n* cuchicheo, *m;* susurro, *m;* (gossip) murmurio, *m.* **w. gallery,** galería de los murmullos, *f. Inf.* sala de los secretos, *f*

whistle /ˈwɪsəl/ *n* (sound) silbido, silbo, *m;* (instrument) pito, silbato, *m; Inf.* gaznate, *m.* —*vi* and *vt* silbar. **blast on the w.,** pitido, *m.* **to w. for,** llamar silbando; *Inf.* esperar sentado, buscar en vano

whistler /ˈwɪslər/ *n* silbador (-ra)

whistling /ˈwɪslɪŋ/ *n* silbido, *m, a* silbador

whit /wɪt/ *n* pizca, *f,* bledo, *m.* **not a w.,** ni pizca

white /wait/ *a* blanco; pálido; puro. —*n* color blanco, blanco, *m;* (pigment) pintura blanca, *f;* (whiteness) blancura, *f;* (of egg) clara (del huevo), *f;* (person) blanco, *m.* **Elizabeth went w.,** Isabel se puso pálida. **the w.,** (billiards) la blanca. **the w. of the eye,** lo blanco del ojo. **w. ant,** hormiga blanca, termita, *f.* **w. cabbage,** repollo, *m.* **w. caps,** (of waves) cabrillas, *f pl;* (of mountains) picos blancos, *m pl.* **w. clover,** trébol blanco, *m.* **w. corpuscle,** glóbulo blanco, *m.* **w. currant,** grosella blanca, *f.* **w. elephant,** elefante (-ta) blanco (-ca). **w. ensign,** pabellón blanco, *m.* **w.-faced,** de cara pálida. **w. fish,** pescado blanco, *m.* **w. flag,** bandera blanca, *f.* **w.-haired,** de pelo blanco. **w. heat,** calor blanco, *m,* candencia, *f;* ardor, *m.* **w. horses,** cabrillas, palomas, *f pl.* **w.-hot,** incandescente. **W. House, the,** la Casa Blanca, *f.* **w. lead,** albayalde, *m.* **w. lie,** mentira inocente, mentira oficiosa, mentira piadosa, la mentirilla, *f.* **w. man,** blanco, hombre de raza blanca, *m.* **the white man's burden,** la misión sagrada de la civilización blanca, *f.* **w. meat,** carne blanca, pechuga, *f.* **w. paper,** libro blanco, *m.* **w. sauce,** salsa blanca, *f.* **w. slave,** víctima de la trata de blancas, *f.* **w. slavery,** trata de blancas, *f.* **w. sugar,** azúcar blanco, azúcar de flor, *m.* **w. woman,** mujer de raza blanca, *f*

whiten /ˈwaitn̩/ *vt* blanquear. —*vi* blanquearse

whiteness /ˈwaitnɪs/ *n* blancura, *f;* palidez, *f;* pureza, *f; Poet.* nieve, *f*

whitening /ˈwaitn̩ɪŋ/ *n* blanqueo, *m;* blanco de España, *m;* blanco para los zapatos, *m*

whitewash /ˈwaitˌwɒʃ/ *vt* blanquear, jalbegar, encalar; (*Fig.* of faults) disculpar, justificar

whitewashing /ˈwaitˌwɒʃɪŋ/ *n* blanqueo, *m,* encaladura, *f*

whither /ˈwɪðər/ *adv* (interrogative) adónde; (with a clause) adonde

whithersoever /ˌwɪðərsouˈɛvər/ *adv* adondequiera

whiting /ˈwaitɪŋ/ *n* blanco de España, *m;* blanco para los zapatos, *m;* (fish) pescadilla, *f,* merlango, *m*

whitish /ˈwaitɪʃ/ *a* blanquecino

whitlow /ˈwɪtlou/ *n* panadizo, *m*

Whitsun /ˈwɪtsən/ *a* de Pentecostés.

Whitsunday /ˈwɪtˈsʌndei/ *n* domingo de Pentecostés, *m*

Whitsuntide /ˈwɪtsənˌtaid/ *n* pascua de Pentecostés, *f*

whittle /ˈwɪtl̩/ *n* navaja, *f.* —*vt* cercenar, cortar; (sharpen) afilar, sacar punta (a); tallar; *Fig.* reducir. **to w. away, down,** *Fig.* reducir a nada

whizz /wɪz/ *n* silbido, zumbido, *m, vi* silbar, zumbar

whizzing /ˈwɪzɪŋ/ *n* silbido, *m, a* que zumba

who /hu/ *pron* (interrogative) quién, *mf;* quiénes, *mf pl;* (relative) quien, *mf;* quienes, *mf pl;* que; (in elliptical constructions the person that, etc.) el que, *m;* la que, *f;* los que, *m pl;* las que, *f pl*

whoa /wou/ *interj* ¡so!

whoever /huˈɛvər/ *pron* quienquiera (que); cualquiera (que); quien.

whole /houl/ *a* (healthy) sano; (uninjured) ileso, entero; todo. —*n* todo, *m;* total, *m;* totalidad, *f;* conjunto, *m.* **on the w.,** por regla general, en general; en conjunto. **the w. week,** la semana entera, toda la semana. **w.-hearted,** sincero, genuino; entusiasta. **w.-heartedly,** de todo corazón. **w.-heartedness,** sinceridad, *f;* entusiasmo, *m.* **w. length,** *a* de cuerpo entero. **w. number,** número entero, *m*

wholemeal /ˈhoulˈmil/ *n* harina de trigo entero, *f, a* de trigo entero

wholeness /ˈhoulnɪs/ *n* totalidad, *f;* integridad, *f;* todo, *m*

wholesale /ˈhoulˌseil/ *a Com.* al por mayor; en grueso; *Fig.* general; en masa. —*n* venta al por mayor, *f.* **w. price,** precio al por mayor, *m.* **w. trade,** comercio al por mayor, *m*

wholesaler /ˈhoulˌseilər/ *n* comerciante al por mayor, *mf* mercader de grueso, *m*

wholesome /ˈhoulsəm/ *a* sano; saludable; (edifying) edificante

wholesomeness /ˈhoulsəmnɪs/ *n* sanidad, *f;* lo sano; lo saludable

wholly /ˈhouli/ *adv* completamente, enteramente, totalmente; integralmente; del todo

whom /hum/ *pron* quien; a quien, *mf;* a quienes, *mf pl;* (interrogative) a quién, *mf;* a quiénes, *mf pl;* al que, *m;* a la que, *f;* a los que, *m pl;* a las que, *f pl.* **from w.,** de quien; (interrogative) de quién. **the man w. you saw,** el hombre a quien viste

whoop /wup, wʊp/ *n* alarido, grito, *m;* estertor de la tos ferina, *m.* —*vi* dar gritos, chillar; /hup/ (whooping-cough) toser

whooping cough /ˈhupɪŋ/ *n* tos ferina, coqueluche, *f*

whore /hɔr/ *n* puta, ramera, *f*

whorl /wɜrl, wɔrl/ *n* (of a shell) espira, *f; Bot.* verticilo, *m;* (of a spindle) tortera, *f*

whorled /wɜrld, wɔrld/ *a Bot.* verticilado; (of shells) en espira

whose /huz/ *pron* cuyo, *m;* cuya, *f;* cuyos, *m pl;* cuyas, *f pl;* de quien, *mf;* de quienes, *mf pl;* (*interrogative*) de quién, de quiénes; **W. daughter is she?** ¿De quién es ella la hija? **This is the writer w. name I always forget,** Este es el autor cuyo nombre siempre olvido

whosoever /ˌhusouˈɛvər/ *pron.* See **whoever**

why /wai/ *adv* (*interrogative*) por qué; (on account of which) por el cual, *m;* por la cual, *f;* por lo cual, *neut;* por los cuales, *m pl;* por las cuales, *f pl;* (how) cómo. —*n* ni porqué, *m, interj* ¡qué!; ¡cómo!; ¡toma!; sí. **not to know the why or wherefore,** no saber ni el porqué ni el cómo, no saber ni el qué ni el por

qué. **Why! I have just come,** ¡Si no hago más de llegar! **Why not?** ¿Por qué no? ¡Cómo no!
wick /wɪk/ *n* mecha, torcida, *f*
wicked /'wɪkɪd/ *a* malo; malvado, perverso; pecaminoso; malicioso; (mischievous) travieso
wickedly /'wɪkɪdli/ *adv* mal; perversamente; maliciosamente
wickedness /'wɪkɪdnɪs/ *n* maldad, *f;* perversidad, *f;* pecado, *m;* (mischievousness) travesura, *f*
wicker /'wɪkər/ *n* mimbre, *m, a* de mimbre
wicket /'wɪkɪt/ *n* postigo, portillo, *m;* (half-door) media puerta, *f;* (at cricket) meta, *f.* **w.-keeper,** guardameta, *m*
wide /waid/ *a* ancho; (in measurements) de ancho; vasto; extenso; grande; amplio; (loose) holgado; (distant) lejos; liberal; general, comprensivo. —*adv* lejos, completamente. **far and w.,** por todas partes. **to be too w.,** ser muy ancho; estar muy ancho; (of garments) venir muy ancho. **two feet w.,** dos pies de ancho. **w.-awake,** muy despierto; despabilado; vigilante. **w.-eyed,** con los ojos muy abiertos; asombrado. **w.-open,** abierto de par en par
widely /'waidli/ *adv* extensamente; generalmente; (very) muy
widen /'waidn̩/ *vt* ensanchar, extender. —*vi* ensancharse; extenderse
widening /'waidn̩ɪŋ/ *n* ensanche, *m;* extensión, *f*
widespread /'waid'sprɛd/ *a* universal, generalizado; extenso; esparcido. **to become w.,** generalizarse
widow /'wɪdou/ *n* viuda, *f.* —*vt* dejar viuda; dejar viudo; *Fig.* privar. **to be a grass w.,** estar viuda. **to become a w.,** enviudar, perder al esposo. **widow's pension,** viudedad, *f.* **widow's weeds,** luto de viuda, *m*
widowed /'wɪdoud/ *a* viudo
widower /'wɪdouər/ *n* viudo, *m.* **to become a w.,** perder a la esposa, enviudar
widowhood /'wɪdouˌhʊd/ *n* viudez, *f*
width /wɪdθ/ *n* anchura, *f;* (of cloth) ancho, *m;* (of mind) liberalismo, *m.* **double w.,** (cloth) doble ancho, *m*
wield /wild/ *vt* (a scepter) empuñar; (power, etc.) ejercer; (a pen, sword) manejar
wife /waif/ *n* esposa, mujer, *f;* mujer, *f;* comadre, *f.* **husband and w.,** los cónyuges, los esposos. **old wives' tale,** cuento de viejas, *m.* **The Merry Wives of Windsor,** Las alegres comadres de Windsor. **to take to w.,** contraer matrimonio con, tomar como esposa (a)
wifely /'waifli/ *a* de esposa, de mujer casada; de mujer de su casa; conyugal
wig /wɪg/ *n* peluca, *f;* (hair) cabellera, *f.* **top wig,** peluquín, *m.* **wigmaker,** peluquero, *m*
wigged /wɪgd/ *a* con peluca, de peluca
wigging /'wɪgɪŋ/ *n* (scolding) peluca, *f*
wigwam /'wɪgwɒm/ *n* tienda de indios, *f*
wild /waild/ *a* (of animals, men, land) salvaje; (barren) desierto, yermo; (mountainous) riscoso, montañoso; (of plants, birds) silvestre; montés; (disarranged) en desorden, desarreglado; (complete) absoluto, completo; (dissipated) disipado; vicioso; (foolish) alocado; (of the sea) bravío; (of weather, etc.) borrascoso; (mad with delight, etc.) loco; (frantic, mad) frenético, loco; (with "talk,' etc.) extravagante; insensato, desatinado; (shy) arisco; (incoherent) inconexo, incoherente; (frightened) alarmado, espantado; (wilful) travieso, indomable. —*n* tierra virgen, *f;* desierto, *m;* soledad, *f.* **It made me w.,** (angry) Me hizo rabiar. **to run w.,** volver al estado silvestre; (of persons) llevar una vida de salvajes; volverse loco. **to shoot w.,** errar el tiro. **to spread like w. fire,** propagarse como el fuego. **w. beast,** fiera, *f.* **w. boar,** jabalí, *m.* **w. cat,** gato montés, *m.* **w. duck,** pato silvestre, *m.* **w. goat,** cabra montesa, *f.* **w.-goose chase,** caza infructuosa, *f;* empresa quimérica, *f.* **w. oats,** avenas locas, *f pl; Fig.* indiscreciones de la juventud, *f pl.* **to sow one's w. oats,** andarse a la flor del berro
wilderness /'wɪldərnɪs/ *n* desierto, *m;* yermo, páramo, despoblado, *m;* soledad, *f;* (jungle) selva, *f;* (maze) laberinto, *m;* infinidad, *f*
wildly /'waildli/ *adv* en un estado salvaje; sin cultivo; (rashly) desatinadamente; sin reflexión, sin pensar; (incoherently) incoherentemente; (stupidly, of looking, etc.) tontamente; (in panic) con ojos espantados, con terror en los ojos, alarmado
wildness /'waildnɪs/ *n* salvajez, *f;* estado silvestre, *m;* naturaleza silvestre, *f;* (ferocity) ferocidad, *f;* (of the wind, sea) braveza, *f;* (of the wind) violencia, *f;* (impetuosity) impetuosidad, *f;* (of statements, etc.) extravagancia, *f;* (incoherence) incoherencia, *f;* (disorder) desorden, *m;* (wilfulness, of children) travesuras, *f pl;* (of the expression) gesto espantado, *m*
wile /wail/ *n* estratagema, *f,* engaño, *m,* ardid, *f*
wilily /'wailɪli/ *adv* astutamente
wiliness /'wailinɪs/ *n* astucia, *f*
will /wɪl/ *n* voluntad, *f;* albedrío, *m;* (wish) deseo, *m;* (pleasure) discreción, *f,* placer, *m;* (legal document) testamento, *m.* **against my w.,** contra mi voluntad. **at w.,** a voluntad; a gusto; a discreción. **free w.,** libre albedrío, *m.* **of one's own free w.,** por su propia voluntad. **iron w.,** voluntad de hierro, *f.* **last w. and testament,** última disposición, última voluntad, *f.* **to do with a w.,** hacer con toda el alma, hacer con entusiasmo. **to make one's w.,** otorgar (hacer) su testamento. **w.-power,** fuerza de voluntad, *f*
will /wɪl/ *vt* querer; disponer, ordenar; (bequeath) legar, dejar en testamento, mandar; (oblige) sugestionar (a una persona) para que haga algo; hipnotizar. —*vi aux* querer; (As a sign of the future it is not translated separately in Spanish) **I w. come tomorrow,** Vendré mañana. **John does not approve, but I w. go,** Juan no lo aprueba pero yo quiero ir. **Do what you w.,** Haga lo que a Vd. le parezca bien, Haga lo que Vd. quiera; Haga lo que haga. **Boys w. be boys,** Los niños son siempre niños. **He w. not (won't) do it,** No lo hará; No quiere hacerlo
willful /'wɪlfəl/ *a* rebelde, voluntarioso; (of children) travieso; (of crimes, etc.) premeditado
willfully /'wɪlfəli/ *adv* voluntariosamente; intencionadamente; (of committing crimes) con premeditación
willfulness /'wɪlfəlnɪs/ *n* rebeldía, *f;* (obstinacy) terquedad, obstinación, *f*
William the Silent /'wɪlyəm/ Guillermo el Taciturno
willing /'wɪlɪŋ/ *a* dispuesto, inclinado; (serviceable) servicial; deseoso; espontáneo; complaciente; gustoso; (willingly) de buena gana. **to be w.,** estar dispuesto (a), querer; consentir (en)
willingly /'wɪlɪŋli/ *adv* de buena gana, con gusto
willingness /'wɪlɪŋnɪs/ *n* buena voluntad, *f;* deseo de servir, *m;* complacencia, *f;* (consent) consentimiento, *m*
will-o'-the-wisp /'wɪləðə'wɪsp/ *n* fuego fatuo, *m*
willow /'wɪlou/ *n* sauce, *m.* **weeping w.,** sauce llorón, *m.* **w.-pattern china,** porcelana de estilo chino, *f.* **w. tree,** sauce, *m*
willowy /'wɪloui/ *a* lleno de sauces; (slim) cimbreño, esbelto, alto y delgado
willy nilly /'wɪli 'nɪli/ *adv* de buen o mal grado, mal que bien
wilt /wɪlt/ *vi* (of plants) marchitarse, secarse; *Fig.* languidecer; ajarse. —*vt* marchitar; *Fig.* ajar; hacer languidecer
wily /'waili/ *a* astuto, chuzón
wimple /'wɪmpəl/ *n* toca, *f*
win /wɪn/ *vt* ganar; (reach) alcanzar, lograr; (a victory, etc.) llevarse; conquistar. —*vi* ganar; triunfar. —*n* triunfo, *m.* **to win back,** volver a ganar; recobrar
wince /wɪns/ *vi* retroceder, recular; (flinch) quejarse; (of a horse) respingar. —*n* respingo, *m.* **without wincing,** sin quejarse; estoicamente
winch /wɪntʃ/ *n* cabria, *f;* (handle) manubrio, *m*
wind /wɪnd/ *n* viento, *m;* aire, *m;* (flatulence) flatulencia, *f;* (breath) respiración, *f,* aliento, *m;* (idle talk) paja, *f.* **breath of w.,** soplo de viento, *m.* **following w.,** viento en popa, *m.* **high w.,** viento alto, viento fuerte, *m.* **land w.,** viento terrenal, *m.* **It's an ill w. that blows nobody good,** No hay mal que por bien no venga. **There is something in the w.,** Hay algo en el aire, Se trama algo. **to get w. of,** husmear. **to sail before the w.,** navegar de viento en popa. **The w. stiffened,** Refrescó el viento. **You took the w. out of his sails,** Le deshinchaste las velas. **w.-instrument,** instrumento de viento, *m.* **w.-proof,** a

prueba del viento. **w.-swept,** expuesto a todos los vientos. **w. storm,** ventarrón, *m*

wind /waind/ *vi* serpentear; desfilar lentamente; torcerse. *—vt* (turn) dar vueltas (a); (a handle) manejar, mover; (a watch) dar cuerda (a); (wool, etc.) devanar, ovillar; (wrap) envolver; (of arms, embrace) rodear (con); (a horn) tocar. **to w. off,** devanar; desenrollar. **to w. round,** (wrap) envolver; (skirt) rodear; (embrace) ceñir con (los brazos); (pass by) pasar por; deslizarse por; (of snakes) enroscarse. **to w. up,** (a watch) dar cuerda (a); (thread) devanar; (conclude) concluir; *Com.* liquidar; (excite) agitar, emocionar

windbag /ˈwɪndˌbæg/ *n* pandero, *m,* sacamuelas, *mf*

winder /ˈwaindər/ *n* (person) devanador (-ra); (machine) devanadera, *f;* (of a clock) llave, *f*

windfall /ˈwɪndˌfɔl/ *n* fruta caída del árbol, *f;* (good luck) breva, *f;* ganancia inesperada, lotería, *f*

windiness /ˈwɪndinɪs/ *n* tiempo ventoso, *m;* situación expuesta a todos los vientos, *f;* (of speech) pomposidad, verbosidad, *f*

winding /ˈwaindɪŋ/ *a* tortuoso; (e.g., road) sinuoso; serpentino; en espiral. *—n* tortuosidad, *f;* meandro, recoveco, *m,* vuelta, curva, *f.* **w. sheet,** mortaja, *f,* sudario, *m.* **w. stair,** escalera de caracol, *f.* **w.-up,** conclusión, *f; Com.* liquidación, *f*

windlass /ˈwɪndləs/ *n* torno, *m*

windless /ˈwɪndlɪs/ *a* sin viento

windmill /ˈwɪndˌmɪl/ *n* molino de viento, *m*

window /ˈwɪndou/ *n* ventana, *f;* (of a shop) escaparate, *m;* (in a train, car, bank, etc.) ventanilla, *f;* (booking office) taquilla, *f;* (of a church) vidriera, *f.* **casement w.,** ventana, *f.* **sash w.,** ventana de guillotina, *f.* **small w.,** ventanilla, *f.* **stained glass w.,** vidriera, *f.* **to lean out of the w.,** asomarse a la ventana. **to look out of the w.,** mirar por la ventana. **w. blind,** (Venetian) persiana, *f;* transparente, *m;* (against the sun) toldo, *m.* **w.-dresser,** decorador (-ra) de escaparates. **w. frame,** marco de ventana, *m.* **w.-pane,** cristal (de ventana), *m.* **w.-shutter,** contraventana, *f.* **w.-sill,** repisa de la ventana, *f,* alféizar, *m*

windpipe /ˈwɪndˌpaip/ *n* tráquea, *f*

windscreen /ˈwɪndˌskrin/ *n* parabrisas, guardabrisa, *m.* **w.-wiper,** limpiaparabrisas, limpiavidrios, *m*

windward /ˈwɪndwərd/ *n* barlovento, *m. —a* de barlovento. *—adv* a barlovento

windy /ˈwɪndi/ *a* ventoso; expuesto al viento; (of style) hinchado, pomposo. **It is w.,** Hace viento

wine /wain/ *n* vino, *m;* zumo fermentado (de algunas frutas), *m. —a* de vino; de vinos; para vino. **in w.,** *Cul.* en vino; (drunk) ebrio, borracho. **heavy w.,** vino fuerte, *m.* **light w.,** vino ligero, *m.* **local w.,** vino del país, *m,* **matured w.,** vino generoso, *m.* **red w.,** vino tinto, *m.* **thin w.,** vinillo, *m.* **white w.,** vino blanco, *m.* **w.-cellar,** bodega, cueva, *f.* **w.-colored,** de color de vino. **w.-cooler,** cubo para enfriar vinos, *m.* **w. country,** tierra de vino, *f.* **w. decanter,** garrafa para vino, *f.* **w.-grower,** vinicultor (-ra). **w.-growing,** *n* vinicultura, *f. —a* vinícola. **w. lees,** zupia, *f.* **w. merchant,** comerciante en vinos, *mf.* vinatero, *m.* **w.-press,** lagar, *m.* **w.-taster,** catavinos, *m.* **w. waiter,** bodeguero, *m*

wineskin /ˈwainˌskɪn/ *n* bota, *f,* odre, pellejo, *m*

wing /wɪŋ/ *n* (of a bird and *Zool. Archit. Aer. Mil. Bot.*) ala, *f;* (flight) vuelo, *m; Theat.* bastidor, *m; Fig.* protección, *f. —vt* dar alas (a); llevar sobre las alas; (wound) herir en el ala; herir en el brazo; volar por. *—vi* volar. **beating of wings,** batir de alas, aleteo, *m.* **in the wings,** *Theat.* entre bastidores. **on the w.,** al vuelo. **to clip a (person's) wings,** cortar (*or* quebrar) las alas (a). **under his w.,** bajo su protección. **w.-case,** élitro (de un insecto), *m.* **w. chair,** sillón con orejas, *m.* **w.-commander,** teniente coronel de aviación, *m.* **w.-span,** (*Zool.* and *Aer.*) envergadura, *f.* **w.-spread,** extensión del ala, *f.* **w.-tip,** punta del ala, *f*

winged /wɪŋd; *esp. Literary* ˈwɪŋɪd/ *a* alado, con alas; (in compounds) de alas...; (swift) alado; (of style) elevado, alado

wink /wɪŋk/ *vi* (blink) pestañear; (as a signal, etc.) guiñar; (of stars, etc.) titilar, parpadear, centellear. *—vt* guiñar (el ojo). *—n* pestañeo, *m;* guiño, *m.* **not to sleep a w.,** no pegar los ojos. **to take forty winks,** echar una siesta. **to w. at,** guiñar el ojo (a); (ignore) hacer la vista gorda

winking /ˈwɪŋkɪŋ/ *n* (blinking) parpadeo, *m;* (as a signal) guiños, *m pl;* (of stars, etc.) titilación, *f,* pestañeo, *m. —a* (of stars, etc.) titilante. **like w.,** en un abrir y cerrar de ojos.

winner /ˈwɪnər/ *n* ganador (-ra); vencedor (-ra)

winning /ˈwɪnɪŋ/ *a* ganador; vencedor; (attractive) encantador. *—n* ganancia, *f.* **w. number,** número galardonado, número premiado, número vencedor, *m.* **w.-post,** meta, *f.* **w. side,** *Sports.* equipo vencedor, *m;* (politics, etc.) partido vencedor, *m*

winnings /ˈwɪnɪŋz/ *n* ganancias, *f pl*

winnow /ˈwɪnou/ *vt* aventar, abalear; *Fig.* separar

winnower /ˈwɪnouər/ *n* aventador (-ra)

winnowing /ˈwɪnouɪŋ/ *n* abaleo, aventamiento, *m; Fig.* separación, *f.* **w. fork,** bieldo, *m.* **w. machine,** aventador mecánico, *m*

winsome /ˈwɪnsəm/ *a* sandunguero; dulce, encantador

winsomeness /ˈwɪnsəmnɪs/ *n* sandunga, *f;* encanto, *m,* dulzura, *f*

winter /ˈwɪntər/ *n* invierno, *m. —a* de invierno; hiemal. *—vi* pasar el invierno, invernar. *—vt* (of cattle, etc.) guardar en invierno. **in w.,** en invierno, durante el invierno. **w. clothes,** ropa de invierno, *f.* **w. palace,** palacio de invierno, *m.* **w. quarters,** invernadero, *m.* **w. season,** invierno, *m;* temporada de invierno, *f.* **w. sleep,** invernada, *f.* **w. solstice,** solsticio hiemal, *m.* **w. sports,** deportes de nieve, *m pl.* **w. wheat,** trigo de invierno, *m*

wintry /ˈwɪntri/ *a* de invierno; invernal; (of a smile, etc.) glacial

wipe /waip/ *vt* limpiar; (rub) frotar; (dry) secar; (remove) quitar. *—n* limpión, *m;* (blow) golpe de lado, *m.* **to w. one's eyes,** enjugarse las lagrimas. **to w. off, out,** limpiar; (remove) quitar; (erase) borrar; (kill) destruir completamente, exterminar; (a military force) destrozar; (a debt) cancelar

wire /waiᵊr/ *n* alambre, *m;* hilo metálico, *m;* telégrafo (eléctrico), *m; Inf.* telegrama, *m. —vt* atar con alambre; (fence) alambrar; (snare) coger con lazo de alambre; (of electrical equipment, etc.) instalar; (telegraph) telegrafiar. *—vi* (telegraph) telegrafiar. **barbed w.,** alambre espinoso, *m.* **live w.,** alambre cargado (de electricidad), *m;* (person) fuerza viva, *f.* **w.-cutters,** cortaalambres, *m pl.* **w.-entanglement,** *Mil.* alambrada, *f.* **w. fence,** alambrera, *f,* cercado de alambre, *m.* **w. gauze,** tela metálica, *f.* **w. nail,** punta de París, *f.* **w.-netting,** malla de alambre, *f;* alambrado, *m.* **w.-pulling,** influencias secretas, *f pl;* intrigas políticas, *f pl*

wiredraw /ˈwaiᵊrˌdrɔ/ *vt* estirar (alambre), tirar (el hilo de hierro, plata, etc.); (arguments, etc.) sutilizar

wiredrawer /ˈwaiᵊrˌdrɔər/ *n* estirador, *m*

wiredrawing /ˈwaiᵊrˌdrɔɪŋ/ *n* tirado, *m; Fig.* sutileza, *f*

wireless /ˈwaiᵊrlɪs/ *a* sin hilos; (of a message) radiotelegráfico; por radio. *—n* telegrafía sin hilos, *f;* radiotelefonía, *f;* (telegram) radiocomunicación, *f;* (broadcasting) radio, *f. —vt* radiotelegrafiar. **Let's listen to the w.,** Vamos a escuchar la radio. **portable w.,** radio portátil, *f.* **w. engineer,** ingeniero radiotelegrafista, *m.* **w. enthusiast,** radioaficionado (-da). **w. licence,** permiso de radiorreceptor, *m.* **w. operator,** radiotelegrafista, *mf.* **w. room,** cuarto de telegrafía sin hilos, *m.* **w. set,** aparato de radio, *m.* **w. station,** estación de radiotelegrafía, *f;* (broadcasting) radioemisora, *f.* **w. telegraph,** telégrafo sin hilos, *m.* **w. telegraphy,** telegrafía sin hilos, radiotelegrafía, *f.* **w. telephony,** telefonía sin hilos, *f.* **w. transmission,** radioemisión, *f*

wiretap /ˈwaiᵊrˌtæp/ *vi* poner escucha. *—vt* poner escucha a

wiring /ˈwaiᵊrɪŋ/ *n* instalación de alambres eléctricos, *f*

wiry /ˈwaiᵊri/ *a* semejante a un alambre; (of persons) nervudo

wisdom /ˈwɪzdəm/ *n* sabiduría, *f;* (learning) saber, *m;* (judgment) juicio, *m.* **Book of W.,** Libro de la Sabiduría, *m.* **w.-tooth,** muela del juicio, *f*

wise /waiz/ *a* sabio; juicioso, prudente; (informed) enterado, informado. **a w. man,** un sabio. **in no w.,** de ningún modo. **the W. Men of the East,** los magos. **w. guy,** *Inf.* toro corrido, *m*

wisely /'waizli/ *adv* sabiamente; prudentemente, con prudencia

wish /wɪʃ/ *n* deseo, *m.* **Best wishes for the New Year,** Los mejores deseos para el Año Nuevo. **w.-bone,** espoleta, *f*

wish /wɪʃ/ *vt* querer; desear; ansiar; (with "good morning', etc.) dar. **I w. he were here!** ¡Ojalá que estuviera aquí! **Theresa wishes us to go,** Teresa quiere que vayamos. **I w. it had happened otherwise,** Quisiera que las cosas hubiesen pasado de otra manera. **I w. you would make less noise,** Me gustaría que hicieses menos ruido. **I only w. one thing,** Solamente deseo una cosa. **I w. you good luck,** Te deseo mucha suerte. **I wished him a merry Christmas,** Le deseé unas Pascuas muy felices, Le felicité las Pascuas. **to w. a prosperous New Year,** desear un próspero Año Nuevo. **to w. good-by,** despedirse (de). **to w. good day,** dar los buenos días. **to w. for,** desear

wisher /'wɪʃər/ *n* el que, *m,* (*f,* la que) desea, deseador (-ra)

wishful /'wɪʃfəl/ *a* deseoso; ansioso; ávido. **w. thinking,** ilusiones, *f pl*; optimismo injustificado, optimismo exagerado, *m*

wisp /wɪsp/ *n* mechón, *m;* jirón, *m;* trozo, pedazo, *m*

wistaria /wɪ'stɪəriə, -'stɛər-/ *n* vistaria, *f*

wistful /'wɪstfəl/ *a* ansioso; triste; patético; (envious) envidioso; (regretful) de pesar; (remorseful) de remordimiento; (thoughtful) pensativo

wistfully /'wɪstfəli/ *adv* con ansia; tristemente; patéticamente; con envidia; con pesar; con remordimiento; pensativo

wistfulness /'wɪstfəlnɪs/ *n* ansia, *f;* tristeza, *f;* (envy) envidia, *f;* (regret) pesar, *m;* (remorse) remordimiento, *m;* (thoughtfulness) lo pensativo, lo distraído

wit /wɪt/ *n* (reason) juicio, *m;* agudeza, gracia, *f,* rasgo de ingenio, *m;* ingenio, *m;* inteligencia, *f,* talento, *m;* (person) hombre de ingenio, *m;* mujer de ingenio, *f.* **my five wits,** mis cinco sentidos. **to be at one's wits' end,** no saber qué hacer. **to live by one's wits,** ser caballero de industria. **to lose one's wits,** perder el juicio

witch /wɪtʃ/ *n* bruja, *f.* **witches' sabbath,** aquelarre, *m.* **w.-doctor,** hechizador, mago, *m.* **witch-hazel,** carpe, *m;* loción de carpe, *f*

witchcraft /'wɪtʃˌkræft/ *n* brujería, *f;* sortilegio, encantamiento, *m*

witchery /'wɪtʃəri/ *n* brujería, *f; Fig.* encanto, *m,* magia, *f*

with /wɪθ, wɪð/ *prep* con; en compañia de; en casa de; (against) contra; (among) entre; en; (by) por; (towards) hacia; para con; (according to) según; (notwithstanding) a pesar de; a; (concerning) con respecto a; en el caso de. **Rose is w. Antony,** Rosa está con Antonio. **He was w. his dog,** Estaba acompañado por su perro. **He pulled at it w. both hands,** Lo tiró con las dos manos. **filled w. fear,** lleno de miedo. **to shiver w. cold,** temblarse de frío. **the girl w. golden hair,** la muchacha del pelo dorado. **They killed it w. one blow,** Lo mataron de un solo golpe. **It rests w. you to decide,** Tú tienes que decidirlo; Te toca a tí decidirlo. **to begin w.,** *adv* para empezar; *v* empezar por. **w. all speed,** a toda prisa. **to part w.,** desprenderse de; (of people) despedirse de; separarse de. **w. that...,** (at once) en esto... (disease and poverty, etc.) **are still with us,** están todavía en el mundo

withal /wɪð'ɔl, wɪθ-/ *adv* además; al mismo tiempo. —*prep* con

withdraw /wɪð'drɔ, wɪθ-/ *vt* retirar; (words) retractar; (remove) quitar, privar (de); (a legal action) apartar. —*vi* retirarse; retroceder; apartarse; irse

withdrawal /wɪð'drɔəl, wɪθ-/ *n* retirada, *f;* (retirement) retiro, *m;* apartamiento, *m*

withdrawn /wɪð'drɔn, wɪθ-/ *a* (abstracted) ensimismado, meditabundo

wither /'wɪðər/ *vi* marchitarse, secarse, ajarse. —*vt* marchitar, secar, ajar; *Fig.* hacer languidecer, matar; (snub) avergonzar

withered /'wɪðərd/ *a* marchito, mustio; muerto; (of persons) acartonado, seco

witheredness /'wɪðərdnɪs/ *n* marchitez, *f;* sequedad, *f*

withering /'wɪðərɪŋ/ *a* que marchita; (scorching) abrasador, ardiente; (scornful) despreciativo, desdeñoso; (biting) mordaz, cáustico

withers /'wɪðərz/ *n* cruz, *f*

withhold /wɪθ'hould, wɪð-/ *vt* retener; detener; (restrain) refrenar; apartar; (refuse) negar; abstenerse de; (refuse to reveal) ocultar

withholding /wɪθ'houldɪŋ, wɪð-/ *n* detención, *f;* (refusal) negación, *f*

within /wɪð'ɪn, wɪθ-/ *adv* dentro, adentro; en el interior; en casa; *Fig.* en su interior. **He stayed w.,** Se quedó dentro. **Is Mrs. González w.?** ¿Está en casa la Sra. González?

within /wɪð'ɪn, wɪθ-/ *prep* dentro de; el interior de; en; entre; (within range of) al alcance de; a la distancia de; (near) cerca de; a poco de; (of time) en el espacio de, en; dentro de; (almost) por poco, casi. **He was w. an inch of being killed,** Por poco le matan. **to be w. hearing,** estar al alcance de la voz. **seen from w.,** visto desde dentro. **twice w. a fortnight,** dos veces en quince días. **w. himself,** por sus adentros, entre sí. **w. an inch of,** *Fig.* a dos dedos de. **w. a few miles of Edinburgh,** a unas millas de Edimburgo. **w. a short distance,** en una corta distancia; a poca distancia

without /wɪð'aut, wɪθ-/ *prep* sin; falto de; (outside) fuera de; (beyond) más allá de. —*adv* exteriormente; por fuera; hacia afuera; fuera. **It goes w. saying,** No hay que decir. **w. more ado,** sin más ni más. **w. my knowledge,** sin que yo lo supiese. **w. regard for,** sin miramentos por. **w. saying more,** sin decir más. **without batting an eyelash,** sin sobresaltos

withstand /wɪθ'stænd, wɪð-/ *vt* resistir, oponerse (a); soportar

withstanding /wɪθ'stændɪŋ, wɪð-/ *n* resistencia, oposición (a), *f*

witless /'wɪtlɪs/ *a* sin seso, tonto, necio

witness /'wɪtnɪs/ *n* (evidence) testimonio, *m;* (person) testigo, *mf;* espectador (-ra). **in w. whereof,** en fe de lo cual. **to bear w.,** atestiguar, dar testimonio. **to bring forward witnesses,** hacer testigos. **w. my hand,** en fe de lo cual, firmo. **w.-box,** puesto de los testigos, *m.* **w. for the defence,** testigo de descargo, *mf.* **w. for the prosecution,** testigo de cargo, *mf*

witness /'wɪtnɪs/ *vt* (show) mostrar, señalar; (see) ser testigo de, ver, presenciar; *Law.* atestiguar. —*vi* dar testimonio; servir de testigo

witticism /'wɪtəˌsɪzəm/ *n* rasgo de ingenio, donaire, *m,* agudeza, *f*

wittily /'wɪtli/ *adv* ingeniosamente, donairosamente, agudamente

wittiness /'wɪtinɪs/ *n* viveza de ingenio, donosura, *f*

witty /'wɪti/ *a* salado, gracioso. **w. sally,** agudeza, *f*

wizard /'wɪzərd/ *n* mago, hechicero, *m*

wizardry /'wɪzərdri/ *n* magia, *f*

wizened /'wɪzənd/ *a* seco, arrugado; (of persons) acartonado

wobble /'wɒbəl/ *vi* tambalearse, balancearse; (quiver) temblar; oscilar; *Mech.* galopar; (stagger) titubear; *Fig.* vacilar

wobbly /'wɒbli/ *a* que se bambolea; inestable; *Fig.* vacilante

woe /wou/ *n* dolor, *m,* congoja, aflicción, *f,* mal, desastre, infortunio, *m.* **Woe is me!** ¡Ay de mí! ¡Desdichado de mí!

woebegone /'woubɪˌgɔn/ *a* angustiado

woeful /'woufəl/ *a* triste; doloroso; funesto

woefully /'woufəli/ *adv* tristemente; dolorosamente

wolf /wʊlf/ *n* lobo (-ba). **a w. in sheep's clothing,** un lobo en piel de cordero. **to cry w.,** gritar «el lobo!» **to keep the w. from the door,** ponerse a cubierto del hambre. **w.-cub,** lobezno, *m.* **w.-hound,** perro lobo, *m.* **w. pack,** manada de lobos, *f*

wolfish /'wʊlfɪʃ/ *a* lobuno, de lobo

wolfram /'wʊlfrəm, 'vɔl-/ *n* volframio, *m*

woman /'wʊmən/ *n* mujer, *f;* hembra, *f;* (lady-in-waiting) dama de servicio, *f.* **a fine figure of a w.,** una real hembra. **w. doctor,** médica, *f.* **w.-hater,** misógino, *m.* **w. of the town,** mujer de la vida airada, *f.* **w. of the world,** mujer de mundo, *f*

womanhood /'wʊmən,hʊd/ *n* feminidad, *f;* sexo femenino, *m*

womanish /'wʊmənɪʃ/ *a* afeminado

womankind /'wʊmən,kaind/ *n* el sexo femenino, las mujeres

womanliness /'wʊmənlinɪs/ *n* feminidad, *f;* carácter femenino, *m*

womanly /'wʊmənli/ *a* femenino, de mujer

womb /wum/ *n* útero, *m,* matriz, *f; Fig.* seno, *m*

women's dormitory /'wɪmɪnz/ *n* residencia para señoritas, *f*

wonder /'wʌndər/ *n* maravilla, *f;* prodigio, *m;* portento, milagro, *m;* (surprise) sorpresa, *f;* admiración, *f;* asombro, *m;* (problem) enigma, *m;* misterio, *m.* —*vi* admirarse, asombrarse, maravillarse; sorprenderse. —*vt* (ask oneself) preguntarse; desear saber. **I wondered what the answer would be,** Me preguntaba qué sería la respuesta. **It is no w. that...,** No es mucho que..., No es sorprendente que... **It is one of the wonders of the world,** Es una de las maravillas del mundo. **to work wonders,** hacer milagros. **to w. at,** asombrarse de, maravillarse de; sorprenderse de. **w.-working,** milagroso

wonderful /'wʌndərfəl/ *a* maravilloso; magnífico; asombroso; *Inf.* estupendo

wonderfully /'wʌndərfli/ *adv* maravillosamente; admirablemente

wondering /'wʌndərɪŋ/ *a* de asombro, sorprendido; perplejo

wonderingly /'wʌndərɪŋli/ *adv* con asombro

wonderland /'wʌndər,lænd/ *n* mundo fantástico, *m;* reino de las hadas, *m;* país de las maravillas, *m.* **"Alice in W.,"** Alicia en el país de las maravillas

wonderment /'wʌndərmənt/ *n.* See **wonder**

wondrous /'wʌndrəs/ *a* maravilloso. —*adv* extraordinariamente

wont /wɔnt, wount/ *n* costumbre, *f.* —*vi* soler. **as he was w.,** Como solía

won't /wount/. See **will not**

wonted /'wɔntɪd, 'woun-/ *a* sólito, acostumbrado

woo /wu/ *vt* galantear; hacer la corte (a), solicitar amores a; cortejar; *Fig.* solicitar; perseguir

wood /wʊd/ *n* bosque, *m;* madera, *f;* (for the fire, etc.) leña, *f;* (cask) barril, *m.* —*a* de madera; (of the woods) selvático. **dead w.,** ramas muertas, *f pl; Fig.* paja, *f.* **w. alcohol,** alcohol metílico, *m.* **w.-anemone,** anémona de los bosques, *f.* **w.-block floor,** entarimado, *m.* **w.-borer,** xiló-fago, *m.* **w.-carver,** tallista, *mf* **w.-carving,** talla en madera, *f.* **w.-craft,** conocimiento del campo, *m.* **w.-cut,** grabado en madera, *m.* **w.-cutter,** leñador, *m.* **w.-engraver,** grabador (-ra) en madera. **w.-engraving,** grabado al boj, *m.* **w.-fibre,** fibra de madera, *f.* **w.-louse,** cochinilla, *f.* **w.-nymph,** ninfa de los bosques, *f.* **w.-pigeon,** paloma torcaz, *f.* **w.-pile,** pila de leña, leñera, *f.* **w.-pulp,** pulpa de madera, *f.* **w.-shaving,** acepilladura, *f.* **w.-splinter,** tasquil, *m,* astilla, *f.* **w.-wind,** *Mus.* madera, *f.* **w.-worm,** carcoma, *f*

wooded /'wʊdɪd/ *a* provisto de árboles, plantado de árboles, arbolado

wooden /'wʊdn̩/ *a* de madera; de palo; (of smiles) mecánico; (stiff) indiferente, sin emoción; (clumsy) torpe; (of character) inflexible. **He has a w. leg,** Tiene una pata de palo. **w. beam,** madero, *m;* viga de madera, *f.* **w. bridge,** pontón, *m.* **w. galley,** *Print.* galerín, *m*

woodland /*n.* 'wʊd,lænd; *a* -lənd/ *n* bosques, *m pl.* —*a* de bosque; silvestre

woodpecker /'wʊd,pɛkər/ *n* pájaro carpintero, picamaderos, *m*

woodshed /'wʊd,ʃɛd/ *n* leñera, *f*

woodwork /'wʊd,wɜrk/ *n* maderaje, *m;* molduras, *f pl;* carpintería, *f*

woody /'wʊdi/ *a* leñoso; arbolado, con árboles. **w. tissue,** tejido leñoso, *m*

wooer /'wuər/ *n* pretendiente, galanteador, *m*

woof /wʊf/ *n* trama, *f*

wooing /'wuɪŋ/ *n* galanteo, *m*

wool /wʊl/ *n* lana, *f.* —*a* de lana; lanar. **to go w.-gathering,** estar distraído. **to pull the w. over a person's eyes,** engañar como a un chino. **w.-bearing,** lanar. **w.-carding,** cardadura de lana, *f.* **w.-growing,** cría de ganado lanar, *f.* **w. merchant,** comerciante en lanas, *mf,* lanero, *m.* **w.-pack,** fardo de lana, *m.* **w. trade,** comercio de lana, *m*

woollen /'wʊlən/ *a* de lana; lanar. —*n* paño de lana, *m;* género de punta de lana, *m*

woolliness /'wʊlinɪs/ *n* lanosidad, *f*

woolly /'wʊli/ *a* lanudo, lanoso; de lana; *Bot.* velloso; (of hair) lanoso, crespo. —*n* género de punta de lana, *m;* (sweater) jersey, *m*

word /wɜrd/ *n* palabra, *f; Gram.* vocablo, *m; Theol.* verbo, *m;* (maxim) sentencia, *f,* dicho, *m;* (message) recado, *m;* (news) aviso, *m,* noticias, *f pl;* (*Mil.* command) voz de mando, *f;* (order) orden, *f;* (password) contraseña, *f;* (term) término, *m.* —*vt* expresar; formular; (draw up) redactar; escribir. **He was as good as his w.,** Fue hombre de palabra. **I do not know how to w. this letter,** No sé cómo redactar esta carta. **in a w.,** en una palabra; en resumidas cuentas. **by w. of mouth,** de palabra. **I give you my w. for it,** Le doy mi palabra de honor. **in other words,** en otros términos; en efecto. **the W.** (**of God**), el Verbo (de Dios). **to have a w. with,** hablar con; conversar con; entablar conversación con. **to leave w.,** dejar recado. **to have words with,** tener palabras con. **to keep one's w.,** cumplir su palabra

word index *n* índice de vocablos, *m*

wordiness /'wɜrdinɪs/ *n* palabrería, verbosidad, *f*

wording /'wɜrdɪŋ/ *n* fraseología, *f;* expresión, *f;* estilo, *m;* (terms) términos, *m pl;* (drawing up) redacción, *f*

word processing /'wɜrd ,prɒsɛsɪŋ/ *n* tratamiento de textos, procesamiento de textos, *m*

wordy /'wɜrdi/ *a* verboso, prolijo

work /wɜrk/ *n* trabajo, *m;* (sewing) labor, *f;* (literary, artistic production and theological) obra, *f;* (behavior) acción, *f,* acto, *m;* (employment) empleo, *m;* (business affairs) negocios, *m pl; pl* **works,** obras, fortificaciones, *f, pl;* obras públicas, *f pl;* construcciones, *f pl;* (of a machine) mecanismo, *m;* motor, *m;* (factory) fábrica, *f,* taller, *m.* **w. of art,** obra de arte. **w. accident,** accidente del trabajo, *m.* **w.-bag,** bolsa de costura, *f,* saco de labor, *m.* **w.-box,** (on legs) costurero, *m;* (small) neceser de costura, *m.* **w.-people,** obreros (-as). **w.-room,** taller, *m;* (study) estudio, *m;* (for sewing) cuarto de costura, *m.* **w.-table,** banco de taller, *m;* (for writing) mesa de escribir, *f*

work /wɜrk/ *vi* trabajar; *Sew.* hacer labor de aguja, coser; (embroider) bordar; *Mech.* funcionar, marchar; (succeed) tener éxito; ser eficaz; (be busy) estar ocupado; (be employed) tener empleo; (of the face) demudarse, torcerse; (ferment) fermentar; (operate) obrar *vt* trabajar; operar, hacer funcionar; mover; (control) manejar; (a mine) explotar; (embroider) bordar; (wood) tallar; (a problem) resolver; calcular; (iron, etc.) labrar; (the soil) cultivar; (a ship) maniobrar; (do) hacer; (bring about) efectuar; traer consigo; producir; (agitate oneself) agitarse, emocionarse, excitarse. **to w. in repoussé,** repujar. **to w. loose,** desprenderse. **to w. one's passage,** trabajar por el pasaje. **to w. overtime,** trabajar horas extraordinarias. **to w. two ways,** ser espada de dos filos. **to w. at,** trabajar en; ocuparse en; dedicarse a; elaborar. **to w. in,** *vt* introducir; insinuar. —*vi* combinarse. **to w. into,** penetrar en. **to w. off,** usar, emplear; (get rid of) deshacerse de, librarse de. **to w. on, upon,** influir en; obrar sobre; estar ocupado en. **to w. out,** *vt* calcular; resolver; (a mine, topic, etc.) agotar; (develop) elaborar, desarrollar; trazar, planear; (find) encontrar. —*vi* llegar (a); resultar; venir a ser. **to w. up,** crear; (promote) fomentar; producir; (excite) agitar, excitar; (fashion) dar forma (a), labrar; (finish) terminar

workable /'wɜrkəbəl/ *a* laborable; factible, practicable; (of a mine) explotable

workableness /'wɜrkəbəlnɪs/ *n* practicabilidad, *f*

workaday /'wɜrkə,dei/ *a* de todos los días; prosaico

workbench /'wɜrk,bɛntʃ/ banco de mecánico, *f,*

banco de taller, banco de trabajo, *m*, mesa de trabajo, *f*

workday /'wɜrk,dei/ *n* día de trabajo, día laborable, *m*

worker /'wɜrkər/ *n* trabajador (-ra); (manual) obrero (-ra); (of a machine) operario (-ia). **w.-ant,** hormiga obrera, *f.* **w.-bee,** abeja obrera, *f*

workhouse /'wɜrk,haus/ *n* asilo, *m*

working /'wɜrkɪŋ/ *a* de trabajo; (of capital) de explotación; trabajador, que trabaja; obrero. —*n* trabajo, *m;* (of a machine, organism, institution) funcionamiento, *m;* explotación, *f;* (of a mine) laboreo, *m;* (of a ship) maniobra, *f;* (of metal, stone, wood) labra, *f;* operación, *f;* (result) efecto, resultado, *m;* (calculation) cálculo, *m.* **"Not w.,"** «No funciona.» **to be in w. order,** funcionar bien. **w.-class,** clase obrera, *f;* pueblo, *m.* **w.-clothes,** ropa de trabajo, *f.* **w.-day,** día de trabajo, *m.* **w.-hours,** horas de trabajo, horas hábiles, *f pl.* **w. hypothesis,** postulado, *m.* **w.-man,** obrero, *m;* trabajador, *m.* **w.-out,** elaboración, *f;* ensayo, *m.* **w.-plan,** plan de trabajo, *m.* **w.-woman,** obrera, *f;* trabajadora, *f*

workless /'wɜrklɪs/ *a* sin trabajo

workman /'wɜrkmən/ *n* obrero, *m;* (agricultural) labrador, *m*

workmanlike /'wɜrkmən,laik/ *a* bien hecho, bien acabado; (clever) hábil

workmanship /'wɜrkmən,ʃɪp/ *n* trabajo, *m;* manufactura, *f;* hechura, *f;* (cleverness) habilidad, *f*

works /wɜrks/ *n* fábrica, *f*

workshop /'wɜrk,ʃɒp/ *n* taller, *m*

world /wɜrld/ *n* mundo, *m.* **For all the w. as if...,** Exactamente como si... **to see the w.,** ver mundo. **to treat the w. as one's oyster,** ponerse el mundo por montera. **w. without end,** por los siglos de los siglos. **w.-power,** potencia mundial, gran potencia, *f.* **w.-wide,** mundial, universal

world almanac *n* compendio mundial, *m*

worldliness /'wɜrldlinɪs/ *n* mundanería, *f,* conocimiento del mundo, *m;* frivolidad, vanidad mundana, *f;* egoísmo, *m;* prudencia, *f*

worldly /'wɜrldli/ *a* de este mundo; mundano; humano; profano; frívolo. **to be w.-wise,** tener mucho mundo

worm /wɜrm/ *n* gusano, *m;* lombriz, *f; Chem.* serpentín, *m;* (of a screw) tornillo sinfín, *m;* (person) gusano, *m; Fig.* gusano roedor, remordimiento, *m.* **Intestinal w.,** lombriz intestinal, *f,* gusano de la conciencia. **w.-eaten,** carcomido. **w.-hole,** picadura de gusano, lombriguera, *f.* **w.-powder,** polvos antihelmínticos, *m pl.* **w.-shaped,** vermiforme

worm /wɜrm/ *vt* (a dog) dar un vermífugo (a). —*vi* arrastrarse como un gusano. **to w. one's way into,** deslizarse en; *Fig.* insinuarse en, introducirse en. **to w. out,** (secrets, information) sonsacar

wormwood /'wɜrm,wʊd/ *n* ajenjo, *m*

wormy /'wɜrmi/ *a* gusanoso, lleno de gusanos

worn /wɔrn/ *a* (of garments) raído; estropeado; gastado; (of paths) trillado; (of the face) arrugado, cansado. **w. out,** acabado; muy usado; (tired) rendido; (exhausted) agotado

worrier /'wɜriər/ *n* inquietador (-ra); receloso (-sa); aprensivo (-va)

worry /'wɜri/ *n* preocupación, inquietud, ansiedad, *f;* problema, cuidado, *m.* —*vt* (prey) zamarrear; preocupar, inquietar; molestar; importunar. —*vi* estar preocupado, estar intranquilo, inquietarse. **Don't worry,** Pierda cuidado, No pase cuidado

worrying /'wɜriɪŋ/ *a* inquietante, perturbador; molesto

worse /wɜrs/ *a compar* peor; inferior. —*adv* peor; menos. —*n* lo peor. **so much the w.,** tanto peor. **to be w. off,** estar peor; estar en peores circunstancias; ser menos feliz. **to be the w. for wear,** ser muy usado; estar ajado; ser ya viejo. **to grow w.,** empeorarse; (of an ill person) ponerse peor. **w. and w.,** de mal en peor, peor que peor. **w. than ever,** peor que nunca

worsen /'wɜrsən/ *vt* agravar, hacer peor; exasperar. —*vi* agravarse, empeorarse; exasperarse

worsening /'wɜrsənɪŋ/ *n* agravación, *f,* empeoramiento, *m;* exasperación, *f*

worship /'wɜrʃɪp/ *n* culto, *m;* adoración, *f;* veneración, *f.* —*vt* adorar; reverenciar. —*vi* adorar; rezar; dar culto (a). **place of w.,** edificio de culto, *m.* **Your W.,** vuestra merced

worshipful /'wɜrʃɪpfəl/ *a* venerable, respetable

worshipper /'wɜrʃɪpər/ *n* adorador (-ra); *pl* **worshippers,** (in a church, etc.) fieles, *m pl,* congregación, *f*

worshipping /'wɜrʃɪpɪŋ/ *n* adoración, *f,* culto, *m*

worst /wɜrst/ *a* el (la, etc.) peor; más malo. —*adv* el (la, etc.) peor. —*n* el (la, etc.) peor; lo peor. —*vt* vencer, derrotar; triunfar sobre **If the w. comes to the w.,** En el peor de los casos. **The w. of it is that...,** Lo peor es que... **to have the w. of it,** salir perdiendo, llevar la peor parte

worsted /'wʊstɪd, 'wɜrstɪd/ *n* estambre, *m, a* de estambre

worth /wɜrθ/ *n* valor, *m;* precio, *m;* mérito, *m, a* (que) vale; de precio de; cuyo valor es de; equivalente a; (que) merece; digno de. **He bought six hundred pesetas w. of sweets,** Compró seiscientas pesetas de dulces. **He sang for all he was w.,** Cantó con toda su alma. **It is w. seeing,** Es digno de verse, Vale la pena de verse. **to be w.,** valer. **to be w. while,** valer la pena, merecer la pena

worthily /'wɜrðɪli/ *adv* dignamente

worthiness /'wɜrðinɪs/ *n* mérito, valor, *m*

worthless /'wɜrθlɪs/ *a* sin valor; sin mérito; inútil; malo; (of persons) vil, despreciable, indigno

worthlessness /'wɜrθlɪsnɪs/ *n* falta de valor, *f;* falta de mérito, *f;* inutilidad, *f;* (of persons) bajeze, vileza, *f*

worthy /'wɜrði/ *a* digno de respeto, benemérito, respetable; digno, merecedor; meritorio. —*n* varón ilustre, hombre célebre, *m;* héroe, *m;* (*Inf. Ironic.*) tío, *m.* **to be w. of,** ser digno de, merecer

would /wʊd; *unstressed* wəd/ *preterite* and *subjunctive* of **will.** (indicating a conditional tense) **They w. come if...,** Vendrían si...; (indicating an imperfect tense) **Often he w. sing,** Muchas veces cantaba, **Now and then a blackbird w. whistle,** De vez en cuando silbó un mirlo; (expressing wish, desire) **What w. they?** ¿Qué quieren? **The place where I w. be,** El lugar donde quisiera estar. **W. I were at home!** ¡Ojalá que estuviese en casa! **I thought that I w. tell you,** Se me ocurrió la idea de decírselo. **It w. seem that...,** Parece ser que..., Según parece...; Se diría que... **He said that he w. never have done it,** Dijo que no lo hubiera hecho nunca. **They w. have been killed if he had not rescued them,** Habrían sido matados si él no los hubiese salvado. **He w. go,** Se empeñó en ir. **He w. not do it,** Rehusó hacerlo, Se resistió a hacerlo; No quiso hacerlo. **This w. probably be the house,** Sin duda esta sería la casa. **W. you be good enough to...,** Tenga Vd. la bondad de..., Haga el favor de...

would-be /'wʊdbi/ *a* supuesto; llamado; aspirante (a); en esperanza de (followed by infin.); (frustrated) frustrado, malogrado

wound /wund/ *n* herida, *f.* —*vt* herir; (the feelings) lastimar, lacerar. **deep w.,** herida penetrante, *f.* **the wounded,** los heridos.

wounding /'wundɪŋ/ *n* herida, *f, a Fig.* lastimador

wraith /reiθ/ *n* fantasma, espectro, *m,* sombra, *f*

wrangle /'ræŋgəl/ *vi* discutir; altercar, disputar acaloradamente; reñir; (bargain) regatear. —*n* argumento, *m;* disputa, *f,* altercado, *m;* riña, *f*

wrangler /'ræŋglər/ *n* disputador (-ra); (Cambridge University) laureado en matemáticas, *m*

wrangling /'ræŋglɪŋ/ *n* disputas, *f pl,* altercación, *f;* (bargaining) regateo, *m*

wrap /ræp/ *vt* envolver; arrollar; cubrir; abrigar; (conceal) ocultar. —*n* envoltorio, *m;* abrigo, *m; pl* **wraps,** abrigos y mantas de viaje, *m pl.* **W. yourself up well!** ¡Abrígate bien! **to be wrapped up in,** estar envuelto en; *Fig.* estar entregado a, estar absorto en; (a person) estar embelesado con

wrapper /'ræpər/ *n* envoltura, *f;* embalaje, *m;* (of a newspaper) faja, *f;* (of a book) sobrecubierta, *f;* (dressing-gown) bata, *f,* salto de cama, *m*

wrapping /'ræpɪŋ/ *n* envoltura, cubierta, *f.* **w.-paper,** papel de envolver, *m*

wrath /ræθ/ *n* ira, *f*

wrathful /'ræθfəl/ *a* airado

wreak /rik/ *vt* ejecutar; (anger, etc.) descargar. **to w. one's vengeance,** vengarse

wreath /riθ/ *n* guirnalda, *f;* corona, *f;* trenza, *f.* **funeral w.,** corona funeraria, *f*

wreathe /rið/ *vt* trenzar; (entwine) entrelazar (de); (garland) coronar (de), enguirnaldar (con); (encircle) ceñir, rodear; (a face in smiles) iluminar

wreck /rɛk/ *n* naufragio, *m;* buque naufragado, *m;* destrucción, *f; Fig.* ruina, *f;* (remains) restos, *m pl;* (person) sombra, *f.* —*vt* hacer naufragar; destruir; *Fig.* arruinar; hacer fracasar. **I am a complete w.,** *Inf.* Estoy hecho una ruina. **to be wrecked,** irse a pique, naufragar; *Fig.* arruinarse; frustrarse

wreckage /'rɛkɪdʒ/ *n* naufragio, *m;* restos de naufragio, *m pl;* ruinas, *f pl;* (of a car, plane, etc.) restos, *m pl;* accidente, *m*

wrecked /rɛkt/ *a* naufragado

wrecker /'rɛkər/ *n* destructor (-ra); (of ships) raquero, *m*

wren /rɛn/ *n* reyezuelo, *m*

wrench /rɛntʃ/ *n* (jerk) arranque, *m;* (pull) tirón, *m;* (sprain) torcedura, *f;* (tool) llave, *f;* (pain) dolor, *m.* —*vt* arrancar; forzar; torcer, dislocar. **He has wrenched his arm,** Se ha torcido el brazo

wrest /rɛst/ *vt* arrebatar, arrancar

wrestle /'rɛsəl/ *vi* luchar. —*n* lucha grecorromana, *f; Fig.* lucha, *f.* **to w. with,** *Fig.* luchar con; luchar contra

wrestler /'rɛslər/ *n* luchador, *m*

wrestling /'rɛslɪŋ/ *n* lucha grecorromana, *f.* **all-in-w.,** lucha libre, *f.* **w.-match,** lucha, *f*

wretch /rɛtʃ/ *n* infeliz, *mf;* (ruffian) infame, *m;* (playful) picaruelo (-la). **a poor w.,** un pobre diablo

wretched /'rɛtʃɪd/ *a* (unhappy) infeliz, desdichado; miserable; pobre; (ill) enfermo; horrible; malo; mezquino; despreciable; lamentable

wretchedly /'rɛtʃɪdli/ *adv* tristemente; pobremente; muy mal; ruinmente

wretchedness /'rɛtʃɪdnɪs/ *n* infelicidad, desdicha, *f;* miseria, pobreza, *f;* escualidez, *f;* ruindad, *f*

wriggle /'rɪgəl/ *vi* agitarse, moverse; menearse; serpear, culebrear; retorcerse. —*n* See under **wriggling. to w. into,** insinuarse en, deslizarse dentro (de). **to w. out,** escaparse. **to w. out of a difficulty,** extricarse de una dificultad

wriggling /'rɪglɪŋ/ *n* meneo, *m;* retorcimiento, *m;* serpenteo, culebreo, *m*

wring /rɪŋ/ *vt* torcer; estrujar; exprimir; arrancar; (force) forzar. **to w. one's hands,** restregarse las manos. **to w. the neck of,** torcer el pescuezo (a). **to w. out,** exprimir; estrujar

wringer /'rɪŋər/ *n* torcedor (-ra); (for clothes) exprimidor de ropa, *m*

wringing /'rɪŋɪŋ/ *n* torsión, *f.* **w.-machine,** exprimidor de ropa, *m*

wrinkle /'rɪŋkəl/ *n* arruga, *f;* pliegue, *m; Inf.* noción, *f.* —*vt* arrugar. —*vi* arrugarse. **to w. one's brow,** (frown) fruncir el ceño; (in perplexity) arrugar la frente

wrinkling /'rɪŋklɪŋ/ *n* arrugamiento, *m*

wrinkly /'rɪŋkli/ *a* arrugado

wrist /rɪst/ *n* muñeca, *f.* **w.-band,** tira del puño de la camisa, *f.* **w. bandage,** pulsera, *f*

wristlet /'rɪstlɪt/ *n* pulsera, *f;* manguito elástico, *m.* **w. watch,** reloj de pulsera, *m*

writ /rɪt/ *n* escritura, *f; Law.* decreto judicial, mandamiento, *m;* orden, *f;* título ejecutorio, *m;* hábeas corpus, *m.* **Holy W.,** la Sagrada Escritura. **to issue a w.,** dar orden. **to serve a w.,** notificar una orden. **w. of privilege,** auto de excarcelación, *m*

write /rait/ *vt* and *vi* escribir; *Fig.* mostrar. **He writes a good hand,** Tiene buena letra. **I shall w. to them for a list,** Les escribiré pidiendo una lista. **to w. back,** contestar por escrito; contestar a una carta. **to w. down,** poner por escrito; anotar, apuntar; describir. **to w. for,** escribir para; escribir para pedir algo; escribir algo en vez de otra persona. **to w. off,** escribir; escribir rápidamente; cancelar. **to w. on,** seguir escribiendo; escribir sobre. **to w. out,** copiar; redactar. **to w. over again,** escribir de nuevo, escribir otra vez, volver a escribir. **to w. up,** redactar; *Com.* poner al día; (praise) escribir alabando

writer /'raitər/ *n* escritor (-ra); autor (-ra). **the present w.,** el que, *m,* (*f,* la que) esto escribe. **writer's cramp,** calambre del escribiente, *m*

writhe /raið/ *vi* retorcerse

writhing /'raiðɪŋ/ *n* retorsión, *f*

writing /'raitɪŋ/ *n* escritura, *f;* (work) escrito, *m;* inscripción, *f;* documento, *m;* (style) estilo, *m;* (hand) letra, *f;* el arte de escribir; trabajo literario, *m.* **in one's own w.,** de su propia letra. **in w.,** por escrito. **w.-case,** escribanía, *f.* **w.-desk,** escritorio, *m.* **w.-pad,** taco de papel, *m.* **w.-paper,** papel de escribir, *m.* **w.-table,** mesa de escribir, *f*

written /'rɪtn̩/ *a* escrito

wrong /rɔŋ/ *a* injusto; mal; equivocado, erróneo; inexacto; falso; incorrecto; desacertado; inoportuno. **It is the w. one,** No es el que hacía falta; No es el que quería. **to be in the w. place,** estar mal situado; estar mal colocado. **to be w.,** estar mal; no tener razón; (mistaken) estar equivocado; (of deeds or things) estar mal hecho; (be unjust) ser injusto; (of clocks) andar mal. **to do w.,** hacer mal; obrar mal. **to get out of bed on the w. side,** levantarse del izquierdo. **to go w.,** (of persons) descarriarse; (of affairs) ir mal; salir mal; frustrarse; (of apparatus) estropearse, no funcionar. **We have taken the w. road,** Nos hemos equivocado de camino. **You were very w. to...,** Has hecho muy mal en... **w.-headed,** terco, obstinado; disparatado. **w.-headedness,** terquedad, obstinación, *f.* **w. number,** (telephone) número errado, *m.* **w. side,** revés, *m;* lado malo, *m.* **w. side out,** al envés; al revés

wrong /rɔŋ/ *adv* mal; injustamente; sin razón; incorrectamente; equivocadamente; (inside out) al revés. **to get it w.,** (a sum) calcular mal; (misunderstand) comprender mal

wrong /rɔŋ/ *n* mal, *m;* injusticia, *f;* perjuicio, *m;* ofensa, *f,* agravio, *m;* culpa, *f;* error, *m.* **to be in the w.,** no tener razon; haber hecho mal. **to put one in the w.,** echar la culpa (a), hacer responsable (de)

wrong /rɔŋ/ *vt* hacer mal (a); perjudicar; ser injusto con; ofender

wrongdoer /'rɔŋˌduər/ *n* malhechor (-ra); pecador (-ra); perverso (-sa)

wrongdoing /'rɔŋˌduɪŋ/ *n* maldad, maleficencia, *f;* pecado, *m;* injusticia, *f*

wrongful /'rɔŋfəl/ *a* injusto; perjudicial; falso

wrongfully /'rɔŋfəli/ *adv* injustamente; falsamente

wrongly /'rɔŋli/ *adv* injustamente; erróneamente, equivocadamente; perversamente; mal

wrongness /'rɔŋnɪs/ *n* mal, *m;* injusticia, *f;* falsedad, *f;* inexactitud, *f,* error, *m*

wrought /rɔt/ *a* forjado; labrado; (hammered) batido; trabajado. **w. iron,** hierro dulce, hierro forjado, *m.* **w. up,** muy excitado, muy agitado, muy nervioso

wry /rai/ *a* torcido; tuerto; triste; pesimista; desilusionado; irónico. **wry face,** mueca *f,* de desengaño, de ironía, de disgusto, etc. **make a wry face,** torcer el gesto. **wry neck,** *Ornith.* torcecuello, *m*

wryly /'raili/ *adv* tristemente; irónicamente

Wuthering Heights /'wʌðərɪŋ/ Cumbres borrascosas

wye /wai/ *n* (letter) ye, i griega, *f;* horquilla, cosa en forma de Y, *f*

XYZ

x /ɛks/ *n* equis, *f*
x-ray /ˈɛksˌrei/ *vt* tomar una radiografía (de). **x-ray,** rayo x, *m pl.* **x-ray examination,** examen con rayos x, *m.* **x-ray photograph,** radiografía, *f*
xylophone /ˈzailəˌfoun/ *n* xilófono, *m*
y /wai/ *n* (letter) i griega, ye, *f*
yacht /yɒt/ *n* yate, *m.* **y. club,** club marítimo, *m.* **y. race,** regata de yates, *f*
yachting /ˈyɒtɪŋ/ *n* navegación en yate, *f,* paseo en yate, *m*
yachtsman /ˈyɒtsmən/ *n* deportista náutico, balandrista, balandrismo, *m*
yank /yæŋk/ *n* tirón, *m,* sacudida, *f.* —*vt* dar un tirón (a); sacar de un tirón
Yankee /ˈyæŋki/ *a* and *n* yanqui, *mf*
yap /yæp/ *vi* ladrar. —*n* ladrido, *m*
yapper /ˈyæpər/ *n* (yapping dog) gozque, gozquejo, *m*
yapping /ˈyæpɪŋ/ *n* ladridos, *m pl, a* que ladra
yard /yɑrd/ *n* (measure) yarda, *f; Naut.* verga, *f;* corral, *m;* (courtyard) patio, *m.* —*vt* acorralar. **goods y.,** estación de mercancías, *f.* **y.-arm,** penol (de la verga), *m.* **y.-stick,** vara de medir de una yarda, *f*
yarn /yɑrn/ *n* hilaza, *f;* hilo, *m;* (story) historia, *f,* cuento, *m.* **to spin a y.,** contar una historia
yaw /yɔ/ *vi Naut.* guiñar; *Aer.* serpentear. —*n Naut.* guiñada, *f; Aer.* serpenteo, *m*
yawl /yɔl/ *n* yola, *f;* bote, *m*
yawn /yɔn/ *vi* bostezar; quedarse con la boca abierta; (of chasms, etc.) abrirse. —*n* bostezo, *m.* **to stifle a y.,** ahogar un bostezo
yawning /ˈyɔnɪŋ/ *a* abierto. —*n* bostezos, *m pl*
ye /ði; *spelling pron.* yi/ *pers pron* vos, vosotros
yea /yei/ *adv* en verdad, ciertamente; y aun... no sólo... sino. —*n* si, *m*
year /yɪər/ *n* año, *m; pl* **years,** años, *m pl,* edad, *f.* **We are getting on in years,** Nos vamos haciendo viejos. **He is five years old,** Tiene cinco años. **all the y. round,** todo el año, el año entero. **by the y.,** al año. **every other y.,** cada dos años, un año sí y otro no. **in after years,** en años posteriores. **last y.,** el año pasado. **next y.,** el año próximo. el año que viene. **y. after y.,** año tras año. **New Y.,** Año Nuevo, *m.* **to see the New Y. in,** ver empezar el Año Nuevo. **New Year's Day,** día de Año Nuevo, *m.* **(A) Happy New Y.!** ¡Feliz Año Nuevo! **y.-book,** anuario, *m*
yearling calf /ˈyɪərlɪŋ/ *n* becerra *f*
yearly /ˈyɪərli/ *a* anual. —*adv* anualmente, cada año; una vez al año
yearn /yɜrn/ *vi* anhelar, suspirar (por); desear vivamente
yearning /ˈyɜrnɪŋ/ *n* sed, ansia, *f;* anhelo, deseo vehemente, *m.* —*a* ansioso; anhelante; (tender) tierno
yeast /yist/ *n* levadura, *f*
yell /yɛl/ *vi* and *vt* chillar; gritar. —*n* chillido, *m;* grito, *m*
yelling /ˈyɛlɪŋ/ *n* chillidos, *m pl;* gritos, *m pl,* gritería, *f*
yellow /ˈyɛlou/ *a* amarillo; (of hair) rubio; (cowardly) cobarde; (newspaper) amarillista, sensacionalista. **to turn y.,** *vi* ponerse amarillo; amarillear. —*vt* volver amarillo. **y. fever,** fiebre amarilla, *f.* **y. hammer,** *Ornith.* emberizo, *m*
yellowing /ˈyɛlouɪŋ/ *n* amarilleo, *m*
yellowish /ˈyɛlouɪʃ/ *a* amarillento
yellowness /ˈyɛlounɪs/ *n* amarillez, *f*
yellow pages *n* páginas amarillas, páginas doradas, *f pl*
yelp /yɛlp/ *vi* gañir. —*n* gañido, *m*
yelping /ˈyɛlpɪŋ/ *n* gañidos, *m pl*
yen /yɛn/ *n* (currency) yen, *m;* (desire) deseovivo, *m*
yeoman /ˈyoumən/ *n* pequeño propietario rural, *m;* soldado de caballería, *m.* **Y. of the Guard,** alabardero de la Casa Real, *m*
yes /yɛs/ *adv* sí. **Yes?** ¿De verdad? ¿Y qué pasó después? ¿Y entonces? **to say yes,** decir que sí; dar el sí. **yes-man,** amenista, sacristán de amén, *m*
yesterday /ˈyɛstərˌdei/ *adv* ayer. —*n* ayer, *m.* **the day before y.,** anteayer
yet /yɛt/ *adv* aún, todavía. **as yet,** hasta ahora; todavía. **He has not come yet,** No ha venido todavía. **yet again,** otra vez
yet /yɛt/ *conjunc* sin embargo, no obstante, con todo; pero. **The book is well written and yet I do not like it,** El libro está bien escrito, y sin embargo no me gusta
yew /yu/ *n* tejo, *m;* madera de tejo, *f*
Yiddish /ˈyɪdɪʃ/ *n* yídis, yídish, yídico, *m; a* yídico
yield /yild/ *vt* producir; dar; (grant) otorgar; (afford) ofrecer; (surrender) ceder. —*vi* producir; (submit) rendirse, someterse; (of disease) responder; (give way) flaquear, doblegarse; dar de sí; (consent) consentir (en); (to circumstances, etc.) ceder (a), sucumbir (a). —*n* producción, *f,* producto, *m; Com.* rédito, *m;* (crop) cosecha, *f.* **to y. to temptation,** ceder a la tentación. **to y. up,** entregar; devolver
yielding /ˈyildɪŋ/ *a* flexible; (soft) blando; dócil, sumiso; fácil; condescendiente
yogurt /ˈyougərt/ *n* yogur, *m*
yoke /youk/ *n* yugo, *m;* (of oxen) yunta, *f;* (for pails) balancín, *m;* (of a garment) canesú, *m; Fig.* férula, *f,* yugo, *m.* —*vt* uncir, acoplar. **to throw off the y.,** sacudir el yugo
yokel /ˈyoukəl/ *n* patán, rústico, *m*
yolk /youk/ *n* (of an egg) yema, *f*
yonder /ˈyɒndər/ *a* aquel, *m;* aquella, *f;* aquellos, *m pl;* aquellas, *f pl.* —*adv* allí; allí a lo lejos
yore /yɔr/ *n* **in days of y.,** antaño; en otro tiempo
you /yu; *unstressed* yʊ, yə/ *pers pron nominative* (polite form) usted (Vd.), *mf;* ustedes (Vds.), *mf pl;* (familiar form) *sing* tu, *mf;* (*pl*) vosotros, *m pl;* vosotras, *f pl;* (one) uno, *m;* una, *f;* se (followed by 3rd pers. sing. of verb). —*pers pron acc* (polite form) le, *m;* la, *f;* les, *m pl;* las, *f pl;* a usted, a ustedes; (informal form) te, *mf,* os, *mf pl;* (after most prepositions) ti, *mf;* vosotros, *m pl;* vosotras, *f pl.* **Are you there?** (telephone) ¡Oiga! **I gave the parcel to you,** Te (os) di el paquete; Di el paquete a usted (a ustedes). **I shall wait for you in the garden,** Te (os) esperaré en el jardín; Esperaré a Vds. (a Vd.) en el jardín. **This present is for you,** Este regalo es para tí (para vosotros, para Vd. (Vds.)). **Away with you!** ¡Vete! ¡Marchaos! **Between you and me,** Entre tú y yo. **you can't eat your cake and have it too,** no hay rosa sin espinas. **You never can tell,** No se sabe nunca, Uno no sabe nunca
young /yʌŋ/ *a* joven; nuevo, reciente; inexperto; poco avanzado. —*n* cría, *f,* hijuelos, *m pl.* **y. blood,** *Inf.* pollo pera, *m.* **y. girl,** jovencita, *f.* **y. man** joven, *m.* **y. people,** jóvenes, *m pl.* **in his y. days,** en su juventud. **The night is y.,** La noche está poca avanzada. **to grow y. again,** rejuvenecer. **with y.,** (of animals) preñada *f*
younger /ˈyʌŋgər/ *a* más joven; menor. **Peter is his y. brother,** Pedro es su hermano menor. **to look y.,** parecer más joven
youngish /ˈyʌŋgɪʃ/ *a* bastante joven
youngster /ˈyʌŋstər/ *n* jovencito, chico, muchacho, *m;* nino, *m*
your /yʊr, yɔr; *unstressed* yər/ *a poss* (polite form) su (*pl* sus), de usted (Vd.), (*pl* de ustedes (Vds.)); (familiar form) tu (*pl* vuestro). **I have y. papers,** Tengo tus (vuestros) papeles; Tengo los papeles de Vd. (*or* de Vds.). **How is y. mother?** ¿Cómo está su (tu) madre? **It is y. turn,** Te toca a ti, Le toca a Vd.
yours /yʊrz, yɔrz/ *pron poss* (polite form) (el) suyo, *m;* (la) suya, *f;* (los) suyos, *m pl;* (las) suyas, *f pl;* el, *m;* la, *f;* lo, *neut;* los, *m pl;* las, *f pl;* de usted (Vd.), *mf sing* or de ustedes (Vds.), *mf pl;* (familiar form) (el) tuyo, *m;* (la) tuya, *f;* (los) tuyos, *m pl;* (las) tuyas, *f pl;* (el) vuestro, *m;* (la) vuestra, *f;* (los) vuestros, *m pl;* (las) vuestras, *f pl.* **This is a picture of y.,**

(addressing one person), Este es uno de los cuadros de usted (Vd.), Este es uno de tus cuadros. **This hat is mine, it is not y.,** Este sombrero es el mío, no es el tuyo. **The horse is y.,** El caballo es tuyo (de Vd.). **Y. affectionately,** Un abrazo de tu amigo... **Y. faithfully,** Queda de Vd. su att. (atentísimo) s.s. (seguro servidor). **Y. sincerely,** Queda de Vd. su aff. (afectuoso)

yourself /yʊr'sɛlf, yɔr- yər-/ *pers pron* (familiar form *sing*) tú mismo, *m;* tú misma, *f;* (after a preposition) ti, *mf;* (polite form) usted (Vd.) mismo, *m;* usetd misma, *f; pl* **yourselves,** (familiar form) vosotros mismos, *m pl;* vosotras mismas, *f pl;* (polite form) ustedes (Vds.) mismos, *m pl;* ustedes mismas, *f pl.* **This is for y.,** Esto es para ti; Esto es para Vd.

youth /yuθ/ *n* juventud, *f;* (man) joven, chico, mozalbete, *m;* (collectively) jóvenes, *m pl,* juventud, *f*

youthful /'yuθfəl/ *a* joven, juvenil; de la juventud

yowl /yaul/ *n* gañido, aullido, *m.* —*vi* gañir, aullar

Yucatan /ˌyukə'tæn/ *a* yucateco

yucca /'yʌkə/ *n Bot.* yuca, *f*

Yugoslav /'yugouˌslɑv/ *n* yugoeslavo (-va). —*a* yugoeslavo

Yugoslavia /ˌyugou'slaviə/ Yugoeslavia, *f*

Yukon, the /'yukɒn/ el Yukón, *m*

Yule /yul/ *n* Navidad, *f.* **y.-log,** leño de Navidad, *m.* **y-tide,** Navidades, *f pl*

z /zi/ *n* (letter) zeda, zeta, *f*

zeal /zil/ *n* celo, entusiasmo, *m;* ardor, fervor, *m*

zealot /'zɛlət/ *n* fanático (-ca)

zealous /'zɛləs/ *a* celoso, entusiasta

zealously /'zɛləsli/ *adv* con entusiasmo

zebra /'zibrə/ *n* cebra, *f*

zenith /'zinɪθ/ *n* cenit, *m; Fig.* apogeo, punto culminante, *m*

zephyr /'zɛfər/ *n* céfiro, *m,* brisa, *f*

zero /'zɪərou/ *n* cero, *m.* **below z.,** bajo cero. **z. hour,** hora cero, *f*

zest /zɛst/ *n* sabor, gusto, *m;* entusiasmo, *m.* **to eat with z.,** comer con buen apetito. **to enter on with z.,** emprender con entusiasmo

zigzag /'zɪgˌzæg/ *n* zigzag, *m.* —*a* and *adv* en zigzag. —*vi* zigzaguear, hacer zigzags, serpentear; (of persons) andar haciendo eses

Zimbabwe /zɪm'bɑbwei/ Zimbabue

zinc /zɪŋk/ *n* cinc, *m.* **z. oxide,** óxido de cinc, *m*

Zion /'zaiən/ *n* Sión, *m*

Zionism /'zaiəˌnɪzəm/ *n* sionismo, *m*

Zionist /'zaiənɪst/ *n* and *a* sionista

zip /zɪp/ *n* (of a bullet) silbido, *m; Inf.* energía, *f.* **zip fastener,** cierre de cremallera, *m*

zip code *n* código postal, *m*

zipper /'zɪpər/ *n* cremallera, *f,* cierre relámpago, cierre, cerrador, *m*

zircon /'zɜrkɒn/ *n* circón, *m*

zither /'zɪθər/ *n* cítara, *f*

zodiac /'zoudiˌæk/ *n* zodiaco, *m*

zone /zoun/ *n* zona, *f;* faja, *f*

zoo /zu/ *n* jardín zoológico, *m*

zoological /ˌzouə'lɒdʒɪkəl/ *a* zoológico. **Z. garden,** jardín zoológico, *m*

zoologist /zou'ɒlədʒɪst/ *n* zoólogo, *m*

zoology /zou'ɒlədʒi/ *n* zoología, *f*

zoom /zum/ *n* zumbido, *m.* —*vi* zumbar; *Aer.* empinarse

Zulu /'zulu/ *a* and *n* zulú *mf*

Zuyder Zee, the /'zaidər 'zei, 'zi/ el Zuyderzée, *m*

Spanish Irregular Verbs

Infinitive	Present	Future	Preterit	Past Part.
andar	ando	andaré	anduve	andado
caber	quepo	cabré	cupe	cabido
caer	caigo	caeré	caí	caído
conducir	conduzco	conduciré	conduje	conducido
dar	doy	daré	di	dado
decir	digo	diré	dije	dicho
estar	estoy	estaré	estuve	estado
haber	he	habré	hube	habido
hacer	hago	haré	hice	hecho
ir	voy	iré	fui	ido
jugar	juego	jugaré	jugué	jugado
morir	muero	moriré	morí	muerto
oir	oigo	oiré	oí	oído
poder	puedo	podré	pude	podido
poner	pongo	pondré	puse	puesto
querer	quiero	querré	quise	querido
saber	sé	sabré	supe	sabido
salir	salgo	saldré	salí	salido
ser	soy	seré	fui	sido
tener	tengo	tendré	tuve	tenido
traer	traigo	traeré	traje	traído
valer	valgo	valdré	valí	valido
venir	vengo	vendré	vine	venido
ver	veo	veré	vi	visto

Las formas del verbo inglés

1. Se forma la 3ª persona singular del tiempo presente exactamente al igual que el plural de los sustantivos, añadiendo **-es** o **-s** a la forma sencilla según las mismas reglas, así:

(1)	teach	pass	wish	fix	buzz		
	teaches	passes	wishes	fixes	buzzes		
(2)	place	change	judge	please	freeze		
	places	changes	judges	pleases	freezes		
(3a)	find	sell	clean	hear	love	buy	know
	finds	sells	cleans	hears	loves	buys	knows
(3b)	think	like	laugh	stop	hope	meet	want
	thinks	likes	laughs	stops	hopes	meets	wants
(4)	cry	try	dry	carry	deny		
	cries	tries	dries	carries	denies		

Cinco verbos muy comunes tienen 3ª persona singular irregular:

(5)	go	do	say	have	be
	goes	does	says	has	is

2. Se forman el tiempo pasado y el participio de modo igual, añadiendo a la forma sencilla la terminación **-ed** o **-d** según las reglas que siguen:

(1) Si la forma sencilla termina en **-d** o **-t,** se le pone **-ed** como sílaba aparte:

end	fold	need	load	want	feast	wait	light
ended	folded	needed	loaded	wanted	feasted	waited	lighted

(2) Si la forma sencilla termina en cualquier otra consonante, se añade también **-ed** pero sin hacer sílaba aparte:

(2a)	bang	sail	seem	harm	earn	weigh
	banged	sailed	seemed	harmed	earned	weighed
(2b)	lunch	work	look	laugh	help	pass
	lunched	worked	looked	laughed	helped	passed

(3) Si la forma sencilla termina en **-e,** se le pone sólo **-d:**

(3a)	hate	taste	waste	guide	fade	trade
	hated	tasted	wasted	guided	faded	traded
(3b)	free	judge	rule	name	dine	scare
	freed	judged	ruled	named	dined	scared
(3c)	place	force	knife	like	hope	base
	placed	forced	knifed	liked	hoped	based

(4) Una **-y** final que sigue a cualquier consonante se cambia en **-ie** al añadir la **-d** del pasado/participio:

cry	try	dry	carry	deny
cried	tried	dried	carried	denied

3. Varios verbos muy comunes forman el tiempo pasado y el participio de manera irregular. Pertenecen a tres grupos.

(1) Los que tienen una sola forma irregular para tiempo pasado y participio, como los siguientes:

bend	bleed	bring	build	buy	catch	creep	deal
bent	bled	brought	built	bought	caught	crept	dealt
dig	feed	feel	fight	find	flee	get	hang
dug	fed	felt	fought	found	fled	got	hung
have	hear	hold	keep	lead	leave	lend	lose
had	heard	held	kept	led	left	lent	lost
make	mean	meet	say	seek	sell	send	shine
made	meant	met	said	sought	sold	sent	shone
shoot	sit	sleep	spend	stand	strike	sweep	teach
shot	sat	slept	spent	stood	struck	swept	taught

(2) Los que tienen una forma irregular para el tiempo pasado y otra forma irregular para el participio, como los siguientes:

be	beat	become	begin	bite
was	beat	became	began	bit
been	beaten	become	begun	bitten

blow	break	choose	come	do
blew	broke	chose	came	did
blown	broken	chosen	come	done

draw	drink	drive	eat	fall
drew	drank	drove	ate	fell
drawn	drunk	driven	eaten	fallen

fly	forget	freeze	give	go
flew	forgot	froze	gave	went
flown	forgotten	frozen	given	gone

grow	hide	know	ride	ring
grew	hid	knew	rode	rang
grown	hidden	known	ridden	rung

rise	run	see	shake	shrink
rose	ran	saw	shook	shrank
risen	run	seen	shaken	shrunk

sing	sink	speak	steal	swear
sang	sank	spoke	stole	swore
sung	sunk	spoken	stolen	sworn

swim	tear	throw	wear	write
swam	tore	threw	wore	wrote
swum	torn	thrown	worn	written

(3) Los que no varían del todo, la forma sencilla funcionando también como pasado/participio; entre éstos son de mayor frecuencia:

bet	burst	cast	cost	cut
hit	hurt	let	put	quit
read	set	shed	shut	slit
spit	split	spread	thrust	wet

Numbers/Números

Cardinal/Cardinales

one	1	uno, una
two	2	dos
three	3	tres
four	4	cuatro
five	5	cinco
six	6	seis
seven	7	siete
eight	8	ocho
nine	9	nueve
ten	10	diez
eleven	11	once
twelve	12	doce
thirteen	13	trece
fourteen	14	catorce
fifteen	15	quince
sixteen	16	dieciséis
seventeen	17	diecisiete
eighteen	18	dieciocho
nineteen	19	diecinueve
twenty	20	veinte
twenty-one	21	veinte y uno (*or* veintiuno)
twenty-two	22	veinte y dos (*or* veintidós)
thirty	30	treinta
thirty-one	31	treinta y uno
thirty-two	32	treinta y dos
forty	40	cuarenta
fifty	50	cincuenta
sixty	60	sesenta
seventy	70	setenta
eighty	80	ochenta
ninety	90	noventa
one hundred	100	cien
one hundred one	101	ciento uno
one hundred two	102	ciento dos
two hundred	200	doscientos, -as
three hundred	300	trescientos, -as
four hundred	400	cuatrocientos, -as
five hundred	500	quinientos, -as
six hundred	600	seiscientos, -as
seven hundred	700	setecientos, -as
eight hundred	800	ochocientos, -as
nine hundred	900	novecientos, -as
one thousand	1,000	mil
two thousand	2,000	dos mil
one hundred thousand	100,000	cien mil
one million	1,000,000	un millón
two million	2,000,000	dos millones

Ordinal/Ordinales

first	1st / 1°	primero
second	2nd / 2°	segundo
third	3rd / 3°	tercero
fourth	4th / 4°	cuarto
fifth	5th / 5°	quinto
sixth	6th / 6°	sexto
seventh	7th / 7°	séptimo
eighth	8th / 8°	octavo
ninth	9th / 9°	noveno
tenth	10th / 10°	décimo

Days of the Week/Días de la Semana

Sunday	domingo
Monday	lunes
Tuesday	martes
Wednesday	miércoles
Thursday	jueves
Friday	viernes
Saturday	sábado

Months/Meses

January	enero
February	febrero
March	marzo
April	abril
May	mayo
June	junio
July	julio
August	agosto
September	septiembre
October	octubre
November	noviembre
December	diciembre

Weights and Measures/Pesos y Medidas

1 centímetro	= .3937 inches		1 kilolitro	=	264.18 gallons
1 metro	= 39.37 inches		1 inch	=	2.54 centímetros
1 kilómetro	= .621 mile		1 foot	=	.305 metros
1 centigramo	= .1543 grain		1 mile	=	1.61 kilómetros
1 gramo	= 15.432 grains		1 grain	=	.065 gramos
1 kilogramo	= 2.2046 pounds		1 pound	=	.455 kilogramos
1 tonelada	= 2.204 pounds		1 ton	=	.907 toneladas
1 centilitro	= .338 ounces		1 ounce	=	2.96 centilitros
1 litro	= 1.0567 quart (liquid);		1 quart	=	1.13 litros
	.908 quart (dry)		1 gallon	=	4.52 litros

Signs/Señales

Caution	Precaución	**No smoking**	Prohibido fumar
Danger	Peligro	**No admittance**	Entrada prohibida
Exit	Salida	**One way**	Dirección única
Entrance	Entrada	**No entry**	Dirección prohibida
Stop	Alto	**Women**	Señoras, Mujeres, Damas
Closed	Cerrado	**Men**	Señores, Hombres, Caballeros
Open	Abierto	**Ladies' Room**	El cuarto de damas
Slow	Despacio	**Men's Room**	El servicio

Useful Phrases/Locuciones Útiles

Good day, Good morning. Buenos días.
Good afternoon. Buenas tardes.
Good night, Good evening. Buenas noches.
Hello. ¡Hola!
Welcome! ¡Bienvenido!
See you later. Hasta luego.
Goodbye. ¡Adiós!
How are you? ¿Cómo está usted?
I'm fine, thank you. Estoy bien, gracias.
I'm pleased to meet you. Mucho gusto en conocerle.
May I introduce . . . Quisiera presentar . . .
Thank you very much. Muchas gracias.
You're welcome. De nada *or* No hay de qué.
Please. Por favor.
Excuse me. Con permiso.
Good luck. ¡Buena suerte!
To your health. ¡Salud!

Please help me. Ayúdeme, por favor.
I don't know. No sé.
I don't understand. No entiendo.
Do you understand? ¿Entiende usted?
I don't speak Spanish. No hablo español.
Do you speak English? ¿Habla usted inglés?
How do you say . . . in Spanish? ¿Cómo se dice . . . en español?
What do you call this? ¿Cómo se llama esto?
Speak slowly, please. Hable despacio, por favor.
Please repeat. Repita, por favor.
I don't like it. No me gusta.
I am lost. Ando perdido; Me he extraviado.

What is your name? ¿Cómo se llama usted?
My name is . . . Me llamo . . .
I am an American. Soy norteamericano.
Where are you from? ¿De dónde es usted?
I'm from . . . Soy de . . .

How is the weather? ¿Qué tiempo hace?
It's cold (hot) today. Hace frío (calor) hoy.
What time is it? ¿Qué hora es?

How much is it? ¿Cuánto es?
It is too much. Es demasiado.
What do you wish? ¿Qué desea usted?
I want to buy . . . Quiero comprar . . .
May I see something better? ¿Podría ver algo mejor?
May I see something cheaper? ¿Podría ver algo menos caro?
It is not exactly what I want. No es exactamente lo que quiero.

I'm hungry. Tengo hambre.
I'm thirsty. Tengo sed.
Where is there a restaurant? ¿Dónde hay un restaurante?
I have a reservation. Tengo una reservación.
I would like . . . Quisiera . . .; Me gustaría . . .
Please give me . . . Por favor, déme usted . . .
Please bring me . . . Por favor, tráigame usted . . .
May I see the menu? ¿Podría ver el menú?
The bill, please. La cuenta, por favor.
Is service included in the bill? ¿El servicio está incluido en la cuenta?
Where is there a hotel? ¿Dónde hay un hotel?
Where is the post office? ¿Dónde está el correo?
Is there any mail for me? ¿Hay correo para mí?
Where can I mail this letter? ¿Dónde puedo echar esta carta al correo?

Take me to . . . Lléveme a . . .
I believe I am ill. Creo que estoy enfermo.
Please call a doctor. Por favor, llame al médico.
Please call the police. Por favor, llame a la policía.
I want to send a telegram. Quiero poner un telegrama.
As soon as possible. Cuanto antes.

Round trip. Ida y vuelta.
Please help me with my luggage. Por favor, ayúdeme con mi equipaje.
Where can I get a taxi? ¿Dónde puedo coger un taxi?
What is the fare to . . . ¿Cuánto es el pasaje hasta . . . ?
Please take me to this address. Por favor, lléveme a esta dirección.
Where can I change my money? ¿Dónde puedo cambiar mi dinero?
Where is the nearest bank? ¿Dónde está el banco más cercano?
Can you accept my check? ¿Puede aceptar usted mi cheque?
Do you accept traveler's checks? ¿Aceptan cheques de viaje?
What is the postage? ¿Cuánto es el franqueo?
Where is the nearest drugstore? ¿Dónde está la farmacia más cercana?
Where is the men's (women's) room? ¿Dónde está el servicio de caballeros (de señoras)?
Please let me off at. . . Por favor, déjeme bajar en . . .
Right away. ¡Pronto!
Help. ¡Socorro!
Who is it? ¿Quién es?
Just a minute! ¡Un momento no más!
Come in. ¡Pase usted!
Pardon me. Dispense usted.
Stop. ¡Pare!
Look out. ¡Cuidado!
Hurry. ¡De prisa! *or* ¡Dése prisa!
Go on. ¡Siga!
To (on, at) the right. A la derecha.
To (on, at) the left. A la izquierda.
Straight ahead. Adelante.